Chilton's auto repair manual 1977

american cars from 1970 to 1977

President	William A. Barbour
Executive Vice President	K. Robert Brink
Vice President and General Manager	William D. Byrne
Associate Editorial Director	Glen Ruh
Managing Editor	John H. Weise, S.A.E.
Assistant Managing Editor	Peter J. Meyer, S.A.E.
Editorial Staff	Arthur I. Birney
	Robert J. Brown
	Byron P. Collins
	Stephen Davis, S.A.E.
	Kerry Freeman
	Martin J. Gunther
	Martin W. Kane
	Dominic Magazino
	John G. Mohan
	Richard J. Rivele
	Ronald L. Sessions
Production Manager	Warren Owens
Assistant	Timothy Frelick

CHILTON BOOK COMPANY Radnor, Pennsylvania

Copyright⁵ Chilton Book Company 1976
Published in Radnor by Chilton Book Company
Chilton Way, Radnor, Pa. 19089   215-687-8200
ISBN: 0-8019-6499-7 Library of Congress Catalog Card No. 76-648878
Manufactured in the U.S.A.

Contents

Car Section

AMERICAN MOTORS

American Motors Section C1

Ambassador C1	Gremlin C1	Javelin C1	Pacer C1
AMX C1	Hornet C1	Matador C1	Rebel C1

CHRYSLER CORPORATION

Barracuda, Challenger, Dart, Valiant, Aspen, Volare Section C105
Chrysler, Cordoba, Imperial Section C421
Dodge, Plymouth Section C511

Aspen C105	Charger SE C511	Duster C105	Polara C511
Barracuda C105	Cordoba C421	Fury, Gran Fury C511	Satellite C511
Belvedere C511	Coronet C511	GTX C511	Swinger C105
Chrysler C421	Dart C105	Imperial C421	Valiant C105
Challenger C105	Dodge C511	Plymouth C511	Volare C105
Charger C511	Demon C105	Monaco; Gran Monaco C511	

FORD MOTOR COMPANY

Bobcat, Mustang II, Pinto Section C148
Comet, Cougar, Elite, Fairlane, Falcon, Granada, Maverick, Monarch, Montego, Mustang, Torino Section C441
Ford, Mercury, Thunderbird Section C549
Lincoln Continental, Mark III, Mark IV, Mark V Section C593

Bobcat C148	Elite C441	Mark IV C593	Monterey C549
Comet C441	Galaxie C549	Mark V C593	Mustang C441
Continental C593	Granada C441	Marquis C549	Mustang II C148
Cougar C441	Lincoln C593	Maverick C441	Pinto C148
Fairlane C441	LTD C549	Mercury C549	Thunderbird C549
Falcon C441	LTD II C441	Monarch C441	Thunderbird, 1977 C441
Ford C549	Mark III C593	Montego C441	Torino, Gran Torino C441

GENERAL MOTORS

Astre, Firebird, Grand AM, GTO, LeMans, Tempest, Ventura, Sunbird Section C48
Buick Section C191
Buick Apollo, Century, Gran Sport, Regal, Skyhawk, Skylark, Special Section C219
Cadillac, Seville Section C252
Cadillac, Eldorado Section C289
Camaro, Chevelle, Monte Carlo, Nova Section C313
Chevette Section C399
Chevrolet, Corvette Section C356
Monza, Vega Section C619
Oldsmobile, Cutlass, F-85, 4-4-2, Omega, Starfire Section C659
Oldsmobile Toronado Section C709
Pontiac, Grand Prix Section C727

Apollo C219	Chevrolet C356	GTO C48	Seville C252
Astre C48	Corvette C356	LeMans C48	Skyhawk C219
Buick C191	Cutlass C659	Malibu C313	Skylark C219
Buick Special C219	Delmont C659	Monte Carlo C313	Starfire C659
Cadillac C252	Eldorado C289	Monza C619	Stingray C356
Camaro C313	F-85 C659	Nova C313	Sunbird C48
Caprice C356	Firebird C48	Oldsmobile C659	Tempest C48
Catalina C727	Grand Am C48	Omega C659	Toronado C709
Century C219	Grand Prix C727	Pontiac C727	Vega C619
Chevelle C313	Grandville C727	Regal C219	Ventura C48
Chevette C399	Gran Sport C219	Riviera C191	

Unit Repair Section

Anti-Freeze Charts U369	Drive Axles, Differential Information U285	Fusebox and Flasher Location Chart U367
Brakes U299	Electronic Ignition Systems U34	Manual Steering U328
Carburetors U50	Emission Controls U145	Manual Transmissions U231
Charging & Starting Systems U2	Engine Rebuilding U209	Metric Conversion Charts U359
Dash Gauges U350	Engine Troubleshooting U194	Power Brakes U299
Diagnostic Charts U355	Front End Alignment U292	Power Steering U328

INDEX

American Motors

Automatic Transmission in-car service	**C32**
Band Adjustments	C35
Downshift Solenoid Removal and Installation	C34
Identification	C33
Kick-down Band Adjustment	C34
Shift Linkage Adjustment	C34
Neutral Safety Switch Replacement and Adjustment	C33
Filter Removal and Installation	C35
Pan Removal and Installation	C35
Brakes	**C41, U299**
Master Cylinder Removal and Installation	C41
Parking Brake Adjustment	C42
Parking Brake Cable Replacement	C42
Power Brake Unit Removal and Installation	C42
Charging System	**C12 U2**
Alternator Removal and Installation	C12
Regulator Removal	C12
Clutch	**C30**
Clutch Removal and Installation	C30
Pedal Free Play Adjustment	C30
Cooling System	
Radiator Removal	C17
Thermostat Removal	C18
Water Pump Removal	C17
Emission Controls	**C18, U145**
Engine	**C21, U209**
Cylinder Head Removal and Installation	C25
ENGINE Removal and Installation	C22
LUBRICATION	C28
Oil Pan Removal and Installation	C28
Oil Pump Service	C29
Rear Main Bearing Oil Seal Removal and Installation	C30
MANIFOLDS	C22
Exhaust Manifold Removal and Installation	C23
Intake Manifold Removal and Installation	C22
Pistons and Rings	**C28**
Piston Removal	C28

Ring Replacement	C28
Rod and Piston Installation	C28
TIMING COVER, CHAIN, AND CAMSHAFT	C25
Camshaft Removal and Installation	27
Timing Case Cover Removal and Installation	C26
Timing Chain and Sprocket Removal and Installation	C26
Valve Timing	C27
Vibration Damper Removal	C25
VALVE SYSTEM	C24
Rocker Assembly Removal and Installation	C24
Valve Guide Service	C24
Front Suspension	**C37, U292**
Ball Joint Inspection and Replacement	C39
Control Arm Removal and Installation	C38
Spring Removal and Installation	C37
Shock Absorber Removal and Installation	C37
Wheel Bearing Inspection and Adjustment	C40
Fuel System	**C15, U50**
Carburetor Adjustments	C15
Dashpot Adjustment	C17
Fuel Filter Removal and Installation	C15
Fuel Pump Removal and Installation	C15
Heater	**C45**
Heater Core Removal and Installation	C45
Heater Blower Removal and Installation	C47
Ignition System	**C13**
Distributor Removal and Installation	C13
Firing Order	C3
Ignition Timing Adjustment	C15
Point Replacement	C13
Instrument Panel	**C43, U350**
Headlight Switch Removal and Installation	C44
Ignition Switch Removal and Installation	C43
Lock Cylinder Removal and Installation	C43
Jacking, Hoisting	**C37**
Manual Transmission	**C31, U231**
Shift Linkage Adjustment	C32
Transmission Removal and Installation	C31

Radio	**C45**
Removal and Installation	C45
Rear Axle	**C36**
Axle Shaft, Bearing, and Seal Removal and Installation	C36
Rear Suspension	**C40**
Spring Removal and Installation	C41
Shock Absorber Removal and Installation	C41
Seat Belts	**C47**
Disabling the Interlock System	C47
Specifications	**C2, U255**
Capacities	C8
Crankshaft and Connecting Rod	C11
Engine Identification Code	C4
General Engine	C5
Piston Clearance	C12
Rings	C11
Serial Number Location	C4
Torque	C11
Tune-Up	C6
Valve	C10
Wheel Alignment	C12
Year Identification	C2
Starting System	**C12, U2**
Starter Removal	C13
Steering	**C42, U328, U336**
Power Steering Pump Removal and Installation	C42
Steering Wheel Removal and Installation	C42
Turn Signal Switch Removal and Installation	C42
U-Joints	**C37**
Driveshaft Removal and Installation	C37
Universal Joint Repairs	C37
Windshield Wipers	**C44**
Motor Removal and Installation	C44
Linkage Removal and Installation	C44

YEAR IDENTIFICATION

SERIES 10, REBEL AND MATADOR

1970 Rebel

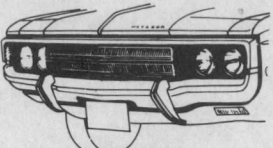

1971 Matador

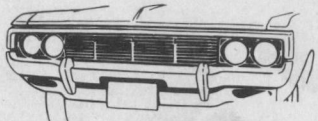

1972 Matador

1973 Matador

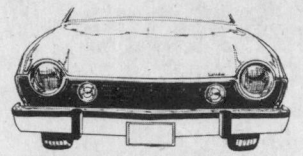

1974-1975 Matador Coupe

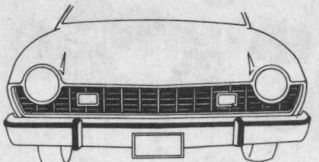

1975 Matador Coupe

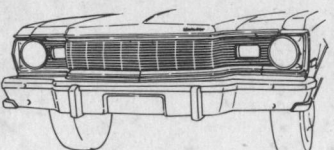

1977 Matador

1977 Matador Coupe

SERIES 80, AMBASSADOR AND MATADOR

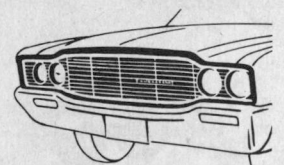

1970 Ambassador

1971 Ambassador

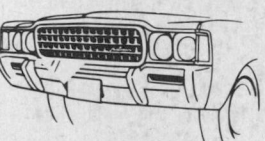

1972 Ambassador

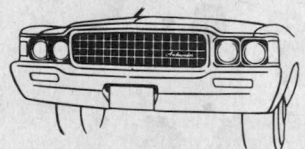

1973 Ambassador

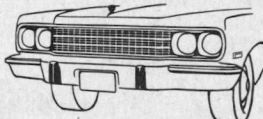

1974 Ambassador

1975 Matador Sedan, Wagon

1976 Matador Sedan, Wagon

SERIES 01 AND 40, GREMLIN AND HORNET

1970-72 Hornet

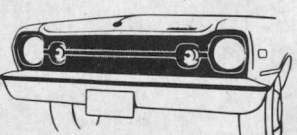

1973 Hornet

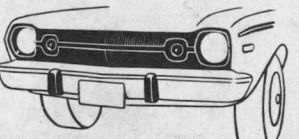

1974 Hornet

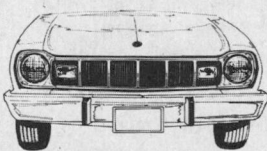

1975-76 Hornet

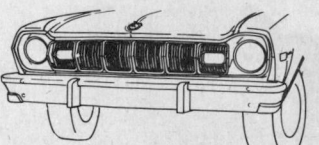

1977 Hornet

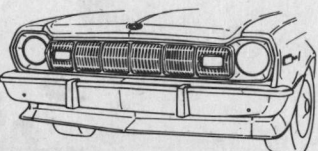

1977 Hornet AMX

1971-72 Gremlin

1973 Gremlin

1974 Gremlin

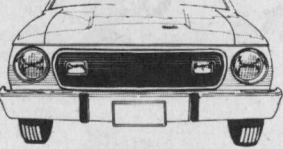

1975 Gremlin

1976 Gremlin

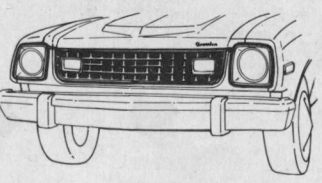

1977 Gremlin

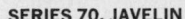

SERIES 70, JAVELIN

1970 Javelin

1971 Javelin SST

1972 Javelin SST

1973 Javelin

1974 Javelin

1971 Javelin AMX

1972 Javelin AMX

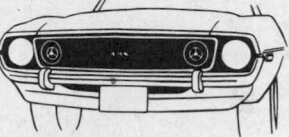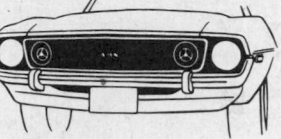

1973 Javelin AMX

1974 Javelin AMX

SERIES 30, AMX

1970 AMX

SERIES 60, PACER

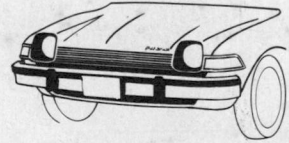

1975 Pacer

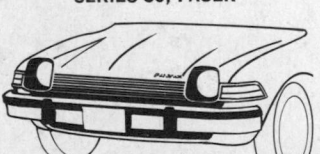

1976 Pacer

1977 Pacer

FIRING ORDER

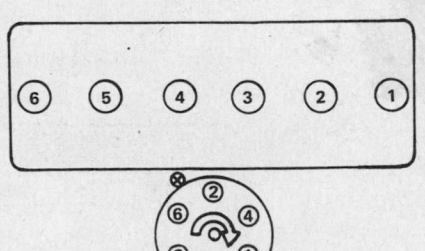

CLOCKWISE ROTATION
1-5-3-6-2-4

6 cylinder
(© American Motors Corp)

FRONT →

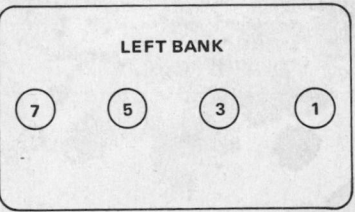

LEFT BANK

7 5 3 1

CLOCKWISE ROTATION
1-8-4-3-6-5-7-2

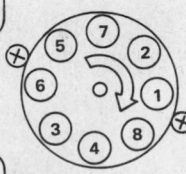

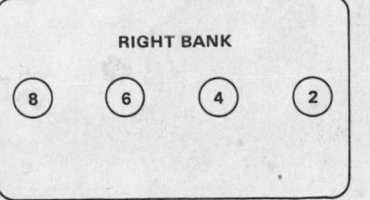

RIGHT BANK

8 6 4 2

FRONT →

V8
(© American Motors Corp)

VEHICLE IDENTIFICATION NUMBER LOCATION

The thirteen digit vehicle identification number is stamped on a plate mounted to the left top of the dashboard, visible through the windshield. This number also can be found on a non-removable safety sticker on the rear of the left front door.

Engine Identification Code

Six—Stamped on right upper side of block.

V8—Stamped on a tag attached to righthand front of valve cover.

NOTE: All V8 engines have their cubic inch displacement cast into block, on both banks, between the first and second core plugs. This is the best way to tell engine displacement, because valve covers are interchangeable between engines.

6 cyl. engine code location
(© American Motors Corp.)

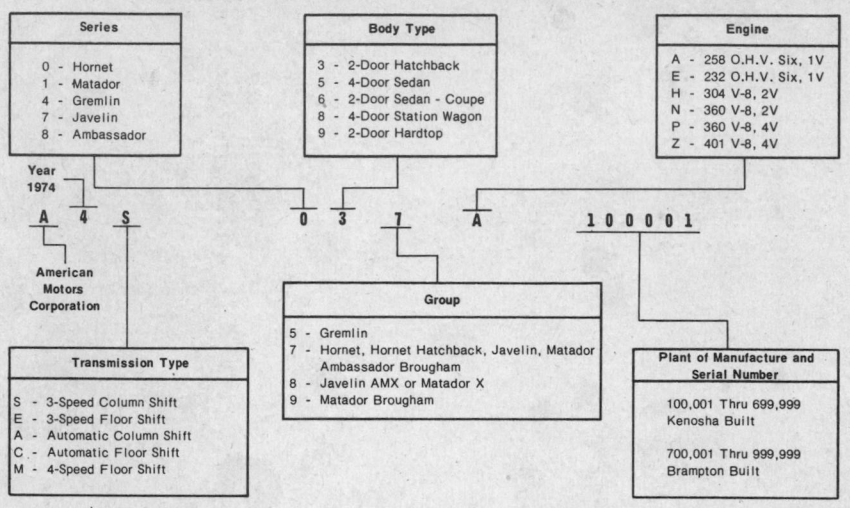

Series

0 -	Hornet
1 -	Matador
4 -	Gremlin
7 -	Javelin
8 -	Ambassador

Body Type

3 -	2-Door Hatchback
5 -	4-Door Sedan
6 -	2-Door Sedan - Coupe
8 -	4-Door Station Wagon
9 -	2-Door Hardtop

Engine

A -	258 O.H.V. Six, 1V
E -	232 O.H.V. Six, 1V
H -	304 V-8, 2V
N -	360 V-8, 2V
P -	360 V-8, 4V
Z -	401 V-8, 4V

Year 1974

A   4   S   0   3   7   A   1 0 0 0 0 1

American Motors Corporation

Transmission Type

S -	3-Speed Column Shift
E -	3-Speed Floor Shift
A -	Automatic Column Shift
C -	Automatic Floor Shift
M -	4-Speed Floor Shift

Group

5 -	Gremlin
7 -	Hornet, Hornet Hatchback, Javelin, Matador Ambassador Brougham
8 -	Javelin AMX or Matador X
9 -	Matador Brougham

Plant of Manufacture and Serial Number

100,001 Thru 699,999
Kenosha Built

700,001 Thru 999,999
Brampton Built

Typical vehicle Identification Number (VIN) decoding chart (© American Motors Corp)

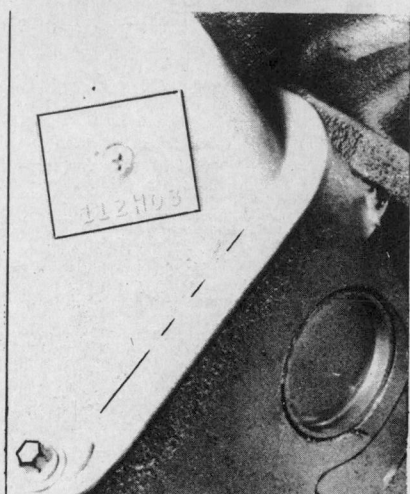

V8 engine code location
(© American Motors Corp)

ENGINE CODE

The engine code is the 4th digit of the engine build code stamped on a machined surface of the cylinder block between No. 2 and No. 3 cylinders on 6 cylinder engines and stamped on a tag attached to the right bank valve cover on V8 engines. In addition, the engine code is the 7th digit of the Vehicle Identification Number. (V.I.N.) The V.I.N. is stamped on a plate located at the left side of the instrument panel visible through the windshield.

Disp	Carb. No. Bbls.	■ Hp	'70	'71	'72	'73	'74	'75	'76	'77
6-Cylinder Models										
199	1	128	A							
232	1	90							E	E
232	1	100			E	E	E	E		
232	1	135		E						
232	1	145	E							
232	2	155	G							
258	1	95							A	A
258	1	110		A	A	A	A			
258	2	120							C	C
258	1	150	A							

Disp	Carb. No. Bbls.	■ Hp	'70	'71	'72	'73	'74	'75	'76	'77
8-Cylinder Models										
304	2	120							H	H
304	2	150			H	H	H	H		
304	2	210	H	H						
360	2	140							N	N
360	2	175			N	N	N	N		
360	4	180							P	P
360	4	195, 220#			P	P	P	P		
360	2	245	N	N						
360	4	290	P	P						
390	4	325	X							
390	4	340	Y							
401	4	215							Z	Z
401	4	225			Z	Z	Z	Z		
401	4	330	Z							

\# With dual exhaust

■ Beginning 1972, horsepower and torque are SAE net figures. They are measured at the rear of the transmission with all accessories installed and operating. Since the figures vary when a given engine is installed in different models, some are representative rather than exact.

GENERAL ENGINE SPECIFICATIONS

Year	Engine No. Cyl. Displacement Cu. In.	Carburetor Type	Horsepower @ rpm ■	Torque @ rpm (ft lbs) ■	Bore and Stroke (in.)	Compression Ratio	Oil Pressure @ 2000 rpm
'70	6-199	1 bbl	128 @ 4400	182 @ 1600	3.750 x 3.000	8.5:1	46
	6-232	1 bbl	145 @ 4300	215 @ 1600	3.750 x 3.500	8.5:1	46
	6-232	2 bbl	155 @ 4400	222 @ 1600	3.750 x 3.500	8.5:1	46
	8-304	2 bbl	210 @ 4400	305 @ 2800	3.750 x 3.440	9.0:1	46
	8-360	2 bbl	245 @ 4400	365 @ 2400	4.080 x 3.440	9.0:1	46
	8-360	4 bbl	290 @ 4800	395 @ 3200	4.080 x 3.440	10.0:1	46
	8-390	4 bbl	325 @ 5000	420 @ 3200	4.165 x 3.574	10.0:1	46
	8-390	4 bbl	340 @ 5100	430 @ 3600	4.165 x 3.574	10.0:1	46
'71	6-232	1 bbl	135 @ 4000	210 @ 1600	3.750 x 3.500	8.0:1	46
	6-258	1 bbl	150 @ 3800	240 @ 1800	3.750 x 3.900	8.0:1	46
	8-304	2 bbl	210 @ 4400	300 @ 2600	3.750 x 3.444	8.4:1	46
	8-360	2 bbl	245 @ 4400	365 @ 2600	4.080 x 3.444	8.5:1	46
	8-360	4 bbl	285 @ 4800	330 @ 5000	4.080 x 3.444	8.5:1	46
	8-401	4 bbl	330 @ 5000	430 @ 3400	4.650 x 3.680	9.5:1	46
'72	6-232	1 bbl	100 @ 3600	185 @ 1800	3.750 x 3.500	8.0:1	46
	6-258	1 bbl	110 @ 3500	195 @ 2000	3.750 x 3.900	8.0:1	46
	8-304	2 bbl	150 @ 4200	245 @ 2500	3.750 x 3.440	8.4:1	46
	8-360	2 bbl	175 @ 4000	285 @ 2400	4.080 x 3.440	8.5:1	46
	8-360	4 bbl	195 @ 4400	295 @ 2900	4.080 x 3.440	8.5:1	46
	8-401	4 bbl	255 @ 4600	345 @ 3300	4.165 x 3.680	8.5:1	46
'73	6-232	1 bbl	100 @ 3600	185 @ 1800	3.750 x 3.500	8.0:1	46
	6-258	1 bbl	110 @ 3500	195 @ 2000	3.750 x 3.900	8.0:1	46
	8-304	2 bbl	150 @ 4200	245 @ 2500	3.750 x 3.440	8.3:1	46
	8-360	2 bbl	175 @ 4000	285 @ 2400	4.080 x 3.440	8.3:1	46
	8-360	4 bbl	195 @ 4400	295 @ 2900	4.080 x 3.440	8.3:1	46
	8-360①	4 bbl	220 @ 4400	315 @ 3100	4.080 x 3.440	8.3:1	46
	8-401	4 bbl	255 @ 4600	345 @ 3300	4.165 x 3.680	8.5:1	46
'74	6-232	1 bbl	100 @ 3600	185 @ 1800	3.750 x 3.500	8.0:1	46
	6-258	1 bbl	110 @ 3500	195 @ 2000	3.750 x 3.900	8.0:1	46
	8-304	2 bbl	150 @ 4200	245 @ 2500	3.750 x 3.440	8.4:1	46
	8-360	2 bbl	175 @ 4000	285 @ 2400	4.080 x 3.440	8.25:1	46
	8-360	4 bbl	195 @ 4400	295 @ 2900	4.080 x 3.440	8.25:1	46
	8-360①	4 bbl	220 @ 4400	315 @ 3100	4.080 x 3.440	8.25:1	46
	8-401	4 bbl	255 @ 4600	345 @ 3300	4.165 x 3.680	8.25:1	46
'75	6-232	1 bbl	100 @ 3600	185 @ 1800	3.750 x 3.500	8.0:1	46
	6-258	1 bbl	110 @ 3500	195 @ 2000	3.750 x 3.900	8.0:1	46
	8-304	2 bbl	150 @ 4200	245 @ 2500	3.750 x 3.440	8.4:1	46
	8-360	2 bbl	175 @ 4000	285 @ 2400	4.080 x 3.440	8.25:1	46
	8-360	4 bbl	195 @ 4400	295 @ 2900	4.080 x 3.440	8.25:1	46
	8-360①	4 bbl	220 @ 4400	315 @ 3100	4.080 x 3.440	8.25:1	46
	8-401②	4 bbl	255 @ 4600	345 @ 3300	4.165 x 3.680	8.25:1	46

GENERAL ENGINE SPECIFICATIONS (Cont'd)

Year	Engine No. Cyl. Displacement Cu. In.	Carburetor Type	Horsepower @ rpm ■	Torque @ rpm (ft lbs) ■	Bore and Stroke (in.)	Compression Ratio	Oil Pressure @ 2000 rpm
'76-'77	6-232	1 bbl	90 @ 3050	170 @ 2000	3.750 x 3.500	8.0:1	46
	6-258	1 bbl	95 @ 3050	180 @ 2100	3.750 x 3.900	8.0:1	46
	6-258	2 bbl	120 @ 3400	200 @ 2000	3.750 x 3.900	8.0:1	46
	8-304	2 bbl	120 @ 3200	220 @ 2200	3.750 x 3.440	8.4:1	46
	8-360	2 bbl	140 @ 3200	260 @ 1600	4.080 x 3.440	8.25:1	46
	8-360	4 bbl	180 @ 3600	280 @ 2800	4.080 x 3.440	8.25:1	46
	8-401②	4 bbl	215 @ 4200	320 @ 2800	4.165 x 3.680	8.25:1	46

■ Beginning 1972, horsepower and torque are SAE net figures. They are measured at the rear of the transmission with all accessories installed and operating. Since the figures vary when a given engine is installed in different models, some are representative rather than exact.
① Dual exhaust
② Police only

Ambassador, Gremlin, Hornet, Rebel, Matador, Pacer

TUNE-UP SPECIFICATIONS

When analyzing compression test results, look for uniformity among cylinders rather than specific pressures.

	ENGINE		SPARK PLUGS		DISTRIBUTOR		IGNITION TIMING (deg) ▲		VALVES	Fuel	IDLE SPEED ● (rpm) ▲	
Year	No. Cyl Displacement (cu in.)	hp	Type §	Gap (in.)	Point Dwell (deg)	Point Gap (in.)	Man Trans ●	Auto Trans	Intake Opens ■ (deg)	Pump Pressure (psi)	Man Trans	Auto Trans *
'70	6-199	128	N-14Y	.035	33	.016	3B	3B	12½	4-5½	600	550
	6-232	145	N-14Y	.035	33	.016	3B	3B	12½	4-5½	600	550
	6-232	155	N-14Y	.035	33	.016	3B	3B	12½	4-5½	600	550
	8-304	210	N-12Y	.035	30	.016	5B	5B	18½	4-5½	650	600
	8-360	245	N-12Y	.035	30	.016	5B	5B	18½	4-5½	650	600
	8-360	290	N-12Y	.035	30	.016	5B	5B	18½	4-5½	650	600
	8-390	325	N-12Y	.035	30	.016	5B	5B	18½	4-5½	650	600
	8-390	340	N-12Y	.035	30	.016	5B	5B	18½	4-5½	650	600
'71	6-232	135	N-12Y	.035	33	.016	3B	5B	12½	4-5½	700	600
	6-258	150	N-12Y	.035	33	.016	5B	5B	12½	4-5½	700	600
	8-304	210	N-12Y	.035	30	.016	2½B	2½B	14¾	4-5½	750	650
	8-360	245	N-12Y	.035	30	.016	2½B	2½B	14¾	4-5½	750	650
	8-360	285	N-12Y	.035	30	.016	2½B	2½B	14¾	4-5½	750	650
	8-401	330	N-12Y	.035	30	.016	2½B	2½B	25½	4-5½	750	650
'72	6-232	100	N-12Y	.035	33	.016	5B(3B)	5B(3B)	12	4-5½	600(700)	550(600)
	6-258	110	N-12Y	.035	33	.016	5B(3B)	5B(3B)	12	4-5½	600(700)	550(600)
	8-304	150	N-12Y	.035	30	.016	5B	5B	14¾	4-5½	750	650(700)
	8-360	175	N-12Y	.035	30	.016	5B	5B	14¾	4-5½	750	700
	8-360	195	N-12Y	.035	30	.016	5B	5B	14¾	4-5½	750	700
	8-401	255	N-12Y	.035	30	.016	5B	5B	25½	4-5½	750	650(700)
'73	6-232	100	N-12Y	.035	33	.016	5B(3B)	5B(3B)	12	4-5½	700	600
	6-258	110	N-12Y	.035	33	.016	5B(3B)	5B(3B)	12	4-5½	700	600
	8-304	150	N-12Y	.035	30	.016	5B	5B	14¾	4-5½	750	700
	8-360	175	N-12Y	.035	30	.016	5B	5B	14¾	4-5½	750	700
	8-360	195	N-12Y	.035	30	.016	5B	5B	14¾	4-5½	750	700
	8-401	255	N-12Y	.035	30	.016	5B	5B	25½	4-5½	750	700

TUNE-UP SPECIFICATIONS (Cont'd)

When analyzing compression test results, look for uniformity among cylinders rather than specific pressures.

Year	No. Cyl Displacement (cu in.)	hp	Type §	Gap (in.)	Point Dwell (deg)	Point Gap (in.)	Man Trans •	Auto Trans	Intake Opens ■ (deg)	Fuel Pump Pressure (psi)	Man Trans	Auto Trans *
'74	6-232	100	N-12Y	.035	33	.016	5B(3B)	5B(3B)	12	4-5½	700	600
	6-258	110	N-12Y	.035	33	.016	5B(3B)	5B(3B)	12	4-5½	700	600
	8-304	150	N-12Y	.035	30	.016	5B	5B (2½ B)	14¾	5-6½	750	700
	8-360	175	N-12Y	.035	30	.016	5B	5B	14¾	5-6½	750	700
	8-360	195	N-12Y	.035	30	.016	5B	5B	14¾	5-6½	750	700
	8-401	255	N-12Y	.035	30	.016	5B	5B	25½	5-6½	750	700
'75	6-232	100	N-12Y	.035	electronic		5B	5B	12	4-5	600	550(700)
	6-258	110	N-12Y	.035	electronic		3B	3B	12	4-5	600	550(700)
	8-304	150	N-12Y	.035	electronic		5B	5B	14¾	5-6½	750	700
	8-360	175	N-12Y	.035	electronic		5B	5B	14¾	5-6½	750	700
	8-360	195	N-12Y	.035	electronic		5B	5B	14¾	5-6½	750	700
	8-401	255	N-12Y	.035	electronic		5B	5B	25½	5-6½	750	700
'76	6-232	90	N-12Y	.035	electronic		8B	8B	12	4-5	850	550(700)
	6-258	95	N-12Y	.035	electronic		6B	8B	12	4-5	850①	550(700)
	6-258	120	N-12Y	.035	electronic		6B	8B	12	4-5	850	550(700)
	8-304	120	N-12Y	.035	electronic		5B	10B(5B)	14¾	5-6½	750	700
	8-360	140	N-12Y	.035	electronic		—	10B(5B)	14¾	5-6½	—	700
	8-360	180	N-12Y	.035	electronic		—	10B(5B)	14¾	5-6½	—	700
	8-401	215	N-12Y	.035	electronic		—	10B(5B)	25½	5-6½	—	700
'77	All				See Underhood Specifications Sticker							

▲ See text for procedure
• Figure in parentheses indicates California engine
■ All figures Before Top Dead Center
* With transmission in Drive
§ All spark plug listings are original equipment numbers
B Before Top Dead Center

TDC Top Dead Center (zero degrees)
  — Not applicable
① 600 rpm for Matador coupe and sedan
NOTE: The underhood specifications sticker often reflects tune-up specification changes made in production. Sticker figures must be used if they disagree with those in this chart.

AMX-Javelin   TUNE-UP SPECIFICATIONS

When analyzing compression test results, look for uniformity among cylinders rather than specific pressures.

Year	No. Cyl Displacement (cu in.)	hp	Type §	Gap (in.)	Point Dwell (deg)	Point Gap (in.)	Man Trans •	Auto Trans	Intake Opens ■ (deg)	Fuel Pump Pressure (psi)	Man Trans •	Auto Trans
'70	6-232	145	N-14Y	.035	31-34	.016	3B	3B	12½	4-5½	600	550
	8-304	210	N-12Y	.035	29-31	.016	5B	5B	18½	5-6½	650	600
	8-360	245	N-12Y	.035	29-31	.016	5B	5B	18½	5-6½	650	600
	8-360	290	N-12Y	.035	29-31	.016	5B	5B	18½	5-6½	650	600
	8-390	325	N-12Y	.035	29-31	.016	TDC①	TDC①	18½	5-6½	650	600
'71	6-232	135	N-12Y	.035	31-34	.016	3B	5B	12½	4-5½	700	600
	6-258	150	N-12Y	.035	31-34	.016	—	5B	12½	4-5½	—	600
	8-304	210	N-12Y	.035	29-31	.016	2½B	2½B	14¾	5-6½	750	650
	8-360	245	N-12Y	.035	29-31	.016	2½B	2½B	14¾	5-6½	750	650
	8-360	285	N-12Y	.035	29-31	.016	2½B	2½B	14¾	5-6½	750	650
	8-401	330	N-12Y	.035	29-31	.016	2½B	2½B	25½	5-6½	750	650

TUNE-UP SPECIFICATIONS (Cont'd)

When analyzing compression test results, look for uniformity among cylinders rather than specific pressures.

Year	ENGINE No. Cyl Displacement (cu in.)	hp	SPARK PLUGS Type §	Gap (in.)	DISTRIBUTOR Point Dwell (deg)	DISTRIBUTOR Point Gap (in.)	IGNITION TIMING (deg) ▲ Man Trans ●	IGNITION TIMING (deg) ▲ Auto Trans	VALVES Intake Opens ■ (deg)	Fuel Pump Pressure (psi)	IDLE SPEED (rpm) ▲ Man Trans ●	IDLE SPEED (rpm) ▲ Auto Trans
'72	6-232	100	N-12Y	.035	31-34	.016	5B	5B	12½	4-5½	600(700)	550(600)
	6-258	110	N-12Y	.035	31-34	.016	—	3B	12½	4-5½	—	550(600)
	8-304	150	N-12Y	.035	29-31	.016	5B	5B	14¾	5-6½	750	650(700)
	8-360	175	N-12Y	.035	29-31	.016	—	5B	14¾	5-6½	—	700
	8-360	195	N-12Y	.035	29-31	.016	5B	5B	14¾	5-6½	750	700
	8-401	255	N-12Y	.035	29-31	.016	5B	5B	25½	5-6½	750	650(700)
'73	6-232	100	N-12Y	.035	31-34	.016	5B	5B	12½	4-5½	700	600
	6-258	110	N-12Y	.035	31-34	.016	—	3B	12½	4-5½	—	600
	8-304	150	N-12Y	.035	29-31	.016	5B	5B	14¾	5-6½	750	700
	8-360	175	N-12Y	.035	29-31	.016	—	5B	14¾	5-6½	—	700
	8-360	190	N-12Y	.035	29-31	.016	5B	5B	14¾	5-6½	750	700
	8-401	255	N-12Y	.035	29-31	.016	5B	5B	25½	5-6½	750	700
'74	6-232	100	N-12Y	.035	31-34	.016	5B	5B	12½	4-5½	600(700)	550(600)
	6-258	110	N-12Y	.035	31-34	.016	—	3B	12½	4-5½	—	550(600)
	8-304	150	N-12Y	.035	29-31	.016	5B	5B (2½ B)	14¾	5-6½	750	650(700)
	8-360	175	N-12Y	.035	29-31	.016	—	5B	14¾	5-6½	—	700
	8-360	190	N-12Y	.035	29-31	.016	5B	5B	14¾	5-6½	750	700
	8-401	255	N-12Y	.035	29-31	.016	5B	5B	25½	5-6½	750	650(700)

▲ See text for procedure
■ All figures Before Top Dead Center
● Figure in parentheses indicates California engine
§ All spark plug listings are original equipment numbers
NOTE: The underhood specifications sticker often reflects tune-up specification changes made in production. Sticker figures must be used if they disagree with those in this chart.

① For vehicles prior to engine code No. 209X26, adjust ignition timing to 5 degrees before Top Dead Center
B Before Top Dead Center
TDC Top Dead Center
— Not applicable

CAPACITIES

Year	ENGINE No. Cyl Displacement (cu in.)	MODEL	Engine Crankcase Add 1 Qt For New Filter	TRANSMISSION Pts To Refill After Draining Manual 3-Speed	TRANSMISSION Manual 4-Speed	TRANSMISSION Automatic	Drive Axle (pts)	Gasoline Tank (gals)	COOLING SYSTEM (qts) With Heater	COOLING SYSTEM With A/C
'70	6-199		4	1.5	—	18.5	3	See	10.5	10.5
	6-232		4	1.5①	—	18.5	3	chart	10.5	10.5
	8-304		4	3	2.5	18.5	4	below	14	14
	8-360		4	—	2.5	20	4		13	13
	8-390		4	—	2.5	20	4		13	13
'71	6-232		4	1.5①	—	18.5	3③		10.5	10.5
	6-258		4	2.5	—	18.5	3③		10.5	10.5
	8-304		4	2.5	2.5	18.5	4		14	14
	8-360		4	3	2.5	20	4		13	13
	8-401		4	—	2.5	20	4		13	13
'72	6-232		4	1.5①	—	17	3③		10.5	10.5
	6-258		4	2.5	—	17	3③		10.5	10.5
	8-304		4	2.5	2.5	17	4		14	14
	8-360		4	2.5	2.5	19	4		13	13
	8-401		4	2.5	2.5	19	4		13	13

CAPACITIES (Cont'd)

Year	ENGINE No. Cyl. Displacement (cu in.)	MODEL	Engine Crankcase Add 1 Qt For New Filter	TRANSMISSION Pts To Refill After Draining			Drive Axle (pts)	Gasoline Tank (gals)	COOLING SYSTEM (qts)	
				Manual		Automatic			With Heater	With A/C
				3-Speed	4-Speed					
'73	6-232		4	2.5	—	17	3③		10.5	10.5
	6-258		4	2.5	—	17	3③		10.5	10.5
	8-304		4	2.5	2.5	17	4		14	14
	8-360		4	2.5	2.5	19	4		13	14
	8-401		4	2.5	2.5	19	4		13	14
'74	6-232		4	2.5	—	17	3③		11	11.5
	6-258		4	2.5	—	17	3③		11	11.5
	8-304		4	2.5	2.5	17	4		16④	16④
	8-360		4	2.5	2.5	19	4		15.5⑤	15.5⑤
	8-401		4	2.5	2.5	19	4		15.5⑤	15.5⑤
'75	6-232		4	3.5②	—	17	3③		11⑧	11.5⑥
	6-258		4	3.5②	—	17	3③		11⑧	11.5⑥
	8-304		4	3.5	—	17	4		16.5④	16④⑦
	8-360		4	—	—	19	4		15.5⑤	15.5⑤
	8-401		4	—	—	19	4		15.5⑤	15.5⑤
'76-'77	6-232	Gremlin, Hornet	4	2.5②	—	17	3		11	11.5
	6-232	Pacer	4	3.5②	3.5	17	3		14	14
	6-258	Gremlin, Hornet	4	2.5②	—	17	3		11	11.5
	6-258	Pacer	4	3.5②	3.5	17	3		14	14
	6-258	Matador coupe	4	3.5	—	17	4		11	13.5
	6-258	Matador sedan, wagon	4	3.5	—	17	4		11	11.5
	8-304	Gremlin, Hornet	4	3.5	—	17	4		16	16
	8-304	Matador coupe	4	3.5	—	17	4		18.5	18.5
	8-304	Matador sedan, wagon	4	3.5	—	17	4		16.5	16.5⑨
	8-360, 401	Matador coupe	4	—	—	19	4		17.5	17.5
	8-360, 401	Matador sedan, wagon	4	—	—	19	4		15.5	15.5⑨

① Fully synchronized transmission 2.25 pts
② 4 pts with overdrive
③ 8.875 ring gear—4 pts
④ Matador Coupe—18.5 qts, with coolant recovery system—20.5 qts; Hornet and Gremlin—16 qts
⑤ Matador Coupe—17.5 qts, with coolant recovery system—19.5 qts
⑥ 13.5 qts in Matador Coupe, 15.5 qts in Matador Coupe with coolant recovery system, 14.5 qts in Pacer
⑦ 16.5 qts in Matador Sedan and Wagon
⑧ 14.5 qts in Pacer
⑨ 2 qts more with coolant recovery system
—— Not applicable

GASOLINE TANK CAPACITIES (gals)

Model	'70	'71	'72	'73	'74	'75	'76	'77
Ambassador	21.5	19.5	19.5	19.5	24.9			
AMX	19							
Javelin	19	16	16	16	16			
Rebel	21.5							
Gremlin		21	21	21	21	21	21	21
Hornet		16	16	16	16	22	22	22
Matador		19.5	19.5	19.5	24.9	24.5	24.5	24.5
Matador Wagon	19	17	20	20	21	21	21	21
Pacer						22	22	22

VALVE SPECIFICATIONS

Year	Engine No. Cyl. Displacement (cu in.)	Seat Angle (deg) ■	Face Angle (deg) ●	Spring Test Pressure (lbs @ in.)	Spring Installed Height (in.)	STEM TO GUIDE Clearance (in.) Intake	Exhaust	STEM Diameter (in.) Intake	Exhaust
'70	6-199	45	44	195 @ 1.44	1 13/16	.0010-.0030	.0010-.0027	.3720	.3720
	6-232	45	44	195 @ 1.44	1 13/16	.0010-.0030	.0010-.0027	.3720	.3720
	8-304	45	44	200 @ 1.39	1 13/16	.0010-.0030	.0010-.0030	.3720	.3720
	8-360	45	44	200 @ 1.39	1 13/16	.0010-.0030	.0010-.0030	.3720	.3720
	8-390	45	44	189 @ 1.37	1 13/16	.0010-.0030	.0010-.0030	.3720	.3720
	8-390①	45	44	250 @ 1.33	1 13/16	.0010-.0030	.0010-.0030	.3720	.3720
'71	6-232	45	44	195 @ 1.44	1 13/16	.0010-.0030	.0010-.0027	.3720	.3720
	6-258	45	44	195 @ 1.44	1 13/16	.0010-.0030	.0010-.0027	.3720	.3720
	8-304	45	44	189 @ 1.37	1 13/16	.0010-.0030	.0010-.0030	.3720	.3720
	8-360	45	44	189 @ 1.37	1 13/16	.0010-.0030	.0010-.0030	.3720	.3720
	8-401	45	44	189 @ 1.37	1 13/16	.0010-.0030	.0010-.0030	.3720	.3720
	8, All①	45	44	250 @ 1.33	1 13/16	.0010-.0030	.0010-.0030	.3720	.3720
'72	6-232	45	44	195 @ 1.44	1 13/16	.0010-.0030	.0010-.0027	.3720	.3720
	6-258	45	44	195 @ 1.44	1 13/16	.0010-.0030	.0010-.0027	.3720	.3720
	8-304	45	44	218 @ 1.37	1 13/16	.0010-.0030	.0010-.0030	.3720	.3720
	8-360	45	44	218 @ 1.37	1 13/16	.0010-.0030	.0010-.0030	.3720	.3720
	8-401	45	44	218 @ 1.37	1 13/16	.0010-.0030	.0010-.0030	.3720	.3720
	8, All①	45	44	250 @ 1.33	1 13/16	.0010-.0030	.0010-.0030	.3720	.3720
'73	6-232	45	44	195 @ 1.44	1 13/16	.0010-.0030	.0010-.0027	.3720	.3720
	6-258	45	44	195 @ 1.44	1 13/16	.0010-.0030	.0010-.0027	.3720	.3720
	8-304	45	44	218 @ 1.37	1 13/16	.0010-.0030	.0010-.0030	.3720	.3720
	8-360	45	44	218 @ 1.37	1 13/16	.0010-.0030	.0010-.0030	.3720	.3720
	8-401	45	44	218 @ 1.37	1 13/16	.0010-.0030	.0010-.0030	.3720	.3720
'74	6-232	45	44	195 @ 1.44	1 13/16	.0010-.0030	.0010-.0027	.3720	.3720
	6-258	45	44	195 @ 1.44	1 13/16	.0010-.0030	.0010-.0027	.3720	.3720
	8-304	45	44	213 @ 1.37	1 13/16	.0010-.0030	.0010-.0030	.3720	.3720
	8-360	45	44	213 @ 1.37	1 13/16	.0010-.0030	.0010-.0030	.3720	.3720
	8-401	45	44	213 @ 1.37	1 13/16	.0010-.0030	.0010-.0030	.3720	.3720
'75	6-232	44.5	44	195 @ 1.44	1 13/16	.0010-.0030	.0010-.0027	.3720	.3720
	6-258	44.5	44	195 @ 1.44	1 13/16	.0010-.0030	.0010-.0027	.3720	.3720
	8-304	44.5	44	213 @ 1.38	1 13/16	.0010-.0030	.0010-.0030	.3720	.3720
	8-360	44.5	44	213 @ 1.38②	1 13/16	.0010-.0030	.0010-.0030	.3720	.3720
	8-401	44.5	44	223 @ 1.35②	1 13/16	.0010-.0030	.0010-.0030	.3720	.3720
'76-'77	6-232, 258	44.5	44	195 @ 1.44	1 13/16	.0010-.0030	.0010-.0027	.3720	.3720
	8-304, 360	44.5	44	213 @ 1.38②	1 13/16	.0010-.0030	.0010-.0030	.3720	.3720
	8-401	44.5	44	223 @ 1.35②	1 13/16	.0010-.0030	.0010-.0030	.3720	.3720

● Exhaust valve face angles are shown
  All intake valve face angles are 29°
■ Exhaust valve seat angles are shown
  All intake valve seat angles are 30°
① With high-performance camshaft; optional 1970,
  dealer-installed 1971-72

② 1974-75 Police 360, 401:
intake—270 @ 1.38;
exhaust—270 @ 1.19,
exhaust installed height—1⅝ in.

TORQUE SPECIFICATIONS
All readings in ft lbs

Year	Engine	Cylinder Head Bolts	Rod Bearing Bolts	Main Bearing Bolts	Crankshaft Vibration Damper Bolt	Crankshaft Flywheel to Bolts	MANIFOLD Intake	MANIFOLD Exhaust
'70-'77	6-All	80③	26-30	75-85	48-64	95-120	18-28	18-28
	8-All	100-120	①	90-105	48-64②	95-120	37-47	20-30

① 1970-75 304, 360—26-30; All 390, 401—35-40; 1976 and later 304, 360—30-35 ft. lbs.
② 1975 and later—70-90 ft. lbs.
③ 1973 and later—95-115 ft. lbs.

CRANKSHAFT AND CONNECTING ROD SPECIFICATIONS
All measurements are given in inches

Year	Engine	CRANKSHAFT Main Brg. Journal Dia	CRANKSHAFT Main Brg. Oil Clearance	Shaft End-Play	Thrust on No.	CONNECTING ROD Journal Diameter	CONNECTING ROD Oil Clearance	Side Clearance
'70-'71	6-All	2.4986-2.5001	.001-.002	.002-.007	3	2.0934-2.0955	.001-.002	.008-.010
'72-'77	6-All	2.4986-2.5001	.001-.003	.002-.007	3	2.0934-2.0955	.001-.003	.005-.014
'70-'71	8-All	2.7474-2.5001①	.001-.002②	.003-.008	3	③	.001-.002	.009-.015
'72-'73	8-All	2.7474-2.5001①	.001-.002②	.003-.008	3	③	.001-.002	.009-.015
'74	8-All	2.7474-2.5001①	.001-.003	.003-.008	3	③	.001-.002	.009-.015
'75-'77	8-All	2.7474-2.5001①	.001-.003	.003-.008	3	③	.001-.003	.006-.018

① No. 5—2.7464-2.7479
② Rear main—.002-.003
③ 390, 401 through 1974—2.2471-2.2485; All 304, 360—2.0934-2.0955; 1975 and later 401—2.2464-2.2485

RING GAP
All measurements are given in inches

Year	Engine	Top Compression	Bottom Compression
'70-'77	All engines	.010-.020	.010-.020

Year	Engine	Oil Control
'70-'71	All engines	.015-.055
'72-'77	6-232, 258, 8-304	.010-.025
'72-'77	8-360	.015-.045
'72-'77	8-401	.015-.055

RING SIDE CLEARANCE
All measurements are given in inches

Year	Engine	Top Compression	Bottom Compression
'70-'71	6-199, 232, 258	.0015-.0035	.0015-.0035
'70-'71	8-304, 360, 390, 401	.002-.004	.002-.004
'72-'73	All engines	.0015-.0035	.0015-.0035
'74-'77	6-232, 258	.0015-.0030	.0015-.0030
'74-'77	8-304	.0015-.0035	.0015-.0030
'74-'77	8-360, 401	.0015-.0030	.0015-.0035

Year	Engine	Oil Control
'70-'71	All engines	.0000-.0050
'72-'77	6-232, 258, 8-304	.0011-.0080
'72-'77	8-360, 401	.0000-.0070

PISTON CLEARANCE

Year	Engine	Piston-to-Bore Clearance (in.)
'70	6-199, 232	.0005-.0013
	V8-304, 390	.0010-.0018
	V8-360	.0012-.0020
'71	6-232, 258	.0005-.0013
	V8-304, 401	.0010-.0018
	V8-360	.0012-.0020

Year	Engine	Piston-to-Bore Clearance (in.)
'72-'77	6-232, 258	.0009-.0017
	V8-304, 401	.0010-.0018②
	V8-360	.0012-.0020①

① 1974 and later police 360—.0016-.0024
② 1974 and later police 401—.0014-.0022

WHEEL ALIGNMENT SPECIFICATIONS

Year	Model	CASTER Range (deg)	CASTER Pref Setting (deg)	CAMBER Range (deg)	CAMBER Pref Setting (deg)	Toe-in (in.)	Steering Axis Inclin. (deg)	WHEEL PIVOT RATIO (deg) Inner Wheel	WHEEL PIVOT RATIO (deg) Outer Wheel
'70-'71	All	½P to 1½P	1P	⅜N to ⅜P	0	¹⁄₁₆ to ³⁄₁₆	7¾	25	22
'72	All	½P to 1½P	1P	①	②	¹⁄₁₆ to ³⁄₁₆	7¾	25	22
'73-'74	Hornet, Gremlin	½N to ½P	0	①	②	¹⁄₁₆ to ³⁄₁₆	7¾	25	22
	Matador, Javelin, Ambassador	½P to 1½P	1P	①	②	¹⁄₁₆ to ³⁄₁₆	7¾	25	22
'75-'77	Hornet, Gremlin	½N to ½P	0	①	②	¹⁄₁₆ to ³⁄₁₆	7¾	25	22
	Matador, Pacer	½P to 1½P	1P	①	②	¹⁄₁₆ to ³⁄₁₆	7¾	25	22

① Left: ⅛P to ⅝P; Right: 0 to ½P
② Left ⅜P; Right: ⅛P
N Negative   P Positive

CHARGING SYSTEM

Information on alternator and regulator repair and troubleshooting can be found in the Unit Repair Section.

Regulator Removal

Disconnect plug to the regulator. Remove the metal screws which hold the regulator to the sheet metal and lift off the regulator.

NOTE: Starting 1975, the Delco-Remy alternator has a solid state voltage regulator built into the end frame. The unit is integral with the alternator assembly and cannot be adjusted.

Alternator Removal and Installation

1. Disconnect battery cables.
2. Disconnect alternator wires or plug, then loosen adjusting bolt.
3. Remove V-belt, mounting bolts and alternator.
4. To install, reverse removal procedure.
5. There are several methods used for tightening the belt. Some alternator brackets have a hole through which you can insert a bar to pry out on the front alternator housing, others have a hole into which you can insert a ½ in. square socket drive to pullout on the alternator, and others have a square boss around the adjusting bolt which takes a 1 in. open end wrench. If there are none of these systems, use a bar to pry against the front alternator housing. The longest run of belt should deflect about ½ in. under moderate thumb pressure.

Alternator Precautions

Caution Since the alternator and regulator are designed for use on only one polarity system, the following precautions must be observed:

1. The polarity of the battery, generator and regulator must be matched and considered before making any electrical connections in the system.
2. When connecting a booster battery, be sure to connect the negative battery terminals respectively and the positive battery terminals respectively.
3. When connecting a charger to the battery, connect the charger positive lead to the battery positive terminal. Connect the charger negative lead to the battery negative terminal.
4. Never operate the alternator on open circuit. Be sure that all connections in the circuit are clean and tight.
5. Do not short across or ground any of the terminals on the alternator regulator.
6. Do not attempt to polarize the alternator.
7. Do not use test lamps of more than 12 volts for checking diode continuity.
8. Avoid long soldering times when replacing diodes or transistors. Prolonged heat is damaging to these units.
9. Disconnect the battery ground terminal when servicing any AC system. This will prevent the possibility of accidental reversing of polarity.
10. If electronic welding equipment is used on the car, be sure to completely disconnect the alternator.

STARTING SYSTEM

American Motors cars are equipped with an integral positive engagement drive starter and a separate starter relay.

Starter repair procedures can be found in the Unit Repair Section.

Starter Removal

6 Cylinder

Disconnect the battery lead from the starter and the solenoid lead from the starter. From underneath the vehicle, remove the bolts which hold the starter to the bell housing and lift off the starter.

V8

Disconnect the battery wire and the solenoid wire at the starter. From underneath the vehicle, remove the bolts which hold the starter to the flywheel housing and lift off the starter.

IGNITION SYSTEM

On all cars with emission control systems, the point type distributor uses a cam lubricator. The lubricator should be rotated one-half turn at every tune-up and replaced at every other tune-up. Never oil the lubricator; always replace it at the proper interval. It is a good idea, however, to apply a small amount of high-melting-point lubricant to the breaker cam itself, when the points are replaced.

Starting 1975, all American Motors cars are equipped with the Breakerless Inductive Discharge (BID) ignition system. The system consists of an electronic ignition control unit, a standard type ignition coil, a distributor that contains an electronic sensor and trigger wheel instead of a cam, breaker points and condenser, and the usual high tension wires and spark plugs. There are no contacting (and thus wearing) surfaces between the trigger wheel and the sensor. The dwell angle remains the same and

never requires adjustment. The dwell angle is determined by the control unit and the angle between the trigger wheel spokes. For more information and repair procedures, see the "Electronic Ignition systems" Unit Repair Section.

Distributor Removal

1. Remove the distributor cap, mark the position of the rotor relative to the distributor body and mark the body relative to the block. Remove the carburetor air cleaner if necessary, the distributor primary wire and the distributor vacuum lines.
2. Remove the hold-down bolt and take the distributor up out of the block.

The rotor and body are marked so that they can be returned to the position from which they were removed. Do not turn the engine after the distributor has been taken off.

Distributor Installation

Engine Not Disturbed— Timing Retained

Install the distributor in the reverse order of removal. Be sure that the rotor and distributor are installed with the marks, which were made during removal, in alignment. Adjust the timing as required.

Engine Disturbed—Timing Lost

If the rotor position was not noted during removal, or if the engine was cranked with the distributor out, install it as follows:

1. Remove the spark plug from the no. one cylinder and position a compression gauge or a thumb over the spark plug hole.
2. Slowly crank the engine, until compression pressure starts to build up.
3. Continue cranking the engine so that the timing mark or pointer aligns with the TDC mark.
4. Install the distributor with its drive meshed, so that the rotor points to the no. one terminal on the distributor cap with engine at TDC.
5. Complete installation in the reverse order of removal and adjust the timing as required.

Breaker Points and Condenser Replacement, Dwell Angle Adjustment

The usual procedure is to replace the condenser each time the point set is replaced. Although this is not always necessary, it is easy to do at this time and the cost is negligible. Every time you adjust or replace the breaker points, the ignition timing must be checked and, if necessary, adjusted. No special equipment other

than a feeler gauge is required for point replacement or adjustment, but a dwell meter is strongly advised.

1. Push down on the spring-loaded V8 distributor cap retaining screws and give them a half-turn to release. Unscrew the captive six-cylinder cap retaining screws. Remove the cap. You might have to unclip or detach some or all of the plug wires to remove the cap.
2. Clean the cap inside and out with a clean rag. Check for cracks and carbon paths. A carbon path shows up as a dark line, usually from one of the cap sockets or inside terminals to a ground. Check the condition of the carbon button inside the center of the cap and the inside terminals. Replace the cap as necessary.
3. Pull the six-cylinder rotor up and off the shaft. Remove the two screws and lift the round V8 rotor off. There is less danger of losing the screws if you just back them out all the way and lift them off with the rotor. Clean off the metal outer tip if it is burned or corroded. Don't file it. Replace the rotor as necessary or if one came with your tune-up kit.
4. The factory says that the points don't need to be replaced if metal transfer from one contact to the other doesn't exceed 0.020 in. However, experience shows that it is more economical and reliable in the long run to replace the point set while the distributor is open, than to have to do this at a later (and possibly more inconvenient) time.
5. Pull off the two wire terminals from the point assembly. One wire comes from the condenser and the other comes from within the distributor. The terminals are usually held in place by spring tension only. There might be a clamp screw securing the terminals on some older versions. There is now available a one-piece point/condenser assembly. Loosen the point set hold-down screws(s). Be very careful not to drop any of these little screws inside the distributor. If this happens, the distributor will probably have to be removed to get at the screw. If the hold-down screw is lost elsewhere, it must be replaced with one that is no longer than the original to avoid interference with the distributor workings. Remove the point set, even if it is to be reused.
6. If the points are to be reused, clean them with a few strokes of a special point file. This is done with the points removed to prevent tiny metal filings getting into the distributor.
7. Loosen the condenser hold-down

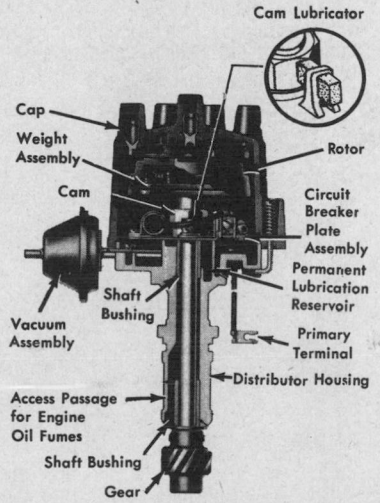

Cam Lubricator
Cap
Weight Assembly
Cam
Rotor
Circuit Breaker Plate Assembly
Permanent Lubrication Reservoir
Shaft Bushing
Vacuum Assembly
Primary Terminal
Distributor Housing
Access Passage for Engine Oil Fumes
Shaft Bushing
Gear

Distributor—all V8 through 1974
(© American Motors Corp.)

screw and slide the condenser out of the clamp. This will save you a struggle with the clamp, condenser, and the tiny screw when you install the new one. If you have the type of clamp that is permanently fastened to the condenser, remove the screw and the condenser. Don't lose the screw.

8. Attend to the distributor cam lubricator. If you have the round kind, turn it around on its shaft at the first tune-up and replace it at the second. If you have the long kind, switch ends at the first tune-up and replace it at the second. On models beginning 1971, the lubricator is supposed to be replaced at every tune-up.

NOTE: Don't oil or grease the lubricator. The foam is impregnated with a special lubricant.

If you didn't get any lubricator at all, or if it looks like someone took it off, don't worry. You don't really need it. Just rub a matchhead size dab of high melting point grease on the cam lobes.

9. Install the new condenser. If you left the clamp in place, just slide the new condenser into the clamp.

10. Replace the point set and tighten the screws on a V8. Leave the screw slightly loose on a six. Replace the two wire terminals, making sure that the wires don't interfere with anything. Some V8 distributors have a ground wire that must go under one of the screws.

11. Check that the contacts meet squarely. If they don't, bend the tab supporting the fixed contact.

NOTE: If you are installing preset points on a V8, go ahead to Step 16. If they are preset, it will say so on the package.

12. Turn the engine until a high point on the cam that opens the points contacts the rubbing block on the point arm. You can turn the engine by hand if you can get a wrench on the crankshaft pulley nut, or you can grasp the fan belt and turn the engine with the spark plugs removed.

CAUTION: *If you try turning the engine by hand, be very careful not to get your fingers pinched in the pulleys.*

On a stick-shift car, you can push it forward in High gear. Another alternative is to bump the starter switch or use a remote starter switch.

13. On a six, there is a screwdriver slot near the contacts. Insert a screwdriver and lever the points open or closed until they appear to be at about the gap specified in the "Tune-Up Specifications." On a V8, simply insert a 1/8 in. allen wrench into the adjustment screw and turn. The wrench

sometimes comes with a tune-up kit.

14. Insert the correct size feeler gauge and adjust the gap until you can push the gauge in and out between the contacts with a slight drag, but without disturbing the point arm. Check by trying the gauges 0.001-0.002 larger and smaller than the setting size. The larger one should disturb the point arm, while the smaller one should not drag at all. Tighten the six-cylinder point set holddown screw. Recheck the gap, because it often changes when the screw is tightened.

15. After all the point adjustments are complete, pull a white business card through (between) the contacts to remove any traces of oil. Oil will cause rapid contact burning.

NOTE: You can adjust six-cylinder dwell at this point, if you wish. Refer to Step 18.

16. Push the rotor firmly down into place. It will only go one way. Tighten the V8 rotor screws. If the rotor is not installed properly, it will probably break when the starter is operated.

17. Replace the distributor cap.

18. If a dwell meter is available, check the dwell. The dwell meter hookup is shown in the "Engine Troubleshooting" Section.

NOTE: This hookup does not necessarily apply to electronic, capacitive discharge, or other special ignition systems. Some dwell meters won't work at all with such systems.

Dwell can be checked with the engine running or cranking. Decrease dwell by increasing the point gap; increase by decreasing the gap. Dwell angle is simply the number of degrees of distributor shaft rotation during

which the points stay closed. Theoretically, if the point gap is correct, the dwell should also be correct or nearly so. Adjustment with a dwell meter produces more exact, consistent results since it is a dynamic adjustment. If dwell varies more than 3 degrees from idle speed to 1,750 engine rpm, the distributor is worn.

19. To adjust dwell on a six, trial and error point adjustments are required. On a V8, simply open the metal window on the distributor and insert a 1/8 in. allen wrench. Turn until the meter shows the correct reading. Be sure to snap the window closed.

20. An approximate dwell adjustment can be made without a meter on a V8. Turn the adjusting screw clockwise until the engine begins to misfire, then turn it out 1/2 turn.

21. If the engine won't start, check:
    a. That all the spark plug wires are in place.
    b. That the rotor has been installed.
    c. That the two (or three) wires inside the distributor are connected.
    d. That the points open and close when the engine turns.
    e. That the gap is correct and the hold-down screw (on a six) is tight.

22. After the first 200 miles or so on a new set of points, the point gap often closes up due to initial rubbing block wear. For best performance, recheck the dwell (or gap) at this time.

23. Since changing the gap affects the ignition point setting, the timing should be checked and adjusted as necessary after each point replacement or adjustment.

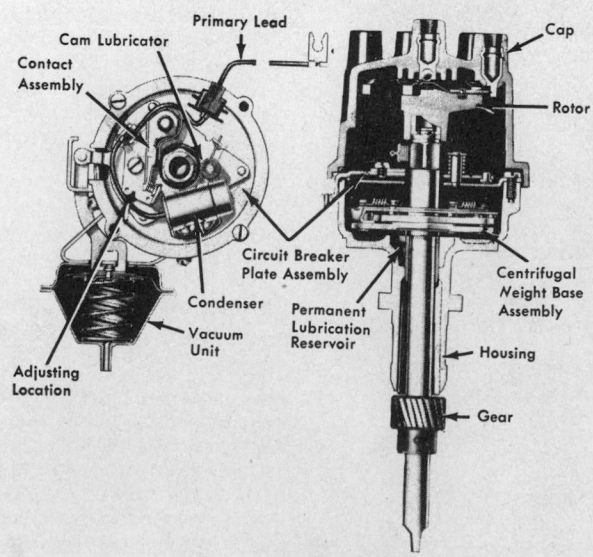

Distributor—6 cylinder through 1974
(© American Motors Corp.)

Ignition Timing Adjustment

A scale located on the timing chain cover and a notch milled into the vibration damper are used as references to set ignition timing.

NOTE: Connect a tachometer to the BID ignition system in the conventional way; to the negative (distributor) side of the coil and to a ground. Some tachometers may not work with a BID ignition system and there is a possibility that some could be damaged. Check with the manufacturer of the tachometer to make sure it can be used.

1. Disconnect the vacuum hose, at the distributor vacuum unit. Plug the vacuum line to prevent leakage.
2. Connect a timing light and a tachometer in accordance with the manufacturer's instructions. If the timing light has an advance control, be sure that it is in the "off" position.
3. Start the engine. Adjust the carburetor curb idle screw so that the engine idles at 500 rpm. If there is a throttle stop solenoid, disconnect it electrically. Aim the timing light at the Pointer marks.
4. Adjust the timing by loosening the distributor clamp nut and rotating the distributor. Set the timing to the proper specification.

NOTE: On some models, a white paint mark is applied to the scale for the specified, initial timing setting. Do not mistake this mark for TDC.

5. Check the timing again after tightening the distributor clamp.
6. Connect the vacuum hose and set the idle speed to normal specifications.

FUEL SYSTEM

On cars equipped with vacuum-operated windshield wipers (through 1971) a double-action, vacuum booster fuel pump is used. If the car is equipped with an electric wiper motor, a conventional single-action fuel pump is fitted.

Emission controls are covered in the sections which deal with them, except when their service is part of the carburetor adjustment. In this case, their adjustment is covered in this section.

Fuel Pump Removal and Installation

Disconnect both gas lines from the fuel pump, disconnect the vacuum line, if it is a vacuum pump. Remove the two bolts which hold it to the block and lift off the pump.

Installation is the reverse of removal.

Fuel Pump Removal and Installation

These models use an inline fuel filter in the line from the carburetor to the fuel pump. Some V8 and all 1976 and later models also have a vapor return line from the filter to the tank. To replace it:

1. Remove the air cleaner as necessary.
2. Put an absorbent rag under the filter to catch spillage.
3. Remove the hose clamps.
4. Remove the filter and short attaching hoses.
5. Assemble the new filter and hoses.

NOTE: The original equipment type hose clamps can't be reused with much success. It is much better to replace them with screw type clamps. If there is an arrow on the new filter, it must point toward the carburetor. 1976 and later four barrel models also have a check valve with flow indicating arrows.

6. Fit the filter in place, tighten the clamps, start the engine, and check for leaks. Discard the rag safely.

Carburetor Adjustments

1970-71

Adjust with air cleaner installed.
NOTE: Do not allow the engine to idle for more than three minutes at a time. If the idle mixture adjustment is not completed at the end of three minutes, run the engine at 2000 rpm for one minute. Continue the adjustments at the specified rpm.

1. Start engine and allow it to warm up to operating temperature. Connect a tachometer. *On engine with air pumps, disconnect air bypass hose at valve.*
2. Adjust carburetor idle speed screw to obtain 600 rpm for 6-cylinder manual, 550 rpm for 1970 6-cylinder automatic (in Drive), 650 rpm for V8 manual, or 600 rpm for 1970 V8 automatic (in Drive), 700 rpm for six-cylinder manual, 600 rpm for 1971 six-cylinder automatic, 750 rpm for the 1971 V8 manual, and 650 rpm for the 1971 V8 automatic.
3. Starting from full rich stop/s (or two turns from seated on 4-BBL. manual V8) turn mixture screw/s clockwise until engine speed drops off.
4. Turn mixture screw/s counterclockwise until engine speed picks up to former level. The highest idle speed obtainable within the range of the limiter caps (or between the rich drop-off and lean drop-off points for 4-BBL. manual V8) is the "lean best idle setting." Both

mixture screws should be turned equally unless the engine definitely demands otherwise.

5. If idle speed changes more than 30 rpm during mixture adjustment, reset carburetor idle speed screw and readjust mixture.
6. On cars with air pumps, reconnect air bypass valve hose.

NOTE: if idle quality is poor within the range of the limiter caps, the caps may be removed and the idle speed set using the corrective procedure. Keep in mind that a combustion gas analyzer is necessary to meet the critical federal exhaust emission standards. All cars should have a 14:1 air/fuel ratio except 4-BBL. manual transmission V8's, which should be set up at 13.5:1 (air bypass hose disconnected).

Idle Quality Corrective Procedure

1. Remove idle limiter caps by inserting a sheet metal screw into the center of the cap.
2. Adjust carburetor idle speed screw to obtain 50 rpm less than specified idle speed for all 6-cylinder, and all V8 automatic. Manual transmission V8's should be set to specified idle speed.
3. Turn in the mixture screw(s) until they are gently seated, then back out one turn. Connect a tachometer.

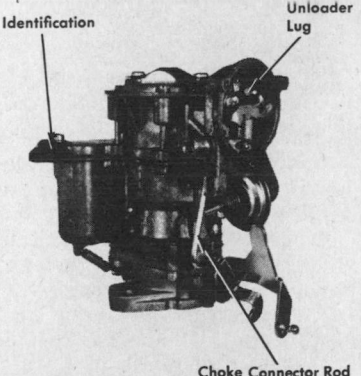

Carter YF carburetor adjustments
(© American Motors Corp)

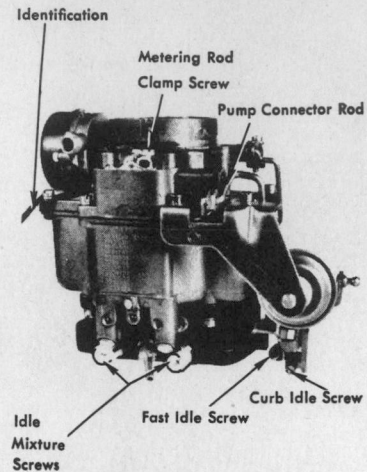

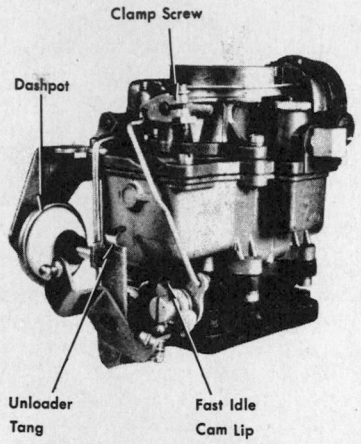

WCD carburetor adjustments
(© American Motors Corp)

4. Start the engine and turn the mixture screw(s) counterclockwise until the engine speed drops off slightly. On 2 bbl and 4 bbl carburetors, turn both mixture screws equally unless the engine definitely demands otherwise.
5. Turn the mixture screw(s) inward until the speed is regained, then continue inward until the speed begins to fall off again.
6. Turn the mixture screw(s) outward until the speed is regained. This is the "lean best idle" setting.
7. Readjust the idle speed screw to obtain the proper idle speed. Disconnect the tachometer.
8. Install new service idle limiter caps with ears against full rich stops.

1972

The basic procedure for adjusting the 1972 emission control carburetors is the same as that for 1969–71, above. There are, however, some variations.

1. Six-cylinder engines use the following rpm settings for idle speed:
   a. Manual transmissions — 600 rpm/National; 700 rpm/California.
   b. Automatic transmissions — 500 rpm (in Drive)/National; 600 rpm (in Drive)/California.
2. V8 engines use the following idle settings:
   a. Manual transmissions — 750 rpm/all engines.
   b. Automatic transmissions — set the 304 and 401 cu in. engines at 650 rpm (in Drive)/National; at 700 rpm (in Drive)/California. The 360 cu in. engine is set at 700 rpm/National and California.
3. On 360 and 401 cu in. V8 engines, with automatic transmissions, set the idle speed by adjusting the throttle stop solenoid, if so equipped, to the specified figure. Then adjust the engine idle to 500 rpm with the idle stop solenoid disconnected. Reconnect the solenoid.

Caution When adjusting the idle speed on a car equipped with an automatic transmission, set in the Drive range, be sure that the parking brake is firmly on and that the front wheels are blocked.

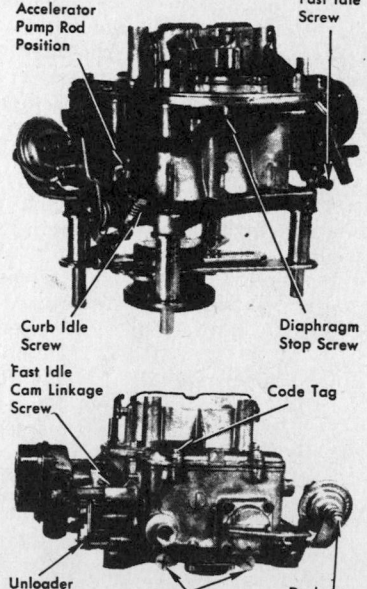

Autolite/Motorcraft 2100 carburetor adjustments (© American Motors Corp)

1973-74

Adjust with air cleaner installed.
NOTE: Do not allow the engine to idle more than three minutes at a time. If the idle/mixture adjustment is not completed by the end of three minutes, run the engine for one minute at 2,000 rpm. Return to specified rpm and continue the adjustment.

1. Remove the idle limiter cap(s) by inserting a screw in its center. Turn the cap clockwise to remove it.
2. Discard the old cap(s).
3. Start the engine and allow it to reach normal operating temperature.
4. Install a tachometer of known accuracy, in accordance with its manufacturer's instructions.
5. Adjust the idle speed to 30 rpm above the speed specified in the "Tune-Up Specifications" chart.
NOTE: On 1973-74 V8, automatic transmission equipped cars and 1974 California sixes with automatic transmission, adjust the idle speed by turning the hex screw on the throttle stop solenoid.
6. Turn the mixture screws until they are seated against their full-rich stops.
7. Then turn the mixture screws clockwise (leaner) until a drop in engine idle speed is noted.
8. Turn the mixture screws counterclockwise from this position until the highest rpm is obtained.
NOTE: When adjusting the idle mixture on a carburetor which has two mixture screws, turn both screws equally unless satisfactory idle cannot be obtained in this manner.
9. If the idle speed changes more than 30 rpm during the mixture adjusting procedure, set the idle to 30 rpm above specification and repeat steps 6-8 again.
10. After completing steps 1-9 satisfactorily, turn the mixture screws clockwise until the engine idle speed drops the amount specfied below:

Engine/Transmission	RPM
6 cyl/manual	35
6 cyl/automatic	20
V8/All	40

11. Install new service idle limiter caps.

Caution When adjusting the idle speed/mixture on a car with its automatic transmission set in Drive range, be sure that the parking brake is firmly on and that the front wheels are blocked.

1975-76

NOTE: This adjustment is performed with the air cleaner installed. Do not allow the engine to idle more than three minutes at a time. If the idle/mixture adjustment is not completed by the end of three minutes, run the engine for one minute at 2,000 rpm. Return to the specified rpm and continue the adjustment.

1. Adjust the idle screw(s) to the full rich stop(s). Note the position of the screw head slot inside the limiter cap slots.
2. Carefully remove the idle limiter cap(s) by installing a sheet

metal screw in the center of the cap and turning clockwise. Discard the old caps. Return the screws to their original positions.

3. Install a tachometer on the engine.

4. Start the engine and allow it to reach normal operating temperature.

5. Adjust the idle speed to 30 rpm above the specified idle speed. See the Tune-Up Specifications chart.

NOTE: On most engines the idle speed is adjusted with the throttle stop solenoid.

CAUTION: *On the Carter BBD 2bbl., the curb idle and fast idle screws are side by side; it is easy to get the wrong one when setting idle speed on cars without a throttle stop solenoid. The screw for idle speed is the longer of the two.*

6. Starting from the full rich stop position, as noted in step 1, turn the mixture screw(s) clockwise (leaner) until the engine looses speed.

7. Turn the mixture screw(s) counterclockwise until the highest rpm reading is obtained.

NOTE: On engines with two mixture screws, turn both of the screws an equal number of turns unless the engine demands otherwise.

8. If the idle speed has changed more than 30 rpm during the mixture adjustment, reset the idle to 30 rpm above the specified idle rpm as indicated in the "Tune-Up Specifications" chart.

9. Turn the mixture adjustment screw(s) clockwise until the rpm drops as follows:

1975-76 Six cylinder automatic	25 rpm
1975 Six cylinder manual	25 rpm
1976 Six cylinder manual	50 rpm
1975 Six cylinder manual with EGR and catalytic converter	35 rpm
1975 Six cylinder manual with EGR	50 rpm
1975-76 V8 automatic	20 rpm
1975 V8 manual	40 rpm
1976 V8 manual	100 rpm

10. Install new blue service idle limiter cap(s) over the idle mixture screw(s) with the limiter cap tang(s) positioned against the full rich stop(s). Be careful not to disturb the idle mixture setting while installing the cap(s). Press the cap(s) firmly into place.

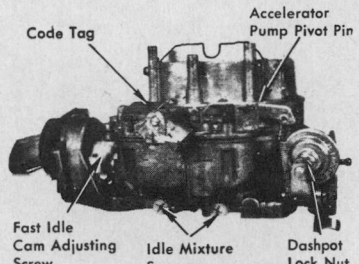

Autolite/Motorcraft 4300 carburetor (© American Motors Corp)

Dashpot Adjustment

Some carburetors are equipped with a dashpot to prevent stalling. The dashpot adjustment procedure for these carburetors is as follows:

1. Be sure that the throttle valves are closed (curb idle position) and that the diaphragm stem is fully depressed.

2. Measure the clearance between the dashpot stem and the throttle lever with a feeler gauge. For the proper clearance specification see the chart below.

3. If the clearance is not correct, adjust it by loosening the locknut and rotating the dashpot until the proper clearance is obtained. Tighten the locknut.

Year	Carburetor		Clearance (Gauge size in.)
1970	YF(1-V)	4768S	0.120
		4770S	0.095
	WCD(2-V)	All	0.095
	2100(2-V)	All	0.125
	4300(4-V)	All	0.125
1971	YF(1-V)	All	0.110
	2100(2-V)	All	0.125
	4300(4-V)	1TM4	0.065
		1TA4	0.125
1972-74	YF(1-V)	All	0.095
	2100(2-V)	2DM2	0.110
		2DA2, 3DM2, 4DM2	0.140
	4300(4-V)	All	0.140
1975	YF (1-V)	All	0.075
	2100 (2-V)	All	0.093
1976	YF(1-V)	All	0.075
	2100(2-V)	All	0.075
	BBD(2-V)	All	0.104

COOLING SYSTEM

American Motors cars are equipped with a conventional cooling system which utilizes a vertical flow radiator, a water pump, and a thermostat. The Pacer has a crossflow radiator. An internal by-pass port is used on the six-cylinder engine, which allows water to flow through the engine when the thermostat is closed. The V8 engine uses an external hose to perform the same function.

Information on the water temperature gauge can be found in the Unit Repair Section.

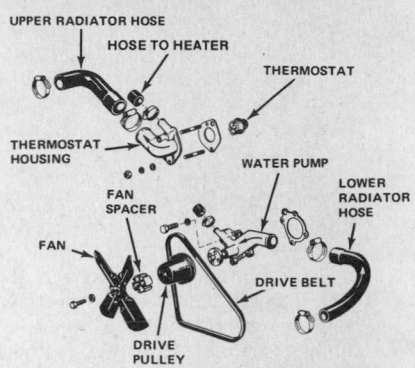

Cooling system components and coolant flow for 6 cylinder engines (© American Motors Corp)

Radiator Removal

Raise the hood, drain the radiator, remove the upper and lower radiator hose. On models equipped with the optional coolant recovery system, disconnect its hose from the radiator. Remove the radiator shroud, if so equipped. Take out the bolts which hold the radiator to its cradle and, if the car is fitted with an automatic transmission, disconnect the fluid cooler lines and lift the core up and out. You may have to remove the fan.

Water Pump Removal and Installation

The water pump is a centrifugal unit having a non-adjustable packless seal. It is non-serviceable and must be replaced if defective—no maintenance is required.

6 Cylinder

1. Drain the cooling system. Disconnect the negative (—) cable from the battery.

2. Unfasten the radiator and the heater hoses at the pump.

3. Loosen the adjustment bolts from the alternator and the power steering pump (if so equipped). Remove the V-belts.

4. Unfasten the fan ring securing bolts. Remove the fan and pump pulley assembly. Withdraw the fan ring (or shroud).

5. Remove the securing bolts from the water pump. Withdraw the pump along with its gasket.

Installation is the reverse order of removal. Always use a new pump gasket. Bleed the radiator by running the engine and opening the heater control valve. Run the engine long enough so that the thermostat opens. Check the coolant level.

The water pump securing bolts should be tightened to 10–15 ft lbs.

V8

1. Drain the cooling system at the radiator. Remove the upper hose from the radiator. Disconnect the negative (—) cable from the battery.
2. Remove the air cleaner.
3. Remove the fan shroud. Remove the drive belts, the fan, and hub assembly by withdrawing the attaching bolts.
4. If the car is equipped with power steering, remove the pump assembly.
5. If the car is equipped with an emission control air pump, remove the pump.
6. Loosen the bolts attaching the alternator bracket. Leave one bolt in position, so that the alternator may be swung to one side. Do not disconnect the wire from the alternator.
7. Disconnect the heater hose at the water pump.
8. On cars equipped with A/C, disconnect the compressor bracket and set it and the compressor out of the way. Do not discharge the air conditioning system.
9. Remove the by-pass and the lower radiator hoses from the pump.
10. Remove the pump and clean the gasket areas.

Installation is the reverse of removal. Always install a new pump gasket. Tighten the pump bolts to 18 ft lbs. Bleed the cooling system by starting the engine and opening the heater valve. Leave it open until the thermostat opens. Check the coolant level.

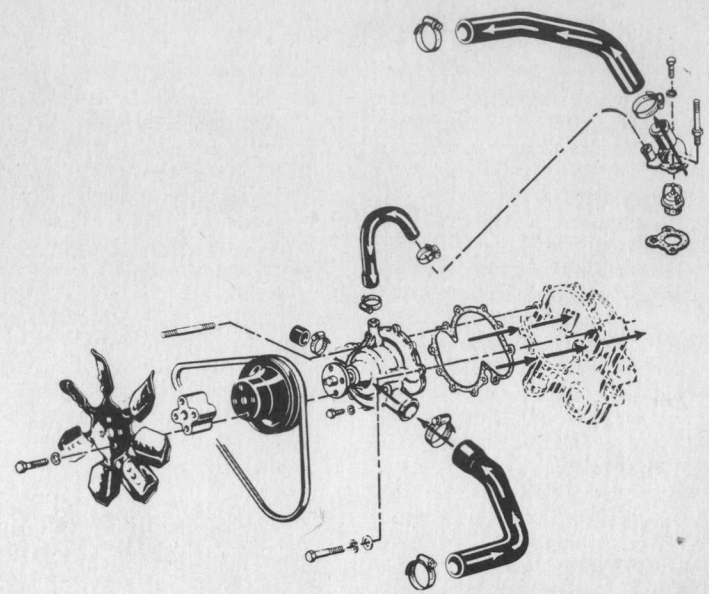

V8 Water pump components and coolant flow
(© American Motors Corp.)

Drain the coolant to a point below the thermostat. Disconnect the upper radiator hose and remove the bolts which hold the water outlet neck to the engine. Remove the thermostat.

When installing the thermostat, be sure that the pellet or coil spring are facing the engine. Thermostats are marked on the outer flange with the proper installing direction. Replace the gasket.

The bleed hole on the thermostats used on six-cylinder engines must be installed up (at 12 o'clock), to prevent "burping" caused by air trapped in the block.

Caution Tightening the housing bolts unevenly, or with the thermostat cocked in its recess, will cause the housing to crack.

Refill the cooling system and run the engine for a while with the heater on to bleed the system of air. Recheck the coolant level.

Thermostat Removal and Installation

The thermostat is located in the water outlet housing at the top of the cylinder head, or on V8 models in front of the manifold.

EMISSION CONTROLS

See the "Unit Repair Section" for testing and repair of the various emission control system components.

1970

An air injection system (Air-Guard) was used.

This system consists of:

1. A belt-driven, vane-type pump which feeds air through a manifold and into each exhaust port via a stainless steel nozzle. The air mixes with the hot exhaust gases and aids in burning them completely in the exhaust manifold.
2. A carburetor with a different flow characteristic and a dashpot which is used to control throttle closing speed (except on six-cyl-

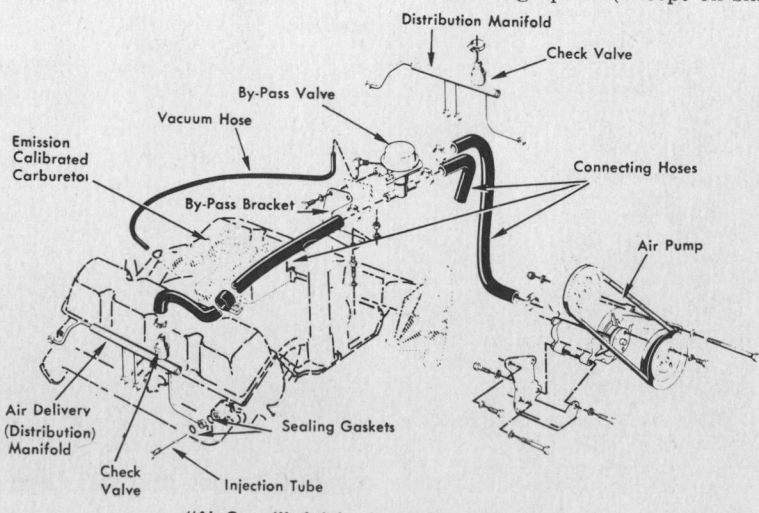

"Air-Guard" air injection system components
(© American Motors Corp)

inder models with automatic transmissions).

3. A distributor with a different advance curve and a special cam lubricator.
4. A positive crankcase ventilation system (PCV) retained from earlier models.

All other engines used a system of "engine modifications" to meet the new Federal emissions standards.

These engine modifications consist of:

1. A composition head gasket to replace the steel head gasket.
2. An emission-calibrated carburetor, equipped with idle limiter caps to prevent the fuel/air mixture from being set over rich.
3. A distributor with a centrifugal advance curve designed to retard the timing only at idle speed, while still retaining normal performance characteristics.
4. A positive crankcase ventilation system (PCV) retained from earlier models.
5. A "low-quench" combustion chamber on six-cylinder engines.
6. A thermostatically controlled air cleaner (TAC) on V8s. The TAC allows only air heated by a stove on the exhaust manifold to enter the air cleaner when the under hood temperature is less than 120°F. When the air is above this temperature, the valve opens allowing under-hood air to be drawn through the air cleaner snorkle, in a conventional manner.

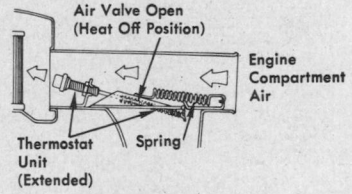

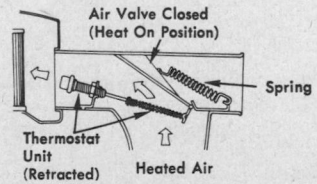

Thermostatically controlled air cleaner (TAC) —6 cylinder application
(© American Motors Corp)

In addition, the following controls are added:

1. A deceleration valve is added to the 199, 232, and 390 cu. in. engines when equipped with manual transmissions. When the car is decelerating and intake manifold pressure rises to a specific value, the valve closes off the vacuum spark port opening. Direct intake manifold vacuum is supplied to the advance diaphragm (dual-diaphragm dis-

tributor). This permits maximum ignition timing advance, to prevent afterburning in the engine exhaust system.

2. A dual-diaphragm distributor is used on all engines equipped with a deceleration valve and on the 304 and 360 cu in. V8 engines. It is not used on the 232 or 390 cu in. engines with automatic transmissions. It has a retard (secondary) diaphragm in addition to the advance (primary) diaphragm. The secondary diaphragm permits additional timing retardation during closed throttle deceleration and idle, thus reducing hydrocarbon emissions.

1970 California Models

In addition to the above modifications, all cars sold in California, starting with 1970 models, have to be equipped with an evaporative emission control system (EEC).

The American Motors EEC System consists of:

1. A fuel expansion tank that is integral with the fuel tank.
2. A closed vent system on the fuel tank.
3. A fuel check valve used to prevent the flow of *liquid* fuel through the closed vent system (not used on Gremlin models).
4. A special pressure and vacuum relief filler cap.

The EEC system routes raw fuel vapor into the PCV system, where it is burned along with regular crankcase emissions and the fuel-air mixture.

1971

The use of the evaporative emission control (EEC) system has been extended to the nationwide emission control package. All other systems have been retained, except for the dual-diaphragm distributor and the deceleration valve.

In addition, a charcoal canister has been added to the EEC system, on V8 engines equipped with automatic transmissions. The canister is used for fuel vapor storage.

1971 California

To meet oxides of nitrogen (NO_x) emission standards for California, a transmission-controlled spark (TCS) has been adapted, in addition to the other emission control systems. The TCS system is also used nationally on the 304 and 360 cu in. V8 engines, when equipped with an automatic transmission.

The TCS system functions to lower peak combustion temperature and pressures, thus reducing exhaust emissions of oxides of nitrogen.

The TCS system consists of:

1. A transmission control switch which opens or closes, depending upon car speed and the gear selected.
2. A solenoid vacuum valve that is activated by the transmission switch. It vents ported vacuum into the atmosphere, resulting in no distributor vacuum advance, when it is energized.
3. A temperature override switch, mounted on the front crossmember, is used to complete the circuit to the battery if the ambient temperature is more than 63° F. If the temperature is lower than this, the TCS system does not function.

The TCS system prevents vacuum advance from occurring when the car is in a low or intermediate gear and the ambient temperature is above 63° F. When the car is in high gear (or above 34 mph—automatic transmission) or the temperature is higher than 63° F, full vacuum advance is supplied to the distributor.

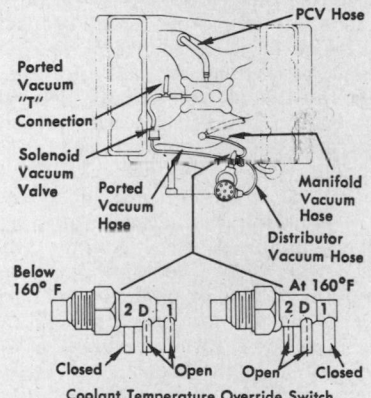

TCS hose routing, when equipped with a coolant temperature override switch
(© American Motors Corp)

1972

The 1972 emission controls have remained similar to those used in 1971. Several detail improvements have been incorporated. These consist of:

1. A charcoal canister is used on the EEC system of all V8 models with automatic transmissions, for fuel vapor storage. A "purge valve" is used to empty the canister into the PCV system at normal cruising speed.
2. The thermostatically controlled air cleaner (TAC) is extended in use to all engines in 1972. The TAC used on the V8 engines has a vacuum assist motor to operate the door in the air cleaner snorkle. The six-cylinder engine TAC works by spring tension against a thermostatically controlled door.
3. A coolant temperature operated vacuum valve is used on cars

equipped with V8 engines and automatic transmissions. If the coolant temperature is above 160° F, intake manifold vacuum is blocked off and carburetor ported vacuum is sent through a hose to the distributor advance diaphragm, thus decreasing the amount of vacuum advance. On cars equipped with TCS, the distributor vacuum advance is controlled by the TCS system once 163° F is reached.

1973

All six cylinder models are equipped with TCS. A description of this system can be found above under "1972 California."

New in 1973 is an Exhaust Gas Recirculation (EGR) system which is used on all V8s and six cylinder Matadors. This system directs a portion of the exhaust gases back into the intake manifold where they combine with the incoming mixture. This diluting of the mixture lowers peak combustion temperatures and reduces NO_x. The EGR valve, which is controlled by carburetor vacuum, controls the amount of exhaust gas, if any, that is recycled into the engine. Two ambient temperature switches and one coolant temperature valve control the flow of vacuum to the valve. The low temperature ambient valve is mounted in the radiator support, near the grille, and opens at temperatures below 60°F to vent carburetor vacuum to the atmosphere. The high temperature ambient valve is mounted on the firewall and opens when ambient temperature rises above 115°F. When either of these valves is open the EGR valve will be closed, preventing exhaust gas from entering the engine. The coolant temperature valve is mounted in either the intake manifold or engine block and is closed to block vacuum when coolant temperature is below 115°F (160° on 304 V8 with manual transmssion).

Also new for 1973 is an electrically-assisted automatic choke used on V8 models equipped with 4-bbl carburetors.

Once under-hood temperatures reach 95°F (± 15°F), a bimetallic switch located in the choke cap closes, allowing a ceramic heating element to draw power from a special tap on the alternator.

This causes the choke valve to open faster than normal, thus reducing CO emission during engine warm-up.

After the engine is shut off, the bimetallic switch remains closed until under-hood temperature drops below 65°F. Thus, if the engine is turned off for only a short time or if the ambient temperature is above 65°F, the choke will function for only a limited period of time.

All Matador wagons and all V8s are equipped with an air pump.

1973½—74

Starting with vehicles made on or after 15 March 1973, the ambient temperature overrides were dropped from both the TCS and EGR systems.

Dropping these overrides on six-cylinder engines caused driveability problems, so a spark temperature override was added. This override provides normal vacuum advance below a coolant temperature of 160°F. Addition of the spark temperature override meant that the EGR coolant temperature override had to be dropped from the six-cylinder engines.

At the same time these changes were made, a new transmission controlled spark (TCS) was incorporated on all models equipped with automatic transmissions.

NOTE: The new TCS switch was used on Kenosha-built cars after VIN A3AXXXX229935 and on Brampton-built cars after VIN A3AXXXX723815 (6 cyl) or VIN A3AXXXX726274 (V8).

An adjustable TCS solenoid control switch, which is operated by transmission governor oil pressure, is mounted at the right rear of the block on sixes or at the rear of the right-hand valve cover on V8s. The switch is preset at the factory and should not normally require adjustment. If adjustment becomes necessary, the procedure for it may be found in the emission control unit repair section.

For 1974, most of the changes made in March are retained, except that the EGR coolant temperature override has been returned to the six-cylinder engines.

In addition, 1974 cars also have the following:

1. A back pressure sensing device to prevent EGR from occurring during idle, is used on all California six-cylinder engines when equipped with EGR valves, and V8s with automatic transmissions (except for the 401 cu in. V8).
2. Exhaust gas recirculation (EGR) has been extended to all six-cylinder engines, as well as V8s, except for the following:

   232 cu in. six—all Hornet sedans, Hornet hatchback, and Gremlin.

   258 cu in. six—Hornet 2-door sedan, Hornet hatchback, and Gremlin.
3. A new style diverter valve is used with air injection. The relief valve is now part of the diverter valve, rather than being mounted on the pump.
4. All engines for 1974 use a char-

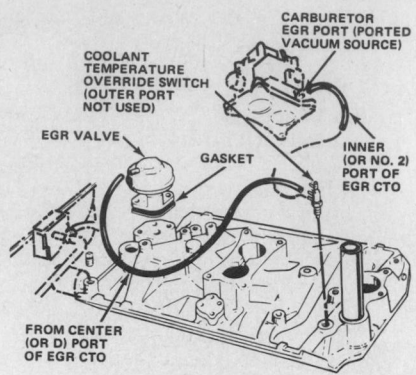

1974 V8 EGR system without backpressure sensor
(© American Motors Corp)

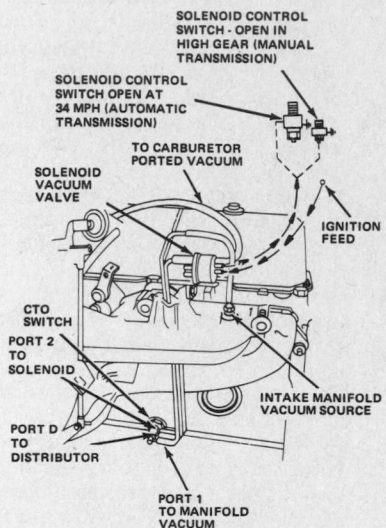

1974 TCS system—6 cylinder
(© American Motors Corp)

coal canister which is purged through the air cleaner snorkel. There is no purge valve on the canister.
5. The electrically assisted choke is retained on all 4-bbl V8 engines.

1975

All American Motors cars built for sale in California are equipped with the following emission control equipment:

a. Air guard air injection system
b. Catalytic converter (all V8s have two converters)
c. Exhaust gas recirculation (EGR)
d. Fuel tank vapor control system (FTVC)
e. Fuel vapor return system
f. Positive crankcase ventilation system (PCV)
g. Thermostatically controlled air cleaner (TAC)
h. Transmission controlled spark (TCS)
i. Exhaust back-pressure sensor (BPS)

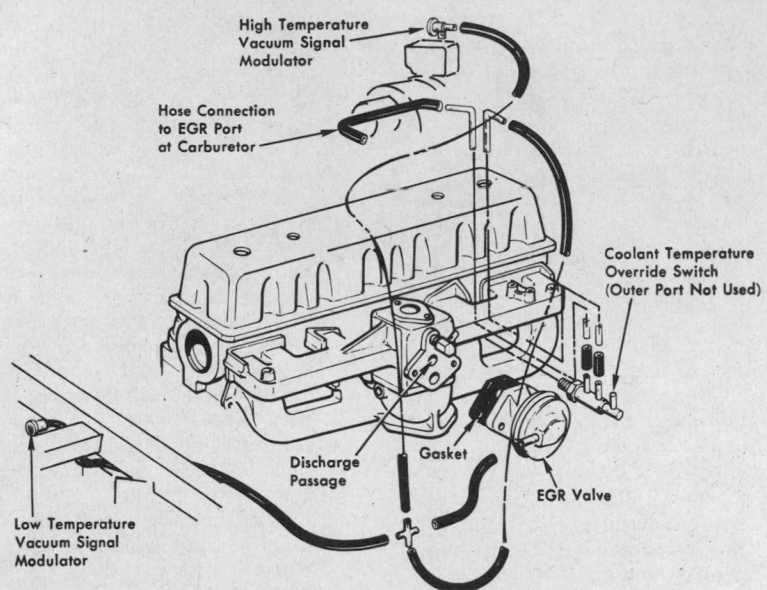

EGR valve installation and hose routing—6 cylinder
(© American Motors Corp)

Labels on figure:
High Temperature Vacuum Signal Modulator
Hose Connection to EGR Port at Carburetor
Coolant Temperature Override Switch (Outer Port Not Used)
Low Temperature Vacuum Signal Modulator
Discharge Passage
Gasket
EGR Valve

j. EGR coolant temperature override switch
k. Vacuum advance (distributor) coolant temperture override switch

American Motors cars built for sale in the remaining 49 states are equipped with all of the emission control devices California cars have with the following exceptions:

a. All six cylinder vehicles except manual transmission Matadors, do not have catalytic converters. All V8s and the 258 Matador Six with manual transmission have one catalytic converter; the 360 4 bbl V8 has two converters.
b. All Gremlin sixes and automatic transmission Hornet sixes and Pacers do not have the Air Guard air injection system.
c. All six cylinder vehicles except the Matador and Pacer automatic do not have the Fuel Vapor Return System.

See the "Emission Controls Unit Repair Section" for more information.

1976

No new emission control devices were introduced for 1976, but applications were changed as follows:
Air pump
49 States
Used on all V8 engines
Pacer and Hornet 6 cylinder Manual Transmission only.
Matador, all 6 cylinder
California
All models
Closed positive crankcase ventilation
Emission calibrated carburetor
Emission calibrated distributor

Single diaphragm vacuum advance
Exhaust gas recirculation
Vapor control, canister storage
Heated air cleaner
Transmission controlled spark
49 States
Not used
California
All models
Catalytic converter, single
49 States
Matador 258 1 bbl. Manual Transmission only.
All 2 bbl. V8
California
All 6 cylinder
Catalytic converter, dual
49 States
All 4 bbl. V8
California
All V8
Electric choke
49 States

Hornet 6 cylinder manual transmission only.
Pacer 1 bbl. 6 cylinder manual transmission only.
Matador 6 cylinder manual transmission only.
All 4 bbl. V8
California
Hornet 6 cylinder automatic transmission only.
Gremlin 6 cylinder automatic transmission only.
Pacer 1 bbl. 6 cylinder automatic transmission only.
All 4 bbl. V8

ENGINE

Six-Cylinder

The base AMC engine is the 199 or 232 cubic inch six. Although American Motors has used this same engine since 1966, it is of relatively modern design. It has a seven main bearing crankshaft and overhead valves with hydraulic lifters. In engineer's parlance, this is an "oversquare" engine; the bore dimension exceeds that of the stroke. The 232 was offered with either a one or a two-barrel carburetor in 1970. The 199 was dropped in 1972. Beginning 1971, the 232 two-barrel was replaced by a very similar 258 cubic inch six, using a one barrel carburetor. A two-barrel 258 was introduced in 1976. The 258 is slightly "undersquare"; the stroke dimension exceeds the bore.

V8

All the AMC V8s, are similar in design, having five main bearing crankshafts and overhead valves with hydraulic lifters.

The most common sizes are the 304 and 360. Two 390 V8s were offered in 1970, one of them a 340 horsepower brute available only in the Rebel "Machine," a red, white, and blue

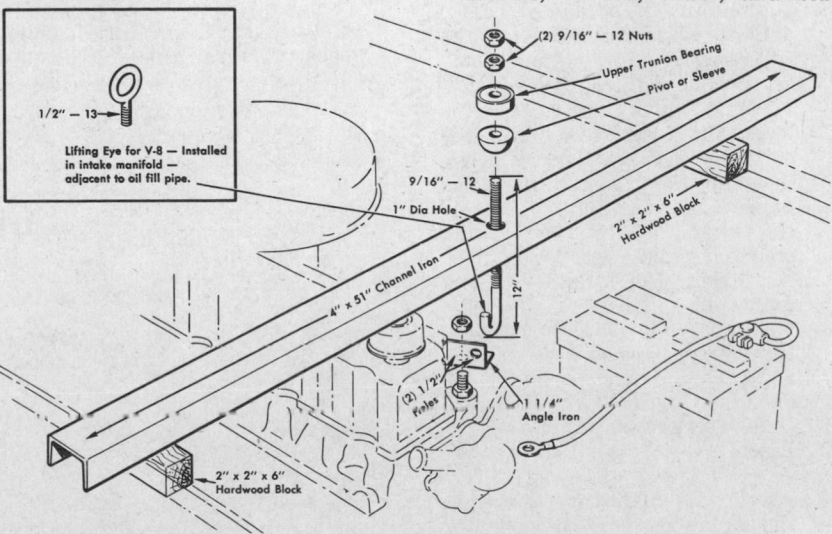

Lifting fixture can be fabricated as illustrated to facilitate oil pan and motor mount removal
(© American Motors Corp)

striped musclecar. In 1971, the 390 was replaced by a similar 401. All of these V8 engines are "oversquare" or "short stroke" designs; their bore dimension exceeds that of the stroke. The base V8, the 304, has been offered only with a two-barrel carburetor. The 390 and 401 have been offered only with four-barrel carburetors. The 360 has been available with a choice of two or four-barrel carburetion. Starting 1975, the 401 is available only to law enforcement agencies.

Engine Removal and Installation

The engine and transmission should be removed as a unit.

1. Remove the hood after marking the hinge location.
2. Remove the battery and the air cleaner.
3. Drain the engine oil and the cooling system.
4. On automatic transmission models, drain the transmission fluid and detach the cooler lines.
5. Remove the fan, power steering pump, air pump, and air conditioner compressor and condenser.
   CAUTION: *Don't disconnect the air conditioning or power steering lines. Just set the compressor aside out of the way.*
   On the Pacer, you will have to bleed the air conditioning system and remove the condenser for clearance.
   CAUTION: *Do not attempt this if you are at all unsure. Have it done by an air conditioning shop or a dealer. Compressed refrigerant will freeze any surface it contacts, including your eyes, on expansion. It also forms a poisonous gas in the presence of a flame.*
   All line openings must be capped to prevent the entry of moisture.
6. Disconnect the exhaust pipe(s) at the manifold.
7. Disconnect the speedometer cable and the shift linkage from the transmission. On a manual floorshift, remove the shift lever. Remove the boot and unbolt the lever. On some Hurst units, the shift lever can be removed by inserting a 0.015-0.020 in. feeler gauge along the driver's side of the lever, between the spring steel barb and the lower part of the lever. Pull the lever and gauge out together.
8. Disconnect all hoses, tubes, linkage, and wiring connecting the engine and transmission to the chassis.
9. Remove the radiator.
10. Remove the starter and oil filter on the Pacer.
11. Attach the lifting apparatus to the engine. Support the weight of the engine and transmission.
12. Remove the driveshaft.
13. Remove the rear crossmember. On the Pacer, remove the carburetor, rocker cover, and crankshaft vibration damper.
14. Disconnect the front motor mounts and pull the engine and transmission out as a unit. On the Pacer, you must first raise the front of the car with a floor jack under the front crossmember, so that the bottom of the front bumper is three feet off the floor. Support the car with jackstands.
15. On installation, lower the engine and transmission approximately into place. Attach the rear crossmember, then lift it into place with a floor jack. Lower the front of the engine until the front motor mounts are in place. Bolt the crossmember and motor mounts down.
16. The remainder of the installation procedure involves replacing and filling all the items removed or drained in Steps 1-14.

Engine Manifolds

Intake Manifold Removal and Installation

6 Cylinder

The intake manifold is mounted on the left-hand side of the engine and bolted to the cylinder head. A gasket is used between the intake manifold and the head, none is required for the exhaust manifold.

1. Remove the air cleaner and carburetor.
2. Disconnect the accelerator cable from the accelerator bellcrank.
3. Disconnect the PCV vacuum hose from the intake manifold and the TCS solenoid and bracket, if so equipped.
4. Remove the spark CTO switch and EGR valve (or exhaust back-pressure sensor) vacuum lines from each of these components.
5. Disconnect the hoses from the air pump and the injection manifold check valve. Disconnect the vacuum line from the diverter valve and remove the diverter valve with hoses, if so equipped.
6. Remove the air pump and power steering bracket (if so equipped) and remove the air pump. Move the power steering pump aside, out of the way, without disconnecting the hoses.
7. Remove the air conditioning drive belt idler assembly from the cylinder head, if so equipped. On some models it is necessary to remove the A/C compressor. Do not discharge the A/C system; just lie the compressor aside.
8. Remove the EGR valve (and exhaust back-pressure sensor) from the exhaust manifold.
9. Disconnect the exhaust pipe from the manifold.
10. Remove the manifold attaching bolts, nuts, and clamps and remove the intake and exhaust manifolds as an assembly. Discard the gasket. The two manifolds are separated at the heat riser.

To install the intake and exhaust manifolds:

1. Clean all of the mating surfaces on the cylinder head and the manifolds.
2. Assemble the two manifolds to-

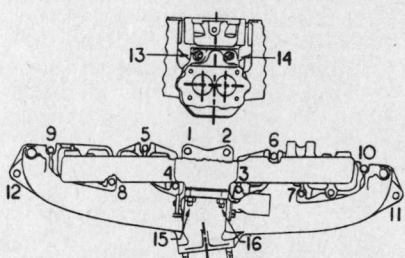

Intake manifold torque sequence—6 cylinder
(© American Motors Corp)

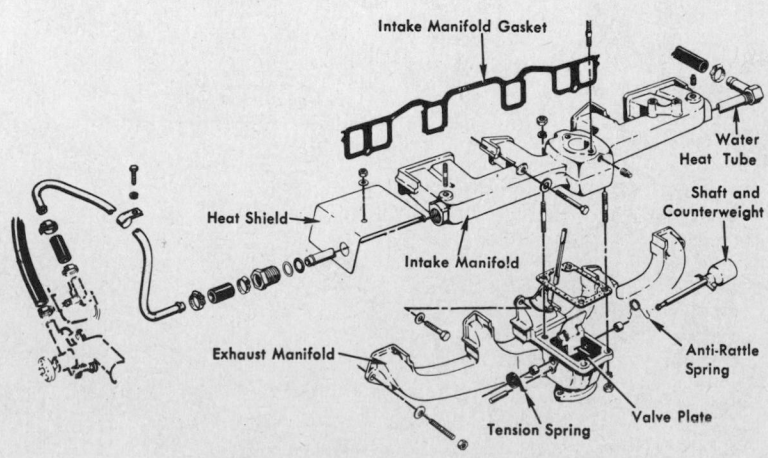

6 cylinder intake and exhaust manifold
(© American Motors Corp)

gether and tighten the heat riser retaining nuts to 5 ft lbs.

3. Position the manifold to the engine together with a new intake manifold gasket and tighten the manifold attaching bolts and nuts in the proper sequence to the specified torque.

4. Install the remaining components in the reverse order of removal. Adjust the automatic transmission throttle linkage, if so equipped. Adjust the drive belt(s) tension.

V8

The cast iron manifold completely encloses and seals the tappet valley between the cylinder heads. The manifold contains water passages, a crankcase vent passage, exhaust crossover, induction, and in some cases, EGR passages. A one-piece metal gasket seals the intake manifold to cylinder head joint and also serves as an oil splash baffle. The left-hand carburetor bores supply cylinders No. 1, 7, 4 and 6; the right-hand bores cylinders No. 3, 5, 2 and 8.

1. Drain the cooling system.
2. Remove the air cleaner assembly from the carburetor.
3. Mark and remove the spark plug wires.
4. Remove the spark plug wire guides from the rocker cover, ignition coil and by-pass valve brackets.
5. Disconnect the radiator upper hose and the by-pass hoses from their fittings on the intake manifold. Disconnect the temperature

gauge sending unit electrical lead.

6. Remove the ignition coil and bracket. Set the coil/bracket assembly out of the way.
7. Remove the TCS solenoid, if so equipped, from the right-hand valve cover.
8. Disconnect any of the emission control wiring or hoses as necessary. Disconnect the heater hose from the rear of the intake manifold.
9. Disconnect the throttle linkage and fuel and vacuum lines from the carburetor.
10. On cars equipped with air injection, remove the by-pass (diverter) valve bracket. Set the valve assembly (with hoses) out of the way, forward of the engine.
11. If the car is equipped with "Cruise Command" (automatic speed control), remove the vacuum servo mounting bracket and set the servo assembly aside.
12. Remove the carburetor assembly from the manifold.
13. Remove the intake manifold assembly complete with gasket and end seals.

Always use a new gasket when installing the intake manifold. Use a good commercial sealer on both sides of the metal gasket and on the rubber end seals. Align the gasket at the rear first, then at the front.

The rest of the installation procedure is the reverse of removal. Torque the manifold bolts evenly to the specified torque, working from the center out.

Exhaust Manifold Removal and Installation

V8—Except Gremlin and Hornet w/Air Pump

NOTE: The mating surfaces of both the exhaust manifold and the cylinder head are machined smooth, thus eliminating any need for a gasket between them.

1. Disconnect the wires from the spark plugs after marking them for firing order.
2. On models equipped with air injection, disconnect the air delivery hoses from the injection manifold. Remove the injection manifold and nozzles from the exhaust manifold.
3. Disconnect the exhaust pipe from the exhaust manifold flange.
4. Remove the bolts and washers used to retain the manifold.
5. Remove the shields from the spark plugs.
6. Remove the exhaust manifold from the cylinder head.
7. Clean the machined surfaces of the manifold and head. Installation is the reverse of removal.

Gremlin and Hornet V8 with Air Pump

The exhaust manifold on the left-side may be removed in the same manner as detailed for other V8 engines, however, the right side manifold on Gremlins and Hornets equipped with air pumps, must be removed in the following order:

1. Raise the car and securely support it with jackstands.
2. Disconnect the exhaust pipe from the manifold flange.
3. Support the engine at the vibration damper, by placing a jack with a block of wood on its lifting pad underneath it.
4. Remove the bolts which secure the engine mounting bracket on the right-side.
5. Remove the air cleaner assembly, including the tube which runs to the manifold heat stove.
6. Disconnect the battery cables. Remove the spark plug leads after marking them for installation.
7. Disconnect the air supply hose from the air injection manifold.
8. Remove the air injection tubes from the exhaust manifold.
9. On cars with automatic transmissions, remove the dipstick and the screw which secures the transmission dipstick tube.
10. Working from the rear, unscrew the exhaust manifold mounting bolts.
11. Raise the engine. Remove the exhaust manifold and the air injection manifold as an assembly.

Prior to installation, clean the join-

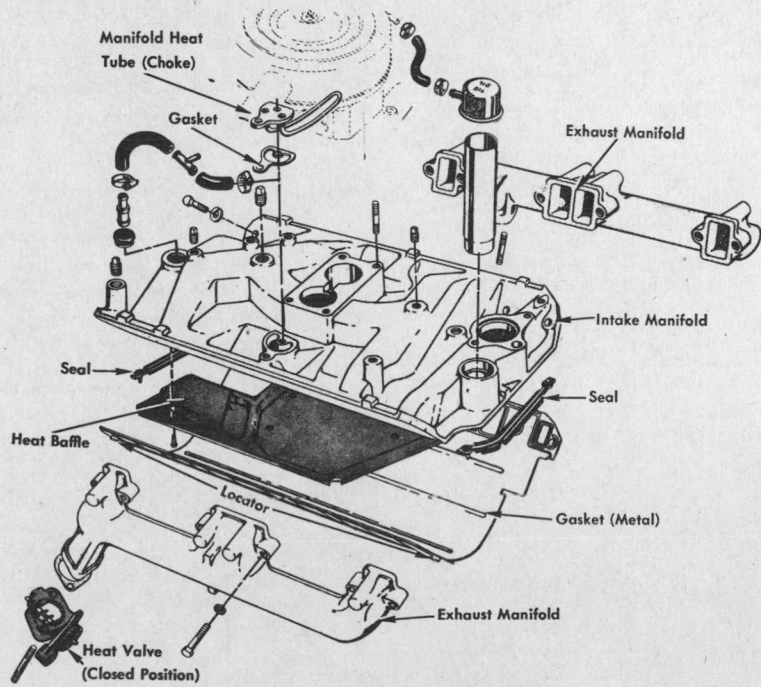

Manifold Heat Tube (Choke)

Gasket

Exhaust Manifold

Intake Manifold

Seal

Seal

Heat Baffle

Locator

Gasket (Metal)

Exhaust Manifold

Heat Valve (Closed Position)

Two-barrel intake manifold—V8
(© American Motors Corp)

ing surfaces of the manifold and cylinder head. Be careful not to nick or scratch either surface.

The rest of installation is the reverse of removal. Torque the manifold securing bolts to specification, starting from the rear and working forward.

6 Cylinder

Exhaust manifold is removed along with *intake* manifold; see previous instructions.

Valve System

American Motors cars use hydraulic tappets; thus, no mechanical valve adjustment is necessary. Special tappets to permit higher sustained rpm are used in police engines. The valve guides are integral with the head on all engines.

The valve stem oil deflectors should be replaced whenever valve service is performed.

American Motors engines do not have replaceable valve guides. If stem to guide clearance is excessive, guides must be reamed to the proper oversize. Three oversize valves are available with stems 0.003, 0.015 and 0.030 in. larger than standard diameter.

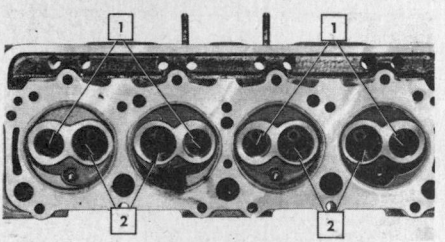

Valve sequence V8
(© American Motors Corp)
1 Exhaust valves
2 Intake valves

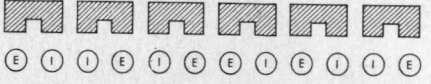

I = INTAKE VALVE
E = EXHAUST VALVE

Valve sequence—6 cylinder —bottom view
(© American Motors Corp)

Valve Margin

Correct Valve Facing

Incorrect Valve Facing

(© American Motors Corp)

Rocker Assembly Removal and Installation

There are three basic types of

rocker arm systems used in these engines. Make sure that you have the procedure for the type you are working on; there may have been some substitutions due to parts shortages.

1970-72 All V8, and 1973 360, 401 V8—Pivot Ball Type

Individually mounted, pressed steel rocker arms operate the valves. These rockers are mounted on threaded studs and are held by a pivot ball and locknut. The hollow pushrods conduct oil from each hydraulic tappet to the rockers. There is a metering system in each tappet, consisting of a stepped lower pushrod cap surface and a flat plate. Any loss of lubrication to the rockers usually can be traced to failure of this part, or to a blocked pushrod oil passage. The pushrods rub against the cylinder head during operation and serve to maintain the correct rocker to valve stem angle.

1. Remove valve covers, after first removing any accessories and the air cleaner preheat tube.
2. Loosen and remove the retaining locknuts, ball pivots and rocker arms. It is a good idea to lay them out in order, along with their respective pushrods.
3. Installation is the reverse of removal.

NOTE: when installing new threaded studs, make sure hex nut is fully seated and tightened to 65-70 ft lbs. Retaining locknuts are tightened to 20-25 ft lbs.

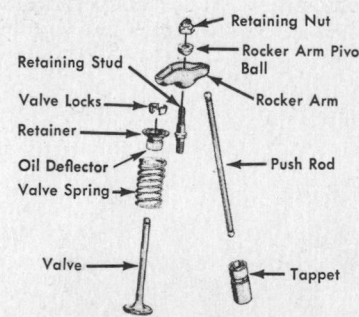

Retaining Nut
Retaining Stud
Rocker Arm Pivot Ball
Valve Locks
Rocker Arm
Retainer
Oil Deflector
Push Rod
Valve Spring
Valve
Tappet

V8 rocker arm assembly—Pivot ball type
(© American Motors Corp)

1970-72 and 1974 6 Cylinder—Shaft Type

The rocker arms on these engines are mounted on a common shaft. Oil pressure for rocker lubrication is

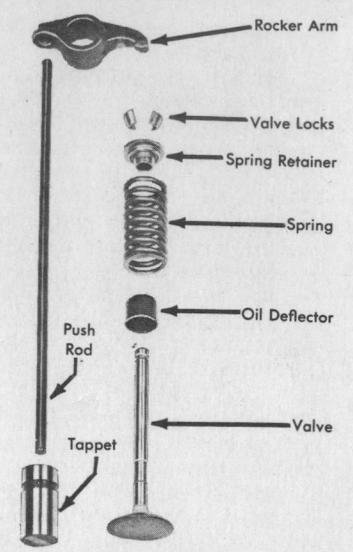

Rocker Arm
Valve Locks
Spring Retainer
Spring
Push Rod
Oil Deflector
Tappet
Valve

Valve assembly sequence—shaft type
(© American Motors Corp)

supplied via No. 3 camshaft bearing from the main oil gallery to No. 5 rocker support.

1. Remove valve cover.
2. Unbolt cap bolts and remove rockers and shaft.
3. Installation is the reverse of removal. Torque mounting bolts to 18-26 ft lbs.

NOTE: hold rockers in place using large rubber bands.

1973 and 1975-77 6 Cylinder, 304 V8 and All 1974-77 V8s —Bridged Pivot Type

The intake and exhaust rocker arms for each cylinder pivot on a bridged pivot assembly bolted to the cylinder head. The pushrods are hollow to supply lubrication to the rocker arms. The pushrods act as guides to keep the rocker arms in alignment, so it is not abnormal for them to rub slightly on the cylinder head.

NOTE: Be careful when ordering new valve train components, not to get parts for the wrong year. Some 1973 sixes may have come from the factory with the wrong tappets installed; check for this fault on any car which has noisy valves.

1. Remove any accessories which are in the way and remove the valve cover, complete with gasket.
2. Unscrew the rocker arm cap-

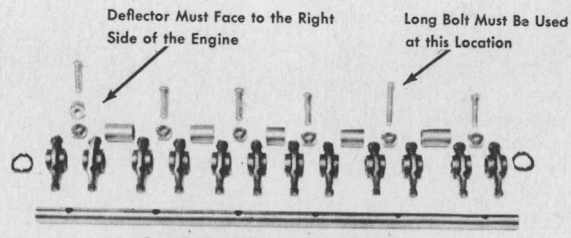

Deflector Must Face to the Right Side of the Engine

Long Bolt Must Be Used at this Location

6 cylinder rocker shaft assembly
(© American Motors Corp)

screws evenly to avoid breaking the bridge.

3. Remove the pivot assemblies, rocker arms, and pushrods.

NOTE: Be sure to keep all parts in the same order in which they were removed.

4. Clean all parts in solvent. Blow all oil passages in the rocker arms and pushrods dry with compressed air.

Replace any deeply pitted rocker arms and scuffed or worn pushrods. If the pushrod is worn from lack of oil, replace it, its valve lifter and rocker arm, as well.

Installation is performed in the following order:

1. Insert the pushrods in their bores, be sure to center the bottom of each rod in the plunger cap of the hydraulic valve lifter.

2. Install the rocker arms, pivot assemblies and capscrews. Tighten the capscrews evenly to 21 ft lbs.

NOTE: Be sure that the pushrods, pivot assemblies, and capscrews are returned to exactly the same places from which they were removed.

3. Install the valve cover and gasket; secure them with retaining screws and washers.

4. Install anything which was removed to gain access to the valve covers.

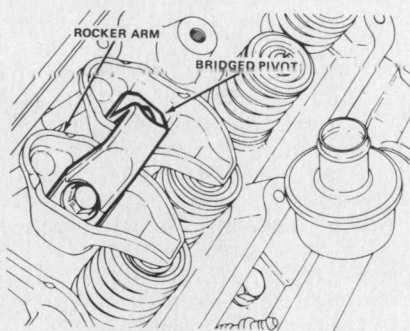

Bridged pivot type rocker arms
(© American Motors Corp.)

Cylinder Head Removal and Installation

CAUTION: *Don't loosen the head bolts until the engine is thoroughly cool, to prevent warping.*

If the head sticks, operate the starter to loosen it by compression or rap it upward with a soft hammer. Do not force anything between the head and the block.

NOTE: Resurfacing (milling or grinding) the cylinder head will increase the compression ratio, and can affect the emission output, as well as the fuel octane requirement. For this reason, the factory recommends replacing, rather than resurfacing cylinder heads.

Cylinder head bolts should be retorqued after the first 500 miles or so unless a special AMC gasket is used.

The special gasket doesn't require retorquing.

CAUTION: *Make sure to blow any coolant out of the cylinder head bolt holes before reassembly to prevent inaccurate torque readings.*

6 Cylinder

1. Drain the cooling system. Disconnect throttle linkage, fuel lines, water hoses, spark plug wires and vacuum line. Remove the air cleaner, PCV hose, and the temperature sender.

2. Remove the valve cover and its gasket. Remove the rocker arm assembly and the push-rods. Keep the pushrods in order.

3. Remove the intake and exhaust manifold assembly from the head.

4. Disconnect the spark plug wires and remove the plugs.

5. Disconnect the battery ground cable, the coil, and the coil bracket from the head. Disconnect the temperature sending unit wire.

6. If the vehicle is equipped with air conditioning, remove the drive belt idler pulley bracket from the cylinder head. Loosen the alternator drive belt and remove the bolts from the compressor mounting bracket and set the compressor aside.

7. Remove the bolts and remove the cylinder head from the block.

8. Clean the gasket surfaces of both the head and the block. Remove the carbon deposits from the top of each piston and from the combustion chambers.

9. Check the head for straightness. If the head (or the block) is 0.008 in. out of true over its entire length, 0.001 in. in 1 in., or

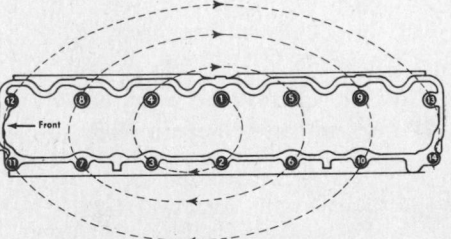

Cylinder head torque sequence for all 6 cylinder engines

0.003 in. in 6 in., the head requires resurfacing.

Installation of the cylinder head is performed in the following order:

1. Use a new head gasket and coat both of its sides with sealer. The word "top," on the gasket, faces upward.

2. Tighten the head bolts in three stages and proper sequence, see the illustration, to the proper torque specification.

3. The rest of installation is the reverse of the removal. Refill the cooling system when completed.

V8

Maximum out of true is 0.006 in. for the entire length of head, 0.001 in every 1 in., or 0.003 in. in 6 in.

1. Remove oil filler tube, rocker covers, air pump, power steering pump, alternator, exhaust manifolds and air conditioner. Move air conditioner compressor out of the way without disconnecting its hoses.

2. Drain the cooling system. Remove rockers and pushrods.

3. Disconnect water hoses, fuel lines, wiring, vacuum lines; remove distributor and intake manifold.

4. Remove cylinder head bolts and lift off heads carefully.

Apply a commercial sealing compound to both sides of the head gasket. The word "top" should always face upward when installing the gasket. Tighten the head bolts to specifications in three steps in the sequence illustrated. The rest of removal is the reverse of installation.

Timing Cover, Chain, and Camshaft
Vibration Damper Removal

All Models

Remove the radiator core and the fan. Remove the nut from the center of the pulley. The best way to do this is to affix a heavy wrench and rap it with a substantial hammer. The nut must be unscrewed in the opposite direction of normal engine rotation. Using a puller, remove the pulley from the front of the crankshaft.

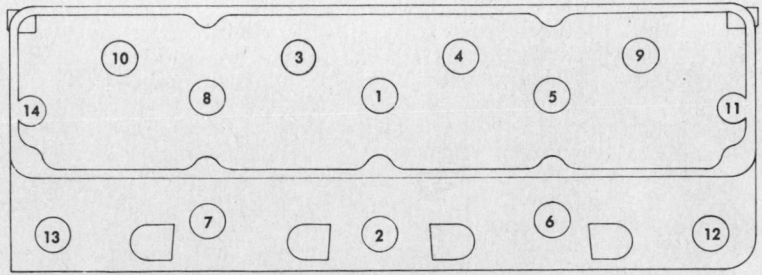

Cylinder head torque sequence for all V8 engines

Timing Case Cover Removal and Installation

6 Cylinder

1. Remove all V-belts, fan blades and pulley.
2. Remove vibration damper.
3. Remove oil pan to cover bolts and cover to block bolts.
4. Raise cover and pull oil pan front seal up far enough to extract the tabs from the holes in cover.

CAUTION: *If this isn't done, the oil pan will have to be removed to get the seals into place.*

5. Remove cover gasket from block; cut off seal tab flush with front face of block.
6. Clean all mating surfaces and remove oil seal.
7. Install a new front oil seal.
8. Install new neoprene front oil pan seal, cutting off protruding tabs to match original. Use sealer on the end tabs.
9. Position cover on block and install bolts. Tighten cover bolts to 4-6 ft. lbs.; four lower bolts to 10-12 ft. lbs. Use sealer on the gasket.
10. Install vibration damper, tightening the bolt to the specified torque.

NOTE: front oil seal can be installed with cover in place only if proper tool or duplicate is available.

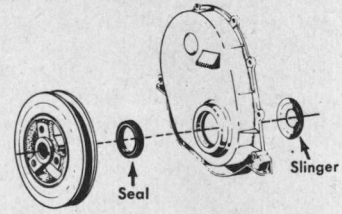

Timing chain cover assembly—6 cylinder
(© American Motors Corp.)

V8

The die-cast timing cover incorporates an oil seal at the vibration damper hub. This seal must be installed from the rear; therefore the cover must be removed from engine in every case to replace front seal.

1. Drain coolant and remove hoses from water pump.
2. Remove distributor, fuel pump, alternator drive belt, accessory drive belts, fan and hub assembly.
3. Remove the vibration damper bolt, then pull off the damper.
4. Remove air conditioner compressor and power steering pump, if so equipped, and swing them out of the way *without* disconnecting hoses.
5. Remove the two front oil pan bolts from beneath the car, then remove the cover bolts.

NOTE: The timing case cover attaching bolts are of different lengths

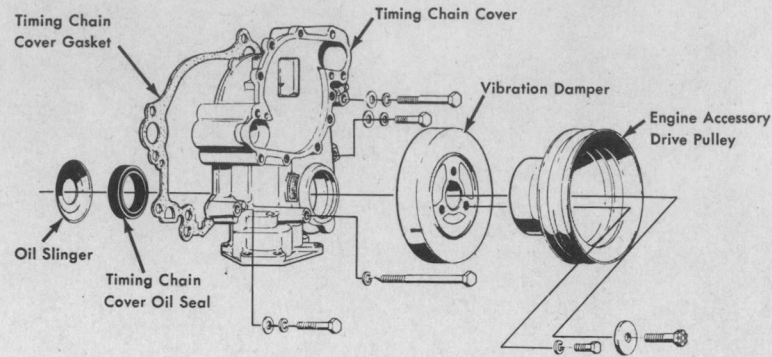

Timing chain cover assembly—V8
(© American Motors Corp.)

and must be replaced in their original locations.

6. Remove cover from block, then clean all parts and mating surfaces and remove oil seal.
7. Coat new seal lips with Petroleum jelly and seal surface with sealer, then drive seal into cover bore until it seats against the outer cover face. Use a proper size arbor for this job.
8. Remove lower dowel pin from cylinder block; this must be replaced when cover is in position but before bolts are installed.
9. Cut the oil pan gasket flush with the block on both sides of the oil pan.
10. Cut corresponding pieces of gasket from another oil pan gasket and cement them to cover. Install neoprene oil pan front seal into cover and align gasket tabs with pan seal.
11. Apply sealant to gaskets, then position cover. Install oil pan bolts and tighten evenly until cover lines up with upper dowel pin.
12. Install lower dowel pin, then cover to block bolts; tighten to 20-30 ft. lbs.
13. Install all removed pieces and adjust ignition timing.

Timing Chain and Sprocket Removal and Installation

6 Cylinder

1. Remove the drive belt (s).
2. Remove the engine fan and hub assembly.
3. Remove the vibration damper pulley and remove the vibration damper.
4. Remove the timing case cover. Remove the seal from the timing case cover, because the seal should be replaced every time the cover is removed from the engine.
5. Remove the camshaft sprocket retaining bolt and washer.
6. Turn the crankshaft until the 0 timing mark on the crankshaft sprocket is closest to and on a centerline with the timing pointer of the camshaft sprocket.

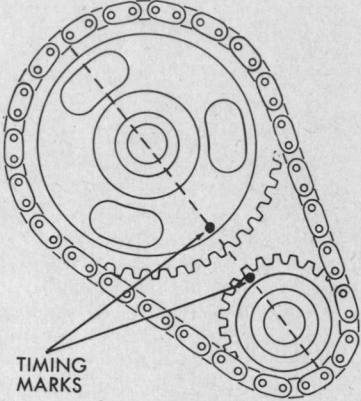

TIMING MARKS

Six-cylinder timing chain and sprockets

7. Remove the crankshaft sprocket, camshaft sprocket and timing chain as an assembly. Disassemble the chain and sprockets.

To install the timing chain and sprockets.

8. Assemble the timing chain, crankshaft sprocket, and camshaft sprocket with the timing marks aligned as shown in the illustration.
9. Install the assembly to the crankshaft and camshaft.
10. Install the camshaft sprocket retaining bolt and washer and tighten the bolt to 50 ft lbs.
11. To ensure the correct installation of the timing chain, locate the timing mark of the camshaft sprocket at about the 1 o'clock position. This should place the

7-1/2 Links or 15 Pins

Correct timing chain installation— 6 cylinder
(© American Motors Corp.)

timing mark on the crankshaft sprocket where the sprocket teeth mesh with the chain. There should be 15 timing chain pins between the timing marks of both sprockets.

V8

1. Remove the timing case cover and gasket.
2. Remove the crankshaft oil slinger.
3. Remove the camshaft sprocket retaining bolt and washer.
4. Remove the distributor drive gear and the fuel pump eccentric.
5. Turn the crankshaft until the 0 timing mark on the crankshaft sprocket is closest to and on a center line with the 0 timing mark on the camshaft sprocket.

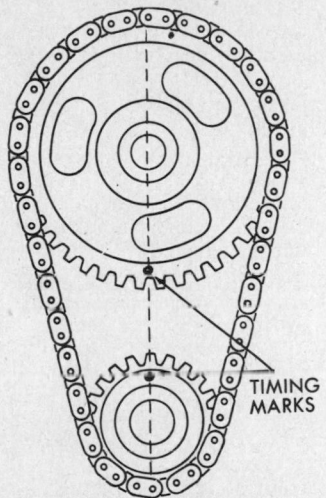

V8 timing chain and sprockets

6. Remove the crankshaft sprocket, camshaft sprocket and the timing chain as an assembly.

To install the timing chain and sprockets:

7. Assemble the timing chain, and the two sprockets with the timing marks aligned vertically, and install the assembly to the crankshaft and camshaft.
8. Install the fuel pump eccentric and the distributor drive gear. The fuel pump eccentric is installed with the word "REAR" toward the camshaft sprocket.
9. Install the camshaft sprocket, washer, and retaining bolt, tightening the bolt to 30 ft lbs.
10. To ensure the timing chain is installed correctly, turn the crankshaft until the timing mark on the camshaft sprocket is placed horizontally at the 3 o'clock position. Starting with the timing chain pin directly opposite the camshaft sprocket timing mark, count the number of pins down to the timing mark on the crankshaft sprocket. There should be

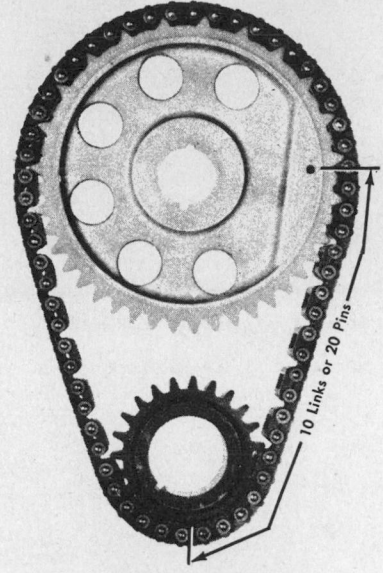

Correct timing chain installation—V8
(© American Motors Corp)

20 pins between the two timing marks. The crankshaft timing mark must be between the 20th and 21st pin.

11. Install the crankshaft oil slinger.
12. Install the timing case cover together with a new gasket.

Camshaft Removal and Installation

6 Cylinder

1. Drain the cooling system and remove the radiator.
2. If the car is equipped with air conditioning, remove the condenser and the receiver unit as a *charged assembly*, only.

NOTE: Do not discharge the A/C system.

3. Remove the valve cover and gasket.
4. Remove the rocker arm assembly and the cylinder head. Remove the tappets.

NOTE: Pushrods and tappets should be kept in the proper order. They must be returned to their original places during assembly.

5. Remove the drivebelt(s), fan assembly, accessory pulley(s), vibration damper, and the timing chain cover.
6. Remove the fuel pump. Take off the distributor assembly, including spark plug wires.
7. Turn the crankshaft until the "0" timing mark on the crankshaft sprocket is nearest to, on a centerline with, and aligns with the timing pointer on the camshaft sprocket.
8. Remove the sprockets and the timing chain as an assembly.
9. Remove the front bumper and/or grille as necessary. Withdraw the camshaft through the

opening. On the Pacer, unbolt the front engine mounts from the crossmember and raise the engine.

10. Inspect the bearing journals, distributor drive, cam lobes, and tappets for wear or damage. Replace parts, as required.

Camshaft installation is performed in the following order:

1. Use a generous amount of a suitable engine oil supplement on the camshaft. Install it in the block, using care not to damage any surfaces.
2. Install the timing chain and sprocket assembly.
3. Install the timing chain cover and a new oil seal.
4. Install the vibration damper and the accessory drive pulley(s).
5. Install the engine fan assembly and the drive belt(s). Tighten the belts to the proper tension.
6. Install the fuel pump.
7. With the number one piston at TDC of its compression stroke, fit the distributor so that the rotor is aligned with the no. one terminal on the cap (distributor fully seated on the block). Install the cap and the spark plug wires.
8. Install the tappets, cylinder head, its gasket, valve train (pushrods in the same order, as removed), valve cover and its gasket.

NOTE: All valve train components must be lubricated with engine oil supplement. The supplement must remain in the engine for at least the first 1000 miles. It does not require draining until the next regular oil change.

9. Install the air conditioner receiver and condenser, without discharging any coolant (if so equipped).
10. Install the radiator and top up the cooling system.
11. Install the front bumper and/or grille. Bolt down the Pacer engine mounts.

V8

1. Disconnect the battery cable.
2. Drain the radiator and both banks of the cylinder block. Remove the radiator, the hoses, and the thermostat housing. Remove the air conditioning condenser and receiver assembly as a charged unit, if so equipped.
3. Remove the distributor, complete with spark plug wires and the coil from the intake manifold.
4. Remove the intake manifold as a complete assembly.
5. Take off the valve cover and take out the valve train, including the hydraulic tappets.

NOTE: Keep the valve train components in proper order. They must be returned to their original place during assembly.

6. Remove the power steering pump from its bracket, without disconnecting the hoses. Set it out of the way.
7. Remove the fan assembly and then the fuel pump. Disconnect heater hose at the water pump.
8. Unbolt the alternator bracket and set it out of the way, complete with the alternator. Do not disconnect the alternator wiring.
9. Remove the crankshaft pulley and the vibration damper.
10. With the timing marks in vertical alignment, remove the front cover, distributor/oil pump drive gear, fuel pump eccentric, sprockets, and the timing chain.
11. Remove the hood latch upper support bracket attachment screws. Move the bracket, as necessary, to permit removal of the camshaft. Remove the bumper and grille if necessary.
12. Use care during camshaft removal, so that the journal bearings are not damaged.
13. Inspect all parts for wear and damage. Replace them as required.

Installation of the cam is the reverse of removal. Install the timing chain and cover. Adjust the belt tension and fill up the cooling system.

NOTE: Lubricate the camshaft, tappets, and the valve train with a suitable engine oil supplement. Add the remaining supplement to the crankcase, and leave it in the engine for at least the first 1000 miles. It does not require draining until the next regular oil change.

Rod and Piston Assembly

The piston and rod assemblies are installed in the engine from the top

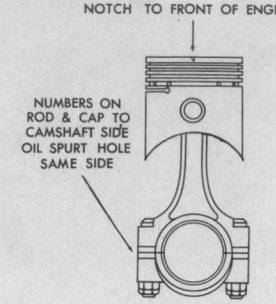

NOTCH TO FRONT OF ENGINE

NUMBERS ON ROD & CAP TO CAMSHAFT SIDE OIL SPURT HOLE SAME SIDE

Piston and rod assembly 6 cylinder engine

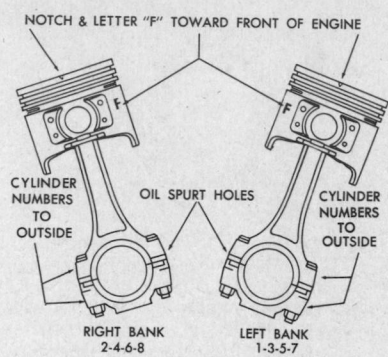

NOTCH & LETTER "F" TOWARD FRONT OF ENGINE

CYLINDER NUMBERS TO OUTSIDE

OIL SPURT HOLES

CYLINDER NUMBERS TO OUTSIDE

RIGHT BANK 2-4-6-8

LEFT BANK 1-3-5-7

Piston and rod assembly—V8 engines

and the dimple, notch, or dot, on the top of the piston goes toward the front. On sixes, the connecting rod numbers must go toward the camshaft; on V8s, they must go toward the outside of the cylinder.

Engine Lubrication

Oil Pan Removal and Installation

NOTE: It is much easier to remove the engine in most cases.

6 Cylinder (Except Pacer)

1. Disconnect front cushions from engine bracket and remove right bracket from engine.
2. Disconnect ground strap.
3. Disconnect idler arm from side sill.

4. If equipped, disconnect stabilizer bar.
5. Remove bolts retaining crossmember, and, with weight of car on wheels, pry down crossmember and insert wooden blocks to hold it down.
6. Drain oil and remove pan.
7. To install, reverse removal procedure. Use a new gasket with sealer.

Pacer

1. Drain the engine oil.
2. Install an engine lifting device and support the weight of the engine.
3. Disconnect the steering shaft flexible joint and hold it aside with a length of wire.
4. Raise and support the car.
5. Remove the front engine support through bolts.
6. Disconnect the front brake lines at the wheel cylinders.
7. Disconnect the upper ball joints from the spindles. Make sure the shock absorbers are attached securely.
8. Remove the upper control arm and move it aside.
9. Support the front crossmember with a jack.
10. Remove the nuts from the front crossmember rear mounts and swing the crossmember down and forward.
11. Remove the starter motor.
12. Remove the oil pan attaching screws and then the oil pan.
13. Remove the oil pan front and rear neoprene oil seals and thoroughly clean the gasket mating surfaces and inside of the oil pan.
14. Install a new oil pan front seal to the timing chain cover and apply a generous amount of silicone sealer to the end tabs.
15. Cement a new oil pan side gasket set into position on the engine block, applying a generous amount of silicone sealer to the gasket ends.

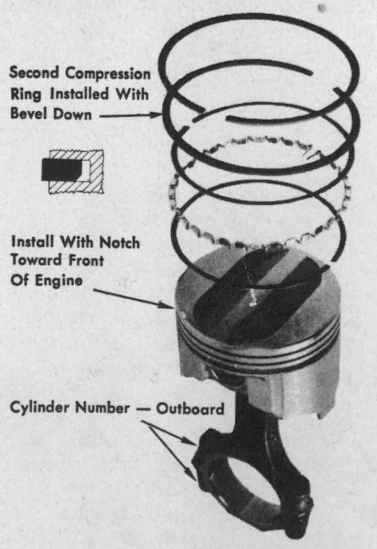

Second Compression Ring Installed With Bevel Down

Install With Notch Toward Front Of Engine

Cylinder Number — Outboard

Squirt Hole — Inboard

Piston ring assembly sequence
(© American Motors Corp)

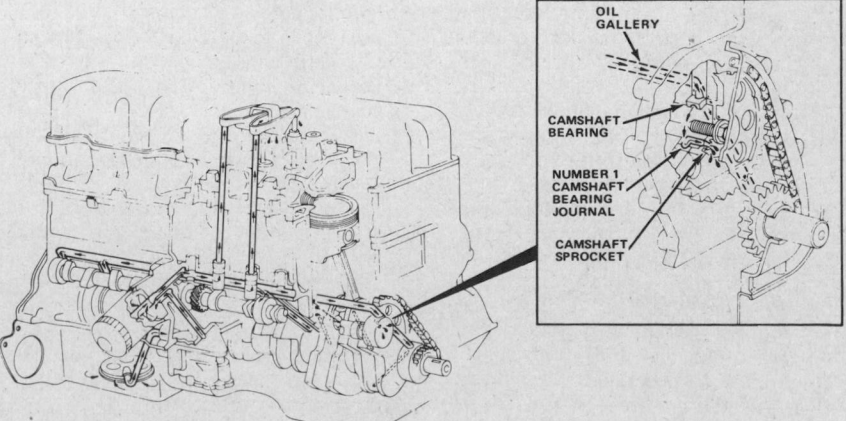

OIL GALLERY

CAMSHAFT BEARING

NUMBER 1 CAMSHAFT BEARING JOURNAL

CAMSHAFT SPROCKET

Six cylinder oiling system (© American Motors Corp.)

16. Coat the inside curved surface of the new oil pan rear seal with soap and apply silicone sealer to the side gasket contacting surface of the seal end tabs.

17. Install the seal in the recess of the rear main bearing cap, making sure it is fully seated.

18. Apply engine oil to the contacting surface of the front and rear oil pan seals.

19. Install and assemble the remaining components in the reverse order of removal, tightening the ¼ in. oil pan screws to 7 ft lbs, the 5/16 in. oil pan screws to 11 ft lbs, the crossmember attaching nuts to 50 ft lbs, the upper control arm cross shaft bolt and nut to 60 ft lbs, brake lines-to-wheel cylinders to 100 in. lbs, and the engine mount and steering shaft nuts to 25 ft lbs. Fill the crankcase with oil and bleed the brakes.

V8

1. Disconnect engine cushion mounts from crossmember.
2. Disconnect battery and engine ground strap.
3. Remove starter motor.
4. Remove idler arm at frame.
5. Disconnect the stabilizer bar brackets at the side rails.
6. Loosen strut rod bolts at lower control arms; remove crossmember side sill bolts.
7. With car weight on front wheels, pry crossmember down far enough for clearance. Use wood blocks for support between crossmember and side sills.
8. Remove oil pan bolts and oil pan.

Reverse the removal procedure to install the oil pan. Use new oil pan-to-timing chain cover front seal. Coat the end tabs with sealer. Use new side and rear gaskets, coat them, as well.

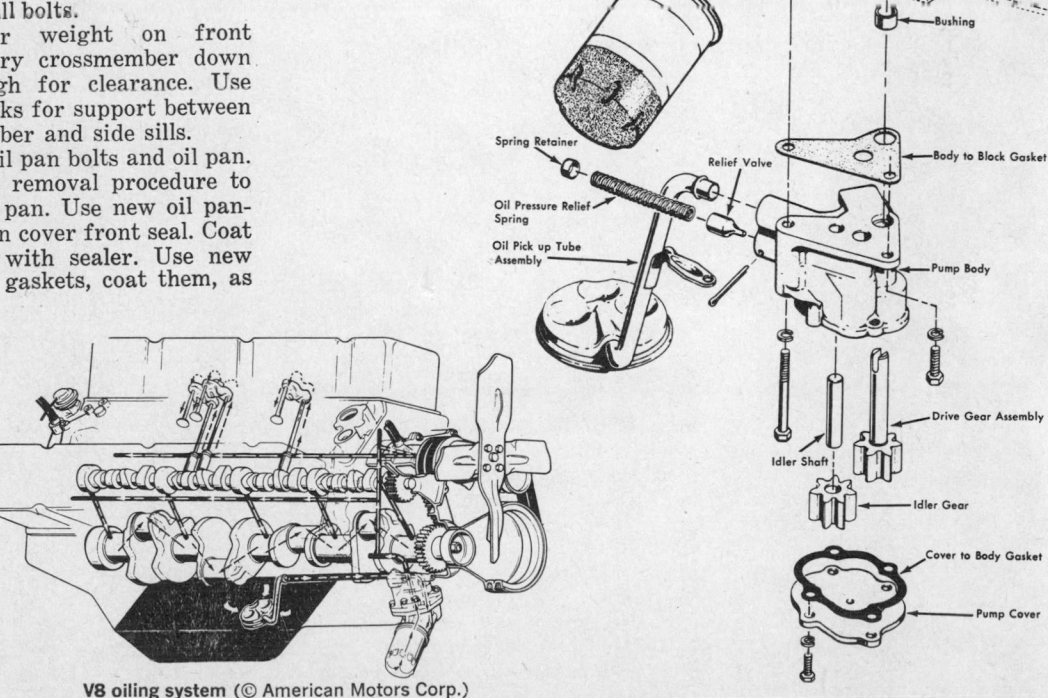

V8 oiling system (© American Motors Corp.)

Oil Pump Service

CAUTION: *Anytime the oil pump cover is removed or the pump disassembled, the pump must be primed. Do this by filling the spaces around the gears with petroleum jelly. Do not use grease.*

6 Cylinder

The oil pump is driven by the distributor drive shaft. Oil pump R&R does not, however, affect distributor timing because the drive gear remains in mesh with the camshaft gear.

1. Drain the oil and remove the oil pan.
2. Remove the oil pump attaching screws. Remove the pump and gasket from the engine block.
3. Remove the pump cover.

With a straightedge across the pump body and gears, clearance should be 0.000-0.004 in. through 1971 and .002-.006 in. 1972 and later (gears should project above body). Do not disturb the location of the tube in the pump body. If the tube is moved, a new tube and screen must be installed. Now, measure clearance between gears and wall of gear cavity opposite point of gear mesh; should be 0.0005-0.0025 in. The oil pressure relief valve is set at the factory and is not adjustable.

Installation is the reverse of removal.

V8

The oil pump is located in, and as part of, the timing cover. The pump is driven by the distributor drive shaft. Oil pump R&R does not, however, affect distributor timing.

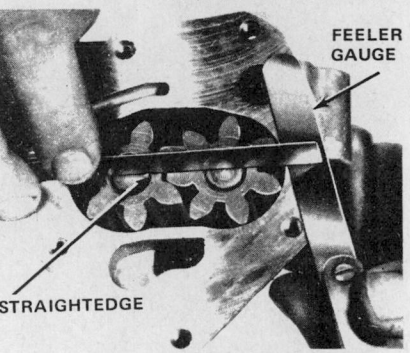

FEELER GAUGE

STRAIGHTEDGE

Oil pump gear end clearance measurement
(© American Motors Corp.)

Remove pump cover and place a straightedge across pump body and gears. Clearance should be 0.002-0.006 in. (gears projecting above body). Measure clearance between gears and wall of gear cavity opposite point of gear mesh; should be 0.002-0.004 in. through 1971 and 0.0005-0.0025 in. for 1972 and later. The oil pressure relief valve is not adjustable.

Valve Spring
Filter Connector
Raised Seat Must Face Valve
Retainer
By-Pass Valve
Bushing
Spring Retainer
Relief Valve
Body to Block Gasket
Oil Pressure Relief Spring
Oil Pick up Tube Assembly
Pump Body
Drive Gear Assembly
Idler Shaft
Idler Gear
Cover to Body Gasket
Pump Cover

6 cylinder oil pump assembly
(© American Motors Corp.)

Rear Main Bearing Oil Seal Replacement

1. Remove oil pan, as previously described.
2. Scrape clean all gasket surfaces, then remove rear main cap.
3. Discard lower portion of seal; drive out upper portion, using a brass drift, until it can be grasped with pliers.
4. Clean main cap, then *loosen* all remaining main cap bolts.

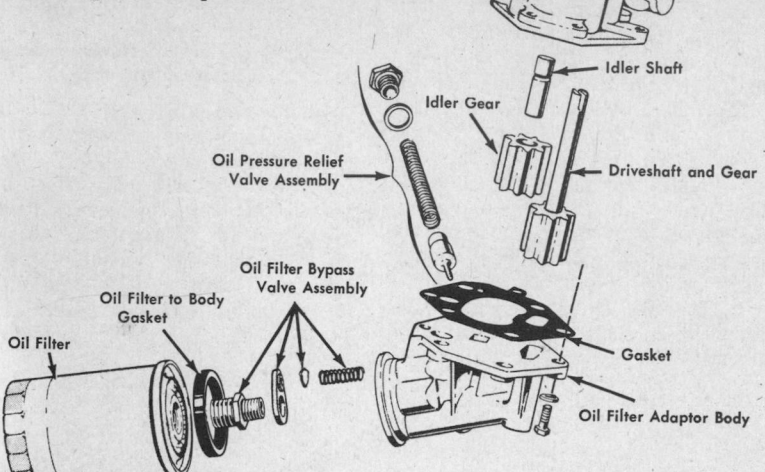

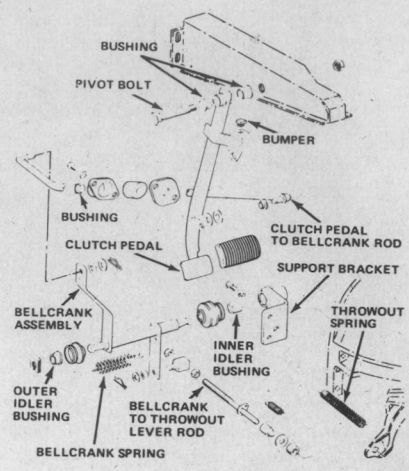

Typical clutch linkage
(© American Motors Corp.)

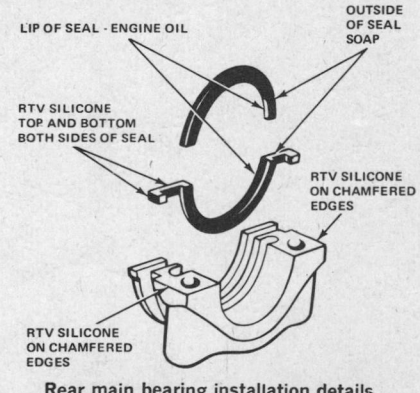

Rear main bearing installation details
(© American Motors Corp.)

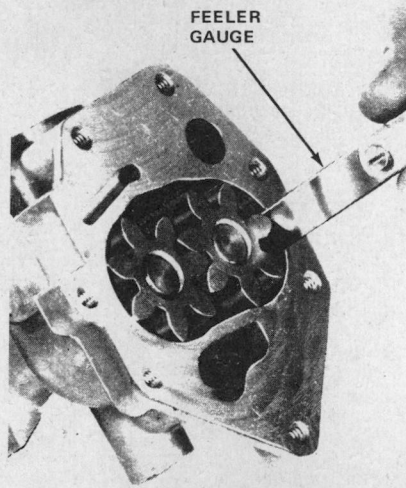

Oil pump gear to body clearance measurement
(© American Motors Corp.)

5. Coat the lip of the new upper seal with SAE 40 engine oil.
6. Install upper seal portion with the lip facing the front.
7. Coat both sides of the lower seal end tabs with sealant.
8. Coat the back surface of new lower seal with soap, the lip with SAE 40 engine oil. Install lower seal firmly into main cap.
9. Coat both chamfered edges of rear main cap with sealant install bearing inserts (if removed) and tighten all cap bolts to the specified torque.
10. Install the pan.

V8 oil pump assembly
(© American Motors Corp)

CLUTCH

The clutch is a single-plate, dry-disc, coil spring type. A semi-centrifugal 11 inch diameter clutch assembly is used with 360 and larger V8s through 1974. A 10 inch direct spring pressure type is used with the 304 V8, while a 9 1/4 inch indirect spring pressure type is used on sixes.

Pedal travel decrease due to normal wear of the linings can be compensated for by adjusting the clutch pedal free-play.

Pedal Free Play Adjustment

Adjust the free-play of the clutch pedal to 7/8-1 1/8 in. This is done by changing the length of the link between the throwout lever rod and the bellcrank assembly.

Clutch Removal

Remove the transmission and starter motor, then disconnect the clutch linkage at the release lever and remove the capscrews that hold the bellhousing (clutch housing) to the engine. It may be necessary to move the rear of the engine up or down to gain wrench clearance.

Any shims between the housing and engine must be replaced in exactly the same place to prevent misalignment.

Matchmark the clutch cover, pressure plate and flywheel before removal to ensure proper balance. Loosen each clutch cover capscrew a few turns at a time until spring tension is released, then remove the cover, pressure plate, and disc.

Check the pilot bushing in the end of the crankshaft for scoring or looseness. If it is necessary to replace the bushing, use either an expanding-end slidehammer or a suitable tap. Screwing the tap into the bore until it bottoms will force the bushing out.

Lubricate the busing with high temperature grease before installing the clutch. If there is a lubricating wick, soak it in engine oil.

Inspect the flywheel surface for heat cracks, scoring, or blue heat marks. Check the flywheel capscrews for proper torque. It will be necessary to lock-up the flywheel ring gear with a block or flywheel holding clamp tool before tightening these capscrews.

The throwout (release) linkage consists of a forked, pivoted lever contacting the bearing at one end and the linkage pushrod on the other. A return spring keeps the lever in contact with the ball pivot.

The throwout bearing itself is pre-lubricated and cannot be re-packed if dry. The slots in the inner groove of the throwout bearing sleeve should be filled with high temperature grease. Failure is evidenced by uneven clutch pedal pressure and a grinding, rattling noise when the pedal is depressed. Replace any noisy throwout bearings as soon as is practicable to prevent disintegration and possible transmission or clutch damage.

Clutch Installation

Slide the new clutch disc onto the transmission input shaft to check for binding. Remove any burrs from either the splines or hub using emery paper, then clean with a safe solvent. Place the clutch disc against the flywheel and secure it by inserting a dummy pilot shaft (such shafts, made of wood, are available from automotive jobbers) or an old transmission input shaft.

Place the new pressure plate (it is always good policy to replace the pressure plate when installing a new disc) in position, after first making sure that the clutch disc is facing the proper direction (flywheel side is so marked), and that matchmarks are aligned if old pressure plate is used.

Install all the capscrews finger-tight. Tighten the screws a little at a time, working around the pressure plate to avoid distorting it, to 28 ft. lbs on 6 cylinder engines and 38 ft. lbs on V8s. Remove the pilot shaft.

Do not depress clutch pedal until transmission is installed or throwout bearing will fall out.

Install the clutch housing, throwout bearing and tranmission. Hook up clutch linkage and check adjustment.

MANUAL TRANSMISSION

Most American Motors cars through 1974 use Warner manual transmissions. Starting 1975, they are used only in a few light duty applications, such as six-cylinder Gremlins without overdrive. The four-speed used through 1974 is the Warner T-10. A lightweight Warner four-speed was introduced in the Pacer in late 1976. An identification tag, containing Warner and American Motors part numbers, is located at the rear of the transmission. The Warner model number is also usually cast into the side of the case.

A few 1974, and most 1975 and later models, use the model 150T three-speed transmission. A nine-character identification code is stamped on the left front case flange, but does not give the model number.

The 150T can readily be identified by its nine-bolt top cover which is narrower in the front. Unlike the Warner transmissions, it does not have a drain plug; lubricant is

drained by removing the lower extension housing bolt. Warner three-speeds have a rectangular top cover, usually with four or six bolts.

See the Manual Transmission Unit Repair Section for further applications and overhaul procedures.

Transmission Removal and Installation

NOTE: Open the hood to avoid damage when the rear crossmember is removed. If the overdrive and transmission are to be separated, first engage then disengage the overdrive with the clutch pedal depressed and the engine running.

1. Split the rear universal joint and slide the driveshaft off the back of the transmission. (See U-Joints.)
2. Detach the column shift mechanism linkage to the transmission, and disconnect the clutch linkage and speedometer cable; disconnect the back-up light switch wiring, and TCS switch wiring, also.

On a floorshift, remove the shift lever. Remove the boot and unbolt the lever. Detach the column reverse lockup rod. On some Hurst units, the shift lever can be removed by inserting a 0.015-0.020 in. feeler gauge along the driver's side of the lever, between the spring steel barb and the lower part of the lever. Pull the lever and gauge out together. Support the engine.

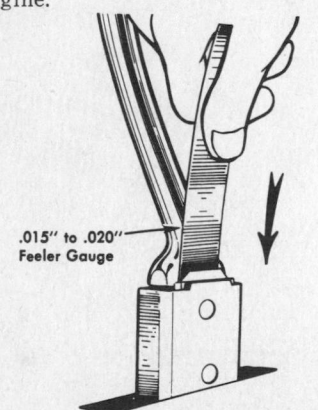

.015" to .020" Feeler Gauge

Removing lever from Hurst shifter (© American Motors Corp)

3. Disconnect the overdrive wiring. Remove the rear transmission support cushion bolts.
4. On Pacers with overdrive, remove the cotter pin from the parking brake equalizer and disconnect the front cable from the equalizer. Remove the cable adjuster and hooks from the floorpan bracket and lower equalizer and rear brake cables to provide clearance. Also, remove the ground strap from the floorpan.

NOTE: on V8 models with dual exhaust or dual catalytic converters,

exhaust pipes must be disconnected from manifolds and lowered so to gain working clearance. On Javelin and AMX models having Hurst shifter, entire shifter should be removed so that transmission can slide back far enough for removal.

5. Remove the transmission support crossmember, remove the two lower studs which hold the transmission to the bell housing and replace these two studs with two long pilot studs.
6. Remove the two top studs and slide the transmission assembly along the pilot studs and out of the car.

Installation is as follows:

1. Fill the slots in the inner groove of the throwout bearing with high temperature grease and soak the crankshaft pilot bushing wick in engine oil. Fit the throwout bearing and the sleeve assembly in the clutch fork. Center the bearing over the clutch lever.
2. Install two pilot studs in the clutch housing, instead of the lower clutch housing cap screws.
3. Carefully slide the transmission into place. Be careful not to damage the clutch driven plate splines while mating them with the transmission input shaft.
4. Install the upper screws, which attach the case to the housing.

Remove the pilot studs and install the lower cap screws.

5. If the car is equipped with a floor shift, install the shift mechanism or lever.
6. Attach the speedometer cable, connect the back-up light switch wires and the transmission controlled spark (TCS) wire, if so equipped.
7. Raise the transmission. Attach the rear crossmember and support to the transmission. Fasten the crossmember to the side sills. Install the parking brake cables and ground strap on Pacer with overdrive.
8. Attach the exhaust pipes to the exhaust manifolds, on V8 engines, if they were removed.
9. Install the front U-joint yoke on the transmission. Do the same for the rear U-joint at the differential.
10. Connect the shift rods on the column shift transmissions and the reverse lockup rod on the floorshift transmission. Check the transmission oil level and add lubricant, as needed.
11. Remove the supports and lower the car.
12. Install the shift lever if the car has a floorshift transmission.
13. Adjust the shift linkage, if it was disturbed.

Shift Linkage Adjustment

Column Shift

1. Disconnect the shift rods from the transmission shift levers. Insert a 3/16 in. drill through the column shift lever holes.
2. Shift into Reverse and lock the column with the ignition key. Position the transmission First/Reverse shift lever in Reverse.
3. Adjust the shift rod trunnion to a free pin fit in the transmission shift lever. Tighten the trunnion locknuts.
4. Unlock the column and move the gearshift to Neutral. Both of the transmission shift levers should be in the Neutral detent.
5. Repeat step three for the Second/Third shift rod trunnion.
6. Remove the drill from the column levers. Shift through all gears and check for a free crossover into Neutral.
7. Shift into Reverse and lock the column. The column should lock without any binding.

Aligning shift levers on column shift models
(© American Motors Corp.)

Three-Speed Floorshift

1. Place the transmission shift levers in their neutral positions.
2. Loosen the second-third lever adjuster.
3. Keeping the first-reverse shift rod and transmission lever in the neutral position, align the second-third rod so the shift notch is

exactly aligned with the first-reverse shift notch. Tighten the adjuster.

4. Operate the linkage and check for full engagement of all gears and a smooth crossover from first to second.
5. If there is a reverse lockup rod to the steering column, loosen both of the locknuts about ½ in. each. Shift into reverse and lock the column. You may have to rotate the lever at the bottom of the column up into the locked position. Tighten the lower locknut until it contacts the trunnion. Tighten the upper locknut while holding the trunnion centered. Unlock the column and shift through the gears. Shift into reverse and lock the binding.

Four-Speed Hurst Floorshift— 1970-74

NOTE: It may be necessary to lower the rear of the transmission to install the shift lever aligning pin.

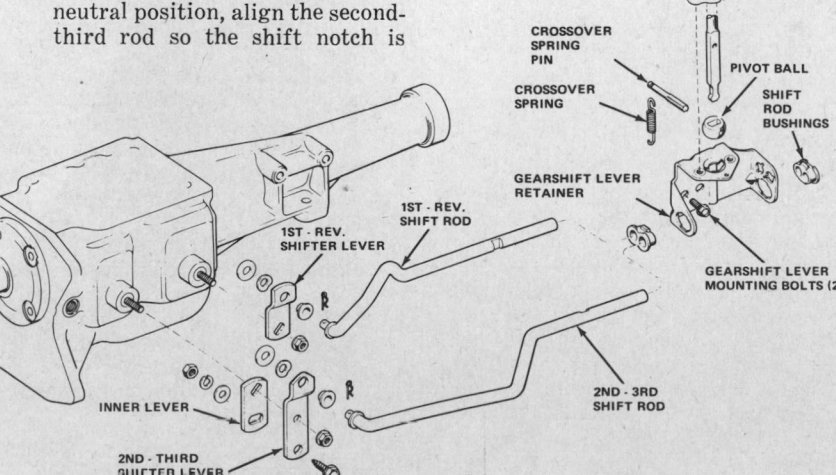

Three-speed floorshift linkage (© American Motors Corp.)

Before lowering the transmission, open the hood and remove the air cleaner. Then disconnect the exhaust system and the rear crossmember. It would probably be easier to cut an access hole.

Remove the boot assembly or plug and loosen the lower nuts and bolts on the two transmission forward speed shift levers. Loosen the two self-locking nuts at the center of the shift levers. Loosen the two locknuts on the reverse shift rod trunnion.

With the shifter in neutral position, insert a ¼ in. diameter aligning pin into the shifter housing and through the center of the three shifter levers. Make sure that the pin enters the notch in the far side of the housing. Check that the transmission levers are in their neutral positions. Remove and reinsert the aligning pin. The pin should slide in freely. If it does not, the shifter is not correctly aligned in the neutral position.

Tighten the lower bolts and nuts at the transmission forward speed shift levers. Tighten the self-locking nuts to 10 ft. lbs. Make sure the transmission reverse lever is in the neutral position. Tighten the trunnion nuts, being careful not to bind the trunnion in the reverse lever, then remove the aligning pin.

Loosen the steering column reverse lock-up rod trunnion locknuts about ½ in. each. Shift into reverse and lock the column. It may be necessary to move the lower column lever upward until it is in the locked position. Tighten the lower trunnion locknut until it contacts the trunnion. Tighten the upper locknut while holding the trunnion centered in the column lever. Unlock the column and check for proper shifting. The column should lock without binding.

AUTOMATIC TRANSMISSION

The Borg-Warner automatic transmission is used through model year 1971 and is called Shift Command. Shift-Command transmissions use a modified valve body to enable the driver to manually select a gear and hold the transmission in that gear.

Starting 1972, American Motors used Chrysler Corporation Torqueflite automatic transmissions in all their cars. These transmissions are the same as the equivalent Chrysler units, the only differences being in case design required by the difference in American Motors' bell-housing configuration and driveshafts.

Identification
Shift Command

All Shift Command automatic transmissions are similar in appearance, construction, design, and operation. The only difference is in calibration for different engine application.

There is a transmission identification tag located on the left side of the transmission that will show the model number, serial number and the American Motors part number.

Shift-Command automatic transmission identification tags
(© American Motors Corp)

SHIFT COMMAND TRANSMISSION IDENTIFICATION

Year	Transmission (Model)	Engine (cu. in.)
1970	42	199
	43	232
	43	232
	44	304
	11B	360
	12	390
1971	43	232
		258
	44	304
	11B	360
	12	401

Torque Command

There are three models of Torque Command automatic transmissions; 904, 998, and 727. The 727 model is physically larger than the other two models, being designed for use with V8 engines and heavy duty applications. Physical identification of the 727 model transmission is assisted by the fact that the slope of the converter housing is much more gradual than the other two.

The 904 and 998 models are similar in size and are designed for lighter duty applications. The 998 model has reinforcing ribs on the top of the rear servo boss on the case which distinguish it from the 904 model.

A seven-digit part number is stamped on the case on the left side above the oil pan mating surface. Following the part number is a coded, four-digit number which indicates the date of manufacture. The last group of numbers stamped on the case is the serial number.

Torque-Command automatic transmission identification numbers
(© American Motors Corp)

TORQUE COMMAND TRANSMISSION IDENTIFICATION

Year	Transmission (Model)	Engine (cu. in.)
1972	904	232
		258
	998	304
	727	360
		401
1973-77	904	232[1]
		258
	998	304[1]
	727	360
		401

① Model 727 optional on 258 six and all V8s except Pacer

Neutral Safety Switch Replacement and Adjustment

Column Shift—through 1971

The neutral safety switch is combined with the back-up light switch, thus, adjustment of the neutral safety switch will automatically adjust the back-up light switch. The switch is mounted in the steering column jacket, below the instrument panel.

NOTE: Engage the parking brake fully before beginning adjustment procedures.

1. Loosen the two screws that attach the switch to the steering column jacket.
2. Select Neutral with the gear lever.
3. Insert a 3/32 in. punch in the hole on the switch face. Turn the

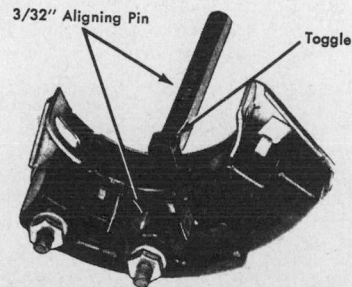

3/32" Aligning Pin   Toggle

Steering column mounted neutral safety switch adjustment—through 1971
(© American Motors Corp.)

switch until the pin freely enters the hole in the toggle.
4. Tighten the two mounting screws. Remove the punch. Be sure that the switch tang entered the channel on the operating shaft, *before* tightening the screws. Check the switch for proper operation.
5. Remove the mounting screws to remove the switch.

Console Shift—through 1971

The neutral safety switch is combined with the back-up light switch and is located in the center console. Before starting adjustment procedures be sure that the parking brake is firmly set.

1. Place the selector in Neutral.
2. Take the selector knob off the shift lever, except on 1971 Javelin models.
3. Remove the attachment screws from the console, raise it up and over the selector lever.
4. On the 1971 Javelin models, remove the console cover attaching screws and slide the cover up the selector lever.
5. Loosen the two switch attaching screws.
6. Insert a 3/32 in. punch in the hole in the face of the switch. Move the switch as necessary to freely fit the punch through the hole in the toggle.
7. Tighten the two screws and remove the punch. Check for proper switch operation. The car should only start in Park or Neutral.
8. If the switch is to be completely removed, take out the screws and remove the switch.
9. When adjustments are completed, assemble the console and shift selector.

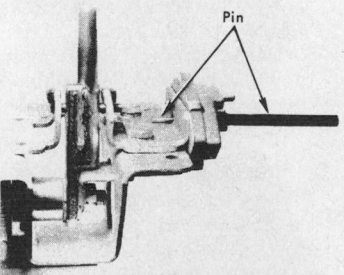

Pin

Console mounted neutral safety switch adjustment—through 1971
(© American Motors Corp.)

1972 and later

A combination back-up light-neutral safety switch is mounted on the left side of the transmission case. This switch cannot be adjusted; failure requires replacement.

To test the switch, proceed in the following manner:
1. Disconnect the wiring connector from the switch.

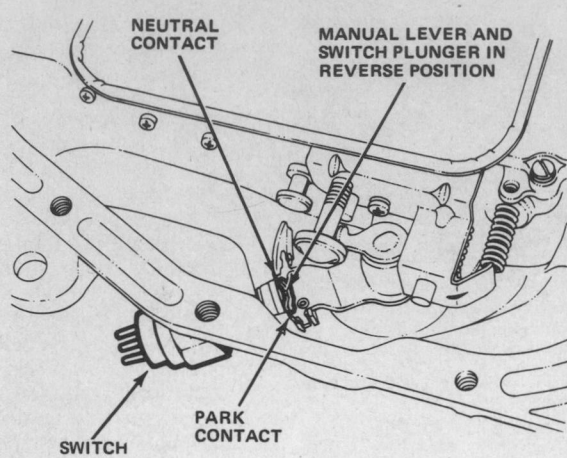

NEUTRAL CONTACT

MANUAL LEVER AND SWITCH PLUNGER IN REVERSE POSITION

PARK CONTACT

SWITCH

Torque-Command neutral start and backup light switch, pan removed - looking up
(© American Motors Corp.)

2. Use a 12V test lamp to check for continuity between the center pin of the switch and the transmission case. The lamp should only light in Park or Neutral.
3. If the lamp lights up in other positions, check the transmission linkage adjustments before replacing the switch.
4. To test the back-up light function of the switch repeat step two, by bridging the outside pins to test continuity. The light should only light in Reverse. No continuity should be present from either of the pins to the case.

To remove the switch, proceed as follows:

1. Place a container under the switch to catch transmission fluid. Unscrew the switch.
2. Select Park and then Neutral while checking to see that the operating fingers for the switch are centered in the case opening.
3. Screw a new switch and a *new* seal into the transmission. Tighten the switch to 24 ft. lbs.
4. Retest continuity. Replenish the transmission fluid, as required.

Shift Linkage Adjustment

Column Shift—through 1971
1. Place selector in Neutral.
2. Push shift rod against Neutral stop on shift gate.
3. Push selector lever forward to remove free play, then adjust clevis for free pin fit.
4. Connect linkage and check action, then test drive car.
5. Place selector in Park and check column lock operation.

Console Shift—through 1971
1. Loosen park lockup rod trunnion locknuts.
2. Place console lever in Neutral.
3. Place transmission shift lever in neutral position.

4. Adjust shift rod for a free pin fit.
5. Place console lever in Park. Lock the steering column. It may be necessary to move the lower column lever upward until it is in the locked position.
6. Tighten the lower trunnion locknut until it contacts the trunnion. Tighten the upper locknut while holding the trunnion centered in the column lever.

1972 and later
1. With the engine off, place the selector in Park and the transmission shift lever in the Park detent.
2. Adjust the shift rod, as necessary, for a free pin fit.
3. See that the steering column lock and the neutral safety switch operate properly.

Throttle Linkage Adjustment
This adjustment positions a valve which controls shift speed, shift firmness, and part-throttle downshift sensitivity. The linkage runs from the carburetor to the left side of the transmission.

1972-73
1. Make sure that the idle speed is correct.
2. Hook a spring in the hole on the transmission throttle lever.
3. Pull the spring forward and fasten it so that about 8-10 lbs tension is exerted on the throttle lever.
4. Unfasten the retaining clip which holds the adjustable throttle rod link at its slotted end.
5. Take the tab washer out of the slot in the rod and loosen, but don't remove, the slip-joint retaining screw.
6. On sixes, lengthen the adjustable rod to remove all slack. On V8s, shorten the adjustable rod to remove all slack.

7. Tighten the retaining screw on the slip-joint.
8. On sixes place the rod slot over the bellcrank lever. On V8s, place it over the carburetor throttle lever.
9. Install the tab washer and the retaining clip, making sure that the tabs on the washer are inserted in the slot.
10. Remove the spring.

1974 and later
1. Detach the throttle control rod spring and hook it so that the throttle control lever is held forward against its stop.
2. Block the choke open and set the carburetor throttle linkage off the fast idle cam.
NOTE: On models with a throttle solenoid valve, energize the solenoid and open the throttle halfway so that the solenoid will lock and then return the throttle to the idle position.
3. Loosen, but do not remove, the retaining bolt on the throttle control rod adjusting link.
4. On V8s, remove the spring clip and nylon washer; leave them in place on sixes.
5. On sixes, pull on the end of the link to remove all lash. On V8s, push on the end of the link to remove all lash.
6. Tighten the retaining bolt while performing Step 5.
7. Replace the throttle control rod spring in its original location. On V8s, install the nylon washer and spring clip on the retaining rod before replacing the spring.

Downshift Solenoid Replacement

Through 1971
1. Drain the fluid and remove pan, then disconnect solenoid wire from transmission case terminal.
2. Push in on the solenoid, while twisting, to disconnect it from the control valve. Take care not to lose the downshift valve spring.
3. To install, reverse the removal procedure, using a new O-ring.

Band Adjustments

Kickdown Band—1972-73
The adjustment screw for the kick-down band is located on the left side of the transmission, above the throttle and shift linkage levers.
1. Loosen the locknut. Back off the screw five turns.
2. Using a torque wrench tighten the screw to 72 in. lbs.
3. Back off two turns on the adjustment screw on the 904 and 998 series transmission.
4. Back off two and one-half turns

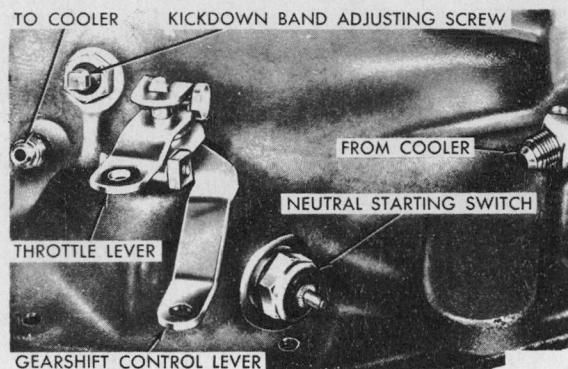

Torque-Command external adjustments
(© Chrysler Corp)

with the 360 cu. in. engines or two turns with the 401 cu. in. engine when used with the 727 series transmission.

5. Hold the adjusting screw and tighten the locknut to 29 ft lbs.

Kickdown Band—1974 and later

The basic adjustment procedures are the same as for 1972-73 transmissions. However, the adjustment screw on all 998 and all 727 transmissions should be backed off two and one-half turns in Step 4. On all transmissions, hold the adjusting screw and tighten the lock-nut to 35 ft lbs, after completing the adjustment.

Front Band—through 1971

1. Drain transmission fluid and remove pan.
2. Check for debris, "scorched" smelling fluid, and loose parts.
3. Check pick up screen for clogging, then check that all valve body cap screws and servo bolts are tight.
4. Check that delivery tubes are in place and snug.
5. To adjust, insert a ¼ in. gauge block between the front servo, adjusting screw and the piston rod, then tighten adjusting screw to 10 in. lbs.

NOTE: The adjusting screw on M11, M11B and M12 transmissions has a left-hand thread.

6. Inspect the adjuster wire for proper clearance—one screw thread must be exposed between the wire and the servo actuating lever.
7. Clean and install the pan, using a new gasket, then install proper quantity of approved fluid.

Rear Band—through 1971

1. Place a hydraulic jack under the transmission, then remove the four crossmember fasteners and the crossmember.

NOTE: Not necessary to remove crossmember on most Ambassador models. On AMX and Javelin equipped with power steering, lift the hood before lowering transmission to

keep the power steering fluid reservoir wingnut from hitting the hood.

2. Lower the transmission, then loosen the rear band adjusting screw locknut and tighten the adjusting screw to 10 ft. lbs.
3. Back off adjusting screw ¾ turn for M36, M37, M40, M43, and M44 transmissions, 1¼ turns for M11, M11B, and M12 transmissions. Tighten locknut to 28 ft. lbs.
4. Raise transmission and replace crossmember.

Low and Reverse Band 904—1972-73; 998 and 727—1972 and later

1. Remove the pan.
2. Loosen the locknut on the adjustment screw and back the screw off five turns.
3. Tighten the screw to 72 in. lbs.
4. Make the following adjustments:
   a. Series 904 transmission—back off three and one-quarter turns on the screw
   b. Series 998 transmission—back off four turns on the screw
   c. Series 727 transmission—back off two turns on the screw
5. Hold the adjusting screw while tightening the locknut to 35 ft. lbs.

6. Install the pan and a new gasket. Refill the transmission with DEXRON fluid.

Low and Reverse Band 904—1974 and later

1. Drain the fluid and remove the pan as detailed above.
2. Check the fluid for particles or burning.
3. Remove the locknut from the adjusting screw.
4. With a torque wrench and a ¼ in. socket, tighten the adjusting screw to 41 in. lbs.
5. Back off 7 turns on the adjusting screw.
6. While holding the adjusting screw, install the locknut and tighten it to 35 ft lbs.
7. Install the pan and a new gasket. Refill with DEXRON transmission fluid.

Pan Removal, Fluid and Filter Change

Through 1971

1. Drive the car until it is thoroughly warm.
2. Unbolt the pan on aluminum case models. It holds three or more quarts, so be ready.

NOTE: If the fluid removed smells burnt, serious transmission troubles, probably due to overheating should be suspected.

3. On cast iron case models, disconnect the filler tube first to drain the fluid. Then unbolt and remove the pan.
4. On aluminum case models, remove and clean the screen and magnet.
5. Clean out the pan, being extremely careful not to leave any lint from rags inside.
6. Replace the pan using a new gasket. Tighten the bolts to 15 ft lbs in a criss-cross pattern.
7. Replace the filler tube if it was removed.
8. Add 3 quarts of DEXRON or

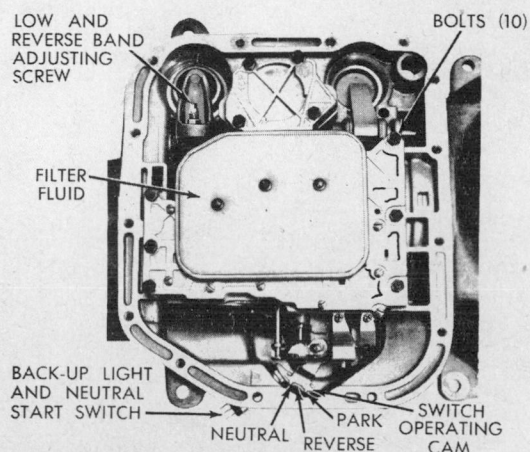

Torque-Command adjustments with the pan removed
(© Chrysler Corp)

AMC automatic transmission fluid through the dipstick tube.

9. Shift into Neutral and start the engine.

CAUTION: *Don't race the engine.*

10. Add fluid until the level is about ¼ in. below the L mark on the dipstick.

11. Operate the car until the transmission is thoroughly warmed up, then check the level. It should be at the F mark.

12. If the level is at or below the L mark, add fluid through the dipstick tube to bring the level up to the F mark. One pint brings the level from L to F. Be very cautious not to overfill the transmission.

1972 and Later

The manufacturer says that the transmission fluid doesn't ever have to be changed, unless the car is used for heavy work such as trailering. In this case, the fluid is to be changed every 25,000 miles. A band adjustment is also required at the same interval for these cars.

1. Drive the car until it is thoroughly warm.

2. Unbolt the pan. It holds six or more quarts so be ready.

NOTE: If the fluid removed smells burnt, serious transmission troubles, probably due to overheating should be suspected.

3. Unscrew and discard the filter.

4. Install a new filter. The proper torque is 28 in. lbs.

5. Clean out the pan, being extremely careful not to leave any lint from rags inside.

6. Replace the pan with a new gasket. Tighten the bolts to 11 ft lbs in a criss-cross pattern.

7. Pour six quarts of DEXRON or AMC automatic transmission fluid through the dipstick tube.

8. Start the engine in Neutral and let it idle for two minutes or more.

9. Hold your foot on the Brake and shift through D, 2, and R and back to N.

10. Add enough fluid to bring the level to the ADD ONE PINT mark.

11. Operate the car until the transmission is thoroughly warmed up, then check the level. It should be between the FULL and ADD ONE PINT mark.

12. If the level is at or below the ADD ONE PINT mark, add fluid through the dipstick tube to bring the level up to the FULL mark. One pint brings the level from ADD ONE PINT to FULL. Be very cautious not to overfill the transmission.

REAR AXLE

Axle Shaft, Bearing and Seal

Removal and Installation

1. The hub and drum are separate units and are removed after the wheel is removed. The hub and axle shaft are serrated together on the taper. An axle shaft key assures proper alignment during assembly.

2. Attach a puller to the rear hub and remove the hub. The use of a "Knock-out" puller should be discouraged, since it may result in damage to the axle shaft or wheel bearings.

3. Disconnect the parking brake cable at the equalizer.

4. Disconnect the brake tube at the wheel cylinder and remove the brake support plate assembly, oil seal, and axle shims. Note that the axle shims are located on the left side only.

5. Using a screw type puller, remove the axle shaft and bearings from the axle housing.

6. Remove the axle shaft inner oil seal and install new seals at assembly.

7. The bearing is a press fit and should be removed with an arbor press.

8. The axle shaft bearings have no provision for lubrication after assembly. Before installing the bearings, they should be packed with a good quality wheel bearing lubricant.

9. Press the axle shaft bearings onto the axle shaft with the small diameter of the cone toward the outer (tapered) end of the shaft.

10. Soak the inner axle shaft seal in light lubricating oil. Coat the outer surface of the seal retainer with sealant.

11. Install the inner oil seal with suitable installer.

12. Install the axle shafts, indexing

the splined end with the differential side gears.

13. Install the outer bearing cup.

14. Install the brake support plate. Sealant should be applied to the axle housing flange and brake support mounting plate.

15. Install the original shims, oil seal and brake support plate. Torque the nuts to 30-35 ft lbs.

NOTE: The oil seal and retainer go between the axle housing flange and the brake support plate on 9 in. brakes. On 10 in. brakes, they go on the outside of the brake support plate.

16. To adjust the axle shaft end-play, strike the axle shafts with a lead mallet to seat the bearings. Install a dial indicator on the brake support plate and check the play while pushing and pulling the axle shaft. End-play should be 0.004-0.008 in., with 0.006 in. desirable. Add shims to the left side only to decrease the play and remove shims to increase the play.

17. Slide the hub onto the axle shafts aligning the serrations and the keyway on the hub with the axle shaft key.

18. Replace the hub and drum, install the wheel, lower the car onto the floor and tighten the axle shaft nut to 250 ft lbs. If the cotter pin hole is not aligned with a castellation on the nut, tighten the nut to the next castellation.

NOTE: a new hub must be installed whenever a new axle shaft is installed. Tighten the new hub onto the shaft until the hub is 1.17 in. from the end of the shaft on 7-9/16 in. differentials, and 1.30 in. on 8⅞ in. models. Loosen the nut and torque to 250 ft. lbs. 7 9/16 in. axles can be identified by the cover mounted filler plug; the 8⅞ axle has a front filler.

19. Connect the parking brake cable at the equalizer.

20. Connect the brake tube at the wheel cylinder and bleed the brakes.

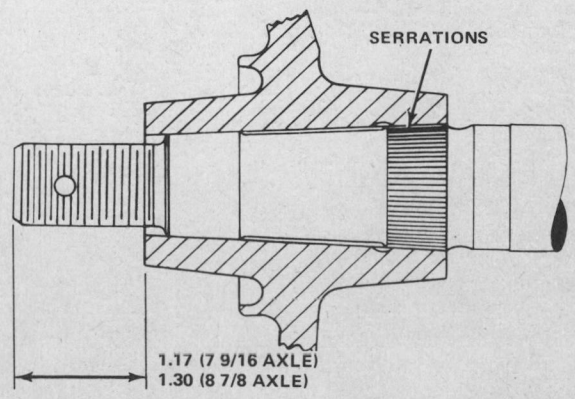

SERRATIONS

1.17 (7 9/16 AXLE)
1.30 (8 7/8 AXLE)

Measurements for installing a new rear axle hub (© American Motors Corp.)

U-JOINTS

A one-piece, tubular driveshaft is used.

Removal and Installation

1. Matchmark and disassemble rear U-joint by removing nuts.
2. Drop rear of driveshaft and slide front yoke out of transmission.
3. To install, reverse removal procedure, tightening U-joint nuts to 15 ft lbs.

Universal Joint Repairs

1. Remove the lock rings from the inner side of two opposite bearings and press on the outer side of one of the bearings, forcing the cross over. This will force the bearing on the opposite side out of its yoke.
2. Remove the bearing which was forced out of the yoke, then press the cross in the opposite direction to force the other bearing out.
3. Repeat this procedure on the third and fourth bearing.
4. When installing the new bearings in the universal joint yoke, press them into place.

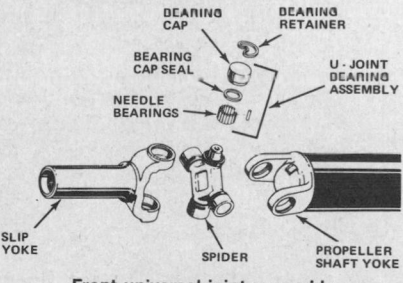

Front universal joint assembly
(© American Motors Corp)

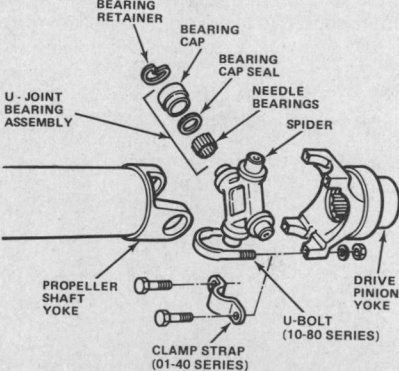

Rear universal joint assembly
(© American Motors Corp)

JACKING, HOISTING

1. Jack car, at front, under lower support arms and, at rear, under rear axle housing.

2. To lift, contact car at rear lift pads marked lift just forward of rear wheels (at the rear spring hangers on Gremlin, Hornet, and Pacer). Front lift points are on underbody sill just to the rear of strut rod-to-sill mounting bracket. On a Pacer, the front lift points are located just to the rear of the dash panel on the front wheelwell sill.

FRONT SUSPENSION

The front suspension on all models is an independent linked type with the coil springs located between seats in the wheelwell panels and seats in the upper control arms. Rubber insulators between the springs and seats reduce noise transmission to the body.

Direct acting, telescopic shock absorbers are located inside the coil springs and the control arms are attached to the body via rubber bushings.

The suspension system is a double ball joint design, both upper and lower control arms each having one joint.

On all models, strut rods serve to support the lower control arms. Stabilizer bars are used on some models.

The Pacer front suspension is different from all other AMC cars. The coil spring is mounted between the two control arms; seated at the bottom on the lower control arm and at the top in the suspension/engine mount crossmember. The crossmember is isolated from the rest of the body structure by rubber mounting points. The shock absorbers are mounted inside the coil spring. The steering knuckle is attached to the upper and lower control arms by upper and lower ball joints. A front stabilizer bar is optional.

NOTE: The front end alignment must be checked after any disassembly procedure.

Shock Absorber Replacement

NOTE: When installing new shock absorbers, purge them of air by extending them in their normal position and compressing them while inverted. Do this several times. It is normal for there to be more resistance to extension than to compression.

All Except Pacer

1. Remove the two lower shock absorber attaching nuts. Remove the washers and the grommets.
2. Remove the upper mounting bracket nuts and bolts.
3. Remove the bracket, complete with shock.
4. Remove the upper attaching nut

and separate the shock from the mounting bracket.

Install the shock as follows:

1. Fit the grommets, washers, upper mounting bracket and nut on the shock, in the reverse order of removal. Tighten the nut to 30 ft lbs (through 1972) or to 8 ft lbs (1973 and later).
2. Fully extend the shock and install two grommets on the lower mounting studs.
3. Lower the shock through the hole in the wheel arch. Fit the lower attachment studs through the lower spring seat.
4. Install the grommets, washers, and nuts. Tighten the nuts to 8 ft lbs (through 1973) or 15 ft lbs (1974 and later).
5. Secure the upper mounting bracket with its attachment nuts and bolts. Tighten them to 20 ft lbs.

Pacer

1. Raise the front of the car and support it. Remove the wheels.
2. Remove the two lower shock absorber attaching bolts.
3. Remove the upper shock absorber attaching nut through the opening in the upper control arm.
4. Remove the shock absorber through the bottom of the lower control arm.

To install the front shock absorbers:

5. Install the rubber grommets and spacers to the shock absorber and install the shock up through the opening in the lower control arm. Place the rubber grommets and washers over the stud protruding through the mounting hole. Install the attaching nut and tighten the nut just enough to slightly compress the rubber grommets (8 ft lbs.)
6. Position the lower shock mounting to the lower control arm and install the rubber grommets, washers and attaching nuts. Tighten the nuts to 20 ft lbs.

Front Spring Removal and Installation

All Except Pacer

Jack up the car far enough to reach the two lower shock absorber nuts. Remove the nuts, washers and grommets, then remove the upper mounting bracket screws and bolts from the wheelwell. Lift the bracket and shock absorber from the panel.

Lower the car to the floor, then install a spring compressor through the upper spring seat opening and bolt it to the lower spring seat using the lower shock absorber mounting holes. Remove the lower spring seat pivot retaining nuts, then tighten the compressor tool to compress the spring about 1 in.

Jack up the front of the car and support it on axle stands at the subframe (allowing the control arms to hang free). Remove the front wheel and pull the lower spring seat out away from the car, then slowly release the spring tension and remove the coil spring and lower spring seat.

To install, place the spring compressor through the coil spring and tape the rubber spring cushion to the small-diameter end of the spring (upper). Place the lower spring seat against the spring with the end of the coil against the formed shoulder in the seat. The shoulder and coil end face inwards, toward the engine, when the spring is installed.

Place the spring up against the upper seat, then align the lower spring seat pivot so that the retaining studs will enter the holes in the upper control arm. Compress the coil spring and install the spring, then install the wheel and tire and lower the car to the floor (to place weight on suspension). Install and tighten lower spring seat spindle retaining nuts and tighten them to 35 ft. lbs. Remove the spring compressor and install the shock absorber.

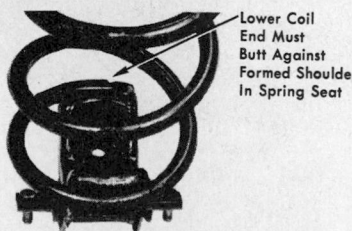

Lower spring seat installation— front coil springs, except Pacer (© American Motors Corp)

Pacer

1. Disconnect the upper end of the shock absorber.
2. Raise the front end of the car and support it.
3. Disconnect the lower end of the shock absorber and remove it.
4. Disconnect the stabilizer bar at the lower control arm, if so equipped.
5. Remove the wheel, brake drum, or caliper and rotor. Do not allow the brake hose to support the weight of the caliper; use a length of wire to suspend the caliper from the frame.
6. Remove the two bolts that attach the steering arm to the steering knuckle and move the steering arm aside.
7. Use a spring compressor to compress the coil spring.
8. Remove the cotter pin and nut from the lower ball joint stud and disengage the stud from the

steering knuckle with a puller.
9. Move the steering knuckle, steering spindle, and support plate, or anchor plate assembly, aside to provide working clearance. Do not allow the brake hose to support the weight of these components. Use wire to hang the components from the upper control arm.
10. Move the lower control arm aside and remove the spring.

To install the front coil spring:
11. Position the upper end of the spring in the spring seat of the front crossmember. Align the cut-off end of the bottom coil with the formed shoulder in the spring seat. The top coil is flat and does not use an insulator. Use a floor jack or jack stand to support the spring until the spring compressor is installed. Install the spring compressor.
12. Assemble the remaining components of the front suspension in the reverse order of removal. Tighten the ball joint stud nut to 75 ft lbs, the steering arm-to-knuckle attaching bolts to 80 ft lbs, the shock absorber lower mounting nuts to 20 ft lbs, and the stabilizer bar locknut to 8 ft lbs.

Control Arm Removal and Installation

Upper Control Arm— Except Pacer

Remove the shock absorber and compress the coil spring approximately 2 in. using the procedure under Front Spring Removal and Installation.

Jack up the front of the car and support the body on jackstands placed under the subframes (allow the control arms to hang free).

Remove the wheel and the upper ball joint cotter pin and retaining nut. Separate the ball joint stud from the steering knuckle using a ball joint removal tool. Remove the inner pivot bolts then remove the control arm.

To install, reverse the removal procedure. Do not tighten the pivot bolt nuts until the full weight of the car is on the wheels. The ball joint stud nut must be tightened to 40 ft lbs., the lower spring seat pivot retaining nuts to 35 ft. lbs, and the control arm inner pivot bolts to 45 ft lbs.

Upper Control Arm—Pacer

1. Raise and support the front of the vehicle.
2. Remove the wheel and tire.
3. Remove the cotter pin, locknut, and retaining nuts from the upper ball joint stud.
4. Loosen the stud from the steering knuckle with a ball joint removal tool.
5. Support the lower control arm with a floor jack.
6. Disengage the stud from the steering knuckle.
7. Remove the retaining nuts that attach the crossshaft to the front crossmember and remove the upper control arm assembly.
8. Install the upper control arm in the reverse order of removal, tightening the cross-shaft retaining nuts to 80 ft lbs, the upper ball joint stud nut to 75 ft lbs, and if new bushings were installed, tighten the nuts to 60 ft lbs. after the car is lowered to the floor.

Lower Control Arm—Except Pacer

The inner end of the lower control arm is attached to a removable crossmember. The outer end is attached to

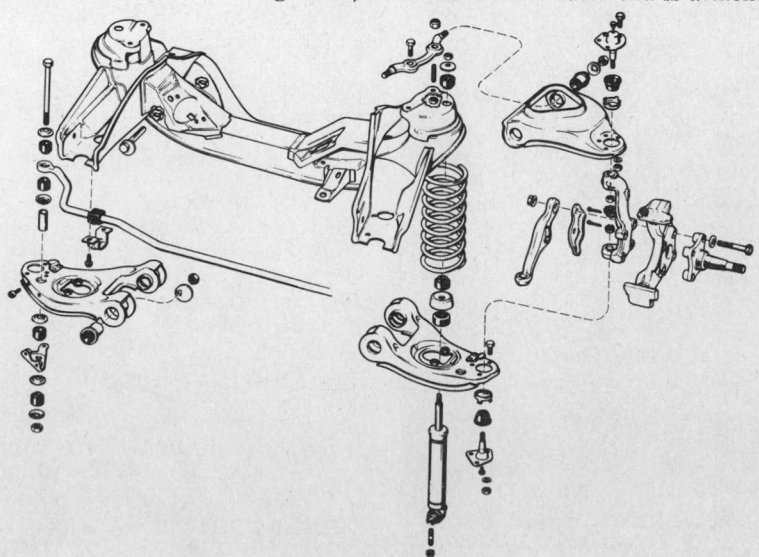

Exploded view of the Pacer front suspension

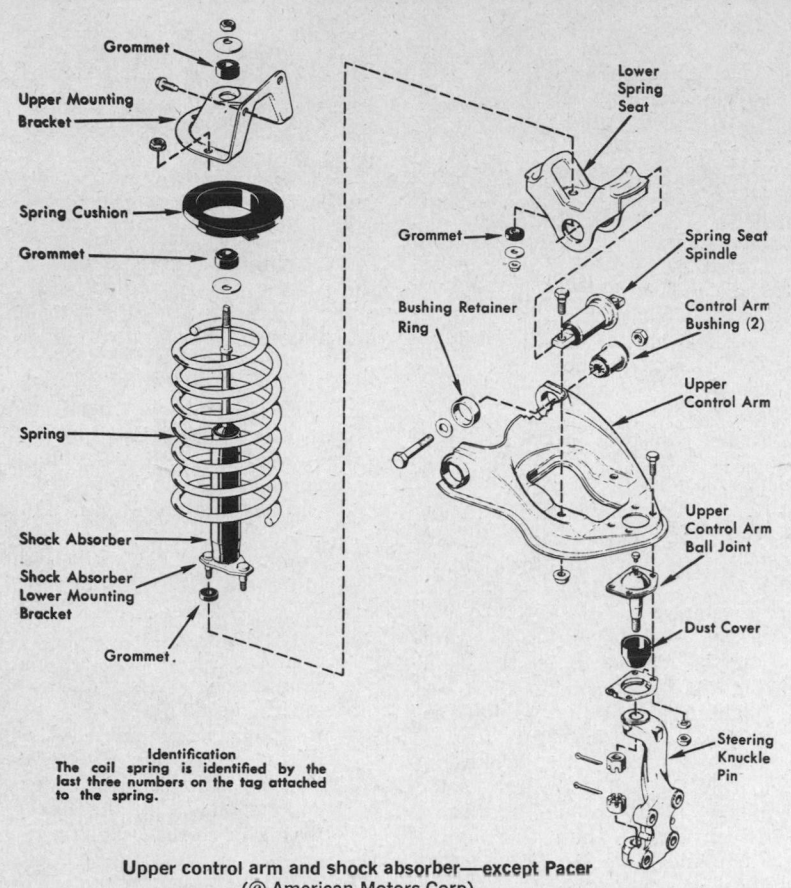

Identification
The coil spring is identified by the last three numbers on the tag attached to the spring.

Upper control arm and shock absorber—except Pacer
(© American Motors Corp.)

the steering knuckle pin and ball joint assembly.

To remove, jack up the car and support it on axle stands under the subframes. Remove the brake drum or caliper and rotor from the spindle, then disconnect the steering arm from the knuckle pin. Remove the lower ball joint stud cotter pin and nut. Separate the ball joint from the knuckle pin using a ball joint removal tool.

Disconnect the sway bar from the control arm, then unbolt the strut rod. Remove the inner pivot bolt and the control arm.

To install, reverse the removal procedure; do not tighten inner pivot bolt until car weight is on wheels. Tighten ball joint retaining nut to 40 ft lbs., strut rod bolts to 75 ft lbs., sway bar bolts to 8 ft lbs, steering arm bolts to 65 ft. lbs., and control arm inner pivot bolt to 95 ft lbs.

Lower Control Arm—Pacer
1. Disconnect the upper end of the shock absorber, raise the front

end of the car and disconnect the lower end of the shock absorber and remove the shock absorber.
2. Disconnect the stabilizer bar at the lower control arm, if so equipped.
3. Remove the wheel, brake drum, or caliper and rotor. Do not allow the brake hose to support the weight of the caliper. Use wire to support it from the frame.
4. Remove the two bolts attaching the steering arm to the steering knuckle and move the steering arm aside.
5. Install a spring compressor and compress the spring.
6. Remove the cotter pin and nut from the lower ball joint stud. Remove the ball joint from the steering knuckle using a ball joint removal tool.
7. Move the steering knuckle assembly out of the way. Support the assembly with wire from the upper control arm.
8. Remove the two pivot bolts that attach the lower arm to the front crossmember and remove the lower control arm.
9. Install the lower control arm in the reverse order of removal, tightening the ball joint stud nut to 75 ft lbs, the steering arm attaching bolts to 80 ft lbs, the shock absorber lower attaching nuts to 20 ft lbs, the stabilizer bar locknut to 8 ft lbs, and lastly, after the car has been lowered to the ground with the wheel and tire installed, tighten the lower control arm pivot bolts to 95 ft lbs.

Ball Joints

Inspection

All Except Pacer
NOTE: Be sure that the front wheel bearings are adjusted to specification before checking the upper ball joint.
1. Jack up the front of the car and place jackstands under the frame side sills.
NOTE: The control arms must hang free if an accurate reading is to be obtained.
2. Check the lower ball joints by grasping the lower portion of the wheel and pulling it in and out.
3. If there is noticeable lateral freeplay, the lower ball joint is worn and must be replaced.
4. To check the condition of the upper ball joint, place a dial indicator with its plunger against the tire scrub bead (just outside the whitewall).
5. Move the upper portion of the wheel and tire toward the car's

STABILIZER BAR
STRUT ROD MOUNTING BRACKET
BUSHING (2 PIECE)
STRUT ROD
BUSHING (2 PIECE)
BUMPER MOUNTING BRACKET
LOWER CONTROL ARM
CROSSMEMBER
LOWER CONTROL ARM
LOWER BALL JOINT ASSEMBLY
BUMPER

Lower control arm details—models except Pacer (© American Motors Corp.)

center, while watching the dial indicator.

6. Move the wheel and tire back out while watching the indicator.
7. The upper ball joint should be replaced if its *total* movement is greater than 0.160 in.

Pacer

1. Check that the front wheel bearings are adjusted properly.
2. Remove the lubrication plug from the lower ball joint. Insert a piece of stiff wire until it contacts the ball. Mark the wire even with the edge of the plug hole.
3. Measure from the end of the wire to the mark. If it exceeds 7/16 in., the ball joint should be replaced.
4. Place a jack under the lower control arm and lift the wheel off the floor.
5. Push the top of the tire in and out. If there is any looseness, replace the upper ball joint.
6. Pry the upper control arm up and down. If there is any looseness, replace the upper ball joint.

Removal and Installation

Lower Ball Joint

1. On all vehicles except Pacer, place a 2 x 4 x 5 in. block of wood on the side sill so that it supports the control arm.
2. Jack up the front end of the car and place jackstands underneath the frame side sills to support the body.
3. Remove the wheel and the brake drum. On cars equipped with disc brakes, remove the caliper and rotor.
4. Disconnect the lower control arm strut rod, on models other than Pacer. Disconnect the stabilizer bar, if so equipped.
5. Separate the steering arm from the steering knuckle.
6. Remove the ball stud retaining nut, after removing its cotter pin.
7. Install a ball joint removal tool then loosen the ball stud in the knuckle pin. Leave the tool in place on the stud.

8. Place a jackstand under the lower control arm.
9. Chisel the heads off the rivets which secure the ball joint to the control arm. Use a punch to remove the rivets.
10. Remove the tool from the ball stud.
11. Remove the ball stud from the knuckle pin and remove the joint from the control arm.

Installation of a new lower ball joint is as follows:

1. Position the new ball joint so that its securing holes align with the rivet holes in the control arm.
2. Install the special 5/16 in. bolts, used to secure the ball joint, loosely.

Caution Use only the hardened 5/16 in. bolts supplied with the ball joint replacement kit; standard bolts are not strong enough.

3. Install the steering strut and stop on the lower control arm. Tighten their bolts to 75 ft lbs.
4. Tighten the 5/16 in. ball joint securing bolts to 25 ft lbs.
5. Fit the knuckle pin and retaining nut on the ball stud; tighten the nut to 40 ft lbs (75 ft lbs on Pacer) Install the cotter pin.
6. Complete the installation procedure in the reverse order of removal and then check front end alignment.

Upper Ball Joint

1. Perform Steps 1-3 of the "Lower Ball Joint Removal" procedure.
NOTE: It is not necessary to remove the brake drum in Step 3.
2. Next, perform Steps 6-9 of the "Lower Ball Joint Removal" procedure to the upper ball joint.
3. Separate the upper ball joint from the control arm.
4. Remove the ball joint puller from the knuckle pin.

Installation of a new upper ball joint is as follows:

1. Perform Steps 1-2 of the "Lower Ball Joint Installation" procedure.
2. Skip Step 3 and go on to Steps

4-5 of the "Lower Ball Joint Installation" procedure.
3. Complete the installation in the reverse order of removal and check front end alignment.

Wheel Bearings

Inspection

Check to see that the inner cones of the bearings are free to "creep" on the spindle. Polish and lubricate the spindle to allow "creeping" movement and to keep rust from forming.

Adjustment

1. With the tire and wheel removed and the car supported by a suitable and safe means, remove the dust cover from the spindle.
2. Remove the cotter pin and nut retainer.
3. Rotate the wheel while tightening the spindle nut to 20-25 ft lbs.
4. Loosen the spindle nut 1/3 of a turn.
5. Rotate the wheel while tightening the spindle nut to 12 in. lbs. for models through 1973 and 6 in. lbs. for 1974 and later.
6. Fit the nut retainer over the spindle and align the slots in it with the cotter pin hole. Insert the cotter pin.
7. Install the dust cover.

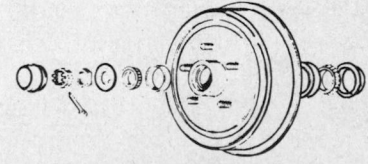

Front wheel bearing components
(ⓒ American Motors Corp)

REAR SUSPENSION

All Pacers, Javelin, Hornet, Gremlin and AMX models use a four or five-leaf semi-elliptic spring, and live axle rear suspension. Shock absorbers are mounted at their lower ends to studs and are bayonet type at their upper ends. Upper shock nuts are accessible by removing cover plates or by removing trunk floormat; except for Pacer and AMX models. The upper ends of the shocks in these models are mounted to bolted-on brackets, which must be removed in order to remove the shocks.

The rear suspension on Rebel, Ambassador, and Matador models is a four-trailing arm, coil spring type. The two lower control arms are attached to the outer ends of the axle tubes and to the body side sills, while the two upper control arms are attached to the differential housing and to a rear crossmember. Rubber bush-

Place a wooden block between the underside of the upper control arm and the top of the subframe when removing ball joints on models other than *Pacer*
(ⓒ American Motors Corp.)

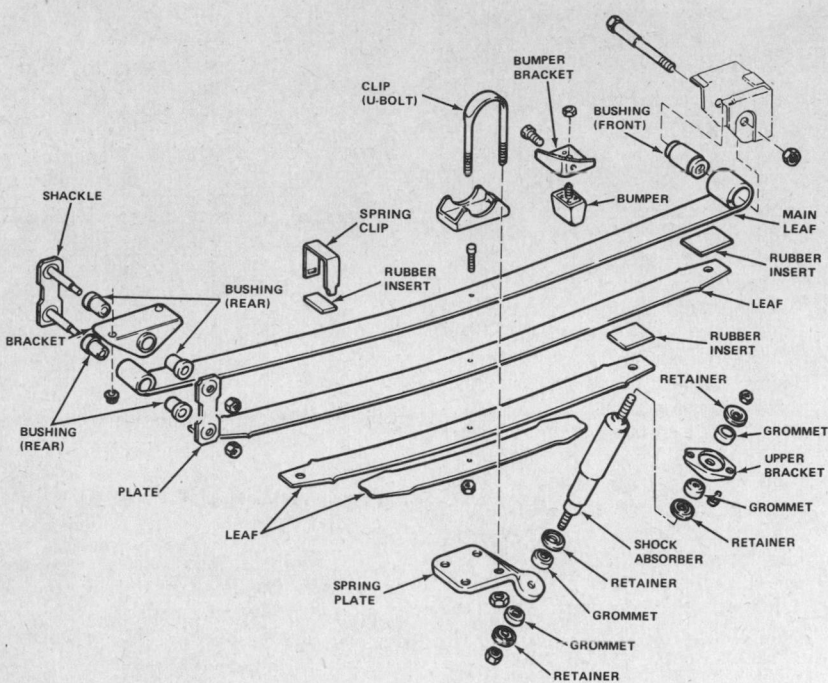

Typical leaf spring rear suspension (© American Motors Corp.)

axle with jacks or a lift to take the load off the rear springs.
2. Disconnect the rear shock from the lower mounting stud.
3. Disconnect the axle U-bolts.
4. Remove the nut from the bolt which attaches the eye of the spring to the front mount. Remove the bolt.
5. Remove the nuts from the rear shackle. Remove the shackle.
6. Installation is the reverse of removal.

Ambassador, Rebel, and Matador

1. Raise the rear of the car and support the rear axle with jacks or a lift to take the load off the rear springs.
2. Disconnect the shock from the axle tube. Lower the axle to the fullest extent of its travel (limited by the control arms). Detach the upper control arms at the axle on 1975 and later models.
3. Pull down the axle tube to completely release the spring.
4. Reverse the above to install the spring. Torque the control arm pivot bolts to 45-80 ft lbs. with the weight of the car on the springs.

ings are used on the lower arms and on the crossmember ends of the upper arms. The lower ends of the upper arms are attached to pressed in bushings in ears on the differential case. Shock absorbers are accessible at their upper ends by removing cover plates in the body or by removing brackets from underneath the car.

Shock Absorber Replacement

NOTE: When installing new shocks, purge them of air by repeatedly extending them in their normal position and compressing them while inverted. It is normal for there to be more resistance to extension than to compression.

1. Support the rear axle with jacks or a lift; this allows the weight of the car to compress the rear spring.

2. Remove the lower shock attachment.
3. Remove the access plate on the rear underbody panel and remove the upper securing nut. It may be necessary to hold the top of the shock while unfastening the nut.
NOTE: Some models do not have an access plate. On these cars, remove the upper attachment plate complete as an assembly.
4. Remove the shock from under the car.
5. Installation is the reverse of removal.

Rear Spring Removal and Installation

Pacer, Javelin, Hornet, and Gremlin

1. Raise the car. Support the rear

BRAKES

All American Motors cars come equipped with dual tandem master cylinders. This allows one set of brakes to operate, should the other set fail. A switch in the system, connected to a warning light on the instrument panel, indicates a difference in pressure between the front and rear brake lines, thus indicating the failure of one brake system. Repair procedures for both the master cylinder and the switch are found in the "Unit Repair Section."

All drum brakes have automatic brake adjusters. These automatically compensate for lining wear, by operating when the brakes are applied while the car is backing up. The automatic mechanism is attached to the star wheel adjuster, which it works through.

Information on brake adjustments, lining replacement, bleeding procedure, master and wheel cylinder overhaul can be found in the Unit Repair Section.

Master Cylinder Removal and Installation

1. Disconnect the front and rear brake lines from the master cylinder. On cars equipped with drum brakes, the check valves will keep the fluid from draining out of the cylinder. If the car is equipped with disc brakes, one or both of the outlets must be plugged, to prevent fluid loss.

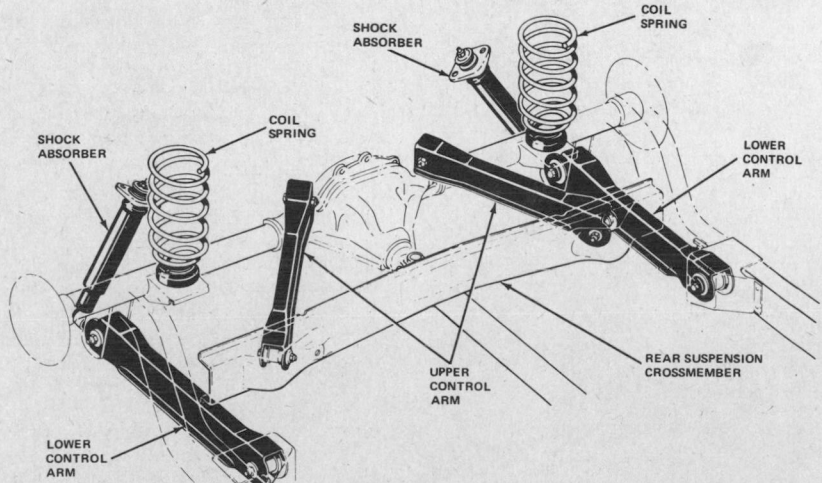

Typical coil spring rear suspension (© American Motors Corp.)

2. Remove the nuts which attach the master cylinder to the firewall or the power brake booster (if so equipped).
3. On cars that have manual brakes, disconnect the pedal push rod from the brake pedal.
4. Remove the master cylinder from the car.

Installation is the reverse of removal. Remember to bleed the brake system once the master cylinder has been installed. (See the "Unit Repair Section.")

Power Brake Unit Removal and Installation

Remove the clevis pin from the power-unit operating rod. Disconnect the vacuum line and the hydraulic lines from the power unit, remove the stop light wires, remove the mounting bolts and lift off the power cylinder.

Installation is the reverse order of the above.

Parking Brake Cable Replacement

1. Disconnect the lower end of the cable at the cross-shaft or equalizer, disconnect it at the hand-brake end.
2. Remove the brackets which retain it to the body and firewall and thread it out of the vehicle.

When a new cable is to be installed, it is always a good idea to tie the new one to the end of the old one so that it will thread through in the same route as the old cable. This, sometimes, will require the service of a helper to guide it.

Parking Brake Adjustment

1. Apply the brakes several times while backing up to adjust the drum brakes. Set the pedal on the first notch from the released position.
2. Block the front wheels and raise the rear wheels.
3. Tighten the cable at the equalizer so that the wheels can just barely be turned forward.
4. Release the parking brake and check for rear brake drag. The wheels should rotate freely with the parking brake off.

STEERING

Power Steering Pump Removal and Installation

1. Remove the fan belt.
2. Place a container under the pump to catch fluid. Remove the fuel vapor storage canister and six-cylinder air cleaner if necessary.
3. Disconnect the hoses and cap the outlets, so that the power steering unit does not loose fluid. Remove the air pump belt on 1975 and later models.
4. On 1975 and later sixes with air conditioning, loosen the idler pulley adjusting bolt and idler pulley, air pump adjusting strap mounting bolt and remove the compressor drive belt from the idler pulley. Loosen the two nuts that attach the upper leg of the aluminum idler pulley mounting bracket to the cylinder head and remove the bolt that attaches the lower leg of the mounting bracket to the engine front cover.
5. On sixes through 1974, loosen the pump bracket pivot bolts. On V8s through 1974, remove the front pump mounting bracket. Remove the pump drive belt and the pump. On 1975 and later sixes, remove the nut from the air pump mounting stud, remove the power steering pump to engine front cover front adapter plate (do not unbolt the adapter plate from the pump), remove the long adjusting bolt that passes through the adapter plate, and remove the bolt hidden behind the flange in the rear adapter plate. Remove the pump, adapter plate and mounting bracket together.

On 1975 and later V8s, remove the two pump mounting stud nuts at the rear of the two-piece mounting bracket. Remove the pump support strap bolts and the front half of the pump mounting bracket. Remove the nut from the stud holding the front half of the pump bracket. Remove the pump and the front half of the mounting bracket.

6. After installation, fill the system with DEXRON or AMC automatic transmission fluid. Bleed the system of air by raising the front of the car and turning the wheels from side to side without hitting the stops several times. Check the level frequently.

Steering Wheel Removal and Installation

1. Disconnect the battery and remove the horn button by one of the following methods:
   a. center button—lift upward.
   b. trim cover—remove the screws, which hold the cover on, from the rear. On "rim-blow" wheels, remove the center contact.
2. Remove the steering wheel center nut and washer. Before removing the wheel, note the position of the index marks on the wheel and the steering shaft.
3. Remove the wheel with a puller.

Installation is the reverse of removal. Tighten the steering wheel nut to 20 ft lbs.

NOTE: Do not hammer on the end of the steering shaft; you could shear the plastic retainers which maintain the rigidity of the energy-absorbing steering column.

Turn Signal Switch Replacement

1. Disconnect the ground cable from the battery. Remove the steering wheel.
2. Loosen the anti-theft cover attaching screws and remove the cover from the column. Do not remove the screws from the cover; they are attached to it with plastic retainers.
3. To remove the lockplate, a special compressor is required. This tool is an inverted U-shape with a hole for the shaft. The shaft nut is used to force it down. Depress the lockplate and pry the snap-ring from the groove in the steering shaft. Remove the tool, snap-ring, plate, turn signal cam, upper bearing preload spring, and the thrust washer from the shaft.
4. Place the turn signal lever in the right turn position and remove it.
5. Depress the hazard warning

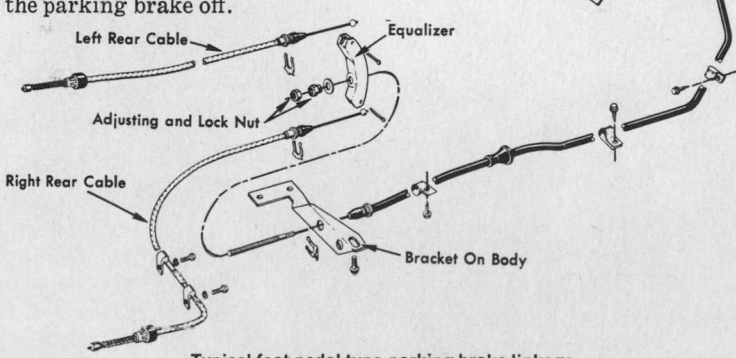

Cable Clevis

Left Rear Cable

Equalizer

Adjusting and Lock Nut

Right Rear Cable

Bracket On Body

Typical foot pedal type parking brake linkage
(© American Motors Corp)

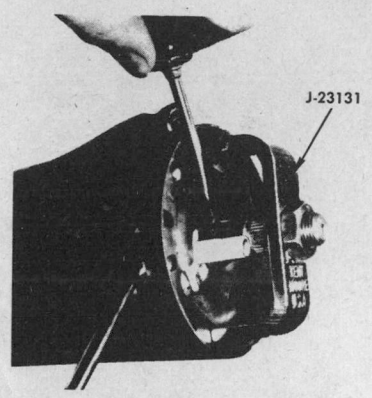

Using the special lockplate removal tool
(© American Motors Corp)

switch button and remove it, by rotating it counterclockwise.

6. Disconnect the wire harness connector block at its mounting bracket, which is located on the right side of the lower column.

7. If the car (Gremlin and Hornet only, after 1973) is equipped with a column-mounted automatic transmission selector, use a paper clip to depress the locktab that holds the shift quadrant light wire in the connector block (the grey wire at terminal "D").

8. Remove the switch attaching screws. Withdraw the switch and wire harness from the column. You may have to remove the package tray, lower trim panel, and wire harness protector.

Install the new switch in the reverse order of removal.

INSTRUMENT PANEL

Current is supplied to the instruments and the instrument panel lights through a printed circuit which is attached to the rear of the instrument cluster. The disconnect plug is part of the panel wiring harness and connects to pins attached to the printed circuit. A keyway located on the printed circuit board insures that the plug is always mounted correctly. **Caution** Never pry under the plug to remove it, or damage to the printed circuit will result.

An instrument voltage regulator is wired in series with the gauges to supply a constant five volts to them. On the Hornet and Gremlin it is integral with the temperature gauge; on other models it is a separate unit.

Ignition Switch Replacement

Through 1971

The ignition switch on all models is mounted on the lower steering column tube and is connected to the lock cylinder via a lock rod.

1. Place key in "OFF-LOCK".
2. Remove switch mounting screws.
3. Disconnect lock rod, remove harness connector and switch.
4. To install, first place both key and switch slide in "OFF-LOCK" positions.
5. Insert a 3/32 in. drill bit into switch alignment hole.
6. With drill in place, hook up lock rod and remove all slack by sliding switch toward steering wheel.
7. Install mounting bolts and tighten securely. Remove drill and hook up wires.

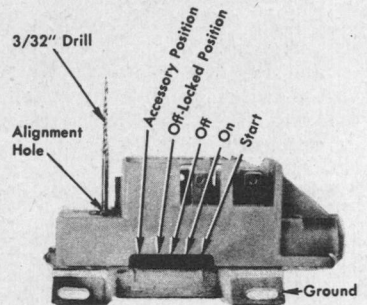

Ignition switch positions through 1971
(© American Motors Corp)

1972 and later

Removal of the column mounted ignition switch is the same as for the models through 1971. However, installation is slightly different:

1. On the standard column, move the switch slide to the left, as far as it will go (toward the wheel) On the tilt-column, push the slide to the extreme right (away from the wheel).
2. Position the lock rod into the hole on the switch slide.
3. Install the switch on the steering column. Be sure that the slide stays in its detent.
4. On the tilt-column, do not tighten the mounting screws. Instead, push the switch down the column, away from the steering wheel. This will remove any slack from the lock rod.
5. Tighten the switch mounting screws.

Lock Cylinder Replacement

1. Remove the battery ground cable and the steering wheel. Loosen anti-theft cover screws and remove cover from column.
2. Depress lock plate as far as possible, using a spacer and steering wheel nut.
3. Remove wire snap-ring from shaft groove, then remove compressor tool, snap-ring, lock plate, turn signal cam, upper bearing preload spring and thrust washer.
4. Place turn signal lever in "right turn" position and remove lever.
5. Depress hazard warning switch and remove button by turning counterclockwise.
6. Remove turn signal switch retaining screws and pull switch and wires out of column, as far as wiring will allow.
7. Place key in "LOCK" position, then depress the lock cylinder retaining tab in the rectangular slot in the column housing and remove the cylinder.

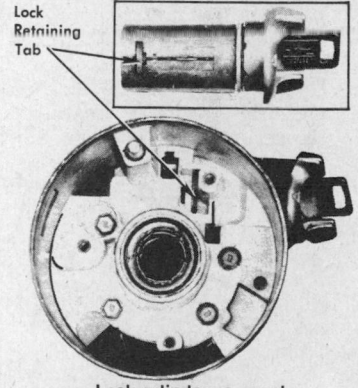
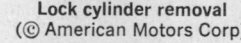

Lock cylinder removal
(© American Motors Corp)

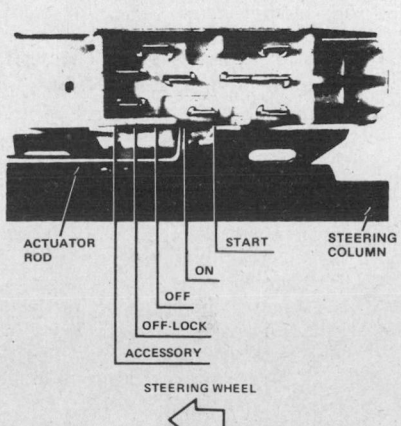
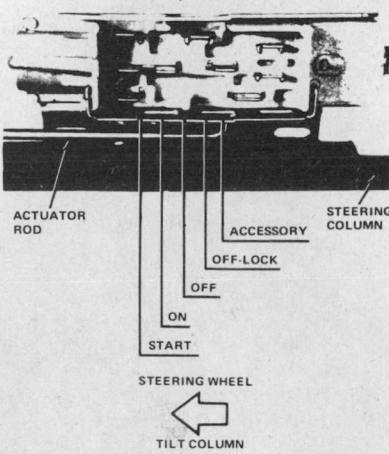

Ignition switch slider positions starting 1972 (© American Motros Corp.)

To install the lock cylinder, proceed in the following manner:

1. Hold the lock cylinder sleeve and turn the lock cylinder clockwise until it contacts the stop.
2. Align the lock cylinder key with the keyway in the housing and slip the cylinder into the housing.
3. Lightly depress the cylinder against the sector, while turning it counterclockwise, until the cylinder and sector are engaged.
4. Depress the cylinder until the retaining tab engages, and the lock cylinder is secured.
5. Install the turn signal switch. Be sure that the actuating lever pivot is properly seated and aligned in the top of the housing boss, before installing it with its screws.
6. Install the turn signal stalk and check the operation of the switch.
7. Install the thrust washer, spring and turn signal cancelling cam on the steering shaft.
8. Align the lockplate and steering shaft splines, and position the lockplate so that the turn signal camshaft protrudes from the "dogleg" opening in the lockplate.
9. Use snap-ring pliers to install the snap-ring on the end of the steering shaft.
10. Secure the anti-theft cover with its screws.
11. Install the button on the hazard warning switch. Install the steering wheel, as detailed above.

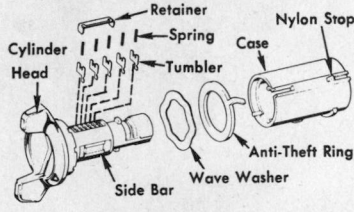

Ignition lock cylinder
(© American Motors Corp)

Headlight Switch Replacement

All except Javelin

Light switches are similar in all models. Some variation occurs in the shape and position of the nut mounting the switch to dash.

1. Disconnect battery and remove the switch overlay cover attaching screws so the cover can be pulled forward.
2. With the switch in the on position press the release button on the switch and remove the knob and shaft.
3. Remove screws, attaching switch or bracket to panel.
4. Reverse for installation, positioning switch so that the shaft is

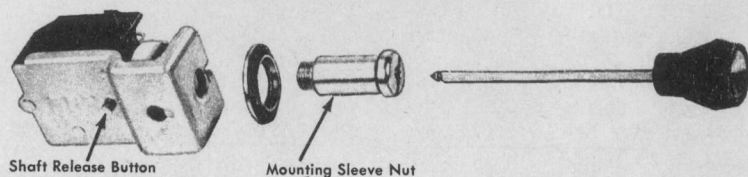

Shaft Release Button   Mounting Sleeve Nut
Light switch assembly (© American Motors Corp)

lined up properly before tightening the bracket screws.

Javelin and AMX

1. Remove the toggle switch knob by inserting a screwdriver in the groove on its left side. Pry upward, toward the knob, to release the spring clip that retains the knob.
2. Remove the screws that secure the lower cover to the steering column and withdraw the cover.
3. Disconnect the wire connectors and the retaining screws from the switch. Remove the switch.
4. Install the switch in the reverse order of removal.

WINDSHIELD WIPERS

Motor Removal and Installation

AMX, Javelin, Hornet, Gremlin through 1974; 1973-74 Ambassador, Matador (except 1974 Coupe)

The wiper motor is mounted on the engine side of the firewall and is easily accessible from under the hood.

1. Remove four screws that hold motor to firewall.
2. Remove hose and control cable, if equipped with vacuum wipers.
3. Unplug harness plug under dash, if equipped with electric wipers.
4. Disconnect motor link and remove motor.
5. To install, reverse removal procedure.

1975 and later; Gremlin, Hornet; Matador Sedan and Wagon

1. Remove the wiper arms and blades.
2. Remove the screws holding the motor adapter plate to the dash panel.
3. Separate the wiper wiring harness connector at the motor.
4. Pull the motor and linkage out of the opening to expose the drive link-to-crank stud retaining clip. Raise up the lock tab of the clip with a screwdriver and slide the clip off the stud.
5. Install the windshield wiper motor in the reverse order of removal.

Rebel, Matador, and Ambassador through 1972

1. Remove wiper arms and blades and the cowl air intake cover.
2. Slide the link-to-motor retainer clip off of the motor arm stud. Remove the link from the motor.
3. Disconnect control cable and vacuum hose or wiring harness from the motor.
4. Remove the motor and mounting plate-to-dash screws, and the motor assembly.
5. Install by reversing removal procedure.

1974 and later Matador Coupe

1. Remove the wiper arm/blade assemblies.
2. Open the hood and remove the cowl screen from the cowl opening.
3. Separate the linkage drive arm from the motor arm crankpin, by unfastening the retaining clip.
4. Disconnect the two multiconnectors from the motor.
5. Remove the wiper motor securing screws and withdraw the motor from the opening.

NOTE: If the output arm hangs up on the dash panel during motor removal, rotate the arm clockwise by hand, so that it clears the panel opening.

Installation is performed in the reverse order of removal. Prior to installation, make sure that the output arm is in the "park" position. Tighten the motor securing screws to 90-120 in lbs.

Pacer

1. Remove the vacuum canister mounting bracket and canister.
2. Disconnect the linkage drive arm from the motor output arm crankpin by removing the retaining clip.
3. On vehicles equipped with air conditioning:
   a. Remove the two nuts on the left side of the heater housing.
   b. Remove the one nut on the right side of the heater housing.
   c. Remove the screw from the heater housing support.
4. On vehicles not equipped with air conditioning:
   a. Remove the two nuts and one screw on the left side of the heater housing.

b. Remove the one nut on the right side of the heater housing.

c. Remove the screw from the heater housing support. Pull the heater housing forward.

5. Remove the wiper motor mounting plate attaching screws and remove the wiper motor assembly from the cowl.

6. Disconect the two wire connectors from the wiper motor.

7. Remove the wiper motor attaching screws and remove the wiper motor.

8. Install the wiper motor in the reverse order of removal.

RADIO

The following precautions should be observed when working on a car radio:

1. Always observe the proper polarity of the power connections; i.e., positive (+) goes to the power source and negative (−) to ground (negative ground electrical system).

2. Never run the radio without a speaker; damage to the output transistors will result. If a replacement (or additional) speaker is used, be sure that it is the correct impedance (ohms) for the radio. The proper impedance is stamped on the case of American Motors radios.

3. If a new antenna or antenna cable is used, adjust the antenna trimmer for the best reception of a weak AM station around 1400kc; the trimmer is located behind or above the tuning knob or in the radio case near the antenna lead. On tape player radios, it is in the cartridge slot.

Removal and Installation

Rebel, Matador, and Ambassador through 1973

1. Disconnect the battery ground cable.

2. Disconnect the antenna, power, ground, and speaker wires from the radio.

3. Remove the radio bracket from the dash panel flange.

4. Remove the cluster overlay.

5. Remove the radio mounting screws and withdraw the radio.

Installation is the reverse of removal.

1974 and later Matador and Ambassador

1. Remove the knobs from the radio and unfasten the control shafts retaining nuts.

2. Remove the bezel securing screws, and remove the bezel.

3. Loosen, but do not remove, the upper radio securing screw.

4. Raise the rear of the radio to separate its bracket from the upper securing screw.

5. Pull the radio forward slightly, and disconnect all of the leads from it. Remove the radio.

Radio installation is performed in the reverse order of removal. Adjust the antenna trimmer.

1970 Javelin and AMX

1. Disconnect the battery ground cable.

2. Remove the ash tray. Remove the bolt from inside the ash tray which attaches to the radio (if so equipped).

3. Remove the radio knobs and remove the shaft retaining nuts. Remove the bezel retaining screws and the bezel on 1970 Javelin/AMX models.

4. Disconnect all of the leads from the radio.

5. Tip the back of the radio up, toward the toe board. Withdraw it from the rear edge of the center instrument panel pad.

NOTE: If equipped with A/C, remove the discharge duct to gain clearance for radio removal.

Installation is the reverse of removal.

Hornet and Gremlin

1. Disconnect the battery ground cable. Remove the package tray.

2. Remove the ash tray and bracket.

3. Pull off the radio knobs and remove shaft retaining nuts.

4. Remove the bezel retaining screws and remove the bezel.

5. Disconnect the speaker, antenna, and power leads, and remove the radio.

Installation is the reverse of removal.

1971-74 Javelin

1. Disconnect the battery ground lead.

2. Remove the upper crash pad retaining screws, which are located next to the windshield.

3. Open the passenger-side door and remove the two panel securing screws from the door pillar area.

4. Remove the five securing screws from the upper flange of the instrument cluster bezel.

5. Remove the molding attaching screws and the passenger assist handle.

6. Remove the map light to gain access to the crash pad mounting stud which is located behind it. Remove the nut from the stud.

7. Remove the entire crash pad assembly.

8. Remove the three speaker mounting plate screws. Remove the speaker.

9. Slide the radio rearward and lift it up, in order to disconnect the speaker and light bulb leads.

10. Disconnect the radio power lead at the fuse block. Tie a string to the power lead, to aid in pulling it back through to the fuse block during assembly.

11. Remove the radio, complete with power lead.

Installation is the reverse of removal. Be sure to install the upper radio attaching screws and the speaker bracket mounting bolts, as these are part of the ground system.

Pacer

1. Disconnect the negative battery cable.

2. Remove the radio knobs, attaching nuts, cluster bezel, and overlay cover.

3. Loosen the radio-to-instrument panel attaching screw.

4. Lift the rear of the radio and pull forward slightly. Disconnect the electrical connections and the antenna and remove the radio.

5. Install in the reverse order of removal.

HEATER

NOTE: It is recommended, unless you are trained in air conditioning servicing procedures, that you not disconnect any of the air conditioning refrigerant lines or vessels.

Heater Core Removal and Installation

Rebel, Matador and Ambassador —through 1973

1. Disconnect hoses from core and plug hoses and tubes. It will not be necessary to drain entire cooling system. On A/C equipped cars disconnect vacuum hoses at damper vacuum motor.

2. Remove lower blower housing attaching nuts and washers in engine compartment.

3. Remove glove compartment door and glove compartment.

4. Remove remaining heater housing screws in passenger compartment, and remove core and housing as an assembly.

5. Slide core from housing.

6. Install in reverse order of above.

1974 Matador and Ambassador

1. Drain about two quarts of coolant from the cooling system.

2. Disconnect and plug the hoses which run to the heater core tubes in the engine compartment.

3. Disconnect the cable from the

negative (—) battery terminal.

4. Remove the instrument panel lower finish panel and the glove compartment as follows:

   a. Remove the screws which secure the instrument cluster bezel and remove the bezel.

   b. Remove the screws from the lower glove compartment opening, which secure the crash padding.

   c. On cars without A/C, remove the mounting screws and remove the fresh air vent cable assemblies from the left and right-sides of the lower panel.

   d. On models with an optional inside hood release, remove the screws retaining its cable assembly to the lower panel and remove the assembly.

   e. Remove the lower finish panel-to-bracket retaining screws.

   f. Pull the panel down, disconnect any electrical connections, and remove the panel.

   g. Working from underneath the instrument panel, remove the nuts securing the glove compartment door hinge, and remove the door and hinge as assembly.

   h. Remove the fuse panel retaining screws, disconnect the electrical leads (mark them for installation first), and lift out the fuse panel.

   i. Remove the sheet metal screws which secure the glove compartment liner and remove the liner.

5. Disconnect the air blend door cable at the heater core housing.

6. On cars equipped with A/C, remove the hoses from the vacuum motors.

7. Remove the screws which secure the heater core housing. On models without A/C, unfasten the fresh air door cable.

8. Remove the housing and core as an assembly. Separate the core from the housing, as necessary.

Installation is the reverse of removal. Adjust the cable on the air blend door for proper operation. Refill the cooling system to capacity.

1975 and later Matador

1. Disconnect the negative battery cable.

2. Drain about 2 quarts of coolant from the cooling system.

3. Disconnect the heater hoses from the heater core in the engine compartment and plug the core tubes.

4. On air conditioned cars, disconnect the blend-air damper cable at the heater core housing and remove the fuse panel. On non-A/C cars, disconnect the blend-air damper door and fresh air door cables.

5. Remove the lower instrument finish panel and remove the glove box door and liner.

6. Remove the right windshield pillar and corner finish mouldings for access to the upper right heater core housing mounting screws.

7. On air conditioned cars, remove the vacuum motor hoses.

8. Remove the remaining heater core housing attaching screws.

9. On air conditioned cars, remove the capscrew retaining the instrument panel to the right body pillar. Pull the right side of the instrument panel slightly rearward.

10. Remove the heater core housing and heater core. Remove the heater core from the housing.

11. Install the heater core and housing in the reverse order of removal.

Javelin and AMX

1. Drain 1½ qts. (2 qts. beginning '70) of coolant from system.

2. Disconnect hoses from heater core tubes in engine compartment. Install corks in hoses and tubes.

3. Disconnect blower motor wires.

4. Remove housing attaching nuts at blower motor opening in dash.

5. Remove glove compartment door and glove compartment.

NOTE: on Javelin and AMX, remove glove box hinge bracket.

6. Disconnect air and defroster cables from damper levers.

7. Remove assembly.

8. Remove the core, defroster, and blower housing assembly from the car.

9. Remove the core from the housing assembly.

Installation is the reverse of removal.

Gremlin and Hornet

1. Disconnect the negative battery cable and drain 2 qts. of coolant.

2. Disconnect heater hoses and plug hoses and core fittings.

3. Disconnect blower wires and remove motor and fan assembly.

4. On 1975 and later models, remove the housing attaching nut from the stud in the engine compartment.

5. Remove package shelf, if so equipped.

6. Disconnect wire at resistor, located below glove box.

7. Remove instrument panel center bezel, air outlet and duct, on A/C models.

8. Disconnect air and defroster cables from damper levers.

9. Remove right-side windshield pillar molding, the instrument panel upper sheet metal screws and the capscrew at the right door post.

10. Remove the right cowl trim panel on 1975 and later models.

11. Remove right kick panel and heater housing attaching screws.

12. Pull right side of instrument panel outward slightly and remove housing.

13. Remove core, defroster and blower housing.

14. Remove core from housing.

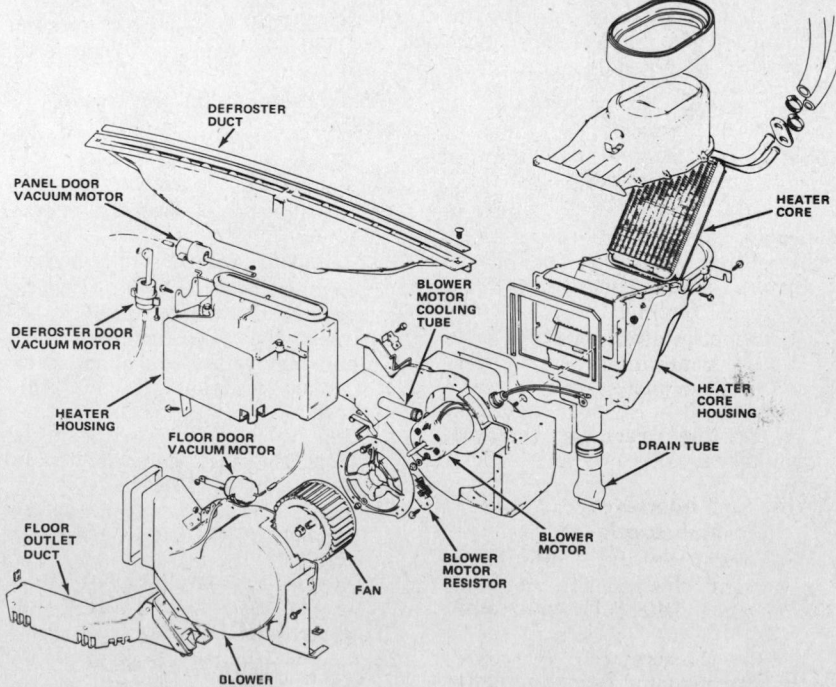

Pacer heater assembly (without air conditioning) (© American Motors Corp.)

Installation is the reverse of removal.

Pacer

1. Drain about two quarts of coolant from the radiator.
2. Disconnect the heater hoses from the heater core tubes and install plugs in the heater hoses and core tubes.
3. Remove the vacuum hoses from the heater core housing cover clip and move the lines aside. With A/C, disconnect the outside air door vacuum hose from the vacuum motor.
4. Remove the heater core housing cover screws.
5. Disconnect the overcenter spring from the cover and remove the cover.
6. Remove the heater core-to-housing attaching screws and remove the heater core.
7. Install the heater core in the reverse order of removal.

Heater Blower Removal and Installation

Rebel, Matador, Ambassador through 1973

1. Remove water valve from blower housing. It is not necessary to disconnect hoses and control cable.
2. Remove nuts, washers and screws attaching blower housing to dash panel in engine compartment.
3. Remove motor and fan, then separate fan from motor.

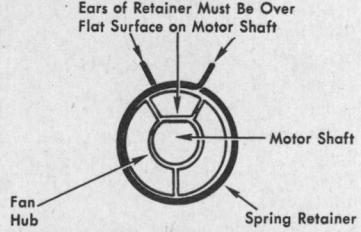

Ears of Retainer Must Be Over Flat Surface on Motor Shaft

Motor Shaft — Fan Hub — Spring Retainer

Blower retaining clip installation
(© American Motors Corp)

4. Install in reverse of above.

Javelin, AMX, Hornet, and Gremlin

1. Disconnect blower wires.
2. Remove retaining nut for cover and remove motor and fan assembly.
3. To install, reverse removal procedure.

1974 and later Matador and Ambassador

1. Working from the engine compartment side of the firewall, disconnect the blower motor leads.
2. Remove the screws which secure the blower motor mounting plate to the blower motor housing.

3. Remove the motor, mounting plate, and fan as an assembly.
Installation is the reverse of removal.

Pacer without A/C

1. Disconnect the negative battery cable.
2. Remove the right side windshield finish moulding.
3. Remove the instrument panel crash pad.
4. Remove the right scuff plate and cowl trim panel.
5. Remove the lower instrument panel-to-right A-pillar attaching screws.
6. Pull the instrument panel to the rear and replace the lower attaching screw in the right A-pillar. Allow the instrument panel to rest on the screw.
7. Remove the heater core housing attaching nuts and screw.
8. Remove the vacuum hoses from the heater core housing clip and set the lines aside.
9. Disconnect the blend-air door cable from the heater core housing.
10. Pull the heater core housing forward and set atop the upper control arm.
11. Remove the blower motor ground wire. Remove the blower motor housing attaching screw.
12. Disconnect the wires at the blower motor resistor.
13. Remove the blower motor housing brace.
14. Loosen the heater housing-to-dash panel attaching nuts.
15. Pull the blower housing to the rear and downward.
16. Disconnect the vacuum hoses from the vacuum motors.
17. Remove the blower housing.
18. Remove the blower housing cover.
19. Disconnect the white blower wire inside the housing.
20. Remove the blower motor mounting plate-to-housing screws and remove the blower motor assembly.
21. Remove the blower fan from the motor shaft and remove the mounting plate from the motor housing.
22. Install the blower motor in the reverse order of removal.

Pacer with A/C

1. Disconnect the negative battery cable.
2. Remove the right scuff plate and cowl trim panel.
3. Remove the radio overlay cover.
4. Remove the instrument panel crash pad.
5. Remove the instrument panel-to-right A-pillar attaching screws.
6. Remove the two upper instru-

ment panel-to-lower instrument panel attaching screws above the glove box.
7. Disconnect the blend-air door cable from the heater core housing.
8. Remove the housing brace-to-floorpan screw.
9. Disconnect the wire at the blower motor resistor.
10. Disconnect the vacuum hoses from the vacuum motors.
11. Remove the heater core housing attaching nuts and screw.
12. Remove the vacuum hoses from the housing clip and set the lines aside.
13. Pull the heater core housing forward and set it atop the upper control arm.
14. Remove the floor outlet duct.
15. Disconnect the wires from the blower motor relay.
16. Remove the blower housing attaching screw located in the engine compartment on the dash panel.
17. Loosen the evaporator housing-to-dash panel attaching nuts.
18. Remove the blower housing-to-dash panel attaching screw.
19. Pull the blower housing to the rear and downward.
20. Pull the right side of the instrument panel to the rear and remove the blower housing from under the panel.
21. Remove the floor door vacuum motor attaching screws and motor to gain access to the blower housing cover attaching screws.
22. Remove the blower housing cover attaching screws and remove the cover.
23. Remove the blower motor mounting plate and remove the blower motor assembly.
24. Remove the blower fan from the motor shaft and the mounting plate from the body of the motor.
25. Install the motor in the reverse order of removal.

SEAT BELTS

Disabling the Interlock System

Since the legal requirement for seat belt/starter interlock systems was dropped during the 1975 model year, those systems installed on cars built earlier may now be legally disabled. However, the warning light is still required. To disable the system:

1. Locate the interlock override relay under the hood, next to the starter solenoid on the right inner fender panel.
2. Unplug the relay.
3. Splice the green wire to the green with tracer wire.

INDEX

Astre · Firebird · Grand Am · GTO · LeMans · Tempest · Ventura · Sunbird

Automatic Transmission
In-Car Service C92, U369
Downshift cable adjustment C94
Band adjustments C93
Neutral safety/Backup light switch
  adjustment C94
Pan Removal and Installation, Fluid
  and Filter Change C92
Shift linkage adjustment C93
Throttle valve linkage adjustment C95
Vacuum modulator Removal and
  Installation C92

Brakes C99, U299
Master cylinder Removal and Installation .. C99
Parking brake adjustment C99
Power brake booster Removal and
  Installation C99

Charging System C66, U2
Alternator Removal and Installation C66
Voltage regulator Removal and
  Installation C66

Clutch C89
Clutch adjustment C90
Clutch Removal and Installation C89

Cooling System C72, U367
Radiator Removal and Installation C72
Thermostat Removal and Installation C73
Water pump Removal and Installation C72

Emission Controls C73, U145

Engine C76, U194
CYLINDER HEAD REMOVAL AND
  INSTALLATION C81
Engine Removal and Installation C76
LUBRICATION C87
Oil pan Removal and Installation C87
Oil pump Removal and Installation C88
Rear main bearing oil seal C88
MANIFOLDS C78
Intake manifold Removal and Installation . C78
Intake and exhaust manifold Removal
  and Installation Inline 6 cyl C79
Exhaust manifold Removal and
  Installation C79
PISTON AND CONNECTING ROD C86
TIMING CASE C83
OHC 4 cylinder timing cover, belt and
  camshaft C84
Front cover Removal and Installation C84

Timing belt and sprocket
  Removal and Installation C84
Camshaft Removal and Installation C84
VALVE SYSTEM C80
Rocker arm Removal and Installation C80
Valve adjustment C80
Valve guides C80

Front Suspension C96, U292
Ball joint inspection C97
Upper ball joint Removal and Installation C97
Coil spring Removal and Installation C97
Lower control arm and ball joint
  Removal and Installation C97
Shock absorber Removal and Installation .. C96
Upper control arm Removal and
  Installation C97
Wheel bearing inspection and
  adjustment C98

Fuel System C68, U50
Fuel filter Removal and Installation C69
Fuel pump Removal and Installation C68
Hot idle compensator C69
Idle speed and mixture adjustments C69
Idle stop solenoid C69

Heater C102
Heater blower Removal and Installation
  air-conditioned cars C103
Heater blower Removal and Installation
  non air-conditioned cars C102
Heater core Removal and Installation
  air-conditioned cars C103
Heater core Removal and Installation
  non air-conditioned cars C102

Ignition System C67, U34
Contact point and condenser adjustment
  and replacement C68
Distributor Removal and Installation C67
Distributor installation if engine
  has been disturbed C67
Firing order C49
Ignition timing C68

Instrument Panel C101, U350
Light switch replacement C110

Jacking, Hoisting C96

Manual Transmission C90, U231
Five speed C92
  Transmission Removal and Installation .. C92
Four speed C91
  Linkage adjustment C91

Transmission Removal and
  Installation C91
Three speed C90
  Linkage adjustment C90
  Transmission Removal and
    Installation C90

Radio C102
Radio Removal and Installation C102

Rear Axle C95
Axle shaft, bearing and seal
  Removal and Installation C95

Rear Suspension C98
Coil spring Removal and Installation C98
Leaf spring Removal and Installation C98
Shock absorber Removal and Installation .. C98

Seat Belts C104
Disabling the interlock system C104

Specifications C50, U359
Capacities C59
Car serial number location C50
Crankshaft and connecting rod C64
Engine identification C50
General engine C54
Piston clearance C65
Ring C65
Torque C64
Tune-up C55
Valve C61
Wheel alignment C66
Year identification C49

Starting System C66, U2
Starter Removal and Installation C66

Steering C100, U328
Ignition switch Removal and
  Installation C101
Lock cylinder replacement C101
Power steering pump Removal and
  Installation C100
Power steering system bleeding C100
Steering wheel Removal and
  Installation C100
Tie-rod end Removal and Installation C100
Turn signal switch Removal and
  Installation C100

U-Joints C95
Driveshaft Removal and Installation C95
U-Joint Removal and Installation C95

Windshield Wipers C101
Motor Removal and Installation C101

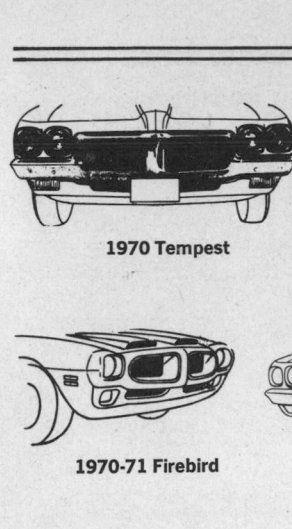

1970 Tempest

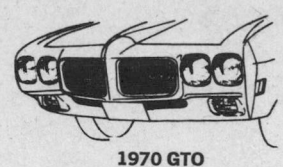

1970 GTO

1971 Tempest

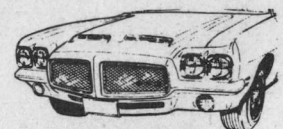

1971 GTO

1970-71 Firebird

1972 Tempest

1972 GTO

1971-72 Ventura II

1973 LeMans

1973 Firebird

1973 Ventura II

1973 Grand Am

1974 Firebird

1974 Ventura

1974 LeMans

1974 Grand Am

1975-76 Astre

1975 Ventura

1975 Firebird

1975 Grand LeMans

1975 Grand Am

1976 Ventura

1976 Firebird

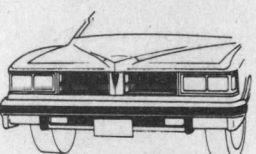

1976 LeMans

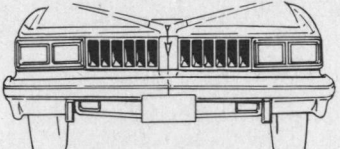

1977 LeMans

1977 Grand LeMans

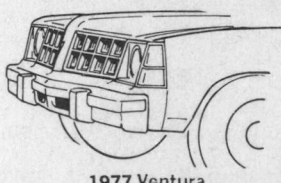

1977 Ventura

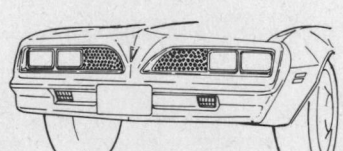

1977 Firebird

1977 Astre

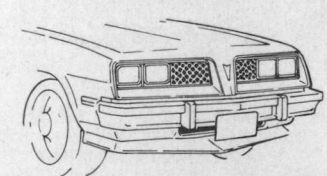

1977 sunbird

FIRING ORDER

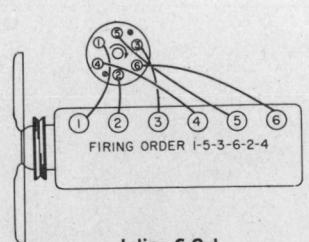

Inline 6 Cyl
(© Pontiac Div., G.M. Corp)

FIRING ORDER 1-5-3-6-2-4

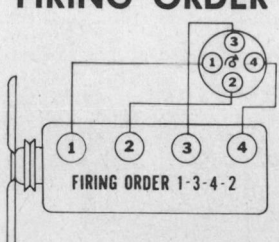

OHC 4 cylinder engine

FIRING ORDER 1-3-4-2

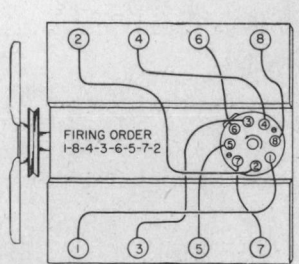

Pontiac design 302, 350, 400, 455 V8

FIRING ORDER 1-8-4-3-6-5-7-2

FIRING ORDER

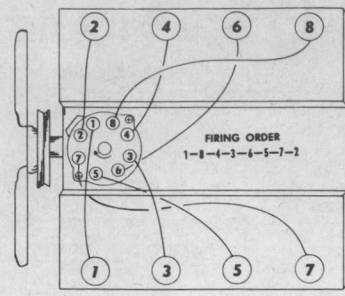

307 V8

1975-76 Ventura 350

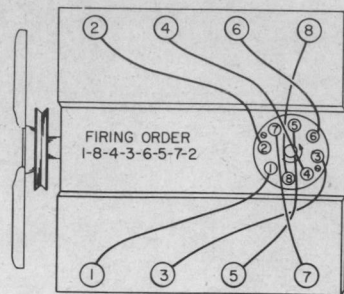

Oldsmobile design 260, 350, 403 V8

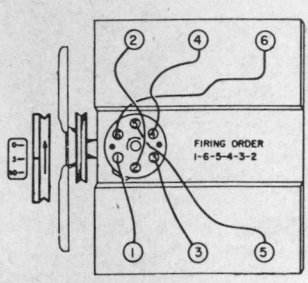

231 V6 (© Pontiac Div, G.M. Corp)

Inline 6-cyl engine number location
(© Pontiac Div., G.M. Corp)

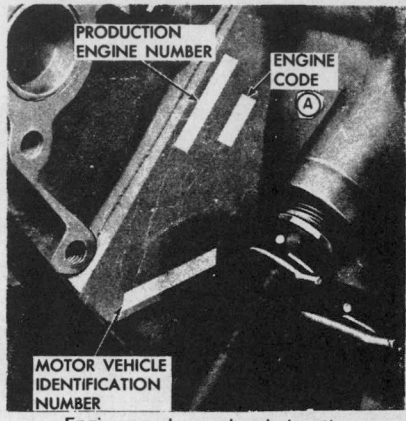

Engine number and code location—
—1970 and later Pontiac design 350
400, 455 V8 engines
(© Pontiac Div., G.M. Corp)

CAR SERIAL NUMBER LOCATION

The car serial number is located on a plate attached to the top of the instrument panel, left-hand side, visible through the windshield. The number is interpreted as follows:

1970-71
First digit: Car division
Second and third digits: Series number
Fourth and fifth digits: Body style code

Sixth digit: Year manufactured
Seventh digit: Plant
Eighth digit: Engine used.
Ninth to thirteenth digits—sequential serial number

1972-74
First digit: Car division
Second digit: Series number
Third and fourth digits: Body style code
Fifth digit: Engine used
Sixth digit: Year manufactured

Seventh digit: Plant
Eighth to thirteenth digits: Sequential serial number

1975-77
First digit: 2, for Pontiac division
Second, third, and fourth digits: Body style
Fifth digit: Engine used
Sixth digit: Year manufactured, 5 for 1975, 6 for 1976
Seventh digit: Assembly plant
Eighth to thirteenth digits: Sequential serial number

ENGINE IDENTIFICATION

Engine identification is made by means of a letter/number code stamped on the distributor mounting pad at the right-side of the block or on the left rear side of the block on OHV six-cylinder engines; stamped on a machined pad, on the right side, above the starter motor on the OHC four-cylinder engine; located to the left of the water pump housing on the V6; and located on the machined face of the cylinder block, below and in front of the right cylinder head on all V8 engines.

Displacement (cu. in.)	Carburetor (no. Bbls.)	Hp.	'70	'71	'72	'73	'74	'75	'76	'77
4 Cylinder Models										
140 OHC	1	78 (net)						BB BC		
140 OHC	2	87 (net)						AM AS AR AT	CBS CBT CBK CBL	
140 OHC	1	69 (net)							CHB CHJ	

ENGINE IDENTIFICATION

Engine identification is made by means of a letter/number code stamped on the distributor mounting pad at the right-side of the block or on the left rear side of the block on OHV six-cylinder engines; stamped on a machined pad, on the right side, above the starter motor on the OHC four-cylinder engine; located to the left of the water pump housing on the V6; and located on the machined face of the cylinder block, below and in front of the right cylinder head on all V8 engines.

Displacement (cu. in.)	Carburetor (no. Bbls.)	Hp.	'70	'71	'72	'73	'74	'75	'76	'77
6 Cylinder Models										
250	1	155	ZB ZG							
250	1	145		CAA CAB ZB ZG						
250	1	110 (net)			CBA CBC CBG CBJ W6 Y6					
250	1	100 (net)				CCA CCB CCC CCD	CCR CCW CCX	JU JT JL		
231 V6	2	110 (net)							FM FH FK FI FO FJ	
8 Cylinder Models										
260	2	110 (net)						QA QD QE QJ TE TJ	QA QD QB QC TE TJ	
307	2	200		CCA CCC						
307	2	130 (net)			CAY CAZ CKG CKH					
350	2	255	WU YU							
350	2	250			WR WU YU XR					
350	2	160, 175# (net)			WR YR YV					
350	2	150, 175# (net)				XR XV Y2 YL YR YV ZR ZV				

ENGINE IDENTIFICATION (con't.)

Engine identification is made by means of a letter/number code stamped on the cylinder head contact surface of the block behind the oil filler pipe on 250 OHC six-cylinder engines; stamped on the distributor mounting pad at the right-side of the block or on the left rear side of the block on OHV six-cylinder engines; stamped on a machined pad, on the right side, above the starter motor on the OHC four-cylinder engine; and located on the machined face of the cylinder block, below and in front of the right cylinder head on all V8 engines.

Displacement (cu. in.)	Carburetor (no. Bbls.)	Hp.	'69	'70	'71	'72	'73	'74	'75	'76
8 Cylinder Models										
350	2	145 (net)						YA YB		
350	2	155, 170# (net)					AA WA WB YA YB YC ZA ZB	RS RI	YA YP YB YR PA PB PO	
350	4	165 (net)						RW RX RN RO		
350	4	170, 200# (net)					WN WP YN YP YS ZP	WN YN ZP	PE PF PP ZX PM PN	
400	2	265	XX	WS XX						
400	2	175, 200# (net)			YX ZX					
400	2	170, 185# (net)				YP YX YZ ZK ZX			YC YJ	
400	2	175, 190# (net)					AH YH ZH ZJ	YH		
400	4	330	WT XV YS							
400	4	335								
400	4	350	WT YS							
400	4	366	WS YZ							
400	4	370	WW XP WH XN							
400	4	300		WK WT YS						
400	4	200, 250# (net)			WK WS YS					

ENGINE IDENTIFICATION (con't.)

Engine identification is made by means of a letter/number code stamped on the cylinder head contact surface of the block behind the oil filler pipe on 250 OHC six-cylinder engines; stamped on the distributor mounting pad at the right-side of the block or on the left rear side of the block on OHV six-cylinder engines; stamped on a machined pad, on the right side, above the starter motor on the OHC four-cylinder engine; and located on the machined face of the cylinder block, below and in front of the right cylinder head on all V8 engines.

Displacement (cu. in.)	Carburetor (no. Bbls.)	Hp.	'69	'70	'71	'72	'73	'74	'75	'76
8 Cylinder Models										
400	4	230 (net)				WK WP WS Y3 YS YT YY ZS				
400	4	225 (net)					AT WT YT YZ ZT			
400	4	210 (net)						YT ZT WT YS		
400	4	185 (net)							Y6 Y7 YT YY WT YS ZA ZK	
455	4	370	WA YC							
455	4	325		YC						
455	4	335		WC WL YE						
455	4	230, 250# (net)			YA YC					
455HO	4	300 (net)			WM YB					
455	4	250 (net)				WT WW YA YC YD YK ZA ZC	AU YY YW ZU ZW			
455	4	215 (net)						YW ZU		
455SD	4	310 (net)				W8 Y8				
455SD	4	290 (net)					W8 Y8			
455	4	200 (net)							Y3 Y8 Z3 Y4 WX Z4 ZB	

With dual exhaust

GENERAL ENGINE SPECIFICATIONS

Year	Engine No. Cyl. Displacement Cu. In.	Carburetor Type	Horsepower @ rpm ■	Torque @ rpm (ft lbs) ■	Bore x Stroke (in.)	Compression Ratio	Oil Pressure @ 2000 rpm
'70	6-250	1 bbl	155 @ 4200	235 @ 1600	3.8762 x 3.530	8.5:1	53①
	8-350	2 bbl	255 @ 4600	355 @ 2800	3.8762 x 3.750	8.8:1	35
	8-400	2 bbl	265 @ 4600	397 @ 2400	4.1212 x 3.750	8.8:1	35
	8-400	4 bbl	330 @ 4800	430 @ 3000	4.1212 x 3.750	10.25:1②	35
	8-400 Ram Air	4 bbl	345 @ 5000	430 @ 3400	4.1212 x 3.750	10.5:1	35
	8-400	4 bbl	350 @ 4800	445 @ 2900	4.1212 x 3.750	10.0:1	35
	8-400	4 bbl	366 @ 5100	445 @ 3600	4.1212 x 3.750	10.5:1	35
	8-400	4 bbl	370 @ 5500	445 @ 3900	4.1212 x 3.750	10.5:1	35
	8-455	4 bbl	360 @ 4600	500 @ 3100	4.1522 x 4.210	10.25:1	35
'71	6-250	1 bbl	145 @ 4200	230 @ 1600	3.8750 x 3.530	8.5:1	38③
	8-307	2 bbl	200 @ 4600	300 @ 2400	3.8750 x 3.530	8.5:1	40①
	8-350	2 bbl	250 @ 4400	350 @ 2400	3.8762 x 3.750	8.0:1	35
	8-400	2 bbl	265 @ 4400	400 @ 2400	4.1212 x 3.750	8.2:1	58
	8-400	4 bbl	300 @ 4800	400 @ 3600	4.1212 x 3.750	8.2:1	58
	8-455	4 bbl	325 @ 4400	455 @ 3200	4.1522 x 4.210	8.2:1	35
	8-455 HO	4 bbl	335 @ 4800	480 @ 3600	4.1522 x 4.210	8.4:1	35
'72	6-250	1 bbl	110 @ 3800	185 @ 1600	3.8750 x 3.530	8.5:1	40①
	8-307	2 bbl	130 @ 4400	230 @ 2400	3.8750 x 3.250	8.5:1	40①
	8-350	2 bbl	160 @ 4400	270 @ 2000	3.8762 x 3.750	8.2:1	35
	8-400	2 bbl	175 @ 4000	310 @ 2400	4.1212 x 3.750	8.2:1	35
	8-400	4 bbl	200 @ 4000	295 @ 2800	4.1212 x 3.750	8.2:1	35
	8-400	4 bbl	250 @ 4400	325 @ 3200	4.1212 x 3.750	8.2:1	35
	8-455	4 bbl	250 @ 3600	375 @ 2400	4.1522 x 4.210	8.2:1	35
	8-455	4 bbl	300 @ 4000	415 @ 3200	4.1522 x 4.210	8.4:1	35
'73	6-250	1 bbl	100 @ 3600	175 @ 1600	3.8750 x 3.530	8.2:1	50-65①
	8-350 SE	2 bbl	150 @ 4000	270 @ 2000	3.8762 x 3.750	7.6:1	55-60④
	8-350 DE	2 bbl	175 @ 4400	280 @ 2400	3.8782 x 3.750	7.6:1	55-60④
	8-400 SE	2 bbl	170 @ 3600	320 @ 2000	4.1212 x 3.750	8.0:1	55-60④
	8-400 DE	2 bbl	185 @ 4000	320 @ 2400	4.1212 x 3.750	8.0:1	55-60④
	8-400 DE	4 bbl	230 @ 4400	325 @ 3200	4.1212 x 3.750	8.0:1	55-60④
	8-455 DE	4 bbl	250 @ 4000	370 @ 2800	4.1522 x 4.210	8.0:1	55-60④
	8-455 S.D. DE	4 bbl	310 @ 4000	390 @ 3600	4.1522 x 4.210	8.4:1	75-80④
'74	6-250	1 bbl	100 @ 3600	175 @ 1600	3.8750 x 3.530	8.2:1	36-41①
	8-350 SE	2 bbl	155 @ 4000	275 @ 2400	3.8762 x 3.750	7.6:1	55-60④
	8-350 DE	2 bbl	170 @ 4400	290 @ 2400	3.8762 x 3.750	7.6:1	55-60④
	8-350 SE	4 bbl	170 @ 4000	280 @ 2000	3.8762 x 3.750	7.6:1	55-60④
	8-350 DE	4 bbl	200 @ 4000	295 @ 2800	3.8762 x 3.750	7.6:1	55-60④
	8-400 SE	2 bbl	175 @ 3600	315 @ 2000	4.1212 x 3.750	8.0:1	55-60④
	8-400 DE	2 bbl	190 @ 4000	330 @ 2400	4.1212 x 3.750	8.0:1	55-60④
	8-400 DE	4 bbl	225 @ 4000	330 @ 2800	4.1212 x 3.750	8.0:1	55-60④
	8-455 SE	4 bbl	215 @ 3600	355 @ 2400	4.1522 x 4.210	8.0:1	55-60④
	8-455 DE	4 bbl	250 @ 4000	380 @ 2800	4.1522 x 4.210	8.0:1	55-60④
	8-455 S.D. DE	4 bbl	290 @ 4000	395 @ 3200	4.1522 x 4.210	8.4:1	75-80④
'75	4-140 OHC	1 bbl	78 @ 4200	120 @ 2000	3.501 x 3.625	8.0:1	40⑤
	4-140 OHC	2 bbl	87 @ 4400	122 @ 2800	3.501 x 3.625	8.0:1	40⑤
	6-250	1 bbl	100 @ 3600	175 @ 1600	3.8750 x 3.530	8.5:1	36-41①
	8-260	2 bbl	110 @ 3400	205 @ 1600	3.500 x 3.385	7.5:1	30-45③

GENERAL ENGINE SPECIFICATIONS

Year	Engine No. Cyl. Displacement Cu. In.	Carburetor Type	Horsepower @ rpm ■	Torque @ rpm (ft lbs) ■	Bore x Stroke (in.)	Compression Ratio	Oil Pressure @ 2000 rpm
	8-350	2 bbl	155 @ 4000	275 @ 2400	3.8762 x 3.750	8.0:1	55-60④
	8-350	4 bbl	170 @ 4000	280 @ 2000	3.8762 x 3.750	8.0:1	55-60④
	8-350 Ventura	2 bbl	145 @ 3200	270 @ 2000	3.800 x 3.850	8.0:1	37⑥
	8-350 Ventura	4 bbl	165 @ 3800	260 @ 2200	3.800 x 3.850	8.0:1	37⑥
	8-400	2 bbl	175 @ 3600	315 @ 2000	4.1212 x 3.750	8.0:1	55-60④
	8-400	4 bbl	210 @ 4000	315 @ 2800	4.1212 x 3.750	8.0:1	55-60④
	8-455	4 bbl	215 @ 3600	355 @ 2400	4.1522 x 4.210	8.0:1	55-60④
'76-'77	4-140 OHC	1 bbl	69 @ 4000	113 @ 2400	3.501 x 3.625	7.9:1	40⑤
	4-140 OHC	2 bbl	87 @ 4400	122 @ 2800	3.501 x 3.625	7.9:1	40⑤
	4-151	—	—	—	4.000 x 3.000	—	—
	V6-231	2 bbl	110 @ 4000	175 @ 2000	3.800 x 3.400	8.0:1	40⑤
	6-250	1 bbl	100 @ 3600	175 @ 1600	3.875 x 3.530	8.3:1	36-41
	8-260	2 bbl	110 @ 3400	205 @ 1800	3.500 x 3.385	7.5:1	30-45④
	8-350 Ventura	2 bbl	135 @ 3200	280 @ 1600	3.800 x 3.850	8.0:1	37⑥
	8-350 Ventura	4 bbl	155 @ 3800	280 @ 1400	3.800 x 3.850	8.0:1	37⑥
	8-350	2 bbl	155 @ 4000	280 @ 2000	3.876 x 3.750	7.6:1	55-60④
	8-350	4 bbl	175 @ 4000	280 @ 2000	3.876 x 3.750	7.6:1	55-60④
	8-400	2 bbl	170 @ 4000	305 @ 2000	4.121 x 3.750	7.6:1	55-60④
	8-400	4 bbl	185 @ 3600	310 @ 1600	4.121 x 3.750	7.6:1	55-60④
	8-455	4 bbl	200 @ 3500	330 @ 2000	4.152 x 4.210	7.6:1	55-60④

■ Beginning 1972 horsepower and torque are SAE net figures. They are measured at the rear of the transmission with all accessories installed and operating. Since the figures vary when a given engine is installed in different models, some are representative, rather than exact.
① Oil pressure at 2000 rpm
② For vehicles equipped with automatic transmissions, compression ratio is 10.0:1

③ Oil pressure at 1500 rpm
④ Oil Pressure above 2600 rpm
⑤ Pressure at 1000 rpm
⑥ Pressure at 2400 rpm
HO High Output
OHC Overhead Cam
SE Single Exhaust
DE Dual Exhaust

TUNE-UP SPECIFICATIONS

Tempest, GTO through 1973, LeMans, Grand Am

When analyzing compression test results, look for uniformity among cylinders rather than specific pressures.

	ENGINE		SPARK PLUGS		DISTRIBUTOR		IGNITION TIMING (deg) ▲		VALVES	Fuel Pump	IDLE SPEED • (rpm) ▲	
Year	No. Cyl Displacement (cu in.)	hp	Orig. Type	Gap (in.)	Point Dwell (deg)	Point Gap (in.)	Man Trans •	Auto Trans	Intake Opens ■ (deg)	Pressure (psi)	Man Trans	Auto Trans
'70	6-250	155	R-46T	.035	32½	.019	TDC	4B	16	4-5	830/750①	630/600①
	8-350	255	R-46S	.035	30	.016	9B	9B	22	5-6½	800	650
	8-400	265	R-46S	.035	30	.016	9B	9B	22	5-6½	800	650
	8-400	330	R-45S	.035	30	.016	9B	9B	30	5-6½	950	650
	8-400	350	R-46S	.035	30	.016	9B	9B	23	5-6½	950	650
	8-400 Ram Air	366	R-46S	.035	30	.016	9B	9B	31	5-6½	950	650
	8-400 Ram Air	370	R-46S	.035	30	.016	15B	15B	40	5-6½	1000①/650	750①/500
	8-455	360	R-46S	.035	30	.016	9B	9B	31/23	5-6½	950	650
'71	6-250	145	R-45T	.035	32½	.019	4B	4B	16	4-5	850/550①	650/500①
	8-350	250	R-47S	.035	30	.016	12B	12B	26/30	5-6½②	800	600
	8-400	265	R-47S	.035	30	.016	—	8B	26	5-6½②	—	600
	8-400	300	R-46S	.035	30	.016	12B	12B	23	5-6½②	1000/600①	700

TUNE-UP SPECIFICATIONS

Tempest, GTO through 1973, LeMans, Grand Am

When analyzing compression test results, look for uniformity among cylinders rather than specific pressures.

	ENGINE		SPARK PLUGS		DISTRIBUTOR		IGNITION TIMING (deg) ▲		VALVES	Fuel Pump	IDLE SPEED • (rpm) ▲	
Year	No. Cyl Displacement (cu in.)	hp	Orig. Type	Gap (in.)	Point Dwell (deg)	Point Gap (in.)	Man Trans •	Auto Trans	Intake Opens ■ (deg)	Pressure (psi)	Man Trans	Auto Trans
	8-455	325	R-46S	.035	30	.016	—	12B	23	5-6½②	—	650
	8-455	335	R-46S	.035	30	.016	12B 12B	31		5-6½②	1000/600①	700
'72	6-250	110	R-45T	.035	32½	.019	4B	4B	16	4-5	700/450①	600/450①
	8-350	160	R-46TS	.035	30	.016	8B	10B	26/30③	5-6½	800	625
	8-400	175	R-46TS	.035	30	.016	—	10B	23/26③	5-6½	—	625
	8-400	200	R-46TS	.035	30	.016	8B	10B	23	5-6½	1000/600①	700/500①
	8-455	250	R-45TS	.035	30	.016	—	10B	23	5-6½	—	650/500①
	8-455	300	R-45TS	.035	—		8B	10B	31	5-6½	1000/600①	700/500①
'73	6-250	100	R-46T	.035	32½	.019	6B	6B	16	4-5	700/450①	600
	8-350 SE	150	R-46TS	.040	30	.016	10B	12B	26/30③	5-6½	900/600①	650
	8-350 DE	175	R-46TS	.040	30	.016	10B	12B	26/30③	5-6½	900/600①	650
	8-400 SE	170	R-46TS	.040	30	.016	10B	12B	26	5-6½	—	650
	8-400 DE	185	R-46TS	.040	30	.016	10B	12B	23/30③	5-6½	—	650
	8-400 DE	230	R-45TS	.040	30	.016	10B	12B	23/30③	5-6½	1000/600①	650
	8-455 DE	250	R-45TS	.040	30	.016	10B	12B	23	5-6½	—	650
	8-455 S.D. DE	310	R-44TS	.040	30	.016	10B	12B	42	5-6½	1000/600①	750/500①
'74	6-250	all	R-46T	.035	32½	.019	6B	6B	16	4-5	850/450①	600/450①
	8-350 2 bbl	all	R-46TS	.040	30	.016	10B	12B(10B)	26	5-6½	900/600①	650(625)
	8-350 4 bbl	all	R-46TS	.040	30	.016	10B	12B(10B)	26	5-6½	1000/600	650(625)
	8-400 2 bbl	all	R-46TS	.040	30	.016	10B	12B(10B)	26	5-6½	—	650(625)
	8-400 4 bbl	all	R-45TS	.040	30	.016	10B	12B(10B)	23/30③	5-6½	1000/600①	650(625)
	8-455	all	R-45TS	.040	30	.016	10B	12B(10B)	23	5-6½	—	650(625)
'75	6-250	100	R-46TX	.060	Electronic		10B	10B	16	4-5	850	550(600)
	8-350 2 bbl	155	R-46TSX	.060	Electronic		—	16B	26	5-6½	—	600
	8-350 4 bbl	170	R-46TSX	.060	Electronic		—	16B(12)	26	5-6½	—	650(625)
	8-400 2 bbl	175	R-46TSX	.060	Electronic		—	16B	26	5-6½	—	650
	8-400 4 bbl	210	R-45TSX	.060	Electronic		—	16B(12)	30	5-6½	—	650(600)
	8-455 4 bbl	215	R-45TSX	.060	Electronic		—	16B(10)	23	5-6½	—	650(675)
'76	6-250	100	R-46TX	.035	Electronic		6B	10B	16	4½-5½	850	550④(600)
	8-260	110	R-46SX	.080	Electronic		16B	18B⑤ (14B)	14	7-8½	750	550(600)
	8-350	155	R46TSX	.060	Electronic		—	16B	22	7-8½	—	550
	8-350	175	R45TSX	.060	Electronic		—	16B	26	7-8½	—	600
	8-400	170	R46TSX	.060	Electronic		—	16B	26	7-8½	—	550
	8-400	185	R46TSX	.060	Electronic		—	16B	30	7-8½	—	575
	8-455	200	R45TSX	.060	Electronic		—	16B(12B)	23	7-8½	—	550(600)
'77	6-231	All	R-46TSX (R-45TSX)	.060	Electronic		12B	12B	17	4¼-5¾	800	600
	8-301	All	R-46TSX	.060	Electronic		—	12B	27	7-8½	—	550,650⑥
	8-350	170	R-45TSX	.060	Electronic		—	16B	29	7-8½	—	575,650⑥
	8-350	Calif., Alt.	R-45SX (R-46SZ)	.080	Electronic		—	20B@1100	—	5½-6½	—	575,650⑥
	8-400	All	R-45TSX	.060	Electronic		—	16B	29	7-8½	—	575,650⑥
	8-403	All	R-45SX (R-46SZ)	.080	Electronic		—	20B@1000	—	5½-6½	—	600,650⑥

SE Single Exhaust   DE Dual Exhaust   ▲ See text for procedure

• Figure in parentheses indicates California engine

■ All figures are in degrees Before Top Dead Center. Where two figures appear, the first represents timing with manual transmission, the second with automatic transmission.

① Lower figure indicates idle speed with solenoid disconnected
② 6½-8 with A/C
③ Lower figure represents manual transmission models; higher figure indicates automatic transmission.

④ 575 w/air conditioning
⑤ Some early models may be 16B
⑥ Higher figure for air conditioned cars, set with A/C on
B Before Top Dead Center

Firebird — TUNE-UP SPECIFICATIONS

When analyzing compression test results, look for uniformity among cylinders rather than specific pressures.

Year	No. Cyl Displacement (cu in.)	hp	Orig. Type	Gap (in.)	Point Dwell (deg)	Point Gap (in.)	Man Trans •	Auto Trans	Intake Opens ■ (deg)	Fuel Pump Pressure (psi)	Man Trans	Auto Trans
'70	6-250	155	R-46T	.035	32½	.019	TDC	4B	16	4-5½	850/500①	650/500①
	8-350	255	R-46S	.035	30	.016	9B	9B	22	5-6½	800	650
	8-400	265	R-46S②	.035	30	.016	9B	9B	22	5-6½	800	650
	8-400	330	R-45S	.035	30	.016	9B	9B	30	5-6½	950	650
	8-400 Ram Air	345	R-44S	.035	30	.016	9B	9B	30	5-6½	950	650
	8-400 Ram Air	370	R-44S	.035	30	.016	15B	15B	30	5-6½	1000/650①	750/500①
'71	6-250	145	R-45T	.035	32½	.019	4B	4B	16	4-5	850/550①	650/500①
	8-350	250	R-47S	.035	30	.016	12B	12B	26/30④	③5-6½	800	600
	8-400	265	R-47S	.035	30	.016	—	8B	26	③5-6½	—	600
	8-400	300	R-46S	.035	30	.016	12B	12B	23	③5-6½	1000/600①	700
	8-455	325	R-46S	.035	30	.016	—	12B	23	③5-6½	—	650
	8-455	335	R-46S	.035	30	.016	12B	12B	31	③5-6½	1000/600①	700
'72	6-250	110	R-45T	.035	32½	.019	4B	4B	16	4-5	700①/450	600①/450
	8-350	160	R-46TS	.035	30	.016	8B	10B	26/30④	5-6½	800	625
	8-400	175	R-46TS	.035	30	.016	—	10B	23/26④	5-6½	—	625
	8-400	250	R-45TS	.035	30	.016	8B	10B	23	5-6½	1000/600①	700/500①
	8-455	300	R-45TS	.035	30	—	8B	10B	31	5-6½	1000/600①	700/500①
'73	6-250	100	R-46T	.035	32½	.019	6B	6B	16	4-5	700/450	600/450
	8-350 SE	150	R-46TS	.040	30	.016	10B	12B	26/30④	5-6½	900/600①	1500/650
	8-350 DE	175	R-46TS	.040	30	.016	10B	12B	26/30④	5-6½	900/600①	650
	8-400 SE	170	R-46TS	.040	30	.016	10B	12B	26	5-6½	—	650
	8-400 DE	230	R-45TS	.040	30	.016	10B	12B	23/30④	5-6½	1000/600①	650
	8-455 DE	250	R-45TS	.040	30	.016	10B	12B	23	5-6½	1000/600①	650
	8-455 S.D. DE	310	R-44TS	.040	30	.016	10B	12B	42	5-6½	1000/600①	750/500①
'74	6-250	all	R-46T	.035	32½	.019	6B	6B	16	4-5	850/450①	600/450①
	8-350 2 bbl	all	R-46TS	.040	30	.016	10B	12B(10B)	26	5-6½	900/600①	650(625)
	8-350 4 bbl	all	R-46TS	.040	30	.016	10B	12B(10B)	26	5-6½	1000/600	650(625)
	8-400 2 bbl	all	R-46TS	.040	30	.016	10B	12B(10B)	26	5-6½	—	650(625)
	8-400 4 bbl	all	R-45TS	.040	30	.016	10B	12B(10B)	23/30④	5-6½	1000/600①	650(625)
	8-455	all	R-45TS	.040	30	.016	10B	12B(10B)	23	5-6½	—	650(625)
	8-455 S.D.	290	R-45TS	.040	30	.016	10B	12B	38	5-6½	1000/600①	750/500①
'75	6-250	100	R-46TX	.060	Electronic		10B	10B	16	4-5	850	550(600)
	8-350 2 bbl	155	R-46TSX	.060	Electronic		—	16B	26	5-6½	—	600
	8-350 4 bbl	170	R-46TSX	.060	Electronic		12B	16B(12)	26	5-6½	775	650(625)
	8-400 4 bbl	210	R-45TSX	.060	Electronic		12B	16B(12)	30	5-6½	775	650(600)
	8-455 4 bbl	215	R-45TSX	.060	Electronic		16B	—	23	5-6½	675	
'76	6-250	100	R46TX	.035	Electronic		6B	10B	16	4-5	850	550(600)
	8-350	155	R-46TSX	.060	Electronic		—	16B	22	5-6½	—	550
	8-350	175	R-45TSX	.060	Electronic		—	16B	26	5-6½	—	600
	8-400	185	R-45TSX	.060	Electronic		12B	16B	30	5-6½	775	575
	8-455	200	R-45TSX	.060	Electronic		12B	16B	23	5-6½	775	550(600)
'77	6-231	all	R-46TSX (R-45TSX)	.060	Electronic		12B	12B	17	4¼-5¾	800	600

Firebird — TUNE-UP SPECIFICATIONS

When analyzing compression test results, look for uniformity among cylinders rather than specific pressures.

Year	No. Cyl Displacement (cu in.)	hp	Orig. Type	Gap (in.)	Point Dwell (deg)	Point Gap (in.)	Man Trans ●	Auto Trans	Valves Intake Opens ■ (deg)	Fuel Pump Pressure (psi)	Man Trans	Auto Trans
	8-301	all	R-46TSX	.060	Electronic		16B	12B	27⑥	7-8½	⑦	550
	8-350	170	R-45TSX	.060	Electronic		—	16B	29	7-8½	—	575
	8-350	Calif., Alt.	R-45SX (R-46SZ)	.080	Electronic		—	20B@1100	—	5½-6½	—	600,650⑧
	8-400	all	R-45TSX	.060	Electronic		—	16B	29	7-8½	⑦	600,650⑧
	8-403	all	R-45SX (R-46SZ)	.080	Electronic		—	20B@1100	—	5½-6½	—	600,650⑧

② AC-R-45S with automatic transmission.
③ 6½-8 with A/C
④ Lower figure represents manual transmission models; higher figure indicates automatic transmission.
⑤ See engine compartment sticker
⑥ 31 with manual transmission
⑦ See underhood specifications sticker
⑧ Higher figure for air conditioned cars, set with A/C on

Ventura, 1974 GTO, Astre, Sunbird

Year	No. Cyl Displacement (cu in.)	hp	Orig. Type	Gap (in.)	Point Dwell (deg)	Point Gap (in.)	Man Trans ●	Auto Trans	Valves Intake Opens ■ (deg)	Fuel Pump Pressure (psi)	Man Trans	Auto Trans
'71	6-250	145	R-45T	.035	31-34	.019	4B	4B	16	4-5	500	500
	8-307	200	R-45TS	.035	29-31	.019	4B	8B	28	5½-7½	600	550
'72	6-250	110	R-45T	.035	31-34	.019	4B	4B	16	4-5	700①/450	600①/450
	8-307	130	R-45TS	.035	29-31	.019	4B	8B	28	5½-7½	900①/450	600①/450
	8-350	160	R-46TS	.035	29-31	.019	10B	10B	16	5-6½	800	625
'73	6-250	110	R-46T	.035	31-34	.019	6B	6B	16	4-5	700/450①	600
	8-350 SE	150	R-46TS	.040	29-31	.019	10B	12B	16	5-6½	900/600①	650
	8-350 DE	175	R-46TS	.040	29-31	.019	10B	12B	16	5-6½	900/600①	650
'74	6-250	all	R-46T	.035	32½	.019	6B	6B	16	4-5	850/450①	600/450①
	8-350 2 bbl	all	R-46TS	.040	30	.019	10B	12B(10B)	26	5-6½	900/600①	650(625)
	8-350 4 bbl	all	R-46TS	.040	30	.019	10B	12B(10B)	26	5-6½	1000/600①	650(625)
'75	4-140 1 bbl	78	R-43TSX	.060	Electronic		8B	10B	22③	3-4½	1000	750
	4-140 2 bbl	87	R-43TSX	.060⑥	Electronic		10B	12B	28③	3-4½	1000	750
	6-250	100	R-46TX	.060	Electronic		10B	10B	16	4-5	850	550(600)
	8-260	110	R-46SX	.080	Electronic		16B	18B(16)	14	5-6½	—	600
	8-350 2 bbl	145	R-45TSX	.060	Electronic		—	12B	19	5-6½	—	600
	8-350 4 bbl	165	R-45TSX	.060	Electronic		—	12B	19	5-6½	—	650(625)
'76	4-140	69	R-43TSX	.035	Electronic		8B	10B	22	3-4½	700	750
	4-140	87	R-43TSX	.035	Electronic		8B	10B	28	3-4½	700	750
	V6-231	110	R44SX	.060	Electronic		12B	12B	17	3-4½	800	600
	6-250	100	R-46TX	.035	Electronic		6B	10B	10	4-5	850	550(600)
	8-260	110	R-46SX	.080	Electronic		16B	18B⑤ (14B)	14	5-6½	750	550(600)
	8-350	All	R-45TSX	.060	Electronic		—	12B	19	5-6½	—	600
'77	4-140	All	R-43TS	.035	Electronic		④	④	34	3-4½	④	④
	4-151	All	R-44TSX	.060	Electronic		14B	14B	33	4-5½	1000	650
	6-231	All	R-46TSX (R-45TSX)	.060	Electronic		12B	12B	17	3-4½②	800	600
	8-301	All	R-46TSX	.060	Electronic		16B	12B	27⑦	7-8½	750, 850⑧	550,650⑧
	8-350	All	R-46SX (R-46SZ)	.080	Electronic		—	20B @ 1100	—	5½-6½	—	600,650⑧

SE Single Exhaust
DE Dual Exhaust
▲ See text for procedure
■ All figures Before Top Dead Center
① Lower figure indicates idle speed with solenoid disconnected
② 4¼-5¾ in Ventura
③ See text for valve lash adjustment
④ See underhood specifications sticker
⑤ Some Venturas may be set at 16B
⑥ R-43TS at .035 if missing or hard starting.
⑦ 31 with manual transmission
⑧ Higher figure for air conditioned cars, set with A/C on

Tempest, GTO through 1973, LeMans, Grand Am — CAPACITIES

Year	ENGINE No. Cyl. Displacement (Cu. In.)	Engine Crankcase Add I Qt For New Filter	TRANSMISSION Pts To Refill After Draining Manual 3-Speed	4/5 Speed	Automatic •	Drive Axle (pts)	Gasoline Tank (gals)	COOLING SYSTEM (qts) With Heater	With A/C
'70	6-250	4	3.5	——	6	3③	20①	13	——
	8-350	5	3.5②	2.5	6	3③	20①	19.9	19.9
	8-400	5	2.5	2.5	7.5	3③	20①	18.3	18.3
	8-455	5	2.5	2.5	7.5	3③	20①	17.5	17.5
'71	6-250	4	3.5	——	6	3③	19	13	12.4
	8-350	5	3.5②	2.5	6	3③	19	20	20.5
	8-400	5	2.8	2.5	7.5	3③	19	18.6	20.8
	8-455	5	2.8	2.5	7.5	3③	19	17.9	16.8
'72	6-250	4	3.5	——	6	3③	20①	13	12.4
	8-350	5	3.5	2.5	6	3③	20①	20	20.5
	8-400	5	2.8	2.5	7.5	3③	20①	18.6	20.8
	8-455	5	——	2.5	7.5	3③	20①	17.9	19
'73	6-250	4	3.5	——	7.5	4.25	21.8	13.3	——
	8-350	5	3.5	2.5	7.5	4.25⑤	21.8⑥	22.0	23.1
	8-400	5	2.8/3.5④	2.5	7.5	4.25⑤	21.8⑥⑦	22.0/23.0⑧	23.1/24.0⑧
	8-455	5	——	2.5	7.5	4.25⑤	21.8⑦	21.1	22.2
'74	6-250	4	3.5	——	7.5	4.25	21.8	13.3	——
	8-350	5	2.8/3.5④	2.5	7.5	4.25⑤	21.8⑥	22.0	23.2
	8-400	5	——	2.5	7.5	4.25⑤	21.8⑥⑦	22.0/23.0⑧	23.2/24.0⑧
	8-455	5	——	——	7.5	4.25⑤	21.8⑦	21.2	21.3
'75-'77	6-250	4	3.5	——	7.5	3	21.0	14.8	14.8
	8-260	4	——	3.5	7.5	3	21.0	23.5	26
	8-350	5	——	——	7.5⑩	3⑨	21.0⑥	21.8	21.8
	8-400	5	——	——	7.5⑩	3⑨	21.0⑥⑦	23.8⑪	21.8⑪
	8-455	5	——	——	7.5⑩	4.9	21.0⑦	21.6	21.6

- • Specifications do not include torque converter
- ① Station wagons: '70—22.5 gals, '72—23 gals less 1 gal for California cars—'70
- ② 2.8 pts with heavy duty 3-speed transmission
- ③ 5 pts with 8.875 in. ring gear
- ④ Lower figure represents 3-speed Muncie transmission; higher figure indicates 3-speed Saginaw transmission
- ⑤ 5.5 pts with 8.875 in. ring gear (station wagon)
- ⑥ 22 gals station wagon
- ⑦ 25 gals Grand Am
- ⑧ Lower figure indicates 2 bbl engine; higher figure indicates 4 bbl engine
- ⑨ 4.9 on wagon, optional on sedans
- ⑩ on M-40; M-38, 8.0
- ⑪ 1976-77: 22 with A/C; 21.4 without
- —— Not applicable

Firebird — CAPACITIES

Year	ENGINE No. Cyl. Displacement (Cu. In.)	Engine Crankcase Add I Qt For New Filter	TRANSMISSION Pts To Refill After Draining Manual 3-Speed	4/5 Speed	Automatic •	Drive Axle (pts)	Gasoline Tank (gals)	COOLING SYSTEM (qts) With Heater	With A/C
'70	6-250	4	3.5	——	6	3②	19.5③	13	——
	8-350	5	3.5①	2.5	6	3②	19.5③	19.9	19.9
	8-400	5	2.5	2.5	7.5	3②	19.5③	18.3	18.3
	8-455	5	2.5	2.5	7.5	3②	19.5③	17.5	17.5
'71	6-250	4	3.5	——	6	4.25	17	12	12.4
	8-350	5	3.5①	2.5	6	4.25	17	20	20.5
	8-400	5	2.8	2.5	7.5	4.25	17	18.6	18.7
	8-455	5	2.8	2.5	7.5	4.25	17	17.9	16.8

Firebird CAPACITIES

Year	ENGINE No. Cyl. Displacement (Cu. In.)	Engine Crankcase Add 1 Qt For New Filter	TRANSMISSION Pts To Refill After Draining			Drive Axle (pts)	Gasoline Tank (gals)	COOLING SYSTEM (qts)	
			Manual 3-Speed	4/5 Speed	Automatic •			With Heater	With A/C
'72	6-250	4	3.5	——	6	4.25	17	12	12.4
	8-350	5	3.5	2.5	6	4.25	17	20	20.5
	8-400	5	2.8	2.5	7.5	4.25	17	18.6	18.7
	8-455	5	——	2.5	7.5	4.25	17	17.9	19
'73	6-250	4	3.5	——	7.5	4.25	18	12.5	——
	8-350	5	3.5	2.5	7.5	4.25	18	22.4	22.7
	8-400	5	——	2.5	7.5	4.25	18	22.4	22.7/23.5④
	8-455	5	——	2.5	7.5	4.25	18	20.9	21.8
'74	6-250	4	3.5	——	7.5	4.25	20.2	12.5	——
	8-350	5	3.5	2.5	7.5	4.25	20.2	22.4	22.8
	8-400	5	——	2.5	7.5	4.25	20.2	22.4	22.7/23.6④
	8-455	5	——	2.5	7.5	4.25	20.2	20.9	21.9
'75-'76	6-250	4	3.5	——	8.0	4.25	21.5	13.5	13.5
	8-350	5	——	2.5	8.0	4.25	21.5	21.2	21.6
	8-400	5	——	2.5	8.0	4.25	21.5	21.6	23.5
	8-455	5	——	2.5	8.0	4.25	21.5	23.3	23.3

- specifications do not include torque converter
① 2.8 pts with heavy duty 3-speed transmission
② 4 pts with heavy duty axle
③ California cars—18.5 gals

④ Lower figure indicates 2 bbl model; higher figure indicates 4 bbl engine
—— Not applicable

Ventura, 1974 GTO, Astre, Sunbird CAPACITIES

Year	ENGINE No. Cyl. Displacement (Cu. In.)	Engine Crankcase Add 1 Qt For New Filter	TRANSMISSION Pts To Refill After Draining			Drive Axle (pts)	Gasoline Tank (gals)	COOLING SYSTEM (qts)	
			Manual 3-Speed	4/5 Speed ▲	Automatic •			With Heater	With A/C
'71	6-250	4	3	——	6	3.75	16	12	——
	8-307	4	3	——	6①	3.75	16	15	16
'72	6-250	4	3	——	6	3.75	16	12	16
	8-307	4	3	——	6①	3.75	16	15	16
	8-350	5	——		5	3.75	16	19.4	20.3
'73	6-250	4	3.5	——	6	4.25	21.5	12.1	——
	8-350	5	3.5	2.5	5	4.25	21.5	12.1	12.1
'74	6-250	4	3.5	——	6	4.25	20.5	12.1	——
	8-350	5	3.5	2.5	7.5	4.25	20.5	19.2	19.3
'75-'77	4-140 OHC	3	2.4	2.4②	5.0	2.8	16③	7.0	7.5
	V6-231	3	2.4	2.4②	5.0	2.25	16③	7.0	7.5
	6-250	4	3.5	——	5.0	3.75	20.5	13.5	13.5
	8-260	4	3.5	——	5.0	3.75	20.5	18.5	19.5
	8-350	4	——	——	5.0	3.75	20.5	18.5	19.5

▲ 5-speed uses Dexron®
• Specifications do not include torque converter
① 5 pts with 3-speed transmission
② 3.5 with 5-speed
③ 18.5 with Sunbird
—— Not applicable

Tempest, GTO, through 1973 Lemans, Grand Am

VALVE SPECIFICATIONS

Year	Engine No. Cyl. Displacement (cu in.)	Seat Angle (deg) ■	Face Angle (deg) ●	Outer Spring Test Pressure ▲ (lbs @ in.)	Spring Installed Height (in.)	STEM TO GUIDE Clearance (in.) Intake	Exhaust	STEM Diameter (in.) Intake	Exhaust
'70	6-250 1 bbl	46③	45④	60 @ 1.66	1 21/32	.0010-.0027	.0021-.0027	.3414	.3414
	8-350 2 bbl	45	44	63 @ 1.58	1 37/64	.0010-.0033	.0021-.0038	.3416	.3416
	8-400 2 bbl	45	44	63 @ 1.58	1 37/64	.0016-.0033	.0021-.0038	.3416	.3411
	8-400① 4 bbl	30	29	61 @ 1.59	1 19/32	.0016-.0033	.0021-.0038	.3416	.3411
	8-400② 4 bbl	30	29	66 @ 1.56	1 9/16	.0016-.0033	.0021-.0038	.3416	.3416
	8-400 R.A. IV	30	29	76 @ 1.82	1 13/16	.0016-.0033	.0021-.0038	.3416	.3411
	8-455	30	29	66 @ 1.56	1 9/16	.0016-.0033	.0021-.0038	.3416	.3411
'71	6-250 1 bbl	46③	45④	61 @ 1.66	1 21/32	.0010-.0027	.0010-.0027	.3414	.3414
	8-350 2 bbl	45	44	61 @ 1.59	1 19/32	.0016-.0033	.0012-.0038	.3416	.3411
	8-400⑤	30	29	60 @ 1.60	1 19/32	.0016-.0033	.0021-.0038	.3416	.3411
	8-400 2 bbl	45	44	61 @ 1.59	1 19/32	.0016-.0033	.0021-.0038	.3416	.3411
	8-400 4 bbl	30	29	65 @ 1.57	1 9/16	.0016-.0033	.0021-.0038	.3416	.3411
	8-455	30	29	65 @ 1.57	1 9/16	.0016-.0033	.0021-.0038	.3416	.3416
	8-455 H.O.	30	29	66 @ 1.56	1 9/16	.0016-.0033	.0021-.0038	.3416	.3416
'72	6-250	46③	45④	60 @ 1.66	1 21/32	.0010-.0027	.0010-.0027	.3414	.3414
	8-350	45	44	61 @ 1.59	1 19/32	.0016-.0033	.0021-.0038	.3416	.3411
	8-400⑥	30	29	60 @ 1.60	1 19/32	.0016-.0033	.0021-.0038	.3416	.3411
	8-400 2 bbl	45	44	61 @ 1.59	1 19/32	.0016-.0033	.0021-.0038	.3416	.3411
	8-400 4 bbl	30	29	65 @ 1.57	1 9/16	.0016-.0033	.0021-.0038	.3416	.3411
	8-455	30	29	64 @ 1.57	1 9/16	.0016-.0033	.0021-.0038	.3416	.3416
	8-455 H.O.	30	29	66 @ 1.56	1 9/16	.0016-.0033	.0021-.0038	.3416	.3416
'73	6-250	46③	45④	60 @ 1.66	1 21/32	.0010-.0027	.0010-.0027	.3414	.3414
	8-350	45	44	61 @ 1.59	1 19/32	.0016-.0033	.0021-.0038	.3416	.3411
	8-400 4 bbl	30	29	60 @ 1.60	1 19/32	.0016-.0033	.0021-.0038	.3416	.3411
	8-400 2 bbl	45	44	61 @ 1.59	1 19/32	.0016-.0033	.0021-.0038	.3416	.3411
	8-400 4 bbl auto.	30	29	65 @ 1.57	1 9/16	.0016-.0033	.0021-.0038	.3416	.3411
	8-455	30	29	64 @ 1.57	1 9/16	.0016-.0033	.0021-.0038	.3416	.3411
	8-455 S.D.	45	44	70 @ 1.82	1 9/16	.0016-.0033	.0021-.0038	.3416	.3416
'74	6-250	46③	45④	60 @ 1.66	1 21/32	.0010-.0027	.0010-.0027	.3414	.3414
	8-350	45	44	61 @ 1.59	1 19/32	.0016-.0033	.0021-.0038	.3416	.3411
	8-400 4 bbl	30	29	60 @ 1.60	1 19/32	.0016-.0033	.0021-.0038	.3416	.3411
	8-400 2 bbl	45	44	61 @ 1.59	1 19/32	.0016-.0033	.0021-.0038	.3416	.3411
	8-400 4 bbl auto.	30	29	65 @ 1.57	1 9/16	.0016-.0033	.0021-.0038	.3416	.3411
	8-455		29	64 @ 1.57	1 9/16	.0016-.0033	.0021-.0038	.3416	.3411
'75-'77	6-250	46③	45④	57 @ 1.66	1 21/32	.0010-.0027	.0010-.0027	.3414	.3414
	8-260	46⑥	45⑦	70 @ 1.67	1 31/32	.0010-.0027	.0015-.0032	.3429	.3424
	8-350	30	29	66 @ 1.56	1 19/32	.0016-.0033	.0021-.0038	3416	.3411
	8-400 2 bbl	30	29	70 @ 1.54	1 19/32	.0016-.0033	.0021-.0038	3416	.3411
	8-400 4 bbl	30	29	70 @ 1.54	1 9/16	.0016-.0033	.0021-.0038	3416	.3411
	8-455	30	29	65 @ 1.57	1 9/16	.0016-.0033	.0021-.0038	3416	.3411

■ Intake valve seat angles are shown. All exhaust valve seat angles are 45° unless otherwise indicated.

● Intake valve face angles are shown. All exhaust valve face angles are 44° unless otherwise indicated.

① Standard and Ram Air GTO with manual transmission

② Standard GTO with automatic transmission

③ Exhaust valve seat angle 46°

④ Exhaust valve face angle 45°

⑤ All 400 cu in. engines with manual transmission

⑥ Exhaust valve seat: 31

⑦ Exhaust valve face: 30

— Not specified

▲INNER SPRING TEST PRESSURE

'70	8-350 2 bbl	35 @ 1.54
	8-400 2 bbl	35 @ 1.54
	8-400⑧ 4-bbl	57 @ 1.52
	8-400⑨ 4 bbl	38 @ 1.52
	8-400 RA IV	40 @ 1.75
	8-455	38 @ 1.52
'71	8-350 2 bbl	33 @ 1.55
	8-400⑩	56 @ 1.53
	8-400 2 bbl	33 @ 1.55
	8-450 4 bbl	36 @ 1.53
	8-455	37 @ 1.53
	8-455 HO	38 @ 1.52
'72	8-350	33 @ 1.55
	8-400⑩	56 @ 1.53
	8-400 2 bbl	33 @ 1.55
	8-400 4 bbl	36 @ 1.53
	8-455	37 @ 1.53
	8-455 HO	38 @ 1.52

'73	8-350	33 @ 1.55
	8-400 4 bbl	56 @ 1.53
	8-400 2 bbl	33 @ 1.55
	8-400 4 bbl auto.	36 @ 1.53
	8-455	37 @ 1.53
	8-455 S.D.	40 @ 1.75
'74	8-350	33 @ 1.55
	8-400 4 bbl	56 @ 1.53
	8-400 2 bbl	33 @ 1.55
	8-400 4 bbl auto.	36 @ 1.53
	8-455	37 @ 1.53
'75-'77	8-350	38 @ 1.52
	8-400 2 bbl	41 @ 1.50
	8-400 4 bbl	41 @ 1.50
	8-455	36 @ 1.53

⑧ Standard GTO with manual transmission and all Ram Air
⑨ Standard GTO with automatic transmission
⑩ All 400 cu in. engines with manual transmission

Firebird, Ventura, 1974 GTO, Astre, Sunbird   VALVE SPECIFICATIONS

Year	Engine No. Cyl. Displacement (cu in.)	Seat Angle (deg) ■	Face Angle (deg) •	Outer Spring Test Pressure ▲ (lbs @ in.)	Spring Installed Height (in.)	STEM TO GUIDE Clearance (in.) Intake	Exhaust	STEM Diameter (in.) Intake	Exhaust
'70	6-250 1 bbl	46③	45③	60 @ 1.66	1 21/32	.0010-.0027	.0010-.0027	.3414	.3414
	8-350 2 bbl	45	44	63 @ 1.58	1 37/64	.0016-.0033	.0021-.0038	.3416	.3416
	8-400 2 bbl	45	44	63 @ 1.58	1 37/64	.0016-.0033	.0021-.0038	.3416	.3411
	8-400① 4 bbl	30	29	61 @ 1.59	1 19/32	.0016-.0033	.0021-.0038	.3416	.3411
	8-400② 4 bbl	30	29	66 @ 1.56	1 9/16	.0016-.0033	.0021-.0038	.3416	.3416
	8-400 Ram Air	30	29	61 @ 1.59	1 19/32	.0016-.0033	.0021-.0038	.3416	.3411
'71	6-250 1 bbl	46③	45③	61 @ 1.66	1 21/32	.0010-.0027	.0010-.0027	.3414	.3414
	8-307 2 bbl	46③	45③	80 @ 1.70	1 45/64	.0010-.0027	.0010-.0027	.3414	.3414
	8-350 2 bbl	45	44	61 @ 1.57	1 19/32	.0016-.0033	.0021-.0058	.3416	.3411
	8-400①	30	29	60 @ 1.60	1 19/32	.0016-.0033	.0021-.0038	.3416	.3411
	8-400 2 bbl	45	44	61 @ 1.59	1 19/32	.0016-.0033	.0021-.0038	.3416	.3411
	8-400 4 bbl	30	29	65 @ 1.57	1 9/16	.0016-.0033	.0021-.0038	.3416	.3411
	8-455	30	29	65 @ 1.57	1 9/16	.0016-.0033	.0021-.0038	.3416	.3416
	8-455 H.O.	30	29	66 @ 1.56	1 9/16	.0016-.0033	.0021-.0038	.3416	.3416
'72	6-250 1 bbl	46③	45③	60 @ 1.66	1 21/32	.0010-.0027	.0010-.0027	.3414	.3414
	8-307 2 bbl	46③	45③	81 @ 1.70	1 45/64	.0010-.0027	.0010-.0027	.3414	.3414
	8-350④ 2 bbl	46③	45③	60 @ 1.66	1 21/32	.0010-.0027	.0010-.0027	.3414	.3414
	8-350⑤ 2 bbl	45	44	61 @ 1.59	1 19/32	.0016-.0033	.0021-.0038	.3414	.3411
	8-400①	30	29	60 @ 1.60	1 19/32	.0016-.0033	.0021-.0038	.3416	.3411
	8-400 2 bbl	45	44	61 @ 1.59	1 19/32	.0016-.0033	.0021-.0038	.3416	.3411
	8-400 4 bbl	30	29	65 @ 1.57	1 9/16	.0016-.0033	.0021-.0038	.3416	.3411
	8-455 H.O.	30	29	66 @ 1.56	1 9/16	.0016-.0033	.0021-.0038	.3416	.3416

Firebird, Ventura, 1974 GTO, Astre, Sunbird — VALVE SPECIFICATIONS

Year	Engine No. Cyl. Displacement (cu in.)	Seat Angle (deg) ■	Face Angle (deg) ●	Outer Spring Test Pressure▲ (lbs @ in.)	Spring Installed Height (in.)	STEM TO GUIDE Clearance (in.) Intake	STEM TO GUIDE Clearance (in.) Exhaust	STEM Diameter (in.) Intake	STEM Diameter (in.) Exhaust
'73	6-250 1 bbl	46③	45③	60 @ 1.66	1 21/32	.0010-.0027	.0010-.0027	.3414	.3414
	8-350 2 bbl	45	44	61 @ 1.59	1 19/32	.0016-.0033	.0021-.0038	.3414	.3411
	8-400①	30	29	60 @ 1.60	1 19/32	.0016-.0033	.0021-.0038	.3416	.3411
	8-400 2 bbl	45	44	61 @ 1.59	1 19/32	.0016-.0033	.0021-.0038	.3416	.3411
	8-400 4 bbl	30	29	65 @ 1.57⑥	1 9/16	.0016-.0033	.0021-.0038	.3416	.3411
	8-455	30	29	66 @ 1.56⑦	1 9/16	.0016-.0033	.0021-.0038	.3416	.3411⑦
'74	6-250 1 bbl	46③	45③	60 @ 1.66	1 21/32	.0010-.0027	.0010-.0027	.3414	.3414
	8-350	45	44	61 @ 1.59	1 19/32	.0016-.0033	.0021-.0038	.3414	.3411
	8-400 2 bbl	45	44	61 @ 1.59	1 19/32	.0016-.0033	.0021-.0038	.3416	.3411
	8-400 4 bbl	30	29	65 @ 1.57⑧	1 9/16	.0016-.0033	.0021-.0038	.3416	.3411
	8-455	30	29	66 @ 1.56	1 9/16	.0016-.0033	.0021-.0038	.3416	.3411
	8-455 SD	45	44	70 @ 1.82	1 9/16	.0016-.0033	.0021-.0038	.3416	.3416
'75-'77	4-140	46③	45③	75 @ 1.75	1 ¾	.0010-.0027	.0017-.0027	.3414	.3414
	V6-231	45③	45③	64 @ 1.72	1 47/64	.0015-.0032	.0015-.0032	.3409	.3409
	6-250	46③	45③	57 @ 1.66	1 21/32	.0010-.0027	.0010-.0027	.3414	.3414
	8-260	46⑨	45⑩	80 @ 1.67	1 31/32	.0010-.0027	.0015-.0032	.3429	.3424
	8-350	30	29	66 @ 1.56	1 19/32	.0016-.0033	.0021-.0038	.3416	.3411
	8-350 Ventura	45③	45③	75 @ 1.73	1 23/32	.0015-.0035	.0015-.0032	.3725	.3727
	8-400	30	29	70 @ 1.54	1 9/16	.0016-.0033	.0021-.0038	.3416	.3411
	8-455	30	29	65 @ 1.27	1 9/16	.0016-.0033	.0021-.0038	.3416	.3411

■ Intake valve seat angles are shown. All exhaust valve seat angles are 45° unless otherwise indicated.

● Intake valve face angles are shown. All exhaust valve face angles are 44° unless otherwise indicated.

① Manual transmission with 400 cu in. engine

② Automatic transmission with 400 cu in. engine

③ Exhaust valve seat and face angles are the same as intake valve seat and face angles

④ Ventura II only

⑤ Firebird only

⑥ 59 @ 1.50 with manual transmission

⑦ .3416 in. for 455 S.D. engine

⑧ 60 @ 1.60 with manual transmission

⑨ Exhaust—31

⑩ Exhaust—30

— Not specified

▲INNER SPRING TEST PRESSURE (lbs @ in.)

Year	Engine No. Cyl Displacement (cu in.)	Test Pressure
'70	8-350 2 bbl	35 @ 1.54
	8-400 2 bbl	35 @ 1.54
	8-400 4 bbl	57 @ 1.52①
	8-400 4 bbl	45 @ 1.52②
	8-400 Ram Air	57 @ 1.52
'71	8-350 2 bbl	33 @ 1.55
	8-400	56 @ 1.53①
	8-400 2 bbl	33 @ 1.55
	8-400 4 bbl	36 @ 1.53
	8-455	37 @ 1.53
	8-455 H.O.	38 @ 1.52

Year		Test Pressure
'72	8-400	56 @ 1.53①
	8-400 2 bbl	33 @ 1.55
	8-400 4 bbl	36 @ 1.53
	8-455 H.O.	38 @ 1.52
'73	8-350	33 @ 1.55
	8-400	56 @ 1.53①
	8-400 2 bbl	33 @ 1.55
	8-400 4 bbl	36 @ 1.53
	8-455	36 @ 1.53③
'74	8-350④	33 @ 1.55
	8-400	56 @ 1.53①
	8-400 2 bbl	33 @ 1.55
	8-400 4 bbl	36 @ 1.53
	8-455	36 @ 1.53③

Year		Test Pressure
'75-'77	8-350	38 @ 1.52
	8-400	41 @ 1.50
	8-455	36 @ 1.53

① 400 cu in. engine with manual transmission

② 400 cu in. engine with automatic transmission

③ 40 @ 1.75 for 455 S.D.

④ Except '75-'76 Ventura 350

TORQUE SPECIFICATIONS
All readings in ft lbs

Year	Engine No. Cyl. Displacement (cu in.)	Cylinder Head Bolts	Rod Bearing Bolts	Main Bearing Bolts	Crankshaft Damper or Pulley Bolt	Flywheel to Crankshaft Bolts	MANIFOLD Intake	MANIFOLD Exhaust
'70-'74	6-250	95	35	65	Pressed on	60	25-30①	25
	8-350, 400, 455	95	43②	90-110④	160	95	40	30
	8-307 ('71-'72)	65	45	75	60	60	30	25
'75-'77	4-140 OHC	60	35	65	80	60	30	30
	V6-231	75	40	115	150	55	45	25
	6-250	95	35	65	Pressed on	60	25-30①	25③
	8-260	85	42	120	310	90	40	25
	8-350, 400, 455	95	43	100④	160	95	40	30
	8-350 Ventura	80	40	115	140	60	45	28

① End bolts 15-20 ft. lbs.
② 63 ft lbs on 455 S.D. engine

③ With integral intake manifold cast into head—18-23 for four end bolts, 30-35 for all others
④ Rear cap—120

CRANKSHAFT AND CONNECTING ROD SPECIFICATIONS
All measurements are given in inches

Year	Engine No. Cyl. Displacement (cu in.)	CRANKSHAFT Main Brg. Journal Dia	CRANKSHAFT Main Brg. Oil Clearance	Shaft End-Play	Thrust on No.	Journal Diameter	CONNECTING ROD Oil Clearance	CONNECTING ROD Side Clearance
'70	6-250	2.30	.0003-.0029	.002-.006	7	2.000	.0007-.0027	.009-.013
	8-350	3.00	.0002-.0017	.0035-.0085	4	2.250	.0005-.0025	.012-.017①
	8-400	3.00	.0002-.0017③	.0035-.0085	4	2.250	.0005-.0026②	.012-.017①
	8-455	3.25	.0005-.0021	.0035-.0085	4	2.250	.0010-.0031	.012-.017①
'71-'74	6-250	2.30	.0003-.0029	.002-.006	7	2.000	.0007-.0027	.009-.014⑦
	8-307 ('71-'72)	④	⑤	.002-.006	5	2.099-2.100	.0013-.0035	.002-.006①
	8-350	3.00	.0002-.0017	.003-.009	4	2.250	.0005-.0025	.012-.017①
	8-400	3.00	.0002-.0017	.003-.009	4	2.250	.0005-.0025	.012-.017①
	8-455	3.25	⑥⑧⑨	.003-.009	4	2.250	.0005-.0025⑩	.012-.017①
'75-'77	4-140 OHC	2.30	.0003-.0027⑫	.002-.007	4	2.000	.0007-.0038	.009-.014
	V6-231	2.50	.0004-.0015	.004-.008	2	2.000	.0002-.0023	.006-.014
	6-250	2.30	.0003-.0029	.002-.006	7	2.000	.0007-.0027	.009-.014
	8-260	2.50	.0005-.0021⑬	.004-.008	3	2.124	.0005-.0026	.006-.020
	8-350, 400	3.00	.0002-.0017	.003-.009	4	2.250	.0005-.0025	.012-.017①
	8-350 Ventura	3.00	.0004-.0015	.003-.009	3	2.000	.0005-.0026	.006-.020
	8-455	3.25	.0005-.0021	.003-.009	4	2.250	.0005-.0025	.012-.017①

① Total for 2 connecting rods
② .0015-.0031 on Ram Air IV engine option
③ No.'s 1, 2, 3, 4 on Ram Air IV option—.0012-.0028
No.'s 1, 2, 3, 4 on Ram Air IV option—.0012-.0028
No. 5 on Ram Air IV option—.0007-.0022
④ No.'s 1, 2, 3, 4—2.4484-2.493
No. 5—2.4479-2.4488
⑤ No. 1—.0008-.0020
No.'s 2, 3, 4—.0011-.0023

⑥ No. 1 bearing cap w/small valve—.0003-.0019
All others—.0005-.0021
⑦ .007-.016 in 1973
⑧ 1973-74—.0005-.0021 (455); .0010-.0026 (455 S.D.)
⑨ No. 1 on 1974 455—.0035-.0020
⑩ .0015-.0031 in 455 SD
⑪ Not used
⑫ .0003-.0020 for no. 1
⑬ .0005-.0031 for no. 5

RING SIDE CLEARANCE
All measurements are given in inches

Year	Engine No. Cyl. Displacement (cu. in.)	Top Compression	Bottom Compression
'70-'76	6-250, 8-307 ('71-'72)	.0012-.0027	.0012-.0032
'70-'77	8-350, 400, 455	.0015-.0050	.0015-.0050
'75-'77	4-140 OHC	.0012-.0027	.0012-.0027
'75-'77	8-350 Ventura	.0030-.0050	.0030-.0050
'75-'77	8-260	.0020-.0040	.0020-.0040
'76-'77	V6-231	.003-.005	.003-.005

Year	Engine	Oil Control
'70-'77	6-250	.001-.005
'71-'72	8-307	.0020-.0070
'70-'77	8-350, 400, 455	.0015-.0050
'75-'77	4-140 OHC	.0000-.0050
'75-'77	8-350 Ventura	.0035 (max.)
'75-'77	8-260	.0010-.0050
'76-'77	V6-231	.0035 (max.)

RING GAP
All measurements are given in inches

Year	Engine No. Cyl. Displacement (cu. in.)	Top Compression	Bottom Compression
'71-'72	8-307	.010-.020	.010-.020
'70-'77	8-350, 400, 455	.010-.030	.010-.030
'70-'77	6-250	.010-.020	.010-.020
'76-'77	V6-231	.013-.023	.013-.023
'75-'77	4-140 OHC	.015-.025	.009-.019
'75-'77	8-350 Ventura	.010-.020	.010-.020
'75-'77	8-260	.010-.023	.010-.023

Year	Engine	Oil Control
'70-'74	All engines	.015-.055
'75-'77	4-140 OHC	.010-.030
'75-'77	6-250	.015-.055
'75-'77	8-350 Ventura	.015-.035
'75-'77	8-350, 400, 455	.015-.055
'75-'77	8-260	.015-.055

PISTON CLEARANCE

Year	Engine No. Cyl. Displacement (cu. in.)	Piston-to-Bore Clearance (in.)
'70	6-250	.0005-.0015
	8-350, 400	.0025-.0033
	8-400 Ram Air	.0055-.0061
'71	6-250	.0005-.0015
	8-350, 400	.0025-.0033
	8-307	.0005-.0011
'72	6-250	.0005-.0015
	8-350, 400, 455	.0025-.0033
	8-307	.0005-.0011

Year	Engine No. Cyl. Displacement (cu. in.)	Piston-to-Bore Clearance (in.)
'73-'77	6-250	.0005-.0015
	8-350, 400	.0029-.0037
	8-455	.0021-.0029①
	8-455 S.D.	.0060-.0068②
'75-'77	4-140 OHC	.0018-.0028
	8-260	.0010-.0020
	8-350 Ventura	.0008-.0014
	V6-231	.0008-.0014

① .0025-.0033 for 1973
② .0064-.0072 for 1974

WHEEL ALIGNMENT SPECIFICATIONS

Year	Model	CASTER Range (deg)	Pref Setting (deg)	CAMBER Range (deg)	Pref Setting (deg)	Toe-in (in.)	Steering Axis Inclin. (deg)	WHEEL PIVOT RATIO (deg) Inner Wheel	Outer Wheel
'70-'71	Tempest, LeMans	1N to 2N	1½N	¼N to ¾P	¼P	0 to ⅛	9	20	22
	Station Wagon	1½N to 2½N	2N	¼N to ¾P	¼P	0 to ⅛	9	20	22
	Firebird	½N to 1½N	1N	¼P to 1¼P	¾P	⅛ to ¼	8.25 to 9.25	20	22
'71-'72	Tempest, LeMans	2N to 1N	1½N	½N to ½P	0	1/16 to 3/16	9	20	22
	Firebird	½N to ½P	0	½P to 1½P	1P	⅛ to ¼	8.25 to 9.25	20	22
	Ventura II	0 to 1P	½P	¼ to ¾P	¼P	⅛ to ¼	N.A.	20	22
'73-'74	LeMans, Grand Am	③	④	①	②	0 to ⅛	10.35	20	22
	Firebird	½N to ½P	0	½P to 1½P	1P	⅛ to ¼	10.35	20	22
	Ventura II	0 to 1P	½P	¼N to ¾P	¼P	⅛ to ¼	8.5 to 9.5	20	22
'74	LeMans, Grand Am	③	④	①	②	0 to ⅛	10.35	20	22
	Firebird	1N to 1P	0	¾P to 1¾P	1P	1/16 to 5/16	10.35	20	22
	Ventura	½N to 1½P	½P	½N to 1P	¼P	1/16 to 5/16	9	20	22
'75-'77	Astre/Sunbird	1¼N to ¼N	¾N	¾N to ¾P	¼P	0 to ⅛	8.55	—	—
	Ventura	⑦	⑧	¼P to 1¼P	¾P	0 to ⅛	8.75	—	—
	Firebird	½N to ½P	0	½P to 1½P	1P	0 to ⅛	9.50	—	—
	LeMans, Grand Am	⑥	⑤	①	②	0 to ⅛	10.50	—	—

N Negative P Positive
① LH: ½P to 1½P; RH: 0 to 1P
② LH: 1P; RH: ½P
③ Manual steering—1½N to ½N
  Power steering—½N to ½P
④ Manual steering—1N
  Power steering—0
⑤ Manual steering—1P
  Power steering—2P

⑥ Manual steering—½P to 1½P
  Power steering—1½P to 2½P
⑦ Manual steering—½N to 1½N
  Power steering—½P to 1½P
⑧ Manual steering—1N
  Power steering—1P
— Not specified

CHARGING SYSTEM

Alternator Removal and Installation

1. Disconnect the battery cables.
2. Remove the alternator wires or connector.
3. Loosen the adjusting and pivot bolts.
4. Remove the V-belt.
5. Remove the alternator adjusting and pivot bolts.
6. Remove the alternator.
7. To install, reverse the removal procedure.

Adjust the belt tension so that the longest span of belt between pulleys can be depressed about ½ in. in the middle by moderate thumb pressure.

Caution Pull out on the alternator by hand to avoid damage to the housing and overtightening, which could damage the bearings.

Tighten first the adjuster bolt, then the pivot bolt.

1970 Voltage Regulator Removal and Installation

1. Disconnect the battery cables.
2. Disconnect the wiring from the voltage regulator.
3. Remove the screws holding the regulator to the firewall or front bulkhead, depending on the car.
4. Reverse the removal procedure for installation.

Voltage Regulator Removal and Installation beginning 1971

The voltage regulator is inside the alternator. See "Charging and Starting Systems" in the "Unit Repair Section."

STARTING SYSTEM

Repair procedures can be found in the "Charging and Starting Systems" section of the "Unit Repair Section."

Starter Removal and Installation

OHC Four and Inline Six

1. Disconnect negative battery cable.
2. Disconnect solenoid wires.
3. Disconnect starter brace, if so equipped.
4. Remove starter-to-engine bolts and starter.

V8

1. Jack up car and support on axle stands.
2. Follow Steps 1-4 of six-cylinder procedure, working from underneath car.

V6 with Manual Transmission

1. Disconnect the negative battery cable.
2. Raise the car and safely support it.
3. Remove the engine front crossmember to body bolts, then remove the right and left crossmember brace bolts.
4. Loosen all the brace bolts to let the crossmember braces hang

down enough to allow removal of the crossmember.

5. Remove the crossmember and follow steps 2-4 under OHC 4 and Inline six Starter Removal.

V6 with Automatic Transmission

1. Raise the car and disconnect the negative battery cable.
2. Remove the exhaust crossover pipe and the flywheel cover.
3. Remove the two transmission mount to transmission bolts and place a jack under the extension housing of the transmission.
4. Remove the right transmission support bracket pivot down.
5. Disconnect and plug the fluid cooler lines and lower the transmission enough to get at the two starter to engine block bolts.
6. Remove those two bolts, the terminals on the starter, and the starter.
7. Installation is the reverse of removal.

IGNITION SYSTEM

Three types of distributors are used: a 12 volt aluminum internal point adjustment distributor used on six-cylinder engines, a 12 volt aluminum external point adjustment distributor used on eight-cylinder engines, and a 12 volt aluminum unitized transistor ignition distributor. During the 1974 model year, the unitized distributor was replaced by the similar HEI (High Energy Ignition) distributor used on other GM products. V8 and V6 HEI distributors have the coil mounted in the distributor cap. On the OHC four and inline six, the coil is mounted separately.

NOTE: There is a tachometer connecting terminal next to the ignition switch connector on the V8 and V6 HEI or unitized distributor cap. On the OHC four and the inline six, connect the tachometer to the terminal opposite the battery terminal on the remote-mounted coil. Most tachometers will work when connected to this terminal and to a ground. Some must connect from this terminal to the positive battery terminal. Some tachometers won't work at all with this system or may require a special hookup.

Never ground the tachometer terminal; the system will be damaged.

Distributor Removal

1. Disconnect the distributor primary wire (the thin wire) from the coil on breaker point systems. On OHC four and inline six HEI systems, detach the wiring harness connector from the coil. On V8 HEI systems, disconnect the ignition switch battery feed wire from the distributor cap. Don't use a screwdriver or other tool to release the lock tab.
2. Remove the distributor cap. Unlatch the cap by using a screwdriver to disengage the spring-loaded latches. Sixes with breaker points have captive retaining screws.
3. Make reference marks on the block and the distributor housing that align with the tip of the rotor. Do not crank the engine after these marks have been made.
4. Disconnect the vacuum line at distributor.
5. Remove the distributor clamp screw and hold-down clamp.
6. Lift out the distributor. Notice the slight rotation of the rotor as the distributor is removed from the block.

Distributor Installation

Installation procedure is the reverse of the removal procedure. It should be noted, however, that while inserting a gear-driven distributor into the block, the rotor should be moved slightly to one side. This is necessary because of the helical cut of the distributor and camshaft gears. As the distributor seats in its bore, the rotor will turn slightly so the reference marks will once again be in line.

Installation—If Engine Has Been Disturbed

Inline Six, V6, and V8

1. With No. 1 piston coming up on

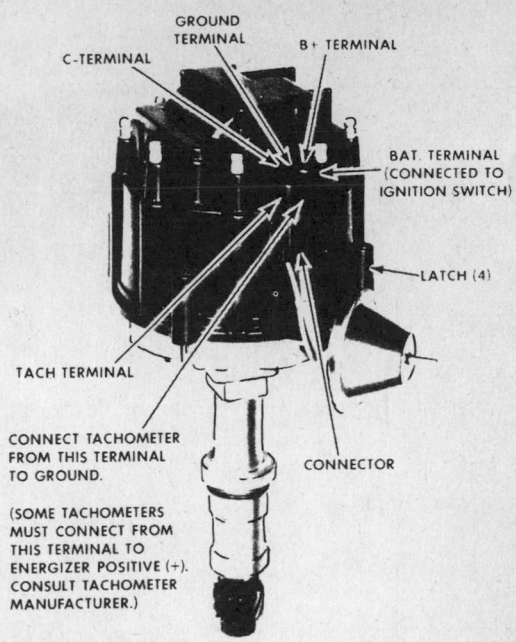

Tachometer hookup for V8 HEI system (© Pontiac Div., G.M. Corp)

compression stroke, continue cranking the engine until the pulley timing mark indexes with the zero (0) mark on the engine timing scale. There are devices available which will screw into the number one cylinder spark plug opening and indicate when TDC is reached.

2. Replace the distributor.
3. Install the distributor in the block so that the vacuum diaphragm faces the left side of the engine on V8 engines, and to the front of the engine on inline six-cylinder engines. The rotor should point toward the contact in the cap for no. 1 cylinder. Move the rotor slightly to the side because, as the distributor is pressed into its bore, it will turn a small amount.
4. Reverse the removal procedure to complete installation.

OHC 4 Cylinder

1. Remove No. 1 spark plug and place a finger over the plug hole. Remove the center coil wire and crank the engine until compression is felt in No. 1 cylinder. Rotate the engine until the timing pulley pointer is aligned with the 0° TDC mark.
2. Install the distributor with the vacuum advance unit pointing toward the front of the engine and the punchmarks on the drive gear (if any) in line with the No. 1 cap tower. The rotor must point to the No. 1 distributor cap tower.
3. Install the hold-down clamp. Tighten the clamp bolt.
4. Install the rotor, cap and vacuum line.

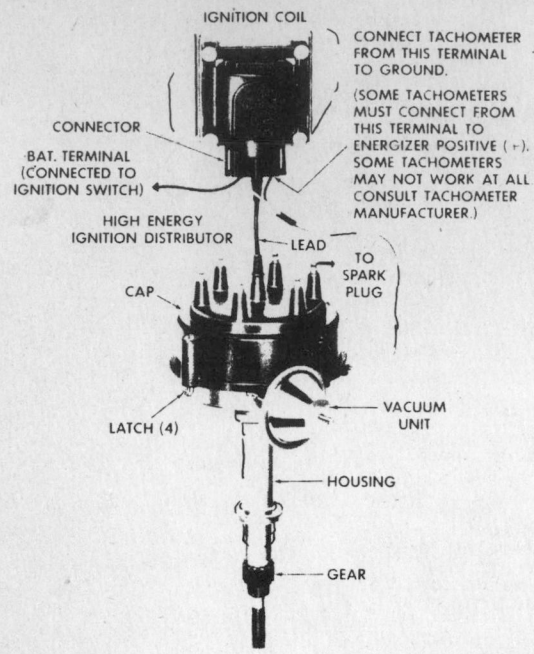

IGNITION COIL

CONNECT TACHOMETER FROM THIS TERMINAL TO GROUND.

(SOME TACHOMETERS MUST CONNECT FROM THIS TERMINAL TO ENERGIZER POSITIVE (+). SOME TACHOMETERS MAY NOT WORK AT ALL CONSULT TACHOMETER MANUFACTURER.)

CONNECTOR

BAT. TERMINAL (CONNECTED TO IGNITION SWITCH)

HIGH ENERGY IGNITION DISTRIBUTOR

LEAD

CAP

TO SPARK PLUG

LATCH (4)

VACUUM UNIT

HOUSING

GEAR

Tachometer hookup for OHC four and inline six HEI system (© Pontiac Div., G.M. Corp)

5. Connect the wiring connector to the coil.
6. Check and adjust the ignition timing.

Contact Point and Condenser Replacement and Adjustment

1. Remove the distributor cap and the rotor.
2. Remove the V8 radio frequency interference (R.F.I.) shield, if so equipped.
3. Remove the screws holding the points in place.
4. Remove the condenser lead and ignition primary lead from the points. Loosen the clamp and slide the condenser out. Remove the point set.
5. Install a new set of points and tighten the attaching screws.
6. Slide the new condenser into the clamp. Connect the condenser and primary leads to the points.
7. Apply a very small amount of high temperature grease to the distributor breaker cam.
8. On sixes, adjust the point gap after turning the engine so that the fiber rubbing block of the point set is on the high point of the breaker cam. Set the dwell with the engine cranking. You don't have to adjust the gap on V8s at this point if you are installing preset points.
9. Install the V8 R.F.I. shield. (The half covering the points should be installed first.) You don't need the shield if the unitized point and condenser set is being used on V8s.
10. Install the rotor and distributor cap.

11. Set the V8 dwell using a dwell meter with the engine running. Using a 1/8 in. allen wrench, rotate the adjusting screw through the cap window until the dwell meets specifications.

Ignition Timing

Timing marks are located on the front engine cover and harmonic balancer or pulley.

1. Disconnect and plug the distributor vacuum advance hose.
2. Make sure that the dwell is adjusted to specifications on models with breaker points.
NOTE: it may be necessary to put a small amount of white paint or chalk on the timing marks to make them more visible.
3. Connect a timing light to no. 1 spark plug.
4. Loosen the distributor hold-down clamp.
5. Start the engine and rotate the distributor until the correct mark on the cover lines up with the pulley or harmonic balancer mark. Tighten the distributor clamp, and recheck the timing.

FUEL SYSTEM

Information on the fuel gauge and carburetors will be found in the Unit Repair Section.

The inline six, V6, and V8 fuel pump is of the single action diaphragm-type, equipped with a pulsation dampening chamber for stabilizing fuel flow.

A vapor diverter is incorporated

into the fuel pumps used on air conditioned V8 and 4-BBL. models. The fuel pump is not repairable and must be replaced as a unit if defective.

The Astre uses an in-tank electric pump.

Fuel Pump Removal and Installation

All models except OHC 4

1. Disconnect fuel inlet, outlet and vapor return lines at pump and plug pump inlet line.
2. Remove two pump mounting bolts and lockwashers; remove pump and gasket.
3. On Ventura 307 V8 engines, if rocker arm pushrod is to be removed: take out the two adapter bolts and lockwashers and remove adapter and gasket.
4. Install pump with new gasket coated with sealer. Coat mounting bolt threads with sealer and tighten bolts.

NOTE: on Ventura 307 V8 engines, mechanical fingers or heavy grease can be used to hold pump pushrod in place during installation. Coat pipe plug threads or adapter gasket with sealer if pushrod was removed.

5. Connect inlet and outlet lines, start engine and check for leaks.

Chilton's TIME SAVER

When replacing a fuel pump on a 307 cu. in. engine, considerable time can be saved as follows:

1. **Before removing the old pump, remove the upper bolt from the engine's right front mounting boss. This bolt hole is in direct alignment with the fuel pump pushrod. The threaded bolt hole continues into the pump pushrod bore. The bolt acts as an oil plug.**
2. **Temporarily insert a longer bolt, (about 3/8—16 x 2 in.) into the hole. Screw the bolt into the bore until it bottoms against the pump pushrod. (Don't tighten the bolt with a wrench or the rod can be damaged.)**
3. **The mechanic is now free to remove and install the fuel pump without worrying about fuel pump pushrod misalignment.**
CAUTION: don't forget to reinstall original motor bolt.

OHC 4 Cylinder

The electrical fuel pump is an integral part of the fuel tank unit assembly, which includes the fuel gauge metering unit. The fuel pump is energized by the ignition switch when the key is in the start position. After the engine starts, the pump receives current through the engine oil pressure safety switch as long as there is approximately 2 psi oil pressure.

1. Disconnect the battery ground cable and siphon the fuel from the tank.
2. Disconnect the gauge sending-unit and pump wires at the rear harness connector.
3. Raise the car. Disconnect the fuel line at the gauge unit pickup line.
4. Disconnect the tank vent line to the vapor separator, which is mounted in the tank.
5. Disconnect the gauge wire ground screw from the floorpan.
6. Remove the tank strap bolts and, very carefully, lower the tank.
7. Use a special wrench, or a suitable substitute, to unscrew the retaining cam ring. Do not strike any part of the tank with a metal tool, such as a hammer; there is a danger of explosion from sparks.
8. Remove the gauge sending-unit and fuel pump assembly.
9. Remove the flat wire conductor from the plastic clip on the fuel tube.
10. While squeezing the clamp, pull the pump straight back 1/2 in. for access to the terminals. Remove the two nuts, lockwashers, and wires from the pump.
11. Squeeze the clamp and pull the pump straight back to completely remove it from the sending unit.

Caution Be careful not to bend the circular support bracket.

12. Slide the replacement pump through the circular support bracket until it rests against the rubber coupling. Be sure that the rubber isolator and saran strainer, supplied in the service package, are attached to the pump.
13. Attach the two pump terminals, using lockwashers and nuts. Be sure that the flat conductor is attached to the terminal farthest away from the float arm.
14. Squeeze the clamp and push the pump into the rubber coupling.
15. Replace the flat wire conductor in the plastic clip on the fuel tube.
16. Install the pump and gauge unit into the tank opening. Tighten the cam ring.

17. Install the fuel tank using a reverse of the removal procedure.

Fuel Filter Removal and Installation

1. Disconnect fuel line connection at inlet of carburetor.
2. Remove inlet fuel filter nut from carburetor using a box wrench.
3. Remove filter element and spring.
4. If a bronze element, blow through cone end—element should allow air to pass freely.
5. Install element spring and new element into carburetor. Bronze elements are installed with small section of cone facing outward.
6. Install new gasket on fitting nut and install nut.
7. Install fuel line and tighten securely. Start engine and check for leaks.

Idle Stop Solenoid

The idle stop solenoid is used on some engines to prevent after-run when the ignition is turned off. The solenoid has an adjustable plunger and is electrically operated. When the ignition is turned on, the plunger is extended and contacts the carburetor throttle lever opening the throttle plate wide enough for the engine to idle properly. When the ignition is turned off, the plunger retracts and the throttle lever falls back on the lever stop. When the throttle lever is on its stop, the throttle plate opening is very small and will not allow enough air-fuel mixture to pass to run the engine with the ignition turned off.

Some 1976 California engines without air conditioning have non-functional idle stop solenoids. These are not connected to the engine wiring, and no attempt should be made to attach them. Also, some 1976 Firebird and LeMans models with V8s are equipped with an idle speed-up solenoid which is used to maintain the idle speed when the air conditioning is turned on. Check the tune-up sticker in the engine compartment to see if such a solenoid is used on your engine.

Hot Idle Compensator

The hot idle compensator is used with automatic transmissions. Its purpose is to offset the enriching effects caused by changes in air density and fuel vapors generated during hot engine operation. It is in a chamber on the float bowl casting. The compensator is a temperature-sensitive unit which opens and closes a passage leading from the atmosphere to an orifice below the throttle valve.

Idle Speed and Mixture Adjustments

1970

Adjust with air cleaner installed.

1. On California cars, remove fuel filler cap.
2. Disconnect and plug distributor vacuum advance hose.
3. Plug hot idle compensator on all automatic transmission V8's with Quadrajet (4 MV) carburetor *except* Ram Air III and IV. Also plug compensator on all L-6 and V8 2-BBL. with automatic and A/C.
4. With automatic in Drive, manual in Neutral, adjust curb idle speed as follows:

Inline six and Ram Air IV

a. With idle stop solenoid energized, adjust solenoid screw to obtain 830 rpm for L-6, 1,000 rpm for R.A. IV, 630 rpm for automatic L-6, and 750 rpm for automatic R.A. IV.
b. Adjust mixture screws equally to obtain lean best idle at 1,000 rpm for manual R.A. IV, 750 rpm for automatic R.A. IV, 750 rpm for manual L-6, and 600 rpm for automatic L-6.
c. Disconnect solenoid wire and adjust carburetor idle speed screw to obtain 400 rpm for L-6, 500 rpm for R.A. IV automatic, and 650 rpm for R.A. IV manual.

350, 400, 455 Engines

a. Back out mixture screws 3-5 turns from lightly seated positions.
b. Adjust carburetor idle speed screw to obtain 850 rpm for manual 350 and 400 2-BBL., 1,050 rpm for manual 400 and 455 4-BBL., or 675 rpm for all automatic 350, 400, 455 engines.
c. Lean mixture screws equally (turn in) to obtain 800 rpm for manual 350 and 400 2-BBL., 950 rpm for manual 400 and 455 4-BBL., or 650 rpm for all automatic 350, 400, 455 engines.

1971-72

Adjust with air cleaner installed.
On some models, the idle stop solenoid is no longer used, having been replaced by the combination emission control valve. This valve is energized through the transmission to increase idle speed under conditions of high gear deceleration and to provide full vacuum spark advance during high gear operation. The valve is de-energized at curb idle and in the lower gears to provide a retarded spark un-

FUEL BOWL
VENT TO AIR
CLEANER

PUMP
LEVER

VACUUM
BREAK
DIAPHRAGM

TO VACUUM
MODULATOR
(AUTO. ONLY)

SECONDARY VALVES
ACTUATING ROD

IDLE SPEED SCREW

VACUUM PURGE
TO CANNISTER

PUMP LEVER
RETAINING PIN

IDLE MIXTURE LIMITER

Rochester 4 bbl (© Pontiac Div., G.M. Corp)

der these conditions, the result of which is lower hydrocarbon emission. *The valve need not be adjusted unless the solenoid or throttle body is removed, or the carburetor overhauled.*

V-8 Idle Speed

1. Disconnect carburetor "EVAP" hose from vapor storage canister.
2. Disconnect and plug carburetor-to-vacuum (distributor vacuum) solenoid hose at solenoid. Disconnect throttle solenoid wire on 4-BBL. manual transmission engines.
3. Set dwell and timing (in that order) at specified idle speed.
4. Adjust carburetor speed screw to obtain specified idle speed, automatic in Drive, manual in Neutral.
5. On 4-BBL. manual transmission models, reconnect throttle solenoid wire, manually extend solenoid screw and adjust to specified idle rpm.
6. Place automatic in Park, manual in Neutral and check fast idle speed with screw on top step of cam. Adjust fast idle screw to obtain 1,700 rpm.
   NOTE: 2-BBL. carburetors are not adjustable for fast idle.
7. Reconnect distributor vacuum and vapor storage hoses.

Inline 6 Cyl. Idle Speed

1. Disconnect fuel tank "EVAP" hose from vapor storage canister.
2. Disconnect and plug distributor vacuum advance hose.
3. Set dwell and timing (in that order) at specified idle speed.
4. Adjust carburetor idle speed screw to obtain 550 rpm for manual, 500 rpm for automatic

(in Drive). Do not adjust solenoid screw.
5. Place automatic in Park and manual in Neutral, then place fast idle tang on top step of fast idle cam and check fast idle speed. Adjust to obtain 2,400 rpm.

V-8 and Inline 6 Cyl. Idle Mixture

If the carburetor has been overhauled, or the plastic locks removed from the mixture screws, the following procedure must be used to adjust idle speed and mixture. It must be emphasized that the manufacturer does not recommend this procedure as a substitute for the preceding methods, in that exhaust emission quality can be adversely affected unless the proper test equipment is available.

1. Turn in mixture screw/s until lightly seated, then back out 3½ turns.
2. Start engine and adjust carburetor idle speed screw to obtain a speed 25 rpm above specified idle (automatic), 75 rpm higher for L-6 and 2-BBL. V8 (manual), or 100 rpm higher for 4-BBL. V8 (manual).
3. Turn mixture screw/s in equally until specified idle speed is obtained. At this point, a CO meter should be employed to adjust mixture. A reading of 1.0% or less must be maintained.
4. Shut off engine and install new limiter caps.
5. Adjust fast idle speed, as described previously.

1973-74

Inline Six-Cylinder Idle Speed

1. Disconnect the fuel tank "evap" hose from the vapor canister in

the engine compartment. Plug the line.
2. Disconnect and plug the distributor vacuum line.
3. Check that dwell and timing are correct.
4. Detach the idle stop solenoid wire (not the C.E.C. solenoid wire) and set the low idle speed to 450 rpm by using a ⅛ in. allen wrench inside the six-sided nut on the solenoid.
   NOTE: The engine must be at normal operating temperature.
5. Reconnect the idle stop solenoid wire.
6. Set the normal idle speed to that specified in the Tune-Up Specifications chart. Adjust by turning the six-sided nut on the solenoid.
   NOTE: The automatic transmission must be in Drive. Block the wheels.
7. On 1973 manual transmission models, pull the C.E.C. solenoid plunger out as far as it will go. The plunger should contact the throttle lever and produce an 850 rpm idle speed. Adjust by turning the plunger.
8. Set the automatic transmission in Park and the manual transmission in Neutral. Set the fast idle tang on the top step of the fast idle cam. The fast idle speed should be 2,400 rpm for 1973 and 1,800 rpm for 1974. Bend the tang to adjust.

V8 Idle Speed

1. Disconnect and plug the carburetor hose from the vapor canister.
2. Disconnect and plug the distributor and EGR valve vacuum hoses. Plug any open vacuum tubes on the carburetor.
3. Check the dwell and timing.
4. Disconnect the idle stop solenoid wire.
5. Adjust the carburetor idle speed screw to the low rpm specified in the Tune-Up Specifications chart.
6. Reconnect the solenoid wire and adjust the solenoid plunger screw to obtain the specified idle speed.
   NOTE: You might have to work the throttle linkage by hand first, since the solenoid isn't always powerful enough to move it.
7. On four-barrel carburetors, check the fast idle speed with the fast idle speed screw on the top step of the fast idle cam. Adjust the speed by turning the fast idle screw. Fast idle speed is 1,500 rpm for all engines except the 1974 455 S.D., which is 2,000 rpm.
   NOTE: The fast idle speed screw is NOT the same one used in Step 5. You can't make this adjustment on two-barrel carburetors.

Idle Mixture

1. Set the parking brake and block the wheels.
2. Disconnect and plug the carburetor hose from the vapor canister in the engine compartment. Disconnect and plug the distributor vacuum hose.
3. If the idle mixture limiter caps are intact and a CO meter is available, attempt to obtain an idle setting of 0.2% CO by adjusting the mixture screws. If this doesn't work, remove the caps and proceed to the next step.

NOTE: The engine must be at normal operating temperature.

4. Remove the idle mixture limiter caps. If you have a CO meter, adjust the mixture screws equally to get a reading of 0.2% CO.
5. Run the screws in until they are lightly seated, then back them out six turns for 1973 and seven for 1974.

NOTE: Sixes have only one screw.

6. Turn the air conditioner off, place the automatic transmission in Drive (block the wheels), place the manual transmission in Neutral, leave the air cleaner off and plug the air cleaner manifold vacuum fitting. Adjust the idle speed screw or the idle stop solenoid to obtain the following temporary idle speed:

Engine	Year	Manual	Automatic
6-250	1973	800	700
8-350, 2 bbl.	1973	1100	700
8-400, 2 bbl.	1973	—	700
8-400, 455, 4 bbl.	1973	1200	700
6-250	1974	950	650
6-250, Calif.	1974	950	630
8-350, 2 bbl.	1974	1150	750
8-350, 2 bbl., Calif.	1974	—	720
8-350, 4 bbl.	1974	1200	730
8-350, 4-bbl., Calif.	1974	—	720
8-400, 2 bbl.	1974	—	720
8-400, 2 bbl., Calif.	1974	—	690
8-400, 4 bbl.	1974	1310	720
8-400, 4 bbl., Calif.	1974	—	685
8-455, 1974	—	680
4 bbl. 8-455, 1974	—	675
4 bbl., Calif. 8-455, 1974	1420	825
S.D.			

CHOKE ROD GUAGE NOTCH — **FAST IDLE LEVER** — **IDLE SPEED SCREW** — **IDLE MIXTURE LIMITERS**

Carter 2 bbl (© Pontiac Div., G.M. Corp)

7. Turn the mixture screws in equally to get the highest idle speed. Then set the speed back to that listed in Step 6.
8. Turn the mixture screws in equally until the engine speed drops to the normal idle speed given in the Tune-Up Specifications chart.
9. Install the air cleaner. If the idle speed changes, adjust the mixture screws slightly to compensate.

1975-76

OHC Four-Cylinder, 1-Bbl. Carburetor

1. The adjustment must be made with the engine at normal operating temperature, with the air conditioner off, and the air cleaner in place. Automatic transmissions must be in Drive and manual transmissions in neutral.
2. Set the parking brake and block the wheels.
3. Disconnect the fuel tank vent hose at the vapor canister. Detach and plug the distributor vacuum hose to prevent any vacuum advance.
4. Use pliers to break off the plastic mixture screw limiter cap.
5. Adjust the idle solenoid screw to get the specified idle speed. The tachometer hookup for the HEI ignition system is covered earlier under Ignition System.
6. Back out the mixture screw to get the fastest possible idle.
7. Use the solenoid screw to return to the specified idle speed.
8. Turn the mixture screw in until the idle speed drops 50 rpm for automatic, and 100 rpm for manual transmission.
9. Correct the idle speed using the solenoid screw.
10. Replace the distributor and canister hoses.

OHC Four-Cylinder, 2-Bbl. Carburetor

1. The adjustment must be made with the engine at normal operating temperature, with the air conditioner off, and the air cleaner removed. Automatic transmissions must be in Drive and manual transmissions in Neutral.
2. Set the parking brake and block the wheels.
3. Disconnect the fuel tank vent hose at the vapor canister. Detach and plug the distributor vacuum hose to prevent any vacuum advance.
4. Use pliers to break off the plastic mixture screw limiter cap.
5. Adjust the idle speed screw to get an idle speed of 830 rpm. On California manual transmission cars, adjust the solenoid screw to get an idle speed of 820 rpm. The tachometer hookup for the HEI ignition system is covered earlier under Ignition System.

6. Back out the mixture screw to get the fastest possible idle.
7. Correct the idle speed to that specified in Step 5.
8. Turn the mixture screw in until the idle speed drops to 750 rpm with automatic and 700 with manual transmission.
9. Correct the idle speed.
10. Replace the distributor and canister hoses, and the air cleaner.

Inline Six-Cylinder, OHC 4, V6, and V8

1. The adjustment must be made with the engine at normal operating temperature, with the air conditioner off, and the air cleaner removed. The air cleaner vacuum fitting in the manifold should be plugged. Automatic transmissions should be in Drive and manual transmissions in neutral.
2. Set the parking brake and block the wheels.
3. On all models, disconnect and plug the hose going to the carburetor from the vapor cannister. On 1975 350 V8 2-bbl except in the Ventura, detach and plug the distributor vacuum hose to block vacuum advance. On 1975 260 V8s with manual transmission, the distributor vacuum hose comes from the same carburetor port. Disconnect the EGR hose while leaving the distributor vacuum hoses connected. On 1976s, disconnect and plug the EGR hose to the carburetor at the EGR valve end. On the models indicated below, disconnect and plug the distributor vacuum hose; on all other models, leave it alone.
Firebird with 400/455 (except H.O.) and manual trans.
All Ventura with 350 V8
All Sunbird and Astres
All Calif. 250 inline sixes
On all 140 OHC fours with a 1-bbl carburetor and manual transmission, and all California 140 OHC fours with a 2-bbl and manual transmission, disconnect the idle stop solenoid.
4. Use pliers to break off the plastic idle mixture screw limiter caps. Sixes have only one screw. Turn in the mixture screws until they seat lightly, then back them out five turns. Back out six turns on manual transmission Ventura 260 V8 and 455 H.O.
5. Adjust the idle speed screw or idle solenoid screw to get the "before lean drop idle" speed listed on the underhood specifications sticker. The tachometer hookup for the HEI ignition system is covered earlier under Ignition System.

6. Adjust the mixture screws equally (quarter-turn increments are recommended) to obtain the highest possible idle speed. Check the adjustment by shifting into Neutral, running the engine at 2,000 rpm for 5-10 seconds, returning to idle, shifting back into Drive, and letting the speed stabilize for 10 seconds.
7. Return the idle speed to that set in Step 5.
8. Repeat Steps 6 and 7, until no further speed increase is possible.
9. Turn in the mixture screws equally until the normal idle speed is reached.
10. Place the automatic transmission in Park and the manual in neutral. Check the tune-up sticker and adjust the fast idle with the fast idle speed screw. If there is no speed shown, you do not have to adjust the fast idle. For 4MC and 1MV carburetors, adjust with the fast idle speed screw on the high step of the cam; for the 5210-C carburetor, set the fast idle screw on the second step.
11. If there is an idle speed-up solenoid, place the transmission in Drive, disconnect the terminal connector at the air conditioner compressor clutch and adjust the solenoid to give 675 RPM; when finished reconnect the terminal connector.
12. If there is a dashpot, adjust it so that at idle, there is .040 in. clearance between the tip of the plunger (compressed) and the throttle lever.
13. Replace and connect the air cleaner. Use the mixture screws to make any slight idle speed correction necessary.
14. Replace the distributor and canister hoses.

COOLING SYSTEM

To refill and bleed the cooling system after repair, first fill the radiator with coolant mixture. Leave the cap off and run the engine with the heater on until the thermostat opens. Then fill the radiator as necessary, with the engine running. Replace the radiator cap. If there is a coolant reservoir, add coolant mixture until the level is between the two marks.

Radiator Removal and Installation

All Except Astre, Sunbird

1. Drain coolant.

2. Remove fan shield assembly on the six. Remove the fan.
3. Disconnect upper and lower hoses.
4. Disconnect and plug oil cooler lines, if equipped with automatic transmission.
5. Lift radiator and shroud straight up and out of car.
6. To install, reverse removal procedure, making sure lower cradles are properly located and automatic transmission is full.

Astre, Sunbird

There are two radiators: a standard type and a larger heavy duty radiator equipped with a fan shroud.
1. Drain the radiator.
2. On models with the heavy duty radiator, remove the fan shroud.
3. Disconnect the intake and outlet hoses and the coolant recovery hose. Disconnect the coolant level indicator lead.
4. Remove the upper mounting panel or bracket.
5. Lift the radiator up and out of the lower brackets.
6. To install, reverse the removal procedure.

Water Pump Removal and Installation

Inline Six, V6, and V8

This is a centrifugal-type waterpump. It is die cast, with sealed bearings and is pressed together. Therefore, it is serviced as a unit.
1. Disconnect the battery and drain the radiator.
2. Loosen the alternator and remove the fan belt.
3. Remove the power steering and air conditioning belts, if so equipped.
4. Remove the fan and water pump pulley.
5. Remove the V8 front alternator bracket.
6. Remove the heater hose and radiator hose at the pump.
7. Remove the water pump retaining bolts and the pump.
8. Install the pump by reversing the above steps. Make sure that all gasket surfaces are clean and smooth. Always use a gasket sealer on both sides of the gasket. Tighten the retaining bolts.

OHC 4 Cylinder

The water pump is located on the front of the engine block immediately above the crankshaft pulley. The pump bearings are permanently lubricated during manufacture and do not require periodic maintenance other than keeping the air vent (top of housing) and drain holes (bottom of housing) free of dirt and grease.
The pump components cannot be

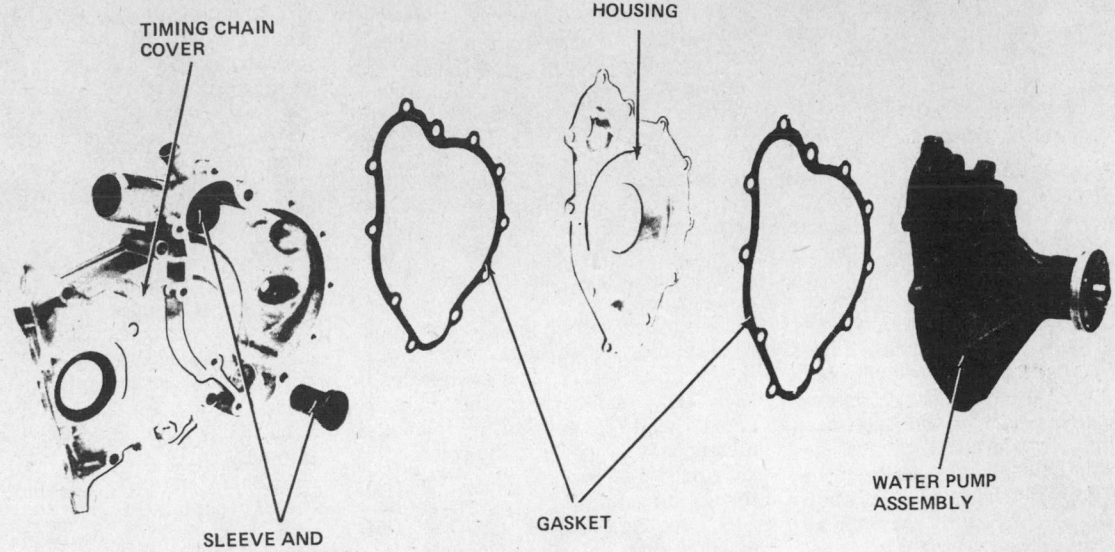

TIMING CHAIN COVER

HOUSING

SLEEVE AND SEAL ASSEMBLY

GASKET

WATER PUMP ASSEMBLY

Pontiac design V8 water pump assembly
(© Pontiac Div., G.M. Corp)

serviced separately and, in the event of pump failure, the complete assembly must be replaced as a unit, as follows:

1. Raise the hood and install a bolt through the hood hold-open link.
2. Disconnect the battery negative cable.
3. Remove the fan and spacer.

Caution No attempt should be made to repair a bent or damaged fan. The fan assembly must be in proper balance and an improperly balanced fan may cause extensive damage.

4. Loosen, but do not remove, the two lower timing belt cover retaining screws. The holes in the cover are slotted so that the cover is easily removed.
5. Remove the two upper timing belt cover retaining screws and remove the cover.
6. Drain the coolant.
7. Loosen the water pump bolts to relieve the tension on the timing belt.
8. Remove the hoses from the water pump.
9. Remove the water pump bolts, pump and gasket.
10. Thoroughly clean the old gasket material from the pump and block.
11. To install, position the water pump on the block using a new gasket and loosely install the water pump bolts. Make sure that the V grooves of the belt are aligned with the grooves in the water pump.
    NOTE: use an anti-seize compound on the water pump bolt threads.
12. A special tool is available to adjust the timing belt. It fits into the round hole in the square lug to the upper right (facing) of

the water pump and bears against the pump housing midway between the bolt holes. If this tool is available, apply 15 ft lbs of torque against the water pump (and belt). If the tool is not available, apply a force to the pump in a similar manner. Tighten the pump bolts to 15 ft lbs.
13. Install the radiator and heater hoses to the pump.
14. Install the timing belt cover, lowering the cover lower screw slots over the screws. Loosely tighten the screws against the cover.
15. Install the two upper timing cover screws, then tighten the upper and lower screws to 50 in. lbs.
16. Install the fan spacer and fan, tightening the bolts to 20 ft lbs.
17. Fill the cooling system, connect the battery negative cable, start the engine and check for leaks.
18. Remove the bolt from the hood hold-open link and close the hood.

Thermostat Removal and Installation

Inline Six, V6, and V8

1. Drain coolant to below thermostat level.
2. Disconnect upper hose and remove water outlet assembly.
3. Replace by reversing the above steps. Clean the gasket surfaces and use a gasket sealer and a new gasket.
4. Refill and bleed cooling system.

OHC 4 Cylinder

The thermostat is located in a housing at the cylinder head water outlet adjacent to the intake mani-

fold.
1. Drain the cooling system.
2. Disconnect the upper radiator hose at the engine.
3. If the alternator is attached to the water outlet, loosen the swivel bolt attachment and move it out of the way.
4. Unbolt the housing and remove the housing, gasket, and thermostat.
5. Replace the thermostat and housing, using a new gasket.
6. Install the alternator and adjust the drive belt.
7. Replace the radiator hose, fill the cooling system, start the engine, and check for leaks.

EMISSION CONTROLS

There are three types of emissions to be controlled: crankcase emissions, carburetor and gas tank gas vapor emissions, and exhaust emissions. See the "Unit Repair Section" for troubleshooting and repair information.

1970

Crankcase emissions are controlled by the Positive Crankcase Ventilation System, and exhaust emissions by the engine Controlled Combustion System (C.C.S.), in conjunction with the new Transmission Controlled Spark System (T.C.S.)

In addition, cars sold in California are equipped with an Evaporation Control System that limits the amount of gasoline vapor discharged into the atmosphere (usually from the carburetor and fuel tank).

The T.C.S. system consists of a transmission switch, a solenoid valve, and a temperature switch. Under normal conditions, the system permits the vacuum distributor (spark) advance to operate only in high gear (both manual and automatic transmissions) and reverse.

The transmission switch is located on the transmission and senses when the transmission is in one of the lower gears. When it is in a lower gear, the switch activates the vacuum solenoid valve. This valve is located in the vacuum line that runs from the carburetor to the distributor and it shuts off vacuum to the distributor advance when it is activated. There is also an engine-temperature sensing switch which overrides the transmission switch. It will allow vacuum advance in the lower gears when engine temperature is below 85° or above 220°. There is always vacuum advance in high gear and reverse.

The Combustion Control System (C.C.S.) utilizes engine modification. Essentially the C.C.S. increases combustion efficiency through carburetor and distributor calibrations and by increasing engine operating temperature.

Carburetors are calibrated leaner and initial ignition timing is retarded. Another carburetor feature is the idle fuel mixture limiting orifice. It is located at the base of the idle mixture screw and makes sure that, even if the idle mixture screw is turned too far, the fuel enrichment will not greatly affect exhaust emissions.

1971

In 1971, the Combination Emission Control System (C.E.C.), was introduced. It uses the C.C.S. of 1968–69 and incorporates several, but not all, of the features in the T.C.S. of 1970. Although distributor vacuum advance is eliminated in the lower gears, as in the T.C.S. system, it is eliminated in a different manner. A C.E.C. solenoid valve is used to regulate distributor vacuum advance.

The C.E.C. solenoid valve is mounted on the carburetor. Vacuum from the intake manifold passes through a port at the base of the solenoid before it reaches the distributor. When the solenoid receives an electrical signal, the plunger extends, opening the port, which allows vacuum to the distributor. At the same time, the plunger head contacts the carburetor throttle lever increasing the idle speed. When the solenoid is de-energized, the spring-loaded plunger returns to its unextended position closing the port and allowing the throttle lever to rest against the idle speed adjusting screw.

The switch is energized by two switches and one relay.

The time-delay relay is used to energize the C.E.C. solenoid and provide vacuum advance for the first 15 seconds after the ignition is turned on.

One of the controlling switches is an engine temperature switch. It allows vacuum advance in all gears, by energizing the C.E.C. solenoid, when the engine temperature is below 82° or above 220°. In between 82° and 220°, this switch will allow no vacuum advance and the solenoid will be de-energized.

The other switch is the transmission switch. When the transmission is in the lower gears, this switch keeps the C.E.C. solenoid in the de-energized position eliminating vacuum advance. In high gear, the solenoid is energized by current from the battery and vacuum advance is supplied.

On air-conditioned (A/C), automatic transmission cars, a solid-state time device engages the A/C compressor for about three seconds after the ignition is turned off. The load from the compressor effectively stalls the engine and prevents dieseling or overrun.

The evaporation control system was added to all cars in 1971. This system limits the amount of gasoline vapor discharged into the air from the gas tank and carburetor. The fuel tank has a non-vented cap. As vapors are generated in the fuel tank, they flow through a liquid vapor separator to a canister where they are stored. From the canister, the vapors are routed to the carburetor where they are burned when the engine is running.

1972

All six-cylinder models with manual transmissions, and all models with a 307 V8—regardless of type of transmission—use the C.E.C. system. All six-cylinder models with automatic transmissions use the A.I.R. system. All V8s equipped with a manual four-speed transmission use the T.C.S. system. All V8 models equipped with a three-speed manual transmission or an automatic transmission use the new Speed Control Spark System (S.C.S.)

The Speed Controlled Spark (S.C.S.), system uses a solenoid valve in the vacuum line running between the carburetor and the distributor. This valve is the same as the transmission-controlled spark valve. The difference in this system is that the valve is regulated by vehicle speed using a speed control spark switch. The S.C.S. solenoid valve is energized below 38 mph in any gear, under normal operating temperature, allowing no vacuum advance. Above 38 mph, in any gear, or any time engine temperature is higher or lower than normal operating temperature, the solenoid valve is de-energized allowing

full vacuum advance to the distributor.

Normal S.C.S. engine operating temperatures range from 95° to 230°. An engine-temperature sensing switch is located in the head and de-energizes the solenoid until operating temperature is reached regardless of vehicle speed.

1973

The Controlled Combustion System (C.C.S.) is standard on all engines. The C.E.C./E.G.R. (Exhaust Gas Recirculation) system is used on all 6 cyl engines with manual transmission. The Air Injection Reactor (A.I.R.) is used on all 6 cyl, 350 with manual transmission, and 350/400 California engines. A combination of the Transmission Controlled Spark and Exhaust Gas Re-circulation (E.G.R.) is found on all V8 engines.

E.G.R. is a system used to reduce nitrous oxide (NO_x) emissions. It

1973½

Mid-year A.I.R. cylinder heads can usually be identified by the absence of a drilled passage and metal sealing ball at the nos. 3 and 6 cylinder locations.

The new engines have a relocated vacuum source for the air cleaner. Vacuum is supplied through a tee in the hose feeding vacuum to the distributor vacuum spark thermal valve.

The mid-year EGR system operates basically on the same principle as the 1973 system, except for two major differences:
1. The EGR and TCS systems now work completely independent of each other.
2. A new EGR thermal vacuum valve is used to sense the temperature of the intake manifold coolant. Below 95°F, no EGR; above 95°F, EGR.

In the TCS system, full vacuum advance is provided below 62°F. When the temperature rises above 62°F, the distributor vacuum spark thermal valve closes and from this point on the distributor solenoid must be energized to get vacuum advance. The upper temperature limit for vacuum advance cut-in is now 240°F.

The Start-Up Relay Switch gives full advance (ported for manual transmission) in any gear for 20 seconds after all engine starts. After the 20 seconds has elapsed, the switch breaks ground and the distributor solenoid is de-energized, shutting off the vacuum advance.

1974

The A.I.R. system is carried over from 1973 and is used on all manual transmission and California six-cylinder engines, 350 2 bbl manual transmission V8s, all 350 cu in. California

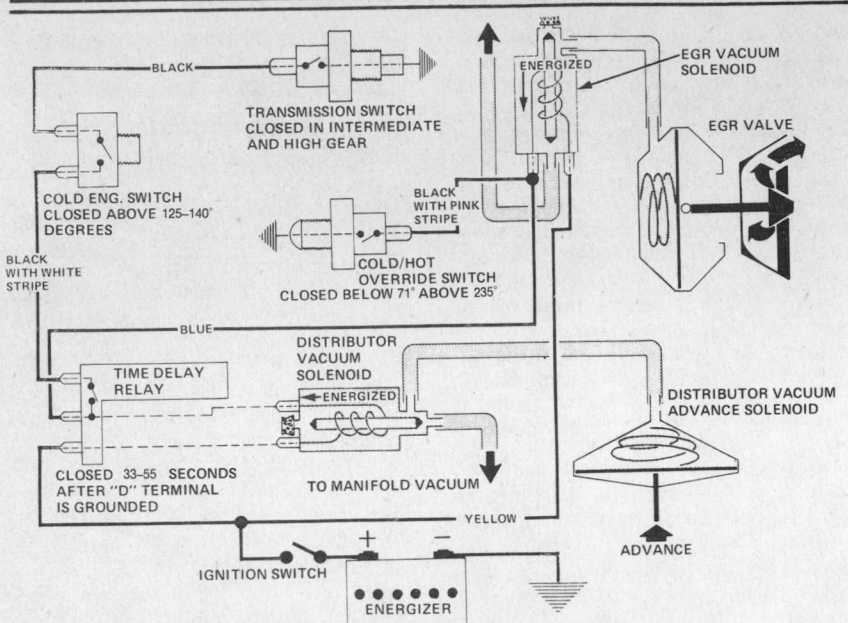

1973 combined TCS and EGR system (© Pontiac Div., G.M. Corp)

engines and 400 cu in. 2 bbl California engines.

The EGR/TCS system is once again together, as in pre-1973½ systems, and consists of a thermal vacuum valve, vacuum advance solenoid, EGR valve, hot coolant switch, cold feed switch and a time-delay relay for engine starting. The system is found on all V8s. Pontiac six-cylinder engines use the Chevrolet system without any changes.

On the EGR/TCS system, the distributor spark-EGR thermal vacuum valve senses the temperature of the air/fuel mixture inside the intake manifold. Below 62°F, EGR is off and functions by allowing a small amount of exhaust gas into the air fuel mixture in the intake manifold, under certain conditions.

The EGR TCS system consists of a temperature switch which senses when the engine temperature is under 71° or over 230°, a second temperature switch sensing engine temperature between 140° and 230°, an EGR solenoid, a vacuum advance solenoid, a transmission switch, and a time delay relay.

The under 71° and over 230° switch is mounted on the left cylinder head. The 140° to 230° switch is mounted in the right cyl head. The time delay relay is mounted on the vacuum advance solenoid.

The 71° to 230° switch grounds the circuit for the solenoids below 71° and above 230°. The 140° switch passes current to the transmission switch when engine temperature is between 140° and 230°. The transmission switch then grounds the circuit for the solenoids in first gear only. Between 71° and 140° the temperature switches are both open and the solenoids are in the normal posi-

tions.

The vacuum advance solenoid is normally closed, allowing no vacuum advance. The EGR solenoid is normally open, allowing exhaust gas recirculation.

Below 71° there is a complete circuit and both solenoids are energized, allowing vacuum advance and cutting off EGR.

From 71° to 140° there is an open circuit, the solenoids return to their normal positions, and vacuum advance is cut off and EGR is allowed.

From 140° to 230°, in first gear, there is an open circuit and the solenoids are in their normal positions. The time delay relay maintains the open circuit for 33 to 55 seconds after the transmission shifts into second gear. However, after the time delay in second and third gear, the solenoids are energized to allow vacuum advance and cut off EGR.

Over 235° the solenoids are energized and vacuum advance occurs and there is no EGR.

The C.E.C. system operates as previously, except that the time-delay relay now provides 20 seconds of vacuum advance before the solenoid is de-energized, and the engine temperature switch provides vacuum ad-

EXHAUST GAS RECIRCULATION (EGR)

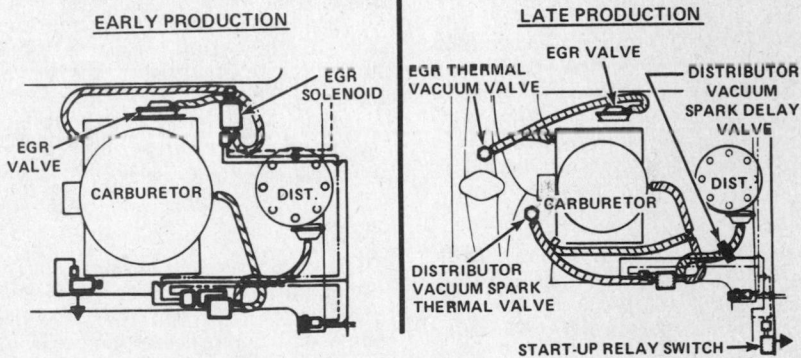

EGR system—1973 mid-year changes (© Pontiac Div, G.M. Corp)

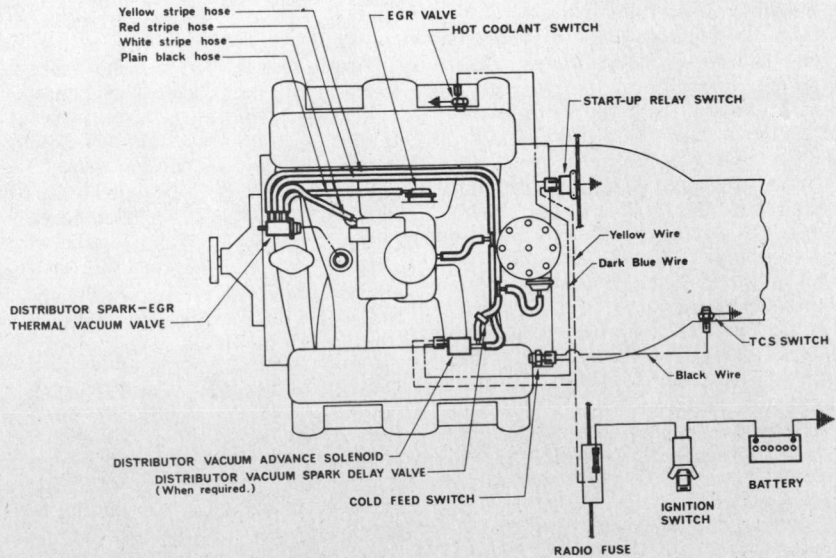

1974 Emissions Control System (© Pontiac Div., G.M. Corp)

vance when engine coolant temperature is below 93°F.

full vacuum advance is provided. When the temperature rises above 62°F, EGR is on (operated by a port above the throttle blade, so that it only comes on above idle). From this point on the distributor vacuum advance solenoid must be energized by the other components and switches to provide vacuum advance.

When the cylinder head metal temperature goes above 125°, 140°, 155°F (depending on use), the cold feed switch closes. This sends the 12V current to the TCS switch looking for a ground. The TCS switch provides a ground only when the transmission shifts into high gear. There is no time delay after shifting into high gear.

Any time the coolant temperature goes over 240°F, the hot coolant switch provides a ground for the distributor solenoid. Since the hot coolant switch will ground whether the TCS switch does or not, vacuum advance will be supplied to the distributor in any gear when the coolant temperature reaches 240°F or above.

There is a distributor vacuum spark delay valve on some models, between the distributor solenoid and the distributor acting as a restrictor on vacuum supplied to the distributor. This merely slows down the rate vacuum is initially supplied to the distributor. Full vacuum is eventually supplied.

The function of the start-up relay switch is identical to 1973½. See Pontiac section for further details.

1975

The Controlled Combustion System (C.C.S.) is continued on all non-California engines. It introduces preheated carburetor intake air during engine warmup.

The Air Injection Reactor (A.I.R.), or air pump system is continued in some applications.

E.G.R. (Exhaust Gas Recirculation) is used with the exhaust gas introduced into the intake mixture in the intake manifold and modulated by an exhaust backpressure modulating valve.

All models have high energy ignition (H.E.I.) to prevent any possible catalyst damage caused by ignition miss. Refer to the "Electronic Ignition" Unit Repair Section for details.

Catalytic converters are used on all models to control hydro-carbons and carbon monoxide. Refer to the "Emission Control" Unit Repair Section for details on this system.

All engines have outside air intakes. The cooler outside air improves driveability.

A heat valve on the exhaust manifold diverts exhaust gases through the intake manifold for a faster warmup. Starting 1975, 350, 400, and 455 V8s, (except in the Ventura), are equipped with primary and secondary choke vacuum breaks. This dual choke break system ensures better driveability in both cold and hot weather. The system works as follows: When an engine is off or cold, the choke coil holds the choke valve in the carburetor closed. While cranking the engine, the choke allows the choke valve to be opened a little to ensure a rich starting mixture for easy starting. Once the engine is running, full manifold vacuum is applied to the primary vacuum break.

The fast idle cam follower is pulled off the high step of the fast idle cam (coming to rest on the second step), and the choke valve is opened, allowing the car to be driven without stalling. When the engine is thoroughly warmed up, the choke is opened fully. In hot weather, the secondary choke vacuum break opens the choke valve a little further than normal.

The thermal vacuum valve in the air cleaner (which controls the secondary vacuum break) senses the temperature is above 62 and opens, allowing vacuum to flow to the secondary vacuum break, which opens the choke plate more than the primary vacuum break. This is accomplished after a slight time delay to allow the engine to stabilize at the leaner mixture. The leaning out of the mixture accomplished by the secondary vacuum break, permits better driveability and reduced emissions.

1976

The 1976 Pontiac emission control systems are basically the same as those used in 1975. In a few cases the components have been changed, but the action of the system has remained the same. Examples of this are the EGR system and the vacuum advance circuit.

In the EGR system, the thermal vacuum valve has been replaced with a heat sensitive snap disc valve, attached to the intake manifold. This senses the engine radiant heat, and denies vacuum to operate the EGR valve when the engine is cold.

In the vacuum advance circuit, the spark retard delay valve has been replaced with a spark delay restrictor. The restrictor allows full manifold vacuum to the distributor except under full acceleration or deceleration. In these cases, it delays vacuum for a few seconds.

Pontiac has added a distributor vacuum valve to the 260 V8, and testing procedures for this are the same as for other Pontiac distributor vacuum valves.

ENGINE

Inline Six-Cylinder Engine

This engine has a cast iron block and cylinder head, uses hydraulic valve lifters, and is similar in construction to the Chevrolet engine. Starting 1975, the intake manifold is integral with the cylinder head. This engine was last used in 1976.

V8 Engine

Pontiac has used seven different V8 engines from 1970-77. These have included four of Pontiac design: the 350, the 400, the 455, and the 455 with four bolt main bearing caps last used in 1973. The Ventura line *only* has used both a 307 similiar to the Chevrolet engine in 1971-72, and a Buick designed 350 starting 1975. Another engine, the Oldsmobile design 260, is also used in the Ventura only in 1975-76.

V6

Starting 1976, Pontiac used the Buick design V6 as the optional engine in the Sunbird line. This engine is similiar to the one last used by Buick in 1967, a cast iron OHV V6 with four main bearings.

4 Cylinder Engines

The Astre engine is a Chevrolet design single overhead camshaft, four-cylinder design using a die cast aluminum cylinder block and a cast iron cylinder head. The iron-plated aluminum pistons ride directly on honed and electro-chemically treated aluminum bores. The cylinder block is cast of an alloy containing silicon which, after suitable etching, provides a proper bore surface for the pistons and rings.

Pontiac is using, a cast iron pushrod model of its own design for 1977. It has overhead valves with very long connecting rods. Using a short stroke (3 in.) and long connecting rods allows the inherent four cylinder roughness to be avoided.

Engine Removal and Installation

Inline Six V6 and V8

1. Disconnect battery.
2. Drain cooling system.
3. Scribe alignment marks on hood and remove hood from hinges.
4. Disconnect the engine wiring harness and ground straps, alternator wires, and the engine-temperature and oil-pressure sending-unit wires.
5. Remove air cleaner and fan shield or shroud.
6. Disconnect radiator and heater hoses.

7. Remove radiator.

NOTE: On some models you can do the job by removing only the radiator or the fan, but it is generally easier to remove them both.

8. Remove fan and fan pulley.

NOTE: if equipped with power steering and/or air conditioning, disconnect and swing aside pump/compressor *without* disconnecting hoses.

9. Disconnect accelerator linkage.
10. Disconnect all vacuum lines at the carburetor and disconnect the throttle cable.
11. Raise the front of the car and drain the engine oil.
12. Disconnect fuel lines at pump.
13. Disconnect exhaust pipes.
14. Disconnect the starter wires and remove the starter on inline six-cylinder models.
15. If equipped with automatic transmission, remove converter cover and three converter retaining bolts, then slide converter to the rear. Make a mark on the flywheel and converter for later realignment.
16. If equipped with manual transmission, disconnect clutch linkage and remove clutch cross-shaft.

NOTE: remove starter and lower flywheel cover on V8s.

17. Remove four lower bellhousing bolts (two per side). Remove the three right side bolts on the 260 V8.
18. Disconnect transmission filler tube support (automatic) and starter wire shield from cylinder heads.
19. Remove two front motor mount-to-frame bracket bolts.
20. Lower car to floor then, using a jack and a wood block, support the transmission. Support the engine with a hoist.
21. Remove two remaining bellhousing bolts. Remove the three left side bolts on the 260 V8.
22. Raise transmission slightly, using the jack and wood block, then, using a chain hoist, remove the engine.
23. To install, reverse removal procedure. Install the two upper bellhousing bolts first (with jack still under transmission).

NOTE: do not lower engine completely until jack and wood block are removed.

OHC 4 Cylinder

1. Raise the hood and install a bolt in the hold-open link.
2. Disconnect the battery cables.
3. Drain the cooling system and disconnect the hoses at the radiator.
4. Disconnect the heater hoses at the water pump and at the heater inlet (bottom hose).
5. Disconnect the following emission hoses:

a. PCV at the cam cover.
b. The canister vacuum hose at the carburetor.
c. PCV vacuum hose at the intake manifold.
d. Bowl vent at the carburetor.

6. Remove the radiator, fan, fan spacer and air cleaner.
7. Disconnect the following electrical leads:

a. Alternator.
b. Ignition coil.
c. Starter solenoid.
d. Oil pressure sending unit.
e. Temperature sending unit.
f. Ground strap at the firewall.

8. Disconnect:

a. Turbo Hydra-Matic detent cable.
b. Fuel line at the rubber hose, rearward of the carburetor.
c. Automatic transmission vacuum modulator and air conditioning vacuum line at the intake manifold.
d. Throttle cable at the manifold bellcrank.

9. On cars with air conditioning, disconnect the compressor at the front support, rear support, rear lower bracket and remove the drive belt from the compressor.

NOTE: Do not disconnect any air conditioning lines or fittings.

10. Being careful not to crimp or bend the hoses, move the compressor slightly forward, allowing the front of the compressor to rest on the frame forward brace. Secure the rear of the compressor to the engine compartment so that it does not interfere with the engine removal.
11. If so equipped, disconnect the power steering pump and position it out of the way.
12. Raise the car on a hoist.
13. Disconnect the exhaust pipe at the exhaust manifold.
14. Remove the engine flywheel lower cover or the torque converter underpan.
15. On vehicles equipped with automatic transmission:

a. Mark the converter-to-flywheel relationship for reassembly.
b. Remove the converter to flywheel retaining bolts and install a converter safety strap, to keep the converter from falling out.
c. Remove the converter housing to engine retaining bolts.
d. Loosen the engine front mount retaining bolts at the frame attachment and lower the vehicle on the hoist.
e. Install a floor jack under the transmission and an engine hoist to raise the engine slightly from its mounts.
f. Remove the engine front

mount retaining bolts.
g. Remove the engine from the vehicle. Pull the engine forward enough to clear the transmission while slowly lifting the engine.

16. On vehicles with manual transmission:

a. Remove the flywheel housing to engine retaining bolts.
b. Proceed with Step 15, parts d, e, f, and g.

To install engine:

17. Install two guide pins into the upper bolt holes in the engine block. Guide pins can be fabricated by cutting the heads off two bolts and sawing screwdriver slots into them.
18. Lower the engine into place, aligning the engine with the transmission.
19. Install the front mount bolts hand-tight.
20. Install the converter or clutch housing-to-engine bolts, replacing the guide pins. Remove the torque converter retaining strap, if one was used.
21. Torque the clutch housing-to-engine bolts to 25 ft lbs and the converter housing-to-engine bolts to 35 ft lbs.
22. After checking to make sure that the front engine mounts are aligned and not making metal-to-metal contact, tighten them to 20 ft lbs.
23. Align the previously made converter and flywheel marks, and torque the bolts to 35 ft lbs.
24. Install the flywheel dust cover or torque converter underpan.
25. Connect the exhaust pipe at the manifold.
26. If so equipped, install the air conditioning compressor and power steering pump. Adjust the alternator belt.
27. Reconnect:

a. the accelerator cable,
b. the automatic transmission vacuum modulator line and the air conditioning vacuum line,
c. the fuel line, and
d. the Turbo Hydra-Matic detent cable.

28. Attach the following electrical connections:

a. alternator
b. coil
c. starter solenoid
d. oil pressure switch
e. temperature switch
f. engine ground strap

29. Replace the air cleaner and install these hoses:

a. vent tube at the air cleaner base
b. carburetor bowl vent
c. PCV vacuum line
d. vacuum canister hose

30. Install the radiator, radiator

31. Connect the heater and radiator hoses. Fill the cooling system.
32. Connect the battery cables. Start the engine and check for leaks. Remember to remove the bolt from the hood hold-open link.

Manifolds

Intake Manifold Removal and Installation

NOTE: Pontiac doesn't recommend a specific manifold bolt torque sequence, for some engines. However, one of the torque sequences shown should be adopted.

V6 and V8 Except Ventura 307

1. Remove the EGR valve. Drain the radiator and block.

NOTE: You can drain most of the coolant through the radiator drain if you raise the rear of the car 15-18 in.

2. Remove air cleaner and upper radiator hose. On the 260 V8, remove the thermostat bypass hose and the heater hose.
3. Disconnect heater hose.
4. Disconnect temperature gauge wire, then remove two spark plug wire brackets from manifold. On the 260 V8, remove the coil mounting bolt.
5. Disconnect power brake vacuum and distributor vacuum lines. On the 1975 and later Buick design 350 engine, remove the compressor bracket bolt, loosen the compressor bolt, and slide the bracket out.

NOTE: vacuum retard line is located at lower rear of vacuum unit on some exhaust emission distributors.

6. Disconnect fuel line at carburetor.

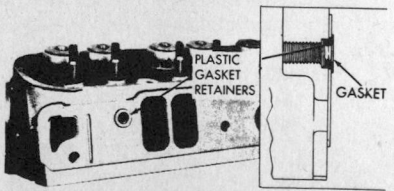

Pontiac design V8 intake manifold gaskets can be held in place by using plastic retainers, available at Pontiac dealers
(© Pontiac Div., G.M. Corp)

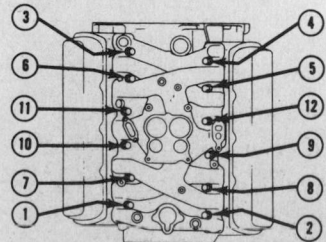

Oldsmobile design 260, 350, 403 V8 intake manifold bolt torque sequence
(© G.M. Corp)

V6 Intake Manifold Torque sequence (© Pontiac Div, G.M. Corp)

7. Disconnect crankcase vent hose and accelerator linkage.
8. Remove bolts that secure accelerator linkage bracket, then remove intake manifold bolts and nuts. If the intake manifold will not clear the distributor, remove the distributor after noting the position of the rotor and the distributor housing. On the V6, remove the distributor cap and rotor to gain access to the bolt below. This bolt requires a special socket.
9. Remove manifold and gasket.

Caution Make sure the O-ring between the intake manifold and timing chain cover is in place, where used.

10. To install, reverse removal procedure, tightening timing chain cover to manifold bolts to 10-20 ft. lbs., manifold hold-down bolts and nuts evenly to the specified torque.

1971-72 Ventura 307 V8

1. Drain water from radiator and both sides of block.
2. Disconnect battery cables, upper radiator hose, accelerator linkage, carburetor fuel line, coil and temperature sender wires.
3. Disconnect power brake hose at carburetor base and spark advance hose at distributor.
4. Disconnect PCV hoses, then remove distributor cap and matchmark rotor and housing.
5. Remove distributor hold-down clamp and pull out distributor.
6. Remove upper alternator bracket and coil.
7. Remove manifold-to-head bolts, then remove manifold from engine.
8. To install, reverse removal procedure. Stick manifold end seals in position with sealer and tighten manifold bolts to 30 ft. lbs.

OHC 4 Cylinder

1. Raise the hood and install a bolt through the hold-open link.
2. Disconnect the negative battery cable.
3. Drain the cooling system.
4. Remove the EGR tube retaining clamps from both the intake and exhaust manifolds. Remove the EGR tube by carefully driving it off.
5. Disconnect the heater hose at the fitting on the intake manifold.
6. Disconnect the vent tube at the base of the air cleaner, then remove the air cleaner.
7. Remove the air cleaner silencer.
8. Disconnect:
   a. The choke rod at the carburetor.
   b. PCV valve at the cam cover.
   c. Fuel line at the carburetor.
   d. The carburetor bowl vent line at the carburetor.
   e. Throttle linkage and the transmission throttle valve linkage.
   f. Power steering pump brace at the manifold.
9. Remove the alternator to thermostat housing through-bolt and loosen the alternator swivel bolt. Move the alternator aside to gain access to the manifold bolt.
10. Remove the four intake manifold bolts and remove the manifold.
11. Remove from the manifold:
    a. The carburetor and carburetor linkage.
    b. Pipe plug.
    c. Vacuum fittings.
    d. Hot water nipple.
12. Install the items removed in Step 10 above to the new manifold.
13. Clean the gasket surfaces on the manifold and the cylinder head.
14. Position a new gasket over the dowels on the cylinder head, then carefully install the mani-

1975-76 Ventura 350 V8 intake manifold bolt torque sequence (© Pontiac Div., G.M. Corp)

fold. Make sure that the gasket remains in place.

15. Install the manifold bolts, tightening to 30 ft. lbs. The stud goes in the hole nearest No. 3 intake port.
16. Connect the power steering pump brace to the manifold.
17. Install the alternator to thermostat housing through bolt and adjust the belt tension.
18. Connect:
    a. The choke rod at the carburetor.
    b. The PCV valve at the cam cover.
    c. Fuel line at the carburetor.
    d. Carburetor bowl vent line at the carburetor.
    e. The throttle and transmission throttle valve linkage.
    f. Vacuum connections at the carburetor.
19. Install the air cleaner silencer and secure it to the heat stove tube.
20. Install the air cleaner. Connect the vent tube at the base of the air cleaner.
21. Connect the heater hose to the intake manifold fitting and fill the cooling system.
22. Raise the car. Install the EGR tube on the intake and exhaust manifolds.
23. Install the EGR tube retaining clamps. Lower the car.
24. Connect the negative battery cable and start the engine. Check for leaks and adjust the carburetor.

Inline Six Cylinder Intake and Exhaust Manifold Removal and Installation through 1974

1. Remove air cleaner.
2. Disconnect accelerator linkage and return spring.
3. Disconnect fuel and vacuum lines at carburetor; disconnect choke rod.
4. Disconnect exhaust pipe at manifold flange.
5. Remove manifold bolts and clamps, then remove manifolds.
   NOTE: intake manifold can be separated from exhaust manifold by removing one bolt and two nuts. These fasteners should be tightened to 25 ft. lbs. after the manifolds are bolted to the engine.

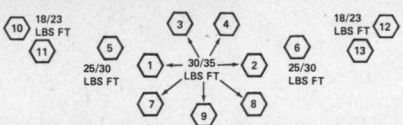

Torque sequence for exhaust manifold on inline six-cylinder with integral intake manifold (© G.M. Corp)

6. To install, reverse removal procedure, tightening center clamp bolts to 30 ft. lbs., end bolts to 15-20 ft. lbs. (for OHV engines), or all bolts to 30 ft. lbs. (for OHC engines).

Inline Six Cylinder Exhaust Manifold Removal and Installation 1975-76

This procedure is for inline sixes with the intake manifold integral with the cylinder head.

1. Remove the air cleaner.
2. Remove the power steering and air pump brackets.
3. Remove the heat riser bracket.
4. Disconnect the throttle controls and the throttle return spring.
5. Detach the exhaust pipe at the manifold flange.
6. Unbolt and remove the manifold.
7. Replace the manifold with a new gasket. Torque the bolts to specifications in the illustrated sequence.
8. Replace the exhaust pipe.
9. Connect the throttle controls and return spring.
10. Replace the air cleaner and heat riser.

V6 and V8 Right-Side Exhaust Manifold Removal and Installation

1. On 307 engines, disconnect the battery ground cable.
2. On 307 engines, remove the air cleaner pre-heater stove.
3. Disconnect the exhaust pipes from the manifolds. On 1975-76 Buick design manual transmission 350 remove the clutch equalizer shaft.
4. Straighten the tabs on the manifold bolts, if used, and remove the manifold bolts, manifold, and gasket.
5. Clean the gasket surfaces.
6. Replace the exhaust manifold, using a new gasket; the holes in

the end of the gasket are slotted.
NOTE: the installation of the gasket may be simplified by first installing the manifold using only the front and rear bolts to retain the manifold. Allow clearance of about 3/16 in. between the cylinder head and the exhaust manifold. After inserting the gasket between the head and the manifold, the remaining bolts may be installed.

7. On the 307 engine, torque the center bolts to 30 ft lbs, and the end bolts to 20 ft lbs. On all other engines, torque all bolts evenly to 30 ft lbs. (28 ft lbs on the V6).
8. Bend the tabs against the sides of the bolt heads.
9. Attach the exhaust pipe, using a new gasket.
10. Connect the battery ground cable on the 307 (only).
11. Install air cleaner pre-heater stove on the 307 (only).

V6 and V8 Left-Side Exhaust Manifold Removal and Installation

1. Remove the alternator belt, alternator and mounting bracket as an assembly.
2. Remove the spark plugs from 307 engines. On the 1975 and later Buick design 350, remove the left front engine mount bolt and loosen the right one, in order to raise the engine.
3. Disconnect the exhaust pipes from the manifolds.
4. Remove the air pre-heater shroud from 260 and 307 engines.
5. Straighten the tabs, if used, on the manifold bolt locks and remove the bolts and manifold.
6. Clean the gasket surfaces.
7. Reverse the removal procedures for installation. The notes for the right-side apply here.

OHC 4 Cylinder Exhaust Manifold Removal and Installation

1. From under the car, disconnect the exhaust pipe from the manifold.
2. Remove the intake manifold.
3. Disconnect the oil dipstick bracket at the exhaust manifold.
4. Remove the exhaust manifold bolts, then remove the manifold and carburetor heater assembly.
5. Install the carburetor heater assembly on the new manifold.
6. Install the exhaust manifold and manifold bolts (loosely). The upper bolts are shorter.
7. Tighten the manifold bolts to 30 ft. lbs.
8. Connect the exhaust pipe to the manifold.

9. Connect the oil dipstick bracket to the exhaust manifold.
10. Install the intake manifold as described above.

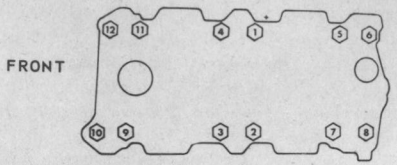

307 V8 intake manifold torque sequence
(© Pontiac Div., G.M. Corp)

Valve System

Valve Guides

Pontiac engines have integral valve guides. Pontiac offers valves with oversize stems for worn guides (0.003 and 0.005 in. being available for most engines). The correct valve stem to guide clearance is given in the Valve Specifications table at the beginning of this section. As an alternate procedure, some local automotive machine shops fit replacement guides that use standard stem valves.

NOTE: Some 1975 Astres with the 140 OHC engine are experiencing a rough idle and loss of power due to the valves not seating properly. To determine if this is the cause of power loss and rough idle, first do a compression check. If any cylinder has less than 120 PSI and will not increase with oil added, the problem is probably caused by valves not seating properly.

Rocker Arm Removal and Installation

Inline Six and Pontiac Design 350, 400, 455 V8

1. Remove the valve covers.
2. Remove the rocker arm nut and rocker arm ball.
3. Lift the rocker arm off the rocker arm stud. Always keep the rocker arm assemblies to-

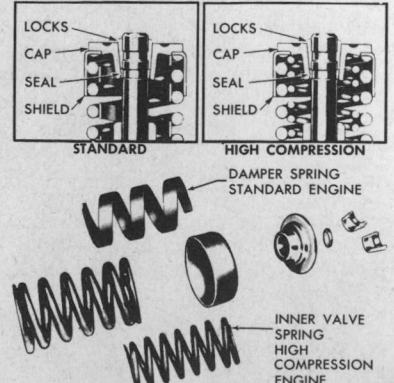

Typical Pontiac design 302, 350, 400, 455 V8
valve spring assemblies
(© Pontiac Div., G.M. Corp)

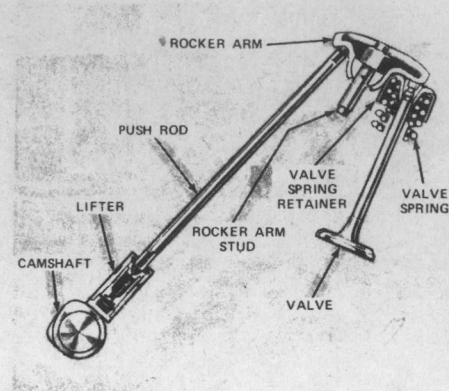

Pontiac design 302, 350, 400, 455 V8 valve train assembly (© Pontiac Div, G.M. Corp.)

gether and assemble them on the same stud.
4. Remove the pushrod from its bore. Make sure the rods are returned to their original bores, with the same end in the block.
5. Reverse the removal procedure to install the rocker arms. On V8s, tighten the rocker arm ball retaining nut to 20 ft lbs. On inline sixes, tighten the rocker arm nut with the lifter on the base circle of the camshaft lobe until

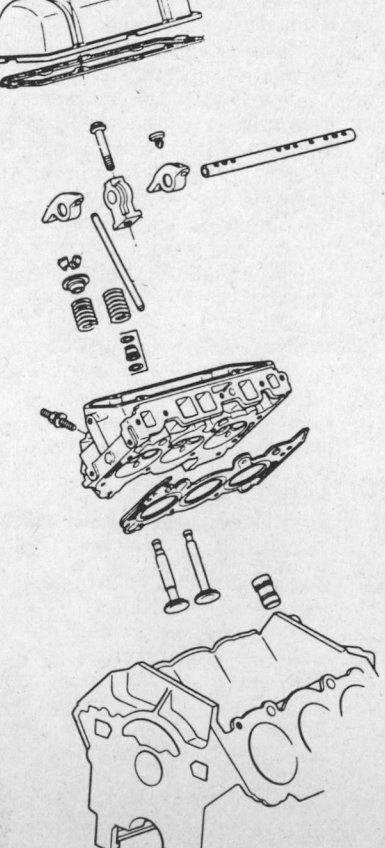

V6 Valve and cylinder head assembly
(© Pontiac Div., G.M. Corp)

valve train play is removed, then tighten a full turn further.

1975 and later Buick Design 350 V8 and 231 V6

1. Remove the rocker arm cover.
2. Remove the rocker arm shaft assembly bolts and the assembly.
3. Remove the nylon arm retainers by breaking them below their head with a chisel.
4. Remove the rocker arms.

NOTE: Each pair of rocker arms must be installed so that the external rib on each arm points away from the rocker arm shaft bolt that is located between each pair of rocker arms.

5. Install the rocker arms on the shaft and lubricate them with oil.
6. Center each arm on the 1/4 in. hole in the shaft. Install new nylon rocker arm retainers in the holes using a 1/2 in. drift.
7. Locate the push rods in the rocker arms and insert the shaft-to-cylinder head bolts. Tighten the bolts a little at a time until they are tight.
8. Install the rocker cover and use a new gasket.

260 V8

Remove the valve covers. Remove the two bolts that attach the rocker arm pivot to the cylinder head. Remove the rocker arms in pairs. Install the pairs of rocker arms for each cylinder only when the lifters are off the cam lobe and the valves are closed. Lubricate all pivot and rocker arm wear points with white grease. Torque the hardened flanged retaining bolts to 25 ft. lbs.

Valve Adjustment

OHC 4 Cylinder (1975 Only)

1. Mark the locations of No. one and four spark plug wires on the side of the distributor with chalk. (Refer to the firing order illustration.)
2. Remove the distributor cap, air cleaner, and valve cover.

3. Turn the engine until the rotor points to the no. one position. The no. one intake and exhaust, no. two intake and no. three exhaust valves are adjusted at this position. The intake valve is the front valve for each cylinder, and the exhaust valve is the rear one.

4. Insert the correct size feeler gauge between the camshaft lobe and the valve tappet. If the clearance is between 0.014 and 0.017 in. for intakes or 0.029 and 0.032 in. for exhausts, no adjustment is necessary. This is due to the fact that the adjusting mechanism only allows adjustments in increments of 0.003 in.

5. If lash is 0.003 in. or more out of adjustment, insert a ⅛ in. allen wrench into the tappet adjusting screw and turn it one full turn. Turning clockwise tightens; turning counterclockwise loosens.

6. Check the lash again and adjust further if necessary. Always turn the adjuster screw one full turn. You can feel the flat spot by pressing down on the tappet while adjusting.

7. Turn the engine so that the rotor points to no. four. Adjust no. two exhaust, no. three intake, and no. four intake and exhaust valves in this position.

8. Replace the valve cover, air cleaner, and distributor cap.

NOTE: 1976 and later 2300 cc engines use hydraulic lifters which do not require adjustment. The cylinder head and lifters on these engines are not interchangeable with older models.

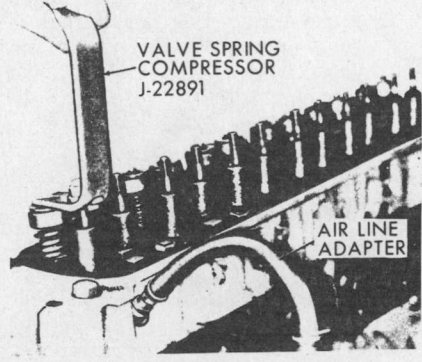

OHV Valve spring removal
(© Pontiac Div., G.M. Corp)

Cylinder Head

Inline 6 Cylinder

Removal

1. Drain cooling system, remove air cleaner. Disconnect radiator hoses.
2. Disconnect accelerator pedal rod at bellcrank, fuel and vacuum lines at carburetor. Disconnect

Chilton's TIME SAVER

The following is a method for replacing valve springs, oil seals or spring retainers without removing the cylinder head.
1. Obtain a spark plug hole airchuck adapter from an auto parts store.
2. To this adapter add an airchuck so that the hose from an air compressor can be attached. This assembly will be used later to pressurize the cylinder.
3. Remove the valve rocker cover. Remove the rocker arm from the valve to be worked on.
4. Remove the spark plug from the cylinder to be worked on.
5. Turn the crankshaft to bring the piston of this cylinder down, away from possible contact with the valve head. Sharply tap the valve retainer to loosen the valve lock.
6. Then turn the crankshaft to bring the piston in this cylinder to the Exact Top of its Compression Stroke.
7. Screw in the chuck-equipped tool.
8. Hook up an air hose to the chuck and turn on the pressure (about 200 lbs.).
9. With a strong and constant supply of air holding the valve closed, compress the valve spring and remove the lock and retainer.
10. Make the necessary replacements and reassemble.
NOTE: it is important that the operation be performed exactly as stated, in this order. The piston in the cylinder must be on exact top-center to prevent air pressure from turning the crankshaft.

exhaust pipe at manifold flange.
3. Remove manifold-to-cylinder head attaching bolts and manifolds.
4. Remove rocker arm cover assembly, temperature sender and coil wires.
5. Loosen rocker arm nuts and rotate rocker arms so the pushrods can be removed.
6. Remove pushrods and store them so they can be installed in their original locations.

7. Disconnect spark plug wires. Remove the spark plugs.
8. Remove cylinder head bolts.
9. Lift off the head.
10. Remove cylinder head gasket.

Installation

1. Position new cylinder head gasket on block, on locating dowels.
2. Place cylinder head in position.
3. Install cylinder head attaching bolts. Tighten to specifications in three stages.
4. Install pushrods in original location and position.
5. Position rocker arm with lifter on base circle of camshaft and tighten rocker arm nuts until valve train play is removed. Tighten one more turn.
6. Install rocker arm cover.
7. Install manifold-to-cylinder head bolts and torque to specifications.
8. Install pushrod cover and crankcase breather outlet pipe.
9. Connect all wires, hoses and linkage; fill cooling system and check for leaks.
10. Replace the spark plugs and connect spark plug wires.

V6 and V8

Removal

NOTE: drain the cooling system, including the block.
1. Remove intake manifold, and rocker arm cover. Position the alternator and air conditioner compressor out of the way.
2. Loosen all rocker arm retaining nuts and pivot rockers off pushrods. Remove the rocker shaft on the 1975-76 Ventura 350 and 231 V6. To remove the 1975-76 Ventura 350 and 231 V6 left head, remove the dipstick, power steering pump and air pump.
3. Remove pushrods and place in order.
4. On the 260, V6, and 1975-76 350 Ventura V8, remove the exhaust manifolds. On all others, remove the exhaust pipe-to-manifold attaching bolts. In order to remove the left head of the 455 S.D., it is necessary to remove the exhaust manifold attaching nuts and drop the manifold. Remove the inner panel of the carburetor heat stove from the two center cylinder head bolts.
NOTE: on 1970 air-conditioned Firebird models, remove compressor hold-down bolts and move compressor aside *without* disconnecting hoses.
5. Remove battery ground strap and engine ground strap on left head; engine ground strap and automatic transmission oil filler tube bracket on right head.
6. Remove cylinder head bolts and head, with exhaust manifold attached.

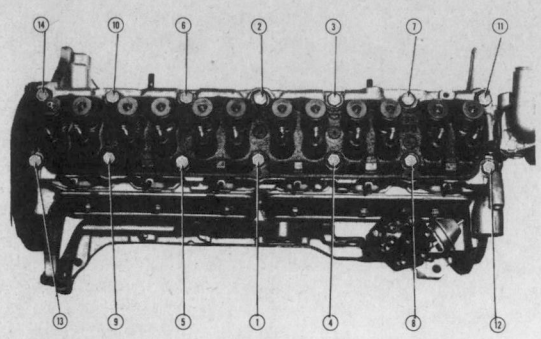

Cylinder head torque sequence—inline 6 cyl
(© Pontiac Div., G.M. Corp)

V6 cylinder head torque sequence (© Pontiac Div, G.M. Corp)

NOTE: left head must be maneuvered to clear power steering and power brake units except on Ventura II.

NOTE: on 1970, air-conditioned Firebird models, the right motor mount-to-frame bolt must be removed and the engine jacked up about 2 in. to gain access to the right rear rocker arm cover bolt and cylinder head bolt.

Installation

1. Check head surface for straightness, then place a new head gasket on block.
   CAUTION: on 1970 air-conditioned Firebird models, install right rear head bolt into head *before placing* head on block.
   NOTE: bolts are of three different lengths on 350 (except 1975 and later Ventura and V6), 400, and 455 V8s. When bolts are properly installed, they will project an equal distance from head.
2. Install all bolts and tighten evenly to specified torque. Tighten the bolts to specifications in three stages.
3. Install pushrods in original positions.

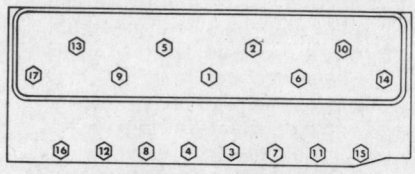

Cylinder head torque sequence—1971-72 307 V8 (© Pontiac Div., G.M. Corp)

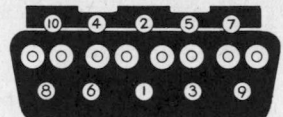

1975-76 Ventura 350 head bolt torque sequence

4. Install the rocker assembly. Adjust as explained under Rocker Arm R & R.
5. Replace rocker arm cover.
6. Replace ground straps, oil filler tube bracket, intake manifold, and right motor mount bolt (on A/C Firebird models).
7. Install exhaust pipe flange nuts. Install the exhaust manifolds, with new gaskets.
   NOTE: 350 (except 1975 and later Ventura), 400, and 455 left and right cylinder heads are interchangeable within a single year; large- and

Oldsmobile design 260, 350, 403 V8 cylinder head bolt torque sequence (© G.M. Corp)

Cylinder head torque sequence—Pontiac design 302, 350, 400, 455 V8
(© Pontiac Div., G.M. Corp)

small-valve heads should not be used on the same engine.

OHC 4 Cylinder Removal and Installation

NOTE: Cylinder head gasket R&R does not require separating the intake and exhaust manifolds from the cylinder head.

1. Remove the timing belt cover and camshaft cover. Drain the cooling system.
2. Remove the timing belt and camshaft sprocket.
3. Remove the intake and exhaust manifolds.
4. Disconnect the water hose at the thermostat housing (outlet).
5. Remove the cylinder head bolts, then the head and gasket.
   NOTE: If the head sticks, bump the starter a few times to loosen it with compression. Do not insert any tools between the head and block to pry them apart.
6. Using a new gasket (smooth side up), carefully position the cylinder head on the block.
7. Install the cylinder head bolts finger-tight. Use an anti-seize compound on the threads. Install

OHC four-cylinder head bolt torque sequence
(© Pontiac Div., G.M. Corp)

the lifting bracket under the second head bolt from the front on the spark plug side. The 6-3/8 in. bolts are installed on the manifold side and the 5-5/8 in. bolts are installed on the spark plug side.
8. Tighten the head bolts to 60 ft. lbs. (in steps), using the recommended sequence.
9. Connect the water hose to the

thermostat housing.

10. Install the intake and exhaust manifolds.
11. Install the timing bolt and sprocket.
12. Install the front cover and camshaft cover.

Timing Case

Timing Gear or Chain Cover and Oil Seal Removal and Installation

Inline 6 Cylinder

1. Drain cooling system and disconnect radiator hoses at radiator.
2. Remove fan and water pump pulley.
3. Remove radiator and fan belt.
4. Remove harmonic balancer, using a puller.
5. Remove the two oil pan-to-front cover bolts. Remove or lower the oil pan on 1970-73 models.
6. Remove timing gear cover bolts, pull the cover forward and, on 1974 and later models, cut off the oil pan seal flush with the block, then remove cover and gasket.
7. Pry out oil seal using a screwdriver.
   NOTE: seal can be replaced with cover installed.
8. Install new seal, with lip toward inside of cover. Drive it into place, using proper seal installer or an old wheel bearing outer race.
9. Inspect oil nozzle for damage and replace if necessary, then clean all gasket surfaces.
10. On 1974 and later models, cut the tabs from a new oil pan front seal and install the seal to the front cover, pressing the tips into the holes in the cover. Use sealer at the joints. Install cover and gasket (stick gasket to block with grease), making sure cover is centered properly on crankshaft end. Replace the two oil pan bolts, on 1974 and later models.
11. Tighten cover bolts, then install harmonic balancer. Replace the oil pan on 1970-73 models.

Pontiac Design 350, 400, 455 V8

1. Drain radiator and cylinder block.
2. Loosen alternator adjusting bolts.
3. Remove fan, fan pulley, and accessory drive belts.
4. Disconnect radiator hoses. Remove the water pump.
5. Remove fuel pump.
   NOTE: not necessary if only seal is being replaced.
6. Remove harmonic balancer bolt and washer.

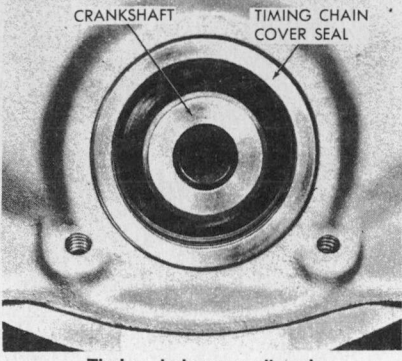

CRANKSHAFT   TIMING CHAIN COVER SEAL

Timing chain cover oil seal
(© Pontiac Div., G.M. Corp)

7. Remove harmonic balancer.
   NOTE: do not pry on rubber-mounted balancers. Seal can be removed, using a screwdriver, at this point. Install new seal with lip inward.
8. Remove front four oil pan to timing cover bolts.
9. Remove timing cover bolts and nuts, and cover to intake manifold bolt.
10. Pull cover forward and remove.
11. Remove O-ring from recess in intake manifold, then clean all gasket surfaces.
12. To replace seal, pry it out of the cover using a screwdriver. Install the new seal with lip inwards.
    NOTE: seal can be replaced with cover installed.
13. To install, reverse removal procedure, making sure all gaskets are replaced. Tighten four oil pan bolts to 12 ft. lbs., harmonic balancer bolt to 160 ft. lbs., and fan pulley bolts to 20 ft. lbs.

1971-72 Ventura 307 V8

NOTE: Removal is similar to Pontiac design 350, 400, and 455 V8 engines with the exceptions noted.
1. Remove oil pan, as outlined in the Lubrication Section.
2. Lower engine back onto motor mounts.
3. Remove harmonic balancer, using a puller.
4. Remove water pump, as outlined previously.
5. Remove timing cover bolts and cover.
6. Install by reversing removal procedure. Tighten cover bolts to 80 in. lbs.

260 V8

The timing case cover and the water pump housing are a one-piece casting.
1. Drain the cooling system and disconnect the radiator and heater hoses, remove the radiator core, the fan blades and pulley.
2. Remove the vibration damper and crankshaft pulley.

3. Drain the oil and remove the oil pan (see Engine Lubrication section).
4. Remove the front cover attaching bolts and remove the cover, timing indicator and water pump from the front of the engine.
5. Install in the reverse order of removal using a new gasket with sealing compound. Tighten self-tapping water pump attaching screws to 13 ft. lbs., 5/16 in. front cover attaching bolts to 22 ft. lbs. and the four bottom bolts (cover plate) to 35 ft. lbs. Torque the pulley hub bolt to 310 ft lbs, crankshaft pulley bolts to 10 ft lbs, and fan bolts to 20 ft lbs.

1975 and later Buick Design 350 and V6

1. Drain cooling system and remove radiator, shroud, fan, pulleys, and belts.
2. Remove crankshaft pulley, fuel pump and distributor.
3. Remove alternator and power steering pump, if necessary.
4. Loosen and slide rearward front clamp on thermostat by-pass hose. Remove harmonic balancer.
5. Remove bolts attaching timing chain cover to cylinder block and oil pan to timing chain cover bolts. Remove timing chain cover assembly and gasket. Clean cover thoroughly, being careful not to damage the gasket surface.
6. Turn the crankshaft so that the timing marks on the sprockets are adjacent to each other on a line with the shaft centers.
7. Remove crankshaft oil slinger.
8. Remove bolt, special washer, distributor drive gear, and fuel pump eccentric from camshaft.
9. Pry camshaft and crankshaft sprockets forward until camshaft sprocket is free. Then remove both sprockets and chain.
   If oil seal appears worn or has been leaking, replace as follows:
10. Use a punch to drive out the old seal and retainer. Drive from front to rear of the timing chain cover.
11. Coil new packing around opening so that ends are at top. Drive in retainer. Stake the retainer in at least three places. Size the packing by rotating a hammer handle, etc. around the packing until the balancer hub fits through the packing.
    If engine has been disturbed since chain and sprockets were removed:
12. Turn crankshaft until No. 1 piston is at top dead center.
13. Mount sprocket temporarily and turn camshaft so that timing

14. Assemble chain and sprockets and mount on shafts with their timing marks closest to each other.
15. Mount slinger on sprocket with the concave side to the front.
16. Reinstall fuel pump eccentric with oil groove forward, distributor drive gear, special washer, and bolt on camshaft. Tighten the bolt to 50 ft lbs.
17. Remove oil pump cover and pack the space around the oil pump gears full of petroleum jelly, leaving no air spaces. Reinstall oil pump cover with new gasket. This step is very important. If it is not done the oil pump will not begin to pump oil as soon as the engine is started.
18. Reinstall timing chain cover with new gasket. Replace the harmonic balancer.

Keep engine speed low for a short time after installation of a new oil seal.

OHC 4 Cylinder Timing Cover, Belt and Camshaft

Front Cover Removal and Installation

1. Raise the hood and install a bolt in the hood hold-open link.
2. Disconnect the negative battery cable.
3. Remove the fan and spacer.
4. Loosen the two lower cover retaining screws.
5. Remove the top cover retaining screw and nut and remove the cover, lifting it until the slots clear the lower screws.
6. To install, position the cover, lowering it until the slots are over the lower screws. Loosely tighten the lower screws.
7. Install the upper screw and nut, then tighten all four screws to 50 in lbs.
8. Install the spacer and fan, tightening the bolts to 20 ft. lbs.
9. Connect the battery cable and remove the bolt from the hood hold-open link.

Timing Belt and Sprocket Removal and Installation

1. Raise the hood and install a bolt in the hood hold-open link.
2. Disconnect the negative battery cable.
3. Loosen the air conditioner and alternator as necessary and remove the drive belts.
4. Remove the crankshaft pulley and four pulley-to-sprocket bolts. Remove the pulley and damper or washer as applicable.

NOTE: it is not necessary to remove the pulley if only the camshaft sprocket is being removed.

5. Drain the engine coolant and loosen the water pump bolts to relieve the tension on the timing belt.
6. Remove the timing belt lower cover.
7. Remove the timing belt.
8. Align one of the holes in the camshaft timing sprocket with the bolt behind the sprocket. Using a socket on the bolt to keep the sprocket from rotating, remove the sprocket retaining bolt and washer.
9. Remove the camshaft sprocket.
10. The crankshaft sprocket may be removed with a puller.
11. Press the crankshaft sprocket back on. Make sure that the timing mark is facing out and that the key is installed.
12. To install the camshaft sprocket, align the dowel in the camshaft with the locating hole in the end of the camshaft.
13. Install the sprocket retaining bolt, tightening to 80 ft. lbs.
14. Align the timing mark on the camshaft sprocket with the notch on the timing belt upper cover and the crankshaft sprocket timing mark with the cast rib on the oil pump cover.
15. Install the timing belt on the crankshaft sprocket, then with the back of the belt positioned in the water pump track, install the belt on the camshaft sprocket.

Make sure that both sprockets maintain their indexed positions.

16. Install the lower timing belt cover, using anti-seize compound on the threads of the bolts and tightening them to 50 in. lbs.
17. Adjust the timing belt tension as described under Water Pump R&R.
18. Fill the cooling system.
19. Install the accessory drive pulley to the crankshaft sprocket, aligning the tang on the pulley with the keyway on the crankshaft. Install the damper locating dowel in the locating hole of the sprocket.
20. Loosely install the four sprocket bolts, then install the crankshaft (center) bolt. Tighten the crankshaft bolt to 80 ft. lbs. and the four sprocket bolts to 15 ft. lbs.
21. Install the alternator and air conditioning compressor as applicable and adjust the belts.
22. Install the engine front cover, fan and fan spacer.
23. Connect the battery cable and remove the bolt from the hood hold-open link.

Camshaft Removal and Installation

Inline 6 Cylinder

1. Drain cooling system.
2. Remove radiator, fan, and water pump pulley.
3. Remove grill.
4. Remove valve cover and gasket, then loosen rocker arm nuts and pivot rockers out of the way.
5. Remove pushrods. Keep them in order.

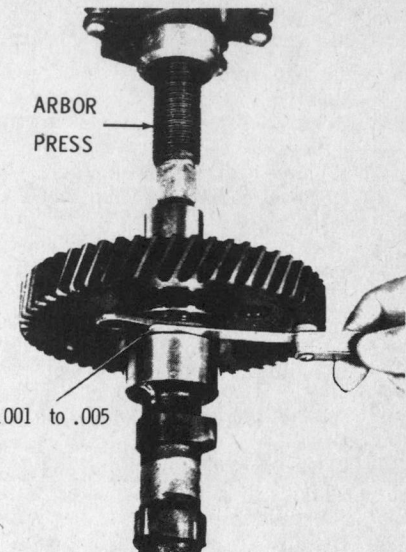

Installing Inline 6 camshaft gear and checking thrust plate end-play
(© Pontiac Div., G.M. Corp)

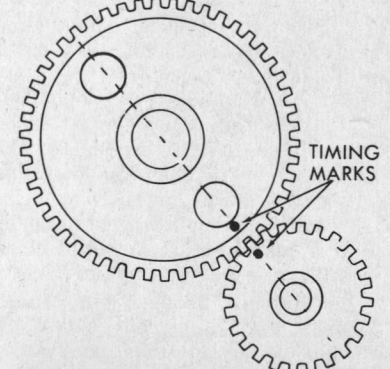

Inline 6 cyl timing mark alignment

Checking inline 6 camshaft gear runout
(© Pontiac Div., G.M. Corp)

6. Remove distributor, fuel pump, and spark plugs.
7. Remove coil, pushrod (tappet gallery) covers and gasket; reach in and remove tappets, keeping them in order.
8. Pull off the harmonic balancer, then loosen the oil pan bolts and allow the pan to drop.
9. Remove timing gear cover.
10. Remove two camshaft thrust plate bolts by rotating cam gear holes to gain clearance.
11. Remove the camshaft by pulling it straight forward.

NOTE: support the camshaft; the cam bearings could be dislodged.

12. If cam gear is to be replaced, press it from the shaft using an arbor press.

CAUTION: thrust plate must be positioned so that Woodruff key does not damage it during removal.

13. New cam gear must be pressed onto the shaft, with the shaft supported in back of the front bearing journal.

NOTE: the thrust plate end-play should be 0.001-0.005 in. If less than 0.001 in., replace spacer ring; if greater than 0.005 in., replace thrust plate.

14. Carefully install the camshaft into the engine, then turn crankshaft and camshaft so that timing marks coincide; tighten thrust plate bolts to 5-8 ft. lbs.
15. Check camshaft and crankshaft gear runout using a dial indicator. Cam gear runout should not exceed 0.004 in., crank gear should not exceed 0.003 in.

NOTE: if runout is excessive, remove gear and clean burrs from shaft.

16. Check gear backlash using a dial indicator; it should not exceed 0.006 in. and should not be less than 0.004 in.
17. To complete installation, reverse Steps 1-9.

NOTE: install distributor with No. 1 piston at TDC on compression stroke as indicated by the damper timing mark so that vacuum diaphragm faces forward and rotor points to No. 1 spark plug wire cap tower. Make sure oil pump drive shaft is properly indexed with distributor drive shaft.

Pontiac design 350, 400, 455 V8

1. Drain cooling system and remove air cleaner.
2. Disconnect all water hoses, vacuum lines and spark plug wires. Remove the radiator.
3. Disconnect accelerator linkage, temperature gauge wire, and fuel lines.
4. Remove hood latch brace.
5. Remove PCV hose, then remove rocker covers.

NOTE: on air-conditioned models, remove alternator and bracket.

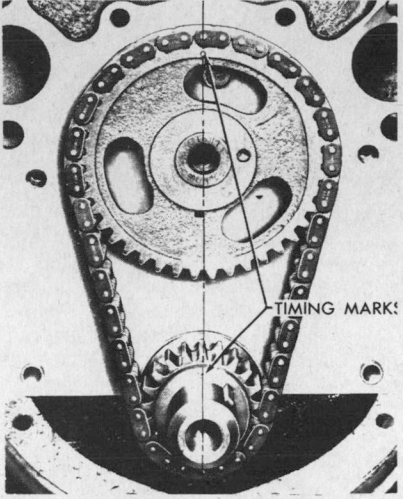

Pontiac design 302, 350, 400, 455 V8 timing gear alignment marks
(© Pontiac Div., G.M. Corp)

6. Remove distributor, then remove intake manifold.
7. Remove valley cover.
8. Loosen rocker arm nuts and pivot rockers out of the way.
9. Remove pushrods and lifters (keep them in proper order).
10. Remove harmonic balancer, fuel pump, and four oil pan to timing cover bolts.
11. Remove timing cover and gasket, then remove fuel pump eccentric and bushing.
12. Align timing marks, then remove timing chain and sprockets.
13. Remove camshaft thrust plate.
14. Remove camshaft by pulling straight forward, being careful not to damage cam bearings in the process.

NOTE: it may be necessary to jack up the engine slightly to gain clearance, especially if motor mounts are worn.

15. Install new camshaft, with lobes and journals coated with heavy (SAE 50-60) oil, into the engine, being careful not to damage cam bearings.

NOTE: most specialty cams come with a special "break-in" lubricant for the lobes and journals; if such lubricant is available, use it instead of heavy oil.

16. Install camshaft thrust plate and tighten bolts to 20 ft. lbs.
17. To install, reverse Steps 1-12, tightening camshaft sprocket bolt to 40 ft lbs, timing cover bolts and nuts to 30 ft. lbs., oil pan bolts to 12 ft. lbs., and harmonic balancer bolt to 160 ft. lbs.

1971-72 Ventura 307 V8

1. Remove intake manifold, valve lifters and timing chain cover (requires oil pan removal).
2. Remove the two center bolts and the one lower bolt that secure the hood latch support. This will

give adequate clearance for the cam. Remove radiator.
2. Remove fuel pump and pump pushrod.
4. Remove camshaft sprocket bolts, sprocket and timing chain. A light blow to the lower edge of a tight sprocket should free it (use a plastic mallet).
5. Install two 5/16—18 x 4 in. bolts in cam bolt holes and pull cam from block.
6. To install, reverse removal procedure, aligning timing marks as illustrated.

NOTE: cam lobes must be lubricated with Molykote® or equivalent before installation. All cam journals are the same diameter, so make sure cam bearings are not dislodged during installation.

260 V8

1. Disconnect the battery ground cable.
2. Drain the coolant. Remove the radiator.
3. Disconnect the fuel pump line.
4. Remove the air cleaner; disconnect the throttle cable.
5. Remove the alternator belt. Move the alternator and power steering pump aside. Move the air conditioning compressor to one side, but don't disconnect the refrigerant lines.
6. At the water pump, disconnect the thermostat bypass hose and heater hose.
7. Detach all engine electrical and vacuum connections.
8. Remove the distributor, exhaust crossover pipe, starter, and detach the exhaust pipe from the manifold.
9. Remove the crankshaft pulley and balancer bolt. Use a puller to remove the balancer.
10. Support the engine with a hoist. Remove the engine mount to bracket bolts, raise the engine as far as possible, and unbolt the

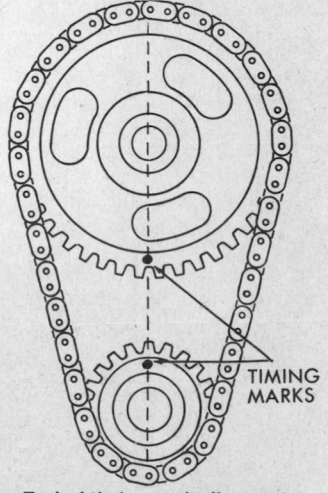

Typical timing mark alignment—
—V8 and V6 except Pontiac design

mounts from the engine.

11. Remove the flywheel inspection cover and the oil pan.

12. Place wood blocks between the exhaust manifolds and the front crossmember to support the engine. Remove the hoist.

12. Remove the timing chain cover.

13. Remove the rocker covers. Remove the intake manifold.

14. Remove the oil filler pipe and the water temperature sender.

15. Remove the rocker arms, pushrods, and lifters. Keep all these parts in order so that they can be replaced in their original locations.

16. Remove the bolt, fuel pump eccentric, camshaft gear, oil slinger, and timing chain.

17. Carefully slide the camshaft out of the front of the engine.

18. On installation, coat the camshaft with special lubricant.

Make sure to install the timing indicator before the power steering pump bracket. Install the flywheel inspection cover after the starter.

1975 and later Buick design 350 V8 and 231 V6

1. Remove the intake manifold and rotate the crankshaft to TDC for cylinder number 1.

2. Remove the rocker covers. Remove the rocker shafts, pushrods, and lifters. Keep these components in order so they can be replaced in their original locations.

3. Remove the timing chain cover and the chain and sprockets.

4. Slide the camshaft out carefully.

5. Reverse the procedure for installation.

OHC 4 Cylinder

NOTE: A special valve tappet depressing tool is necessary for camshaft removal. The procedure given here uses the factory tool; it may vary slightly with those produced by tool companies.

1. Remove the hood.

2. Remove the camshaft timing sprocket.

3. Remove the three screws securing the camshaft seal and retainer assembly and timing cover to the cylinder head.

4. Inspect the seal, prying it out and replacing it if necessary.

5. Remove the camshaft cover.

6. Disconnect the fuel line at the carburetor.

7. Remove:
   a. Idle solenoid from its bracket.
   b. The choke coil, cover and rod assembly.
   c. Ignition distributor.

8. Raise the vehicle on a hoist, dis-

connect the front engine mounts at the body attachment, raise the front of the engine and install wood blocks, about 1-½ in. thick, between the engine mounts and the body.

9. Install camshaft removal tool on the cylinder head to hold down the lifters so that the camshaft may be removed.
   a. Position the tool so that the attaching holes are aligned with the lower cam cover bolt holes and the tappet levers of the tool are aligned to depress both valves of each cylinder.
   b. Back off the bolts in the bottom of the tool so that they are not contacting the bosses beneath the tool.
   c. Install the tool attaching bolts, tightening them securely.
   d. Tighten the bolts in the bottom of the tool until they just touch the bosses of the cylinder head. Before depressing the tappets, rotate the crankshaft pulley timing mark 90° clockwise from the timing mark on the tab. This assures that the pistons are not at TDC and will prevent valve-to-piston contact.
   e. Grease the ball end of the lever depressing bolts and tighten the bolts to depress the tappets.

   NOTE: torque the lever bolts to 10 ft. lbs. If more tightening is required, check to see that the tool is properly installed, then proceed cautiously to prevent damaging the depressing lever.

10. Slide the camshaft forward until it clear the head.

   NOTE: the camshaft bearings may be removed. It is not necessary to remove the camshaft end plug. Gently tap out the bearings, starting at the forward end. Tap out the rear bearing slowly into the distributor housing, being careful not to unseat the end plug. Crush the rear bearing to remove it from the distributor housing. Install, starting with the rear bearing. The oil holes in the three rear bearings must align with the oil holes in the case. On the first two bearings the oil holes are at 11 o'clock (as seen from the front of the engine) and the oil groove in the number one bearing toward the front of the engine.

11. Install the camshaft with the journals seated in the bores.

12. With the car up on a hoist, raise the front of the engine and remove the wood blocks from the engine mounts.

13. Install the front engine mounts, then lower the vehicle.

14. Using a new gasket, install the timing belt upper cover and retainer plate and seal assembly. Tighten the retaining bolts to 15 ft. lbs.

15. Using a dial indicator, measure the camshaft end-play. If it is not 0.004-0.012 in., select a camshaft retainer (according to cam locator thickness) which will provide more or less end-play as required.

16. Remove the tappet depressing tool by first releasing the tappet depressing lever bolts, and then removing the tool attaching bolts.

17. Install:
    a. Camshaft timing sprocket.
    b. The timing belt.
    c. Front engine cover.
    d. Distributor.
    e. Vehicle hood.

18. Adjust the valve tappets.

19. Install the camshaft cover.

20. Install and adjust the carburetor choke coil, cover and rod assembly.

21. Connect the carburetor fuel line.

22. Install the idle solenoid to the bracket.

23. Check and adjust the ignition timing and idle speed.

Piston and Connecting Rod

The letter F, or the notches in the edge of the piston, goes to the front of the engine. The oil spurt holes on the connecting rod must face the camshaft. Some 1973, and all 1974 and later Pontiac design 350, 400, and 455, V8 engines don't have these holes. These connecting rods have three dimples on one side of the rod and a single dimple on the connecting rod

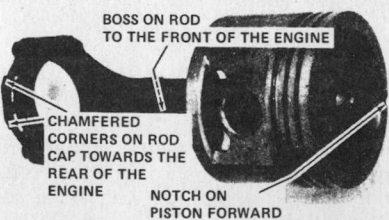

1975-76 Ventura 350 V8 piston rod assembly, right bank (© Pontiac Div., G.M. Corp)

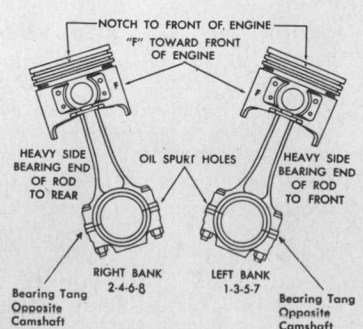

307 V8 piston and rod assembly

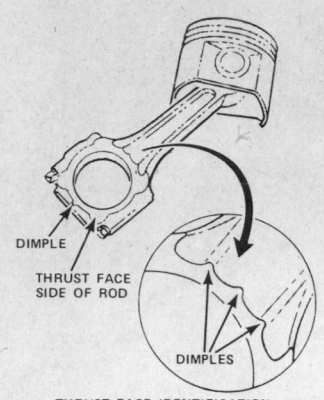

THRUST FACE IDENTIFICATION

The dimples identify the connecting rod thrust faces on some V8 engines
(© Pontiac Div., G.M. Corp)

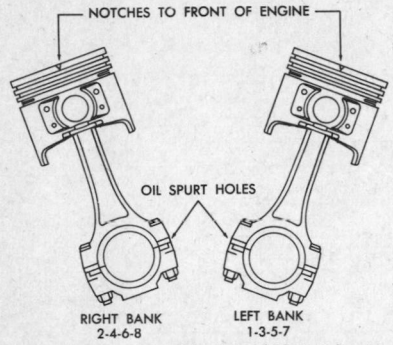

NOTCHES TO FRONT OF ENGINE

OIL SPURT HOLES

RIGHT BANK 2-4-6-8

LEFT BANK 1-3-5-7

Oldsmobile design 260, 350, 403 and Pontiac design 302, 350, 455 V8 piston and rod assembly (© Pontiac Div., G.M. Corp)

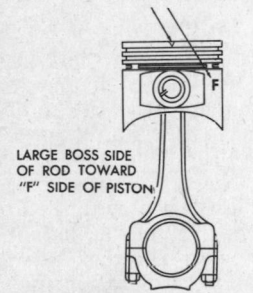

NOTCH & "F" TOWARD FRONT OF ENGINE

LARGE BOSS SIDE OF ROD TOWARD "F" SIDE OF PISTON

Piston and rod assembly—inline 6 cyl
(© Pontiac Div., G.M. Corp)

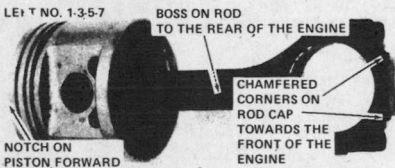

LEFT NO. 1-3-5-7

BOSS ON ROD TO THE REAR OF THE ENGINE

CHAMFERED CORNERS ON ROD CAP TOWARDS THE FRONT OF THE ENGINE

NOTCH ON PISTON FORWARD

1975-76 Ventura 350 V8 piston and rod assembly, left bank
(© Pontiac Div., G.M. Corp)

cap. The dimples must face forward on the left bank, and to the rear on the right.

On the 231 cu in. V6 and Buick design 350 V8 used in the Ventura, the boss on the connecting rod faces the front of the engine and the chamfered corners of the rod cap face toward the rear of the engine on the right bank of cylinders. On the left

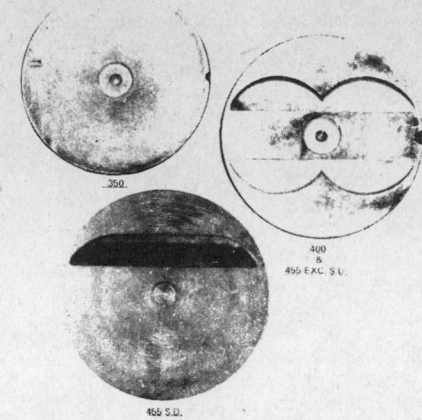

350

400 & 455 EXC. S.D.

455 S.D.

Pontiac design 350, 400, 455 piston identification
(© Pontiac Div., G.M. Corp)

bank, the boss on the rod faces the rear of the engine and the chamfered corners of the cap face the front of the engine.

Lubrication

Oil Pan Removal and Installation

1970 V8 and 1971 Tempest V8 with Manual Transmission
1. Remove engine from car.
2. Remove oil pan bolts.
3. Remove oil pan.

1970½ Firebird and All 1971-77 V8 Models
1. On the 260 V8, remove the distributor cap and align the rotor with the no. 1 plug wire in the cap.
2. Disconnect battery cables.
3. Remove the fan and fan shroud. Tilt the power steering pump out of the way. Tilt the 1975-76 Ventura 350 air conditioning compressor in as far as possible. Remove the 260 V8 dipstick.
4. Move all water hoses and wiring out of the way.
5. Raise car and drain engine oil. Disconnect idler arm from frame and pitman arm from shaft on Firebird.
6. Disconnect exhaust pipe/s at manifold.
7. Remove starter and bracket, then remove flywheel inspection cover.
8. Support engine with a wood-padded jack.
9. Remove both frame-to-motor mount bolts.
10. Jack up engine for clearance, then remove oil pan bolts and pan.
11. To install, reverse the removal procedure. Silicone sealer is recommended at all gasket joints. Tighten pan bolts, and then

tighten the rear bolts, through the reinforcement straps.

Inline 6 Cylinder
1. Remove upper radiator shield assembly.
2. Disconnect battery ground cable.
3. Jack up front of car and drain engine oil.
4. Disconnect exhaust pipe at manifold flange.
5. Remove starter motor and flywheel cover.
6. Raise engine slightly, using a chain hoist, then remove both front motor mount to frame bolts and right motor mount.
7. Remove oil pan bolts, then raise engine and remove oil pan.
8. To install, reverse removal procedure.

NOTE: bolts into timing gear cover should be installed last. They are installed at an angle and holes line up after rest of oil pan bolts are tightened finger-tight.

V6
1. Drain the oil.
2. Remove the flywheel cover and crossover pipe.
3. Remove the oil pan.
4. Installation is the reverse of removal.

OHC 4 Cylinder
1. Raise the vehicle and drain the engine oil. Support the front of the engine, being careful not to distort the pan.
2. Remove the frame crossmember and both front crossmember braces.
3. Disconnect the steering idler arm at the frame side rail. On vehicles with air conditioning, disconnect the idler arm at the relay rod.
4. Mark the position of the steering linkage pitman arm to the steering gear pitman shaft and remove the pitman arm.

NOTE: do not rotate the steering gear pitman shaft while the linkage is disconnected, because the steering wheel alignment will be changed.

5. Remove the flywheel cover or converter underpan.
6. Remove the oil pan bolts, tap the oil pan to break the seal, then remove the pan.
7. Remove the pick-up screen-to-support retaining bolt and the pick-up screen-to-baffle support bolts, then remove the support from the baffle.
8. Remove the bolt which secures the oil drain back tube to the baffle, then rotate the baffle 90° toward the left side of the car and remove the baffle from the pick-up screen.
9. The oil pump screen and pick up tube may be removed as follows:

a. Remove the two self-locking mounting bolts (in block).

b. Lightly tap on the U section of the pick-up tube to remove the tube from the casting.

c. If damaged, the tube and screen assembly are replaced as a unit. It is recommended that once the assembly has been removed, it should not be reused.

d. Apply sealing compound to the pick-up tube sealing surface.

e. Install the tube into its bore, using an open end wrench on the tube boss, tapping the wrench with a mallet. Make sure that the retaining brackets are aligned with the bolt holes.

f. Using anti-seize compound on the threads, install the retaining bolts. Tighten the bolts to 25 ft. lbs.

10. Install the oil pan and baffle in the reverse order of removal. Use sealing compound on the oil pump gasket surface. Tighten the oil pan bolts to 15 ft. lbs. Tighten frame crossmember and brace bolts to 35 ft. lbs.

Oil Pump Removal and Installation

V8 and Inline 6 Cylinder Engines

1. Remove engine oil pan. (See previous procedure.)
2. Remove pump attaching screws and carefully lower the pump.
3. Reinstall in reverse order.

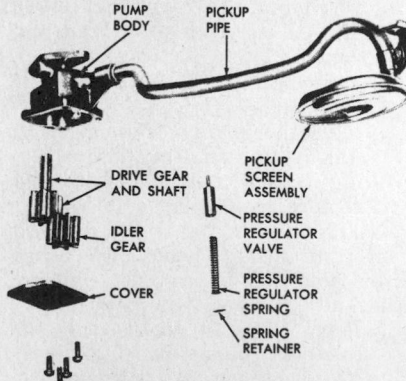

Inline 6 oil pump
(© Pontiac Div., G.M. Corp)

1975 and later Buick Design 350 V8 and 231 V6

1. Remove the oil filter.
2. Remove the screws which attach the oil pump cover assembly to the timing chain cover. Remove the cover assembly and slide out the oil pump gears.
3. To install, reverse the removal procedure, being sure to check the clearance between the gear faces and the pump gasket sur-

face. Clearance should be between 0.002 and 0.006 in.

NOTE: Pack the pump gears with petroleum jelly only. Unless the pump is packed with petroleum jelly, it may not prime itself when the engine is started.

OHC 4 Cylinder

1. Remove:
   a. Front engine cover.
   b. Accessory drive pulley.
   c. Timing belt.
   d. Timing belt lower cover.
   e. Crankshaft sprocket.
2. Raise the vehicle on a hoist and drain the engine oil.
3. Remove the oil pan and baffle.
4. Remove the oil pump bolts and the pump.
5. Inspect the oil pump for wear. The pump gears and body are not serviced separately. Replacement of the entire oil pump is required. Check the pressure regulator for free operation.
6. When installing, clean all gasket surfaces. Be sure that the pump drive key is installed properly. Use anti-seize compound on the threads of the pump mounting bolts, tightening them to 15 ft. lbs. The stud is installed in the upper right (facing pump) and tightened to 30 ft. lbs. Install the oil pan before tightening the timing cover bolts.

Oil Pump (Front Cover) Seal Removal and Installation

1. Remove the following:
   a. Engine front cover.
   b. Accessory drive pulley.
   c. Timing belt.
   d. Timing belt lower cover.
   e. Crankshaft timing sprocket.
2. Pry out the old seal, being careful not to damage the housing seal surfaces.
3. Coat the lips of the new seal with oil and apply sealing compound to the outside diameter of the seal.
4. Install the seal with the closed end outward.
5. Install all components removed in Step 1 above.

Rear Main Bearing Oil Seal

Inline 6 Cylinder Engine

Always replace both upper and lower seal halves. It is not necessary to remove the crankshaft to install the seal.

1. Remove the engine oil pan.
2. Remove the rear main bearing cap.
3. Remove the oil seal from the groove in the cap by prying from the bottom with a small screwdriver.
4. Insert a new seal, well lubricated with engine oil, into the bearing cap groove.

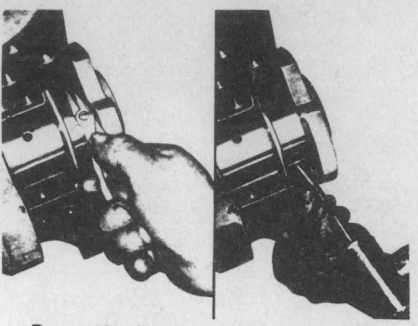

Rear main oil seal removal—upper half
(© Pontiac Div., G.M. Corp)

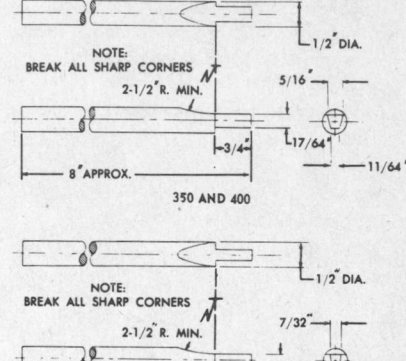

Pontiac design V8 rear main bearing upper seal tool. bottom tool is for the 455
(© Pontiac Div., G.M. Corp)

5. Remove the upper half of the seal. Use a small hammer and brass pin and tap one end of the oil seal until it protrudes far enough to be removed with pliers.
6. Install a new seal with the lip toward the front of the engine.
7. Install the bearing cap and torque it to specifications.

V6 and V8 Except 307

1. Remove the oil pan and baffle.
2. Remove the rear main bearing cap.
3. Make a seal tool as illustrated.
4. Insert the tool against one end of the oil seal in the block and drive the seal gently into the groove until it bottoms. Repeat on the other end of the seal.
5. Form a new seal in the cap. Cut four 3/8 in. long pieces from this seal.
6. Work two of the pieces into each of the gaps which have been made at the end of the seal in the block. Do not cut off any material to make them fit.
7. Form a new seal in the bearing cap.
8. Apply a 1/16 in. bead of silicone sealer from the center of the seal across to the external gasket

groove.

9. Reassemble the cap and torque to specifications.

307 V8 Engine

1. Remove the oil pan, baffle, oil pump, and rear main bearing cap.
2. Remove the upper half of the seal with a hammer and brass punch.
3. Install a new upper seal.
4. Remove the lower seal half from the bearing cap.
5. Install a new lower seal in the bearing cap.
6. Install the bearing cap and torque it to specifications.

OHC 4 Cylinder

NOTE: This repair can be made without removing the engine, but the transmission must be removed so that the crankshaft can be lowered.

1. Remove the oil pan and baffle.
2. Remove the rear main bearing cap and discard the lower seal.
3. Loosen the remaining bearing caps to allow the crankshaft to be lowered.
4. Push the upper seal on one end enough so that the other end can be grasped with pliers. It may help to turn the crankshaft. Pull out the upper seal.
5. Cut and form a new braided fabric upper seal in the bearing cap. Taper the end of the seal and insert a piece of soft wire through the seal about $1/4$ in. from the end. Wrap the wire around the seal to form a secure attachment.
6. Thread the wire through the upper seal groove, then start the seal and pull it into position.
7. Tighten all the bearing caps except the rear cap to 65 ft. lbs.
8. Cut the seal flush to 1/64 in. below the bearing edge, making a clean cut and leaving no raveled edges.
9. Install and cut a seal flush in the rear main bearing cap.
10. Install the rear main bearing cap and measure the clearance with Plastigage, tightening the cap bolts to 65 ft. lbs. If the bearing clearance is within specifications, the seal is properly seated.
11. Install the bearing cap, tightening to 65 ft. lbs.
12. Install rear main bearing cap side sealant. This is available in a kit, complete with plunger applicator. Force the compound firmly into place to ensure that there are no air bubbles.
13. Install the oil pan and baffle.

CLUTCH

Clutch Replacement

All except Astre and Sunbird

1. Raise car and support on jackstands. Disconnect the battery.
2. Support rear of engine.
3. Remove driveshaft.
4. Remove rear crossmember bolts from frame and transmission mounts, and remove crossmember.
5. Disconnect transmission shift linkage, speedometer cable and clutch return spring. Clutch fork pushrod will now hang free.
6. Remove clutch housing cover plate screws and let plate hang from starter gear housing.
7. Lower engine enough to gain access to clutch housing bolts at engine block, then remove all but uppermost bolt.
8. Hold transmission and clutch housing assembly against block over dowel pins while removing last bolt. Remove transmission and clutch housing as an assembly.
9. Matchmark pressure plate and flywheel with paint to make sure correct balance is maintained.
10. Loosen the cover plate attaching screws, a little at a time, until clutch diaphragm spring tension is released. Remove bolts and clutch assembly.
11. The pilot bearing is an oil-impregnated type bearing press-into the crankshaft. Inspect and renew, if necessary.
12. Install clutch disc with long hub forward (toward flywheel).
13. Install pressure plate and cover assembly, then align clutch disc by inserting pilot tool, or old transmission mainshaft, into splines. Align mark on clutch cover with mark on flywheel, then align nearest bolt holes.
14. Install the bolts in the cover and tighten them alternately. Tighten them to 25 ft. lb. (35 for Ventura through 1973).
15. Remove clutch pilot tool and check to see that it can be reinserted and moved freely.
16. Instal clutch fork and dust boot into clutch housing. Lubricate throwout bearing with high melting poit greast.
17. Complete the reassembly of clutch housing and transmission by reversing removal method. Tighten housing bolts to 40 ft. lbs. (30 for Ventura through 1973). Begining 1974, tighten all models to 35 ft lbs.
18. Adjust shifter and clutch release linkage.

Astre and Sunbird

1. Raise vehicle on hoist.
2. Remove transmission.
3. Remove clutch fork cover then disconnect clutch return spring and control cable from clutch fork.
4. Remove main drive gear oil seal from clutch release bearing sleeve.
5. Remove flywheel housing lower cover.
6. Remove flywheel housing from engine.
7. To remove the release bearing from clutch fork and sleeve, slide lever off ball stud against spring action. If necessary to replace ball stud, remove cap, locknut and stud from housing.
8. If assembly marks on clutch assembly and flywheel are not distinguishable, remark with paint or center-punch.
9. Loosen clutch cover to flywheel attaching bolts one turn at a time until spring pressure is released, to avoid bending clutch cover flange.
10. Support the pressure plate and cover assembly then remove the bolts and clutch assembly.

Caution Do not disassemble the clutch cover, spring and pressure plate for repair. If defective replace complete assembly.

11. Index alignment marks on clutch assembly and flywheel. Place driven plate on pressure plate with long end of splined end facing forward, damper springs inside pressure plate, and insert a dummy clutch gear shaft through the cover and driven plate.
12. Position the complete assembly against the flywheel and insert the dummy shaft into the pilot bearing in the crankshaft.
13. Index the alignment marks and install clutch cover to flywheel bolts finger-tight.

Caution Tighten all bolts evenly and gradually until tight to avoid possible clutch distortion. Torque bolts 18 ft. lbs. and remove dummy shaft.

14. Lubricate the clutch fork ball socket and the fingers at the release bearing with high melting poit grease.
15. Lubricate the recess on the inside of the throwout bearing collar and the fork groove with high melting point grease. Install fork in housing but not on stud.
16. Install bearing on sleeve, then position clutch fork over bearing in housing and slide fork onto ball stud.
17. Install flywheel housing and lower cover. Tighten bolts to 25

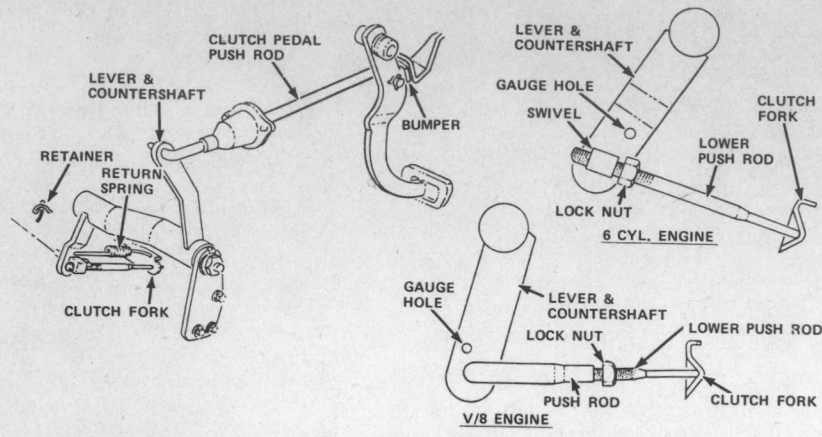

Typical clutch linkage and adjustment points, models through 1971 don't have the gauge hole
(© Pontiac Div., G.M. Corp)

ft. lbs.
18. Install transmission.
19. Adjust clutch.
20. Lower and remove vehicle from hoist.

Clutch Adjustment

Through 1971

1. Remove the return spring.
2. With the pedal against the stop, loosen the locknut on the clutch fork pushrod.
3. Turn the rod until the release bearing contacts the pressure plate fingers lightly.
4. Rotate the pushrod 3½ turns in.
5. Tighten the locknut.
6. Replace the spring.
7. There should be 1 in. free play at the pedal.

1972 and later Except Astre and Sunbird

1. Disconnect the clutch fork return spring.
2. Loosen the pushrod locknut.
3. Detach the swivel or pushrod from the countershaft lever.
4. Install the swivel or pushrod in the gauge hole on the countershaft lever.
5. Push on the countershaft lever so that the clutch pedal is up against the stop.
6. Hold the clutch fork to the rear so that the release bearing lightly contacts the release levers.
7. Adjust the pushrod length to remove all lash from the linkage.
8. Reinstall the swivel or pushrod in the original hole on the countershaft lever. Tighten the locknut.
9. Replace the spring. Pedal free travel should now be ¾-1¼ in.

Astre and Sunbird

Adjustment for normal clutch wear is accomplished by turning the clutch fork ball stud counterclockwise to give .90 ± .25 in. free-play at clutch pedal.

1. Remove ball stud cap and loosen locknut on ball stud end located to the right of the transmission on the clutch housing.
2. Adjust ball stud to obtain .90 ± .25 in. free travel.
3. Tighten locknut being careful not to change adjustment and install ball stud cap.
4. Check operation of clutch.

MANUAL TRANSMISSION

Three-Speed

Two different three-speed manual transmissions have been used in these cars. All light and normal-duty models, and the Astre and Sunbird, use a Saginaw transmission, which can be identified by having only one bolt boss casting "ear" at the center top of the side cover. For 1970-74, the heavy-duty three-speed is a Muncie unit. This is similar in appearance to the Saginaw, but has two bolt boss casting "ears" at the top of the side cover.

NOTE: Some 1975 Saginaw 3 and 4 speed manual transmissions built before Febuary 1975, may slip out of second or third gear due to a synchronizer sleeve which was machined incorrectly. If this condition exists, first make sure the linkage is adjusted correctly, then replace the synchronizer assembly.

Three-Speed Transmission Removal and Installation

All except Astre and Sunbird

1. Disconnect the battery and release the parking brake before raising the car.
2. Disconnect the speedometer cable.
3. Disconnect the transmission shifter levers from the transmission shifter shafts. On six-cylinder engines, disconnect the electrical lead from the T.C.S. switch. On floor-shift models, remove the two shifter assembly-to-shifter support bolts and remove the shifter from the transmission. If it is not necessary to remove the shifter from the car, it may be left hanging from its floor seal. Mark the differential flange and the driveshaft yoke to assure proper reassembly. Remove the driveshaft.
4. Support the rear of the engine and remove the transmission mount.
5. Remove the four crossmember bolts and slide the member rearward.
6. Remove the four transmission-to-bell housing bolts. It is a good idea to remove the upper bolts first and replace them with headless guide pins. This prevents any possible damage caused by the transmission hanging by its input shaft.
7. Slide the transmission rearward until it clears the clutch assembly and bell housing, then remove the transmission.
8. Reverse the removal procedure to install the transmission. Put the transmission in gear and turn the output shaft as necessary to start the splines into the clutch plate.

Three-Speed Linkage Adjustment—Column Shift

Except Ventura

1. Place gearshift lever in Reverse and lock ignition.
2. On the Tempest, loosen the swivel clamp bolt at the rear transmission shift lever (First and Reverse) and the bolt at the equalizer shaft and lever assembly.
3. On the Firebird, loosen the swivel clamp nut at the rear transmission shift lever (First and Reverse) then loosen the nut (D) at the idler lever.
4. Position the front transmission shift lever (Second and Third) in Neutral and the rear transmission shift lever (First and Reverse) in Reverse.
5. Tighten the First and Reverse swivel clamp bolt or nut, then unlock the steering column and shift into Neutral. On the Firebird, tighten both swivel clamp nuts, unlock the steering column, and check the complete shift pattern.
6. Unlock the column and align the lower gearshift levers (on column) in Neutral position, then

insert a 0.185 in. diameter gauge pin through the hole in the lower control levers.

7. Tighten the swivel clamp bolt or nut, then remove the gauge pin and check the shift pattern.

Ventura

1. Set the shift lever in Reverse and lock the column. Loosen the swivel clamp nuts at both shifter levers.
2. Pull down slightly on 1st-Rev rod to remove slack, then tighten swivel clamp nut at 1st-Rev lever.
3. Unlock steering column and shift into Neutral. Align column levers and insert a .185-.186 in. gauge pin through alignment holes.
4. Position 2nd-3rd transmission lever in Neutral, then tighten swivel clamp nut.
5. Remove gauge pin and check shift pattern and ignition lock. With lever in Reverse, key must move to LOCK freely. This should not be possible in any other gear.

Three-Speed Linkage Adjustment—Floor Shift

1. Place gearshift lever in Neutral.
2. Loosen swivel clamp on gearshift control rod.
3. Loosen trunnion locknuts on 1st-Reverse and 2nd-3rd transmission control rods.
4. Insert a 1/4 in. drill rod into shifter assembly.
5. If gearshift lever is not properly aligned with floor opening:
   a. *Console*—loosen two shifter to support bolts and align shifter. Tighten bolts.
   b. *Without console*—loosen two shifter to support bolts and center shifter in boot; tighten bolts.
6. Position both transmission shift levers in Neutral and tighten locknuts.
7. Remove gauge pin and check shift pattern.
8. Place gearshift lever in Reverse, then place steering column lower lever in Lock position and lock ignition.
9. Push up on gearshift control rod to take up lash in column lock mechanism, then tighten adjusting swivel clamp.

Four-Speed

The Saginaw is used as the standard four-speed on the Astre and all other models. The four-speed Muncie is used in heavy duty applications through 1974. Both transmissions are fully synchronized in all forward gears. They can easily be identified by their shift linkage. On the Muncie, two shift rods go to levers on the side cover and one rod (reverse) goes to a lever on the case extension housing. On the Saginaw, all three shift rods go to levers on the side cover. Starting 1975, the heavy duty transmission, used only in the Firebird, is the Warner Gear T-10, which can be identified by a 9 bolt curved bottom side cover. It also has a reverse shift lever on the extension housing.

The GM 70 mm. 4-speed is offerred as an option on models using the 2300 cc OHC 4 cylinder. The linkage is internal, with the shift lever attached to the extension housing; because of this, no linkage adjustments are necessary.

Four-Speed Transmission Removal and Installation

All except Astre and Sunbird

The procedures for these four-speed transmissions are the same as for three-speed units.

Astre and Sunbird—Three and Four-Speed Saginaw Transmission

1. Raise the car and drain the transmission.
2. Remove the driveshaft.
3. Disconnect the speedometer cable, TCS switch, and the back-up light switch.
4. Detach the control rods and levers from the transmission, tie them together, and position them out of the way.
5. Remove the crossmember-to-transmission mounting bolts.
6. Support the engine and remove the crossmember-to-frame bolts. Remove the crossmember.
7. Remove the top transmission-to-clutch housing bolts and install guide pins in the holes.
8. Remove the lower bolts and pull the transmission back and out of the car.
9. On installation, guide the input shaft through the throwout bearing and into the pilot bearing.
10. Install the transmission retaining bolts and lockwashers. Tighten the bolts to 40 ft lbs.
11. Position the crossmember on the frame and install the retaining bolts hand-tight.
12. Install the crossmember-to-transmission bolts and then tighten all bolts to 28 ft lbs.
13. Remove the engine support.
14. Install the transmission control rods to the shifter. Adjust the linkage.
15. Connect the speedometer cable, TCS switch, and back-up light switch.
16. Install the driveshaft.
17. Fill the transmission to the level of the filler plug.

18. Lower the car and check transmission operation.

Astre and Sunbird—GM 70 mm. 4-Speed Transmission

1. Remove the shift lever by pulling down on the lever boot and loosening the locknut; then unscrew the upper part of the lever with the gearshift knob attached.
2. Raise the car on a hoist and drain the lubricant from the transmission.
3. Remove the driveshaft.
4. Disconnect the speedometer cable and TCS-back-up light switch.
5. Disconnect the return spring and clutch cable at the clutch release fork.
6. Remove the crossmember-to-transmission mount bolts.
7. Remove the exhaust manifold nuts and converter-to-tailpipe bolts and nuts. Remove the converter-to-transmission bracket bolts and remove the converter.
8. Remove the crossmember-to-frame bolts and the transmission damper if any.
9. Remove the crossmember.
10. Remove the clutch housing-to-engine retaining bolts, slide the transmission and clutch housing to the rear, and remove the transmission.

To install

11. Place the transmission in gear, position the transmission and clutch housing, and slide forward. Turn the output shaft to align the input shaft splines with the clutch hub.
12. Install the clutch housing retaining bolts and lockwashers. Torque the bolts to 25 ft lbs.
13. Install the converter to transmission bracket and the transmission damper.
14. Position the crossmember to the frame and loosely install the retaining bolts. Install the crossmember-to-transmission mounting bolts. Torque the center nuts to 33 ft lbs; the end nuts to 21 ft lbs. Torque the crossmember-to-frame bolts to 40 ft lbs.
15. Install the exhaust pipe to the manifold and the converter bracket on the transmission. Torque the converter bracket rear support nuts to 150 in. lbs.

Four-Speed Linkage Adjustment

All except Astre and Sunbird

1. Place gearshift lever in Neutral and ignition switch in "off".
2. Loosen adjusting swivel clamp on gearshift control rod.
3. Loosen locknuts for all others.
4. Insert a 1/4 in. drill rod into

gauge pin hole in shifter.

5. If Muncie or Warner gearshift lever is not properly aligned with floor opening:
   a. *Console*—loosen two shifter to support bolts and align shifter. Tighten bolts.
   b. *Without console*—loosen two shifter to support bolts and center shifter in boot; tighten bolts.
6. Place transmission shift levers in Neutral and tighten locknuts.
7. Remove gauge pin and check shift pattern.
8. Place gearshift lever in Reverse, set steering column lower lever in Lock position and lock ignition.
9. Push up on gearshift control rod to take up lash in steering column lock mechanism, then tighten adjusting swivel clamp nut.

Astre and Sunbird Three and Four-Speed Saginaw Linkage Adjustment

1. Turn the ignition switch to "Off" and place the shift lever in neutral.
2. Raise the car.
3. Loosen the lock nuts on the control rods. Position the transmission side cover levers in their neutral detents.
4. With the floor shift lever in neutral, align the shifter levers and insert a gauge pin into the levers and bracket.
5. Tighten the First/Reverse (First/Second on four-speed) control rod lock nut against its swivel.
6. Tighten the Second/Third (Third/Fourth on four-speed) control rod lock nut against its swivel.
7. On four-speeds, tighten the Reverse control rod lock nut against its swivel.
8. Remove the gauge pin and check shifter operation.

5-Speed

Starting 1976, a Borg Warner five speed is an option in Astre, Sunbird, LeMans and Ventura. Fifth gear in the transmission is an overdrive. The shift linkage is contained within the transmission and requires no adjustment.

Five Speed Transmission Removal and Installation

1. Remove the boot retainer and slide the boot upward on the shift lever.
2. Remove the foam insulator over the control assembly bolts.
3. Remove the four control lever bolts and remove the control lever.
4. Raise the car and remove the driveshaft.

5. Remove the damper assembly, the torque converter bracket, and the torque arm bracket.
6. Disconnect the speedometer cable and the back-up light switch.
7. Remove the nut from the front of the torque arm, the catalytic converter bracket bolts, and the transmission damper, if any. Remove the bolts holding the transmission rubber mount to the support then place a transmission jack under the transmission and remove the transmission support.
8. Remove the transmission-to-clutch housing bolts and slide the exhaust bracket forward. After this the transmission can be moved rearward and removed from the car.
9. Installation is the reverse of removal, but take note of the following: make sure the drive gear splines are clean and dry; use guidebolts in the bellhousing holes to aid in aligning the transmission to the engine; shift the lever through all the gears to make sure nothing is binding.

AUTOMATIC TRANSMISSION

The M-35 two speed Powerglide transmission was used from 1970-73. There are three three-speed automatic transmissions used. The Astre uses a Turbo Hydra-Matic 250, sixes and smaller V8s use a Turbo Hydro-Matic 350 (M-38), and the larger V8s use a Turbo Hydra-Matic (M-40) 400. The 350 can readily be identified by its downshift cable between the accelerator linkage and the transmission. The 400 uses an electrical downshift switch at the accelerator pedal.

NOTE: Some 1974-75 models with the M-38 transmission may give symptoms indicating a defective torque converter when the fault is actually a failed intermediate servo piston. Before overhauling the transmission, make this check. Accelerate in Drive from a standing stop to see if performance is sluggish. Shift into L2 and do it again. If the performance is not sluggish, check the servo piston for damage.

Some 1975 M-38 transmissions may click or rattle in first gear because the intermediate steel clutch plates are flat instead of cone shaped. New clutch plates should be installed.

Pan Removal, Fluid and Filter Change

The fluid should be drained with the transmission warm.

1. Support the Astre or Sunbird transmission at the vibration

damper. Remove the crossmember.
2. Prepare a large pan to catch the transmission fluid.
3. Loosen all the pan screws, then pull one corner down to drain most of the fluid.
4. Remove the pan screws and empty out the pan. The pan can be cleaned out with solvent but it must be dried thoroughly before replacement. Be very careful not to leave any lint or threads from rags in the pan.
5. Remove the filter or strainer retaining bolt (two on Turbo Hydra-Matic 250 and 350). A reusable strainer is used on two-speed transmissions and the Turbo Hydra-Matic 250. The strainer may be cleaned in solvent and air-dried thoroughly. Filters are to be replaced.
6. Assemble a new O-ring and filter to the intake pipe on the Turbo Hydra-Matic 400. Use a new gasket on all other models.
7. Install the new filter or cleaned strainer.
8. Install the pan with a new gasket. Tighten the bolts evenly (12 ft lbs) in a criss-cross pattern.
9. Replace the Astre or Sunbird crossmember.
10. Add DEXRON or DEXRON II transmission fluid through the dipstick tube. Add 5 pts for Turbo Hydra-Matic 250, 3 for the 350, and 7 for the 400.
11. Start the engine and let it idle. Do not race the engine. Shift through all the indicator positions, holding the brakes. Check the fluid level with the engine idling in Park. The level should be between the two dimples on the dipstick, about 1/4 in. below the ADD mark. Add fluid as necessary.
12. Check the fluid level after the car has been driven enough to thoroughly warm up the transmission. The level should be at the FULL mark on the dipstick. If the transmission is overfilled, the excess must be drained off. Overfilling causes aerated fluid, resulting in transmission slippage and probable damage.

Vacuum Modulator Replacement

1. Disconnect the vacuum hose from the modulator.
2. Remove the modulator bolt and retainer.
3. Slide the modulator out of the case.
4. Reverse the removal procedure to install. Use a new O-ring seal and check the fluid level.

Band Adjustments

Low Band—Two-Speed (M-35)

This adjustment is required at fluid change intervals, or whenever slippage is evident.

1. Place the shifter lever in Neutral and raise the vehicle.
2. Remove the adjusting screw protecting cap.
3. Loosen the adjusting screw locknut ¼ turn.

    Be sure to hold the adjusting screw locknut at ¼ turn loose during the adjusting procedure.

4. Tighten the adjusting screw to 70 in. lbs. and then back off *exactly* four complete turns for a band with 6,000 miles or more of use, three turns for a band with less than 6,000 miles of use.
5. Tighten the locknut and install the protective cap.

Turbo Hydra-Matic 350, 400

Band adjustments are made during overhaul and cannot be accomplished without disassembly of the transmission.

Intermediate Band—Turbo Hydra-Matic 250

This adjustment is required at fluid change intervals, or whenever slippage is evident.

1. Position the shift lever in Neutral.
2. Loosen the locknut on the right side of the transmission and tighten the adjusting screw to 30 in lbs.
3. Back the screw out three turns and then tighten the locknut.

Shift Linkage Adjustment through 1975

All Column Shift

1. Loosen screw (nut on Firebird) on adjusting swivel clamp.
2. Place gearshift lever in Park and lock ignition.
3. Place transmission shift lever in Park detent.
4. Push up on gearshift control rod until lash is taken up in steering column lock mechanism, then tighten screw or nut on swivel clamp.
5. Readjust the transmission neutral start switch if necessary.

Turbo Hydra-Matic Floorshift, except Astre and 1971-74 Ventura TH-M 350

1. Disconnect shift cable from transmission shift lever by removing nut from pin.
2. Adjust back drive linkage (as in Step 4, above).
3. Unlock ignition and rotate transmission shift lever counterclockwise two detents.
4. Place console lever in Neutral and move against forward Neutral stop.
5. Assemble shift cable and pin to transmission shift lever so that no binding exists, then tighten nut.
6. Readjust the transmission neutral start switch if necessary.

Two-Speed Floorshift

1. Place console lever in Park and lock ignition.
2. Disconnect shift cable from transmission shift lever pin. Loosen the screw on the adjusting swivel at the shaft lever.
3. Rotate transmission shift lever clockwise to Park position and push up on control rod to take up slack.
4. Tighten swivel.
5. Unlock ignition and rotate range lever on transmission counterclockwise two positions.
6. Place shift lever in Neutral and move forward against Neutral stop.
7. Assemble shift cable and pin to transmission lever (free fit) and tighten pin nut.
8. Readjust the transmission neutral start switch if necessary.

Ventura Turbo Hydra-Matic 350 Floorshift, through 1974

1. Loosen both swivel nuts on the shift control rod.
2. Place transmission lever in Drive position.
3. Set pawl rod into Drive notch.
4. Apply a forward load on actuating lever until pawl rod contacts detent.
5. Place a 0.094 in. spacer between front swivel nut and swivel. Run in front nut until it hits spacer, then release load and tighten rear nut to 40 in. lbs.
6. Place transmission shift lever in Park position and lock ignition.
7. Loosen not at the bottom of idler lever, then remove play by rotating shift lever downward. Tighten nut to 20 ft. lbs.

Astre Turbo Hydra-Matic 250 Floorshift

1. Loosen the nut and swivel at the transmission lever.
2. Set the transmission lever in Neutral by moving it counterclockwise to the L1 detent and then clockwise three detent positions to Neutral.
3. Position the shift lever in the Neutral notch of the detent plate.
4. Place the flat of the swivel into the slot of the control rod. Install the washer and cotter pin.
5. Tighten the locknut. Adjust the neutral safety switch, if necessary.

Shift Linkage Adjustment 1976 and Later

All Column Shift

1. Place the shift lever in the Neutral position, and then from underneath the car, loosen the screw on the shift linkage swivel clamp.
2. Put the transmission selector lever in the neutral detent.
3. Hold the swivel clamp flush against the shaft lever assembly and hand tighten the clamp screw against the gearshift control rod. While you are doing this make sure you do not force the control rod or the shaft lever assembly.
4. Tighten the clamp screw and check the shifting against the requirements listed below.

All Console Shift

1. Place the console shift lever in the Park position, and then from underneath the car, loosen the pin from the selector lever.
2. Loosen the screw on the swivel clamp.
3. With the pin fitting freely in the selector lever, tighten the attaching nut.
4. Turn the ignition key to the Lock position, and then from underneath the car, pull the control rod down against the lock-stop to remove all the free play. Hold the swivel clamp flush against the shaft and lever assembly, and tighten the clamp screw against the control rod.
5. Check the shifting of the transmission against the requirements listed below.

Shift Linkage Requirements

1. Move the shift lever from Park to Low to make sure all the stops are available.
2. With the transmission in Drive there should be clearance between the shift lever and the gate; with the transmission in Reverse, there should also be clearance between the shift lever and gate.
3. Turn the ignition key to the On position and place the shift lever into Reverse; you should not be able to remove the key, but the steering will not be locked.
4. On column shift controls, with the key in Lock and the shift lever in Park, the key will be removeable, but the wheel will not turn and the shift lever will not move from Park.
5. On console shift cars, with the key in Lock and the shift lever in

Park, the key will be removeable and the steering wheel will be locked.

Neutral Safety/Backup Light Switch Adjustment

Through 1971

NOTE: The switch is on the steering column. This procedure applies to switches marked "ADJUST" and "RESET".

Caution After the switch has been adjusted, but before starting the engine to test the shifting pattern, make sure that the brakes are securely locked. This is necessary because a misadjusted switch will allow the engine to start in any of the forward or reverse gears.

1. Place the shifter lever in Park.
2. Loosen the switch retaining screws. Make sure that the switch drive tang is engaged in the shifter tube slot and that it stays engaged during adjustment.
3. Rotate the switch in its slot until it is in the Park position and then tighten the screws.
4. After observing the above caution, check the shifter pattern by placing the shifter lever in Neutral. If the transmission does not shift into Neutral, place the lever back in Park and rotate the switch slightly until the shift pattern is correct.
5. If it is possible to move the shift lever a large distance without having the transmission respond, check for a worn switch drive tang or bad electrical contacts inside the switch. In either case, replace the switch.

1972 and later Floorshift, 1971 and later Column Shift— except Astre and Sunbird

NOTE: This procedure applies to all switches with an adjusting pin hole in the back.

1. Place the shift lever in Neutral, except for 1971 models which must be placed in Drive. 1972 floorshift models must be in Park, except for Ventura, which must be in Drive.
2. Loosen the switch mounting screws.
3. Move the switch until you can insert a 0.092 (0.082 beginning 1975) in. diameter adjusting pin into the hole in the back of the switch about ⅜ in.
4. Tighten the screws and remove the pin.
5. Step on the brake pedal and check that the engine will start only in Neutral or Park.

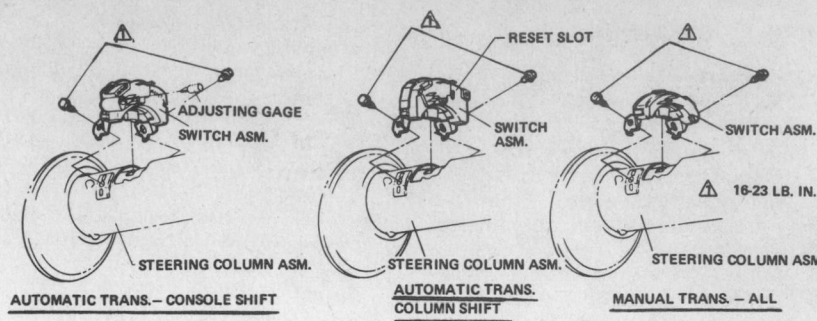

Neutral start switch (© Pontiac Div., G.M. Corp)

AUTOMATIC TRANS.– CONSOLE SHIFT

AUTOMATIC TRANS. COLUMN SHIFT

MANUAL TRANS.– ALL

Astre and Sunbird

1. Remove screws securing floor console.
2. Disconnect the electrical plugs on the back-up, seat belt warning, neutral start, and seat belt buzzer contacts of the neutral safety switch.
3. Place shift lever in Neutral.
4. Remove two screws securing shift indicator plate.
5. Remove two screws securing shift lever curved cover.
6. Remove two screws securing neutral start switch to lever assembly.

NOTE: screws are hidden beneath lever cover.

7. Tilt switch assembly to right as you lift switch out of lever hole.
8. Make sure shift lever is in Neutral before installing switch assembly.
9. Assemble switch assembly to control lever bracket by inserting drive tang into hole in neutral start switch lever.

NOTE: When installing the same neutral switch, align the contact support slot with the service adjustment hole in the switch and insert a 3/32 in. drill to hold the switch in neutral. Remove the drill after the switch is fastened to the shift lever mounting bracket.

10. Tighten two mounting screws securing switch assembly to lever bracket.
11. Install curved shift lever cover and secure with two screws.
12. Install shift indicator plate and attach with two screws.
13. Moving control lever out of Neutral will shear the new switch plastic locating pin.
14. Plug electrical connectors into switch assembly; apply parking brake and start vehicle—check for starting in Neutral and Park only. Also check for back-up lamps in Reverse.
15. Turn off ignition and install console cover securing with four screws.

Downshift Cable Adjustment —Turbo Hydra-Matic 250, 350

Tempest, LeMans

1. With engine off and throttle butterflies closed (off fast idle), position retainer against insert on cable (from inside car).
2. To adjust, grasp accelerator pedal lever adjacent to downshift cable and pull carburetor cable to wide open throttle position. Check for full cable travel.

Firebird

1. With engine off and throttle butterflies closed (off fast idle), position the retainer (under the hood) rearward against washer and insert (or Snap Lock up).
2. To adjust, push carburetor extension lever to wide open throttle position and push the Snap Lock down. Check for full cable travel.

Ventura

1. Disengage the Snap Lock on the detent cable.
2. Place carburetor lever at wide open position, against stop.
3. With detent cable through detent, push Snap Lock downward until its top is flush with the cable.

Astre and Sunbird

1. Remove the air cleaner.
2. Insert a screwdriver on each side of the snap-lock on the bracket at the front of the transmission and pry up to release the lock.
3. Compress the lock tabs and disconnect the snap-lock assembly from the bracket.
4. Position the carburetor lever in the wide open throttle position.
5. Hold the carburetor lever in position and push the Snap Lock on the cable down until the top is flush with the cable.

NOTE: The cable should not be lubricated.

6. Install the air cleaner.

Throttle Valve (TV) Linkage Adjustment—Two-Speed 1970-73

Inline 6 Cylinder Models

1. Remove air cleaner.
2. Disconnect TV control rod swivel and clip from carburetor lever, then disconnect TV return spring from bellhousing.
3. Push TV control rod rearward until transmission TV lever is against internal transmission stop.
4. Holding TV control rod in this position, hold carburetor lever in wide open throttle position and adjust TV control rod swivel so that pin freely enters hole in carburetor lever without binding.
5. Secure swivel, connect return spring and check linkage action for binding.
6. Install air cleaner.

V8 Models

1. Remove air cleaner.
2. Disconnect accelerator linkage at carburetor.
3. Disconnect throttle and TV rod return springs.
4. Pull TV rod forward until transmission is through detent, hold in this position and open carburetor butterflies to wide open position.
5. The butterflies must reach wide open position at the same time that the ball stud contacts end of slot in upper TV rod ($\pm$ 1/32 in.).
6. If necessary, adjust swivel end of upper TV rod.
7. Connect linkage and springs, then check linkage for binding.
8. Install air cleaner.

U-JOINTS

A splined yoke and universal assembly and a rear universal joint are used to accommodate changes in length and orientation of the driveshaft as the car moves over bumps.

Driveshaft Removal and Installation

1. Mark the driveshaft rear yoke and the differential flange to assure correct alignment upon reassembly.
2. Remove the U-bolts and nuts from the differential flange.
3. Remove the driveshaft assembly by first sliding the driveshaft sufficiently forward to disengage the differential flange, then slide the shaft downward and rearward to disengage the front splined yoke from the transmission output shaft.

4. Installation is the reverse of removal. Be sure to align the match mark made before disassembly.

U-Joint Replacement—All Front and Rear U-Joints

Removal

1. Remove the driveshaft.
   NOTE: the universal may have snap-rings that are used to retain the bearing cups in the yokes. These snap-rings may be located at the outside of each yoke or in a groove at the base or open end of each bearing cap. In both cases, there are four snap-rings for each universal joint and they must be removed before proceeding further.
2. Support the splined yoke (front universal) or the journal (rear universal) in a manner that will allow the fixed yoke on the driveshaft to be moved. Support the opposite end so that the driveshaft will be in a horizontal position.
3. Using a piece of pipe, or a similar tool with a large enough diameter, apply force to the fixed yoke until the bearing is almost completely pushed out of the yoke and into the pipe. Remove the bearing completely by insert-

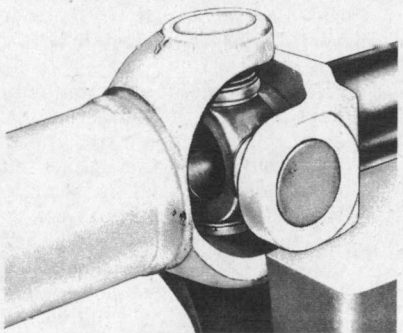

Supporting splined yoke
(© Pontiac Div., G.M. Corp)

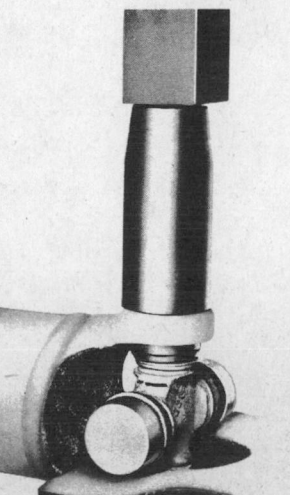

Bearing removal
(© Pontiac Div., G.M. Corp)

ing a spacer between the seal and the bearing cup and finish pressing the bearing out of its yoke, or by tapping around the circumference of the exposed portion of the bearing with a punch and small hammer.

Installing journal
(© Pontiac Div., G.M. Corp)

NOTE: The plastic which retains the bearing will be sheared when the bearing cup is pressed out. Be sure to remove the remains of the plastic retainer from the ears of the yoke. It is easier to remove the remains if a small pin or punch is first driven through the injection holes in the yoke. Failure to remove all of the plastic remains may prevent the bearing cups from being pressed into place and the bearing retainers from being properly seated.

4. Remove the rest of the bearings following the same procedure.

Installation

1. Install a bearing one-quarter of the way into one side of the splined yoke (front universal) or fixed yoke (rear universal).
2. Insert the journal into the yoke so that an arm of the journal seats into the bearing.
3. Press in the bearing the remaining distance.
4. Install the opposite bearing. Do not allow the bearing rollers to jam. Continually check for free movement of the journal in the bearings as they are pressed into the yoke.
5. Install the rest of the bearings in the same manner.

REAR AXLE

Axle Shaft, Bearing, and Seal

Removal and Installation

These cars use two different types of drive axle, the C- and the non C-type. Axle shafts in the C-type are retained by C-shaped locks, which fit grooves at the inner end of the shaft. Axle shafts in the non C-type are retained by the brake backing plate, which is bolted to the axle housing. Bearings in the C-type axle consist of an outer race, bearing rollers and a roller cage, retained by snap-rings. The non C-type axle uses a unit roller bearing (inner race, rollers and outer race), which is pressed onto the shaft, up to a shoulder. When servicing C- or non C-type axles, it is imperative to determine the axle service The Astre uses the C-type axle.

Non C—Type

Caution Before attempting any service to the drive axle or axle shafts, remove the axle carrier cover and visually determine if the axle shafts are retained by C-shaped locks at the inner end, or by the brake backing plate at the outer end. If the shafts are *not* retained by C-locks, proceed as follows.

Design allows for maximum axle shaft end-play of 0.022 in., which can be measured with a dial indicator. If end-play is found to be excessive, the bearing should be replaced. Shimming the bearing is not recommended as this ignores end-play of the bearing itself and could result in improper seating of the bearing.

1. Remove the wheel, tire and brake drum.
2. Remove the nuts holding the retainer plate to the backing plate. Disconnect the brake line.
3. Remove the retainer and install nuts, fingertight, to prevent the brake backing plate from being dislodged.
4. Pull out the axle shaft and bearing assembly, using a slide hammer.
5. Using a chisel, nick the bearing retainer in three or four places. The retainer does not have to be cut, merely collapsed sufficiently, to allow the bearing retainer to be slid from the shaft.
6. Press off the bearing and install the new one by pressing it into position.
7. Press on the new retainer.

NOTE: do not attempt to press the bearing and the retainer on at the same time.

8. Assemble the shaft and bearing in the housing, being sure that the bearing is seated properly in the housing.
9. Install the retainer, drum, wheel and tire. Bleed the brakes.

C—Type

Caution Before attempting any service to the drive axle or axle shafts, remove the

carrier cover and visually determine if the axle shafts are retained by C-shaped locks at the inner ends or by a brake backing plate at the outer end. If they *are* retained by C-shaped locks, proceed as follows.

1. Raise the vehicle and remove the wheels.
2. The differential cover has already been removed (see Caution note above). Remove the differential pinion shaft lockscrew and the differential pinion shaft.
3. Push the flanged end of the axle shaft toward the center of the vehicle and remove the C-lock from the end of the shaft.
4. Remove the axle shaft from the housing, being careful not to damage the oil seal.
5. Remove the oil seal by inserting the button end of the axle shaft behind the steel case of the oil seal. Pry the seal loose from the bore.
6. Seat the legs of the bearing puller behind the bearing. Seat a washer against the bearing and hold it in place with a nut. Use a slide hammer to pull the bearing.
7. Pack the cavity between the seal lips with wheel bearing lubricant and lubricate a new wheel bearing with the same.
8. Use a suitable driver and install the bearing until it bottoms against the tube. Install the oil seal.
9. Slide the axle shaft into place. Be sure that the splines on the shaft do not damage the oil seal. Make sure that the splines engage the differential side gear.
10. Install the axle shaft C-lock on the inner end of the axle shaft and push the shaft outward so that the C-lock seats in the differential side gear counterbore.
11. Position the differential pinion shaft through the case and pinions, aligning the hole for the case with the hole for the lockscrew.

12. Install the pinion shaft lockscrew.
13. Use a new gasket and install the carrier cover. Be sure that the gasket surfaces are clean before installing the gasket and cover.
14. Fill the axle with lubricant to the bottom of the filler hole.
15. Install the brake drum and wheels and lower the car. Check for leaks and road test the car.

JACKING, HOISTING

Jack car at front spring seats of lower control arms. Jack car at rear under axle housing, or under a frame member.

FRONT SUSPENSION

Front Shock Absorber Replacement

New shock absorbers must be purged of air before installation. This is done by repeatedly extending the shock in its normal mounted position, inverting, and compressing it.

Except Astre and Sunbird

1. Remove the nut, retainer, and grommet which are attached to the upper end of the shock absorber and seat against the frame bracket.

NOTE: it may be necessary to hold the shock absorber shaft to remove the nut. This may be done with a wrench on the end of the shaft.

2. Raise the car to allow the shock to be dropped from the lower control arm.
3. Remove the two shock absorber lower attaching screws and lower the shock from the control arm.

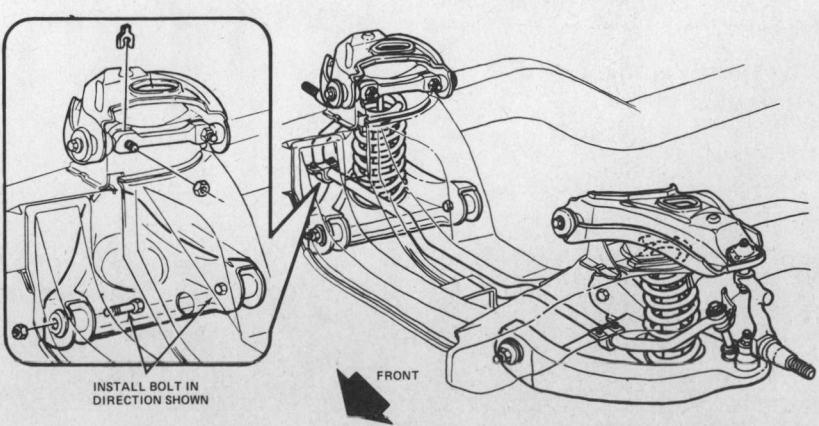

INSTALL BOLT IN DIRECTION SHOWN

FRONT

Front suspension—Ventura (© Pontiac Div., G.M. Corp)

4. Install the shock absorber by reversing the removal steps.
5. Make sure all grommets are in the correct position. Tighten the upper nut to 10 ft. lbs.

Astre and Sunbird

1. Pry out the access plug in the engine compartment so that the upper mount is visible.
2. Raise the front of the car and safely support it.
3. Turn the wheels for clearance.
4. Hold the upper shock stud with a wrench. Loosen and remove the locknut.
5. Unbolt the lower end and pull the shock down and out.
6. Place the lower retainer and rubber grommet on the shock stud.
7. Put the shock in place and tighten the lower bolts. Torque to 20 ft lbs.
8. Place the upper grommet, retainer, and nut on the shock stud.
9. Hold the stud with a wrench and tighten the nut. Torque to 120 in. lbs

Coil Spring R &

Except Astre and Sunbird

1. Jack up car and support on jack stands at frame side rails.
2. Remove shock absorber.
3. Disconnect stabilizer bar at lower control arm.
4. Support lower control arm with a hydraulic floor jack, then remove the two inner control arm to front crossmember pivot bolts.
5. Carefully lower the control arm, allowing the spring to relax.

Caution Allow the spring to completely expand before attempting to remove it.

6. Reach in and remove spring.
7. To install, reverse the removal procedure. Tighten the lower control arm pivot bolts to 105 ft. lbs. or the nuts to 95 ft. lbs. with the weight of the car on the springs.

Astre and Sunbird

1. Raise the front of the car and support it with jackstands placed under the front crossmember braces.
2. Remove the wheel, shock absorbers, and stabilizer bar.
3. Support the lower control arm outer end with a hydraulic floor jack and a block of wood.
4. Securely fasten the spring to the lower control arm with a heavy chain.
5. To detach the tie rod, remove the cotter pin and nut, and tap on the steering arm (not the tie-rod end) with a hammer. Hold another hammer behind the steering arm to take the force of the tapping. The tie rod should then

fall free.
6. Remove the lower ball joint stud from the steering knuckle.
7. Very cautiously lower the jack until the spring is fully expanded.
8. Place the spring in its pads on the lower control arm and shock tower. Secure it with a chain as in step four.
9. Carefully raise the jack.
10. Place the lower ball joint stud in the steering knuckle. Torque the stud nut to 60 ft lbs. If the cotter pin does not align, tighten it further 1/6 of a turn and insert a new cotter pin.
11. Install the tie-rod end to the steering arm. Torque the nut to 35 ft lbs. If the cotter pin hole does not align, tighten further up to a maximum of 50 ft lbs. Insert a new cotter pin.
12. Replace the shock absorber. Do not attach the top end of the shock at this point.
13. Install the stabilizer bar. Tighten the bracket bolts to 30 ft lbs and the control arm bolts to 10 ft lbs.
14. Replace the wheel and lower the car. Install the upper end of the shock absorber.

Upper Control Arm Removal

1. Support car weight at outer end of lower control arm.
2. Remove wheel and tire.
3. Remove cotter pin and loosen the nut on the upper control arm ball stud.
4. Remove the stud from the knuckle with a pry bar, while tapping with a hammer. The preferred method of doing this is to use a ball joint stud remover tool to push the stud out.
5. Remove two nuts that hold the upper control arm cross-shaft to front crossmember. Count number of shims at each bolt.

Upper Control Arm Installation

1. Install bolts through holes and install upper control arm to crossmember.
2. Secure two nuts and washers to the bolts holding the upper control arm shaft to front crossmember. Install same number of shims as removed at each bolt. Torque bolts to 50 ft. lbs. on all 1970-71 and 1975-77 models and 1972-77 Ventura. On 1972-74 Firebird, LeMans and Grand Am, tighten the bolts to 80 ft lbs. Torque the bolts to 60 ft lbs. on the Astre and Sunbird.
3. Lubricate ball joint with chassis lube.
4. Install ball joint stud through knuckle. Install nut, and torque to 50 ft. lbs. (40 ft. lbs.—1972-74, 30 ft. lbs.—Astre and Sunbird). Insert cotter pin.

Caution Care should be taken to insure that the steering knuckle hole, ball stud, and nut are free of dirt and grease before tightening the nut. Turn the nut only in the tightening direction to align the slot with the hole to insert the cotter pin. DO NOT BACK OFF THE NUT. Maximum torque to align the slot with the hole, except on Astre and Sunbird should not exceed 70 ft. lbs. (100 for 1975 and later).

5. Install wheel and tire assembly.
6. Lower car to floor.
7. Be sure to recheck caster and camber.

Ball Joint Inspection

NOTE: before performing this inspection, make sure the wheel bearings are adjusted correctly and that the A arm bushings are in good condition.

1. Jack the car up under the front lower control arm at the spring seat.
2. Raise the car until there is 1–2 in. of clearance under the wheel.
3. Insert a bar under the wheel and pry upward. If the wheel raises more than 1/8 in., the ball joints are worn. Determine whether the upper or lower ball joint is worn by visual inspection while prying on the wheel.

NOTE: due to the distribution of forces in the suspension, the lower ball joint is usually the defective joint.

Lower Ball Joint Wear Indicators —1974 and later Firebird and LeMans, All Models beginning 1975

These cars have a visual wear indicator on the lower ball joint. Wear is indicated by the position of the 1/2 in. nipple into which the grease fitting is screwed. On a new joint, the nipple should project .050 in. beyond the ball joint cover surface. If the nipple is flush or inside the cover surface, replace the ball joint.

Upper Ball Joint Removal

1. Perform Steps 1-4 of Upper Control Arm Removal. Prickpunch the center of the four rivets.

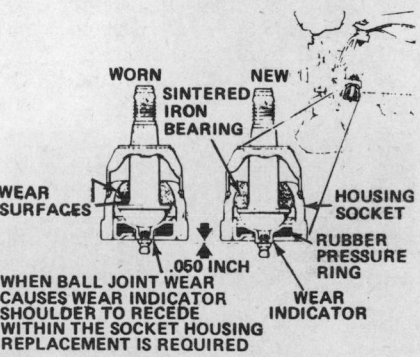

Lower ball joint wear indicator
(© Pontiac Div., G.M. Corp)

2. Drill through the heads of these rivets.

3. Chisel off rivet heads and tap out rivets with a punch.

Upper Ball Joint Installation

1. Install new ball joint against top side of upper control arm. Secure joint to control arm with the four special alloy bolts and nuts furnished with the replacement part.

2. Torque these bolts and nuts to 9 ft. lbs.

Lower Control Arm and Ball Joint Removal and Installation

1. Remove coil spring and lower control arm inner bolts.

2. Separate lower ball joint from steering knuckle by prying, while hammering sharply on steering knuckle.

3. Press lower ball joint from lower control arm using suitable arbors and a large bench vise.

4. To install, reverse removal procedure, tightening lower ball joint stud nut to 85-90 ft. lbs. (70 ft. lbs—1972 and later. Tighten the nut to 60 ft. lbs. on the Astre and Sunbird.

NOTE: if only ball joint is to be removed, remove brake caliper or hub and backing plate, with jack under lower arm. Begin with Step 2.

Wheel Bearing Adjustment

1. Lift the wheel off the ground by jacking under the lower control arm.

2. Remove the dust cap from the hub.

3. Remove the cotter pin and discard it.

4. Snug up the spindle nut while spinning the wheel to seat the bearings (12 ft. lbs). Then back off the nut ¼-½ turn.

5. Retighten the nut by hand until it is finger-tight.

6. Loosen the nut until the nearest hole in the spindle lines up with a slot in the spindle nut and then insert a new cotter pin. When the bearing is properly adjusted, there will be 0.001-0.005 in. end-play.

NOTE: under no circumstances is the final bearing nut adjustment to be even finger-tight.

7. Replace the dust cover and lower the car.

REAR SUSPENSION

Shock Absorber Replacement

New shock absorbers must be purged of air before installation. This is done by repeatedly extending the shock in its normal mounted position,

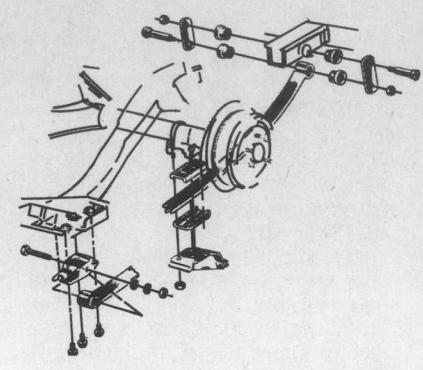

Rear spring installation—Ventura with single leaf springs (© Pontiac Div., G.M. Corp)

inverting, and compressing it.

Except Astre and Sunbird

1. Raise the car at the axle housing.

2. Remove the nut, retainer, and grommet, or nut, and lock-washer, which attach the lower end of the shock absorber to its mounting.

3. Remove the two shock absorber upper attaching screws and the shock absorber.

4. Reverse the removal procedures to install. Tighten the lower nut to 65 ft lbs. on LeMans and Grand Am, to 10 ft lbs. on Firebird and to 55 (45 beginning 1975) ft lbs. on Ventura.

Astre and Sunbird

1. Raise the vehicle and support the rear axle.

2. Remove upper attaching bolts and lower through-bolt.

3. Remove the shock absorber.

4. Install retainer and rubber grommet onto the new shock.

5. Place shock absorber into installed position and install upper retaining bolts.

6. Install the through bolt and a rubber grommet on each side of the shock eye.

7. Lower the car.

Rear Coil Spring Replacement

Tempest, LeMans, Grand Am

1. Raise the rear of the car and support it solidly on the frame rails.

2. Remove the clip that attaches the brake hose to its bracket on the frame crossmember.

3. Support the rear axle with a jack.

4. Remove the nut and lockwasher from the shock absorber and disconnect the shock from the axle. It may be necessary to adjust the height of the jack to disconnect the shock. On models beginning 1973, disconnect the upper control arms from the axle housing.

5. Carefully lower the jack until the spring is free and remove the

spring. Note the position of the spring and replace it with the lower coil pointing in the same direction.

6. Reverse the removal steps to install the spring.

Astre and Sunbird

1. Raise vehicle and support the rear axle, with a hydraulic jack.

2. Disconnect both shock absorbers from lower brackets.

3. Lower axle and remove springs and spring insulators.

NOTE: one or both springs may be removed at this point.

Caution When lowering axle do not stretch brake hose running from frame to axle.

4. Install insulators on top and bottom of springs and position on axle.

5. Raise axle and reconnect shock absorbers. Torque the bottom stud or bolt nuts to 42 in. lbs.

6. Lower the vehicle.

Rear Leaf Spring Replacement

Firebird, Ventura

1. Jack up the car at the rear axle. Then support the major portion of the weight of the car on the frame rails, leaving the jack in place under the axle. At this point the jack should be supporting the axle only; there should be no tension on the spring.

2. Disconnect the shock at the axle and move it out of the way.

3. Remove the spring and shock absorber anchor plate nuts and remove the anchor plate and lower spring cushion pad.

4. Raise the axle with the jack and remove the upper spring cushion pad.

5. Loosen the upper and lower spring shackle pin nuts.

6. Loosen the front spring eye bolt.

7. Remove the screws securing the spring front mounting bracket to the floor pan and carefully let the spring swing down.

8. Remove the lower shackle pin from the rear of the spring and remove the spring from the car.

9. Install the front spring mounting bracket on the front spring eye and loosely insert the bolt and nut. Do not tighten the spring eyebolt until the weight of the car is on the springs.

10. Place the spring into the shackles at the rear of the car and loosely install the lower shackle pin and nut. Do not tighten them.

11. Raise the front end of the spring and install the spring mounting bracket to the floor pan and torque the bolts to 30 ft lbs. Make sure the tab on the spring mounting bracket is indexed in

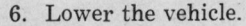
the slot in the floor pan and that the parking brake cables are on the top side of the spring.

12. Place the upper spring cushion pan on the spring and lower the axle onto spring.

13. Install the lower spring cushion and shock absorber anchor plate and torque the anchor plate nuts to 40 ft lbs.

14. Install the shock absorber.

15. Put the weight of the car on the springs and torque the shackle pin nuts to 50 ft lbs. Tighten front eyebolt to 80 ft lbs.

BRAKES

Information on brake service can be found in the Unit Repair Section.

Parking Brake Adjustment

Except Astre and Sunbird

The automatic self-adjusting feature incorporated in the rear brake mechanism normally maintains proper parking brake adjustment. For this reason, the rear brake adjustment must be checked before any adjustment of the parking brake cables is done. Check the parking brake mechanism and cables for free movement and lubricate all working surfaces before proceeding.

Caution It is very important that the parking brake cables are not too tight. If the cables are too tight, they create a drag and position the secondary shoes so that the self-adjusters continue to operate in compensation for drag wear. The result is rapidly worn rear brake linings.

1. Jack up both rear wheels.
2. Push parking brake pedal 5-7 notches from full release position for Tempest and GTO in 1970, 2 notches for Firebird in 1970 and 1975 and later Firebird and Ventura, 3 notches for 1975 and later LeMans and Grand Am, 4-8 notches for all series 1971-72, 8 notches for all series 1973-74.
3. Loosen rear equalizer locknut and adjust forward nut until light rear brake drag is felt as wheels are rotated by hand. On 1975 and later models, you should be able to turn the wheels backwards using two hands, but not forward.
4. Tighten locknut and release parking brake pedal; no drag should be felt.

Astre and Sunbird

1. Raise and support the rear of the car.
2. Apply the parking brake one notch from the fully released position.
3. Loosen the adjusting locknut at the cable equalizer and tighten the adjusting nut until a slight drag is felt when the rear wheels are rotated.
4. Tighten the locknut securely.
5. The rear wheels should rotate freely when the parking brake is fully released.

6. Lower the vehicle.

Master Cylinder Removal and Installation

1. Disconnect hydraulic line/s at master cylinder; disconnect clevis at pedal (except on power brakes).
2. Remove the two retaining nuts and lockwashers that hold cylinder to the firewall or power booster.
3. Remove the master cylinder, gasket and rubber boot.
4. Position master cylinder on firewall; reconnect pushrod clevis to brake pedal.
5. Install nuts and lockwashers.
6. Install hydraulic line/s, then check brake pedal free play.
7. Bleed brakes, as described in Unit Repair Section.

NOTE: cars having disc brakes do not have a check valve in the front outlet port of the master cylinder. If one is installed, front discs will immediately wear out due to residual hydraulic pressure holding pads against rotor.

Power Brake Booster Removal and Installation

1. Remove the vacuum hose from the front housing and discard the grommet. Remove the master cylinder and position away from the booster. It is not necessary to disconnect the lines from the master cylinder if it is not to be repaired.
2. Remove the clevis pin retainer from the brake pedal inside the car.
3. Remove the nuts from the vacuum cylinder studs under the dash and remove the vacuum power section.
4. Reverse the removal procedure to install the booster.

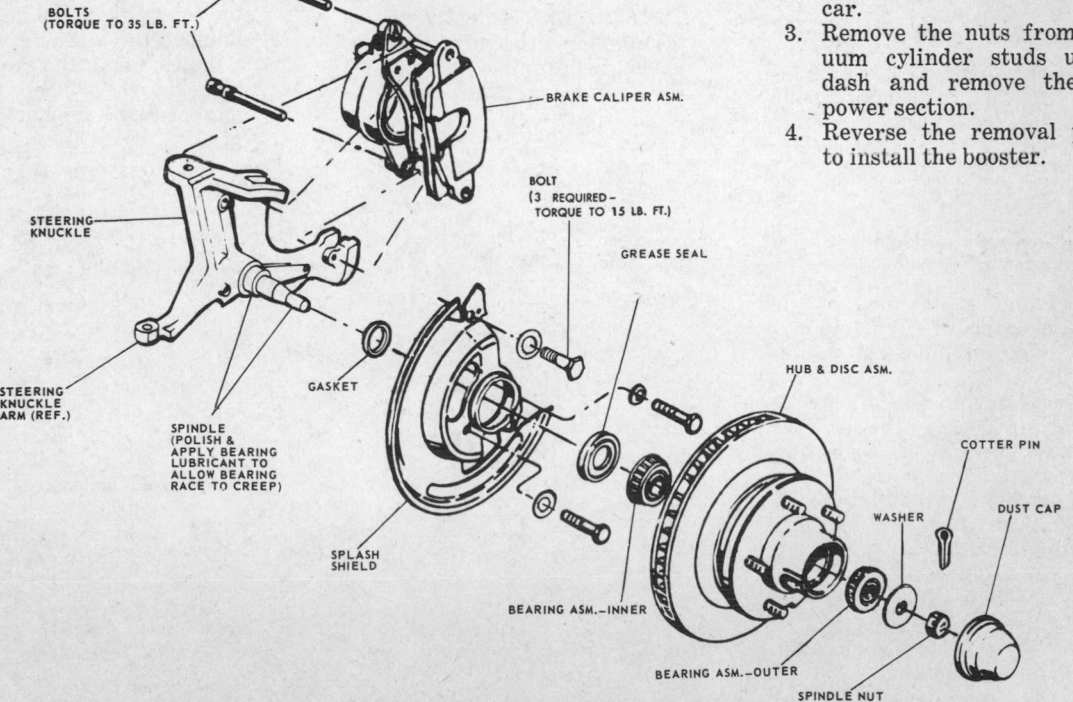

Steering knuckle, hub and disc assembly—Firebird, 1973 and later LeMans and Grand Am (© Pontiac Div., G.M. Corp)

STEERING

Tie Rod End Replacement

1. Loosen the tie rod adjuster sleeve clamp nuts.
2. Remove the tie rod stud nut cotter pin and nut.
3. Remove the tie rod stud from the steering arm or intermediate rod. This is a taper fit. Removal is accomplished by using a ball joint removal tool.
4. Unthread the tie rod from the adjuster sleeve. Outer tie rods have right-hand threads and inner tie rods have left-hand threads. Count the number of turns the tie rod must be rotated to remove it from the adjusting sleeve. This will allow a reasonably accurate realignment upon reassembly.
5. Reverse the removal procedures for installation. Clean all rust and dirt from the threads. Check the alignment and adjust if necessary.

Power Steering Pump Removal and Installation

1. Disconnect the hoses at the pump.
2. Remove the drive pulley attaching nut.
3. Loosen the bracket-to-pump mounting bolts and remove the drive belt.
4. Slide the pulley from the shaft with a gear puller. Do not hammer on the pulley.
5. Remove the bracket-to-pump mounting bolts and remove the pump.
6. Reverse the removal steps for installation. Bleed the pump of air by turning the pulley counterclockwise until no bubbles appear in the reservoir.
7. Bleed the system.

Power Steering System Bleeding

The system must be bled of air whenever any parts of the pump circuit have been disconnected or replaced.

1. Fill the reservoir. Be careful not to overfill, because the level is normally checked at operating temperature after expansion has taken place. Allow the fluid to remain undisturbed for at least two minutes.
2. Start the engine and run it for only about two seconds.
3. Fill again as necessary.
4. Repeat Steps 1 to 3 until the level remains constant.
5. Raise the front wheels off the ground.
6. Run the engine at about 1,500

POSITION OF TIE ROD ADJUSTER SLEEVE & CLAMP

INCORRECT ASSEMBLY

CORRECT ASSEMBLY

NOTE: SLOT IN TIE ROD ADJUSTER SLEEVE MAY BE IN ANY POSITION EXCEPT AT EDGES OF CLAMP JAWS.

Tie rod clamp installation
(© Pontiac Div., G.M. Corp.)

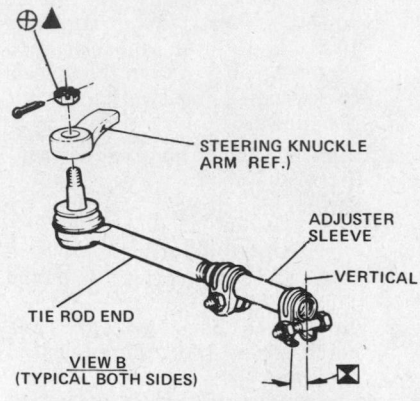

STEERING KNUCKLE ARM REF.)
ADJUSTER SLEEVE
VERTICAL
TIE ROD END
VIEW B (TYPICAL BOTH SIDES)

Tie rod assembly—typical
(© Pontiac Div., G.M. Corp)

rpm and turn the wheels gently against the stops in either direction.
7. Fill again as necessary.
8. Lower the car to the ground. Turn the wheels gently against the stops in either direction with the engine running.
9. Fill again as necessary.

Steering Wheel Removal and Installation

Except Astre and Sunbird

1. On deluxe models, remove the screws holding the trim cover to the wheel, or if equipped with a horn button, lift the button off.
2. Remove the snap-ring and steering wheel nut from the steering shaft.
3. Position the wheels in the straight-ahead position and make match marks on the steering shaft and steering wheel.
4. Using a puller, remove the steering wheel.

Caution Don't pound on the steering wheel or the steering shaft. The collapsible column could be damaged enough to require replacement.

5. Disconnect the horn wire insulator by rotating the insulator counterclockwise to the unlock position and then pull up.
6. Reverse the removal procedures for installation. Make sure the match marks are lined up when installing the wheel.

Astre and Sunbird

1. Disconnect the battery ground cable.
2. Remove the two screws from the back of the wheel, allowing the shroud (horn actuator bar) to be removed. Lift the Formula wheel horn button off.
3. Set the wheel straight ahead. Mark the relationship of the wheel to the shaft and remove the snap-ring and nut.
4. Remove the steering wheel with a puller, using the two threaded holes in the wheel. Disconnect the horn wire insulator by rotat-

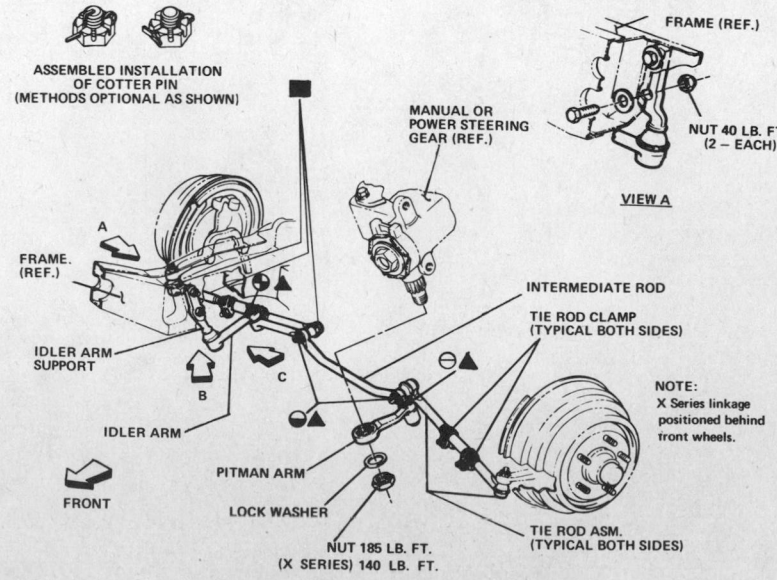

ASSEMBLED INSTALLATION OF COTTER PIN (METHODS OPTIONAL AS SHOWN)
FRAME (REF.)
MANUAL OR POWER STEERING GEAR (REF.)
NUT 40 LB. FT (2 – EACH)
VIEW A
FRAME. (REF.)
INTERMEDIATE ROD
TIE ROD CLAMP (TYPICAL BOTH SIDES)
IDLER ARM SUPPORT
IDLER ARM
FRONT
PITMAN ARM
LOCK WASHER
NUT 185 LB. FT. (X SERIES) 140 LB. FT.
TIE ROD ASM. (TYPICAL BOTH SIDES)
NOTE: X Series linkage positioned behind front wheels.

Steering linkage (© Pontiac Div., G.M. Corp)

ing the insulator counterclockwise to the unlock position and then pulling up.

5. Install the wheel, aligning the previously made marks. Make sure that the turn signal switch is in the neutral position. Torque the nut to 30 ft lbs.
6. Make sure that the lower horn insulator, eyelet, and spring are in place.
7. Position the shroud, seating the pin on the right side of the wheel in the hole in the shroud. Replace the formula wheel horn button.
8. Replace the two screws in the rear of the wheel. Connect the battery cable.

Turn Signal Switch Replacement

1. Remove the steering wheel.
2. Remove the three cover screws and lift the cover off the shaft.
3. Depress the lockplate and remove the snap-ring. All 1976 and later steering columns have a redesigned lock plate which is removed by inserting a screwdriver in the cover slot and prying out. This is done in at least two of the slots to avoid breaking the plate. Remove the retaining ring and lockplate.
4. Slide the upper bearing spring and turn signal cam off the shaft. Remove the thrust washer.
5. Remove the turn signal lever screw and lever.
6. Push the hazard warning switch in and remove the knob.
7. Pull the wiring connector out of the bracket and disconnect it. Wrap it with tape to prevent snagging.
8. Pull the switch straight up and remove it from the housing.
9. Reverse the removal procedures for installation.

Ignition Switch Replacement

The ignition and steering wheel locking switch is located just below the gear selector lever on the steering column.

1. Disconnect battery.
2. Loosen toe pan screws.
3. Remove column to panel nuts, lower steering column, and disconnect switch wire connectors.

Caution Be extremely careful with the steering column. Never let it hang unsupported.

4. Remove switch attaching screws and switch.
5. To install, move key lock to OFF-LOCK position.
6. Move actuator rod hole in switch to OFF-LOCK position.
7. Install switch, with rod in hole, then reverse removal procedure.

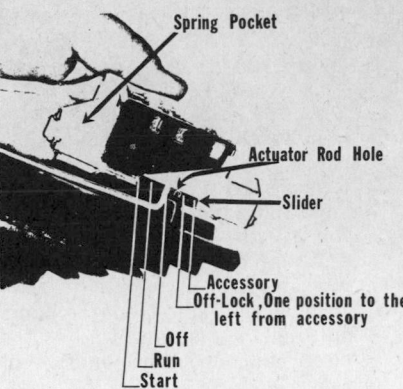

Adjusting ignition switch—tilt column
(© Pontiac Div., G.M. Corp)

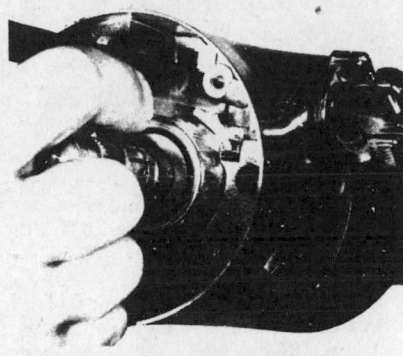

Depressing lock cylinder spring latch
(© Pontiac Div., G.M. Corp)

Switch Adjustment—Standard Column

1. Place switch in OFF position.
2. Position switch on column, then move slider to extreme left (toward wheel).
3. Move slider back two positions to the right of ACCESSORY position.
4. Place key in any run position and shift transmission into any position but Park for automatics or Reverse for manual.
5. Position lock toward ACCESSORY with a light finger pressure and secure switch.

Switch Adjustment—Tilt Column

1. Place key in ACCESSORY position; leave key in lock.
2. Loosen switch mounting screws.
3. Push switch upward toward wheel to make certain it is in ACCESSORY detent.
4. Hold key in full counter clockwise ACCESSORY position and tighten switch mounting screws.
5. Switch is properly adjusted if: it will go into ACCESSORY position, the key can be removed when in lock, and switch will go into START position.

Lock Cylinder Replacement

1. Remove steering wheel.
2. Pull turn signal switch up far enough to allow access to spring

latch slot.

3. Place key in RUN position, insert a thin screwdriver into the slot next to the switch mounting screw boss and depress spring latch.

NOTE: there is a casting flash over this slot if the lock has never before been removed. It is necessary sometimes to use substantial force to break it. Be careful not to damage anything beneath the flashing when penetrating the slot.

4. Remove lock from housing.
5. To install, first hold lock cylinder sleeve and rotate knob clockwise against stop, looking at the key end.
6. Lay a 1/16 in. drill on housing surface next to housing bore. This isn't necessary on 1975 and later models, except Astre.

NOTE: the 1/16 in. drill prevents forcing the lock cylinder inward beyond its normal latched position. The buzzer switch and spring latch can hold the lock cylinder too far inward. Complete disassembly of the upper bearing housing is necessary to release an improperly installed lock cylinder.

7. Insert cylinder into housing bore, aligning keyway, and push in to abutment.
8. Rotate knob counterclockwise, pushing in slightly, until cylinder mates with sector.
9. Push in until spring latch pops into groove, then remove drill.

INSTRUMENT PANEL

Light Switch Replacement

1. Disconnect battery.
2. Pull knob to on position.
3. Reach under instrument panel and depress the switch shaft retainer, then remove knob and shaft assembly.

NOTE: disconnect vacuum hose on vacuum-operated headlamp models.

4. Remove retaining ferrule nut.
5. Remove switch from instrument panel.
6. Disconnect multi-plug connector from switch.
7. Install in reverse of above. (In checking lights before installation, switch must be grounded to test dome lights on some models).

WINDSHIELD WIPERS

Motor Replacement

1. Remove hoses and wire terminals that are connected to wiper unit.
2. Remove clip or nut that secures

wiper crank to wiper linkage arm.

NOTE: this clip is under leaf screen on depressed-park (hidden wiper) motors, and accessible only after firewall bolts are removed on some standard motors. On some models, the wiper arm must be removed to facilitate motor removal.

3. Remove screws that secure wiper motor assembly to firewall.
4. Position wiper assembly on firewall and secure.
5. Connect wire terminals and hoses.
6. Connect wiper crank with wiper linkage arm.

RADIO

Radio Removal and Installation

1970 All Except Firebird

1. Disconnect antenna and power leads, remove tape deck and multiplex.
2. Loosen hex screws and remove knobs.
3. Remove escutcheon retaining nuts.
4. Remove screw that holds receiver to panel bracket, then remove ash tray.
   NOTE: with air conditioner, outlet duct and bezel must be removed.
5. Remove speaker by disconnecting output connector and mounting bracket screws.
6. Reverse above procedure to reinstall.
   NOTE: this procedure is very general, and some combinations of accessories may require slight modifications.

Firebird

1. Disconnect battery.
2. Remove glove box, glove box door and lower right A/C duct.
3. Remove radio knobs, nuts and trim plate.
4. Disconnect antenna and power lines.
5. Disconnect speaker leads, then remove radio bracket and radio from passenger side of dashboard.
6. To install, reverse removal procedure.

1971-72 LeMans and GTO, 1971 and later

1. Disconnect battery. Remove lower A/C duct on Tempest.
2. Remove radio knobs, bezels and hex nuts.
3. Remove support bracket bolt. Remove the Ventura radio side-brace screw.
4. Disconnect electrical and antenna leads; remove radio from under dash.

5. To install, reverse removal procedure.

1973 and later LeMans

1. Disconnect the battery.
2. Remove the radio knobs and bezels.
3. Remove the upper and lower instrument panel trim plates.
4. Remove the two radio side (two front on 1974 and later) retaining screws.
5. Remove the radio from the panel opening, disconnecting the electrical connections and the antenna lead.
6. To install, reverse the removal procedure. If the radio is to be replaced, remove the bushing from the rear of the radio and install it on the replacement radio.

1973 and later Grand Am and Grand LeMans

1. Disconnect the battery.
2. Remove the radio knobs and bezels and the retaining hex nut from the right-hand radio tuning shaft.
3. Remove the four retaining screws and the trim plate.
4. Remove the two side (one front on 1974 and later) retaining screws and the mounting bracket screw.
5. Remove the radio and the mounting bracket from the dash, disconnecting the electrical connections and the antenna lead.
6. To install, reverse the removal procedure.

Astre and Sunbird

1. Remove battery ground cable.
2. Remove knobs, controls, washers and nuts from radio bushings.
3. Disconnect antenna lead, power connector, and speaker connectors from rear of receiver.
4. Remove two screws securing radio mounting bracket to instrument panel lower reinforcement and lift out radio receiver.
5. To install, reverse the removal procedure.

HEATER

Heater Blower Removal and Installation
Non Air-Conditioned Cars

1970-72 Tempest and LeMans, 1970 and later Firebird

1. Jack up front of car and remove right front wheel.
2. Cut access hole along stamped outline on right fender skirt, using an air chisel.
3. Disconnect blower power wire.

4. Remove blower.
5. To install, reverse removal procedure, covering access hole with a metal plate secured with sealer and sheet metal screws.

1973 and later LeMans & Grand Am

1. Disconnect the blower motor feed wire and the ground wire.
2. Remove the blower motor retaining screws and remove the motor.
3. To replace, reverse the removal procedure.

Ventura

1. Disconnect the battery.
2. Detach the heater hoses from the clips on the right front fender skirt.
3. Raise the car and remove all fender skirt attaching bolts except those which attach the skirt to the radiator support.
4. Pull down on the skirt and block the skirt to all clearance for removal of the blower motor.
5. Disconnect the electrical wiring from the motor.
6. Remove the attaching screws and remove the blower motor. Pry the motor flange gently if the sealer acts as an adhesive.
7. Remove the blower impeller retaining nut and separate the motor from the impeller.
8. To replace, reverse the removal procedure.

Astre and Sunbird

1. Disconnect the battery ground cable, and remove the coolant recovery tank.
2. Disconnect the blower motor lead wire. Disconnect the motor cooling tube on air-conditioned models.
3. Scribe the blower motor flange to case position.
4. Remove the blower to case attaching screws and remove the blower wheel and motor assembly. Pry the flange gently if the sealer is retaining the assembly.
5. Remove the blower wheel retaining nut and separate the motor and wheel.
6. To install, reverse Steps 1-5, lining up the match-marks on the motor flange and case which were made at removal.
   NOTE: assemble the blower wheel to the motor with the open end of the blower away from the motor. Reseal the motor flange, if necessary.

Heater Core Removal and Installation
Non Air-Conditioned Cars

Tempest, GTO, LeMans, and Firebird

1. Drain radiator.

2. Disconnect heater hoses at air inlet assembly.

3. Remove nuts from core studs on firewall (under hood). Remove the glove box.

NOTE: on Firebird, remove glove box and door, then remove heater outlet from case. Remove defroster duct screw on all 1971 and later models.

4. From inside the car, pull the heater assembly from the firewall.

5. Disconnect control cables and wires, then remove heater assembly.

6. To remove core, unhook retaining springs or strips.

7. To install, reverse removal procedure, making sure core is properly sealed during installation.

Ventura

1. Disconnect battery.

2. Drain radiator, disconnect heater hoses at core and plug core tubes.

3. Remove nuts from core case studs on firewall.

4. Remove glove box and glove box door.

5. From inside car, drill out lower right hand heater case stud with ¼ in. drill.

6. Pull entire heater case, with core, from firewall.

7. Disconnect cables and blower resistor connector, then remove case from car.

8. Remove core from case.

9. To install, reverse removal procedure. Use sealer around core and replace drilled stud with new screw and stamped nut.

Astre and Sunbird

1. Disconnect the battery ground cable.

2. Disconnect the blower motor lead wire.

3. Place a pan under the vehicle. Disconnect the heater hoses at the core connections and secure the ends of the hoses in a raised position.

4. It may be necessary to remove the coil bracket to dash panel stud nut and move the coil out of the way.

5. Remove the blower intake to dash panel screws and nuts and remove the blower intake, blower motor and wheel as an assembly.

6. Remove the core retaining strap screws and remove the core from the vehicle.

7. To install, reverse Steps 1-6.

NOTE: be sure that the blower intake sealer is intact, replace if necessary.

Heater Blower Replacement— Air-Conditioned Cars

This procedure is the same as for non air-conditioned cars.

Heater Core and Case Removal and Installation— Air-Conditioned Cars

Tempest, GTO, LeMans, and Grand Am

1. Drain the coolant.

2. Disconnect the water hoses at the heater core tubes to prevent spilling coolant during removal.

3. Remove the glove compartment.

4. Remove the cold air duct and heater outlet.

5. Remove the defroster duct attaching screw.

6. Remove the screws and nuts which retain the case to the dash. Remove the blower motor resistor to gain access to the upper retaining nut inside the evaporator case.

7. Move the core and case assembly rearward to free the attaching studs from the cowl and remove the core and case assembly.

8. Disconnect the temperature cable and vacuum hoses from the core and case assembly.

9. Remove the core and case assembly from the car.

10. Remove the heater core retaining screws and core.

11. Reverse the above steps for installation.

Firebird

1. Drain the coolant.

2. Remove the glove box and door.

3. Remove the cold air duct on the lower right-hand side.

4. Remove the left and center lower A/C ducts.

5. Raise the car and remove the rocker panel trim on the right side and remove the screws holding the forward trim brackets.

6. Remove the three lower fender bolts at rear of the fender.

7. Remove the four fender-to-skirt bolts at the rear of the wheel opening.

8. Remove the two fender skirt bolts near the blower motor area.

9. Pry the rear portion of the fender out at the bottom to gain access to the hose clamp on the water valve-to-core hose and disconnect the hose at the heater core.

10. Disconnect the water pump hose at the heater core.

11. Remove the two heater case retaining nuts under the hood at the dash.

12. Remove the two heater case retaining bolts inside the car.

13. Remove the console and tape player if equipped.

14. Disconnect the temperature cable at the heater case.

15. Remove the heater outlet duct.

16. Remove the lower defroster duct screw at the heater case.

17. Remove the right kick panel, and the heater core and case as an assembly.

18. Disconnect the vacuum hoses from the heater case and remove the core from the case.

19. Reverse the above steps for installation.

Ventura

1. Disconnect the battery and drain the coolant.

2. Disconnect the upper heater hose at the core pipe and remove the accessible heater core and case assembly attaching nuts.

3. Remove the right front fender skirt bolts and lower the skirt to gain access to the lower heater hose clamp. Loosen the clamp and disconnect the hose.

4. Remove the lower right-hand heater core and case assembly attaching nut.

5. Remove the glove compartment and door.

6. Remove the recirculation vacuum diaphragm at the right-hand kick panel.

7. Remove the heater outlet and cold air distributor duct.

8. Remove the heater case extension screws and separate the extension from the heater case on models through 1974.

9. Disconnect the heater cables and electrical connectors, and remove the case and core as an assembly.

10. Separate the core from the case.

11. Reverse the above steps for installation.

Astre

1. Disconnect the battery ground cable.

2. Disconnect the heater hoses at the core and plug them.

3. Remove the firewall selector stud nuts, the glove box, and door.

4. Disconnect the left-side flexible dash outlet hose from the center distributor duct.

5. Remove the right-side dash outlet and hose assembly.

6. Remove the steering column lower plastic retainer, insulation, and screws. Remove the column instrument panel stud nuts and let the column rest on the seat.

Caution Be extremely careful with the steering column. Never let it hang unsupported.

7. Remove the instrument panel bezel, ash tray, and tray retainer.

8. Take out the air conditioning

9. Disconnect the radio and antenna leads.
10. Remove the instrument cluster to panel screws, cover the column to prevent scratches, and let the cluster rest on the column. Detach the speedometer cable.
11. Push the air conditioning controls forward and let them rest on the floor.
12. Remove the center distributor duct screws at the selector duct. Remove the duct instrument panel upper retainer and remove the duct by sliding it to the left to clear the lower instrument panel to cluster tab, and then to the right.
13. Remove the defroster duct-to-selector duct screw. Remove the remaining selector duct-to-dash screws and pull the duct back far enough to allow the electrical and vacuum lines to be disconnected.
14. Disconnect the lines and the control cable and remove the selector duct assembly.
15. Pry off the temperature door bellcrank, being careful not to bend the arm or damage the selector case.
16. Remove the temperature door. Remove the backing plate and temperature door cable retainer screws.
17. Remove the heater core and backing plate as an assembly. Remove the core retaining straps and withdraw the core.
18. Reverse the removal procedure to install the core.

Sunbird

1. Have the air conditioning system purged of refrigerant.
2. Disconnect the negative battery cable.
3. Disconnect the inlet and outlet lines and the oil bleed line from

the VIR (receiver-dryer) assembly.
4. Remove the VIR to blower case strap screw, and remove the VIR unit. Cap all the open connections immediately.
5. Remove the blower and case assembly.
6. Remove and plug the heater hoses at the core tubes and then hang them out of the way.
7. Remove the evaporator to dash panel cover plate screws and remove the plate.
8. Remove (from inside the car), the floor outlet duct, the glove compartment assembly and the dash outlets on both sides. To remove the dash outlets, use a putty knife and pry them out.
9. Remove the eleven instrument panel pad screws and pry the pad off.
10. Remove the right side instrument panel to dash and kick pad screws, then loosen the left side instrument cluster to instrument panel screws.
11. Pull out on the right side of the instrument cluster to gain the necessary clearance to remove the right side instrument panel and lower duct.
12. Disconnect the vacuum hoses on the left side of the heater unit and tag them for later reinstallation.
13. Remove the modulator duct to heater unit screw, then pull the carpet and pad to the rear to make room for the heater unit removal.
14. Pull the heater unit toward you until the core tubes clear the firewall, then pull it to the right until there is enough clearance to disconnect the control cable.
15. After disconnecting the control cable, disconnect the wiring harness and remove the heater as-

sembly.
16. Remove the screws and separate the heater case, then remove the core to case screws and remove the core.
17. Installation is the reverse of the above procedure, but before assembly, add 3 oz. of refrigerant oil to the evaporator core.
18. When installing the refrigerant lines, coat all the O-rings with refrigerant oil.

SEAT BELTS

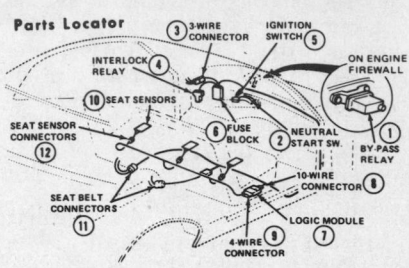

Seat belt/starter interlock component location
(© Pontiac Div., G.M. Corp)

Disabling the Interlock System

Since the requirement for the interlock system was dropped during the 1975 model year, those systems installed on cars built earlier may now be legally disabled. The seat belt warning light is still required.

1. Disconnect the negative battery cable.
2. Locate the interlock harness connector under the left side of the instrument panel on or near the fuse block.
3. Cut and tape the ends of the green wire on the body side of the connector.
4. Remove the buzzer from the fuse block or connector.

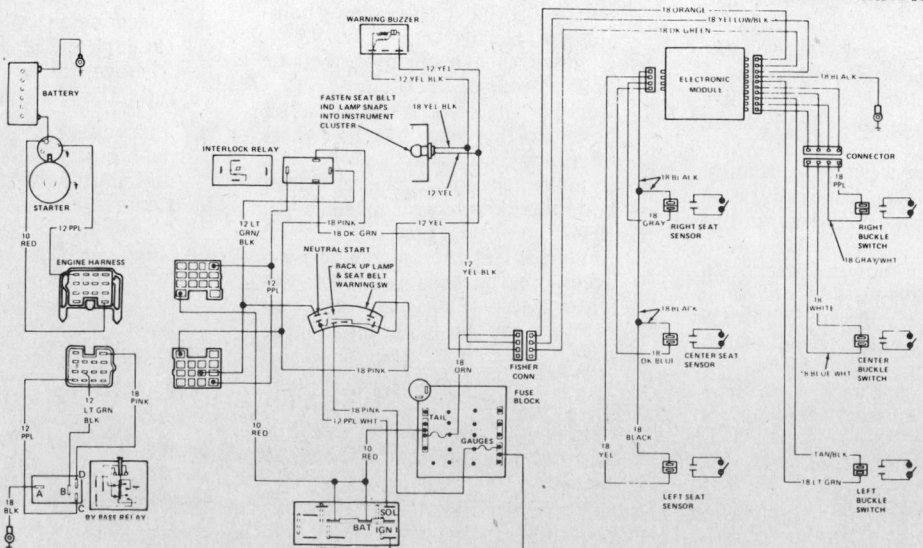

Ventura interlock system schematic, automatic transmission (© Pontiac Div., G.M. Corp)

Barracuda · Challenger · Dart · Valiant · Aspen · Volare

Automatic Transmission
In-car service C133, U369
Band adjustments C133
Draining, refilling, filter service ... C134
Neutral safety/backup light switch
Removal and Installation C133
Shift linkage adjustment C133

Brakes C141, U299
Master cylinder Removal and
Installation C141
Parking brake adjustment C141
Power brake booster Removal and
Installation C141

Charging System C115, U2
Alternator Removal and Installation ... C115
Regulator Removal and Installation ... C115

Clutch C130
Clutch linkage (height and free-play)
adjustment C130
Clutch Removal and Installation C130
Gearshift interlock adjustment C131

Cooling System C118, U367
Radiator Removal and Installation ... C118
Thermostat Removal and Installation ... C119
Water pump Removal and Installation ... C119

Emission Controls C119, U145
Air injection system C120
CAS C119
Catalytic Converter C121
Coolant control Idle enrichment
(CCIE) system C121
Evaporative control system C119
Electrically assisted choke C120
Exhaust gas recirculation system ... C120
Ignition retard solenoid C119
NOx control system C120
Orifice spark advance control
(OSAC) valve C120
Positive Crankcase Ventilation
(PCV) C119

Engine C121, U194
Special engine markings C122
CYLINDER HEAD Removal and Installation ... C125
Cylinder head bolt tightening sequences C126
ENGINE Removal and Installation ... C122
LUBRICATION C128
Oil pan Removal and Installation ... C128
Oil pump Removal and Installation ... C129

Rear main bearing oil seal
Removal and Installation C129
MANIFOLDS C122
6 cylinder combination manifold
Removal and Installation C122
V8 Intake manifold Removal and
Installation C123
V8 Exhaust manifold Removal and
Installation C123
Pistons and Connecting Rods C128
TIMING COVER, CHAIN AND CAMSHAFT ... C126
Camshaft Removal and Installation ... C127
Timing chain and cover Removal
and Installation C126
Timing chain cover seal replacement ... C127
VALVE SYSTEM C123
Rocker shaft Removal and Installation C123
Valve adjustment C124

Front Suspension C136, U292
Control arm Removal and Installation ... C138
Front height adjustment C140
Shock absorber Removal and
Installation C137
Torsion bar Removal and Installation ... C139
Upper and lower ball joints C137
Wheel bearing adjustment C140

Fuel System C117, U50
Carburetors C117
Fuel filter Removal and Installation ... C118
Fuel pump Removal and Installation ... C118
Idle speed and mixture adjustments ... C117
Idle speed solenoid adjustment ... C118

Heater C144
Heater assembly Removal and Installation
without A/C C144
Heater blower motor Removal and
Installation without A/C C145
Heater blower motor Removal
and Installation with A/C C145
Heater core Removal and Installation
with A/C C146
Heater core Removal and Installation
without A/C C145

Ignition System C115, U34
Contact point replacement and
adjustment C116
Distributor Removal and Installation ... C115
Firing order C107
Ignition timing C117

Instrument Panel C143, U350
Headlight switch Removal and
Installation C143

Manual Transmission C131, U231
Linkage adjustment C131
Transmission Removal and Installation ... C131

Jacking, Hoisting C136

Radio C144
Radio Removal and Installation C144

Rear Axle C134
Axle shaft, bearing, and
seal Removal and Installation C135

Rear Suspension C140
Shock absorber Removal and
Installation C140
Spring Removal and Installation ... C140

Seat Belts C147
Seat belt/starter interlock system ... C147

Specifications C107, U359
Capacities C110
Crankshaft and connecting rod C113
Engine identification and code C107
General engine C108
Piston ring C113
Piston clearance C113
Torque C112
Tune-up C109
Valve C111
Wheel alignment C114
Year Identification C106

Starting System C115, U2
Starter Removal and Installation ... C115

Steering C141, U328
Ignition switch and/or Lock cylinder
Removal and Installation C142
Power steering pump Removal and
Installation C141
Steering wheel Removal and
Installation C141
Tie-Rod end Removal and Installation ... C141
Turn signal hazard warning switch
Removal and Installation C142

U-Joints C134
Driveshaft Removal and Installation ... C134
U-joint overhaul C134

Windshield Wipers C143
Motor Removal and Installation C143

YEAR IDENTIFICATION

1970-72 Valiant and Duster

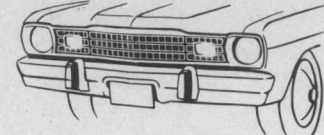

1973 Valiant and Duster

1974 Valiant and Duster

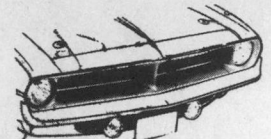

1970 Plymouth Cuda

1971 Cuda

1972 Cuda

1973 Cuda

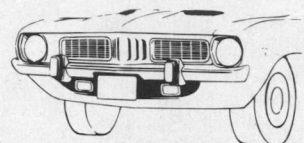

1974 Cuda

1970 Dart

1970-71 Challenger

1971 Demon

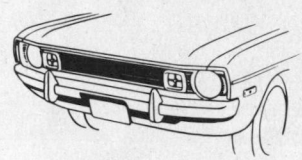

1972 Dart and Demon

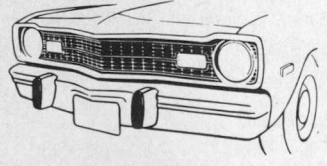

1973 Dart

1972 Challenger

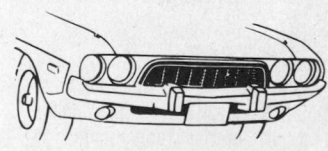

1973 Challenger

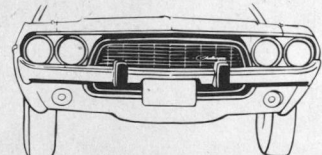

1974 Challenger

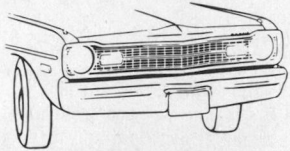

1974 Dart

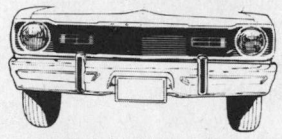

1975-76 Dart

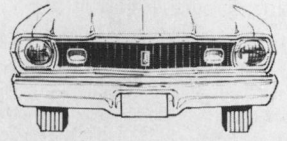

1975-76 Valiant

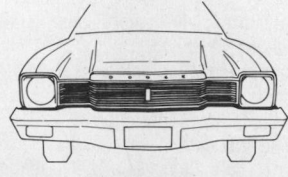

1976 Aspen

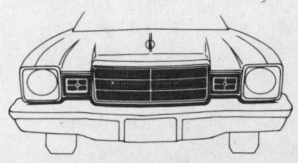

1976 Volare

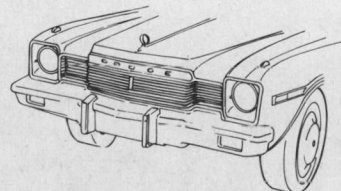

1977 Aspen SE

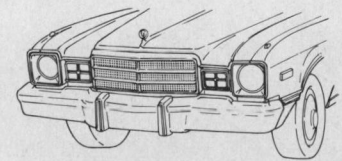

1977 Volare Premier

FIRING ORDER

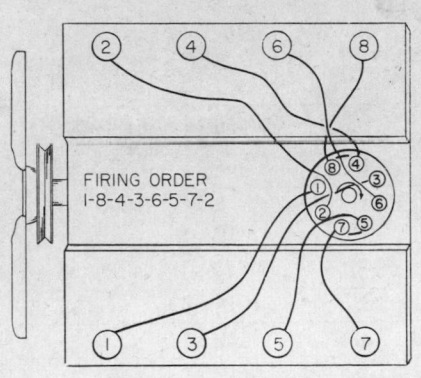

360 cu. in. and smaller V8

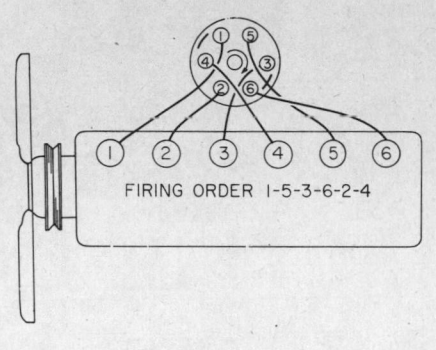

Six Cylinder

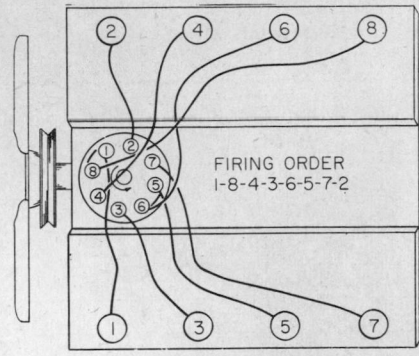

383 cu. in. and larger V8

ENGINE IDENTIFICATION

The engine that the factory installed in the car can be identified by the fifth digit of the Vehicle Identification Number, as explained under Engine Code. The engine itself can be identified by the engine serial number. The cubic inch displacement is given by either the second, third, and fourth, or the third, fourth, and fifth digits of the engine serial number, depending on the year and engine.

Six cylinder engines have their serial number stamped on the joint face of the block, just behind the ignition coil. V8s through 360 cu. in. have the number on the front of the block, just below the left cylinder head. 383 and larger V8s have the number on the oil pan rail, below the starter opening, at the left rear corner of the block. 360 cu. in. and smaller (small block) V8s can quickly be identified as having the distributor at the rear of the engine, while 383 and larger versions have it at the front.

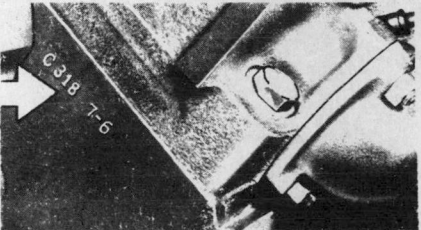

Engine code location—360 and smaller V8
(© Chrysler Corp)

ENGINE CODE

The engine code designation is the 5th digit of the vehicle identification number (V.I.N.). The V.I.N. is stamped on a plate located at the left side of the instrument panel visible through the windshield and located to the rear of the right engine mount on the oil pan rail on V8 engines. It is below the rear spark plug on sixes.

Displacement	Bbl	'70	'71	'72	'73	'74	'75	'76	'77
6-Cylinder Models									
198	1	B	B	B	B	B			
225	1	C	C	C	C	C	C	C	C
8-Cylinder Models									
318	2	G	G	G	G	G	G	G	G
340 HP	4	H	H	H	H				
340 Six Pack	3 x 2	H	H						
360	2							K	K
360 HP	4					L	L	L	L
383	2	L	L						
383	4	L							
383 HP	4	N							
426 Hemi	2 x 4	R							
426 Hemi	4		R						
440 HP	4	U							
440 Six Pack	3 x 2	V	V						

HP High Performance

GENERAL ENGINE SPECIFICATIONS

Year	Engine No. Cyl. Displacement (Cu. In.)	Carburetor Type	Horsepower @ rpm ■	Torque @ rpm (ft lbs) ■	Bore x Stroke (in.)	Compression Ratio	Oil Pressure @ 2000 rpm
'70	6-198	1 bbl	125 @ 4400	180 @ 2000	3.406 x 3.640	8.4:1	55
	6-225	1 bbl	145 @ 4000	215 @ 2400	3.406 x 4.125	8.4:1	55
	8-318	2 bbl	230 @ 4400	320 @ 2000	3.910 x 3.310	8.8:1	55
	8-340 HP	4 bbl	275 @ 5000	340 @ 3200	4.040 x 3.310	10.5:1	55
	8-340 Six Pack	3 x 2 bbl	290 @ 5000	340 @ 3200	4.040 x 3.310	10.3:1	55
	8-383	2 bbl	290 @ 4400	390 @ 2800	4.250 x 3.375	8.7:1	55
	8-383	4 bbl	330 @ 5000	425 @ 3200	4.250 x 3.375	9.5:1	55
	8-383 HP	4 bbl	335 @ 5200	425 @ 3400	4.250 x 3.375	10.5:1	55
	8-426 Hemi	2 x 4 bbl	425 @ 5000	490 @ 4000	4.250 x 3.750	10.2:1	55
	8-440 HP	4 bbl	375 @ 4600	480 @ 3200	4.320 x 3.750	9.7:1	55
	8-440 Six Pack	3 x 2 bbl	390 @ 4700	490 @ 3200	4.320 x 3.750	10.5:1	55
'71	6-198	1 bbl	125 @ 4400	180 @ 2000	3.406 x 3.640	8.4:1	55
	6-225	1 bbl	145 @ 4000	215 @ 2400	3.406 x 4.125	8.4:1	55
	8-318	2 bbl	230 @ 4400	320 @ 2000	3.910 x 3.310	8.6:1	55
	8-340 HP	4 bbl	275 @ 5000	340 @ 3200	4.040 x 3.310	10.3:1	55
	8-340 Six Pack	3 x 2 bbl	290 @ 5000	340 @ 3200	4.040 x 3.310	10.3:1	55
	8-383	2 bbl	275 @ 4400	375 @ 2800	4.250 x 3.375	8.5:1	55
	8-383 HP	4 bbl	300 @ 4800	410 @ 3400	4.250 x 3.375	8.5:1	55
	8-426 Hemi	4 bbl	425 @ 5000	490 @ 4000	4.250 x 3.750	10.2:1	55
	8-440 Six Pack	3 x 2 bbl	385 @ 4700	490 @ 3200	4.320 x 3.750	10.3:1	55
'72	6-198	1 bbl	100 @ 4400	160 @ 2400	3.406 x 3.640	8.4:1	55
	6-198 Calif.	1 bbl	94 @ 4400	158 @ 2400	3.406 x 3.640	8.4:1	55
	6-225	1 bbl	110 @ 4000	185 @ 2000	3.406 x 4.125	8.4:1	55
	6-225 Calif.	1 bbl	97 @ 4000	180 @ 2000	3.406 x 4.125	8.4:1	55
	8-318	2 bbl	150 @ 4000	260 @ 1600	3.910 x 3.310	8.6:1	55
	8-340 HP	4 bbl	240 @ 4800	290 @ 3600	4.040 x 3.310	8.5:1	55
'73	6-198	1 bbl	95 @ 4000	155 @ 1600	3.406 x 3.640	8.4:1	55
	6-225	1 bbl	105 @ 4000	185 @ 1600	3.406 x 4.125	8.4:1	55
	8-318	2 bbl	150 @ 3600	265 @ 2000	3.910 x 3.310	8.6:1	55
	8-340HP	4 bbl	240 @ 4800	295 @ 3600	4.040 x 3.310	8.5:1	55
'74	6-198	1 bbl	95 @ 4000	145 @ 2000	3.406 x 3.640	8.4:1	55
	6-225	1 bbl	105 @ 3600	180 @ 1600	3.406 x 4.125	8.4:1	55
	8-318	2 bbl	150 @ 4000	255 @ 2200	3.910 x 3.310	8.6:1	55
	8-360HP	4 bbl	245 @ 4800	320 @ 3600	4.000 x 3.580	8.4:1	55
'75	6-225	1 bbl	95 @ 3600	170 @ 1600	3.406 x 4.125	8.4:1	55
	6-225 Calif.	1 bbl	90 @ 3600	165 @ 1600	3.406 x 4.125	8.4:1	55
	8-318	2 bbl	145 @ 4000	255 @ 1600	3.910 x 3.310	8.5:1	55
	8-318 Calif.	2 bbl	140 @ 3600	255 @ 1600	3.910 x 3.310	8.5:1	55
	8-360 HP	4 bbl	230 @ 4400	300 @ 3600	4.000 x 3.580	8.4:1	55
	8-360 HP Calif.	4 bbl	190 @ 4000	270 @ 3200	4.000 x 3.580	8.4:1	55
'76-'77	6-225	1 bbl	100 @ 3600	170 @ 1600	3.406 x 4.125	8.4:1	55
	6-225 Calif.	1 bbl	90 @ 3600	165 @ 1600	3.406 x 4.125	8.4:1	55
	8-318	2 bbl	150 @ 4000	255 @ 1600	3.910 x 3.310	8.5:1	55
	8-318 Calif.	2 bbl	140 @ 3600	250 @ 2000	3.910 x 3.310	8.5:1	55
	8-360	2 bbl	170 @ 4000	280 @ 2400	4.000 x 3.580	8.4:1	55
	8-360 HP	4 bbl	220 @ 4000	280 @ 3200	4.000 x 3.580	8.4:1	55

■ Beginning 1972, horsepower and torque are SAE net figures. They are measured at the rear of the transmission with all accessories installed and operating. Since the figures vary when a given engine is installed in different models, some figures are representative rather than exact.

HP High Performance

Valiant, Dart, Aspen, Volare TUNE-UP SPECIFICATIONS

When analyzing compression test results, look for uniformity among cylinders rather than specific pressures.

Year	ENGINE No. Cyl Displacement (cu in.)	hp	SPARK PLUGS Orig. Type	Gap (in.)	DISTRIBUTOR Point Dwell (deg)	Point Gap (in.)	IGNITION TIMING (deg) ▲ Man Trans ●	Auto Trans	VALVES Intake Opens ■ (deg)	Fuel Pump Pressure (psi)	IDLE SPEED (rpm) ▲ Man Trans ●	Auto Trans
'70	6-198	125	N-14Y	.035	41-46	.020	2½B	TDC	10	3½-5	750	750①
	6-225	145	N-14Y	.035	41-56	.020	TDC	TDC	10	3½-5	700	650①
	8-318	230	N-14Y	.035	30-34	.017	TDC	TDC	10	5-7	750	700
	8-340 HP	275	N-9Y	.035	27-32③	.017	5B	5B	22	5-7	900	900
'71	6-198	125	N-14Y	.035	41-46	.020	2½B	2½B	16	3½-5	800	800
	6-225	145	N-14Y	.035	41-46	.020	TDC(2½B)	TDC(2½B)	16	3½-5	750	750
	8-318	230	N-14Y	.035	30-34	.017	TDC	TDC	10	5-7	750	700
	8-340 HP	275	N-9Y	.035	27-32③	.017	5B	5B	22	5-7	900	900
'72	6-198	100	N-14Y	.035	41-46	.020	2½B	2½B	16	2½-5	800(700)	800(700)
	6-225	110	N-14Y	.035	41-46	.020	TDC(2½B)	TDC(2½B)	16	2½-5	750(700)	750(700)
	8-318	150	N-13Y	.035	30-34	.017	TDC	TDC	10	5-7	750	750(700)
	8-340 HP	240	N-9Y	.035	30-34	.017	TDC(2½B)	2½B	22	5-7	900(850)	750
'73	6-198	95	N-14Y	.035	Electronic		2½B	2½B	16	4-5½	800	750
	6-225	105	N-14Y	.035	Electronic		TDC	TDC	16	4-5½	750	750
	8-318	150	N-13Y	.035	Electronic		2½B	TDC	10	6-7½	750	700
	8-360 HP	245	N-9Y	.035	Electronic		5B	2½B	22	6-7½	850	850
'74	6-198	95	N-14Y	.035	Electronic		2½B	2½B	16	3½-5	800	750
	6-225	105	N-14Y	.035	Electronic		TDC	TDC	16	5-7	800	750
	8-318	150	N-13Y	.035	Electronic		TDC	TDC	10	5-7	750	750
	8-360 HP	245	N-12Y	.035	Electronic		5B(2½B)	5B	22	5-7	850	850
'75	6-225	95	RL-13Y	.035	Electronic		TDC	TDC	16	3½-5	800	750
	8-318	145	N-13Y	.035	Electronic		2B	2B	10	5-7	750	750
	8-360 HP	230	N-12Y	.035	Electronic		—	2B	22	5-7	—	750
'76	6-225	100	RBL-13Y	.035	Electronic		6B(4B)	2B	16	3½-5	750(800)	750
	6-225④	100	RBL-13Y	.035	Electronic		12B	12B	16	3½-5	750(800)	750
	8-318	150	RN-12Y	.035	Electronic		2B	2B(TDC)	10	5-7	750	750
	8-318⑤	150	RN-12Y	.035	Electronic		—	2A	10	5-7	—	900
	8-360	170	RN-12Y	.035	Electronic		—	2B	18	5-7	—	850
	8-360 HP	230	RN-12Y	.035	Electronic		—	2B	22	5-7	—	850
'77	6-225	All	RBL-15Y (RBL-13Y)	.035	Electronic		12B(8B)	12B(8B)	16	4-5½	700(750)	700(750)
	8-318	All	RN-12Y	.035	Electronic		8B	8B	10	5¾-7¼	700	700(850)
	8-360	All	RN-12Y	.035	Electronic		—	10B	18	5¾-7¼	—	700

MECHANICAL VALVE LIFTER CLEARANCE

Engine	Intake (Hot) In.	Exhaust (Hot) In.
All six cylinder	.010	.020

▲ See text for procedure
■ All figures Before Top Dead Center
● Figure in parentheses indicates California engine

① A/C on
② Dart only
③ Adjust both sets of points to this figure. With both sets connected, total reading should be 37-42 degrees.
④ in Feather Duster/Dart Lite
⑤ with air pump, no converter
A After Top Dead Center
B Before Top Dead Center
TDC Top Dead Center
HP High Performance

NOTE: The underhood specifications sticker often reflects tune-up specification changes made in production. Sticker figures must be used if they disagree with those in this chart.

Barracuda, Challenger TUNE-UP SPECIFICATIONS

When analyzing compression test results, look for uniformity among cylinders rather than specific pressures.

ENGINE No. Cyl Displacement Year (cu in.)	hp	SPARK PLUGS Orig. Type	Gap (in.)	DISTRIBUTOR Point Dwell (deg)	Point Gap (in.)	IGNITION TIMING (deg) ▲ Man Trans	Auto Trans	VALVES Intake Opens ■ (deg)	Fuel Pump Pressure (psi)	IDLE SPEED (rpm) ▲ Man Trans	Auto Trans
'70 6-225	145	N-14Y	.035	44	.020	TDC	TDC	10	3½-5	700	650
8-318	230	N-14Y	.035	32	.017	TDC	TDC	10	5-7	750	700
8-340 HP	275	N-9Y	.035	30②	.017	5B	5B	22	5-7	900	900
8-340 Six Pack	290	N-9Y	.035	29½②③	.017	2½B	2½B	22	5-7	950	1000
8-383	290	J-14Y	.035	30½	.019	TDC	2½B	18	3½-5	750	650
8-383	330	J-11Y	.035	30½	.019	TDC	2½B	18	3½-5	750	700
8-383 HP	335	J-11Y	.035	30½	.019	TDC	2½B	21	3½-5	750	750
8-426 Hemi	425	N-10Y	.035	30②	.017	TDC	2½B	36	7-8½	900	900
8-440 HP	375	J-11Y	.035	30½	.019	TDC	2½B	21	3½-5	900	800
8-440 Six Pack	390	J-11Y	.035	30②	.017	5B	5B	21	6-7½	900	900
'71 6-198	125	N-14Y	.035	44	.020	2½B	2½B	16	3½-5	800	800
6-225	145	N-14Y	.035	44	.020	TDC(2½B)	TDC(2½B)	16	3½-5	750	750
8-318	230	N-14Y	.035	32	.017	TDC	TDC	10	5-7	750	700
8-340 HP	275	N-9Y	.035	32②	.017	5B	5B	22	5-7	900	900
8-340 Six Pack	290	N-9Y	.035	29½②③	.017	2½B	2½B	22	5-7	950	1000
8-383	275	J-14Y	.035	30½	.019	TDC	2½B	18	3½-5	750	700
8-383	300	J-11Y	.035	30½	.019	TDC	2½B	21	3½-5	900	800
8-426 Hemi	425	N-10Y	.035	30	.017	TDC	2½B	36	7-8½	900	900
8-440 Six Pack	385	J-11Y	.035	30	.017	5B	5B	21	6-7½	950	950
'72 6-225	110	N-14Y	.035	44	.020	TDC(2½B)	TDC(2½B)	16	2½-5	750(700)	750(700)
8-318	150	N-13Y	.035	32	.017	TDC	TDC	10	5-7	750	750(700)
8-340 HP	240	N-9Y	.035	Electronic		TDC(2½B)	2½B	22	5-7	900(850)	750
'73 8-318	150	N-13Y	.035	Electronic		2½B	TDC	10	6-7½	750	700
8-340 HP	240	N-9Y	.035	Electronic		5B	2½B	22	6-7½	850	850
'74 8-318	150	N-13Y	.035	Electronic		TDC	TDC	10	5-7	750	750
8-360 HP	245	N-12Y	.035	Electronic		5B(2½B)	5B	22	5-7	850	850

▲ See text for procedure
● Figure in parentheses indicates California engine
■ All figures Before Top Dead Center
① Not used
② Adjust both sets of points to this figure. With both sets connected, the total reading should be 40 degrees.
③ 32 degrees with automatic
A After Top Dead Center
B Before Top Dead Center
TDC Top Dead Center
HP High performance

MECHANICAL VALVE LIFTER CLEARANCE

Engine	Intake (Hot) In.	Exhaust (Hot) In.
All 6 cylinder	.010	.020

NOTE: The underhood specifications sticker often reflects tune-up specification changes made in production. Sticker figures must be used if they disagree with those in this chart.

CAPACITIES

Year	Engine No. Cyl. Displacement (Cu. In.)	Engine Crankcase Add 1 Qt For New Filter	TRANSMISSION Pts To Refill After Draining Manual 3-Speed	4-Speed	Automatic	Drive Axle (pts)	Gasoline Tank (gals)	COOLING SYSTEM (qts) With Heater	With A/C
'70 6-198		4	6.5①	—	17	2	18	13	14
6-225		4	6.5①	—	17	2	18	13	14
8-318		4	4.75	7.5	16	4	18	16	17

CAPACITIES

Year	Engine No. Cyl. Displacement (Cu. In.)	Engine Crankcase Add 1 Qt For New Filter	TRANSMISSION Pts To Refill After Draining Manual 3-Speed	Manual 4-Speed	Automatic	Drive Axle (pts)	Gasoline Tank (gals)	COOLING SYSTEM (qts) With Heater	With A/C
'70	8-340	4	4.75	7	16	4	18	15.5	15.5
	8-383	4	4.75	7.5	19③	4	18	14.5	15
	8-426 Hemi	6	—	7.5	17	5.5	18	17	—
	8-440	6	—	7.5	19	5.5	18	17	—
'71	6-198	4	6.5①	—	17	2⑥	17⑦	13	14
	6-225	4	6.5①	—	17	2⑥	17⑦	13	14
	8-318	4	4.75	—	17	4.5	17⑦	16	17.5
	8-340	4	4.75	7	16.3	4.5	17⑦	15.5	15.5
	8-383	4	4.75	7.5	19③	4.5	18	14.5	15
	8-426 Hemi	6	—	7.5	16.3	5.5	18	17	—
	8-440 Six Pack	6	—	7.5	19	5.5	18	15.5	17
'72	6-198	4	6.5	—	17	2	16	13	14
	6-225	4	6.5①	—	17	2	16⑧	13	14
	8-318	4	4.75	—	17	4.5	16⑧	16	17
	8-340 HP	4	4.75	7②	16.3	4.5	16⑧	15	15
'73	6-198	4	6.5	—	17	2	16	13	13
	6-225	4	6.5	—	17	2	16	13	14
	8-318	4	4.75	—	17	4.5	16⑧	16	17.5
	8-340 HP	4	4.75	7②	16.3	4.5	16⑧	15.5⑨	15.5
'74	6-198	4	6.5	—	17	2	16⑦	13	—
	6-225	4	4.75	—	17	2	16⑦	13	14.0
	8-318	4	4.75	7.0②	17	4.5	16⑦	16	17.5
	8-360 HP	4	4.75	7.0②	16.5	4.5	16⑦	16	16.0
'75	6-225	4	3.5	7.0	17	2	16	13	14
	8-318	4	4.75	7.0	17	4.5	16	16	17.5
	8-360 HP	5	—	—	16.5	4.5	16	16	16
'76-'77	6-225	4	3.5	7.0	17	2	16/18④	13	17.5
	8-318	4	4.75	7.0	17	4.5	16/18④	16	17.5
	8-360	4	—	—	17	4.5	18	16	16
	8-360 HP	5	—	—	16.5	4.5	16	16	16

① Barracuda, Challenger—4.75 pts
② Barracuda, Challenger—7.5 pts
③ Hi-performance—16 pts
④ Valiant, Dart/Aspen, Volare
⑤ Not used
⑥ Barracuda, Challenger—4.5 pts
⑦ Barracuda, Challenger—18 gals
⑧ Barracuda—16.5 gals, Challenger—18 gals
⑨ Barracuda, Challenger—15 qts
— Not applicable

VALVE SPECIFICATIONS

Year	Engine No. Cyl. Displacement (cu in.)	Seat Angle (deg)	Face Angle (deg)	Spring Test Pressure (lbs @ in.)	Spring Installed Height (in.)	STEM TO GUIDE Clearance (in.) Intake	Exhaust	STEM Diameter (in.) Intake	Exhaust
'70	6-198	45	①	144 @ 1.31	1 11/16	.0010-.0030	.0020-.0040	.3725	.3715
	6-225	45	①	144 @ 1.31	1 11/16	.0010-.0030	.0020-.0040	.3725	.3715
	8-318	45	①	177 @ 1.31	1 11/16	.0010-.0030	.0020-.0040	.3725	.3715
	8-340	45	①	242 @ 1.22	1 11/16	.0015-.0035	.0025-.0045	.3720	.3710
	8-383 2 bbl	45	45	200 @ 1.44	1 7/8	.0010-.0030	.0020-.0040	.3727	.3717

VALVE SPECIFICATIONS

Year	Engine No. Cyl. Displacement (cu in.)	Seat Angle (deg)	Face Angle (deg)	Spring Test Pressure (lbs @ in.)	Spring Installed Height (in.)	STEM TO GUIDE Clearance (in.)		STEM Diameter (in.)	
						Intake	Exhaust	Intake	Exhaust
'70	8-383 4 bbl	45	45	246 @ 1.72	1 7/8	.0015-.0032	.0025-.0042	.3722	.3712
	8-426	45	45	310 @ 1.38	1 7/8	.0020-.0040	.0030-.0050	.3090	.3080
	8-440	45	45	310 @ 1.38	1 7/8	.0015-.0032	.0025-.0042	.3725	.3715
'71	6-198	45	①	144 @ 1.31	1 11/16	.0010-.0030	.0020-.0040	.3725	.3715
	6-225	45	①	144 @ 1.31	1 11/16	.0010-.0030	.0020-.0040	.3725	.3715
	8-318	45	①	177 @ 1.31	1 11/16	.0010-.0030	.0020-.0040	.3725	.3715
	8-340	45	①	238 @ 1.31	1 11/16	.0015-.0035	.0025-.0045	.3720	.3710
	8-383 2 bbl	45	45	200 @ 1.44	1 7/8	.0010-.0030	.0020-.0040	.3727	.3717
	8-383 4 bbl	45	45	246 @ 1.72	1 7/8	.0015-.0032	.0025-.0042	.3722	.3712
	8-426	45	45	310 @ 1.38	1 7/8	.0020-.0040	.0030-.0050	3090	.3080
	8-440	45	45	200 @ 1.44	1 7/8	.0010-.0030	.0020-.0040	.3727	.3717
'72	6-198	45	①	144 @ 1.31	1 11/16	.0010-.0030	.0020-.0040	.3725	.3715
	6-225	45	①	144 @ 1.31	1 11/16	.0010-.0030	.0020-.0040	.3725	.3715
	8-318	45	①	177 @ 1.31	1 11/16	.0010-.0030	.0020-.0040	.3725	.3715
	8-340 HP	45	①	208 @ 1.31	1 11/16	.0015-.0035	.0025-.0045	.3720	.3710
'73	6-198	45	①	143 @ 1.31	1 21/32	.0010-.0030	.0020-.0040	.3725	.3715
	6-225	45	①	143 @ 1.31	1 21/32	.0010-.0030	.0020-.0040	.3725	.3715
	8-318	45	①	177 @ 1.31	1 21/32	.0010-.0030	.0020-.0040	.3725	.3715
	8-340 HP	45	①	208 @ 1.31	1 21/32	.0015-.0035	.0025-.0045	.3720	.3710
'74	6-198	45	①	143 @ 1.31	1 21/32	.0010-.0030	.0020-.0040	.3725	.3715
	6-225	45	①	143 @ 1.31	1 21/32	.0010-.0030	.0020-.0040	.3725	.3715
	8-318	45	①	177 @ 1.31	1 21/32	.0010-.0030	.0020-.0040	.3725	.3715
	8-360 HP	45	①	208 @ 1.31	1 21/32	.0010-.0030	.0025-.0045	.3725	.3715
'75	6-225	45	45	143 @ 1.31	1 21/32	.0010-.0030	.0020-.0040	.3725	.3715
	8-318	45	①	177 @ 1.31	1 21/32	.0010-.0030	.0020-.0040	.3725	.3715
	8-360 HP	45	①	208 @ 1.31	1 21/32	.0010-.0030	.0020-.0040	.3725	.3715
'76-'77	6-225	45	45	143 @ 1.31	1 21/32	.0010-.0030	.0020-.0040	.3725	.3715
	8-318	45	①	177 @ 1.31	1 21/32	.0010-.0030	.0020-.0040	.3725	.3715
	8-360	45	①	182 @ 1.31	1 21/32	.0010-.0030	.0020-.0040	.3725	.3715
	8-360 HP	45	①	238 @ 1.22	1 11/16	.0020-.0040	.0030-.0050	.3720	.3710

① Intake 45°, Exhaust 43°
HP High Performance

TORQUE SPECIFICATIONS
All readings in ft lbs

Year	Engine No. Cyl. Displacement (cu in.)	Cylinder Head Bolts	Rod Bearing Bolts	Main Bearing Bolts	Crankshaft Pulley Bolt	Flywheel to Crankshaft Bolts	MANIFOLD Intake	Exhaust
'70-'77	6-All	70	45	85	Press fit	55	10①	10
'70-'73	8-318, 340	95	45	85	135	65	40	30
'74-'77	8-318, 360	95	45	85	100	55	35	15/20⑤
'70-'71	8-383, 440	70	45	85	135	55	40	30
'70-'71	8-426 Hemi	75	75	100③	135	70	④	35

① Intake to exhaust manifold bolts—20 ft. lbs., studs—30 ft. lbs.
② Not used
③ Cross bolt mains—45 ft. lbs.
④ Torque the four center bolts on either side to 6 ft. lbs., all others to 4 ft. lbs.
⑤ Nuts/screws

CRANKSHAFT AND CONNECTING ROD SPECIFICATIONS

All measurements are given in inches

Year	Engine No. Cyl. Displacement (cu in.)	CRANKSHAFT Main Brg. Journal Dia	Main Brg. Oil Clearance	Shaft End-Play	Thrust on No.	CONNECTING ROD Journal Diameter	Oil Clearance	Side Clearance*
'70-'77	6-198, 225	2.7495-2.7505	.0005-.0015	.002-.007	3	2.1865-2.1875	.0005-.0015	.006-.012
'70-'74	8-318, 340	2.4995-2.5005	.0005-.0015	.002-.007	3	2.124-2.125	.0005-.0020	.006-.014
'70-'71	8-383	2.6245-2.6255	.0005-.0015	.002-.007	3	2.3740-2.3750	.0005-.0015	.009-.017
'70-'71	8-440	2.7495-2.7505	.0005-.0015	.002-.007	3	2.3740-2.3750	.0010-.0020	.009-.017
'70	8-426 Hemi	2.7495-2.7505	.0015-.0025	.002-.007	3	2.374-2.375	.0015-.0025	.009-.017
'71	8-426 Hemi	2.7490-2.7500	.0015-.0030	.002-.007	3	2.3738-2.3745	.0015-.0025	.013-.017
'75-'77	8-318	2.4495-2.5005	.0005-.0015	.002-.007	3	2.124-2.125	.0005-.0025	.006-.014
'74-'77	8-360	2.8095-2.8105	.0005-.0020	.002-.007	3	2.124-2.125	.0005-.0020	.006-.014

*Total for two rods

RING GAP

All measurements are given in inches

Year	Engine No. Cyl. Displacement (cu. in.)	Top Compression	Bottom Compression		Year	Engine No. Cyl. Displacement (cu. in.)	Oil Control
'70-'72	6-198, 225 8-318, 340	.010-.020	.010-.020		'70-'77	All	.015-.055
'70-'71	8-383, 440	.013-.023	.013-.023				
'70	8-426	.013-.023	.013-.023				
'71	8-426	.013-.025	.013-.025				
'73	All engines except 8-340	.010-.020	.010-.020				
'73	8-340	.013-.023	.013-.023				
'74-'77	6-198, 225 8-318, 360	.010-.020	.010-.020				

RING SIDE CLEARANCE

All measurements are given in inches

Year	Engine No. Cyl. Displacement (cu. in.)	Top Compression	Bottom Compression		Year	Engine No. Cyl. Displacement (cu. in.)	Oil Control
'70-'77	All engines	.0015-.0030	.0015-.0030		'70-'77	6-198, 225, 8-318, 340, 360, 426	.0002-.0050
					'70-'71	8-383, 440	.0000-.0050

PISTON CLEARANCE

All measurements are given in inches

Year	Engine No. Cyl. Displacement (cu. in.)	Piston-to-Bore Clearance (in.)*		Year	Engine No. Cyl. Displacement (cu. in.)	Piston-to-Bore Clearance (in.)*
'70-'74	6-198	0.0005-0.0015		'70-'71	8-383	0.0003-0.0013
'70-'77	6-225	0.0005-0.0015		'70-'71	8-426	0.0025-0.0035
'70-'77	8-318	0.0005-0.0015		'70-'71	8-440	0.0003-0.0013
'73	8-340	0.0005-0.0015		'74-'77	8-360	0.0005-0.0015

* At top of skirt

WHEEL ALIGNMENT SPECIFICATIONS

Year	Model	Caster Range (deg)	Caster Pref Setting (deg)	Camber Range (deg)	Camber Pref Setting (deg)	Toe-in (in.)	Steering Axis Inclin. (deg.)	Wheel Pivot Ratio (deg) Inner Wheel	Wheel Pivot Ratio (deg) Outer Wheel
'70	Valiant Manual	1/2N ± 1/2	1/2N	①	②	1/8 ± 1/32	7 1/2	20	17.5
	Valiant Power	3/4P ± 1/2	3/4P	①	②	1/8 ± 1/32	7 1/2	20	17.5
	Dart Manual	0 to 1N	1/2N	①	②	1/8 ± 1/32	7 1/2	20	17.6
	Dart Power	1/4P to 1 1/4P	3/4P	①	②	1/8 ± 1/32	7 1/2	20	17.6
	Barracuda Manual	1 5/16N to 15/16N	1N	①	②	3/32 to 5/32	7 1/2	20	17.5
	Barracuda Power	15/16P to 3/8N	1/16N	①	②	3/32 to 5/32	7 1/2	20	17.5
	Challenger Manual	1 5/16N to 15/16N	1N	①	②	3/32 to 5/32	7 1/2	20	17.8
	Challenger Power	15/16P to 3/8N	1/16N	①	②	3/32 to 5/32	7 1/2	20	17.8
'71-'72	Manual	1N to 0	1/2N	①	②	3/8 ± 5/32	7 1/2	20	17.5
	Power	1/4P to 1 1/4P	3/4P	①	②	3/8 ± 5/32	7 1/2	20	17.5
'73	Valiant, Dart, Barracuda, Challenger								
	Manual	0 to 1N	1/2N	③	④	3/32 to 5/32	7 1/2	20	17.5
	Power	1/4P to 1 1/4P	3/4P	③	④	3/32 to 5/32	7 1/2	20	17.5
'74-'77	Valiant, Dart, Barracuda, Challenger								
	Manual	1 3/4N to 1/2P	1/2N	⑦	⑧	1/16 to 1/4	7 1/2	20	18.5
	Power	1/2N to 1 3/4P	3/4P	⑦	⑧	1/16 to 1/4	7 1/2	20	18.5
'76-'77	Aspen, Volare	1 1/2P to 3 3/4P	2 1/2P	⑦	④	1/16 to 1/4	8	20	18

① Left wheel—1/2P ± 1/4; Right wheel—1/4P ± 1/4
② Left wheel—1/2P; Right wheel—1/4P
③ Left wheel—1/4P to 3/4P; Right wheel—0 to 1/2P
④ Left wheel—1/2P; Right wheel—1/4P
⑤ Not used
⑥ Not used
⑦ Left wheel—0 to 1P; Right wheel—1/4N to 3/4P
⑧ Left wheel—1/2P; Right wheel—1/4P
N Negative P Positive

FRONT END HEIGHT

Year	Model	Front End Height
'70	M.S.—Valiant, Dart	2 1/8 ± 1/8
	P.S.—Valiant, Dart	2 1/8 ± 1/8
	M.S.—Barracuda, Challenger	1 3/16 ± 1/8
	P.S.—Barracuda, Challenger	1 3/16 ± 1/8
'71-'72	All M.S.	②
	All P.S.	②
'73	All	③

Year	Model	Front End Height
'74	Dart, Valiant,	1 7/8 ± 1/8
	Barracuda, Challenger	1 1/8 ± 1/8
'75-'77	Valiant, Dart	10 15/16 ± 1/8
'76-'77	Aspen, Volare	10 1/4 ± 1/8

① Not used
② Dart, Valiant 4DR—2 1/8 ± 1/8
Dart, Valiant 2DR—1 5/8 ± 1/8
Barracuda, Challenger—1 ± 1/8
③ Dart, Valiant 4DR—2 1/8 ± 1/8
Dart, Valiant 2DR—1 7/8 ± 1/8
Barracuda, Challenger—1 1/8 ± 1/8
M.S. Manual Steering
P.S. Power Steering

CHARGING SYSTEM

Caution Because alternator design is unique, special care must be taken when servicing the charging system.

1. Battery polarity should be checked before any connections, such as jumper cables or battery charger leads, are made. Reversed battery connections will damage the diodes. It is recommended that the battery cables be disconnected before connecting a battery charger.
2. The battery must *never* be disconnected while the alternator is running because the regulator will be damaged.
3. Always disconnect the battery ground lead before replacing the alternator.
4. Do not attempt to polarize an alternator.
5. Do not short across or ground any alternator terminals.
6. Always disconnect the battery ground lead before removing the alternator output cable, whether the engine is running or not.
7. If electric arc welding has to be done on the car, first disconnect the battery and alternator cables. Never start the car with the welding unit attached.

NOTE: See Unit Repair Section for charging system troubleshooting and repairs.

Alternator Removal and Installation

1. Disconnect battery ground cable.
2. Disconnect BAT and FLD leads from alternator. Disconnect the ground wire.
3. Remove alternator by removing two mounting bolts and belt tensioner bracket bolt.
4. To reinstall, reverse above. Tighten the belt so that it can be depressed about ½ in. by moderate thumb pressure in the center of the longest span between pulleys. Some alternator brackets have a square hole into which

you can insert a ½ in. square socket drive to tension the belt.
NOTE: Never attempt to polarize an alternator, nor short the regulator.

Regulator Removal and Installation

All models have a solid-state (silicon transistor) voltage regulator which is not adjustable. The regulator is in the engine compartment and clearly labeled.

1. Release the spring clips and pull off the regulator wiring plug.
2. Unbolt and remove the regulator.
3. Installation is the reverse of removal. Be sure that the spring clips engage the wiring plug and that the unit has a good ground.

STARTING SYSTEM

All models are equipped with either a reduction-gear starter, with a 3.5:1 or 2:1 reduction gear set, or a direct-drive starter. Both types have solenoids which are mounted on the starter assembly.

See the Unit Repair Section for starting system troubleshooting and repair.

Starter Removal and Installation

1. Disconnect the ground cable at the battery.
2. Remove the cable from the starter.
3. Disconnect the solenoid leads at their solenoid terminals.
4. Remove the starter securing bolts and withdraw the starter from the engine flywheel housing. On some models with automatic transmissions, the oil cooler tube bracket will interfere with starter removal. In this case, remove the starter securing

bolts, slide the cooler tube bracket off the stud, and then withdraw the starter.
5. Installation is the reverse of the above. Be sure that the starter and flywheel housing mating surfaces are free of dirt and oil. When tightening the bolt and nut, hold the starter away from the engine to ensure proper alignment.

IGNITION SYSTEM

The ignition system used on early models is of conventional design using primary and secondary ignition circuits. A separate ballast resistor unit is wired in the primary circuit between the battery and the coil. This resistor controls the current flow in the primary circuit, according to engine speed, reducing the current flow at low engine speeds and increasing the current flow at higher engine speeds. The ballast resistor is bypassed during starter operation to allow full battery voltage to flow to the ignition primary circuit.

Some 1971 and 1972 models are equipped with the Chrysler Electronic Ignition System. Beginning 1973, electronic ignition is standard on all models. For further details, refer to the section on electronic ignition systems in the "Unit Repair Section."

NOTE: Dwell/tachometer hookup with electronic ignition is the same as with conventional point-type systems. One tachometer lead connects to the negative primary coil terminal and the other to ground. Some meters will not work at all with this system.

Distributor Removal

1. Disconnect the vacuum advance line at the distributor.

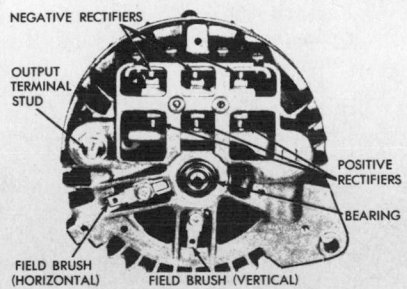

Rear view of the alternator
(© Chrysler Corp)

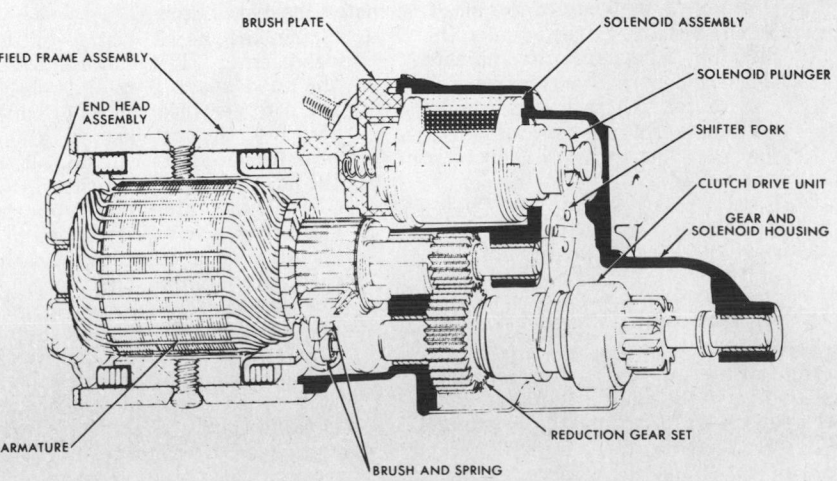

Starter motor details (© Chrysler Corp.)

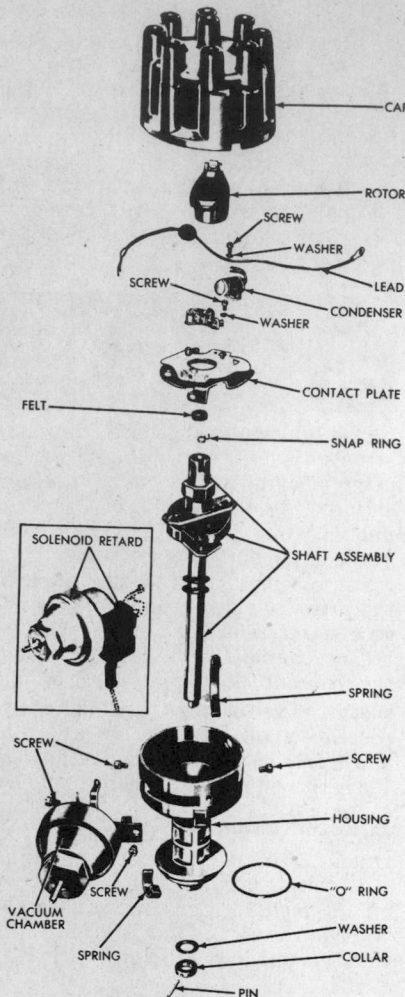

Chrysler distributor components—conventional ignition (© Chrysler Corp)

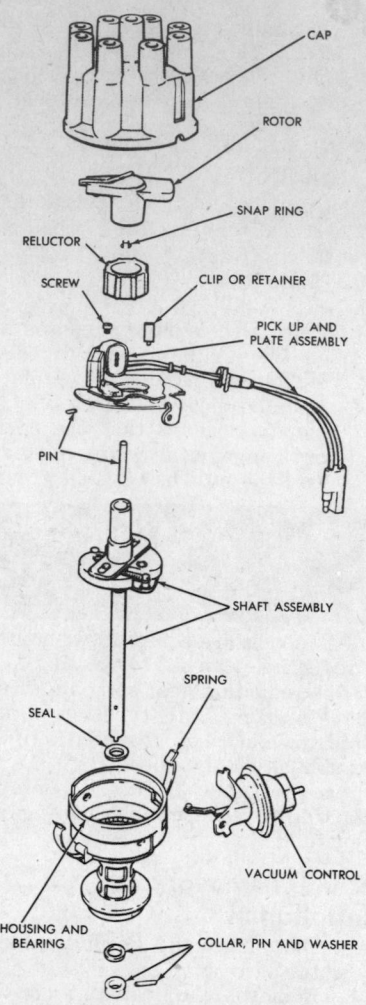

Exploded view of the V8 electronic ignition distributor. The six-cylinder distributor has a drive gear on the end of the shaft. (© Chrysler Corp.)

2. Disconnect the primary wire at the coil. On electronic ignition, disconnect the lead wire at the harness connector.
3. Unfasten the distributor cap retaining clips and lift off the cap.
4. Mark the distributor body and the engine block to indicate the position of the body in the block. Scribe a mark on the edge of the distributor housing to indicate the position of the rotor on the distributor. These marks can be used as guides when installing the distributor in a correctly timed engine.
5. Remove the distributor hold-down clamp screw and clamp.
6. Carefully lift the distributor out of the block.

Distributor Installation

If the crankshaft has not been rotated while the distributor was removed from the engine, installation is the reverse of the removal procedure. (See step two or three of the procedure below.) Use the reference marks that were made before removal to correctly position the distributor in the block. Check the point gap and, before connecting the vacuum advance line, adjust the ignition timing.

If the crankshaft has been rotated or otherwise disturbed (as during engine rebuilding) after the distributor was removed, proceed as follows to install the distributor.

1. Bring the no. 1 piston to top dead center (TDC) by removing the no. 1 spark plug and inserting a finger into the hole, while rotating the crankshaft. Compression pressure can be felt as the no. 1 piston approaches TDC. The TDC timing mark on the crankshaft vibration damper should now be opposite the indicator on the timing chain case.
2. *For six-cylinder engines*: Note the position of the distributor cap (which should be connected to the engine by the spark plug cables). Hold the distributor so that the rotor will be in position *just ahead* of the distributor cap terminal for the no. 1 spark plug when the distributor is installed.

Now lower the distributor into its engine block opening, engaging the distributor gear with the camshaft drive gear. Be sure that the rubber O-ring seal is in the groove in the distributor shank. When the distributor is properly seated, the rotor should be under the no. 1 distributor cap terminal with the contact points just opening. Proceed with step four.

3. *For eight-cylinder engines*: Clean the top of the engine block around the distributor opening to ensure a good seal between the distributor base and the block. Note the position of the distributor cap (which should be connected to the engine by the spark plug cables). Hold the distributor so that the rotor will be in position *directly under* the distributor cap terminal for the no. 1 spark plug when the distributor is installed. Now lower the distributor into its engine block opening, engaging the tongue of the distributor shaft with the slot in the distributor and oil pump drive gear. Proceed with step four.
4. Install the distributor hold-down clamp and tighten its retaining screw finger-tight.
5. Check the point gap and refit the distributor cap. Connect the primary wire to the coil or the lead wire to the harness.
6. Check and adjust the point dwell and the ignition timing.
7. Connect the vacuum advance line to the distributor.

Contact Point Replacement and Adjustment

Single Point Distributor

Use the procedure described below to remove, install, and adjust a single-contact point set.

1. Pull back the spring clips and lift off the distributor cap. Remove the rotor.
2. Loosen the terminal screw nut and remove the primary and condenser leads.
3. Remove the stationary contact lockscrew and remove the contact point set.
4. Remove the condenser and the retaining screw. Lift out the condenser.
5. Install the new condenser and tighten its retaining screw.
6. Install the point set but do not fully tighten its lockscrew.
7. Connect the condenser and primary leads.
8. If necessary, align the contacts by bending the stationary contact bracket only. *Never bend the movable contact arm to correct alignment.*

9. With the rubbing block of the movable contact arm resting on a peak of the cam lobe, adjust the point gap by inserting a screwdriver in the vee notch of the stationary contact base and using the screwdriver to move the stationary contact.

10. Tighten the lockscrew and recheck the gap setting. Reset if necessary.

11. Install the new rotor and refit the distributor cap.

12. Connect a dwell meter to the engine.

13. Start the engine and run it at idle speed. Note the dwell meter reading. If it is not within specifications, the point gap may be incorrect or the movable contact arm may be distorted. Readjust the contact points and recheck the dwell. Be sure that the correct point set has been installed.

Dual Point Distributor

Removal and installation of dual contact points is the same as for a single point set. However, adjustment of dual points using a dwell meter is slightly different because one set of contacts must be blocked open with a clean insulator while the opposite point set is adjusted to specifications, using the single point set adjustment procedure. When adjusted correctly, tighten the lockscrew. Then block open this contact set and adjust the other set in the same manner as the first. Check the total point dwell.

Ignition Timing

Ignition timing must be checked only when the engine is hot and running at its correct idle speed.

1. Disconnect the vacuum line at the distributor (on all models).

2. Connect a stroboscopic timing light, start the engine, and adjust the idle speed to specification.

3. Loosen the distributor hold-down screw so the housing can be rotated.

4. Check the ignition timing with the strobe light. If necessary, advance or retard the timing by rotating the distributor housing, until the correct timing is obtained.

5. Tighten the distributor hold-down screw and connect the vacuum line. Stop the engine and disconnect the timing light.

FUEL SYSTEM

Carburetors

All carburetors incorporate modifications to reduce engine exhaust emissions. These include limiter stops

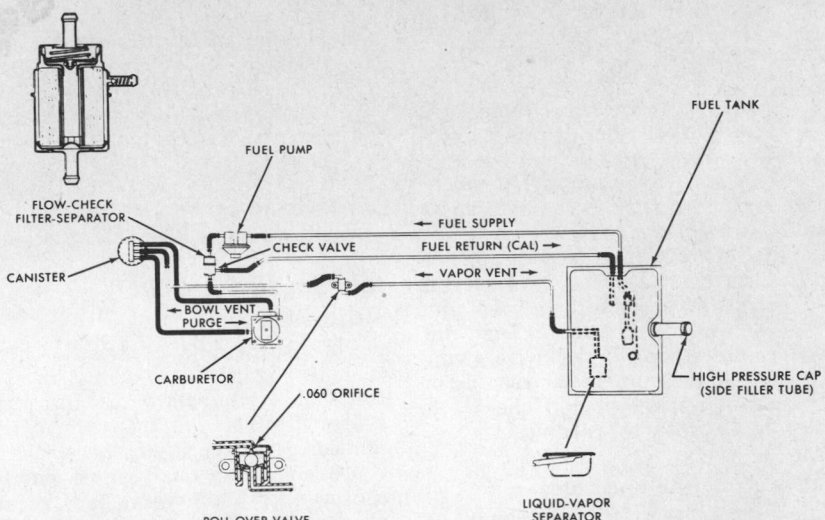

Fuel system with roll-over protection introduced in 1976 (© Chrysler Corp.)

on the carburetor idle mixture adjustment screws, leaner carburetor mixtures, faster acting chokes, and on some models, solenoid operated throttle stops and distributor retard mechanisms. The throttle stop raises the engine idle speed to reduce engine emissions, but de-energizes when the ignition is shut off to prevent the engine from dieseling. The distributor retard solenoid (1971 only) is activated when the idle speed adjustment screw returns to the curb idle position and contacts a sensor, mounted on the carburetor, which retards ignition timing while the engine is at idle. These carburetors also incorporate an internally mounted hot idle compensator which opens to induct additional air into the carburetor during low speed-high temperature operation.

The 426 Hemi and the 340 and 440 engines were available with multiple carburetor options. The 1970 426 Hemi was equipped with two Carter AFB carburetors. Both carburetors had complete idle systems which must be adjusted and synchronized. The 340 and 440 Six-Pack engines were equipped with three Holley 2300 two-venturi carburetors. Only the center carburetor on these engines was equipped with an idle system and the inboard and outboard carburetors contained no idle adjustments.

Idle Speed and Mixture Adjustments (See Illustrations in Dodge Section)

NOTE: These procedures all require the use of sophisticated testing equipment to ensure that the results are within legal limits. There is no way to avoid the need for this equipment; however, the procedures are given for those with access to the equipment.

Through 1974

Adjust with air cleaner installed.

1. Run engine at fast idle to stabilize engine temperature.

2. Make sure choke plate is fully released.

3. Attach a tachometer to the engine. With electronic ignition, connect one tachometer lead to the negative coil primary lead and the other to a good ground.

4. Connect an exhaust analyzer to the engine and insert the probe as far into the tailpipe as possible. On vehicles with dual exhaust, insert the probe into the left tailpipe as this is the side without the heat riser valve.

5. Check ignition timing and adjust it as required.

6. If equipped with air conditioning, turn the air conditioner OFF. On models with six-cylinder engines, turn the headlights on high beam.

7. Place the transmission in the Neutral position. Make sure the hot idle compensator valve is fully seated in the closed position.

8. Turn the engine idle speed adjustment screw in or out to adjust idle speed to specification. If equipped with an electric solenoid, turn the solenoid adjusting screw in or out to obtain specified rpm. Then, adjust the curb idle speed screw until it just touches the stop on the carburetor body. Now, back the curb idle speed adjusting screw out one full turn.

9. Turn each idle mixture adjustment screw 1/16 turn richer (counterclockwise). Wait 30 seconds and observe the reading on the exhaust gas analyzer. Continue this procedure until the meter indicates a definite in-

crease in the richness of the mixture.

NOTE: this step is very important. A carburetor that is set too lean wil cause the exhaust gas analyzer to give a false reading indicating a rich mixture. Because of this, the carburetor must first be known to have a rich mixture to verify the reading on the exhaust gas analyzer.

10. After verifying the reading obtained on the meter, adjust the mixture screws to get an air/fuel ratio of 14.2:1. Turn the mixture screws clockwise (leaner) to raise the meter reading or counterclockwise (richer) to lower the meter reading.

1975 and Later

1. The engine must have been off at least one hour.
2. Start the engine and run it in Neutral or Park on step 2 of the fast idle cam for about 5-10 minutes or until the thermostat opens and the engine warms up thoroughly. The top of the radiator should be hot.
3. Check the underhood sticker. Disconnect and plug the distributor vacuum line if it is required by the sticker for idle mixture setting. This is usually not required on 225 and 318 engines outside California.
4. Stop the engine. If there is an air pump, disconnect and plug the air tube on the engine.
5. If there is a catalytic converter, insert the probe of an emission analyzer into the exhaust system ahead of the converter. Use the left pipe on dual systems.
6. Start the engine and run it up to 2000 rpm for 10 seconds or more. Let it idle and wait at least 30 seconds but no more than 60 seconds, for the meters to stabilize. The transmission must be in Neutral or Park with the air conditioner and headlights off.
7. Adjust the idle speed and air/fuel mixture screws to get the percentage of carbon monoxide specified on the sticker and either the lowest hydrocarbon reading or the smoothest possible idle.
8. Disconnect and plug the EGR vacuum line at the valve. On the 225 and 318 outside California, disconnect and plug the distributor vacuum hose. Adjust the fast idle speed with the screw on the second highest cam step.
9. If there is a problem with rough idle or low speed surge on 2 or 4-barrel carburetors, proceed as follows. Remove the plastic idle mixture limiter caps. Seat both idle speed screws gently, then back them both out 1½ or so turns. Start the engine and ad-

just the screws out equally (richer) 1/16 turn at a time, checking the air/fuel ratio each time. Adjust to get both the specified air/fuel ratio and a smooth surgeless idle. Install new caps.

Multiple Carburetor Engines

See the Dodge/Plymouth Section.

Idle Speed Solenoid Adjustment

This solenoid is energized whenever the ignition circuit is on. Its function is to allow the throttle plates to close farther when the ignition is switched off, thereby preventing running on. It must not be confused with the very similar catalyst protection system throttle position solenoid used on some 1975 models. This solenoid is energized only on deceleration. Further details on the catalyst protection system will be given in the Emission Control Systems Unit Repair Section, but it is not adjusted as part of tune-up.

1. Bring the engine to operating temperature and attach a tachometer.
2. With the engine running, adjust the solenoid screw to the proper rpm.
3. Adjust the slow curb idle screw until the screw end just contacts the stop on the carburetor body. Back the screw off one full turn.
4. Test the above procedure by disconnecting the solenoid wire at the connector. Be sure not to let the lead short to the engine. The solenoid should de-energize and idle speed should drop down below normal. Now reconnect the wire. After you reconnect the solenoid, move the throttle linkage by hand since the solenoid isn't strong enough to move it.

Fuel Filter

Removal and Installation

Locate the filter in the fuel line between the fuel pump and the carburetor. Using hose-clamp pliers, remove the attaching clamps and pull the filter off. Reverse this procedure for installation. Be sure that the arrow on the filter is pointing toward the carburetor (direction of fuel flow).

The 1973 six-cylinder engine has a filter element screwed into the top of the fuel pump. This is not meant to be cleaned; it should be replaced.

Fuel Pump

The fuel pump used on the six-cylinder, 383 and 440 V8 engines are driven by a small cam eccentric cast into the main camshaft. On the 318, 340, and 360 V8 engines, the pump

is driven by a pressed steel eccentric secured on the gear end of the camshaft. On the six-cylinder and 318, 340, and 360 V8 engines, the pump is driven directly by the pump rocker arm pressing on the cam eccentric. On the 383, 426, and 440 big block V8s, there is a pushrod located between the pump rocker arm and the driving eccentric.

Removal and Installation

1. Wipe the pump exterior to remove all dirt and oil.
2. Taking note of positions, remove the pump fuel lines.
3. Remove the bolts securing the pump to the block and remove the pump.
4. Remove all gasket material from machined surfaces. Using a sealer of good quality, coat both sides of the pump gasket.
5. Install the pump to the block. If difficulty is encountered engaging the pump drive, rotate slightly.
6. Connect the fuel lines and tighten the pump bolts. Start the engine and check it for leaks.

COOLING SYSTEM

Radiator Removal and Installation

1. Drain the cooling system.
2. On cars with automatic transmissions, disconnect the fluid cooler lines at the radiator bottom tank. To avoid fluid loss or dirt contamination, plug the cooler lines.
3. Remove the upper and lower radiator hoses.
4. Remove the fan shroud securing screws and separate the shroud from the radiator. Move the shroud toward the engine as far as possible to obtain maximum clearance for removing the radiator.
5. Remove the radiator mounting screws.
6. Lift the radiator out of the engine compartment.

Caution Extreme care should be taken not to damage the radiator cooling fins or water tubes during removal.

7. Reverse the above to install the radiator. Fill the cooling system to 1 ¼ in. below the filler neck with the correct water and antifreeze mixture. Warm up the engine with the heater on and check the coolant level. On cars with automatic transmissions, check the fluid level after warm-up and add fluid as required.

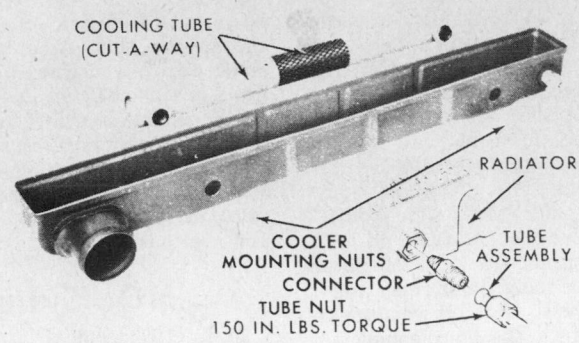

Internal details of the in-radiator transmission fluid cooler (© Chrysler Corp.)

Water Pump Removal and Installation

NOTE: the water pump is serviced only as an assembly. When replacing the water pump, do not install a standard water pump on an air-conditioned car or vice versa.

1. Drain the cooling system.
2. Remove the fan shroud securing screws and move the shroud out of the way.
3. It may be necessary to remove the radiator on some models to obtain the working clearance necessary to remove the water pump.
4. Loosen the alternator mounting bolts. Loosen the mounting bolts for the power steering pump, idler pulley, air conditioning compressor, and air pump (if so equipped). Remove all the accessory belts.
5. Remove the fan, spacer or fluid drive, and the pulley.

Caution For fluid-coupled fan drives, do not position the drive unit with its shaft pointing downward. This will prevent the silicone fluid from draining into the fan-drive bearing and thereby contaminating the grease.

6. On some models, it may be necessary to remove the alternator or compressor mounting bracket bolts from the water pump to swing the alternator or compressor out of the way.
7. Detach the hoses from the water pump. Remove the bolts which secure the water pump body to its engine block housing. Remove the water pump and discard the gasket.
8. Install the water pump with a new gasket, using sealer, on its housing. Torque its securing bolts to 30 ft lbs.
9. Rotate the pump shaft by hand to be sure that it rotates freely. Refit the alternator or compressor mounting bracket to the pump if either was removed. Install the pulley, spacer or fluid drive, and the fan. Torque their retaining nuts to 15 ft lbs.

10. Refit all the accessory drive belts.
11. Install the radiator if it was removed.
12. Install the fan shroud. Fill the cooling system to 1 ¼ in. below the filler neck with correct water and antifreeze mixture. Warm up the engine with the heater on and inspect the water pump for any leaks. Check the coolant level and add as required.

Thermostat Removal and Installation

All 1974 and later engines use a 195°F thermostat; 1971-73 engines use a 185°F unit; most 1970 engines use a 190°F unit. The 1970 318 and 383 2-barrel and 440 manual transmission engines use a 195°F thermostat.

1. Drain the cooling system to below the level of the thermostat.
2. Remove the upper radiator hose from the thermostat housing flange. Remove the housing bolts and take out the thermostat and housing.
3. To install the thermostat, use a new gasket. On V8s, be sure that the pellet end is facing toward engine. Six-cylinder models must have the vent hole facing up.
4. Refill the system. Let the engine warm up with the heater on and recheck the level.

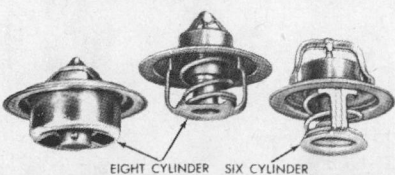

EIGHT CYLINDER   SIX CYLINDER

The part pointed out by the arrow goes into the engine when installing a thermostat (© Chrysler Corp.)

EMISSION CONTROLS

Positive Crankcase Ventilation

All models are equipped with a positive crankcase ventilation (PCV) system which draws air into the engine through the air cleaner and circulates it through the engine. The air combines with vapors in the crankcase and exits the engine through a metering valve mounted in the rocker arm cover. The air vapor mixture then re-enters the engine through the carburetor or intake manifold and passes into the combustion chambers where it is burned.

Cleaner Air System (CAS)

All 1970 models are equipped with this type of exhaust emission control. This system consists of: heated carburetor air cleaner intake ducts, carburetor modifications, ignition timing controls, and reduced engine compression ratios.

Ignition Retard Solenoid—1971

The function of this unit is to retard the ignition timing at closed throttle. Located on the distributor side, this solenoid must be operating when the ignition timing is adjusted. To be sure that the solenoid is operating, disconnect the ground lead after the timing is set. If the engine idle speed increases noticeably, the solenoid is functioning properly.

Disconnect the solenoid when checking the dwell. If this is not done, the dwell meter will not read accurately.

Evaporative Control System

All 1970 vehicles sold in California and all 1971 and later vehicles have an Evaporation Control System to reduce evaporation losses from the fuel system. The system has an expansion tank in the main fuel tank. This prevents spillage due to expansion of warm fuel. A special filler cap with a two-way relief valve is used. An internal presure differential, caused by thermal expansion, opens the valve, as does an external pressure differential caused by fuel usage. Fuel vapors from the carburetor and fuel tank are routed to the crankcase ventilation system. A separator is installed to prevent liquid fuel from entering the crankcase ventilation system.

Evaporation control systems used on 1972 and later vehicles also include a charcoal canister and an overflow limiting valve.

The limiting valve prevents the fuel tank from being overfilled by trapping fuel in the filler when the tank is full. When pressure in the tank becomes greater than the valve operating pressure, the valve opens and allows the gasoline vapors to flow into the charcoal canister.

The charcoal canister is mounted in the engine compartment. It absorbs vapors and retains them until clean air is drawn through a line from it that runs to the PCV valve. Absorption occurs while the car is parked and cleaning occurs when the car engine is running.

Air Injection System (Air Pump)

In 1972-73 the air injection system was used on all six cylinder engines sold in California only. All 1975 and later California and most other 1975 and later engines, except those with catalytic converters, use air pumps.

A belt-driven air pump, mounted on the front of the engine, is used to inject air into the exhaust ports. This causes oxidation of these gases and a considerable reduction in carbon monoxide and hydrocarbons. The system consists of the pump, a check valve to protect the hoses and pump from hot gases, and a diverter-pressure relief valve assembly.

Exhaust Gas Recirculation

In order to reduce the emission of oxides and nitrogen (NOx), exhaust gases are ducted from the intake manifold crossover passage to dilute (with inert, oxygen-free gas) the fuel/air mixture. These gases are introduced to the intake manifold floor by small jets on 1972 models. Starting 1973, all engines have floor jets. In addition to the floor jets, all 1973 engines except the 340 use an EGR control valve. This valve directs exhaust gas from the crossover passage into the intake manifold. By using either ported-vacuum (varies with

throttle opening) or venturi-vacuum signals, the EGR valve is able to proportion the exhaust gas flow to the amount of vacuum present in the carburetor. A thermal switch is used to deenergize the EGR valve when the outside temperature is below 58° F, or the coolant temperature below 62°F, to provide better driveability. Floor jets were dropped from all 1974 and later engines. All 1974 and later models have a delay timer relay and a solenoid valve to shut off vacuum to the system until the engine has run 30-40 seconds after startup.

Electrically Assisted Choke

During warm weather a heating element, located in the automatic choke well, comes on to shorten the period of choke operation and thus reduce hydrocarbon emissions on 1973 and later models. The heating element is operated by a time-delay control switch located next to the choke well. The assist choke draws about three amps of current during operation. A two-stage electric assist choke is used for 1974. The two-stage choke may be identified by its external resistor:

Blue resistor 5 ohm—V8-318
White resistor 10 ohm—All other V8s

Below 58° F, the heating element gets full, low amperage current from the choke control. Above 58° F, the resistor cuts the current in half. After several minutes of operation above 58° F, the control opens the circuit so that the heating element gets no current at all. Most engines use a 20-watt heating element, except for four barrel carburetors which use a 40 watt element. The 40-watt choke has a white paint spot on the choke cover. Most 1975 models have a

single-stage electric choke which is similar to that used on 1973 models. However, there are two exceptions to this; 318 cu in. with manual transmissions and 360 cu in. with 4-bbl carburetors have a two-stage electric assist choke which is similar to that used on 1974 models. Starting 1976, sixes have a single-stage unit and V8s have a two-stage choke.

NO$_x$ System

Many 1971 and 1972 vehicles sold in California have a NO$_x$ system to control the emission of oxides of nitrogen. Engines with this system all have a special camshaft and a 185° F thermostat.

The manual transmission NO$_x$ system uses a transmission switch, a thermal switch, and a solenoid vacuum valve. The transmission switch is screwed into the transmission housing and is closed, except in high gear. The thermal switch, mounted on the firewall, is open whenever the ambient temperature is above 70° F. With the transmission in any gear except high and the temperature above 70°, the solenoid vacuum valve is energized. This shuts off the distributor vacuum advance line preventing vacuum advance. Below 70°, the vacuum advance functions normally.

The NO$_x$ system for automatic transmissions is more complex than the manual transmission system. It prevents vacuum advance when the ambient temperature is above 70° F, speed is below 30 mph, or the car is accelerating. The solenoid vacuum valve is interchangeable with that used in the manual transmission system. The speed switch senses vehicle speed and is driven by the speedometer cable. The control unit is mounted on the firewall. It contains a control module, thermal switch, and a vacuum switch. The control unit senses ambient temperature and manifold vacuum.

OSAC Valve

Starting with the 1973 models, an orifice spark advance control (OSAC) valve is used to delay distributor vacuum advance for about 15 seconds during acceleration.

NOTE: The amount of time-delay varies slightly from one engine size to another.

To aid in cold weather engine operation, a temperature sensing switch is built in to the OSAC valve so that it will not function when the air temperature is below 68° F.

Some time after 1 March and before 15 March 1973, the temperature sensor was removed from the OSAC valve, but the general appearance and location of the valve were not changed. The valve can be recognized by a white

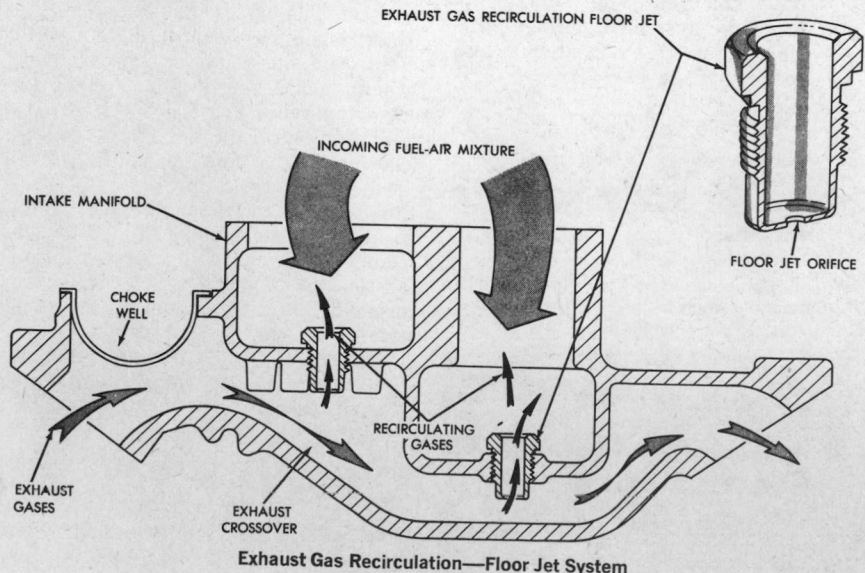

EXHAUST GAS RECIRCULATION FLOOR JET

INCOMING FUEL-AIR MIXTURE

INTAKE MANIFOLD

CHOKE WELL

FLOOR JET ORIFICE

RECIRCULATING GASES

EXHAUST GASES

EXHAUST CROSSOVER

Exhaust Gas Recirculation—Floor Jet System
(© Chrysler Corp)

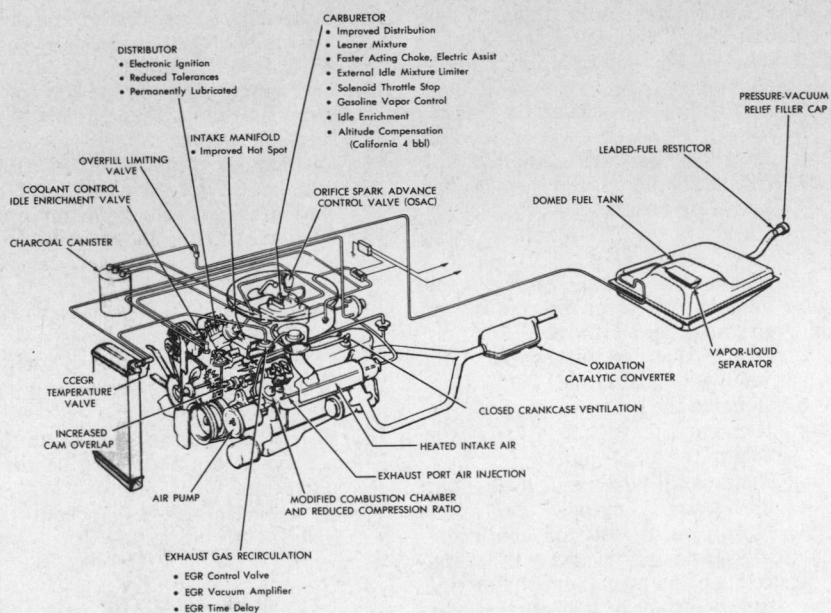

DISTRIBUTOR
• Electronic Ignition
• Reduced Tolerances
• Permanently Lubricated

CARBURETOR
• Improved Distribution
• Leaner Mixture
• Faster Acting Choke, Electric Assist
• External Idle Mixture Limiter
• Solenoid Throttle Stop
• Gasoline Vapor Control
• Idle Enrichment
• Altitude Compensation (California 4 bbl)

PRESSURE-VACUUM RELIEF FILLER CAP

INTAKE MANIFOLD
• Improved Hot Spot

LEADED-FUEL RESTRICTOR

OVERFILL LIMITING VALVE

COOLANT CONTROL IDLE ENRICHMENT VALVE

ORIFICE SPARK ADVANCE CONTROL VALVE (OSAC)

DOMED FUEL TANK

CHARCOAL CANISTER

VAPOR-LIQUID SEPARATOR

CCEGR TEMPERATURE VALVE

OXIDATION CATALYTIC CONVERTER

INCREASED CAM OVERLAP

CLOSED CRANKCASE VENTILATION

HEATED INTAKE AIR

AIR PUMP

EXHAUST PORT AIR INJECTION

MODIFIED COMBUSTION CHAMBER AND REDUCED COMPRESSION RATIO

EXHAUST GAS RECIRCULATION
• EGR Control Valve
• EGR Vacuum Amplifier
• EGR Time Delay

1975 Emission control systems (© Chrysler Corp)

gasket and a stick-on label with the new part number (3755499).

The OSAC valve was moved from the firewall to the air cleaner in 1974 and the temperature control restored. There are six different time delay and operating temperature combinations for the valve. These combinations are identified by a color code tape on the top of the valve.

Catalytic Converter

All 1975-76 Chrysler products sold in California except the 360 HP V8, and all sold nationwide except some 318-2V and all 360 HP V8 applications, are equipped with catalytic converters. These devices are used to oxidize excess carbon monoxide (CO) and hydrocarbons (HC) in the exhaust system before they can escape out the tailpipe and into the atmosphere. The converter is installed in front of the mufflers, underneath the car, and protected by a heat shield.

The expected catalyst life is 50,000 miles, provided that the engine is kept in tune and unleaded fuel is used.

To keep the catalyst from being overheated by an overly rich mixture during deceleration, a catalyst protection system (CPS) is used on some 1975 models. The system consists of a throttle positioner solenoid (not to be confused with the idle stop solenoid), a control box, and an engine rpm sensor.

Any time that the engine speed is more than 2,000 rpm while decelerating from highway speeds, the solenoid is energized and keeps the throttle butterfly from fully closing, thus preventing the mixture from becoming too rich.

Coolant Control Idle Enrichment (CCIE) System

The CCIE system is used on 1975 and later models with automatic

transmissions. The system consists of a vacuum-operated valve built into the carburetor, which shuts off the idle circuit air bleeds when vacuum is supplied to its diaphragm.

Depending upon engine application, vacuum is either routed through a coolant controlled vacuum valve and an EGR vacuum control solenoid.

Vacuum is passed to the valve diaphragm below a predetermined temperature, and on models with an EGR control solenoid for only 35 seconds after the engine is started. The CCIE valve action closes off the air bleed passages, which richens the mixture, and allows a smoother cold idle.

ENGINE

The standard equipment engine in most Chrysler Corporation compacts is the slant six. Although this engine has a long stroke by modern standards (it is/was available in 198, and 225 cu in. versions), it presents a low profile because the entire block is canted 30 degrees to the right.

The 318, 340 and 360 cu in. engines are Chrysler's "A" block series of V8s. All of the V8s utilize hydraulic tappets. They are of the valve-in-head type, and they vary in compression ratio, piston displacement, camshafts, valve springs, carburetors, intake manifolds, and exhaust systems. Of some interest is the 340 Six Pack high-performance engine. With modified valve train, different heads, and three Holley 2-BBL 2300 carburetors, this engine was Chrysler's hottest small-block offering.

Chrysler's "B" block series consists of the 383 and 440 cu in. engines. Actually, these may be divided into two types: the 383 low-block engine and a 440 high-block entry. Basically, the difference is a larger, deeper block on the 440 to accommodate a longer stroke crank. In addition, main journal diameter, connecting rod length, pushrod length, and intake manifolds are different. Otherwise, these engines are similar and many parts will interchange. The 440 was available in both 4-BBL and 6-BBL versions.

In 1970, the 426 Hemi was added to the Barracuda/Challenger option list. It is basically a "B" series, raised-block engine, but with so many differences that it must be treated as a completely separate engine. It has hemispherical combustion chambers with 2.25 in. intake and 1.95 in. exhaust valves actuated by rocker arms mounted on separate intake and exhaust rocker shafts. The spark plugs are centrally located in the combustion chambers, and aluminum tubes protect the plugs and wires from oil where they pass through the rocker covers. Because of the huge intake

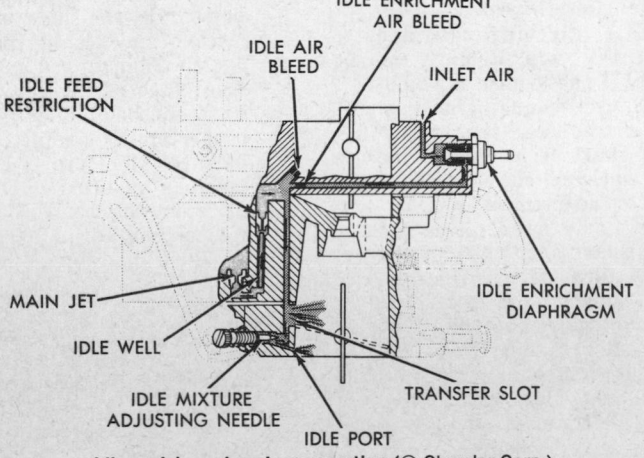

IDLE ENRICHMENT AIR BLEED

IDLE AIR BLEED

INLET AIR

IDLE FEED RESTRICTION

MAIN JET

IDLE WELL

IDLE ENRICHMENT DIAPHRAGM

IDLE MIXTURE ADJUSTING NEEDLE

IDLE PORT

TRANSFER SLOT

Idle enrichment system operation (© Chrysler Corp.)

ports, there is no room for head bolts on the intake side. Instead studs are mounted in the head which extend down into the valley between the cylinder heads. To reduce piston side thrust, Hemis use longer connecting rods than other raised-block "B" engines, and to strengthen the lower end, the main caps are crossbolted. The Hemi engine was discontinued in 1971 and is no longer available.

See the Dodge/Plymouth section for all repair procedures for the 426 Hemi engine.

Special Engine Markings

Over and undersize engine components such as crankshaft and connecting rod journals, cylinder bores, tappets, and valve stems are identified by various marks. These marks may be located on top front engine pads, following the serial number, or on the crankshaft counterweights. In addition, some engines may have oversize valve stem markings stamped on cylinder head ends. For explanation of the meanings of the various markings, consult your local Dodge/Plymouth dealership.

Engine Removal and Installation

6 Cylinder

1. Scribe the hood hinge outlines on the underside of the hood, then remove the hood.
2. Drain the cooling system, remove the battery and carburetor air cleaner.
3. Remove radiator and heater hoses, then the radiator. Remove PCV and evaporative control system (if so equipped).
4. Remove the outlet vent pipe from the cylinder head cover.
5. Disconnect fuel lines, linkage and wiring to the engine.
6. Disconnect exhaust pipe at exhaust manifold.
7. Raise car on hoist.
8. If equipped with automatic transmission, it must be drained. Remove the oil cooler lines, filler tube and shift cable.
9. Remove the clutch torque shaft, and rods.
10. Remove the speedometer cable and gear shift rods.
11. Disconnect driveshaft and tie out of the way.
12. Install an engine support fixture to the rear of the engine.
13. Remove the engine rear support crossmember.
14. Remove transmission mounting bolts from clutch housing.
15. Remove the transmission.
16. Lower the car.
17. Position engine lifting fixture onto the engine, and attach chain hoist to the fixture eyebolt.

18. Remove the engine support fixture.
19. Remove the engine front mounting bolts.
20. Lift the engine out of the engine compartment and lower it onto a substantial work stand.
21. To install the engine, reverse the above procedure.

V8

1. Scribe the outline of the hood hinge brackets on the bottom of the hood and remove the hood.
2. Drain the cooling system and remove the radiator.
3. Remove the battery.
4. Remove the fuel line from the fuel pump and plug the line.
5. Remove all wires and hoses that attach to the engine.
6. If equipped with air conditioning and/or power steering, remove the unit from the engine and position it out of the way *without disconnecting the lines.*
7. Attach lifting sling to the engine. On models equipped with a 426 Hemi engine, never attempt to remove the engine with the lifting sling attached to the intake manifold.
8. Raise the vehicle on a hoist and install an engine support fixture to support the rear of the engine.
9. On automatic transmission models, drain the transmission. On

standard transmission models, disconnect the clutch torque shaft from the engine.
10. Disconnect the exhaust pipe/s from the exhaust manifold/s.
11. Remove the driveshaft.
12. Disconnect the transmission linkage and any wiring or cables that attach to the transmission.
13. Remove the engine rear support crossmember and remove the transmission.
14. Remove the bolts that attach the motor mounts to the chassis.
15. Lower the vehicle and attach a chain hoist or other lifting device to the engine.
16. Raise the engine and carefully remove it from the engine compartment.
17. Reverse the above procedure to install the engine.

Manifolds

6 Cylinder Combination Manifold

Removal
1. Remove air cleaner.
2. Remove vacuum control tube at carburetor and distributor. Remove the EGR line at the carburetor.
3. Remove fuel line and carburetor.
4. Disconnect the exhaust pipe at the flange.

TIME SAVER

To remove the engine without removing the transmission, perform Steps 1-7 and 10 of the engine removal operation. If the vehicle is equipped with an automatic transmission, attach a remote starter switch to the engine, remove the inspection plate from the bellhousing, crank the engine to gain access to the torque converter-to-driveplate attaching nuts and remove the nuts. Remove the starter. If the vehicle is equipped with a manual transmission, disconnect the clutch torque shaft from the engine block and the clutch linkage from the adjustment rod. Remove the bolt that attaches the transmission filler tube to the engine (automatic transmission). Support the transmission and remove the bolts that attach the transmission to the engine or clutch bell housing. When removing the engine, place a block of wood on the lifting point of a floor jack and

position the jack under the transmission. As the engine is removed from the vehicle, raise and lower the jack as required so the angle of the transmission duplicates as nearly as possible the angle of the engine. Use a clamp so that the torque converter doesn't fall out of the transmission.

When installing the engine into a vehicle with an automatic transmission, keep in mind that the crankshaft flange bolt circle, the inner and outer circle of holes in the driveplate, and the four tapped holes in the front face of the converter all have one hole offset. To insure proper engine-torque converter balance, the torque converter must be mounted to the driveplate in the same location it was originally installed.

When installing the engine into a vehicle with a manual transmission, it may be necessary to turn the crankshaft pulley, with the transmission in gear, to get the transmission input shaft spline to mesh with the inner hub on the clutch disc.

5. Remove nuts and washers holding the intake and exhaust manifolds to the cylinder head.
6. Remove the assembly from the head.
7. Remove three bolts holding the intake and exhaust manifolds together.
8. Clean manifold mating and attaching surfaces with a straight edge and feeler gauge. All mating surfaces should be flat and plane within .008 in.

Installation

1. Place a new gasket between intake and exhaust manifolds and install three attaching bolts, loosely.
2. With a new gasket in place, position the complete manifold combination on the cylinder head.
3. Install conical washers (cupped side away from the nut) and nuts. Torque alternately to a final 10 ft. lbs.
4. Now, torque the three intake-to-exhaust manifold bolts to 20 ft. lbs. and studs to 30 ft. lbs.
5. Connect the exhaust pipe to the manifold flange and torque these two bolts to 35 ft. lbs.
6. Install carburetor and connect line, vacuum line and throttle linkage.
7. Install air cleaner. Start engine and check for intake and exhaust leaks.

V8 Intake Manifold Removal and Installation

All Engines Except 426 Hemi

1. Drain the cooling system. Disconnect the negative battery cable.
2. Remove the air cleaner and disconnect the fuel line from the carburetor.
3. Disconnect all vacuum lines that attach to the carburetor or intake manifold.
4. Disconnect the spark plug wires from the plugs and remove the distributor cap and wires as an assembly.
5. Disconnect the wires from the coil and the temperature sending unit.
6. Disconnect the heater hose and bypass hose from the intake manifold.
7. Remove the intake manifold attaching bolts and remove the manifold, carburetor and coil from the engine as an assembly.
8. Clean all gasket mounting surfaces and firmly cement new gaskets to the engine.

NOTE: Do not use sealer on the composition side gaskets used on 1973 and later 340 and 360 engines.

9. Reverse above precedure to install.

Intake manifold tightening sequence for V8 engines (except 426 Hemi)
(© Chrysler Corp)

426 Hemi
See Dodge-Plymouth section.

V8 Exhaust Manifold Removal and Installation

Disconnect the exhaust manifold at the pipe flange. Access to these bolts is underneath the vehicle. If so equipped, disconnect the Air Injection nozzles and carburetor heated air stove. Disconnect any components of the EGR system which are in the way. Remove the exhaust manifold by removing the securing bolts and washers. To reach these bolts, it may be necessary to jack the engine slightly off its front mounts. When the exhaust manifold is removed, sometimes the securing studs will come out with the nuts. If this occurs, studs must be replaced with the aid of sealing compound on the coarse thread ends. If this is not done, water leaks may develop at the studs. To install the exhaust manifold, reverse the removal procedure. On the center branch of the 318, 340, and 360 manifold, no conical washers are used.

Valve System

All valves used in Chrysler engines (except 426 Hemi) are arranged in line in the cylinder head; they ride in guides that are integrally cast with the head. Service valves with oversize stems are available; therefore, valve guides may be reamed if required.

Rocker Shaft Removal and Installation

Six Cylinder

1. Remove the closed ventilation system.
2. Remove the evaporative control system.
3. Remove the valve cover with its gasket.
4. Take out the rocker arm and shaft assembly securing bolts and remove the rocker arm and shaft.
5. Reverse the above for installation. The flat (through 1973) or the oil hole (1971 and later) on the end of the shaft must be on the top and point toward the front of the engine to provide proper lubrication to the rocker arms. The special bolt goes to the rear. Torque the rocker arm bolts to 25 ft lbs and be sure to adjust the valves.

All V8s Except 426 Hemi

The stamped steel rocker arms are arranged on one rocker arm shaft per cylinder head. To remove the rocker arms and shaft:

1. Disconnect the spark plug wires.
2. Disconnect the closed ventilation and evaporative control system.
3. Remove the valve covers with their gaskets.
4. Remove the rocker shaft bolts and retainers, and lift off the rocker arm assembly.
5. Reverse the above procedure to install. The notch on the end of both rocker shafts on the 318, 340, and 360 should point to the engine centerline and toward the front of the engine on the left cylinder head, or toward the rear on the right cylinder head. On the 383 and 440, the rocker arm lubrication holes must point down and toward the valves. Torque the rocker shaft bolts to 17 ft lbs on the 318, 340, and 360, and 25 ft lbs on the 383 and 440.

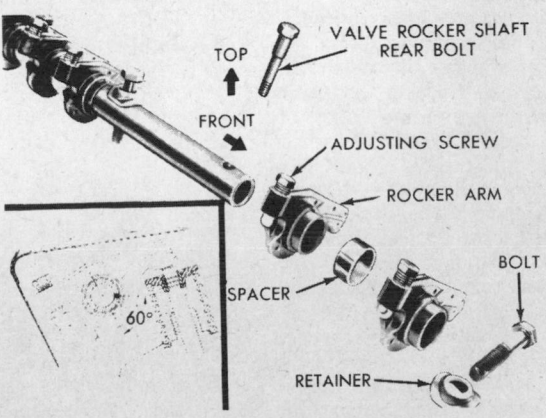

Six-cylinder rocker shaft details (© Chrysler Corp.)

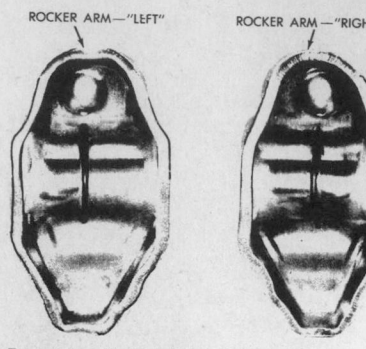

Proper location and installation of rocker arms on the shaft—V8 engines (except 426 Hemi) (© Chrysler Corp)

426 Hemi

See the Dodge/Plymouth section.

Valve Adjustment

This adjustment is required only on the six cylinder engines, the 340 Six Pack, and the 426 Hemi. The sixes use solid lifters and adjustable rocker arms; the Six Pack and Hemi use hydraulic lifters and adjustable rocker arms. All other V8s use hydraulic lifters and non-adjustable rocker arms; the lifters take up lash automatically and no adjustment is possible. After engine reassembly, these lifters adjust themselves shortly after oil pressure builds up.

Adjustment is recommended at tune-up intervals for the sixes; no specific intervals are specified for the high performance engines. Valve lash should be adjusted whenever there is excessive noise from the valve mechanism.

CAUTION: *Do not set the valve lash closer than specified in an attempt to quiet the valve mechanism. This will cause burnt valves.*

Six Cylinder Engines

1. Warm up the engine until it reaches its normal operating temperature (water temperature of about 185°F).
2. Set the engine idle speed to 550 rpm and run the engine at this speed for five minutes.
3. Remove the valve cover by withdrawing its securing bolts. Be careful of the hot oil which will splash off the rocker assembly when the cover is removed.
4. Using the proper thickness feeler gauge, measure the clearance between the valve stem tip and the end of the rocker arm adjusting screw at each valve. If necessary, turn the adjusting screw to obtain the correct valve clearance.
5. After all of the valves have been checked and adjusted, stop the engine and replace the valve cover, using a new gasket between the cover and cylinder

Chilton's TIME SAVER

The factory recommends adjusting the valves on six cylinder engines with the engine running, but the amateur mechanic will have better luck with the following procedure.

1. The engine must be at normal operating temperature. Mark the crankshaft pulley into three equal 120° segments, starting at the timing mark.
2. Remove the valve (rocker) cover and the distributor cap.
3. Set the engine at TDC on the No. 1 cylinder by aligning the mark on the crankshaft pulley with the 0° mark on the timing cover pointer. The distributor rotor should point at the position of the No. 1 spark plug wire in the distributor cap. Both rocker arms on No. 1 cylinder should be free to move slightly. If all this isn't the case, you have No. 6 cylinder at TDC and will have to turn the engine 360° in the normal direction of rotation.
4. The cylinders are numbered from front to rear. The intake and exhaust valves are in the following sequence, starting at the front: E-I, E-I, E-I, I-E, I-E, I-E. Note that intake and exhaust valves have different settings.

5. The lash is measured between the rocker arm and the end of the valve.
6. To check the lash, insert the correct size feeler gauge between the rocker arm and the valve. Press down lightly on the other end of the rocker arm. If the gauge cannot be inserted, loosen the self-locking adjustment nut on top of the rocker arm. Tighten the nut until the gauge can just be inserted and withdrawn without buckling.
7. After both valves for the No. 1 cylinder are adjusted, turn the engine so that the pulley turns 120° in the normal direction of rotation (clockwise). The distributor rotor will turn 60°, since it turns at half engine speed.
8. Check that the rocker arms are free and adjust the valves for the next cylinder in the firing order, No. 5. The firing order is 1-5-3-6-2-4.
9. Turn the engine 120° to adjust each of the remaining cylinders in the firing order. When you are done the engine will have made two complete revolutions (720°) and the rotor one complete revolution (360°).
10. Replace the rocker cover with a new gasket. Replace the distributor cap. Start the engine and check for leaks.

head. If much oil was lost during the valve adjustment procedure, check the oil level in the crankcase.

340 Six Pack and 426 Hemi

1. Adjust ignition timing to TDC.
2. Mark crankshaft damper with chalk at TDC and 180° opposite TDC.
3. Rotate crankshaft until No. 1 cylinder is at TDC and points are just opening.
4. Adjust intake rocker arms on No. 2 and No. 7 cylinders and exhaust rocker arms on No. 4 and No. 8 cylinders. Adjust the valves to have zero lash, then tighten the adjustment screw an additional 1½ turns. Tighten the locknuts to 25 ft lbs.
5. Rotate crankshaft 180° in normal direction of rotation until points open to fire No. 4 cylinder.
6. Adjust intake rocker arms on

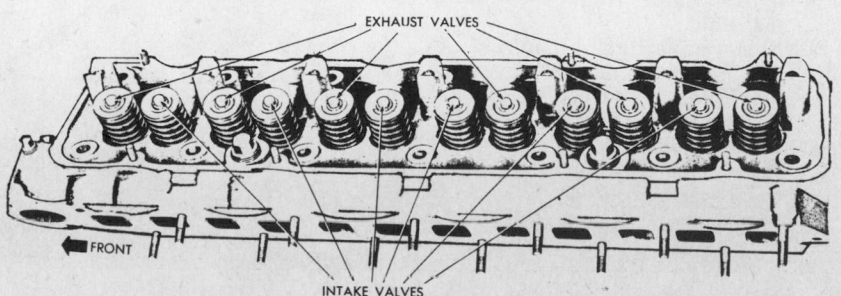

Cylinder head, showing valve sequence—six cylinder engines (© Chrysler Corp)

No. 1 and No. 8 cylinders and exhaust rocker arms on No. 3 and No. 6 cylinders as in Step 4.

7. Rotate crankshaft 180° in normal direction of rotation until points open to fire No. 6 cylinder.
8. Adjust intake rocker arms on No. 3 and No. 4 cylinders and exhaust rocker arms on No. 5 and No. 7 cylinders as in Step 4.
9. Rotate crankshaft 180° in normal direction of rotation until points open to fire No. 7 cylinder.
10. Adjust intake rocker arms on No. 5 and No. 6 cylinders and exhaust rocker arms on No. 1 and No. 2 cylinders as in Step 4.
11. Set ignition timing to operating specifications and install rocker covers.

Cylinder Head

CAUTION: *Don't loosen the head bolts until the engine is thoroughly cool, to prevent warping the head. If the head sticks to the block, operate the starter to loosen it by compression or rap it upward with a soft hammer. Do not force anything between the head and the block. Cylinder head bolts should be retorqued after the first 500 miles, unless a special gasket is used.*

6 Cylinder Removal

1. Drain the cooling system.
2. Remove carburetor air cleaner and fuel lines.
3. Disconnect accelerator linkage.
4. Remove all of the vacuum lines from the carburetor.
5. Carefully disconnect spark plug wires by pulling straight, in line with plug.
6. Disconnect heater hose and clamp holding the by-pass hose.
7. Disconnect the heat indicator-sending-unit wire.
8. Disconnect exhaust pipe at the exhaust manifold flange. If so equipped, disconnect the diverter valve vacuum line from the intake manifold; also remove the air injection assembly (if applicable).
9. Remove the intake and exhaust manifold and carburetor as an assembly.
10. Remove the outlet vent tube, evaporative control system, and cylinder head cover.
11. Remove the rocker arms and shaft.
12. Remove the pushrods and place them in order.
13. Remove the head bolts and lift off the cylinder head.
14. Place cylinder head on bench and remove the spark plugs and tubes.

6 Cylinder Installation

1. Clean carbon from the combustion area. Clean all gasket surfaces of both head and cylinder block. Install spark plugs (the aluminum plug shields used through 1974 act as satisfactory gasket material between spark plug body and cylinder head.)
2. If there is any cause to suspect leakage, check all surfaces with a straightedge. If out of flatness exceeds 0.00075 times the span length in any direction, replace head or machine head gasket surface. For example, on a 12 in. span the maximum allowable out of flat is 12 x 0.00075 or 0.009 in.
3. Apply a reliable sealer to the new gasket and install the gasket and cylinder head.
4. Install the 14 cylinder head bolts. Starting at the top center, tighten all cylinder head bolts to specification in three steps.
5. Inspect all push rods for bends or wear. Replace if necessary.
6. Insert the pushrods, small ends down into the tappets.
7. Install rocker arms and shaft assembly with flat or oil hole on the end of the shaft on top and pointing toward the front of the engine. This is necessary to provide lubrication to the rocker assemblies. Torque the attaching bolts to 25 ft. lbs.
8. Loosen the three bolts that connect the intake and exhaust manifolds. (This is necessary to obtain proper alignment.)
9. Position intake and exhaust manifold and carburetor assembly onto the cylinder head. Put the cup side of the conical washers against the manifolds, install the attaching nuts and torque to specifications.
10. Retighten the three intake-to-exhaust manifold bolts to specifications. Be sure to torque the inner bolt first.
11. Connect the heater hose and by-pass hose clamp.
12. Connect the heat indicator sending-unit wire, the accelerator linkage and the spark plug wires. If applicable, install vacuum control tube at the carburetor, the air injection assembly, and the diverter valve.
13. Install carburetor vacuum line(s).
14. Connect exhaust pipe to the exhaust manifold.
15. Install the fuel line and carburetor air cleaner.
16. Refill the cooling system.
17. Start the engine and let run until operating temperatures have been reached.
18. Adjust valve tappet clearance to .010 in. (intake) and .020 in. (exhaust.) The adjusting screw in the pushrod end of the rocker arm should have a minimum of 3 ft. lbs. (36 in. lbs.) tension as it is turned. If less, replace the adjusting screw and the rocker arm.
19. Place the new cylinder head cover gasket in position and install cylinder head cover. Torque attaching nuts to 40 in. lbs. (3 1/3 ft. lbs.).
20. Install outlet vent tube, and evaporative control system (if applicable).

All V8 except 426 Hemi
Removal and Installation

1. Drain cooling system and disconnect battery.
2. Remove alternator, air cleaner and fuel line.
3. Disconnect accelerator linkage.
4. Remove vacuum hose(s) from the carburetor.
5. Remove distributor cap and wires. If removing heads in vehicle, remove plugs to prevent breaking them.
6. Disconnect coil wires, temperature sending wire, heater hoses, and bypass hose.
7. Remove closed ventilation system (PCV), evaporative control system if so equipped, and valve covers.
8. Remove intake manifold, ignition coil, and carburetor as an assembly. Remove the tappet chamber cover.
9. Remove exhaust manifolds.
10. Remove rocker arm and shaft assemblies. Remove pushrods and identify to ensure installation in original location.
11. Remove the head bolts from each cylinder head and lift off heads.
12. Clean all surfaces.
13. Inspect all surfaces with straight edge if there is any reason to suspect leakage. If out of flatness exceeds 0.00075 times span length in any direction, replace head or machine mating surface. For example, if span length is 12 in., maximum out of flatness is 12 x 0.00075 or 0.009 in.
14. Reverse procedure to install. Be sure to use sealer and torque the cylinder head to specifications in three stages.

NOTE: *318 cylinder heads were changed during the 1976 model year. A new type gasket must be used with the new heads.*

426 Hemi
See Dodge-Plymouth Section.

TIME SAVER

If only one head is to be removed, it is possible to leave the intake manifold on the engine while removing the head:

1. Remove the head bolts from the intake manifold on the side from which the head is to be removed.
2. Loosen, but do not remove, the bolts on the opposite side of the manifold 1½-2 turns.
3. Perform steps 9-11 of the V8 head removal procedure.
4. Slip the head out from under the intake manifold.
5. Perform steps 12-14 of the V8 head removal procedure.

TIME SAVER

Frequently valves become bent or warped or their seats become blocked with carbon or other material. Left unattended, this can cause burnt valves, damaged cylinder heads and other expensive troubles. To detect leaking valves early, perform this test whenever the cylinder head is removed.

1. After removing head, replace sparkplugs. Removing sparkplugs before removing heads eliminates breakage.
2. Place head on bench with valves, springs, retainers and keys installed and combustion chambers up.
3. Pour enough gasoline in each combustion chamber to completely cover both valves. Watch combustion chambers for two minutes for any leakage.

Cylinder Head Bolt Tightening Sequences

NOTE: torque to specifications in three steps.

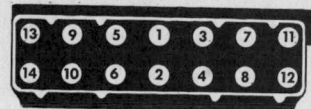

6 cylinder

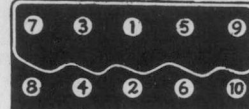

360 cu. in. and smaller V8

383 cu. in. and larger V8

STUD NUTS UNDER MANIFOLD

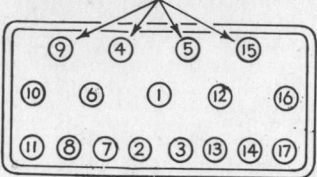

426 Hemi V8

Timing Cover, Chain, and Camshaft

Timing Chain and Cover Replacement

NOTE: It is normal to find particles of neoprene between the seal retainer and the crankshaft oil slinger after the seal has been in service on sixes through 1973 and V8s through 1974.

Six-Cylinder

1. Drain the cooling system and disconnect the battery.
2. Remove the radiator and fan.
3. With a puller, remove the vibration damper.
4. Loosen the oil pan bolts to allow clearance and remove the timing case cover and gasket.
5. Slide the crankshaft oil slinger off the front of the crankshaft.
6. Remove the camshaft sprocket bolt.
7. Remove the timing chain with the camshaft sprocket.
8. On installation: Turn the crankshaft to line up the timing mark

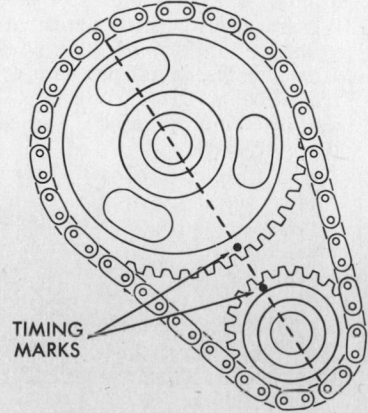

Alignment of timing marks—6 cylinder

TIMING MARKS

on the crankshaft sprocket with the centerline of the camshaft (without the chain).

9. Install the camshaft sprocket and chain. Align the timing marks.
10. Torque the camshaft sprocket bolt to 35 ft lbs.
11. Replace the oil slinger.
12. Reinstall the timing case cover with a new gasket and torque the bolts to 17 ft lbs. Retighten the engine oil pan to 17 ft lbs.
13. Press the vibration damper back on.
14. Replace the radiator and hoses.
15. Refill the cooling system.

V8

1. Disconnect the battery and drain the cooling system.
2. Remove the vibration damper pulley. Unbolt and remove the vibration damper with a puller. On 318, 340, and 360 engines, remove the fuel lines and fuel pump, then loosen the oil pan bolts and remove the front bolt on each side.
3. Remove the timing gear cover and the crankshaft oil slinger.
4. On 318, 340, and 360 engines, remove the camshaft sprocket lockbolt, securing cup washer, and fuel pump eccentric. Remove the timing chain with both sprockets. On 383, 426, and 440 engines, remove the camshaft sprocket lockbolt and remove the timing chain with the camshaft and crankshaft sprockets.
5. To begin the installation procedure, place the camshaft and crankshaft sprockets on a flat surface with the timing indicators on an imaginary centerline through both sprocket bores. Place the timing chain around both sprockets. Be sure that the timing marks are in alignment.

CAUTION: When installing the timing chain, have an assistant support the camshaft with a screwdriver to prevent it from contacting the freeze plug in the rear of the engine block. Remove the distributor and the oil pump/distributor drive gear. Position the screwdriver against the rear side of the cam gear and be careful not to damage the cam lobes.

6. Turn the crankshaft and camshaft to align them with the keyway location in the crankshaft sprocket and the keyway or dowel hole in the camshaft sprocket.
7. Lift the sprockets and timing chain while keeping the sprockets tight against the chain in the correct position. Slide both sprockets evenly onto their respective shafts.
8. Use a straightedge to measure the alignment of the sprocket

timing marks. They must be perfectly aligned.

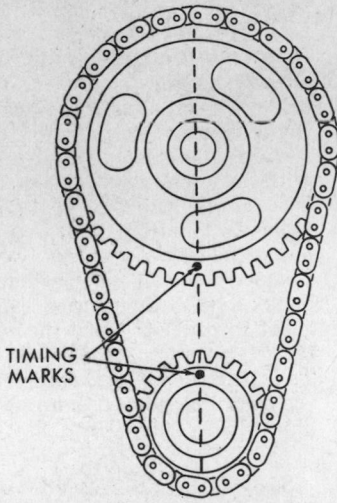

Alignment of timing marks—V8

9. On 318, 340, and 360 engines, install the fuel pump eccentric, cup washer, and camshaft sprocket lockbolt, and torque to 35 ft lbs. If camshaft end play exceeds 0.010 in., install a new thrust plate. It should be 0.002-0.006 in. with the new plate.

On 383, 426, and 440 V8s, install the washer and camshaft sprocket lockbolt and then torque the lockbolt to 35 ft lbs. Check to make sure that the rear face of the camshaft sprocket is flush with the camshaft end.

On the 426 Hemi, install the washers and camshaft lockbolt. Torque the lockbolt to 40 ft lbs.

Timing Cover Seal Replacement

NOTE: A seal remover and installer tool is required to prevent seal damage.

Measuring timing chain stretch
(© Chrysler Corp)

1. Using a seal puller, separate the seal from the retainer.
2. Pull the seal from the case.
3. To install the seal place it face down in the case with the seal lips downward.
4. Seat the seal tightly against the cover face. There should be a maximum clearance of .0014 in. between the seal and the cover. Be careful not to overcompress the seal.

Camshaft Removal and Installation

NOTE: Whenever a new camshaft and/or new tappets are installed, the manufacturer recommends that one qt of their engine oil supplement, or equivalent, be added to the engine oil to aid break-in. This oil mixture should be left in the engine for a minimum of 500 miles.

The manufacturer recommends that the engine be removed from the vehicle before removing the camshaft. However, in some cases it may be possible to remove the camshaft from the engine with the engine still in the car by removing the radiator and grille and sliding the camshaft out through the front of the vehicle.

6 Cylinder

1. Remove the cylinder head, timing gear cover, camshaft sprocket, and timing chain.
2. Remove the valve tappets, keeping them in order to ensure installation in their original location.
3. Remove the crankshaft sprocket.
4. Remove the distributor and the oil pump.
5. Remove the fuel pump.
6. Fit a long bolt into the front of the camshaft to facilitate camshaft removal.

7. Remove the camshaft, being careful not to damage the cam bearings with the cam lobes.
8. Lubricate the camshaft lobes and bearing journals with camshaft lubricant. Insert the camshaft into the engine block.
9. Install the fuel pump and oil pump.
10. Install the distributor. (Refer to the "Distributor Installation" procedure.)
11. Inspect the crowns of all the tappet faces with a straightedge. Replace any tappets that have dished or worn surfaces. Install the tappets.
12. Replace the timing gear and timing gear cover.

V8

1. Remove the cylinder heads. Remove the timing gear cover, camshaft and crankshaft sprocket, and the timing chain.
2. Remove the valve tappets, keeping them in order to ensure installation in their original location.
3. Remove the distributor and lift out the oil pump and distributor driveshaft.
4. Remove the camshaft thrust plate (318, 340, 360).
5. Fit a long bolt into the front of the camshaft and remove the camshaft, being careful not to damage the cam bearings with the cam lobes.
6. Lubricate the camshaft lobes and bearing journals with camshaft lubricant. Insert the camshaft into the engine block within 2 in. of its final position in the block.
7. Have an assistant support the camshaft with a screwdriver to prevent the camshaft from contacting the freeze plug in the rear of the engine block. Remove the distributor and the oil pump distributor drive gear. Position the screwdriver against the rear side of the cam gear and be careful not to damage the cam lobes.
8. Replace the camshaft thrust plate. If camshaft end play exceeds 0.010 in., install a new thrust plate. Play should be 0.002-0.006 in. with the new plate.
9. Install the oil pump and the distributor driveshaft. Install the distributor. (Refer to the "Distributor Installation" procedure.)
10. Inspect the crown of all the tappet faces with a straightedge. Replace any tappets that have dished or worn surfaces. Install the tappets.
11. Install the timing chain, cover, and cylinder heads.

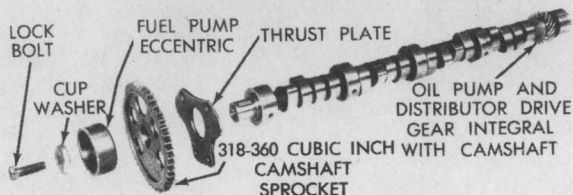

Camshaft and sprocket assembly—V8 through 360 cu. in.
(© Chrysler Corp)

Pistons and Connecting Rods

For all models except the 426 Hemi, the notch on the top of each piston must face the front of the engine. On 426 Hemi engines, the arrow on the piston top points toward the front of the engine.

To position the connecting rod correctly, the oil squirt hole should point to the right-side on all six-cylinder engines. On all V8 engines except the 426 Hemi, the larger chamfer of the lower connecting rod bore must face toward the crankpin journal fillet (toward the front on the left bank and toward the rear on the right bank). On the 426 Hemi, the connecting rod locating tang must face outboard.

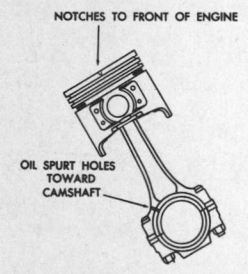

Piston and connecting rod assembly —six-cylinder

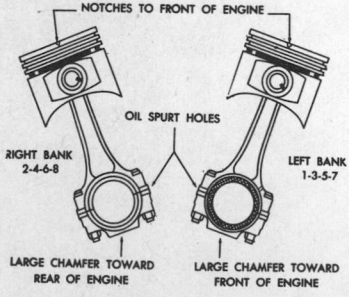

V8 piston and connecting rod assembly

Engine Lubrication

Oil Pan Removal and Installation

Slant Six—Dart, Valiant, Aspen, Volare

1. Disconnect the battery and drain the radiator. Disconnect the upper and lower radiator hoses, and remove the oil dipstick.

2. Remove the radiator shroud attaching screws and position it rearward on the engine.
3. Jack up the vehicle and drain the oil.
4. Remove the steering center link from the steering and idler arms.
5. Position a jack stand at the right front corner of the engine oil pan. Be sure not to support the engine at the crankshaft pulley or vibration damper.
6. Remove the front engine mount bolts. Raise the engine about 1½–2 in.
7. Remove the oil pan bolts, rotate the engine crankshaft to clear the counterweights, and remove the oil pan.
8. Using a new pan gasket set, install the oil pan and torque it to 200 in. lbs.
9. Lower the engine into its original position and install the front engine mount bolts. Torque to specifications.
10. Connect the steering and idler arms to the center link. Torque to specification; be sure to install the cotter pins.
11. If removed, install the radiator hoses and replace the fan shroud.
12. Fill the cooling system, install the dipstick, replace the oil, and check for leaks. Connect the battery and start the vehicle. Run

for five minutes with the heater on, then check again for leaks.

Slant Six— Barracuda and Challenger

1. Disconnect the battery and remove the oil dipstick. Jack up the vehicle and drain the oil.
2. Remove the steering center link with the idler arm attached.
3. Disconnect the exhaust pipe from its manifold and secure it out of the way.
4. Remove the oil pan attaching bolts. Rotate the engine crankshaft in order to clear the counterweights. Remove the oil pan.
5. To install the oil pan, reverse the removal procedure. Torque the pan bolts to 200 in. lbs.

318, 340, and 360 V8 —All Models

1. Disconnect the battery and remove the dipstick.
2. Jack up the vehicle and drain the oil. If so equipped, remove the torque converter-to-engine left housing strut.
3. Disconnect the steering center link from the steering and idler arms.
4. Disconnect the exhaust pipes from the manifolds and secure them out of the way.
5. Visually check to see if there is sufficient clearance to reach all of the oil pan bolts. If there is not, it will be necessary to raise the engine about 1½–2 in. Do this by loosening the motor mounts and jacking or hoisting the engine until the bolts in question become accessible. Be sure to raise the engine only the minimum amount necessary to reach these bolts. Remove the distri-

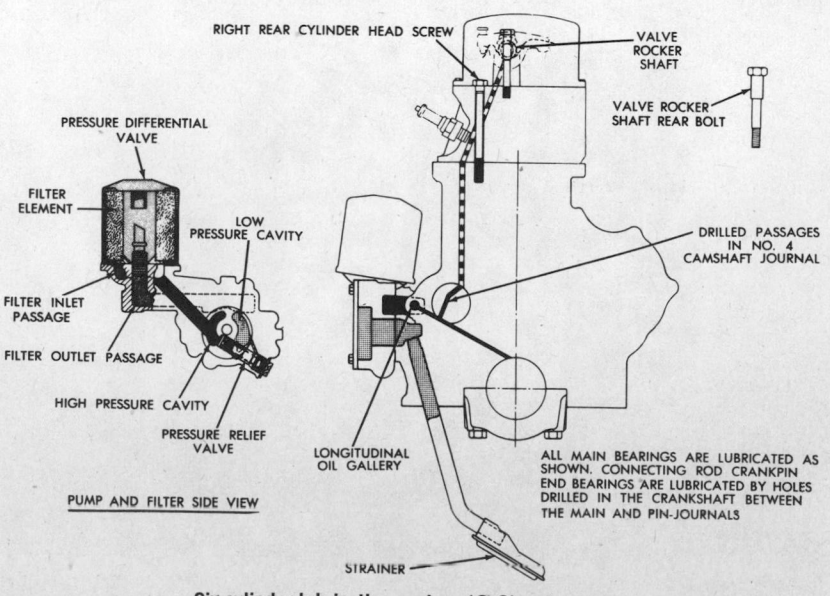

Six-cylinder lubrication system (© Chrysler Corp.)

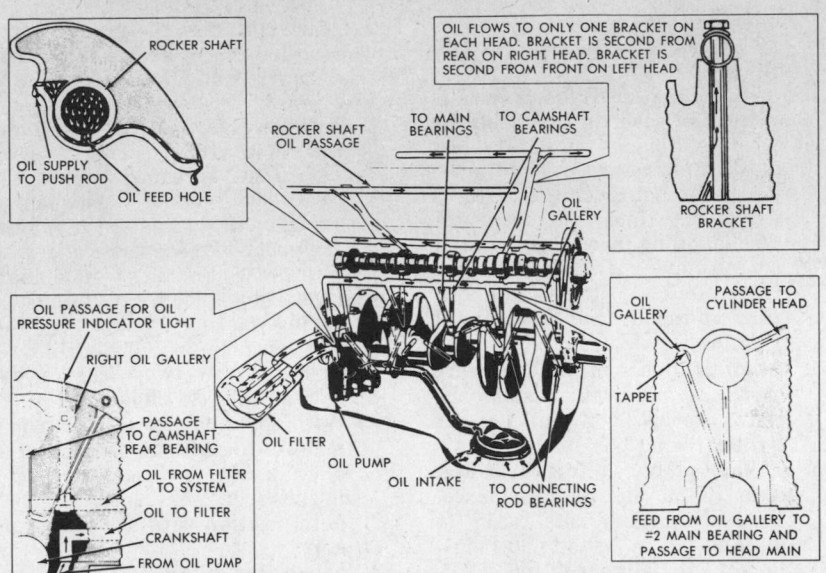

V8 (through 360 cu. in.) Lubrication system (© Chrysler Corp.)

butor cap for clearance. Remove the oil pan bolts, rotate the engine crankshaft to clear the counterweights, and remove the pan with a twisting motion. On 1976 and later models, unbolt the transmission mount and raise the transmission till the pan clears. On 1975 and later 360 hp engines, raise first the transmission to clear the rear of the pan, then the front of the engine to remove the pan.

6. When installing the oil pan, be sure that the oil strainer will be parallel with and will contact the pan bottom. Use a new gasket and torque the pan bolts to 200 in. lbs.

7. If it was necessary to jack the engine from its mounts, return it to its proper position at this time. Torque the engine mount bolts to specifications.

8. Install the engine-to-converter housing strut (if so equipped).

9. From this point, reverse the removal procedure.

383, 426, and 440 V8 —All Models

1. Disconnect the battery and remove the dipstick.

2. Jack up the vehicle and remove the center steering link from the steering and idler arms.

3. Disconnect the exhaust pipes from the manifolds and secure them out of the way.

4. If there is not sufficient clearance for the oil pan to clear the exhaust pipe, remove the clamp attaching the exhaust pipe to the extension and remove the exhaust pipe.

5. Drain the oil.

6. Remove the dust shield from the torque converter.

7. Extract the oil pan bolts. On some models, it may be necessary to jack the engine off its mounts (1½–2 in.) to reach the oil pan bolts. Do this by loosening the motor mounts and jacking or hoisting the engine. Raise the engine only the minimum amount required to reach the bolts in question. When removing the oil pan, be sure to rotate the crankshaft to clear the counterweights. Remove the pan with a twisting motion.

8. When installing the oil pan, be sure to use a new gasket. Torque the pan bolts to 200 in. lbs.

9. If it was necessary to jack the engine, lower it now and torque the engine mounts to specifications. To proceed, reverse the order of removal. After completion, be sure to start the vehicle and idle for at least five minutes. Check for leaks.

Oil Pump Removal and Installation

Six Cylinder

1. Drain radiator, disconnect upper and lower hoses, and remove fan shroud.

2. Raise vehicle on hoist, support front of engine with jack stand placed under right front corner of oil pan, and remove engine mount bolts. Do not support engine at crankshaft pulley or vibration damper.

3. Raise engine approximately 1½ —2 in.

4. Remove oil filter, oil pump attaching bolts, and pump assembly.

318, 340, and 360 V8

1. Remove oil pan.

2. Remove oil pump from rear main bearing cap.

383, 426, and 440 V8

1. The oil pump is located on the bottom side of the engine block at the filter.

2. Removal consists of taking out the attaching bolts and removing the pump and filter as an assembly.

3. To install the pump, reverse the removal procedure.

Rear Main Bearing Oil Seal

Service replacement seals are of split rubber type composition. This type of seal makes it possible to replace the upper half of the rear main oil seal without removing the engine from the car, or the crankshaft from the engine. When installing rubber seals, they must be replaced as a set and cannot be combined with the rope type rear main seal. The following procedure is for removing the rope type seal and replacing it with the rubber type seal.

NOTE: on vehicles with a 426 Hemi engine, remove the transmission and vibration damper in addition to the procedure listed below.

Replacement

1. Remove the oil pan.

2. Remove the rear seal retainer and the rear main bearing cap.

3. Remove the lower rope seal by prying from the side with a small screwdriver.

4. To remove the upper rope seal, drive up on either exposed end of the seal with a 6 in. piece of 3/16 in. brazing rod. When the opposite end of the seal starts to protrude from the block, have an assistant grasp it with pliers and gently pull it from the block while the opposite end is being driven.

5. Wipe crankshaft clean and lightly oil crankshaft and new seal before installing seal.

6. If necessary, loosen all main bearing caps slightly to lower the crankshaft which will ease installation.

Caution Do not allow the crankshaft to drop enough to permit the main bearings to become displaced on the crankshaft.

7. Hold the seal tightly against the crankshaft with the thumb (with paint stripe to the rear) and install the seal in the block groove. Rotate the crankshaft if necessary while installing the seal in the groove. *Make sure the sharp edges on the block groove do not cut or nick the rear of the seal.*

8. Install lower half of seal (with paint stripe to the rear) into the lower seal retainer.

9. Install rear main bearing cap.
10. Tighten all main bearing caps to specification.

NOTE: make sure all main bearings are located in their proper position before tightening the main bearing caps.

CLUTCH

All models utilize a single, dry plate clutch operated by a pedal suspended under the dash. All models are equipped with a return spring; some models have centrifugal rollers assembled between the pressure plate and cover.

NOTE: It is normal for the centrifugal rollers to rattle before the cover is installed.

Clutch Removal

1. Remove the transmission.
2. Remove the clutch housing pan.
3. Disconnect the fork return spring from the clutch housing and release fork.
4. Remove the spring washer fastening the fork rod to the torque shaft lever pin. Remove the pin from the rod and release fork.
5. On models with the A-903 or A-250 three-speed transmission, remove the clip and plain washer securing the interlock rod to the torque shaft lever and remove the washers and rod from the torque shaft.
6. Remove the sleeve assembly and clutch release bearing from the clutch release fork.
7. Punch-mark the clutch cover and flywheel so they may be installed in the same relative positions.
8. Loosen the clutch cover attaching screws one or two turns at a time, in rotation, to avoid bending the cover.
9. Remove the clutch assembly. Be careful not to contaminate the clutch with grease or oil.

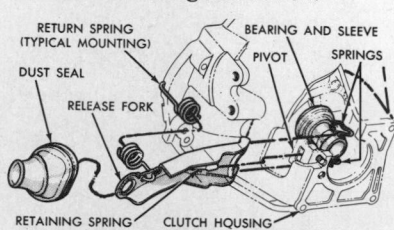

Clutch release fork, bearing and sleeve
(© Chrysler Corp)

Clutch Installation

1. Lightly lubricate the drive pinion bushing in the end of the crankshaft. Use about ½ teaspoonful of long-life chassis grease. Lubricant should be inserted in the cavity in front of the bushing.
2. Thoroughly clean the surfaces of the flywheel and pressure plate

with fine sandpaper. All oil or grease must be removed at this time.
3. Position the clutch disc, pressure plate, and cover in the mounting position. Springs on disc damper must be facing away from the flywheel. Do not touch the disc facing at any time. Insert a clutch disc aligning arbor or suitable substitute (such as a spare transmission drive pinion) through the disc hub and into the bushing.
4. Align the punch marks that were made at removal. Install the clutch cover bolts but do not tighten them.
5. Tighten all bolts a few turns at a time in an alternate sequence. Torque 5/16 in. bolts to 17 ft lbs. and 3/8 in. bolts to 30 ft lbs. Remove the alignment tool.

NOTE: 11 in. clutches don't use lockwashers on the bolts.

6. Pack the bearing sleeve cavity with high temperature grease. Apply the same lubricant to the release fork pads of the sleeve.
7. Insert the release bearing and sleeve assembly into the clutch housing as far forward as possible. Lightly lubricate the fork fingers and retaining spring.
8. Insert the fork fingers under the clutch sleeve retaining springs. Retaining springs on the sleeve must have lateral freedom.

9. Make sure that the groove in the seal is properly seated in the seal opening flange in the clutch housing. Replace the pedal rod on the torque shaft lever pin and secure it with a spring washer.
10. Insert the threaded end of the fork rod assembly in the opening provided in the end of the release fork rod. Replace the eye end of the fork rod on the torque shaft lever pin and lock it with a spring washer.
11. If applicable, install the fork return spring between the release fork and the clutch housing.
12. With the A-903 or A-250 transmission install the spring and plain washer with interlock rod in the torque shaft lever and lock it in position with a washer and clip.
13. When installing the transmission, be sure not to allow grease to settle on the splines or pilot end of the transmission drive pinion.
14. Install the transmission and adjust the clutch pedal free-play.

Clutch Linkage (Height and Free-Play) Adjustment

1. If the vehicle is equipped with a gearshift interlock rod (A-903 or A-250 transmission), disconnect it by loosening the rod swivel clamp screw.

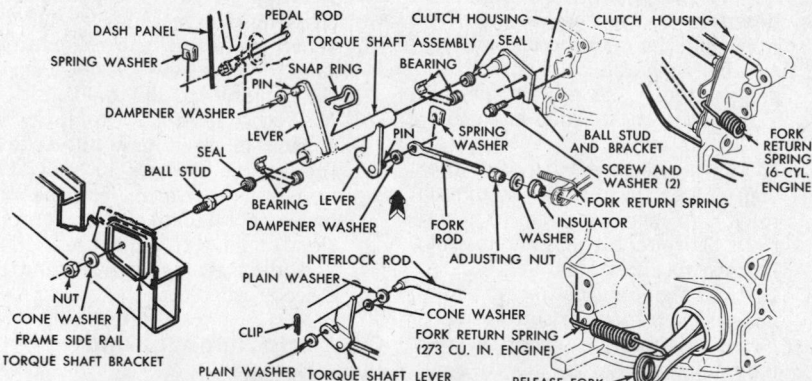

Typical clutch linkage (© Chrysler Corp)

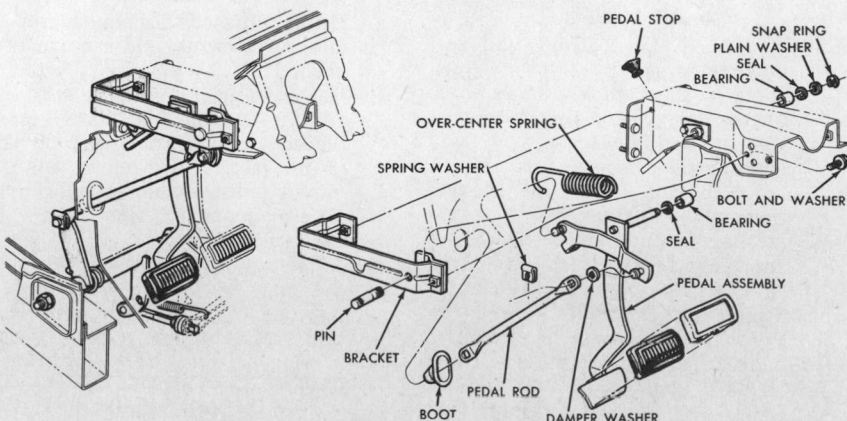

Typical clutch pedal and linkage (© Chrysler Corp)

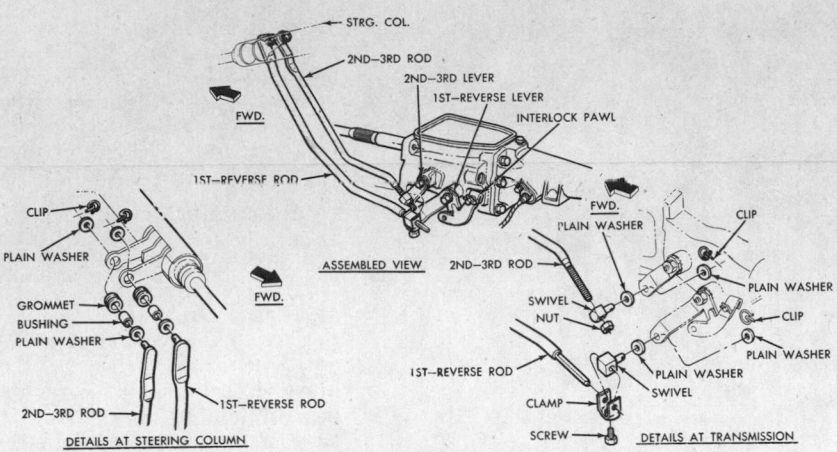

3-speed column shift linkage—sixes with A-903 or A-250 transmission with clutch/gearshift interlock
(© Chrysler Corp)

2. Adjust the fork rod by rotating the self-locking nut to provide 5/32 in. free-play at the fork end. This adjustment will result in the proper 1 in. free-play at the clutch pedal.
3. Adjust the gearshift interlock.

Gearshift Interlock Adjustment
Six Cylinder with A-903 or A-250 Transmission

1. Disconnect the interlock pawl from the clutch rod swivel on the side of the transmission.
2. Adjust the clutch pedal free-play.
3. With the first-reverse lever on the transmission in the neutral (middle detent) position, the interlock pawl should enter the slot in the first-reverse lever.
4. Loosen the swivel clamp bolt and move the swivel on the rod to enter the pawl. Install the washers with a clip. Hold the interlock pawl forward and torque the swivel clamp bolt to 100-125 in. lbs. The clutch pedal must be in the fully returned position during this adjustment.
NOTE: Under no circumstances should the clutch rod be pulled rearward to engage the pawl swivel.
5. Shift the clutch through all gear positions at least three times. Clutch action should be normal.
6. Disengage the clutch and shift halfway to first or reverse gear. The clutch pedal should be held down by the interlock to within 1-2 in. of the floor.

MANUAL TRANSMISSION

Manual transmission applications are as follow: a top cover three-speed A-903 with synchromesh on second and third gears only used on 6-cylinder models through 1972; a top cover three-speed A-250 with synchromesh on second and third gears only used on 1973-74 6-cylinder models; a side cover fully synchronized three-speed A-230 used on 1970 and later V8 and 6-cylinder heavy duty models; a top cover fully synchronized three-speed A-390 used on 1975 and later 6-cylinder models; a side cover fully synchronized four-speed A-833 transmission. The A-833 transmission was offered with V8s only through 1975, and with both sixes and V8s with an overdrive fourth gear beginning 1976.

All manual transmissions have a serial number stamped on a pad on the right side of the case. The third, fourth, and fifth digits are the transmission model number.

Removal and Installation

1. Raise and support the car safely.
2. Remove the shift rods and the clutch interlock rod (A-903 and A-250 only) from the transmission levers.
3. After marking both parts for reassembly, detach the driveshaft and the rear universal joint.
CAUTION: *Don't nick or scratch the ground surface on the sliding spline yoke.*
4. Disconnect the speedometer cable, transmission controlled spark switch, and back-up light switch. Remove the console, if necessary, and unbolt the shifter from the extension housing on floor-shift models. The shift lever unbolts from the shifter, except on 1970 4-speed and 1976 and later Overdrive—4 models. On these, insert a 0.014 in. feeler gauge alongside the driver's side of the lever and pull the lever out.
5. Unfasten the transmission extension housing from the center crossmember and jack up the engine and transmission about 1 in.

6. Remove the center crossmember.
7. On some models it may be necessary to disconnect or loosen the exhaust system and position it to one side to gain clearance in order to remove the transmission.
8. Support the transmission on a jack. Remove the bolts which secure the transmission to the clutch housing.
9. Slide the transmission toward the rear until the input shaft clears the clutch disc. Lower the transmission and remove it from the car.
10. Installation is the reverse of removal. Lubricate the input shaft pilot bearing in the flywheel and the bearing retainer pilot (for the clutch release sleeve). Do not lubricate the clutch splines or the clutch release levers.
11. Position the transmission so that the drive pinion is centered in the clutch housing bore. Push the transmission forward until the pinion shaft enters the clutch disc. Place the transmission in gear. Twist the output shaft until the splines are in alignment. Push the transmission forward until it is seated against the clutch housing.

Caution The transmission must not hang after the pinion is inside the clutch.

12. Replace the transmission housing bolts. Torque them to 50 ft lbs. With a drift, align the crossmember bolt holes and install the bolts. Torque them to 40-50 ft lbs. Remove the engine support fixture. Tighten the engine mount-to-crossmember bolt. Install and perform the gearshift linkage adjustment. Connect the driveshaft and universal joints. Connect the exhaust system and fill the transmission with lubricant.

Linkage Adjustment
Column Shift through 1974

1. Loosen both shift rod swivels at the ends of the two long rods from the column. Be sure that the transmission shift levers are in the neutral (middle) positions.
2. Move the column shift lever into reverse to line up the locating slots in the bottom of the steering column shift housing and the bearing housing. Place a tool in the slot to hold the lever in place.
3. Place a screwdriver between the crossover blade (between the two column levers) and the second-third lever (the top one) at the steering column so that both lever pins are engaged by the cross-over blade.

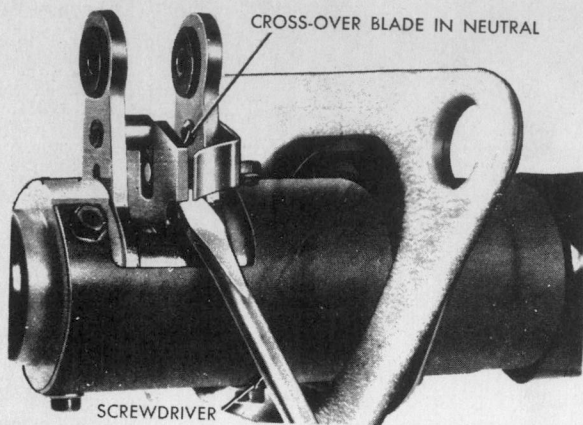

Holding cross-over blades in neutral (© Chrysler Corp)

4. Set the first-reverse lever (the back one) on the transmission to the reverse position (rotate it clockwise).
5. Adjust the first-reverse rod swivel by sliding the swivel along the rod. Tighten the swivel bolt.
6. Remove the gearshift housing locating tool and shift the column lever into the neutral position.
7. Adjust the second-third rod swivel by sliding the swivel along the rod. Tighten the swivel bolt.
8. Remove the screwdriver from the crossover blade at the steering column, and shift through all gears to check adjustment and cross-over (through neutral) smoothness.
9. Check that the ignition switch will lock with the shift lever in reverse only, without applying pressure to the shift lever.

1975 and later Column Shift

1. Loosen both shift rod swivels at the ends of the two long rods from the column.
2. Make sure the transmission levers are in the neutral or middle positions.
3. Move the column shift lever into neutral to line up the locating slots in the bottom of the steering column shift housing and the bearing housing. Install a tool into the slot to hold the lever in place.
4. Place a screwdriver between the crossover blade (between the two column levers) and the second-third (the upper one) lever so that both lever pins are engaged by the crossover blade.
5. Tighten both swivel bolts.
6. Remove the gearshift housing locating tool.
7. Remove the screwdriver.
8. Shift through all gears to check the adjustment and cross-over (through neutral) smoothness.
9. Check that the ignition switch will lock with the shift lever in reverse only, without applying any pressure to the shift lever.

Three-Speed Floorshift

1. Make an alignment tool out of 1/16 in. thick metal. It should be 5/8 in. wide and 2 3/8 in. long.
2. Detach the shift rod swivels.
3. From under the car, insert the alignment tool through the shifter levers and the shifter to hold the levers in the neutral positions.
4. Place both shift levers on the transmission side cover in the neutral or middle position.
5. Adjust the swivels so that they can be installed freely in the shifter lever holes.
6. Remove the alignment tool and check the shifting action.

Four-Speed Floorshift

1. Remove all the shift rods from the transmission shift levers.

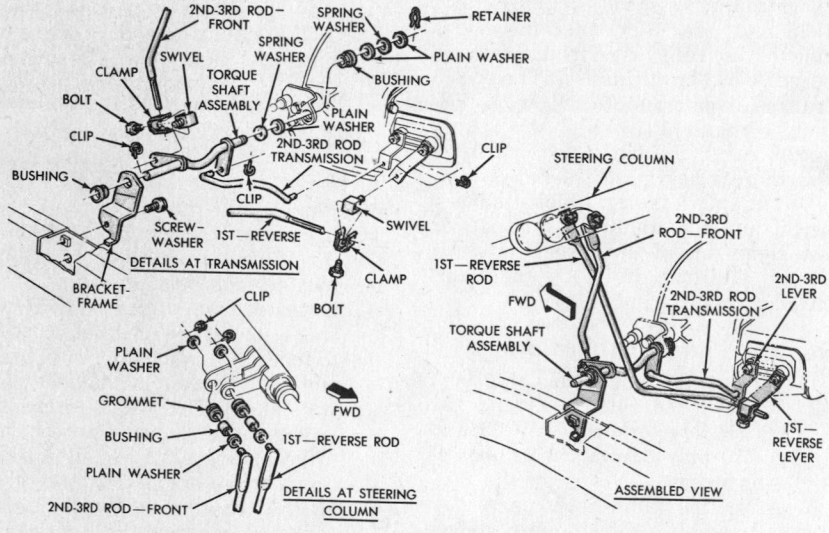

Typical three-speed column shift linkage (© Chrysler Corp)

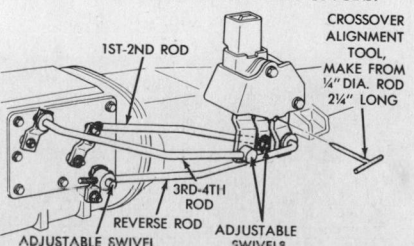

Four-speed floor shift linkage adjustment (© Chrysler Corp)

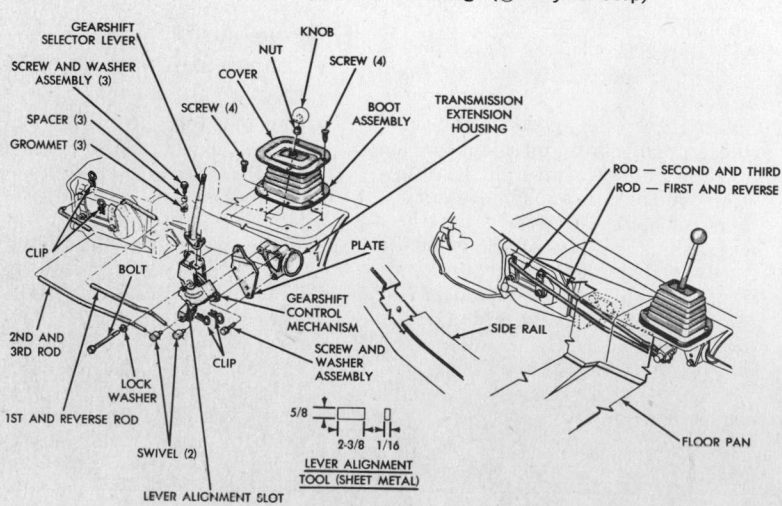

Three-speed floor shift linkage—Barracuda and Challenger; Valiant and Dart similar (© Chrysler Corp)

2. Place all the transmission shift levers in their neutral positions.

3. From under the car, insert a ¼ in. rod or drill bit about 2¼ in. long through the shifter levers and the shifter to hold the levers in the neutral positions.

4. Adjust the shift rods so that they can be installed freely in the shifter lever holes.

5. Remove the aligning tool and check the shifting action.

AUTOMATIC TRANSMISSION

Two different transmission models are used in all models. On models through 1971, the model may be identified by the model number, which is embossed on the lower left side of the bell housing. On 1972 and later models, the model may be identified by the part number, which is stamped on a pad on the left side of the case oil pan flange. The A-727 transmission has a more gradual slope to the converter housing than does the A-904. Generally speaking, all 6 cylinder and 318 V8 engines for normal use are equipped with a model A-904 Torqueflite, while all larger V8s use the model A-727. Starting 1976, normal duty 360 V8s (except HP) use an A-904 torqueflite. Fleet, police, and taxi service 6 cylinder and 318 V8 engines use the A-727 also.

Neutral Safety/Backup Light Switch Replacement

The neutral safety switch is mounted in the transmission case. When the gearshift lever is placed in either the Park or Neutral position, a cam, which is attached to the transmission lever inside the transmission, contacts the neutral safety switch and provides a ground to complete the starter solenoid circuit.

The back-up lamp switch is incorporated into the neutral safety switch The center terminal is for the neutral safety switch and the two outer terminals are for the back-up lamps.

There is no adjustment for the switch. If a malfunction occurs, first check to make sure that the transmission gearshift linkage is properly adjusted. If the malfunction continues, the switch must be removed and replaced.

To remove the switch, disconnect the electrical leads and unscrew the switch from the transmission. Use a drain pan to catch the transmission fluid that drains out of the mounting hole. Install a new switch using a new seal and refill the transmission to the proper level.

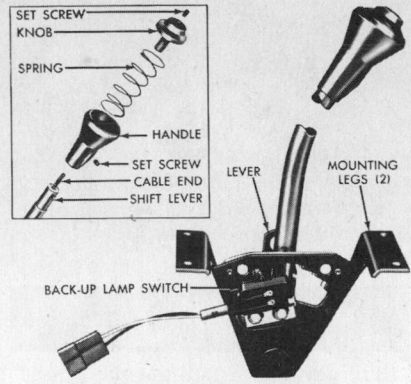

Automatic console shift unit disassembled
(© Chrysler Corp)

Shift Linkage Adjustment

1. Under the car, loosen the adjustable rod swivel lock bolt.
2. Put the floorshift or column shift shift lever into Park.
3. Move the transmission shift lever all the way to the rear.
4. Tighten the swivel lock bolt without putting any pressure on the linkage.
5. The shift effort must be free and the detents should feel crisp. All gate stops must be positive. It should be possible to start the engine in Park and Neutral only.

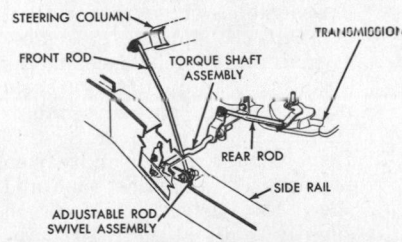

Column shift linkage—Barracuda and Challenger
(© Chrysler Corp)

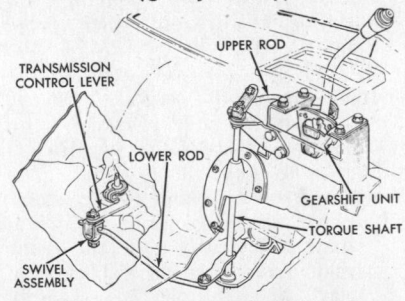

Typical automatic console shift linkage
(© Chrysler Corp)

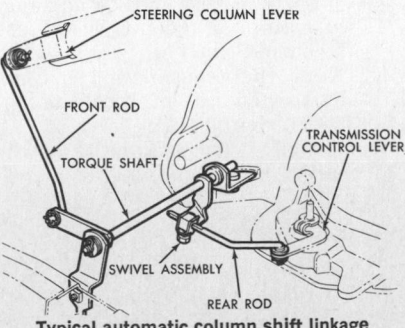

Typical automatic column shift linkage
(© Chrysler Corp)

Band Adjustments
Kickdown Band

The kickdown band adjusting screw is located on the left-hand side of the transmission case near the throttle lever shaft.

1. Loosen the locknut and back off about five turns. Be sure the adjusting screw is free in the case.
2. Torque the adjusting screw to 72 in. lbs.
3. Back off the adjusting screw exactly to specification. Keep the screw from turning, and tighten the locknut to 29 ft. lbs. through 1973 and to 35 ft. lbs. on later models.

Kickdown Band Adjustment

A-904	2 turns
A-727	2½ turns
Hemi V-8 and 440-6	1½ turns
1971 440 w/dual exhaust	2 turns

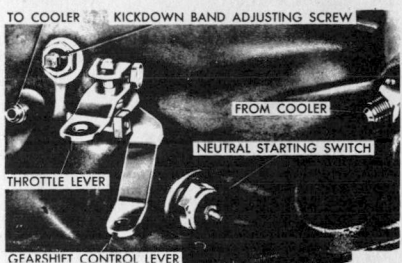

Torqueflite external controls
(© Chrysler Corp)

Low and Reverse Band

Access to the low and reverse band requires pan removal.

1. Raise the car, drain transmission and remove the transmission pan.
2. Loosen the band adjusting screw locknut and back it off about five turns. Be sure the adjusting screw turns freely in the lever.
3. Tighten the adjusting screw to 72 in. lbs. On 1974 and later A-904 transmissions with a six-cylinder engine, torque the adjusting screw to 41 in. lbs.
4. Back off the adjusting screw exactly to specification. Keep the screw from turning and torque the locknut to 35 ft. lbs. through 1973 and to 30 ft. lbs. for later models.
5. Reinstall pan, using new gasket, and torque the pan bolts to 150 in. lbs.
6. Refill transmission.

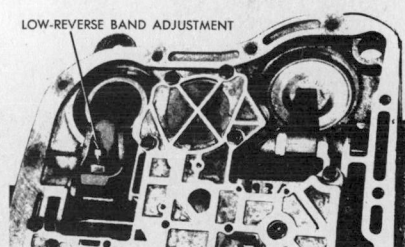

Low-Reverse band adjustment screw location
(© Chrysler Corp)

Low and Reverse Band Screw Adjustment

A-904
Six (through 1973)	3½ turns
Six (1974 and later)	7 turns
318, 360 V8	4 turns
A-727	2 turns

Pan Removal and Installation, Fluid and Filter Change

1. Drive the car until it is thoroughly warm.
2. Unbolt the pan. It holds six or more quarts, so be ready with a large container.

NOTE: If the fluid removed smells burnt, serious transmission troubles, probably due to overheating should be suspected.

3. Remove the access plate in front of the torque converter. With the aid of a socket wrench on the vibration damper bolt, rotate the engine clockwise to bring the converter drain to the bottom. Position the container under the converter, remove the drain plug, and allow the fluid to drain.

Replace the converter drain plug and torque it to 110 in. lbs for a 7/16 in. head plug and 90 in. lbs for a 5/16 in. plug. Install the access plate.

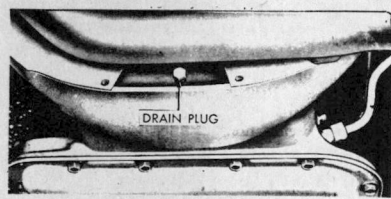

DRAIN PLUG

Converter drain plug
(© Chrysler Corp)

4. Unscrew and discard the filter.
5. Install a new filter. The proper torque is 35 in. lbs.
6. Clean out the pan, being extremely careful not to leave any lint from rags inside.
7. Replace the pan with a new gasket. Tighten the bolts to 150 in. lbs in a crisscross pattern.
8. Pour six quarts of DEXRON® automatic transmission fluid through the dipstick tube.
9. Start the engine in Neutral and let it idle for two minutes or more.
10. Hold your foot on the Brake and shift through D, 2, 1, and R and back to N.
11. Add enough fluid to bring the level to the ADD ONE PINT mark.
12. Operate the car until the transmission is thoroughly warmed up, then check the level. Engage the parking brake and place the selector lever in the Neutral position. After the engine has idled for about two minutes, move the selector lever slowly through all the gear positions, pausing momentarily in each and ending with the lever in the Neutral position. When the fluid is hot, the fluid level should be at the FULL mark, or slightly below. Add fluid as necessary.

NOTE: The manufacturer recommends MOPAR automatic transmission sealer be added to reduce fluid leakage resulting from hardening or shrinking of the seals in high-mileage vehicles.

U-JOINTS

The driveshaft is a one-piece tubular shaft with two universal joints, one at each end. The front joint yoke serves as a slip yoke on the transmission output shaft. The rear universal joint is the type that must be disassembled to be removed.

Driveshaft and U-Joints

Removal and Installation

You can avoid loss of lubricant from the rear of the transmission by raising the rear of the car before removing the driveshaft.

1. Match mark the driveshaft, U-joint and pinion flange before disassembly. These marks must be realigned during reassembly to maintain the balance of the driveline. Failure to align them may result in excessive vibration.
2. Remove both of the clamps from the differential pinion yoke and slide the driveshaft forward slightly to disengage the U-joint from the pinion yoke. Tape the two loose U-joint bearings together to prevent them from falling off.

CAUTION: Do not disturb the bearing assembly retaining strap. Never allow the driveshaft to hang from either of the U-joints. Always support the unattached end of the shaft to prevent damage to the joints.

3. Lower the rear end of the driveshaft and gently slide the front yoke/driveshaft assembly rearward disengaging the assembly from the transmission output shaft. Be careful not to damage the splines or the surface which the output shaft seal rides on.
4. Check the transmission output shaft seal for signs of leakage.
5. Installation is the reverse of removal. Be sure to align the match marks. The torque for the clamp bolts is 14 ft. lbs.

U-Joint Overhaul

1. Remove the driveshaft.
2. To remove the bearings from the yoke, first remove the bearing retainer snap rings located at the base or open end of each bearing cap.
3. Pressing on one of the bearings, drive the bearing in toward the center of the joint. This will force the cross to push the opposite bearing out of the universal joint. This step may be performed using a hammer and drift or a vise and sockets or pieces of pipe. However installation of bearings must be done using the vise or a press.
4. After the bearing has been pushed all the way out of the yoke, pull up the cross slightly and pack some washers under it. Then press on the end of the cross from which the bearing was just removed to force the first bearing out of the yoke. Repeat steps 3 and 4 to remove the remaining two bearings.
5. If a grease fitting is supplied with the new U-joint assembly, install it. If no fitting is supplied, make sure that the joint is amply greased. Pack grease in the recesses in the end of the cross.
6. To reassemble start both bearing cups into the yoke at the same time and hold the cross carefully in the fingers in its installed position. Be careful not to knock any rollers out of position.
7. Squeeze both bearings in a vise or press, moving the bearings into place. Continually check for free movement of the cross in the bearings as they are pressed into the yoke. If there is a sudden increase in the force needed to press the bearings into place, or the cross starts to bind, the bearings are cocked in the yoke. They must be removed and restarted in the yoke. Failure to do so will greatly reduce the life of the bearing. Repeat steps 6 and 7 to reinstall the remaining two bearings.

REAR AXLE

Four different rear axle assemblies have been used. A 7¼ in. (ring gear diameter) unitized carrier axle is used with all six cylinder applications and on some late production 318 V8 models. An 8¼ in. unitized carrier axle is installed in most mid 1972 and later models with 318, 340, or 360 V8s. An 8¾ in. removable differential carrier axle is used on models through 1974 with 318, 340, or 383 engines. A 9¾ in. unitized carrier axle is installed in 1970-71 Barracuda and Challenger models equipped with the high-performance 426 Hemi or 440 V8s.

These axles can be visually identified as follows:

The 7¼ in. axle has a 9 bolt rear cover with a filler plug. The 8¼ in. has a 10 bolt rear cover without a filler plug. The 8¾ in. has a welded rear cover. The 9¾ in. has a 10 bolt rear cover with a filler plug.

All axles, except the 7¼ in. unit through 1973, have a ratio identification tag under one of the cover or carrier bolts. The 7¼ in. axle through 1973 has an axle ratio code marking on the front of the pad at the bottom of the housing.

Axle Shaft, Bearing, and Seal

Removal and Installation

Because the axle shafts are slightly different from one rear axle assembly to another, individual service procedures are required for each axle shaft assembly. Two very important points to remember when servicing any rear axle assembly are:

1. Always elevate *both* rear wheels when performing any rear axle service, or when using the engine or other means to rotate the axle.
2. On those cars that are equipped with a Sure-Grip differential, you must never rotate one axle shaft without rotating the other. If it is necessary to rotate one of the axle shafts, *both* shafts must be in position and both must be rotated. Otherwise, alignment of the axle shafts will be very difficult.

NOTE: This procedure also covers axle shaft end-play adjustment, on those axles on which it is possible.

7¼ In. Axle

NOTE: Whenever this axle assembly is serviced, both the break support plate gaskets and the inner axle shaft oil seal must be renewed. There is no provision for adjusting axle shaft end-play.

1. Support the rear of the car and remove the rear wheels.
2. Detach the clips which secure the brake drum to the axle shaft studs and remove the brake drum.
3. Disconnect the brake lines at the wheel cylinders and block off the lines.
4. Through the access hole in the axle shaft flange, remove the axle shaft retaining nuts.
5. Attach a puller or slide hammer to the axle shaft flange and remove the axle shaft.
6. Remove the brake assembly from the axle housing.
7. Remove the axle shaft oil seal from the axle housing.

CAUTION: *Never use a torch or other heat source as an aid in removing any axle shaft components as this will result in serious damage to the axle assembly.*

8. Place the axle shaft housing retaining collar in a vise. With a chisel, cut deeply into the retaining collar at 90° intervals.
9. To assemble and install the axle shaft, replace the retainer plate bearing, and bearing retainer collar on the axle shaft, using a press.
10. Insert new axle shaft oil seals in the axle housing and lightly grease the outside diameter of the bearing.
11. Replace the foam gasket on the studs of the axle housing and install the brake support plate assembly on the axle housing studs. Refit the outer gasket.
12. Very carefully slide the axle shaft assembly through the oil seal and engage the splines of the differential slide gear. Using a non-metallic hammer, lightly tap the end of the axle shaft to position the axle shaft bearing in the recess of the axle housing. Install the retainer plate over the axle housing studs and torque the securing nuts to 35 ft lbs.
13. Reconnect the brake lines to the wheel cylinders and bleed the hydraulic system.
14. Install the brake drum and retaining clips.
15. Refit the rear wheels and lower the car.

8¼ In. Axle

NOTE: There is no provision for adjusting axle shaft endplay on this axle.

1. Raise the vehicle and remove the wheels.
2. Clean all dirt from the housing cover and remove the cover to drain the lubricant.
3. Remove the brake drum.
4. Rotate the differential case until the differential pinion shaft lockscrew can be removed. Remove the lockscrew and pinion shaft.
5. Push the axle shaft toward the center of the vehicle and remove the C-lock from the groove on the axle shaft.
6. Pull the axle shaft from the housing, being careful not to damage the bearing which remains in the housing.
7. Inspect the axle shaft bearings and replace any doubtful parts. Whenever the axle shaft is replaced, the bearings should also be replaced.
8. Remove the axle shaft seal from the bore in the housing, using the button end of the axle shaft.
9. Remove the axle shaft bearing from the housing. Do not reuse the bearing or the seal.
10. Check the bearing shoulder in the axle housing for imperfec-

tions. These should be corrected with a file or polish.
11. Clean the axle shaft bearing cavity.
12. Install the axle shaft bearing in the cavity. Be sure that the bearing is not cocked and that it is seated firmly against the shoulder.
13. Install the axle shaft bearing seal. It should be seated beyond the end of the flange face.
14. Insert the axle shaft, making sure that the splines do not damage the seal. Be sure that the splines are properly engaged with the differential side gear splines.
15. Install the C-locks in the grooves on the axle shafts. Pull the shafts outward so that the C-locks seat in the counterbore of the differential side gears.
16. Install the differential pinion shaft through the case and pinions. Install the lockscrew and secure it in position.
17. Clean the housing and gasket surfaces. Install the cover and a new gasket.

NOTE: Replacement gaskets may not be available for differential covers. In this case, the use of a gel type nonsticking sealant is recommended.

Be sure that the rear axle ratio identification tag is replaced under one of the cover bolts. Refill the axle with the specified lubricant.

18. Install the brake drum and wheel.
19. Lower the vehicle.

8 ¾ and 9¾ In. Axles

NOTE: Whenever this axle assembly is serviced, both the brake support plate gaskets and the inner axle shaft oil seal must be renewed.

1. Jack up the rear of the car and remove the rear wheels.
2. Detach the clips which secure the brake drum to the axle shaft studs, and remove the brake drum.
3. Through the access hole in the axle shaft flange, remove the axle shaft retaining nuts. The right-side axle shaft has a threaded adjuster in the retainer plate and a lock under one of its studs which should be removed at this time.
4. Remove the parking brake strut.
5. Attach a puller to the axle shaft. Remove the shaft.
6. Remove the brake assembly from the axle housing.
7. Remove the axle shaft oil seal from the axle housing.

CAUTION: *It is advisable to position some sort of a protective sleeve over the axle shaft seal surface next to the bearing collar to protect the seal surface. Never use a torch or other heat source as an aid in removing any axle shaft components as this will result in serious damage to the axle assembly.*

8. Wipe the axle housing seal bore clean. Install a new axle shaft oil seal.

NOTE: All 8¾ in. axle shaft bearings are factory packed with a special lubricant. If the roller bearing must be repacked, the factory lubricant must be washed out; it is not compatible with the other lubricants.

9. Place the axle shaft housing retaining collar in a vise. With a chisel, cut deeply into the retaining collar at 90° intervals. Remove the bearing with a puller.
10. Remove the bearing roller retainer flange by cutting off the lower edge with a chisel.
11. Grind or file a section off the flange of the inner bearing cone and remove the bearing rollers.
12. Pull the bearing roller retainer down as far as possible and cut it off with side cutters.
13. Remove the roller bearing cup with its protective sleeves.
14. To prevent damage to the seal journal when the bearing cone is removed, protect the journal with a single wrap of shim stock that is 0.002 in. thick and is held in place by a rubber band.
15. Using a puller, remove the bearing cone. Remove the seal in the bearing retainer plate and replace it with a new seal.
16. To assemble the axle, first install the retainer plate and seal assembly on the axle shaft.
17. Grease the wheel bearings and install them.
18. Install a new axle shaft bearing cup, cone and collar on the shaft. Check the axle shaft seal journal for imperfections and if necessary, polish with no. 600 crocus cloth.
19. Thoroughly clean the axle housing flange face and brake support. Install a new rubber/asbestos gasket onto the axle housing studs. Next, install the brake support plate assembly on the left side of the axle housing.
20. Lightly grease the outside edge of the bearing cup. Install the bearing cup in the bearing bore.
21. Replace the foam gasket on the studs of the left-side axle housing and very carefully slide the axle shaft assembly through the oil seal and engage the splines of the differential side gear.
22. Using a non-metallic hammer, lightly tap the end of the axle shaft to position the axle shaft bearing in the recess of the axle housing. Install the retainer plate over the axle housing studs and, starting with the bottom

securing nut, torque the nuts to 30–35 ft lbs.
23. Repeat step 19 for the right-side axle housing.
24. At the right side of the axle housing, back off the threaded adjuster until the inner face of the adjuster is flush with the inner face of the retainer plate. Very carefully slide the axle shaft assembly through the oil seal and engage the splines of the differential side gear. Repeat step 22.
25. Mount a dial indicator on the left brake support. Turn the adjuster clockwise until both wheel bearings are seated and there is zero end-play in the axle shafts. Back off the adjuster about four notches to establish an end-play of 0.008-0.018 in. on 8¾ in. axles and 0.008-0.012 for the 9¾.
26. Lightly tap the end of the left shaft with a non-metallic hammer. This will seat the right wheel bearing cup against the adjuster. Turn the axle shaft several times so that a true end-play reading is obtained.
27. Remove one retainer plate nut and install the adjuster lock. If the lock tab does not mate with the notch in the adjuster, turn the adjuster slightly until it does. Refit the nut and torque it to 30–35 ft lbs.
28. Recheck the axle shaft end-play. If it is not correct, repeat the adjustment. When the adjustment is complete, remove the dial indicator.
29. Install the parking brake strut.

Refit the brake drum and retaining clips.
30. Install the rear wheels and lower the car.

JACKING, HOISTING

Jack car at front control arms and at rear under axle housing.

To lift at frame use adapters, so that contact will be made at points shown. Lifting pads must extend beyond sides of supporting structure.

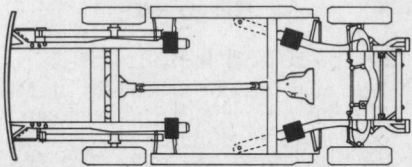

Positioning lift adapter (© Chrysler Corp)

FRONT SUSPENSION

All Chrysler vehicles utilize a torsion bar type front suspension. Aspen and Volare have transverse torsion bars; all others have longitudinal (parallel to the frame) bars. Compression type lower ball joints are located in the steering knuckles. When servicing the front suspension, it should be kept in mind that rubber bushings must not be lubricated at any time. In addition, any front sus-

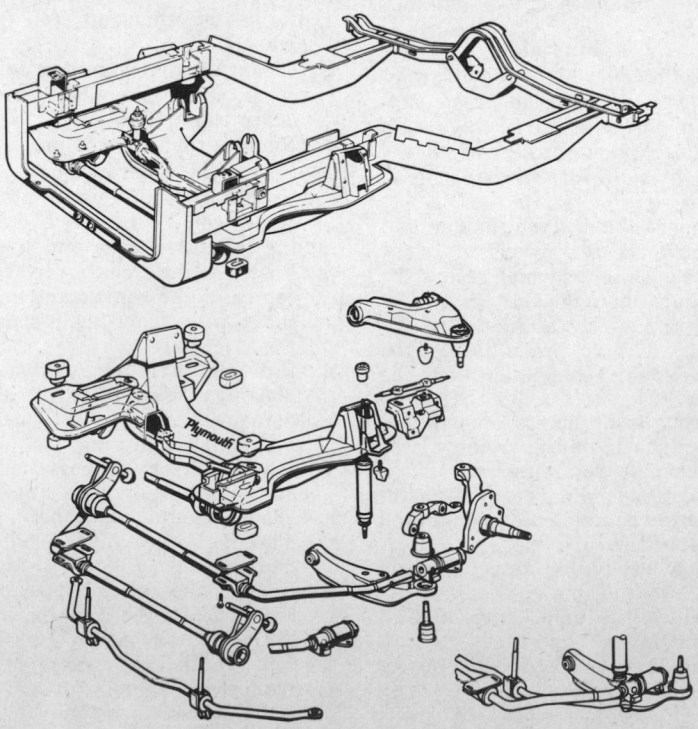

Aspen, Volare isolated front suspension with transverse torsion bars
(© Chrysler Corp.)

pension adjustments or servicing that is required on any part that contains rubber should be tightened with the suspension at the proper height and with full vehicle weight on the point in question.

Shock Absorber
Removal and Replacement

1. Remove the washer and nut from shock absorber upper end. Be sure to note the positions of all small parts.
2. Jack the vehicle until the wheels clear the floor. Remove the shock absorber lower attaching bolt or nut. Allow the control arm to lower itself.
3. Fully compress the shock absorber by pushing upward. Pull the shock firmly and remove it from the vehicle.
4. Purge the new shock of air by repeatedly extending it in its normal position and compressing it while inverted. It is normal for there to be more resistance to extension than to compression. Fully compress the new shock absorber. Insert the mount through the upper bushing and install the retainer and nut. Torque the nut to 25 ft lbs. Be sure that all the retainers are installed with the concave side in contact with rubber.
5. Position and align the lower mount of shock absorber. Install the bolt (from the rear) or nut and finger-tighten it. Lower the vehicle and torque the nut to 50 ft lbs. (35 on Aspen/Volare) with the full weight of the vehicle on the wheels.

Ball Joints
Inspection

NOTE: Before performing the inspection, make sure the wheel bearings are adjusted correctly and that the control arm bushings are in good condition.

1. Place a jack under the lower control arm as close to the wheel as possible.
2. Raise the car until there is 1-2 in. of clearance under the wheel.
3. Insert a bar under the wheel and pry upward. If the wheel raises noticeably the ball joints are worn. Determine if the upper or lower ball joint is worn by visual inspection while prying on the wheel.
4. You can make a more accurate measurement by clamping a dial indicator to the lower control arm and measuring the lower ball joint stud movement.

NOTE: Due to the distribution of forces in the suspension the lower ball joint is usually the defective joint.

The manufacturer's limit for lower ball joint play, measured at the joint, is 0.020 in. for Aspen and Volare and 0.070 in. for all others. This limit may not agree with your state's inspection regulations.

Removal and Installation
Upper Ball Joint

1. Raise the car by placing a jack stand under the lower control arm as close to the wheel as possible. Remove the wheel.
2. Remove the nut that attaches the upper ball joint to the steering knuckle. Loosen the ball joint stud from the steering knuckle. Press the ball joint stud out with a ball joint removal tool. Never strike the ball joint stud.
3. Unscrew the upper ball joint from the upper control arm and remove it from the vehicle.
4. Position a new ball joint on the upper control arm and screw the joint into the arm. Be careful not to cross thread the joint in the arm. Torque it to 125 ft lbs.
5. Position a new seal on the ball joint stud and install the seal in the ball joint making sure the seal is fully seated on the ball joint housing.
6. Position the ball joint stud in the steering knuckle and install the retaining nut. Torque the nut to 100 ft lbs. Install a new cotter pin
7. Lubricate the ball joint. Adjust the wheel alignment.

Lower Ball Joint—Valiant, Dart, Barracuda, Challenger

The lower ball joint and the steering arm are an integral unit. Because of this, they cannot be replaced separately.

1. Take the upper control arm rebound bumper off.
2. Raise the car. Be sure that the suspension is under no load (full rebound).

CAUTION: *If jacks are used, there must be a support placed between the K-member and the jack.*

3. Back-off (counterclockwise) the torsion bar adjuster to remove the load on the torsion bar.
4. Remove the wheel, tire, and the drum or disc brake.
5. Unfasten the two lower bolts from the brake support which secure the ball joint/steering arm assembly to the steering knuckle.
6. Remove the end of the tie rod from the steering arm with a puller or removal tool.
7. Use a ball joint stud puller to remove the ball joint stud from the lower control arm. The ball joint/steering arm assembly may now be removed.

8. Position a new seal over the new ball joint, being certain that the lip of the seal is fully seated in the housing.
9. Attach the ball joint/steering arm assembly to the steering knuckle and tighten the attachment bolts to 110 ft lbs. through 1972 and to 160 ft lbs. starting 1973.
10. Fit the ball joint stud into the opening in the lower control arm. Tighten the stud retaining nut to 100 ft lbs starting 1976, or 85 ft lbs (through 1975). Install the cotter pin. Lubricate the ball joint.
11. Check the tie rod seal for signs of damage and replace it if necessary. Attach the tie rod end to the steering knuckle arm. Torque its securing nut to 40 ft lbs. Install the cotter pin.
12. Load the torsion bar by rotating its adjusting nut clockwise.
13. Install the wheel and brake assembly. Adjust the front wheel bearing.
14. Lower the car. Install the upper control arm rebound bumper and tighten its securing nut.
15. Adjust the front end height and wheel alignment.

Lower Ball Joint—Aspen, Volare

1. Remove the lower control arm rebound bumper.
2. Raise the vehicle so that the front suspension drops to the downward limit of its travel. Position jackstands beneath the front frame for extra support.
3. Remove the wheel and tire assembly.
4. Remove the brake caliper from its mounts and tie it up out of the way so that there is no strain on the flexible brake hose.
5. Remove the hub and rotor assembly, splash shield, and lower shock absorber mounting nut and bolt.
6. Unload the torsion bar by rotating the adjusting bolt counterclockwise.
7. Remove the upper ball joint stud cotter pin and nut. Use a ball joint removal tool to press the ball joint out. Never strike the ball joint stud.
8. Press the ball joint out of the lower control arm.
9. Press the new ball joint into the lower control arm.
10. Place a new seal over the ball joint. Press the retainer portion of the seal down over the ball joint housing until it locks into position.
11. Insert the ball joint stud through the opening in the knuckle arm and install the stud retaining nut. Tighten to 100 ft lbs. Install

the cotter pin and lubricate the ball joint.

12. Load the torsion bar by rotating the adjusting bolt clockwise.

13. Install the shock absorber nut and bolt, the splash shield, hub and rotor assembly, and brake caliper. Install the wheel and tire assembly.

14. Adjust the front wheel bearings. Remove the jackstands and lower the car. Install the rebound bumper. Adjust the front suspension height and alignment.

Upper Control Arm Removal and Installation

1. Follow Steps 1-2 of the Upper Ball Joint Removal and Installation Procedure.

2. On Valiant, Dart, Barracuda, and Challenger, remove the nuts, lockwashers, cams, and cam bolts holding the upper control arm to the support bracket. On installation, tighten the adjusting bolts to 70 ft lbs.

3. On Aspen and Volare, remove the rubber splash shield and remove the pivot shaft nuts. Remove the control arm and pivot shaft assembly. On installation, tighten the pivot shaft nuts to 150 ft lbs.

4. Follow Steps 3-7 of the Upper Ball Joint Removal and Installation procedure.

Lower Control Arm Removal and Installation

Valiant, Dart, Barracuda, Challenger

1. Raise the car and support it under the frame. Let the suspension hang down. Remove the wheel, tire and brake drum or disc. Remove the rebound bumper.

2. Remove the shock absorber at the bottom attachment and swing it up out of the way. Remove the torsion bar from its mount-

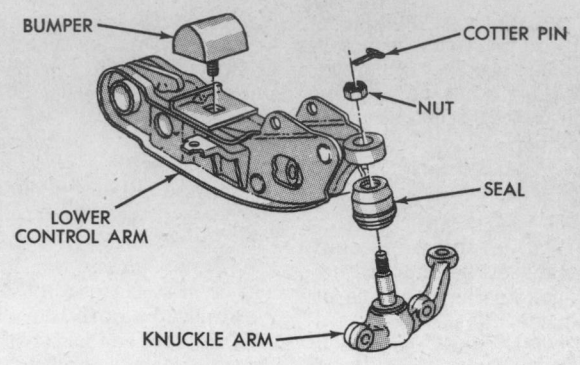

Typical Valiant, Dart, Barracuda, Challenger lower control arm (© Chrysler Corp.)

ing at the lower control arm after releasing its tension.

3. Remove the tie rod end from the steering knuckle arm. Be careful not to damage the seal.

4. Remove the sway bar link from the lower control arm. Remove the steering knuckle arm-to-brake support bolts and remove the steering knuckle arm, as in Lower Ball Joint Removal.

5. At the forward end of the crossmember, remove the strut spring pin, nut, and bushings, taking note of their positions. Remove the nut and washer from the lower control arm shaft.

6. Using a soft hammer, tap the end of the lower control arm shaft and remove it from the crossmember.

7. Remove the lower control arm, strut and shaft as an assembly.

8. On installation, position the front strut bushing half and sleeve into the crossmember and install the control arm, strut, and shaft assembly. Replace the shaft bushing outer retainer and finger tighten the nut.

9. Replace the lower control arm shaft washer and finger tighten the nut.

10. Replace the lower ball joint stud into the lower control arm and tighten it to 85 ft lbs through 1975, and to 100 ft lbs starting

1976. Install a new cotter pin.

11. Install the brake support to steering knuckle and replace the two upper bolts and finger tighten them.

12. Install the steering knuckle on the steering knuckle arm and insert the two lower bolts. Tighten the upper bolts to 55 ft lbs and the lower ones to 110 ft lbs through 1972 and to 160 ft lbs starting 1973.

13. Install the tie rod end to the steering knuckle arm. Tighten the nut to 40 ft lbs and install a new cotter pin.

14. Connect the shock absorber and finger tighten the bolt.

15. Replace the torsion bar assembly.

16. Install the brake, wheel, and tire.

17. Lower the car. Tighten the strut nut to 70 ft lbs, the lower control arm shaft nut to 145 ft lbs, and the shock absorber lower mounting to 50 ft lbs Readjust the front suspension height and realign the front end.

Aspen, Volare

1. Raise the car and remove the wheel.

2. Remove the brake caliper and wire it up.

3. Remove the lower shock absorber attachment.

4. Remove the hub, rotor and splash shield.

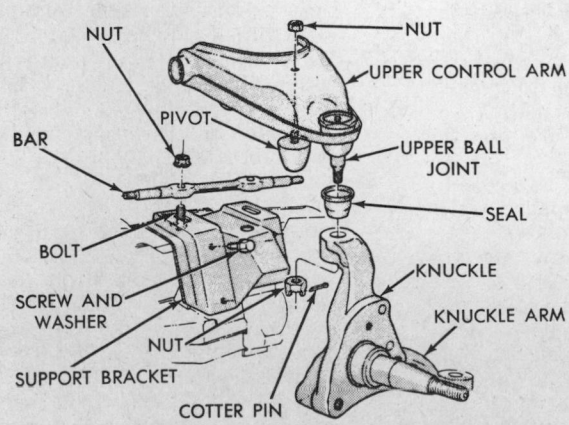

Typical Valiant, Dart, Barracuda, Challenger upper control arm and steering knuckle (© Chrysler Corp.)

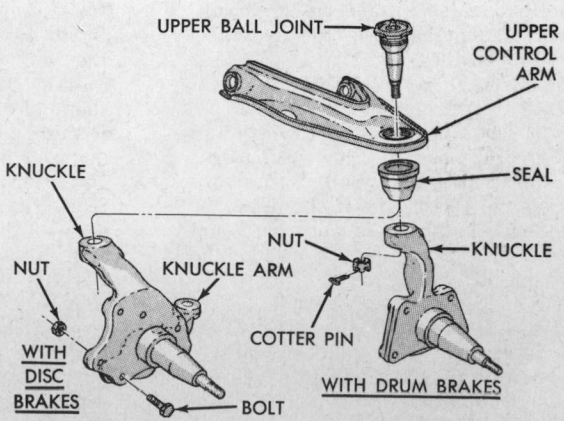

Steering knuckle and upper control arm details—Aspen, Volare (© Chrysler Corp.)

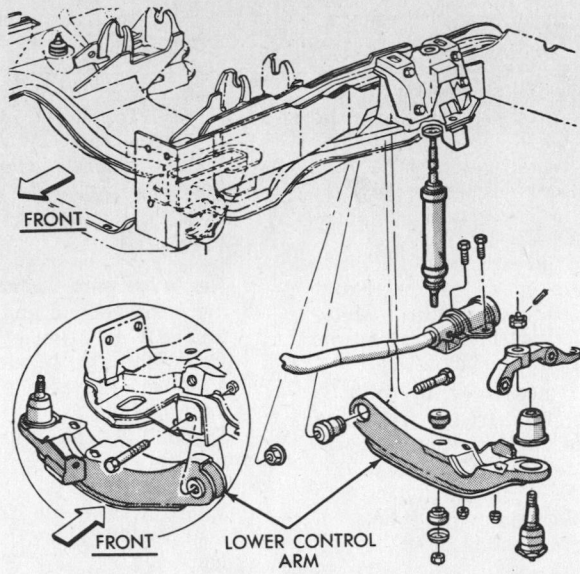

Aspen, Volare lower control arm details (© Chrysler Corp.)

5. Unload both torsion bars by turning the adjusting bolts counterclockwise.
   CAUTION: *Unload both bars even if you are removing only one control arm.*
6. Raise the lower control arm until there is 2⅞ in. clearance between the crossmember ledge at the jounce bumper and the torsion bar bushing on the lower control arm. Unbolt the torsion bar bushing from the control arm.
7. Separate the lower ball joint from the steering knuckle arm.
8. Remove the lower control arm pivot bolt and the control arm.
9. Position the control arm, install the pivot bolt, and make the flange nut finger tight.
10. Install the ball joint stud in the steering knuckle arm, tighten the nut to 100 ft lbs, and install a new cotter pin.
11. Hold the control arm at the height used in Step 6. Tighten the torsion bar bushing bolts to 50 ft. lbs. Tighten the control arm pivot bolt to 100 ft. lbs.
12. Replace the shock absorber and tighten the lower nut to 35 ft lbs.
13. Replace the brake assembly. Tighten the caliper bolts to 15 lbs.
14. Turn the adjusting screws clockwise to load the torsion bars.
15. Lower the car and adjust suspension height and wheel alignment.

Torsion Bar Removal and Installation

The torsion bars are not interchangeable from right to left. They are marked with an R or an L, according to their location.

Valiant, Dart, Barracuda, Challenger

1. Remove the upper control arm rebound bumper before raising the car.
2. Lift the car high enough to free the front suspension of all load.
3. Release load from torsion bar by backing off anchor adjusting nuts counterclockwise.
4. Remove the lock ring from the rear of torsion bar rear anchor. Remove the automatic transmission torque shaft on 1974 and later models, if necessary.
5. Remove the torsion bar from its mounts. A special tool is available for this job, it clamps to the bar and provides a striking surface for driving the bar out.
   CAUTION: *The torsion bar may be under some load so be careful when removing it. Never use heat to ease removal of the bar as this will destroy the temper of the bar.*
6. It may be necessary to move the rear balloon seal out of the way to ease removal. Slide the torsion bar out through the rear mounting. Be careful not to damage the balloon seal.
7. Inspect the torsion bar and lightly dress any sharp edges. Coat the dressed area with a rust preventive. Clean and lightly lubricate the bar.
8. Start replacement by sliding the bar into the rear anchor. Slide the balloon seal over the bar with the cupped end toward the rear of the bar. Coat both hex ends of the bar with waterproof grease.
9. Insert the torsion bar through the hex opening of the lower control arm. Replace the lockring in the rear anchor.
10. Fully pack the ring opening in the rear anchor with waterproof grease.
11. Install the balloon seal on the rear anchor so the seal lip engages the anchor grove.
12. Rotate the adjusting bolt clockwise to load the torsion bar. Lower the vehicle and adjust the front suspension height. Replace the upper control arm rebound bumper.

Aspen, Volare

1. Raise the car so that the front suspension hangs down.
2. Release the load on the torsion bar by turning the anchor adjusting bolts counterclockwise.
3. Remove the adjusting bolt on the bar to be removed.
4. Raise the lower control arms until there is 2⅞ in. clearance between the crossmember ledge at the jounce bumper and the torsion bar bushing on the lower control arm.
5. Unbolt the sway bar from the control arm.
6. Unbolt the torsion bar pivot bushing from the crossmember. Remove the bar and anchor assembly from the crossmember.
7. Check the seals on the bar for damage. If corrosion is evident, replace the bar assembly. Touch up any paint nicks or scratches. Check the adjusting bolt and swivel for corrosion or damage. Replace them if necessary.
8. Slide the balloon seal over the end of the bar with the cupped end toward the hex.
9. Coat the hex end of the bar with high-temperature waterproof grease.
10. Install the hex end of the bar into the anchor bracket. The ears of the bracket should be nearly straight up.
11. Install the bar anchor bracket assembly into the crossmember anchor retainer. Install the adjusting bolt and bearing. Attach the pivot bushing to the crossmember, finger tight.
12. Support the lower control arms at the height specified in Step 4 and install the torsion bar bushing to lower control arm bolts. Tighten them to 50 ft lbs.
13. Check that the anchor bracket is fully seated in the crossmember. Tighten the pivot bushing bolts to 75 ft lbs.
14. Put the balloon seal over the anchor bracket.
15. Install a new sway bar end bolt and tighten to 50 ft lbs.
16. Load the bar by turning the adjusting bolt clockwise. Lower the car and adjust the front end height.

Wheel Bearing Adjustment

Through 1972

1. Raise the front of the car and remove the hub caps and grease caps from the front wheels. Remove the cotter pin from the spindle and remove the adjusting nut lock.
2. The wheel must be rotated while the bearing adjusting nut is tightened. The adjusting nut should be tightened to 90 in. lbs.
3. Place the lock over the nut so that one pair of slots aligns with the cotter pin hole.
4. Back the nut and lock assembly off one slot. Install the cotter pin. This adjustment should yield 0.0–0.003 in. end-play.
5. Clean the grease cap. Coat, but do not fill, the cap with grease. Install it on the hub.
6. Lower the car and road-test it.

1973 and later

1. Jack up or hoist the car, so that the front wheels are off the floor.
2. Remove the hub caps, grease cup, cotter pin and nut lock.
3. Back off on the adjusting nut.
4. Check for free wheel rotation. If binding is present, repair the threads as required.
5. While rotating the wheel, tighten the wheel bearing adjustment nut to 240–300 in. lbs.
6. Release the torque. Retighten the nut so that it is finger tight.
7. Position the nut lock so that one pair of slots is in line with the cotter pin hole and install the cotter pin.
8. Install the rest of the items removed. Repeat the procedure for the other wheel and lower the car.

Front Height Adjustment

Through 1974

1. Jounce the car and measure from the lowest point, at the centerline, of the lower ball joint to the floor (measurement B).
2. Measure from the lowest area of the torsion bar adjusting blade to the floor (measurement A).
3. Subtract B from A. This is the front end height.
4. Measure the other side in the same way. Compare figures obtained with figure given in the Wheel Alignment Specifications table in the front of this section.
5. Adjust, if necessary, by turning the torsion bar adjusting bolt, in to raise; out to lower.

1975 and later

1. Jounce the car several times, releasing it in the downward motion.

2. Measure the distance between the lowest point of the lower control arm torsion bar anchor (at a point one inch forward of the rear face of the anchor) and the ground. On Aspen and Volare, measure from the lowest point of the lower control arm inner pivot bushing to the floor. This is measurement "A".
3. Compare measurement "A" with the figure given under Front End Height in the Wheel Alignment Specifications chart at the beginning of this car section.
4. Adjust, if necessary, by rotating clockwise to increase front end height, or rotating counterclockwise to decrease the height.
5. Check the adjustment on both sides. Maximum variation of front end height is ⅛ in.

REAR SUSPENSION

All Dodge and Plymouth models utilize rear springs of the semi-elliptical leaf type. They are engineered to operate with little or no camber under conditions of small or no load. Heavy-duty springs are offered as an option on all models. They serve to increase the stability of the vehicle under conditions of heavy load. All vehicles with leaf springs are constructed with zinc interleaves between the normal leaves. They have the purpose of reducing spring corrosion and lengthening spring life.

Rear Shock Absorbers

Removal and Installation

1. Jack the vehicle under the axle assembly in such a manner as to relieve load from the shock absorbers.
2. Remove the nut attaching the shock to the spring mounting plate.
3. At the upper mount, remove the shock attaching bolt or nut and the shock. On Barracuda and Challenger, access is through a rubber plug in the trunk.
4. Purge the new shock of air by repeatedly extending it in its normal position and compressing it while inverted. It is normal for there to be more resistance to extension than to compression. To install the shock, position it so the upper bolt or nut may be replaced. Hand-tighten only.
5. Align the shock with the spring mounting plate and install the bolt or nut. Hand-tighten only.
6. Lower the vehicle and tighten

the shock absorber mounting bolts. Torques are 50 ft lbs at the bottom, except for Aspen and Volare stud nuts, which are 35 ft lbs. Top bolt torques are 70 ft lbs, except on Valiant and Dart stud nuts, which are 50 ft lbs.

Rear Springs

Removal and Installation

1. Jack the vehicle and remove the wheels. Position jack stands under the axle in such a manner so as to relieve weight from the rear springs.
2. Disconnect the rear shock absorbers at the bottom. Lower the axle assembly to allow the rear springs to hang free. Disconnect the rear sway bar links, if so equipped.
3. Remove U-bolt nuts and withdraw bolts and spring plates. Remove the nuts securing the front spring hanger to the body mounting bracket.
4. Remove the rear spring hanger bolts and allow the spring to drop enough to allow the front spring hanger bolts to be removed. On the Barracuda and Challenger, loosen and remove the rear shackle nuts and plate and remove the shackle.
5. Remove the front pivot bolt from the front spring hanger.
6. Remove the shackle nuts and shackle from the rear spring.
7. To begin installation, assemble the shackle and bushings in the rear of the spring and hanger. Start the shackle bolt nut. Do not lubricate rubber bushings to ease installation. Do not tighten the bolt nut.
8. Install the front spring hanger to the front spring eye and insert the pivot bolt and nut. Do not tighten them.
9. Install the rear spring hanger-to-body bracket and torque the bolts to 30 ft lbs.
10. With the aid of a helper, raise the spring and insert the bolts in the spring hanger mounting bracket holes. Install the nuts and torque them to 30 ft lbs.
11. Position the axle assembly so it is correctly aligned with the spring center bolt.
12. Position the center bolt over the lower spring plate. Insert the U-bolt and nut. Tighten the U-bolts to 45 ft. lbs. (40 ft lbs with 2½ in. diameter axle tube). Connect the rear shock absorbers.
13. Lower the vehicle. Torque the pivot bolts to 125 ft lbs (85 on Dart and Valiant through 1972). Tighten the shackle nuts to 30 ft lbs on Valiant and Dart, 40 ft lbs on all others.

BRAKES

A dual (tandem) master cylinder is used. In operation, this type master cylinder provides braking even if one section of the system should develop a leak.

Both drum and disc type brake systems are hydraulically operated. Power assist is offered as an option.

With the exception of heavy-duty fleet units, brakes are self-adjusting.

Beginning 1973, front disc brakes are standard on all models with the exception of six-cylinder Valiants and Darts.

Master Cylinder Removal and Installation

1. Disconnect the brake lines from the master cylinder. Plug the brake line outlets to prevent fluid loss.
2. Remove the nuts that attach the master cylinder to the cowl panel or brake booster.
3. On models with standard brakes, disconnect the pushrod from the brake pedal.
4. Slide the master cylinder straight out and off the cowl panel or brake booster.
5. Reverse above procedure to install and bleed brake system.

Power Brake Booster Removal and Installation

1. Remove the nuts that attach the master cylinder to the brake booster and position the master cylinder out of the way without disconnecting the lines. Use care not to kink the brake lines.
2. Disconnect the vacuum hose from the brake booster.
3. Working under the dash, remove the nut and bolt that attaches the brake booster pushrod to the brake pedal.
4. Remove the brake booster attaching nuts and washers.
5. Remove booster assembly from the vehicle.

6. Reverse above procedure to install.

Parking Brake Adjustment

1. Apply the brakes several times while backing up to adjust the rear drum brakes. Release the parking brake lever and clean and lubricate the parking brake cable adjusting nut and threads. Loosen the cable adjusting nut.
2. Tighten the cable adjusting nut until a slight drag is felt in the rear wheels when the rear wheels are rotated. Loosen the cable adjusting nut until the rear wheels can be rotated freely. Back off the cable adjusting nut two additional turns.
3. Apply and release the parking brake several times and check to verify that the rear wheels rotate freely, without any brake drag.

STEERING

A worm and recirculating ball type steering gear is used with the manual steering system.

Power steering is an option on all models. Hydraulic power is provided by a belt-driven pump. Some power steering pumps were equipped from the factory with oil coolers. These were used on vehicles with high-performance engines and/or special axle ratios.

Tie-Rod End Removal and Installation

1. Loosen the tie rod adjuster sleeve clamp nuts.
2. Remove the tie rod end stud nut and cotter pin.
3. If the outer tie rod end is being removed, remove the stud from the steering knuckle. If the inner tie rod end is being removed, remove the stud from the center link. The studs on all the tie rod ends fit in a tapered hole. They can be removed with a ball joint stud removal tool.
4. Unscrew the tie rod end from the threaded sleeve. The threads may be left or right-hand threads. Count the number of turns required to remove it.

5. To install, reverse the above. Turn the tie rod end in as many turns as was needed to remove it. This will give approximately correct toe-in.
6. Tighten the stud nuts to 40 ft lbs and install new cotter pins.
7. Set the toe-in.

Power Steering Pump Removal and Installation

1. Back off the pump mounting and locking bolts, and remove the pump drive belt.
2. Disconnect all hoses at the pump.
3. Remove the pump bolts and pump with the bracket.
4. To install the pump, place the pump in position and install the mounting bolts.
5. Install the pump drive belt and adjust. There should be no more than 1/2 in. of play, under moderate thumb pressure, on the longest run of belt. Some pump brackets have a 1/2 in. square hole for use in tensioning the belt. Torque the mounting bolts to 30 ft lbs.
6. Connect the pressure and return hoses. Replace the pressure hose O-ring, if there is one.
7. Fill the pump with power steering fluid.
8. Start the engine and rotate the steering wheel from stop to stop several times. This will bleed the system. Check the pump fluid level and fill as required.
9. Be certain the hoses are away from the exhaust manifolds and are not kinked or twisted.

Steering Wheel Removal and Installation

NOTE: All models are equipped with collapsible steering columns. A sharp blow or excessive pressure on the column will cause it to collapse. Do not hammer on the steering wheel.

1. Disconnect the ground cable from the battery.
2. Remove the padded center assembly. This center assembly is often held on only by spring clips. There are usually holes in the back of the wheel so the pad can be pushed off. However, on some deluxe interiors it is held on by screws behind the arms of the wheel.
3. On the tilt and telescoping steering column remove the locking lever knob by releasing the clip on its underside. Remove the locking lever screws and the lever.
4. Remove the large center nut. Mark the steering wheel and steering shaft so that the wheel may be replaced in its original position. In most cases, the wheel can only go on one way.

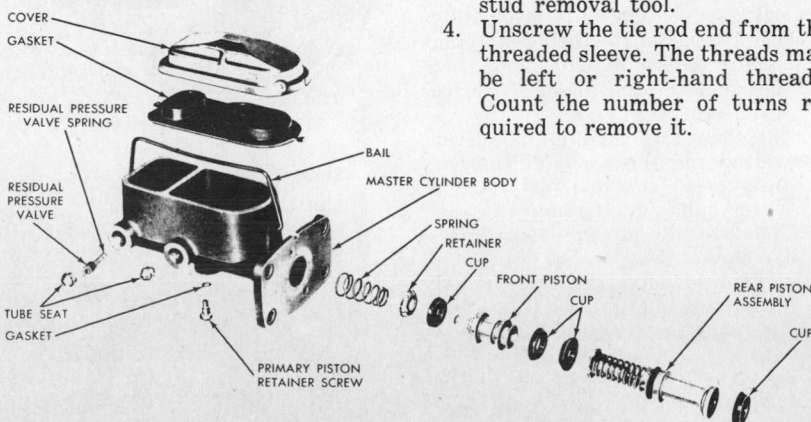

COVER
GASKET
RESIDUAL PRESSURE VALVE SPRING
RESIDUAL PRESSURE VALVE
TUBE SEAT
GASKET
BAIL
MASTER CYLINDER BODY
SPRING
RETAINER
CUP
FRONT PISTON
CUP
REAR PISTON ASSEMBLY
CUP
PRIMARY PISTON RETAINER SCREW

Dual type master cylinder (disc brakes) (© Chrysler Corp)

5. Using a puller, pull the steering wheel from the steering shaft.

6. Reverse the procedure to install the wheel. When placing the wheel on the shaft, make sure the tires are straight ahead and the match marks are aligned. Tighten the nut to 28 ft lbs on models through 1972, and 60 ft lbs on 1973 and later models.

TIME SAVER

A steering wheel puller can be made by drilling two holes in a piece of steel the same distance apart as the two threaded holes in the steering wheel. Sometimes an old spring shackle will have the right dimensions. Drill another hole in the center. Place a center bolt with the head against the steering shaft and a nut against the bottom of the homemade puller bar. Thread the two outer bolts into the holes in the wheel. Unscrew the nut on the center bolt to draw the wheel off the shaft.

Turn Signal/Hazard Warning Switch Removal and Installation

Through 1971

1. Disconnect the negative battery ground cable.

2. Disconnect the wiring connectors at the base of the steering column.

3. Remove the steering wheel. Tie a string to the turn signal switch wires. Before proceeding further, see if the switch wiring will pull out of the switch without removing the wiring from the column.

4. Remove the turn signal lever. On tilting columns, the lever unscrews. Otherwise, it is held by a screw.

NOTE: On models with cruise control, do not remove the turn signal lever, allow it to hang by the wire.

5. Disconnect the switch wiring multiconnector at the base of the column jacket.

6. Unfasten the screws which secure the switch to the column. Remove the switch and its wiring from the column, leaving the string in the column as an installation aid.

Installation is the reverse of removal. Attach the switch wiring to the string which was left in the column and pull the wiring through the column with the string.

1972-75

1. Perform steps 1 through 4 of the "Through 1971 Turn Signal Switch Removal" procedure; it is unnecessary to tie a string to the switch wiring, however. The lever is held on by a nut.

2. Remove the screws which attach the turn signal switch upper bearing retainer and remove the retainer.

3. If the column has a cover, remove it.

4. Unfasten the wire which holds the horn wire on its mounting stud.

5. Remove the nuts which attach the mounting bracket to the steering column.

6. Separate the wiring harness trough from the column by unfastening its screws. Remove the tape from the harness and unfasten the harness multiconnector.

7. Pull the switch out of the column, while carefully guiding its wires through the column.

8. Work the connector through the column opening and completely remove the switch from the column.

Installation is the reverse of removal.

1976 and Later

1. Disconnect the battery ground cable.

2. Remove the steering wheel.

3. Remove the steering column cover.

4. With tilting steering wheel, remove the shift position indicator, unbolt the steering column from the lower instrument panel reinforcement and the mounting bracket from the column, and remove the column wiring trough.
CAUTION: *Support the steering column to prevent damage.*

5. With standard column, unsnap the wiring trough from the column.

6. Position the automatic transmission column shift lever fully clockwise. Set the tilting steering wheel at its midpoint.

7. Disconnect the harness wire connector.

8. Remove the turn signal lever screw and the lever. If the car has speed control, just let the lever hang; don't remove it.

9. Remove the upper bearing retainer screws.

10. Pull the switch gently from the column while guiding the wires through the column opening.

11. Installation is the reverse of removal. Tighten the mounting bracket to steering column bolts to 10 ft lbs and the bracket bolts to 9 ft lbs.

Ignition Switch and/or Ignition Lock Cylinder Removal and Installation

Standard Steering Column

1. Disconnect the negative battery cable. Remove the steering wheel.

2. Remove the screw that attaches the turn signal lever to the steering column.

3. Remove the three screws that attach the upper bearing retainer to the turn signal switch.

4. Pull the turn signal switch as far upward as possible.

5. Using snap-ring pliers, remove the upper bearing housing snapring from the steering shaft.

6. Remove the screw that attaches the ignition key light assembly to the upper bearing housing.

7. Using care not to damage any components, pry the upper bearing housing off the steering shaft by lifting upward on alternate sides of the bearing housing with screwdrivers.

8. Lift upward as far as possible on the steering shaft lockplate and place a screwdriver or other object under it to hold it in the raised position. If this operation does not provide adequate working room under the lockplate, it will be necessary to press out the pin that attaches the lockplate to the steering shaft and remove the lockplate from the steering shaft. If the ignition switch is being replaced, the lockplate must be removed.

9. Using an offset screwdriver, remove the two screws that attach the lock lever guide plate to the steering column.

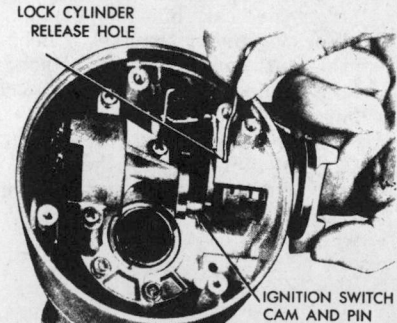

LOCK CYLINDER RELEASE HOLE

IGNITION SWITCH CAM AND PIN

Lock cylinder removal
(© Chrysler Corp)

10. With the ignition lock cylinder in the "lock" position and the ignition key removed, insert a stiff wire into the lock cylinder release hole in the steering column. Push in on the wire to release the spring-loaded lock retainer and pull the lock cylinder out of the steering column.

11. If the ignition switch is being replaced, remove the two screws that attach the ignition key

buzzer switch to the steering column and the three screws that attach the ignition switch to the steering column. Lift the ignition switch out of the housing.

12. Reverse the above procedure for installation.

Tilt Steering Column

1. Disconnect the negative battery cable.
2. Remove the steering wheel.
3. Remove the three attaching screws and the shaft lock cover.
4. Remove the screws that attach the tilt control lever and the turn signal lever to the steering column and remove the levers.
5. Push the hazard warning knob in and unscrew the knob from the turn signal switch. Remove the ignition key lamp assembly.
6. Using a suitable tool, depress the lockplate to gain access to the lockplate retaining snap-ring. Remove the snap-ring from the steering shaft.
7. Remove the lockplate, cancelling cam, and spring.
8. Remove the three turn signal switch attaching screws, place the shift lever in the low position, and pull the switch and wires as far upward as possible.
9. With the ignition lock cylinder in the "lock" position, insert a small screwdriver into the lock release slot in the housing cover.
10. Press down with the screwdriver to release the spring latch at bottom of the slot and pull the lock cylinder from the housing.

The following steps are for ignition switch replacement only.

11. Remove the three screws that attach the upper steering column housing to the steering column and remove the housing.
12. Install the column tilt control lever and move the column to the full "up" position.
13. Insert a screwdriver into the slot in the spring retainer and press the retainer in approximately 3/16 in. Turn the retainer approximately 1/8 turn to the left until the ears align with the grooves in the housing. Remove the spring retainer, spring, and guide.
14. Push the steering shaft inward to enable removal of the inner race and seat. Remove the race and seat.
15. Make sure the ignition switch is in the "lock" position, then remove the wire connector from the ignition switch and remove the screws that attach the ignition switch to the outside of the dash steering column.
16. Lift the ignition switch from the column and twist it to disengage the switch actuating rod from

the rack. Remove the switch.
17. To install the ignition lock cylinder, insert the cylinder into the housing with the cylinder in the lock position and the key removed.
18. Move the cylinder into the housing until it contacts the switch actuator. Move the switch actuator rod up and down to align the parts. When the parts are aligned the cylinder will move inward and lock into place.

The following steps are for ignition switch installation only.

19. With the ignition switch in the "lock" position, insert the actuating rod into the steering column.
20. Twist the switch and rod assembly as required to engage the actuating rod with the rack. Make sure the ignition lock cylinder is in the "lock" position.
21. Install the ignition switch mounting screws but do not tighten them.
22. Move the ignition switch downward away from the steering wheel and tighten the switch mounting screws. Make sure the ignition switch has not moved out of the lock detent.
23. Attach the switch wiring connector.

INSTRUMENT PANEL

Headlight Switch Removal and Installation

Valiant and Dart

1. On models through 1973, remove the fuse box attaching screw and position the fuse box out of the way.
2. Press the release button on the body of the headlight switch and pull the control knob and shaft from the switch.
3. Disconnect the multiple connector from the rear of the headlight switch.
4. Remove the bezel nut that attaches the headlight switch to the dash and remove the switch.
5. Reverse above procedure to install.

Barracuda and Challenger

1. Disconnect the negative battery cable.
2. Remove the six lamp panel mounting screws and carefully slide the lamp panel out of the dash and lay it on top of the instrument panel. It is not necessary to disconnect the wiring harness.

3. Remove the four switch bezel mounting screws. Carefully slide the switch bezel out and to the right, overlapping the center instrument cluster, then lower it until it is free of the instrument panel and disconnect the wiring harness.
4. Remove the two headlight switch mounting screws and remove the switch from the bezel assembly.
5. Install in reverse order.

Aspen, Volare

1. Remove the instrument cluster bezel by removing the four screws along the lower edge, placing the automatic transmission selector in 1, and pulling out to detach the top edge clips.
2. Remove the switch module assembly mounting screws, pull the assembly out, and let it hang.
3. Depress the switch stem, release the button on the switch, and pull out the knob and stem.
4. Insert a Phillips screwdriver through the stem opening in the switch bezel and remove the switch mounting nut.
5. Disconnect the switch wiring connector. Remove the switch.
6. Reverse the procedure for installation, making sure the stem locks into place.

WINDSHIELD WIPERS

Motor Removal

Valiant and Dart

1. Disconnect battery.
2. Disconnect wiper motor wiring harness.
3. Remove three wiper motor mounting nuts. On vehicles without air conditioning it is easier to remove crank arm nut and crank arm from under instrument panel first and omit steps 4 and 5.
4. Work motor off mounting studs far enough to gain access to crank arm mounting nuts.

CAUTION: *Do not force or pry motor from mounting studs as drive link can be easily distorted.*

5. Using an open end wrench, remove the motor crank arm nut while holding the motor crank arm with a second wrench. Carefully pry arm off shaft.
6. Remove wiper motor.

Barracuda and Challenger

1. Disconnect battery.
2. Carefully remove wiper arm and blade assemblies.
3. Remove left cowl screen.

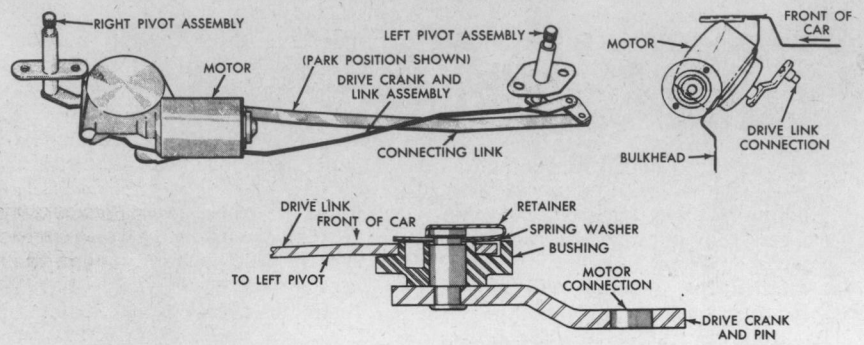

Valiant and Dart windshield wiper linkage (© Chrysler Corp)

4. Remove drive crank arm retaining nut and drive crank. Disconnect wiring to motor.
5. Remove three wiper motor mounting nuts and remove motor.

Aspen, Volare

1. Disconnect the battery ground cable.
2. Remove the wiper arms.
3. Remove the cowl screen.
4. Hold the motor crank with a wrench while removing the crank arm nut.
5. Remove the three mounting nuts and the motor.

RADIO

Removal

Valiant, Dart, Barracuda, and Challenger

1. Disconnect battery.
2. From under panel, disconnect speaker, antenna, and wiring leads at radio.
3. Pull off the knobs and remove the shaft nuts.
4. Remove two radio mounting nuts from panel and remove radio to lower support bracket mounting screw. Hold radio in position and remove radio bracket.
5. Move radio toward the front of the car, down, and out from under instrument panel.

NOTE: If the car is equipped with air conditioning, it will be necessary to remove the two air outlet assembly-to-instrument panel mounting nuts from the underside of the panel and drop the assembly down and remove it from under the instrument panel. It will also be necessary to remove the ash tray and ash tray housing.

1970-71 Dart and Valiant with Rallye Dash

1. Disconnect the negative battery cable.
2. Remove the control knobs from the front of the radio.
3. On models equipped with air conditioning, remove the two air conditioner outlet duct retaining nuts and remove the duct. Disconnect the right-side defroster hose and hose bracket and position them out of the way of the radio.
4. Remove the bottom screw from the radio mounting bracket.
5. Remove the left-side defroster hose.
6. Loosen the top screw on the radio mounting bracket and remove the bracket.
7. Disconnect the speaker and antenna leads.
8. Remove the radio mounting nuts from the front of the radio.
9. Remove the radio bezel.
10. Lower the radio and disconnect the radio power lead.
11. Remove the radio from under the instrument panel.

Volare, Aspen

1. Disconnect the battery ground cable. Remove the instrument cluster bezel by removing the four screws along the lower edge, placing the automatic transmission selector in 1, and pulling out to detach the top edge clips.
2. Remove the radio mounting screws.
3. Pull the radio from the panel and disconnect the wiring and antenna.
4. Remove the radio.

HEATER

Heater Assembly Removal— Non Air-Conditioned Cars

Heater assembly removal is required in order to service the blower motor or heater core on cars without A/C.

Valiant and Dart

1. Drain radiator and disconnect battery.
2. Disconnect heater hoses from heater and remove heater hoses to dash retainer plate. Disconnect heater motor wires.
3. Remove heater motor seal retainer plate from dash panel.
4. Disconnect heater-defroster and temperature control cables from heater assembly.
5. Remove the heater motor resistor wire from the resistor at the top of the unit. Remove the three mounting nuts.
6. Remove defroster tubes from heater assembly.
7. Disconnect heater housing support rod from fresh air duct.
8. Remove heater assembly.

Barracuda and Challenger

1. Disconnect battery.
2. Drain coolant.
3. Disconnect heater hoses from core tubes at dash panel. Plug core tubes to prevent spilling coolant on interior of car.
4. Remove three mounting nuts from studs around blower motor and remove flange and air seal.
5. Unplug antenna from radio and place wire to one side.
6. Remove screw from housing to plenum support rod on right side of housing above fresh air opening.
7. Disconnect three air door cables.
8. Disconnect wires from blower motor resistor.
9. Tip unit down and out from under instrument panel.

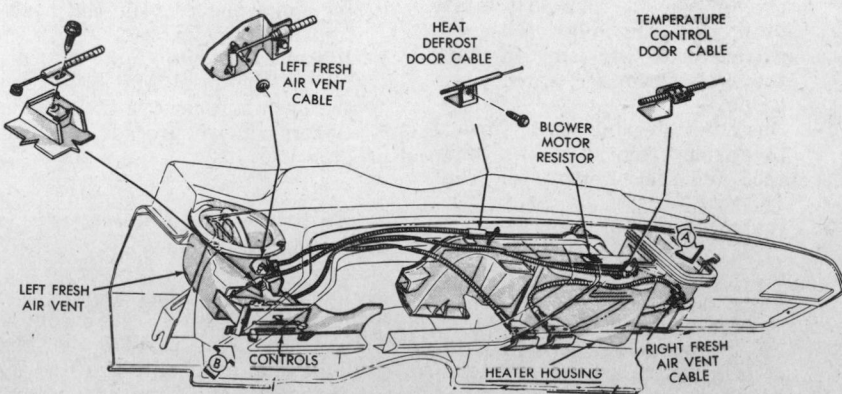

Barracuda and Challenger heater assembly
(© Chrysler Corp)

Aspen, Volare

CAUTION: *This is a major disassembly operation.*

1. Disconnect the battery ground cable and drain the coolant.
2. Disconnect the heater hoses at the firewall. Plug the core tubes to prevent spillage.
3. Slide the front seat all the way back.
4. Remove the core tube firewall seals and retainer.
5. Remove the instrument cluster bezel by removing the four screws along the lower edge, placing the automatic transmission selector in 1, and pulling out to detach the upper edge clips.
6. Remove the instrument panel upper cover by removing the mounting screws at the top inner surface of the glove box, at the brow above the instrument cluster, at the left end cap mounting, at the right side of the pad brow, and in the defroster outlets.
7. Remove the steering column cover (the instrument panel piece under the column).
8. Remove the right intermediate side cowl trim panel. Remove the lower instrument panel (the part with the glove box). Remove the instrument panel center to lower reinforcement.
9. Remove the right vent control cable, the temperature, and heating mode door control cables from the unit.
10. Disconnect the blower motor resistor block wiring.
11. Remove the mounting nuts on the engine side of the firewall.
12. Remove the heater support-to-plenum bracket.
13. Remove the heater unit.

Heater Blower Motor Removal —Non Air-Conditioned Cars

Valiant and Dart

1. Remove the heater assembly.
2. Remove the seal from around the heater blower motor mounting studs.
3. Remove the spring clips that retain the spacers and the blower motor to the heater housing on models through 1972. On later models, remove the backplate from the housing and the fan from the motor.
4. Remove the blower motor from the heater housing.

Barracuda and Challenger

1. Remove heater assembly from car.
2. Disconnect blower motor lead from resistor block and ground wire from mounting plate.
3. Remove six sheet metal screws and six retaining clips holding blower motor assembly from housing.
4. Remove blower wheel from motor shaft.
5. Remove two retaining nuts and separate motor from mounting plate.

Aspen, Volare

1. Remove the heater assembly from the car.
2. Remove the retainer clips and separate the housing halves.
3. Remove the screw attaching the seal retainer and seal around the core tubes. Remove the core tube support clamp.
4. Slide the core out.
5. Remove the blower vent tube and the blower mounting nuts. Remove the blower motor.

Heater Core Removal—Non Air-Conditioned Cars

Valiant and Dart

1. Remove the heater assembly and the heater blower motor as outlined above. Remove the motor resistor assembly.
2. Remove the fresh air door seal from either the inner or outer heating housing half only.
3. Remove the clips that retain the heater housing halves together.
4. Separate the heater housing halves.
5. Remove the screw that attaches the seal retainer and seal around the heater core tubes.
6. Remove the heater core tube support clamp.
7. Remove the screws that attach the heater core to the heater housing and remove the heater core.
8. Reverse above procedure to install.

Barracuda and Challenger

1. Remove the heater assembly.
2. Remove the nine spring clips and four screws that hold the front cover to the heater housing.
3. Cut the sponge rubber plenum-to-heater housing air seal in two places where the front cover separates the cover from the housing.
4. Remove the core tube retaining screw from behind the housing, between the core tubes.
5. Remove the two sponge rubber gaskets from the heater core tubes and remove the core from the heater housing.

Aspen, Volare

This procedure is the same as for Heater Blower Motor Removal.

Heater Blower Motor Removal —Air-Conditioned Cars

Valiant, Dart, Barracuda, and Challenger

The blower motor can be removed from the engine compartment.

1. Detach the motor wiring. Remove the air tube, if any.
2. Remove the nuts holding the mounting plate.
3. Remove the mounting plate and blower motor.

Aspen, Volare

The blower motor is removed from inside the car.

1. Disconnect the motor wiring.
2. Remove the motor mounting nuts from the bottom of the recirculation housing.
3. Separate the lower blower motor housing from the upper housing.
4. Remove the mounting plate screws and remove the mounting plate and blower motor.

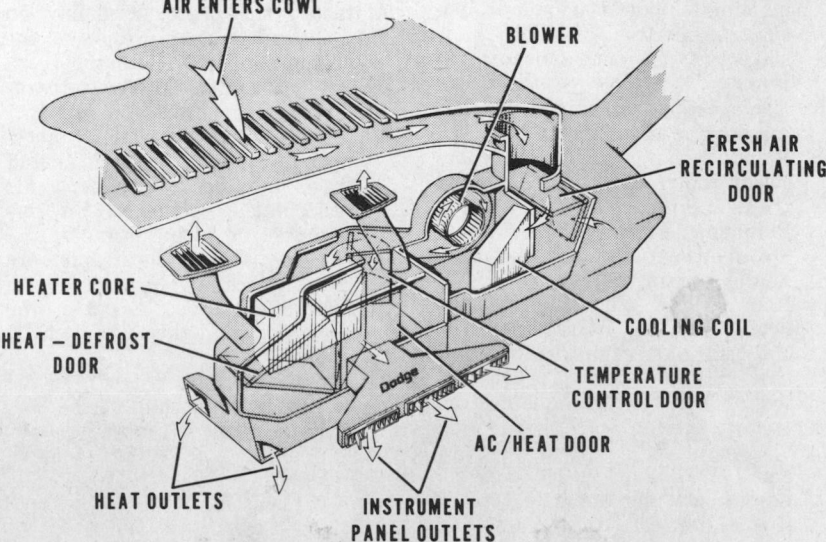

Dart and Valiant heater and air conditioner assembly through 1973
(© Chrysler Corp)

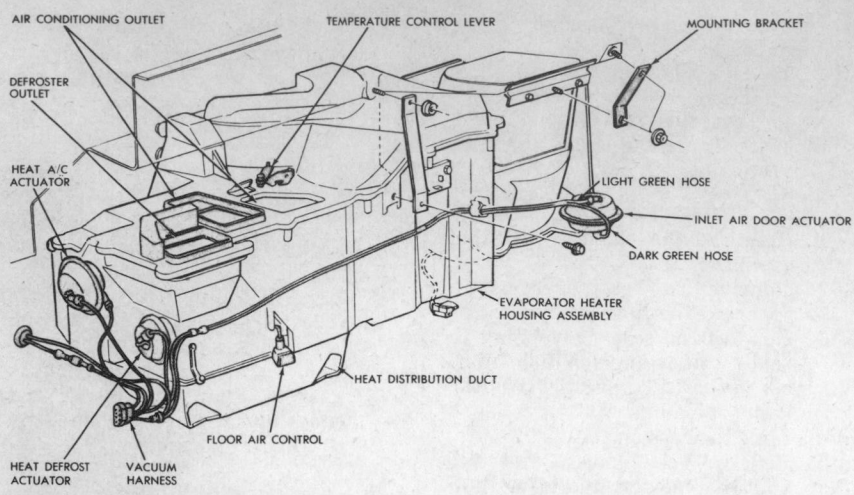

AIR CONDITIONING OUTLET — TEMPERATURE CONTROL LEVER — MOUNTING BRACKET
DEFROSTER OUTLET
HEAT A/C ACTUATOR
LIGHT GREEN HOSE
INLET AIR DOOR ACTUATOR
DARK GREEN HOSE
EVAPORATOR HEATER HOUSING ASSEMBLY
HEAT DISTRIBUTION DUCT
FLOOR AIR CONTROL
HEAT DEFROST ACTUATOR — VACUUM HARNESS

Aspen, Volare heater/air-conditioner unit (© Chrysler Corp.)

Heater Core Removal—Air-Conditioned Cars

Dart and Valiant through 1973

1. The core and cover are serviced as an assembly. They are located just forward of the instrument panel.
2. Disconnect the battery and remove the air cleaner. Remove glove box, the air outlet assembly, and the right defroster tube.
3. Drain the cooling system and remove the heater hoses at the core.
4. Disconnect the vacuum hoses from the fresh air recirculating actuator, the electrical wires from the resistor block, the temperature control cable, the evaporator temperature control switch control cable, and the ground wire from the heater core.
5. Extract the screws holding the heater to the evaporator assemblies. Disconnect the heater housing support rod from its position at the fresh air duct.
6. Take out the entire heater assembly.
7. Remove the fresh air recirculating door actuator.
8. Remove the operating link between the recirculating door and the bellcrank.
9. Remove the fresh air intake seal from either the front or rear heater housing halves only.
10. Remove the clips holding the heater housing halves together. Pull the halves apart. Take out the screws which secure the heater core to the housing and remove the core.
11. To begin installation, place a small amount of sealer into the heater housing flange. Replace the heater core in the housing and install the attaching screws.
12. Place weatherseal on the inner

lip of the heater core flange. Squeeze a small amount of sealer onto the heater housing cover.
13. Install the two housing halves together and install their retaining clips. Wipe off any excess sealer.
14. Install the link between the recirculating door and the bellcrank. It may require some adjustment; the fresh air door should be fully open when the recirculating door is closed. Replace the fresh air door recirculating actuator.
15. Place the heater assembly in the vehicle. Replace the temperature control cable on the outer operating arm; position it so that it is in the full heat position with the end of the cable housing $\frac{1}{4}$ in. beyond the edge of the retainer clip.
16. Replace the evaporator temperature control switch cable on the inner operating arm. In the full heat position, the end of the cable housing should be $\frac{1}{4}$ in. beyond the edge of the cable clip.
17. Install the heater assembly on the dash panel. Replace the heater support rod to the fresh air duct and install the evaporator assembly screw.
18. Replace the electrical connections to the resistor block. Install the vacuum hoses to the fresh air recirculating actuator. Be certain the red stripe is facing the rod side. Install the heater core ground wire.
19. Install the defroster tube, the glove box, and the air outlet assembly.
20. Replace the heater hoses, fill the cooling system, connect the battery and replace the air cleaner.
21. Start engine and bring to operating temperature. Test operation of the heater.

1974 and later Valiant and Dart

1. Disconnect the battery.

2. Drain the cooling system and disconnect the heater hose from the unit.
3. Remove the core tube seal nut, bracket and seal.
4. Remove the air conditioning duct.
5. Remove the ash tray and housing.
6. Remove the radio.
7. Remove the heat-defrost vacuum actuator pot and let it hang by its rod.
8. To remove the heat distribution duct, remove the three screws on the front cover, two on each end and work the housing out of the lip and remove it to the left-side.
9. Remove the left defroster duct. Remove the right defroster duct from the unit and let it hang from the top.
10. Remove the rear distribution housing. You may reach through the radio opening for some of the screws; three on top, three on the bottom, and one at the left end.
11. With the distribution housing off, the heater core will be loose. Separate it from the seal and lift it out.

Barracuda and Challenger
NOTE: This procedure requires evacuation of the air conditioner refrigerant. Use proper safety precautions.
1. Remove the air cleaner and disconnect the battery.
2. Drain the cooling system. Disconnect the heater hoses at the dash panel. Plug the core tubes to prevent spillage.
3. Discharge refrigerant from the system.
4. Disconnect the refrigerant lines at the dash panel (use two wrenches for this procedure). Leave the expansion valve attached to the line. Plug all refrigerant openings.
5. Disconnect the blower motor electrical connections. Remove the motor cooling tube and remove the blower motor.
6. Remove the glove box assembly.
7. Remove the appearance shield from the lower edge of the instrument panel.
8. Remove the left spot cooler duct and the air distribution housing.
9. Disconnect all wires from the blower motor resistor, and the antenna wire from the radio bottom.
10. Remove the radio.
11. Disconnect the vacuum harness from the control switch rear.
12. Remove the water valve cable from the bracket on the housing left end.
13. In the engine compartment, re-

move the nuts from the housing mounting studs.

14. Remove the rubber drain tube.
15. Take the support bracket from the plenum-to-housing panel.
16. Remove the unit from beneath the instrument panel.
17. With the unit removed from the vehicle, remove the plenum air seal.
18. Remove the vacuum hose from the fresh air door actuator and bypass door actuator. Remove the air seal from the evaporator core tubes and heater.
19. Remove the 18 screws securing the front and rear covers, extract one screw from between the evaporator core tubes. Pull the housings apart.
20. Extract the three screws from the evaporator core access plate and remove the plate. With access now clear to the 2 evaporator core mounting screws, remove them. In addition, remove the four screws securing the evaporator core to the front cover and remove the core.
21. Carefully lift the left housing half seal from the rear cover. Do not remove the entire seal; the lower portion acts as a water seal.
22. Remove the two core retaining screws from the mounting plate. From the back of the rear cover, remove one screw from between the core tubes. Lift the heater core from the housing.
23. To begin assembly and installation, place the heat door in the "up" position. Place the heater core into the rear cover. Install its retaining screws.
24. Apply rubber cement to the bottom of the raised portion of the housing seal; carefully replace it in its original position over the heater core.
25. Insert the evaporator core into the front cover and replace its four securing screws.
26. Place the front and rear covers together. Make sure the cover seal is seated properly. Replace the 18 securing screws (and the screw between the evaporator core tubes at the back of the rear cover).
27. Replace the air seal over the heater and evaporator core tubes.
28. Connect all vacuum hoses to their respective actuators. Connect the hose with the red tracer to the actuator rod side.
29. Install the evaporator core access cover plate to the housing front and replace its three sheet metal screws.
30. Apply rubber cement to the plenum air seal and install it in position.
31. Position the housing up under the instrument panel. Connect the housing-to-plenum support bracket.
32. In the engine compartment, install four retaining nuts on the housing mounting studs; torque them to 24 in. lbs.
33. Install the vacuum harness to the rear of the control switch. Install the water valve control cable in its retaining bracket.
34. Install the radio.
35. Install all blower motor resistor wiring. Plug the antenna lead into the radio bottom.
36. Replace the center outlet air distribution housing. Replace the left spot cooler duct.
37. Replace the appearance shield at the instrument panel bottom.
38. Replace the glove box.
39. Replace the blower motor and connect its wiring. Install the blower motor cooling tube and replace the evaporator drain tube.
40. Connect the refrigerant lines to the evaporator core tubes. Freely lubricate the fittings and O-rings with refrigerant oil. Use two wrenches to avoid twisting the tubes.
41. Connect the heater hoses to the core tubes. Fill the cooling system.
42. Sweep the system. Evacuate the system. Charge the system and check for leaks.

Aspen, Volare

CAUTION: *This procedure requires evacuation of the air conditioner refrigerant. Do not attempt this yourself unless you are familiar with air conditioning service. This is also a major disassembly operation.*

1. Discharge the air conditioning system.
2. Disconnect the battery ground cable, drain the coolant, remove the air cleaner, and disconnect the heater hoses. Plug the core tubes to prevent spillage.
3. Remove the H-type expansion valve.
4. Slide the front seat all the way back.
5. Remove the instrument cluster bezel assembly by removing the four screws along the lower edge, placing the automatic transmission selector in 1, and pulling out to detach the upper edge clips.
6. Remove the instrument panel upper cover by removing the mounting screws at the top inner surface of the glove box, at the brow above the instrument cluster, at the left end cap mounting, at the right side of the pad brow, and in the defroster outlets.
7. Remove the steering column cover (the instrument panel piece under the column).
8. Remove the right intermediate side cowl trim panel. Remove the lower instrument panel (the part with the glove box). Remove the instrument panel center to lower reinforcement.
9. Remove the floor console, if any.
10. Remove the right center air distribution duct. Detach the locking tab on the defroster duct.
11. Disconnect the temperature control cable from the housing. Disconnect the blower motor resistor block wiring.
12. Detach the vacuum lines from the water valve and tee in the engine compartment. Detach the wiring from the evaporator housing. Remove the vacuum lines from the inlet air housing and disconnect the vacuum harness coupling.
13. Remove the drain tube in the engine compartment. Remove the mounting nuts from the firewall.
14. Remove the hanger strap from the rear of the evaporator and plenum stud.
15. Roll the unit back so that the pipes clear and remove it.
16. Remove the blend air door lever from the shaft. Remove the screws and lift off the top cover. Lift the heater core out.
17. Reverse the procedure for installation. Sweep, leak test, and charge the air conditioning system. Refill the cooling system.

SEAT BELTS

Seat Belt/Starter Interlock System

All 1974 and some 1975 models are equipped with Chrysler Corporation's seat belt/starter interlock system, which prevents starting of the car engine until front seat belts are fastened. For information on this system refer to the Dodge/Plymouth and Chrysler/Cordoba/Imperial car sections.

INDEX

Bobcat · Mustang II · Pinto

Automatic Transmission
In-car service **C179, U355**
Band adjustments C180
Downshift linkage adjustment C179
Shift linkage adjustment C179
Neutral start switch adjustment,
Removal and Installation C180
Pan Removal and Installation, Fluid
and Filter Change C181
Brakes **C184, U299**
Master cylinder Removal and
Installation C184
Parking brake adjustment C185
Vacuum brake booster Removal and
Installation C184
Charging System **C154, U2**
Alternator precautions C154
Alternator Removal and Installation C154
Regulator Removal and Installation C154
Clutch **C178**
Clutch, clutch housing and
transmission Removal and
Installation C178
Adjustment C178
Cooling System **C159**
Radiator Removal and Installation C159
Thermostat Removal and Installation ... C159
Water pump Removal and Installation ... C159
Emission Controls **C160, U145**
Catalytic Converter C160
CRANKCASE EMISSION CONTROLS C161
DISTRIBUTOR CONTROLS C160
Coolant temperature control valve C160
Dual-diaphragm distributor C160
Electronic spark control C160
Spark delay valve C160
Exhaust Gas Recirculation C160
FUEL SYSTEM CONTROLS C160
Carburetors C160
Deceleration valve C161
Evaporative emission control system ... C161
Heated air intake air cleaner C161
Thermactor (air pump) C160
Engine **C161, U145**
Engine Removal and Installation C161
CAMSHAFT, AUXILIARY SHAFT, AND
TIMING BELT—2000 AND 2300 CC C171
Auxiliary shaft Removal and Installation C173
Camshaft Removal and Installation C173
Timing Belt Removal and Installation ... C172
CYLINDER HEAD Removal and Installation C169

LUBRICATION C175
Crankshaft rear main oil seal
Removal and Installation C177
Oil pan Removal and Installation C175
Oil pump Removal and Installation C176
MANIFOLDS C164
Exhaust manifold Removal and
Installation C166
Intake manifold Removal and
Installation C164
TIMING CASE AND CAMSHAFT—V6 and V8 C173
Front oil seal Removal and Installation .. C173
TIMING COVER, CHAIN AND CAMSHAFT
—1600 CC C171
Camshaft and valve lifter Removal
and Installation C171
Timing cover and chain Removal
and Installation C171
VALVE SYSTEM C167
Rocker arm or shaft Removal
and Installation C168
Valve adjustment C167

Front Suspension **C182, U292**
Lower ball joint inspection and
replacement C182
Lower control arm Removal and
Installation C182
Shock absorber Removal and
Installation C183
Upper control arm Removal
and Installation C182
Upper ball joint inspection and
replacement C182
Wheel bearing adjustment C184

Fuel System **C157, U50**
Carburetor C157
Fuel filter Removal and Installation ... C157
Fuel pump Removal and Installation ... C157
Idle speed and mixture adjustment ... C158

Heater **C187**
AIR CONDITIONED CARS C187
Blower motor Removal and Installation C189
Heater assembly Removal and
Installation C187
Heater core Removal and Installation .. C189
NON AIR-CONDITIONED CARS C187
Blower motor Removal and
Installation C187
Heater assembly Removal and
Installation C187
Heater core Removal and Installation .. C187

Ignition System **C155, U34**
Contact point replacement and
adjustment C156
Distributor Removal and Installation ... C155
Firing order C149
Ignition timing C157
Tachometer Hookup for Solid
state ignition C155
Instrument Panel **C186, U350, U368**
Headlight switch Removal and
Installation C186
Ignition lock cylinder Removal and
Installation C186
Ignition switch Removal and
Installation C186
Jacking, Hoisting **C182**
Manual Transmission **C179, U231**
Transmission Removal and Installation .. C179
Radio **C187**
Radio Removal and Installation C187
Rear Axle **C181**
Axle shaft, bearing, and seal Removal
and Installation C181
Rear Suspension **C184**
Shock absorber Removal and
Installation C184
Spring Removal and Installation C184
Seat Belts **C190**
Disabling the interlock system C190
Specifications **C149**
Capacities C152
Crankshaft and connecting rod C153
Engine identification and code C150
General engine C150
Piston clearance C152
Piston ring C153
Serial Number Location C150
Torque C152
Tune-up C151
Valve C151
Wheel alignment C154
Year Identification C149
Starting System **C154, U2**
Starter Removal and Installation C154
Steering **C185, U328, U336**
Power steering pump Removal and
Installation C185
Steering wheel Removal and Installation C185
Turn signal and flasher switch
Removal and Installation C186
U-Joints **C181**
U-Joint Removal and Installation C181
Windshield Wipers **C187**
Motor Removal and Installation C187

YEAR IDENTIFICATION

1971-72 Pinto

1973 Pinto

1974 Pinto

1975 Pinto

1976 Pinto

1977 Pinto

1974 Mustang II

1975-76 Mustang II

1977 Mustang II

1976 Bobcat

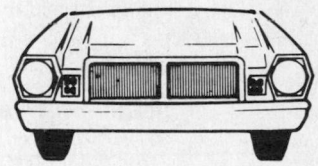

1977 Bobcat

FIRING ORDER

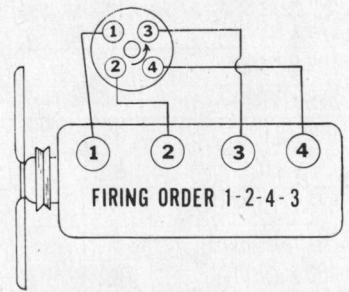

1600 cc

FIRING ORDER 1-2-4-3

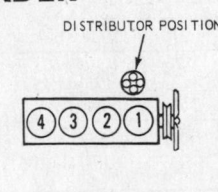

DISTRIBUTOR POSITION

CAP CLIP POSITION

CLOCKWISE

FIRING ORDER –1–3–4–2

2000 cc (© Ford Motor Co.)

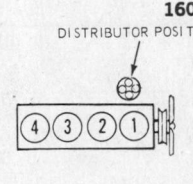

DISTRIBUTOR POSITION

POSITION OF CAP ATTACHING SCREWS

CLOCKWISE

FIRING ORDER –1–3–4–2

2300 cc (© Ford Motor Co)

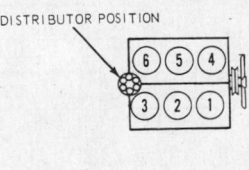

DISTRIBUTOR POSITION

CAP CLIP POSITION

CLOCKWISE

FIRING ORDER – 1–4–2–5–3–6

2800 cc V6 (© Ford Motor Co)

FIRING ORDER 1-5-4-2-6-3-7-8

302 V8

CAR SERIAL NUMBER LOCATION

Vehicle Identification Number

The Vehicle Identification Number is located on a tab mounted on the upper left-hand corner of the dashboard, visible through the windshield. The VIN also appears on the Vehicle Certification Label.

The Vehicle Certification Label is located on the rear edge or lock pillar of the driver's door.

Vehicle Certification Label

The Vehicle Certification Label is located on the rear edge or lock pillar of the driver's door. Alteration or removal of this label will result in its destruction, or the appearance of the word VOID.

■ Beginning 1972, horsepower and torque are SAE net figures. They are measured at the rear of the transmission with all accessories installed and operating. Since the figures vary when a given engine is installed in different models, some are representative rather than exact.

ENGINE CODE

The engine code designation is the 5th digit of the vehicle identification number (V.I.N.). The V.I.N. is stamped on a plate located at the left side of the instrument panel visible through the windshield on all models.

Disp	Bbl	Hp ■	'71	'72	'73	'74	'75	'76	'77
4-Cylinder Models									
98 (1600cc)	1	54		W	W				
98 (1600cc)	1	75	W						
122 (2000cc)	2	80				X			
122 (2000cc)	2	85, 86		X	X				
122 (2000cc)	2	100	X						
140 (2300cc)	2	82, 88				Y			
140 (2300cc)	2	83					Y		
140 (2300cc)	2	92						Y	Y
6-Cylinder Models									
171 (2800cc)	2	105				Z			
171 (2800cc)	2	97					Z		
171 (2800cc)	2	103, 100, 99						Z	Z
8-Cylinder Models									
302 (4900cc)	2	129					F		
302 (4900cc)	2	134						F	F

GENERAL ENGINE SPECIFICATIONS

Year	Engine No. Cyl. Displacement (Cu. In., cc.)	Carburetor Type	Horsepower @ rpm ■	Torque @ rpm (ft lbs) ■	Bore x Stroke (in.)	Compression Ratio	Oil Pressure @ 2000 rpm
'71	4-97.6 (1600 cc)	1 bbl	75 @ 5000	96 @ 3000	3.188 x 3.056	8.0:1	38
	4-122 (2000 cc)	2 bbl	100 @ 5600	120 @ 3600	3.575 x 3.029	8.6:1	50①
'72	4-97.6 (1600 cc)	1 bbl	54 @ 4600	80 @ 2400	3.188 x 3.056	8.0:1	38
	4-122 (2000 cc)	2 bbl	86 @ 5400	103 @ 3200	3.575 x 3.029	8.2:1	50①
'73	4-97.6 (1600 cc)	1 bbl	54 @ 4600	80 @ 2400	3.188 x 3.056	8.0:1	38
	4-122 (2000 cc)	2 bbl	86 @ 5400	103 @ 3200	3.575 x 3.029	8.2:1	50①
'74	4-122 (2000 cc)	2 bbl	80 @ 5400	98 @ 3000	3.575 x 3.029	8.2:1	50①
	4-140 (2300 cc)	2 bbl	88 @ 5000②	116 @ 2600	3.781 x 3.126	8.4:1	50
	6-170.8 (2800 cc)	2 bbl	105 @ 4600	140 @ 3200	3.660 x 2.700	8.2:1	40-55①
'75	4-140 (2300 cc)	2 bbl	83 @ 4800	109 @ 2800	3.781 x 3.126	8.4:1	50
	6-170.8 (2800 cc)	2 bbl	97 @ 4400	138 @ 3200	3.660 x 2.700	8.2:1	40-55①
	8-302 (4900 cc)	2 bbl	129 @ 4000	213 @ 1800	4.000 x 3.000	8.0:1	50-70
'76-'77	4-140 (2300 cc)	2 bbl	92 @ 5000	121 @ 3000	3.781 x 3.126	9.0:1	40-60
	6-170.8 (2800 cc)	2 bbl	103 @ 4300	149 @ 2800	3.660 x 2.700	8.7:1	40-60
	6-170.8 (2800 cc) Calif.	2 bbl	99 @ 4400	144 @ 2200	3.660 x 2.700	8.7:1	40-60
	6-170.8 (2800 cc) Mustang II, Auto.	2 bbl	100 @ 4600	143 @ 2600	3.660 x 2.700	8.7:1	40-60
	6-170.8 (2800 cc) Mustang II, Auto., Calif.	2 bbl	100 @ 4400	143 @ 2600	3.660 x 2.700	8.7:1	40-60
	8-302 (4900 cc)	2 bbl	134 @ 3600	247 @ 1800	4.000 x 3.000	8.0:1	40-60

■ Beginning 1972, horsepower and torque are SAE net figures. They are measured at the rear of the transmission with all accessories installed and operating. Since the figures vary when a given engine is installed in different models, some are representative rather than exact.
① Oil pressure at 1500 rpm.
② 88 hp in Mustang II; 82 hp in Pinto

TUNE-UP SPECIFICATIONS

When analyzing compression test results, look for uniformity among cylinders rather than specific pressures.

| | ENGINE | SPARK PLUGS | | DISTRIBUTOR | | IGNITION TIMING (deg) ▲ | | VALVES | Fuel Pump | IDLE SPEED (rpm) ▲ | |
| | No. Cyl. | Orig. | Gap | Point Dwell | Point Gap | Man | Auto | Intake | Pressure | Man | Auto |
Year	Displacement (cu in.)	Type	(in.)	(deg)	(in.)	Trans ●	Trans	Opens ■ (deg)	(psi)	Trans	Trans
'71	4-97.6 (1600 cc)	AGR-22	.030	40	.025	12B	—	17	3½-5½	800/500③	—
'71	4-122 (2000 cc)	BRF-32①	②	40	.025	6B-10B	6B-10B	24	3½-5½	750/500③	650/500③
'72	4-97.6 (1600 cc)	AGR-22	.030	40	.025	12B	—	17	3½-5½	800/500③	—
'72	4-122 (2000 cc)	BRF-42	.034	40	.025	6B-10B	6B-10B	24	3½-5½	750/500③	650/500③
'73	4-97.6 (1600 cc)	AGR-32	.034	40	.025	12B	—	17	3½-5½	800/500③	—
	4-122 (2000 cc)	BRF-42	.034	40	.025	6B-10B	6B-10B	24	3½-5½	750/500③	650/500③
'74	4-122 (2000 cc)	BRF-42	.034	39	.025	6B(3B)	6B(3B)	24	3½-4½	750	750
	4-140 (2300 cc)	AGRF-52	.034	38	.027	6B	6B	22	3½-4½	750④	650④
	6-170.8 (2800 cc)	AGR-42	.044	38	.025	12B	12B	20	3½-4½	750	650
'75	4-140 (2300 cc)	AGRF-52	.034	Electronic		6B	6B(10B)	22	3½-5½	550	550
	6-170.8 (2800 cc)	AGR-42	.034	Electronic		10B(8B)	12B(6B)	20	3½-5½	850	700
	8-302	ARF-42	.044	Electronic		—	6B	20	5-7	—	650
'76	4-140 (2300 cc)	AGRF-52	.034	Electronic		6B	20B	22	5-7	750	650
	6-170.8 (2800 cc)	AGR-42	.034	Electronic		10B(8B)	12B(6B)	20	3½-6	850	700
	8-302	ARF-42	.044	Electronic		12B	6B(8B)	16	6-8	800	700
'77	4-140 (2300 cc)	AGRF-52	.034	Electronic		⑤	⑤	22	5½-6½	⑤	⑤
	6-170.8 (2800 cc)	AGR-42	.034	Electronic		⑤	⑤	20	3½-8	⑤	⑤
	8-302 (4900 cc)	ARF-52 (ARF-52-6)	.050(.060)	Electronic		⑤	⑤	16	5½ 6½	⑥	⑤

▲ See text for procedure
■ All figures Before Top Dead Center
● Figure in parentheses is for California
B Before Top Dead Center
— Not applicable
① BRF-42 recommended service replacement plug
② For BRF-32, set gap to .025 inches and for BRF-42, set gap to .034 inches

③ First figure is for idle speed with solenoid energized and automatic transmission In Drive, while the second figure is for idle speed with solenoid disconnected and automatic transmission in Neutral. Cars without a solenoid use higher figure.

④ 850 man, 750 auto in Pinto

NOTE: The underhood specifications sticker often reflects tune-up specification changes made in production. Sticker figures must be used if they disagree with those in this chart.

VALVE SPECIFICATIONS

Year	Engine No. Cyl. Displacement (cu in.)	Seat Angle (deg)	Face Angle (deg)	Spring Test Pressure (lbs @ in.)	Spring Installed Height (in.)	STEM TO GUIDE Clearance (in.) Intake	Exhaust	STEM Diameter (in.) Intake	Exhaust
'71	4-97.6 (1600 cc)	45	45	47 @ 1.26	1 17/64	.0008-.0030	.0017-.0039	.3100	.3100
	4-122 (2000 cc)	45	45	67 @ 1.42	1 13/32	.0015-.0015	.0015-.0025	.3149	.3149
'72	4-97.6 (1600 cc)	45	45	50 @ 1.26	1 17/64	.0008-.0027	.0017-.0036	.3102	.3093
	4-122 (2000 cc)	45	46	69 @ 1.42	1 13/32	.0008-.0025	.0018-.0035	.3163	.3153
'73	4-97.6 (1600 cc)	45	44	47 @ 1.263	1 17/64	.0008-.0027	.0017-.0036	.3102	.3093
	4-122 (2000 cc)	45	44	69 @ 1.418	1 13/32	.0008-.0025	.0018-.0035	.3163	.3153
'74	4-122 (2000 cc)	45	46	69 @ 1.418	1 47/64	.0008-.0025	.0018-.0035	.3163	.3153
	4-140 (2300 cc)	45	46	75 @ 1.560	1 53/64	.0010-.0027	.0015-.0022	.3419	.3415
	6-170.8 (2800 cc)	45	44	64 @ 1.585	1 29/32	.0008-.0025	.0018-.0035	.3162	.3153
'75-'77	4-140 (2300 cc)	45	46	75 @ 1.56	1 9/16	.0006-.0023	.0015-.0032	.3424	.3415
	4-170.8 (2800 cc)	45	46	64 @ 1.59	1 19/32	.0008-.0025	.0018-.0035	.3162	.3153
	8-302	45	46	80 @ 1.60	1 39/64	.0010-.0027	.0015-.0032	.3420	.3415

CAPACITIES

Year	ENGINE No. Cyl. Displacement (Cu. In.)	Engine Crankcase Add 1 Qt For ■ New Filter	TRANSMISSION Pts To Refill After Draining Manual 3-Speed	Manual 4-Speed	Automatic	Drive Axle (pts)	Gasoline Tank (gals)	COOLING SYSTEM (qts) With Heater	With A/C
'71-'72	4-97.6 (1600 cc)	3	——	2.5	——	2.2	11①	7.75	——
	4-122 (2000cc)	4	——	2.5	16	2.2	11①	8.50	8.50
'73	4-97.6 (1600 cc)	3	——	2.8	——	2.2	11①	7.80	——
	4-122 (2000cc)	4	——	2.8	16	2.2	11①	8.50	8.50
'74	4-122 (2000 cc)	4	——	2.8	16	3	13①	8.50	8.50
	4-140 (2300 cc)	4	——	4④	16	3	13①	8.80③	9.20③
	6-170.8 (2800 cc)	5	——	4	16	3	13	12.5	12.8
'75	4-140 (2300 cc)	4	——	3.5④	16	3⑧	13⑤⑥	8.7	9.0
	6-170.8 (2800 cc)	4.5	——	3.5④	15⑦	4	13⑤⑥	12.5	13.2
	8-302	4	——	——	15	4	13⑥	16.3	16.3
'76-'77	4-140 (2300 cc) Pinto, Bobcat	4	——	2.8	16/14②	2.2/4.5⑨	13⑤	8.7	9.0
	4-140 (2300 cc) Mustang II	4	——	3.5	16	3/4.5⑨	13⑥	8.5	9.1
	6-170.8 (2800 cc) Pinto, Bobcat	4.5	——	3.5	16/14②	2.2/4.5⑨	13⑤	12.5	13.2
	6-170.8 (2800 cc) Mustang II	4.5	——	3.5	15	3/4.5⑨	13⑥	12.3	13.2
	8-302	4	——	3.5	15	4.5	13⑥	16.3	16.3

■ ½ quart for 1600, 2300, 2800
—— Not applicable
① Wagon—12 gals
② C3/C4
③ 8.5 qt in Pinto
④ 2.8 pt in Pinto

⑤ 14 gals on station wagon
⑥ 16.5 gals with auxiliary tank in Mustang II
⑦ 14 pt in Pinto
⑧ 2.3 pt in Pinto
⑨ 6.75/8.00 in. axle

TORQUE SPECIFICATIONS
All readings in ft lbs

Year	Engine No. Cyl. Displacement (cu in.)	Cylinder Head Bolts	Rod Bearing Bolts	Main Bearing Bolts	Crankshaft Pulley Bolt	Flywheel to Crankshaft Bolts	MANIFOLD Intake	Exhaust
'71-'77	4-97.6 (1600 cc)	65-70	30-35	65-70	24-28	50-55	12-15	15-18
	4-122 (2000 cc)	65-80	29-34	65-75	39-43	47-51	12-15	12-15①
	4-140 (2300 cc)	80-90	30-36	80-90	80-114②	54-64	14-21	16-23
	6-170.8 (2800 cc)	65-80	21-25	65-75	92-103②	47-51	15-18	14-18③
	8-302	65-72	19-24	60-70	70-90②	75-85	23-25	18-24

① 15-18 in 1974
② Crankshaft damper bolt
③ 16-23 starting 1975

PISTON CLEARANCE

Year	Engine	Piston-to-Bore Clearance (in.)
'71-'73	4-1600 cc	.0016-.0022* .0019-.0025**
'71-'74	4-2000 cc	.0010-.0020
'74-'77	4-2300 cc	.0014-.0022
'74-'77	6-2800 cc	.0011-.0019
'75-'77	8-302	.0018-.0026

* No. 1, 2, and 3
** No. 4

CRANKSHAFT AND CONNECTING ROD SPECIFICATIONS

All measurements are given in inches

| Year | Engine No. Cyl. Displacement (cu in.) | CRANKSHAFT | | | | CONNECTING ROD | | |
		Main Brg. Journal Dia	Main Brg. Oil Clearance	Shaft End-Play	Thrust on No.	Journal Diameter	Oil Clearance	Side Clearance
'71	4-97.6 (1600 cc)	2.1253-2.1261	.0004-.0018	.003-.011	3	1.9368-1.9376	.0004-.0024	.004-.010
	4-122 (2000 cc)	2.2432-2.2440	.0005-.0015	.004-.008	3	2.0464-2.0472	.0006-.0026	.004-.010
'72-'73	4-97.6 (1600 cc)	2.1253-2.1261	.0005-.0016	.003-.011	3	1.9368-1.9376	.0004-.0024	.004-.010
	4-122 (2000 cc)	2.2432-2.2440	.0006-.0016	.003-.011	3	2.0464-2.0472	.0006-.0026	.004-.010
'74	4-122 (2000 cc)	2.2432-2.2440	.0006-.0016	.003-.011	3	2.0464-2.0472	.0006-.0015	.004-.011
	4-140 (2300 cc)	2.3982-2.3990	.0008-.0015	.004-.012	3	2.0465-2.0472	.0006-.0027	.0008-.0026
	6-170.8 (2800 cc)	2.2433-2.2441	.0006-.0019	.003-.011	3	2.0464-2.0472	.0006-.0022	.004-.011
'75	4-140 (2300 cc)	2.3982-2.3990	.0008-.0015	.004-.008	3	2.0464-2.0472	.0008-.0015	.0035-.0105
	6-170.8 (2800 cc)	2.2433-2.2441	.0005-.0016	.004-.008	3	2.1252-2.1260	.0005-.0015	.004-.011
	8-302	2.2482-2.2490	.0005-.0015①	.004-.008	3	2.1228-2.1236	.0008-.0015	.010-.020
'76-'77	4-140 (2300 cc)	2.3982-2.3990	.0008-.0015	.004-.008	3	2.0464-2.0472	.0008-.0015	.0035-.0105
	6-170.8 (2800 cc)	2.2433-2.2441	.0008-.0015	.004-.008	3	2.1252-2.1560	.0006-.0015	.004-.011
	8-302	2.2482-2.2490	.0008-.0015	.004-.008	3	2.1228-2.1236	.0008-.0015	.010-.020

① .0001-.0005 on No. 1

RING GAP

All measurements are given in inches

Year	Engine	Top Compression	Bottom Compression		Year	Engine	Oil Control
'71-'73	4-97.6 (1600 cc)	.009-.014	.009-.014		'71-'73	1600 cc	.009-.014
'71-'72	4-122 (2000 cc)	.019-.021	.019-.021		'71-'74	2000 cc	.016-.055
'73-'74	4-122 (2000 cc)	.015-.023	.015-.023		'74	2300 cc	.015-.055
'74	4-140 (2300 cc)	.010-.020	.010-.020		'74	2800 cc	.015-.055
'74	6-170.8 (2800 cc)	.015-.023	.015-.023		'75-'77	2300 cc	.015-.055
'75-77	4-140 (2300 cc)	.010-.020	.010-.020		'75-'77	2800 cc	.015-.055
'75-'77	6-170 (2800 cc)	.015-.023	.015-.023		'75-'77	8-302	.015-.055
'75-'77	8-302	.010-.020	.010-.020				

RING SIDE CLEARANCE

All measurements are given in inches

Year	Engine	Top Compression	Bottom Compression		Year	Engine	Oil Control
'71-'73	4-97.6 (1600 cc)	.0016-.0036	.0016-.0036		'71-'73	1600 cc	.0018-.0038
'71-'74	4-122 (2000 cc)	.0019-.0038	.0019-.0038		'71-'74	2000 cc	Snug
'74-'77	4-140 (2300 cc)	.0020-.0040	.0020-.0040		'74-'77	2300 cc	Snug
'74-'77	6-170.8 (2800 cc)	.0020-.0033	.0020-.0033		'74-'77	2800 cc	Snug
'75-'77	8-302	.002-.004	.002-.004		'75-'77	8-302	Snug

WHEEL ALIGNMENT SPECIFICATIONS

Year	Model	CASTER Range (deg)	CASTER Pref Setting (deg)	CAMBER Range (deg)	CAMBER Pref Setting (deg)	Toe-in (in.)	Steering Axis Inclin.	WHEEL PIVOT RATIO (deg) Inner Wheel	WHEEL PIVOT RATIO (deg) Outer Wheel
'71	All models	1P to 2P	1½P	0 to 1½P	¾P	0 to ¼	8.968	20	18.95
'72	All models	½N to 3½P	1½P	¼N to 1¾P	¾P	1/16 to 7/16	8.968	20	18.94
'73	All models	1N to 3P	1P	¼N to 1¾P	¾P	0 to ¼	8.968	20	18.94
'74-'77	Pinto, Bobcat	½P to 2P	1¼P	0 to 1½P	¾P	⅛ to ⅜	10.018	20	18.84
'74-'77	Sta. Wag.	¾P to 2¼P	1½P	0 to 1½P	¾P	⅛ to ⅜	10.018	20	18.84
'74-'77	Mustang II	⅛N to 1⅝P	⅞P	¼N to 1¼P	½P	0 to ¼	9.763	20	18.84

N Negative   P Positive

NOTE: The Mustang II, beginning 1974, is in this section. Mustang models through 1973 are in the Comet car section.

CHARGING SYSTEM

Testing and adjustment of the alternator and regulator are covered in the "Unit Repair Section."

Alternator Removal

1. Disconnect the battery negative cable.
2. Disconnect the electrical leads.
3. Loosen the mounting bolts and tilt the alternator in toward the engine.
4. Remove the fanbelt, then remove the mounting bolts and the alternator.

Alternator Installation

1. Position the alternator and loosely install the mounting bolts.
2. Install fanbelt, pry on the front of the alternator so as to place tension on the belt (¼ in. deflection at belt midpoint), then tighten mounting bolts.
3. Connect alternator wires and the battery cable.

Regulator Replacement

1. Disconnect the battery ground cable.
2. Remove the wiring harness from the regulator.
3. Remove the regulator retaining screws and remove the regulator.
4. Position the regulator on the car and install the retaining screws.
5. Attach wiring to the regulator and connect the ground cable.

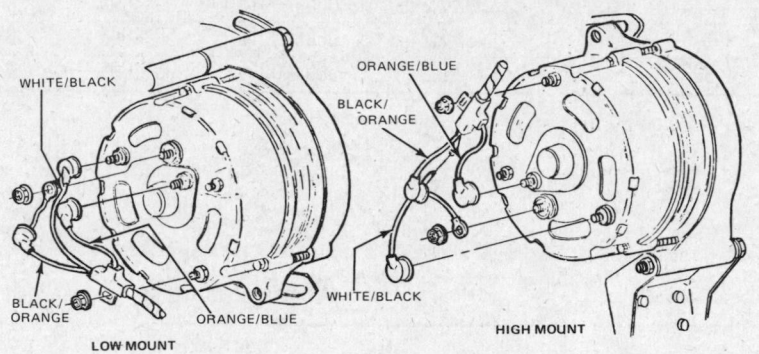

Typical connector details for the rear terminal alternator (© Ford Motor Co.)

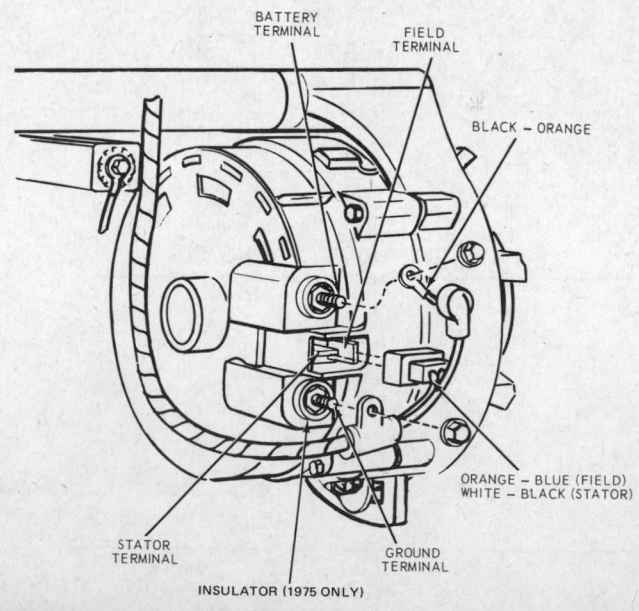

Typical connector details for the side terminal alternator (© Ford Motor Co.)

STARTING SYSTEM

The engine is equipped with a positive engagement starter. Internal starter repair procedures can be found in the Unit Repair Section.

Starter Removal and Installation

Through 1973

1. Remove the ground cable from the battery.
2. Raise the car on a hoist and dis-

connect the starter cable. On the 1600, remove the right steering gear housing clamp and grommet from the crossmember, and loosen the left clamp bolts.

3. Remove the 3 starter retaining bolts. Remove the starter. On the 2000, you may have to turn the steering gear bellows clamp.
4. Position the starter motor to the engine.
5. Install the 3 retaining bolts and connect the starter cable. Tighten the steering clamps and bolts.
6. Lower the car and install the battery ground cable.

1974 and later

1. Disconnect the battery ground cable.
2. Raise the car on a hoist and remove the four bolts retaining the crossmember under the bellhousing.
3. Remove the flex coupling clamping screw at the attachment point to the steering gear.
4. Remove the 3 nuts and bolts which attach the steering gear to the crossmember.
5. Disengage the steering gear from the flex coupling and pull the steering gear down to provide access to the starter motor.
6. Disconnect the starter cable from the starter motor.
7. Remove the starter motor attaching bolts and remove the starter.
8. Install the starter motor in the reverse order of removal.

IGNITION SYSTEM

All distributors are the dual advance type; that is, they have both centrifugal and vacuum advance. Some models are equipped with a vacuum retard mechanism which retards ignition timing during deceleration and idling.

Beginning 1975, all Ford engines have electronic ignition which does not use replaceable contacts. This system, while retaining most of the features of the conventional system, uses a unique armature and magnetic pickup coil assembly inside the distributor and a solid state amplifier module.

Tachometer Hookup for Solid State Ignition

The new solid state ignition coil connector allows a tachometer test lead with an alligator clip type tip to be connected to the distributor electronic control terminal without removing the connector.

Connect the clip to the Tach Test

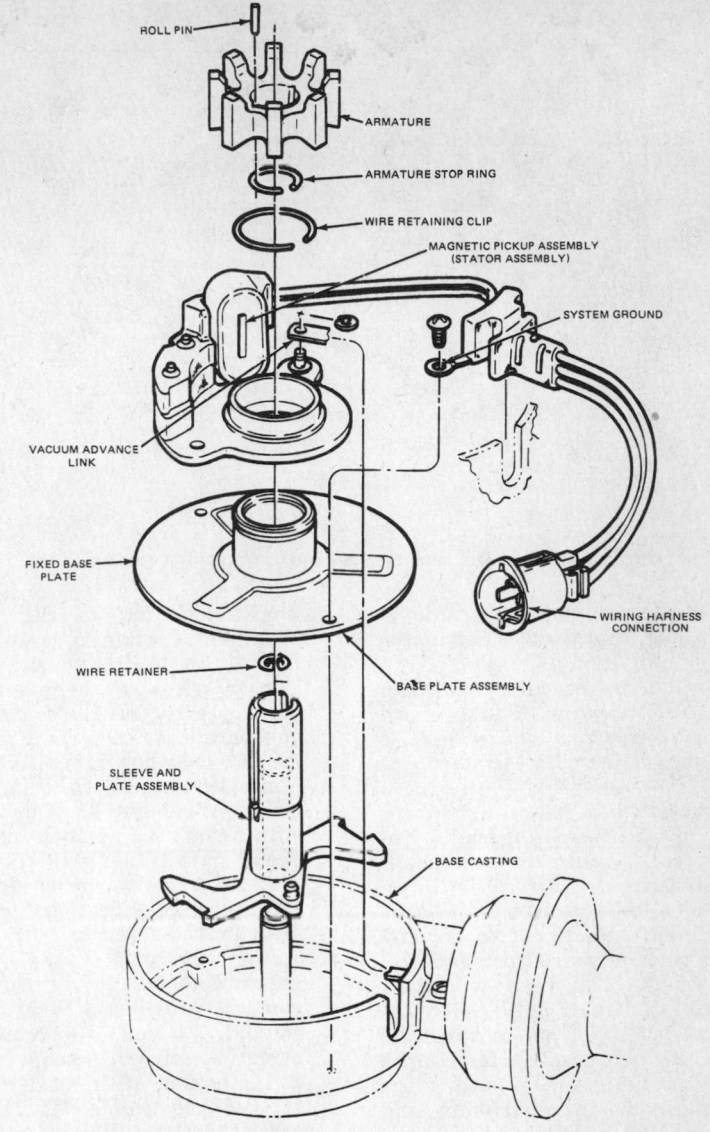

Exploded view of solid state ignition distributor (© Ford Motor Co.)

cavity. If the coil connector must be removed pull it out straight until it disconnects.

Distributor Removal and Installation

1. Remove the air cleaner on V6 and V8 engines. On the 4 cylinder engines equipped with an air pump, remove the one mounting bolt and the drive belt, then swing the pump to one side to gain access to the distributor. It may be necessary to disconnect the air pump system air filter and lines. Unsnap the two clips or loosen the two screws and remove the distributor cap.
2. Note their positioning, and then disconnect the vacuum lines from the distributor. Disconnect the electronic ignition wiring harness.
3. Matchmark the distributor hous-

ing and the engine block, then scribe another mark on the housing to indicate the rotor position.
4. Remove the bolt that holds the distributor, then carefully pull out the unit.

NOTE: The hex shaft which drives the oil pump may stick in the distributor shaft and be withdrawn from the pump. When installing the distributor coat one end of the hex shaft

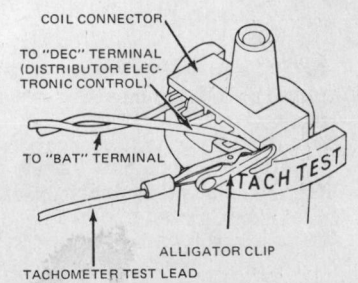

Electronic ignition test tachometer hookup (© Ford Motor Co.)

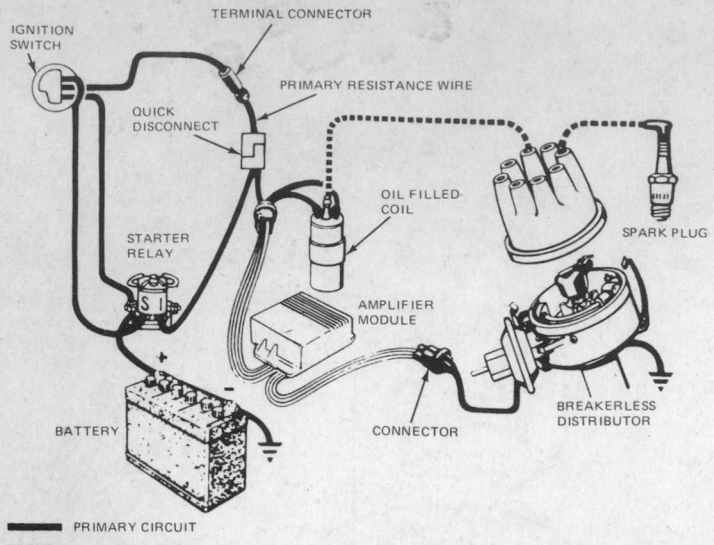

PRIMARY CIRCUIT

SECONDARY CIRCUIT

Typical electronic ignition system schematic (© Ford Motor Co.)

with heavy grease and insert that end into the hex hole in the distributor shaft.

On the V8, make sure the oil pump intermediate shaft is fully engaged with the distributor. You may have to turn the engine with the starter to get full engagement.

Installation is as follows:

1. Align matchmarks, if engine has not been disturbed, and install distributor.

NOTE: keep in mind that the helical gear will tend to rotate the distributor as it is pushed down.

2. If engine has been disturbed, turn crankshaft until No. 1 piston is at TDC on compression stroke and crankshaft damper timing marks are aligned. Place the cap on the distributor and scribe the location of No. one spark plug tower. Install the distributor so that the rotor points toward No. one. Tighten the hold-down bolt.

3. Tighten the hold-down bolt and connect the primary and high-tension wires. Adjust contact breaker points, if any, and ignition timing. Connect the vacuum line(s).

Contact Point Replacement and Adjustment

1600 cc

1. Remove the distributor cap. Remove the screw that retains the primary and condenser wires to the point set.

2. Remove the two retaining screws and lift out the point set. It is best to replace the condenser and point set at the same time.

3. Lubricate the cam with silicone cam lube. Place the point set on the breaker plate, making sure the tab on the bottom engages

the indentation in the plate. Tighten the retaining screw.

4. Install the primary and condenser wires to the point set, making sure that the connectors are parallel to each other and to the ground when tightened.

5. Turn the engine to bring the point set rubbing block onto one of the cam's high points. Insert a feeler gauge, thickness equal to the point gap specified in the "Tune-Up Specifications" chart, between the contacts.

6. Adjust the gap if the feeler gauge does not fit between the contacts with just a slight drag. Partially loosen the retaining screws and insert a screwdriver in the breaker plate notch at the top of the points. Twist the screwdriver until the correct gap is obtained, and then tighten the retaining screws.

7. Install the distributor cap, aligning the tab in the cap with the notch in the distributor. Check the dwell angle with a meter.

2000 cc, 2300 cc, and 2800 cc V6

1. Remove the distributor cap. Pull the breaker point wire from the condenser connector near the outside edge of the distributor body.

2. Remove the retaining screws and lift out the point set.

3. To replace the condenser: remove the attaching screw, grasp the condenser and wire, and work the rubber grommet out of the distributor body. Disconnect the ignition wire connector from the coil and disconnect the coil wire from the condenser.

The condenser is mounted inside the distributor on the 2300 cc engine. Remove it by disconnecting the condenser lead, removing the retaining screw, and lifting the condenser from the distributor.

4. To install the condenser: place the condenser and wire assembly on the side of the distributor and work the grommet into the distributor body. Install the retaining screw and position the end of the wire attached to the condenser on the "dist" coil post. Install the ignition wire on the coil post over the condenser wire.

Install the condenser on the 2300 cc engine by placing the condenser in position in the distributor, installing the hold-down screw and connecting the condenser lead to the points terminal.

5. Position the point set on the breaker plate and tighten the retaining screw. Connect the breaker point wire to the condenser. Lubricate the cam with silicone cam lube.

6. Turn the engine to bring the point set rubbing block onto one of the cam's high points. Insert a feeler gauge, the thickness of which is equal to the point gap specified in the "Tune-Up Speci-

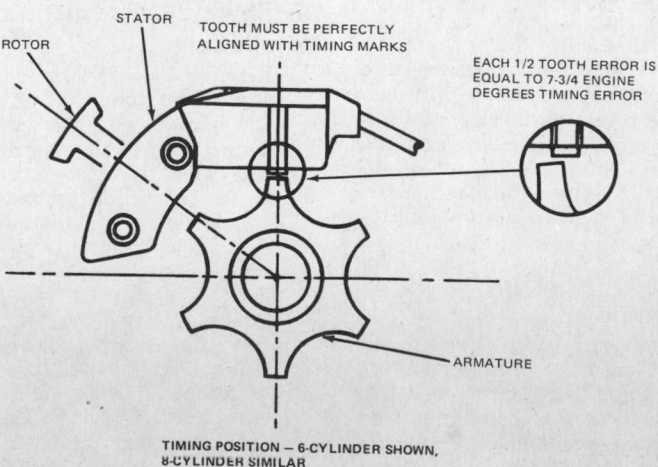

Distributor firing position with electronic ignition (© Ford Motor Co.)

fications" chart, between the contacts.

Caution When rotating the engine manually, never turn the overhead camshaft engine pulley counterclockwise or the camshaft drive belt may slip and alter the timing.

7. Adjust the gap if the feeler gauge does not fit between the contacts with just a slight drag. Slightly loosen the retaining screw and insert a screwdriver between the boss on the breaker plate and the notch on the points. Twist the screwdriver until the correct gap is obtained, and then tighten the retaining screw.

8. Install the distributor cap, aligning the tab in the cap with the notch in the distributor. Check the dwell angle with a meter.

Ignition Timing

1. Locate the timing marks and pointer on the lower engine pulley and front cover. Clean the marks and pointer, and then scribe the mark and pointer with chalk. (See "Tune-Up Specifications" chart for the correct timing.)

2. Hook up a timing light to no. one spark plug according to the manufacturer's instructions. Disconnect the one or two vacuum lines and plug the open end(s).

3. Attach a tachometer and adjust the engine idle speed to 600 rpm or the timing speed specified on the underhood specifications sticker. (See "Idle Speed Adjustment".)

4. Aim the timing light at the pulley marks. If the marks do not align, loosen the distributor hold-down screw or bolt and slowly rotate the distributor until the marks align. Tighten the hold-down screw or bolt. *NOTE: A variance of plus or minus two degrees from the specified timing is acceptable.*

5. Recheck the timing, and then adjust the engine to normal idle speed.

FUEL SYSTEM

Carburetor

The carburetor used on the 1600 cc engine is an Autolite 1250 single-barrel downdraft unit.

All other four-cylinder engines are equipped with an Autolite model 5200 carburetor. The 5200 model is a two stage, two venturi carburetor. The primary stage venturi bore is of smaller diameter than the secondary stage venturi bore. The secondary stage is actuated by mechanical linkage when the primary throttle plates

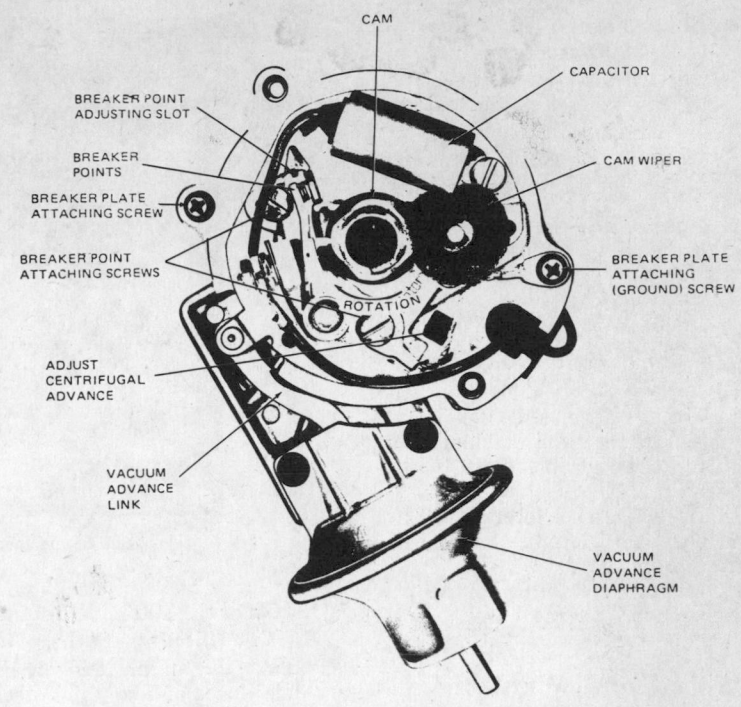

View of the inside of the 2300 cc point-type distributor (© Ford Motor Co)

reach an opening of approximately 45°.

V6 and V8 engines use the Motorcraft 2150 two-barrel carburetor. This is a non-progressive two-barrel; both barrels operate simultaneously.

Fuel Pump

All of the engines use a diaphragm-type mechanical fuel pump. All of the fuel pumps are mounted on the front, left-side of the engine, except on the 1600 cc engine where it is on the right-side.

The fuel pump is operated by a lever running on an eccentric on the camshaft on the 1600 cc, the 1974 and later 2000 and 2300 cc, and the 302 V8. All 1971-73 2000 cc, and the 2800 cc V6 engines have a pushrod operated fuel pump driven by an eccentric on the auxiliary shaft.

All of the fuel pumps are sealed and must be replaced when defective.

Removal and Installation

1. Disconnect the fuel lines from the fuel pump and plug the inlet

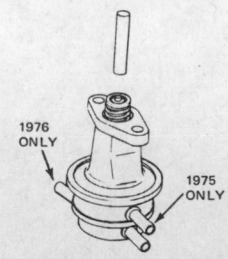

The configuration of the V6 fuel pump is changed, starting 1976 (© Ford Motor Co.)

line from the gas tank to prevent gas leakage.

2. Remove the fuel pump retaining screws and remove the pump.

3. Remove the fuel pump actuating rod, if so equipped.

4. Clean all gasket mounting surfaces.

5. Install the fuel pump actuating rod, if so equipped.

6. Apply oil-resistant sealer to the fuel pump, position the pump on the engine and install the retaining screws. *NOTE: Make sure the fuel pump rocker arm or rod is riding on the camshaft or intermediate shaft eccentric.*

7. Connect the fuel lines to the fuel pump, start the engine and check for leaks.

Fuel Filter Removal and Installation

1600 cc

The fuel filter is located in the fuel line beneath the battery; therefore, it is necessary to remove the battery to replace the filter.

1. Disconnect the battery cables. Remove the hold-down retaining nut and remove the battery.

Caution Be careful not to spill electrolyte from the battery as you are removing it.

2. Loosen the filter clamps, remove the lines from the old filter, and install the replacement filter.

3. Tighten the filter clamps and replace the battery.

2000 cc through 1973 and 2800 cc V6

The fuel filter is located in the fuel line between the fuel pump and the carburetor.

1. Squeeze the tabs on the fuel filter clamps together and remove the old filter.
2. Compress the clamp tabs and install the replacement filter, positioning the clamps near the ends of the filter.

1974 and later 2000 cc and 2300 cc, 302 V8

1. Remove the air cleaner.
2. Loosen the retaining clamp securing the fuel inlet hose to the fuel filter.
3. Unscrew the fuel filter from the carburetor. Disconnect the fuel filter from the hose.
4. Install the fuel filter in the reverse order of removal.

Idle Speed and Mixture Adjustment

NOTE: The factory recommended procedure for adjusting the idle mixture on 1975 and later models requires the addition of an artificial mixture enrichment substance (propane) to the air intake. This method requires special tools not generally available to the public. The procedures that follow are specifically recommended by the factory only for models through 1974.

1600 cc

1. Check the idle speed with the air cleaner removed and the headlights on high beam. If it is necessary to make an adjustment, turn the nut on the bottom of the carburetor solenoid to correct the speed.
2. When the idle speed is correct, disconnect the solenoid at the quick-disconnect.
3. Idle speed should equal the lower figure in the "Tune-Up Specifications" chart. Turn the carburetor idle screw if an adjustment is necessary.
4. Reconnect the solenoid. Open the throttle slightly and check to see that the solenoid plunger extends. Idle speed should be increased to the higher figure given in the "Tune-Up Specifications" chart.
5. Adjust the idle mixture screw until a smooth idle is obtained.
6. Turn the engine off and install the air cleaner. Recheck the idle speed and, if it is not correct, remove the air cleaner and readjust the idle speed. Repeat this operation until the idle speed is correct.

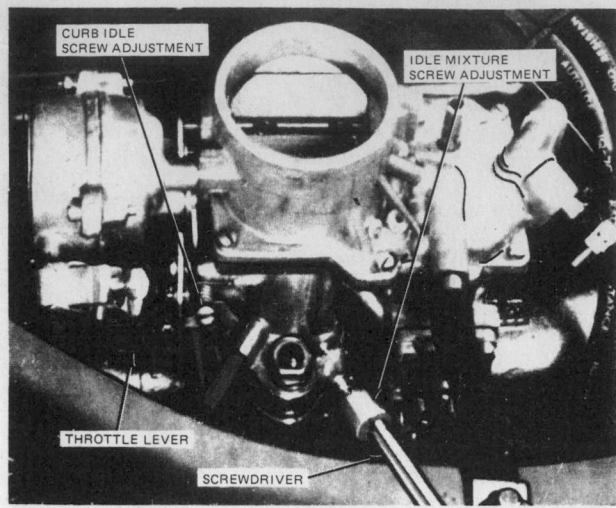

1600 cc idle speed and mixture adjustment screws
(© Ford Motor Co)

2000 cc, 2300 cc Without Air Conditioning, and all V6

1. Start the engine and check the idle speed. Make this check on automatic-equipped cars with the selector in Drive and the wheels blocked.
2. Turn the carburetor curb idle screw in or out as necessary to correct the idle speed to the figure in the "Tune-Up Specifications" chart.
3. Adjust the carburetor idle mixture adjusting screw to obtain the smoothest idle.
4. Turn off the engine and install the air cleaner. Restart the engine and check the idle speed. If the idle speed has changed, remove the air cleaner and readjust the idle speed. Repeat this operation until the idle speed is correct.

2000 cc, 2300 cc With Air Conditioning

1. Turn the air conditioner on and, if equipped with automatic transmission, block the wheels and place the selector in Drive.

2. Check the idle speed and, if it isn't equal to the higher figure given in the "Tune-up Specifications" chart, turn the adjusting nut on the bottom of the carburetor solenoid to correct it.
3. Disconnect the solenoid at the quick-disconnect. Turn the air conditioner off and, on automatic-equipped cars, put the selector in neutral.
4. Check the idle speed. If it does not conform with the lower figure in the "Tune-Up Specifications" chart, adjust the carburetor curb idle screw to correct it.
5. Reconnect the solenoid. Open the throttle slightly and check to see that the solenoid plunger extends. The idle speed should be increased to the higher figure listed in the "Tune-Up Specifications" chart.
6. Turn the carburetor idle mixture screw until the smoothest idle is obtained.
7. Turn the engine off and install the air cleaner. Restart the engine and check the idle speed

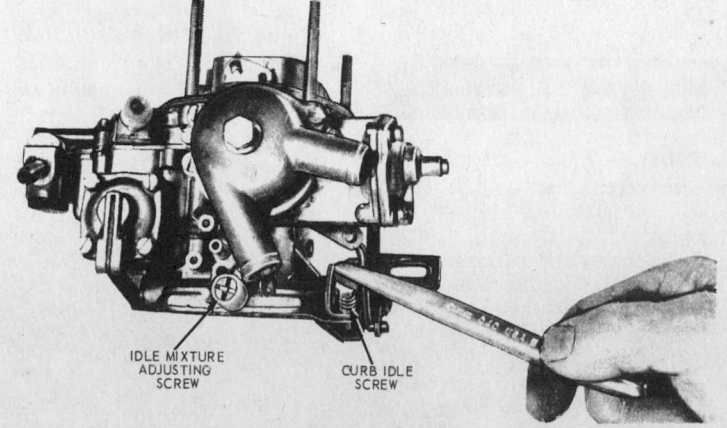

Autolite 5200 carburetor idle adjustments
(© Ford Motor Co)

(A/C on, automatic transmission in Drive). If an adjustment is necessary, turn the engine off and remove the air cleaner. Start the engine and adjust the idle speed. Repeat this operation as many times as necessary.

302 V8

1. Warm up the engine to normal operating temperature.
2. Check timing and adjust if necessary.
3. If applicable, remove the spark delay valve and connect the part throttle vacuum line to the advance side of the distributor. Leave the manifold vacuum line connected to the retard side.
4. Disconnect the EGR valve and plug the line.
5. With the dashpot set at 0.080 in. (manual transmission models only), manual transmission in neutral; automatic in Drive, set the idle speed to that specified with the idle speed screw.
6. In neutral, raise the engine speed to 2200 RPM for about 5 seconds.
7. Let the engine return to normal idle and readjust if necessary, remembering to check the dashpot setting on manual transmission models.
8. Replace the spark delay valve and reconnect the vacuum line to the EGR valve.

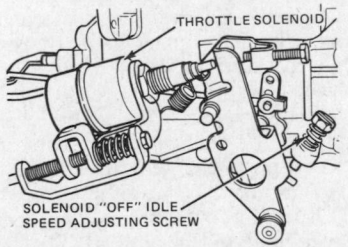

Model 2150 carburetor idle speed adjustment
(© Ford Motor Co.)

COOLING SYSTEM

Coolant is circulated from the bottom of the radiator up through the water pump and into the cylinder block and cylinder head to the thermostat. If the engine is at operating temperature (or hotter), the coolant is returned to the radiator top tank, from where it flows down through the radiator tubes to be cooled by air. If the engine is cold, the coolant flows through a bypass hose to allow the coolant in the block and head to warm up quickly.

NOTE: Early 1975 models require that air be bled from the cooling system to prevent overheating at low speeds. Fill the engine block through the upper radiator hose; to bleed the system, detach the heater core return hose momentarily with the engine running. Do not attempt this with the engine at normal operating temperature; serious burns could result.

Overheating at high speeds on the early 1975 V8 Mustang II may be caused by incorrect radiator air deflectors. The top deflector should be removed and the lower one replaced with the updated part.

Radiator Removal and Installation

1. Remove the radiator cap and drain the coolant.
2. Disconnect the charcoal canister line from the clip on the radiator.
3. Disconnect the radiator hoses from the radiator.
4. Disconnect the transmission oil cooler lines from the bottom of the radiator, if so equipped.
5. Place a block of wood under the radiator for support and remove the mounting bolts. Position the fan shroud, if so equipped, rearward over the fan. Remove the radiator.
6. Reverse the removal procedure to install the radiator. Refill the cooling system.

Water Pump Removal and Installation

1. Drain the cooling system.
2. Disconnect the lower radiator hose and heater hose from the water pump.
3. Loosen the alternator retaining and adjusting bolt, and remove the drive belt.
4. Remove the fan shroud, fan and water pump pulley. On 2000 and 2300 cc engines, remove the camshaft drive belt cover first.
5. Remove the water pump retaining bolts and remove the pump from the engine.

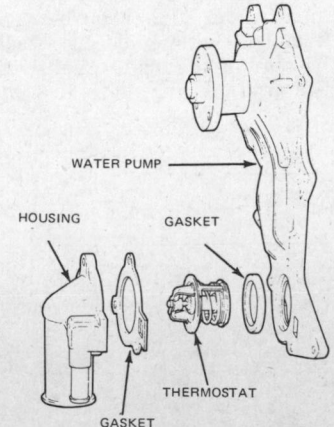

2300 cc engine thermostat installation
(© Ford Motor Co.)

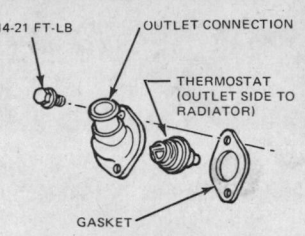

V6 engine thermostat installation
(© Ford Motor Co.)

6. Clean all mating surfaces and install the pump with a new gasket coated with sealer. If a new pump is being installed, transfer the heater hose fitting from the old pump.
7. Reverse the removal steps to install the pump. Refill the cooling system.

Thermostat Removal and Installation

1. Drain the cooling system.
2. Remove the thermostat housing attaching bolts.

NOTE: On the 2800 cc V6, the thermostat is located on the bottom of the water pump housing. The thermostat housing connects to the radiator lower hose, instead of the upper hose.

3. On 1600 cc, 2300 cc, and 302 V8 engines, lift the thermostat housing from the engine and remove the thermostat and gasket.
4. On 2000 cc engines, remove the retaining clip, thermostat, thermostat seal, and gasket from the housing.
5. Clean the gasket mating surfaces and the thermostat housing.
6. Install the thermostat, gasket, seal, and retaining clip (2000 cc only) in the thermostat housing. On the 2300 cc and V8 engines, twist the thermostat to lock it into place in the housing. Coat the gasket with sealer.
7. Install the attaching bolts and tighten them to 12–15 ft lbs.
8. Refill the cooling system.

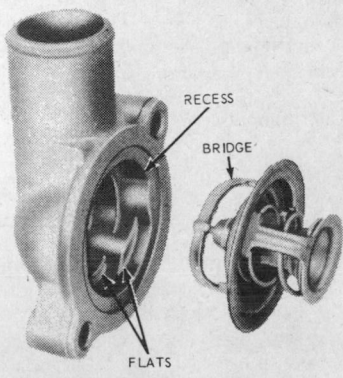

V8 engine thermostat installation
(© Ford Motor Co.)

EMISSION CONTROLS

Testing and diagnosis of emission control equipment is included in the "Emission Control Systems" section of the "Unit Repair Section."

Distributor Controls

Dual-Diaphragm Distributor

Certain models use a dual-diaphragm distributor. This distributor has a normal set of centrifugal advance weights and vacuum diaphragm advance, with the addition of another diaphragm controlled by manifold vacuum. This second diaphragm acts to retard the spark under deceleration and idle, when manifold vacuum is greatest. While this decreases the power of the engine at these times, there is an increase in the braking effect of the engine and hydrocarbon emissions are reduced.

Coolant Temperature Control Valve

Certain models use a coolant temperature control valve which screws into the water jacket. Vacuum lines connect it to the carburetor, outer distributor vacuum chamber (advance), and the intake manifold. This valve helps prevent overheating by connecting intake manifold vacuum to the distributor and allowing vacuum advance during idling when the coolant temperature reaches a certain point.

Cold Start Spark Advance System

On some 1975 and later engines, a cold start spark advance system is added to the distributor control system. Intake manifold vacuum is routed to the distributor when the coolant temperature is below 125°F or above 235°F. Thus full advance is provided when the engine is cold or overheated at idle.

Spark Delay Valve

Some models utilize a spark delay in the vacuum line to the vacuum advance chamber of the distributor. This valve cuts off vacuum advance during certain heavy throttle applications for a period of seconds.

Electronic Spark Control

This system, used in 1972 only, blocks carburetor vacuum to the distributor vacuum advance mechanism under certain speed and temperature conditions. It consists of a temperature sensor, a speed sensor, an amplifier, and a distributor modulator vacuum valve. This system prevents ignition advance by blocking carburetor vacuum from the distributor advance mechanism until the car reaches 35 mph when the ambient temperature is over 65°F.

The temperature sensor monitors outside air temperature and relays this information to the amplifier. The amplifier controls the distributor modulator vacuum valve, which is connected into the carburetor-to-distributor vacuum line and is normally open. When the temperature is over 65°F, the sensor sends a signal to the amplifier which relays the signal to the distributor vacuum modulator. The modulator closes, cutting off ignition advance, until vehicle speed reaches 35 mph as signaled by the speed sensor in the speedometer cable. When the ambient temperature is below 49° the system does not function.

Exhaust Gas Recirculation

Some models, starting 1974, utilize an Exhaust Gas Recirculation System (EGR) to control oxides of nitrogen. On V6 and V8 engines, exhaust gases travel through the exhaust gas crossover passage in the intake manifold. A portion of these gases are diverted into a spacer which is mounted under the carburetor. The EGR control valve, which is attached to the rear of the spacer, consists of a vacuum diaphragm with an attach-ed plunger which normally blocks off exhaust gases from entering the intake manifold. On 4 cylinder engines, an external tube carries exhaust manifold gases to the carburetor spacer. The EGR valve is controlled by a vacuum line from the carburetor.

The vacuum diaphragm opens the EGR valve permitting exhaust gases to flow through the carburetor spacer and enter the intake manifold where they combine with the fuel mixture and enter the combustion chambers. The exhaust gases are relatively oxygen-free, and tend to dilute the combustion charge. This lowers peak combustion temperature thereby reducing oxides of nitrogen.

Thermactor

From 1974 on, some models are equipped with an air injection system. The thermactor system consists of an air pump, check valves, antibackfire valve, and air distribution and injection tubes. The belt driven air pump injects air into the exhaust manifold near the cylinder head. The air combines with the gases leaving the cylinders and burns off some of the harmful exhaust gases.

Catalytic Converter

Starting 1975, some Pintos, Bobcats, and Mustang IIs and all California cars, are equipped with catalytic converter units. All 1976 models have them. While the unit does not require servicing until replacement, there are some precautions that must be observed.

1. Use unleaded fuel; the use of leaded fuel in a converter equipped car will invalidate the warranty.
2. Running out of gas may cause damage to the catalyst.
3. Proper engine maintenance is important. Misfires and other malfunctions can cause overheating and converter damage.
4. Do not run the engine for more than 30 seconds with a plug wire off or shorted.
5. Do not run an overly rich mixture for a long period of time.
6. Check ignition performance with an oscilloscope rather than by pulling a plug wire off.

Fuel System Controls

Carburetors

Carburetors are calibrated for leaner mixtures to decrease unburned hydrocarbon emissions. Idle mixture adjusting screws are equipped with limiter caps to prevent their being adjusted for excessively rich air-fuel mixtures at idle. The 1600 cc engine and 2000 cc engines equipped with

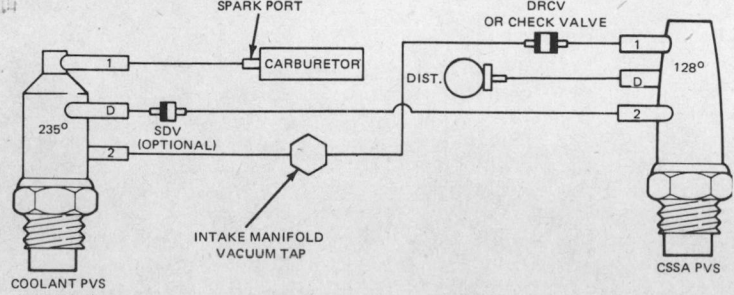

CSSA system, PVS means ported vacuum switch (© Ford Motor Co.)

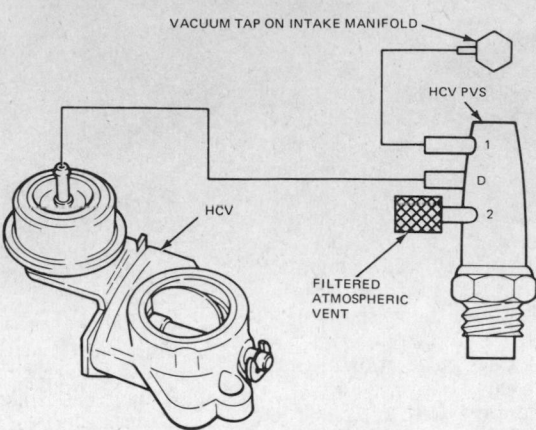

VACUUM TAP ON INTAKE MANIFOLD

HCV PVS

HCV

FILTERED
ATMOSPHERIC
VENT

Vacuum operated heat riser valve system (© Ford Motor Co.)

air conditioning have a throttle positioning solenoid, which raises the idle speed when energized and retracts from the throttle lever when de-energized to prevent dieseling.

Heat Riser Valve

Starting 1975, some engines use a vacuum operated heat riser valve. The valve preheats the fuel-air mixture by directing exhaust gases through passages in the intake manifold. The heat riser operates only during engine warmup.

Deceleration Valve

This valve is a vacuum-actuated valve which is attached to the intake manifold and connected to the carburetor with an air-fuel line. High vacuum during deceleration opens the valve and draws a metered air-fuel mixture through the hose from the carburetor. This enters the intake manifold and then the combustion chamber, where it is burned. This extra mixture slows the engine's deceleration rate and reduces the usually high exhaust emissions during slow-down.

Heated Air Intake Air Cleaner

The air cleaner is equipped with a thermostatically controlled door in the air cleaner snorkel. When the underhood temperature is under about 90°F, the door is closed, blocking off cooler underhood air from the air cleaner and allowing heated air from a shroud over the exhaust manifold to enter. When the temperature is over about 130°F, the door opens allowing the cooler underhood air to enter the air cleaner.

Evaporative Emission Control System

All models are equipped with a fuel vapor control system. The system has three major components—the fuel tank, the vapor separator, and the vapor absorbing charcoal canister.

The fuel tank is equipped with a pressure-vacuum relief filler cap and has the vapor separator mounted on the top.

Fuel vapors are stored in the vapor canister to be drawn into the engine to be consumed.

Crankcase Emission Controls

Crankcase emission control equipment consists of an oil separator (mounted on the side of the four-cylinder engine block), a positive crankcase ventilation (PCV) valve (mounted on the top of the oil separator on four-cylinders, in the intake manifold on 1974 V6s, and in the rocker cover on 1975 and later V6 and V8), a closed oil filler cap, and connecting hoses.

ENGINE

The standard engine used in the Pinto through 1973 is a 1600 cc, four-cylinder, inline overhead valve unit having a cross-flow cylinder head and piston-shaped combustion chambers. The cylinder bores are machined in the cast-iron block and cooled by full-length water jackets.

The crankshaft is made of cast iron and runs in five main bearings. End-play is controlled by half thrust washers on each side of the center main bearing.

The connecting rods are forged steel and pistons are solid skirt aluminum alloy with two compression rings and one oil ring. Piston pins are full-floating.

The camshaft is driven in a conventional manner, at one-half engine speed, by a single-row roller chain. A helical gear on the cam drives the distributor and oil pump, while an eccentric operates the fuel pump.

The cast-iron cylinder head has integral valve guides; although guide replacement is possible and sleeves

are available. Intake valves are aluminum coated, and cannot be refaced.

The 2000 and 2300 cc, overhead camshaft, four-cylinder engine is of cast-iron construction. The crankshaft is supported by five main bearings and the camshaft by three bearings. The camshaft is belt driven by the crankshaft. Belt tension is adjusted by a spring loaded idler pulley.

The pistons are made from an aluminum alloy and forged steel connecting rods are used.

The 2800 cc engine is a V6 overhead valve design. The cylinder heads and engine block are made of cast iron. Four main bearings support the crankshaft. The distributor and the oil pump are driven by an eccentric at the front of the camshaft. The connecting rods are forged steel with replaceable copper-lead alloy insert bearings. The intake manifold is made from aluminum and has individual passages to the openings in the cylinder heads. The V6 has a full pressure lubrication system fed by a rotor type oil pump mounted at the rear of the crankcase.

Starting 1975, the Mustang II was offered with an optional 302 cubic inch V8. This is the same engine as used in other Ford cars, an overhead valve design with wedge shaped combustion chambers.

Caution Metric and standard thread bolts are used in the four and six cylinder engines and transmissions. Only metric tools should be used to remove metric bolts.

If any repair operation requires the removal of a component of the air conditioning system (on vehicles so equipped), do not disconnect the refrigerant lines. If it is impossible to move the component out of the way with the lines attached, have the system evacuated. Air conditioning systems contain pressurized Freon, which is very dangerous to the untrained.

Engine Removal—1600 cc

1. Remove hood, after scribing matchmarks around hinges.
2. Disconnect battery cables.
3. Drain the cooling system.
   NOTE: drain engine block as well as radiator.
4. Disconnect radiator hoses and remove radiator.
5. Remove air cleaner assembly.
6. Disconnect heater hoses from water pump and intake manifold.
7. Disconnect throttle linkage.
8. Disconnect oil pressure and temperature sender wires, then disconnect alternator wires. Disconnect the carburetor solenoid and coil battery wires.
   NOTE: it is a good idea to tag these wires.

9. Disconnect exhaust pipe from manifold and remove hot air tubes.
10. Disconnect fuel inlet line at fuel pump.
   NOTE: plug the line so that gas does not siphon from tank.
11. Disconnect coil wires, then remove spark plug wires and distributor cap.
12. Jack up the front of the car and support on axle stands.
13. Disconnect starter wires, remove starter and oil pan shield.
14. Remove clutch cover. Drain the oil.
15. Lower the car to the floor.
16. Remove clutch housing-to-engine bolts, then install lifting brackets and chain hoist.
17. Disconnect the front motor mounts, while supporting engine with chain hoist.
18. Place an axle stand or wooden block under the transmission.
19. Raise the engine slightly, while pulling forward to separate the transmission input shaft from the clutch; lift engine out of car.

Engine Installation—1600 cc

1. Position the engine assembly in the engine compartment and start the input shaft into the clutch disc. It may be necessary to adjust the position of the transmission if the input shaft doesn't enter the clutch disc properly. If the engine won't move after the shaft enters the clutch, turn the crankshaft pulley slowly with the transmission in gear until the splines on the input shaft align with those on the clutch disc.
2. Slide the engine rearward, making sure the flywheel upper cover plate engages the dowels on the clutch housing. Align the front motor mounts and the exhaust manifold with the exhaust pipe.
3. Install the front motor mount nuts and tighten them to 20–30 ft lbs.
4. Install and tighten the upper clutch housing-to-engine attaching bolts. Make sure that the engine ground strap is secured by the upper left bolt.
5. Install the distributor cap and wires. Connect the fuel line to the fuel pump.
6. Connect the oil pressure water temperature sending unit wires. Connect the carburetor solenoid and distributor battery wires.
7. Connect the alternator wires.
8. Connect the exhaust pipe to the exhaust manifold and install the heat duct on the manifold.
9. Connect the throttle linkage to the carburetor.
10. Connect the heater hoses to the

engine.
11. Install the radiator and connect the hoses.
12. Install the air cleaner.
13. Jack the front of the car up and support it with stands.
14. Install the starter and connect the cable.
15. Install the lower clutch housing cover.
16. Install the oil pan drain plug and the cooling system drain plug in the block. Close the radiator petcock.
17. Remove the jack stands and lower the car.
18. Fill the engine with oil and the cooling system with coolant.
19. Connect the negative battery cable.
20. Start the engine and allow it to idle. Check for leaks and perform any necessary adjustments.
21. Install the hood.

Engine Removal—2000 cc

1. Drain the engine of coolant and oil. Remove the hood.
2. Remove the air cleaner and the exhaust manifold shroud.
3. Disconnect the battery ground cable.
4. Remove the upper and lower hoses from the radiator.
5. Remove the radiator and fan.
6. Disconnect the heater hose from the water pump and carburetor choke fitting.
7. Disconnect the wires from the alternator and starter. It is good practice to tag these wires to prevent confusion during installation.
8. Disconnect the carburetor accelerator cable. If the vehicle is equipped with air conditioning, remove the compressor from the mounting bracket and lay it aside.
   NOTE: leave the refrigerant lines attached.
9. Disconnect the flexible fuel line from the fuel tank line and plug the fuel tank line.
10. Disconnect the coil primary wire and the water temperature and oil temperature sending units.
11. Jack up vehicle and remove the starter.
12. Remove the flywheel (or converter housing) upper mounting bolts.
   NOTE: Two 10 mm $\times$ 3/8 in. studs are used to attach the upper housing to the engine. If the studs are removed, make sure they are reinstalled with the metric threads in the engine block.
13. Disconnect the exhaust pipe at the exhaust manifold. Unbolt the engine right and left mount at the underbody bracket. Remove the flywheel (or converter housing) cover.

14. On vehicles equipped with manual transmissions, remove the flywheel housing lower mounting bolts. On automatic transmission vehicles, disconnect the converter from the flywheel and remove the converter housing lower mounting bolts. It is necessary to turn the crankshaft pulley to gain access to the four converter - to - flywheel attaching nuts.
15. Lower the vehicle and support the transmission or converter housing with a hydraulic jack.
16. Attach the engine lifting apparatus and carefully pull the engine from the engine compartment.
17. On automatic transmission-equipped vehicles, match-mark the flywheel and the torque converter so they can be rejoined correctly.

Engine Installation—2000 cc

1. Place a new gasket over the exhaust pipe.
2. Carefully, lower the engine into the engine compartment. Be sure that the exhaust manifold studs are aligned with the holes in the exhaust pipe flange. On a vehicle with automatic transmission, start the converter pilot shaft into the crankshaft. On manual transmission cars, start the transmission drive gear into the clutch disc. It may be necessary to adjust the position of the transmission with relation to the engine if the input shaft fails to enter the clutch disc. If the engine hangs up after the shaft enters, turn the crankshaft slowly with the transmission in gear, until the input shaft splines mesh with the clutch disc splines.
3. Remove the lifting apparatus and install the flywheel (or converter housing) upper mounting bolts.
4. Remove the jack from the transmission and jack up vehicle.
5. Install the flywheel (or converter housing) lower mounting bolts. On an automatic transmission car, attach the converter to the flywheel and torque to 23-28 ft. lbs.
6. Install the flywheel (or converter housing) dust cover.
7. Install the engine left and right mounting brackets to the underbody.
8. Unplug the fuel tank line and connect it to the flexible line. Tighten the exhaust pipe and exhaust manifold.
9. Lower the vehicle and connect the water and oil temperature sending units, coil primary wire and accelerator cable.

10. Install and connect the starter. Connect the alternator wires, and heater hose to the water pump and carburetor choke fitting.
11. Install the fan pulley, fan and drive belt. On vehicles equipped with air conditioning, install the compressor on the mounting bracket and adjust the belt tension. Drive belt should sag approximately ½ in. under thumb pressure at the middle of the longest side.
12. Install the radiator and connect the upper and lower hoses. Fill and bleed the cooling system. Fill the engine with the proper amount and grade of engine oil.
13. Connect the battery ground cable and operate the engine at fast idle, checking all gaskets and hoses for leaks.
14. On automatic transmission vehicles, adjust the transmission control linkage.
15. Install the air cleaner and connect the crankcase ventilation hose.
16. Install the hood.

Engine Removal—2300 cc

1. Raise the hood and fasten it up.
2. Drain the coolant from the radiator and the oil from the crankcase.
3. Remove the air cleaner and the exhaust manifold shroud.
4. Disconnect the ground cable from the battery.
5. Remove the radiator upper and lower hoses.
6. Remove the radiator and fan.
7. Disconnect the heater hose from the water pump and carburetor choke fitting.
8. Disconnect the alternator wires from the alternator, starter cable from the starter, and the accelerator cable from the carburetor. With air conditioning, remove the compressor from the mounting bracket, and position it out of the way, leaving the refrigerant lines attached.
9. Disconnect the flexible fuel line at the fuel pump line and plug the fuel line.
10. Disconnect the coil primary wire at the coil. Disconnect the oil pressure and the water temperature sending unit wires at the sending units.
11. Remove the starter.
12. Raise the vehicle. Remove the flywheel or converter housing upper attaching bolts.
13. Disconnect the headpipe at the exhaust manifold. Disconnect the engine right and left mounts at the underbody bracket. Remove the flywheel or converter housing cover. With automatic transmission,

disconnect the converter from the flywheel. Remove the converter housing lower attaching bolts.

With manual transmission, remove the flywheel housing lower attaching bolts.
14. Lower the vehicle. Support the transmission and the flywheel or converter housing with a jack.
15. Attach the engine lifting device to the existing lifting brackets.
16. Carefully lift the engine out of the engine compartment.

Engine Installation—2300 cc

1. Carefully lower the engine into the engine compartment.
2. Make sure that the studs on the exhaust manifold are aligned with the holes in the lead pipe.

With automatic transmission, start the converter pilot into the crankshaft.

With manual transmission, start the transmission main drive gear into the clutch disc. It may be necessary to adjust the position of the transmission in relation to the engine if the input shaft will not enter the clutch disc. If the engine hangs up after the shaft enters, turn the crankshaft slowly clockwise, with the transmission in gear, until the shaft splines mesh with the clutch disc splines.
3. Install the flywheel or converter housing upper attaching bolts. Remove the engine lifting sling hooks.
4. Remove the jack from the transmission. Raise the vehicle.
5. Install the flywheel or converter housing lower attaching bolts.

With automatic transmission, attach the converter to the flywheel.
6. Install the flywheel or converter housing dust cover.
7. Install the engine left and right mount to the underbody bracket.
8. Remove the plug from the fuel line and connect the flexible fuel line to the fuel pump line. Install the exhaust manifold to headpipe nuts.
9. Lower the vehicle. Connect the oil pressure and engine temperature sending unit wires. Connect the coil primary wire. Connect the accelerator cable.
10. Install the starter motor. Connect the starter cable. Connect the alternator wires. Connect the heater hose at the water pump and carburetor for the choke fitting.
11. Install the pulley, fan, and drive belt. Adjust the drive belt tension. With air conditioning, install the compressor on the mounting bracket, and adjust the belt tension. Install the radi-

tor. Connect the radiator upper and lower hoses. Fill and bleed the cooling system. Fill the crankcase with the proper type and quantity of motor oil.
12. Connect the battery ground cable.
13. Operate the engine at fast idle and check all gaskets and hose connections for leaks.

With an automatic transmission, adjust the transmission control linkage, as necessary.
14. Install the air cleaner and connect the PCV hose.

Engine Removal—2800 cc V6

1. Remove any interfering air pump system components. Disconnect the battery, drain the cooling system and remove the hood.
2. Remove the air cleaner and intake duct assembly.
3. Disconnect the upper and lower hoses at the radiator.
4. Remove the fan shroud attaching bolts and position the shroud over the fan. Remove the radiator and shroud.
5. Remove the alternator and bracket. Position the alternator out of the way. Disconnect the alternator ground wire from the cylinder block.
6. Disconnect the heater hoses at the block and water pump.
7. Remove the ground wires from the cylinder block.
8. Disconnect the fuel line at the fuel pump. Plug the fuel tank line.
9. Disconnect the accelerator cable or linkage at the carburetor and intake manifold. Disconnect the automatic transmission downshift linkage.
10. Disconnect the engine wire loom at the ignition coil. Disconnect the brake booster vacuum line.
11. Raise the vehicle on a hoist.
12. Disconnect the headpipes at the exhaust manifolds.
13. Disconnect the starter cable and remove the starter.
14. Remove the engine front support through-bolts.
15. With automatic transmission, remove the converter inspection cover and disconnect the flywheel from the converter.

Remove the downshift rod.

Remove the converter housing-to-engine block bolts and the adapter plate-to-converter housing bolt.

With manual transmission, remove the clutch linkage and remove the bellhousing-to-engine block bolts.
16. Lower the vehicle.
17. Attach an engine lifting device to the lifting brackets at the exhaust manifolds.

18. Position a jack under the transmission.
19. Raise the engine slightly and carefully pull it from the transmission. Carefully lift the engine out of the engine compartment so that the rear cover plate is not bent or parts damaged.

Engine Installation—2800 cc V6

1. Lower the engine carefully into the engine compartment. Make sure that the exhaust manifolds are properly aligned with the headpipes.

   With manual transmission, start the transmission main driveshaft into the clutch disc. It may be necessary to adjust the position of the transmission in relation to the engine if the input shaft will not enter the clutch disc. If the engine hangs up after the shaft enters, turn the crankshaft slowly, with the transmission in gear, until the shaft splines mesh with the clutch disc splines.

   With automatic transmission, start the converter pilot into the crankshaft.
3. Install the bellhousing or converter housing upper bolts, making sure that the dowels in the cylinder block engage the flywheel housing. Remove the jack from under the transmission.
4. Remove the lifting device from the engine.
5. With automatic transmission, position the downshift rod on the transmission and engine.
6. Raise the vehicle on a hoist.
7. With automatic transmission, position the transmission linkage bracket and install the remaining converter housing bolts. Install the adapter plate-to-converter housing bolts. Install the converter-to-flywheel nuts and install the inspection cover. Connect the downshift rod on the transmission.

   On manual transmission cars, install the lower bellhousing bolts and connect the clutch linkage to the engine block.
8. Install the starter and connect the cable.
9. Connect the muffler inlet pipes at the exhaust manifolds.
10. Install the engine front support through-bolts.
11. Lower the vehicle.
12. Install the ground wire. Install the engine wire loom and connect it to the ignition coil, then install the water temperature sending unit and oil pressure sending unit. Connect the brake booster vacuum line.
13. Install the accelerator linkage and connect the automatic transmission downshift rod. Connect

the vacuum lines. Connect the fuel tank line at the fuel pump.
14. Connect the ground wire at the cylinder block. Install the heater hoses at the water pump and cylinder block.
15. Install the alternator and bracket. Connect the alternator ground wire to the cylinder block. Install the drive belt and adjust the belt tension.
16. Position the fan shroud over the fan. Install the radiator and connect the upper and lower radiator hoses. Install the fan shroud attaching bolts.
17. Fill and bleed the cooling system. Fill the crankcase with oil. Adjust the automatic transmission downshift linkage. Connect the battery.
18. Operate the engine at fast idle until it reaches normal operating temperature and check all gaskets and hose connections for leaks. Adjust the ignition timing and idle speed.
19. Install the air cleaner and intake duct. Install and adjust the hood.

Engine Removal and Installation—V8

1. Remove or disconnect any interfering air pump system components.
2. Drain the coolant. Remove the hood. Disconnect the battery and alternator ground cables.
3. Remove the air cleaner assembly.
4. Detach the upper radiator hose from the engine and the lower hose from the pump.
5. Detach the automatic transmission cooler lines from the radiator. Unbolt the fan shroud and remove the shroud, radiator fan pulley and spacer.
6. Unbolt the alternator and set it aside.
7. Disconnect and plug the fuel line. Detach any gauge wires from the engine.
8. Disconnect the accelerator rod at the carburetor. With automatic transmission, disconnect the throttle valve vacuum line and shift linkage. Remove the filler tube bracket from the engine.
9. Set the air conditioner assembly aside without disconnecting any lines. See the Caution at the beginning of this section.
10. Unbolt and set the power steering pump aside without disconnecting the lines.
11. Detach the power brake vacuum line.
12. Detach the heater hoses at the water pump and intake manifold.
13. Remove the upper flywheel or converter housing to engine bolts.
14. Detach the ignition system wir-

ing harness at the coil. Detach the engine ground strap.
15. Raise and support the car safely. Remove the starter.
16. Unbolt the headpipes from the engine manifolds. Detach the engine mount insulators from the frame brackets.
17. With manual transmission, unbolt the clutch linkage from the frame and the engine. Remove the rest of the flywheel housing bolts.
18. With automatic transmission, remove the converter housing cover. Unbolt the flywheel from the converter. Remove the rest of the converter housing bolts. Arrange a strap or clamp to keep the converter in the housing.
19. Lower the car to the floor and support the transmission. Attach the hoist to the engine and raise it slightly, carefully pulling it from the transmission.
20. Installation is the same as that shown previously for the V6 engine. Flywheel housing to engine bolt torque is 28-32 ft lbs. Converter housing to engine and flywheel to converter bolt torques are 28-38 ft lbs.

Engine Manifolds

Intake Manifold Removal

1600 cc

1. Drain the cooling system.
2. Remove the air cleaner and disconnect the throttle shaft at the carburetor throttle lever.
3. Disconnect the fuel line and vacuum line from the carburetor. Disconnect the carburetor solenoid wire at the quick-disconnect.
4. Remove the choke thermostatic spring and water housing.
5. Disconnect the water outlet hose and crankcase ventilation hose from the intake manifold.
6. Disconnect the decel valve-to-carburetor hose at the carburetor.
7. Remove the intake manifold attaching bolts and remove the manifold.
8. Remove all gasket material.
9. If the intake manifold is to be replaced, transfer all necessary components to the new manifold. Loosen the union fitting on the manifold and remove the decel valve from the intake manifold. Remove the decel valve adaptor from the manifold by inserting a large allen wrench into the adaptor and turning the adaptor out of the manifold.

2000 and 2300 cc

1. Remove the air cleaner assembly.

2. Disconnect the fuel line from the carburetor.

3. Disconnect the two vacuum lines from the distributor at the intake manifold.

4. Disconnect the crankcase ventilation hose at the intake manifold.

5. Remove the intake manifold attaching bolts and remove the manifold, carburetor, and decel valve from the studs, as an assembly.

Intake Manifold Installation

1600 cc

1. Clean the cylinder head and intake manifold mating surfaces thoroughly.

2. Carefully coat the mating surfaces with sealer and position a new gasket on the studs. Install the manifold and torque the nuts alternately and evenly.

3. Further installation is the reverse of removal.

2000 and 2300 cc

1. Clean all dirt and gasket material from the surfaces on the cylinder head and intake manifold.

2. Position a new gasket and the manifold on the studs. Torque the bolts and nuts to the specified torque.

3. Connect the crankcase ventilation hose to the manifold.

4. Connect the distributor vacuum lines to the manifold.

5. Connect the fuel line to the carburetor.

6. Install the air cleaner assembly.

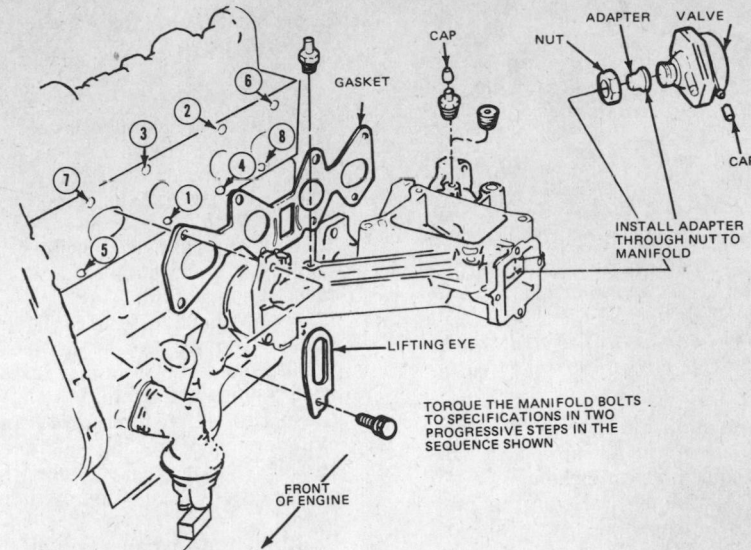

Intake manifold tightening sequence—2300 cc engine (© Ford Motor Co.)

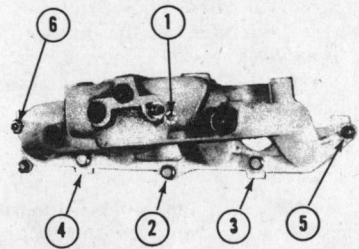

Intake manifold tightening sequence—2000 cc engine (© Ford Motor Co.)

Intake Manifold Removal and Installation

2800 cc V6

1. Remove the air cleaner assembly and disconnect the battery.

2. Disconnect the throttle cables.

3. Drain the cooling system. Disconnect and remove the hose from the water outlet to the radiator and the hoses and line from the water outlet to the water pump.

4. Remove the distributor cap and spark plug wires as an assembly. Disconnect the distributor wire and the vacuum line.

5. Mark the position of the distrib-

utor and remove it.

6. Remove the fuel line and filter between the fuel pump and the carburetor and then remove the rocker arm covers.

7. Remove the intake manifold bolts and nuts. Tap the manifold lightly with a plastic hammer to break the gasket seal, and then lift off the manifold.

8. Remove all the gasket material and dirt from the manifold and cylinder heads.

9. Apply sealing compound to the joining surfaces. Place the manifold gasket in place. (Make sure that the tap on the right bank of the cylinder head gasket fits into the cutout of the manifold gasket.)

10. Install the intake manifold. Tighten the attaching bolts until they are hand tight, and then tighten them, in sequence, to the proper torque.

NOTE: Tightening bolt no. 7 with a torque wrench will require an attachment called a "crow's foot."

11. Install the distributor so the rotor is pointing to the mark made previously.

12. Connect the distributor wire and vacuum line.

13. Install the carburetor, fuel line, fuel filter, and the rocker arm covers.

14. Install the distributor cap and wires.

15. Install and adjust the carburetor linkage.

16. Install the air cleaner assembly and air cleaner tube to the carburetor. Connect the battery.

17. Adjust the ignition timing.

302 V8

1. Drain the cooling system, remove the air cleaner assembly and disconnect the crankcase ventilation hose and choke heated air inlet hose.

2. Disconnect the throttle linkage from the carburetor; remove the automatic transmission and brake booster lines from the intake manifold.

3. Remove the air pump; remove the spark plug wires and distributor cap assembly with wires attached.

4. Remove the EGR vacuum amplifier, gas inlet line and automatic choke heat tube.

5. Remove the distributor and thermostat upper hose and sending unit assembly; remove the hose

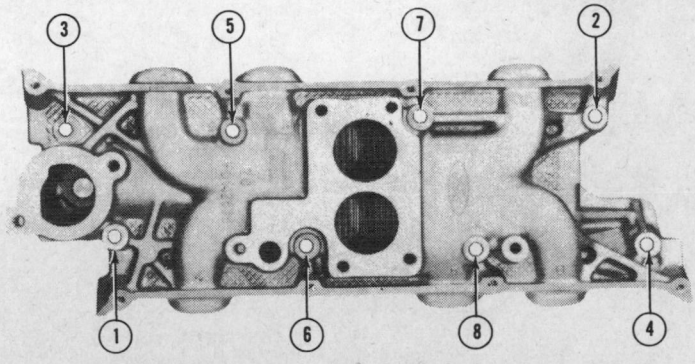

V6 intake manifold bolt torque sequence (© Ford Motor Co.)

from the choke assembly to the intake manifold.

6. Remove the water pump bypass hose, and crankcase vent hose at the rocker arm cover.
7. Remove the air conditioner compressor-to-intake manifold brackets.
8. Remove the carburetor and intake manifold as an assembly.

NOTE: It may be necessary to pry the manifold away from the cylinder heads. Use caution to avoid damaging the sealing surfaces. Discard the intake manifold attaching bolt sealing washers.

9. If the manifold is to be disassembled, mark all vacuum hoses before disconnecting them.
10. For installation, clean the mating surfaces of the manifold and engine block.
11. Put new gaskets on the cylinder head and new seals on the engine block, checking to make sure they interlock. Apply sealer to the outside of each seal.

NOTE: Most sealers set up quickly so it is important that the rest of the operation be done as quickly as possible.

12. Lower the manifold to the block. When it is in place, run your finger around the seals to make sure they are in place.
13. Install the attaching nuts and bolts and torque to specifications in sequence.
14. Replace the distributor.
15. To complete the operation, reverse the procedure in the Steps 1-7.

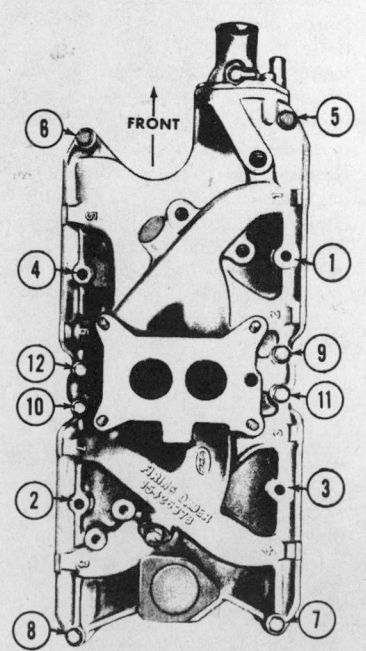

Intake manifold tightening sequence—302 V8 (© Ford Motor Co.)

Exhaust Manifold Removal and Installation

1600 cc
1. Remove the air cleaner.
2. Place a block of wood under the front of the exhaust pipe and disconnect the exhaust pipe from the manifold.
3. Remove the exhaust manifold attaching nuts and bolts, and remove the manifold.
4. If a new manifold is to be installed, remove the heat shroud from the old manifold and install it on the new manifold.
5. Clean the exhaust manifold and cylinder head mating surfaces.
6. Install a new gasket over the center studs on the cylinder head.
7. Position the exhaust manifold near the cylinder head and install the end exhaust manifold gaskets between the manifold and the head.
8. Install the attaching nuts and bolts and tighten them to the proper torque.
9. Connect the exhaust pipe to the manifold, remove the wood support, and install the air cleaner.

2000 and 2300 cc
1. Remove the air cleaner. Remove the heat shroud from the exhaust manifold.
2. Place a block of wood under the exhaust pipe, and then disconnect it from the manifold.

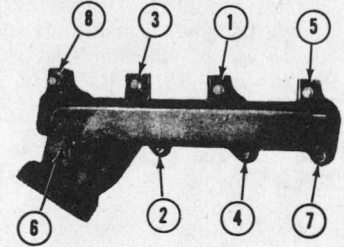

Exhaust manifold tightening sequence—2000 cc engine (© Ford Motor Co)
RIGHT SIDE

3. Remove the attaching nuts and remove the manifold from the head. Clean the mating surfaces.
4. Install a light coat of graphite grease on the exhaust manifold mating surface and position the manifold on the cylinder head.
5. Install the attaching nuts and tighten them to the proper torque.
6. Connect the exhaust pipe to the manifold and remove the wood support from under the pipe.
7. Install the air cleaner.

2800 cc
1. Remove the air cleaner.
2. Remove the four attaching nuts from the exhaust manifold shroud (right side only).
3. Disconnect the attaching nuts from the muffler inlet pipe.
4. Remove the exhaust manifold attaching nuts and remove the manifold.
5. These manifolds do not use gaskets. When installing the manifold, smear a light coat of graphite grease on the mating surfaces.
6. Position the manifold on the studs and install the bolts hand-tight then torque them evenly to the proper torque.
7. Install a new inlet pipe gasket and the attaching nuts.
8. Position the exhaust manifold shroud on the manifold and install the attaching nuts (right side).
9. Install the air cleaner.

302 V8
1. On the right exhaust manifold, remove the air cleaner, automatic choke heat tube and air cleaner heat ducts.
2. Disconnect the exhaust manifold(s) from the muffler inlet pipe(s).
3. Remove the manifold attaching bolts and remove the manifold(s).

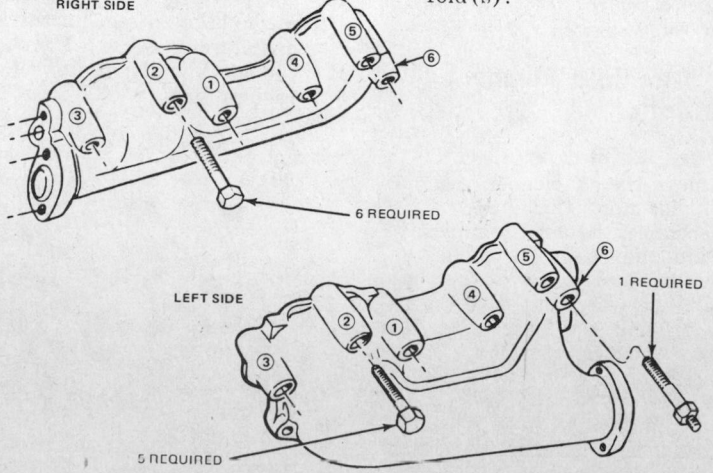

V6 exhaust manifold torque sequence (© Ford Motor Co.)

4. Reverse the procedure to reinstall, using new inlet pipe gaskets.

Valve System

1600 cc

The valves are mounted vertically in the cylinder head, the intake valve heads being larger than the exhaust valve heads. The exhaust valves are stellite-coated for better heat and wear resistance, while the intake valves are coated with diffused aluminum for the same reason. *The factory does not recommend grinding the intake valves or lapping the intake valve seats, because the grinding operation removes the coating and shortens the life of the valve.* Exhaust valves, on the other hand, may be ground if necessary.

Valve stems are phosphate-coated for better wear resistance. Valve guides are cast integral with the head, although sleeves are available if guides become worn. In addition, valves are available with 0.003 and 0.015 in. oversize stem diameters.

The valve keepers do not grip the stem, allowing the valves to rotate freely during operation.

Valve Adjustment

1600 cc

Valves are set with the engine at normal operating temperature and turned off.
1. Remove the air cleaner. Disconnect the carburetor solenoid wire at the connector near the rear of the valve cover.
2. Remove the throttle cable retaining screw, pry the end of the throttle cable off the carburetor stud, and position the cable out of the way.
3. Remove the valve cover. Identify the spark plug wires and disconnect them.
4. Turn the engine to depress the proper valves by turning the crankshaft pulley.

Valve Clearance Adjustment

1600 cc Engine—Set Hot

Valve Depressed	Valves to Adjust to .010	.017
No. 1	No. 3	No. 8
No. 2	No. 7	No. 5
No. 3	No. 6	No. 1
No. 5	No. 2	No. 4

5. Insert a feeler gauge of the specified thickness between the tip of the rocker arm and the top of the valve. If an adjustment is necessary, turn the adjusting screw in or out as necessary.
6. Install the removed or disconnected components in a reverse order of removal. Tighten the

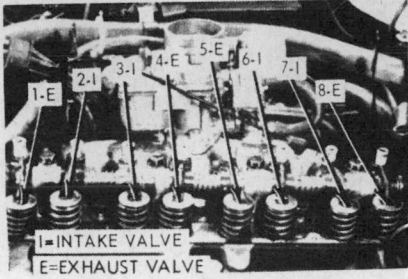

1600 cc engine valve identification
(© Ford Motor Co.)

valve cover retaining screws to 2.5–3.5 ft lbs.

2000 cc

Valves are set with engine cold.
1. Remove the air cleaner. Identify the spark plug wires and remove them, positioning them out of the way.

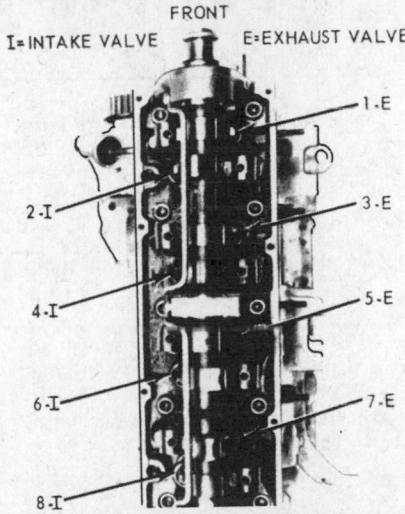

2000 cc engine valve identification
(© Ford Motor Co.)

2. On non-air-conditioned models, move the heater hose attached to the carburetor choke housing off the valve cover and out of the way. On air-conditioned models, disconnect the carburetor choke heater hose from the heater hot water valve and position it out of the way.

3. Remove the valve cover retaining screw (note the position of the screws with rubber coated washers) and remove the valve cover.
4. Turn the crankshaft pulley to depress the valves specified in the chart.

Caution Never turn the pulley in a counterclockwise direction, as the camshaft drive belt may slip and alter the timing.

5. Check clearance according to the following chart:

Valve Clearance Adjustment

2000 cc Engine—Set Cold

Valve Depressed	Valves to Adjust to .008	.010
No. 1	No. 6	No. 7
No. 2	No. 8	No. 3
No. 3	No. 2	No. 5
No. 6	No. 4	No. 1

Clearance is checked between the rocker arm and the cam. Use a screwdriver to snap the retaining spring off the rocker arm until it hangs loose. Use a feeler gauge of the specified thickness to check the clearance.

6. If an adjustment is necessary, loosen the locknut and turn the adjusting screw in or out as necessary. When the adjustment is correct, tighten the locknut and snap the retaining spring back into place.
7. Replace the removed or disconnected components in a reverse order of removal. Tighten the rear valve cover cap screws to 4–6 ft lbs. from the back forward, the two vertical cap screws to 1–2 ft lbs, the two lateral cap screws to 4–6 ft lbs, and retighten the two vertical cap screws to 4–6 ft lbs.

2300 cc

This engine uses hydraulic lash adjusters. Thus, no routine valve adjustment is required.

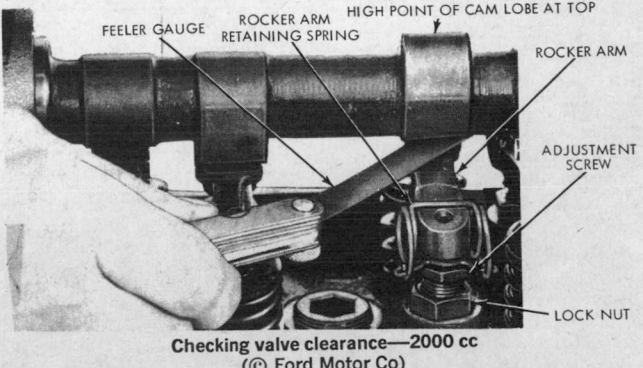

Checking valve clearance—2000 cc
(© Ford Motor Co)

2800 cc

If the valves are being adjusted for tune-up, the engine must be at normal operating temperature. If the valves are being adjusted after engine assembly, the engine must not be started until a preliminary adjustment has been made. Final adjustment can then be made after the engine is warmed up.

1. Remove the air cleaner assembly and disconnect the negative battery cable.
2. Remove the Thermactor air by-pass valve and its mounting bracket.
3. Remove the two engine lifting eyes; remove the alternator drive belt, loosen the alternator mounting bolts and swing the alternator outward toward the fender.
4. Remove the plug wires and remove the rocker covers.

NOTE: Some 1975 engines were assembled so that the distributor diaphragm housing interferes with rocker cover removal. This can be corrected by removing the distributor and resetting it one tooth clockwise.

5. When removing the rocker covers, remove or reposition any wires or hoses which block the removal of the rocker covers.
6. Torque the rocker arm support bolts to 46 ft lbs.
7. Reconnect the battery cable, place the transmission in Neutral (manual) or Park (automatic), and apply the parking brake.
8. Place a finger on the adjusting screw of the intake valve rocker arm for cylinder No. 5. Cylinder numbering is shown under Firing Order at the start of the section. Valve arrangement, from front to rear, on the left bank is I-E-E-I-E-I; on the right it is I-E-I-E-E-I. You will be able to feel the rocker arm begin to move.
9. Use a remote starter switch or manual means to turn the engine until you can just feel the valve begin to open. Now the engine is in position to adjust the intake and exhaust valves on the No. 1 cylinder.
10. Adjust the No. 1 cylinder intake valve so that a 0.014 in. feeler gauge has a slight drag while a 0.015 in. feeler gauge is a tight fit. To decrease lash, turn the adjusting screw clockwise; to increase lash, turn the adjusting screw counterclockwise. There are no locknuts to tighten; the adjusting screws are self-locking.

CAUTION: Do not use a step-type, "go-no go" feeler gauge. When checking lash, insert the feeler gauge and move it parallel with the crankshaft.

The following is a method for replacing valve springs, oil seals or spring retainers without removing the cylinder head.

1. **Obtain an air hose spark plug hole adaptor.**
2. **Remove the valve rocker cover.**
3. **Remove the rocker arm from the valve to be worked on.**
4. **Remove the spark plug from the cylinder to be worked on.**
5. **Turn the crankshaft to bring the piston of this cylinder down, away from possible contact with the valve head. Sharply tap the valve retainer to loosen the valve lock.**
6. **Then turn the crankshaft to bring the piston in this cylinder to the Exact Top of its Compression Stroke.**
7. **Screw in the spark plug hole adaptor.**
8. **Hook up an air hose to the chuck and turn on the pressure.**
9. **With a strong and constant supply of air holding the valve closed, compress the valve spring and remove the lock and retainer.**
10. **Make the necessary replacements and reassemble.**

NOTE: it is important that the operation be performed exactly as stated, in this order. The piston in the cylinder must be on exact top-center to prevent air pressure from turning the crankshaft.

Do not move it in and out perpendicular with the crankshaft: this will give an erroneous feel which will result in overtightened valves.

11. Adjust the exhaust valve the same way so that an 0.018 in. feeler gauge has a slight drag, while a 0.019 in. gauge is a tight fit.
12. The rest of the valves are adjusted in the same way, in their firing order (1-4-2-5-3-6), by positioning the engine according to the following chart:

V6 Valve Clearance Adjustment

Intake valve just opening in cylinder No.:	Adjust both valves in this cylinder: (Intake—0.014 in.; Exhaust—0.018 in.)
5	1
3	4
6	2
1	5
4	3
2	6

13. Remove all the old gasket material from the cylinder heads and rocker cover gasket surfaces, and disconnect the negative cable from the battery.
14. Remove the spark plug wires and reinstall the rocker arm covers.
15. Reinstall any hoses and wires which were removed.
16. Reinstall the spark plug wires, the alternator drive belt, and the Thermactor air by-pass valve and its mounting bracket.
17. Reconnect the battery cable, replace the air cleaner assembly, start the engine, and check for leaks.

302 V8

This rocker arm nut tightening procedure is needed only if the valve train has been disturbed, as in cylinder head removal and replacement. It is not a normal tune-up procedure.

1. Crank the engine until no. 1 cylinder is at TDC of the compression stroke and the timing pointer is aligned with the 0 mark on the crankshaft damper.
2. Tighten the following rocker arms: no. 1, 7, and 8 intake; no. 1, 5, and 4 Exhaust. Tighten the nut until it contacts the shoulder of the rocker and then torque to 18-20 ft lbs.
3. Rotate the crankshaft 180° clockwise and tighten the following valves: no. 5 and 4 intake; no. 2 and 6 exhaust.
4. Rotate the crankshaft 270° clockwise and tighten the following valves: no. 2, 3, and 6 intake; no. 7, 3, and 8 exhaust.

Rocker Arm or Shaft Replacement

1600 cc

1. Remove the valve cover as described under "Valve Adjustment." Disconnect the spark plug wires and move them out of the way.
2. Loosen each rocker shaft attaching bolt one turn at a time until all the bolts are loose.
3. Remove the rocker shaft.
4. To install, position the rocker

shaft on the head and align the pushrods with the rocker arm adjusting screws.

5. Starting from the front of the engine and working back, tighten each bolt one turn at a time until the shaft is mounted on the head. Finally, tighten each bolt to 25-30 ft lbs.

6. Adjust the valves as previously described. Install the valve cover and spark plug wires.

2000 cc

1. Remove the valve cover as described under "Valve Adjustment."

2. Rotate the crankshaft in a clockwise direction until the cam lobe for the rocker arm that is to be removed is pointing straight up.

3. Remove the retaining spring from the rocker arm.

4. Depress the valve spring that corresponds to the rocker arm that is to be removed just enough to remove the rocker arm.

5. To install, position the rocker arm on the valve and adjusting screw and install the rocker arm retaining spring.

6. Adjust the valve clearance as previously described.

7. Install the valve cover, air cleaner, and any other components that were removed or disconnected in a reverse order of removal.

2300 cc

1. Remove the valve cover and associated parts as required.

2. Rotate the camshaft so that the base circle of the cam is against the cam follower you intend to remove.

3. Remove the retaining spring from the cam follower, if so equipped.

4. Using special tool T74P-6565-B or a valve spring compressor tool for a 2300 cc engine, collapse the lash adjuster and/or depress the valve spring, as necessary, and slide the cam follower over the lash adjuster and out from under the camshaft.

5. Install the cam follower in the reverse order of removal. Make sure that the lash adjuster is collapsed and released before rotating the cam shaft.

2800 cc

1. Remove any emission control equipment as necessary to remove the rocker cover(s), remove the spark plug wires, remove the throttle linkage to the carburetor as necessary, and remove the valve rocker cover(s).

2. Remove the rocker arm shaft stand retaining bolts; loosen them each 2 turns at a time in sequence. Lift off the rocker arm and shaft assembly and the oil baffle.

3. Before installing the rocker shaft assemblies, back off the adjusting screws on the rockers a few turns. Install the rocker shafts in the reverse order of removal; tighten the rocker shaft stand retaining bolts 2 turns at a time in sequence until they are tightened to 46 ft lbs.

302 V8

The 302 V8 is equipped with individual stud-mounted rocker arms. Use the following procedure to remove the rocker arms:

1. On the right cylinder head, disconnect the choke heat chamber air hose.

2. Remove the air cleaner and inlet duct assembly, the choke heat tube, PCV valve and hose, and the EGR hoses. Remove the Thermactor by-pass valve and air supply hoses.

3. Label and disconnect the spark plug wires at the plugs. Remove the plug wires from the harness.

4. Remove the valve cover attaching bolts and remove the covers.

5. Remove the valve rocker arm stud nut, fulcrum seat, and then the rocker arm.

6. Reverse the above procedure to install. Tighten each stud nut to 17-23 ft lbs. after the nut contacts the shoulder. Install and tighten the nuts in the sequence given under Valve Adjustment.

Cylinder Head

NOTE: To prevent distortion or warping of the cylinder head, allow the engine to cool completely before removing the head bolts.

If the head sticks, operate the starter to loosen it by compression or rap it upward with a soft hammer. Do not force anything between the head and the block.

Removal—1600 cc

1. Remove the air cleaner, then disconnect the fuel line at the pump and the carburetor.

2. Drain the cooling system.

3. Disconnect spark plug wires, then disconnect heater and vacuum hoses from the intake manifold and choke housing.

4. Disconnect temperature sender wire, then disconnect exhaust pipe at manifold flange.

5. Disconnect throttle linkage and distributor vacuum line at carburetor. Disconnect the carburetor solenoid wire.

6. Remove thermostat housing and thermostat.

7. Remove rocker arm cover and gasket, then remove the rocker shaft bolts, evenly, and the rocker shaft assembly.

8. Remove pushrods and place them aside in proper order for correct installation.

9. Remove cylinder head bolts, head, and gasket.

Installation—1600 cc

1. Place a new head gasket on the block.

2. Position the cylinder head and install the bolts. Tighten evenly in sequence to proper torque.

NOTE: manifolds may be installed prior to placing head on block.

3. Install pushrods in correct order, then place rocker arms and shaft assembly on head and locate pushrods in rocker arm screws. Tighten rocker arm bolts to 25-30 ft lbs.

4. Adjust valve clearance, then install rocker arm cover and gasket.

5. Continue installation by reversing Steps 1-6 of removal procedure.

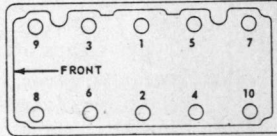

1600 cc cylinder head bolt tightening sequence
(© Ford Motor Co.)

Removal—2000 cc and 2300 cc

1. Drain the cooling system.

2. Remove the air cleaner and the valve rocker cover.

3. Remove the intake and exhaust manifolds. The intake manifold, decel valve and carburetor can be removed as an assembly.

4. Remove the camshaft drive belt cover.

5. Loosen the drive belt tensioner and remove the drive belt.

6. Remove the water outlet from the cylinder head.

7. Remove the cylinder head bolts evenly, and remove the cylinder head.

NOTE: A special 12-point allen wrench is necessary to remove the head bolts on the 2000 cc engine.

Installation—2000 cc and 2300 cc

1. Position a new cylinder head gasket on the block.

2. Position the cylinder head and camshaft assembly on the block. Install the bolts finger tight, then torque according to specifications.

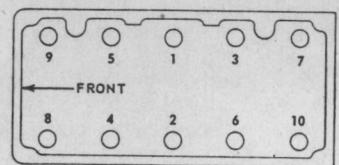

Cylinder head bolt tightening sequence 2000 cc and 2300 cc (© Ford Motor Co.)

NOTE: If difficulty in positioning the head on the block is encountered, guide pins may be fabricated by cutting the heads off two extra cylinder head bolts.

3. Set the crankshaft at TDC and be sure that the camshaft drive gear and distributor are positioned correctly as explained under Timing Belt Replacement.
4. Install the camshaft drive belt and release the tensioner. Rotate the crankshaft two full turns to remove all slack from the belt. The timing marks should again be aligned. Tighten the tensioner lockbolt and pivot bolt.
5. Install the camshaft drive belt cover.
6. Apply sealer to the water outlet and new gasket, and install.
7. Install the intake and exhaust manifolds.
8. Adjust the valve clearance.
9. Install a new valve cover gasket and install the valve cover.
10. Install the air cleaner and crankcase ventilation hose.
11. Refill the cooling system.

Removal and Installation— 2800 cc

1. Remove the air cleaner assembly and disconnect the battery and accelerator linkage. Drain the cooling system.
2. Remove the distributor cap with the spark plug wires attached. Remove the distributor vacuum line and distributor. Remove the hose from the water pump to the water outlet which is on the carburetor.
3. Remove the valve covers, fuel line and filter, carburetor, and the intake manifold.
4. Remove the rocker arm shaft and oil baffles. Remove the push-

rods, keeping them in the proper sequence for installation.
5. Remove the exhaust manifold, referring to the appropriate procedures.
6. Remove the cylinder head retaining bolts and remove the cylinder heads and gaskets.
7. Remove all gasket material and carbon from the engine block and cylinder heads.
8. Place the head gaskets on the engine block.
NOTE: The left and right gaskets are not interchangeable.
9. Install guide studs in the engine block. Install the cylinder head assemblies on the engine block one at a time. Tighten the cylinder head bolts in sequence, and in steps, to the specified torque.
10. Install the intake and exhaust manifolds.
11. Install the pushrods (ends lubricated) in the proper sequence. Install the oil baffles and the rocker arm shaft assemblies. Adjust the valve clearances.
12. Install the valve covers with new gaskets.
13. Install the distributor and set the ignition timing.
14. Install the carburetor and the distributor cap with the spark plug wires.
15. Connect the accelerator linkage, fuel line, with fuel filter installed, and distributor vacuum line to the carburetor. Fill the cooling system.

302 V8

1. Drain the cooling system.
2. Remove the intake manifold and the carburetor as an assembly, following the procedures under "Intake Manifold Removal."
3. Disconnect the spark plug wires, marking them as to placement. Position them out of the way of the cylinder head. Remove the spark plugs.
4. Disconnect the exhaust pipes at the manifolds.
5. Remove the rocker arm covers.
6. On cars with air conditioning, remove the mounting bolts and the drive belt, and position the compressor out of the way of the

Cylinder head bolt tightening sequence 302 V8 (© Ford Motor Co.)

left cylinder head. Remove the compressor upper mounting bracket from the cylinder head.
CAUTION: If the compressor refrigerant lines do not have enough slack to permit repositioning of the compressor without first disconnecting the refrigerant lines, the air conditioning system will have to be evacuated by a trained air conditioning serviceman. Under no circumstances should an untrained person attempt to disconnect the air conditioning refrigerant lines.

7. In order to remove the left cylinder head, on cars equipped with power steering, it may be necessary to remove the steering pump and bracket remove the drive belt, and wire or tie the pump out of the way, but in such a way as to prevent the loss of its fluid.
8. In order to remove the right head it may be necessary to remove the alternator mounting bracket bolt and spacer, the ignition coil, and the air cleaner inlet duct from the right cylinder head.
9. In order to remove the left cylinder head on a car equipped with a Thermactor air pump system, disconnect the hose from the air manifold on the left cylinder head.
10. If the right cylinder head is to be removed on a car equipped with a Thermactor system, remove the Thermactor air pump and its mounting bracket. Disconnect the hose from the air manifold on the right cylinder head.
11. Loosen the rocker arm stud nuts enough to rotate the rocker arms to the side, in order to facilitate the removal of the pushrods. Remove the pushrods in sequence, so that they may be installed in their original positions. Remove the exhaust valve stem caps.
12. Remove the cylinder head attaching bolts, noting their positions. Lift the cylinder head off the block. Remove and discard the old cylinder head gasket.

Installation is as follows:
1. Position the new cylinder head gasket over the dowels on the block. Position new gaskets on the muffler inlet pipes at the exhaust manifold flange.
2. Position the cylinder head to the block, and install the head bolts, each in its original position. On engines on which the exhaust

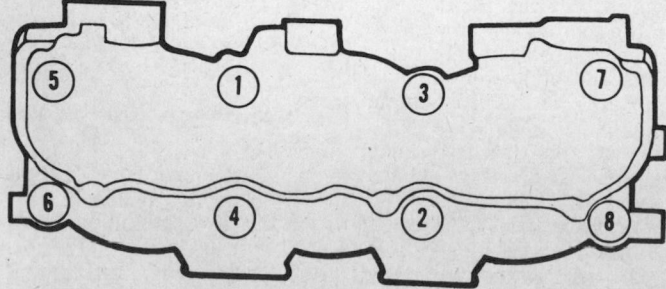

V6 cylinder head bolt torque sequence (© Ford Motor Co.)

manifold has been removed from the head to facilitate removal, it is necessary to properly guide the exhaust manifold studs into the muffler inlet pipe flange when installing the head.

3. Step-torque the cylinder head retaining bolts first to 50 ft lbs. then to 60 ft lbs, and finally to the torque specification listed in the "Torque Specifications" chart. Tighten the exhaust manifold-to cylinder head attaching bolts to specifications.

4. Tighten the nuts on the exhaust manifold studs at the muffler inlet flanges to 18 ft lbs.

5. Clean and inspect the pushrods one at a time. Clean the oil passage within each pushrod with solvent and blow the passage out with compressed air. Check the ends of the pushrods for nicks, grooves, roughness, or excessive wear. Visually inspect the pushrods for straightness, and replace any bent ones. Do not attempt to straighten pushrods.

6. Install the pushrods in their original positions. Apply Lubriplate® or a similar product to the valve stem tips and to the pushrod guides in the cylinder head. Install the exhaust valve stem caps.

7. Apply Lubriplate® or a similar product to the fulcrum seats and sockets. Turn the rocker arms to their proper position and tighten the stud nuts enough to hold the rocker arms in position. Make sure that the lower ends of the pushrods have remained properly seated in the valve lifters. Tighten the stud nuts to 17-23 ft lbs. in the order given under Valve Adjustment.

8. Install the valve covers.

9. Install the intake manifold and carburetor, following the procedure under "Intake Manifold Installation."

10. Replace all other items removed.

Timing Cover, Chain, and Camshaft—1600 cc

Timing Cover and Chain Replacement

1. Drain coolant.
2. Disconnect radiator hoses at the engine, then remove radiator.
3. Remove fanbelt, fan, and water pump pulley.
4. Remove the water pump.
5. Remove the crankshaft pulley, using a puller only.
6. Remove the front cover.

NOTE: cover is secured by four oil pan bolts as well.

Perform steps 7 through 13 to remove and install the timing chain.

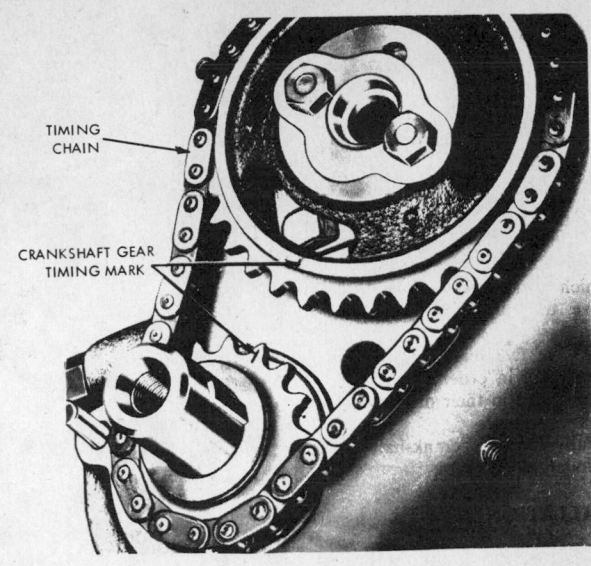

Valve timing mark alignment—1600 cc
(© Ford Motor Co)

7. With the transmission in Neutral, have an assistant tap the starter to align the cam and crankshaft sprockets.
8. Remove the timing chain tensioner.
9. Remove the timing chain sprocket attaching bolts.
10. Slide the timing chain and the camshaft sprocket off the engine as an assembly.

NOTE: The timing chain tensioner pad is designed so that two grooves are gradually worn into it. Do not alter the grooves. Replace the chain and tensioner as a unit.

11. Install the replacement timing chain on the camshaft and crankshaft sprockets and align the timing marks.
12. Position the sprockets and timing chain on the engine. Be sure that the timing marks on the sprockets are aligned as shown in the figure.
13. Install the camshaft sprocket attaching bolts.
14. Coat the front cover gasket with sealer and position it and the cover on the engine.
15. Using a large socket wrench or other suitable tool to center the cover on the engine, install the cover attaching bolts.
16. Tighten the bolts to 5–7 ft lbs and remove the centering tool.
17. Install the four front oil pan bolts and tighten them to 7–9 ft lbs.
18. Install the lower engine pulley and the water pump. Adjust the engine drive belts.
19. Install the radiator and fill the cooling system.

Camshaft and Valve Lifter Replacement

The 1600 cc engine utilizes mushroom lifters, i.e., the bottom diameter is larger than the top diameter. For this reason, it is necessary to remove the engine, remove most of its external components, and invert it to remove the camshaft and/or lifters.

1. Remove the engine from the car and mount it securely on a stand.
2. Remove the fuel and oil pumps.
3. Remove the distributor.
4. Remove the valve cover, rocker shaft, and pushrods.
5. Remove the front cover and timing chain.
6. Place a pan under the engine and invert it on the stand.
7. Remove the oil pan.
8. Remove the camshaft thrust plate and remove the camshaft.
9. Remove the lifters.
10. Install the camshaft and/or lifters using a reverse of the removal procedure. Be sure to utilize the specific instructions on installing the timing chain and distributor. Adjust the valve clearance as previously described.

Camshaft, Auxiliary Shaft and Timing Belt —2000 cc and 2300 cc

Should the camshaft drive belt jump timing by a tooth or two, the engine could still run; but very poorly. To visually check for correct timing of the crankshaft, auxiliary shaft, and the camshaft on the 2000 cc and 2300 cc engines, follow this procedure:

On 2000 cc engines, turn the crankshaft until the two round locating holes in the camshaft pulley are visible from the rear side of the pulley, looking forward from the left-side of the car. When these two holes are parallel to the ground, the timing pointer on the crankshaft pulley

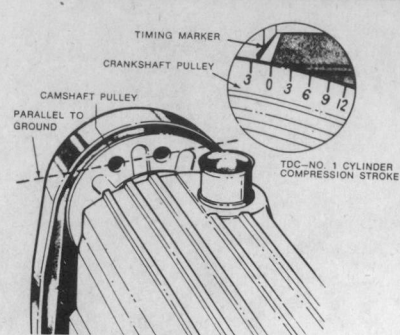

Checking 2000 cc overhead camshaft timing
(© Ford Motor Co)

should point to TDC. If the drive belt is dislocated, the crankshaft damper will be retarded or advanced 19° per cog on the belt.

If the engine you are working on does not have the two locating holes on the rear side of the camshaft pulley, then you will have to remove the drive belt cover and observe that when the crankshaft timing marks are aligned to TDC of the compression stroke of the No. 1 cylinder, the distributor rotor is pointing to the index mark on the upper lip of the distributor housing which coincides with No. 1 spark plug tower, and the pointer on the camshaft pulley is aligned with the index mark on the cylinder head.

On 2300 cc engines, there is an access plug provided in the cam drive belt cover so that the camshaft timing can be checked without removing the drive belt cover. Remove the access plug, turn the crankshaft until the timing mark on the crankshaft damper indicates TDC, and observe that the timing mark on the camshaft drive sprocket is aligned with the pointer on the inner belt cover. Also, the rotor of the distributor must align with the No. 1 cylinder firing position.

NOTE: Never turn the crankshaft of any of the overhead cam engines in the opposite direction of normal rotation. Backward rotation of the crankshaft may cause the timing belt to slip and alter the timing.

CAUTION: *After any procedure requiring removal of the rocker arms on the 2300, each lash adjuster must be fully collapsed after assembly, then released. This must be done before the camshaft is turned.*

Timing Belt Replacement

1. Remove the camshaft drive belt cover.
2. Remove the distributor cap from the distributor and position it out of the way.
3. Turn the engine clockwise until:
   a. The timing pointer is aligned with the "0" mark on the crankshaft pulley.
   b. The pointer on the camshaft

Crankshaft, camshaft, and distributor timing marks—2000 cc engine
(© Ford Motor Co)

sprocket is aligned with the ball in the belt guide plate.
   c. The distributor rotor is aligned with the timing mark on the upper lip of the distributor housing.

NOTE: If the drive belt has slipped and is out of timing, disregard this step.

4. Loosen the drive belt tensioner bolt and move the tensioner as far left as possible. Tighten the tensioner adjustment bolt.

5. Remove the belt from the pulleys.
6. Conditions should be as in step three. Install the belt on the three sprockets, making sure that the cogs in the belt engage the slots in the sprockets.
7. Loosen the tensioner adjustment bolt and allow the full spring pressure of the tensioner to force the tensioner against the belt.
8. Turn the crankshaft pulley clockwise two complete turns to

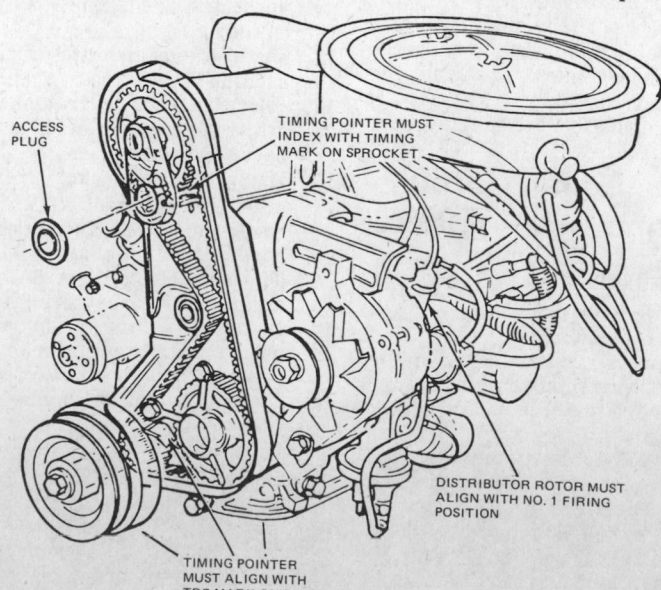

Crankshaft, camshaft, and distributor timing marks—2300 cc engine
(© Ford Motor Co)

remove all slack from the belt.

9. Continue to turn the pulley until the marks described in step three are aligned. If the belt has slipped, remove the belt and repeat the installation procedure.

10. Position the drive belt tensioner so there is no free-play in the drive belt and tighten the tensioner pivot bolt to 34 ft lbs. and the adjustment bolt to 17 ft lbs. Be careful not to overtighten the belt.

Camshaft Replacement

1. Remove the cylinder head as previously described.
2. Remove the rocker arms.
3. Remove the camshaft drive gear attaching bolt and washer, and remove the gear and belt guide plate.
4. Carefully slide the camshaft out of the rear of the cylinder head on the 2000 cc engine.

   On the 2300 cc engine, the camshaft is removed through the front of the cylinder head.
5. Reverse the removal procedure to install the camshaft and cylinder head.

NOTE: Coat the camshaft with oil before sliding it into the cylinder head.

CAUTION: *After any procedure requiring removal of the rocker arms on the 2300, each lash adjuster must be fully collapsed after assembly, then released. This must be done before the camshaft is turned.*

Auxiliary Shaft Replacement

1. Remove the camshaft drive belt cover.
2. Remove the drive belt. Remove the auxiliary shaft sprocket. A puller may be necessary to remove the sprocket.
3. Remove the distributor and fuel pump.
4. Remove the auxiliary shaft cover and thrust plate.
5. Withdraw the auxiliary shaft from the block.

NOTE: The distributor drive gear and the fuel pump eccentric on the auxiliary shaft must not be allowed to touch the auxiliary shaft bearings during removal and installation. Completely coat the shaft with oil before sliding it into place.

6. Slide the auxiliary shaft into the housing and insert the thrust plate to hold the shaft.
7. Install a new gasket and auxiliary shaft cover.
8. Fit a new gasket into the fuel pump and install the pump.
9. Insert the distributor and install the auxiliary shaft sprocket.
10. Align the timing marks and install the drive belt.
11. Install the drive belt cover.
12. Check the ignition timing.

Timing Case, Gears, and Camshaft—V6

Front Cover Removal and Installation

1. Remove the oil pan as described in the following section.
2. Remove the radiator and any other necessary parts such as the water pump, to allow clearance.
3. Remove the alternator and drive belts. Remove the water pump and water lines.
4. Remove the fan.
5. Remove the crankshaft pulley with a puller.
6. Remove the front cover retaining bolts and remove the front cover. If the front cover plate gasket needs replacement, remove the two screws and the plate to replace the gasket. If necessary, remove the guide sleeves from the cylinder block.
7. To install, reverse the procedures, cleaning all surfaces of gasket material and installing new gaskets and sealing compound.

NOTE: If the guide sleeves were removed, install them with new seal rings but do not use sealing compound.

Front Oil Seal Removal and Installation

1. Remove the timing cover.
2. Drive out the old seal with a punch and make sure that the inside rim is clean.
3. Coat a new seal with grease and place it into position on the case.
4. Drive the seal in until fully seated; check to make sure that the spring is properly positioned in the seal.
5. Reinstall the timing cover.

Camshaft Removal and Installation

1. Drain the cooling system.
2. Remove the radiator.
3. Remove the distributor cap with the spark plug wires attached. Remove the distributor vacuum line, distributor, alternator, rocker arm covers, fuel line and filter, carburetor, and intake manifold.
4. Remove the rocker arm and shaft assemblies. Lift out the pushrods and mark them so they can be replaced in the same location.
5. Remove the oil pan. (See the following sections.)
6. Remove the timing chain cover and water pump as an assembly.
7. Remove the camshaft gear retaining bolt and slide the gear off the camshaft. Remove the camshaft thrust plate.

V6 timing gear alignment
(© Ford Motor Co)

8. Remove the valve lifters from the engine block with a magnet. Lifters should be identified to permit installation in the same location.
9. Carefully pull the camshaft from the engine block, avoiding damage to the camshaft bearings. Remove the key and spacer ring.
10. Coat the camshaft with a cam lubricant or heavy engine oil.
11. Install the camshaft, carefully avoiding damage to the bearings.

NOTE: When installing the camshaft, do not push it hard into the engine. There is an oil plug at the rear of the engine block called the "bore plug." If the camshaft is forced into the engine, it could push this plug out, resulting in oil leaking on the clutch and pressure plate.

12. Install the spacer ring with the chamfered side toward the engine. Insert the camshaft key. Install the thrust plate. Camshaft end-play should be 0.001-0.004 in. The spacer ring and thrust plate are available in two sizes for adjustment.
13. Install the camshaft timing gear and align the timing marks. Install the retaining washer and bolt.
14. Install the valve lifters.
15. Install the timing cover.
16. Install the belt drive pulley and secure it with the washer and retaining bolt.
17. Install the oil pan.
18. Install the pushrods in the same locations from which they were removed. Install the intake manifold.
19. Install the oil baffles and rocker arm shaft assemblies. Adjust the valves.
20. Install the carburetor, fuel line and filter, alternator, distributor cap, and wires.
21. Fill the cooling system.
22. Install the rocker arm covers but not permanently. Run the engine, check for leaks, and set the

ignition timing.

23. Set the valves at their hot setting. Install the valve covers permanently.

Timing Cover, Chain, and Camshaft—V8

Timing Cover and Chain Removal and Installation

1. Drain the cooling system and the crankcase. Disconnect the negative battery cable.
2. Remove the fan shroud retaining bolts and position the shroud to the rear. Remove the bolts attaching the spacer to the water pump and remove the fan and spacer (or fan drive clutch) from the water pump shaft. Remove the fan shroud.
3. Remove the air conditioner drive belt and idler pulley bracket. Remove the alternator and alternator drive belt. Remove the power steering pump and drive belt. Remove the Thermactor air pump and drive belt.
4. Remove the water pump pulley.
5. Disconnect the radiator hose, heater hose, and the water pump by-pass hose from the water pump.
6. Remove the crankshaft pulley from the crankshaft vibration damper. After removing the damper retaining screw and washer, install a universal gear puller on the damper and pull it off.
7. Disconnect the fuel pump outlet line at the fuel pump. Remove the fuel pump retaining bolts and position the pump to one side with the flexible fuel line still attached.
8. Remove the engine dip-stick.
9. Remove the bolts attaching the oil pan to the front cover. Using a thin-bladed knife, cut the oil pan gasket flush with the cylinder block face prior to separating the cover from the cylinder block. Then remove the front cover and water pump as an assembly.
10. Discard the old front cover gasket, and remove the crankshaft front oil slinger.
11. Check the timing chain deflection. Gently rotate the crankshaft in a clockwise direction until all slack is removed from the left-side of the timing chain. Scribe a mark on the engine block parallel to the present position of the left-side of the chain. Turn the crankshaft in a counterclockwise direction to remove all the slack from the right-side of the chain. Force the left-side of the chain outward with the fingers and measure the distance between the

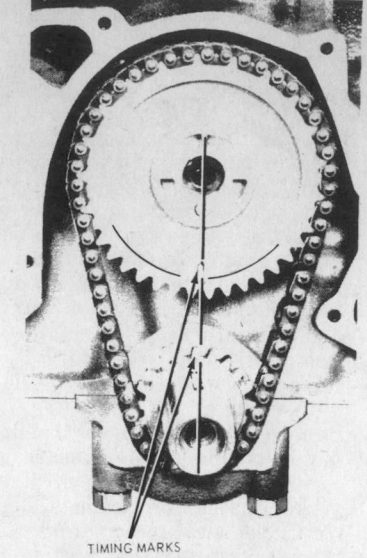

TIMING MARKS

Aligning the camshaft timing marks—302 V8 (© Ford Motor Co.)

reference point and the present position of the chain. If the distance exceeds ½ in., replace the chain and sprockets.
12. Turn the engine in the normal direction of rotation until the timing sprocket marks are positioned "dot-to-dot."
13. Remove the camshaft sprocket capscrew, washers and the fuel pump eccentric. Slide both sprockets and the timing chain forward, and remove them as an assembly.

To install:

1. Position the sprockets and timing chain on the camshaft and crankshaft simultaneously, aligning the marks.
2. Install the fuel pump eccentric, washers and camshaft sprocket capscrew. Tighten the capscrew to 30-35 ft lbs. Install the front oil slinger.
3. Clean the front cover, oil pan and cylinder block mating surfaces to remove all old gasket material.
4. Replace the cover oil seal.
5. Lubricate the timing chain with engine oil.
6. Coat the gasket surface of the oil pan with oil-resistant sealer. Cut and position the required sections of a new gasket on the oil pan and apply oil-resistant sealer at the corners. Install the oil pan seal. Coat the gasket surfaces of the block and front cover with oil-resistant sealer, and position the new gasket on the block.
7. Place the front cover on the block, taking care to avoid seal damage or gasket mislocation.
8. Install the front cover. To align the holes in the block with those

in the cover, it may be necessary to insert two phillips head screwdrivers in two of the bolt holes and force the cover downward, compressing the new pan gasket. Then, with the attaching bolts coated with oil for ease of installation, install the bolts, tightening them diagonally, in rotation, to a final torque of 12-15 ft lbs.
9. Apply white grease to the rubbing surface of the vibration damper inner hub to prevent damage to the seal. Apply a light coating of graphite and engine oil to the front of the crankshaft for damper installation. Then, align the vibration damper keyway. Install the vibration damper on the crankshaft and install the capscrew and washer. Tighten the screw to 70-90 ft lbs. Install the crankshaft pulley.
10. Using a new gasket, install the fuel pump to the block. Connect the fuel outlet line.
11. Install the dipstick.
12. Connect the radiator hose, heater hose, and the water pump by-pass hose at the water pump.
13. Install the Thermactor air pump and drive belt. Install the power steering pump and drive belt. Install the alternator and drive belt. Install the air conditioner idler pulley and drive belt.
14. Position the fan shroud over the water pump pulley. Install the fan and spacer (or fan clutch drive). Install the fan shroud retaining bolts.
15. Adjust all drive belts.
16. Fill the crankcase and cooling system. Connect the battery cable. Bleed the cooling system.
17. Start the engine and operate it at a fast idle. Check for coolant and oil leaks.
18. Adjust the ignition timing.

Front Oil Seal Removal and Installation

This procedure is identical to that shown for the V6.

Camshaft Removal and Installation

1. Drain the cooling system. Disconnect the radiator hoses and the automatic transmission cooler lines. Remove the fan shroud retaining bolts. Remove the radiator. If equipped with air conditioning, remove the bolts securing the air conditioning condenser and position the condenser to one side. CAUTION: *Do not disconnect the refrigerant lines.*
2. Remove the intake manifold as outlined under "Intake Manifold Removal and Installation."

3. Remove the front cover timing chain and sprockets as outlined under "Timing cover and chain Removal and Installation."

4. Remove the crankcase ventilation valve and hoses. Remove the rocker arm covers. Loosen the rocker arm stud nuts and rotate the rocker arms to one side (away from the pushrods).

5. Lift out the pushrods, keeping them in order so that they may be installed in their original positions. Using a magnet, remove the valve lifters, also keeping them in order. If the lifters become stuck in their bores, use a claw-type tool to remove them.

6. Remove the camshaft thrust plate and remove the camshaft by carefully pulling it to the front of the engine. Take care not to damage the camshaft lobes or the cam bearing journals while removing the camshaft from the engine.

7. Prior to installing the camshaft, coat the cam lobes with a camshaft lubricant, and the bearing journals and all valve parts with heavy engine oil.

8. Reverse the above procedure to install, taking care to tighten the rocker arm nuts in the order specified under valve adjustment before starting the engine. Permissible camshaft end-play is 0.001-0.007 in., adjusted by replacement of the thrust plate.

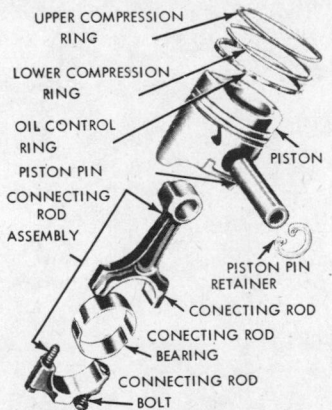

UPPER COMPRESSION RING
LOWER COMPRESSION RING
OIL CONTROL RING
PISTON PIN
CONNECTING ROD ASSEMBLY
PISTON
PISTON PIN RETAINER
CONECTING ROD
CONECTING ROD BEARING
CONNECTING ROD BOLT

Connecting rod and piston assembly for the 1600 cc engine (© Ford Motor Co)

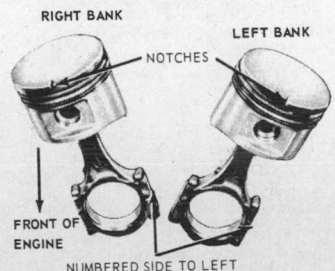

RIGHT BANK
LEFT BANK
NOTCHES
FRONT OF ENGINE
NUMBERED SIDE TO LEFT

Piston and rod positioning for installation—2800 cc V6
(© Ford Motor Co.)

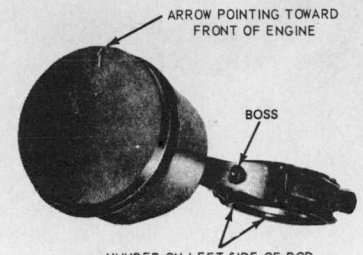

ARROW POINTING TOWARD FRONT OF ENGINE
BOSS
NUMBER ON LEFT SIDE OF ROD

Piston and rod positioning for installation in 2000 cc and 2300 cc engines
(© Ford Motor Co)

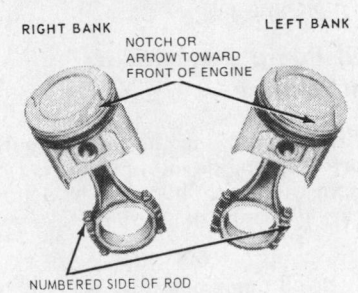

RIGHT BANK
LEFT BANK
NOTCH OR ARROW TOWARD FRONT OF ENGINE
NUMBERED SIDE OF ROD

Piston and connecting rod positioning for installation—302 V8 (© Ford Motor Co.)

Engine Lubrication

NOTE: The Brazilian-built 2300 cc engine has an oil restrictor pin in the oil gallery behind the pressure sender. This pin restricts oil pressure to the tappets during cold and full throttle operation. If the pin is removed, the valves will not seat properly. The Brazilian engine has a 900 through 922 series number on the white engine timing belt cover tag.

Oil Pan Removal and Installation

1600, 2000, and 2300 cc

1. Drain the crankcase.
2. Remove the oil dipstick.
3. On 1600 cc engines, disconnect the negative battery cable, remove the starter motor retaining bolts and remove the starter from the engine.
4. Disconnect the steering shaft connection from the rack and pinion.

5. Disconnect the rack and pinion from the crossmember and move it forward to provide clearance.
6. Remove the flywheel housing inspection cover.
7. Remove the oil pan attaching bolts and remove the pan.
8. Clean the gasket mounting surface of the block and the pan.
9. Coat the block surface and the oil pan gasket with oil resistant sealer and position the gasket on the block. The 2000 has a two piece gasket.
10. Coat the oil pan front oil seal and the front cover with oil resistant sealer and position the seal on the front cover, making sure the ends of the seal contact the oil pan gasket.
11. Coat the rear oil pan seal with oil resistant sealer and install it in the rear main bearing cap.
12. Position the pan on the block and tighten the bolts to specification. Tighten all bolts to 7-9 ft lbs., except 8 mm bolts on the 2300. Tighten these to 11-13 ft lbs.
13. Reverse steps 1-6 to complete installation.

2800 cc V6

1. Remove the dipstick. Remove the bolts attaching the fan shroud to the radiator. Position the shroud over the fan. Disconnect the battery ground cable at the battery. Loosen the alternator bracket and adjusting bolts. Drain the coolant and remove the radiator hoses and automatic transmission cooler lines.
2. Raise the vehicle on a hoist. Disconnect the steering gear and set it out of the way. Disconnect the sway bar ends.
3. Drain the crankcase.
4. Remove the splash shield. Remove the starter.
5. Remove the engine front support nuts.
6. Raise the engine and place wood blocks between the engine front supports and the chassis brackets. Remove the clutch or converter housing cover.

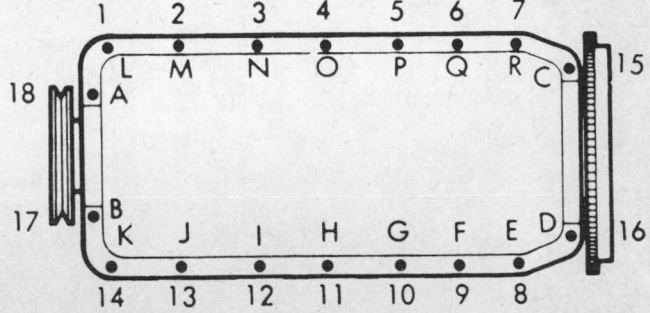

1600 cc engine oil pan torque sequence—use the alphabetical pattern first, then the numerical (© Ford Motor Co.)

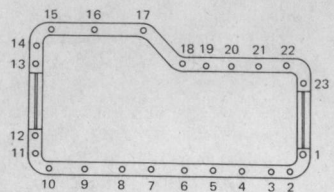

2000 cc engine oil pan torque sequence (© Ford Motor Co.)

7. Remove the oil pan attaching bolts and remove the oil pan.
8. Clean the gasket surfaces of the block and the oil pan. The oil pan has a two-piece gasket.
9. Coat the block surface and the oil pan gasket with sealer. Position the oil pan gaskets on the cylinder block.
10. Position the oil pan front seal on the cylinder front cover. Be sure that the tabs on the seal are over the oil pan gasket.
11. Place the end seals in position flush with the cylinder block oil pan rail, if previously removed. Position the oil pan rear seal on the rear main bearing cap. Be sure that the tabs on the seal are over the oil pan gasket.
12. Position the oil pan centered on the cylinder block. Install two bolts at both ends (front and rear) of the oil pan, then install the remaining bolts and tighten them to 5-7 ft lbs, starting with the bolt at the left front corner on the leading edge of the oil pan and working clockwise around the circumference of the pan.
13. Replace the converter housing or clutch cover.
14. Raise the engine and remove the wood blocks from between the engine supports and chassis brackets. Lower the engine and install the engine support nuts.
15. Replace the starter and splash shield, steering gear, and sway-bar.
16. Lower the vehicle.
17. Install the alternator.
18. Connect the battery ground wire.
19. Install the fan shroud.
20. Install the dipstick. Fill the crankcase with oil. Start the engine and check for leaks.

302 V8
1. Disconnect the battery ground cable.
2. Unbolt the fan shroud and place it over the fan.
3. Raise the car cafely.
4. Drain the oil.
5. Remove the four bolts and the crossmember.
6. Remove the steering shaft flex joint attaching screw. Unbolt the steering gear from the cross-member.

7. Unbolt the sway bar from the chassis and move it down.
8. Disconnect the battery cable at the starter and remove the starter.
9. Remove the pan bolts and the pan.
10. On installation, clean the gasket surfaces. Cement the pan gasket and seals to the block. Install the pan.
11. Replace all the other items removed. Torque the steering gear to crossmember bolts to 80-100 ft lbs. and the coupling bolt to 20-30 ft lbs.

Oil Pump Removal and Installation
When installing an oil pump, prime it by filling the inlet or outlet port with engine oil and rotating the pump by hand. This must be done to prevent engine damage.

1600 cc
The oil pump and filter assembly is bolted to the left side of the block and can be serviced with the engine installed in the car.

Two types of oil pump have been installed during production—an eccentric bi-rotor type and a sliding vane type. These pumps are readily identified by their end covers—the eccentric bi-rotor type has four recesses cast into its cover while the sliding vane type has a flat cover. These two pumps are interchangeable, although their internal parts are not.
1. Lift the hood and place a drain pan under the oil pump.
2. Remove the three bolts which hold the pump and filter assembly.
NOTE: *Tighten these bolts to 13-15 ft. lbs. when installing pump.*
3. Remove filter from pump.
4. To install, reverse removal procedure.

2000 and 2300 cc
The oil pump, of bi-rotor design, is

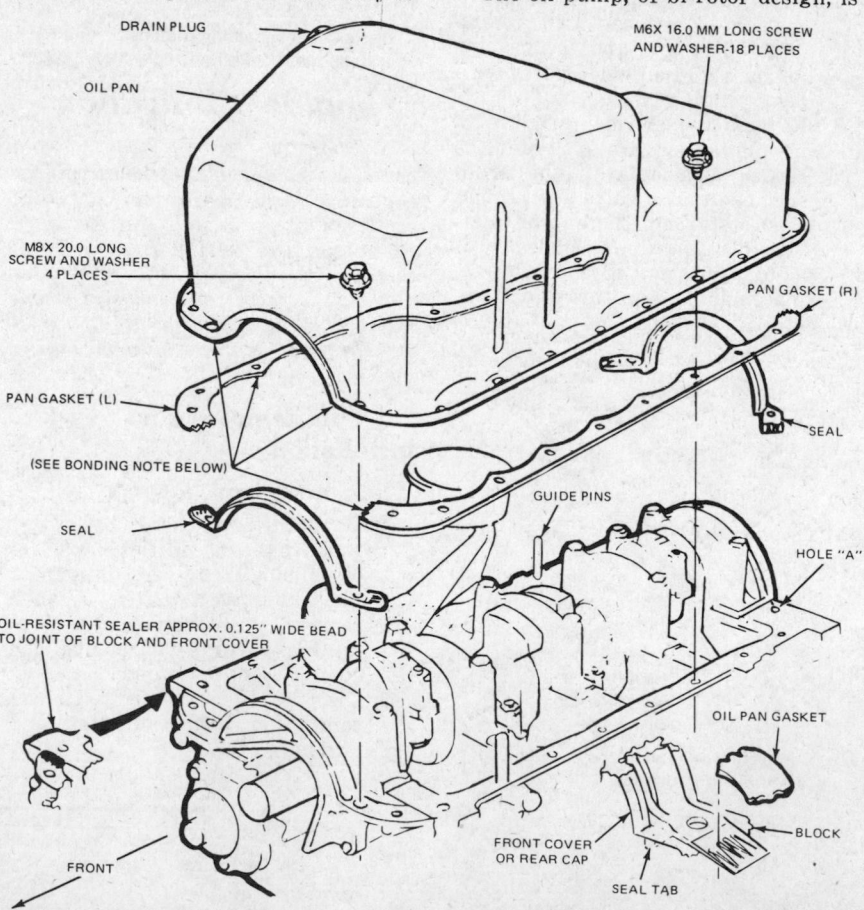

1. APPLY GASKET ADHESIVE EVENLY TO OIL PAN FLANGE AND TO PAN SIDE GASKETS. ALLOW ADHESIVE TO DRY PAST WET STAGE, THEN INSTALL GASKETS TO OIL PAN.
2. APPLY SEALER TO JOINT OF BLOCK AND FRONT COVER. INSTALL SEALS TO FRONT COVER AND REAR BEARING CAP AND PRESS SEAL TABS FIRMLY INTO BLOCK. BE SURE TO INSTALL THE REAR SEAL BEFORE THE REAR MAIN BEARING CAP SEALER HAS CURED.
3. POSITION 2 GUIDE PINS AND INSTALL THE OIL PAN. SECURE THE PAN WITH THE FOUR M8 BOLTS SHOWN ABOVE.
4. REMOVE THE GUIDE PINS AND INSTALL AND TORQUE THE EIGHTEEN M6 BOLTS, BEGINNING AT HOLE "A" AND WORKING CLOCKWISE AROUND THE PAN.

2300 cc engine oil pan torque sequence (© Ford Motor Co.)

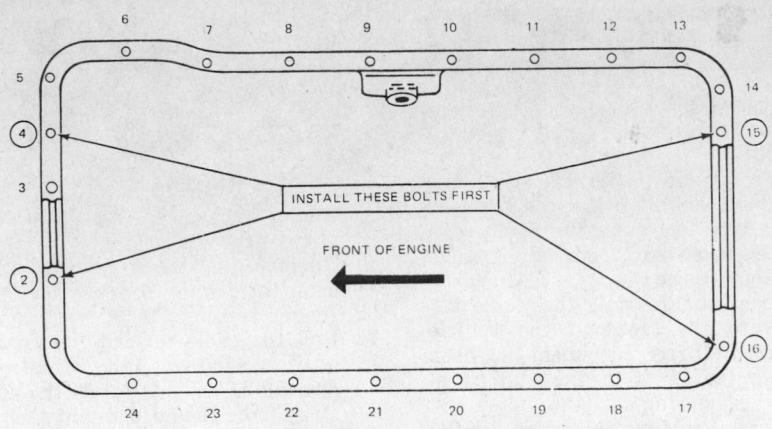

V6 oil pan bolt torque sequence (© Ford Motor Co.)

mounted to the bottom of the cylinder block, inside the oil pan. To remove the pump, remove the oil pan and remove the two bolts that mount the oil pump to the block.

NOTE: Under no circumstances should the three-bolt cover oil pump on a 2300 cc engine be disassembled. If the pump is found to be defective, it should be replaced as a unit. Four-bolt cover pumps (introduced in 1976) may be disassembled.

V6

1. Remove the oil pan and unbolt the oil pickup screen from the main bearing cap.
2. Remove the pump bolts.
3. Remove the pump and pump drive shaft.
4. On installation, prime the pump. Insert the driveshaft into the engine block with the pointed end inward. The pointed end is closest to the pressed-on flange.
5. Install the pump with a new gasket and tighten the mount-screws; install the inlet tube and screen assembly with a new gasket.
6. Replace the oil pan, start the engine, and check for leaks.

302 V8

1. Remove the oil pan. Remove the pump inlet tube and screen assembly.
2. Unbolt and remove the pump, gasket, and driveshaft.
3. On installation, prime the pump. Insert the driveshaft in the distributor socket. The stop on the shaft should touch the roof of the crankcase. Remove the shaft and position the stop if necessary.
4. Insert the driveshaft into the pump. Install the pump and shaft as an assembly. If the pump won't go into place, the driveshaft is probably not correctly aligned with the distributor shaft.
5. Tighten the pump bolts and re-

place the inlet and screen assembly. Replace the pan.

Crankshaft Rear Main Oil Seal Replacement

1600 cc

1. Remove transmission and unbolt the right and left engine mounts from the cylinder block.
2. Raise and support the engine above the engine mounts.
3. Remove the pressure plate bolts in sequence, a few turns at a time, and remove the pressure plate and clutch disc.
4. Remove the flywheel.
5. Remove the oil pan and gaskets.
6. Remove the rear oil seal carrier.
7. Remove the seal from the carrier and install a new one.

8. Locate a new gasket on the rear oil seal carrier. Fit the carrier to the block rear face. Tighten the bolts evenly to 12-15 ft lbs.
9. Position new gaskets on the block flange. Position the cork packing strips with the chamfered ends into the grooves. Install the oil pan.
10. Assemble the clutch, transmission, and motor mounts in the reverse order of removal.

2000 cc and 2800 cc V6

1. Remove the transmission. Remove the clutch pressure plate and clutch disc, if so equipped.
2. Remove the flywheel, flywheel housing and rear plate.
3. Punch two holes in the crankshaft rear oil seal on opposite sides of the crankshaft just above the bearing cap-to-cylinder block split line. Install a sheet metal screw in each of the holes and pry the crankshaft rear main oil seal from the block.

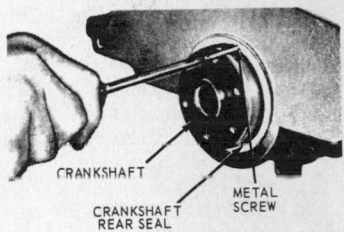

Removing the crankshaft rear main oil seal—2000 cc and 2800 cc V6 (© Ford Motor Co)

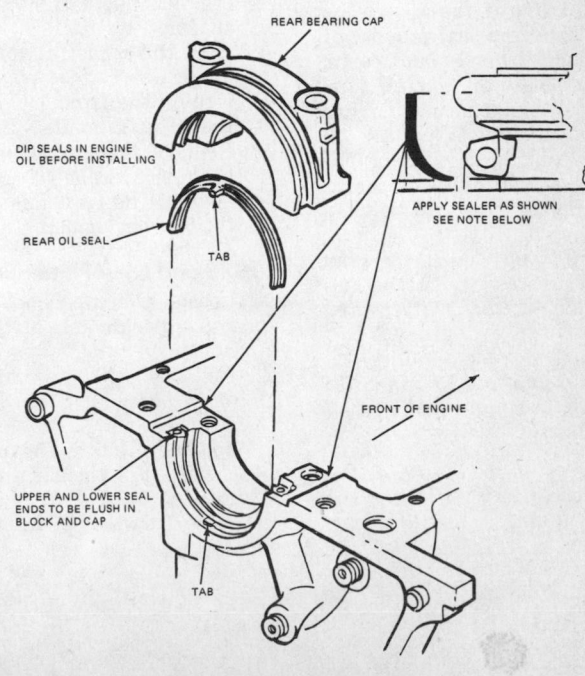

SEALER NOTE: CLEAN THE AREA WHERE SEALER IS TO BE APPLIED BEFORE INSTALLING THE SEALS. USE FORD SPOT REMOVER B7A-19521-A OR EQUIVALENT. AFTER THE SEALS ARE IN PLACE, APPLY A 1/16 INCH BEAD OF C3AZ-19562-A OR -B SEALER AS SHOWN. SEALER MUST NOT CONTACT SEALS.

Replacement of the crankshaft rear main oil seal—2300 cc engine (© Ford Motor Co)

NOTE: Use extreme caution not to scratch the crankshaft oil seal surface.

Clean the oil seal recess in the cylinder block and main bearing cap.

4. Coat the seal and all of the seal mounting surfaces with oil and install the seal in the recess, driving it in place with an oil seal installation tool or a large socket.
5. Install the clutch and/or transmission in the reverse order of removal.

2,300 cc and 302 V8

1. Remove the oil pan and oil pump, if required.
2. Loosen all the main bearing cap bolts, thereby lowering the crankshaft slightly but not more than 1/32 in.
3. Remove the rear main bearing cap, and remove the oil seal from the bearing cap and the cylinder block. Install a small sheet metal screw in one end of the cylinder block half of the seal, and pull on the screw to remove the seal.
4. Clean the seal grooves in the cap and block with a brush and solvent. Dry the area thoroughly. No solvent should come in contact with the seal.
5. Dip the seal halves in clean engine oil.
6. Carefully install the upper seal (block half) into its groove with the undercut side of the seal toward the front of the engine, by rotating it on the seal journal of the crankshaft until about 3/8 in. protrudes below the parting surface. Be sure that no rubber has been shaved off. Wipe all oil from the mating surface of the bearing cap and cylinder block.
7. Tighten the bearing cap bolts to specifications.
8. Install the lower seal in the rear main bearing cap with the undercut side of the seal toward the front of the engine. Allow the seal to protrude about 3/8 in. above the parting surface to mate with the upper seal when the cap is installed.

NOTE: Install the seals so that the locating tab faces the rear of the engine. (2300 cc only).

9. Apply a *small* amount of sealer to the mating surface of the bearing cap. No sealer compound should come in contact with the rubber seals when the bearing cap is installed and tightened.
10. Install the oil pump (if removed) and oil pan. Fill the crankcase with oil, and operate the engine, checking for leaks.

CLUTCH

Adjustment

Pinto Built Before 10/1/70

1. From under the car, pull the clutch cable toward the front of the vehicle until the C-clip can be removed from the cable. Remove the clip.
2. Continue to pull the cable toward the front of the vehicle until all free movement has been eliminated from the clutch release bearing.
3. While holding the cable in the zero free play position, insert a 0.135 in. spacer against the flywheel boss on the engine side and install the C-clip in the closest possible groove next to the spacer.
4. Remove the spacer and release the cable.

Pinto Built from 10/1/70 through 1974

1. Working under the car, loosen the clutch adjusting nut, the front locknut and the rear locknut (if so equipped).
2. Pull the clutch cable toward the front of the car until all free-play is removed from the clutch release lever.
3. Holding the cable in this position, place a 1/4 in. spacer against the engine side of the flywheel housing and tighten the adjusting nut finger-tight against the spacer.
4. Hold the adjusting nut so that it maintains its position and tighten the front locknut against the adjusting nut.
5. Remove the spacer and tighten the rear locknut (if so equipped) against the transmission side of the flywheel housing.

1975 and Later Pinto and Bobcat

1. Loosen the cable locknut on the transmission side of the flywheel housing.
2. Pull the cable toward the front of the car until the tabs on the adjuster nut are clear of the housing. Rotate the nut toward the front of the car about 1/4 in.
3. Release the cable. Then pull the cable forward again until there

is no release lever free movement. Rotate the adjusting nut toward the housing until the tabs touch the housing, then drop the tabs into the nearest groove.
4. Tighten the locknut.

Mustang II

1. Remove the cable retaining clip at the firewall.
2. Remove the screw holding the cable attaching bracket on the fender apron.
3. Pull the cable toward the front of the vehicle until the adjusting nut can be turned. Rotate the nut away from the adjustment sleeve about 1/4 in.
4. Release the cable, and then pull the cable again until free movement of the release lever is eliminated.
5. Rotate the adjusting nut toward the adjustment sleeve until contact is made, then index it into the next notch.
6. Reinstall the cable retaining clip and cable attaching bracket, and the screw on the fender apron.

Clutch, Clutch Housing, and Transmission

Removal, Pinto and Bobcat

1. Place the gearshift lever in the neutral position. Raise the car and remove the back-up light switch from the transmission extension housing.
2. Loosen the shift lever locknut. Remove the knob and the locknut from the shift lever. Remove the four rubber boot attaching screws and remove the boot.
3. Compress the corrugated rubber spring, then remove the retaining snap-ring and slide the spring upward on the lever.
4. Bend the shift lever locktabs up, then thread the plastic dome nut from the extension housing.
5. Lift the shift lever from the extension housing.
6. Working from under the hood, remove the upper flywheel housing-to-engine attaching bolts.
7. Raise the vehicle and match-mark the driveshaft and the rear axle pinion flange.
8. Disconnect and remove the driveshaft. Place rags in the extension housing to prevent loss of lubricant.

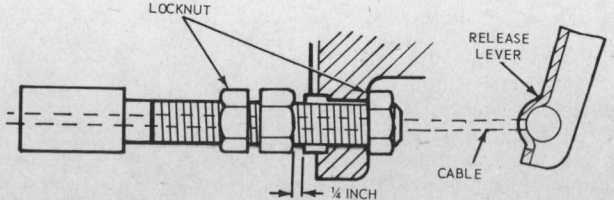

Pinto clutch linkage adjustment, 1971-74 models—see text for specific dates
(© Ford Motor Co.)

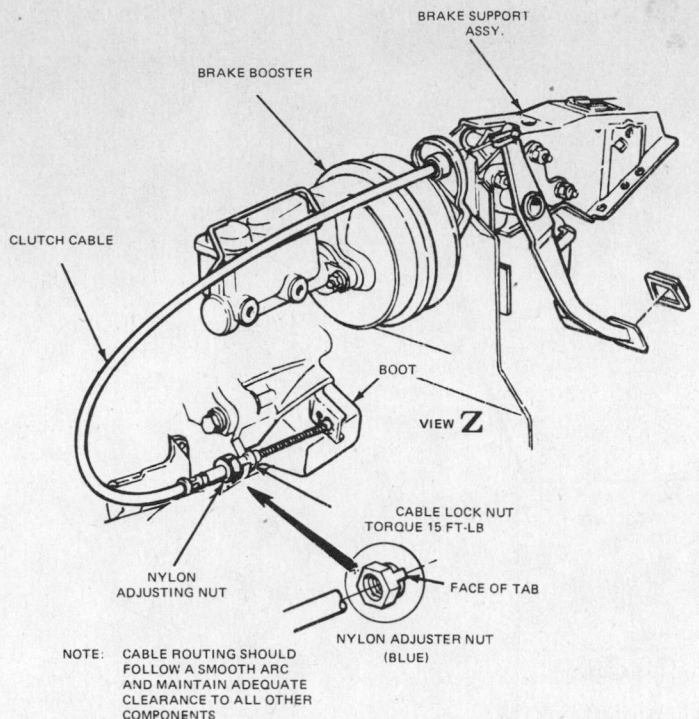

BRAKE BOOSTER

BRAKE SUPPORT ASSY.

CLUTCH CABLE

BOOT

VIEW Z

CABLE LOCK NUT
TORQUE 15 FT-LB

NYLON
ADJUSTING NUT

FACE OF TAB

NYLON ADJUSTER NUT
(BLUE)

NOTE: CABLE ROUTING SHOULD FOLLOW A SMOOTH ARC AND MAINTAIN ADEQUATE CLEARANCE TO ALL OTHER COMPONENTS

1975 and later Pinto and Bobcat clutch linkage (© Ford Motor Co.)

9. Remove the clutch release lever dust cover.
10. Disconnect the clutch cable from the clutch release lever.
11. Remove the starter motor attaching bolts and position the motor out of the way.
12. Remove the speedometer cable-to-transmission attaching screw and remove the cable and gear from the transmission. Plug the opening in the transmission to prevent lubricant spillage.
13. Support the rear of the engine with a jack and remove the crossmember-to-body attaching bolts.
14. Remove the bolts that attach the crossmember to the transmission extension housing and remove the crossmember from the car.
15. Lower the engine to gain working room, and remove the remaining flywheel housing-to-engine attaching bolts.
16. Slide the transmission rearward and remove it from the car.
17. If the clutch is to be removed loosen the six pressure plate attaching bolts evenly to release spring pressure gradually. If the same pressure plate and cover are to be reused, mark the position of the pressure plate and flywheel so they can be returned to their original location.
18. Remove the pressure plate attaching bolts and remove the pressure plate and clutch from the car.

Removal, Mustang II

1. Place the shift lever in neutral.

Remove the carpet and boot. Remove the three metric lever base bolts and remove the shift lever.
2. Raise the car safely. Remove the driveshaft, after matchmarking its location, and plug the end of the transmission.
3. Disconnect the seat belt sensing switch, if any, and the backup light wires.
4. Remove the attaching screw and pull out the speedometer cable. Plug the hole.
5. The remainder of the procedure is the same as for Pinto and Bobcat, starting with Step 9. The major difference is that the transmission is removed separately, leaving the clutch housing in place.

Installation, Pinto, Bobcat, Mustang II

1. Position the clutch and pressure plate on the flywheel and install the attaching bolts loosely.

NOTE: the three dowel pins on the flywheel must be aligned with the pressure plate.

2. Align the clutch assembly, using a pilot shaft or other suitable tool, and alternately tighten the bolts.
3. Position the transmission and flywheel assembly on the studs on the cylinder block and install the retaining bolts.
4. Reverse removal procedure to install remaining equipment. The shift lever must be installed before the back-up light switch.

MANUAL TRANSMISSION

A four-speed manual transmission is standard equipment on all models. Some 1600 cc Pintos have an English built transmission. The majority of 1600 cc Pintos and all other Pintos and Bobcats use a German built transmission. These transmissions can be identified from the transmission ID code on the identification tag at the left front of the extension housing. The Mustang II uses an American built transmission. See the Manual Transmissions Unit Repair section for further details.

Transmission Removal and Installation

See *Clutch, Clutch Housing, and Transmission Removal and Installation* in this car section.

AUTOMATIC TRANSMISSION

All models use a C4 automatic transmission, except for those with the 2300 cc engine and 1975 and later V6. These models use a C3 transmission. The Vehicle Certification Label gives the transmission code letter, V for C3, and W for C4.

NOTE: Perform the adjustments in the order listed below.

Downshift Linkage Adjustment

1. Disconnect the downshift lever return spring on models through 1972.
2. Hold the throttle shaft lever in the wide open position. Hold the downshift rod against the through detent stop. Adjust the downshift screw to obtain 0.050-0.070 in. clearance (0.010-0.080 in. starting 1973) between the screw tip and the throttle shaft lever tab.
3. Connect the downshift lever return spring.

Shift Linkage Adjustment

1. Place the transmission floor selector lever in the Drive position against the rear stop.
2. Raise the vehicle and loosen the linkage shift rod at the selector lever.
3. Move the transmission lever to the Drive position (fourth detent position from the rear of the transmission).
4. Tighten the adjustment on the linkage.
5. Lower the car and check transmission operation.

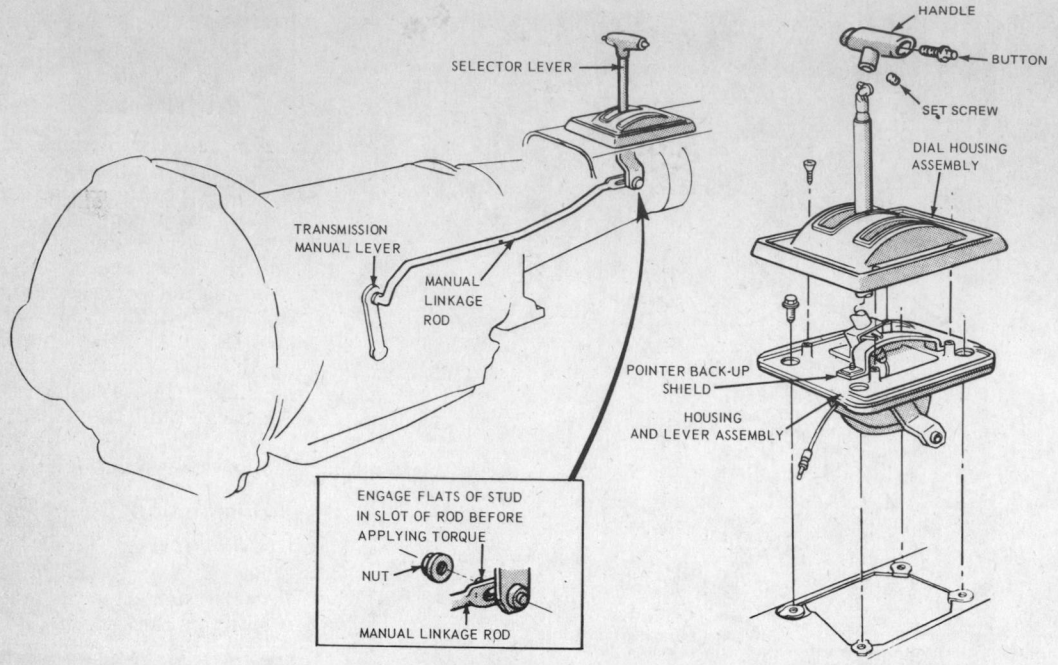

Automatic transmission shift linkage (© Ford Motor Co.)

Neutral Start Switch Adjustment

C4

1. Place the transmission selector lever in the Neutral position.
2. Raise the vehicle on a hoist and loosen the two bolts that attach the neutral switch to the transmission.
3. Rotate the switch until a gauge pin (shank end of a #43 drill bit) can be inserted through the gauge pin holes in the switch. The gauge pin must be inserted a full 31/64 in. into the switch through all three holes in the switch.
4. Tighten the switch retaining bolts and remove the pin.

Neutral Start Switch Replacement

C4

1. Raise the car, with the transmission in neutral, and disconnect the downshift linkage.
2. Remove the neutral switch attaching bolts and remove the switch and disconnect the wires.
3. Install the replacement switch and adjust it as described above.
4. Install the downshift outer lever.
5. Connect the downshift linkage rod to the downshift lever.

C3

1. Unplug the connector from the switch and unscrew the switch from the transmission case.
2. Replace the switch with a new O-ring.
3. Carefully check that the back-up lights work only in Reverse and that the engine will start only in Neutral and Park. No adjustment is required.

Band Adjustments

Caution The torque figures and numbers of turns given in these procedures must be exactly correct to prevent transmission damage.

NOTE: The only band adjustment required on the C3 transmission is on the front band.

Intermediate (Front) Band

1. Wipe clean the area around the adjusting screw on the side of the transmission, near the left-front corner of the transmission.
2. Remove the adjusting screw locknut and discard it.
3. Install a new locknut on the adjusting screw but do not tighten it.
4. Tighten the adjusting screw to *exactly 10 ft lbs.*
5. Back off the adjusting screw *exactly 1¾ turns; 1½ turns on the C3.*
6. Hold the adjusting screw so that it *does not turn* and tighten the adjusting screw locknut to 35–45 ft lbs.

Low-Reverse Band

1. Wipe clean the area around the adjusting screw on the side of the transmission, near the right-rear corner.
2. Remove the adjusting screw locknut and discard it.
3. Install a new locknut on the adjusting screw but do not tighten it.
4. Tighten the adjusting screw to *exactly 10 ft lbs.*

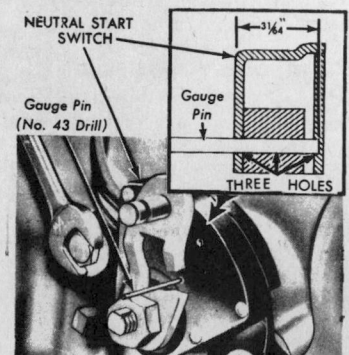

C4 Neutral start switch adjustment (© Ford Motor Co)

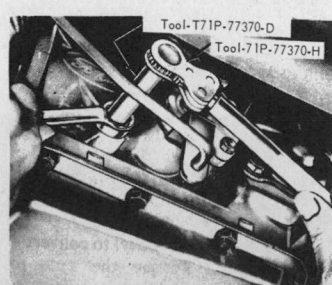

Intermediate band adjustment (© Ford Motor Co)

C4 Low-reverse band adjustment (© Ford Motor Co)

5. Back off the adjusting screw *exactly 3 full turns*.
6. Hold the adjusting screw so that it *does not turn* and tighten the adjusting screw to 35–45 ft lbs.

Pan Replacement, Fluid and Filter Change

1. Raise the car up on a lift.
2. Some C4 models require that the transmission fluid filler tube be disconnected to drain the pan; all others can be drained by loosening the pan bolts and letting the fluid drain out when the pan is lowered.
3. After the fluid has drained out, remove the rest of the attaching bolts, the pan and the gasket.
4. Remove the bolts holding the filter in place, remove the filter, clean, and replace it. The filter may be reused after cleaning in a non-detergent solution, such as new transmission fluid.
5. Replace the filter and gasket and attach the mounting bolts. Clean the edge of the transmission pan before installing the new gasket; bolt the pan to the transmission, and reattach the fluid filler tube if applicable.
6. Refill the transmission with the proper amount of Type F fluid (See Capacities Chart in the front of this section), and check for leaks around the pan.

Caution Add a little less than the specified amount of fluid at first, run the engine, shift through all positions, and check the level. It should be between ADD and FULL. The level should be at FULL after the transmission is fully warmed up. Be very cautious not to overfill.

U-JOINTS

Driveshaft and U-Joint

Removal and Installation

1. Raise the vehicle.
2. Mark the position of the rear driveshaft yoke in relation to the pinion flange so the driveshaft can be returned to its original location.
3. Disconnect the rear U-Joint from the pinion flange and remove the loose bearing caps. Pull the driveshaft rearward until it clears the transmission extension housing. Plug the extension housing. Remove the driveshaft from the car.
4. Place the driveshaft in a vise and remove the snap-rings from the U-Joint to be removed.
5. Press one of the bearing caps on the U-Joint to be removed toward the center of the driveshaft.
6. Remove the opposite bearing cap from the one being pressed as it emerges from the driveshaft.
7. Repeat Step 6 until all bearing caps have been removed.
8. Remove the U-Joint spider from the driveshaft.
9. To install, position the spider in the driveshaft and press the new bearing caps onto the spider.
10. Install the snap-rings.
11. Reinstall the driveshaft using a reverse of the removal procedure. Make sure that the yoke and pinion flange marks are aligned.

REAR AXLE

Axle Shaft, Bearing and Seal

Removal and Installation

NOTE: Bearings must be pressed on and off the shaft with an arbor press.

1. Remove the wheel, tire, and the brake drum.
2. Working through the axle shaft flange access hole, remove the nuts holding the axle retainer plate to the backing plate.
3. Remove the retainer and install the nuts fingertight to prevent the backing plate from being dislodged.
4. Using a slide hammer, remove the axle shaft and bearing assembly. If the end play is excessive, replace the bearing.
5. Using a chisel, nick the bearing retainer in three or four places.
6. Press off the old bearing and install the new one by pressing it into position.
7. Press on the new retainer.
8. With a slide hammer, remove the seal from the axle housing; when removed, clean the seal recess in the axle housing.
9. Place a new seal in position and drive it into place with a seal installation tool. The right and left seals are not interchangeable, so make sure that the seal is on the proper axle.
10. Assemble the shaft and bearing in the housing and make sure that the bearing is seated properly.

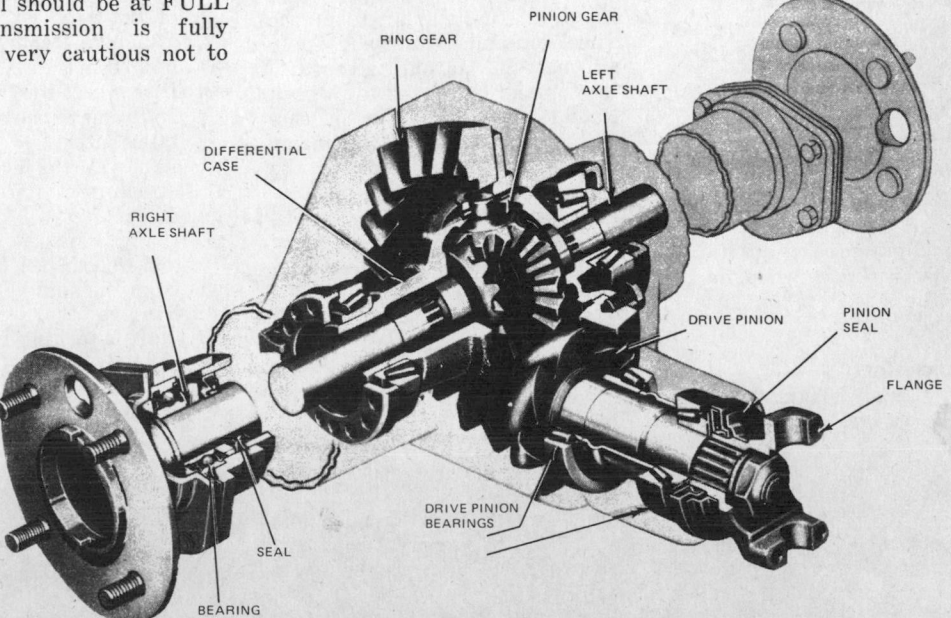

Cutaway view of rear axle (© Ford Motor Co.)

Removing the rear wheel bearing retainer ring
(© Ford Motor Co.)

11. Install the retainer, the drum, the wheel, and the tire.

Lift and jacking points are shown in the figure. A floor jack may also be used under the center of the number two crossmember or under the differential housing.

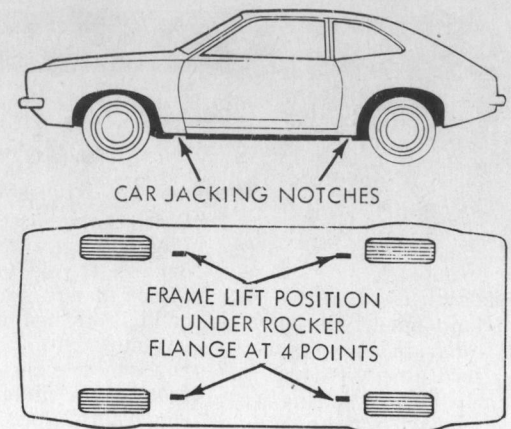

Lifting and jacking points
(© Ford Motor Co)

Upper Ball Joint

Inspection

1. Raise the vehicle by placing a floor jack under the lower arm. Do not allow the lower arm to hang freely with the vehicle on a hoist or bumper jack.
2. Have an assistant grasp the bottom of the tire and move the wheel in and out.
3. As the wheel is being moved, observe the upper control arm where the spindle attaches to it. Any movement between the upper part of the spindle and the upper ball joint indicates a bad ball joint which must be replaced.

NOTE: during this check the lower ball joint will be unloaded and may move; this is normal and not an indication of a bad ball joint. Also, do not mistake a loose wheel bearing for a defective ball joint.

Replacement

1. Raise the vehicle and allow the front wheels to fall into their full down position.
2. Drill a 1/8 in. hole completely through each ball joint attaching rivet.
3. Using a large chisel, cut off the head of each rivet and drive them from the upper arm.
4. Place a jack under the lower arm and lower the vehicle about

6 in.
5. Remove the cotter pin and attaching nut from the ball joint stud.
6. Using a ball joint stud removal tool, loosen the ball joint stud from the spindle and remove the ball joint from the upper arm.
7. Clean all metal burrs from the upper arm and install the new ball joint, using the service part nuts and bolts to attach the ball joint to the upper arm. Do not attempt to re-rivet the ball joint once it has been removed.
8. Check front end alignment.

Lower Ball Joint

Inspection

1. Raise the vehicle by placing a floor jack under the lower arm; or, raise the vehicle on a hoist and place a jack stand under the lower arm and lower the vehicle onto it to remove the preload from the lower ball joint.
2. Have an assistant grasp the wheel top and bottom and apply alternate in and out pressure to the top and bottom of the wheel.
3. Radial play of 1/4 in. is acceptable measured at the inside of the wheel adjacent to the lower arm.

NOTE: this radial play is multiplied at the outer circumference of the tire and should be measured only at the inside of the wheel.

Replacement

1. Raise the vehicle and allow the front wheels to fall to their full down position.
2. Drill a 1/8 in. hole completely through each ball joint attaching rivet.
3. Use a 3/8 in. drill in the pilot hole to drill off the head of the rivet.
4. Drive the rivets from the lower arm.
5. Place a jack under the lower arm and lower the vehicle about

6 in.
6. Remove the lower ball joint stud cotter pin and attaching nut.
7. Using a ball joint stud removal tool, loosen the ball joint from the spindle and remove the ball joint from the lower arm.
8. Clean all metal burrs from the lower arm and install the new ball joint, using the service part nuts and bolts to attach the ball joint to the lower arm. Do not attempt to re-rivet the ball joint once it has been removed.
9. Check front end alignment.

Upper Control Arm

Replacement

1. Raise the vehicle on a hoist.
2. If equipped with drum brakes, remove the tire, wheel and brake drum as an assembly. If equipped with disc brakes, remove the tire and wheel, remove the caliper attaching bolts and position the caliper out of the way with the brake hose attached. Remove the rotor and hub from the spindle.
3. Disconnect the lower control arm and remove the coil spring as detailed later.
4. Remove the cotter pin and attaching nut from the ball joint stud.
5. Using a ball joint stud removal tool, loosen the upper ball joint from the spindle.
6. Remove the upper arm inner shaft attaching bolts and remove the arm and shaft from the chassis as an assembly.
7. Reverse above procedure to install. Torque the arm to frame bolts to 95-120 ft lbs and the ball joint stud to 75-90 ft lbs.
8. Adjust front end alignment.

Lower Control Arm

Replacement

1. Raise the car and support it with

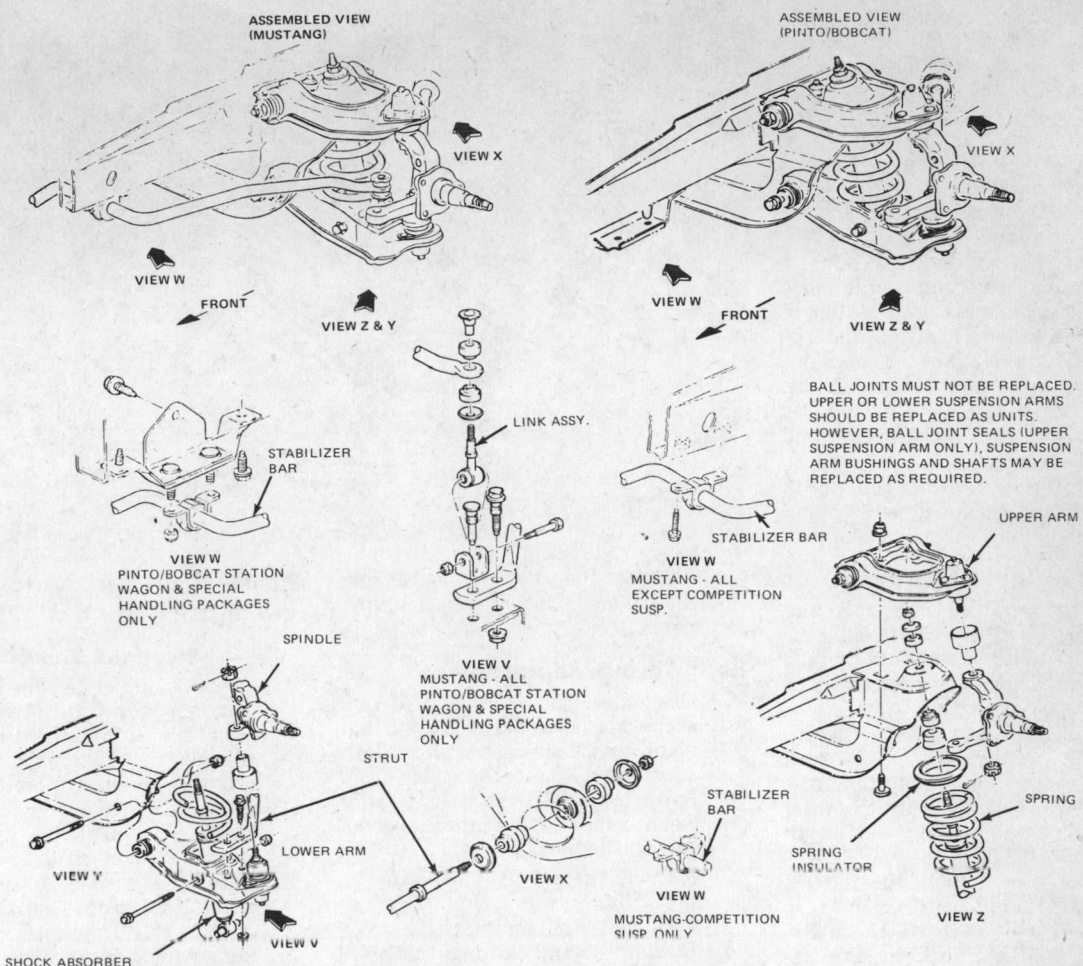

ASSEMBLED VIEW (MUSTANG)

ASSEMBLED VIEW (PINTO/BOBCAT)

VIEW X

VIEW W

FRONT

VIEW Z & Y

LINK ASSY.

STABILIZER BAR

VIEW W
PINTO/BOBCAT STATION WAGON & SPECIAL HANDLING PACKAGES ONLY

SPINDLE

VIEW V
MUSTANG - ALL
PINTO/BOBCAT STATION WAGON & SPECIAL HANDLING PACKAGES ONLY

STRUT

BALL JOINTS MUST NOT BE REPLACED. UPPER OR LOWER SUSPENSION ARMS SHOULD BE REPLACED AS UNITS. HOWEVER, BALL JOINT SEALS (UPPER SUSPENSION ARM ONLY), SUSPENSION ARM BUSHINGS AND SHAFTS MAY BE REPLACED AS REQUIRED.

UPPER ARM

STABILIZER BAR

VIEW W
MUSTANG - ALL EXCEPT COMPETITION SUSP.

STABILIZER BAR

SPRING INSULATOR

SPRING

LOWER ARM

VIEW Y

VIEW X

VIEW W
MUSTANG-COMPETITION SUSP. ONLY

VIEW Z

SHOCK ABSORBER

VIEW V

Front suspension details (© Ford Motor Co.)

stands placed under the frame.

2. If equipped with drum type brakes, remove the wheel and brake drums as an assembly. Remove the brake backing plate attaching bolts and remove the backing plate from the spindle. Wire the assembly back out of the way.

3. If equipped with disc brakes, remove the wheel from the hub. Remove the caliper from the rotor and wire it back out of the way. Remove the hub and rotor from the spindle.

4. Disconnect the shock absorber and remove it.

5. Remove the cotter pins from the upper and lower ball joint stud nuts.

6. Remove the two bolts and nuts holding the strut to the lower arm.

7. Loosen the lower ball joint stud nut two turns. Do not remove this nut.

8. Install a spreader tool between the upper and lower ball joint studs.

9. Expand the tool until the tool exerts considerable pressure on the studs. Tap the spindle near the lower stud with a hammer to

loosen the stud in the spindle. Do not loosen the stud with tool pressure only.

10. Position a floor jack under the lower arm and remove the lower ball joint and nut.

11. Lower the floor jack and remove the spring and insulator.

12. Remove the A arm-to-crossmember attaching parts, and remove the arm from the car.

13. Reverse the above procedure to install. Torque the arm to crossmember bolts to 95-120 ft lbs, the strut bolts to 40-60 ft lbs, and the ball joint stud nut to 75-90 ft. lbs. Have front-end alignment checked.

Spring Replacement

1. Jack up the front of the car and support it with jackstands.

2. Remove the shock absorber.

3. Disconnect the strut bar and sway bar from the lower control arm.

4. Place a floor jack under the lower control arm.

5. Remove the nut and bolt that attach the lower control arm to the front crossmember.

6. Carefully lower the jack, slowly, to relieve the spring pressure

from the lower arm.

7. Remove the spring and upper insulator.

8. Place the upper insulator on the spring and secure it in place with tape.

9. Position the spring on the lower control arm. Make sure that the bottom of the spring properly engages the seat on the lower control arm.

10. Raise the lower control arm with the floor jack and guide the lower control arm and the top of the spring into place. Install the lower control arm attaching bolt and nut. Tighten the lower control arm attaching bolt to 75–110 ft lbs after the car is resting on its wheels.

11. Install the shock absorber after removing the jack.

12. Remove the jack stands and lower the car.

Shock Absorber Replacement

1. Remove the nut, washer, and bushing from the upper end of the shock. If the shaft of the shock absorber turns while you are attempting to remove the nut, hold the shaft in place with an adjustable wrench while re-

moving the nut.

2. Raise the front end of the car and install jackstands.

3. Disconnect the bottom of the shock absorber from the lower control arm. It may be necessary to raise the lower arm to remove the bottom bolt.

4. Remove the shock absorber from under the car.

5. Purge the new shock of air by repeatedly extending it in its normal position and compressing it while inverted. Position the replacement shock absorber on the lower control arm and install the attaching bolts.

6. Remove the jackstands and lower the car.

7. Connect the top of the shock absorber to the upper spring pad.

Wheel Bearing Adjustment

1. Jack the front of the car up and support it with jackstands.

2. Remove the dust cap and spindle nut cotter pin. Slide the nut lock off. Discard the pin.

3. With disc brakes, loosen the adjusting nut three turns and rock the wheel in and out to push the brake pads away from the disc. Tighten the adjusting nut on all models to 17-25 ft lbs while turning the wheel. Back the nut off one-half turn.

4. Tighten the nut to 10–15 in. lbs.

5. Install the nut lock on the adjusting nut so that two of the slots align with the hole in the spindle.

6. Install a new cotter pin and bend back its ends.

7. Install the dust cap and lower the car.

REAR SUSPENSION

Rear Shock Absorber Replacement

1. Disconnect the lower end of the shock absorber from the spring plate.

2. Remove the three bolts retaining the shock absorber mounting bracket at the upper end of the shock. Station wagons have two stud nuts holding the top of the shock to the body.

3. Compress and remove the shock from the car.

4. Purge the new shock of air by repeatedly extending it in its normal position and compressing it while inverted. Transfer the mounting bracket to the new shock except on the station wagon.

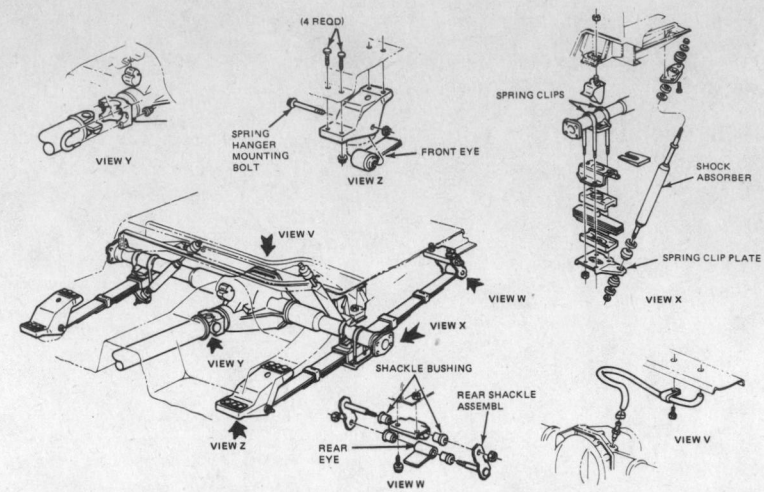

Mustang II rear suspension (© Ford Motor Co)

5. Position the shock absorber on the car and install the attaching parts.

Rear Spring Replacement

1. Disconnect the lower end of the shock absorber from the spring plate and position the shock out of the way.

2. Raise the vehicle on a hoist and place supports under the axle and the underbody.

3. Remove the spring plate attaching nuts from the U-bolts. Remove the spring plate.

4. Disconnect and remove the rear shackle from the spring.

5. Remove the front hanger bolt and nut from the eye of the spring. Remove the spring from the car.

6. Reverse above procedure to install.

BRAKES

The drum brake system incorporates single anchor, internal expanding and self adjusting brake assemblies. The brake hydraulic system employs a dual reservoir master cylinder, a control valve and a single cylinder, dual piston wheel cylinder mounted on each backing plate. Front disc brakes are available as an option on early Pintos, and standard on later models.

The parking brake is operated through a floor-mounted lever located between the front seats. Pulling the lever transmits force through a cable linkage to operate the rear drum brakes. A self-adjusting feature operates when there is excessive clearance between the brake shoes and drums.

Replacement, overhaul, and bleeding procedures are included in the "Unit Repair Section."

Master Cylinder Removal and Installation

Standard Brakes

1. Working under the dash, disconnect the stop light switch wires from the stop light switch and remove the switch and master cylinder pushrod from the brake pedal. Use care not to damage the stop light switch during removal.

2. Raise the hood and remove the brake lines from the master cylinder.

3. Remove the capscrews and lockwashers that attach the master cylinder to the firewall and remove the master cylinder.

4. Reverse above procedure to install, but, leave the brake lines loose on the master cylinder.

5. Fill the master cylinder with Extra Heavy Duty Brake Fluid.

6. Bleed the master cylinder by slowly depressing the foot pedal.

7. Refill master cylinder and bleed the front, then the rear, brakes. The rear of the cover is held by two screws on 1975 and later models.

Power Brakes

1. Disconnect the brake lines from the master cylinder.

2. Remove the nuts holding the master cylinder to the booster.

3. Remove the master cylinder. Reverse the procedure for installation. Bleed the system.

Vacuum Brake Booster Removal and Installation

1. From inside the car, remove the stoplight switch connector from the switch; remove the pin retainer and washer from the pedal pin and slide the stoplight switch far enough to clear the pin and remove the switch. Slide

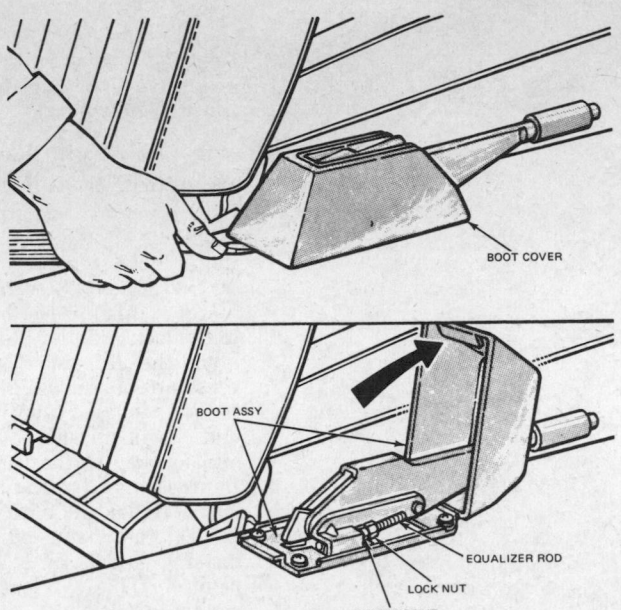

BOOT COVER

BOOT ASSY

EQUALIZER ROD

LOCK NUT

ADJUSTING NUT

Parking brake adjustment; starting 1975 the rear of the boot cover has two hold-down screws. (© Ford Motor Co)

the booster push rod, bushing and washer off the brake pin.

2. On four and six cylinder models, remove: air cleaner, accelerator cable (at carburetor), accelerator cable bracket, choke water inlet hose (at thermostat), and vacuum hose from EGR valve.

3. Disconnect the manifold vacuum hose from the booster.

4. Remove the primary and secondary brake lines from the outlet ports on the master cylinder. Cap the lines and the master cylinder ports.

5. Remove the master cylinder retaining nuts and remove the master cylinder.

6. From inside the car, remove the booster to firewall retaining nuts. From the engine side, pull the booster until the pushrod clears the firewall, rotate the booster ninety degrees, and pull up until it comes clear.

7. To install, put the booster in position with the check valve on the upper right side. Replace the booster pushrod assembly on the brake pedal pin; secure the booster to the firewall and tighten the bolts.

8. Place the stoplight switch on the booster push rod with the slot toward the pedal and the hole just clearing the pin. Be careful not to damage the switch. Install the retaining washer and pin and connect the wiring connector.

9. Reconnect the manifold vacuum hose to the booster unit.

10. Reattach the master cylinder assembly, reconnect the items removed in Step 2 and bleed the brakes.

Parking Brake Adjustment

1. Fully release the parking brake.
2. Place the transmission in Neutral and raise the rear axle until the rear wheels clear the floor. The weight of the car must be on the springs.
3. Pry the handle cover up inside the car. The rear of the cover is held by two screws on 1975 and later models. Tighten the adjusting nut until the rear brakes drag when the rear wheels are turned.
4. Loosen the adjusting nut until the rear wheels can be turned without the rear brakes dragging.
5. Lower the rear of the vehicle and check the operation of the parking brake.

STEERING

The steering gear is of the rack and pinion type. The gear input shaft is connected to the steering shaft by a flexible coupling. A pinion gear, machined on the input shaft, engages the rack and rotation of the input shaft pinion causes the rack to move laterally.

The tie-rod is attached at each end of the rack joint. This allows the tie-rods to move with the front suspension. The gear is sealed at each end with rubber bellows. The steering gear is filled with approximately 5-8 oz. of SAE-90 E.P. type oil at initial assembly and checking or refilling is not required unless fluid leakage is evident or repairs become necessary.

Couplings attaching the tie-rods are retained on the rack, are pinned and cannot be disassembled in ser-

vice. Replacement of inner tie-rods, rack, housing, or upper pinion bearing requires installation of a new steering gear assembly.

Integral power rack and pinion steering is a hydraulic-mechanical unit, which uses an integral piston and rack design. Internal valving directs the flow of fluid from the pump and controls the pressure, as required. The unit contains a rotary hydraulic fluid control valve integrated to the input shaft of the steering gear and a boost cylinder integrated with the rack. See the Power Steering Unit Repair Section for details.

Caution When the front wheels of the vehicle are suspended completely off the ground, do not turn the wheels quickly or forcefully from lock to lock. This could cause a build-up of hydraulic pressure within the steering gear which could damage or blow out the bellows.

Power Steering Pump Removal and Installation

1. Disconnect the fluid return hose at the reservoir, and drain the fluid from the pump.
2. Disconnect the pressure hose from the pump.
3. Remove the bolts or nuts from the pump attaching it to the mounting bracket. Disconnect the belt from the pulley and remove the pump.
4. Install the pump in the reverse order of removal.
5. Fill the reservoir with fluid.
6. Turn the steering wheel from stop-to-stop several times. Do not hold the steering wheel in the far left or right position.
7. Recheck the fluid level and add fluid as necessary.
8. Start the engine and allow it to run for several minutes.
9. Stop the engine and recheck the fluid level in the reservoir; add fluid, as necessary.

Steering Wheel Removal and Installation

1. Disconnect the battery ground cable.
2. On models with a small horn button, remove the horn button by pushing down and turning it counterclockwise.
3. On deluxe steering wheels, remove the pad by removing the two screws from behind the steering wheel. Disconnect the horn wires from the pad.
4. Remove the steering wheel attaching nut and, using a puller, remove the steering wheel.
5. Align the mark on the hub with the mark on the shaft and install the wheel on the shaft.
6. Install the attaching nut and tighten it to 30-40 ft lbs.
7. Install the horn button or pad.

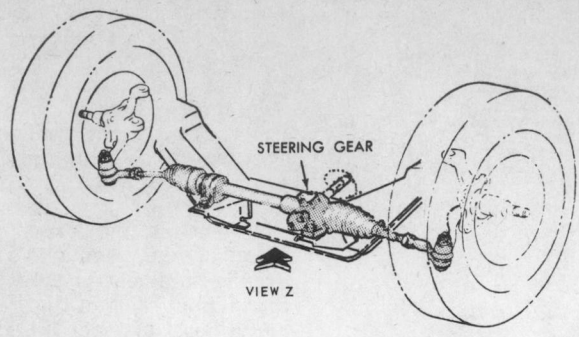

STEERING GEAR

VIEW Z

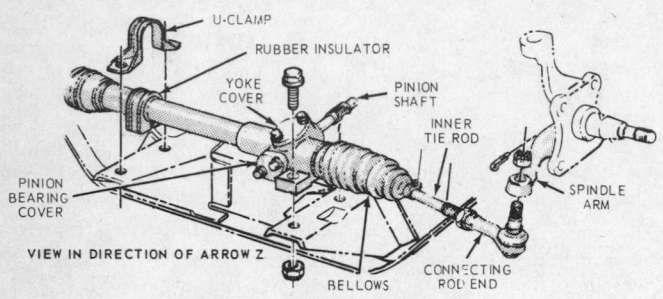

U-CLAMP
RUBBER INSULATOR
YOKE COVER
PINION SHAFT
INNER TIE ROD
PINION BEARING COVER
SPINDLE ARM
VIEW IN DIRECTION OF ARROW Z
BELLOWS
CONNECTING ROD END

Rack and pinion steering
(© Ford Motor Co)

Turn Signal and Flasher Switch Removal and Installation

1. Remove the steering wheel as previously outlined.
2. Remove the turn signal lever by unscrewing it from the steering column.
3. Remove the lower steering column shroud.
4. Disconnect the steering column wiring connectors from the steering column by lifting up on the tabs and removing the connectors from the brackets.
6. Remove the three screws that attach the head of the switch to the top of the steering column.
7. Pull the switch and wire assembly up and out of the steering column. A thin wire attached to the connector will make it easy to pull it down through the column on installation.
8. With speed control, transfer the ground brush to the new switch. To install the switch, position it and the wires in the steering column and work the wires down the steering column.
9. Secure the wires and connectors to the base of the steering column.
10. Connect the wire connectors at the base of the column.
11. Install the switch head attaching screws.
12. Install the turn signal lever and steering wheel.

Ignition Switch

Removal

1. To gain access to the switch,

remove the steering column shroud and disconnect and lower the steering column from the brake support bracket.
2. Disconnect the negative battery cable.
3. Disconnect the switch wiring at the multiple connector.
4. Remove the two nuts that retain the ignition switch to the steering column.
5. Remove the pin that connects the switch plunger to the actuating rod and remove the switch.

Installation

1. When installing the ignition switch, both the switch and the ignition lock must be in the LOCK position. The parts can be held in place by turning the ignition lock cylinder to the LOCK position with the transmission in Park (automatic transmission) or reverse (standard transmission). To hold the switch in the Lock position, insert a pin in the hole on the top of the switch, after manually moving the switch to the lock position. New switches are already pinned in Lock.
2. Position the hole in the end of the switch plunger to the hole in the actuator and install the connecting pin.
3. Position the ignition switch on the steering column, and install, but do not tighten the retaining nuts.
1. Move the switch up and down on the steering column to find the mid-point of the actuating rod

lash, then tighten the switch retaining nuts.
5. Remove the locking pin from the switch and install the steering column and shroud.

Ignition Lock Cylinder Removal and Installation

1. Disconnect the negative battery cable.
2. Remove the steering wheel as described under "Steering." Insert a stiff wire into the hole located in the lock cylinder housing.
3. Place the gearshift lever in Reverse on standard shift cars and in Park on cars with an automatic transmission, and turn the ignition key to the Run position.
4. Depress the wire and remove the lock cylinder and wire.
5. Insert the new cylinder into housing and turn it to the Off position. This will lock the cylinder into position.
6. Reinstall the steering wheel and pad.
7. Connect the negative battery cable.

INSTRUMENT PANEL

Headlight Switch Removal and Installation

Pinto and Bobcat

1. Disconnect the battery ground cable.
2. Remove the instrument cluster. There are two retaining screws at the top.
3. Remove the headlight switch control knob, shaft and retaining nut.
4. Disconnect the multiple connector from the switch and remove the switch from instrument cluster opening.
5. Reverse above procedure to install.

Mustang II

1. Disconnect the battery ground cable.
2. Through the hole in the underside of the instrument panel, press the release button with a screwdriver, and remove the knob and shaft assembly.
3. Remove the bezel nut, lower the switch and disconnect the multiple connector.
4. Remove the switch.
5. Install the headlight switch in the reverse order of removal.

WINDSHIELD WIPERS

Motor Removal and Installation

1. Loosen the two nuts and disconnect the wiper pivot shaft and link assembly from the motor drive arm ball. A link retaining clip is used on the Mustang II.
2. Remove the three motor attaching screws and lower the motor away from the left side of the instrument panel.
3. Disconnect the wiper motor wires and remove the motor.
4. To install, position the motor and install the wires. Operate the motor to ensure it is in Park position.
5. Position the motor and install the retaining screws.
6. Position the wiper pivot shaft and link assembly to the motor drive arm ball and tighten the two nuts. On the Mustang II, install the retaining clip.

RADIO

Removal and Installation

1. Disconnect the negative battery cable from the battery.
2. Remove the control knobs, discs, control shaft nuts and washers on Mustang II. Remove the panel trim brace cover on Pinto or Bobcat.
3. On the Mustang II, pull the ash tray out to expose the lower mounting bolt. Remove the bolt.
4. Remove the radio rear support attaching nut or bolt.
5. On Pinto or Bobcat, remove the four screws attaching the bezel to the instrument panel opening.
6. Remove the radio from the instrument panel; out through the front on Pinto, or Bobcat, or down from behind the instrument panel on Mustang II.
7. Disconnect the electrical lead, antenna lead, and speaker leads from the radio and remove the radio from the vehicle.
8. Install the radio in the reverse order of removal.

HEATER

Heater Assembly Removal and Installation, Non-Air Conditioned Cars

1. Drain the cooling system and disconnect the negative battery cable.
2. Disconnect the blower motor ground wire (black) at the engine side of the firewall.
3. Disconnect the heater hoses at the engine block.
4. Remove the four nuts that attach the heater assembly to the firewall, from the engine side.
5. Working inside the car, remove the glove box.
6. Disconnect the control cables from the heater. Disconnect the motor lead. Remove the radio.
7. Remove the snap-rivet that attaches the forward side of the defroster air duct to the heater assembly. Move the air duct back into the defroster nozzle and disengage it from the tabs on the heater box. Tilt the forward edge of the duct up and forward to disengage it from the nozzle, and remove it from the left side of the heater assembly.
8. Remove the heater assembly to instrument panel support bracket mounting screw and remove the heater assembly. At the same time, pull the heater hoses through the firewall. Then, disconnect the hoses from the heater core in the case.
9. Install in the reverse order of removal.

Blower Motor Removal and Installation, Non-Air Conditioned Cars

1. Remove the heater assembly.

2. Disconnect the blower motor lead wire from the resistor.
3. Remove the four blower motor mounting plate attaching nuts and remove the motor and wheel.
4. Install in the reverse order.

Heater Core Removal and Installation, Non-Air Conditioned Cars

1. Remove the heater assembly.
2. Remove the compression gasket from the cowl air inlet and remove the eleven clips from the case. Separate the case and remove the heater core.
3. Install in the reverse order.

Heater Assembly Removal and Installation, Air Conditioned Cars

1971-72 Pinto

NOTE: This procedure requires evacuation of the air conditioning refrigerant. Failure to exercise proper safety precautions could cause personal injury.

1. Disconnect the negative battery cable and drain the cooling system.
2. Evacuate the air conditioning system.
3. Disconnect the heater hose from the heater housing.
4. Remove the expansion valve from the evaporator core and tape the openings on the core closed.
5. Disconnect the green and brown vacuum hoses from the hot water valve and remove the two screws that attach the hot water valve and vacuum motor to the firewall.
6. Remove the three heater housing attaching nuts from the engine side of the firewall.
7. Remove the glove box door and the glove box. On models equipped with a console, remove the console.
8. Remove the radio and the kick panel from under the right side of the instrument panel.
9. Remove the three bolts that attach the right pillar brace to the lower edge of the instrument panel.
10. Disconnect the temperature control cable from the heater housing, and the purple and green vacuum hoses from the water valve vacuum switch on the heater housing.
11. Disconnect the white hose from the vacuum motor and the electrical leads from the blower motor resistor.
12. Disconnect the blower motor ground wire from the cowl and the red and yellow vacuum hoses from the vacuum motor above

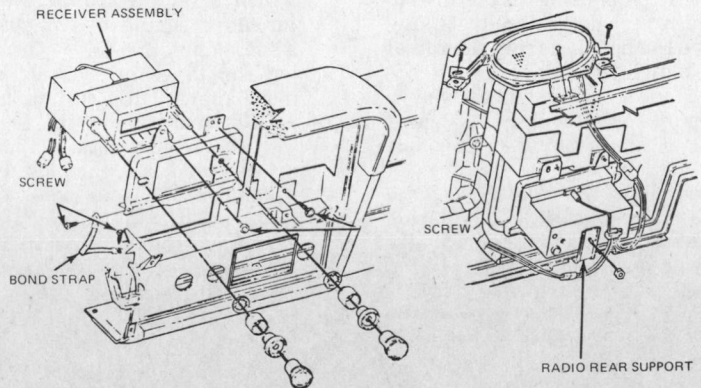

RECEIVER ASSEMBLY

SCREW

BOND STRAP

SCREW

RADIO REAR SUPPORT

Radio installation Mustang II (© Ford Motor Co.)

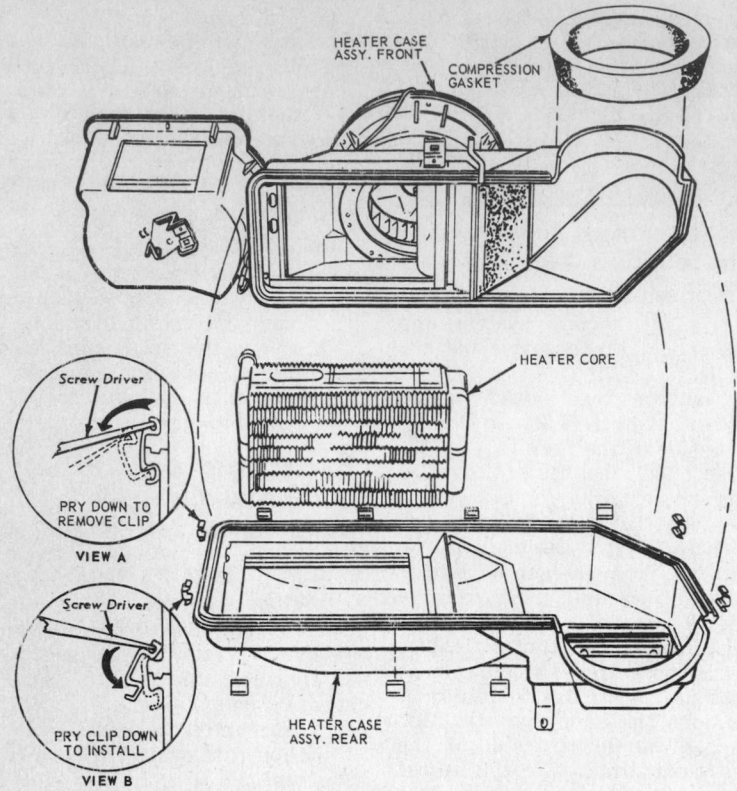

Heater core removal—non-air conditioned models
(© Ford Motor Co)

VIEW A

Screw Driver

PRY DOWN TO
REMOVE CLIP

VIEW B

Screw Driver

PRY CLIP DOWN
TO INSTALL

the heater blower motor.

13. Remove the cover plate from the bottom of the defroster duct that runs out of the blower motor.

14. Remove the two screws that attach the air distribution duct to the blower motor and remove the duct.

15. Reach through the opening left by the removal of the air distribution duct and remove the nut and lock plate that attaches the blower housing to the heater housing.

16. Turn the blower housing counterclockwise to disconnect it from the heater housing. Position the blower housing out of the way on the transmission tunnel.

17. Remove the drain hose from the heater housing and remove the screw that attaches the right side of the heater housing to the cowl upper support.

18. Remove the heater housing from under the instrument panel.

19. Reverse the above procedure to install the heater housing. After installation, charge the refrigerant system.

1973 Pinto

NOTE: This procedure requires evacuation of the air conditioning refrigerant. Failure to exercise proper safety precautions could cause personal injury.

1. Disconnect the negative battery cable and drain the cooling system.

2. Evacuate the air conditioning system.

3. Disconnect the heater hoses from the heater core tubes.

4. Disconnect the expansion valve from the evaporator core tubes and plug the openings in the core tubes.

5. Remove the three nuts that attach the heater assembly to the firewall.

6. Remove the glove box and disconnect the right and left air ducts from the heater housing.

7. Disconnect the blue vacuum hose from the A/C-defroster distribution housing. Open the access door in the bottom of the housing and remove the two screws that attach the housing to the instrument panel defroster ducts. Remove the housing from the top of the blower motor housing.

8. Disconnect the red and the yellow vacuum hoses from the A/C-heat door vacuum motor (upper left side of housing).

9. Disconnect the white vacuum hose from outside recirculation door vacuum motor (upper right side of housing).

10. Disconnect the multiple vacuum connector from the rear of the A/C-heater control on the instrument panel.

11. Disconnect the control cable from the temperature control

door crank arm.

12. Disconnect the purple and the green vacuum hoses from the water valve switch. The water valve switch is located on the heater housing just above the temperature door crank arm.

13. Remove the bracket that attaches the heater housing to the underside of the instrument panel.

14. Move the heater assembly rearward until it clears its mounting studs, then detach the vacuum hoses that are taped or clipped to the top of the housing.

15. Tag and disconnect the wiring that attaches to the heater housing.

16. Remove the heater housing from the car.

17. Reverse the above procedure to install the heater housing. Charge the refrigerant system.

1974 Mustang II, 1974 and later Pinto and Bobcat

NOTE: This procedure requires evacuation of the air conditioning refrigerant. Failure to exercise proper safety precautions could cause personal injury.

1. Drain the engine coolant, discharge the air conditioning system and disconnect the battery.

2. Remove the A/C refrigerant lines and the front half of the refrigerant manifold.

3. Remove the manifold mounting stud to provide clearance when removing the evaporator case assembly.

4. Disconnect the two heater hoses from the core tubes in the engine compartment.

5. Remove the A/C condensate drain hose in the engine compartment.

6. Remove the glove box.

7. Disconnect the vacuum hoses from the evaporator case.

8. Disconnect the temperature control cable from the blend door crank arm.

9. Remove the heat distribution duct. On the Mustang II, remove the mode door vacuum motor which is retained to the evaporator case assembly by two nuts and a spring nut.

10. On the Pinto or Bobcat, to remove the A/C defrost plenum:

   a. Cut and remove the two staples which retain the fold down door in the closed position on the plenum.

   b. Bend the fold down door away from the locating tabs on each side of the plenum to allow removal of the adaptor duct.

   c. Remove the adapter duct.

On the Mustang II, remove the lower section of the A/C defrost plenum which is retained by 3 screws and two retaining tabs.

11. Remove the blower motor and wheel from the blower scroll.
12. Install one 1/4-20 hex-washer head screw to the mounting tab on the inlet duct to upper cowl bracket to hold the duct in place. Leave this screw in place when installing the case assembly.
13. Remove the three inlet duct-to-evaporator case attaching screws through the blower scroll opening.
14. Remove the one upper case-to-inlet duct attaching screw located under the outside-recirculating motor mounting bracket.
15. Remove the two evaporator-to-upper cowl bracket attaching screws.
16. Remove the four evaporator-to-dash panel attaching nuts in the engine compartment.
17. Rotate the evaporator assembly down and away from the dash panel and out from under the instrument panel.
18. Install the heater/evaporator case in the reverse order of removal. During installation, position the fold down door of the defrost plenum between the locating tabs on each side of the plenum and tape it in position with two pieces of black tape 1 in. wide by 4 in. long.

1975 and Later Mustang II

NOTE: This procedure requires evacuation of the air conditioning system. This should not be attempted by untrained persons; personal injury may result. This is also a major disassembly operation.

1. Remove the battery, drain the coolant, and discharge the air conditioner.
2. Remove the instrument panel pad, the radio speaker, both A-pillar moldings, both side kick panel assemblies, and the lower steering column cover.
3. Remove the steering column to cowl panel brace.
4. Remove the accelerator pedal. Disconnect the heater control cables.
5. Remove the bottom bolt holding the center brace to the instrument panel.
6. Disconnect the radio antenna lead. Detach the five connectors at the left cowl panel. Unplug the dimmer switch. Disconnect the blower motor resistor.
7. Disconnect the temperature control cable. Remove the two upper cowl bracket screws.
8. Detach the main wiring harness in the engine compartment. Push the harness into the passenger compartment. Do the same with the last three connectors.

9. Disconnect the turn signal switch. Remove the four steering column nuts, unplug the ignition switch, unplug the stoplight switch, and remove the column center support bracket.
10. Remove the four retaining bolts and the instrument panel.
11. Detach the heater hoses from the core tubes. Disconnect the two lines at the evaporator manifold assembly. Remove the manifold from the bracket. Remove the outer manifold.
12. Remove the nuts and remove the assembly from the firewall.
13. Installation is carried out in the reverse order of removal. Fill the cooling system and charge the air conditioner.

Blower Motor Removal and Installation, Air Conditioned Cars

1971-72

1. Disconnect the negative battery cable. If equipped with a console, remove the console from the car.
2. Remove the radio.
3. Remove the fuse panel attaching screw, disconnect the multiple connector from the fuse panel and remove the fuse panel from the fuse panel support bracket which is attached to the brake pedal support bracket.
4. Remove the fuse panel support bracket from the brake pedal support bracket and position it out of the way.
5. Remove the instrument panel-to-cowl brace and position the fuse panel on the lower edge of the instrument panel.
6. Disconnect the lead wires from the blower motor resistor and the blower motor ground wire from the cowl.
7. Remove the red and yellow vacuum hoses from the vacuum motor over the blower motor.
8. Remove the cover plate from the bottom of the defroster outlet duct of the blower motor.
9. Remove the two screws that attach the air distribution duct to the blower motor housing.
10. Reach through the opening left by the removal of the air distribution duct and remove the nut and lock plate that attaches the blower motor housing to the heater housing.
11. Turn the blower motor counterclockwise to disconnect it from the heater housing and position the blower motor on the transmission tunnel.
12. Remove the steering column-to-instrument panel brace. It may be necessary to move the blower housing slightly rearward to gain access to the upper brace

attaching bolt.
13. Cut the blower housing-to-heater housing gasket at the break in the two blower housing pieces.
14. Disconnect the A/C-heat door rod from the A/C-heat door.
15. Remove the seven clips and separate the two halves of the blower housing.
16. Remove the left half of the blower housing with the blower motor attached.
17. Remove the three blower motor mounting nuts and remove the blower motor and wheel.
18. Reverse the above procedure to install the blower motor.

1973

1. Disconnect the negative battery cable.
2. Remove the two screws that attach the hot air distribution duct to the bottom of the blower housing and remove the duct.
3. Open the access door in the bottom of the A/C-defroster distribution housing and remove the two screws that attach the distribution housing to the instrument panel defroster ducts.
4. Working through the opening left by removal of the bottom heat distribution duct, remove the nut and lock plate that attaches the blower housing to the heater housing.
5. Turn the blower motor housing clockwise to disengage the two locking tabs on the blower housing from the pin on the heater housing.
6. Remove the blower housing from the car.
7. Cut the blower outlet gasket at the blower housing seams.
8. Remove the clips that secure the two halves of the blower housing, and separate the housing.
9. Remove the three blower motor attaching nuts and the motor.

1974 and Later

The blower motor and wheel is integrally located within the scroll portion of the evaporator assembly on the right-side of the evaporator case. To remove the blower motor and wheel, remove the glove box and remove the four screws retaining the blower motor and wheel in the blower scroll. Install the blower motor and wheel in the reverse order of removal.

Heater Core Removal and Installation, Air Conditioned Cars

1971-73

1. Remove the heater housing and remove the rubber seal from the housing.
2. Remove the eleven clips that hold

the two halves of the heater housing together and separate the housing.

3. Remove the A/C thermostatic de-icing switch from the top of the housing.

4. Remove four screws and remove the evaporator core from the upper housing.

5. Remove four screws and the temperature blend door upper frame.

6. Remove the spring clip and crank arm and remove the temperature blend door from the housing.

7. Remove four screws and the temperature blend door lower frame.

8. Remove the heater core and gasket from the lower housing.

1974 and Later

1. Remove the evaporator case assembly from the vehicle.

2. Remove the eight upper-to-lower case attaching screws.

3. Remove the rubber seal from the heater core tubes.

4. Remove the upper half of the evaporator case.

5. Move the rubber seal on the evaporator core forward to clear the case mounting stud and pull the core out of the lower case.

6. Install in the reverse order of removal. Be sure to install new rope sealer around the flange of

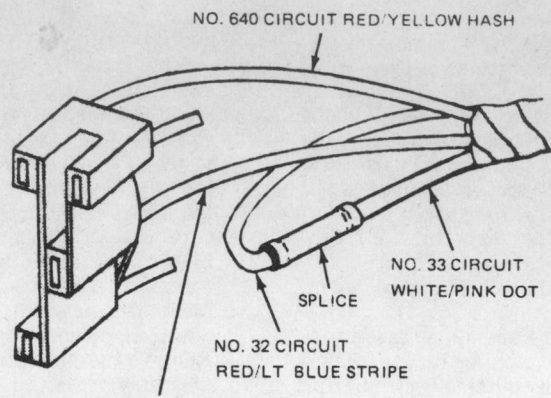

Seatbelt interlock override switch terminal connector and wires (© Ford Motor Co.)

the lower case before installing the upper half of the case. Install new O-rings on the manifold plate. Dip the new O-rings in refrigerant oil before installing them.

SEAT BELTS

Disabling the Interlock System

New automobiles are no longer required to have the interlock system. The system may legally be disabled on cars that do have it, but the following procedure must be used.

1. Locate the override switch and terminal connector attached to it.

2. Remove the no. 32 (red with a light blue stripe) wire(s) and no. 33 (white with pink dots), wire(s) and splice them together.

3. To remove the buzzer, remove the terminal connector from the buzzer, and tape it to the wiring harness to prevent rattling; then remove the buzzer unit.

4. To remove the warning light, remove the bulb from its socket, and replace the empty socket.

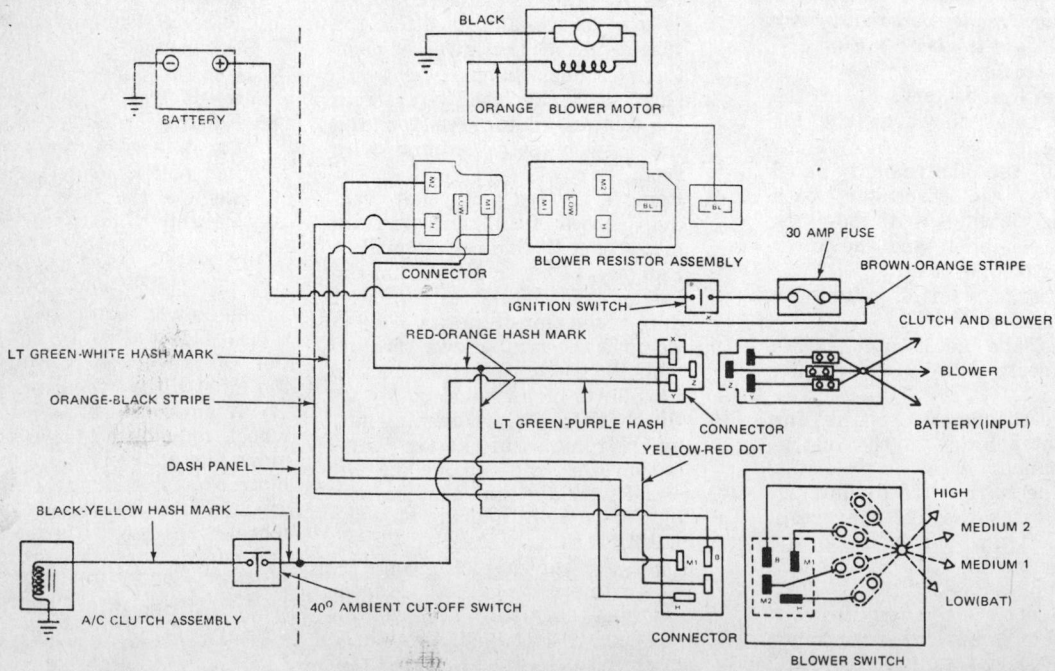

Air Conditioning Electrical Circuit

(© Ford Motor Co.)

Buick

Automatic Transmission
In-car service **C207, U355**
Detent switch adjustment C208
Identification C207
Neutral start switch adjustment C207
Pan Removal and Installation,
fluid and filter change C208
Shift linkage adjustment C208

Brakes **C213, U299**
Master cylinder Removal and
Installation C213
Parking brake adjustment C213
Power brake unit Removal and
Installation C213

Charging System **C198, U2**
Alternator Removal and Installation   C198
Voltage regulator Removal and
Installation C198

Clutch **C206**
Clutch pedal adjustment C207
Clutch assembly Removal and
Installation C206

Cooling System **C201**
Radiator core Removal and Installation C201
Thermostat Removal C201
Water pump Removal C201

Emission Controls **C201, U145**

Engine **C202, U194**
Engine Removal and Installation C202
CONNECTING RODS, RINGS, AND PISTONS C205
CYLINDER HEAD Removal and Installation C203
LUBRICATION C205
Oil pan Removal and Installation C205
Oil pump Removal and Installation C205
Rear main bearing oil seal replacement C206
MANIFOLDS C203
Exhaust manifold Removal and
Installation C203
Intake manifold Removal and
Installation C203
TIMING CASE COVER, TIMING CHAIN
AND CAMSHAFT C204
Camshaft Removal and Installation C205

Timing chain and front oil seal
replacement C204
Virbration damper Removal and
Installation C204
VALVE SYSTEM C203
Rocker arm Removal and Installation C203
Valve adjustment C203
Valve guide replacement C203

Front Suspension **C210, U292**
Ball joint inspection C211
Control arm, ball joint, and and spring
Removal and Installation C211
Shock absorber Removal and
Installation C211
Wheel bearing adjustment C212

Fuel System **C200, U50**
Fuel filter replace C200
Fuel pump Removal and Installation ..C200
Idle speed and mixture adjustment ..C200

Heater **C217**
Blower motor Removal and Installation
with A/C C217
Blower motor Removal and Installation
without A/C C217
Blower and heater core assembly
Removal and Installation without A/C C217
Heater core Removal and Installation
with A/C C218
Heater core Removal and Installation
without A/C C217

Ignition System **C198, U34**
Contact point replacement and
adjustment C199
Distributor Removal and Installation ...C198
Firing order C193
Ignition timing C199
Solid state ignition C199

Instrument Panel **C216, U350, U368**
Light switch replacement C216

Manual Transmission **C207, U231**
Shift linkage adjustment C207
Transmission Removal and Installation C207

Jacking, Hoisting **C210**

Radio **C216**
Radio Removal and Installation C216

Rear Axle **C210**
Axle/shaft, bearing, and seal,
Removal and Installation C210

Rear Suspension **C212**
Coil spring Removal and Installation C212
Leaf spring Removal and Installation C212
Shock absorber Removal and
Installation C212

Seat Belts **C218**
Disabling the interlock system C218

Specifications
Capacities C195
Crankshaft and connecting rod C195
Engine identification and code C193
General engine C194
Piston clearance C197
Ring C197
Serial number location C193
Torque C197
Tune-up C195
Valve C196
Wheel alignment C198
Year identification C192

Starting Systems **C198, U2**
Starter Removal and Installation C198
Starter drive C198

Steering **C213, U328, U336**
Ignition switch/lock cylinder
Removal and Installation C214
Power steering pump Removal and
Installation C213
Steering wheel Removal and
Installation C214
Turn signal switch Removal and
Installation C214

U-Joints **C209**
Driveshaft disassembly C210
Driveshaft Removal and Installation ..C209

Windshield Wipers **C216**
Motor Removal and Installation C216

YEAR IDENTIFICATION

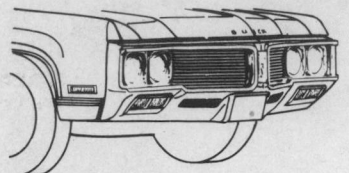

1970 Le Sabre

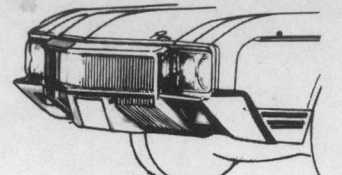

1970 Riviera

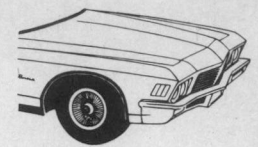

1971 Riviera

1971 Le Sabre

1971 Electra

1971 Centurion

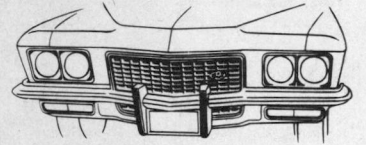

1972 Riviera

1972 Electra

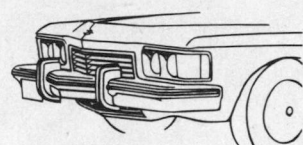

1973 Riviera

1973 Buick

1974 Riviera

1974 Electra

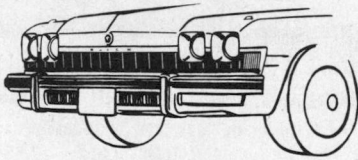

1974 Le Sabre

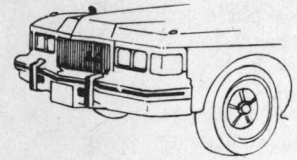

1975 Riviera

1975 Electra

1975 LeSabre

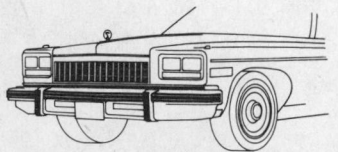

1976 Electra

1976 Electra Limited

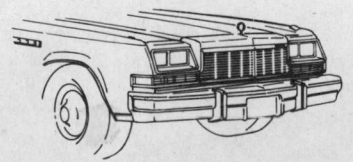

1977 LeSabre

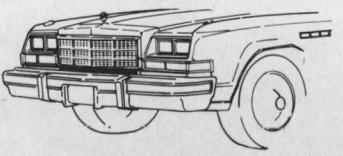

1977 Electra

FIRING ORDER

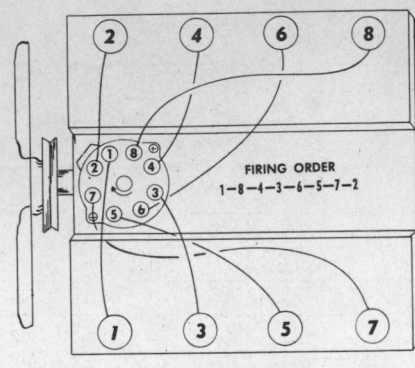

FIRING ORDER
1—8—4—3—6—5—7—2

350, 455 cu in.

CAR SERIAL NUMBER LOCATION AND ENGINE IDENTIFICATION

The car serial number is used for registration and other legal records. This number is unique to the individual car. The production code number identifies the type of engine and its production date. The Engine Production Code chart can be used to determine the type of engine in the particular vehicle. The engine number also appears on the vehicle identification plate following model and series identification.

1970-71

The serial number identification plate is attached to the top of the instrument panel on the left side.

On the 350 cu. in. engine, the serial number is on the front of the left cylinder bank just below the cylinder head. The production code number is between the left exhaust manifold and the two front spark plugs on the left bank.

On the 455 cu. in. engine, the serial number is between the two front spark plugs and the exhaust manifold on the left side. The production code number is between the two rear spark plugs and the exhaust manifold, also on the left side.

1972 and later

The car serial number identification plate is attached to the top of the instrument panel on the left-side.

On the V6 engine, the engine serial number is just below the front of the left cylinder head. The production code number is between the front and middle branches of the right exhaust manifold.

ENGINE PRODUCTION CODE

Disp	Bbl	Hp ■	'70	'71	'72	'73	'74	'75	'76
6-Cylinder Models									
231	2	105							
8-Cylinder Models									
350	2	150, 165#				XC	XC	AB	
350	2	155			WC				
350	4	155							PT PU PK PL PR PS
350	4	160, 165						AM	
350	4	175, 195#				XB	XB		
350	4	180			WB				
350	2	230		TC TO					
350	2	260	SO						
350	4	260		TB TD					
350	4	285	SB						
350	4	315	SP						
455	4	205					AF	SA SB	
455	4	225, 210, 230#	RD		WF	XF XF			
455	4	260 (net)			WA	XA			
Stage 1									
455	4	245					XA		
455	4	315		TR					
455	4	330		TA					
455	4	350	SR						
455	4	370	SF						

\# Dual exhaust

■ Beginning 1972, horsepower and torque are SAE net figures. They are measured at the rear of the transmission with all accessories installed and operating. Since the figures vary when a given engine is installed in different models, some are representative rather than exact.

On the 350 cu. in. engine, the engine serial number is on the front of the right cylinder bank. The production code number is between the left exhaust manifold and the two front spark plugs.

On the 455 cu. in. engine, the engine serial number is on the front of the right cylinder bank. The production code number is between the left exhaust manifold and the two rear spark plugs.

GENERAL ENGINE SPECIFICATIONS

Year	Engine No. Cyl. Displacement (cu. in.)	Carburetor Type	Horsepower @ rpm ■	Torque @ rpm (ft lbs) ■	Bore x Stroke (in.)	Compression Ratio	Oil Pressure @ 2000 rpm (psi)
'70	8-350	2 bbl	260 @ 4600	360 @ 2600	3.800 x 3.850	9.0:1	37
	8-350	4 bbl	285 @ 4600	375 @ 3200	3.800 x 3.850	10.25:1	37
	8-350	4 bbl	315 @ 4800	410 @ 3200	3.800 x 3.850	10.25:1	37
	8-455	4 bbl	370 @ 4600	510 @ 2800	4.3125 x 3.900	10.0:1	40
'71	8-350	2 bbl	230 @ 4400	350 @ 2400	3.800 x 3.850	8.5:1	37
	8-350	4 bbl	260 @ 4600	360 @ 3000	3.800 x 3.850	8.5:1	37
	8-455	4 bbl	315 @ 4400	450 @ 2800	4.3125 x 3.900	8.5:1	40
	8-455	4 bbl	330 @ 4600	455 @ 2800	4.3125 x 3.900	8.5:1	40
'72	8-350	2 bbl	155 @ 3800	270 @ 2400	3.800 x 3.850	8.5:1	37
	8-350 Calif.	2 bbl	150 @ 3800	265 @ 2400	3.800 x 3.850	8.5:1	37
	8-350	4 bbl	180 @ 3800	275 @ 2400	3.800 x 3.850	8.5:1	37
	8-350 Calif.	4 bbl	175 @ 3800	270 @ 2400	3.800 x 3.850	8.5:1	37
	8-455	4 bbl	225 @ 4000	360 @ 2600	4.3125 x 3.900	8.5:1	40
	8-455 DE	4 bbl	250 @ 4000	375 @ 2800	4.3125 x 3.900	8.5:1	40
	8-455	4 bbl	260 @ 4400	380 @ 2800	4.3125 x 3.900	8.5:1	40
'73	8-350	2 bbl	150 @ 3800	265 @ 2400	3.800 x 3.850	8.5:1	37
	8-350	4 bbl	175 @ 3800	270 @ 2400	3.800 x 3.850	8.5:1	37
	8-455	4 bbl	225 @ 4000	360 @ 2600	4.3125 x 3.900	8.5:1	37
	8-455 DE	4 bbl	250 @ 4000	375 @ 2800	4.3125 x 3.900	8.5:1	37
	8-455	4 bbl	260 @ 4400	380 @ 2800	4.3125 x 3.900	8.5:1	37
'74	8-350 SE	2 bbl	150 @ 3600	270 @ 2000	3.800 x 3.850	8.5:1	37
	8-350 DE	2 bbl	165 @ 3800	285 @ 2000	3.800 x 3.850	8.5:1	37
	8-350 SE	4 bbl	175 @ 3800	260 @ 2000	3.800 x 3.850	8.5:1	37
	8-350 DE	4 bbl	195 @ 4000	280 @ 2000	3.800 x 3.850	8.5:1	37
	8-455 SE	2 bbl	175 @ 3400	355 @ 2000	4.3125 x 3.900	8.5:1	37
	8-455 DE	2 bbl	190 @ 3600	370 @ 2000	4.3125 x 3.900	8.5:1	37
	8-455 SE	4 bbl	210 @ 3600	335 @ 2200	4.3125 x 3.900	8.5:1	37
	8-455 DE	4 bbl	230 @ 3800	355 @ 2200	4.3125 x 3.900	8.5:1	37
	8-455 DE Stage I	4 bbl	245 @ 4000	360 @ 2400	4.3125 x 3.900	8.5:1	37
'75	8-350	4 bbl	165 @ 3800	260 @ 2200	3.800 x 3.850	8.0:1	37
	8-350 Calif.	4 bbl	160 @ 3800	260 @ 2200	3.800 x 3.850	8.0:1	37
	8-455	4 bbl	205 @ 3800	345 @ 2000	4.3125 x 3.900	7.9:1	40
'76-'77	6-231	2 bbl	105 @ 3400	185 @ 2000	3.800 x 3.400	8.0:1	37
	8-350	4 bbl	155 @ 3400	280 @ 1800	3.800 x 3.850	8.0:1	34
	8-455	4 bbl	205 @ 3800	345 @ 2000	4.3125 x 3.900	7.9:1	40

■ Beginning 1972, horsepower and torque are SAE net figures. They are measured at the rear of the transmission with all accessories installed and operating. Since the figures vary when a given engine is installed in different models, some are representative rather than exact.

SE Single Exhaust
DE Dual Exhaust

TUNE-UP SPECIFICATIONS

Year	ENGINE No. Cyl Displacement (cu in.)	hp	SPARK PLUGS Orig. Type	Gap (in.)	DISTRIBUTOR Point Dwell (deg)	DISTRIBUTOR Point Gap (in.)	IGNITION TIMING (deg) ▲ ● Man Trans	IGNITION TIMING Auto Trans	VALVES Intake Opens ■ (deg) ●	Fuel Pump Pressure (psi)	IDLE SPEED (rpm) ▲ ● Man Trans	IDLE SPEED Auto Trans
'70	8-350	260	R-45TS	.030	30	.016	6B	6B	24	4¼-5¾	700	600
	8-350	285	R-45TS	.030	30	.016	6B	6B	24	4¼-5¾	700	600
	8-350	315	R-45TS	.030	30	.016	6B	6B	24	4¼-5¾	700	600
	8-455	350	R-44TS	.030	30	.016	6B	6B	18	4¼-5¾	700	600
	8-455	370	R-44TS	.030	30	.016	6B	6B	18	4¼-5¾	700	600
'71	8-350	230	R-45TS	.030	30	.016	6B	10B①	24	4¼-5¾	1100/800②	600
	8-350	260	R-45TS	.030	30	.016	6B	4B	28	4¼-5¾	1100/800②	600
	8-455	315	R-45TS	.030	30	.016	6B	4B	12	4¼-5¾	1100/700②	600
	8-455	330	R-44TS	.030	30	.016	10B	10B	12	4¼-5¾	1100/700②	600
'72	8-350	155	R-45TS	.040	30	.016	4B	4B	24	4¼-5¾	800②/600	650②/500
	8-350	180	R-45TS	.040	30	.016	4B	4B	24	4¼-5¾	800②/600	650②/500
	8-455	225	R-45TS	.040	30	.016	4B	4B	12(14)	4¼-5¾	900②/600	650②/500
	8-455	250	R-45TS	.040	30	.016	4B	4B	12(14)	4¼-5¾	900②/600	650②/500
	8-455	260	R-45TS	.040	30	.016	4B	4B	12(14)	4¼-5¾	900②/600	650②/500
'73	8-350	150	R-45TS	.040	30	.016	—	4B	24	4¼-5¾	—	600/500②
	8-350	175	R-45TS	.040	30	.016	—	4B	24	4¼-5¾	—	600/500②
	8-455	225	R-45TS	.040	30	.016	—	4B	14	4¼-5¾	—	650/500②
	8-455	250	R-45TS	.040	30	.016	—	4B	14	4¼-5¾	—	650/500②
	8-455	260	R-45TS	.040	30	.016	—	4B	14	4¼-5¾	—	650/500②
'74	8-350	All⑤	R-45TS	.040	30	.016	—	4B	19(25)④	4¼-5¾	—	650/500②
	8-455	All⑤	R-45TS	.040	30	.016	—	4B	10④	4¼-5¾	—	650/500②
'75	8-350	165	R-45TSX	.060	Electronic		—	12B	19④	4¼-5¾	—	600
	8-455	205	R-45TSX	.060	Electronic		—	12B	10④	4¼-5¾	—	600
'76	V6-231	105	R-44SX	.060	Electronic		—	12B	17	4¼-5¾	—	600
	8-350	155	R-45TSX	.060	Electronic		—	12B	13.5	5-6½	—	600
	8-455	205	R-45TSX	.060	Electronic		—	12B	10	7½-9	—	600
'77	All					See Underhood Specifications Sticker						

▲ See text for procedure
■ All figures Before Top Dead Center
● Figure in Parentheses indicates California engine
① 4B for LeSabre
② Lower figure indicates idle speed with solenoid disconnected
③ Not used
④ These figures do not represent a change from 1973; however, the reference point is changed from .004 in. valve lift to .004 in. cam lift to be consistent with information required for government certification.

⑤ See underhood specifications sticker on engines with H.E.I. electronic ignition system.
B Before Top Dead Center
N.A. Not available
TDC Top Dead Center
— Not applicable

NOTE: The underhood specifications sticker often reflects tune-up specification changes made in production. Sticker figures must be used if they disagree with those in this chart.

CAPACITIES

Year	ENGINE No. Cyl. Displacement (cu. in.)	Engine Crankcase Add 1 Qt For New Filter	TRANSMISSION Pts To Refill After Draining Manual 3-Speed	4-Speed	Automatic ●	Drive Axle (pts)	Gasoline Tank (gals)	COOLING SYSTEM (qts) With Heater	With A/C
'70	8-350	4	3.5	——	6	3	25	16.2	16.6
	8-455	4	3.5	——	7	4.25	25①	19.7	20
	Riviera	4	——	——	7	4.25	21	19.7	20

CAPACITIES

Year	ENGINE No. Cyl. Displacement (cu. in.)	Engine Crankcase Add 1 Qt For New Filter	TRANSMISSION Pts To Refill After Draining Manual 3-Speed	4-Speed	Automatic •	Drive Axle (pts)	Gasoline Tank (gals)	COOLING SYSTEM (qts) With Heater	With A/C
'71	8-350	4	3.5	—	6	4.25	25	16.2	16.6
	8-455	4	3.5	—	7	5.5	25②	18.7	19
	Riviera	4	—	—	7	5.5	24	19.7	20
'72	8-350	4	—	—	6	4.25	25	19	19.3
	8-455	4	—	—	7	5.5	25②	18.7	19
	Riviera	4	—	—	7	5.5	24	18.7	19
'73	8-350	4	—	—	6	4.25	26	18.9	19.3
	8-455	4	—	—	7	5.4	26③	18.7	19④
'74	8-350	4	—	—	6	4.25	26	18.9	19.3
	8-455	4	—	—	7⑤	5.4	26③	18.7	19④
'75	8-350	4	—	—	6	4.25	26	16.9	17.2
	8-455	4	—	—	7⑤	5.4	26③	19.6	21.4
'76-'77	6-231	4	—	—	6	4.25	26	16.9	17.2
	8-350	4	—	—	6	4.25	26	16.9	17.2
	8-455	4	—	—	7	5.4	26③	19.7	20

• Specifications do not include torque converter
① Estate wagon—24 gals
② Estate wagon—23 gals
③ Estate wagon—22 gals
④ 20.2 with H.D. cooling
⑤ LeSabre 455—6 pts
— Not applicable

VALVE SPECIFICATIONS

Year	Engine No. Cyl. Displacement (cu in.)	Seat Angle (deg)	Face Angle (deg)	Spring Test Pressure (lbs @ in.)	Spring Installed Height (in.)	STEM TO GUIDE Clearance (in.) Intake	Exhaust	STEM Diameter (in.) Intake	Exhaust
'70	8-350	45	45	180 @ 1.34	1 23/32	.0015-.0025	.0015-.0032	.3725	.3725
	8-455	45	45	177 @ 1.45	1 29/32	.0015-.0035	.0015-.0032	.3725	.3725
'71	8-350	45	45	180 @ 1.34	1 23/32	.0015-.0035	.0015-.0032	.3725	.3725
	8-455	45	45	177 @ 1.45	1 29/32	.0015-.0035	.0015-.0032	.3725	.3727
'72	8-350	45	45	180 @ 1.34	1 23/32	.0015-.0035	.0015-.0032	.3725	.3727
	8-455	45	45	177 @ 1.45	1 29/32	.0015-.0035	.0015-.0032	.3725	.3727
'73	8-350	45	45	180 @ 1.34	1 23/32	.0015-.0035	.0015-.0032	.3725	.3730
	8-455	45	45	177 @ 1.45	1 29/32	.0015-.0035	.0015-.0032	.3725	.3730
'74	8-350	45	45	180 @ 1.34	1 23/32	.0015-.0035	.0015-.0032	.3725	.3730
	8-455	45	45	177 @ 1.45	1 29/32	.0015-.0035	.0015-.0032	.3725	.3730
'75-'77	6-231	45	45	164 @ 1.34	1 47/64	.0015-.0035	.0015-.0032	.3407	.3409
	8-350	45	45	180 @ 1.34①	1 47/64	.0015-.0035	.0015-.0032	.3725	.3727
	8-455	45	45	177 @ 1.45	1 57/64	.0015-.0035	.0015-.0032	.3725	.3727

① Exhaust—175 @ 1.34

TORQUE SPECIFICATIONS

All readings in ft lbs

Year	Engine Displacement (cu in.)	Cylinder Head Bolts	Rod Bearing Bolts	Main Bearing Bolts	Crankshaft Pulley or Balancer Bolt	Flywheel to Crankshaft Bolts	MANIFOLD Intake	Exhaust
'70-'72	350	75	35	95	120	60	55	18
	430, 455	100	35①	110	200	60	55②	18
'73	350	80	35③	115	140	60	55	18
	455	100	45	115	200	60	65	18
'74-'75	350	80	40	115	140	60	45	28
	455	100	45	115	200	60	45	28
'76-'77	231, 350	80	40	115	175	60	45	25
	455	100	45	115	225	60	45	25

① 1970 455 cu in.—45 ft. lbs.
② 1970-72 455 cu in.—65 ft. lbs.
③ 40 with cap screws

CRANKSHAFT AND CONNECTING ROD SPECIFICATIONS

All measurements are given in in.

Year	Engine Displacement (cu in.)	CRANKSHAFT Main Brg. Journal Dia	Main Brg. Oil Clearance	Shaft End-Play	Thrust on No.	CONNECTING ROD Journal Diameter	Oil Clearance	Side Clearance
'70-'72	350	2.9995	.0004-.0015	.003-.009	3	2.0000	.0002-.0023	.006-.014
	455	3.2500	.0007-.0018	.003-.009	3	2.2495	.0002-.0023	.005-.012
'73	350	2.9995	.0004-.0015	.003-.009	3	2.0000	.0002-.0023	.006-.020
	455	3.2500	.0007-.0018	.003-.009	3	2.2495	.0002-.0023	.005-.012
'74	350	3.0000	.0004-.0015	.003-.009	3	2.0000	.0002-.0023	.006-.020
	455	3.2500	.0007-.0018	.003-.009	3	2.2495	.0002-.0023	.005-.012
'75-'77	231	2.4995	.0004-.0015	.004-.008	2	1.9995	.0002-.0023	.006-.014
	350	2.9995	.0004-.0015	.002-.006	3	1.9995	.0005-.0026	.006-.026
	455	3.2500	.0007-.0018	.003-.009	3	2.2491	.0005-.0026	.005-.025

RING GAP

All measurements are given in inches

Year	Engine No. Cyl Displacement (cu in.)	Top Compression	Bottom Compression	Oil Control
'70	8-350	.010-.020	.010-.020	.015-.035
	8-455	.013-.023	.013-.023	.015-.055
'71-'72	8-350	.013-.023	.013-.023	.015-.035
	8-455	.013-.023	.013-.023	.015-.055
'73-'74	8-350	.010-.020	.010-.020	.015-.035
	8-455	.013-.023	.013-.023	.015-.055
'75-'77	6-231, 8-350	.013-.023	.013-.023	.015-.035
	8-455	.013-.023	.013-.023	.015-.035

PISTON CLEARANCE

Year	Engine No. Cyl. Displacement (cu. in.)	Piston to Bore Clearance (in.)
'70-'74	8-350	.0008-.0020
	8-455	.0010-.0016
'75-'77	6-231, 8-350	.0008-.0014
	8-455	.0010-.0016

RING SIDE CLEARANCE

All measurements are given in inches

Year	Engine	Top Compression	Bottom Compression	Oil Control
'70-'72	All	.003-.005	.003-.005	.0035-.0095
'73-'77	All	.003-.005	.003-.005	.0035 Maximum

WHEEL ALIGNMENT SPECIFICATIONS

Year	Model	CASTER Range (deg)	CASTER Pref Setting (deg)	CAMBER Range (deg)	CAMBER Pref Setting (deg)	Toe-in (in.)	Steering Axis Inclin. (deg)	WHEEL PIVOT RATIO (deg) Inner Wheel	WHEEL PIVOT RATIO (deg) Outer Wheel
'70	All exc. Riviera	¼P to 1¼P	¾P	½N to ½P	0	³⁄₁₆ to ⁵⁄₁₆	10.5	20	19½
	Riviera	½P to 1½P	1P	¼N to ¾P	¼P	⅛ to ¼	10.5	20	16¾
'71	All	½P to 1½P	1P	¼N to ¾P	¼P	⅛ to ¼	10.5	20	18½
'72	All	½P to 1½P	1P	0 to 1P	½P	⅛ to ¼	10.5	20	18½
'73	All	½P to 1½P	1P	¼N to ¾P	¼P	⅛ to ¼	10.5	20	18½
'74	All	½P to 1½P	1P	½P to 1½P LH 0 to 1P RH	1P LH ½P RH	0 to ⅛	10.5	20	18½
'75-'77	All	1P to 2P	1½P	½P to 1½P LH 0-1P RH	1P LH ½ RH	0 to ⅛	10.5	20	18½

N Negative P Positive
LH Left-hand side
RH Right-hand side

NOTE: All procedures concerning the 231 cu. in. V6 will be found in the Buick Apollo section.

CHARGING SYSTEM

Voltage Regulator Removal and Installation—1970

1. Disconnect the battery cables.
2. Disconnect the wiring from the voltage regulator.
3. Remove the screws holding the regulator to the firewall or front bulkhead depending on the car.
4. Reverse the removal procedures to install.

Voltage Regulator Removal and Installation 1971 and later

Starting 1971, all Buicks are equipped with a Delcotron 10 SI alternator with internal voltage regulator. The regulator requires no adjustment and is not servicable without overhauling the alternator.

Alternator Removal and Installation

Remove the bolt holding the tension bar to the alternator. On some models, it may be necessary to loosen and rotate the fan shroud to get at the pivot bolt. Push the alternator in toward the engine to release the drive belt. Remove the alternator mounting bolt to release the alternator from the engine.

When reinstalling, adjust the alternator drive belt to allow ½ in. play on the longest run between pulleys.

NOTE: on A/C models, remove the compressor brace.

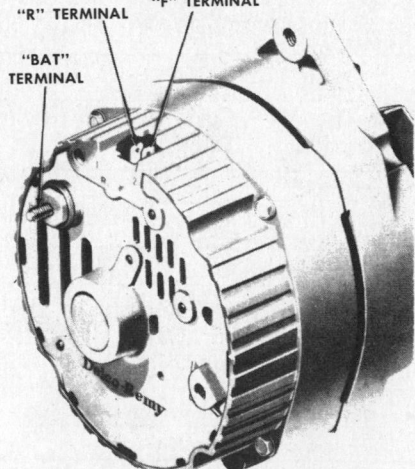

"R" TERMINAL   "F" TERMINAL

"BAT" TERMINAL

Delcotron wire connections
(© Buick Div., G.M. Corp)

STARTING SYSTEM

See the "Unit Repair Section" for rebuilding procedures and troubleshooting.

Starter Removal and Installation

1. Disconnect battery negative cable.
2. Jack up car and remove the four flywheel inspection cover screws.
3. Disconnect wires from solenoid.
4. Remove the starter bolts.
5. Remove starter.
NOTE: On some models, it may be necessary to move exhaust pipe to gain clearance.
6. Reverse the above steps to install.

IGNITION SYSTEM

Distributor Removal

Disconnect the distributor primary wire from the coil and the hose from the vacuum unit. On the HEI system, first disconnect the battery ground cable, then disconnect the terminal connectors from the distributor and remove the vacuum advance hose. Remove distributor cap by inserting a screwdriver into upper slotted end of cap latches, pressing down and turning 90° counterclockwise.

Make a mark on the distributor body in line with the rotor. Match-mark position of vacuum unit to the engine.

Remove clamp to release distributor and remove from crankcase.

NOTE: 1970-73 distributors have a radio interference shield over the contact points. Only snap-lock point sets can be used because screw-type connectors will hit this shield and short ignition. The shield isn't necessary if a unitized point and condenser set is installed. The unitized set is standard equipment for 1974.

Distributor Installation

If engine was inadvertently turned over while distributor was out, proceed as follows:

Remove right rocker arm cover. Using a wrench on the crankshaft pulley bolt, turn the engine over until both valves for No. 1 cylinder are closed. The timing mark on the harmonic balancer behind the crankshaft pulley should be aligned with the zero degree mark. No. 1 cylinder is now at firing point.

Install distributor in engine with rotor in position to fire No. 1 cylinder. The vacuum unit should align with the match-mark made when distributor was removed. Press down lightly on distributor if it does not seat correctly. Use starter to turn engine until the tang on the distributor shaft slips into the slot in the oil pump shaft. This will not disturb the relationship between the distributor and the camshaft because the drive gear engages before the tang. However, it will be necessary to return the engine to the No. 1 firing point and check that rotor is also at No. 1 firing point. Reconnect vacuum tube and primary wire. Rotate the distributor body slightly until contacts just start to open. Install and tighten distributor

clamp. Install distributor cap. Start engine and adjust point dwell.

If the engine has not been disturbed since the distributor was removed proceed as follows:

Insert distributor into the block so that the rotor is pointing to the mark made on distributor housing and the vacuum advance unit is aligned with the match-mark made on the engine. Connect the vacuum tube, primary wire, and install the distributor cap. Install distributor clamp. Check that spark plug wires are correctly routed. Start engine and adjust point dwell and then adjust ignition timing. Rotate distributor body counterclockwise to advance the timing.

Contact Point Replacement and Adjustment

NOTE: the condenser should be replaced when the points are replaced.

1. Remove the distributor cap and rotor. If equipped with an interference shield, remove the shield.
2. Loosen the two screws holding the contact point set in place and remove the point set.
3. Disconnect the condenser and primary leads from their terminals on the points.
4. Connect the wires to a new set of points and install them into the distributor.
5. Put a small amount of grease on the breaker cam or turn the lubricator.
6. Reinstall the shield, rotor, and cap. Install the shield half that covers the points first.
7. Adjust the dwell to specification.
8. Check the timing.

Ignition Timing

Timing marks are located on the front engine cover and on the harmonic balancer.

1. Disconnect the distributor vacuum advance hose from the distributor and plug the hose.
2. Make sure the dwell is correct.

NOTE: it may be necessary to put a small amount of white paint or chalk on the timing marks to make them more visible.

3. Connect a timing light to No. 1 cylinder.
4. Loosen the distributor clamp.
5. Start the engine and rotate the distributor until the correct marks line up. Tighten the distributor clamp and recheck the timing.
6. Reconnect the vacuum hose.

Solid State Ignition

Beginning 1974, a solid state, high energy ignition (HEI) system is offered as an option on all Buick engines. Beginning 1975, the HEI system is standard equipment on all models. There are no points or condenser to replace, nor any cam or rubbing block to wear out.

There is a convenient tachometer terminal at the top of the distributor cap on HEI systems. The terminal is marked "TACH". Connect the positive tachometer lead to the distributor terminal and the negative

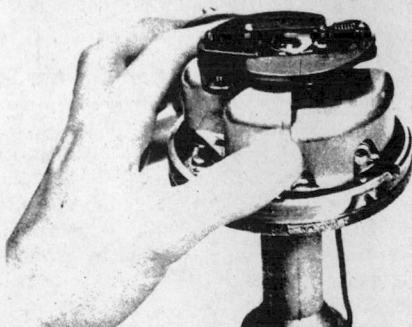

Installing RFI shield 1970-73
(© Buick Div., G.M. Corp)

Distributor—exploded view

- Distributor Cap
- Screw
- Washer — Lockwasher
- Rotor
- Springs
- Shaft — Weights
- Camweight Base
- Condenser
- Contact Point Assembly
- Spring Retainer
- Breaker Plate
- Vacuum Advance Unit
- Felt Washer
- Primary Lead
- "O" Ring Seal
- Gear — Pin

Distributor—exploded view
(© Buick Div., G.M. Corp)

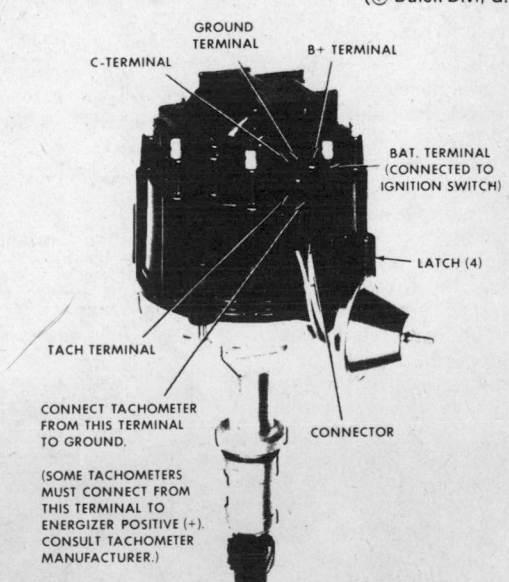

- GROUND TERMINAL
- C-TERMINAL
- B+ TERMINAL
- BAT. TERMINAL (CONNECTED TO IGNITION SWITCH)
- LATCH (4)
- TACH TERMINAL
- CONNECT TACHOMETER FROM THIS TERMINAL TO GROUND.
- (SOME TACHOMETERS MUST CONNECT FROM THIS TERMINAL TO ENERGIZER POSITIVE (+). CONSULT TACHOMETER MANUFACTURER.)
- CONNECTOR

Tachometer connection for the HEI system (© Buick Div., G.M. Corp)

tachometer lead to a ground. Some tachometers must connect from the distributor terminal to the positive terminal of the battery. Follow the tachometer manufacturer's instructions.

Note: Never ground the HEI tachometer terminal.

The procedure for checking the timing on this system is the same as for conventional ignition systems.

FUEL SYSTEM

Fuel Pump

These models use a single action fuel pump mounted on the lower side of the engine front cover. Flexible gas lines are used.

The fuel pump is not rebuildable.

1970 Riviera Only

These models have a turbine type electric fuel pump mounted at the bottom of the fuel tank. This pump maintains a steady pressure whenever the engine is running. The electrical circuit to the pump is completed by an oil pressure switch which is bypassed for starting. If oil pressure fails, the fuel pump will not operate.

All Engines with Air Conditioners, All 455 Cu. In.

All air-conditioner equipped cars have a special fuel pump with a metering outlet for a vapor return system. Hot fuel and fuel vapor is returned to the fuel tank. The fuel pump is continuously cooled by circulating fuel from the tank, thus greatly reducing the possibility of vapor lock.

Fuel Pump Removal and Installation

1. Disconnect the fuel inlet, outlet, and vapor return hoses.
2. Remove the two bolts holding the pump to the engine.
3. Remove the old fuel pump.
To install:
1. Install a new pump and gasket.
2. Install the two bolts.
3. Reconnect the hoses to the pump. Do not force the threaded fittings, use very light pressure until it is obvious that the threads are started properly.
4. Start the engine and check for leaks.

Fuel Filter Replacement

The filter is located in the carburetor inlet behind the large hex nut. This is a small pleated paper or sintered bronze filter.
1. Remove the fuel inlet line from the carburetor.
2. Remove the large nut from the

carburetor body.
3. Remove the old filter.
4. Install a new filter with the spring inserted before the filter.
5. Install the large hex nut and fuel line.
6. Start the engine and check for leaks.

Idle Speed and Mixture Adjustments

1970

NOTE: The air cleaner must be in place for idle mixture adjustment.
1. Check PCV system for proper operation.
2. Connect tachometer; warm engine to normal operating temperature.
3. Place manual transmission in N, automatic in D (wheels blocked).
4. To make sure the Thermo Vacuum switch does not switch distributor vacuum over to full manifold vacuum due to overheated coolant, remove the hose from the distributor and plug.
NOTE: check that the compressor for the Automatic Level Control. if so equipped, is not running. The compressor now has a regulating valve to shut off vacuum at idle speed. If the compressor is running, this valve is faulty and must be replaced before a good idle can be obtained.
5. Adjust throttle stop screw to obtain an idle speed 20 rpm faster than specified.
6. Turn in each mixture needle, alternately, to obtain an idle speed 10 rpm less *per needle* than the basic idle setting of Step 5 (for a total of 20 rpm less).
7. Press down on the hot idle compensator, if so equipped. If idle drops, valve is open and should be unstuck and idle reset.

1971

NOTE: The air cleaner must be in place to get the proper idle mixture.
1. Check PCV system for proper operation.
2. Connect tachometer; warm en-

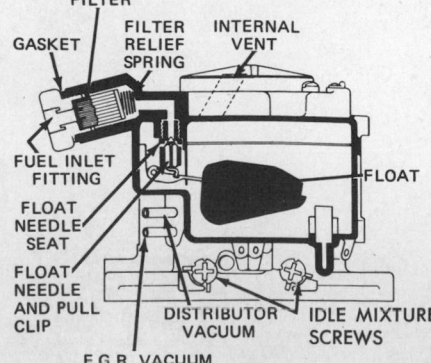

2 bbl carburetor
(© Buick Div., G.M. Corp)

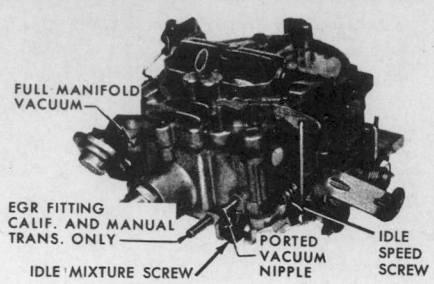

4 bbl carburetor
(© Buick Div., G.M. Corp)

gine to normal operating temperature.
3. Place manual transmission in N, automatic in D (wheels blocked).
4. Remove distributor hose and plug.
NOTE: check that the compressor for the Automatic Level Control, if so equipped, is not running. The compressor has a regulating valve to shut off vacuum at idle speed. If the compressor is running, this valve is faulty and must be replaced before a good idle can be obtained.
5. Adjust throttle stop screw to obtain specified idle speed.
6. Adjust idle mixture needles, alternately, to obtain highest tachometer reading.
7. Readjust throttle stop and mixture screws as required to obtain an idle speed 50 rpm faster than specified, then turn in each screw (leaner) to reduce idle speed 25 rpm *per needle* (for a total reduction of 50 rpm).
8. Adjust fast idle speed.

1972-73

1. Connect a tachometer to the engine.
2. Start the engine and run it until it is warmed up.
3. Remove and plug the vacuum hose to the distributor.
4. Place manual transmissions in neutral and automatic transmissions in D.
5. Open the throttle sufficiently to allow the solenoid to extend and contact the throttle lever pad in the idle position.
6. Adjust the solenoid set screw to obtain the specified rpm. This is the higher figure in the specification chart.
7. Disconnect the solenoid wire to disengage solenoid.
8. Adjust the carburetor idle screw to obtain specified idle speed, which is the lower figure in the specification chart.
9. Reconnect the solenoid wire.
10. Adjust the idle mixture needles, one at a time, to obtain the highest tachometer reading. After the highest reading is reached, readjust the solenoid plunger to obtain 50 rpm over the specified

idle speed. Turn each mixture needle in to reduce the idle speed 25 rpm for each needle. This reduces the idle speed to the recommended rpm.

11. Adjust the fast idle speed on all four-barrel carburetors. Fast idle must be adjusted after slow idle speed and mixture have been adjusted. Automatic transmission cars are adjusted on the low step of the fast idle cam in Drive to 700 RPM. Manual transmission cars are adjusted on the low cam step to 820 RPM for 350 engines, and 920 RPM for 455 engines.

12. Connect the distributor vacuum hose.

13. Install the "red" service idle needle limiter caps on the mixture screws.

1974-76

NOTE: Idle speed and mixture must be set with the engine at normal operating temperature, the air conditioner off, the air cleaner on, and the transmission in drive. If a CO meter is available, set the idle mixture to that specified on the underhood specifications sticker.

1. Set the parking brake and block the wheels.

2. Disconnect the evaporative emission hose at the air cleaner. Disconnect and plug the distributor vacuum line at the distributor. Disconnect and plug the EGR vacuum line at the EGR valve.

3. Adjust the idle speed to that specified in the "Tune-Up Specifications" chart. On 1974-75 models, first adjust the idle speed screw with the solenoid disconnected to get the lower speed, then adjust the solenoid screw with the solenoid connected to get the higher speed. On 1976 models, adjust the idle speed with the idle speed screw.

4. Cut the tabs off the mixture screw caps, then equally richen (turn out) the mixture screws until the maximum idle speed is achieved.

5. Using the solenoid screw or idle speed screw, adjust, if necessary, the idle speed to 70 rpm above the specified speed for 455 engines, and 60 rpm above for the 350 (1974). On 1975-76 vehicles, adjust the idle speed to 80 rpm above specification.

6. Turn in (lean) the mixture screws equally until the engine returns to the specified idle speed.

7. Reconnect all the hoses removed in Step 2.

COOLING SYSTEM

Radiator Removal and Installation

On models equipped with a fan shroud, remove the shroud from the radiator and position it rearward over the fan.

Remove the capscrews that hold the fan blades to the fan hub and take off the blades, spacer and pump pulley. Drain the cooling system and remove the top and bottom radiator hoses and the two automatic transmission oil coder lines from the radiator. Remove the bolts that hold the radiator core to the cradle and lift the core straight up. Reverse the above steps to install.

Water Pump Removal and Installation

It is possible to remove and replace the water pump on all Buicks without disturbing the radiator core. This is accomplished by removing the fan belt, fan blades, and pulley, disconnecting the hoses and removing the water pump attaching bolts. Reverse the removal procedure to install. Use a new gasket and make sure all gasket surfaces are clean.

Thermostat Removal and Installation

The thermostat is contained in the water outlet elbow mounted on the front of the intake manifold.

To replace the thermostat, disconnect the upper radiator hose, remove the water outlet attaching bolts, lift off the outlet and take out the thermostat.

Caution When installing a thermostat always place the end of the thermostat with the spring inside the engine.

EMISSION CONTROLS

There are three types of emissions to be controlled: crankcase emissions, carburetor and gas tank fuel vapor emissions, and exhaust emissions. See the "Unit Repair Section" for troubleshooting and repair information.

1970-71

Crankcase emissions are controlled by the Closed Positive Crankcase Ventilation System, and exhaust emissions by the engine Controlled Combustion System (CCS), in conjunction with the new Transmission Controlled Spark System (TCS).

The CCS system reduces emissions by increasing combustion efficiency through carburetor (limiter caps on the mixture screws), and distributor (retarding the timing over earlier years) calibrations. The system also uses a higher temperature thermostat ($195°F$) to increase engine operating temperature and a thermostatically controlled air cleaner to regulate the temperature of the air entering the carburetor.

In addition, cars sold in California are equipped with an Evaporation Control System that limits the amount of gasoline vapor discharged into the atmosphere (usually from the carburetor and fuel tank).

The TCS system consists of a transmission switch, a solenoid valve, and a temperature switch. Under normal conditions, the system permits the vacuum distributor (spark) advance to operate only in high gear (both manual and automatic transmissions) and reverse.

The transmission switch is located on the transmission and senses when the transmission is in one of the lower gears. When in a lower gear, the switch activates the vacuum solenoid valve. This valve is located in the vacuum line that runs from the carburetor to the distributor and shuts off vacuum to the distributor advance when it is activated. There is also an engine-temperature sensing switch which overrides the transmission switch. It will allow vacuum advance in the lower gears when engine temperature is below $85°F$ or above $220°F$. There is always vacuum advance in high gear and reverse.

The Evaporative Emission Control System was introduced in 1970. Vapors generated in the gas tank while the car is at rest are transferred to an activated charcoal canister located in the engine compartment. When the car is running the vapors are removed from the canister and burned by the engine.

1972

In 1972, all engines are equipped with positive crankcase ventilation, transmission controlled vacuum spark advance (TCS) and the controlled combustion system (CCS). The air injection reactor system is standard on all engines except the non-California 350 cu in. with automatic transmissions. All California cars and all cars with manual transmissions have Exhaust Gas Recirculation (EGR).

CCS and TCS are explained in the 1970-71 section.

The EGR system is used to reduce oxides of nitrogen emissions. To lower the formation of nitrogen oxides, it is necessary to reduce combustion temperatures. This is done by introducing exhaust gases into the in-

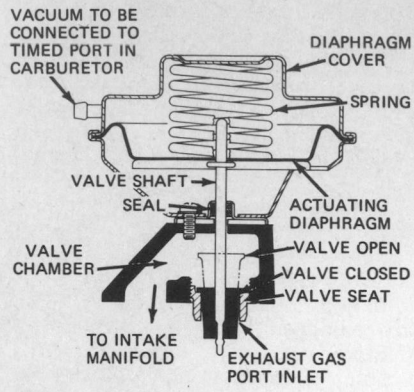

EGR valve
(© Buick Div., G.M. Corp)

take manifold to be burned.

An EGR valve is mounted on the right rear of the intake manifold and is used to regulate the amount of exhaust gases and the time the exhaust gases enter the intake manifold. As the engine speeds up, carburetor vacuum is applied to the valve which opens a port connecting the intake manifold to the exhaust gas passage that is cast in the intake manifold. This allows exhaust gases to pass into the intake manifold. The EGR system is not in operation during engine idle.

1973

All engines are equipped with Positive Crankcase Ventilation, Controlled Combustion, Air Injection Reactor System, Exhaust Gas Recirculation, Transmission Controlled Vacuum Spark Advance System and Evaporative Emission Control. With the exception of a low temperature cut-out valve that was added to the EGR system, the emission control systems remain unchanged from previous years.

The EGR system is the same one that was used on 1972 California cars with a new temperature valve. This black and white plastic valve is

located in the vacuum line to the EGR valve and it senses ambient temperature above the engine intake manifold. At temperatures below 55°F, the temperature valve closes to prevent carburetor vacuum from opening the EGR valve. When the temperature above the manifold rises above 60°F, the valve opens and allows carburetor vacuum to control the operation of the EGR valve. Whenever installing a new valve, always make sure the side of the valve marked EGR faces toward the EGR valve.

1974

The 1974 Buick emission control system is unchanged from 1973, except for a change in the EGR temperature sensor. Instead of ambient temperature, it measures coolant temperature. Although the system design remains unchanged, there has been an extensive refinement and recalibration of components to insure greater efficiency.

1975—76

All 1975-76 models are equipped with a catalytic converter. Details on this system will be found in the Emission Control Systems Unit Repair Section. A fast warm-up system is used to heat incoming fuel by directing exhaust gas flow through the intake manifold crossover passage be-

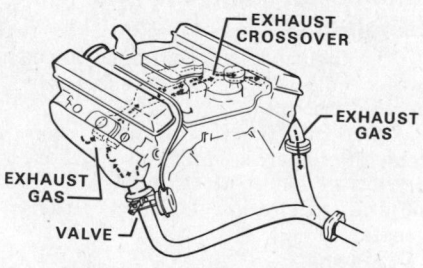

Beginning 1975 Fast warm-up system
(© Buick Div., G.M. Corp)

low the carburetor when engine temperatures are low. A choke modulator is used to keep the choke on longer in cold weather by restricting the flow of exhaust gas warmed air to the choke. In warm weather, the modulator allows normal choke operation. High Energy Ignition became standard equipment in 1975. For 1976, the emission control systems are the same as 1975, but air cleaner cold air ducts on some engines have been dropped.

ENGINE

NOTE: All procedures concerning the 231 cu. in. V6 will be found in the Buick Apollo section.

Engine Removal and Installation

1. Drain cooling system.
2. Scribe hinge outline on underside of hood. Remove hood attaching bolts and remove hood.
3. Disconnect battery cables.
4. Remove radiator and heater hoses and remove the air cleaner.
5. Disconnect transmission oil cooler lines. Remove fan shroud, fan belts, and pulleys.
6. Remove attaching bolts and lift out radiator.
7. Disconnect exhaust pipe or pipes at the exhaust manifold/s.
8. Disconnect vacuum line to power brake unit.
9. Disconnect accelerator to carburetor linkage.
10. Disconnect all engine component wiring that would interfere with engine removal, such as generator wires, gauge sending unit wires, primary ignition wires, engine-to-body ground strap, etc.
11. Disconnect gas line at fuel pump.
12. Detach power steering pump and position to the left. Do not disconnect the hoses.
13. Detach air conditioner compressor at bracket and position to the right. Do not disconnect hoses.

Caution If the compressor refrigerant lines do not have enough slack to position the compressor out of the way without disconnecting the refrigerant lines, the air conditioning system will have to be removed by a trained air conditioning specialist. Under no conditions should an untrained person attempt to disconnect the air conditioning refrigerant lines. These lines contain pressurized freon which can be extremely dangerous to the untrained.

14. Disconnect transmission control linkage.
15. Disconnect vapor emission lines.
16. Attach lifting device to the en-

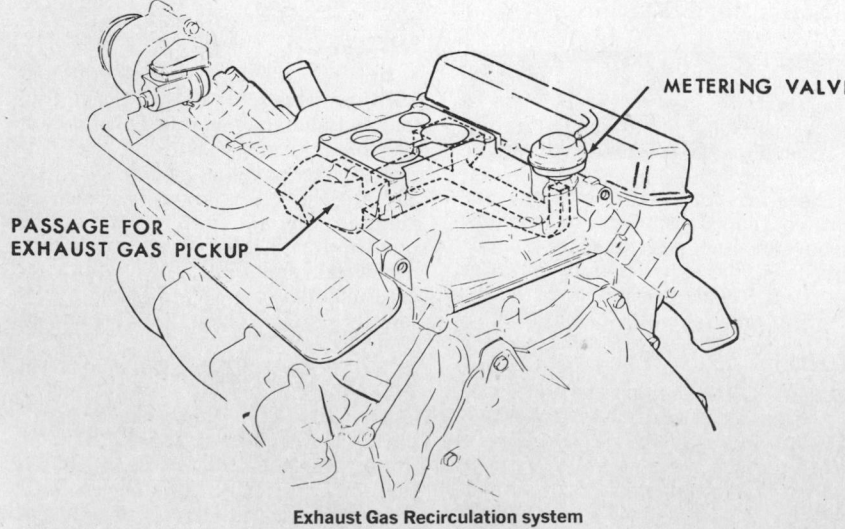

Exhaust Gas Recirculation system
(© Buick Div., G.M. Corp)

gine and raise enough to support the engine weight.

17. Remove flywheel cover pan. On cars equipped with an automatic transmission, remove the flywheel to-torque converter bolts. Match-mark the flywheel and torque converter for reassembly.
18. Separate engine from transmission at bell housing on cars equipped with automatic transmission. On cars equipped with a manual transmission, separate the transmission from the bellhousing.
19. Remove engine attachment thru-bolts at the engine mounts.
20. Lift engine forward and upward to clear engine compartment.
21. Install by reversing above procedure. When installing an engine, the front mounting pad to frame bolts should be the last mounting bolts to be tightened. Note that there are dowel pins in the block that have matching holes in the bellhousing. These pins must be in almost perfect alignment before the engine will go together with the transmission.

Manifolds

Intake Manifold Removal and Installation

1. Drain the cooling system and disconnect the battery.
2. Remove carburetor air cleaner. Disconnect all tubes and hoses from the carburetor. Disconnect and remove the coil.
3. Disconnect temperature indicator wire from sending unit.
4. Disconnect accelerator and transmission linkage at carburetor. Disconnect throttle return spring.
5. Slide front thermostat by-pass hose clamp back on the hose. Disconnect upper radiator hose at outlet.
6. Disconnect heater hose at the temperature control valve inlet. Force the end of the hose down to permit coolant to drain from intake manifold.
7. Loosen the air conditioning compressor bracket bolt and swing the bracket out of the way.
8. Remove manifold attaching bolts.
9. Remove intake manifold and carburetor as an assembly by sliding rearward to disengage the thermostat by-pass hose from the water pump. Remove intake manifold gasket.
10. Reverse the above steps to install. Torque the bolts in the sequence shown.

NOTE: New intake manifold gasket and seals must be used whenever a manifold is removed.

Intake manifold tightening sequence—350 and 455 V8 beginning 1971
(© Buick Div., G.M. Corp)

Exhaust Manifold Removal and Installation

1. Jack up car and support on jack stands.
2. Disconnect exhaust pipe from manifolds on both sides of engine and lower. If equipped with dual exhaust, disconnect and lower only on the side being worked on.
3. If equipped with manual transmission, remove equalizer shaft.

Note: On right side, it may be necessary to remove A/C, power steering, or alternator. On 1971-1972 left-side exhaust manifolds on models other than LeSabre, the pitman arm must be removed and the steering linkage pushed out of the way.

4. Remove exhaust manifold-to-cylinder head bolts.
5. Remove manifold from beneath car.
6. Reverse the above steps to install.

Valve System

Rocker Arm Removal and Installation

Removal

1. Remove the rocker arm cover.
2. Remove the rocker arm shaft assembly bolts and then the assembly.
3. Remove the nylon arm retainers by prying them out with pliers or breaking them with a chisel.
4. Remove the rocker arms. Remove any retainer pieces from the inside of the shaft.

Installation

1. Install the rocker arms on the shaft and lubricate them with oil.
2. Center each arm on the ¼ in. hole in the shaft. Install new nylon rocker arm retainers in the holes using a drift 1⁄2 in. in diameter.

NOTE: On V8 engines through 1972, each pair of rocker arms must be in-

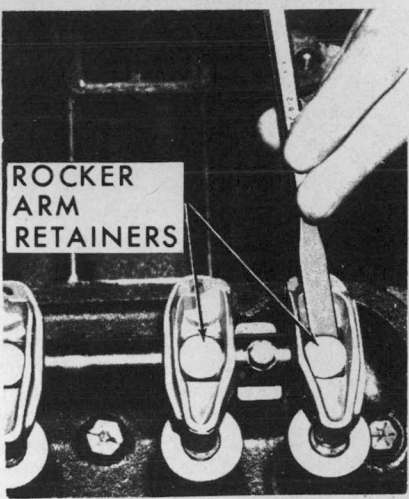

Removing nylon rocker arm retainers—350 and 455 beginning 1971
(© Buick Div., G.M. Corp)

stalled so that the external rib on each arm points away from the rocker arm shaft bolt that is located between each pair of rocker arms. On 1973 and later engines, replacement rocker arms are marked R and L. From the front of the engine on the left bank, the sequence should be L-R, L-R, L-R, L-R. On the right bank, it should be R-L, R-L, R-L, R-L.

3. Locate the push rods in the rocker arms and insert the shaft-to-cylinder head bolts. Tighten the bolts a little at a time to 25-30 ft lbs.
4. Install the rocker cover and use a new gasket.

Valve Adjustment

After the shaft assembly-to-cylinder head bolts are torqued to specification, the valves are automatically-properly adjusted.

Valve Guide Replacement

Valve guides are cast into the cylinder heads of all engines. The valve guides must be reamed and fitted with valves with oversize stems to be repaired.

NOTE: All 350 and some 455 engines use progressively wound valve springs. The coils are closer together at one end than at the other. The close wound end must go against the cylinder head. 0.010 in. oversize lifters are sometimes installed at the factory. These are identified by an O on the lifter bore and two grooves on the lifter body.

Cylinder Head

Cylinder Head Removal and Installation

1. Disconnect the battery.
2. Drain the coolant.
3. Remove the air cleaner.

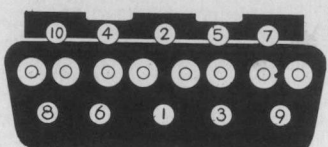

Cylinder head torque sequence
for 350, 455 cu in.

4. Remove the air conditioning from the engine, but do not disconnect any lines.
5. Remove the intake manifold.
6. When removing the right cylinder head, loosen the alternator belt and remove the alternator; if equipped with an air conditioning compressor, remove the compressor from the mounting bracket and position it out of the way WITH THE HOSES CONNECTED, then remove the alternator with the mounting bracket; finally, disconnect the metal temperature indicator wire (1973 and later models only).
7. When removing the left cylinder head, remove the dipstick and the power steering pump without disconnecting any hoses.
8. Disconnect the plug wires.
9. Disconnect the exhaust manifold from the head being removed.
10. Remove the rocker arm cover and rocker shaft assembly. Lift out the push rods. Disconnect the AIR hoses from the cylinder head.
11. Remove the cylinder head bolts.
12. Remove the cylinder head and gasket.
13. Reverse the above steps to install. Torque the head bolts to specifications in three steps.

Timing Case Cover, Timing Chain and Camshaft

Vibration Damper Removal

Remove the radiator core and take out the cap screws that hold the fan pulley to the vibration damper. Remove the large bolt from the center of the crankshaft and insert a bolt type puller into the holes which held the fan pulley. Pull off the vibration damper.

Timing Chain and Front Oil Seal Replacement

350 Cu. In.

1. Drain cooling system and remove radiator, shroud, fan, pulleys, and belts.
2. Remove crankshaft pulley, fuel pump and distributor.
3. Remove Delcotron and power steering pump, if necessary.
4. Loosen and slide rearward front clamp on thermostat by-pass

hose. Remove harmonic balancer.
5. Remove bolts attaching timing chain cover to cylinder block and oil pan to timing chain cover bolts. Remove timing chain cover assembly and gasket. Clean cover thoroughly, being careful not to damage the gasket surface.
6. Turn the crankshaft so that the timing marks on the sprockets are adjacent to each other on a line with the shaft centers.
7. Remove crankshaft oil slinger.
8. Remove bolt, special washer, distributor drive gear, and fuel pump eccentric from camshaft.
9. Alternately pry camshaft and crankshaft sprockets forward until camshaft sprocket and chain are free. Then remove the crankshaft sprocket.
   If oil seal appears worn or has been leaking, replace as follows:
10. Use a punch to drive out the old seal and retainer. Drive from front to rear of the timing chain cover.
11. Coil new packing around opening so that ends are at top. Drive in retainer. Stake the retainer in at least three places. Size the pack-

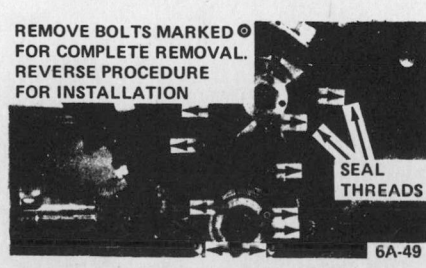

REMOVE BOLTS MARKED ⊙ FOR COMPLETE REMOVAL. REVERSE PROCEDURE FOR INSTALLATION

SEAL THREADS

6A-49

350 timing cover bolts (© Buick Div., G.M. Corp)

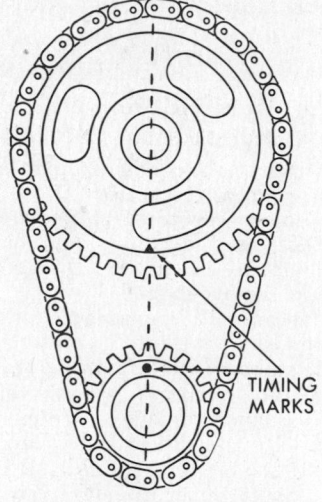

Timing chain and sprocket marks

ing by rotating a hammer handle, etc. around the packing until the balancer hub fits through the packing.

If engine has been disturbed since chain and sprockets were removed:
12. Turn crankshaft until No. 1 piston is at top dead center of the compression stroke.
13. Mount sprocket temporarily and turn camshaft so that timing mark is straight down.
14. Assemble chain and sprockets and mount on shafts with their timing marks closest to each other and aligned vertically.
15. Mount slinger on sprocket with the concave side to the front.
16. Reinstall fuel pump eccentric, distributor drive gear, special

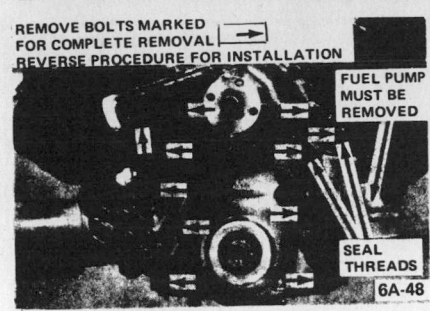

REMOVE BOLTS MARKED FOR COMPLETE REMOVAL REVERSE PROCEDURE FOR INSTALLATION

FUEL PUMP MUST BE REMOVED

SEAL THREADS

6A-48

455 timing cover bolts
(© Buick Div., G.M. Corp)

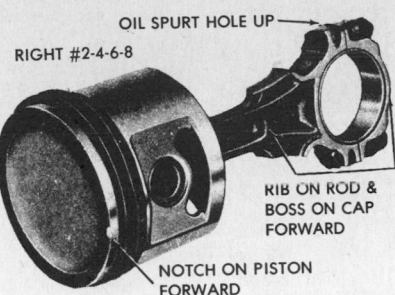

OIL SPURT HOLE UP

RIGHT #2-4-6-8

RIB ON ROD & BOSS ON CAP FORWARD

NOTCH ON PISTON FORWARD

350 piston and connecting rod assembly —right bank
(© Buick Div., G.M. Corp)

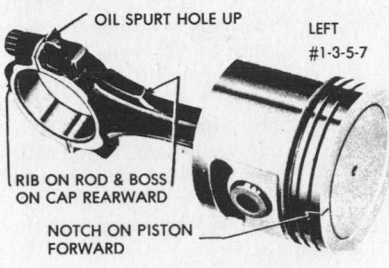

OIL SPURT HOLE UP

LEFT #1-3-5-7

RIB ON ROD & BOSS ON CAP REARWARD

NOTCH ON PISTON FORWARD

350 piston and connecting rod assembly —left bank
(© Buick Div., G.M. Corp)

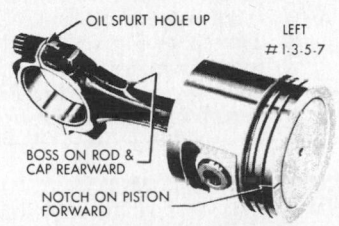

OIL SPURT HOLE UP

LEFT #1-3-5-7

BOSS ON ROD & CAP REARWARD

NOTCH ON PISTON FORWARD

455 piston and connecting rod assembly—left bank
(© Buick Div., G.M. Corp)

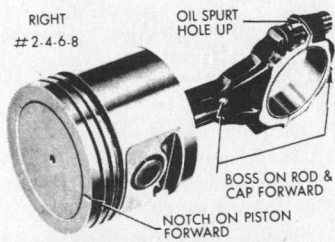

RIGHT #2-4-6-8

OIL SPURT HOLE UP

BOSS ON ROD & CAP FORWARD

NOTCH ON PISTON FORWARD

455 piston and connecting rod assembly—right bank
(© Buick Div., G.M. Corp)

washer, and bolt on camshaft. Reinstall Woodruff key with oil groove forward.

17. Remove oil pump cover and pack the space around the oil pump gears full of petroleum jelly, leaving no air spaces. Reinstall oil pump cover with new gasket. This step is very important. If it is not done the oil pump will not begin to pump oil as soon as the engine is started.

18. Reinstall timing chain cover with new gasket.

Keep engine speed low for a short time after installation of a new oil seal.

455 Cu. In.

This procedure is identical to that outlined for 350 cu. in. engines with the substitution of the following steps:

8. Remove oil pan. Remove camshaft sprocket bolts.
16. Reinstall oil pan. Reinstall camshaft sprocket bolts.

Camshaft Removal and Installation

1. Remove the intake manifold, distributor, radiator, air conditioning condenser and grille.
2. Remove the rocker arm covers.
3. Remove the rocker arm and shaft assemblies, push rods, and valve lifters.
4. Remove the timing chain cover, timing chain, and camshaft sprocket.
5. Slide the camshaft forward, through the grille opening, and out from the bearing bores. Carefully avoid marring the bearing surfaces.
6. Reverse the above steps to install.

Connecting Rods, Rings And Pistons

When the rod assemblies are replaced in the engine, the connecting rod bearing oil spurt hole must point up toward the camshaft.

Engine Lubrication

Oil Pan Removal and Installation

1. Disconnect the battery.
2. Remove the fan shroud-to-radiator tie bar screws.
3. Remove the air cleaner and disconnect the throttle linkage.
4. Raise the car and support it on jackstands.
5. Drain the oil.
6. On cars equipped with manual transmission, loosen the clutch equalizer bracket - to - frame at-

taching bolts and remove the exhaust crossover pipe.

7. On cars equipped with automatic transmissions, remove the lower flywheel housing, remove the shift linkage attaching bolt and swing it out of the way, and disconnect the exhaust crossover pipe at the engine.
8. On 1970-72 models, disconnect the idler arm at the frame and push the steering linkage forward to the crossmember.
9. Remove the front engine mounting bolts.
10. Raise the engine by placing a jack under the crankshaft pulley mounting.

Caution On air conditioned cars, place a support under the right-side of the transmission before raising the engine. If you don't do this, the engine and transmission will cock to the right due to the weight of the air conditioning equipment.

11. Remove the oil pan bolts and remove the pan. It may be necessary to rotate the crankshaft to get enough clearance to remove the pan. Remove the rear main seal on the 455.
12. Reverse the above steps to install. Use gasket sealer and new gaskets. Tighten the bolts evenly to 14 ft lbs.

Oil Pump Removal

The oil pump is located in the timing chain cover on the right-hand side. It is connected by a drilled passage in the crankcase to an oil screen housing and pipe assembly. The screen is submerged in the oil supply in the oil pan.

The pump can be disassembled as follows:

1. Remove the oil filter.
2. Unbolt the pump cover assembly from the timing chain cover.
3. Remove the cover assembly and slide out the pump gears.
4. Remove the oil pressure relief valve cap, spring, and valve. Do not remove the oil filter by-pass valve and spring.
5. Check that the relief valve spring isn't worn on its side or collapsed. Check that the relief valve is no more than an easy slip fit in its bore in the cover. If there is any perceptible side-play, replace the valve. If there is still side-play, replace the cover.
6. Check the filter by-pass valve for good condition.

To assemble the pump:

7. Lubricate and install the pressure relief valve and spring in the cover bore. Install the gasket and cap, torquing the cap to 35 ft. lbs.

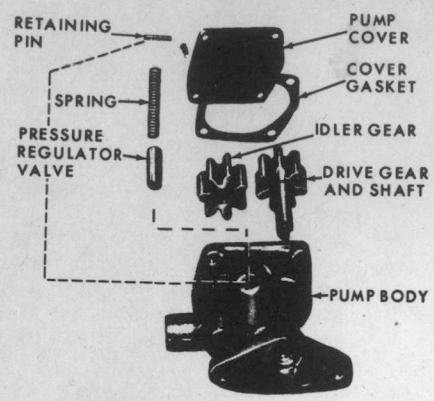

Typical oil pump assembly
(© Buick Div., G.M. Corp)

8. Install the gears and check that gear-to-cover end clearance is between 0.002-0.006 in. If the clearance is less, check the timing cover gear pocket for wear.
9. Remove the gears and pack the gear pocket full of petroleum jelly. Don't use grease.
   Unless the pump is primed this way, it won't produce any oil pressure when the engine is started.
10. Install the gears. Install a new gasket and the cover. Torque the bolts evenly to 10 ft lbs. Replace the filter.

Rear Main Bearing Oil Seal Replacement

Buick uses an oil slinger and groove, a braided fabric seal and two neoprene strips to seal the rear main bearing. The braided fabric seal can be installed in the crankcase half (upper) only when crankshaft is removed. However, the seal can be replaced in the lower half whenever the lower half (cap) has been removed. To renew the seals in the cap proceed as follows:

Remove the oil pan. Remove the old seals and clean the cap. Place new braided seal in groove with both ends projecting above parting surface of cap. Force seal into groove by rubbing down with a hammer handle or other smooth tool until seal is seated in groove and ends project above the parting face of the cap not more than 1/16 in. Using a razor blade, cut off ends flush with parting surface.

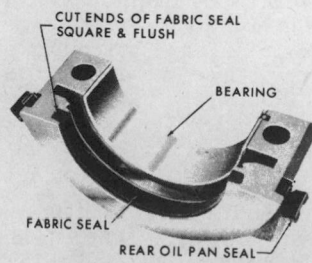

Rear main bearing cap—455 cu in.
(© Buick Div., G.M. Corp)

Chiltm's TIME SAVER

Top Half, Rear Main Bearing Oil Seal Replacement

1. Drain engine oil and remove oil pan.
2. Remove rear main bearing cap.
3. With a 6 in. length of 3/16 in. brazing rod, drive up on either exposed end of the top half oil seal. When the opposite end of the seal starts to protrude, have a helper grasp it with pliers and pull gently while the driven end is being tapped. It is surprising how easily most of these seals can be removed by this method.

To replace the woven fabric-type seal:

1. Obtain a 12 in. piece of copper wire (about the same gauge as that used in the strands of an insulated battery cable).
2. Thread one strand of this wire through the new seal, about ½ in. from the end, bend back and make secure.

On 350 cu in. engines only, just before installing the bearing cap, lightly lubricate the neoprene side seals and install in bearing cap with the upper ends protruding about 1/16 in. The seals must not be cut to length.
NOTE: The neoprene side seals may fit loosely in the side grooves of the rear main bearing cap when first installed, and may even leak for a short time. However, the seals swell considerably when they come in contact with oil and heat and will soon seal properly if installed correctly.

After installing the cap, force the seals up into the cap with a blunt instrument to insure a seal at the line between the cap and the case.

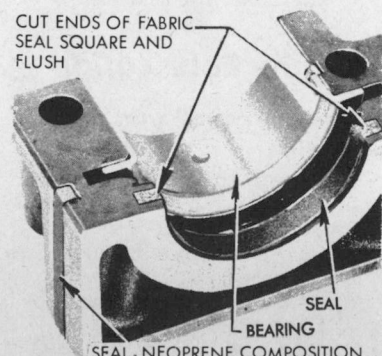

Rear main bearing cap—except 455 cu in.
(© Buick Div., G.M. Corp)

3. Thoroughly saturate the new seal with engine oil.
4. Push the copper wire up through the oil seal groove until it comes down on the opposite side of the bearing.
5. Pull (with pliers) on the protruding copper wire while the crankshaft is being turned and the new seal is slowly fed into place.
   CAUTION: this snaking operation slightly reduces the diameter of the new seal and care will have to be used to keep the seal from slipping too far through the top half of the bearing.
6. When an equal amount of seal is extending from each side, cut off the copper wire close to the seal and tamp both ends of the seal up into the groove (this will tend to expand the seal again).
   NOTE: don't worry about the copper wire left in the groove, it is too soft to cause damage.
7. Replace the seal in the cap in the usual way and replace the oil pan.

NOTE: the 455 cu. in. engines use a rear bearing cap which does not have the neoprene side seals. These engines are sealed at this point by a rear oil pan seal.

Caution The engine must be operated at slow speed when first started after installation of new braided seals.

CLUTCH

On models through 1971, there is a safety switch attached to the clutch pedal arm inside the car to prevent the engine from being started unless the clutch pedal is depressed.

Clutch Removal and Installation

Through 1971

1. Remove transmission.
2. Remove pedal return spring from clutch fork. Disconnect rod assembly from clutch fork.
3. Remove flywheel housing.
4. Remove throwout bearing from clutch fork.
5. Disconnect clutch fork from ball stud by moving toward center of flywheel housing.
6. Mark clutch cover and flywheel so that cover can be reinstalled in the same position. This is important to proper balance.

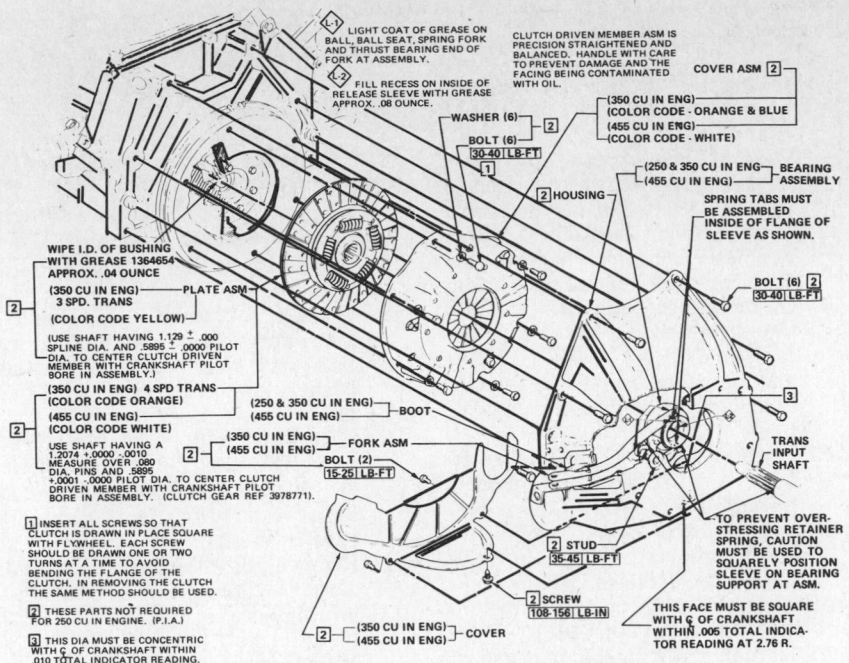

LIGHT COAT OF GREASE ON BALL, BALL SEAT, SPRING FORK AND THRUST BEARING END OF FORK AT ASSEMBLY.

CLUTCH DRIVEN MEMBER ASM IS PRECISION STRAIGHTENED AND BALANCED. HANDLE WITH CARE TO PREVENT DAMAGE AND THE FACING BEING CONTAMINATED WITH OIL.

FILL RECESS ON INSIDE OF RELEASE SLEEVE WITH GREASE APPROX. .08 OUNCE.

COVER ASM 2

WASHER (6) 2
BOLT (6) 2 30-40 LB-FT
(350 CU IN ENG) (COLOR CODE - ORANGE & BLUE)
(455 CU IN ENG) (COLOR CODE - WHITE)

2 HOUSING
(250 & 350 CU IN ENG) (455 CU IN ENG) BEARING ASSEMBLY

SPRING TABS MUST BE ASSEMBLED INSIDE OF FLANGE OF SLEEVE AS SHOWN.

WIPE I.D. OF BUSHING WITH GREASE 1364654 APPROX. .04 OUNCE
PLATE ASM
(350 CU IN ENG) 3 SPD. TRANS (COLOR CODE YELLOW)

BOLT (6) 2 30-40 LB-FT

(USE SHAFT HAVING 1.129 ± .000 SPLINE DIA. AND .5895 ± .0000 PILOT DIA. TO CENTER CLUTCH DRIVEN MEMBER WITH CRANKSHAFT PILOT BORE IN ASSEMBLY.)

(350 CU IN ENG) 4 SPD TRANS (COLOR CODE ORANGE)
(455 CU IN ENG) (COLOR CODE WHITE)
(250 & 350 CU IN ENG)
BOOT

USE SHAFT HAVING A 1.2074 +.0000 -.0010 MEASURE OVER .080 DIA. PINS AND .5895 +.0001 -.0000 PILOT DIA. TO CENTER CLUTCH DRIVEN MEMBER WITH CRANKSHAFT PILOT BORE IN ASSEMBLY. (CLUTCH GEAR REF 3978771.)

(350 CU IN ENG) (455 CU IN ENG) FORK ASM
BOLT (2) 15-25 LB-FT

3 TRANS INPUT SHAFT

1 INSERT ALL SCREWS SO THAT CLUTCH IS DRAWN IN PLACE SQUARE WITH FLYWHEEL. EACH SCREW SHOULD BE DRAWN ONE OR TWO TURNS AT A TIME TO AVOID BENDING THE FLANGE OF THE CLUTCH. IN REMOVING THE CLUTCH THE SAME METHOD SHOULD BE USED.

2 THESE PARTS NOT REQUIRED FOR 250 CU IN ENGINE. (P.I.A.)

3 THIS DIA MUST BE CONCENTRIC WITH C OF CRANKSHAFT WITHIN .010 TOTAL INDICATOR READING.

2 STUD 35-45 LB-FT

TO PREVENT OVER-STRESSING RETAINER SPRING, CAUTION MUST BE USED TO SQUARELY POSITION SLEEVE ON BEARING SUPPORT AT ASM.

2 SCREW 108-156 LB-IN

THIS FACE MUST BE SQUARE WITH C OF CRANKSHAFT WITHIN .005 TOTAL INDICATOR READING AT 2.76 R.

2 (350 CU IN ENG) (455 CU IN ENG) COVER

Typical clutch assembly sequence—1971 illustrated (© Buick Div., G.M. Corp)

7. Loosen clutch cover to flywheel attaching bolts one turn at a time to maintain even spring pressure.
8. Support pressure plate and cover assembly while removing bolts. Remove pressure plate and driven plate. Caution should be used to keep the driven plate clean.
9. Reinstall by receiving the removal procedure. Use a dummy shaft to align the clutch plate. Tighten pressure plate to 30-40 ft lbs.

Clutch Pedal Adjustment

Through 1971

Clutch pedal clearance is adjusted under the car at the link between the clutch throwout fork and the equalizer. There should be 5/8-7/8 in. freeplay of the clutch pedal before the throwout bearing strikes the fingers (or diaphragm).

MANUAL TRANSMISSION

See the "Unit Repair Section" for overhaul procedures.

The backup light switch is mounted on the steering column under the instrument panel in the same location as the neutral start and backup light switch on automatic transmission models. The switch is operated by the movement of the column shift tube. The mounting bracket has slotted holes for adjustment.

Transmission Removal

Through 1971

1. Mark universal joint and transmission shaft companion flange for proper indexing at time of installation. Remove two U-bolts and disconnect driveshaft at the front joint. Slide the driveshaft rearward as far as possible and remove.
2. Disconnect shift linkage from transmission.
3. Disconnect speedometer cable at transmission. Remove driven gear and sleeve.
4. Loosen all three exhaust pipe ball joints to permit transmission and rear of engine to be lowered.
5. Remove two bolts holding transmission mounting pad to transmission support. Leave mounting pad bolted to transmission.
6. With a padded jack under the engine, raise the unit until the transmission mounting pad clears the transmission support.
7. Remove four bolts holding transmission support to body members. Remove support, then lower the jack to allow transmission to clear the underbody.
8. Remove the two top transmission-to-flywheel housing bolts and insert guide pins.
NOTE: If guide pins are not used, damage to the clutch driven plate can result.
9. Remove the two lower transmission attaching bolts. Slide the transmission back until the drive gear shaft disengages the clutch disc and clears the flywheel hous-

ing. Lower the transmission.
10. Install transmission by reversing the above procedure.

Shift Linkage Adjustment— Three-Speed Column Shift

Through 1971

1. Place column selector lever in reverse position. Loosen first-reverse adjusting clamp bolts.
2. Shift first-reverse transmission lever into reverse. Tighten first-reverse adjusting clamp bolt to 17-23 ft. lbs.
3. Shift transmission levers into neutral positions. Loosen second-third adjusting clamp.
4. Install 3/16 in. rod into alignment holes. Tighten second-third adjusting clamp bolt to 17-23 ft. lbs.

AUTOMATIC TRANSMISSION

Turbo Hydra-Matic 350, 375B, and 400 transmissions are used on Buicks. The most notable distinguishing feature between them is the kickdown arrangement. The 350 and 375 kickdown linkage is by a cable attached to the accelerator linkage. The 400 kickdown is done electrically by a switch at the accelerator pedal. The only difference between the 350 and 375B transmissions is that the 375 has more direct clutch plates, to increase torque capacity. There is no way to differentiate between the two externally.

Neutral Start Switch Adjustment

This safety switch prevents starting except in Neutral or Park positions. The switch combines function with the back-up light switch and is actuated by the transmission linkage. On column shift cars, the switch is on the steering column under the instrument panel. On console shift cars, the switch is inside the console in 1970, on the column thereafter. To check switch adjustment:
1. Turn on ignition switch.
2. Place shift control lever in Reverse, and make sure back-up lights are on.
3. Set parking brake. Hold foot brake. Place shift control in Neutral and make sure engine will start. Repeat in Park, Drive, and Reverse. Engine must start only in Neutral or Park.
4. To adjust the switch, place the shift lever in the Neutral position and insert a 3/32 in. (No. 41) drill bit through the hole marked N in 1972 and later models, in the back of the switch.

Move the switch until the bit goes in about ⅜ in. Tighten the mounting screws.

5. Check the adjustment as in Step 3.

Shift Linkage Adjustment

Column Shift—1970

1. Place the manual control lever against the Drive stop.
2. Loosen the adjusting clamp bolt at the transmission.
3. Place the transmission lever in the Drive position (the third detent from the back).
4. Tighten the adjusting clamp bolt to 17-23 ft lbs. Overtightening will cause hard shifting.

1971 and later Column Shift

1. Loosen adjusting clamp bolt.
2. Place selector lever in Neutral.
3. Place transmission lever, at transmission, in Neutral.
4. Tighten adjusting clamp bolt to 17-23 ft. lbs.
5. Start engine. Check for proper shifting into all ranges.

Floorshift

These units are operated by a cable linkage. Adjust as follows:
1. Loosen the trunnion bolt at the transmission end of the cable on models through 1971. On 1972 and later models, pull the clip from the cable housing at the side of the transmission.
2. Set the console shift lever against the Drive stop on models through 1971. On 1972 and later models, set it in the Park detent.
3. Set the transmission shift lever in the Drive position on models through 1971. This is the third position from the back. On 1972 and later models, set it in the Park, or most forward, position.
4. On models through 1971, tighten the trunnion bolt against the cable end to 6-9 ft lbs. On 1972 and later models, replace the clip to hold the cable housing in position.
5. Place the console shift lever in the Park position on models through 1971.
6. Loosen back drive rod clamp screw or nut.
7. Push back drive rod (from linkage to steering column) up and hold lightly against stop.
8. Tighten screw in clamp at end of back drive rod to 17-23 ft. lbs.
9. Start engine. Check for proper shifting into all ranges.

Detent Switch Adjustment

Turbo Hydra-Matic 400

On 1972 and later models, the initial adjustment on installation is made by pushing the switch lever all the way toward the firewall. The final adjustment is made automatically the first time the accelerator pedal is fully depressed.

Pan Replacement, Fluid and Filter Change

Turbo Hydra-Matic 350 and 375

1. Raise the car and support it with jack stands.
2. Place a container under one of the pan corners and loosen the pan attaching screws. Pull the corner down to drain some of the fluid.
3. After the fluid has drained, remove the pan, clean and dry it thoroughly. Be very careful not to leave any lint from cleaning rags in the pan.
4. Remove the filter assembly and gasket by removing the two retaining screws.
5. Install a new filter-to-valve body gasket on the filter and install the filter. Tighten the retaining screws.
6. Install the pan with a new gasket. Tighten the retaining screws to 13 ft lbs.
7. Lower the car and add 3 pints of transmission fluid through the filler neck.
8. With the shift lever in Park,

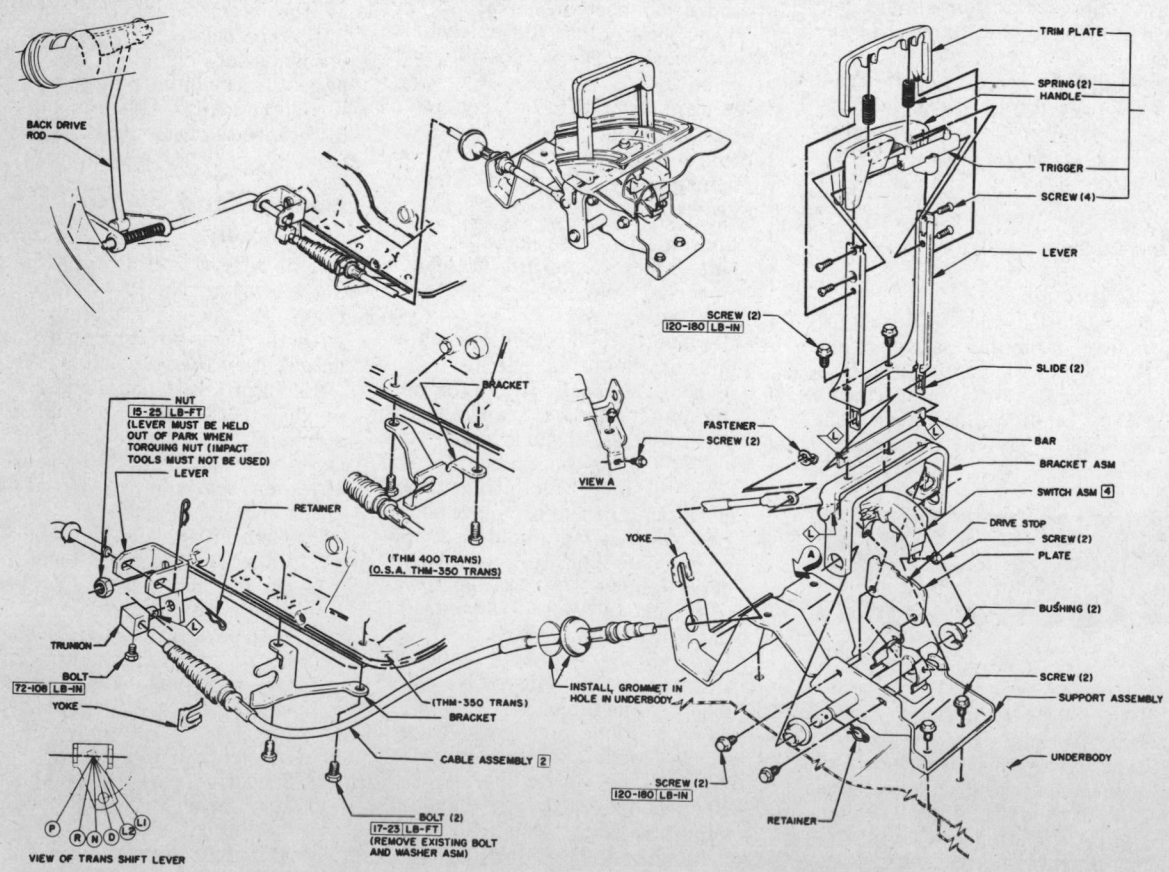

Cable type console shift linkage—Turbo-Hydramatic 400, through 1971
(© Buick Div., G.M. Corp)

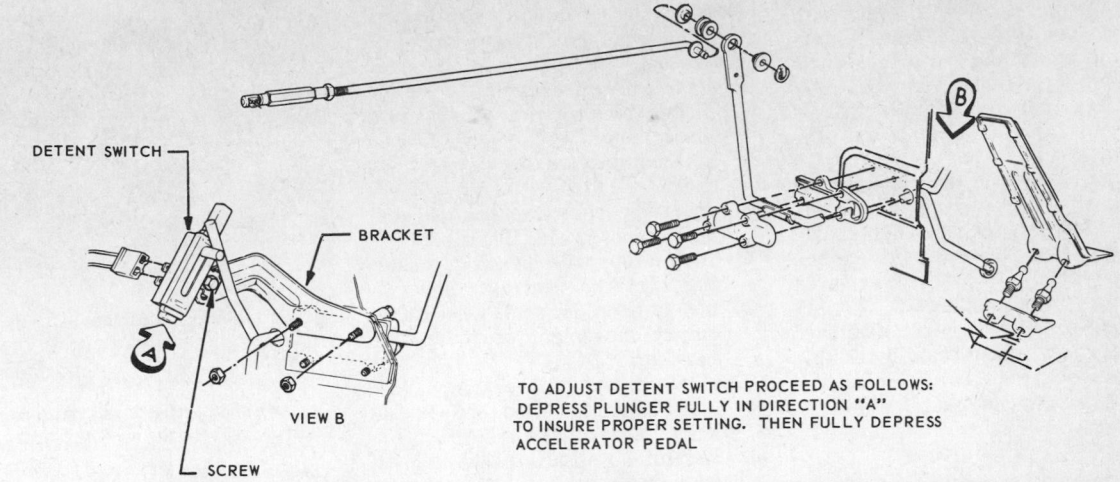

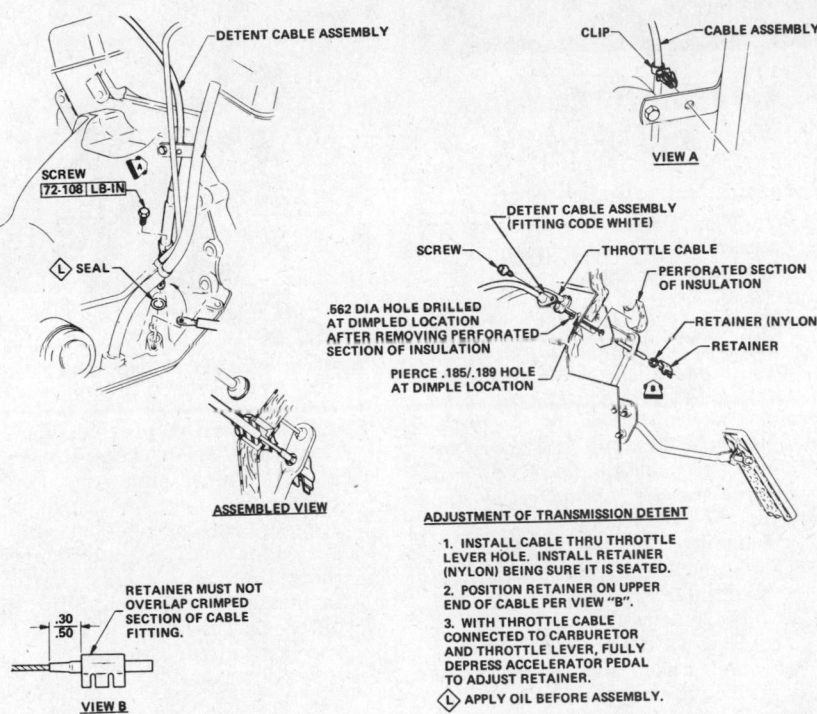

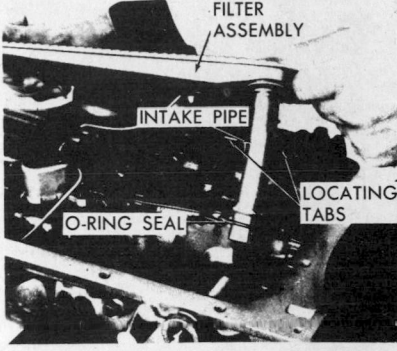

TO ADJUST DETENT SWITCH PROCEED AS FOLLOWS:
DEPRESS PLUNGER FULLY IN DIRECTION "A"
TO INSURE PROPER SETTING. THEN FULLY DEPRESS
ACCELERATOR PEDAL

Detent switch adjustment—1971 (© Buick Div., G.M. Corp)

ADJUSTMENT OF TRANSMISSION DETENT

1. INSTALL CABLE THRU THROTTLE LEVER HOLE. INSTALL RETAINER (NYLON) BEING SURE IT IS SEATED.
2. POSITION RETAINER ON UPPER END OF CABLE PER VIEW "B".
3. WITH THROTTLE CABLE CONNECTED TO CARBURETOR AND THROTTLE LEVER, FULLY DEPRESS ACCELERATOR PEDAL TO ADJUST RETAINER.
Ⓛ APPLY OIL BEFORE ASSEMBLY.

1970 Turbo-Hydramatic 400 detent switch adjustment
(© Buick Div., G.M. Corp)

Removing/installing the filter and O-ring
seal on a 400 automatic transmission
(© Buick Div., G.M. Corp)

filter and intake pipe. Install a new O-ring. Tighten the filter retaining bolt to 12 ft lbs. Add 5 pints of fluid through the filler tube.

U-JOINTS

Driveshaft Removal

1970 Riviera

1. Mark pinion flange and rear joint for reassembly. At rear pinion flange, remove U-bolt clamps from rear universal; on

start the engine, but do not race it. Move the shift lever through each range.

9. Immediately check the fluid level with the selector lever in Park, and the engine running. Make sure the vehicle is resting on a level surface.

10. Add additional fluid as necessary to bring the level to ¼ in. below the "ADD" mark on the dipstick. Do not overfill.

Turbo Hydra-Matic 400

The procedure for removing the pan and changing the fluid and filter are the same as for the 350 and 375. The filter of the 400 is attached by one bolt and has an O-ring seal on the end of the intake pipe. Make sure

that the O-ring is removed from its seat if it does not come out with the

Removing/installing the filter and gasket on a 350 or 375 automatic transmission
(© Buick Div., G.M. Corp)

Riviera, remove four rear constant velocity joint to pinion flange bolts. Use tape to secure bearings on the spider.

2. Remove four center bearing attaching bolts; two bolts on Riviera.
3. Support rear end of shaft. Slide assembly rearward until front yoke is free of transmission shaft splines. On Riviera, slide complete shaft assembly rearward through frame tunnel.
4. Protect the oil seal surface on the front yoke from dirt or marring.
   NOTE: do not bend constant velocity joint to its extreme angle at any time.

1970, Except Riviera, All 1971 and later

1. Mark shaft and pinion flange for reassembly.
2. Remove U-bolts from rear pinion flange. Use tape to secure bearings on the spider.
3. Remove shaft assembly by sliding rearward to disengage splines on transmission shaft.

Driveshaft Disassembly

Single Universal Joint

Nylon-injected composite universal joints are used.

1. Remove the driveshaft.
2. By using a piece of pipe or similar tool, slightly larger than 1⅛ in. to encircle the bearing shell, apply force on the yoke until downward movement of the yoke and stationary position of journal force the bearing assembly almost out of the top of the yoke (the force applied on the yoke will shear nylon retainers which lock bearings in place).
3. Rotate propeller shaft 180° and repeat preceding step to partially remove the opposite bearing.
4. Complete removal of these bearings by tapping around the circumference of exposed portion of bearing.
5. Remove journal from driveshaft rear yoke.
6. Remove bearings and journal from splined yoke in the same way.

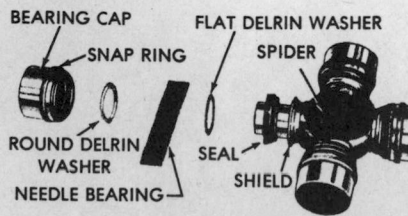

Typical U-joint
(© Buick Div., G.M. Corp)

BEARING CAP
SNAP RING
ROUND DELRIN WASHER
NEEDLE BEARING
FLAT DELRIN WASHER
SPIDER
SEAL
SHIELD

NOTE: New bearings and journal assembly kits must be used upon reassembly. The kit includes snap-rings and Delrin washers.

7. Install by inserting one bearing one-quarter way in one side of splined yoke, using brass hammer.
8. Insert journal into splined yoke (with dust shields installed).
9. Install opposite bearing, ensuring that the bearing rollers do not jam on journal. Check free rotary movement of journal in bearing.
10. Now, press both bearings into place (just far enough to install snap rings).
11. Assemble opposite end universal in the same way.

REAR AXLE

Axle Shaft, Bearing and Seal

Removal and Installation

1. Jack up the vehicle and remove the wheel and brake drum on the side to be serviced.
   NOTE: There are two types of axles installed in Buicks; one with the axle shafts attached to the differential side gears with C-clips and the other with the axle shafts held in by retainer plates attached to the brake backing plate. The only way to be sure of which type you are working on is to remove the differential cover and look for the C-clips.
2. On models with the C-clips:
   a. Remove the bolts and differential carrier cover and allow the lubricant to drain out.
   b. Remove the pinion shaft lock bolt and pinion shaft from the differential.
   c. Push the axle shafts inward to permit the removal of the C-clips and remove the axle shafts.
3. On models with retainer plates:
   a. Remove the nuts holding the retainer plates to the brake backing plates.
   b. Pull the retainers clear of the bolts and reinstall two opposite nuts finger tight to hold the brake backing plate in position.
   c. Pull the axle shaft out using an axle puller (slide hammer).
4. On axles with C-clips, the bearing and seal are removed and installed from the axle housing with special bearing and seal tools.
5. On axles with the retainer plates, and axle bearing retainer ring must be cracked with a chisel,

Axle shaft C-clips inside the differential
(© Buick Div., G.M. Corp)

AXLE SHAFT "C" LOCK

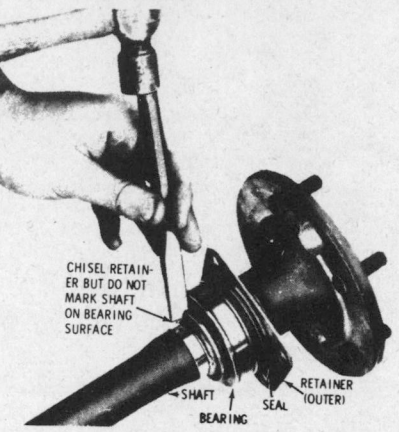

Breaking the bearing retainer with a chisel
(© Buick Div., G.M. Corp)

CHISEL RETAINER BUT DO NOT MARK SHAFT ON BEARING SURFACE
SHAFT
BEARING
SEAL
RETAINER (OUTER)

and the bearing pressed off and on with an arbor press. Press on a new retainer ring.

6. Install the axle shafts in the reverse order of removal. Apply a small amount of lubricant to the splines of the axle shaft to facilitate installation. If the differential is a limited slip type, use a limited slip differential type lubricant.

JACKING, HOISTING

Jack car at front spring seat of lower control arm or center of crossmember.

Jack car at rear, at axle housing.

To lift at frame, use side rails in front of body floor pan and at rear side rail at lower control arm front pivot.

FRONT SUSPENSION

Figures covering the caster, camber, toe-in, king pin inclination, and turning radius can be found in the Wheel Alignment table.

Shock Absorber Replacement

1. Remove the upper shock absorber attaching nut, grommet retainer, and grommet.
2. Remove the lower retaining screws. Lower the shock through the hole in the lower control arm.
3. Reverse the above steps to install.

Ball Joints

Inspection

Through 1972

NOTE: before performing this inspection, make sure that the wheel bearings are adjusted correctly and that the A-arm bushings are in good condition. Due to the distribution of forces in the suspension, the lower ball joint is usually the defective joint.

1. Jack the car up under the front lower control arm at the spring seat.
2. Raise the car until there is 1–2 in. of clearance under the wheel.
3. Insert a bar under the wheel and pry upward. If the wheel raises more than 1/8 in., the ball joints are worn. Determine whether the upper or lower ball joint is worn by visual inspection while prying on the wheel.

Beginning 1973

The lower ball joints contain a visual wear indicator. The lower ball joint grease plug screws into the wear indicator which protrudes from the bottom of the ball joint housing. As long as the wear indicator extends out of the ball joint housing, the ball joint is not worn. If the tip of the wear indicator is parallel with, or recessed into the ball joint housing, the ball joint is defective.

Control Arms, and/or Ball Joint, Spring—Removal and Installation

Upper Control Arm

1. Raise car with jack under the frame. Remove wheel and tire.
2. Remove cotter pin from upper ball joint stud.
3. Loosen, but do not remove nut.

Caution If the nut is removed, the full force of the coil spring could be released.

Rap the knuckle sharply in the area of the tapered stud to free the stud from the knuckle.

4. With another jack, support the car weight under the outer edge of the lower control arm. Raise jack enough to free upper control arm from upper ball stud.
5. Wire brake and knuckle in place to prevent brake hose damage, then, lift upper arm from knuckle.

NOTE: If only ball joints are to be replaced, stop at this point. Center punch and drill out the four rivets, then chisel off their heads. Remove old ball joint—the new joint comes with four specially hardened bolts, which must be torqued to 8 ft. lbs. The nut goes on top.

6. Remove the upper control arm shaft-to-bracket nuts and lock washers. Carefully note the number, thickness, and location of the adjusting shims. Remove control arm assembly.
7. Reverse the above steps to install.

Caution When installing the cotter pin, never

CASTER AND CAMBER ADJUSTMENT

FOR CASTER AND CAMBER DIMENSIONS, SEE WHEEL ALIGNMENT AND SPEC CHART.

FOR INCREASED OR POSITIVE CASTER, DECREASE SHIMS AT BOLT "A" AND INCREASE SHIMS AT BOLT "B" BY TWICE THIS AMOUNT

FOR DECREASED OR NEGATIVE CASTER, INCREASE SHIMS AT BOLT "A" AND DECREASE SHIMS AT BOLT "B" BY TWICE THIS AMOUNT.

FOR INCREASED CAMBER, DECREASE SHIMS AT BOTH "A" AND "B" BOLTS. SHIMMING GREATER THAN .750 NOT PERMISSIBLE.

SHIM THICKNESS AT "A" AND "B" LOCATION TO BE WITHIN .40 OF EACH OTHER

SHIM AS REQUIRED - AT LEAST ONE OF THESE SHIMS MUST BE USED AT EACH BOLT.
.030 THICK
.060 THICK
.120 THICK

BOLT "B"-REAR

BOLT "A"-FRONT

VIEW A

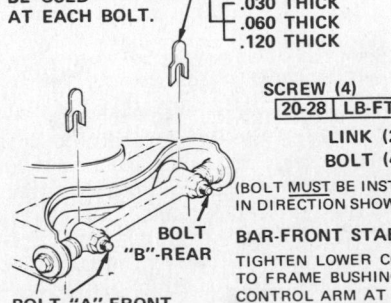

INSTALL PIN HEAD TIGHT IN NUT SLOT & BEND APPROX AS SHOWN, AT BOTH UPPER & LOWER BALL STUDS.

AXIS OF COTTER PIN HOLES IN JOINT STUDS SHOULD BE LOCATED APPROX PARALLEL TO ℄ CAR WITH FRONT WHEELS STRAIGHT AHEAD.

VIEW B

NUT (2) | 60-120 LB-IN
RETAINER (4)
GROMMET (4)
BOLT (4)
BUSHING (2)
BRACKET (2)

SCREW (4) | 20-28 LB-FT
LINK (2)
BOLT (4)
(BOLT MUST BE INSTALLED IN DIRECTION SHOWN)
BAR-FRONT STABILIZER
TIGHTEN LOWER CONTROL ARM TO FRAME BUSHINGS WITH CONTROL ARM AT CURB POSITION.
TIGHTEN STABILIZER TO FRAME BRACKETS WITH STABILIZER IN CURB POSITION.

NUT (4) | 90-115 LB-FT
BUMPER (2)
SPACER (2)
RETAINER (8)
GROMMET (8)
NUT (2) | 14-20 LB-FT
NUT (2) | 10-15 LB-FT
SCREW (4) | 15-25 LB-FT
NUT (4)
ARM ASM-LOWER

NUT (4) | 65-85 LB-FT
ARM ASM-UPPER
INSULATOR (2)
BUMPER (2)
PERM ANTI-FREEZE MAY BE USED TO ASSIST INSTALLATION OF BUMPER
COTTER PIN (4)
STEERING KNUCKLE AND FT WHEEL HUB ASM
NUT (2) | 40-60 LB-FT
WHEN CHECKING TORQUE, TIGHTEN TO NEXT COTTER PIN HOLE. THIS TORQUE NOT TO EXCEED 90 LB-FT.
NUT (2) | 60-105 LB-FT
WHEN CHECKING TORQUE, TIGHTEN TO NEXT COTTER PIN HOLE. THIS TORQUE NOT TO EXCEED 125 LB-FT.

WITH SUSPENSION ASSEMBLED, THE BOTTOM END OF COIL SPRING MUST SHOW IN FIRST HOLE AND NOT COVER SECOND HOLE.

VIEW C

Front suspension—starting 1971 (© Buick Div., G.M. Corp)

loosen the nut to align the cotter pin holes. Always tighten the nut to the next slot that lines up with the hole.

Lower Control Arm, or Spring

1. Raise the front of the car and remove the tires, wheels, hub and drum or rotor.
2. Disconnect and remove shock absorber.
3. Remove front stabilizer rod link from lower control arm.
4. Disconnect brake reaction rod from lower control arm but leave it attached to the front frame crossmember on 1970 models.
5. Remove control arm bumper on 1970 models.
6. As a safety precaution and to gain maximum leverage, place a jack about ½ in. below the lower ball joint stud. Now, remove the ball stud cotter pin and loosen the nut about ⅛ in. Do not remove the nut.
7. Rap the steering knuckle in the area of the stud to separate the stud from the knuckle.
8. After the stud has broken loose from the knuckle, raise the jack against the control arm. Remove nut and separate the steering knuckle from the tapered stud.
9. Carefully lower jack under the control arm and release the spring. With the jack entirely lowered, it may be necessary to pry the spring off its seat on the lower control arm with a pry bar.
10. After the spring is removed, the lower control arm may be removed by removing the lock nut attaching the control arm to the frame.
11. Install by reversing removal procedure. Tighten castellated nut to 85 ft. lbs.

Lower Ball Joint Replacement

1. Perform steps two through eight, inclusive, in the "Lower Control Arm R&R" procedure.
2. Remove the ball joint by pressing the joint from the lower control arm. It may be necessary to remove the ball joint and lower control arm as an assembly and have the ball joint removed in a press if suitable tools are not available.
3. Install a new ball joint and reverse the removal procedure.

Front Wheel Bearing Adjustment

1970

Adjustment of freshly cleaned and repacked roller bearings is as follows:

1. Torque spindle nut to 19 ft. lbs. while rotating the wheel.
2. Back off the nut until bearings are loose.
3. Retorque spindle nut to 11 ft. lbs. while rotating the wheel.
4. If either cotter pin hole in spindle lines up with nut castellations, back off the nut one-twelfth turn and install cotter pin. Otherwise, back off the nut to the first position that will accept a horizontal or vertical cotter pin.
5. Install cotter pin and lock spindle nut into position.

NOTE: .002-.006 in. end-play is normal.

1971 and Later

1. Lift the wheel off the ground by jacking under the lower control arm.
2. Remove the dust cap from the hub.
3. Remove the cotter pin and discard.
4. Snug up the spindle nut to seat the bearings. Then back off the nut 1/4-1/2 turn.
5. Retighten the nut by hand until it is finger-tight.
6. Loosen the nut 1/12 of a turn (no more than 1/6) and line up the hole in the spindle with the nearest slot in the spindle nut, and insert a new cotter pin. There should be 0.001-0.005 in. end-play.

NOTE: Under no circumstances is the final bearing nut adjustment to be even finger-tight.

7. Replace the dust cover and lower the car.

REAR SUSPENSION

Shock Absorber Replacement

1. Raise the car at the axle housing.
2. Remove the nut, retainer, and grommet or nut, and lockwasher, as equipped, which attach the lower end of the shock absorber to its mounting.
3. Remove the two shock absorber upper attaching screws and remove the shock absorber.
4. Reverse the removal procedures to install. On 1973 and later models the upper attaching nut should be tightened to 10-15 ft lbs.

Rear Leaf Spring Replacement —1971 and later Station Wagon

1. Jack up car at axle housing. Make sure you don't crush exhaust pipe.
2. Support car at both frame side rails in front of and behind the springs, using axle stands.
3. Remove nut and lockwasher from lower shock stud.
4. Move shock out of the way.
5. Disconnect the right side exhaust system by removing the screw that attaches the exhaust pipe hanger to the rear frame crossmember. Support the exhaust system to prevent damage from bending.
6. Remove spring anchor plate nuts, then remove anchor plate and cushion.
7. Jack axle housing up and remove upper cushion.
8. Loosen upper and lower spring shackle nuts.
9. Loosen spring eye bolt.
10. Remove eye bolt and carefully lower spring.
11. Support spring and remove lower shackle pin.
12. Remove spring.
13. To install, reverse removal procedure. Tighten front eye bolt to 80-100 ft lbs., shackle nuts to 75-95 ft lbs., anchor plate nuts to 35-50 ft lbs, and lower shock nut to 55-75 ft lbs.

Rear Coil Spring Replacement

1. Jack up the back of the car and support both sides on stand jacks on the frame, in front of the rear axle. Disconnect shock absorbers.

NOTE: It may be necessary to disconnect the rear brake line in order to obtain sufficient axle drop to remove the spring. If this is done, first depress and secure the brake pedal at least 1 in. from the relaxed position to prevent the master cylinder from draining when the rear brake line is disconnected.

2. Place a jack under the lower control arms and remove the bolts which hold the upper control arms to the rear axle housing.

NOTE: Spring can often be removed without disconnecting lower control arm.

3. Slowly, and very carefully, let the trailing arms come down until the tension is released from the rear coil springs. Then, take off the coil spring. Note the direction the end of the last coil is pointing. Reinstall the spring in the same position.
4. When starting a new coil spring, make certain that the bottom of the coil is properly inserted into the socket in the frame and into the form plate on the trailing arm.
5. Jack the trailing arms into place and reinstall but do not tighten the bolts yet.
6. Lower the car to rest on its wheels.
7. Tighten the bolts to 65-85 ft lbs.

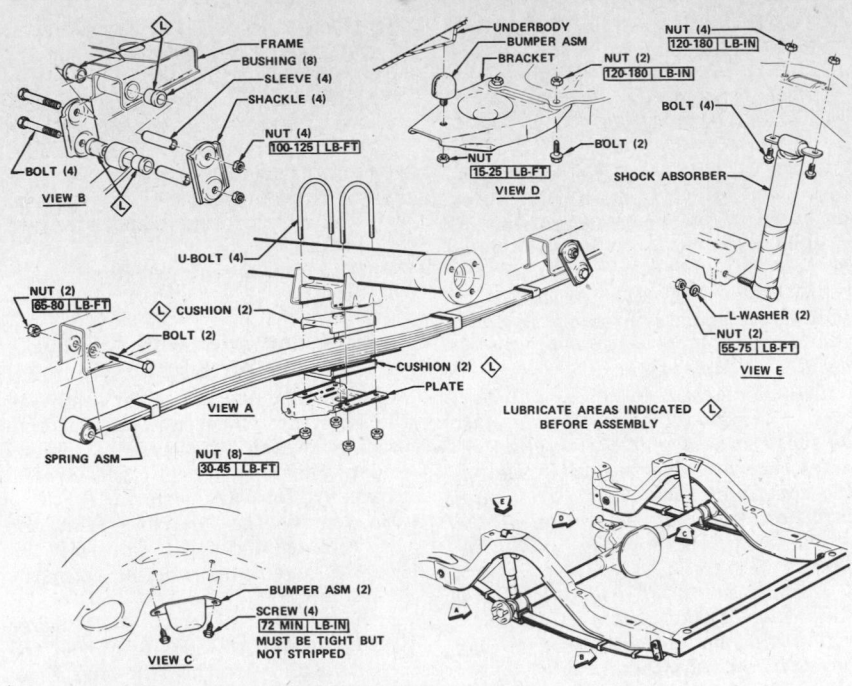

Rear suspension details—Estate Wagon with leaf springs, 1971 and later
(© Buick Div., G.M. Corp)

Power Brake Unit Removal and Installation

1. Unbolt the master cylinder from the power unit. Being careful not to kink or bend the brake lines, pull the master cylinder away from the power unit without disconnecting the brake lines.
2. Disconnect and plug the vacuum hose.
3. Disconnect the power brake pushrod from the brake pedal.
4. Unbolt the power brake unit from the firewall.
5. Remove the unit.
6. Mount the unit to the firewall.
7. Install the master cylinder to the power unit and torque the nuts to 25 ft lbs.
8. Connect the vacuum hose.
9. Connect the power brake pushrod to the brake pedal.

Parking Brake Adjustment

Adjustment of the parking brake is necessary whenever the rear brake cables have been disconnected or the parking brake pedal can be depressed more than sixteen rachet clicks (13 on 1974 and later models) under foot pressure. The car should first be raised on a lift.

1. Make sure that service brakes are properly adjusted.
2. Depress parking brake pedal three ratchet clicks (six on 1974 and later Estate wagons).
3. Loosen jam nut on equalizer adjusting nut. Tighten adjusting nut until rear wheels can just be turned rearward by hand but not forward.
4. Release rachet one click; the rear wheels should rotate rearward freely and forward with a slight drag.
5. Release rachet fully; the rear wheels should turn freely in either direction.

NOTE: be sure that the parking brake does not drag. An overtightened, dragging parking brake on a car with automatic brake adjusters will result in an extremely short life for rear brake linings.

BRAKES

A dual master cylinder is used on all models. Information on the system and brake adjustments, lining replacement, bleeding procedure, master and wheel cylinder overhaul can be found in the Unit Repair Section.

Master Cylinder Removal and Installation

1. Disconnect brake pipe or pipes from master cylinder and tape

end of pipe or pipes to prevent entrance of dirt.
2. Disconnect brake pedal from master cylinder at the pushrod.

NOTE: Step 2 is not necessary with power brakes.

3. Remove master cylinder-to-dash or booster retaining bolts. Remove the master cylinder.
4. Reverse the above steps to install. Bleed the brakes and check for leaks after installation.

STEERING

Power Steering Pump Removal and Installation

Disconnect the drive belt and remove the pump pulley with a suitable puller. On some models, the pulley has bolt access holes which make pulley removal unnecessary. Disconnect the hoses from the pump and unbolt the pump from the bracket. Use caps or tape to cover the hose connectors, unions, and hose ends to keep out dirt.

Reinstall by reversing procedure.

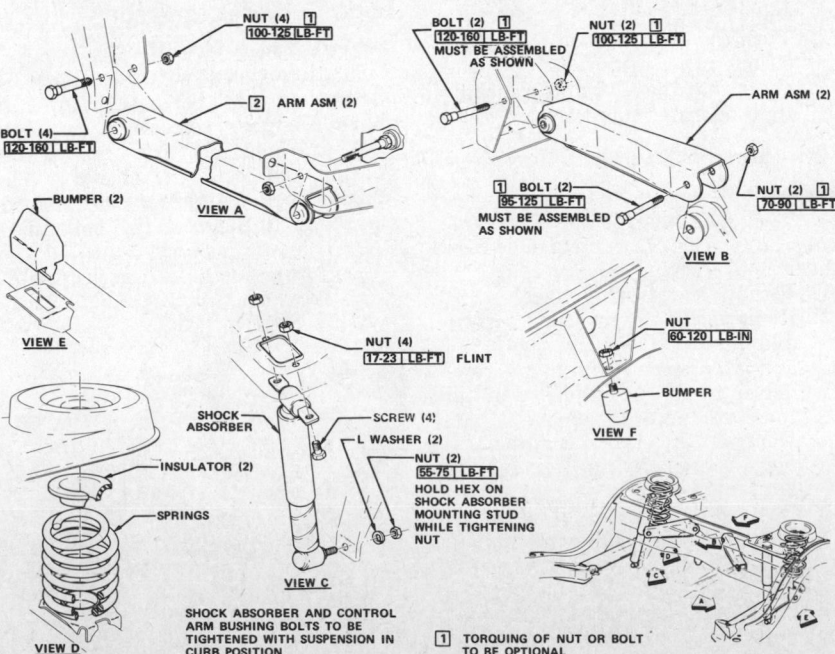

Rear suspension details—typical with coil springs (© Buick Div., G.M. Corp)

The drive belt should be adjusted to have about ½ in. play on the longest run between pulleys. After replacing pump, fill reservoir and bleed pump by idling engine for three minutes before moving the steering wheel. Then rotate steering wheel slowly throughout its entire range. Recheck level.

Steering Wheel Removal and Installation

1. Unplug the horn wire connector from the steering column.
2. On cars with standard wheel or optional wood-rim wheel, pull off cap, remove three screws and bushing spacer, receiver cup, and Belleville spring. On cars with bar-type horn actuator remove screws securing actuator from underside of steering wheel, pull out lead connector plug, and remove actuator assembly.
3. Remove the retaining ring. On tilt wheel models, remove the flange and lever retaining bolts and remove the flange and lever. Loosen the steering wheel nut several turns but do not remove it.
4. Apply steering wheel puller and pull wheel up to the nut. Now remove puller, nut and steering wheel.

Caution Don't pound on the steering wheel in either direction or the collapsible steering column will collapse, requiring replacement.

5. Install wheel with the location mark aligned with that of the shaft.

NOTE: Location marks are provided on the steering wheel and shaft to simplify proper indexing at the time of installation.

6. Install the wheel nut and torque to 30 ft lbs.
7. Reinstall horn button or actuator assembly.

Special Procedure for Cars with A.C.R.S. (Air Bags)

Some 1974 and later models have an air cushion, or air bag, restraint system. One of the elements of this complex system is an air cushion module in the top of the steering wheel. The steering wheel can be removed in the manner described in this section after the module has been removed.

To remove the module:
1. Turn the ignition lock to the LOCK position.
2. Disconnect the battery ground cable and tape the end to prevent any possibility of a complete circuit.
3. Remove the 4 module-to-steering wheel screws. A special tool is available to do this.

4. Lift up the module and disconnect the horn wire.
5. Disconnect the module wire connector. A special tool is available to do this, too.

WARNING: The driver air cushion module should always be carried with the vinyl cover away from all parts of one's body and should always be laid on a flat surface with the vinyl side up. This is necessary so that a free space is provided to allow the air cushion to expand in case of accidental deployment.

Do not attempt to repair any portion of the module. The module must be serviced as a unit. Attempting repairs such as soldering wires, changing covers, etc. may cause accidental inflation or impair operation of the driver module and cause serious injury.

Do not dispose of a module in any way. The highly inflammable material in the module can cause serious burns if ignited. Modules must be exchanged at an authorized dealer's parts department.

To install the module:
6. Hold the module with the emblem in the lower right corner.
7. Loop the air cushion harness clockwise from the 11 O'clock position to the 6 O'clock position.
8. Install the module connector by pushing it onto the column circuit firmly. Check that it is fully seated.
9. Install the horn wire.
10. Position the module, making sure that the wiring is still in place, and install the 4 screws. Torque them to 40 in. lbs.
11. Reconnect the battery ground cable.
12. Turn the ignition lock to any position other than LOCK and check that the restraint indicator light operates correctly.

Turn Signal Switch Replacement

NOTE: The steering wheel must always be supported. Use extreme care not to bend steering column.
1. Remove the steering wheel.
2. Remove the three cover screws and remove the cover. On 1976 and later models, insert a screwdriver in the slot and pry up on the cover plate to remove it.
3. Depress the lockplate and remove the snap-ring. Remove the lockplate.
4. Remove the spring and horn contact signal cancelling cam. Remove the thrust washer from the upper steering shaft.
5. Remove the turn signal lever, depress and remove the hazard warning knob, and tilt column lever, if equipped.

6. Tape the wiring harness connector to the wires so it will slip easily up the steering column.
7. Remove the three turn signal switch mounting screws. Pull the connector out from the bracket on the column.
8. Pull the switch straight up with the wire protector and wire harness.
9. Reverse the above steps to install.

1974 and later with A.C.R.S. (Air Bags)

Follow the procedure for removing the steering wheel and air cushion module which appears previously under "Steering Wheel R&R, Special Procedure for Cars with A.C.R.S."
1. Remove the 3 screws from the retainer and cover. Carefully lift the cover and retainer from the column.
2. Carefully insert a screwdriver blade into the locking tab at the side and lift the slip ring from the column.
3. Now proceed with Steps 3-8 of the "Tilt and Non-Tilt Column Turn Signal Switch R & R" procedure.
4. To replace the slip ring, align the slip ring locating tab with the slot in the bowl and push the slip ring into position. Make sure that all 3 locking tabs are securely positioned.
5. Install the cover and retainer, aligning the cover over the locating tab. Torque the screws to 15 in. lbs.

Ignition Switch

Lock Cylinder and/or Switch Replacement

The ignition switch occupies a position on the steering column, just above the gear selector lever. This lock prevents shifting the transmission and locks the steering. The ignition lock cylinder cannot be removed until the steering column is

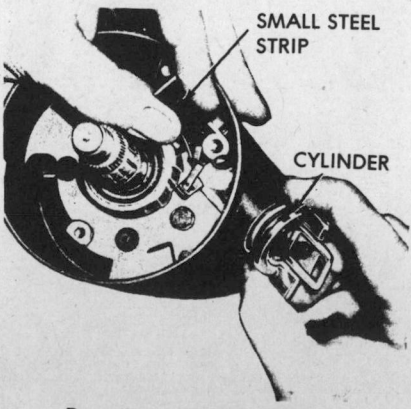

SMALL STEEL STRIP

CYLINDER

Removing ignition lock cylinder
(© Buick Div., G.M. Corp)

partially disassembled to gain access to the internal lock cylinder retainer. The steering wheel, lock plate, and turn signal switch assembly must be removed first.

Standard Column

1. Remove steering wheel using proper puller.
2. Remove three cover screws and cover; remove retainers.
3. Depress lock plate, then remove wire snap-ring and lock plate.
4. Slide upper bearing preload spring and cancelling cam off shaft.
5. Slide thrust washer off shaft, then remove turn signal lever screw and lever.
6. Push in four-way flasher switch; remove knob.
7. Remove three turn signal switch mounting screws, pull connector out of its bracket on the column and tape the upper part of connector and wires together.
8. Pull turn signal switch out of column jacket.
9. Insert a small screwdriver into the slot next to the turn signal switch mounting screw boss (right-hand slot), depress spring latch and remove key lock.
10. Pull buzzer switch straight out, depressing switch clip with pliers. If the ignition switch is to be removed, disconnect the steering column mounting bracket from the lower edge of the instrument panel and lower the steering column. Support the column so that it does not flex.
11. Place ignition switch in accessory position by pulling up on connecting rod until there is a definite stop or detent felt.
12. Remove two attaching screws and ignition switch.

LOCK PLATE

RETAINER RING

SCREWDRIVER

Depress the lock plate to remove the retaining ring (© Buick Div., G.M. Corp)

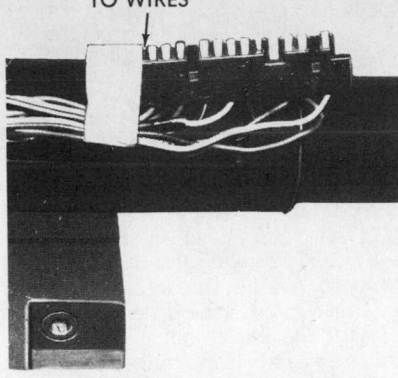

TAPE CONNECTOR TO WIRES

Tape the connector to the wires so that it will slip easily up the steering column (© Buick Div., G.M. Corp)

13. Assembly is the reverse of the above. However, note the following steps before proceeding with the reassembly.
14. To install the steering lock, hold the lock cylinder sleeve and rotate the knob clockwise against the stop. Insert the cylinder into the cover bore with the key on the cylinder sleeve aligned with the keyway in the housing. Then push the cylinder in until it bottoms. Maintaining a light inward pressure, rotate the knob counterclockwise until the drive section of the cylinder mates with the drive shaft. Push in until the snap ring pops into the groove and the lock cylinder is secured in the cover. Check for free rotation.
15. When installing the ignition switch, be sure the lock cylinder is in the lock position. Put the shift bowl or shroud in the park position. Make sure the ignition switch is in the lock position. Then insert the actuator rod into the switch and assemble the switch to the column.
16. The neutral start switch is adjusted with the shift lever in the drive position.

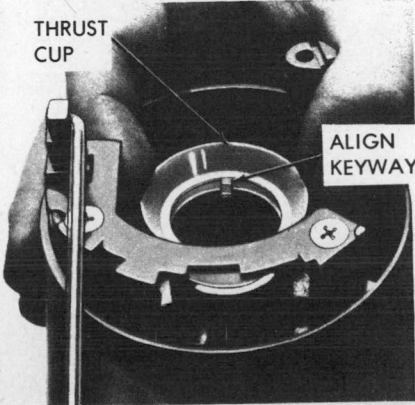

THRUST CUP

ALIGN KEYWAY

Removing the buzzer switch on a standard steering column (© Buick Div., G.M. Corp)

Tilt Column

1. Remove column mounting bracket from column.
   NOTE: be careful not to damage the "breakaway" capsules.
2. Remove steering wheel using proper puller.
3. Remove turn signal wire protector (lower column).
4. Remove three column cover screws and cover.
5. Remove tilt release lever, turn signal switch lever, push four-way flasher knob in and remove knob, and remove upper shift lever.
6. Depress lock plate and remove the snap-ring; remove lock plate.
7. Remove cancelling cam and spring.
8. Remove three turn signal switch screws, tape wires to wire connector at upper end and place shift bowl in Low. Pull switch straight up and out.
9. Insert a small screwdriver into the slot next to the turn signal switch mounting screw boss (right-hand slot), depress spring latch and remove key lock.
10. If ignition switch is to be replaced, remove buzzer switch straight out, depressing switch clip with pliers.
11. Remove three housing cover screws and cover.
12. Install tilt release lever and place column in full UP position.
13. Place screwdriver in slot of tilt spring retainer, press in about 3/16 in. and turn counterclockwise. Remove spring and guide.

NOTE: spring is very strong—be careful.

14. Place column in neutral position, push in on upper steering shaft, remove inner race seat and race.
15. Remove upper flange pinch bolt, place ignition switch in accessory position, remove two switch mounting screws and switch.

BUZZER SWITCH

Removing the buzzer switch on a tilt steering column (© Buick Div., G.M. Corp)

NOTE: neutral start switch can be removed at this time, if necessary.

16. Assembly is the reverse of the above. However, note the following steps before proceeding with the reassembly.

17. To install the steering lock, hold the lock cylinder sleeve and rotate the knob clockwise against the stop. Insert the cylinder into the cover bore with the key on the cylinder sleeve aligned with the keyway in the housing. Then push the cylinder in until it bottoms. Maintaining a light inward pressure, rotate the knob counterclockwise until the drive section of the cylinder mates with the drive shaft. Push in until the snap ring pops into the groove and the lock cylinder is secured in the cover. Check for free rotation.

18. When installing the ignition switch, be sure the lock cylinder is in the lock position. Put the shift bowl or shroud in the park position. Make sure the ignition switch is in the lock position. Then insert the actuator rod into the switch and assemble the switch to the column.

19. The neutral start switch is adjusted with the shift lever in the drive position.

INSTRUMENT PANEL

Light Switch

Replacement

1. Disconnect battery.
2. Starting 1975 remove the left side trim panel by moving the steering column rubber ring up and prying the trim panel off; then remove the three screws and lift the switch out of the instrument panel. Disconnect the terminal connector.
3. Pull switch knob to last notch and depress spring loaded latch button on top of switch, while pulling knob and rod out of switch.
4. Remove escutcheon and retaining nut. Remove switch from cluster.
   NOTE: remove left trim plate on 1973 and later models.
4. Disconnect multiple connector.
5. Install in reverse of above.

WINDSHIELD WIPERS

Motor Removal and Installation

1970

1. Disconnect wire connectors from motor and pump.
2. Remove washer hoses from the pump.
3. Remove left side air intake grille.
4. Remove spring retainer clip from wiper motor shaft lever.
5. Lift transmission drive links off motor shaft lever.
6. Remove motor attaching bolts, then lift out motor.
7. Install by reversing the above procedure.

1971 and Later

1. Raise the hood and remove the cowl screen.
2. Loosen the transmission drive link-to-crankarm attaching nuts through the cowl screen opening.
3. Remove the transmission drive link(s) from the motor crank arm.
4. Disconnect the wiring and washer hoses.
5. Remove the motor attaching screws.
6. Remove the motor while guiding the crank arm through the hole.
7. Install the wiper motor in the reverse order of removal. The motor must be in the Park position when assembling the crank arm to the transmission drive link(s).

RADIO

Always disconnect the battery ground cable before working on any part of the instrument panel.

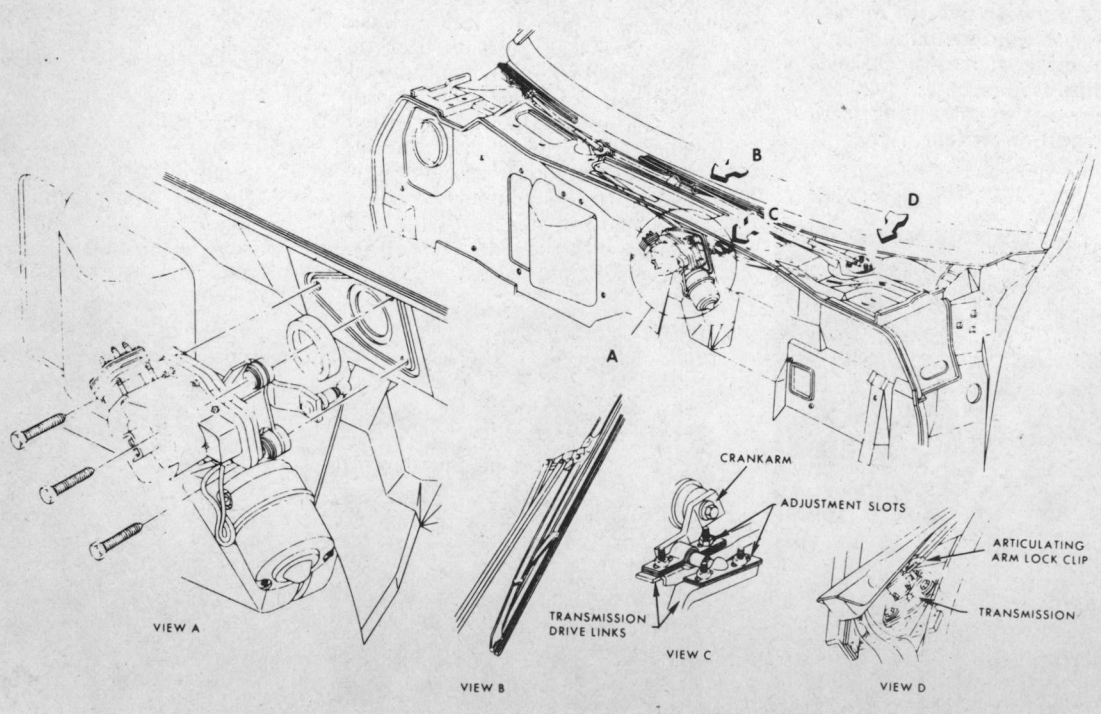

Windshield wiper system—1971 and later (© Buick Div., G.M. Corp)

Removal and Installation

1970 Riviera

1. Remove ash tray assembly.
2. Remove knobs, escutcheons, and hex nuts.
3. Unplug antenna and wiring leads.
4. Remove radio downward.
5. Install by reversing procedure.

1970 Except Riviera

1. Remove center air-conditioning duct.
2. Remove right instrument trim panel and screw in bottom of radio.
3. Remove radio knobs, escutcheons, and two hex nuts.
4. Unplug antenna and wiring leads.
5. Remove radio downward.
6. Install by reversing procedure.

1971 and Later

1. Remove knobs and escutcheons from radio. If equipped with Trip-Set and/or Speed-Alert, remove cone-shaped knobs.
2. Remove face plate by pulling outward. Disconnect terminal connector before completely removing face plate, if equipped with Trip-Set/Speed-Alert.
3. Remove the two hex nuts from the control shafts.
4. Remove ash tray and frame.
5. Disconnect the two connectors behind dash and unplug antenna.
6. Unscrew the support bracket nuts and remove radio to the rear and downwards.
7. Install by reversing removal procedure.

1974 and later with A.C.R.S. (Air Bags)

1. Turn the ignition lock to the LOCK position.
2. Disconnect the battery ground cable and tape its end thoroughly to prevent any possibility of a circuit.
3. Remove both lower instrument panel cover trim plates after prying them out.
4. Disconnect the parking brake release cable and remove the lower left instrument panel cover assembly by removing the 8 retaining screws.
5. Remove:
   a. 2 horizontal screws below the instrument panel
   b. 4 vertical screws on the upper horizontal instrument panel surface.
   c. 2 screws from the outside of the glove box door hinge
   d. 1 screw from the right-side of the instrument panel cover.

6. Disconnect the radio, speakers, convector (remote unit) connectors, and antenna lead cable from the radio.
7. Release the 4 clips behind the instrument panel by grasping the tongue of the far right-side clip, squeezing, and pulling forward.
8. Remove the radio knobs and escutcheons from the shafts.
9. Carefully pull the trim plate off the instrument panel housing.
10. Remove the retaining nuts from the shafts.
11. Unscrew and remove the power antenna relay.
12. Loosen the nut on the left radio support. Remove the right support nut.
13. Lower the radio from beneath the instrument panel.
14. If the car has a radio/tape unit, remove the two convector (remote unit) mounting screws and remove the convector from the right-side of the instrument panel housing support.
15. Reverse all these steps on installation.

HEATER

NOTE: On procedures which call for removal of fender in order to gain access to the blower motor, it is possible to cut a trap door in the inner fender panel to gain access to the blower motor. Using a torch or sheet metal cutter, cut the door on three sides and bend it out of the way. Remove and install the motor. Bend the trap door back and weld it in place. Then, spray the welds and door with undercoating.

Blower and Heater Core Removal and Installation w/o A/C

1970 Riviera

1. Remove the right front fender.
2. Disconnect the vacuum hoses.
3. Disconnect the wire that is attached to the motor and remove the connector from the blower resistor. If just the blower motor is to be replaced, remove the blower motor attaching screws and the blower.
4. Disconnect the control wire attached to the temperature door lever.
5. Drain the coolant and remove the heater hoses at the firewall.
6. Remove the 12 screws securing the blower and heater assembly to the firewall and remove the assembly.
7. Reverse the above steps to install.

Blower Motor Removal and Installation w/o A/C

All 1970 Models Except Riviera

1. Remove the right front fender.
2. Disconnect the blower motor wire.
3. Remove the blower motor attaching screws and remove the motor.
4. Reverse the above steps to install.

1971 and Later

1. Support the hood and loosen the hood hinge from the extension and plate assembly.
2. Remove the extension and plate assembly.
NOTE: Steps 1 and 2 are only necessary on the 1974-76 Riviera.
3. Disconnect the blower motor wire.
4. Remove the blower motor attaching screws and the motor.

Heater Core Removal and Installation w/o A/C

All Models Except 1970 Riviera

1. Drain the radiator and disconnect the heater inlet and outlet hoses at the dash.
2. Disconnect the control wires from the defroster door and vacuum hose diverter door actuator diaphragm and control cable from the temperature door lever.
3. Remove the 4 nuts securing the heater assembly to the dash.
4. Remove the screw securing the defroster outlet tab to the heater assembly.
5. Remove the heater from the car.
6. Reverse the above steps to install.

Blower Motor Removal and Installation with A/C

1970 Riviera

1. Remove the right front fender inner panel.
2. Remove the motor wires.
3. Remove the five blower motor securing screws and remove the motor.
4. Reverse the above steps to install.

1970 All Models Except Riviera

1. Remove the blower motor wires.
2. Remove the five blower motor securing screws and remove the motor.
3. Reverse the above steps to install.

1971 and Later

1. Support the hood and loosen the hood hinge from the extension and plate assembly.

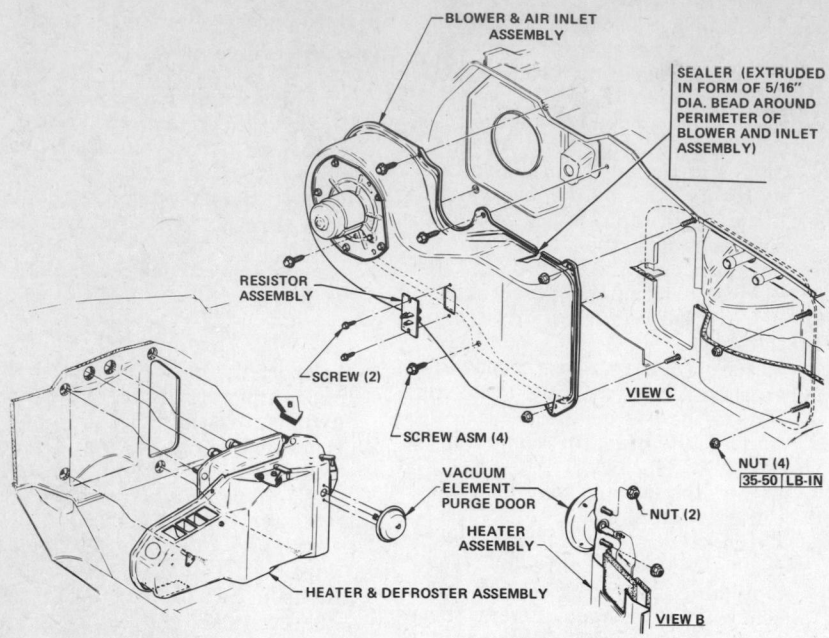

Heater blower removal—beginning 1971 (© Buick Div., G.M. Corp)

2. Remove the extension and plate assembly.

   NOTE: Steps 1 and 2 are not necessary on the 1974 and later models.

3. Disconnect the blower motor wires.

4. Remove the blower motor securing screws and remove the motor.

Heater Core Removal and Installation with A/C

1970 Riviera

1. Drain the radiator and disconnect the heater hoses from the heater core.

2. Disconnect the temperature door control cable and blower wires.

3. Remove the six screws securing the air conditioner assembly to the firewall and remove the assembly.

4. Reverse the above steps to install.

1970 All Models except Riviera

1. Drain the radiator and disconnect the hoses from the heater core.

2. Remove the instrument panel cover with the center A/C outlet and right A/C outlet with hose attached.

3. Remove the center A/C duct, A/C distributor duct and defroster outlet manifold assembly.

4. Disconnect the defroster and temperature control wires and the pink hose from the mode door diaphragm.

5. Remove the seven screws from the inside and the two screws from the engine compartment and remove the core assembly.

1971 and Later

NOTE: This procedure does not apply to those models with the A.C. R.S. (air bag) system. For those models with air bags, it is advisable to take the car to a dealer for proper servicing.

1. Drain the radiator and disconnect the hoses from the core.

2. Disconnect the wires from the defroster door, diverter door and temperature door.

3. Remove the four nuts securing the core assembly to the dash.

4. Remove the screw securing the defroster outlet tab to the heater assembly.

5. Remove the core assembly.

6. Reverse the above steps to install.

SEAT BELTS

Disabling the Seat Belt/ Starter Interlock System

It is legal to disconnect the seat belt interlock, but not the seat belt warning light. Disconnect the system as follows:

1. Disconnect the negative battery cable.

2. Locate the interlock wiring harness under the left side of the instrument panel on or near the fuse block. The connector has orange, yellow and green wires.

3. Cut and tape the ends of the green wire on the body side of the harness.

4. Disconnect the seat belt warning buzzer from the installed position under the left side of the instrument panel by removing the buzzer from the fuse block or connector and removing the two yellow wires with black tracers from the multiple connector into which the buzzer is plugged. Tape the terminal and reinstall the buzzer.

5. Connect the battery ground cable.

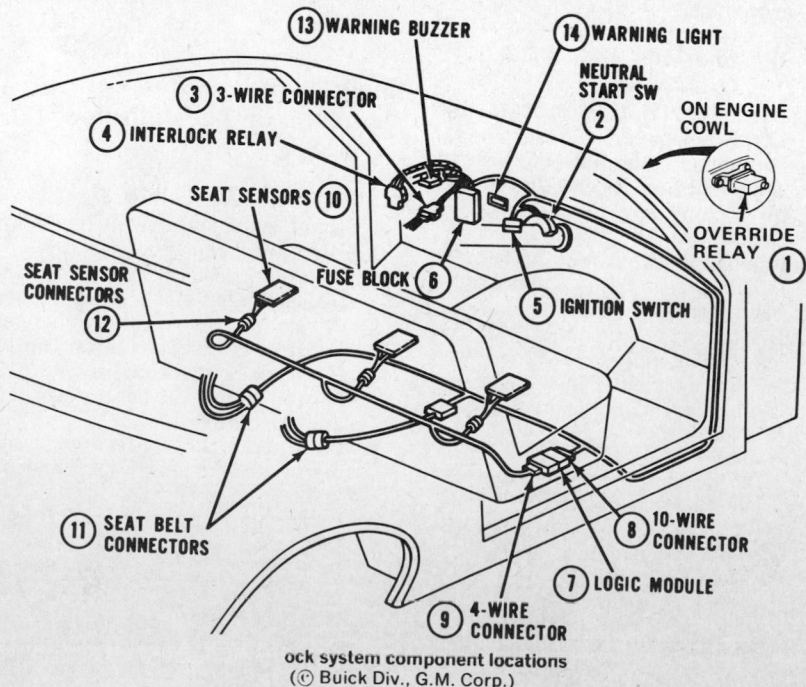

ock system component locations
(© Buick Div., G.M. Corp.)

INDEX

Buick Apollo · Century · Gran Sport · Regal · Skyhawk · Skylark · Special

Automatic Transmission
In-car Service **C240, U369**
Detent Cable or Switch Adjustment C241
Shift Linkage Adustment C241
Neutral Safety Switch Adjustment C242
Pan Removal and Installation,
  Fluid and Filter Change C242

Brakes **C246, U299**
Master Cylinder Removal and
  Installation C246
Parking Brake Adjustment C247
Power Brake Unit Removal and
  Installation C247

Charging System **C226, U2**
Alternator Removal and Installation C226
Voltage Regulator Removal and
  Installation C226

Clutch **C239**
Clutch Removal and Installation C239
Linkage Adjustment C239

Cooling System **C230, U367**
Radiator Removal and Installation C231
Thermostat Removal and Installation ... C230
Water Pump Removal and Installation .. C231

Emission Controls **C231, U145**

Engine **C232, U194**
Engine Removal and Installation C232
CYLINDER HEAD Removal and
  Installation C234
LUBRICATION C237
Oil Pan Removal and Installation C238
Oil Pump Removal and Installation C237
Rear Main Bearing Oil Seal Replacement C238
MANIFOLDS C232
Exhaust Manifold C233
Intake Manifold C233
PISTON ASSEMBLY C237
TIMING COVER, CHAIN, AND CAMSHAFT C235
Camshaft Removal and Installation C236
Timing Chain, Cover Oil Seal, and
  Cover Removal and Installation C235

VALVE SYSTEM C233
Adjustment C233
Rocker Arm Removal and Installation ... C233

Front Suspension **C244, U292**
Ball Joint Inspection C244
Upper Control Arm, Ball Joint, and
  Spring Removal and Installation C244
Lower Ball Joint Removal and
  Installation C245
Shock Absorber Removal and
  Installation C245
Wheel Bearing Adjustment C245

Fuel System **C220, U50**
Fuel Filter Replacement C230
Fuel Pump Removal and Installation ... C230
Idle Speed and Mixture Adjustment C228

Heater **C249**
Heater Blower Removal and Installation
  without A/C C250
Heater Core Removal and Installation
  without A/C C249
Heater Blower Removal and Installation
  with A/C C250
Heater Core Removal and Installation
  with A/C C250

Ignition System **C227, U34**
Contact Point Replacement and
  Adjustment C227
Distributor Removal and Installation ... C227
Firing Order C220
High Energy Ignition System,
  Tachometer Hookup C228
Ignition Timing C228

Instrument Panel **C249, U350**
Light Switch Replacement C249
Speedometer Cable Replacement C249

Manual Transmission **C239, U231**
Linkage Adjustment C240
Transmission Removal and Installation .. C239

Jacking, Hoisting **C244**

Radio **C249**
Removal and Installation C249

Rear Axle **C243, U285**
Axle Shaft, Bearing, and Seal Removal
  and Installation C243

Rear Suspension **C245**
Spring Replacement C245
Shock Absorber Removal and
  Installation C245

Seat Belts **C251**
Disabling the Interlock System C251

Specifications **C221, U359**
Capacities C224
Crankshaft and Connecting Rod C225
Engine Identification and Code C221
General Engine C222
Piston Clearance C226
Ring C225
Torque C224
Tune-Up C223
Valve C225
Wheel Alignment C226
Year Identification C220

Starting System **C226, U2**
Starter Removal and Installation C226

Steering **C247, U328**
Ignition Switch and Lock Cylinder
  Removal and Installation C248
Power Steering Pump Removal and
  Installation, System Bleeding C247
Steering Wheel Removal and
  Installation C247
Tie-Rod End Removal and Installation .. C247
Turn Signal Switch Removal and
  Installation C247

U-Joints **C242**
Driveshaft Removal and Installation ... C243
Universal Joint Removal and Installation C243

Windshield Wipers **C249**
Motor Removal and Installation C249

YEAR IDENTIFICATION

1970 Buick Special

1971 Skylark

1971 G.S.

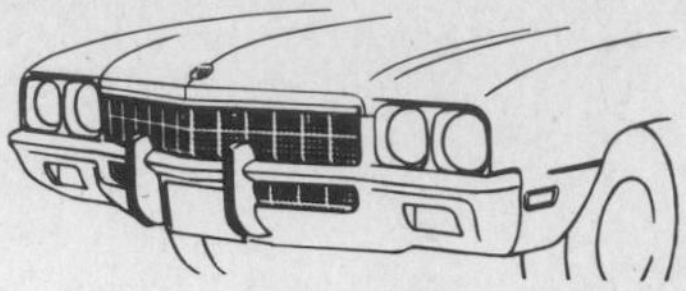

1972 Skylark

1972 Buick Gran Sport

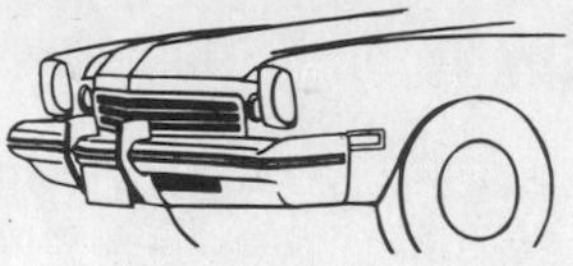

1973 Buick Century

1973 Buick Regal

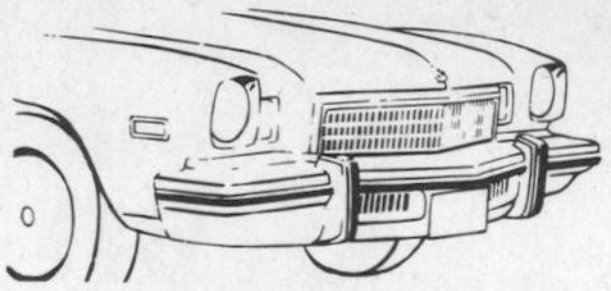

1974 Buick Regal

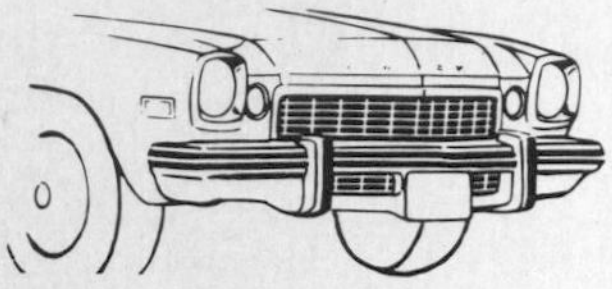

1974 Buick Century

1974 Apollo

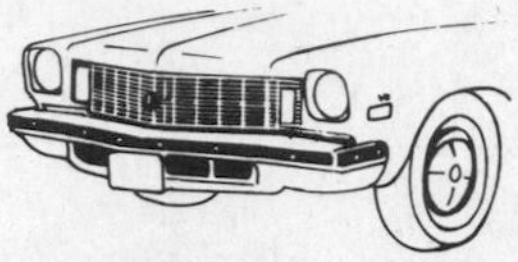

1975 Century

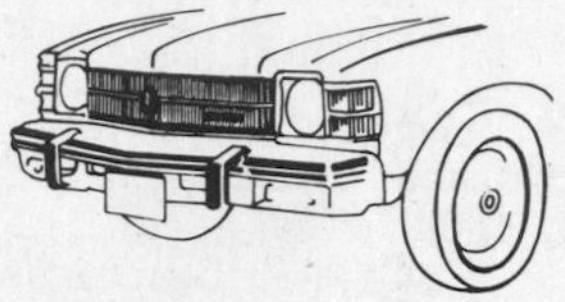

1975 Skylark, Apollo

1975 Skyhawk

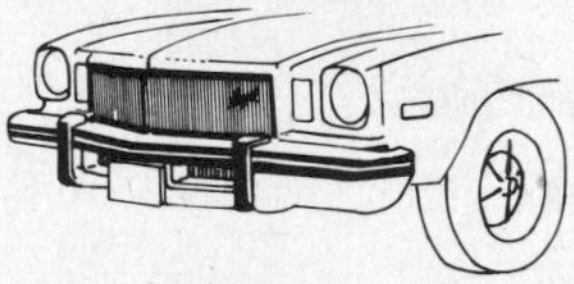

1975 Regal

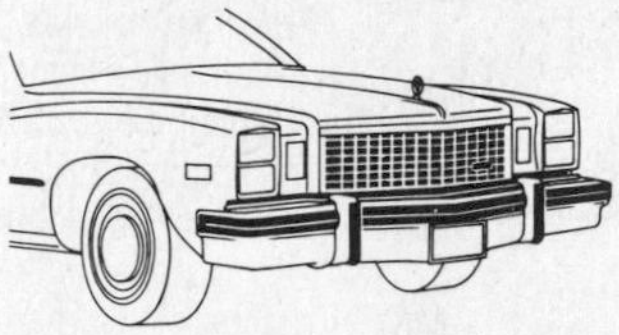

1976 Century

1976 Skylark, Apollo

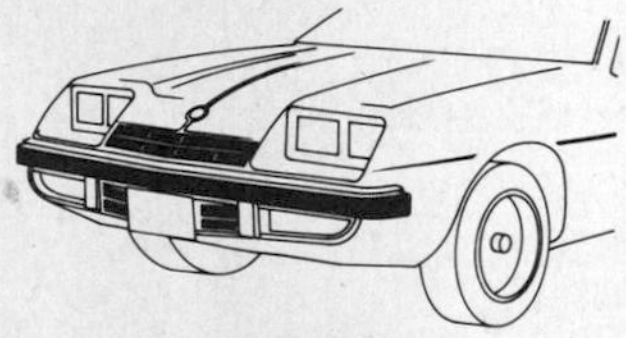

1976 Skyhawk

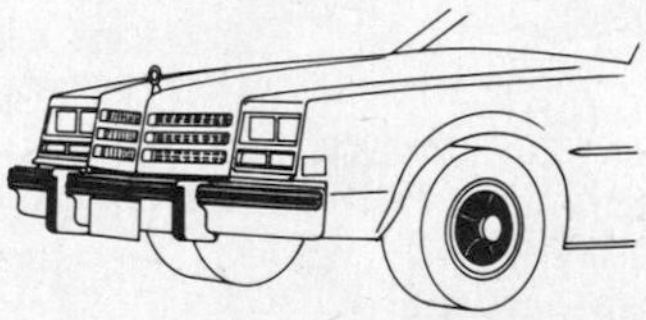

1976 Century Special

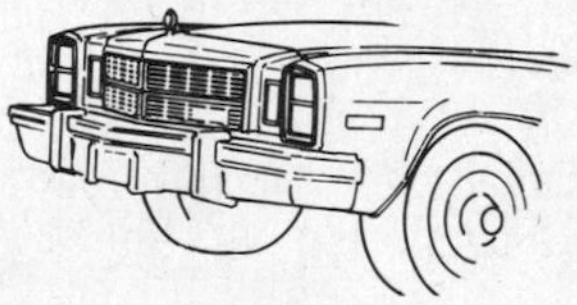

1977 Century

1977 Skylark

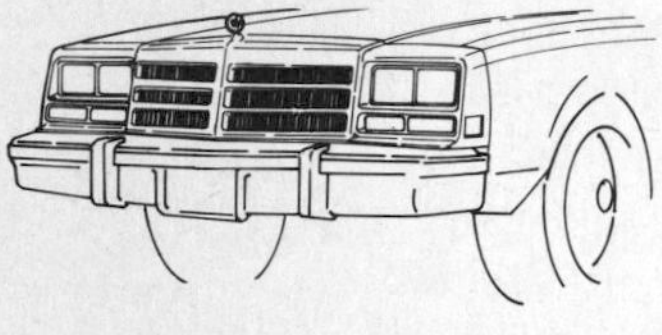

1977 Century Special

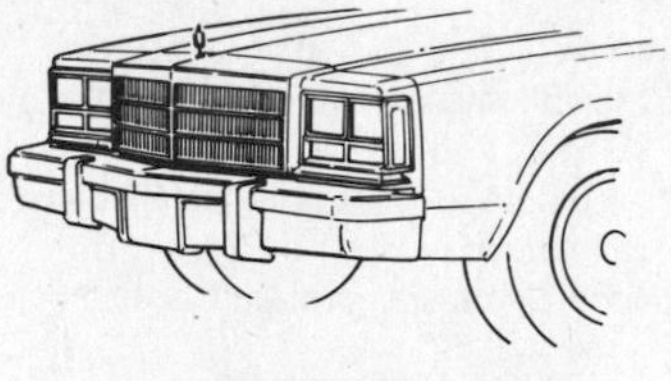

1977 Regal

1977 Skyhawk

FIRING ORDER

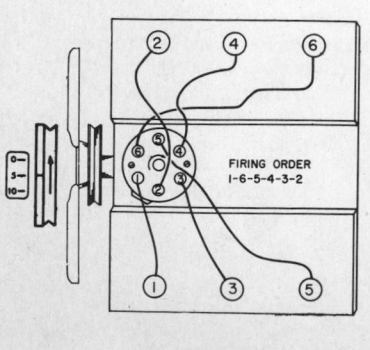

FIRING ORDER
1-6-5-4-3-2

V6 engine

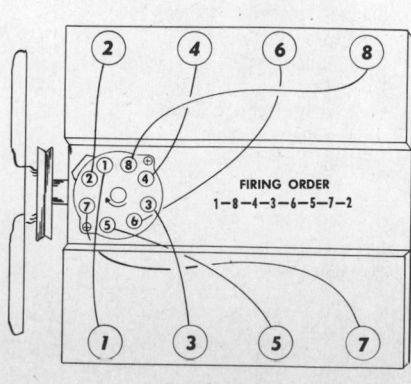

FIRING ORDER
1-8-4-3-6-5-7-2

350, 455 cu in.

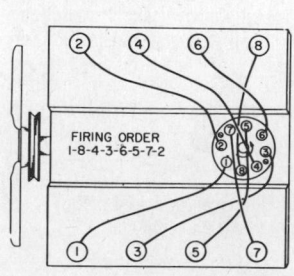

FIRING ORDER
1-8-4-3-6-5-7-2

260 V8

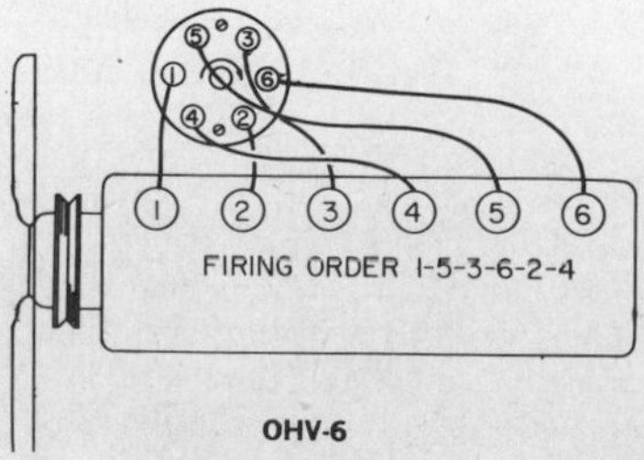

FIRING ORDER 1-5-3-6-2-4

OHV-6

ENGINE IDENTIFICATION

The production code number identifies the type of engine and its production date. The Engine Identification Code chart can be used to determine the type of engine installed in the vehicle.

1970-71

The serial number identification plate is attached to the top left of the instrument panel. It can be seen through the windshield.

On the 250 cu. in. OHV6 engine, the engine number and production code number are on the right side, to the rear of the distributor.

On the 350 cu. in. V8 engine, the engine number is on the front of the left bank of cylinders. The production code number is between the left exhaust manifold and the two front spark plugs.

On the 455 cu. in. engine, the production code number is between the two rear spark plugs and the left exhaust manifold. The engine number is between the two front spark plugs and the exhaust manifold.

1972 and later

The car serial number identification plate is attached to the top of the instrument panel on the left-side.

On the 250 cu in. six-cylinder engine, the engine number and production code number are on the right-side, to the rear of the distributor.

On the V6 engine, the production code number is between the front and middle branches of the right exhaust manifold. The engine serial number is just below the front of the left cylinder head.

On the 260 cu in. engine, the engine serial and production code is on the oil filler tube on the front of the engine.

On the 350 cu in. engine, the engine serial number is on the front of the right cylinder bank. The production code number is between the left exhaust manifold and the two front spark plugs.

On the 455 cu in. engine, the engine serial number is on the front of the right cylinder bank. The production code number is between the left exhaust manifold and the two rear spark plugs.

On most 1975 and later engines, the production code can be found with the serial number.

■ Beginning 1972, horsepower and torque are SAE net figures. They are measured at the rear of the transmission with all accessories installed and operating. Since the figures vary when a given engine is installed in different models, some are representative rather than exact.

ENGINE PRODUCTION CODE

Disp	Bbl	Hp ■	'70	'71	'72	'73	'74	'75	'76	'77
6-Cylinder Models										
231	2	110						AD		
231	2	105								FA, FB, FC, FD, FE, FR, FP, FF, FG, FH, FI, FJ, FO
250	1	145	ZB	ZG						
250	1	155	SA	SB						
250	1	100 (net)					CCR, CCW, CCK, CCX			
8-Cylinder Models										
260	2	110							QA, QD, QB, QC, TE, TJ	
350	2	140								PA, PB, PC, PD
350	2	145						AB		
350	4	165						AM		
350	2	150, 165#				XC	XC			
350	2	155			WC					
350	4	155								PE, PF, PN, PM, PT, PU, PK, PL, PR, PS
350	4	175, 190#				XB	XB			
350	4	180, 195#			WB					
350	2	230	TC, TO							
350	2	260	SO							
350	4	260	TB, TD							
350	4	285	SB							
350	4	315	SP							
403	4	—								
455	2	190						—		
455	4	225			WF, WA	XF	XF			
Stage 1										
455	4	255						XS		
455	4	270			WS	XS				
Stage 1										
455	4	315	TR							
455	4	345	TS							
Stage 1										
455	4	450	SR							
455	4	360	SS							
Stage 1										

Dual exhaust

GENERAL ENGINE SPECIFICATIONS

Year	Engine Displacement (Cu. In.)	Carburetor Type	Advertised Horsepower @ rpm ■	Advertised Torque @ rpm (ft lbs) ■	Bore and Stroke (in.)	Advertised Compression Ratio	Oil Pressure @ 2400 rpm
'70	6-250	1 bbl	155 @ 4200	235 @ 1600	3.875 x 3.530	8.5:1	37①
	8-350	2 bbl	260 @ 4600	360 @ 2600	3.800 x 3.850	9.0:1	37
	8-350	4 bbl	285 @ 4600	375 @ 3000	3.800 x 3.850	9.0:1	37
	8-350	4 bbl	315 @ 4800	410 @ 3200	3.800 x 3.850	10.25:1	37
	8-455	4 bbl	350 @ 4600	510 @ 2600	4.3125 x 3.900	10.0:1	40
	8-455 Stage 1	4 bbl	360 @ 4600	510 @ 2600	4.3125 x 3.900	10.5:1	40
'71	6-250	1 bbl	145 @ 4000	235 @ 2400	3.875 x 3.530	8.5:1	37①
	8-350	2 bbl	230 @ 4400	350 @ 2400	3.800 x 3.850	8.5:1	37
	8-350	4 bbl	260 @ 4600	360 @ 3000	3.800 x 3.850	8.5:1	37
	8-455	4 bbl	315 @ 4400	450 @ 2800	4.3125 x 3.900	8.5:1	40
	8-455 Stage 1	4 bbl	345 @ 5000	460 @ 3000	4.3125 x 3.900	8.5:1	40
'72	8-350	2 bbl	155 @ 3800	270 @ 2400	3.800 x 3.850	8.5:1	37②
	8-350	4 bbl	180 @ 3800	275 @ 2400	3.800 x 3.850	8.5:1	37②
	8-350 DE	4 bbl	195 @ 4000	290 @ 2800	3.800 x 3.850	8.5:1	37②
	8-455	4 bbl	225 @ 4000	360 @ 2600	4.3125 x 3.900	8.5:1	40
	8-455 Stage 1	4 bbl	270 @ 4400	390 @ 3000	4.3125 x 3.900	8.5:1	40
'73	8-350	2 bbl	150 @ 3800	265 @ 2400	3.800 x 3.850	8.5:1	37
	8-350	4 bbl	175 @ 3800	270 @ 2400	3.800 x 3.850	8.5:1	37
	8-350	4 bbl	190 @ 4000	285 @ 2800	3.800 x 3.850	8.5:1	37
	8-455	4 bbl	225 @ 4000	360 @ 2600	4.3125 x 3.900	8.5:1	37
	8-455	4 bbl	270 @ 4400	390 @ 3000	4.3125 x 3.900	8.5:1	37
'74	6-250	1 bbl	100 @ 3600	175 @ 1600	3.875 x 3.530	8.3:1	40④
	8-350	2 bbl	150 @ 3600	270 @ 2000	3.800 x 3.850	8.5:1	37
	8-350	4 bbl	175 @ 3800	260 @ 2000	3.800 x 3.850	8.5:1	37
	8-455 DE	2 bbl	190 @ 3600	370 @ 2000	4.3125 x 3.900	8.5:1	40
	8-455 DE	4 bbl	230 @ 3300	355 @ 2200	4.3125 x 3.900	8.5:1	40
	8-455 DE③	4 bbl	255 @ 4400	370 @ 2800	4.3125 x 3.900	8.5:1	40
'75	V6-231	2 bbl	110 @ 4000	175 @ 2000	3.800 x 3.400	8.0:1	37
	6-250	1 bbl	105 @ 3800	185 @ 1200	3.875 x 3.530	8.25:1	36-41④
	8-260	2 bbl	110 @ 3400	210 @ 1600	3.550 x 3.385	8.5:1	30-45
	8-350	2 bbl	145 @ 3200	270 @ 2000	3.800 x 3.850	8.1:1	37
	8-350	4 bbl	165 @ 3800	260 @ 2200	3.800 x 3.850	8.0:1	37
'76-'77	V6-231	2 bbl	105 @ 3400	185 @ 2000	3.800 x 3.400	8.0:1	37
	8-260	2 bbl	110 @ 3400	210 @ 1600	3.550 x 3.385	8.5:1	30-45④
	8-350	2 bbl	140 @ 3400	280 @ 1600	3.800 x 3.850	8.0:1	37
	8-350	4 bbl	155 @ 3400	280 @ 1800	3.800 x 3.850	8.0:1	37
	8-403⑤	4 bbl	—	—	4.351 x 3.385	—	—

■ Beginning 1972, horsepower and torque are SAE net figures. They are measured at the rear of the transmission with all accessories installed and operating. Since the figures vary when a given engine is installed in different models, some are representative rather than exact.

① Oil pressure at 1500 rpm
② Oil pressure at 2600 rpm
③ Stage I Gran Sport
④ Oil pressure at 2000 rpm
⑤ Wagon only
DE Dual exhaust

TUNE-UP SPECIFICATIONS

When analyzing compression test results, look for uniformity among cylinders rather than specific pressures.

Year	ENGINE No. Cyl Displacement (cu in.)	hp	SPARK PLUGS Orig. Type	Gap (in.)	DISTRIBUTOR Point Dwell (deg)	Point Gap (in.)	IGNITION TIMING (deg) ▲ Man Trans ●	Auto Trans	VALVES Intake Opens ■ (deg) ●	Fuel Pump Pressure (psi)	IDLE SPEED (rpm) ▲ Man Trans ● *	Auto Trans
'70	6-250	155	R-46T	.035	32½	.019	TDC	4B	16	4-5	750/400	600/400
	8-350	260	R-45TS	.030	30	.016	6B	6B	24	4¼-5¾	700	600
	8-350	285	R-45TS	.030	30	.016	6B	6B	24	4¼-5¾	700	600
	8-350	315	R-45TS	.030	30	.016	6B	6B	24	4¼-5¾	700	600
	8-455	350	R-44TS	.030	30	.016	6B	6B	18	4¼-5¾	700	600
	8-455 Stage 1	360	R-44TS	.030	30	.016	10B	10B	18	4¼-5¾	700	600
'71	6-250	145	R-46T	.035	32½	.019	4B	4B	16	4-5	550	600
	8-350	230	R-45TS	.030	30	.016	6B	10B	24	4¼-5¾	800	600
	8-350	260	R-45TS	.030	30	.016	6B	6B	28	4¼-5¾	800	600
	8-455	315	R-45TS	.030	30	.016	6B	6B	12	4¼-5¾	700	600
	8-455 Stage 1	270	R-45TS	.030	30	.016	10B	10B	28	4¼-5¾	700	600
'72	8-350	155	R-45TS	.040	30	.016	4B	4B	24	4¼-5¾	800/600	650/500
	8-350	180	R-45TS	.040	30	.016	4B	4B	24	4¼-5¾	800/600	650/500
	8-350	195	R-45TS	.040	30	.016	4B	4B	24	4¼-5¾	800/600	650/500
	8-455	225	R-45TS	.040	30	.016	4B	4B	24(14)	4¼-5¾	900/600	650/500
	8-455 Stage 1	360	R-45TS	.040	30	.016	8B	10B	24(14)	4¼-5¾	900/600	650/500
'73	8-350	150	R-45TS	.040	30	.016	4B	4B	24	4¼-5¾	800/600	650/500
	8-350	175	R-45TS	.040	30	.016	4B	4B	24	4¼-5¾	800/600	650/500
	8-350	190	R-45TS	.040	30	.016	4B	4B	24	4¼-5¾	800/600	650/500
	8-455	225	R-45TS	.040	30	.016	4B	4B	24	4¼-5¾	900/600	650/500
	8-455 Stage 1	270	R-45TS	.040	30	.016	8B	10B	24	4¼-5¾	900/600	650/500
'74	6-250	All	R-46T	.035	31-34	.019	8B	6B	16④	4-5	950/450	600/450
	8-350	All	R-45TS	.040	30	.016	—	4B	19(25)④	4¼-5¾	—	650/500
	8-455	All	R-45TS	.040	30	.016	—	4B	10④	4¼-5¾	—	650/500
	8-455 Stage 1	255	R-45TS	.040	30	.016	—	10B	10④	4¼-5¾	—	650/500
'75	V6-231	175	R-44SX	.060	Electronic		12B	12B	17	3-4½⑤	800/600	700
	6-250	100	R-46TX	.060	Electronic		10B	10B	14	4-5	850	550
	8-260	110	R-465X	.060	Electronic		—	18B(14B)	22	4¼-5¾	—	650
	8-350	All	R-45TSX	.060	Electronic		12B	12B	19	4¼-5¾	—	600
'76	V6-231	105	R-44SX	.060	Electronic		12B	12B	17	3-4½⑤	800/600	600
	8-260	110	R-46SX	.080	Electronic		18B(14B) @ 1100	18B(14B) @ 1100	22	4½-5¾	—	650/550 (650/600)
	8-350	All	R-45TSX	.060	Electronic		12B	12B	13½	5-6½	—	600
'77	All				See Underhood Specifications Sticker							

NOTE: The underhood specifications sticker often reflects tune-up specification changes made in production. Sticker figures must be used if they disagree with those in this chart.

▲ See text for procedure
● Figure in parentheses indicates California engine
■ All figures Before Top Dead Center
* Lower figure indicates idle speed with solenoid disconnected

① Not used
② Not used
④ These figures do not represent a change from 1973; however, the reference point is changed (from .004 inch valve lift to .004 inch cam lift) to be consistent with information required for Government certification.
⑤ 4¼-5¾ on mechanical pumps
B Before Top Dead Center
TDC Top Dead Center

CAPACITIES

Year	ENGINE No. Cyl. Displacement (cu. in.)	Engine Crankcase Add 1 Qt For New Filter	TRANSMISSION Pts To Refill After Draining Manual 3-Speed	Manual 4/5-Speed	Automatic •	Drive Axle (pts)	Gasoline Tank (gals)	COOLING SYSTEM (qts) With Heater	With A/C
'70	6-250	4	3.4	——	6	3	20	16	16
	8-350	4	3.4	——	6	3	20①	16.5	16.5
	8-350 Gran Sport	4	3.5	3	7	3	20	16.5	16.5
	8-455	4	3.5	3	7	4.25	20	19.2	19.7
'71	6-250	4	3.4	——	6	4.25	20	16	16
	8-350	4	3.4	——	6	4.25	20①	16.5	16.5
	8-350 Gran Sport	4	3.4	3	6	4.25	20	16.5	16.5
	8-455	4	——	3	7	5.5	20	19.2	19.7
'72	8-350	4	3.4	——	6	4.25	20①	16.5	16.9
	8-350 Gran Sport	4	3.4	3	6	4.25	20	16.2	16.6
	8-455	4	——	3	7	5.5	20	19.2	19.7
'73	8-350	4	3.4	——	6	4.25	22	16.5	16.9
	8-350 Gran Sport	4	3.4	3.4	6	4.25	22	16.5	16.9
	8-455	4	——	3.4	6	4.25	22	16.2	16.6
'74	6-250	4	3.5	——	6	4.25	21	14.0	②
	8-350 Apollo	4	——	——	6	4.25	21	18.9	19.3
	8-350	4	——	——	6	4.25	22	16.5	16.9
	8-455	4	——	——	6	4.25	22	16.2	16.6
'75-'77	V6-231, Skyhawk	4	——	3.5③	6	2.8	18.5	13.35	14.19
	V6-231, Skylark	4	3.5		6	4.25	21	16.6	16.7
	V6-231, Other	4	3.5		6	4.25	22	15.5	15.4
	6-250	4	3.5		6	4.25	21	16.92	17.0
	8-260	4	——	——	6	4.25	21	22.4	22.9
	8-350, Apollo/Skylark	4	——	——	6	4.25	21	18.9	19.3
	8-350, Other	4	——	——	6	4.25	22	17.9	18.5

• Specifications do not include torque converter   —— Not applicable
① Sportwagon—23 gals
② Optional—16 qts
③ 5-speed uses Dexron® II ATF

TORQUE SPECIFICATIONS

All readings in ft lbs

Year	Engine No. Cyl. Displacement (cu. in.)	Cylinder Head Bolts	Rod Bearing Bolts	Main Bearing Bolts	Crankshaft Pulley or Balancer Bolts	Flywheel to Crankshaft Bolts	MANIFOLD Intake	Exhaust
'70-'77	6-250	95	35	60-70	60	55-65	35	②
	6-231	75	40	115	150③	55⑥	45	25
	8-260	85	42	120	200③	60	40	25
	8-350	80	35④	115	140③	60	45	28
	8-455	100	45	115	200③	60	45	28

① Not used
② Center Bolts 25-30; End Bolts 15-20
③ Minimum
④ 40 with capscrews
⑤ 80—1976 and later
⑥ 60—1976 and later

CRANKSHAFT AND CONNECTING ROD SPECIFICATIONS

All measurements are given in inches

Year	Engine No. Cyl. Displacement (cu in.)	CRANKSHAFT Main Brg. Journal Dia	Main Brg. Oil Clearance	Shaft End-Play	Thrust on No.	Journal Diameter	CONNECTING ROD Oil Clearance	Side Clearance
'70-'74	6-250	2.3004	.0003-.0029	.002-.006	7	2.0000	.0007-.0027	.009-.014
	8-350	2.9995②	.0004-.0015	.002-.006①	3	2.0000	.0002-.0023	.006-.020
	8-455	3.2500	.0007-.0018	.003-.009	3	2.2500	.0002-.0023	.005-.019
'75-'77	V6-231	2.4995	.0004-.0015	.004-.008	2	2.0000	.0002-.0023	.006-.014
	6-250	2.2999	.0003-.0029	.002-.006	7	2.0000	.0007-.0027	.007-.016
	8-260	2.4995	.0005-.0021	.004-.008	3	2.1240	.0005-.0026	.006-.020
	8-350	2.9995	.0004-.0015	.002-.006	3	2.0000	.0005-.0026	.006-.026

① 1972 and later V8—350; .003-.009 in.   ② 3.0000 for 1974 and later

VALVE SPECIFICATIONS

Year	Engine No. Cyl. Displacement (cu in.)	Seat Angle (deg)	Face Angle (deg)	Spring Test Pressure (lbs @ in.)	Spring Installed Height (in.)	STEM TO GUIDE Clearance (in.) Intake	Exhaust	STEM Diameter (in.) Intake	Exhaust
'70	6-250	46	45	186 @ 1.27	1 21/32	.0010-.0027	.0010-.0027	.3414	.3414
	8-350	45	45	180 @ 1.34	1 23/32	.0015-.0025	.0015-.0032	.3725	.3727
	8-455	45	45	177 @ 1.45	1 29/32	.0015-.0035	.0015-.0032	.3725	.3727
'71	6-250	46	45	186 @ 1.27	1 21/32	.0010-.0027	.0010-.0027	.3414	.3414
	8-350	45	45	180 @ 1.34	1 23/32	.0015-.0035	.0015-.0032	.3725	.3727
	8-455	45	45	177 @ 1.45	1 29/32	.0015-.0035	.0015-.0032	.3725	.3727
'72	8-350	45	45	180 @ 1.34	1 23/32	.0015-.0035	.0015-.0032	.3725	.3727
	8-455	45	45	198 @ 1.45	1 29/32	.0015-.0035	.0015-.0032	.3725	.3727
'73	8-350	45	45	180 @ 1.34	1 23/32	.0015-.0035	.0015-.0032	.3720	.3730
	8-455	45	45	198 @ 1.45	1 29/32	.0015-.0035	.0015-.0032	.3725	.3727
'74	6-250	46	45	186 @ 1.27	1 21/32	.0010-.0027	.0010-.0027	.3413	.3413
	8-350	45	45	180 @ 1.34	1 29/32	00015-.0035	.0015-.0032	.3725	.3727
	8-455	45	45	178 @ 1.45	1 29/32	.0015-.0035	.0015-.0032	.3725	.3727
'75-'77	V6-231	45	45	164 @ 1.34②	1 47/64	.0015-.0035	.0015-.0032	.3407	.3407
	6-250	46	45	186 @ 1.27	1 21/32	.0010-.0027	.0010-.0020	.3413	.3413
	8-260	45④	46④	187 @ 1.27	—	.0010-.0027	.0015-.0032	.3428	.3424
	8-350	45	45	180 @ 1.34③	1 47/64	.0015-.0035	.0015-.0032	.3725	.3727

① Not used
② Exhaust—182 @ 1.34

③ Exhaust—175 @ 1.34
④ Exhaust—59 seat, 60 face

RING GAP

All measurements are given in inches

Year	Engine No. Cyl. Displacement (cu. in.)	Top Compression	Bottom Compression	Year	Engine No. Cyl. Displacement (cu. in.)	Oil Control
'70-'74	8-455	.013-.023	.013-.023	'70-'77	8-400, 455	.015-.055
'71-'75	6-250	.010-.020	.010-.020	'70-'72	8-350	.015-.035
'71-'72	8-350	.013-.023	.013-.023	'73-'74	8-455	.015-.035
'73-'77	8-350	.010-.020	.010-.020	'70-'71	6-250	.015-.025
'75-'77	V6-231	.010-.020	.010-.020	'75-'77	6-250	.015-.055
'75-'77	8-260	.010-.023	.010-.023	'75-'77	V6-231	.015-.035
				'75-'77	8-260	.015-.055

RING SIDE CLEARANCE

All measurements are given in inches

Year	Engine No. Cyl. Displacement (cu. in.)	Top Compression	Bottom Compression	Oil Control
'70-'72	8-350, 400, 455	.003-.005	.003-.005	.0035-.0095
'73-'77	6-231, 8-350, 455	.003-.005	.003-.005	.0035 Max.
'70-'77	6-250	.0012-.0027	.0012-.0032	.0000-.0050
'75-'77	8-260	.002-.004	.002-.004	.001-.005

PISTON CLEARANCE

Year	Engine No. Cyl. Displacement (cu. in.)	Piston to Bore Clearance (in.)
'70-'71	6-250	.0005-.0011
	8-350	.0008-.0020
	8-455	.0010-.0016
'72-'77	V6-231	.0008-.0020
	6-250	.0005-.0015
	8-260	.0010-.0020
	8-350	.0008-.0020
	8-455	.0010-.0016

WHEEL ALIGNMENT SPECIFICATIONS

Year	Model	CASTER Range (deg)	CASTER Pref Setting (deg)	CAMBER Range (deg)	CAMBER Pref Setting (deg)	Toe-in (in.)	Steering Axis Inclin. (deg)	WHEEL PIVOT RATIO (deg) Inner Wheel	WHEEL PIVOT RATIO (deg) Outer Wheel
'70-'72	All	1N to 0	½N	0 to 1P	½P	⅛ to ¼	8	20	18½
'73	All	0 to 1P	½P	0 to 1P①	½P	1/16 to ⅛	8	—	—
'74	Apollo	½N to 1½P	½P	½N to 1P	¾P	1/16 to 5/16	9	—	—
	Century, Regal, Luxus	1N to 1P	0	¼N to 1¼P RH ¼P to 1¾P LH	½P RH 1P LH	0 to 3/16	8	—	—
'75-'77	Skyhawk	1¼N to ¼N	¾N	½N to ¾P	¼P	0 to ⅛	8.55	—	—
	Apollo/Skylark, manual steer.	½N to 1½N	1N	¼P to 1¼P	¾P	0 to ⅛	10	—	—
	Apollo/Skylark, power steer.	½P to 1½P	1P	¼P to 1¼P	¾P	0 to ⅛	10	—	—
	Century, Regal	1½P to 2½P	2P	0-1P ½P to 1½P LH	½P RH 1P LH	0 to ⅛	8	—	—

① Right wheel given, left wheel is 0 to 2P, preferred 1P
N Negative   P Positive

RH Right hand side
LH Left hand side

—Not specified

CHARGING SYSTEM

Complete information on charging system troubleshooting and repairs can be found in the "Unit Repair Section."

Alternator Removal and Installation

Remove bolt holding tension bar to unit. Release drive belt. Unfasten mounting bolt to release Delcotron from engine. When reinstalling, adjust drive belt to allow ½ in. play on the longest run between pulleys.

NOTE: on some models, it may be necessary to loosen and rotate fan shroud. On all A/C models, remove compressor bracket.

Voltage Regulator Removal and Installation, 1970

1. Disconnect the battery negative cable.
2. Disconnect the wiring from the voltage regulator.
3. Remove the screws holding the regulator to the firewall or front bulkhead, depending on the car.
4. Reverse the removal procedures to install.

Voltage Regulator Removal and Installation beginning 1971

The voltage regulator is inside the alternator. For additional procedures see "Charging and Starting Systems" in the "Unit Repair Section."

STARTING SYSTEM

Starter Removal and Installation

Inline Six Cylinder

1. Disconnect battery and solenoid wires.
2. Remove the flywheel inspection cover.
3. On 1974 models, disconnect the starter support bracket.
4. Remove attaching bolts and lift out starter.

V6

Disconnect the negative battery cable from the battery. Note the locations of the wiring connections and disconnect the electrical leads from the starter. Remove the capscrew which secures the starter motor to the angle bracket on the side of the engine. Remove the two capscrews which secure the drive end of the starter motor to the cylinder block and remove the starter. Install the starter in the reverse order of removal.

V8

1. Disconnect battery.
2. Jack up car.
3. Remove four screws (3/8 in.) that hold flywheel inspection cover.
4. Disconnect wires from solenoid.
5. Remove one bolt from starter bracket to engine block, then remove two rear starter bolts using a 9/16 in. socket.
NOTE: the bracket bolt is hidden and must be removed using a short 1/2 in. open-end wrench. This bolt must be started by hand when installing. The bracket was used only through 1972.
6. Remove starter motor.

Skyhawk, Automatic Transmission

1. Disconnect the battery and raise the car.
2. Remove the exhaust crossover pipe and flywheel cover.
3. Remove the two transmission mount to transmission bolts and support the transmission extension housing.
4. Remove the right transmission support bolt and loosen the left bolt enough to let the transmission support pivot down.
5. Lower the transmission and disconnect the oil cooler lines at the transmission.
6. Remove the starter mounting bolts; remove the starter wires, and lower the starter from the engine.
7. Installation is the reverse of removal.

IGNITION SYSTEM

Distributor Removal

1. Remove distributor cap, primary wire and vacuum line at the distributor. On inline sixes with HEI, remove No. 1 and 2 spark plug wires and the coil connectors. Unplug the V6 and V8 distributor cap HEI connectors.
2. Scribe a mark on the distributor body, locating the position of the rotor and scribe another mark on the engine block, showing the position of the body in the block.
3. Remove the hold-down clamp and lift the distributor out of the block.

Distributor Installation

For firing order and cylinder numbering, see specifications.
1. If engine has been disturbed, rotate the crankshaft to bring the piston of No. 1 cylinder to the top of its compression stroke. If the engine has not been disturbed, insert the distributor into the engine, making sure the tip of the rotor is aligned with the marks that were scribed on the distributor housing and the engine block.
2. Position the distributor in the block with the rotor at No. 1 firing position. Make sure the oil pump intermediate drive shaft is properly seated in the oil pump.
3. Install the distributor lock but do not tighten.
4. Rotate the distributor body clockwise until the breaker points are just starting to open. Tighten the retaining screw.
5. Connect the primary wire and the vacuum line to the distributor, then install distributor cap.
6. Start the engine and check the timing with a timing light.

Contact Point Replacement and Adjustment
Inline Six-Cylinder through 1974

1. Loosen the captive distributor cap retaining screws and remove the cap.
2. Pull off the rotor.
3. Disconnect the primary and condenser leads from the point set.
4. Remove the retaining screw and the point set.
5. Remove the condenser and clamp.
6. Rotate the sponge cam lubricator or apply a trace of petroleum jelly or distributor lubricant to the cam.
7. Insert the new point set and the attaching screw.
8. Install the new condenser and clamp.
9. Connect the leads to the point set.
10. Turn the engine so that the points are open their maximum.
11. Adjust the gap with a feeler gauge. Use the screwdriver slot to lever the points open or closed.
12. Check the dwell with the engine either cranking or running. Set the dwell by adjusting the point gap.
13. Check the timing.

V8 through 1974
NOTE: the condenser should be replaced when the points are replaced.
1. Remove the distributor cap and rotor. If equipped with an interference shield, remove the shield.

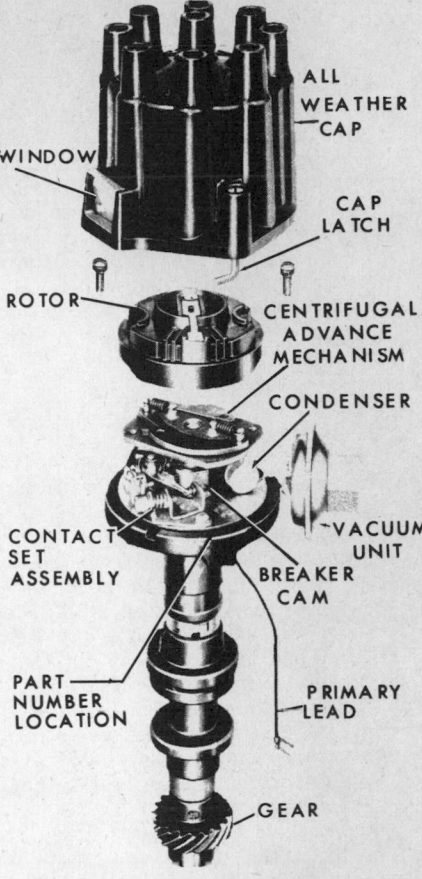

Distributor assembly, R.F.I. shield was used 1970-73 (© Buick Div., G.M. Corp)

2. Disconnect the condenser and primary leads from their terminal on the points.
3. Loosen the two screws holding the contact point set in place and remove point set.
4. Connect the wires to a new set of points and install them into the distributor.
NOTE: 1970-73 distributors have a radio interference shield over the contact points. Only snap-lock point sets can be used because screw-type connectors will hit this shield and short the ignition. The shield isn't needed if the later type unitized point/condenser set is installed.

Installing R.F.I. shield (© Buick Div., G.M. Corp)

5. Put a small amount of grease on the breaker cam or rotate the lubricator.
6. Reinstall the shield, rotor, and cap. Install the shield half that covers the points first. The shield isn't necessary if a unitized point and condenser set is installed. The unitized set is standard equipment beginning 1974. It can be installed in all General Motors V8 distributors.
7. Adjust the dwell to specifications using a 1/8 in. allen wrench through the cap window.
8. Check the timing.

Ignition Timing

Timing marks are located on the front engine cover and on the harmonic balancer.
1. Disconnect the distributor vacuum advance hose from the distributor and plug the hose.
2. Make sure the dwell is adjusted and the timing marks are clean and readable.

NOTE: it may be necessary to put a small amount of white paint or chalk on the timing marks to make them more visible.
3. Connect a timing light to no. 1 cylinder.
4. Loosen the distributor clamp.
5. Start the engine and rotate the distributor until the correct marks line up. Tighten the distributor clamp and recheck the timing.
6. Reconnect the vacuum hose.

High Energy Ignition System

Beginning 1974, a solid state, high energy ignition system is offered as an option on all Buick V8 engines. On 1975 and later Buicks, it is standard equipment. There are no points or condenser to replace, nor any cam or rubbing block to wear out.

High Energy Ignition System Tachometer Hookup

Some 1974, and all 1975 and later Buicks are equipped with the High Energy Ignition System which uses a different tachometer hookup than was used in previous years.

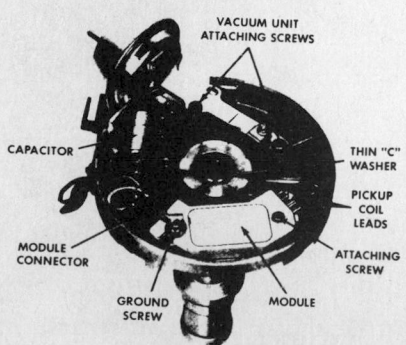

Internal components of HEI distributor
(© Buick Div., G.M. Corp)

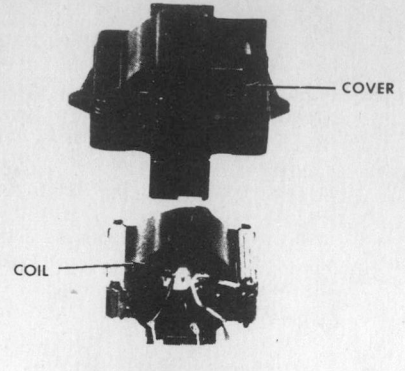

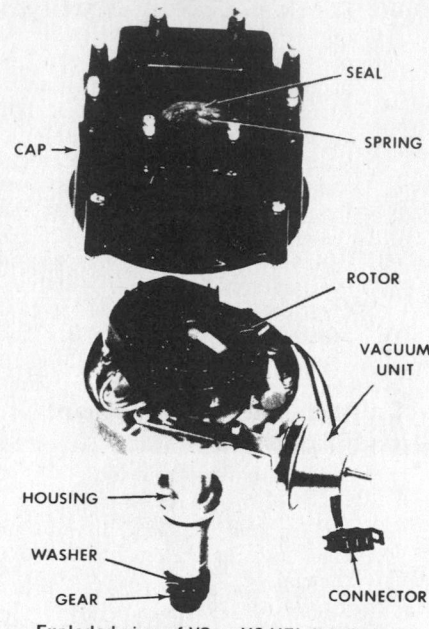

Exploded view of V8 or V6 HEI distributor
(© Buick Div., G.M. Corp)

1. On the V6 and V8 engines, connect the tachometer to the TACH terminal on the distributor and to a suitable ground.

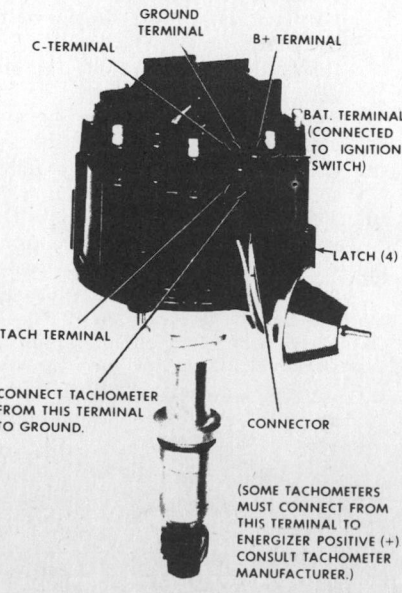

V8 HEI system distributor tachometer hookup
(© Buick Div., G.M. Corp)

NOTE: Some tachometers must connect to the TACH terminal on the distributor and to the positive terminal on the battery. If there is any doubt check the tachometer manufacturer's instructions.
2. On the inline six cylinder, connect the tachometer to the TACH terminal on the coil, opposite the BAT terminal, and to a ground.

FUEL SYSTEM

Idle Speed and Mixture Adjustment

1970 V8

1. Connect a tachometer to the engine.
2. Run the engine until it is warmed up.
3. Remove and plug the vacuum hose to the distributor.
4. Place a manual transmission in neutral, and an automatic transmission in Drive.

NOTE: check to see that the compressor for the Automatic Level Control, if equipped, is not running. The compressor now has a regulating valve to turn off vacuum at idle speed. If the compressor is running, this valve is faulty and must be adjusted or replaced before a good idle can be obtained.
5. Adjust the throttle stopscrew to set the idle speed according to specifications.
6. Adjust the idle mixture needles, one at a time, to obtain the highest tachometer reading. Readjust the throttle stopscrew to obtain 20 revolutions per minute (rpm) faster than specified idle speed. Turn each mixture needle to reduce engine speed 10 rpm. This reduces idle speed to specifications.

1970 Inline 6 Cyl.

See the note in the 1970 V8 section on Automatic Level Control.
1. Connect a tachometer to the engine.
2. Start the engine and warm it up.
3. Remove and plug the vacuum hose to the distributor.
4. Place manual transmissions in Neutral and automatics in Drive. Make sure the wheels are blocked and the brakes are securely set.
5. Adjust the solenoid plunger screw to set the specified idle speed. This is the higher figure in the specification table.
6. Stop the engine and turn the mixture screw in until it contacts the seat lightly, then turn it out four turns. Restart the engine.

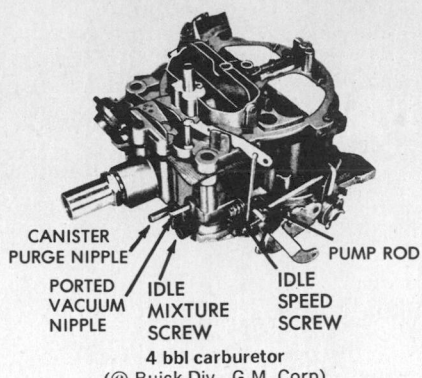

CANISTER PURGE NIPPLE — **PUMP ROD**
PORTED VACUUM NIPPLE — **IDLE MIXTURE SCREW** — **IDLE SPEED SCREW**

4 bbl carburetor
(© Buick Div., G.M. Corp)

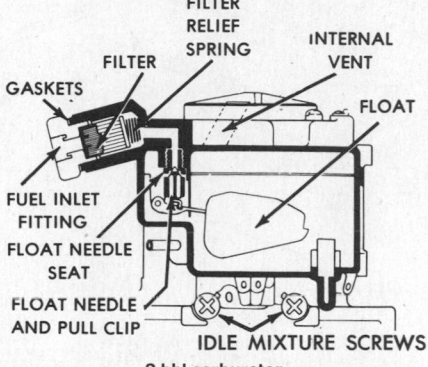

FILTER RELIEF SPRING — **INTERNAL VENT**
FILTER — **FLOAT**
GASKETS
FUEL INLET FITTING
FLOAT NEEDLE SEAT
FLOAT NEEDLE AND PULL CLIP — **IDLE MIXTURE SCREWS**

2 bbl carburetor
(© Buick Div., G.M. Corp)

7. Readjust the solenoid screw to get 830 rpm for manual transmissions and 630 rpm for automatics.
8. Adjust the mixture screw in to achieve the specified idle speed.
9. Disconnect the wire from the idle stop solenoid to de-energize the solenoid.
10. Adjust the carburetor throttle stopscrew to obtain specified slow-idle speed. This is the lower figure in the specification table. Reconnect the solenoid wire and check the fast-idle speed.

1971 All

NOTE: On models with a V8 engine and manual transmission, the relay and solenoid located near the carburetor are emission control devices and should not be adjusted. See the note in the 1970 V8 procedure on automatic level control.

1. Connect a tachometer to the engine.
2. Start the engine and warm it up.
3. Remove the hose to the distributor and plug it up.
4. Adjust the throttle stopscrew to set the specified idle speed.
5. Adjust the idle mixture screws (one screw on 6 cyl) to obtain the highest idle within the limited travel of the screws.
6. Readjust the throttle stopscrew to obtain the specified idle speed.

1972-73 All

See the note in the 1970 V8 procedure on automatic level control.

1. Connect a tachometer to the engine.
2. Start the engine and run it until it is warmed up.
3. Remove and plug the vacuum hose to the distributor.
4. Place manual transmissions in Neutral and automatic transmissions in Drive.
5. Open the throttle sufficiently to allow the solenoid to extend and contact the throttle lever pad in the idle position.
6. Adjust the solenoid plunger to obtain the specified rpm. This is the higher figure in the specification chart.
7. Disconnect the solenoid wire to disengage solenoid.
8. Adjust the carburetor idle screw to obtain specified idle speed, this is the lower figure in the specification chart.
9. Reconnect the solenoid wire.
10. Adjust the idle mixture needles, one at a time, to obtain the highest tachometer reading. After the highest reading is reached, readjust the solenoid plunger to obtain 50 rpm over the specified idle speed. Turn each mixture needle in to reduce the idle speed 25 rpm for each needle. This reduces the idle speed to the recommended rpm.
11. Adjust the fast idle speed on all four-barrel carburetors. Fast idle must be adjusted after the slow idle speed and mixture have been adjusted. Automatic transmission cars are adjusted on the low step of the fast idle cam, in Drive, to 700 rpm. Manual transmission cars are adjusted on the low cam step to 820 rpm for 350 engines, and 920 rpm for 455 engines.
12. Connect the distributor vacuum hose.
13. Install the red service idle needle limiter caps on the mixture screws.

1974-75 Inline Six-Cylinder

NOTE: Idle speed and mixture must be set with the engine at normal operating temperature, the air conditioner off, the air cleaner on, and the automatic transmission in Drive.

1. Set the parking brake and block the wheels.

2. Disconnect the fuel tank vent hose at the vapor canister. Disconnect and plug the distributor vacuum line at the distributor.
3. Adjust the idle speed to the higher figure specified in the "Tune-Up Specifications" chart. Adjust the solenoid screw with the solenoid connected.
4. Cut the tab off the idle mixture screw cap.
5. Using the solenoid screw, set the idle speed to the higher speed specified on the underhood sticker. This is usually 30-350 rpm above normal idle speed.
6. Adjust the mixture screw (usually out) until the maximum engine idle speed is reached.
7. Lean the mixture by turning the mixture screw in until the engine slows to the idle speed you started with in Step 3. Adjust the idle speed to the lower figure from the "Tune-Up Specifications" chart with the solenoid disconnected.
8. Reconnect all the hoses removed in Step 2.

1974 and later V6 and V8 (except 260)

NOTE: Idle speed and mixture must be set with the engine at normal operating temperature, the air conditioner off, the air cleaner on, and the transmission in Drive.

1. Set the parking brake and block the wheels.
2. Disconnect the evaporative emission hose at the air cleaner. Disconnect and plug the distributor vacuum line at the distributor. Disconnect and plug the EGR vacuum line at the EGR valve on all 1974 models, and all 1975-76 V6s.
3. Adjust the idle speed to that specified in the "Tune-Up Specifications" chart. First adjust the idle speed screw with the solenoid disconnected to get the lower speed, then adjust the solenoid screw with the solenoid connected to get the higher speed on models so equipped. If there is no solenoid, adjust the idle speed with the idle speed screw.
4. Cut the tabs off the mixture screw caps then turn them out to obtain the maximum idle speed.

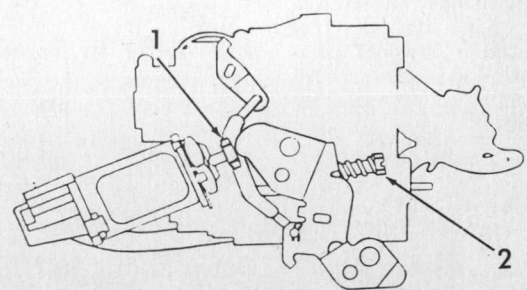

Idle speed screw (2) and idle solenoid screw (1)

5. Using the solenoid screw (if equipped), or the idle speed screw, adjust the idle speed to the higher speed specified on the underhood sticker, which is usually 60-100 rpm above the normal idle speed.

6. Turn in the mixture screws equally until the engine returns to the normal idle speed. On the V6, reset the idle speed with the solenoid deenergized if necessary.

7. Reconnect all the hoses removed in Step 2.

260 V8

1. Follow the first two steps under the 1974 and later V6 and V8 procedure, but plug the EGR line at the carburetor.

2. Remove the caps on the mixture screws and then lightly seat each screw.

3. Back out each screw *exactly* five turns.

4. Adjust the idle speed screw to obtain 610 rpm for non-California models or 700 rpm for California models.

5. Turn in the mixture screws ½ turn at a time until the idle speed is 550 rpm for non-California models or 600 rpm for California models.

6. If the car is equipped with air conditioning, it may have an idle speed-up solenoid on the carburetor which must be adjusted when adjusting the idle speed. Turn on the air conditioning and disconnect the terminal connector at the compressor clutch. With the solenoid energized, adjust the screw to obtain 650 rpm with the transmission in Drive. When completed, reconnect the connector at the compressor clutch.

Fuel Pump

A mechanical fuel pump is used on all except Skyhawk. The pump lever works from the underside of a camshaft eccentric. It is of the single-action diaphragm type. Fuel pumps are sealed units. They are not to be repaired.

All air conditioned cars with V8 engines and all cars with 400 and 455 cu. in. engines have a special fuel pump. This pump has a vapor return line which returns hot fuel and fuel vapor to the fuel tank. The possibility of vapor lock is thus greatly reduced by keeping cool fuel circulating through the pump.

Fuel Pump Replacement

All except Skyhawk

1. Disconnect the fuel inlet hose from the pump. Disconnect the vapor return hose, if equipped. Disconnect the outlet hose.

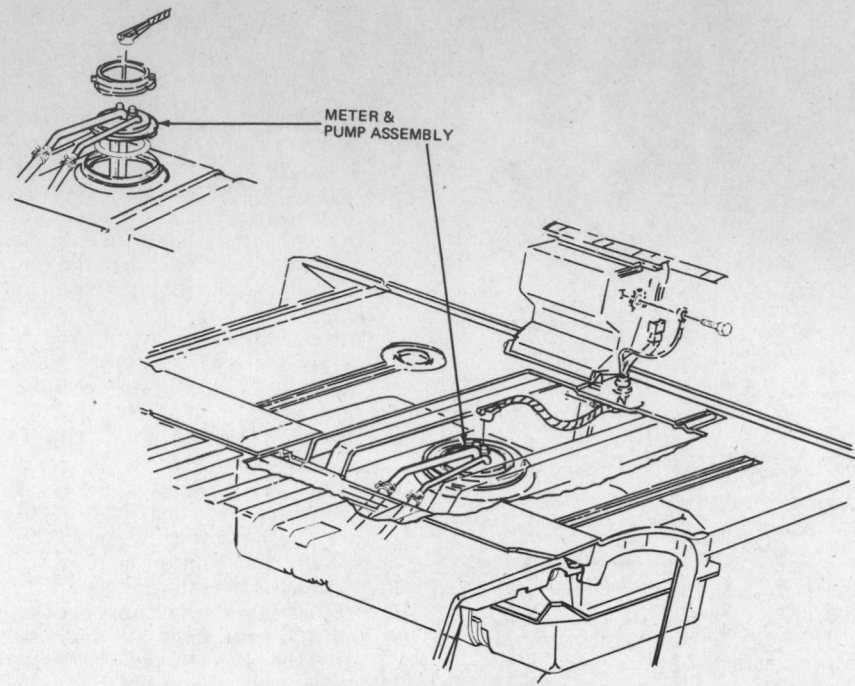

Skyhawk fuel pump location
(© Buick Div., G.M. Corp)

2. Remove the two ½ inch (in.) bolts.
3. Remove the fuel pump.
4. Install a new gasket.
5. Install a new pump and bolts.
6. Tighten the bolts alternately and evenly.
7. Reconnect the hoses, start the engine, and check for leaks.

Skyhawk

The fuel pump used in the Skyhawk is an electric pump, mounted in the gas tank.

1. Disconect the fuel pump wires at the rear wiring harness connector.
2. Raise the car on a hoist and drain the gas tank.
3. Disconnect the gas line hose at the tank, and the vent hose.
4. Remove the gas gauge ground wire from the bottom of the tank.
5. Remove the tank retaining straps, and lower the tank carefully.
6. A special spanner wrench is needed to unscrew the pump retaining ring.
7. Installation is the reverse of removal.

Fuel Filter Replacement

1. Disconnect the fuel line connection at the inlet of the carburetor.
2. Remove the inlet fuel filter nut from the carburetor with a box wrench.
3. Remove the filter element and spring.
4. If a bronze element, blow through the cone end—the ele-

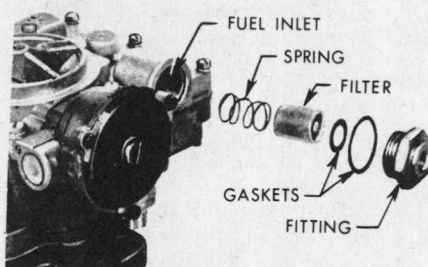

Fuel filter
(© Buick Div., G.M. Corp)

ment should allow air to pass freely.

5. Install the element spring and a new element into the carburetor. Bronze elements are installed with the small section of the cone facing outward.
6. Install a new gasket on the fitting nut and install the nut.
7. Install the fuel line and tighten it securely. Start the engine and check for leaks.

COOLING SYSTEM

Thermostat Replacement

To replace the thermostat, remove the two bolts holding the water neck in place. Remove the water neck and the thermostat will lift out. Use a new gasket when reinstalling a new thermostat.

Caution Be sure the thermostat is not reversed in its installed position. The spring should extend toward the rear or down.

Water Pump Removal and Installation

Inline Six-Cylinder

1. Drain the radiator.
2. Disconnect the heater hose and the lower radiator hose from the pump.
3. Loosen the alternator bolt and remove the belt.
4. Remove the fan blades and pulley.
5. Unbolt the power steering pump from the water pump. Unbolt the water pump from the engine.
6. Remove the pump. Be careful to pull it straight out, to avoid impeller damage.
7. On installation, use a new, sealer coated gasket.
8. Reverse the procedure for installation.

V6 and V8 Removal

1. Drain the cooling system; on all 1975-76 models, the fan shroud must be removed. On the Skyhawk, the fan shroud and fan must be removed together.
2. Loosen belt or belts, then remove fan blades and pulley or pulleys from hub on water pump shaft. Remove belt or belts.
3. Disconnect hose from water pump inlet and heater hose from nipple. Remove bolts, then remove pump and gasket from the timing case cover.

V6 and V8 Installation

1. Install pump assembly with new gasket. Bolts and lock washers must be torqued evenly.
2. Connect radiator hose to pump inlet and heater hose to nipple. Fill cooling system and check all points of possible coolant leaks.
3. Install fan pulley or pulleys and fan blade. Install belt or belts and adjust for correct tension.

Radiator Removal and Installation

The radiator mounting is a four-point system using rubber inserts on U-shaped brackets for the lower mounting. The radiator upper mounting points are part of the upper radiator panel. The radiator is removed by removing the upper radiator panel, disconnecting the hoses and automatic transmission lines if equipped, and lifting the radiator out of the car. On models equipped with a fan shroud, remove the shroud from the radiator and position it rearward over the fan. Installation is the reverse of removal.

EMISSION CONTROLS

There are three types of emissions to be controlled: crankcase emissions, carburetor and gas tank gas vapor emissions, and exhaust emissions. See the "Unit Repair Section" for troubleshooting and repair information.

1970-71

The more stringent 1970 laws require tighter control of emissions. Crankcase emissions are controlled by the Closed Positive Crankcase Ventilation System; exhaust emissions are controlled by the engine Controlled Combustion System (CCS), in conjunction with the new Transmission Controlled Spark System (TCS).

In addition, cars sold in California in 1970 and all 1971 models are equipped with an Evaporation Control System that limits the amount of gasoline vapor discharged into the atmosphere (usually from the carburetor and fuel tank).

The CCS system reduces emissions by increasing combustion efficiency through carburetor (limiter caps on the mixture screws), and distributor (retarding the timing over earlier years) calibrations. The system also uses a higher temperature thermostat (195°F) to increase engine operating temperature and a thermostatically controlled air cleaner to regulate the temperature of the air entering the carburetor.

The TCS system consists of a transmission switch, a solenoid valve, and a temperature switch. Under normal conditions, the system permits the vacuum distributor (spark) advance to operate only in high gear (both manual and automatic transmissions) and reverse.

The transmission switch is located on the transmission and senses when the transmission is in one of the lower gears. When in a lower gear, the switch activates the vacuum solenoid valve. This valve is located in the vacuum line that runs from the carburetor to the distributor and shuts off vacuum to the distributor advance when it is activated. There is also an engine-temperature sensing switch which overrides the transmission switch. It will allow vacuum advance in the lower gears when the engine temperature is below 85° or above 220°. There is always vacuum advance in high gear and reverse.

The Evaporative Emission Control System was introduced in 1970. Vapors generated in the gas tank while the car is at rest are transferred to an activated charcoal canister located in the engine compartment. When the car is running the vapors are removed from the canister and burned by the engine.

1972

In 1972, all engines are equipped with Positive Crankcase Ventilation, Transmission Controlled Vacuum Spark Advance, and the Controlled Combustion System. See the 1970-71 section for an explanation of TCS. The Air Injection Reactor System is standard on all engines except non-California 350 cu in. engines with automatic transmissions. All California cars and all cars with manual transmissions have Exhaust Gas Recirculation (EGR).

The EGR System is used to reduce oxides of nitrogen emissions. To lower the formation of nitrogen oxides, it is necessary to reduce combustion temperatures. This is done by introducing exhaust gases into the intake manifold to be burned.

An EGR valve is mounted on the right rear of the intake manifold and is used to regulate the amount of exhaust gases and the time the exhaust gases enter the intake manifold. As the engine speeds up, carburetor vacuum is applied to the valve which opens a port connecting the intake manifold to the exhaust gas passage that is cast in the intake manifold. This allows exhaust gases to pass into the intake manifold. The EGR system is not in operation during engine idle.

1973

All engines are equipped with Positive Crankcase Ventilation, Controlled Combustion, Air Injection Reactor System, Exhaust Gas Recirculation, Transmission Controlled Vacuum Spark Advance System, and Evaporative Emission Control. With the exception of a low temperature cut-out valve that added to the EGR system, the emission control systems remain unchanged from previous years.

The EGR system is the same one that was used on 1972 California cars with a new temperature valve. This black and white plastic valve is located in the vacuum line to the EGR valve and it senses ambient temperature above the engine intake manifold. At temperatures below 0°F, the temperature valve closes to prevent carburetor vacuum from opening the EGR valve. When the temperature above the manifold rises above 60°F, the valve opens and allows carburetor vacuum to control the operation of the EGR valve. Whenever installing a new valve, always make sure the side of the valve marked EGR faces toward the EGR valve.

1974

The 1974 Buick emission control system is unchanged from 1973, except for a required change in the EGR temperature sensor. The EGR temperature sensor now records coolant temperature rather than ambient (engine compartment) temperature. Although the system design remains unchanged, there has been an extensive refinement and recalibration of components to insure greater efficiency.

1975

The 1975 Buick emission control system has three additions to the 1974 system, while dropping the Transmission Controlled Spark system used since 1970. The additions are: a catalytic converter, a choke air modulator, and an early fuel evaporation system (EFE).

The catalytic converter is a device used to reduce hydrocarbons and carbon monoxide in the exhaust system. See the Unit Repair Section for more details.

The choke air modulator, located in the bottom of the air cleaner, provides heated air to the choke thermostatic coil housing to improve drivability and performance.

The EFE valve promotes quick heating of the incoming fuel to the carburetor by directing the flow of exhaust gas through the intake manifold crossover passage underneath the carburetor.

1976

The 1976 emission control system is a carryover from 1975. The only changes are the addition of spark advance vacuum modulator to the distributor advance circuit on the 260 V8 to more closely match timing to engine demand, and the dropping of the cold air intake snorkel to the air cleaner.

ENGINE

There are five different engines designed by three different GM divisions used in these models. The 231 V6, and the 350 and 455 V8s are all Buick designed engines using a front mounted distributor and a valve rocker shaft rather than individual rocker arms. The 260 V8 is based on an Oldsmobile design. Additional information can be found in the Oldsmobile section. The 250 Inline Six cylinder is based on a Chevrolet design and was dropped after 1975; additional information can be found in the Camaro section.

Engine Removal

1. Scribe marks at the hood hinges and the hinge brackets. Remove the hood.
2. Disconnect the battery and drain the coolant.
3. Remove the air cleaner.
4. On cars with air conditioning (A/C), disconnect the compressor ground wire from the bracket. Remove the electrical connector from the compressor. Remove the compressor and position the compressor out of the way. Do not disconnect any hoses.

Caution If the compressor refrigerant lines do not have enough slack to position the compressor out of the way without disconnecting the refrigerant lines, the air conditioning system will have to be removed by a trained air conditioning specialist. Under no conditions should an untrained person attempt to disconnect the air conditioning refrigerant lines. These lines contain pressurized freon, which can be extremely dangerous to the untrained.

5. Remove the fan blade, pulley, and belts.
6. Disconnect the radiator and heater hoses. Remove the radiator and shroud assembly.
7. Remove the power steering pump and move it out of the way. Do not disconnect any hoses.
8. Remove the fuel pump hoses and plug them.
9. Disconnect the vapor emission lines, on 1970 and later models, from the carburetor, the vacuum supply hose from the carburetor to the vacuum manifold, and the power brake vacuum hoses, if equipped.
10. Disconnect the throttle linkage at the carburetor.
11. Disconnect the oil and coolant switch.
12. Disconnect the engine-to-body ground strap.
13. Raise the car and disconnect the starter wires.
14. Disconnect the pipe from the exhaust manifold and support the exhaust system.
15. Remove the flywheel and converter cover.
16. On cars equipped with automatic transmissions, remove the flywheel-to-converter attaching bolts. Match-mark the converter to the flywheel. On standard transmission models, disconnect the clutch linkage.
17. Remove the transmission-to-engine attaching bolts.

NOTE: On inline sixes, leave the engine and transmission bolted together. They are removed as a unit. Unbolt the transmission rear mount from the crossmember and remove the driveshaft before removing the engine.

18. Support the transmission.
19. Remove the thru-bolts from the motor mounts.
20. Lower the car, making sure the transmission is adequately supported.
21. Disengage the engine from the transmission and remove the engine from the car.

Engine Installation

Install the engine in the reverse order of removal.

Note that there are dowel pins in the block that have matching holes in the bellhousing. These dowel pins must be in almost perfect alignment before the engine will go together with the transmission.

Manifolds

1970-74 Inline Six-Cylinder

This engine uses a combined intake and exhaust manifold, equipped with a heat-riser.

To remove the manifold assembly, disconnect the exhaust pipe flange and remove all connections to the carburetor. Take off the vacuum lines at the manifold and also at the carburetor. Remove power steering pump and bracket. Remove the EFE valve bracket.

Remove the carburetor. Unbolt the manifold from the side of the cylinder head. The intake manifold can be separated from the exhaust manifold by removing one bolt and two nuts. These fasteners should be tightened to 15-30 ft lbs after the manifolds are bolted to the engine.

1975 Inline Six-Cylinder

Some 1975 inline sixes have an intake manifold which is integral with

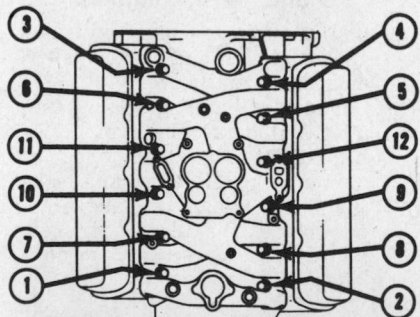

260 V8 intake manifold torque sequence
(© Buick Div., G.M. Corp)

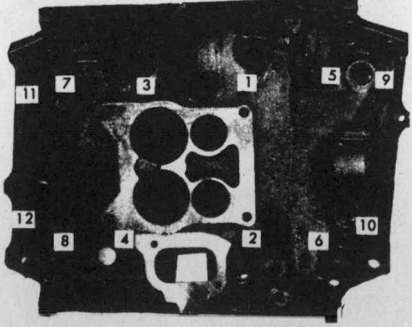

V8 (except 260) intake manifold torque sequence
(© Buick Div., G.M. Corp)

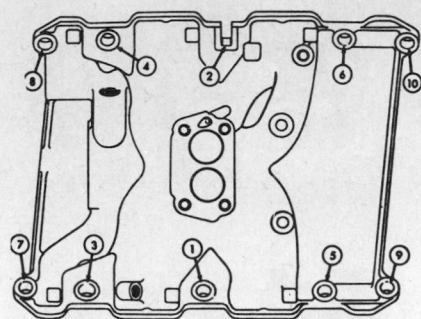

V6 intake manifold torque sequence
(© Buick Div., G.M. Corp)

the cylinder head. To remove the intake manifold, you must remove the cylinder head assembly.

Intake Manifold Removal and Installation

V8

The manifold incorporates an exhaust heat passage to warm the carburetor throttle body. Engine coolant flows out of the engine through the water passages in the manifold and through the thermostat and water outlet elbow located at the front of the manifold.

1. Drain cooling system and disconnect the battery.
2. Remove the air cleaner and disconnect all lines, wires and hoses from the carburetor. On V8s, remove the spark plug wires, and on models without HEI, disconnect and remove the coil.
3. Disconnect temperature indicator wire from sending unit. Loosen the air conditioning compressor bracket bolt and alternator bracket and swing the bracket out of the way.
4. Disconnect accelerator and transmission linkage at carburetor. Disconnect throttle return spring.
5. Slide front thermostat by-pass hose clamp back on the hose. Disconnect upper radiator hose at outlet.
6. Disconnect heater hose at the temperature control valve inlet. Force the end of the hose down to permit coolant to drain from intake manifold.
7. Remove the vacuum hoses from distributor thermal vacuum switch, the EFE valve pipe and the vacuum tank hose.
8. Remove manifold-to-heat attaching bolts. On the V6, remove the distributor cap rotor to get at the left manifold torx head bolt which requires a special wrench for removal. After removing this bolt, remove the V6 plug wires.
9. Remove intake manifold and carburetor as an assembly by sliding rearward to disengage the thermostat by-pass hose from

the water pump. Remove intake manifold gasket. Reverse the above steps to install, torquing the bolts in the sequence illustrated.

Exhaust Manifold Removal and Installation

1975 Inline Six with Integral Intake Manifold

1. Remove the air cleaner.
2. Remove the power steering and air pump brackets.
3. Remove the EFE valve bracket.
4. Disconnect the throttle linkage and return spring.
5. Unbolt the exhaust pipe from the flange.
6. Unbolt and remove the manifold.
7. Reverse the procedure for installation. Tighten the four end bolts to specifications last.

All V6 and V8

1. Jack up car and support on axle stands.
2. Disconnect the exhaust crossover pipe from the manifolds on both sides of the engine and lower it. On the V6, disconnect the choke pipe if you are working on the right side, the EFE line if you are working on the left side. On the Apollo or Skylark; to remove the left manifold, you must remove the engine left mounting bracket through bolt, loosen the right one and jack the engine up enough to provide the clearance to remove the manifold.
3. If equipped with manual transmission, remove equalizer shaft.
   NOTE: on right side, it may be necessary to remove A/C, power steering, or alternator.
4. Remove exhaust manifold-to-cylinder head bolts.
5. Remove manifold from beneath car.
6. Reverse the above to install. Always use the bolt locks.

Valve System

All V8 and V6 engines, except the 260, use rocker arm shafts while the inline six and the 260 V8 use rocker arm studs. All lifters are the hydraulic type.

Valve Adjustment

The V6 and V8 valves cannot be adjusted. If there is excessive clearance in the valve train, look for worn push rods, rocker arms, valve springs or collapsed or stuck lifters. For procedures on the inline six, see the Camaro section.

NOTE: All 250, 350, and some 455 engines use progressively wound valve springs. The coils are closer together at one end than at the other. The close wound end must go against the cylinder head.

Rocker Arm Removal and Installation

Inline Six-Cylinder

NOTE: these rocker arms are of the individual pedestal design and need not be removed to remove head.

1. Remove rocker arm cover.
2. Remove rocker arm nuts, rocker arm balls, rocker arms, and push rods. These should be reinstalled in their original locations.

1970 and later V8 and V6

1. Remove the rocker arm cover.
2. Remove the rocker arm shaft assembly bolts and the assembly.
3. Remove the nylon arm retainers by breaking them below their head with a chisel.
4. Remove the rocker arms.

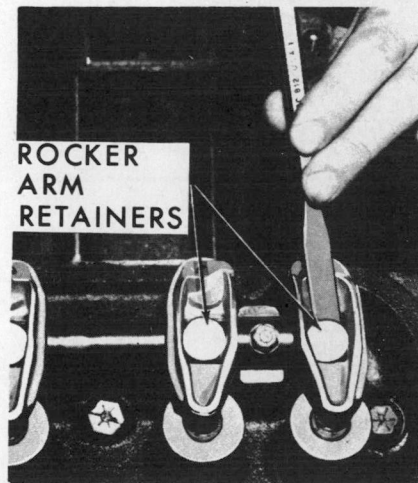

Removing nylon rocker arm retainer
(© Buick Div., G.M. Corp)

Rocker arms and shaft, 455 cu in. through 1972   (© Buick Div., G.M. Corp)

NOTE: On 1970-72 engines, each pair of rocker arms must be installed so that the external rib on each arm points away from the rocker arm shaft bolt that is located between each pair of rocker arms. On 1973 and later engines, the rocker arms are marked R and L. From the front of the engine on the left bank, the sequence should be L-R, L-R, L-R, L-R. On the right bank, it should be R-L, R-L, R-L, R-L.

5. Install the rocker arms on the shaft and lubricate them with oil.
6. Center each arm on the ¼ in. hole in the shaft. Install new nylon rocker arm retainers in the holes using a 1/2 in. drift.
7. Locate the push rods in the rocker arms and insert the shaft-to-cylinder head bolts. Tighten the bolts a little at a time until they are tightened to 30 ft lbs.
8. Install the rocker cover and use a new gasket.

260 V8

1. Remove the valve cover.
2. Remove the rocker arm bolts, and the rocker arm pivot.
3. Remove the rocker arm assembly. Remove each rocker arm assembly as a unit before proceeding to the next one.
4. Place a rocker arm assembly in the proper position, and lubricate the rocker arms and pivot assembly.
5. Install the rocker arm bolts, alternately tightening them to 25 ft lbs.

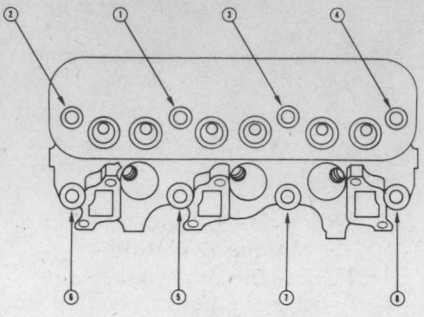

V6 cylinder head bolt torque sequence
(© Buick Div., G.M. Corp)

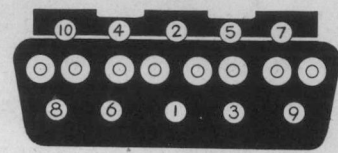

350, 455 cu in. cylinder head torque sequence

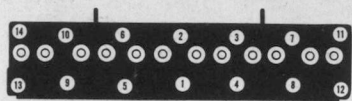

Inline six-cylinder engine head torque sequence

260 V8 cylinder head bolt torque sequence
(© Buick Div., G.M. Corp)

6. Proceed to the next rocker arm assembly until installation is complete; install the rocker arm cover.

Cylinder Head Removal and Installation

Removal Inline Six

1. Drain coolant.
2. Disconnect the exhaust pipe at the manifold flange, then remove the manifold bolts and clamps and remove the manifolds and carburetor as an assembly on those engines with removeable intake manifolds.

3. Remove the air conditioning compressor, if equipped, *but do not disconnect any lines.* Disconnect the air pump hose at the check valve.
4. Disconnect the spark plug wires from the plugs.
5. Disconnect the fuel and vacuum lines from the retaining clip at the water outlet. Disconnect the wires from the temperature sending unit, and accelerator pedal at bellcrank.
6. Remove the upper radiator hose.
7. Remove the coil and rocker arm cover.
8. Loosen the rocker arm nuts and rotate the rocker arms so the pushrods can be removed, then remove the pushrods and store them so they can be installed in their original locations.
9. Remove the cylinder head bolts, cylinder head, and gasket.

Installation Inline Six

1. Clean all gasket surfaces, install a new gasket, and place the head on the block.
2. Install the head bolts. Torque the head bolts to specifications in three stages.
3. Reverse steps one through eight to finish installation.

V6 and V8

1. Disconnect the battery.
2. Drain the coolant.
3. Remove the air cleaner.
4. Remove the air conditioning compressor, *but do not disconnect any lines.*
5. Remove the intake manifold.
6. When removing the right cylinder head, loosen the alternator belt and remove the alternator.
7. When removing the left cylinder head, remove the dipstick, power

TIME SAVER

The following is a method for replacing valve springs, oil seals, or spring retainers without removing the cylinder head.

1. Obtain a spark plug hole air chuck adapter from an auto parts store.
2. Add an air chuck to this adaptor so the hose from an air compressor can be attached. This assembly will be used later to pressurize the cylinder.
3. Remove the valve rocker cover. Remove the rocker arm from the valve to be worked on.
4. Remove the spark plug from the cylinder to be worked on.
5. Turn the crankshaft to bring the piston of this cylinder down, away from

possible contact with the valve head. Sharply tap the valve retainer to loosen the valve lock.
6. Turn the crankshaft to bring the piston in this cylinder to the exact top of its compression stroke.
7. Screw in the chuck-equipped tool.
8. Hook up an air hose to the chuck and turn on the pressure (about 200 lbs).
9. With a strong and constant supply of air holding the valve closed, compress the valve spring and remove the lock and retainer.
10. Make the necessary replacements and reassemble.

NOTE: it is important that the operation be performed exactly as stated, in this order. The piston in the cylinder must be on exact top-center to prevent air pressure from turning the crankshaft.

steering pump and AIR pump if so equipped.
8. Disconnect the plug wires.
9. Disconnect exhaust manifold from the head being removed.
10. Remove the rocker arm cover and rocker shaft assembly. Lift out the push rods.
11. Remove the cylinder head bolts.
12. Remove the cylinder head and gasket.
13. Reverse the above steps to install. Torque the head bolts to specifications in three steps.

Timing Cover, Chain, and Camshaft

Timing Chain, Cover Oil Seal, & Cover

Removal and Installation Inline Six

This engine uses timing gears instead of sprockets and chain. The factory recommends that the engine be removed for this operation, but the following procedure should allow you to save a lot of time by leaving it in place.

1. Drain the cooling system and disconnect the radiator hoses at the radiator.
2. Remove the fan and water pump pulley.
3. Remove the radiator and fan belt.
4. Remove the harmonic balancer, using a puller.
5. Loosen the oil pan bolts and allow the pan to rest against the front crossmember.
6. Remove the timing gear cover bolts, then remove the cover and gasket.
7. Pry out the oil seal using a screwdriver.
   NOTE: The seal can be replaced with the cover installed.
8. Install a new seal with the lip toward the inside of the cover. Drive it into place, using the proper seal installer or an old wheel bearing outer race.
9. Inspect the oil nozzle for damage and replace it if necessary, then clean all gasket surfaces.
10. Install the cover and gasket (stick the gasket to the block with Petroleum jelly or wheel bearing grease), making sure the cover is centered properly on the crankshaft end.
11. Tighten the cover bolts to 7 ft lbs, then install the oil pan and harmonic balancer.

Removal 455 Cu. In.

1. Drain cooling system.
2. Remove radiator, fan, fan pulley and belt, and crankshaft pulley and pulley reinforcement.
2. Remove fuel pump and Delcotron alternator.

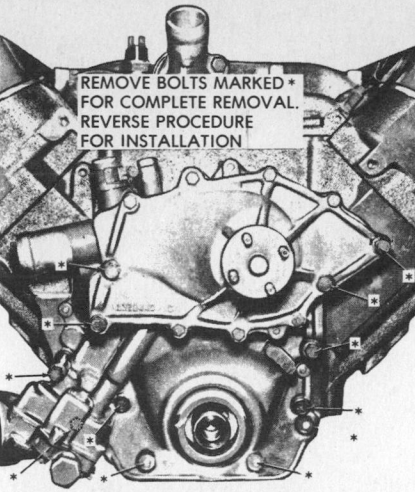

455 timing chain cover
(© Buick Div., G.M. Corp)

REMOVE BOLTS MARKED →
FOR COMPLETE REMOVAL.
REVERSE PROCEDURE FOR INSTALLATION

FUEL PUMP MUST BE REMOVED

350 timing chain cover
(© Buick Div., G.M. Corp)

4. Remove distributor.
5. Loosen clamp on thermostat bypass hose.
6. Remove harmonic balancer.
7. Remove timing chain cover to crankcase bolts. Remove oil pan to timing chain cover bolts. Thoroughly clean cover and crankcase surface. Pry the seal out with a screwdriver. Do not distort the cover.
8. Align timing marks on sprockets.
9. Remove oil pan.
10. Remove crankshaft oil slinger. Remove camshaft sprocket bolts.
11. Use two large screwdrivers to alternately pry the camshaft sprocket, then the crankshaft sprocket, forward and off their respective shafts.

Removal 231 and 350 Cu. In.

This procedure is the same as that detailed above for the 455 cu. in. engine with the substitution of the following steps:
9. Delete Step 9.
10. Remove bolt, special washer, camshaft distributor drive gear, and fuel pump eccentric from camshaft. Remove crankshaft oil slinger.

Installation 231 and 350 Cu. In.

1. Make sure, with sprockets temporarily installed, that No. 1 piston is at top dead center and the camshaft sprocket O-mark is straight down and on the centerline of both shafts.
2. Remove the camshaft sprocket and assemble the timing chain on both sprockets. Then slide the sprockets-and-chain assembly on the shafts with the O-marks in their closest together position and on a centerline with the sprocket hubs.
3. Assemble slinger on crankshaft with I.D. against the sprocket,

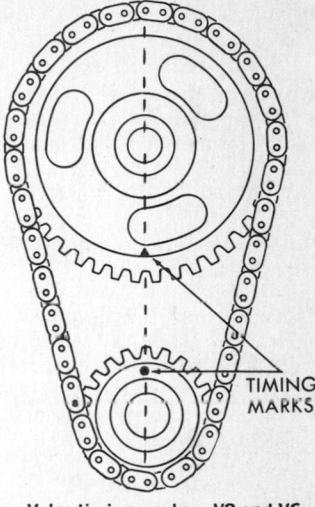

Valve timing marks—V8 and V6

(concave side toward front of engine).
4. Slide fuel pump eccentric on camshaft and Woodruff key with oil groove forward.
5. Install distributor drive gear.
6. Install drive gear and eccentric bolt and retaining washer. Torque to 40-55 ft. lbs.
7. Reinstall timing case cover. Install a new seal by lightly tapping it in place. The lip of the seal faces inward. By reversing removal procedure, paying particular attention to the following points.
   A. Remove oil pump cover and pack space around the oil pump gears completely full of petroleum jelly. There must be no air space left inside the pump. Reinstall the pump cover using new gasket.
   B. The gasket surface of the block and timing chain cover must be clean and smooth. Use a new gasket correctly positioned.
   C. Install chain cover being certain the dowel pins engage

the dowel pin holes before starting the attaching bolts.
D. Lube the bolt threads before installation and install them.
E. If the car has power steering, the front pump bracket should be installed at this time.
F. Lube the O.D. of the harmonic balancer hub before installation to prevent damage to the seal when starting the engine.

Installation 455 Cu. In.

This procedure is similar to that above for 350 V8, with the substitution of the following steps:
4. Delete Step 4.
5. Reinstall oil pan.
6. Install camshaft sprocket bolts. Torque to 22 ft. lbs.

Removal 260 V8

The removal procedure for the 260 V8 is the same as the procedure for the 455 V8 except for the following: Steps 4, 10, and 11, do not apply. In place of Steps 10 and 11, use the following:

Remove the fuel pump eccentric from the camshaft.

Remove the oil slinger, the camshaft sprocket and timing chain. Remove the key from the crankshaft sprocket then remove the sprocket. Because of the close fit of the crankshaft sprocket, it may be necessary to use a gear puller to remove it.

Installation 260 V8

1. Install the camshaft and crankshaft sprockets, and the timing chain together, and align their timing marks. When the two marks are in alignment. No. 6 cylinder is at TDC. To obtain TDC for No. 1 cylinder, rotate the camshaft one revolution. This will bring No. 1 to TDC.
2. Install the fuel pump eccentric on the camshaft gear.
3. Install the key into the crankshaft sprocket.
4. Reinstall the oil slinger.
5. Install a new cover gasket, and install the front cover assembly. Tighten the bolts evenly in a criss-cross pattern.
6. Install the oil pan; lubricate the pulley hub seal surface and install the pulley hub and bolt, torquing the bolt to 255 ft lbs.
7. From this point on, reverse the removal procedure to finish installing the components.

Camshaft Removal and Installation

Inline Six-Cylinder

1. Drain cooling system.
2. Remove radiator, fan, and water pump pulley.

3. Remove grille.
4. Remove valve cover and gasket, then loosen rocker arm nuts and pivot rockers out of the way.
5. Remove pushrods.
6. Remove distributor, fuel pump, and spark plugs.
7. Remove coil, pushrod (tappet gallery) covers and gasket; reach in and remove tappets, keeping them in order.
8. Remove harmonic balancer, then loosen oil pan bolts and allow pan to drop.
9. Remove timing gear cover.
10. Align the timing marks. Remove two camshaft thrust plate bolts by rotating cam gear holes to gain clearance.

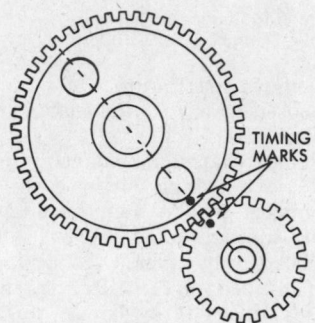

Valve timing marks—inline 6

11. Remove the camshaft by pulling it straight forward.
    NOTE: do not wiggle the camshaft; cam bearings could be dislodged.
12. If cam gear is to be replaced, press it from the shaft using an arbor press.
    NOTE: thrust plate must be positioned so that Woodruff key does not damage it during removal.
13. New cam gear must be pressed onto the shaft, with the shaft supported in back of the front bearing journal.
    NOTE: the thrust plate end-play should be 0.001-0.005 in. If less than 0.001 in., replace spacer ring; if greater than 0.005 in., replace thrust plate.
14. Carefully install the camshaft into the engine, then turn crankshaft and camshaft so that timing marks coincide; tighten thrust plate bolts to 5–8 ft. lbs. Lubricate the camshaft lobes and bearings with heavy oil.
15. Check camshaft and crankshaft gear runout using a dial indicator. Cam gear runout should not exceed 0.004 in., crank gear runout should not exceed 0.003 in.
    NOTE: if runout is excessive, remove gear and clean burrs from shaft.
16. Check gear backlash using a dial indicator; it should not exceed 0.006 in. and should not be less than 0.004 in.

17. To complete installation, reverse Steps 1-9.
    NOTE: install distributor with No. 1 piston at TDC on compression stroke so that vacuum diaphragm faces forward and rotor points to No. 1 spark plug wire cap tower. Make sure oil pump drive shaft is properly indexed with distributor drive shaft.

V6 and V8

1. Drain the cooling system.
2. Remove the radiator, fan, and water pump pulley.
3. Remove the grille.
4. Remove the valve cover, rocker shaft assemblies, and push rods. Keep these parts in order. They must be reassembled in the same order.
5. Remove the distributor and fuel pump.
6. Remove the harmonic balancer, water pump timing chain cover assembly, timing chain, and sprocket.
7. Remove the intake manifold.
8. Remove the hydraulic lifters and keep them in order.
   NOTE: 0.010 in. oversize lifters are sometimes installed. These are identified by an O on the lifter bore and two grooves on the lifter body.
9. Slide the camshaft forward out of the bearing bores. Do this very carefully to avoid marring the bearing surfaces.
10. Reverse the above steps to install. Clean all gasket surfaces and use new gaskets. Make sure the camshaft timing marks are aligned. Lubricate the camshaft lobes and bearings with heavy oil.

260 V8

1. Disconnect the battery.
2. Drain the radiator, remove all radiator hoses, disconnect the transmission cooler lines, remove the fan shroud, and remove the radiator.
3. Disconnect the fuel line at the pump, remove the air cleaner and disconnect the throttle cable.
4. Remove the alternator belt and move the alternator to one side; remove the power steering pump and belt and set it aside out of the way.
5. Remove the air conditioner compressor mounting bracket and move the assembly out of the way. Do not disconnect the lines.
6. Remove the thermostat bypass hose and all heater hoses; disconnect any electrical and vacuum connections that are in the way; disconnect the sparkplug wires.
7. Remove the distributor, engine oil pan, starter and exhaust crossover pipe.

8. Remove the harmonic balancer and pulley; remove the flywheel inspection cover, the engine front cover, both valve covers and the intake manifold.

9. Remove the rocker arm assembly.

10. If the car is equipped with air conditioning move the condensor to the side.

11. Remove the fuel pump eccentric, the camshaft sprocket, the oil slinger and the timing chain.

12. Remove the camshaft by carefully sliding it out of the front of the engine.

Installation is the reverse of removal but note the following points:

1. Make sure that the camshaft and bearings are liberally coated with heavy oil.

2. Make sure that the camshaft and crankshaft sprockets are properly aligned.

3. Before installing the power steering pump make sure that the timing indicator attaching stud is installed and properly torqued (35 ft lbs.).

4. Install the flywheel inspection cover after installing the starter.

5. The left side rear oil gallery plug, just behind the distributor, is used for distributor lubrication. There is a cup plug on top of the threaded plug which has to be removed before lubricant can be added. The front oil gallery plug is on the right side and provides lubrication for the timing chain and gears.

Piston Assembly

All V8 engines are numbered 1-3-5-7, left bank; and 2-4-6-8, right bank. The inline 6 engine is numbered 1-2-3-4-5-6, front to rear.

On the V6, starting at the front end of the crankcase, the cylinders in the right bank are numbered 2-4-6 and in the left bank are numbered 1-3-5.

All compression rings are marked with a dimple, a letter "T", a letter "O", or the word "TOP" to identify the side of the ring which must face toward the top of the piston.

When the piston and connecting rod assembly is properly installed, the oil spurt hole in the connecting rod will face the camshaft. The rib on the edge of the bearing cap will be on the same

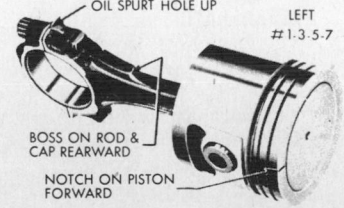

Piston and rod assembly, left bank—350, 455
(© Buick Div., G.M. Corp)

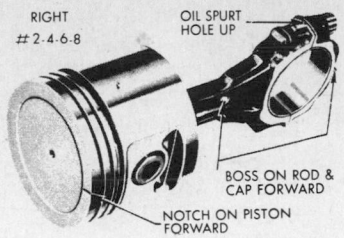

Piston and rod assembly, right bank—350, 455
(© Buick Div., G.M. Corp)

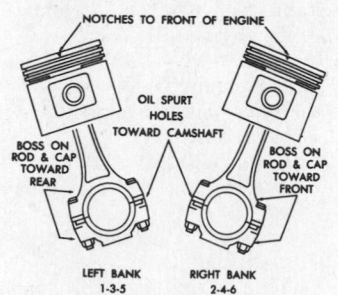

Piston and rod assembly—V6

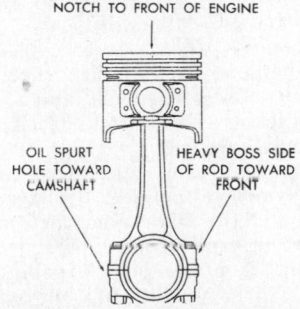

Piston and rod assembly—inline 6

side as the conical boss on the connecting rod web. These marks on the rib and the boss will be toward the other connecting rod on the same crankpin. The notch on the piston will face the front of the engine.

Lubrication

Oil Pump Removal and Installation

On the inline 6, the oil pump is located in the oil pan and mounted to the front section of the cylinder block where it is connected to an oil screen housing and pipe assembly. On the V6 and V8s, the oil pump is located in the left side of the timing chain cover, where it is connected by a drilled passage in the cylinder crankcase to an oil screen housing and standpipe assembly.

Inline Six-Cylinder

1. Drain the oil and remove the oil pan.

2. Remove the two flange mounting bolts and the pickup pipe bolt and remove the pump and screen as an assembly.

3. To install, reverse the above pro-

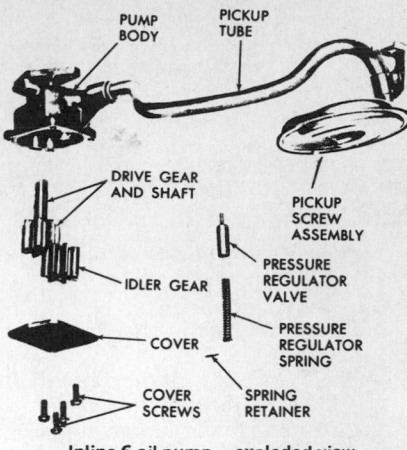

Inline 6 oil pump—exploded view
(© Buick Div., G.M. Corp)

cedure, being sure to tighten the mounting bolts to 9 ft lbs.

NOTE: The oil pump should slide easily into place. If not, remove it and relocate the slot.

V6 and V8 except 260

The pump can be disassembled as follows:

1. Remove the oil filter.

2. Unbolt the pump cover assembly from the timing chain cover.

3. Remove the cover assembly and slide out the pump gears.

4. Remove the oil pressure relief valve cap, spring, and valve. Do not remove the oil filter by-pass valve and spring.

5. Check that the relief valve spring isn't worn on its side or collapsed. Check that the relief valve is no more than an easy slip fit in its bore in the cover. If there is any perceptible side-play, replace the valve. If there is still side-play, replace the cover.

6. Check the filter by-pass valve for good condition.

To assemble the pump:

7. Lubricate and install the pressure relief valve and spring in the cover bore. Install the gasket and cap, torquing the cap to 35 ft lbs.

8. Install the gears and check that gear-to-cover end clearance is between 0.002-0.006 in. If the clearance is less, check the timing cover gear pocket for wear.

9. Remove the gears and pack the gear pocket full of petroleum jelly. Don't use grease.

Caution
Unless the pump is primed this way, it won't produce any oil pressure when the engine is started.

10. Install the gears. Install a new gasket and the cover. Torque the bolts evenly to 10 ft lbs. Replace the filter.

260 V8

1. Remove the oil pan.

2. Remove the oil pump to rear main bearing cap mounting bolts.
3. Remove the pump and drive shaft extension.
4. Installation is the reverse of removal.

Oil Pan Removal and Installation

V6 and V8 Engines except 260

1. Disconnect the battery ground cable.
2. Remove the fan shroud-to-radiator screws.
3. Remove the air cleaner and disconnect the throttle linkage.
4. Raise the front end and support it on jackstands.
5. Drain the oil.
6. Disconnect the exhaust crossover pipe at the engine. The clutch equalizer bracket will have to be unbolted from the frame on some earlier models.
7. Remove the lower flywheel housing cover.
8. Remove the shift linkage bolt and swing it out of the way.
9. Remove the front engine mount bolts.
10. Raise the front of the engine, either by placing a block of wood and a jack under the crankshaft pulley mounting or lifting it with a hoist.

Caution On air conditioned cars, place a support under the right-side of the transmission before raising the engine. If you don't do this, the engine and transmission will flop to the right due to the weight of the air conditioning equipment.

11. On 1974 and later Apollo and Skylark disconnect the idler arm at the frame and swing the assembly down.
12. Unbolt and remove the pan. It may be necessary to turn the crankshaft so that it doesn't interfere with the front of the pan.
13. Reverse the procedure for installation.

260 V8

1. Remove distributor cap and place rotor at TDC for No. 1 cylinder by turning crankshaft pulley.
2. Disconnect the battery cable; remove the dipstick.
3. Put the car on a lift and drain the oil.
4. Remove the flywheel cover and starter assembly.
5. Disconnect the exhaust and exhaust crossover pipes.
6. Jack up the engine to disconnect the engine mounts then raise the front of the engine as far as possible.
7. Remove the oil pan mounting bolts and remove the pan.

8. Install the front and rear seals, the pan gasket, and replace the pan.
9. Reverse the removal steps to install.

Inline Six-Cylinder

1. Disconnect battery, remove air cleaner and disconnect throttle linkage.
2. Remove fan shroud-to-radiator screws.
3. Jack up car and support on axle stands under lower A-frames.
4. Drain engine oil.
5. If equipped with automatic transmission:
   a. Remove flywheel housing inspection cover.
   b. Remove shift linkage bolt and swing linkage out of way.
   c. Disconnect exhaust pipe at manifold.
6. Remove front motor mount bolts.
7. Jack up engine as far as it will go, with padded jack under crank pulley mounting.
8. Remove front motor mounts completely to gain clearance. Remove the left mount and frame bracket, on 1974 and later Apollo and Skylark.
9. On 1974 and later Apollo and Skylark, disconnect the steering rod at the idler lever, then move the linkage to one side.
10. On 1974 and later Apollo and Skylark, unbolt and move the brake line away from the front crossmember.
11. Turn the crankshaft until the timing mark on the damper is at the bottom.
12. Unbolt the pan. On 1974 and later Apollo and Skylark, lower it slightly and roll it into the area from which you removed the left engine mount, tilt the front of the pan up and pull it down and out to the rear.
13. Reverse the procedure on installation. Tighten the bolts to 7-10 ft lbs, except for those that go into the front cover. These must be installed last and tightened to 5 ft lbs.

Rear Main Bearing Oil Seal Replacement

Inline Six-Cylinder

1. The rear main bearing oil seal can be replaced without removing the crankshaft. Remove the oil pan and rear main bearing cap.
2. Remove the seal from the bearing cap and clean the groove.
3. Remove the upper seal half by tapping the seal out with a brass punch until it can be grasped with pliers.

4. To replace the bearing cap seal, lubricate the groove in the cap and lightly press the seal in place. Do not cut the end of the seal. Do not get any oil on the parting line surface.
5. To replace the upper seal, lubricate the new seal with oil. Gradually push the seal in the groove in the block, while turning the crankshaft, until the seal is rolled into place.
6. Install the rear main bearing cap and torque it to specifications. Be sure the cross seal tabs are in place and properly seated. Make sure there is no oil on the parting line between the bearing cap and the block. Run the engine slowly for the first few minutes.

Chilton's TIME SAVER

Top Half, Rear Main Bearing Oil Seal Replacement

Although the factory recommends removing the crankshaft to replace the top half of the oil seal, the following procedure can be used without removing the crankshaft.

1. Remove the oil pan and rear main bearing cap.
2. Loosen the rest of the crankshaft main bearings and allow the crankshaft to drop about 1/16 in.
3. Remove the old upper half of the oil seal.
4. Wrap some soft copper wire around the end of the new seal and leave about 12 in. on the end. Generously lubricate the new seal with oil.
5. Slip the free end of the copper wire into the oil seal groove and around the crankshaft. Pull the wire until the seal protrudes an equal amount on each side. Rotate the crankshaft as the seal is pulled into place.
6. Remove the wire. Push any excess seal that may be protruding back into the groove.
7. Before tightening the crankshaft bearing caps, visually check the bearings to make sure they are in place. Torque the bearing cap bolts to specifications. Make sure there is no oil on the parting surfaces.
8. Replace the oil pan. Run the engine slowly for the first few minutes of operation.

V6 and V8

1. Braided fabric seals are used. The upper seal half cannot be replaced without removing the crankshaft, unless you use the Time Saver in this section.
2. Remove the oil pan and rear main bearing cap.
3. Remove the old seal from the bearing cap and place a new seal in the groove with both ends projecting above the parting surface of the cap.
4. Force the seal into the groove by rubbing down with a hammer handle or smooth tool, until the seal projects above the groove not more than 1/16 in. Cut the ends off flush with the surface of the cap. Use a razor blade.
5. Use the same procedure to install a new upper seal half after removing the engine from the car and the crankshaft from the engine.

CLUTCH

Clutch Removal

1. Remove pedal return spring from clutch fork. On the Skyhawk, remove the clutch fork cover, then disconnect the clutch return spring and control cable from the clutch fork. Remove the transmission.
2. Remove flywheel housing.
3. Remove throw-out bearing from clutch fork.
4. Disconnect clutch fork from ball stud.
5. Mark clutch cover and flywheel to assure proper balance on reassembly.
6. Loosen clutch cover to flywheel bolts one turn at a time until spring pressure is released.
7. Support pressure plate and cover assembly while removing last bolts, then remove cover assembly and driven plate.

Clutch Installation

Install clutch by reversing removal procedure. Use a clutch aligning pilot or a spare main drive gear through the hub of driven plate and into the pilot bushing. Be sure to align the clutch cover-to-flywheel index marks.

Clutch Linkage Adjustment

Through 1974

Check pedal lash (free-play) by pushing down on the pedal by hand. Lash should be approximately ¾ in. measured at the pedal pad.

1. Make sure the pedal is at full release position, contacting the rubber bumper stop. Remove return spring.
2. Adjust clutch release rod underneath car to give zero lash at the clutch pedal.
3. Back off release rod adjustment 2-3 turns to give ¾ in. lash at pedal pad. (Equals 1/16-⅛ in. at pushrod.)
4. Tighten locknut on clutch release rod.

1975 and later except Skyhawk

1. Disconnect the return spring at the clutch operating fork.
2. Use the linkage to push the clutch pedal up against its rubber bumper stop.
3. Push the end of the clutch operating fork to the rear until the release bearing can just be felt to contact the pressure plate fingers.
4. Detach the front end of the operating rod from the clutch pivot shaft arm and place it in the gauge hole on the arm.
5. Loosen the locknut and lengthen the rod just enough to take all the play out of the linkage. Tighten the locknut.
6. Replace the operating rod in its original location.
7. Replace the return spring and check the free play at the pedal pad. It should be ¾-1 in.

Skyhawk

1. Make sure that the pedal is at full release position, contacting the rubber bumper stop. Remove the return spring.
2. Push the clutch fork forward until the throwout bearing just touches the clutch spring (about 1¾ in.).
3. Tighten the screw pin on the cable to obtain about ¼ in. fork free play; this will produce ¾-1 in. free play at the clutch pedal.
4. Attach the return spring

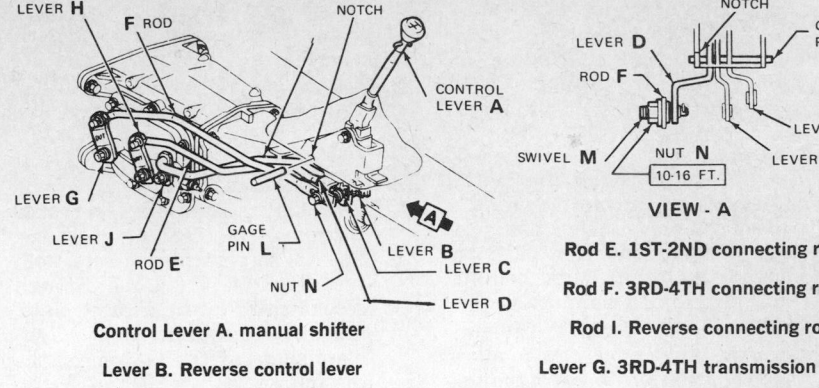

Control Lever A. manual shifter

Lever B. Reverse control lever

Lever C. 1ST-2ND control lever

Lever D. 3RD-4TH control lever

Rod E. 1ST-2ND connecting rod

Rod F. 3RD-4TH connecting rod

Rod I. Reverse connecting rod

Lever G. 3RD-4TH transmission lever

Lever H. 1ST-2ND transmission lever

Lever J. Reverse transmission lever

Skyhawk 4 speed transmission linkage
(© Buick Div., G.M. Corp)

MANUAL TRANSMISSION

Two different, fully-synchronized three-speed transmissions have been available in these cars. A Muncie transmission was used in 1970-71 GS models. It can be identified by the two casting "ears" or bolt bosses on the case at the top of the side cover. A Saginaw transmission is used on all other models. It can be identified by the single casting "ear" or bolt boss on the case at the top of the side cover. The production code and transmission serial number are on the right side of the transmission case.

The Muncie 4-speed is the only 4-speed transmission used in cars made before 1975.

In the Skyhawk, a fully synchronized, four speed Saginaw transmission is used. The production code and transmission serial number are stamped on the right side of the transmission case.

Starting 1976, the Skyhawk was available with the Borg-Warner 5-speed transmission. The linkage on this model is internal and does not require any adjustment.

For repair procedures, see the Unit Repair Section.

Removal and Installation

All except 5-speed

1. Mark the universal joint and transmission shaft companion flange for proper indexing at the time of installation. Remove the two U-bolts and disconnect the driveshaft at the rear joint. Slide the driveshaft rearward as far as possible and remove it.
2. Disconnect the shift linkage from the transmission.
3. Disconnect the speedometer cable at the transmission.
4. Loosen all exhaust pipe joints to permit the transmission and the

rear of the engine to be lowered if necessary.

5. Remove the two bolts holding the transmission mounting pad to the transmission support. Leave the mounting pad bolted to the transmission.

6. With a padded jack under the engine, raise the unit until the transmission mounting pad just clears the transmission support.

7. Remove the four bolts holding the transmission support to the body members. Remove the support, then lower the jack to allow the transmission to clear the underbody.

8. Remove the two top transmission-to-flywheel housing bolts and install guide pins.

NOTE: If guide pins are not used, damage to the clutch driven plate can result.

9. Remove the other transmission attaching bolts. Slide the transmission back until the drive gear shaft disengages the clutch disc and clears the flywheel housing. Lower the transmission.

10. On installation, install the guide pins in the upper and lower right-side bolt holes for alignment. If the guide pins aren't used, the clutch plate might be damaged.

5-Speed

1. Remove the boot retainer and slide the boot upward on the shift lever.

2. Remove the foam insulator over the control assembly bolts.

3. Remove the four control lever bolts and remove the control lever.

4. Raise the car and remove the driveshaft.

5. Remove the damper assembly, the torque converter bracket, and the torque arm bracket.

6. Disconnect the speedometer cable and the back-up light switch.

7. Place a transmission jack under the transmission and remove the transmission support.

8. Remove the transmission-to-clutch housing bolts and slide the exhaust bracket forward; after this the transmission can be moved rearward and removed from the car.

9. Installation is the reverse of removal. Make sure that the main drive gear splines are clean and dry.

Linkage Adjustment

Three-Speed Column Shift

1. Place the column shift lever in Reverse. Turn the ignition lock to the LOCK position.

2. Loosen first-reverse clamp bolt.

3. Place the transmission first-reverse lever (the rear one) into the reverse (forward) position. Pull down on the shift rod and tighten the clamp bolt to 17-23 ft. lbs.

4. Unlock the ignition lock and shift the transmission levers into their neutral (center) positions.

5. Loosen second-third clamp bolt.

6. Install a 3/16 in. dia. rod through second-third lever, selector plate, first-reverse lever, and alignment plate at the bottom of the column.

7. Tighten second-third clamp bolt to 17-23 ft. lbs.

8. With the shift lever in Reverse, the key must move freely to the LOCK position. You should not be able to get into the LOCK position in any gear position other than Reverse.

Three-Speed Floorshift

1. Place transmission levers into neutral.

2. Loosen shift rod adjusting clamp bolts.

3. Place a 5/16 in. dia. rod in notch in rear portion of shift bracket assembly.

4. Move both shift levers back against rod.

5. Tighten shift rod adjusting bolts to 17-23 ft. lbs.

Four-Speed Floorshift

All except Skyhawk

1. Place transmission levers in neutral positions.

2. Place a 5/16 in. dia. rod in rear lower portion of shift bracket assembly.

3. Adjust all three shift levers back against rod.

4. Tighten adjusting clamp bolts to 17-23 ft. lbs.

Skyhawk

1. Loosen the rod retaining nuts at the base of the shift lever; set the third and fourth, first and second, and reverse gear levers into neutral. This can be done by moving the levers counterclockwise one detent and then clockwise one detent.

2. Move the shift lever into neutral and then align the holes of the reverse, first and second, and third and fourth gear levers with the notch on the shifter assembly. When they are aligned, insert a pin to hold them in place.

3. Attach the third and fourth gear rod to the third and fourth gear lever.

4. Attach the third and fourth gear rod and retaining nut loosely to the swivel on the third and fourth gear lever. When installed, tighten the retaining nut.

5. Repeat steps 3 and 4 for the first and second, and for the reverse gear adjustment.

6. When the adjustments have been completed, remove the pin.

AUTOMATIC TRANSMISSION

All the Buick models covered in this section except the Gran Sport through 1971, use the 350-375B Turbo Hydra-Matic transmission. The identification number for this transmission is located on the lower left side. The Gran Sport through 1971

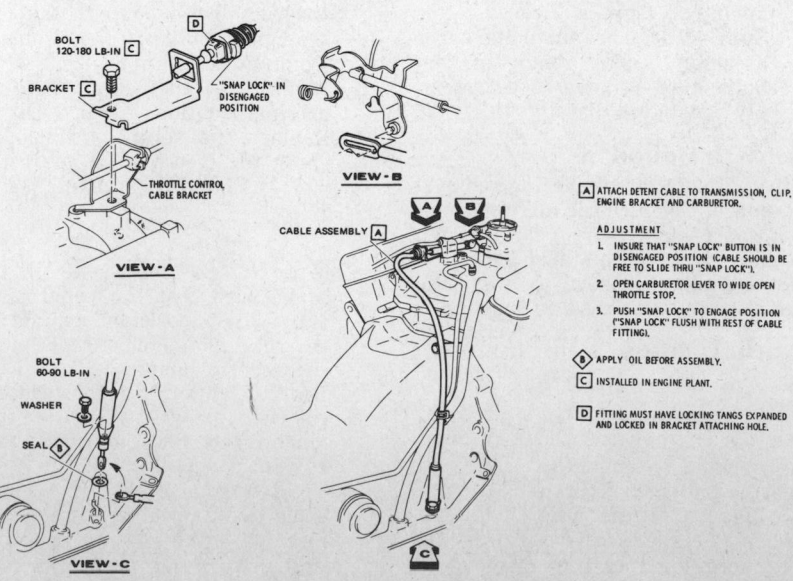

Apollo/Skylark Turbo Hydra-Matic 350 detent switch installation and adjustment
(© Buick Div., G.M. Corp)

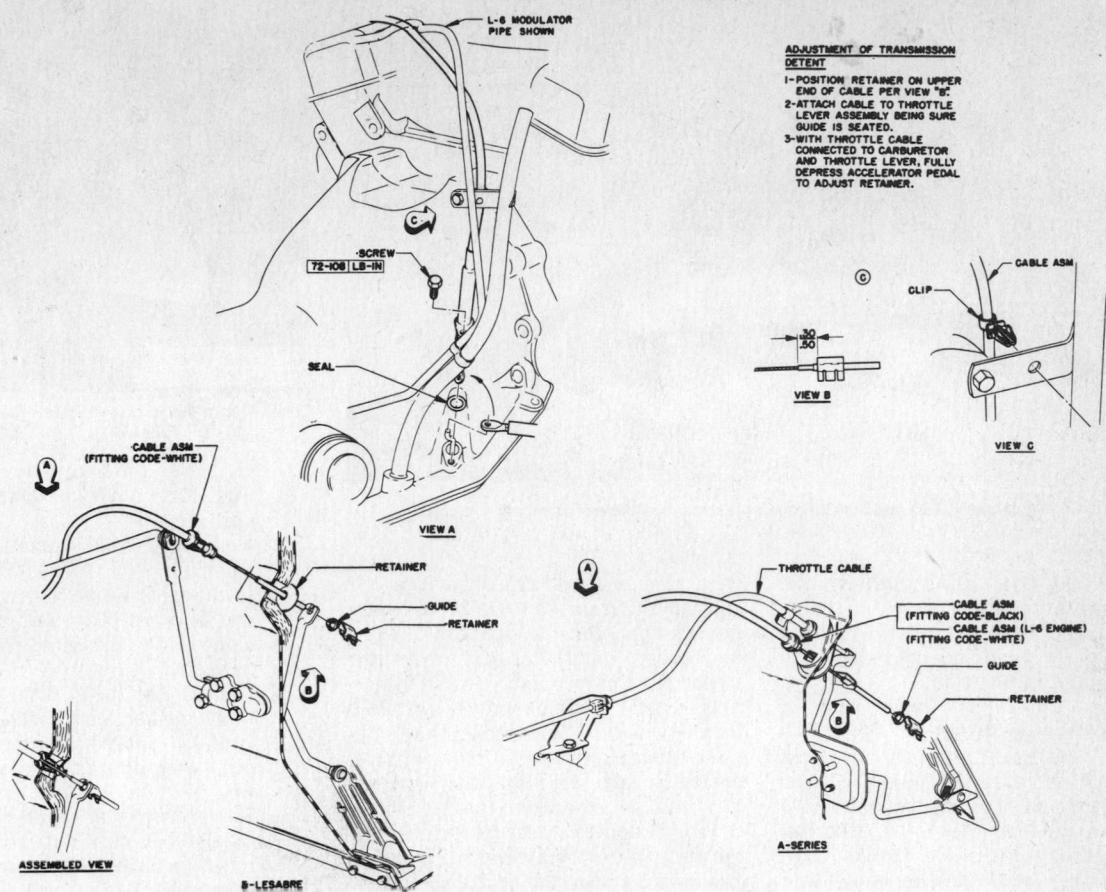

Transmission detent cable adjustment—Turbo Hydra-Matic 350 (© Buick Div., G.M. Corp)

uses a Turbo Hydra-Matic 400 transmission with its identification number in the same place as the 350-375B transmission.

One way to tell the difference between the 350-375B transmission and the 400 transmission is the detent switch. On the 350-375B series, the detent cable runs from the throttle linkage down to the right side of the transmission. On the 400 series, there is an electrically operated detent switch in the engine compartment, on the firewall, next to the throttle lever.

Detent Cable Adjustment— Turbo Hydra-Matic 350 and 375B

Refer to the accompanying illustration for this procedure.

Detent Switch Adjustment— Turbo Hydra-Matic 400

The switch is on the firewall, inside the car, near the accelerator pedal. The initial adjustment on installation is made by pushing the switch lever all the way toward the firewall. The final adjustment is made automatically the first time the accelerator pedal is floorboarded.

Shift Linkage Adjustment

Column Shift

1. Place selector lever in Drive (Neutral for 1971 up).
2. Loosen adjusting clamp bolt.
3. Place lever at transmission in drive (Neutral for 1971 up) position.
4. Tighten clamp bolt to 17-23 ft. lbs.

Floorshift except Skyhawk

There are two procedures that can be used, depending on the shape of the transmission end of the shifter cable. On early models, the cable ends in a straight rod with a clamp (trunnion) bolt. On later models, the cable ends in a flattened eye with a fixed bolt through it.

1. Loosen the trunnion bolt at the transmission end of the cable on early models. On later models, pull the clip from the cable housing at the side of the transmission.
2. Set the console shift lever against the Drive stop on early models. On later models, set it in the Park detent.
3. Set the transmission shift lever in the Drive position on early models and on the Apollo and Skylark. This is the third position from the back. On later models, set it in the Park, or most forward, position.

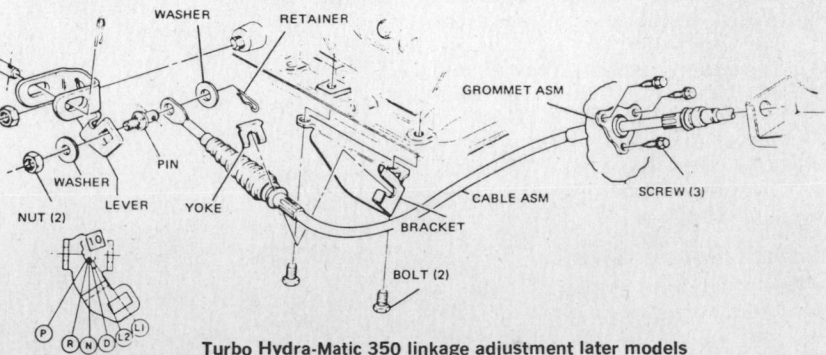

Turbo Hydra-Matic 350 linkage adjustment later models
(© Buick Div., G.M. Corp)

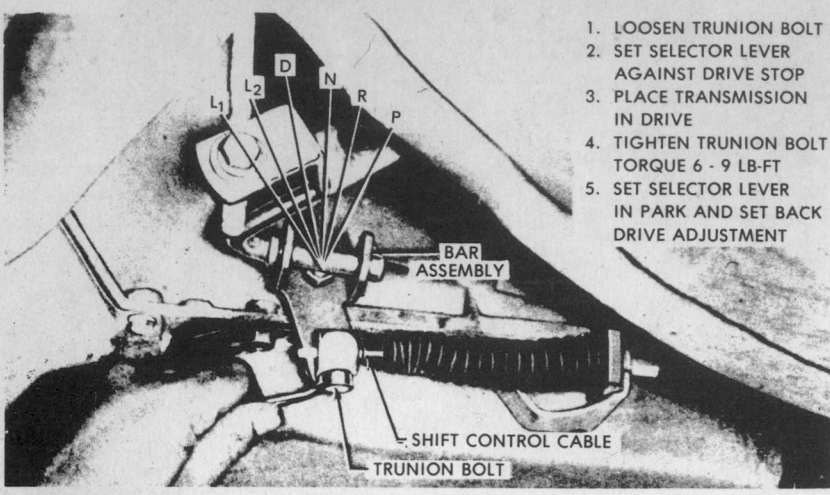

1. LOOSEN TRUNION BOLT
2. SET SELECTOR LEVER AGAINST DRIVE STOP
3. PLACE TRANSMISSION IN DRIVE
4. TIGHTEN TRUNION BOLT TORQUE 6 - 9 LB-FT
5. SET SELECTOR LEVER IN PARK AND SET BACK DRIVE ADJUSTMENT

Turbo Hydra-Matic 350 and 400 linkage adjustment console shifter (early models)
(© Buick Div., G.M. Corp)

Turbo Hydra-Matic transmission filter and gasket
(© Buick Div., G.M. Corp)

4. On early models, tighten the trunnion bolt against the cable end to 6-9 ft lbs. On later models, replace the clip to hold the cable housing in position.
5. Place the console shift lever in the Park position.
6. Set the console shift lever in Park. Loosen the clamp at the bottom of the back drive rod (the one that goes to the steering column). Push the back drive rod up against the stop and tighten the clamp screw.

1975 Skyhawk Floorshift

1. Loosen the nut and swivel at the transmission lever.
2. Place the transmission lever in Neutral by moving it counterclockwise to the L1 detent and then clockwise three detent positions to Neutral.
3. Position the shift lever in the Neutral notch of the detent plate.
4. Place the flat of the swivel into the slot of the control rod. Install the washer and cotter pin.
5. Tighten the locknut and adjust the neutral safety switch if necessary.

1976 and later Skyhawk Floorshift

1. Loosen the nut on the transmission lever, with the control cable on the pin and connected to the shifter assembly and the cable bracket.
2. Place the shifter in Neutral, and the transmission lever in Neutral. You can find neutral on the transmission lever by moving it to the L1 detent, and then forward four stops.
3. Tighten the nut.

Neutral Safety Switch

This switch prevents the engine from being started in any transmission position except Neutral or Park. The back-up light switch is combined with the neutral safety switch. On column shift cars and 1971 and later models with console shift, the switch is located on the steering column under the instrument panel. On earlier console shift cars, the switch is located inside the console. When the neutral start portion of the switch is correctly adjusted, the back-up portion is adjusted automatically. Slotted mounting screw holes permit switch movement for adjustment. To adjust the switch, place the shift lever in the Neutral position and insert a 3/32 in. drill bit through the hole in the back of the switch. Move the switch until the bit goes in about 3/8 in. Tighten the mounting screws and check the adjustment.

Caution when checking to see if engine will start in transmission positions other than Neutral or Park, always hold the service brake firmly.

Pan Removal and Installation, Fluid and Filter Change

Turbo Hydra-Matic 350, 375 B

1. Raise the car on a lift, remove the pan bolts and washers. Loosen the bolts gradually so that the fluid can drain out of one corner of the pan without spilling.
2. Remove the old gasket and clean the pan.
3. Remove the two screws holding the filter in place and remove it, remove the filter to valve body gasket.
4. Install the new filter to valve body gasket on the filter and install the assembly. Replace the pan, torquing the bolts to 13 ft lbs.
5. Lower the car and add three pints of Dexron automatic transmission fluid; then start the car and shift it through each gear.
6. Check the transmission fluid level and add if necessary.

Turbo Hydra-Matic 400

The procedure is the same, but when the filter is removed, the intake pipe O-ring seal must be replaced. The pan bolts are torqued to 10 ft lbs.

U-JOINTS

The driveshaft is a one piece unit with a splined slip yoke and a universal joint at the transmission end, and a second universal joint at the differential end. The shaft, depending on application, can be a one-piece solid

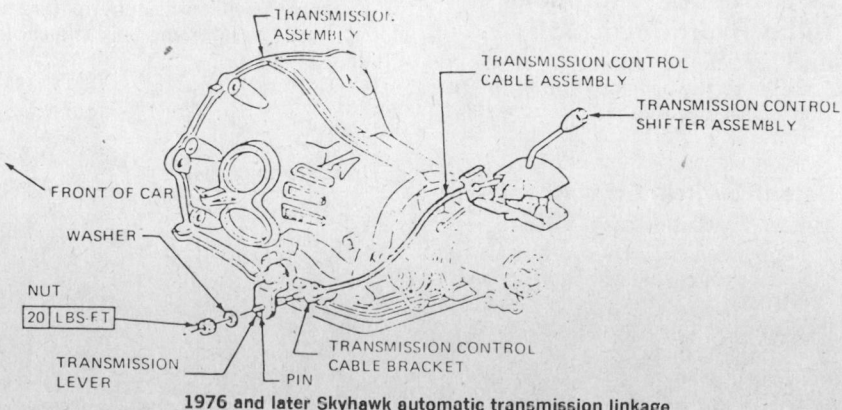

1976 and later Skyhawk automatic transmission linkage
(© Buick Div., G.M. Corp)

steel unit, or can be composed of two concentric tubes damped with rubber.

Driveshaft Removal and Installation

1. Mark the driveshaft rear yoke and the differential flange to assure correct alignment upon reassembly.
2. Remove the bolts and straps from the differential flange.
3. Remove the driveshaft assembly by first sliding the driveshaft sufficiently forward to disengage the differential flange and then slide the shaft downward and rearward to disengage the front splined yoke from the transmission output shaft.
4. Installation is the reverse of removal. Be sure to align the match marks made before disassembly.

Universal Joint Removal and Installation

Nylon-injected composite universal joints are used. To replace universal joints:
1. Remove the driveshaft.
2. By using a piece of pipe or similar tool, slightly larger than 1⅛ in. to encircle the bearing shell, apply force on the yoke until downward movement of the yoke and stationary position of journal force the bearing assembly almost out of the top of the yoke (the force applied on the yoke will shear nylon retainers which lock bearings in place).
3. Rotate the shaft 180° and repeat preceding step to partially remove the opposite bearing.
4. Complete removal of these bearings by tapping around the circumference of exposed portion of bearing.
5. Remove journal from driveshaft rear yoke.
6. Remove bearings and journal from splined yoke in the same way.
   NOTE: new bearings and journal assembly kits must be used upon reassembly. The kit includes snap-rings and Delrin washers.
7. Install by inserting one bearing one-quarter way in one side of splined yoke, using brass hammer.
8. Insert journal into splined yoke (with dust shields installed).
9. Install opposite bearing, ensuring that the bearing rollers do not jam on journal. Check free rotary movement of journal in bearing.
10. Now, press both bearings into place (just far enough to install snap rings).
11. Assemble opposite end universal in the same way.

REAR AXLE

Axle, Shaft, Bearing, and Seal

Removal and Installation

These cars use two different types of drive axle, the C- and the non C-type. Axle shafts in the C-type are retained by C-shaped locks, which fit grooves at the inner end of the shaft. Axle shafts in the non C-type are retained by the brake backing plate, which is bolted to the axle housing. Bearings in the C-type axle consist of an outer race, bearing rollers and a roller cage, retained by snap-rings. The non C-type axle uses a unit roller bearing (inner race, rollers and outer race), which is pressed onto the shaft up to a shoulder. When servicing C or non C type axles, it is imperative to determine the axle type before attempting any service.

Non C-Type

Caution Before attempting any service to the drive axle or axle shafts, remove the axle carrier cover and visually determine if the axle shafts are retained by C-shaped locks at the inner end, or by the brake backing plate at the outer end. If the shafts are *not* retained by C-locks, proceed as follows.

Design allows for maximum axle shaft end-play of 0.022 in., which can be measured with a dial indicator. If end-play is found to be excessive, the bearing should be replaced. Shimming the bearing is not recommended as this ignores end-play of the bearing itself and could result in improper seating of the bearing.
1. Remove the wheel, tire and brake drum.
2. Remove the nuts holding the retainer plate to the backing plate. Disconnect the brake line.
3. Remove the retainer and install nuts, fingertight, to prevent the brake backing plate from being dislodged.
4. Pull out the axle shaft and bearing assembly, using a slide hammer.
5. Using a chisel, nick the bearing retainer in three or four places. The retainer does not have to be cut, merely collapsed sufficiently, to allow the bearing retainer to be slid from the shaft.
6. Press off the bearing and install the new one by pressing it into position.
7. Press on the new retainer.
   NOTE: do not attempt to press the bearing and the retainer on at the same time.
8. Assemble the shaft and bearing in the housing, being sure that

the bearing is seated properly in the housing.
9. Install the retainer, drum, wheel and tire. Bleed the brakes.

C-Type

Caution Before attempting any service to the drive axle or axle shafts, remove the carrier cover and visually determine if the axle shaft(s) are retained by C-shaped locks at the inner ends or by a brake backing plate at the outer end. If they *are* retained by C-shaped locks, proceed as follows.
1. Raise the vehicle and remove the wheels.
2. The differential cover has already been removed (see Caution note above). Remove the differential pinion shaft lockscrew and the differential pinion shaft.
3. Push the flanged end of the axle shaft toward the center of the vehicle and remove the C-lock from the end of the shaft.
4. Remove the axle shaft from the housing, being careful not to damage the oil seal.
5. Remove the oil seal by inserting the button end of the axle shaft behind the steel case of the oil seal. Pry the seal loose from the bore.
6. Seat the legs of the bearing puller behind the bearing. Seat a washer against the bearing and

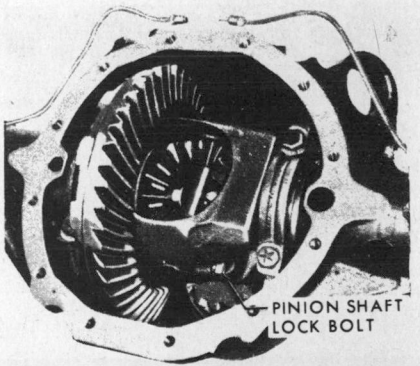

Removing pinion shaft lock bolt from differential
(© Buick Div., G.M. Corp)

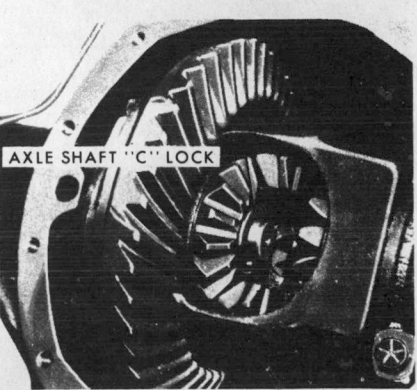

Removing the axle shaft C lock
(© Buick Div., G.M. Corp)

hold it in place with a nut. Use a slide hammer to pull the bearing.

7. Pack the cavity between the seal lips with wheel bearing lubricant and lubricate a new wheel bearing with same.

8. Use a suitable driver and install the bearing until it bottoms against the tube. Install the oil seal.

9. Slide the axle shaft into place. Be sure that the splines on the shaft do not damage the oil seal. Make sure that the splines engage the differential side gear.

10. Install the axle shaft C-lock on the inner end of the axle shaft and push the shaft outward so that the C-lock seats in the differential side gear counterbore.

11. Position the differential pinion shaft through the case and pinions, aligning the hole in the case with the hole for the lockscrew.

12. Install the pinion shaft lockscrew.

13. Use a new gasket and install the carrier cover. Be sure that the gasket surfaces are clean before installing the gasket and cover.

14. Fill the axle with lubricant to the bottom of the filler hole.

15. Install the brake drum and wheels and lower the car. Check for leaks and road test the car.

JACKING, HOISTING

Jack car at front spring seat of lower control arm or center of cross member.

Jack car at rear at axle housing.

To lift at frame, use side rails in front of body floor pan and at rear side rail at lower control arm front pivot.

FRONT SUSPENSION

Ball Joint Inspection

Through 1972

NOTE: before performing this inspection, make sure the wheel bearings are adjusted correctly and that the A arm bushings are in good condition.

1. Jack up the car under the front lower control arm at the spring seat.

2. Raise the car until there is 1–2 in. of clearance under the wheel.

3. Insert a bar under the wheel and pry upward. If the wheel raises

more than 1/8 in. the ball joints are worn. Determine if the upper or lower ball joint is worn by visual inspection while prying on the wheel.

NOTE: due to the distribution of forces in the suspension, the lower ball joint is usually the defective joint.

1973 and later

Beginning 1973, on all cars except the 1973-74 Apollo, lower ball joints have a visual wear indicator. The lower ball joint grease plug screws into the wear indicator which protrudes from the bottom of the ball joint housing. As long as the wear indicator extends out of the ball joint housing, the ball joint is not worn. If the tip of the wear indicator is parallel with, or recessed into the ball joint housing, the ball joint is defective.

All Models through 1972 and 1973-74 Apollo

1. Place a jack under the lower control arm spring seat. Raise the wheel off the floor.

2. Measure the distance from the tip of the grease fitting to the end of the ball joint stud with calipers. What you are measuring here is the total length of the ball joint.

3. Insert a bar under the tire and pry up. Measure the length of the ball joint, with the wheel raised.

4. If there is a difference in the two measurements of more than 1/16 in., the joint is worn.

Control Arm, and/or Ball Joint, Spring—Removal and Installation

Upper Control Arm

1. Raise the car and place a jack under the frame. Remove the wheel and tire.

2. Remove the cotter pin from the upper ball joint stud.

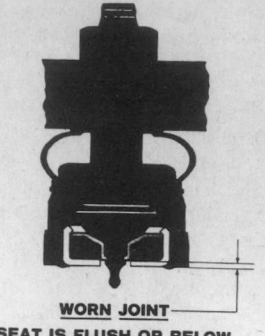

WORN JOINT
SEAT IS FLUSH OR BELOW SURFACE OF COVER

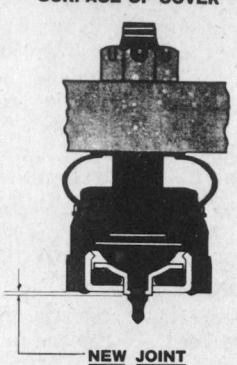

NEW JOINT
SEAT EXTENDS PAST COVER

The wear indicating lower ball joint is used beginning 1973 on all models except Apollo, and beginning 1975 on Apollo
(© Buick Div., G.M. Corp)

3. Loosen, but do not remove, the nut.

Caution If the nut is removed, the full force of the coil spring could be released.

Rap the knuckle sharply in the area of the tapered stud or use a ball joint removal tool to free the stud from the knuckle.

4. With another jack, support the car weight under the outer edge of the lower control arm. Raise the jack enough to free the upper control arm from the upper ball stud.

5. Wire the brake and knuckle in place to prevent brake hose damage, then lift the upper arm from the knuckle.

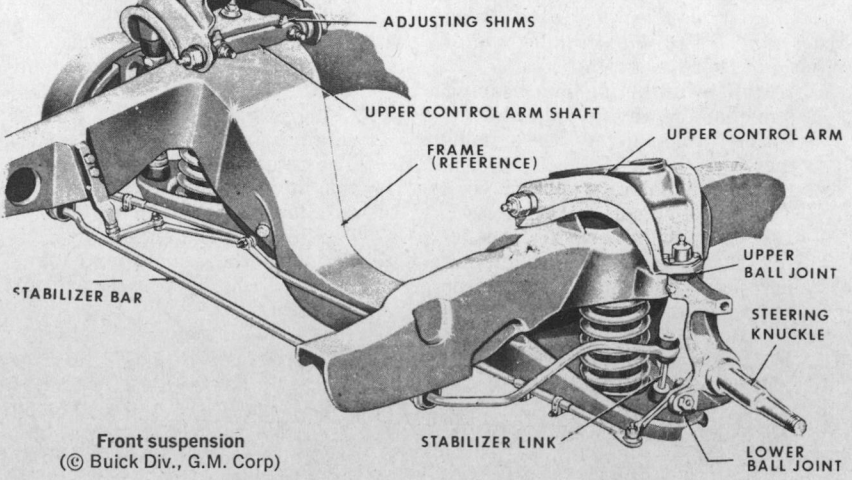

Front suspension
(© Buick Div., G.M. Corp)

ADJUSTING SHIMS

UPPER CONTROL ARM SHAFT

FRAME (REFERENCE)

UPPER CONTROL ARM

UPPER BALL JOINT

STEERING KNUCKLE

LOWER BALL JOINT

STABILIZER LINK

STABILIZER BAR

NOTE: If only the ball joints are to be replaced, stop at this point. Center punch and drill out the four rivets, then chisel off their heads. Remove the old ball joint. The new joint comes with four specially hardened bolts which must be torqued to 8 ft lbs. The nut goes on top.

6. Remove the upper control arm shaft-to-bracket nuts and lock washers. Carefully note the number, thickness, and location of the adjusting shims. Remove the control arm assembly.
7. Reverse the above steps to install.

Caution

When installing the cotter pin, never loosen the nut to align the cotter pin holes. Always tighten the nut to the next slot that lines up with the hole.

Lower Control Arm or Spring

1. Raise the front of the car and remove the tires, wheels, hub, and drum or rotor.
2. Disconnect and remove the shock absorber.
3. Remove the front stabilizer rod link from the lower control arm.
4. Disconnect the brake reaction rod from the lower control arm but leave it attached to the front frame crossmember up to 1970 models. On the Skyhawk, mark the position of the front alignment cam bolts to aid in reassembly.
5. Remove the control arm bumper up to 1970 models.
6. As a safety precaution and to gain maximum leverage, place a jack about ½ in. below the lower ball joint stud. Now, remove the ball stud cotter pin and loosen the nut about ⅛ in. Do not remove the nut.

Caution

If the nut is removed, the full force of the coil spring could be released.

7. Rap the steering knuckle in the area of the stud or use a ball joint removal tool to separate the stud from the knuckle.
8. After the stud has broken loose from the knuckle, raise the jack against the control arm. Remove the nut and separate the steering knuckle from the tapered stud.
9. Carefully lower the jack under the control arm and release the spring. With the jack entirely lowered, it may be necessary to pry the spring off its seat on the lower control arm with a pry bar.
10. After the spring is removed, the lower control arm may be removed by removing the lock nut which attaches the control arm to the frame.
11. Install by reversing the removal procedure. Tighten the castellated nut to 85 ft lbs.

Lower Ball Joint Removal and Installation

1. Perform Steps 1-8, inclusive, as in the "Lower Control Arm" procedure. In Step 1, the brake drum or rotor does not have to be removed.
2. Remove the ball joint by pressing the joint from the lower control arm. It may be necessary to remove the ball joint and lower control arm as an assembly and have the ball joint removed in a press if suitable tools are not available.
3. Install a new ball joint and reverse the removal procedure.

Front Wheel Bearing Adjustment

1970

Adjustment of freshly cleaned and repacked roller bearings is as follows:

1. Torque the spindle nut to 19 ft lbs while rotating the wheel.
2. Back off the nut until the bearings are loose.
3. Retorque the spindle nut to 11 ft lbs while rotating the wheel.
4. If either cotter pin hole in the spindle lines up with the nut castellations, back off the nut ½ turn and install the cotter pin. Otherwise, back off the nut to the first position that will accept a horizontal or vertical cotter pin.
5. Install the cotter pin and lock spindle nut into position.

NOTE: 0.002-0.006 in. end-play is normal.

1971 and later

1. Lift the wheel off the ground by jacking under the lower control arm.
2. Remove the dust cap from the hub.
3. Remove the cotter pin and discard it.
4. Snug up the spindle nut to seat the bearings while turning the wheel. Then back off the nut ¼-½ turn.
5. Retighten the nut by hand until it is finger-tight.
6. Loosen the nut until the nearest hole in the spindle lines up with a slot in the spindle nut, and insert a new cotter pin.

NOTE: Under no circumstance is the final bearing nut adjustment to be even finger-tight.

7. Feel the looseness in the hub assembly. There will be 0.001-0.005 in. end-play.
8. Replace the dust cover and lower the car.

Shock Absorber Removal and Installation

1. Remove the upper shock absorber attaching nut, grommet retainer, and grommet.
2. Remove the lower retaining screws. Lower the shock through the hole in the lower control arm.
3. Reverse the above steps to install.

REAR SUSPENSION

Shock Absorber Removal and Installation

1. Raise car at the axle housing.
2. Remove the nut, retainer, and grommet or nut and lockwasher, as equipped, which attach the lower end of the shock absorber to its mounting.
3. Remove the two shock absorber upper attaching screws and remove the shock absorber.
4. Reverse the removal procedures to install.

Rear Leaf Spring Replacement

1. Raise the rear of the car on stands.

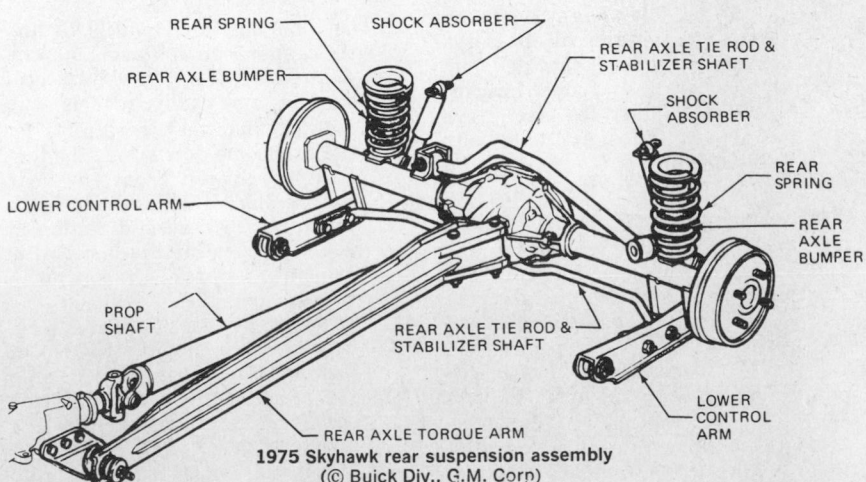

1975 Skyhawk rear suspension assembly
(© Buick Div., G.M. Corp)

2. Support the rear axle to take its weight off the springs.

3. Disconnect the bottom of the shock absorber.

4. Loosen the front spring eye bolt.

5. Unbolt the spring front bracket from the underbody.

6. Lower the axle slightly and remove the front bracket from the spring.

7. Pry the parking brake cable out of its retainer bracket on the axle spring mounting plate.

8. Unbolt the spring from the axle.

9. Remove the spring plate and cushion from the bottom of the spring. There should also be a cushion between the axle and the spring.

10. Remove the upper bolt from the rear spring shackle. Lower the spring and remove the bottom bolt.

11. On installation, attach the front bracket to the spring eye. The head of the bolt should be toward the center of the car.

12. Assemble the shackle loosely to the rear spring eye.

13. Raise the rear end of spring and install the upper shackle bolt loosely, making sure that the parking brake cable goes under the spring.

14. Raise the front end of the spring and loosely attach the front bracket to the underbody. Make sure that the bracket tab goes into its slot.

15. Make sure that the upper and lower spring cushions are aligned properly. The upper one has locating ribs and the lower one, a locating dowel.

16. Install the spring lower mounting plate over the locating dowel and loosely install the nuts. Don't forget the parking brake cable bracket.

17. Attach the bottom of the shock absorber.

18. Attach the parking brake cable to the bracket on the lower spring plate.

19. Let the vehicle weight down on the springs. Tighten all the bolts. Torques are: rear shackle bolts —40-60 ft lbs, front bracket screws—25-35 ft lbs, front eye bolt—65-80 ft lbs, and axle bolts —35-50 ft lbs.

Rear Coil Spring Replacement

1. Jack up the back of the car and support both sides on stand jacks on the frame, in front of the rear axle. Disconnect the shock absorber.

NOTE: *It may be necessary to disconnect the rear brake line in order to obtain sufficient axle drop to remove the spring. If this is done, first depress and secure the brake pedal at*

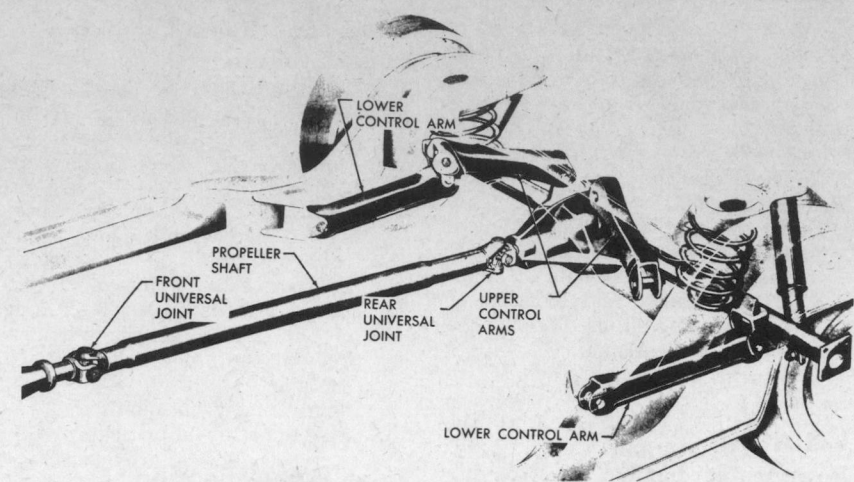

Rear suspension, except Apollo/Skylark and Skyhawk

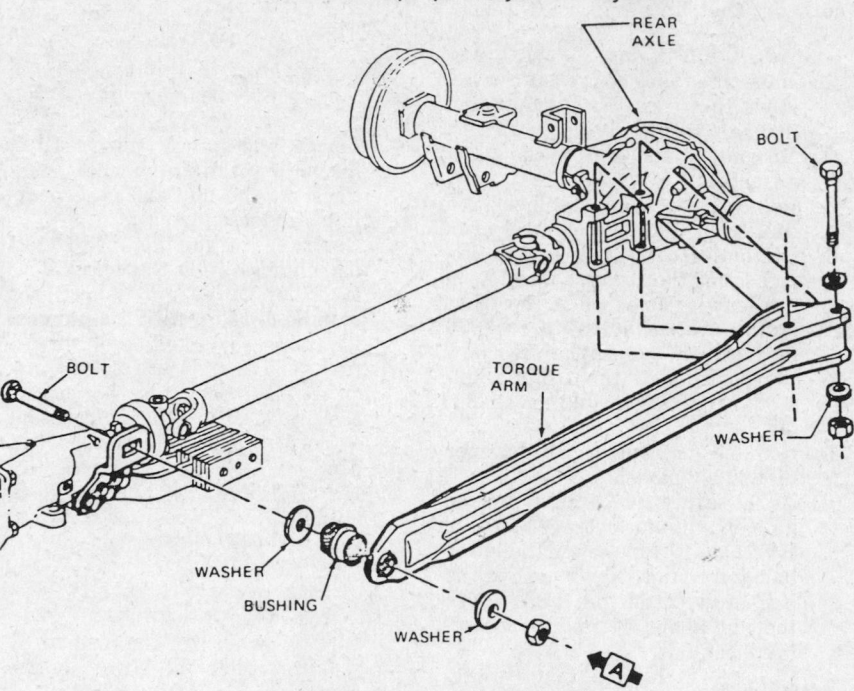

1976 and later Skyhawk rear suspension
(© Buick Div., G.M. Corp)

least 1 in. from the relaxed position to prevent the master cylinder from draining when the rear brake line is disconnected.

2. On 1973 and later models, detach the upper control arms at the differential. This may be necessary on some earlier models also.

3. Slowly, and very carefully, let the axle come down until the tension is released from the rear coil spring. Then, take off the coil spring. Note the direction in which the end of the last coil is pointing. Reinstall the spring in the same position.

4. When starting a new coil spring, make certain that the bottom of the coil is properly inserted into the socket in the frame and into the form plate on the trailing arm.

5. Jack the axle into place and rein-

stall the control arm bolt. Tighten the bolts to 75-95 ft lbs with the car's weight on the springs.

BRAKES

For detailed brake service information, see Unit Repair Section.

Master Cylinder Removal

1. Disconnect brake pipe or pipes from master cylinder and tape end of pipe or pipes to prevent entrance of dirt.

2. Disconnect brake pedal from master cylinder at the pushrod. NOTE: *This step isn't required with power brakes.*

3. Remove master cylinder-to-dash retaining bolts. Remove the master cylinder. Reverse the above steps to install. Bleed the master cylinder after it is reinstalled.

Power Brake Unit Removal and Installation

1. Unbolt the master cylinder from the power unit. Being careful not to kink or bend the brake lines, pull the master cylinder away from the power unit without disconnecting the brake lines. On the Skyhawk, you must also remove the combination valve mounting bolt so you can move the valve with the master cylinder.
2. Disconnect and plug the vacuum hose.
3. Disconnect the power brake pushrod from the brake pedal.
4. Unbolt the power brake unit from the firewall.
5. Remove the unit.
6. Mount the unit to the firewall.
7. Install the master cylinder to the power unit and torque the nuts to 25 ft lbs.
8. Connect the vacuum hose.
9. Connect the power brake pushrod to the brake pedal.

Parking Brake Adjustment

Except Skyhawk

Adjustment of the parking brake is necessary whenever the rear brake cables have been disconnected or the parking brake pedal can be depressed more than eight rachet clicks under heavy foot pressure. The car should first be raised on a lift.

1. Make sure that service brakes are properly adjusted.
2. Depress parking brake pedal three rachet clicks, two on Apollo.
3. Loosen jam nut on equalizer adjusting nut. Tighten adjusting nut until rear wheels can just be turned rearward by hand but not forward.
4. Release rachet one click; the rear wheels should rotate rearward freely and forward with a slight drag.
5. Release rachet one more click; rear wheels should turn freely in either direction.

NOTE: be sure that the parking brake does not drag. An overtightened, dragging parking brake on a car with automatic brake adjusters will result in an extremely short life for rear brake linings.

Skyhawk

1. Raise and support the rear of the car.
2. Apply the parking brake one notch from the fully released position.
3. Loosen the adjusting locknut at the cable equalizer and tighten the adjusting nut until a slight drag is felt when the rear wheels are rotated.
4. Tighten the locknut securely.

5. The rear wheels should rotate freely when the parking brake is fully released.
6. Lower the vehicle.

STEERING

See the "Unit Repair Section" for rebuilding procedures.

Refer to the Unit Repair Section for adjustments and repairs to steering gear, both manual and power-assisted.

Power Steering Pump Removal and Installation

1. Remove the hoses at the pump and tape the openings shut to prevent contamination. Position the disconnected lines in a raised position to prevent leakage.
2. Remove the pump belt.
3. Loosen the retaining bolts and any braces, and remove the pump.
4. Install the pump on the engine with the retaining bolts hand-tight.
5. Connect and tighten the hose fittings.
6. Refill the pump with fluid and bleed by turning the pulley counterclockwise (viewed from the front). Stop the bleeding when air bubbles no longer appear.
7. Install the pump belt on the pulley and adjust the tension.

Power Steering System Bleeding

The system must be bled of air whenever any parts of the pump circuit have been disconnected or replaced.

1. Fill the reservoir. Be careful not to overfill, because the level is normally checked at operating temperature after expansion has taken place. Allow the fluid to remain undisturbed for at least two minutes.
2. Start the engine and run it for only about two seconds.
3. Fill again as necessary.
4. Repeat Steps 1 to 3 until the level remains constant.
5. Raise the front wheels off the ground.
6. Run the engine at about 1,500 rpm and turn the wheels gently against the stops in either direction.
7. Fill again as necessary.
8. Lower the car to the ground. Turn the wheels gently against the stops in either direction with the engine running.
9. Fill again as necessary.

Steering Wheel

Removal

1. Unplug the horn wire connector from the steering column.

2. On cars with standard wheel or optional wood-rim wheel, pull off cap, remove three screws and contact, insulator, and spring. On cars with bar-type horn actuator, remove screws securing actuator from underside of steering wheel, pull out lead connector plug, and remove actuator assembly.
3. Loosen steering wheel nut.
4. Apply steering wheel puller and pull wheel up to the nut. Now remove puller, nut and steering wheel.

Caution Don't pound on the steering wheel in either direction or the collapsible steering column will collapse, requiring replacement.

Installation

NOTE: location marks are provided on the steering wheel and shaft to simplify proper indexing at the time of installation.

1. Install wheel with the location mark aligned with that of the shaft.
2. Install the wheel nut and torque to 30 ft. lbs.
3. Reinstall horn button or actuator assembly.

Tie-Rod End Removal and Installation

1. Loosen the tie-rod adjuster sleeve clamp nuts.
2. Remove the tie-rod stud nut cotter pin and nut.
3. Remove the tie-rod stud from the steering arm or intermediate rod. This is a taper fit. Removal is accomplished using a ball joint removal tool or by hitting the steering arm sharply with a hammer, while using a heavy hammer as a backup. If the joint is to be reused the removal tool must be used.
4. Unthread the tie rod from the adjuster sleeve. Outer tie rods have right-hand threads and inner tie rods have left-hand threads. Count the number of turns the tie rod must be rotated to remove it from the adjusting sleeve. This will allow a reasonably accurate realignment upon reassembly.
5. Reverse the removal procedures to install. Clean rust and dirt from the threads. Check the alignment and adjust if necessary.

Turn Signal Switch Removal and Installation

NOTE: the steering wheel must always be supported. Use extreme care not to bend the steering column.

1. Remove the steering wheel.

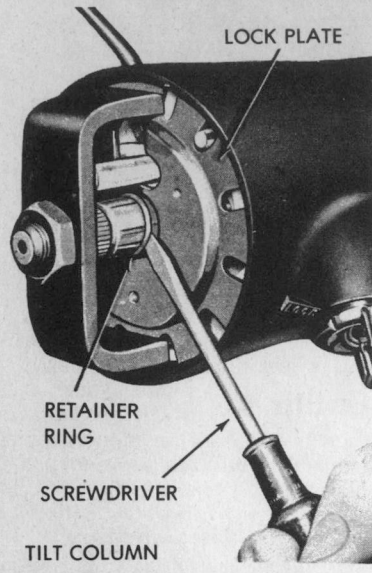

LOCK PLATE

RETAINER
RING

SCREWDRIVER

TILT COLUMN

Removing lock plate
(© Buick Div., G.M. Corp)

2. Remove the three cover screws and the cover. All 1976 and later steering columns have a redesigned lock plate which is removed by inserting a screwdriver in the cover slot and prying out. This is done in at least two of the slots to avoid breaking the plate.
3. Depress the lockplate and remove the snap-ring. Remove the lockplate.
4. Remove the spring and horn contact signal cancelling cam. Remove the thrust washer.
5. Remove the turn signal lever, depress the hazard warning knob, and remove the knob and tilt column lever—if equipped.
6. Remove the three turn signal switch mounting screws. Pull the connector out of the bracket on the column.
7. Pull the switch straight up with the wire protector and wire harness.
8. Reverse the above steps to install.

Ignition Switch and Lock Cylinder Removal and Installation

Standard Column

1. Remove steering wheel using proper puller.
2. Remove three cover screws and cover; remove retainers. All 1976 and later steering columns have a redesigned lock plate which is removed by inserting a screwdriver in the cover slot and prying out. This is done in at least two of the slots to avoid breaking the plate.
3. Depress lock plate, then remove wire snap-ring and lock plate.
4. Slide upper bearing preload spring and cancelling cam off shaft. Remove the steering

column-to-instrument panel attaching bolts (2), and carefully lower the column.
NOTE: steering shaft is now unsupported and could slide out the bottom of the column.
5. Slide thrust washer off shaft, then remove turn signal lever screw and lever.
6. Push in four-way flasher switch; remove knob.
7. Remove three turn signal switch mounting screws, pull connector out of its bracket on the column and tape the upper part of connector and wires together.
8. Pull turn signal switch out of column jacket.
9. Insert a small screwdriver into the slot next to the turn signal switch mounting screw boss (right-hand slot), depress spring latch and remove key lock.
10. Pull buzzer switch straight out, depressing switch clip with pliers.
11. Place ignition switch in accessory position by pulling up on connecting rod until there is a definite stop or detent felt.
12. Remove two attaching screws and ignition switch.
13. Assembly is the reverse of the above. However, note the following steps before proceeding with the reassembly.
14. To install the steering lock, hold the lock cylinder sleeve and rotate the knob clockwise against the stop. Insert the cylinder into the cover bore with the key on the cylinder sleeve aligned with the keyway in the housing. Then push the cylinder in until it bottoms. Maintaining a light inward pressure, rotate the knob counterclockwise until the drive section of the cylinder mates with the drive shaft. Push in until the snap-ring pops into the groove and the lock cylinder is secured in the cover. Check for free rotation.
15. When installing the ignition switch, be sure the lock cylinder is in the LOCK position. Put the shift bowl or shroud in the PARK position. Make sure the ignition switch is in the LOCK position. Then insert the actuator rod into the switch and assemble the switch to the column.
16. The neutral start switch is adjusted with the shift lever in the Drive position.

Tilt Column

1. Remove column mounting bracket from column.
NOTE: be careful not to damage the "breakaway" capsules.
2. Remove steering wheel using proper puller.

3. Remove turn signal wire protector (lower column).
4. Remove three column cover screws and cover. All 1976 and later steering columns have a redesigned lock plate which is removed by inserting a screwdriver in the cover slot and prying out. This is done in at least two of the slots to avoid breaking the plate.
5. Remove tilt release lever, turn signal switch lever, push four-way flasher knob in and remove knob, and remove upper shift lever.
6. Depress lock plate and remove the snap-ring; remove lock plate.
7. Remove cancelling cam and spring.
8. Remove three turn signal switch screws, tape wires to wire connector at upper end and place shift bowl in Low. Pull switch straight up and out.
9. Insert a small screwdriver into the slot next to the turn signal switch mounting screw boss (right-hand slot), depress spring latch and remove key lock.
10. Remove buzzer switch straight out, depressing switch clip with pliers.
11. Remove three housing cover screws and cover.
12. Install tilt release lever and place column in full UP position.
13. Place screwdriver in slot of tilt spring retainer, press in about 3/16 in. and turn counterclockwise. Remove spring and guide.
NOTE: spring is very strong—be careful.
14. Place column in neutral position, push in on upper steering shaft, remove inner race seat and race.
15. Remove upper flange pinch bolt, place ignition switch in accessory position, remove two switch mounting screws and switch.
NOTE: neutral start switch can be removed at this time, if necessary.
16. Assembly is the reverse of the above. However, note the following steps before proceeding with the reassembly.
17. To install the steering lock, hold the lock cylinder sleeve and rotate the knob clockwise against the stop. Insert the cylinder into the cover bore with the key on the cylinder sleeve aligned with the keyway in the housing. Then push the cylinder in until it bottoms. Maintaining a light inward pressure, rotate the knob counterclockwise until the drive section of the cylinder mates with the drive shaft. Push in until the snap-ring pops into the groove and the lock cylinder is secured in the cover. Check for free rotation.
18. When installing the ignition switch, be sure the lock cylinder

is in the LOCK position. Put the shift bowl or shroud in the PARK position. Make sure the ignition switch is in the LOCK position. Then insert the actuator rod into the switch and assemble the switch to the column.

19. The neutral start switch is adjusted with the shift lever in the Drive position.

INSTRUMENT PANEL

Light Switch Replacement

1. Disconnect battery.
2. Disconnect multiple connector from switch.
3. Pull switch knob to last notch and depress spring loaded latch button on top of switch while pulling knob and rod out of switch.
NOTE: on A/C cars, remove left duct if so equipped.
4. Remove escutcheon and switch.
5. Install in reverse of above.

Speedometer Cable Replacement

1. Reach up underneath the dash and disconnect the cable housing from the cluster housing. On some models you might first have to remove the left air conditioning duct.
2. Carefully bend the cable housing down and pull out the cable.
3. Hold the cable vertically and turn it slowly between your fingers. If it is kinked, you will notice it flopping around. Replace any kinked cable.
4. Install the new cable in the cable housing after lubricating it.

WINDSHIELD WIPERS

Windshield Wiper Motor Removal and Installation

Non-hidden Wipers

1. Disconnect the battery.
2. Remove the cowl screen. Beginning 1974, this is necessary only on Apollo.
3. Loosen the two nuts on the adjustable motor drive link at the crank arm and slip the drive link off.
4. Remove the electrical connectors from the washer motor and pump.
5. Disconnect the washer pump hoses.
6. Remove the three bolts securing the motor to the cowl and care-

fully lift the motor away from the cowl.
7. Reverse the above steps for installation.

Hidden Wipers

1. Disconnect the battery.
2. Remove the hoses from the washer nozzles.
3. Remove the rubber weatherstrip and cowl screen.
4. Loosen the two nuts on the adjustable motor drive link at the crank arm and slip the drive link off.
5. Disconnect the washer hoses and electrical connectors.
6. Remove the three wiper motor-to-cowl retaining screws and the motor.
7. Reverse the above steps to install.

Wiper Blade Removal and Installation

Any one of three methods of blade attachment may be used on these models. If there is a small tab on top of the blade, depress it and slide off the blade. If there is a small spring visible in the top of the blade, insert a screwdriver in the opening, press down and slide the blade off. If there is a clip on the under side of the arm, press down on the clip and slide the blade off.

RADIO

Radio Removal and Installation

1970-72

NOTE: if equipped with stereo tape, remove tape player before starting Step 2.
1. Disconnect battery ground lead.
2. Remove radio knobs, escutcheons, and hex nuts.
3. Remove two screws from radio filler plate and remove plate.
4. Remove ashtray assembly.
5. Remove center air conditioning duct, if so equipped.
6. Remove radio bracket.
7. Remove two instrument panel attaching nuts at radio face.
8. Disconnect wiring and remove radio downward.
9. Install in reverse order of removal.

1973 and later, except Skyhawk

NOTE: Use Steps 1, 2, 5, and 6 on the Apollo and Skylark.
1. Disconnect the battery ground cable.
2. Remove the radio knobs and escutcheons.
3. Remove the two screws and remove the center air conditioning

duct assembly control. Disconnect the left air conditioning hose.
4. Disconnect the antenna, power, and speaker leads.
5. Loosen the support nut or screw at the side of the radio.
6. Remove the radio shaft nuts and slide the radio back and down.
7. Reverse the procedure on installation, adjusting the trimmer screw before replacing the right knob.

Caution Don't turn on the radio without the speaker connected. Failure will result.

1975 Skyhawk

1. Disconnect the battery; remove the clock knob and trim panel.
2. Remove the instrument panel cover, glove compartment, and four attaching nuts from above the glove compartment door.
3. Lower the steering column by removing the nuts holding the column to the upper bracket guide.

Caution Be extremely careful not to let the column drop or hang unsupported.
4. Disconnect the speedometer cable from the speedometer; remove the instrument cluster assembly.
5. Remove all the knobs and escutcheons from the radio; remove the radio support bracket retaining screw from the lower dash.
6. Disconnect the electrical connections and antenna lead wire, remove the radio.
7. Installation is the reverse of removal.

1976 and later Skyhawk

1. Disconnect the battery negative cable and pull off the radio control knobs and bezels.
2. With a deep well socket, remove the control shaft nuts and washers.
3. Remove the antenna wire, and remove the two screws holding the radio to the instrument panel.
4. Lower the radio with the mounts attached and remove the lead wires.
5. Remove the radio mounts and put them on the new radio, then install the radio reversing Steps 1 through 4.

HEATER

Heater Core Removal and Installation without A/C

1970-72

1. Remove right front inner fender panel.
2. Drain radiator.

3. Disconnect control cables from defroster door and outside air inlet door. Disconnect temperature control cable from temperature door.
4. Remove nuts from heater assembly studs.
5. Disconnect inlet and outlet hoses.
6. Remove connector from blower motor resistor.
7. Remove screws securing defroster outlet assembly to top of heater assembly.
8. Work heater assembly rearward until studs clear dash. Remove heater assembly.
9. Install in reverse of above.

1973 and later, except Apollo/ Skylark

1. Drain the radiator and disconnect the heater inlet and outlet hoses at the dash. On the Skyhawk, remove the blower inlet to dash screws, remove the blower inlet, motor and wheel as an assembly.
2. Disconnect the control wires from the defroster door and vacuum hose diverter door actuator diaphragm and control cable from the temperature door lever, except on the Skyhawk.
3. Remove the four nuts securing the heater assembly to the dash. On the Skyhawk, remove the core retaining strap screws and remove the core.
4. Remove the screw securing the defroster outlet tab to the heater assembly, except on the Skyhawk.
5. Remove the heater from the car.
6. Reverse the above steps to install.

Apollo/Skylark

1. Disconnect the battery ground cable.
2. Drain the radiator.
3. Disconnect the heater hoses and plug the tubes to prevent spillage, when you remove the assembly from inside the car.
4. Remove the retaining nuts from the studs on the engine side of the firewall.
5. Remove the glove compartment and door.
6. Drill out the lower right heater case stud from inside the car.
7. Pull the core and case assembly from below the instrument panel.
8. Detach the cables and wiring from the case and remove the case from the car.
9. Remove the core from the case.
10. Reverse the procedure on installation, replacing the drilled out stud with a new screw and stamped nut.

Heater Blower Removal and Installation without A/C
1970-72

1. Remove right front inner fender panel.
2. Remove nuts and screws securing blower and air inlet assembly to cowl.
3. Disconnect blower motor wire and remove assembly.
4. Install in reverse of above.

1973 and later, except Apollo/ Skylark, Skyhawk

1. Disconnect the blower motor wire.
2. Remove the blower motor attaching screws and the motor.

Apollo/Skylark

1. Disconnect the battery ground cable.
2. Raise the car. Remove all the fender skirt bolts except those holding the skirt to the radiator support.
3. Pull out and down on the fender skirt. Put a wood block between the skirt and fender to allow clearance for removing the motor.
4. Disconnect the motor wiring.
5. Remove the screws and the motor.
6. Reverse the procedure on installation.

Skyhawk

See Heater Core Removal and Installation without A/C, 1973 and later, except Apollo/Skylark.

Blower Motor Removal and Installation with A/C
1970

1. On 1970 cars, remove the right front inner fender panel. On 1969 models, remove the fender.
2. Disconnect the motor wiring.
3. Remove the five securing screws and remove the motor.

4. Reverse the above steps to install.

1971-72

1. Support the hood and remove the extension and plate assembly from the hood hinge.
2. Disconnect the motor wiring.
3. Remove the screws securing the motor to the firewall and remove the motor.
4. Reverse the above steps to install.

1973 and later

1. Follow the same procedures as described in the .Blower R&R without A/C.

Heater Core Removal and Installation with A/C
1970

1. Drain the radiator and disconnect the heater hoses from the heater core.
2. Remove the instrument panel cover with the right-side A/C outlet and hose still attached.
3. Remove the center A/C duct, left A/C outlet duct, A/C distributor duct, and the defroster assembly.
4. Disconnect the defroster and temperature control wires.
5. Remove the four nuts and two screws securing the air conditioner heater assembly to the dash and remove the assembly.
6. Reverse the above steps to install.

1971-72

1. Drain the radiator and disconnect the heater inlet and outlet hoses from the dash.
2. Disconnect the control wires from the defroster door and vacuum hose diverter door actuator diaphragm and control cable from the temperature door lever.
3. Remove the four nuts securing the heater assembly to the dash.

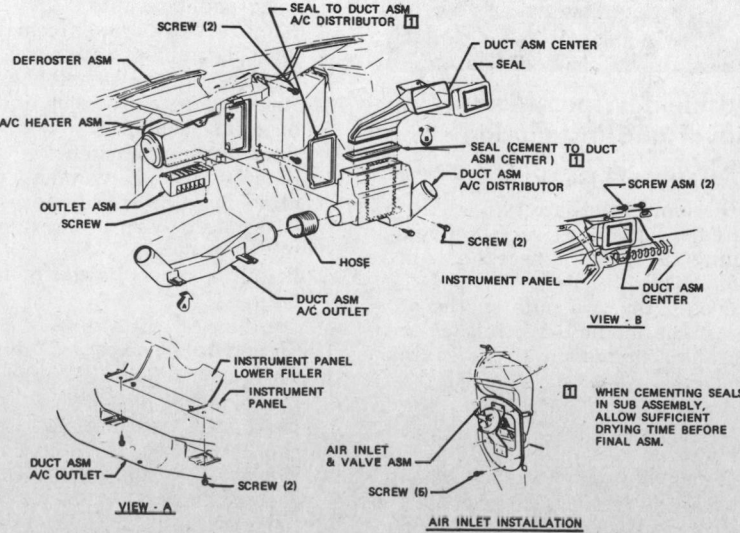

1972 air conditioning ducts (© Buick Div., G.M. Corp)

4. Remove the screw securing the defroster outlet tab to the heater assembly.

5. Move the heater assembly rearward until the studs clear the dash and then remove the heater assembly.

6. Reverse the above steps to install.

1973 and later, except Apollo/ Skylark, Skyhawk

1. Drain the radiator and disconnect the heater hoses.

2. Disconnect the temperature control cable and the vacuum hoses.

3. Remove the resistor assembly. Reach through the opening and remove the attaching nut. Remove the attaching nut directly over the transmission and the two attaching nuts to the upper and lower inboard evaporator case half.

4. From inside the car, remove the screw in the lower right corner on the passenger side.

5. Remove the lower attaching outlets. Work the assembly to the rear until the studs clear. Remove the heater assembly.

6. On installation, adjust the control cable to get about 1/8 in. springback in the hot position.

Apollo/Skylark

1. Disconnect the battery ground cable.

2. Drain the coolant.

3. Disconnect the upper heater hose and remove all the heater case assembly nuts you can reach.

4. Remove the right front fender skirt bolts and lower the skirt to remove the lower heater hose clamp. Remove the lower right case nut while you're in there.

5. Plug the heater core tubes to prevent spillage inside the car.

6. Remove the glove compartment and door.

7. Remove the diaphragm at the right kick panel.

8. Remove the heater outlet at the bottom of the heater case.

9. Remove the cold air duct from the heater case.

10. Remove the heater case extension screws and separate the extension from the case.

11. Disconnect the heater cables and wiring.

12. Remove the core and case assembly.

13. Reverse the whole procedure on installation.

1975 Skyhawk

Caution This procedure requires purging the air conditioning system of refrigerant. Do not attempt this unless you are a qualified air conditioning technician.

1. Disconnect the battery and purge the refrigerant from the air conditioning system.

2. Remove the glove compartment, the right side air outlet duct, the instrument bezel and pad, and air outlet duct on the left side.

3. Lower the steering column.

NOTE: Make sure that the steering column is adequately supported when lowered to avoid major damage.

4. Remove the instrument panel assembly and heater-air conditioner control assembly from the instrument panel.

5. Remove the radio and the defroster duct.

6. Remove the large center distributor duct, and the heater hoses at the core pipes.

7. Clean the VIR (receiver vessel) of any dirt which may have accumulated on it. Disconnect the compressor inlet line, oil bleed line and condenser outlet line; cap all these lines.

8. Loosen the evaporator inlet and outlet lines; remove the VIR mounting clamp and slide the VIR off the evaporator, outlet line first.

9. Remove and discard all the old O ring gaskets and plug all open lines to prevent contamination.

10. Remove the heater to cowl attaching nuts and remove the heater-distributor assembly, disconnect all electrical and vacuum connections.

11. Separate the heater case from the distributor assembly; separate the heater core from the heater case.

12. Installation is the reverse of removal, but when raising the steering column to its proper position, be careful not to damage any if its components. If the mounting bracket for the steering column is damaged, replace it.

1976 and later Skyhawk

1. Have the air conditioning system purged of refrigerant.

2. Disconnect the negative battery cable.

3. Disconnect the inlet and outlet lines and the oil bleed line from the VIR (receiver-dryer) assembly.

4. Remove the VIR to blower case strap screw, and remove the VIR unit. Cap all the open connections immediately.

5. Remove the blower and case assembly.

6. Remove and plug the heater hoses at the core tubes and then hang them out of the way.

7. Remove the evaporator to dash panel cover plate screws and remove the plate.

8. Remove (from inside the car), the floor outlet duct, the glove compartment assembly and the dash outlets on both sides. Use a putty knife to pry out the dash outlets.

9. Remove the eleven instrument panel pad screws and pry the pad off.

10. Remove the right side instrument panel to dash and kick pad screws, then loosen the left side instrument cluster to instrument panel screws.

11. Pull out on the right side of the instrument cluster to gain the necessary clearance to remove the right side instrument panel and lower duct.

12. Disconnect the vacuum hoses on the left side of the heater unit and tag them for later reinstallation.

13. Remove the modulator duct to heater unit screw, then pull the carpet and pad to the rear to make room for the heater unit.

14. Pull the heater unit toward you until the core tubes clear the firewall, then pull it to the right until there is enough clearance to disconnect the control cable.

15. After disconnecting the control cable, disconnect the wiring harness and remove the heater assembly.

16. Remove the screws and separate the heater case, then remove the core to case screws and remove the core.

17. Installation is the reverse of the above procedure, but before assembly, add 3 oz. of refrigerant oil to the evaporator core.

18. When installing the refrigerant lines, coat all the O-rings with refrigerant oil.

SEAT BELTS

Disabling the Interlock System

The seat belt interlock and warning buzzer are no longer mandatory. These may now be disabled, but the seat belt warning light must remain in operation.

1. Disconnect the battery, and locate the interlock terminal connector. This is a connector with orange, yellow and green wires, located under the left side of the instrument panel, near the fuse box.

2. Cut and tape the green wire on the body harness side of the connector.

3. Remove the warning buzzer from the fuse block or terminal connector on all Skyhawk, Skylark, and Apollo models.

4. On all other models, remove and tape the terminal with two yellow wires with black stripes. This terminal is located near the fuse block.

INDEX

Cadillac · Seville

Automatic Transmission
In car service **C273**
Neutral safety switch C274
Shift linkage adjustment C274
Kickdown adjustment C274
Pan Removal and Installation,
  fluid and filter change C274

Brakes **C281, U299**
Power brake unit Removal and
  Installation C281
Parking brake adjustment C282
Master cylinder Removal and
  Installation C282

Charging System **C257, U2**
Alternator Removal and Installation C257

Cooling System **C265, U367**
Radiator Removal and Installation C265
Water Pump Removal and Installation .. C265
Thermostat Removal and Installation .. C266

Emission Controls **C266, U145**
PCV system C266
Air injection C266
Thermostatically controlled air cleaner C266
TCS C266
ELC C267
EGR C267
Catalytic Converter C267
EFE C267
Component Removal and Installation .. C268
Model usage C268

Engine **C269, U194**
ENGINE REMOVAL AND INSTALLATION C269
CYLINDER HEAD REMOVAL AND
  INSTALLATION C270
LUBRICATION C272
Oil pump Removal and Installation C272
Oil pan Removal and Installation C273
Rear main seal Removal and Installation C273
MANIFOLDS
Exhaust C269
Intake C270
PISTON AND ROD INSTALLATION C272
TIMING CASE COVER—CHAIN, AND
  CAMSHAFT 271
Timing chain cover, chain and sprocket
  removal 271
Timing cover oil seal Removal and
  Installation C271

Camshaft Removal and Installation C272
VALVE SYSTEM C270
Rocker arm Removal and Installation .. C270

Front Suspension **C276, U292**
Shock absorber Removal and
  Installation C277
Lower control arm and coil spring
  Removal and Installation C277
Ball joint inspection C277
Lower ball joint Removal and
  Installation C279
Upper ball joint Removal and
  Installation C279
Wheel Bearing adjustment C280

Fuel System **C259, U50**
Fuel pump and filter Removal and
  Installation C261
Speed-up control adjustment C264
Idle speed and mixture adjustments C264
Electronic fuel injection C259
Electronic fuel injection troubleshooting C260
Electronic fuel injection component
  removal C263
Throttle position switch adjustment C265

Heater **C287**
Heater blower removal and
  installation—Non-air-conditioned cars C287
Heater blower Removal and Installation
  Air-conditioned cars C287
Heater core Removal and Installation
  —Non-air-conditioned cars C287
Heater core Removal and Installation
  —Air-conditioned cars C287

Ignition System **C257, U34**
Point replacement C257
Distributor Removal and Installation C258
Thermal vacuum switch C258
Ignition timing C259
Firing order C253

Instrument Panel **C285, U350**
Headlight switch Removal and
  Installation C285

Jacking, Hoisting **C276**

Radio **C286**
Removal and Installation C286

Rear Axle **C276, U285**
Axle Shaft, Bearing, and Seal Removal
  and Installation C276

Rear Suspension **C280**
Shock absorber Removal and
  Installation C280
Coil spring Removal and
  Installation C280
Leaf spring Removal and Installation ... C281

Seat Belts **C288**
Disabling, the interlock and buzzer C288

Specifications **C253, U359**
Capacities C255
Crankshaft and Connecting Rod C256
Engine identification C253
General engine C254
Rings C256
Piston clearance C256
Serial number location C253
Torque C255
Tune-Up C254
Valve C255
Wheel Alignment C257
Year Identification C253

Starting System **C257, U2**
Starter Removal and Installation C257

Steering **C282, U328**
Ignition switch Removal and
  Installation C284
Lock cylinder replacement C284
Steering wheel Removal and
  Installation C282
Turn signal switch Removal and
  Installation C282
Steering linkage Removal and
  Installation C284
Power steering pump Removal and
  Installation C284

U-Joints **C275**
Shaft Removal and Installation C275
U-Joint Removal and Installation C275

Windshield Wipers **C286**
Wiper and washer motor Removal and
  Installation C286

YEAR IDENTIFICATION

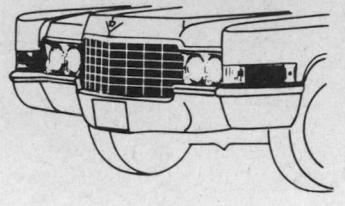

1970

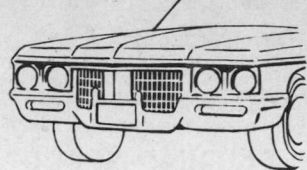

1971

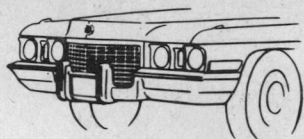

1972

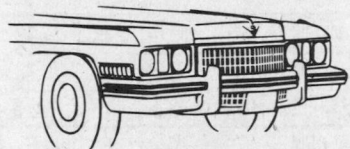

1973

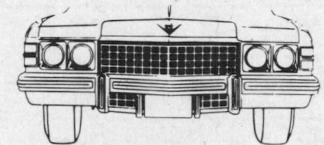

1974

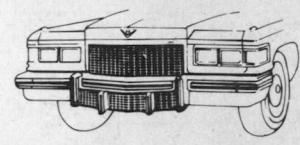

1975-76

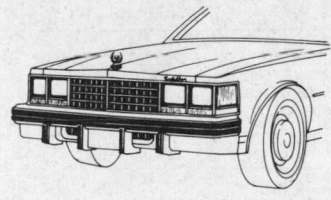

1976 Seville

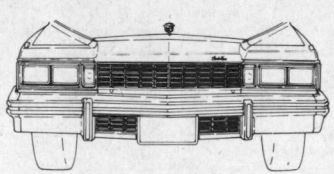

1977

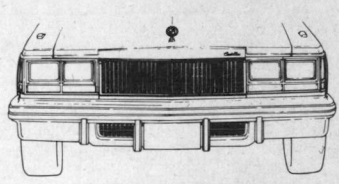

1977 Seville

FIRING ORDER

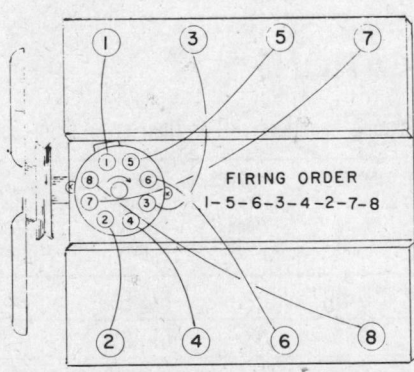

FIRING ORDER
1-5-6-3-4-2-7-8

425, 472, 500 Cadillac V8

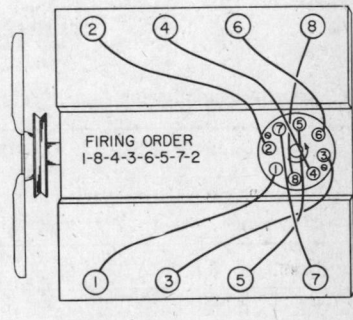

FIRING ORDER
1-8-4-3-6-5-7-2

350 Seville V8

CAR SERIAL NUMBER LOCATION AND ENGINE IDENTIFICATION

1970

The vehicle identification plate is located on the top left side of the dashboard, and is visible through the windshield. The eight digit serial number consists of a sales code letter. the last digit of the model year (0), and a six digit sequential serial number.

All models utilize a 472 cu. in. V8 engine. The vehicle identification number, less sales code, is stamped on the top rear of the engine block, adjacent to the transmission.

1971-77

The vehicle identification plate is located on the top left side of the dashboard, and is visible through the windshield. The thirteen digit serial number consists of the G.M. Division Code (6), a three digit series and model number, engine code, the last digit of the model year, plant designation, and a six digit sequential serial number.

All full-size models utilize a 472 cu in. V8 engine through 1974, a 500 cu. in. V8 in 1975-76, and a 425 cu in. V8 beginning 1977. A derivative of

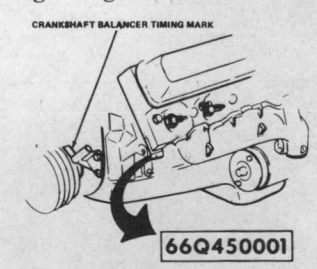

CRANKSHAFT BALANCER TIMING MARK

66Q450001

Engine identification number location on the Seville 350 V8 (© G.M. Corp.)

the vehicle identification number is stamped on the top rear of the engine block behind the intake manifold.

1972-77 models have the engine code located on the left rear of the engine block behind the left cylinder head.

The engine number on the 1976-77 350 cu in. Seville V8 is on a boss at the left front side of the cylinder block directly below the front spark plug.

GENERAL ENGINE SPECIFICATIONS

Year	Engine Displacement Cu. In.	Carburetor Type	Horsepower @ rpm ■	Torque @ rpm (ft lbs) ■	Bore x Stroke (in.)	Compression Ratio	Oil Pressure @ 2000 rpm
'70	8-472	4 bbl	375 @ 4400	525 @ 3000	4.300 x 4.060	10.0:1	38
'71	8-472	4 bbl	345 @ 4400	500 @ 2800	4.300 x 4.060	8.5:1	38
'72	8-472	4 bbl	220 @ 4000	365 @ 2400	4.300 x 4.060	8.5:1	35
'73	8-472	4 bbl	220 @ 4000	365 @ 2400	4.300 x 4.060	8.5:1	35
'74	8-472	4 bbl	220 @ 4000	365 @ 2400	4.300 x 4.060	8.25:1	35
'75	8-500	4 bbl	235 @ 3800	386 @ 2400	4.300 x 4.304	8.5:1	35
'76	8-500	4 bbl	190 @ 3600	360 @ 2000	4.300 x 4.304	8.5:1	35
	8-500	EFI	215 @ 3600	400 @ 2000	4.300 x 4.304	8.5:1	35
	8-350	EFI	180 @ 4400	275 @ 2000	4.057 x 3.385	8.0:1	35
'77	8-425	4 bbl	180 @ 3600	260 @ 2000	4.082 x 4.060	8.5:1	35
	8-425	EFI	215 @ 3600	260 @ 2000	4.082 x 4.060	8.5:1	35
	8-350	EFI	180 @ 4400	275 @ 2000	4.057 x 3.385	8.0:1	35

■ Beginning 1972 horsepower and torque are SAE net figures. They are measured at the rear of the transmission with all accessories installed and operating. Since the figures vary when a given engine is installed in different models, some are representative rather than exact.
EFI Electronic fuel injection

TUNE-UP SPECIFICATIONS

When analyzing compression test results, look for uniformity among cylinders rather than specific pressures.

Year	ENGINE No. Cyl Displacement (cu in.)	hp	SPARK PLUGS Orig. Type	Gap (in.)	DISTRIBUTOR Point Dwell (deg)	Point Gap (in.)	IGNITION TIMING (deg) ▲ Man Trans	Auto Trans	VALVES Intake Opens ■ (deg)	Fuel Pump Pressure (psi)	IDLE SPEED (rpm) ▲ Man Trans	Auto Trans
'70	8-472	375	R-46-N	.035	30	.016	—	7½B	18	5¼-6½	—	600①
'71	8-472	345	R-46-N	.035	30	.016	—	8B	38	5¼-6½	—	600②/400
'72	8-472	220	R-46-N	.035	30	.016	—	8B	34	5¼-6½	—	600②/400
'73	8-472	220	R-46-N	.035	30	.016	—	8B	34	5¼-5¾	—	600②/400
'74*	8-472	220	R-45-NS	.035	30	.016	—	10B	21	5¼-6½	—	600②/400
'75	8-500	235	R-45NSX	.060	Electronic		—	6B③	34	5¼-6¼	—	600②/400
'76	8-500	190	R-45NSX	.060	Electronic		—	6B	21	5¼-6½	—	600
	8-500 EFI	215	R-45NSX	.060	Electronic		—	12B	21	39 min.	—	600
	8-350 EFI	180	R-46SX	.080	Electronic		—	10B④	22	39 min.	—	600
'77	All					See Underhood Specifications Sticker						

▲ See text for procedure
■ All figures Before Top Dead Center
* No point gap or dwell with electronic ignition
① Adjust idle to 900-950 rpm with idle speed-up on. See text for special procedure.
② Lower figure indicates idle speed with solenoid disconnected
③ 12B for fuel injected engines

④ 6B for California engines
B Before Top Dead Center
EFI Electronic fuel injection
— Not applicable

NOTE: The underhood specifications sticker often reflects tune-up specification changes made in production. Sticker figures must be used if they disagree with those in this chart.

CAPACITIES

Year	ENGINE No. Cyl. Displacement (Cu. In.)	Engine Crankcase Add 1 Qt For New Filter	TRANSMISSION Pts To Refill After Draining Manual 3-Speed	4-Speed	Automatic ●	Drive Axle (pts)	Gasoline Tank (gals)	COOLING SYSTEM (qts) With Heater	With A/C
'70	All	4	—	—	8	5	26①	21.3	21.8②
'71	All	4	—	—	8	5	27.5	21.3	21.8②
'72	All	4	—	—	8	5	27.5	21.3	21.8②③
'73	All	4	—	—	8	5	27.5	21.3	21.8②③
'74	All	4	—	—	8	5	27.5	21.3	23.8④
'75-'77	8-500	4	—	—	8	5	27.5	21.3	23.0②
	8-350	4	—	—	8	5	21	18.9	18.9
	8-425	4	—	—	8	5	27.5	21.3	23.0②

- ● Specifications do not include torque converter
- ① Fleetwood—20 gals
- ② Fleetwood—25.8 qts
- ③ Trailer package—2 qts additional
- ④ Fleetwood—26.8 qts

VALVE SPECIFICATIONS

Year	Engine No. Cyl. Displacement (cu In.)	Seat Angle (deg)	Face Angle (deg)	Spring Test Pressure (lbs @ in.)	Spring Installed Height (in.)	STEM TO GUIDE Clearance (in.) Intake	Exhaust	STEM Diameter (in.) Intake	Exhaust
'70	8-472	45	44	160 @ 1.50	1 15/16	.0005-.0025	.0010-.0025	.3420	.3418
'71	8-472	45	44	160 @ 1.50	1 15/16	.0010-.0027	.0010-.0025	.3420	.3418
'72	8-472	45	44	168 @ 1.50	1 15/16	.0010-.0027	.0012-.0027	.3420	.3418
'73	8-472	45	44	168 @ 1.50	1 15/16	.0010-.0027	.0012-.0027	.3420	.3418
'74	8-472	45	44	165 @ 1.50	1 15/16	.0010-.0027	.0016-.0027	.3420	.3418
'75-'77	8-500	45	44	168 @ 1.50	1 15/16	.0010-.0027	.0010-.0027	.3418	.3416
	8-350	①	②	187 @ 1.27	1 43/64	.0010-.0027	.0015-.0032	.3429	.3424
	8-425	45	44	168 @ 1.50	1 15/16	.0010-.0027	.0010-.0027	.3418	.3416

- ① Intake 45°; exhaust 31°
- ② Intake 44°; exhaust 30°

TORQUE SPECIFICATIONS

All readings in ft lbs

Year	Engine Displacement (cu in.)	Cylinder Head Bolts	Rod Bearing Bolts	Main Bearing Bolts	Crankshaft Pulley Bolt	Flywheel to Crankshaft Bolts	MANIFOLD Intake	Exhaust
'70-'76	472,500	115	40	90	Press fit①	75	30	35
'76-'77	350	85	42	80②	310③	60	40	25
'77	425	115	40	90	Press fit①	75	30	35

NOTE—Some bolts and nuts are marked on the heads to indicate the grade of steel used. Do not use bolts of a lower grade than those originally installed. The marks consist of lines: SAE5—3 lines; SAE7—5 lines; SAE8—6 lines

- ① Pulley-to-harmonic damper screw—17 ft lbs
- ② 120 ft lbs. on No. 5
- ③ Balancer-to-crankshaft

CRANKSHAFT AND CONNECTING ROD SPECIFICATIONS

All measurements are given in inches

| Year | Engine Displacement (cu in.) | CRANKSHAFT | | | | CONNECTING ROD | | |
		Main Brg. Journal Dia	Main Brg. Oil Clearance	Shaft End-Play	Thrust on No.	Journal Diameter	Oil Clearance	Side Clearance
'70-'73	472	3.250	.0003-.0026	.002-.012	3	2.5000	.0005-.0035	.008-.016
'74	472	3.250	.0013-.0026	.002-.012	3	2.0250	.0005-.0028	.011-.021
'75-'76	500	3.250	.0010-.0026	.002-.012	3	2.5000	.0005-.0028	.008-.020
'76-'77	350	2.4985-2.4995①	.0005-.0021②	.004-.008	3	2.1238-2.1248	.0004-.0033	.006-.020
'77	425	3.250	.0010-.0026	.002-.012	3	2.5000	.0005-.0028	.008-.020

① No. 1—2.4988-2.4998 in.
② No. 5—.0015-.0031 in.

RING GAP

All measurements are given in inches

Year	Engine	Top Compression	Bottom Compression
'70-'76	472, 500	.013-.025	.013-.025
'76-'77	350	.010-.023	.010-.023
'77	425	.013-.025	.013-.025

Year	Engine	Oil Control
'70-'77	All engines	.015-.055

RING SIDE CLEARANCE

All measurements are given in inches

Year	Engine	Top Compression	Bottom Compression
'70-'74	472	.0017-.0040	.0017-.0040
'75-'76	500	.0017-.0040	.0017-.0040
'76-'77	350	.0020-.0040	.0020-.0040
'77	425	.0017-.0040	.0017-.0040

Year	Engine	Oil Control
'70-'76	472, 500	None (side sealing)
'76-'77	350	.0006-.0096
'77	425	None (side sealing)

PISTON CLEARANCE

Year	Engine	Piston to Bore Clearance (in.)
'70	472	.0006-.0010
'71	472	.0006-.0010
'72	472	.0006-.0010
'73	472	.0006-.0010
'74	472	.0006-.0010
'75-'76	500	.0006-.0010
'76-'77	350	.0010-.0020
'77	425	.0006-.0010

WHEEL ALIGNMENT SPECIFICATIONS

Year	Model	CASTER Range (deg)	CASTER Pref Setting (deg)	CAMBER Range (deg)	CAMBER Pref Setting (deg)	Toe-in (in.)	Steering Axis Inclin. (deg)	WHEEL PIVOT RATIO (deg) Inner Wheel	WHEEL PIVOT RATIO (deg) Outer Wheel
'70	All Series	1½N to ½N	1N	⅜N to ⅜P	0	⅛ to ¼	6	20	18
'71-'73	All Series	1½N to ½N	1N	①	①	⅛ to ¼	6	20	18
'74-'77	Cadillac	②	②	①	①	1/16 to 3/16	6	20	18
'76-'77	Seville	1½P to 2½P	2P	③	③	0 to ⅛	—	—	—

① Left ⅜P to ⅜N; zero preferred
   Right ⅛P to ⅝N; ¼N preferred
② All except Fleetwood—½N to ½P; zero preferred
   Fleetwood 75 models—1½N to ½N; 1N preferred

N Negative   P Positive

③ Left—⅛P to ⅞P; ½P preferred
   Right—⅛N to ⅝P; ¼P preferred

CHARGING SYSTEM

For charging system trouble shooting and repair information, consult the "Unit Repair Section."

Alternator Removal and Installation

1970-72
Disconnect the battery. Disconnect the wire leads at the alternator. Remove alternator adjusting strap drive belt. Remove alternator.

NOTE: heavy duty alternator used on commercial chassis is slid backwards off its lower mounting bolts, after first loosening belt tensioner and removing fan belt and upper bolt.

1973-77
1. Disconnect the negative battery cable.
2. Disconnect the electrical leads from the alternator.
3. Remove the screw from the alternator adjusting link.
4. Remove the screw from the rear of the alternator, retaining the shims for reinstallation.
5. Loosen the alternator pivot bolt and remove the drive belt.
6. Remove the AIR pump pulley for access to the AIR pump bolt behind the pulley.
7. Loosen the two screws securing the front bracket to the engine.
8. Remove the alternator, spacer and lower through bolt by twisting the alternator toward the fender for clearance.
9. Install the alternator in the reverse order of removal.

STARTING SYSTEM

Cadillac starter motors are located on the right hand side of the engine, except on the Seville 350 V8 where it is on the left side.

Information on starter overhaul can be found in the Unit Repair Section.

Starter Removal and Installation

1. Disconnect battery cable and jack up car.
2. Disconnect battery lead and two wires from solenoid.
3. Remove bolt that holds support bracket to starter.
4. Remove two starter-to-engine bolts.
5. Remove motor by pulling it forward and down, or toward right front wheel and over the steering linkage.
6. To install, reverse removal procedure, tightening starter-to-engine bolts to 46 ft. lbs., bracket bolt to 12 ft lbs. and nut to 6 ft lbs.

IGNITION SYSTEM

The distributor used in full-size Cadillacs is a single-point type using clockwise rotation. It is constructed of aluminum alloy and is located at the top left front of the engine. Seville HEI distributors rotate counterclockwise.

The High Energy Ignition system was optional in 1974 and became standard equipment in 1975. The HEI system consists of an ignition coil, electronic module and a magnetic pick-up assembly all within the distributor.

A terminal in the top of the distributor cap is provided for the connection of a tachometer. The terminal is marked "TACH".

Distributor Point Replacement

1. Remove distributor cap by depressing and turning the retaining screws.
2. Remove two screws securing rotor cap and remove cap.
3. Remove condenser and primary leads from nylon insulated connection.

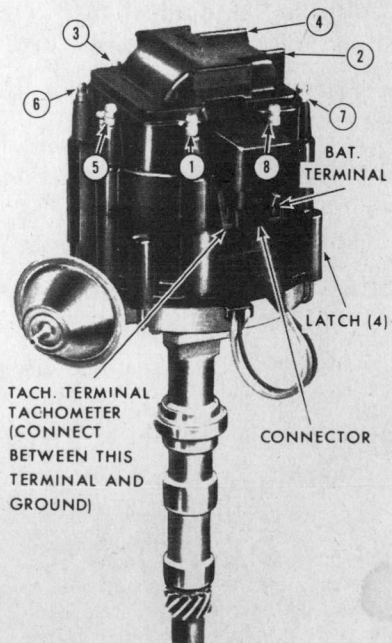

Tachometer connection on HEI system
(© Cadillac Div., G.M. Corp.)

4. Loosen two screws holding base of contact assembly in place and remove points.

5. Inspect weight assembly, replace or lubricate as required.

6. Place new points under the two screws and tighten screws.

7. Connect the condenser and primary leads at the nylon insulated connection.

NOTE: be sure leads do not interfere with cap, weight base, or breaker advance.

8. Install rotor cap. Square and round lugs must be properly aligned.

9. With ⅛ in. Allen wrench inserted, turn until points close while rubbing block is on high point of lobe. Then turn screw counterclockwise one-half turn.

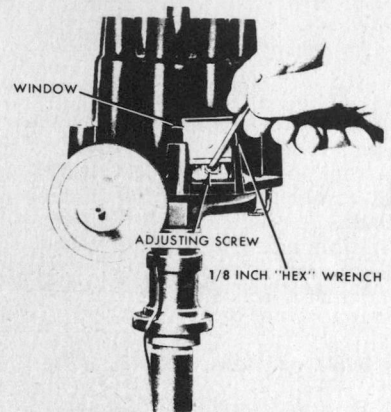

Distributor point adjustment
(© Cadillac Div., G.M. Corp)

10. Replace distributor cap.
11. With engine warmed up and off fast idle, set points to get proper dwell angle.

Distributor Removal

Unplug (HEI) and remove distributor cap. Disconnect vacuum line. Disconnect primary lead at distributor.

Turn the engine to top dead center for No. 1 cylinder so that the rotor points to the No. 1 cylinder tower in the distributor cap and the pointer on the timing case cover points to the O-mark on the crankshaft pulley.

Using a scribe mark, index the vacuum advance unit to the cylinder block, and the tip of the rotor to the distributor housing so that the distributor body will be correctly replaced at reassembly. Remove clamp bolt and distributor.

Distributor Installation

Install the distributor so that the vacuum advance unit aligns with the match-mark made at removal. Turn the rotor slightly left of center so that as the gear engages the camshaft it will revolve into the proper position, pointing to the No. 1 contact in the cap.

NOTE: if the engine has been cranked, remove the No. 1 spark plug. Crank the engine until the No. 1 piston is in firing position with the pointer and the O-mark on the crank-shaft pulley aligned. Then proceed as above.

Install the hold-down clamp. Connect the primary lead and install the cap.

Fill the distributor oiler tube with 10W oil or rotate lubricator.

Plug the distributor vacuum line to the carburetor.

Insert an adapter pin alongside the No. 1 wire in the distributor cap and connect a timing light.

Clean the crankshaft pulley markings and the pointer.

Set the timing to specifications.

Tighten clamp bolt to 18 ft. lbs.

Remove plug and adapter pin and reconnect the vacuum line to the advance unit.

Distributor Installation (If Engine Has Been Disturbed)

If the engine has been disturbed (cranked) after removing the distributor, perform the following procedure for installation:

1. Crank the engine until no. 1 piston is at the top of its compression stroke. The compression stroke can be determined by removing the spark plug from no. 1 cylinder and placing your thumb over the hole while an assistant slowly cranks the engine. Crank until compression is felt at the hole and then continue cranking slowly until the timing mark on the crankshaft pulley lines up with the zero degrees (0°) timing mark located on the timing chain cover.

2. Position the distributor in the block but do not, at this time, allow it to engage with its drive gear at the base of the mounting hole. Observe the position of the vacuum control unit on the distributor. If the distributor is located correctly, the vacuum unit will be positioned normally so that the vacuum hose can easily connect to it.

3. Rotate the distributor shaft so that the rotor points to the front of the engine, turn the rotor counterclockwise about ⅛ turn toward the left (driver's side), and push the distributor down to engage the camshaft. It may be necessary to turn the rotor a small amount in either direction in order to achieve this engagement. If installed correctly, the rotor should point toward the no. 1 spark plug terminal in the distributor cap.

4. Press firmly downward on the distributor housing. This will ensure that the distributor shaft engages the oil pump shaft, thereby allowing the distributor to fully contact the engine block.

5. Install the hold-down clamp and tighten the bolt until it is snug.

6. Turn the distributor slightly until the points just open and then tighten down on the bolt.

7. Install the distributor cap, making sure that the rotor points to no. 1 terminal in the cap.

8. Attach all wires and the vacuum advance hose.

9. Start the engine. If it fails to start, or runs roughly, the distributor is 180° out of time. Lift up on the distributor, turn the rotor one-half revolution, and install the distributor. Repeat steps 1–9 if the engine continues to run poorly.

10. Check the timing and change it as necessary.

Thermal Vacuum Switch

The thermal vacuum switch was added to the distributor vacuum circuit to prevent engine overheating in heavy traffic. This switch is so designed to provide full vacuum advance in prolonged idling, or high temperature, situations. Under these conditions, the switch sends full manifold vacuum, instead of the normal carburetor vacuum, to the advance unit. Vacuum switch units having four ports, instead of the normal three, allow manifold vacuum to operate an idle speed-up device (the adjustment of which is found under *Fuel System*). The cut-off temperature of the switch is 220°F. An overheating condition may be due to a faulty switch.

To check the switch, proceed as follows:

1. Idle engine at 600 rpm and at normal operating temperature.

2. With an assistant in the car with his foot on the brake, and transmission in Reverse, disconnect the line from the distributor advance unit and check that vacuum is available (from port D). If vacuum is not available, the separate vacuum solenoid may be at fault.

3. Remove the line between the switch and the vacuum break T at carb. Vacuum still should be available at distributor line (from port D) and should not be available at the line just removed from port MT.

4. Block radiator with a piece of cardboard until "Engine Temp" light comes on.

5. Reconnect line removed in Step 3 and disconnect line between carburetor and switch port C. Vacuum now should be available at distributor line (from port D) and should not be available

at line disconnected from port C.
6. If the previous checks indicate a faulty switch, replace the unit.

Ignition Timing

1. Loosen the distributor hold-down bolt so that the distributor can be turned without it being too loose.
2. Remove the hose from the vacuum advance and tape the free end closed. The end must be taped as a manifold leak will affect the timing.
3. Remove the vacuum hose from the parking brake and tape the end.
4. Connect the timing light. With HEI, connect it at the No. 1 distributor terminal. Make certain that the timing marks are visible.
5. Connect a tachometer to the engine and, after securing the parking brake, start the engine and place the selector lever in Drive.
6. Adjust the idle speed to the specified rpm, then place the transmission in Park or Neutral.
7. Point the timing light at the pulley and observe the notch in the pulley in relation to the notches on the front cover. Check the specification chart for the correct timing setting.
8. If the setting is not correct, rotate the distributor until the correct timing is obtained then tighten the distributor clamp nut to 18 ft lbs and recheck the timing.
9. Untape and reconnect the vacuum hoses on the parking brake and the vacuum advance.

FUEL SYSTEM

Carbureted Engines

The standard Cadillac fuel system (except Seville) includes the fuel pump, fuel filter, lines, carburetor and intake manifold.

Fuel Injected Engines

Electronic Fuel Injection (EFI) is standard on Seville and optional on 1976-77 full size models except the Fleetwood, Limousine, and Commercial Chassis vehicles.

EFI provides a means of precisely controlling the air/fuel mixture for combustion by monitoring selected engine operating conditions and electronically metering the fuel requirements to meet those conditions.

The EFI system consists of four basic subsystems; the fuel delivery system, air induction system, the network of sensors, and the electronic control unit (ECU).

Fuel Delivery System

The fuel delivery subsystem is made up of an in-tank fuel pump and a chassis mounted fuel pump, fuel filter, a fuel pressure regulator, fuel rails, an injector for each cylinder, and supply and return lines.

Fuel Pumps

The electric fuel pumps are connected in parallel to the ECU and are activated by the ECU when the ignition is turned on and the engine is cranking or operating. If the engine stalls or if the starter is not engaged, the fuel pumps will stop in about one second. The fuel is pumped from the fuel tank, through the supply line and filter, through the pressure regulator, fuel rails and to the injectors, with excess fuel being returned to the fuel tank.

The in-tank boost pump is located in the fuel tank and is an integral part of the fuel gauge tank unit. This pump supplies fuel to the chassis mounted fuel pump and helps prevent vapor lock on the suction side of the system.

The chassis mounted fuel pump is a constant-displacement, roller-vane

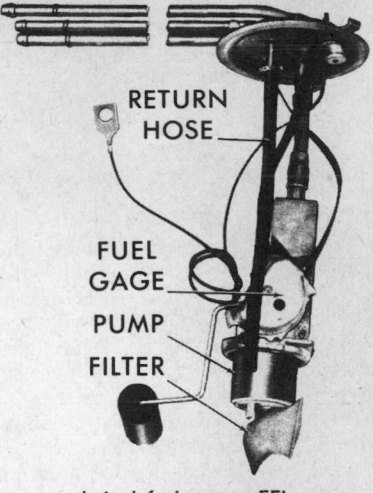

In-tank fuel pump—EFI
(© Cadillac Div., G.M. Corp.)

pump with a check valve to prevent fuel from flowing back into the tank. This pump has a flow rate of 33 gallons per hour and maintains a minimum presure of 39 psi. An internal relief valve opens at 55-95 psi to protect the system from excessive pressure. The pump is mounted under the vehicle, forward of the left rear wheel on all vehicles except the Eldorado, where it is mounted in front of the right rear wheel.

Fuel Filter

The fuel filter is located on a bracket on the lower left front of the engine. The filter consists of a casing with an internal throwaway type paper filter element.

Fuel Pressure Regulator

The fuel pressure regulator, located on the fuel rail at the front of the engine, maintains a constant 39 psi pressure across the fuel injectors. The regulator contains an air chamber and fuel chamber separated by a spring-loaded diaphragm. The air chamber is connected by a hose to the throttle body assembly. The pressure in the air chamber of the regulator is

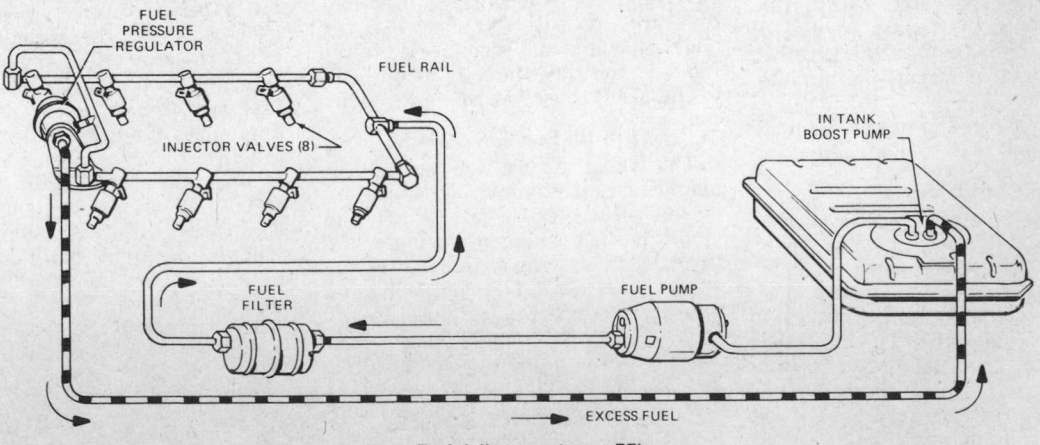

Fuel delivery system—EFI
(© Cadillac Div., G.M. Corp.)

identical to the pressure in the intake manifold. The changing manifold pressure and the spring control the action of the diaphragm valve, opening or closing an orifice in the fuel chamber of the regulator. At this point excess fuel is routed out of the regulator and back to the fuel tank.

Fuel Injector

The fuel injector is a solenoid operated pintle valve that meters fuel to each cylinder. The injectors are controlled by an electronic pulse signal from the ECU. When energized, the valve opens for precisely the proper amount of time to spray the exact amount of fuel droplets required by the engine. When the injector is deenergized, it prevents any futher fuel flow to the engine.

The eight injectors are divided into two groups of four each. Cylinders 1, 2, 7, and 8 form group 1 and the remaining injectors form group 2. All four injectors in each group are opened and closed simultaneously; while the two groups operate alternately.

The injectors are located on the intake manifold above the intake valve of each cylinder.

Air Induction System

The air induction system is made up of the throttle body assembly, fast idle valve assembly, and the intake manifold.

Throttle Body

Air for combustion enters the throttle body and is controlled by the throttle valves which are connected to the accelerator pedal linkage, much like a conventional carburetor. The throttle body consists of a housing with two bores and two shaft mounted throttle valves. The throttle valves are pre-set slightly open when the throttle lever is resting against the idle stop position. *The adjustment is not to be tampered with.* An adjustable set screw on the front of the throttle body adjusts an idle by-pass air passage incorporated within the throttle body and allows a regulated amount of air to by-pass the throttle valves, adjusting warm engine idle speed.

A large port on top of the throttle body contains the fast idle valve.

Fast Idle Valve

The fast idle valve, installed on the top of the throttle body, consists of a plastic body that houses an electric heater, a spring and plunger, and a temperature sensitive unit.

The fast idle valve is connected electrically to the fuel pump circuit through the ECU. When the engine is started cold, the open valve allows extra air to bypass the throttle valves. The heater warms the thermal ele-

ment which expands and forces the spring and plunger toward the air orifice, restricting the flow of extra air and gradually reducing the engine speed to the normal idle rpm. The fast idle valve has no effect after the thermal element reaches about 140°F. The rate at which the valve closes is a function of time and temperature. The warmer the air, the faster the valve closes. At 68°F the valve will close in about 90 seconds and at −20°F the valve will require about 5 minutes to close.

Intake Manifold

The intake manifold is basically the same as those installed on carbureted engines. There are, however, a few minor differences: Only air travels through the intake manifold. There is a hole above each cylinder for injector installation. A port is made available for the installation of the air temperature sensor. There is no exhaust heat cross-over passage. The exhaust passage from the right cylinder head is for EGR only.

Engine Sensors

All of the engines sensors are electrically connected to the Electronic Control Unit (ECU). Each of the sensors operates independently, monitors a specific engine operating condition, and transmits this information via electronic signal to the ECU. The sensors continuously send information signals to the ECU while the ignition switch is in the On or Start position.

Manifold Absolute Pressure Sensor

The manifold absolute pressure (MAP) sensor monitors pressure changes within the intake manifold which are the direct result of engine load, speed, and barometric pressure. As pressure in the intake manifold increases, additional fuel is required. The MAP sensor sends this information to the ECU so that the length of time the injectors are energized is increased or decreased accordingly.

The sensor is mounted within the electronic control unit. A manifold pressure line is routed with the engine harness and is connected to the front of the throttle body at one end to the MAP sensor at the other end.

Throttle Position Switch

The throttle position switch is mounted to the throttle body, connected to the throttle valve shaft, and monitors the opening or closing of the throttle valves. The switch senses the shaft movement and position and transmits electrical signals to the ECU. The ECU processes these signals to determine the fuel requirement for the engine.

Temperature Sensors

The two air and coolant temperature sensors vary electrical current

resistance as a function of temperature. Low temperatures provide low resistance and vice versa. Voltage changes across each sensor is monitored by the ECU.

The air temperature sensor is located on the rear of the intake manifold and is connected to the engine harness. The coolant temperature sensor is located on the heater hose fitting at the rear of the right cylinder head.

The sensors are identical and completely interchangeable.

Speed Sensor

The speed sensor is incorporated within the ignition distributor, and consists of two components. The first is a plastic housing containing two reed switches. The second is a rotor with two magnets attached to it and rotating with the distributor shaft.

The rotation of the magnets past the reed switches causes them to open and close, providing two bits of information: one for synchronization of the ECU and the proper injector group with the intake valve timing; and the engine rpm for fuel scheduling.

Electronic Control Unit

The electronic control unit (ECU), installed above the glove box in the passenger compartment on big Cadillacs and below the radio in the Seville, is a preprogrammed analog computer. The ECU is electrically connected to the vehicle's power supply, all of the EFI system electrical components, plus the EGR activation solenoid by a harness routed through the firewall.

When the ECU is energized by the ignition switch being turned to the On or Crank position, it continuously receives information from all of the engine sensors, and activates the fuel pumps, fast idle valve, fuel injectors, and the EGR solenoid.

The commands for proper air/fuel ratios for various driving and atmospheric conditions are designed into the ECU. As the electronic signals are received from the sensors, the ECU analyzes the signals and computes the exact fuel requirement for the engine. The ECU then causes the fuel injectors to open for a specific amount of time. The duration of time the injectors are open varies as the engine operating conditions change.

The electronic control units are calibrated differently depending on where the car is sold (California or 49 states) and in which vehicle the unit is installed. Each ECU is labeled for its intended use. The proper unit must be used for each application.

Troubleshooting

NOTE: Because a special electronic tester is necessary to diagnose problems in the ECU, this section will deal with troubleshooting only mechanical and basic electrical problems of the EFI system. If the ECU is diagnosed as being the possible cause of a problem, the car should be taken to a Cadillac dealer where the special electronic tester and trained personnel are available.

NOTE: Before disconnecting any part of the fuel delivery system on EFI equipped vehicles, the pressure within the fuel lines must be bled off. On early model cars without a pressure fitting in the rear fuel rail, cover the fitting to be removed with a shop towel while loosening. Dispose of the gasoline soaked cloth safely.

On models with the "Schrader" pressure relief valve in the rear fuel rail, arrange a shop towel or suitable container at the valve so the fuel will be contained. Remove the protective cap, depress the valve, and bleed the pressure out of the system. Dispose of the fuel or fuel soaked cloth safely. Replace the protective cap on the valve and proceed with the service.

ELECTRONIC FUEL INJECTION TROUBLE-SHOOTING CHART

PROBLEM: Engine cranks but will not start
POSSIBLE CAUSE:
NOTE: The following possible causes assume that the rest of the vehicle electrical system is functioning properly.

1. Blown 10 amp in-line fuel pump fuse (located under the instrument panel near the ECU wiring harness connectors). To check, listen for the whine of the chassis-mounted fuel pump when the ignition key is turned to the On position. The fuel pump should only operate for one second before shutting off. Do not turn the ignition key to the Start position.
2. Poor connection of the green wire at the fuel pump wiring harness near the ECU harness below the instrument panel. Check the operation of the fuel pump in the same manner as in POSSIBLE CAUSE 1 above.
3. Malfunction in the chassis-mounted pump.
4. Open circuit in the purple wire between the starter solenoid and the ECU.
4. Open circuit in the green wire between the alternator BAT terminal and the ECU.
6. Poor connection at the engine coolant sensor or an open circuit in the wiring or the sensor, with the engine cold only. To check, connect an ohmmeter to the temperature sensor connector ter-

minals. If the resistance in the sensor is greater than 1600 ohms, replace the sensor.
7. Poor connection of the ECU wiring harness.
8. Poor connection at the speed sensor on the distributor.
9. The speed sensor trigger is stuck closed.
10. The wide-open-throttle section of the throttle position switch is shorted. To check, disconnect the switch; the engine should start.
11. A restriction in the fuel delivery system.

PROBLEM: Hard starting
POSSIBLE CAUSE:
1. Open circuit in the engine coolant temperature sensor. This should occur only when the engine is cold or partially warm. The engine should start satisfactorily when hot.
2. The wide-open-throttle section of the throttle position switch is shorted. To check, disconnect the switch; the engine should start.
3. The fuel pressure regulator is malfunctioning.
4. The chassis-mounted fuel pump is malfunctioning.

PROBLEM: Poor fuel economy
POSSIBLE CAUSE:
1. The manifold absolute air pressure sensor is disconnected or leaking.
2. The vacuum hose at the fuel pressure regulator or throttle body is disconnected.
3. The air temperature or coolant temperature sensors are malfunctioning. Check the coolant temperature sensor as outlined under "Engine cranks but will not start", number 6. Check the air temperature sensor by connecting an ohmmeter to the sensor connector terminals; if the sensor resistance is less than 700 ohms, replace the sensor.

PROBLEM: Engine stalls after being started
POSSIBLE CAUSE:
1. A poor connection or open circuits in the black and yellow ignition signal wire between the fuse block and the ECU.
2. A poor connection or open circuit in the wiring or body of the engine coolant temperature sensor; cold or warm engine only. Check as outlined under "Engine cranks but will not start", number 6.

PROBLEM: Rough idle
POSSIBLE CAUSE:
1. Disconnected, leaking, or pinched manifold absolute air pressure sensor vacuum hose.
2. Poor connection or an open cir-

cuit in the air temperature sensor or wiring; cold engine only. See "Poor fuel economy", number 3.
3. Poor connection or short in the sensor or wiring of the engine coolant temperature sensor. See "Engine cranks but will not start", number 6.
4. Poor connection at the injectors.

PROBLEM: Fast idle condition is prolonged
POSSIBLE CAUSE:
1. Throttle position switch needs adjusting.
2. Poor connection at the fast idle valve or an open circuit in the heating element.
3. A vacuum leak in or around the throttle body.

PROBLEM: Hesitation of the engine under acceleration
POSSIBLE CAUSE:
1. Leaking, restricted, or disconnected manifold absolute air pressure sensor vacuum hose.
2. Throttle position switch needs adjusting or is malfunctioning.
3. Poor connecton of the ECU wiring harness at the ECU.
4. Poor connection at the EGR valve solenoid or the solenoid is stuck open; cold engine only.
5. Intermittent malfunction of the speed sensor trigger at the distributor.

PROBLEM: High speed performance is poor
POSSIBLE CAUSE:
1. The wide-open-throttle section of the throttle position switch needs adjusting or the switch is malfunctioning.
2. The fuel filter is blocked or restricted.
3. The chassis-mounted fuel pump is malfunctioning.
4. Intermittent malfunction of the speed sensor trigger.
5. An open circuit in the purple wire between the starter solenoid and the ECU.

Fuel Pump and Filter

The fuel pump on carbureted engines is mounted on the left-hand side of the engine. The pump is operated by an eccentric on the camshaft. The fuel filter is mounted inside the fuel pump on models through 1974. Beginning 1975, the fuel filter is mounted in the carburetor behind the fuel inlet nut. Beginning 1976, a check valve is included in the fuel filter. On air conditioned cars, the fuel filter has a passage and a connecting line to the fuel tank to return fuel vapors to the tank under high temperature conditions.

Vehicles with EFI have two electric fuel pumps; one is mounted in the fuel tank and is integral with the fuel level sending unit and the other, a chassis-mounted pump located in front of the rear axle either on the right or left side. A fuel filter is mounted on a bracket at the lower left front of the engine. On Seville models the fuel filter is mounted on the left side of the frame near the fuel pump.

Pump Removal and Installation

Carbureted Engines

NOTE: on air conditioned cars, be sure to disconnect the flexible line connecting the fuel filter to the vapor return line from the tank.

1. If equipped with A.I.R. system, it may be necessary to remove air pump and bracket for clearance.
2. Remove center coil wire. Jack up front of car and support on axle stands so that pump can be removed from underneath.
3. Loosen one bolt and one stud nut.
4. Turn over engine so that tension on mounting bolts is relieved.
5. Disconnect pump inlet line and pump outlet line. Plug inlet line. Disconnect the vapor return line.
6. Remove two mounting bolts and pump.
7. To install, reverse removal procedure. Make sure pump arm is properly positioned on cam eccentric; tighten bolts to 15 ft. lbs.

Fuel Injected Engines

Chassis-Mounted Pump

1. Relieve the pressure in the fuel lines and remove the fuel inlet and outlet hoses from nipples on the pump.

2. Peel back the rubber boot and remove the two nuts, one from each electrical terminal. Remove the electrical leads.
NOTE: These nuts have metric threads.
3. Remove the two screws and flat washers holding the fuel pump to the bracket and remove the pump assembly.
4. Install the fuel pump in the reverse order of removal. Connect the green wire to the positive terminal on the pump and the black wire to the negative terminal. Check to make sure the fuel pump is resting evenly on its two mounts and not grounding against the bracket or frame.

In-Tank Pump

1. Disconnect the battery, open the fuel tank filler door and disconnect the tan sending unit feed wire.
2. Siphon the fuel from the fuel tank. If the rear of the car is raised one foot higher than the front, more fuel can be taken out.
3. Raise the rear of the car and remove the screw securing the ground wire to the cross member.
4. Disconnect the fuel line, evaporative emission lines and the fuel return lines at the front of the tank.
5. Support the tank with a jack and wooden block and remove one screw on each side securing the fuel tank support straps to the body at the front of the tank.
6. Lower the jack and tank enough so that the fuel pump electrical lead can be disconnected. Disconnect the wire.
7. Remove the fuel tank from the car.

8. Remove the locknuts securing the fuel gauge tank unit and fuel pump feed wires to the tank unit.
9. Turn the cam locking ring counterclockwise with a soft non-ferrous punch and hammer. When the lock ring is disengaged, remove it and lift the gauge/pump unit from the tank.
10. Install in the reverse order of removal. Tighten the fuel tank retaining strap screws to 25 ft lbs.

Filter Removal and Installation

Carbureted Engines

Models Through 1974

1. Jack up car and support on stands.
2. Clamp or plug rubber section of inlet hose.
3. Disconnect fuel pump outlet line at fuel pump.
4. Remove fuel outlet nut and remove filter.
NOTE: use two wrenches to prevent loosening of nut welded to pump cover.
5. Install in reverse of above.

1975 and Later

1. Disconnect the fuel line at the carburetor inlet.
2. Remove the fuel inlet nut from the carburetor using a box wrench.
3. Remove the fuel filter element and spring.
4. Install the filter spring and new fuel filter element into the carburetor.
5. Install a new gasket on the fuel inlet nut and install the nut.
6. Connect the fuel line to the fuel inlet nut and tighten securely. Start the engine and check for leaks.

Fuel Injected Engines

NOTE: *The fuel filter element can be replaced by unscrewing the bottom cover and removing it.*

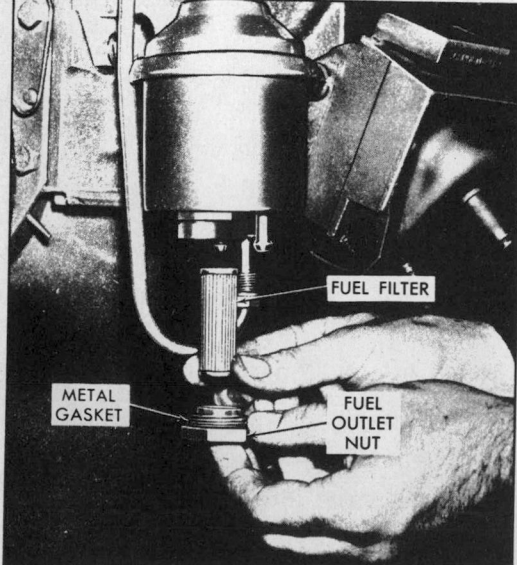

Fuel filter—models through 1974
(© Cadillac Div., G.M. Corp.)

Fuel filter—1975 and later models
(© Cadillac Div., G.M. Corp.)

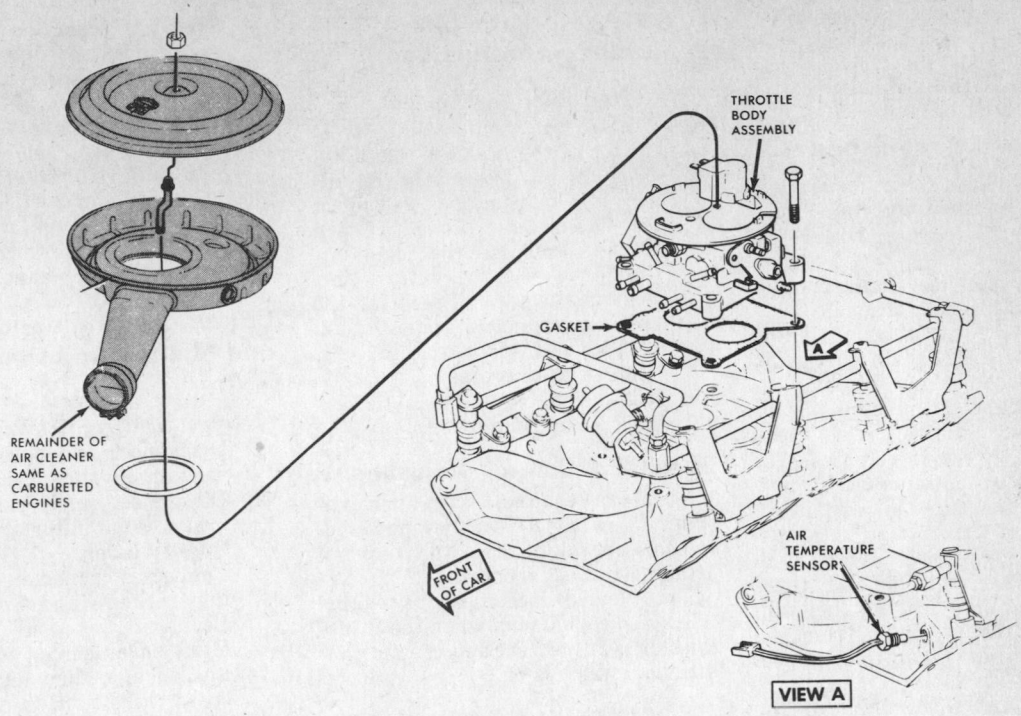

Mounting of the throttle body assembly and air temperature sensor—EFI
(© Cadillac Div., G.M. Corp.)

1. Bleed the pressure from the fuel delivery system and remove the fuel inlet and outlet hoses from the fuel filter.
2. Remove the two screws retaining the fuel filter to the bracket and remove the filter from the engine or frame.
3. Remove the inlet and outlet fittings from the filter assembly if they are needed for the new filter.
4. Install the fittings to the new filter, using a sealer on the threads.
5. Attach the filter to the bracket and tighten the retaining screws to 12 ft lbs.
6. Connect the inlet and outlet line, using new clamps.

NOTE: It may require considerable cranking before the engine starts due to the drained fuel lines.

Throttle Body Assembly Removal and Installation

Fuel Injected Engines

1. Remove the air cleaner.
2. Disconnect the two throttle return springs from the throttle lever.
3. Remove the cruise control chain retainer and chain, if so equipped.
4. Remove the clip and disconnect the throttle cable from the throttle lever.
5. Remove the left rear throttle body mounting screw and remove the one screw holding the throttle bracket to the intake manifold.

6. Remove the downshift switch from the throttle lever and position bracket. Move the switch and linkage aside.
7. Disconnect the throttle position and fast idle valve electrical connectors. Slide the fast idle valve wiring out of the notch in the throttle body.
8. Disconnect the vacuum lines from the throttle body.
9. Remove the remaining throttle body retaining screws and remove the throttle body.
10. Remove all gasket material from the intake manifold and the throttle body.
11. Install the throttle body in the reverse order of removal. Install the throttle return springs between the throttle lever and pressure regulator bracket with the open end of the spring on the outside of the throttle lever.

Throttle Position Switch Removal and Installation

Fuel Injected Engines

1. Remove the throttle body from the engine.
2. Remove the two mounting screws and remove the switch from the throttle body.
3. Install the switch on the right side of the throttle body so that the tab on the switch engages the flat on the throttle shaft.
4. Install the two mounting screws and tighten the screws so that the switch will move but is still firmly attached.

5. Adjust the throttle position switch as outlined under "Adjustments".
6. Reinstall the throttle body.

Fast Idle Valve Removal and Installation

Fuel Injected Engines

1. Remove the air cleaner and disconnect the fast idle valve heater electrical connection.
2. Remove the air cleaner mounting stud.
3. Push down and twist the fast idle valve heater counterclockwise 90° to remove it.
4. Remove the fast idle valve, spring and seat from the throttle body.
5. Install the fast idle valve seat, spring and valve in the throttle body.
6. Position the heater on top of the fast idle valve and push it down to compress the spring. Be careful to avoid damaging the micro-switch contact arm on the bottom of the heater housing.
7. Align the tabs on the fast idle valve heater with the cut-out portion of the throttle body and compress the spring further.

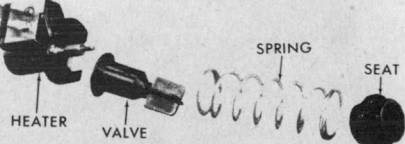

Fast idle valve assembly—exploded view—EFI
(© Cadillac Div., G.M. Corp.)

C263

8. Rotate the heater clockwise 90° to secure it in position.

9. Connect the electrical lead and install the air cleaner stud and air cleaner.

Fuel Injector Removal and Installation

Fuel Injected Engines

1. Remove the front and rear fuel rails.

2. Remove the electrical conduit from the injector brackets.

3. Remove the two screws holding each injector bracket to the intake manifold and remove the brackets and grommets.

4. Disconnect the electrical lead from all of the injectors on the fuel rail being removed.

5. Remove the fuel rail and injectors from the engine as an assembly. Some injectors may stick to the intake manifold and others will come off with the fuel rail. Remove the injectors from the fuel rail and manifold as required.

6. Remove and discard all of the used O-rings used to seal the injectors at the fuel rail and intake manifold.

7. Before installing the new O-ring seals, lubricate them with a suitable lubricant and install the O-rings on the fuel rail end of each injector.

8. Install the injectors into the fuel rail with the electrical connector facing inward.

9. Install new O-rings into each injector port in the intake manifold.

10. Install the fuel rail/injector assembly to the intake manifold. Make certain that each injector is properly positioned in the manifold O-ring.

11. Install the rubber grommets, flanges down, on the fuel rail and install the injector brackets in position.

12. Install and tighten the bracket retaining screws to 5 ft lbs.

13. Route and secure the electrical harness along the bracket. Connect all eight injectors as follows: the two front and two rear cylinders' injectors are connected to the red/black wires; the four center cylinders' injectors are connected to the black/white wires.

14. Install the front and rear fuel rails.

15. Turn the ignition On and Off a few times to build up fuel pressure in the system and check for leaks.

16. Start the engine and check for leaks. It may require considerable cranking to start the engine due to the drained condition of the fuel lines.

Fuel Pressure Regulator Removal and Installation

Fuel Injected Engines

1. Remove the vacuum hose from the top of the pressure regulator.

2. Bleed off the pressure in the fuel delivery system and disconnect the flexible fuel hose between the fuel rail and the regulator. Disconnect the fuel return line.

3. Remove the one nut securing the pressure regulator to the bracket. This nut has metric threads.

4. Remove the regulator.

5. Install the regulator in the reverse order of removal.

Speed-Up Control Adjustment

Some cars equipped with air conditioning have a vacuum-powered, solenoid-operated speed-up control attached to the carburetor.

This device increases the engine idle speed to 900 rpm when the transmission is in neutral and the air conditioner switch is on.

1970 Fleetwood 75 Sedan and Limousine

The idle speed-up control is acuated only when radiator water temperature reaches 220°F. The air conditioner does not have to be on for the speed-up device to function.

1. Set curb and fast idle.

2. Stop engine and remove air cleaner and heat duct.

3. Disconnect and plug distributor advance hose.

4. Disconnect vacuum hose at vacuum break tank and connect it to distributor advance unit.

5. Disconnect vacuum hose that goes from Thermo Vacuum switch to reducing nipple, at the reducing nipple.

6. Disconnect vacuum hose connector at carburetor vacuum break T.

7. Connect a 25 in. section of 3/16 in. vacuum hose between T and reducing nipple.

8. Turn A/C to HIGH and set dial to 65°F.

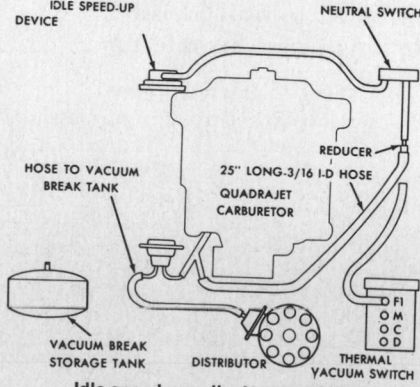

Idle speed-up adjustment—1970
(© Cadillac Div., G.M. Corp)

9. Start and warm up engine, then adjust idle speed-up in Neutral. Turn adjusting screw, as illustrated, to maintain 900-950 rpm.

NOTE: pull rod on idle speed-up unit should move when selector lever is moved to Park or Neutral. If it does not, check neutral switch or for vacuum leaks.

10. Turn off engine, reconnect hoses and install air cleaner.

Carbureted Engine Idle Speed and Mixture Adjustments

1970

Adjust with air cleaner removed.

1. Disconnect and plug distributor vacuum advance line.

2. Disconnect and plug parking brake vacuum line at vacuum release cylinder.

3. Connect a tachometer, set parking brake and remove air cleaner.

4. Make sure dashpot is not touching linkage, then turn slow idle speed screw in approximately 1½ turns after it contacts primary throttle lever. Turn in both mixture screws until they seat gently, then unscrew them approximately 6 turns.

5. Place car in Drive after warming up engine. Turn off Air Conditioning.

NOTE: press down on hot idle compensator pin while making adjustments.

6. Adjust slow idle screw to obtain 620 rpm.

7. Turn one mixture screw clockwise until speed falls off 10 rpm, then repeat Steps 6 and 7 for other mixture screw. Idle speed now should be 600 rpm, indicating a 10 rpm drop per mixture needle.

8. Install air cleaner, shut off engine and disconnect tach.

9. Connect parking brake vacuum line and distributor vacuum line.

1971-74

Adjust with air cleaner removed.
Idle speed is adjusted at a new anti-dieseling solenoid located where the dashpot was located in previous years. The throttle must be opened slightly to allow the plunger to move out all the way, then it must be closed against the now-extended solenoid plunger before making the idle speed adjustment. The solenoid plunger will retract when the ignition is shut off.

1. Disconnect and plug distributor vacuum advance hose and parking brake vacuum hose (at the release cylinder). If equipped with "self-leveling", remove and plug the air leveling compressor hose at the air cleaner. Remove

the air cleaner but keep the vacuum hoses connected.

2. Connect a tachometer and set the parking brake with transmission in Neutral.
3. Turn in mixture screws until they seat gently, then turn the screws out approximately 6 turns 1971-73 or 4 turns—1974.
4. Start engine and allow it to warm up. Make sure choke is off.
5. Place car in Drive (DR) with A/C off.

NOTE: *Press down on hot idle compensator pin while making adjustments. This applies to Fleetwood 75 and Commercial models only.*

6. Set idle speed to 620 rpm—1971-73 or 640 rpm—1974 by adjusting anti-dieseling solenoid. Tighten jam nut.
7. Turn each mixture screw clockwise ¼ turn at a time alternately until idle speed of 600 rpm is obtained.
8. Install limiter caps, then disconnect wire that energizes solenoid. The plunger should retract to allow a slower idle speed of 350-400 rpm.
9. Shut off engine, disconnect tach, connect vacuum lines and solenoid wire and install air cleaner.

1975-77

Adjust with air cleaner removed.

Normal engine idle speed is adjusted with the idle speed screw located at the throttle lever side of the carburetor.

1. Disconnect and plug the distributor vacuum advance hose and parking brake vacuum hose (at the release cylinder). Disconnect the air leveling compressor hose at the air cleaner and plug it. Remove the air cleaner, but keep the vacuum hoses connected.
2. Connect a tachometer to the engine, set the parking brake, and block the wheels. Place the transmission in Neutral.
3. Turn in the mixture screws until they seat gently, then turn them out 5 turns.
4. Start and warm the engine to normal operating temperature. Be sure that the choke is off and that the throttle lever stop tang is contacting the carburetor idle speed screw (slow idle position).
5. Place the transmission in Drive with A/C off.
6. Set the idle speed to 650 rpm (49 states) or 620 rpm (Calif.) by adjusting the idle speed screw located at the throttle lever side of the carburetor.

NOTE: *Do not depress the brake pedal on cars equipped with the Hydro-boost brake system as engine speed will be decreased.*

7. Alternately turn each mixture

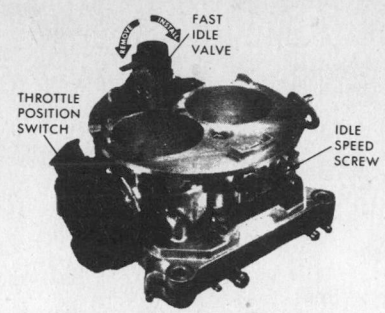

Throttle body adjustments—EFI
(© Cadillac Div., G.M. Corp.)

screw inward ¼ turn at a time until 600 rpm is reached.

8. Install replacement mixture screw limiter caps and recheck idle speed.
9. Stop the engine, remove the tachometer, connect all vacuum lines, and install the air cleaner.

Idle Speed Adjustment

Fuel Injected Engines

1. Adjust the ignition timing to the correct specifications.
2. Disconnect and plug the distributor vacuum line, the parking brake release cylinder vacuum line, and the air leveling compressor hose at the air cleaner.
3. Connect a tachometer to the engine, start it, allow the engine to reach normal operating temperature.
4. Place the transmission selector in Drive, and turn the air conditioning Off.
5. Loosen the lock nut on the idle by-pass adjusting screw on the front of the throttle body.
6. Adjust the idle by-pass adjusting screw to obtain an idle speed of 600 rpm.
7. Tighten the lock nut on the adjusting screw, stop the engine, remove the tachometer, and install the air cleaner and vacuum hoses.

Adjusting the idle speed—EFI
(© Cadillac Div., G.M. Corp.)

Throttle Position Switch

Fuel Injected Engines

1. Loosen the two throttle position switch mounting screws.
2. While holding the throttle valves in the idle position, turn the throttle position switch counterclockwise carefully until the endstop is reached.
3. Tighten the mounting screws.
4. Check and make sure that the throttle valves close to the throttle stop. Readjust, if necessary.

COOLING SYSTEM

Cadillac uses a sealed cooling system. The sealed system is designed to remain sealed at all times. A coolant reservior allows the pressurized system to be kept sealed even when fresh coolant is added. There is no need to open the radiator cap.

Information on the water temperature gauge can be found in the Unit Repair Section.

Radiator Removal and Installation

1. Disconnect battery cable.
2. Drain cooling system.
3. Disconnect air conditioning compressor, if so equipped, and position out of the way without disconnecting hoses.
4. Remove clamp that holds A/C high pressure vapor line to cradle.
5. Loosen hose clamps and disconnect upper and lower radiator hoses.
6. Disconnect two transmission oil cooler lines and plug them.

NOTE: *disconnect heater return hose, if so equipped.*

7. Remove two top radiator cradle clamps or straps and fan shroud. Disconnect reservoir hose from the filler neck.
8. Remove vacuum hoses, if so equipped. Mark for proper installation.
9. Pull radiator straight up and out of car.

Water Pump Removal and Installation

1. Disconnect negative battery cable.
2. Drain radiator and remove fan shroud.
3. Remove fan assembly. The screws cannot be removed entirely due to lack of clearance between fan and radiator. Slide loosened assembly near power steering pump to remove bolts and spacer.

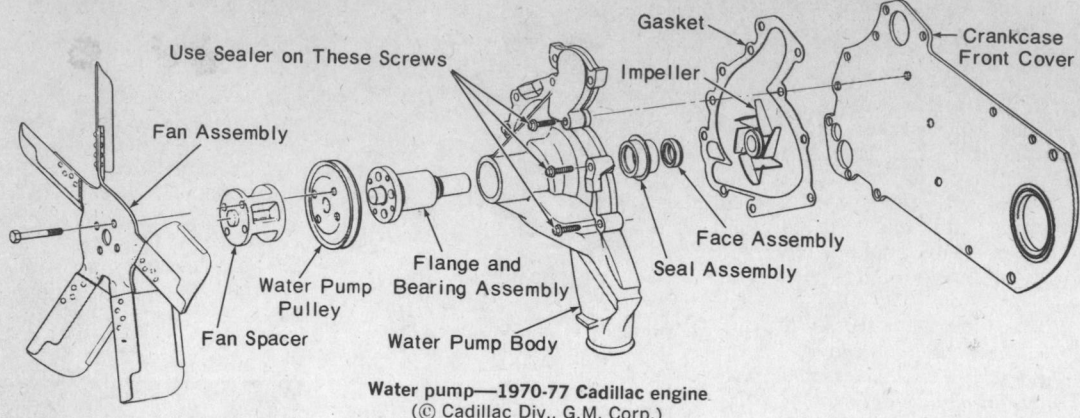

Water pump—1970-77 Cadillac engine.
(© Cadillac Div., G.M. Corp.)

4. Loosen alternator mounting screws and remove generator belt.
5. Loosen power steering pump mounting screws and remove belts.
6. On applicable models, remove A.I.R. pump and belt.
7. Remove water pump pulley, disconnect water inlet and remove 11 screws and pump.

Thermostat Removal and Installation

Removal
1. Drain the cooling system until the coolant level is below the level of the thermostat.
2. Remove the upper radiator hose at the thermostat housing.
3. Remove the thermostat housing.
4. Pull the thermostat from the engine block.

Installation
1. Position the thermostat in the block with the valve up.
2. Install a new gasket coated with sealer onto the engine block.
3. Position and secure the thermostat housing; tighten screws to 10 ft lbs.
4. Connect the radiator hose and refill the system to the proper level.

EMISSION CONTROLS

Positive Crankcase Ventilation (PCV) System

A simple valve, operated by intake manifold vacuum, is used to meter the flow of air and vapors through the crankcase. Air is drawn in through the breather assembly, located between the left rocker cover and the carburetor air cleaner

(closed system). When the car is decelerating or the engine is idling, high manifold vacuum opens the valve; this allows full flow of the crankcase vapor into the intake manifold. During acceleration or at a constant speed, the intake manifold vacuum drops. the valve spring forces the valve closed and restricts the flow of vapors into the intake manifold from the crankcase. If a backfire occurs the valve closes, preventing the vapor in the crankcase from being ignited.

Air Injection

The Air Injection Reactor (AIR) system consists of an engine-driven air pump which forces air into the exhaust port of each cylinder to promote further oxidation and reduce the concentration of hydrocarbons.

The 1970 models did not use the AIR system but substituted the Controlled Combustion System (CCS). The PCV system was retained on all 1970 models. The CCS system is composed of a thermac air cleaner and a transmission-controlled spark advance.

Thermostatically Controlled Air Cleaner

The Thermac air cleaner regulates the air temperature at the air cleaner inlet so that it maintains a constant temperature of 105°F. A damper in the air cleaner, when the engine is cold (85°F or below) allows the intake air to be heated by the exhaust manifold before it enters the carburetor. As the engine reaches operating temperature, the damper opens and allows a mixture of outside cool air and heated air to mix to obtain the 105° F intake air.

The Thermac air cleaner is not used on fuel injected engines.

Transmission Controlled Spark (TCS)

The transmission-controlled spark system is composed of a transmission

switch, a thermal vacuum switch, and a vacuum solenoid. The switch is positioned in the block with vacuum lines from the intake manifold, the distributor and the carburetor running to it. The line between the carburetor and the thermal vacuum switch has the solenoid attached to it. The solenoid has a wire which connects it with the transmission. Inside the thermal vacuum switch there is a ball check valve system which opens and closes the ports in the switch.

The vacuum switch has two vacuum sources attached to it: intake manifold vacuum and carburetor vacuum. In the normal running position, the ball check blocks the passage of vacuum from the intake manifold to the distributor and allows vacuum to pass from the carburetor to the distributor. This vacuum is regulated by the transmission solenoid. If the engine should overheat at idle speed, the ball check valve blocks the carburetor-to-distributor vacuum and allows the intake manifold-to-distributor vacuum port to be uncovered allowing the stronger intake manifold vacuum to advance the ignition timing and cool the engine.

The vacuum solenoid is a type of regulator between the carburetor vacuum line, the thermal vacuum switch, the distributor, and the transmission.

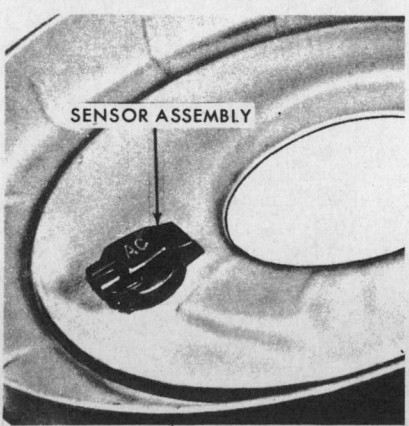

Location of the Thermac air cleaner sensor
(© Cadillac Div., G.M. Corp)

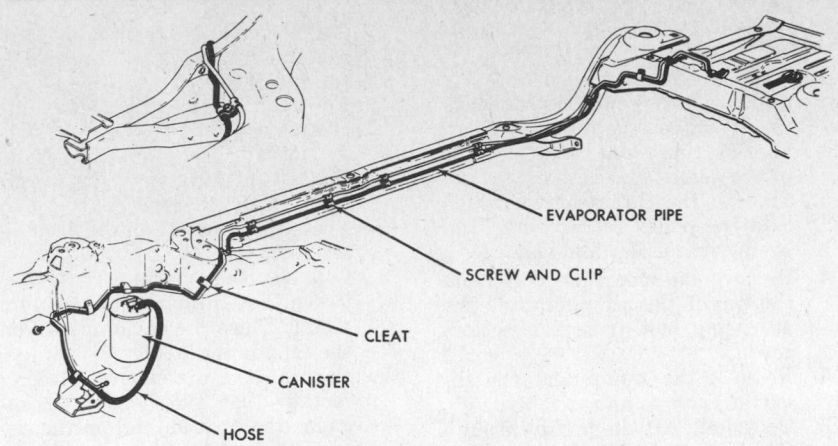

Evaporative control system (© Cadillac Div., G.M. Corp)

When the transmission is in neutral, first, or second gear, the solenoid is energized which eliminates vacuum advance to the distributor. When the transmission shifts into third gear the solenoid is de-energized allowing the vacuum advance to pass to the distributor.

Evaporative Loss Control (ELC)

Evaporative Loss Control (ELC), also known as evaporative control system (E.C.S.), was used in California cars in 1970 and nationally starting in 1971. The concept of this system is, the venting of the fuel tank through a canister containing charcoal. Both liquid fuel and fuel vapors from the tank are fed into the liquid vapor separator which is located ahead of the fuel tank. The vapors are collected in the charcoal canister which is mounted on the front of the radiator. The vapors are drawn from the canister by a vacuum line which is connected to the air cleaner. The liquid fuel which is ducted to the separator is returned to the fuel tank.

Exhaust Gas Recirculation (EGR)

The Exhaust Gas Recirculation System (EGR), used from 1973 on, is a control system used to reduce nitrous oxides released into the air. The basic function of the system is to reduce the temperature in the combustion chambers. This will lessen nitrogen oxidation and reduce pollution. It is accomplished by recirculating a small amount of engine exhaust through ports in the intake manifold and into the carburetor for reburning.

This channeling of exhaust is governed by the EGR valve which is mounted at the rear of the intake manifold. As the engine speed increases, vacuum is applied to the vacuum diaphragm in the valve and this

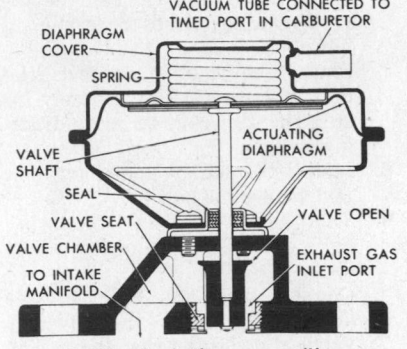

E.G.R. valve in the open position
(© Cadillac Div., G.M. Corp)

opens the exhaust port allowing exhaust gases to enter. As vacuum decreases at idle speed and wide open throttle, the valve closes and the gases are cut off.

Temperature overrides are used to prevent exhaust gas recirculation from occurring when the engine is cold. Prior to March 15, 1973, these overrides depended upon ambient temperature; overrides used after this date were enclosed in shrouds, making them dependent upon engine temperature. The temperature override switch blocks vacuum to the EGR valve at temperature below 60°F.

All 1974-76 models sold in California use an exhaust backpressure transducer which is connected to the EGR valve to prevent exhaust gases from being recirculated at idle, and wide open throttle because the higher volume of gas recirculated on these models would cause poor performance.

The EGR system is slightly different on EFI engines. The EGR vacuum solenoid valve is controlled by the ECU and installed in the signal line to the EGR valve. The ECU keeps the solenoid valve closed when coolant temperatures are below about 130°F, blocking the signal to the EGR valve. This is to improve cold starting and engine warm up. When the coolant temperature goes above 130°F, ported vacuum is directed to the EGR valve and exhaust pressure transducer. A thermal delay valve is not used.

Catalytic Converter

Catalytic converters are used on 1975 and later Cadillac and Seville models. The converter is located in the exhaust pipe, under the floor on the passenger's side.

For more information on how the converter works, as well as service procedures for it, see the "Emission Controls" Unit Repair Section.

Early Fuel Evaporation (EFE)

Early Fuel Evaporation (EFE) is used on 1975 and later Cadillacs (except fuel injected models). The system consists of a valve installed on the right-hand exhaust manifold which is controlled by a thermostatic vacuum switch (TVS), located in the upper left front of the cylinder block.

Below approximately 150 F engine coolant temperature, the TVS routes intake manifold vacuum to the EFE valve. The vacuum closes the EFE valve, forcing exhaust gases through the exhaust crossover passage in the intake manifold to heat the intake manifold for better fuel vaporization.

Exhaust pressure transducer and EGR valve—1974 and later
(© Cadillac Div., G.M. Corp.)

At approximately 150°F coolant temperature, the TVS blocks manifold vacuum to the EFE valve. This causes the EFE valve to open, ending heating of the intake manifold.

Model Usage

The 1970 models use PCV, Controlled Combustion System (CCS), and, on California models only, Evaporative Loss Control (ELC). CCS includes the Thermac air cleaner and Transmission Controlled Spark (TCS).

In 1971 transmission controlled spark (TCS) and the thermostatically controlled air cleaner were used. The ELC system was expanded to include cars sold nationally and PCV was continued.

In the 1971 model year all cars were equipped with the PCV, AIR, and ELC systems.

The 1972 cars use the PCV, AIR, ELC, and a Speed Control Spark (SCS) which controls the spark advance to the distributor at low speeds. The switch is mounted within the transmission and connected to the speedometer gear. The switch is closed prior to 33 mph, allowing no vacuum advance to the distributor during speeds from 0 to 33 mph. When the vehicle reaches 33 mph, the contacts in the switch separate, allowing the vacuum port to be uncovered. Once the port is uncovered the vacuum causes the distributor to advance.

1973-74 models use EGR, PCV, AIR, and ELC.

1975 models use PCV, AIR (Calif. cars and Commercial Chassis), EGR, EFE, ECS, and catalytic converters.

1976 Cadillac models use PCV, AIR (Calif. cars and fuel injected models), EGR, EFE (except fuel injected models), ECS, and catalytic converters.

All 1976 Seville models use PCV, AIR, EGR, ECS, and catalytic converters.

Component Removal and Installation

PCV Valve

1. Disconnect the valve from its connection in the valve cover.
2. Remove the hose clamp and the hose from the ventilator valve grommet.
3. To install, place a small amount of silicone sealer on both ends of the new valve and install the small end of the valve into the hose. Secure with the clamp.
4. Place the large end of the valve into the grommet in the valve cover.

AIR Pump

NOTE: *Pump service should be limited to replacement of the entire unit. At no time should the pump be opened.*

1. Raise and support the vehicle.
2. Remove the air hose from the diverter valve and disconnect the vacuum line from the other side of the valve.
3. Remove the three screws which hold the pulley to the pump and remove the pulley and belt.
4. Remove the mounting bolt from the top of the air pump and the adjusting bolt from the bottom rear.
5. Remove the pump and the diverter valve as an assembly.
6. To install, lift the pump through the space between the lower radiator hose and the oil filter. Turn the pump so that the diverter valve passes over the oil filter.
7. Place the pump against the mounting bracket and loosely install the upper screw and adjusting bolt.
8. Install the pulley and drive belt and adjust the belt.
9. The adjusting and mounting bolts should be torqued to 25 ft lbs.
10. Connect the air hose to the larger fitting of the diverter valve and tighten the clamp. The vacuum hose is installed on the small fitting of the valve.

Centrifugal Filter Fan R & R

NOTE: *Never attempt to clean the filter fan. It is impossible to remove the fan without destroying it.*

1. Remove the air pump from the car, as detailed above.
2. Gently pry the outer disc off and pull off the remaining portion. Be careful that no fragments from the fan enter the pump air intake.
3. Install a new filter fan pulling it into place with the pump pulley and attaching belts.
4. Alternately torque the bolts so that the fan is drawn down *evenly*. Be sure that the outer edge of the fan fits into the pump housing.

Caution
Never hammer or press the fan into place; damage to it and the pump will result.

5. Install the pump on the car.

NOTE: *For the first 20-30 miles of operation, the fan may squeal until its lip has worn in. This is normal and does not indicate a damaged pump.*

Thermac Temperature Sensor

1. Remove the hose from between the sensor and the manifold fitting.
2. Remove the air cleaner.
3. Remove the hose between the sensor and the vacuum motor.
4. Pull the retainer from the sensor vacuum fittings and remove the retainer.
5. Pull the sensor from the air cleaner.
6. To install, place the gasket on the sensor and install the sensor into the air cleaner.
7. Press the retainer on the vacuum connections.
8. Connect the vacuum hose between the sensor and the vacuum motor. Place the vacuum hose on the remaining fitting.
9. Position the air cleaner making certain that the heat tube engages the heat shroud on the exhaust manifold.
10. Connect the vacuum hose between the sensor and the manifold.

Exhaust Gas Recirculation Valve

1. Remove the air cleaner and the vacuum hoses from the air cleaner and the front of the carburetor.
2. Remove the valve attaching nuts and the vacuum signal line and remove the valve.
3. To install, place the valve on the manifold studs and install the attaching nuts.
4. Connect the vacuum signal line to the E.G.R. valve and the two vacuum hoses to the air cleaner.
5. Install the air cleaner.

Evaporative Control System Canister

1. Remove the hoses from the top of the canister.
2. Remove the canister strap bracket from the radiator cradle.
3. Remove both the strap and the canister from the cradle.
4. To install, position the canister onto the radiator cradle bracket with the fittings on the top facing toward the engine.
5. Tighten the hold-down strap and connect the two hoses to the top of the canister. The smaller diameter hose is connected to the carburetor while the larger diameter hose goes to the tank.

Evaporative Control System Canister Filter

1. Remove the canister from its cradle.
2. Pull out the element by squeezing it under the retainer bar.
3. To install, push the element under the bar and locate it evenly around the entire bottom of the canister.
4. Install the canister.

For troubleshooting and adjustment of the Cadillac emission control systems consult the "Unit Repair Section."

ENGINE

Engine Removal and Installation

Except Seville

1. Disconnect negative battery cable.
2. Remove hood, after scribing hood hinge outline for proper alignment.
3. Remove air cleaner and heat shroud.
4. Drain cooling system. Unfasten the fender struts from the radiator shroud.
5. Remove radiator hose bracket, radiator cover and fan.
6. Remove upper radiator hose.
7. Disconnect throttle and Cruise Control linkage at carburetor.
8. Remove Cruise Control power unit on cars so equipped.
9. Disconnect power steering pump bracket and swing pump out of way with hoses still connected. Position power steering fluid cooler out of the way.
10. Remove A/C compressor bracket bolts and swing compressor out of way with hoses still connected.
11. Disconnect temperature sender wire, idle speed-up wire (if so equipped), ignition primary wire, downshift switch wire, S.C.S. or T.C.S. solenoid (if so equipped) and anti-dieseling solenoid wires, electronic ignition connector, block temperature sender lead, and all ground straps. On fuel injected engines, disconnect the EFI manifold harness and move it out of the way.
12. Bend back clips and position wiring harness out of the way.
13. Disconnect all vacuum hoses, and purge hose from E.L.C. canister. Disconnect the automatic level control line, on models, so equipped.
14. Disconnect alternator, heater switch and oil pressure sender wires.
15. Remove wiring harness from clips.
16. Remove water hose from fitting at rear of right-hand cylinder head.

NOTE: on A/C cars up to 1969, remove blower relay, power servo, and master switch from heater air selector.

17. Loosen and remove alternator and A.I.R. pumps and remove belts.
18. Disconnect tie struts and swing out of the way.
19. Remove upper two transmission-to-engine bolts. Remove two screws that secure right air deflector to lower radiator cradle.
20. Jack up car and support on axle stands.
21. Remove starter motor, then disconnect exhaust pipes from manifolds.
22. Remove front engine mount bolts, then disconnect and plug vapor return line at fuel pump (A/C cars only) and fuel inlet line. Remove oil filter, after draining engine oil.
23. Disconnect lower radiator hose and remove flywheel housing cover.
24. Remove the three screws that secure flex plate to converter. Engine must be rotated for access.
25. Remove four transmission-to-engine bolts.
26. Lower the car to the ground.
27. Connect a lifting bracket to the engine.
28. Support transmission with a wood-padded floor jack.
29. Raise engine slightly and pull forward to disengage from transmission, then pull engine up and out.
30. Reverse the above procedure to install the engine.

Seville

1. Disconnect the negative battery cable.
2. Drain the cooling system.
3. Remove the hood. Scribe marks on the hinges and their mounting points for installation.
4. Remove the air cleaner assembly.
5. Remove the struts from both right and left wheelhousings.
6. Remove the radiator cover.
7. Disconnect the power brake hose at the point where it joins the steel tube to the rear of the left cylinder head.
8. Disconnect the left and right side section of the wiring harness and position them out of the way.
9. Disconnect the heater hose from the rear of the intake manifold.
10. Disconnect the upper and lower radiator hoses from the engine and remove the fan assembly from the water pump.
11. Remove the distributor cap and spark plug wires.
12. Disconnect the two ground wires from the compressor bracket and position the harness out of the way.
13. Disconnect the accelerator linkage and vapor canister hose from the throttle body.
14. Disconnect the fuel inlet line from the fuel rail and plug the line.
15. Disconnect the power steering hoses at the steering gear and plug the hoses and gear. Secure hoses to engine.
16. Disconnect the fuel return line from the pressure regulator outlet fitting.
17. Remove the air conditioner compressor from the engine without disconnecting the refrigerant lines and move it out of the way.
18. Raise the car on a hoist.
19. Disconnect the exhaust pipe and exhaust crossover pipe from the exhaust manifolds.
20. Remove the torque converter cover.
21. Remove the starter motor.
22. Remove the screw and clip securing the transmission oil cooler lines to the engine oil pan.
23. Remove the three screws securing the flexplate to the convertor.
24. Remove the through-bolt from each engine mount.
25. Remove the screws holding the engine and transmission together.
26. Lower the car.
27. Remove the screws securing the heater water valve to the evaporator and move the valve out of the way.
28. Support the transmission with a jack and a block of wood placed between the jack and the transmission case.
29. Install a suitable lifting device on the engine and raise the engine off of the motor mounts. Reposition the transmission support.
30. Raise the engine carefully, pull it forward and lift it from the car.
31. Install the engine in the reverse order of removal.

Manifolds

Exhaust Manifold Removal

1. In order to remove the left exhaust manifold remove the air cleaner assembly, then remove the air cleaner bracket and heat stove from the manifold, by unfastening the manifold nuts from the studs on the Nos. 2 and 8 cylinders.
2. Unfasten the nuts which secure the downpipes to either manifold. Remove the two studs retaining the EFE valve to the right-side manifold and remove the EFE valve.
3. Remove the bolts which secure the manifold to the cylinder heads.

NOTE: It may not be possible to remove the fifth bolt from the front of the cylinder head completely. Back the bolt all the way out and remove it with the manifolds.

4. Lift the manifold out of the engine compartment.

Installation is performed in the reverse order of removal. Lubricate the cylinder head installation surface with moly grease. Install the fifth screw from the front prior to installing the manifold. Tighten the bolts to specifications. On the right-side manifold, position the EFE valve on the manifold with the actuator toward the engine block. Tighten the two stud bolts to 35 ft lbs.

Intake Manifold Removal
Carbureted Engines

1. Remove the negative battery cable, air cleaner, heat tube, and crankcase vent.
2. Disconnect the throttle linkage and the Cruise Control.
3. Remove the coil leads and the connector from the SCS solenoid.
4. Disconnect the downshift switch and the temperature sender. On some models it is necessary to remove the anti-dieseling solenoid and the SCS solenoid.
5. Disconnect all vacuum lines. Remove the carburetor fuel line.
6. On cars with air conditioning, it is necessary to partially remove the compressor.
7. Remove the manifold hold-down bolts and lift the manifold from the engine.
8. To install the intake manifold, reverse the above procedure. The intake manifold bolts are torqued to 30 ft lbs, using a diagonal torque pattern beginning from the center of the manifold and working toward the ends.

Fuel Injected Engines

1. Disconnect the negative battery cable and remove the air cleaner and crankcase filter.
2. Disconnect the throttle cable and cruise control linkage at the throttle body. Remove the cable from the bracket and move it aside.
3. Disconnect the coolant temperature switch wire, the HEI wire, speed sensor wire, downshift switch wire, and the injector wiring harness from the fuel rail brackets and move the harness out of the way.
4. Disconnect the two vacuum hoses from the throttle body to the thermal vacuum switch (TVS).
5. Disconect the vacuum hoses and power brake pipe from the rear of the throttle body.
6. Bleed the pressure from the fuel delivery system and disconnect the fuel line from the fuel rail.
7. Disconnect the EGR solenoid wires, air temperature sensor wire and the MAP sensor vacuum hose.
8. Remove the PCV valve from the rocker cover and move it out of the way.

9. Remove the spark plug wires and the distributor cap.
10. Remove the front fuel rail.
11. Remove the air conditioner compressor from the engine. Do not disconnect the refrigerant lines.
12. Remove the fuel return line hose from the fuel pressure regulator.
13. Remove the 12 intake manifold retaining screws and remove the manifold. Do not pry or lift the manifold by the fuel rails or their mounting brackets.
14. Clean all gasket material from the mating surfaces of the manifold, cylinder heads and block.
15. Place new rubber intake manifold seals over the rails at the front and rear of the cylinder block. The tabs on the gasket should be positioned in the holes in the rails and the beveled ends of the gasket tucked into the slot at the mating of the head and rail.
16. Apply gasket sealer to the sheet metal gasket-shield on the engine. The holes in the gasket should engage the dowel pins on the cylinder heads. Be careful not to use too much sealer near the injector tips.
17. Carefully position the manifold on the top of the engine. Install and tighten the intake manifold retaining screws to the specified torque.
18. Assemble and install the remaining components in the reverse order of removal.

Valve System

All Cadillacs use hydraulic lifters. Valve systems with hydraulic lifters operate with zero clearance in the valve train. The rocker arms are non-adjustable. The lifter itself will compensate if there is slack in the system but if there is excessive play, the entire system should be examined.

If the valve guides are found to be worn past allowable limits, the valve guides will have to be rebored and valves with oversize stems installed.

Three oversize valves of different stem diameters are available for each engine.

Sometimes a valve guide bore is made oversize at the factory. Oversize valve guide bores from the factory are marked on the inboard side of the cylinder heads on a machined surface just above the intake manifold surface on the 350 V8 in the Seville and on the cylinder head gasket surface in line with the oversize valve on the 472 and 500 V8 in the full-size Cadillacs.

NOTE: Some 350 V8 Seville engines have both standard and .010 in. oversize valve lifters. The oversize lifters have "O" etched on the side of the lifter and the same marking on the lifter housing boss on the cylinder block.

Rocker Arm Removal and Installation

The rocker arms are mounted in pairs (four pairs to each cylinder head). They are of the modified pedestal-mounted type.

Rocker arms may be removed in pairs and do not require cylinder-head removal.

Torque rocker arm mounting screws to 60 ft lbs—1970-73; 70 ft lbs—1974 and later Cadillac models; or 25 ft lbs—1976 and later Seville models.

Cylinder Head
Removal and Installation

Care must be used when replacing Cadillac engine cylinder-head bolts. They are different lengths.
1. Remove intake manifold.
2. Drain engine coolant.
3. Disconnect ground strap at rear of cylinder heads from cowl. Disconnect wiring connector for high engine temperature warning system from sending unit at rear of left cylinder head.
4. Remove alternator, if working on the right cylinder head, or

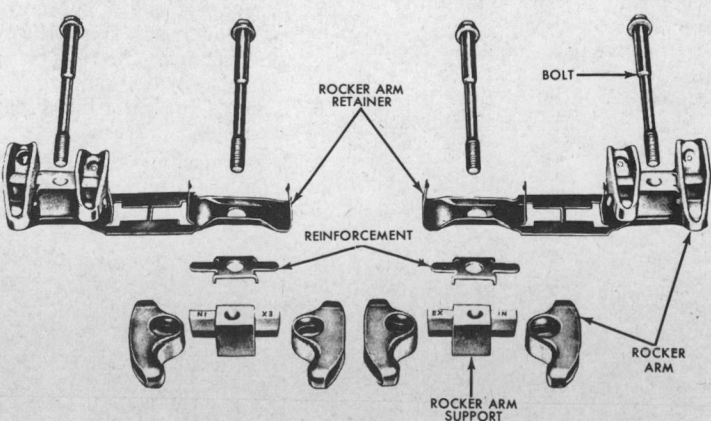

Cadillac engine rocker arm assembly (© Cadillac Div., G.M. Corp)

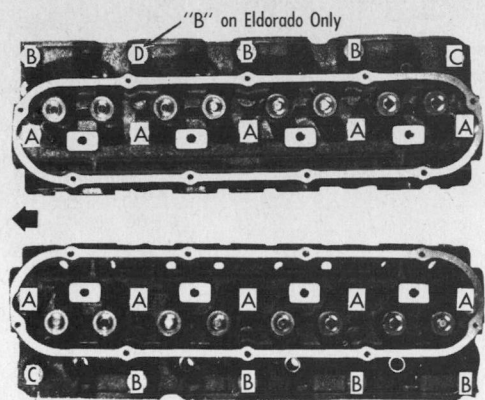

"B" on Eldorado Only

Cylinder head bolt location and length—1970-77 Cadillac engine

Bolt Location	Length
A (Bolt)	4.36"
B (Bolt)	4.77"
C (Bolt)	3.02"
D (Bolt/Stud)	3.02"

(© Cadillac Div., G.M. Corp.)

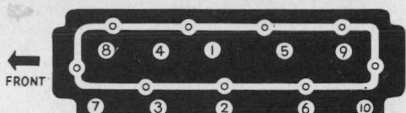

Cylinder head bolt tightening sequence
—Cadillac engine

Cylinder head bolt tightening sequence
—Seville 350 V8 (© G.M. Corp.)

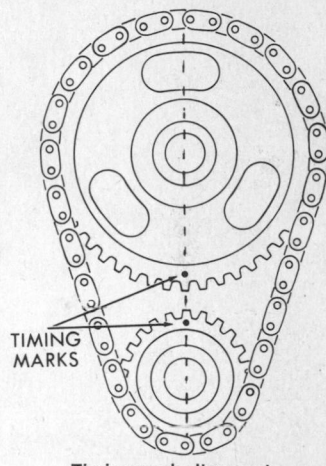

Timing mark alignment

partially remove the steering pump if working on the left head. Remove the heater hose from the rear of the right cylinder head.

5. Disconnect A.I.R. injection pump tubes from cylinder heads.
6. Remove clamps holding the wire harness to the cylinder heads and tie harness back out of the way.
7. Remove screws holding exhaust manifolds to cylinder heads.
8. Remove screws holding the rocker arm cover to the heads.
9. Remove the rocker cover.
10. Remove screws holding each rocker arm support to cylinder head, then remove rocker arm assemblies. Store these assemblies so that they may be reinstalled in their correct locations.
11. Remove pushrods and store them with their respective rocker arm assemblies.
12. Install two 7/16 x 6 in. screws to be used as lifting handles in two of the rocker arm support screw holes.
13. Remove ten cylinder-head bolts.
14. Lift cylinder head off the block.
15. Remove all gasket material from the cylinder head and block mating surfaces.
16. Install by reversing removal procedures.

When torquing the head bolts, use the three-step method. Starting from the middle of the center row of bolts and working outward (toward each end), torque the bolts to 1/3 of the total torque listed. Once this is done, repeat the same procedure, this time torquing all the bolts to 2/3 of the total listed torque. Finally torque the bolts to the recommended torque.

Timing Case Cover—Chains and Camshaft

Timing Chain Cover, Chain, and Sprocket Removal

1. Disconnect negative battery cable and drain cooling system.
2. Detach upper radiator hose retainer from cradle and position hose out of the way.
3. Remove fan, generator belt and power steering belts.
4. Remove four capscrews that secure crank pulley to harmonic balancer, then remove both pulley and balancer.
5. Remove plug from end of crankshaft, and install balancer puller pilot in one bore in the end of the crankshaft and remove balancer hub from the end of the crankshaft.
6. Drain engine oil and remove oil pan.
7. Disconnect lower radiator hose from water pump, then remove the ten screws that hold front cover to engine. Remove cover with water pump attached.
8. Remove distributor and fuel pump.
9. Remove oil slinger and fuel pump eccentric.
10. Remove two capscrews that secure camshaft sprocket.
11. Remove camshaft sprocket along with timing chain.
12. To install, reverse removal procedure.

Mount the timing chain over the camshaft and the crankshaft sprocket and start the camshaft sprocket over the shaft, being certain the aligning dowel is in a position where it will enter the hole in the camshaft freely. Make certain that the timing marks

on the sprockets are in line between shaft centers.

Camshaft sprockets sometimes install a little stiffly. However, a comparatively easy way to install a tight-fitting sprocket is to draw it on carefully with two bolts somewhat longer than the regular mounting bolts. By drawing alternately against each bolt, and tapping gently with a plastic hammer, even a very tight camshaft gear sprocket can be installed.

When the camshaft is secured, turn the engine two full revolutions until the timing marks again assume the original position. Check to make certain that the punch marks, which are stamped into the front face of the sprockets, are in line between the shaft centers.

Timing Cover Oil Seal Removal and Installation

All models are equipped with a molded-type front cover crankshaft oil seal. The seal may be replaced without removing the engine front cover.

1. Disconnect the battery and remove carburetor air cleaner.
2. Remove power steering pump drive belt.
3. Remove generator drive belt.
4. On air conditioned cars, and cars equipped with the A.I.R. system. remove the pump drive belts.
5. Raise and support the front of

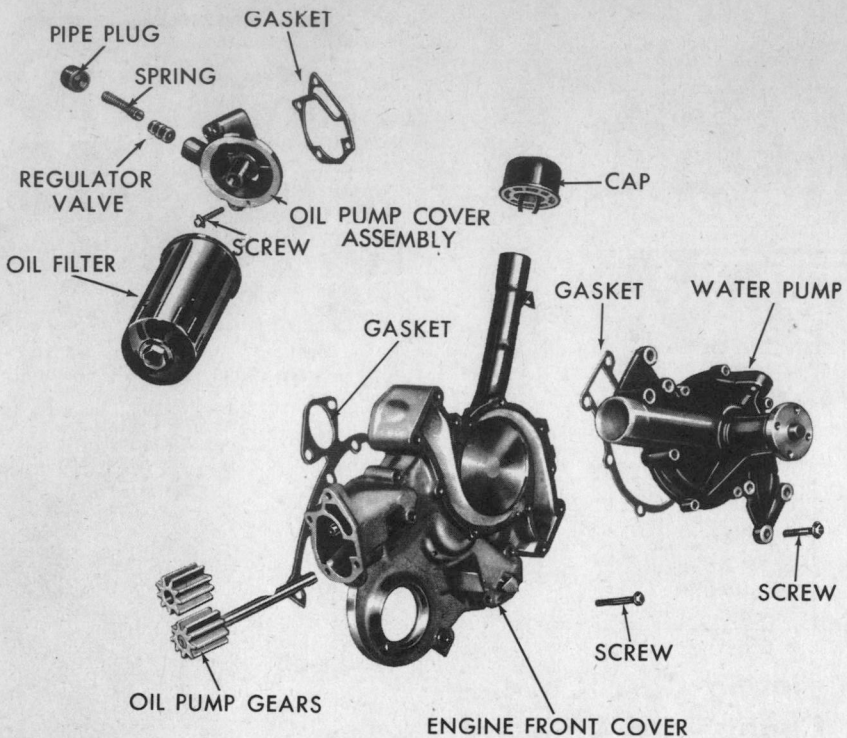

Engine front cover disassembled—Cadillac engine
(© Cadillac Div., G.M. Corp)

PIPE PLUG GASKET SPRING REGULATOR VALVE OIL FILTER SCREW OIL PUMP COVER ASSEMBLY GASKET GASKET WATER PUMP CAP SCREW SCREW OIL PUMP GEARS ENGINE FRONT COVER

the car on stands. Remove the fan.

6. Remove pulley and harmonic balancer, as outlined in Timing Chain and Sprocket Removal.

7. With a thin blade screwdriver, pry out front cover oil seal.

8. Lubricate new dual-lip oil seal with wheel bearing grease. Position seal on end of crankshaft with garter spring side toward engine.

9. Using a seal installer drive the front seal into the front cover until it bottoms.

10. Assemble and install the remaining parts in reverse order of disassembly.

Camshaft Removal and Replacement

1. Remove the radiator.
2. Remove the engine front cover and the distributor.
3. Remove the oil pump and the oil slinger from the crankshaft.
4. Remove the fuel pump and the fuel pump eccentric from the camshaft.
5. Remove the camshaft sprocket and the timing chain.

NOTE: Make certain that the aligning marks on the two sprockets are correctly aligned before removing the timing chain.

6. Remove the lifters and slide the camshaft carefully out of the engine block.

NOTE: Do not allow the camshaft lobes to scratch the camshaft bearings.

7. To install the camshaft, reverse the above procedure. Before installation, the camshaft should be lubricated with a thin coat of rear axle lubricant and then carefully inserted to avoid bearing damage.

8. The camshaft sprocket screws should be torqued to 18 ft lbs while the fuel pump eccentric screw is tightened to 35 ft lbs.

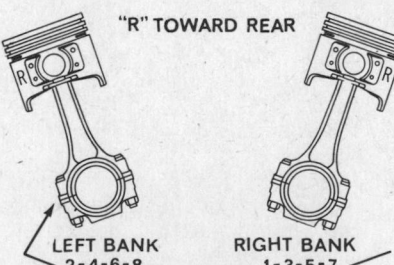

"R" TOWARD REAR

LEFT BANK 2-4-6-8   RIGHT BANK 1-3-5-7

Piston to connecting rod relationship —Cadillac engine

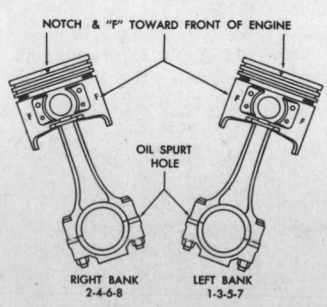

NOTCH & "F" TOWARD FRONT OF ENGINE

OIL SPURT HOLE

RIGHT BANK 2-4-6-8   LEFT BANK 1-3-5-7

Piston and connecting rod positioning —Seville 350 V8

Piston and Rod Installation

The numbers on the connecting rods face away from the camshaft; that is, the numbers on the left bank, (even) face to the left; the numbers on the right bank, (odd) face to the right. As a double check, the word *rear*, (or "R"), stamped on the piston, faces the rear of the engine on both banks and an arrow on the piston top points to the front of the engine. The rod nuts are torqued to 40 ft lbs.

On the 350 Seville V8, the piston is placed in the cylinder with the notch in the top of the piston and the "F" on the side of the piston facing toward the front of the engine. The oil spurt hole in the connecting rod faces toward the camshaft.

Lubrication

Oil Pump Removal and Installation

472, 500 V8

1. Jack up car and remove oil filter.
2. Remove five capscrews that secure oil pump to engine.

NOTE: Remove screw nearest pressure regulator last.

3. Slide drive shaft, drive gear and driven gear out of housing.
4. Remove plug from housing cover, using 5/16 in. wrench. Remove pressure regulator valve and spring.
5. Check free length of regulator spring—it should be 2.57-2.69 in.
6. Inspect gears and housing for burrs or scoring.
7. Check pump clearance limits.
8. On installation, pack the pump with petroleum jelly. Use a new gasket, engage the pump driveshaft with the distributor drive, and install screw nearest pressure regulator first. Install remaining screws and tighten all five screws to 15 ft lbs. Install oil filter, add one quart oil to engine, run engine and check for leaks.

350 V8

1. Remove the oil pan.
2. Remove the oil pump-to-rear main bearing cap attaching bolts and remove the oil pump and drive shaft extension.
3. Remove the drive shaft extension. Do not attempt to remove the washers from the shaft. The shaft extension and washers must be serviced as an assembly if the washers are not 1-11/32 in. from the end of the shaft.
4. Remove the cotter pin, spring and the pressure regulator valve. Place your thumb over the pressure regulator bore before removing the cotter pin to contain the spring.

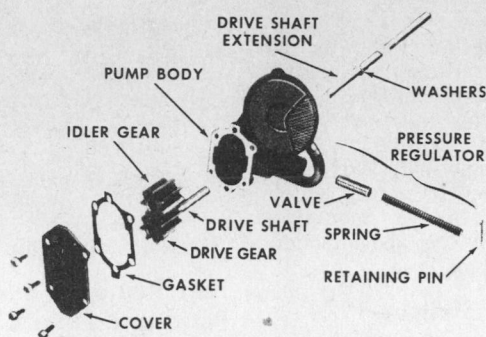

Exploded view of 350 Seville V8 oil pump
(© Cadillac Div., G.M. Corp.)

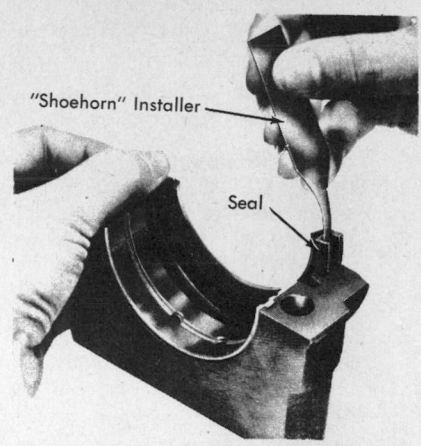

Installing rear main bearing oil seal
(© Cadillac Div., G.M. Corp)

5. Remove the oil pump cover attaching screws and remove the cover and gasket.
6. Remove the idler gear and drive gear from the pump body.
7. Check the gears for scoring and any other damage. Install new gears, if necessary.
8. Assemble and install the oil pump in reverse order of removal. The end of the drive shaft extension nearest the washers is inserted into the drive shaft.

Oil Pan Removal and Installation

472, 500 V8

1. Drain engine oil and disconnect positive battery cable.
2. Disconnect exhaust crossover pipe at exhaust manifold.
3. Disconnect exhaust support bracket at transmission extension housing, and position exhaust system to one side.
4. Remove starter motor.
5. Remove two idler arm support mounting screws from frame side member, and lower support.
6. Disconnect pitman arm at drag link, and lower steering linkage.
7. Remove transmission lower cover.
8. Remove engine oil pan.
9. When reinstalling, reverse above procedure and torque oil pan screws and nuts to 10 ft lbs. The transmission cover screws should be torqued to 20 ft lbs.

350 V8

1. Remove the wheelhousing struts from the fenders.
2. Remove the radiator cover.
3. Raise the car.
4. Remove the through-bolt from each motor mount.
5. Remove the exhaust crossover pipe.
6. Remove the starter motor.
7. Remove the torque converter cover.
8. Drain the crankcase and remove the oil pan attaching screws.
9. Raise the engine as far as necessary with a jack placed under the crankshaft pulley and remove the oil pan.

10. Clean all of the gasket material from the oil pan and engine block mating surfaces and install the oil pan in the reverse order of removal, using a new gasket kit and sealer. The rubber front and rear seals cover the tabs on the oil pan gaskets at the front cover. Torque the oil pan screws to 10 ft lbs.

Rear Main Seal Removal and Installation

472, 500 V8

1. Remove the oil pan, after removing spark plug wires and plugs.
2. Remove the rear main bearing cap and loosen the bolts holding the other four bearings about three turns each. Remove the old rear main bearing seals.
3. Clean the groove in the cap and in the block. Lubricate seals with engine oil.
4. Make an installation tool, as illustrated.
5. Start the upper half into the groove in the block with the lip facing forward and rotate it into position, using the tool as a guide. Press firmly on both ends to be sure it is protruding uniformly on each side.
6. Install the lower half of the seal into the bearing cap with the lip facing forward and one end of the seal over the ridge and flush with the split line. Hold one finger over this end to prevent it from slipping, and push the seal into seated position by applying pressure to the other end. Be sure the seal is firmly seated and protrudes evenly on each side. Do not apply pressure to the lip. This may damage the effectiveness of the seal.
7. Apply rubber cement to the mating surfaces of the block and

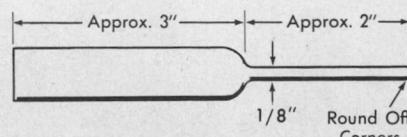

Rear main bearing oil seal installation tool

cap being careful not to get any cement on the bearing, the crankshaft or the seal. The cement coating should be about .010 in. thick.
8. Install the bearing cap, tightening the bolts with the fingers only.
9. Move the crankshaft forward and rearward by pounding on the counterweight with a plastic hammer to assure alignment of the rear main bearing thrust surfaces.
10. Tighten the bearing bolts to 90-100 ft. lbs. Be sure to tighten the bolts of the other four bearings also.
11. Reinstall the oil pan.

350 V8

The crankshaft need not be removed to replace the rear main bearing upper oil seal.

1. Drain the crankcase and remove the oil pan and rear main bearing cap.
2. Using a blunt-ended tool, drive the upper seal into its groove on each side until it is tightly packed. This is usually 1/4-3/4 in.
3. Cut pieces of new seal 1/16 in. longer than required to fill the grooves and install, packing into place.
4. Carefully trim any protruding seal, being sure not to scratch or damage the bearing surface.
5. Install a new seal in the bearing cap and install cap, tightening bolts to 120 ft lbs. Install the oil pan.

AUTOMATIC TRANSMISSION

All Cadillac cars use a Turbo Hydra-matic 400 automatic transmission.

Neutral Safety Switch through 1973

NOTE: switch is on steering column under dash.

Removal

1. Position the gear selector in the Neutral position.
2. Release the clamp and remove the switch without moving the contact carrier. The position of the carrier should be marked.
3. Remove the vacuum hoses after they have been marked and disconnect the wires from the switch.

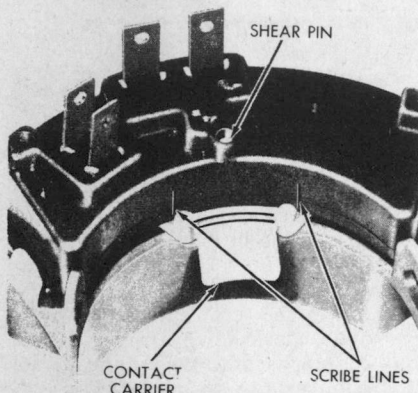

Neutral safety switch
(© Cadillac Div., G.M. Corp)

4. Installation is accomplished by reversing the above procedure.

Adjustment

1. Check that the gear lever is correctly adjusted and that the neutral safety switch is properly positioned by this check.
2. Set the handbrake. Put the hand lever on the steering column in drive. Hold the ignition key on and slowly move the hand lever toward Neutral or Park until the starter cranks and the engine runs.
3. Without moving the lever farther, press the accelerator to determine whether the transmission is really in Neutral or Park.
4. If all is correct, the engine will have started when the hand lever got to the neutral position and the transmission will not be in gear. Also, back-up lights will go on with transmission in Reverse.
NOTE: a vacuum leak that can be corrected by moving shift lever is an indication that the switch only needs adjustment and is not defective.
5. Adjust the neutral safety switch by turning it and its mounting bracket until the above conditions are met.

Neutral Safety Switch—1974 and later

On all models 1974 and later, the neutral safety switch works mechanically, rather than electrically. When the transmission selector is any position other than Park or Neutral, the key cannot be turned to "Start."

Shift Linkage Adjustment

1. Loosen nut on steering column manual lever on full-size Cadillacs and the adjustment screw on the relay lever on Seville.
2. From under the car, pull relay rod up, positioning transmission shift valve in Park, then push rod down to the Neutral third step.
3. Position selector lever in Neutral.
4. Tighten nut on steering column manual lever on full-size Cadillacs and the adjustment screw on the relay lever on Seville.
5. Check that positions selected on selector lever correspond with appropriate detents on transmission.

Kickdown Adjustment

1. Remove the air cleaner.
2. Make certain that the idle speed is set correctly and that the carburetor is operating on the low-speed circuit.
3. Loosen the switch mounting screws and insert 0.094 in. wire gauge into the hole in the lower wire terminal.
4. With the gauge in place, adjust the position of the switch so that the lever just touches the carburetor adaptor plate arm. The switch should make contact above 60° of throttle opening.
5. After adjusting, tighten the mounting screws and remove the gauge.
6. Reinstall the air cleaner.

Pan Removal and Installation, Fluid and Filter Change

1. Either use a suction gun to remove two quarts of fluid through the oil filler tube, or raise the vehicle and loosen one corner of the transmission pan and allow the fluid to drain into a container.
2. Remove the remaining pan attaching screws and remove the pan and gasket. Discard the gasket.
3. Clean the pan with solvent and dry it throughly.
4. Remove the filter retaining bolt.
5. Remove the intake pipe and filter assembly. Remove the intake pipe O-ring and discard the filter and O-ring.
6. Install the new intake pipe O-ring on the pipe and install the intake pipe into the new filter assembly.

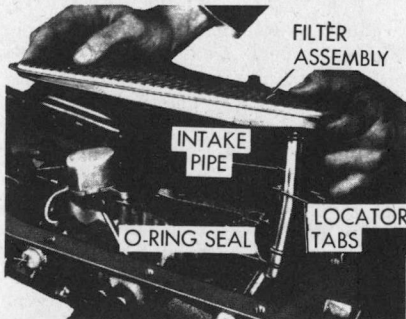

Removing the transmission filter assembly
(© Cadillac Div., G.M. Corp.)

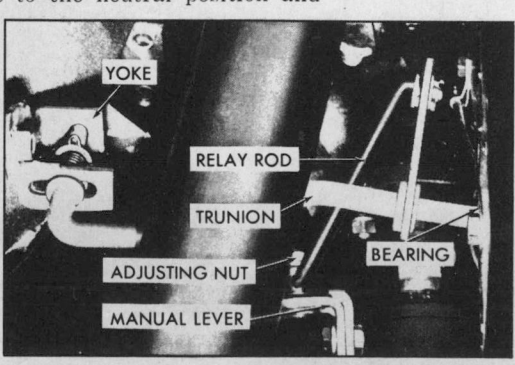

Manual linkage adjustment—1970-72
(© Cadillac Div., G.M. Corp.)

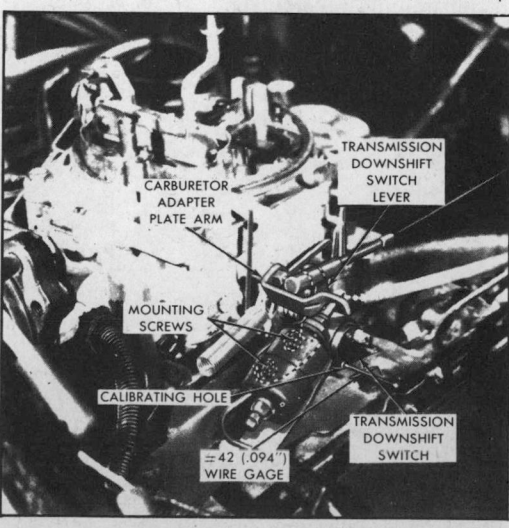

Downshift switch adjustment
(© Cadillac Div., G.M. Corp.)

7. Install the intake pipe and filter assembly into the case bore. Install the filter retaining bolt.

8. Install a new gasket on the pan and install the pan, tightening the retaining screws to 12 ft lbs.

9. Lower the car and add 4 quarts of Dexron automatic transmission fluid through the filler tube. If the filter was not replaced, only add 2 quarts.

10. Start the engine and allow it to run at normal idle speed for 1½ minutes with the gear selector in Park.

11. Check the fluid level. With the fluid below normal operating temperature the level should be ¼ in. below the ADD mark on the dip stick. Add fluid as necessary.

U-JOINTS

Universal joints and driveshafts can be divided into two groups: single-piece shaft models (full-size Cadillac and Seville models except Fleetwood 75 sedan and limousine and Commercial Chassis), and two-piece shaft models (Fleetwood 75 sedan and limousine and Commercial Chassis models only).

Single-Piece Shaft Removal and Installation

Full-Size Cadillac

1. Place transmission in Neutral and jack up car; support on axle stands.
2. Remove the two accessible rear U-joint flange capscrews.
3. Rotate driveshaft and remove other two capscrews, after supporting rear of shaft on a chain. Never let the full weight of the driveshaft be supported only by the front constant velocity joint.
4. Push shaft forward to clear pinion flange, then pull rearward to disengage slip yoke from transmission. Plug transmission to prevent oil leak.
5. Lubricate slip yoke inside diameter with gear lube, outside of splines with A.T.F.
6. To install, reverse removal procedure, tightening rear U-joint fasteners to 70 ft. lbs. Place transmission in Park to hold shaft while tightening capscrews.

Seville

1. Raise the vehicle with the transmission in Park and the front of the car slightly lower than the rear, if possible.
2. Mark the position of the ball support yoke in relation to the axle pinion flange.
3. Remove the ball support yoke attaching screws. Support the drive shaft as the last screw is being removed.
4. Remove the drive shaft by pushing it forward into the rear of the transmission until the ball support yoke clears the differential pinion flange, and then pulling it rearward out of the transmission. Fluid could leak out of the rear of the transmission if the front isn't lowered enough. Plug the opening with a clean lint free cloth, if necessary.
5. Install the drive shaft in the reverse order of removal. Tighten the ball support yoke attaching screws to 70 ft lbs.

Two-Piece Shaft Removal and Installation

1. Follow Steps 1-6 of *Single-Piece Shaft Removal and Installation*, with the addition of the following step:
1A. Remove center bearing support after matchmarking it and crossmember. When installing, tighten the bolts to 16 ft. lbs.

U-Joint Removal and Installation

1. Remove the drive shaft.
2. Remove the lockrings from the bearings. If the original universal joints are being replaced, the nylon ring will sear off when the bearing is removed.
3. Match-mark the yoke and the shaft so that the shaft parts can be reassembled easily.
4. Position the yoke or bearing trunnion on vise jaws. Using a bearing remover, or a similar tool, and a hammer tap the remover until the bearing is driven out of the yoke about ½ in.
5. Place the tool in the vise and then drive the yoke away from the tool until the bearing is removed. (See illustration.)
6. Use the no. 4 and 5 procedures for all other bearings.
7. To install the bearings lubricate the cross arm ends with universal joint grease and install the joint cross into position.
8. Start the bearings into the driveshaft yoke and press them into position using a vise.

NOTE: If the bearings are not positioned with normal vise pressure, there is a possibility that one of the needle bearings has fallen out of place.

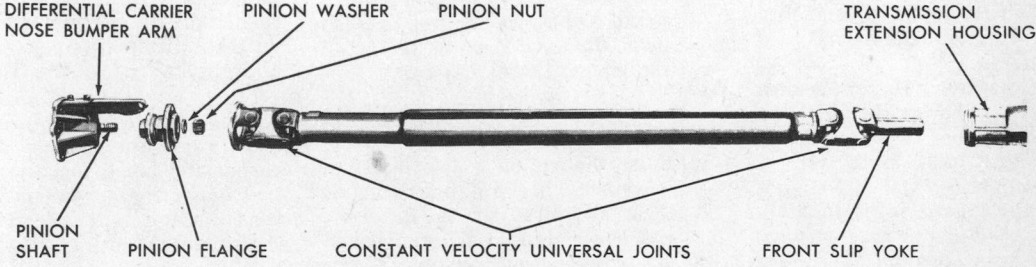

Single-piece driveshaft (ⓒ Cadillac Div., G.M. Corp)

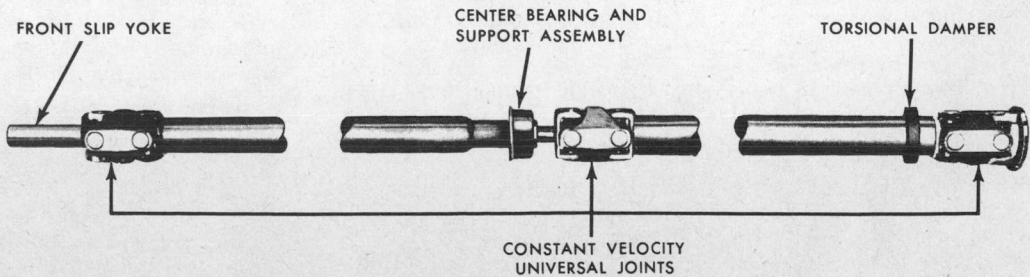

Two-piece driveshaft with C.V. joints (ⓒ Cadillac Div., G.M. Corp)

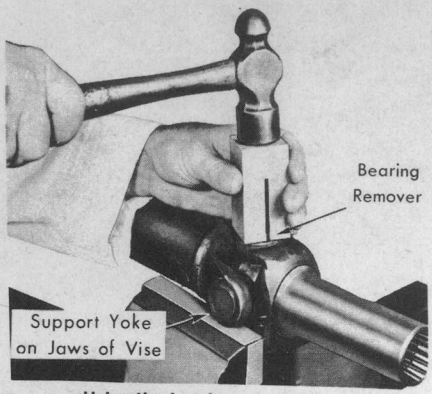

Using the bearing removal tool
(© Cadillac Div., G.M. Corp)

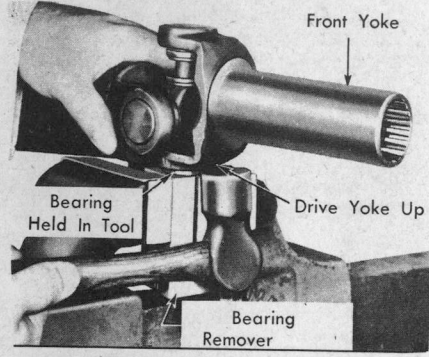

Removing the universal joint bearing
(© Cadillac Div., G.M. Corp)

9. Use the same installation procedure for the other bearings.
10. Install the lock rings.

REAR AXLE

Axle Shaft, Bearing, and Seal

Removal and Installation
Full-Size Cadillac

1. Raise the rear of the car and support it. Remove the wheel and brake drum.
2. Remove the four nuts that secure the retainer and backing plate to the axle housing.
3. Remove the axle shaft with a slide hammer.

NOTE: When the axle shaft is removed the outer bearing race may remain in the axle housing. This does not indicate bearing failure. If the bearing is to be replaced, make sure the old outer bearing race is removed from the axle housing.

4. Using a chisel and hammer, split the bearing retainer next to the bearing. Be careful not to damage the bearing of the axle shaft. Remove and discard the retainer.
5. Stand the axle shaft upright on the flanged end and use two screwdrivers to pry the oil seal away from the bearing.
6. Remove axle bearing from the axle shaft with a press.

7. Make sure that the axle shaft and bearing are clean and install the bearing seal onto the axle shaft. The oil seal is properly installed when it can't be pushed on any further.
8. Apply a light coat of wheel bearing grease to the bearing.
9. If a tapered roller bearing is used, position the bearing on the axle shaft with the narrow ring of the bearing facing the flanged end of the axle shaft. If a straight roller bearing is installed, the loose ring at one end of the inner race must be installed toward the flange.
10. Press the bearing onto the axle shaft until the bearing bottoms against the shoulder on the shaft.
11. Press the retainer on the axle shaft until the retainer bottoms against the bearing.
12. If the axle bearing has been replaced because of bearing failure, inspect the axle housing and differential carrier for metal chips and clean thoroughly.
13. Apply a thin film of wheel bearing grease to the wheelbearing bore in the axle housing. Also, lubricate the oil seal and the outer race of the bearing with wheel bearing grease.
14. Install a new gasket on the brake backing plate.
15. Install the axle shaft onto the axle housing, using extreme care to align the oil seal cover with the axle housing mounting bolts. Rotate the axle shaft so the axle shaft splines engage the differential side gear splines.
16. Install the four nuts on the axle housing flange bolts to hold the gasket, brake backing plate, and oil seal cover in place. Tighten the nuts to 50 ft lbs. Install the brake drum and one nut to push it on. Remove the nut to install the wheel. Lower the car.

Seville

1. Raise the car on a hoist and remove the wheel and brake drum.
2. Clean any dirt from the differential cover and loosen the cover attaching screw, allowing the lubricant to drain out into a suitable container.
3. Remove the pinion shaft lockscrew and remove the pinion shaft.
4. Push in on the flanged end of the axle shaft and remove the "C" lock from the splined end of the axle shaft.
5. Remove the axle shaft from the housing, being cautious not to damage the oil seal.
6. Use a screwdriver to pry the oil seal out of the bore. Use an axle shaft bearing puller on a slide

hammer to remove the axle bearing from the bearing bore.
7. Install the new bearing in the bearing bore until it is 0.550 in. from the end of the axle tube. Use a block of wood and a hammer to tap the bearing in place. Install the axle shaft bearing seal until it is flush with the end of the axle tube.
8. Slide the axle shaft into the housing until the splines on the end of the shaft engage the splines of the differential side gear. Handle the shaft gently when trying to engage the splines.
9. Install the axle shaft "C" lock on the splined end of the axle shaft in the differential. Push the shaft outward so that the shaft lock seats in the counterbore of the differential side gear.
10. Install the pinion cross shaft through the differential case and pinion gears. Align the lock screw hole and install the lock screw, tightening it to 25 ft lbs.
11. Clean the differential housing and cover mating surfaces and install the cover with a new gasket.
12. Fill the differential with lubricant, install the brake drum and wheel, and lower the car.

JACKING, HOISTING

All Except Seville

When jacking under front suspension arms, make sure lift is made from the flattened portion on the flange of the lower arms.

When lifting on frame area, make sure of solid contact at the corners of the perimeter of the frame with the lift points close to the bend at front and rear of the frame.

Seville

To raise the car on a twin-post suspension hoist, place the lift adapters under the lower control arms at the front and under the axle tube near the spring mounting pads at the rear.

When using a framehoist, place the lift adapters under the front sub-frame members just in front of the rear cross member and under the rear sub-frame members opposite the front rear spring shackles.

FRONT SUSPENSION

All Cadillacs use the same front suspension system (except Eldorado). The system is a coil spring suspension which consists of two upper and two lower control arm assemblies, shock absorbers, front struts, a stabilizer bar and two steering knuckles, and a pair of steel coiled springs.

For further information on front suspension alignment consult the "Unit Repair Section."

Shock Absorber Removal and Installation

1. Open the hood. Remove the retaining nut from the frame spring tower. Use a box wrench to prevent the shock stem from turning while the nut is being unfastened.
2. Take off the bolt, nut, and lockwasher which secure the lower end of the shock to the suspension arm.
3. Remove the shock through the bottom of the lower arm.

Installation is performed in the following order:

If you are replacing the grommet, dip it in soapy water and twist it through the frame hole.

NOTE: Don't use silicone lubricant.

4. Install the retainer in the upper stem.
5. Extend the shock rod as far as it will go.
6. Install the shock up through the coil spring and guide the stem into the grommet.
7. Position the lower end of the shock on the lower control arm. Install the bolt lockwasher and nut. Tighten the bolt to 55 ft lbs (19 ft lbs on Seville).
8. Tighten the retaining nut on the upper stem to 15 ft lbs, while holding the stem with a box wrench to keep it from turning. On Seville, tighten the nut to the end of the threads (about 1⅛ in. of stud is above the nut).

Lower Control Arm and Coil Spring Removal and Installation

1. Disconnect front shock at its upper mount.
2. Raise car and support under front frame side rails.
3. Remove wheel and tire assembly.
4. Disconnect stabilizer link from lower arm or spring to be removed.
5. Disconnect tie-strut at lower arm.
6. Remove bolt holding shock to lower arm, and remove shock from car.
7. Remove nut from pivot bolt in lower arm at frame mount.
8. Position jack under outboard end of lower suspension arm so that jack is supporting the arm.
9. Remove locknut from lower ball joint stud. Install standard nut on joint stud and run nut to within two threads of knuckle.

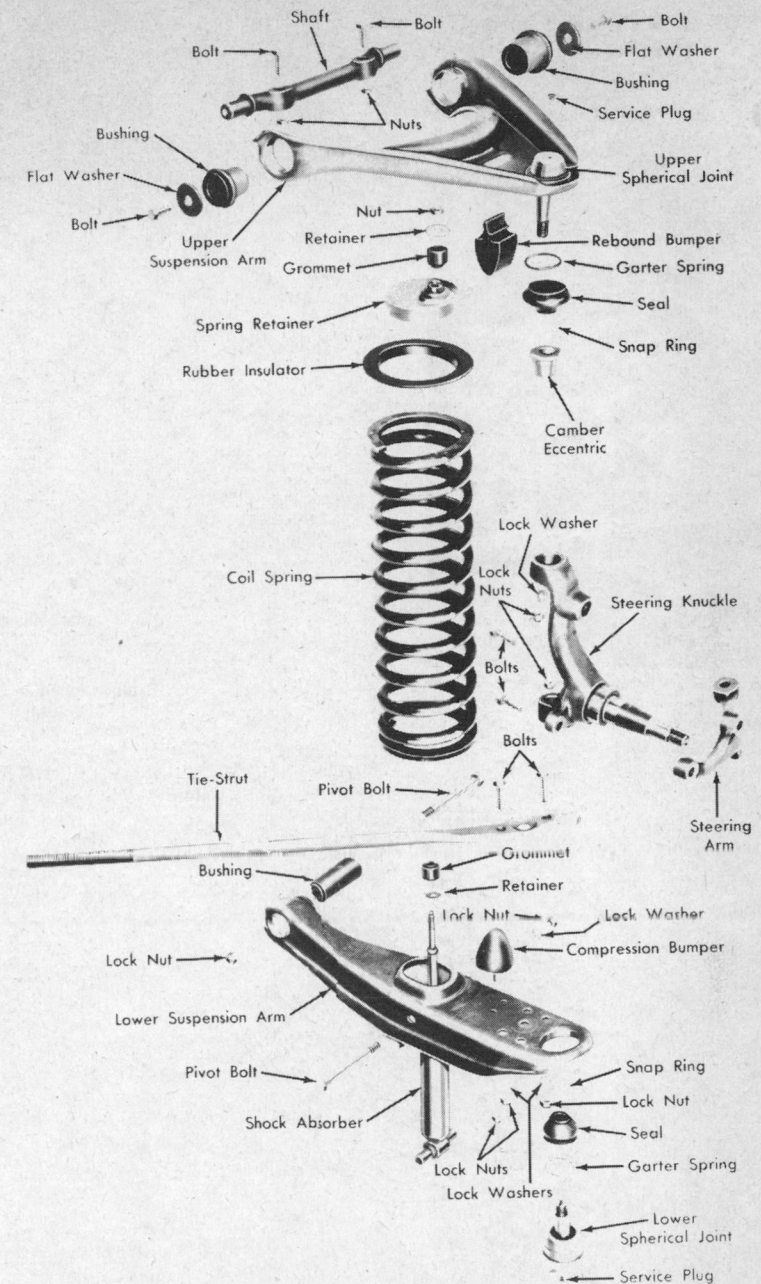

Typical front suspension—1970
(© Cadillac Div., G.M. Corp.)

10. Strike knuckle with a hammer in area of ball joint stud to loosen the joint. Raising the opposite rear corner of the car will help compress the spring and assist in removing the joint stud from the knuckle.
11. Use jack to lift spring load from nut and remove nut from joint stud. Wrap a chain around the spring and through the lower control arm as a safety measure.
12. Slowly lower jack and remove spring.
13. Remove pivot bolt from lower arm at frame mount and remove the arm.
14. Install by reversing the removal procedure.

Ball Joint Inspection

NOTE: Before performing this inspection, make sure the wheel bearings are adjusted correctly and that the A-arm bushings are in good condition.

1. Jack the car up under the front lower control arm at the spring seat.
2. Raise the car until there is 1–2 in. of clearance under the wheel.
3. Insert a bar under the wheel and pry upward. If the wheel raises more than ⅛ in. the ball joints are worn. Determine if the upper or lower ball joint is worn by visual inspection while prying on the wheel.

NOTE: Due to the distribution of forces in the suspension, the lower ball joint is usually the defective joint. Also, 1973 and later Cadillacs and Sevilles are equipped with wear indicators on the lower ball joint. As long as the wear indicator neck extends below the ball stud seat, replacement is unnecessary.

COIL SPRING
1" ½"
TIE STRUT
LOWER CONTROL ARM

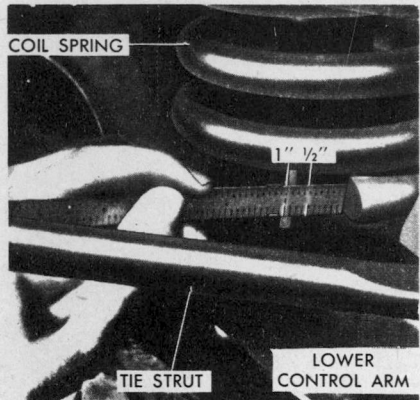

Install the front coil spring on a full size Cadillac so that the end of the coil is ½ to 1 in. from the edge of the lower control arm
(© Cadillac Div., G.M. Corp.)

SHIM
SHAFT
SPHERICAL JOINT
UPPER SUSPENSION ARM
BUSHING
WASHER
NUT
BUMPER
COIL SPRING
BUSHING
FRAME
SPLASH SHIELD
BRAKE CALIPER
STEERING KNUCKLE
STABILIZER BAR
SPHERICAL JOINT
NUT
HUB AND ROTOR ASSEMBLY
CAP
LINK BOLT
BEARING CUP
BEARING
SHOCK ABSORBER
WASHER

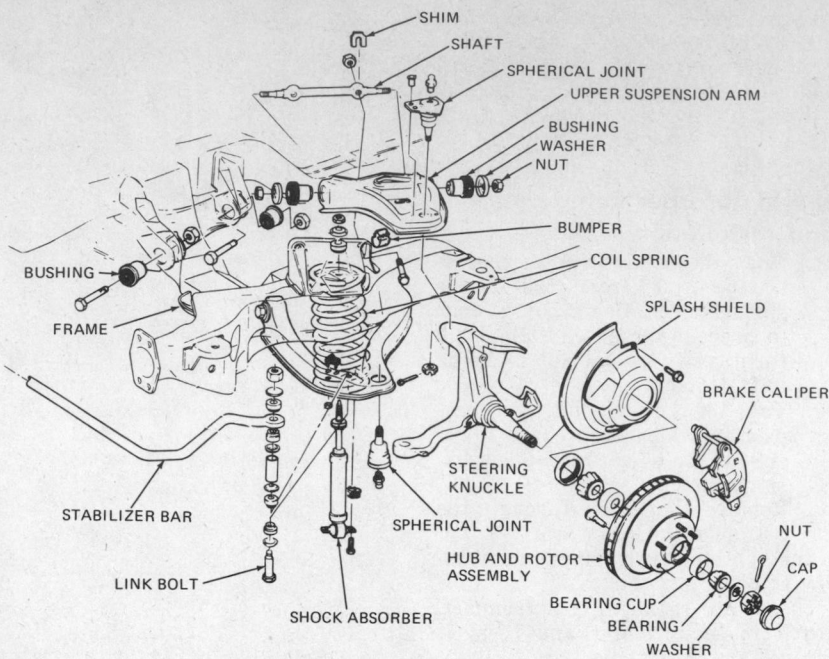

Exploded view of Seville front suspension
(© Cadillac Div., G.M. Corp.)

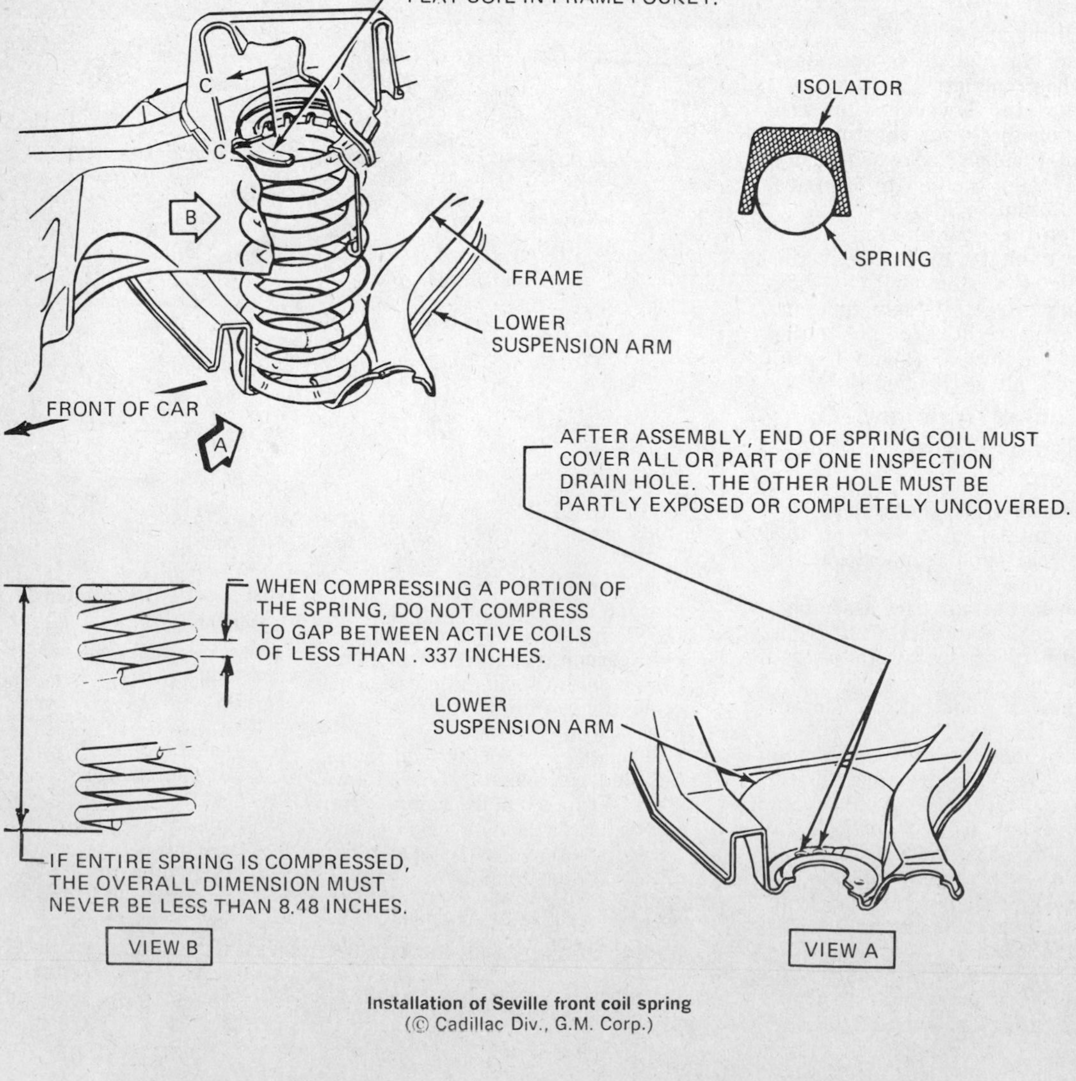

SPRING TO BE INSTALLED WITH FLAT COIL IN FRAME POCKET.
C
C
B
FRAME
LOWER SUSPENSION ARM
FRONT OF CAR
A
ISOLATOR
SPRING
AFTER ASSEMBLY, END OF SPRING COIL MUST COVER ALL OR PART OF ONE INSPECTION DRAIN HOLE. THE OTHER HOLE MUST BE PARTLY EXPOSED OR COMPLETELY UNCOVERED.
WHEN COMPRESSING A PORTION OF THE SPRING, DO NOT COMPRESS TO GAP BETWEEN ACTIVE COILS OF LESS THAN . 337 INCHES.
LOWER SUSPENSION ARM
IF ENTIRE SPRING IS COMPRESSED, THE OVERALL DIMENSION MUST NEVER BE LESS THAN 8.48 INCHES.
VIEW B
VIEW A

Installation of Seville front coil spring
(© Cadillac Div., G.M. Corp.)

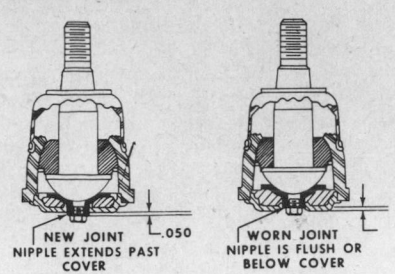

NEW JOINT NIPPLE EXTENDS PAST COVER ⌐.050

WORN JOINT NIPPLE IS FLUSH OR BELOW COVER

Lower ball joint wear indicator—1973 and later (© Cadillac Div., G.M. Corp.)

Lower Ball Joint Removal and Installation

Full-Size Cadillac

1. Follow Steps 1-12 of *Lower Control Arm and Coil Spring Removal and Installation*.
2. Remove band and seal from ball joint.
3. If ball joint vertical movement exceeds 1/16 in. (.062 in.), press old ball joint out of lower control arm, using press tool.
4. Press new joint into arm until it bottoms on flange, using standard nut and flat washer to pull joint into position.
5. Reverse Steps 1-12 of *Lower Control Arm and Coil Spring Removal and Installation*, tightening stud nut to 85 ft lbs.

Seville

1. Raise the car and remove the wheel and tire.
2. Remove the lower ball joint stud cotter pin. Loosen (not more than one turn), but do not remove, the stud nut.
3. Install a ball joint removal tool between the studs and turn the threaded end of the tool until the stud is free of the steering knuckle.

Caution

If a hoist is not used, the lower control arm must be supported so that the spring cannot force the arm down.

4. Remove the lower stud nut. Pull out on bottom of tire and simultaneously push tire up to free steering knuckle from ball joint stud.
5. Lift up on upper control arm (with steering knuckle and hub attached), and place a block of wood between the frame and the upper arm. Be careful not to pull on the brake hose when lifting the knuckle and hub.

NOTE: Remove the tie-rod end from the steering knuckle only if necessary.

6. Use a ball joint removal tool to push the ball joint from the lower control arm.
7. To install, place the lower ball joint in the lower control arm and seat it. Position the bleed vent in the rubber boot of the new ball joint facing inward.
8. Turn the ball joint stud cotter pin hole fore and aft. Remove the wood block holding the upper control arm.

NOTE: Examine the tapered hole in the steering knuckle. Clean the area. The knuckle MUST be replaced if any out-of-roundness, deformation, or damage is found.

9. Attach the ball joint stud to the steering knuckle and install the stud nut. Torque the nut to 80 ft lbs and install a new cotter pin.

NOTE: 125 ft lbs or 1/6 turn maximum is allowed to align the cotter pin slot. Do not back off the nut to install the cotter pin.

10. Lubricate the ball joint. If removed, install the tie-rod end and torque the nut to 35 ft lbs. Install the cotter pin.
11. Install the wheel and tire and lower the car. Have the front wheel alignment checked and adjusted as necessary.

Upper Ball Joint Removal and Installation

Full-Size Cadillac

The upper ball joints on 1970 and later full-size models are pressed into the upper control arms and are tack-welded to the arms at two places. Do not attempt to remove the upper ball joints as any rewelding could damage the joint seals or weaken the control arms. The upper control arms and ball joints are replaced as an assembly.

Seville

1. Raise the car on a hoist.
2. Remove the wheel and tire.
3. Remove the upper ball joint stud cotter pin.
4. Remove the brake caliper assembly and support it from the frame with a length of wire.
5. Loosen the stud nut, but not more than one turn.
6. Strike the top of the steering knuckle until the ball joint is free of the steering knuckle.
7. Support the lower control arm with a jack so that the steering knuckle can be disconnected from the ball joint.
8. Remove upper ball joint stud nut and remove the joint from the steering knuckle and allow the knuckle to swing out of the way.
9. Lift the upper control arm and place a block of wood between it and the frame as a support.
10. If the ball joint has any perceptible side-to-side shake or can be turned in its socket with your fingers, then it should be replaced.
11. Remove the rivets from the upper control arm with either a chisel or a grinding wheel. Drive them out with a punch after removing the heads. Do not damage the ball joint seat.

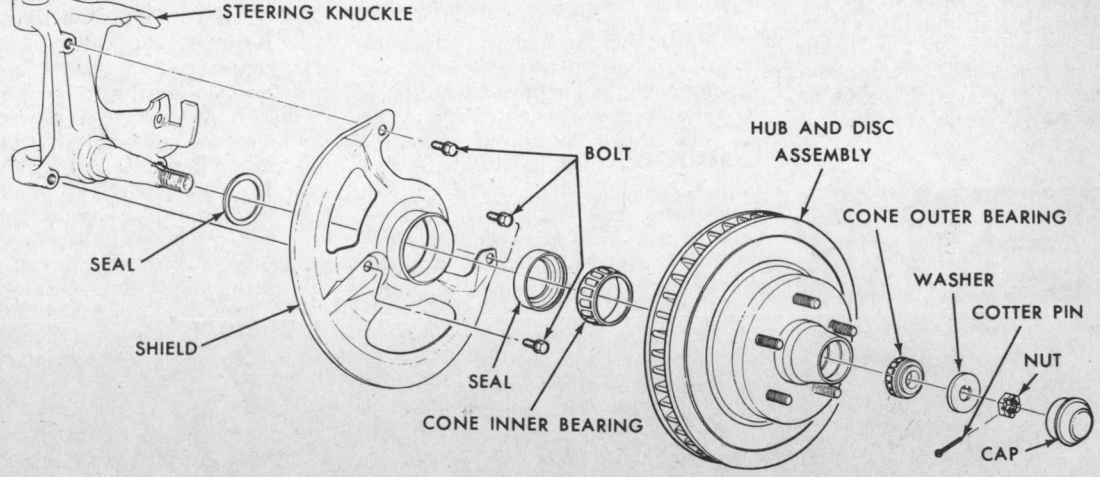

STEERING KNUCKLE

BOLT

HUB AND DISC ASSEMBLY

CONE OUTER BEARING

SEAL

WASHER

COTTER PIN

SHIELD

SEAL

NUT

CONE INNER BEARING

CAP

Front disc brake hub assembly (© Cadillac Div., G.M. Corp)

C279

12. Install the new ball joint in the upper control arm and attach it with the nuts and bolts provided. Insert the bolts from the bottom and tighten them to 25 ft lbs.
13. Turn the ball joint stud so the cotter pin hole runs front-to-rear.
14. Remove the block of wood from between the frame and the upper control arm.
15. Before installing the ball joint stud in the steering knuckle, check the tapered hole and remove any dirt or debris. If the hole is distorted or damaged, the steering knuckle must be replaced.
16. Install the ball joint stud in the hole in the top of the steering knuckle. Install the castellated nut and tighten it to 60 ft lbs. Tighten the nut to a maximum of 100 ft lbs to install the cotter pin. Do not back the nut off in order to install the cotter pin.
17. Install the brake caliper assembly.
18. Grease the ball joint.
19. Install the wheel and tire and lower the car.

Wheel Bearing Adjustment

1970-71 Full-Size Cadillac

1. Tighten the adjusting nut to 30 ft lbs while rotating the wheel.
2. Back off ¼ turn (90°) and insert the cotter pin. If the pin cannot be inserted, loosen the adjusting nut until it can be installed.
3. Peen the cotter pin over so that it cannot be moved within its hole.

1972 and Later Full-Size Cadillac, 1976 and Later Seville

1. Rotate the wheel and tighten the adjusting nut to 15 ft lbs.
2. Back off the nut until it is free and then tighten it finger tight.
3. Insert the cotter pin. If the pin cannot be installed in this position, back off the nut until the holes align. Make certain that the pin fits tight. If it can be moved with your fingers, it should be replaced.

REAR SUSPENSION

All Except Commercial and Seville

A four-link rear suspension system, consisting of upper and lower control arms, coil springs and shock absorbers is used. The coil springs are placed on brackets on the rear axle housing at their lower ends, the upper ends being seated in the frame

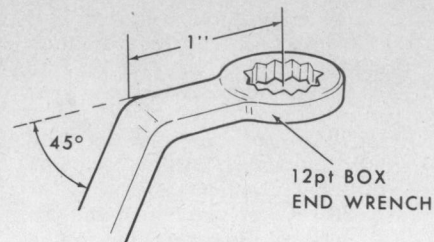

Rear shock absorber wrench
(© Cadillac Div., G.M. Corp)

crossmember. Cars can be equipped with Automatic Level Control.

Commercial Chassis and Seville

The Commercial Chassis and Seville use semi-elliptic leaf springs. Automatic Level Control is standard on Seville models and optional on Commercial Chassis.

Shock Absorber Removal and Installation

Full-Size Cadillac

1. Raise the rear of the vehicle and support both the frame and the axle with separate jacks.
2. If the vehicle is equipped with Automatic Level Control, remove the air lines at the shocks.

Caution The shocks act as rebound stops for the rear suspension and under no circumstances should the rear end be raised excessively high while disconnecting the shocks, unless both the rear axle and the frame are supported.

3. Remove the upper retaining bolts and nuts. To perform this, bend a ½ in. box end wrench to form a 45° angle at a point one inch from the center of the box diameter. This is used to hold the upper mounting nut.
4. Remove the lower retaining nut while holding the stem by the grommet to keep the stem from turning. Pull the shock off.
5. Installation is the reverse of removal.

Seville

1. Raise the car and support both the frame and rear axle.
2. Remove the air lines at the shock absorbers.

Caution The shocks act as rebound stops for the rear suspension and under no circumstances should the rear end be raised excessively high while disconnecting the shocks, unless both the rear axle and the frame are supported.

3. Remove the shock absorber upper and lower retaining bolts and remove the shock absorber.
NOTE: The left-hand shock absorber has two air line connections; the right has only one.

4. To install, position the crossbar of the upper mount to the underbody so that the shock angles toward the lower mount. The line connections are to the front on the left-side; to the rear on the right-side.
5. Install and tighten the upper retaining bolts to 12 ft lbs.
6. Place the shock absorber lower mount into the mounting bracket. Install and tighten the retaining bolt and nut to 45 ft lbs.
7. Install the air line fittings at the shocks. (The line with the black and white stripe goes to the lower port on the left-hand shock). Tighten the fittings to 35 in. lbs.
8. Inflate the reservoir through the service valve to 140 psi.
9. Disconnect the overtravel lever at the underbody bracket and push the arm up to inflate the shock absorbers. Do not put the car weight on the shocks until they are inflated as they may be damaged.
10. Return the overtravel lever to the normal position and reconnect it to the axle bracket.
11. Lower the car and check system for proper operation.

Coil Spring Removal and Installation

1970

1. Jack up rear of car and place axle stands under frame side rails.
2. Place a jack under the differential housing.
3. Remove tire and wheel assemblies.
4. If car has A.L.C., disconnect link at overtravel lever and position it in center position.

Caution The shock absorbers act as stops for the suspension. Make certain that both the axle and frame are supported before proceeding further.

5. Remove shock absorber lower retaining nuts and washers.
6. Remove rear bolts from upper control arms, then free links from mountings.
NOTE: it may be necessary to place another jack under differential pinion housing to facilitate bolt removal.
7. If removing right spring, disconnect brake hose at crossmember bracket and disconnect parking brake cable strap. Lower jacks under differential.

Caution Do not allow the differential to wind up as it is lowered as the spring may fly out.

8. Place floor jack under control arm opposite of spring being removed. (If removing right spring, place jack under left control arm and vice-versa.)

9. Jack up on lower control arm until spring can be removed.
10. To install, reverse removal procedure. Tighten upper and lower control arm bolts to 75 ft. lbs.

1971-77

1. Follow Steps 1-5 of previous procedure.
2. Position container to catch brake fluid, then disconnect brake hose from steel line at frame.
3. Remove brake hose and clip from frame.
4. Disconnect rear U-joint and support driveshaft on a chain.
5. Remove nuts and bolts that secure both upper control arms to axle brackets.
6. Lower rear axle assembly slowly until springs are free.

Caution Do not allow the differential to wind up as it is lowered as the spring may fly out.

7. To install, reverse removal procedure. Tighten upper and lower control arm bolts to 75 ft. lbs.

Leaf Spring Removal and Installation

Commercial Chassis

1. Jack up car and support on axle stands at frame side rails.
2. Place axle stands under axle housing, after jacking up housing.
3. Remove front eye bolt nut and drive out bolt.
4. Disconnect shock absorber from U-bolt plate.
5. Remove rear shackle nuts.
6. Remove U-bolt plate nuts, plate and insulators.
7. Disconnect rear shackle links and lower spring.
8. To install, reverse removal procedure. Tighten shackle nuts to 70 ft. lbs., U-bolt nuts to 45 ft. lbs., and lower shock nuts to 50 ft. lbs.

Seville

1. Raise the rear of the car and support it so the axle can be raised or lowered. Raise the axle so that all tension is relieved from the spring.
2. Disconnect the rear automatic leveling valve overtravel lever from its link and hold the lever in the exhaust position (down) to deflate the shock absorbers.
3. Disconnect the lower half of the shock absorbers and move them out of the way.
4. Loosen the parking brake adjustment at the equalizer and remove the parking brake cable clip from the front retaining bracket

on the spring. Remove the cable clamps from the under side of the springs.
5. Loosen the spring front eye bushing-to-retaining bracket bolt.
6. Remove the bolts retaining the front spring bracket to the underbody.
7. Lower the axle enough to permit access to the front eye bolt and remove the bracket from the spring.

NOTE: The front eye bushing can be replaced at this time.

8. Remove the U-bolt and T-bolt nuts retaining the lower spring plate to the axle and stabilizer bar brackets.
9. Remove the upper and lower spring pads and spring plate.
10. Support the spring with a jack stand and remove the two nuts from the rear shackle.
11. Separate the shackle and remove the spring from the vehicle.
12. If the spring is being replaced, remove the spring damper for installation on the new spring by removing the clamp bolt and bending the bottom half of the clamp down about 2 in. Slide the clamp rearward over the damper and remove the damper from the spring.
13. Position the spring damper on the new spring and position it $\frac{1}{8}$ in. from the front spring eye. Slide the clamp forward over the damper and position the clamp at the second leaf of the spring.

NOTE: The clamp must face upward and the nut must be on the outside of the spring.

Install the clamp bolt pointing up and tighten to 20 ft lbs.

NOTE: Do not tighten any of the attaching hardware to specifications until step 25. Allow the retaining nuts and bolts to remain only finger tight until the entire spring is assembled; before lowering the car.

14. Position the front eye of the spring to the front mounting bracket and install the attaching bolt with the head on the inside. Tighten the bolt to 105 ft lbs.
15. Install the upper shackle bushings in the frame. Position the shackles to the bushings and install the bolt and nut, tightening to 50 ft lbs.
16. Install the bushing halves in the rear spring eye and install the spring to the shackle, tightening the lower shackle bolt and nut to 50 ft lbs.
17. Raise the front end of the spring and position the bracket to the underbody. Make sure the tab on the bracket is aligned in the slot in the underbody.
18. Install the screws retaining the front spring bracket to the underbody and tighten to 30 ft lbs.

19. Position the spring upper cushion between the spring and the axle bracket so the cushion ribs align with the bracket locating ribs.
20. Position the lower mounting plate over the locating dowel on the lower spring pad and install the retaining nuts, tightening them to 45 ft lbs.
21. Position the stabilizer brackets to the lower spring plate and tighten the retaining bolts and nuts to 30 ft lbs.
22. Connect the lower shock absorber mount to the lower spring bracket and tighten to 45 ft lbs.
23. Install the parking brake cable under the leaf spring and secure it at the front of the spring with the wire clip and clamp. Adjust the parking brake cable.
24. Connect the rear leveling valve overtravel lever to its link.
25. Tighten all of the attaching hardware to the specifications given in the preceding text.
26. Lower the vehicle.

BRAKES

All Cadillacs have power-assisted, hydraulic front and rear brakes. They also use a vacuum-release operated parking brake. All cars are equipped with single-piston, sliding-caliper front disc brakes and the rear drum system.

For information relating to brake shoe replacement and adjustment, wheel cylinder and caliper overhaul, and brake bleeding refer to the brake "Unit Repair Section."

Beginning 1976, "Hydro-boost" is installed on Fleetwood 75 limousine models and the Commercial Chassis. Hydro-boost is a hydraulically-assisted power brake booster. The power steering pump provides the hydraulic fluid pressure to operate both the power brake booster and the power steering gear.

Refer to the "Cadillac Eldorado" car section for Hydro-boost service procedures.

Power Brake Unit Removal and Installation

Full Size Cadillac

1. Disconnect and cap hydraulic lines from master cylinder.
2. Disconnect vacuum line from vacuum check valve on unit.
3. Remove steering column lower cover.
4. Remove cotter pin, washer and spring spacer that secure power unit pushrod to brake pedal arm.
5. Remove the four nuts that secure power unit to firewall, then remove power unit.

6. To install, reverse removal procedure. The torque on the brake lines should be no greater than 20 ft lbs. Bleed the hydraulic system.

Seville

1. Remove any vacuum from the booster by depressing the brake pedal several times.
2. Disconnect the two front and one rear brake outlet lines and electrical connector from the combination valve. Plug the lines and outlets to prevent entry of dirt.
3. Remove the two attaching nuts securing the master cylinder to the booster, and discard the nuts. Remove the master cylinder and combination valve assembly from the car.
4. Disconnect the booster vacuum hose from the check valve.
5. From under the instrument panel, remove the clip and washer from the brake pedal push rod pin. Do not remove the push rod from the brake pedal assembly yet.
6. Remove the two screws retaining the twilight sentinel amplifier, if so equipped, to the brake pedal bracket. Lower the amplifier and discard the connectors.
7. Remove the four booster-to-cowl retaining nuts and discard the nuts. Slide the studs through the cowl. Move the booster toward the engine and keep the mounting surface parallel to the cowl. Slide the push rod from the brake pedal pin and remove the booster from the car.
8. Install the booster in the reverse order of removal, using new attaching nuts. Tighten the booster-to-cowl nuts to 15 ft lbs, and the master cylinder-to-booster nuts to 20 ft lbs.
9. Bleed the brake hydraulic system. Start the engine and check the brake vacuum system for leaks and operation.

Parking Brake Adjustment

NOTE: make certain that the rear brakes are properly adjusted before adjusting the parking brake.

1. Make a check of the parking brake linkage for the free movement of all the cables. Lubricate, if necessary.
2. Depress the parking brake pedal as follows: 1¾ in.— through 1972; 1 in.—1973-75; 1½ in.— 1976-77; and 1 in.—1976-77 Seville.
3. Raise the rear wheels off the ground.
4. While holding the cable stud to keep it from turning, tighten the equalizer nut until a light drag is felt on either wheel when they are spun in the forward direction.
5. When the parking brake is released there should be no brake shoe drag.
6. After adjustment the brake pedal should travel the following amounts when 50 lbs force is applied. 1¾-2¾ in.—through 1971; 1⅛-2⅛ in.—1972. The next figures are measured at 125 lbs (heavy foot pressure): 2-3 in.—1973-75; 4-5 in.—1976-77; or 5-6 in.—1976-77 Seville.

Master Cylinder Removal and Installation

NOTE: It is possible to remove the master cylinder unit without removing the power booster from the vehicle.

1. Disconnect and plug the front and rear brake lines at the master cylinder.
2. Remove the two securing nuts which hold the master cylinder to the power booster.
3. Remove the master cylinder.
4. To install, reverse the removal procedure. Bleed the hydraulic system.

STEERING

Steering Wheel Removal

NOTE: For models equipped with air bags, perform the special procedure detailed below, prior to removing steering wheel.

1. Remove the screws on the underside of the steering wheel spokes near the center and remove the pad assembly.
2. Remove the horn contact wire from the plastic tower by pushing in on the wire and turning it counterclockwise.
3. Remove the nut holding the steering wheel to the steering shaft.
4. On tilt wheels, remove locking lever and flange and screw assembly.
5. Note the match-marking of the shaft and wheel and use a puller to remove the steering wheel.
6. On installation, tighten the steering shaft nut to 30 ft lbs— 1970 models; 20 ft lbs—1971 models; 30 ft lbs—1972-77 full-size and Seville models.

Special Procedure for Cars with A.C.R.S. (Air Bags)

Some 1974 and later models have an air cushion, or air bag, restraint system. One of the elements of this complex system is an air cushion module in the top of the steering wheel. The steering wheel can be removed in the manner described in this section after the module has been removed.

To remove the module:
1. Turn the ignition lock to the LOCK position.
2. Disconnect the battery ground cable and tape the end to prevent any possibility of a complete circuit.
3. Remove the 4 module-to-steering wheel screws. A special tool is available to do this.
4. Lift up the module and disconnect the horn wire.
5. Disconnect the module wire connector. A special tool is available to do this, too.

WARNING: The driver air cushion module should always be carried with the vinyl cover away from all parts of one's body and should always be laid on a flat surface with the vinyl side up. This is necessary so that a free space is provided to allow the air cushion to expand in case of accidental deployment.

Do not attempt to repair any portion of the module. The module must be serviced as a unit. Attempting repairs such as soldering wires, changing covers, etc. may cause accidental inflation or impair operation of the driver module and cause serious injury.

Do not dispose of a module in any way. The highly inflammable material in the module can cause serious burns if ignited. Modules must be exchanged at an authorized dealer's parts department.

To install the module:
6. Hold the module with the emblem in the lower right corner.
7. Loop the air cushion harness clockwise from the 11 o'clock position to the 6 o'clock position.
8. Install the module connector by pushing it onto the column circuit firmly. Check that it is fully seated.
9. Install the horn wire.
10. Position the module, making sure that the wiring is still in place, and install the 4 screws. Torque them to 40 in. lbs.
11. Reconnect the battery ground cable.
12. Turn the ignition lock to any position other than LOCK and check that the restraint indicator light operates correctly.

Turn Signal Switch Removal and Replacement
Full Size Cadillac
Models w/o A.C.R.S. (Air Bags)

1. Remove the steering wheel.
2. Remove the lockplate cover assembly.
3. After compressing the lockplate spring, remove the snap-ring from the groove in the shaft.

Caution When the snap-ring is removed do not allow the shaft to slide out the bottom of the column.

"C" RING

LOCK PLATE AND SPRING COMPRESSOR

Removing the C-ring (© Cadillac Div., G.M. Corp)

4. Remove the lockplate and slide the turn signal cam and the upper bearing preload spring off the upper steering shaft. Remove horn contact carrier.
5. Remove the thrust washer from the shaft.
6. Remove the hazard warning switch from the column along with the turn signal lever.
7. Use the following procedure if the car is equipped with Cruise Control.
   a. Attach a length of wire to the connector on the Cruise Control switch harness.
   b. Gently pull the harness up and out of the column.
8. Remove the two vertical bolts at the steering column upper support. Remove the shim packs. Keep the shims in order for reinstallation.
9. Remove the four screws securing the column upper mounting bracket to the column and remove the bracket.
10. Remove the turn signal switch mounting screws.
11. Slide the switch connector out of the bracket on the steering column.
12. If the switch is known to be bad, cut the wires and discard the switch. Tape the connector of the new switch to the old wires, and pull the new harness down through the steering column while removing the old wires.

If the original switch is to be reused, wrap tape around the wire and connector and pull the harness up through the column. It may be helpful to attach a length of wire or string to the harness connector before pulling it up through the column to facilitate installation.

13. After freeing the switch wiring protector from its mounting, pull the turn signal switch straight up and remove the switch, switch harness, and the connector from the column.
14. To reassemble reverse the removal procedure.

1974 and Later Full Size Cadillac Models with A.C.R.S. (Air Bags)

Follow the procedure for removing the steering wheel and air cushion module which appears previously under "Steering Wheel Removal, Special Procedure for Cars with A.C.R.S."

1. Remove the 3 screws from the retainer and cover. Carefully lift the cover and retainer from the column.
2. Carefully insert a screwdriver blade into the locking tab at the side and lift the slip-ring from the column.
3. Now proceed with Steps 3-10 of the "Turn Signal Switch Removal and Replacement" procedure.
4. To replace the slip-ring, align the slip-ring locating tab with the slot in the bowl and push the slip-ring into position. Make sure that all 3 locking tabs are securely positioned.
5. Install the cover and retainer, aligning the cover over the locating tab. Torque the screws to 15 in. lbs.

LOCK BOLT

SPRING

Turn signal switch
(© Cadillac Div., G.M. Corp.)

Seville

1. Disconnect the battery and remove the steering wheel.
2. Remove the rubber sleeve bumper from the steering shaft.
3. Remove the plastic retainer with a screwdriver, disengaging the tabs on the retainer from the C-ring.
4. Compress the upper steering shaft preload spring with a compressor and remove the C-ring.
5. Remove the spring compressor and remove the upper steering shaft lock plate, horn contact carrier and the preload spring.
6. Remove the steering column lower cover.
7. Unscrew and remove the turn signal lever. If equipped with cruise control:
   a. Disconnect the cruise control wire from the harness near the bottom of the steering column.
   b. Slide the protector off the cruise control wire and wind the wire around the turn signal lever until the lever is disconnected. Do not remove the wire from the column.
8. Remove the two nuts and shim packs from the upper column support. Keep the shims together as a unit for reinstallation.
9. Remove the bracket from the steering column.
10. Disconnect the turn signal wiring harness from the car harness and remove the wires from the plastic protector.
11. Remove the turn signal switch retaining screws and pull the switch up out of the steering column.
12. If the switch is to be replaced, cut the wires from the switch and tape the new switch connector to the old wires. Carefully pull the new harness down through the column as the old wires are removed.
13. If the old switch is to be reused, tape the connector to the wires and carefully pull the harness up out of the column.
14. Feed the wiring harness down through the steering column to replace the old switch.
15. Secure the switch in the steering column.
16. Install the upper shaft preload spring.
17. Install the lock plate and carrier assembly. Make sure that the flat on the lower end of the steering shaft is pointing up and that the small plastic tab on the carrier is up or nearest the top of the column. The flat surface of the lock plate must be installed facing down against the turn signal switch.
18. Install the spring compressor, compress the preload spring and lock plate and install the C-ring with the wide side toward the keyway.
19. Remove the spring compressor and install the plastic retainer on the C-ring.
20. Install the rubber sleeve bumper over the steering shaft and install the steering wheel.
21. Install the turn signal lever. If the vehicle is equipped with cruise control:
   a. Turn the turn signal lever clockwise exactly 6 turns to wind the harness tightly around the lever.
   b. Position the lever to the switch and screw it in, unwinding the harness as the lever is installed.

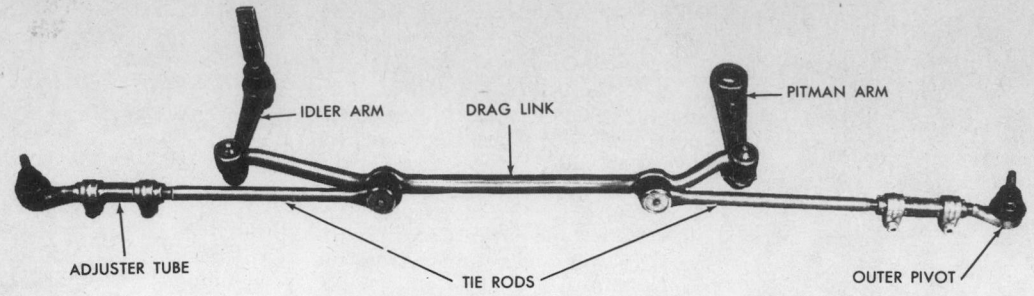

IDLER ARM   DRAG LINK   PITMAN ARM

ADJUSTER TUBE   TIE RODS   OUTER PIVOT

Cadillac Steering linkage (© Cadillac Div., G.M. Corp)

22. Remove the tape from the end of the harness and connect the switch and cruise control, if so equipped, to the car harness.
23. Cover both harnesses with the plastic protector and position it to the column. The turn signal connector slides on the tabs of the column.
24. Position the steering column upper bracket over the turn signal switch harness plastic protector.
25. Install the mounting bracket nuts and shims in their original positions.
26. Install the steering column lower cover.

Steering Linkage Removal and Replacement

1. Remove cotter pins and nuts from outer tie-rod pivots.
2. Remove outer tie rod pivots from steering knuckles using tie-rod end puller.
3. Remove idler arm screws and lockwashers from side member.
4. Remove pitman arm cotter pin, nut and washer at steering linkage.
5. Remove steering linkage from pitman arm.
6. Remove drag link with tie-rods and idler arm attached.
7. Remove cotter pins and nuts from idler arm pivot and inner tie-rod pivots.
8. Remove tie-rod.
9. Remove idler arm from drag link.
10. Remove dust seals from pitman arm and idler arm pivot studs.
11. Remove outer tie-rod pivots by loosening nuts on outer clamp bolts and unscrewing the pivot from adjuster tubes.
12. To install, reverse removal procedure. Tighten the idler arm nuts to 40 ft lbs and install the cotter pin. Do not tighten above 50 ft lbs.

Power Steering Pump Removal and Installation

1. On a Seville, remove the alternator and bracket.
2. Disconnect the pump lines and seal them to prevent fluid loss.

3. Remove the pump mounting from the engine block. Remove the drive belt.
4. By releasing the bottom pivot screw the pump can be removed with the mounting bracket attached.
5. The installation procedure is the reverse of the removal. Remember to adjust the pump belt tension and bleed the hydraulic line system.
NOTE: To adjust power steering pump belt, loosen pump to mounting bracket screws, move pump upward until belt is tight. Tighten mounting bracket screws. Run the engine faster than idle speed, turn steering wheel full right or left. If belt squeals, it is too loose and should be tightened more.

Ignition Switch Replacement

1. Disconnect battery.
2. Position lock cylinder in "lock" position.
3. Remove steering column lower cover.
4. Loosen two nuts on upper steering column, allowing column to drop.

Caution   Do not remove nuts, as column may bend under its own weight.

5. Disconnect ignition switch connector at switch.
6. Remove two screws securing ignition switch to steering column. Remove switch.
7. To install, first assemble ignition switch on actuator rod and adjust to "lock" position, as follows:
   a. *Standard Column*—Hold switch actuating rod stationary with one hand while moving switch toward bottom of column until switch reaches end of travel (Acc. position). Back off one detent, then, with key also in "lock" position, tighten two switch mounting screws to 35 in. lbs.
   b. *Tilt column*—Hold switch actuating rod stationary with one hand while moving switch toward upper end of column until switch reaches end of travel (Acc. position).

Back off one detent, then, with key also in "lock" position, tighten two switch mounting screws to 35 in. lbs.
8. Connect wires, tighten two steering column nuts, install lower cover and reconnect battery.

Lock Cylinder Replacement

NOTE: On 1974 and later models, equipped with air bags (A.C.R.S.), perform the special procedure for removing the air bag module from the steering wheel, prior to removing the lock cylinder.

Standard Steering Column

1. Remove the steering wheel.
2. Remove the lockplate cover assembly.
3. After compressing the lockplate spring, remove the snap-ring from the groove in the shaft.

Caution   When the snap-ring is removed do not allow the shaft to slide out the bottom of the column.

4. Remove the lockplate and slide the turn signal cam and the upper bearing preload spring off the upper steering shaft.
5. Remove the thrust washer from the shaft.
6. Remove the hazard warning switch from the column along with the turn signal lever.
7. Use the following procedure if the car is equipped with Cruise Control.
   a. Attach a piece of stiff wire to the connector on the Cruise Control switch harness.
   b. Gently pull the harness up and out of the column.
8. Remove the turn signal switch mounting screws.
9. Slide the switch connector out of the bracket on the steering column.
10. After freeing the switch wiring protector from its mounting, pull the turn signal switch straight up and remove the switch, switch harness and the connector from the column.
11. Turn the ignition switch to "on" or "run" and then insert a small screwdriver into the slot next to the switch mounting screw boss. Push the lock cylinder tab and remove the lock cylinder.

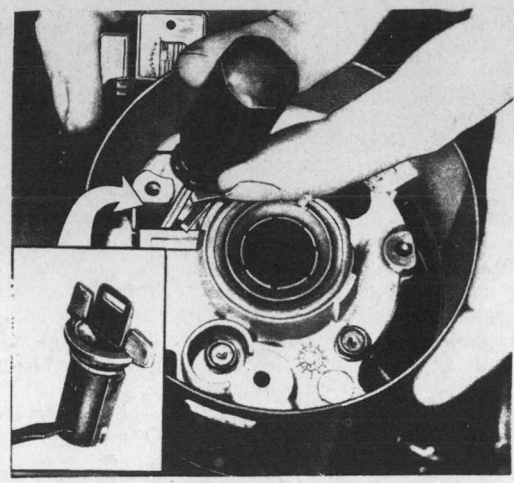

Removing the lock cylinder (© Cadillac Div., G.M. Corp)

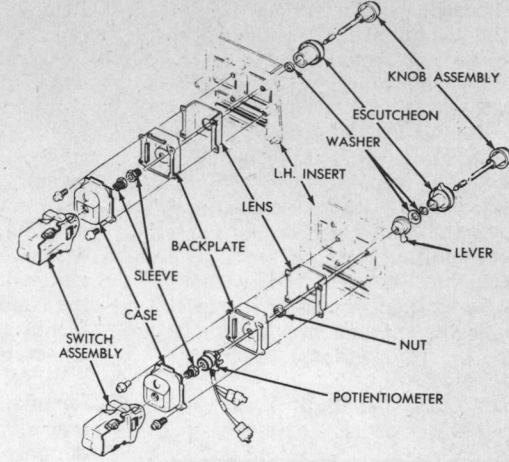

Seville headlight switch components
(© Cadillac Div.. G.M. Corp.)

Tilt Column

1. Remove the steering wheel.
2. Remove the rubber sleeve bumper from the steering shaft.
3. Using a small screwdriver remove the plastic retainer.
4. Using a spring compressor, compress the upper steering shaft spring and remove the C-ring. Release the steering shaft lockplate, the horn contact carrier, and the upper steering shaft pre load spring.
5. Remove the four screws which hold the upper mounting bracket and then remove the bracket.
6. Slide the harness connector out of the bracket on the steering column. Tape the upper part of the harness and connector.
7. Disconnect the hazard button and position the shift bowl in Park. Remove the turn signal lever from the column.
8. Use the following procedure for cars with Cruise Control.
   a. Remove the harness protector from the harness.
   b. Attach a piece of piano wire to the switch harness connector.
   c. Before removing the turn signal lever, loop a piece of piano wire and insert it into the turn signal lever opening. Using the wire, pull the Cruise Control harness out through the opening.
   d. Pull the rest of the harness up through and out of the column.
   e. Remove the guide wire from the connector and secure the wire to the column.
   f. Remove the turn signal lever.
9. Pull the turn signal switch up until the end connector is within the shift bowl. Remove the hazard flasher lever. Allow the switch to hang.

10. Place the ignition key in the "run" position.
11. Depress the center of the lock cylinder retaining tab with a screwdriver and then remove the lock cylinder.
12. To install reverse the above procedure.

INSTRUMENT PANEL

Headlight Switch Removal and Installation

Full Size Cadillac

1. Disconnect the negative battery cable and remove the lower cover of the steering column.
2. Release the wiring harness retainer which runs below the headlight switch.
3. Depress the knob release button which is located on the top of the headlight switch. While the button is depressed, remove the rod and knob.
4. Remove the two mounting screws and the ground wire which is located at the bottom of the switch housing.
5. Pull the headlight switch assembly down and rearward, disconnect the wiring harness connectors, and the two bulbs, and then remove the assembly.
6. Unfasten the hex-head sleeve which holds the headlight switch to the housing case, then remove the switch from the case.
7. On units with Guide-Matic or Twilight Sentinel, use the following additional procedure.
   a. Remove the two screws securing the backplate and the lens to the bezel. Then re-

move the backplate and the lens.
   b. Remove the control ring and the washer on units equipped with one of the systems only. On cars with both systems, a dual control with an inner and outer shaft is used.
   c. Remove the hex nut securing the control switch and then remove the switch from the backplate.
8. To reassemble reverse the removal procedure.

Seville

1. Disconnect the negative battery cable.
2. Remove the lower steering column cover and instrument cluster bezel.
3. Remove the trim screw from the left side of the lower panel.
4. Remove the 2 screws securing the left lower instrument panel to the top cover.
5. Loosen the screw securing the lower panel to the reinforcement.
6. Pull the left lower instrument panel out to gain access to the connectors. Disconnect the climate control electrical and vacuum connectors, cruise control and headlight connectors, illumination bulbs and sockets, and ground wires.
7. Pull the knob on the headlight switch On and depress the spring loaded button on the bottom of the switch. Remove the headlight switch knob and rod.
8. Remove the headlight switch case-to-instrument panel insert screws and separate the headlight switch assembly from the left lower instrument panel assembly.
9. Remove the sleeve that secures the switch to the case.

C285

10. Without Guide-Matic and/or Twilight Sentinel, remove the sleeve that secures the escutcheon, washer and lens to the backplate.
   If the vehicle is equipped with Guide-Matic and/or Twilight Sentinel, remove the Guide-Matic knob, wave washer and Twilight Sentinel lever by carefully pulling straight out. The lens may be removed without any further disassembly. Remove the spanner nut to remove the potentiometer(s) from the backplate.

11. Install the headlight switch in the reverse order.

WINDSHIELD WIPERS

Wiper and Washer Motor Removal and Installation

1970

1. Disconnect negative battery cable.
2. Disconnect three washer hoses from control valve. Matchmark hoses and valve nipples for proper assembly sequence.
3. Disconnect two-way connector at washer unit and three-way connector at wiper unit.
4. Remove rubber grommet or cover plate above wiper motor on firewall.
5. Loosen two locknuts that secure crank arm to ball socket. Disengage arm from socket, without removing the locknuts.
6. Remove three screws that secure wiper/washer to firewall and remove assembly.
7. To install, reverse removal procedure, making sure wiper crank is in Park position.

1971-77

1. Disconnect negative battery cable, after raising hood.
2. Remove cowl screen.
3. Reach through opening and disengage transmission drive link from wiper crank arm by loosening two nuts.
4. Disconnect wiring and washer hoses.
5. Remove three screws that secure wiper/washer unit to firewall.
6. Remove entire assembly.
7. To install, reverse removal procedure, making sure wiper crank arm is in Park position.

RADIO

Removal and Installation

1970 Full Size Cadillac

1. Remove steering column lower cover.

2. Remove defroster hose behind radio.
3. Remove radio knobs, washers and rings by pulling straight out.
4. Using spanner nut wrench, remove spanner nuts securing control shafts to instrument panel.
5. Disconnect wire connectors and antenna lead-in cable. On cars with stereos, disconnect the single lead to the rear speaker and the four-way connector to the front speaker. Disconnect the two-way speaker connector on AM/FM units.
6. Remove screws securing support bracket to radio and panel center support and remove bracket.
7. Pull radio rearward and down.
8. Disconnect dial bulb socket and remove radio.
9. Install in reverse order.

1971-73 Full Size Cadillac

This procedure is the same as 1970 procedure, except that Step 2 can be eliminated.

Seville

1. Remove the electronic fuel injection electronic control unit.
2. Remove the screw holding the climate control outlet extension to the heater case.
3. Disconnect the antenna.
4. Remove the nut retaining the rear radio support rod to the radio and move it out of the way.
5. Remove the control knobs, springs, control rings and both hex nuts from the control shafts at the front of the radio. The control knobs on radios with 8-track tape players are secured by set screws with 5/64 in. allen heads.
6. Slide the radio forward and pivot the rear downward to disconnect the electrical connectors.
7. Remove the radio from the vehicle.
8. Install in the reverse order.

1974 and later Full Size Cadillacs w/o Air Bags (A.C.R.S.)

1. Remove the 4 screws each which secure the lower steering column cover to its reinforcement and the instrument panel support.
2. Take the lower cover off.
3. Unfasten the screws which secure the lower ash tray bracket, and then remove the two screws from the left-hand ash tray bracket.
4. Unfasten the right-hand ash tray securing screw. Remove the ash tray assembly from the dash panel.
5. Remove the knobs, washers, outer rings, and shaft retaining nuts.
6. Remove the radio-to-dash panel

lower support brace nut from the back of the radio.
7. Loosen, but don't remove, the screw which secures the brace to the support, and turn the brace clockwise.
8. Slide the radio back from the instrument panel. Detach the speaker connector, power connector, and antenna lead from it.
9. Turn the dial side of the radio (front) so that it is facing down, and lower the left-side of the receiver. Withdraw it through the ash tray opening.

Installation is performed in the reverse order of removal.

1974 and later Full Size Cadillacs with Air Bags (A.C.R.S.)

1. Turn the ignition switch to "Lock."
2. Remove the negative (—) battery cable and tape its terminal end.

Caution If the battery cable is not disconnected and taped, there is a chance that the air bag could accidently deploy.

3. Remove the 3 screws which retain the glovebox in the dash, but don't remove the two striker screws.
4. Remove the glovebox partition screws, and set the glovebox aside, without disconnecting the wiring.
5. Remove the tape storage compartment retaining screws and remove the compartment.
6. Remove the ash tray assembly retaining screws, pull the assembly out partway, unfasten the electrical leads, and remove the assembly.
7. Remove the knee restraint left trim screw.
8. Remove the screws, and loosen, but don't remove, the fifth screw (under the steering column) from the bottom of the knee restraint.
9. Remove the 4 knee restraint securing screws working from the tape storage compartment and ash tray openings.
10. Perform Steps 5-7 of the radio removal procedure for 1974 and later Cadillacs without air bags.
11. Through the knee restraint opening, disconnect the antenna lead, depress the locktabs and push the electrical connections upwards to disengage them.
12. Clear the instrument panel support by turning the radio to the left. Slide the radio away from you, lower the front of the radio (dial), and withdraw it, front first, through the knee restraint opening.

Installation is the reverse of removal.

HEATER

Heater Blower—
Non-Air-Conditioned Cars

1970

1. Disconnect negative battery cable.
2. Drain cooling system.
3. Remove one screw that secures antenna bracket to wheelhousing.
4. Disconnect blower electrical connector.
5. Remove five screws that secure blower to case and remove blower motor by rotating it 180° while pulling out.
6. Remove heater hoses.
7. Disconnect green vacuum hose at vacuum power unit.
8. Disconnect temperature valve cable and remove cable clamp.
9. Remove screw that secures check valve and position valve out of the way.
10. Position power brake vacuum line out of the way.
11. Disconnect three-way connector at blower resistor.
12. Remove seat warmer relay, if so equipped.
13. Remove wiring harness from clip.
14. Remove seven screws that secure the bottom of the blower assembly to cowl.
15. Remove five screws and one nut that secure top of blower assembly to cowl.
16. Remove blower case assembly.
17. To install, reverse removal procedure.

1971-75

1. Disconnect negative battery cable.
2. Disconnect electrical connector.
3. Remove five blower-to-case screws and blower motor.

Heater Blower—
Air-Conditioned Cars

1. Disconnect negative battery cable.
2. On 1970 models only, remove screw that secures antenna bracket to wheelhousing.
3. Remove rubber cooling hose from nipple and blower motor.
4. Disconnect electrical connector.
5. Remove screws that secure motor to case, then twist motor 180° and pull out.

Heater Core—
Non-Air-Conditioned Cars

1970

1. Disconnect the negative battery cable.

---

2. Drain the cooling system.
3. Disconnect the electrical connector lead to the heater blower motor.
4. Remove the attaching screws of the blower motor and remove the motor.
5. Remove screws from each side of heater core, securing wire retaining clamps to blower case, then remove clamps.
6. Pull core out of case and remove grommets from inlet and outlet fittings.
7. Install in reverse of above.

1971-75

1. Drain cooling system.
2. Remove heater hoses from core nipples. Plug the nipples.
3. Remove instrument panel top cover.
4. Remove screws and position center ventilator duct and sleeve out of the way.
5. Remove vacuum hoses from diverter door and defroster door vacuum actuators.
6. Unfasten the bowden cable from temperature door and case and move out of way.
7. Take out the screws, securing heater case to cowl.
8. Work heater case from position under instrument panel.
9. Remove the screws and clips securing the core to heater case, and lift out core.
10. To install, reverse removal procedure.

Heater Core—
Air-Conditioned Cars

1970

1. Disconnect negative battery cable.
2. Remove air cleaner.
3. Drain coolant.
4. Disconnect two heater hoses at heater air selector.
5. Remove blower relay connector.
6. Remove connector from power servo.
7. Remove neutral switch, vacuum storage tank, and Automatic Level Control hoses from vacuum check valve.
8. Remove right and left tie struts.
   NOTE: if equipped with Automatic Level Control, position left tie strut out of the way in the engine compartment.
9. Disconnect Thermal Vacuum Switch hose.
10. Disengage wiring harness from clips, then remove white vacuum hose at water valve.
11. Remove vacuum harness connector from cowl, then remove six air selector to cowl screws.
12. Remove one nut and blower relay ground wire from air selector stud.

---

13. Remove fuse block and position it out of the way.
14. Remove four mode selector screws.
15. Pull vacuum harness connector into passenger compartment and disconnect.
16. Guide heater and air modulator assembly from engine compartment.
17. Remove four screws that secure heater core frame to case.
18. Remove gasket, then pull heater core and frame away from case.
19. Remove rubber grommets from air inlet and outlet fittings.
20. Remove four screws, retaining clamps and heater core.
21. To install, reverse removal procedure.

1971-77 Full Size Cadillac

NOTE: On 1974 and later models equipped with air bags (A.C.R.S.), the passenger air bag restraint assembly must be removed first. This dangerous procedure is best left to a dealer shop.

1. Drain cooling system.
2. Remove hoses from heater core nipples. Plug the nipples.
3. Remove instrument panel top cover.
4. Remove right and left A/C outlet hoses and center outlet connector.
5. Remove screws securing A/C distributor to heater case and lift off distributor.
6. Remove defroster nozzle.
7. Remove glove box.
8. Disconnect vacuum hoses at recirculator door, water valve, control head supply hose, and programmer (if equipped).
9. Disconnect aspirator hose from in-car sensor.
10. Take off instrument panel braces.
11. On engine side of cowl remove the nuts securing heater case to cowl.
12. Work the heater case out from under dash.
13. Remove rubber seals from around core nipples.
14. Remove the screw and clip from beneath the seal.
15. Take out screws and clip from opposite end of core and remove core.
16. Reverse the above procedure for installation.

Seville

NOTE: In order to remove the heater core, the air conditioning system must be discharged and the evaporator case assembly removed from the car. If you are not knowledgeable about or properly equipped to service automotive air conditioning systems, do not attempt to discharge the system.

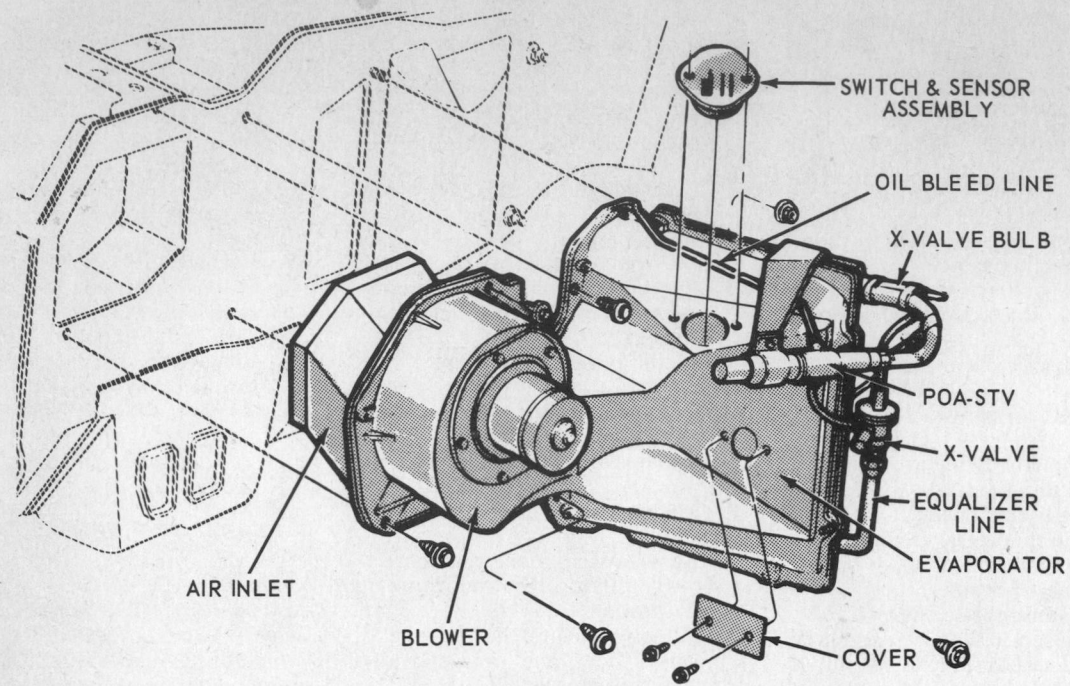

SWITCH & SENSOR ASSEMBLY

OIL BLEED LINE

X-VALVE BULB

POA-STV

X-VALVE

EQUALIZER LINE

EVAPORATOR

COVER

AIR INLET

BLOWER

1971-73 blower, air inlet, and evaporator (© Cadillac Div., G.M. Corp)

1. Discharge the air conditioning system.
2. Drain the cooling system and remove the right side wheelhousing strut.
3. Support the front of the hood and tape a pad to the right rear corner of the hood. Remove the right hood hinge.
4. Remove the electrical connections from the components mounted on the evaporator assembly and move the wiring harness out of the way.
5. Remove the heater hose at the heater core side of the hot water valve. Remove the two screws securing the valve to the evaporator case and move the valve out of the way.
6. Jack up the front of the car and support it with jackstands. Remove the right front wheel.
7. Remove the five screws securing the wheelhousing to the fender at the wheel opening.
8. Remove the two screws attaching the wheelhousing at the front.
9. Remove the three plastic retainers securing the wheel housing seal at the rear of the wheelwell, front of the wheelwell, and at the fender, forward of the wheel opening.
10. Remove the two screws behind the wheelwell securing the wheelhousing to the cowl brace.
11. Remove the battery and battery tray.
12. Remove the three screws and retainer securing the wheelhousing to the radiator support under the horns.
13. Remove the wheelhousing damper upper mounting bolt and move the damper out of the way.
14. Remove the wheelhousing from the car. Some prying and bending may be necessary.
15. Remove the heater hoses from the heater core nipples.
16. Disconnect and plug the refrigeration lines at the receiver.
17. Remove the screws and nuts retaining the evaporator case and remove the case from the vehicle.
18. Separate the case and remove the heater core.
19. Install in the reverse order. Use new O-rings at the connection of the refrigeration lines to the receiver. Fill the cooling system and evacuate and recharge the refrigeration system of the air conditioning.

SEAT BELTS

Disabling the Seat Belt Interlock and Buzzer

It is now legal to disconnect the seat belt interlock and buzzer system, but not the seat belt warning light.

1. Disconnect the negative battery cable.
2. Locate the interlock harness connector under the left side of the instrument panel on or near the fuse block with orange, yellow and green wires.
3. Cut and tape the green wire on the body harness side of the interlock connector.
4. Disconnect the seat belt warning buzzer from its position under the left side of the instrument panel by removing the lower steering column cover. Remove the connector and seat belt buzzer from the left body bracket and disconnect the buzzer from the harness and reinstall the connector to the bracket. Install the lower steering column cover.

Cadillac Eldorado

Automatic Transmission In-Car Service **C299**
Kickdown adjustment C299
Shift linkage adjustment C299
Neutral safety switch C299
Pan Removal and Installation, fluid
change C299
Filter replacement C300

Brakes **C308, U299**
Master cylinder Removal and Installation 308
Parking brake adjustment C310
Power brake booster Removal and
Installation C308
Hydraulic power brake booster
Removal and Installation C308
Hydro-Boost system bleeding C309
Rear disc brake pad replacement C309

Charging System **C294, U2**
Alternator Removal and Installation C294

Cooling System **C296, U367**
Radiator Removal and Installation C296
Water pump and Thermostat Removal
and Installation C296

Drive Axles **C300**
Drive axle left side Removal and
Installation C301
Drive axle right side Removal and
Installation C300
DIFFERENTIAL C301
Final Drive Removal and Installation C301

Emission Controls **C296, U145**

Engine **C297, U194**
ENGINE Removal and Installation C297
CYLINDER HEAD REMOVAL AND
INSTALLATION C297
LUBRICATION C298
Rear main bearing oil seal Removal
and Installation C299
Oil pan Removal and Installation C298
MANIFOLDS C297
Exhaust manifold Removal and
Installation C297
Intake manifold Removal and
Installation C297

PISTONS AND RODS C298
TIMING COVER, CHAIN, AND CAMSHAFT .. C298
Camshaft Removal and Installation C298
Timing cover, chain, and
sprockets Removal and Installation C298

Front Suspension **C303**
Alignment procedures C305
Ball joint checks C305
Lower control arm Removal and
Installation C305
Lower ball joint Removal and
Installation C305
Lower control arm ball joint seal
Removal and Installation C305
Shock absorber Removal and
Installation C305
Torsion bar Removal and Installation C303
Upper control arm Removal and
Installation C304
Wheel bearing adjustment C306
Wheel hub Removal and Installation C303

Fuel System **C295, U50**
Electric Fuel Pump C295
Electronic Fuel Injection C296
Fuel filter Removal and Installation C295
Mechanical Fuel pump Removal and
Installation C295
Idle speed and mixture adjustment C295

Heater **C312**
Blower motor Removal and Installation .. C312
Heater core Removal and Installation C312

Ignition System **C294, U34**
Distributor Removal and Installation C295
Firing order C290
Ignition timing C295
Point replacement and adjustment C295
HEI Tachometer hookup C295

Instrument Panel **C312, U350**
Headlight switch Removal and
Installation C312

Jacking, Hoisting **C301**

Radio **C312**

Rear Suspension **C306**
Automatic level control C307
Axle assembly C307
Coil spring Removal and Installation C307
Leaf spring removal C307
Lower control arm Removal and
Installation C307
Upper control arm Removal and
Installation C307
Wheel bearing adustment C307

Seat Belts **C312**
Disabling the interlock system C312

Specifications **C290, U359**
Capacities C291
Crankshaft and connecting rod C292
Engine Identification C290
General engine C291
Piston clearance C293
Rings C293
Serial number location C290
Torque C292
Tune-up C291
Valve C292
Wheel alignment C293
Year Identification C290

Starting System **C294, U2**
Starter Removal and Installation C294

Steering **C311, U328**
Ignition switch replacement C311
Ignition lock cylinder replacement C312
Power steering pump Removal and
Installation C311
Steering linkage Removal and
Installation C311
Steering wheel Removal and Installation C311
Turn signal switch Removal and
Installation C311

U-Joints **C320**

Windshield Wipers **C312**
Motor Removal and Installation C312

YEAR IDENTIFICATION

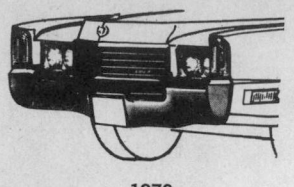

1970

1971

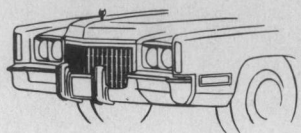

1972

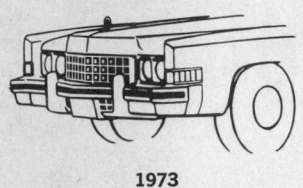

1973

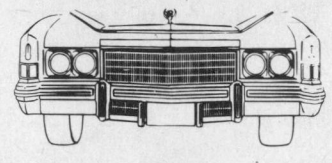

1974

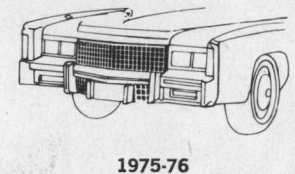

1975-76

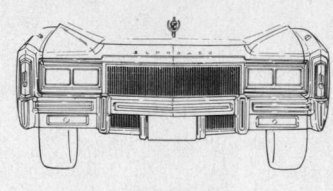

1977

FIRING ORDER

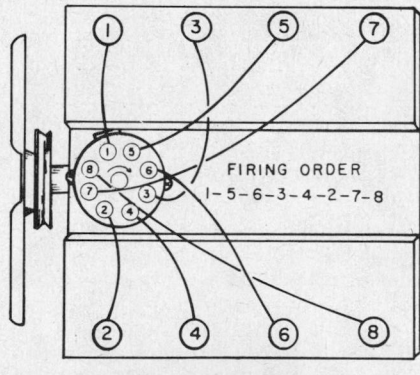

FIRING ORDER
1-5-6-3-4-2-7-8

425, 500 V8

CAR SERIAL NUMBER LOCATION AND ENGINE IDENTIFICATION

1970

The vehicle identification plate is located on the top left side of the dashboard, and is visible through the windshield. The eight digit serial number consists of a sales code letter. The last digit of the model year (0), and a six digit sequential number.

A 500 cu. in. engine is used in 1970. The vehicle identification number, less sales code, is stamped on the top rear of the engine block, adjacent to the transmission.

1971 and later

The vehicle identification plate is located on the top left side of the dashboard, and is visible through the windshield. The thirteen digit serial number consists of the G.M. Division Code (6), a three digit series and model number, the engine code, the last digit of the model year, plant designation, and a six digit sequential serial number.

All models utilize a 500 cu in. V8 engine through 1976. Beginning 1977, a 425 cu in. V8 is used. A derivative of the vehicle identification number is stamped on the top rear of the engine block, adjacent to the transmission.

1972 and later models have the engine code located on the left rear of the engine block, behind the intake manifold.

GENERAL ENGINE SPECIFICATIONS

Year	Engine No. Cyl Displacement (cu in.)	Carburetor Type	Horsepower @ rpm ■	Torque @ rpm (ft lbs) ■	Bore and Stroke (in.)	Compression Ratio	Oil Pressure @2000 rpm
'70	8-500	4 bbl	400 @ 4400	550 @ 3000	4.300 x 4.304	10.0:1	38
'71	8-500	4 bbl	365 @ 4400	535 @ 2800	4.300 x 4.304	8.5:1	38
'72	8-500	4 bbl	235 @ 3800	385 @ 2400	4.300 x 4.304	8.5:1	35
'73	8-500	4 bbl	235 @ 3800	385 @ 2400	4.300 x 4.304	8.5:1	35
'74	8-500	4 bbl	210 @ 3600	380 @ 2000	4.300 x 4.304	8.25:1	35
'75	8-500	4 bbl	210 @ 3600	380 @ 2000	4.300 x 4.304	8.25:1	35
	8-500	EFI	210 @ 3600	380 @ 2000	4.300 x 4.304	8.25:1	35
'76	8-500	4 bbl	190 @ 3600	360 @ 2000	4.300 x 4.304	8.5:1	35
	8-500	EFI	215 @ 3600	400 @ 2000	4.300 x 4.304	8.5:1	35
'77	8-425	4 bbl	180 @ 3600	260 @ 2000	4.082 x 4.060	8.5:1	35
	8-425	EFI	215 @ 3600	260 @ 2000	4.082 x 4.060	8.5:1	35

■ Beginning 1972 horsepower and torque are SAE net figures. They are measured at the rear of the transmission with all accessories installed and operating. Since the figures may vary when a given engine is installed in different models, some are representative rather than exact.
EFI—Electronic Fuel Injection

TUNE-UP SPECIFICATIONS

When analyzing compression test results, look for uniformity among cylinders rather than specific pressures.

Year	ENGINE No. Cyl Displacement (cu in.)	hp	SPARK PLUGS Orig. Type	Gap (in.)	DISTRIBUTOR Point Dwell (deg)	Point Gap (in.)	IGNITION TIMING (deg) ▲ Man Trans	Auto Trans	VALVES Intake Opens ■ (deg)	Fuel Pump Pressure (psi)	IDLE SPEED (rpm) ▲ Man Trans *	Auto Trans
'70	8-500	400	R-46-N	.035	30	.016	—	7½B	18	5¼ 6½		600/400
'71	8-500	365	R-46-N	.035	30	.016	—	8B	38	5¼-6½	—	600/400
'72	8-500	235	R-46-N	.035	30	.016	—	8B	34	5¼-6½	—	600/400
'73	8-500	235	R-46-N	.035	30	.016	—	8B	34	5¼-6½	—	600/400
'74	8-500	210	R-45NS	.035	30	.016	—	10B	21	5¼-6½	—	600/400
	8-500 (H.E.I.)	210	R-45NS	.035	Electronic		—	10B	21	5¼-6½	—	600/400
'75	8-500	210	R-45NSX	.060	Electronic		—	6B	21	5¼-6½	—	600
	8-500 (EFI)	210	R-45NSX	.060	Electronic		—	6B	21	39 min.	—	600
'76	8-500	190	R-45NSX	.060	Electronic		—	6B	21	5¼-6½	—	600
	8-500 (EFI)	215	R-45NSX	.060	Electronic		—	12B	21	39 min.	—	600
'77	All				See Underhood Specifications Sticker							

NOTE: The underhood specifications sticker often reflects tune-up specification changes made in production. Sticker figures must be used if they disagree with those in this chart.
▲ See text for procedure
■ All figures Before Top Dead Center

* Lower figure indicates idle speed with solenoid disconnected
B Before Top Dead Center
— Not applicable
H.E.I.—High Energy Ignition
EFI—Electronic Fuel Injection

CAPACITIES

Year	ENGINE No. Cyl. Displacement (cu. in.)	Engine Crankcase Add 1 Qt For New Filter	TRANSMISSION Pts To Refill After Draining Manual 3-Speed	4-Speed	Automatic ●	Drive Axle (pts)	Gasoline Tank (gals)	COOLING SYSTEM (qts) With Heater	With A/C
'70	All	5	—	—	11.9	4.5	24①	21.3	21.8
'71	All	5	—	—	11.9	4.0	27.5	21.3	21.8

CAPACITIES

Year	ENGINE No. Cyl. Displacement (cu. in.)	Engine Crankcase Add 1 Qt For New Filter	TRANSMISSION Pts To Refill After Draining Manual 3-Speed	4-Speed	Automatic ●	Drive Axle (pts)	Gasoline Tank (gals)	COOLING SYSTEM (qts) With Heater	With A/C
'72	All	5	—	—	11.9	4.0	27.5	21.3	21.8②
'73	All	5	—	—	11.9	4.0	27.5	21.3	21.8②
'74	All	5	—	—	11.9	4.0	27.5	21.3	21.8②
'75	All	5	—	—	10.0	4.0	27.5	25.8	25.8
'76-'77	All	5	—	—	11.5	4.0	27.5	23.0	23.0

● Specifications do not include torque converter
① California cars—22 gals
② Trailer package—2 qts additional
— Not applicable

VALVE SPECIFICATIONS

Year	Engine No. Cyl. Displacement (cu in.)	Seat Angle (deg)	Face Angle (deg)	Spring Test Pressure (lbs @ in.)	Spring Installed Height (in.)	STEM TO GUIDE Clearance (in.) Intake	Exhaust	STEM Diameter (in.) Intake	Exhaust
'70	8-500	45	44	160 @ 1.50	1 15/16	.0005-.0025	.0010-.0025	.3420	.3418
'71	8-500	45	44	160 @ 1.50	1 15/16	.0010-.0027	.0010-.0025	.3420	.3418
'72	8-500	45	44	168 @ 1.50	1 15/16	.0010-.0027	.0012-.0027	.3418	.3416
'73	8-500	45	44	168 @ 1.50	1 15/16	.0010-.0027	.0012-.0027	.3418	.3416
'74	8-500	45	44	168 @ 1.50	1 15/16	.0010-.0027	.0012-.0029	.3418	.3416
'75	8-500	45	44	160 @ 1.50	1 15/16	.0010-.0027	.0010-.0027	.3416	.3416
'76	8-500	45	44	160 @ 1.50	1 15/16	.0010-.0027	.0010-.0027	.3416	.3416
'77	8-425	45	44	160 @ 1.50	1 15/16	.0010-.0027	.0010-.0027	.3416	.3416

TORQUE SPECIFICATIONS

All readings in ft lbs

Year	Engine Displacement (cu in.)	Cylinder Head Bolts	Rod Bearing Bolts	Main Bearing Bolts	Crankshaft Pulley Bolt	Flywheel to Crankshaft Bolts	MANIFOLD Intake	Exhaust
'70-'76	500	115	40	90	Press fit	75	30	35
'77	425	115	40	90	Press fit	75	30	35

NOTE—Some bolts and nuts are marked on the heads to indicate the grade of steel used. Do not use bolts of a lower grade than those originally installed. The marks consist of lines: SAE 5—3 lines; SAE 7—5 lines; SAE 8—6 lines

CRANKSHAFT AND CONNECTING ROD SPECIFICATIONS

All measurements are given in inches

Year	Engine Displacement (cu in.)	CRANKSHAFT Main Brg. Journal Dia	Main Brg. Oil Clearance	Shaft End-Play	Thrust on No.	CONNECTING ROD Journal Diameter	Oil Clearance	Side Clearance
'70-'73	500	3.250	.0003-.0026	.002-.012	3	2.500	.0005-.0035	.008-.016
'74	500	3.250	.0003-.0026	.002-.012	3	2.500	.0005-.0028	.011-.021
'75-'76	500	3.250	.0001-.0026	.002-.012	3	2.500	.0005-.0028	.008-.020
'77	425	3.250	.0001-.0026	.002-.012	3	2.500	.0005-.0028	.008-.020

RING GAP

All measurements are given in inches

Year	Engine No. Cyl. Displacement (cu in.)	Top Compression	Bottom Compression
'70-'76	8-500	.013-.025	.013-.025
'77	8-425	.013-.025	.013-.025

Year	Engine	Oil Control
'70-'76	All engines	.015-.055
'77	8-425	.015-.055

RING SIDE CLEARANCE

All measurements are given in inches

Year	Engine	Top Compression	Bottom Compression
'70-'76	8-500	.0017-.0040	.0017-.0040
'77	8-425	.0017-.0040	.0017-.0040

Year	Engine	Oil Control
'70-'76	All engines	None (side sealing)
'77	8-425	None (side sealing)

PISTON CLEARANCE

Year	Engine	Piston to Bore Clearance (in.)
'70	500	.0006-.0010
'71	500	.0006-.0010
'72	500	.0006-.0010
'73	500	.0006-.0010
'74	500	.0006-.0010
'75-'76	500	.0006-.0010
'77	425	.0006-.0010

WHEEL ALIGNMENT SPECIFICATIONS

Year	CASTER Range (deg)	CASTER Pref Setting (deg)	CAMBER Range (deg)	CAMBER Pref Setting (deg)	Toe-in (in.)	Steering Axis Inclin.	WHEEL PIVOT RATIO (deg) Inner Wheel	WHEEL PIVOT RATIO (deg) Outer Wheel
'70	1½N to 2½N	2N	⅜N to ⅜P	0	0 to ⅛	11	20	18⅙
'71-'73	½N to 1½N	1N	⅜N to ⅜P	0	¹⁄₁₆N to ¹⁄₁₆P	11	20	18⅙
'74-'77	½N to ½P	0	LH—⅜N to ⅜P RH—⅝N to ⅛P	0 ¼N	¹⁄₁₆N to ¹⁄₁₆P	11	20	18⅙

N Negative   P Positive
LH—Left-hand
RH—Right-hand

CHARGING SYSTEM

Alternator Removal and Installation

Except 80 Amp Alternator

1. Disconnect negative battery cable.
2. Disconnect A.I.R. hose at check valve and remove heater hose clip from adjusting link (if so equipped).
3. Remove cap, if installed, from "+" terminal.
4. Disconnect wires from "+" terminal.
5. Unplug multiple connector.
6. Disconnect black wire from ground terminal (if used).
7. Remove link adjusting screw and raise link, then loosen lower alternator mounting screw and remove V-belt.
8. Remove lower mounting screw, spacer and washer.

NOTE: it may be necessary to twist alternator towards fender to do this.

9. Remove alternator.
10. To install, reverse removal procedure. Tighten mounting screw to 17-20 ft lbs.

80 Amp H. D. Alternator

1. Disconnect the negative battery cable.
2. Disconnect all wiring connections from the alternator.
3. Loosen the belt tension adjusting bolts and remove the belt.
4. Remove the 2 nuts and lockwashers from the lower mounting bolts, leaving the bolts in place.
5. Remove the upper mounting bolt and remove the alternator by sliding it rearward off the lower mounting bolts.
6. Installation is the reverse of removal. Adjust the belt tension.

STARTING SYSTEM

For detailed testing and repair procedures consult the "Unit Repair Section."

Starter Removal and Installation

1. Disconnect the negative battery cable.
2. Disconnect the starter harness which is located at the right rear of the engine.
3. Raise the front of the car.
4. Remove the spring clip securing wire which is attached to the solenoid housing.

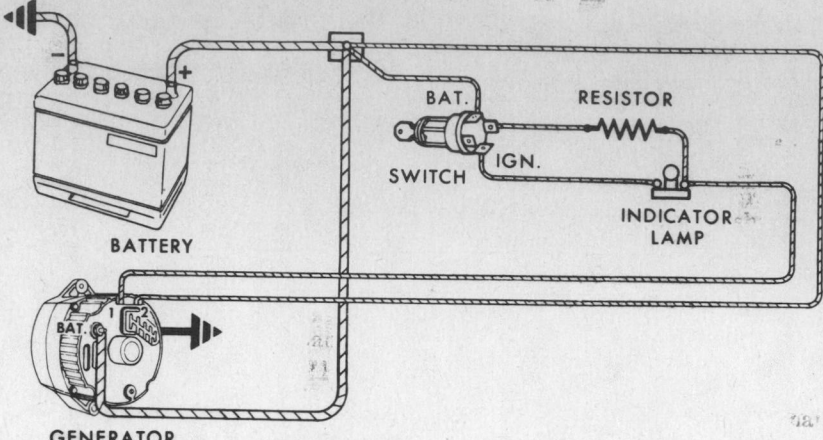

Charging system diagram (© Cadillac Div., G.M. Corp)

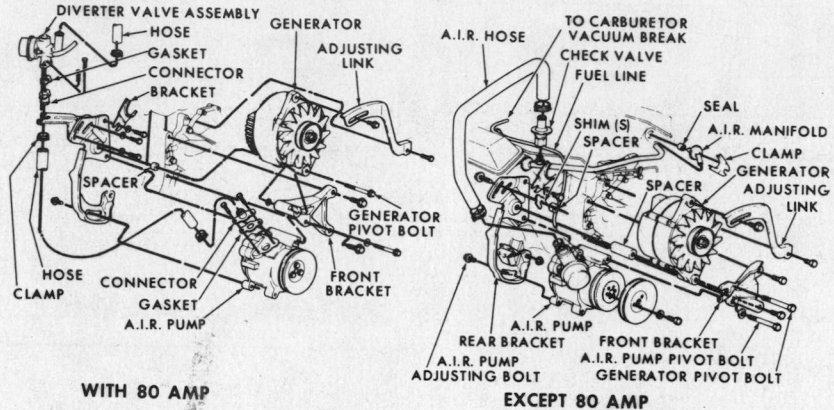

Alternator mounting positions (© Cadillac Div., G.M. Corp)

5. Remove the support bracket which holds the starter to the crankcase.
6. Remove the two screws which attach the starter to the crankcase.
7. Remove the starter from the car by first pulling it forward and then toward the right front wheel and then up over the steering linkage.
8. To install the unit, position it properly onto the engine crankcase and then tighten the attaching screws to 46 ft lbs.
9. Install the support bracket. Tighten the screws to 12 ft lbs and the nut to 6 ft lbs.
10. Install the spring clip and lower the car. Connect the starter harness and the negative battery cable.

IGNITION SYSTEM

In 1974, GM "High Energy Ignition" (HEI) was offered as an option; it became standard equipment starting in 1975.

HEI is a breakerless system which has the coil and the control module

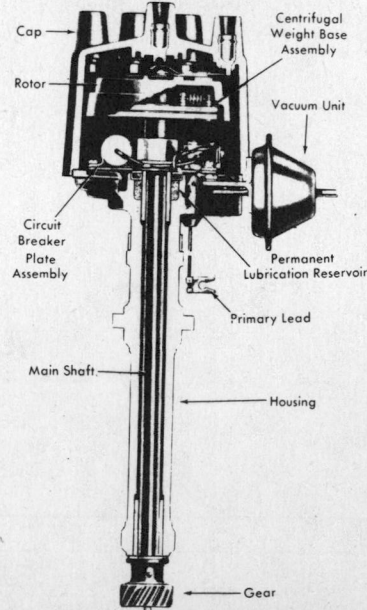

Conventional distributor showing major components (© Cadillac Div., G.M. Corp)

integral with the distributor. For futher description as well as repair procedures, see "Electronic Ignition" in the Unit Repair Section.

Contact Point Replacement and Adjustment through 1974

1. Remove distributor cap by depressing and turning the retaining screws.
2. Remove the two rotor screws.
3. Remove condenser and primary leads from nylon insulated connection.
4. Loosen two screws holding base of contact assembly in place and remove points.
5. Inspect weight assembly, replace or lubricate as required.
6. Place new points under the two screws and tighten screws.
7. Connect the condenser and primary leads at the nylon insulated connection.
   NOTE: be sure leads do not interfere with cap, weight base, or breaker advance.
8. Install rotor. Square and round lugs must be properly aligned.
9. With 1/8 in. Allen wrench, turn until points close while rubbing block is on high point of lobe. Then turn screw counterclockwise one-half turn.
10. Replace distributor cap.
11. With engine warmed up and at idle, set points to proper dwell angle.

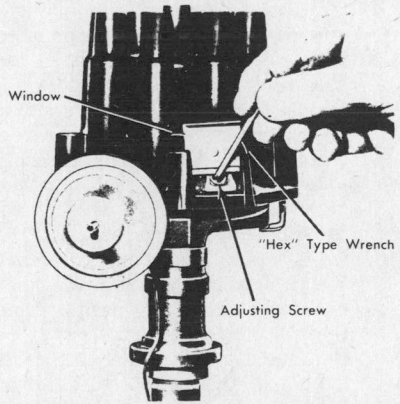

Adjusting distributor points
(© Cadillac Div., G.M. Corp.)

Distributor Removal

1. Remove distributor cap. Disconnect vacuum hose. Disconnect primary lead at the coil.
2. Crank the engine to top dead center for No. 1 cylinder. The pointer on the timing case cover will point to the O-mark on the crankshaft pulley and the rotor will face No. 1 plug wire on the cap.
3. Match-mark the vacuum advance unit to the cylinder block so that the distributor body will be correctly replaced at reassembly.
4. Remove hold-down clamp and lift the distributor straight up.

Distributor Installation

1. Install rubber seal-ring below distributor housing mounting flange.
2. Install the distributor so that the vacuum advance unit aligns with the match-mark made at removal. Turn the rotor slightly left of center so that as the gear engages the camshaft it will revolve into the proper position, pointing to No. 1 contact in the cap.
3. Install the distributor hold-down and connect the distributor lead to the coil.
4. Check the condition of the contact points and the breaker gap.
5. Install the cap and set the timing. (See "Ignition Timing.")
6. Reconnect the vacuum hose to the vacuum advance unit.
   NOTE: if the engine has been cranked, remove No. 1 spark plug. Crank the engine until No. 1 piston is in firing position with the pointer and the O-mark on the crankshaft pulley aligned. Lower the distributor into position with the rotor pointing to No. 1 contact on the distributor cap.

Tachometer Hook-up to HEI Ignition

In the distributor cap, there is a "tach" terminal. Connect the tachometer to this terminal and to ground. Some tachometers must connect from the "tach" terminal to the battery positive (+) terminal; follow the manufacturer's instructions.

Caution Grounding the "tach" terminal could damage the HEI electronic module.

Ignition Timing

1. Loosen the distributor clamp enough to allow the distributor to be turned by hand without excessive looseness.
2. Disconnect the vacuum advance at the distributor and tape the end of the hose to prevent any air leaks.
3. Disconnect the parking brake vacuum hose at the diaphragm and tape the end.
4. Connect a timing light to the engine.
5. Connect a tachometer to the engine.
   NOTE: *Make sure that the timing mark on the pulley and the aligning plate on the front cover are clean.*
6. Disconnect the automatic level control hose on cars so equipped.
7. Allow the engine to reach operating temperature.
8. Set the idle speed with the selector lever in Drive.
9. Set the timing to specifications with transmission in Park or Neutral. At the correct setting

tighten the hold-down bolt of the distributor to 18 ft lbs. and recheck the timing.
10. Connect the 3 vacuum hoses and remove both the timing light and the tachometer from the engine.

FUEL SYSTEM

Mechanical Fuel Pump

The fuel pump is mounted on the left-front of the engine and is driven by an eccentric on the camshaft. The fuel filter is an integral part of the fuel pump on models through 1974. A strainer is also located behind the fuel inlet nut on the carburetor. Beginning 1975, the fuel filter is located behind the fuel inlet nut. Starting 1976, a check valve is included in the fuel filter element.

See the Cadillac section for filter replacement.

All air conditioned cars have a provision to return excess fuel vapor to the gasoline tank to prevent vapor lock under high temperature conditions. The line runs directly from the fuel pump.

Fuel Pump Removal and Installation

1. If equipped with A.I.R. system, it may be necessary to remove air pump and bracket for clearance.
2. Remove center coil wire.
3. Jack up the front of the car and support on axle stands so that pump can be removed from underneath.
4. Loosen two mounting bolts, or one bolt and one nut.
5. Turn over engine to relieve tension on pump arm.
6. Disconnect pump inlet and outlet lines. Plug inlet line.
7. Disconnect vapor return line.
8. Remove mounting bolts and fuel pump.
9. To install, reverse removal procedure.

Fuel Filter

See Cadillac section.

Electric Fuel Pump

Models equipped with electronic fuel injection (EFI) have two electric fuel pumps. For fuel pump service on cars so equipped, see the Cadillac section.

Carburetor

Idle Speed and Mixture Adjustments

1970

Adjust with air cleaner removed.

1. Disconnect and plug distributor vacuum advance line.
2. Disconnect and plug parking brake vacuum line at vacuum release cylinder.
3. Connect a tachometer, set parking brake and remove air cleaner.
4. Make sure dashpot is not touching linkage, then turn slow idle speed screw in approximately 1½ turns after it contacts primary throttle lever. Turn in both mixture screws until they seat gently, then unscrew them approximately 6 turns.
5. Place car in Drive after warming up engine. Turn off A/C.
   NOTE: press down on hot idle compensator pin while making adjustments.
6. Adjust slow idle screw to obtain 620 rpm.
7. Turn one mixture screw clockwise until speed falls off 10 rpm, then repeat Steps 6 and 7 for other mixture screw. Idle speed now should be 600 rpm, indicating a 10 rpm drop per mixture needle.
8. Install air cleaner, shut off engine and disconnect tach.
9. Connect parking brake vacuum line and distributor vacuum line.

1971-74

Adjust with air cleaner removed.

Idle speed is adjusted at a new anti-dieseling solenoid located where the dashpot was located in previous years. The throttle must be opened slightly to allow the plunger to move out all the way, then it must be closed against the now-extended solenoid plunger before making the idle speed adjustment. The solenoid plunger will retract when the ignition is shut off.

1. Disconnect and plug distributor vacuum advance hose and parking brake vacuum hose (at the release cylinder).
2. Connect a tachometer and set the parking brake with transmission in Neutral.
3. Remove the air cleaner and turn in mixture screws until they seat gently, then turn the screws out approximately 6 turns (4 turns, 1974).
4. Start engine and allow it to warm up.
5. Place car in Drive with A/C off.
6. Set idle speed to 620 rpm (640 rpm, 1974) by adjusting anti-dieseling solenoid. Tighten jam nut.
7. Alternately, turn each mixture screw clockwise ¼ turn at a time until idle speed reaches 600 rpm.
8. Disconnect wire that energizes solenoid. The plunger should re-

tract to allow a slower idle speed of 350-400 rpm.
9. Shut off engine, disconnect tach, connect vacuum lines and solenoid wire and install air cleaner.

1975-76

1. Disconnect the hose from the parking brake vacuum release cylinder. Plug the hose.
2. Apply the parking brake. Block the wheels. Remove and plug the air leveling compressor hose at the air cleaner.
3. Connect a tachometer. Allow the engine to reach normal operating temperature. The choke should fully open and the cam follower should be off the fast idle cam completely.

Caution
Do not allow the engine to idle or fast idle for excessive periods of time; catalyst damage could result.

4. Place the transmission in Drive and shut-off the air conditioner.
5. Adjust the idle speed screw to obtain 600 rpm (unless the mixture is to be adjusted).
   NOTE: Do not depress the brake pedal when adjusting idle speed on 1976 models. These cars are equipped with "Hydro-boost" power brake system; brake application will decrease engine speed.
6. Remove the air cleaner but leave its vacuum hoses connected.
7. Remove the limiter caps and screw both mixture screws out 5 turns from fully seated.
8. Set the idle speed to 650 rpm on 49-state cars or 620 rpm on California cars with the idle speed screw.
8. Use a hex-driver with an extension to turn in each mixture screw ¼-turn at a time until the normal idle speed of 600 rpm is obtained.
9. Shut off the engine. Install service replacement limiter caps on the idle mixture screws and install the air cleaner.
10. Remove the tachometer. Connect all the vacuum hoses.

Electronic Fuel Injection (EFI)

Starting 1975, electronic fuel injection (EFI) was offered as an option on all Cadillacs, including Eldorado models.

For a description of the EFI system, as well as adjustment and service procedures, see the Cadillac section.

COOLING SYSTEM

Eldorados use a sealed cooling system which maintains 15 lbs maximum

pressure. The radiator is constructed with two vertical tanks that connect to the enclosed cross-flow tubing. The coolant enters the upper left-hand inlet tank and circulates through the cross-flow tubes and enters the right return tank. A coolant reservoir is attached to the radiator filler neck by a hose. The reservoir allows for coolant expansion and indicates the need for additional coolant. Coolant should be added to the reservoir, not the radiator.

Further information on the cooling system may be found in the Cadillac section under the same year model. Also, system capacities can be found in the "Capacities" chart.

Radiator Removal and Installation

1. Remove the negative battery cable.
2. Open the drain plug on the radiator and drain the coolant. Remove the radiator cap so that the liquid drains faster.
3. Remove the hose clamps and remove the upper hose.
4. Remove the heater return hose which is located at the right radiator tank.
5. Disconnect the two transmission cooler lines from the bottom of the radiator. Plug the ends of the lines to prevent loss of fluid.
6. On the 1970 cars, remove the two top cradle clamps and then the three screws which fasten the finger guard to the cradle.
7. On 1971 and later cars it is necessary to remove the screw which holds the upper radiator hose to the cover panel and then remove the cover panel by removing the six panel screws.
8. On 1971 and later cars, remove the reservoir hose from the filler neck and the two straps from the top of the radiator.
9. Remove the radiator, being careful not to damage the radiator or the fan. Pull the unit straight up.
10. Installation is the reverse of removal.

Water Pump and Thermostat Removal and Installation

See the Cadillac section under the specific year.

EMISSION CONTROLS

The Cadillac Eldorado uses the same emission control systems as the rest of the Cadillac line.

For a description of these controls, as well as their removal and installation (where applicable), see "Emission Controls" in the Cadillac car section.

For emission control tests and adjustments, see "Emission Control Systems" in the Unit Repair Section.

ENGINE

On the Eldorado, special mounting brackets welded to the frame provide the front attaching points and a special crossmember is used for the rear mount.

Engine Removal and Installation

Caution If it is necessary to reposition the air conditioner compressor or the lines, do not disconnect the lines.

1. Follow Steps 1-16 of procedure in Cadillac Section.
2. Disconnect left exhaust pipe at manifold flange.
3. Remove screw that holds transmission cooler lines to motor mount.
4. Remove nut that secures dipstick tube to manifold. Remove the upper screw holding the steering gear flex coupling shroud to the frame.
5. Jack up car and remove the steering gear flex coupling shroud.
6. Remove starter motor.
7. Disconnect right exhaust pipe at manifold flange.
8. Remove transmission inspection cover.
9. Disconnect and plug vapor return line and fuel inlet at fuel pump.
10. Remove lower radiator hose at water pump.
11. Remove three screws that secure flex plate to converter.
12. Remove four screws that secure engine to transmission.
13. Remove front motor mount bolts and bolt that secures final drive to mount.
14. Remove right drive axle spindle nut and cotter pin.
15. Remove drive axle-to-output shaft screws and lockwashers.
   NOTE: discard screws and washers. Have an assistant hold brake pedal to prevent shaft from turning.
16. Remove shaft support-to-engine bolts, and one support-to-brace screw.
17. Rotate inboard end of drive axle rearward toward starter motor.
18. Pull output shaft straight out, then lower and remove from underside of car. Proceed with engine removal procedure.
19. Lower car, install lifting bracket and chain hoist and place a wood-padded jack under the transmission pan.
20. Raise engine and pull forward to disengage transmission. Lift engine out of car.
21. To install, reverse removal procedure. See Cadillac Section for flex-plate alignment.

Manifolds

Intake Manifold Removal and Installation

With Carburetor

1. Remove the negative battery cable.
2. Remove the air cleaner, heat tube, crankcase breather, carburetor linkage, and the Cruise Control linkage.
3. Remove the coil wires or HEI connector and disconnect the SCS solenoid.
4. Remove the primary coil wire (if so equipped) and then remove the distributor cap.
5. Disconnect the single connector near the ignition coil and the green wire to the temperature sender.
6. Remove the two orange wires from the downshift switch and disconnect the antidieseling solenoid.
7. Remove the ignition coil (if so equipped) antidieseling solenoid, and the SCS solenoid.
8. Remove the power brake vacuum hose and the vacuum modulator hose which is located at the rear of the carburetor.
9. On air-conditioned cars, disconnect the compressor clutch electrical connection. Remove the vacuum hose for the air conditioner from the rear of the manifold.
10. Remove the fuel line from the carburetor and remove the distributor vacuum advance hose at the carburetor.
11. Disconnect the PCV valve from the right valve cover and the automatic level control (ALC) vacuum hose. Remove the 12 manifold retaining bolts.
12. Remove the manifold. Also remove the inner manifold shield and gasket and the front and rear gaskets.
13. To reassemble reverse the above procedure.

With Electronic Fuel Injection (EFI)

For intake manifold removal and installation on 1975-77 models with electronic fuel injection, see the Cadillac section.

Exhaust Manifold Removal and Installation

1. If the work is to be done on the left-side manifold, remove the carburetor air cleaner and the heat duct. Remove the nuts from no. 2 and no. 6 cylinders and the heat shroud from around the manifold.
2. Remove the dipstick tube.
3. Release the eight securing screws, disconnect the manifold from the exhaust pipe, and remove the manifold. The 5th screw from the front may not be removable due to frame interference. Back it out and remove it with the manifold.
4. Use the same procedure for removing the right-side manifold except remove the two studs retaining the EFE valve (if equipped) to the manifold and remove the valve.
5. Reassembly is the reverse of the above procedure. Right manifold with EFE valve: Install the EFE valve on the manifold with the actuator toward engine block. Tighten stud bolts to 35 ft lbs.

Cylinder Head

Cylinder Head Removal

NOTE: Care must be used when replacing cylinder-head bolts. They are of different lengths.

1. Remove intake manifold.
2. Drain engine coolant.
3. Disconnect ground strap at rear of cylinder heads from cowl. Disconnect wiring connector for high engine temperature warning system from sending unit at rear of left cylinder head.
4. Remove alternator and heater hose, if working on the right cylinder head, or partially remove the steering pump if working on the left head.
5. Disconnect AIR injection pump tubes from cylinder heads.
6. Remove clamps holding the wire harness to the cylinder heads and tie harness back out of the way.
7. Remove screws holding exhaust manifolds to cylinder heads.
8. Remove screws holding the rocker arm cover to the heads.
9. Remove the cover.
10. Remove the screws holding each rocker arm support to cylinder head, then remove rocker arm assemblies. Store these assemblies so that they may be reinstalled in their correct locations.
11. Remove pushrods and store them with their respective rocker arm assemblies.
12. Install two 7/16 x 6 in. screws to be used as lifting handles in two of the rocker arm support screw holes.
13. Remove ten cylinder-head bolts.
14. Lift cylinder head off the block.
15. Remove all gasket material from

the cylinder head and block mating surfaces.

Cylinder Head Installation

When torquing the head bolts, use the three-step method. Starting from the middle of the center row of bolts and working outward (toward each end), torque the bolts to 1/3 of the total torque listed. Once this is done, repeat the same procedure, this time torquing all the bolts to 2/3 of the total listed torque. Finally torque the bolts to the recommended torque.

By using this procedure, head warping is eliminated. It ensures equal pressure on the head gasket over its entire surface.

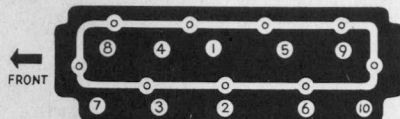

Cylinder head bolt tightening sequence
See text in "Cadillac" section for bolt location and length

Assembling Rod and Piston Assemblies to the Block

The numbers on the connecting rods face away from the camshaft; that is, the numbers on the left bank face to the left; the numbers on the right bank face to the right. As a double check, the word *rear*, (or "R"), stamped on the piston, faces the rear of the engine on both banks and an arrow or notch on the piston top points to the front of the engine.

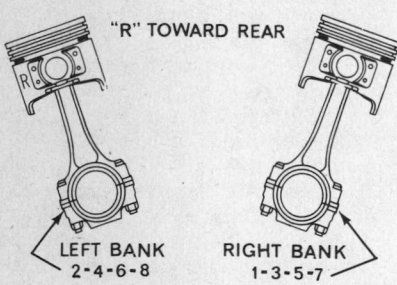

Piston-to-connecting rod relationship

Timing Cover, Chain and Camshaft

Timing Cover, Chain and Sprockets Removal and Installation

Through 1974

The engine must be removed from the car before the front cover can be removed. The procedure is otherwise identical to that for the same year Cadillac as found in the Cadillac Section.

1975 and Later

The front cover may be removed with the engine in the car. This procedure eliminates the necessity of removing the oil pan.

1. Disconnect the negative battery cable.
2. Drain the crankcase and the radiator.
3. Loosen the radiator inlet (top) hose clamp and remove the one screw retaining the hose to the radiator cover. Place the hose out of the way.
4. Remove the fan assembly and the alternator and power steering pump drive belts.
5. Remove the four capscrews retaining the crankshaft pulley and the plug from the end of the crankshaft.
6. Use suitable puller tools to remove the crankshaft hub. It may be necessary to hold one piston within its compression stroke with compressed air to avoid turning the crankshaft. Remove a spark plug and use the proper adapter to apply air pressure to the cylinder.
7. Loosen the starter enough to gain access to the oil pan screws. Loosen the oil pan nuts and screws and lower the front of the oil pan.
8. Loosen the hose clamp at the water pump inlet and remove the lower radiator hose from the water pump.
9. Remove the 10 screws retaining the front cover to the block. Remove the cover with the water pump attached and discard the gasket.
10. Inspect the oil pan front seal to make sure that it was not damaged on removal. Replace the seal if damaged. If the seal is satisfactory, remove any oil and coat the sealing surface with gasket cement.
11. Place a new front cover gasket over the locating dowels on the block. Hold the gasket in place with a small amount of gasket cement.
12. Position the front cover over the end of the crankshaft and down over the oil pan lip. Align the holes in the cover with the dowels on the block. Tighten the retaining screws.
13. Lubricate the bore of the hub and seal with E.P. lubricant to prevent seizure to crankshaft. Position the hub on the crankshaft aligning the slot in the hub with the key on the crankshaft.
14. Press the hub onto the crankshaft with the proper tools. Again use of compressed air may be necessary to avoid turning the crankshaft. Install the crankshaft pulley onto the hub. Tighten the four capscrews to 15 ft lbs.

15. If used, exhaust air pressure from the cylinder, remove the adapter, and install the spark plug.
16. Install the fan assembly on the water pump and install the power steering pump and alternator drive belts. Adjust drive belt tension.
17. Connect the upper radiator hose at the radiator inlet and secure with the hose clamp. Secure the hose to the radiator cover with one screw.
18. Tighten the oil pan nuts and screws to 10 ft lbs; tighten the starter motor mounting bolts to 45 ft lbs.
19. Connect the lower radiator hose to the water pump inlet and secure with hose clamp. Refill the cooling system and add engine oil. Connect the negative battery cable. Start the engine and check for coolant and oil leaks.

Camshaft Removal and Installation

See Cadillac section.

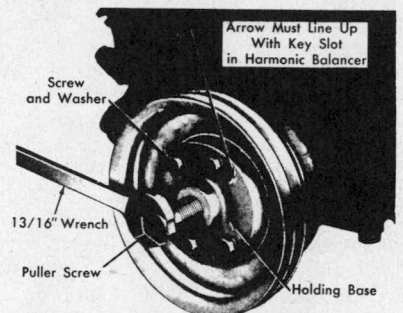

Balancer assembly removal
(© Cadillac Div., G.M. Corp.)

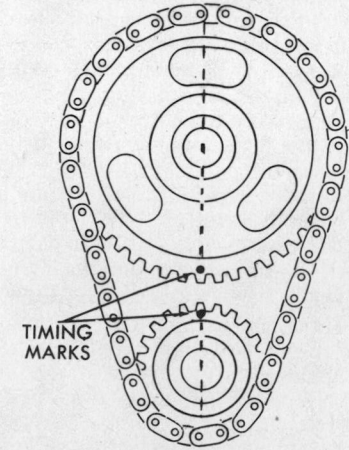

Timing sprocket location marks

Lubrication

Oil Pan Removal and Installation

1. Remove engine as previously de-

scribed in "Engine Removal and Installation."
2. Drain engine oil.
3. Remove the transmission lower cover.
4. Remove two brackets-to-block bolts on each side of engine front mounting support.
5. Remove nuts and cap screws that hold oil pan to cylinder block and engine front cover, then remove the oil pan.
6. Remove side gaskets and rubber front and rear seals from oil pan. Discard the gaskets and seals.
7. Install by reversing the removal procedure. Torque to 10 ft lbs.

Rear Main Bearing Oil Seal Replacement

1. Remove the oil pan, after removing spark plug, wires and plugs.
2. Remove the rear main bearing cap and loosen the bolts holding the other four bearings about three turns each. Remove the old rear main bearing seals.
3. Clean the groove in the cap and in the block. Lubricate seals with engine oil.
4. Make an installation tool, as illustrated.
5. Start the upper half into the groove in the block with the lip facing forward and rotate it into position, using the tool as a guide. Press firmly on both ends to be sure it is protruding uniformly on each side.
6. Install the lower half of the seal into the bearing cap with the lip facing forward and one end of the seal over the ridge and flush with the split line. Hold one finger over this end to prevent it from slipping, and push the seal into seated position by applying pressure to the other end. Be sure the seal is firmly seated and protrudes evenly on each side. Do not apply pressure to the lip. This may damage the effectiveness of the seal.
7. Apply rubber cement to the mating surfaces of the block and cap being careful not to get any cement on the bearing, the crankshaft or the seal. The cement coating should be about .010 in. thick.
8. Install the bearing cap, tightening the bolts with the fingers only.
9. Tighten the bearing bolts to specifications. Be sure to tighten the bolts of the other four bearings also.
10. Reinstall the oil pan.

AUTOMATIC TRANSMISSION

The Turbo Hydra Matic transmission used on the Eldorado is a fully automatic transmission used for front wheel drive applications. It consists primarily of a three-element hydraulic torque converter, dual sprocket and link assembly, compound planetary gear set, three multiple-disc clutches, a sprag clutch, a roller clutch, two band assemblies, and an hydraulic control system.

Neutral Safety Switch— Through 1973

NOTE: switch is on steering column under dash.

Removal

1. Position the gear selector in the Neutral positon.
2. Release the clamp and remove the switch without moving the contact carrier. The position of the carrier should be marked.
3. Remove the vacuum hoses after they have been marked and disconnect the two wires from the switch.
4. Installation is accomplished by reversing the above procedure.

Adjustment

1. Check that the gear lever is correctly adjusted and that the neutral safety switch is properly positioned by this check.
2. Set the handbrake. Put the hand lever on the steering column in drive. Hold the ignition key on and slowly move the hand lever toward Neutral or Park until the starter cranks and the engine runs.
3. Without moving the lever farther, press the accelerator to determine whether the transmission is really in Neutral or Park.
4. If all is correct, the engine will start wih the lever in Park. The transmission will not be in gear. Also, back-up lights will go on with transmission in Reverse.
NOTE: a vacuum leak that can be corrected by moving shift lever is an indication that the switch only needs adjustment and is not defective.
5. Adjust the neutral safety switch by turning it and its mounting bracket until the above conditions are met.

Neutral Safety Switch—1974 and Later

On all models from 1974, the neutral safety switch works mechanically rather than electrically. When the transmission selector is in any position other than Park or Neutral, the key cannot be turned to "Start."

This mechanical system is contained within the steering column and is identified by a yellow and black instruction label attached to the jacket adjacent to the ignition switch.

Shift Linkage Adjustment

1. Place the transmission shift valve into the Park position and then move the relay rod to the Neutral step which is the third one in the downward position.
2. Loosen the adjusting screw on the relay lever and place the selector lever in the Neutral detent position.
3. Tighten the relay rod adjusting screw with the shift lever held against the neutral stop.
4. Check the adjustment by:
   a. Moving the selector lever to the Neutral detent making sure that the lever fits securely into the notch on the steering column.
   b. Move the lever to Drive. Make sure that the lever is secure in this gear. Move the lever to Reverse and check for gear security.

Caution When the linkage is adjusted check the operation of the Neutral Safety Switch, parking brake release and the back-up lights.

Kickdown Adjustment

1. Remove the air cleaner.
2. Make certain that the idle speed is set correctly and that the carburetor is operating on the low-speed circuit.
3. Loosen the switch mounting screws and insert a 0.094 in. wire gauge into the hole in the lower wire terminal.
4. With the gauge in place, adjust the position of the switch so that the lever just touches the carburetor adapter plate stud. The switch should make contact above 60° of throttle opening.
5. After adjusting, tighten the mounting screws and remove the gauge.
6. Reinstall the air cleaner.

Pan Removal and Installation, Fluid Change

1. Remove the transmission dipstick.
2. Insert a rubber hose attached to a suction gun into the filler tube. Remove enough fluid to prevent the pan from overflowing when it is removed.
3. Raise the car and support it securely. Place a container under the transmission pan to catch fluid.
4. Remove the pan and gasket.

Throw the old gasket away. Drain and clean the pan.

Installation is as follows:

1. Place a new gasket on the pan and install the pan. Tighten the attaching screws to 12 ft lbs.
2. Lower the car.
3. Add 4 qts of DEXRON® transmission fluid through the filler tube.
4. Start the engine and run it at 800 rpm for 1½ minutes with the gear selector in Park (P).
5. Return the engine speed to idle. Check the level and add fluid as necessary. The level should be between *add* and *full*.

Filter Replacement

1. Remove the transmission pan.
2. Remove the intake pipe/filter assembly.
3. Remove the intake pipe O-ring and discard it.
4. Insert a new O-ring in the pipe bore.
5. Install a new intake pipe/filter assembly in the pipe bore.
6. Install the pan and add 5 quarts of transmission fluid. Add fluid as necessary to correct level.

DRIVE AXLES

Drive axles are a complete flexible assembly and consist of an axle shaft and an inner tri-pot joint and outer constant velocity joint. The inner tri-pot joint has complete flexibility, plus inward and outward movement. The outer constant velocity joint has complete flexibility at the angle of operation.

The constant velocity joints are to be replaced as a unit and are only disassembled for repacking and replacement of seals.

Drive Axle—Right Side

Removal—through 1971

1. Hoist car under lower control arms.
   NOTE: battery should be disconnected.
2. Remove drive axle, cotter pin, nut and washer.
3. Using a wood-padded hammer, tap on end of drive axle to unseat axle at hub assembly.
   NOTE: install a piece of rubber hose over torsion bar connector at lower control arm to prevent *seal* damage.
4. Remove inner constant velocity joint attaching bolts.
   NOTE: Disconnect tie-rod end at steering knuckle and disconnect upper ball joint before proceeding to Step 5.
5. Remove two output shaft support-to-engine bolts and one support-to-brace screw.
6. Rotate inboard end of axle rearward toward starter motor.
7. Slide output shaft straight out and remove.
8. Rotate drive axle inboard and toward front of car, guiding over front crossmember.

Removal—1972 and later

1. Remove the negative battery cable and the wheel disc.
2. If the drive axle is to be removed, release the cotter pin and loosen but do not remove the spindle nut.
3. Raise the car at the lower control arms.
4. Loosen but do not remove the right front shock absorber lower mounting nut. Then pry the shock absorber along the lower mounting stud until it reaches the nut. Do not remove the shock absorber from the lower mount.
5. To keep the torsion bar connec-

tors from being damaged, cover them with a short length of rubber hose.
6. Remove the screws securing the drive axle to the output shaft.
7. Position the inside end of the drive axle toward the starter motor to gain access to the output shaft. Then remove the screw which supports the output shaft to the final drive housing.
8. Remove the two screws which support the right output shaft support to the engine.
9. Remove the output shaft, support, and strut as an assembly in the following manner.
   a. Slide the output shaft outward to disengage the splines.
   b. Move the inside end of the assembly forward and downward until it is clear of the car.
10. If the drive axle is to be removed, use the following procedure.
    a. Using a hammer and a wooden block tap the end of the drive axle to unseat the axle at the hub.

NOTE: The spindle nut should be loosened but not removed.

   b. Rotate the axle inward and toward the front of the car positioning the axle over the front crossmember and out from under the car.

Caution Care must be exercised so that constant velocity joints do not turn to full extremes, and that seals are not damaged against shock absorber or stabilizer bar.

Installation

1. Carefully place right-hand drive axle assembly into lower control arm and enter outer race splines into knuckle.
2. Lubricate final drive output shaft seal, with wheel bearing grease.
3. Install right-hand output shaft into final drive and attach the support bolts to engine and brace. Torque the bolts to 50 ft. lbs.
4. Install brace.
5. Move right-hand drive axle assembly toward front of car and align with right-hand output shaft. Install attaching bolts and torque to 65 ft. lbs.
6. Install washer and nut on drive axle.
7. Remove floor stands and lower hoist.
8. Tighten wheel lugs to 105 ft lbs —through 1972; 130 ft lbs—1973 and later, and drive axle nut to 110 ft. lbs., (1972-73 to 150 ft lbs.) Install cotter pin.

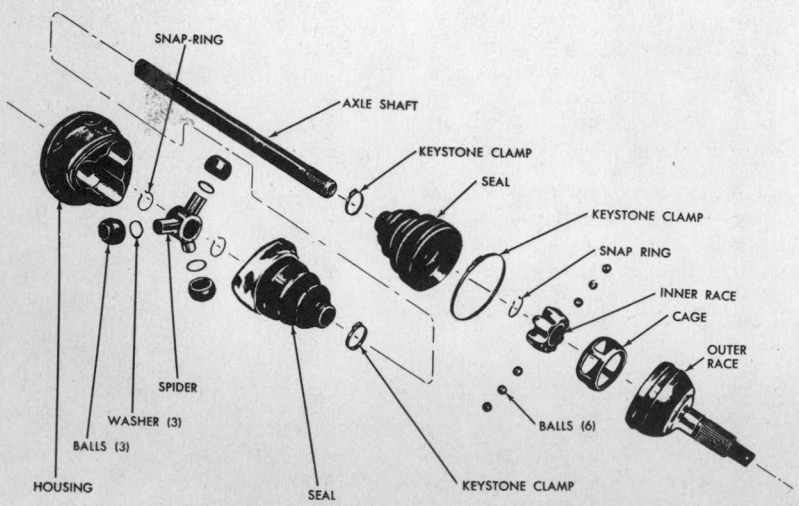

SNAP-RING
AXLE SHAFT
KEYSTONE CLAMP
SEAL
KEYSTONE CLAMP
SNAP RING
INNER RACE
CAGE
OUTER RACE
BALLS (6)
KEYSTONE CLAMP
SPIDER
WASHER (3)
BALLS (3)
HOUSING
SEAL

Drive axle—exploded view (© Cadillac Div., G.M. Corp)

Drive Axle—Left Side

Removal and Installation

1. Hoist car under lower control arms.
2. Remove wheel and tire.
3. Remove drive axle cotter pin, nut and washer.
4. Install a piece of rubber hose over lower control arm torsion bar connector.
5. Remove six drive axle-to-output shaft screws and washers.
6. Loosen upper shock mounting bolt. Disconnect stabilizer bar link on 1970 models.
7. Remove upper control arm ball joint cotter pin and nut.
8. Using hammer and brass drift, drive on knuckle until upper ball joint stud is free.
9. Remove brake hose bracket.
10. Tip upper part of knuckle and support outward so that brake hose is not damaged.
11. Carefully guide drive axle assembly outboard. Remove left output shaft retaining bolt by installing two screws in the shaft flange to prevent shaft rotation. Pull the shaft straight out toward side of car.
    NOTE: care must be exercised so that constant velocity joints do not turn to full extremes and that seals are not damaged against shock absorber or stabilizer bar.
12. To install, reverse removal procedure. Tighten output shaft retaining bolt to 40 ft lbs, output shaft-to-axle screws to 65 ft lbs, upper ball joint stud nut to 60 ft lbs, upper shock absorber bolt to 75 ft lbs. Tighten wheel lug nuts to 105 ft lbs—through 1972; 130 ft lbs—1973 and later. Tighten drive axle nut to 110 ft lbs (150 ft lbs—1972-73).

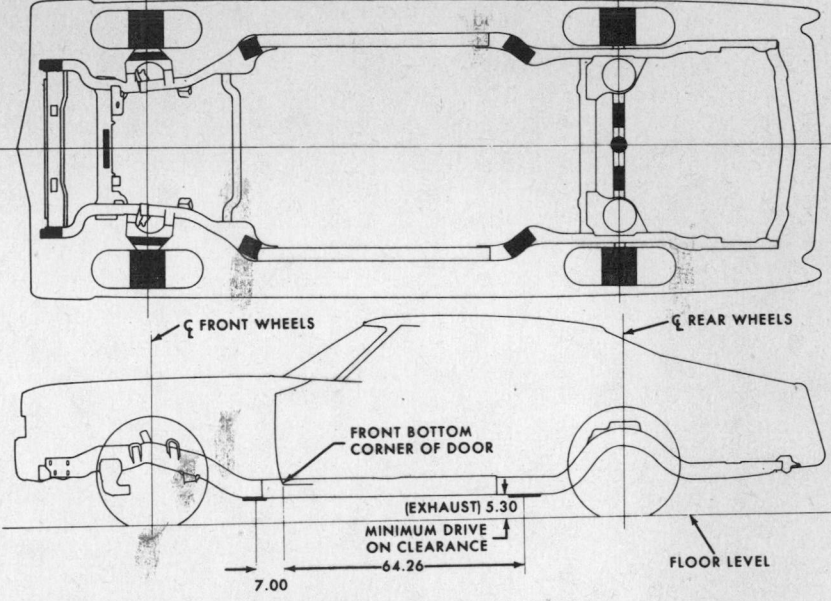

Lift points (© Cadillac Div., G.M. Corp)

JACKING, HOISTING

When jacking the front of the vehicle, make certain that the jack is placed so that it contacts the lower suspension arm just inside the stabilizer bar. If the vehicle is lifted from the rear, place the jack as far in to the middle of the frame as possible so that the Automatic Level Control and the fuel and brake lines are not damaged.

Ideally, the best lift is one which contacts both the front and rear suspension at the same time.

Caution The rear lower control arm should never be used as a lift point for the vehicle.

When working on the vehicle in the raised position, it is recommended that two jackstands be placed under the front frame crossmember. Also, the

Front jacking position
(© Cadillac Div., G.M. Corp)

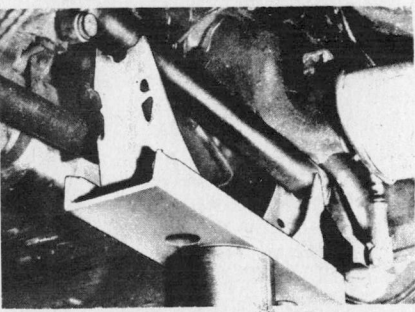

Rear jacking position
(© Cadillac Div., G.M. Corp.)

vehicle should never be supported at the very ends of the frame with anything other than the jack provided with the car.

DIFFERENTIAL

A bevel gear-type differential is used on all front wheel drive models. This design supersedes the original planetary-type final drive. While unit removal and installation procedures are typical, the assembly, or its components are not interchangeable with the earlier design.

Overhauling the differential as-sembly is not recommended. Cadillac recommends that the unit be serviced by replacement only.

Final Drive

Cadillac recommends that the final drive unit not be serviced. It should be serviced by replacement only.

Removal—through 1971

1. Disconnect battery.
2. Pump about one gallon of transmission fluid out of filler tube. Remove bolt on the bracket that secures filler tube and remove filler tube, plugging the filler tube hole.
3. Remove bolts A and B and nut H. (See illustration.)
4. Remove the bolt holding the transmission cooler line to the final drive support bracket.
5. Remove the nut from the large through-bolt and remove the final drive support bracket from the final drive unit.
6. Remove the nut and bolt securing the left front engine mount support bracket to the engine.
7. Remove the bolt securing the final drive support bracket to the left front engine mount support.
8. Raise car and remove wheels and tires.
9. Install lengths of rubber hose on both lower torsion bar connectors.
10. Loosen twelve screws and washers that secure drive axles to output shafts.
11. Loosen, BUT DO NOT REMOVE, lower shock nut on right side.
12. Remove the brace from the final drive case and right-hand output shaft support.

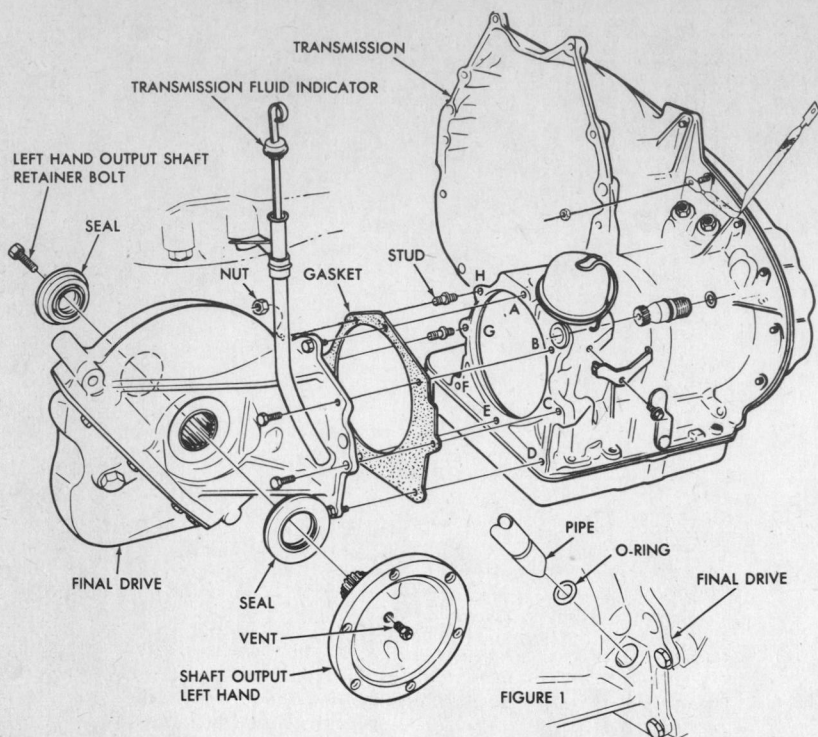

LEFT HAND OUTPUT SHAFT RETAINER BOLT

TRANSMISSION FLUID INDICATOR

TRANSMISSION

SEAL

NUT GASKET

STUD

FINAL DRIVE

SEAL

VENT

SHAFT OUTPUT LEFT HAND

PIPE O-RING

FINAL DRIVE

FIGURE 1

Final drive-to-transmission assembly (© Cadillac Div., G.M. Corp)

13. Remove the battery clip attached to the frame above the right-hand drive axle.
14. Remove the 2 bolts securing the right-hand output shaft support to the engine.
15. Rotate the drive axle rearward toward the starter to gain access to the output shaft.
16. Remove right output shaft.
17. Remove six screws and lock-washers that secure left output shaft to axle.
18. Raise and block the steering gear out of the way.
19. Loosen screws that secure final drive cover to final drive. Allow lubricant to drain then remove screws and cover.
20. Compress left drive axle inner constant velocity joint and secure drive axle to frame.
21. Remove final drive support bracket.
22. Remove bolts C, D, E, and F and nut G.
23. Disengage final drive splines from transmission.
24. Remove final drive unit, permitting ring gear to rotate up over steering gear.
25. Remove transmission to final drive gasket and discard.

Installation—through 1971

1. Positioning new gasket on transmission, install final drive unit, permitting ring gear to rotate up over steering linkage.
2. Align final drive splines with splines in transmission.

3. Align bolt studs G and H on transmission with holes in final drive.
4. Install bolts C, D, E and F and nut G finger tight.
5. Install support bracket on final drive unit.
6. Install other support brackets.
7. Install bolt in oil cooler lines clamp and tighten to 8 ft. lbs.
8. Tighten bolts C, D, E and F and nut G to 25 ft. lbs.
9. Reposition left drive axle and install screws to 65 ft. lbs.
10. Install right output shaft and axle.
11. Position final drive cover to final drive and install screws to 30 ft lbs—through 1973; 13 ft lbs—1974 and later.
12. Fill final drive unit. Tighten lower shock nut to 75 lbs.
13. Install wheels and tires, tightening nuts finger tight.
14. Lower car and tighten wheel nuts to 105 ft lbs—through 1972; 130 ft lbs—1973 and later.
15. Install bolts A and B and nut H, tightening to 25 ft. lbs.
16. Install new O-ring on transmission filler tube, remove plug in filler tube hole and install filler tube.
17. Position the transmission cooler line clips and secure the support bracket with the screw torqued to 8 ft lbs.
18. Connect battery.
19. Check engine oil and transmission fluid. Start engine and add fluid as needed.

20. After running check the seals for leaks.

Removal—1972 and later

1. Disconnect the negative battery cable.
2. Unbolt the transmission filler tube bracket and remove the filler tube.
3. Remove screws A, B and the nut H.
4. Disconnect the transmission cooler lines from the final drive support bracket and slide the clip out of the way.
5. Remove the locknut, washer and long through-bolt holding the final drive support brace to the engine mount bracket.
6. Remove the right-hand output shaft.

Caution The shock absorbers act as rebound stops. Before performing the following Step, be sure that the right-hand shock absorber lower sleeve cannot be dislodged from the stud.

7. Place jackstands under the front frame side rails and lower the hoist that was used when removing the right-hand output shaft.
8. Remove the final drive cover and allow the lubricant to drain into a drain pan.
9. Remove the 6 screws holding the left-hand drive axle to the output shaft. Compress the drive axle inner C.V. joint and hold it in this position to remove the final drive unit with the left-hand output shaft installed.
10. Remove the bolt, washer, and nut holding the left tie strut to the frame crossmember. Loosen the bolt holding the strut to the side rail and rotate the strut outboard until the strut is clear of the final drive area.
11. Remove the large through-bolt nut and washers, securing the final drive support bracket to the final drive.
12. Remove the final drive support bracket.
13. Remove the final drive cover and gasket(s).
14. Remove the final drive with a transmission lift and adapter. The adapter should have a rotating feature to ease removal and installation.
15. Place a drain pan under the transmission and remove screws C, D, E, F and nut G.
16. Disengage the final drive splines from the transmission and let the unit drain.
17. Remove the final drive unit from under the car by sliding the unit toward the front of the car and permitting the ring gear to rotate over the steering linkage. Lower the housing from the car.

18. Remove and discard the final drive-to-transmission gasket.

Installation—1972 and later
See "Installation—through 1971."

FRONT SUSPENSION

The front suspension consists of control arms, stabilizer bar, shock absorbers and a right and left torsion bar. Torsion bars are used in place of conventional coil springs. The front end of the torsion bar is attached to the lower control arm. The rear of torsion bar is mounted into an adjustable arm at the torsion bar crossmember. The carrying height of the car is controlled by this adjustment.

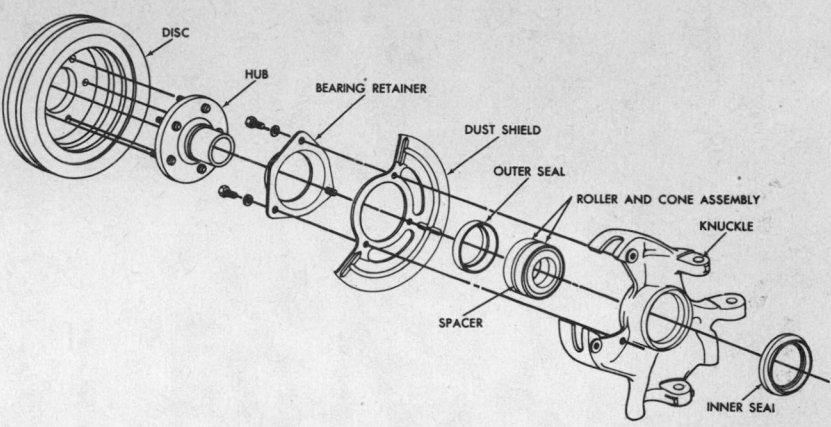

Front hub, bearing, and retainer (© Cadillac Div., G.M. Corp)

Wheel Hub (Front)
Removal and Installation

1. Remove hub cap, loosen wheel nuts, remove drive axle cotter pin and loosen drive axle nut.
2. Jack up car and place axle stands under lower control arms.
3. Remove axle nut and wheel and tire assembly.
4. Remove brake hose and caliper.
   NOTE: Match-mark disc and hub, then remove disc.
5. Remove upper ball joint cotter pin and loosen stud nut.
6. Strike steering knuckle near upper joint to separate it from taper.
7. Cover the lower control arm torsion bar connector with a short piece of rubber hose to avoid damaging the inboard tri pot joint seal when the hub and knuckle are removed.
8. Remove tie-rod end cotter pin and nut.
9. Separate tie-rod end from steering knuckle using a tie-rod splitter.
10. Remove lower ball joint cotter pin and stud nut.
11. Disconnect lower ball joint.
12. Remove hub, backing plate and steering knuckle as an assembly.
13. To install, reverse removal procedure. Tighten both ball joint stud nuts to 85 ft lbs—through 1971. 1972 and later models: Tighten upper ball joint stud to 60 ft lbs; tighten lower ball joint stud to 80 ft lbs. Tighten tie-rod end nut as follows: 30 ft lbs—1970; 38 ft lbs—1971; 40 ft lbs—1972 and later models. Tighten drive axle nut to 110 ft lbs (150 ft lbs—1972-73). Tighten wheel lug nuts to 105 ft lbs—through 1972; 130 ft lbs—1973 and later models.

Torsion Bar

Removal—1970

1. Raise car and place jack under rear axle. Raise front of car and place jacks under front lower control arms.
2. Install torsion bar remover and installer on torsion bar cross-

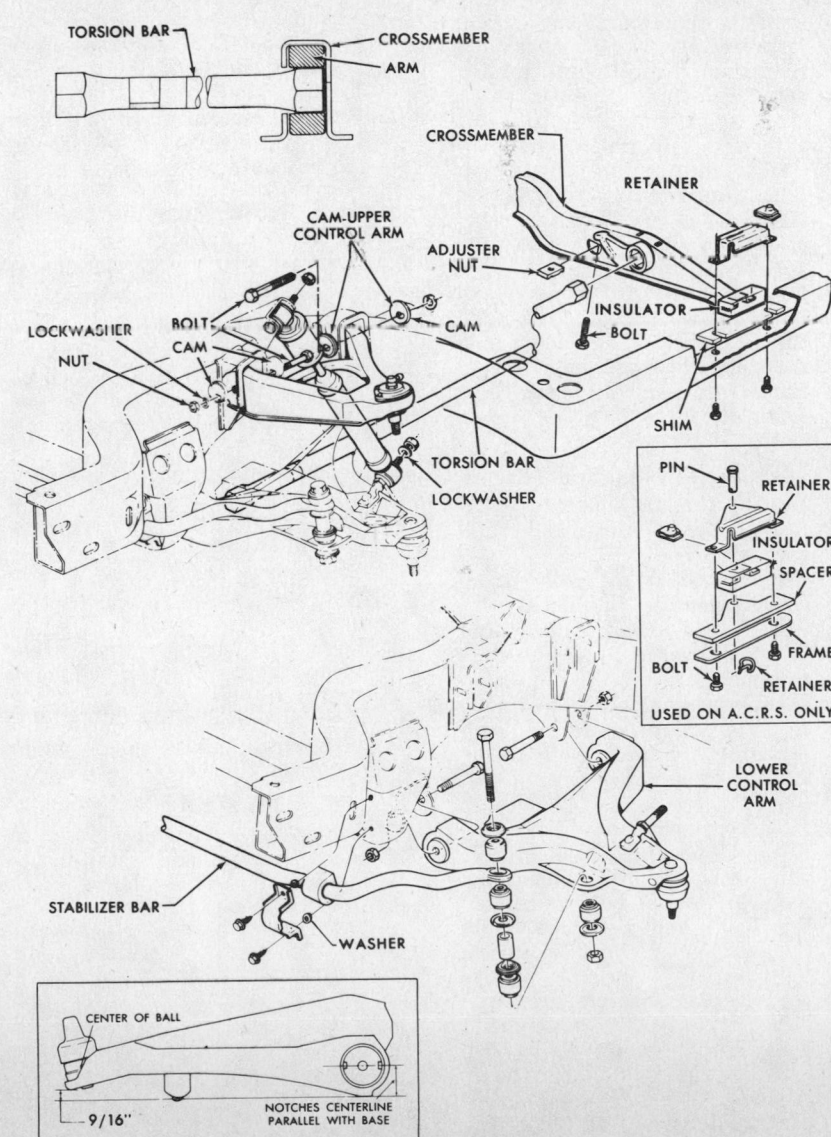

Front suspension disassembled—1975 shown. Right inset shows crossmember lockpins and retainers used on cars equipped with air bags (ACRS).
(© Cadillac Div., G.M. Corp.)

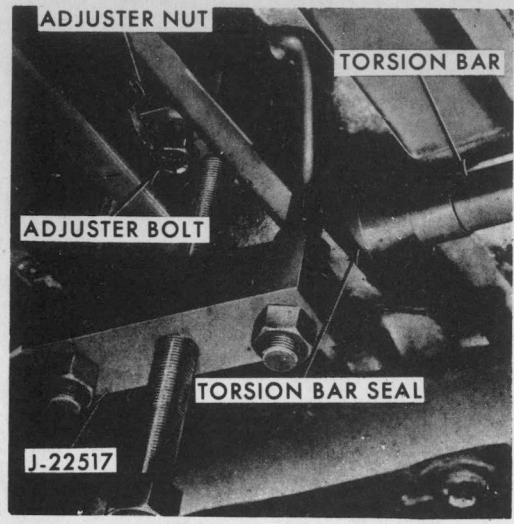

ADJUSTER NUT

TORSION BAR

ADJUSTER BOLT

TORSION BAR SEAL

J-22517

Torsion bar remover and installer (© Cadillac Div., G.M. Corp)

member. Tighten center bolt on this tool until torsion bar adjusting arm is raised enough to permit removal of adjusting bolt and lock nut. Remove adjusting bolt and lock nut.

3. Remove torsion bar installer and remover and install on other end of torsion bar crossmember and repeat Step 2. Remove tool.

4. Remove torsion bar crossmember mounting bolts, bushings, retainers and parking brake cable clip.

5. Drive crossmember down, then rearward until both torsion bars are free. Adjusting arms will fall out.

6. Lift up on crossmember. Remove torsion bars by sliding them out of lower control arm connectors.

Installation—1970

1. Lubricate both ends of torsion bar for approximately 3 in. with extreme pressure chassis lubricant.

2. Place torsion bar in retainer at chassis crossmember.

3. Lubricate lower control arm torsion bar connector and slide torsion bar into connector.

NOTE: The torsion bars are stamped "L" and "R" for left and right. The end which is stamped is inserted in the lower control arm torsion bar connector.

4. Repeat procedure for other torsion bar.

5. Place torsion bar adjusting arm in crossmember, then slide torsion bar toward rear of car until seated in adjusting arm.

6. Repeat for other torsion bar.

7. Install bushings and retainers between crossmember and frame on both sides.

8. Raise front of car, positioning jacks under lower control arms.

9. Install crossmember mounting

bolts and tighten to 40 ft. lbs.

10. Install torsion bar remover and installer on crossmember and tighten center bolt until torsion bar adjusting arm is high enough to permit installation of adjusting bolt and locknut. Install locknut and adjusting bolt.

11. Remove torsion bar remover and installer and install on other end of crossmember and repeat Step 10 for other torsion bar.

12. Remove torsion bar remover and installer.

13. Check the standing height and the front wheel alignment.

14. Raise car, removing jacks, and lower car.

Removal—1971 and later

1. Jack up car and support so that front suspension hangs at full rebound.

2. Remove adjusting bolt from both torsion bar locknuts.

3. Install torsion bar remover and installer tool on torsion bar crossmember.

4. Tighten center bolt of tool until adjusting arm is raised high enough to permit removal of locknut. Remove locknut.

5. Repeat Steps 3 and 4 on other side of crossmember.

6. Remove parking brake cable guide at right side of underbody.

7. Remove torsion bar crossmember bolts and retainers from both sides. On 1974-77 models with air bags (ACRS), remove the lock pins and retainers from either end of the crossmember.

8. Move crossmember toward side opposite the torsion bar being removed. One side of crossmember should clear frame at this point.

9. Lower the free end on the crossmember and drive it rearward until torsion bar is free. It may

be necessary to loosen parking brake adjuster nut to gain slack in cable.

NOTE: although both torsion bars can be removed at this point, it has been found much easier to do only one side at a time.

10. Remove torsion bar from lower control arm.

NOTE: nicks or scratches in torsion bar can cause its failure.

Installation—1971 and later

1. Lubricate 3 in. of each end of torsion bar. Bars are marked L or R for left and right sides—do not interchange.

2. Slide torsion bar into lower control arm as far as it will go after installing the torsion bar seal.

3. Position adjusting arm in crossmember. Holding arm in place, slide torsion bar rearward until it is seated in adjusting arm. The torsion bars are stamped "L" for left and "R" for right. The stamped end is installed in the lower control arm.

4. Position crossmember to frame and reverse Steps 1-7 of *Removal* procedure.

Upper Control Arm
Removal

NOTE: the upper control arm can be serviced as an assembly, although bushings and upper ball joint kits are available.

1. Hoist car and remove wheel. Support the car on jackstands as close to the ball joints as possible.

2. Remove upper shock absorber attaching bolt.

3. Remove cotter pin and nut on upper ball joint.

4. Disconnect brake hose clamp from ball joint stud. Remove caliper.

5. Using hammer and a drift, drive on spindle until upper ball joint stud is disengaged.

6. Remove upper control arm cam assemblies and remove control arm from car.

Installation

1. Guide upper control arm over shock absorber and install bushing ends into frame horns.

2. Install cam assemblies.

NOTE: Front cam is mounted up, rear cam is mounted down—through 1971; both cams are mounted with bolt holes downward—1972 and later models.

3. Install ball joint stud into knuckle. Install caliper.

4. Install brake hose clip on ball joint stud.

5. Install ball joint nut. Torque to 85 ft. lbs. for 1970-71 and 60 ft. lbs. in 1972 and later, and insert cotter pin, crimp.

NOTE: cotter pin must be crimped toward upper control arm to prevent interference with outer C. V. joint seal.

6. Install upper shock attaching bolt and nut. Torque to 75 ft. lbs.
7. Install wheel.
8. Lower hoist.
9. Check camber, caster and toe-in, and adjust if necessary.

Lower Control Arm

Removal

1. Remove wheel disc and loosen wheel mounting nuts.
2. Remove hub cotter pin. Loosen nut.
3. Raise car and remove wheel and tire.
4. Remove torsion bar, as described previously.
5. Remove hub nut and washer, and brake line clips attached to frame.
6. Remove cotter pin, nut and brake line clip from upper ball joint and remove joint from steering knuckle with a hammer and drift.
7. Disconnect shock absorber and remove.
8. Disconnect tie-rod end at steering knuckle with tie-rod end puller.
9. Disconnect stablizer bar and nut and link bolt.
10. Disconnect lower ball joint with ball joint puller and adapter.
11. Disengage hub, knuckle and disc as an assembly and secure to upper control arm with wire.
12. Remove lower control arm to frame nuts and bolts and disengage arm from frame mounts.

Installation

1. Install hub, disc and knuckle assembly on drive axle.
2. Install lower control arms into mounts at chassis.
   NOTE: do not tighten nuts now.
3. Install lower control arm ball joint into steering knuckle. Tighten nut to 85 ft. lbs. to 1971 and 80 ft. lbs. in 1972 and later. Install the cotter pin.
4. Tighten lower control arm bolts to 75 ft lbs (80 ft lbs 1972 and later).
5. Install shock absorber and tighten nut to 75 ft. lbs.
6. Install upper control arm ball joint into steering knuckle and install brake line clip. Tighten nut to 85 ft. lbs. from 1970 to 1971 and 60 ft. lbs from 1972 and later. Install cotter pin.
7. Install brake line clip to chassis.
8. Install tie-rod end in steering knuckle, tightening nut to 30 ft lbs—1970; 38 ft lbs—1971; or 40 ft lbs—1972 and later.

9. Install stabilizer bar.
10. Install hub to drive axle washer and nut.
11. Install torsion bar.
12. Install wheel and tire.
13. Lower car.
14. Tighten hub-to-drive axle nut to 110 ft !bs (150 ft lbs—1972-73), and install cotter pin. Tighten wheel lug nuts to 105 ft lbs—through 1972; 130 ft lbs—1973 and later.
15. Install wheel disc.

Ball Joint Checks

Vertical Check

1. Raise the car and position floor stands under the left and right lower control arm, as near as possible to each lower ball joint. Car must be stable and should not rock on floor stands.
2. Position dial indicator to register vertical movement at wheel hub.
3. Place a pry bar between the lower control arm and the outer race, and pry down on the bar. Very little pressure is necessary. Often the weight of the bar is sufficient. Care must be used so that the drive axle seal is not damaged. The vertical reading must not exceed 0.125 in.

Horizontal Check

1. Place car on floor stands as outlined in Step 1 in the Vertical Check.
2. Position dial indicator at the rim of the wheel, to indicate side play.
3. Grasp wheel, top and bottom, and push in on the bottom of the tire while pulling out at the top. Read gauge, then reverse the push-pull procedure. Horizontal deflection on the gauge should not exceed 0.125 in. at the wheel rim.

Lower Control Arm Ball Joint

Removal

1. Remove the lower control arm.
2. Using chisel, cut the three rivet heads off.
3. By using a 7/32 in. drill bit, drill side rivets 3/16 in. deep.
4. Using hammer and punch, drive center rivet of joint, until joint is out of the control arm.

Installation

1. Install service ball joint into control arm and torque bolts and nut.
2. Reverse lower control arm removal.

Lower Control Arm Ball Joint Seal

The lower ball joint seal can be installed with lower control arm either in or out of the car.

Removal

1. Remove steering knuckle.
2. Using hammer and chisel, tap lightly on the seal retainer.
3. Work the retainer off the joint with a small screwdriver.
4. Wipe grease from ball joint and stud.

Installation

1. Position new seal over ball joint stud.
2. Lubricate jaws of camber adjusting wrench and carefully slide jaw between seal and retainer.
3. Tap lightly with hammer on center bolt of the wrench until retainer is fully seated.
4. Install knuckle.
5. Lubricate the ball joint fitting until grease is apparent in seal.

Front Shock Absorber

Replacement

The front shock absorbers should be removed with the car on a platform type hoist, so that the vehicle weight is supported on the front suspension. If a platform hoist is available, ignore Steps 1 3. If no platform hoist is available, support the car as indicated in Steps 1-3.

1. Remove wheel disc and loosen wheel mounting nuts.
2. Raise car, place on jacks, and remove wheel and tire.
3. Place a hydraulic jack under lower control arm and raise so that load is taken off shock absorber.
4. Disconnect shock absorber at upper and lower mount.
5. Compress shock absorber, working lower mount free from mount bolt.
6. Remove shock absorber.
7. Install by reversing procedure above, tightening shock absorber nuts to 75 ft. lbs. and wheel mounting nuts to 105 ft lbs. (130 ft lbs 1973 and later).

Alignment Procedures Setting Camber & Caster

1. Check camber. The preferred setting for camber is in the specifications. To adjust proceed as follows:
   A. Loosen nut on upper control arm front and rear cam bolts.
   B. Note camber reading and rotate front bolt to correct for one-half of the incorrect reading or as near to that amount as possible. Tighten front nut.
   C. Loosen nut on upper control arm rear cam bolt and rotate

rear cam bolt to bring camber reading to 0°. Tighten rear nut.

D. Check caster. Preferred reading is in the specifications.

NOTE: if caster requires adjustment, proceed with Step E; if not, move to Step I.

E. Loosen front cam bolt nut.

F. Using camber scale on alignment equipment, rotate front bolt so that the camber changes an amount equal to one-quarter of the desired caster change.

NOTE: if adjusting to correct for excessive negative caster, rotate front bolt to increase positive camber. If adjusting to correct for excessive positive caster, rotate front bolt to increase negative camber.

G. Tighten front nut.

H. Loosen nut on rear cam bolt and rotate the rear bolt until camber setting returns to 0°. This results in the correct caster setting.

I. Tighten upper control arm cam nuts to 95 ft. lbs. Hold head of bolt securely; any movement of the cam will affect final setting and will require a recheck of the camber and caster adjustments.

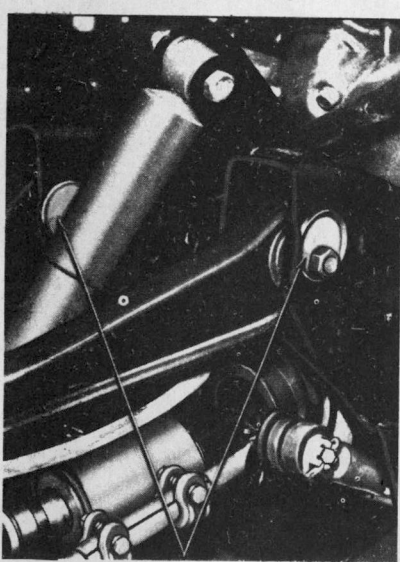

Caster and camber cam locations
(© Cadillac Div., G.M. Corp.)

Relationship of Front and Rear Cams

When setting camber and caster, remember this relationship:

Front cams. If turned for more positive camber, then caster also becomes more positive.

In other words, when turning the front cams to obtain a more positive setting for camber, caster will follow to a more positive setting.

The same is true when turning for more positive caster: more positive camber will follow.

Rear cams. If turned for more positive camber, then caster becomes more negative.

When turning the rear cams to obtain a more positive setting for camber, caster will advance in the opposite direction toward a more negative setting.

Toe-in Adjustment

A. Center steering wheel, raise car and check wheel runout.

B. Loosen tie-rod adjuster nuts, and adjust to proper setting.

C. Tighten tie-rod adjuster nuts. Torque nuts 22 ft. lbs. Position tie-rod clamps so opening of clamps are facing UP. This is a very necessary setting. Interference and a possible tie up of front end linkage could occur, if clamps hit anything while turning.

Front Wheel Bearing Adjustment

1. Raise the front of the car and remove the wheel covers from the wheels and the dust covers, nut locks and cotter pins from the spindles.

2. On 1970 to 1971 models tighten the adjusting nut to 30 ft lbs. while on 1972 to 1977 models torque the nut to 15 ft lbs.

3. Once the correct torque is obtained, on 1970 to 1971 models back the nut off to 0 pounds of torque. 1972 to 1977 models require that the nut be backed off until it is just loose (1 flat).

4. Tighten the nut on 1970 to 1971 models to 6 ft lbs of torque. 1972-77 models are tightened finger tight only.

5. Install cotter pin.

NOTE: If the cotter pin cannot be installed, back the adjusting nut off to the next hole. DO NOT tighten the nut over 6 lbs on 1970 to 1971 models.

REAR SUSPENSION

1970

The rear suspension on the Cadillac Eldorado consists of two single leaf, semi-elliptical springs, two vertical and two horizontal shock absorbers.

1971 and later

A new rear suspension system, introduced in 1971, has replaced the old leaf spring type used previously. This new system is a four-link, coil spring suspension having no components interchangeable with other Cadillac models. Instead of two vertical and two horizontal shock absorbers, as used on earlier models, Automatic Level Control Superlift shock absorbers are used exclusively.

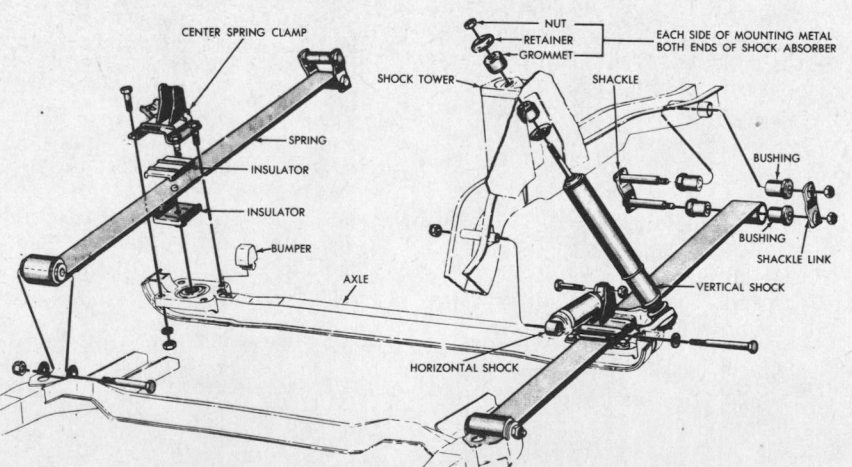

Rear suspension—1970 (© Cadillac Div., G.M. Corp.)

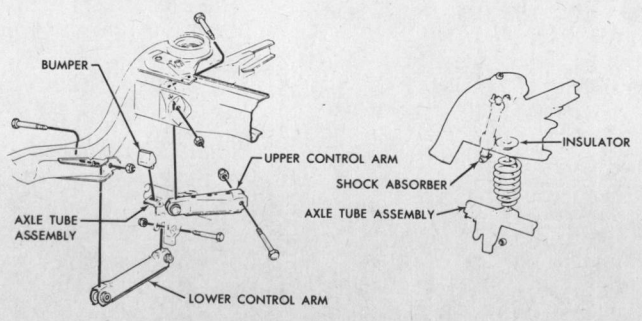

Rear suspension—1971 and later
(© Cadillac Div., G.M. Corp.)

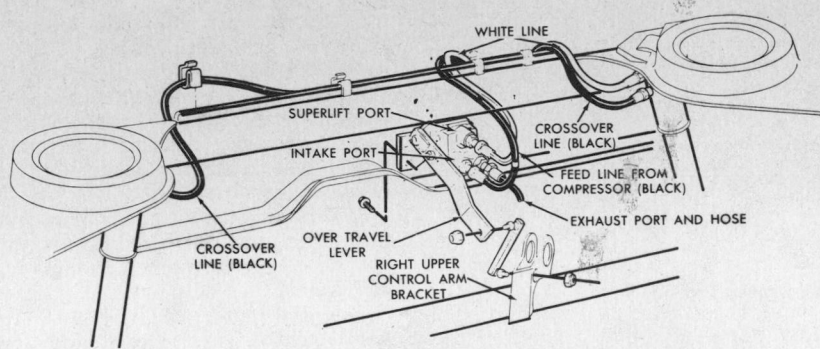

Location of the automatic level control components (© Cadillac Div., G.M. Corp)

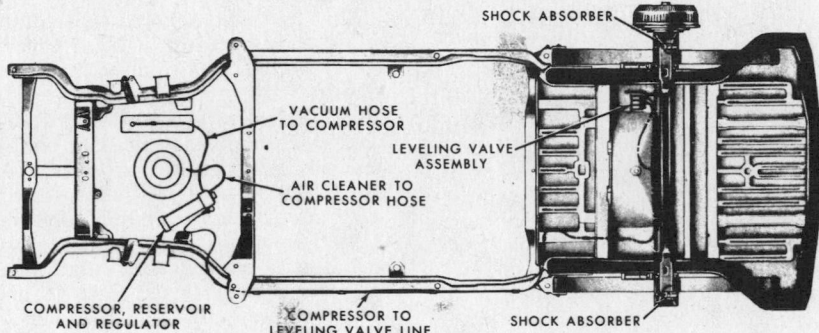

Automatic leveling system (© Cadillac Div., G.M. Corp)

Automatic Level Control

This system is basically the same as that used on other Cadillac models and functions identically. However, the on-car location of major components is different. Procedures will be found in the Cadillac section.

Rear Leaf Spring Removal —1970

1. Raise car.
2. Support rear axle at center with hydraulic jack.
3. Remove rear wheel from side being worked on.
4. Remove nut that secures Automatic Level Control link to axle bracket and remove link.
5. Remove nut that secures front of spring to frame bracket.
   NOTE: do not remove bolt now.
6. Remove two nuts at rear shackle outer link and remove link.
7. Remove four nuts and lockwashers that secure center spring clamp to rear axle and position out of the way.
8. Lower hydraulic jack until axle is free from spring.
9. Remove rear shackle assembly from spring and body.
10. Remove bolt from front of spring and remove spring.

Upper Control Arm Removal and Installation—1971 and Later

1. Jack up car and support rear on axle stands under frame side members.
2. Disconnect Automatic Level Control system over-travel link at right upper control arm axle bracket, then position lever in "center" position.
3. Disconnect lower shock bolt and position shock out of the way.
4. Jack up under rear axle to unload upper control arm.
5. Remove bolt and nut that secures upper arm to axle bracket.
6. Remove bolt and nut that secures upper arm to crossmember; remove arm.
   NOTE: bushings can be replaced at this point.
7. Install upper arm to brackets and install bolts and nuts. Do not tighten nuts at this time.
8. Install lower shock bolt and shock.
9. Jack up on rear axle and remove axle stands under frame side members.
10. With weight of car on axle only, tighten upper arm-to-crossmember nuts to 100 ft lbs (145 ft lbs 1973 and later) and lower axle bracket nuts to 75 ft lbs (110 ft lbs 1973 and later).
11. Install A.L.C. overtravel lever, lower car and inflate system to 140 psi.
    NOTE: control arm pivot bolts must be tightened at standing height or ride rate will be affected.
12. Inspect brake lines for damage.

Lower Control Arm Removal and Installation—1971 and Later

1. Jack up car.

2. Remove bolts and nuts that secure lower arm to axle and frame.
3. Remove lower control arm.
4. Install lower arm and tighten bolts to 100 ft lbs (145 ft lbs 1973 and later).

Rear Coil Spring Removal and Installation—1971 and Later

1. Remove both upper control arms from their axle mountings.
2. Disconnect both rear shocks at lower ends.
3. Disconnect brake hose and cap brake line.
4. Lower axle carefully, using a floor jack, until springs can be removed.

Caution If axle is lowered beyond full rebound, springs can jump from their seats with considerable force. For this reason, lower axle only far enough to allow springs to be lightly compressed by hand and removed.

5. Inspect rubber insulators for damage.
6. Insert springs and jack up axle until springs are compressed.
7. Reconnect shocks and upper control arms.
8. Connect brake hose and bleed rear brake circuit.

Rear Axle Assembly

1970

The rear axle consists of a welded beam-type, drop center axle having spindles pressed into and bolted to the axle flanges. The rear wheels run on tapered roller bearings very similar to those used on the front wheels of Cadillac models other than the Eldorado.

1971 and later

The rear axle was changed in 1971 to a straight, hollow tube design. The spindles still are pressed and bolted to the axle flanges and tapered roller bearings are used. The Track Master system, optional on 1971 and later Eldorado models, uses a hollow spindle through which the drive cables for the speed sensors run.

Rear Wheel Bearing Adjustment

Regularly scheduled wheel bearing repacking is not required. When major brake service is required, it is recommended that the rear wheel bearings be cleaned and repacked with a high melting point grade 2 lithium grease.

Through 1972

1. Adjustment should be made while revolving the wheel at

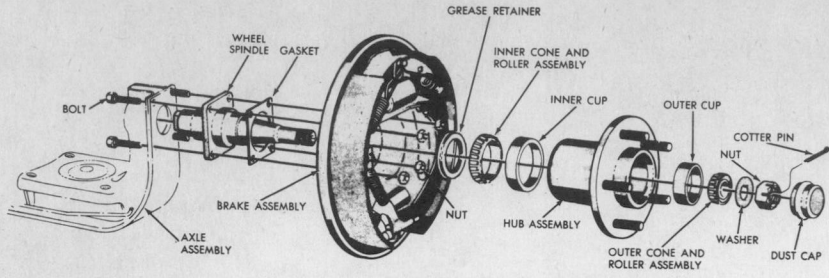

Rear axle disassembled—1970 (© Cadillac Div., G.M. Corp)

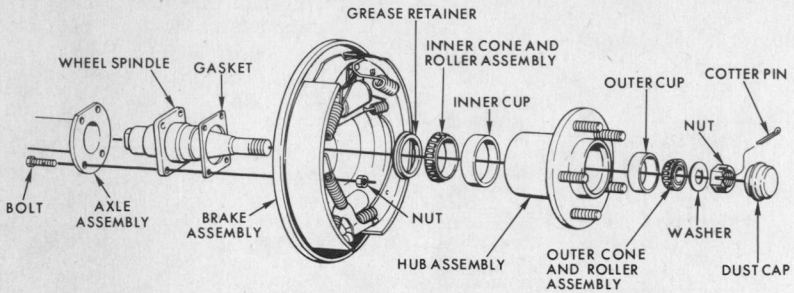

Rear axle disassembled—1971 and later (© Cadillac Div., G.M. Corp)

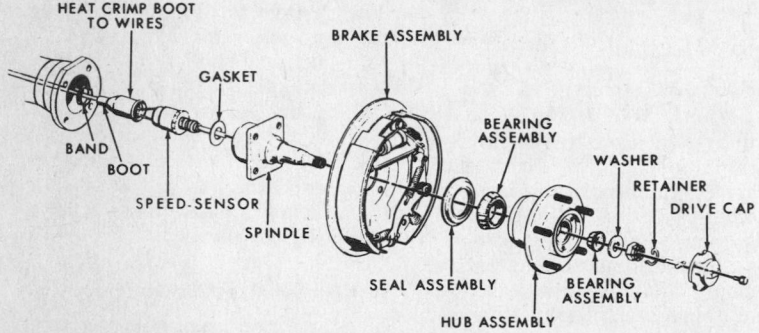

Rear axle disassembled—1971-72 with Track Master (© Cadillac Div., G.M. Corp)

least 3 times the speed of nut rotation through at least 3 revolutions.

2. Check to be sure that the hub is completely seated on the spindle.

3. While rotating the wheel assembly, tighten the spindle nut to 30 ft lbs (through 1971) or 15 ft lbs (1972).

4. On models through 1971, back off the spindle nut 90°. On 1972 models, back the nut off until it is free.

5. On models through 1971, insert the cotter pin after backing the nut off 90°. On 1972 models, tighten the nut finger-tight and insert the cotter pin.

6. If the cotter pin cannot be inserted in either of the 2 holes, back the nut off until it can be inserted.

7. Peen the end of the pin securely.

8. If equipped with Track Master, insert the pin into the end of the sensor assembly using pliers, and install insulators on each end of the pin. The pin should protrude equally from each end of the sensor.

9. Install the dust cap, or if equipped with Track Master, install the drive cap.

1973 and later

1. Adjustment should be made while rotating the wheel at least 3 times the speed of the nut rotation through at least 3 revolutions.

2. While rotating the hub, tighten the spindle nut to 25-30 ft lbs.

3. Back the nut off ½ turn and tighten it to 24 in. lbs. Install the cotter pin.

4. If the cotter pin cannot be installed, back the nut off until it can be installed.

5. The final adjustment should be 24 in. lbs nut torque to 0.004 in. bearing play.

6. Peen the end of the cotter pin and install the dust cap.

BRAKES

Single-piston, sliding caliper Delco-Moraine disc brakes are standard equipment on the front wheels of all Eldorado models. The master cylinders used with these brakes are the same as for the same year Cadillac,

even though the Eldorado uses tandem power **booster** units.

A foot-operated, vacuum-released parking brake working on the rear drums via mechanical linkage is used. This is virtually identical to the parking brake used on other Cadillac models.

Beginning 1976, hydraulically-assisted four-wheel disc brakes are standard. 11 in. diameter single-piston disc brakes with integral parking brake and automatic adjusters are used on the rear. Front and rear brake calipers and pads are not interchangeable.

The hydraulic power booster is called "Hydro-boost." The booster uses power steering pump fluid pressure to assist or multiply brake pedal force applied to the master cylinder. The booster unit is mounted on the firewall in the same location as previous vacuum boosters. A larger capacity power steering pump reservoir is used in addition to a fluid cooler and filter. A reserve accumulator system stores pressurized fluid to provide a minimum of three power-assisted brake applications should pump fluid be stopped. Non-assisted braking is available when the reserve system is exhausted.

For brake service, see the Unit Repair Section of this manual.

Master Cylinder Removal and Installation

See Cadillac section.

Power Brake Booster Removal and Installation

1. Disconnect hydraulic lines from master cylinder.
2. Disconnect vacuum line from vacuum check valve on unit.
3. Remove steering column lower cover.
4. Remove cotter pin, washer and spring spacer that secure power unit pushrod to brake pedal arm.
5. Remove the four nuts that secure power unit to firewall, then remove power unit.
6. To install, reverse removal procedure.

Hydraulic Power Brake Booster Removal and Installation

Caution *Power steering fluid and brake fluid are incompatible. If brake seals contact steering fluid or steering seals contact brake fluid, the seals will be damaged.*

1. With engine off, pump brake pedal four or five times to empty accumulator of pressurized fluid.
2. Remove the two master cylinder-to-booster attaching nuts and move the master cylinder away from the booster with brake lines attached.

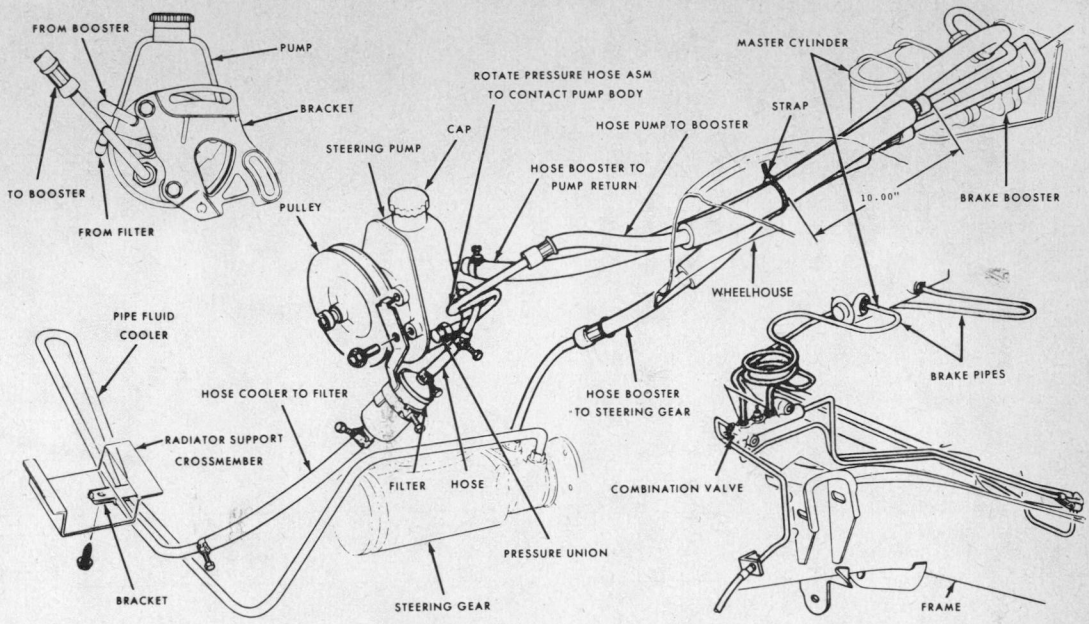

Hydro-boost system components (© Cadillac Div., G.M. Corp.)

3. Remove and plug the three hydraulic lines from the booster. Remove the washer and retainer that secures the booster pedal rod to the brake pedal arm.

4. Remove the four nuts which attach the booster to the firewall.

NOTE: *To avoid damaging the booster, never pry the pedal rod off the pedal arm.*

5. Loosen the booster from the firewall and move the booster pedal rod inboard until it disconnects from the brake pedal arm. Remove the spring washer from the brake pedal arm and remove the booster.

6. To install, reverse the removal procedure. Tighten the booster mounting nuts to 15 ft lbs and the master cylinder-to-booster mounting nuts to 20 ft lbs. Bleed the Hydro-boost system.

Hydro-Boost System Bleeding

The system should be bled whenever the booster is removed and installed.

1. Fill the power steering pump until the fluid level is at the base of the pump reservoir neck. Disconnect the battery lead from the HEI distributor.

2. Jack up the front of the car, turn the wheels all the way to the left, and crank the engine for a few seconds.

3. Check steering pump fluid level. If necessary, add fluid to the "Add" mark on the dipstick.

4. Lower the car, connect the battery lead, and start the engine. Check fluid level and add fluid to the "Add" mark if necessary. With the engine running, turn the wheels from side to side to bleed air

from the system. Make sure that the fluid level stays above the internal pump casting.

5. The Hydro-boost system should now be fully bled. If the fluid is foaming after bleeding, stop the engine, let the system set for one hour, then repeat the second part of Step 4.

The preceding procedure should be effective in removing excess air from the system, however sometimes air may still remain trapped. When this happens the booster may make a "gulping" noise when the brake is applied. Lightly pumping the brake pedal with the engine running should cause this noise to disappear. After the noise stops, check the pump fluid level and add as necessary.

Rear Disc Brake Pad Replacement

1976 and Later Models

1. Remove and discard 2/3 of the brake fluid in the forward master cylinder reservoir. This will prevent overflow when removing the rear calipers.

2. Raise the car and remove the wheel and tire. Install one wheel lug nut with the flat side toward the rotor to secure the rotor when the caliper is removed.

3. Loosen the tension on the parking brake cable at the equalizer. Remove the cable from the parking brake lever.

4. Remove the return spring, locknut, lever, lever seal, and anti-friction washer.

NOTE: *The lever must be held in place while removing the nut.*

5. Clean any dirt from the caliper surface in the area of the lever

seal. Using a 7 in. or larger C-clamp with the solid end on the lever stop and screw end on the back of the outboard pad, turn the clamp until the piston bottoms in the caliper.

NOTE: *Do not position the C-clamp on the actuator screw.*

6. Before removing the clamp, lubricate the caliper housing surface (under the lever seal), with silicone.

7. Install the anti-friction washer, lever seal, and lever, using new parts if necessary.

NOTE: *Install the lever on the hex with the arm pointing downward.*

8. Rotate the lever toward the front of the car, hold in this position, install the nut, and torque to 25 ft lbs. Then rotate the lever back to stop.

9. Install the lever return spring and remove the C-clamp.

NOTE: *Return springs are color coded—red for right-hand caliper, black for left-hand.*

10. Remove the brake line from the caliper and plug the opening.

NOTE: *If the brake line nut is seized, the brass bolt and block on the caliper can be removed with the brake line attached by removing the bolt and block copper washers after removing the caliper mounting bolts. Plug the openings.*

11. Remove the caliper mounting bolts, remove the caliper with the brake pads, then remove the pads.

12. Clean the face of the piston. Inspect the piston and check valve area for fluid leaks evidenced by excessive moisture around boot area. Check the dust boot for cuts, cracks, or other damage

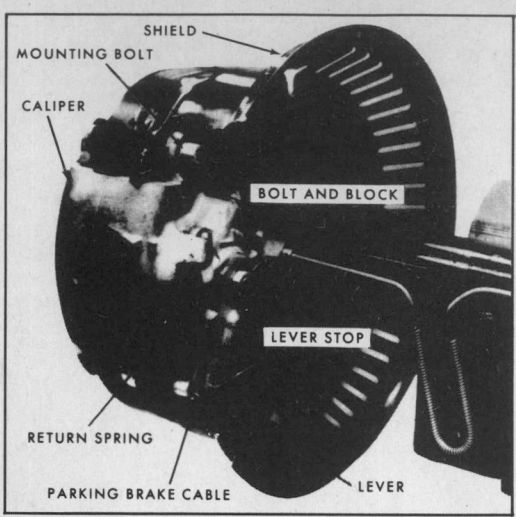

Inboard view of rear disc brake assembly
(© Cadillac Div., G.M. Corp.)

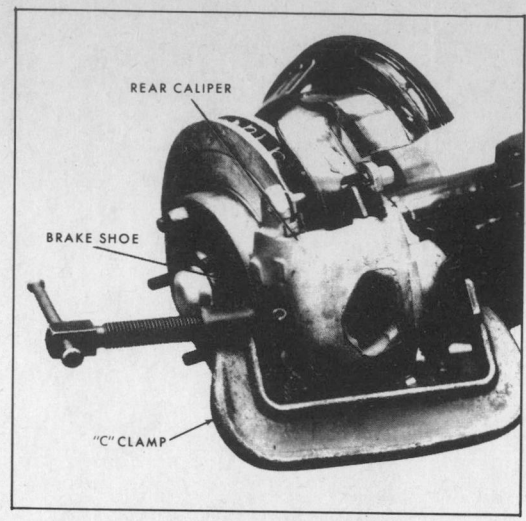

C-clamp installed on rear caliper
(© Cadillac Div., G.M. Corp.)

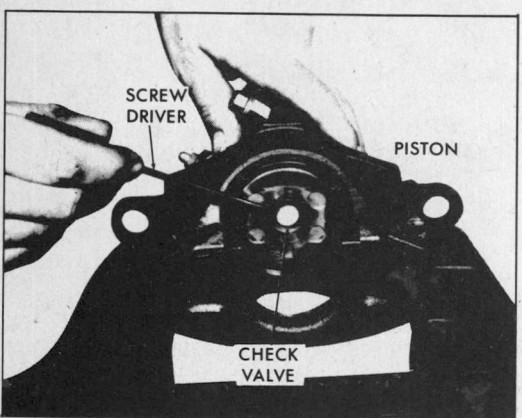

Removing the piston check valve
(© Cadillac Div., G.M. Corp.)

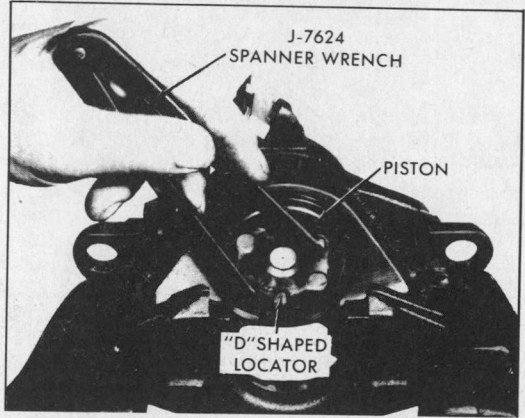

Rotating caliper piston with special tool. Note D-shaped indentation in piston.
(© Cadillac Div., G.M. Corp.)

which would affect its sealing ability. Replace if leaks are present.

Caution *Do not use compressed air to clean the caliper to avoid the possibility of unseating the dust boot.*

13. Check the piston boot seal for leaks. If leaks are present, replace the piston seal and the boot seal.
14. Check for leaks at the threaded end of the actuator screw. If leaks are present, replace the seal. Replace the caliper if the bore is scratched or nicked.
15. Remove and discard the two caliper mounting sleeves and four bushings. Install new bushings and sleeves using silicone lube.

NOTE: *The sleeves are installed in the inner bushings.*

16. Remove and discard the piston check valve. Install a new piston check valve.

IMPORTANT: *Do not use front brake pads on the rear calipers.*

17. Position a new inboard pad on the piston. The D-shaped tab MUST fit in the identation present in the piston. Should the

piston need rotation, use the special tool.

18. Install the new outboard pad.
19. Remove all dirt from the caliper mounting bolts. Do not use sandpaper or a wire brush as this will damage the plating. Replace the bolts if corroded or damaged.

NOTE: *If the brass bolt and block was removed with the brake line, unplug the fittings and install the bolt and block using two new copper gaskets. Torque the bolt to a maximum of 30 ft lbs.*

20. Slide the caliper over the rotor and install the mounting bolts. Make sure that all sleeves, bushings, and pins are well lubricated with silicone.

NOTE: *The mounting bolt should go under the inboard shoe ears.*

21. Torque the caliper mounting bolts to 30 ft lbs.
22. Unplug the fittings and install the brake line tube nut into the caliper. Pump the brake pedal to seat the pad against the rotor.
23. Clinch the upper ear of the outboard pad by placing a 12 in. pliers with one jaw on top of the upper ear and the other jaw in

the notch on the bottom of the pad, opposite the upper ear. After clinching there should be no radial clearance between the pad ears and the caliper housing. If any radial clearance exists, repeat the clinching procedure.

24. Connect the parking brake cables and adjust the parking brake.
25. Bleed the rear brake system. After bleeding, apply the service brake several times to ensure adjustment.
26. Remove the one wheel lug nut used to retain the rotor and install the wheel and tire. Lower the car and tighten the wheel lug nuts to 130 ft lbs.

Parking Brake Adjustment

Through 1975
See *Cadillac section.*

1976 and Later Models

1. Lubricate the parking brake cables at the equalizer hooks and underbody rub points. Check for free movement of all cables.
2. With the parking brake in the fully released position, jack the

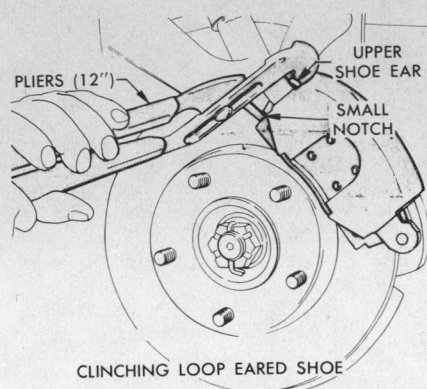

CLINCHING LOOP EARED SHOE

Clinching outer brake pad
(© Cadillac Div., G.M. Corp.)

rear of the car to raise the rear wheels off the floor.

3. Hold the brake cable stud from turning and tighten the equalizer nut until slack is removed.

4. Make sure that the caliper levers are against their stops on the caliper housings. If the levers are off their stops, loosen the cable until the levers return to their stops.

5. Operate the parking brake pedal several times to check the adjustment. After adjustment, the parking brake pedal should travel 4-5 in. with an approximate force of 125 lbs on the pedal.

6. Lower the car.

NOTE: *The caliper levers must be on their stops after adjustment.*

STEERING

The steering linkage on the Eldorado is composed of a pitman arm, idler arm, a pair of tie rod assemblies, a drag link, and a shock absorber. The pitman arm connects the left side of the drag link to the steering gear while the idler arm connects the right side of the drag link to the frame. The small shock absorber connects the drag link to the frame and serves to dampen the vibrations in the linkage. The tie rods connect the drag link with the steering knuckles.

For steering gear overhaul see the "Unit Repair Section."

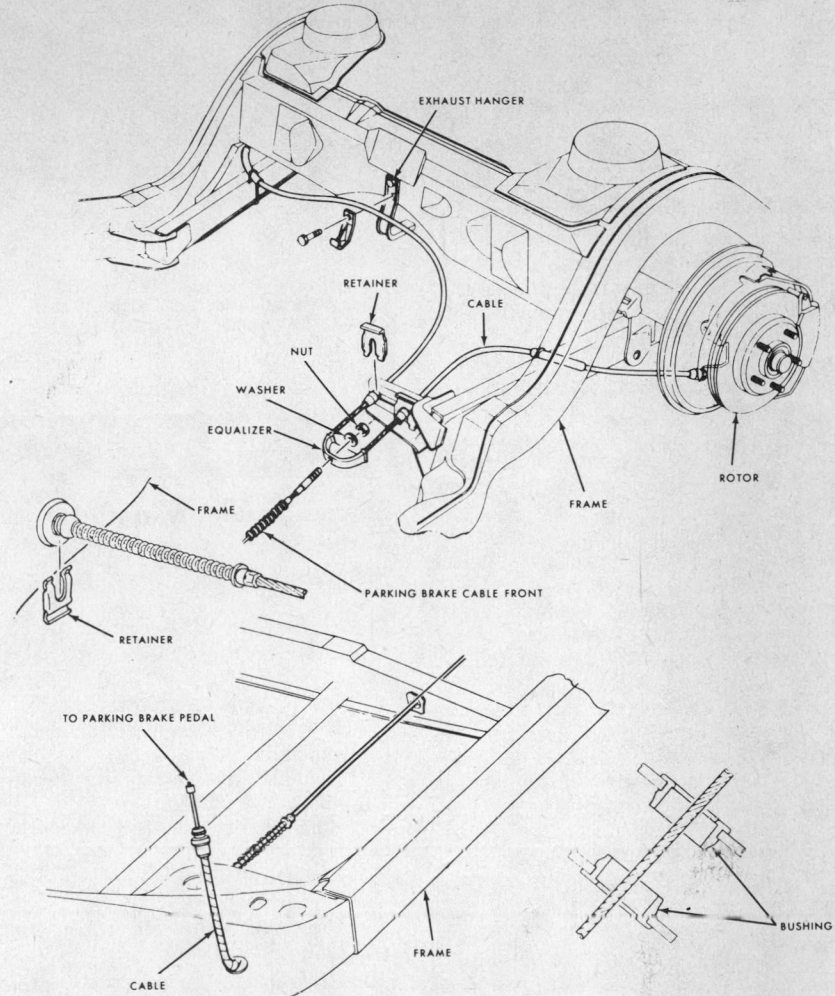

Parking brake cables—1976 and later (© Cadillac Div., G.M. Corp.)

Steering Linkage Removal and Installation

1. Remove the front wheels.
2. Remove the steering damper from the frame.
3. Remove all the cotter pins and nuts from the pitman arm and the idler arm pivots on the drag link.
4. Using a puller, remove both the idler and pitman arm pivots from the drag link.

NOTE: *It may be necessary to loosen the steering gear from the* frame *to remove the drag link from the pitman arm.*

5. The cotter pins and nuts from the outer tie rod pivots should be removed at the steering knuckles. Then separate the tie rod pivots from the steering knuckles.
6. The linkage can be removed from the frame.
7. If the idler arm is to be removed, loosen the locknut and bolt which fastens it to the frame.
8. Installation is accomplished by reversing the removal procedure. The torque on the damper should be 40 ft lbs while the tie rod torque is 60 ft lbs. When installing the idler arm on the frame tighten the bolt to 95 ft lbs.

Power Steering Pump, Steering Wheel, and Turn Signal Switch Removal and Installation

See *Cadillac Section.*

Ignition Switch Removal and Installation

See *Cadillac Section.*

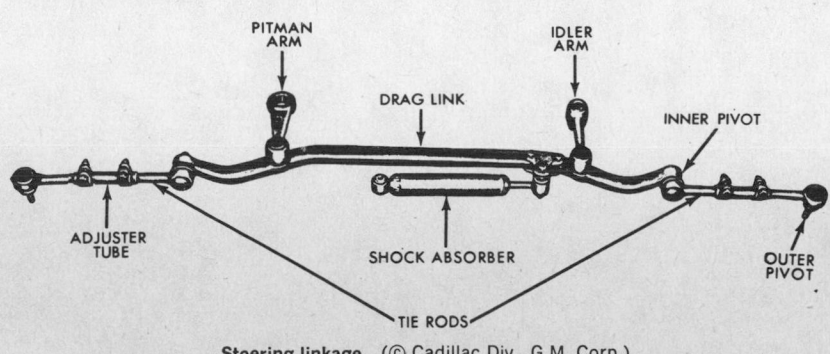

Steering linkage (© Cadillac Div., G.M. Corp.)

Ignition Lock Cylinder Removal and Installation

See *Cadillac Section.*

INSTRUMENT PANEL

Basically the instrument panel of the Eldorado is the same as that of the Cadillac. For a general description of the instrument panel see the Cadillac section.

Headlight Switch Removal and Installation

1. Disconnect negative battery cable. Remove steering column lower cover.
2. Disconnect wiring harness retainer below headlight switch assembly.
3. Depress spring loaded release button on top of headlight switch and remove switch, knob and rod assembly (switch "on").
4. Remove screw with ground wire at bottom of switch housing.
5. Pull assembly down and rearward, disconnect wiring harness connectors, two bulbs and remove assembly.
6. Install in reverse of above.

WINDSHIELD WIPERS

The windshield wiper system is similar to that used on other Cadillac models.

Motor Removal and Installation

See *Cadillac Section.*

RADIO

See *Cadillac Section.*

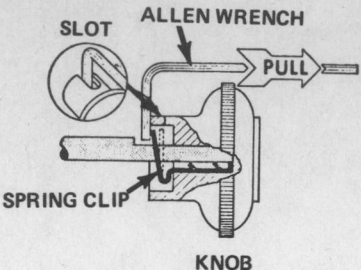

1971 and later radio knob removal
(© Cadillac Div., G.M. Corp.)

HEATER

Blower Assembly and Motor Removal and Installation

1970

1. Drain cooling system.
2. Remove rubber cooling hose from nipple and blower motor.
3. Disconnect blower motor electrical connector.
4. Remove five attaching screws and blower motor.
5. Remove left cowl-to-fender strut rod.
6. Remove heater hoses from blower case.
7. Disconnect Bowden cable from temperature door.
8. Disconnect connector from motor resistor.
9. Disconnect vacuum hoses, then remove twelve screws from blower case.
10. Pull blower assembly away from cowl and remove from car.
11. To install, reverse removal procedure, using a new gasket.

1971 and later

See *Cadillac Section.*

Heater Core Removal and Installation

1970

1. Remove heater blower motor and assembly.
2. Remove four screws, two on each side, that secure retaining clamps.
3. Remove retaining clamps and heater core.

1971 and later

See *Cadillac Section.*

SEAT BELTS

Disabling the Seat Belt/ Starter Interlock and Buzzer

The seat belt/starter interlock was used only on early production 1975s.

It is now legal to disable the seat belt/starter interlock, but *not* the warning light. To do this, proceed as follows:

1. Disconnect the negative (−) battery cable.
2. Locate the interlock harness connector, which is on or near the fuse block. The connector has orange, yellow, and green leads running to it.
3. Cut and tape the green lead on the body harness side of the interlock connector.
4. Remove the steering column lower cover.
5. Remove the buzzer connector from its mounting bracket and separate the buzzer from it. Install the connector back on the bracket.
6. Replace the steering column lower cover.
7. Connect the negative battery cable.
8. Check system operation by starting the car with the seat belt unfastened.

☐ PARTS SPECIFIC TO F.I. VEHICLES

*ELDORADO WITH CARBURETOR AND ALL WITH FUEL INJECTION

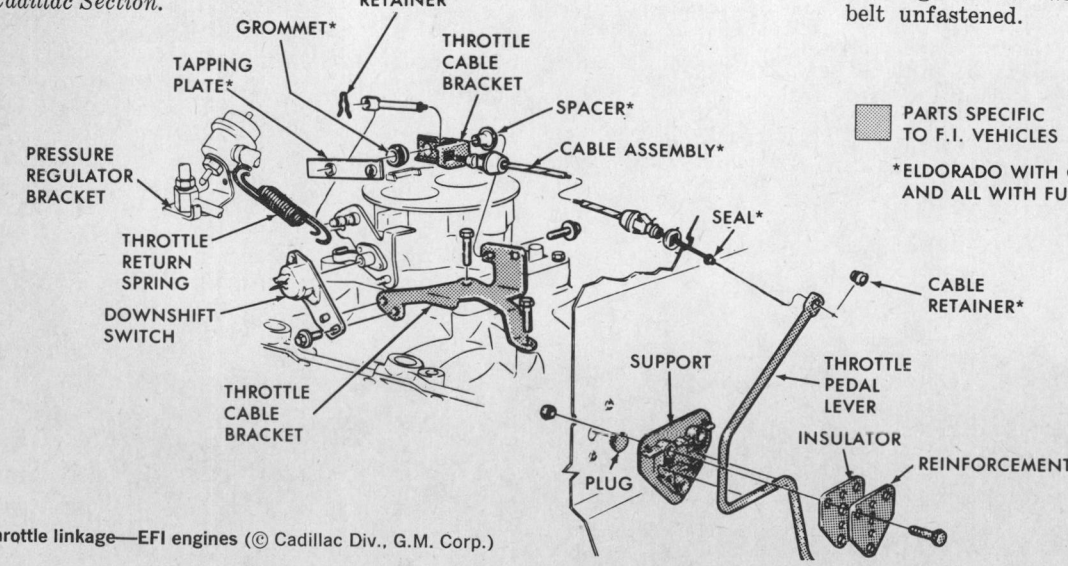

Throttle linkage—EFI engines (© Cadillac Div., G.M. Corp.)

INDEX

Camaro · Chevelle · Monte Carlo · Nova

Automatic Transmission in-car service   **C344**
Band adjustments   C347
Neutral safety switch adjustment   C347
Pan Removal and Installation, fluid and
    filter change   C347
Powerglide throttle valve linkage
    adustment   C346
Shift linkage adjustment   C345
Turbo Hydra-Matic detent adjustment   C346

Brakes   **C351, U299**
Master cylinder Removal and
    Installation   C351
Parking brake adjustment   C352
Power brake booster Removal and
    Installation   C351

Charging System   **C329, U2**
Alternator Removal and Installation   C329
Regulator Removal and Installation   C329

Clutch   **C342**
Free-play adjustment   C343
Removal and Installation   C342

Cooling System   **C334, U367**
Radiator Removal and Installation   C334
Thermostat Removal and Installation   C335
Water pump Removal and Installation   C335

Emission Controls   **C335, U145**
Air injection reactor   C335
Catalytic converter   C336
Controlled combustion system   C335
Early fuel evaporation system   C336
Evaporative emission control   C335
Exhaust gas recirculation   C336
Positive crankcase ventilation   C335
Transmission controlled spark   C335

Engine   **C336, U194**
ENGINE Removal and Installation   C337
CYLINDER HEAD REMOVAL AND
    INSTALLATION   C338
LUBRICATION   C341
Oil pan Removal and Installation   C341
Oil Pump Removal and Installation   C341
Rear main seal Removal and
    Installation   C342
MANIFOLDS   C337

PISTONS and CONNECTING RODS
TIMING COVER, CHAIN AND CAMSHAFT   C337
Camshaft Removal and Installation   C340
Cover Removal and Installation   C339
Cover oil seal Removal and Installation   C340
Timing chain replacement   C340
VALVE SYSTEM   C337
Valve adjustment   C337

Front Suspension   **C349, U292**
Ball joint inspection   C349
Ball joint Removal and Installation   C349
Control arm Removal and Installation   C350
Coil spring Removal and Installation   C349
Shock absorber Removal and
    Installation   C349
Wheel bearing adjustment   C349

Fuel System   **C332, U50**
Fuel filter Removal and Installation   C332
Fuel pump Removal and Installation   C332
Idle speed and mixture adjustment   C332

Heater   **C354**
Heater blower Removal and Installation   C354
Heater core Removal and Installation   C355

Ignition System   **C330, U34**
Breaker point adjustment   C331
Distributor Removal and Installation   C330
Firing Order   C315
HEI system tachometer hookup   C330
Ignition timing   C331

Instrument Panel   **C354, U350**
Light switch replacement   C354

Manual Transmission   **C343, U231**
Shift linkage adjustment   C343
Transmission Removal and Installation   C343

Jacking, Hoisting   **C348**

Radio   **C354**
Radio Removal and Installation   C354

Rear Axle   **C348, U285**
Axle shaft, bearing, and seal
    Removal and Installation   C348

Rear Suspension   **C350**
Spring Removal and Installation   C351
Shock absorber Removal and
    Installation   C350

Seat Belts   **C355**
Disabling the interlock system   C355

Specifications   **C314, U359**
Capacities   C324
Crankshaft and connecting rod   C326
Engine identification   C315
General engine   C319
Piston clearance   C328
Ring   C328
Tune-up   C321
Torque   C327
Valve   C325
Wheel alignment   C329
Year identification   C314

Starting System   **C329, U2**
Starter Removal and Installation   C329

Steering   **C352, U328**
Bleeding power steering system   C352
Ignition Switch replacement   C353
Lock cylinder replacement   C353
Steering wheel Removal and Installation   C353
Turn signal switch Removal and
    Installation   C353
Tie rod Removal and Installation   C352
Power steering pump Removal and
    Installation   C352

U-Joints   **C347**
Driveshaft Removal and Installation   C348
Universal joint Removal and Installation   C348
    Dana and Cleveland type   C348
    Saginaw type   C348

Windshield Wipers   **C354**
Motor Removal and Installation   C354

YEAR IDENTIFICATION

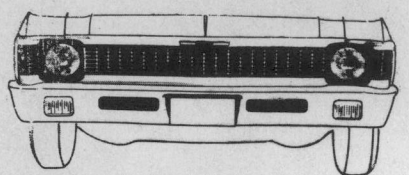

1970-72 Nova

1973 Nova

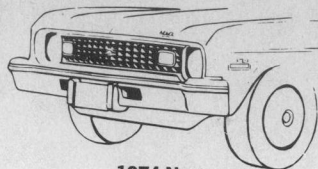

1974 Nova

1975 Nova LN

1976 Nova LN

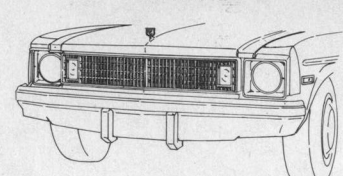

1977 Nova

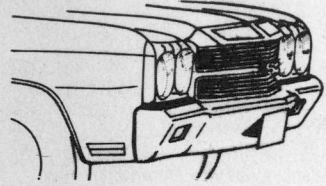

1970 Chevelle

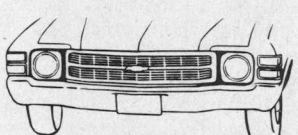

1971 Chevelle

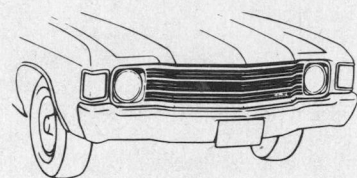

1972 Chevelle

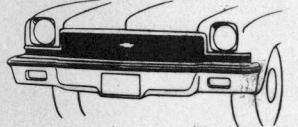

1973 Chevelle

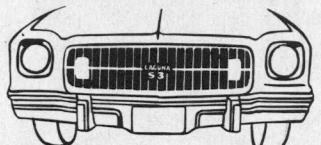

1974 Chevelle Laguna

1975 Malibu Classic

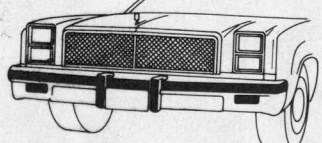

1976 Malibu Classic

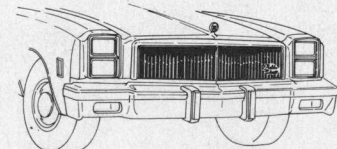

1977 Malibu Classic

1970-71 Camaro

1972 Camaro

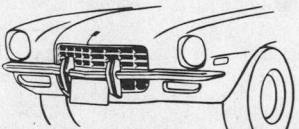

1973 Camaro

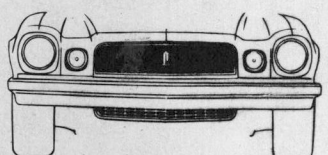

1974 Camaro

1975 Camaro

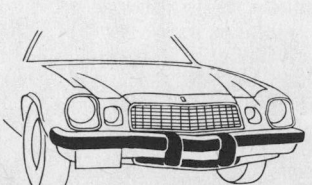

1976-77 Camaro

1970 Monte Carlo

1971 Monte Carlo

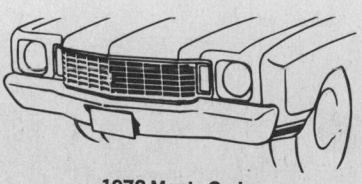

1972 Monte Carlo

YEAR IDENTIFICATION

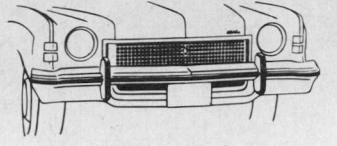

1973 Monte Carlo

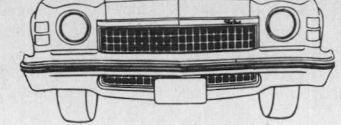

1974 Monte Carlo

1975 Monte Carlo

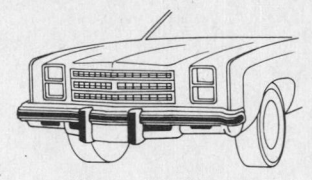

1976 Monte Carlo

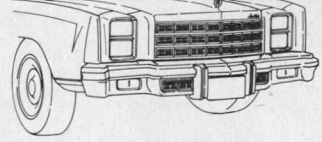

1977 Monte Carlo

FIRING ORDER

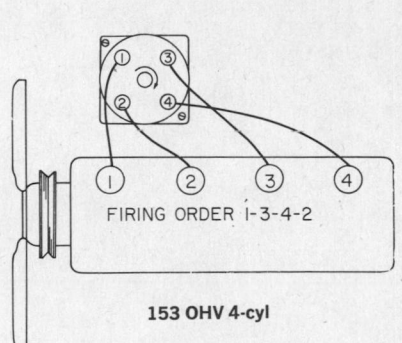

FIRING ORDER 1-3-4-2

153 OHV 4-cyl

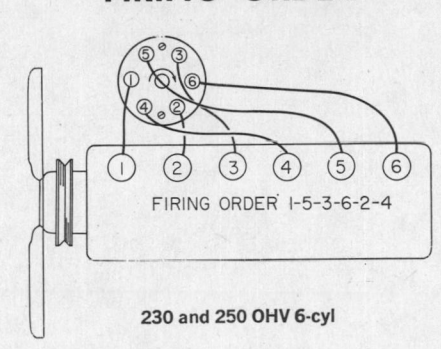

FIRING ORDER 1-5-3-6-2-4

230 and 250 OHV 6-cyl

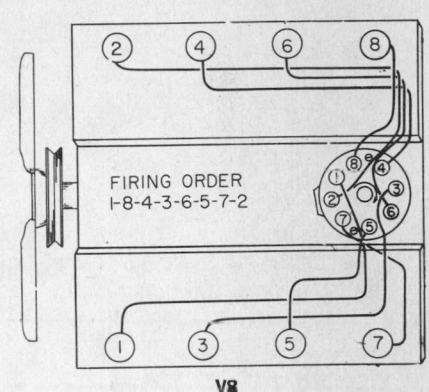

FIRING ORDER 1-8-4-3-6-5-7-2

V8

ENGINE IDENTIFICATION

Engine identification code letters follow engine serial number.
4-6 Cyl.—Pad at front right-hand side of cylinder block at rear of distributor.
V8—Pad at front right-hand side of cylinder block.

Nova

No. Cyls.	Cu. In. Displ.	Type	1970	1971	1972	1973	1974	1975	1976	1977
						YEAR AND CODE				
4	153	M.T.	CCA							
4	153	PG, Torque Dr.	CCB							
6	230	Torque Dr.	CCD							
6	250	M.T.	CCG, CRF	CCI, CCL	CBG, CDM	CCC	CCR			
6	250	PG, w/ex. EM	CCM		CSD	CCA				
6	250	PG, AC								
6	250	T.H. 350	CCK				CCK			
6	250	M.T.	CAA							
6	250	PG, TD	CAB							
6	250	M.T., w/NB2				CCD				
6	250	PG, w/NB2				CCB				
6	250	T.H. California					CCW			
6	250							CJL, CJS, CJM, CJT, KJR, CJU	CCB, CCC, CCD, CCF	
8	262							CZF, CZH, CZJ, CZK, CZL, CZM	CZL, CZM	
8	305								CPA, CPB, CPC	
8	307	M.T.			CKG	CHB				
8	307	PG			CKH					
8	307	T.H.			CTK	CHH				

C315

ENGINE IDENTIFICATION (Continued)

Nova

No. Cyls.	Cu. In. Displ.	Type	1970	1971	1972	1973	1974	1975	1976	1977
8	307	M.T., w/ex. EM			CAR					
8	307	PG, w/ex. EM			CAZ					
8	307	T.H., w/ex. EM			CMA					
8	307	M.T., w/NB2				CHD				
8	307	T.H., w/NB2				CHC				
8	307	M.T.	CNC							
8	307	PG	CNE							
8	307	T.H. 350	CNF							
8	307	4-spd.	CND							
8	307	M.T.	CCA	CCA						
8	307	PG	CCC	CCC						
8	350	M.T.	CNI(250), CNJ(300)		CKA CKK	CKA, CKB				
8	350	T.H.	CNN(250), CRE(300)		CTL CKD	CKW CKW				
8	350	2-BBL.								
8	350	PG	CNK, CNM							
8	350	PG, 2-BBL.								
8	350	PG	CGB(250)	CGB						
8	350	M.T.	CGK(300)	CGK						
8	350	T.H. 350	CGL(300), CJD(300)	CGL	CDD CMD					
8	350	M.T.	CJG(300)		CDG					
8	350	M.T., w/NB2				CKC, CKH	CKH			
8	350	A.T., w/NB2				CKK, CKD	CKD			
8	350	3-spd., 2-BBL.					CMC			
8	350	4-spd., 4-BBL.					CKB			
8	350	T.H., 2-BBL.					CMA			
8	350	T.H., 4-BBL.					CKD			
8	350							CMU, CMY, CRC, CRD, CRT, CRU, CRX, CUH, CUJ, CRZ, CUM, CUS	CMB, CHW, CML, CKJ, CKK, PA, PB, PE, PF, PM, PN, PO, PP	
8	396	T.H. 400	CTW(350), CTY(375), CKN(325)							
8	396	M.T.	CTX(350), CKO(375)							
8	396	T.H. 400#	CKP(375)							
8	396	M.T., HDC	CTZ(350), CKQ(375)							
8	396	B.T., HDC#	CKU(375)							
8	396	M.T.#	CKT(375)							
8	402	M.T.	CKR(330)							
8	402	M.T., HDC	CKS(300)							

AC—air conditioned
HDC—heavy duty clutch
HP—high performance engine
w/ex. EM, or EM—with exhaust emission
M.T.—manual transmission

PG—Powerglide transmission.
3-spd.—three speed transmission
4-spd.—four speed transmission
T.H.—Turbo Hydra-Matic
#—Aluminum heads

TD—Torque Drive
NB2—Calif. only
MK. IV—Big block

ENGINE IDENTIFICATION (Continued)

Engine identification code letters follow engine serial number.
6 Cyl.—Pad at front right-hand side of cylinder block at rear of distributor.
V8—Pad at front right-hand side of cylinder block.

Chevelle and Monte Carlo

No. Cyls.	Cu. In. Displ.	Type	YEAR AND CODE							
			1970	1971	1972	1973	1974	1975	1976	1977
6	250	3-spd.	CCL							
6	250	PG	CCM		CBJ					
6	250	T.H.	CCK			CCA	CCX			
6	250	T.H., AC								
6	250	M.T.		CAA	CBG	CCC	CCR			
6	250	M.T., w/NB2				CCD				
6	250	T.H., w/NB2				CCB	CCW			
6	250							CJL, CJR, CJT, CJU, CJS	CCD CCC CCF CPB	
8	305									
8	307	T.H.	CNF		CTK	CMA				
8	307	M.T.	CNC			CHB				
8	307	4-spd.	CND							
8	307	PG	CNE		CKH					
8	307	M.T.		CCA	CKG					
8	307	T.H., w/NB2				CHC				
8	350	M.T.			CKK, CKA	CKA, CKB				
8	350	2-BBL., M.T.					CMC			
8	350	2-BBL., T.H.					CMA			
8	350	PG	CNM(250)							
8	350	M.T.	CNI(250)							
8	350	M.T.	CNJ(300)							
8	350	PG	CNK(300)		CKB, CDB					
8	350	T.H.	CRE(300)		CT, CKD	CKL, CKJ				
8	350	M.T.		CGA(245)						
8	350	PG		CGB(245)						
8	350	M.T.		CGK(270)						
8	350	T.H. 350		CGL(270) CJD(270)						
8	350	M.T.		CJJ(270)						
8	350	M.T., w/NB2			CKC, CKH					
8	350	T.H., w/NB2			CKD, CKK		CKD			
8	350	3-spd., 4-BBL.					CKH			
8	350							CMY, CRU, CMJ, CMH, CRX, CR2, CUS, CMM	CMJ, CHH, CMM	
8	396	M.T.	CTX(350) CKT(375) CKO(375)							
8	396	T.H. 400	CTW(350)							
8	396	SHP, T.H. 400 ('#—CKP only)	CTY(375), CKP(375) CKU(375)							
8	396	M.T.								
8	396	T.H. 400	CKN(325)							
8	396	M.T., HDC	CTZ(350), CKQ(375)							
8	400	T.H., 4-BBL.					CTC			
8	400	T.H., 4-BBL., California					CTA			
8	400							CTU, CTX, CTB	CTX, CTU, CSB, CSF	
8	402	M.T.	CKR							
8	402	M.T., HDC (330 hp)	CKS		CLA, CLS					

ENGINE IDENTIFICATION (Continued)

Chevelle and Monte Carlo

No. Cyls.	Cu. In. Displ.	Type	1970	1971	1972	YEAR AND CODE 1973	1974	1975	1976	1977
8	402	T.H. 350 (Mk. IV)								
8	402	T.H. 400 (Mk. IV)		CLB	CLB					
8	402	M.T. (Mk. IV)								
8	402	4-spd. (Mk. IV)		CLL						
8	402	M.T. Police (Mk. IV)		CLR						
8	402	M.T. (Mk. IV)		CLS						
8	402	M.T. (Mk. IV)		CPR						
8	400	M.T. (Mk. IV)		CPA CPG CPD CPP	CPA					
8	454	M.T. (390 hp)	CRN, CRT							
8	454	T.H. 400	CRQ							
8	454	T.H. 400 (450 hp)	CRR		CPD					
8	454	T.H. 400# (450 hp)	CRS							
8	454	M.T.	CRV			CWA	CWA			
8	454	T.H.				CWB	CWX			
8	454	M.T., w/NB2				CWC				
8	454	T.H. w/NB2				CWD	CWD			
8	454							CXW		

AC—air conditioned
HP—high performance
M.T.—manual transmission
PG—powerglide transmission

w/ex. EM—with exhaust emission
w/T. Ign.—with transistor ignition
4-BBL.—four-barrel carburetor
T.H.—Turbo Hydra-Matic

#—Aluminum heads
NB2—Calif. only
MK. IV—Big block

Engine identification code letters follow engine serial number.
6 Cyl.—Pad at front right-hand side of cylinder block at rear of distributor.
V8—Pad at front right-hand side of cylinder block.

Camaro

No. Cyls.	Cu. In. Displ.	Type	1970	1971	1972	YEAR AND CODE 1973	1974	1975	1976	1977
6	230	3 or 4-spd.	CCC							
6	230	PG, Torque Dr.	CCD							
6	250	M.T.		CAA	CBG	CCC	CCR			
6	250	PG		CCA	CBJ					
6	250	T.H.				CCA	CCX			
6	250	M.T., w/NB2				CCP				
6	250	T.H., w/NB2				CCB	CCW			
6	250							CJL, CJT, CJU	CCC, CCD, CCF	
8	305							CPA, CPB, CPC, 9W		
8	307	M.T.	CNC							
8	307	P.G.	CNE							
8	307	T.H. 350	CNF		CTK	CHH				
8	307	4-spd.	CND							
8	307	M.T.		CCA	CKG	CHB				
8	307	PG		CCA	CKH					
8	307	M.T., w/NB2				CHJ				
8	307	T.H., w/NB2				CHK				
8	327	3 or 4-spd.(210)								
8	327	PG (210 hp)								

ENGINE IDENTIFICATION (Continued)

Camaro

No. Cyls.	Cu. In. Displ.	Type	1970	1971	1972	1973	1974	1975	1976	1977
						YEAR AND CODE				
8	350	3 or 4-spd.	CNJ(300)							
8	350	PG	CNK(300)							
8	350	T.H.	CRE(300)		CKD					
8	350	2-BBL.	CNJ(250)							
8	350	T.H., 2-BBL.	CNM(250)				CMA			
8	350	PG, 2-BBL.	CNN(250)							
8	350	PG		CGB(245)						
8	350	T.H. 400		CGR(330)		CLK	CLK			
8	350	M.T.		CGK(270)	CKA	CKB				
				CJG(270)	CRG					
8	350	T.H. 350		CGL(270)	CTL	CKU	CKU			
				CJD(270)	CRD	CKW				
8	350	M.T.		CJG(330)	CKK					
8	350	M.T., 4-spd., Z28				CLJ, CKA	CLJ			
8	350	M.T., w/NB2				CLM, CKY	CKH			
8	350	T.H., w/NB2				CKH, CLL, CKX, CKD	CKD			
8	350	M.T., 2-BBL.					CMC			
8	350	M.T., 4-BBL.					CKB			
8	350							CMU, CRX, CML	CMB, CHW, CML	CMB, CHW, CML, 7X	
8	396	T.H. 400	CJI(350)							
8	396	SHP, T.H. 400	CJL(375)							
8	396	M.T.	CJF(350)							
8	396	M.T., SHP	CJH(375)							
8	402	T.H.	CTW(350), CKN(325), CTY(375)		CTB					
8	402	M.T.	CTX(350), CKO(375)		CLA, CTA					
8	402	T.H.		CLD(300)	CLB					
8	402	M.T.		CLC(300)						

AC—air conditioned
HDC—heavy duty clutch
HP—high performance
SHP—special high performance

M.T.—manual transmission
PG—Powerglide transmission
w/ex. EM—with exhaust emission
4-BBL.—four-barrel carburetor

2-BBL.—two-barrel carburetor
T.H.—Turbo Hydra-Matic
#—Aluminum heads
NB2—Calif. only

GENERAL ENGINE SPECIFICATIONS

Year	Engine No. Cyl. Displacement (cu in.)	Carburetor Type	Horsepower @ rpm ■	Torque @ rpm (ft lbs) ■	Bore x Stroke (in.)	Compression Ratio	Oil Pressure @ 2000 rpm
'70	4-153	1 bbl	90 @ 4000	152 @ 2400	3.875 x 3.250	8.5:1	40
	6-230	1 bbl	140 @ 4400	220 @ 1600	3.875 x 3.250	8.5:1	40
	6-250	1 bbl	155 @ 4200	235 @ 1600	3.875 x 3.530	8.5:1	40
	8-307	2 bbl	200 @ 4600	300 @ 2400	3.875 x 3.250	9.0:1	40
	8-350	2 bbl	250 @ 4800	345 @ 2800	4.000 x 3.480	9.0:1	40
	8-350	4 bbl	300 @ 4800	380 @ 3200	4.000 x 3.480	10.25:1	40
	8-400	2 bbl	265 @ 4400	400 @ 2400	4.125 x 3.760	9.0:1	40
	8-402	4 bbl	330 @ 4800	410 @ 3200	4.126 x 3.760	10.25:1	40
	8-402	4 bbl	350 @ 5200	415 @ 3400	4.126 x 3.760	10.25:1	40
	8-454	4 bbl	360 @ 4400	500 @ 3200	4.251 x 4.000	10.25:1	40

GENERAL ENGINE SPECIFICATIONS

Year	Engine No. Cyl. Displacement (cu in.)	Carburetor Type	Horsepower @ rpm ■	Torque @ rpm (ft lbs) ■	Bore x Stroke (in.)	Compression Ratio	Oil Pressure @ 2000 rpm
'71	6-250	1 bbl	145 @ 4200	230 @ 1600	3.875 x 3.530	8.5:1	40
	8-307	2 bbl	200 @ 4600	300 @ 2400	3.875 x 3.250	8.5:1	40
	8-350	2 bbl	245 @ 4800	350 @ 2800	4.000 x 3.480	8.5:1	40
	8-350	4 bbl	270 @ 4800	360 @ 3200	4.000 x 3.480	8.5:1	40
	8-350	4 bbl	330 @ 5000	275 @ 5600	4.000 x 3.480	9.0:1	40
	8-402	4 bbl	300 @ 4800	400 @ 3200	4.126 x 3.760	8.5:1	40
	8-454	4 bbl	365 @ 4800	465 @ 3200	4.251 x 4.000	8.5:1	40
	8-454	4 bbl	425 @ 5600	475 @ 4000	4.251 x 4.000	9.0:1	40
'72	6-250	1 bbl	110 @ 3800	185 @ 1600	3.875 x 3.530	8.5:1	40
	8-307	2 bbl	130 @ 4000	230 @ 2400	3.875 x 3.250	8.5:1	40
	8-350	2 bbl	165 @ 4000	280 @ 2400	4.000 x 3.480	8.5:1	40
	8-350	4 bbl	200 @ 4400	300 @ 2800	4.000 x 3.480	8.5:1	40
	8-350	4 bbl	255 @ 5600	280 @ 4000	4.000 x 3.480	9.0:1	40
	8-402	4 bbl	240 @ 4400	345 @ 3200	4.126 x 3.760	8.5:1	40
	8-454	4 bbl	220 @ 4000	390 @ 3200	4.251 x 4.000	8.5:1	40
'73	6-250	1 bbl	100 @ 3800	175 @ 1600	3.875 x 3.530	8.25:1	40
	8-307	2 bbl	115 @ 4000	205 @ 2000	3.875 x 3.250	8.5:1	40
	8-350	2 bbl	145 @ 4000	255 @ 2400	4.000 x 3.480	8.5:1	40
	8-350	4 bbl	175 @ 4400	270 @ 2400	4.000 x 3.480	8.5:1	40
	8-350	4 bbl	245 @ 5200	280 @ 4000	4.000 x 3.480	9.0:1	40
	8-454	4 bbl	245 @ 4000	375 @ 2800	4.251 x 4.000	8.5:1	40
'74	6-250	1 bbl	100 @ 3600	175 @ 1800	3.875 x 3.530	8.25:1	40
	8-350	2 bbl	145 @ 3600	250 @ 2200	4.000 x 3.480	8.5:1	40
	8-350	4 bbl	160 @ 3800	245 @ 2400	4.000 x 3.480	8.5:1	40
	8-350	4 bbl	185 @ 4000	270 @ 2600	4.000 x 3.480	8.5:1	40
	8-350	4 bbl	245 @ 5200	280 @ 4000	4.000 x 3.480	9.0:1	40
	8-400	2 bbl	150 @ 3200	295 @ 2600	4.126 x 3.750	8.5:1	40
	8-400	4 bbl	180 @ 3800	290 @ 2400	4.126 x 3.750	8.5:1	40
	8-454	4 bbl	235 @ 4000	360 @ 2800	4.251 x 4.000	8.25:1	44
'75	6-250	1 bbl	105 @ 3800	185 @ 1200	3.875 x 3.530	8.25:1	40
	8-262	2 bbl	110 @ 3600	200 @ 2000	3.671 x 3.10	8.5:1	40
	8-350	2 bbl	145 @ 3800	250 @ 2200	4.000 x 3.480	8.5:1	40
	8-350	4 bbl	155 @ 3800	245 @ 2400①	4.000 x 3.480	8.5:1	40
	8-400	4 bbl	175 @ 3600	305 @ 2000	4.126 x 4.000	8.5:1	40
	8-454	4 bbl	215 @ 4000	350 @ 2400	4.251 x 4.000	8.15:1	44
'76-'77	6-250	1 bbl	105 @ 3800	185 @ 1200	3.875 x 3.530	8.25:1	40
	8-305	2 bbl	140 @ 3800	245 @ 2000	3.736 x 3.480	8.5:1	40
	8-350	2 bbl	145 @ 3800	250 @ 2200	4.000 x 3.480	8.5:1	40
	8-350	4 bbl	165 @ 3800	260 @ 2400	4.000 x 3.480	8.5:1	40
	8-400	4 bbl	175 @ 3600	305 @ 2000	4.126 x 4.000	8.5:1	40

■ Starting 1972, horsepower and torque are SAE net figures. They are measured at the rear of the transmission with all accessories installed and operating. Since the figures vary when a given engine is installed in different models, some are representative rather than exact.

① 250 @ 2400 in wagon

Camaro

TUNE-UP SPECIFICATIONS

When analyzing compression test results, look for uniformity among cylinders rather than specific pressures.

Year	ENGINE No. Cyl. Displacement (cu in.)	hp	SPARK PLUGS Orig. Type	Gap (in.)	DISTRIBUTOR Point Dwell (deg)*	Point Gap (in.)	IGNITION TIMING (deg) ▲ • Man Trans	Auto Trans	VALVES Intake Opens ■ (deg) •	Fuel Pump Pressure (psi)	IDLE SPEED (rpm) ▲ Man Trans	• * Auto Trans.
'70	6-250	155	R-46T	.035	31-34	.019	TDC	4B	16	3½-4½	750	600/400
	8-307	200	R-43	.035	28-30	.019	2B	8B	28	5-6½	700	600/450
	8-350	250	R-44	.035	28-32	.019	TDC	4B	28	5-6½	750	600/450
	8-350	300	R-44	.035	28-32	.019	TDC	4B	28	5-6½	700	600
	8-350	360	R-43	.035	29-31	.019	8B	8B	42½	7-8½	800	750/500
	8-396	350	R-44T	.035	29-31	.019	TDC	4B	56	5-8½	700	600
	8-396	375	R-43T	.035	29-31	.019	4B	4B	N.A.	5-8½	750	700
'71	6-250	145	R-46TS	.035	31-34	.019	4B	4B	16	3½-4½	550	550②
	8-307	200	R-45TS	.035	29-31	.019	4B	8B	28	5-6½	600	550②
	8-350	245	R-45TS	.035	29-31	.019	2B	6B	28	7-8½	600	550②
	8-350	270	R-44TS	.035	29-31	.019	4B	8B	28	7-8½	600	550②
	8-350	300	R-43TS	.035	29-31	.019	8B	12B	42⅔	7-8½	700	700
	8-402	300	R-44TS	.035	28-30	.019	8B	8B	28	7-8½	600	600
'72	6-250	110	R-46T	.035	31-34	.019	4B	4B	16	3½-4½	700	600
	8-307	130	R-44T	.035	29-31	.019	4B	8B	28	5-6½	900	600
	8-350	165	R-44T	.035	29-31	.019	6B	6B	28(44)	7-8½	900	600
	8-350	200	R-44T	.035	29-31	.019	4B	8B	28(44)	7-8½	800	600
	8-350	255	R-44T	.035	29-31	.019	8B	12B	43	7-8½	900	700
	8-402	240	R-44TS	.035	28-30	.019	8B	8B	28	7-8½	800	600
'73	6-250	100	R-46T	.035	31-34	.019	6B	6B	16	3½-4½	700/450	600/450
	8-307	115	R-44T	.035	29-31	.019	4B	8B	28	5-6½	900/450	600/450
	8-350	145	R-44T	.035	29-31	.019	8B	8B	28	7½-8½	900/450	600/450
	8-350	175	R-44T	.035	29-31	.019	8B	12B	28	7½-8½	900/450	600/450
	8-350	245	R-44T	.035	29-31	.019	8B	12B	52	7½-8½	900/450	700/450
'74	6-250	100	R-46T	.035	31-34	.019	6B	6B	16	4-5	800/450	600/450
	8-350	145	R-44T	.035	29-31	.019	4B	8B	28	7½-9	900/450	600/450
	8-350	160	R-44T	.035	29-31	.019	4B	8B	44	7½-9	900/450	600/450
	8-350	185	R-44T	.035	29-31	.019	4B	8B	28	7½-9	900/450	600/450
	8-350	245	R-44T	.035	29-31	.019	8B	8B	52	7½-9	900/450	700/450
'75	6-250	105	R-46TX	.060	Electronic		10B	10B	16	4-5	800/425	550/425① (600/425)
	8-350	145	R-44TX	.060	Electronic		6B	6B	28	7½-9	800	600
	8-350	155	R-44TX	.060	Electronic		6B	8B(6B)	28	7½-9	800	600
'76	6-250	105	R-46TS	.035	Electronic		6B	6B	16	4-5	850	550②(600)
	8-305	140	R-45TS	.045	Electronic		6B	8B(TDC)	28	7½-9	800	600
	8-350	165	R-45TS	.045	Electronic		8B(6B)	8B(6B)	28	7½-9	800	600
'77	6-250	All	R-46TS	.035	Electronic		6B	8B(10B)	16	4-5	850	550(600)
	8-305	All	R-45TS	.045	Electronic		6B	6B(TDC)	28	7½-9	800	600
	8-350	All	R-45TS	.045	Electronic		8B	8B(6B)	28	7½-9	800	600

▲ See text for procedure.
• Figure in parentheses indicates California engine
■ All figures Before Top Dead Center
* When two idle speed figures are separated by a slash, the lower figure is with the idle speed solenoid disconnected.
① Without intake manifold integral with head—600/450
② A/C on
A After Top Dead Center
B Before Top Dead Center
N.A. Not available
TDC Top Dead Center
— Not applicable

NOTE: The underhood specifications sticker often reflects tune-up specification changes made in production. Sticker figures must be used if they disagree with those in this chart.

MECHANICAL VALVE LIFTER CLEARANCE

Year	Engine	Intake (Hot) In.	Exhaust (Hot) In.
1970	V8-350 360 hp	.024	.030
1971	V8-350 300 hp	.024	.030
1972	V8-350 255 hp	.024	.030

Nova

TUNE-UP SPECIFICATIONS

When analyzing compression test results, look for uniformity among cylinders rather than specific pressures.

Year	ENGINE No. Cyl. Displacement (cu in.)	hp	SPARK PLUGS Orig. Type	Gap (in.)	DISTRIBUTOR Point Dwell (deg)	Point Gap (in.)	IGNITION TIMING (deg) ▲ • Man Trans	Auto Trans	VALVES Intake Opens ■ (deg) ●	Fuel Pump Pressure (psi)	IDLE SPEED (rpm) ▲ Man Trans • *	Auto Trans.
'70	4-153	90	R-46N	.035	31-34	.019	TDC	4B	17½	4-5	750	650
	6-230	140	R-46N	.035	31-34	.019	TDC	4B	16	4-5	700	600/400
	6-250	155	R-46T	.035	31-34	.019	TDC	4B	16	3½-4½	700	600/400
	8-307	200	R-43	.035	28-32	.019	2B	8B	28	5-6½	700	600/450
	8-350	250	R-44	.035	28-32	.019	TDC	4B	28	5-6½	750	600/450
	8-350	300	R-44	.035	28-32	.019	TDC	4B	28	5-6½	700	600
'71	6-250	145	R-46TS	.035	31-34	.019	4B	4B	16	4-5	550	500
	8-307	200	R-45TS	.035	29-31	.019	4B	8B	28	5½-7½	600	550②
	8-350	245	R-45TS	.035	29-31	.019	2B	6B	28	7½-9	600	550②
	8-350	270	R-44TS	.035	29-31	.019	4B	8B	28	7½-9	600	550②
'72	6-250	110	R-46T	.035	31-34	.019	4B	4B	16	4-5	700	600
	8-307	130	R-44T	.035	29-31	.019	4B	8B	28	5½-7½	900	600
	8-350	165	R-44T	.035	29-31	.019	6B	6B	28(44)	7½-9	900	600
	8-350	200	R-44T	.035	29-31	.019	4B	8B	28(44)	7½-9	800	600
'73	6-250	100	R-46T	.035	31-34	.019	6B	6B	16	3½-4½	700/450	600/450
	8-307	115	R-44T	.035	29-31	.019	4B	8B	28	5-6½	900/450	600/450
	8-350	145	R-44T	.035	29-31	.019	8B	8B	28	7-8½	900/450	600/450
	8-350	175	R-44T	.035	29-31	.019	8B	12B	28	7-8½	900/450	600/450
'74	6-250	100	R-46T	.035	31-34	.019	6B	6B	16	4-5	800/450	600/450
	8-350	145	R-44T	.035	29-31	.019	4B	8B	28	7½-9	900/450	600/450
	8-350	160	R-44T	.035	29-31	.019	4B	8B	44	7½-9	900/450	600/450
	8-350	185	R-44T	.035	29-31	.019	4B	8B	28	7½-9	900/450	600/450
'75	6-250	105	R46TX	.060	Electronic		10B	10B	16	4-5	800/425	550/425③ (600/425)
	8-262	110	R-44TX	.060	Electronic		8B	8B	26	7½-9	800	600
	8-350	145	R-44TX	.060	Electronic		6B	6B	28	7½-9	800	600
	8-350	155	R-44TX	.060	Electronic		6B	8B(6B)	28	7½-9	800	600
'76	6-250	105	R-46TS	.035	Electronic		6B	6B	16	3½-4½	850	550(600)
	6-250①	105	R-46TS	.035	Electronic		6B	8B	16	3½-4½	850	600
	8-305	140	R-45TS	.045	Electronic		6B	8B(TDC)	28	7-8½	800	600
	8-350	165	R-45TS	.045	Electronic		8B(6B)	8B(6B)	28	7-8½	800	600
'77	6-250	All	R-46TS	.035	Electronic		④	④	16	4-5	850	550(600)
	8-305	All	R-45TS	.045	Electronic		④	④	28	7½-9	800	600
	8-350	All	R-45TS	.045	Electronic		④	④	28	7½-9	800	600

NOTE: The underhood specifications sticker often reflects tune-up specification changes made in production. Sticker figures must be used if they disagree with those in this chart.
▲ See text for procedure
• Figure in parentheses indicates California engine
■ All figures before top dead center
* When two idle speed figures are separated by a slash, the lower figure is with the idle speed solenoid disconnected.

① Without integral intake manifold
② A/C on
③ Without intake manifold integral with head—600/450
④ See underhood specifications sticker
A After Top Dead Center
B Before Top Dead Center
TDC Top Dead Center
— Not applicable

Chevelle, Monte Carlo

TUNE-UP SPECIFICATIONS

When analyzing compression test results, look for uniformity among cylinders rather than specific pressures.

Year	ENGINE No. Cyl. Displacement (cu in.)	hp	SPARK PLUGS Orig. Type	Gap (in.)	DISTRIBUTOR Point Dwell (deg)	Point Gap (in.)	IGNITION TIMING (deg) ▲ ● Man Trans	Auto Trans	VALVES Intake Opens ■ (deg) ●	Fuel Pump Pressure (psi)	IDLE SPEED (rpm) ▲ Man Trans *	Auto Trans.
'70	6-250	155	R-46T	.035	31-34	.019	TDC	4B	16	3-4½	750	600/400
	8-307	200	R-43	.035	28-32	.019	2B	8B	28	5-6½	700	600/450
	8-350	250	R-44	.035	28-32	.019	TDC	4B	28	5-6½	750	600/450
	8-350	300	R-44	.035	28-32	.019	TDC	4B	28	5-6½	700	600
	8-396	350	R-44T	.035	28-32	.019	TDC	4B	56	5-8½	700	600
	8-396	375	R-43T	.035	28-32	.019	4B	4B	N.A.	5-8½	750	700
	8-400	265	R-44	.035	28-32	.019	4B	8B	28	5-8½	700	600/450
	8-400	330	R-44T	.035	28-32	.019	4B	4B	28	5-8½	700	600
	8-454	360	R-43T	.035	28-32	.019	6B	6B	56	5-8½	700	600
'71	6-250	145	R-46TS	.035	31-34	.019	4B	4B	16	3½-4½	550	500
	8-307	200	R-45TS	.035	29-31	.019	4B	8B	28	5-6½	600	550
	8-350	245	R-45TS	.035	29-31	.019	2B	6B	28	7-8½	600	550
	8-350	270	R-44TS	.035	29-31	.019	4B	8B	28	7-8½	600	550
	8-400	255	R-44TS	.035	29-31	.019	4B	8B	28	7-8½	600	550
	8-402	300	R-44TS	.035	29-31	.019	8B	8B	28	7-8½	600	600
	8-454	365	R-42TS	.035	29-31	.019	8B	8B	56	7-8½	600	600
	8-454	425	R-42TS	.035	29-31	.019	8B	12B	44	7-8½	700	700
'72	6-250	110	R-46TS	.035	31-34	.019	4B	4B	16	3½-4½	700	600
	8-307	130	R-44T	.035	29-31	.019	4B	8B	28	5-6½	900	600
	8-350	165	R-44T	.035	29-31	.019	6B	6B	28	7-8½	900	600
	8-350	175	R-44T	.035	29-31	.019	4B	8B	28	7-8½	800	600
	8-402	240	R-44T	.035	29-31	.019	8B	8B	30	7-8½	750	600
	8-454	270	R-44T	.035	29-31	.019	8B	8B	56	7-8½	750	600
'73	6-250	100	R-46T	.035	31-34	.019	6B	6B	16	3½-4½	700/450	600/450
	8-307	115	R-44T	.035	29-31	.019	4B	8B	28	5-6½	900/450	600/450
	8-350	145	R-44T	.035	29-31	.019	8B	8B	28	7-8½	900/450	600/450
	8-350	175	R-44T	.035	29-31	.019	8B	12B	28	7-8½	900/450	600/450
	8-454	245	R-44T	.035	29-31	.019	10B	10B	55	7-8½	900/450	600/450
'74	6-250	100	R-46T	.035	31-34	.019	6B	6B	16	4-5	800/450	600/450
	8-350	145	R-44T	.035	29-31	.019	4B	8B	28	7½-9	900/450	600/450
	8-350	160	R-44T	.035	29-31	.019	4B	8B	44	7½-9	900/450	600/450
	8-400	150	R-44T	.035	29-31	.019	—	8B	28	7½-9	—	600/450
	8-400	180	R-44T	.035	29-31	.019	—	8B	44	7½-9	—	600/450
	8-454	235	R-44T	.035	29-31	.019	10B	10B	55	7½-9	800/450	600/450
'75	6-250	105	R-46TX	.060	Electronic		10B	10B	16	4-5	850/425	550/425 (600/425)
	8-350	145	R-44TX	.060	Electronic		6B	6B	28	7½-9	800	600
	8-350	155	R-44TX	.060	Electronic		—	6B	28	7½-9	—	600
	8-400	175	R-44TX	.060	Electronic		—	8B	28	7½-9	—	600
	8-454	215	R-44TX	.060	Electronic		—	16B	55	7½-9	—	600/500

NOTE: The underhood specifications sticker often reflects tune-up specification changes made in production. Sticker figures must be used if they disagree with those in this chart.

  ▲ See text for procedure
  ● Figure in parentheses indicates California engine
  ■ All figures Before Top Dead Center
  * When two idle speed figures are separated by a slash, the lower figure is with the idle speed solenoid disconnected

A After Top Dead Center
B Before Top Dead Center
TDC Top Dead Center
— Not applicable

Chevelle, Monte Carlo · TUNE-UP SPECIFICATIONS

When analyzing compression test results, look for uniformity among cylinders rather than specific pressures.

Year	ENGINE No. Cyl. Displacement (cu in.)	hp	SPARK PLUGS Orig. Type	Gap (in.)	DISTRIBUTOR	IGNITION TIMING (deg) ▲ ● Man Trans	Auto Trans	VALVES Intake Opens ■ (deg) ●	Fuel Pump Pressure (psi)	IDLE SPEED (rpm) ▲ Man Trans	Auto Trans.
'76	6-250	105	R-46TS	.035	Electronic	6B	6B	16	3½-4½	850	550(600)
	8-305	140	R-45TS	.045	Electronic	—	8B(TDC)	28	7-8½	—	600
	8-350	145	R-45TS	.045	Electronic	—	6B	28	7-8½	—	600
	8-350	165	R-45TS	.045	Electronic	—	8B(6B)	28	7-8½	—	600
	8-400	175	R-45TS	.045	Electronic	—	8B	28	7-8½	—	600
'77	6-250	All	R-46TS	.035	Electronic	①	①	16	4-5	①	①
	8-305	All	R-45TS	.045	Electronic	①	①	28	7½-9	①	①
	8-350	All	R-45TS	.045	Electronic	①	①	28	7½-9	①	①

NOTE: The underhood specifications sticker often reflects tune-up specification changes made in production. Sticker figures must be used if they disagree with those in this chart.

▲ See text for procedure
● Figure in parentheses indicates California engine
■ All figures Before Top Dead Center
* When two idle speed figures are separated by a slash, the lower figure is with the idle speed solenoid disconnected
① See underhood specifications sticker
A After Top Dead Center
B Before Top Dead Center

TDC Top Dead Center
— Not applicable

MECHANICAL VALVE LIFTER CLEARANCE

Year	Engine		Intake (Hot) in.	Exhaust (Hot) in.
1970-71	V8-396	375 hp	.024	.028
1971	V8-454	425 hp	.024	.028

CAPACITIES

Year	ENGINE No. Cyl. (Cu. In.) Displacement	Engine Crankcase Add 1 Qt For New Filter*	TRANSMISSION Pts To Refill After Draining Manual 3-Speed	4-Speed	Automatic ●	Drive Axle (pts)	Gasoline Tank (gals)	COOLING SYSTEM (qts) With Heater	With A/C
'70	4-153	3.5	3	——	6	3.75①		9	9
	6-230	4	3	——	6⑤	3.75①		12	13
	6-250	4	3	——	6⑤	3.75①		12	13
	8-307	4	3	——	6⑤	3.75①		15	16
	8-350	4	3	3	6.5②⑤	3.75①		16	16
	8-400	4	3	3	8	3.75①		16	16
	8-396	4	3	3	8	3.75①		23	24
	8-400	4	3	3	8	3.75①		23	24
	8-454	4	3	3	8	3.75①		22	23
'71	6-250	4	3	——	6	3.75		12	——
	8-307	4	3	——	6⑤	3.75		15	16
	8-350	4	3	3	6.5⑤	3.75		16	16
	8-400	4	3	3	8	3.75		23	23
	8-454	4	——	3	8	3.75		22	23
'72	6-250	4	3	——	6⑤	4.25		12	——
	8-307	4	3	——	6⑤	4.25		15	16
	8-350	4	3	3	6.5③⑤	4.25		16	16
	8-402	4	——	.3	8	4.25④		24	24
	8-454	4	——	3	8	4.25④		23	24
'73	6-250	4	3	——	6⑤	4.25		12.5	——
	8-307	4	3	——	5	4.25		16⑥	17⑦
	8-350	4	3	3	5③	4.25		16⑥	17⑦
	8-454	4	——	3	8	4.25④		23	24

CAPACITIES

Year	ENGINE No. Cyl. (Cu. In.) Displacement	Engine Crankcase Add 1 Qt For New Filter*	TRANSMISSION Pts To Refill After Draining Manual 3-Speed	4-Speed	Automatic •	Drive Axle (pts)	Gasoline Tank (gals)	COOLING SYSTEM (qts) With Heater	With A/C
'74	6-250	4	3	——	8	4.25		12.5	——
	8-350	4	3	3	8	4.25		16⑥	17⑦
	8-400	4	——	——	8	4.25④		16	17
	8-454	4	——	3	9	4.9		23	24
'75	6-250	4	3	——	8	4.25		14⑨	15⑧
	8-262	4	3	——	8	4.25		17	18
	8-350	4	3	3	8	4.25		17	18⑩
	8-400	4	——	——	8	4.25④		17⑪	18
	8-454	4	——	3	9	4.9		23	23
'76-'77	6-250	4	3	——	8	4.25		15⑫	17⑨
	8-305	4	3	——	8	4.25		17	18
	8-350	4	——	3	8	4.25		17	18
	8-400	4	——	——	8	4.25		17	18

* Add ½ qt with filter change on 4 cyl engine
• Specifications do not include torque converter
① 4.25 pts with 8⅞ in. ring gear
② 8 pts with 360 hp engine
③ 8 pts with Z-28 350
④ 4.9 pts in Monte Carlo or Chevelle with 8⅞ in. ring gear
⑤ 5 pts with Turbo Hydramatic 350
⑥ 15.5 Nova
⑦ 16.5 Nova
⑧ 16 Chevelle
⑨ 15 Nova
⑩ 17 Nova
⑪ 18 Monte Carlo
⑫ 14 Nova
—— Not applicable

GAS TANK CAPACITIES (Gals)

Year	Nova	Chevelle, Monte Carlo	Camaro
'70	18	20①	19
'71	16	19①	17
'72	16	19①	18
'73	21	22	18
'74	21	22	21
'75-'77	21	22	21

① 18 gals in station wagon

VALVE SPECIFICATIONS

Year	Engine No. Cyl. Displacement (cu in.)	Seat Angle (deg)	Face Angle (deg)	Spring Test Pressure (lbs @ in.)	Spring Installed Height (in.)	STEM TO GUIDE Clearance (in.) Intake	Exhaust	STEM Diameter (in.) Intake	Exhaust
'70	4-153	46①	45	81 @ 1.66	1 21/32	.0010-.0037	.0015-.0052	.3414	.3414
	6-230	46①	45	59 @ 1.66	1 21/32	.0010-.0037	.0015-.0052	.3414	.3414
	6-250	46①	45	59 @ 1.66	1 21/32	.0010-.0037	.0015-.0052	.3414	.3414
	8-307	46①	45	80 @ 1.70	1 23/32	.0010-.0037	.0012-.0049	.3414	.3414
	8-350	46①	45	80 @ 1.70	1 23/32	.0010-.0037	.0012-.0049	.3414	.3414
	8-400	46①	45	80 @ 1.70	1 7/8	.0010-.0037	.0012-.0047	.3414	.3414
	8-402	46①	45	75 @ 1.88②	1 7/8	.0010-.0037	.0012-.0047	.3719	.3717
	8-454	46①	45	75 @ 1.88②	1 7/8	.0010-.0037	.0012-.0047	.3717	.3719
'71	6-250	46	45	60 @ 1.66	1 21/32	.0010-.0037	.0015-.0052	.3414	.3414
	8-307	46	45	80 @ 1.70	1 23/32	.0010-.0037	.0012-.0049	.3414	.3414
	8-350	46	45	80 @ 1.70	1 23/32	.0010-.0037	.0012-.0049	.3414	.3414
	8-402	46	45	75 @ 1.88②	1 7/8	.0010-.0037	.0012-.0047	.3719	.3717
	8-454	46	45	75 @ 1.88②	1 7/8	.0010-.0037	.0012-.0047	.3719	.3717

VALVE SPECIFICATIONS

Year	Engine No. Cyl. Displacement (cu in.)	Seat Angle (deg)	Face Angle (deg)	Spring Test Pressure (lbs @ in.)	Spring Installed Height (in.)	STEM TO GUIDE Clearance (in.) Intake	Exhaust	STEM Diameter (in.) Intake	Exhaust
'72	6-250	46	45	60 @ 1.66	1 21/32	.0010-.0037	.0015-.0052	.3414	.3414
	8-307	46	45	80 @ 1.70	1 23/32	.0010-.0037	.0012-.0049	.3414	.3414
	8-350	46	45	80 @ 1.70	1 23/32	.0010-.0037	.0012-.0049	.3414	.3414
	8-402	46	45	75 @ 1.88②	1 7/8	.0010-.0037	.0012-.0047	.3719	.3717
	8-454	46	45	75 @ 1.88②	1 7/8	.0010-.0037	.0012-.0047	.3719	.3717
'73	6-250	46	45	60 @ 1.66	1 21/32	.0010-.0027	.0015-.0032	.3414	.3414
	8-307	46	45	80 @ 1.61③	1 5/8	.0010-.0027	.0012-.0029	.3414	.3414
	8-350	46	45	80 @ 1.70③	1 23/32④	.0010-.0027	.0012-.0027	.3414	.3414
	8-454	46	45	80 @ 1.88	1 7/8	.0010-.0027	.0012-.0027	.3719	.3417
'74	6-250	46	45	60 @ 1.66	1 21/32	.0010-.0027	.0010-.0027	.3414	.3414
	8-350	46	45	80 @ 1.70③	1 23/32④	.0010-.0027	.0010-.0027	.3414	.3414
	8-400	46	45	80 @ 1.70③	1 23/32④	.0010-.0027	.0010-.0027	.3414	.3414
	8-454	46	45	80 @ 1.88	1 7/8	.0010-.0027	.0010-.0027	.3719	.3719
'75-'77	6-250	46	45	60 @ 1.66	1 21/32	.0010-.0027	.0010-.0027⑤	.3414	.3414
	8-262	46	45	80 @ 1.70③	1 23/32④	.0010-.0027	.0010-.0027	.3414	.3414
	8-305	46	45	80 @ 1.70	1 23/32	.0010-.0027	.0010-.0027	.3414	.3414
	8-350	46	45	80 @ 1.70③	1 23/32④	.0010-.0027	.0010-.0027	.3414	.3414
	8-400	46	45	80 @ 1.70③	1 23/32④	.0010-.0027	.0010-.0027	.3414	.3414
	8-454	46	45	90 @ 1.80	1 51/64	.0010-.0027	.0010-.0027	.3719	.3719

① 45° on aluminum heads
② Inner spring—30 @ 1.78
③ 80 @ 1.61 for exhaust
④ 1 39/64 for exhaust
⑤ 1976 and later—.0015-.0032
⑥ 1976 and later—82 @ 1.66

CRANKSHAFT AND CONNECTING ROD SPECIFICATIONS

All measurements are given in inches

Year	Engine No. Cyl. Displacement (cu in.)	CRANKSHAFT Main Brg. Journal Dia	Main Brg. Oil Clearance	Shaft End-Play	Thrust on No.	CONNECTING ROD Journal Diameter	Oil Clearance	Side Clearance
'70	4-153	2.2983-2.2993	.0003-.0029	.002-.006	5	1.999-2.000	.0007-.0027	.009-.013
	6-230	2.2983-2.2993	.0003-.0029	.002-.006	7	1.999-2.000	.0007-.0027	.009-.013
	6-250	2.2983-2.2993	.0003-.0029	.002-.006	7	1.999-2.000	.0007-.0027	.009-.013
	8-307, 350	2.4484-2.4493①	.0003-.0015③	.002-.006	5	2.099-2.100	.0007-.0028	.008-.014
	8-350 (Z28)	2.4484-2.4493①	.0013-.0025④	.002-.006	5	2.099-2.100	.0013-.0035	.008-.014
	8-400 (Monte Carlo)	2.6584-2.6493⑧	.0008-.0020⑪	.002-.006	5	2.099-2.100	.0009-.0025	.008-.014
	8-402	2.7487-2.7496⑤	.0007-.0019⑥	.006-.010	5	2.199-2.200	.0009-.0025	.013-.023
	8-454	2.7485-2.7494②	.0013-.0025⑦	.006-.010	5	2.199-2.200	.0009-.0025	.015-.021
'71	6-250	2.2983-2.2993	.0003-.0029	.002-.006	7	1.999-2.000	.0007-.0027	.009-.014
	8-307, 350	2.4484-2.4493⑩	.0008-.0020⑪	.002-.006	5	2.099-2.100	.0013-.0035	.008-.014
	8-350 (Z28)	2.4484-2.4493⑩	.0013-.0025④	.002-.006	5	2.099-2.100	.0013-.0035	.008-.014
	8-402	2.7487-2.7496⑤	.0007-.0019⑥	.006-.010	5	2.199-2.200	.0009-.0025	.013-.023
	8-454 (365 H.P.)	2.7485-2.7494②	.0013-.0025⑦	.006-.010	5	2.199-2.200	.0009-.0025	.015-.021
	8-454 (425 H.P.)	2.7481-2.7490①	.0013-.0025⑨	.006-.010	5	2.1985-2.1995	.0009-.0025	.019-.025
'72	6-250	2.2983-2.2993	.0003-.0029	.002-.006	7	1.999-2.000	.0007-.0027	.009-.014
	8-307, 350	2.4484-2.4493⑩	.0008-.0020⑪	.002-.006	5	2.099-2.100	.0013-.0035	.008-.014
	8-350 (Z28)	2.4484-2.4493⑩	.0013-.0025④	.002-.006	5	2.099-2.100	.0013-.0035	.008-.014
	8-402	2.7487-2.7496⑤	.0007-.0019⑥	.006-.010	5	2.199-2.200	.0009-.0025	.013-.023
	8-454	2.7485-2.7494②	.0013-.0025⑦	.006-.010	5	2.199-2.200	.0009-.0025	.015-.021

CRANKSHAFT AND CONNECTING ROD SPECIFICATIONS (Continued)

All measurements are given in inches

Year	Engine No. Cyl. Displacement (cu in.)	CRANKSHAFT Main Brg. Journal Dia	Main Brg. Oil Clearance	Shaft End-Play	Thrust on No.	CONNECTING ROD Journal Diameter	Oil Clearance	Side Clearance
'73	6-250	2.3004	.0003-.0029	.002-.006	7	1.999-2.000	.0007-.0027	.009-.014
	8-307, 350	2.4502⑫	.0008-.0020⑪	.002-.007	5	2.099-2.100	.0013-.0035	.008-.014
	8-454	2.7492⑬	.0007-.0019⑭	.006-.010	5	2.199-2.200	.0009-.0025	.015-.023
'74-'77	6-250	2.2988	.0003-.0029	.002-.006	7	1.9928-2.000	.0007-.0027	.007-.016
	8-262	2.4489⑮	④	.002-.006	5	2.099-2.100	.0012-.0035	.008-.014
	8-305	2.4489⑮	④	.002-.006	5	2.099-2.100	.0013-.0035	.008-.014
	8-350	2.4489⑮	④	.002-.006	5	2.099-2.100	.0035-.0035	.008-.014
	8-400	2.6489⑯	.0008-.0002⑰	.002-.006	5	2.099-2.100	.0035-.0035	.008-.014
	8-454	2.7490	.0013-.0025⑱	.006-.010	5	2.199-2.200	.0009-.0025	.015-.021

① No. 5—2.4478-2.4488
② No. 1—2.7484-2.7493
    Nos. 2-4—2.7481-2.7490
    No. 5—2.7478-2.7488
③ Nos. 2-4—.0006-.0018
    No. 5—.0008-.0023
④ w/Man. trans.—No. 5—.0023-.0033
    w/Auto. trans.—No. 1—.0019-.0031
                Nos. 2-4—.0013-.0025
                No. 5—.0023-.0033
⑤ Nos. 3-4—2.7481-2.7490
    No. 5—2.7473-2.7483
⑥ Nos. 2-4—.0013-.0025
    No. 5—.0019-.0035
⑦ No. 5—.0024-.0040
⑧ No. 5—2.6479-2.6488

⑨ No. 5—.0029-.0045
⑩ Nos. 2-4—2.4481-2.4490
    No. 5—2.4479-2.4488
⑪ Nos. 2-4—.0011-.0023
    No. 5—.0017-.0033
⑫ No. 5—2.4508
⑬ Nos. 2-4—2.7504
    No. 5—2.7499
⑭ Nos. 2-4—.0013-.0028
    No. 5—.0019-.0035
⑮ No. 2-4: 2.4486
    No. 5: 2.4485
⑯ No. 5: 2.6485
⑰ No. 2-4: .001-.0023
    No. 5: .0017-.0033
⑱ No. 5: .0024-.0070

TORQUE SPECIFICATIONS

All readings in ft lbs

Year	Engine No. Cyl. Displacement (cu in.)	Cylinder Head Bolts	Rod Bearing Bolts	Main Bearing Bolts	Crankshaft Pulley or Damper Bolt	Flywheel to Crankshaft Bolts	MANIFOLD Intake	Exhaust
'70-'77	4-153, 6-230, 250	95	35	65	—	60	35⑦	30⑥⑨
'70-'77	8-262, 302, 307, 350, 400	70⑩	45	75②⑪	60⑤	60	30	④
'70-'77	8-396, 402	80①	50	110	85⑤	65	30	30
'70-'75	8-454	80①	50③	110	85⑧	65	30	20

① Aluminum Heads—Short bolts 65, Long bolts 75
② Engines with 4-bolt mains—Outer bolts 65
③ 7/16 Rod bolts—70
④ Center bolts—30, end bolts 20
⑤ Where applicable
⑥ Exhaust-to-intake

⑦ Manifold-to-head
⑧ 65 starting 1975
⑨ With intake manifold integral with head—30 center, 20 on four end bolts
⑩ 65 starting 1976
⑪ 70 starting 1976

RING GAP

All measurements are given in inches

Year	Engine	Top Compression	Bottom Compression
'70-'77	4-153, 6-230, 250, 8-307, 396, 400, 402, 454	.010-.020	.010-.020
'70-'72	8-350①	.010-.020	.013-.025
'73-'75	8-350	.010-.020	.013-.025
'75	8-262	.010-.020	.013-.025
'76-'77	8-305	.010-.020	.010-.025
	8-350 2 bbl	.010-.020	.010-.020
	8-350 4 bbl	.010-.020	.013-.025

Year	Engine	Oil Control
'70-'77	All	.015-.055

① 255, 330 hp Top .010-.020   2nd .013-.023

RING SIDE CLEARANCE

All measurements are given in inches

Year	Engine	Top Compression	Bottom Compression
'70-'77	4-153, 6-230, 250, 307, 400	.0012-.0027 ③	.0012-.0032 ③
'70-'77	8-262, 305, 350	.0012-.0032①	.0012-.0027②
'70-'75	8-402, 454	.0017-.0032	.0017-.0032

Year	Engine	Oil Control
'70-'77	4-153, 6-230, 250, 8-262, 302, 305, 307, 350, 400	.0000-.0050④
'70-'75	8-396, 402, 454	.0005-.0065

① .0012-.0027 on 1975 2 bbl. 350
② 145, 155, 165, 245, 250 hp 350 cu in. engine .0012-.0032
③ 330 hp 400 cu in. engine
Top .0017-.0032
2nd .0017-.0032
④ .002-.007 for 1970-74 350 2 bbl and 1974-77 350 4 bbl, except 1974 Z28

PISTON CLEARANCE

Year	Engine	Horsepower	Piston to Bore Maximum Service Clearance (in.)
'70	4-153, 6-230, 250, 8-307	All	.0025
	8-302	All	.0061
	8-350	250, 300	.0027
	8-400	265	.0034
	8-402	All	.0038
	8-454	360	.0049
'71-'72	6-250, 8-307	All	.0025
	8-350	245, 270	.0027
	8-350	330	.0061
	8-402	All	.0035
	8-454	365	.0049
	8-454①	425	.0065
'73	6-250, 8-307	All	.0025
	8-350	145, 175	.0027
	8-350	245	.0061
	8-454	All	.0035
'74	6-250	100	.0025
	8-350	145, 160, 185	.0027
	8-350	245	.0051
	8-400	150, 180	.0034
	8-454	235	.0035
'75-'77	6-250	105	.0025
	8-262, 305, 350	All	.0027
	8-400	175	.0034
	8-454	215	.0035

① 1971 Only

WHEEL ALIGNMENT SPECIFICATIONS

Year	Model	CASTER Range (deg)	Pref Setting (deg)	CAMBER Range (deg)	Pref Setting (deg)	Toe-in (in.)	Steering Axis Inclination (deg)	WHEEL PIVOT RATIO (deg) Inner Wheel	Outer Wheel
'70-'71	Nova	0 to 1P	½P	¼N to ¾P	½P	⅛ to ¼	8¼ to 9¼	20	N.A.
	Chevelle, Monte Carlo	1½N to ½N①	1N	0 to 1P	½P	⅛ to ¼	7¾ to 8¾	20	N.A.
	Camaro	0 to 2P	1P	¼N to 1¾P	¾P	⅛ to ¼	10 to 11	20	N.A.
'72	Nova	0 to 1P	½P	¼N to ¾P	¼P	⅛ to ¼	8¾ to 9¼	—	—
	Chevelle	1½N to ½N	1N	¼P to 1¼P	¾P	⅛ to ¼	7¾ to 8¾	—	—
	Monte Carlo	½N to ½P	0	¼P to 1¼P	¾P	⅛ to ¼	7¾ to 8¾	—	—
	Camaro	½N to ½P	0	½P to 1½P	1P	⅛ to ¼	9 to 10	—	—
	Camaro Z28	1½N to ½N	1N	¼P to 1¼P	¾P	⅛ to ¼	9¼ to 10¼	—	—
'73	Nova	½N to 1½P	½P	½N to 1P	¾P	1/16 to 5/16	9	—	—
	Chevelle	1¾N to ¾N	1¼N	½P to 1½P	1P②	⅛ to ¼	9½	—	—
	Monte Carlo	4¼P to 5¼P	4¾P	½P to 1½P	1P②	0 to ⅛	9½	—	—
	Camaro	1N to 1P	0	¼P to 1¾P	1P	1/16 to 5/16	10½	—	—
	Camaro Z28	2N to 0	1N	1½N to 0	¾N	1/16 to 5/16	10½	—	—
'74	Nova	0 to 1P	½P	¼P to ¾P	¼P	⅛ to ¼	8¾	—	—
	Chevelle③	1½ to ½N	1N	½P to 1½P	1P	0 to ⅛	10½	—	—
	Chevelle④	½N to ½P	0	½P to 1½P	1P	0 to ⅛	10½	—	—
	Monte Carlo	4½ to 5½P	5	½P to 1½P	1P	0 to ⅛	10½	—	—
	Camaro	½N to ½P	0	½P to 1½P	1P	⅛ to ¼	9½	—	—
	Camaro Z28	1½N to ½N	1N	¼P to 1¼P	¾P	⅛ to ¼	9¾	—	—
'75-'77	Nova③	1½N to ½N	1N	¼P to 1¼P	¾P	0 to ⅛	10	—	—
	Nova④	½P to 1½P	1P	¼P to 1¼P	¾P	0 to ⅛	10	—	—
	Chevelle	1½P to 2½P	2P	0 to 1P②	½P	0 to ⅛	9 19/32	—	—
	Monte Carlo	4½P to 5½P	.5P	0 to 1P②	½P	0 to ⅛	9 19/32	—	—
	Camaro	½N to ½P⑤	0⑥	½P to 1½P	1P	0 to ⅛	10 11/32	—	—

N Negative   P Positive
① SS 396—0 to 1P
② Left wheel given, right wheel is ½P ± ½
③ Manual steering
④ Power steering
⑤ '76 and later—½P to 1½P
⑥ '76 and later—1P
N.A. Not available
— Not specified

CHARGING SYSTEM

Alternator and regulator troubleshooting and repair are covered in the Unit Repair Section.

Alternator Removal and Installation

1. Disconnect battery ground cable to prevent diode damage.
2. Disconnect the alternator wiring.
3. Remove brace bolt. If power steering equipped, loosen pump brace and mount nuts. Detach drive belt (s).
4. Support the alternator and remove mount bolt(s). Remove unit from vehicle.
5. Reverse procedure to install. Adjust drive belt to have ¼-½ in. play on longest run of belt.

Regulator Removal and Installation through 1972

1. Disconnect the ground cable at the battery.
2. Disconnect the wiring harness from the regulator.
3. Remove the mounting screws and remove the regulator.
4. Make sure that the regulator base gasket is in place before installation.
5. Clean the attaching area for proper grounding.
6. Install the regulator. Do not overtighten the mounting screws, as this will cancel the cushioning effect of the rubber grommets.

Integral Voltage Regulator

An alternator with an integral voltage regulator has been optional. It became standard equipment in 1973. There are no adjustments possible with this unit; any testing procedures will be found in the Charging And Starting Systems Unit Repair Section.

STARTING SYSTEM

Starter motor troubleshooting and repairs are covered in the Unit Repair Section.

Starter Removal and Installation

1. Disconnect battery ground cable.
2. Raise and support vehicle.
3. Disconnect all wires at solenoid terminals. Note color coding of wires for reinstallation.
4. Remove starter front bracket and two mount bolts. On engines with solenoid heat shield,

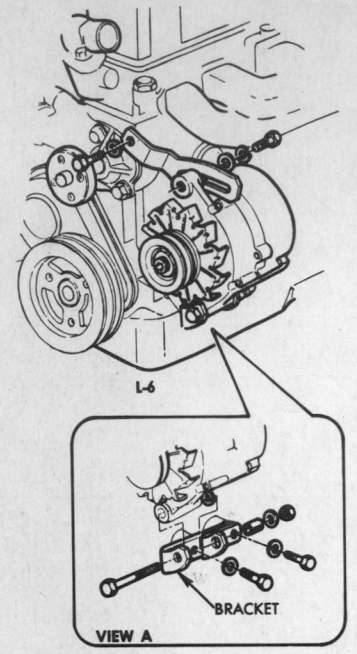

L-6

VIEW A

BRACKET

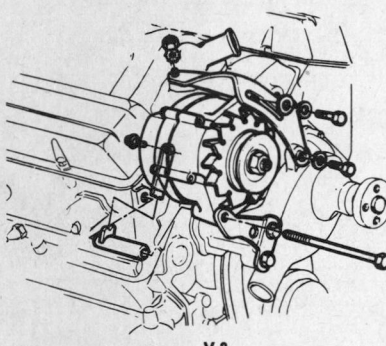

V-8

Delcotron installation
(© Chevrolet Div., G.M. Corp)

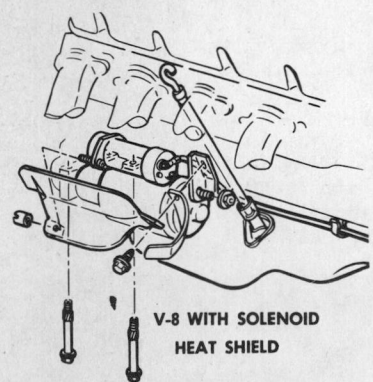

V-8 WITH SOLENOID
HEAT SHIELD

Starter motor installation
(© Chevrolet Div., G.M. Corp)

IGNITION SYSTEM

All models are equipped with the HEI distributor and ignition system starting 1975. This system uses no points and is, therefore, maintenance free. See the Electronic Ignition section for unit description.

Caution
When using an auxiliary starter switch the primary distributor lead on point-type systems must be disconnected from the negative post of the ignition coil and the ignition switch must be on. On HEI systems, the distributor BATT lead must be disconnected. Failure to do this may cause damage to the grounding circuit in the ignition switch.

HEI System Tachometer Hookup

There is a terminal marked TACH on the side of the V8 HEI distributor. Connect one tachometer lead to this terminal and the other to ground. On some tachometers, the leads must be connected to the TACH terminal and to the battery positive terminal. The hookup is the same for the six-cylinder HEI system, except that the TACH terminal is opposite the BAT terminal on the connector plug on the remote-mounted coil.

Caution
Never ground the TACH terminal; serious system damage will result. If there is any doubt as to the correct tachometer hookup, check with the tachometer manufacturer.

Distributor Removal and Installation

The drive gear is attached to the distributor shaft. If it becomes necessary to remove the distributor, carefully mark the position of the rotor in relation to the engine block and the distributor housing so that, if the engine is not turned after the distributor is taken out, the rotor can be returned to the position from which it was removed without difficulty.

To remove the distributor, take off the V8 carburetor air cleaner, disconnect the coil primary wire and the vacuum line, remove the distributor cap, take out the distributor body.

With a pencil, mark the position of the body relative to the block, and then work the distributor up out of the block.

When installing the distributor, turn the rotor about ⅛ turn counter clockwise past the alignment mark before pushing the distributor into place. The marks should align when the distributor seats. Check the timing.

Distributor Installation (Engine Disturbed)

1. Turn the crankshaft until the No. 1 cylinder is at the top of its compression stroke. Remove the No. 1 spark plug to feel the compression.
2. Align the timing mark on the vibration damper with the TDC indicator or 0 mark on the timing scale.
3. With distributor body oriented in its normal position, hold the rotor pointing toward the No. 1 plug wire location, then turn the rotor approximately ⅛ turn counterclockwise and push the distributor down until it engages the camshaft, rotating the shaft slightly if necessary.

NOTE: on Mark IV (big block) V8 engines there is a punch mark on the distributor drive gear which indicates the rotor position. Thus, the distributor may be installed with the cap in place. Align the punch mark 2° clockwise from the No. 1 cap terminal, then rotate the distributor body ⅛ turn counterclockwise and push the distributor down into the block.

4. Press down on the distributor and crank the engine to make sure the oil pump shaft is engaged.
5. Return the crankshaft to No. 1 cylinder compression stroke with the timing marks aligned.
6. Turn the distributor body counterclockwise until the points are just beginning to open, then tighten the distributor clamp bolt.
7. Install the distributor cap, checking that the rotor points to the No. 1 terminal. Make sure that the spark plug wires are in

remove front bracket upper bolt and detach bracket from starter motor.
5. Remove front bracket bolt or nut. Rotate bracket clear. Lower starter front end first. Remove starter.
6. Reverse procedure to install. Torque mount bolts to 25-35 ft. lbs.

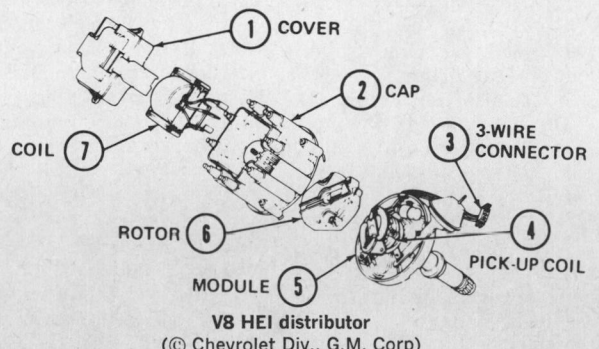

1 COVER
2 CAP
3 3-WIRE CONNECTOR
7 COIL
4 PICK-UP COIL
6 ROTOR
5 MODULE

V8 HEI distributor
(© Chevrolet Div., G.M. Corp)

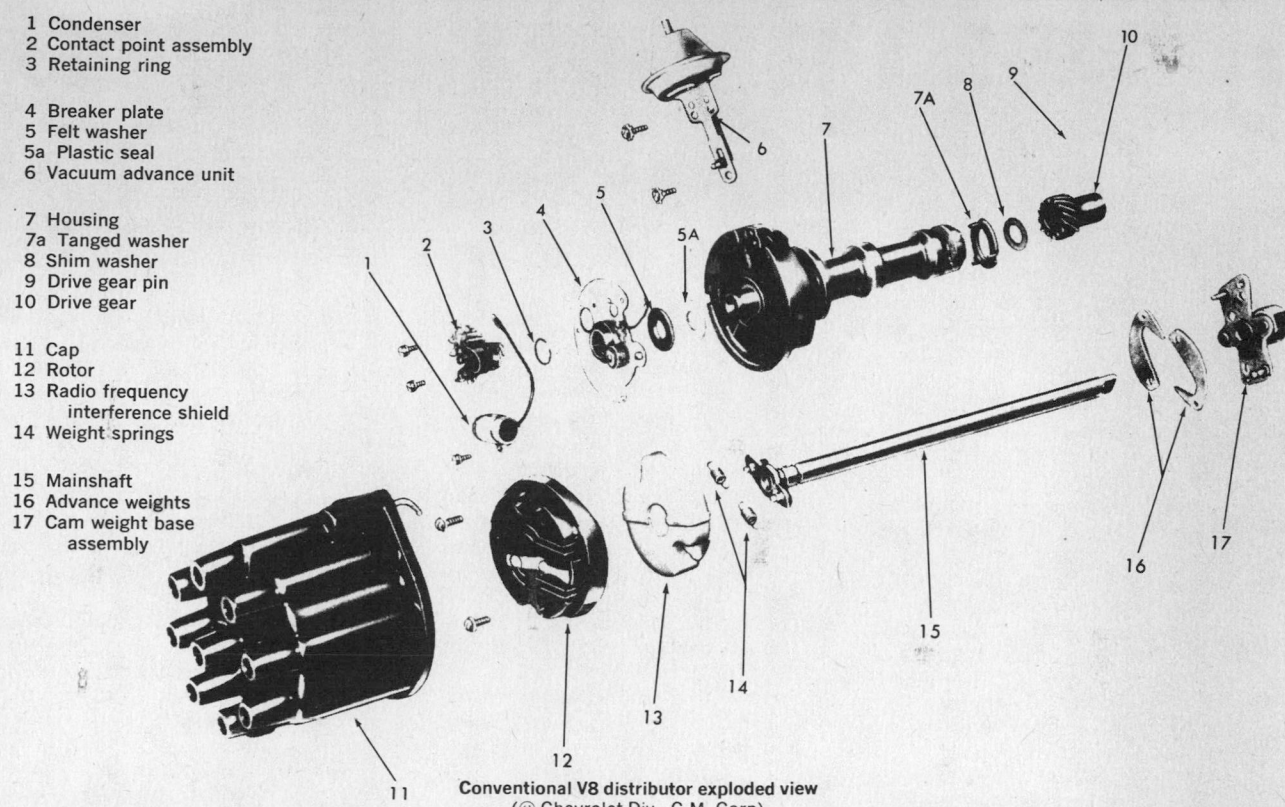

1 Condenser
2 Contact point assembly
3 Retaining ring

4 Breaker plate
5 Felt washer
5a Plastic seal
6 Vacuum advance unit

7 Housing
7a Tanged washer
8 Shim washer
9 Drive gear pin
10 Drive gear

11 Cap
12 Rotor
13 Radio frequency
    interference shield
14 Weight springs

15 Mainshaft
16 Advance weights
17 Cam weight base
    assembly

Conventional V8 distributor exploded view
(© Chevrolet Div., G.M. Corp)

their supports and are securely connected.

8. Connect distributor vacuum line and primary wire.
9. Start engine and set the timing.

Breaker Point Adjustment

NOTE: 1970-73 distributors are equipped with a radio static-shield which must be removed for access to the points. If a unitized point and condenser set is used, the shield isn't needed.

Breaker point gap (dwell) adjustment is accomplished for four and six

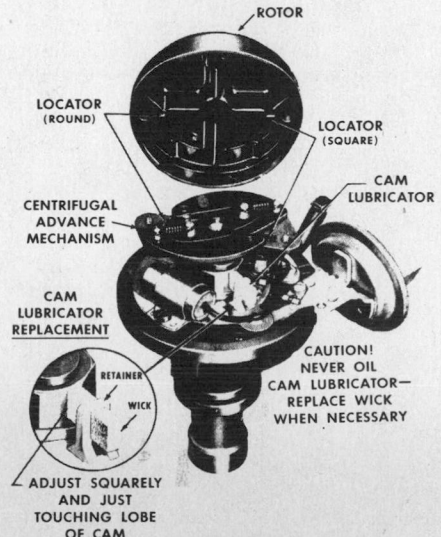

ROTOR
LOCATOR (ROUND)
LOCATOR (SQUARE)
CENTRIFUGAL ADVANCE MECHANISM
CAM LUBRICATOR
CAM LUBRICATOR REPLACEMENT
CAUTION! NEVER OIL CAM LUBRICATOR—REPLACE WICK WHEN NECESSARY
RETAINER
WICK
ADJUST SQUARELY AND JUST TOUCHING LOBE OF CAM

V8 distributor cam lubricator
(© Chevrolet Div., G.M. Corp)

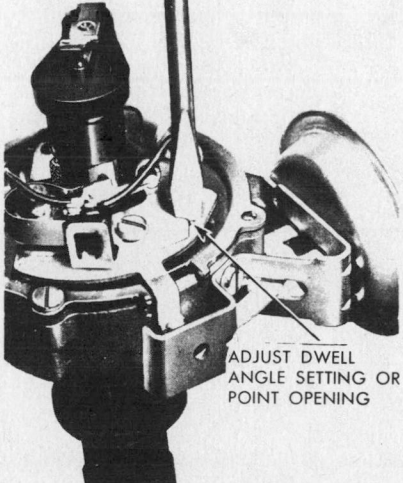

ADJUST DWELL ANGLE SETTING OR POINT OPENING

Inline six-cylinder point adjustment
(© Chevrolet Div., G.M. Corp)

cylinder engines by loosening the point assembly attaching screw and adjusting the points with a screwdriver until the correct gap clearance is obtained (use a feeler gauge). Tighten the point assembly attaching screw and install the distributor cap. Use a dwell meter to check the dwell angle, readjusting if necessary. Dwell can be checked with the engine cranking or running.

On V8 models there is a window in the distributor cap so that the dwell angle may be set while the engine is running. Use an allen (hex) wrench to make the adjustment.

See Tune-Up Specifications at the beginning of this section for correct breaker point gap and dwell angle.

The distributor cam lubricator should be rotated 180° or switched end-for-end every 12,000 miles, and replaced every 24,000 miles. Do not oil these lubricator wicks.

Caution On V8 models the distributor body is involved in the engine lubricating system. The lubricating circuit to the right-bank valve train can be interrupted by mis-alignment of the distributor body. This can cause serious trouble and may be hard to diagnose. See Firing Order and Timing illustrations for correct distributor positioning.

Ignition Timing

Remove the spark plug wire from No. 1 plug and attach a timing light between the wire and the plug. With HEI, use an adapter at the no. 1 distributor terminal. Disconnect the distributor spark advance hose and plug the vacuum opening. Start the engine and run it at idle speed. Aim the timing light at the degree scale just over the harmonic balancer. Adjust the timing by loosening the securing clamp and rotating the distributor until the desired ignition advance is achieved, then tighten the clamp. To advance the timing, rotate the distributor opposite to the normal direction of rotor rotation. Retard the timing by rotating the distributor in the normal direction of rotor rotation.

FUEL SYSTEM

Fuel Pump

The fuel pump is the single action AC diaphragm type.

The pump is actuated by an eccentric located on the engine camshaft. On inline engines, the eccentric actuates the pump rocker arm. On V8 engines, a pushrod between the camshaft eccentric and the fuel pump actuates the pump rocker arm.

Fuel Pump Removal and Installation

1. Disconnect fuel inlet and outlet lines at pump and plug pump inlet line.
2. Remove two pump mounting bolts and lockwashers; remove pump and gasket.
3. On all small-block engines, if rocker arm pushrod is to be removed: take out the two adapter bolts and lockwashers and remove adapter and gasket.
4. On big-block V8 engines, if rocker arm pushrod is to be removed: take out pipe plug.
5. Install pump with new gasket coated with sealer. Coat mounting bolt threads with sealer and tighten bolts.
   NOTE: on V8 engines, mechanical fingers or heavy grease can be used to hold pump pushrod in place during installation. Coat pipe plug threads or adapter gasket with sealer if pushrod was removed.
6. Connect inlet and outlet lines, start engine and check for leaks.

Paper fuel filter
(© Chevrolet Div., G.M. Corp)

3. Remove filter element and spring.
4. If a bronze element, blow through cone end—element should allow air to pass freely.
5. Install element spring and new element into carburetor. Bronze elements are installed with small section of cone facing outward.
6. Install new gasket on fitting nut and install nut.
7. Install fuel line and tighten securely. Start engine and check for leaks.

Idle Speed and Mixture Adjustments

1970

Adjust with air cleaner installed.
1. Disconnect "FUEL TANK" line from vapor canister (E.E.C.).
2. Connect a tachometer to engine, start engine and allow it to come up to operating temperature. Make sure choke and preheater valves are fully open.

Chilton's TIME SAVER

When replacing a fuel pump on small block V8 engines, considerable time can be saved as follows:

1. Before removing the old pump, remove the upper bolt from the engine's right front mounting boss. This bolt hole is in direct alignment with the fuel pump pushrod. The threaded bolt hole continues into the pump pushrod bore.

The bolt acts as an oil plug.
2. Temporarily insert a longer bolt, (about 3/8—16 x 2 in.) into the hole. Screw the bolt into the bore until it bottoms against the pump pushrod. (Don't tighten the bolt with a wrench or the rod can be damaged.)
3. The mechanic is now free to remove and install the fuel pump without worrying about fuel pump pushrod misalignment.
CAUTION: don't forget to reinstall original motor bolt.

Fuel Filter Removal and Installation

All 1976 and later fuel filters use a check valve to prevent fuel spillage in an accident. When you replace the filter, make sure the new one has a check valve.

1. Disconnect fuel line connection at inlet of carburetor.
2. Remove inlet fuel filter nut from carburetor using a box wrench.

3. Turn off A/C and set parking brake. Disconnect and plug distributor vacuum line.
4. Make the following adjustments:

4 cylinder 153
  a. Set mixture screw to obtain maximum idle rpm.
  b. Adjust idle speed screw to obtain 750 rpm for manual transmission (in Neutral),

650 rpm for automatic (in Drive).
  c. Adjust mixture screw to obtain a 20 rpm drop in idle speed, then back out 1/4 turn from this point.
  d. Readjust idle speed to obtain specified rpm, then reconnect vacuum line.

6 cylinder 230/250
  a. Turn in mixture screw until it gently seats, then back out screw four turns.
  b. Adjust solenoid screw to obtain 830 rpm for manual transmission (in Neutral) or 630 rpm for automatic (in Drive).
  c. Adjust mixture screw to obtain 750 rpm for manual transmission (in Neutral) or 600 rpm for automatic (in Drive).
  d. Disconnect solenoid wire and set idle speed to 400 rpm, then reconnect.
  e. Reconnect distributor vacuum line.

V8 307 and 400 (265 H.P.)
  a. Turn in mixture screws until they seat gently, then back out four turns.
  b. Adjust carburetor idle speed screw to obtain 800 rpm for manual transmission (in Neutral), or adjust solenoid screw to obtain 630 rpm for automatic transmission (in Drive).
  c. Adjust both mixture screws equally inward to obtain 700 rpm for manual transmission, 600 rpm for automatic (in Drive).
  d. On cars with automatic, disconnect solenoid wire, set carburetor idle screw to obtain 450 rpm and reconnect solenoid.
  e. Reconnect distributor vacuum line.

V8 350 (250 H.P.)
  a. Turn in mixture screws until they gently seat, then back out four turns.
  b. Adjust solenoid screw to obtain 830 rpm for manual transmission (in Neutral), 630 rpm for automatic (in Drive).
  c. Adjust both mixture screws equally inward to obtain 750 rpm for manual transmission or 600 rpm for automatic (in Drive).
  d. Disconnect solenoid wire, set carburetor idle screw to obtain 450 rpm and reconnect solenoid.
  e. Reconnect distributor vacuum line.

V8 350 (300 H.P.) and 400 (330 H.P.)

a. Turn in both mixture screws until they gently seat, then back out four turns.

b. Adjust carburetor idle screw to obtain 775 rpm for manual transmission, 630 rpm for automatic (in Drive).

c. Adjust mixture screws equally to obtain 700 rpm for manual transmission, 600 rpm for automatic (in Drive).

d. Reconnect distributor vacuum line.

V8 396 (350 H.P.) and 454 (360 H.P.)

a. Turn in both mixture screws until they gently seat, then back out four turns.

b. Adjust carburetor idle screw to obtain 700 rpm for manual transmission or 630 rpm for automatic (in Drive).

c. For cars with automatic transmission: adjust mixture screws equally to obtain 600 rpm with transmission in Drive.

d. For cars with manual transmission: turn in *one* mixture screw until speed drops to 400 rpm, then adjust carburetor idle screw to obtain 700 rpm. Turn in the *other* mixture screw until speed drops 40 rpm, then regain 700 rpm by adjusting carburetor idle screw.

e. Reconnect distributor vacuum line.

5. Disconnect tachometer and reconnect fuel vapor line.

1971

Adjust with air cleaner installed. The idle stop solenoid is no longer used, having been replaced by the combination emission control valve. This valve is energized through the transmission to increase idle speed under conditions of high gear deceleration and to provide full vacuum spark advance during high gear operation. The valve is de-energized at curb idle and in the lower gears to provide a retarded spark under these conditions, the result of which is lower hydrocarbon emission. *The valve need not be adjusted unless the solenoid or throttle body is removed, or the carburetor overhauled.*

On all 1971 vehicles except those with solid lifter cams, i.e., 350/330 (Z28) and 454/425 (LS-6), idle limiter caps are installed on the mixture screws of the carburetors. Chevrolet does not recommend removing these caps, and does not recommend adjusting the mixture. Adjusting the mix-

ture without the proper test gear will result in hydrocarbon emission levels in excess of the specified minimum.

1. Follow Steps 1-3 of 1970 procedure.
2. Make the following adjustments:

6 cylinder 250

a. Adjust carburetor idle speed screw to obtain 550 rpm for manual transmission (in Neutral) or 500 rpm for automatic (in Drive). *Do not adjust solenoid screw.*

b. Reconnect vapor line and distributor vacuum advance line.

V8 307 (200 H.P.) and 350 (245 H.P.)

a. Adjust carburetor idle speed screw to obtain 600 rpm for manual transmission (in Neutral) with A/C off, or 550 rpm for automatic (in Drive) with A/C on. *Do not adjust solenoid screw.*

b. Reconnect vapor line and distributor vacuum advance line.

V8 350 (270 H.P.)

a. Adjust carburetor idle speed screw to obtain 600 rpm for manual transmission (in Neutral) with A/C off, or 550 rpm for automatic (in Drive) with A/C on. *Do not adjust solenoid screw.*

b. Place fast idle cam follower on second step of fast idle cam, turn A/C off and adjust fast idle to 1,350 rpm for manual transmission (in Neutral) or 1,500 rpm for automatic (in Park).

c. Reconnect vapor line and distributor vacuum advance line.

V8 350 (330 H.P. Z28) and 454 (425 H.P.)

a. Adjust mixture screws to obtain maximum speed (rpm at idle), then adjust carburetor idle speed screw to obtain 700 rpm (manual in Neutral and automatic in Drive).

b. Turn in one mixture screw to obtain a 20 rpm drop in speed, then back out 1/4 turn.

c. Repeat Step "b" for other mixture screw, then reset idle to 700 rpm. *Do not adjust solenoid screw.*

d. Reconnect vapor line and distributor vacuum line.

V8 396 (300 H.P.) and 454 (365 H.P.)

a. Turn off A/C and adjust carburetor idle speed screw

to obtain 600 rpm with manual transmission in Neutral and automatic in Drive. *Do not adjust solenoid screw.*

b. Place fast idle cam follower on second step of fast idle cam, turn off A/C and adjust fast idle to 1,350 rpm for manual transmission (in Neutral) or 1,500 rpm for automatic (in Park).

c. Reconnect vapor line and distributor vacuum line.

1972

Disconnect the fuel tank line from the vapor canister. Disconnect the distributor vacuum hose and plug the opening. All carburetors are equipped with idle mixture limiter caps. Do not try to adjust the mixture or remove the caps. Adjust the idle speed with the engine running at its normal temperature, choke open, and parking brake set. Turn the air conditioner off, if so equipped. Chock the wheels on automatic transmission cars. Manual transmissions should be in Neutral, and automatic transmissions in Drive.

250 cu in. 6 cylinder

Adjust the idle stop solenoid (not the C.E.C. solenoid, which is the larger of the two carburetor-mounted solenoids) for a speed of 700 rpm (M.T.) or 600 rpm (A.T.).

307, 350 and 400 cu in V8s (two-barrel carburetor)

Adjust the idle stop solenoid screw for 900 rpm (M.T.) or 600 rpm (A.T.). Set the carburetor fast idle cam screw for 1850 rpm on 307 engines and 2200 rpm on 350 and 400 engines.

350 cu in. V8 (Quadrajet four-barrel carburetor)

Adjust the idle stop solenoid screw to obtain 800 rpm (M.T.) or 600 rpm (A.T.). Position the fast idle follower on the second step of the fast idle cam and set the fast idle to 1350 rpm (M.T.) or 1500 rpm (A.T.).

350 cu in. V8 (Holley four-barrel carburetor)

Adjust the idle stop solenoid screw for 900 rpm.

402 and 454 cu in. V8s (Quadrajet four-barrel carburetor)

Adjust the idle stop solenoid screw for 800 rpm (M.T.) or 600 rpm (A.T.). Position the fast idle follower on the second step of the fast idle cam and set the fast idle at 1350 rpm (M.T.) or 1500 rpm (A.T.).

1973

All models are equipped with idle limiter caps and idle solenoids. Disconnect the fuel tank line from the evaporative canister. The engine must be running at operating temperature, choke off, parking brake on, and rear wheels blocked. Disconnect the distributor vacuum hose and plug it. After adjustment, reconnect the vacuum and evaporative hoses.

250 cu. in. 6 cylinder

Adjust the idle stop solenoid for 700 rpm on manual transmission models or 600 rpm on automatics. On manual models, make no attempt to adjust the CEC solenoid (the larger of the two carburetor solenoids) or a decrease in engine braking could result.

Two-barrel 307, 350, and 400 cu. in. V8's

1. With air conditioning switched off, if so equipped, adjust the idle stop solenoid screw for a speed of 900 rpm on manual models; 600 rpm on automatics.
2. De-energize the idle stop solenoid and adjust the idle speed screw (screw resting on lower step of the cam) for 450 rpm on 307, 400 rpm on 350 and 400 engines with automatic transmission, or 500 rpm on 350 engines with a manual transmission.

Four-barrel 350 and 454 cu. in V8's

1. Adjust the idle stop solenoid screw for 900 rpm on manual transmission models; 600 rpm on automatics.
2. Connect the distributor vacuum hose and position the fast idle cam follower on the top step of the fast idle cam (turn air conditioning off if so equipped) and adjust the fast idle to 1300 rpm on manual transmission 350 engines; 1600 on manual 454 engines and all automatics (in Park).

Z28

1. Adjust the idle stop solenoid screw (air conditioning off if so equipped) for a speed of 900 rpm on manual transmission; 700 rpm on automatic (in Drive).
2. Connect the distributor vacuum hose and position the fast idle cam follower on the top step of the cam (turn air conditioning off if so equipped) and adjust the fast idle to 1300 rpm on manual models; 1600 rpm on automatics.

1974

The same preconditions as 1973 apply.

250 cu. in. 6 cylinder

Adjust the idle stop solenoid hex nut for 850 rpm on manual transmission; 600 rpm on automatics (in Drive).

Two-barrel 350 and 400 cu. in. V8s

1. Turn the air conditioning off, if so equipped. Adjust the idle stop solenoid screw for 900 rpm on manual transmission models; 600 rpm on automatics (in Drive).
2. De-energize the solenoid and adjust the carburetor idle cam screw (on low step of cam) for 400 rpm on automatic models (in Drive); 500 rpm on 350 engines with manual transmission.

Four-barrel 350 and 400 cu. in. V8s

1. Turn the air conditioning off, if so equipped. Adjust the idle stop solenoid screw for 900 rpm on manual transmission models; 600 rpm on automatics (in Drive).
2. Connect the distributor vacuum hose. Position the fast idle cam follower on the top step of the fast idle cam and adjust the fast idle speed to 1300 rpm on manual transmission models; 1600 on automatics (in Park).

Z28

1. Turn the air conditioning off, if so equipped. Adjust the idle stop solenoid for 900 rpm on manual transmission models; 700 rpm on automatics (in Drive).
2. Connect the distributor vacuum hose. Position the fast idle cam follower on the top step of the cam and adjust the fast idle to 1300 rpm on manual transmission cars; 1500 rpm on automatics (in Park).

454 cu. in. V8

1. Shut off the air conditioning, if so equipped. Adjust the idle stop solenoid screw for 800 rpm on manual transmission models; 600 rpm on automatics (in Drive).
2. Connect the distributor vacuum hose and position the fast idle cam follower on the top step of the cam and adjust the fast idle to 1600 rpm on manual transmission cams; 1500 rpm on automatics (in Park).

1975-76

The engine must be at normal operating temperature with the air cleaner on, the choke open, the air conditioner off, and the timing correctly set.
1. Set the brake and block the wheels.
2. Set the automatic transmission in Drive and the manual in neutral. Disconnect the fuel tank hose from the vapor canister in the engine compartment.
3. Use needle nose pliers to break off the mixture screw cap or caps.

1 bbl

Adjust the idle speed by turning the solenoid in or out to obtain the higher of the two speeds listed on the sticker. Disconnect the electrical connector from the solenoid and turn the 1/8 in. allen screw in the end of the solenoid body to lower the idle speed to the second figure on the sticker.

2 bbl

Adjust the idle speed with the idle speed screw to obtain the higher idle speed shown on the sticker.

4 bbl

Disconnect the electrical connector at the idle solenoid, and adjust the idle speed to the lower of the two figures given on the sticker. Reconnect the electrical connector, open the throttle to extend the solenoid plunger, then turn the solenoid plunger screw to obtain the higher of the two idle speed figures. For 1976, the idle solenoid has been dropped; the idle is adjusted with an idle speed screw.

4. On all but the 2 bbl., turn out the mixture screws until the highest possible idle speed is reached. If the idle speed becomes excessive (more than that set in Step 4), reset the idle speed to that set in Step 4. On the 2 bbl., turn out the mixture screws to obtain the highest idle and then, turn in the mixture screws to obtain the lower of the two figures listed on the sticker.
5. Turn in the mixture screws equally until the normal idle speed is reached.
6. Replace the vapor canister hose.

COOLING SYSTEM

A standard pressure cooling system is used on all models. The radiator cap is designed to maintain a cooling system pressure of about 13 or 15 psi above atmospheric. The water pump requires no attention except to make certain the air vent at the top of the housing and the drain holes in the bottom do not become clogged.

Radiator Removal and Installation

1. Drain radiator.
2. Disconnect hoses and oil cooler lines.
3. Remove radiator upper panel and shroud (if so equipped).
4. Remove radiator attaching bolts and lift radiator out of car.
5. Slide radiator into position.
6. Install attaching bolts, shroud, and upper panel.

7. Install hoses and close drain.
8. Fill cooling system, run engine with radiator cap off until operating temperature has been reached. Again fill cooling system and check for leaks.

Water Pump Removal and Installation

1. Drain the radiator and loosen the fan pulley bolts.
2. Disconnect the heater hose, lower radiator hose and, if applicable, the bypass hose at the water pump.
3. On V8 engines, remove the alternator upper brace. Loosen the swivel bolt and remove the fan belt.
4. On Mark IV (big block) engines, disconnect the power steering and air conditioning belts and swivel the power steering pump to one side.
5. Remove the fan blade and pulley.
   NOTE: thermostatic fan clutches must be kept in an "in-car" position. When removed from the car the assembly should be supported so that the clutch disc remains in a vertical plane to prevent silicone fluid leakage.
6. Remove the water pump attaching bolts and, if applicable, the power steering-to-pump bolts and remove the pump and gasket.
   NOTE: on four and six-cylinder engines, pull the pump straight out of the block first to avoid damage to the impeller.
7. Install the pump assembly using a new gasket. Coat the gasket on both sides with sealer. Tighten the 5/16 in. bolts to 15 ft lbs. (four and six-cylinder) and the 3/8 in. bolts (V8) to 30 ft lbs.
8. Install the pulley and fan.
9. On big block engines, install the power steering and air conditioning bolts.
10. Connect the hoses and fill the cooling system.
11. On V8 engines, install the alternator upper brace and fan belt. Install the power steering pump bolt.
12. Adjust the belts, then start the engine and check for leaks.

Thermostat Removal and Installation

The thermostat is located inside a housing on the front of the cylinder head on four and six-cylinder engines and inside the front of the intake manifold casting on V8 engines. It is not necessary to remove the radiator hose from the thermostat housing when removing the thermostat.

1. Remove the two retaining bolts from the thermostat housing and lift up the housing with the hose attached. Remove the thermostat.
2. Insert the new thermostat, spring end down, and install the housing with a new gasket. Tighten the housing retaining bolts to 30 ft lbs.

EMISSION CONTROLS

NOTE: see the Unit Repair Section for emission control systems troubleshooting.

Positive Crankcase Ventilation

In this system, crankcase vapors are drawn into the intake manifold and burned as part of engine combustion. The system draws clean air from the carburetor air cleaner. The ventilation flow is regulated by the PCV valve.

Air Injection Reactor

The AIR system injects air into the exhaust system, near enough to the exhaust valves to continue the burning of the normally unburned segment of the exhaust gases. To do this it employs an air injection pump and a system of hoses, valves, tubes, etc., necessary to carry the compressed air from the pump to the exhaust manifolds. Carburetors and distributors for AIR engines have specific modifications to adapt them to the air injection system; those components should not be interchanged with those intended for use on engines that do not have the system.

A diverter valve is used to prevent backfiring. The valve senses sudden increases in manifold vacuum and ceases the injection of air during fuel-rich periods. During coasting, this valve diverts the entire air flow through the pump muffler and during high engine speeds, expels it through a relief valve. Check valves in the system prevent exhaust gases from entering the pump.

Controlled Combustion System

C.C.S. increases combustion efficiency through leaner carburetor adjustments and revised distributor calibration. Thermostatically controlled air intakes are also used on most models. A higher temperature thermostat is used on C.C.S. cars.

Evaporative Emission Control

Introduced on California cars in 1970, and nationwide in 1971, this system reduces the amount of escaping gasoline vapors. Float bowl emissions are controlled by internal carburetor modifications. Redesigned bowl vents, reduced bowl capacity, heat shields, and improved intake manifold-to-carburetor insulation serve to reduce vapor loss into the atmosphere. The venting of fuel tank vapors into the air has been stopped. Fuel vapors are now directed through lines to a canister containing an activated charcoal filter. Unburned vapors are trapped here until the engine is started. When the engine is running, the canister is purged by air drawn in by manifold vacuum. The air and fuel vapors are then directed into the engine to be burned. All 1973 into the engine to be burned. Most 1973 and later models have integral vapor separators within the fuel tank.

Transmission Controlled Spark

Introduced in 1970, this system controls exhaust emissions by eliminating vacuum advance in the lower forward gears.

The 1970 system consists of a transmission switch, solenoid vacuum switch, time delay relay, and a thermostatic water temperature switch. The solenoid vacuum switch is energized in the lower gears via the transmission switch and closes off distributor vacuum. The two-way transmission switch is activated by the shifter shaft on manual transmissions, and fluid pressure on automatic transmissions. The switch de-energizes the solenoid in high gear, the plunger extends and uncovers the vacuum port, and the distributor receives full vacuum. The temperature switch overrides the system when engine temperature is below 63° or above 232°. This allows vacuum advance in all gears. A time delay relay opens 15 seconds after the ignition is switched on. Full vacuum advance during this delay eliminates the possibility of stalling.

The 1971 system is similar, except that the vacuum solenoid (now called a Combination Emissions Control or CEC solenoid) serves two functions. One function is to control distributor vacuum; the added function is to act as a deceleration throttle stop in high gear. This cuts down on emissions when the vehicle is coming to a stop in high gear. The CEC solenoid is controlled by a temperature switch, a transmission switch, and a 20 second time delay relay. This system also contains a reversing relay, which energizes the solenoid when the transmission switch, temperature switch or time delay completes the CEC circuit to ground. This system is directly opposite the 1970 system in operation. The 1970 vacuum solenoid was normally open to allow vacuum advance and when energized, closed to block vacuum. The 1971 system is normally closed blocking vacuum advance and when energized, opens to allow vacuum advance. The temperature switch completes the CEC circuit to ground when engine temperature is below 82°. Some Camaros also have a high temperature terminal on the switch to complete the CEC circuit when coolant temperature reaches 232°. The time delay relay allows vacuum advance (and raised idle speed) for 20 seconds after the ignition key is turned to the "on" position. Models with an automatic transmission and air conditioning also have a solid state timing device which engages the air conditioning compressor for three seconds after the ignition key is turned to the "off" position to prevent the engine from running-on.

The 1972 6 cylinder system is similar to that used in 1971, except that an idle stop solenoid has been added to the system. In the energized position, the solenoid maintains engine speed at a predetermined fast idle. When the solenoid is de-energized by turning off the ignition, the solenoid allows the throttle plates to close beyond the normal idle position; thus cuting off the air supply and preventing engine run-on. The 6 cylinder is the only 1972 engine with a C.E.C. valve, which serves the same deceleration function as in 1971. The 1972 time delay relay delays full vacuum 20 seconds after the transmission is shifted into high gear. V8 engines use a vacuum advance solenoid similar to that used in 1970. This relay is normally closed to block vacuum and opens when energized to allow vacuum advance. The solenoid controls distributor vacuum advance and performs no throttle positioning function. The idle stop solenoid used operates in the same manner as the one on 6 cylinder engines. All air-conditioned cars have an additional anti-diesel (run-on) solenoid which engages the compressor clutch for three seconds after the ignition is switched off. The 1973 TCS system differs from the 1972 system in three ways. The 32 second upshift delay has been replaced by a 20 second starting relay. This relay closes to complete the TCS circuit and open the TCS solenoid, allowing vacuum advance, for 20 seconds after the key is turned to the "on" position. The operating temperature of the temperature overide switch has been raised to 93°, and the switch that was used to engage the A/C compressor when the key was turned "off" has been eliminated. All models are equipped with an electric throttle control solenoid to prevent run-on. The 1973 TCS system is used on all models equipped with a 307 engine, all V8 models equipped with a manual transmission, and all full-size station wagons equipped with a 165 hp 350 or a 170 hp 400.

The 1974 TCS system is used only on manual transmission models. System components remain unchanged from 1973. The vacuum advance solenoid is located on the coil bracket.

For diagnosis procedures, see the Unit Repair Section. Any of the methods of exhaust emission control requires close and frequent attention to tune-up factors of engine maintenance.

Early Fuel Evaporation System

1975 and later models are equipped with this system to reduce engine warm-up time, improve driveability, and reduce emissions. On start-up, a vacuum motor acts to close a heat valve in the exhaust manifold which causes exhaust gases to enter the intake manifold heat riser passages. Incoming fuel mixture is then heated and more complete fuel evaporation is provided during warm-up.

Catalytic Converter

All 1975 and later models are equipped with a catalytic converter. The converter is located midway in the exhaust system. Stainless steel exhaust pipes are used ahead of the converter. The converter is stainless steel with an aluminized steel cover and a ceramic felt blanket to insulate the converter from the floorpan. The catalyst pellet bed inside the converter consists of noble metals which cause a reaction that converts hydrocarbons and carbon monoxide into water and carbon monoxide into water and carbon dioxide. See the "Unit Repair" section for a complete description.

Exhaust Gas Recirculation

All 1973 and later engines are equipped with exhaust gas recirculation (EGR). This system consists of a metering valve, a vacuum line to the carburetor, and cast-in exhaust gas passages in the intake manifold. The EGR valve is controlled by carburetor vacuum, and accordingly opens and closes to admit exhaust gases into the fuel/air mixture. The exhaust gases lower the combustion temperature, and reduce the amount of oxides of nitrogen (NO_x) produced. The valve is closed at idle and wide open throttle, but is open between the two extreme throttle positions.

Some California engines are equipped with a dual diaphragm EGR valve. This valve further limits the exhaust gas opening (compared to the single diaphragm EGR valve) during high intake manifold vacuum periods, such as high-speed cruising, and provides more exhaust gas recirculation during acceleration when manifold vacuum is low. In addition to the hose running to the thermal vacuum switch, a second hose is connected directly to the intake manifold.

ENGINE

Four, six, and eight cylinder engines are used. The 1970 four cylinder engine is a 153 cu. in. inline design with five main bearings. The six cylinder engines are also of the inline type, with seven main bearings. They have been built in 230 and 250 cu. in. displacements. V8 engines are of two basic types. All engines of each type are generally similar in design and have some interchangeability of parts. The first type is the small block V8 series. This includes the 262, 302, 305, 307, 350, and 400 cu. in. engines. The second type is the big block or Mark IV, V8 series. This in-

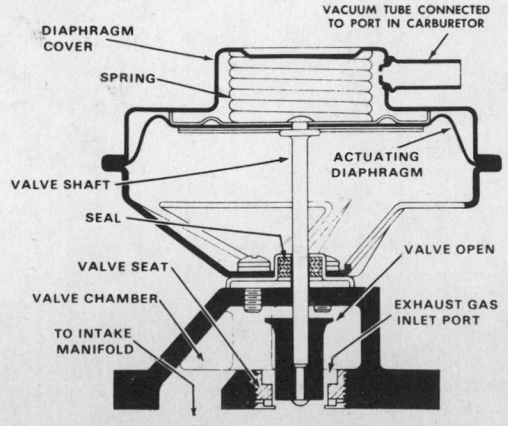

Cutaway view of an EGR valve
(© Chevrolet Div., G.M. Corp)

cludes engines of 396, 402, and 454 cu. in. displacement.

The big block 402 was last offered in 1972. The small block 400 was offered starting 1974.

Engine Removal and Installation

NOTE: unless otherwise stated, the following operations cover the 4 cylinder, 6 cylinder and V8 engines.

Caution Do not discharge the compressor or disconnect the A/C lines. Damage to the A/C system or personal injury could result.

Removal

1. Raise car and place on jackstands.
2. Drain cooling system, transmission, and crankcase.
3. Scribe alignment marks on underside of hood and around hood hinges, and remove hood from hinges.
4. Disconnect coolant and heater hoses at engine attachment.
5. Disconnect battery cables at battery.
6. Remove radiator and shroud assembly. Remove fan and pulley.
7. Remove air cleaner.
8. Disconnect coil, starter and alternator wires, engine-to-body ground strap, oil pressure and engine temperature sender wires, C.E.C. wire, and any other wires.
9. Disconnect gas line at fuel pump.
10. Disconnect accelerator control linkage at firewall.
11. Disconnect hand choke linkage (4 cylinder), and power brake vacuum line.
12. Disconnect exhaust pipe from manifold. Disconnect the crossover pipe on V8 models, if so equipped.
13. Disconnect clutch shaft bracket at frame and disconnect clutch linkage. On automatic transmission models, remove transmission oil filler tube and plug the opening.
14. Attach engine lifting apparatus. Attach to hoist and secure the engine.
15. Remove driveshaft.
16. Remove and set aside power steering pump and air conditioning compressor. Do not disconnect hoses.
17. Remove engine rear mounting bolts.
18. Disconnect speedometer cable, transmission control rod linkage lower ends, T.C.S. switch, and transmission oil cooler lines.
19. Loosen front engine mounting bolts.
20. Raise engine slightly and remove bolts.
21. Remove transmission crossmember and free the transmission rear mounting.
22. Remove engine and transmission as a unit from the car.

Installation

1. Bolt engine lifting tool to engine and lower engine and transmission into chassis as a unit. Guide engine to align front engine mounts with mounts on frame.
2. Install one rear transmission crossmember side bolt, swing crossmember up under transmission mount and install bolt in opposite side rail.
3. Align and install rear mount bolts.
4. Install engine front mount bolts and remove lifting tool from engine.
5. Install and connect all items in reverse order of engine removal procedure.

Manifolds

Refer to the Chevrolet section for intake and exhaust manifold removal and installation procedures for both inline and V8 engines. Use the following procedure for exhaust manifold removal and installation on sixes with the intake manifold integral with the cylinder head.

Exhaust Manifold Removal and Installation, 1975 and Later Six Cylinder Engine with Integral Intake Manifold

1. Remove the air cleaner.
2. Remove the power steering and air pump brackets.
3. Remove the EFE valve bracket.
4. Disconnect the throttle linkage and return spring.
5. Unbolt the exhaust pipe from the flange.
6. Unbolt and remove the manifold.
7. Reverse the procedure for installation. Tighten the four end bolts to specifications last.

Valve System

Chevrolet uses a hydraulic tappet system with adjustable rocker mounting nuts to obtain zero lash.

A few high-performance V8s

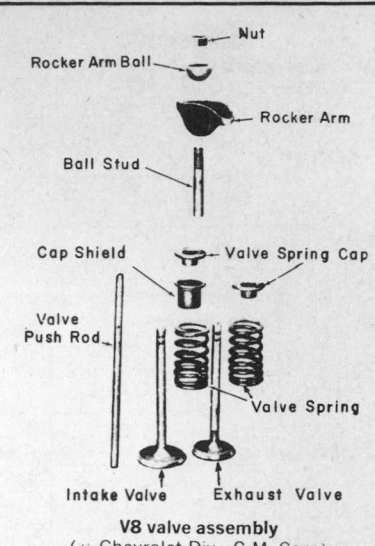

V8 valve assembly
(© Chevrolet Div., G.M. Corp)

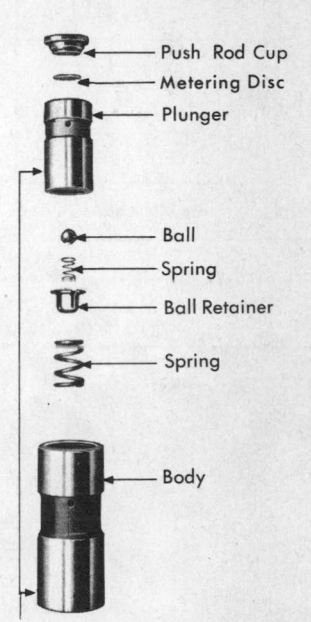

Hydraulic lifter plunger and body are fitted pairs and must not be mismated
(© Chevrolet Div., G.M. Corp)

through 1972 use mechanical tappets (valve lifters) which require periodic adjustment.

Hydraulic Valve Lifter Adjustment

Preliminary Adjustment

In the case of disassembly, or any other cause for valve tappet adjustment, proceed as follows:

1. Remove the rocker arm covers.

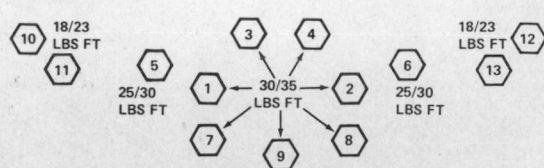

Exhaust manifold torque sequence— inline six cylinder with integral intake manifold
(© Chevrolet Div., G.M. Corp.)

VALVE ARRANGEMENT

FRONT ← | E I I E E I I E |

OHV 4 cylinder

FRONT ← | E I I E E I I E E I I E |

6 cylinder

FRONT ← | E I I E E I I E |
| E I I E E I I E |

Small block V8s

FRONT ← | E I E I E I E I |
| E I E I E I E I |

Big block V8s

Adjusting valve clearance—6 cyl hydraulic lifters
(© Chevrolet Div., G.M. Corp)

2. Remove distributor cap and crank engine until distributor rotor points to No. 1 cylinder terminal, with points open. The crankshaft damper timing marks should be aligned.

The following valves can be adjusted with the engine in No. 1 firing position:

OHV 4—Intake No. 1, 2, Exhaust No. 1, 3

OHV 6—Intake No. 1, 2, 4, Exhaust No. 1, 3, 5

V8—Intake No. 1, 2, 5, 7, Exhaust No. 1, 3, 4, 8

3. Turn the rocker arm mounting nut until all lash is removed from each valve train. This can be determined by rotating the pushrod while turning the ad-justment. When all play has been removed, turn adjusting nut one more turn. This will place the lifter plunger in the center of its travel.

4. Turn the engine 360° clockwise. The following valves can be adjusted with the engine in the No. 6 firing position (No. 4 on OHV 4):

OHV 4—Intake No. 3, 4, Exhaust No. 2, 4

OHV 6—Intake No. 3, 5, 6, Exhaust No. 2, 4, 6

V8—Intake No. 3, 4, 6, 8, Exhaust No. 2, 5, 6, 7

Running Adjustment

Adjust the lifters as follows with the engine hot and running.

1. Remove rocker arm covers and gaskets.
2. Place oil deflector clips on rocker arms.
3. With engine running at idle, back off rocker arm nut until it starts to clatter.
4. Turn nut down until clatter stops. This is the zero lash position.
5. Tighten nut down one-quarter turn. Pause ten seconds. Repeat additional quarter turns and ten second pauses until nut has been tightened down one full turn from the zero lash position.
6. Repeat steps 3, 4, and 5 for all rocker arms.
7. Remove oil deflector clips and replace rocker arm covers.

Mechanical Valve Lifter Adjustment

1. Set engine in No. 1 firing position.
2. Adjust the clearance between the valve stems and the rocker arms using a feeler gauge. Adjust the rocker arm mounting nut. Check the Tune-Up Specifications table for the proper clearance. Adjust the following Valves in No. 1 firing position: Intake No. 2, 7, Exhaust No. 4, 8.

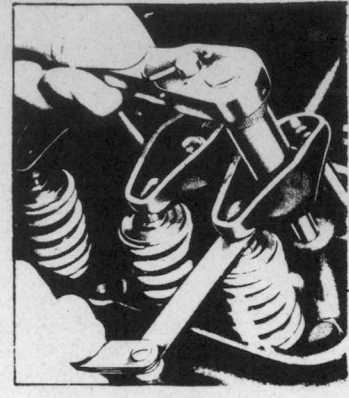

Adjusting valve clearance—V8 w/mechanical lifters
(© Chevrolet Div., G.M. Corp)

3. Turn crankshaft one-half revolution (180°) clockwise. Adjust the following valves: Intake No. 1, 8, Exhaust No. 3, 6.
4. Turn crankshaft one-half revolution clockwise to No. 6 firing position. Adjust the following valves in No. 6 firing position: Intake No. 3, 4, Exhaust No. 5, 7.
5. Turn crankshaft one-half revolution clockwise. Adjust the following valves: Intake No. 5, 6, Exhaust No. 1, 2.
6. Run engine until normal operating temperature is reached. Reset all clearances, hot and running, using oil deflectors.

Cylinder Head

Removal and Installation

Caution Do not discharge the compressor or disconnect the A/C lines. Damage to the A/C system or personal injury could result.

4 and 6 Cylinder Engines

1. Drain cooling system and remove air cleaner. Disconnect P.C.V. hose.
2. Disconnect choke cable (4 cylinder), accelerator pedal rod at

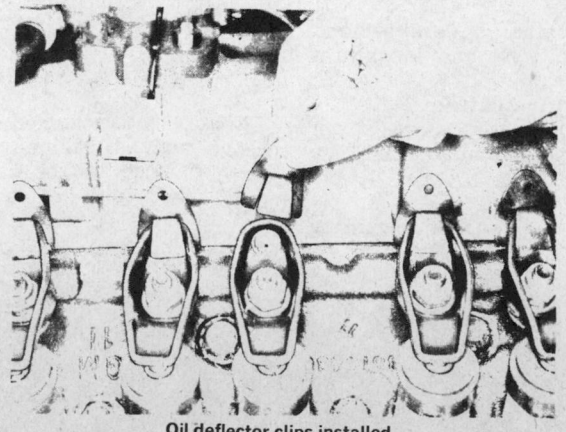

Oil deflector clips installed
(© Chevrolet Div., G.M. Corp)

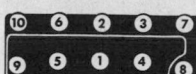

OHV 4 cylinder engine cylinder head torque sequence

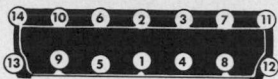

6 cylinder engine cylinder head torque sequence

bell crank on manifold, and fuel and vacuum lines at carburetor.

3. Disconnect exhaust pipe at manifold flange, then remove manifold bolts and clamps and remove manifolds and carburetor as an assembly.

4. Remove fuel and vacuum line retaining clip from water outlet. Then disconnect wire harness from heat sending unit and coil, leaving harness clear of clips on rocker arm cover.

5. Disconnect radiator hose at water outlet housing and battery ground strap at cylinder head.

6. Disconnect wires and remove spark plugs. On the 6 cylinder engine disconnect coil to distributor primary wire lead at coil and remove the coil.

7. Remove rocker arm cover. Back off rocker arm nuts, pivot rocker arms to clear push rods and remove push rods.

8. Remove cylinder-head bolts, cylinder head and gasket.

9. Place a new cylinder-head gasket over dowel pins in cylinder block.

10. Guide and lower cylinder head into place over dowels and gasket.

11. Oil cylinder-head bolts, install and run them down snug.

12. Tighten the cylinder-head bolts a little at a time with a torque wrench in the correct sequence. Final torque should be as specified.

13. Install valve pushrods down through the cylinder-head openings and seat them in their lifter sockets.

14. Install rocker arms, balls and nuts and tighten rocker arm nuts until all pushrod play is taken up.

15. Install thermostat, thermostat housing and water outlet using new gaskets. Then connect radiator hose.

16. Install heat sending switch and torque to 15–20 ft. lbs.

17. Clean spark plugs or install new ones.

18. Torque 13/16 in. hex plugs to 20 ft lbs and 5/8 in. hex plugs to 15 ft lbs. Tapered seat plugs are used on some engines starting in 1970 and all engines beginning in 1971.

19. Install coil (on six cylinder en-

gine) then connect heat sending unit and coil primary wires, and connect battery ground cable at the cylinder head.

20. Clean surfaces and install new gasket over manifold studs. Install manifold. Install bolts and clamps and torque as specified.

21. Connect throttle linkage, and choke wire (on four cylinder engine).

22. Connect P.C.V., fuel and vacuum lines and secure lines in clip at water outlet.

23. Fill cooling system and check for leaks.

24. Adjust valve lash.

25. Install rocker arm cover and position wiring harness in clips.

26. Clean and install air cleaner.

V8 Engines

Removal and Installation

1. Drain coolant. Remove air cleaner.

2. Disconnect:
   a. battery
   b. radiator and heater hose from manifold
   c. throttle linkage
   d. fuel line
   e. coil wires
   f. temperature sending unit
   g. power brake hose, distributor vacuum hose, and crankcase vent hoses.

3. Remove:
   a. distributor, marking position
   b. alternator upper bracket
   c. coil and bracket
   d. manifold attaching bolts
   e. intake manifold and carburetor.

4. Remove:
   a. rocker arm covers
   b. rocker arm nuts, balls, rocker arms, and push rods. These items must be replaced in their original locations.

5. Remove cylinder head bolts, cylinder head, and gasket.

6. Reverse procedure to install. Tighten head bolts evenly to the specified torque. On engines having steel gasket, use sealer on both sides. No sealer should be used on steel-asbestos gaskets. Adjust the valve lash.

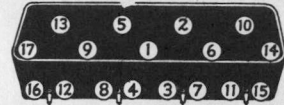

Small block V8 cylinder head torque sequence

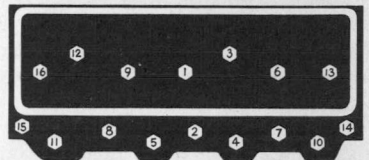

Big block V8 cylinder head torque sequence

Timing Cover, Chain, and Camshaft

All 4 and 6 cylinder engines have gear driven camshafts, while all V8 camshafts are driven by a timing chain. 4 or 6 cylinder timing gear replacement requires camshaft removal.

NOTE: the 6 cylinder engine uses a harmonic balancer that closely resembles the Chevrolet V8-type. The removal procedure for this damper will be the same as that for the Chevrolet V8. Driving the damper back onto the crankshaft without supporting the pulley can cause damage. A replacement tool must be used during the reassembly operation.

Cover Removal and Installation

1. Drain and remove radiator.

2. Remove harmonic balancer, (6 and 8 cylinder) or a crankshaft pulley, (4 cylinder) using a puller.

3. Drain the engine oil and remove the oil pan on all engines through 1972, and on small block V8s

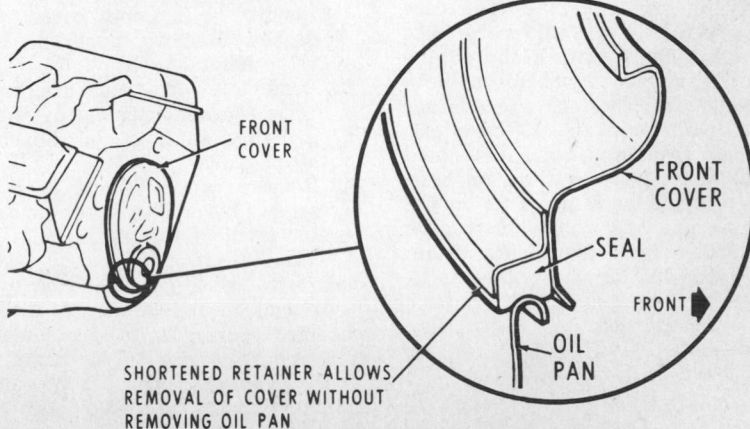

On 1975 and later small block V8s, it is no longer necessary to remove or lower the oil pan to remove the timing cover. The seal retainer is shortened enough to clear the pan

(© Chevrolet Div., G.M. Corp)

through 1974. Remove the V8 water pump. If the oil pan isn't to removed, cut the pan seal off flush with the block.

4. Remove timing gear cover attaching screws, and cover and gasket.
5. Reverse procedure to install. Use silicone sealer at the oil pan to cylinder block joint.

Caution The 6 and 8 cylinder engines use a harmonic balancer. Breakage may occur if the balancer is hammered back onto the crankshaft.

This balancer must be drawn back into place.

TIME SAVER

When replacing the crankshaft damper, it has been found that lightly polishing the inside diameter with crocus cloth will greatly ease replacement. This procedure will also assist in any future removals, as it is sometimes difficult to pull a damper even with a puller. Be sure that the polishing is not overdone, or the damper will wobble on the crankshaft.

Oil Seal Removal and Installation

1. After removing gear cover, pry oil seal out of front of cover with large screwdriver.
2. Install new lip seal with lip (open side of seal) inside and drive or press seal carefully into place.

Timing Chain Replacement

V8

V8 models are equipped with a timing chain. To replace the chain, remove the radiator, water pump harmonic balancer, and the crankcase front cover. This will allow access to the timing chain. Crank the engine until the marks punched on both sprockets are closest to one another and in line between the shaft centers. Take out the three bolts that hold the camshaft gear to the camshaft. This gear is a light press fit on the camshaft and will come off readily. It is located by a dowel. The chain comes off with the camshaft gear. A gear puller will be required to remove the crankshaft gear.

Without disturbing the position of the engine, mount the new crank gear on the shaft, then mount the chain over the camshaft gear. Arrange the camshaft gear in such a way that the timing marks will line up between the shaft centers and the camshaft

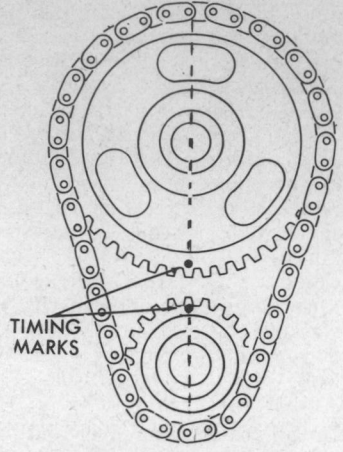

V8 engine timing marks

locating dowel will enter the dowel hole in the cam sprocket.

Place the cam sprocket, with its chain mounted over it, in position on the front of the camshaft and pull up with the three bolts that hold it to the camshaft.

After the gears are in place, turn the engine two full revolutions to make certain that the timing marks are in correct alignment between the shaft centers.

Camshaft Removal and Installation

4 and 6 Cylinder engines

The manufacturer recommends that the engine be removed from the car to remove the camshaft. However, in most cases the following procedure can be used. You may also have to raise the front of the engine for clearance.

1. In addition to removing the timing gear cover, remove the grille assembly.
2. Remove valve cover and gasket, loosen all the valve rocker arm nuts and pivot the arms clear of the pushrods.
3. Remove distributor and fuel pump.
4. Remove coil, side cover and gasket. Remove pushrods and valve lifters.
5. Remove the two camshaft thrust plate retaining screws by working through holes in the camshaft gear.
6. Remove camshaft and gear assembly by pulling it out through the front of the block.

NOTE: if renewing either camshaft or camshaft gear, the gear must be pressed off the camshaft. The replacement parts must be assembled in the same manner (under pressure). In placing the gear on the camshaft, press the gear onto the shaft until it bottoms against the gear spacer ring. The end clearance of the thrust plate should be .001 to .005 in.

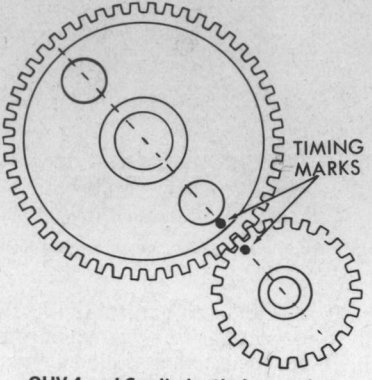

OHV 4 and 6 cylinder timing marks

7. Install camshaft assembly in the engine.
8. Turn crankshaft and camshaft to align and bring the timing marks together. Push the camshaft into this aligned position. Install camshaft thrust plate-to-block screws and torque them to 6-7½ ft. lbs.
9. Runout on either crankshaft or camshaft gear should not exceed .003 in.
10. Backlash between the two gears should be between .004 and .006 in.
11. Install timing gear cover and gasket.
12. Install oil pan and gaskets.
13. Install harmonic balancer.
14. Line up keyway in balancer with key on crankshaft and drive balancer onto shaft until it bottoms against crankshaft gear.
15. Install valve lifters and pushrods. Install side cover with new gasket. Attach coil wires; install fuel pump.
16. Install distributor and set timing as described under distributor at the beginning of the section.
17. Pivot rocker arms over pushrods and adjust the valves.
18. Add oil to the engine. Install and adjust fan belt.
19. Install radiator or shroud.
20. Install grille assembly.
21. Fill cooling system, start engine and check for leaks.
22. Check and adjust timing.

V8 Engines

1. Remove intake manifold, valve lifters and timing chain cover as described in this section.
2. Remove grille, except on Nova. On this model, remove both front motor mount bolts and right motor mount, then lower engine until it rests on frame.
3. On Nova, remove the two center bolts and the one lower bolt that secure the hood latch support. This will give adequate clearance for the cam.
4. Remove fuel pump and pump pushrod.
5. Remove camshaft sprocket bolts,

sprocket and timing chain. A light blow to the lower edge of a tight sprocket should free it (use a plastic mallet).

6. Install two 5/16—18 x 4 in. bolts in cam bolt holes and pull cam from block.
7. To install, reverse removal procedure aligning the sprocket timing marks.

NOTE: cam lobes must be lubricated with Molykote® or SAE 90 gear oil before installation. All cam journals are the same diameter, so be careful that the cam bearings are not dislodged during installation.

Lubrication

Oil Pan Removal and Installation

Nova, Camaro—4 and 6 Cylinder

1. Disconnect battery ground cable.
2. Remove front engine mount bolts. Remove upper radiator panel or side mount bolts.
3. Drain coolant. Remove radiator hoses.
4. Remove fan.
5. Drain engine oil.
6. On all 1970-74 models, and 1975 and later models with manual transmission, disconnect and remove the starter.
7. Disconnect oil cooler lines and remove converter or flywheel housing underpan.
8. On Nova through 1974 and Camaro through 1972, disconnect steering rod at idler lever. Swing linkage to one side for pan clearance.
9. Rotate crankshaft until timing mark on torsional damper is at 6:00 o'clock position.
10. On Camaro, raise engine enough to insert 2 X 4 in. blocks under engine mounts.
11. Unbolt oil pan. On some models it may be necessary to remove the oil pump and intake pipe for clearance. On Nova, remove the left engine mount and frame bracket. Lower the pan slightly and roll it into the area where the mount was. Then tilt the front of the pan up and pull it down and to the rear. Lower pan.

1970-72 Chevelle—6 Cylinder

1. Disconnect battery ground cable.
2. Remove radiator upper mounting panel. Place a piece of heavy cardboard between fan and radiator.
3. Remove starter. Disconnect fuel line.
4. Drain engine oil; disconnect brake line from front crossmember.
5. Remove converter housing underpan and splash shield.

Installing blocks for oil pan removal—V8
(© Chevrolet Div., G.M. Corp)

6. Rotate crankshaft until timing mark on torsional damper is at 6:00 o'clock position.
7. Remove front engine mount through bolts.
8. Raise engine approximately three inches, remove engine mounts, and lower oil pan.

Camaro, Nova, Chevelle, Monte Carlo—V8

See the next procedure for Chevelle and Monte Carlo through 1972 with big block V8.

1. Disconnect battery ground cable.
2. Remove distributor cap.
3. Remove radiator upper mounting panel.
4. Remove fan. On big block (Mark IV) engine models, place a piece of heavy cardboard between the radiator and fan.
5. Drain engine oil.
6. Disconnect exhaust or crossover pipes.
7. Remove converter housing underpan and splash shield.
8. On Camaro through 1972, disconnect steering idler lever at the frame. Swing linkage down.
9. Rotate crankshaft until timing mark on torsional damper is at 6:00 o'clock position.
10. Remove starter.
11. On 1970 small V8, remove fuel pump. On 1973-74 big block Chevelles with a 4-speed, remove the transmission mount to crossmember nut and raise the rear of the transmission.
12. Remove front engine mount through bolts.
13. Raise engine and insert blocks under engine mounts. Block thickness should be 2 in. for Nova and Camaro, and 3 in. for Chevelle.
14. Remove oil pan.

Chevelle and Monte Carlo —396, 402, 454 V8

1. Disconnect battery ground cable.
2. Remove:
   a. air cleaner
   b. dipstick
   c. distributor cap

d. radiator shroud and upper mounting panel.
3. On 396 engines place a piece of heavy cardboard between radiator and fan.
4. Disconnect engine ground straps.
5. Disconnect accelerator control cable.
6. Drain oil.
7. Remove driveshaft and plug rear of transmission.
8. Remove starter.
9. Disconnect transmission linkage at transmission or remove floor-shift lever.
10. Disconnect speedometer cable and back-up switch connector.
11. On manual transmission vehicles disconnect clutch shaft at frame. On automatic transmission vehicles, disconnect cooler lines, detent cable, rod or switch wire, and modulator pipe.
12. Remove crossmember bolts. Jack up engine. Move crossmember rearward.
13. Remove crossover or disconnect dual exhaust pipes.
14. Remove:
    a. flywheel housing cover
    b. transmission
    c. flywheel housing and throw-out bearing (manual transmission)
    d. front engine mount through bolts.
15. Raise rear of engine approximately 4 inches. Support engine by hoist.
16. Raise front of engine approximately 4 inches and insert 2 in. blocks under front engine mounts.
17. Rotate crankshaft until timing mark on torsional damper is at 6:00 o'clock position.
18. Unbolt and remove oil pan.

Oil Pump Removal and Installation

1. Remove oil pan.
2. Remove pump and pickup tube and screen assembly on inline engine and pump to rear main bearing cap bolt on V8. Remove

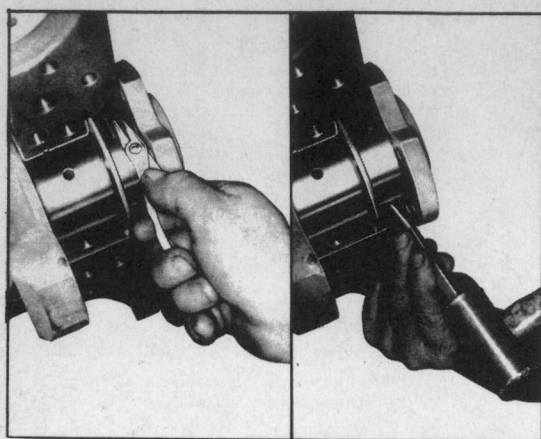

Rear main seal installation
(© Chevrolet Div., G.M. Corp)

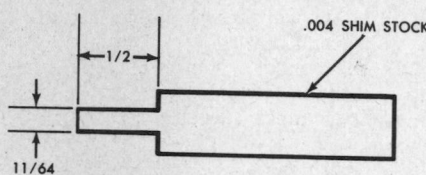

Rear main bearing seal installation tool
(© Chevrolet Div., G.M. Corp)

the pump and extension shaft on the V8.

3. To install, reverse removal procedure.

Rear Main Seal Removal and Installation

The rear main bearing seal may be replaced without removing the crankshaft. Seals should only be replaced as a pair. Fabrication of a seal installation tool as shown in the figure will prevent damaging the bead on the cylinder block. The seal lips should face the front of the engine when properly installed.

1. Remove the oil pan and pump as previously outlined, and remove the rear main bearing cap.
2. Pry the lower seal out of the bearing cap with a screwdriver, being careful not to gouge the cap surface.
3. Remove the upper seal by lightly tapping on one end with a brass pin punch until the other end can be grasped and pulled out with pliers.
4. Clean the bearing cap, cylinder block, and crankshaft mating surfaces with solvent. Inspect all these surfaces for gouges, nicks, and burrs.
5. Apply light engine oil on the seal lips and bead, but keep the seal ends clean.
6. Insert the tip of the installation tool between the crankshaft and the seal seat of the cylinder block. Place the seal between the tip of the tool and the crankshaft, so that the bead contacts the tip of the tool.

7. Be sure that the seal lip is facing the front of the engine, and work the seal around the crankshaft, using the installation tool to protect the seal from the corner of the cylinder block.

NOTE: do not remove the tool until the opposite end of the seal is flush with the cylinder block surface.

8. Remove the installation tool, being careful not to pull the seal out at the same time.
9. Using the same procedure, install the lower seal into the bearing cap. Use your finger and thumb to lever the seal into the cap.

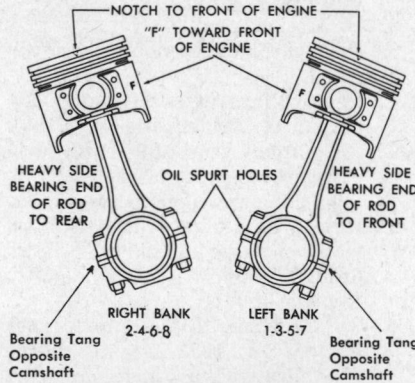

Piston-to-rod relationship—small block V8

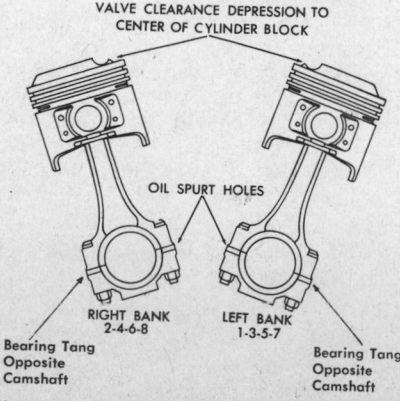

Piston-to-rod relationship—Mk IV (big block) V8

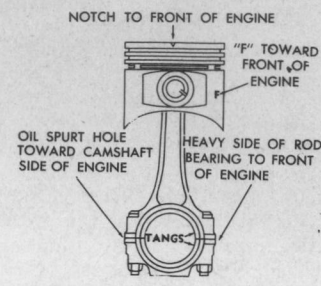

Piston and rod assembly—OHV 4 and 6 cylinder

10. Apply sealer to the cylinder block only where the cap mates to the surface. Do not apply sealer to the seal ends.
11. Install the rear cap and torque the bolts to specifications. Install the oil pan and pump as previously described.

CLUTCH

The only service adjustment necessary on the clutch is to maintain the correct pedal free play. Clutch pedal free play, or throwout bearing lash, decreases with driven disc wear.

Removal

1. Support engine and remove transmission.
2. Disconnect clutch fork push rod and spring.
3. Remove flywheel housing.
4. Slide clutch fork from ball stud and remove fork from dust boot. Ball stud is threaded into clutch housing and may be replaced, if necessary.
5. Install an alignment tool (dummy shaft) to support the clutch assembly during removal. Mark flywheel and clutch cover for reinstallation, if they do not already have X marks.
6. Loosen clutch to flywheel attaching bolts evenly, one turn at a time, until spring pressure is released. Remove bolts and clutch assembly.

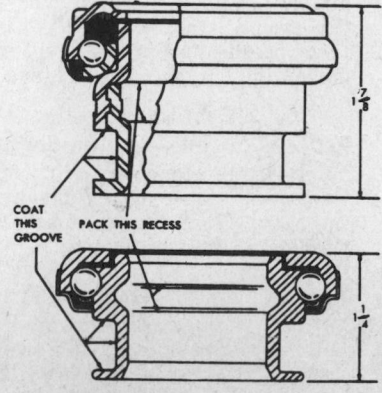

Clutch release bearing lubrication, flat finger type at top, bent finger type at bottom
(© Chevrolet Div., G.M. Corp)

C342

Single disc diaphragm clutch assembly (© Chevrolet Div., G.M. Corp)

MANUAL TRANSMISSION

The normal-duty three-speed transmission is the Saginaw unit, while the heavy-duty three-speed used through 1974 is the Muncie. The Saginaw has one bolt boss casting "ear" at the center top of the side cover, while the Muncie has two such "ears".

The normal-duty four-speed is the Saginaw, while the heavy-duty unit used through 1974 is the Muncie. During 1974, the Muncie four-speed was phased out and the Warner T-10 heavy-duty four-speed introduced in the Camaro only. On the Saginaw, all three shift linkage rods go to the levers on the side cover. On the Muncie, two shift rods go to levers on the side cover and one rod (reverse) goes to a lever on the case extension housing. The Warner T-10 linkage is similar to that on the Muncie, but the transmission has a 9 bolt curved bottom side cover.

Installation

1. Clean pressure plate and flywheel face.
2. Support clutch disc and pressure plate with alignment tool. The driven disc is installed with the damper springs on the transmission side. The grease slinger is always on the transmission side.
3. Turn clutch assembly until mark on cover lines up with mark on flywheel, then install bolts. Tighten down evenly and gradually to avoid distortion.
4. Remove alignment tool.
5. Lubricate ball socket and fork fingers at release bearing end with high melting point grease. Lubricate recess on inside of throwout bearing and throwout fork groove with a light coat of graphite or other high melting point grease.
6. Install clutch fork and dust boot into housing. Install throwout bearing to throwout fork. Install flywheel housing. Install transmission.
7. Connect fork push rod and spring. Lubricate spring and pushrod ends.
8. Adjust shift linkage and clutch pedal free play.

Free Play Adjustment

This adjustment must be made under the vehicle on the clutch operating linkage. Free play is measured at the clutch pedal.

1970 Chevelle, Monte Carlo, and Camaro, Nova through 1971

1. Disconnect the return spring at the clutch operating fork.
2. Use the linkage to push the clutch pedal up against its rubber bumper stop.
3. Loosen the operating rod locknut and lengthen the adjustable rod until it pushes the fork back enough that the release bearing can just be felt to contact the pressure plate fingers.
4. Shorten the rod three turns and tighten the locknut.
5. Replace the spring and check the free play at the pedal pad. It should be about 1 in. or more.

1971 Chevelle, Monte Carlo, and Camaro, All Models starting 1972

You can also use this procedure on any earlier models that have a gauge hole in the clutch pivot shaft arm.

1. Disconnect the return spring at the clutch operating fork.
2. Use the linkage to push the clutch pedal up against its rubber bumper stop. On the 1973 Chevelle, more clearance can be obtained by loosening the rubber bumper bracket and moving the bracket.
3. Push the end of the clutch operating fork to the rear until the release bearing can just be felt to contact the pressure plate fingers.
4. Detach the front end of the operating rod from the clutch pivot shaft arm and place it in the gauge hole on the arm.
5. Loosen the locknut and lengthen the rod just enough to take all the play out of the linkage. Tighten the locknut.
6. Replace the operating rod in its original location.
7. Replace the return spring and check the free play at the pedal pad. It should be about 1 in. or more.

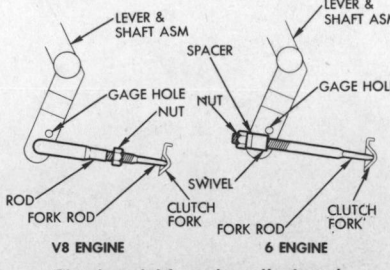

Clutch pedal free-play adjustment
(© Chevrolet Div., G.M. Corp)

Transmission Removal and Installation

1. On floorshift models, remove the shift knob, and the spring and T handle on four-speeds. Remove the boot.
2. Raise the car.
3. Disconnect the speedometer cable and TCS switch wiring at the transmission.
4. Remove the driveshaft.
5. On models through 1972, remove the crossmember to shifter brace.
6. Support the rear of the engine and remove the crossmember. On models through 1972, the crossmember may be slid rearward.
7. Detach the shift rods from the transmission levers.
8. On floorshift models, remove the shifter from the transmission.
9. Remove the upper transmission to clutch housing bolts and replace them with headless guide pins. Remove the lower bolts.
10. Slide the transmission back along the guide pins until the input shaft clears the clutch. Remove the transmission.
11. Reverse the procedure for installation. If the input shaft won't engage the clutch splines, put the transmission in gear and turn the output shaft slightly. Torque the transmission to clutch housing bolts to 55 ft lbs through 1972, and to 75 ft lbs beginning 1973.

Shift Linkage Adjustment
Column Shift

1. With transmission in Reverse,

C343

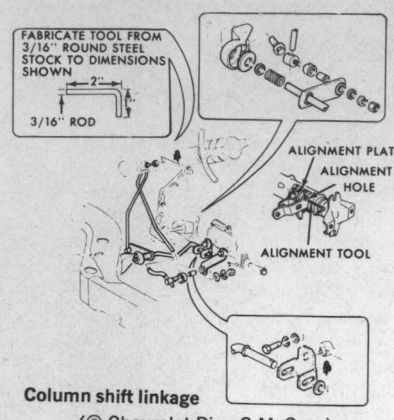

Column shift linkage
(© Chevrolet Div., G.M. Corp)

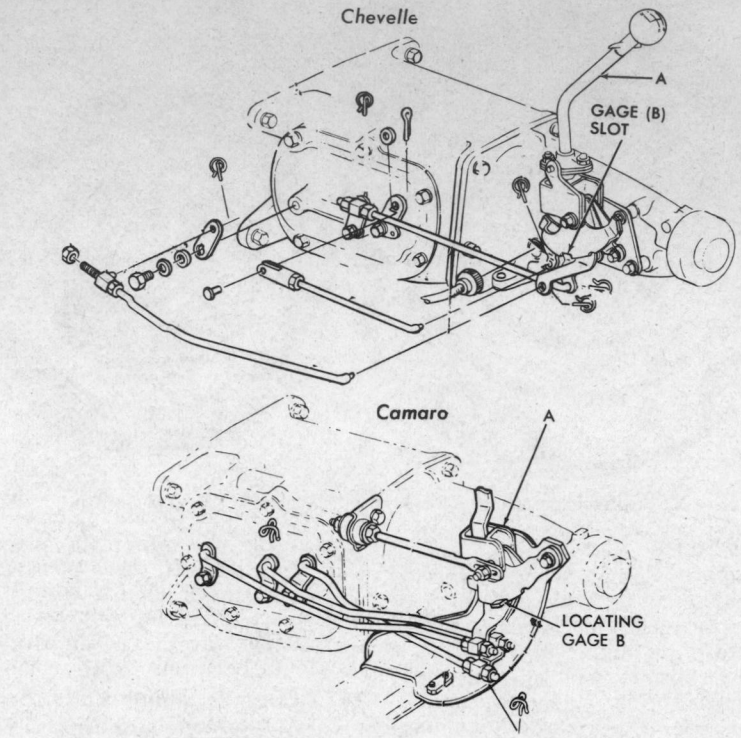

Chevelle

GAGE (B) SLOT

Camaro

LOCATING GAGE B

Typical four speed floorshift linkage (© Chevrolet Div., G.M. Corp)

place ignition switch in Off position for 1970 models. Lock for 1971 and later.

2. Loosen shift rod lock nuts.

3. Set transmission first-reverse lever in reverse position. Push up on first-reverse control rod to 1970, pull down for 1971 and later until column lever is in reverse detent position. Tighten first-reverse lock nut.

4. Unlock the switch and shift the column and transmission levers to neutral position. Insert a 3/16 in. dia. rod into alignment holes in levers.

5. Tighten second-third locknut.

6. Remove alignment rod. Shift column lever to reverse. Turn key to Lock. Ignition switch must move freely to Lock position and it must not be possible to turn key to Lock when in any transmission position other than reverse. If this interlock binds, leave switch in Lock position and readjust first-reverse rod.

7. Check shifting.

Floorshift

1. Turn ignition switch to Lock position up to 1970, Off starting 1971.

2. Loosen locknuts on shift rods and back drive rod.

3. Set transmission levers in neutral positions.

4. Set floorshift lever in neutral. Install locating gauge, 1/8 in. thick, 41/64 in. wide, 3 in. long, into control lever bracket assembly alignment slot. Some later models may take a locating pin.

5. Adjust length of shift rods. Tighten locknuts.

6. Remove locating gauge. Shift into reverse and lock the switch.

7. Pull down slightly on back drive rod to remove any slack and tighten locknut. Ignition switch must move freely to Lock position and it must not be possible to turn key to Lock when in any transmission position other than reverse. If this interlock binds, leave the switch in Lock position

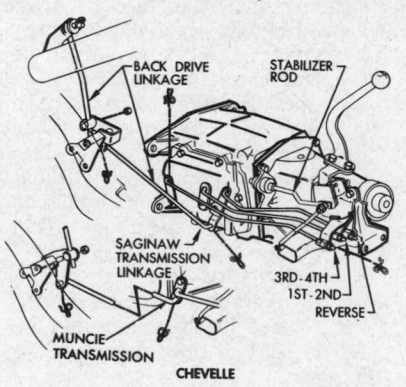

BACK DRIVE LINKAGE — STABILIZER ROD — SAGINAW TRANSMISSION LINKAGE — 3RD-4TH 1ST-2ND REVERSE — MUNCIE TRANSMISSION

CHEVELLE

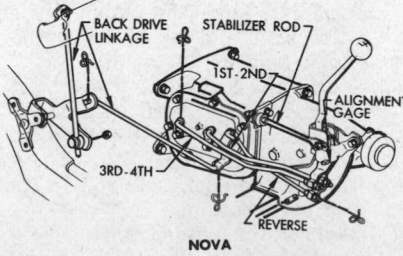

BACK DRIVE LINKAGE — STABILIZER ROD — 1ST-2ND — ALIGNMENT GAGE — 3RD-4TH — REVERSE

NOVA

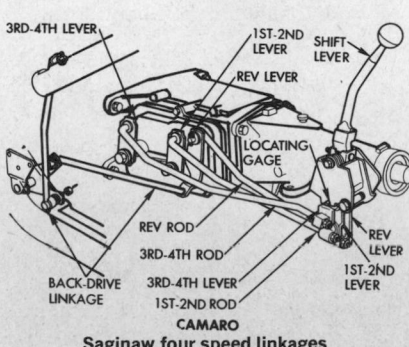

3RD-4TH LEVER — 1ST-2ND LEVER — SHIFT LEVER — REV LEVER — LOCATING GAGE — REV ROD — 3RD-4TH ROD — BACK-DRIVE LINKAGE — 3RD-4TH LEVER — 1ST-2ND ROD — REV LEVER — 1ST-2ND LEVER

CAMARO
Saginaw four speed linkages
(© Chevrolet Div., G.M. Corp)

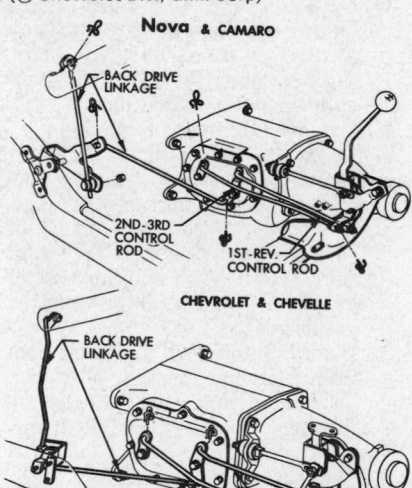

Nova & CAMARO

BACK DRIVE LINKAGE — 2ND-3RD CONTROL ROD — 1ST-REV. CONTROL ROD

CHEVROLET & CHEVELLE

BACK DRIVE LINKAGE — 2ND-3RD CONTROL ROD — 1ST-REV. CONTROL ROD

Typical three speed floorshift linkage
(© Chevrolet Div., G.M. Corp)

and readjust back drive rod.

8. Check shifting operation.

AUTOMATIC TRANSMISSION

There are two basic automatic transmissions. The first is the two speed Powerglide. A variation on the Powerglide, dropped in 1971, is the Torque Drive transmission. The Torque Drive unit is a Powerglide with the automatic shifting provisions removed. Torque Drive is shifted manually, but has no clutch. The Powerglide transmission was dropped in mid-1973. The second type is the three speed Turbo Hydra-Matic. several load capacities, the Turbo Hydra-Matic 250, 350, 375, and 400.

The Turbo Hydra-Matic 250 is used only in 1974 and later six-cylinder models. The 250 may be identified by the intermediate band adjusting screw on the right side of the case. The intermediate band replaces the intermediate clutch on the larger capacity models. The 250 and 350 have a cable operated downshift linkage running from the accelerator linkage to the right side of the transmission, while the 375 and 400 have a downshift solenoid activated by a switch on the accelerator linkage. There is no external difference between the 375 and 400; they differ internally in numbers of clutch plates and other items related to torque capacity.

Powerglide Shift Linkage Adjustment

Column Shift through 1972

1. Loosen adjustment clamp at cross-shaft. Set transmission lever in drive by rotating lever counterclockwise to low detent, then clockwise one detent to drive.
2. Set selector lever in Drive. Remove any free play by holding cross-shaft upward and pulling shift rod downward.
3. Tighten the clamp and check the adjustment.
4. Place shift lever in Park and ignition switch in Lock. Loosen back drive rod clamp nut. Remove column lash and tighten clamp nut.
5. With selector lever in Park, the ignition key should move freely to Lock position. Lock position should be obtainable only when transmission is in Park.

Torque Drive through 1971

1. Loosen swivel at idler lever.
2. Place transmission lever in Hi position.
3. Set shift lever at lower end of column up against first position stop.
4. Adjust rod in swivel and tighten retaining nut.
5. Place shift lever in Park and ignition switch in Lock. Loosen back drive rod clamp nut. Remove column lash and tighten clamp nut.
6. With selector lever in Park, the ignition key should move freely to Lock position. Lock position should be obtainable only when transmission is in Park.

Nova Floorshift 1970

This is a rod operated linkage.
1. Loosen adjustment nuts at

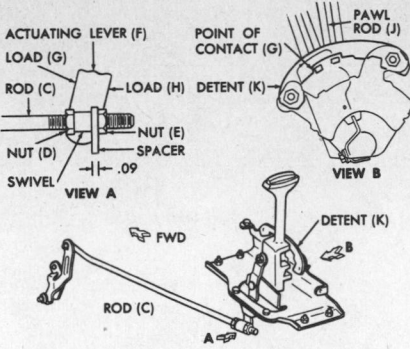

Automatic transmission rod operated floorshift linkage, Nova   (© Chevrolet Div., G.M. Corp)

swivel. Set transmission lever in drive position by moving counterclockwise to low detent, then clockwise one detent to drive.
2. Set floorshift lever in Drive. Hold floorshift unit lower operating lever forward against shift lever detent.
3. Place a 3/32 (.0094 in.) spacer between rear nut and swivel. Tighten rear nut against spacer.
4. Remove spacer and tighten front nut against swivel, locking swivel between nuts.
5. Place shift lever in Park position. Adjust column (back drive) rod. With shift lever in Park, the ignition key must move freely to Lock, and Lock position must not be obtainable in any transmission position other than Park.

Camaro, Chevelle, Monte Carlo Floorshift through 1972

These models use a cable operated linkage.
1. Place shift lever in Drive position.
2. Disconnect cable from transmission lever. Place transmission lever in drive by rotating lever counterclockwise to low detent, then clockwise one detent to drive.
3. Measure distance from rearward face of attachment bracket to center of cable attachment pin. Adjust this dimension to 5.5 in. by loosening and moving cable end stud nut.
4. Place shift lever in Park and ignition switch in Lock position.
5. Loosen and adjust column (back drive) rod.
6. With selector lever in Park position, the ignition key should move freely to Lock position. Lock position should not be obtainable in any transmission position other than Park.

Turbo Hydra-Matic Shift Linkage Adjustment
Column Shift

1. Loosen the swivel at the lower

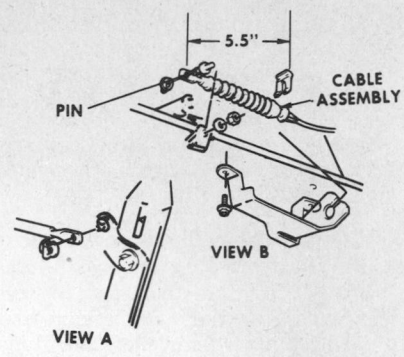

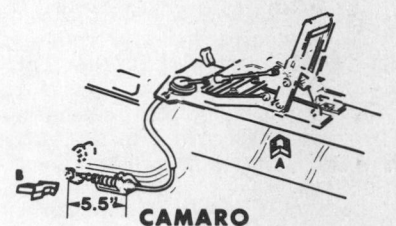

CAMARO

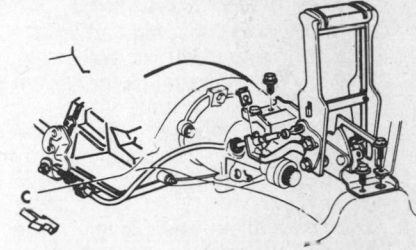

CHEVELLE

Automatic transmission cable operated floorshift linkage, Camaro and Chevelle
(© Chevrolet Div., G.M. Corp)

end of the rod that comes from the column.
2. On 1973 and later models, set the transmission lever in the Neutral detent by turning the lever counterclockwise to the L1 detent, then clockwise three positions. On models through 1972, set the lever in the Drive detent by turning the lever counterclockwise to the L1 detent, then clockwise two positions.
3. Put the column lever in Neutral for 1973 and later models, and in Drive for models through 1972. The important thing here is not where the indicator points but that the lever be in the correct position.
4. Tighten the swivel.
5. Check that the key cannot be removed and that the wheel is not locked with the key in RUN. Check that the key can be removed in LOCK with the lever in Park, and that the steering wheel is locked.

Nova Floorshift through 1974

This is a rod operated linkage, very similar to the rod operated linkage used on the 1970 Nova Powerglide floorshift. The adjustment procedure is the same, except that 1972 and later models are adjusted in Neutral, rather than Drive. The Turbo Hydra-Matic Drive position is obtained by turning the transmission lever counterclockwise to the L1 detent, then clockwise two positions. The Neutral position is obtained by turning the level clockwise three positions from the L1 detent.

Camaro, Chevelle, Monte Carlo Floorshift through 1972

This is a cable operated linkage, very similar to the cable linkage used on the Camaro, Chevelle, and Monte Carlo Powerglide floorshift through 1972. The adjustment procedure is the same, except that the Turbo Hydra-Matic Drive position is obtained by turning the transmission lever counterclockwise to the L1 detent, then clockwise two positions.

Camaro, Chevelle, Monte Carlo Floorshift 1973 and later; Nova Floorshift 1975 and later

This is a cable operated linkage.
1. Loosen the swivel at the lower end of the rod that comes from the steering column.
2. Loosen the pin at the transmission end of the cable.
3. Set the floorshift lever in the Drive detent.
4. Set the transmission lever in the Drive detent by moving it counterclockwise to the L1 detent, then clockwise three detent positions.
5. Tighten the nut on the pin at the transmission end of the cable.
6. Put the floorshift lever in Park and the ignition switch in LOCK.
7. Pull down lightly on the rod from the column and tighten its clamp nut.

Powerglide Throttle Valve Linkage Adjustment

Inline Engines through 1973
1. Fully depress the accelerator pedal.
2. Bellcrank must be at wide open throttle position.
3. On models through 1971, the dash lever at the firewall must be 1/64-1/16 in. off the lever stop.
4. Transmission lever must be against transmission internal stop.
5. Adjust linkage to simultaneously obtain conditions in Steps 1-4, above.

V8 Engines through 1972
1. Remove air cleaner.
2. Disconnect accelerator linkage at carburetor.
3. Disconnect both return springs.
4. Pull throttle valve upper rod forward until transmission is through detent.
5. Open carburetor to wide open

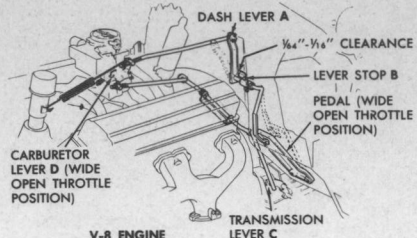

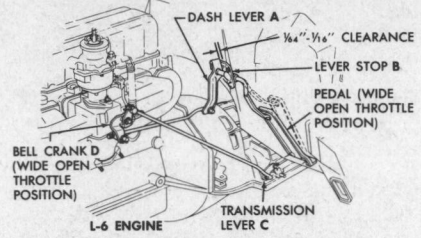

Powerglide throttle valve adjustment V8, 1970-73 inline engines
(© Chevrolet Div., G.M. Corp)

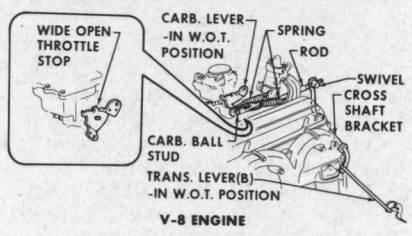

Powerglide throttle valve linkage—1970-73
(© Chevrolet Div., G.M. Corp)

throttle position. Adjust swivel on end of upper throttle valve rod so carburetor reaches wide open throttle position at the same time that the ball stud contacts the end of the slot in the upper throttle valve rod. A tolerance of 1/32 in. is allowable.

Turbo Hydra-Matic 250 and 350 Detent Cable Adjustment

The Turbo Hydra-Matic 250 and 350 have a detent, or downshift, cable between the carburetor linkage and the transmission.

1970 and later Nova and Camaro, Chevelle and Monte Carlo through 1972
1. Remove air cleaner.
2. Loosen detent cable screw or disengage snap lock.
3. Place carburetor lever in wide open throttle position. Make sure lever is against stop. On vehicles with Quadrajet carburetors, disengage the secondary lock out before placing lever in wide open throttle position.
NOTE: detent cable must be pulled through detent position.
4. Engage snap lock or tighten detent screw.

1973 and Later Chevelle and Monte Carlo
On these models, the cable adjusts itself the first time the accelerator pedal is floorboarded.

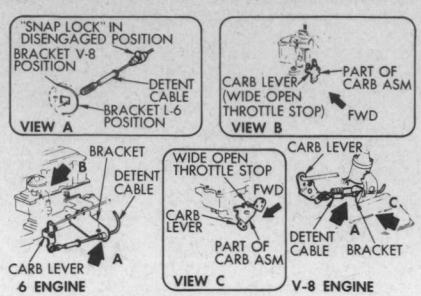

Turbo Hydra-Matic 350 detent cable adjustment
(© Chevrolet Div., G.M. Corp)

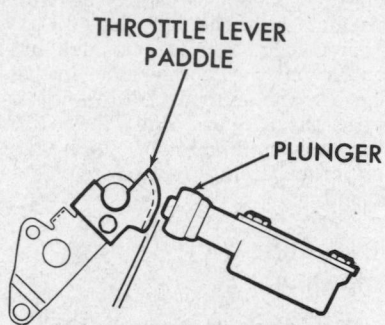

Turbo Hydra-Matic 400 detent switch adjustment—Nova and Camaro
(© Chevrolet Div., G.M. Corp)

Turbo Hydra-Matic 375 and 400 Detent Switch Adjustment

The Turbo Hydra-Matic 375 and 400 transmission has an electrical detent, or downshift, switch operated by the throttle linkage.

Nova and Camaro through 1972
1. Loosen the switch mounting bolts. Place the carburetor lever in the wide open throttle position.
2. Make sure the choke is off.
3. Depress the switch plunger all the way.
4. Adjust switch mounting to obtain distance between depressed switch plunger and throttle lever paddle of .22-.24 in.
5. Tighten the switch mounting bolts.

Chevelle and Monte Carlo through 1972
1. Pull detent switch driver rearward until hole in switch body aligns with hold in driver. Insert a .092 in. dia. pin through the aligned holes to hold the driver in position.
2. Loosen mounting bolt.
3. Depress accelerator to wide open throttle position. Move switch forward until driver contacts accelerator lever.
4. Tighten mounting bolt. Remove pin.

1973 and Later
After installation, the switch adjusts itself the first time the accelerator is floorboarded.

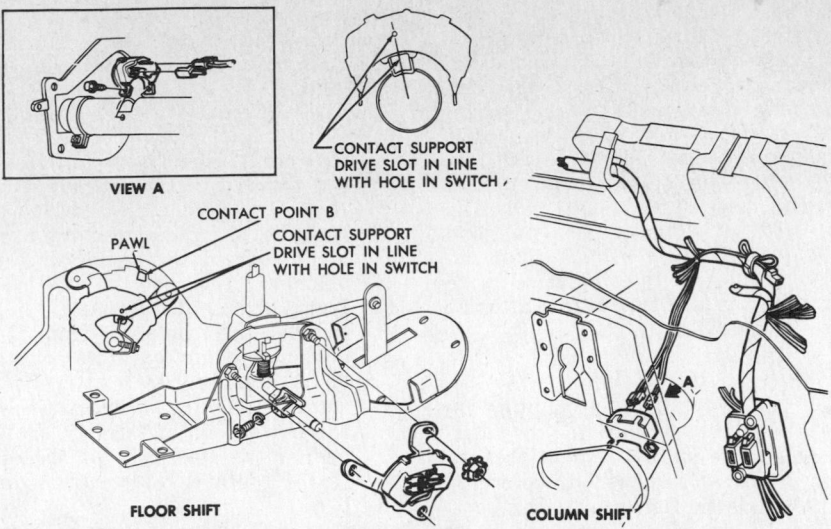

Typical neutral safety switch installation (© Chevrolet Div., G.M. Corp.)

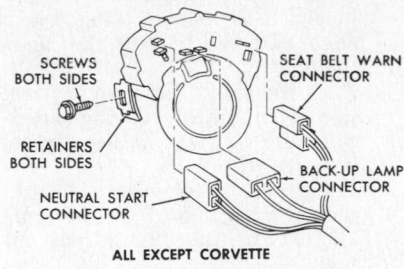

1973 combination neutral start switch connections
(© Chevrolet Div., G.M. Corp)

Neutral Safety Switch Adjustment

The neutral safety switch prevents the engine from being started in any transmission position except Neutral or Park. On all column shift models and floorshift models from late 1972, the switch is located on the upper side of the steering column under the instrument panel. On floorshift models thru early 1972, the switch is located inside the shift console.

1. Remove console for access on early floorshift models.
2. Disconnect wiring connectors.
3. Remove switch.
4. Position the shift lever in Neutral on column shift models from late 1972. Put it in Drive on earlier column shift models, and in Park on floorshift models with the column mounted switch. On column shift models, locate lever tang against transmission selector plate.
5. Align slot in contact support with hole in switch. Insert 3/32 in. dia. pin to hold support in place. Switch is now aligned.

NOTE: 1973 and later neutral safety switches have a shear-pin installed to aid in proper new switch alignment so that insertion of a pin is unnecessary. Moving the shift lever shears the pin.

6. Place contact support drive slot over drive tang. Install screws.
7. Remove pin. Connect wiring. Replace console.
8. Set parking brake and footbrake. Check to see that engine will start only in Drive or Neutral.

Band Adjustments

There are no band adjustments possible or required for the Turbo Hydra-Matic 350, 375, or 400.

Low Band—Powerglide and Torque Drive

The low band must be adjusted at the first required fluid change or whenever there is slippage.

1. Position the shift lever in Neutral.
2. Remove the protective cap from the adjusting screw on the left side of the transmission.
3. Loosen the locknut ¼ turn and hold it with a wrench during the entire adjusting procedure.
4. Tighten the adjusting nut to 70 in. lbs, using a 7/32 allen wrench.
5. Back off the adjusting nut exactly three turns for a band used less than 6,000 miles. Back off exactly four turns for a band used 6,000 miles or more.
6. Torque the locknut to 15 ft lbs. and replace the cap.

Intermediate Band— Turbo Hydra-Matic 250

The intermediate band must be adjusted with every required fluid change or whenever there is slippage.

1. Position the shift lever in Neutral.
2. Loosen the locknut on the right side of the transmission and tighten the adjusting screw to 30 in lbs.
3. Back the screw out three turns and then tighten the locknut to 15 ft lbs.

Pan Removal and Installation, Fluid and Filter Change

The fluid should be changed with the transmission warm. If you are not sure which transmission is in your car, refer to the pan gasket illustrations in the Chevrolet Section.

1. Raise and support the vehicle, preferably in a level attitude.
2. On Nova with Turbo Hydra-Matic 250 or 350, support the transmission and remove the support crossmember.
3. Place a large pan under the transmission pan. Remove all the front and side pan bolts. Loosen the rear bolts about four turns.
4. Pry the pan loose and let it drain.
5. Remove the pan and gasket. Clean the pan throughly with solvent and air dry it. Be very careful not to get any lint from rags in the pan.
6. Remove the strainer to valve body screws, the strainer, and the gasket. Most 350 transmissions will have a throw-away filter instead of a strainer. On the 400 transmission, remove the filter retaining bolt, filter, and intake pipe O-ring.
7. If there is a strainer, clean it in solvent and air dry.
8. Install the new filter or cleaned strainer with a new gasket. Tighten the screws to 12 ft lbs. On the 400, install a new intake pipe O-ring and a new filter, tightening the retaining bolt to 10 ft lbs.
9. Install the pan with a new gasket. Tighten the bolts evenly to 12 ft lbs (8 for Powerglide and Torque Drive).
10. Lower the car and add 5 pts (3 on Powerglide and Torque Drive) of DEXRON® or DEXRON II® automatic transmission fluid through the dipstick tube.
11. Start the engine in Park and let it idle. Do not race the engine. Shift into each shift lever position, shift back into Park, and check the fluid level on the dipstick. The level should be ¼ in. below. ADD. Be very careful not to overfill. Recheck the level after the car has been driven long enough to thoroughly warm up the transmission. Add fluid as necessary. The level should then be at FULL.

U-JOINTS

The universal joints are lubricated and sealed at the factory and require no periodic maintenance. Two basic universal joints are used. The Dana or Cleveland type uses snapring bearing cap retainers. The Saginaw uses injection molded plastic to retain the bearing caps. On the Saginaw type there is a snap-ring groove in the bearing housing inboard of the yoke to facilitate installation of a repair kit.

Driveshaft Removal and Installation

Disconnect the rear universal joint flange. On some models, the bearing caps are bolted directly to the differential flange with clamps or U-bolts. Pull the front yoke from the transmission. Watch for oil leaks from the transmission output housing. Install in the reverse order of removal.

Universal Joint Removal and Installation

Dana and Cleveland Type

1. Remove the driveshaft.
2. Remove the snap-rings from the trunnion yoke.
3. Using a vise and suitably sized sockets, press on the trunnion until the bearing cap is almost out. Grasp the cap in the vise and work it out of the yoke. Repeat the above procedure for the rest of the bearing caps.
4. Pack the rollers in grease and fill the grease reservoir.
5. To install, position the trunnion in the yoke and partially install one bearing cap. Start the trunnion in the bearing cap and partially install the other cap. Align the trunnion with the caps and press into place.
6. If necessary, repeat Step 5 above for the other yoke.
7. Install the snap-rings.
8. Install the driveshaft in the vehicle.

Saginaw Type

Remove and install the bearing caps and trunnion as described for the Dana and Cleveland type universal joints. On an original universal joint, however, the bearing caps will be secured in the yokes with injected plastic. The plastic will shear when the bearing caps are pressed. Service snap-rings are installed in the groove on the inside (of yoke) of the installed caps.

REAR AXLE

Axle Shaft, Bearing and Seal

Removal and Installation

These cars use, basically, two different types of drive axle, the C- and the non C-type. Axle shafts in the C-type are retained by C-shaped locks, which fit grooves at the inner end of the shaft. Axle shafts in the non C-type are retained by the brake backing plate, which is bolted to the axle housing. Bearings in the C-type axle consist of an outer race, bearing rollers and a roller cage, retained by snap-rings. The non C-type axle uses a unit roller bearing (inner race, rollers and outer race), which is pressed onto the shaft, up to a shoulder. When servicing C or non C-type axles, it is imperative to determine the axle type before attempting any service.

Non C Type

Caution Before attempting any service to the drive axle or axle shafts, remove the axle carrier cover and visually determine if the axle shafts are retained by C-shaped locks at the inner end, or by the brake backing plate at the outer end. If the shafts are *not* retained by C-locks, proceed as follows.

Design allows for maximum axle shaft end-play of 0.022 in., which can be measured with a dial indicator. If end-play is found to be excessive, the bearing should be replaced. Shimming the bearing is not recommended as this ignores end-play of the bearing itself and could result in improper seating of the bearing.

1. Remove the wheel, tire and brake drum.
2. Remove the nuts holding the retainer plate to the backing plate. Disconnect the brake line.
3. Remove the retainer and install nuts, fingertight, to prevent the brake backing plate from being dislodged.
4. Pull out the axle shaft and bearing assembly, using a slide hammer.
5. Using a chisel, nick the bearing retainer in three or four places. The retainer does not have to be cut, merely collapsed sufficiently, to allow the bearing retainer to be slid from the shaft.
6. Press off the bearing and install the new one by pressing it into postion.
7. Press on the new retainer.

NOTE: do not attempt to press the bearing and the retainer on at the same time.

8. Assemble the shaft and bearing in the housing, being sure that the bearing is seated properly in the housing.
9. Install the retainer, drum, wheel and tire. Bleed the brakes.

C—Type

Caution Before attempting any service to the drive axle or axle shafts, remove the carrier cover and visually determine if the axle shaft(s) are retained by C-shaped locks at the inner ends or by a brake backing plate at the outer end. If they *are* retained by C-shaped locks, proceed as follows.

1. Raise the vehicle and remove the wheels.
2. The differential cover has already been removed (see Caution note). Remove the differential pinion shaft lock-screw and the differential pinion shaft.
3. Push the flanged end of the axle shaft toward the center of the vehicle and remove the "C" lock from the end of the shaft.
4. Remove the axle shaft from the housing, being careful not to damage the oil seal.
5. Remove the oil seal by inserting the button end of the axle shaft behind the steel case of the oil seal. Pry the seal loose from the bore.
6. Seat the legs of the bearing puller behind the bearing. Seat a washer against the bearing and hold it in place with a nut. Use a slide hammer to pull the bearing.
7. Pack the cavity between the seal lips with wheel bearing lubricant and lubricate a new wheel bearing with same.
8. Use a suitable driver and install the bearing until it bottoms against the tube. Install the oil seal.
9. Slide the axle shaft into place. Be sure that the splines on the shaft do not damage the oil seal. Make sure that the splines engage the differential side gear.
10. Install the axle shaft, C-lock on the inner end of the axle shaft and push the shaft outward so that the C-lock seats in the differential side gear counterbore.
11. Position the differential pinion shaft through the case and pinions, aligning the hole in the case with the hole for the lock-screw.
13. Use a new gasket and install the carrier cover. Be sure that the gasket surfaces are clean before installing the gasket and cover.
14. Fill the axle with lubricant to the bottom of the filler hole.
15. Install the brake drum and wheels and lower the car. Check for leaks and road test the car.

JACKING, HOISTING

1. Jack car at front spring seat of lower control arm. Jack car at rear axle housing except when equipped with rear stabilizer bar. On these models, jack at frame rails.
2. To lift at frame, use side rails in front of body floor pan and at

rear corner at squared off corner of box ahead of rear wheel.

FRONT SUSPENSION

Coil Spring Removal and Installation

1. Remove the shock absorber. Disconnect the stabilizer bar.
2. Suport the car at the frame so the control arms hang free.
3. Support the inner end of the control arm with a floor jack. (dealers have a device that cradles the inner bushings).
4. Raise the jack enough to take the tension off the lower control arm pivot bolts.
5. Chain the spring to the lower control arm, for safety's sake.
6. Remove first the rear, then the front pivot bolt.
7. Cautiously lower the jack until all spring tension is released.
8. Note the way in which the spring is installed to the control arm and remove it.
9. On installation, position the spring to the control arm and raise it into place.
10. Install the pivot bolts and torque the nuts to 100 ft lbs for all 1974 and later models except for 1974 Nova. Torque the 1974 Nova and all models through 1973 to 85 ft lbs.
11. Replace the shock absorber and stabilizer bar.

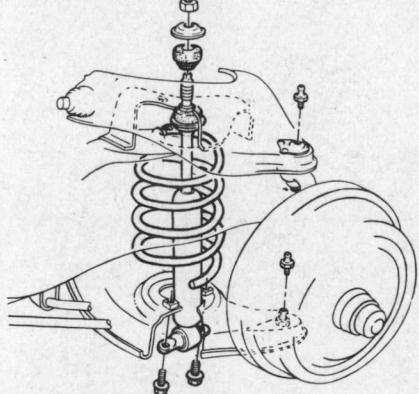

Chevelle and Camaro shock absorber installation
(© Chevrolet Div., G.M. Corp)

Shock Absorber Removal and Installation

1. Remove the upper stem nut while holding the stem to keep it from turning.
2. Remove the two bolts holding the shock absorber to the lower control arm, and pull the shock through the arm.
3. Extend the new shock absorber

and insert it up through the lower control arm. Make sure that the upper stem goes through the hole in the upper control arm frame bracket.
NOTE: Purge new shocks of air by repeatedly compressing them while inverted and extending them in their normal installed position.
4. Install the grommet, retainer cup, and nut to the shock absorber upper stem.
5. Hold the shock absorber stem and tighten the upper nut to 8 ft lbs.
6. Install the lower control arm retaining bolts and tighten to 20 ft lbs.

Front Wheel Bearing Adjustment

1. Jack the car up and support it at the lower arm.
2. Remove the hub dust cover and spindle cotter pin. Loosen the nut.
3. While spinning the wheel, snug the nut down to seat the bearings. Do not exert over 12 ft lbs of force on the nut.
4. Back the nut off ¼–½ a turn or until it is just loose. Line up the cotter pin hole in the spindle with the hole in the nut.
5. Insert a new cotter pin. End-play should be between 0.001 and 0.005 in. If play exceeds this tolerance, the wheel bearings should be replaced.

Ball Joints

Ball Joint Inspection

NOTE: before performing this inspection, make sure the wheel bearings are adjusted correctly and that the A-arm bushings are in good condition.
1. Jack the car up under the front

lower control arm at the spring seat.
2. Raise the car until there is 1–2 in. of clearance under the wheel.
3. Insert a bar under the wheel and pry upward. If the wheel raises more than ⅛ in., the ball joints are worn. Determine if the upper or lower ball joint is worn by visual inspection while prying on the wheel.
4. The upper ball joint can be further inspected after partial suspension disassembly. If the stud has any detectable side-to-side movement or if it can be twisted with your fingers it should be replaced.
NOTE: due to the distribution of forces in the suspension, the lower ball joint is usually the defective joint. Because of this, 1974 and later Chevelle, Camaro, and Monte Carlo and 1975 and later Nova models are equipped with wear indicators on the lower ball joint. As long as the indicator extends below the ball stud seat, replacement is unnecessary.

Upper Ball Joint Removal and Installation

1. Raise the car on a hoist.
2. Remove the tire and wheel assembly.
3. Support the lower control arm with a jack.
4. Remove the upper ball stud nut.
5. Remove the ball stud from the knuckle.
6. Chisel or grind off the ball joint mounting rivets.
7. Drill out the ball stud attaching holes to accept the service ball joint attaching bolts.
8. Install the ball joint with the nuts and bolts supplied with the new joint, nuts on top.
9. Install the lube fitting in the new joint.

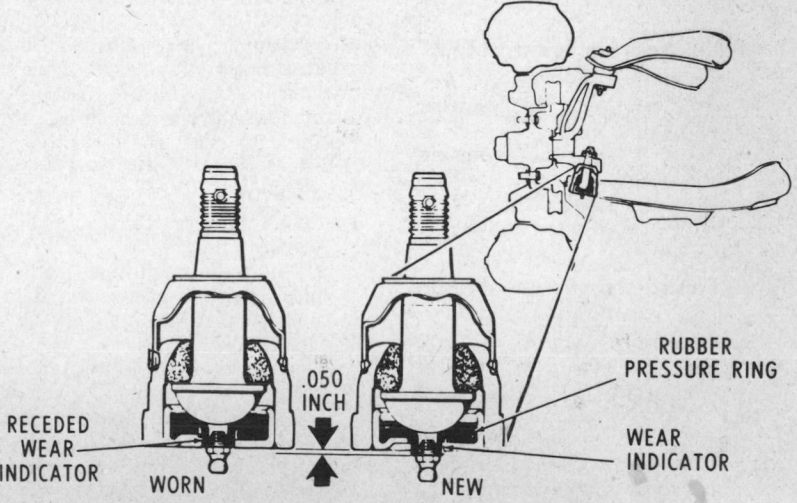

1974 and later Chevelle, Monte Carlo, and Camaro and 1975 and later Nova models are equipped with wear indicators on the lower ball joint
(©Chevrolet Div., G.M. Corp)

10. Mate the upper control arm to the steering knuckle and install the ball stud through the knuckle boss.
11. Tighten the ball stud nut to 55 ft lbs. plus whatever is necessary to align the cotter pin holes. Install the cotter pin.

NOTE: Do not back off on the nut to align the cotter pin.

12. Install the wheel and lower the vehicle.

Lower Ball Joint Removal and Installation

1. Raise the vehicle on a hoist and remove the wheel.
2. Support the lower control arm with a jack.
3. Loosen the lower ball stud nut. Break the ball stud loose. Remove the ball stud nut.
4. Remove the ball stud from the steering knuckle.
5. The ball joint in 1970 models is attached with rivets which must be chiseled or ground off. Beginning with 1971 models, the ball joint is pressed in and must be pressed out.
6. Install the new ball joint, using the bolts supplied with the service ball joint (drill out the rivet holes to accommodate the mounting bolts) on 1970 models. The thick-headed bolt is installed on the forward side of the control arm. Press in the ball joint on 1971 and later models.
7. Install the ball stud in the steering knuckle boss. This may be done by raising the lower control arm with the jack.
8. Install the nut on the ball stud, tightening to 50 ft lbs on all models through 1973 and 1974 Nova; 60 ft lbs on 1974 Chevelle, Monte Carlo, and Camaro, and 83 ft lbs on all 1975 and later models.
9. Install the lube fitting.

Lower Control Arm Removal and Installation

1. Remove the spring as described earlier.
2. Remove the ball stud from the steering knuckle.
3. Remove the control arm.
4. To install, reverse the above procedure.

Upper Control Arm Removal and Installation

1. Raise the vehicle on a hoist.
2. Support the outer end of the lower control arm with a jack.
3. Remove the wheel.
4. Separate the upper ball joint from the steering knuckle as described above under "Upper Ball Joint R&R".
5. Remove the control arm shaft to frame nuts.

NOTE: tape the shims together and identify them so that they can be installed in the positions from which they were removed.

6. Remove the bolts which attach the control arm shaft to the frame and remove the control arm. Note the positions of the bolts.
7. Install in the reverse order of removal. Make sure the shaft to frame bolts are installed in the same position they were in before removal and that the shims are in their original positions. Tighten the shaft to frame bolts to 55 ft lbs on Nova through 1974 and Chevelle and Monte Carlo through 1972; 75 ft lbs on all 1975 and later models; 80 ft lbs on Camaro through 1973; and 90 ft lbs on 1973-74 Chevelle and Monte Carlo, and 1974 Camaro. The control arm shaft nuts are torqued to 40 ft lbs on Chevelle and Monte Carlo through 1973 and Nova through 1974; 65 ft lbs on Camaro through 1974 and 1974 Chevelle and Monte Carlo; and 75 ft lbs on all 1975 and later models.

REAR SUSPENSION

The Chevelle and Monte Carlo have a coil spring rear suspension located by two lower control arms and two diagonally mounted upper control arms. Fore and aft axle movement is prevented by the lower control arms. Lateral movement is prevented by the upper control arms and the axle-to-frame tie-rod.

The Camaro and Nova have a leaf spring rear suspension.

All models use staggered shock absorbers to prevent axle hop on hard acceleration. The right shock absorber is mounted forward of the axle and the left shock absorber is mounted behind the axle.

Shock Absorber Removal and Installation

1. Jack the car to a convenient working height.
2. If the car is equipped with superlift shock absorbers, disconnect the air line.
3. On Chevelle and Monte Carlo: remove the two retaining bolts from the upper mounting bracket. Hold the hex on the bottom stud and disconnect the lower mounting. Remove the shock absorber.
4. On Camaro: with the rear axle supported, remove the lower shock absorber nut, retainer, and

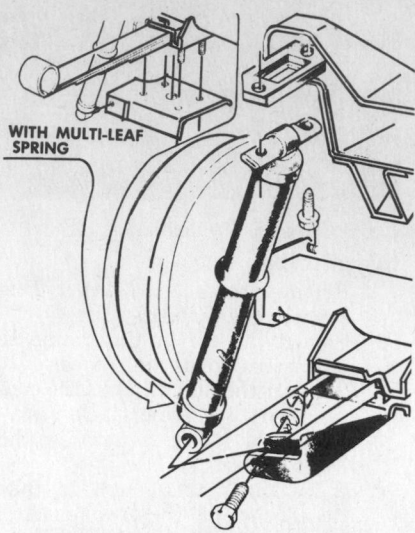

WITH MULTI-LEAF SPRING

Nova rear shock absorber mounting
(© Chevrolet Div., G.M. Corp)

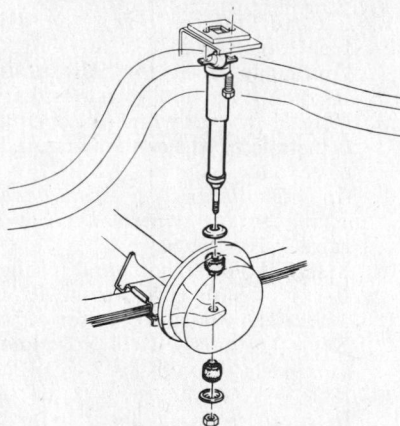

Camaro rear shock absorber mounting
(© Chevrolet Div., G.M. Corp)

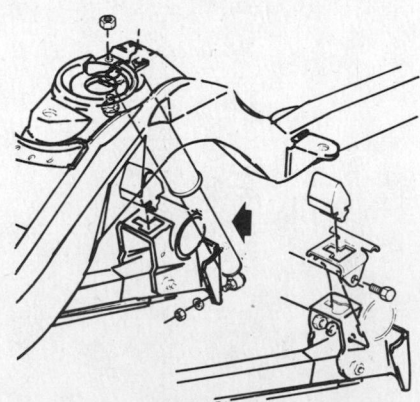

STATION WAGON

Chevelle rear shock absorber mounting
(© Chevrolet Div., G.M. Corp)

grommet. Remove the upper bolts, and remove the shock.
5. On Nova: remove the lower shock absorber eye bolt. Remove the upper bolts, and remove the shock absorber.

NOTE: Purge new shocks of air by repeatedly compressing them while inverted and extending them in their normal installed position.

6. Install the shock absorbers in a reverse of the removal procedure. Torque the upper fasteners: 12 ft lbs on Chevelle and Monte Carlo and 18 ft lbs on Nova and Camaro. Torque the bottom fasteners: 65 ft lbs on Chevelle and Monte Carlo, 45 ft lbs on Nova (60 ft lbs with performance suspension) and 8 ft lbs on Camaro.

Spring Removal and Installation

Chevelle and Monte Carlo

If the springs have been in use for any length of time, it will probably be necessary to replace both to maintain an even ride height.

1. Raise the car by the frame so that the rear axle can be independently raised and lowered.
2. Support the rear axle with a floor jack.
3. Disconnect the shock absorber from the axle. You don't have to disconnect both shocks unless you are removing both springs.
4. On 1973 and later models, disconnect the brake line at the axle housing junction block. Disconnect the upper control arm at the axle. You don't have to disconnect both unless you are removing both springs.
NOTE: This step makes the job easier on earlier models, too.
5. Lower the axle to the limits of its travel, being careful of the brake lines.
6. Pry the lower end of the spring over the axle bracket vertical retainer. Remove the spring and insulator. Reverse the procedure for installation. Torque the upper control arm to axle mount to 80 ft lbs.

Nova and Camaro

1. Raise the car by the frame so that the rear axle can be independently raised and lowered.
2. Support the rear axle with a floor jack.
3. Disconnect the shock absorber lower mount.
4. Loosen the retaining bolt through the front spring eye. Unbolt the front bracket from the body.
5. Lower the axle enough to remove the bracket and retaining bolt from the front spring eye.
6. Pry the parking brake cable from the spring mounting plate retainer.
7. Remove the U-bolt nuts, the spring plate, and the upper and lower spring pads.
8. Remove the lower rear shackle bolt. Remove the spring.
9. On installation, install the front bracket to the spring eye, install

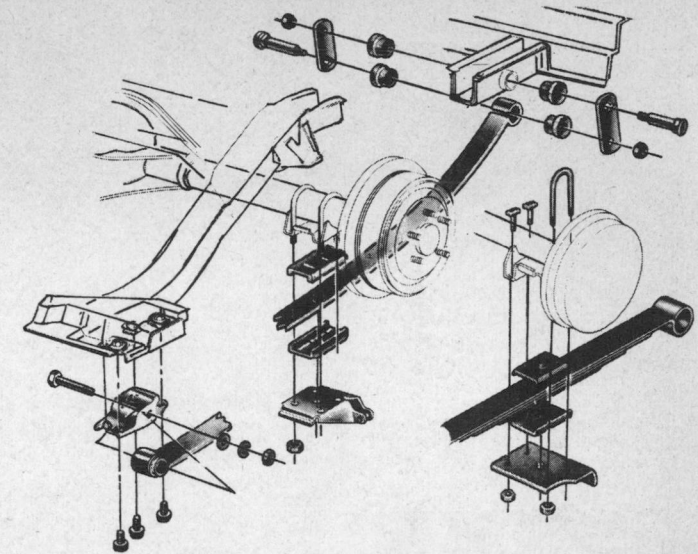

Rear spring mounting—Nova and Camaro
(© Chevrolet Div., G.M. Corp)

the rear shackle, bolt the front bracket in place, install the U-bolts, and replace the shock absorber. Tighten the bolts with the weight of the car on the springs. Torque the front bracket mounting bolts to 25-30 ft lbs, the front eye bolt to 75 ft lbs, the U-bolts to 40 ft lbs, and the rear shackle bolts to 50 ft lbs.

BRAKES

Brake lining replacement and adjustment, wheel and master cylinder overhaul and brake bleeding procedures can be found in the Unit Repair Section.

Master Cylinder Removal and Installation

1. Disconnect hydraulic line/s at master cylinder.
2. Remove the retaining nuts and lockwashers that hold cylinder to firewall. Disconnect pushrod at brake pedal.
3. Remove the master cylinder, gasket and rubber boot.
4. Position master cylinder on firewall, making sure pushrod goes through the rubber boot into the piston. Reconnect pushrod clevis to brake pedal.
5. Install nuts and lockwashers.
6. Install hydraulic line/s, then check brake pedal free play.
7. Bleed brakes, as described in Unit Repair Section.
NOTE: cars having disc brakes do not have a check valve in the front outlet port of the master cylinder. If one is installed, front discs will immediately wear out due to residual hydraulic pressure holding pads against rotor.

Power Brake Booster Removal and Installation

Except the Following Chevelle and Monte Carlo Models

1. Disconnect vacuum hose from vacuum check valve.
2. Disconnect hydraulic lines at master cylinder.
3. Disconnect pushrod at brake pedal assembly.
NOTE: Some Nova-Camaro brake boosters may also be held on with a sealant. This can be easily removed with tar remover.
4. Remove nuts and lockwashers that secure booster to firewall and remove booster from engine compartment.
5. Install by reversing removal procedure. Make sure to check operation of stop lights and bleed brakes. Allow engine vacuum to build before applying brakes.

1970 Chevelle Station Wagon, 1971-77 Chevelle and Monte Carlo—All

1. Remove master cylinder from vacuum booster.
2. Remove vacuum line from vacuum check valve.
3. On 1971 and later models, remove brake line clip from booster.
4. From inside vehicle, remove nuts and lockwashers that secure booster to firewall.
5. Push brake pedal to the floor. This will disengage booster from firewall and adequate clearance for removal of the pushrod pivot pin will be gained.
6. Remove clip from pivot pin, then remove power unit from car.
7. Install by reversing removal procedure. Make sure to check operation of stop lights and

bleed brakes. Allow engine vacuum to build before applying brakes.

Parking Brake Adjustment

1. Jack up rear of car and support with both rear wheels off floor.
2. Apply parking brake two notches from fully released position.
3. Loosen the equalizer locknut, then tighten the adjusting nut until a light to moderate drag is felt when the rear wheels are rotated.
4. Tighten the locknut.
5. Fully release parking brake and rotate rear wheels—no drag should be felt.

STEERING

Tie-Rod Removal and Installation

1. Remove the cotter pins and nuts from the tie-rod end studs.
2. Tap on the steering arm near the tie-rod end (use another hammer as backing) and pull down on the tie-rod, if necessary, to free it.
3. Remove the inner stud in the same manner as the outer.
4. Loosen the clamp bolts and unscrew the ends if they are being replaced.
5. Lubricate the tie-rod end threads with chassis grease if they were removed. Install each end assembly an equal distance from the sleeve.
6. Ensure that the tie-rod end stud threads and nut are clean. Install new seals and install the studs into the steering arms and relay rod.
7. Install the stud nuts. Tighten to 35 ft lbs. If necessary, you can tighten the nuts to as much as 50 ft lbs to install the cotter pins.
8. Adjust the toe-in.

NOTE: before tightening the sleeve clamps, ensure that the clamps are positioned so that adjusting sleeve slot is covered by the clamp.

Power Steering Pump Removal and Installation

All models use an integral type of power steering gear. A pump delivers hydraulic pressure through two hoses to the steering gear itself.

Detailed service coverage is found in the Unit Repair Section.

1. Remove the hoses at the pump and tape the openings shut to prevent contamination. Position the disconnected lines in a raised position to prevent leakage.
2. Remove the pump belt.
3. Loosen the retaining bolts and

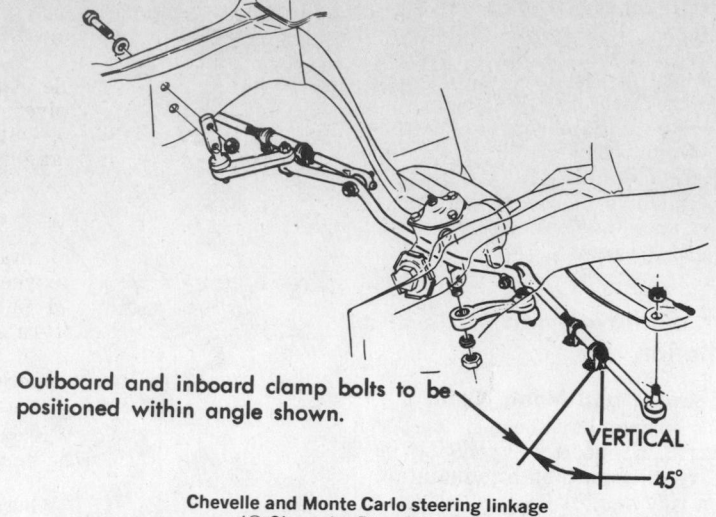

Outboard and inboard clamp bolts to be positioned within angle shown.

VERTICAL
45°

Chevelle and Monte Carlo steering linkage
(© Chevrolet Div., G.M. Corp)

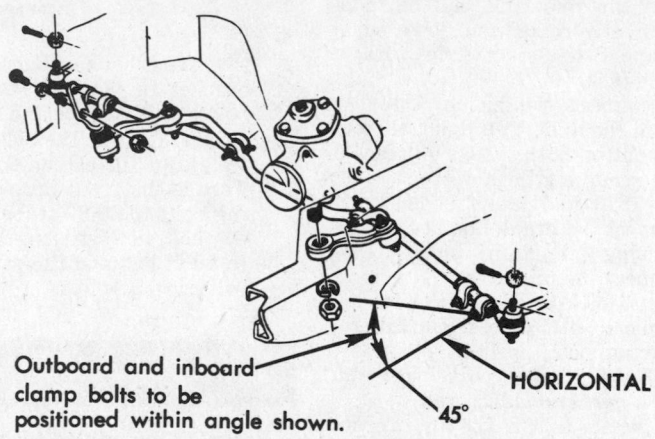

Outboard and inboard clamp bolts to be positioned within angle shown.

HORIZONTAL
45°

Camaro steering linkage
(© Chevrolet Div., G.M. Corp)

HORIZONTAL
30°
30°

Outboard and inboard clamps bolts to be positioned within angle shown.

Nova steering linkage
(© Chevrolet Div., G.M. Corp)

any braces, and remove the pump.
4. Install the pump on the engine with the retaining bolts hand-tight.
5. Connect and tighten the hose fittings.
6. Refill the pump with fluid and bleed by turning the pulley counterclockwise (viewed from the front). Stop the bleeding when air bubbles no longer appear.
7. Install the pump belt on the pul-

ley and adjust the tension. Bleed the system.

Bleeding Power Steering System

1. Fill the fluid reservoir.
2. Let the fluid stand undisturbed for two minutes, then crank the engine for about two seconds. Refill reservoir if necessary.
3. Repeat Steps 1 and 2 above until the fluid level remains constant after cranking the engine.

4. Raise the front of the car until the wheels are off the ground, then start the engine. Increase the engine speed to about 1,500 rpm.

5. Turn the wheels lightly against the stops to the left and right, checking the fluid level and refilling if necessary.

Steering Wheel Removal and Installation

Caution Disconnect the battery ground cable before removing the steering wheel. When installing a steering wheel, always make sure that the turn signal lever is in the neutral position.

Padded Rim Wheel

1. Pry out the center cap and retainer. Remove the shaft snapping ring on 1975 and later models.

NOTE: On the tilt-telescope wheel, remove the three upper contact retaining screws, the contact and shim if used. Then remove the center star screw and lever.

2. Remove the steering wheel nut and washer.

3. Remove the three receiving cup screws and remove the cup, belleville spring, bushing, and pivot ring.

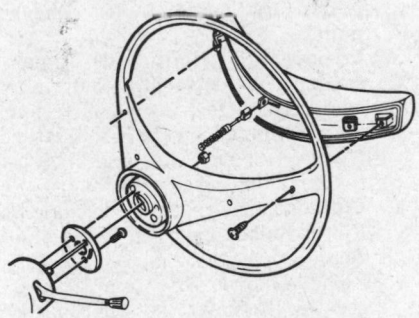

Standard steering wheel
((©)Chevrolet Div., G.M. Corp)

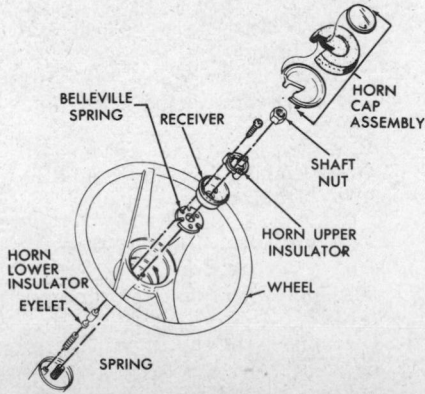

Cushioned rim steering wheel assembly
(© Chevrolet Div., G.M. Corp)

4. Mark the wheel-to-shaft relationship, and then remove the wheel with a puller.

5. Install the wheel on the shaft, aligning the previously made marks. Tighten the nut to 30 ft lbs.

6. Install the belleville spring (dished side up), pivot ring, bushing, and receiving cup. Install the center cap and reconnect the battery.

Standard Wheel

1. Remove the trim retaining screws from behind the wheel.

2. Lift the trim off and pull the horn wires from the turn signal cancelling cam.

NOTE: On the tilt-telescope wheel, remove the three upper contact retaining screws, the contact and shim if used. Then remove the center star screw and lever.

3. Remove the steering wheel nut.

4. Mark the wheel-to-shaft relationship, and then remove the wheel with a puller.

5. Install the wheel on the shaft, aligning the previously made marks. Tighten the nut to 30 ft lbs.

6. Insert the horn wires into the cancelling cam.

7. Install the center trim and reconnect the battery cable.

Turn Signal Switch Removal and Installation

1. Remove the steering wheel as previously outlined. Remove the trim cover.

2. Loosen the cover screws (on 1976 and later models, pry the cover off with a screwdriver), and lift the cover off the shaft.

3. Position the U-shaped lockplate compressing tool on the end of the steering shaft and compress the lock plate by turning the shaft nut clockwise. Pry the wire snap-ring out of the shaft groove.

4. Remove the tool and lift the lockplate off the shaft.

5. Slip the cancelling cam, upper bearing preload spring, and thrust washer off the shaft.

6. Remove the turn signal lever. Push the flasher knob in and unscrew it.

7. Pull the switch connector out of the mast jacket and tape the upper part to facilitate switch removal. Attach a long piece of wire to the turn signal switch connector. When installing the turn signal switch, feed this wire through the column first, and then use this wire to pull the switch connector into position. On tilt wheels, place the turn signal and shifter housing in Low position and remove the harness cover.

8. Remove the three switch mounting screws. Remove the switch by pulling it straight up while

guiding the wiring harness cover through the column.

9. Install the replacement switch by working the connector and cover down through the housing and under the bracket. On tilt models, the connector is worked down through the housing, under the bracket, and then the cover is installed on the harness.

10. Install the switch mounting screws and the connector on the mast jacket bracket. Install the column-to-dash trim plate.

11. Install the flasher knob and the turn signal lever.

12. With the turn signal lever in neutral and the flasher knob out, slide the thrust washer, upper bearing preload spring, and cancelling cam onto the shaft.

13. Position the lock plate on the shaft and press it down until a new snap-ring can be inserted in the shaft groove.

14. Install the cover and the steering wheel.

Ignition Switch Replacement

All models have the ignition lock cylinder located on the upper right side of the steering column. The ignition switch is inside the channel section of the brake pedal support. The switch is inaccessible unless the steering column is lowered.

1. Lower steering column. The column must be carefully supported to prevent damage.

2. Remove lock cylinder.

NOTE: pull actuating rod for switch up until a definite stop is felt, then push it down one detent to Lock position.

3. Remove two switch screws and switch assembly.

4. When replacing switch, make sure switch and lock are in Lock position. Do not use switch screws longer than the originals, or the compressibility feature of the column may be lost.

Lock Cylinder Replacement

1. Remove steering wheel and directional signal switch as previously outlined in "Steering."

2. Place lock cylinder in Lock position up to 1970, Run position starting 1971.

Caution Do not remove the ignition key buzzer.

3. Insert a small screwdriver into the turn signal housing slot. Keeping the screwdriver to the right side of the slot, break the housing flash loose and depress the spring latch at the lower end of the lock cylinder. Remove the lock cylinder.

NOTE: considerable force may be necessary to break this casting flash, but be careful not to damage any other parts. When ordering a new lock cylinder, specify a cylinder assembly. This will save assembling the cylinder, washer, sleeve, and adaptor.

4. To install, hold the lock cylinder sleeve and rotate the knob clockwise against the stop. Insert the cylinder into the housing, aligning the key and keyway. Hold a .070 in. drill between the lock bezel and housing. Rotate the cylinder counterclockwise, maintaining a light pressure until the drive section of the cylinder mates with the sector. Push in until the snap ring pops into the grooves. Remove drill. Check cylinder operation.

Caution The drill prevents forcing the lock cylinder inward beyond its normal position. The buzzer switch and spring latch can hold the lock cylinder in too far. Complete disassembly of the upper bearing housing is necessary to release an improperly installed lock cylinder.

INSTRUMENT PANEL

Light Switch Replacement

Nova

1. Disconnect battery.
2. Pull knob out to on position.
3. Reach under instrument panel and depress the switch shaft retainer, and remove knob and shaft assembly.
4. Remove the retaining ferrule nut.
5. Remove switch from instrument panel.
6. Disconnect the multi-plug connector from the switch.
7. Reverse the procedure to install.

Chevelle, Monte Carlo

1. Disconnect battery ground cable.
2. Remove six screws and instrument panel pad.
3. Remove left radio speaker.
4. Pull knob to on position.
5. Reach behind instrument panel and depress switch shaft retainer. Remove knob and shaft assembly.
6. Remove ferrule nut and switch assembly from instrument panel.
7. Reverse procedure to install.

Camaro

1. Disconnect battery negative cable.
2. Remove steering column lower cover (six screws).
3. Reach up under cluster on the left side and depress light switch shaft retainer, while pulling gently on shaft.

4. Remove nut that secures switch to cluster carrier.
5. Remove four cluster carrier screws in front and two from rear, then tilt right side of cluster out. Cigarette lighter grounding ring may have to be freed.
6. Unplug harness connector from switch.
7. Remove switch.
8. To install, reverse removal procedure. Make sure all ground connections are refastened.

WINDSHIELD WIPERS

Motor Removal and Installation

1. Make sure wiper motor is in park position.
2. Disconnect washer hoses and electrical connectors.
3. Remove the plenum chamber grille or access cover. Disconnect the drive link from the motor crank arm.
4. Remove the retaining screws or nuts and remove motor.
5. Reverse procedure to install, checking sealing gaskets at motor.

RADIO

Radio Removal and Installation

through 1972

1. Disconnect battery ground cable.
2. Remove ash tray and ash tray housing as necessary.
3. Remove knobs, controls, washers, trim plate, and nuts from radio.
4. Remove hoses from center air conditioning duct as necessary.
5. Disconnect all wiring leads.
6. Remove screw from radio rear mounting bracket and lower radio.
7. To install, reverse above procedure.

1973 and Later Chevelle and Monte Carlo

1. Disconnect the battery ground cable.
2. Remove the left air conditioner lap cooler duct.
3. Pull off the knobs and bezels.
4. Remove the control shaft nuts and washers. You will probably need a deep well socket.
5. Remove the support bracket stud nut. Disconnect the antenna, speaker, and power wires.
6. Move the radio back until the shafts clear the instrument panel. Lower it from behind the panel.

7. Reverse the procedure for installation. Make sure to hook up the speaker leads before turning the radio on; operating without a speaker will damage the transistors.

1973 and Later Nova and Camaro

1. Disconnect the battery ground cable.
2. Pull off the knobs and bezels.
3. Remove the control shaft nuts and washers. A deep well socket will be needed on the Camaro.
4. Remove the mounting bracket screws or nuts.
5. Move the radio back until the shafts clear the instrument panel. Lower it and disconnect the antenna, speaker, and power wires.
6. Remove the radio. Reverse the procedure for installation. Make sure to hook up the speaker leads before turning the radio on; operating without a speaker will damage the transistors.

HEATER

Heater Blower Removal and Installation

1970-72 Chevelle and Monte Carlo, 1970 and later Nova and Camaro

1. Disconnect battery ground cable.
2. Disconnect hoses and wiring from right side inner fender panel.
3. Remove all right side inner fender panel attaching bolts except those attaching panel to radiator support. On 1974 and later Nova, remove the eight rear fender skirt screws instead.
4. Pull out, then down, on panel. Place a block between panel and fender.
5. Remove blower to case attaching screws. Remove the air-cooling hose from the motor on air-conditioned cars. Remove blower assembly. On 1974 and later Nova, separate the blower wheel and motor first.
6. Remove blower wheel retaining nut and separate the motor and wheel.
7. Reverse procedure to install. Open end of blower should be away from motor.

1973 and Later Chevelle and Monte Carlo

1. Disconnect the battery ground cable.
2. Disconnect the motor lead wire.
3. Remove the blower to case screws and the blower.
4. Remove the retaining nut to separate the motor and wheel.
5. Reverse the procedure for installation. The open end of the blower wheel should be away from the motor.

Heater Core Removal and Installation

All Non Air-Conditioned Models

1. Disconnect battery ground cable.
2. Drain radiator.
3. Disconnect heater hoses. Plug core inlet and outlet. *Note: The larger hose goes to the water pump.*
4. Remove nuts from air distributor duct studs on firewall.
5. On Nova, remove glove compartment and door assembly.
6. From under Nova dash, drill out lower right hand distributor duct stud with a ¼ in. drill.
7. On 1970 and later Camaro: remove glove box and radio, then defroster duct to distributor duct screw.
8. Pull distributor duct from firewall mounting. Remove resistor wires.
9. Remove core assembly from distributor duct.
10. Reverse procedure to install.

Chevelle and Monte Carlo with Air Conditioning through 1972

1. Drain the cooling system and disconnect the battery ground cable. It is not necessary to purge the A/C refrigerant.
2. Remove the heater hoses at the firewall and plug the openings.
3. Remove the case stud nuts from the firewall.
4. Remove the glove compartment on 1969 models.
5. Remove the right kick pad cover and the recirculating air valve.
6. Remove the center duct from the distributor, and remove the floor distributor duct.
7. From inside the passenger compartment, drill the lower right distributor duct stud out.
8. Remove the remaining air distributor-to-firewall screws, electrical connectors, and control cables.
9. Scribe the temperature door camming plate-to-distributor duct relationship and remove the plate.
10. Remove the heater core housing and core.
11. Reverse the removal procedure to install the core. Replace the drilled-out stud with a screw and speed nut.

1973 and Later Chevelle and Monte Carlo with Air Conditioning

1. Disconnect the battery ground cable and drain the radiator.
2. Detach the heater hoses and plug the core tubes.
3. Remove the nuts from the firewall distributor case studs inside the car.
4. Remove the resistor assembly, reach through the opening, and remove the last distributor stud nut.
5. Remove the screws holding the right lap cooler duct to the instrument panel. Remove the duct.
6. Remove the center duct.
7. Remove the glove box strap screw, strap, and glove box.
8. Remove the floor outlet.
9. Remove the defroster to distributor duct screw at the lower distributor duct screw at the lower right of the duct.
10. Pull the distributor assembly back far enough that the studs and core tubes clear. Lower it and detach the electrical and vacuum connections.
11. Disconnect the temperature door cable.
12. Remove the distributor assembly.
13. Remove the screws holding the core clamps to the distributor assembly and remove the core.
14. Reverse the procedure for installation.

Nova with Air Conditioning

1. Disconnect the battery ground cable and drain the cooling system. It is not necessary to purge the refrigerant from the A/C system.
2. Disconnect the heater hose from the upper pipe at the firewall.
3. Remove the nuts from the heater studs in the firewall.
4. Remove the right front inner fender panel screws and lower the panel onto the tire.
5. Remove the remaining stud nut and the lower heater hose.
6. Remove the glove compartment.
7. Remove the right kick pad recirculating air valve.
8. Detach the center duct from the selector duct.
9. Remove the floor duct and separate the two selector halves.
10. Remove the selector duct from the firewall.
11. Disconnect the control cables and electrical wires.
12. Scribe the temperature door camming plate-to-selector duct relationship and remove the plate.

13. Place the selector duct on the floor and remove the heater core housing and core.
14. Reverse the removal steps to install the core.

Camaro with Air Conditioning

1. Disconnect the battery ground cable and drain the cooling system. It is not necessary to purge the refrigerant from the cooling system. On 1974 and later models, remove the 8 to 10 rearmost inner fender skirt screws and block the skirt out with a 4 in. wood block for access.
2. Disconnect the heater hoses at the firewall and plug the openings.
3. Remove the nuts from the heater studs protruding through the firewall.
4. Remove the glove compartment and radio.
5. Remove the defroster duct-to-distributor duct screw and pull the defroster duct rearward.
6. Pull the distributor duct from its dash mounting. Disconnect the control cables and electrical wires when there is sufficient clearance.
7. Remove the distributor duct and core from the car.
8. Remove the retainers and remove the heater core.
9. Reverse the removal procedure to install the heater core.

SEAT BELTS

Disabling the Interlock System

Since the requirement for the interlock system was dropped during the 1975 model year, those systems installed on cars built earlier may now be legally disabled. The seat belt warning light is still required.

1. Disconnect the negative battery cable.
2. Locate the interlock harness connector under the left side of the instrument panel on or near the fuse block. It has orange, yellow, and green leads.
3. Cut and tape the ends of the green wire on the body side of the connector.
4. Remove the buzzer from the fuse block or connector.

INDEX

Chevrolet · Corvette

Automatic Transmission in-Car Service ... **C386, C420**
Turbo Hydra-Matic detent adjustment .. C388
Band adjustment, Pan Removal and Installation, fluid & filter change C388
Shift linkage adjustment C387
Neutral safety switch adjustment C386
Powerglide throttle valve adjustment ... C388

Brakes **C393, U299**
Parking brake adjustment C393
Master cylinder Removal and Installation C393
Power brake unit Removal and Installation C393

Charging System **C368**
Alternator Removal and Installation C368
Regulator Removal and Installation C368

Clutch **C384**
Clutch Removal and Installation C384
Clutch adjustment C384

Cooling System **C374, U367**
Radiator Removal and Installation C374
Thermostat Removal and Installation ... C375
Water pump Removal and Installation .. C374

Emission Controls **C375, U145**
Air injection reactor C375
Anti-dieseling solenoid C375
Catalytic converter C377
Controlled combustion system C375
Early fuel evaporation system C376
Evaporative emission control C375
Exhaust gas recirculation C376
Positive crankcase ventilation C375
Transmission controlled spark C375

Engine **C377, U194**
ENGINE REMOVAL AND INSTALLATION C377
CYLINDER HEAD REMOVAL AND INSTALLATION C380
LUBRICATION C383
Oil pan Removal and Installation C383
Oil pump Removal and Installation C384
Rear main bearing oil seal replacement C384
MANIFOLDS C378
Exhaust manifold Removal and Installation V8 .... C379
Intake manifold Removal and Installation V8 .... C378
6 cylinder combination manifold Removal and Installation C378

PISTONS AND CONNECTING RODS C383
Assembling piston to connecting rod ... C383
TIMING CASE C381
Camshaft Removal and Installation C382
Crankshaft pulley replacement C381
Timing case cover and front oil seal replacement C381
Timing chain or gear replacement C381
VALVE SYSTEM C379
Rocker arm Removal and Installation ... C379
Valve arrangement C380
Valve guides C379
Valve clearance adjustment C379

Front Suspension **C389, U292**
Ball joint inspection C390
Spring Removal and Installation C389
Ball joint Removal and Installation C390
Control arm Removal and Installation .. C390
Shock absorber Removal and Installation C389
Wheel bearing adjustment C390

Fuel System **C370, U50**
Fuel filter Removal and Installation C371
Fuel pump Removal and Installation C370
Carburetor adjustments C371

Heater **C397**
Heater blower Removal and Installation C397
Heater core Removal and Installation .. C397

Ignition System **C368, U34**
Breaker point adjustment C369
Distributor installation (engine disturbed) C369
Distributor Removal and Installation ... C368
Firing order C357
Hei system Tachometer hookup C369
Ignition timing C370

Instrument Panel **C432, U350**
Headlight switch replacement C396

Jacking, Hoisting **C389**

Manual Transmission **C385, U231**
Shift linkage adjustment C385
Transmission Removal and Installation C385

Radio **C396**
Radio Removal and Installation C396

Rear Axle **C388, U285**
Corvette rear axle Removal and Installation C388

Rear Suspension **C390**
Coil spring Removal and Installation ... C391
Leaf spring Removal and Installation (station wagon) C392
Shock absorber Removal and Installation C391
Strut rod and bracket (Corvette) C392
Rear wheel camber adjustment C392
Rod and bracket Removal and Installation C392
Torque control arm Removal and Installation (Corvette) C392
Transverse leaf spring (Corvette) Removal and Installation C391

Seat Belts **C398**
Disabling the interlock system C398

Specifications **C357, U359**
Capacities C363
Crankshaft and connecting rod C366
Engine identification C357
General engine C360
Piston clearance C367
Ring gap and side clearance C366
Torque C365
Tune-up C362
Valve C365
Wheel alignment C367
Year identification C367

Starting System **C368, U2**
Starter Removal and Installation C368

Steering **C393, U328**
Bleeding power steering system C394
Ignition switch replacement C393
Lock cylinder Removal and Installation C395
Power steering pump Removal and Installation C394
Steering wheel Removal and Installation C394
Tie rod Removal and Installation C394
Turn signal switch Removal and Installation C394

U-Joints **C388**

Windshield Wipers **C396**
Motor Removal and Installation C396

YEAR IDENTIFICATION

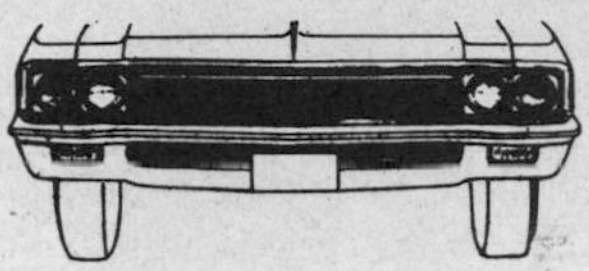

1970

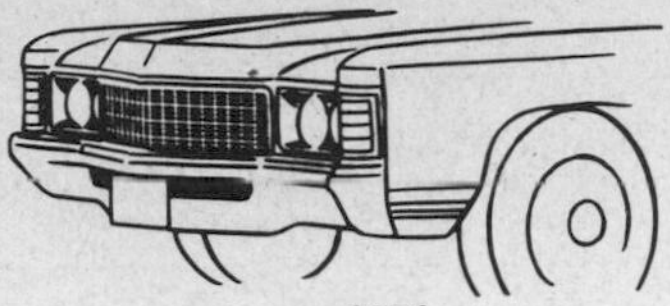

1971

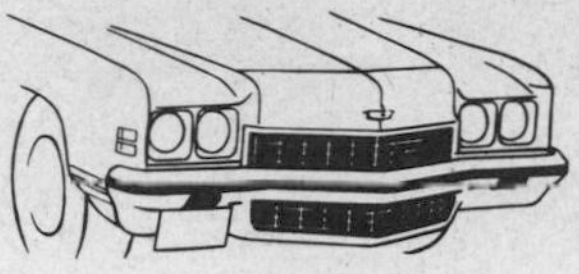

1972 Caprice

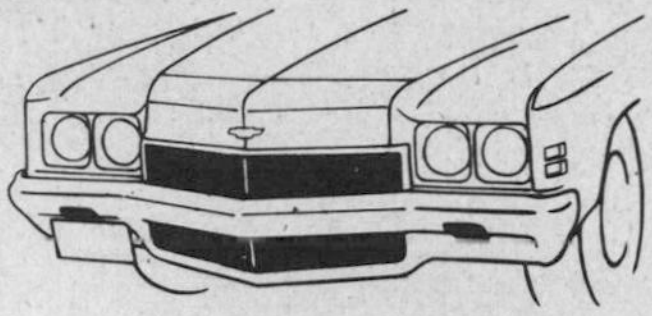

1972 Impala

1973 Impala

1974 Impala

1974 Caprice

1975 Caprice

1976 Impala

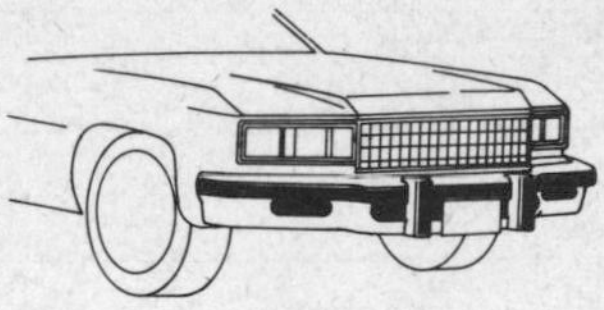

1976 Caprice

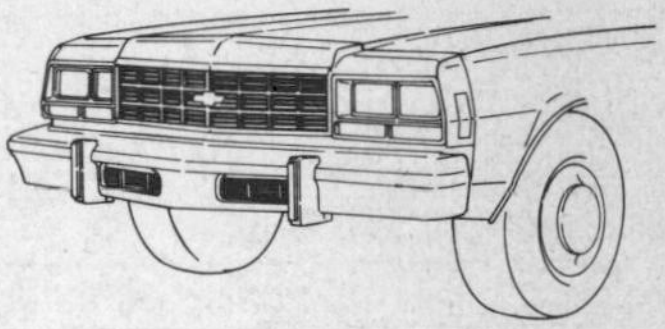

1977 Impala

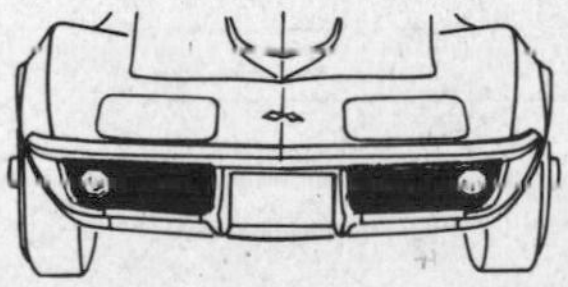

1970-71

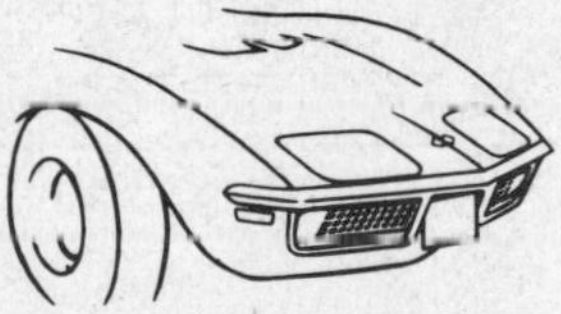

1972

1973

1974

1975 Corvette

1976 Corvette

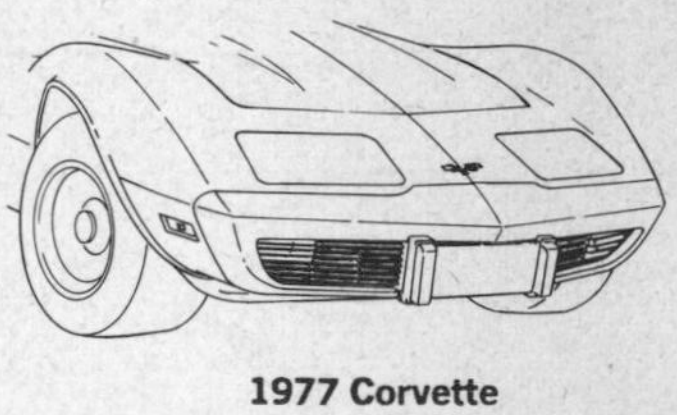

1977 Corvette

FIRING ORDER

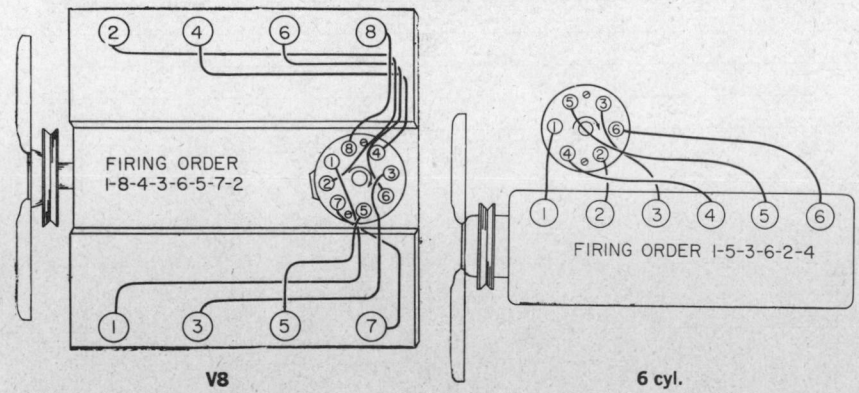

FIRING ORDER
1-8-4-3-6-5-7-2

V8

FIRING ORDER 1-5-3-6-2-4

6 cyl.

Engine Identification

Six Cylinder Engines

The production code letters immediately follow the engine serial number. The number is found on a pad at the front right-hand side of the cylinder block, just to the rear of the distributor.

V8 Engines

The production code letters immediately follow the engine serial number. The number is found on a pad at the front right-hand side of the cylinder block.

C357

Chevrolet — ENGINE IDENTIFICATION

No. Cyls.	Cu. in. Displ.	Type	1970	1971	1972	1973	1974	1975	1976	1977
6	250	M.T.	CCG, CCH, CCZ, CRF, CRG	CAA	CNJ					
6	250				CDL	CCL				
6	250	M.T. California				CCM				
6	250	M.T., AC			CBH					
6	250	Taxi, Police, M.T.	CCL	CAC	CBJ					
6	250	PG		CAB	CBK					
6	250	PG, Taxi, Police	CCM	CAD						
6	250	T.H. 350, Police		CCK						
8	350	M.T.	CND (250)	CGA (245), CNQ (300)	CSJ					
8	350	T.H. 400		CKB						
8	350	T.H. 350	CNR (300), CNV (250)							
8	350	PG	CNS (300), CNU (250)	CGB						
8	350	T.H. 350, Taxi, 2-BBL.		CGJ			CMD			
8	350	T.H., 2-BBL.				CKL	CMA			
8	350	T.H., 2-BBL., California				CKK				
8	350	T.H., 2-BBL., Wagon				CLU				
8	350	T.H., 2-BBL., Wagon, Calif.				CLT				
8	350	T.H., 4-BBL., California Police and Taxi					CMK			
8	350	T.H., 4-BBL., Police					CMJ			
8	350							CRS, CRZ, CRF, CRX, CRY, CRU, CRW, CMX, CMY	CMJ, CLF, CMH, CLH, CMM, CKM	
8	350	M.T., Taxi, Police	CNP (250)	CJB, CJH						
8	350	PG, Taxi, Police	CNW (250)		CAR, CSH					
8	350	T.H. 350, Taxi	CNT (300), CNX (250)	CGJ						
8	350	T.H., 4-BBL.				CKJ	CMH			
8	350	T.H., 4-BBL., California				CKD	CKD			
8	400	M.T. (265 hp)	CGR							
8	400	T.H. 350	CLK (265)		CDL, CDM					
8	400	T.H.				CSA				
8	400	T.H., California				CSD				
8	400	T.H., Wagon				CSK				
8	400	T.H., Wagon, California				CSM				
8	400	T.H., 2-BBL.					CTA			
8	400	T.H., 2-BBL., Police					CTB			
8	400	T.H., 4-BBL.					CTD, CTJ			
8	400	T.H., 4-BBL., California					CTC			
8	400	T.H., 4-BBL., California Police					CTK			
8	400							CSH, CSR, CSS, CST, CTL, CTM, CTR, CTS	CTY, CTW, CTL, CTZ, CSF, CTL, CTU, CTM, CSJ	
8	402	T.H. 350 (Mk. IV)	CLP (300)							
8	402	M.T., Police (Mk. IV)	CLR (330)		CLR, CTB					
8	402	M.T.			CLB					
8	402	M.T., w/AIR, Police			CTJ					

Chevrolet ENGINE IDENTIFICATION

No. Cyls.	Cu. in. Displ.	Type	1970	1971	1972	1973	1974	1975	1976	1977
				YEAR AND CODE						
8	454	M.T.	CGV (345), CGU (390)	CPD (365)						
8	454	M.T., Police	CGS (345), CGT (390)	CPG (365)						
8	454	T.H.			CPD	CWL				
8	454	T.H., Police			CPG					
8	454	T.H., w/AIR			CRW					
8	454	T.H., Police, w/AIR			CRY					
8	454	T.H., California				CWD				
8	454	T.H., 4-BBL.					CXA, CWY			
8	454	T.H., 4-BBL., Police					CWU			
8	454	T.H., 4-BBL., California Police					CWW			
8	454							CXK, CXL CXX, CXY	CXX CXY	

AC—Air conditioned
M.T.—Manual transmission
PG—Powerglide transmission
T.H.—Turbo-Hydramatic transmission

Corvette ENGINE IDENTIFICATION

No. Cyls.	Cu. in. Displ.	Type	1970	1971	1972	1973	1974	1975	1976	1977
				YEAR AND CODE						
8	350	HP, AC	CTN							
8	350	HP	CTO							
8	350	M.T.	CTL							
8	350	T.H. 400	CTM							
8	350	HP, T. Ign.	CTP							
8	350	HP, T. Ign., AC	CTQ							
8	350	SHP	CTR							
8	350	SHP, T. Ign.	CTU							
8	350	SHP, T. Ign., M.T.	CTV							
8	350	M.T. (270 hp)		CGS						
8	350	M.T. (330 hp)		CGZ						
8	350	M.T. (200 hp)			CKW					
8	350	M.T., w/ex. EM (200 hp)			CDH					
8	350	T.H. (200 hp)			CKX					
8	350	T.H., w/ex. EM (200 hp)			CDJ					
8	350	M.T. (255 hp)			CKY					
8	350	HDMT (255 hp)			CKZ					
8	350	M.T., w/AIR (255 hp)			CRT					
8	350	T.H., w/AIR (255 hp)			CRS					
8	350	Hyd. 400 (270 hp)		CGT						
8	350	4-Spd. (330 hp)		CGY						
8	350	M.T. (190 hp)				CKZ	CKZ			
8	350	M.T., California (190 hp)				CLB	CLB			
8	350	T.H. (190 hp)				CLA	CLA			
8	350	T.H., California (190 hp)				CLC	CLC			
8	350	M.T. (250 hp)				CLR	CLR			
8	350	M.T., California (250 hp)				CLS	CLS			
8	350	T.H. (250 hp)				CLD	CLD			
8	350	T.H., California (250 hp)				CLH	CLH			

Corvette ENGINE IDENTIFICATION

No. Cyls.	Cu. in. Displ.	Type	1970	1971	1972	1973	1974	1975	1976	1977
					YEAR AND CODE					
8	350	4-Spd.						CRJ, CUA CUB		
8	350	T.H. 400						CRK		
8	350	4-Spd. HP						CRL, CUT CUD		
8	350	T.H. 400 HP						CRM		
8	350								CLM, CHC CLR, CHR CLS, CKC	
8	454	HP, 4-BBL., T.H. 400	CGW							
8	454	HP, 4-BBL.	CZU							
8	454	Heavy duty, 4-BBL.	CZL							
8	454	T.H. 400, 4-BBL.	CZN							
8	454	HP, 4-BBL., T. Ign.	CRI							
8	454	T.H. 400 (365 hp)		CPJ						
8	454	M.T. (365 hp)		CPH						
8	454	M.T. (425 hp)		CPW						
8	454	T.H. 400 (425 hp)		CPX						
8	454	M.T. (270 hp)			CPH					
8	454	T.H. (270 hp)			CPJ					
8	454	w/AIR (270 hp)			CSR CSS					
8	454	M.T.				CWM	CWM			
8	454	M.T., California				CWT	CWT			
8	454	T.H.				CWR	CWR			
8	454	T.H., California				CWS	CWS			

AC—Air conditioned
HP—High performance
SHP—Special high performance
M.T.—Manual transmission

w/ex. EM—With exhaust emission
T. Ign.—With transistor ignition
4-BBL.—Four barrel carburetor

T.H.—With Turbo-Hydramatic
HDMT—Heavy duty 4-speed
w/AIR—With Air Injection Reactor

GENERAL ENGINE SPECIFICATIONS

Year	Engine No. Cyl. Displacement Cu. In.	Carburetor Type	Horsepower @ rpm ■	Torque @ rpm (ft lbs) ■	Bore X Stroke (in.)	Compression Ratio	Oil Pressure @ 2000 rpm
'70	6-250	1 bbl	155 @ 4200	235 @ 1600	3.875 x 3.530	8.5:1	58
	8-350	2 bbl	250 @ 4800	345 @ 2800	4.000 x 3.480	9.0:1	58
	8-350	4 bbl	300 @ 4800	380 @ 3200	4.000 x 3.480	10.25:1	58①
	8-350	4 bbl	350 @ 5600	380 @ 3600	4.000 x 3.480	11.0:1	40
	8-350	4 bbl	370 @ 6000	380 @ 4000	4.000 x 3.480	11.0:1	40
	8-400	2 bbl	265 @ 4400	400 @ 2400	4.125 x 3.750	9.0:1	58
	8-454	4 bbl	345 @ 4400	500 @ 3000	4.251 x 4.000	10.25:1	62
	8-454	4 bbl	390 @ 4800	500 @ 3400	4.251 x 4.000	10.25:1	62①
	8-454	4 bbl	460 @ 5600	490 @ 3600	4.251 x 4.000	11.25:1	62①
'71	6-250	1 bbl	145 @ 4200	230 @ 1600	3.875 x 3.530	8.5:1	40
	8-350	2 bbl	245 @ 4800	350 @ 2800	4.000 x 3.480	8.5:1	40
	8-350	4 bbl	270 @ 4800	360 @ 3200	4.000 x 3.480	8.5:1	40
	8-350	4 bbl	330 @ 5600	360 @ 4000	4.000 x 3.480	9.0:1	40
	8-400	2 bbl	255 @ 4400	390 @ 2400	4.125 x 3.750	8.5:1	40
	8-400 (402 Cu. In.)	4 bbl	300 @ 4800	400 @ 3200	4.126 x 3.760	8.5:1	40
	8-454	4 bbl	365 @ 4800	465 @ 4000	4.251 x 4.000	8.5:1	40
	8-454	4 bbl	425 @ 5600	475 @ 4000	4.251 x 4.000	9.0:1	40

GENERAL ENGINE SPECIFICATIONS

Year	Engine No. Cyl. Displacement Cu. In.	Carburetor Type	Horsepower @ rpm ∎	Torque @ rpm (ft lbs) ∎	Bore X Stroke (in.)	Compression Ratio	Oil Pressure @ 2000 rpm
'72	6-250	1 bbl	110 @ 3800	185 @ 1600	3.875 x 3.530	8.5:1	40
	8-350	2 bbl	165 @ 4000	280 @ 2400	4.000 x 3.480	8.5:1	40
	8-350	4 bbl	200 @ 4400	300 @ 2800	4.000 x 3.480	8.5:1	40
	8-350	4 bbl	255 @ 5600	280 @ 4000	4.000 x 3.480	9.0:1	40
	8-400	2 bbl	170 @ 3400	325 @ 2000	4.126 x 3.750	8.5:1	40
	8-402	4 bbl	210 @ 4400	320 @ 2400	4.126 x 3.760	8.5:1	40
	8-454	4 bbl	270 @ 4000	390 @ 3200	4.251 x 4.000	8.5:1	40
'73	6-250	1 bbl	100 @ 3600	175 @ 1600	3.875 x 3.530	8.25:1	40
	8-350	2 bbl	145 @ 4000	255 @ 2400	4.000 x 3.480	8.5:1	40
	8-350	4 bbl	175 @ 4000	260 @ 2800	4.000 x 3.480	8.5:1	40
	8-350	4 bbl	190 @ 4400	270 @ 2800	4.000 x 3.480	8.5:1	40
	8-350	4 bbl	250 @ 5200	285 @ 4000	4.000 x 3.480	9.0:1	40
	8-400	2 bbl	150 @ 3200	295 @ 2000	4.126 x 3.750	8.5:1	40
	8-454	4 bbl	245 @ 4000②	375 @ 2800③	4.251 x 4.000	8.25:1	40
	8-454	4 bbl	275 @ 4400	395 @ 2800	4.251 x 4.000	8.25:1	40
'74	8-350	2 bbl	145 @ 3600	250 @ 2200	4.000 x 3.480	8.5:1	40
	8-350	4 bbl	160 @ 3800	245 @ 2400	4.000 x 3.480	8.5:1	40
	8-350	4 bbl	195 @ 4400	275 @ 2800	4.000 x 3.480	8.5:1	40
	8-350	4 bbl	250 @ 5200	285 @ 4000	4.000 x 3.480	9.0:1	40
	8-400	2 bbl	150 @ 3200	295 @ 2000	4.126 x 3.750	8.5:1	40
	8-400	4 bbl	180 @ 3800	290 @ 2400	4.126 x 3.750	8.5:1	40
	8-454	4 bbl	235 @ 4000	360 @ 2800	4.251 x 4.000	8.25:1	40
	8-454	4 bbl	270 @ 4400	380 @ 2800	4.251 x 4.000	8.25:1	40
'75	8-350	2 bbl	145 @ 3800	250 @ 2200	4.000 x 3.480	8.5:1	40
	8-350	4 bbl	155 @ 3800	250 @ 2400	4.000 x 3.480	8.5:1	40
	8-350	4 bbl	165 @ 3800	255 @ 2400	4.000 x 3.480	8.5:1	40
	8-350	4 bbl	205 @ 4800	255 @ 3600	4.000 x 3.480	9.0:1	40
	8-400	4 bbl	175 @ 3600	305 @ 2000	4.126 x 3.750	8.5:1	40
	8-454	4 bbl	215 @ 4000	350 @ 2400	4.251 x 4.000	8.15:1	40
'76-'77	6-250	1 bbl	105 @ 3800	185 @ 1200	3.875 x 3.530	8.25:1	40
	8-305	2 bbl	140 @ 3800	245 @ 2000	3.736 x 3.480	8.5:1	40
	8-350	2 bbl	145 @ 3800	250 @ 2200	4.000 x 3.480	8.5:1	40
	8-350	4 bbl	165 @ 3800	260 @ 2400	4.000 x 3.480	8.5:1	40
	8-350	4 bbl	180 @ 4000	270 @ 2400	4.000 x 3.480	8.5:1	40
	8-350	4 bbl	210 @ 5200	255 @ 3600	4.000 x 3.480	9.0:1	40
	8-400	4 bbl	175 @ 3600	305 @ 2000	4.126 x 3.750	8.5:1	40
	8-454	4 bbl	225 @ 3800	360 @ 2400	4.251 x 4.000	8.25:1	46

∎ Beginning 1972, horsepower and torque are SAE net figures. They are measured at the rear of the transmission with all accessories installed and operating. Since the figures vary when a given engine is installed in different models, some are representative rather than exact.

① For Corvettes, oil pressure is 40 psi
② 215 in wagon
③ 345 in wagon

C361

Chevrolet — TUNE-UP SPECIFICATIONS

When analyzing compression test results, look for uniformity among cylinders rather than specific pressures.

Year	No. Cyl Displacement (cu in.)	hp	Orig. Type	Gap (in.)	Point Dwell (deg)	Point Gap (in.)	Man Trans	Auto Trans	Intake Opens (deg)	Fuel Pump Pressure (psi)	Man Trans	Auto Trans
'70	6-250	155	R46T	.035	31-34	.019	TDC	4B	16	4-5	750/400②	600/400①
	8-350	250	R44	.035	29-31	.019	TDC	4B	28	7½-9	700/450②	600/450②
	8-350	300	R44	.035	29-31	.019	TDC	4B	28	7½-9	700	600
	8-400	265	R44	.035	29-31	.019	4B	8B	28	7½-9	700	600/450①
	8-454	345	R44T	.035	28-30	.019	6B	6B	30	7½-9	700	600
	8-454	390	R43T	.035	28-30	.019	6B	6B	56	7½-9	700	600
'71	6-250	145	R46TS	.035	31-34	.019	4B	4B	16	4-5	550	500①
	8-350	245	R44TS	.035	29-31	.019	2B	6B	28	7½-9	600	550①
	8-350	270	R44TS	.035	29-31	.019	4B	8B	28	7½-9	600	550①
	8-400	255	R44TS	.035	29-31	.019	4B	8B	28	7½-9	600	550①
	8-402	300	R44TS	.035	29-31	.019	8B	8B	28	7½-9	600	600①
	8-454	365	R43TS	.035	28-30	.019	8B	8B	56	7½-9	600	600
'72	6-250	110	R46T	.035	31-34	.019	4B	4B	16	4-5	700	600
	8-350	165	R44T	.035	29-31	.019	6B	6B	28(44)	7½-9	900	600
	8-400	170	R44T	.035	29-31	.019	2B	6B	28(44)	7½-9	900	600
	8-402	210	R44T	.035	29-31	.019	8B	8B	30(44)	7½-9	750	600
	8-454	270	R44T	.035	29-31	.019	8B	8B	56	7½-9	750	600
'73	6-250	100	R46T	.035	31-34	.019	6B	—	16	3½-4½	700/450②	—
	8-350	145	R44T	.035	29-31	.019	—	8B	28	7½-9	—	600/450②
	8-350	175	R44T	.035	29-31	.019	—	12B	28	7½-9	—	600/450②
	8-400	140	R44T	.035	29-31	.019	—	8B	28	7½-9	—	600/450②
	8-454	245	R44T	.035	29-31	.019	—	10B	55	7½-9	—	600/450②
'74	8-350	145	R44T	.035	29-31	.019	—	8B	28(44)	7½-9	—	600
	8-350	160	R44T	.035	29-31	.019	—	12B(8B)	28(44)	7½-9	—	600
	8-400	150	R44T	.035	29-31	.019	—	8B	28(44)	7½-9	—	600
	8-400	180	R44T	.035	29-31	.019	—	8B	28(44)	7½-9	—	600
	8-454	235	R44T	.035	29-31	.019	—	10B	55	7½-9	—	600
'75	8-350	145	R-44TX	.060	Electronic		—	6B	28	7½-9	—	600
	8-350	155	R-44TX	.060	Electronic		—	6B	28	7½-9	—	600
	8-400	175	R-44TX	.060	Electronic		—	8B	28	7½-9	—	600
	8-454	215	R-44TX	.060	Electronic		—	16B	55	7½-9	—	650
'76	8-350	145	R-45TS	.045	Electronic		—	6B	28	7½-9	—	600
	8-350	165	R-45TS	.045	Electronic		—	8B (6B)	28	7½-9	—	600
	8-400	175	R-45TS	.045	Electronic		—	8B	28	7½-9	—	600
	8-454	225	R-45TS	.045	Electronic		—	12B	55	7½-9	—	550
'77	6-250	All	R-46TS	.035	Electronic		③	③	16	4-5	③	③
	8-305	All	R-45TS	.045	Electronic		③	③	28	7½-9	③	③
	8-350	All	R-45TS	.045	Electronic		③	③	28	7½-9	③	③

▲ See text for procedure
● Figure in parentheses indicates California engine
■ All figures Before Top Dead Center
① A/C on
② Lower figure with Idle Solenoid disconnected
③ See underhood specifications sticker
B Before Top Dead Center
TDC Top Dead Center
— Not applicable

Corvette   TUNE-UP SPECIFICATIONS

When analyzing compression test results, look for uniformity among cylinders rather than specific pressures.

Year	ENGINE No. Cyl Displacement (cu in.)	hp	SPARK PLUGS Orig. Type	Gap (in.)	DISTRIBUTOR Point Dwell (deg)	Point Gap (in.)	IGNITION TIMING (deg) ▲ Man Trans •	Auto Trans	VALVES Intake Opens ■ (deg)	Fuel Pump Pressure (psi)	IDLE SPEED • (rpm) ▲ Man Trans	Auto Trans
'70	8-350	300	R44	.035	29-31	.019	4B	4B	28	7½-9	700	600
	8-350	350	R44	.035	29-31	.019	4B	—	52	7½-9	750	—
	8-350	370	R43T	.035	—	—	8B	12B	42½	7½-9	700	—
	8-454	390	R43T	.035	28-30	.019	6B	6B	56	7½-9	800	600
	8-454	460	R43XL	.035	—	—	4B	4B	62	7½-9	750	600
'71	8-350	270	R44TS	.035	29-31	.019	8B	8B	28	7½-9	600	550
	8-350	330	R43TS	.035	—	—	8B	12B	42½	7½-9	700	700
	8-454	365	R43TS	.035	28-30	.019	8B	8B	56	7½-9	600	600
	8-454	425	R44TS	.035	—	—	8B	12B	44	7½-9	700	700
'72	8-350	200	R44T	.035	29-31	.019	8B	8B	28(44)	7½-9	800	600
	8-350	255	R44T	.035	29-31	.019	4B	8B	42½	7½-9	900	700
	8-454	270	R44T	.035	29-31	.019	8B	8B	56	7½-9	800	600
'73	8-350	190	R44T	.035	29-31	.019	12B	12B	28	7½-9	900/450①	600/450
	8-350	250	R44T	.035	29-31	.019	8B	8B	52	7½-9	900/450①	700/450
	8-454	275	R44T	.035	29-31	.019	10B	10B	55	7½-9	900/450①	600/450
'74	8-350	195	R44T	.035	29-31	.019	8B(4B)	8B	28(44)	7½-9	900	600
	8-350	250	R44T	.035	29-31	.019	8B	8B	52	7½-9	900	700
	8-454	270	R44T	.035	29-31	.019	10B	10B	55	7½-9	800	600
'75	8-350	165	R-44TX	.060	Electronic		6B	6B	28	7½-9	800	600
	8-350	205	R-44TX	.060	Electronic		12B	12B	52	7½-9	900	700
'76	8-350	180	R-45TS	.045	Electronic		8B	8B(6B)	28	7½-9	800	600
	8-350	210	R-45TS	.045	Electronic		12B	12B	52	7½-9	1000	700
'77	8-350	180	R-45TS	.045	Electronic		②	②	28	7½-9	②	②
	8-350	210	R-45TS	.045	Electronic		②	②	52	7½-9	②	②

▲ See text for procedure
• Figure in parentheses iindicates California engine
■ All figures Before Top Dead Center
① Lower figure with Idle Solenoid disconnected
② See underhood specifications sticker
B Before Top Dead Center
— Not applicable

MECHANICAL VALVE LIFTER CLEARANCE

Year	Engine		Intake (Hot) In.	Exhaust (Hot) In.
1970	V8-350	370 hp	.024	.030
1970	V8-454	460 hp	.024	.028
1971	V8-350	330 hp	.024	.030
1971	V8-454	425 hp	.024	.028
1972	V8-350	255 hp	.024	.030

Chevrolet

CAPACITIES

Year	ENGINE No. Cyl. (Cu. In.) Displacement	Engine Crankcase Add 1 Qt For New Filter	TRANSMISSION Pts To Refill After Draining Manual 3-Speed	4-Speed	Automatic •	Drive Axle (pts) ▲	Gasoline Tank (gals) ■	COOLING SYSTEM (qts) With Heater	With A/C
'70	6-250	4	3	—	6	3.5	25	12	12
	8-350	4	3	—	6.5③	3.5	25	16	16①
	8-400	4	—	—	5②	3.5	25	16	17
	8-454	4	—	—	8	3.5	25	22	22

Chevrolet CAPACITIES

Year	ENGINE No. Cyl. (Cu. In.) Displacement	Engine Crankcase Add 1 Qt For New Filter	TRANSMISSION Pts To Refill After Draining Manual 3-Speed	4-Speed	Automatic ●	Drive Axle (pts) ▲	Gasoline Tank (gals) ■	COOLING SYSTEM (qts) With Heater	With A/C
'71	6-250	4	3	——	6	3.5	24	12	——
	8-350	4	3	——	6.5③	3.5	24	16	17
	8-400	4	3	——	5②	3.5	24	16	17
	8-402	4	——	——	8	3.5	24	23	24
	8-454	4	——	——	8	3.5	24	22	23
'72	6-250	4	3	——	6	4.25	23	12	——
	8-350	4	——	——	5	4.25	23	16	17
	8-400	4	——	——	5	4.25	23	16	17
	8-402	4	——	——	8	4.25	23	23	24
	8-454	4	——	——	8	4.25	23	22	23
'73	6-250	4	3	——	5	4.25	26	12	12
	8-350	4	——	——	5	4.25	26	16	17
	8-400	4	——	——	5	4.25	26	16.5	17.5
	8-454	4	——	——	8	4.25	26	23	24
'74	8-350	4	——	——	8	4.25	26	16	16
	8-400	4	——	——	8④	4.25	26	16	16
	8-454	4	——	——	9	4.25	26	22	23
'75	8-350	4	——	——	8	4.25	26	16	16
	8-400	4	——	——	9	4.25	26	16	16
	8-454	4	——	——	9	4.25	26	22	23
'76-'77	6-250	4	3	——	5	4.25	26	12	12
	8-305	4	——	——	8	4.25	26	18	20
	8-350	4	——	——	8	4.25	26	18	20
	8-400	4	——	——	9	4.25	26	18	20
	8-454	4	——	——	9	4.25	26	23	25

- ● Specifications do not include torque converter
- ■ Station wagons: '70—22 gals, '71—23 gals, '72-'77—22 gals
- ▲ With 8.875 diameter ring gear: '70-'71: 4 pts. '72 and later: 4.9 pts.
- ① 17 qts with 300 hp engine
- ② 8 pts with 3-speed Turbo Hydramatic 400
- ③ 5 pts with 3-speed Turbo Hydramatic 350
- ④ 9 with 400 4 bbl
- —— Not applicable

Corvette CAPACITIES

Year	ENGINE No. Cyl. (Cu. In.) Displacement	Engine Crankcase Add 1 Qt For New Filter	TRANSMISSION Pts To Refill After Draining Manual 3-Speed	4-Speed	Automatic ●	Drive Axle (pts) ▲	Gasoline Tank (gals) ■	COOLING SYSTEM (qts) With Heater	With A/C
'70	8-350	4	——	3	8	4	20	15①	18
	8-454	5	——	3	8	4	20	22	22
'71	8-350	4	——	3	8	4	18	15②	18
	8-454	5	——	3	8	4	18	22	22
'72	8-350	4	——	3	8	4	18	15②	18
	8-454	5	——	3	8	4	18	22	24
'73	8-350	4	——	3	8	4	18	18	18
	8-454	5	——	3	8	4	18	24	24
'74	8-350	4	——	3	8	4	18	17	17
	8-454	5	——	3	8	4	18	22	23
'75	8-350	4	——	3	8	4	18	17	17
'76-'77	8-350	4	——	3	8	4	18	18	18

- ● Specifications do not include torque converter
- ① 18 qts with 370 hp
- ② 18 qts with 330 hp
- —— Not applicable

VALVE SPECIFICATIONS

Year	Engine No. Cyl. Displacement (cu in.)	Seat Angle (deg)	Face Angle (deg)	Spring Test Pressure (lbs @ in.)	Spring Installed Height (in.)	STEM TO GUIDE Clearance (in.) Intake	Exhaust	STEM Diameter (in.) Intake	Exhaust
'70	6-250	46	45	60 @ 1.66	1 21/32	.0010-.0037	.0010-.0047	.3414	.3414
	8-350	46	45	80 @ 1.70	1 23/32	.0010-.0037	.0010-.0047	.3414	.3414
	8-400	46	45	80 @ 1.70	1 7/8	.0010-.0037	.0010-.0047	.3414	.3414
	8-454	46	45	75 @ 1.88⑥	1 7/8	.0010-.0037	.0010-.0047	.3718	.3718
	8-454⑦	46	45	75 @ 1.88⑧	1 7/8	.0010-.0037	.0010-.0047	.3718	.3718
'71	6-250	46	45	60 @ 1.66	1 21/32	.0010-.0037	.0010-.0047	.3414	.3714
	8-350	46	45	80 @ 1.70	1 23/32	.0010-.0037	.0010-.0047	.3414	.3714
	8-400	46	45	80 @ 1.70	1 23/32	.0010-.0037	.0010-.0047	.3414	.3714
	8-400⑨	46	45	75 @ 1.88⑥	1 7/8	.0010-.0037	.0010-.0047	.3719	.3717
	8-454	46	45	75 @ 1.88⑥	1 7/8	.0010-.0037	.0010-.0047	.3719	.3717
'72	6-250	46	45	60 @ 1.66	1 21/32	.0010-.0037	.0010-.0047	.3414	.3414
	8-350	46	45	80 @ 1.70	1 23/32	.0010-.0037	.0010-.0047	.3414	.3414
	8-400	46	45	80 @ 1.70	1 23/32	.0010-.0037	.0010-.0047	.3414	.3414
	8-402	46	45	90 @ 1.88	1 7/8	.0010-.0037	.0010-.0047	.3719	.3717
	8-454	46	45	75 @ 1.88⑥	1 7/8	.0010-.0037	.0010-.0047	.3719	.3717
'73	6-250	46	45	60 @ 1.66	1 21/32	.0010-.0027	.0010-.0027	.3414	.3414
	8-350	46	45	80 @ 1.70⑩	1 23/32	.0010-.0027	.0010-.0027	.3414	.3414
	8-400	46	45	80 @ 1.70⑩	1 23/32	.0010-.0027	.0010-.0027	.3414	.3414
	8-454	46	45	80 @ 1.88	1 7/8	.0010-.0027	.0010-.0027	.3719	.3717
'74	8-350	46	45	80 @ 1.70⑩	1 23/32	.0010-.0027	.0010-.0027	.3414	.3414
	8-400	46	45	80 @ 1.70⑩	1 23/32	.0010-.0027	.0010-.0027	.3414	.3414
	8-454	46	45	80 @ 1.88	1 7/8	.0010-.0027	.0010-.0027	.3719	.3717
'75-'77	6-250	46	45	60 @ 1.66	1 21/32	.0010-.0027	.0015-.0032	.3414	.3414
	8-305	46	45	80 @ 1.70	1 23/32	.0010-.0027	.0010-.0027	.3414	.3414
	8-350	46	45	80 @ 1.70⑩	1 23/32	.0010-.0027	.0010-.0027	.3414	.3414
	8-400	46	45	80 @ 1.70⑩	1 23/32	.0010-.0027	.0010-.0027	.3414	.3414
	8-454	46	45	80 @ 1.88	1 7/8	.0010-.0027	.0010-.0027	.3719	.3717

② 45° on engines with aluminum heads
③ 430 hp
④ Inner spring 41 @ 1.78
⑤ 350 hp
⑥ Inner spring 30 @ 1.78
⑦ 460 hp
⑧ Inner spring 41 @ 1.78
⑨ 300 hp
⑩ Intake, 80 @ 1.61 for exhaust spring

TORQUE SPECIFICATIONS

All readings in ft lbs

Year	Engine No. Cyl. Displacement (cu in.)	Cylinder Head Bolts	Rod Bearing Bolts	Main Bearing Bolts	Crankshaft Pulley Bolt	Flywheel to Crankshaft Bolts	MANIFOLD Intake	Exhaust
'70-'73	6-250	95	35	65	——	60	30⑧	25⑦
'77	6-250	95	35	65	——	60		③
'70-'77	8-305, 350, 400	70⑥	45	75②	60	60	30	⑤
'70-'77	8-402 (Big Block)	80①	50	105	85	65	30	30
	8-454	80①	50④	110	85	65	30	30

① Aluminum Heads—Short bolts 65, Long bolts 75
② Engines with 4-bolt mains—Outer bolts 65; 70 starting 1976
③ 30 center, 20 on four end bolts
④ 7/16 Rod bolts—70
⑤ Center bolts—30, end bolts 20
⑥ 65 starting 1976
⑦ Exhaust-to-intake
⑧ Manifold-to-head

CRANKSHAFT AND CONNECTING ROD SPECIFICATIONS

All measurements are given in in.

Year	Engine No. Cyl. Displace. (cu in.)	CRANKSHAFT				CONNECTING ROD		
		Main Brg. Journal Dia	Main Brg. Oil Clearance	Shaft End-Play	Thrust on No.	Journal Diameter	Oil Clearance	Side Clearance
'70	6-250	2.2983-2.2993	.0003-.0029	.002-.006	7	1.9990-2.0000	.0007-.0027	.009-.014
	8-350	2.4484-2.4493⑦	.0003-.0015⑧	.002-.006	5	2.0990-2.1000	.0007-.0028	.008-.014
	8-400 (265 H.P.)	2.6509	.0008-.0020⑨	.002-.006	5	2.0990-2.1000	.0009-.0030	.008-.014
	8-454	2.7485-2.7494③	.0013-.0025⑩	.006-.010	5	2.1990-2.2000	.0009-.0025	.015-.021
	8-454 (460 H.P.)	2.7481-2.7490⑤	.0013-.0025⑪	.006-.010	5	2.1985-2.1995	.0014-.0030	.019-.025
'71	6-250	2.2983-2.2993	.0003-.0029	.002-.006	7	1.9990-2.0000	.0007-.0027	.009-.014
	8-350	2.4484-2.4493⑦	.0008-.0020⑨	.002-.006	5	2.0990-2.1000	.0013-.0035	.008-.014
	8-350 (330 H.P.)	2.4484-2.4493⑦	.0013-.0025⑬	.002-.006	5	2.0990-2.1000	.0013-.0035	.008-.014
	8-400 (255 H.P.)	2.6484-2.6493⑭	.0008-.0020⑨	.002-.006	5	2.0990-2.1000	.0013-.0035	.008-.014
	8-402 (300 H.P.) (Mk. IV)	2.7487-2.7496⑮	.0007-.0019⑯	.006-.010	5	2.1990-2.2000	.0009-.0025	.013-.023
	8-454 (365 H.P.)	2.7485-2.7494⑰	.0013-.0025⑩	.006-.010	5	2.1990-2.2000	.0009-.0025	.015-.021
	8-454 (425 H.P.)	2.7481-2.7490⑤	.0013-.0025⑪	.006-.010	5	2.1985-2.1995	.0009-.0025	.019-.025
'72	6-250	2.2983-2.2993	.0003-.0029	.002-.006	7	1.9990-2.0000	.0007-.0027	.009-.014
	8-350	2.4484-2.4493⑫	.0008-.0020⑨	.002-.006	5	2.0990-2.1000	.0013-.0035	.008-.014
	8-350 (255 H.P.)	2.4484-2.4493⑫	.0013-.0025⑬	.002-.006	5	2.0990-2.1000	.0013-.0035	.008-.014
	8-400 (170 H.P.)	2.6484-2.6493⑭	.0008-.0020⑨	.002-.006	5	2.0990-2.1000	.0013-.0035	.008-.014
	8-402 (210 H.P.)	2.7487-2.7496⑮	.0007-.0019⑯	.006-.010	5	2.1990-2.2000	.0009-.0025	.013-.023
	8-454 (270 H.P.)	2.7485-2.7494⑰	.0013-.0025⑩	.006-.010	5	2.1990-2.2000	.0009-.0025	.015-.021
'73-'77	6-250 All	2.2983-2.2993	.0003-.0029	.002-.006	7	1.9990-2.000	.0007-.0027	.009-.014
	8-305, 350 145, 175 HP	2.4484-2.4493⑱	.0008-.0020⑨	.002-.006	5	2.0990-2.1000	.0013-.0035	.008-.014
	8-350 245, 250 HP auto. trans	2.4484-2.4493⑱	.0019-.0031	.002-.006	5	2.0990-2.1000	.0013-.0035	.008-.014
	8-350 245, 250 HP Manual Trans	2.4484-2.4493⑱	.0013-.0025	.002-.006	5	2.0990-2.1000	.0013-.0035	.008-.014
	8-400	2.6484-2.6493⑲	.0008-.0020⑨	.002-.006	5	2.0990-2.1000	.0013-.0035	.008-.014
	8-454	2.7485-2.7494⑰	.0013-.0025⑩	.006-.010	5	2.1990-2.2000	.0009-.0025	.015-.021

① Not used
② Not used
③ No.'s 3, 4—2.7481-2.7490; No. 5—2.7478-2.7488
④ Not used
⑤ No. 5—2.7478-2.7488
⑥ Not used
⑦ No. 5—2.4479-2.4488
⑧ No.'s 2, 3, 4—.0006-.0018; No. 5—.0008-.0023
⑨ No.'s 2, 3, 4—.011-.0023; No. 5—.0017-.0033
⑩ No. 5—.0024-.0040
⑪ No. 5—.0029-.0045

⑫ No.'s 2, 3, 4—2.4481-2.4490; No. 5—2.4479-2.4488
⑬ No. 5—.0023-.0033; with auto. trans. No. 1—.0019-.0031
⑭ No. 5—2.6479-2.6488
⑮ No.'s 3, 4—2.7481-2.7490; No. 5—2.7473-2.7483
⑯ No.'s 2, 3, 4—.0013-.0025; No. 5—.0019-.0035
⑰ No.'s 2, 3, 4—2.7481-2.7490; No. 5—2.7478-2.7488
⑱ No. 5—2.4508
⑲ No. 5—2.6509
⑳ No.'s 1, 5—2.7499
㉑ No. 1—2.7499; No. 5—2.7505

RING GAP

All measurements are given in inches

Year	Engine No. Cyl.	Top Compression	Bottom Compression
'70-'77	6-250	.010-.020	.010-.020
'77	8-305	.010-.020	.010-.025
'70-'71	8-350	.010-.020①	.013-.025①
'70-'77	8-400, 402, 454	.010-.020	.010-.020
'73-'77	8-350	.010-.020	.013-.025②

Year	Engine No. Cyl.	Oil Control
'70-'77	All	.015-.055

① 250, 300 hp 350 cu in. Top .013-.023
2nd .013-.025
② 210, 250, 255 hp 350 cu in. .013-.023

RING SIDE CLEARANCE
All measurements are given in inches

Year	Engine No. Cyl.	Top Compression	Bottom Compression
'70-'77	6-250	.0012-.0027	.0012-.0032
'70-'77	8-350 2 bbl	.0012-.0032	.0012-.0032
'70-'77	8-305, 8-350 4 bbl	.0012-.0032	.0012-.0027
'70-'77	8-400	.0012-.0027②	.0012-.0032②
'70-'77	8-402, 454	.0017-.0032	.0017-.0032

Year	Engine No. Cyl.	Oil Control
'70-'77	6-250, 8-305, 400	.000-.005③
'70-'77	8-350 2 bbl	.002-.007
'70-'77	8-350 4 bbl	.000-.005
'70-'77	8-402, 454	.0005-.0065

① 250, 275 hp 327 cu in.
Top .0012-.0027
2nd .0012-.0032

② 330 hp 400 cu in.
Top .0017-.0032
2nd .0012-.0032

③ 330 hp 400 cu in.
.0005-.0065

PISTON CLEARANCE

Engine Displacement cu in.	Advertised H.P.	Piston to Bore Clearance (in.) ●
250		.0005-.0025
	145, 155, 165, 175, 185, 190, 195, 200, 250	.0007-.0027

Engine Displacement cu in.	Advertised H.P.	Piston to Bore Clearance (in.) ●
305, 350	300, 350	.0020-.0036
	205, 210, 245, 255, 370	.0036-.0061
400	150, 175, 180, 265	.0014-.0034
	330	.0018-.0038

Engine Displacement cu in.	Advertised H.P.	Piston to Bore Clearance (in.) ●
454	215, 235, 245, 275	.0018-.0035
	345	.0024-.0049
	360	.0024-.0049
	390	.0024-.0049
	450	.0040-.0065

● Service range—minimum to maximum

WHEEL ALIGNMENT SPECIFICATIONS

Year	Model	CASTER Range (deg)	CASTER Pref Setting (deg)	CAMBER Range (deg)	CAMBER Pref Setting (deg)	Toe-in (in.)	Steering Axis Inclin. (deg)	WHEEL PIVOT RATIO (deg) Inner Wheel	WHEEL PIVOT RATIO (deg) Outer Wheel
'70	Chevrolet	¼P to 1¼P	¼P	¼N to ¾P	¼P	⅛ to ¼	7 to 8	20	18
	Corvette	½P to 1½P①	1P	½P to 1¼P②	¾P	3/16 to 5/16②	6½ to 7½	20	18½
'71	Chevrolet	1½N to ½N	1N	0 to 1P	½P	⅛ to ¼	9½ to 10½	N.A.	N.A.
'71-'72	Corvette	½P to 1½P①	1P	¼P to 1¼P	¾P	3/16 to 5/16	6½ to 7½	N.A.	N.A.
'72	Chevrolet	½P to 1½P	1P	0 to 1P	½P	3/16 to 5/16	9½ to 10½	N.A.	N.A.
'73	Chevrolet	0 to 2P	1P	¼P to 1¾P⑤	1P	1/16N to 3/16P	10½	N.A.	N.A.
	Corvette	0 to 2P③	1P	0 to 1½P④	¾P	⅛ to ⅜④	6⅞	N.A.	N.A.
'74	Chevrolet	½-1½P	1P	½-1½P⑤	1P⑥	1/16 to 3/16	9½	N.A.	N.A.
	Corvette	½P-1½P①	1P	¼P-1¼P④	¾P	3/32 to 5/32④	7¾	N.A.	N.A.
'75-'77	Chevrolet	½P-2½P⑧	1½P	½-1½P⑤	1P⑥	1/16 to 3/16	97/64	N.A.	N.A.
	Corvette⑦⑨	½P-1½P①	1P	¼P-1¼P	¾P	1/32 to 3/32	7¾	N.A.	N.A.

① W/power steering—1¾P to 2¾P
② Rear wheel alignment: camber 1⅛N to ⅝N to toe-in 1/32 to 3/32
③ W/power steering—1¼P to 3¼P, 2¼ preferred
④ Rear wheel alignment: camber ⅞N ± ¼. toe-in 2/32 ± 1/32
⑤ Left wheel given, right wheel is ¼N to 1¼P, preferred ½P
⑥ Left wheel given, right wheel is ½P

⑦ Rear wheel alignment through 1975: Camber—11/16N ± ¼; Toe-in—0 ± 1/32
⑧ ½P-1½P W/bias belted tires
⑨ 1976-77 Rear Wheel Alignment: Camber, ⅞N ± ¼; Toe-In, 1/32-3/32

N Negative   P Positive

CHARGING SYSTEM

Repair and test details can be found in the Unit Repair Section.

Alternator Removal and Installation

1. Disconnect the battery cables from the battery terminals.
2. Disconnect and identify the wire leads from the alternator.
3. Remove the alternator brace bolt, then remove belt(s).
4. Remove the alternator pivot attaching bolt and remove alternator from vehicle.
5. To install, reverse the above procedure and adjust belt tension.

Regulator Removal and Installation

1. Disconnect the ground cable at the battery.
2. Disconnect the wiring harness from the regulator.
3. Remove the mounting screws and remove the regulator.
4. Make sure that the regulator base gasket is in place before installation.
5. Clean the attaching area for proper grounding.
6. Install the regulator. Do not overtighten the mounting screws, as this will cancel the cushioning effect of the rubber grommets.

NOTE: An integral alternator/regulator is used starting 1973. Separate removal or adjustment of the regulator is not possible with this unit. This unit is described in the "Unit Repair Section."

STARTING SYSTEM

More information on starters can be found in the Unit Repair Section under Charging and Starting Systems.

Starter Removal and Installation

1. Disconnect the battery and the wires from the solenoid.
NOTE: 1975 and later models do not have a solenoid-to-ignition coil wire, thus eliminating the R terminal on the solenoid.
2. Remove the starter mounting bolt and lock washers. On V8s, a stud nut and lock washer are at the front of the starter.
3. Pull starter forward and out of car.
4. To install, reverse the above procedure.

IGNITION SYSTEM

Three types of ignition systems have been available: a conventional breaker type, an optional Corvette magnetic pulse system, and a High Energy Ignition (HEI) system. The magnetic pulse distributor, which was discontinued in 1972, requires no maintenance.

A resistance wire connects the ignition switch and the coil on the breaker type system. The magnetic pulse system utilizes two; one between the negative coil terminal and ground, the other resistance wire provides a voltage drop for the engine run circuit. The HEI system doesn't use a resistance wire.

The HEI system was used starting in 1974 on 454 cu. in. Chevrolets. All 1975 and later models are equipped with HEI. Description and trouble-shooting for both the magnetic pulse and HEI systems are found in the Electronic Ignition Unit Repair Section.

Distributor Removal

6 Cylinder

The distributor assembly is mounted on the right side of the block and is driven directly from the camshaft.

To remove the distributor, first detach the vacuum lines from the vacuum advance unit and lift off the distributor cap.

The distributor body is fastened to the block by a single cap screw which holds the octane selector plate down against the block. Scribe marks so that the distributor body and rotor can be installed in their original locations. Do not turn engine while the distributor is removed. Remove the retaining screw and lift the distributor out of the block.

V8—Standard Distributor

The distributor is located between the two banks of cylinders at the back of the block.

The drive gear is attached to the distributor shaft; therefore, if it becomes necessary to remove the distributor, carefully mark the position of the rotor. Then, if the engine is not turned after the distributor is taken out, it can be installed in the same position from which is was removed.

To remove the distributor, disconnect the carburetor air cleaner, disconnect the coil primary wire and the vacuum line, remove the distributor cap, take out the single hold-down

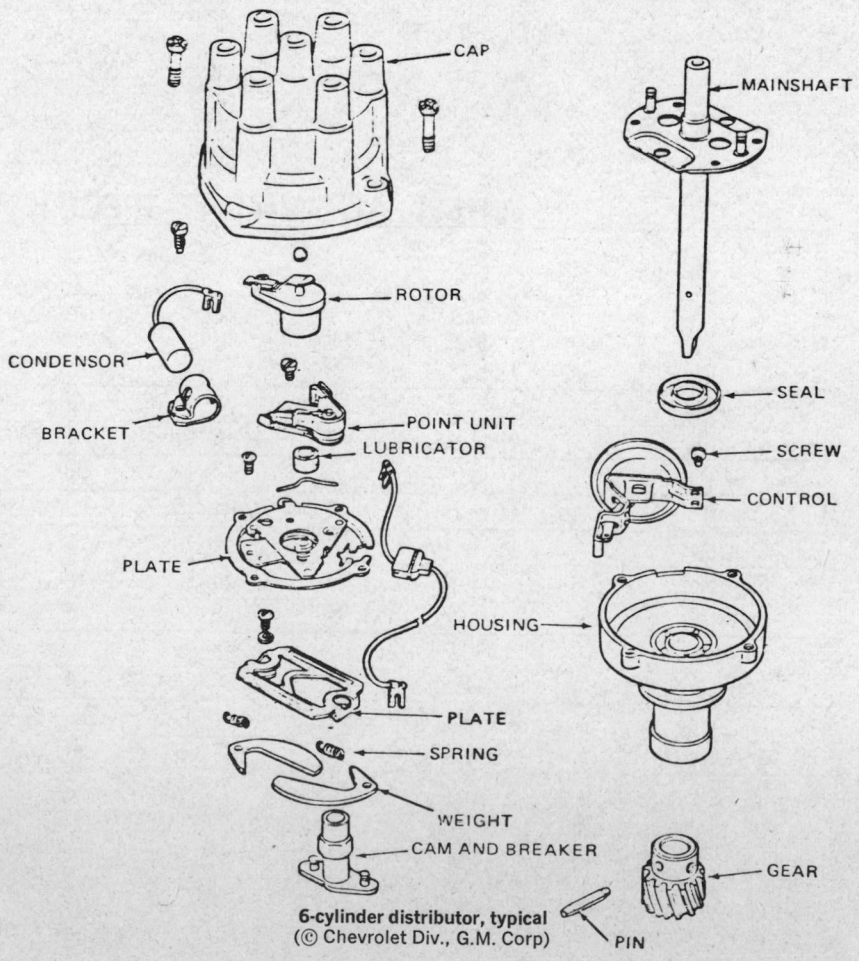

6-cylinder distributor, typical
(© Chevrolet Div., G.M. Corp)

bolt located under the distributor body, mark the position of the body relative to the block and then work the distributor up out of the block.

Magnetic Pulse and HEI Distributor

1. Disconnect pick-up coil connector.
2. Remove distributor cap.
3. Crank engine so that rotor points to No. 1 cylinder plug tower and timing mark on crankshaft pulley is indexed with pointer. Mark the position of the tip of the rotor on the engine block.
4. Remove distributor vacuum line.
5. Remove distributor hold-down bolt and clamp, then remove distributor.
6. When installing the distributor, align the tip of the rotor with the mark that was made on the block.

Distributor Installation (Engine Disturbed)

1. Turn crank until the No. 1 cylinder is at the top of its compression stroke. Remove the No. 1 spark plug to feel the compression.
2. Align the timing mark on the fly-wheel or vibration damper with the indicator.
3. With distributor body oriented in its normal position, hold the rotor pointing toward the front of the engine, then turn the rotor approximately ⅛ turn counterclockwise and push the distributor down until it engages the camshaft, rotating the shaft slightly if necessary.

NOTE: on Mark IV engines there is a punch mark on the distributor drive gear which indicates the rotor position. Thus, the distributor may be installed with the cap in place. Align the punch mark 2° clockwise from the No. 1 cap terminal, then rotate the distributor body clockwise ⅛ turn counterclockwise and push the distributor down into the block.

4. Press down on the distributor and crank the engine to make sure the oil pump shaft is engaged.
5. Return the crankshaft to No. 1 cylinder compression stroke with the timing marks aligned.
6. Turn the distributor body counterclockwise until the points are just beginning to open, then tighten the distributor clamp bolt.
7. Install the distributor cap, checking that the rotor points to the No. 1 terminal. Make sure that the spark plug wires are in their supports and are securely connected.

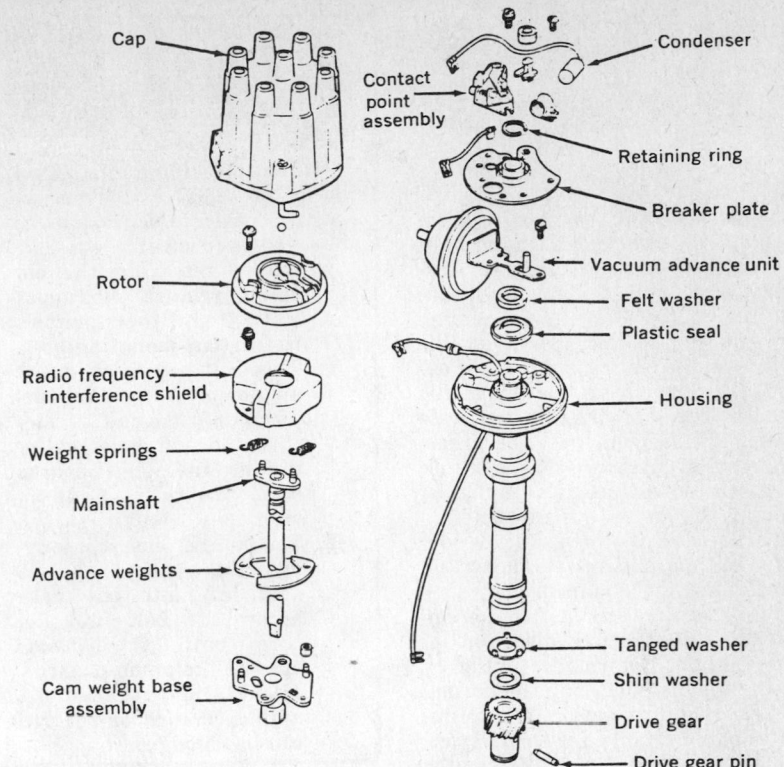

Typical V8 distributor (© Chevrolet Div., G.M. Corp)

8. Connect distributor vacuum line and primary wire.
9. Start engine and set the timing.

Caution When using an auxiliary starter switch for bumping the engine into position for timing, the primary distributor lead must be disconnected from the negative post of the ignition coil and the switch must be in the on position. Failure to do this may cause damage to the grounding circuit in the ignition switch.

Breaker Point Adjustment

NOTE: 1970-72 distributors are equipped with a radio static shield, which must be removed for access to the points.

Breaker point gap (dwell) adjustment is accomplished for 6-cylinder engines by loosening the point assembly attaching screw and adjusting it with a screwdriver until correct gap clearance is obtained (use a feeler gauge). Tighten the point assembly attaching screws and install the distributor cap. Use a dwell meter, if available, to check the dwell angle, readjusting if necessary.

On V8 models there is a window in the distributor cap so that the dwell angle may be set while the engine is running. Use a ⅛ in. Allen (hex) wrench to make the adjustment.

See Tune-Up Specifications at the beginning of this section for correct breaker point gap and dwell angle.

Caution On V8 models the distributor body is involved in the engine lubricating sys-

ADJUST DWELL ANGLE SETTING OR POINT OPENING

6 cylinder point adjustment (© Chevrolet Div., G.M. Corp)

tem. The lubricating circuit to the right-bank valve train can be interrupted by mis-alignment of the distributor body. This can cause serious trouble and may be hard to diagnose. See Firing Order and Timing illustrations for correct distributor positioning.

HEI System Dwell/Tachometer Hookup

Connect one dwell/tach lead to the TACH terminal on the side of the distributor and the other to ground. Some tachometers must be connected to the TACH terminal and the battery positive terminal. Not all tachometers will operate correctly with the HEI system. Check with the manufacturer if there is any doubt.

Caution

The TACH terminal should never be connected to ground.

When hooking up a remote starter switch, disconnect the BATT terminal.

Ignition Timing

Remove the spark plug wire from no. one plug and attach a timing light between the wire and the plug. Disconnect the distributor spark advance hose and plug the vacuum opening. Start the engine and run it at idle speed. Aim the timing light at the degree scale just over the harmonic balancer. The markings on the scale are in 2° increments with the greatest number of markings on the *before* side of the 0. Adjust the timing by loosening the securing clamp and rotating the distributor until the desired ignition advance is achieved, then tighten the clamp. To advance the timing, rotate the distributor opposite to the normal direction of rotor rotation. Retard the timing by rotating the distributor in the normal direction of rotor rotation. When timing an engine equipped with HEI, use an adapter at the No. 1 distributor terminal.

Chilton's TIME SAVER

305, 350, 400 cu. in.

When replacing a fuel pump on a 305, 350, or 400 cu. in. engine, considerable time can be be saved as follows:

1. Before removing the old pump, remove the upper bolt from the engine's right front mounting boss. This bolt hole is in direct alignment with the fuel pump pushrod. The threaded bolt hole continues into the pump pushrod bore. The bolt acts as an oil plug.
2. Temporarily insert a longer bolt, (about ⅜—16 x 2 in.) into the hole. Screw the bolt into the bore until it bottoms against the pump pushrod. (Don't tighten the bolt with a wrench or the rod can be damaged.)

3. The mechanic is now free to remove and install the fuel pump without worrying about fuel pump pushrod misalignment.
   CAUTION: don't forget to reinstall original motor bolt.

402 and 454 cu. in.

The design of these engines prevents the use of the method of simplifying fuel pump pushrod positioning while installing a fuel pump. However, to hold the pump pushrod in position while installing the fuel pump, the following works satisfactorily;

1. Clean oil from pushrod.
2. Pack a small quantity of non-fibrous grease in the area around the fuel pump pushrod to hold it in suspension long enough to position the fuel pump.
3. Install and check pump action, then torque attaching bolts.

FUEL SYSTEM

Data on capacity of the gas tank can be found in the Capacities table. Data on correct engine idle speed and fuel pump pressure can be found in the Tune-up Specifications table.

Information covering operation and troubles of the fuel gauge is in the Unit Repair Section.

Fuel Pump Removal and Installation

To remove the fuel pump, disconnect the input line and the output line to the carburetor. The fuel pump then can be unbolted from the side of the block and lifted off. On V8 models, the pump is actuated by a pushrod in the block.

Caution

A fuel pump may fail to function at the time of replacement as a result of error in positioning or damage to the fuel pump pushrod of the V8 engine. This pushrod can slip out of place during the process of pump replacement and result in no pump action from the newly replaced unit. Before tightening the fuel pump to the engine, have someone spin the engine with the starter while feeling the fuel pump body for movement. If the pump and pushrod are in correct position, movement will be felt in the

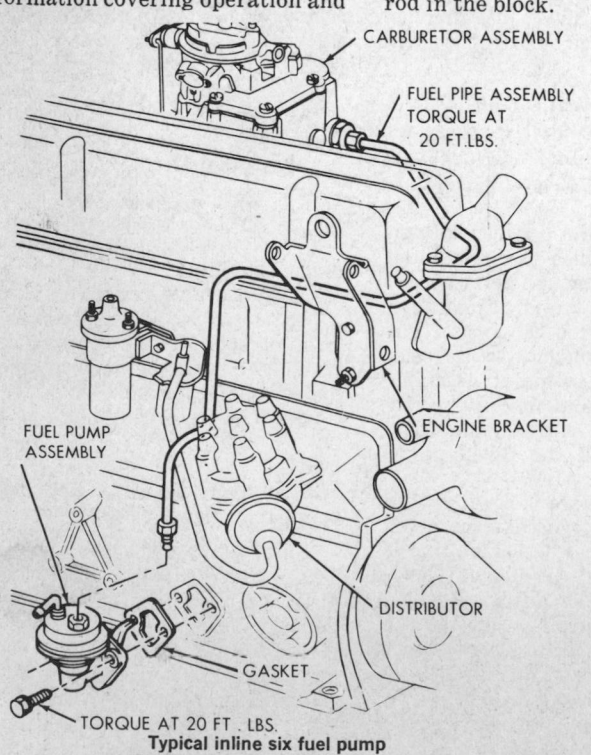

Typical inline six fuel pump
(© Chevrolet Div., G.M. Corp.)

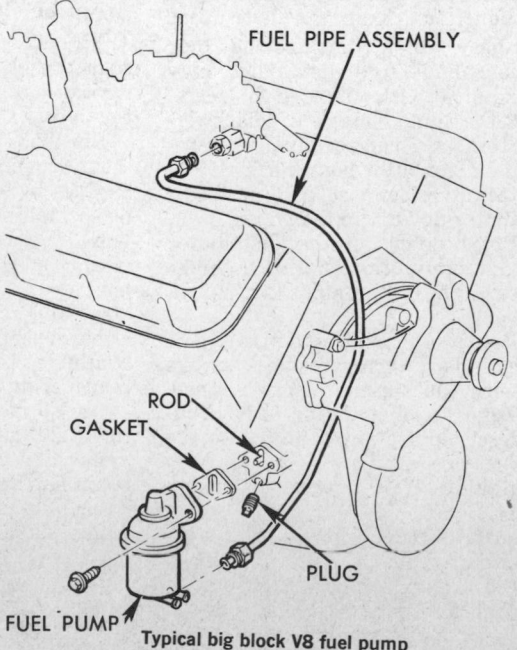

Typical big block V8 fuel pump
(© Chevrolet Div., G.M. Corp.)

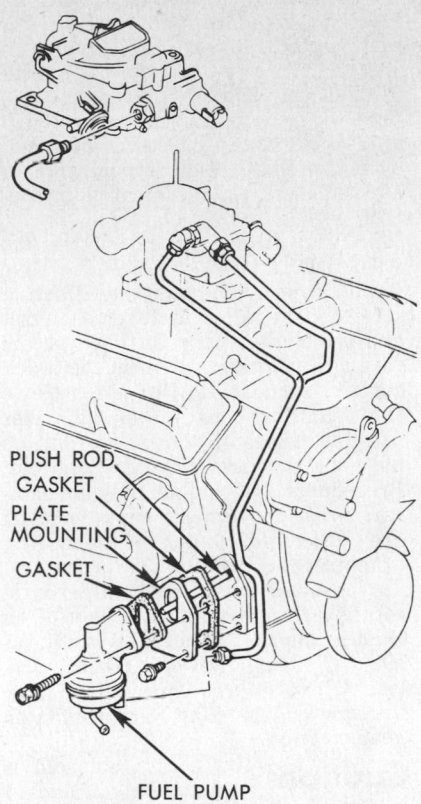

PUSH ROD
GASKET
PLATE
MOUNTING
GASKET

FUEL PUMP

Typical small block V8 fuel pump installation
(© Chevrolet Div., G.M. Corp.)

pump as the pushrod pressure is applied and released from the pump arm.

Fuel Filter Removal and Installation

Fuel filters are integral with the carburetor body. The filter element can be replaced as follows:
1. Disconnect the fuel line.
2. Remove the fuel filter nut from the carburetor.
3. Remove the filter element and spring. Blow through the filter end. If the air does not flow freely, replace the element. Do not attempt to clean the filter element.
4. Install the spring, then the element. Bronze filters in Holley carburetors must have the small section of the cone facing out.
5. Install the inlet fitting using a new gasket.
6. Install the fuel line.

Carburetor Adjustments

When adjusting a carburetor with two idle mixture screws, adjust them alternately and evenly, unless otherwise stated.

See the Unit Repair Section for illustrations and adjustment specifications of Carter, Holley and Rochester carburetors. In the following adjustment procedures the term

"lean roll" means turning the mixture adjusting screws in (clockwise) from optimum setting to obtain an obvious drop in engine speed (usually 20 rpm).

1970 Chevrolet

Adjust with air cleaner installed. If the vehicle is equipped with Evaporative Emission, disconnect the fuel tank line from the vapor canister while making the idle speed and mixture adjustments. Warm up the engine and leave it running with the choke and, if applicable, air cleaner damper door fully open and the air conditioning off.

250 Engine

1. Disconnect and plug the distributor vacuum hose at the distributor end.
2. Turn the idle mixture screw in until it lightly contacts the seat, back it out 4 turns.
3. Adjust the solenoid plunger to obtain 830 rpm (manual transmission in Neutral) or 630 rpm (automatic transmission in Drive).
4. Adjust mixture screw in to obtain 750 rpm (manual transmission in Neutral) or 600 rpm (automatic transmission in Drive).
5. Disconnect the solenoid wire and, with the solenoid plunger depressed, adjust the carburetor idle speed screw to obtain 400 rpm.
6. Reconnect the solenoid wire and distributor vacuum hose.

400 (265 H.P.) Engine

1. Disconnect and plug the distributor vacuum hose at the distributor end.
2. Turn the idle mixture screws in until they lightly contact the seats, then back them out 4 turns.
3. With manual transmission in Neutral, adjust the carburetor idle speed screw to obtain 800 rpm. With automatic transmission in Drive, adjust the solenoid plunger to obtain 630 rpm.
4. Adjust the idle mixture screws in equally to obtain 700 rpm (manual transmission in Neutral) or 600 rpm (automatic transmission in Drive).
5. If equipped with automatic transmission, disconnect the solenoid wire and, with solenoid plunger depressed, set the carburetor idle speed screw to obtain 450 rpm.
6. Reconnect the solenoid wire and the distributor vacuum hose.

350 (250 H.P.) Engine

1. Disconnect and plug the dis-

tributor vacuum hose at the distributor end.
2. Turn the idle mixture screws in until they lightly contact the seats, then back them out 4 turns.
3. With manual transmission in Neutral, adjust the solenoid plunger to obtain 830 rpm. With automatic transmission in Drive, adjust the solenoid plunger to obtain 630 rpm.
4. Adjust the idle mixture screws in equally to obtain 750 rpm (manual transmission in Neutral) or 600 rpm (automatic transmission in Drive).
5. Disconnect the solenoid wire and, with the solenoid plunger fully depressed, set the carburetor idle speed screw to obtain 450 rpm.
6. Reconnect the solenoid wire and distributor vacuum hose.

350 (300 H.P.) Engine

1. Disconnect the vacuum hose at the distributor and plug the hose.
2. Turn the idle mixture screws in until they lightly contact the seats, then back them out 4 turns.
3. With manual transmission in Neutral, adjust the carburetor idle speed screw to obtain 775 rpm. With automatic transmission in Drive, adjust the carburetor idle speed screw to obtain 630 rpm.
4. Adjust the mixture screws in equally to obtain 700 rpm (manual transmission in Neutral) or 600 rpm (automatic transmission in Drive).
5. Reconnect the distributor vacuum hose.

454 (450 H.P.) Engine

1. *Remove the air cleaner.*
2. Disconnect the distributor vacuum hose at the distributor and plug the hose.
3. Adjust the mixture screws for maximum idle speed.
4. With manual transmission in Neutral, adjust the carburetor idle speed screw to obtain 750 rpm. With automatic transmission in Drive, adjust the carburetor idle speed screw to obtain 700 rpm.
5. Turn one idle mixture screw to obtain a 20 rpm drop in idle speed, then back the screw out 1/4 turn. Repeat for the second idle mixture screw.
6. Repeat Step 4 above.
7. Reconnect the distributor vacuum hose and install the air cleaner.

454 (345 H.P.) and 454 (390 H.P.) Engines

1. Disconnect the distributor vac-

uum hose at the distributor and plug the hose.

2. Turn the idle mixture screws in they are lightly seated, then back them out 4 turns.

3. With automatic transmission in Drive, adjust the carburetor idle speed screw to obtain 630 rpm. Adjust the idle mixture screws in equally to obtain 600 rpm.

4. With manual transmission in Neutral, adjust the carburetor idle speed screw to obtain 700 rpm. Turn one of the mixture screws in until the engine speed drops to 400 rpm. Readjust the idle speed screw to obtain 700 rpm. Turn in the other mixture screw until the engine speed drops 40 rpm. Readjust the idle speed screw to obtain 700 rpm.

5. Reconnect the distributor vacuum hose.

1970 Corvette
Adjust with air cleaner installed. If the vehicle is equipped with Evaporative Emission, disconnect the fuel tank line from the vapor canister while making the idle speed and mixture adjustments. Warm up the engine and leave it running while adjusting. The choke valve and, if applicable, air cleaner damper door should remain open. Leave the air conditioning off.

350 (300, 350 and 370 H.P.) Engines

1. Adjust the idle mixture screws equally to obtain maximum idle speed.

2. On the 300 H.P. engine with manual transmission in Neutral adjust the idle speed screw to obtain 700 rpm. On the 300 H.P. engine with automatic transmission in Drive, adjust the idle speed screw to obtain 600 rpm.

3. On the 350 and 370 H.P. engines, adjust the idle speed screw to obtain 750 rpm with the manual transmission in Neutral.

427 (390 H.P. and 400 H.P.) Without Air Conditioning

1. Adjust the idle mixture screws to obtain the maximum idle rpm.

2. On the 390 H.P. engine with manual transmission in Neutral, adjust the idle speed screw to obtain 800 rpm. On the 390 engine with automatic transmission in Drive, adjust the idle speed screw to obtain 600 rpm.

3. On the 400 H.P. engine with manual transmission in Neutral, adjust the idle speed screw to obtain 750 rpm. On the 400 H.P. engine with automatic transmission in Drive, adjust the idle speed screw to obtain 600 rpm.

427 (390 and 400 H.P.) With Manual Transmission and Air Conditioning

1. Turn the air conditioning off and disconnect the wire from the idle-stop solenoid.

2. Adjust the idle mixture screws to obtain the maximum idle speed.

3. With transmission in Neutral, adjust the idle speed screw to obtain 550 rpm.

4. Turn each idle mixture screw in to obtain a 20 rpm drop, then back out each screw ¼ turn.

5. Turn on the air conditioning and reconnect the wire to the idle-stop solenoid.

6. Adjust the solenoid plunger to obtain 1,000 rpm.

427 (390 and 400 H.P.) with Automatic Transmission and Air Conditioning

1. Turn the air conditioning on.

2. Adjust the mixture screws to obtain the maximum idle speed.

3. Adjust the solenoid plunger to obtain 650 rpm with the transmission in Drive.

4. Adjust each mixture screw to obtain a 20 rpm drop in engine speed, then back out each screw ¼ turn.

5. Readjust the solenoid plunger to obtain 650 rpm.

6. Disconnect the solenoid wire and, with the plunger depressed, adjust the carburetor idle speed screw to obtain 500 rpm.

7. Reconnect the solenoid wire.

427 (430 and 435 H.P.) Engines

1. Adjust the idle mixture screws alternately and evenly to obtain the maximum smooth idle speed.

2. With the automatic transmission in Drive, adjust the solenoid plunger to obtain 750 rpm.

3. With the manual transmission in Neutral, adjust the carburetor idle speed screw to obtain 750 rpm (435 H.P.) or 1,000 rpm (430 H.P.).

4. Disconnect the solenoid wire (automatic transmission models only) and, with the solenoid plunger fully depressed, adjust the carburetor idle speed screw to obtain 500 rpm.

5. If necessary, readjust the carburetor idle screw (manual transmission) or the solenoid plunger (automatic transmission) to obtain the speeds specified in Steps 2 and 3.

All 1971—Initial Adjustments
Adjust with air cleaner installed. The following initial idle adjustments are part of the normal engine tune-up. There is a tune-up decal placed conspicuously in the engine compartment outlining the specific procedure and settings for each engine application. Follow all of the instructions when adjusting the idle. These tuning procedures are necessary to obtain the delicate balance of variables for the maintenance of both reliable engine performance and efficient exhaust emission control.

NOTE: all engines except the 350 (330 H.P.) and 454 (425 H.P.) have limiter caps on the mixture adjusting screws. The idle mixture is preset and the limiter caps installed at the factory in order to meet emission control standards. Do not remove these limiter caps unless all other possible causes of poor idle condition have been thoroughly checked out. Procedures for setting the idle mixture with the limiter caps removed are described under the heading "Complete Adjustment" later on.

The solenoid used on 1971 carburetors is different from the one used on earlier models. Combination Emission Control System (C.E.C. solenoid) valve regulates distributor vacuum as a function of transmission gear position.

Caution The C.E.C. solenoid is adjusted only after: 1) replacement of the solenoid, 2) major carburetor overhaul, or 3) after the throttle body is removed or replaced. Instructions for C.E.C. solenoid plunger adjustment are contained in the Unit Repair Section.

All initial adjustments described below are made:

1. With the engine warmed up and running.

2. With the choke fully open.

3. With the fuel tank line disconnected from the Evaporative Emission canister on all models except the Corvette.

4. With the fuel tank gas cap removed on the Corvette.

5. With the vacuum hose disconnected at the distributor and plugged.

Be sure to reconnect the distributor vacuum hose and to connect the fuel tank to evaporative emission canister line or install the gas cap when idle adjustments are complete.

350 (4-bbl Quadrajet) Engines

Adjust the carburetor idle speed screw (NOT the solenoid plunger) to obtain 550 rpm (manual transmission in Neutral) or 500 rpm (automatic transmission in Drive).

350 and 400 (2-bbl) and 350 (4-bbl Quadrajet) Engines

Adjust the carburetor idle speed screw (NOT the solenoid plunger) to obtain 600 rpm (manual transmission in Neutral with the air conditioner off) or 550 rpm (automatic transmission in Drive with the air conditioner on).

*350 and 454 (4-bbl Holley) Engines
—Corvette*

1. Adjust the carburetor idle speed screw (NOT the solenoid plunger) to obtain 700 rpm (manual transmission in Neutral or automatic transmission in Drive).
2. Adjust the idle mixture screws alternately to obtain the maximum smooth idle speed.
3. Adjust one of the idle mixture screws to obtain a 20 rpm drop ("lean roll"), then back it out ¼ turn.
4. Repeat Step 4 above for the other idle mixture screw.
5. Readjust the carburetor idle speed screw to obtain 700 rpm if necessary.

402 and 454 (4-bbl Quadrajet) Engines

Turn the air conditioner off. Adjust the carburetor idle speed screw (NOT the solenoid plunger) to obtain 600 rpm (manual transmission in Neutral or automatic transmission in Drive).

All 1971—Complete Adjustment

The adjustment of the idle mixture requiring the removal of the limiter caps is only made after carburetor overhaul, throttle body part replacement, mixture needle part replacement or limiter cap and needle removal. Before proceeding, follow the tuning instructions on the tune-up decal (refer to "All 1971—Initial Adjustment").

1. Turn the idle mixture screw/s in until lightly contact the seat, then back out 4 turns.
2. Referring to the chart ("Idle Mixture Adjustment"), adjust the idle speed screw (NOT the solenoid plunger) to obtain the "initial idle speed" listed in Column #1.
3. Hook-up a CO (carbon monoxide) gas analyzer to the vehicle.
4. Adjust the idle mixture screw (both screws equally on 2- and 4-BBL carburetors) to obtain the specified %CO reading (Column #3).
5. Readjust the idle speed screw (NOT the solenoid plunger) to obtain the specified "final idle speed" (Column #2).
6. Install service idle mixture screw limiter cap/s on the idle mixture screws (except on Holley carburetors).
7. Reconnect the distributor vacuum hose.
8. Reconnect the fuel tank vapor hose or, on Corvettes, install the fuel tank cap.
NOTE: if a CO analyzer is unavailable, the following alternate procedure may be used to adjust the idle mixture.

1. Turn the idle mixture screw/s in until lightly seated, then back out 4 full turns.
2. Adjust the carburetor idle speed screw (NOT the solenoid plunger) to obtain the "initial idle speed" (see Column #1 of "Idle Mixture Adjustment" chart).
3. Adjust the idle mixture screw/s to obtain the "final idle speed" (see Column #2 in the "Idle Mixture Adjustment" chart).
4. Install service idle limiter cap/s on mixture screws.
5. Reconnect the distributor vacuum hose and fuel vapor line.

1972

NOTE: all carburetors are equipped with idle limiter caps and idle mixture is preset at the factory and should not require adjustment.

1. On Chevrolet models, disconnect the fuel tank line from the vapor storage canister. On Corvettes, remove the fuel filler cap but do not remove the vapor line.
2. Detach the distributor vacuum hose and plug the hose.
3. Set the parking brake and turn the air conditioner (if so equipped) off. On cars equipped with an automatic transmission, chock the wheels.
4. Allow the engine to reach normal operating temperature. Be sure that the choke is open.
5. If the car has an automatic transmission, set the selector in Drive. If the car has a manual transmission keep the transmission in Neutral.
6. Adjust the anti-dieseling solenoid to the *higher* of the two rpm figures given in the specifications.

Caution Do not turn the solenoid more than one complete turn unless the electrical lead is disconnected (solenoid de-energized).

7. Disconnect the solenoid lead and set the idle speed to the *lower* of the two figures given in the specifications. Use an allen wrench in the end of the solenoid for this adjustment, on six cylinder engines. On V8's use the normal idle speed adjusting screw.
NOTE: if no lower figure is given, adjust the idle to 450 rpm.
8. Reconnect all of the wires and hoses which were disconnected in order to perform these adjustments.

1973

All models are equipped with idle limiter caps and idle solenoids. Disconnect the fuel tank line from the evaporative canister. The engine must be running at operating temperature, choke off, parking brake on,

and rear wheels blocked. Disconnect the distributor vacuum hose and plug it. After adjustment, reconnect the vacuum and evaporative hoses.

250 cu in. Six-Cylinder

Adjust the idle stop solenoid for 700 rpm on manual transmission models or 600 rpm on automatics. On manual models, make no attempt to adjust the CEC solenoid (the larger of the two carburetor solenoids) or a decrease in engine braking could result.

Two-barrel 350 and 400 cu in. V8s

1. With air conditioning switched off, adjust the idle stop solenoid screw for a speed of 900 rpm on manual models; 600 rpm on automatics.
2. De-energize the idle stop solenoid and adjust the idle speed screw (screw resting on lower step of the cam) for 400 rpm on 350 and 400 engines with automatic transmission, or 500 rpm on 350 engines with manual transmission.

Four-barrel 350 and 454 cu in. V8s

1. Adjust the idle stop solenoid screw for 900 rpm on manual, 600 rpm on automatic.
2. Connect the distributor vacuum hose and position the fast idle cam follower on the top step of the fast idle cam (turn air conditioning off) and adjust the fast idle to 1300 rpm on manual transmission 350 engines; 1600 on manual 454 engines and all automatics (in Park).

Optional Corvette 350 cu in. (L82) V8

1. Adjust the idle stop solenoid screw (air conditioning off) for a speed of 900 rpm on manual transmission; 700 rpm on automatic (in Drive).
2. Connect the distributor vacuum hose and position the fast idle cam follower on the top step of the cam (turn air conditioning off) and adjust the fast idle to 1300 rpm on manual; 1600 rpm on automatic.

1974

The same preconditions as for 1973 apply.

Two-barrel 350 and 400 cu in. V8s

1. Turn the air conditioning off. Adjust the idle stop solenoid screw for 900 rpm on manual; 600 rpm on automatic (in Drive).
2. De-energize the solenoid and adjust the carburetor idle cam screw (on low step of cam) for 400 rpm on automatic models (in Drive); 500 rpm on 350 engines with manual transmission.

Four-barrel 350 and 400 cu in. V8s

1. Turn the air conditioning off. Adjust the idle stop solenoid screw for 900 rpm on manual transmission models; 600 rpm on automatic (in Drive).
2. Connect the distributor vacuum hose. Position the fast idle cam follower on the top step of the fast idle cam and adjust the fast idle speed to 1300 rpm on manual; 1600 on automatic (in Park).

Optional Corvette 350 cu in. (L82) V8

1. Turn the air conditioning off. Adjust the idle stop solenoid for 900 rpm on manual; 700 rpm on automatic (in Drive).
2. Connect the distributor vacuum hose. Position the fast idle cam follower on the top step of the cam and adjust the fast idle to 1300 rpm on manual; 1600 rpm on automatic (in Park).

454 cu in. V8

1. Shut off the air conditioning. Adjust the idle stop solenoid screw for 800 rpm on manual; 600 rpm on automatic (in Drive).
2. Connect the distributor vacuum hose and position the fast idle cam follower on the top step of the cam and adjust the fast idle to 1600 rpm on manual; 1500 rpm on automatic (in Park).

1975-76

The engine must be at normal operating temperature with the air-cleaner on, the choke open, the air conditioner off, and the timing correctly set.

1. Set the brake and block the wheels.
2. Set the automatic transmission in Drive and the manual in neutral. Disconnect the fuel tank hose from the vapor canister in the engine compartment.
3. Use needle nose pliers to break off the mixture screw cap or caps.

2 bbl

4. Adjust the idle speed with the idle speed screw to obtain the higher idle speed shown on the sticker.

4 bbl

Disconnect the electrical connector at the idle solenoid, and adjust the idle speed to the lower of the two figures given on the sticker. Reconnect the electrical connector, open the throttle to extend the solenoid plunger, then turn the solenoid plunger screw to obtain the higher of the two idle speed figures. For 1976, the idle solenoid has been dropped; the idle is adjusted with an idle speed screw.

5. On the 4 bbl, turn out the mixture screws until the highest possible idle speed is reached. If the idle speed becomes excessive (more than that set in Step 4), reset the idle speed to that set in Step 4. On the 2 bbl., turn out the mixture screws to obtain the highest idle and then, turn in the mixture screws to obtain the lower of the two figures listed on the sticker.
6. Turn in the mixture screws equally until the normal idle speed is reached.
7. Replace the vapor canister hose.

COOLING SYSTEM

Cooling system capacities for the various models can be found in the Capacities table at the beginning of this section. Information on the water temperature gauge can be found in the Unit Repair Section.

Radiator Removal and Installation

Chevrolet

1. Drain the cooling system.
2. Disconnect the radiator upper and lower hoses and, if applicable, transmission coolant lines. Remove the coolant recovery system line, if so equipped.
3. Remove the radiator upper panel if so equipped.
4. If there is a radiator shroud in front of the radiator, the radiator and shroud are removed as an assembly.
5. If there is a fan shroud, remove the shroud attaching screws let the shroud hang on the fan.
6. Remove the radiator attaching bolts and remove the radiator.
7. Installation is the reverse of the removal procedure.

Corvette Through 1974

1. Drain the radiator.
2. Raise the hood and insert a bolt in the hole of the hood support. Remove the hood.
3. Remove the radiator inlet and outlet hoses and, if applicable, the transmission coolant hoses.
4. If applicable, remove the supply tank hose at the radiator connection.
5. Remove the shroud to radiator support bracket screws (the L88 engine does not have a fan shroud).
6. Remove the shroud to radiator baffle bracket screws and let the shroud rest on the fan.
7. Remove the radiator upper support bracket screws and care-

fully lift the radiator from the car.

8. Install in the reverse order of removal.

1975 and later Corvette

1. Drain the radiator and disconnect the battery ground cable. Disconnect cooler lines on automatic transmission models.
2. Remove the hood. This is a two man job.
3. Remove the radiator support brackets attached to the fan shroud.
4. Remove the two front hood hinge bolts.
5. From inside the wheel well, remove the six radiator side support bolts.
6. Remove the two bottom radiator support bolts and the center brace.
7. Pull the radiator support forward and use a clamp to retain it to the right hood hinge.
8. Disconnect the two radiator hoses and the overflow hose.
9. Carefully lift the radiator out of the car.
10. If replacing the radiator, remove the shrouds and mount them on the new unit.
11. Installation is the reverse of removal.

Water Pump Removal and Installation

1. Drain the radiator and loosen the fan pulley bolts.
2. Disconnect the heater hose, lower radiator hose and, if applicable, the bypass hose at the water pump.
3. On V8 engines, remove the Delcotron upper brace. Loosen the swivel bolt and remove the fan belt.
4. On big block engines, disconnect the power steering and air conditioning belts and swivel the power steering pump to one side.
5. Remove the fan blade and pulley. Replace a bent or damaged fan.

NOTE: thermostatic fan clutches must be kept in an "in-car" position. When removed from the car the assembly should be supported so that the clutch disc remains in a vertical plane to prevent silicone fluid leakage.

6. Remove the water pump attaching bolts and, if applicable, the power steering-to-pump bolts and remove the pump and gasket.

NOTE: on six-cylinder engines, pull the pump straight out of the block first to avoid damage to the impeller.

7. Install the pump assembly using a new gasket. Coat the gasket on both sides with sealer. Tighten

the 5/16 in. bolts to 15 ft. lbs. (six-cylinder) and the 3/8 in. bolts (V8) to 30 ft. lbs.

8. Install the pulley and fan.
9. On big block engines, install the power steering and air conditioning bolts.
10. Connect the hoses and fill the cooling system.
11. On V8 engines, install the Delcotron upper brace and fan belt. Install the power steering pump bolt.
12. Adjust the belts, then start the engine and check for leaks.

Thermostat Removal and Installation

The thermostat is located inside a housing on the front of the cylinder head on six-cylinder engines and between the intake manifold and the cylinder head (forward) on V8 engines. It is not necessary to remove the radiator hose from the thermostat housing.

1. Remove the two retaining bolts from the thermostat housing and lift up the housing with the hose attached. Remove the thermostat.
2. Insert the new thermostat, spring end down, and install the housing with a new gasket.

EMISSION CONTROLS

Positive Crankcase Ventilation

In this system, crankcase vapors are drawn into the intake manifold and burned as part of the engine combustion. The "closed positive" system draws clean air from the carburetor air cleaner. The ventilation flow is regulated by a PCV valve located in the valve cover.

Air Injection Reactor

The A.I.R. system injects compressed air into the exhaust system, close enough to the exhaust valves to continue the burning of the normally unburned segment of the exhaust gases. To do this it employs an air injection pump and a system of hoses, valves, tubes, etc., necessary to carry the compressed air from the pump to the exhaust manifolds. Carburetors and distributors for A.I.R. engines have specific modifications to adapt them to the air injection system; these components should not be interchanged with those intended for use on engines that do not have the system.

A diverter valve is used to prevent backfiring. The valve senses sudden increases in manifold vacuum and ceases the injection of air during fuel-rich periods. During coasting, this valve diverts the entire air flow through the muffler and during high engines speeds, expels it through a relief valve. Check valves in the system prevent exhaust gases from entering the pump.

On models with catalytic converters, it is not necessary to inject the air close to the exhaust valves. For this reason, not all models are equipped with manifolds on the exhaust manifolds for air injection as in previous years. Instead, one large pipe is used to inject air into the exhaust pipe ahead of the converter. Some models use part of the old system, but utilize only two or three of the injection nozzles on the exhaust manifold.

Controlled Combustion System

This system increases combustion efficiency by means of leaner carburetor mixtures and revised distributor calibration. On most installations, thermostatically controlled air cleaner intakes draw warm air from an exhaust manifold shroud. This allows leaner carburetor settings and improves engine warm-up. A higher temperature thermostat is employed on C.C.S. cars.

Particular attention must be paid to the tuning of C.C.S. equipped engines to maintain performance and efficient exhaust emission control.

Evaporative Emission Control

Introduced on California cars in 1970, and nationwide in 1971, this system reduces the amount of escaping gasoline vapors. Float bowl emissions are controlled by internal carburetor modifications. Redesigned bowl vents, reduced bowl capacity, heat shields, and improved intake manifold-to-carburetor insulation serve to reduce vapor loss into the atmosphere. The venting of fuel tank vapors into the air has been stopped. Fuel vapors are now directed through lines to a canister containing an activated charcoal filter. Unburned vapors are trapped here until the engine is started. When the engine is running, the canister is purged by air drawn in by manifold vacuum. The air and fuel vapors are then directed into the engine to be burned. This system is designed to reduce fuel vapor emission. The canister filter should be replaced every 12 months or 12,000 miles. To replace the filter, proceed as follows:

The filter is located in the bottom of the canister. Pull out the old filter and work the new filter into place. It may be necessary, on earlier models, to remove the bottom of the canister for access.

Anti-Dieseling Solenoid

Some models may have an idle speed solenoid on the carburetor. All 1972-74 models have idle solenoids. Due to the leaner carburetor settings required for emission control, the engine may have a tendency to "diesel" or "run-on" after the ignition is turned off. The carburetor solenoid, energized when the ignition is on, maintains the normal idle speed. When the ignition is turned off, the solenoid is de-energized and permits the throttle valves to fully close, thus preventing run-on. For adjustment of carburetors with idle solenoids see Carburetor Adjustments.

Transmission Controlled Spark

Introduced in 1970, this system controls exhaust emissions by eliminating vacuum advance in the lower forward gears.

1970

The 1970 system consists of a transmission switch, solenoid vacuum switch, time delay relay, and a thermostatic water temperature switch. The solenoid vacuum switch is energized in the lower gears via the transmission switch and closes off distributor vacuum. The two-way transmission switch is activated by the shifter shaft on manual transmissions, and by oil pressure on automatic transmissions. The switch de-energizes the solenoid in high gear, the plunger extends and uncovers the vacuum port, and the distributor receives full vacuum. The temperature switch overrides the system when engine temperature is below 63° or above 232°. This allows vacuum advance in all gears. A time delay relay opens 15 seconds after the ignition is switched on. Full vacuum advance during this delay eliminates the possibility of stalling.

1971

The 1971 system is similar, except that the vacuum solenoid (now called a Combination Emissions Control solenoid) serves two functions. One function is to control distributor vacuum; the added function is to act as a deceleration throttle stop in high gear. This cuts down on emissions when the vehicle is coming to a stop in high gear. The CEC solenoid is controlled by a temperature switch, a transmission switch, and a 20 second time delay relay. This system also contains a reversing relay, which energizes the solenoid when the transmission switch, temperature switch or time delay completes the CEC circuit to ground. This system is directly opposite the 1970 system in operation. The 1970 vacuum solenoid was normally open to allow vacuum advance and when energized, closed to block vacuum. The 1971 system is normally closed blocking vacuum advance and when energized, opens to allow vacuum advance. The temperature switch completes the CEC circuit to ground when engine temperature is below 82°. Some Camaros and Corvettes also have a high temperature terminal on the switch to complete the CEC circuit when coolant temperature reaches 232°. The time delay relay allows vacuum advance (and raised idle speed) for 20 seconds after the ignition key is turned to the "on" position. Models with an automatic transmission and air conditioning also have a solid state timing device which engages the air conditioning compressor for three seconds after the ignition key is turned to the "off" position to prevent the engine from running-on. Two throttle settings are necessary; one for curb idle and one for emission control on coast. Both settings are described in the tune-up section.

1972-74

The 1972-73 L6 system is similar to that used in 1971, except that an idle stop solenoid has been added to the system. In the energized position, the solenoid maintains engine speed at a predetermined fast idle. When de-energized the solenoid allows the throttle plates to close beyond the normal idle position; thus cutting off the air supply and preventing engine run-on. The L6 is the only 1972-74 engine with a CEC valve, which serves the same deceleration function as in 1971. The 1972 time delay relay delays full vacuum 20 seconds after the transmission is shifted into high gear. On 1973-74 models, the delay relay is replaced by a time relay which energizes the CEC valve for 20 seconds after the key is turned to the On position. This relay is not used on 1973 V8 engines with small blocks. V8 engines use a vacuum advance solenoid similar to that used in 1970. This relay is normally closed to block vacuum and opens when energized to allow vacuum advance. The solenoid controls distributor vacuum advance and performs no throttle positioning function. The idle stop solenoid used operates in the same manner as the one on L6 engines. All air-conditioned cars have an additional anti-diesel (run-on) solenoid which engages the compressor clutch for three seconds after the ignition is switched off. The 1973-74 Chevrolet TCS system differs from the 1972 system in three ways. The 23 second upshift delay has been replaced by a 20 second starting relay. This relay closes to complete the TCS circuit and open the TCS solenoid, allowing vacuum advance, for 20 seconds after the key is turned to the "on" position. The operating temperature of the temperature override switch has been raised to 93°, and the switch that was used to engage the A/C compressor when the key was

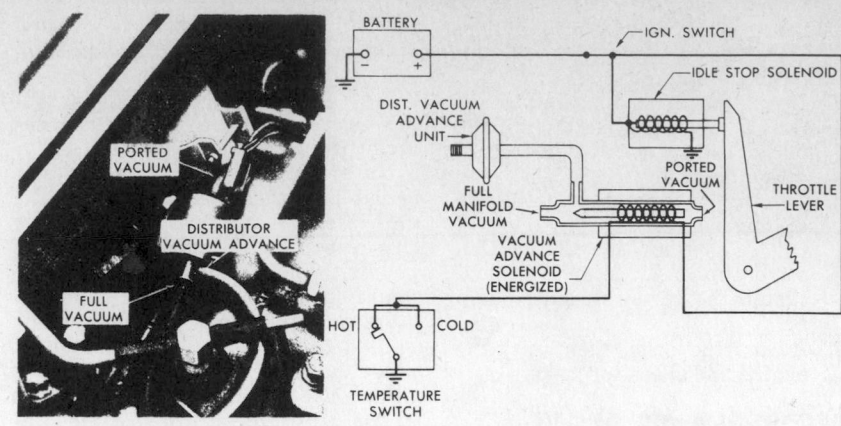

1973-74 Corvette Thermo-Override System (© Chevrolet Div., G.M. Corp)

turned "off" has been eliminated. All models are equipped with an electric throttle control solenoid to prevent run-on. The 1973 TCS system is used on all full-size station wagons equipped with a 165 hp 350 or a 170 hp 400. The 1974 TCS system is used only on manual transmission models. System components remain unchanged from 1973. The vacuum advance solenoid is located on the coil bracket.

1973-74 Corvette models are equipped with a Thermo-Override system instead of the normal TCS system. This system consists of a three-position temperature switch, which is mounted in the right cylinder head and a two-position vacuum advance solenoid. Three vacuum lines are connected to the solenoid, a ported vacuum line from the carburetor, a vacuum line from the intake manifold, and a vacuum line that runs to the distributor vacuum advance unit. When the engine temperature is between 93°F and 232°F, the temperature switch contacts are open and the vacuum solenoid is de-energized. This causes carburetor-ported vacuum to control the operation of the distributor vacuum advance unit. When the engine temperature is below 93°F or above 232°F, the temperature switch contacts are closed and the vacuum solenoid is energized. This moves the plunger in the solenoid to block the ported vacuum opening and connect manifold vacuum to the distributor. When the engine reaches normal temperature, the temperature switch contacts open and ported vacuum is restored to the distributor.

For diagnosis procedures, see the Unit Repair Section. Any of the methods of exhaust emission control requires close and frequent attention to tune-up factors of engine maintenance. TCS is not used on 1975 and later models.

Exhaust Gas Recirculation

All 1973 and later engines are equipped with exhaust gas recircula-

tion (EGR). This system consists of a metering valve, a vacuum line to the carburetor, and cast-in exhaust gas passages in the intake manifold. The EGR valve is controlled by carburetor vacuum, and accordingly opens and closes to admit exhaust gases into the fuel/air mixture. The exhaust gases lower the combustion temperature, and reduce the amount of oxides of nitrogen (NOx) produced. The valve is closed at idle and wide open throttle, but is open between the two extreme throttle positions.

As the car accelerates, the carburetor throttle plate uncovers the vacuum port for the EGR valve. At 3–5 in. Hg, the EGR valve opens and then some of the exhaust gases are allowed to flow into the air/fuel mixture to lower the combustion temperature. At full-throttle the valve closes again.

400 cu. in. California engines are equipped with a dual diaphragm EGR valve. This valve further limits the exhaust gas opening (compared to the single diaphragm EGR valve) during high intake manifold vacuum periods, such as high-speed cruising, and provides more exhaust gas recirculation during acceleration when manifold vacuum is low. In addition to the hose running to the thermal vacuum switch, a second hose is connected directly to the intake manifold.

Early Fuel Evaporation System

1975 models are equipped with this system to reduce engine warm-up time, improve driveability, and reduce emissions. On start-up, a vacuum

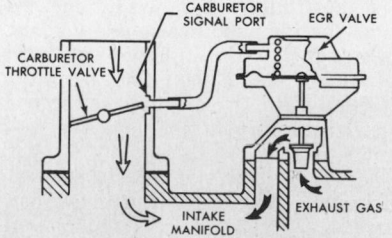

EGR system schematic (© Chevrolet Div., G.M. Corp)

motor acts to close a heat valve in the exhaust manifold which causes exhaust gases to enter the intake manifold heat riser passages. Incoming fuel mixture is then heated and more complete fuel evaporation is provided during warm-up.

Catalytic Converter

All 1975 and later models are equipped with a catalytic converter. The converter is located midway in the exhaust system. Stainless steel exhaust pipes are used ahead of the converter. The converter is stainless steel with an aluminized steel cover and a ceramc felt blanket to insulate the converter from the floorpan. The catalyst pellet bed inside the converter consists of noble metals which cause a reaction that converts hydrocarbons and carbon monoxide into water and carbon dioxide.

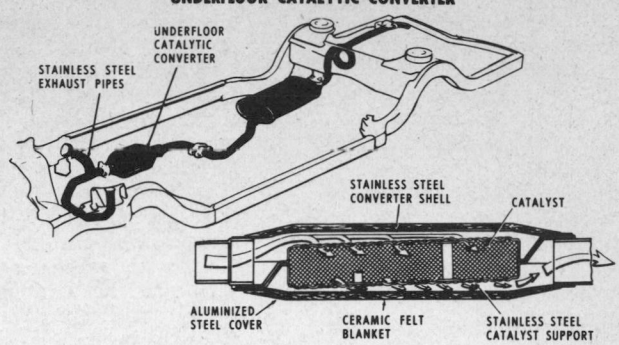

UNDERFLOOR CATALYTIC CONVERTER

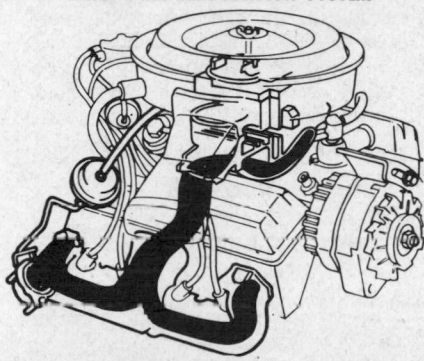

EARLY FUEL EVAPORATION SYSTEM

ENGINE

Engine application and specification tables may be found at the beginning of this section.

The following service procedures apply to all engines, except where differences are specified. The 402 and 454 V8 (big blocks) are essentially the same engine. Similarly, the 305, 350 and 400 small block series engines utilize the same design. The big block 402 was last offered in 1972. The small block 400 was offered in 1974 in both two and four-barrel form.

Engine Removal and Installation

Chevrolet

1. Remove the hood. Scribe lines around the hinges so that the hood can be installed in its original location.
2. Remove the air cleaner.
3. Disconnect the battery cables at the battery.
4. Remove the radiator and shroud.

5. Remove the fan blade and pulley.
6. Disconnect wires at:
   a. C.E.C. solenoid.
   b. Coil.
   c. Temperature switch.
   d. Delcotron.
   e. Starter solenoid.
   f. Oil pressure sending unit.
7. Disconnect:
   a. Accelerator linkage at the pedal.
   b. Oil pressure gauge line, if so equipped.
   c. Exhaust pipes at the manifold flanges.
   d. Engine cooler lines, if so equipped.
   e. Vacuum line to the power brake unit, if so equipped.
   f. Fuel line (front tank) at the fuel pump.
8. Remove the power steering pump, leaving the hoses attached to the pump.
9. Raise the car on a hoist.
10. Drain the cooling system and the crankcase.
11. Remove the driveshaft.

NOTE: if a plug for the driveshaft opening in the transmission is not available, drain the transmission.

12. Disconnect:
    a. Shift linkage at the transmission.
    b. Speedometer cable at the transmission.
    c. Transmission cooler lines, if so equipped.
    d. TCS switch at the transmission.
13. On vehicles with synchromesh transmissions, disconnect the clutch linkage at the cross-shaft then remove the cross-shaft at the frame bracket.

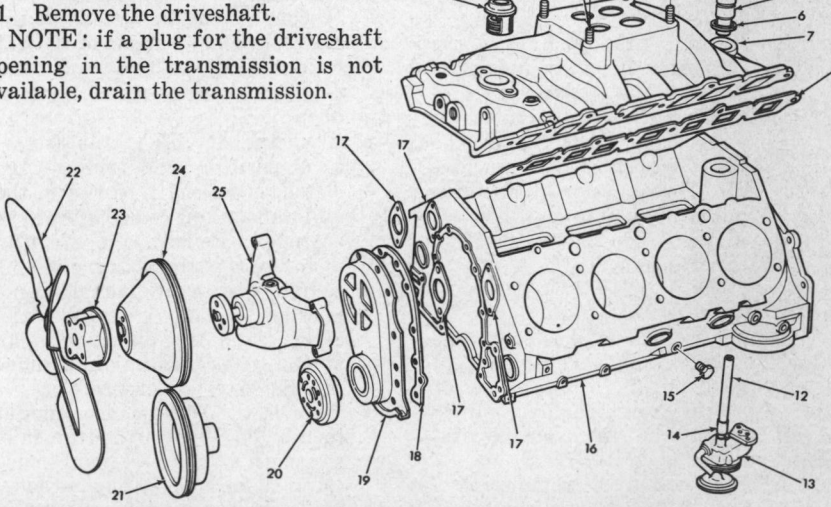

Mark IV (big block) exploded view (© Chevrolet Div., G.M. Corp)

1 Cap nipple	14 Sleeve	24 Pulley
2 Rotor	15 Drain plug	25 Water pump
3 Spring clip	16 Cylinder block	26 Thermostat
4 Distributor	17 Gasket	27 Water neck
5 Distributor gear	18 Gasket	28 Carburetor stud
6 Gasket	19 Timing cover	29 Gasket
7 Intake manifold	20 Damper	30 Shaft
8 Gasket	21 Pulley	31 Vacuum unit
12 Oil pump shaft	22 Fan	32 Distributor cap
13 Oil pump	23 Spacer	

14. Lower the vehicle and remove the rocker arm covers and install engine lifting adapter on the cylinder heads.
15. Raise the engine enough to take the weight off the front mounts, then remove the front mount through bolts.
16. Remove the rear mount to crossmember bolts.
17. Raise the engine enough to take the weight off the rear mount, then remove the crossmember.

NOTE: on Chevrolets it is necessary to remove the mount from the transmission before the crossmember can be removed.

18. Remove the engine/transmission assembly as a unit.
19. To remove the clutch and transmission from the engine:
    a. Remove the clutch housing cover plate screws.
    b. Remove the clutch housing to engine attaching bolts, then, remove the transmission and clutch housing as a unit.

Caution Do not let the weight of the transmission hang on the spline because the clutch disc may be easily damaged.

    c. Remove the starter and clutch housing rear cover plate.
    d. Loosen the clutch mounting bolts one turn at a time (to prevent distortion of the clutch cover) until the spring pressure is released. Remove all the bolts, clutch disc and pressure plate assembly.
20. To remove the automatic transmission:
    a. Remove the starter and the converter housing underpan.
    b. Remove the flywheel to converter attaching bolts.
    c. Supporting both the engine and transmission, remove the transmission to engine mounting bolts.
    d. Slowly guide the engine from the transmission.

Corvette

This procedure is basically the same for all engines regardless of size and model year. Certain pieces of optional equipment require minor specific changes but the overall operation remains the same.

1. The engine may be removed separately from the transmission, through the top of the engine compartment. Begin by draining the cooling system and the engine crankcase.
2. Disconnect the battery cables from the battery terminals and remove the air cleaner and ignition shields. Cover the carburetor.

3. Disconnect wiring at the alternator, temperature sending unit, oil pressure switch, primary coil lead, and CEC solenoid when applicable. Also disconnect the engine ground wires and the accelerator rod at the bellcrank.
4. Disconnect the power brake hose at the manifold end when applicable. Disconnect the tachometer drive cable at the distributor and the throttle valve if so equipped. Scribe the hood hinge locations on the support brackets and remove the hood.
5. Remove the radiator shroud and radiator, then the fan and fan assembly. If the car is equipped with power steering, remove the pump mounting bolts and push the pump into the vacant radiator opening. An alternate method is to disconnect the pump lines and plug both ends.
6. Remove the heater hose from the clip at the alternator bracket, then disconnect the hose from the engine connections and move back for extra clearance. Remove the rocker arm covers and place the vehicle on jack stands.
7. Remove the center head bolt on each head, and install the lift tool to the engine. Unhook the distributor cap and move it forward. Cover the distributor with a clean cloth.
8. Disconnect the exhaust pipes at the manifold flanges. On cars equipped with large block engines, the front stud on each manifold must be removed before the exhaust pipes can be removed.
9. Disconnect the wire leads at the starter solenoid. Remove the gas tank line at the fuel pump and plug the line to prevent fuel siphoning.
10. Block the clutch pedal in the return position and remove the clutch cross-shaft. Remove the oil filter and oil cooler lines if so equipped. Remove the starting motor. If the Corvette is equipped with a manual transmission, remove the flywheel cover plate. If equiped with an automatic transmission, remove the converter underpan.
11. Remove the front engine mount thru-bolts. Support the transmission with a floor jack and remove the transmission-to-engine bolts. If the car has an automatic transmission, remove the converter-to-flywheel bolts and install the converter holding bracket to the transmission.
12. Move the engine forward and upward as needed to clear the engine compartment.
13. Replacement is the reversal of this procedure.

Manifolds

Combination Manifold Used on 6 Cylinder Engines

Most Chevrolet six cylinder engines are equipped with a combination intake and exhaust manifold. See the Camaro section for details on the six with integral head and intake manifold. The exhaust manifold is equipped with a heat riser valve which, when the engine is cold, deflects the hot exhaust gases against the intake manifold to assist in rapid warm up.

To remove the manifold assembly, disconnect the exhaust pipe flange and remove all connections to the carburetor. Take off the vacuum lines at the manifold and at the carburetor.

Remove the carburetor, and the manifold may be unbolted from the side of the cylinder head using socket wrenches and box wrenches. If necessary to remove either exhaust or intake manifolds they may be separated by removing one bolt and two nuts at center of assembly.

Before reinstalling the manifold, thoroughly clean all mating surfaces.

Intake Manifold Removal and Installation—V8

1. Remove the air cleaner.
2. Drain the radiator.
3. Disconnect:
   a. Battery cables at the battery.
   b. Upper radiator and heater hoses at the manifold.
   c. Crankcase ventilation hoses as required.
   d. Fuel line at the carburetor.
   e. Accelerator linkage at the pedal lever.
   f. Vacuum hose at the distributor.
   g. Power brake hose at the carburetor base or manifold, if applicable.
   h. Ignition coil and temperature sending switch wires.
4. Remove the distributor cap and scribe the rotor position relative to distributor body.
5. Remove the distributor.
6. If applicable, remove the Delcotron upper bracket.
7. Remove the manifold to head attaching bolts, then remove the manifold and carburetor as an assembly.
8. If the manifold is to be replaced, transfer the carburetor (and mounting studs), water outlet and thermostat (use a new gasket), heater hose adapter and, if applicable, the choke coil and EGR valve with its vacuum line.
9. Before installing the manifold, thoroughly clean the gasket and seal surfaces of the cylinder heads and manifold.
10. Install the manifold end seals, folding the tabs if applicable,

and the manifold/head gaskets, using a sealing compound around the water passages. Make sure the gaskets are firmly cemented in place before installing the manifold.

11. When installing the manifold, care should be taken not to dislocate the end seals. It is helpful to use a pilot in the distributor opening. Tighten the manifold bolts to 30 ft. lbs. in the sequence illustrated.
12. Install the ignition coil.
13. Install the distributor with the rotor in its original location as indicated by the scribe line. If the engine has been disturbed, refer to "Distributor Removal and Installation."
14. If applicable, install the Delcotron upper bracket and adjust the belt tension.
15. Connect all components disconnected in Step 3 above.
16. Fill the cooling system, start the engine, check for leaks and adjust the ignition timing and carburetor idle speed and mixture.

Exhaust Manifold Removal and Installation—V8

1970-73

1. If equipped with A.I.R., remove the air injector manifold assembly. The ¼ in. pipe threads in the manifold are straight threads. Do not use a ¼ in. tapered pipe tap.
2. Disconnect the battery.
3. If applicable, remove the air cleaner pre-heater shroud.
4. Remove the exhaust pipe flange nuts, then hang the pipe with wire.
5. Remove the manifold mounting bolts (end bolts first), then remove the manifold.
6. To install, clean the mating surfaces, then install the manifold with the center bolts first. Install the end bolts, then tighten all bolts to 20 ft. lbs.
7. To complete installation, reverse Steps 1 through 3.

1974 and later Left Side

1. Disconnect the battery ground cable and raise the car. Disconnect the exhaust pipe at the manifold.
2. Remove the front manifold to exhaust pipe flange stud, and then remove the rear spark plug shield; lower the car.
3. On all models except the Corvette, remove the air conditioning compressor and set it aside. DO NOT DISCONNECT ANY AIR CONDITIONING LINES.
4. Disconnect the spark plug wires and their holder, the tempera-

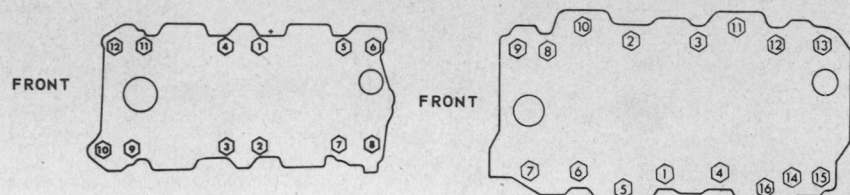

Intake manifold tightening sequence (left—small block V8; right—Mk. IV (big block) V8)
(© Chevrolet Div., G.M. Corp)

ture sending unit lead and the dipstick.
5. Remove the attaching bolts and remove the manifold.
6. To install, reverse the removal procedure.

1974 and later Right Side

1. Disconnect the ground cable, and remove the fan shroud upper bolts and loosen the fan shroud. Remove the air cleaner intake pipe. On the Corvette, remove and set aside the air conditioning compressor and then remove the compressor lower mounting bracket. DO NOT DISCONNECT ANY AIR CONDITIONING LINES. On models to 1974, if equipped with an air pump, remove the air injector manifold assembly.
2. Raise the car and disconnect the exhaust pipe at the manifold.
3. Remove the right side engine mounting bracket through bolt, and loosen the left side mounting bracket through bolt. Jack up the right side of the engine, reinstall the right side through bolt, and lower the engine until the through bolt is resting on the mounting bracket.
4. Remove the rear spark plug shield bolt. On the Corvette only, disconnect the AIR tube from the exhaust pipe and move it aside; also remove the rear spark plug shield and the three rear manifold attaching bolts.
5. Lower the vehicle and remove the spark plug wires, air cleaner heat stove pipe, and the air cleaner intake pipe. Remove the rear spark plug shield.
6. Remove the manifold to engine bolts, and remove the manifold, the EFE valve and the vacuum can.
7. To install, reverse the removal procedure.

Valve System

Valve Guides

Valve guides are integral with the cylinder head. Valve guide bores may be reamed to accommodate oversize valve stems or the guides may be knurled (if wear permits) to allow the retention of standard size valves.

Rocker Arm Removal and Installation

Rocker arms are removed by removing the adjusting nut. Be sure to adjust valve lash after replacing rocker arms.

NOTE: when replacing an exhaust rocker, move an old intake rocker to the exhaust rocker arm stud and install the new rocker arm on the intake stud.

Rocker arm studs that have damaged threads or are loose in the cylinder heads may be replaced with new studs available in 0.003 in. and 0.013 in. oversize or the bores may be tapped and screw-in replacement studs used. Do not attempt to install an oversize stud without reaming the stud bore. Studs are press-fit. Mark IV and late high-performance small-block engines use screw-in studs and pushrod guide plates.

NOTE: if engine is equipped with the A.I.R. exhaust emission control system, the interfering components of the system must be removed. Disconnect the lines at the air injection nozzles in the exhaust manifolds.

Valve Clearance Adjustment

Hydraulic Lifters

On six-cylinder engines, crank the engine until the distributor rotor points to the No. 1 firing position and the breaker points are just opening. The following valves may be adjusted:

No. 1	exhaust	intake
No. 2		intake
No. 3	exhaust	
No. 4		intake
No. 5	exhaust	

To adjust the rest of the valves, crank the engine until the distributor rotor points to the No. 6 firing position and the breaker points are just opening. The following valves may be adjusted:

No. 2	exhaust	
No. 3		intake
No. 4	exhaust	
No. 5		intake
No. 6	exhaust	intake

On V8 engines, crank the engine until the No. 1 piston is at TDC of its compression stroke (the compression can be felt by placing a finger over the spark plug hole or by feeling the

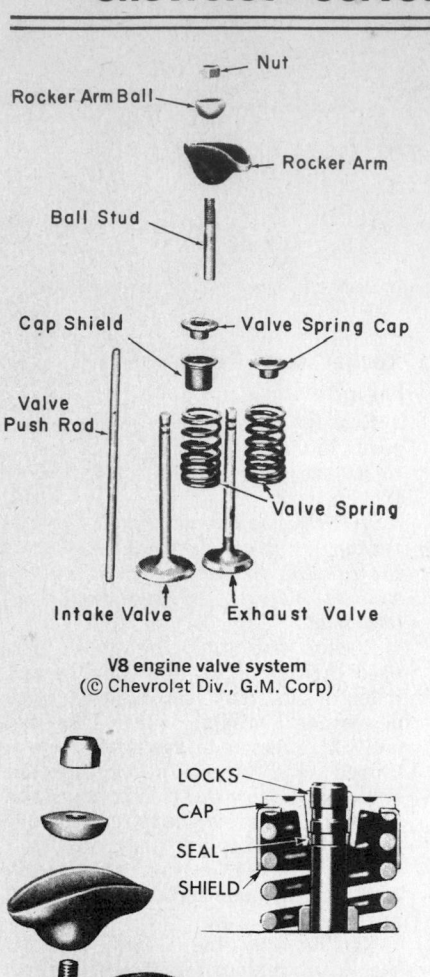

V8 engine valve system
(© Chevrolet Div., G.M. Corp)

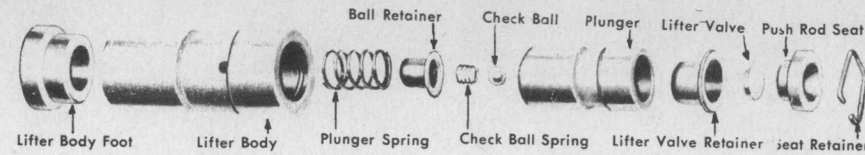

Typical hydraulic lifter exploded (© Chevrolet Div., G.M. Corp)

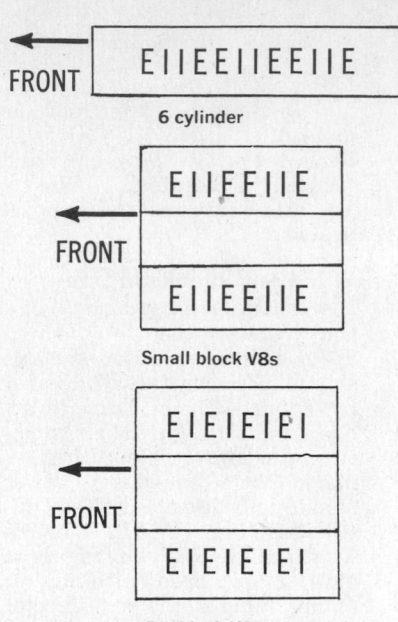

FRONT ← E I I E E I I E E I I E

6 cylinder

FRONT ← E I I E E I I E / E I I E E I I E

Small block V8s

FRONT ← E I E I E I E I / E I E I E I E I

Big block V8s

6-cylinder head and rocker arm assembly,
250 cu. in. engine
(© Chevrolet Div., G.M. Corp)

valves as the timing mark passes "0"—if the valves don't move, the No. 1 piston is at the top of its compression stroke). With the crankshaft in this position the following valves may be adjusted:

Exhaust—1, 3, 4, 8
Intake—1, 2, 5, 7

Rotate the crankshaft one full revolution until the timing pointer is again aligned with the "0". With the crankshaft thus in No. 6 cylinder firing position, the following valves may be adjusted:

Exhaust—2, 5, 6, 7
Intake—3, 4, 6, 8

Adjustment is made by backing off the rocker arm adjusting nut until there is play in the pushrod. Tighten the nut to remove the pushrod clear-ance (this can be felt by rotating the pushrod with the fingers while tightening the adjusting nut). When the pushrod cannot be freely turned, tighten the nut one additional turn to place the hydraulic lifter in the center of its travel. No further adjustment is required.

Mechanical Lifters

Position the crankshaft for No. 1, then No. 6 cylinder firing positions as described for adjusting hydraulic lifters above. In the case of mechanical lifters, however, use a feeler gauge between the rocker arm and the valve

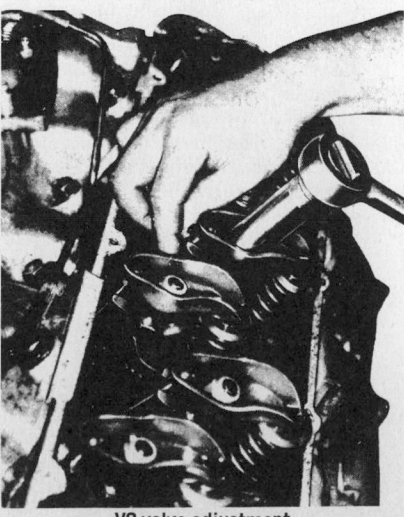

V8 valve adjustment
(© Chevrolet Div., G.M. Corp)

stem to obtain the correct clearance. The final valve lash setting is made with the engine running at normal operating temperature. Specified valve lash (hot) can be found in the Tune-Up Specifications at the beginning of this section.

Cylinder Head

Removal and Installation

6 Cylinder

To remove the cylinder head, detach the air cleaner and all rods, lines and vacuum tubes at the carburetor and manifold.

NOTE: if the engine is equipped with an exhaust emission control system, the injector connections must be disconnected at the cylinder head. Disconnect any interfering components and tie back out of the way.

When installing, do not use sealer on the composition steel asbestos gasket. Coat the threads of the head bolts with sealing compound before installation. Tighten the head bolts in sequence (see the illustration at the beginning of this section) a little at a time until each is torqued to 95 ft. lbs. Install all components which were removed. Adjust the valve mechanism as described later.

Caution The ¼ in. pipe threads at the cylinder head air injection nozzles are a straight pipe thread. Do not use a ¼ in. tapered pipe tap. Hoses used in this air injection system are of special material. Do not substitute.

1. Unbolt the manifold from the cylinder head, but not from the exhaust pipe flange. The manifold is simply pulled away from the head.
2. Remove the engine side plate covers and the gas lines at the fuel pump. Unbolt and lift off the rocker cover, disconnect the oil line leads to the rockers.
3. The rocker arms are supported separately and may be left intact until the head is removed.
4. Unbolt and lift off the cylinder head.

V8

1. Remove the intake manifold as described above.
2. Remove the exhaust manifolds as described above.
3. Back off the rocker arm nuts and pivot the rocker arms out of the way so that the pushrods

can be removed. Identify the pushrods so that they can be reinstalled in their original locations.

4. Remove the cylinder head bolts and cylinder heads.
5. Install using new gaskets. The head gasket is installed with the bead up.

NOTE: coat a STEEL gasket on both sides with sealer. If a STEEL ASBESTOS gasket is used, do not apply sealer. Clean the bolt threads, apply sealing compound and install the bolts finger tight.

6. Tighten the head bolts a little at a time in the sequence illustrated in the Specifications at the beginning of this section.
7. Install the exhaust and intake manifolds as described previously.
8. Adjust the valves as described later.

Timing Case

Crankshaft Pulley Replacement

NOTE: to prevent vibration damper damage, it is important that a puller be used to draw the pulley on the crankshaft.

6 Cylinder

1. Remove the radiator core and the fan belt. Remove accessory drive pulley and belt, if so equipped.
2. Use a screw-type puller to remove the balancer-pulley assembly.

V8

1. Drain radiator and disconnect the hoses. Take off the fan belt, and the fan pulley assembly. Remove the battery.
2. Remove the fan shroud. Remove the radiator core. Unbolt the pulley portion of the balancer-pulley assembly.

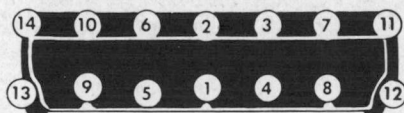

OHV 6 cylinder

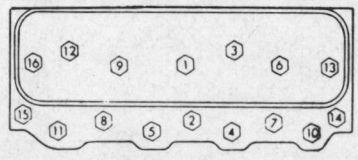

Big block V8

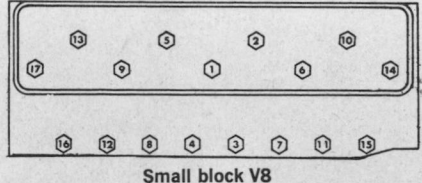

Small block V8

When replacing the crankshaft damper, it has been found that lightly polishing the crankshaft damper with crocus cloth will greatly ease replacement. This procedure will also assist in any future removals, as it is sometimes difficult to pull a damper even with a puller. Be sure that the polishing is not overdone, or the damper will wobble on the crankshaft.

3. Install screw-type puller and remove the balancer portion from the crankshaft.

Timing Case Cover and Front Oil Seal Replacement

NOTE: the timing case cover oil seal may be replaced without removing the case cover on all Corvettes and Chevrolets.

After gaining access to the oil seal, pry the old seal out of the cover with a screwdriver. Then, lubricate the new seal and drive it into place with a seal installer.

6 Cylinder, 402 and 454 V8

1. Remove the radiator, fan belts and, using a puller, remove the crankshaft pulley. On V8 engines, remove the water pump.
2. Remove the timing case-to-engine attaching bolts and remove the two oil pan-to-timing case bolts. The front cover is changed, beginning 1974.
3. Slide the front cover forward until a knife can be positioned behind the cover, then cut the ends of the oil pan front seal off flush with the cylinder block on the two ends of the front cover.
4. Remove the front cover and clean all gasket mounting surfaces on the front cover, the block and the exposed portion of the oil pan.
5. Temporarily position a new oil pan front seal on the front of the oil pan and trim off the edges of the new seal so that it will fit flush with the engine block.
6. Remove the new front seal, coat it with sealer and install it on the front cover. Apply a bead of silicone rubber sealer to the

Cutting oil pan front seal
(© Chevrolet Div., G.M. Corp)

place on the front of the oil pan where the cut off portion of the old seal will mate with the new oil pan front seal.

7. Install a centering tool in the crankshaft snout hole in the front cover and install the front cover on the engine.
8. Install the front cover bolts finger tight, remove the centering tool and tighten the cover bolts. Install the pulley, fan belts and radiator.

305, 350 and 400 V8

1. Remove the crankshaft pulley. Remove the oil pan. The pan need not be removed on 1975 and later engines. Remove the water pump. Remove the screws holding the timing case cover to the block and remove the cover and gaskets.
2. Use a large screwdriver to pry the old seal out of the front face of the cover.
3. Install the new seal so that open end is toward the inside of the cover.
4. Check that the timing chain oil slinger is in place against the crankshaft sprocket.
5. Install the cover carefully onto the locating dowels.
6. Tighten the attaching screws to 6-8 ft. lbs.

Timing Chain Replacement

6 Cylinder

Chevrolet timing gears are arranged so that (unless deliberately

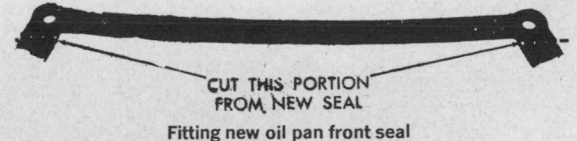

CUT THIS PORTION FROM NEW SEAL
Fitting new oil pan front seal
(© Chevrolet Div., G.M. Corp)

disturbed) the valve timing will remain as set at the factory. Unless the gears are badly worn or seriously damaged, the valve timing will remain constant within reasonable limits.

If it becomes necessary to replace the timing gears due to wear or damage, remove the radiator core, disconnect the front motor mounts and jack up the front of the engine. Remove the fan belt, fan pulley, oil pan and timing case cover.

NOTE: the manufacturer recommends that the camshaft be removed from the car in order to remove and replace the gear in an arbor press.

Sometimes when the gear is being pressed on in place on the car, damage results to the thrust washer in back of the cam gear. Unfortunately, this damage is not noticed until the engine is started.

To replace the gear by removing the camshaft, remove the rocker arm assemblies and the distributor, take out all of the pushrods and all of the lifters. The camshaft may then be pulled out toward the front of the engine. It will be necessary to retime the ignition.

Runout of the timing gear should not exceed .004 in. Backlash between the two gears should not be less than .004 in. nor more than .006 in. End clearance of the thrust plate should be .001 to .005 in.

Caution

The use of a dial indicator will reduce the possibility of driving the gear too far onto the camshaft. This would alter the desired camshaft thrust clearance of .001 to .005 in. Use care when approaching the final position of the gear on the shaft, because it is impossible to increase the thrust clearance without pulling the new gear. In the absence of a dial indicator, this end thrust can be measured with a feeler gauge. In this case, the thrust clearance is to be measured between the camshaft gear hub and the thrust plate. A feeler gauge strip, inserted in either of the two large gear holes, will reach this point.

V8

To replace the chain, remove the radiator core, water pump, the harmonic balancer and the crankcase front cover. This will allow access to the timing chain. Crank the engine until the timing marks on both sprockets are nearest each other and in line between the shaft centers. Then take out the three bolts that hold the camshaft gear to the camshaft. This gear is a light press fit on the camshaft and will come off easily. It is located by a dowel.

The chain comes off with the camshaft gear.

A gear puller will be required to remove the crankshaft gear.

Without disturbing the position of the engine, mount the new crankshaft gear on the shaft, and mount the chain over the camshaft gear. Arrange the camshaft gear in such a way that the timing marks will line up between the shaft centers and the camshaft locating dowel will enter the dowel hole in the cam sprocket.

Place the cam sprocket, with its chain mounted over it, in position on the front of the car and pull up with the three bolts that hold it to the camshaft.

After the gears are in place, turn the engine two full revolutions to make certain that the timing marks are in correct alignment between the shaft centers.

End-play of the V8 camshaft is zero.

Camshaft Replacement

6 Cylinder

Due to the length of the six cylinder camshaft, a large amount of working room will be required in front of the engine to remove the camshaft. There are two ways to go about this task: either remove the engine assembly from the car, or remove the radiator, grille and supports that are mounted directly in front of the engine, disconnect the motor mounts and raise the front of the engine as required to gain enough clearance to remove the cam from the engine. In either case the following equipment will have to be removed from the engine:

1. Remove the valve cover. Loosen each rocker arm mounting stud enough to turn it sideways and remove the pushrods. Keep the pushrods in their proper order.
2. Remove the fuel pump.
3. Remove the inspection plates from the side of the engine and remove the valve lifters. Keep the lifters in order when they are removed.
5. Remove the timing case cover.
6. Turn the crankshaft until the timing marks on the camshaft and crankshaft gears are aligned.

7. Remove the distributor cap and mark the position of the distributor rotor relative to the distributor body and the position of the distributor body relative to the engine block. Remove the distributor.
8. Remove the camshaft from the engine.

V8

1. Drain the cooling system and remove the radiator. On Corvettes, remove the hood.
2. Remove the water pump and the timing case cover.
3. Turn the crankshaft until the timing marks on the camshaft and crankshaft gears are aligned.
4. Remove the valve covers and loosen each rocker arm nut enough to turn the rocker to the side and remove the pushrods. Keep the pushrods in order when they are removed from the engine.
5. Remove the distributor cap and mark the position of the rotor relative to the distributor body and the position of the distributor body relative to the engine. Remove the distributor.
6. Remove the intake manifold, then remove the valve lifters from the engine. Keep the lifters in order when they are removed from the engine.
7. Remove the fuel pump.
8. Remove the timing chain and sprockets from the engine.
9. Install two 5/16 in. 18x4 bolts in the holes in the front of the cam and carefully slide it out of the engine.

NOTE: On some engine and model combinations it will be necessary to disconnect the motor mounts and jack up the front of the engine or remove the grille from the car in order to gain adequate clearance in front of the engine to get the camshaft out of the engine.

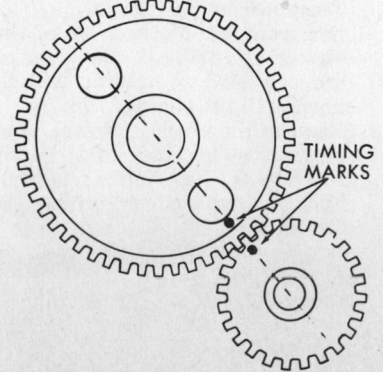

Timing mark alignment, 6 cylinder

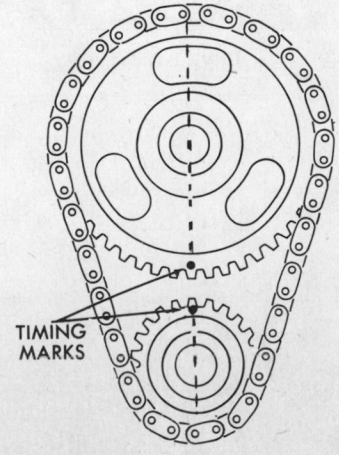

Timing mark alignment, V8

Pistons and Connecting Rods

NOTE: complete engine rebuilding procedures are contained in the "Engine Rebuilding Section."

Assembling Piston to Connecting Rod

6 Cylinder

Where split skirt-type pistons are being installed, the split in the skirt of the piston should be placed opposite the clamp screw of the wrist-pin. This is also opposite the number on the bottom of the connecting rod.

Where solid skirt slipper-type pistons are being replaced, it is unimportant which way the piston is mounted onto the connecting rod. However, if the old pistons are being reinstalled, the piston should be carefully marked before it is detached from the connecting rod in order that it may be replaced on the same side from which it was removed.

When assembling the rods to the pistons and installing the pistons in their respective bores, be sure that the flange, or heavy side of the rod at the bearing end, is toward the front of the piston (cast depression in top of piston head). The oil hole in the connecting rod goes toward the camshaft side of the engine.

V8

Pistons are marked with a cast depression at the top of the piston and also the letter F on the piston strut. This depression and F always go toward the front.

For the left bank, pistons Nos. 1, 3, 5, and 7, the heavy flange at the bottom of the connecting rod goes on the side of the piston having the depression and F mark. For the right bank, cylinders Nos. 2, 4, 6, and 8, the heavy flange on the connecting rod goes to the side opposite the stamped letter F and the cast depression in the top of the piston.

Place the piston and rod assemblies into the cylinder so that the depression cast into the top of the piston (and the letter F stamped on the boss of the piston) face front. Double

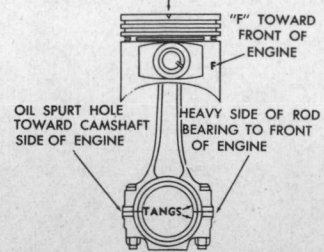

NOTCH TO FRONT OF ENGINE

"F" TOWARD FRONT OF ENGINE

OIL SPURT HOLE TOWARD CAMSHAFT SIDE OF ENGINE

HEAVY SIDE OF ROD TO FRONT OF ENGINE

TANGS

Correct relation of piston to rod, 6-cylinder 250 cu. in. engine

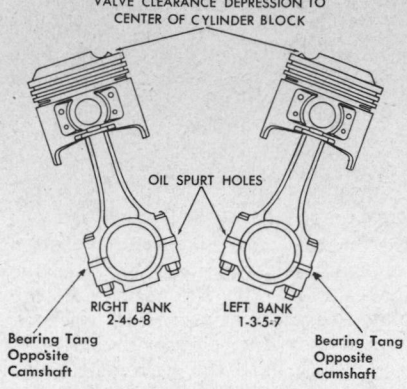

VALVE CLEARANCE DEPRESSION TO CENTER OF CYLINDER BLOCK

OIL SPURT HOLES

RIGHT BANK 2-4-6-8

LEFT BANK 1-3-5-7

Bearing Tang Opposite Camshaft

Bearing Tang Opposite Camshaft

Piston-to-rod relationship—Mk. IV (big block) V8

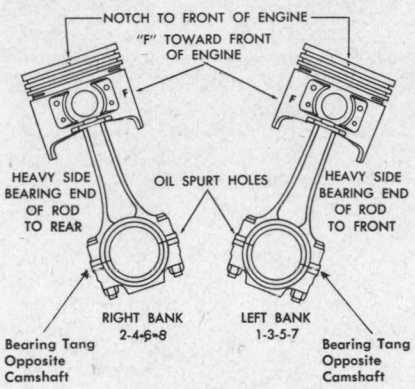

NOTCH TO FRONT OF ENGINE

"F" TOWARD FRONT OF ENGINE

HEAVY SIDE BEARING END OF ROD TO REAR

OIL SPURT HOLES

HEAVY SIDE BEARING END OF ROD TO FRONT

RIGHT BANK 2-4-6-8

LEFT BANK 1-3-5-7

Bearing Tang Opposite Camshaft

Bearing Tang Opposite Camshaft

Picton-to-rod relationship—small block V8

check that the pistons are in the correct bank by noting that on the left bank, pistons Nos. 1, 3, 5 and 7, the heavy flange on the connecting rod will also face forward, but on the right bank, cylinders Nos. 2, 4, 6 and 8, the heavy flange on the connecting rod will face toward the rear.

Lubrication

Oil Pan Removal

6 Cylinder

The oil pan can be removed, either after removing engine, or as follows:
1. Drain radiator and oil pan.
2. Disconnect gas tank line at fuel pump and upper and lower radiator hoses.
3. Remove clutch housing-to-engine block bolt above dowel on right side.
4. Raise vehicle on hoist or place on jack stands.
5. Rotate engine to align distributor rotor between No. 3. and No. 5 plug wire. (This locates No. 6 crank throw part way up.)
6. Remove starter and flywheel front cover plate (or converter housing shield).
7. Remove front mount through bolts.
8. Jack up front of engine. Raise as far as possible always using care

by checking various dash and body tunnel clearances.
9. Remove front engine mount frame bracket on right side and remove oil filter where necessary.
10. Remove oil pan screws and lower pan to frame.
11. Remove oil pump to gain clearance, then remove oil pan by sliding and rotating front to right and then to rear, and down at an angle. (On certain earlier models, these procedures may be varied in some self-evident areas.)
12. Install in reverse of above.

NOTE: gasket can be replaced by completely removing pan from vehicle.

Chevrolet—V8

1. Disconnect battery negative cable.
2. Remove distributor cap from distributor to prevent breakage against firewall.
3. Drain cooling system. Remove radiator hoses, and remove oil dipstick and tube, where necessary.
4. Remove fan blade assembly.
5. Raise car, and drain engine oil.
6. Remove bolts from engine front mounts. Disconnect and remove starter.
7. On cars with automatic transmissions, remove converter housing underpan.
8. Disconnect the exhaust Y pipe from the manifolds.
9. Rotate crankshaft until timing mark on the damper is at six o'clock position.
10. Using a block of wood and a suitable jack, raise engine enough to insert 2 x 4 in. wood blocks under engine mounts then lower engine onto blocks.
11. Remove engine oil pan.
12. Install by reversing removal procedures.

NOTE: the 402, and 454 cu. in. engines use three 1/4 in. attaching bolts at crankcase front cover; one at each corner, and one at the lower center.

Corvette

1. Disconnect battery, and remove dipstick and tube.
2. Raise car and support on stands. Drain engine oil.
3. Remove starter and flywheel underpan.
4. Disconnect steering idler arm and lower steering linkage.
5. Remove oil pan and discard gaskets and seals.
6. On high performance engines, the oil baffle must be removed before additional operations can be performed.

NOTE: on the 454 cu. in. engine, the oil pan has three 1/4 in. attaching bolts at crankcase front cover; one at each front corner, and one at lower center.

7. Install by reversing removal procedure.

Oil Pump Replacement

On all Chevrolet engines, the oil pump is located in the oil pan, and it is driven by a tang from the distributor shaft.

On six-cylinder engines, the pump is flange-mounted to the under side of the crankcase with two cap screws.

On V8 models, the oil pump is bolted to the rear, main bearing cap. Oil is fed from the pump up through the rear, main bearing cap.

Rear Main Bearing Oil Seal

Removal and Installation

1. Remove rear main bearing cap and pry old seal from groove. Insert new seal with lubricant only on the lip. Do not get oil on the glue-treated parting line surfaces. Lip faces front of engine.
2. Using a hammer and small punch, revolve the upper half of the seal until it protrudes far enough to remove with pliers.
3. Oil the seal except at the glue-treated ends and, using a hammer handle, roll the seal into place in the block.
4. These seals are made to size and require no trimming. Install the lower half over the crankshaft and in place onto the block.

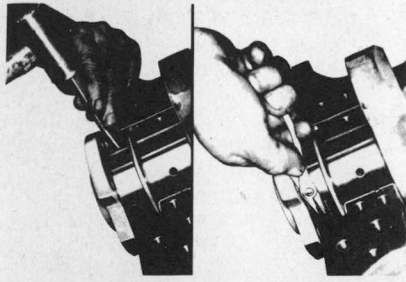

Rear main seal removal
(© Chevrolet Div., G.M. Corp)

CLUTCH

Clutches are of the diaphragm spring type. The throwout bearing is a ball bearing with no provision for lubrication. The throwout fork pivots on a ball stud which is mounted in the rear face of the bellhousing.

Clutch Removal and Installation

1. Support the engine and remove the transmission as described in "Manual Transmission."
2. Disconnect the clutch fork pushrod and spring.

3. Remove the flywheel housing.
4. Slide the clutch fork from the ball stud and remove the fork from the dust boot. The ball stud is threaded into the clutch housing and is easily replaced, if necessary.
5. Install a clutch pilot tool.

NOTE: look for the assembly markings "X" on the flywheel and the clutch cover (pressure plate assembly). If there are none, scribe marks to identify the position of the clutch cover relative to the flywheel.

6. Loosen the clutch cover bolts evenly until the spring pressure is relieved, then remove the bolts and clutch assembly.
7. Before installing, clean the pressure plate and the flywheel face.
8. Position the disc and pressure plate assembly on the flywheel and install a pilot tool.

NOTE: the disc on six cylinder engines is installed with the springs facing the flywheel. On V8 engines, the grease slinger must face the transmission.

9. Install the pressure plate assembly bolts. Make sure the mark on the cover is aligned with the mark on the flywheel. Tighten the bolts alternately and evenly to 35 ft. lbs.
10. Remove the pilot tool.
11. Remove the release fork and lubricate the ball socket and the fork fingers at the throwout bearing with graphite or Moly Grease. Reinstall the release fork.
12. Lubricate the inside recess and the fork groove of the throwout bearing with a light coat of graphite or Moly Grease.
13. Install the clutch release fork and dust boot in the clutch housing and the throwout bearing on the fork, then install the flywheel housing. Tighten flywheel housing bolts to 30 ft. lbs.
14. Connect the fork pushrod and spring.
15. Adjust the shift linkage as described later.
16. Adjust the clutch pedal free play as described previously.

Clutch Adjustment

1970 Chevrolet and Corvette through 1974

1. Disconnect the spring between the clutch push rod and cross shaft lever.
2. While holding the clutch pedal against the stop, loosen the two locknuts enough to allow the adjusting rod to move against the clutch fork until the throwout bearing light touches the pressure plate springs.
3. Turn the upper nut against the swivel and then back it off $4\frac{1}{2}$

turns. Tighten the bottom locknut to lock the swivel against the top nut.

4. Reinstall the return spring. Pedal free travel, the distance the pedal can be moved before the throwout bearing contacts the pressure plate spring, should be:

1970 Chevrolet 1-1½ in.
1970-71 Corvette 1¼-2 in.
1970 Corvette with HD clutch 2-2½ in.
1972 Corvette 1¼-1¾ in.
1973 Corvette 1¼-1½ in.
1974 Corvette 1-1½ in.

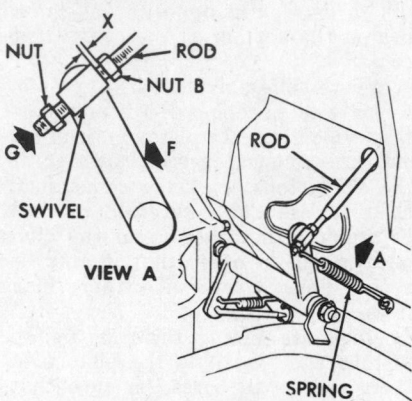

1970 Chevrolet clutch linkage
(© Chevrolet Div., G.M. Corp)

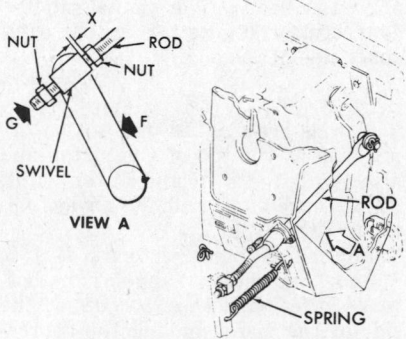

Corvette clutch linkage through 1974
(© Chevrolet Div., G.M. Corp)

1971-73 Chevrolet

1. Disconnect the return spring at the clutch fork.
2. Push the clutch lever and shaft assembly until the clutch pedal is tight against the rubber stop under the dash.
3. Push the outer end of the clutch fork backward until the throwout bearing just touches the pressure plate
4. Install the pushrod into the upper hole on the lever and increase its length until all play is removed.
5. Remove the rod from the upper hole and reinsert it into the lower hole.
6. Tighten the locknut, being careful not to change the length of the push rod.
7. Install the return spring.

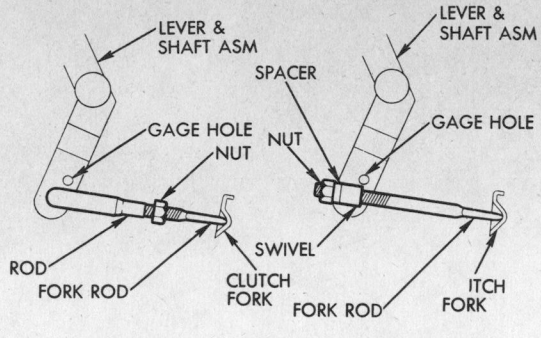

V8 ENGINE   L6 ENGINE

1971-73 Chevrolet clutch linkage
(© Chevrolet Div., G.M. Corp)

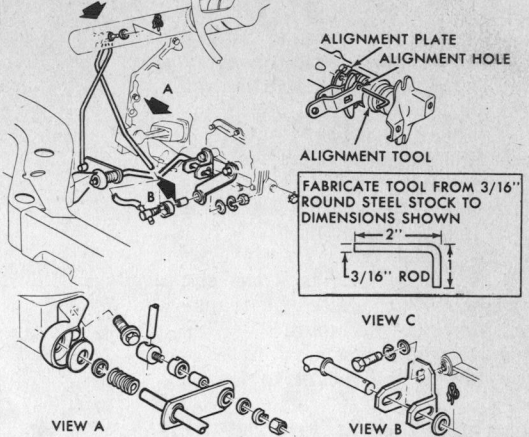

3-speed column shift linkage adjustment through 1973
(© Chevrolet Div., G.M. Corp)

8. Check the pedal free travel. It should be 1¼-1¾ in.

1975 and later Corvette

1. Disconnect the return spring between the floor and the cross shaft.
2. Push the clutch lever and shaft assembly until the clutch pedal is tightly against the rubber stop under the dash.
3. Loosen the two locknuts on the shaft.
4. Push the shaft until the throwout bearing just touches the pressure plate spring.
5. Tighton tho top locknut towards the swivel until the distance between it and the swivel is 0.4 in.
6. Tighten the bottom locknut against the swivel.
7. Check pedal free travel. It should be 1-1½ in.

MANUAL TRANSMISSION

Transmission refill capacities are in the Capacities table of this section.

Manual transmissions used in these models are the Muncie 3-speed, Saginaw 3-speed, Saginaw 4-speed, Muncie 4-speed, and Warner 4-speed. The Warner was installed in Corvettes beginning in mid-year 1974. All 1975 and later 4-speed Corvettes are equipped with the Warner unit. Identification is determined by side cover design and linkage. The 3-speed Muncie side cover has two ears on the case at the top and the Saginaw 3-speed one. The Saginaw 4-speed linkage arms are all mounted through the side cover. The Muncie and Warner 4-speeds have the reverse fork mounted in the tailshaft. These two may be differentiated by the shape of the side cover; the Warner has a nine bolt curved bottom and the Muncie a seven bolt straight bottom.

Troubleshooting and repair of manual transmissions is covered in the Unit Repair Section.

Shift Linkage Adjustment

Three-Speed Column Shift through 1973

1. With transmission in Reverse, place ignition switch in Off position for 1970, Lock for 1971-73.
2. Loosen shift rod lock nuts.
3. Set transmission first-reverse lever in reverse position. Push up on first-reverse control rod for 1970, pull down for 1971-73 until column lever is in reverse detent position. Tighten first-reverse lock nut.
4. Shift column and transmission levers to neutral position. Insert a 3/16 in. dia. rod into alignment holes in levers and alignment plate.
5. Tighten second-third locknut.
6. Remove alignment rod. Shift column lever to reverse. Turn key to Lock. Ignition switch must move freely to Lock position and it must not be possible to turn key to Lock when in any transmission position other than reverse. If this interlock binds, leave switch in Lock position and readjust first-reverse rod.
7. Check shifting.

Corvette Four-Speed

1. Place the ignition switch in "lock."
2. Loosen locknuts at swivels on shift rods and back drive control rod.
3. Set transmission shift levers in neutral positions.
4. Shift lever into neutral. Insert locating gauge, ⅛ thick X 41/64 wide X 3 in. long, into control lever bracket assembly.
5. Hold each lever against the gauge and adjust in turn. Tighten shift rod locknuts and remove gauge.
6. Loosen the interlock bracket assembly bolts at the bottom of the steering column. Make sure that

the bracket is not stuck to the dash and then tighten the bracket again.
7. Move the ignition key through "off" and "lock" positions. If there is any binding, readjust the interlock linkage.

Transmission Removal

Chevrolet

1. Raise the car on a hoist and drain the transmission. Disconnect the speedometer cable and the control levers. Disconnect the propeller shaft. Remove two bolts attaching the center bearing to the frame. Remove nuts and U-bolts retaining the rear universal joint bearing to the differential pinion drive flange. Move the propeller shaft rearward to the left and under the rear axle housing to withdraw the front universal joint from the transmission output shaft. Remove the transmission rear mounting pad bolts and unbolt the support member from the frame.
2. On all models, remove the two top transmission-to-clutch housing cap screws, and insert guide pins to keep the weight of the transmission from falling on the clutch assembly.
3. Remove the lower transmission-to-clutch housing cap screws. Slide the transmission straight back on the guide pins until the input shaft of the transmission is free of the clutch.
4. Remove the transmission from under the car.
5. Install in reverse order of removal.

Corvette

1. Disconnect the battery ground cable.
2. Remove the shifter ball and "T" handle.
3. Remove the console trim plate.

4. Raise the vehicle on a hoist.
5. Remove the right and left exhaust pipes. It may be necessary to remove the catalytic converter and its mounting bracket to gain sufficient clearance to remove the transmission.
6. Disconnect the driveshaft at the transmission, lower the driveshaft and remove the slip yoke from the transmission.
7. Remove the rear mount to bracket bolts, then jack the engine enough to raise the transmission from the mount.
8. Remove the transmission linkage mounting bracket to frame bolts.
9. Disconnect the shift levers at the transmission.
10. Remove the bolts attaching gearshift assembly to mounting bracket and remove the mounting bracket. Remove the shifter mechanism with the rods attached.
11. Disconnect the speedometer cable and the TCS switch wiring.
12. Remove the transmission mount bracket.
13. Remove the transmission to clutch housing retaining bolts and the lower left extension bolt.
14. Pull the transmission rearward until it is clear of the clutch housing, then rotate it clockwise while pulling to the rear. Carefully lower the rear of the engine until the tachometer drive cable at the distributor just clears the firewall.

Caution The tachometer cable is easily damaged if it hits the firewall. Slide the transmission rearward until it clears the clutch, then tilt the front of it down and lower it from the car.

15. Installation is the reverse of removal. Adjust the shift linkage.

AUTOMATIC TRANSMISSION

Four automatic transmissions have been used. Powerglide was available only in Chevrolets. This 2-speed transmission was used for the last time in 1972. Three Turbo Hydra-Matics have been available, the 350, 375, and the 400. All are 3-speed transmissions. Identification can be made by the shape of the pan.

Neutral Safety Switch Adjustment

Through 1971
In all models the adjustment is made with the shift lever in Drive

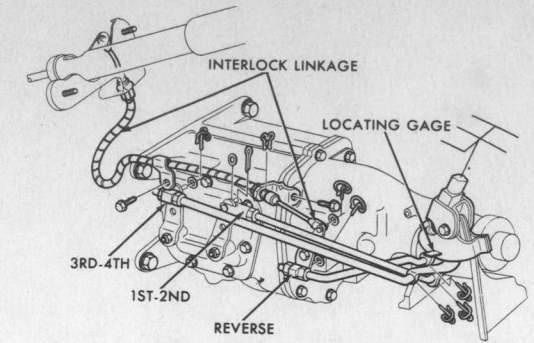

Corvette 4-speed linkage adjustment
(© Chevrolet Div., G.M. Corp)

Powerglide pan

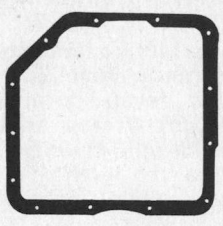

Turbo Hydra-Matic 350 pan

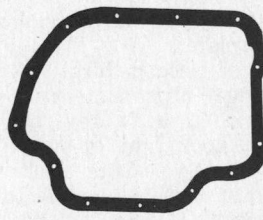

Turbo Hydra-Matic 375 and 400 pan

position. Loosen the switch mounting screws. Align the slot in the contact support with the hole in the switch and insert a 3/32 in. pin to hold the support in place.

On column shift models, place the contact support drive slot over the shifter tube drive tang and tighten the screws.

On Corvettes, the shift control lever must be disconnected from the control rod and the shift control knob removed. Then remove the trim plate to get at the switch. Proceed as described in the first paragraph above, then place the contact support drive slot over the drive tang. Tighten the switch mounting screws, then remove the pin. Reinstall the shift control lever and trim plate.

On Chevrolet models with floor shift, the ash tray, trim plate assembly and indicator lens and housing

must be removed from the console before proceding as described in the first paragraph above. Clamp the control lever pawl against the contact point of the detent. Tighten the switch mounting screws, then remove the pin and reinstall all the console components which were removed.

1972

Column Shift
1. Disconnect the wiring at the switch.
2. Remove the retaining screws and remove the switch from the steering column.
3. Put the shift level in neutral when installing the switch
4. Align the slot in the contact support with the hole in the switch and insert a 3/32 in. pin to hold the support in position. The switch is now in the Drive position.
5. Put the contact support drive slot over the shifter tube drive tang and tighten the screws. Remove the clamp and the pin.
6. Connect the wiring and check the switch for proper operation.

Floorshift
1. Disconnect the shift control lever arm from the control rod.
2. Remove the shift knob.
3. Remove the trim plate.
4. Remove the control assembly retaining screws and lift the assembly away from the seal.
5. Remove the neutral switch from the control assembly.
To install:
6. On early 1972 models put the shifter into Drive. Park on later Chevrolets (with neutral switch on column), or Neutral on later Corvettes.
7. Align the hole in the contact support with the hole in the switch and insert a 3/32 in. pin to hold the support in place.
8. Place the contact support drive slot over the drive tang and tighten the switch mounting screws. Remove the pin.
9. Install the control assembly

mounting screws. Connect the switch wiring and check the switch operation.

10. Install the trim plate and shift knob.
11. Connect the shift lever arm to the transmission control rod.

1973 and Later

Use the procedure outlined previously except that during installation, the shift lever is positioned in Neutral on column shift or Drive on floor shift models. It is only necessary to use the 3/32 in. pin for alignment when the original switch pin has been sheared off.

Shift Linkage Adjustment

Column Shift through 1972

1. Make sure that the shift lever works freely in the mast jacket.
2. Check for proper linkage adjustment:
   a. Pull the selector lever back and allow the lever to be positioned in Drive by the transmission detent.
   NOTE: do not use the indicator pointer as a reference. The indicator pointer will be adjusted after the linkage.
   b. Release the lever. The lever should not go into Low range unless it is lifted.
   c. Lift the shift lever and allow the lever to be positioned in Neutral by the transmission detent.
   d. Release the lever. The lever should not go into Reverse unless it is lifted.
   e. If the selector lever can move beyond the Neutral and Drive detents without being lifted, then the mechanical stops in the steering column are not coordinated with the transmission detents and adjustment is required.
3. To adjust, place the selector lever in Drive as determined by the transmission detent.
4. Loosen the adjustment clamp or swivel at the cross-shaft and position the selector lever in Drive.
5. With the selector lever in Drive and the transmission lever in Drive detent position, tighten the clamp or swivel bolt.
6. Repeat Step 2 above to check for proper adjustment.
7. If necessary, readjust the selector pointer to agree with the transmission detents.
8. Readjust the neutral safety switch if necessary.
9. When properly adjusted:
   a. From Reverse to Drive position travel, the transmission detent must be noted and related to the indicated position on the dial.
   b. In Drive and Reverse positions, the selector lever must drop back into position freely when lifted.

1973 and later Column Shift

1. Follow steps 1 and 2 of the preceding procedure.
2. Remove the retaining screw and spring washer from the linkage swivel.
3. Set the lever on the transmission in neutral by moving it counterclockwise to the L1 detent and then clockwise three detent positions to neutral.
4. Place the transmission selector lever in Neutral as determined by the stop in the steering column. Don't use the indicator pointer for reference. The pointer will be adjusted last.
5. Assemble the swivel, spring washer, and screw to the lever and tighten to 20 ft lbs.
6. Readjust the indicator needle, if necessary, to match the transmission detent positions. Readjust the neutral switch.

7. Make sure that the key cannot be removed with the key in the run position and the transmission in reverse. When the key is in the Lock position and shift lever in Park, be sure that the key can be removed, the steering is locked, and that the transmission remains in Park when the steering column is locked.

Corvette Through 1972 (Turbo Hydra-Matic)

1. Disconnect the pushrod at the transmission lever.
2. With the transmission lever in Drive detent and the selector lever in Drive, rotate the pushrod until the hole lines up with the lever pin.
3. Install the pushrod on the pin and install the retainer clip.
4. Check operation of the linkage in all positions.

1973 and later Corvette (Turbo Hydra-Matic 400)

1. Loosen the nut on the transmission lever so that the pin can

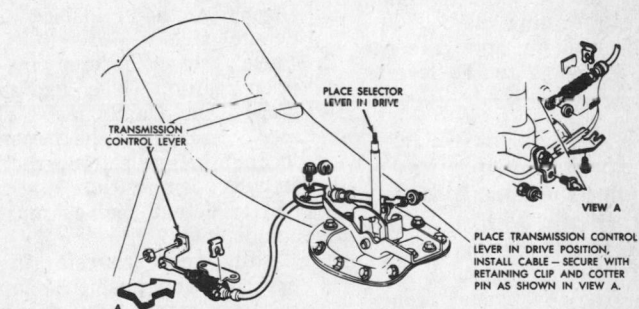

Corvette Turbo Hydra-Matic linkage adjustment
(© Chevrolet Div., G.M. Corp)

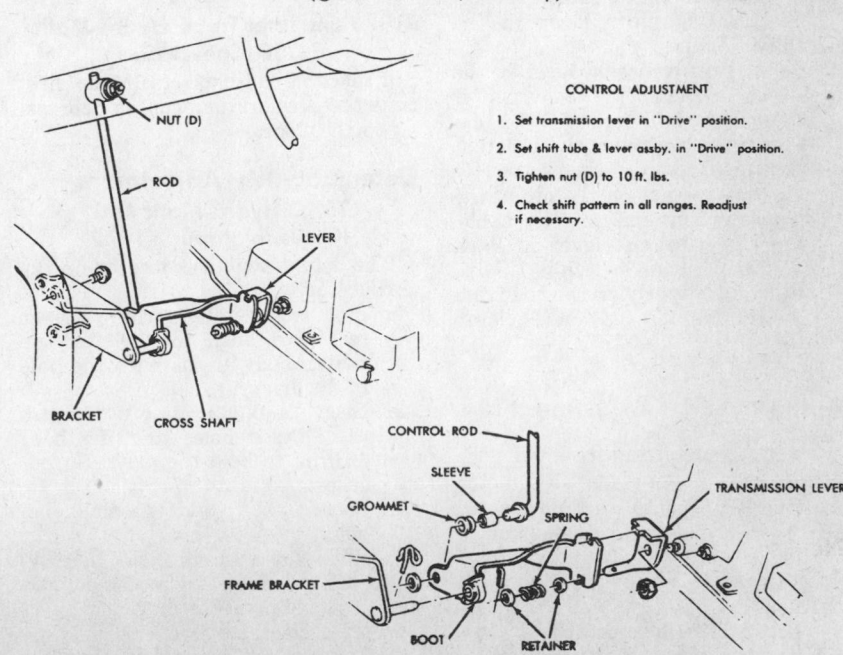

Turbo Hydra-Matic column linkage adjustment (© Chevrolet Div., G.M. Corp)

move in the slot. Remove the console cover.

2. Move the transmission lever counter-clockwise to the L1 position and then clockwise five detents to Park.
3. Place the shift lever in Park and insert a 0.40 in. spacer in front of the pawl.
4. Tighten the nut on the transmission lever to 20 ft. lbs.
5. Turn the ignition switch to Lock with the shift lever in Park.
6. Remove the cotter pin and washer from the backdrive cable at the column lever. Disconnect the cable.
7. Working under the dash, remove the two nuts at the steering column-to-dash bracket.
8. Turn the lock tube lever counterclockwise (when viewed from the front of the column) to remove any free-play from the column.
9. Move the bracket until the cable eye passes freely over the retaining pin on the bracket.
10. While holding the bracket in place, have an assistant tighten the bracket retaining nuts.
11. Install the cotter pin and washer to retain the cable to the lever retaining pin.

1976 and later Corvette Turbo Hydra-Matic 350

This is a cable operated linkage.
1. Loosen the swivel at the lower end of the rod that comes from the steering column.
2. Loosen the pin at the transmission end of the cable.
3. Set the floorshift lever in the Drive detent.
4. Set the transmission lever in the Drive detent by moving it counterclockwise to the L1 detent, then clockwise three detent positions.
5. Tighten the nut on the pin at the transmission end of the cable.
6. Put the floorshift lever in Park and the ignition switch in LOCK.
7. Pull down lightly on the rod from the column and tighten its clamp nut.

Throttle Valve Adjustment

6-Cylinder through 1973

Adjustment is made with the throttle pedal completely depressed and the bellcrank in wide open position.

Adjust the length of the linkage to obtain a 1/64 in. to 1/16 in. clearance between the lever on the firewall and its stop when the transmission lever is against its stop.

V8 Powerglide through 1972

1. Remove the air cleaner and disconnect:
   a. Accelerator linkage at the carburetor.
   b. Accelerator return spring.
   c. Throttle valve rod return spring.
2. Pull the throttle valve upper rod forward until the transmission is through detent and place the carburetor in wide open position. The carburetor must reach wide open position at the same time that the ball stud contacts the end of the slot in the upper throttle valve rod.
3. Adjust the swivel on the end of the upper throttle valve rod to obtain the setting described in Step 2 above. Allowable tolerance is approximately 1/32 in.
4. Connect and adjust the carburetor linkage.

Detent Cable Adjustment
Turbo Hydra-Matic 350 Chevrolet through 1972, 1976 and later Corvette

1. Disengage the snap lock on the detent cable.
2. Place the carburetor in wide open position (lever against the stop). On Quadrajet carburetors, disengage the secondary locknut before placing the lever in wide open position.
NOTE: detent cable must be through detent.
3. Holding the carburetor in wide open position, push the snap lock on the detent cable downward until the top is flush with the cable.

1973 and later Turbo-Hydra-Matic 350 (Chevrolet)

The cable adjusts itself the first time the accelerator pedal is depressed to the floor.

Detent Switch Adjustment
Turbo Hydra-Matic 400 (Corvette) through 1972

The detent switch is located on the carburetor.
1. Pull the detent switch driver rearward until the hole in the switch body aligns with the hole in the driver.
2. Insert a 0.092 in. pin through the aligned holes to a depth of 0.10 in. to hold the driver in position.
3. Loosen the switch mounting bolt.
4. With the throttle held in wide open position, move the switch forward until the driver contacts the accelerator lever.
5. Tighten the mounting bolt and remove the pin.

Turbo-Hydra-Matic 400 (Chevrolet) Through 1972

The detent switch is located on the carburetor.
1. Loosen the switch mounting bolt.
2. Holding the throttle in wide open position (choke fully open), depress the detent switch plunger until it bottoms in the switch. Move the switch toward the throttle lever paddle until there is a clearance of 0.23 ± 0.01 in. between the face of the lever paddle and the depressed detent switch plunger.
3. Tighten the switch mounting bolts.

1973 and later Turbo Hydra-Matic 375 and 400 (Chevrolet and Corvette)

The switch is located over the accelerator pedal. After installing a new switch, adjustment is made by pressing the plunger in. This presets the switch and it will self-adjust the first time the pedal is fully depressed.

Band Adjustment, Pan Removal and Installation, Fluid and Filter Change

Follow the procedures given in the Camaro section.

U-JOINTS

For driveshaft and U-joint procedures, see the Camaro section.

REAR AXLE

For Chevrolet axle shaft, bearing, and seal service, refer to the Camaro section.

Corvette Differential Removal and Installation

Corvette is equipped with an independent rear suspension. The differential is solidly attached to the car frame, the rear wheels being driven through tubular rear axles, each fitted with two universal joints. A transverse, multiple leaf rear spring provides rear suspension. Brake torque and driving forces are transmitted through radius arms to the frame. The spring supports vertical loads, while lateral forces, on turns etc., are taken by the axles and control rods to the fixed differential and to the frame.
1. Raise the vehicle on a hoist.
2. Disconnect the spring and link bolts.
3. Disconnect the axle shafts at the carrier by removing the U-bolts on the universal joint trunnions.
4. Disconnect the carrier front support bracket at the frame crossmember.

5. Disconnect the driveshaft at the companion flange.

6. Scribe marks indicating the cam and bolt relative location on the strut rod bracket and loosen the cam bolts.

7. Remove the four bolts which secure the bracket to the carrier lower surface and drop the bracket. Remove the camber cam bolts and swing the strut rods up and out of the way.

8. Remove the eight carrier to cover bolts, loosening the bolts gradually to permit the lubricant to drain out.

9. Pull the carrier partially out of the cover, drop the nose to clear the crossmember, then gradually work the carrier down and out.

10. To install, clean the carrier cover and grease the gasket surface.

11. Using a new gasket and two ½-13 x 1-¼ in. studs as aligning studs, raise the carrier into position.

12. Install the carrier to cover bolts, tightening securely.

13. Install the driveshaft to the companion flange, tightening the clamp bolts securely.

14. Install the rubber cushion on the bracket and position to the frame crossmember. Install the nut, tightening to 50 ft. lbs.

15. Install the axle trunnions to the yokes with the U-bolts.

16. Assemble the strut rods to the bracket and raise the bracket into position under the carrier. Install the four bolts, tightening to 35 ft. lbs.

17. Move the camber cams to the marked locations and tighten the cam nuts.

18. Connect the spring end link bolts.

19. Fill the housing with lubricant to the level of the filler hole.

JACKING, HOISTING

When jacking the car, place the jack at the spring seat of the lower control arm in the front and at the axle housing in the rear. A bumper jack may be used on Chevrolet models, but not Corvettes.

To hoist the car, position the hoist arms at the frame side rails immediately in front of the rear wheels and immediately behind the front wheels.

FRONT SUSPENSION

Both Chevrolet and Corvette utilize conventional short-long arm suspension, with coil springs and tube shocks. A stabilizer bar is used between the lower arms to reduce roll.

Shock Absorber Removal and Installation

1. Remove the upper stem nut while holding the stem to keep it from turning.

2. Remove the two bolts holding the shock absorber to the lower control arm and pull the shock through the arm.

3. Extend the shock absorber and insert it up through the lower control arm. Make sure that the upper stem goes through the hole in the upper control arm frame bracket.

4. Install the grommet, retainer cup, and nut to the shock absorber upper stem.

5. Hold the shock absorber stem and tighten the upper nut to 8 ft lbs.

6. Install the lower control arm retaining bolts and tighten to 20 ft lbs. (Chevrolet) or 13 ft lbs. (Corvette).

Spring Removal and Installation

1970 Chevrolet

1. Remove shock absorber upper stem retaining nut and grommet.

2. Support the car by the frame so that the control arms hang free. Remove the wheel assembly, shock absorber, stabilizer to lower control arm link, strut rod to lower control arm attaching nuts, bolts and lockwashers, and the tie-rod end.

3. Scribe the position of the inner pivot camber adjusting cam bolt and then remove the nut, lock washer and outer cam.

4. Install a steel bar through the shock absorber mounting hole in the lower control arm so that the notch in the bar seats over the

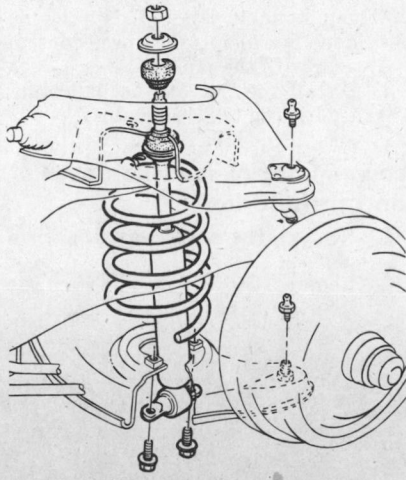

Installing shock absorbers—typical
(© Chevrolet Div., G.M. Corp)

bottom spring coil and the bar extends inboard and under the inner bushing. Fit a 5 in. wood block between the bar and the lower arm inner support bushing.

5. With a floor jack, raise the end of the steel bar enough to remove tension from the inner pivot cam bolt. The bolt can then be removed.

6. Carefully lower the inner end of the control arm. Tension on the spring must be removed before the spring can be taken out of the car.

7. Remove the spring.

8. Install by reversing removal procedure.

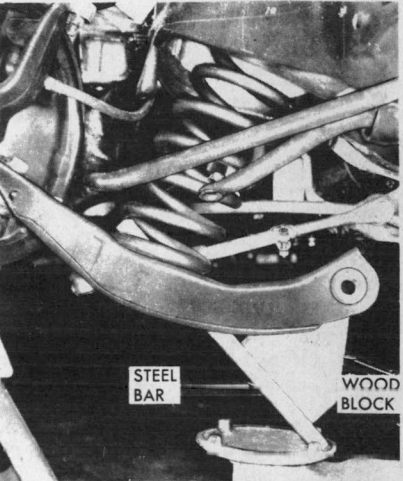

Chevrolet front spring removal
(© Chevrolet Div., G.M. Corp)

1971 and later Chevrolet, All Corvette

1. Raise car on hoist and remove nut, retainer and grommet from top of shock absorber. Support car so that control arms swing free.

2. Disconnect stabilizer bar from lower control arm and remove shock absorber.

3. Bolt spring remover tool (J-22944) to a suitable jack and place it under the lower control arm bushings so that the bushings seat in the grooves of the tool.

NOTE: This tool is a cradle which, when fastened to a hydraulic jack, allows the lowering of the control arm and slow decompression of the spring. A similar tool can be fabricated in the shop. Always safety-chain the spring and control arm when using this method.

4. Remove cross shaft rear retaining nut and the two front retaining bolts.

5. Slowly release jack, swing control arm forward, then remove spring.

6. Install by reversing procedure above.

Corvette front spring removal
(© Chevrolet Div., G.M. Corp)

NOTE: Chevrolet recommends this cradle spring removal tool for all models, beginning in 1971. Either of the other two methods may be used, depending on the availability of tools.

Ball Joint Inspection

NOTE: before performing this inspection, make sure the wheel bearings are adjusted correctly and that the A arm bushings are in good condition.

1. Jack the car up under the front lower control arm at the spring seat.
2. Raise the car until there is 1-2 in. of clearance under the wheel.
3. Insert a bar under the wheel and pry upward. If the wheel raises more than ⅛ in. the ball joints are worn. Determine if the upper or lower ball joint is worn by visual inspection while prying on the wheel.

NOTE: due to the distribution of forces is the suspension, the lower ball joint is usually the defective joint. Also, 1973 and later Chevrolets are equipped with wear indicators on the lower ball joint. As long as the wear indicator neck extends below the ball stud seat, replacement is unnecessary.

Upper Ball Joint Removal and Installation

1. Raise the car on a hoist.
2. Remove the tire and wheel assembly.
3. Support the lower control arm with a jack.
4. Loosen the upper ball stud nut.
5. Install a ball joint remover tool and unseat the upper joint from the steering knuckle. Remove the upper stud nut and install a block of wood under the upper A-arm.
6. Chisel or grind off the ball joint mounting rivets.
7. Drill out the ball stud attaching

holes to accept the service ball joint attaching bolts.
8. Install the ball joint with the nuts and bolts supplied with the new joint.
9. Install the lube fitting in the new joint.
10. Mate the upper control arm to the steering knuckle and install the ball stud through the knuckle boss.
11. Tighten the ball stud nut to 50 ft. lbs. plus whatever is necessary to align the cotter pin holes. Install the cotter pin.
12. Install the wheel and lower the vehicle.

Lower Ball Joint Removal and Installation

NOTE: On the 1971 and later Corvette, the lower ball joint removal and installation is the same as that described for the upper ball joint above. For all others:

1. On 1970 models raise the vehicle on a hoist and remove the wheel. On vehicles equipped with disc brakes, remove the caliper assembly.
2. Support the lower control arm with a jack.
3. Loosen the lower ball stud nut. Break the ball stud loose. Remove the ball stud nut.
4. Remove the ball stud from the steering knuckle.
5. The ball joint in 1970 models is attached with rivets which must be chiseled or ground off. Beginning with 1971 models, the ball joint is pressed in and must be pressed out.
6. Install the new ball joint, using the bolts supplied with the service ball joint (drill out the rivet holes to accommodate the mounting bolts) on 1970 models. The thick-headed bolt is installed on the forward side of the control arm. Press in the ball joint on 1971 and later models.
7. Install the ball stud in the steering knuckle boss. This may be done by raising the lower control arm with the jack.
8. Install the nut on the ball stud, tightening to 80-90 ft. lbs.
9. Install the lube fitting.

Lower Control Arm Removal and Installation

1. Remove the spring as described above.
2. Remove the ball stud from the steering knuckle as described above.
3. Remove the control arm pivot bolts and remove the control arm. On some Corvettes, the pivot bolt is secured to the frame with two bolts.
4. To install, reverse the above procedure.

Upper Control Arm Removal and Installation

1. Raise the vehicle on a hoist.
2. Support the outer end of the lower control arm, with a jack.
3. Remove the wheel.
4. Separate the upper ball joint from the steering knuckle as described above under "Upper Ball Joint Removal and Installation."
5. Remove the control arm shaft to frame nuts.

NOTE: tape the shims together and identify them so that they can be installed in the positions from which they were removed.

6. Remove the bolts which attach the control arm shaft to the frame and remove the control arm. Note the positions of the bolts.
7. Install in the reverse order of removal. Make sure the shaft to frame bolts are installed in the same position they were in before removal and that the shims are in their original positions. Tighten the shaft to frame bolts to 85 ft. lbs. on the Chevrolet and to 55 ft. lbs. on the Corvette. The control arm shaft nuts are torqued to 60 ft. lbs.

Front Wheel Bearing Adjustment

1. Jack the car up and support it at the lower arm.
2. Remove the hub dust cover and spindle cotter pin.
3. While spinning the wheel, snug the nut down to seat the bearings. Do not exert over 12 ft lbs of force on the nut.
4. Back the nut off ¼–½ a turn. Tighten the nut *finger-tight* (if the roller bearings are preloaded with the wheel off the ground, the inner edges of the bearings will be forced against the bearing cage), then *loosen* the nut as required to line up the cotter pin hole in the spindle with the hole in the nut.
5. Insert the cotter pin. End-play should be between 0.001 and 0.008 in. If play exceeds this tolerance, the wheel bearings should be replaced.

REAR SUSPENSION

The Chevrolet uses a coil sprung axle located by two trailing arms on each side, except the 1971 and later station wagon which has semi-elliptical leaf springs. The Corvette uses a three-link, independent suspension with a nine-leaf, transverse spring.

Shock Absorber Removal and Installation

Chevrolet

1. Jack the car to a convenient working height.
2. If the car is equipped with superlift shock absorbers, disconnect the air line.
3. Remove the two retaining bolts from the upper mounting bracket.
4. Hold the hex on the bottom stud and disconnect the lower mounting. Remove the shock absorber.
5. Install the top two bolts hand-tight.
6. Install the lower stud into the axle bracket and install the lockwasher and nut hand-tight.
7. Torque the upper bolts to 12 ft lbs.
8. While holding the hex stud, torque the nut to 65 ft lbs.
9. Attach the air line, if so equipped, and lower the car.

Corvette

1. Jack the car to a convenient working height.
2. Remove the upper bolt and nut.
3. Remove the lower mounting nut and washers.
4. Pivot the top of the shock absorber out the frame bracket and pull the bottom off the strut shaft.
5. Slide the upper shock absorber eye into the frame bracket and install the bolt, lockwasher, and nut.
6. Install the rubber grommets on the lower shock eye and place the shock over the strut shaft. Install the washers and nut.
7. Torque the upper bolt to 50 ft lbs and the lower nut to 35 ft lbs. Lower the car.

Coil Spring Removal and Installation (Chevrolet)

1. Raise rear of vehicle and place jack stands under frame. Support weight of vehicle at rear axle housing separately from above frame position.

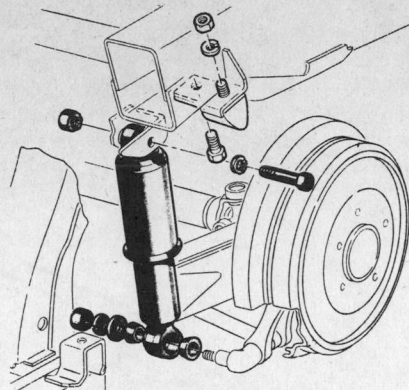

Shock absorber installation, Corvette
(© Chevrolet Div., G.M. Corp)

2. Remove both rear wheels.
3. With car supported as in Step 1, and springs compressed by weight of vehicle:
   a. Disconnect both rear shocks from anchor pin lower connection.
   b. Loosen the upper control arm(s) rear pivot bolt (do not remove the nut).
   c. Loosen both left and right lower control arm rear attachment (do not disconnect from axle brackets).
   d. Remove rear suspension tie rod from stud on axle tube.
4. Slightly loosen the nut on the bolt that retains the spring and seat to control arm at lower seat of both rear springs. When bolt has been backed off the maximum distance, all threads of the nut should still be engaged on the bolt.

Caution Under no condition should the nut, at this time, be removed from the bolt in the seat of either spring.

5. Slowly lower the rear axle assembly, allowing the axle to swing down, carrying the springs out of the upper seat. This provides access for spring removal.
6. Remove the lower seat attaching parts from each spring, then remove springs from vehicle.
7. Position springs in upper seat and install lower seat parts on control arm. Install nut of spring retaining bolt finger-tight.

NOTE: Omit lockwasher under the special high carbon bolt, so that sufficient threads will be available to start the nut. Lockwashers will be installed later.

8. Alternately raise the axle slightly and retighten the nut on each spring lower seat bolt. Continue in until the weight is fully supported on the jack or lift. With spring now completely compressed to approximate curb position, completely position the springs in the lower seats by torquing the nut on the lower seat bolt.
9. Reconnect shock absorbers, torque rear attachment of upper and lower control arms, and reconnect the axle tie-rod.
10. While still jacked under axle, remove the nut from the lower seat bolt of one rear spring and install lockwasher and replace nut and tighten. Similarly install lockwasher at other spring.
11. Install rear wheels and lower car to floor.

Transverse Leaf Spring Removal and Installation (Corvette)

1. Raise car and support it by the frame, slightly forward of torque control pivot points. Remove wheel assemblies.
2. Place floor jack under spring near link bolt, and raise spring until nearly flat.
3. Tie the end of the spring to the suspension crossmember to hold this flat attitude, with a ¼ in. or 5/16 in. chain and grab hook wrapped around the spring and crossmember. To prevent chain slipping, use a C-clamp on the spring adjacent to the chain.
4. Remove link bolt and rubber bushings.
5. Support and raise spring end, as before, and remove chain.
6. Carefully lower jack to completely relax spring.
7. Repeat foregoing procedure on the other side of car.
8. Remove four bolts and washers attaching the spring at the center.

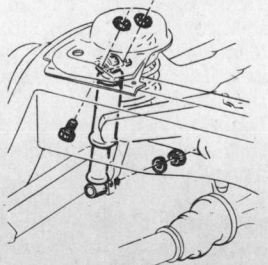

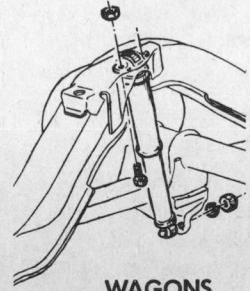

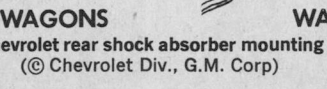

EXCEPT WAGONS   **WAGONS**
Chevrolet rear shock absorber mounting
(© Chevrolet Div., G.M. Corp)

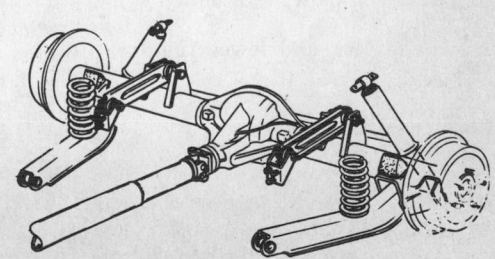

Chevrolet rear suspension except 1971 and later station wagon
(© Chevrolet Div., G.M. Corp)

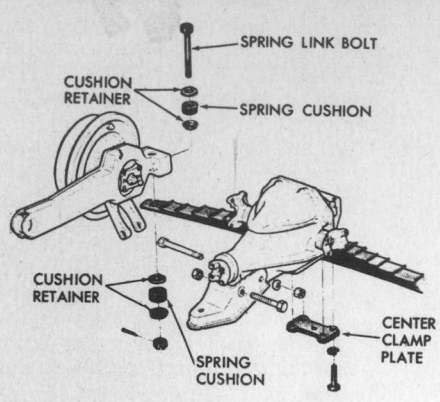

Spring mounting, Corvette
(© Chevrolet Div., G.M. Corp)

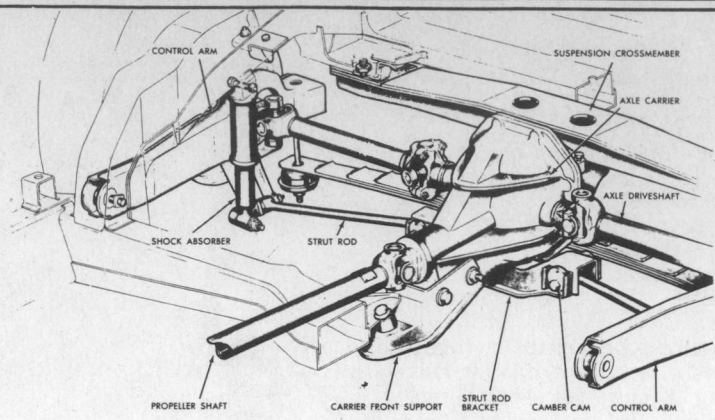

Corvette rear suspension
(© Chevrolet Div., G.M. Corp)

9. Remove the spring by sliding it over the exhaust pipes and out one side of the car.
10. Install by reversing removal procedure.

Leaf Spring Removal and Installation 1971 and later Chevrolet Station Wagon

1. Raise the vehicle on a hoist and place an adjustable jack under the axle.
2. Raise the axle until all tension is relieved from the spring.
3. Disconnect the shock absorber from the spring retainer plate.
4. Remove the upper shackle retaining bolt, then the front spring eye bolt.
5. Remove the spring/axle U-bolts, lower plate, spring pads, and spring.
6. Remove the shackle from the spring.
7. Before installing the spring, install the shackle on the rearward end.
8. Place the upper cushion on the spring, then insert the front of the spring into the frame and attach the rear shackle, leaving the bolt loose.
9. Install the lower spring pad and retainer plate, tightening the U-bolt nuts to 40 ft. lbs.
10. Tighten the rear shackle bolts to 115 ft. lbs.
11. Tighten the front eye bolt to 80 ft. lbs.
12. Attach the shock absorber to spring retainer plate, tightening to 65 ft. lbs.
13. Remove the jack and lower the vehicle.

Strut Rod and Bracket (Corvette)

Rear Wheel Camber Adjustment

Due to the design of this rear suspension, it is important that the strut rod and rear wheel camber adjusting specifications and procedures be included.

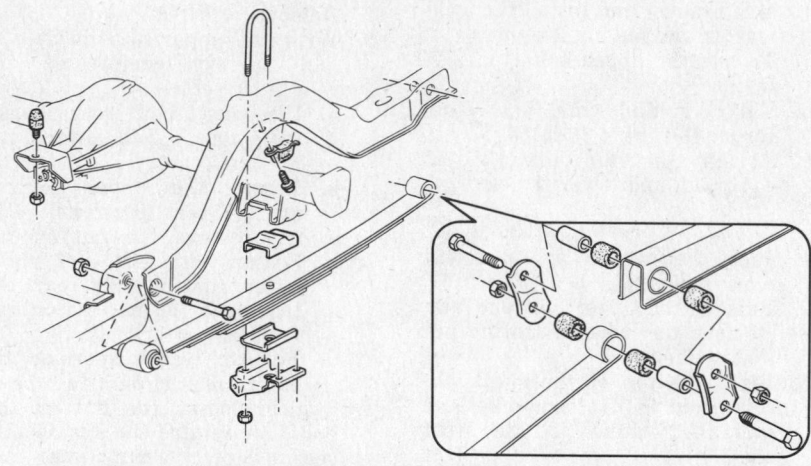

1971 and Later station wagon rear suspension (© Chevrolet Div., G.M. Corp)

Rod and Bracket—Removal

1. Raise car on a hoist.
2. Disconnect shock absorber lower eye from strut rod shaft.
3. Remove strut rod shaft cotter pin and nut. Withdraw shaft by pulling toward the front of the car.
4. Mark related position of camber adjustment, so that adjustment is maintained upon reassembly.
5. Loosen camber bolt and nut. Remove four bolts holding strut rod bracket to carrier and lower the bracket.
6. Remove cam bolt and cam bolt assembly. Pull strut down out of bracket and remove bushing caps.
7. Inspect strut rod bushings for wear and replace where necessary. Replace strut rod if it is bent or damaged in any way.
8. Install by reversing removal procedure.
9. Check rear wheel camber and adjust to specifications. Removal and Installation.

Torque Control Arm Removal and Installation (Corvette)

1. Disconnect spring on the side from which the torque arm is to be removed. Follow procedure for Spring Removal and Installation.

NOTE: if so equipped, disconnect stabilizer rod from torque arm.

2. Remove shock absorber lower eye from strut rod shaft.
3. Disconnect and remove strut rod shaft and swing strut rod down.
4. Remove four bolts holding the axle driveshaft to spindle flange and disconnect drive shaft.
5. Disconnect brake line at wheel cylinder inlet or caliper and from torque arm. Disconnect parking brake cable.
6. Remove torque arm pivot bolt and toe-in shims, then pull torque arm out of frame. Tape shims together to assure relationship for reassembly.
7. To install, place torque arm in frame opening.
8. Position toe-in shims in original location on both sides of torque arm. Install pivot bolt and lightly tighten at this time.
9. Raise axle driveshaft into position and install to drive flange. Torque bolts to 75 ft. lbs.
10. Raise strut into position and insert strut rod shaft so that flat lines up with flat in spindle support fork. Install nut and torque to 80 ft. lbs.
11. Install shock absorber lower eye and tighten nut to 35 ft. lbs.

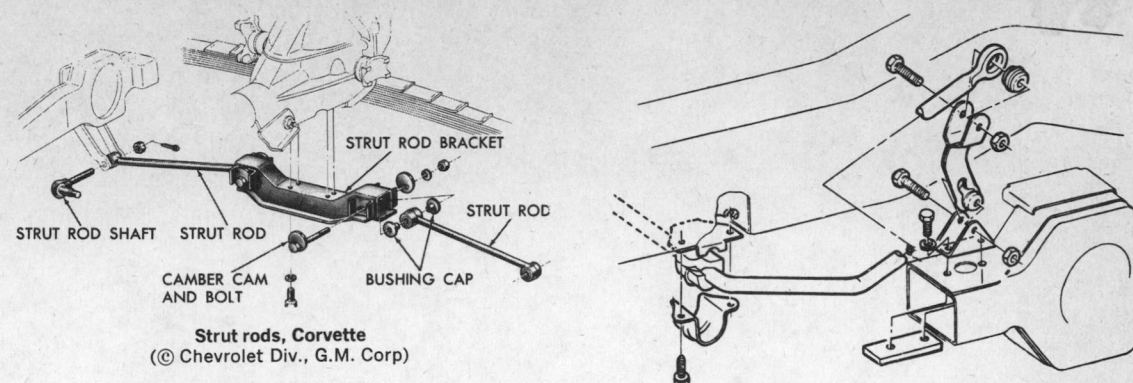

Strut rods, Corvette
(© Chevrolet Div., G.M. Corp)

Stabilizer shaft installation, Corvette
(© Chevrolet Div., G.M. Corp)

12. Connect spring end as outlined under Leaf Type Rear Spring Removal and Installation.
NOTE: if car is so equipped, connect stabilizer shaft.

13. Install brake drum or disc and caliper, and wheel. Then lower the car. Tighten torque pivot bolt to 50 ft. lbs.

14. Bleed brakes and check camber and toe-in.

BRAKES

Brake adjustments, lining replacement, bleeding procedure, master and wheel cylinder overhaul can be found in the Unit Repair Section.

A dual hydraulic brake system is employed. The front and rear brakes are each separate systems with a common tandem master cylinder. In the event of a failure in either of the systems, the other will remain operable.

Parking Brake Adjustment

Corvette

1. Jack the rear wheels off the ground and remove the wheels.
2. Rotate the disc until the adjusting screw can be seen through the hole in the disc.
3. Insert a screwdriver and adjust with an up-and-down motion.
4. Tighten the adjuster until the disc cannot move, then back off 6 to 8 notches.

5. Apply the parking brake to the fourth notch. Tighten the cables at the equalizer to give a light drag with the wheel mounted.
6. Release the parking brake and check for a no drag condition.

Chevrolet

Adjustment is made at the equalizer while the parking brake pedal is applied two notches from the full release position. Loosen the forward equalizer adjusting nut, tighten the rear nut until slight brake drag is obtained, then tighten the forward adjusting nut. Check operation after adjustment.

Power Brake Unit Removal

1. Remove vacuum hose from vacuum check valve.
2. Disconnect hydraulic lines at unit.
3. Disconnect push rod at brake pedal assembly.
4. Remove nuts and lockwashers that secure unit to firewall and remove unit.

Master Cylinder Removal

The pedals are pivoted from underneath the dash panel. The master cylinder is located on the engine side of the firewall.

1. To remove the master cylinder, disconnect the hydraulic lines, remove the clevis that connects the brake pushrod to the brake pedal from under the dash.
2. Remove the mounting bolts that hold the master cylinder to the firewall and lift off the master cylinder.
3. To install, reverse the above procedure, and bleed the brake system when installation is complete.

STEERING

Caution *On 1973 Chevrolets equipped with the air bag restraint system, refer to the Buick section for steering wheel and turn signal switch service.*

Manual steering gear on both the Chevrolet and Corvette is of the recirculating ball type. Relay-type steering linkage is used on all models, with a pitman arm connected to one end of a relay rod and a frame-mounted idler arm at the other end. Two tie-rods assemblies connect the relay rod to the steering arms. The tie-rod ends are threaded into sleeves to provide adjustment.

Chevrolet power steering is the integral-gear type. The only external hydraulic lines on this system are the pressure and return hoses to the pump. The Corvette uses a linkage

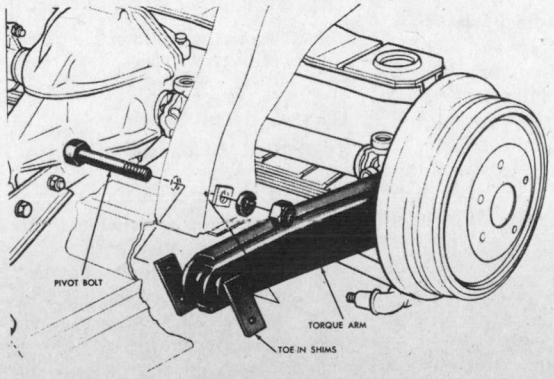

Torque control arm, Corvette
(© Chevrolet Div., G.M. Corp)

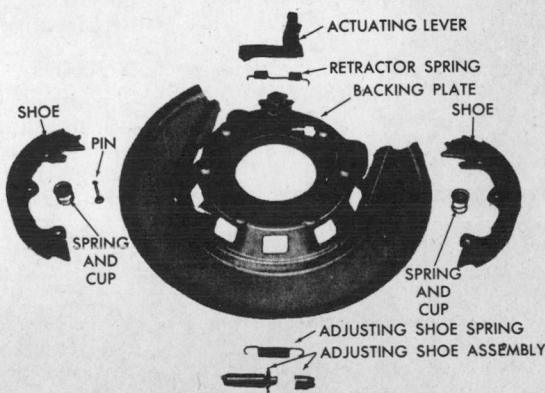

Corvette parking brake components
(© Chevrolet Div., G.M. Corp)

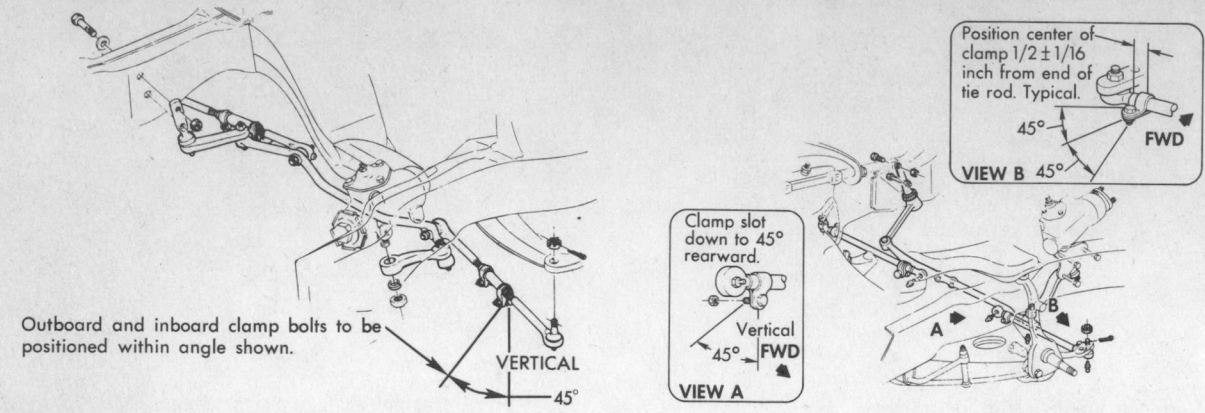

Outboard and inboard clamp bolts to be positioned within angle shown.

VERTICAL
45°

Clamp slot down to 45° rearward.
Vertical
45° FWD
VIEW A

Position center of clamp 1/2 ± 1/16 inch from end of tie rod. Typical.
45°
FWD
VIEW B 45°

A ▲   ▲ B

Chevrolet steering linkage
(© Chevrolet Div., G.M. Corp)

Corvette steering linkage
(© Chevrolet Div., G.M. Corp)

assist system. A valve attached to the linkage modulates pressure according to power requirements. A power cylinder supplies the actual assist.

Tie-Rod Removal and Installation

1. Remove the cotter pins and nuts from the tie-rod end studs.
2. Tap on the steering arm near the tie-rod end (use another hammer as backing) and pull down on the tie rod, if necessary, to free it.
3. Remove the inner stud in the same manner as the outer.
4. Loosen the clamp bolts and unscrew the ends if they are being replaced.
5. Lubricate the tie-rod end threads with chassis grease if they were removed. Install each end assembly an equal distance from the sleeve.
6. Ensure that the tie-rod end stud threads and nut are clean. Install new seals and install the studs into the steering arms and relay rod.
7. Install the stud nuts. Tighten the outer end nut to 35 ft lbs and the inner nut to 60 ft lbs (35 ft lbs on Corvette)
8. Adjust the toe-in as described in the "Front End Alignment" section.

NOTE: before tightening the sleeve clamps, ensure that the clamps are positioned so that the adjusting sleeve slot is covered by the clamp.

Power Steering Pump Removal and Installation

1. Remove the hoses at the pump and tape the openings shut to prevent contamination. Position the disconnected lines in a raised position to prevent leakage.
2. Remove the pump belt. On 427 and 454 Corvettes, loosen the alternator and remove the pump-to-alternator belt.

3. Loosen the retaining bolts and any braces, and remove the pump.
4. Install the pump on the engine with the retaining bolts hand-tight.
5. Connect and tighten the hose fittings.
6. Refill the pump and bleed by turning the pulley counterclockwise (viewed from the front). Stop the bleeding when air bubbles no longer appear.
7. Install the pump belt on the pulley and adjust the tension.

Bleeding Power Steering System

1. Fill the fluid reservoir.
2. Let the fluid stand undisturbed for two minutes, then crank the engine for about two seconds. Refill reservoir if necessary.
3. Repeat Steps 1 and 2 above until the fluid level remains constant after cranking the engine.
4. Raise the front of the car until the wheels are off the ground, then start the engine. Increase the engine speed to about 1,500 rpm.
5. Turn the wheels to the left and right, checking the fluid level and refilling if necessary.

Steering Wheel Removal and Installation

Caution Disconnect the battery ground cable before removing the steering wheel. When installing a steering wheel, always make sure that the turn signal lever is in the neutral position.

1975 and later models have a snap ring on the steering column which must be removed for steering wheel service.

1. Remove the four trim retaining screws from behind the wheel.
2. Lift the trim off and pull the horn wires from the turn signal cancelling cam.

3. Remove the steering wheel nut.
4. Mark the wheel-to-shaft relationship, and then remove the wheel with a puller.
5. Install the wheel on the shaft, aligning the previously made marks. Tighten the nut to 30 ft lbs.
6. Insert the horn wires into the cancelling cam.
7. Install the center trim and reconnect the battery cable.

NOTE: The 1973 Chevrolet cushioned rim wheel, and the Corvette wheel do not require pulling for removal. Pry off the center cap and horn contact assembly. On the tilt/telescope Corvette wheel, remove the shim, center lock-screw, lock lever or knob, and the spacer. The wheel is held to the hub by phillips screws. Reverse the disassembly procedure to install the wheel.

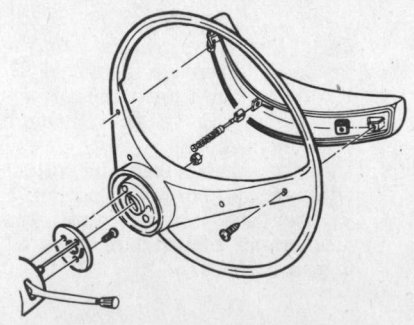

Chevrolet standard steering wheel
(© Chevrolet Div., G.M. Corp)

Turn Signal Switch Removal and Installation

Chevrolet and Corvette

1. Remove the steering wheel as previously outlined.
2. Loosen the three cover screws and lift the cover off the shaft. On 1976 and later models, use a screwdriver blade to pry the cover from the lock plate.
3. Position the special lockplate compressing tool on the end of

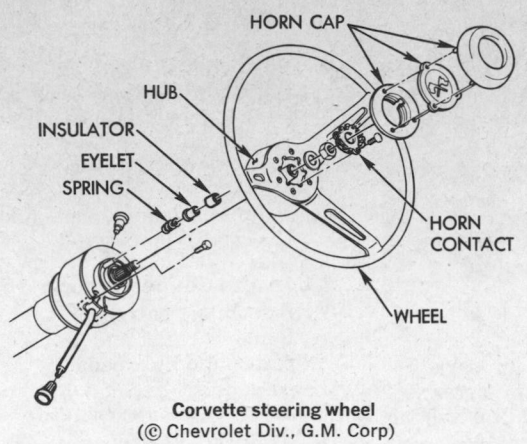

Corvette steering wheel
(© Chevrolet Div., G.M. Corp)

Compressing steering wheel lockplate and removing snap-ring
(© Chevrolet Div., G.M. Corp)

the steering shaft and compress the lockplate by turning the shaft nut clockwise. Pry the wire snap-ring out of the shaft groove.

4. Remove the tool and lift the lockplate off the shaft.
5. Slip the cancelling cam, upper bearing pre-load spring, and thrust washer off the shaft.
6. Remove the turn signal lever. Push the flasher knob in and unscrew it.
7. Pull the switch connector out of the mast jacket and tape the upper part to facilitate switch removal. On tilt wheels, place the turn signal and shifter housing in Low position and remove the harness cover.
8. Remove the three switch mounting screws. Remove the switch by pulling it straight up while guiding the wiring harness cover through the column.
9. Install the replacement switch by working the connector and cover down through the housing and under the bracket. On tilt models, the connector is worked down through the housing, under the bracket, and then the cover is installed on the harness.
10. Install the switch mounting screws and the connector on the mast jacket bracket. Install the column-to-dash trim plate.
11. Install the flasher knob and the turn signal lever.
12. With the turn signal lever in neutral and the flasher knob out, slide the thrust washer, upper bearing pre-load spring, and cancelling cam onto the shaft.
13. Position the lockplate on the shaft and press it down until a new snap-ring can be inserted in the shaft groove.
14. Install the cover and the steering wheel.

Corvette Tilt-Telescope

1. Remove the steering wheel as previously outlined and press off the hub with a puller.

2. Remove the steering column dash trim cover.
3. Remove the C-ring plastic retainer, if so equipped.
4. Install the special lockplate compressing tool over the steering shaft. Position a 5/16 in. nut under each tool leg and reinstall the star screw to prevent the shaft from moving.
5. Compress the lockplate by turning the shaft nut clockwise until the C-ring can be removed.
6. Remove the tool and lift out the lock plate, horn contact carrier, and the upper bearing preload spring.
7. Pull the switch connector out of the mast jacket and tape the upper part to facilitate switch removal.
8. Remove the turn signal lever. Push the flasher in and unscrew it.
9. Position the turn signal and shifter housing in Low position. Remove the switch by pulling it straight up while guiding the wiring harness out of the housing.
10. Install the replacement switch by working the harness connector down through the housing and under the mounting bracket.
11. Install the harness cover and clip the connector to the mast jacket.
12. Install the switch mounting screws, signal lever, and the flasher knob.
13. With the turn signal lever in neutral and the flasher knob out, install the upper bearing pre-load spring, horn contact carrier, and lockplate onto the shaft. Horn contact carrier is last on 1969 models.
14. Position the tool as in step four and compress the plate far enough to allow the C-ring to be installed.
15. Remove the tool. Install the plastic C-ring retainer.
16. Install the column/dash trim cover. Install the steering wheel.

Ignition Switch Replacement

The switch is located inside the channel section of the brake pedal support and is completely inaccessible without first lowering the steering column. The switch is actuated by a rod and rack assembly. A gear on the end of the lock cylinder engages the toothed upper end of the rod.

1. Lower the steering column; be sure to properly support it.
2. Put the switch in "Lock" position. With the cylinder removed, the rod is in "Lock" position when it is in the next to the uppermost detent.
3. Remove the two switch screws and remove the switch assembly.
4. Before installing, place the new switch in "Lock" position and make sure the lock cylinder and actuating rod are in "Lock" position (second detent from the top).
5. Install the activating rod into the switch and assemble the switch on the column. Tighten the mounting screws. Use only the specified screws since overlength screws could impair the collapsibility of the column.
6. Reinstall the steering column.

Lock Cylinder Removal and Installation

1. Remove steering wheel and directional signal switch.
2. Place lock cylinder in Lock position for 1970, Run position starting 1971.

Caution Do not remove the ignition key buzzer.

3. Insert a small screwdriver into the turn signal housing slot. Keeping the screwdriver to the right side of the slot, break the housing flash loose and depress the spring latch at the lower end of the lock cylinder. Remove the lock cylinder.

NOTE: Considerable force may be necessary to break this casting flash, but be careful not to damage any other parts. When ordering a new lock cylinder, specify a cylinder assembly. This will save assembling the cylinder, washer, sleeve and adaptor.

4. To install, hold the lock cylinder sleeve and rotate the knob clockwise against the stop. Insert the cylinder into the housing, aligning the key and keyway. Hold a .070 in. drill between the lock bezel and housing. Rotate the cylinder counterclockwise, maintaining a light pressure until the drive section of the cylinder mates with the sector. Push in until the snap ring pops into the grooves. Remove drill. Check cylinder operation.

Caution The drill prevents forcing the lock cylinder inward beyond its normal position. The buzzer switch and spring latch can hold the lock cylinder in too far. Complete disassembly of the upper bearing housing is necessary to release an improperly installed lock cylinder.

INSTRUMENT PANEL

Headlight Switch Replacement

Chevrolet
1. Disconnect battery.
2. Pull knob out to On position.
3. Reach under instrument panel and depress the switch shaft retainer. Remove knob and shaft assembly.
4. Remove the retaining ferrule nut. (Tool J-4880 will assist.)
5. Remove switch from instrument panel.
6. Disconnect the multi-plug connector from the switch.
7. Replace in reverse of above. (In checking lights before installation, switch must be grounded to test dome light.)

Corvette
1. Disconnect the battery.
2. Remove mast jacket trim covers.
3. Unclip and remove the left forward console side trim panel.
4. Lower the steering column.
5. Remove the screws and washers which secure the left instrument panel to the door opening, the top of the dash and the left side of the center instrument cluster.
6. Pull the cluster assembly down and tilt it forward.
7. Depress the switch shaft retainer and remove the knob and shaft assembly.
8. Remove the switch retaining bezel.
9. Disconnect the vacuum lines,

identifying them for correct reconnection.
10. Pry the connector from the switch.
11. Install in the reverse order of removal.

WINDSHIELD WIPERS

Motor Removal and Installation

1. With wiper motor in park position and hood open, disconnect the washer hoses and all wiring from the motor assembly.
2. Remove the plenum chamber grill on Corvettes or the access cover on Chevrolet models.
3. Loosen the nuts which retain the drive link to the crank arm ball stud on Chevrolet models. Remove the nut which retains the crank arm to the motor assembly on Corvette models.
4. On Corvettes, remove the ignition shield and distributor cap. Remove and identify the left bank spark plug leads.
5. Remove the motor mounting screws or nuts and remove the motor.
6. To install, reverse the above procedure.

RADIO

Removal and Installation
Chevrolet through 1972
1. Disconnect battery.
2. Remove ash tray, retainer attaching screws and retainer.
3. Remove heater control panel retaining screws and push panel assembly from console.

NOTE: if interference between control panel and radio is met, loosen radio retaining nuts.

4. Remove radio control knobs, bezels and retaining nuts.
5. Disconnect radio wiring harness, and antenna lead-in.
6. Remove radio rear brace attaching screw, and remove radio from the car.
7. Remove speaker retaining bolt and remove speaker.
8. To install, reverse removal procedure.

1973 and later Chevrolet
1. Disconnect the negative battery cable.
2. On cars with A/C, remove the lap cooler duct.
3. Turn the radio control knobs until the slots in the bottom of the knobs are visible. Depress the metal retainers with a screwdriver and remove the knobs and bezels.

4. Remove the control shaft nuts and washers.
5. Remove the right side bracket-to-instrument panel bolt and the stud nut on the left side of the radio.
6. Pull the radio forward and disconnect the wiring from the radio and remove the radio from the car.

Corvette Coupe through 1971
1. Disconnect battery.
2. Remove right and left door sill plates and kick pads.
3. Disconnect right and left side radio-to-speaker connectors.
4. Remove right side dash pad.
5. Remove right and left console forward trim pads.
6. Remove bolt and remove the heater floor outlet duct by pulling it through left hand opening.
7. From front of console, tape radio push buttons in depressed position. From rear of console, disconnect electrical connector, brace and antenna lead-in.
8. Remove radio knobs and bezel retaining nuts. Push radio assembly forward and remove from rear through right side opening.
9. Install by reversing procedure above.

Corvette Convertible through 1971
1. Disconnect battery.
2. Remove right instrument panel pad.
3. Disconnect speaker connectors.
4. Remove wiper switch trim plate screws to gain access to switch connector and remove connector and trim plate from cluster assembly.
5. Unclip and remove right and left console forward trim pads and remove forwardmost screw on right and left side of console.
6. Inserting a flexible drive socket between the console and metal horseshoe brace, remove the nuts from the two studs on the lower edge of the console cluster. Remove the remaining screws that retain the cluster assembly to the instrument panel.
7. From rear of console, disconnect electric connector, brace and antenna lead-in.
8. Remove radio knobs and bezel retaining nuts.
9. Pull radio assembly forward and remove through right side opening.
10. Install by reversing procedure above.

1973 and later Corvette
1. Disconnect the negative battery cable and remove the right instrument panel pad.

2. Disconnect the radio speaker connectors.
3. Remove the wiper switch trim plate screws and tip the plate forward to gain access to the switch connector. Remove the switch connector and trim plate from the dash.
4. Unclip and remove the right and left forward console trim pads. Remove the forwardmost screw on the left and right sides of the console.
5. Working with a flexible drive socket between the console and the metal horseshoe brace, remove the nuts from the studs on the lower edge of the console cluster.
6. Remove the remaining console attaching screws and disconnect the radio electrical connectors, antenna wire and radio brace from the rear of the console. Remove the radio knobs and nuts.
7. Pull the top of the console rearward and separate the radio from the console and remove it from the right side opening.

NOTE: The center instrument cluster trim panel is designed to collapse under impact. Do not deflect the panel to gain access to the radio. Also, the remotely located radio heat sink should be removed with the radio when servicing is required.

HEATER

Heater Blower Removal and Installation

Chevrolet
1. Disconnect battery.
2. Unclip hoses from fender skirt.
3. Disconnect electrical feed from motor. Disconnect the motor air-cooling hose on air-conditioned cars.
4. Turn vehicle front wheels to extreme right.
5. Remove right front fender skirt bolts and allow skirt to drop, resting it on top of tire. It may be wedged away from fender lower flange with block of wood to provide better access to bolts.
6. Remove screws attaching motor mounting plate to air inlet housing.
7. Remove screws attaching motor to mounting plate.
8. Remove clip attaching cage to shaft and remove blower motor.
9. Install in reverse of above.

Corvette (Non-Air Conditioned)
1. Remove the radiator supply tank from its retaining straps. Move it out of the way. Disconnect the battery.
2. Remove blower motor electrical connectors.

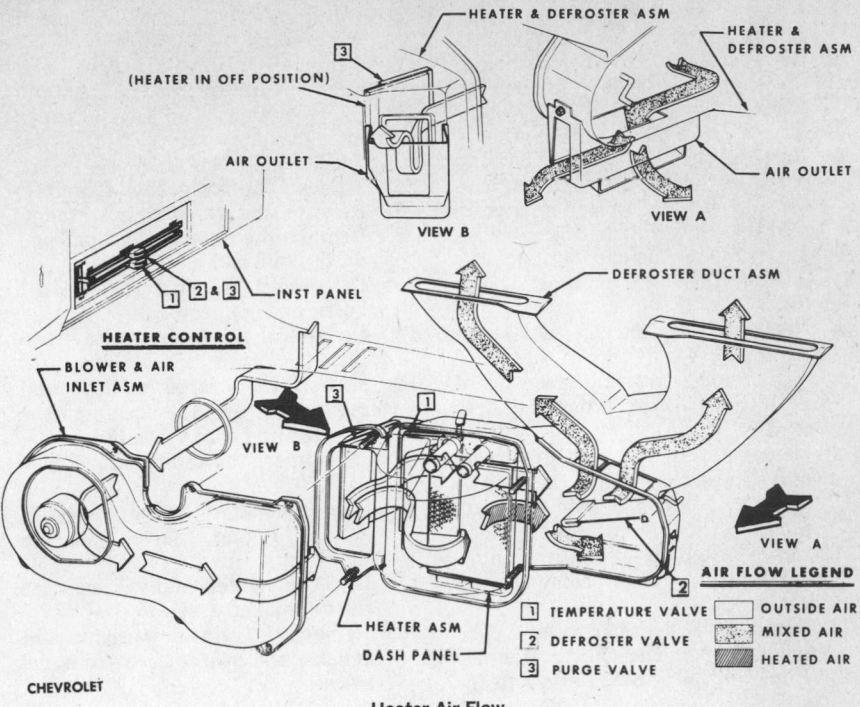

Heater Air-Flow
(© Chevrolet Div., G.M. Corp.)

3. Scribe a reference mark on the blower motor mounting plate and the blower motor.
4. Remove the five screws that mount the blower mounting plate to the blower inlet assembly.
5. Withdraw the blower assembly from the inlet assembly.
6. Install in reverse of removal procedure.

Corvette with Air Conditioning
1. Remove the battery ground cable.
2. Disconnect the air cooling tube and electrical wire from the blower motor.
3. Remove the first three sill molding screws and pry the molding out to allow access to the right splash shield bolts.
4. Remove the splash shield.
5. Remove the motor retaining screws and drop the motor out through the splash shield opening. Pry on the mounting flange gently, if necessary to break the motor loose.
6. Reverse the removal steps to install the motor.

Heater Core Removal and Installation

All Except Air Conditioned Cars
1. Drain radiator.
2. Remove heater hoses at connections beside air inlet assembly.
3. Remove cable and electrical connectors from heater and defroster assembly.
4. On engine side of dash, remove screws and nuts holding air inlet to dash panel.

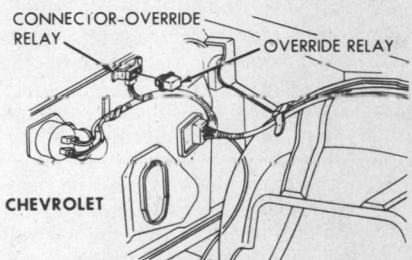

Override relay location
(© Chevrolet Div., G.M. Corp)

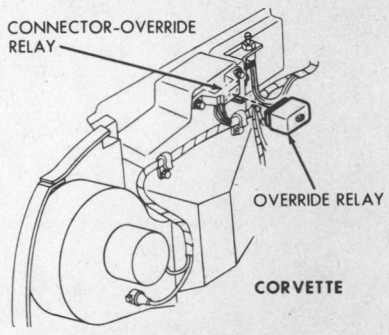

Override relay location
(© Chevrolet Div., G.M. Corp)

5. Inside vehicle, pull entire assembly from firewall and remove assembly from vehicle.
6. Remove core assembly retaining springs and remove core.
7. Install in reverse of above.

Chevrolet with Air Conditioning through 1971
1. Remove the battery ground cable.
2. Drain the cooling system. It is not necessary to evacuate the A.C. refrigerant.

3. Remove the heater hoses at the firewall.
4. Remove the nuts from the heater distributor studs protruding through the firewall.
5. Remove the glove compartment.
6. Remove the five center distributor duct hoses, duct cables, center duct-to-selector duct screws, and the center duct.
7. From inside the car, drill out the lower case stud using a 1/4 in. drill.
8. Remove the floor distributor duct.
9. Remove the firewall screws and pull the selector from the firewall.
10. Remove all wires, vacuum lines, and cables attached to the assembly, and remove it from the car.
11. Scribe the temperature door camming plate-to-selector duct relationship and remove the plate.
12. Remove the heater core and core housing from the selector duct.
13. Reverse the removal steps to install.

1972 and later Chevrolet with Air Conditioning

1. Drain the cooling system. It is not necessary to evacuate the A.C. refrigerant.
2. Disconnect the battery ground cable and compressor clutch connector.
3. Disconnect the vacuum line from the vacuum check valve and push the grommet through the firewall into the passenger compartment.

4. Disconnect the heater hoses at the firewall.
5. Remove the three screws and nuts retaining the heater and selector duct. The inner fender must be pried out from the firewall to gain access to one screw.
6. Remove the lap cooler assembly.
7. Remove the glove compartment.
8. Remove the floor outlet duct and dash panel pad.
9. Disconnect the distributor duct hoses and connector.
10. Remove the duct from the selector.
11. Loosen the defroster duct and move it to provide access to the selector and core assembly.
12. Disconnect the temperature door cable.
13. Separate the inline vacuum connector and the outside air diaphragm line.
14. Lift the heater and air selector duct out as an assembly.
15. Remove the retaining screws and remove the heater core from the selector.

Corvette with Air Conditioning

1. Disconnect the battery ground cable.
2. Drain the cooling system. It is not necessary to evacuate the A.C. refrigerant.
3. Disconnect the heater hoses at the firewall and plug the pipes.
4. Remove the nuts from the distributor studs protruding through the firewall.
5. Remove the right side dash pad

and center dash cluster (described under "Instruments").
6. Disconnect the right dash outlet from the center duct.
7. Remove the center duct from the selector duct.
8. Remove the selector duct to the dash panel and pull it to the right and to the rear.
9. Remove the cables and wiring connectors from the selector and remove it from the car.
10. Remove the temperature door cam plate from the selector duct.
11. Remove the heater core and housing from the selector.
12. Reverse the removal procedure to install.

SEAT BELTS

Disabling the Interlock System

Since the requirement for the interlock system was dropped during the 1975 model year, these systems may now be legally disabled. The seat belt warning light is still required.
1. Disconnect the battery ground cable.
2. Locate the interlock harness connector under the left side of the instrument panel on or near the fuse block. It has orange, yellow, and green leads.
3. Cut and tape the ends of the green wire on the body side of the connector.
4. Remove the buzzer from the fuse block or connector.

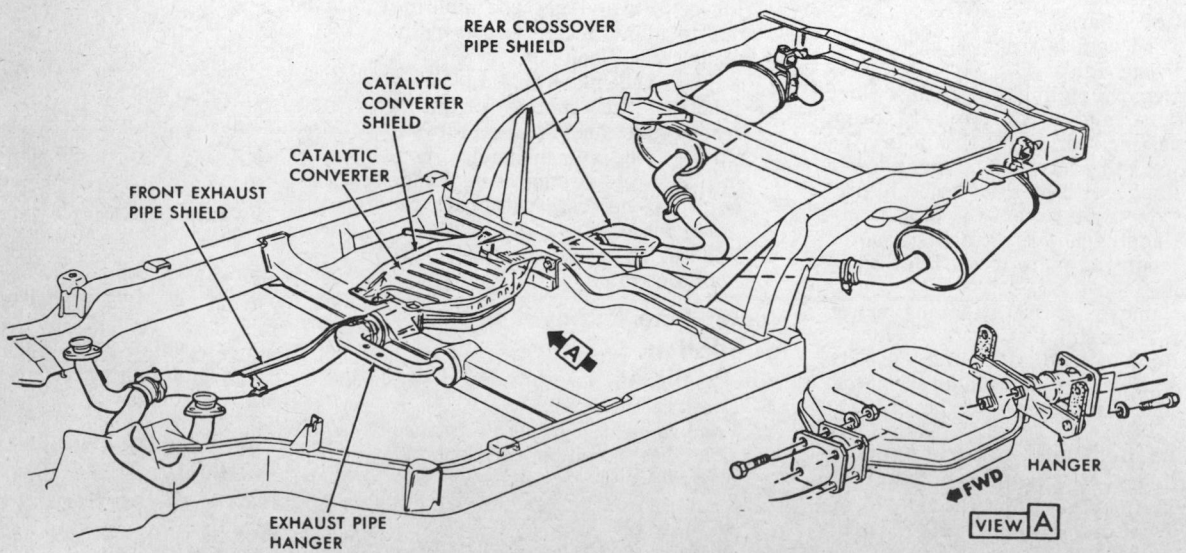

REAR CROSSOVER PIPE SHIELD

CATALYTIC CONVERTER SHIELD

CATALYTIC CONVERTER

FRONT EXHAUST PIPE SHIELD

EXHAUST PIPE HANGER

HANGER

FWD

VIEW A

1975 Corvette exhaust system and catalytic converter
(© Chevrolet Div., G.M. Corp)

Chevette

Automatic Transmission In-Car Service .. **C412**
Neutral safety switch replacement C412
Shift linkage adjustment C413
Downshift cable adjustment C413
Pan removal and installation, fluid and
filter change C413

Brakes **C417, U299**
Master cylinder removal and installation C417
Parking brake adjustment C417

Charging System **C402, U2**
Alternator removal and installation   C402

Clutch **C411**
Clutch disc removal and installation ... C411
Clutch pedal free-play adjustment C411

Cooling System **C405, U367**
Radiator removal and installation C405
Water pump removal and installation   C405
Thermostat removal and installation C406

Emission Controls **C406, U145**
Positive crankcase ventilation C406
Exhaust gas recirculation C406
Air injector reactor C406
Evaporative emission control C407
Controlled combustion system C407
Catalytic converter C407

Engine **C407, U194**

ENGINE REMOVAL AND INSTALLATION C407

CYLINDER HEAD REMOVAL AND
INSTALLATION C408

LUBRICATION C410
Oil pan removal and installation C410
Oil pump removal and installation C411
Rear main oil seal replacement C411

PISTONS AND CONNECTING RODS C410

TIMING COVER, BELT, AND CAMSHAFT ... C408
Timing belt cover removal and
installation C408

Timing belt and sprocket removal and
installation C409
Crankcase front cover removal and
installation C409
Camshaft removal and installation C410

VALVE SYSTEM C408
Rocker arm removal and installation ... C408
Valve guides C408

Front Suspension **C415, U292**
Shock absorber removal and installation C415
Lower ball joint removal and installation C415
Lower control arm and coil spring
removal and installation C415
Upper ball joint removal and installation C416
Upper control arm removal and
installation C416
Front wheel bearing adjustment C416

Fuel System **C404, U50**
Fuel pump removal and installation C404
Fuel filter removal and installation C404
Idle speed adjustment C405
Idle mixture adjustment C405

Heater **C420**
Blower motor removal and installation ... C420
Heater core removal and installation ... C420

Ignition System **C403, U34**
HEI system tachometer hookup C404
Distributor removal and installation C404
Ignition timing C404
Firing Order C400

Instrument Panel **C419, U350**
Instrument cluster replacement C419
Headlight switch removal and
installation C419

Jacking, Hoisting **C414**

Manual Transmission **C412, U231**
Transmission removal and installation   C412
Shift lever removal and installation C412

Radio **C420**
Removal and installation C420

Rear Axle **C414, U285**
Axle shaft, bearing, and seal removal
and installation C414

Rear Suspension **C416**
Shock absorber removal and
installation C416
Spring removal and installation C416

Specifications **C400, U359**
Capacities C401
Car serial number C400
Crankshaft and connecting rod C366
Engine identification C400
General engine C400
Piston clearance C402
Ring gap and side clearance C401
Torque C402
Tune-Up C400
Valve C401
Wheel alignment C402
Year identification C400

Starting System **C402, U2**
Starter removal and installation C402
Starter drive removal and installation C403

Steering **C417, U328**
Steering wheel removal and installation C417
Turn signal switch removal and
installation C418
Wiper/washer switch removal and
installation C418
Ignition key buzzer switch removal
and installation C418
Lock cylinder removal and installation ... C419
Ignition switch and dimmer switch
removal and installation C419

U-Joints **C414**
Driveshaft removal and installation C414
Universal joint removal and installation C414

Windshield Wipers **C420**
Motor removal and installation C420

YEAR IDENTIFICATION

CHEVROLET Chevette 4-cyl. engine (1.4 & 1.6 liters)

Engine firing order: 1-3-4-2

Distributor rotation: clockwise

FIRING ORDER

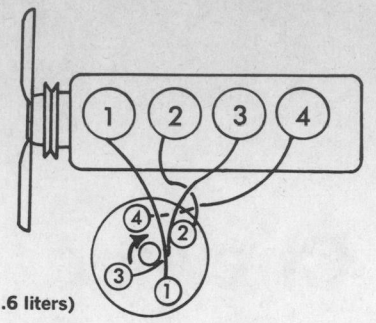

CAR SERIAL NUMBER LOCATION

Car serial number is located on the top left-hand side of the instrument panel, visible through the windshield.

Car Serial Number Interpretation

A typical vehicle serial number tag yields manufacturer's identity, vehicle type, model year assembly plant and production unit number when broken down as shown in the following chart.

Engine Identification Number

The engine identification number is located on a pad on the right-side of the cylinder block below the No. 1 spark plug.

1976 and Later

Mfr. Identity[1]	Series Code Letter[2]	Body Style[3]	Engine Model[4]	Model Year[5]	Assy. Plant[6]	Unit No.[7]
1	B	08	A	6	Y	100025

1 Manufacturer's identity number assigned to all Chevrolet vehicles.
2 Series.
3 Body style.
4 Engine code

5 Last number of model year (1976)
6 Assembly plant (Y—Wilmington).
7 Unit numbering will start at 100001.

GENERAL ENGINE SPECIFICATIONS

Year	Engine No. Cyl. Displacement liters (cu in.)	Carburetor Type	Horsepower @ rpm ■	Torque @ rpm (ft lbs) ■	Bore x Stroke (in.)	Compression Ratio	Oil Pressure @ 2000 rpm
'76-'77	4-1.4 (85)	1 bbl	52 @ 5300	67 @ 3400	3.228 x 2.606	8.5:1	39-46
	4-1.6 (97.6)	1 bbl	60 @ 5300	77 @ 3200	3.228 x 2.980	8.5:1	39-46

■ Horsepower and torque are SAE net figures. They are measured at the rear of the transmission with all accessories installed and operating. Since the figures vary when a given engine is installed in different models, some are representative rather than exact.

TUNE-UP SPECIFICATIONS

When analyzing test results, look for uniformity among cylinders rather than specific pressures.

Year	ENGINE No. Cyl. Displacement (liters)	SPARK PLUGS Type	SPARK PLUGS Gap (in.)	DISTRIBUTOR Point Dwell (deg)	DISTRIBUTOR Point Gap (in.)	IGNITION TIMING (deg) ▲ Man Trans	IGNITION TIMING (deg) ▲ Auto Trans	VALVES Intake Opens ■ (deg) ●	Fuel Pump Pressure (psi)	IDLE SPEED (rpm) ▲ Man Trans •	IDLE SPEED (rpm) ▲ Auto Trans.
'76	4-1.4	R43TS	.035	Electronic		10B	10B	32	5-6.5	800(1000)	800(850)
	4-1.6	R43TS	.035	Electronic		8B	10B	32	5-6.5	800(1000)	800(850)
'77	4-1.4	R43TS	.035	Electronic		①	①	32	5-6.5	800(1000)	800(850)
	4-1.6	R43TS	.035	Electronic		①	①	32	5-6.5	800(1000)	800(850)

▲ See text for procedure
• Figure in parentheses indicates California engine
■ All figures Before Top Dead Center
B Before Top Dead Center

NOTE: The underhood specifications sticker often reflects tune-up specification changes made in production. Sticker figures must be used if they disagree with those in this chart.
① See underhood specifications sticker

CAPACITIES

Year	ENGINE No. Cyl. Displacement (liters)	Engine Crankcase Add ½ Qt For New Filter	TRANSMISSION Pts To Refill After Draining Manual 4-Speed	Automatic •	Drive Axle (pts)	Gasoline Tank (gals)	COOLING SYSTEM (qts) With Heater	With A/C
'76-'77	4-1.4	4	3	7	2.8	13	8.5	8.5
	4-1.6	4	3	7	2.8	13	9.0	9.0

• Specifications do not include torque converter

VALVE SPECIFICATIONS

Year	Engine No. Cyl. Displacement (liters)	Seat Angle (deg)	Face Angle (deg)	Spring Test Pressure (lbs @ in.)	Spring Installed Height (in.)	STEM TO GUIDE Clearance (in.) Intake	Exhaust	STEM Diameter (in.) Intake	Exhaust
'76-'77	4-1.4	46	45	68 @ 1.26	1.26	.0018-.0021	.0026-.0029	.3141	.3133
	4-1.6	46	45	68 @ 1.26	1.26	.0018-.0021	.0026-.0029	.3141	.3133

CRANKSHAFT AND CONNECTING ROD SPECIFICATIONS

All measurements are given in inches

Year	Engine No. Cyl. Displacement (liters)	Main Brg. Journal Dia	CRANKSHAFT Main Brg. Oil Clearance	Shaft End-Play	Thrust on No.	Journal Diameter	CONNECTING ROD Oil Clearance	Side Clearance
'76-'77	4-1.4	2.0075-2.0085	.0009-.0025	.004-.008	4	1.809-1.810	.0014-.0030	.004-.012
	4-1.6	2.0075-2.0085	.0009-.0025	.004-.008	4	1.809-1.810	.0014-.0030	.004-.012

RING GAP

All measurements are given in inches

Year	Engine No. Cyl. Displacement (liters)	Top Compression	Bottom Compression	Year	Engine No. Cyl. Displacement (liters)	Oil Control
'76-'77	4-1.4	.009-.019	.008-.018	'76-'77	4-1.4	.015-.055
	4-1.6	.009-.019	.008-.018		4-1.6	.015-.055

RING SIDE CLEARANCE

All measurements are given in inches

Year	Engine No. Cyl. Displacement (liters)	Top Compression	Bottom Compression	Year	Engine No. Cyl. Displacement (liters)	Oil Control
'76-'77	4-1.4	.0012-.0027	.0012-.0032	'76-'77	4-1.4	.0000-.0050
	4-1.6	.0012-.0027	.0012-.0032		4-1.6	.0000-.0050

PISTON CLEARANCE

Year	Engine No. Cyl. Displacement (liters)	Piston① to Bore Clearance (in.)
'76-'77	4-1.4	.0008-.0016
	4-1.6	.0008-.0016

① Measured 1½ in. from top of piston

TORQUE SPECIFICATIONS

All readings in ft lbs

Year	Engine No. Cyl. Displacement (liters)	Cylinder Head Bolts	Rod Bearing Bolts	Main Bearing Bolts	Crankshaft Pulley or Damper Bolt	Flywheel to Crankshaft Bolts	MANIFOLD Intake	MANIFOLD Exhaust
'76-'77	4-1.4, 1.6	70-80	34-40	40-52	65-85	40-52	13-18	①

① Center bolts—13-18; end bolts—19-25

WHEEL ALIGNMENT SPECIFICATIONS

Year	Model	CASTER Range (deg)	CASTER Pref Setting (deg)	CAMBER Range (deg)	CAMBER Pref Setting (deg)	Toe-in (in.)	Steering Axis Inclination (deg)	WHEEL PIVOT RATIO (deg) Inner Wheel	WHEEL PIVOT RATIO (deg) Outer Wheel
'76-'77	All	4P to 5P	4½P	¼N to ¾P	¼P	1/16	7½	NA	NA

N Negative
P Positive
NA Not available

CHARGING SYSTEM

A Delcotron 10-SI series alternator is used. This unit also contains a solid state, integrated circuit voltage regulator. The alternator is nonadjustable and requires no periodic maintenance. Refer to the "Unit Repair Section" for applicable testing and overhaul procedures.

Alternator Removal and Installation

1. Disconnect the negative battery cable.
2. Disconnect the alternator wiring.
3. Remove the adjustment brace bolt and remove the drive belt.
4. Support the alternator, remove the alternator mounting bolt, and remove the alternator.
5. Installation is the reverse of removal. Adjust drive belt deflection to ½ in. under moderate thumb pressure.

STARTING SYSTEM

Engine cranking is accomplished by a solenoid-actuated starter motor powered by the vehicle battery. The motor is a Delco-Remy unit similar to previous Chevrolet starters. No periodic lubrication of the motor or solenoid is necessary. Testing and overhaul procedures can be found in the "Unit Repair Section."

Starter Removal and Installation

Cars Without Power Brakes

1. Disconnect the negative battery cable and remove the air cleaner.
2. Disconnect the electrical connector from the oil pressure sending unit and remove the sending unit.
NOTE: The oil pressure sending unit has a harness lock. To disconnect the electrical connector, lift the tab on the collar of the lock and remove the lock assembly.
3. Disconnect the wires from the starter solenoid.
4. Remove the brace screw from the bottom of the starter housing.
5. Remove the two starter-to-flywheel housing mounting screws.
6. Hold the starter with both hands and tip it past the engine mount bracket, then upward between the intake manifold and wheelarch.
7. Installation is the reverse of removal.

Cars With Power Brakes (Without Air Conditioning)

1. Disconnect the battery negative cable and remove the air cleaner.
2. Remove the distributor cap and place it aside.
3. Remove the fuel line from the fuel pump to the carburetor.
4. Disconnect the electrical connector from the ignition coil. Remove the three coil bracket retaining screws and remove the coil with bracket.
5. Disconnect the vacuum hose to the distributor vacuum advance unit.
6. Disconnect the electrical con-

nector from the oil pressure sending unit and remove the sending unit. See the preceding "Note" concerning the oil pressure sender harness lock.

7. Disconnect the wires from the starter solenoid.
8. Remove the brace screw from the bottom of the starter housing.
9. Remove the two starter-to-flywheel housing mounting screws.
10. Hold the starter with both hands and remove it by sliding it toward the front of the car.
11. Installation is the reverse of removal.

Cars With Power Brakes and Air Conditioning

1. Disconnect the negative battery cable and remove the air cleaner.
2. Remove the upper starter-to-flywheel housing mounting screw.
3. Remove the two steering column lever cover screws.
4. Remove the mast jacket lower bracket screw.
5. Remove the upper steering column mounting bracket.
6. Disconnect the four electrical connectors from the steering column.
7. Raise the car on a hoist.
8. Disconnect the steering flexible coupling (rag joint) and push it aside.
9. Disconnect the wires from the starter solenoid.
10. Remove the brace screw from the bottom of the starter housing.
11. Remove the lower starter-to-flywheel housing mounting screw.
12. To gain clearance, raise the engine 1/2 in. with a jack placed under the left-side of the engine.
13. Remove the starter by lowering it through the opening at the bottom of the engine.
14. Installation is the reverse of removal.

Starter Drive Removal and Installation

1. Disconnect the field coil connector(s) from the starter solenoid terminal and remove the starter through-bolts.
2. Remove the commutator end frame, field frame assembly, and the armature from the drive housing.
3. Remove the starter drive by sliding the two-piece thrust collar off the armature shaft. Install a 1/2 in. pipe coupling or other suitable cylinder into the shaft to butt against the edge of the retainer. Using a hammer, tap the coupling to force the retainer toward the armature end of the snap-ring.
4. Use pliers to remove the snap-ring from the groove in the

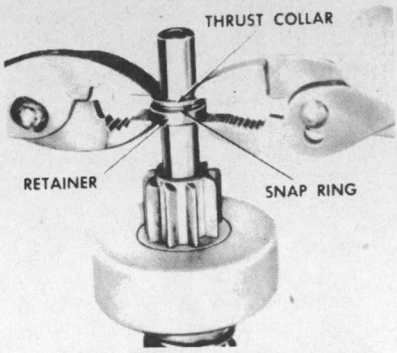

Forcing the snap-ring into the retainer
(© Chevrolet Div., G.M. Corp)

shaft. If the snap-ring becomes distorted, use a new one upon assembly. Remove the retainer and starter drive from the armature.

Inspect all parts, replacing where necessary. Do not use grease dissolving solvent when cleaning starter parts—the drive mechanism and internal electrical insulation will be damaged.

To install:

5. Apply silicone lubricant to the drive end of the armature and slide the drive asembly onto the armature with the pinion outward. Install the retainer on the armature with its cupped surface facing away from the pinion.
6. Install the snap-ring on the shaft by standing the armature on a wood surface (commutator end down), placing the snap-ring on the end of the shaft held in position with a wood block, and tapping the wood block with a hammer. Slide the snap-ring into its groove on the shaft. Place the thrust collar on the shaft with its shoulder against the snap-ring.
7. With the armature on a flat surface, place the retainer and thrust collar next to the snap-ring. Using pliers on both sides

of the shaft at the same time, grip the retainer and thrust collar and squeeze until the snap-ring is forced into the retainer.
8. Apply silicone lubricant to the drive housing bushing. With the thrust collar in place against the snap-ring and retainer, slide the armature and starter drive assembly into the drive housing. Engage the solenoid shift lever with the drive assembly.
9. Place the field frame over the armature and apply sealing compound between the frame and the solenoid case. Using care to avoid damage to the brushes, position the field frame against the drive housing.
10. Use silicone lubricant to lubricate the commutator end frame bushing. Install the leather washer onto the armature shaft and slide the commutator end frame onto the armature shaft.
11. Install the through-bolts and reconnect the field coil connector(s) to the starter solenoid terminal.

IGNITION SYSTEM

All Chevette models are equipped with High Energy Ignition (HEI). This is a pulse triggered transistor-controlled, inductive discharge ignition system that uses no breaker points. The HEI distributor contains a pick-up assembly and an electronic module which perform the function of breaker points. Centrifugal and vacuum advance mechanisms are basically the same as those in breaker point distributors. The capacitor in the distributor only serves to reduce radio noise. The ignition coil is mounted externally.

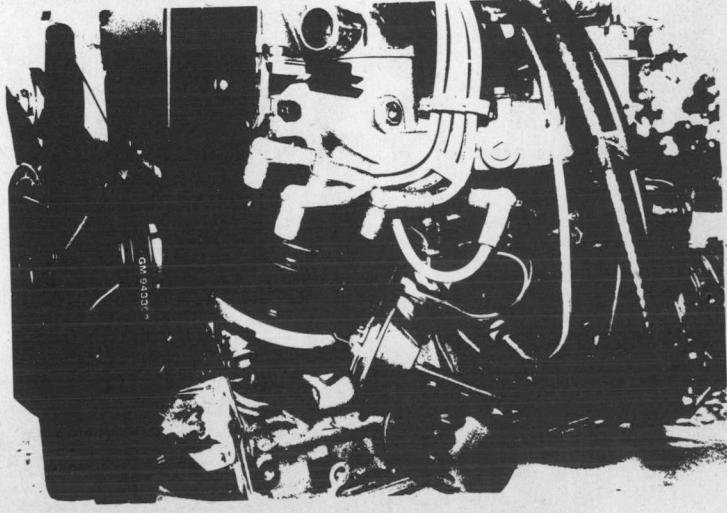

Chevette HEI distributor with remote-mounted coil

Distributor mounting is at the front of the engine on the left-side.

HEI System Tachometer Hookup

Connect tachometers to the "TACH" terminal in the distributor cap and to ground. However, some tachometers must connect to the "TACH" terminal and the battery positive terminal. Check the tachometer manufacturer's instructions.

CAUTION: *Never ground the "TACH" terminal as the HEI electronic module could be damaged.*

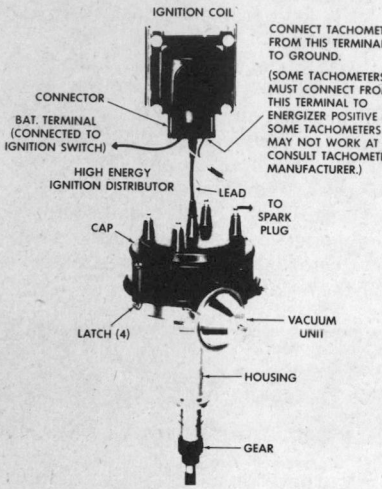

HEI distributor with remote-mounted coil

Distributor Removal

1. Disconnect the wiring harness connector from the distributor cap, remove the cap, and position it out of the way.
2. Disconnect the vacuum line from the vacuum advance mechanism.
3. Scribe marks indicating rotor position in relation to distributor and distributor position in relation to the engine.
4. Remove the distributor hold-down nut and clamp and remove the distributor from the engine.

Distributor Installation

1. Turn the rotor approximately ⅛ turn clockwise past the alignment mark.
2. Push the distributor into position while moving the rotor slightly to mesh the drive gears.
3. Install the hold-down clamp and nut.
4. Install the distributor cap by aligning the tab in the cap with the notch in the housing and securing the four latches.
5. Connect the wiring harness connector to the terminals on the side of the cap. Reconnect the vacuum advance line.

6. Check ignition timing and adjust if necessary.

Installation—Engine Disturbed

1. Remove the No. 1 spark plug and place a finger over the spark plug hole. Turn the engine until compression is felt in the No. 1 cylinder.
2. Install the distributor with the distributor body scribe mark aligned with the mark on the engine and with the rotor pointing toward the distributor cap No. 1 spark plug tower.
3. Install the hold-down clamp and nut, but do not tighten them securely.
4. Install the distributor cap by aligning the tab in the cap with the notch in the housing and securing the four latches.
5. Connect the wiring harness connector to the terminals on the side of the cap. The connector will attach one way only. Reconnect the vacuum advance line.
6. Check and adjust the ignition timing. Securely tighten the distributor hold-down clamp.

Ignition Timing

NOTE: Use an adapter to make timing light connections at the distributor No. 1 terminal.

1. Bring the engine to normal operating temperature. Stop the engine and connect a tachometer. Disconnect and plug the PCV hose at the vapor canister and the vacuum hose at the distributor vacuum advance unit. Start the engine and check curb idle speed. Adjust as necessary.
2. Stop the engine, clean the timing marks and mark them with chalk. Connect a timing light.
3. Start the engine and aim the timing light at the timing marks. If the marks align, stop the engine, reconnect the PCV and vacuum hoses, and remove the timing light.
4. If adjustment is necessary, loosen the distributor clamp and rotate

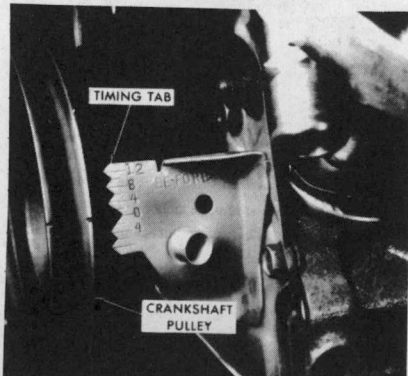

Ignition timing marks
(© Chevrolet Div., G.M. Corp)

the distributor to align the marks. Tighten the clamp and recheck the timing.

NOTE: *Air conditioned models require removal of the compressor, bracket, and belt to reach the distributor clamp.*

5. Reset the curb idle speed if necessary, stop the engine, and remove the tachometer and timing light. Reconnect the PCV and vacuum hoses.

FUEL SYSTEM

All Chevette models use a Rochester 1ME Monojet carburetor. The carburetor has an electrically heated choke coil, an aluminum throttle body, and an electrically-operated idle speed solenoid. All models use dual throttle return springs and idle mixture screw limiter caps. An EGR vacuum port is located in the throttle body.

Fuel is filtered by an internal paper element located in the fuel bowl behind the fuel inlet nut. Also in the fuel inlet is a check valve to prevent fuel spillage in the event of a roll over accident.

The fuel pump is located on the left side of the engine under the intake manifold.

Fuel Pump Removal and Installation

NOTE: Air conditioned cars require the removal of the rear compressor bracket to gain working room.

1. Working from under the car, remove the ignition coil.
2. Disconnect the fuel inlet and outlet lines at the pump and plug the inlet line.
3. Remove the two pump mounting bolts and lockwashers and remove the fuel pump and gasket.
4. Install the fuel pump with a new gasket coated with sealer. Tighten the two mounting bolts.
5. Connect the fuel inlet and outlet lines at the pump. Install the ignition coil.
6. Start the engine and check for leaks.

Fuel Filter Removal and Installation

1. Disconnect the fuel line fitting at the carburetor fuel inlet nut.
2. Remove the fuel inlet nut from the carburetor.
3. Remove the fuel filter element and spring from the carburetor.
4. Install the spring and the fuel filter element into the carburetor.
5. With a new gasket on the fuel inlet nut, install the nut into the carburetor and tighten it securely.

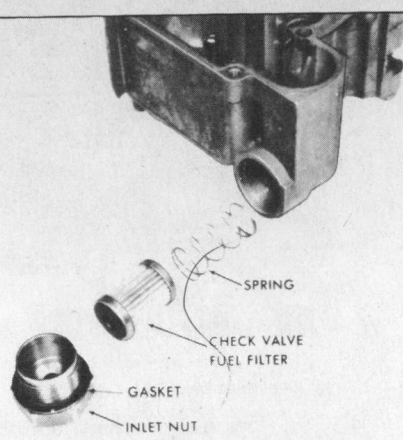

Fuel filter and check valve assembly
(© Chevrolet Div., G.M. Corp)

6. Install the fuel line fitting into the fuel inlet nut and tighten securely.

Idle Speed Adjustment

Two idle speeds are controlled by a solenoid on models without both automatic transmission and air conditioning. One is normal curb idle speed (solenoid energized). The second is low idle speed (solenoid de-energized) which prevents dieseling when the ignition is turned off. On cars with both automatic transmission and air conditioning the solenoid is energized when air conditioning is on to maintain curb idle speed.

1. With engine at normal operating temperature, air cleaner on, choke open, and air conditioning off, attach a tachometer to the engine. Apply parking brake, block the rear wheels, and disconnect and plug the PCV hose at vapor canister and vacuum advance hose at the distributor.
2. For cars without both automatic transmission and air conditioning, turn the idle solenoid in or out to obtain the curb idle speed stated on the underhood specifications sticker, then disconnect the wire from the solenoid.
3. With automatic transmission in Drive or manual transmission in Neutral set the low idle speed to the specified rpm by turning the 1/8 in. hex screw located in the end of the solenoid. Reconnect the wire to the solenoid.
4. Cars with both automatic transmission and air conditioning must have a green wire with a double white strip, NOT a brown wire, connected to the idle solenoid. Correct if necessary.
5. With air conditioning off and automatic transmission in Drive, turn the 1/8 in. hex screw in the end of the solenoid in until fully bottomed.
6. Turn the solenoid assembly to obtain 950 rpm.

7. Adjust curb idle speed by turning the hex screw out to obtain the specified curb idle speed.
8. Check ignition timing and adjust if necessary. Readjust solenoid assembly and curb idle speed if necessary.
9. Stop engine, remove tachometer, and connect PCV and vacuum hoses.

Idle Mixture Adjustment

Carburetor idle mixture is present at the factory and a plastic limiter cap is mounted on the idle mixture screw. The cap limits the mixture screw to approximately one turn leaner (clockwise) without breaking the cap. Idle mixture should be adjusted at major carburetor overhaul.

1. With engine at normal operating temperature, air cleaner on, choke open, and air conditioning off, attach a tachometer to the engine. Apply parking brake, block the rear wheels, and disconnect and plug the PCV hose at vapor canister and vacuum advance hose at the distributor.
2. Start the engine and check ignition timing. Adjust timing as necessary. Replace vacuum advance hose.
3. Place automatic transmission in Drive or manual transmission in Neutral.

NOTE: If the mixture screw is removed from the carburetor, gently seat it, then back it out 3 turns. Continue with Step 4.

4. Remove the air cleaner and cut the tab off the limiter cap, but do not remove the cap from the screw. Replace the air cleaner. Obtain the maximum idle speed by turning the mixture screw clockwise (leaner) or counterclockwise (richer).
5. Turn the idle speed solenoid in or out to obtain the higher idle speed stated on the underhood tune-up specifications sticker.
6. While turning the idle mixture screw clockwise (leaner), watch the tachometer to obtain the lower idle speed stated on the underhood specifications sticker.
7. Stop engine, remove the tachometer, and replace the PCV and vacuum advance hoses.

COOLING SYSTEM

A standard pressurized water cooling system is used. A permanently-lubricated impeller-type water pump forces coolant through engine and cylinder head water jackets and into a cross-flow radiator. Some models use a heavy-duty radiator with a fan

shroud. The pressure-type radiator cap pressurizes the cooling system to 15 psi. A 190°F thermostat in the coolant outlet passage is used to control coolant flow. A translucent plastic coolant recovery reservoir is used to provide for coolant expansion. Coolant level is checked by observing the amount present in the reservoir with the engine at normal operating temperature. Add coolant to the reservoir, not the radiator. A 50/50 mixture of ethylene glycol antifreeze and water yielding freeze protection to −20°F should be used as coolant.

Radiator Removal and Installation

1. Drain the radiator.
2. Disconnect the upper and lower radiator hoses and the coolant recovery reservoir hose.
3. Remove the radiator baffle or shroud. Remove the baffle by removing the four baffle-to-radiator support screws. Remove the shroud by removing the two upper screws and the two middle screws. Remove the upper radiator shroud. The lower shroud is removed from its mounting clips.
4. Disconnect and plug the transmission cooler lines if necessary.
5. Remove the radiator upper mounting panel or brackets and lift the radiator out of the lower brackets.
6. To install, reverse the removal procedure.

Water Pump Removal and Installation

1. Disconnect the battery negative cable and remove the engine drive belt(s).
2. Remove the engine fan, spacer (air conditioned models), and the pulley.

CAUTION: *A bent or damaged fan assembly should always be replaced. Do not attempt repairs as fan balance is critical. If unbalanced, the fan could fail and break apart while in use.*

3. Remove the timing belt front cover by removing the two upper bolts, center bolt, and two lower nuts.
4. Drain the coolant from the engine.
5. Remove the lower radiator hose and the heater hose at the water pump.
6. Turn the crankshaft pulley so that the mark on the pulley is aligned with the 0 mark on the timing scale and that a 1/8 in. drill bit can be inserted through the timing belt upper rear cover and cam gear.
7. Remove the idler pulley and pull the timing belt off the gear. Don't disturb crankshaft position.

Timing belt idler pulley
(© Chevrolet Div., G.M. Corp)

8. Remove the water pump retaining bolts and remove the pump and gasket from the engine.
9. Clean all the old gasket material from the cylinder case.
10. With a new gasket in place on the water pump, position the water pump in place on the cylinder case and install the water pump retaining bolts.
11. Install the timing belt onto the cam gear.
12. Apply sealer to the idler pulley attaching bolt and install the bolt and the idler pulley. Turn the idler pulley counterclockwise on its mounting bolt to remove the slack in the timing belt.
13. Use a tension gauge to adjust timing belt tension. Check belt tension midway between the tensioner and the cam sprocket on the idler pulley side. Correct belt tension is 55 lbs. Torque the idler pulley mounting bolt to 13-18 ft lbs.
14. Remove the 1/8 in. drill bit from the upper rear timing belt cover and cam gear.
15. Install the lower radiator hose and the heater hose to the water pump.
16. Install the timing belt front cover.
17. Install the water pump pulley, spacer (if equipped), and engine fan.
18. Install the engine drive belt(s).
19. Refill the cooling system.
20. Connect the battery negative cable.
21. Start the engine and check for leaks.

Thermostat Removal and Installation

1. Drain the radiator and remove the upper radiator hose at the water outlet.
2. Remove the thermostat housing bolts and remove the housing, gasket, and thermostat.
3. Install the thermostat. Use a new gasket on the thermostat housing

and install the thermostat housing bolts.
4. Install the upper radiator hose at the water outlet.
5. Fill the cooling system.

CONTROLS EMISSION

Positive Crankcase Ventilation

Positive Crankcase Ventilation (PCV) reroutes combustion blow-by gases from the crankcase through the intake manifold for reburning. The system consists of a hose connecting the air cleaner to the cam cover and another hose connecting the PCV valve, mounted in a grommet in the cam cover, and the intake manifold.

The PCV valve regulates the flow of combustion gases through the system. During engine idle and deceleration when intake manifold vacuum is high, the PCV valve restricts vapor flow to the intake manifold. When the engine is accelerated or is at constant speed, intake manifold vacuum is low and the PCV valve allows crankcase gases to flow into the intake manifold. Should the engine backfire, the plunger inside the valve is forced against its seat preventing the backfire from traveling through the PCV valve and into the engine crankcase.

The PCV valve is checked for proper operation simply by removing it from the grommet in the cam cover and shaking. If the plunger in the valve rattles, the valve is good and can be replaced. At 24 month or 30,000 mile intervals, install a new PCV valve and use compressed air to blow out the PCV valve hose to eliminate any restrictions.

Exhaust Gas Recirculation

Exhaust Gas Recirculation (EGR) is used to reduce oxides of nitrogen (NO_x) exhaust emissions. NO_x formation occurs at very high combustion temperatures so that the EGR system reduces combustion temperature slightly by introducing small amounts of inert exhaust gas into the intake manifold. The result is reduced formation of NO_x.

An EGR valve is mounted on the intake manifold. It contains a vacuum diaphragm and is operated by intake manifold vacuum to control the flow of exhaust gases. A vacuum signal supply port is located in the throttle body of the carburetor above the throttle plate. Vacuum is supplied to the EGR valve (causing recirculation), at part-throttle condi-

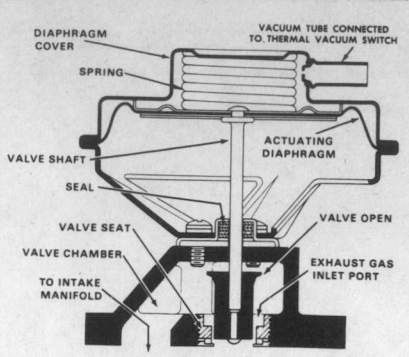

EGR valve cutaway
(© Chevrolet Div., G.M. Corp)

tions. EGR does not occur at idle or at wide open throttle. A 0.030 in. orifice in the EGR valve vacuum tube further regulates vacuum.

Some models also use a thermal vacuum switch (TVS), mounted in the outlet water housing to block vacuum to the EGR valve until engine coolant temperature is approximately 100°F.

Air Injection Reactor

The Air Injection Reactor (AIR) system reduces carbon monoxide and unburned hydrocarbon emissions by injecting air into the exhaust system at the rear of the exhaust valves. The AIR system is used on California cars only. The system consists of an air pump, air injection tubes (one for each cylinder), a vacuum differential valve, an air by-pass valve, a differential vacuum delay and separator valve, a check valve, and the required hoses to connect the components.

The air pump (with an integral filter), compresses and injects the air through the air manifolds into the exhaust system to the rear of the exhaust valves. The additional air brings about further combustion of hydrocarbons and carbon monoxide in the exhaust manifold. The vacuum differential valve stops air injection to prevent backfiring during engine deceleration by activating the air by-pass valve. The vacuum differential valve is triggered by sharp increases in manifold vacuum. On engine deceleration total air pump output is vented to the atmosphere through a muffler in the air by-pass valve. Also in the air by-pass valve is a pressure relief valve which vents excess air from the air pump at high engine speeds. The by-pass valve also vents air through its muffler at times of low intake manifold vacuum (engine acceleration). This low manifold vacuum venting is controlled by the differential vacuum delay and separator valve which blocks this venting for very short periods of 20 seconds or less, to prevent possible overheating of the catalytic converter. The check valve prevents exhaust gases from entering the air pump.

Evaporative Emission Control

The Evaporative Control System (ECS) limits gasoline vapor escape into the atmosphere. A domed fuel tank and pressure-vacuum filler cap is used with a plastic, charcoal-filled storage canister.

Fuel vapors travel from the fuel tank vent pipe (located above fuel level in the dome of the fuel tank), by way of steel tubing and fuel-resistant rubber hose to the plastic vapor storage canister in the engine compartment. Fuel vapors are routed into the PCV system for burning when ported carburetor vacuum operates a valve in the canister. As fuel is pumped from the tank, a relief valve in the tank cap opens to allow air to enter the fuel tank.

Controlled Combustion System

The Controlled Combustion System (CCS) increases combustion efficiency by way of leaner carburetor mixtures and revised distributor calibration. Also, a thermostatically-controlled damper in the air cleaner snorkel maintains warm air intake to the carburetor to optimize fuel vaporization.

An air intake duct routes air from the radiator support to the air cleaner snorkel, then to the 50,000 mile, one-piece air cleaner. Air temperature is automatically controlled by a thermostatic damper inside the air cleaner snorkel. The damper selects warm air from the exhaust manifold heat stove when air temperature is below 50°F. When air temperature is above 110°F, the damper selects outside air from the air intake duct.

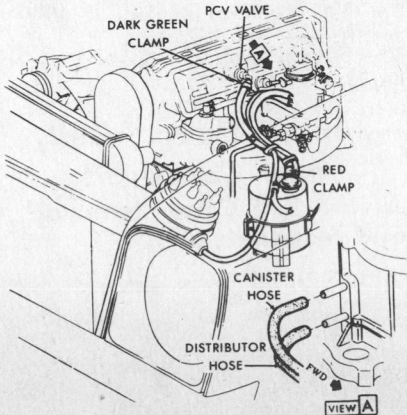

ECS canister and lines

(© Chevrolet Div., G.M. Corp)

When replacing the 50,000 mile air cleaner, remove the air cleaner from the air intake snorkel and the carburetor and throw it away. Check the carburetor air horn gasket and replace it if damaged or cracked, and install a new air cleaner.

Catalytic Converter

All models are equipped with an underfloor catalytic converter. The converter contains pellets coated with the catalyst material containing platinum and palladium. The converter reduces hydrocarbon and carbon monoxide emissions by transforming them into carbon dioxide and water through a chemical reaction which takes place at great heat.

Unleaded fuel only must be used with converter equipped cars because lead in leaded fuel is not consumed in the combustion process and will enter the converter and coat the pellets, eventually rendering the catalytic converter useless for emission control. To ensure the use of unleaded fuel only, all models have a small diameter fuel inlet filler which will accept only the smaller unleaded fuel nozzle.

See the "Emission Control Systems" in the Unit Repair Section for additional information on emission controls.

ENGINE

All Chevette models are powered by a 1.4 or optional 1.6 liter inline four-cylinder overhead camshaft engine of 85 or 98 cu in. respectively.

The belt-driven camshaft is supported on five bearings and is housed in an aluminum carrier on top of the cast iron cylinder head. The cross-flow cylinder head has induction-hardened exhaust valve seats for greater durability. Rocker arms bridge hydraulic valve lifters and the valve stems and open the valves via camshaft depression.

The distributor and oil pump are simultaneously gear driven by a gear on the crankshaft next to the front main bearing. A cam on the distributor shaft drives the fuel pump.

The cast iron cylinder block supports the crankshaft in five main bearings. The aluminum intake manifold is heated by engine coolant.

Engine Removal and Installation

Caution *Do not discharge the air conditioning compressor or disconnect any air conditioning lines. Personal injury could result.*

1. Remove the engine hood from the car.
2. Disconnect the positive and negative battery cables.
3. Remove the battery cable clips from the right frame rail.
4. Drain the cooling system. Disconnect the radiator hoses from the engine and the heater hoses at the heater.
5. Disconnect the engine wiring harness at the firewall connector.
6. Remove the radiator upper support and remove the radiator and engine fan.
7. Remove the air cleaner assembly.
8. Disconnect the following items:
   a. Fuel line at the rubber hose along the left frame rail.
   b. Automatic transmission throttle valve linkage.
   c. Accelerator cable.
9. On air conditioned cars, remove the compressor from its mount and lay it aside.
10. Raise the car on a hoist.
11. Disconnect the exhaust pipe at the exhaust manifold.
12. Remove the flywheel dust cover on manual transmission cars or the torque converter underpan on automatic transmission cars.
13. On automatic transmission cars, remove the torque converter-to-flywheel bolts.
14. Remove the converter housing or flywheel housing-to-engine retaining bolts and lower the car.
15. Position a floor jack or other suitable support under the transmission.
16. Remove the safety straps from the front engine mounts and remove the mount nuts.
17. Install the engine lifting apparatus.
18. Remove the engine by pulling forward to clear the transmission while lifting slowly. Check to make sure that all necessary disconnections have been made and that proper clearance exists with surrounding components. Remove the lifting apparatus.

To install the engine:
19. Install the engine lifting apparatus and install guide pins in the engine block.
20. Install the engine in the car by aligning the engine with the transmission housing.
21. Install the front engine mount nuts and safety straps.
22. Raise the car on a hoist.
23. Install the engine-to-transmission housing bolts.
24. On automatic transmission cars, install the torque converter to the flywheel.
25. Install the flywheel dust cover or torque converter underpan as applicable.
26. Install the exhaust pipe to the exhaust manifold and lower the car.

27. Install the air conditioning compressor if necessary, and adjust drive belt tension.
28. Connect the following items:
    a. Fuel line at the rubber hose along the left frame rail.
    b. Automatic transmission throttle valve linkage.
    c. Accelerator cable.
29. Install the air cleaner.
30. Install the engine fan, radiator, and radiator upper support.
31. Connect the engine wiring harness at the firewall connector.
32. Connect the radiator and heater hoses and fill the cooling system.
33. Install the battery cable clips along the right frame rail.
34. Install the engine hood.
35. Connect the battery cables, start the engine and check for leaks.

Valve System

Valve operation is accomplished by rocker arms bridging hydraulic lash adjusters and the valve stems being depressed by the camshaft.

Periodic adjustment of the hydraulic valve lash adjusters is not necessary.

Cleanliness should be exercised when handling the valve lash adjusters. Before installation of lash adjusters, check the lash adjuster hole in the cylinder head to make sure that it is free of foreign matter and fill the lash adjusters with oil.

Rocker Arm Removal and Installation

NOTE: A special valve spring compressor is necessary for this procedure. Also prelubricate new rocker arms with Molykote® or its equivalent.

1. Remove the camshaft cover.
2. Using the special valve spring compressor, compress the valve springs and remove the rocker arms. Keep the rocker arms and guides in order so that they can be installed in their original locations.
3. To install the rocker arms, compress the valve springs and in-

Compressing the valve springs
(© Chevrolet Div., G.M. Corp)

stall the rocker arm guides.
4. Position the rocker arms in the guides and on the valve lash adjusters.
5. Install the camshaft cover.

Valve Guides

Valves with oversize stems are available. To install, remove the cylinder head and remove the camshaft from the cylinder head. Remove the valves and ream the valve guides with an appropriate oversize reamer.

Cylinder Head

Cylinder Head Removal and Installation

1. Remove the timing belt.
2. Drain the cooling system and disconnect the upper radiator hose and heater hose at the intake manifold.
3. Remove the air cleaner and snorkel (silencer) assembly.
4. Remove the accelerator cable support bracket.
5. Disconnect the spark plug wires.
6. Disconnect the wires from the idle solenoid, choke, temperature sender, and alternator.
7. Raise the car on a hoist and disconnect the exhaust pipe from the exhaust manifold.
8. Lower the car.
9. Remove the dipstick tube bracket-to-manifold attaching bolt.
10. Disconnect the fuel line at the carburetor.
11. Remove the coil bracket bolts and lay the coil aside.
12. Remove the camshaft cover.
13. Remove the camshaft cover-to-camshaft housing attaching studs.
14. Remove the rocker arms, rocker arm guides, and valve lash adjusters. Keep the parts in order so that they can be installed in their original locations.
15. Remove the camshaft carrier bolts and remove the camshaft carrier. A sharp wedge may be necessary to separate the camshaft carrier from the cylinder head.
16. With an assistant, remove the manifold and cylinder head assembly.
To install the cylinder head:
17. Install a new cylinder head gasket with the words "This Side Up" facing up over dowel pins in the block. Make sure that the gasket is absolutely clean.
18. With an assistant, install the manifold and cylinder head assembly.
19. Apply a light, thin continuous bead of Loctite® #75 or its equivalent to the joining surfaces of the cylinder head and the camshaft carrier and install the

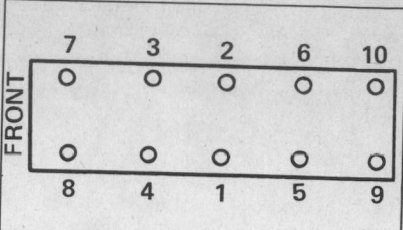

1.4 and 1.6 liter cylinder head torque sequence
(© Chevrolet Div., G.M. Corp)

camshaft carrier. Clean any excess sealer from the cylinder head. Apply sealing compound to the camshaft carrier/cylinder head bolts and install the bolts finger-tight. Tighten the bolts a little at a time and in the proper sequence until the final specified torque figure is reached.
20. Install the camshaft cover-to-camshaft housing attaching studs.
21. Install the valve lash adjusters and rocker arm guides. Prelube the rocker arms with Molykote® or its equivalent and install the rocker arms.
22. Using new gaskets, install the camshaft covers.
23. Install the coil bracket mounting bolt.
24. Connect the fuel line to the carburetor.
25. Install the dipstick tube bracket-to-manifold attaching bolt.
26. Raise the car on a hoist and attach the exhaust pipe to the exhaust manifold.
27. Lower the car.
28. Connect the wires to the idle solenoid, choke, temperature sender, and alternator.
29. Connect the spark plug wires.
30. Apply Teflon tape or its equivalent to the threads of the accelerator cable support bracket attaching bolts and install the bracket.
31. Install the air cleaner and snorkel (silencer) assembly.
32. Connect the upper radiator hose and heater hose to the intake manifold.
33. Fill the cooling system.
34. Install the timing belt.

Timing Cover, Belt, and Camshaft

Timing Belt Cover Removal and Installation

Upper Front Cover

1. Disconnect the negative battery cable.
2. Remove engine accessory drive belts.
3. Remove the engine fan.
4. Remove the cover retaining screws and nuts and remove the cover.

To install the cover:

5. Align the screw slots on the upper and lower parts of the cover.
6. Install the cover retaining screws and nuts. Torque the nuts to 80-105 in. lbs.
7. Install the engine fan.
8. Install the engine accessory drive belts.
9. Connect the negative battery cable.

Lower Front Cover

1. Disconnect the negative battery cable.
2. Remove the crankshaft pulley.
3. Remove the upper front timing belt cover.
4. Remove the one cover-to-block retaining nut.
5. To install the cover, align the cover with the studs on the engine block.
6. Install the lower front cover retaining nut and torque to 80-105 in. lbs.
7. Install the upper front timing belt cover.
8. Install the crankshaft pulley. Torque the retaining bolt to 65-85 ft lbs.

Upper Rear Cover

1. Disconnect the negative battery cable.
2. Remove the upper and lower front cover, the timing belt, and the camshaft timing sprocket.
3. Remove the three screws retaining the camshaft sprocket cover to the camshaft carrier.
4. Inspect the condition of the cam seal.
5. Position and align a new gasket over the end of the camshaft and against the camshaft carrier.
6. Install the three camshaft sprocket cover retaining screws.
7. Install the camshaft sprocket, timing belt, and the upper and lower front covers.
8. Connect the negative battery cable.

Timing Belt and Sprockets Removal and Installation

Caution *Do not discharge the air conditioning compressor or disconnect the air conditioning lines. Personal injury could result.*

1. Disconnect the negative battery cable.
2. Remove the alternator and air conditioning compressor (if equipped) drive belts.
3. Remove the engine fan and pulley.
4. Remove the engine upper and lower front timing belt covers.
5. Remove the crankshaft pulley and timing belt idler pulley.
6. Remove the timing belt from

Correct distributor rotor alignment for timing belt installation
(© Chevrolet Div., G.M. Corp)

the camshaft and crankshaft timing sprockets.
7. With the distributor cap off, mark the location of the rotor in the No. 1 spark plug firing position on the distributor housing. On air conditioned cars, remove the compressor and lower its mounting bracket.
8. Remove the camshaft timing sprocket bolt and washer and remove the camshaft sprocket.
9. Remove the crankshaft timing sprocket.

To install:

10. Place the crankshaft timing sprocket on the crankshaft making sure that the locating tabs face outward.
11. Install the crankshaft timing sprocket.
12. Align the camshaft sprocket dowel with the hole in the end of the camshaft and install the sprocket on the camshaft.
13. Apply Loctite® sealer or its equivalent to the camshaft sprocket retaining bolt and washer and torque to 65-85 ft lbs.
14. Position the timing belt over the crankshaft sprocket.
15. Install the crankshaft pulley. Torque to 65-85 ft lbs.
16. Align the crankshaft pulley timing mark with the 0 mark on the timing scale and the distributor rotor with the scribed

Correct camshaft sprocket alignment for timing belt installation
(© Chevrolet Div., G.M. Corp)

mark on the distributor housing.
17. Align the hole in the camshaft sprocket with the hole in the upper rear timing belt cover.
18. Install the timing belt on the camshaft and crankshaft sprockets.
19. Adjust timing belt tension as follows:
   a. Remove the upper radiator support. On air conditioned cars, also remove the upper part of the fan shroud.
   b. Turn the crankshaft clockwise a minimum of one revolution and place the No. 1 cylinder at top dead center. A 1/8 in. drill bit should fit through the hole in the rear of the upper rear timing belt cover and the hole in the camshaft sprocket. Do not turn the crankshaft counterclockwise.
   c. Remove the idler pulley attaching bolt. Apply Loctite® sealer or its equivalent to the bolt threads and install the bolt and idler pulley, but do not fully tighten.
   d. Turn the idler pulley counterclockwise on its attaching bolt to remove slack in the timing belt.
   e. Using a belt tension gauge, check timing belt tension with the gauge located midway between the idler pulley and the camshaft sprocket on the idler pulley side. Timing belt tension should be 55 lbs. Tighten the idler pulley attaching bolt to 13-18 ft lbs.
   f. Remove the 1/8 in. drill bit from the timing belt upper rear cover and the camshaft sprocket. Install the upper radiator support and on air conditioned cars, the upper part of the fan shroud.
20. Install the distributor cap. On air conditioned cars, install the lower compressor bracket and the compressor.
21. Install the upper and lower front timing belt covers.
22. Install the engine fan and pulley.
23. Install the alternator and, if necessary, the air conditioning compressor drive belts.
24. Connect the negative battery cable.

Crankcase Front Cover Removal and Installation

NOTE: An oil seal alignment tool is required for this procedure.

1. Disconnect the negative battery cable.
2. Remove the upper and lower front timing belt covers, crankshaft pulley, idler pulley, timing belt, and the crankshaft timing sprocket.

3. Remove three oil pan bolts and the cover attaching bolts.
4. Remove the old cover gasket and the front portion of the oil pan gasket.
5. Inspect the crankshaft front oil seal and replace if necessary.

To install:

6. Replace the crankcase cover gasket, cut the front portion of the oil pan gasket, and apply RTV sealer or its equivalent to the cutoff portion of the oil pan gasket.
7. Using an oil seal alignment tool, install the front cover. Torque the cover bolts to 75-110 in. lbs.
8. Install the crankshaft timing sprocket, timing belt, idler and crankshaft pulleys. Adjust timing belt tension following Step 19 in "Timing Belt and Sprockets Removal and Installation." Install the upper and lower front timing belt covers.
9. Connect the negative battery cable.

Camshaft Removal and Installation

NOTE: A special valve spring compressor is necessary for this procedure. If replacing the camshaft or rocker arms, prelube new parts with Molykote® or its equivalent.

1. Disconnect the negative battery cable.
2. Remove engine accessory drive belts.
3. Remove the engine fan and pulley.
4. Remove the upper and lower front timing belt covers.
5. Loosen the idler pulley and remove the timing belt from the camshaft sprocket.
6. Remove the camshaft sprocket attaching bolt and washer and remove the camshaft sprocket.
7. Remove the camshaft cover. Using the special valve spring compressor, remove the valve arms and guides. Keep the rocker arms and guides in order so that they can be installed in their original locations.
8. Remove any components necessary to gain working clearance.

NOTE: The heater assembly will probably have to be removed from the firewall to gain working clearance.

9. Remove the upper rear timing belt cover from the camshaft carrier.
10. Remove the camshaft thrust plate bolts. Slide the camshaft slightly to the rear and remove the thrust plate.
11. Remove the engine mount nuts and wire retainers.
12. Using a floor jack, raise the engine.

13. Remove the camshaft from the camshaft carrier.

To install:

14. Install the camshaft into the camshaft carrier.
15. Lower the engine.
16. Install the engine mount nuts and attach the retaining wires.
17. Slide the camshaft slightly to the rear and install the thrust plate.
18. Position and align a new gasket over the end of the camshaft, against the camshaft carrier, and install the upper rear timing belt cover.
19. Install any components which were removed to gain working clearance.
20. Install the valve rocker arms and guides in their original locations using the special valve spring compressor. Install the camshaft covers.
21. Align the dowel in the camshaft sprocket with the hole in the end of the camshaft and install the sprocket.
22. Apply Loctite® sealer or its equivalent to the sprocket retaining bolt threads and install the bolt and washer. Torque the sprocket retaining bolt to 65-85 ft lbs.
23. Turn the crankshaft clockwise to bring the No. 1 cylinder to top dead center. Make sure that the distributor rotor is in position to fire the No. 1 spark plug. Align the hole in the camshaft sprocket with the hole in the upper rear timing belt cover and install the timing belt on the camshaft sprocket.
24. Adjust timing belt tension following Step 19 in "Timing Belt and Sprockets Removal and Installation."
25. Install the upper and lower front timing belt covers.
26. Install the engine fan and pulley.
27. Install the engine accessory drive belts.
28. Connect the negative battery cable.

Pistons and Connecting Rods

Install piston and connecting rod assemblies into their original cylin-

Piston locating notch
(© Chevrolet Div., G.M. Corp)

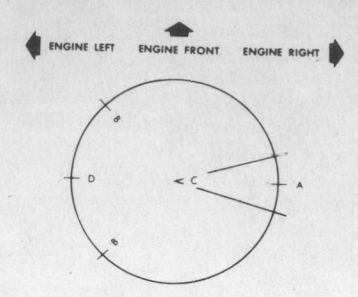

A OIL RING SPACER GAP   C 2ND COMPRESSION RING GAP
B OIL RING RAIL GAPS   D TOP COMPRESSION RING GAP

Ring gap locations
(© Chevrolet Div., G.M. Corp)

ders. Install the piston and rod assemblies with the notch on the piston crown facing to the front of the engine. The numbers on the connecting rods and bearing caps must be on the same side when installing pistons and connecting rods.

Lubrication

Oil Pan Removal and Installation

1. Remove the heater housing assembly from the firewall and rest it on top of the engine.
2. Remove the engine mount nuts and pull back on the engine mount wire retainers.
3. Remove the radiator upper support. On air conditioned cars, remove the upper fan shroud.
4. Disconnect the fuel vapor line from the charcoal canister.
5. Raise the car on a hoist and drain the engine oil.
6. Remove the flywheel splash shield.
7. On cars with manual transmission, remove the rack and pinion-to-front crossmember attaching bolts and lay it aside.
8. Loosen the rear converter-to-exhaust pipe clamp bolts.
9. Install an engine lifting tool and raise the engine.
10. Remove the oil pan bolts.
11. On cars with manual transmission, lower the oil pan approximately one inch, turn the front of the pan to the right and the rear to the left. Then tilt the pan 45° to remove it. Throw away the old oil pan gasket.

To install:

12. Clean all gasket surfaces thoroughly.
13. Apply RTV sealer or its equivalent to the areas where the crankcase front cover and the rear main bearing cap join the engine block and install a new oil pan gasket.
14. Tilt the pan 45° and turn it so that its front is to the right and the rear is to the left.

15. Align the oil pan with the engine block and install the bolts. Torque the bolts to 45-60 in. lbs.
16. Tighten the rear converter-to-exhaust pipe clamp bolts.
17. On manual transmission cars, install the rack and pinion to the front crossmember.
18. Install the flywheel splash shield.
19. While aligning the engine mount bolts with the engine mount brackets on the engine, lower the engine.
20. Install the engine mount nuts and their wire retainers.
21. Install the upper radiator support. On air conditioned cars, install the upper fan shroud.
22. Install the heater housing assembly on the firewall.
23. Connect the fuel vapor line to the charcoal canister.
24. Fill the crankcase with the proper type and quantity of oil, start the engine, and check for leaks.

Oil Pump Removal and Installation

1. Remove the ignition coil attaching bolts and lay the coil aside.
2. Raise the car and remove the fuel pump, pushrod, and gasket.
3. Lower the car and remove the distributor. On air conditioned cars, remove the compressor mounting bolts and lay it aside. Do not disconnect any refrigerant lines.
4. Raise the car and remove the oil pan.
5. Remove the oil pump pipe and screen assembly clamp and remove the bolts attaching the pipe and screen assembly.
6. Remove the pipe and screen assembly from the oil pump.
7. Remove the pick-up tube seal from the oil pump.
8. Remove the oil pump attaching bolts and remove the oil pump.
   To install:
9. Install the oil pump. Torque the oil pump bolts to 45-60 in. lbs.

NOTE: Make certain that the pilot on the oil pump engages the case.

10. Install the pick-up tube seal in the oil pump.
11. Install the pick-up pipe and screen assembly in the oil pump and install the pick-up pipe and screen clamp. Torque the clamp bolt to 70-95 in. lbs. Torque the pick-up tube and screen mounting bolt to 19-25 ft. lbs.
12. Install the oil pan.
13. Lower the car and install the distributor.
14. Raise the car and install the fuel pump with gasket and pushrod.
15. Lower the car and install the ignition coil.

Rear Main Oil Seal Replacement

1. Remove the engine from the car and place it in a stand.
2. Remove the oil pan.
3. Remove the rear main bearing cap.
4. Clean the bearing cap and case.
5. Check the crankshaft seal for excessive wear, etc.
6. Install a new crankshaft seal. Make sure that it is properly seated against the rear main bearing seal bulkhead.
7. Apply RTV sealer or its equivalent to the bearing cap horizontal split line.
8. With the sealer still wet, install the rear main bearing cap. Torque the cap bolts to 40-52 ft lbs.
9. Apply RTV sealer or its equivalent in the vertical grooves of the rear main bearing cap.
10. Remove any excess sealer and install the oil pan. Torque the oil pan bolts to 45-60 in. lbs.
11. Install the engine in the car.

CLUTCH

Chevette manual transmission models use a cable-operated diaphragm spring-type clutch. The clutch cable is attached to the clutch pedal at its upper end and is threaded at its lower end where it attaches to the clutch fork. The clutch release fork pivots on a ball stud located opposite the clutch cable attaching point. The pressure plate, clutch disc, and throwout bearing are of conventional design.

Clutch Disc Removal and Installation

1. Raise the car on a hoist.
2. Remove the transmission.
3. Remove the throwout bearing from the clutch fork by sliding the fork off the ball stud against spring tension. If the ball stud is to be replaced, remove the locknut and stud from the bellhousing.
4. If the balance marks on the pressure plate and the flywheel are not easily seen, remark them

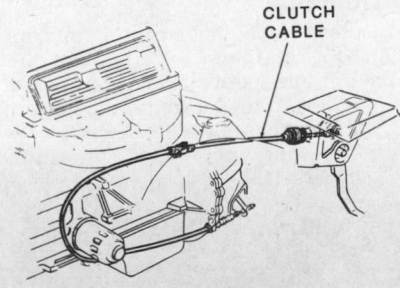

CLUTCH CABLE

Clutch control cable
(© Chevrolet Div., G.M. Corp)

with paint or centerpunch.
5. Alternately loosen the pressure plate-to-flywheel attaching bolts one turn at a time until spring tension is released.
6. Support the pressure plate and cover assembly, then remove the bolts and the clutch assembly.

Caution *Do not disassemble the clutch cover and pressure plate for repair. If defective, replace the assembly.*

7. Align the balance marks on the clutch assembly and the flywheel. Place the clutch disc on the pressure plate with the long end of the splined hub facing forward and the damper springs inside the pressure plate. Insert a dummy shaft through the cover and clutch disc.
8. Position the assembly against the flywheel and insert the dummy shaft into the pilot bearing in the crankshaft.
9. Align the balance marks and install the pressure plate-to-flywheel bolts finger-tight.

Caution *Tighten all bolts evenly and gradually until tight to avoid possible clutch distortion. Torque the bolts to 18 ft lbs and remove the dummy shaft.*

10. Pack the groove on the inside of the throwout bearing with graphite grease. Also coat the fork groove and ball stud depression with the lubricant.
11. Install the throwout bearing and release fork assembly in the bellhousing with the fork spring hooked under the ball stud and the fork spring fingers inside the bearing groove.
12. Position the transmission and clutch housing and install the clutch housing attaching bolts and lockwashers. Torque the bolts to 25 ft lbs.
13. Complete the transmission installation.

Caution *Check position of the engine in the front mounts and realign as necessary.*

NOTE: A special gauge (Part No. J-23644) is necessary to adjust ball stud position if it has been removed.

14. Adjust clutch pedal free-play if necessary.
15. Lower the car and check operation of the clutch and transmission.

Clutch Pedal Free-Play Adjustment

Adjustment for normal wear is made by turning the release fork ball stud counterclockwise to give 0.812 ± 0.25 in. (20.6 ± 6 mm) lash at the clutch pedal.

1. Loosen the locknut on the ball stud end located to the right of the transmission on the clutch housing.

2. Adjust the ball stud to obtain the correct free-play.
3. Tighten the locknut to 25 ft lbs,

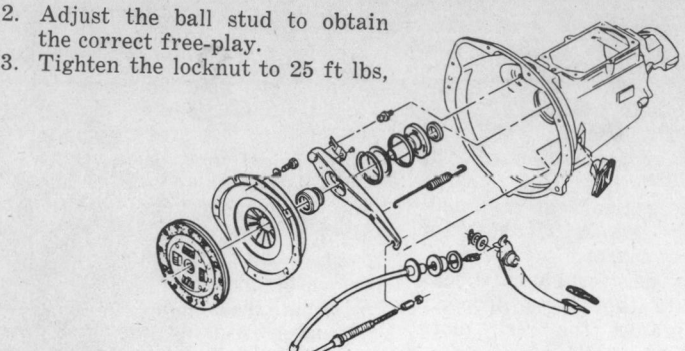

Clutch assembly (© Chevrolet Div., G.M. Corp)

being careful not to change the adjustment.
4. Check for proper clutch operation.

MANUAL TRANSMISSION

Chevette models use a four-speed fully synchronized transmission. This transmission is identified as the "70 mm" four-speed transmission. Helical gears are used throughout the transmission. The mainshaft gears are free to rotate independently on the mainshaft and are in constant mesh with the countershaft gears. The countershaft gears are integral with the shaft and rotate at all times of clutch engagement being in constant mesh with the main drive gear. The reverse idler gear is carried on a bushing and is not synchronized. The synchronizer assemblies consist of a hub, sleeve, two key energizer springs, and three synchronizer keys. The synchronizer hubs are splined to the mainshaft and are retained by snaprings. Gear shifting is accomplished by an internal shifter shaft. No adjustment of the mechanism is possible.

Transmission Removal and Installation

1. Remove the shift lever.
2. Raise the car on a hoist and drain the lubricant from the transmission.
3. Remove the driveshaft.
4. Disconnect the speedometer cable and back-up light switch.
5. Disconnect the return spring and clutch cable at the clutch release fork.
6. Remove the crossmember-to-transmission mount bolts.
7. Remove the exhaust manifold nuts and converter-to-tailpipe bolts and nuts. Remove the converter-to-transmission bracket bolts and remove the converter.
8. Remove the crossmember-to-frame bolts and remove the crossmember.

9. Remove the dust cover.
10. Remove the clutch housing-to-engine retaining bolts, slide the transmission and clutch housing to the rear, and remove the transmission.
    To install:
11. Place the transmission in gear, position the transmission and clutch housing, and slide forward. Turn the output shaft to align the input shaft splines with the clutch hub.
12. Install the clutch housing retaining bolts and lockwashers. Torque the bolts to 25 ft lbs.
13. Install the dust cover.
14. Position the crossmember to the frame and loosely install the retaining bolts. Install the crossmember-to-transmission mounting bolts. Torque the center nuts to 33 ft. lbs; the end nuts to 21 ft. lbs. Torque the crossmember-to-frame bolts to 40 ft. lbs.
15. Install the exhaust pipe to the manifold and the converter bracket on the transmission. Torque the converter bracket rear support nuts to 150 in. lbs.
16. Connect the clutch cable. Adjust clutch pedal free-play.
17. Connect the speedometer cable and back-up light switch.
18. Install the driveshaft.
19. Fill the transmission to the correct level with SAE 80W or SAE 80W-90 GL-5 gear lubricant. Lower the car.
20. Install the shift lever and check operation of the transmission.

Shift Lever Removal and Installation

1. Remove the floor console and/or boot retainer.
2. Raise the shift lever boot to gain access to the locknut on the lever. Loosen the locknut and unscrew the upper portion of the shift lever with the knob attached.
3. Remove the foam insulator to gain access to the control assembly bolts.
4. Remove the three bolts on the extension and remove the control assembly.

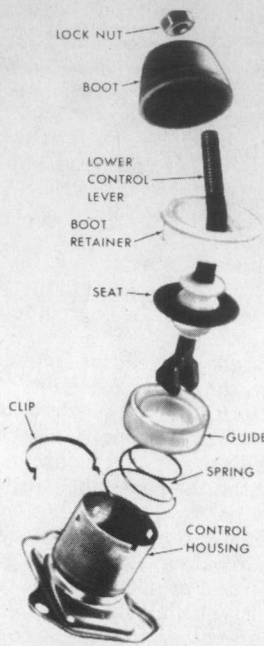

Shift lever components
(© Chevrolet Div., G.M. Corp)

5. Use caution when removing the clip on the control housing as the internal components are under spring pressure.
6. Remove the locknut, boot retainer, and seat from the threaded end of the shift lever.
7. Remove the spring and guide from the forked end of the shift lever.
8. To assemble the shift lever, install the spring and guide on the forked end of the lever.
9. Install the seat, boot retainer, and the locknut over the threaded end of the lever.
10. Assemble the components in the control housing and install the clip on the control housing.
11. Install the control assembly on the extension making sure that the fork at the lower end of the lever engages the shifter shaft lever arm pin. Torque the shift lever retaining bolts to 35 in. lbs.
12. Install the foam insulator, boot, retainer, and/or floor console.
13. Slide the boot below the threaded portion of the shift lever and install the upper shift lever. Tighten the locknut.

AUTOMATIC TRANSMISSION

Chevette models use the Turbo Hydra-Matic 200 transmission. The transmission is a fully automatic unit providing three forward speeds and reverse.

Neutral Safety Switch Replacement

1. Remove the floor console cover.

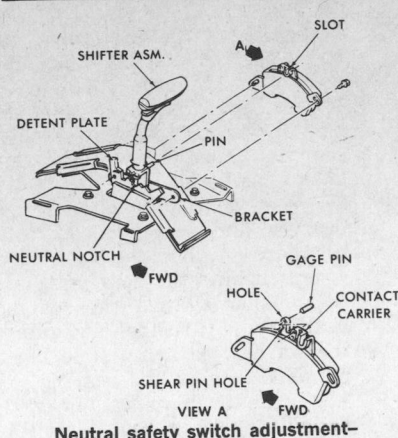

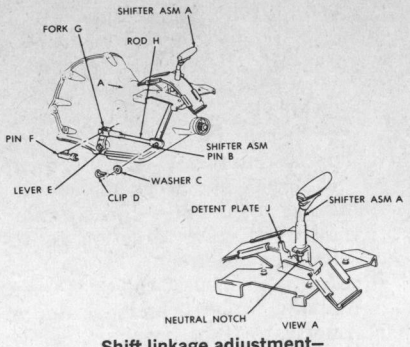

**Neutral safety switch adjustment—
—Turbo Hydra-Matic 200**
(© Chevrolet Div., G.M. Corp)

2. Disconnect the electrical connectors on the back-up, seat belt warning, and neutral starter contacts on the switch.
3. Place the shift lever in Neutral.
4. Remove the two switch attaching screws and remove the switch.
5. Make sure that the shift lever is in the Neutral position before installing the switch assembly.
6. Place the neutral start switch assembly in position on the shift lever making sure that the pin on the lever is in the slot of the switch.
NOTE: When replacing the original switch, align the contact support slot with the service adjustment hole in the switch and insert a 3/32 in. drill bit to hold the switch in Neutral. Remove the drill bit after the switch is fastened to the shift lever mounting bracket.
7. Install the two switch attaching screws.
8. Move the shift lever out of Neutral to shear the plastic pin.
9. Connect the electrical connectors to the switch contacts. Apply the parking brake and start the engine. Check to make sure that the engine starts only in Park or Neutral. Make sure that the back-up lights work only in Reverse. Check that the seat belt warning system operates.
10. Stop the engine and install the floor console cover.

Shift Linkage Adjustment

1. Place the shift lever in the Neutral position of the detent plate.
2. Disconnect the rod from the lower end of the shift lever. Place the transmission lever in the Neutral position. Do this by moving the lever clockwise to the maximum detent (Park), then moving the lever counterclockwise two (2) detent positions (Neutral).
3. Adjust the rod until the hole in the rod aligns with the pin on

**Shift linkage adjustment—
—Turbo Hydra-Matic 200**
(© Chevrolet Div., G.M. Corp)

the lower end of the shift lever. Install the rod on the pin and secure it by adding the washer and spring clip.

Downshift Cable Adjustment

The Turbo Hydra-Matic 200 transmission has a cable between the carburetor linkage and the transmission which controls transmission downshifting.
1. Remove the air cleaner.
2. Disengage the snap lock. (The cable should be free to slide through the snap lock).
3. With the cable installed in the support and attached to the transmission and carburetor levers, move the carburetor lever to the wide open throttle position.
4. Push the snap lock flush and return the carburetor lever to the closed position.
5. Install the air cleaner.

Pan Removal and Installation, Fluid and Filter Change

Transmission fluid should be drained while at normal operating temperature.

Caution *Transmission fluid temperature can exceed 350°F.*

1. Raise the car and support the transmission with a jack at the transmission vibration damper.
2. Place a receptacle of at least three quarts capacity under the transmission pan. Remove the pan attaching bolts from the front and side of the pan.
3. Loosen the rear pan attaching bolts approximately four turns.
4. Drain the fluid by carefully prying the pan loose with a screwdriver.
5. After the fluid has drained, remove the remaining pan attaching bolts. Remove the pan and gasket. Throw the old gasket away.
6. Drain the remaining fluid from the pan. Thoroughly clean the pan with solvent and dry with compressed air.
7. Remove the two screen-to-valve body bolts and remove the screen and gasket. Discard the gasket.
8. Thoroughly clean the screen in solvent and dry with compressed air.
9. Install a new gasket on the screen and install the screen. Tighten the screen attaching bolts to 6-10 ft lbs.
10. Install the pan using a new gasket. Tighten the pan bolts and washers to 10-13 ft lbs.
11. Lower the car and add approximately six pints of DEXRON® or DEXRON® II automatic transmission fluid through the filler tube.
12. With the transmission in Park, apply the parking brake, start the engine and let it idle (not fast idle). Do not race the engine.
13. Move the gear selector lever slowly through all positions, return the lever to Park, and check the transmission fluid level.
14. Add fluid as necessary to raise the level between the dimples

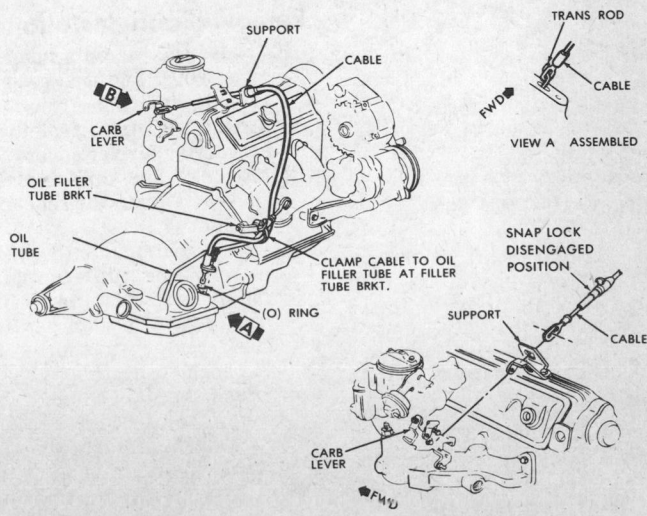

Downshift cable adjustment—Turbo Hydra-Matic 200 (© Chevrolet Div., G.M. Corp)

on the dipstick. Be careful not to overfill the transmission; approximately one pint of fluid will raise the level to the correct amount.

U-JOINTS

A one-piece driveshaft is mounted to the companion flange with a conventional universal joint at the rear. The driveshaft is connected to the transmission output shaft with a splined slip yoke. The slip yoke contains a thrust spring which seats against the end of the transmission output shaft. The thrust spring MUST be installed for proper operation.

The universal joints are of the long-life design and do not require periodic inspection or lubrication. When the joints are disassembled, repack the bearings and lubricate the reservoirs at the end of the trunnions with chassis grease and replace the dust seals.

Driveshaft Removal and Installation

1. Raise the car on a hoist. Scribe matchmarks on the driveshaft and the companion flange and disconnect the rear universal joint by removing the trunnion bearing straps.
2. Move the driveshaft to the rear under the axle to remove the slip yoke from the transmission. Watch for oil leakage from the transmission output shaft housing.

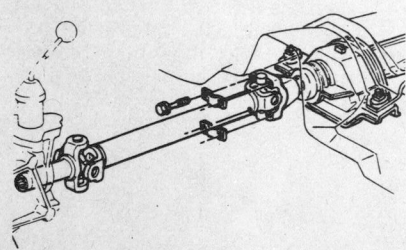

Chevette driveshaft assembly
(© Chevrolet Div., G.M. Corp)

3. Install the driveshaft in the reverse order of removal. Tighten the trunnion strap bolts to 16 ft lbs.

Universal Joint Removal and Installation

1. Remove the driveshaft.
2. For reassembly purposes, scribe a line on the transmission end of the driveshaft and on the slip yoke. Remove the snap-rings

from the trunnion yoke.
3. Support the trunnion yoke on a piece of 1¼ in. ID pipe on an arbor press or bench vise. Use a suitable socket or rod to press on the trunnion until the bearing cup is almost out. Grasp the cup in the vise and work the cup out of the yoke. Press the trunnion in the opposite direction to remove the other cup.
4. Clean and inspect the dust seals, bearing rollers, and trunnions. Lubricate the bearings. Make sure that the lubricant reservoir at the end of each trunnion is completely filled with lubricant. A squeeze bottle is recommended to fill the reservoirs from the bottom to prevent air pockets.
5. When installing a U-joint rebuilding kit, place the dust seals on the trunnions with the cavities of the seals toward the end of the trunnions. Use caution when pressing the seals onto the trunnions to prevent seal distortion and to assure proper seal seating.
   NOTE: Install the transmission yoke on front of the driveshaft as marked in Step 2. If this is not done, driveline vibration may result.
6. To assemble, position the trunnion into the yoke. Partially install one bearing cup into the yoke and start the trunnion into the bearing cup. Partially install the other cup, align the trunnion into the cup, and press the cups into the yoke.
7. Install the snap-rings.
8. Install the driveshaft.

REAR AXLE

Axle Shaft, Bearing, and Seal

Removal and Installation

1. Raise the car on a hoist. Remove the wheel and tire assembly and the brake drum.
2. Clean the area around the differential carrier cover.
3. Remove the differential carrier cover to drain the rear axle lubricant.
4. Use a metric allen wrench to unscrew the differential pinion shaft lockscrew and remove the differential pinion shaft. It may be necessary to shorten the allen wrench to do this.
5. Push the flanged end of the axle shaft toward the center of the car and remove the "C" lock from the button end of the shaft.
6. Remove the axle shaft from the housing making sure not to damage the oil seal.

7. If replacing the seal only, remove the oil seal by using the button end of the axle shaft. Insert the button end of the shaft behind the steel case of the oil seal and carefully pry the seal out of the bore.
8. To remove bearings, insert a bearing and seal remover into the bore so that the tool head grasps behind the bearing. Slide the washer against the seal or bearing and turn the nut against the washer. Attach a slide hammer and remove the bearing.
9. Lubricate a new bearing with hypoid lubricant and install it into the housing with a bearing installer tool. Make sure that the tool contacts the end of the axle tube to make sure that the bearing is at the proper depth.
10. Lubricate the cavity between the seal lips with a high melting point wheel bearing grease. Place a new oil seal on the seal installation tool and position the seal in the axle housing bore. Tap the seal into the bore flush with the end of the housing.
11. To install the axle shaft, slide the axle shaft into place making sure that the splines on the end of the shaft do not damage the oil seal and that they engage the splines of the differential side gear. Install the "C" lock on the button end of the axle shaft and push the shaft outward so that the shaft lock seats in the counterbore of the differential side gear.
12. Position the differential pinion shaft through the case and pinions, aligning the hole in the shaft with the lockscrew hole. Install the lockscrew.
13. Clean the gasket mounting surfaces on the differential carrier and the carrier cover. Install the carrier cover using a new gasket and tighten the cover bolts in a crosswise pattern to 22 ft lbs.
14. Fill the rear axle with lubricant to the bottom of the filler hole.
15. Install the brake drum and the wheel and tire assembly.
16. Lower the car.

JACKING, HOISTING

The accompanying illustration shows the recommended areas for jacking and hoisting. When using a twin post hoist, be sure that it is positioned properly on the rear axle to avoid damaging the rear stabilizer. Never lift the car by the rear lower control arms.

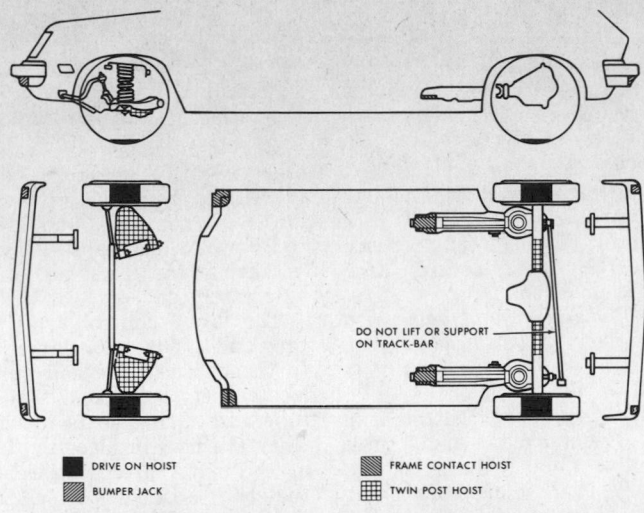

■ DRIVE ON HOIST
▨ BUMPER JACK

▨ FRAME CONTACT HOIST
▦ TWIN POST HOIST

Lift points (© Chevrolet Div., G.M. Corp)

When jacking or lifting on the frame side rails be certain that the lift pads do not contact the catalytic converter.

FRONT SUSPENSION

The Chevette front suspension is of conventional long and short control arm design with coil springs. The control arms attach with bolts and bushings at the inner pivot points and to the steering knuckle/front wheel spindle assembly at the outer pivot points. Lower ball joints are the wear indicator type. A front stabilizer bar is used.

Shock Absorber Removal and Installation

1. Hold the shock absorber upper stem and remove the nut, upper retainer, and rubber grommet
2. Raise the car on a hoist.
3. Remove the bolt from the lower end of the shock absorber and remove the shock absorber.

To install:

4. With the lower retainer and rubber grommet in position, extend the shock absorber stem and install the stem through the wheelhouse opening.
5. Install and torque the lower bolt to 35-50 ft lbs.
6. Lower the car.
7. Install the upper rubber grommet, retainer, and nut to the shock absorber stem.
8. Hold the shock absorber upper stem and torque the nut to 60-120 in. lbs.

NOTE: Torque is produced by running the nut to the unthreaded part of the stud.

Lower Ball Joint Removal and Installation

1. Raise the car on a hoist.
2. Remove the tire and wheel.
3. Support the lower control arm with a hydraulic floor jack.
4. Loosen, but do not remove the lower ball stud nut.
5. Install a ball joint removal tool with the cup end over the upper ball stud nut.
6. Turn the threaded end of the ball joint removal tool until the ball stud is free of the steering knuckle.
7. Remove the ball joint removal tool and remove the nut from the ball stud.
8. Remove the ball joint.

NOTE: Inspect the tapered hole in the steering knuckle. Clean the area. If any out-of-roundness, deformation, or damage is found, the steering knuckle MUST be replaced.

9. To install the lower ball joint, mate the ball stud through the lower control arm and into the steering knuckle.

NOTE: The ball joint studs use a special nut which must be discarded whenever loosened and removed. On assembly, use a standard nut to draw the ball joint into position on the knuckle, then remove the standard nut and install a new special nut for final installation.

10. Install and torque the ball stud nut to 41-54 ft lbs.
11. Install the tire and wheel.
12. Lower the car.

Lower Control Arm and Coil Spring Removal and Installation

1. Raise the car on a frame contact hoist.
2. Remove the wheel and tire.
3. Disconnect the stabilizer bar from the lower control arm and disconnect the tie-rod from the steering knuckle.
4. Support the lower control arm with a jack.
5. Remove the nut from the lower ball joint, then use a ball joint removal tool to press out the lower ball joint.
6. Swing the knuckle and hub aside and attach them securely with wire.
7. Loosen the lower control arm pivot bolts.
8. As a safety precaution, install a chain through the coil spring.
9. Slowly lower the jack.
10. When the spring is extended as far as possible, use a pry bar to carefully lift the spring over the lower control arm seat. Remove the spring.
11. Remove the pivot bolts and remove the lower control arm.

To install:

12. Install the lower control arm and pivot bolts to the underbody brackets. Torque the lower control arm pivot bolts to 49 ft lbs.
13. Position the spring correctly and install it in the upper pocket. Use tape to hold the insulator onto the spring.
14. Install the lower end of the spring onto the lower control arm. An assistant may be necessary to compress the spring far enough to slide it over the raised area of the lower control arm seat.

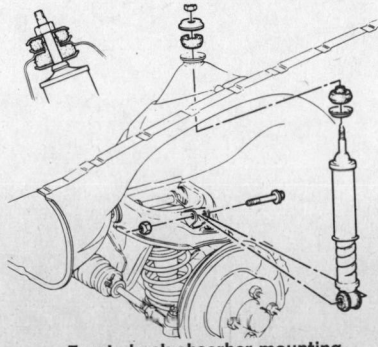

Front shock absorber mounting
(© Chevrolet Div., G.M. Corp)

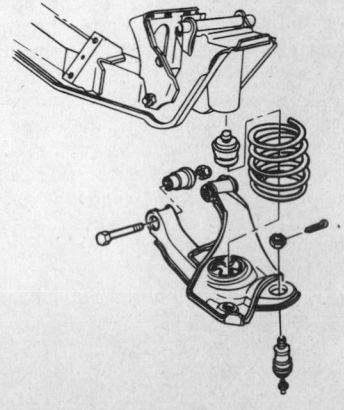

Correct position for front spring installation
(© Chevrolet Div., G.M. Corp)

15. Use a jack to raise the lower control arm and compress the coil spring.

NOTE: The ball joint studs use a special nut which must be discarded whenever loosened and removed. On assembly, use a standard nut to draw the ball joint into position on the knuckle, then remove the standard nut and install a new special nut for final installation.

16. Install the ball joint through the lower control arm and into the steering knuckle. Install the nut on the ball stud nut and torque to 41-54 ft lbs.

17. Connect the stabilizer bar to the lower control arm and torque its attaching bolt to 15 ft lbs. Connect the tie-rod to the steering knuckle. Install the wheel and tire.

18. Lower the car.

Upper Ball Joint Removal and Installation

1. Raise the car on a hoist.
2. Remove the tire and wheel.
3. Support the lower control arm with a floor jack.
4. Loosen, but do not remove the upper ball stud nut.
5. Install a ball joint removal tool with the cup end over the lower ball stud nut.
6. Turn the threaded end of the ball joint removal tool until the upper ball stud is free of the steering knuckle.
7. Remove the ball joint removal tool and remove the nut from the ball stud.
8. Remove the two nuts and bolts attaching the ball joint to the upper control arm and remove the ball joint.

NOTE: Inspect the tapered hole in the steering knuckle. Clean the area. If any out-of-roundness, deformation, or damage is found, the steering knuckle MUST be replaced.

9. To install the upper ball joint, install the nuts and bolts attaching the ball joint to the upper control arm. Torque the nuts to 29 ft lbs. Then mate the upper control arm ball stud to the steering knuckle.

NOTE: The ball joint studs use a special nut which must be discarded whenever loosened and removed. On assembly, use a standard nut to draw the ball joint into position on the knuckle, then remove the standard nut and install a new special nut for final installation.

10. Install and torque the ball stud nut to 29-36 ft lbs.
11. Install the tire and wheel.
12. Lower the car.

Upper Control Arm Removal and Installation

1. Raise the car on a hoist.

2. Remove the tire and wheel.
3. Support the lower control arm with a floor jack.
4. Remove the upper ball joint from the steering knuckle as previously described.
5. Remove the upper control arm pivot bolts and remove the upper control arm.
6. To install the upper control arm, install the upper control arm with its pivot bolts.

NOTE: The inner pivot bolt must be installed with the bolt head toward the front.

7. Install the pivot bolt nut.
8. Position the upper control arm in a horizontal plane and torque the nut to 43-50 ft lbs.

NOTE: The ball joint studs use a special nut which must be discarded whenever loosened and removed. On assembly, use a standard nut to draw the ball joint into position on the knuckle, then remove the standard nut and install a new special nut for final installation.

9. Install the ball joint to the upper control arm and to the steering knuckle as previously described. Torque the ball joint-to-upper control arm attaching bolts to 29 ft lbs. Torque the ball stud nut to 29-36 ft lbs.
10. Install the tire and wheel.
11. Lower the car.

Front Wheel Bearings

Adjustment

1. Raise the car and support at the front lower control arm.
2. Remove the hub cap or wheel cover from the wheel. Remove the dust cap from the hub.
3. Remove the cotter pin from the spindle and spindle nut.
4. Spin the wheel forward by hand and tighten the spindle nut to 12 ft lbs. This will fully seat the bearings.
5. Back off the nut to the "just loose" position.
6. Hand-tighten the spindle nut. Loosen the spindle nut until either hole in the spindle aligns with a slot in the nut, but not more than ½ flat.
7. Install a new cotter pin, bend the ends of the pin against the nut, and cut off any extra length to avoid interference with the dust cap.
8. Measure the end-play in the hub. Proper bearing adjustment should give 0.001-0.005 in. of end-play.
9. Install the dust cap on the hub and the hub cap or wheel cover on the wheel.
10. Lower the car.
11. Adjust the opposite front wheel bearings.

REAR SUSPENSION

Chevette models use a solid rear axle and coil springs. The axle is attached to the body by two tubular lower control arms, a straight track rod, two shock absorbers, and a bracket at the front end of the rear axle extension.

The lower control arms maintain fore and aft relationship of the axle to the chassis. The coil springs are located between brackets on the axle tube and spring seats in the frame. They are held in place by the weight of the car and, during rebound, by the shock absorbers which limit axle movement. The shock absorbers are angle-mounted on brackets behind the axle housing and the rear spring seats in the frame. A rear stabilizer bar is used.

When using a hoist contacting the rear axle, be sure that the stabilizer links and the track rod are not damaged.

Shock Absorber Removal and Installation

1. Raise the car on a hoist.
2. Support the rear axle.
3. Remove the shock absorber upper attaching nut and lower attaching bolt and nut, and remove the shock absorber.

To install:

4. Install the retainer and the rubber grommet onto the shock absorber.
5. Place the shock absorber into its installed position and install and tighten the upper retaining nut to 7 ft lbs.
6. Install the lower shock absorber nut and bolt and torque to 33 ft lbs.
7. Remove the rear axle supports and lower the car.

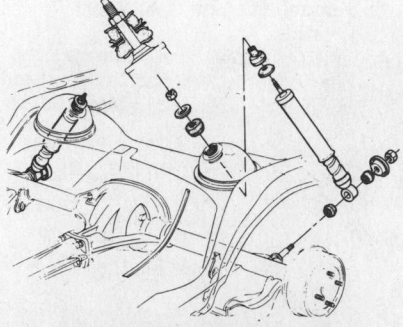

Rear shock absorber mounting
(© Chevrolet Div., G.M. Corp)

Rear Spring Removal and Installation

1. Raise the car on a hoist.
2. Support the rear axle with a hydraulic jack.

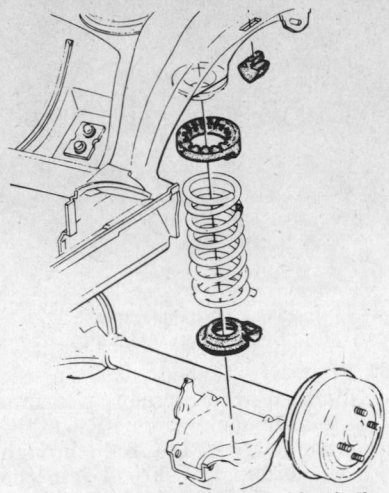

Rear spring installation—position both insulators as shown
(© Chevrolet Div., G.M. Corp)

3. Disconnect both shock absorbers from their lower brackets.
4. Disconnect the rear axle extension center support bracket from the underbody. Use caution when disconnecting the extension and safely support it when disconnected.
5. Lower the rear axle and remove the springs and spring insulators.

NOTE: One or both springs can be removed now.

Caution *Do not stretch the rear brake hoses when lowering the rear axle.*

6. To install, place the insulators on top and on the bottom of the springs and position the springs between their upper and lower seats.
7. Raise the rear axle. Connect the rear axle extension center support bracket to the underbody. Torque the bolts to 37 ft·lbs.
8. Connect the shock absorbers to their lower brackets. Torque the nuts to 33 ft·lbs.
9. Remove the hydraulic jack from the axle.
10. Lower the car.

BRAKES

Front disc brakes are standard equipment on all models. Power brakes are available as an option. The disc is 9.68 in. in diameter, ½ in. thick, and is a one-piece casting with the hub. Single-piston sliding calipers are used.

The rear brakes are of conventional leading-trailing shoe design. Brake drum diameter is 7.87 in. Automatic adjusters are used in the rear brakes which provide adjustment when needed whenever the brakes are applied.

The front and rear brake lines are routed through a distributor and switch assembly located on the left-hand engine compartment side panel. The switch is a pressure differential type which lights the brake warning light on the instrument panel if either the front or rear hydraulic system fails. The switch is nonadjustable and nonserviceable; it must be replaced if defective.

Master Cylinder Removal and Installation

1. Disconnect the master cylinder pushrod from the brake pedal.
2. Remove the pushrod boot.
3. Remove the air cleaner.
4. Thoroughly clean all dirt from the master cylinder and the brake lines. Disconnect the brake lines from the master cylinder and plug them to prevent the entry of dirt.
5. Remove the master cylinder securing nuts and remove the master cylinder.
6. Install the master cylinder with its spacer. Tighten the securing nuts to 150 in. lbs.
7. Connect the brake lines to their proper ports. Tighten the nuts to 150 in. lbs.

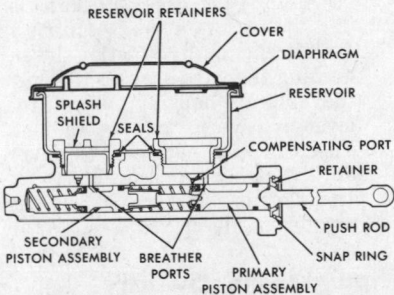

Dual piston master cylinder with common reservoir (© Chevrolet Div., G.M. Corp)

8. Place the pushrod boot over the end of the pushrod. Secure the pushrod to the brake pedal with the pin and clip.
9. Fill the master cylinder and bleed the entire hydraulic system. After bleeding, fill the master cylinder to within ¼ in. from the top of the reservoir. Check for leaks.
10. Install the air cleaner.
11. Check brake operation before moving the car.

Parking Brake Adjustment

1. Raise the car on a hoist.
2. Apply the parking brake one notch from the fully released position.
3. Tighten the parking brake cable equalizer adjusting nut until a light drag is felt when the rear wheels are rotated forward.
4. Fully release the parking brake and rotate the rear wheels. There should be no drag.
5. Lower the car.

STEERING

All Chevette models use manual rack and pinion steering which encloses the steering gear and linkage in one unit. Power steering is not available.

Rotary motion of the steering wheel is converted into linear motion to turn the wheels by the meshing of the helical pinion with the teeth of the rack. The pinion and a major portion of the rack are encased in a die cast aluminum housing. Inner tie-rod assemblies are threaded and staked to the rack. The inner tie-rods contain a belleville spring-loaded ball joint which permits both rocking and rotating tie-rod movement. The outer tie-rods thread onto the inners and are held in position by jam nuts. Two convoluted boots are secured by clamps to the housing and inner tie-rods to prevent the entrance of dirt. The rack and pinion assembly is secured to the front suspension crossmember with two clamps and bushings.

The energy-absorbing steering column has a "smart" switch which operates the turn signals (up and down movement), the headlight dimmer switch (front and back movement), the windshield wipers (rotation), and the windshield washers (by pushing the lever into the column).

Steering Wheel Removal and Installation

1. Disconnect the negative battery cable.
2. Remove the two steering wheel shroud screws at the underside of the steering wheel and remove the shroud.
3. Remove the wheel nut retainer and the wheel nut.

Caution *Do not overexpand the retainer.*

4. Using a steering wheel puller, thread the puller anchor screws into the threaded holes in the steering wheel. With the center bolt of the puller butting against the steering shaft, turn the center bolt to remove the steering wheel.

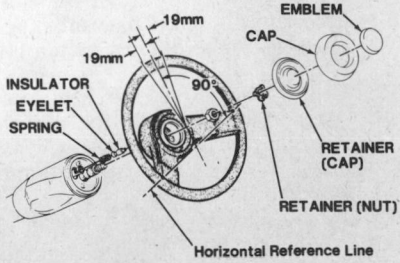

Chevette steering wheel assembly
(© Chevrolet Div., G.M. Corp)

5. To install, place the turn signal lever in the neutral position and install the steering wheel. Torque the steering wheel nut to 30 ft lbs and install the nut retainer. Use caution not to overexpand the nut retainer.
6. Connect the negative battery cable.

Turn Signal Switch Removal and Installation

1. Remove the steering wheel as previously described.
2. Position a screwdriver blade into one of the three cover slots. Pry up and out (at least two slots) to free the cover.
3. Place the U-shaped lockplate compressing tool on the end of the steering shaft and compress the lockplate, but the full load of the spring should not be relieved because the ring will rotate and make removal difficult. Pry the round wire snap-ring out of the shaft groove and discard it. Remove the lockplate compressing tool and lift the lockplate off the end of the shaft.
4. Slide the turn signal cancelling cam, upper bearing preload spring, and thrust washer off the end of the shaft.
5. Remove the multi-function lever by rotating it clockwise to its stop (off position), then pull the lever straight out to disengage it.

J-23653

Removing the lockplate snap-ring
(© Chevrolet Div., G.M. Corp)

6. Push the hazard warning knob in and unscrew the knob.
7. Remove the two screws, pivot arm, and spacer.
8. Wrap the upper part of the connector with tape to prevent snagging the wires during switch removal.
9. Remove the three switch mounting screws and pull the switch straight up, guiding the wiring harness through the column housing.

Caution *On installation it is extremely important that only the specified screws, bolts, and nuts be used. The use of overlength screws could prevent the*

steering column from compressing under impact.
10. Position the switch into the housing.
11. Install the three switch mounting screws. Replace the spacer and pivot arm. Be sure that the spacer protrudes through the hole in the arm and that the arm finger encloses the turn signal switch frame. Tighten the truss head screw (secures the spacer to the signal switch) to 20 in. lbs and the flat head screw to 35 in. lbs.
12. Install the hazard warning knob.
13. Make sure that the turn signal switch is in the neutral position and that the hazard warning knob is out. Slide the thrust washer, upper bearing preload spring, and the cancelling cam into the upper end of the shaft.
14. Place the lockplate and a NEW snap-ring onto the end of the shaft. Using the lockplate compressing tool, compress the lockplate as far as possible. Slide the new snap-ring into the shaft groove and remove the lockplate compressing tool.
On assembly, always use a new snap-ring.
15. Install the multi-function lever, guiding the wire harness through the column housing. Align the lever pin with the switch slot. Push on the end of the lever until it is seated securely.
16. Install the steering wheel as previously described.

Wiper/Washer Switch Removal and Installation

The wiper/washer switch is located on the left-side of the column under the turn signal switch.
1. Remove the steering wheel and turn signal switch as previously described. The ignition switch is mounted on top of the mast jacket near the front of the dash.
2. Remove the upper attaching screw on the ignition and dimmer switch; this releases the dimmer switch and actuator rod assembly.

NOTE: Do not move the ignition switch. If this happens, refer to the switch adjustment procedure in "Ignition Switch and Dimmer Switch Removal and Installation."

3. The wiper/washer switch and pivot assembly now can be removed from the column housing.
4. To install, place the wiper/washer switch and pivot assembly into the housing and guide the connector down through the bowl and shroud assembly.
5. Install the turn signal switch as previously described.

Installing the dimmer switch
(© Chevrolet Div., G.M. Corp)

6. Fit the pinched end of the dimmer switch actuator rod into the dimmer switch. Feed the other end of the rod through the hole in the shroud into the hole in the wiper/washer switch and pivot assembly drive, but do not tighten the attaching screw. Depress the dimmer switch slightly to insert a 3/32 in. drill bit to lock the switch to the body. Push the switch up to remove the lash between both the ignition and dimmer switches and the actuator rod. Install the wiper/washer switch mounting screw and tighten it to 35 in. lbs. Remove the drill bit and check dimmer switch operation with the actuating lever.

Ignition Key Buzzer Switch Removal and Installation

1. Remove the steering wheel and turn signal switch as previously described.
2. Make a right angle bend in a short piece of small wire about ¼ in. from one end. The wire should be inserted in the exposed loop of the wedge spring, then a straight pull on the wire will remove both the spring and the switch.

Caution *Do not attempt to remove the switch separately as the clip may fall into the column. If this happens, the clip must be found before assembly.*
NOTE: The lock cylinder must be in the "Run" position if it is in the housing. Also, if the lock cylinder is in place, the buzzer switch actuating button on the lock cylinder must be depressed before the buzzer switch can be installed.

3. Install the buzzer switch with the contacts toward the upper end of the steering column and with the formed end of the spring clip around the lower end of the switch. Push the switch and spring assembly into the hole with the internal switch contacts toward the lock cylinder bore.
4. Install the turn signal switch and the steering wheel as previously described.

Lock Cylinder Removal and Installation

The lock cylinder is located on the right-side of the steering column and should be removed only in the "Run" position. Removal in any other position will damage the key buzzer switch. The lock cylinder cannot be disassembled; if replacement is required, a new cylinder coded to the old key must be installed.

1. Remove the steering wheel and turn signal switch as previously described.
2. Do not remove the buzzer switch or damage to the lock cylinder will result.
3. Insert a small screwdriver or similar tool into the turn signal housing slot to the upper right of the steering shaft. Keep the tool to the right-side of the slot and depress the retainer at the bottom to release the lock cylinder. Remove the lock cylinder.
4. To install the lock cylinder, hold the cylinder sleeve in the left hand and rotate knob (key in) clockwise to stop. (This retracts the actuator). Insert the cylinder into the housing bore with the key on the cylinder sleeve aligned with the keyway in the housing. Push the cylinder in until it bottoms. Rotate the knob counterclockwise while maintaining a light pressure inward until the drive section of the cylinder mates with the sector.

Removing the lock cylinder
(© Chevrolet Div., G.M. Corp)

Push the cylinder in fully until the retainer pops into the housing groove.

5. Install the turn signal switch and the steering wheel as previously described.

Ignition Switch and Dimmer Switch Removal and Installation

The ignition switch is mounted on top of the mast jacket near the front of the dash. The switch is located inside the channel section of the brake pedal support and is completely inaccessible without first lowering the steering column.

1. Disconnect the negative battery cable.

2. Remove the steering wheel as previously described.
3. Move the driver's seat as far back as possible.
4. Remove the floor pan bracket screw.
5. Remove the two column bracket-to-instrument panel nuts and lower the column far enough to disconnect the ignition switch wiring harness.

Caution *Be sure that the steering column is properly supported before proceeding.*

6. The switch should be in the "Lock" position before removal. If the lock cylinder has already been removed, the actuating rod to the switch should be pulled up until there is a definite stop, then moved down one detent which is the "Lock" position.
7. Remove the two mounting screws and remove the ignition and dimmer switch.
8. Refer to the installation procedure previously described in "Lock Cylinder Removal and Installation."
9. Turn the cylinder clockwise to stop and then counterclockwise to stop, then counterclockwise again to stop ("Off-Unlock" position).

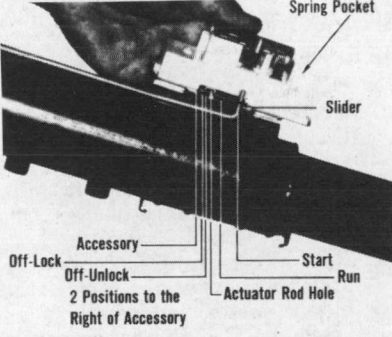

Positioning the ignition switch for installation
(© Chevrolet Div., G.M. Corp)

10. Place the ignition switch in the "Off-Unlock" position by positioning the switch as shown in the accompanying illustration. Move the slider two positions to the right from "Accessory" to the "Off-Unlock" position.
11. Fit the actuator rod into the slider hole and install the switch on the column. Be sure to use only the correct screws. Tighten only one bottom screw to 35 in. lbs. Be careful not to move the switch out of its detent.
12. Perform the dimmer switch adjustment procedure previously outlined in "Wiper/Washer Switch Removal and Installation."
13. Connect the ignition switch wiring harness.
14. Loosely install the column

bracket-to-instrument panel nuts.
15. Install the floor pan bracket screw and tighten it to 20 ft lbs.
16. Tighten the column bracket-to-instrument panel nuts to 20 ft lbs.
17. Install the steering wheel as previously outlined.
18. Connect the battery negative cable.

INSTRUMENT PANEL

The standard instrument cluster contains a speedometer and fuel gauge with warning lights for oil pressure, coolant temperature, alternator, brakes, and seat belts. The optional cluster adds a tachometer, but retains all warning lights.

Instrument Cluster Replacement

The instrument cluster must be removed to replace light bulbs, gauges, and printed circuit.

1. Disconnect the negative battery cable.
2. Remove the clock stem knob.
3. Remove the four screws and remove the instrument cluster bezel and lens.
4. Remove the two nuts securing the instrument cluster to the instrument panel and pull the cluster slightly forward.
5. Disconnect the electrical connector and speedometer cable from the cluster and remove it.
6. Installation is the reverse of removal.

Headlight Switch Removal and Installation

1. Disconnect the negative battery cable.
2. Pull the headlight switch control knob to the "On" position.
3. Reach up under the instrument panel and depress the switch

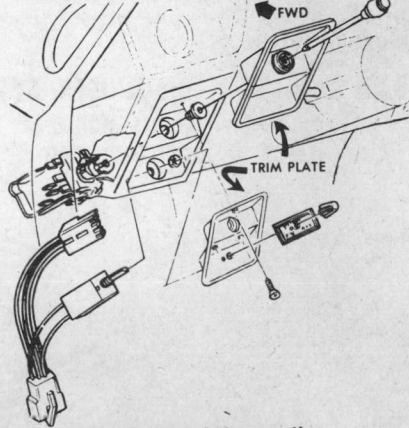

Headlight switch mounting
(© Chevrolet Div., G.M. Corp)

shaft retainer button while pulling on the switch control shaft knob.

4. Remove the three screws and remove the headlight switch trim plate.
5. Use a large-bladed screwdriver to remove the light switch ferrule nut from the front of the instrument panel.
6. Disconnect the multi-contact connector from the bottom of the headlight switch. (A small screwdriver will aid removal).
7. Installation is the reverse of removal.

WINDSHIELD WIPERS

Motor Removal and Installation

1. Working inside the car, reach up under the instrument panel above the steering column and loosen, but do not remove, the transmission drive link-to-motor crank arm attaching nuts.
2. Disconnect the transmission drive link from the motor crank arm.
3. Raise the hood and disconnect the motor wiring.
4. Remove the three motor attaching bolts.
5. Remove the motor while guiding the crank arm through the hole.
6. To install, align the sealing gasket to the base of the motor and reverse the rest of the removal procedure. Tighten the motor attaching bolts to 30-45 in. lbs. Tighten the transmission drive link-to-motor crank arm attaching nuts to 25-35 in. lbs.

NOTE: If the wiper motor-to-dash panel sealing gasket is damaged during removal, it should be replaced with a new gasket to prevent possible water leaks.

BASE EQUIPMENT DIAGNOSTIC SYSTEM
ADDITIONAL CIRCUITS MONITOR
MAJOR OPTIONAL EQUIPMENT

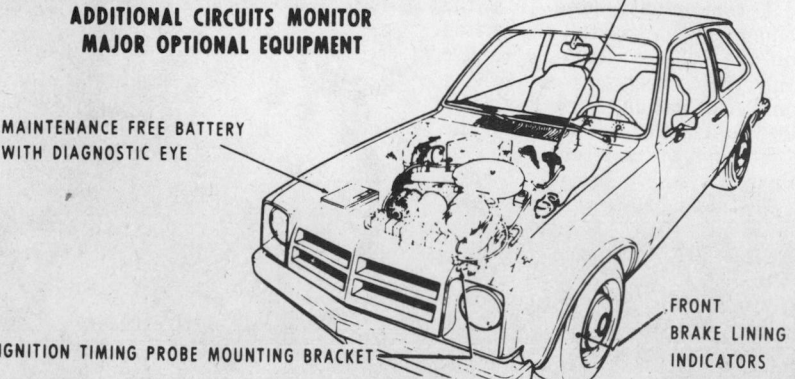

MAINTENANCE FREE BATTERY WITH DIAGNOSTIC EYE

MASTER DIAGNOSTIC CONNECTOR (IGNITION PERFORMANCE)

IGNITION TIMING PROBE MOUNTING BRACKET

FRONT BRAKE LINING INDICATORS

RADIO

Radio Removal and Installation

1. Disconnect the negative battery cable.
2. Remove the nut from the mounting stud on the bottom of the radio.
3. Remove all control knobs and/or spacers from the right and left radio control shafts.
4. Remove the four screws from the center trim plate and pull the trim plate and the radio forward slightly.
5. Disconnect the antenna lead from the rear of the radio.
6. Disconnect the speaker and electrical connectors from the radio harness.
7. Disconnect the electrical connectors from the rear window defogger and cigarette lighter.
8. Use a deep well socket to remove the retaining nuts from both control shafts and remove the radio.
9. To install, reverse the removal procedure.

HEATER

Blower Motor Removal and Installation

1. Disconnect the negative battery cable.
2. Disconnect the electrical lead from the blower motor.
3. Scribe a mark to reference the blower motor flange-to-case position.
4. Remove the blower motor-to-case attaching screws and remove the blower motor and wheel as an assembly. Pry the flange gently if the sealer acts as an adhesive.
5. Remove the blower wheel retaining nut and separate the motor and wheel.
6. Reverse Steps 1-5 to install. Be sure to align the scribe marks made during removal.

Blower motor assembly
(© Chevrolet Div., G.M. Corp)

NOTE: Assemble the blower wheel to the motor with the open end of the wheel away from the motor. If necessary, replace the sealer at the motor flange.

Heater Core Removal and Installation

1. Disconnect the negative battery cable.
2. Drain the radiator.
3. Disconnect the heater hoses at the heater core tube connections. Use care when removing the hoses as the core tube attachment seams can be easily damaged if too much force is used on them. When the hoses are removed, install plugs in the core tubes to avoid spilling coolant when removing the core.

NOTE: The larger diameter hose goes to the water pump; the smaller diameter hose goes to the thermostat housing.

4. Remove the screws around the perimeter of the heater core cover on the engine side of the dash panel.
5. Pull the heater core cover from its mounting in the dash panel.
6. Remove the core from the distributor assembly.
7. Reverse the removal procedure to install. Be sure that the core-to-case sealer is intact before replacing the core; use new sealer if necessary. When installation is complete, check for coolant leaks.

Diagnostic System

The Chevette maintenance-free battery and front brake lining wear indicators give direct indications if service is required. An underhood master electronic diagnostic connector and ignition probe bracket are used to speed diagnosis of malfunctions.

A special do-it-yourself owner maintenance booklet is included with each Chevette.

INDEX

Chrysler · Cordoba · Imperial

Automatic Transmission In-car
  service **C429**
  Band Adjustments C429
  Neutral safety/backup light Switch C429
  Pan Removal and Installation,
    fluid change C429
  Shift Linkage Adjustment C429

Brakes **C435, U299**
  Master Cylinder Removal and
    Installation C435
  Parking Brake Adjustment C435
  Power Brake Booster Removal and
    Installation C435

Charging System
Clutch
Cooling System
Emission Controls
Engine
  See Dodge-Plymouth section

Front Suspension **C431, U292**
  Lower Ball Joint Inspection,
    Removal and Installation C432
  Height Adjustment C431
  Shock Absorber Removal and
    Installation C431
  Upper Ball Joint Removal and
    Installation C434
  Torsion Bar Removal and Installation .. C434
  Wheel Bearing Adjustment C432

FUEL SYSTEM
  See Dodge-Plymouth section

Heater **C438**
  Blower Motor Removal and

Installation with A/C C439
Blower Motor Removal and Installation
  without A/C C438
Heater Core Removal and Installation
  with A/C C439
Heater Core Removal and Installation
  without A/C C438

Ignition System
  See Dodge-Plymouth section

Instrument Panel **C437, U350**
  Headlight Switch Replacement C437

Jacking, Hoisting **C431**

Manual Transmission ....
  See Dodge-Plymouth section

Radio **C437**
  Radio Removal and Installation C437

Rear Axle **C431, U285**
  Axle Shaft, bearing and seal
    Removal and Installation C431

Rear Suspension **C435**
  Shock Absorber Removal and
    Installation C435
  Spring Removal and Installation C435

Seat Belts
  See Dodge-Plymouth section

Specifications **C444, U359**
  Capacities C426
  Crankshaft and Connecting Rod C427
  Engine Code, Identification C423
  Firing Order C423
  General Engine C424
  Piston Clearance C428
  Piston Ring gap and side clearance C428
  Torque C426
  Tune-up C425
  Valve C427
  Wheel Alignment C428
  Year Identification C422

Starting System
  See Dodge-Plymouth section

Steering **C436, U328**
  Ignition Lock Cylinder Replacement C437
  Ignition Switch Replacement C437
  Power Steering Pump Removal
    and Installation C436
  Steering Wheel Removal and
    Installation C436
  Turn Signal Hazard Warning Switch
    Removal and Installation C437

U-Joints **C429**
  Constant Velocity U-Joint Disassembly C429
  Cross and Roller Bearing U-Joint
    Disassembly C430
  Driveshaft Removal and Installation C429

Windshield Wipers **C437**
  Wiper Motor Removal and Installation .. C437

YEAR IDENTIFICATION
Chrysler

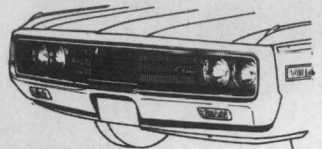

1970 Newport Custom

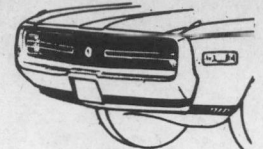

1970 "300"

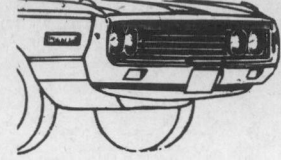

1970 New Yorker

1971 Newport

1972 Newport

1972 New Yorker

1973 Newport

1973 New Yorker

1974 New Yorker

1975 Newport

1975 Cordoba

1975 New Yorker Brougham

1976 Newport

1976 Cordoba

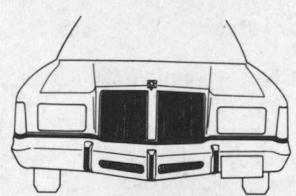

1976 New Yorker Brougham

1977 Newport

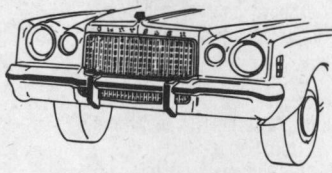

1977 Cordoba

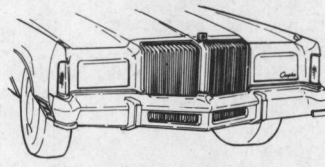

1977 New Yorker Brougham

Chrysler Imperial

1970 LeBaron

1971 LeBaron

1972 LeBaron

YEAR IDENTIFICATION

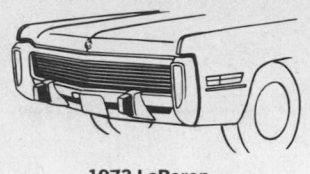

1973 LeBaron

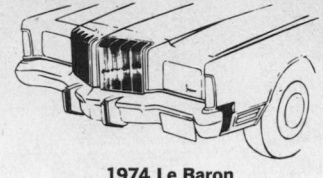

1974 Le Baron

1975 Imperial LeBaron

FIRING ORDER

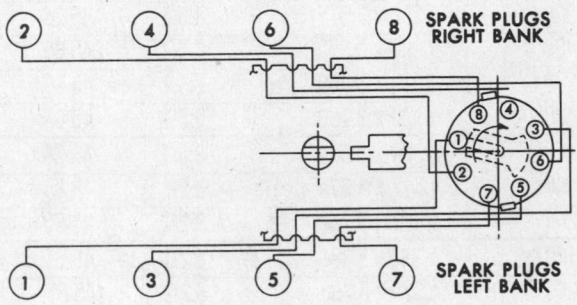

318, 360 (© Chrysler Corp.)

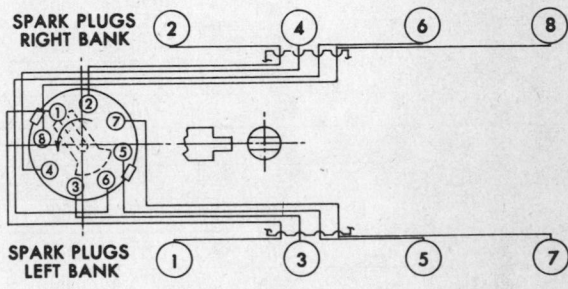

383, 400, 440 (© Chrysler Corp.)

ENGINE CODE

The engine code designation is the 5th digit of the vehicle identification number (V.I.N.). The V.I.N. is stamped on a plate located at the left side of the instrument panel visible through the windshield, and located to the rear of the right engine mount on the oil pan rail on V8 engines.

Displacement	Bbl	'70	'71	'72	'73	'74	'75	'76	'77
318	2						G	G	G
360	2		K	K			K	K	K
360	4					J	J	J	J
383	2	L	L						
383	4	N	N						
400	2			M	M	M	M	M	M
400	4					N	N	N	N
400 HP	4						P	P	P
440	4	T	T	T	T	T	U	T	T
440 HP	4	U	U				T	U	U

HP High Performance

ENGINE IDENTIFICATION

The engine that the factory installed in the car can be identified by the fifth digit of the Vehicle Identification Number, as explained under Engine Code. The engine itself can be identified by the engine serial number. The cubic inch displacement is given by either the second, third, and fourth, or the third, fourth, and fifth digits of the engine serial number, depending on the year and engine.

V8s through 360 cu. in. have the serial number on the front of the block, just below the left cylinder head. 383 and larger V8s have the number on the oil pan rail, below the starter opening, at the left rear corner of the block; in front of the distributor; or along the left front tappet rail. 360 cu. in. and smaller (small block) V8s can quickly be identified as having the distributor at the rear of the engine, while 383 and larger versions have it at the front.

GENERAL ENGINE SPECIFICATIONS

Year	Engine No. Cyl. Displacement (Cu. In.)	Carburetor Type	Horsepower @ rpm ■	Torque @ rpm (ft lbs) ■	Bore X Stroke (in.)	Compression Ratio	Oil Pressure @ 2000 rpm
'70	8-383	2 bbl	290 @ 4400	390 @ 2800	4.250 x 3.375	8.7:1	45-65
	8-383	4 bbl	330 @ 5000	425 @ 3200	4.250 x 3.375	9.5:1	45-65
	8-440	4 bbl	350 @ 4400	480 @ 2800	4.320 x 3.750	9.7:1	45-65
	8-440 HP	4 bbl	375 @ 4600	480 @ 3200	4.320 x 3.750	9.7:1	45-65
'71	8-360	2 bbl	255 @ 4000	360 @ 2400	4.000 x 3.580	8.7:1	45-65
	8-383	2 bbl	275 @ 4400	375 @ 2800	4.250 x 3.375	8.5:1	45-65
	8-383	4 bbl	300 @ 4800	410 @ 3400	4.250 x 3.375	8.5:1	45-65
	8-440	4 bbl	335 @ 4400	460 @ 3200	4.320 x 3.750	8.5:1	45-65
	8-440 HP	4 bbl	370 @ 4600	480 @ 3200	4.320 x 3.750	9.5:1	45-65
'72	8-360	2 bbl	175 @ 4000	285 @ 2400	4.000 x 3.580	8.8:1	45-65
	8-400	2 bbl	190 @ 4400	310 @ 2400	4.342 x 3.375	8.2:1	45-65
	8-440	4 bbl	225 @ 4400	345 @ 3200	4.320 x 3.750	8.2:1	45-65
'73	8-400	2 bbl	185 @ 3600	310 @ 2400	4.340 x 3.380	8.2:1	45-65
	8-440	4 bbl	215 @ 3600	345 @ 2000	4.320 x 3.750	8.2:1	45-65
	8-440 Calif.	4 bbl	208 @ 3600	340 @ 2000	4.320 x 3.750	8.2:1	45-65
'74	8-360	4 bbl	200 @ 4000	290 @ 3200	4.000 x 3.580	8.4:1	45-65
	8-400	2 bbl	185 @ 4000	315 @ 2400	4.340 x 3.380	8.2:1	45-65
	8-400	4 bbl	205 @ 4400	310 @ 2400	4.340 x 3.380	8.2:1	45-65
	8-440	4 bbl	230 @ 4000	350 @ 3200	4.320 x 3.750	8.2:1	45-65
	8-440 Calif.	4 bbl	220 @ 4000	345 @ 3200	4.320 x 3.750	8.2:1	45-65
'75	8-318	2 bbl	150 @ 4000	255 @ 1600	3.910 x 3.310	8.5:1	45-65
	8-318 Calif.	2 bbl	135 @ 3600	245 @ 1600	3.910 x 3.310	8.5:1	45-65
	8-360	2 bbl	180 @ 4000	290 @ 2400	4.000 x 3.580	8.4:1	45-65
	8-360	4 bbl	190 @ 4000	270 @ 3200	4.000 x 3.580	8.4:1	45-65
	8-400	2 bbl	175 @ 4000	300 @ 2400	4.340 x 3.380	8.2:1	50-75
	8-400 Cordoba	2 bbl	165 @ 4000	295 @ 3200	4.340 x 3.380	8.2:1	50-75
	8-400	4 bbl	195 @ 4000	285 @ 3200	4.340 x 3.380	8.2:1	50-75
	8-400 Cordoba	4 bbl	190 @ 4000	290 @ 3200	4.340 x 3.380	8.2:1	50-75
	8-400 Cordoba Calif.	4 bbl	185 @ 4000	285 @ 3200	4.340 x 3.380	8.2:1	50-75
	8-400 HP	4 bbl	235 @ 4200	320 @ 3200	4.340 x 3.380	8.2:1	50-75
	8-440	4 bbl	215 @ 4000	330 @ 3200	4.320 x 3.750	8.2:1	50-75
	8-440 Calif.	4 bbl	210 @ 4000	320 @ 3200	4.320 x 3.750	8.2:1	50-75
	8-440 HP	4 bbl	260 @ 4400	355 @ 3200	4.320 x 3.750	8.2:1	50-75
	8-440 HP Calif.	4 bbl	250 @ 4000	350 @ 3200	4.320 x 3.750	8.2:1	50-75
'76-'77	8-318	2 bbl	150 @ 4000	255 @ 1600	3.910 x 3.310	8.5:1	45-65
	8-318 Calif.	2 bbl	140 @ 3600	250 @ 2000	3.910 x 3.310	8.5:1	45-65
	8-360	2 bbl	170 @ 4000	280 @ 2400	4.000 x 3.580	8.4:1	45-65
	8-360 Calif.	4 bbl	175 @ 4000	270 @ 1600	4.000 x 3.580	8.4:1	45-65
	8-400	2 bbl	175 @ 4000	300 @ 2400	4.340 x 3.380	8.2:1	50-75
	8-400	4 bbl	210 @ 4400	305 @ 3200	4.340 x 3.380	8.2:1	50-75
	8-400 Calif.	4 bbl	185 @ 3600	285 @ 3200	4.340 x 3.380	8.2:1	50-75
	8-400 HP	4 bbl	240 @ 4400	325 @ 3200	4.340 x 3.380	8.2:1	50-75
	8-440	4 bbl	205 @ 3600	320 @ 2000	4.320 x 3.750	8.2:1	50-75
	8-440 Calif.	4 bbl	200 @ 3600	310 @ 2400	4.320 x 3.750	8.2:1	50-75

HP High Performance
■ Starting 1972, horsepower and torque are SAE net figures. They are measured at the rear of the transmission with all accessories installed and operating. Since the figures vary when a given engine is installed in different models, some are representative rather than exact.

TUNE-UP SPECIFICATIONS

When analyzing compression test results, look for uniformity among cylinders rather than specific pressures.

Year	ENGINE No. Cyl Displacement (cu in.)	hp	SPARK PLUGS Orig. Type	Gap (in.)	DISTRIBUTOR Point Dwell (deg)	Point Gap (in.)	IGNITION TIMING (deg) ▲ ● Man Trans	Auto Trans	VALVES Intake Opens ■ (deg)	Fuel Pump Pressure (psi) ●	IDLE SPEED (rpm) ▲ ● Man Trans		Auto Trans
'70	8-383	290	J-14Y	.035	28½-32½	.018	TDC	2½B	18	3½-5	750		650
	8-383	330	J-11Y	.035	28½-32½	.018	TDC	2½B	18	3½-5	—		700
	8-440	350	J-13Y	.035	28½-32½	.018	—	5B	18	3½-5	—		650
	8-440 HP	375	J-11Y	.035	28½-32½	.018	TDC	2½B	21	3½-5	900		800
'71	8-360	255	J-13Y	.035	30-34	.017	2½B	2½B	16	3½-5	750		700
	8-383	275	J-14Y	.035	30-34	.017	TDC	2½B	18	3½-5	750		700
	8-383	300	J-14Y	.035	28½-32½	.017	TDC	2½B	21	3½-5	900		800
	8-440	335	J-13Y	.035	28½-32½	.017	—	5B	18	3½-5	—		750
	8-440 HP	370	J-11Y	.035	28½-32½	.017	TDC	2½B	21	3½-5	900		900
'72	8-360	175	N-13Y	.035	28½-32½	.017	—	TDC	16	5-7	—		700
	8-400	255	J-13Y	.035	28½-32½	.018	—	①5B(2½B)	18	3½-5	—		700
	8-440	280	J-11Y	.035	28½-32½	.018	—	10B(5B)	18	3½-5	—		900
'73	8-400	185	J-13Y	.035	Electronic		—	10B	18	3½-5	—		700
	8-440	215	J-11Y	.035	Electronic		—	10B	18	3½-5	—		700
'74	8-360	200	N-12Y	.035	Electronic		—	5B	22	5-7	—		750
	8-400	185	J-13Y	.035	Electronic		—	10B(5B)	18	3½-5	—		750
	8-400	205	J-11Y	.035	Electronic		—	10B(2½B)	21	3½-5	—		900
	8-440	230	J-11Y	.035	Electronic		—	10B	21	3½-5	—		750
'75	8-318	150, 135	N-13Y	.035	Electronic		—	2B	10	5-7	—		750
	8-360	180	N-12Y	.035	Electronic		—	6B	18	5-7	—		750
	8-360	190	N-12Y	.035	Electronic		—	6B	18	5-7	—		750
	8-400	2 bbl	J-13Y	.035	Electronic		—	10B	18	6-7½	—		750
	8-400	4 bbl	J-13Y	.035	Electronic		—	8B	18	3½-5(6-7½)	—		750
	8-440	4 bbl	RY-87P	.040	Electronic		—	8B	18	4-5½	—		750
'76	8-318	150, 140	RN-12Y	.035	Electronic		—	2B(TDC)	10	5-7	—		750
	8-360	170, 175	RN-12Y	.035	Electronic		—	6B	18	5-7	—		700(750)
	8-400	175	RJ-13Y	.035	Electronic		—	10B	18	5-7	—		700
	8-400	210, 185	RJ-13Y	.035	Electronic		—	6B(8B)	18	5-7	—		850(750)
	8-400 HP	240	RJ-86P	.035	Electronic		—	6B	18	5-7	—		850
	8-440	205, 200	RJ-13Y	.035	Electronic		—	8B	18	5-7	—		750
'77	8-318	All	RN-12Y	.035	Electronic		—	8B	10	5¾-7¼	10	—	700(750)
	8-360	All	RN-12Y	.035	Electronic		—	10B(6B)	18	5¾-7¼	18	—	700(750)
	8-400	All	RJ-13Y	.035	Electronic		—	10B	20	5¾-7¼②	20	—	750
	8-440	All	RJ-13Y	.035	Electronic		—	8B	20	5¾-7¼	20	—	750

▲ See text for procedure
● Figure in parentheses indicates California engine
■ All figures Before Top Dead Center
① Non-California cars built after Feb. 2, 7½B
② 5¼-6¾ on Cordoba
A After Top Dead Center

B Before Top Dead Center
TDC Top Dead Center
— Not applicable

NOTE: The underhood specifications sticker often reflects tune-up specification changes made in production. Sticker figures must be used if they disagree with those in this chart.

CAPACITIES

Year	ENGINE No. Cyl. Displacement (Cu. In.)	Engine Crankcase Add 1 Qt For New Filter	TRANSMISSION Pts To Refill After Draining			Drive Axle (pts)	Gasoline Tank (gals)	COOLING SYSTEM (qts)	
			Manual 3-Speed	4-Speed	Automatic			With Heater ▲	With A/C
'70	8-383	4	4.75	——	19.0①	4	24	14.5②	16②
	8-440	4	——	——	19.0	4	24	15.5	17
	Town & Country	4	——	——	19.0①	4	23	16	17
	Imperial	4	——	——	19.0	4.4	24	18	18
'71	8-360	4	4.75	——	16.3	4.5	23	15.5	16
	8-383	4	4.75③	——	19.0①	4.5	23	14.5	15
	8-440	4	——	——	19.0	4.5	23	15.5	17
	Town & Country	4	——	——	19.0①	4.5	23	16	17
	Imperial	4	——	——	19.0	4.5	23	17.5	17.5
'72	8-360	4	——	——	16.3	4.4	23	15.5	16.5
	8-400	4	——	——	19.0	4.4	23	14.5	15.5
	8-440	4	——	——	19.0	4.4	23	17.5	17.5
	Town & Country	4	——	——	19.0	4.4	23	16	17
	Imperial	4	——	——	19.0	4.4	23	17.5	17.5
'73	8-400	4	——	——	19.0	4.5	23	16	16
	8-440	4	——	——	19.0	4.5	23	15.5	15.5
	Imperial	4	——	——	19.0	4.5	23	18	18
'74	8-360	4	——	——	16.1	4.5	26.5④	16	16
	8-400	4	——	——	18.9	4.5	26.5④	16.5	16.5
	8-440	4	——	——	18.9	4.5	26.5④	16	16
	Imperial	4	——	——	16.5	4.5	26.5	17	17
'75	8-318	4	——	——	16.5	4.5	25.5	16.5	18
	8-360	4	——	——	16.5	4.5	26.5④	16.0	16.0
	8-400	4	——	——	16.5	4.5	26.5④	16.5	16.5
	8-400 HP	4	——	——	16.5	4.5	20.5	16.5	16.5
	8-440	4	——	——	16.5	4.5	26.5④	16.0	16.0
	Imperial	4	——	——	16.5	4.5	26.5	17.0	17.0
'76-'77	8-318	4	——	——	17	4.5	25.5	16.5	18
	8-360	4	——	——	19	4.5	26.5④	16	16
	8-400	4	——	——	19	4.5	26.5④	16.5	16.5
	8-400 HP	5	——	——	19	4.5	20.5	16.5	16.5
	8-440	4	——	——	19	4.5	26.5	16	16

▲ Add 1.5 qts if equipped with rear seat heater
① 4 bbl carb—16 pts
② 4 bbl carb—15.5-17 pts
③ 2 bbl only
④ Wagons—24 gals, Cordoba—25.5 gals
—— Not applicable

TORQUE SPECIFICATIONS
All readings in ft lbs

Year	Engine No. Cyl. Displacement (cu in.)	Cylinder Head Bolts	Rod Bearing Bolts	Main Bearing Bolts	Crankshaft Pulley Bolt	Flywheel to Crankshaft Bolts	MANIFOLD Intake	Exhaust
'71-'72	8-360	95	45	85	135	55	40	20
'74-'77	8-318, 360	95	45	85	100	55	40	20/15①
'70-'77	8-383, 400, 440	70	45	85	135	55	45	30

① Screw/nut

VALVE SPECIFICATIONS

	Engine No. Cyl. Displacement (cu. in.)	Seat Angle (deg)	Face Angle (deg)	Spring Test Pressure (lbs @ in.)	Spring Installed Height (in.)	STEM TO GUIDE Clearance (in.)		STEM Diameter (in.)	
						Intake	Exhaust	Intake	Exhaust
'70	8-383	45	45	200 @ 1.44	1 7/8	.0010-.0030	.0020-.0040	.3725	.3715
	8-440	45	45	200 @ 1.44	1 7/8	.0010-.0030	.0020-.0040	.3725	.3715
	8-440 HP	45	45	246 @ 1.36	1 7/8	.0010-.0030	.0020-.0040	.3725	.3715
'71	8-360	45	④	177 @ 1.31	1 11/16	.0010-.0030	.0020-.0040	.3725	.3715
	8-383 2 bbl	45	45	200 @ 1.44	1 7/8	.0010-.0030	.0020-.0040	.3727	.3715
	8-383 4 bbl	45	45	246 @ 1.36	1 7/8	.0015-.0032	.0025-.0042	.3722	.3712
	8-440	45	45	200 @ 1.44	1 7/8	.0010-.0030	.0020-.0040	.3727	.3717
	8-440 HP	45	45	246 @ 1.36	1 7/8	.0015-.0032	.0025-.0042	.3722	.3712
'72	8-360	45	④	177 @ 1.31	1 11/16	.0010-.0030	.0020-.0040	.3725	.3715
	8-400	45	45	200 @ 1.44	1 7/8	.0010-.0030	.0020-.0040	.3725	.3715
	8-440	45	45	200 @ 1.44	1 7/8	.0010-.0030	.0020-.0040	.3725	.3715
'73	8-400	45	45	200 @ 1.42	1 55/64	.0015-.0032	⑤	.3722	⑥
	8-440	45	45	200 @ 1.42	1 55/64	.0015-.0032	⑤	.3722	⑥
'74	8-360	45	④	208 @ 1.31	1 43/64	.0010-.0030	.0020-.0040	.3725	.3720
	8-400	45	45	200 @ 1.43	1 55/64	.0010-.0027	⑤	.3727	⑥
	8-440	45	45	234 @ 1.40	1 55/64	.0015-.0032	⑥	.3722	⑥
'75	8-318	45	④	177 @ 1.31	1 21/32	.0010-.0030	.0020-.0040	.3725	.3715
	8-360	45	④	177 @ 1.31	1 21/32	.0010-.0030	.0020-.0040	.3725	.3715
	8-400	45	45	200 @ 1.43	1 55/64	.0010-.0027	⑤	.3726	⑥
	8-400 HP	45	45	246 @ 1.36	1 55/64	.0015-.0032	③	.3722	②
	8-440	45	45	200 @ 1.43	1 55/64	.0010-.0027	⑤	.3726	⑥
'76-'77	8-318	45	④	177 @ 1.31	1 21/32	.0010-.0030	.0020-.0040	.3725	.3715
	8-360	45	④	177 @ 1.31	1 21/32	.0010-.0030	.0020-.0040	.3725	.3715
	8-400	45	45	200 @ 1.43	1 55/64	.0011-.0028	⑤	.3726	⑥
	8-400 HP	45	45	246 @ 1.36	1 55/64	.0016-.0033	③	.3722	②
	8-440	45	45	200 @ 1.43	1 55/64	.0011-.0028	⑤	.3726	⑥

① not used
② Hot end—.3712, cold end—.3722
③ Hot end—.0026-.0043, cold end—.0016-.0033
④ Intake valve face angle 45°
  Exhaust valve face angle 43°

⑤ Hot end—.0020-.0037, cold end—.0010-.0027
⑥ Hot end—.3716, cold end—.3726
⑦ Hot end—.0025-.0042, cold end—.0015-.0040
HP High Performance

CRANKSHAFT AND CONNECTING ROD SPECIFICATIONS
All measurements are given in inches

Year	Engine No. Cyl. Displacement (cu in.)	CRANKSHAFT Main Brg. Journal Dia	Main Brg. Oil Clearance	Shaft End-Play	Thrust on No.	CONNECTING ROD Journal Diameter	Oil Clearance	Side Clearance*
'74-'77	8-318	2.4995-2.5005	.0005-.0020	.002-.007	3	2.124-2.125	.0005-.0025	.006-.014
'71-'77	8-360	2.8095-2.8105	.0005-.0020	.002-.007	3	2.124-2.125	.0005-.0025	.006-.014
'70-'71	8-383	2.6245-2.6255	.0005-.0015	.002-.007	3	2.3740-2.3750	.0005-.0030	.009-.017
'72-'74	8-400 2 bbl	2.6245-2.6255	.0005-.0020	.002-.007	3	2.374-2.375	.0005-.0020	.009-.017
'75-'77	8-400 2 bbl	2.6245-2.6255	.0005-.0020	.002-.007	3	2.375-2.376	.0005-.0025	.009-.017
'74	8-400 4 bbl	2.6245-2.6255	.0005-.0020	.002-.007	3	2.374-2.375	.0010-.0025	.009-.017
'75-'77	8-400 4 bbl	2.6245-2.6255	.0005-.0020	.002-.007	3	2.375-2.376	.0010-.0030	.009-.017
'70-'77	8-440	2.7495-2.7505	.0005-.0020	.002-.007	3	2.3750-2.3760	.0005-.0030	.009-.017

* Total for two rods

RING GAP
All measurements are given in inches

Year	Engine No. Cyl. Displacement (cu. in.)	Top Compression	Bottom Compression
'70-'77	8-383, 440	.013-.025	.013-.025
'71-'77	8-360, 318	.010-.020	.010-.020
'72-'77	8-400	.013-.023	.013-.023

Year	Engine No. Cyl. Displacement (cu. in.)	Oil Control
'70-'77	All engines	.015-.055

RING SIDE CLEARANCE
All measurements are given in inches

Year	Engine No. Cyl. Displacement (cu. in.)	Top Compression	Bottom Compression
'70-'77	All engines	.0015-.0030	.0015-.0030

Year	Engine No. Cyl. Displacement (cu. in.)	Oil Control
'70-'77	8-383, 400, 440	.0002-.005
'71-'77	8-360, 318	.0000-.005

PISTON CLEARANCE

Year	Engine	Piston to bore clearance (in.)*
'70	383, 440	.0003-.0013
'71	360	.0005-.0015
	383, 440	.0003-.0013
'72-'77	318, 360 2 bbl	.0005-.0015
	360 4 bbl	.0010-.0020
	400, 440	.0003-.0013

* at top of skirt

FRONT END HEIGHT▲

Year	Model	Front End Height
'70-'73	Chrysler	$1\frac{1}{8} \pm \frac{1}{8}$
	Imperial	$1\frac{3}{4} \pm \frac{1}{8}$
'74	Chrysler	$1 \pm \frac{1}{8}$
	Imperial	$1 \pm \frac{1}{8}$
'75-'77	Chrysler	$10\frac{1}{8} \pm \frac{1}{8}$
	Imperial	$10\frac{1}{8} \pm \frac{1}{8}$
	Cordoba	$10\frac{3}{4} \pm \frac{1}{8}$

▲ See text for procedure

WHEEL ALIGNMENT SPECIFICATIONS

Year	Model	CASTER Range (deg)	CASTER Pref Setting (deg)	CAMBER Range (deg)	CAMBER Pref Setting (deg)	Toe-in (in.)	Steering Axis Inclin. (deg.)	WHEEL PIVOT RATIO (deg) Inner Wheel	WHEEL PIVOT RATIO (deg) Outer Wheel
'70	Manual Steering Chry.	$\frac{1}{2}$N $\pm$ $\frac{9}{16}$	$\frac{1}{2}$N	④	⑤	$\frac{3}{32}$ to $\frac{5}{32}$	$7\frac{1}{2}$	20	18.8
	Power Steering Chry.	$\frac{1}{2}$N $\pm$ $\frac{9}{16}$	$\frac{1}{2}$N	④	⑤	$\frac{3}{32}$ to $\frac{5}{32}$	$7\frac{1}{2}$	20	18.8
	Imperial	$\frac{3}{4}$P $\pm$ $\frac{9}{16}$	$\frac{3}{4}$P	④	⑤	$\frac{3}{32}$ to $\frac{5}{32}$	9	20	17.9
'71-'72	Manual Steering Chry.	0 to 1P	$\frac{1}{2}$N	④	⑤	$\frac{3}{32}$ to $\frac{5}{32}$	$7\frac{1}{2}$	20	18.8
	Power Steering Chry.	$\frac{1}{4}$P to $1\frac{1}{4}$P	$\frac{3}{4}$P	④	⑤	$\frac{3}{32}$ to $\frac{5}{32}$	$7\frac{1}{2}$	20	18.8
	Imperial	$\frac{1}{4}$P to $1\frac{1}{4}$P	$\frac{3}{4}$P	④	⑤	$\frac{3}{32}$ to $\frac{5}{32}$	9	20	17.9
'73	Chrysler	$\frac{1}{16}$N to $1\frac{5}{16}$P	$\frac{5}{8}$P	⑦	⑤	$\frac{1}{8} \pm \frac{3}{32}$	$7\frac{1}{2}$	20	18.8
	Imperial	$\frac{1}{16}$N to $1\frac{5}{16}$P	$\frac{5}{8}$P	⑦	⑤	$\frac{1}{8} \pm \frac{3}{32}$	9	20	17.9
'74	Chrysler, Imperial	$\frac{1}{2}$N to $1\frac{3}{4}$P	$\frac{3}{4}$P	⑧	⑤	$\frac{1}{16}$ to $\frac{1}{4}$	9	20	18.3
'75	Cordoba	$\frac{1}{2}$N to $1\frac{3}{4}$P	$\frac{3}{4}$P	⑦	⑤	$\frac{1}{16}$ to $\frac{1}{4}$	8	20	18.0
	Chrysler, Imperial	$\frac{1}{2}$N to $1\frac{3}{4}$P	$\frac{3}{4}$P	⑦	⑤	$\frac{1}{16}$ to $\frac{1}{4}$	9	20	18.3
'76-'77	Cordoba	$\frac{1}{2}$N to $1\frac{3}{4}$P	$\frac{3}{4}$P	⑧		$\frac{1}{2}$P $\frac{1}{16}$ to $\frac{1}{4}$	8	20	18
	Chrysler	$\frac{1}{2}$N to $1\frac{3}{4}$P	$\frac{3}{4}$P	⑧		$\frac{1}{2}$P $\frac{1}{16}$ to $\frac{1}{4}$	9	20	18.3

① not used
② not used
③ not used
④ Left side—$\frac{1}{2}$P $\pm$ $\frac{1}{4}$; Right side—$\frac{1}{4}$P $\pm$ $\frac{1}{4}$
⑤ Left side—$\frac{1}{2}$P; Right side—$\frac{1}{4}$P
⑥ not used
⑦ Left side—$\frac{1}{8}$P to $\frac{7}{8}$P
Right side—$\frac{1}{8}$N to $\frac{5}{8}$P
⑧ Left side—0 to 1P
Right side—$\frac{1}{4}$N to $\frac{3}{4}$P
N Negative   P Positive

NOTE: Service procedures for the Charging System, Starting System, Ignition System, Fuel System, Cooling System, Emission Control System, Engine, and Clutch on Chrysler, Cordoba, and Imperial cars can be found in the Dodge-Plymouth section.

AUTOMATIC TRANSMISSION

On models through 1971, model identification appears in large letters embossed on the lower side of the bell housing. On 1972 and later models, the model may be identified by the part number, which is stamped on a pad on the left side of the case fluid pan flange. All models use the A-727 transmission, except for those with the 318 engine, which use the smaller A-904. The A-727 transmission can be visually identified as having a more gradual slope to the converter housing than the A-904.

Neutral Safety/Backup Light Switch Replacement
Shift Linkage Adjustment
Pan Removal and Installation, Fluid Change

These procedures are covered for all Chrysler Corporation cars in the Barracuda, Challenger Dart, Valiant, Aspen, Volare car section.

Band Adjustments

Kick-down Band

The kick-down band adjusting screw is located on the left-hand side of the transmission case near the throttle lever shaft.

1. Loosen the locknut and back it off about five turns. Be sure that the adjusting screw is free in the case.
2. Using an inch pounds torque wrench torque the adjusting screw to 72 in. lbs.
3. Back off the adjusting screw the exact number of turns specified below. Keep the screw from turning and tighten the locknut.

1970 . . . . .2 turns
1971 and later . . . . 2½ turns
1975 and later 318 (A-904) . .2 turns

Low and Reverse Band

The pan must be removed from the transmission to gain access to the low and reverse band adjusting screw.

1. Drain the transmission and remove the pan.
2. Loosen the band adjusting screw locknut and back it off about five turns. Be sure that the adjusting screw turns freely in the lever.
3. Using an inch pounds torque wrench, tighten the adjusting screw to 72 in. lbs.
4. Back off the adjusting screw the exact number of turns specified below. Keep the screw from turning and tighten the locknut.

1970 and later . . . . .2 turns
1975 and later 318 (A-904) . .4 turns

5. Using a new gasket, install the pan and tighten the attaching bolts to 150 in. lbs.
6. Fill the transmission.

U-JOINTS

All models use one-piece driveshafts with two U-joints. All full size Chrysler, Cordoba, and 1974-75 Imperial models have two cross-and-roller joints with a slip spline at the front U-joint. There are two constant-velocity U-joints on Imperials through 1973.

Driveshaft Removal and Installation

You can avoid loss of lubricant from the rear of the transmission by raising the rear of the car before removing the driveshaft.

1. Scribe alignment marks on the driveshaft, rear U-joint, and the drive pinion flange. This is necessary to ensure proper drive train balance upon installation of the various parts.
2. Remove both of the U-joint roller and bushing assembly clamps from the rear axle drive pinion flange. Be sure not to disturb the retaining strap (if so equipped) which holds the bushing assemblies on the U-joint cross. Do not allow the driveshaft to hang loose while removing either U-joint.
3. Slide the driveshaft with the front yoke from the transmission output shaft. Be careful not to damage the splines on the output shaft and the yoke. Do not disturb the yoke seal unless it is damaged or leaking. Remove the driveshaft and protect the sliding yoke from damage.
4. To install the driveshaft, clean the sliding yoke and inspect its machined surface. File off burrs if necessary. Carefully engage the yoke splines with the splines on the end of the transmission output shaft.
5. At the rear, align the scribe marks and install the U-joint cross and roller bushings into the drive pinion flange. Fit the bushing clamps and securing screws.

Constant Velocity Universal Joint—Imperial through 1973

Disassembly

Remove the driveshaft and, before disassembling any parts, mark the joints for proper indexing at the time of assembly.

1. Remove four screws and lockwashers. Remove spline yoke.
2. Remove two loose bearings from centering socket yoke.
3. Remove snap-rings holding the bearing assemblies in the center socket yoke shaft, and center yoke bores.

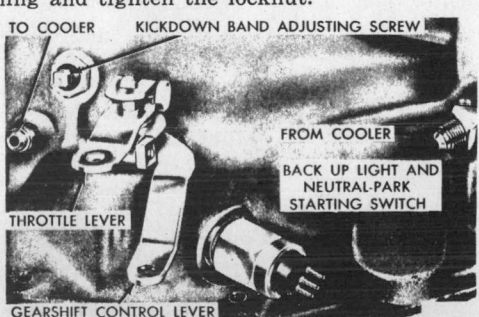

TorqueFlite transmission external controls, showing the location of the kick-down band adjustment
(© Chrysler Corp)

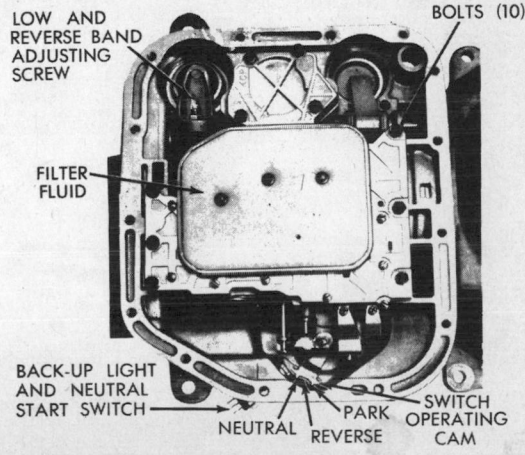

TorqueFlite transmission bottom view with the pan removed. Note the low and reverse band adjusting screw location
(© Chrysler Corp)

C429

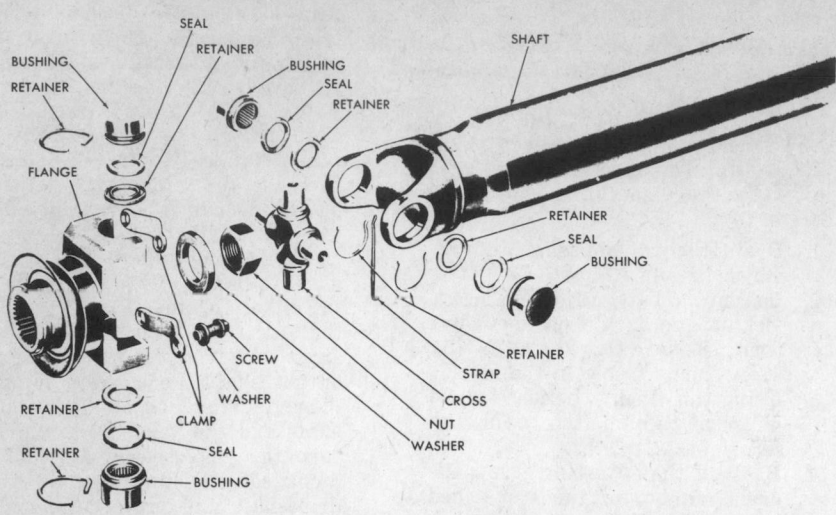

Rear cross and roller U-joint—All Chrysler, Cordoba, and 1974-75 Imperial

4. Press bearing assemblies from the yokes by using a ¾ in. socket as a remover and a pipe or socket with an inside diameter of not less than 1 1/16 in. as a receiver on the opposite bearing. With the aid of a press or vise, press one of the rear yoke bearings about ⅜ in. out of the yoke.

5. Clamp the exposed bearing in the vise and drive the yoke from the bearing with a brass drift.

6. Using the same procedure, press the exposed end of the cross to force the bearing on the opposite end about ⅜ in. out of the yoke. Remove the bearing from the yoke as previously described in Step 5.

7. Remove the remaining set of bearings from the propeller shaft yoke in the same way.

8. With the shaft held in the vise, press in on the yoke shaft and work the center joint off the cross.

9. Remove the cross from the propeller shaft yoke. Remove centering stud spring from the propeller shaft.

10. Remove the four roller bearing assemblies to separate the yoke shaft from the center yoke, as

previously described.

If it is necessary to remove the centering ball and socket assembly, proceed as follows:

11. Carefully pry the centering ball seal assembly from the yoke shaft.

12. Remove seal from the centering stud seal retainer and the bearing rollers from the centering ball.

13. Fill the cavity behind the centering ball and inside the ball with lithium base grease.

14. Insert a rod, slightly smaller than the inside diameter of the centering ball, into the ball, then strike it sharply with a hammer. The force applied should force the ball and retainer from the yoke.

Assembly

1. Position the centering assembly in the yoke with the large diameter hole up, and press it firmly into its seat.

2. Apply grease on the inside surface of the centering ball. Install the 34 rollers. Install the centering stud seal in the ball.

3. Install centering ball seal assembly on the yoke and press firmly into place.

4. Coat the inside surfaces of the bearing races with the same grease, and install the 32 rollers. Also, pack the reservoirs in the ends of the cross with the same grease.

5. Place the cross in the shaft yoke. Insert one bearing assembly in the bearing bore of the shaft yoke. With the bar stock or socket used as a remover when disassembling, press the bearing into the bore. At the same time, guide the cross into the bearing. Press the bearing into the yoke far enough to install the snap-ring. Install the snap-ring. Reverse the position of the yoke and install the opposite bearing and snapping in th same manner.

6. Place the center yoke on the cross installed in the shaft yoke. Install the two bearings and snap-rings in the yoke, as previously described.

7. Install the cross and two bearings in the shaft yoke, in the same manner as previously described. Install snap-rings.

8. Install centering stud spring on the centering stud, (large end first). Apply grease to the stud.

9. Position the cross in the center universal joint of the propeller shaft while guiding the centering ball on the centering stud, applying pressure at the same time. Work the center yoke over the cross. Don't damage the cross seals.

10. Install the two bearing assemblies in the rear bores of the center yoke as previously described. Install snap-rings.

11. Coat the splines of the center socket yoke with grease.

12. Install slip spline yoke on the constant velocity joints with screws and lockwashers. Torque to specifications.

Cross and Roller Bearing U-Joints—Chrysler, Cordoba, and 1974-75 Imperial

Disassembly and Assembly

1. To disassemble the joint, remove the four bolts that hold the two bearing assemblies to the companion flange and knock the bearings off the flange.

2. To remove the bearings from the yoke, first remove the bearing retainer lock washers or C-washers, then pressing on one of the bearings, drive the bearing in toward the center of the joint. This will force the cross to push the opposite bearing out of the universal joint yoke. After it

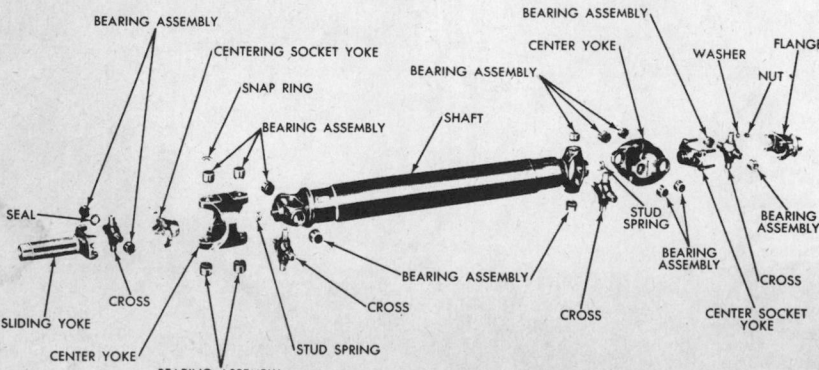

Constant Velocity U-joints and drive shaft—Imperial through 1973
(© Chrysler Corp)

has been pushed all the way out of the yoke, pull up the cross slightly and pack some washers under it. Then press on the end of the cross from which the bearing was just removed to force the first bearing out of the yoke.

3. Perhaps the easiest way to reassemble is to start both bearing retainers into the yoke at the same time, hold the cross carefully in the fingers and squeeze both bearings in a vise or heavy C-clamp. Driving the bearings into place usually cocks the rollers, greatly reducing the life of the bearings.

4. Install the locking devices.

REAR AXLE

Three different rear axle assemblies are being used on Chrysler, Imperial and Cordoba models. A removable carrier axle with an 8¾ in. ring gear diameter differential was installed on all models through 1972. Beginning 1973, two integral carrier axles are used; an 8¼ and a 9¼ in. unit. Both the 8¼ and 9¼ in. axles use C-clips to retain the axle shafts.

These axles can be visually identified as follows:

The 8¼ in. axle has a 10 bolt rear cover without a filler plug, the 8¾ in. axle has a welded nonremovable rear cover, and the 9¼ in. axle has a 12 bolt rear cover with a filler plug.

All axles have a ratio identification tag under one of the cover or carrier bolts.

Axle Shaft, Bearing and Seal Removal and Installation

See the Dodge/Plymouth section for these procedures. They are arranged by differential ring gear diameter size.

JACKING, HOISTING

Jack car at front under lower control arm and at rear under axle housing.

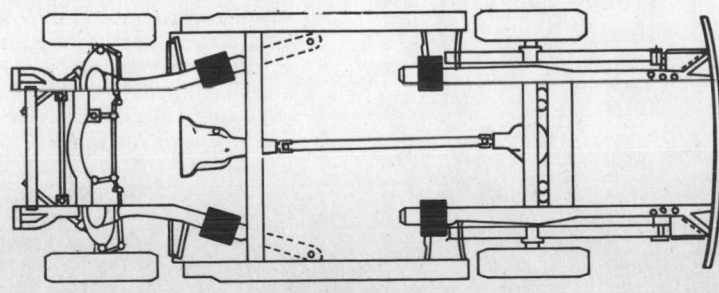

Positioning lift adapter
(© Chrysler Corp)

To lift at frame, use adapters so that contact will be made at points shown. Lifting pad must extend beyond sides of supporting structure.

FRONT SUSPENSION

Front Shock Absorber Removal and Installation

1. Remove the nut and retainer from the shock absorber top.
2. Jack up the front of the vehicle. It is sometimes necessary to remove the tire and wheel assembly and perform the removal operation from beneath the fender.
3. Remove the shock absorber lower attaching bolt or stud nut. Remove the bolt from the shock absorber eye.
4. Push upward on the shock absorber and fully compress it; pull the shock downward and out of its upper mounting bushings and remove from the vehicle. On Imperial models through 1973, the dust shield is removed with the shock absorber. It may be necessary to remove the upper control arm bumper, on some models, to obtain enough clear-

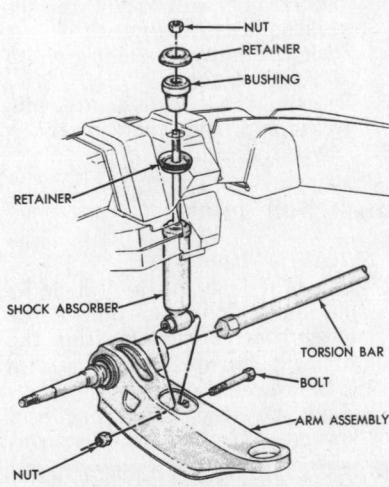

Front shock absorber and lower control arm assembly—Cordoba
(© Chrysler Corp)

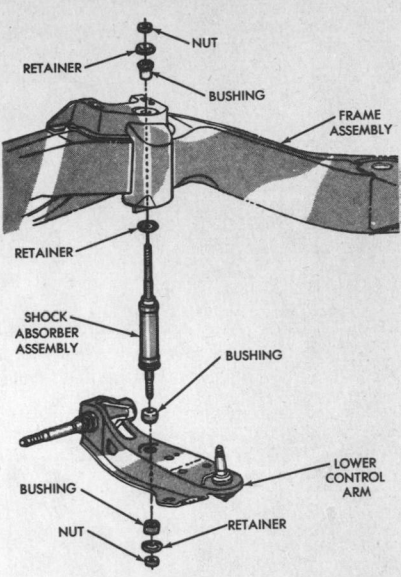

**Front shock absorber components
—1974 and later
Chrysler and Imperial**
(© Chrysler Corp)

ance to remove the shock absorber assembly.

5. Purge the new shock of air by repeatedly extending it in its normal position and compressing it while inverted. To begin the installation procedure fully compress the shock. Insert the rod through the upper bushing, install the retainer and nut, and tighten the nut. On Imperial models through 1973, place the retainer on the shock absorber upper rod; then install the dust shield. Install the rod to the upper bushing with its nut and retainer and tighten the nut. *NOTE: All retainers must be installed with the concave (sunken) side in contact with the rubber.* Align the shock lower eye or shaft with its lower control arm mountings. Install its retaining nut and bolt finger tight. Lower the vehicle and tighten the nut with the full weight of the vehicle on the wheels.

Front Height Adjustment

Through 1974

1. Jounce vehicle several times, releasing it on downward motion.
2. Measure distance A. For Chrysler models through 1973, the measurement is taken from the lowest point of the adjusting blade. For all Imperial models and 1974 Chrysler models measure from the lowest point of the front torsion bar anchor at the rear of the lower control arm flange.
3. Measure distance B. This is the distance between the lowest point of the lower ball joint

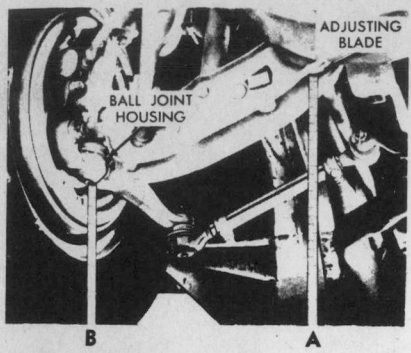

Measuring front suspension height—Chrysler through 1973 (© Chrysler Corp)

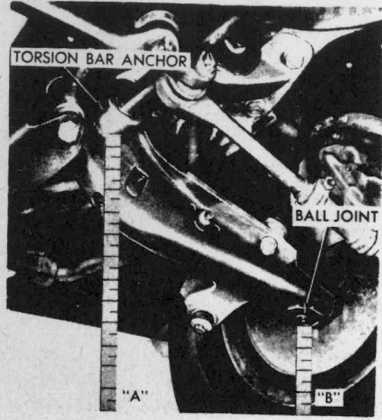

Measuring front suspension height—Imperial and 1974 and later Chrysler (© Chrysler Corp)

housing and the floor.

4. Subtract distance A from distance B to obtain front suspension height. Check this figure against the figure listed in the front end alignment table in the front of this section.

5. Measure the other side. There should be no more than 1/8 in. difference in height from one side to the other.

6. Adjust height, as necessary, by turning torsion bar adjusting bolt clockwise to increase height and counterclockwise to decrease height.

1975 and Later

1. Jounce the vehicle several times, releasing it in the downward position.

2. Measure distance "A". The measurement is taken from the lowest point of the lower control arm torsion bar anchor at a point 1 inch forward of the rear face of the anchor, to the ground. Check this figure against that listed in the "Front End Height" table in the front of this section.

3. Measure the other side. Maximum allowable variation in height from one side to another is 1/8 in.

4. Adjust height, as necessary, by rotating the torsion bar adjust-

ing bolt clockwise to increase height and counterclockwise to decrease height.

Wheel Bearing Adjustment

Through 1972

1. Jack the vehicle and remove the hub cap and grease cup. Take out the cotter pin, remove the nut lock and loosen the adjusting nut.

2. While rotating the wheel, tighten the wheel bearing adjusting nut to 90 in. lbs.

3. Align the nut lock on the nut so that one pair of slots is in line with the cotter pin hole.

4. Back off the adjusting nut lock assembly one slot and install a new cotter pin. This should yield an adjustment between zero (no preload) and 0.003 in. end-play.

5. Clean the grease cup. Coat, but do not fill, the inside of the cup with wheel bearing lubricant and install it on the vehicle. Install the hub caps and lower the vehicle.

1973 and Later

1. Raise the front of the car to allow the wheels to spin freely.

2. Remove the wheel cover, grease cup, cotterpin, and lock nut.

3. Tighten the wheel bearing adjusting nut to 240-300 in. lbs while spinning the wheel.

4. Back the nut off and retighten to finger tight.

5. Reinstall the lock nut, cotter pin, grease cup, and wheel cover.

6. Lower the car.

Lower Ball Joint

Inspection

1. Raise the front of the vehicle by placing a floor jack under the lower control arm. Position the lifting point of the jack as close to the wheel as possible.

2. Have an assistant raise and lower the tire and wheel assem-

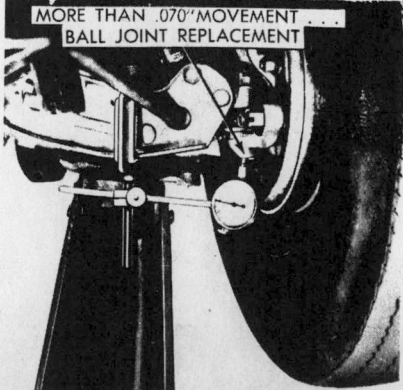

Measuring lower ball joint play; see text for specifications (© Chrysler Corp)

bly and observe any movement at the lower ball joint.

3. On Chryslers through 1973, replace the ball joint if the axial play exceeds 0.070 in. On all Cordobas, Imperials, and 1974 and later Chryslers, the lower ball joints are preloaded and, if any free-play exists in excess of 0.020 in., the lower ball joint control arm assembly must be removed for service.

Removal—Chrysler through 1973

The compression-type lower ball joint is integral with the steering arm and is not serviced separately.

1. Remove the upper control arm rebound bumper. Raise the vehicle on a hoist so the front suspension will drop to the downward limit of its travel.

2. Place a jack stand under the lower control arm, near the ball joint.

3. Lower the vehicle onto the jack stand. Off-load the torsion bars by rotating the adjusting bolts counterclockwise.

4. Remove the tire, wheel, and brake drum from the vehicle as an assembly. If equipped with disc brakes, remove the tire and wheel. Remove the brake pads, and remove the caliper from the steering knuckle and position it out of the way with the brake line attached. Remove the rotor from the spindle.

5. Remove the two lower bolts that attach the steering arm-ball joint assembly to the brake assembly mounting plate.

6. Using a suitable tool, disconnect the tie rod end from the steering arm, taking care not to damage the seal.

7. Remove the ball joint stud retaining nut and cotter pin.

8. Using a suitable tool, separate and remove the ball joint from the lower control arm.

Installation

1. Position ball joint-steering arm assembly on the steering knuckle and install the two retaining bolts.

2. Insert the ball joint stud in the lower control arm and install the retaining nut and cotter pin.

3. Position the tie rod end in the steering knuckle and install the retaining nut and cotter pin.

4. Place a load on the torsion bar by turning the adjusting bolt in a clockwise direction.

5. Install the tire, wheel and brake drum assembly. If equipped with disc brakes, install the rotor, caliper, brake pads and tire and wheel assembly.

6. Lower vehicle and install upper

control arm rebound bumper if so equipped.

7. Check and adjust front suspension height as required.

Removal—Imperial through 1973

Lower ball joints on Imperial models are serviced only as ball joint-control arm assemblies.

1. Raise the vehicle on a hoist so the front suspension drops to the downward limit of its travel.
2. Remove the wheel and tire as an assembly.
3. Remove the load from *both* torsion bars by turning the adjusting bolts in a counterclockwise direction.
4. Disconnect the shock absorber from the lower control arm and position the shock out of the way. Disconnect the strut bar from the lower control arm.
5. Disconnect the brake hose from the caliper.
6. Remove the lower ball joint retaining nut and cotter pin.
7. Using a suitable tool, separate the ball joint stud from the steering knuckle.
8. Remove the nut and washer that attaches the lower control arm pivot shaft to the frame.
9. Using a brass drift and hammer, tap the end of the pivot shaft to loosen it (the shaft is a tapered fit in the front crossmember).
10. Remove the lower control arm and shaft from the vehicle as an assembly.
11. Position the control arm assembly in a press with the hex opening for the torsion bar in the up position and place a support under the outer edge of the control arm.
12. Insert a brass drift in the hex opening and press the shaft out of the control arm. The bushing inner arm will remain on the shaft.
13. Remove the torsion bar adjusting bolt and swivel from the control arm.

Installation

1. Position a new bushing on the pivot shaft (flange end of the bushing first) and seat the bushing on the shoulder of the pivot shaft.
2. Press the shaft and bushing assembly into the new control arm.
3. Install the torsion bar adjusting bolt and swivel on the new control arm.
4. Position a new seal on the ball joint and install the seal. To ease installation of the seal, the ball joint stud should be perpendicular to the body of the ball joint.
5. Position the control arm assembly on the crossmember in approximate operating position

and install the nut and washer. *Do not tighten the nut until the full weight of the vehicle is on the wheels.*

6. Insert the lower ball joint stud in the steering knuckle and install the retaining nut and cotter pin.
7. Install the strut bar rear bushing and retainer on the strut bar and insert the strut bar through the crossmember.
8. Install the front strut bar bushing and retainer on the strut bar and install the retaining nut finger tight only.
9. Position the rear of the strut bar over the lower control arm and install the bumper and plate.
10. Connect the shock absorber to the lower control arm and install the retaining nut finger tight. Place a load on each torsion bar by turning the adjusting bolt clockwise.
11. Connect the brake line to the disc brake caliper and bleed the brakes.
12. Install the tire and wheel assembly.
13. Lower the vehicle to the floor. Tighten the strut bar, shock absorber and lower control arm attaching nuts.
14. Check and adjust front end height and alignment.

Removal—1974 and Later Chrysler, Cordoba, and Imperial

Lower ball joints on these models may be serviced separately. The ball joints are a press-fit.

1. Place the ignition switch in the "off" or "unlocked" position.
2. Remove the rebound bumper.
3. Raise the vehicle on a hoist so that the front suspension drops to the downward limit of its travel. Position jackstands beneath the front frame for extra support.
4. Remove the wheel and tire assembly.
5. Remove the caliper from its mounts and tie it up out of the way so that there is no strain on the flexible brake hose.

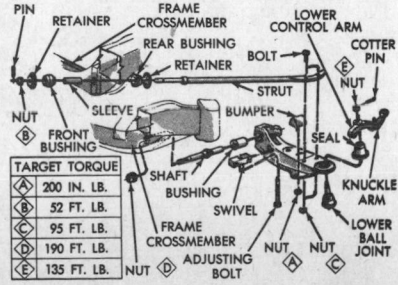

Lower control arm assembly exploded view—1974 and later Chrysler and Imperial
(© Chrysler Corp)

PIN RETAINER FRAME CROSSMEMBER LOWER CONTROL ARM
REAR BUSHING COTTER PIN
RETAINER BOLT NUT
STRUT
NUT SLEEVE BUMPER
FRONT BUSHING SEAL

TARGET TORQUE	
A	200 IN. LB.
B	52 FT. LB.
C	95 FT. LB.
D	190 FT. LB.
E	135 FT. LB.

SHAFT BUSHING
FRAME CROSSMEMBER SWIVEL
NUT NUT
ADJUSTING BOLT
KNUCKLE ARM
LOWER BALL JOINT

Removing ball joint stud with a stud remover tool
(© Chrysler Corp)

6. Remove the hub and rotor assembly, splash shield, lower shock absorber mounting nut, retainer and insulator.
7. Off-load the torsion bars by rotating the adjusting bolts counterclockwise.
8. Remove the upper and lower ball joint stud cotter pins and nuts. Using a ball joint press tool, slide the tool over the upper stud until the tool rests on the steering knuckle.
9. Then, turn the threaded portion of the tool so that it locks snugly against the lower stud. Tighten the tool enough to load the lower ball joint stud, and then strike the steering knuckle arm with a hammer to loosen the stud. Under no circumstances should you attempt to force the stud from the knuckle using the tool alone.
10. Using a press, press the ball joint out of the lower control arm.

Installation

1. Using the press, press the new ball joint into the lower control arm.
2. Place a new seal over the ball joint (as necessary). Press the retainer portion of the seal down over the ball joint housing until it locks into position.
3. Insert the ball joint stud through the opening in the knuckle arm and install the stud retaining nut. Tighten the stud nut to 100 ft. lbs. for Chrysler through 1973 and Cordoba, and to 135 ft. lbs. for 1974 and later Chrysler and all Imperial. Install the cotter pins and lubricate the ball joint.
4. Load the torsion bar by rotating the adjusting bolt clockwise.
5. Install the shock absorber retaining nut, retainer and insulator,

the splash shield, hub and rotor assembly, and brake caliper. Install the wheel and tire assembly.

6. Adjust the front wheel bearings.
7. Remove the jackstands and lower the car. Install the rebound bumper. Adjust the front suspension height.

Upper Ball Joint

Replacement

1. Place the ignition in the "off" or "unlocked" position. Raise the vehicle by placing a floor jack under the lower control arm. Place the lifting point of the jack as close as possible to the wheel.
2. Remove the wheel, tire and drum as an assembly. On models with disc brakes, remove the tire and wheel, remove the disc brake pads, remove the disc brake caliper from the steering knuckle and position the caliper out of the way with the brake line attached. Remove the brake rotor from the steering knuckle.
3. Remove the nut that attaches the upper ball joint to the steering knuckle and, using a ball joint stud removal tool, loosen the ball joint stud from the steering knuckle.
4. Unscrew the upper ball joint from the upper control arm and remove it from the vehicle.

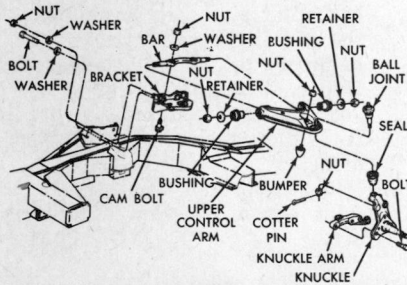

Imperial upper control arm—through 1973
(© Chrysler Corp)

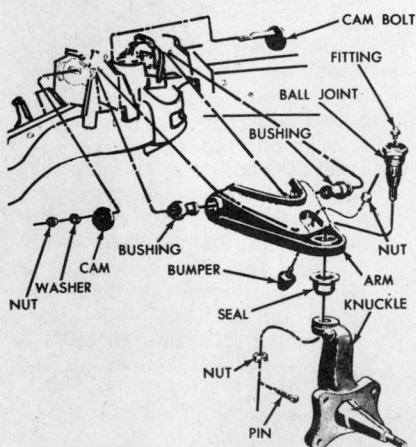

Chrysler upper control arm—through 1973
(© Chrysler Corp)

5. Position new ball joint on the upper control arm, screw the ball joint into the control arm until it bottoms and tighten the ball joint to a minimum of 125 ft. lbs. for Cordoba, 150 ft. lbs. for Imperial and Chrysler models.

NOTE: when installing a ball joint, make certain the ball joint threads engage those of the upper control arm squarely if the original control arm is being used.

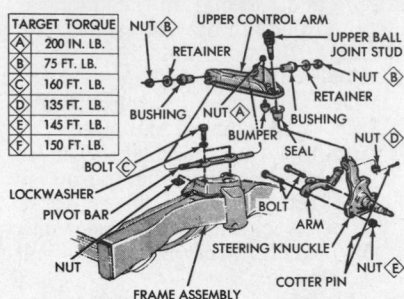

Upper control arm assembly exploded view—1974 and later Chrysler and Imperial
(© Chrysler Corp)

6. Position a new seal on the ball joint stud and install the seal in the ball joint making sure the seal is fully seated on the ball joint housing.
7. Position ball joint stud in the steering knuckle and install the retaining nut. Tighten the stud nut to 100 ft. lbs. for Chrysler through 1973 and Cordoba, and to 135 ft. lbs. for 1974 and later Chrysler and all Imperial.
8. Lubricate ball joint and, if replacement ball joint is equipped with knock-off type grease fitting, break off that portion of the fitting over which the lubrication gun was installed.
9. If equipped with disc brakes, install the rotor, caliper and brake pads. Install the tire and wheel.
10. Lower the vehicle and adjust the wheel alignment.

Torsion Bar Removal and Installation

The torsion bars are not interchangeable from right to left. They are marked with an R or an L.

Removal

1. Raise the vehicle so the front suspension drops to the limit of its downward travel.
2. Remove the upper control arm rebound bumper if so equipped.
3. On all models except Imperials through 1973, remove the tension from the torsion bar to be replaced by turning the anchor adjusting bolt in a counterclockwise direction. On Imperials through 1973, release the load on both torsion bars by turning each anchor adjusting bolt in a counterclockwise direction. This is necessary because the rubber insulator rear crossmember would be under load and could possibly cause severe damage or personal injury.
4. Slide rear anchor balloon seal off the rear anchor and remove the lockring from the anchor. On Imperial models remove the balloon seal clamp. Remove the automatic transmission torque shaft on 1974 and later models, if necessary.
5. On all models, remove the torsion bar from the vehicle by sliding it rearward and out of the torsion bar rear anchor. A special tool is available for this job; it clamps to the bar and provides a striking surface for driving the bar out.

Installation

1. Position the torsion bar in the chassis and apply a coating of chassis lubricant to both ends.
2. Install the lockring in the anchor, making sure it is seated in the groove.
3. Pack the annular opening in the rear anchor completely full of

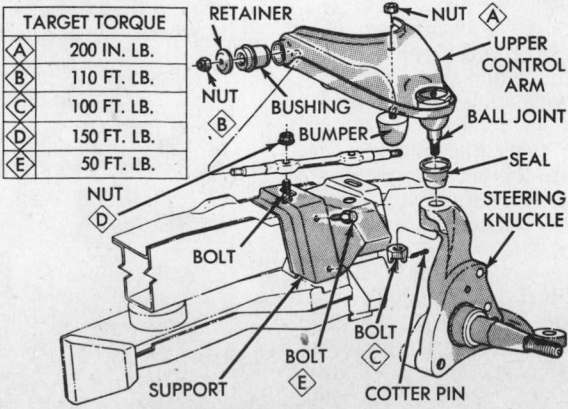

Cordoba upper control arm assembly
(© Chrysler Corp.)

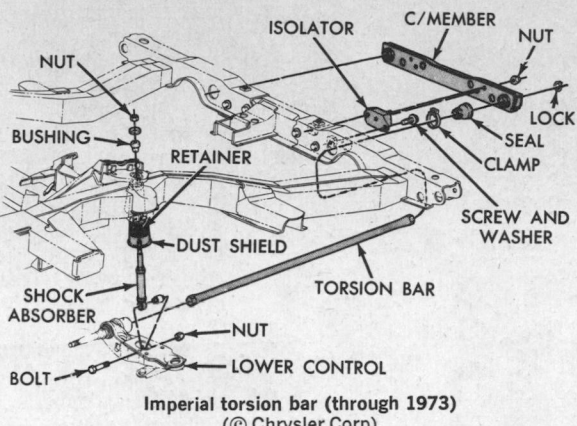

Imperial torsion bar (through 1973)
(© Chrysler Corp)

chassis lubricant and position the lip of the balloon seal in the groove of the anchor. On Imperial models, install the balloon seal clamp.

4. On all Chrysler, Cordoba, and 1974-75 Imperial models, turn torsion bar. On Imperial models through 1973, turn both adjusting bolts to load both torsion bars.

5. Lower the vehicle to the floor and adjust front end height as required.

REAR SUSPENSION

All models use a leaf-spring rear suspension and double-acting shock absorbers. The springs are of the semi-elliptical type, with zinc interleaves between the normal leaves to increase spring life and reduce corrosion. On most models, rubber insulators are used where the springs attach to the body to reduce road noise and vibration.

Shock Absorber Removal and Installation

1. Jack the vehicle under the rear axle. Position the jackstands in such a manner that the shock absorbers are under no load.

2. At the bottom mount, remove the nut and retainer securing the shock to the spring seat isolator retainer plate; remove the shock from the stud.

3. At the top mount, remove the retaining bolt and nut and washer and then remove the shock. To replace the shock absorber, reverse the removal procedure. Remember that the shock absorber mounting bolts must not be fully tightened until the full vehicle weight is resting on the wheels.

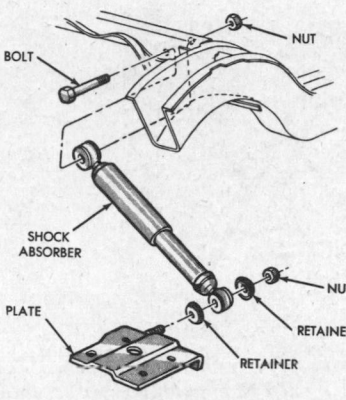

Rear shock absorber components—1974 and later Chrysler and Imperial
(© Chrysler Corp)

Spring Removal and Installation

1. Raise the vehicle on a hoist.
2. Place jack stands under the differential and lower the vehicle until the weight is removed from the rear springs.
3. Disconnect the rear shock absorber. If so equipped, remove the sway bar.
4. Loosen and remove the U-bolt nuts and U-bolts. Remove the spring plate.
5. Loosen and remove the nuts holding the front spring hanger to the front body mounting bracket.

Caution 1974 and later full-size models have preloaded rear springs. A special spring stretcher (tool no. C-4211) must be installed before releasing either end of the spring. Do not try to remove the spring without the stretcher; its sudden release could cause serious injury.

6. Remove the rear spring hanger bolts and let the spring drop far enough to pull the front spring hanger bolts out of the body mounting bracket.
7. Remove the front pivot bolt from the front spring hanger.

8. Loosen and remove rear shackle nuts and remove the rear shackle from the spring.
9. Remove rear spring from the vehicle.
10. Reverse above procedure to install. When installing the front and rear pivot nuts and bolts, do not tighten the bolts until the vehicle has been lowered to the floor and weight is on the wheels.

BRAKES

The 1974-75 Imperial uses rear disc brakes. The system is similar to that employed on domestic sportscars, with internal drum brake shoes for the parking brake.

NOTE: Procedures for brake shoe or pad replacement and adjustment, wheel and master cylinder overhaul, and brake bleeding can be found in the "Unit Repair Section."

Master Cylinder Removal and Installation

1. Disconnect fluid lines. On disc brake cylinders, plug brake outlets to prevent leakage.
2. Remove nuts attaching master cylinder to firewall or to power brake unit.

NOTE: it is not necessary to disconnect the pedal push rod as it is possible to separate the master cylinder from the rod by pulling them apart after the master cylinder attaching nuts have been removed.

3. Disconnect pedal push rod (non-power brakes) from brake pedal.
4. Remove master cylinder from vehicle.
5. Reverse procedure to install.
6. Bleed brake system.

Power Brake Booster Removal and Installation

1. Remove the nuts attaching the master cylinder to the brake booster and position the master cylinder out of the way. If the brake lines do not have enough slack to allow the master cylinder to be moved without kinking the brake lines, it will be necessary to disconnect the brake lines.
2. Disconnect the vacuum hose from the brake booster.
3. Working under the dash, remove the attaching nut and bolt from the brake booster pushrod and disconnect the pushrod from the brake pedal.
4. Remove the nuts and washers that attach the brake booster to the firewall.
5. Remove the booster from under the hood.

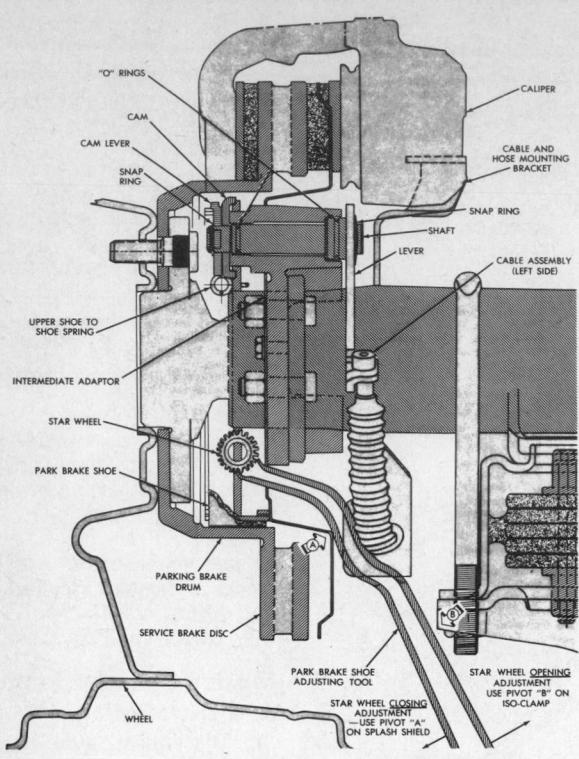

"O" RINGS

CAM

CAM LEVER

SNAP
RING

UPPER SHOE TO
SHOE SPRING

INTERMEDIATE ADAPTOR

STAR WHEEL

PARK BRAKE SHOE

CALIPER

CABLE AND
HOSE MOUNTING
BRACKET

SNAP RING

SHAFT

LEVER

CABLE ASSEMBLY
(LEFT SIDE)

PARKING BRAKE
DRUM

SERVICE BRAKE DISC

PARK BRAKE SHOE
ADJUSTING TOOL

STAR WHEEL CLOSING
ADJUSTMENT
— USE PIVOT "A"
ON SPLASH SHIELD

WHEEL

STAR WHEEL OPENING
ADJUSTMENT
USE PIVOT "B" ON
ISO-CLAMP

Parking brake shoe adjustment—1974-75 Imperial
(© Chrysler Corp)

6. Reverse above procedure to install.
7. If the brake lines were disconnected, bleed the brake system.

Parking Brake Adjustment

NOTE: On 1974-75 Imperials, the internal drum parking brake is first adjusted by inserting an adjusting spoon through an opening in the intermediate adapter (from the in-

1. Housing assembly
2. Bleeder valve
3. Parking brake assembly with backing plate
4. Bracket assembly with cable and hose mounting
5. Caliper mounting bolts
6. Gasket
7. Hose

board side) and turning the starwheel until the parking brake shoes seat against the drum/disc surface. Then, back off the starwheel exactly 12 clicks so that the disc turns freely. Finally, adjust the cable as described below.

1. Apply the brakes several times while backing up to adjust the rear drum brakes. Raise and support vehicle. Release parking

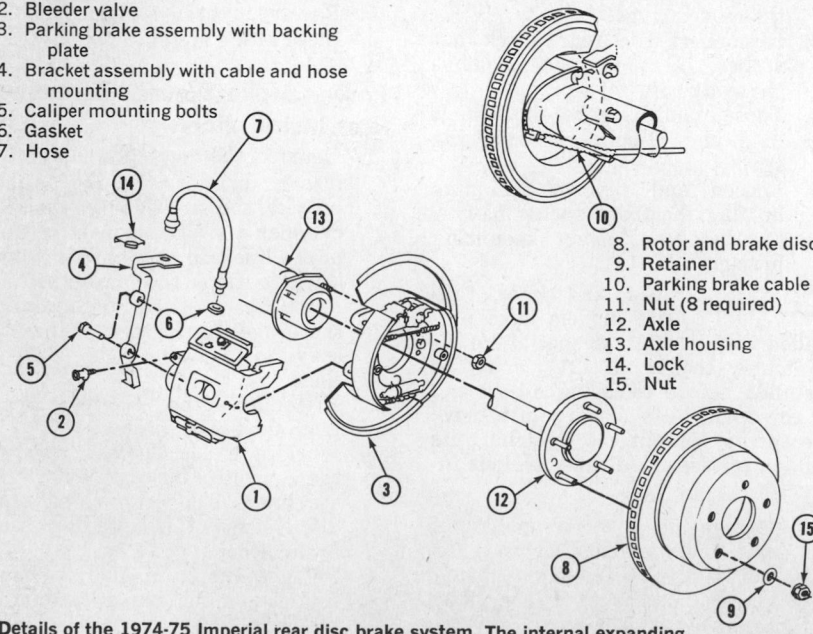

8. Rotor and brake disc
9. Retainer
10. Parking brake cable
11. Nut (8 required)
12. Axle
13. Axle housing
14. Lock
15. Nut

Details of the 1974-75 Imperial rear disc brake system. The internal expanding shoes are the parking brake
(© Chrysler Corp)

brake lever. Loosen cable adjusting nut.
2. Tighten cable adjusting nut until a slight drag is felt while rotating wheel.
3. Loosen cable adjusting nut until both rear wheels can be rotated freely. Back off cable adjusting nut two full turns.
4. Apply parking brake several times. Check to see that rear wheels rotate freely without dragging.

STEERING

A worm and recirculating ball type steering gear is used with the manual steering system. Constant-Control power steering is an option on all models. Hydraulic power is provided by a belt-driven pump. Some power steering pumps were equipped from the factory with fluid coolers. These were used on vehicles with air conditioning, high-performance engines, and/or vehicles equipped with special axle ratios.

Power Steering Pump Removal and Installation

1. Before beginning the removal procedure, carefully take note of the exact hose routing. The hoses must be installed in the exact same position as before removal.
2. Back off the pump mounting and locking bolts and remove the pump drive belt.
3. Disconnect all hoses at the pump.
4. Remove the pump bolts and remove the pump with its bracket.
5. To install the pump, place it in position and install the mounting bolts.
6. Install the pump drive belt and adjust. There should be no more than ½ in. of play, under moderate thumb pressure, on the longest run of belt. Some pump brackets have a ½ in. square hole for use in tensioning the belt. Torque the pump mounting bolts 30 ft lbs.
7. Connect the pressure and return hoses. Install a new pressure-hose O-ring if there is one.
8. Fill the pump with power steering fluid.
9. Start the engine and rotate the steering wheel from stop to stop several times. This will bleed the system. Check the pump fluid level and fill as required.
10. Be certain the hoses are away from the exhaust manifolds and are not kinked or twisted.

Steering Wheel Removal and Installation

NOTE: Be careful when removing the steering wheel from vehicles that are equipped with a collapsible steering column. A sharp blow or excessive pressure on the column could cause it to collapse.

1. Disconnect the battery.
2. Remove the padded center assembly. This center assembly is often held on only by spring clips. There are usually holes in the back of the wheel so the pad can be pushed off. On some deluxe interiors, and with the rim blow horn, it is held on by screws behind the arms of the wheel. On the tilt and telescoping steering column, remove the locking lever knob by releasing the clip on its underside. Remove the locking lever screws and the lever.
3. Remove the large center nut. Remove the steering wheel from the column with a puller.
4. Reverse the procedure to install.

Turn Signal/Hazard Warning Switch Removal and Installation
Ignition Switch and/or Ignition Lock Cylinder Removal and Installation

These procedures are covered for all Chrysler Corporation cars in the Barracuda, Challenger, Dart, Valiant, Aspen, Volare car section.

INSTRUMENT PANEL

Headlight Switch Replacement

1970

1. Disconnect the battery. Remove instrument cluster.
2. Remove headlamp switch from rear of cluster.
3. Install in reverse of above.

1971-73

1. Disconnect the battery. If equipped with air conditioning,

Chilton's TIME SAVER

Although the Chrysler service literature calls for the removal of the instrument cluster to remove the headlight switch, the switch may be removed with the cluster in place. Working from under the instrument panel, remove the wires from the switch. Remove the switch retaining screws using a stubby screwdriver. Remove the switch from the panel.

remove the left air conditioning duct.
2. Remove the headlight switch shaft and knob by pulling the switch to the On position, reaching under the dash, and depressing the button on the bottom of the headlight switch case. Pull the knob and shaft from the switch.
3. Remove the sentinel and automatic dimmer control knobs if equipped with automatic headlight dimmer.
4. Remove the headlight switch attaching nut.
5. Remove the headlight switch from under the dash and disconnect the wires.
6. Reverse above procedure to install.

1974 and Later Chrysler and Imperial

1. Disconnect the battery ground cable. Remove the instrument cluster bezel.
2. Pull the air conditioner outlet housing seal loose at the top to get at the lower switch bracket mounting screws. Remove the screws.
3. Pull the assembly out from the carrier housing and disconnect all the wires.
4. Pull the light switch to the on position and depress the release button on the side of the switch. Pull the knob and stem from the switch.
5. Remove the sentinel and dimmer control knobs, if any.
6. Remove the illumination lamp assembly mounting screw and the lamp.
7. Remove the mounting clips and the headlight switch lens.
8. Remove the switch to mounting plate nut and remove the switch.
9. Reverse the procedure for installation.

Cordoba

1. Disconnect the battery ground cable. Remove the instrument cluster upper bezel.
2. Remove the escutcheon mounting screw.
3. Remove the screws holding the switch mounting plate to the cluster housing.
4. Detach the wires.
5. Depress the switch stem release button and pull the knob and stem from the switch.
6. Remove the escutcheon and switch mounting nut. Remove the switch.
7. Reverse the procedure for installation.

WINDSHIELD WIPERS

Wiper Motor Removal and Installation

1970

1. Disconnect battery ground cable.
2. Lift the wiper arm and insert a .090 pin or drill. Pull wiper arm from shaft with a rocking motion.
3. Remove windshield lower moulding.
4. Remove cowl screen.
5. Remove drive crank arm retaining nut and drive crank. To prevent damage to the gears, hold the crank arm nut with a wrench when removing the crank arm from the motor. Disconnect motor wiring.
6. Remove three mounting nuts. Remove motor.
7. Reverse procedure to install.

1971 and Later

1. Disconnect the negative battery cable.
2. Lift the latch on each wiper arm and remove the arms and blades as an assembly.
3. Remove the cowl screen.
4. Remove the drive crank retaining nut and drive crank. To prevent damage to the gears, hold the crank arm with a wrench when removing the crank nut from the motor. Disconnect motor wiring.
5. Disconnect the lead wires from the wiper motor.
6. Remove the three wiper motor mounting bolts and remove the motor from the vehicle.
7. Reverse above procedure to install. When installing the wiper arms and blades, make sure the wiper motor is in the Park position.

RADIO

Removal and Installation

Through 1973

1. Disconnect battery ground cable.
2. Remove left ash tray.
3. On models through 1971 remove the steering column cover.
4. Unscrew stereo tape reset knob, if so equipped.
5. Disconnect radio wiring.
6. Move defroster vacuum actuator to facilitate radio removal.
7. Remove two radio mounting screws through access openings in lower instrument panel. On search-tune and AM radios, remove knobs, bezels, and nuts.

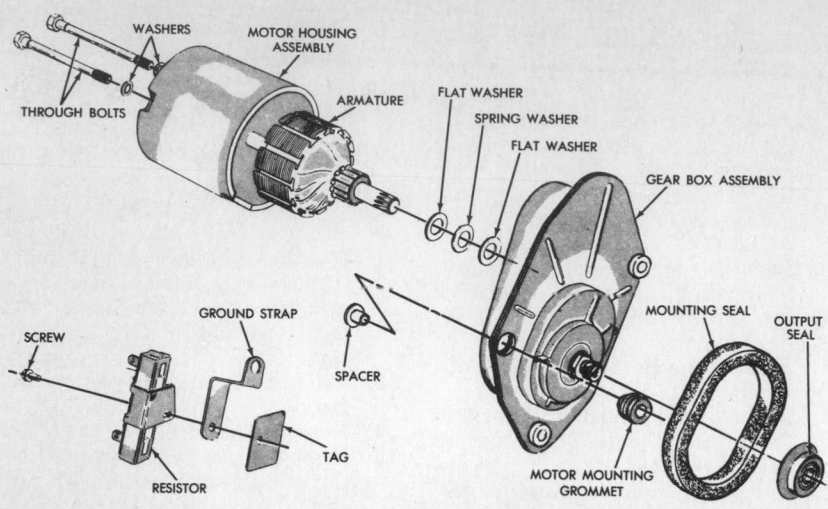

Two-speed wiper motor—exploded view (©Chrysler Corp)

8. Remove radio support bracket (if so equipped) mounting screw from lower reinforcement. Support radio.
9. Remove radio support bracket or mounting screws through the access openings in the lower instrument panel. Remove radio from under instrument panel.
10. Reverse procedure to install.

1974 and Later Chrysler and Imperial

1. Disconnect the battery ground cable.
2. Remove the instrument cluster bezel.
3. On monaural radios, remove the lamp assembly from the front of the radio.
4. Remove the radio to panel screws.
5. Remove the instrument panel upper cover. Work through the access hole in the top of the instrument panel to disconnect the antenna and speaker leads. Remove the bracket mounting nut.
6. Remove the radio and detach the electrical lead.
7. Reverse the procedure for installation.

Cordoba

1. Disconnect the battery ground cable.
2. Remove the instrument cluster lower bezel.
3. Disconnect the antenna, speaker, and electrical leads.
4. Remove the nut holding the radio to the support bracket. The nut is at the back of the radio and on the side of tape player/radios.
5. Remove the screws holding the radio to the cluster housing from the front.
6. Remove the radio.
7. Reverse the procedure for installation.

HEATER

Blower Motor Removal and Installation— Non-Air Conditioned Models

Chrysler and Imperial

The blower motor is mounted to the housing under the right front fender between the inner fender shield and the fender. The inner fender shield must be removed to service the blower motor.

Cordoba

1. Disconnect the negative battery cable.
2. Remove the entire heater assembly from the car, as outlined under "Heater Core Removal and Installation, Non-Air Conditioned Models."
3. Disconnect the blower motor lead from the resistor block, and the ground wire from the mounting plate.
4. Remove the 6 sheet metal screws and clips retaining the blower mount to the housing. Separate the mount and blower from the housing.
5. Remove the blower wheel from the motor shaft.
6. Remove the two retaining nuts and separate the motor from its mount.
7. Reverse the procedure to install.

Heater Core Removal and Installation— Non-Air Conditioned Models

Through 1973

1. Disconnect battery ground cable. Drain coolant.
2. Disconnect heater hoses and plug fittings.
3. Slide front seat back. Unplug antenna from radio.

4. Remove vacuum hoses from trunk lock, if so equipped.
5. Disconnect blower motor resistor block.
6. Remove vacuum hoses from defroster actuator and heater shut off door actuator.
7. Swing support bracket up out of the way.
8. Remove four retaining nuts from studs on engine side housing.
9. Remove locating bolt from bottom center of passenger side housing.
10. Roll or tip housing out from under instrument panel.
11. Remove temperature control cable retaining clip and cable from heat shut off door crank.
12. From inside housing, remove two retaining nuts from right side of heater core and four screws from outside of housing.
13. Remove core tube locating metal screw from top of housing.
14. Carefully pull heater core out of housing.
15. Reverse procedure to install.

1974 and Later Chrysler and Imperial

1. Disconnect the battery ground cable and drain the coolant.
2. Detach the heater hoses at the firewall and plug the core tubes.
3. Slide the front seat back. Remove the instrument panel lower cover.
4. Unplug the antenna from the radio. Disconnect the upper level ventilation actuator vacuum line.
5. Remove the screw holding the upper level vent ducts to the heater housing and the screw holding the bracket to the instrument panel. Swing back the duct.
6. Disconnect the blower motor resistor connectors at the lower right end of the housing.
7. Detach the mode cable from the clip and crank on the front of the housing.
8. Remove the bottom retaining nut and swing the support bracket out of the way.
9. On the engine side, remove the five nuts.
10. Tip the housing out from under the instrument panel.
11. Detach the temperature control cable at the top.
12. Remove the core tube locating screw between the tubes. Remove the six nuts holding the front and rear housings together. Remove the four core retaining screws and separate the housings. Slide the core out.
13. Reverse the procedure for installation.

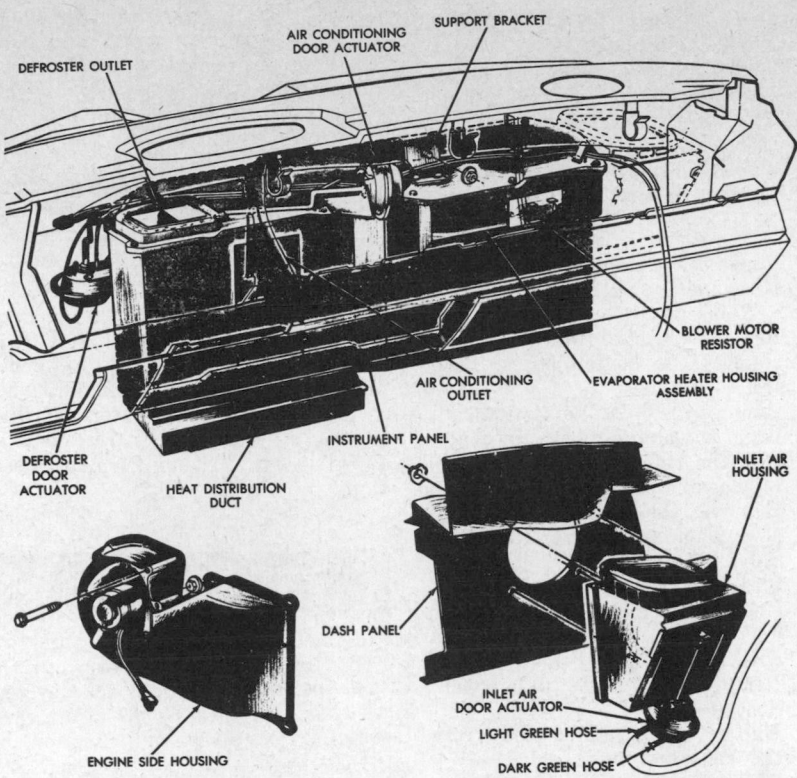

Air conditioning-heater housing assembly—1974 and later Chrysler and Imperial
(© Chrysler Corp)

Labels on diagram: DEFROSTER OUTLET; AIR CONDITIONING DOOR ACTUATOR; SUPPORT BRACKET; BLOWER MOTOR RESISTOR; AIR CONDITIONING OUTLET; EVAPORATOR HEATER HOUSING ASSEMBLY; INSTRUMENT PANEL; DEFROSTER DOOR ACTUATOR; HEAT DISTRIBUTION DUCT; DASH PANEL; INLET AIR HOUSING; INLET AIR DOOR ACTUATOR; LIGHT GREEN HOSE; DARK GREEN HOSE; ENGINE SIDE HOUSING

Cordoba

1. Disconnect the battery ground cable and drain the coolant.
2. Disconnect the heater hoses at the firewall and plug the core tubes.
3. Remove the three mounting nuts around the blower motor and the one near the center.
4. Remove the lower instrument panel bezel, glove box, and glove box door.
5. Unplug the antenna from the radio.
6. Remove the screw from the housing to plenum support rod on the right side above the outside air opening.
7. Detach the two air door cables and the blower motor resistor wires.
8. Tip the unit out from under the instrument panel.
9. Remove the front cover screws. Cut the plenum to housing air seal in two places where the front cover separates the cover from the housing.
10. Remove the core tube retaining screw between the tubes. Remove the heater core.
11. Reverse the procedure for installation. Seal the plenum air seal with rubber cement.

Blower Motor Removal and Installation—Air Conditioned Models

Chrysler and Imperial

1. The blower motor is mounted on the engine side housing, under the right front fender, between the inner fender shield and the fender. To service the motor, it is necessary to remove the inner fender panel by extracting its securing bolts. If the vehicle is equipped with a power antenna, it is necessary to disconnect it before the inner fender panel is removed.
2. For all models, disconnect the battery and feed wires and remove the air tube (if so equipped). Remove its mounting bolts and remove the blower assembly.
3. Installation is the reverse of the above.

Cordoba

1. Disconnect the feed wire at its connector. Remove the air tube.
2. Remove the three nuts retaining the blower mount to the firewall (from the engine side.)
3. Lift out the blower motor and fan assembly.
4. Reverse the procedure to install.

Heater Core Removal and Installation—Air Conditioned Models

Chrysler and Imperial Through 1973

1. The heater core is located in the front cover of the passenger side housing. The air conditioning system need not be discharged to remove the heater core.
2. Disconnect the battery and drain the cooling system. Remove the air cleaner and disconnect the heater hoses. Plug the heater core tubes to prevent fluid loss.
3. Remove the left spot cooler duct and the steering column cover. On 1972 models, remove the linkage shield.
4. Disconnect the two actuator rods at the linkage on the left side of the housing. Remove the two cover retaining screws.
5. Remove the heat distribution duct securing screws, the duct, and the now-exposed screws in the bottom lip of the front cover.
6. Remove the glove box and the center spot cooler duct; also the right spot cooler duct and the air distribution housing.
7. Working in the glove box opening, remove the top and right side retaining screws from the housing. On vehicles with Auto-Temp, remove the aspirator tube from its clip before performing the above.
8. Disconnect all electrical leads at the resistor block. Remove the vacuum hoses from the recirculating housing actuator. On cars with Auto-Temp, remove the wires from the plastic strips and metal clip; remove the amplifier, master, and compressor switches.
9. Remove the nut from the housing end of the support bracket. Swing the bracket upward and out of the way, and carefully roll the heater core and front cover out from beneath the instrument panel. On 1972-73 models, remove the core from the housing by cutting the adhesive away, grasping it at the top, and pulling it from the housing.
10. (This step applies to models through 1971 only.) To begin the installation procedure, install the heater core in the front cover and place the core and cover on the evaporator housing. Hold the front cover in position and swing the support bracket down over the stud on the front cover face. Install its retaining nut.
11. (This step applies to 1972-73 models only). To begin the installation procedure, remove the condensate seal from the heater

core flange and cement a new seal in position. Install the heater core in the rear housing and secure with a screw at either end. Install the core and rear housing to the front housing. Hold the rear housing in position and swing the support bracket down and over the stud on the rear housing face; install its retaining nut.

12. Working through the glove box opening, install the housing top retaining screws and the screws at the right side of the front cover (through 1971) or the screws at the right side of the rear housing (1972-73).

13. Working beneath the instrument panel, replace all the screws securing the housings together. On 1972-73 models, install the two screws on the left side of the rear housing. (On these models, it is not necessary to reinstall the linkage shield.)

14. Install the heat distribution duct to the bottom of the housing.

15. Connect the actuator rods.

16. Connect all of the vacuum hoses to the actuators; install all electrical connections to the resistor block. On cars with Auto-Temp, secure the wires with the plastic straps and metal clip. Install the aspirator tube in the clip.

17. Working through the glove box opening, replace the air distribution housing, the center spot cooler duct, and the right spot cooler duct.

18. Install the steering column cover and the left spot cooler duct. Replace the glove box assembly. On Auto-Temp equipped vehicles, install the amplifier, master, and compressor switches.

19. From this point, reverse the removal procedure.

1974 and Later Chrysler and Imperial

NOTE: *This procedure requires evacuation of the refrigerant in the air conditioning system. Therefore, it should not be attempted by persons not having the special tools and training required to perform the job safely.*

1. Purge the system of refrigerant.
2. Disconnect the battery ground cable. Drain the coolant.
3. Remove the air cleaner and disconnect the heater hoses. Plug the core tubes.
4. Remove the 5/16" bolt in the center of the plumbing sealing plate.
5. Pull the refrigerant line assembly toward the front of the car.
6. Remove the two 1/4-20 Allen screws and remove the "H" valve.
7. Slide the front seat back, out of the way. Remove the lap cooler and lower instrument panel cover.
8. Remove the A/C distribution duct.
9. Unplug the antenna lead from the radio.
10. Disconnect the wires and vacuum lines from unit.
11. Remove the drain tube. With automatic temperature control (ATC), remove the electrical connections and vacuum connector from the servo. Disconnect the amplifier wires. Disconnect the wires and vacuum hoses from the master and compressor switches. Disconnect the aspirator tube.
12. Remove the temperature control cable from the clip on the unit.
13. Remove the retaining nut from the support bracket.
14. Remove the six retaining nuts from the studs in the engine compartment.

15. Remove the housing from under the instrument panel, and place it on a work table.
16. Remove the mode door and the blend air door levers from the shaft. Remove the screws and lift off the top cover.
17. Remove the 4 retaining screws and the 3 screws for the core tube seal. Lift out the core.
18. Reverse the procedure to install.

Cordoba

See the "Heater Core Removal" procedure (for air-conditioned models) for 1971 and later Satellite, Coronet, Charger and 1975 and later Fury" in the Dodge-Plymouth section.

SEAT BELTS

For information concerning the seat belt/starter interlock system used on Chrysler Corporation cars, see the Dodge-Plymouth section.

Seat belt interlock override switch—1974-75 models; pushing the switch button will permit the car to be started once for servicing purposes, without an occupant using the seat restraint system
(© Chrysler Corp)

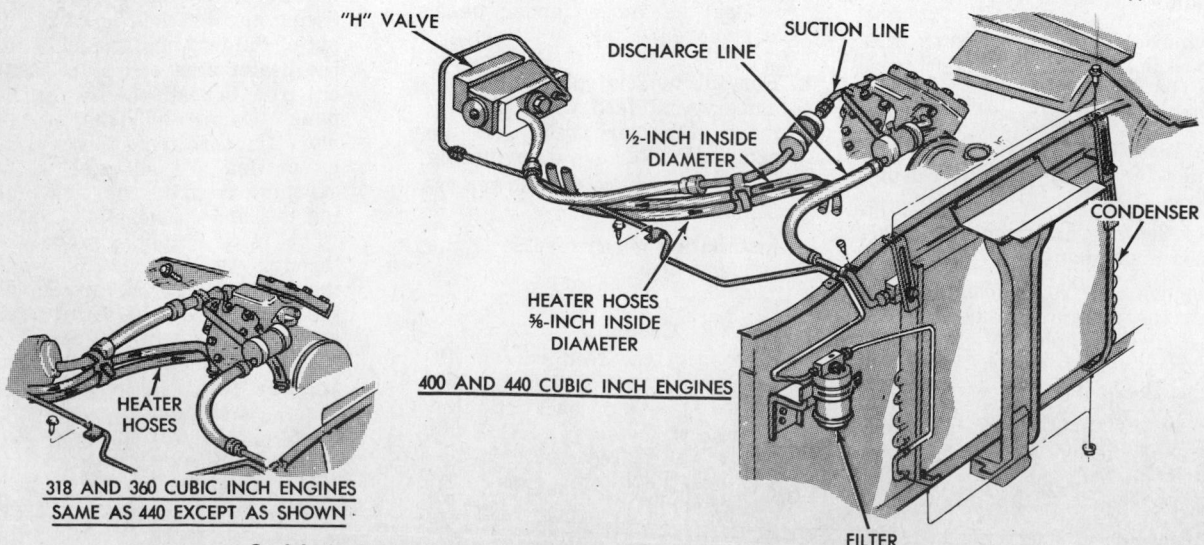

Cordoba heating and air conditioning plumbing (© Chrysler Corp.)

Comet · Cougar · Elite · Fairlane · Falcon · Granada · Maverick · Monarch · Montego · Mustang · Torino · LTD II · 1977 Thunderbird

Automatic Transmission in-car service **C482**
  Pan Removal and Installation, fluid & filter change C482
C4 .... C482
  Band adjustment C486
  Lock Rod adjustment C486
  Shift linkage adjustment C482
  Throttle linkage adjustment C482
C6 .... C486
  Band adjustment C487
  Throttle and downshift linkage adjustment C486
FMX TRANSMISSION C487
Brakes **C496, U299**
  Disc brakes C496
  Hydro-Boost Power Unit Removal and Installation C497
  Master cylinder Removal and Installation C496
  Parking brake adjustment C497
  Power brake vacuum unit Removal and Installation C496
  Wheel bearing adjustment C498
Charging System **C459, U2**
  Alternator Removal and Installation C459
  Voltage regulator Removal and Installation C459
Clutch **C479**
  Clutch and/or transmission Removal and Installation C489
  Pedal adjustment C479
Cooling System **C463, U367**
  Radiator Removal and Installation C463
  Thermostat Removal and Installation C464
  Water pump Removal and Installation ... C464
Emission Controls **C464, U145**
Engine **C471, U194**
  Engine Removal and Installation C471
CYLINDER HEAD REMOVAL AND INSTALLATION C475
LUBRICATION C477
  Oil pan Removal and Installation C477
  Oil pump Removal and Installation C478
  Rear crankshaft oil seal Removal and Installation C478
MANIFOLDS C472
  Exhaust manifold Removal and Installation C473
  Intake manifold Removal and Installation C472
TIMING CHAIN COVER, CHAIN, AND CAMSHAFT C476

Camshaft Removal and Installation C477
Cover & Chain Removal and Installation C476
Cover seal Removal and Installation C477
VALVE SYSTEM C473
  Preliminary valve adjustment C474
  Valve guides C474
  V8 mechanical valve lifter final adjustment C474
Front Suspension **C489, U292**
COIL SPRING ON LOWER ARM C492
  Coil spring and lower arm Removal and Installation C492
  Lower ball joint Inspection and Replacement C493
  Shock absorber Removal and Installation C492
  Upper ball joint Inspection and Replacement C493
  Shock absorber Removal and Installation C489
  Upper ball joint Inspection and Replacement C491
  Upper control arm Removal and Installation C493
COIL SPRING ON UPPER ARM C489
  Spring Removal and Installation C490
  Lower ball joint Inspection and Replacement C491
  Upper control arm Removal and Installation C492
Fuel System **C462, U50**
  Dashpot adjustment C463
  Fuel filter Removal and Installation C462
  Fuel pump Removal and Installation C462
  Idle speed and mixture adjustment C462
Heater **C503**
VEHICLES WITH AIR CONDITIONING C504
  Blower motor Removal and Installation ... C508
  Heater-air conditioner housing Removal and Installation C504
  Heater core Removal and Installation C506
VEHICLES WITHOUT AIR CONDITIONING ... C503
  Blower motor Removal and Installation ... C504
  Heater core Removal and Installation C504
  Heater Removal and Installation C503
Ignition System **C459, U34**
  Contact point Removal and Installation ... C461
  Distributor Removal and Installation C460
  Firing order C444
  Ignition timing C461
Instrument Panel **C500, U350**
  Headlight switch Removal and Installation C500

Jacking, Hoisting **C488**
Manual Transmission **C481, U231**
  Linkage adjustment C481
  Transmission lock rod adjustment C482
  Transmission Removal and Installation ... C482
Radio **C501**
  Radio Removal and Installation C501
Rear Axle **C488, U285**
  Axle Shaft Removal and Installation, bearing and seal replacement C488
Rear Suspension **C493**
COIL SPRING SUSPENSION C495
  Shock absorber Removal and Installation C495
  Spring Removal and Installation C495
LEAF SPRING SUSPENSION C494
  Shock absorber Removal and Installation C494
  Spring Removal and Installation C494
Seat Belts **C509**
  Disconnecting the Seat belt/starter interlock system C509
Specifications **C442, U359**
  Capacities C453
  Crankshaft and connecting rod C456
  Engine identification C445
  General engine C446
  Piston clearance C458
  Ring gap and side-clearance C457
  Serial no. location C445
  Torque C457
  Transmission identification C446
  Tune-up C448
  Valve C455
  Wheel alignment C458
  Year identification C442
Starting System **C459, U2**
  Starter Removal and Installation C459
Steering **C498, U328**
  Ignition lock cylinder Removal and Installation C498
  Ignition switch Removal and Installation C498
  Power steering pump Removal and Installation C498
  Steering wheel Removal and Installation C498
  Turn signal switch Removal and Installation C498
U-Joints **C487**
  Front U-joint Removal and Installation ... C488
  Rear U-joint Removal and Installation ... C487
Windshield Wipers **C500**
  Motor Removal and Installation C500

YEAR IDENTIFICATION

FAIRLANE AND TORINO

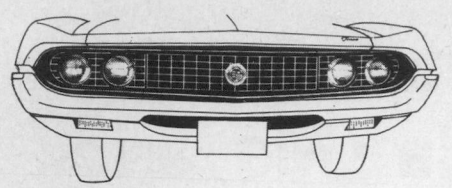

1970

1971

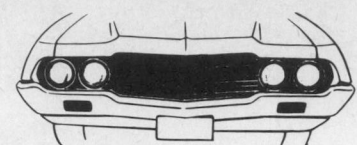

1972 Torino

1972 Gran Torino

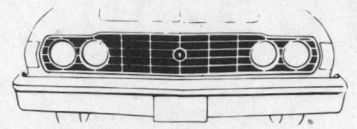

1973 Torino

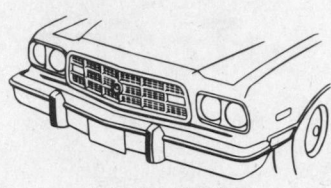

1973 Gran Torino

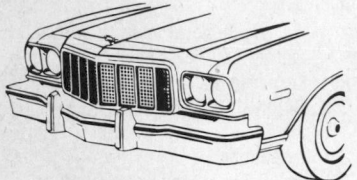

1974 Gran Torino

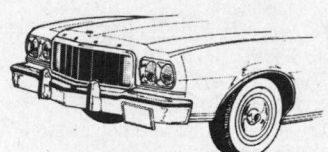

1975 Gran Torino Brougham

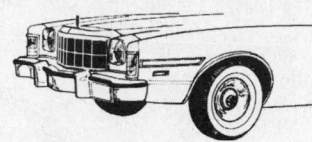

1974-75 Ford Elite

1976 Gran Torino Brougham

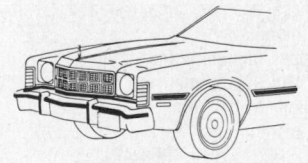

1976 Ford Elite

1977 LTD II

THUNDERBIRD

1977 Thunderbird

FALCON

1970

GRANADA

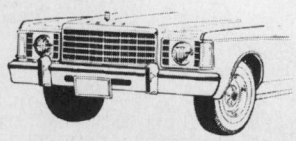

1975

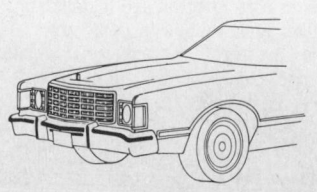

1976

1977 Granada

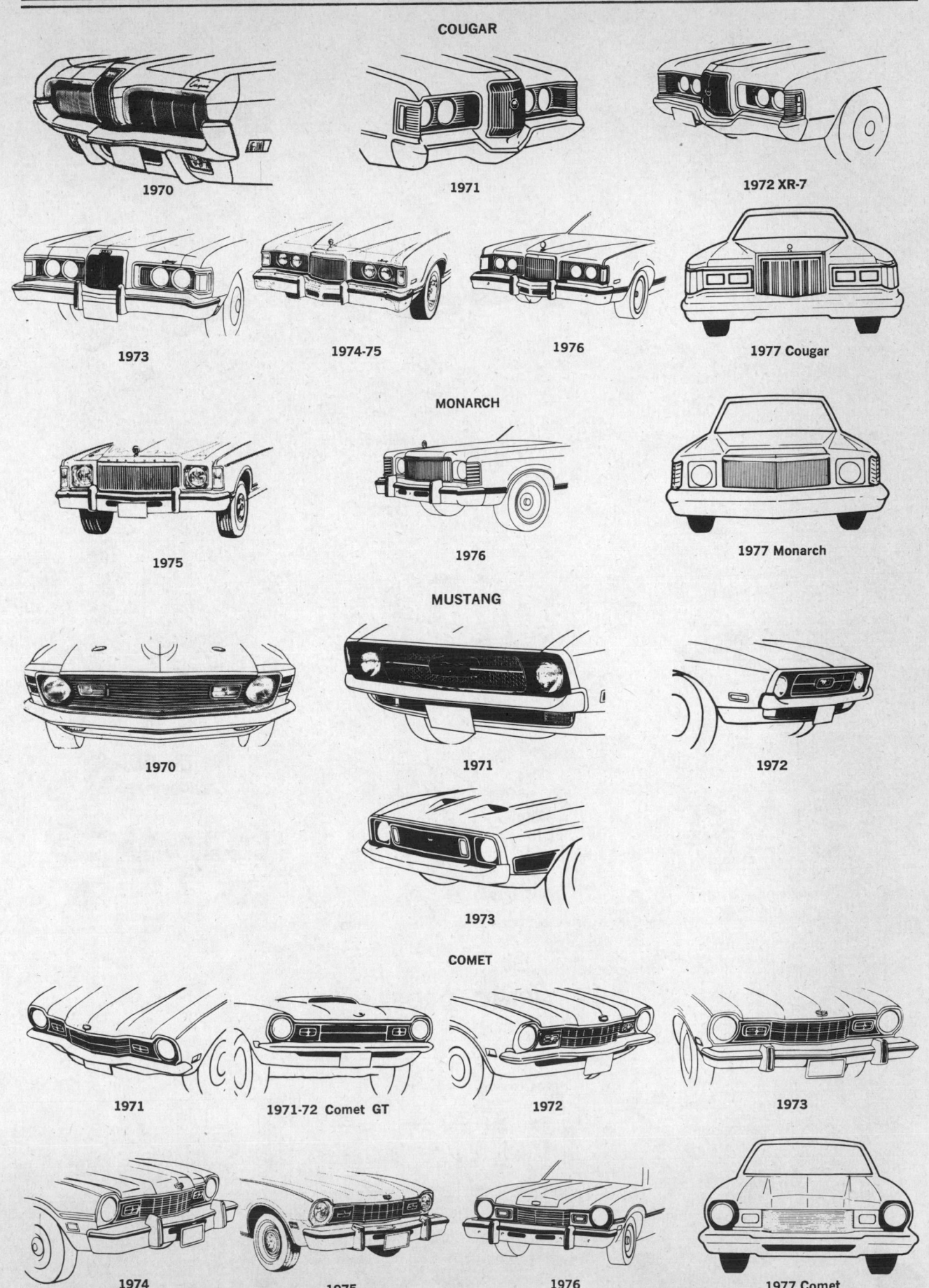

COUGAR

1970

1971

1972 XR-7

1973

1974-75

1976

1977 Cougar

MONARCH

1975

1976

1977 Monarch

MUSTANG

1970

1971

1972

1973

COMET

1971

1971-72 Comet GT

1972

1973

1974

1975

1976

1977 Comet

C443

MONTEGO

1970

1971

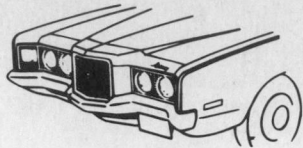

1972

1973

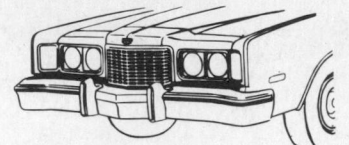

1974

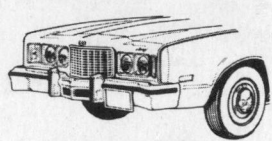

1975

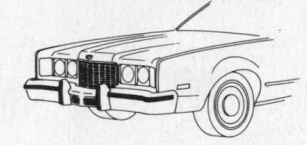

1976

MAVERICK

1970-72

1973

1974

1975

1976

1977 Maverick

FIRING ORDER

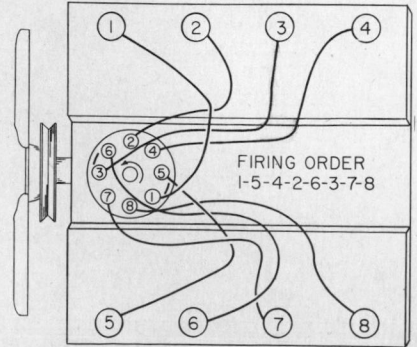

All V8 except 351, 400 V8

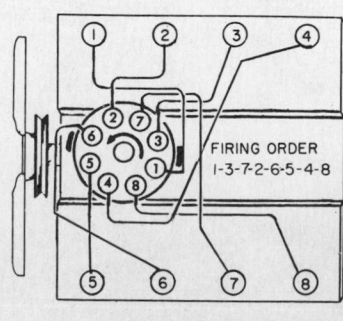

351 and 400 V8

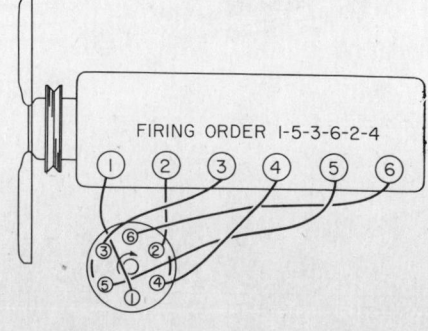

All 6 cylinder

CAR SERIAL NUMBER LOCATION AND ENGINE IDENTIFICATION

Vehicle Identification Number

The serial number is on a plate attached to the top of the instrument panel, visible through the windshield. The plate is interpreted as per the illustrations.

1 CONSECUTIVE UNIT NO.
2 BODY SERIAL CODE
3 MODEL YEAR CODE
4 ASSEMBLY PLANT CODE
5 ENGINE CODE
6 TRIM CODE
7 REAR AXLE CODE
8 COLOR CODE
9 BODY TYPE CODE
10 DISTRICT SPEC EQUIP CODE
11 TRANSMISSION CODE

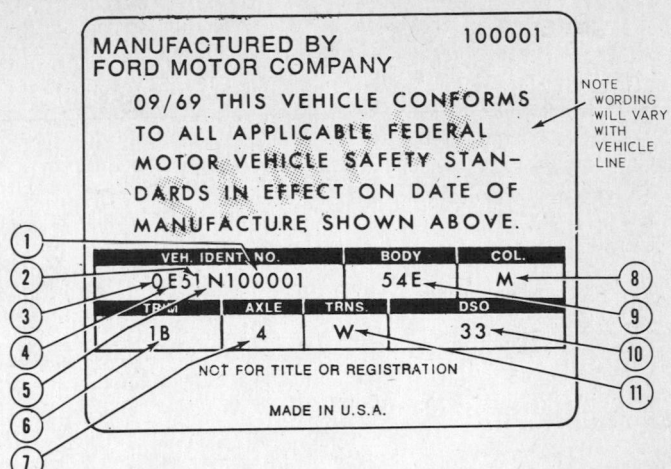

Vehicle certification label

ENGINE CODE

The engine code designation is the 5th digit of the vehicle identification number (V.I.N.). The V.I.N. is stamped on a plate located at the left side of the instrument panel, visible through the windshield.

Disp	Bbl	HP*	'70	'71	'72	'73	'74	'75	'76	'77
6-Cylinder Models										
170	1	82			U					
170	1	100		U						
170	1	105	U							
200	1	74, 75				T	T	T		
200	1	84			T	T				
200	1	91			T					
200	1	115		T						
200	1	120	T							
250	1	70, 79, 72, 85				L	L	L		
250	1	88, 91, 92, 99			L	L				
250	1	95, 98			L					
250	1	145		L						
250	1	155	L							
8-Cylinder Models										
302	2	135, 137, 138, 141					F			
302	2	115, 122, 129						F	F	F
302	2	138, 140, 143				F	F			
302	2	210	F	F						
302	2	220	F							
302 (Boss)	4	290	G							
351W	2	153, 143, 154				H	H	H		
351W	2	156, 162			H	H				
351C	2	154, 159, 163, 177				H	H			
351①	2	161, 164, 177		H	H					
351M	2	150, 148				H	H	Q		
351CJ	4	246, 255, 266			Q	Q	Q			
351HO	4	266		R						
351①	2	240		H						

Disp	Bbl	HP*	'70	'71	'72	'73	'74	'75	'76	'77
351W	2	250	H							
351C	4	280			Q					
351C	4	285			M					
351C	4	300		M						
351 (Boss)	4	330		R						
400	2	144, 158						S	S	S
400	2	163, 168, 170					S	S		
400	2	168, 172			S					
428	4	335	Q							
429	4	197, 201				N				
429	4	205, 208, 212			N					
429	4	360	N	N						
429CJ	4	370	C	C						
429SCJ	4	375	J	J						
429 (Boss)	4	375	Z							
460	4	217, 216						A	A	A
460	4	202, 208, 195, 220					A			
460PI	4	226						C	C	C

① Both Windsor and Cleveland versions of the 351 2V engine have been available. The quickest method of identification, on engines through 1974, is to disconnect a spark plug wire and examine the size of the plug. Windsor engines through 1974 are equipped with standard 18mm spark plugs. Cleveland engines through 1974 and all 1975 and later 351 engines use the smaller 14mm plugs.

* All 1972 and later horsepower ratings are SAE net.

CJ	Cobra Jet	C	Cleveland
HO	High output	SCJ	Super Cobra Jet
W	Windsor	PI	Police Interceptor

TRANSMISSION CODE

The transmission is identified by the code number on the vehicle certification label, attached to the driver's door.

1970-71

1 ....Three speed manual	W ....Automatic C4
5 ..Four speed manual-wide ratio	U ....Automatic C6
6..Four speed manual-close ratio	X ....Automatic FMX
V .....Semi-Automatic stick shift	Z ......Automatic C6 Special for Police and trailer towing

1972-77

1 ....Three speed manual	W ....Automatic C4
5 ....Four speed manual	X ....Automatic FMX
U ....Automatic C6	Z ......Automatic (C6 Special) for Police and trailer towing

Vehicle Certification Label

The vehicle certification label is located on the rear of the driver's door. The upper half of the label contains the name of the manufacturer, the month and year of manufacture, and the certification statement. For interpretation of the lower half of the label, see the illustration.

Typical vehicle identification number (VIN) tab

GENERAL ENGINE SPECIFICATIONS

Year	Engine No. Cyl. Displacement (Cu. In.)	Carburetor Type	Horsepower @ rpm ■	Torque @ rpm (ft lbs) ■	Bore X Stroke (in.)	Compression Ratio	Oil Pressure @ 2000 rpm
'70	6-170	1 bbl	105 @ 4400	158 @ 2400	3.500 x 2.940	8.7:1	35-60
	6-200	1 bbl	120 @ 4400	190 @ 2400	3.680 x 3.130	8.7:1	35-60
	6-250	1 bbl	155 @ 4400	240 @ 1600	3.682 x 3.910	9.0:1	35-60
	8-302	2 bbl	210 @ 4400	295 @ 2400	4.000 x 3.000	9.5:1	35-60
	8-302 BOSS	4 bbl	290 @ 5800	290 @ 4300	4.000 x 3.000	9.5:1	35-60
	8-351 C or W	2 bbl	250 @ 4600	355 @ 2600	4.000 x 3.500	9.5:1	35-60
	8-351 C	4 bbl	300 @ 5400	380 @ 3400	4.000 x 3.500	11.4:1	35-60
	8-428 CJ	4 bbl	335 @ 5200	440 @ 3400	4.130 x 3.984	10.6:1	35-60
	8-429	4 bbl	360 @ 4600	480 @ 2800	4.362 x 3.590	10.5:1	35-60
	8-429 CJ	4 bbl	370 @ 5400	450 @ 3400	4.362 x 3.590	11.3:1	35-60
	8-429 SCJ	4 bbl	375 @ 5600	450 @ 3400	4.362 x 3.590	10.5:1	35-60
	8-429 BOSS	4 bbl	375 @ 5200	450 @ 3400	4.362 x 3.590	10.5:1	45-60
'71	6-170	1 bbl	100 @ 4200	148 @ 2600	3.500 x 2.940	8.7:1	35-60
	6-200	1 bbl	115 @ 4000	180 @ 2200	3.680 x 3.130	8.7:1	35-60
	6-250	1 bbl	145 @ 4000	232 @ 1600	3.682 x 3.910	9.0:1	35-60
	8-302	2 bbl	210 @ 4600	296 @ 2600	4.000 x 3.000	9.0:1	35-60
	8-351 C or W	2 bbl	240 @ 4600	355 @ 2600	4.000 x 3.500	9.5:1	35-60
	8-351 BOSS	4 bbl	330 @ 5800	380 @ 3400	4.000 x 3.500	11.0:1	35-60
	8-351 CJ	4 bbl	280 @ 5800	345 @ 3800	4.000 x 3.500	9.0:1	35-60
	8-351 C	4 bbl	285 @ 5400	370 @ 3400	4.000 x 3.500	10.7:1	35-60
	8-429	4 bbl	360 @ 4600	480 @ 2800	4.362 x 3.590	10.5:1	35-75
	8-429 CJ	4 bbl	370 @ 5400	450 @ 3400	4.362 x 3.590	11.3:1	35-75
	8-429 SCJ	4 bbl	375 @ 5600	450 @ 3400	4.362 x 3.590	11.3:1	35-75
'72	6-170	1 bbl	82 @ 4400	129 @ 1800	3.500 x 2.940	8.3:1	35-60
	6-200	1 bbl	91 @ 4000	154 @ 2200	3.680 x 3.130	8.3:1	35-60
	6-250	1 bbl	99 @ 3600	184 @ 1600	3.680 x 3.910	8.0:1	35-60
	8-302	2 bbl	141 @ 4000	242 @ 2000	4.000 x 3.000	8.5:1	35-60
	8-351 C or W	2 bbl	164 @ 4000	276 @ 2000	4.000 x 3.500	8.6:1	35-60
	8-351 CJ	4 bbl	248 @ 5400	290 @ 3800	4.000 x 3.500	8.6:1	35-85
	8-351 HO	4 bbl	266 @ 5400	301 @ 3600	4.000 x 3.500	8.6:1	35-85
	8-400	2 bbl	168 @ 4200	297 @ 2200	4.000 x 4.000	8.4:1	35-85
	8-429	4 bbl	205 @ 4400	322 @ 2600	4.362 x 3.590	8.5:1	35-75

GENERAL ENGINE SPECIFICATIONS

Year	Engine No. Cyl. Displacement (Cu. In.)	Carburetor Type	Horsepower @ rpm ■	Torque @ rpm (ft lbs) ■	Bore X Stroke (in.)	Advertised Compression Ratio	Oil Pressure @ 2000 rpm
'73	6-200	1 bbl	91 @ 4000	154 @ 2200	3.680 x 3.130	8.3:1	35-60
	6-250	1 bbl	99 @ 3600	184 @ 1600	3.680 x 3.910	8.0:1	35-60
	8-302	2 bbl	141 @ 4000	242 @ 2000	4.000 x 3.000	8.5:1	35-60
	8-351	2 bbl	164 @ 4000	276 @ 2000	4.000 x 3.500	8.6:1	35-85
	8-351	4 bbl	248 @ 5400	290 @ 3800	4.000 x 3.500	8.0:1	35-85
	8-400	2 bbl	168 @ 4200	297 @ 2200	4.000 x 4.000	8.0:1	35-85
	8-429	4 bbl	205 @ 4400	322 @ 2600	4.362 x 3.590	8.5:1	35-75
	8-460 PI	4 bbl	269 @ 4600	388 @ 2800	4.362 x 3.850	8.8:1	35-75
'74	6-200	1 bbl	84 @ 3800	150 @ 1800	3.680 x 3.130	8.3:1	35-55
	6-250	1 bbl	91 @ 3200	190 @ 1600	3.680 x 3.910	8.0:1	35-55
	8-302	2 bbl	140 @ 3800	230 @ 2600	4.000 x 3.000	8.0:1	35-55
	8-351 W	2 bbl	162 @ 4000	275 @ 2200	4.000 x 3.500	8.0:1	50-70
	8-351 C	2 bbl	163 @ 4200	278 @ 2000	4.000 x 3.500	8.0:1	50-70
	8-351	4 bbl	255 @ 5600	290 @ 3400	4.000 x 3.500	7.9:1	50-70
	8-400	2 bbl	170 @ 3400	330 @ 2000	4.000 x 4.000	8.0:1	50-70
	8-460	4 bbl	195 @ 3800	355 @ 2600	4.362 x 3.850	8.0:1	35-75
	8-460	4 bbl	220 @ 4000	355 @ 2600	4.362 x 3.850	8.0:1	35-75
	8-460 PI	4 bbl	260 @ 4400	380 @ 2700	4.362 x 3.850	8.8:1	50-75
'75	6-200 MT	1 bbl	75 @ 3200	145 @ 2000	3.680 x 3.130	8.3:1	30-50
	6-200 AT	1 bbl	74 @ 3400	132 @ 2400	3.680 x 3.130	8.3:1	30-50
	6-250 MT	1 bbl	85 @ 2900	180 @ 2000	3.680 x 3.910	8.0:1	40-60
	6-250 AT	1 bbl	72 @ 2900	180 @ 1400	3.680 x 3.910	8.0:1	40-60
	6-250 MT Cal.	1 bbl	79 @ 2800	177 @ 1600	3.680 x 3.910	8.0:1	40-60
	6-250 AT Cal.	1 bbl	70 @ 2800	175 @ 1400	3.680 x 3.910	8.0:1	40-60
	8-302 Granada, Monarch	2 bbl	129 @ 3800	220 @ 1800	4.000 x 3.000	8.0:1	40-60
	8-302 Maverick, Comet	2 bbl	122 @ 3800	208 @ 1800	4.000 x 3.000	8.0:1	40-60
	8-302 Cal.	2 bbl	115 @ 3600	203 @ 1800	4.000 x 3.000	8.0:1	40-60
	8-351 W Compact	2 bbl	143 @ 3600	255 @ 2200	4.000 x 3.500	8.2:1	40-65
	8-351-W Intermediate	2 bbl	154 @ 3800	268 @ 2200	4.000 x 3.500	8.2:1	40-65
	8-351 W Cal.	2 bbl	153 @ 3400	270 @ 2400	4.000 x 3.500	8.2:1	40-65
	8-351 M 49	2 bbl	148 @ 3800	243 @ 2400	4.000 x 3.500	8.0:1	50-75
	8-351 M Cal.	2 bbl	150 @ 3800	244 @ 2800	4.000 x 3.500	8.0:1	50-75
	8-400 49	2 bbl	158 @ 3800	276 @ 2000	4.000 x 4.000	8.0:1	50-75
	8-400 Cal.	2 bbl	144 @ 3600	255 @ 2200	4.000 x 4.000	8.0:1	50-75
	8-460 49	4 bbl	216 @ 4000	366 @ 2600	4.362 x 3.850	8.0:1	40-65
	8-460 Cal.	4 bbl	217 @ 4000	365 @ 2600	4.362 x 3.850	8.0:1	40-65
	8-460 PI	4 bbl	226 @ 4000	374 @ 2600	4.362 x 3.850	8.0:1	40-65
'76-'77	6-200 MT	1 bbl	81 @ 3400	151 @ 1700	3.682 x 3.126	8.3:1	30-50
	6-200 AT	1 bbl	78 @ 3300	152 @ 1600	3.682 x 3.126	8.3:1	30-50
	6-250 MT①	1 bbl	90 @ 3000	190 @ 2000	3.682 x 3.910	8.0:1	40-60
	6-250 MT②	1 bbl	87 @ 3000	187 @ 1900	3.682 x 3.910	8.0:1	40-60
	6-250 AT①	1 bbl	81 @ 3000	192 @ 2000	3.682 x 3.910	8.0:1	40-60
	6-250 AT②	1 bbl	78 @ 3000	187 @ 1900	3.682 x 3.910	8.0:1	40-60
	6-250 MT Cal.	1 bbl	—	—	3.682 x 3.910	8.0:1	40-60
	6-250 AT Cal.①	1 bbl	78 @ 3000	183 @ 1400	3.682 x 3.910	8.0:1	40-60
	6-250 AT Cal.②	1 bbl	76 @ 3000	179 @ 1300	3.682 x 3.910	8.0:1	40-60

C447

GENERAL ENGINE SPECIFICATIONS

Year	Engine No. Cyl. Displacement (Cu. In.)	Carburetor Type	Horsepower @ rpm ■	Torque @ rpm (ft lbs) ■	Bore X Stroke (in.)	Advertised Compression Ratio	Oil Pressure @ 2000 rpm
	8-302 MT①	2 bbl	138 @ 3600	245 @ 2000	4.000 x 3.000	8.0:1	40-60
	8-302 MT ②	2 bbl	134 @ 3600	242 @ 2000	4.000 x 3.000	8.0:1	40-60
	8-302 AT①	2 bbl	137 @ 3600	246 @ 1800	4.000 x 3.000	8.0:1	40-60
	8-302 AT②	2 bbl	133 @ 3600	243 @ 1800	4.000 x 3.000	8.0:1	40-60
	8-302 AT Cal.①	2 bbl	137 @ 3600	247 @ 1800	4.000 x 3.000	8.0:1	40-60
	8-302 AT Cal.②	2 bbl	130 @ 3600	238 @ 1600	4.000 x 3.000	8.0:1	40-60
	8-351 AT②	2 bbl	143 @ 3200	285 @ 1600	4.000 x 3.500	8.0:1	45-65
	8-351 W	2 bbl	154 @ 3400	286 @ 1800	4.000 x 3.500	8.0:1	45-65
	8-351 M	2 bbl	152 @ 3800	274 @ 1600	4.000 x 3.500	8.0:1	45-65
	8-351 AT Cal.②	2 bbl	140 @ 3400	276 @ 1600	4.000 x 3.500	8.0:1	45-65
	8-400	2 bbl	180 @ 3800	336 @ 1800	4.000 x 4.000	8.0:1	35-65
	8-460	4 bbl	202 @ 3800	352 @ 1600	4.362 x 3.850	8.0:1	35-65
	8-460 PI	4 bbl	—	—	4.362 x 3.850	8.0:1	35-65

■ Beginning 1972 horsepower and torque are SAE net figures. They are measured at the rear of the transmission with all accessories installed and operating. Since the figures vary when a given engine is installed in different models, some are representative rather than exact.

W Windsor
C Cleveland
M Modified Cleveland
PI Police Interceptor

MT Manual Transmission
AT Automatic Transmission
49 49 states only
Cal California only
① Maverick/Comet
② Granada/Monarch

TUNE-UP SPECIFICATIONS

Fairlane, Torino, Montego, Mustang, Cougar, Elite, LTD II, 1977 Thunderbird

When analyzing compression test results, look for uniformity among cylinders rather than specific pressures.

Year	Engine No. Cyl Displacement (cu in.)	hp	Spark Plugs Orig. Type	Gap (in.)	Point Dwell* (deg)	Point Gap (in.)	Ignition Timing (deg) ▲ Man Trans	Auto Trans	Valves Intake Opens ■ (deg)	Fuel Pump Pressure (psi)	Idle Speed (rpm) ▲ ● Man Trans	Trans
'70	6-200	120	BF-82	.035	38	.027	6B	6B	9	4-6	750②	550①
	6-250	155	BF-82	.035	38	.025	6B	6B	10	4-6	750/500	600/500
	8-302	210	BF-42	.035	27	.021	6B	6B	16	4-6	800/500	600/500
	8-302	290	AF-32	.035	32	.020	16B	—	40	4½-6½	800/500	—
	8-351C	250	AF-42	.035	27	.021	6B	6B	12	5-7	700/500	600
	8-351W	250	BF-42	.035	27	.021	10B	10B	11	5-7	700/500	575 600/500
	8-351C	300	BF-32	.035	27/29	.021/ .017	6B	6B	16	5-6	800/500	600 600/500
	8-428	335	BF-32	.035	32	.020	6B	6B	18	4½-6½	725	675 675/500
	8-429	360	BF-42	.035	27/29	.021/ .017	6B	6B	16	5-7	700	600
	8-429CJ	370	AF-32	.035	27/29	.021/ .017	10B	10B	16	6½-8½	700 700/500	650
	8-429	BOSS	AF-32	.035	27/29	.021/ .017	10B	10B	16	6½-8½	650/500	700/500

Fairlane, Torino, Montego, Mustang, Cougar, Elite, LTD II, 1977 Thunderbird

TUNE-UP SPECIFICATIONS

When analyzing compression test results, look for uniformity among cylinders rather than specific pressures.

Year	ENGINE No. Cyl Displacement (cu in.)	hp	SPARK PLUGS Orig. Type	Gap (in.)	DISTRIBUTOR Point Dwell* (deg)	DISTRIBUTOR Point Gap (in.)	IGNITION TIMING (deg) ▲ Man Trans	IGNITION TIMING (deg) ▲ Auto Trans	VALVES Intake Opens ■ (deg)	Fuel Pump Pressure (psi)	IDLE SPEED (rpm) ▲ Man Trans	IDLE SPEED (rpm) ▲ Trans
'71	6-250	145	BRF-82	.034	36	.027/.025	6B	6B	10	4-6	750	600
	8-302	210	BRF-42	.034	27	.021	6B	6B	16	4-6	800/500	575 600/500
	8-351C	240	ARF-42	.034	27	.021	6B	6B	12	5-7	700/500	600
	8-351W	240	BRF-42	.034	27	.021	6B	6B	12	5-7	700/500	575 600/500
	8-351CJ	280	ARF-42	.034	27	.021	6B	6B	18	5-7	800/500	600
	8-351C	285	ARF-32	.034	27/29	.021/.017	6B	6B	18	5-7	800/500	600
	8-351	BOSS	ARF-32	.034	27/29	.021/.017	6B	6B	18	4½-5½	800	590
	8-429	360	BRF-42	.034	27/29	.021/.017	4B	4B	16	5-7	700	600 600/500
	8-429CJ	370	ARF-42	.034	25	.020	10B	10B	32	4½-6½	700	650 650/500
	8-429	SCJ	ARF-42	.034	28	.020	10B	10B	40½	4½-6½	650/500	700/500
'72	6-250	95	BRF-82	.034	37	.027	6B	6B	10(16)	4½-6½	750/500	600/500
	8-302	140	BRF-42	.034	28	.017	6B	6B	16	5½-6½	800/500	575 600/500
	8-351C	165	ARF-42	.034	28	.017	6B	6B	12	5½-6½		575/500 (625/500)
	8-351W	165	BRF-42	.034	28	.017	—	6B	12	5½-6½	—	575 600/500
	8-351CJ	266	ARF-42	.034	28	.017/.020	16B	16B④	14	5½-6½		700/500④ (800/500)
	8-351HO	N.A.	ARF-42	.034	28	.020	10B	—	17½	5½-6½	1000/500	—
	8-400	168	ARF-42	.034	28	.017	—	6B	17	4½-5½	—	625/500
	8-429	205	ARF-42	.034	28	.017	—	10B	8	5½-6½	—	600/500
'73	6-250	95	BRF-82	.034	37	.027/.025	6B	6B	16	4½-6½	750/500	600/500
	8-302	140	BRF-42	.034	28	.017	6B	6B	16	5½-6½	800/500	575 600/500
	8-351C	165	ARF-42	.034	28	.017	—	6B	12	5½-6½	—	625/500
	8-351W	165	BRF-42	.034	28	.017	—	6B	12	5½-6½		575 600/500
	8-351CJ	266	ARF-42	.034	28⑤	.017③	16B	16B④	14	5½-6½	1000/500	800/500④
	8-400	168	ARF-42	.034	28	.017	—	6B	17	5½-6½	—	625/500
	8-429	205	ARF-42	.034	28	.017	—	10B	8	5½-6½	—	600/500
	8-460PI	269	ARF-42	.035	28	.017	—	10B	18	5½-7½	—	600
'74	6-250	91	BRF-82	.044	37⑩	.027	6B	6B	26	5½-6½	800/500	625/500
	8-302	140	BRF-42	.044	28⑩	.017	10B	6B	16⑦	5½-6½	800/500	625/500
	8-351W	162	BRF-42	.044	28⑩	.017	—	6B	15	5½-6½	—	600/500
	8-351C	163	ARF-42	.044	28⑩	.017		14B	11.5	5½-6½	—	600/500
	8-351CJ	255	ARF-42	.044	28⑩	.017		20B⑥	14	5½-6½	—	800/500
	8-400	170	ARF-42	.044	Electronic		—	12B⑥	17	5½-6½	—	625/500
	8-460	195, 220, 260	ARF-42	.054	Electronic		—	14B	8	5½-6½	—	650/500

C449

Fairlane, Torino, Montego, Mustang, Cougar, Elite, LTD II, 1977 Thunderbird

TUNE-UP SPECIFICATIONS

When analyzing compression test results, look for uniformity among cylinders rather than specific pressures.

Year	ENGINE No. Cyl Displacement (cu in.)	hp	SPARK PLUGS Orig. Type	Gap (in.)	DISTRIBUTOR Point Dwell* (deg)	Point Gap (in.)	IGNITION TIMING (deg) ▲ Man Trans	Auto Trans	VALVES Intake Opens ■ (deg)	Fuel Pump Pressure (psi)	IDLE SPEED (rpm) ▲ ● Man Trans	Trans
'75	8-351W	153, 154	ARF-42	.044	Electronic		—	6B	15	5½-6½	—	600/500
	8-351M	148, 150	ARF-42	.044	Electronic		—	6B	19½	5½-6½	—	700/500
	8-400	144, 158	ARF-42	.044	Electronic		—	6B	17	5½-6½	—	625/500
	8-460	216, 217	ARF-52	.044	Electronic		—	14B	8	5½-6½	—	650/500
	8-460PI	226	ARF-52	.044	Electronic		—	14B	18	5½-7	—	700/500
'76	8-351W	All	ARF-42/52⑧	.054	Electronic		—	⑧	15	5½-6½	—	650
	8-351M	All	ARF-42/52⑧	.044	Electronic		—	⑧	19½	5½-6½	—	650 (650/675⑧)
	8-400	All	ARF-42/52⑧	.044	Electronic		—	⑧	17	5½-6½	—	650(625)
	8-460	All	ARF-52	.044	Electronic		—	8/14B⑧⑨ @ 650	8	5½-6½	—	650
	8-460PI	226	ARF-52	.044	Electronic		—	14B⑨ @ 650	18	5½-7	—	650
'77	8-302	All	ARF-52⑪	.050⑫	Electronic		—	⑧	16	5½-6½	—	650
	8-351W	All	ARF-52⑪	.050⑫	Electronic		—	⑧	23	4-6	—	650
	8-351M	All	ARF-52⑪	.050⑫	Electronic		—	⑧	19½	6½-7½	—	⑧
	8-400	All	ARF-52⑪	.050⑫	Electronic		—	⑧	17	7-8	—	⑧

NOTE: The underhood specifications sticker often reflects tune-up specification changes made in production. Sticker figures must be used if they disagree with those in this chart.

* Where two dwell or point gap figures are separated by a slash, the first figure is for engines equipped with dual diaphragm distributors and the second figure is for engines equipped with single diaphragm distributors

▲ See text for procedure

● In all cases where two idle speed figures are separated by a slash, the first is for idle speed with solenoid energized and automatic transmission in Drive, while the second is for idle speed with solenoid disconnected and automatic transmission in Neutral. Figures in parentheses are for California

■ All figures are in degrees Before Top Dead Center

① For air conditioned vehicles, adjust idle speed to 600 rpm with A/C on

② For air conditioned vehicles, adjust, idle speed to 800 rpm with A/C on

③ Figure is .020 for manual transmission with dual point distributor

④ On Cougars with automatic transmission, set ignition timing to 6B and set idle speed to 650 rpm

⑤ Figure is 32°-35° on manual transmission model with dual point distributor with both point sets combined

⑥ At 500 rpm

⑦ 20° BTC for 302 automatic

⑧ Depends on emission equipment; check underhood specifications sticker

⑨ In Drive

⑩ Electronic ignition used on all engines assembled after May, 1974

⑪ ARF-52-6 for Calif. engines

⑫ .060 in. for Calif. engines

B Before Top Dead Center
C Cleveland
M Modified Cleveland
CJ Cobra Jet
HO High Output
N.A. Not available
SCJ Super Cobra Jet
W Windsor
— Not applicable

MECHANICAL VALVE LIFTER CLEARANCE

Year	Engine	Intake (Hot) In.	Exhaust (Hot) In.
1970	302 BOSS	.025	.025
1970	429 BOSS	.013 (Cold)	.013 (Cold)
1970-1971	429 SCJ	.019	.019
1971	351 BOSS	.025	.025
1972	351 HO	.025	.025

Falcon — TUNE-UP SPECIFICATIONS

When analyzing compression test results, look for uniformity among cylinders rather than specific pressures.

Year	ENGINE No. Cyl Displacement (cu in.)	hp	SPARK PLUGS Orig. Type	Gap (in.)	DISTRIBUTOR Point Dwell* (deg)	Point Gap (in.)	IGNITION TIMING (deg) ▲ Man Trans	Auto Trans	VALVES Intake Opens ■ (deg)	Fuel Pump Pressure (psi)	IDLE SPEED (rpm) ▲ Man Trans ●	Trans
'70	6-200	120	BF-82	.035	37	.027	6B	6B	9	4½-5½	750②	550③
	8-302	220	BF-42	.035	27/29	.021/ .017	6B	6B	16	4½-5½	800/500	600/500

* Where two dwell or point gap figures are separated by a splash, the first figure is for engines equipped with dual diaphragm distributors, while the second is for engines equipped with single diaphragm distributors.

▲ See text for procedure

■ All figures Before Top Dead Center

● Where two idle speed figures are separated by a slash, the first is for idle speed with solenoid energized and automatic transmission in Drive; the second is for idle speed with solenoid disconnected and automatic transmission in Neutral

① Not used

② For air conditioned vehicles, adjust idle speed to 800 rpm with A/C off

③ For air conditioned vehicles, adjust idle speed to 600 rpm with A/C off

B Before Top Dead Center

TDC Top Dead Center

NOTE: The underhood specifications sticker often reflects tune-up specification changes made in production. Sticker figures must be used if they disagree with those in this chart.

Maverick, Granada, Comet, Monarch — TUNE-UP SPECIFICATIONS

When analyzing compression test results, look for uniformity among cylinders rather than specific pressures.

Year	ENGINE No. Cyl Displacement (cu in.)	hp	SPARK PLUGS Orig. Type	Gap (in.)	DISTRIBUTOR Point Dwell* (deg)	Point Gap (in.)	IGNITION TIMING (deg) ▲ Man Trans	Auto Trans	VALVES Intake Opens ■ (deg)	Fuel Pump Pressure (psi)	IDLE SPEED (rpm) ▲ Man Trans ●	Trans
'70	6-170	105	BF-82	.034	37/39	.027/ .025	6B	6B	9	4½	750	550
	6-200	120	BF-82	.034	37/39	.027/ .025	6B	6B	9	4½	800/500	600/500
	6-250	155	BF-82	.034	37/39	.027/ .025	—	6B	10	4-6	—	550
'71	6-170	100	BRF-82	.034	35/36	.027/ .025	6B	—	9	4-6	750	—
	6-200	115	BRF-82	.034	35/36	.027/ .025	6B	6B	9	4-6	800/500	600/500
	6-250	145	BRF-82	.034	35/36	.027/ .025	6B	6B	10	4-6	750/500	600/500
	8-302	210	BRF-42	.034	26/28	.021/ .017	6B	6B	16	4-6	800/500	600/500
'72	6-170	82	BRF-82	.034	37	.027/	6B	—	9	4-6	750	—
	6-200	91	BRF-82	.034	37	.027	6B	6B	9	4-6	800/500	600/500
	6-250	98	BRF-82	.034	37	.027	6B	6B	10	4-6	750/500	600/500
	8-302	143	BRF-42	.034	28	.017	6B	6B	16	4-6	800/500	600/500
'73	6-200	91	BRF-82	.034	37	.027/ .025	6B	6B	9	4-6	800/500	600/500
	6-250	98	BRF-82	.034	37	.027/ .025	—	6B	10	4-6	—	600/500
	8-302	143	BRF-42	.034	28	.017	6B	6B	16	4-6	800/500	600/500

Maverick, Granada, Comet, Monarch — TUNE-UP SPECIFICATIONS

When analyzing compression test results, look for uniformity among cylinders rather than specific pressures.

Year	ENGINE No. Cyl Displacement (cu in.)	hp	SPARK PLUGS Orig. Type	Gap (in.)	DISTRIBUTOR Point Dwell* (deg)	Point Gap (in.)	IGNITION TIMING (deg) ▲ Man Trans	Auto Trans	VALVES Intake Opens ■ (deg)	Fuel Pump Pressure (psi)	IDLE SPEED (rpm) ▲ ● Man Trans	Trans
'74	6-200	84	BRF-82	.034⑥	37⑤	.024/.030	6B	6B	28	4½-5½	750/500	550/500
	6-250	91	BRF-82	.044	37⑤	.024/.030	6B	6B	26	4½-5½	750/500	600/500
	8-302	140	BRF-42	.044	27⑤	.014/.020	6B	6B	②	5½-6½	800/500	650/500①
'75	6-200	74, 75	BRF-82	.044	Electronic		6B	6B	20	4½-5½	750/500	600/500
	6-250	70,72,79,85	BRF-82	.044	Electronic		6B	6B	26	4½-5½	850/500	600/500
	8-302	122, 129	ARF-42	.044	Electronic		6B	6B	20	5½-6½	900/500	650/500
	8-302	115	ARF-42	.044	Electronic		6B	8B	20	5½-6½	900/500	650/500
	8-351 W	143	ARF-42	.044	Electronic		—	4B	15	5½-6½	—	700/500
	8-351 W	153	ARF-42	.044	Electronic		—	6B	15	5½-6½	—	650/500
'76	6-200	All	BRF-82	.044	Electronic		③	③	20	4½-5½	800	650
	6-250	All	BRF-82	.044	Electronic		③	③	26	4½-5½	850	600
	8-302	All	ARF-42/52③	.044	Electronic		③	③	20	5½-6½	750	650(700)
	8-351W	All	ARF-52	.044	Electronic		—	8(10B)④ @ 625(650)	15	5½-6½	—	625(650)
'77	6-200	All	BRF-82	.050	Electronic		③	③	20	5½-6½	800	650
	6-250	All	BRF-82	.050	Electronic		③	③	18	5½-6½	850	600
	8-302	All	ARF-52⑦	.050⑧	Electronic		③	③	16	5½-6½	750	650(700)
	8-351	All	ARF-52⑦	.050⑧	Electronic		—	③	23	5½-6½	—	625

* Where two dwell or point gap figures are separated by a slash, the first figure is for engines equipped with dual diaphragm distributors and the second figure is for engines equipped with single diaphragm distributors
▲ See text for procedure
■ All figures Before Top Dead Center
● Where two idle speed figures are separated by a slash, the first figure is for idle speed with solenoid energized and automatic transmission in Drive, while the second is for idle speed with solenoid disconnected and automatic transmission in Neutral. Figures in parentheses are for California
B Before Top Dead Center
— Not applicable

① 600/500 with air conditioning
② 16° B—manual transmission
   20° B—automatic transmission
③ Depends on emission equipment; check underhood specifications sticker
④ In Drive
⑤ Electronic ignition used on all engines assembled after May, 1974
⑥ .044 in. with electronic ignition
⑦ ARF-52-6 for Calif. engines
⑧ .060 in. for Calif. engines
NOTE: The underhood specifications sticker often reflects tune-up specification changes made in production. Sticker figures must be used if they disagree with those in this chart.

CAPACITIES

Year	ENGINE No. Cyl. Displacement (Cu. In.)	Engine Crankcase Add 1 Qt For New Filter	TRANSMISSION Pts To Refill After Draining Manual 3-Speed	4-Speed	Automatic	Drive Axle (pts)	Gasoline Tank (gals)	COOLING SYSTEM (qts) With Heater	With A/C
'70	**FALCON, MAVERICK**								
	6-170, 200	3.5	3.5	—	16	2.5	16	9	9
	MAVERICK								
	6-250	3.5	—		18	2.5	16	10	10
	FAIRLANE, TORINO								
	6-250	3.5	3.5	—	18	4	22	11.5	11.5
	FALCON, FAIRLANE, TORINO								
	8-302	4	3.5	4	18	5	22	15.5	16.5
	FAIRLANE, TORINO								
	8-351	4	3.5	4	22	5	22	15.5	16.5
	8-429	6⑨	—	4	26	5	22	19.5	19.5
	MUSTANG								
	6-200	3.5	3.5	—	16	2.25	22	9	9
	6-250	3.5	3.5	—	18	4	22	10	10
	8-302	4	3.5	4	18	4	22	13.5	15
	8-351	4	3.5	4	22	5	22	14.5	16
	8-428	4		4	26	5	22	19.5	19.5
	MONTEGO								
	6-250	3.5	3.5	—	18	4	22	11.5	11.5
	8-302	3.5	3.5	—	18	4	22	15	15
	MONTEGO, COUGAR								
	8-351	4	3.5	4	22	4	22	15.5	16
	8-429, 428	4⑨	—	4	26	5	22	19.5	19.5
'71	**MAVERICK, COMET**								
	6-170, 200	3.5	3.5	—	16	2.5	15	9	9
	6-250	3.5	3.5	—	18	2.5	15	9.5	9.5
	8-302	4	3.5	—	18	4	15	13.5	14
	TORINO, MONTEGO								
	6-250	3.5	3.5	—	18	4	20⑩	11	11
	8-302	4	3.5	—	18	4	20⑩	15	15.5
	8-351	4	3.5	4	22	5	20⑩	15.5	16.5
	8-429	6⑨	—	4	26	5	20⑩	19.5	19.5
	MUSTANG								
	6-250	3.5	3.5	—	18	4	20	11	11
	8-302	4	3.5	—	18	4	20	15	15.5
	MUSTANG, COUGAR								
	8-351	4	3.5	4	22	5	20	15.5	16
	8-429	6⑨	—	4	26	5	20	19.5	19.5
'72	**MAVERICK, COMET**								
	6-170, 200	3.5	3.5	—	16	4	15	9	9
	6-250	3.5	3.5	—	18	4	15	9.5	10.5
	8-302	4	3.5	—	18	4	15	13.5	14.5
	TORINO, MONTEGO								
	6-250	3.5	3.5	—	18	4	22.5⑩	11.5	11.5
	8-302	4	3.5	—	18	4	22.5⑩	15	15
	8-351	4	—	4	20.5⑪	4	22.5⑩	15.5	16
	8-400	4	—	—	26	4	22.5⑩	17.5	17.5
	8-429	4	—	—	26	5	22.5	19	19

CAPACITIES

Year	ENGINE No. Cyl. Displacement (Cu. In.)	Engine Crankcase Add 1 Qt For New Filter	TRANSMISSION Pts To Refill After Draining			Drive Axle (pts)	Gasoline Tank (gals)	COOLING SYSTEM (qts)	
			Manual 3-Speed	4-Speed	Automatic			With Heater	With A/C
	MUSTANG								
	6-250	3.5	3.5	—	18	4	19.5	11	11
	8-302	4	3.5	—	18	4	19.5	15	15.5
	MUSTANG, COUGAR								
	8-351	4	3.5	4	22⑫	5	19.5	16	16
'73	**MAVERICK, COMET**								
	6-200	3.5	3.5	—	16	4	15	9	9
	6-250	3.5	3.5	—	18	4	15	9.5	10.5
	8-302	4	3.5	—	18	4	15	13.5	14.5
	TORINO, MONTEGO								
	6-250	3.5	3.5	—	18	4	22.5⑩	11.5	11.5
	8-302	4	3.5	—	18	4	22.5⑩	15	15
	8-351	4	—	4	20.5⑪	4	22.5⑩	15.5	16
	8-400	4	—	—	26	4	22.5⑩	17.5	17.5
	8-429	4	—	—	26	5	22.5⑩	19	19
	8-460	6	—	—	26	5	22.5⑩	19.5	19.5
	MUSTANG								
	6-250	3.5	3.5	—	18	4	19.5	11	11
	8-302	4	3.5	—	18	4	19.5	15	15.5
	MUSTANG, COUGAR								
	8-351	4	—	4	22⑫	5	19.5	16	16
'74	**MAVERICK, COMET**								
	6-200	4	3.5	—	16	4	15	9.0	9.0
	6-250	4	3.5	—	18	4	15	9.7	9.7
	8-302	4	3.5	—	18	4	15	13.4	14.2
	TORINO, MONTEGO								
	6-250	4	—	—	⑬	4	26.5⑰	11.5	—
	8-302	4	3.5	—	⑬	4	26.5⑰	15.7	15.7
	TORINO, MONTEGO, COUGAR, ELITE								
	8-351	4	—	—	⑭	4⑯	26.5⑰	⑱	⑲
	8-400	4	—	—	25⑮	5	26.5⑰	17.7	18.3
	8-460	6	—	—	25⑮	5	26.5⑰	18.9	19.5
'75-'77	**MAVERICK, COMET**								
	6-200	4	3.5	—	16	4①	16㉓	9.0	9.0
	6-250	4	3.5	—	18	4①	16㉓	9.7	9.7
	8-302	4	3.5	—	18	4①	16㉓	13.4	14.2
	TORINO, MONTEGO								
	8-351	4	—	—	⑳	4②	26.5⑰	15.9㉑	16.2㉑
	8-400	4	—	—	⑳	5	26.5⑰	17.1	17.5
	8-460	4	—	—	⑳	5	26.5⑰	19.2③	19.2③
	COUGAR, ELITE								
	8-351	4	—	—	㉒	5	26.5	16.3④	16.8⑤
	8-400	4	—	—	㉒	5	26.5	17.7④	18.3⑤
	8-460	4	—	—	㉒	5	26.5	18.9⑥	20.5⑥
	GRANADA, MONARCH								
	6-200	4	3.5	4	—	4⑦	19.2	9.9	9.9
	6-250	4	3.5	4	17.0	4⑦	19.2⑧	10.5	10.7
	8-302	4	3.5	4	17.0	4	19.2⑧	14.6	14.6

CAPACITIES

Year	ENGINE No. Cyl. Displacement (Cu. In.)	Engine Crankcase Add 1 Qt For New Filter	TRANSMISSION Pts To Refill After Draining			Drive Axle (pts)	Gasoline Tank (gals)	COOLING SYSTEM (qts)	
			Manual 3-Speed	4-Speed	Automatic			With Heater	With A/C
	8-351	4	—	—	20.0	4	19.2	15.7	16.7

LTD II, 1977 THUNDERBIRD

Year	ENGINE No. Cyl. Displacement (Cu. In.)	Engine Crankcase Add 1 Qt For New Filter	3-Speed	4-Speed	Automatic	Drive Axle (pts)	Gasoline Tank (gals)	With Heater	With A/C
	8-302	4	—	—	20	5	26㉔	13.5	14.1
	8-351	4	—	—	22	5	26㉔	15.9㉕	16.3㉕ ㉖
	8-400	4	—	—	25	5	26㉔	17.1	17.5

① 4.5 pts in 1976-77
② 5 pts in 1976-77
③ 19.7 qts in 1976-77
④ 17.1 qts in 1976-77
⑤ 17.5 qts in 1976-77
⑥ 19.2 qts in 1976-77
⑦ Some use 5 pts in 1976-77
⑧ 1 gal less on certain 1976-77 models
⑨ 429 4 bbl—4 qts
   428, 429 CJ, SCJ—6 qts
   add 1 qt if equipped with oil cooler
⑩ Less 2 gals—station wagon, Ranchero
⑪ 26 pts for 351 CJ
⑫ Less 1 pt with 4 bbl
⑬ C4—18 or 20 pts; FMX—22 pts
⑭ 351 2V with C-4—20 pts; 351 2V with FMX—22pts; 351 2V with C-6—25 pts; 351-4V (C6)—21 pts

⑮ Cougar—21 pts
⑯ Cougar—5 pts
⑰ Station wagon—21.2 gallons
⑱ 351 W 2V—16.4 qts
   351 C 2V—15.9 qts
   351 C 4V—15.9 qts
⑲ 351 W 2V—16.8 qts
   351 C 2V—16.5 qts
   351 C 4V—16.9 qts
⑳ C4—20 pts; C6—25 pts; FMX—22 pts
㉑ 17.1 qts with heater, 17.5 qts with AC on 351 C 2 bbl
㉒ C4—21 pts; C6—24.5 pts; FMX—22 pts
㉓ 19.2 gals in 1976
㉔ 1977 station wagon—21.3 gals
㉕ 8-351W given; 8-351M—17.1/17.5 qts
㉖ 1977 Thunderbird 8-351W w/AC—17.2 qts
— Not applicable

VALVE SPECIFICATIONS

Year	Engine No. Cyl. Displacement (cu in.)	Seat Angle (deg)	Face Angle (deg)	Spring Test Pressure (lbs @ in.)	Spring Installed Height (in.)	STEM TO GUIDE Clearance (in.) Intake	Exhaust	STEM Diameter (in.) Intake	Exhaust
'70	6-170, 200	45	44	150 @ 1.22	1 19/32	.0008-.0025	.0010-.0027	.3104	.3102
	6-250	45	44	150 @ 1.22	1 19/32	.0008-.0025	.0010-.0027	.3104	.3102
	8-302	45	44	180 @ 1.23	1 21/32	.0010-.0027	.0010-.0027	.3420	.3415
	8-302④	45	44	315 @ 1.31	1 13/16	.0010-.0027	.0015-.0032	.3420	.3415
	8-351⑤	45	44	215 @ 1.34	1 25/32	.0010-.0027	.0010-.0027	.3420	.3415
	8-351⑥	45	44	209 @ 1.42	1 13/16	.0010-.0027	.0015-.0032	.3420	.3415
	8-351⑦	45	44	285 @ 1.31	1 13/16	.0010-.0027	.0015-.0032	.3420	.3415
	8-428	②	③	265 @ 1.31	1 13/16	.0015-.0032	.0015-.0032	.3715	.3710
	8-429	45	44	253 @ 1.33	1 13/16	.0010-.0027	.0010-.0027	.3420	.3420
	8-429④	②	③	315 @ 1.31	1 13/16	.0010-.0024	.0020-.0034	.3715	.3705
	8-429⑧	②	③	306 @ 1.36	1 13/16	.0010-.0024	.0020-.0034	.3420	.3417
'71	6-170, 200	45	44	150 @ 1.22	1 19/32	.0008-.0025	.0010-.0027	.3104	.3102
	6-250	45	44	150 @ 1.22	1 19/32	.0008-.0025	.0010-.0027	.3104	.3102
	8-302	45	44	180 @ 1.23	1 21/32	.0010-.0027	.0015-.0032	.3420	.3415
	8-302④	45	44	315 @ 1.31	1 13/16	.0010-.0027	.0015-.0032	.3420	.3415
	8-351⑤	45	44	215 @ 1.34	1 25/32	.0010-.0027	.0015-.0032	.3420	.3415
	8-351⑥	45	44	210 @ 1.42	1 13/16	.0010-.0027	.0015-.0032	.3420	.3415
	8-351⑦	45	44	285 @ 1.31	1 13/16	.0010-.0027	.0015-.0032	.3420	.3415
	8-429	45	45	229 @ 1.33	1 13/16	.0010-.0027	.0010-.0027	.3420	.3420

VALVE SPECIFICATIONS

Year	Engine No. Cyl. Displacement (cu in.)	Seat Angle (deg)	Face Angle (deg)	Spring Test Pressure (lbs @ in.)	Spring Installed Height (in.)	STEM TO GUIDE Clearance (in.) Intake	Exhaust	STEM Diameter (in.) Intake	Exhaust
'72	6-170, 200	45	44	150 @ 1.22	1 19/32	.0008-.0025	.0010-.0027	.3104	.3102
	6-250	45	44	150 @ 1.22	1 19/32	.0008-.0025	.0010-.0027	.3104	.3102
	8-302	45	44	200 @ 1.23	1 11/16	.0010-.0027	.0015-.0032	.3420	.3415
	8-351⑤	45	44	200 @ 1.34	1 25/32	.0010-.0027	.0015-.0032	.3420	.3415
	8-351⑥	45	44	210 @ 1.42	1 13/16	.0010-.0027	.0015-.0032	.3420	.3415
	8-351⑦	45	44	285 @ 1.23	1 13/16	.0010-.0027	.0015-.0032	.3420	.3415
	8-351④	45	44	315 @ 1.23	1 13/16	.0010-.0027	.0015-.0032	.3420	.3415
	8-400	45	44	226 @ 1.39	1 13/16	.0010-.0027	.0015-.0032	.3420	.3415
	8-429	45	45	229 @ 1.33	1 13/16	.0010-.0027	.0010-.0027	.3420	.3420
'73-	6-200	45	46	150 @ 1.22	1 19/32	.0008-.0025	.0010-.0027	.3104	.3102
'77	6-250	45	46	150 @ 1.22	1 19/32	.0008-.0025	.0010-.0027	.3104	.3102
	8-302	45	46	200 @ 1.22	1 9/16	.0010-.0027	.0015-.0032	.3420	.3415
	8-351⑤	45	46	200 @ 1.34	1 25/32	.0010-.0027	.0015-.0032	.3420	.3415
	8-351⑥	45	46	282 @ 1.32	1 13/16	.0010-.0027	.0015-.0032	.3420	.3415
	8-351⑦	45	46	285 @ 1.32	1 13/16	.0010-.0027	.0015-.0032	.3420	.3415
	8-400	45	46	226 @ 1.39	1 13/16	.0010-.0027	.0015-.0032	.3420	.3415
	8-460	45	46	253 @ 1.33	1 13/16	.0010-.0027	.0010-.0027	.3420	.3420

① Not used
② Intake valve seat angle 30°
   Exhaust valve seat angle 45°
③ Intake valve face angle 29°
   Exhaust valve face angle 44°

④ Boss
⑤ Windsor heads
⑥ Cleveland or modified Cleveland 2 bbl
⑦ Cleveland or modified Cleveland 4 bbl
⑧ Cobra Jet

CRANKSHAFT AND CONNECTING ROD SPECIFICATIONS

All measurements are given in inches

Year	Engine No. Cyl. Displacement (cu in.)	Main Brg. Journal Dia	CRANKSHAFT Main Brg. Oil Clearance	Shaft End-Play	Thrust on No.	Journal Diameter	CONNECTING ROD Oil Clearance	Side Clearance
'70-'77	6-170	2.2482-2.2490	.0005-.0022	.004-.008	3	2.1232-2.1240	.0008-.0024	.003-.010
	6-200	2.2482-2.2490	.0005-.0022	.004-.008	5	2.1232-2.1240	.0008-.0024	.003-.010
	6-250	2.3982-2.3990	.0005-.0022	.004-.008	5	2.1232-2.1240	.0008-.0024	.003-.010
	8-302	2.2482-2.2490	.0005-.0024⑤⑪	.004-.008	3	2.1228-2.1236①	.0008-.0026②	.010-.020
	8-351W	2.9994-3.0002	.0013-.0030⑩	.004-.008	3	2.3103-2.3111	.0008-.0026	.010-.020
	8-351C or M	2.7484-2.7492⑫	.0009-.0026⑦	.004-.008	3	2.3103-2.3111	.0008-.0026	.010-.020
	8-400	2.9994-3.0002	.0011-.0028	.004-.008	3	2.3103-2.3111	.0008-.0026⑦⑨	.010-.020
	8-428	2.7484-2.7492	.0010-.0020	.004-.010	3	2.4380-2.4388	.0011-.0026⑨	.010-.020
	8-429, 460	2.9994-3.0002	.0010-.0020③⑧	.004-.008	3	2.4992-2.5000	.0008-.0028④	.010-.020

① Boss 302—2.1222-2.1230
② Boss 302—.0015-.0025
③ Boss 429—.0010-.0025
④ Boss 429—.0015-.0025
⑤ 302—.0001-.0005 No. 1 bearing only
⑥ Not used

⑦ Boss 351, 351 HO and 351 C or M 4-bbl—.0011-.0015
⑧ No. 1—.0010-.0015
⑨ .008-.0015 in. in 1974-77
⑩ .008-.0026 in. in 1974-77
⑪ .0005-.0015 Falcon in 1974-77
⑫ 8-351C given; 8-351M—2.9994-3.0002

TORQUE SPECIFICATIONS

All readings in ft lbs

Year	Engine No. Cyl. Displacement (cu in.)	Cylinder Head Bolts*	Rod Bearing Bolts	Main Bearing Bolts	Crankshaft Pulley or Damper Bolt	Flywheel to Crankshaft Bolts	MANIFOLD Intake	MANIFOLD Exhaust
'70-'73	6-170, 200, 250	70-75	19-24②	60-70	85-100	75-85	—	13-18
	8-302	65-72	19-24③	60-70④	70-90	75-85	23-25	12-16
	8-351	95-100①	40-45⑥	95-105⑦	70-90	75-85	23-25 (5/16) 28-32 (3/8) 6-9 (1/4)	12-22
	8-400	95-105⑨	40-45	⑩	70-90	75-85	21-25 (5/16) 27-33 (3/8) 6-9 (1/4)	12-16
	8-428	80-90	53-58	95-105	70-90	75-85	32-35	18-24
	8-429, 460	130-140	40-45	95-105⑤	70-90	75-85	25-30	28-33
	8-429 Boss	90-95	85-90	70-80	70-90	75-85	25-30	28-33
'74-'77	6-200	70-75	19-24	60-70	85-100	75-85	—	13-18
	6-250	70-75	21-26	60-70	85-100	75-85	—	13-18
	8-302	65-72	19-24	60-70	70-90	75-85	19-27	12-16
	8-351W	105-112	40-45	95-105	70-90	75-85	19-27	18-24
	8-351C, 351M	95-105⑧	40-45	⑨	70-90	75-85	⑩	12-22
	8-400	95-105⑧	40-45	⑨	70-90	75-85	⑩	12-16
	8-460	130-140	40-45	95-105	70-90	75-85	22-32	28-33

① 351 Boss and HO three steps—40, 80, 120 ft. lbs.
② 250—21-26
③ 302 Boss—40-45
④ 302 Boss—outer bolts 35-40
⑤ 7/16 in. bolts—70-80
⑥ 351 Boss and HO—43-48 ft. lbs.
⑦ 3/8 in. bolts—34-45 ft. lbs.
⑧ Three steps—55, 75, then maximum figure
⑨ 1/2 in—13 bolts, 95-105, 3/8 in—16 bolts, 35-45
⑩ 5/16 in. bolt, 21-25; 3/8 in. bolt, 22-32; 1/4 in. bolt, 6-9
* Tighten cylinder head bolts in three steps

RING GAP

All measurements are given in inches

Year	Engine	Top Compression	Bottom Compression
'70-'73	6-170, 200, 250 8-302, 351, 400, 428, 429, 460	.010-.020	.010-.020
'74-'77	6-200, 250	.008-.016	.008-.016
	8-302, 351, 400, 460	.010-.020	.010-.020

Year	Engine	Oil Control
'70-'77	6-170, 200, 250	.015-.055
'70-'71	8-302, 351	.015-.069
'70-'71	8-428, 429	.010-.035
'72-'77	8-302, 351	.015-.055①
'72-'77	8-400	.015-.069
'72-'77	8-429, 460	.015-.055

① .015-.069 in Cleveland built engine through 1973

RING SIDE CLEARANCE

All measurements are given in inches

Year	Engine	Top Compression	Bottom Compression
'70-'77	All engines	.002-.004	.002-.004

Year	Engine	Oil Control
'70-'77	All engines	Snug

PISTON CLEARANCE

Year	Engine	Piston-to-Bore Minimum	Clearance (in.) Maximum
'70-'77	302, 351W	0.0018	0.0026
'70	428	0.0015	0.0023
'70-'77	170, 200, 250	0.0013	0.0021
'70-'77	351C, 351M, 400, 429, 460	0.0014	0.0022
'70	429CJ, 429SCJ	0.0030	0.0038
'71	429CJ, 429SCJ	0.0042	0.0050
'72	351HO (CJ)	0.0034	0.0042

WHEEL ALIGNMENT SPECIFICATIONS

Year	Model	CASTER Range (deg)	CASTER Pref Setting (deg)	CAMBER Range (deg)	CAMBER Pref Setting (deg)	Toe-in (in.)	Steering Axis Inclin. (deg)	WHEEL PIVOT RATIO (deg) Inner Wheel	WHEEL PIVOT RATIO (deg) Outer Wheel
'70-'71	Montego, Falcon, Torino	1¼N to ¼N	¾N	½N to 1P	¼P	⅛ to ⅜	7⅔②	20	③
	Cougar & Mustang	1N to 1P	0	0 to 1½P⑤	1P	¹⁄₁₆ to ⁵⁄₁₆	6¾	20	18⅔
	Maverick, Comet	1½N to ½P	½N	½N to ¼P	¼P	¹⁄₁₆ to ⁵⁄₁₆	6¾	20	18¾④
'72	Torino, Montego	1¼N to 2¾P	¾P	¼N to 1¾P	¾P	¹⁄₁₆ to ⁷⁄₁₆	7⅔	20	17¾
	Mustang, Cougar	2N to 2P	0	½N to 1½P	½P	¹⁄₁₆ to ⅜	6¾	20	17¾
	Maverick, Comet	2½N to 1½P	½N	¾N to 1¼P	¼P	¹⁄₁₆ to ⅜	6¾	20	18½④
'73	Torino, Montego	¾N to 2¼P	¾P	¼N to 1¾P	¾P	³⁄₁₆ to ⁹⁄₁₆	7⅔	20	17.73
	Mustang, Cougar	2N to 2P	0	½N to 1½P	½P	¹⁄₁₆ to ⅜	6¾	20	17.72
	Maverick, Comet	2½N to 1½P	½N	¾N to 1¼P	¼P	¹⁄₁₆ to ⅜	6¾	20	18.44④
'74	Torino, Montego, Cougar, Elite	½P to 3½P	2P	⑥	⑦	0 to ⅜	9	20	18.11
	Maverick, Comet	2½N to 1½P	½N	¾N to 1¼P	¼P	¹⁄₁₆ to ⅜	6¾	20	18.39④
'75-'77	Torino, Montego, Cougar, Elite, LTD II, 1977 Thunderbird	3¼P to 4¾P	4P	⑨	⑩	0 to ⅜	9⑪	20	18.06⑫
	Maverick, Comet, Monarch, Granada	1¼N to ¼P	½N	½N to 1P	¼P	0 to ⅜	6¾	20	⑧

① Not used
② Falcon—6⅔
③ Falcon—18°6'; others with manual steering—17°19'; power steering—17°49'
④ 18.16° for power steering.
⑤ 1970 models—¼P to 1¾P
⑥ Left—⅜N to 1⅝P
    Right—⅞N to 1⅛P
⑦ Left—⅝P
    Right—⅛P
⑧ Maverick/Comet w/PS—18.13; w/o PS—18.36
    Granada/Monarch w/PS—18.20; w/o PS—18.43
⑨ Left—¼N to 1¼P
    Right—½N to 1P
⑩ Left—½P
    Right—¼P
⑪ Thunderbird—9½
⑫ LTD II—17.73
N Negative   P Positive

NOTE: Mustang models through 1973 are covered in this section. Refer to the Bobcat, Mustang II, Pinto car section for coverage of 1974 and later Mustang II models. Beginning 1977, Thunderbird models are covered in this section. See the Ford, Mercury, Thunderbird car section for coverage of Thunderbird models through 1976.

CHARGING SYSTEM

All Ford cars use alternating current (AC) charging systems.

Charging system troubleshooting and repair procedures can be found in the Unit Repair Section under Charging and Starting Systems.

Alternator

The alternator is covered in the Charging and Starting Systems Unit Repair Section.

Alternator Removal and Installation

1. Disconnect the battery ground cable.
2. Loosen the alternator mounting bolts and remove the adjustment arm to alternator attaching bolt. Disengage the alternator belt.
3. Remove the electrical connectors from the alternator and remove the alternator. On some models it is necessary to remove the alternator mounting bolts and the alternator wiring ground bolt from engine to gain access to the electrical connectors.
4. Reverse above procedure to reinstall.

Voltage Regulator Removal and Installation

1. Disconnect the negative battery cable.
2. Remove the regulator mounting screws.

3. Remove the cable quick-disconnect from the old regulator and attach to the new regulator.
4. Place the mounting bracket for the radio suppression capacitor over the hole for the lower regulator's mounting screw and install the screws.
5. Connect the negative battery cable.
6. Test the system for proper voltage regulation.

STARTING SYSTEM

Starting system troubleshooting and repair procedures can be found in the Charging and Starting Systems Unit Repair Section.

All models, except Torinos, Elites, Montegos, Mustangs, and Cougars through 1976 with 429 or 460 V8 have a positive engagement starter with a self-contained engagement mechanism. The 429 and 460 V8 engined models use a solenoid activated starter to which is mounted an outboard solenoid. There is no difference in procedures for removing or installing these two types of starters.

Starter Removal and Installation

Due to interference of the exhaust inlet pipe on some models, the steering idler arm must be lowered to provide clearance for starter removal.

1. Disconnect the starter cable at the starter terminal, remove the flywheel housing to starter retaining screws. Remove the starter assembly and the rubber dust ring.
2. Position the rubber dust ring on the flywheel housing.
3. Position the starter assembly to the flywheel housing, and begin on the starter retaining screws. On a car with an automatic transmission, the transmission dipstick tube bracket is mounted under the starter side mounting bolt. Snug all bolts, then tighten to 15 ft. lbs., tightening the middle bolt first.

NOTE: Intermittent starter operation on solenoid starter motor equipped 429 and 460 V8s may be due to the loosening of screws and terminals on the solenoid switch assembly. To remedy this, apply a small amount of bolt locking compound.

IGNITION SYSTEM

Beginning 1974, Ford uses a solid state or "breakerless" ignition system on all 200 cu in. and larger engines in the state of California, and on all 400 and 460 cu in. V8s

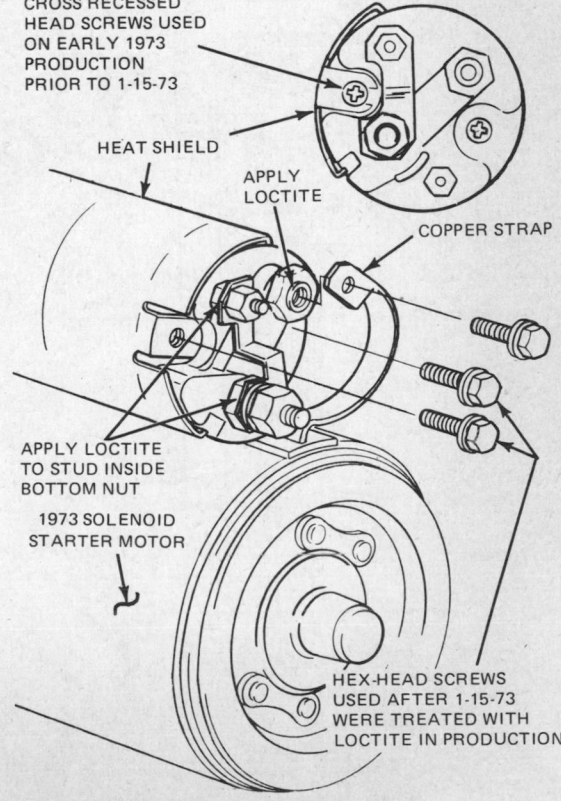

CROSS RECESSED HEAD SCREWS USED ON EARLY 1973 PRODUCTION PRIOR TO 1-15-73

HEAT SHIELD

APPLY LOCTITE

COPPER STRAP

APPLY LOCTITE TO STUD INSIDE BOTTOM NUT

1973 SOLENOID STARTER MOTOR

HEX-HEAD SCREWS USED AFTER 1-15-73 WERE TREATED WITH LOCTITE IN PRODUCTION

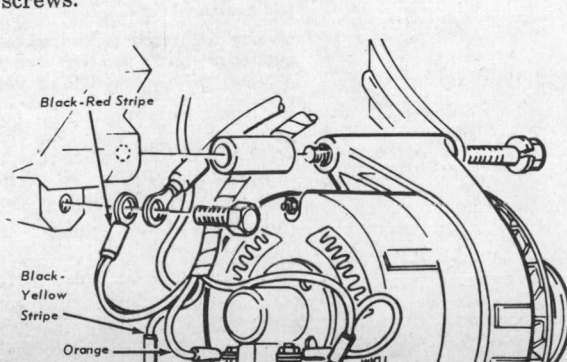

Black-Red Stripe

Black-Yellow Stripe

Orange

Black-Red Stripe

Typical alternator mounting (© Ford Motor Co)

Solenoid-actuated starter motor (© Ford Motor Co)

nationwide. All engines assembled after May, 1974 have the system.

Starting 1975, breakerless ignition is standard on all Ford engines. This system is unique in that it eliminates the contact breaker points, replacing them with a permanent magnet low voltage generator.

Beginning 1977, an improved breakerless ignition system called "DuraSpark" is standard. Two versions of the DuraSpark system are used: one for California cars and one for all other engines. Both utilize higher spark voltages of up to 42,000 volts to allow wider spark plug gaps necessary to fire leaner air/fuel mixtures.

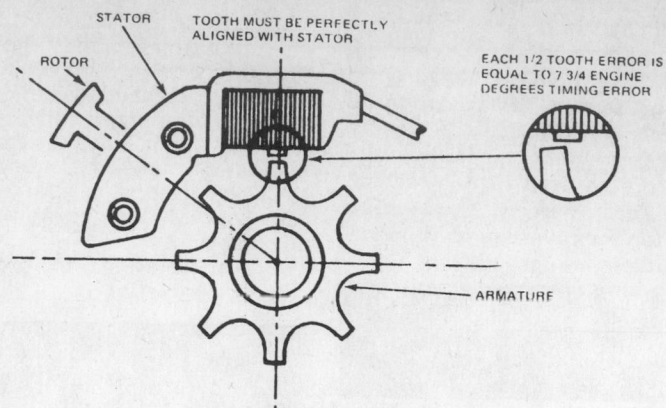

Breakerless ignition distributor static timing position
(© Ford Motor Co)

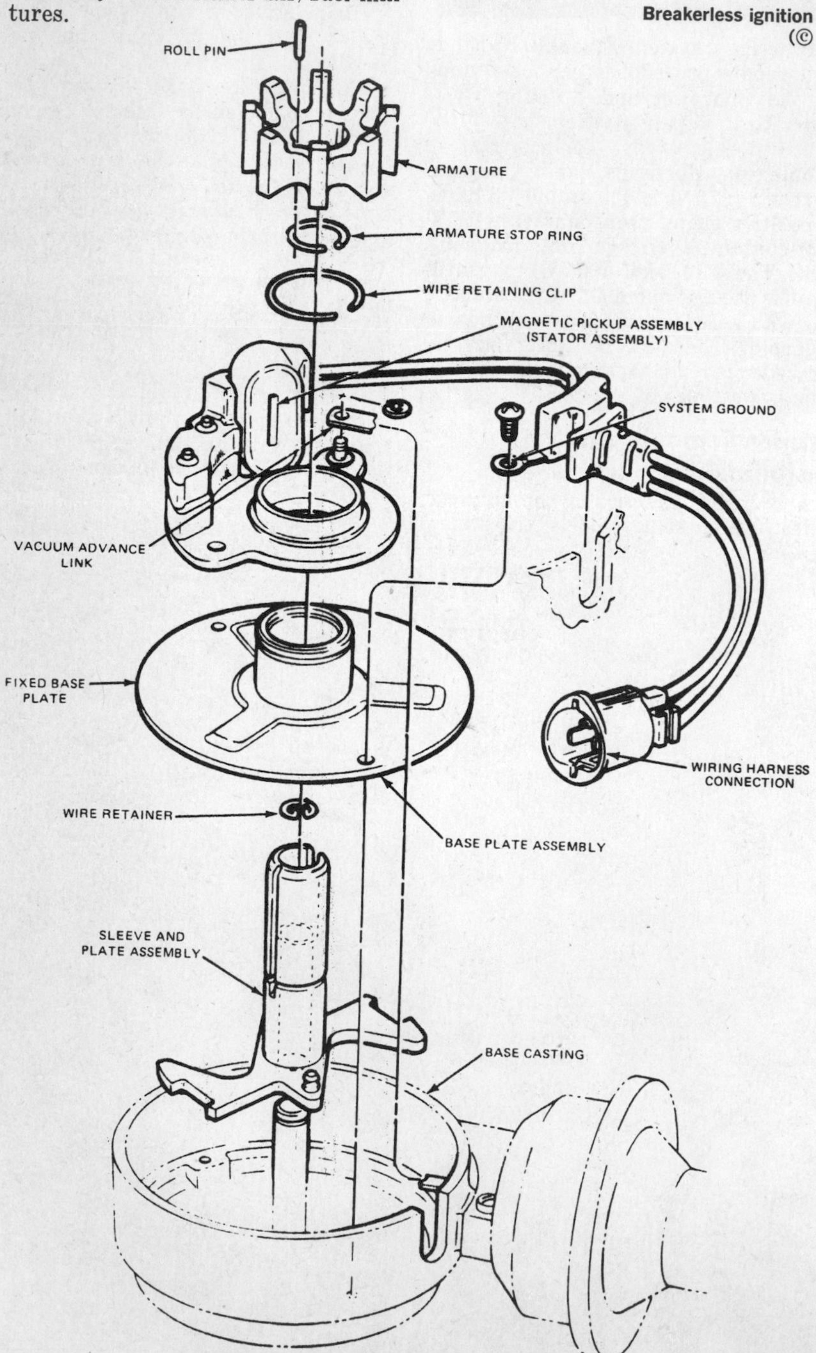

NOTE: On 1975 and later models there is a terminal on the coil provided for connecting a tachometer. The terminal is labeled "Tach Test" and has a small arrowhead pointing to the proper terminal.

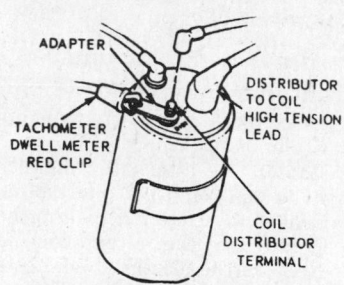

Installing dwell/tachometer adaptor on coil—1974 and earlier models equipped with conventional ignition
(© Ford Motor Co)

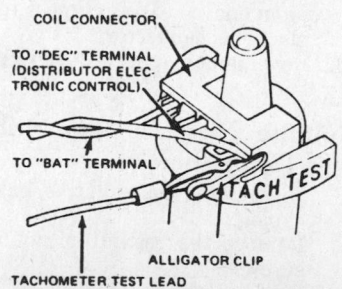

Attaching dwell/tachometer lead to coil connector—1975 and later models equipped with breakerless ignition
(© Ford Motor Co)

Distributor Removal

1. Remove distributor cap. Disconnect the primary wire at the coil and the vacuum control line at the distributor.
2. Scribe a mark on the distributor body, showing position of the rotor. Then, scribe another mark on the distributor body and engine block, showing the position of the body in the block. These marks can be used to advantage when reassembling the distributor in an undisturbed engine.

Breakerless V8 distributor diassembled
(© Ford Motor Co)

3. Remove the screw, lockwasher and hold-down clamp. Pull the distributor out of the block. Do not rotate crankshaft while distributor is out of block because it will then be necessary to re-time ignition.

Distributor Installation

1. If the engine was not cranked while the distributor was removed, install the distributor in the engine, aligning the tip of the rotor with the marks that were made on the distributor body and the engine. Proceed to Step 3. If the engine was cranked while the distributor was removed, rotate the crankshaft to bring No. 1 piston to T.D.C. of its compression stroke.
2. Position distributor in the block with the rotor at No. 1 firing position. Be sure that the oil pump intermediate driveshaft is properly seated in the oil pump.
3. Install, but do not tighten, the distributor retaining clamp and screw.
4. Rotate the distributor body clockwise until the breaker points start to open.
5. Tighten the retaining clamp screw.
6. Install distributor cap.
7. Connect distributor primary wire.
8. Start engine and run long enough to obtain engine operating temperature.
9. Idle engine to 500 rpm. Then, with a timing light, check the timing marks at the front pulley and make necessary corrections.
10. Connect the vacuum control line to the distributor and check advance characteristics with the timing light when the engine is accelerated.

Contact Point Replacement and Adjustment—1974 and earlier models

1. Unsnap the distributor cap retaining clips and position the cap clear of the breaker plate. Remove the rotor by pulling it straight up.
2. Remove the metal point shield, if so equipped.
3. Disconnect the primary lead and condenser wires from the contact point assembly. On dual-point distributors, remove the jumper strap also.
4. Remove the contact point and condenser retaining screws. Lift the contact point assembly and condenser from the distributor.
5. Lightly lubricate the distributor cam with heat-resistant lubricant.
6. Place the new contact point as-

sembly and condenser in the distributor. Install, but do not tighten, the retaining screws.
7. On all V8 engines, except those equipped with a centrifugal advance distributor, place the ground wire under the contact point assembly screw farthest from the contacts. This ground wire is positioned under the condenser retaining screw on all six-cylinder engines.
8. Turn the engine until the rubbing block on the point assembly is resting on the high point of the distributor cam lobe. Insert a feeler gauge of specified thickness between the contact points and adjust the gap. Tighten the retaining screw and remove the feeler gauge.
9. Connect the primary and condenser wires to the contact point assembly in the same order as they were removed. On those distributors with a metal point shield, the wires should be positioned 180 degrees (180°) from

each other. Install the shield.
10. Install the rotor and distributor cap.
11. If a dwell meter is available, check to see that the distributor dwell is within specifications.

Ignition Timing

1. Locate the timing marks and pointer on the lower engine pulley and engine's front cover.
2. Clean the marks and apply chalk or bright-colored paint to the pointer.
3. Attach a timing light according to the manufacturer's specifications.
4. Disconnect and plug all vacuum lines leading to the distributor.
5. If the recommended engine idle speed is in excess of 500 rpm, set the idle at 500 rpm for setting the timing. If the recommended idle speed is below 500 rpm, do not alter it.
6. Aim the timing light at the timing mark and pointer on the front of the engine. If the marks

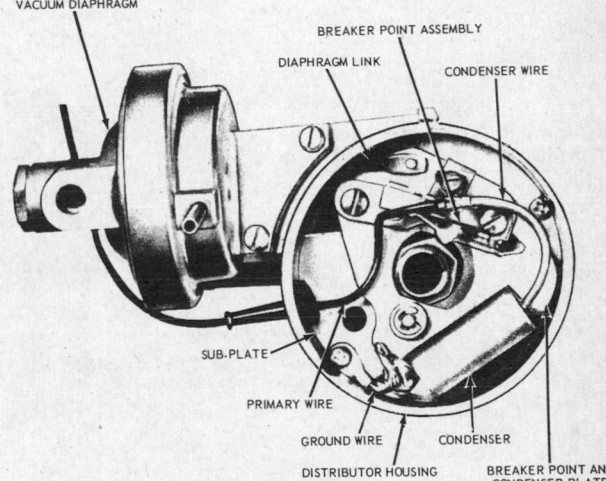

Breaker plate installed—6 cylinder engine, dual diaphragm distributor
(© Ford Motor Co)

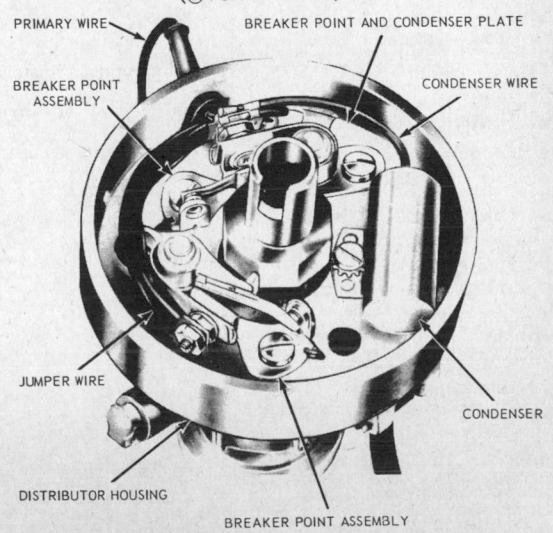

Dual point distributor breaker plate (© Ford Motor Co)

align when the timing light flashes, remove the timing light, set the idle to its proper specification, and connect the vacuum lines at the distributor. If the marks do not align when the light flashes, turn the engine off and loosen the distributor hold-down clamp slightly.

7. Start the engine again, and observe the alignment of the timing marks. To advance the timing, turn the distributor counter-clockwise, on six-cylinder engines, or clockwise, for V8 engines. When altering the timing, it is wise to tap the distributor lightly with a wooden hammer handle to move it in the desired direction. Grasping the distributor with your hand may result in a painful electric shock. When the timing marks are aligned, turn the engine off and tighten the distributor hold-down clamp.

FUEL SYSTEM

Fuel Pump

On 6-cylinder engines the fuel pump is located on the lower, left center of the engine block. The V8 fuel pump is mounted on the left side of the cylinder front cover.

1975-76 Police Interceptor 460 V8s use a tank-mounted electric fuel pump.

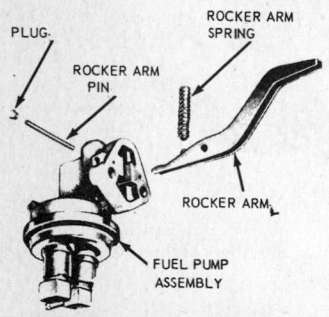

Typical fuel pump—V8 shown

(© Ford Motor Co)

Removal and Installation —All Models except 460 PI V8

1. Remove the inlet and outlet lines from the pump.
2. Remove the fuel pump retaining screws and remove the pump and gasket.
3. Clean all gasket material from the pump mounting surface on the engine, and apply a coat of oil-resistant sealer to the new gasket.
4. Position pump on engine and install retaining screws.
5. Reinstall lines, start engine and check for leaks.

NOTE: if resistance is felt while positioning the fuel pump on the block, the camshaft eccentric is in the high position. To ease installation, connect a remote engine starter switch to the engine and "tap" remote switch until resistance fades.

Fuel Filter

All models use a non-serviceable in-line fuel filter which is located at the carburetor fuel inlet.

Fuel Filter Removal and Installation

The filter is removed by removing the air cleaner, loosening the hose clamp on the inlet line, and unscrewing the filter. When installing, use a new hose clamp to prevent leakage.

Idle Speed and Mixture Adjustments

NOTE: Adjust with air cleaner installed.

Idle Speed Adjustment

This is the procedure for adjusting all carburetors; any exceptions are listed below.

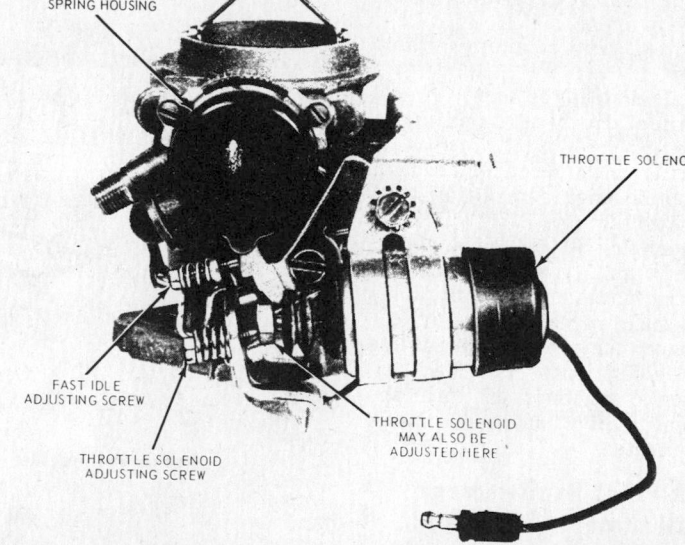

Carburetor adjustments—solenoid equipped Carter RBS IV (© Ford Motor Co)

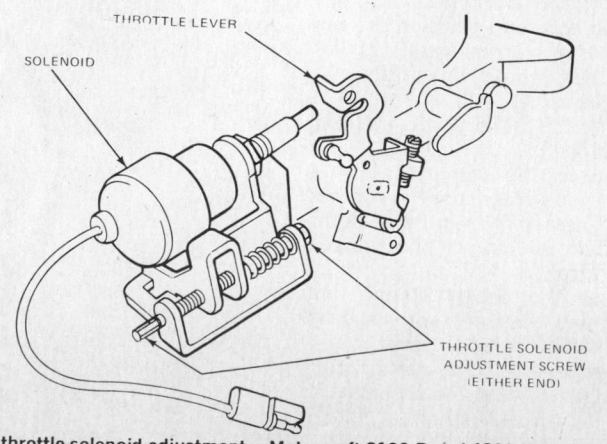

1972-74 throttle solenoid adjustment—Motorcraft 2100-D and 4300 installation shown

(© Ford Motor Co)

NOTE: If the following adjustment fails to produce a satisfactory idle, the following items should be checked: vacuum leaks, ignition wiring continuity, spark plug condition, dwell angle, breaker point condition, ignition timing, carburetor float level, PCV valve condition, valve clearance, cylinder compression, and, failing all else, check for an overly lean air fuel mixture with a CO meter of known accuracy

1. Run engine at fast idle to equalize operating temperature.
2. Make sure the choke plate is fully released.
3. Turn headlights on high beam. On models equipped with an automatic transmission, apply the parking brake and put the transmission selector lever in Drive.
4. If engine is equipped with hot idle compensator valve, make sure it is fully seated in the closed position.
5. Attach tachometer of known accuracy to the engine.
6. On cars equipped with air conditioning, the idle speed is set with

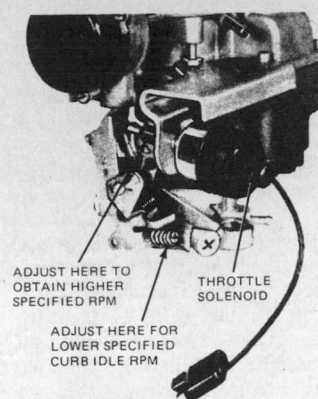

Carburetor adjustments—solenoid equipped Carter YF IV; Carter YFA similar
(© Ford Motor Co)

ADJUST HERE TO OBTAIN HIGHER SPECIFIED RPM

THROTTLE SOLENOID

ADJUST HERE FOR LOWER SPECIFIED CURB IDLE RPM

the air conditioner turned OFF.

7. On models equipped with a temperature sensing valve in the distributor vacuum line, remove and plug the vacuum hoses from the intake manifold to the valve, at the valve located in the intake manifold. Also plug the intake manifold hose fitting on the valve.

8. Make sure the dashpot is working freely and not binding.

9. If it is not possible to adjust the idle speed with the air cleaner installed, the engine idle speed must be rechecked after installing the air cleaner. On cars with vacuum controlled heat ducts in the air cleaner, the vacuum line must be plugged if the carburetor is to be adjusted with the air cleaner removed.

10. On carburetors which do not have an electric throttle solenoid, turn the idle speed adjusting screw inward or outward to obtain the specified idle speed. On 1970-71 models which have a throttle solenoid, turn the solenoid plunger in or out to obtain the higher of the two idle speeds listed in the "Tune-up Specifications" table. On 1972-77 models which are equipped with a throttle solenoid, turn the throttle solenoid adjustment screw inward or outward to obtain the higher of the two idle speeds listed in the "Tune-up Specifications" table.

11. If equipped with a throttle solenoid, disconnect the lead wire from the solenoid and turn the curb idle adjusting screw on the carburetor to obtain the lower of the two idle speeds listed in the "Tune-up Specifications" table. On models equipped with an automatic transmission, place the transmission selector lever in Park or neutral before adjusting the lower idle speed.

NOTE: with the electric solenoid

disengaged, the carburetor adjusting screw must make contact with the throttle shaft to prevent the throttle plates from jamming in the throttle bore when the engine is shut off.

Fuel Mixture Adjustment

Adjust by turning the idle mixture adjusting screw (s) inward to obtain the smoothest idle possible *within the range of the idle limiters. Limiter caps should not be removed*, unless a CO meter is available to bring the emissions within the legal limits.

NOTE: The factory recommended procedure for adjusting the idle mixture on 1975 and later models requires the addition of an artificial mixture enrichment substance (propane) to the air intake. This method requires special tools not generally available to the public. The previous procedure is specifically recommended by the factory only for models through 1974.

Dashpot Adjustment

1. With engine idle speed and mixture properly adjusted and with engine at operating temperature, loosen dashpot lock nut.

2. Hold throttle in closed position and depress dashpot plunger. Measure clearance between plunger and cam. Adjust dashpot nut to give proper clearance.

NOTE: Not all engines have dashpots and not all are adjusted in this manner. This chart applies only to models mentioned.

PLUNGER DEPRESSED

ADJUST TO SPECIFIED CLEARANCE

Anti-stall dashpot adjustment
(© Ford Motor Co)

Year, Model and Engine	Clearance Manual (in.)	Clearance Automatic (in.)
1970-71 170 and 200 six cylinder if so equipped	7/64	7/64
1970-71 Montego, Fairlane, and Mustang 250 six		7/32
1970 302 2V without air conditioning		1/8
1970-71 351 Windsor 2V without air conditioning		1/8
1970-71 351 Cleveland 2V without air conditioning		1/8
1970-71 351 Cleveland 4V without air conditioning		0.080
1970 429 4V Montego and Fairlane	0.070	0.070
1970 428 CJ without air conditioning	0.140	0.200

In the 6-cylinder engine, coolant flows from the cylinder head, past the thermostat (if it is open) and into the radiator upper tank. In the V8 engine, coolant from each cylinder head flows through water passages in the intake manifold, then past the thermostat (if it is open) and into the radiator upper tank.

A single water pump assembly is used. The pump has a sealed bearing integral with the water pump shaft. The bearing requires no lubrication. There is a bleed hole in the water pump housing. This is not a lubrication hole.

Some models are equipped with a coolant recovery or "constant full" system. These systems have a non-vented radiator cap that forces coolant expansion into an expansion reservoir. When adding coolant to these systems, add coolant to the reservoir only, not the radiator.

Radiator

Removal

1. Drain cooling system.
2. Disconnect upper and lower hoses at the radiator.
3. On automatic transmission-equipped cars, disconnect oil cooler lines at radiator.
4. On vehicles equipped with a fan shroud, remove the shroud retaining screws and position the shroud out of the way.
5. Remove radiator attaching bolts and lift out the radiator.

Installation

1. If a new radiator is to be installed, transfer the petcock from the old radiator to the new one. On cars equipped with automatic transmissions, transfer the oil cooler line fittings from the old radiator to the new one.
2. Position the radiator and install, but do not tighten, the radiator support bolts. On cars equipped with automatic transmissions, connect the oil cooler lines. Then tighten the radiator support bolts.
3. On vehicles equipped with a fan shroud, reinstall the shroud.
4. Connect the radiator hoses. Close the radiator petcock. Then fill and bleed the cooling system.
5. Start the engine and bring to operating temperature. Check for leaks.
6. On cars equipped with automatic transmissions, check the cooler lines for leaks and interference. Check transmission fluid level.

Water Pump Removal and Installation

1. Drain cooling system.
2. On 351C, 351M, and 400 V8, disconnect the negative battery cable.
3. On cars with power steering, remove the drive belt. On models with 428 engines, remove the power steering mounting retaining screws and remove the pump and bracket as an assembly and position it out of the way.
4. If the vehicle is equipped with air conditioning, remove the idler pulley bracket and air conditioner drive belt.
5. On engines with Thermactor, remove the belt.
6. Disconnect the lower radiator hose and heater hose from the water pump.
7. On cars equipped with a fan shroud, remove the retaining screws and position the shroud rearward.
8. Remove the fan and spacer from the engine, and if the car is equipped with a fan shroud, remove the fan and shroud from the engine as an assembly.
9. Loosen alternator mounting bolts, remove the alternator belt and remove the alternator adjusting arm bracket from the water pump.
10. Loosen bypass hose at water pump.
11. Remove water pump retaining screws and remove pump from engine.
12. Clean any gasket material from the pump mounting surface, and on 429 V8 remove the water pump backing plate and replace the gasket.

NOTE: The 250 6-cylinder engine originally uses a one-piece gasket for the cylinder front cover and water pump. Trim away the old gasket at the edge of the cylinder cover and replace with service gasket.

13. Remove the heater hose fitting from the old pump and install it on the new pump.
14. Coat both sides of the new gasket with a water-resistant sealer, then re-install pump reversing the above procedure.

Thermostat Removal and Installation

1. Open the drain cock and drain the radiator so the coolant level is below the coolant outlet elbow which houses the thermostat.
2. Remove the outlet elbow retaining bolts and position the elbow sufficiently clear of the intake manifold or cylinder head to provide access to the thermostat.
3. Remove the thermostat by rotating it in a counterclockwise direction and lifting it from the housing.
4. Clean the mating surfaces of the outlet elbow and the engine to remove all old gasket material and sealer. Coat the new gasket with water-resistant sealer and install it on the engine. Install the thermostat in the outlet elbow. On the above-mention engines (step three), the thermostat must be rotated clockwise to lock it in position.
5. Install the outlet elbow and retaining bolts on the engine. Torque the bolts to 12–15 ft lbs.
6. Refill the radiator. Run the engine at operating temperature and check for leaks. Recheck the coolant level.

EMISSION CONTROLS

All Models

All Ford cars covered in this text use positive crankcase ventilation (PCV) systems. The PCV system routes a harmful mixture of blow-by gases and condensation vapors, which were formerly dispelled into the atmosphere, through a modulating valve (PCV valve) and into the intake manifold where they combine with the carburetor air fuel mixture and are burned in the combustion chamber.

1970-71

The fuel evaporative emission control system was used on California models in 1970, and nationwide in 1971. This system eliminates pollution due to evaporating fuel by channeling the breathing of the fuel tank and by the venting of the carburetor float bowl through a canister filled with activated charcoal, condensing the fuel vapors and returning them to the fuel system.

The IMCO system of emission control was further extended in 1970 to become the Distributor Modulator (Dist-O-Vac) System. The Dist-O-Vac system incorporated all of the IMCO features but included three units of equipment which control spark advance in a more sophisticated manner. A speed sensor is located between two sections of the speedometer cable and generates a small current which increases in direct proportion to speed. A thermal switch is located in the right door pillar and activates at outside temperatures of 58° or higher. The impulses of both are fed into the electronic control amplifier. The distributor vacuum advance hose is connected from the carburetor, through the electronic control amplifier, to the distributor. When ambient temperature is above 58°, the contacts in the temperature switch open, and a plunger in the amplifier prevents vacuum from being supplied to the distributor. When vehicle speed reaches approximately 30 mph, the signal from the speed sensor causes the control amplifier to open the vacuum line to the distributor and ignition timing is allowed to advance in the normal manner. When the ambient temperature is below 58°, the temperature switch closes, and normal vacuum is supplied to the distributor regardless of vehicle speed. In the event of engine overheating, the ported vacuum switch (PVS), a carryover from the IMCO system, overrides the electronic control modulator by connecting intake manifold vacuum to the distributor.

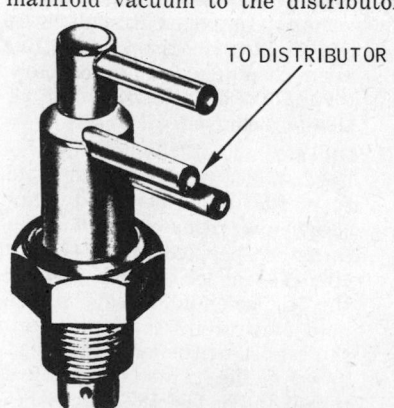

TO DISTRIBUTOR

Distributor vacuum control valve (ported vacuum switch)
(Ford Motor Co)

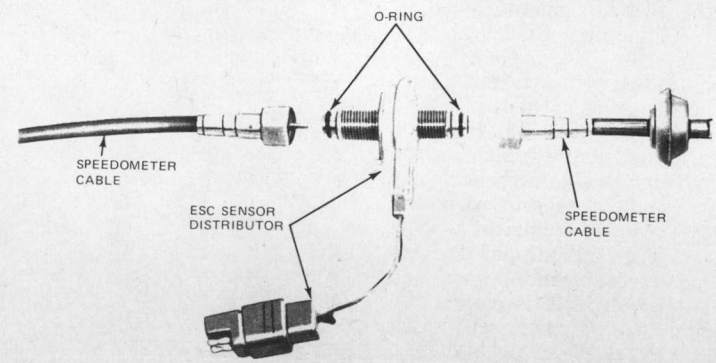

O-RING

SPEEDOMETER CABLE

ESC SENSOR DISTRIBUTOR

SPEEDOMETER CABLE

Speed sensor location (© Ford Motor Co)

1972

For 1972, the Dist-O-Vac system was replaced by two different spark control systems. The Electronic Spark Control (ESC) system is the same as the old Dist-O-Vac system except that the electronic control modulator was separated into two pieces, an amplifier and a distributor modulator valve. The amplifier judges the signals sent to it by the speed and temperature switches and tells the distributor modulator valve when to open and close and thus allow or prevent vacuum to reach the distributor. The Transmission Regulated Spark (TRS) is similar to the ESC system except that the speed sensor is replaced by a transmission switch. The switch is mounted on the side of the transmission and is hydraulically actuated on cars equipped with an automatic transmission and manually actuated on models equipped with a manual transmission. When the ambient temperature is above 55°, the transmission switch is closed whenever the transmission is in any gear other than high gear (manual transmission), or high gear or reverse (automatic transmission). When the transmission switch closes, it signals the distributor modulator valve to close and thus prevents carburetor vacuum from reaching the distributor. As in past systems, neither of these systems is functional below 55–58°, and both are bypassed by the PVS if the engine should overheat.

On most 1972 and later models, a spark delay valve was inserted into the vacuum advance line to the distributor. The valve closes under hard acceleration, blocking carburetor vacuum to the distributor for a predetermined period of seconds. The valves are color coded for identification purposes.

1973

1973 and later models utilize an Exhaust Gas Recirculation System (EGR) to control oxides of nitrogen. On V8 engines, exhaust gases travel through the exhaust gas crossover passage in the intake manifold. A portion of these gases is diverted into a spacer which is mounted under the carburetor The EGR control valve, which is attached to the rear of the spacer, consists of a vacuum diaphragm with an attached plunger which normally blocks off exhaust gases from entering the intake manifold. On 6 cylinder engines, an external tube carries exhaust manifold gases to the carburetor spacer. On all models except those equipped with a 250 six-cylinder and manual transmission, the EGR valve is controlled by a vacuum line from the carburetor which passes through a ported vacuum switch. The EGR ported vacuum

switch provides vacuum to the EGR valve at coolant temperature above 125°F. The vacuum diaphragm then opens the EGR valve permitting exhaust gases to flow through the carburetor spacer and enter the intake manifold where they combine with the fuel mixture and enter the combustion chambers. The exhaust gases are relatively oxygen-free, and tend to dilute the combustion charge. This lowers peak combustion temperature thereby reducing oxides of nitrogen.

1973-74 Torinos and Montegos equipped with a 250 six-cylinder engine and manual transmission have a combined spark control and EGR system called "TRS+1." The spark control portion of this system is identical to the TRS system described under "1972." Operation of the EGR control valve is governed by vacuum from either the distributor vacuum port on the carburetor or the EGR vacuum port. When the TRS system is not in operation. EGR valve vacuum comes from the EGR port on the carburetor. The vacuum passes through a coolant temperature vacuum valve and a three-way solenoid valve. The coolant valve blocks vacuum from the EGR valve until the engine coolant temperature has reached 60° F. The vacuum lines from both the EGR and distributor vacuum ports on the carburetor connect to the three-way solenoid valve. The third line is an outlet line to the EGR valve. When the TRS system is not in operation, the three-way solenoid valve is deenergized. When the TRS system is in operation, the solenoid is energized, blocking the EGR port on the three-way solenoid, and opening the distributor port to the EGR valve. When the transmission is shifted into high gear, the TRS and three-way solenoids are de-energized. This restores normal vacuum to the distributor and the EGR valve.

All models equipped with a 250 six-cylinder engine and automatic transmission and built prior to March 15, 1973, use another system to control

distributor spark advance. The system, known as the Temperature Activated Vacuum (TAV) system, contains a three-way solenoid valve, an ambient temperature switch, and a vacuum bleed line to the air cleaner. The operation of the three-way solenoid valve is identical to the valve described above for 250 manual transmission engines. The only difference is that the output line of the three-way valve is connected to the distributor. When the ambient temperature is above 60°, the contacts in the temperature sensor close and complete the circuit to the three-way solenoid. This energizes the solenoid and connects the EGR vacuum port on the carburetor to the distributor vaccum advance. When the ambient temperature is below 49°, the solenoid is de-energized and the distributor vacuum advance operates in the normal manner.

1973 Torino and Montego station wagons equipped with a 302 or 351W V8 and manual transmission and all 1973 models that are equipped with a 351C, 400, or 429 V8 built prior to March 15, 1973, use a Delay Vacuum By-Pass (DVB) spark control system. This system provides two paths by which carburetor vacuum can reach the distributor vacuum advance. The system consists of a spark delay valve, a check valve, a solenoid vacuum valve, and an ambient temperature switch. When the ambient temperature is below 49°F. the temperature switch contacts and the vacuum solenoid are open (de-energized). Under these conditions, vacuum will flow from the carburetor, through the open solenoid, and to the distributor. Since the spark delay valve resists the flow of carburetor vacuum, the vacuum will always flow through the vacuum solenoid when it is open, since this is the path of least resistance. When the ambient temperature rises above 60°F. the contacts in the temperature switch (which is located in the door post) close. This passes ignition switch current to the

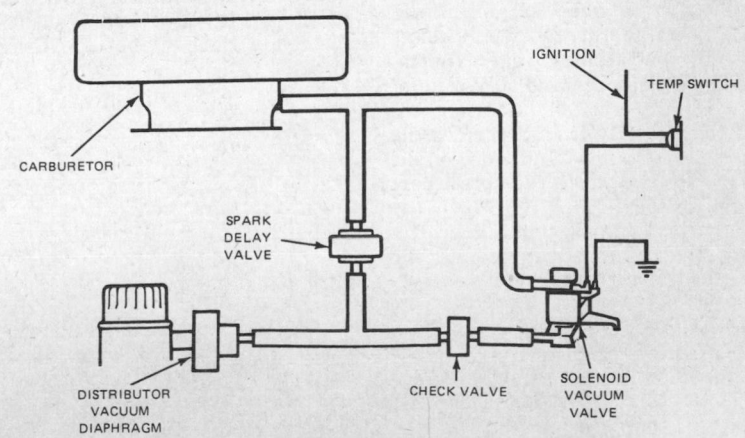

Delay vacuum by-pass system—DVB (© Ford Motor Co)

solenoid, energizing the solenoid. This blocks one of the vacuum paths. All distributor vacuum must now flow through the spark delay valve. When carburetor vacuum rises above a certain level on acceleration, a rubber valve in the spark delay valve blocks vacuum from passing through the valve for 5-30 seconds. After this delay, normal vacuum is supplied to the distributor. When the vacuum solenoid is closed (temperature above 60°), the vacuum line from the solenoid to the distributor is vented to atmosphere. To prevent the vacuum that is passing through the spark delay valve from escaping through the solenoid into the atmosphere, a one-way check valve is installed in the vacuum line from the solenoid to the distributor.

All 1973 and later models use an electric choke heating element. When ambient temperature is above 63°, and the ignition switch is turned on, a heating element in the choke housing raises the temperature of the choke bimetallic spring, thus preventing the choke from engaging.

1974

1974 models sold in California and all 1975 models are equipped with a Thermactor (air injection) system to reduce hydrocarbons and carbon monoxide. This system is used in addition to the previously mentioned EGR and IMCO systems, which are used to reduce oxides of nitrogen.

A Cold Temperature Actuated Vacuum (CTAV) System is installed on some 1973 models manfactured after March 15, 1973 and many 1974 models to control distributor spark advance. It is basically a refinement of the DVB or TAV spark control systems with the temperature switch relocated in the air cleaner and a latching relay added to maintain a strong vacuum signal at the distributor, whether it be EGR port or spark port carburetor vacuum, and to keep the system from intermittently switching vacuum signals when the intake air is between 49 and 60° F. When the temperature switch closes at 60° F, the latching relay (normally off) is energized and stays on until the ignition switch is turned off. The latching relay then overrides the temperature switch and forces the solenoid valve to keep the spark port vacuum system closed and open the EGR port vacuum system. This prevents full vacuum advance, once the engine is warmed-up, thereby lowering emissions.

The EGR/CSC system is used on most 1974 and later models. It regulates both distributor spark advance and EGR valve operation, according to coolant temperature, by sequentially switching vacuum sources.

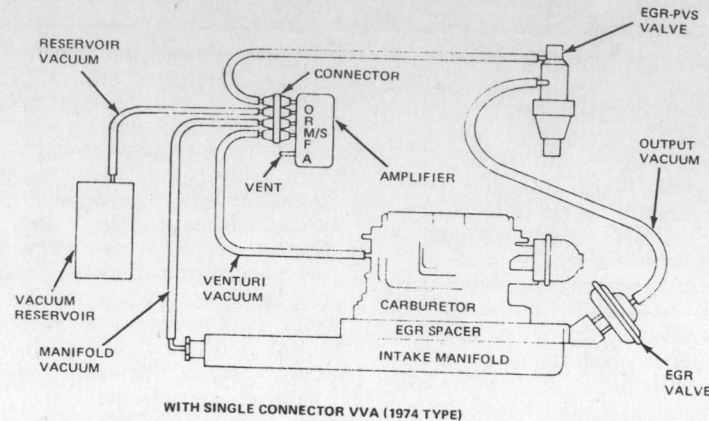

WITH SINGLE CONNECTOR VVA (1974 TYPE)

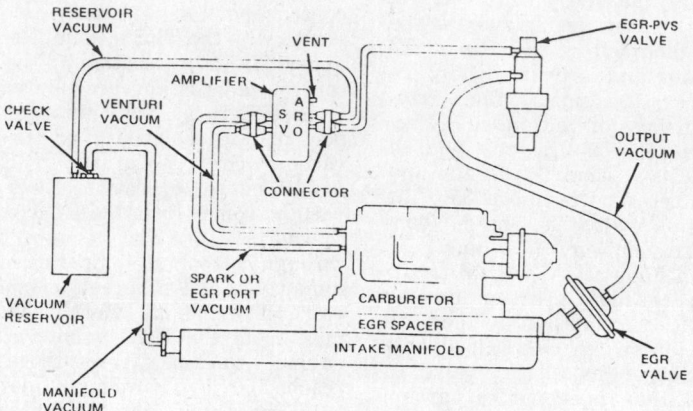

Typical 1974-76 EGR system components
(© Ford Motor Co)

The major components are:
a. 95°F EGR-PVS valve,
b. spark delay valve (SDV), and
c. a vacuum check valve.

When coolant temperature is below 85°F, the EGR-PVS valve admits carburetor EGR port vacuum (at about 2500 rpm) directly to the distributor advance diaphragm through a one-way check valve. At the same time, EGR-PVS valve shuts off carburetor EGR vacuum to the EGR valve and transmission diaphragm.

When coolant temperature is above 95° F, the EGR-PVS valve is actuated and admits carburetor EGR vacuum to the EGR valve and transmission instead of the distributor. At temperatures between 82° and 95°F, the EGR-PVS valve may be open, closed, or in midposition.

1975-76

Catalytic converters are installed in all 1975 and later cars sold in California, and on most 1975 models sold in the 49 states with the following exceptions; 250 six-cylinder and 302 V8 Mavericks and Comets, 250 six-cylinder 2-door Granadas and Monarchs. Torino, Elite, Montego and Cougar models sold in California use dual converters.

All 1976 models use a catalytic converter system.

The catalyst units convert emis-

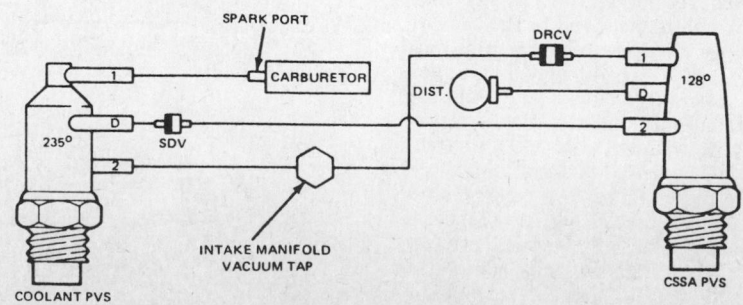

CSSA System schematic
(© Ford Motor Co)

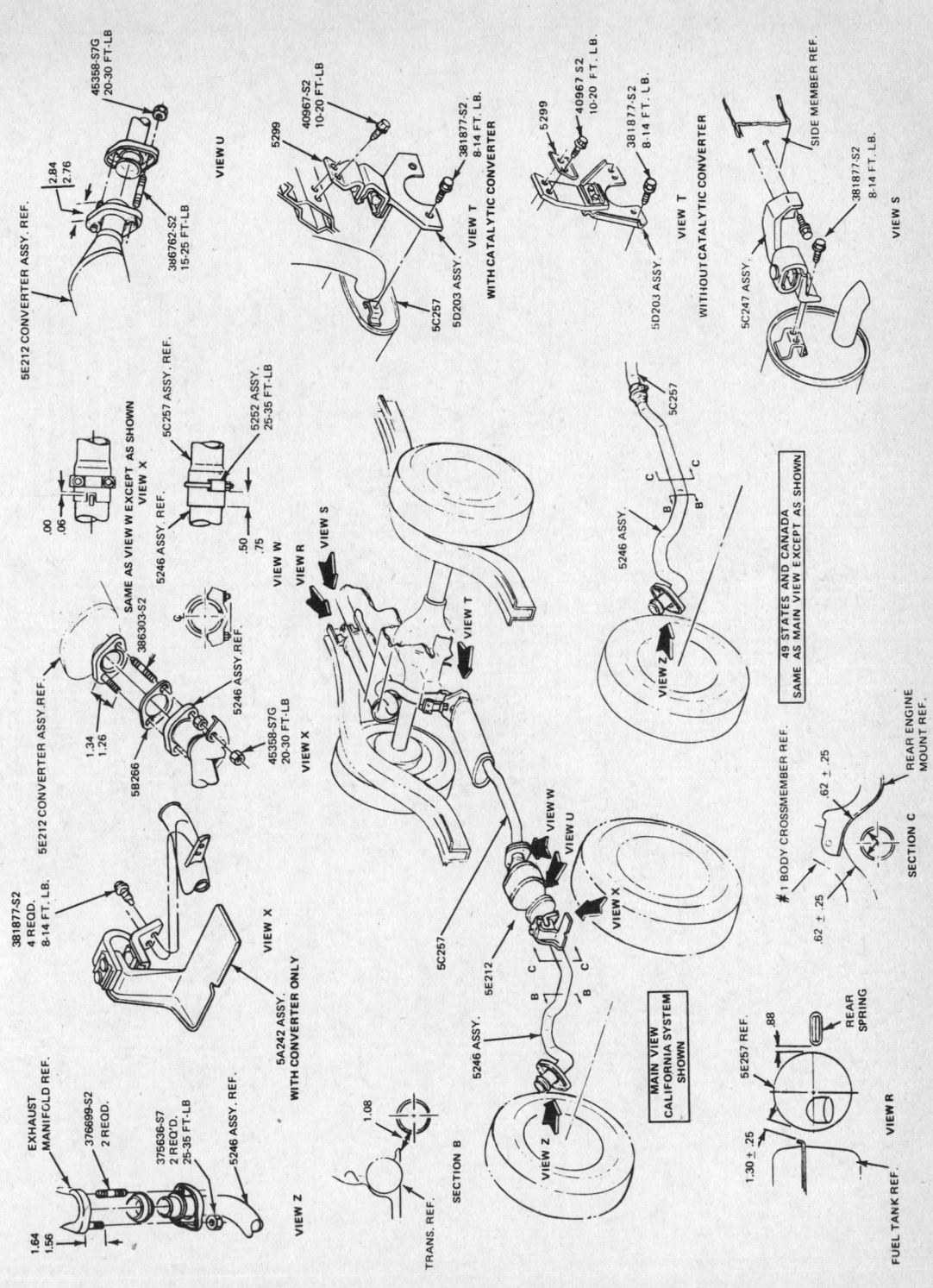

45358-S7G
20-30 FT-LB

5E212 CONVERTER ASSY. REF.

2.84
2.76

386762-S2
15-25 FT-LB

VIEW U

40967-S2
10-20 FT. LB.

5299

381877-S2
8-14 FT. LB.

5C257

5D203 ASSY. REF.

WITH CATALYTIC CONVERTER

VIEW T

40967-S2
10-20 FT. LB.

5299

381877-S2
8-14 FT. LB.

5D203 ASSY. REF.

WITHOUT CATALYTIC CONVERTER

VIEW T

SIDE MEMBER REF.

381877-S2
8-14 FT. LB.

5C247 ASSY.

VIEW S

5C257 ASSY. REF.

5252 ASSY.
25-35 FT-LB

.00
.06

SAME AS VIEW W EXCEPT AS SHOWN

VIEW X

5246 ASSY. REF.

VIEW W

.50
.75

VIEW R

VIEW S

VIEW W

386303-S2

5246 ASSY. REF.

VIEW T

5C257

5246 ASSY.

VIEW Z

5E212 CONVERTER ASSY. REF.

1.34
1.26

5B266

45358-S7G
20-30 FT-LB

VIEW X

49 STATES AND CANADA
SAME AS MAIN VIEW EXCEPT AS SHOWN

VIEW U

VIEW X

381877-S2
4 REQD.
8-14 FT. LB.

VIEW X

5A242 ASSY.
WITH CONVERTER ONLY

5C257

5E212

B
C

5246 ASSY.

VIEW Z

MAIN VIEW
CALIFORNIA SYSTEM
SHOWN

1 BODY CROSSMEMBER REF.

.62 ± .25

.62 ± .25

REAR ENGINE
MOUNT REF.

SECTION C

EXHAUST
MANIFOLD REF.

381877-S2
4 REQD.

376699-S2
2 REQD.

375636-S7
2 REQD.
25-35 FT-LB

5246 ASSY. REF.

1.64
1.56

VIEW Z

1.08

TRANS. REF.

SECTION B

5E257 REF.

.88

REAR
SPRING

1.30 ± .25

FUEL TANK REF.

VIEW R

Maverick and Comet, Granada and Monarch six cylinder exhaust system and catalytic
converter—1975-76 (© Ford Motor Co.)

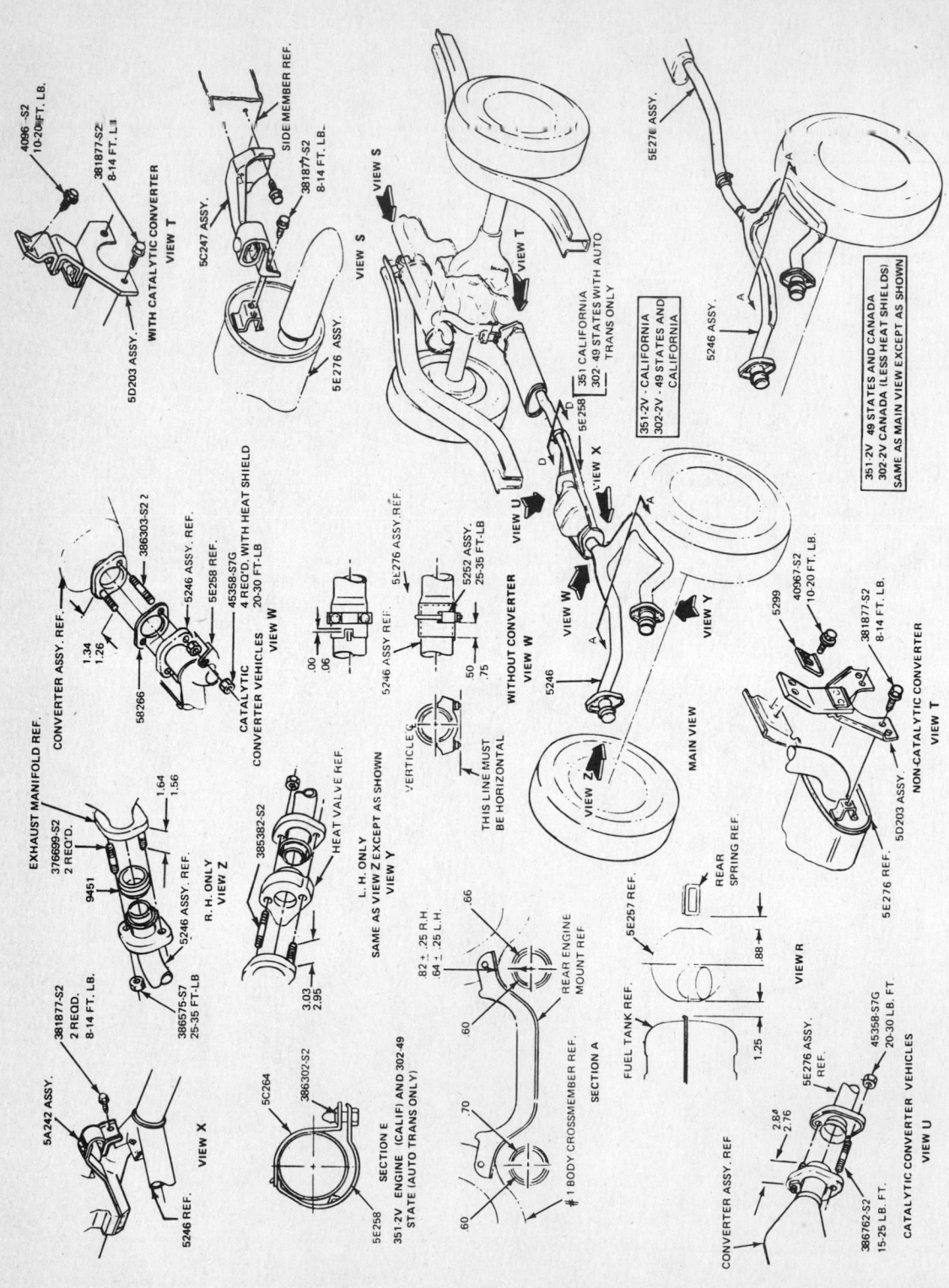

Granada and Monarch 302 V8 single exhaust system and catalytic converter installation —1975-76 (© Ford Motor Co.)

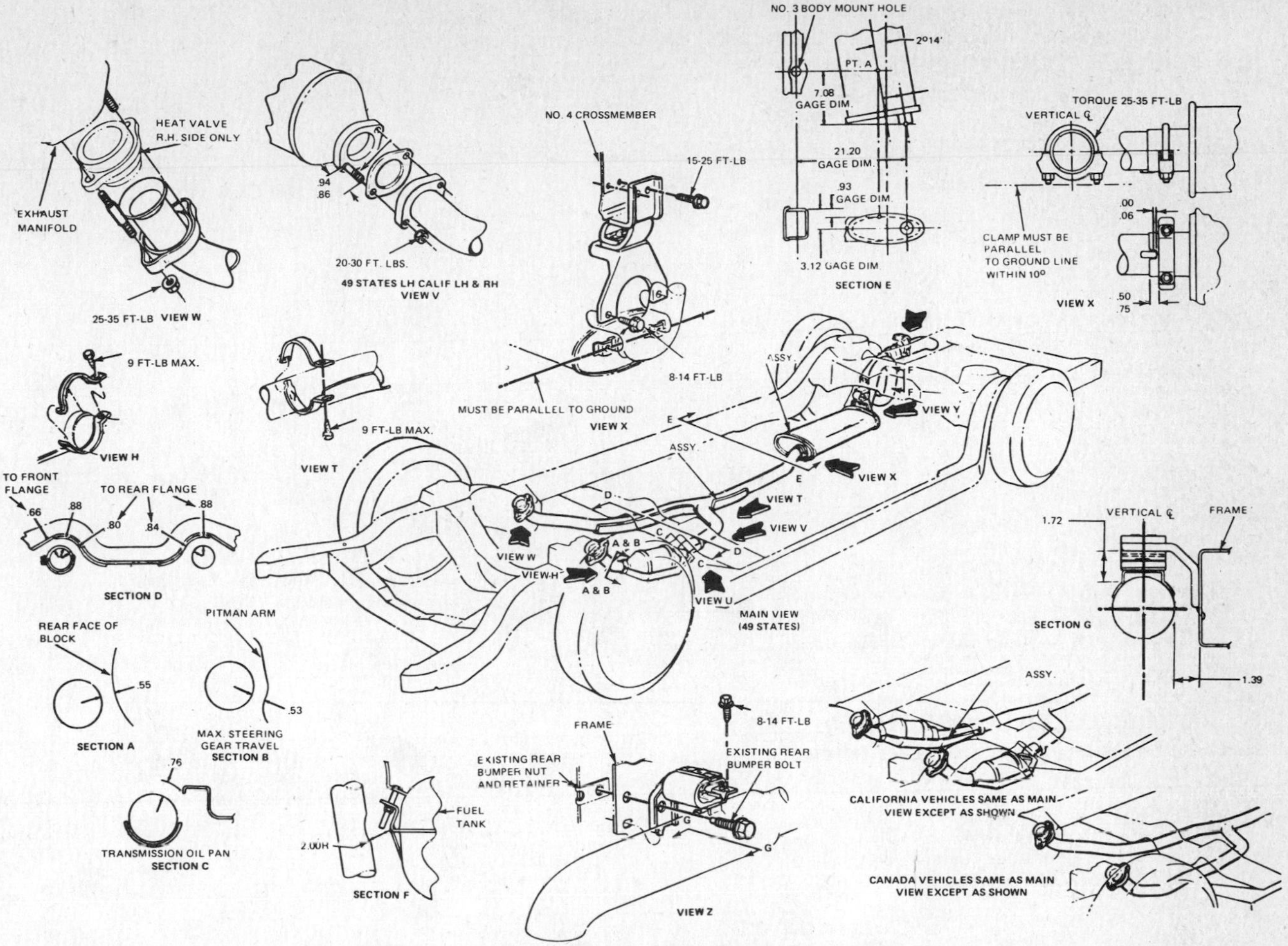

HEAT VALVE R.H. SIDE ONLY

EXHAUST MANIFOLD

25-35 FT-LB VIEW W

.94 .86

20-30 FT. LBS.
49 STATES LH CALIF LH & RH VIEW V

NO. 4 CROSSMEMBER

15-25 FT-LB

MUST BE PARALLEL TO GROUND VIEW X

8-14 FT-LB

NO. 3 BODY MOUNT HOLE
2°14'
PT. A
7.08 GAGE DIM.
21.20 GAGE DIM.
.93 GAGE DIM.
3.12 GAGE DIM
SECTION E

TORQUE 25-35 FT-LB
VERTICAL ℄
CLAMP MUST BE PARALLEL TO GROUND LINE WITHIN 10°
.00 .06
.50 .75
VIEW X

9 FT-LB MAX.
VIEW H

9 FT-LB MAX.
VIEW T

ASSY

VIEW Y
VIEW X
VIEW T
VIEW V

TO FRONT FLANGE
.66 .88
.80 .84 .88
TO REAR FLANGE
SECTION D

REAR FACE OF BLOCK
.55
SECTION A

PITMAN ARM
.53
MAX. STEERING GEAR TRAVEL SECTION B

.76
TRANSMISSION OIL PAN SECTION C

VIEW W
VIEW H
A & B
A & B
D
C
VIEW U
MAIN VIEW (49 STATES)

VERTICAL ℄
1.72
FRAME
SECTION G
1.39

FRAME
8-14 FT-LB
EXISTING REAR BUMPER BOLT
EXISTING REAR BUMPER NUT AND RETAINER
FUEL TANK
2.00H
SECTION F
VIEW Z

ASSY.
G G

CALIFORNIA VEHICLES SAME AS MAIN VIEW EXCEPT AS SHOWN

CANADA VEHICLES SAME AS MAIN VIEW EXCEPT AS SHOWN

Typical catalytic converter installation—1975-76 Torino, Elite, Montego and Cougar (body/frame cars) shown
(© Ford Motor Co)

sions of hydrocarbons and carbon monoxide into harmless carbon dioxide and water, and in some cases, small amounts of possibly harmful sulfur dioxide (rotten egg odor) or (when mixed with water) sulphuric acid. The reaction takes place inside the converters at great heat (1300-1500°F) using platinum and palladium metals as the catalyst. The units are installed in the exhaust system, upstream from the mufflers. They are designed, if the engine is kept in proper tune and *only* unleaded fuel is used, to last 50,000 miles before replacement.

On models using the 460 V8 engine, a Cold Start Spark Advance (CSSA) System is used to improve cold engine operation. When the coolant temperature is below 125° F, carburetor ported vacuum is routed to the distributor through a spark delay valve and coolant temperature operated vacuum valve (PVS).

Another aid to cold engine operation is a "cold weather modulator," which is added to the heated air intake system. When the ambient temperature is below 55° F and the engine is cold, the cold weather modulator prevents the door in the air cleaner snorkel from opening to the fresh air position under hard acceleration. Above 55° F, the door works the same as in other years; i.e., opening under hard acceleration or when the engine has reached normal operating temperatures.

All 1975 engines have a spacer entry EGR valve mounted on a spacer beneath the carburetor. This replaces the "floor entry" system used on some 1974 engines.

Positive crankcase ventilation (PCV) and evaporative emission control systems are carryovers from previous years.

To futher aid cold start driveability during engine warmup, most 1975 engines use a vacuum Operated Heat Valve (VOHV) located between the exhaust manifold and the exhaust inlet (header) pipe.

When the engine is first started, the valve is closed, blocking exhaust gases from exiting from one bank of cylinders. These gases are then diverted back through the intake manifold crossover passage under the carbure-

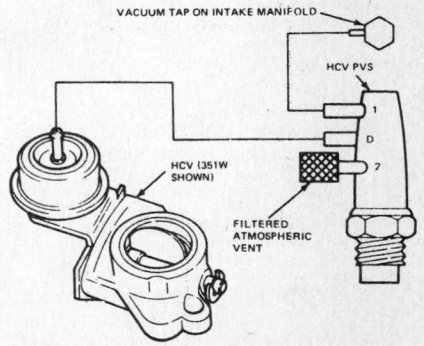

VACUUM TAP ON INTAKE MANIFOLD
HCV PVS
HCV (351W SHOWN)
1
D
7
FILTERED ATMOSPHERIC VENT

VOHV System schematic
(© Ford Motor Co)

tor and choke. The VOHV is controlled by a ported vacuum switch which uses manifold vacuum to keep the vacuum motor on the valve closed until the coolant reaches a predetermined "warm-up" value. When the engine is warmed-up, the PVS shuts off vacuum to the VOHV, and a strong return spring opens the VOHV butterfly.

The complexity of the emission control equipment on all Ford vehicles has been substantially re-

THERMACTOR NON-CATALYST SYSTEM
- Used on vehicles without catalytic converter.
- Same as 1974 except as shown.

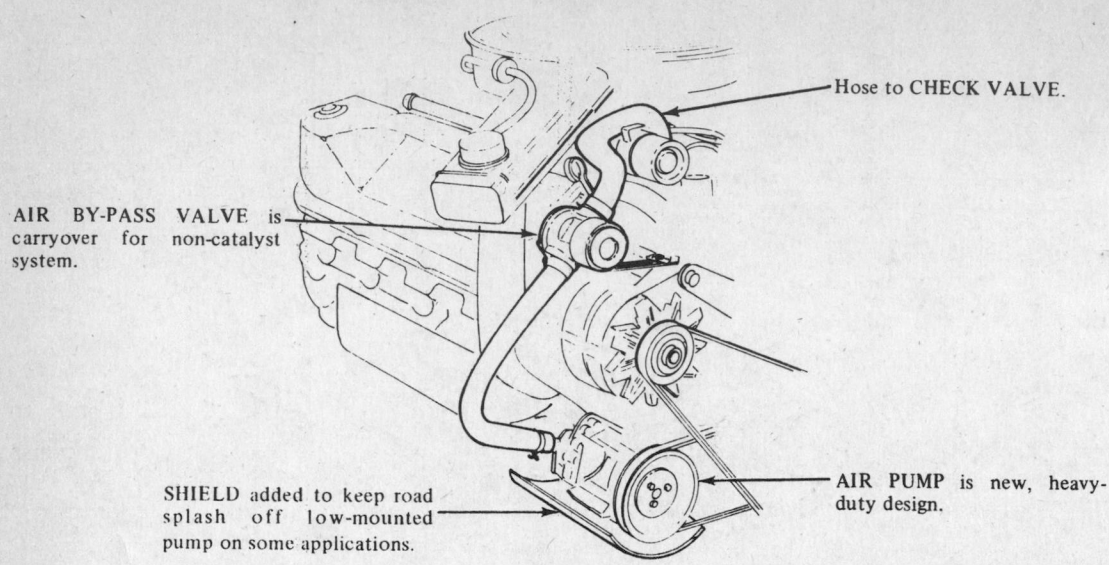

Hose to CHECK VALVE.

AIR BY-PASS VALVE is carryover for non-catalyst system.

SHIELD added to keep road splash off low-mounted pump on some applications.

AIR PUMP is new, heavy-duty design.

THERMACTOR CATALYST SYSTEM
- Used on vehicles with catalytic converter.

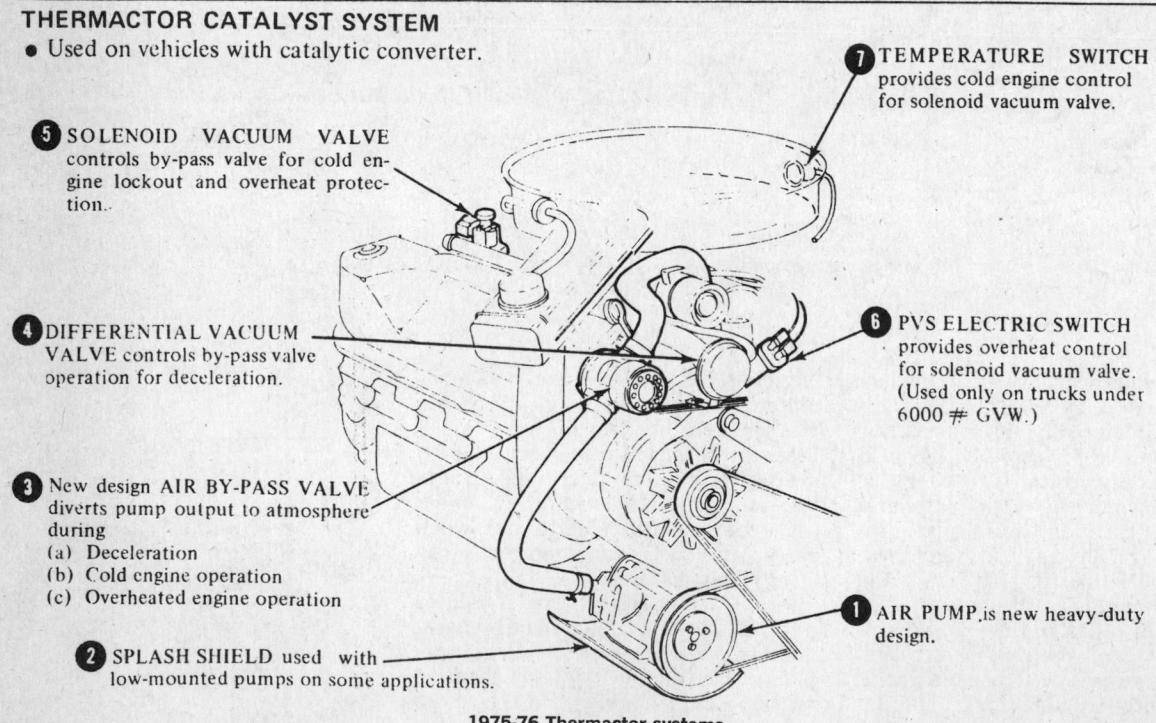

❼ TEMPERATURE SWITCH provides cold engine control for solenoid vacuum valve.

❺ SOLENOID VACUUM VALVE controls by-pass valve for cold engine lockout and overheat protection.

❹ DIFFERENTIAL VACUUM VALVE controls by-pass valve operation for deceleration.

❻ PVS ELECTRIC SWITCH provides overheat control for solenoid vacuum valve. (Used only on trucks under 6000 # GVW.)

❸ New design AIR BY-PASS VALVE diverts pump output to atmosphere during
(a) Deceleration
(b) Cold engine operation
(c) Overheated engine operation

❷ SPLASH SHIELD used with low-mounted pumps on some applications.

❶ AIR PUMP is new heavy-duty design.

1975-76 Thermactor systems
(© Ford Motor Co)

duced in 1976 due to the more extensive use of catalyst and catalytic converters. All 1976 model passenger cars have catalytic converters. The average number of emission control components has been reduced from 25 to 11 on most cars.

In addition, a new exhaust gas recirculation signal vacuum control system is used on all 1976 V8 engines. The new system uses an exhaust back-pressure transducer to regulate the EGR valve spark port vacuum signal which modulates the flow of EGR.

This more accurately matches the amount of EGR to the engine load; improving engine driveability and fuel economy.

For system checks and adjustments, see "Emission Control Systems" in the Unit Repair Section.

1977
1977 models carry over the emission controls used in 1976: air injection, PCV, EGR, evaporative controls, and catalytic converters. However some revisions have been made.

Physically larger catalytic converters are used. Improved breakerless electronic ignition called "Dura-Spark" which generates up to 42,000 volts is standard on all engines. Engine modifications include larger intake valves and revised combustion chambers for the 200 and 250 cu in. six-cylinder engines. The 302 and 351W V8 engines have modified combustion chambers and pistons. Cylinder heads also have larger coolant passages for improved spark plug and exhaust valve cooling. There are reduced size passages in the intake manifolds to increase velocity of the air/fuel mixture which aids combustion and improves performance at low rpm.

Also new is a variable venturi two-barrel carburetor (the Motorcraft 2700 VV), for use on the California 302 V8 engine. This carburetor changes the size of the venturis as a function of speed and load. Tapered metering rods, attached to the venturi valves, slide in the main jets to control fuel flow. Venturi valve position is controlled by a spring (closed), and by control vacuum operating through a rubber diaphragm (open). The venturi valves are not directly linked to the throttle shaft. Throttle plate opening results in a stronger control vacuum signal which causes the venturi valves to open, increasing venturi size. The control vacuum and opposing spring select the precise air/fuel ratio for all speed and load conditions except wide open throttle.

ENGINE

There were three different six-cylinder engines available in compact and intermediate size Ford products through 1972: the 170, the 200 and the 250 cu. in. engines. The 170 engine was dropped from production in 1973. These engines are all of the same family, and the only great difference among them is their bore and stroke. One distinguishing characteristic that makes these engines easily identifiable is the fact that the intake manifold is cast as an integral part of the cylinder head.

Optional V8 engines for these models are very numerous, and like the family of six-cylinder engines, there is a great amount of similarity among them.

The most widely used are the 302 V8s. These are remarkably compact engines with stud-mounted rockers and wedge-shaped combustion chambers.

The 351 Windsor engine has the wedge-shaped combustion chambers and stud-mounted rockers of the small block engine in a new intermediate sized block.

A high-performance version of the 302 engine was called the Boss 302. This engine featured mechanical valve lifters and large valve—small spark plug cylinder heads similar to the ones that were used on the 1970 and later 351 Cleveland engines.

In 1970, Ford Motor Company added the 351 Cleveland engine. The 351 Cleveland engine has the same bore and stroke as the Windsor engine, and there most of the resemblance ends. It has different main bearing size, larger valves, smaller plugs, and semi-hemispherical combustion chambers. It is used concurrently with the Windsor engine and is found in many of the same models. A longer stroke, 400 cu in. version of the 351 Cleveland V8 was introduced in 1972. In 1975, all 351C engines are designated 351M, for modified Cleveland.

The Boss 302 V8 was eliminated from production in 1971, and it was replaced by a high-performance version of the 351 Cleveland engine. It is designated as the 351 HO (High Output) engine, available on 1971-72 models.

Starting in 1970, some Montegos, Cyclones and Torinos used the big block 429 V8. This V8 came in three forms. The first was the 429 engine, which is the same as was used in full sized Mercury and Ford cars. The second was the 429CJ engine which used stronger rods, big valve heads, smaller 14 mm. plugs, and an ignition governor set at 5,800 rpm. The third was the 429 Super CJ, which was similar to the 429 CJ except for forged pistons, four bolt main caps, solid lifters, and a 6,000 rpm governor. The 429 CJ and SCJ were discontinued after the 1971 model year run. The standard performance 429-4V V8 was available through 1973. Beginning 1974, a similar 460 4V V8 is used in some heavy-duty applications.

Engine Removal

1. Scribe the hood hinge outline on the under-hood, disconnect the hood and remove.
2. Drain the entire cooling system and crankcase.
3. Remove the air cleaner, disconnect the battery at the cylinder head. On automatic transmission equipped cars, disconnect oil cooler lines at the radiator.
4. Remove upper and lower radiator hoses and remove radiator. If equipped with air conditioning, unbolt compressor and position compressor out of way with refrigerant lines intact. Unbolt and lay refrigerant radiator forward without disconnecting refrigerant lines.

NOTE: If there is not enough slack in the refrigerant lines to position the compressor out of the way, the refrigerant in the system must be evacuated (using proper safety precautions) before the lines can be disconnected from the compressor.

On some 428 CJ engines and all 429 Super CJ, Boss 302, and Boss 429 engines disconnect inlet and outlet lines from engine oil cooler, remove hold-down bracket and remove cooler.

5. Remove fan, fan belt and upper pully.
6. Disconnect the heater hoses from the engine.

7. Disconnect the alternator wires at the alternator, the starter cable at the starter, the accelerator rod at the carburetor.
8. Disconnect fuel tank line at the fuel pump and plug the line.
9. Disconnect the coil primary wire at the coil. Disconnect wires at the oil pressure and water temperature sending units.
10. Remove the starter and dust seal.
11. On a car equipped with a manual-shift transmission, remove the clutch retracting spring. Disconnect the clutch equalizer shaft and arm bracket at the underbody rail and remove the arm bracket and equalizer shaft.
12. Raise the car. Remove the flywheel or converter housing upper retaining bolts.
13. Disconnect the exhaust pipe or pipes at the exhaust manifold. Disconnect the right and left motor mount at the underbody bracket. Remove the flywheel or converter housing cover.
14. On a car with manual shift, remove the flywheel housing lower retaining bolts.
15. On a car equipped with automatic transmission, disconnect throttle valve vacuum line at the intake manifold (2 lines on 1973 models) disconnect the converter from the flywheel. Remove the converter housing lower retaining bolts. On a car with power steering, disconnect power steering pump from cylinder head. Put drive belt and wire steering pump out of the way.
16. Lower the car. Support the transmission and flywheel or converter housing with a jack.
17. Attach an engine lifting hook. Lift the engine up and out of the compartment and onto an adequate workstand.

Engine Installation

1. Place a new gasket over the studs of the exhaust manifold/s.
2. Attach engine sling and lifting device. Lift engine from workstand.
3. Lower the engine into the engine compartment. Be sure the exhaust manifold/s is in proper alignment with the muffler inlet pipe/s, and the dowels in the block engage the holes in the flywheel housing.

On a car with automatic transmission, start the converter pilot into the crankshaft.

On a car with manual-shift transmission, start the transmission main drive gear into the clutch disc. If the engine hangs up after the shaft enters, rotate the crankshaft slowly (with transmission in gear) until the shaft and clutch disc splines mesh.

4. Install the flywheel or converter housing upper bolts.

5. Install engine support insulator to bracket retaining nuts. Disconnect engine lifting sling and remove lifting brackets.

6. Raise front of car. Connect exhaust line/s and tighten attachments.

7. Position dust seal and install starter.

8. On cars with manual-shift transmissions, install remaining flywheel housing-to-engine bolts. Connect clutch release rod. Position the clutch equalizer bar and bracket, and install retaining bolts. Install clutch pedal retracting spring.

9. On cars with automatic transmissions, remove the retainer holding the converter in the housing. Attach the converter to the flywheel. Install the converter housing inspection cover and the remaining converter housing retaining bolts.

10. Remove the support from the transmission and lower the car.

11. Connect engine ground strap and coil primary wire.

12. Connect water temperature gauge wire and the heater hose at coolant outlet housing. Connect accelerator rod at the bellcrank.

13. On cars with automatic transmission, connect the transmission filler tube bracket. Connect the throttle valve vacuum line.

14. On cars with power steering, install the drive belt and power steering pump bracket. Install the bracket retaining bolts. Adjust drive belt to proper tension.

15. Remove plug from the fuel tank line. Connect the flexible fuel line and the oil pressure sending unit wire.

16. Install the pulley, belt, spacer, and fan. Adjust belt tension.

17. Tighten alternator adjusting bolts. Connect generator wires and the battery ground cable.

18. Install radiator. Connect radiator hoses. On air conditioned cars, install compressor and refrigerant radiator. On some 428 CJ engines, and all 429 Super CJ, Boss 302, and Boss 429 engines, install engine oil cooler and hold-down bracket and connect inlet and outlet lines.

19. On cars with automatic transmission, connect oil cooler lines.

20. Install oil filter. Connect heater hose at water pump, after bleeding the system.

21. Bring crankcase to level with correct grade of oil. Run engine at fast idle and check for leaks. Install air cleaner and make final engine adjustments.

22. Install and adjust hood.
23. Road-test car.

Intake Manifold Removal and Installation

6 Cylinder

170, 200 and 250 cu. in. sixes have intake manifolds that are integral with the cylinder head and cannot be removed.

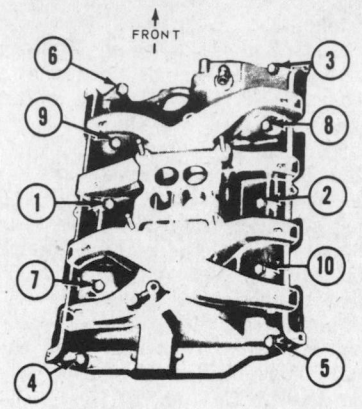

Intake manifold torque sequence—428 V8
(© Ford Motor Co)

302, 351W, 428, 429, 429CJ, 429SCJ, and 460

1. Drain the cooling system.
2. Disconnect the upper radiator hose from the thermostat housing and the bypass hose from the manifold.
3. Remove the air cleaner and ducts.
4. Remove the distributor cap and wires from the engine. Mark the position of the distributor rotor in relationship to the intake manifold, remove the primary wire from the coil, then remove the distributor hold-down bolt and the distributor.
5. Remove all vacuum lines from the intake manifold and remove the temperature sending unit wire.
6. Disconnect the fuel line and any vacuum lines from the carburetor.

7. Remove all carburetor linkage and kickdown linkage that attaches to the intake manifold.

8. On 428 engines, remove the valve covers, the rocker arm assemblies and the pushrods. The rocker arms should be removed by backing off each of the four bolts two turns in sequence from front to back. Keep pushrods in order so that they can be installed in their original position.

9. Remove the manifold attaching bolts and remove the manifold. If it is necessary to pry the manifold to loosen it from the engine, use care not to damage any gasket sealing surfaces.

10. Clean all gasket surfaces and firmly cement new gaskets in place. The gaskets should be securely locked in place before attempting to install the manifold.

11. Reverse above procedure to reinstall.

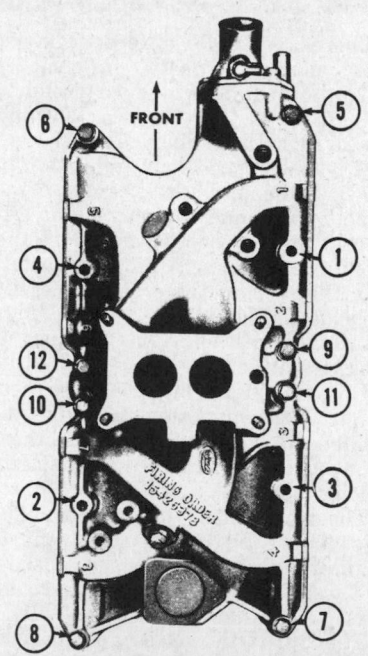

Intake manifold torque sequence—302 V8
(© Ford Motor Co)

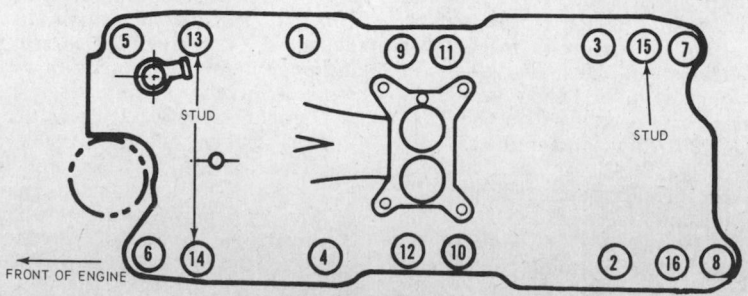

Intake manifold torque sequence—351W V8
(© Ford Motor Co)

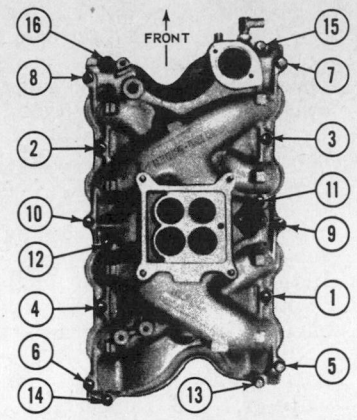

Intake manifold torque sequence—1970-73
429, 1974-76 460 V8
(© Ford Motor Co)

bracket and position out of way.
2. Disconnect accelerator linkage and accelerator downshift linkage, if so equipped, and position out of way. On Boss 302, disconnect choke cable from carburetor.
3. Disconnect high tension lead and wires from coil. Disconnect engine wire loom and position out of way.
4. Disconnect spark plug wires from spark plugs by grasping, twisting, and pulling molded cap only. Remove distributor cap and wire assembly.
5. Remove carburetor fuel inlet line.
6. Disconnect distributor vacuum hoses from distributor. Remove hold-down bolt and remove distributor.
7. Disconnect radiator upper hose from coolant outlet housing and disconnect temperature sender wire.
8. Loosen clamp on water pump by-pass hose at coolant outlet housing and slide hose off outlet housing.
9. Disconnect crankcase vent hose (PCV) at rocker cover.
10. If vehicle is air conditioned, remove compressor to intake manifold brackets.
11. Remove intake manifold and carburetor as an assembly. Dis-

Intake manifold torque sequence—351C,
351M and 400 V8
(© Ford Motor Co)

card all used gaskets and clean all mating surfaces.
12. Reverse procedure to install.

Exhaust Manifold Removal and Installation

6 Cylinder Engines
1. Remove the air cleaner and heat duct body.
2. Disconnect the muffler inlet pipe and remove the choke hot air tube from the manifold.
3. Bend the exhaust manifold attaching bolt lock tabs back, remove the bolts and the manifold.
4. Clean all manifold mating surfaces and place a new gasket on the muffler inlet pipe.
5. Reinstall manifold by reversing above procedure, torque attaching bolts in sequence from the centermost bolt outward.

V8 Engines—Except 428 CJ and 429 Boss
1. On right exhaust manifold, remove the air cleaner, automatic choke heat tube and air cleaner heat ducts.
2. Disconnect the exhaust manifold(s) from the muffler inlet pipe(s).
3. Remove the manifold attaching bolts and remove the manifold(s).
4. Reverse above procedure to reinstall, using new inlet pipe gaskets.

NOTE: To remove the left side exhaust manifold from a car equipped with a 351C, 351M, or 400 engine, it is necessary to remove the oil filter and the transmission selector cross-shaft or clutch linkage and equalizer shaft bracket, depending on transmission type.

428 CJ Engine
This procedure is for removing both manifolds. If only one manifold is to be removed, do not remove any equipment located on or near the opposite side of the engine.
1. Remove the air cleaner, heat tubes, choke and vacuum lines from the manifold.
2. Remove the air cleaner heat tube mounting studs and the three forward attaching bolts from the right-side manifold.
3. Raise the car on a hoist, and remove the idler arm bracket from the frame.
4. Disconnect the starter cable and remove the starter motor.
5. Remove the remaining right-side manifold attaching bolts.
6. Disconnect all exhaust system hangers and lower the exhaust system.
7. Remove the inlet pipes from the manifolds.

8. On vehicles with manual transmission, remove the clutch linkage and equalizer bracket from the engine.
9. Disconnect the Pitman arm from the steering sector shaft and, on vehicles with power steering, remove the steering control valve bracket from the frame.
10. Lower the car, disconnect the steering shaft flex joint, unbolt and remove the steering gear box assembly from the frame.
11. Raise the car again and disconnect and remove both motor mounts and the rear crossmember support attaching bolts.
12. Position a jack under the engine and, using a piece of wood under the oil pan, raise the engine slightly.
13. Remove remaining manifold attaching bolts and remove the manifolds.
14. Clean all gasket surfaces and, using new inlet pipe gaskets, reverse above procedure to reinstall manifolds.

Valve System

V8 engines, except the 429 SCJ, and Boss 302, 351, and 429, use hydraulic tappets. The pushrods in the V8s also transfer oil under pressure to the friction areas of the rocker arms.

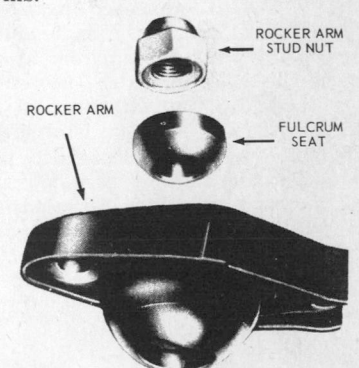

302, and 351 Windsor rocker arm assembly
(© Ford Motor Co)

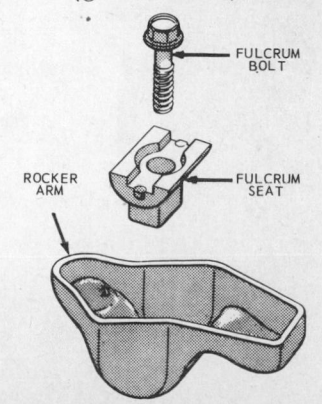

351 Cleveland V8 rocker arm assembly; 351M, 400 V8 similar (with oil deflector)
(© Ford Motor Co)

C473

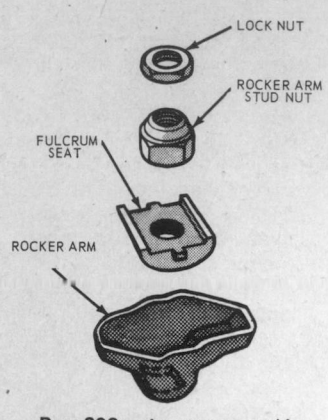

Boss 302 rocker arm assembly
(© Ford Motor Co)

Preliminary Valve Adjustment
V8

NOTE: The early 302 V8 engine has rocker arm mounting studs which do *not* incorporate a positive stop shoulder on the mounting stud. These engines were originally equipped with this kind of stud. However, due to production differences, it is possible some early 302 engines may be encountered that *are* equipped with positive stop rocker arm mounting studs. Before adjusting the valves, verify that the rocker arm mounting studs do not incorporate a positive stop shoulder. On studs without a positive stop, the shank portion of the stud that is exposed just above the cylinder head is the same diameter as the threaded portion, at the top of the stud, to which the rocker arm retaining nut attaches. If the shank portion of the stud is of greater diameter than the threaded portion, this identifies it as a positive stop rocker arm stud and the adjustment specifications for the 351 engine with adjusting nuts should be used.

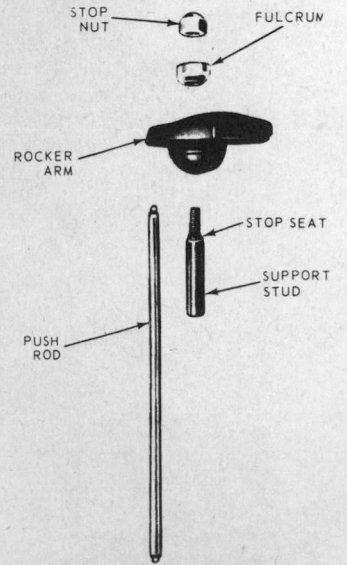

Positive Stop Rocker Arm Stud and Nut
(© Ford Motor Co)

Only the 302, 351W and 1970-71 429 engines require a preliminary valve adjustment. All other V-8s use either a bolt and fulcrum (351C, 351M, 400, 460, and 1972-73 429) or rocker shafts (428). High performance versions of any of these V8s probably will be equipped with rocker arm adjusting nuts.

*302, 351W and 1970-71 429
With Rocker Arm Adjusting Nuts*

1. Crank the engine until #1 cylinder is at TDC of the compression stroke and the timing pointer is aligned with the marks on the crankshaft damper.
2. Scribe a mark on the damper at this point.
3. Scribe three more marks on the damper, dividing the damper into quarters.
4. With the first mark aligned with valves on #1 cylinder by backing off the adjusting nut until the pushrod has free play in it. Then, tighten the nut until there is no free play in the rocker arm. This can be determined by turning the pushrod while tightening the nut; when the pushrod can no longer be turned, all clearance has been removed. After the clearance has been removed, tighten the nut an additional ¾ of a turn (302 V8 w/o positive stop rocker arm studs).
5. Repeat this procedure for each valve, turning the crankshaft ¼ turn to the next mark each time and following the engine firing order.
6. Rocker arm adjusting nut tightening specifications are: 302 (with positive stop rocker arm nut until it contacts the rocker shoulder, then torque it to 18-20 ft lbs; 429—tighten the nut until it contacts the rocker shoulder then tighten the nut to 18-22 ft lbs.

All 6 Cylinder and 428 V8s

These engines are equipped with shaft-mounted rocker arms which do not require a preliminary valve adjustment. In the event of cylinder head or rocker arm removal, the rocker arm shaft bolts are tightened, front to rear, to 30-35 ft-lbs (6 cylinder) or 40-45 ft-lbs (428 V8).

*351C, 351M, 400, 460, and
1972-73 429*

These engines use a bolt and fulcrum rocker arm and require no preliminary valve adjustment. In the event that the valve train is disturbed, install the fulcrum, oil deflector, and tighten the bolt to 18-25 ft. lbs.

*Boss 302, Boss 351 and Boss 429,
429 SCJ*

1. Make primary valve adjustment in the following manner, and continue to install rocker covers and fill cooling system.

NOTE: Tappets must be adjusted while on the low radius of the cam.

2. If the distributor has not been disturbed and ignition timing is reasonably correct, proceed as follows: rotate crankshaft until the distributor rotor points to No. 1 plug wire tower of the distributor cap. Adjust valves in cylinder firing order according to rotor position.
3. If the distributor is out of time or has been removed from the engine: turn the crankshaft until No. 1 piston is at the top of its compression stroke. (intake valve of No. 6 cylinder just beginning to open), and the crankshaft damper is on T.D.C. Make three chalk marks on the crankshaft damper, 120° apart, starting with T.D.C. These marks will divide crankshaft travel into three parts, or six segments, of each engine cycle. Valve adjustment can then be made in firing sequence, beginning with No. 1 on TDC and progressing through the regular order of firing by advancing one chalk mark (120 crankshaft degrees) at a time.

V8 Mechanical Valve Lifter Final Adjustment

1. Run engine to bring to operating temperature.
2. Remove rocker covers.
3. Insert a feeler gauge of specified thickness between the rocker arm and valve, and with engine running, adjust rocker arm to obtain desired clearance.
4. Reinstall rocker cover.

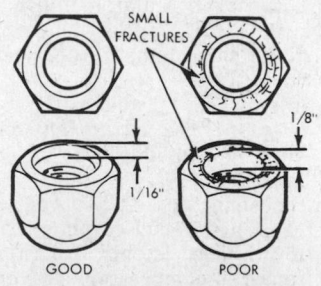

Rocker arm stud nut inspection
(© Ford Motor Co)

Valve Guides

Ford Motor Company engines use integral valve guides. Mercury and Ford dealers offer valves with oversize stems for worn guides. To fit these, enlarge valve guide bores with valve guide reamers to an oversize that cleans up wear. If a large oversize is required it is best to approach that size in stages by using a series of reamers of increasing diameter. This helps to maintain the concentricity of the guide bore with the valve seat. The correct valve guide to stem clearance is at front of this section.

As an alternative, some local automotive machine shops will fit replacement guides that use standard stem valves.

Cylinder Head

6 Cylinder Removal

1. Drain cooling system, remove the air cleaner and disconnect the battery cable at the cylinder head.
2. Disconnect exhaust pipe at the manifold end, spring the exhaust pipe down and remove the flange gasket.
3. Disconnect the fuel and vacuum lines from the carburetor. Disconnect the intake manifold line at the intake manifold.
4. Disconnect the accelerator and retracting spring at the carburetor.
5. Disconnect the carburetor spacer outlet line at the spacer. Disconnect the radiator upper hose and the heater hose at the water outlet elbow. Disconnect the radiator lower hose and the heater hose at the water pump.
6. Disconnect the distributor vacuum control line at the distributor. Disconnect the gas filter line on the inlet side of the filter.
7. Disconnect the spark plug wires and remove the plugs.
8. Remove the rocker arm cover.
9. Back off all of the tappet adjusting screws to relieve tension on the rocker shaft. Loosen the rocker arm shaft attaching bolts and remove the rocker arm and shaft assembly. Remove the valve pushrods, in order, and keep them that way.
10. Remove one cylinder-head bolt from each end of the head (at opposite corners) and install cylinder head guide studs. Remove the remaining cylinder head bolts and lift off the cylinder head.

To help in removal and installation of cylinder head, two 6 in. x 7/16—14 bolts with heads cut off and the head end slightly tapered and slotted for installation and removal, with a screwdriver, will reduce the possibility of damage during head replacement. These guide studs make a handy tool during head removal and gasket and head replacement.

6 Cylinder Installation

1. Clean the cylinder head and block surfaces. Be sure of flatness and no surface damage.
2. Apply cylinder head gasket sealer to both sides of the new gasket and slide the gasket down over the two guide studs in the cylinder block.
   NOTE: apply gasket sealer only to

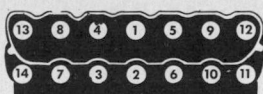

Cylinder head bolt tightening sequence—170, 200, 250 cu. in. 6 cyl

steel shim head gaskets. Steel-asbestos composite head gaskets are to be installed without any sealer.

3. Carefully lower the cylinder head over the guide studs. Place the exhaust pipe flange on the manifold studs (new gasket).
4. Coat the threads of the end bolts for the right side of the cylinder head with a small amount of water-resistant sealer. Install, but do not tighten, two head bolts at opposite ends to hold the head gasket in place. Remove the guide studs and install the remaining bolts.
5. Cylinder head torquing should proceed in three steps and in prescribed order. Tighten to 55 ft. lbs., then give them a second tightening to 65 ft. lbs. The final step is to 75 ft. lbs., at which they should remain undisturbed.
6. Lubricate both ends of the pushrods and install them in their original locations.
7. Apply a petroleum jelly-type lubricant to the rocker arm pads and the valve stem tips and position the rocker arm shaft assembly on the head. Be sure the oil holes in the shaft are in a down position.
8. Tighten all the rocker shaft retaining bolts to 30-35 ft. lbs. and do a preliminary valve adjustment (make sure there are no tight valve adjustments).
9. Hook up the exhaust pipe.
10. Reconnect the heater and radiator hoses.
11. Reposition the distributor vacuum line, the carburetor gas line and the intake manifold vacuum line on the engine. Hook them up to their respective connections and reconnect the battery cable to the cylinder head.
12. Connect the accelerator rod and retracting spring. Connect the choke control cable and adjust the choke.
13. Reconnect the vacuum line at the distributor. Connect the fuel inlet line at the fuel filter and the intake manifold vacuum line at the vacuum pump. Connect the windshield wiper vacuum line to the other side of the vacuum pump.
14. Lightly lubricate the spark plug threads, install them and torque to 25 ft. lbs. Connect spark plug wires and be sure the wires are all the way down in their sockets.
15. Fill the cooling system and bleed. Run the engine to stabilize all

engine parts temperatures.
16. Adjust engine idle speed and idle fuel-air adjustment.
17. Coat one side of a new rocker cover gasket with oil-resistant sealer. Lay the treated side of the gasket on the cover and install the cover. Be sure the gasket seals evenly all around the cylinder head.

Cylinder head bolt tightening sequence—302, 302 Boss, 351W, 351C, 400 V8 shown; 428, 429 Boss V8 have similar bolt pattern

(© Ford Motor Co)

All V8 Except 428 and Boss 429

1. Remove the valve covers and disconnect the negative battery cable.
2. Remove the intake manifold and carburetor assembly.
3. On cars equipped with air conditioning, remove the compressor from the engine and position it to one side, *without disconnecting the refrigerant lines.*
4. If removing the left cylinder head, on cars equipped with power steering, remove the pump, bracket, and drive belt and position to one side *without disconnecting the lines.* On cars with Thermactor emission control system, disconnect the hose from the air manifold on the left cylinder head.
5. If removing the right cylinder head, remove the alternator mounting bracket bolt and spacer, ignition coil, and air cleaner inlet duct. On cars equipped with Thermactor emission control, remove the air pump and bracket. Disconnect the hose from the right cylinder head.
6. Disconnect the exhaust manifold/s from the exhaust pipe/s.
7. Loosen the rocker arm stud nuts so that the arms can rotate to the side to clear the pushrods. Remove the pushrods.
8. Remove the cylinder head bolts and lift off the cylinder head. On some 351 engines, it may be necessary to remove the exhaust manifold to gain access to the lower cylinder head bolts.
9. Reverse the above procedures for installation taking care to follow the specified torque sequence as per the diagrams. Perform a preliminary valve adjustment before starting the engine.

428 V8

1. Remove the intake manifold assembly as previously described.
2. Remove any remaining accessories that may obstruct removal.
3. Disconnect the exhaust manifold/s from the exhaust pipe/s.
4. Unbolt and remove heads.
5. Reverse above procedure for installation taking care to follow the specified torque sequence as per the diagrams.

TIME SAVER

Frequently valves become bent or warped or their seats become blocked with carbon or other material. Left unattended, this can cause burnt valves, damaged cylinder heads and other expensive troubles. To detect leaking valves early, perform this test whenever the cylinder head is removed.

1. After removing head, replace spark plugs. Removing spark plugs before removing heads eliminates breakage.
2. Place head on bench with valves, springs, retainers and keys installed and combustion chambers up.
3. Pour enough gasoline in each combustion chamber to completely cover both valves. Watch combustion chambers for two minutes for any leakage.

Timing Cover, Chain, and Camshaft

6-Cylinder Cover and Chain

Removal

1. Drain the cooling system and crankcase.
2. Disconnect the upper radiator hose from the intake manifold and the lower hose from the water pump. On cars with automatic transmission, disconnect the cooler lines from the radiator.
3. Remove the radiator, fan and pulley, and engine drive belts. On models with air conditioning, remove the condenser retaining bolts and position the condenser forward. *Do not disconnect the refrigerant lines.*
4. On 170 and 200 cu. in. engines remove the cylinder front cover retaining bolts and front oil pan bolts and gently pry the cover away from the block. On 250 en-

gines, it is necessary to remove the oil pan before removing the front cover.
5. Remove the crankshaft pulley bolt and use a puller to remove the vibration damper.
6. With a socket wrench of the proper size on the crankshaft pulley bolt, gently rotate the crankshaft in a clockwise direction until all slack is removed from the left side of the timing chain. Scribe a mark on the engine block parallel to the present position of the left side of the chain. Next, turn the crankshaft in a counterclockwise direction to remove all the slack from the right side of the chain. Force the left side of the chain outward with the fingers and measure the distance between the reference point and the present position of the chain. If the distance exceeds ½ inch, replace the chain and sprockets.
7. Crank the engine until the timing marks are aligned as shown in the illustration. Remove the bolt, slide sprocket and chain forward and remove as an assembly.

Installation

1. Position the sprockets and chain on the engine, making sure that the timing marks are aligned, dot to dot.
2. Reinstall the front cover, applying oil resistant sealer to the new gasket.
   NOTE: on 170 and 200 engines, trim away the exposed portion of the old oil pan gasket flush with front of the engine block. Cut and position the required portion of a new gasket to the oil pan, applying sealer to both sides of it.
3. On 250 engines, reinstall the oil pan.
4. Install the fan, pulley and belts. Adjust belt tension.
5. Install the radiator, connect the radiator hoses and transmission cooling lines. If equipped with air conditioning, install the condenser.
6. Fill the crankcase and cooling system. Start the engine and check for leaks.

V8 Cover and Chain

Removal

1. Drain cooling system, remove air cleaner and disconnect the battery.
2. Disconnect radiator hoses and remove the radiator.
3. Disconnect heater hose at water pump. Slide water pump by-pass hose clamp toward the pump.
4. Loosen alternator mounting bolts at the alternator. Remove the

alternator support bolt at the water pump. Remove Thermactor pump on all engines so equipped.
5. Remove the fan, spacer, pulley, and drive belt.
6. Remove pulley from crankshaft pulley adapter. Remove cap screw and washer from front end of crankshaft. Remove crankshaft pulley adapter with a puller.
7. Disconnect fuel pump outlet line at the pump. Remove fuel pump retaining bolts and lay the pump to the side.
8. Remove the front cover attaching bolts. On the 351C, 351M, and 400 engines, it is necessary to remove the oil pan before the front cover can be removed.
9. Remove the crankshaft oil slinger if so equipped.
10. Check timing chain deflection, using the procedure outlined in Step 6 of the six cylinder cover and chain removal.
11. Crank engine until sprocket timing marks are aligned as shown in valve timing illustration.
12. Remove crankshaft sprocket cap screw, washers, and fuel pump eccentric. Slide both sprockets and chain forward and off as an assembly.

Installation

1. Position sprockets and chain on the camshaft and crankshaft with both timing marks dot to dot on a centerline. Install fuel pump eccentric, washers and sprocket attaching bolt. Torque the sprocket attaching bolt to 30–35 ft lbs.
2. Install crankshaft front oil slinger.
3. Clean front cover and mating surfaces of old gasket material.
4. Coat a new cover gasket with sealer and position it on the block.
   NOTE: On all except 351C, 351M, and 400 engines, trim away the exposed portion of the oil pan gasket flush with the cylinder block. Cut and position the required portion of a new gasket to the oil pan, applying sealer to both sides of it. On 351C, 351M, and 400 engines, after installing the cylinder front cover, install the oil pan using a new gasket.
5. Install front cover, using a crankshaft-to-cover alignment tool. Torque attaching bolts to 12-15 ft. lbs.
6. Install fuel pump, torque attaching bolts to 23-28 ft. lbs., connect fuel pump outlet tube.
7. Install crankshaft pulley adapter and torque attaching bolt to 70-90 ft. lbs. Install crankshaft pulley.
8. Install water pump pulley, drive belt, spacer and fan.
9. Install alternator support bolt at

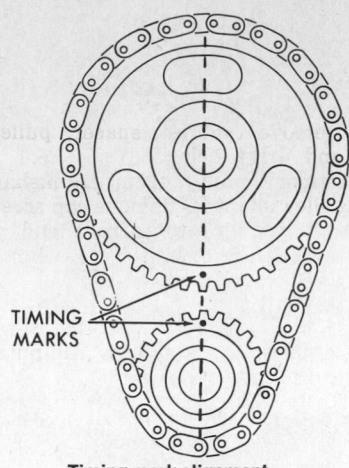

Timing mark alignment

the water pump. Tighten alternator mounting bolts. Adjust drive belt tension. Install Thermactor pump if so equipped.
10. Install radiator and connect all coolant and heater hoses. Connect battery cables.
11. Refill and bleed cooling system.
12. Start engine and operate at fast idle to operating temperature.
13. Check for leaks, install air cleaner. Adjust ignition timing and make all final adjustments.

Cover Seal Removal and Installation

It is a recommended practice to replace the cover seal any time the front cover is removed.
1. With the cover removed from the car, drive the old seal from the rear of cover with a pinpunch. Clean out the recess in the cover.
2. Coat the new seal with grease and drive it into the cover until it is fully seated. Check the seal after installation to be sure the spring is properly positioned in the seal.

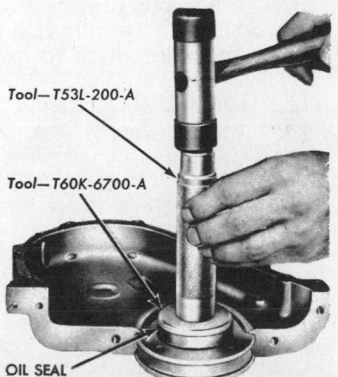

Tool—T53L-200-A
Tool—T60K-6700-A
OIL SEAL

Typical 6 cyl crankshaft front oil seal replacement (© Ford Motor Co)

Camshaft Removal and Installation

6 Cylinder Engines
1. Remove the cylinder head as directed in that section.
2. Remove the cylinder front cover, timing chain and sprockets as outlined in the preceding section.
3. Disconnect and remove the grille. On Mustang models, remove the gravel deflector.
4. Using a magnet, remove the valve lifters and keep them in order so that they can be installed in their original positions.
5. Remove the camshaft thrust plate and remove the camshaft by pulling it from the front of the engine. Use care not to damage the camshaft lobes or journals while removing the cam from the engine.
6. Before installing the camshaft, coat the lobes with Lubriplate and the journals and all valve parts with heavy oil.
7. Reverse above procedure to install, following recommended torque settings and tightening sequences. Perform a preliminary valve adjustment before starting the engine.

V8 Engines
1. Remove the intake manifold as outlined previously.
2. Remove the cylinder front cover, timing chain and sprockets as directed previously.
3. Remove the grille, and, on models with air conditioning, remove the condenser retaining bolts and position it out of the way. *Do not disconnect refrigerant lines.*
4. Remove the rocker arm covers.
5. On 428 engines it is necessary to remove the rocker arm shafts to remove the intake manifold. On all other engines with individually mounted rocker arms, loosen the rocker arm fulcrum bolts and rotate the rocker arms to the side.
6. Remove the pushrods and lifters and keep them in order so that they can be installed in their original positions.
7. Remove the camshaft thrust plate and washer if so equipped. Remove the camshaft from the front of the engine. Use care not to damage camshaft lobes or journals while removing the cam from the engine.
8. Before installing the camshaft, coat the lobes with Lubriplate and the journals and valve parts with heavy oil.
9. Reverse above procedure to install.

NOTE: on engines with individually mounted rocker arms, it is necessary to perform a preliminary valve adjustment before starting the engine.

Lubrication

All engines are equipped with full-flow-type oil filters to condition the oil before it reaches the main bearings. The filter is equipped with an internal, relief, by-pass valve as a safety precaution.

Oil Pan Removal and Installation

NOTE: on certain engine-chassis combinations, interference will be encountered between the oil pan and oil pump while attempting to remove the oil pan. If this occurs, lower the oil pan and reach inside it and remove the two bolts retaining the oil pump and pickup tube to the engine block. Lower the pump and pickup tube assembly into the pan and remove it with the pan. To ensure proper gasket sealing, the oil pan retaining bolts should be tightened from the center outward.

1970 170, 200, and 250 6 Cylinder—All Models
1. Drain the crankcase. Remove the

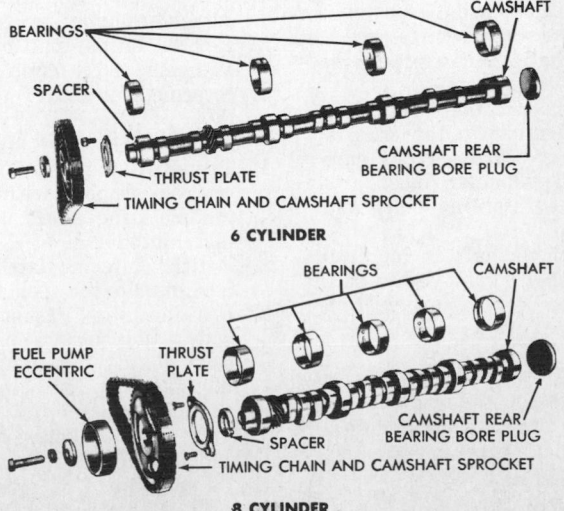

6 CYLINDER

BEARINGS
SPACER
THRUST PLATE
TIMING CHAIN AND CAMSHAFT SPROCKET
CAMSHAFT
CAMSHAFT REAR BEARING BORE PLUG

8 CYLINDER

BEARINGS
FUEL PUMP ECCENTRIC
THRUST PLATE
SPACER
TIMING CHAIN AND CAMSHAFT SPROCKET
CAMSHAFT
CAMSHAFT REAR BEARING BORE PLUG

Camshaft and related parts (© Ford Motor Co)

dipstick and the flywheel inspection plate.

2. In Mustangs and Cougars, disconnect the stabilizer bar and pull downward, out of the way.
3. Remove one bolt, loosen the other and swing no. 2 crossmember out of the way.
4. Remove the retaining bolts and oil pan. Reverse the above procedure to install.

1971-77 Maverick and Comet with 170 and 200 6 Cylinder

1. Drain the crankcase. Remove the dipstick and the flywheel inspection plate.
2. Remove the retaining bolts and oil pan. Reverse the above procedures to install, taking care to place the tabs of the front and rear oil seals over the pan gasket.

1971-77 Torino, Montego, Maverick, Monarch, Granada and Comet with 250 6 Cylinder, 1971-73 Mustang 6 Cylinder

1. Drain the crankcase and cooling system. Remove the dipstick and the flywheel inspection plate.
2. Remove the radiator. On cars with automatic transmissions, the oil cooler lines must be disconnected and plugged.
3. Raise the vehicle. Remove the stabilizer bar.
4. Remove the engine support thru-bolts and nuts.
5. Raise the engine with a jack and place two 2 in. wooden blocks between the engine supports and the chassis brackets.
6. Remove the retaining bolts and the starter motor.
7. Remove the retaining bolts and oil pan. Reverse the above procedures for installation.

1970 Mustang and Cougar 302, Boss 302, 351W, and 351C V8

1. Drain the crankcase. Remove the dipstick. Raise the vehicle.
2. Remove the stabilizer-to-frame retaining bolts.
3. Remove the two bolts retaining the crossmember to the chassis.
4. Remove the starter from cars with 351 Cleveland engines.
5. Remove the retaining bolts and the oil pan.
6. Turn the crankshaft as required for clearance to remove the pan.
7 Install in the reverse order from above.

1970 Falcon, Fairlane, Torino, and Montego with 302 or 351 V8; 1970-76 All Models with 429 or 460 V8; 1971-77 All models with 302, 351 or 400 V8

1. Remove the dipstick.
2. Remove the fan shroud retaining bolts, on models so equipped, and position the shroud over the fan.
3. Raise the vehicle and drain the crankcase.
4. On vehicles with 351C, 351M, 400, and 429 engines, disconnect the negative battery cable and remove the starter.
5. Disconnect the stabilizer bar links and pull the ends down.
6. Remove the engine front support thru-bolts.
7. Install a wooden block on a jack and position the jack beneath the leading edge of the pan.
8. Raise the engine and place 1–1½ in. wood blocks between the engine supports and the chassis. Remove the jack from beneath the engine.
9. Remove the oil pan retaining bolts and lower the pan to the crossmember.
10. If the car is equipped with an automatic transmission, position the oil cooler lines out of the way.
11. Turn the crankshaft as required to obtain clearance to remove the pan.
12. Install in reverse of above.

NOTE: Oil leakage from the rear section of the oil pan gasket (not the rear main seal) has been a problem on some 429 and 460 Police Interceptor V8's. Ford has remedied the situation with a new style seal. However, if the neoprene seal is of the old type, the seal may be prevented from leaking by the application of silicone rubber sealer to the corners of the rear main bearing cap saddle, as shown, prior to installation. Once the silicone sealer is applied, install the oil pan immediately, as the sealer will begin to harden.

Oil Pump

Removal—All Engines

1. Remove oil pan.
2. Remove oil pump inlet tube and screen assembly.
3. Remove oil pump attaching bolts and remove oil pump gasket and intermediate shaft.

Installation—All Engines

1. Prime oil pump by filling inlet and outlet port with engine oil and rotating shaft of pump to distribute it.
2. Position intermediate drive shaft into distributor socket.
3. Position new gasket on pump body and insert intermediate drive shaft into pump body.
4. Install pump and intermediate shaft as an assembly.

NOTE: do not force pump if it does not seat readily. The drive shaft may be misaligned with the distributor shaft. To align rotate intermediate drive shaft into a new position.

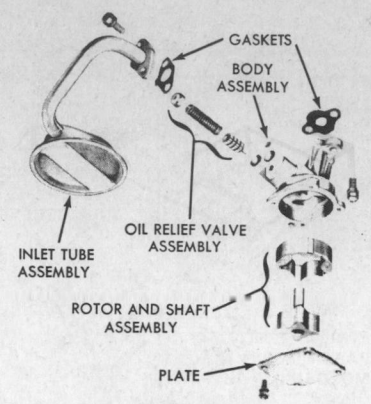

302, Boss 302, and 351 Windsor V8 oil pump
(Ⓒ Ford Motor Co)

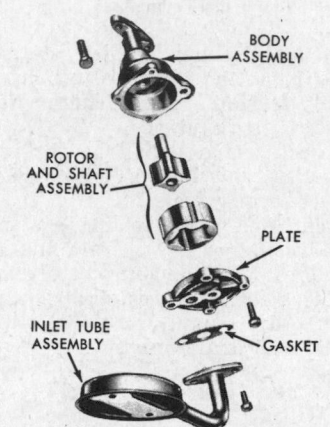

6 cyl oil pump (Ⓒ Ford Motor Co)

5. Install and torque oil pump attaching screws to 12-15 ft. lbs. on six cylinder, 20-25 ft. lbs. on V8s.
6. Install oil pan.

Rear Crankshaft Oil Seal Removal and Installation

NOTE: the rear oil seal installed in these engines is a rubber type seal.

1. Remove the oil pan, and, if required, the oil pump.
2. Loosen all main bearing caps allowing the crankshaft to lower slightly.

NOTE: the crankshaft should not be allowed to drop more than 1/32 in.

3. Remove the rear main bearing cap and remove the seal from the cap and block.
4. Carefully clean the seal grooves in the cap and block with solvent.
5. Soak the new seal halves in clean engine oil.
6. Install the upper half of the seal in the block with the undercut side of the seal toward the front of the engine. Slide the seal around the crankshaft journal until ⅜ in. protrudes beyond the base of the block.
7. Repeat above procedure on lower seal, allowing an equal length of

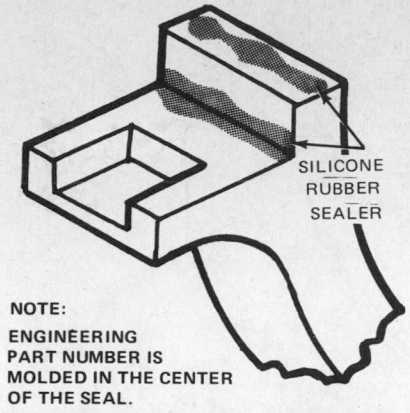

NOTE:
ENGINEERING PART NUMBER IS MOLDED IN THE CENTER OF THE SEAL.

Old style oil pan gasket seal (© Ford Motor Co)

the seal to protrude beyond the opposite end of the bearing cap.

8. Install rear bearing cap and torque all main bearings to specifications. Apply sealer only to the rear of the seals.

9. Dip the bearing cap side seals in oil, then immediately install them. Do not use any sealer on the side seals. Tap the seals into place and do not clip the protruding ends.

10. Install the oil pump and pan. Fill the crankcase with oil, start engine check for leaks.

CLUTCH

The clutch is a single dry disc type and is mechanically engaged. Centrif-ugal weights are used to increase pressure plate grip at high rpm.

Pedal Adjustment

1. Disconnect clutch return spring from release lever.

2. Loosen release lever rod locknut and adjusting nut.

3. Move clutch release lever rear-ward until release bearing lightly contacts clutch pressure plate release fingers.

4. Adjust rod length until rod seats in release lever pocket.

5. Insert specified feeler gauge between adjusting nut and swivel sleeve. Tighten adjusting nut against gauge.

6. Tighten lock nut against adjusting nut, taking care not to disturb adjustment. Torque locknut to 15-20 ft. lbs. and remove feeler gauge.

7. Install clutch return spring.

8. Check free travel at pedal. Readjust if necessary to obtain specified travel. Moving adjusting nut away from swivel sleeve increases travel. Moving adjusting nut toward swivel sleeve decreases travel.

9. As final check, measure pedal free travel with transmission in neutral and engine running at 3,000 rpm. If pedal travel is not minimum of ½ in., readjust free travel.

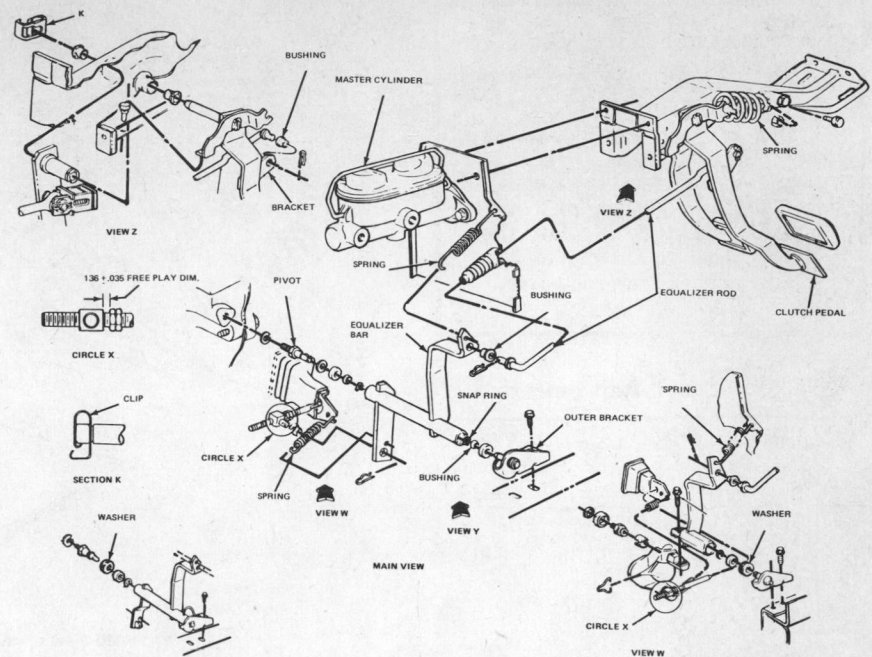

Clutch pedal and linkage adjustment—1970-74 Maverick and Comet
(© Ford Motor Co)

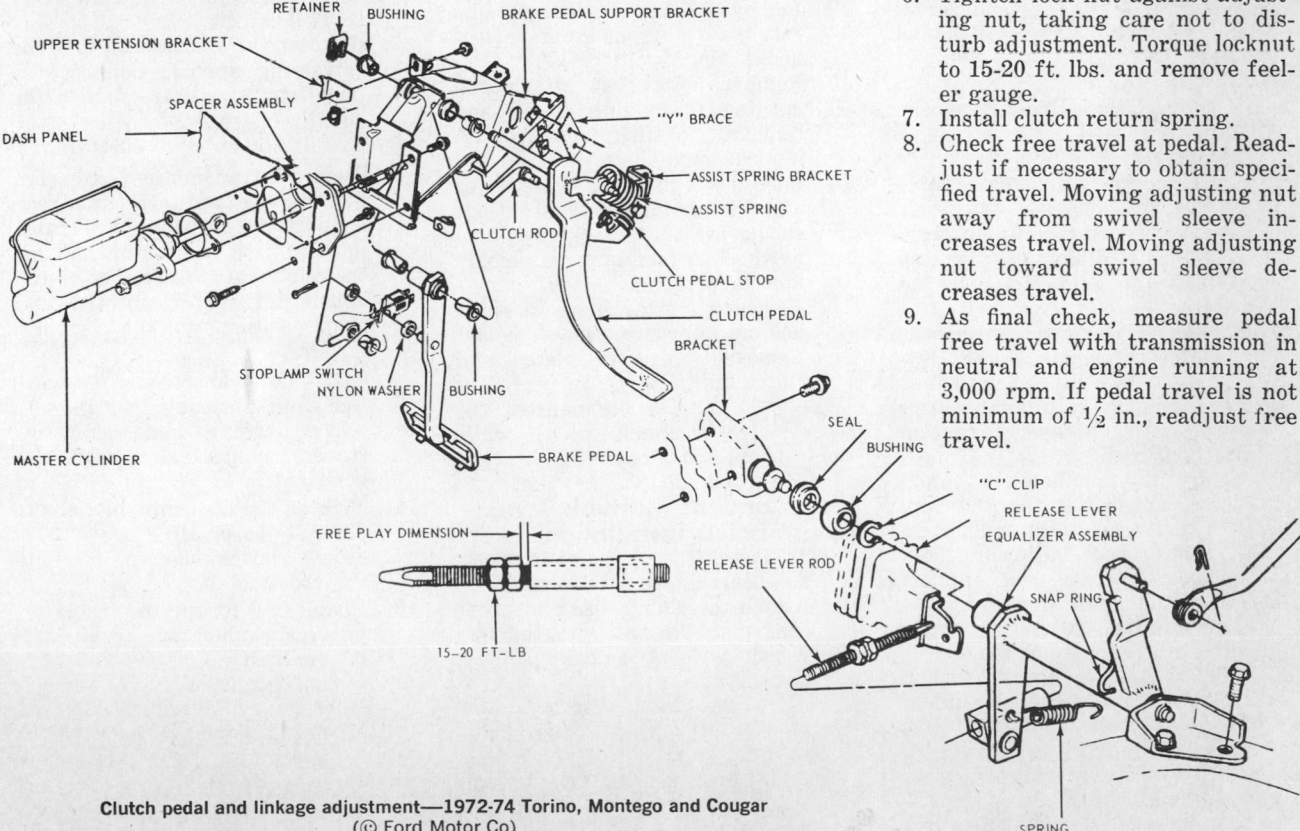

Clutch pedal and linkage adjustment—1972-74 Torino, Montego and Cougar
(© Ford Motor Co)

TIME SAVER

If a problem is encountered with clutch adjustment rods bending, check the clutch equalizer shaft. A bent or distorted equalizer shaft will allow the clutch pedal to travel too far, which will bend the adjustment rod.

Clutch Pedal Adjustment

Year and Engine	Clearance* (in.)	Free Travel (in.)
1970-71 except 428 and 429	0.136	⅞-1⅛
1970-71 428 and 429	0.178	⅞-1⅛
1972-74 Torino, Montego, Cougar and 1972-73 Mustang	0.194	⅞-1⅛
1972-77 Comet, Maverick, Monarch and Granada	0.136	⅞-1⅛

* Between adjusting nut and swivel sleeve

Clutch and/or Manual Transmission Removal

1. Disconnect and remove starter and dust ring, if the clutch is to be removed. On floor-shift models, remove the boot retainer and shifter lever.
2. Raise the car.
3. Disconnect the driveshaft at the rear universal joint and remove the driveshaft.
4. Disconnect the speedometer cable at the transmission extension. On cars with transmission regulated spark, disconnect the lead wire at the connector. Disconnect the seat belt sensor wires.
5. Disconnect the gear shift rods from the transmission shift levers. If car is equipped with four speed, remove bolts that secure shift control bracket to extension housing.
6. Remove the bolt holding the extension housing to the rear support, and remove the muffler inlet pipe bracket to housing bolt.
7. Remove the two rear support bracket insulator nuts from the underside of the crossmember. Remove crossmember.
8. Place a jack (equipped with a protective piece of wood) under the rear of the engine oil pan. Raise the engine, slightly.
9. Remove transmission - to - flywheel-housing bolts.
NOTE: on 429 and 460 cu in. en-

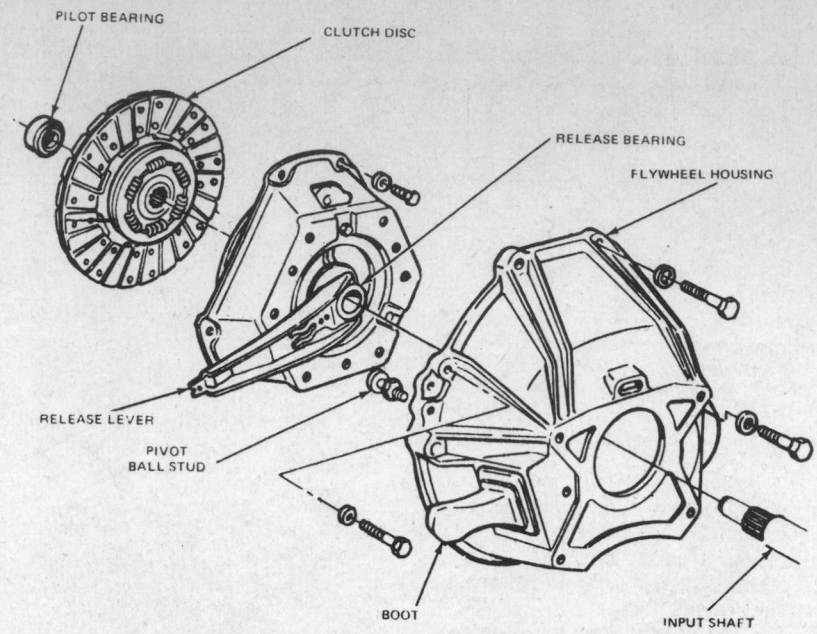

Exploded view of clutch and related parts
(© Ford Motor Co)

gines the upper left-hand transmission attaching bolt is a seal bolt. Carefully note its position so that it may be reinstalled in its original position.
10. Slide the transmission back and out of the car.
11. To remove the clutch, remove release lever retracting spring and disconnect pedal at the equalizer bar.
12. Remove bolts that secure engine rear plate to front lower part of bellhousing.
13. Remove bolts that attach bell housing to cylinder block and remove housing and release lever as a unit.
14. Loosen six pressure plate cover attaching bolts evenly to release spring pressure. Mark cover and flywheel to facilitate reassembly in same position.
15. Remove six attaching bolts while holding pressure plate cover. Remove pressure plate and clutch disc.

Caution Do not depress the clutch pedal while the transmission is removed.

Clutch and/or Manual Transmission Installation

1. To install the clutch, first wash flywheel surface with alcohol.
2. Attach the clutch disc and pressure plate assembly to the flywheel with the bolts finger tight.
3. Align the clutch disc with the pilot bushing. Torque cover bolts to 12-20 ft. lbs.
4. Lightly lubricate the release lever fulcrum ends. Install the release lever in the flywheel

housing and install the dust shield.
5. Apply very little lubricant on the release bearing retainer journal. Attach the release bearing and hub on the release lever.
6. Install the flywheel housing and torque the attaching bolts to 40-50 ft. lbs. on all V8s. Torque sixes to 23-33 ft. lbs. Install the dust cover and torque the bolts to 17-20 ft. lbs.
7. Connect the release rod and the retracting spring. Connect the pedal - to - equalizer - rod at the equalizer bar.
8. Install starter and dust ring.
9. Start the transmission extension housing up and over the rear support. After moving the transmission back just far enough for the pilot shaft to clear the clutch housing, move it upward and into position on the flywheel housing.
10. Move the transmission forward and into place against the flywheel housing, and install the transmission attaching bolts finger-tight.
11. Tighten the transmission bolts to 37-42 ft. lbs. on all cars.
12. Slowly lower the engine onto the crossmember.
13. Install and torque the insulator-to-crossmember nuts to 30-42 ft lbs on 428 CJ Cougars and Mustangs. Torque 1970-77 Torinos, Montegos, Mavericks, Comets, Monarchs, and Granadas to 30-50 ft lbs and 1970-74 Cougars and 1970-73 Mustangs to 25-35 ft lbs.
14. Connect gear shift rods and the

speedometer cable. On transmission regulated spark equipped cars, connect the lead wire at the connector.

15. Hook up the drive shaft.
16. Refill transmission to proper level. On floor-shift models, install the boot retainer and shift lever.

MANUAL TRANSMISSION

There are three manual transmissions used: (1) a heavy-duty, top cover, fully synchromesh three-speed used on all three-speed applications, (2) a heavy-duty, top cover, fully synchromesh, Ford-built four-speed used on V8 engines through 1974. The heavy-duty four-speed manual transmission is not available on 1975 and later models, and (3) beginning 1977, a fully synchromesh four-speed overdrive transmission is available on Granada and Monarch six-cylinder or 302 V8 engines. Designed by Ford, the transmission has a floor shift, cast iron case, and a fourth gear ratio of 0.81 : 1.

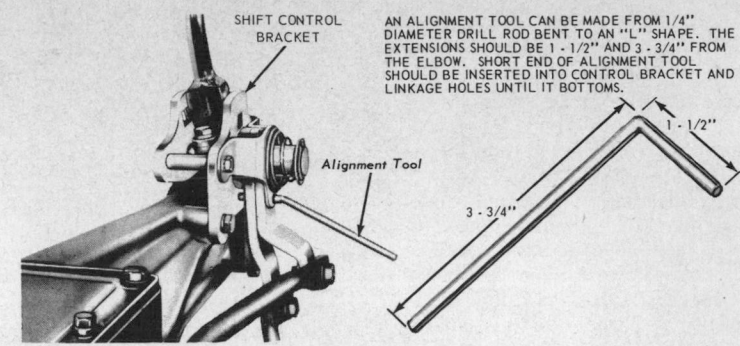

Manual transmission floor or console shift adjustment (© Ford Motor Co)

Linkage Adjustment

Three-Speed Column Shift

With the transmission in neutral, the shift lever should be in a horizontal plane and parallel to the instrument panel line. Corrective adjustments should be made at the gear shift rods.

1. Place lever in neutral.
2. Loosen two gear shift rod adjustment nuts.
3. Insert 3/16 in. diameter alignment pin through first and reverse gear shift lever and second and third gear shift lever. Align levers to insert pin.
4. Tighten gear shift rod adjustment nuts, and remove pin.
5. Check gear lever for smooth crossover.

Three-Speed Floor and Console Shift

1. Loosen three shift linkage adjustment nuts.
2. Install a 1/4 in. diameter alignment pin through control bracket and levers.
3. Tighten three shift linkage adjustment nuts and remove alignment pin.

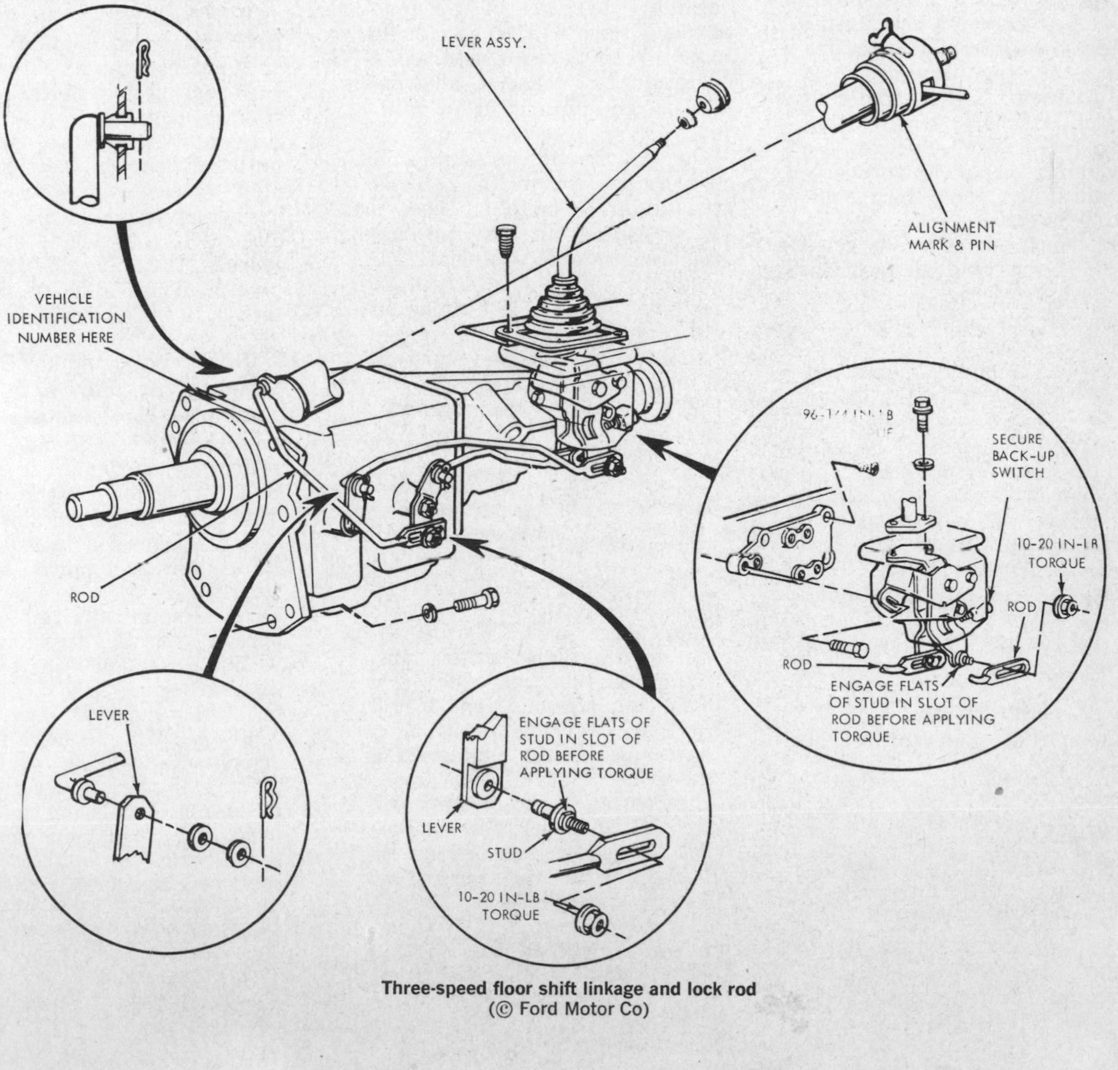

Three-speed floor shift linkage and lock rod (© Ford Motor Co)

4. Check gear lever for smooth crossover.

Four-Speed

1. Place shifter lever in neutral position, then raise car on a hoist.
2. Insert a ¼ in. rod into the alignment holes of the shift levers.
3. If the holes are not in exact alignment, check for bent connecting rods or loose lever lock nuts at the rod ends. Make replacements or repairs, then adjust as follows.
4. Loosen the three rod-to-lever retaining lock nuts and move the levers until the ¼ in. gauge rod will enter the alignment holes. Be sure that the transmission shift levers are in neutral and the reverse shifter lever is in the neutral detent.
5. Install the shift rods and torque the lock nuts to 18-23 ft. lbs.
6. Remove the ¼ in. gauge rod.
7. Operate the shift levers to assure correct shifting.
8. Lower the car and road test.

Transmission Lock Rod Adjustment

Models with floor or console mounted shifters and manual transmissions incorporate a transmission lock rod which prevents the shifter from being moved from the reverse position when the ignition lock is in the OFF position. The lock rod connects the shift tube in the steering column to the transmission reverse lever. The lock rod cannot be properly adjusted until the manual linkage adjustment is correct.

1. With the transmission selector lever in the neutral position, loosen the lock rod adjustment nut on the transmission reverse lever.
2. Insert a .180 in. diameter rod (No. 15 drill bit) in the gauge pin hole located at the 6 o'clock position on the steering column socket casting, directly below the ignition lock.
3. Manipulate the pin until the casting will not move with the pin inserted.
4. Torque the lock rod adjustment rod to 10-20 ft. lbs.
5. Remove the pin and check the linkage operation.

Transmission Removal

See Clutch and/or Transmission Removal.

AUTOMATIC TRANSMISSION

Three different automatic transmissions are used in Ford compact and intermediate cars: a C4, a C6,

and an FMX. The C4 is a light duty transmission used on six cylinder and small block V8 engines. The FMX is an intermediate duty transmission used on medium duty V8s. The C6 is a heavy duty transmission used on high-performance and large displacement V8 engines.

The transmission identification code can be found on the vehicle certification label affixed to the left front door lock panel or door pillar. Interpret the code by the "Transmission Codes" chart at the beginning of this section.

Pan Removal and Installation, Fluid Change

The procedure for a partial drain and refill of the transmission fluid is as follows:

1. Raise the car on a hoist or jack stands.
2. Place a drain pan under the transmission pan.
   NOTE: On some models of the C4 transmission, the fluid is drained by disconnecting the filler tube from the transmission fluid pan.
3. Loosen the pan attaching bolts to allow the fluid to drain.
4. When the fluid has stopped draining to level of the pan flange, remove the pan bolts starting at the rear and along both sides of the pan, allowing the pan to drop and drain gradually.
5. When all the transmission fluid has drained, remove the pan and the fluid filter and clean them.
6. After completing the transmission repairs or adjustments, install the fluid filter screen, a new pan gasket, and the pan on the transmission. Tighten the pan attaching bolts on C4 and C6 transmissions to 12–16 ft lbs. On FMX and CW transmissions, tighten the pan attaching bolts to 10–13 ft lbs.
   NOTE: Be sure to use Type "F" transmission fluid. The use of any other type of fluid such as Type "A" suffix "A," or DEXRON will materially affect the service life of the transmission.
7. Install three quarts of transmission fluid through the filter tube. If the filler tube was removed to drain the transmission, install the filler tube using a new O-ring.
8. Start and run the engine for a few minutes at low idle speed and then at the fast idle speed (about 1,200 rpm) until the normal operating temperature is reached. Do not race the engine.
9. Move the selector lever through all gear positions and place it at the Park position. Check the fluid level, and add fluid until the level is between the "add" and "full"

marks on the dipstick. Do not overfill.

C4

Throttle Linkage Adjustment

Initial Adjustments—All Models

1. Apply parking brake and place selector lever at N.
2. Run engine at normal idle speed. If engine is cold, run engine at fast idle speed (about 1200 rpm) until it reaches normal operating temperature. When engine is warm, slow it down to normal idle speed.
3. Connect tachometer to engine.
4. Adjust engine idle speed to specified rpm with transmission selector lever at D or D_1 or D_2.
5. The carburetor throttle lever must be against hot idle speed adjusting screw at specified idle speed in D or D_1 or D_2.

1970 Mustang, Six Cylinder, and 1970 Montego, Fairlane, Torino and Maverick Six Cylinder— Final Adjustments

1. Disconnect throttle return spring and remove trunnion and cable at bellcrank.
2. Hold transmission in full downshift against stop.
3. Hold carburetor throttle lever wide open against stop.
4. Adjust trunnion at bellcrank until ball stud on shaft and ball stud receiver on cable align. Then turn trunnion one full additional turn to increase length.
5. Release transmission and carburetor to normal free position.
6. Install throttle return spring.

1970-77 Cougar and 1970-73 Mustang V8s, and 1970-77 All Models—Final Adjustments

1. Disconnect throttle and downshift return springs.
2. Hold carburetor throttle lever in wide open position against stop.
3. Hold transmission in full downshift position against internal stop.
4. Turn adjustment screw on carburetor downshift lever to within 0.040-0.080 in. on 1971 and earlier models, 0.050–0.070 in. on 1972 models, and 0.010–0.080 on 1973 and later models, of contacting pickup surface of carburetor throttle lever.
5. Release transmission and carburetor to normal free positions.
6. Install throttle and downshift return springs.

Shift Linkage Adjustment

Column Shift

1. With engine stopped, loosen

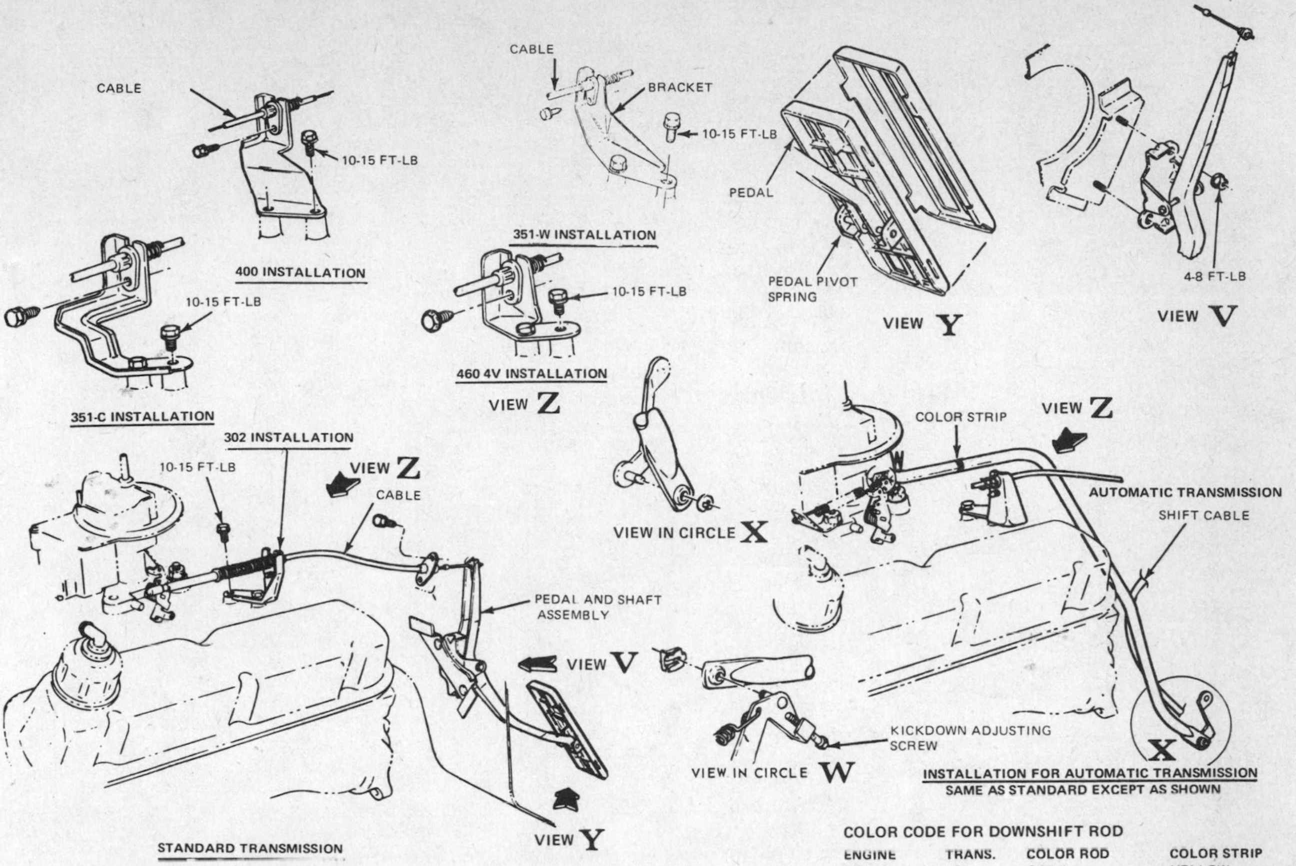

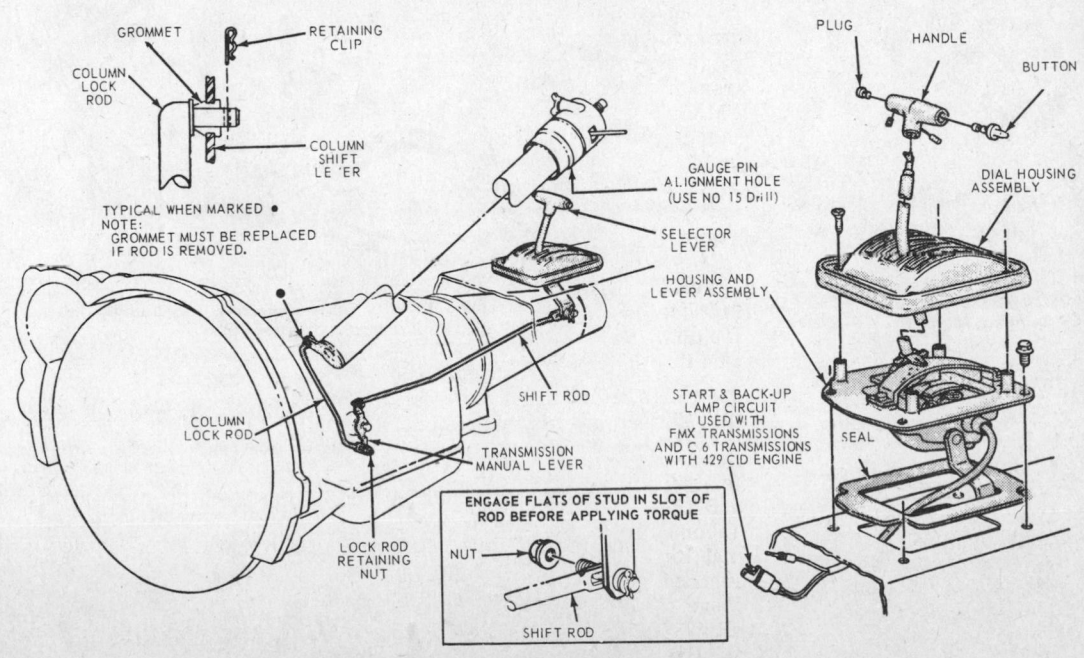

CABLE

CABLE

10-15 FT-LB

400 INSTALLATION

BRACKET

10-15 FT-LB

PEDAL

351-W INSTALLATION

10-15 FT-LB

460 4V INSTALLATION

VIEW **Z**

PEDAL PIVOT SPRING

VIEW **Y**

4-8 FT-LB

VIEW **V**

10-15 FT-LB

351-C INSTALLATION

10-15 FT-LB

302 INSTALLATION

VIEW **Z**

CABLE

VIEW IN CIRCLE **X**

COLOR STRIP

VIEW **Z**

AUTOMATIC TRANSMISSION

SHIFT CABLE

PEDAL AND SHAFT ASSEMBLY

VIEW **V**

KICKDOWN ADJUSTING SCREW

VIEW IN CIRCLE **W**

INSTALLATION FOR AUTOMATIC TRANSMISSION
SAME AS STANDARD EXCEPT AS SHOWN

VIEW **Y**

STANDARD TRANSMISSION

KICK-DOWN CONTROL ADJUSTMENT

A. WITH CARBURETOR HELD AT W.O.T. POSITION AND THE KICKDOWN ROD HELD DOWNWARD AGAINST THE "THROUGH DETENT" STOP, ADJUST THE KICKDOWN ADJUSTING SCREW TO OBTAIN 0.010-0.080 INCH CLEARANCE BETWEEN THE SCREW AND THROTTLE ARM.

B. RELEASE CARBURETOR AND TRANSMISSION LEVERS TO FREE POSITIONS.

COLOR CODE FOR ACCELERATOR CABLE

ENGINE	COLOR
302-2V	YELLOW
351-2V	YELLOW
351-4V	BLUE
400-2V	YELLOW
460-4V P.I.	BLACK

COLOR CODE FOR DOWNSHIFT ROD

ENGINE	TRANS.	COLOR ROD	COLOR STRIP
302-2V	XP3	GOLD	YELLOW
351C-2V	XP3	GOLD	WHITE
351C-2V	XPL	GOLD	VIOLET-WHITE
351C-2V	FMX	GOLD	WHITE-BLUE
351W-2V	XP3	GOLD	RED-YELLOW
351W-2V	XPL	GOLD	BLACK-BLUE
351W-2V	FMX	GOLD	BROWN-SILVER
351-4V	XPL	GOLD	VIOLET
400-2V	XPL	GOLD	VIOLET
460-4V P.I.	XPL	GOLD	SILVER

Throttle and downshift linkage—1972-77 Torino, Elite, Montego and Cougar V8
(© Ford Motor Co)

GROMMET

RETAINING CLIP

COLUMN LOCK ROD

COLUMN SHIFT LEVER

PLUG

HANDLE

BUTTON

GAUGE PIN ALIGNMENT HOLE (USE NO 15 Drill)

SELECTOR LEVER

DIAL HOUSING ASSEMBLY

TYPICAL WHEN MARKED •
NOTE:
GROMMET MUST BE REPLACED IF ROD IS REMOVED.

HOUSING AND LEVER ASSEMBLY

COLUMN LOCK ROD

SHIFT ROD

TRANSMISSION MANUAL LEVER

START & BACK-UP LAMP CIRCUIT USED WITH FMX TRANSMISSIONS AND C 6 TRANSMISSIONS WITH 429 CID ENGINE

SEAL

LOCK ROD RETAINING NUT

ENGAGE FLATS OF STUD IN SLOT OF ROD BEFORE APPLYING TORQUE

NUT

SHIFT ROD

Automatic transmission floor mounted shift linkage and lock rod—1970-73 Mustang and Cougar
(© Ford Motor Co)

C483

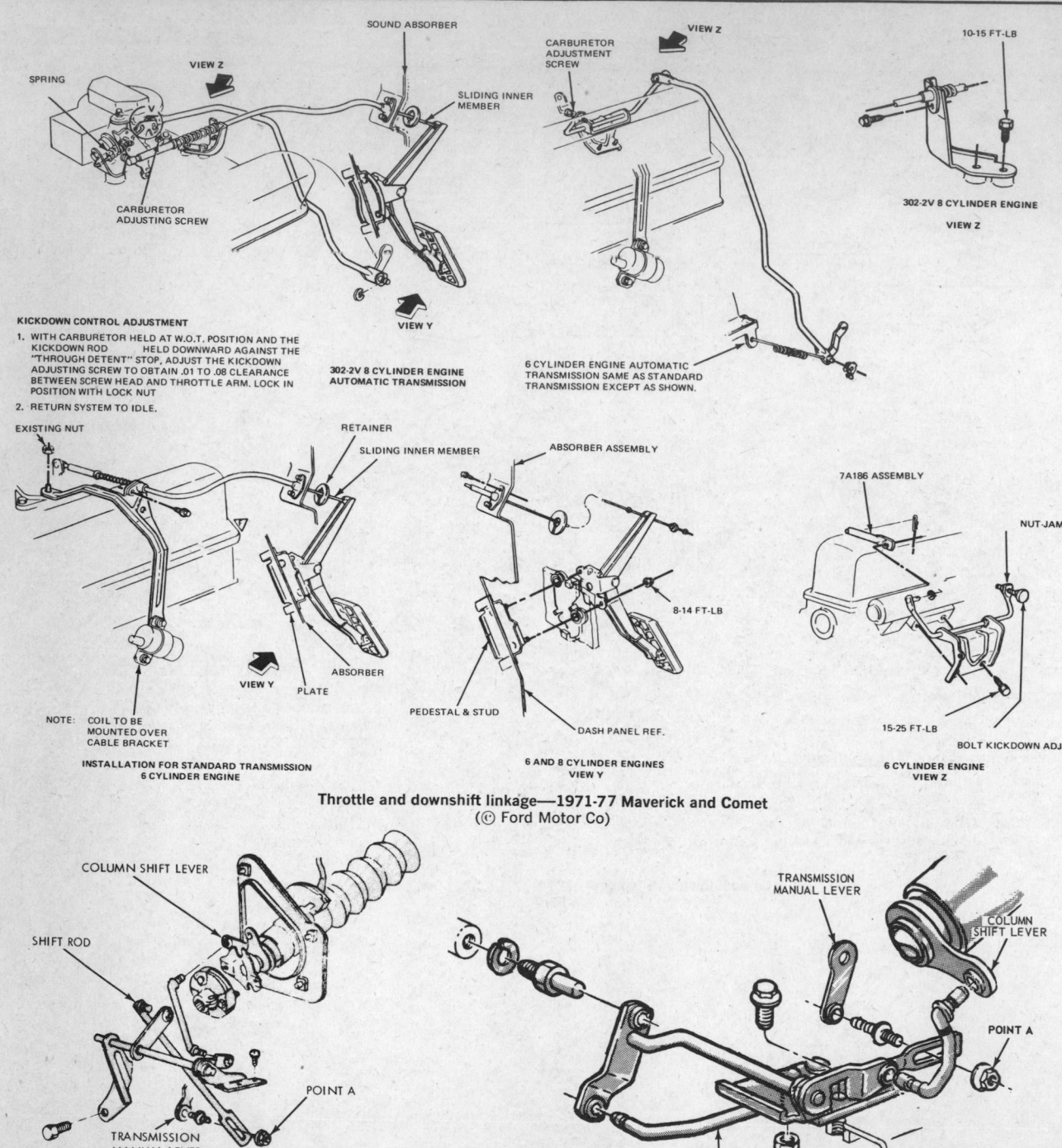

KICKDOWN CONTROL ADJUSTMENT

1. WITH CARBURETOR HELD AT W.O.T. POSITION AND THE KICKDOWN ROD   HELD DOWNWARD AGAINST THE "THROUGH DETENT" STOP, ADJUST THE KICKDOWN ADJUSTING SCREW TO OBTAIN .01 TO .08 CLEARANCE BETWEEN SCREW HEAD AND THROTTLE ARM. LOCK IN POSITION WITH LOCK NUT

2. RETURN SYSTEM TO IDLE.

Throttle and downshift linkage—1971-77 Maverick and Comet
(© Ford Motor Co)

Column shift—1970-77 Maverick and 1971-77 Comet
(© Ford Motor Co)

Column shift—1970   Fairlane, Falcon, Torino and Montego
(© Ford Motor Co)

clamp at shift lever at point A so that shift rod is free to slide in clamp. On vehicles equipped with a shift cable, remove the nut at point A and at manual lever stud.

2. Place transmission shift lever into D or D_1 (large dot) position. On Maverick with semi-automatic transmission, place lever in Hi.

3. Shift manual lever at transmission into D, D_1, or Hi. On transmission through 1971, D or Hi is the third detent from the rear. On 1972 and later transmissions, D is the second detent from the rear.

4. Tighten clamp on shift rod at point A to 10-20 ft. lbs. On vehicles equipped with a shift cable, position the cable end on the transmission manual lever stud, aligning the flats. Start the adjusting nut.

5. Check pointer alignment and transmission operation for all selector lever positions.

Floor or Console Shift

1. Place transmission shift lever in D.

2. Raise vehicle and loosen manual lever shift rod retaining nut. Move transmission lever to D_1 or D position. On all cars through 1970, D is fourth detent from rear. On 1971 cars, D is the third detent from the rear. On 1972 and later cars, D is second from rear.

3. With transmission shift lever

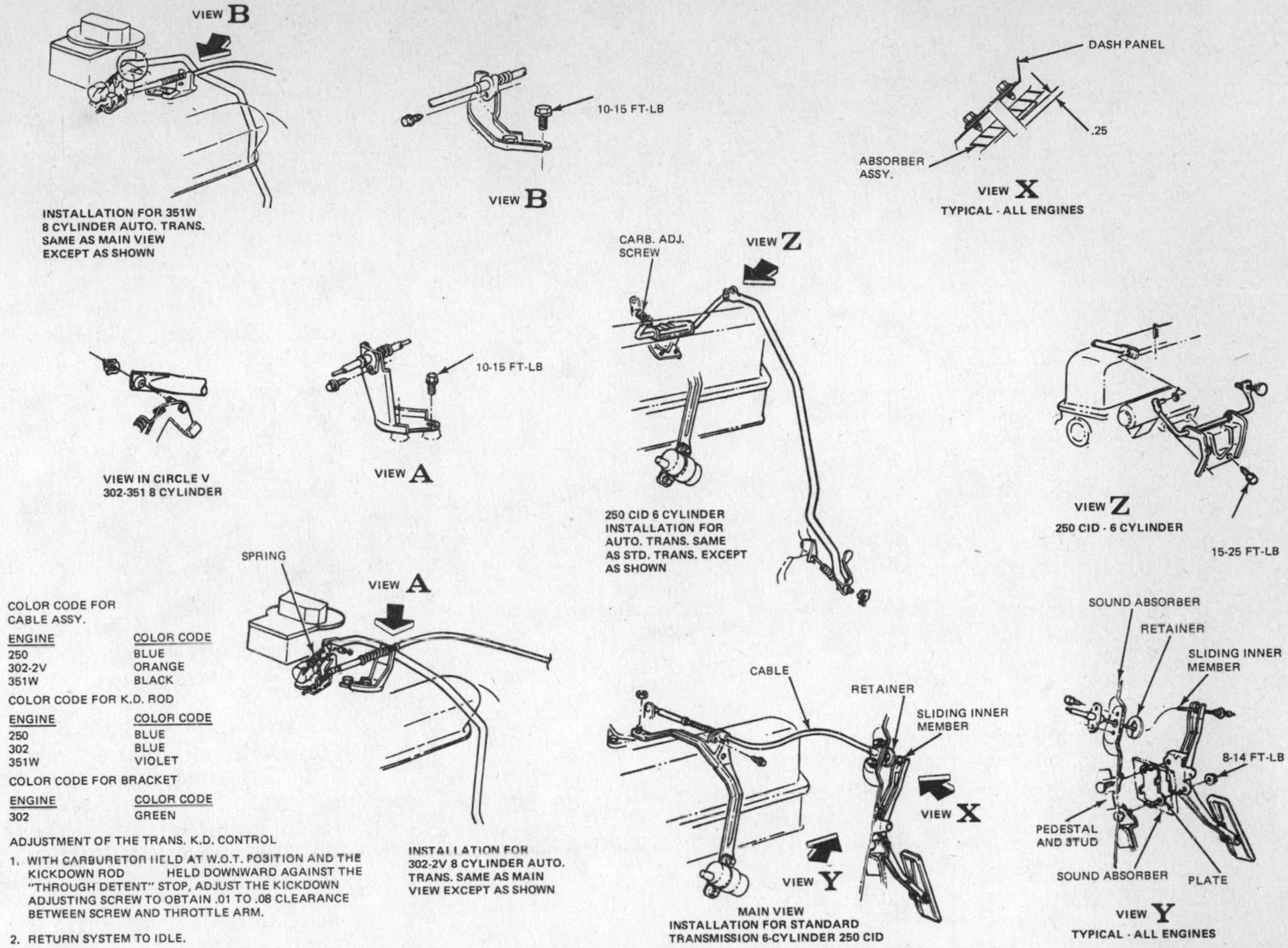

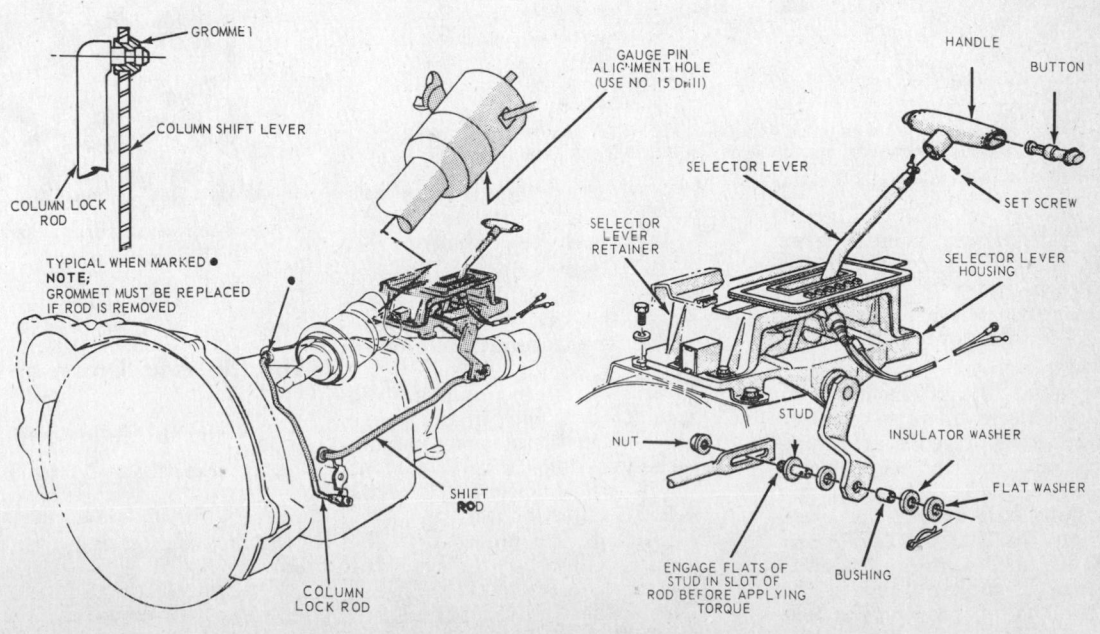

VIEW **B**

INSTALLATION FOR 351W
8 CYLINDER AUTO. TRANS.
SAME AS MAIN VIEW
EXCEPT AS SHOWN

10-15 FT-LB

VIEW **B**

DASH PANEL

.25

ABSORBER
ASSY.

VIEW **X**
TYPICAL - ALL ENGINES

CARB. ADJ.
SCREW

VIEW **Z**

VIEW IN CIRCLE V
302-351 8 CYLINDER

10-15 FT-LB

VIEW **A**

250 CID 6 CYLINDER
INSTALLATION FOR
AUTO. TRANS. SAME
AS STD. TRANS. EXCEPT
AS SHOWN

VIEW **Z**
250 CID - 6 CYLINDER

15-25 FT-LB

SPRING

VIEW **A**

COLOR CODE FOR
CABLE ASSY.

ENGINE	COLOR CODE
250	BLUE
302-2V	ORANGE
351W	BLACK

COLOR CODE FOR K.D. ROD

ENGINE	COLOR CODE
250	BLUE
302	BLUE
351W	VIOLET

COLOR CODE FOR BRACKET

ENGINE	COLOR CODE
302	GREEN

ADJUSTMENT OF THE TRANS. K.D. CONTROL

1. WITH CARBURETOR HELD AT W.O.T. POSITION AND THE
   KICKDOWN ROD   HELD DOWNWARD AGAINST THE
   "THROUGH DETENT" STOP, ADJUST THE KICKDOWN
   ADJUSTING SCREW TO OBTAIN .01 TO .08 CLEARANCE
   BETWEEN SCREW AND THROTTLE ARM.

2. RETURN SYSTEM TO IDLE.

INSTALLATION FOR
302-2V 8 CYLINDER AUTO.
TRANS. SAME AS MAIN
VIEW EXCEPT AS SHOWN

CABLE

RETAINER

SLIDING INNER
MEMBER

VIEW **X**

VIEW **Y**

MAIN VIEW
INSTALLATION FOR STANDARD
TRANSMISSION 6-CYLINDER 250 CID

SOUND ABSORBER

RETAINER

SLIDING INNER
MEMBER

8-14 FT-LB

PEDESTAL
AND STUD

SOUND ABSORBER

PLATE

VIEW **Y**
TYPICAL - ALL ENGINES

Throttle and downshift linkage—1975-77 Granada and Monarch
(© Ford Motor Co)

GROMMET

COLUMN SHIFT LEVER

COLUMN LOCK
ROD

TYPICAL WHEN MARKED •
NOTE:
GROMMET MUST BE REPLACED
IF ROD IS REMOVED

GAUGE PIN
ALIGNMENT HOLE
(USE NO 15 DRILL)

HANDLE

BUTTON

SELECTOR LEVER

SELECTOR
LEVER
RETAINER

SET SCREW

SELECTOR LEVER
HOUSING

SHIFT
ROD

COLUMN
LOCK ROD

NUT

STUD

INSULATOR WASHER

FLAT WASHER

BUSHING

ENGAGE FLATS OF
STUD IN SLOT OF
ROD BEFORE APPLYING
TORQUE

**Automatic transmission floor mounted shift linkage and lock rod—
1970-71 Fairlane, Torino and Montego**
(© Ford Motor Co)

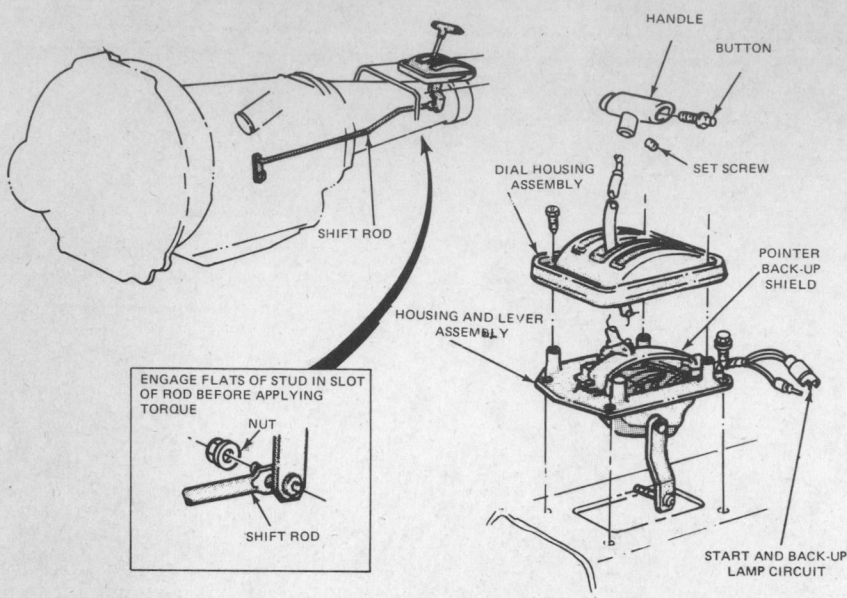

Automatic transmission floor mounted linkage—1972-76 Torino, Elite, and Montego; 1972-77 Cougar; 1977 LTD II and Thunderbird
(© Ford Motor Co)

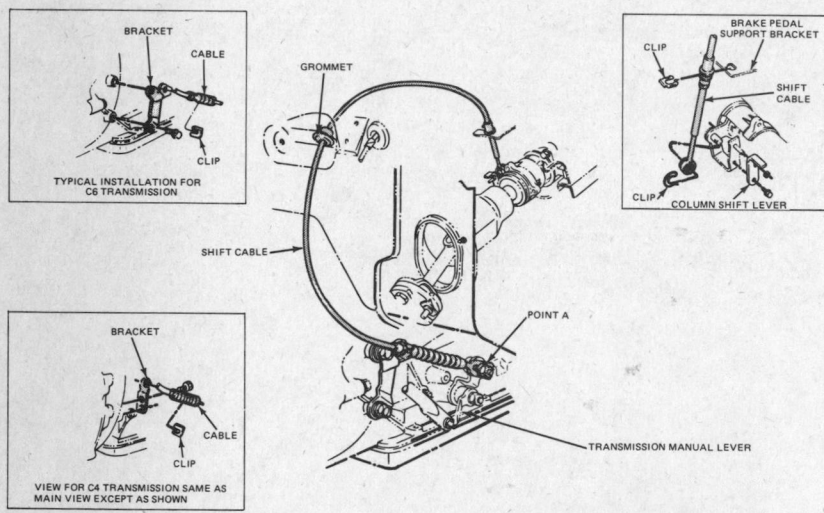

Automatic transmission column mounted linkage—1972-76 Torino, Elite, and Montego; 1972-77 Cougar, Granada, and Monarch; 1977 LTD II and Thunderbird

and transmission manual lever in position, tighten nut at point A to 10-20 ft. lbs.

4. Check transmission operation for all selector lever detent positions.

NOTE: since 1970, all models with a floor or console mounted selector lever have incorporated a transmission lock out rod to prevent the transmission selector from being moved out of the PARK position when the ignition lock is in the OFF position. The lock rod connects the shift tube in the steering column to the transmission manual lever. The lock rod cannot be properly adjusted until the manual linkage adjustment is correct.

Lock Rod Adjustment

1. With the transmission selector lever in the DRIVE position, loosen the lock rod adjustment nut on the transmission manual lever.
2. Insert a .180 in. diameter rod (No. 15 drill bit) in the gauge pin hole in the steering column socket casting, it is located at the 6 o'clock position directly below the ignition lock.
3. Manipulate the pin so that the casting will not move when the pin is fully inserted.
4. Torque the lock rod adjustment nut to 10-20 ft. lbs.
5. Remove the pin and check the linkage operation.

Band Adjustment

Intermediate Band

1. Clean all the dirt from the adjusting screw and remove and discard the locknut.
2. Install a new locknut on the adjusting screw. Using a torque wrench, tighten the adjusting screw to 10 ft lbs.
3. Back off the adjusting screw *exactly* 1¾ *turns*.
4. Hold the adjusting screw steady and tighten the locknut to the proper torque.

C4 Intermediate band adjustment
(© Ford Motor Co)

Low-Reverse Band

1. Clean all dirt from around the band adjusting screw, and remove and discard the locknut.
2. Install a new locknut on the adjusting screw. Using a torque wrench, tighten the adjusting screw to 10 ft lbs.
3. Back off the adjusting screw *exactly* 3 *full turns*.
4. Hold the adjusting screw steady and tighten the locknut to the proper torque.

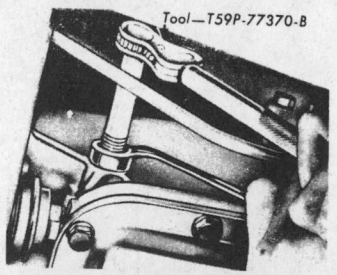

C4 Low-Reverse band adjustment
(© Ford Motor Co)

C6

Throttle and Downshift Linkage

Initial Adjustments

See C4 section.

Final Adjustments

See C4 section under 1970-77 Cougar V8.

Shift Linkage Adjustment, Transmission Lock Rod Adjustment

See C4 section.

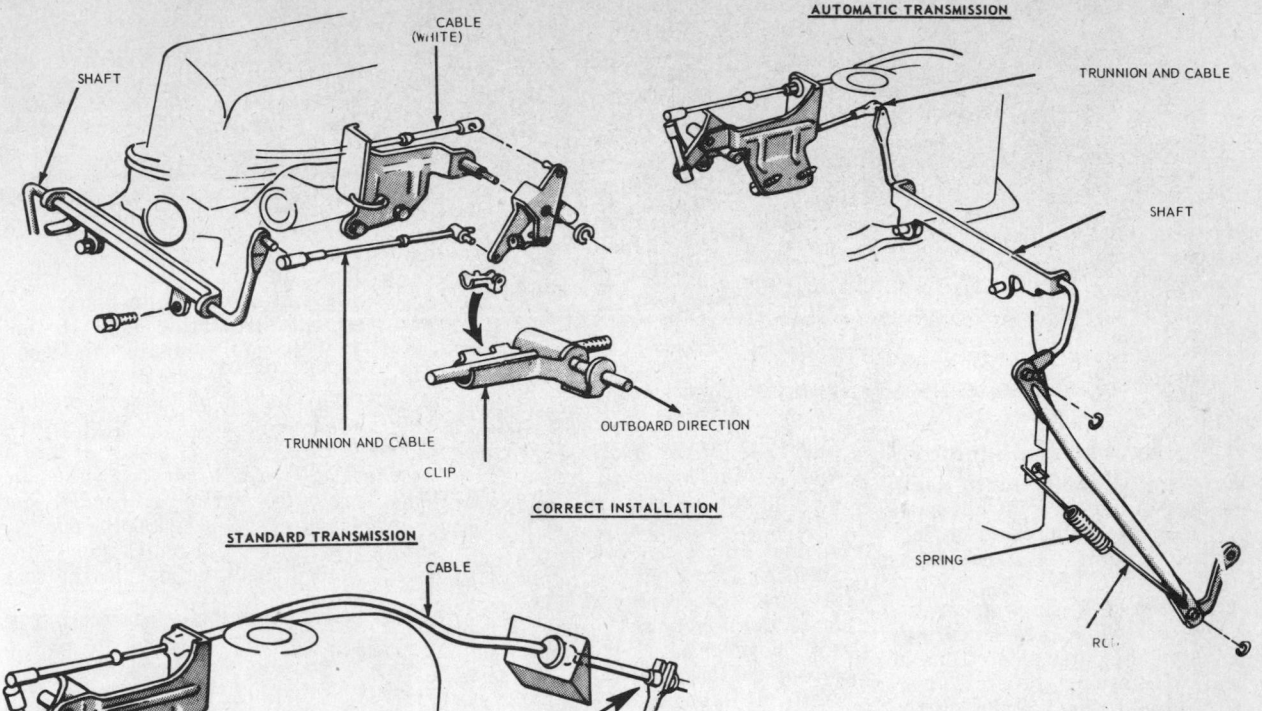

AUTOMATIC TRANSMISSION

SHAFT

CABLE (WHITE)

TRUNNION AND CABLE

SHAFT

TRUNNION AND CABLE

CLIP

OUTBOARD DIRECTION

CORRECT INSTALLATION

SPRING

ROD

STANDARD TRANSMISSION

CABLE

SNAP IN FITTING

MAVERICK CABLE INSTALLATION

Throttle linkage adjustment—1970 Maverick (© Ford Motor Co)

Band Adjustment

Intermediate Band Adjustment

1. Raise the car on a hoist or place it on jackstands.
2. Clean the threads of the inter-mediate band adjusting screw.
3. Loosen the adjustment screw lock nut.
4. Tighten the adjusting screw to 10 ft lbs and back the screw off *exactly 1½ turns.* Tighten the adjusting screw locknut.

FMX

Since 1969, the FMX transmission has been used in some intermediate size Fords. It is usually used in con-junction with the 351 V8 engine. The throttle and downshift linkage ad-justments are the same as used with the C4 transmission.

FMX Band Adjustment

See Ford section.

U-JOINTS

Rear Universal Joint Removal

The rear universal joint has two pillow blocks which are bolted to the pinion shaft flange.

Take out the four bolts that hold the bearing blocks to the pinion shaft and gently tap off the bearing blocks.

Lower the back end of the drive shaft and the front end can be slid out of the back of the transmission to-gether with the transmission yoke portion of the front universal joint.

Carry the assembly—the front uni-versal joint complete, the driveshaft and the rear universal joint—to the bench and remove the cross from the rear universal joint by taking out the lock rings from the inner side of the bearings. Using a large punch or an arbor press, drive one of the bearings in toward the center, which will force out the opposite bearing.

When it is pressed out far enough to grip it with a pair of pliers, grip it and pull it out of the driveshaft yoke.

Now drive the cross in the opposite direction until the opposite bearing has been driven far enough out for gripping with a pair of pliers.

When both bearings have been taken out, the cross can be lifted from between the two yokes.

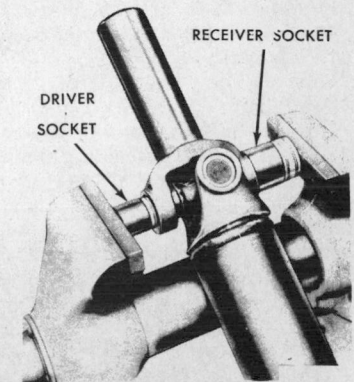

RECEIVER SOCKET

DRIVER SOCKET

U-joint removal (© Ford Motor Co)

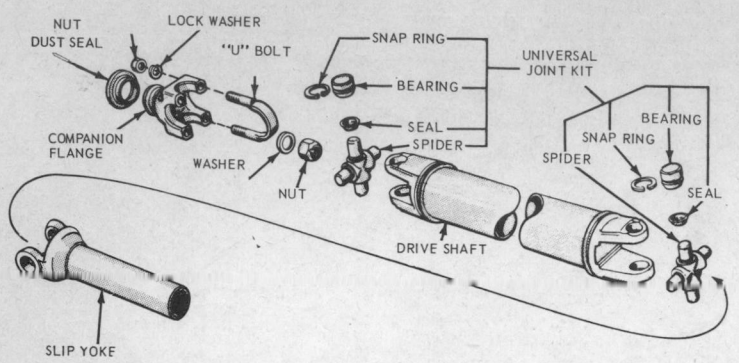

Driveshaft and universal joint assembly (© Ford Motor Co)

Front Universal Joint Removal

Follow the procedure given above for the rear universal joint but leave the rear universal joint cross in place on the driveshaft if it is not to be removed.

Remove the lock rings from the inner side of two opposite bearings and press on the outer side of one of the bearings, forcing the cross over, which will force the bearing on the opposite side out of its yoke.

Remove the bearing which was forced out of the yoke and then press the cross in the opposite direction to press the other bearing out.

Repeat this procedure on the third and fourth bearings.

When installing the new bearings in the universal joint yoke, it is possible to put them in with a driver of some type, but it is recommended that this work be done in an arbor press since a heavy jolt on the needle bearings can very easily misalign them, which will greatly shorten their life.

REAR AXLE

Axle Shaft

Shaft Removal and Installation, Bearing Replacement

NOTE: Bearings must be pressed on and off the shaft with an arbor press. Unless you have access to one, it is inadvisable to attempt any repair work on the axle shaft and bearing assemblies.

1. Remove the wheel, tire, and brake drum.
2. Remove the nuts holding the retainer plate to the backing plate. Disconnect the brake line.
3. Remove the retainer and install nuts, finger-tight, to prevent the brake backing plate from being dislodged.

NOTE: Some late-model cars using the integral carrier or WER axles have C-clips retaining the axle shafts. Prior to removing the shaft, remove the inspection plate and check for C-

clips. The clips must be removed prior to shaft removal.

4. Pull out the axle shaft and bearing assembly, using a slide hammer.

NOTE: If end-play is found to be excessive, the bearing should be replaced. Shimming the bearing is not recommended as this ignores end-play of the bearing itself and could result in improper seating of the bearing.

5. Uusing a chisel, nick the bearing retainer in 3 or 4 places. The retainer does not have to be cut, but merely collapsed sufficiently to allow the bearing retainer to be slid from the shaft.
6. Press off the bearing and install the new one by pressing it into position.

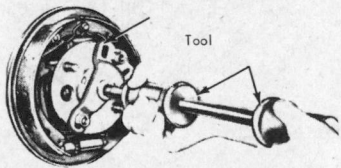

Removing axle shaft
(© Ford Motor Co)

7. Press on the new retainer.

NOTE: Do not attempt to press the bearing and retainer on at the same time.

8. Assemble the shaft and bearing in the housing, being sure that the bearing is seated properly in the housing.
9. Install the retainer, drum, wheel, and tire. Bleed the brakes.

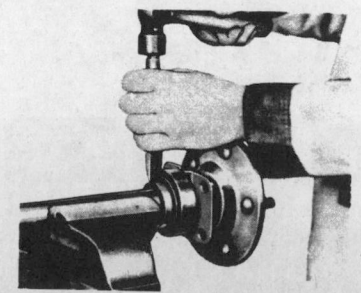

Removing rear wheel bearing retainer ring
(© Ford Motor Co)

Axle Shaft Seal Replacement

1. Remove the axle shaft from the rear axle assembly, following the procedures previously discussed.
2. Using a two-fingered seal puller (slide hammer), remove the seal from the axle housing.
3. Thoroughly clean the recess in the rear axle housing from which the seal was removed.
4. Position a new seal on the housing and drive it into place with a seal installation tool. If this tool is not available, a wood block may be substituted.

NOTE: Although the right and left-hand seals are identical, there are many different types of seals which have been used. It is advisable to have one of the old seals with you when you are purchasing new ones.

5. When the seal is properly installed, install the axle shaft.

JACKING, HOISTING

Jack car at front under spring seat of lower control arm. Jack car at rear axle housing close to differential case.

Twin post lifts—front adapters must be carefully placed, large enough to cover entire spring seat area. On models with leaf spring rear suspension, rear adapters or forks must be placed under axle not more than one in. outboard from welds near differential housing. Do not allow the lifts to contact the steering linkage.

Rear hoist contact area—cars with unitized construction (© Ford Motor Co)

On 1972 and later Torinos and Montegos, as well as 1974 and later Cougars and Elites, and 1977 LTD IIs and Thunderbirds, *do not* position the fork lifts outboard of the rear suspension lower arms. Place the forklifts under the axle housing inboard of the suspension arm brackets.

Frame contact lifts—on all except 1972 Torino and Montego and 1974

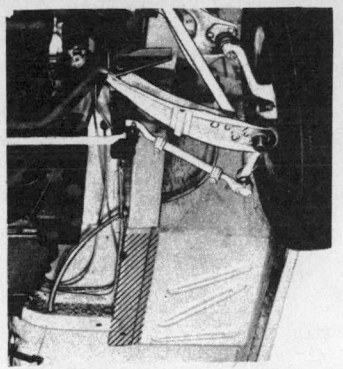

Front hoist contact area—cars with unitized construction (© Ford Motor Co)

and later Cougar and Elite, and 1977 LTD II and Thunderbird, place adapters as shown in diagram. Be sure that pads cover at least 12 sq. in. in area.

FRONT SUSPENSION

On all compact and intermediate Ford Products, except the 1972 and later Torino and Montego and 1974 and later Cougar and Elite, and 1977 LTD II and Thunderbird, the front coil springs are mounted on top of the upper control arm to a tower in the sheet metal of the body. This type of mounting provides good stability. The lower arm and stabilizing strut substitute for the conventional a frame and serve to guide the lower

part of the spindle through its cycle of up-and-down movement. The rod-type stabilizing strut is mounted between two rubber buffer pads at the front end to cushion fore and aft thrust of suspension. The effective length of this rod is variable and must be considered in maintenance. Ball joints are of the usual steel construction.

On 1972 and later Torinos and Montegos and 1974 and later Cougars and Elites, and 1977 LTD IIs and Thunderbirds, the front coil springs are mounted between the upper and lower control arm. This type of mounting, used on standard-sized Fords for many years, aids cornering ability by lowering the roll center.

Front end alignment procedures are given in the Unit Repair Section.

Coil Spring on Upper Arm

Shock Absorber
Removal

1. Raise the hood and remove the three shock absorber-to-spring tower attaching bolts.
2. Raise the front of the vehicle and place jackstands under the lower control arms.
3. Remove the shock absorber lower attaching nuts, washers, and insulators.
4. Lift the shock absorber and upper bracket from the spring tower and remove the bracket

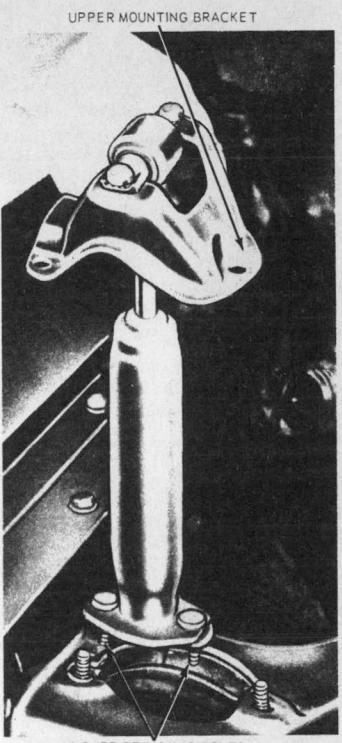

Removing shock absorber and bracket assembly—spring on upper arm (© Ford Motor Co)

from the shock absorber. Remove the insulators from the lower attaching studs.

Installation

1. Install the upper mounting

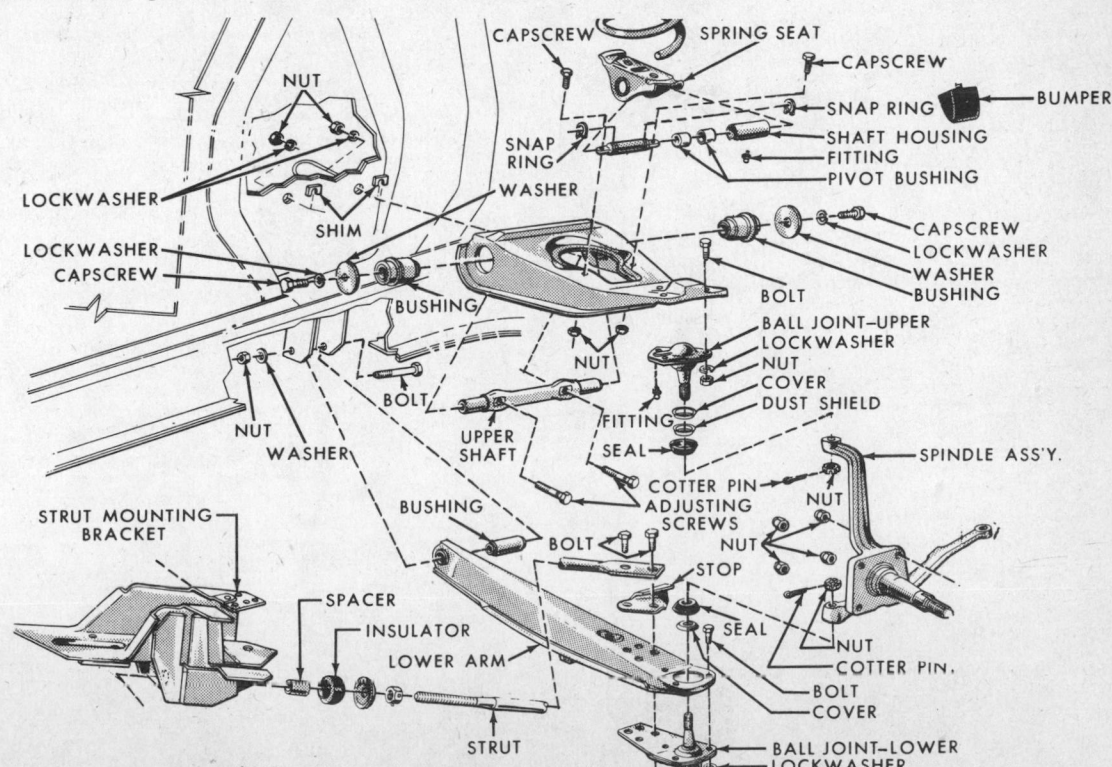

Front suspension—spring on upper arm (© Ford Motor Co)

C489

bracket on the shock absorber. Install the insulators on the lower attaching studs.

2. Place the shock absorber and upper bracket assembly in the spring tower, making sure that the shock absorber lower studs are in the pivot plate holes.

3. Install the two washers and attaching nuts on the lower studs of the shock absorbers.

4. Install the three shock absorber upper mounting bracket attaching nuts.

5. Remove the jackstands and lower the vehicle.

Spring

Removal

1. Raise hood and remove shock absorber upper mounting bracket bolts.

2. Raise front of vehicle, and place safety stands under inboard ends of lower control arms.

3. Remove shock absorber lower attaching nuts, washers and insulators.

4. Lift shock absorber and upper bracket from spring tower.

5. Remove wheel cover on hub cap.

6. Remove grease cap, cotter pin, nut lock, adjusting nut, and outer bearing.

7. Pull wheel, tire and hub and drum off spindle as an assembly. Remove the disc brake assembly, if so equipped.

8. Install spring compressor as shown in figures.

9. Compress spring until all tension is removed from control arms.

10. Remove two upper control arm attaching nuts and swing control arm out board.

11. Release spring compressor and remove.

12. Remove spring.

Installation

1. Place upper spring insulator on spring and secure in place with tape.

2. Position spring in spring tower and compress with spring compressor.

3. Swing upper control arm in board and install attaching nuts.

4. Release spring pressure and guide spring into upper arm spring seat. The end of the spring must be not more than 1/2 in. from tab on spring seat.

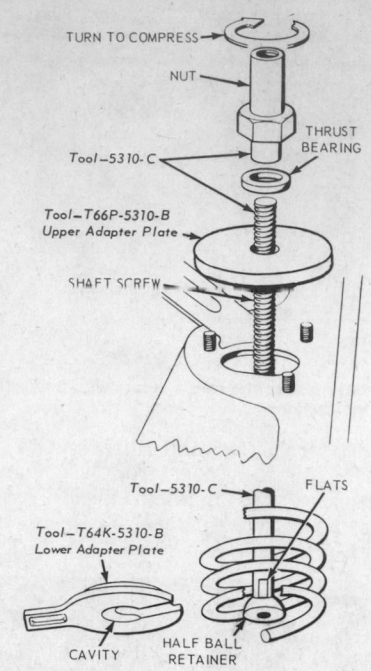

Spring compressor—spring on upper arm (© Ford Motor Co)

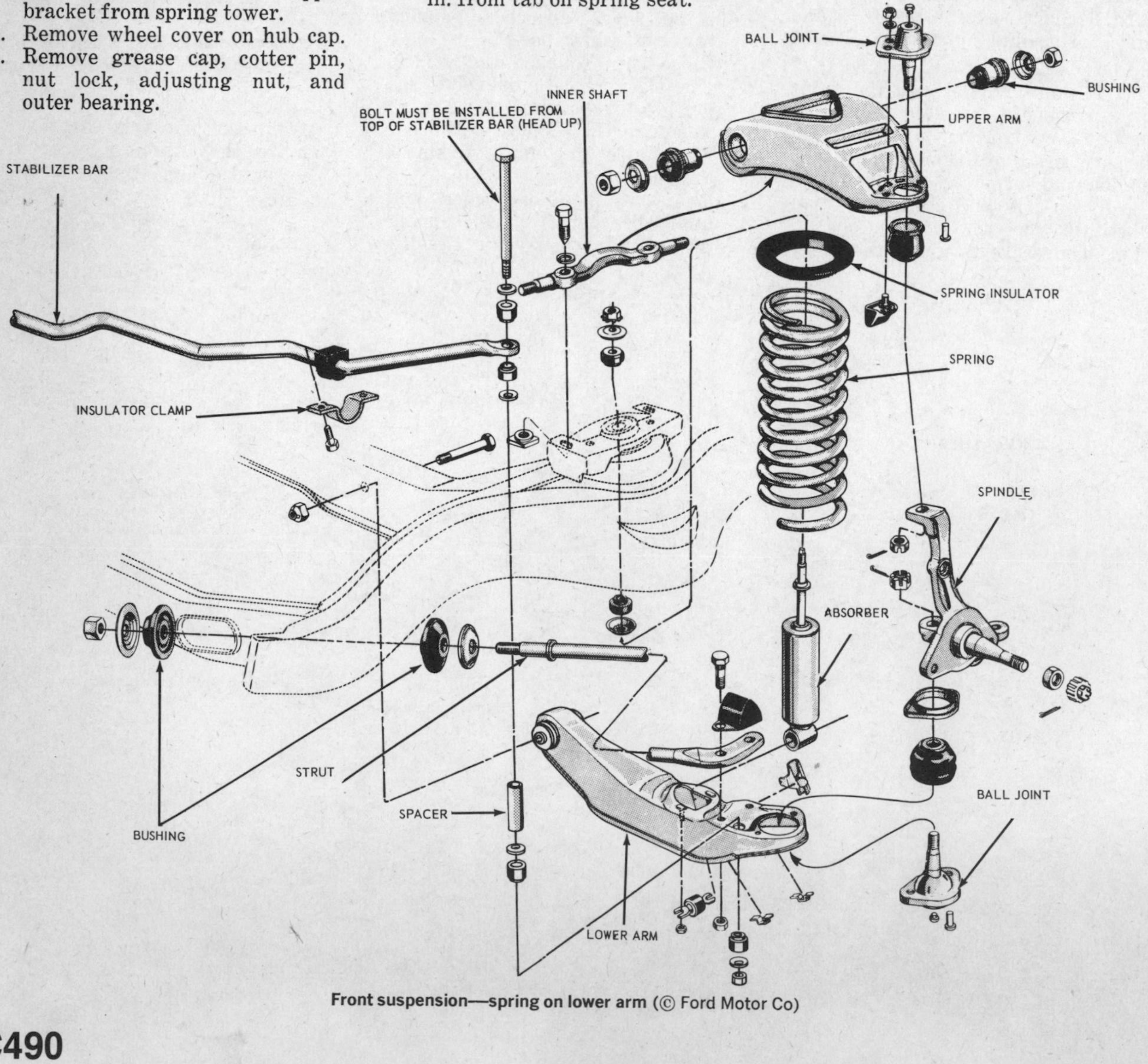

Front suspension—spring on lower arm (© Ford Motor Co)

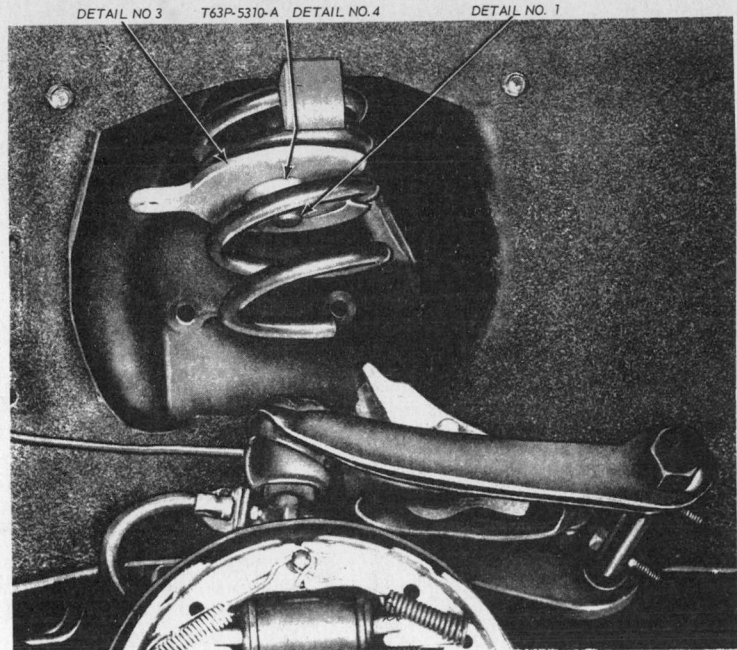

DETAIL NO 3   T63P-5310-A   DETAIL NO. 4   DETAIL NO. 1

Compressing spring—spring on upper arm (© Ford Motor Co)

5. Remove spring compressor and position wheel, tire, and hub and drum on spindle. Install disc brake assembly, if so equipped.
6. Install bearing, washer and adjusting nut.
7. On disc brake cars, loosen adjusting nut three turns, and rock wheel hub and rotor assembly in and out to push disc brake pads away from rotor.
8. While rotating wheel, hub and drum assembly, torque adjusting nut to 17-25 ft. lbs. to seat bearing.
9. With 1⅛ in. box wrench back off adjusting nut ½ turn, and tighten nut to 10-15 in. lbs. or finger tight.
10. Position lock on adjusting nut and install new cotter pin. Bend ends of pin around castellated flange of nut lock.
11. Check front wheel rotation and install grease cap and hub cap.
12. Install shock absorber and upper bracket assembly, making sure shock absorber lower studs have insulators and are in pivot plate holes.
13. Install nuts and washers on lower studs and torque to 8-12 ft. lbs. on 1970 and later models.
14. Install nuts on shock absorber upper bracket.
15. Lower car.

Lower Ball Joint

On all intermediate size Ford cars which have the coil springs mounted on the upper control arm, the lower ball joint is an integral part of the lower control arm. If the lower ball joint is defective the entire lower control arm must be replaced.

Inspection

1. Raise the vehicle on a hoist or floor jack so that the front wheel falls to the full down position.
2. Have an assistant grasp the bottom of the tire and move the wheel in and out.
3. As the wheel is being moved, observe the lower control arm where the spindle attaches to it.
4. Any movement between the lower part of the spindle and the lower control arm indicates a bad control arm which must be replaced.

NOTE: during this check, the upper ball joint will be unloaded and may move; this is normal and not an indication of a bad ball joint. Also, do not mistake a loose wheel bearing for a worn ball joint.

Replacement

1. Position an upper control arm support between the upper arm and side rail as shown in the illustration.
2. Raise the vehicle, position jack stands and remove the wheel and tire.
3. Remove the stabilizer bar to link attaching nut and disconnect the bar from the link.
4. Remove the link bolt from the lower arm.
5. Remove the strut bar to lower attaching nuts and bolts.
6. Remove the lower ball joint cotter pin and back off the nut. Using a suitable tool, loosen the ball joint stud in the spindle.
7. Remove the nut from the arm and lower the arm.
8. Remove the lower arm to underbody cam attaching parts and remove the arm.
9. To install, position the lower arm in the underbody and install the ball joint and cam attaching parts loosely.
10. Install the stabilizer and strut and torque the attaching parts to specifications.
11. Torque the lower arm pivot and ball joint stud to specifications.
12. Lower the car and remove the upper arm support.
13. Front end alignment must be rechecked.

Upper Ball Joint

Inspection

1. Raise the vehicle on a hoist or floor jack so that the front wheels hang in full down position.

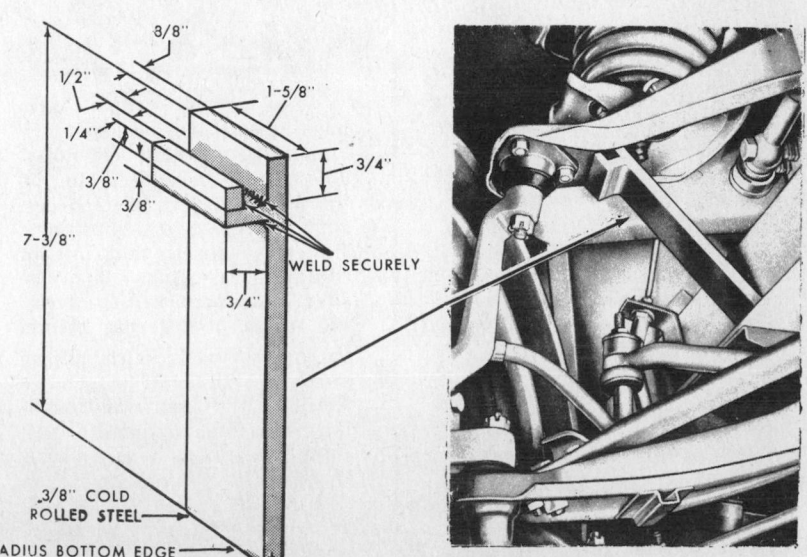

3/8"
1/2"
1/4"
1-5/8"
3/8"
3/8"
3/4"
7-3/8"
WELD SECURELY
3/4"
.3/8" COLD ROLLED STEEL
RADIUS BOTTOM EDGE

Upper control arm support—spring on upper arm (© Ford Motor Co)

C491

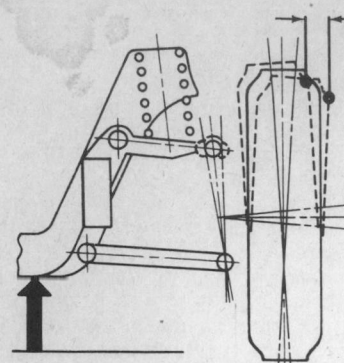

**Measuring upper ball joint radial play
—spring on upper arm**
(© Ford Motor Co)

2. Have an assistant grasp the wheel top and bottom and apply alternate in and out pressure to the top and bottom of the wheel.
3. Radial play of ¼ in. is acceptable measured at the inside of the wheel adjacent to the upper arm.
NOTE: this radial play measurement is multiplied at the outer circumference of the tire and should not be measured here. Measure only at the inside of the wheel.

Replacement

1. Position support between the upper arm and frame rail as shown in illustration.
2. Raise the vehicle and remove the tire and wheel.
3. Remove the upper ball joint cotter pin and loosen the nut.
4. Using a suitable tool, loosen the ball joint in the spindle.
5. Remove the three ball joint retaining rivets using a large chisel.
6. Remove the nut from the ball joint stud and remove the ball joint.
7. Clean and remove all burrs from the ball joint mounting area of the control arm before installing new ball joint.
8. Install the ball joint in the upper arm using the service part nuts and bolts. Do not attempt to rivet a new ball joint to the arm.
9. Install and torque the ball joint stud nut and install the cotter pin.
10. Lubricate the new joint with a hand type grease gun only, using an air pressure gun may loosen the ball joint seal.
11. Install wheel, lower vehicle and remove upper arm support.
12. Check front end alignment.

Upper Control Arm

Replacement

1. Remove the shock absorber and upper mounting bracket from the car as an assembly.
2. Raise the vehicle and remove the wheel and tire as an assembly.

3. Install spring compressor tool.
4. Place a safety stand under the lower arm.
5. Remove the cotter pin from the upper ball joint stud and loosen the nut.
6. Using a suitable tool, loosen the ball joint in the spindle, then, remove the nut and lift the stud from the spindle.
7. Remove the upper arm attaching nuts from the engine compartment, and remove the upper arm.
8. To install the arm, position it on the mounting bracket and install the attaching nuts on the inner shaft attaching bolts.
NOTE: the original equipment keystone-type lockwashers must be used with the inner shaft attaching nuts and bolts.
9. Install the upper ball joint stud in the spindle and tighten the nut to specifications. Install a new cotter pin.
10. Remove spring compressor and position spring on upper arm. Install wheel and check front end alignment.

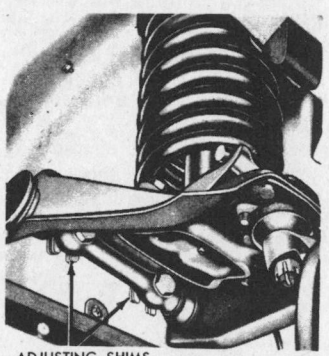

ADJUSTING SHIMS
Upper control arm assembly—spring on upper arm (© Ford Motor Co)

T70P-3068-D

Upper control arm lubricating tool
(© Ford Motor Co)

Coil Spring on Lower Arm

Shock Absorber

Removal and Replacement

1. Remove the nut, washer, and bushing from the upper end of the shock absorber.
2. Raise the vehicle and install jackstands under the frame rails.
3. Remove the two bolts securing the shock absorber to the lower control arm and remove the shock absorber.
4. Install a new bushing and washer on the top of the shock absorber and position the unit inside the front spring. Install the two lower attaching bolts and torque them to 8–15 ft lbs.
5. Remove the jackstands and lower the vehicle.
6. Place a new bushing and washer on the shock absorber top stud and install the attaching nut. Torque to 22–30 ft lbs.

Coil Spring and Lower Control Arm Removal and Installation

1. Raise car and support it with stands placed in back of lower arms.
2. If equipped with drum type brakes, remove the wheel and brake drum as an assembly. Remove the brake backing plate attaching bolts and remove the backing plate from the spindle. Wire the assembly back out of the way.
3. If equipped with disc brakes, remove the wheel from the hub. Remove the bolts and washers that hold the caliper and brake hose bracket to the spindle. Remove the caliper from the rotor and wire it back out of the way. Then, remove the hub and rotor from the spindle.
4. Disconnect lower end of the shock absorber and push it up to the retracted position.
5. Disconnect stabilizer bar link from the lower arm.

6. Remove cotter pins from the upper and lower ball joint stud nuts.

7. Remove two bolts and nuts holding the strut to the lower arm.

8. Loosen the lower ball joint stud nut two turns. Do not remove this nut.

9. Install a spreader tool between the upper and lower ball joint studs.

10. Expand the tool until the tool exerts considerable pressure on the studs. Tap the spindle near the lower stud with a hammer to loosen the stud in the spindle. Do not loosen the stud with tool pressure only.

11. Position floor jack under the lower arm and remove the lower ball joint stud nut.

12. Lower floor jack and remove the spring and insulator.

13. Remove the A-arm to crossmember attaching parts, and remove the arm from the car.

14. Reverse above procedure to install. If lower control arm was replaced because of damage, check front end alignment.

Coil spring and lower arm replacement —spring on lower arm
(© Ford Motor Co)

Lower Ball Joint

Inspection

1. Raise the vehicle by placing a floor jack under the lower arm; or, raise the vehicle on a hoist and place a jack stand under the lower arm and lower the vehicle onto it to remove the preload from the lower ball joint.

2. Have an assistant grasp the wheel top and bottom and apply alternate in and out pressure to the top and bottom of the wheel.

3. Radial play of 1/4 in. is acceptable measured at the inside of the wheel adjacent to the lower arm.

NOTE: this radial play is multiplied at the outer circumference of the tire and should be measured only at the inside of the wheel.

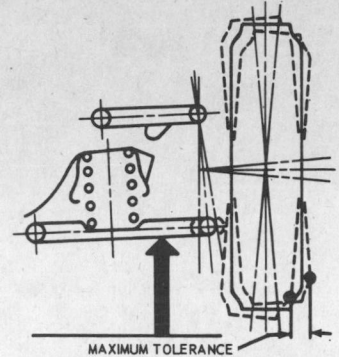

MAXIMUM TOLERANCE

Measuring lower ball joint radial play —spring on lower arm
(© Ford Motor Co)

Replacement

1. Raise the vehicle on a hoist and allow the front wheels to fall to their full down position.

2. Drill a 1/8 in. hole completely through each ball joint attaching rivet.

3. Use a 3/8 in. drill in the pilot hole to drill off the head of the rivet.

4. Drive the rivets from the lower arm.

5. Place a jack under the lower arm and lower the vehicle about 6 in.

6. Remove the lower ball joint stud cotter pin and attaching nut.

7. Using a suitable tool, loosen the ball joint from the spindle and remove the ball joint from the lower arm.

8. Clean all metal burrs from the lower arm and install the new ball joint, using the service part nuts and bolts to attach the ball joint to the lower arm. Do not attempt to rerivet the ball joint once it has been removed.

9. Check front end alignment.

Upper Ball Joint

Inspection

1. Raise the vehicle by placing a floor jack under the lower arm. Do not allow the lower arm to hang freely with the vehicle on a hoist or bumper jack.

2. Have an assistant grasp the bottom of the tire and move the wheel in and out.

3. As the wheel is being moved, observe the upper control arm where the spindle attaches to it. Any movement between the upper part of the spindle and the upper ball joint indicates a bad ball joint which must be replaced.

NOTE: During this check the lower ball joint will be unloaded and may move; this is normal and not an indication of a bad ball joint. Also, do not mistake a loose wheel bearing for a defective ball joint.

Replacement

1. Raise the vehicle on a hoist and allow the front wheels to fall to their full down position.

2. Drill a 1/8 in. hole completely through each ball joint attaching rivet.

3. Using a large chisel, cut off the head of each rivet and drive them from the upper arm.

4. Place a jack under the lower arm and lower the vehicle about 6 in.

5. Remove the cotter pin and attaching nut from the ball joint stud.

6. Using a suitable tool, loosen the ball joint stud from the spindle and remove the ball joint from the upper arm.

7. Clean all metal burrs from the upper arm and install the new ball point, using the service part nuts and bolts to attach the ball joint to the upper arm. Do not attempt to rerivet the ball joint once it has been removed.

8. Check front end alignment.

Upper Control Arm

Replacement

1. Raise the vehicle on a hoist.

2. If equipped with drum brakes remove the tire, wheel and brake drum as an assembly. If equipped with disc brakes, remove the tire and wheel.

3. Remove the cotter pin and attaching nut from the ball joint stud.

4. Using a suitable tool, loosen the upper ball joint from the spindle.

5. Place a jack under the lower arm and lower the vehicle about 6 in.

6. Remove the upper arm inner shaft attaching bolts and remove the arm and shaft from the chassis as an assembly.

7. Reverse above procedure to install.

8. Adjust front end alignment.

REAR SUSPENSION

All intermediate and compact-sized Ford products, except the 1972 and later Torino and Montego, 1974 and later Cougar and Elite, and the 1977 LTD II and Thunderbird, use a leaf-spring rear suspension. A pair of leaf springs support the axle housing, which is secured to the springs by two U-bolts and retaining plates. Each spring is suspended from the underbody side rails by a hanger at the front and a shackle at the rear. The shock absorbers are mounted between the leaf spring retaining plates and brackets bolted to the crossmember. Some 1970-71 high-

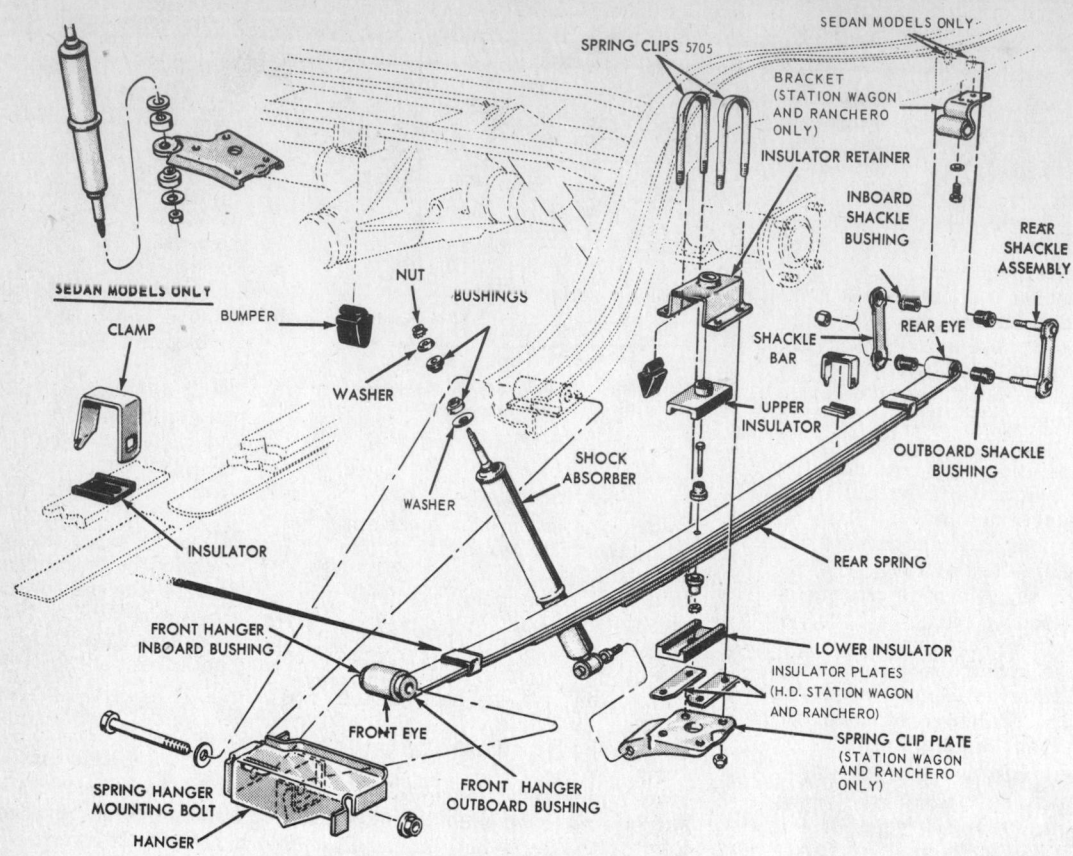

Exploded view of leaf spring rear suspension
(© Ford Motor Co)

performance models are equipped with staggered rear shock absorbers.

1972 and later Torinos and Montegos and 1974 and later Cougars and Elites, and 1977 LTD IIs and Thunderbirds, utilize a coil spring, rear suspension. The axle housing is suspended from the frame by an upper and lower trailing arm, and a shock absorber at each side of the vehicle. These arms pivot in the frame members and the rear axle housing brackets. Each coil spring is mounted between a lower seat which is welded to the axle housing and an upper seat integral with the frame. The shock absorbers are bolted to the spring upper seats at the top and brackets mounted on the axle housing at the bottom. A rear stabilizer, bar attached to the frame side rail brackets and the two axle housing brackets, is available as optional equipment.

Leaf Spring Suspension

Spring Removal and Installation

1. Raise the vehicle and place supports beneath the underbody and axle.
2. Disconnect the lower end of the shock absorber from the spring clip plate and position it out of the way. Remove the supports from under the axle.

3. Remove the spring plate nuts from the U-bolt and remove the spring plate. With a jack, raise the rear axle just enough to remove the weight of the housing from the spring.
4. Remove the two rear shackle attaching nuts, the shackle bar, and the two inner bushings.
5. Remove the rear shackle assembly and the two outer bushings.
6. Remove the nut from the spring mounting bolt and tap the bolt out of the bushing at the front hanger. Lift out the spring assembly.

NOTE: all used attaching components (nuts, bolts, etc.) must be discarded and replaced with new ones prior to assembly.

7. Position the leaf spring under the axle housing and insert the shackle assembly into the rear hanger bracket and the rear eye of the spring.
8. Install the shackle inner bushings, the shackle plate, and the locknuts. Hand-tighten the locknuts.
9. Position the spring eye in the front hanger, slip the washer on the front hanger bolt, and, from the inboard side, insert the bolt through the hanger and eye. Install the locknut on the hanger bolt finger-tight.

10. Lower the rear axle housing so that it rests on the spring. Place the spring plate on the U-bolt and tighten the nuts.
11. Attach the lower end of the shock absorber to the spring plate using a new nut.
12. Place jackstands under the rear axle. Lower the vehicle until the spring is in the approximate curb load position, and tighten the front hanger locknut.
13. Tighten the rear shackle locknuts. Close the hole in the inner rail with a body plug.
14. Remove the jackstands and lower the vehicle.

Shock Absorber Removal and Installation

1970-73 Mustang and Cougar

1. Disconnect the shock absorber at the spring plate.
2. Remove the shock absorber access cover from the trunk. Remove the rear seat from convertibles to reach the access cover.
3. Remove the shock absorber upper retaining nut.
4. Compress and remove the shock absorber. Remove all bushings and washers from the unit.
5. Place new inner bushings and washers on the shock absorber studs.

6. Connect the upper stud to the mounting. Install a new outer bushing, washer, and nut on the stud. Install the access cover.
7. Connect the lower stud to the spring plate. Install a new outer bushing, washer, and nut on the stud. Be sure that the spring plate is free of burrs.

1970 Falcon and Fairlane, 1970-71 Torino and Montego All Models Except Convertible

1. Remove the spare from the trunk. On station wagons, remove the access cover from the opening in the seat riser over the shock absorber. On Rancheros, remove the attaching screws and remove the forward half of the floor panel, then remove the access cover from the opening in the floor pan. On all other models, fold back the trunk floor mat and remove the access cover.
2. Remove the nut, outer washer, and rubber bushing from the top of the shock absorber.
3. Raise the vehicle and remove the attaching nut, outer washer, and bushing from the shock absorber at the spring plate. Compress and remove the shock absorber. Remove all bushings and washers from the unit.
4. Position a new inner washer and bushing on each shock absorber stud.
5. Place the shock absorber between the spring plate and the mounting in the floor pan. Install a new outer bushing, washer, and nut on the lower stud. Make sure that the spring plate is free of burrs. Lower the vehicle.
6. Install the new outer bushing, washer, and nut on the upper stud.
7. On station wagon models, replace the retaining screws and floor bed panel. On Rancheros, install the access cover and the forward half of the bed. On all other models, install the access cover and secure the spare in the trunk.

1970 Fairlane, and 1970-71 Torino and Montego Convertibles

1. Remove the rear seat.
2. Raise the vehicle and install jackstands. Have an assistant hold the shock absorber from underneath the car and remove the nut, washer, and bushing from the top of the shock absorber.
3. Remove the lower shock absorber nut, washer, and bushing. Compress and remove the shock absorber. Remove the inner bushings and washers from the unit.

4. Place the new inner washers and bushings on the shock absorber. Secure the shock absorber at its lower attachment by installing the new outer bushing, washer, and nut on the lower mounting stud.
5. Lower the vehicle and install the new outer bushing, washer, and nut on the top of the shock absorber.
6. Install the rear seat.

1970-77 Maverick and 1971-77 Comet, 1975-77 Granada and Monarch

1. Remove the lower end of the shock absorber from the spring plate.
2. Remove the nut retaining the upper end of the shock absorber to the mounting bracket underneath the car.
3. Compress and remove the shock absorber.
4. Transfer the washers and bushings to the new shock absorber. Insert the upper stud through the mounting bracket, and install the attaching nut finger-tight.
5. Compress and install the shock absorber to the spring plate. Install the washers, bushings, and attaching nuts.
6. Tighten the upper and lower attaching nuts.

Coil Spring Suspension

Spring Removal and Installation

1. Place a jack under the rear axle housing. Raise the vehicle and place jackstands under the frame side rails.
2. Disconnect the lower studs of the shock absorbers from the mounting brackets on the axle housing.
3. Lower the axle housing until the springs are fully released.
4. Remove the springs and insulators from the vehicle.
5. Place the insulators in each upper seat and position the springs between the upper and lower seats.
6. With the springs in position, raise the axle housing until the lower studs of the rear shock absorbers reach the mounting brackets on the axle housing. Connect the lower studs and install the attaching nuts.
7. Remove the jackstands and lower the vehicle.

Shock Absorber Removal and Installation

1. Raise the vehicle and install jackstands.
2. Remove the shock absorber outer attaching nut, washer and insu-

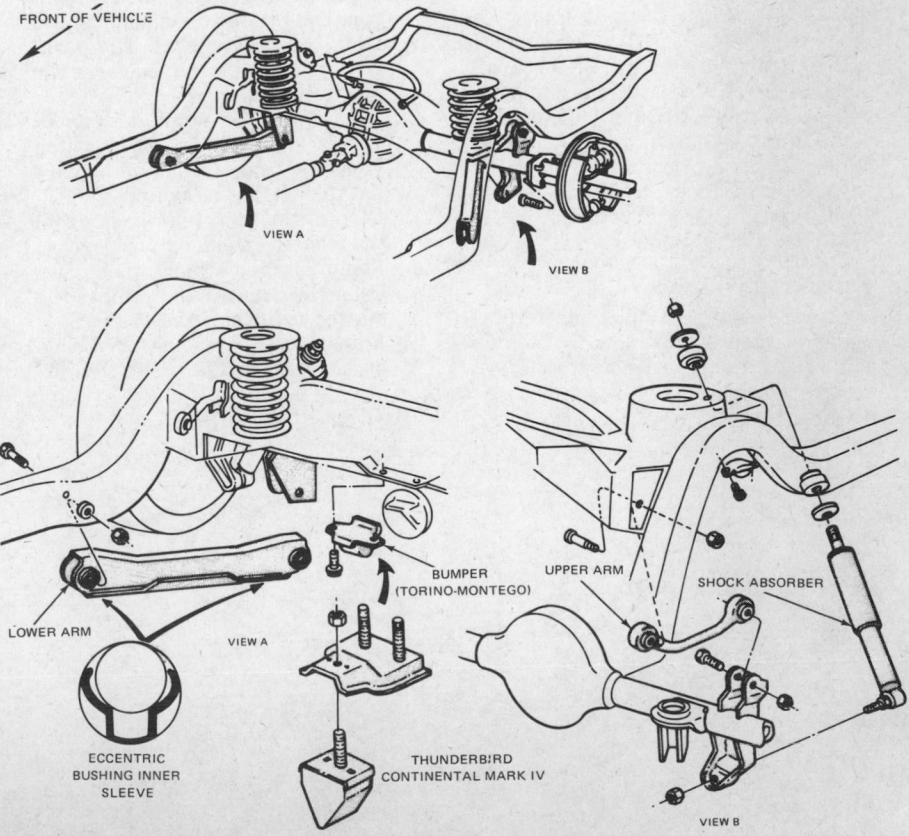

Coil spring rear suspension (© Ford Motor Co)

lator from the stud at the top side of the spring upper seat. Compress the shock sufficiently to clear the spring seat hole, and remove the inner insulator and washer from the upper attaching stud.

3. Remove the locknut and disconnect the shock absorber lower stud at the mounting bracket on the axle housing. Remove the shock absorber.

4. Position a new inner washer and insulator on the upper attaching stud. Place the upper stud in the hole in the upper spring seat. While maintaining the shock in this position, install a new outer insulator, washer, and nut on the stud from the top side of the spring upper seat.

5. Extend the shock absorber. Locate the lower stud in the mounting bracket hole on the axle housing and install the locknut.

Dual master cylinder—disc brakes (© Ford Motor Co)

BRAKES

An independent parking brake operates the rear wheel brake shoes or pads through a mechanical cable linkage. Brake shoe or pad replacement and adjustment procedures as well as wheel cylinder and master cylinder overhaul and brake bleeding procedures can be found in the Unit Repair Section.

Disc Brakes

Front disc brakes have been available on front wheels of most models. Rear disc brakes are available on Granada and Monarch when equipped with the hydraulically assisted Hydro-Boost System. Complete Service Procedures are covered in the Unit Repair Section.

Master Cylinder

A tandem-type (dual) master cylinder is used on all models. This design divides the brake hydraulic system into two independent and hydraulically separated halves. In the event of a single hydraulic failure, 50% braking efficiency is maintained.

Master Cylinder Removal and Installation

Standard Brakes

1. Working under the dash, disconnect the master cylinder pushrod from the brake pedal. The pushrod cannot be removed from the master cylinder.

2. Disconnect the stoplight switch wires and remove the switch from the brake pedal, using care not to damage the switch.

3. Disconnect the brake lines from the master cylinder.

4. Remove the attaching screws from the firewall and remove the master cylinder from the car.

5. Reinstall in reverse of above order, leaving the brake line fittings loose at the master cylinder.

6. Fill the master cylinder, and with the brake lines loose, slowly bleed the air from the master cylinder using the foot pedal.

Power Brakes

1. Disconnect the brake line from the master cylinder.

2. Remove the two nuts and lockwashers that attach the master cylinder to the brake booster.

3. Remove the master cylinder from the booster.

4. Reverse above procedure to reinstall.

5. Fill master cylinder and bleed entire brake system.

6. Refill master cylinder.

Power Brakes

Vacuum Power Unit Removal

1. Working inside the car below the instrument panel, disconnect booster valve operating rod from the brake pedal assembly.

2. Open the hood, and disconnect the wires from the stop light switch at the brake master cylinder.

3. Disconnect the brake line at the master cylinder outlet fitting.

4. Disconnect manifold vacuum hose from the booster unit.

5. Remove the four bracket-to-dash panel attaching bolts.

6. Remove the booster and bracket assembly from the dash panel, sliding the valve operating rod out from the engine side of the dash panel.

Vacuum Power Unit Installation

1. Mount the booster and bracket

1. Source of hydraulic working pressure is power steering pump.

2. Power steering fluid is routed to Hydro-Boost.

3. Fluid from Hydro-Boost is routed to power steering gear.

4. Cooler lines (section of steel tubing) are mounted to radiator support and pass in front of radiator core. Fluid is air cooled before returning to pump reservoir.

Hydro-Boost installation
(© Ford Motor Co)

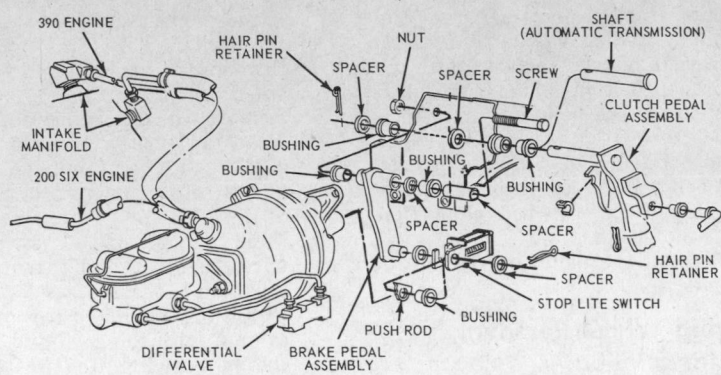

Vacuum brake booster installation (© Ford Motor Co)

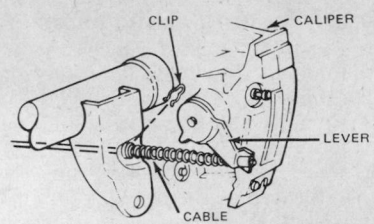

Parking brake cable and lever—Granada and Monarch with rear disc brakes
(© Ford Motor Co)

assembly to the dash panel by sliding the valve operating rod in through the hole in the dash panel, and installing the attaching bolts.

2. Connect manifold vacuum hose to the booster.
3. Connect the brake line to the master cylinder outlet fitting.
4. Connect stop light switch wires.
5. Working inside the car below the instrument panel, install the rubber boot on the valve operating rod at the passenger side of the dash panel.
6. Connect the valve operating rod to the brake pedal with the bushings, eccentric shoulder bolt, and nut.

Hydro-Boost Power Unit Removal and Installation

See the "Lincoln" section.

Parking Brake Adjustment

In most cases, a rear brake shoe adjustment will provide satisfactory parking brake action. However, if parking brake cables are excessively loose after releasing the handbrake, proceed as follows:

1. On handle-actuated systems pull up the handle to the third notch. On pedal-actuated systems, depress the parking brake pedal one notch from its normal released position.
2. Loosen locknut on equalizer rod under the car. Then loosen the nut in front of the equalizer, several turns.
3. Turn the locknut forward against the equalizer until the cables are tight enough so that the rear wheels cannot be turned by hand. Then, back off the adjustment until the rear wheels turn freely.
4. When cables are properly adjusted, tighten both nuts against the equalizer.
5. Release the brake and feel for freeness of rear wheels.

Granada and Monarch with Rear Disc Brakes

1. Fully release the parking brake.
2. Place the transmission in Neutral. If it is necessary to raise the car to reach the adjusting nut and observe the parking brake levers, use an axle hoist or a floor jack positioned beneath the differential. This is necessary so that the rear axle remains at the curb attitude, not stretching the parking brake cables.

Caution *If you are raising the rear of the car only, block the front wheels.*

3. Locate the adjusting nut beneath the car on the driver's side. While observing the parking brake actuating levers on the rear calipers, tighten the adjusting nut until the levers just begin to move. Then, loosen the nut sufficiently for the levers to fully return to the stop position.
4. Check the operation of the parking brake. Make sure the actuating levers return to the stop position by attempting to pull them rearward. If the lever moves rearward, the cable adjustment is too tight, which will cause a dragging rear brake and consequent brake overheating and fade.

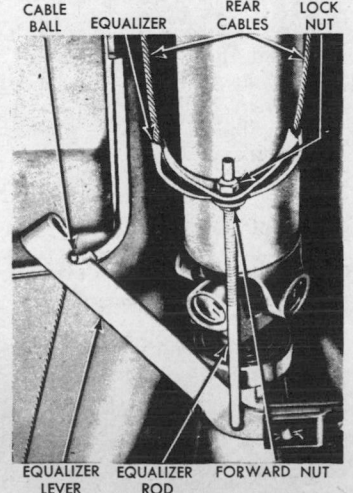

Parking brake linkage (© Ford Motor Co)

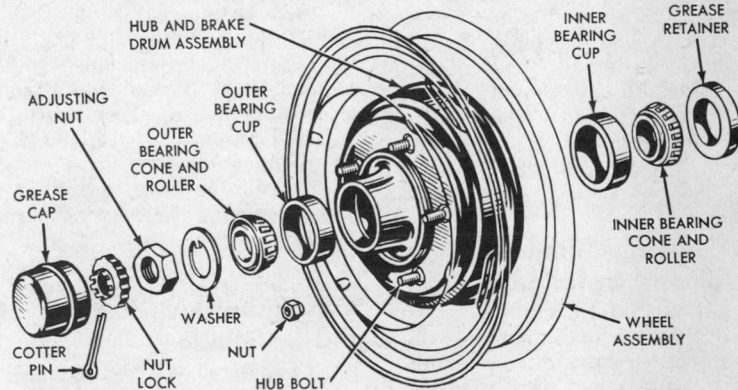

Front hub, bearings, and grease retainers—drum brakes shown, disc brakes similar
(© Ford Motor Co)

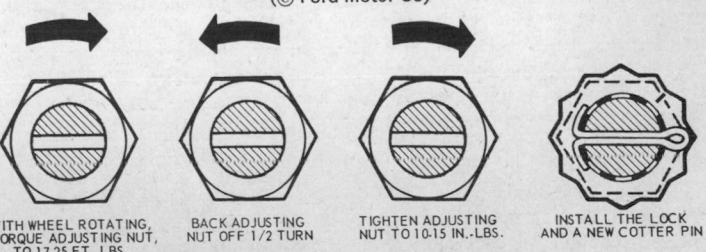

Adjusting wheel bearings (© Ford Motor Co)

Wheel Bearing Adjustment

1. Raise the front of the vehicle.
2. Remove the wheel cover and grease cap.
3. Remove the cotter pin and nut lock.
4. Back off the adjusting nut and retighten the nut to 17–25 ft. lbs. Back off the adjusting nut again ½ turn. Retighten the nut to 10–15 in. lbs. Install the nut lock so that the castellations are aligned with the cotter pin hole. Install the cotter pin and bend the ends around the castellations of the nut lock to prevent interference with the radio static collector in the grease cap.
5. Install the grease cap and wheel cover.
6. Lower the vehicle.

STEERING

The manual steering gear is of the worm and recirculating ball type.

Power steering is available as an option. On all compact and intermediate Ford products, except the 1971–73 Mustang, 1972 and later Torino and Montego, the 1974 and later Cougar and Elite, and the 1977 LTD II and Thunderbird, the power steering system is the Bendix non-integral type. The Bendix system utilizes the manual worm and recirculating ball steering gear. Hydraulic assist is provided externally to the steering linkage via a power steering pump, power cylinder, and control valve. The 1971-73 Mustangs and Cougars use the Saginaw integral system, while the 1972 and later Torinos and Montegos and 1974 and later Cougars and Elites, and 1977 LTD IIs and Thunderbirds use the Ford integral system. On both types, hydraulic assist is directly applied to the steering gear, eliminating all hoses and hardware which were previously mounted under the chassis on the Bendix system.

Power Steering Pump Removal and Installation

1. Drain the fluid from the pump reservoir by disconnecting the fluid return hose at the pump. Then, disconnect the pressure hose from the pump.
2. Remove the mounting bolts from the front of the pump. On eight cylinder engines, there is a nut on the rear of the pump that must be removed. After removal, move the pump inward to loosen the belt tension and remove the belt from the pulley. Then, remove the pump from the car.
3. To reinstall the pump, position on mounting bracket and loosely install the mounting bolts and nuts. Put the drive belt over the pulley and move the pump outward against the belt until the proper belt tension is obtained. Measure the belt tension with a belt tension gauge for the proper adjustment. Only in cases where a belt tension gauge is not available should the belt deflection method be used.
4. Tighten the mounting bolts and nuts.

Steering Wheel Removal and Installation

1. Open the hood and disconnect the negative cable from the battery.
2. On models with safety crash pads, remove the crash pad attaching screws from the underside of the steering wheel spoke and remove the pad. On all models equipped with a horn button, remove the horn button or ring by pressing down evenly and turning it counterclockwise approximately 20° and then lifting it from the steering wheel. Disconnect the horn wires from the crash pad on models so equipped.
3. Remove the nut from the end of the shaft. Install a steering wheel puller on the end of the shaft and remove the wheel.

Caution The use of knock-off type steering wheel puller or the use of a hammer on the steering shaft will damage the column bearing, on collapsible columns, the column itself may be damaged.

4. Lubricate the upper surface of the steering shaft upper bushing with white grease. Transfer all serviceable parts to the new steering wheel.
5. Position the steering wheel on the shaft so that the alignment marks line up. Install a locknut and torque it to 20–30 ft lbs. Connect the horn wires.
6. Install the horn button or ring by turning it clockwise or install the crash pad.

Turn Signal Switch Removal and Installation

1. Open the hood and disconnect the negative battery cable.
2. Remove the steering wheel.
3. Unscrew the turn signal handle from the side of the column. Remove the emergency flasher retainer and knob, if so equipped.
4. Remove the wire assembly cover and disconnect the wire connector plugs. Record the location and color code of each wire and tape the wires together. Make sure that the horn wires are disconnected. Remove the plastic cover from the wiring harness.

Attach a piece of heavy cord to the switch wires to pull them through the column during installation.

5. Remove the retaining clips and attaching screws from the turn signal switch and pull the switch and wire assembly from the top of the column.
6. Tape the ends of the new switch wires together and transfer the pull cord to these wires.
7. Pull the wires down through the column with the cord and attach the new switch to the column hub.
8. Connect the wiring plugs to their mating plugs at the lower end of the column and install the plastic cover at the harness.
9. Install all retaining clips and wire assembly covers that were removed and install the turn signal handle. Install the emergency flasher retainer and knob, if so equipped.
10. Install the steering wheel and retaining nut.
11. Connect the negative battery cable.

Ignition Lock Cylinder Replacement

1. Disconnect the negative battery cable.
2. On cars with a fixed steering column, remove the steering wheel trim pad and the steering wheel. Insert a stiff wire into the hole located in the lock cylinder housing. On cars with a tilt steering wheel, this hole is located on the outside of the steering column near the emergency flasher button and it is not necessary to remove the steering wheel.
3. Place the gear shift lever in Reverse on standard shift cars and in Park on cars with automatic transmission, and turn the ignition key to the ON or RUN position.
4. Depress wire and remove lock cylinder and wire.
5. Insert new cylinder into housing and turn to the OFF position. This will lock the cylinder into position.
6. Reinstall steering wheel and pad.
7. Connect negative battery cable.

Ignition Switch Replacement

1. Disconnect the negative battery cable.
2. Remove shrouding from the steering column, and detach and lower the steering column from the brake support bracket.
3. Disconnect the switch wiring at the multiple plug.
4. Remove the two nuts that retain the switch to steering column.

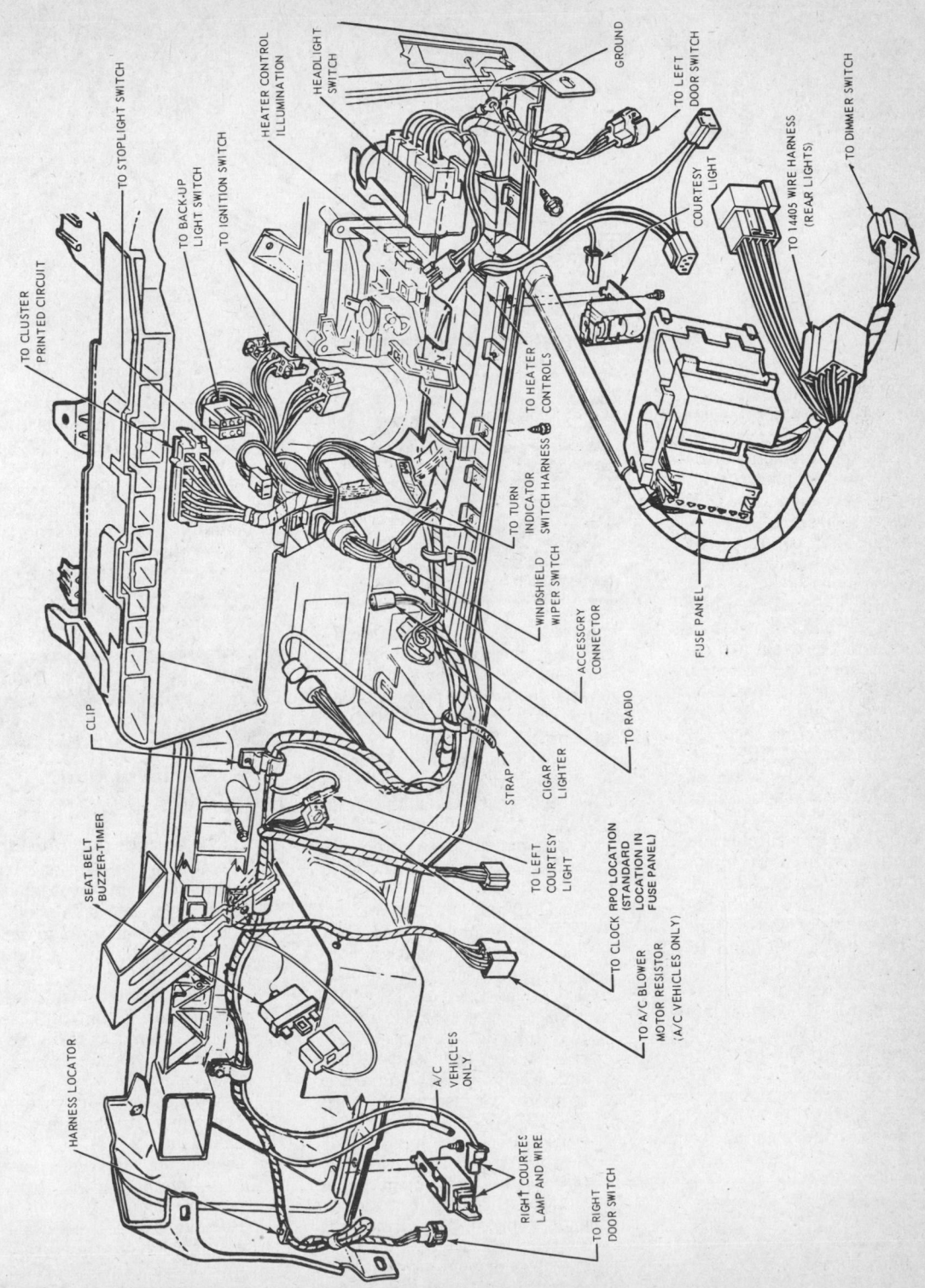

Torino, Elite, Montego, and Cougar instrument panel wiring harness—1975-76
(© Ford Motor Co.)

C499

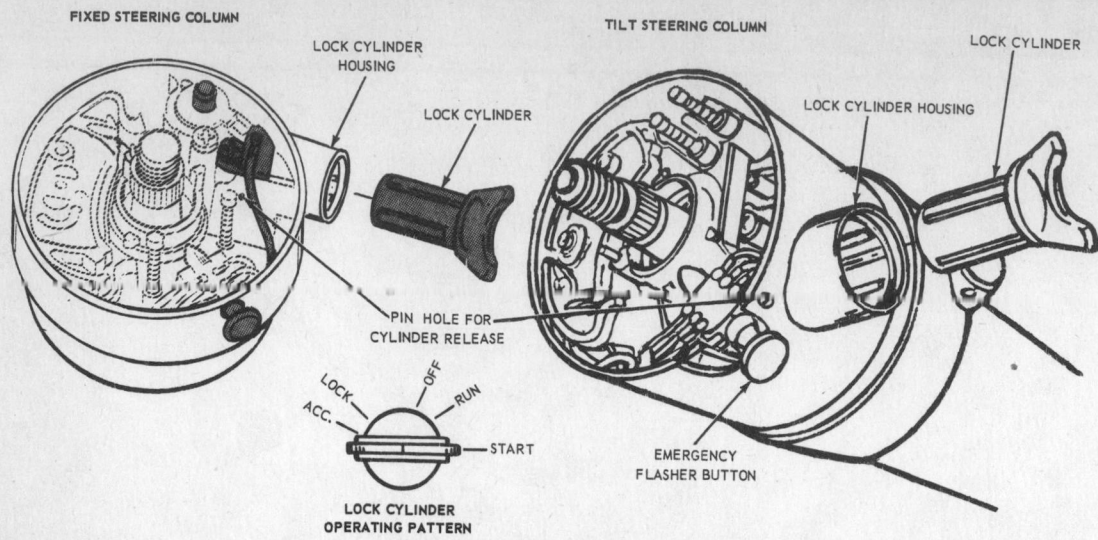

FIXED STEERING COLUMN

TILT STEERING COLUMN

LOCK CYLINDER HOUSING

LOCK CYLINDER

LOCK CYLINDER

LOCK CYLINDER HOUSING

PIN HOLE FOR CYLINDER RELEASE

LOCK · OFF · RUN · ACC · START

EMERGENCY FLASHER BUTTON

LOCK CYLINDER OPERATING PATTERN

Lock cylinder replacement with locking column (© Ford Motor Co)

5. On models with a steering column-mounted gearshift lever, disconnect the ignition switch plunger from the ignition switch actuator rod and remove the ignition switch. On models with a floor mounted gearshift lever, remove the pin that connects the switch plunger to the switch actuator and remove the switch.
6. To re-install the switch, place both locking mechanism at top of column and switch itself in lock position for correct adjustment. To hold column in lock position, place automatic shift lever in PARK or manual shift lever in reverse, and turn to LOCK and remove the key. New switches are held in lock by plastic shipping pins. To pin existing switches, pull the switch plunger out as far as it will go and push back in to first detent. Insert 3/32 in. diameter wire into locking hole in the top of the switch.
7. Connect the switch plunger to the switch actuator rod.
8. Position the switch on the column and install the attaching nuts. Do not tighten them.
9. Move the switch up and down to locate the mid-position of rod lash, and then tighten the nuts.
10. Remove the locking pin or wire.
11. Attach the steering column to the brake support bracket and install the shrouding.

INSTRUMENT PANEL

Headlight Switch Replacement

1. Disconnect the negative battery cable.
2. Remove the headlight switch

KNOB RELEASE BUTTON

Headlight switch (© Ford Motor Co)

control knob and shaft after depressing the release button on the rear of the switch. Some models require special procedures to gain access to the release button. They are:
   a. On Mustangs and Cougars through 1971, remove the two screws that attach the parking brake mechanism to the dash panel and lower the brake control with the vent cable attached to it.
   b. On 1970 and later Mavericks, Comets, Monarchs, and Granadas equipped with air conditioning, disconnect the left A/C duct from the duct-to-register connector, loosen the two nuts that retain the left register to the utility shelf and remove the connector from the register.
   c. On 1972–73 Mustangs and Cougars, insert a screwdriver through the hole in the bottom of the instrument panel beneath the headlight switch and depress the headlight switch release button with the screwdriver.
3. After pulling the switch shaft and knob from the switch, remove the bezel nut that attaches the switch to the instrument panel.
4. Lower the switch and disconnect the lead wires from the switch.

5. On models equipped with headlight doors, disconnect the vacuum hoses from the headlight switch.
6. Reverse the above procedure to install the new switch. When installing the new switch, insert the control knob and shaft into the switch until a distinct click is heard, signifying that the shaft is locked in place.

WINDSHIELD WIPERS

Motor Removal and Installation

1970 Cougar and Mustang

1. Remove wiper arm and blade assemblies from pivot shafts and disconnect left side washer hose at T fitting on cowl grille.
2. Remove eight screws and remove cowl top grille.
3. Motor is located inside left fresh air plenum chamber. Disconnect motor ground wire by removing one screw at forward edge of plenum chamber.
4. Disconnect motor wire at plug and push it back into plenum chamber.
5. Disconnect linkage drive arm from motor output arm crank pin by removing retaining clip.
6. Remove three bolts that retain motor to mounting bracket, rotate motor output arm 180 degrees, and remove motor.
7. Before installing motor, rotate output arm 180 degrees. Before connecting linkage drive arm to motor, turn ignition to ACC position to allow motor to go to park position.

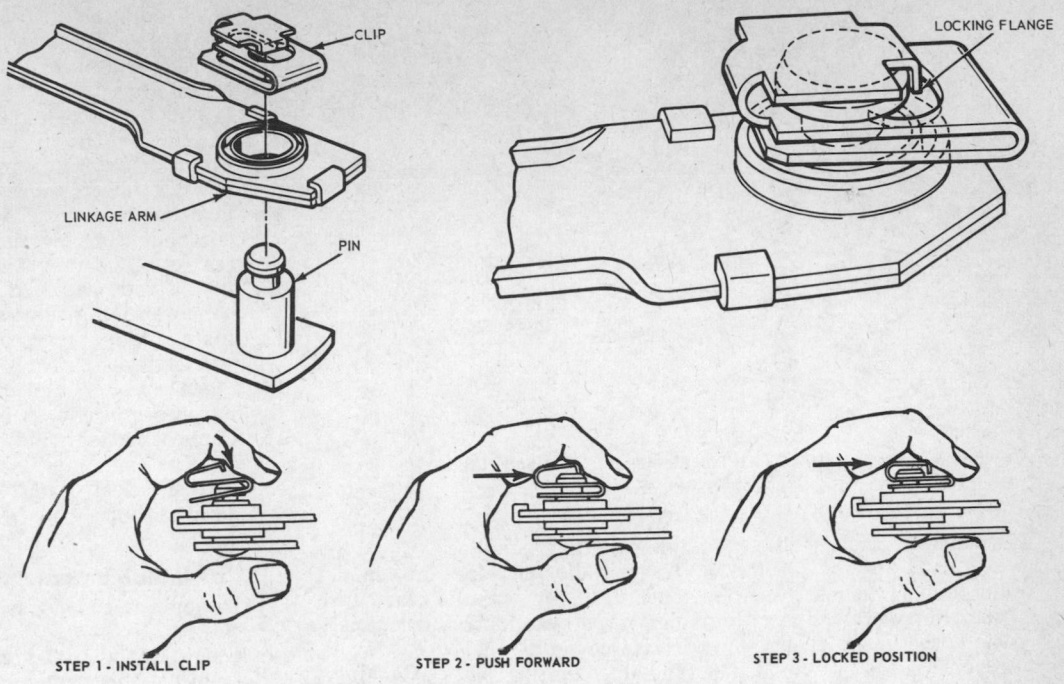

STEP 1 - INSTALL CLIP   STEP 2 - PUSH FORWARD   STEP 3 - LOCKED POSITION

Installation of windshield wiper connecting clips (© Ford Motor Co)

1970-71 Montego, Falcon, Fairlane, and Torino; 1972-76 Torino and Montego, and 1977 LTD II with Non-Hidden Wipers; 1971-73 Mustang and Cougar

1. Disconnect battery and wiper motor connector.
2. Remove cowl top left vent screen by removing four retaining drive pins.
3. Remove wiper link retaining clip from wiper motor arm.
4. Remove three wiper motor retaining bolts, and remove wiper motor and mounting bracket.
5. To install motor, place wiper motor and mounting bracket against dash panel and install three retaining bolts.
6. Position wiper link on motor drive arm, and install connecting clip. Be sure to force clip locking flange into locked position as shown in figure.
7. Install cowl top vent screen and secure with four drive pins.
8. Check motor operation and connect wiring plugs.

Maverick, Comet, Monarch, and Granada

1. Remove instrument cluster.
2. If air conditioned, remove center connector and duct assembly. Remove mounting bracket screw behind center duct, disconnect assembly from plenum chamber and left duct, and pull center connector and duct assembly out through cluster opening.
3. Working through cluster opening, disconnect two pivot shaft links from motor drive arm by removing retaining clip.
4. Disconnect wiring plug at motor, remove three retaining bolts, and remove motor through cluster opening.
5. To install motor, bolt motor to mounting plate with three retaining bolts.
6. Connect right pivot shaft link to motor and then connect left pivot shaft link. Lock clip as shown.
7. On air conditioned vehicles, insert end of center connector and duct assembly near mounting bracket into left duct and opposite end into plenum chamber.
8. Secure assembly with mounting bracket screw.
9. Install instrument cluster, and check operation of wiper motor.

1972-73 Torino and Montego (Hidden Wipers)

1. Disconnect the negative battery cable.
2. Remove the wiper arms from the pivot shafts.
3. Disconnect the linkage drive arm from the motor output arm crankpin by removing the retaining clip.
4. From the engine side of the dash, disconnect the two wire connectors from the motor.
5. Remove the three retaining bolts and the motor from the dash.
6. If the output arm catches on the dash during removal, hand-turn the arm clockwise so it will clear the opening in the dash.
7. Reverse the above procedure for installation, making sure that the output arm is in the "park" position prior to installation.

1974-76 Torino, Elite, and Montego; 1974-77 Cougar; 1977 LTD II and Thunderbird (Hidden Wipers)

1. Disconnect the battery ground cable.
2. Remove the wiper arm and blade assemblies from the pivot shafts.
3. Remove the left cowl screen for access through the cowl opening. Disconnect the linkage drive arm from the motor output arm crankpin by removing the retaining clip. From the engine side of the dash, disconnect the two push-on wire connectors from the motor.
4. Remove the three bolts which retain the motor to the dash and remove the motor. If the output arm catches on the dash during removal, hand turn the arm clockwise, so that it will clear the opening in the dash.
5. Before installing the motor, be sure that the output arm is in the Park position.

RADIO

Removal and Replacement

1970-76 Falcon, Fairlane, Torino, and Montego; 1974-77 Cougar; 1977 LTD II and Thunderbird

1. Disconnect battery.

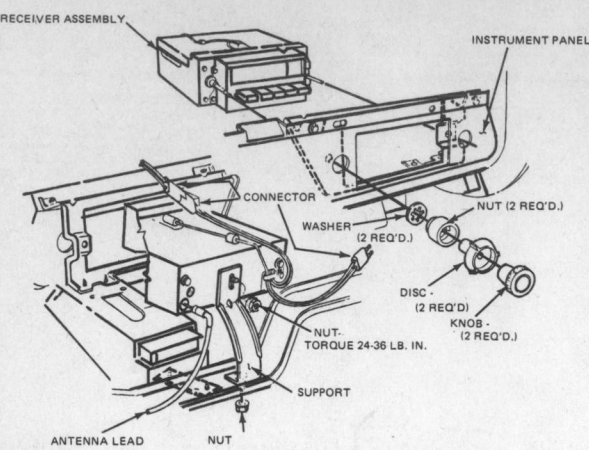

Radio removal—1974-77 Torino, Montego, Cougar and Elite
(© Ford Motor Co)

2. Pull radio control knobs off shafts.
3. Remove radio support to instrument panel attaching screw.
4. Remove two bezel nuts from radio control shafts.
5. Lower radio and disconnect antenna, speaker, and power leads. Remove radio.
6. To install, connect antenna, speaker and power leads to radio.
7. Position radio in instrument panel and install two bezel nuts. Torque bezel nuts to 30-35 in. lbs.
8. Install radio support bracket to instrument panel attaching screw and torque to 30-35 in. lbs.
9. Connect battery.
10. Adjust antenna trimmer, if necessary.
11. Install radio control knobs and set push buttons for desired stations.

1970 Cougar and Mustang

1. Disconnect battery.
2. Pull control knobs, discs, and sleeve from radio control shafts.
3. Remove radio applique from instrument panel.
4. Remove right and left finish panels.
5. Remove two mounting plate attaching screws.
6. Pull radio out of instrument panel and disconnect wires from radio.
7. Remove mounting plate and rear support from radio.
8. Remove radio.
9. To replace, install mounting plate and rear support on radio.
10. Position radio near opening and connect wires to radio.
11. Install jumper wire to ground radio to instrument panel.
12. Connect battery and check operation of radio.
13. Adjust antenna trimmer.
14. Disconnect battery and remove

jumper cable.
15. Insert radio and wires into panel opening. Be sure radio rear support slips over instrument panel reinforcement.
16. Install mounting plate attaching screws.
17. Install left and right finish panels.
18. Install radio applique, sleeve, discs, and control knobs.
19. Connect radio ground cable and set push buttons.

1971-73 Mustang and Cougar

1. Disconnect the negative battery cable.
2. Disconnect the radio antenna wire from the radio.
3. Pull off the radio control knobs and remove the two radio bezel nuts from the radio.
4. Remove the four radio bezel attaching screws.
5. Pull the radio away from the instrument panel and disconnect the lead wires from the radio as they become accessible.
6. To install the radio, position it on the instrument panel and connect the lead wires to it.
7. To complete installation, reverse the removal procedure. When positioning the radio in the instrument panel, make sure the radio support bracket on the rear of the radio engages the tab on the instrument panel.

Maverick and Comet

1. Disconnect battery.
2. Remove radio rear support nut and lock washer.
3. Remove four radio to instrument panel retaining screws.
4. Pull radio from instrument panel and disconnect antenna, speaker, and power leads.
5. Remove radio.
6. Remove knob and disc assemblies from radio shafts.
7. Remove two bezel retaining nuts

and remove bezel.
8. To install radio, position bezel on radio and install two bezel retaining nuts.
9. Install disc and knob assemblies on radio shafts.
10. Connect antenna, speaker, and power connectors.
11. Position radio so that rear support mounting bolt enters hole in rear support mounting bracket.
12. Install four radio to instrument panel retaining screws.
13. Install radio rear support nut and lock washer.
14. Place speaker and power wire harnesses in clip on bezel.
15. Connect battery and check operation of radio.
16. Adjust selector buttons for desired stations.

Granada and Monarch

1. Disconnect the negative battery cable.
2. Remove the headlight switch from the instrument panel. Remove the heater, air conditioner, windshield wiper/washer knobs, and radio knobs and discs.
3. Remove the six screws which attach the applique to the instrument panel and remove the applique. Disconnect the antenna lead-in cable from the radio.
4. Remove the four screws which attach the radio bezel to the instrument panel. Slide the radio and bezel out of the lower rear support bracket and instrument panel opening toward the interior far enough to disconnect the electrical connections, and remove the radio.
5. Remove the nut attaching the rear support bracket to the radio and remove the bracket. Remove the nuts and washer from the radio control shafts and remove the bezel.
6. To install, install the rear support bracket on the radio. Install the bezel and the washers and nuts on the radio shafts.
7. Insert the radio with rear support bracket and bezel through the instrument panel opening far enough to connect the electrical leads and antenna lead-in cable. Install the radio upper rear support bracket into the lower rear support bracket.
8. Center the radio and bezel in the opening and install the four bezel attaching screws.
9. Install the instrument panel applique with its six attaching screws. Install all knobs removed from the instrument panel and radio. Install the headlight switch.
10. Connect the negative battery cable.

HEATER

Vehicles without Air Conditioning

Heater Removal and Installation

1970-73 Cougar and Mustang

1. Disconnect battery and drain coolant.
2. Remove instrument panel pad.
3. Remove glove compartment liner and door.
4. Remove air distribution duct from heater.
5. Disconnect control cables from heater assembly.
6. Disconnect wires from blower motor resistor.
7. Remove right courtesy light located on underside of instrument panel, if so equipped.
8. Remove heater support to dash panel retaining screw.
9. Disconnect vacuum hoses and remove power air vent duct, if so equipped.
10. Remove blower motor ground wire grounding screw.
11. Disconnect heater hoses from heater at dash panel.
12. Working in engine compartment, remove five heater assembly retaining nuts.
13. Remove instrument panel to cowl attaching screws.
14. Remove instrument panel right side brace.
15. Pull heater assembly and right side of instrument panel rear-

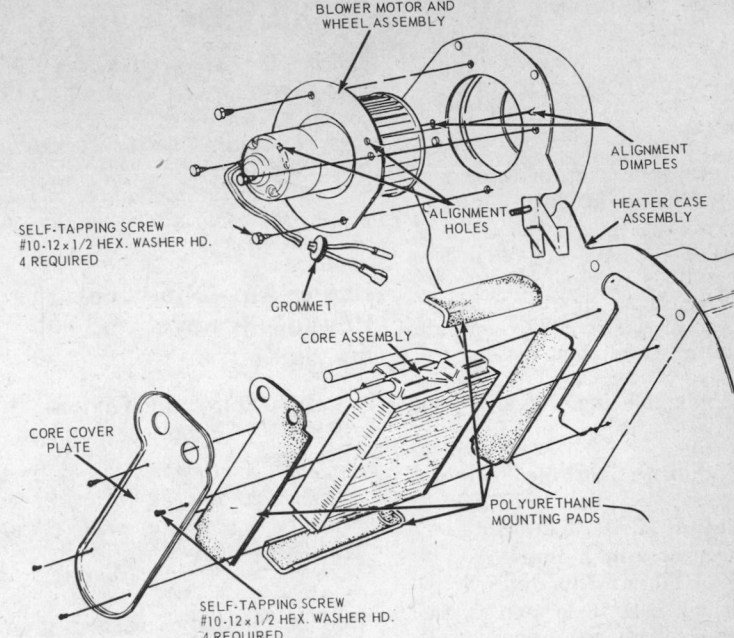

Heater, blower motor and core assemblies—1970 Fairlane and Falcon, 1970-76 Montego and Torino, 1974-77. Cougar and Elite; Granada and Monarch similar
(© Ford Motor Co)

ward, and remove heater assembly. Reverse procedure to install.

1970 Falcon and Fairlane; 1975-77 Granada and Monarch; 1970-76 Torino, Montego, and Elite; 1974-77 Cougar; 1977 LTD II and Thunderbird

1. Drain coolant.
2. Disconnect both heater hoses at dash.
3. Remove nuts retaining heater assembly to dash.
4. Disconnect temperature and defroster cables at heater.
5. Disconnect wires from resistor, and disconnect blower motor wires and clip retaining heater assembly to defroster nozzle.
6. Remove glove box.
7. Remove bolt and nut right air duct control to instrument panel. Remove nuts retaining right air duct and remove duct assembly.
8. Remove heater assembly to bench.

Maverick, Comet

1. Drain the cooling system and disconnect the negative battery cable.
2. Disconnect the blower ground wire (black) from the fender apron.
3. Disconnect the heater hoses from the engine block.
4. Remove the five heater assembly to firewall attaching bolts from the firewall.
5. Working inside the car, remove the ignition switch and plate from the package tray and remove the tray from the dash.
6. Remove the right kick panel and remove the package tray bracket.
7. Disconnect the heater control cables from the heater.
8. Disconnect the defroster air duct from the top of the heater.
9. Disconnect the heater blower motor lead wires from the resistor at the bottom of the heater.
10. Remove the one screw from the bracket that mounts the heater to the dash.
11. Remove the heater from the car by pulling the heater hoses

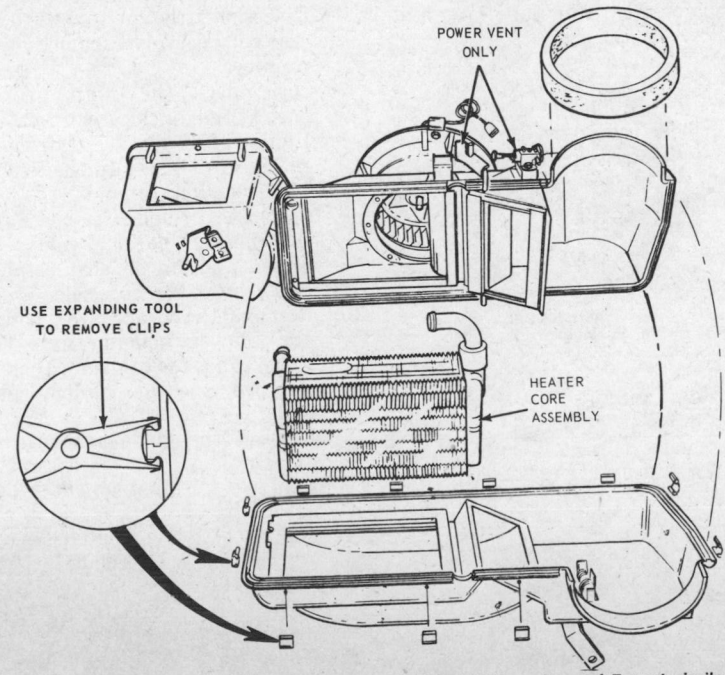

Heater core removal—1970-73 Cougar and Mustang; Maverick and Comet similar
(© Ford Motor Co)

through the firewall, then disconnecting them from the heater.

Heater Core Removal and Installation

1970 Cougar and Mustang, 1970-77 Maverick and Comet

1. Remove heater assembly.
2. Remove air inlet seal from heater assembly.
3. Remove eleven clips from heater assembly flange and separate heater assembly housing.
4. Remove heater core from heater assembly housing. Reverse procedure to install.

1970-76 Falcon, Fairlane, Torino, Montego, and Elite; 1971-73 Mustang; 1971-77 Cougar, Granada, and Monarch; 1977 LTD II and Thunderbird

The heater core is located in the heater case in a diagonal position. It is serviced through an opening in the back plate. With the heater assembly removed from the vehicle, remove heater core cover and pad and remove core. Reverse procedure to install.

Blower Motor Removal and Installation

The blower motor on all models is located inside the heater assembly. To replace the blower motor, remove the heater assembly from the car following the steps in the above procedures. Once the heater assembly is removed, it is a simple operation to remove the motor attaching bolts and remove the motor. On all models, the motor and cage are removed as an assembly.

Vehicles with Integral Heater-Air Conditioning

NOTE: removal of the heater-air conditioner housing requires evacuation of the air conditioner refrigerant. This operation requires special tools and training. Failure to follow proper safety precautions may cause personal injury.

Heater-Air Conditioner Housing Removal and Installation

1970 Falcon and Fairlane, 1970-71 Torino and Montego

Removal

NOTE: to remove the core, it is necessary to remove the entire evaporator assembly.

1. Remove the carburetor air cleaner.
2. Disconnect the battery ground cable.
3. Drain the cooling system.
4. Purge the system of refrigerant.
5. Disconnect the high and low pressure lines at the expansion valve.
6. Remove the two piece seal retainer from the dash panel and the refrigerant hose seal.
7. Disconnect the three heater hoses at the dash panel.
8. Disconnect the two clutch wires from the vacuum switch at the water valve mounting plate.
9. Disconnect the vacuum hoses at the water valves, clutch switch and vacuum supply tank. Push the hose-wire harness into the passenger compartment.
10. Remove the drain tube hose and seal from the evaporator housing.
11. Disengage the defroster nozzle from the plenum.
12. Disconnect the red-stripe hose from the vacuum motor.
13. Remove the plenum chamber.
14. Remove the glove compartment liner.
15. Disconnect the vacuum hose from the right vent motor.
16. Remove the right vent assembly.
17. Disconnect the four vacuum hoses and the temperature control cable from the control assembly.
18. Disconnect the wires from the blower resistor and icing switch.
19. Disconnect the flexible hoses from the center air duct.
20. Remove the center air duct.
21. Remove the defroster nozzle.
22. Remove the evaporator retaining nuts and remove the assembly.

Installation

To install, reverse the removal procedure. Evacuate, leak test, and charge the system with refrigerant.

1970 Mustang and Cougar

Removal

NOTE: to remove the core, it is necessary to remove the entire evaporator assembly.

1. Remove the carburetor air cleaner.
2. Disconnect the battery ground cable.
3. Drain the cooling system.
4. Purge the system of refrigerant.
5. Remove the heat shield from the expansion valve.
6. Disconnect the low pressure hose and service valve from the compressor.
7. Disconnect the high pressure hose at the quick disconnect.
8. Remove the straps retaining the refrigerant hoses to the dash-to-fender apron supports.
9. Disconnect the heater hoses from the heater core. Remove the upper and lower seal retainers and remove the hose seal.
10. Remove the evaporator housing and blower housing nuts from the engine side of dash panel.
11. Remove the instrument panel pad.
12. Remove the glove box assembly and support.
13. Remove the instrument cluster assembly.
14. Disconnect all vacuum hoses.
15. Disconnect the control cable from the temperature blend door, wires from the A/C thermostat switch.
16. Disconnect air ducts from the plenum chamber, remove the air ducts.

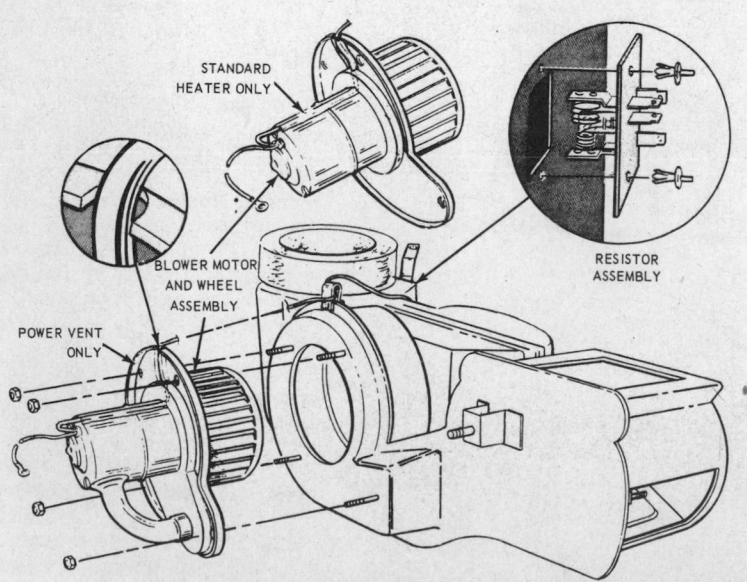

Heater blower and motor installation—1970-73 Mustang and Cougar, 1970-77 Maverick, 1971-77 Comet
(© Ford Motor Co)

17. Remove the A/C defrost plenum chamber.
18. Remove the instrument right side brace, evaporator housing upper rear support.
19. Move the blower housing to the left away from the evaporator housing.
20. Cover carpet and pull drain tube from hole in floor pan.
21. Remove the instrument panel lower finish cover from around the steering column.
22. Remove nuts and bolts retaining the instrument panel to steering column support.
23. Position the instrument panel back and remove the evaporator housing from the vehicle.

Installation

To install, reverse the removal procedure, Evacuate. Leak test. Charge the system.

Maverick, Comet

Removal

NOTE: to facilitate installation, tag vacuum lines and electrical wires, as to their proper location, before disassembling unit. To remove the core, it is necessary to remove the entire evaporator assembly.

1. Disconnect the battery and remove the air cleaner.
2. Drain the cooling system.
3. Connect a manifold gauge set to the compressor, and discharge the system.
4. Remove the expansion valve and disconnect the heater hoses from the heater core. Tape over openings to avoid entry of dirt.

5. Remove the three A/C assembly-to-dash panel mounting stud nuts. Remove the utility shelf and bracket from the lower edge of the instrument panel, and remove the right cowl trim panel and radio. Remove the glove compartment.
6. Disconnect the right and left A/C register air ducts from the plenum chamber.
7. Remove the floor distribution duct from the blower housing.
8. Remove the center register from the instrument panel. Then pull the plenum chamber part way through the register opening to disengage it from the blower housing. Disconnect the (blue) hose from the (7) door motor on the plenum chamber.
9. Disconnect the vacuum hoses from the doormotors.
10. Disconnect the vacuum harness multiple connector from the control assembly.
11. Disconnect the temperature control cable from the evaporator housing, and disconnect the vacuum hoses from the adjacent water valve vacuum switch.
12. Remove the screw which retains the evaporator housing to the cowl upper support and move A/C assembly rearward and away from the dash panel.
13. Remove any remaining hoses and disconnect wires from the blower resistor, the de-icing switch and the blower motor ground wire.
14. Remove the evaporator and

blower housing assembly from the vehicle.

Installation

1. Install assembly into the vehicle by reversing the removal procedures, being careful to correctly connect the vacuum holes. When making connections to the water valve vacuum switch, connect the purple hose to the nipple closest to the switch plunger and attach the green hose to the water valve motor.
2. After installation, adjust the temperature control cable and, if neccessary, the water valve vacuum switch.
3. Evacuate, leak test and charge the system.

1971-73 Mustang and Cougar

Removal

NOTE: to remove the core, it is necessary to remove the entire evaporator assembly.

1. Remove the carburetor air cleaner.
2. Disconnect the battery.
3. Drain the cooling system.
4. Purge the system of refrigerant.
5. Disconnect the evaporator tubes from the expansion valve, disconnect the heater hoses.
6. Remove the housing-to-dash panel mounting stud nuts.
7. Remove the glove box and map light from the lower edge, right side of instrument panel.
8. Disconnect the vacuum hoses at the motor.
9. Disconnect the two hoses from the water valve vacuum switch,

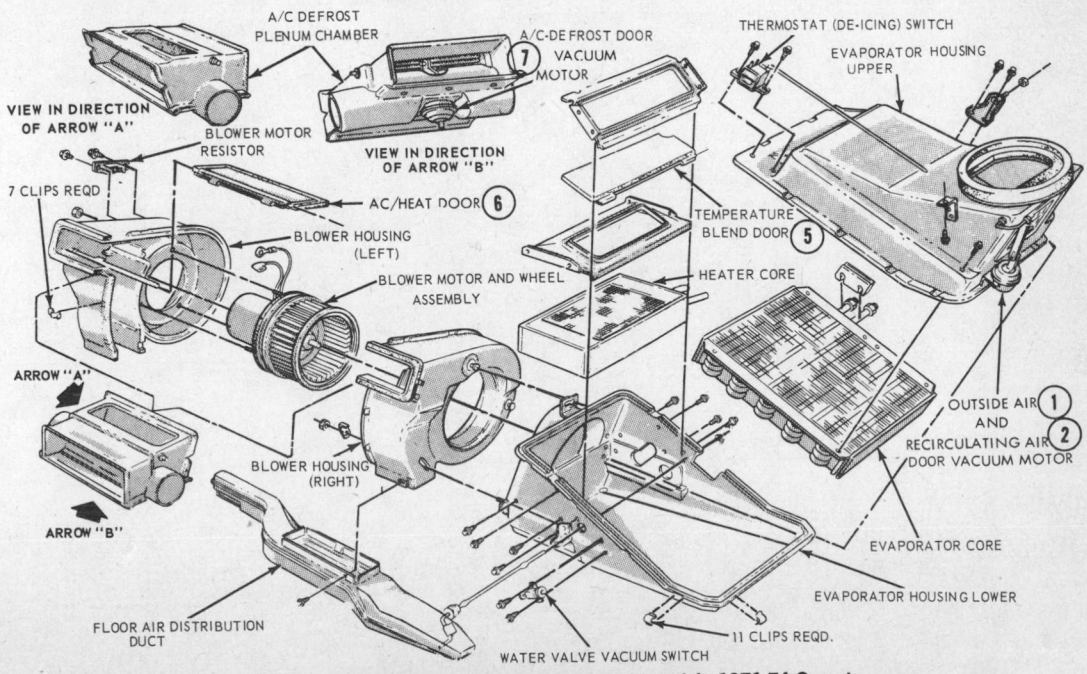

Heater-air conditioner assembly—1970-74 Maverick, 1971-74 Comet, 1975-77 Maverick and Comet similar
(© Ford Motor Co)

and disengage the hoses from the slip at the top of the housing.

10. Disconnect the wires from the thermostatic (de-icing) switch.
11. Disconnect the cable from the door crank arm.
12. Remove the motor from the housing to allow clearance at the lower edge of the instrument panel, and remove the motor bracket.
13. Remove the motor to allow clearance at the right side of the housing during removal.
14. Remove the housing-to-cowl bracket.
15. Pull the drain hose from the hole in the floor pan.
16. Remove the two blower housing-to-cowl attaching screws, lower the blower housing slightly. Pull the housing away from the dash panel, move it to the right to separate it from the blower housing and remove it from the vehicle.

Installation

To install, reverse the removal procedure. Evacuate, Leak test, and Charge the refrigerant system.

1972-76 Torino, Montego, and Elite; 1974-77 Cougar; 1977 LTD II and Thunderbird

Removal

NOTE: to remove the core, it is necessary to remove the entire assembly.

1. Discharge system as outlined under instructions referring to units with six cylinder compressor.
2. Disconnect the heater hoses, and position them so coolant will not escape.

3. Disconnect liquid line to expansion valve, low pressure line to STV valve, and STV valve equalizer line.
4. Remove insulation around capillary tube, and remove tube from suction line. Remove expansion valve from evaporator.
5. Remove STV valve by disconnecting it from the evaporator.
6. Remove the two mounting flange nuts and three mounting flange screws that can be reached from the engine compartment. Remove the sheet metal mounting screws, plenum right lower mounting screws, and blower housing-to-evaporator housing screw from under the instrument panel. Remove the plenum mounting screws and move the plenum to the rear.
7. Remove the evaporator case from the engine compartment.

Installation

1. Reverse the removal procedures, observing the following precautions:
   a. After installing heater hoses, replace any coolant that may have been lost.
   b. Evacuate, leak test, and charge the system.

Heater Core Removal and Installation

1970 Falcon and Fairlane 1970-71 Torino and Montego

1. Remove the heater-air conditioner assembly.
2. Separate the heater housing from the plenum.

3. Slip the heater core out of the plenum.
4. Transfer the old heater core seal to the new core.
5. Slip the new core with seal into the plenum.
6. Install the heater housing to the plenum. Connect the wires at the resistor block, and install the seal and retainer at the evaporator tubes.
7. Install the heater-air conditoner assembly.

1970-73 Mustang and Cougar, 1970-77 Maverick, 1971-77 Comet

1. Remove the heater-air conditioner assembly.
2. Remove the flange clips and upper half of the housing assembly.
3. Remove the water valve vacuum switch from the lower half of the housing.
4. Remove the screw, retaining clip and temperature blend door shaft, the four screws and door upper frame, the door, and the four screws and door lower frame from the lower half of the housing.
5. Lift the heater core from the lower housing.
6. Transfer the pads from the old core to the new core.
7. Reverse the above procedures to install. Leak-test, evacuate and charge the refrigeration system.

1972-76 Torino, Montego, and Elite; 1974-77 Cougar; 1977 LTD II and Thunderbird

1. Drain the cooling system and disconnect the heater hoses at the core.

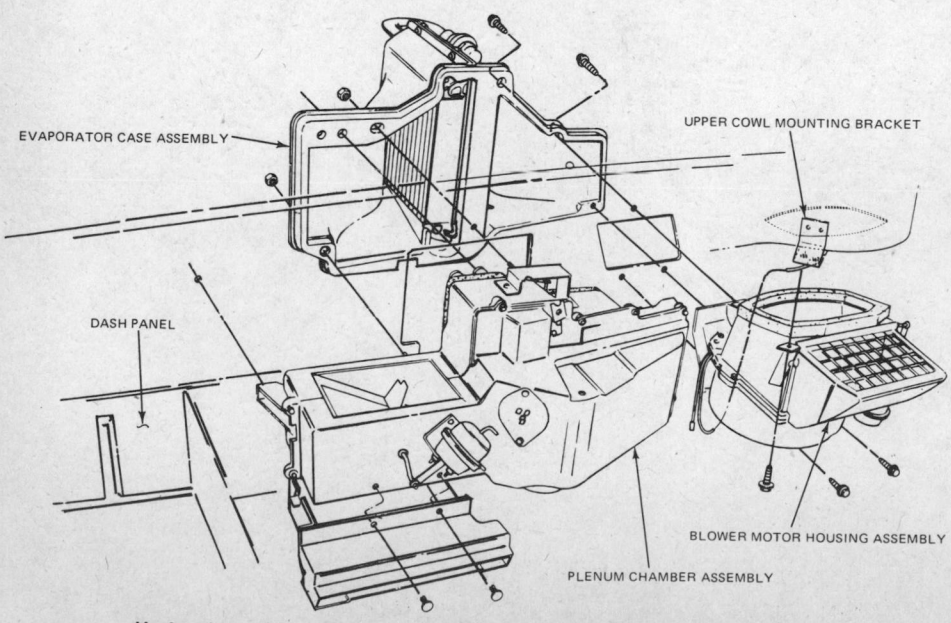

EVAPORATOR CASE ASSEMBLY

UPPER COWL MOUNTING BRACKET

DASH PANEL

BLOWER MOTOR HOUSING ASSEMBLY

PLENUM CHAMBER ASSEMBLY

Heater-air conditioner assembly—1972-77 Torino, Montego, Cougar and Elite
(© Ford Motor Co)

2. Remove the glove box.
3. Remove the two snap clips and the heater air outlet register from the plenum.
4. Remove the temperature control cable assembly mounting screw, and disconnect the end of the cable from the blend door crank arm.
5. Remove the blue and red vacuum hoses from the high-low door vacuum motor; the yellow hose from the panel-defrost door motor, and the brown hose from the inline tee connector.
6. Disconnect the wires at the resistor block.
7. Remove the ten screws and the rear half of the plenum.
8. Remove the mounting nut from the heater core tube support bracket.
9. Reverse the above procedures to install, taking care to apply body sealer around the case flanges to insure a positive seal.

Granada and Monarch

NOTE: The refrigerant system components and charge do not have to be disturbed when removing and installing the heater core.

1. Drain the coolant and disconnect the battery.
2. Disconnect 2 heater hose clamps at the dash panel in the engine compartment. Plug the core tubes to prevent coolant leakage during removal.
3. Remove the heat distribution duct from the instrument panel.
4. Remove the seat belt interlock module and bracket.
5. Remove the glovebox liner.
6. Loosen the right door sill scuff plate, right "A" pillar trim cover and remove the right cowl side trim panel.
7. Loosen instrument panel-to-right cowl side bolt and remove the instrument panel brace bolt at the lower rail, below the glove box.
8. Remove the instrument panel crash pad.
9. Remove the radio speaker or panel cowl brace.
10. Remove the 4 nozzle-to-cowl bracket mounting screws.
11. Lift the defroster nozzle upward through the crash pad opening.
12. Disconnect the vacuum hoses from the A/C-Defrost and Heat/Defrost door motors. Remove the

screw from the clip holding the vacuum harness to the plenum.
13. Remove 2 Heat/Defrost door mounting nuts and swing the motor rearward on the door crankarm.
14. Remove 2 screws attaching the plenum to the left mounting bracket. Then remove the 2 screws and 3 clips securing the plenum to the evaporator case.
15. Swing the bottom of the plenum away from the evaporator case to disengage the S-clip on the forward flange of the plenum. Raise the plenum to clear the tabs on the top of the evaporator case.
16. Move the plenum to the left as far as possible, (about 4 inches) pulling rearward on the instrument panel to gain clearance. Take care when pulling back on the instrument panel to avoid cracking the plastic panel.

NOTE: There is very little clearance between the plenum and the wiper motor assembly.

17. Pull the heater core to the left using the tab molded into the rear heater core seal. As the rear surface of the heater core clears

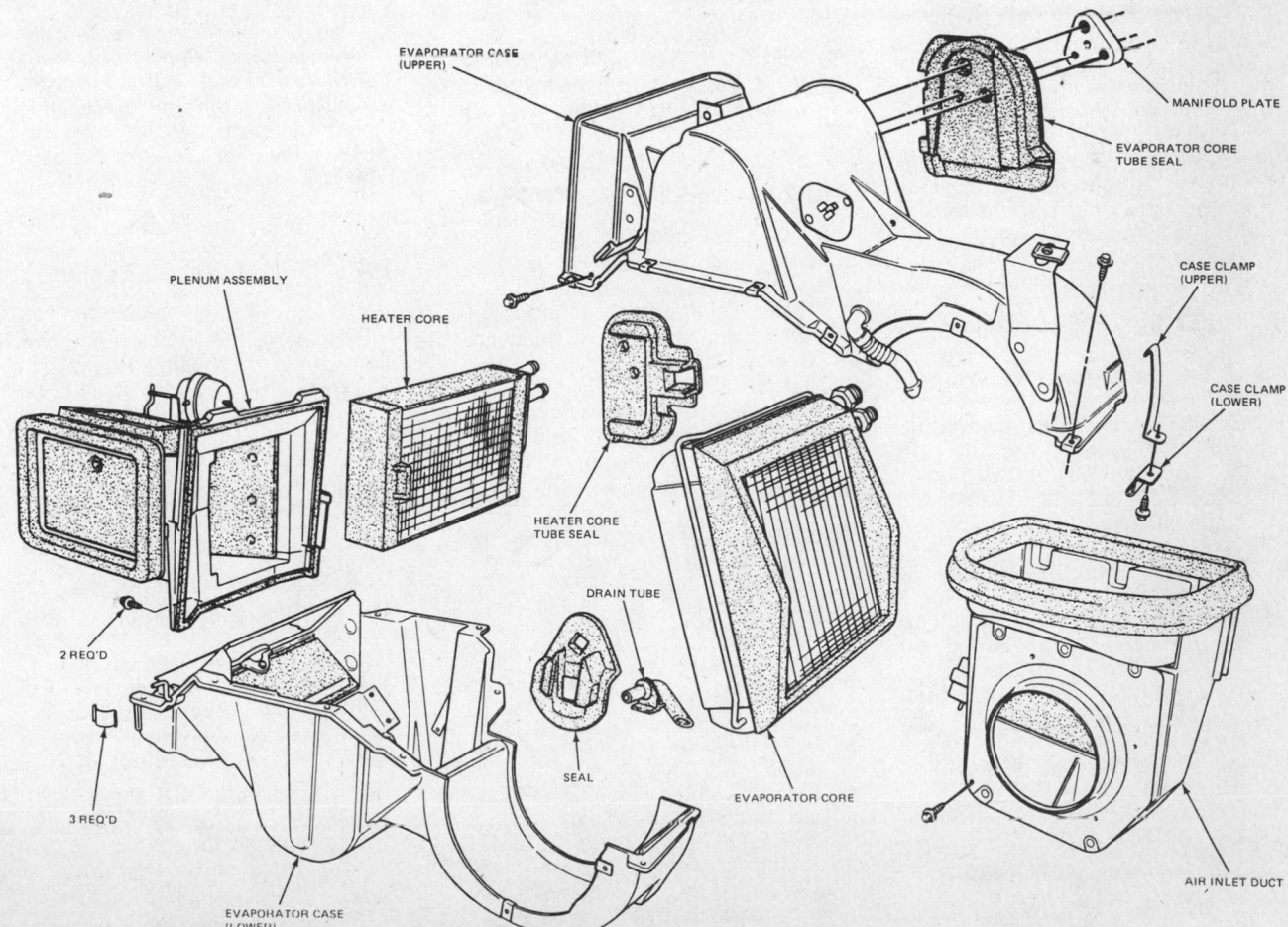

Heater core removal—Granada and Monarch with heater/air conditioner system
(© Ford Motor Co)

C507

the evaporator case, pull the core rearward and downward to clear the instrument panel.

18. Reverse the above procedure to install.

NOTE: Before installing the core, make sure that the heater core tube to dash panel seal is in place between the evaporator case and the dash panel.

Blower Motor Removal and Installation

1970 Falcon and Fairlane; 1970-76 Torino, Montego, and Elite; 1974-77 Cougar; 1977 LTD II and Thunderbird

Removal

1. Disconnect the battery and take out the glove box.
2. On 1971 and earlier models, take out the right hand fresh air duct. On 1972 and later models, remove recirculating air duct.
3. Remove the two screws which attach the blower lower housing to the dash panel.
4. Disconnect the vacuum line from the actuator and move it out of the way.
5. Disconnect the plug from the resistor block and lift out the resistor block.
6. On 1971 and earlier models, take off the blower motor cover and lift out the motor and the blower wheel. On 1972 and later models, remove all blower housing flange screws, separate blower housing halves, and unscrew and remove blower assembly.
7. Remove the blower wheel.

Installation

1. Install the blower wheel on the motor.
2. Install the motor and shell and ground wire in the case.
3. On 1971 and earlier models, install the blower cover. On 1972 and later models, install blower assembly into lower housing, and reassemble housing.
4. Connect the wires.
5. Fasten the resistor block to the plenum.
6. Install the fresh air duct on earlier models, recirculating air duct on 1972 and later models.
7. Install the two screws which attach the blower lower housing to the dash.
8. Install the glove box and connect the battery.

1970 Mustang and Cougar

Removal

1. Disconnect battery ground cable, and drain cooling system.
2. Remove instrument panel pad,

glove compartment liner, and glove compartment door.
3. Remove the heater air distribution duct.
4. Disconnect the control cables, and the wires from the blower motor resistor.
5. Remove the right side courtesy light, if applicable.
6. Remove the heater support mounting screw from the dash.
7. Disconnect the vacuum hoses. If the vehicle is equipped with a power ventilation system, remove the power vent air duct.
8. Disconnect the heater hoses at the dash panel.
9. From the engine compartment, remove the blower motor ground screw, and the five heater assembly retaining nuts.
10. Remove the screws which hold the instrument panel to the cowl, and the instrument panel right side brace. Pull the right side of the instrument panel rearward, and remove the heater assembly.
11. Disconnect blower motor wires where they connect at the resistor.
12. Remove the four mounting plate nuts, and remove the blower and motor assembly.

Installation

1. To install, reverse the procedures, being careful to properly adjust the control cables.

1970-73 Maverick, 1971-73 Comet

Removal

1. Disconnect the battery and remove the radio asembly.
2. Remove the utility shelf, and air ducts from the plenum chamber.
3. Remove the air duct from the bottom of the blower housing.
4. Remove the blower housing mounting stud nut and lock plate.
5. Rotate the blower housing from the evaporator housing.
6. Disconnect the vacuum hoses, resistor and ground wires, and remove the housing.
7. Separate the left and right halves.

Installation

1. Set the motor in place.
2. Install the motor attaching nuts.
3. Set the blower fan on the motor shaft.
4. Install the blower motor and fan assembly.
5. Set the blower housing in place.
6. Install the blower housing attaching nuts, washers, and screws.
7. Install the water valve.
8. Reverse steps 1-3 to complete assembly.

1974-77 Maverick and Comet

1. Disconnect the battery and remove the radio.
2. Remove the floor air distribution duct retaining bolts, and disconnect the right and left A/C register air duct assemblies from the plenum chamber.
3. Remove the floor air distribution duct from the bottom of the blower housing.
4. Remove the blower housing mounting stud nut and lockplate.
5. Rotate the blower housing to unlock the slotted tabs on the blower housing from their lock pins on the evaporator housing. There are two tabs and pins. Disconnect the red and yellow hoses at the vacuum motor on the blower housing. Disconnect the resistor and ground wires, and remove the blower housing.
6. Cut the gaskets around the A/C outlets at the break line.
7. Remove the seven clips, and separate the left and right halves of the blower housing.
8. Remove the three blower motor mounting plate retaining nuts, and remove the motor and wheel assembly from the housing.
9. Assemble and install in the reverse order of removal, making sure that the A/C-Heat door is positioned properly before clipping the right and left housing halves together. Connect the battery.

1971-73 Mustang and Cougar

Removal

1. Disconnect the battery. Remove the blower housing mounting bracket stud nut (engine side of the dash panel.)
2. Remove the two blower housing-to-instrument panel support mounting screws.
3. Disconnect the blower motor ground wire (black) from the resistor.
4. Disconnect the blower motor lead wire (orange-black) from the resistor.
5. Rotate the blower housing to a diagonal position. Remove the blower motor mounting screws, and remove the blower motor and wheel as an assembly.

Installation

1. Position the assembly and secure the mounting screws.
2. Connect the blower motor lead and ground wires.
3. Position the blower motor on the blower housing and install the mounting bracket.
4. Install the battery.

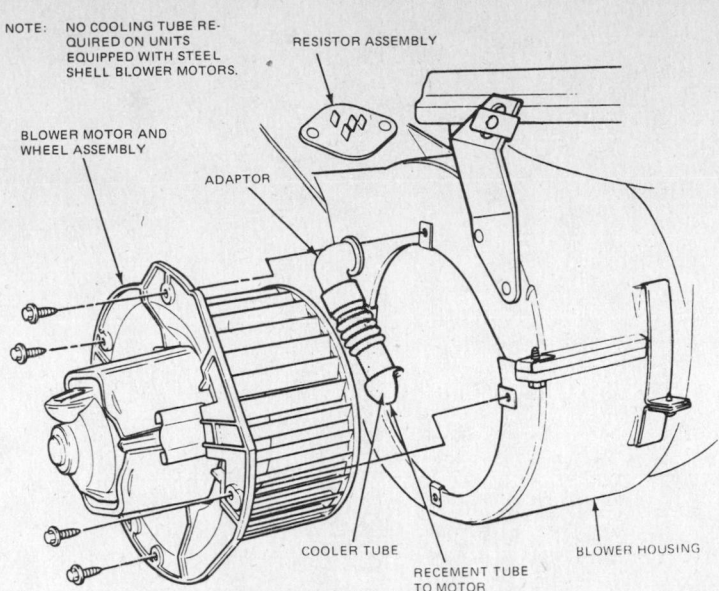

NOTE: NO COOLING TUBE REQUIRED ON UNITS EQUIPPED WITH STEEL SHELL BLOWER MOTORS.

RESISTOR ASSEMBLY

BLOWER MOTOR AND WHEEL ASSEMBLY

ADAPTOR

COOLER TUBE

RECEMENT TUBE TO MOTOR

BLOWER HOUSING

Blower motor removal—Granada and Monarch with heater/air conditioner system
(© Ford Motor Co)

SEAT BELTS

Disconnecting Seat Belt/Starter Interlock

It is now legal to disconnect the seat belt/starter interlock system. However the warning light portion of the system must be left operational.

1. Apply the parking brake and remove the ignition key.
2. Open the hood and locate the system emergency override switch and connector. Remove the connector.
3. Cut the white wire(s) with the pink dots (# 33 circuit) and the red wire(s) with the light blue stripe (#32 circuit).
4. Splice the two (four) wires together and tape the splice. Use a "butt" connector if available.

NOTE: Do not cut and splice the other connector wires. If the red/yellow hash wire is spliced to any of the other wires the car will start in gear.

6. Install the connector back on the override switch. Close the hood.
7. Apply the parking brakes, buckle the seat belt, and turn the key to the "ON" position. If the starter cranks in "ON" or any gear selected, the wrong wires have been cut and spliced. Repeat steps 3-6.
8. Unbuckle the belt and try to start the car. If the car doesn't start, repeat steps 3-6. If the car starts, everything is OK.
9. To stop the warning buzzer from operating, remove it from its connector and throw it away. Tape the connector to the wiring harness so that it can't rattle.

Granada and Monarch

1. Disconnect the negative battery cable.
2. Loosen the passenger side door sill scuff plate and the right "A" pillar trim cover. Remove the right cowl side trim panel.
3. Remove the bolt retaining the lower side of the instrument panel to the cowl. Remove the right cowl side brace bolt.
4. Disconnect the wiring harness connectors at the blower motor.
5. If so equipped, remove the cooling tube from the blower motor.
6. Remove the 4 screws retaining the blower motor and wheel assembly to the scroll. To remove the motor, pull rearward on the lower edge of the instrument panel to provide clearance.
7. Installation is the reverse of removal. If necesary, cement the cooling tube to the blower motor.

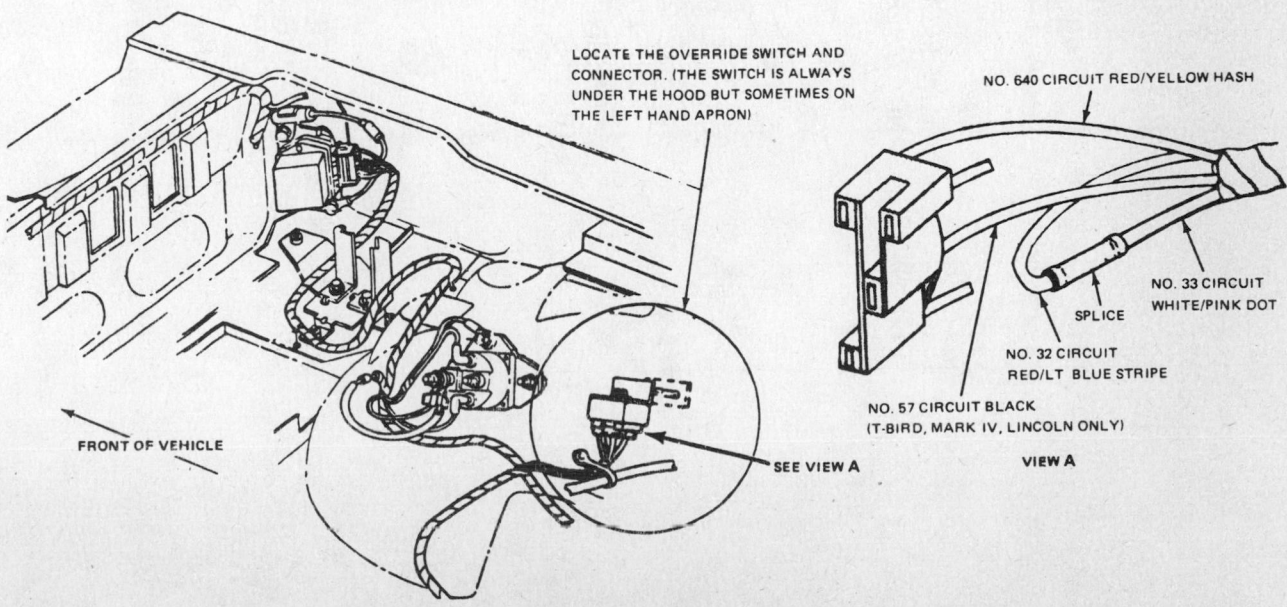

LOCATE THE OVERRIDE SWITCH AND CONNECTOR. (THE SWITCH IS ALWAYS UNDER THE HOOD BUT SOMETIMES ON THE LEFT HAND APRON)

FRONT OF VEHICLE

SEE VIEW A

NO. 640 CIRCUIT RED/YELLOW HASH

SPLICE

NO. 33 CIRCUIT WHITE/PINK DOT

NO. 32 CIRCUIT RED/LT BLUE STRIPE

NO. 57 CIRCUIT BLACK (T-BIRD, MARK IV, LINCOLN ONLY)

VIEW A

Disconnecting seat belt/starter interlock system
(© Ford Motor Co)

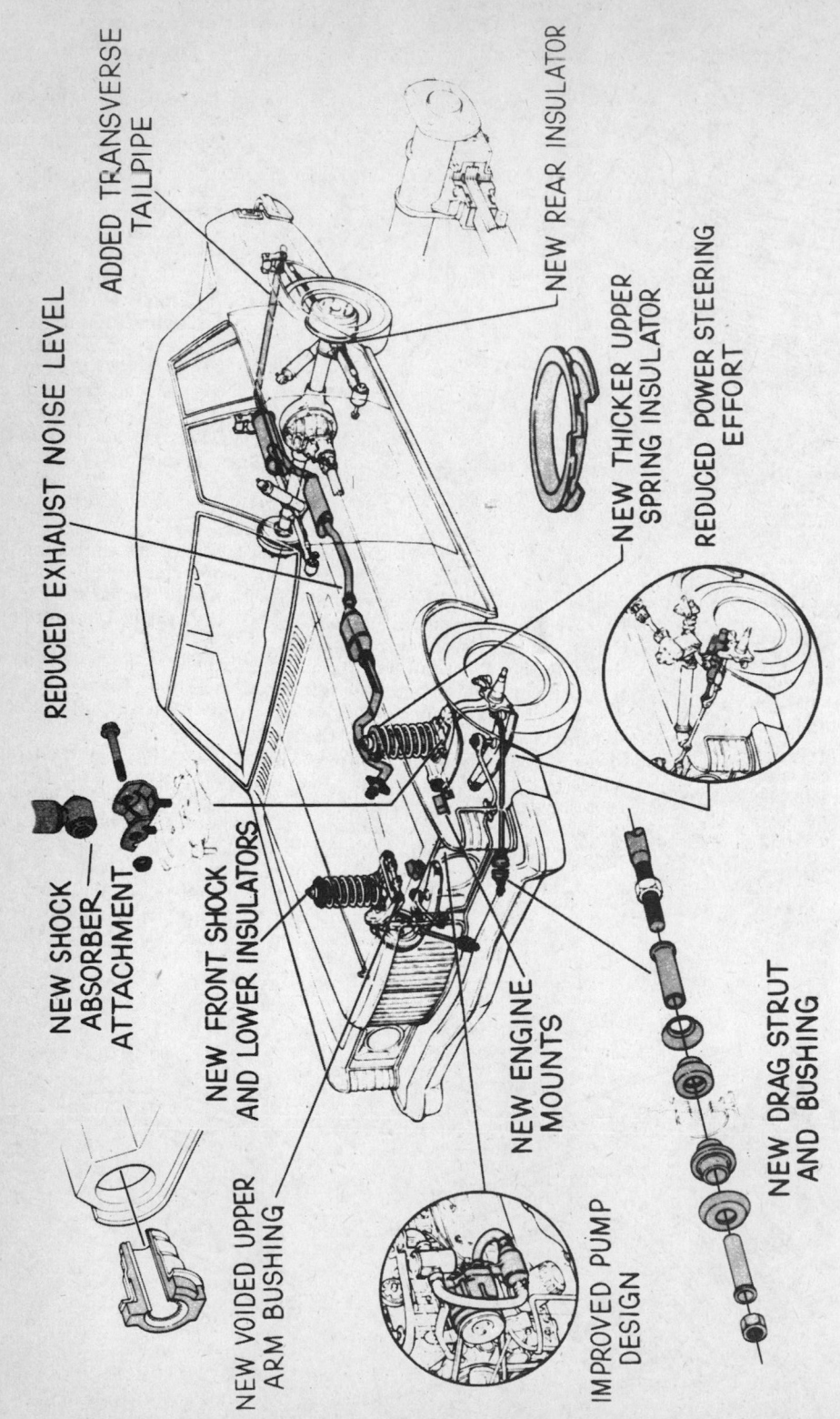

ADDED TRANSVERSE TAILPIPE

NEW REAR INSULATOR

REDUCED EXHAUST NOISE LEVEL

NEW THICKER UPPER SPRING INSULATOR

REDUCED POWER STEERING EFFORT

NEW SHOCK ABSORBER ATTACHMENT

NEW FRONT SHOCK AND LOWER INSULATORS

NEW ENGINE MOUNTS

NEW VOIDED UPPER ARM BUSHING

IMPROVED PUMP DESIGN

NEW DRAG STRUT AND BUSHING

1976 Monarch/Granada ride improvement and noise reduction changes
(© Ford Motor Co.)

INDEX

Dodge · Plymouth

Automatic Transmission
in car service **C535**
Band adjustments C535
Gearshift linkage adjustment C535
Neutral safety/backup light switch
Removal and Installation C535
Pan Removal and Installation, fluid
and filter change C535

Brakes **C541, U299**
Master cylinder Removal and
Installation C541
Parking brake adjustment C541
Power brake booster Removal and
Installation C541

Charging System **C525, U2**
Alternator Removal and Installation C525
Regulator Removal and Installation C525

Clutch **C535**

Cooling System **C530, U367**

Emission Controls **C530, U145**
Lean-Burn System C530

Engine **C532, U194**
426 Hemi Intake Manifold
Removal and Installation C532
426 Hemi Rocker Shaft Removal
and Installation C532
426 Hemi cylinder head
Removal and Installation C534
Oil Pan Removal and Installation C534

Front Suspension **C536, U292**
Shock absorber Removal and
Installation C536
Front suspension height C539
Lower control arm and steering
knuckle Removal and Installation C540

Lower ball joint inspection and
replacement C537
Torsion bar Removal and Installation ... C539
Upper ball joint replacement C538
Wheel bearing adjustment C540

Fuel System **C526, U50**
Balancing multiple carburetors C529
Idle speed solenoid adjustment C528
Fuel filter Removal and Installation C528
Fuel pump Removal and Installation C528
Idle speed and mixture adjustment C528

Heater **C543**
Blower motor Removal and Installation
(Non A/C) C544
Blower motor Removal and Installation
(Air-conditioned) C548
Heater assembly Removal and Installation
(Non A/C) C543
Heater core Removal and Installation
(Non A/C) C544
Heater core Removal and Installation
(Air-conditioned) C545

Ignition System **C525, U34**
Breaker points and condenser
Removal and Installation C526
Distributor Removal and Installation ... C526
Firing order C514
Ignition advance solenoid C525
Ignition retard solenoid C525
Ignition timing C526

Instrument Panel **C541, U350**
Headlight switch Removal and
Installation C541

Jacking, Hoisting **C536**

Manual Transmission **C535, U231**

Radio **C542**
Radio Removal and Installation C542

Rear Axle **C536, U285**
Axle shaft, bearing, and seal
Removal and Installation C536

Rear Suspension **C540**
Shock absorber Removal and
Installation C540
Spring Removal and Installation C541

Seat Belts **C548**
Disabling the interlock system C548

Specifications **C512, U359**
Capacities C519
Car serial number location C514
Crankshaft and connecting rod C522
Engine identification code C514
General engine C514
Piston clearance C523
Ring C523
Torque C523
Tune-up C516
Valve C521
Wheel alignment and front end
height C523
Year Identification C512

Starting System **C525, U2**
Starter Removal and Installation C525

Steering **C541, U328**

U-Joints **C536**
Driveshaft Removal and Installation ... C536
Overhaul C536

Windshield Wipers **C542**
Motor Removal and Installation C542

MODEL IDENTIFICATION

1970 Polara

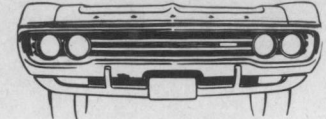

1971 Polara

1972 Polara

1973 Polara

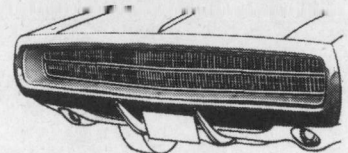

1970 Charger

1971 Charger

1972 Charger

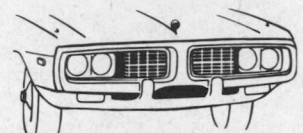

1973 Charger

1974 Charger

1975 Charger S.E.

1976 Charger S.E.

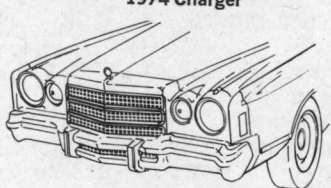

1977 Charger SE

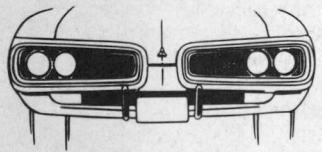

1970 Coronet 440

1970 Coronet 500

1971 Coronet

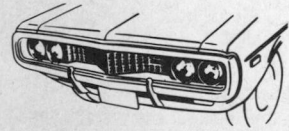

1972 Coronet

1973 Coronet

1974 Coronet

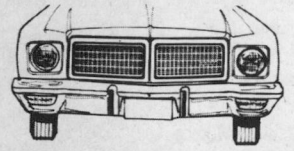

1975-76 Coronet

1975-76 Coronet Brougham

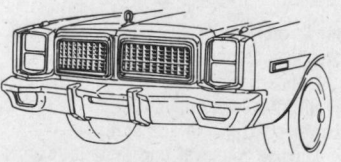

1977 Monaco

1972 Monaco

1973 Monaco

MODEL IDENTIFICATION (con't.)

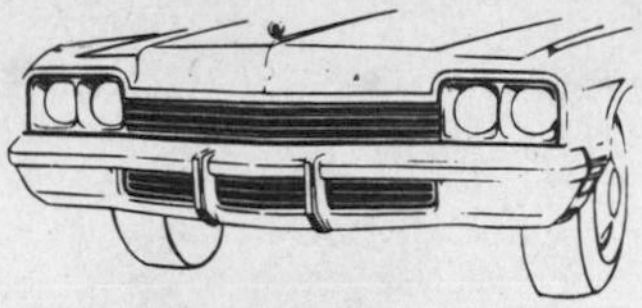

1974 Monaco

1975 Monaco

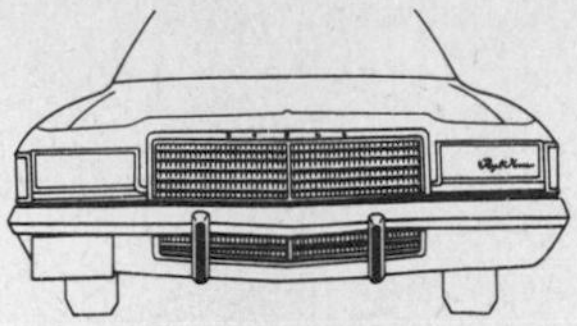

1976 Monaco

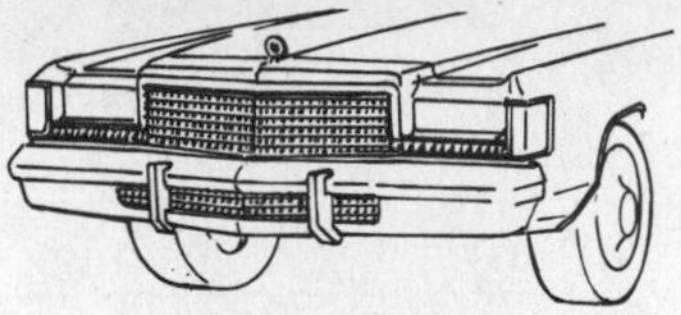

1977 Royal Monaco

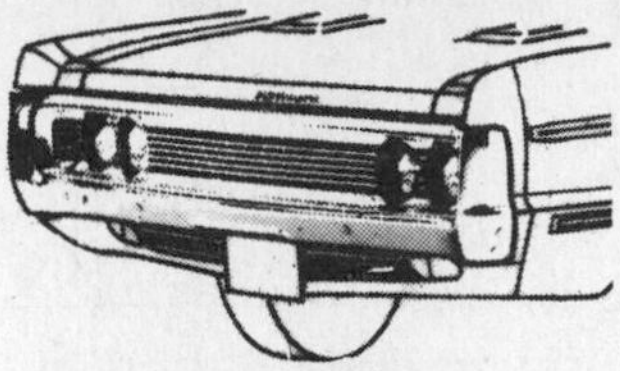

1970 Fury

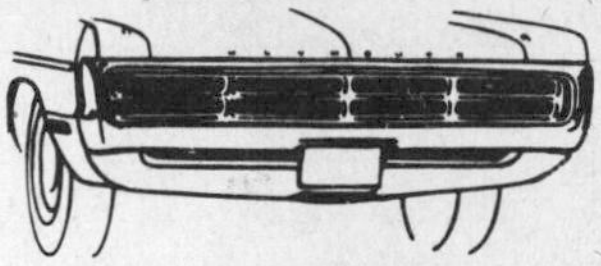

1971 Fury

1972 Fury

1973 Fury

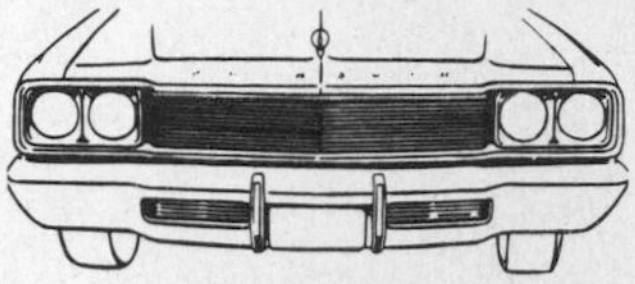

1974 Fury

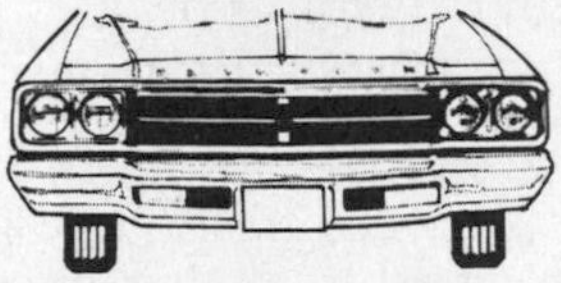

1975 Gran Fury

1975 Gran Fury Brougham

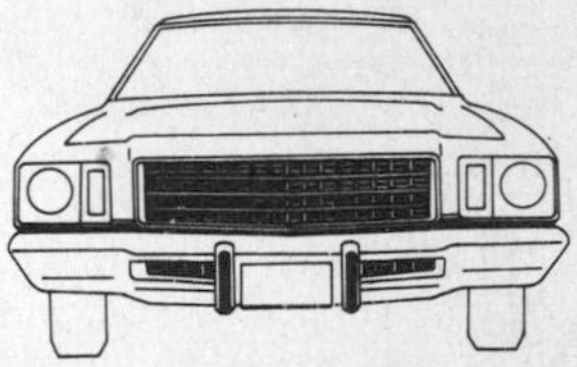

1976 Gran Fury

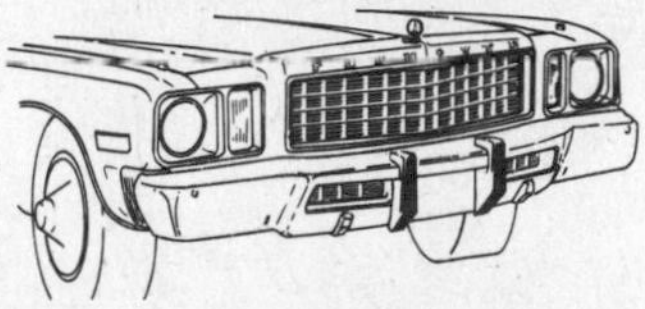

1977 Gran Fury

1970 GTX

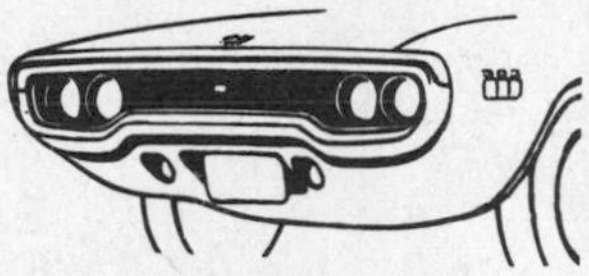

1971 Sebring

1971 Road Runner

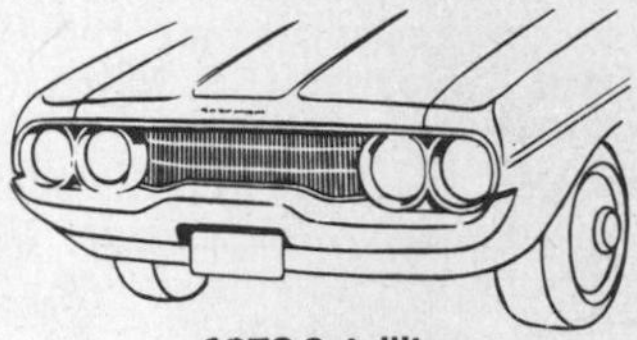

1972 Satellite

1972 Sebring

1972 Road Runner

1973 Satellite

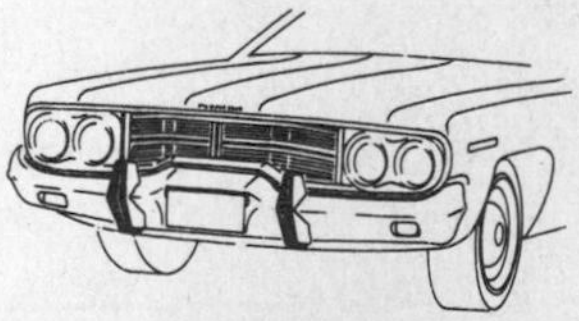

1974 Satellite

1974 Sebring

1974 Road Runner

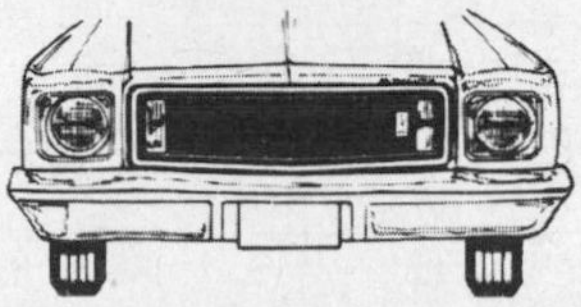

1975-Road Runner

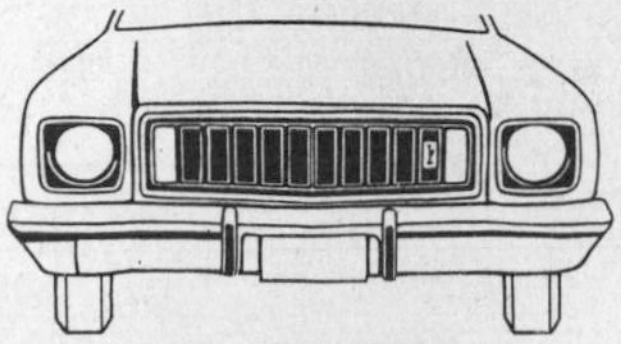

1976 Road Runner

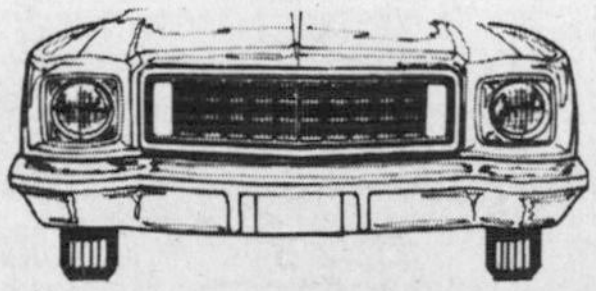

1975-76 Fury

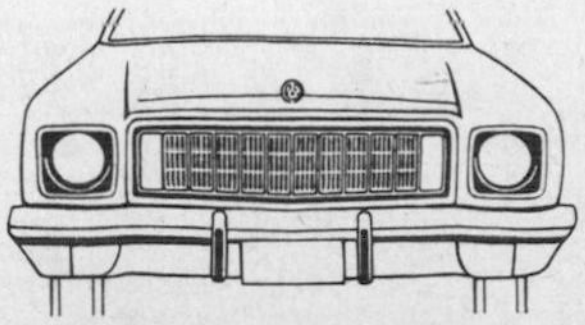

1976 Sport Fury.

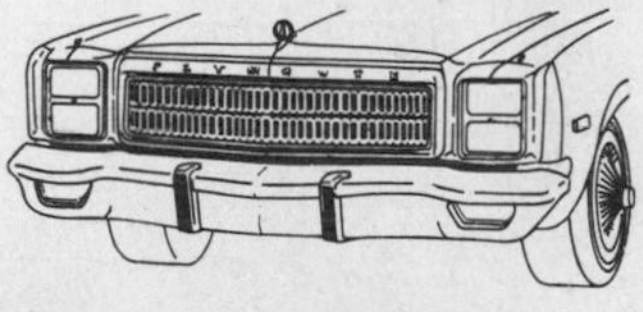

1977 Fury

FIRING ORDER

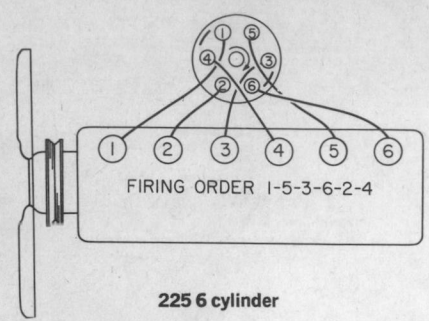

225 6 cylinder

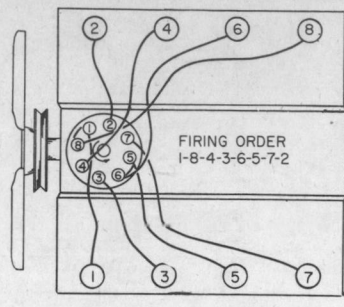

383, 426 Hemi, 400, 440 cu. in.

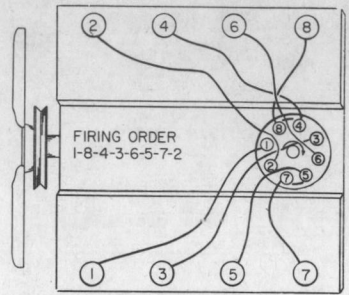

318, 340, 360 cu. in. V8

ENGINE CODE

The engine code designation is the 5th digit of the vehicle identification number (V.I.N.). The V.I.N. is stamped on a plate located at the left side of the instrument panel visible through the windshield and located to the rear of the right engine mount on the oil pan rail on V8 engines. It is below the rear spark plug on sixes.

Disp	Bbl	Hp	'70	'71	'72	'73	'74	'75	'76	'77
6-Cylinder Models										
225	1		C	C	C	C	C	C	C	C
8-Cylinder Models										
318	2		G	G	G	G	G	G	G	G
318 HP	2						G			
340 HP	4				H	H	H			
360	2				K	K	K	K	K	K
360	4							J	J	J	J
360 HP	4						L			
383	2		L	L						
383	4		L							
383 HP	4		N	N						
400	2				M	M	M	M	M	M
400	4						N		N	N
400 HP	4				P	P	P	P	P	P
426 Hemi	2x4		R							
426 Hemi	4			R						
440	4		T	T	T	T	T	T	T	T
440 HP	4		U	U	U	U	U	U	U	U
440	3x2		V	V						

HP High performance

The engine that the factory installed in the car can be identified by the fifth digit of the Vehicle Identification Number, as explained under Engine Code. The engine itself can be identified by the engine serial number. The cubic inch displacement is given fourth, or the third, fourth, and fifth digits of the engine serial number, depending on the year and engine.

Six cylinder engines have their serial number stamped on the joint face of the block, just behind the ignition coil. V8s through 360 cu. in. have the number on the front of the block, just below the left cylinder head. 383 and larger V8s have the number either on the oil pan rail, below the starter opening, at the left rear corner of the block; ahead of the base of the distributor; or on the left bank front tappet rail. 360 cu. in. and smaller (small block) V8s can quickly be identified as having the distributor at the rear of the engine, while 383 and larger versions have it at the front.

GENERAL ENGINE SPECIFICATIONS

Year	Engine No. Cyl. Displacement Cu. In.	Carburetor Type	Horsepower @ rpm ■	Torque @ rpm (ft lbs) ■	Bore x Stroke (in.)	Compression Ratio	Oil Pressure @ 2000 rpm
'70	6-225	1 bbl	145 @ 4000	215 @ 2400	3.400 x 4.125	8.40:1	55
	8-318	2 bbl	230 @ 4400	320 @ 2000	3.910 x 3.310	8.80:1	55
	8-383	2 bbl	290 @ 4400	390 @ 2800	4.250 x 3.375	8.70:1	55
	8-383	4 bbl	330 @ 5000	425 @ 3200	4.250 x 3.375	9.50:1	55
	8-383 HP	4 bbl	335 @ 5200	425 @ 3400	4.250 x 3.375	9.50:1	55
	8-426 Hemi	2 x 4 bbl	425 @ 5000	490 @ 4000	4.250 x 3.750	10.20:1	55
	8-440	4 bbl	350 @ 4400	480 @ 2800	4.320 x 3.750	9.70:1	55
	8-440 HP	4 bbl	375 @ 4600	480 @ 3200	4.320 x 3.750	9.70:1	55
	8-440	3 x 2 bbl	390 @ 4700	490 @ 3200	4.320 x 3.750	10.50:1	55

GENERAL ENGINE SPECIFICATIONS (con't.)

Year	Engine No. Cyl. Displacement Cu. In.	Carburetor Type	Horsepower @ rpm ■	Torque @ rpm (ft lbs) ■	Bore and Stroke (in.)	Compression Ratio	Oil Pressure @ 2000 rpm
'71	6-225	1 bbl	145 @ 4000	215 @ 2400	3.400 x 4.125	8.40:1	55
	8-318	2 bbl	230 @ 4400	320 @ 2000	3.910 x 3.310	8.60:1	55
	8-340 HP	4 bbl	275 @ 5000	340 @ 3200	4.040 x 3.310	10.30:1	55
	8-360	2 bbl	255 @ 4400	360 @ 2400	4.000 x 3.580	8.70:1	55
	8-383	2 bbl	275 @ 4400	375 @ 2800	4.250 x 3.375	8.50:1	55
	8-383 HP	4 bbl	300 @ 4800	410 @ 3400	4.250 x 3.375	8.50:1	55
	8-426 Hemi	4 bbl	425 @ 5000	490 @ 4000	4.250 x 3.750	10.20:1	55
	8-440	4 bbl	335 @ 4400	460 @ 3200	4.320 x 3.750	8.50:1	55
	8-440 HP	4 bbl	370 @ 4600	480 @ 3200	4.320 x 3.750	9.50:1	55
	8-440	3 x 2 bbl	385 @ 4700	490 @ 3200	4.320 x 3.750	10.30:1	55
'72	6-225	1 bbl	110 @ 4000	185 @ 2000	3.400 x 4.125	8.40:1	55
	6-225 Calif.	1 bbl	97 @ 4000	180 @ 2000	3.400 x 4.125	8.40:1	55
	8-318	2 bbl	150 @ 4000	260 @ 1600	3.910 x 3.310	8.60:1	55
	8-340 HP	4 bbl	240 @ 4800	290 @ 3600	4.040 x 3.310	8.50:1	55
	8-360	2 bbl	175 @ 4000	285 @ 2400	4.000 x 3.580	8.80:1	55
	8-400	2 bbl	190 @ 4400	310 @ 2400	4.340 x 3.380	8.20:1	55
	8-400 Calif.	2 bbl	181 @ 4400	305 @ 2400	4.340 x 3.380	8.20:1	55
	8-400 HP	4 bbl	255 @ 4800	340 @ 3200	4.340 x 3.380	8.20:1	55
	8-400 Calif.	4 bbl	246 @ 4800	335 @ 3200	4.340 x 3.380	8.20:1	55
	8-400 HP	4 bbl	265 @ 4800	345 @ 3200	4.340 x 3.380	8.20:1	55
	8-440	4 bbl	225 @ 4400	345 @ 3200	4.320 x 3.750	8.20:1	55
	8-440 Calif.	4 bbl	216 @ 4400	340 @ 3200	4.320 x 3.750	8.20:1	55
	8-440	4 bbl	280 @ 4800	375 @ 3200	4.320 x 3.750	8.20:1	55
	8-440 HP	4 bbl	290 @ 4800	380 @ 3200	4.320 x 3.750	8.20:1	55
'73	6-225	1 bbl	105 @ 4000	185 @ 1600	3.400 x 4.125	8.4:1	55
	8-318	2 bbl	150 @ 3600	265 @ 2000	3.910 x 3.310	8.6:1	55
	8-340 HP	4 bbl	240 @ 4800	295 @ 3600	4.040 x 3.310	8.5:1	55
	8-360	2 bbl	170 @ 4000	285 @ 2400	4.000 x 3.580	8.4:1	55
	8-400	2 bbl	185 @ 3600	310 @ 2400	4.340 x 3.380	8.2:1	55
	8-400 HP	4 bbl	260 @ 4800	335 @ 3600	4.340 x 3.380	8.2:1	55
	8-440	4 bbl	220 @ 3600	350 @ 2400	4.320 x 3.750	8.2:1	55
	8-440 HP	4 bbl	275 @ 4800	380 @ 3200	4.320 x 3.750	8.2:1	55
'74	6-225	1 bbl	105 @ 3600	180 @ 1600	3.400 x 4.125	8.4:1	55
	8-318	2 bbl	150 @ 4000	255 @ 2200	3.910 x 3.310	8.6:1	55
	8-318 HP	2 bbl	170 @ 4000	265 @ 2600	3.910 x 3.310	8.6:1	55
	8-360	2 bbl	180 @ 4000	290 @ 2400	4.000 x 3.580	8.4:1	55
	8-360	4 bbl	200 @ 4000	290 @ 3200	4.000 x 3.580	8.4:1	55
	8-360 HP	4 bbl	245 @ 4800	320 @ 3600	4.000 x 3.580	8.4:1	55
	8-400	2 bbl	185 @ 4000	315 @ 2400	4.340 x 3.380	8.2:1	55
	8-400	4 bbl	205 @ 4400	310 @ 2400	4.340 x 3.380	8.2:1	55
	8-400 HP	4 bbl	250 @ 4800	330 @ 3400	4.340 x 3.380	8.2:1	55
	8-440	4 bbl	230 @ 3600	350 @ 3200	4.320 x 3.750	8.2:1	55
	8-440 Calif.	4 bbl	220 @ 3600	345 @ 3200	4.320 x 3.750	8.2:1	55
	8-440 HP	4 bbl	275 @ 4400	375 @ 3200	4.320 x 3.750	8.2:1	55
'75	6-225	1 bbl	95 @ 3600	170 @ 1600	3.400 x 4.125	8.4:1	55
	6-225 Calif.	1 bbl	90 @ 3600	165 @ 1600	3.400 x 4.125	8.4:1	55
	8-318	2 bbl	150 @ 4000	255 @ 1600	3.910 x 3.310	8.5:1	55
	8-318①	2 bbl	150 @ 4000	260 @ 1600	3.910 x 3.310	8.5:1	55

GENERAL ENGINE SPECIFICATIONS

Year	Engine No. Cyl. Displacement Cu. In.	Carburetor Type	Horsepower @ rpm ■	Torque @ rpm (ft lbs) ■	Bore x Stroke (in.)	Compression Ratio	Oil Pressure @ 2000 rpm
	8-318 Calif.	2 bbl	135 @ 3600	245 @ 1600	3.910 x 3.310	8.5:1	55
	8-318 Calif.①	2 bbl	145 @ 3600	250 @ 1600	3.910 x 3.310	8.5:1	55
	8-360	2 bbl	180 @ 4000	290 @ 2400	4.000 x 3.580	8.4:1	55
	8-360	4 bbl	190 @ 4000	270 @ 3200	4.000 x 3.580	8.4:1	55
	8-400	2 bbl	165 @ 4000	295 @ 3200	4.340 x 3.380	8.2:1	55
	8-400①	2 bbl	175 @ 4000	300 @ 3200	4.340 x 3.380	8.2:1	55
	8-400②	2 bbl	165 @ 4000	295 @ 3200	4.340 x 3.380	8.2:1	55
	8-400	4 bbl	190 @ 4000	290 @ 3200	4.340 x 3.380	8.2:1	55
	8-400①	4 bbl	195 @ 4000	285 @ 3200	4.340 x 3.380	8.2:1	55
	8-400 Calif.	4 bbl	185 @ 4000	285 @ 3200	4.340 x 3.380	8.2:1	55
	8-400 HP	4 bbl	235 @ 4200	320 @ 3200	4.340 x 3.380	8.2:1	55
	8-400 HP①	4 bbl	240 @ 4200	325 @ 3200	4.340 x 3.380	8.2:1	55
	8-440	4 bbl	215 @ 4000	330 @ 3200	4.320 x 3.750	8.2:1	55
	8-440 Calif.	4 bbl	210 @ 4000	320 @ 3200	4.320 x 3.750	8.2:1	55
	8-440 HP	4 bbl	260 @ 4000	355 @ 3200	4.320 x 3.750	8.2:1	55
	8-440 Calif.	4 bbl	250 @ 4000	350 @ 3200	4.320 x 3.750	8.2:1	55
'76-'77	6-225	1 bbl	100 @ 3600	170 @ 1600	3.400 x 4.125	8.4:1	55
	8-318	2 bbl	150 @ 4000	255 @ 1600	3.910 x 3.310	8.5:1	55
	8-318 Calif.	2 bbl	140 @ 3600	250 @ 2000	3.910 x 3.310	8.5:1	55
	8-360	2 bbl	170 @ 4000	280 @ 2400	4.000 x 3.580	8.4:1	55
	8-360	4 bbl	175 @ 4000	270 @ 1600	4.000 x 3.580	8.4:1	55
	8-400	2 bbl	175 @ 4000	300 @ 2400	4.340 x 3.380	8.2:1	55
	8-400	4 bbl	240 @ 4400	325 @ 3200	4.340 x 3.380	8.2:1	55
	8-400 Calif.	4 bbl	185 @ 3600	285 @ 3200	4.340 x 3.380	8.2:1	55
	8-400 Lean Burn	4 bbl	210 @ 4400	305 @ 3200	4.340 x 3.380	8.2:1	55
	8-400 HP	4 bbl	240 @ 4400	325 @ 3200	4.340 x 3.380	8.2:1	55
	8-440	4 bbl	205 @ 3600	320 @ 2000	4.320 x 3.750	8.2:1	55
	8-440 Police	4 bbl	255 @ 4400	355 @ 3200	4.320 x 3.750	8.2:1	55
	8-440 Police Calif.	4 bbl	250 @ 4000	350 @ 3200	4.320 x 3.750	8.2:1	55
	8-440 Calif.	4 bbl	200 @ 3600	310 @ 2400	4.320 x 3.750	8.2:1	55

■ Beginning 1972, horsepower and torque are SAE net figures. They are measured at the rear of the transmission with all accessories installed and operating. Since the figures vary when a given engine is installed in different models, some are representative rather than exact.

① Gran Fury, Monaco
② Charger SE
HP High Performance

Belvedere, Satellite, Coronet, Charger, 1975 and later Fury, 1977 Monaco (intermediate size)

TUNE-UP SPECIFICATIONS

When analyzing compression test results, look for uniformity among cylinders rather than specific pressures.

	ENGINE No. Cyl Displacement		SPARK PLUGS			DISTRIBUTOR		IGNITION TIMING (deg) ▲		VALVES Intake Opens	Fuel Pump Pressure (psi)	IDLE SPEED (rpm) ▲	
Year	(cu in.)	hp	Orig. Type	Gap (in.)	Point Dwell (deg)	Point Gap (in.)		Man Trans ●	Auto Trans	■ (deg)		Man Trans ●	Auto Trans
'70	6-225	145	N-14Y	.035	44	.020	TDC	TDC		10	3½-5	700	650
	8-318	230	N-14Y	.035	32	.017	TDC	TDC		10	5-7	750	700
	8-383	290	J-14Y	.035	30	.018	TDC	2½B		18	3½-5	750	650
	8-383	330	J-11Y	.035	30	.018	TDC	2½B		18	3½-5	750	750
	8-383 HP	335	J-11Y	.035	30	.018	TDC	2½B		21	3½-5	750	750

Belvedere, Satellite, Coronet, Charger, 1975 and later Fury, 1977 Monaco (intermediate size)

TUNE-UP SPECIFICATIONS

When analyzing compression test results, look for uniformity among cylinders rather than specific pressures.

Year	ENGINE No. Cyl Displacement (cu in.)	hp	SPARK PLUGS Orig. Type	Gap (in.)	DISTRIBUTOR Point Dwell (deg)	Point Gap (in.)	IGNITION TIMING (deg) ▲ Man Trans ●	Auto Trans	VALVES Intake Opens ■ (deg)	Fuel Pump Pressure (psi)	IDLE SPEED (rpm) ▲ Man Trans ●	Auto Trans
	8-426 Hemi	425	N-10Y	.035	30①	.017	TDC	5B	36	7-8½	900	900
	8-440 HP	375	J-11Y	.035	30	.018	TDC	2½B	18	3½-5	900	800
	8-440	390	J-11Y	.035	30①	.017	5B	5B	21	6-7½	900	900
'71	6-225	145	N-14Y	.035	44	.020	TDC(2½B)	TDC(2½B)	16	3½-5	750	750
	8-318	230	N-14Y	.035	32	.017	TDC	TDC	10	5-7	750	700
	8-340 HP	275	N-9Y	.035	33②	.017	5B	5B	22	5-7	900	900
	8-383	275	J-14Y	.035	30	.018	TDC	2½B	18	3½-5	750	700
	8-383 HP	300	N-11Y	.035	30	.018	TDC	2½B	21	3½-5	900	800
	8-426 Hemi	425	N-10Y	.035	30①	.017	TDC	2½B	36	7-8½	950	950
	8-440 HP	370	J-11Y	.035	30	.018	TDC	2½B	18	3½-5	900	800
	8-440	385	J-11Y	.035	30①	.017	12½B	12½B	21	6-7½	900	900
'72	6-225	110	N-14Y	.035	44	.020	TDC	TDC	16	3½-5	750(700)	750(700)
	8-318	150	N-13Y	.035	32	.017	TDC	TDC	10	5-7	750	750(700)
	8-340 HP	240	N-9Y	.035	Electronic		2½B	2½B	22	5-7	900(850)	750
	8-400	190	J-13Y	.035	30	.018		5B③	18	3½-5	—	700
	8-400 HP	255, 265	J-11Y	.035	Electronic		TDC(2½B)	10B(5B)	21	3½-5	900(800)	750
	8-440 HP	290	J-11Y	.035	Electronic		2½B	10B(5B)	21	3½-5	900(800)	900
'73	6-225	105	N-14Y	.035	Electronic		TDC	TDC	16	4-5½	750	750
	8-318	150	N-13Y	.035	Electronic		2½B	TDC	10	6-7½	750	700
	8-340 HP	240	N-9Y	.035	Electronic		5B	2½B	22	6-7½	850	850
	8-400	175	J-13Y	.035	Electronic		—	10B	18	4-5½	—	700
	8-400 HP	260	J-11Y	.035	Electronic		2½B	10B	21	4-5½	900	850
	8-440 HP	275	J-11Y	.035	Electronic		—	10B	21	4-5½	—	800
'74	6-225	105	N-14Y	.035	Electronic		TDC	TDC	16	3½-5	800	750
	8-318	150	N-13Y	.035	Electronic		TDC	TDC	10	5-7½	750	750
	8-318 HP	170	N-13Y	.035	Electronic		TDC	TDC	22	5-7½	750	750
	8-360	180	N-12Y	.035	Electronic		—	5B	16	5-7½	—	750
	8-360	200	N-12Y	.035	Electronic		—	5B	16	6-7½	—	750
	8-360 HP	245	N-12Y	.035	Electronic		5B(2½B)	5B	22	6-7½	850	850
	8-400	205	J-13Y	.035	Electronic		—	5B	18	4-5½	—	900
	8-400 HP	250	J-11Y	.035	Electronic		5B	5B(2½B)	21	4-5½	900	900
	8-440	275	J-11Y	.035	Electronic		—	10B(5B)	21	7-8.2	—	800
'75	6-225	95	BL-13Y	.035	Electronic		TDC	TDC	16	3½-5	—	750
	8-318	150	N-13Y	.035	Electronic		2B	2B	10	5-7	—	750
	8-360	All	N-12Y	.035	Electronic		—	6B	18	5-7	—	750
	8-400	All	J-13Y	.035	Electronic		—	8B	18	4-5½	—	750
'76	6-225	100	RN-12Y	.035	Electronic		6B(4B)	2B	16	3½-5	750(800)	750
	8-318	150, 140	RBL-13Y	.035	Electronic		2B	2B(TDC)	10	5-7	750	750
	8-360	170	RN-12Y	.035	Electronic		—	2B	18	5-7	—	850
	8-400	175	RJ-13Y	.035	Electronic		—	10B	18	5-7	—	700
	8-400	4 bbl	RJ-13Y	.035	Electronic		—	8B	18	5-7	—	750
	8-400 HP	240	RJ-86P	.035	Electronic		—	6B	18	5-7	—	850
'77	6-225	All	RBL-15Y	.035	Electronic		12B	12B	16	4-5½	700	700
	8-318	All	RN-12Y	.035	Electronic		8B	8B	10	5¾-7¼	700	700(850)
	8-360	All	RN-12Y	.035	Electronic		—	10B(6B)	18	5¾-7¼④	—	700(750)
	8-400	All	RJ-13Y	.035	Electronic		—	10B	20	5¼-6¾	—	750

C517

▲ See text for procedure
● Figure in parentheses indicates California engine
■ All figures Before Top Dead Center
① Adjust each set of points to this figure. With both sets connected, the total reading should be 40 degrees.
② For vehicles with manual transmission, adjust each set of points to 30 degrees. With both sets connected, the total reading should be 40 degrees.
③ For non-California vehicles built after February 2, 1972, adjust ignition timing to 7½ degrees Before Top Dead Center
④ 5¼-6¾ In wagons
HP—High performance
NOTE: The underhood specifications sticker often reflects tune-up specification changes made in production. Sticker figures must be used if they disagree with those in this chart.

A After Top Dead Center
B Before Top Dead Center
TDC Top Dead Center
— Not applicable

MECHANICAL VALVE LIFTER CLEARANCE

Engine	Intake In.	Exhaust In.
All 6 cylinder	.010 (Hot)	.020 (Hot)

TUNE-UP SPECIFICATIONS

Polara, Monaco through 1976,
1977 Royal Monaco,
Fury through 1974, 1975 and later
Gran Fury (full size)

When analyzing compression test results, look for uniformity among cylinders rather than specific pressures.

Year	ENGINE No. Cyl Displacement (cu in.)	hp	SPARK PLUGS Orig. Type	Gap (in.)	DISTRIBUTOR Point Dwell (deg)	Point Gap (in.)	IGNITION TIMING (deg) ▲ Man Trans ●	Auto Trans	VALVES Intake Opens ■ (deg)	Fuel Pump Pressure (psi)	IDLE SPEED (rpm) ▲ Man Trans ●	Auto Trans
'70	6-225	145	N-14Y	.035	41-46	.020	TDC	TDC	10	3½-5	700	650
	8-318	230	N-14Y	.035	30-34	.017	TDC	TDC	10	5-7	750	700
	8-383	290	J-14Y	.035	28-32	.018	TDC	2½B	18	3½-5	750	650
	8-383	330	J-11Y	.035	28-32	.018	TDC	2½B	18	3½-5	750	750
	8-440	350	J-13Y	.035	28-33	.018	—	12½B	18	3½-5	—	650
	8-440	390	J-11Y	.035	27-32①	.017	5B	5B	21	6-7½	900	900
'71	6-225	145	N-14Y	.035	41-46	.020	TDC(2½B)	TDC(2½B)	16	3½-5	750	750
	8-318	230	N-14Y	.035	30-34	.017	TDC	TDC	10	5-7	750	700
	8-360	255	N-13Y	.035	30-34	.017	2½B	2½B	16	3½-5	750	700
	8-383	275	J-14Y	.035	28-32	.018	TDC	2½B	18	3½-5	750	700
	8-383 HP	300	J-11Y	.035	28-32	.018	TDC	2½B	21	3½-5	900	800
	8-440	335	N-13Y	.035	30.34	.017	—	5B	18	3½-5	—	750
	8-440 HP	370	J-11Y	.035	28-32	.018	TDC	2½B	21	3½-5	900	800
'72	8-318	150	J-11Y	.035	28-32	.018	—	TDC	10	5-7	—	750(700)
	8-360	175	N-13Y	.035	30-34	.017	—	TDC	16	5-7	—	750
	8-400	190	J-13Y	.035	28-32	.018	—	5B②	18	3½-5	—	700
	8-440	225	J-11Y	.035	28-32	.018	—	10B	18	3½-5	—	750(700)
'73	8-318	150	N-13Y	.035	Electronic		—	TDC	10	6-7½	—	700
	8-360	170	N-13Y	.035	Electronic		—	TDC	16	6-7½	—	750
	8-400	185	J-13Y	.035	Electronic		—	10B	18	4-5½	—	700
	8-440	220	J-11Y	.035	Electronic		—	10B	18	4-5½	—	700
'74	8-360	180	N-12Y	.035	Electronic		—	5B	16	5-7½	—	750
	8-400	185	J-13Y	.035	Electronic		—	5B	18	4-5½	—	750
	8-400	205	J-13Y	.035	Electronic		—	5B	18	4-5½	—	900 (750)
	8-440	275	J-11Y	.035	Electronic		—	10B	18	7-8.2	—	750
'75	8-318	150	N-13Y	.035	Electronic		—	2B	10	5-7	—	750
	8-360	All	N-12Y	.035	Electronic		—	6B	18	5-7	—	750
	8-400	175	J-13Y	.035	Electronic		—	10B	18	4-5½	—	750
	8-400	190	J-13Y	.035	Electronic		—	8B	18	4-5½	—	750
	8-440	215	RY-87P	.040	Electronic		—	8B	18	4-5½	—	750
'76	8-318	150	RN-12Y	.035	Electronic		—	2B	10	5-7	—	750
	8-360	170	RN-12Y	.035	Electronic		—	2B	18	5-7	—	850
	8-360	175	RN-12Y	.035	Electronic		—	6B	18	5-7	—	750

TUNE-UP SPECIFICATIONS

Polara, Monaco through 1976, 1977 Royal Monaco, Fury through 1974, 1975 and later Gran Fury (full size)

When analyzing compression test results, look for uniformity among cylinders rather than specific pressures.

ENGINE Year	ENGINE No. Cyl Displacement (cu in.)	ENGINE hp	SPARK PLUGS Orig. Type	SPARK PLUGS Gap (in.)	DISTRIBUTOR Point Dwell (deg)	DISTRIBUTOR Point Gap (in.)	IGNITION TIMING (deg) ▲ Man Trans	IGNITION TIMING (deg) ▲ ● Auto Trans	VALVES Intake Opens ■ (deg)	Fuel Pump Pressure (psi)	IDLE SPEED (rpm) ▲ Man Trans	IDLE SPEED (rpm) ▲ ● Auto Trans
	8-400	175	RJ-13Y	.035	Electronic		—	10B	18	5-7	—	700
	8-400	4 bbl	RJ-13Y	.035	Electronic		—	8B	18	5-7	—	750
	8-440	200, 205	RJ-13Y	.035	Electronic		—	8B	18	5-7	—	750
'77	8-318	All	RN-12Y	.035	Electronic		—	8B	10	5¾-7¼	—	700
	8-360	All	RN-12Y	.035	Electronic		—	10B(6B)	18	5¾-7¼	—	700(750)
	8-400	All	RJ-13Y	.035	Electronic		—	10B	20	5¾-7¼	—	750
	8-440	All	RJ-13Y	.035	Electronic		—	8B	20	5¾-7¼	—	750

▲ See text for procedure
■ Before Top Dead Center
● Figure in parentheses indicates California engine
① Both sets 37°-40°
② Non-California cars built after Feb. 2, 7½B

NOTE: The underhood specifications sticker often reflects tune-up specification changes made in production. Sticker figures must be used if they disagree with those in this chart.

A After Top Dead Center
B Before Top Dead Center
TDC Top Dead Center
HP High Performance

MECHANICAL VALVE LIFTER CLEARANCE

Engine	Intake (Hot) In.	Exhaust (Hot) In.
All six cylinder	.010	.020

CAPACITIES

Year	ENGINE No. Cyl. Displacement (Cu. In.)	Engine Crankcase Add 1 Qt For New Filter	TRANSMISSION Pts To Refill After Draining Manual 3-Speed	Manual 4-Speed	Automatic	Drive Axle (pts)	Gasoline Tank (gals)	COOLING SYSTEM (qts) With Heater	With A/C
'70	6-225	4	4.75	—	17	2④	19⑩	13	15
	8-318	4	4.75	—	16	4	19⑩	16	19
	8-383 2 bbl	4	4.75	—	19	4	19⑩	16	17
	8-383 4 bbl	4	4.75	7.5	16	4	19⑩	16	17
	8-426	6	—	7.5	17	5.5	19	18	—
	8-440	4①	—	7.5	19	5.5⑥	19⑩	17	18
'71	6-225	4	6.5②	—	17	4⑦	21⑪	13	13
	8-318	4	4.75	—	17	4⑦	21⑪	16	16.5
	8-340	4	4.75	7.5	16.3	4	21	15	15
	8-360	4	4.75	—	16	4.5	23	15.5	15
	8-383	4	4.75	7.5	16③	4⑦	21⑪	14.5	15
	8-426	6	—	7.5	17	5.5	21	15.5	—
	8-440	4①	—	7.5	19	5.5⑦	21⑪	15.5	17
'72	6-225	4	6.5	—	17	4.5	21	13	14
	8-318	4	4.75	—	17	4.5	21⑪	16	17.5
	8-340	4	—	7.5	16.3	4.5	21	15	15.5
	8-360	4	—	—	16.3	4.5	23	16	16
	8-400 2 bbl	4	—	—	19	4.5	21⑪	14.5	15
	8-440	4	4.75	7.5	16.3	4.5	21⑪	14.5	14.5

CAPACITIES

| Year | ENGINE No. Cyl. Displacement (Cu. In.) | Engine Crankcase Add 1 Qt For New Filter | TRANSMISSION Pts To Refill After Draining | | | Drive Axle (pts) | Gasoline Tank (gals) | COOLING SYSTEM (qts) | |
| | | | Manual | | Automatic | | | With Heater | With A/C |
			3-Speed	4-Speed					
'73	6-225	4	4.75	——	17	4.5	19.5	13	13
	8-318	4	4.75	7.5	17	4.5	19.5[11][18]	16	17.5
	8-340	4	——	7.5	16.3	4.5	19.5	15	15.5
	8-360	4	——	——	16.3	4.5	19.5[11]	15.5	16
	8-400	4	——	7.5	19[16]	4.5	19.5[11][18]	16	17[19]
	8-440	4	——	——	16.3[17]	4.5	19.5[11]	16.5[20]	16.5[20]
'74	6-225	4	4.75	——	17	4.4	19.5	13	——
	8-318	4	4.75	7.5	17 (17.5)	4.4	19.5[18]	16	18
	8-360 Satellite, Charger, Coronet	4	——	7.5	16.5 (17)	4.4	19.5[18]	16.5	16.5
	8-360 Fury, Polara, Monaco	4	——	——	16.5 (17.5)	4.4[12]	25.0[8]	16	16
	8-400 Satellite, Charger, Coronet	4	——	——	19 (20)	4.4[12]	19.5[18]	16.5	16.5
	8-400 HP Satellite, Charger, Coronet	4	——	7.5	16.5 (17)	4.4[12]	19.5[18]	16.5	17.5
	8-400 Fury, Polara, Monaco	4	——	——	19 (20.5)	4.4[12]	25.0[8]	16.5	16.5
	8-440 HP Satellite, Charger, Coronet	4	——	——	16.5	4.4	19.5	16	16
	8-440 Fury, Polara, Monaco	4	——	——	19 (20.5)	4.5	25.0[8]	16	16
'75	6-225 Charger, Coronet, Fury	4	4.75	——	16.5	4.5	25.5	13.0	——
	8-318 Charger, Coronet, Fury	4	4.75	——	16.5	4.5	25.5[18]	16.5	18.0
	8-318 Gran Fury, Monaco	4	——	——	16.5	4.5	26.5	17.5	17.5
	8-360 Charger, Coronet, Fury	4	——	——	16.5	4.5	25.5[18]	16.0	16.0
	8-360 Gran Fury, Monaco	4	——	——	16.5	4.5	26.5[8]	16.0	16.0
	8-400 Charger, Coronet, Fury	4	——	——	16.5	4.5	25.5[18][21]	16.5	16.5
	8-400 Gran Fury, Monaco	4	——	——	16.5	4.5	26.5[8]	16.5	16.5
	8-440 Gran Fury, Monaco	4	——	——	16.5	4.5	26.5[8]	16.0	16.0
'76-'77	6-225 Charger, Coronet, Fury	4	4.75	——	17	4.5	20.5	13.0	14.5
	8-318 Charger, Coronet, Fury	4	4.75	——	17	4.5	25.5[14]	16.5	18.0
	8-318 Gran Fury, Monaco	4	——	——	19	4.5	26.5	17.5	17.5
	8-360 Charger, Coronet, Fury	4	——	——	17[5]	4.5	25.5[14]	16.0	16.0
	8-360 Gran Fury, Monaco	4	——	——	19	4.5	26.5	16.0	16.0
	8-400 Charger, Coronet, Fury	4	——	——	19	4.5	25.5[14]	16.5	16.5
	8-400 HP Charger	5	——	——	19	4.5	20.5	16.5	16.5

CAPACITIES

Year	ENGINE No. Cyl. Displacement (Cu. In.)	Engine Crankcase Add 1 Qt For New Filter	TRANSMISSION Pts To Refill After Draining			Drive Axle (pts)	Gasoline Tank (gals)	COOLING SYSTEM (qts)	
			Manual 3-Speed	4-Speed	Automatic			With Heater	With A/C
	8-400 Gran Fury, Monaco	4	—	—	19	4.5	26.5⑧	16.5	16.5
	8-440 Gran Fury, Monaco	4	—	—	19	4.5	26.5⑧	16.0	16.0

① 3-2 bbl—6 qts
② Fury, Polara, Monaco—4.75 pts
③ 2 bbl—19 pts
④ Fury, station wagon—4 pts
⑤ Charger SE—19
⑥ Fury, Polara, Monaco—4 pts
⑦ Fury, Polara, Monaco—4.5 pts
⑧ Station wagons—24 gals
⑨ Station wagon—22 gals
⑩ Fury, Polara, Monaco—24 gals, station wagon—23 gals
⑪ Fury, Polara, Monaco—23 gals
⑫ Station wagons—4.5 pts

⑬ Not used
⑭ Station wagons—20.5 leaded, 20 unleaded
⑮ Not used
⑯ Charger, Coronet, Satellite with 4 bbl—16.3 pts
⑰ Fury, Polara, Monaco—19 pts
⑱ Station wagons—21 gals
⑲ Fury, Polara, Monaco—16 qts
⑳ Fury, Polara, Monaco—15.5 qts
㉑ 400 4 bbl w/dual exhaust—20.5 gals.
— Not applicable

VALVE SPECIFICATIONS

Year	Engine No. Cyl. Displacement (cu in.)	Seat Angle (deg)	Face Angle (deg)	Spring Test Pressure (lbs @ in.)	Spring Installed Height (in.)	STEM TO GUIDE Clearance (in.)		STEM Diameter (in.)	
						Intake	Exhaust	Intake	Exhaust
'70	6-225	45	45①	144 @ 1.31	1 11/16	.0010-.0030	.0020-.0040	.3725	.3715
	8-318	45	45①	177 @ 1.31	1 11/16	.0010-.0030	.0020-.0040	.3725	.3715
	8-383 2 bbl	45	45	200 @ 1.44	1 7/8	.0010-.0030	.0020-.0040	.3727	.3717
	8-383 4 bbl	45	45	246 @ 1.72	1 7/8	.0015-.0032	.0025-.0042	.3722	.3712
	8-426	45	45	200 @ 1.44	1 7/8	.0020-.0040	.0030-.0050	.3090	.3080
	8-440	45	45	246 @ 1.72	1 7/8	.0010-.0030	.0020-.0040	.3727	.3717
	8-440 HP	45	45	310 @ 1.38	1 7/8	.0015-.0032	.0025-.0042	.3722	.3712
'71	6-225	45	45①	144 @ 1.31	1 11/16	.0010-.0030	.0020-.0040	.3725	.3715
	8-318	45	45①	177 @ 1.31	1 11/16	.0010-.0030	.0020-.0040	.3725	.3715
	8-340	45	45①	238 @ 1.31	1 11/16	.0015-.0035	.0025-.0045	.3720	.3710
	8-360	45	45①	177 @ 1.31	1 11/16	.0010-.0030	.0020-.0040	.3725	.3715
	8-383 2 bbl	45	45	200 @ 1.44	1 7/8	.0010-.0030	.0020-.0040	.3727	.3717
	8-383 4 bbl	45	45	246 @ 1.72	1 7/8	.0015-.0032	.0025-.0042	.3722	.3712
	8-426	45	45	310 @ 1.28	1 7/8	.0020-.0040	.0030-.0050	.3090	.3080
	8-440	45	45	200 @ 1.44	1 7/8	.0010-.0030	.0020-.0040	.3722	.3717
	8-440 HP	45	45	246 @ 1.72	1 7/8	.0015-.0032	.0025-.0042	.3722	.3712
'72	6-225	45	45①	144 @ 1.31	1 11/16	.0010-.0030	.0020-.0040	.3725	.3715
	8-318	45	45①	177 @ 1.31	1 11/16	.0010-.0030	.0020-.0040	.3725	.3715
	8-340	45	45①	208 @ 1.31	1 11/16	.0015-.0035	.0025-.0045	.3720	.3710
	8-360	45	45①	177 @ 1.31	1 11/16	.0010-.0030	.0020-.0040	.3725	.3715
	8-400 2 bbl	45	45	200 @ 1.44	1 7/8	.0010-.0030	.0020-.0040	.3727	.3717
	8-400 4 bbl	45	45	246 @ 1.72	1 7/8	.0015-.0032	.0025-.0042	.3722	.3712
	8-440	45	45	200 @ 1.44	1 7/8	.0010-.0030	.0020-.0040	.3727	.3717
	8-440 HP	45	45	246 @ 1.72	1 7/8	.0015-.0032	.0025-.0042	.3722	.3712
'73	6-225	45	45②	160 @ 1.24	1 21/32	.0010-.0030	.0020-.0040	.3725	.3715
	8-318	45	45②	189 @ 1.28	1 21/32	.0010-.0030	.0020-.0040	.3725	.3715
	8-340	45	45②	238 @ 1.22	1 21/32	.0015-.0035	.0025-.0045	.3720	.3710

VALVE SPECIFICATIONS

Year	Engine No. Cyl. Displacement (cu in.)	Seat Angle (deg)	Face Angle (deg)	Spring Test Pressure (lbs @ in.)	Spring Installed Height (in.)	STEM TO GUIDE Clearance (in.) Intake	Exhaust	STEM Diameter (in.) Intake	Exhaust
	8-360	45	45②	195 @ 1.24	1 21/32	.0010-.0030	.0020-.0040	.3725	.3715
	8-400 2 bbl	45	45	200 @ 1.42	1 55/64	.0010-.0027	⑦	.3727	⑨
	8-400 4 bbl	45	45	234 @ 1.40	1 55/64	.0015-.0032	⑧	.3722	⑩
	8-440	45	45	200 @ 1.42	1 55/64	.0010-.0027	⑦	.3727	⑨
	8-440 HP	45	45	234 @ 1.40	1 55/64	.0015-.0032	⑧	.3722	⑩
'74	6-225	45	45①	143 @ 1.31	1 21/32	.0010-.0030	.0020-.0040	.3725	.3715
	8-318	45	45①	177 @ 1.31	1 21/32	.0010-.0030	.0020-.0040	.3725	.3715
	8-360	45	45①	208 @ 1.31⑪	1 21/32	.0010-.0030	.0025-.0040	.3725	.3715
	8-400, 440 std.	45	45	200 @ 1.43	1 55/64	.0010-.0027	⑦	.3727	⑨
	8-400 HP	45	45	246 @ 1.36	1 55/64	.0015-.0032	⑧	.3722	⑩
	8-440 HP	45	45	246 @ 1.36	1 55/64	.0015-.0032	⑧	.3722	⑩
'75	6-225	45	45	143 @ 1.31	1 21/32	.0010-.0030	.0020-.0040	.3725	.3715
	8-318	45	①	177 @ 1.31	1 21/32	.0010-.0030	.0020-.0040	.3725	.3715
	8-360	45	①	208 @ 1.31⑪	1 21/32	.0010-.0030	.0020-.0040	.3725	.3715
	8-400, 440 std.	45	45	200 @ 1.44	1 55/64	.0011-.0028	⑦	.3727	⑨
	8-400, 440 HP	45	45	246 @ 1.36	1 55/64	.0016-.0033	⑧	.3722	⑩
'76-'77	6-225	45	45	143 @ 1.31	1 21/32	.0010-.0030	.0020-.0040	.3725	.3715
	8-318	45	①	177 @ 1.31	1 21/32	.0010-.0030	.0020-.0040	.3725	.3715
	8-360	45	①	182 @ 1.31	1 21/32	.0010-.0030	.0020-.0040	.3725	.3715
	8-400, 440 std.	45	45	200 @ 1.44	1 55/64	.0011-.0028	⑦	.3725	⑨
	8-400 HP	45	45	246 @ 1.36	1 55/64	.0016-.0033	⑧	.3722	⑩

① Exhaust 43°
② Exhaust 47°
③ to ⑥ Not used
⑦ Hot end—.0021 .0038, cold end—.0011-.0028
⑧ Hot end—.0026 .0043, cold end—.0016-.0033
⑨ Hot end—.3716, cold end—.3726
⑩ Hot end—.3711, cold end—.3721
⑪ 177 @ 1.31 on 2 bbl engine
HP High Performance

CRANKSHAFT AND CONNECTING ROD SPECIFICATIONS

All measurements are given in inches

Year	Engine Displacement (cu in.)	CRANKSHAFT Main Brg. Journal Dia	Main Brg. Oil Clearance	Shaft End-Play	Thrust on No.	CONNECTING ROD Journal Diameter	Oil Clearance	Side* Clearance
'70-'77	6-225	2.7495-2.7505	.0005-.0015	.002-.007	3	2.1865-2.1875	.0005-.0015	.006-.012
'70-'77	8-318, 340	2.4495-2.5005	.0005-.0015	.002-.007	3	2.124-2.125	.0005-.0020	.006-.014
'71-'77	8-360	2.8095-2.8105	.0005-.0020	.002-.007	3	2.124-2.125	.0005-.0020	.006-.014
'70-'74	8-383, 400	2.6245-2.6255	.0005-.0020	.002-.007	3	2.3740-2.3750	.0005-.0020	.009-.017
'75-'76	8-400	2.6245-2.6255	.0005-.0020	.002-.007	3	2.3750-2.3760	.0005-.0030	.009-.017
'70-'74	8-440	2.7495-2.7505	.0005-.0020	.002-.007	3	2.3740-2.3750	.0010-.0025	.009-.017
'75-'76	8-440	2.7495-2.7505	.0005-.0020	.002-.007	3	2.3750-2.3760	.0005-.0030	.009-.017
'70	8-426 Hemi	2.7495-2.7505	.0015-.0025	.002-.007	3	2.374-2.375	.0015-.0025	.009-.017
'71	8-426 Hemi	2.7490-2.7500	.0015-.0030	.002-.007	3	2.3738-2.3745	.0015-.0025	.013-.017

* Total for two rods

TORQUE SPECIFICATIONS

All readings in ft lbs

Year	Engine Displacement (cu in.)	Cylinder Head Bolts	Rod Bearing Bolts	Main Bearing Bolts	Crankshaft Pulley Bolt	Flywheel to Crankshaft Bolts	MANIFOLD Intake	MANIFOLD Exhaust
'70-'77	6-225	70	45	85	Press fit	55	10①	10
'70	8-318	95	45	85	135	55	35	20
'71-'77	8-318, 340, 360	95	45	85	100	55	40	15/20②
'70-77	8-383, 400, 440	70	45	85	135	55	45	30
'70-'71	8-426 Hemi	75	75	100③	135	70	④	35

① Intake to exhaust manifold bolts—20 ft. lbs., studs—30 ft. lbs.
② Nuts/screws

③ Cross bolt mains—45 ft. lbs.
④ 4 center bolts on either side—6 ft. lbs., others 4 ft. lbs.

RING GAP

All measurements are given in inches

Year	Engine No. Cyl. Displacement (cu. in.)	Top Compression	Bottom Compression
'70-'72	6-225	.010-.020	.010-.020
	8-318, 340, 360, 8-383, 400, 426, 440	.013-.023	.013-.023
'73-'77	6-225, 8-318, 360	.010-.020	.010-.020
'73-'77	8-340, 400, 440	.013-.023	.013-.023

Year	Engine	Oil Control
'69-'77	All engines	.015-.055

PISTON CLEARANCE

Year	Engine No. Cyl. Displacement (cu. in.)	Piston to Bore Clearance (in.)*
'70-'77	6-225, 8-318, 340, 360	.0005-.0015
'70-'77	8-383, 400, 440	.0003-.0013
'70-'71	8-426 Hemi	.0025-.0035

* At top of skirt

RING SIDE CLEARANCE

All measurements are given in inches

Year	Engine No. Cyl. Displacement (cu. in.)	Top Compression	Bottom Compression
'70-'77	All engines	.0015-.0030	.0015-.0030

Year	Engine No. Cyl. Displacement (cu. in.)	Oil Control
'70-'77	6-225 8-318, 426, 340, 360, 400	.002-.005
'70-'77	8-383, 440	.0000-.005

WHEEL ALIGNMENT SPECIFICATIONS

Year	Model	CASTER Range (deg)	CASTER Pref Setting (deg)	CAMBER Range (deg)	CAMBER Pref Setting (deg)	Toe-in (in.)	Steering Axis Inclin. (deg)	WHEEL PIVOT RATIO (deg) Inner Wheel	WHEEL PIVOT RATIO (deg) Outer Wheel
'70-'72	M.S.—Coronet, Charger, Belvedere, Satellite	½N ± ½	½N	①	①	3/32 to 5/32	7½	20	17.8
	P.S.—Coronet, Charger, Belvedere, Satellite	¾P ± ½	¾P	①	①	3/32 to 5/32	7½	20	17.8

WHEEL ALIGNMENT SPECIFICATIONS

Year	Model	CASTER Range (deg)	CASTER Pref Setting (deg)	CAMBER Range (deg)	CAMBER Pref Setting (deg)	Toe-in (in.)	Steering Axis Inclin. (deg)	WHEEL PIVOT RATIO (deg) Inner Wheel	WHEEL PIVOT RATIO (deg) Outer Wheel
	M.S.—Fury, Monaco, Polara	1/2N ± 1/2	1/2N	①	①	3/32 to 5/32	7 1/2	20	18.8
	P.S.—Fury, Monaco, Polara	1/4 to 1 1/4P⑤	3/4P⑤	①	①	3/32 to 5/32	7 1/2	20	18.8
'73	M.S.—Coronet, Charger, Satellite	1 5/16N to 1/16P	5/8N	⑥	⑥	1/8 ± 3/32	7 1/2	20	17.8
	P.S.—Coronet Charger, Satellite	1/16N to 1 5/16P	5/8P	⑥	⑥	1/8 ± 3/32	7 1/2	20	17.8
	P.S.—Fury, Monaco, Polara	1/16N to 1 5/16P	5/8P	⑥	⑥	1/8 ± 3/32	7 1/2	20	18.8
'74	M.S.—Coronet, Charger, Satellite	1 3/4N to 1/2P	5/8N	⑦	⑦	1/16 to 1/4	8	20	18.0
	P.S.—Coronet, Charger, Satellite	1/2N to 1 3/4P	5/8P	⑦	⑦	1/16 to 1/4	8	20	18.0
	P.S.—Fury, Monaco, Polara	1/2N to 1 3/4P	5/8P	⑦	⑦	1/16 to 1/4	9	20	18.3
'75	M.S.—Coronet, Charger, Fury	1 5/16N to 1/16P	1/2N	⑥	⑥	3/32 to 9/32	8	20	18.0
	Charger, P.S.—Coronet, Fury	1/16N to 1 5/16P	3/4P	⑥	⑥	3/32 to 9/32	8	20	18.0
	P.S.—Gran Fury, Monaco	1/16N to 1 5/16P	3/4P	⑥	⑥	3/32 to 9/32	9	20	18.3
'76-'77	M.S.—Coronet, Charger, Fury	1 3/4N to 1/2P	1/2N	⑦	⑦	1/16 to 1/4	—	20	18.0
	P.S.—Coronet, Charger, Fury	1/2N to 1 3/4P	3/4P	⑦	⑦	1/16 to 1/4	—	20	18.0
	P.S.—Gran Fury, Monaco	1/2N to 1 3/4P	3/4P	⑦	⑦	1/16 to 1/4	—	20	18.3

M.S. Manual steering
P.S. Power steering
P Positive
N Negative

① Left—1/4P to 3/4P; 1/2P preferred
Right 0 to 1/2 P; 1/4P preferred
② Heavy duty—2 1/8 ± 1/8
③ Fury sta. wag., Monaco, Polara, Custom 880—1 1/8 ± 1/8
④ Sta. wag.—1 3/4 ± 1/8
⑤ 1970—0 to 1N (1/2N preferred)
⑥ Left—1/8P to 7/8P; 1/2P preferred
Right—1/8N to 5/8P; 1/4P preferred
⑦ Left—0 to 1P; 1/2P preferred
Right—1/4N to 3/4P; 1/4P preferred

FRONT END HEIGHT ▲

Year	Model	Front End Height	Year	Model	Front End Height
'70-'74	Coronet, Charger, Belvedere, Satellite	1 7/8 ± 1/8②	'75-'77	Coronet, Satellite, Charger, Fury	10 3/4 ± 1/8
	Fury, Monaco, Polara	1 3/8 ± 1/8①③		Wagon	11 1/4 ± 1/8
				Gran Fury Monaco	10 1/8 ± 1/8

① Monaco, Polara—1 1/8 ± 1/8
② '71-'73—1 5/8 ± 1/8
③ 1974—1 in.
▲ See text for procedure

NOTE: Service procedures for the Charging System, Starting System, Ignition System, Cooling System, Fuel System, Emission Control Systems, Engine, Clutch and Manual Transmission apply to Chrysler, Cordoba, and Imperial models, as well.

CHARGING SYSTEM

Before undertaking any electrical system service, the battery must be disconnected. Never attempt to polarize or short any component of the system.

Charging System troubleshooting can be found in the Unit Repair Section.

Alternator Removal and Installation

To remove alternator:
1. Disconnect battery.
2. Disconnect Bat. and Fld. leads from alternator.
3. Remove alternator by removing two mounting bolts and belt tensioner bracket bolt.
4. To reinstall: reverse the above. Tighten the belt so that it can be depressed about ½ in. by moderate thumb pressure in the center of the longest span between pulleys. Some alternator brackets have a square hole into which you can insert a ½ in. square socket drive to tension the belt.

NOTE: Never attempt to polarize an alternator, nor short the regulator.

Regulator Removal and Installation

All models have a solid-state (silicon transistor) voltage regulator which is not adjustable. The regulator is in the engine compartment and clearly labeled.
1. Release the spring clips and pull off the regulator wiring plug.
2. Unbolt and remove the regulator.
3. Installation is the reverse of removal. Be sure that the spring clips engage the wiring plug and that the unit has a good ground.

STARTING SYSTEM

All models are equipped with one of two types of starter: a direct-drive type or a 3.5:1 or 2.0:1 reduction gear type. The reduction gear type of starter may be identified by the battery terminal on the starter being installed at an angle; the direct-drive type starter battery terminal is parallel to the starter case. Both types of starters have solenoids which are mounted directly on the starter assembly.

Starter Removal and Installation

1. Disconnect the ground cable at the battery.
2. Remove the cable from the starter.
3. Disconnect the solenoid leads at their solenoid terminals.
4. Remove the starter securing bolts and withdraw the starter from the engine flywheel housing. On some models with automatic transmissions, the oil cooler tube bracket will interfere with starter removal. In this case, remove the starter securing bolts, slide the cooler tube bracket off the stud and then withdraw the starter.
5. Installation is the reverse of the above. Be sure that the starter and flywheel housing mating surfaces are free of dirt and oil. When tightening the bolt and nut, hold the starter away from the engine to ensure proper alignment.

IGNITION SYSTEM

Chrysler used conventional ignition systems on all models to 1971 and most 1972 models.

An electronic ignition system is standard on all 1973 and later Chrysler Corporation vehicles. This type of ignition system has no contact points; consequently, there is no dwell adjustment. The only regular ignition system maintenance required is inspection of the wiring and spark plug replacement (check timing on occasion only). To determine whether a car is equipped with electronic ignition, check for a double primary lead from the distributor, a dual ballast resistor located on the firewall, and a control unit located either on the left wheel housing or the firewall. Further details and troubleshooting on electronic ignition are in the Unit Repair Section.

NOTE: Test tachometer hookup with electronic ignition is the same as with conventional point-type systems. One tachometer lead connects to the negative primary coil terminal and the other to ground. Some meters will not work at all with this system.

1971 Ignition Retard Solenoid

This unit's function is to retard ignition timing at closed throttle. *Located on the distributor side, this solenoid must be operating when ignition timing is checked.* To check

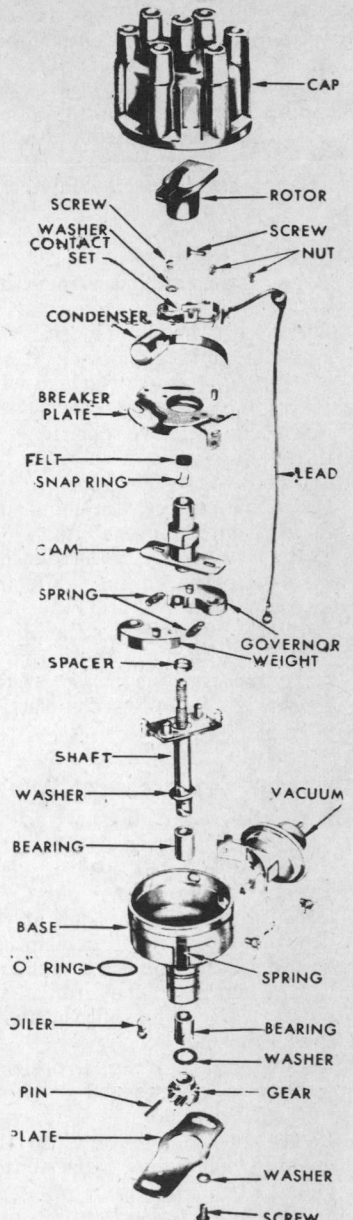

6 cylinder distributor (conventional ignition)
(© Chrysler Corp)

whether the solenoid is operating, disconnect the ground lead after timing is set. If engine idle speed increases noticeably, the solenoid is functioning properly. Disconnect the solenoid when checking dwell.

1972-74 400 or 440 4-V V8 Ignition Advance Solenoid

This solenoid, located on the distributor side, is connected to the starter relay so that it operates only during engine cranking to improve starting.

When the engine fires, this solenoid ceases to operate. If the solenoid is not operating, it will affect starting, but not drivability. A possible sign of non-operation is popping through the carburetor during engine cranking.

To check operation, idle engine and connect a jumper wire from the battery to the solenoid lead. If the solenoid is operating properly, the engine speed will increase noticeably.

Caution Disconnect jumper wire as soon as possible after checking solenoid operation.

Distributor Removal

1. Take off the cap and wire assembly.
2. Disconnect the primary coil wire and vacuum tube. With electronic ignition, disconnect the lead wire at the harness connector.
3. Mark the relative positions of the distributor and rotor on the engine block.
4. Loosen the distributor mounting and lift out the distributor.

NOTE: to simplify reinstallation, do not disturb the engine while the distributor is out.

5. Reinstall by reversing the above procedure, aligning the distributor rotor and the mark on the block when installing the distributor.

Distributor Replacement (When Engine has been Disturbed)

Slant 6 Engine

1. Rotate the engine until No. 1 piston is up on compression at top dead center. This is determined by the pressure on the thumb and the 0 mark on the crankshaft pulley hub being aligned with the timing pointer.
2. Rotate the rotor to a position just ahead of the No. 1 distributor cap terminal.
3. Lower the distributor into the opening, engaging distributor gear with drive gear on camshaft. With distributor fully seated on engine, rotor should be under the cap No. 1 tower with distributor contact points just opening.
4. Install cap, tighten hold-down arm screw and check timing with a timing light.

V8 Engine

Rotate the crankshaft until No. 1 cylinder is at top dead center. The pointer on the chain case cover should be over the 0 mark on the crankshaft pulley. The slot in the intermediate shaft which carries the gear that drives the oil pump and the distributor, should be parallel (or nearly so) with the crankshaft.

Hold the distributor over the mounting pad on the cylinder block so that the distributor body flange coincides with the mounting pad and the rotor points to the No. 1 cylinder firing position.

V8 distributor (conventional ignition)
(© Chrysler Corp)

Install the distributor while holding the rotor in position, allowing it to move only enough to engage the slot in the drive gear.

Breaker Points and Condenser Replacement

Single Point Distributor

1. Remove the distributor cap. Do not pull the wires from the cap. Pull the rotor from the shaft.
2. Carefully note the position of all leads and remove the securing nut. Loosen the point plate lockscrew and remove the points and condenser from the vehicle.
3. With a clean, lint-free rag, wipe any of the old cam grease from the distributor cam. Apply fresh cam lubricant sparingly.
4. Insert a new point set with the contact heel resting on the highest point of the cam lobe. Set

point gap to specifications with a feeler gauge. The setting is correct when the feeler gauge is removed with a light drag. Install the condenser and secure the leads. Lock the point securing screws.

5. Replace the distributor cap and rotor. Check the dwell with a dwell meter. Adjust the point gap as necessary.
6. Road-test vehicle.

Dual Point Distributor

The removal and installation of dual contact points is the same as for a single point set. The point adjustment is also the same, except that each set must be set while its rubbing block is on the high point of the cam lobe. The dwell adjustment of dual points is slightly different because one set of contacts must be blocked open with a clean insulator while the opposite point set is adjusted to specifications. When correctly adjusted, tighten the lockscrew. Block open this contact set and adjust this contact set in the same manner as the first. Check the total point dwell.

Ignition Timing

NOTE: Before timing engine, check information on ignition retard/advance solenoids.

The ignition timing test indicates correct timing of the engine only at idle and with the engine hot. Check timing as follows:

1. Disconnect the vacuum hose at the distributor and plug the line.
2. Connect a timing light to No. 1 spark plug and to the battery terminals.
3. Start the engine and set it to the specified idle speed with the transmission in Neutral.
4. Loosen the distributor locking screw so that the housing can be rotated.
5. Check the timing by aiming the timing light at the vibration damper. If timing is ahead of the mark, turn the distributor housing in the direction of rotor-rotation. This will retard timing. If it is past the mark, rotate the distributor against its direction of rotation to advance the timing. When timing is adjusted to specifications, tighten the distributor lockscrew and reconnect the vacuum hose to the distributor.

FUEL SYSTEM

The fuel pumps used on the six-cylinder and all big blocks (383-440 cu in.) are driven by a small cam eccentric cast into the main camshaft. On the 318, 340, and 360 engines, the pump is driven by a pressed

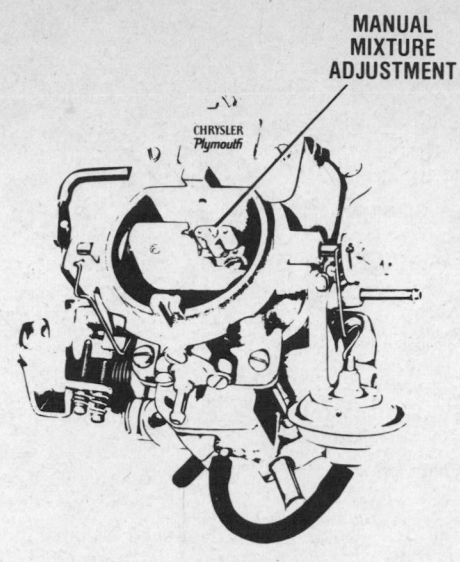

ALTITUDE ADJUSTABLE CARBURETOR
318-CID ENGINE

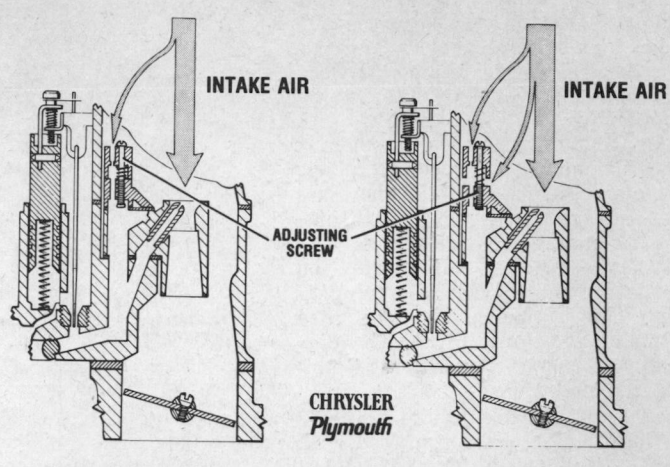

**MANUAL-ADJUSTING
HIGH-ALTITUDE CALIBRATION CARBURETOR**
318 CID ENGINE

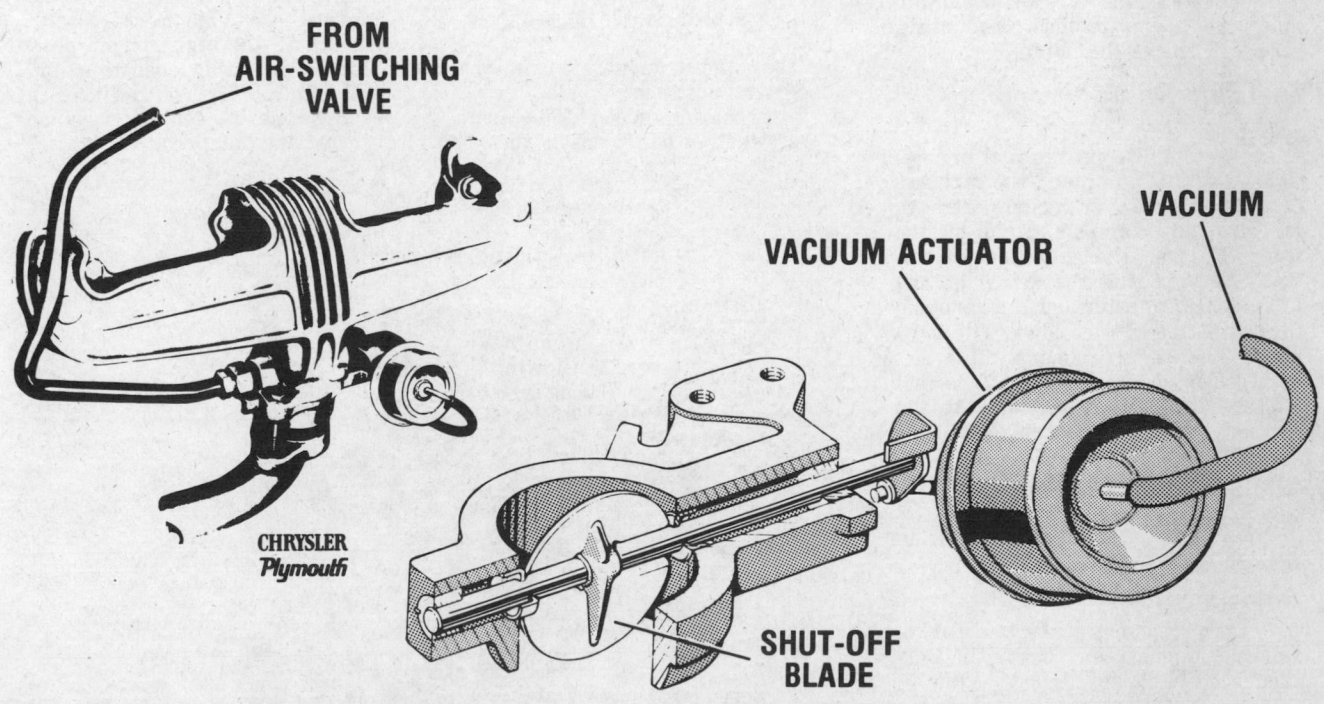

POWER HEAT CONTROL VALVE

steel eccentric secured on the gear end of the camshaft. On the six-cylinder and 318, 340, and 360 engines, the pump is driven directly by the pump rocker arm pressing on the cam eccentric. On the big block engines, there is a push rod located between the pump rocker arm and the driving eccentric.

The carburetor idle speed solenoid raises the engine idle speed to reduce engine emissions, but de-energizes when the ignition is shut off to prevent the engine from dieseling.

Some carburetors incorporate an internally mounted hot idle compensator. This compensator is designed to induct additional air to the carburetor during low-speed, high-temperature operation.

Both the 426 Hemi and the 440 Six-Pack were equipped with multiple carburetors. The 1970 Hemi used two Carter AFBs. Both carburetors were equipped with complete idle systems; they must be adjusted and synchronized to obtain a satisfactory engine idle. The 440 Six Pack was equipped with three Holley 2300 two-barrel carburetors. Only the center carburetor was equipped with an idle system; the inboard and outboard carburetors contained no idle adjustments.

Fuel Pump Removal

Remove all lines at the fuel pump, and the pump-to-block mounting screws. Remove the pump.

Fuel Filter Removal and Installation

Locate the filter in the fuel line between the fuel pump and the carburetor. Using hose-clamp pliers, remove the attaching clamps and pull off the filter. Reverse the procedure to install. Be sure that the arrow on the filter is pointing toward the carburetor (direction of fuel flow). The 1973 six-cylinder engine has a filter element screwed into the top of the fuel pump. This is not meant to be cleaned; it should be replaced.

Idle Speed and Mixture Adjustments

Idle Speed Solenoid Adjustment

These procedures are given for all Chrysler Corporation cars in the Barracuda, Challenger, Dart, Valiant, Aspen, Volare section.

1970 426 Hemi Idle Speed and Mixture Adjustment

Because each carburetor is equipped with a complete idle system, accurate carburetor synchronization is very important. After adjusting the idle speed and mixture, it should

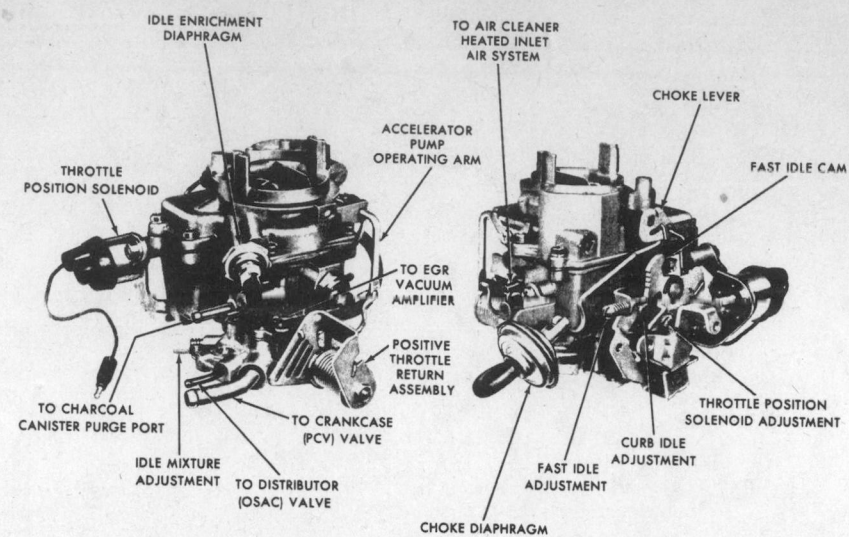

Holley 1945 carburetor adjustments (© Chrysler Corp)

be rechecked and rebalanced as required in the outside ambient temperature after a road test.

Adjust with air cleaner removed.

1. Run engine at fast idle to stabilize engine temperature.
2. Make sure the choke plate is fully released.
3. Attach a tachometer of known accuracy to the engine.
4. If equipped with a hot idle compensator valve, make sure it is fully seated in the closed position.
5. Place the transmission in the Neutral position.
6. Turn the idle speed adjustment screws in or out to adjust the engine idle speed to specification. If equipped with an electric solenoid throttle positioner, turn the solenoid adjusting screw in or out to obtain specified engine idle speed. Then, turn the curb idle speed adjusting screw clockwise until it just touches the stop on the carburetor throttle body. Next, back the curb idle speed adjusting screw out one full turn.
7. Adjust each idle mixture screw to obtain the highest rpm possible. Repeat this operation until all four mixture adjustment screws have been properly adjusted and balanced.

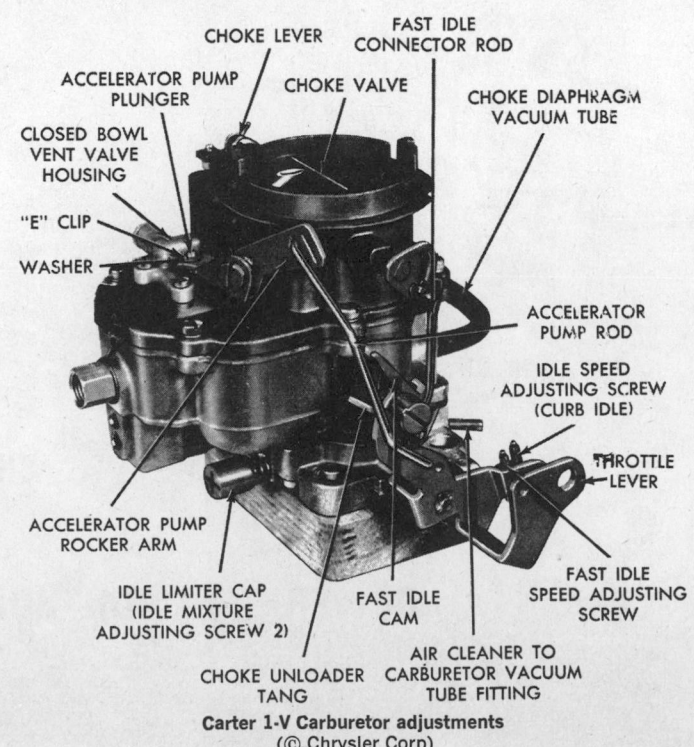

Carter 1-V Carburetor adjustments
(© Chrysler Corp)

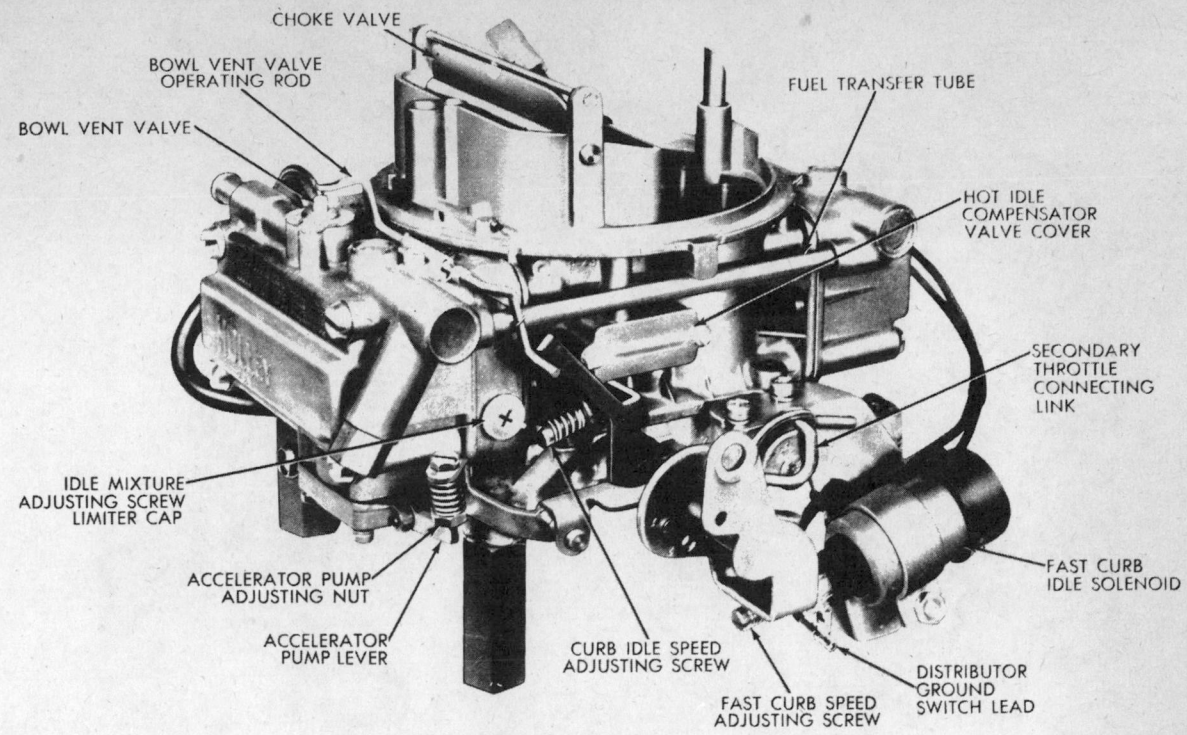

CHOKE VALVE

BOWL VENT VALVE
OPERATING ROD

BOWL VENT VALVE

FUEL TRANSFER TUBE

HOT IDLE
COMPENSATOR
VALVE COVER

SECONDARY
THROTTLE
CONNECTING
LINK

IDLE MIXTURE
ADJUSTING SCREW
LIMITER CAP

ACCELERATOR PUMP
ADJUSTING NUT

ACCELERATOR
PUMP LEVER

CURB IDLE SPEED
ADJUSTING SCREW

FAST CURB SPEED
ADJUSTING SCREW

FAST CURB
IDLE SOLENOID

DISTRIBUTOR
GROUND
SWITCH LEAD

1970-71 Holley 4-V carburetor adjustments (© Chrysler Corp)

8. If the idle mixture adjustment procedure has changed the engine idle speed, adjust the idle speed.

Balancing Multiple-Carburetor Installations

426 Hemi

There is no actual adjustment of the external carburetor linkage to synchronize the twin carburetors.

Proper balancing of the carburetor idle speeds as described in the idle speed for the 1970 426 Hemi will ensure correct and mixture adjustment procedure carburetor synchronization.

440 Six Pack through 1971

Because only the center carburetor has provisions for adjusting the engine idle speed and fuel mixture, these adjustments are performed using the procedure for single-carburetor installations. The throttle rods which connect each outboard carburetor to the center carburetor can be adjusted for correct throttle synchronization using the procedure below.

1. Remove the air cleaner.
2. Remove the outboard throttle rod securing clips and disengage

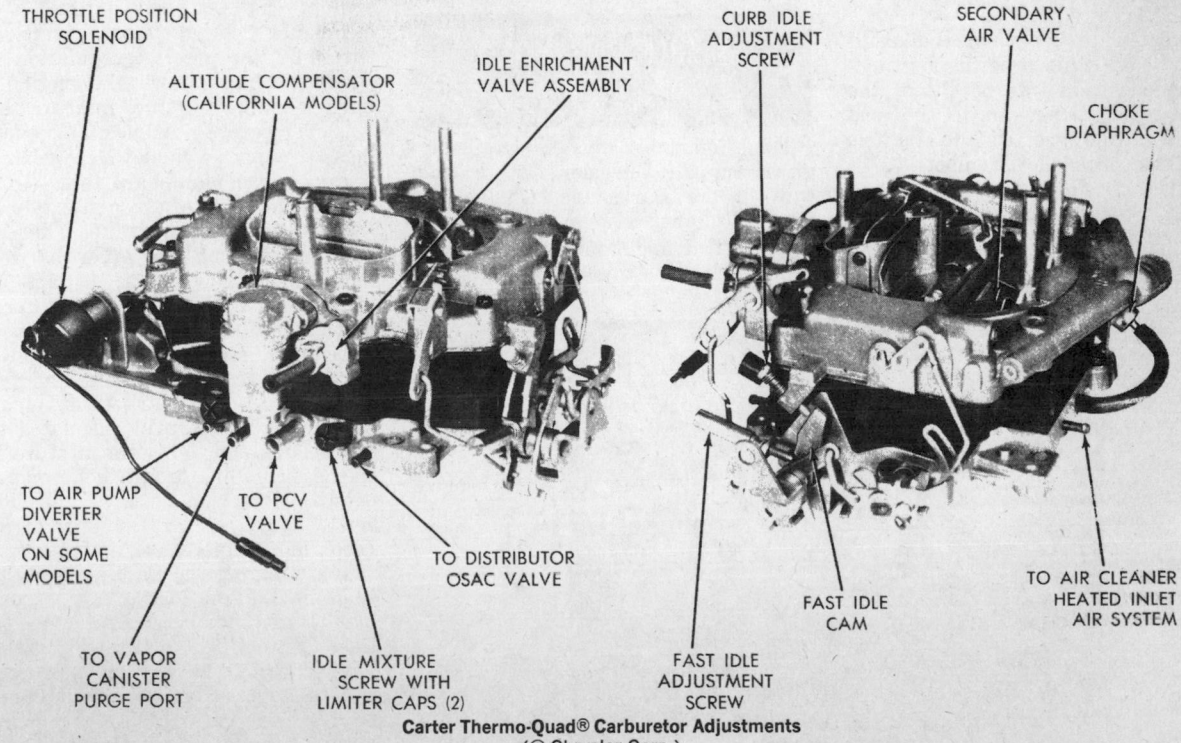

THROTTLE POSITION
SOLENOID

ALTITUDE COMPENSATOR
(CALIFORNIA MODELS)

IDLE ENRICHMENT
VALVE ASSEMBLY

CURB IDLE
ADJUSTMENT
SCREW

SECONDARY
AIR VALVE

CHOKE
DIAPHRAGM

TO AIR PUMP
DIVERTER
VALVE
ON SOME
MODELS

TO PCV
VALVE

TO DISTRIBUTOR
OSAC VALVE

FAST IDLE
CAM

TO AIR CLEANER
HEATED INLET
AIR SYSTEM

TO VAPOR
CANISTER
PURGE PORT

IDLE MIXTURE
SCREW WITH
LIMITER CAPS (2)

FAST IDLE
ADJUSTMENT
SCREW

Carter Thermo-Quad® Carburetor Adjustments
(© Chrysler Corp.)

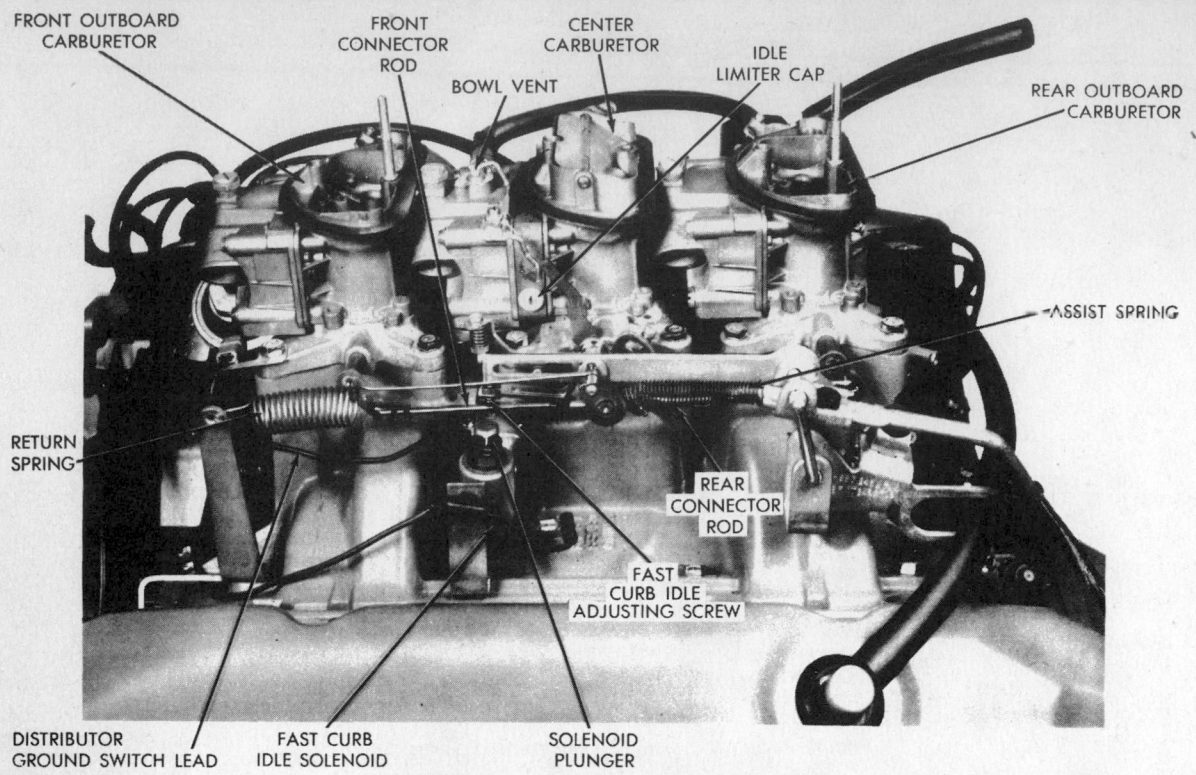

Holley Six Pack carburetor adjustments (© Chrysler Corp)

the front and rear rods from the throttle levers.

3. Be sure that the ignition switch is turned off. (This de-energizes the fast curb idle solenoid so that clearance can be obtained between the plunger and the fast curb idle adjusting screw.)

4. Close the throttle valves of all three carburetors and hold them in the closed position.

5. Shorten or lengthen the front and rear connector rods by turning each rod into or out of the threaded sleeve until the rod end can be inserted into the hole in the throttle lever smoothly.

6. Fit each throttle connector rod into its corresponding throttle lever and secure each rod with a clip.

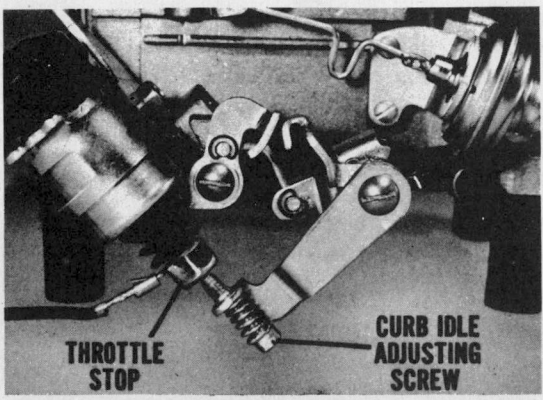

Curb idle speed adjustment
(© Chrysler Corp)

COOLING SYSTEM

Cooling system procedures are given for all Chrysler Corporation cars in the Barracuda, Challenger, Dart, Valiant, Aspen, Volare section.

EMISSION CONTROLS

Emission control system details are given for all Chrysler Corporation cars in the Barracuda, Challenger, Dart, Valiant, Aspen, Volare section. Testing and troubleshooting procedures for all emission controls, including the electronic lean-burn system are given in the Emission Control Systems Unit Repair Section.

Lean-Burn System

Introduced on 1976 Chrysler Corporation cars with the 400-4V engine is the electronic spark advance control or "lean-burn" system. This system (not to be confused with electronic "breakerless" ignition), through its precise regulation of spark timing, allows the engine to burn a leaner air/fuel mixture than was ever before possible on a modern, mass-produced vehicle. Most contemporary powerplants are tuned to an air/fuel mixture of approximately 14-1/2 parts air to one part fuel. The lean-burn engine, on the other hand, is most efficient at about 18 parts air to one part fuel. Six engine compartment-mounted sensors monitor all critical and fast changing factors that affect engine performance, and feed this data to the spark control computer which instantly calculates the precise moment to fire the mixture for the best combination of fuel economy, performance, and low emissions levels. These sensors monitor engine (coolant) temperature, ambient (outside air temperature, intake manifold vacuum (engine load), engine speed (rpm) and position relative to Top Dead Center (TDC), throttle position. With the lean-burn system, the following items of emission control may be dropped; catalytic converter (except California), air injection (air

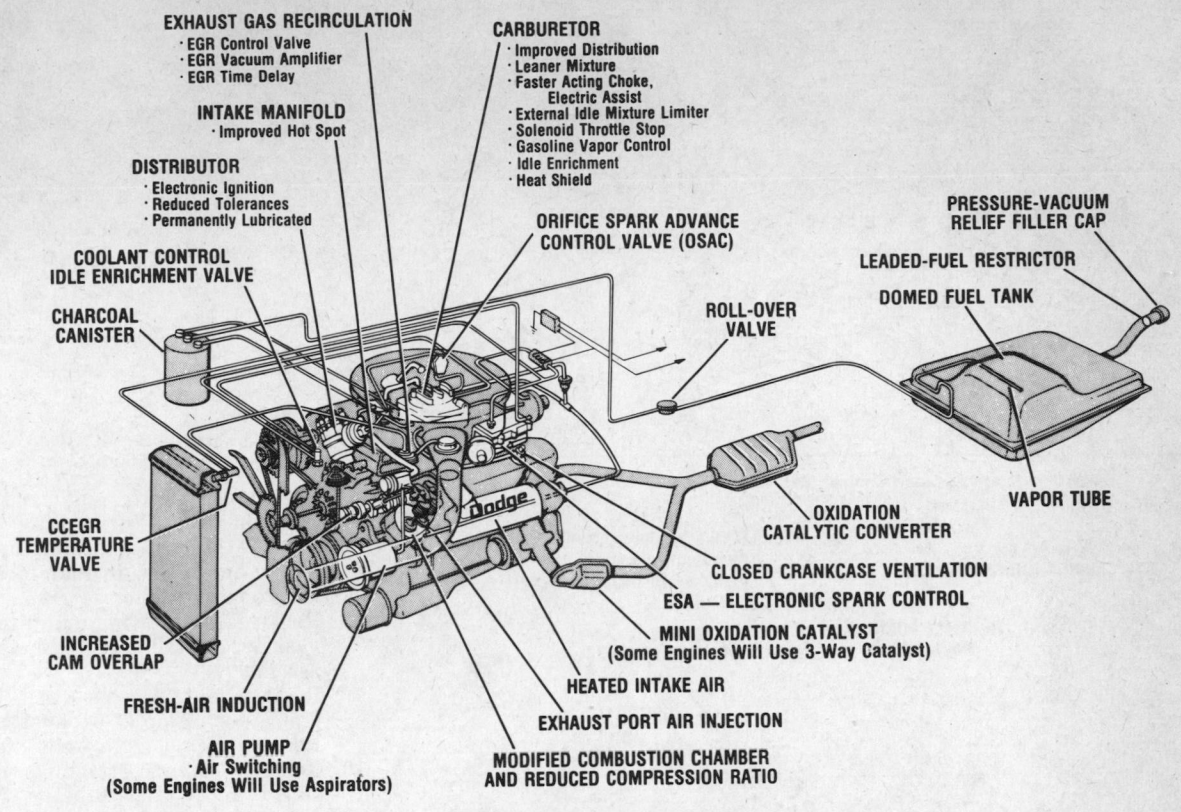

EXHAUST GAS RECIRCULATION
· EGR Control Valve
· EGR Vacuum Amplifier
· EGR Time Delay

INTAKE MANIFOLD
· Improved Hot Spot

DISTRIBUTOR
· Electronic Ignition
· Reduced Tolerances
· Permanently Lubricated

COOLANT CONTROL
IDLE ENRICHMENT VALVE

CHARCOAL
CANISTER

CCEGR
TEMPERATURE
VALVE

INCREASED
CAM OVERLAP

FRESH-AIR INDUCTION

AIR PUMP
· Air Switching
(Some Engines Will Use Aspirators)

CARBURETOR
· Improved Distribution
· Leaner Mixture
· Faster Acting Choke,
  Electric Assist
· External Idle Mixture Limiter
· Solenoid Throttle Stop
· Gasoline Vapor Control
· Idle Enrichment
· Heat Shield

ORIFICE SPARK ADVANCE
CONTROL VALVE (OSAC)

ROLL-OVER
VALVE

PRESSURE-VACUUM
RELIEF FILLER CAP

LEADED-FUEL RESTRICTOR

DOMED FUEL TANK

VAPOR TUBE

OXIDATION
CATALYTIC CONVERTER

CLOSED CRANKCASE VENTILATION

ESA — ELECTRONIC SPARK CONTROL

MINI OXIDATION CATALYST
(Some Engines Will Use 3-Way Catalyst)

HEATED INTAKE AIR

EXHAUST PORT AIR INJECTION

MODIFIED COMBUSTION CHAMBER
AND REDUCED COMPRESSION RATIO

1977 CLEANER AIR SYSTEM
COMPARISONS ARE WITH PRE-CONTROLLED ENGINES

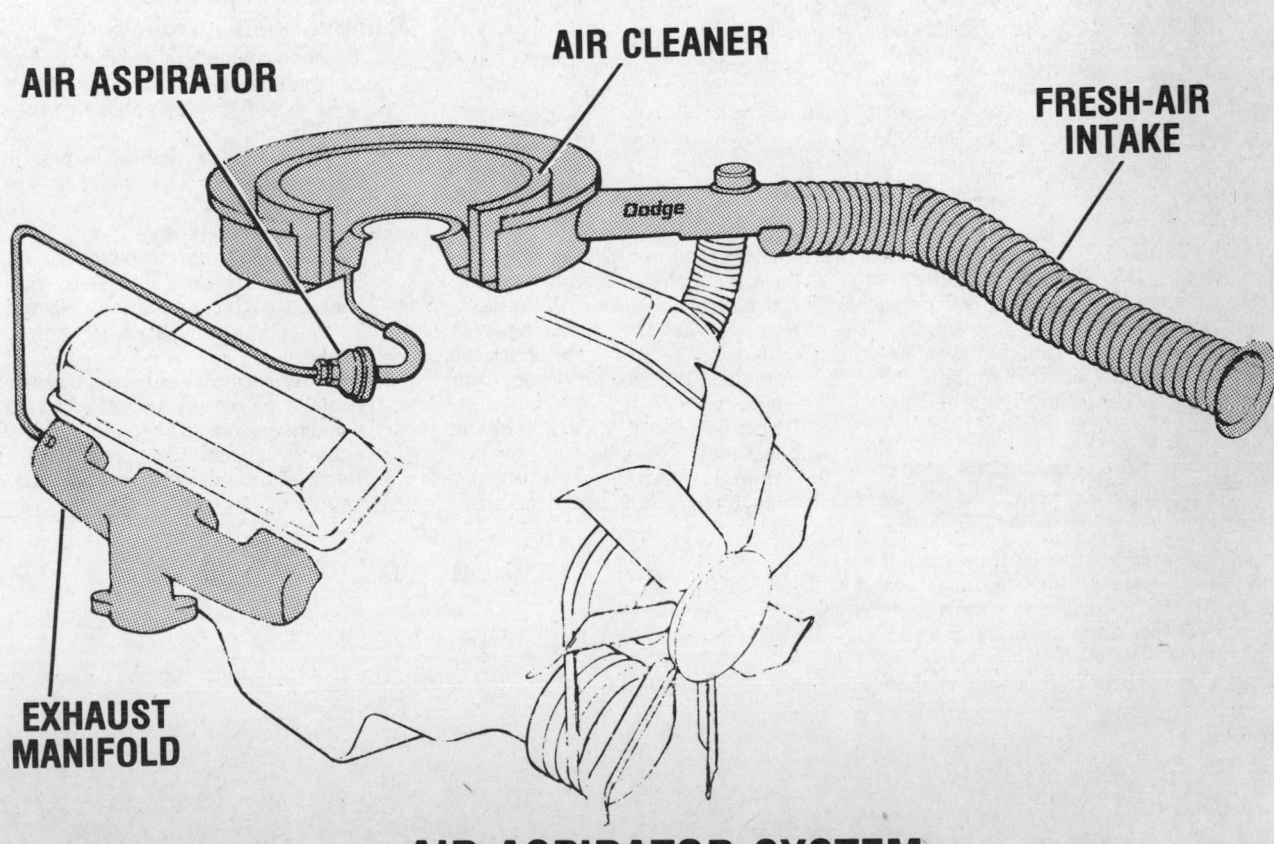

AIR ASPIRATOR

AIR CLEANER

FRESH-AIR
INTAKE

EXHAUST
MANIFOLD

AIR ASPIRATOR SYSTEM

C531

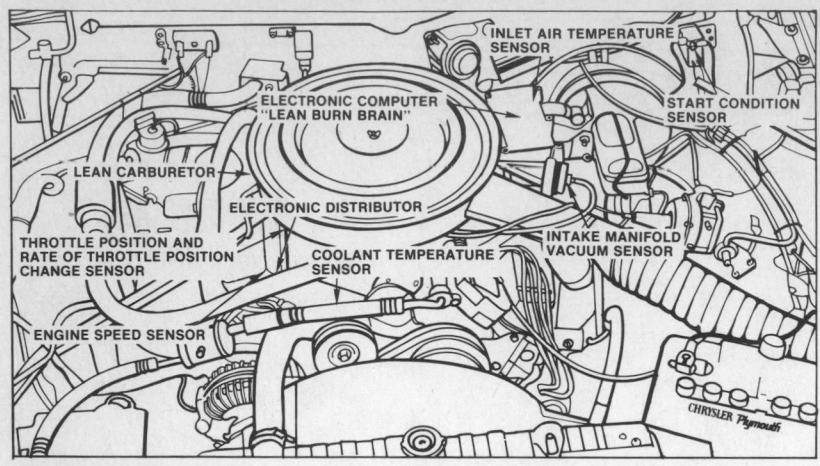

Electronic Spark Advance Control (Lean-Burn) System Components
(© Chrysler Corp.)

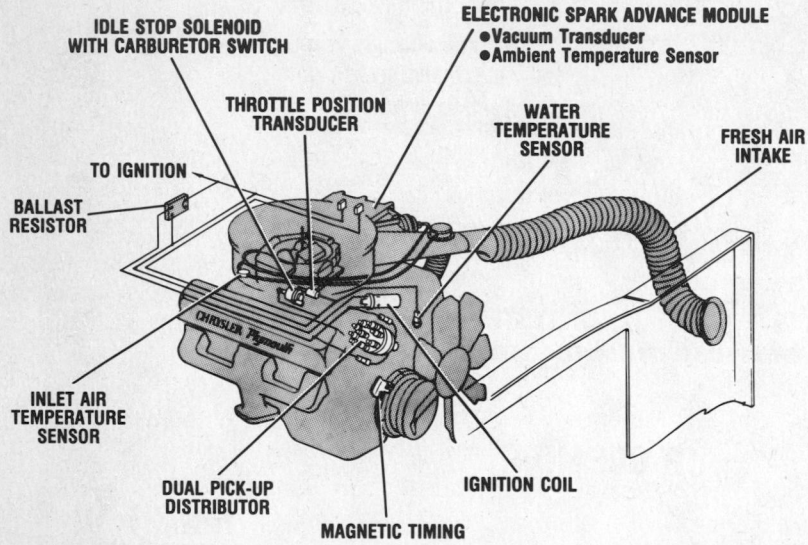

Lean-burn System Schematic
(© Chrysler Corp.)

pump) system, exhaust gas recirculation system, OSAC valve, and distributor vacuum controls. The key is to clean up pollutants in the engine; not with power robbing hang-on devices. Full details on this system are given in the Emission Control Systems Unit Repair Section.

ENGINE

Engine service procedures for all Chrysler Corporation engines are given in the Barracuda, Challenger, Dart, Valiant, Aspen, Volare car section. The only exceptions are 426 Hemi service procedures and oil pan removal procedures which are in this section.

426 Hemi Intake Manifold Removal and Installation

1. Drain cooling system and disconnect battery.

2. Remove the air cleaner and fuel lines from the carburetors.
3. Disconnect accelerator linkage.
4. Remove vacuum control between carburetor and distributor. Remove distributor cap and wires.
5. Disconnect coil wires, heater hoses and bypass hose.
6. Remove two stud nuts and washers which retain intake manifold

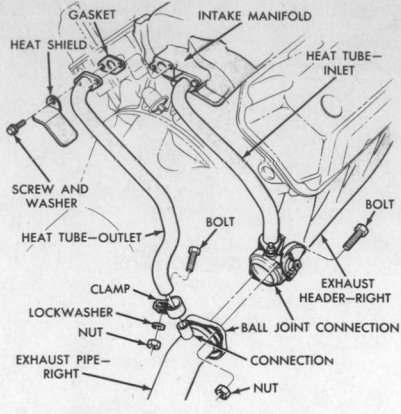

Manifold heat tubes—426 Hemi
(© Chrysler Corp)

inlet heat tube to right hand exhaust header.
7. Remove screws attaching upper end of inlet tube to rear face of intake manifold.
8. Remove inlet tube and discard gaskets. Install new gaskets at assembly.
9. Remove nut, washer, and bolt from tube clamp at exhaust pipe. Remove clamp from outlet tube.
10. Remove screws attaching heat shield and outlet tube to rear face of intake manifold and remove tube and shield.
11. Remove intake manifold, coil and carburetors as an assembly.

426 Hemi Rocker Shaft Removal and Installation

1. Remove air cleaner, and distributor cap with spark plug cables and secondary coil cable as an assembly.
2. Grasp secondary cables at plastic spark covers and pull covers straight out.
3. Remove spark plugs.
4. On left bank, disconnect brake lines at master cylinder, and remove cotter pin and clevis pin from linkage in back of power brake.
5. Remove four nuts attaching booster to mounting bracket and remove power brake and master cylinder assembly.
6. Remove rocker covers and gaskets.

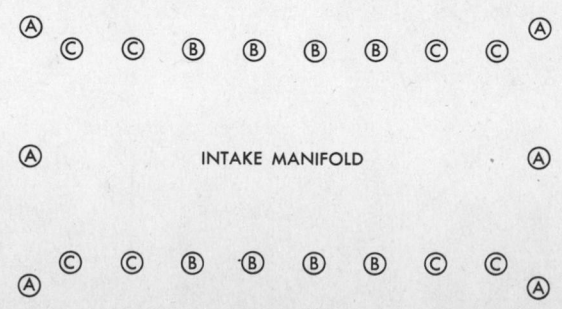

426 Hemi intake manifold tightening sequence, torque in three steps
(© Chrysler Corp)

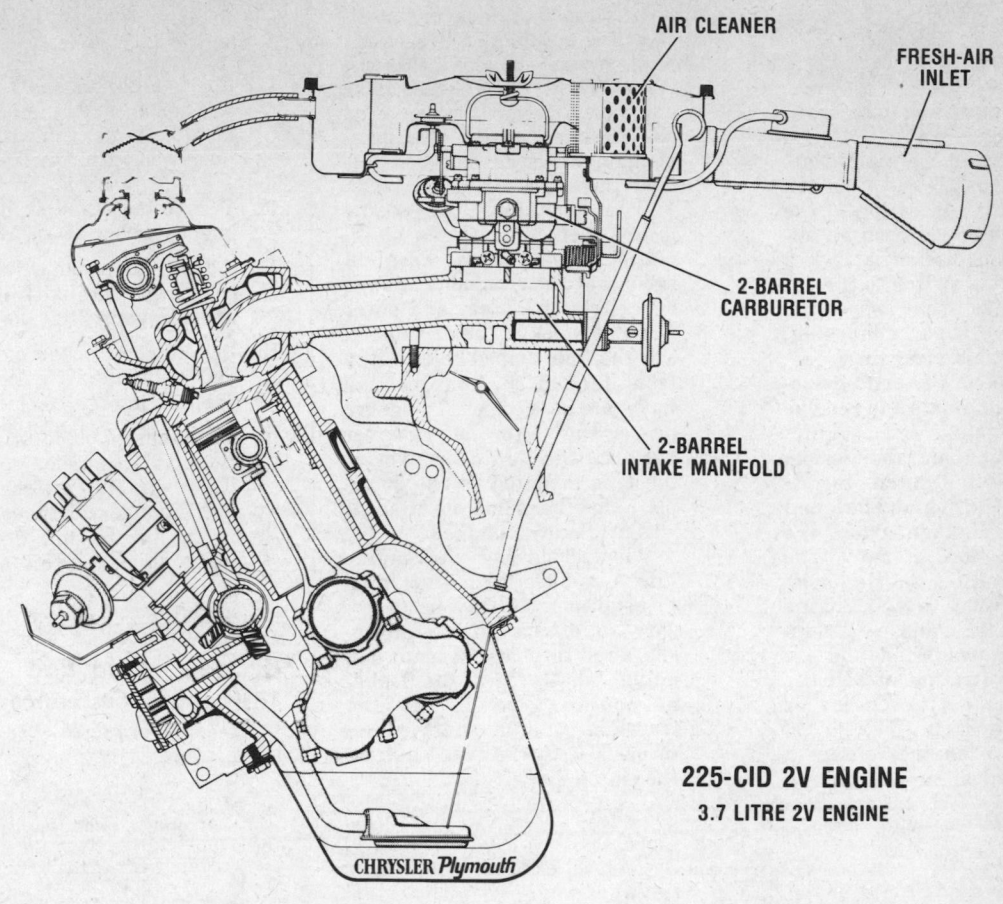

AIR CLEANER

FRESH-AIR INLET

2-BARREL CARBURETOR

2-BARREL INTAKE MANIFOLD

225-CID 2V ENGINE
3.7 LITRE 2V ENGINE

CHRYSLER *Plymouth*

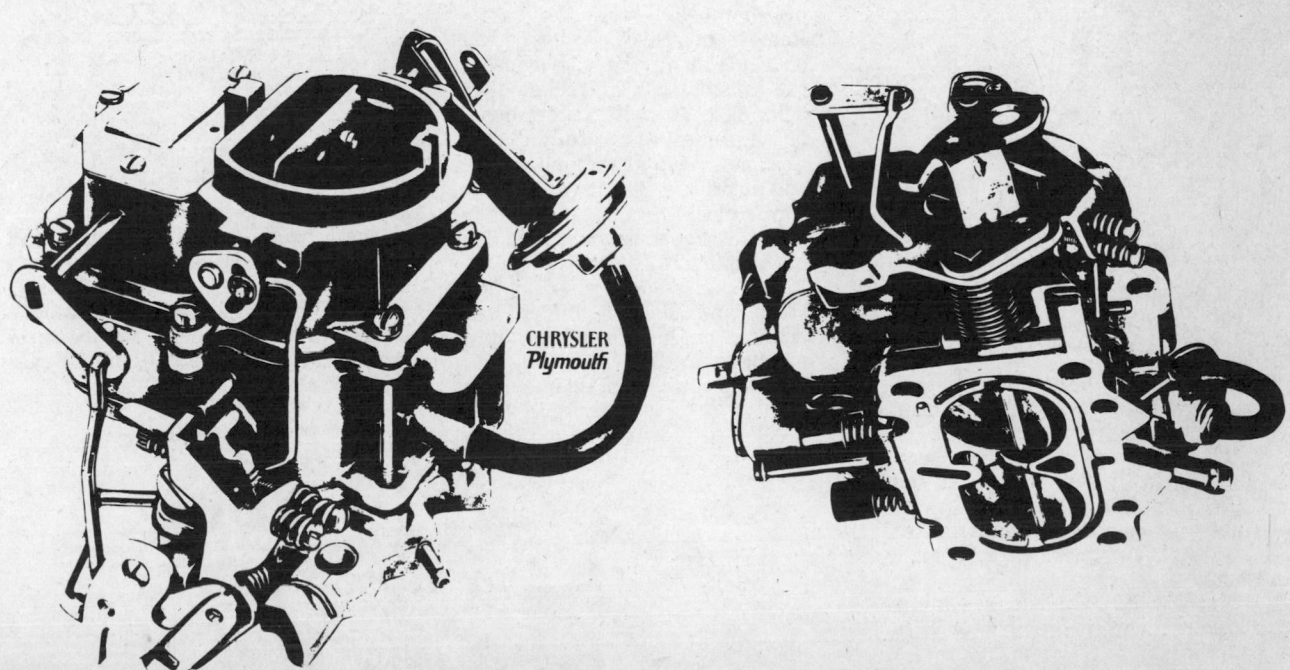

CHRYSLER *Plymouth*

TWO-BARREL CARBURETOR — 225 CID ENGINE

Chilton's TIME SAVER

To remove the engine without removing the transmission, use the following operation. Perform Steps 1-7 and 10 of the "Engine R&R" operation. If the vehicle is equipped with an automatic transmission, attach a remote starter switch to the engine, remove the inspection plate from the bellhousing, crank the engine to gain access to the torque converter-to-driveplate attaching nuts and remove the nuts. If the vehicle is equipped with a manual transmission, disconnect the clutch torque shaft from the engine block and the clutch linkage from the adjustment rod. Remove the bolt that attaches the transmission filler tube to the engine (automatic transmission). Support the transmission and remove the bolts that attach the transmission to the engine or clutch bellhousing. When removing the engine, place a block of wood on the lifting point of a floor jack and position the jack under the transmission. As the engine is removed from the vehicle, raise and lower the jack as required so the angle of the transmission duplicates as nearly as possible the angle of the engine.

When installing the engine into a vehicle with an automatic transmission, keep in mind that the crankshaft flange bolt circle, the inner and outer circle of holes in the driveplate, and the four tapped holes in the front face of the converter all have one hole offset. To ensure proper engine-torque converter balance, the torque converter must be mounted to the driveplate in the same location it was originally installed.

When installing the engine into a vehicle with a manual transmission, it may be necessary to disconnect the driveshaft and turn the transmission output shaft, with the transmission in gear, to get the transmission input shaft splines to mesh with the inner hub on the clutch disc.

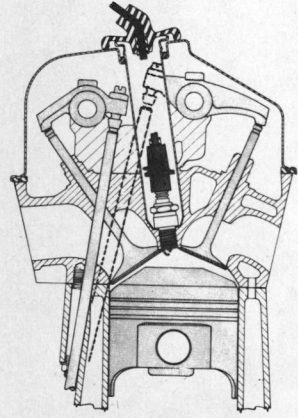

426 Hemi valve gear
(© Chrysler Corp)

7. Remove five bolts that attach rocker shafts assembly on each head.

NOTE: these rocker shaft assembly bolts pass through the head and into the block. Anytime rocker shaft assembly is removed, remove that head, fit a new gasket, reassemble and torque.

8. Lift off rocker shafts assembly.
9. Reverse the procedure for installation.

426 Hemi Cylinder Head Removal and Installation

1. Remove rocker covers.
2. Remove rocker shaft assemblies.
3. Remove intake manifold.
4. Disconnect exhaust headers, and tie out of way.
5. Remove eight lower head bolts. Remove the nuts from the four cylinder studs inside of the tappet chamber.
6. Remove heads. Do not set heads on studs at any time. Because of the unusual use of rocker shaft bolts as head bolts follow installation procedure carefully.
7. Coat new head gasket with sealer and install with raised bead towards block.
8. Install cylinder heads taking care not to damage studs.
9. Install nuts on cylinder head studs and short cylinder head bolts in outer bolt holes, but do not tighten either.
10. Install pushrods in their original bores. The short rods go in the upper holes and the long rods go in the lower holes.
11. Position rocker shafts assemblies on heads and install five long head bolts in each after lining up pushrods with rockers.
12. Torque bolts and stud nuts in sequence given at front of section.
13. Adjust valve lash.
14. Install headers with new gaskets and torque to 35 ft. lbs.
15. Install new rocker cover gaskets and install rocker covers. Tighten nuts to 10 ft. lbs.
16. Gap plugs to 0.035 in. Slide spark plug tube shields over tubes. With six in. extension install spark plugs and tubes. Torque to 30 ft. lbs. Do not drop or bang spark plugs for this may change gap.
17. Install manifold.

Cylinder Head Bolt Tightening Sequence

NOTE: Torque to specifications in three stages.

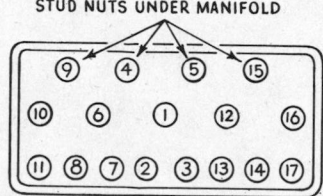

426 Hemi V8

Oil Pan Removal and Installation

These procedures are given for all Chrysler Corporation cars in the Barracuda, Challenger, Dart, Valiant, Aspen, Volare car section. Use the Dart, Valiant, Aspen, Volare procedure for Dodge and Plymouth cars with the slant six.

Torquing Hemi head stud nuts
(© Chrysler Corp)

Chilton's TIME SAVER

The following is a method for replacing valve springs, oil seals or spring retainers without removing the cylinder head.

1. Entirely dismantle a spark plug and save the threaded shell.
2. To this shell, braze or weld an air chuck.
3. Remove the valve rocker cover. Remove the rocker arm from the affected valve.
4. Remove the spark plug from the affected cylinder.
5. Turn the crankshaft to bring the piston of this cylinder down, away from possible contact with the valve head. Sharply tap the valve retainer to loosen the valve lock.
6. Turn the crankshaft to bring the piston in this cylinder to the exact top of its compression stroke.
7. Screw in the chuck-equipped spark plug shell.
8. Hook up an air hose to the chuck and turn on the pressure (about 200 lbs.).
9. With a strong and constant supply of air holding the valve closed, compress the valve spring and remove the lock and retainer.
10. Make the necessary replacements and reassemble.
NOTE: it is important that the operation be performed exactly as stated, in this order. The piston in the affected cylinder must be on exact top center to prevent air pressure from turning the crankshaft.

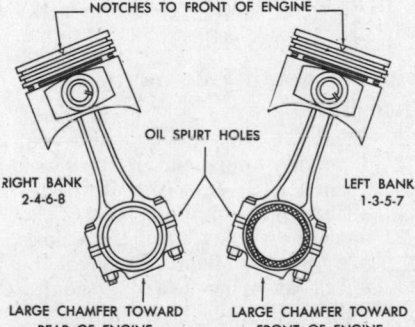

NOTCHES TO FRONT OF ENGINE

OIL SPURT HOLES

RIGHT BANK 2-4-6-8

LEFT BANK 1-3-5-7

LARGE CHAMFER TOWARD REAR OF ENGINE

LARGE CHAMFER TOWARD FRONT OF ENGINE

Relation of piston and rod—all V8s
(© Chrysler Corp)

CLUTCH MANUAL TRANSMISSION

Clutch and manual transmission service procedures for all Chrysler Corporation cars are covered in the Barracuda, Challenger, Dart, Valiant, Aspen, Volare car section.

AUTOMATIC TRANSMISSION

On models through 1971, model indentification appears in large letters embossed on the lower side of the bell housing. On 1972 and later models, the model may be identified by the part number, which is stamped on a pad on the left side of the case pan flange. Visual identification is aided by the fact that the A-727 transmission has a more gradual slope to the converter housing than does the A-904.

As a general rule, the A-904 Torqueflite is used on all 6 cylinder and light duty (318) V8 applications. The A-727 Torqueflite is used on all medium and heavy duty V8 applications. Starting 1976, normal duty 360 V8s in the Fury and Coronet use the A-904.

Neutral Safety/Backup Light Switch Replacement

Shift Linkage Adjustment

Pan Removal and Installation, Fluid Change

These procedures are covered for all Chrysler Corporation cars in the Barracuda, Challenger, Dart, Valiant, Aspen, Volare car section.

Band Adjustments

Kickdown Band

The kickdown band adjusting screw is located on the left-hand side of the transmission case near the throttle lever shaft.

1. Loosen the locknut and back it off about five turns. Be sure that the adjusting screw is free in the case.
2. Torque the adjusting screw to 72 in. lbs.
3. Back off the adjusting screw the exact number of turns specified below. Keep the screw from turning and torque the locknut to 29 ft. lbs. through 1973 and to 35 ft. lbs. on later models.

Kickdown Band Adjustment Specifications

A—904	2 turns
A—727	2 turns
1970	2 turns
1970-71 Hemi and 440 Six Pack	1½ turns
1971-77	2½ turns
1971-77 440 dual exhaust	2 turns

Low and Reverse Band

The pan must be removed from the transmission to gain access to the First and Reverse band adjusting screw.

1. Drain the transmission and remove the pan.
2. Loosen the band adjusting screw locknut and back it off about five turns. Be sure that the adjusting screw turns freely in the lever.
3. Torque the adjusting screw to 72 in. lbs. (1974 and later A-904 six cylinder applications—41 in. lbs)
4. Back off the adjusting screw the exact number of turns specified below. Keep the screw from turning and torque the locknut to 35 ft. lbs. through 1973 and to 30 ft. lbs. for later models.
5. Using a new gasket, refit the oil pan and torque the pan bolts to 150 in. lbs. Refill the transmission to the proper fluid level.

Low and Reverse Band Adjustment Specifications

A—904	
6 Cyl. (through 1973)	3¼ turns

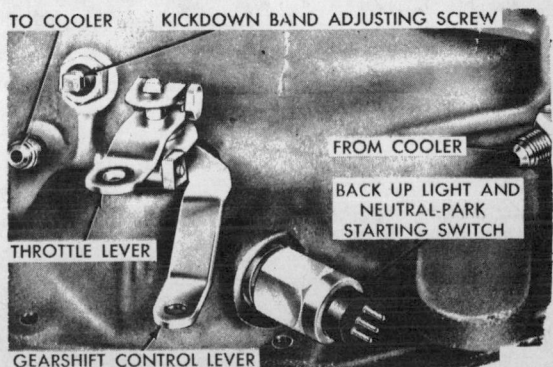

TO COOLER   KICKDOWN BAND ADJUSTING SCREW

FROM COOLER

BACK UP LIGHT AND NEUTRAL-PARK STARTING SWITCH

THROTTLE LEVER

GEARSHIFT CONTROL LEVER

Torqueflite external adjustments and controls
(© Chrysler Corp)

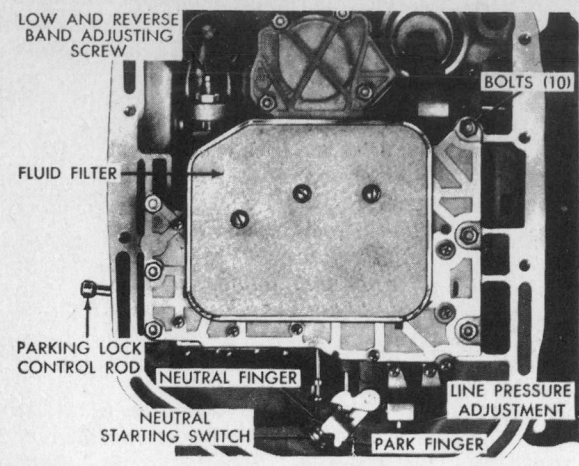

Low and reverse band adjusting screw (except 1974 and later A-904 six cylinder applications) (© Chrysler Corp)

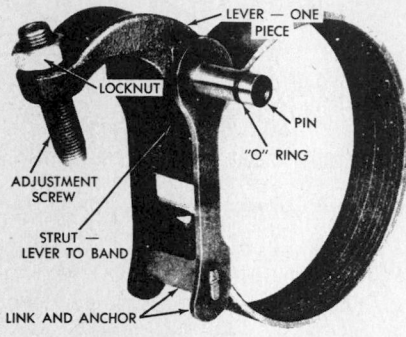

1974 and later A-904 six-cylinder low-reverse band adjustment (© Chrysler Corp)

6 Cyl. (1974 and later)	7 turns
318, 360 V8	4 turns
A—727	2 turns

U-JOINTS

Driveshaft Removal and Installation

U-Joint Overhaul

These procedures are given in the Barracuda, Challenger, Dart, Valiant, Aspen, Volare car section.

REAR AXLE

Five different rear axle assemblies have been used on intermediate and full-sized Dodge and Plymouth models. A 7¼ in. (ring gear diameter) unitized carrier axle is used on most 1970 six cylinder applications. An 8¼ in. unitized carrier axle is installed in many models equipped with the heavy-duty six cylinder or small block (318, 340, 360) V8 engines. An 8¾ in. removable carrier axle is used through 1974 with the heavy-duty six cylinder all small block V8s, and the 383 V8. Starting 1974, a 9¼ in. unitized carrier axle is installed in models equipped with

the 400 or 440 V8. A 9¾ in. unitized carrier axle is used on intermediates through 1972 equipped with the high-performance 426 Hemi or 440 V8s.

These axles can be visually identified as follows: The 7¼ in. axle has a 9 bolt rear cover with a filler plug. The 8¼ in. axle has a 10 bolt rear cover without a filler plug. The 8¾ in. axle has a welded rear cover. The 9¼ in. axle has a 12 bolt rear cover with a filler plug. The 9¾ in. axle has a 10 bolt rear cover with a filler plug.

All axles, except the 7¼ in. unit, have a ratio identification tag under one of the cover or carrier bolts. The 7¼ in. axle has an axle ratio code marking on the front of the pad at the bottom of the housing.

Axle Shaft, Bearing, and Seal

Axle Shaft, Bearing, and Seal Removal and Installation

These procedures are given for all Chrysler Corporation axles in the Barracuda, Challenger, Dart, Valiant, Aspen, Volare car section. Use the 8¼ in. axle procedure for the 9¼ in. axle.

JACKING, HOISTING

Jack car at front lower control arm and at rear under axle housing.

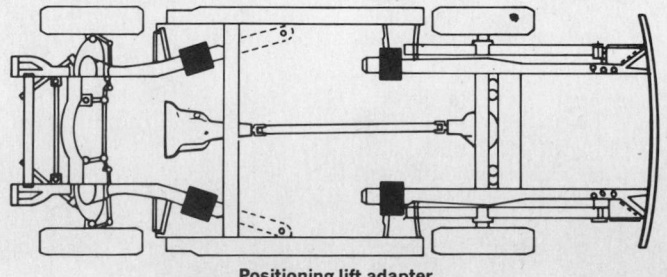

Positioning lift adapter

To lift at frame, use adapters so that contact will be made at points shown. Lifting pads must extend beyond sides of supporting structure.

FRONT SUSPENSION

All Chrysler vehicles utilize a torsion-bar front suspension. Compression-type lower ball joints are located in the steering arms on intermediates through 1972 and full size cars through 1973. 1973 Satellite, Charger and Coronet models use screw-in type lower ball joints. All 1974 and later models utilize serviceable lower ball joints which are *pressed* into the lower control arms. When servicing the front suspension, it should be kept in mind that rubber bushings must not be lubricated at any time. Any front suspension adjustments or servicing that is required on any part that contains rubber should be tightened with the suspension at the proper height and with the full vehicle weight on the wheels.

Shock Absorber Removal and Installation

1. Remove the washer and nut from the upper end of the shock absorber. Be sure to note the positions of all small parts.
2. Jack the vehicle until the wheels are off the floor. Remove the shock absorber lower attaching bolt.
3. Fully compress the shock absorber by pulling upward. Pull the shock firmly and remove it from the vehicle.
4. Check the shock absorber bushings, if they are worn or scored, replace them. Remove and install the bushings with a press or a drift and hammer. To ease installation, lubricate with water.

Caution Do not use oil to ease installation.

5. Purge the new shock of air by repeatedly extending it in its normal position and compressing it while inverted. To install the shock, compress it fully. Insert the mount through the upper bushing, replace the retainer and

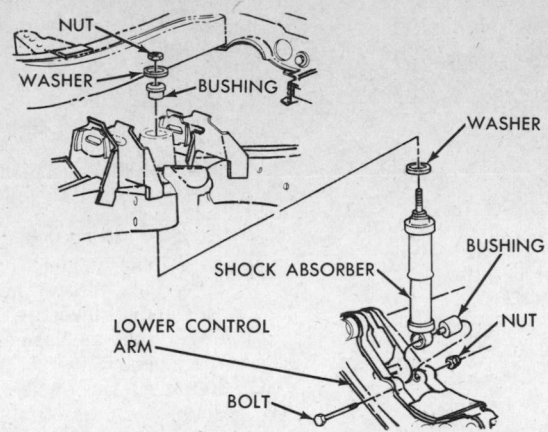

Front shock absorber replacement—Fury through 1973, Polara, Monaco; Satellite, Coronet, Charger 1973 and later; 1975 and later Fury
(© Chrysler Corp)

nut, and torque it to 25 ft lbs. Be sure that all of the retainers are installed with the concave side in contact with the rubber.

6. Position and align the lower mount of the shock absorber. Install the bolt (on some models it must be installed from the rear) with a nut and finger-tighten it. Lower the vehicle and torque the bolt to 50 ft lbs with the full weight of the vehicle on the wheels.

Lower Ball Joint

Inspection

1. Raise the front of the vehicle by placing a floor jack under the lower control arm. Position the lifting point of the jack as close to the wheel as possible.
2. Have an assistant raise and lower the tire and wheel assembly and observe any movement at the lower ball joint.
3. On intermediate models through 1972 and full size models through 1973, replace the ball joint if the axial (up and down) play exceeds 0.070 in. On 1973 and later Satellite, Charger and Coronet models, as well as 1974 and later Fury, Polara and Monaco models, replace the joint if axial play exceeds 0.020 in.

Removal

Intermediates through 1972, Full Size through 1973

The lower ball joint is integral with the steering arm and is not serviced separately.

1. Raise the vehicle on a hoist so the front suspension will drop to the downward limit of its travel.
2. Place a jack stand under the lower control arm.
3. Lower the vehicle onto the jack stand.
4. Remove the tire, wheel, and brake drum from the vehicle as

an assembly. If equipped with disc brakes, remove the tire and wheel, remove the brake pads, and remove the caliper from the steering knuckle and position it out of the way with the brake line attached. Remove the rotor from the spindle.

5. Remove the two lower and upper bolts that attach the steering arm-ball joint assembly to the brake assembly mounting plate and move the backing plate out of the way.
6. Using a suitable tool, disconnect the tie-rod end from the steering arm.
7. Remove the ball joint stud retaining nut and cotter pin.
8. Using a suitable tool, separate and remove the ball joint from the lower control arm.

Installation

Intermediates through 1972, Full Size through 1973

1. Position ball joint-steering arm assembly on the steering knuckle and install the two retaining bolts.
2. Insert the ball joint stud in the lower control arm and install the retaining nut and cotter pin.

Removing ball joint stud—1973 and later intermediates and 1974 and later full size models (© Chrysler Corp)

3. Position the tie-rod end in the steering knuckle and install the retaining nut and cotter pin.
4. Place a load on the torsion bar by turning the adjusting bolt in a clockwise direction. *Note: Loading the torsion bar is only necessary if it was removed.*
5. Install the tire, wheel and brake drum assembly. If equipped with

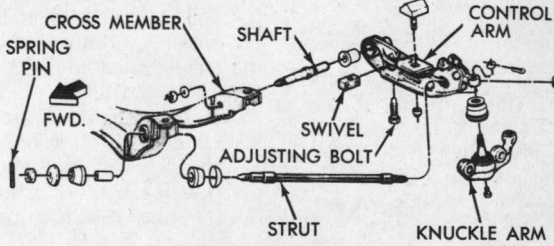

Lower control arm—Belvedere, Satellite, Coronet and Charger through 1972
(© Chrysler Corp)

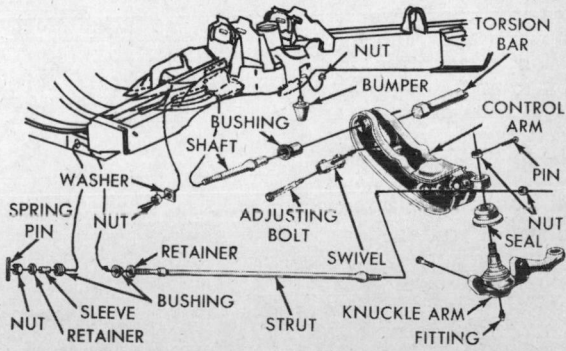

Lower control arm—Fury, Polara and Monaco through 1973
(© Chrysler Corp)

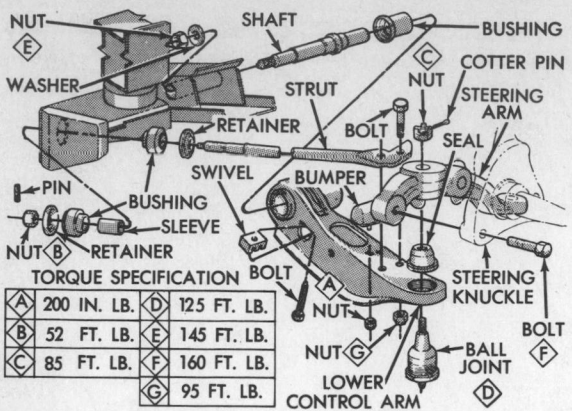

TORQUE SPECIFICATION			
Ⓐ 200 IN. LB.	Ⓓ 125 FT. LB.
Ⓑ 52 FT. LB.	Ⓔ 145 FT. LB.
Ⓒ 85 FT. LB.	Ⓕ 160 FT. LB.
	Ⓖ 95 FT. LB.

1973 and later Satellite, Coronet, Charger, 1975 and later Fury lower control arm assembly
(© Chrysler Corp)

disc brakes, install the rotor, caliper, brake pads and tire and wheel assembly.

6. Lower vehicle and install upper control arm rebound bumper if so equipped and if it was removed.

7. Check and adjust front suspension height and alignment.

Removal

All 1974 and later Models and 1973 Intermediates

Lower ball joints on these models may be serviced separately.

1. Place the ignition switch in the "Off" or "Unlocked" position.

2. Remove the rebound bumper.

3. Raise the vehicle on a hoist so that the front suspension drops to the downward limit of its travel. Position jackstands beneath the front frame for extra support.

4. Remove the wheel and tire assembly.

5. Remove the caliper from its mounts and tie it up out of the way so that there is no strain on the flexible brake hose.

6. Remove the hub and rotor assembly, splash shield, lower shock absorber mounting nut, retainer and insulator.

7. Off-load the torsion bars by rotating the adjusting bolts counterclockwise.

8. Remove the upper and lower ball joint stud cotter pins and nuts. Using a ball joint press tool, slide the tool over the upper stud until the tool rests on the steering knuckle.

9. Then turn the threaded portion of the tool so that it locks snugly against the lower stud. Tighten the tool enough to load the lower ball joint stud, and then strike the steering knuckle arm with a hammer to loosen the stud. Under no circumstances should you attempt to force the stud from the knuckle using the tool

alone.

10. On all 1974 and later models, use a press to press the ball joint out of the lower control arm. On 1973 intermediates, unscrew the ball joint from the lower control arm.

Installation

All 1974 and later Models and 1973 Intermediates

1. On all 1974 and later models, use a press to press the new ball joint into the lower control arm. On 1973 intermediates, screw in the ball joint and tighten to 125 ft lbs.

2. Place a new seal over the ball joint (as necessary). Press the retainer portion of the seal down over the ball joint housing until it locks into position.

3. Insert the ball joint stud through the opening in the knuckle arm and install the stud retaining nuts. Tighten to 100 ft lbs on intermediates and 135 ft lbs on full-size. Install the cotter pins and lubricate the ball joint.

4. Load the torsion bar by rotating the adjusting bolt clockwise.

5. Install the shock absorber retaining nut, retainer and insulator,

splash shield, hub and rotor assembly, and brake caliper. Install the wheel and tire assembly.

6. Adjust the front wheel bearings.

7. Remove the jackstands and lower the car. Install the rebound bumper. Adjust the front suspension height and alignment.

Upper Ball Joint Replacement

1. Raise the vehicle by placing a floor jack under the lower control arm. Place the lifting point of the jack as close as possible to the wheel.

2. Remove the wheel, tire and drum as an assembly. On models with disc brakes, remove the tire and wheel, remove the disc brake pads, remove the disc brake caliper from the steering knuckle and position the caliper out of the way with the brake line attached. Remove the brake rotor from the steering knuckle.

3. Remove the nut that attaches the upper ball joint to the steering knuckle and, using a ball joint stud removal tool, loosen the ball joint stud from the steering knuckle.

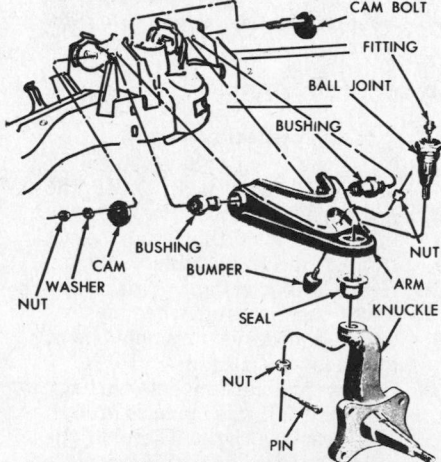

Upper control arm—Fury through 1973, Polara, and Monaco (© Chrysler Corp)

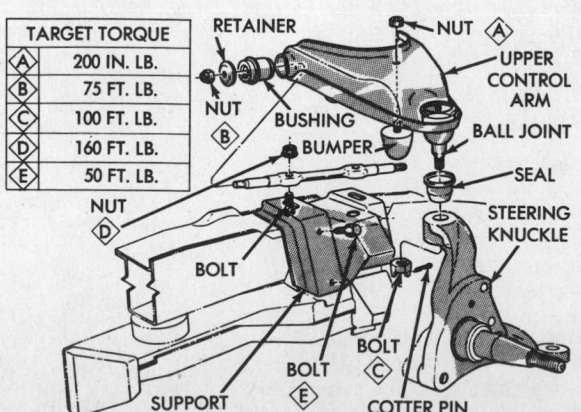

TARGET TORQUE	
Ⓐ	200 IN. LB.
Ⓑ	75 FT. LB.
Ⓒ	100 FT. LB.
Ⓓ	160 FT. LB.
Ⓔ	50 FT. LB.

1973 and later Satellite, Coronet, Charger, 1975 and later Fury upper control arm assemblies
(© Chrysler Corp)

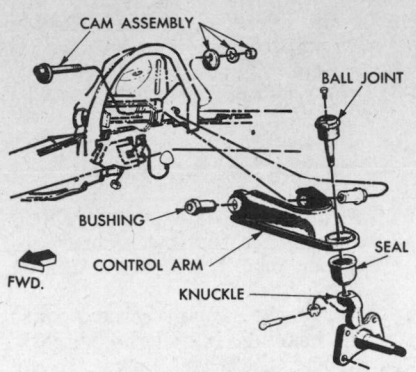

**Upper control arm Belvedere, Satellite, Coronet
and Charger through 1972**
(© Chrysler Corp)

4. Unscrew the upper ball joint from the upper control arm and remove it from the vehicle.
5. Position new ball joint on the upper control arm, screw the ball joint into the control arm until it bottoms on the control arm and tighten the ball joint to a minimum of 125 ft lbs.

NOTE: when installing a ball joint, make certain the ball joint threads engage those of the upper control arm squarely if the original control arm is being used.

6. Position a new seal on the ball joint stud and install the seal in the ball joint making sure the seal is fully seated on the ball joint housing.
7. Position ball joint stud in the steering knuckle and install the retaining nut. Tighten the nut to 100 ft lbs on intermediates and 135 ft lbs on full size.
8. Lubricate ball joint.
9. If equipped with disc brakes, install the rotor, caliper and brake pads. Install the tire and wheel.
10. Lower the vehicle and adjust front suspension height and alignment.

Front Suspension Height Adjustment

Through 1974

1. Check to make sure that the vehicle is fully loaded with fuel, that the tire pressures are correct, and that the vehicle is positioned on a level floor.

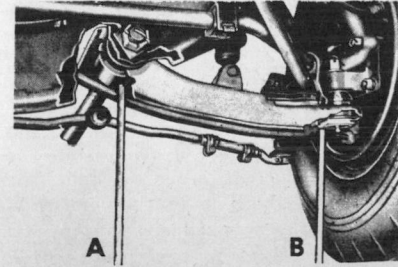

**Checking front suspension height at ball joint
and lower control arm, through 1974**
(© Chrysler Corp)

2. Clean road dirt from the bottom of the steering knuckle arm assemblies. Clean the lowest area of the height-adjusting blades directly below the center of the lower control arm inner pivot assembly.
3. Bounce vehicle at least five times and release on a downward motion.
4. Check the distance from the bottom of one adjusting blade to the floor (refer to illustration measurement A) and from the lowest point of the steering knuckle arm at the centerline on the same side of the vehicle (measurement B). Be sure to measure only one side at a time.
5. The difference in measurement between A and B is the front suspension height.
6. Refer to the specifications and make adjustments as necessary. Do this by rotating the torsion bar adjusting bolt clockwise to increase the height and counterclockwise to decrease the height. After each adjustment, bounce the vehicle as was done previously before checking the height. Both sides must be measured even though only one side may have been adjusted. Be sure that height does not vary more than 1/8 in. from side to side.

1975 and Later

1. Jounce the car several times, releasing it on the downward motion.
2. Measure the distance between the lowest point of the lower control arm torsion bar anchor (at a point one inch forward of the rear face of the anchor) and the ground. This is measurement "A".
3. Compare measurement "A" with the figure given under "Front End Height" in the "wheel Alignment Specifications" chart at the beginning of this car section.
4. Adjust, if necessary, by rotating the torsion bar adjusting bolt clockwise to increase front end height, or rotating counterclockwise to decrease the height.
5. Check the adjustment on both sides. Maximum variation of front end height is 1/8 in.

Torsion Bar Removal and Installation

NOTE: Torsion bars are not interchangable side-for-side. Do not mix them.

1. Remove the upper control arm rebound bumper (if so equipped).
2. If the vehicle is jacked on a hoist, be sure that it is lifted on

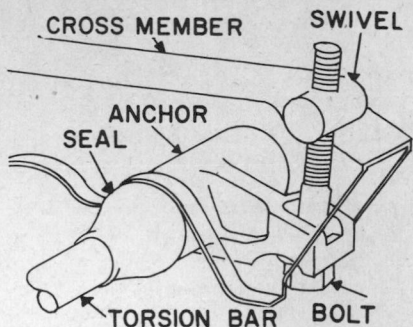

Torsion bar adjustment bolt
(© Chrysler Corp)

the body in such a manner that the front suspension is under no load. If the vehicle is to be lifted with a floor jack, at the center crossmember, first place a support between the jack and the crossmember. The front suspension must be under no load.

3. Remove all load from the torsion bars by rotating the anchor adjusting bolts counterclockwise.
4. At the torsion bar rear anchor, remove the lockring. Remove the automatic transmission torque shaft on 1974 and later models, if necessary.
5. Remove the torsion bar from its mounts. A special tool is available for this job; it clamps to the bar and provides a striking surface for driving the bar out.

Caution The torsion bar may be under some load so be careful when removing it. Heat must never be used to ease bar removal.

6. It may be necessary to move the rear balloon seal out of the way to ease removal of the torsion bar. Slide the torsion out through the rear of the anchor. Be careful not to damage the balloon seal.
7. Inspect the torsion bar and lightly dress all sharp edges. Coat the area of repair with a rust preventive. Clean the bar and lubricate it lightly to ease installation.
8. To begin replacement, slide the torsion bar into the rear anchor. Slide the balloon seal over the bar with the cupped end toward the rear of the bar.
9. Lightly grease the hex ends of the bar. Insert the torsion bar through the hex opening of the lower control arm. Replace the lockring in the rear anchor.
10. Fully pack the ring opening in the rear anchor with grease.
11. Install the balloon seal on the rear anchor so the seal lip engages with the anchor groove.
12. Rotate the adjusting bolt clockwise to load the torsion bar. Lower the vehicle and adjust the front suspension height. Replace

the upper control arm rebound bumper.

Lower Control Arm and Steering Knuckle Removal and Installation

Intermediates through 1972, Full size through 1973

1. Raise the car and support it under the frame; let the suspension hang down. Remove the wheel/tire and drum (or disc) as an assembly.
2. Remove the shock absorber at the bottom attachment and swing it up out of the way. Remove the torsion bar from its attachment at the lower control arm after releasing its tension.
3. Using a puller, remove the tie rod end from the steering knuckle arm. Be careful not to damage the seal during this operation. At this point, it is a good idea to match-mark the wheel alignment cam to act as an aid in assembly.
4. Remove the sway bar link from the lower control arm (or strut attaching straps). Remove the knuckle arm-to-brake support bolts and remove the knuckle arm. Position the brake support assembly to one side.
5. With a puller, remove the ball joint stud from the lower control arm. Be sure not to damage the seal during this operation.
6. At the forward end of the crossmember, remove the strut spring, pin, nut, and retainer, taking note of their relative positions. Remove the nut and washer from the lower control arm shaft.
7. Using a non-metallic object, tap the end of the lower control arm shaft to aid in shaft removal from the crossmember. Take off the lower control arm, strut, and shaft as an assembly.
8. To begin installation (on some models), insert a new strut bushing into the crossmember with a twisting motion. Use water as a lubricant to aid installation—grease or oil must not be used. Position the strut bushing inner retainer on the strut and install the control arm, strut, and shaft assembly. Replace the shaft bushing retainer and finger-tighten the nut.
9. Replace the lower control arm shaft washer and finger-tighten the nut.
10. Replace the lower ball joint stud into the lower control arm and torque it to 85 ft lbs on intermediates and 100 ft lbs on full size. Install the cotter pin.
11. Install the brake support to the

steering knuckle and replace the two upper bolts with nuts. Finger-tighten them only.
12. Install the steering knuckle on the steering knuckle arm and insert the two lower bolts with nuts. Torque the upper bolts to 55 ft lbs and the lower bolts to 120 ft lbs. Inspect the tie rod end seal and replace it if necessary. Install the tie rod end to the steering knuckle arm and torque it to 40 ft lbs. At this point, install the cotter pin.
13. Connect the shock absorber and finger-tighten it.
14. Replace the torsion bar assembly.
15. Install the wheel/tire/brake assembly.
16. Lower the vehicle. Adjust the front suspension height. Torque the strut nut at the crossmember of 52 ft lbs and insert the strut pin. Torque the lower control arm shaft nut to 145 ft lbs on intermediates and 185 ft lbs on full size and complete the installation of the shock absorber.
17. Align the front end.

1973 and Later Intermediates, 1974 and Later Full Size

1. Remove the rebound bumper from the lower control arm.
2. Raise and support the car so that the front suspension hangs down.
3. Remove the wheel and brake caliper. Don't let the caliper hang by the brake line.
4. Remove the hub and brake disc, splash shield, and the lower shock absorber mount.
5. Remove the two strut bar attaching bolts.
6. Remove the automatic transmission gearshift torque shaft on intermediates, if it interferes.
7. Measure and record the torsion bar anchor bolt depth into the lower control arm and release the bar tension.
8. Remove the torsion bar as described earlier.
9. Use a ball joint removal tool to separate the lower ball joint stud from the steering knuckle.
10. Remove the lower control arm shaft nut from the control arm shaft and push the shaft out from the frame cross-member. Tap the threaded end of the shaft with a soft hammer to loosen it.
11. Remove the lower control arm and shaft as an assembly.
12. On installation, position the control arm and shaft in the crossmember. Install the shaft nut finger tight.
13. Install the lower ball joint stud into the steering knuckle and tighten the nut to 100 ft lbs on intermediates and 135 ft lbs on full size. Install a new cotter pin.

14. Install the torsion bar. Tighten the adjusting bolt to its original position.
15. Replace the gearshift torque shaft.
16. Replace the strut bar on the control arm and tighten the bolts to 95 ft lbs.
17. Attach the brake splash shield and replace the lower shock absorber mount, but don't tighten it yet.
18. Attach the hub and rotor. Adjust the bearing. Install the caliper.
19. Replace the wheel. Lower the car to the floor and tighten the lower shock mount. Adjust the suspension height and wheel alignment. Tighten the control arm pivot shaft nut to 145 ft lbs on intermediates and 190 ft lbs on full size.

Wheel Bearing Adjustment

1. The wheel must be rotated while the bearing adjusting nut is tightened. Models through 1972 should be adjusted to 90 in. lbs, and 1973 and later models to 240-300 in. lbs.
2. Place the lock over the nut so that one pair of slots align with the cotter pin hole.
3. On models through 1972, back the nut and lock assembly off one slot. On 1973 and later models, loosen the nut and tighten it finger tight. Install the cotter pin. This adjustment should yield zero to .003 in. end-play.
4. Clean the grease cap. Coat, but do not fill, the cap with grease. Install it on the hub.
5. Lower car and road test.

REAR SUSPENSION

Shock Absorber Removal and Installation

1. Jack up the vehicle under the axle assembly in such a manner as to relieve the load from the shock absorbers.
2. Remove the nut attaching the shock to the spring mounting plate stud.
3. At the upper mount, remove shock attaching bolt and the shock.
4. Purge the new shock of air by repeatedly extending it in its normal position and compressing it while inverted. To install the shock, position it so that the upper bolt may be inserted. Hand-tighten the bolt.
5. Align the shock with the spring mounting plate stud and install the bolt and nut. Hand-tighten only.

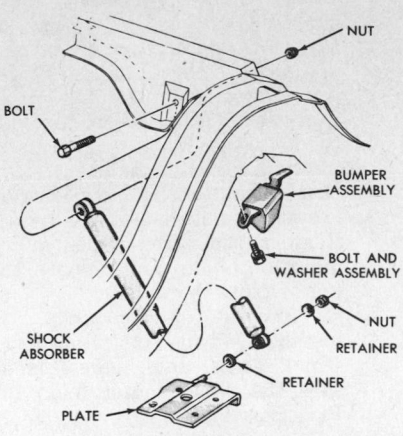

Rear shock absorber installation—Satellite, Coronet, Charger, 1975 and later Fury

6. Lower the vehicle to the ground. Torque the lower nut to 50 ft lbs and the upper nut to 70 ft lbs.

Spring Removal and Installation

1. Jack up the vehicle and remove the wheels. Position jack stands under the axle to relieve the weight on the rear springs.
2. Disconnect the rear shock absorbers at the bottom attaching bolts. Lower the axle assembly to allow the rear springs to hang free.
3. Remove the U-bolt nuts and withdraw the bolts and spring plates. Remove the nuts securing the front spring hanger to the body mounting bracket.

Caution *1974 and later full-size models have pre-loaded rear springs. A special spring stretcher (tool no. C-4211) must be installed before releasing either end of the spring. Do not try to remove the spring without the stretcher; its sudden release could cause serious injury.*

4. Remove the rear spring hanger bolts and allow the spring to drop enough to allow the front spring hanger bolts to be removed.
5. Remove the front pivot bolt from the front spring hanger.
6. Remove the shackle nuts and remove the shackle from the rear spring.
7. To begin installation, assemble the shackle and bushings in the rear of the spring and hanger. Start the shackle bolt nuts. Do not lubricate the rubber bushings to ease installation. Do not tighten the bolt nut.
8. Install the front spring hanger to the front spring eye and insert the pivot bolt and nut. Do not tighten them.
9. Install the rear spring hanger to the body bracket and torque the bolts to 30 ft lbs.

10. With the aid of a helper, raise the spring and insert the bolts in the spring hanger mounting bracket holes. Install the nuts and torque them to 30 ft lbs.
11. Position the axle assembly so it is correctly aligned with the spring center bolt.
12. Position the center bolt over the lower spring plate. Insert the U-bolt and nut. Torque the bolt to 45 ft lbs and connect the shock absorbers.
13. Lower the vehicle. Torque the pivot bolts to 125 ft lbs. Torque the shackle nuts to 40 ft lbs.
14. After this operation, drive the vehicle, check the front suspension height, and make adjustments as necessary.

BRAKES

Information on brake adjustments, lining replacement, disc brakes, bleeding procedure, master and wheel cylinder overhaul can be found in the Unit Repair Section.

Master Cylinder Removal and Installation

Power Brake Booster Removal and Installation

Parking Brake Adjustment

These procedures are covered for all Chrysler Corporation cars in the Barracuda, Challenger, Dart, Valiant, Aspen, Volare car section.

STEERING

A worm and recirculating ball-type steering gear is used with the manual steering system.

Constant-Control power steering is an option or standard on all models. Hydraulic power is provided by a belt-driven pump.

Some power steering pumps were equipped by the factory with oil coolers. These were used on vehicles with high-performance engines and/or special axle ratios. Steering service procedures for all Chrysler Corporation cars are given in the Barracuda, Challenger, Dart, Valiant, Aspen, Volare car section.

INSTRUMENT PANEL

Headlight Switch Replacement
1970 Belvedere, Satellite and Coronet; 1970-71 Fury, Polara and Monaco

1. Disconnect the battery ground cable. Disconnect the multiple connector from the rear of the headlight switch. On models with air conditioning, it may be necessary to disconnect the ducts to gain access to the wiring.
2. Remove the two screws that attach the headlight switch to the dash and remove the headlight switch from the vehicle.
3. Reverse above procedure to install.

1970 Charger

1. Disconnect the negative battery cable.
2. Remove the instrument cluster. See "Instrument Cluster Removal and Replacement."
3. Disconnect the wiring connector from the rear of the headlight switch.
4. Disconnect the two vacuum hoses from the heater switch to gain access to the headlight switch mounting screws.
5. Remove the headlight switch mounting screws and remove the switch.
6. Reverse the above procedure to install the new switch.

1971-74 Coronet, Charger, Satellite; 1972-73 Fury, Polara, Monaco

1. Disconnect the negative battery cable.
2. On cars equipped with air conditioning, disconnect the air duct from the spot cooler on the instrument panel.
3. Reach up under the instrument panel and depress the headlight switch control knob release button on the headlight switch.
4. While depressing the release button, pull the headlight switch control knob and shaft from the front of the instrument panel.
5. Disconnect the electrical leads from the rear of the switch.
6. Using a spanner wrench, remove the spanner nut that attaches the front of the headlight switch to the front of the instrument panel.
7. Remove the headlight switch from the rear of the instrument panel.
8. Reverse the above procedure to install the new switch.

1975 and Later Coronet, Charger, Fury

1. Disconnect the battery ground cable. Remove the instrument cluster upper bezel by removing the screws and pulling out at the top.
2. Remove the escutcheon mounting screw.
3. Remove the screws holding the

switch mounting plate to the cluster housing.

4. Pull the switch assembly from the cluster housing and disconnect the wires.

5. Depress the switch stem release button and pull the knob and stem from the switch.

6. Remove the switch mounting nut and remove the switch from the plate.

7. Reverse the procedure for installation.

1974 and Later Monaco, Gran Fury

1. Disconnect the battery ground cable. Remove the instrument cluster bezel by placing the automatic transmission level in 1 position, removing the ashtray and lighter, removing the screws under the lower bezel edge, pulling the top out, and disengaging the locking tabs.

2. Remove the wiper/washer switch mounting screws.

3. Pull the switch and mounting plate out and disconnect the wires.

4. Pull the switch to the on position and depress the release button on the side of the switch. Pull the knob and stem out.

5. Remove the escutcheon plate screw and remove the escutcheon. Remove the mounting plate nut and the switch.

6. Reverse the procedure for installation.

WINDSHIELD WIPERS

Motor Removal and Installation

1970 Fury, Polara and Monaco

1. Remove the windshield wiper arm and blade assemblies. Insert a 0.090 in. pin in the hole in the base of the wiper arm to release the assemblies from the pivots.

2. Remove the windshield lower moulding.

3. Remove the cowl grille.

4. Remove the nut that attaches the wiper link to the wiper motor drive pin or crank and disconnect the link from the motor.

5. Disconnect the wiper motor wiring at the multiple connector.

6. Remove the nuts that attach the wiper motor to the cowl panel and remove the motor through the cowl grille opening.

1970 Belvedere, Satellite, Coronet, Charger; All 1971-75 with Non-Concealed Wipers

1. Disconnect the negative battery cable.

2. Disconnect the wiper motor wiring at the multiple connector.

3. On models without air conditioning, working under the dash, remove the nut that attaches the drive link to the wiper motor and disconnect the drive link from the motor. Remove the nuts that attach the wiper motor to the studs in the cowl panel and remove the motor from the vehicle.

4. Remove the wiper motor mounting nuts. Work the motor off the mounting studs far enough to gain access to the nut that attaches the drive link to the wiper motor. *Do not force or pry the wiper motor off the mounting studs as this could damage the wiper drive link.* Using a ½ in. open end wrench, remove the motor crank arm nut. Remove the arm from the wiper motor and remove the motor from the vehicle.

1971-75 with Concealed Wipers, All 1976 and later

1. Disconnect the negative battery cable.

2. Lift the latch on each wiper arm and remove the arms and blades as an assembly.

3. Remove the cowl screen.

4. Remove the drive crank retaining nut and drive crank.

5. Disconnect the lead wires from the wiper motor.

6. Remove the three wiper motor mounting bolts and remove the motor from the vehicle.

7. Reverse the above procedure to install. When installing the wiper arms and blades, make sure the wiper motor is in the Park position.

RADIO

Removal and Installation

1970 Charger

1. Disconnect battery.

2. Remove radio finish plate.

3. On air conditioned vehicles, remove lower center air duct, left air duct, and upper center duct.

4. Remove radio mounting bracket.

5. Remove two screws mounting radio to front of instrument panel.

6. Disconnect antenna and speaker leads.

7. Remove radio from under panel. Reverse procedure to install.

1970 Coronet, Belvedere, and Satellite

1. Disconnect battery.

2. Remove radio upper trim panel.

3. Remove radio finish plate.

4. Remove radio rear mounting nut from mounting bracket.

5. Disconnect electrical wiring and antenna lead.

6. Remove two mounting screws from front of instrument panel.

7. Remove radio from instrument panel.

1970 Polara and Monaco

1. Disconnect battery.

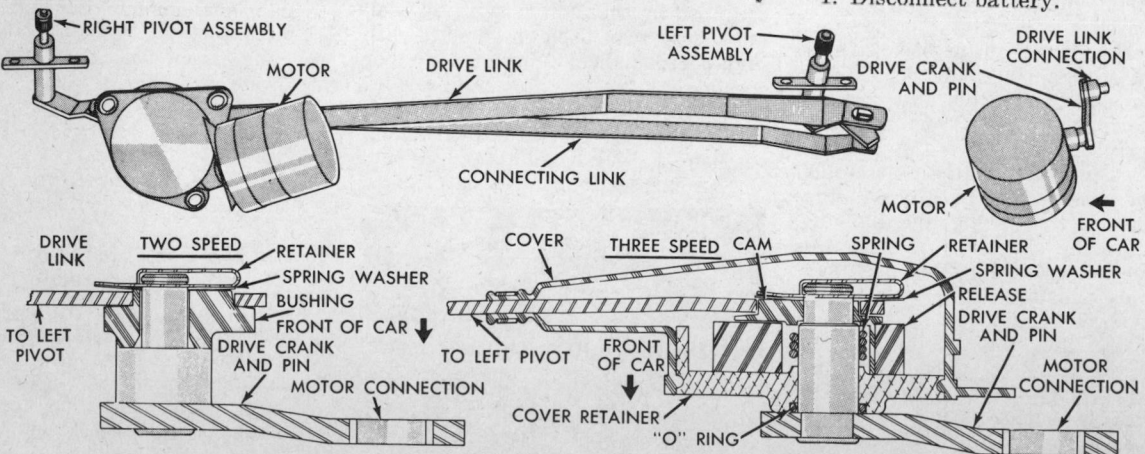

Windshield wiper system—Fury, Polara and Monaco (© Chrysler Corp)

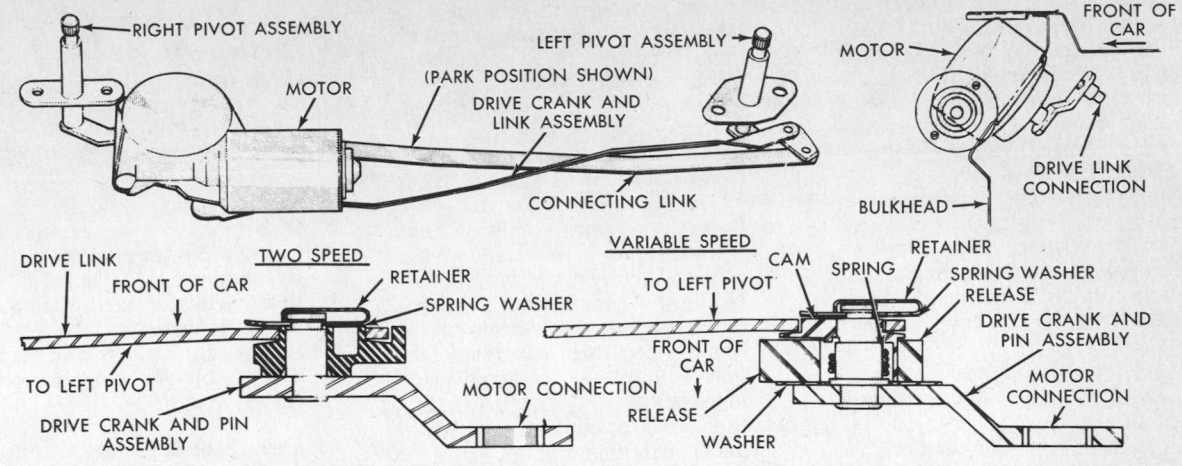

Windshield wiper system—Satellite, Belvedere, Coronet and Charger (© Chrysler Corp)

2. Remove automatic temperature control, if so equipped.
3. Remove radio bezel.
4. Remove two radio mounting bolts at front of instrument panel.
5. Remove air conditioner duct, if so equipped.
6. Disconnect electrical leads and antenna lead.
7. Loosen radio mounting bracket stud nut and slide radio and stud towards front of car from mounting bracket.
8. Carefully remove radio from under panel to avoid damaging electrical leads from main harness or automatic temperature control aspirator tube. Reverse procedure to install.

Fury through 1973; 1971-73 Polara, Monaco

1. Disconnect battery.
2. Remove nine lamp panel mounting screws, lower lamp panel assembly slightly, disconnect lamp harness from main harness, and remove lamp panel from instrument panel.
3. Remove steering column cover.
4. Remove radio trim bezel mounting screws and bezel.
5. Remove center lower air conditioner duct, if so equipped.
6. Disconnect electrical leads and antenna lead at radio.
7. Remove radio support mounting bracket.
8. Remove two radio mounting bolts.
9. Move radio down through bottom of instrument panel carefully to avoid damage to vacuum hoses and electrical leads. Reverse procedure to install.

1974 and Later Monaco, Gran Fury

1. Disconnect the battery ground cable. Remove the instrument cluster bezel by placing the auto-matic transmission lever in 1 position, removing the ashtray and lighter, removing the screws under the lower bezel edge, pulling the top out, and disengaging the locking tabs.
2. Remove the sub bezel by removing the nylon attaching pins with pliers.
3. Remove the lamp assembly from the front of the monaural radio.
4. Remove the radio to panel screws.
5. Remove the instrument panel upper cover, first pulling the rear edge up.
6. Disconnect the antenna and speaker wires. Remove the radio bracket mounting nut.
7. Pull the radio out and disconnect the wire.
8. Reverse the procedure for installation.

1971-73 Satellite, Coronet, Charger

1. Disconnect the negative battery cable.
2. Remove the ash tray (1971 models only).
3. Remove the radio control knobs and retaining nuts. Remove the rear radio support brackets.
4. Disconnect the lead wires from the radio and remove the radio from the vehicle.

1974 Satellite, Coronet, Charger

1. Disconnect the battery ground cable.
2. Remove the ashtray.
3. Remove the right radio mounting screw from the right cluster leg. You can reach the screw through the lower left corner of the ashtray housing.
4. Loosen the support bracket nut on the right side of the radio.
5. Pull the knobs off. Remove the mounting nuts from the panel.

6. Detach the antenna, speaker, and power wires.
7. Remove the radio. Reverse the procedure for installation.

1975 and Later Coronet, Charger, Fury

1. Disconnect the battery ground cable.
2. Remove the instrument cluster lower bezel by removing the right remote control mirror mounting nut, removing the mounting screws, and pulling it off.
3. Disconnect the power, speaker, and antenna leads.
4. Remove the nut holding the radio to the support bracket at the rear. On tape player/radios, it is at the side.
5. Remove the radio mounting screws from the front of the panel.
6. Remove the radio from the front of the panel. Reverse the procedure for installation.

HEATER

Heater Assembly Removal and Installation—Non Air-Conditioned Cars

1970 Belvedere, Satellite, Coronet, Charger

1. Drain radiator and disconnect battery. Remove the glove box.
2. On models equipped with a console, the console must be moved rearward before the heater assembly can be removed. From inside the console storage area, remove the two console mounting bolts and the two screws from the front sides of the console. Remove the two shift indicator bezel screws, move the transmission selector lever to the Drive position, and turn the bezel side-

ways and allow it to rest on the console. Remove the two screws from the rear of the gear selector mounting bracket and disconnect the back up light switch wiring. Remove the gear indicator light bulb, then move the console rearward.

3. Disconnect heater hoses at bulkhead. Plug hose fittings on heater to prevent spilling coolant on trim when removing heater.

4. From under instrument panel remove heater to cowl support bracket.

5. Remove defroster hoses and disconnect wiring from heater motor resistor.

6. Disconnect fresh air vent control and shut off door cables at heater from under instrument panel. Reaching through glove box, disconnect temperature control door cable.

7. From inside engine compartment, remove three nuts that mount heater to bulkhead.

8. Rotate heater assembly until mounting studs are up and carefully remove heater from under instrument panel.

9. Reverse procedure to install.

Polara, Monaco; Fury through 1974, 1975 and Later Gran Fury

NOTE: This is the removal procedure for the heater housing that attaches to the passenger compartment side of the firewall. Do not remove the part of the housing that attaches to the engine side of the firewall.

1. Disconnect battery and drain radiator.

2. Disconnect heater hoses at firewall. Plug hose fittings on heater to prevent spilling coolant.

3. Slide front seat back to allow room. Remove the instrument panel lower cover.

4. Disconnect radio antenna and upper level ventilator actuator vacuum line. Remove the screw holding the vent ducts to the heater housing, detach the bracket, and swing the ducts back.

5. Disconnect electrical conductors from blower motor resistor block on face of housing.

6. Remove vacuum hoses from trunk lock if so equipped.

7. Remove control cables from defroster door crank and heat shut off door crank.

8. Remove bottom retaining nut from support bracket and swing bracket up and out of way.

9. In engine compartment remove retaining nuts from studs.

10. Remove locating bolt from bottom center of passenger side housing.

11. Roll or tip housing out from under instrument panel.

12. Remove temperature control cable.

1971 and Later Satellite, Coronet, Charger; 1975 and Later Fury

1. Disconnect the negative battery cable.

2. Drain the cooling system.

3. Disconnect the heater hoses from the heater core tubes at the firewall. Plug the core tubes to prevent spilling coolant on the interior of the car.

4. Remove the three mounting nuts from the studs around the blower motor, the one nut from the heater housing near the center. On 1975 and later models, remove the lower instrument panel bezel, glove box, and glove box door.

5. Disconnect the antenna lead wire from the radio and position it out of the way.

6. Remove the screw that attaches the housing to the support rod for the plenum. It is located on the right-side of the housing above the outside air opening.

7. Disconnect the air door cables.

8. Disconnect the wires from the blower motor resistor.

9. Tip the heater assembly down and out.

Blower Motor Removal and Installation—Non Air-Conditioned Cars

Belvedere, Satellite, Coronet, Charger; 1975 and Later Fury

1. Remove heater assembly.

2. Disconnect wiring from blower motor to heater assembly.

3. Remove motor cooler tube.

4. Remove heater back plate assembly from heater.

5. Remove fan from motor shaft.

6. Remove blower motor from back plate.

Polara, Monaco; Fury through 1974, 1975 and later Gran Fury

The blower motor is mounted to the engine side housing under the right front fender, between the inner fender shield and the fender. The inner fender shield must be removed to service the blower motor.

1. Raise the hood and remove all brackets and clips that attach to the inner fender shield under the hood.

2. Raise the car on a hoist and remove the right front tire and wheel assembly.

3. From under the fender, remove the bolts that attach the inner fender shield to the fender.

4. Remove the fender shield from the vehicle.

5. Disconnect the blower motor wiring at the multiple connector.

6. Remove the nuts that attach the blower motor to the heater housing and remove the blower motor.

Heater Core Removal and Installation—Non Air-Conditioned Cars

1970 Belvedere, Satellite, Coronet and Charger

1. Remove the heater assembly.

2. Remove the heater cover plate.

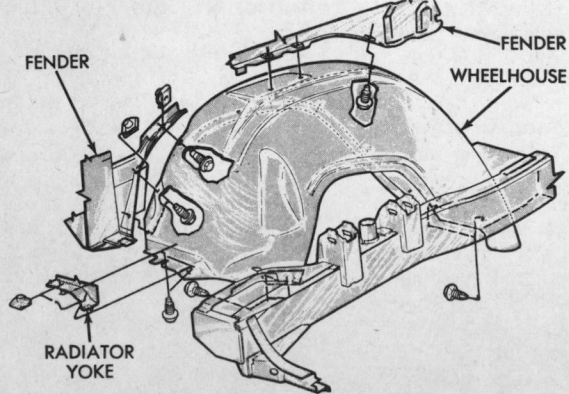

Inner fender shield attaching points—Fury through 1973, Polara, and Monaco
(© Chrysler Corp)

MOUNTING STUDS

Blower motor removal—Coronet, Belvedere, Charger, Satellite, 1975 and later Fury
(© Chrysler Corp)

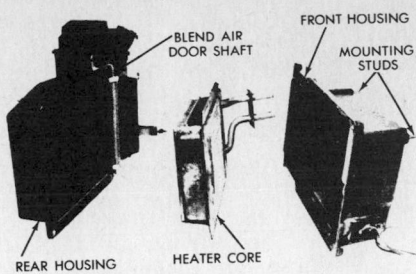

BLEND AIR
DOOR SHAFT

FRONT HOUSING

MOUNTING
STUDS

REAR HOUSING

HEATER CORE

Heater core removal—1974 and later Monaco,
1974 Fury, and 1975 and later Gran Fury

(© Chrysler Corp.)

3. Remove the screws that attach the heater core to the heater assembly and remove the core.

Polara, Monaco; Fury through 1974, 1975 and later Gran Fury

1. Remove the heater assembly.
2. Separate the housing.
3. Remove the heater core attaching screws.
4. Remove the heater core locating screw.
5. Carefully pull the heater core from the heater housing.

1971 and later Satellite, Coronet, Charger; 1975 and later Fury

1. Remove the heater assembly.
2. Remove the screws that attach the front cover to the heater housing.
3. Cut sponge rubber plenum-to-housing air seal in two places, where the front cover separates the cover from the housing.
4. Remove the one core tube retaining screw from behind the heater housing, between the heater core tubes.
5. Remove the sponge rubber gaskets from the heater core tubes. Remove the heater core from the heater housing.

Heater Core Removal and Installation—Air-conditioned Cars

1970 Charger, Coronet, Belvedere, Satellite

The heater core is positioned behind a separate cover attached to the evaporator case. It is located just forward of the instrument panel.

1. Disconnect the battery and drain the cooling system. Remove the air cleaner and disconnect the heater hoses.
2. Remove the distribution housing, glove box, and the heater core intake-outlet tube assembly.
3. Remove the fresh air intake hose. Disconnect the floor air actuator rod.
4. Disconnect the actuator vacuum hoses. Remove the fresh air door

housing assembly.
5. Remove the defroster hoses. Disconnect the resistor block and bypass switch electrical connections.
6. Extract the screws holding the water bypass valve to the heater cover. Remove the operating link attaching screw.
7. At its mounting bracket, disconnect the air conditioning door actuator and remove the supporting braces.
8. Remove the retainer spring clips and screws securing the cover to the case.
9. Pull the lower edge of the cover rearward; lift the assembly 3/8 in. This will release the cover lip from the case. Lower the assembly and remove it from the right side.
10. To begin the installation procedure, install the water bypass valve to the heater core (if it was removed). Be sure to use new O-rings on the intake and outlet tubes.
11. Place the heater core into the evaporator case. Install the cover by hooking the cover lip on the evaporator case and rolling it down into position. Replace the retainer spring clips and screws.
12. Install the water bypass valve to the heater cover. Connect the linkage to the air conditioning door.
13. Replace the air conditioning door actuator with its vacuum hoses. Be sure to replace the hose with the red stripe to the rod side. Install the two support braces.
14. Replace all electrical connections to the resistor block.
15. Connect the vacuum hoses to the floor air actuator and the fresh air recirculating actuator. Be sure the hose with the red stripe is facing the rod side. Replace the fresh air recirculating door housing. Connect the floor air actuator rod to its linkage.
16. Connect the fresh air recirculating air intake hose.
17. Replace the heater core intake-outlet tube assembly. Use a drop of water on the O-rings to ease installation. Replace the temperature control valve capillary tube in the heater core cover.
18. Open the air conditioning door about 1 in. Install the distribution housing.
19. Replace the flexible hoses to the instrument panel outlets.
20. Replace the glove box.
21. Connect the heater hoses and fill the cooling system with the proper amount and type of antifreeze.
22. Install the air cleaner and connect the battery. Test the operation of the heater.

Fury, Polara, Monaco through 1971

The air conditioning heater core is located in the front cover of the passenger side housing. To remove only the heater core, the air conditioning system need not be discharged.

1. Disconnect the battery and drain the cooling system. Disconnect the heater hoses and remove the air cleaner.
2. Plug the heater core tubes to prevent coolant loss when the core is removed.
3. Take off the steering column cover and remove the left spot cooler duct.
4. At the linkage on the left side of the housing, disconnect the two actuator rods. Remove the two cover retaining screws.
5. Remove the screws securing the heat duct in position and remove the duct. With the duct removed, the screws in the bottom of the front cover lip will be exposed. Remove them.
6. Remove the glove box. Remove the center spot cooler duct, the air distribution housing, and the right spot cooler duct.
7. Working in the glove box opening, remove the top retaining screws and the screws from the right side of the housing.
8. At the resistor block, disconnect all electrical connections. Disconnect the vacuum hoses from the recirculating housing actuator.
9. Take off the nut at the housing end of the cover support bracket. Swing the bracket upward and carefully roll the front cover and heater core outward. Remove it from under the instrument panel.
10. To begin installation, replace the heater core in the front cover. Position the core and cover on the evaporator housing. While holding the front cover in position, swing the support bracket downward over the stud on the front cover face. Install its retaining nut.
11. Working in the glove box opening, replace the top housing and right-side screws.
12. Working under the instrument panel, install the screws that retain the housing in position.
13. Replace the heat distribution duct to the housing bottom and connect the actuator rods.
14. Connect all the vacuum hoses to their actuators; install all electrical connections to the resistor block.
15. Through the glove box opening, install the air distribution housing, the center spot cooler duct, and the right spot cooler duct.
16. Replace the steering column

cover and the left spot cooler duct. Replace the glove box assembly.

17. From this point, reverse the removal procedure. Be sure to fill cooling system with proper type and amount of antifreeze.

1971-74 Satellite, Coronet, Charger

NOTE: this procedure requires evacuation of the refrigerant system which requires special tools and training.

1. Remove the air cleaner and disconnect the battery.
2. Drain the cooling system. Disconnect the heater hoses at the dash panel. Plug the core tubes to prevent spillage.
3. Discharge refrigerant from the system.
4. Disconnect the refrigerant lines at the dash panel (use two wrenches for this procedure). Leave the expansion valve attached to the line. Plug all refrigerant openings.
5. Disconnect the blower motor electrical connections. Remove the motor cooling tube and the blower motor.
6. Remove the glove box assembly.
7. Remove the left spot cooler duct and the air distribution housing.
8. Disconnect all wires from the blower motor resistor, and the antenna wire from the radio bottom.
9. Remove the radio.
10. Disconnect the vacuum harness from the control switch rear.
11. Remove the water valve cable from the bracket on the housing left end.
12. In the engine compartment, remove the nuts from the housing mounting studs.
13. Remove the rubber drain tube.
14. Remove the support bracket from the plenum-to-housing panel.
15. Remove the unit from beneath the instrument panel.
16. With the unit removed from the vehicle, remove the plenum air seal.
17. Remove the vacuum hose from the fresh air door actuator and

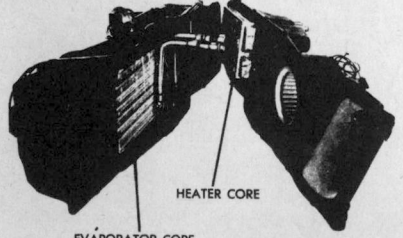

HEATER CORE

EVAPORATOR CORE

Evaporator and heater core mounting—1973 and later Satellite, Coronet, Charger, 1975 and later Fury (© Chrysler Corp)

bypass door actuator. Remove the air seal from the evaporator core tubes and heater.

18. Remove the 18 screws securing the front and rear covers; extract one screw from between the evaporator core tubes. Pull the housings apart.
19. Extract the three screws from the evaporator core access plate; remove the plate. With access now clear to the two evaporator core mounting screws, remove them. In addition, remove the four screws securing the evaporator core to the front cover; remove the core.
20. Carefully lift the left housing half seal from the rear cover. Do not remove the entire seal; the lower portion acts as a water seal.
21. Remove the two core retaining screws from the mounting plate. From the back of the rear cover, remove one screw from between the core tubes. Lift the heater core from the housing.
22. To begin assembly and installation, place the heat door in the up position. Place the heater core into the rear cover. Install its retaining screws.
23. Apply rubber cement to the bottom of the raised portion of the housing seal; carefully replace it in its original position over the heater core.
24. Insert the evaporator core into the front cover and replace its four securing screws.
25. Place the front and rear covers together. Make sure the cover seal is seated properly. Replace the 18 securing screws (and the screw between the evaporator core tubes at the back of the rear cover).
26. Replace the air seal over the heater and evaporator core tubes.
27. Connect all vacuum hoses to their respective actuators. Connect the hose with the red tracer to the actuator rod side.
28. Install the evaporator core access cover plate to the housing front and replace its three sheet metal screws.
29. Apply rubber cement to the plenum air seal and install it in position.
30. Position the housing up under the instrument panel. Connect the housing-to-plenum support bracket.
31. In the engine compartment, install four retaining nuts on the housing mounting studs; torque to 24 in. lbs.
32. Install the vacuum harness to the control switch rear. Install the water valve control cable in its retaining bracket.

33. Install the radio.
34. Install all blower motor resistor wiring. Plug the antenna lead into the radio bottom.
35. Replace the center outlet air distribution housing. Replace the left spot coller duct.
36. Replace the glove box.
37. Replace the blower motor and connect its wiring. Install the blower motor cooling tube and replace the evaporator drain tube.
38. Connect the refrigerant lines to the evaporator core tubes. Freely lubricate fittings and O-rings with refrigerant oil. Use two wrenches to avoid twisting the tubes.
39. Connect the heater hoses to the core tubes. Fill the cooling system.
40. Sweep the system. Evacuate the system. Charge the system and check for leaks.

1975 and Later Coronet, Charger, Fury

1. Remove the carburetor air cleaner.
2. Disconnect the battery ground cable.
3. Drain the coolant. Disconnect the heater hoses at the firewall. Plug the core tubes.
4. Discharge the air conditioning system.

NOTE: This procedure requires evacuation of the air conditioning system which requires special tools and training.

5. Disconnect the refrigerant line assembly at the H-valve. Cover the plumbing sealing plate. Remove the expansion valve attached to the evaporator and cover the evaporator sealing plate and both sealing surfaces of the expansion valve.
6. Disconnect the blower motor wires and remove the blower motor cooling tube.
7. Remove the glove box, the ashtray, and housing.
8. Remove the appearance shield and right lap cooler duct from the lower edge of the instrument panel.
9. Remove the right front passenger side cowl panel.
10. Remove the air distribution duct.
11. Remove the air conditioner mode door vacuum actuator from its mounting bracket and shift the actuator forward 90 degrees.
12. Remove the wiring from the seat belt interlock control unit and leave it hanging from the glove box opening.
13. Disconnect the blower motor resistor wires and the radio antenna wire.
14. Remove the radio.

15. Disconnect the vacuum housing from the extension to the control.
16. Remove the nuts from the housing mounting studs in the engine compartment.
17. Remove the rubber drain tube.
18. Adjust the front seat all the way back.
19. Remove the support bracket from the rear unit to the plenum.
20. Pull the unit back so that it clears the firewall. Rotate it out from under the instrument panel, right end first.
21. Remove the plenum air seal. Disconnect the inlet air door vacuum actuator hose. Remove the air seal from the heater and evaporator core tubes. Remove the clamps and screws holding the housing together and separate them.
22. Remove the three screws from the evaporator coil access plate and remove the plate for access to the two evaporator coil mounting screws. Remove the screws holding the evaporator coil to the front cover and remove the coil.
23. Carefully lift the left half of the housing seal from the rear cover; do not remove the entire seal.
24. Remove the two core retaining screws from the mounting plates and the one between the core tubes. Lift the core out of the housing.
25. Reverse the procedure for installation.

1972-73 Polara, Monaco, Fury

To remove only the heater core, it is not necessary to discharge the air conditioning system. The heater core is positioned in the rear housing of the passenger-side unit.

1. Disconnect the battery and drain the cooling system. Remove the air cleaner and disconnect the heater hoses. Plug the heater core tubes to prevent coolant loss when the core is removed.
2. Remove the steering column cover and remove the left spot cooler duct.
3. On the left side of the housing, remove the linkage shield and disconnect the actuator rods. Remove the screws from the housing left side.
4. Remove the screws holding the heat distribution duct and remove it. With duct removed, the screws in the bottom lip of the rear housing will become visible. Remove them.
5. Remove the glove box. In addition, remove the right spot cooler duct, the air distribution housing, and the center outlet duct.
6. Working in the glove box opening, remove the top retaining screws and the right-side hous-

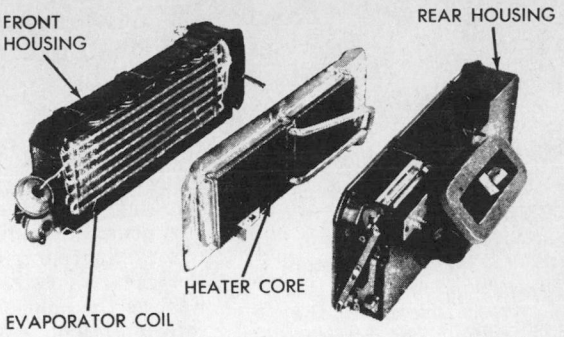

Heater and evaporator core—1972-73 Polara, Monaco and Fury
(© Chrysler Corp)

ing screws. If the vehicle is Auto-Temp equipped, remove the aspirator tube from the clip first and then remove the amplifier and master compressor switches. Now remove the right-side housing screws.
7. Disconnect all electrical connections at the resistor block. On Auto-Temp equipped vehicles, remove the wires from the two plastic straps and the metal clip.
8. Remove the nut from the housing end of the support bracket. Swing the bracket upward and out of the way. Carefully roll the housing out from under the instrument panel. The heater core may be removed by pulling it out from the top. Cut the adhesive along the bottom and sides with a knife to ease removal.
9. To begin installation, scrape all remaining sealer from the heater core flange and fit a new seal. Position the heater core in the rear housing and secure with a screw at either end. Place the front housing in position; hold the rear housing in place and swing the support bracket down. Secure it in position with its retaining nut.
10. Working in the glove box opening, install the top two housing screws and the screws at the right side of the rear housing.
11. From beneath the instrument panel, install the screws along the housing bottom and the screws at the left side of the rear housing. It is not necessary to reinstall the linkage shield.
12. Replace the heat distribution duct to the housing bottom.
13. Connect the actuator rods.
14. Working in the glove box opening, connect the resistor block wires. Tighten the support bracket nuts. On Auto-Temp equipped vehicles, fasten the wires with the plastic straps and metal clip. Install the aspirator tube in the clip.
15. Replace the center outlet duct. the air distribution housing, and

the right spot cooler duct.
16. Install the steering column cover, the left spot cooler duct, and the glove box assembly. On Auto-Temp equipped vehicles, install the amplifier and the master and compressor switches.
17. From this point, reverse the removal procedure. Be sure to fill the cooling system with the proper amount and type of antifreeze.

1974 and later Polara and Monaco, 1974 Fury, 1975 and later Gran Fury

NOTE: *This procedure requires evacuation of the refrigerant in the air conditioning system. Therefore, this operation should not be attempted by persons not having the special tools and training required to perform the job safely.*

1. Purge the system of refrigerant.
2. Disconnect the battery ground cable.
3. Remove the air cleaner and disconnect the heater hoses. Plug the core tubes.
4. Remove the 5/16" bolt in the center of the plumbing sealing plate.
5. Pull the refrigerant line assembly toward the front of the car.
6. Remove the two ¼-20 Allen screws and remove the "H" valve.
7. Slide the front seat back, out of the way. Remove lap cooler and lower instrument panel cover.

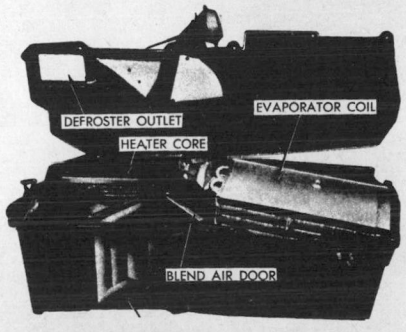

Evaporator and heater core mounting—1974 Fury, 1974 and later Polara, Monaco, and 1975 and later Gran Fury (© Chrysler Corp)

8. Remove the A/C distribution duct.
9. Unplug the antenna lead from the radio.
10. Disconnect wires and vacuum lines from unit.
11. Remove the drain tube. With automatic temperature control (ATC), remove electrical connections and vacuum connector from the servo. Disconnect the amplifier wires. Disconnect the wires and vacuum hoses from the master and compressor switches. Disconnect the aspirator tube.
12. Remove the temperature control cable from the clip on the unit.
13. Remove the retaining nut from the support bracket.
14. Remove the six retaining nuts from the studs in the engine compartment.
15. Remove the housing from under the instrument panel, and place on a work table.
16. Remove the mode door and the blend air door levers from the shaft. Remove the screws and lift off the top cover.
17. Remove the 4 retaining screws and the 3 screws for the core tube seal. Lift out the core.
18. Reverse the procedure to install.

Blower Motor Removal and Installation—Air-Conditioned Cars

Coronet, Charger, and Belvedere, Satellite and 1975 and later Fury

1. Working inside the engine compartment, disconnect the feed wire and ground wire. Remove the air tube (if so equipped).
2. Remove the mounting screws located on the outer surface of the mounting plate.
3. Remove the mounting plate, blower motor, and fan as an assembly.
4. To install motor, if the motor was removed from its mounting plate, be sure mounting grommets are installed at the attaching bolts. In addition, be sure the blower wheel is free and does not rub.
5. Install the blower motor assembly to the evaporator casing with the air tube opening toward the bottom. Install its retaining screws.
6. Install the air tube, ground, and feed wires.
7. Check blower motor operation.

Fury through 1974, 1972 and later Polara, Monaco, and 1975 and later Gran Fury

The blower motor is located under the right front fender between the inner fender shield and the fender. Remove the inner fender shield to provide access to the blower motor. Service consists of removing its electrical leads and attaching screws. The blower motor is not repaired; replace if defective.

SEAT BELTS

Disabling the Interlock System

Since the regulation requiring the interlock system was done away with during the 1975 model year, this device may now be legally disabled. All dealers have received a service bulletin on how to properly accomplish this modification for customers requesting it. It involves disconnecting the buzzer wire (you could easily do this yourself) and making some internal wiring changes to the printed circuit board in the interlock module (the bulletin recommends that this be done by a radio repair shop).

NOTE: *Although the interlock can be disabled by disconnecting the seat sensor wires at the connectors under the seat, this is not the proper method, since it also disables the seat belt warning light. The seat belt warning light is still required.*

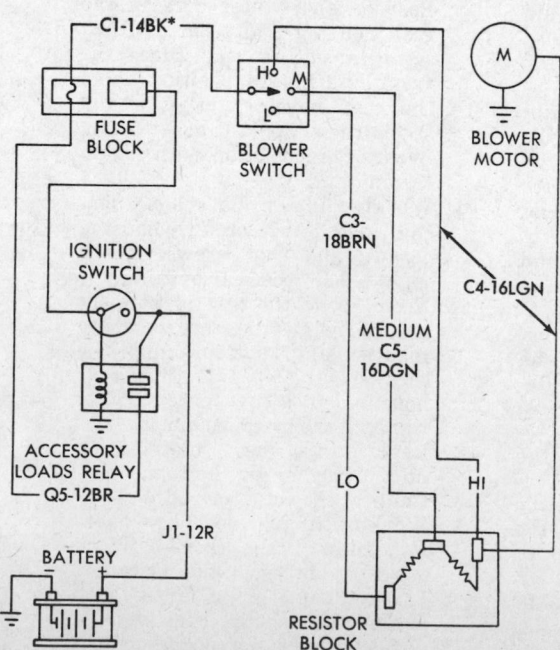

1976 Intermediate-size car heater control circuit (© Chrysler Corp.)

Ford · Mercury · Thunderbird

Automatic Transmission
in car service **C577**
C4 Band adjustment C578
C6 Band adjustment C578
FMX, MX, and CW Band adjustment C578
Shift linkage adjustment C577
Neutral start switch adjustment C577
Pan Removal and Installation,
fluid change C578
Throttle linkage adjustment C578

Brakes **C585, U299**
Brake vacuum booster Removal and
Installation C587
Hydro-boost Accumulator Removal
and Installation C587
Master cylinder Removal and
Installation C585
Parking brake adjustment C587

Charging System **C561, U2**
Alternator Removal and Installation C561
Regulator Removal and Installation C561

Clutch **C576**
Clutch pedal adjustment C576
Clutch and/or transmission
Removal and Installation C576

Cooling System **C565, U367**
Radiator Removal and Installation C565
Water pump Removal and Installation ... C565
Thermostat Removal and Installation ... C565

Emission Controls **C565, U145**

Engine **C568, U194**
CYLINDER HEAD C573
ENGINE REMOVAL AND INSTALLATION ... C568
6 Cylinder head Removal and
Installation C573
V8 Head Removal and Installation C573
LUBRICATION C575
Oil pan removal C575
Oil pump Removal and Installation ... C575
Rear main bearing oil seal C576
MANIFOLDS C570
Intake and exhaust manifold—
6 cylinder C570
Exhaust manifold removal V8 .... C571
Intake manifold removal—V8 .... C571
Piston and Rod Alignment C575
TIMING CASE C574
6 Cylinder timing gear and/or
camshaft Removal and Installation ... C574

6 Cylinder timing gear cover removal ... C574
Timing case oil seal replacement C575
V8 camshaft replacement C575
V8 cover and chain replacement C574
VALVE SYSTEM C571
Preliminary valve adjustment C571
Valve guides C572

Front Suspension **C581, U292**
Coil spring and lower control arm
Removal and Installation C581
Lower ball joint inspection,
Removal and Installation C582
Shock absorber Removal and
Installation C581
Upper ball joint inspection,
Removal and Installation C584
Upper control arm Removal and
Installation C584
Wheel bearing adjustment C584

Fuel System **C563, U50**
Carburetor C563
Dashpot adjustment C565
Fuel filter Removal and Installation ... C563
Fuel mixture adjustment C564
Fuel pump Removal and Installation ... C563
Idle speed adjustment C563

Heater **C591**
VEHICLES WITH AIR-CONDITIONING C591
Blower motor Removal and
Installation C591
Heater core Removal and Installation ... C591
VEHICLES WITHOUT AIR-CONDITIONING ... C592
Blower motor Removal and Installation ... C592
Heater core Removal and Installation ... C592

Ignition System **C562, U34**
Contact point replacement
and adjustment C562
Distributor Removal and Installation ... C562
Ignition retiming C562
Electronic ignition tachometer
connection C562
Firing Order C551
Ignition timing C563
Solid state ignition C562

Instrument Panel **C589, U350**
Headlight switch Removal and
Installation C589

Jacking, Hoisting **C580**

Manual Transmission **C577, U231**
Shift linkage adjustment C577
Lock rod adjustment C577
Transmission Removal and Installation ... C577

Radio **C590**
Removal and Installation C590

Rear Axle **C580, U285**
Axle shaft, bearing and seal
Removal and Installation C580

Rear Suspension **C584**
Shock absorber replacement C585
Spring Removal and Installation C585

Seat Belts **C592**
Disabling the seat belt/starter
interlock C592

Specifications **C550, U359**
Capacities C556
Crankshaft and Connecting Rod C559
Engine Identification C551
General Engine C552
Piston C560
Ring C560
Serial Number Location C551
Torque C559
Transmission Identification C552
Tune-up C553
Valve C558
Wheel Alignment C561
Year Identification C550

Starting System **C562, U2**
Starter Removal and Installation C562

Steering **C587, U328**
Ignition lock cylinder replacement C589
Ignition switch replacement C589
Power Steering Pump Removal and
Installation C587
Steering wheel Removal and
Installation C588
Turn signal switch Removal and
Installation C588

U-Joints **C579**
Double cardan U-Joint Removal and
Installation C579
Front joint removal C579
Rear joint removal C579

Windshield Wipers **C590**
Motor Removal and Installation C590

YEAR IDENTIFICATION

FORD

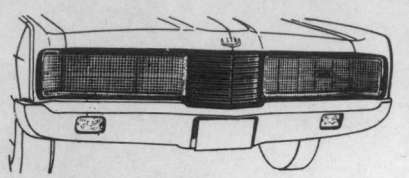

1970 LTD

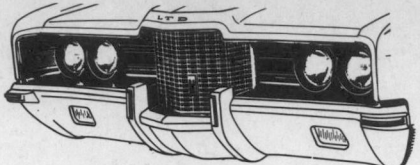

1971 LTD

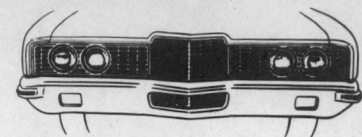

1972 Galaxie

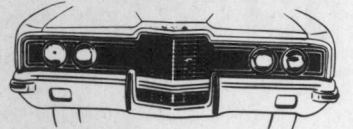

1972 LTD

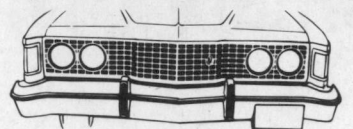

1973 Galaxie

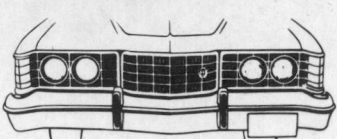

1973 LTD

1974 LTD

1975 Ford LTD Landau

1976 LTD

1977 LTD

THUNDERBIRD

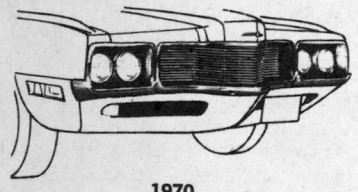

1970

1972

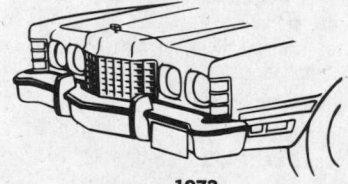

1973

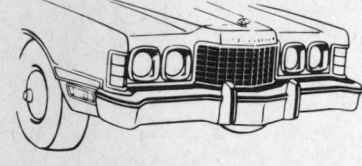

1974

1975

1976

MERCURY

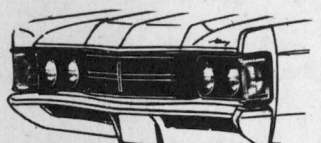

1970 Monterey

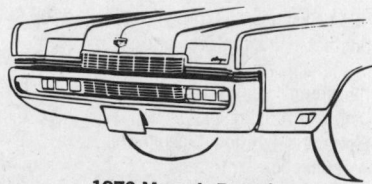

1970 Marquis Brougham

1971 Mercury

1972 Monterey

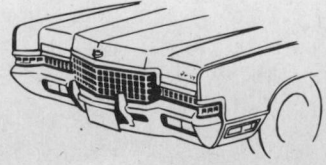

1972 Marquis

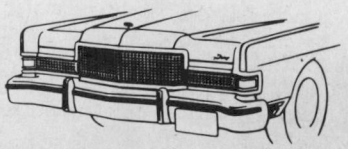

1973 Marquis

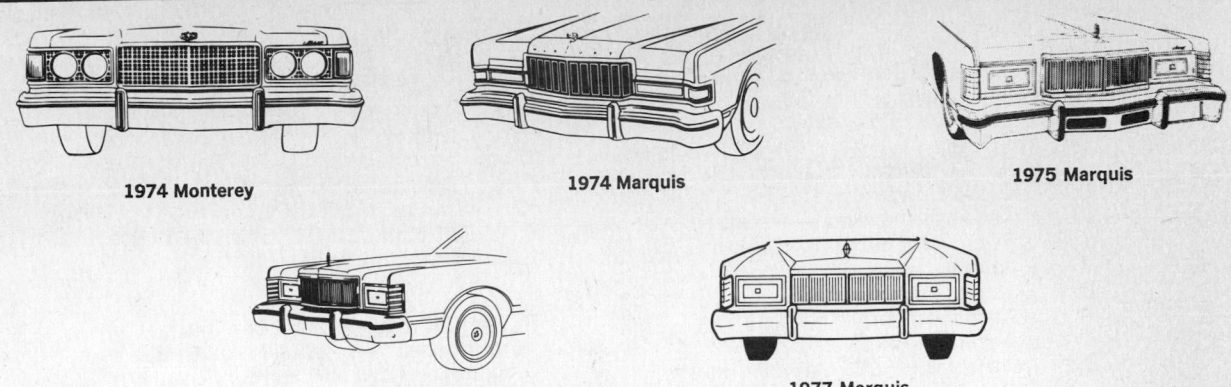

1974 Monterey   **1974 Marquis**   **1975 Marquis**

1976 Mercury   **1977 Marquis**

CAR SERIAL NUMBER

The car serial number is composed of eleven digits. The first digit, the production year code is the last digit of the model year in which the vehicle was produced. The fifth digit, a letter, represents the engine identification code.

The serial number can be found on a plate attached to the top of the instrument panel, visible through the windshield.

FIRING ORDER

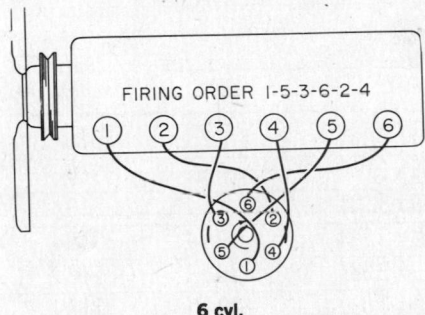

6 cyl.

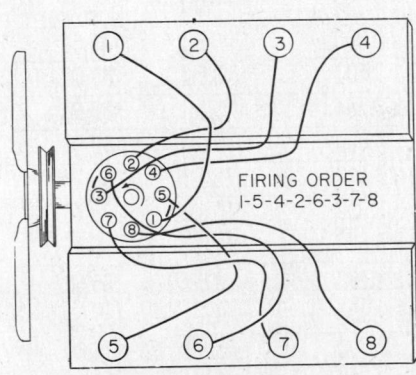

V8 except 351, 400 cu. in.

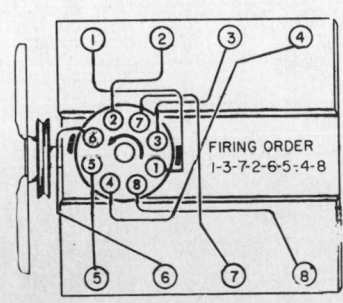

351, 400 cu. in. V8

ENGINE CODE

The engine code designation is the 5th digit of the vehicle identification number (V.I.N.). The V.I.N. is stamped on a plate located at the left side of the instrument panel, visible through the windshield.

Disp (Cu in.)	Carb no. bbls	Hp*	'70	'71	'72	'73	'74	'75	'76	'77
6-Cylinder Models										
240	1	103			V					
240	1	140		V						
240	1	150	V							
8-Cylinder Models										
302	2	140			F					
302	2	210	F	F						
351 W	2	153, 162			H	H	H			
351 C	2	163			H	H	H			
351 M	2	148, 150						H	H	H
351	2	240			H					
351	2	250	H					H		
390	2	255		Y						
390	2	265	Y							
390	2	270	Y							
400	2	144, 158, 170					S	S	S	S
400	2	172			S	S				
400	2	260		S						
428 PI	4	360	P							
429	4	208, 212			N	N				
429 PI	4	N.A.				P				
429	4	320	K	K						
429	4	360	N	N						
429 PI	4	370			P					
460	4	194, 195, 218, 220, 223, 224					A	A	A	A
460	4	200, 208, 212				A	A			
460 PI	4	226, 267, 274, 275				C	C	C	C	C

PI   Police Interceptor

* All 1972 and later horsepower ratings are SAE net figures. The figures vary when a given engine is installed in different models.

TRANSMISSION CODES

The transmission code is found on the vehicle certification label, on the driver's door.

Through 1971
1. Three speed manual
5. Four speed manual—wide ratio
6. Four speed manual—close ratio
W. Automatic C4
U. Automatic C6
X. Automatic FMX
Y. Automatic MX
Z. Automatic C6 special—Police and trailer towing

1972 and Later
W. Automatic C4
U. Automatic C6
X. Automatic FMX
#. Automatic CW
Y. Automatic FMX
Z. Automatic C6 Special—Police trailer towing

\# The CW transmission is a Warner unit used on 1973-74 400 cid equipped Ford and Mercury sedans with a 2.75:1 rear axle ratio only.

GENERAL ENGINE SPECIFICATIONS

Year	Engine No. Cyl. Displacement (cu in.)	Carburetor Type	Horsepower @ rpm ■	Torque @ rpm (ft lbs) ■	Bore X Stroke (in.)	Compression Ratio	Oil Pressure @ 2000 rpm
'70	6-240	1 bbl	150 @ 4000	234 @ 2200	4.000 x 3.180	9.2:1	35-60
	8-302	2 bbl	210 @ 4400	295 @ 2400	4.000 x 3.000	9.5:1	35-60
	8-351	2 bbl	250 @ 4600	355 @ 2600	4.000 x 3.500	9.5:1	35-60
	8-390	2 bbl	270 @ 4400	390 @ 2600	4.050 x 3.784	9.5:1	35-60
	8-428 PI	4 bbl	360 @ 5400	459 @ 3200	4.130 x 3.984	10.5:1	35-60
	8-429	2 bbl	320 @ 4400	460 @ 2200	4.360 x 3.590	10.5:1	35-60
	8-429	4 bbl	360 @ 4600	476 @ 2800	4.360 x 3.590	11.0:1	35-60
'71	6-240	1 bbl	140 @ 4000	230 @ 2200	4.000 x 3.180	8.9:1	35-60
	8-302	2 bbl	210 @ 4600	296 @ 2600	4.000 x 3.000	9.0:1	35-60
	8-351	2 bbl	240 @ 4600	350 @ 2600	4.000 x 3.500	8.9:1	35-60
	8-390	2 bbl	255 @ 4400	376 @ 2600	4.050 x 3.784	9.5:1	35-60
	8-400	2 bbl	260 @ 4400	400 @ 2200	4.000 x 4.000	9.0:1	50-70
	8-429	2 bbl	320 @ 4400	460 @ 2200	4.360 x 3.590	10.5:1	35-75
	8-429	4 bbl	360 @ 4600	480 @ 2800	4.360 x 3.590	10.5:1	35-75
	8-429 PI	4 bbl	370 @ 5400	450 @ 3400	4.360 x 3.590	11.0:1	35-75
'72	6-240	1 bbl	103 @ 3800	170 @ 2200	4.000 x 3.180	8.5:1	35-60
	8-302	2 bbl	140 @ 4000	239 @ 2000	4.000 x 3.000	8.5:1	35-60
	8-351 W	2 bbl	153 @ 3800	266 @ 2000	4.000 x 3.500	8.3:1	35-60
	8-351 C	2 bbl	163 @ 3800	277 @ 2000	4.000 x 3.500	8.6:1	35-60
	8-400	2 bbl	172 @ 4000	298 @ 2200	4.000 x 4.000	8.4:1	50-70
	8-429	4 bbl	208 @ 4400	322 @ 2800	4.362 x 3.590	8.5:1	35-75
	8-429	4 bbl	212 @ 4400	327 @ 2600	4.362 x 3.590	8.5:1	35-75
	8-460	4 bbl	200 @ 4400	326 @ 2800	4.362 x 3.850	8.5:1	35-75
	8-460	4 bbl	212 @ 4400	342 @ 2800	4.362 x 3.850	8.5:1	35-75
'73	8-351 W	2 bbl	153 @ 3800	266 @ 2000	4.000 x 3.500	8.3:1	35-60
	8-351 C	2 bbl	163 @ 3800	277 @ 2000	4.000 x 3.500	8.6:1	35-60
	8-400	2 bbl	172 @ 4000	298 @ 2200	4.000 x 4.000	8.4:1	50-70
	8-429	4 bbl	208 @ 4400	322 @ 2800	4.362 x 3.590	8.5:1	35-75
	8-429	4 bbl	212 @ 4400	327 @ 2600	4.362 x 3.590	8.5:1	35-75
	8-460	4 bbl	200 @ 4400	326 @ 2800	4.362 x 3.850	8.5:1	35-75
	8-460	4 bbl	212 @ 4400	342 @ 2800	4.362 x 3.850	8.5:1	35-75

GENERAL ENGINE SPECIFICATIONS

Year	Engine No. Cyl. Displacement (cu in.)	Carburetor Type	Horsepower @ rpm ■	Torque @ rpm (ft lbs) ■	Bore X Stroke (in.)	Compression Ratio	Oil Pressure @ 2000 rpm
'74	8-351 W	2 bbl	162 @ 4000	275 @ 2200	4.000 x 3.500	8.2:1	45-65
	8-351 C	2 bbl	163 @ 4200	278 @ 2000	4.000 x 3.500	8.0:1	45-75
	8-400	2 bbl	170 @ 3400	330 @ 2000	4.000 x 4.000	8.0:1	45-75
	8-460	4 bbl	195 @ 3800	335 @ 2600	4.362 x 3.850	8.0:1	35-65
	8-460 PI	4 bbl	275 @ 4400	395 @ 2800	4.362 x 3.850	8.8:1	35-65
'75-'77	8-351 M	2 bbl	148 @ 3800	243 @ 2400	4.000 x 3.500	8.0:1	45-75
	8-351 M Calif.	2 bbl	150 @ 3800	244 @ 2800	4.000 x 3.500	8.0:1	45-75
	8-400	2 bbl	158 @ 3800	276 @ 2000	4.000 x 4.000	8.0:1	45-75
	8-400 Calif.	2 bbl	144 @ 3600	255 @ 2200	4.000 x 4.000	8.0:1	45-75
	8-460	4 bbl	218 @ 4000	369 @ 2000	4.362 x 3.850	8.0:1	35-65
	8-460 Calif.	4 bbl	218 @ 4000	367 @ 2600	4.362 x 3.850	8.0:1	35-65
	8-460 T-Bird①	4 bbl	224 @ 4000	370 @ 2600	4.362 x 3.850	8.0:1	35-65
	8-460 T-Bird②	4 bbl	194 @ 3800	347 @ 2600	4.362 x 3.850	8.0:1	35-65
	8-460 T-Bird③	4 bbl	223 @ 4000	366 @ 2600	4.362 x 3.850	8.0:1	35-65
	8-460 PI	4 bbl	226 @ 4000	374 @ 2600	4.362 x 3.850	8.0:1	35-65

■ Beginning 1972, horsepower and torque are SAE net figures. They are measured at the rear of the transmission with all accessories installed and operating. Since the figures vary when a given engine is installed in different models, some are representative rather than exact.

W Windsor Design
C Cleveland Design
M Modified Cleveland Design
PI Police Interceptor

① Dual exhaust
② Single exhaust
③ California

Ford

TUNE-UP SPECIFICATIONS

When analyzing compression test results, look for uniformity among cylinders rather than specific pressures.

Year	ENGINE No. Cyl. Displacement (cu in.)	hp	SPARK PLUGS Orig. Type ●	Gap (in.)	DISTRIBUTOR Point Dwell (deg)	Point Gap (in.)	IGNITION TIMING (deg) ▲ Man Trans ●	Auto Trans	VALVES Intake Opens ■ (deg)	Fuel Pump Pressure (psi)	IDLE SPEED (rpm) ▲ Man Trans * ●	Auto Trans
'70	6-240	150	BF-42	.034	35-40	.027	6B	6B	12	4-6	800/500	500
	8-302	210	BF-42	.034	24-29	.021	6B	6B	16	4-6	575 800/500	575 600/500
	8-351	250	BF-42	.034	24-29	.021	10B	10B	11	5-7	575 700/500	575 600/500
	8-390	270	BF-42	.034	24-29①	.021①	6B	6B	13	5-7	750/500	600/500
	8-428PI	360	BF-32	.034	24-29	.021	—	6B	18	4½-6½	—	600/500
	8-429	320	BRF-42	.034	24-29①	.021①	—	6B	16	5-7	—	600/500
	8-429	360	BRF-42	.034	24-29①	.021①	6B	6B	16	5-7	700/500	600/500
'71	6-240	140	BRF-42	.034	33-38	.027	6B	6B	18	4-6	800/500	600/500
	8-302	210	BRF-42	.034	24-29	.021	6B	6B	16	4-6	575 800/500	575 650/500
	8-351W	240	BRF-42	.034	24-29	.021	6B	6B	11	5-7	575 775/500	575 600/500
	8-351C	240	ARF-42	.034	24-29	.021	—	6B	12	5-7	—	625/550
	8-390	255	BRF-42	.034	24-29	.021	—	6B	13	5-7	—	600/475
	8-400	260	ARF-42	.034	24-29	.021①	—	10B(6B)	17	5-7	—	625/500
	8-429PI	370	ARF-42	.034	27½-29½	.020	—	10B	32	5-7	—	650/500
	8-429	320	BRF-42	.034	24-29①	.021①	—	4B	16	5-7	—	600
	8-429	360	BRF-42	.034	24-29①	.021①	4B	4B	16	5-7	700	600

Ford   TUNE-UP SPECIFICATIONS

When analyzing compression test results, look for uniformity among cylinders rather than specific pressures.

Year	ENGINE No. Cyl Displacement (cu in.)	hp	SPARK PLUGS Orig. Type ●	Gap (in.)	DISTRIBUTOR Point Dwell (deg)	Point Gap (in.)	IGNITION TIMING (deg) ▲ Man Trans ●	Auto Trans	VALVES Intake Opens ■ (deg)	Fuel Pump Pressure (psi)	IDLE SPEED (rpm) ▲ Man Trans * ●	Auto Trans
'72	6-240	103	BRF-42	.034	35-39	.027	—	6B	18	4-6	—	500
	8-302	140	BRF-42	.034	26-30	.017	—	6B	16	5-7	—	575 600/500
	8-351W	153	BRF-42	.034	26-30	.017	—	6B	11	5-7	—	575 600/500
	8-351C	163	ARF-42	.034	26-30	.017	—	6B	12	5-7	—	600/500
	8-400	172	ARF-42	.034	26-30	.017	—	6B	17	5-7	—	625/500
	8-429	208	BRF-42	.034	26-30	.017	—	10B	8	5-7	—	600/500
	8-429PI	N.A.	ARF-42	.034	26-30	.017	—	10B	32	4½-6½	—	650/500
'73	8-351W	153	BRF-42	.034	26-30	.017	—	6B	11	5-7	—	575 600/500
	8-351C	163	ARF-42	.034	26-30	.017	—	6B	12	5-7	—	600/500
	8-400	172	ARF-42	.034	26-30	.017	—	6B	17	5-7	—	625/500
	8-429	208	BRF-42	.034	26-30	.017	—	10B	8	5-7	—	600/500
	8-460PI	267, 274	ARF-42	.034	26-30	.017	—	10B	32	4½-6½	—	650/500
'74	8-351W	162	BRF-42	.034②	26-30③	.014-.020③	—	6B	15	4-6	—	600/500
	8-351C	163	ARF-42	.044	26-30③	.014-.020③	—	14B	19½	5½-6½	—	700/500
	8-400	170	ARF-42	.044 (.054)	Electronic		—	12B	17	5½-6½	—	625/500
	8-460	195	ARF-52	.054 (.044)	Electronic		—	14B	8	5½-6½	—	650(675) 500
	8-460PI	275	ARF-52	.054	Electronic		—	10B	18	Electric	—	700/500
'75	8-351M	148, 150	ARF-42	.044	Electronic		—	8B	19½	5½-6½	—	700
	8-400	144, 158	ARF-42	.044	Electronic		—	6B④	17	5½-6½	—	625
	8-460	218	ARF-52	.044	Electronic		—	14B	8	6.2-7.2	—	650
	8-460PI	226	ARF-52	.044	Electronic		—	14B	18	6.2-7.2	—	650
'76	8-351M	2 bbl	ARF-52	.044	Electronic		—	8B	19½	5½-6½	—	650
	8-351M	4 bbl	ARF-42	.044	Electronic		—	8B	19½	5½-6½	—	650
	8-400	2 bbl	ARF-52	.044	Electronic		—	10B	17	5½-6½	—	650
	8-400	4 bbl	ARF-42	.044	Electronic		—	10B	17	5½-6½	—	650
	8-460	All	ARF-52	.044	Electronic		—	8B(14B)	8	5-7	—	650
	8-460	PI	ARF-52	.044	Electronic		—	14B	18	6-7	—	650
'77	8-351M	All	ARF-52	.050	Electronic		—	⑤	19½	6½-7½	—	650
	8-400	All	ARF-52	.050	Electronic		—	⑤	17	6½-7½	—	625
	8-460	All	ARF-52-6	.060	Electronic		—	⑤	8	7-8	—	650
	8-460	PI	ARF-52-6	.060	Electronic		—	⑤	8	7-8	—	650

NOTE: The underhood specifications sticker often reflects tune-up specification changes made in production. Sticker figures must be used if they disagree with those in this chart.

▲ See text for procedure

● Figure in parentheses indicates California engine

■ All figures Before Top Dead Center

* In all cases where two idle speed figures are separated by a slash, the first is for idle speed with solenoid energized and the automatic transmission in Drive, while the second is for idle speed with solenoid disconnected and automatic transsion in Neutral.

① For engines equipped with single diaphragm distributors adjust point dwell to 26-31 degrees and point gap to .017 inch

② .044 on California models and all cars using Solid State Ignition

③ Solid State Ignition used on all engines nationwide on cars assembled after May, 1974.

④ 8B with 3.25:1 rear axle, Code 9 or R on Certification label, except in California

⑤ See underhood specifications sticker

  B Before Top Dead Center

  C Cleveland

  M Modified Cleveland

  PI Police Interceptor

TDC Top Dead Center

  W Windsor

  — Not applicable

Mercury — TUNE-UP SPECIFICATIONS

When analyzing compression test results, look for uniformity among cylinders rather than specific pressures.

Year	Engine No. Cyl Displacement (cu in.)	hp	Spark Plugs Orig. Type ●	Gap (in.)	Distributor Point Dwell (deg)	Point Gap (in.)	Ignition Timing (deg) ▲ Man Trans	Ignition Timing Auto Trans	Valves Intake Opens ■ (deg)	Fuel Pump Pressure (psi)	Idle Speed (rpm) ▲ Man Trans * ●	Idle Speed Auto Trans
'70	8-390	265	BF-42	.034	27	.021	10B	10B	13	5½-6½	750/500	575
	8-428PI	360	BF-32	.034	27	.021	—	6B	13	5-6	—	600
	8-429	320	BF-42	.034	27	.021	6B	6B	18	5½-6½	850/500	600
	8-429	360	BF-42	.034	27	.021	6B	6B	16	5½-6½	850/500	600
'71	8-351C	240	ARF-42	.034	27	.021	6B	6B	12	5½-6½	700/500	600 600/500
	8-351W	240	BRF-42	.034	27	.021	6B	6B	11	5½-6½	775/500	575 600/500
	8-400	260	ARF-42	.034	27①	.021①	—	10B(6B)	17	5½-6½	—	600/500
	8-429	320	BRF-42	.034	27①	.021①	—	6B	16	5½-6½	—	590 600/500
	8-429	360	BRF-42	.034	27①	0.21①	4B	4B	16	5½-6½	700	650
	8-429PI	370	AF-32	.034	27①	.021①	10B	10B	32	5½-6½	700 700/500	650 650/500
'72	8-351C	163	ARF-42	.034	28	.017	6B	6B	12	5½-6½	750/500	575/500 (625/500)
	8-400	172	ARF-42	.034	28	.017	—	8B(6B)	17	5½-6½	—	625/500
	8-429	208	BRF-42	.034	28	.017	—	10B	8	5½-6½	—	650/500
	8-429PI	N.A.	ARF-42	.034	28	.020	—	10B	32	5½-6½	—	650/500
	8-460	200	BRF-42	.034	28	.017	—	10B(6B)②	8	5½-6½	—	625/500
'73	8-351C	163	ARF-42	.034	28	.017	—	6B	12	5½-6½	—	650/500
	8-400	172	ARF-42	.034	28	.017	—	6B	17	5½-6½	—	650/500
	8-429	208	BRF-42	.034	28	.017	—	10B	8	5½-6½	—	650/500
	8-429PI	N.A.	ARF-42	.034	28	.020	—	10B	32	5½-6½	—	650/500
	8-460	200	BRF-42	.034	28	.017	—	6B	8	5½-6½	—	(625/500)
'74	8-351C	163	ARF-42	.044	28③	.017③	—	14B	19½	5½-6½	—	600/500
	8-400	170	ARF-42	.044 (.054)	Electronic		—	12B	17	5½-6½	—	625/500
	8-460	195	ARF-52	.054	Electronic		—	10B	8	5½-6½	—	625/500
'75	8-400	144, 158	ARF-42	.044	Electronic		—	12B	17	5.5-6.5	—	625
	8-460	218	ARF-52	.044	Electronic		—	14B	8	6.2-7.2	—	650
	8-460PI	226	ARF-52	.044	Electronic		—	14B	18	6.2-7.2	—	650
'76	8-400	2 bbl	ARF-52	.044	Electronic		—	10B	17	5½-6½	—	650
	8-400	4 bbl	ARF-42	.044	Electronic		—	10B	17	5½-6½	—	650
	8-460	All	ARF-52	.044	Electronic		—	8B(14B)	8	5-7	—	650
	8-460	PI	ARF-52	.044	Electronic		—	14B	18	6-7	—	650
'77	8-400	All	ARF-52	.050	Electronic		—	④	17	6½-7½	—	625
	8-460	All	ARF-52-6	.060	Electronic		—	④	8	7-8	—	650
	8-460	PI	ARF-52-6	.060	Electronic		—	④	8	7-8	—	650

NOTE: The underhood specifications sticker often reflects tune-up specification changes made in production. Sticker figures must be used if they disagree with those in this chart.

▲ See text for procedure
● Figure in parentheses indicates California engine
■ All figures Before Top Dead Center
* In all cases where two figures are separated by a slash, the first figure is for idle speed with solenoid energized and automatic transmission in Drive, while the second is for idle speed with solenoid disconnected and automatic transmission in Neutral.

① For single diaphragm distributors, the dwell is 26-31 deg and the gap is .017 in.
② For all vehicles with 3.00 axles, Code 6 or 0 on certification label, figure is 6B
③ Solid State Ignition used on all engines nationwide on cars assembled after May 1974.
④ See underhood specifications sticker
B Before Top Dead Center
C Cleveland
PI Police Interceptor
W Windsor
— Not applicable

Thunderbird

TUNE-UP SPECIFICATIONS

When analyzing compression test results, look for uniformity among cylinders rather than specific pressures.

Year	ENGINE No. Cyl Displacement (cu in.)	hp	SPARK PLUGS Orig. Type ●	Gap (in.)	DISTRIBUTOR Point Dwell (deg)	Point Gap (in.)	IGNITION TIMING (deg) ▲ Man Trans ●	Auto Trans	VALVES Intake Opens ■ (deg)	Fuel Pump Pressure (psi)	IDLE SPEED (rpm) ▲ Man Trans * ●	Auto Trans
'70	8-429	360	BRF-42	.034	26-31	.017	—	6B	16	5½-6½	—	600
'71	8-429	360	BRF-42	.034	26-31	.017	—	4B	16	5½-6½	—	600
'72	8-429	208, 212	BRF-42	.034	26-30	.020	—	10B	8	5½-6½	—	650/500
	8-460	200, 212	BRF-42	.034	26-30	.020	—	10B(6B)	8	5½-6½	—	650/500
'73	8-429	208, 212	BRF-42	.034	26-30	.020	—	10B	8	5½-6½	—	650/500
	8-460	200, 212	BRF-42	.034	26-30	.020	—	6B	8	5½-6½	—	650/500
'74	8-460	195	ARF-52	.044	Electronic		—	14B	8	5½-6½	—	675/500
'75	8-460	194, 223, 224	ARF-52	.044	Electronic		—	14B	8	6½-7½		650
'76	8-460	All	ARF-52	.044	Electronic		—	8B(14B)	8	6-7	—	650

NOTE: The underhood specifications sticker often reflects tune-up specification changes made in production. Sticker figures must be used if they disagree with those in this chart.
▲ See text for procedure
● Figure in parentheses indicates California engine
■ All figures Before Top Dead Center
— Not applicable

* First figure is for idle speed with solenoid energized and automatic transmission in Drive, while the second figure is for idle speed with solenoid disconnected and automatic transmission in Neutral

B Before Top Dead Center

Ford

CAPACITIES

Year	ENGINE No. Cyl. Displacement (Cu. In.)	Engine Crankcase Add 1 Qt For New Filter	TRANSMISSION Pts To Refill After Draining Manual 3-Speed	4-Speed	Automatic	Drive Axle (pts)	Gasoline Tank (gals) ■	COOLING SYSTEM (qts) With Heater	With A/C
'70	6-240	4	3.5	—	See	5	24.5	14.4	14.4
	8-302	4	3.5	—	chart	4.5	24.5	15.4	15.6
	8-351	4	3.5	—	below	4.5	24.5	16.5	16.9
	8-390	4	3.5	—		4.5	24.5	20.1	20.5
	8-428 PI	4	—	—		4.5	24.5	19.7	19.7
	8-429	4	—	—		4.5	24.5	18.6	19.0
'71	6-240	4	3.5	—		5	22.5	14.1	14.1
	8-302	4	3.5	—		4.5	22.5	15.2	15.6
	8-351	4	3.5	—		4.5	22.5	16.3	16.7
	8-390	4	—	—		4.5	22.5	20.3	26.3
	8-400	4	—	—		4.5	22.5	17.6	17.6
	8-429	4	—	—		4.5	22.5	18.8	18.8
'72	6-240	4	—	—		4	22	14.2	14.2
	8-302	4	—	—		4.5	22	15.2	15.2
	8-351	4	—	—		4.5	22	16.3	16.3
	8-400	4	—	—		5	22	17.7	18.3
	8-429	4	—	—		5	22	18.8	19.5
'73	8-351	4	—	—		4.5	22	16.3	16.3
	8-400	4	—	—		5	22	17.7	18.3
	8-429	4	—	—		5	22	18.8	19.5
'74	8-351	4	—	—		4.5	22	16.3	①
	8-400	4	—	—		5	22	18.0	18.0
	8-460	4	—	—		5	22	19.4	19.4

Ford CAPACITIES

Year	ENGINE No. Cyl. Displacement (Cu. In.)	Engine Crankcase Add 1 Qt For New Filter	TRANSMISSION Pts To Refill After Draining — Manual 3-Speed	4-Speed	Automatic	Drive Axle (pts)	Gasoline Tank (gals) ■	COOLING SYSTEM (qts) With Heater	With A/C
'75-'76	8-351 M	4	—	—		4.5④	24.2③	17.1	17.6
	8-400	4	—	—		4.5④	24.2③	17.1	17.6
	8-460	4	—	—		5	24.2③	18.5	18.5
	8-460 PI	6②	—	—		5	24.2③	20.0	20.0
'77	8-351 M	4	—	—		4⑤	24.2③	17.1	17.2
	8-400	4	—	—		4⑤	24.2③	17.1	17.5
	8-460	4	—	—		5	24.2③	19.2	19.2
	8-460 PI	6②	—	—		5	24.2③	19.7	19.7

① 351W—17.1 qts.; 351C—16.3 qts
② 7.5 w/oil cooler
③ With auxiliary fuel tank: sedan—32.3 gals; wagon—29.0 gals.
④ 5 with locker or 3.25:1 ratio
⑤ 5 with locker or 3.0:1 ratio
■ Station wagons:
 '70—20 gals
 '71—22 gals
 '72-'77—21 gals
M Modified Cleveland
PI Police interceptor
—— Not applicable

AUTOMATIC TRANSMISSION REFILL CAPACITIES (Pts)

Year	Code▲	Capacities
'70-'77	X, Y, #	22
'70-'77	W	20.5
'70-'77	U, Z	25

▲ Transmission code can be found on the serial number plate or the vehicle certification label.

Mercury CAPACITIES

Year	ENGINE No. Cyl. Displacement (Cu. In.)	Engine Crankcase Add 1 Qt For New Filter	TRANSMISSION Pts To Refill After Draining — Manual 3-Speed	4-Speed	Automatic	Drive Axle (pts)	Gasoline Tank (gals) ■	COOLING SYSTEM (qts) With Heater	With A/C
'70	8-390	4	3.5	—	25.5	5	24.5	20.1	20.5
	8-428	4	—	—	25.5	5	24.5	19.7	19.7
	8-429	4	—	—	25.5	5	24.5	20.5	21.5
'71	8-351	4	3.5	—	22	5	23	16.3	16.7
	8-400	4	—	—	25	5	23	17.6	17.6
	8-429	4	—	—	25	5	23	18.8	18.8
'72	8-351	4	—	—	22	4	22	15.8	16.3
	8-400	4	—	—	25.5	5	22	17.7	18.3
	8-429	4	—	—	25.5	5	22	18.8	19.5
'73-'74	8-351	4	—	—	22	4	22	15.8	16.3
	8-400	4	—	—	25.5	5	22	17.7	18.3
	8-429	4	—	—	25.5	5	22	18.8	19.5
	8-460	4	—	—	26	5	22	19.5	19.5
'75-'76	8-400	4	—	—	22	4④	24.2②	17.1	17.6
	8-460	4	—	—	25③	4④	24.2②	18.5	18.5
	8-460 PI	6①	—	—	25	4④	24.2②	20.0	20.0
'77	8-400	4	—	—	25	4④	24.2②	17.1	17.5
	8-460	4	—	—	25	5	24.2②	19.2	19.2
	8-460 PI	6①	—	—	25	5	24.2②	19.7	19.7

■ Station Wagons:
 '70 to '71—22 gals
 '72 to '77—21 gals
① 7.5 with oil cooler
② With auxiliary fuel tank: sedan—32.3 gals; wagon—29.0 gals.
③ 22 for FMX
④ 5 for removeable differential thial carrier axle
— Not applicable
PI Police interceptor

Thunderbird — CAPACITIES

Year	ENGINE No. Cyl. Displacement (Cu. In.)	Engine Crankcase Add 1 Qt For New Filter	TRANSMISSION Pts To Refill After Draining — Manual 3-Speed	4-Speed	Automatic	Drive Axle (pts)	Gasoline Tank (gals)	COOLING SYSTEM (qts) With Heater	With A/C
'70	8-429	4	—	—	26	5	24①	19.4	19.4
'71	8-429	4	—	—	26	5	22.5	19.4	19.4
'72-'74	8-429	4	—	—	26	5	22.5	18.8	18.8
	8-460	4	—	—	26	5	22.5	20	20
'75	8-460	4	—	—	25	5	26.5	19.3②	19.3②
'76	8-460	4	—	—	25	5	26.5	—	19.8

① With evaporative emission controls—22.5 gals   ② 19.8 with Class III towing package   —— Not applicable

VALVE SPECIFICATIONS

Year	Engine No. Cyl. Displacement (cu in.)	Seat Angle (deg)	Face Angle (deg)	Spring Test Pressure (lbs @ in.)	Spring Installed Height (in.)	STEM TO GUIDE Clearance (in.) Intake	Exhaust	STEM Diameter (in.) Intake	Exhaust
'70	6-240	45	44	197 @ 1.30	1 11/16	.0010-.0027	.0010-.0027	.3420	.3420
	8-302	45	44	180 @ 1.23	1 21/32	.0010-.0027	.0015-.0032	.3420	.3415
	8-351	45	44	215 @ 1.34	1 25/32	.0010-.0027	.0010-.0027	.3420	.3415
	8-390	①	44	220 @ 1.38	1 13/16	.0010-.0027	.0015-.0032	.3715	.3710
	8-429	45	44	253 @ 1.33	1 13/16	.0010-.0027	.0010-.0027	.3420	.3420
'71	6-240	45	44	197 @ 1.30	1 11/16	.0010-.0027	.0010-.0027	.3420	.3420
	8-302	45	44	180 @ 1.23	1 21/32	.0010-.0027	.0015-.0032	.3420	.3415
	8-351W	45	44	215 @ 1.34	1 25/32	.0010-.0027	.0015-.0032	.3420	.3415
	8-351C	45	44	210 @ 1.42	1 13/16	.0010-.0027	.0015-.0032	.3420	.3415
	8-390	①	44	220 @ 1.38	1 13/16	.0010-.0027	.0015-.0032	.3715	.3710
	8-400	45	44	226 @ 1.39	1 13/16	.0010-.0027	.0015-.0032	.3420	.3415
	8-429	45	45	253 @ 1.33	1 13/16	.0010-.0027	.0015-.0032	.3420	.3415
'72	6-240	45	44	197 @ 1.30	1 11/16	.0010-.0027	.0010-.0027	.3420	.3420
	8-302	45	44	200 @ 1.31	1 11/16	.0010-.0027	.0015-.0032	.3420	.3415
	8-351W	45	44	200 @ 1.34	1 25/32	.0010-.0027	.0015-.0032	.3420	.3415
	8-351C	45	44	210 @ 1.42	1 13/16	.0010-.0027	.0015-.0032	.3420	.3415
	8-400	45	44	226 @ 1.39	1 13/16	.0010-.0027	.0015-.0032	.3420	.3415
	8-429	45	45	229 @ 1.33	1 13/16	.0010-.0027	.0010-.0027	.3420	.3420
	8-460	45	45	229 @ 1.33	1 13/16	.0010-.0027	.0010-.0027	.3420	.3420
'73-'74	8-351W	45	44	200 @ 1.34	1 25/32	.0010-.0027	.0015-.0032	.3420	.3415
	8-351C	45	44	210 @ 1.42②	1 13/16	.0010-.0027	.0015-.0032	.3420	.3415
	8-400	45	44	226 @ 1.39	1 13/16	.0010-.0027	.0015-.0032	.3420	.3415
	8-429	45	45	229 @ 1.33	1 13/16	.0010-.0027	.0010-.0027	.3420	.3420
	8-460	45	45	229 @ 1.33	1 13/16	.0010-.0027	.0010-.0027	.3420	.3420
'75-'76	8-351M	44½-45	45½-45¾	226 @ 1.39	1 13/16	.0010-.0027	.0015-.0032	.3420	.3415
	8-400	44½-45	45½-45¾	226 @ 1.39	1 13/16	.0010-.0027	.0015-.0032	.3420	.3415
	8-460	44½-45	45½-45¾	253 @ 1.33	1 13/16	.0010-.0027	.0010-.0027	.3420	.3420
	8-460 PI	44½-45	45½-45¾	315 @ 1.32	1 13/16	.0010-.0027	.0010-.0027	.3420	.3420
'77	8-351 M	44½-45	45½-45¾	226 @ 1.39	1 13/16	.0010-.0027	.0015-.0032	.3420	.3415
	8-400	44½-45	45½-45¾	226 @ 1.39	1 13/16	.0010-.0027	.0015-.0032	.3420	.3415
	8-460	44½-45	45½-45¾	③	1 13/16	.0010-.0027	.0010-.0027	.3420	.3420
	8-460 PI	44½-45	45½-45¾	③	1 13/16	.0010-.0027	.0010-.0027	.3420	.3420

① Intake valve seat angle 30°   ② 1974 models—226 @ 1.39   C Cleveland engine   PI Police interceptor
Exhaust valve seat angle 45°   ③ Intake: 240 @ 1.33, Exhaust: 253 @ 1.33   M Modified Cleveland engine   W Windsor engine

TORQUE SPECIFICATIONS

All readings in ft lbs

Year	Engine No. Cyl. Displacement (cu in.)	Cylinder Head Bolts	Rod Bearing Bolts	Main Bearing Bolts	Crankshaft Pulley or Damper Bolt	Flywheel to Crankshaft Bolts	MANIFOLD Intake	MANIFOLD Exhaust
'70	6-240	70-75	40-45	60-70	130-150	75-85	25	25
	8-302	65-72	19-24	60-70	70-90	75-85	24	14
	8-351	95-100	40-45	95-105	70-90	75-85	23-25	18-24
	8-390	80-90	③	95-105	70-90	75-85	32-35	18-24
	8-429	130-140	40-45	95-105	70-90	75-85	27½	30½
'71	6-240	70-75	40-45	60-70	130-150	75-85	25	25
	8-302	65-72	19-24	60-70	70-90	75-85	24	14
	8-351	95-100	40-45	95-105	70-90	75-85	23-25	18-24④
	8-390	80-90	40-45	95-105	70-90	75-85	32-35	18-24
	8-400	95-105	40-45	95-105	70-90	75-85	27-33	12-16
	8-429	130-140	40-45	95-105	70-90	75-85	27½	30½
'72	6-240	70-75	40-45	60-70	130-150	75-85	23-28	23-28
	8-302	65-72	19-24	60-70	70-90	75-85	23-25	12-16
	8-351W	105-112	40-45	95-105	100-130	75-85	23-25	18-24
	8-351C, 400	95-105⑤	40-45⑥	⑦	70-90	75-85	⑧	12-16
	8-429, 460	130-140	40-45	95-105	70-90	75-85	25-30	28-33
'73-'77	8-351W	105-112	40-45	95-105	70-90	75-85	23-25	18-24
	8-351C, 351M, 400	95-105⑤	40-45⑥	⑦	70-90	75-85	⑩	18-24⑨
	8-429, 460	130-140	40-45	95-105	70-90	75-85	22-32	28-33

① ② Not used
③ 390—40-45; 428—53-58
④ 351C engine—12-16
⑤ 351 HO—120

⑥ 351 HO—40-45
⑦ ½ x 13 in. bolt—95-105
  ⅜ x 16 in. bolt—35-45
⑧ 5/16 in. bolt—21-25
  ⅜ in. bolt—27-23
  ¼ in. bolt—6-9

⑨ 1973-74 351—12-22
  1973-74 400—12-16
⑩ 5/16 bolt: 21-25
  ⅜ bolt: 22-32
  ¼ bolt: 6-9

CRANKSHAFT AND CONNECTING ROD SPECIFICATIONS

All measurements are given in inches

Year	Engine No. Cyl. Displacement (cu in.)	CRANKSHAFT Main Brg. Journal Dia	CRANKSHAFT Main Brg. Oil Clearance	Shaft End-Play	Thrust on No.	CONNECTING ROD Journal Diameter	CONNECTING ROD Oil Clearance	CONNECTING ROD Side Clearance
'70	6-240	2.3982-2.3990	.0005-.0015	.004-.008	5	2.1228-2.1236	.0008-.0026	.006-.013
	8-302	2.2482-2.2490	.0005-.0015	.004-.008	3	2.1228-2.1236	.0008-.0026	.010-.020
	8-351	2.9994-2.3002	.0013-.0025	.004-.008	3	2.3103-2.3111	.0008-.0026	.010-.020
	8-390	2.7484-2.7492	.0005-.0025	.004-.008	3	2.4380-2.4388	.0008-.0026	.010-.020
	8-428	2.7484-2.7492	.0008-.0020	.004-.008	3	2.4380-2.4388	.0008-.0026	.010-.020
	8-429	2.9994-3.0002	.0005-.0025	.004-.008	3	2.4992-2.5000	.0008-.0026	.010-.020
'71	6-240	2.3982-2.3990	.0005-.0022	.004-.008	5	2.1228-2.1236	.0008-.0026	.006-.013
	8-302	2.2482-2.2490	.0005-.0024①	.004-.008	3	2.1228-2.1236	.0008-.0026	.010-.020
	8-351W	2.9994-3.0002	.0013-.0030	.004-.008	3	2.3103-2.3111	.0008-.0026	.010-.020
	8-351C	2.7484-2.7492	.0009-.0026	.004-.010	3	2.3103-2.3111	.0008-.0026	.010-.020
	8-390	2.7484-2.7492	.0008-.0020	.004-.008	3	2.4380-2.4388	.0010-.0030	.010-.020
	8-400	2.9994-3.0002	.0009-.0026	.004-.010	3	2.3103-2.3111	.0008-.0026	.010-.020
	8-429	2.9994-3.0002	.0005-.0025	.004-.008	3	2.4992-2.5000	.0008-.0028	.010-.020

C559

CRANKSHAFT AND CONNECTING ROD SPECIFICATIONS

All measurements are given in inches

Year	Engine No. Cyl. Displacement (cu in.)	Crankshaft: Main Brg. Journal Dia	Crankshaft: Main Brg. Oil Clearance	Crankshaft: Shaft End-Play	Crankshaft: Thrust on No.	Connecting Rod: Journal Diameter	Connecting Rod: Oil Clearance	Connecting Rod: Side Clearance
'72	6-240	2.3982-2.3990	.0005-.0022	.004-.008	5	2.1228-2.1236	.0008-.0026	.006-.013
	8-302	2.2482-2.2490	.0005-.0024 ①	.004-.008	3	2.1228-2.1236	.0008-.0026	.010-.020
	8-351W	2.9994-3.0002	.0008-.0026	.004-.008	3	2.3103-2.3111	.0008-.0026	.010-.020
	8-351C	2.7484-2.7492	.0011-.0028	.004-.010	3	2.3103-2.3111	.0011-.0026	.010-.020
	8-400	2.9994-3.0002	.0011-.0028	.004-.010	3	2.3103-2.3111	.0011-.0026	.010-.020
	8-429	2.9994-3.0002	.0010-.0020 ②	.004-.008	3	2.4992-2.5000	.0008-.0028	.010-.020
	8-460	2.9994-3.0002	.0010-.0020 ②	.004-.008	3	2.4992-2.5000	.0008-.0026	.010-.020
'73-'74	8-351W	2.9994-3.0002	.0008-.0026	.004-.008	3	2.3103-2.3111	.0008-.0026	.010-.020
	8-351C	2.7484-2.7492	.0011-.0028	.004-.010	3	2.3103-2.3111	.0008-.0015 ④⑤	.010-.020
	8-400	2.9994-3.0002	.0011-.0028	.004-.010	3	2.3103-2.3111	.0011-.0026	.010-.020
	8-429	2.9994-3.0002	.0010-.0020 ②	.004-.008	3	2.4992-2.5000	.0008-.0028	.010-.020
	8-460	2.9994-3.0002	.0010-.0020 ②	.004-.008	3	2.4992-2.5000	.0008-.0026	.010-.020
'75-'76	8-351M	2.7484-2.7492	.0009-.0026 ④	.004-.008	3	2.3103-2.3111	.0008-.0015 ④	.010-.020
	8-400	2.9994-3.0002	.0011-.0028	.004-.008	3	2.3103-2.3111	.0011-.0026	.010-.020
	8-460	2.9994-3.0002	.0012-.0028 ③	.004-.008	3	2.4992-2.5000	.0008-.0028	.010-.020
'77	8-351M	2.9998	.0009-.0026	.004-.008	3	2.3107	.0008-.0026	.010-.020
	8-400	2.9998	.0009-.0026	.004-.008	3	2.3107	.0008-.0026	.010-.020
	8-460	2.9998	.0009-.0027 ⑥	.004-.008	3	2.4992-2.500	.0008-.0028	.010-.020
	8-460 PI	2.9998	.0009-.0027 ⑥	.004-.008	3	2.4992-2.500	.0008-.0028	.010-.020

① #1—.0001-.0018
② #1—.010-.015
③ #1 bearing—.0010-.0015"
④ 4 bbl: .0011-.0015
⑤ 1973: .0008-.0026
⑥ #1 bearing—.0004-.0020

RING GAP

All measurements are given in inches

Year	Engine	Top Compression	Bottom Compression
'70-'77	6-240, 8-302, 351, 429, 400, 460	.010-.020	.010-.020
'70-'71	8-390	.010-.020	.010-.020
'70	8-428	.010-.020	.010-.020

Year	Engine	Oil Control
'70-'72	6-240	.015-.055
'70-'71	8-302	.015-.069
'72	8-302	.015-.055
'70-'74	8-351, 351W	.015-.069
'72-'74	8-351C	.015-.055
'70-'71	8-390	.015-.055
'70-'74	8-351M, 400	.015-.069
'75-'77	8-351M, 400	.015-.055
'70	8-428, 429	.010-.035
'71-'77	8-429, 460	.015-.055

PISTON CLEARANCE

Year	Engine	Piston-to-Bore Clearance (in.)
'70-'72	240 Six	.0014-.0022
'70-'74	302, 351W V8	.0018-.0026
'70-'71	390, 428 V8	.0015-.0023
'70-'77	351C, 351M, 400, 429, 460 V8	.0014-.0022

RING SIDE CLEARANCE

All measurements are given in inches

Year	Engine	Top Compression	Bottom Compression
'70-'77	All engines	.002-.004	.002-.004

Year	Engine	Oil Control
'70-'77	All engines	Snug

WHEEL ALIGNMENT SPECIFICATIONS

Year	Model	CASTER Range (deg)	CASTER Pref Setting (deg)	CAMBER Range (deg)	CAMBER Pref Setting (deg)	Toe-in (in.)	Steering Axis Inclin. (deg)	WHEEL PIVOT RATIO (deg) Inner Wheel	WHEEL PIVOT RATIO (deg) Outer Wheel
'70-'71	Ford, Mercury	0 to 2P	1P	$\frac{1}{4}$N to 1$\frac{1}{4}$P	$\frac{1}{2}$P	$\frac{1}{16}$ to $\frac{5}{16}$	7$\frac{3}{4}$	20	19$\frac{4}{25}$
	T-Bird	0 to 2P	1P	$\frac{1}{4}$N to 1$\frac{1}{4}$P	$\frac{1}{2}$P	$\frac{1}{16}$ to $\frac{5}{16}$	7$\frac{3}{4}$	20	19$\frac{8}{25}$
'72	Ford, Mercury	1N to 3P	1P	$\frac{1}{2}$N to 1$\frac{1}{2}$P	$\frac{1}{2}$P	$\frac{1}{16}$ to $\frac{7}{16}$	7$\frac{3}{4}$	20	19$\frac{4}{25}$
	T-Bird	1N to 3P	1P	$\frac{1}{4}$N to 1$\frac{3}{4}$P	$\frac{3}{4}$P	*$\frac{1}{16}$ to $\frac{7}{16}$	7$\frac{3}{4}$	20	17$\frac{37}{50}$
'73	Ford, Mercury	0 to 4P	2P	1N to 1P	0	$\frac{1}{16}$ to $\frac{7}{16}$	7$\frac{3}{4}$	20	18$\frac{3}{4}$
	T-Bird	$\frac{1}{2}$N to 3$\frac{1}{2}$P	1$\frac{1}{2}$P	$\frac{1}{4}$N to 1$\frac{3}{4}$P	$\frac{3}{4}$P	$\frac{1}{16}$ to $\frac{7}{16}$	7$\frac{3}{4}$	20	17$\frac{3}{4}$
'74	Ford	0 to 4P	2P	①	②	$\frac{3}{16}$	9$\frac{1}{2}$	20	18$\frac{3}{4}$
	Mercury	0 to 4P	2P	③	②	$\frac{3}{16}$	9$\frac{1}{2}$	20	18$\frac{3}{4}$
	T-Bird	$\frac{1}{2}$P to 3$\frac{1}{2}$P	2P	$\frac{1}{4}$N to 1$\frac{3}{4}$P	$\frac{3}{4}$P	$\frac{3}{16}$	9	20	18
'75-'76	Ford, Mercury	0 to 4P	2P	③	②	$\frac{3}{16}$	9$\frac{7}{16}$	20	18$\frac{3}{4}$
	T-Bird	2$\frac{1}{2}$P to 5$\frac{1}{2}$P	4P	④	⑤	$\frac{3}{16}$	9	20	18
'77	Ford, Mercury	1$\frac{1}{4}$P to 2$\frac{3}{4}$P	2P	⑥	⑥	$\frac{1}{16}$ to $\frac{5}{16}$	9.44	20	18.69

① Left wheel—0 to 1P
Right wheel—$\frac{1}{4}$N to $\frac{3}{4}$P

② Left wheel—$\frac{1}{2}$P
Right wheel—$\frac{1}{4}$P

③ Left wheel—$\frac{1}{2}$N to 1$\frac{1}{2}$P
Right wheel—$\frac{3}{4}$N to 1$\frac{1}{4}$P

④ Left wheel—0 to 2P
Right wheel—$\frac{1}{2}$N to 1$\frac{1}{2}$P

⑤ Left wheel—1P
Right wheel—$\frac{1}{2}$P

⑥ Left $\frac{1}{2}$P to $\frac{3}{4}$P
Right $\frac{1}{4}$P to $\frac{3}{4}$P

— Not specified
N Negative   P Positive

NOTE: The Thunderbird through 1976 is in this section. Thunderbird, starting 1977, is in the Comet, Cougar, Elite, Fairlane, Falcon, Granada, Maverick, Monarch, Montego, Mustang, Torino car section.

CHARGING SYSTEM

All Ford cars use alternating-current (AC) charging systems.

Alternator Removal and Installation

1. Disconnect the negative battery cable.

2. Loosen the alternator mounting bolts, remove the alternator to adjusting arm bolt and remove the belt.

3. Remove the alternator mounting bolt and spacer, position the alternator so that the wire connectors can be disconnected and remove the alternator.

NOTE: on alternators with integral regulators mounted on the back of the alternator housing, press the sides of the retainer clip and remove the wire from the regulator.

4. Reverse above procedure to reinstall, applying pressure only to the front of the alternator housing when tightening the drive belt.

Regulator Removal and Installation

1. Disconnect the negative battery cable. The regulator is located behind the battery and it is necessary to remove the battery to remove the regulator.

2. Remove the regulator mounting screws, unlock the wire connectors, then with integral regulator.

3. On vehicles with integral regulator, remove the alternator to adjusting arm bolt and the drive belt.

4. Swing the alternator down, remove the terminal covers from the regulator and remove the regulator attaching nuts.

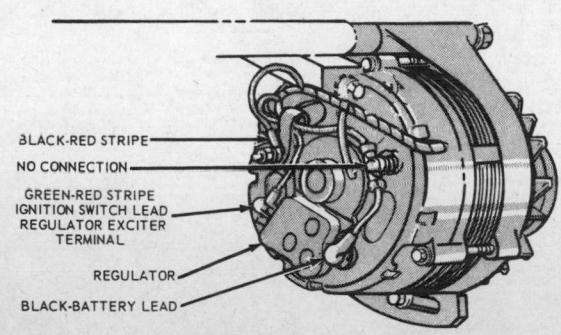

BLACK-RED STRIPE
NO CONNECTION
GREEN-RED STRIPE IGNITION SWITCH LEAD REGULATOR EXCITER TERMINAL
REGULATOR
BLACK-BATTERY LEAD

Typical alternator installation
(© Ford Motor Co)

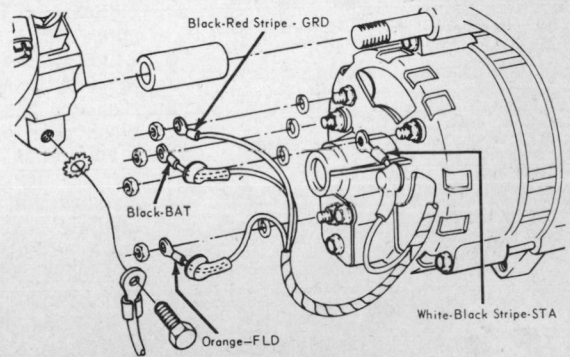

Black-Red Stripe - GRD
Black-BAT
Orange—FLD
White-Black Stripe-STA

Alternator wiring harness—with integral regulator
(© Ford Motor Co)

STARTING SYSTEM

All models, except 429 and 460 V8 engined Thunderbirds, Fords and Mercurys, use positive engagement starters. These medium-duty starters have a self-contained engagement mechanism. The 429 and 460 V8 engined cars are equipped with heavy-duty, solenoid-actuated starters, to which an outboard solenoid is mounted. There is no difference in procedures for removing or installing these two types of starters.

Starting system troubleshooting and repairs may be found in the Unit Repair Section under Charging and Starting Systems.

Starter Removal and Installation

1. Disconnect the negative battery cable.
2. Disconnect the starter cable from the starter.
3. Remove the starter mounting bolts. On Thunderbird, remove the 2 front brace attaching bolts.
4. Manipulate the starter so that it can be lowered through the steering linkage. On some engine/chassis combinations this can be done by turning the steering wheel all the way to the right; on others it will be necessary to remove the idler arm bracket attaching bolts and lower the assembly away from the engine.
5. Reverse above procedure to reinstall.

IGNITION SYSTEM

Solid State Ignition

Beginning 1974, Ford is utilizing a solid state or "breakerless" ignition system on all 351 cubic inch and larger engines in the state of California, and on all 400 and 460 cubic inch V8s nationwide. All engines assembled after May 1974 use this maintenance-saving ignition system. This system is unique in that it eliminates the contact breaker points, replacing them with a permanent magnet, low voltage generator.

Complete service information for the Ford Solid State Ignition System can be found in the "Electronic Ignition" Unit Repair Section.

Tachometer Connection— Electronic Ignition

Install a tachometer alligator clip into the "Tach Test" cavity. If the coil connector must be removed, grasp the wires and pull horizontally until it disconnects from the terminals.

An alligator type clip from the tachometer test lead can also be connected to the DEC (Distributor Electronic Control) without removing the connector.

Distributor Removal and Installation

Remove the distributor cap and mark the position of tip of the rotor in relation to the body of the distributor and the engine block. Disconnect the ignition primary wires, the vacuum line(s) then take out the holddown bolt that holds the distributor down in the block and lift it up out of the block.

Do not disturb the engine after the distributor has been removed. If the engine is cranked with the distributor removed, the engine will have to be retimed.

Ignition Retiming—Except Solid State Distributor

If the timing relationship has been disturbed, proceed to retime the ignition as follows: bring No. 1 cylinder up into the firing position. This can be checked by removing the spark plug, placing your thumb in the spark plug hole, then cranking the engine until the compression attempts to blow by your thumb. Now, slowly bring the crankshaft around until the T.D.C. mark on the crankshaft pulley lines up with the pointer. This is the approximate firing position for No. 1 cylinder.

Scribe a mark on the engine that corresponds with the position of the no. 1 spark plug wire in the distributor cap. Remove the distributor and reinstall it so that the tip of the rotor aligns with the mark on the engine.

Viewed from above, rotation of distributor for six cylinder engine is clockwise; for eight cylinder, counterclockwise.

Ignition Retiming— Solid State Distributor

1. Rotate the engine until No. 1 piston is on TDC of the compression stroke.
2. Align the correct initial timing mark with the pointer.
3. Position the distributor in the block with one of the armature segments as shown and the rotor at No. 1 firing position.
4. Be sure that the oil pump intermediate shaft properly engages the distributor shaft. Install, but do not tighten, the distributor clamp bolt.
5. Rotate the distributor to advance the timing to a point where the armature tooth is properly aligned. Tighen the clamp.

6. Connect the distributor wiring and check the timing with a timing light.

Contact Point Replacement and Adjustment

1. Unsnap the distributor cap retaining clips and position the cap clear of the breaker plate. Remove the rotor by pulling it straight up.
2. Remove the metal point shield, if so equipped.
3. Disconnect the primary lead and condenser wires from the contact point assembly. On dual-point distributors, remove the jumper strap also.
4. Remove the contact point and condenser retaining screws. Lift the contact point assembly and condenser from the distributor.
5. Lightly lubricate the distributor cam with heat-resistant lubricant.
6. Place the new contact point assembly and condenser in the distributor. Install, but do not tighten, the retaining screws.
7. On all V8 engines, place the ground wire under the contact point assembly screw farthest from the contacts. On all six-cylinder engines, this ground wire is positioned under the condenser retaining screw.
8. Turn the engine until the rubbing block on the point assembly is resting on the high point of the distributor cam lobe. Insert a feeler gauge of specified thickness between the contact points and adjust the gap. Tighten the retaining screw and remove the feeler gauge.
9. Connect the primary and condenser wires to the contact point assembly in the same order in which they were removed. On distributors equipped with a metal point shield, the wires should be positioned 180° from each other, then install the shield.
10. Install the rotor and distributor cap.
11. If a dwell meter is available, check to see that the distributor dwell is within specifications.

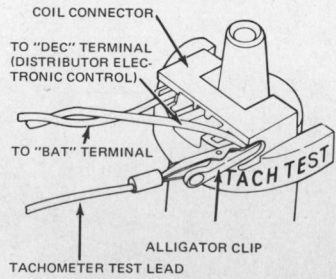

COIL CONNECTOR
TO "DEC" TERMINAL (DISTRIBUTOR ELECTRONIC CONTROL)
TO "BAT" TERMINAL
TACH TEST
ALLIGATOR CLIP
TACHOMETER TEST LEAD

Electronic ignition tach connection
(© Ford Motor Co.)

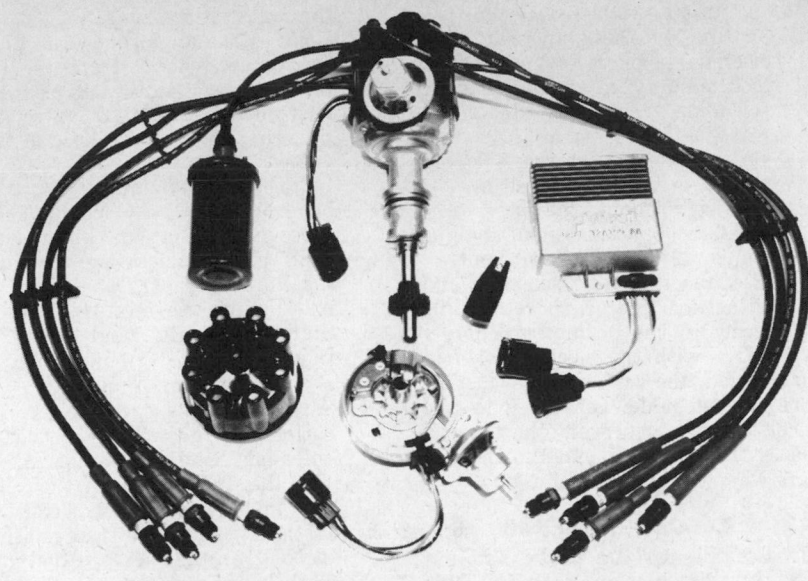

Solid state "breakerless" ignition system components (© Ford Motor Co)

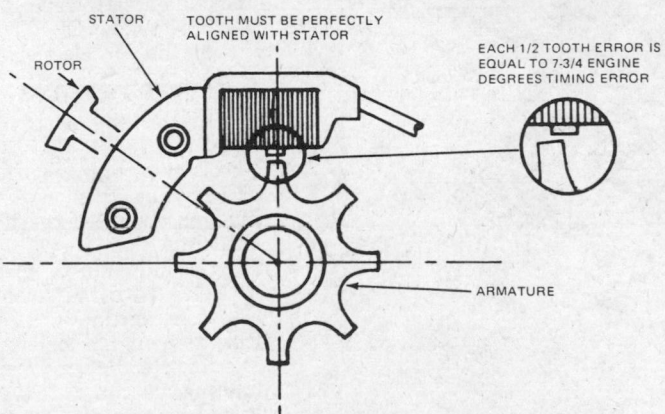

STATOR

ROTOR

TOOTH MUST BE PERFECTLY ALIGNED WITH STATOR

EACH 1/2 TOOTH ERROR IS EQUAL TO 7-3/4 ENGINE DEGREES TIMING ERROR

ARMATURE

Static timing position—electronic ignition (© Ford Motor Co)

5. Press the sides of the retainer clip and remove the retaining clip and supply wire. Remove the regulator.
6. Reverse above procedure to reinstall. On electromechanical regulators, the radio suppression condenser mounts under one screw.

Ignition Timing

1. Locate the timing marks and pointer on the lower engine pulley and engine front cover.
2. Clean the marks and apply chalk or bright-colored paint to the pointer.
3. Attach a timing light according to the manufacturer's specifications.
4. Disconnect and plug all vacuum lines leading to the distributor.
5. If the recommended engine idle speed is in excess of 500 rpm, set the idle at 500 rpm for setting the timing. If the recommended idle speed is below 500 rpm, do not alter it.

6. Aim the timing light at the timing mark and pointer on the front of the engine. If the marks align when the timing light flashes, remove the timing light, set the idle to its proper specification, and connect the vacuum lines at the distributor. If the marks do not align when the light flashes, loosen the distributor hold-down clamp slightly.
7. Start the engine again, and observe the alignment of the timing marks. To advance the timing, turn the distributor counterclockwise on six-cylinder engines and clockwise on V8 engines. When altering the timing, it is wise to tap the distributor lightly with a wooden hammer handle in order to move it in the desired direction. Grasping the distributor with your hand may result in a painful electric shock. When the timing marks are aligned, turn the engine off and tighten the distributor hold-down clamp.

FUEL SYSTEM

Fuel Pump Replacement

A single-action, permanently sealed fuel pump is used on all models. On 6-cylinder engines, the fuel pump is located on the lower left center of the engine block. The V8 fuel pump is mounted on the left side of the cylinder front cover.

1. Remove the inlet and outlet lines from the pump.
2. Remove the fuel pump retaining screws and remove the pump and gasket.
3. Clean all gasket material from the pump mounting surface on the engine, and apply a coat of oil-resistant sealer to the new gasket.
4. Position pump on engine and install retaining screws.
5. Reinstall lines, start engine and check for leaks.

NOTE: if resistance is felt while positioning the fuel pump on the block, the camshaft eccentric is in the high position. To ease installation, connect a remote engine starter switch to the engine and "tap" remote switch until resistance fades.

Fuel Filter Replacement

All models use a non-serviceable inline fuel filter which is located at the carburetor fuel inlet.

1. Remove the air cleaner.
2. Loosen the hose clamp or crimp type clamp at the fuel inlet hose connection.
3. Unscrew the filter from the carburetor.
4. Disconnect the filter from the hose and discard the hose clamp.
5. Reverse the above procedure to install, using a new hose clamp. After installation, start the engine and check for fuel leakage.

Carburetor

See the Carburetor Unit Repair Section for all carburetor adjustments not covered in this section.

Idle Speed Adjustment

Through 1974

This is the procedure for adjusting all carburetors, any exceptions are listed below. Adjust with air cleaner installed.

1. Run engine at fast idle to equalize operating temperature.
2. Make sure the choke plate is fully released.
3. Turn headlights on high beam.
4. If engine is equipped with hot idle compensator valve, make sure it is fully seated in the closed position.
5. Attach tachometer of known accuracy to the engine.

6. The idle speed is set with the air conditioner turned OFF.

7. On models equipped with a temperature sensing valve in the distributor vacuum line, remove and plug the vacuum hoses from the distributor to the valve and from the intake manifold to the valve, at the valve located in the intake manifold.

8. Make sure the dashpot is working freely and not binding.

9. If it is not possible to adjust the idle speed with the air cleaner installed, the engine idle speed must be rechecked after installing the air cleaner. On cars with vacuum controlled heat ducts in the air cleaner, the vacuum line must be plugged if the carburetor is to be adjusted with the air cleaner removed.

10. On 1970 cars for which the specifications list two idle speeds, the first speed listed is obtained by turning the plunger on the electric solenoid. On 1972-74 models equipped with an electric solenoid, the higher idle speed is adjusted by turning the adjusting screw in the solenoid mounting bracket. On all models with a solenoid, the lower idle speed is obtained by putting the transmission in Park or Neutral, disconnecting the solenoid and adjusting the carburetor idle screw in the normal manner.

NOTE: with the electric solenoid disengaged, the carburetor adjusting screw must make contact with the throttle shaft to prevent the throttle plates from jamming in the throttle bore when the engine is shut off.

1975-76 351M and 400 V8

1. Set the parking brake and put the transmission in Drive. Turn the air conditioner OFF.

2. Remove the air cleaner and plug the vacuum hoses from the intake manifold to the air cleaner.

3. Disconnect the EGR valve by plugging the vacuum hose at the valve.

4. If the idle fuel mixture screws have not been previously set, be sure they are at maximum rich (full counterclockwise) against the limiter stops. Otherwise, do not disturb the mixture screws.

5. Start the engine and warm it thoroughly.

6. Set the ignition timing.

7. Adjust the idle speed to specifications with the TSP (throttle solenoid positioner) energized. Use the TSP screw in the solenoid mounting bracket. After adjustment, place the transmission in Neutral and increase the rpm slightly to clear up any loading condition. Return the engine to idle and check the speed in Drive.

8. Reconnect the EGR valve and install the air cleaner.

1975-76 460 V8

1. Warm the engine to operating temperature.

2. Check the timing with the advance line disconnected and plugged. Connect the hose after checking.

3. Set the idle rpm to specification in Drive with the solenoid positioner engaged.

4. Run the engine briefly at fast idle in Neutral and check the idle speed again in Drive.

5. Readjust the idle speed if necessary.

Fuel Mixture Adjustment
Through 1974

1. On models with idle mixture

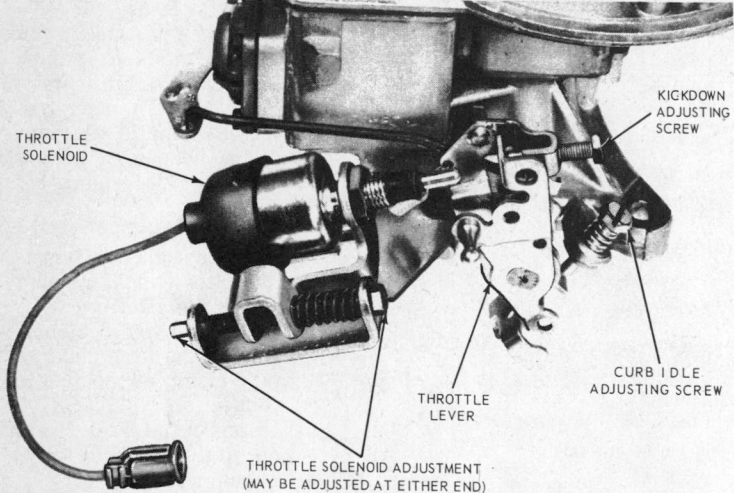

THROTTLE SOLENOID

KICKDOWN ADJUSTING SCREW

THROTTLE LEVER

CURB IDLE ADJUSTING SCREW

THROTTLE SOLENOID ADJUSTMENT (MAY BE ADJUSTED AT EITHER END)

Throttle solenoid adjusting locations—Motorcraft 2100 shown; Motorcraft 4300 similar. (© Ford Motor Co)

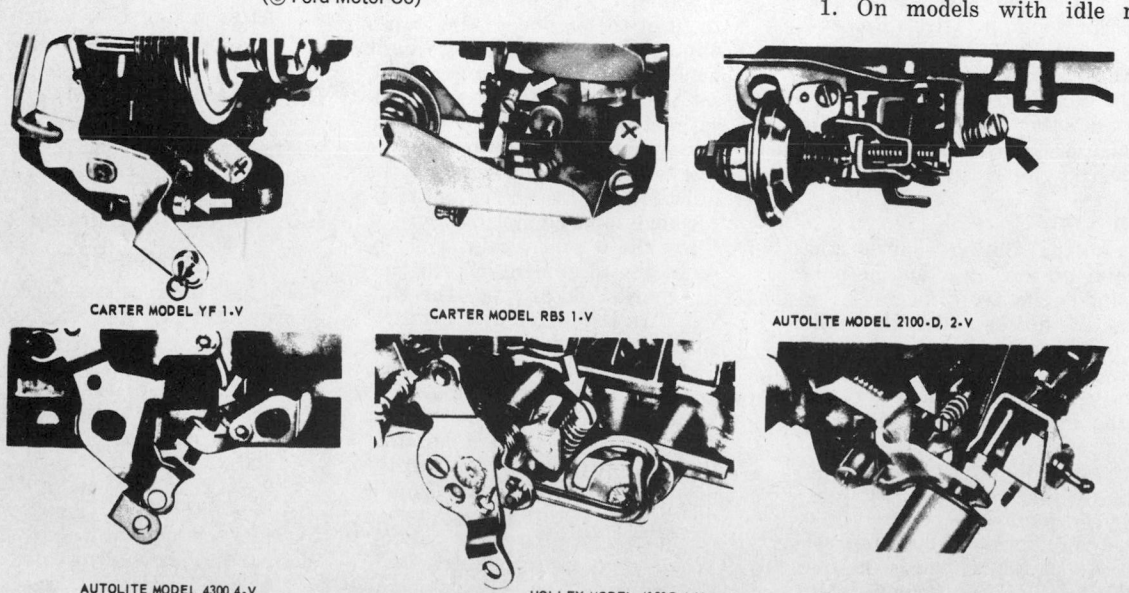

CARTER MODEL YF 1-V

CARTER MODEL RBS 1-V

AUTOLITE MODEL 2100-D, 2-V

AUTOLITE MODEL 4300 4-V

HOLLEY MODEL 4150C 4-V

ROCHESTER MODEL 4 MV

Idle speed adjusting screws (© Ford Motor Co)

Dashpot Adjustment

	Clearance (in.)	
Model	Manual	Automatic
1970 240 1V	—	7/64
1971 240 1V	—	0.100
1970-72 302, 351, 400, 429 2V	—	1/8
1970-71 429 4V	—	0.100
1972 240 1V	—	7/64

limiters, adjust to obtain the highest rpm possible. Limiter caps should not be removed.

1975 and Later

Fuel mixture adjustment requires an artificial enrichment substance (propane). This should not be attempted unless you have the special equipment.

Dashpot Adjustment

1. With engine idle speed and mixture properly adjusted and with engine at operating temperature, loosen dashpot locknut.
2. Hold throttle in closed position and depress dashpot plunger. Measure clearance between plunger and cam. Adjust dashpot adjusting nut to give proper clearance.
3. Tighten locknut and check setting of accelerator pump.

COOLING SYSTEM

Both the 6-cylinder and V8 engines employ cooling systems that are basically similar.

In the 6-cylinder engine, coolant flows from the cylinder head, past the thermostat (if it is open) and into the radiator upper tank. In the V8 engine, coolant from each cylinder head flows through water passages in the intake manifold, then past the thermostat (if it is open) and into the radiator upper tank.

A single water pump assembly is used. The pump has a sealed bearing integral with the water pump shaft. The bearing requires no lubrication. There is a bleed hole in the water pump housing. This is not a lubrication hole.

Radiator Removal and Installation

1. Drain the cooling system.
2. Remove the upper and lower radiator hoses from the radiator.
3. On models with a fan shroud, remove the shroud attaching screws and move the shroud rearward to gain clearance.
4. If equipped with automatic transmission, remove the cooler lines from the radiator.
5. Remove radiator attaching screws and remove radiator from the car.
6. Reverse above procedure to install.
7. Fill cooling system, run engine at fast idle and check for leaks.

Water Pump Removal and Installation

1. Drain the cooling system. Disconnect the negative battery cable.
2. On cars with power steering, remove the drive belt; remove the power steering mounting retaining screws and remove the pump and bracket as an assembly and position it out of the way.
3. If vehicle is equipped with air conditioning, remove the idler pulley and drive belt from the engine.
4. Disconnect the lower radiator hose, heater hose and bypass hose from the water pump.
5. On cars with a fan shroud, remove the shroud retaining screws and position the shroud rearward over the fan.
6. Remove the fan attaching screws and remove the fan, fan spacer and shroud from the engine compartment.
7. Loosen the alternator mounting bolts and remove the belt.
8. Remove the air pump pulley and pivot bolt. Remove the air pump adjusting bracket. Swing the upper bracket aside. Detach the air conditioner compressor and lay it aside.
9. Remove any accessory mounting brackets from the water pump.
10. Disconnect the heater and lower radiator hoses from the water pump.
11. Remove the water pump mounting bolts and remove the pump from the engine.
12. Clean all gasket surfaces, and on 429 and 460 V8 remove the water pump backing plate and replace the gasket.

NOTE: the 240 6-cylinder engine originally had a one-piece gasket for the cylinder front cover and the water pump. Trim away the old gasket at the edge of the cylinder cover and replace with service gasket.

13. Remove the water pump fitting from the old pump and install it in the new pump.
14. Coat both sides of the new gasket with water resistant sealer, then install pump by reversing above procedure.

Thermostat Replacement

1. Drain the radiator so that the coolant level is below the thermostat housing.
2. Remove the outlet elbow retaining bolts and position the elbow clear of the intake manifold or cylinder head sufficiently to provide access to the thermostat.
3. Remove the thermostat and old gasket. The thermostat must be rotated counterclockwise for removal.
4. Clean the mating surfaces of the outlet elbow and the engine to remove all old gasket material and sealer. Coat the new gasket with water-resistant sealer and install it on the engine. Install the thermostat in the outlet elbow. The thermostat must be rotated clockwise to lock it in position.
5. Install the outlet elbow and retaining bolts on the engine. Torque the bolts to 12–15 ft lbs.
6. Refill the radiator. Run the engine at operating temperature and check for leaks. Recheck the coolant level.

EMISSION CONTROLS

All Ford cars use positive crankcase ventilation (PCV) systems. The PCV system routes a harmful mixture of blow-by gases and condensation vapors, which were formerly dispelled into the atmosphere, through a modulating valve (PCV valve) and into the intake manifold where they combine with the carburetor air/fuel mixture and are burned in the combustion chamber. The system is closed to the atmosphere, deriving its fresh air from the air cleaner.

1970-71

On 1970-71 high-performance V8 models, the Thermactor (air injection) system was used. This system, which injects fresh air into the exhaust ports to achieve after-burning of exhaust fumes, consists of an air pump, a bypass and a check valve, and external air manifolds (not an integral part of the engine exhaust manifolds).

The fuel evaporative emission control system was introduced on California models in 1970, and nationwide in 1971. This system eliminates pollution due to evaporating fuel by channeling the breathing of the fuel tank and by the venting of the carburetor float bowl through a canister filled with activated charcoal, condensing the fuel vapors and returning them to the fuel system.

The IMCO system of emission control was further extended in 1970 to become the Distributor Modulator (Dist-O-Vac) System. The Dist-O-Vac system incorporated all of the IMCO features but included three units of equipment which control spark advance in a more sophisticated manner. A speed sensor is located between two sections of the speedometer cable and generates a small current which increases in direct proportion to speed. A thermal switch is located in the right door pillar and activates at outside temperatures of 58°F or higher. The impulses of both are fed into the electronic control amplifier.

The distributor vacuum advance hose is connected from the carburetor, through the electronic control amplifier, to the distributor. When ambient temperature is above 58°F, the contacts in the temperature switch open and a plunger in the amplifier prevents vacuum from being supplied to the distributor. When vehicle speed reaches approximately 30 mph, the signal from the speed sensor causes the control amplifier to open the vacuum line to the distributor and ignition timing is allowed to advance in the normal manner. When the ambient temperature is below 58°F, the temperature switch closes, and normal vacuum is supplied to the distributor regardless of vehicle speed. In the event of engine overheating, the ported vacuum switch (PVS), a carryover from the IMCO system overrides the electronic control modulator by connecting intake manifold vacuum to the distributor.

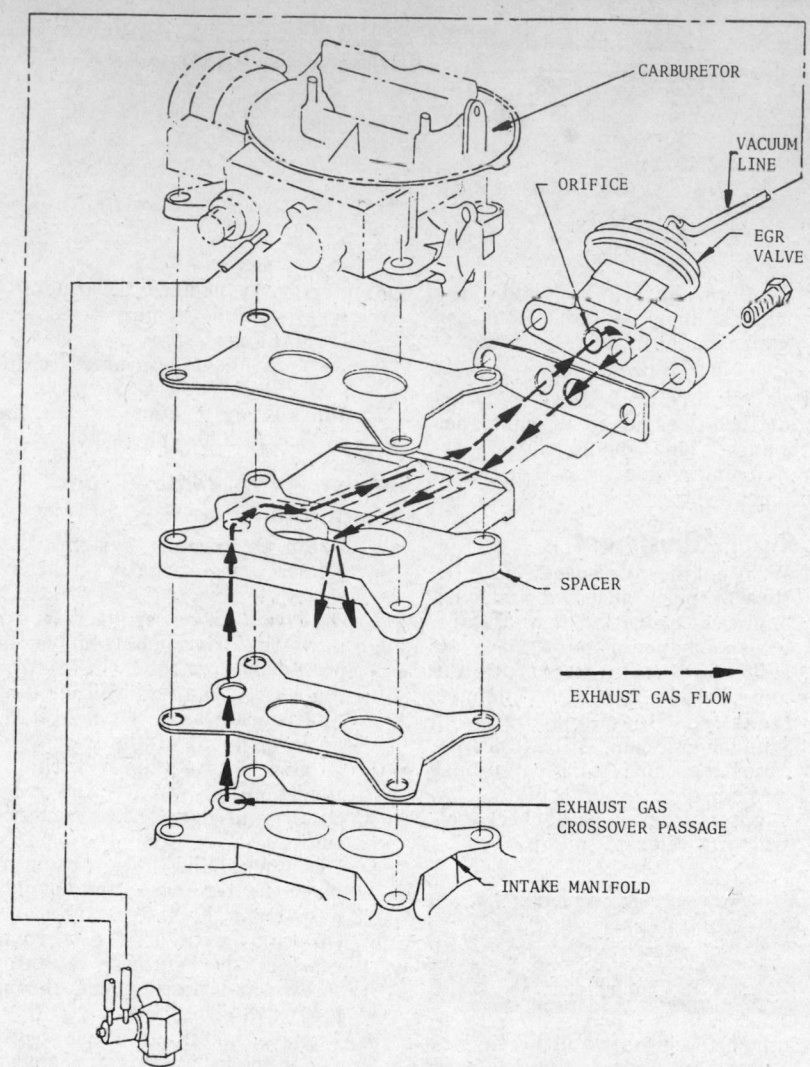

Exhaust Gas Recirculation (EGR) System (© Ford Motor Co)

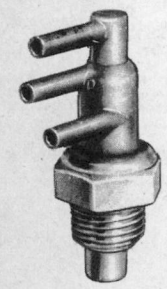

Ported Vacuum Switch (PVS)
(© Ford Motor Co)

1972

For 1972, the Dist-O-Vac system was replaced by two different spark control systems. The Electronic Spark Control (ESC) system is the same as the old Dist-O-Vac system except that the electronic control modulator was separated into two pieces, an amplifier and a distributor modulator valve. The amplifier judges the signals sent to it by the speed and temperature switches and tells the

distributor modulator valve when to open and close and thus allow or prevent vacuum to reach the distributor. The Transmission Regulated Spark (TRS) is similar to the ESC system except that the speed sensor is replaced by a transmission switch. The switch is mounted on the side of the transmission and is hydraulically actuated on cars equipped with an automatic transmission and manually actuated on models equipped with a manual transmission. When the ambient temperature is above 55°F, the transmission switch is closed whenever the transmission is in any gear other than high gear (manual transmission), or high gear or reverse (automatic transmission).

When the transmission switch closes, it signals the distributor modulator valve to close and thus prevent carburetor vacuum from reaching the distributor. As in past systems, neither of these systems is functional below 55–58°F, and both are bypassed by the PVS if the engine should overheat.

On some 1972 models, a spark

delay valve has been inserted into the vacuum advance line to the distributor. The valve closes under hard acceleration, blocking carburetor vacuum to the distributor for a predetermined period of a few seconds. The

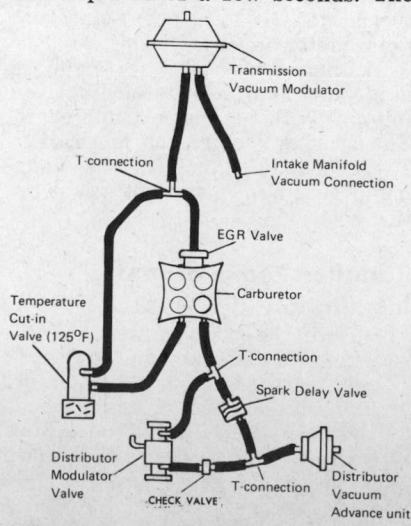

Typical vacuum hose schematic with EGR
(© Ford Motor Co)

valves are color coded for identification purposes.

1973-74

1973-74 models use an Exhaust Gas Recirculation System (EGR) to control oxides of nitrogen. On V8 engines, exhaust gases travel through the exhaust gas crossover passage in the intake manifold. A portion of these gases is diverted into a spacer which is mounted under the carburetor. The EGR control valve, which is attached to the rear of the spacer, consists of a vacuum diaphragm with an attached plunger which normally blocks off exhaust gases from entering the intake manifold. The EGR valve is controlled by a vacuum line from the carburetor which passes through a ported vacuum switch. The EGR ported vacuum switch provides vacuum to the EGR valve at coolant temperatures above 125°F. The vacuum diaphragm then opens the EGR valve permitting exhaust gases to flow through the carburetor spacer and enter the intake manifold where they combine with the fuel mixture and enter the combustion chambers. The exhaust gases are relatively oxygen-free and tend to dilute the combustion charge. This lowers peak combustion temperature thereby reducing oxides of nitrogen.

All models that are equipped with a 351C, 400, 429, or 460 V8 use the new Delay Vacuum By-Pass (DVB) spark control system. This system provides two paths by which carburetor vacuum can reach the distributor vacuum advance. The system consist of a spark delay valve, a check valve, a solenoid vacuum valve, and an ambient temperature switch. When the ambient temperature is below 49°F, the temperature switch contacts are open and the vacuum solenoid is open (de-energized). Under these conditions, vacuum will flow from the carburetor, through the open solenoid, and to the distributor. Since the spark delay valve resist the flow of carburetor vacuum, the vacuum will always flow through the vacuum solenoid when it is open, since this is the path of least resistance. When the ambient temperature rises above 60°F, the contacts in the temperature switch (which is located in the door post) close. This passes ignition switch current to the solenoid, energizing the solenoid. This blocks one of the two vacuum paths. All distributor vacuum must now flow through the spark delay valve. When carburetor vacuum rises above a certain level on acceleration, a rubber valve in the spark delay valve blocks vacuum from passing through the valve for from 5 to 30 seconds. After this time delay has elapsed, normal vacuum is supplied to the distributor. When the vacuum solenoid

CSSA system components

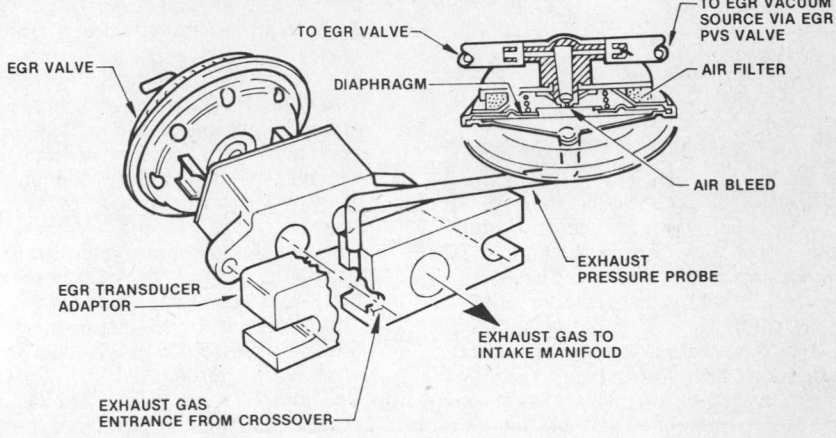

EGR valve with exhaust back pressure transducer (© Ford Motor Co)

is closed, (temperature above 60°), the vacuum line from the solenoid to the distributor is vented to atmosphere. To prevent the vacuum that is passing through the spark delay valve from escaping through the solenoid into the atmosphere, a one-way check valve is installed in the vacuum line from the solenoid to the distributor.

In order to meet 1974 California emission control standards, all 1974 Ford cars sold in that state will be equipped with a Thermactor (air injection) system to control hydrocarbons and carbon monoxide. The EGR and IMCO systems are retained, as in 1973, to control oxides of nitrogen.

1975

All full size Ford Motor Co. cars were equipped with catalytic converters. California models are equipped with two converters, while models sold in the 49 states have only one unit. The converters are needed to meet the 1975 Federal and California emission control standards.

Catalytic converters convert noxious emissions of hydrocarbons (HC) and carbon monoxide (CO) into harmless carbon dioxide and water. The units are installed in the exhaust system ahead of the mufflers and are designed, if the engine is properly

tuned, to last 50,000 miles before replacement.

In addition to the converters, most 1975 Ford, Mercury and Thunderbird cars are equipped with the Thermactor air pumps (air injection system) previously mentioned. The air injection system, which afterburns the uncombusted fuel mixture in the exhaust ports, is needed with the converters to prevent an overly rich mixture from reaching the converter, and to help supply oxygen to aid in converter reaction.

Other emission control equipment for 1975 includes a carryover of the Positive Crankcase Ventilation (PCV) System, the Fuel Evaporative Control System, spacer entry exhaust gas recirculation, and all of the IMCO engine modifications first introduced in 1968.

Emission control related improvements for 1975 include standard Solid State (breakerless) Ignition, induction hardened exhaust valve seats, exhaust manifold redesign, vacuum operated heat riser valves, and improved carburetors with more precise fuel metering control and a mechanical high-speed bleed system.

All cars equipped with the 460 V8 engine use a Cold Start Spark Advance (CSSA) System in 1975 to aid in cold start driveability. Basically, the system will allow full vacuum advance to the distributor until the coolant temperature reaches 125°F.

1976

For 1976, the complexity of emission control equipment has been reduced on Ford products. The average number of emission control components has been reduced from 25 to 11 on most cars. All 1976 models have catalytic converters. In addition, a new proportional exhaust gas recirculation system has been introduced. Exhaust backpressure regulates the EGR valve spark port vacuum signal to modulate the recirculation of gases, matching EGR flow to engine load.

1977

See the Comet car section for details on the 1977 emission control systems.

ENGINE

The only 6-cylinder engine available on full sized Fords through 1972 is the 240 cu. in. version. The intake manifolding on this six is mounted conventionally on the right-hand side and is detachable, unlike the intake manifolding on Ford sixes in smaller cars. The 302, 351W, 351C, 351M and 400 V8 engines are the most popular engines in full sized Fords. The 302 is notably compact, about 20 in. across. The larger displacement 351W is wider and bulkier although nearly identical in layout and conformation. All have trapezoidal shaped valve covers. The 390 and 428 family of engines is recognizable by its unusual intake manifold that extends under valve covers. The engines of this family are identical in exterior appearance. These engines have been widely used in full size Fords. The 351M, a modified 351C, was introduced in 1975.

The 429 engine was the first of a new series of big block Ford engines. It has been available in two-barrel and four-barrel versions. The engine is identifiable by its great bulk, and by the tunnel port configuration noticeable in the shape of its intake manifold. A similar 460 V8 is available on the Thunderbird and Mercury from 1972 and the Ford from 1974. The 240 Six and 302 V8 were discontinued in 1973 Fords, the 351 engine becoming standard equipment. The 429 V8 was dropped after the 1973 model run.

Engine Removal

Remove or disconnect air pump equipment that interferes with removal.

1. Scribe the hood hinge outline on the underside of the hood, disconnect the hood and remove.

2. Drain the entire cooling system and oil from engine oil pan.
3. Remove the air cleaner, disconnect the battery at the cylinder head. On automatic transmission-equipped cars, disconnect oil cooler lines at the radiator.
4. Remove the upper and lower radiator hoses from the engine and, if the engine is equipped with a fan shroud, disconnect the shroud from the radiator and position it rearward. Remove the radiator from the car.
5. Remove the fan attaching screws and remove the fan, fan spacer and shroud from the engine as an assembly. Loosen and remove all drive belts. Remove the water pump pulley.
6. Disconnect the heater hoses from the engine. If the vehicle is equipped with power steering, remove the pump from the engine and position it out of the way.
7. Remove the alternator mounting bolts and ground wire from the block and remove the alternator. Disconnect the carburetor kickdown linkage and speed control wire from the engine.
8. On models with power brakes, remove the vacuum line from the engine. On cars with air conditioning, remove the compressor mounting bracket from the engine and position the compressor out of the way without disconnecting the refrigerant lines.

NOTE: if the compressor lines do not have enough slack to move the compressor out of the way without disconnecting the refrigerant lines, the air conditioning system must be evacuated, using the required tools, before the refrigerant lines can be disconnected.

9. Disconnect fuel tank line at the fuel pump and plug the line. On 460 V8 remove the automatic transmission filler tube.
10. Disconnect the coil primary wire at the coil. Disconnect wires at the oil pressure and water temperature-sending units.
11. Remove the starter and dust seal.
12. On a car equipped with a manual-shift transmission, remove the clutch retracting spring. Disconnect the clutch equalizer shaft and arm bracket at the underbody rail and remove the arm bracket and equalizer.
13. Raise the car. Remove the flywheel or converter housing upper retaining bolts through the access holes in the floor pan.
14. Disconnect the exhaust pipe or pipes at the exhaust manifold. Disconnect the right and left motor mount at the underbody

bracket. Remove the flywheel or converter housing cover.
15. On a car with manual shift, remove the flywheel housing lower retaining bolts.
16. On a car with automatic transmission, disconnect throttle valve vacuum line at the intake manifold, disconnect the converter from the flywheel. Remove the converter housing lower retaining bolts.
17. Lower the car. Support the transmission and flywheel or converter housing with a jack.
18. Attach an engine lifting hook. Lift the engine up and out of the compartment and onto an adequate work stand.

Engine Installation

1. Place a new gasket over the studs of the exhaust manifold/s except on 390 and 428 engines.
2. Attach engine sling and lifting device. Then lift engine from work stand.
3. Lower the engine into the engine compartment. Be sure the exhaust manifold/s properly line up with the muffler inlet pipe/s and the dowels in the block engage the holes in the flywheel housing.
   On a car with automatic transmission, start the converter pilot into the crankshaft.
   On a car with manual-shift transmission, start the transmission main drive gear into the clutch disc. If the engine hangs up after the shaft enters, rotate the crankshaft slowly (with transmission in gear) until the shaft and clutch disc splines mesh.
4. Install the flywheel or converter housing upper bolts.
5. Install engine support insulator to bracket retaining nuts. Disconnect engine lifting sling and remove lifting brackets.
6. Raise front of car. Connect exhaust line/s and tighten attachments.
7. Position dust seal and install starter.
8. On cars with manual-shift transmissions, install remaining flywheel housing-to-engine bolts. Connect clutch release rod. Position the clutch equalizer bar and bracket and install retaining bolts. Install clutch pedal retracting spring.
9. On cars with automatic transmissions, remove the retainer holding the converter in the housing. Attach the converter to the flywheel. Install the converter housing inspection cover. Install the remaining converter housing retaining bolts.

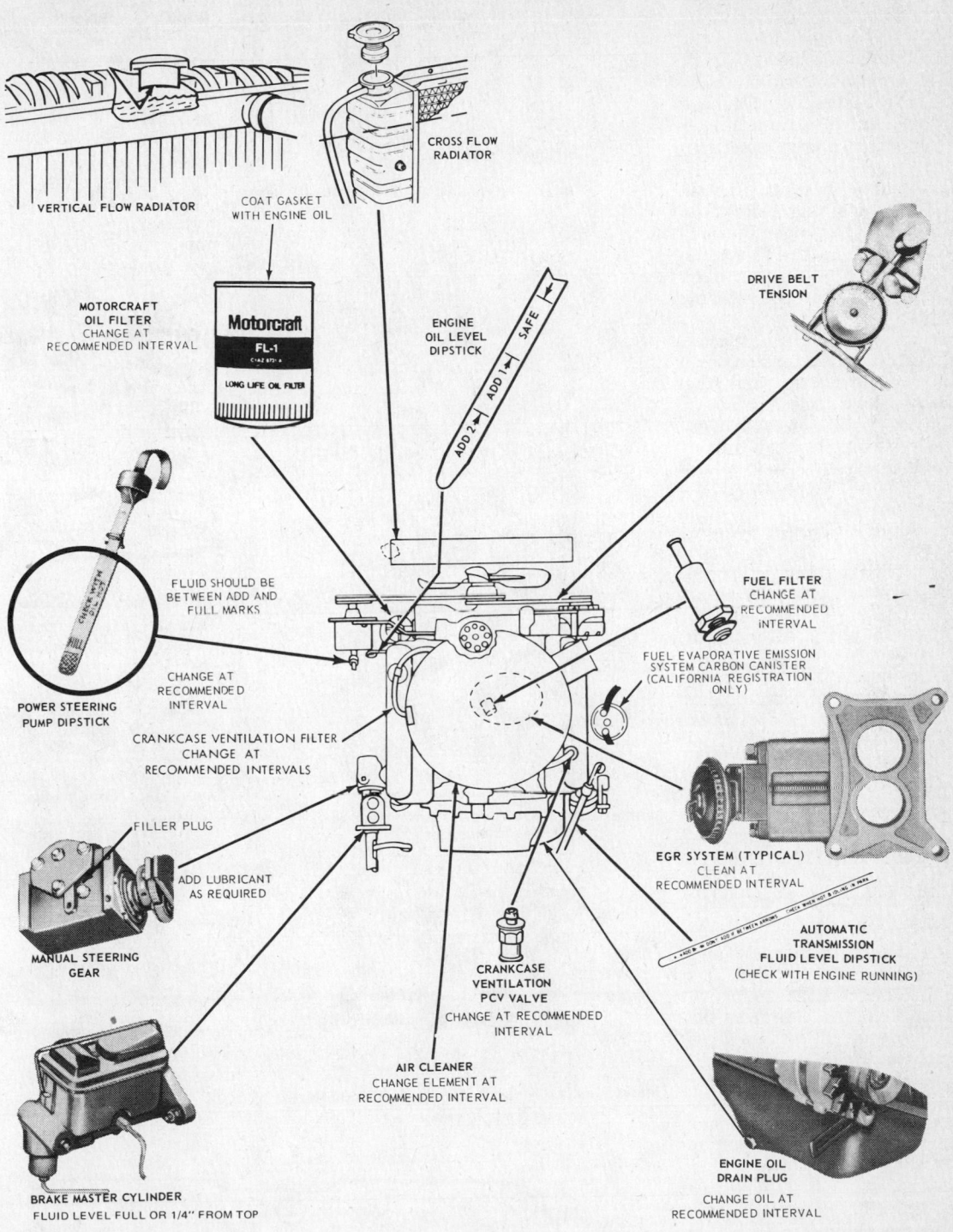

VERTICAL FLOW RADIATOR

CROSS FLOW RADIATOR

COAT GASKET WITH ENGINE OIL

MOTORCRAFT OIL FILTER
CHANGE AT RECOMMENDED INTERVAL

Motorcraft FL-1
LONG LIFE OIL FILTER

ENGINE OIL LEVEL DIPSTICK

SAFE
ADD 1
ADD 2

DRIVE BELT TENSION

FLUID SHOULD BE BETWEEN ADD AND FULL MARKS

POWER STEERING PUMP DIPSTICK

CHANGE AT RECOMMENDED INTERVAL

FUEL FILTER
CHANGE AT RECOMMENDED INTERVAL

FUEL EVAPORATIVE EMISSION SYSTEM CARBON CANISTER (CALIFORNIA REGISTRATION ONLY)

CRANKCASE VENTILATION FILTER CHANGE AT RECOMMENDED INTERVALS

FILLER PLUG

ADD LUBRICANT AS REQUIRED

MANUAL STEERING GEAR

EGR SYSTEM (TYPICAL)
CLEAN AT RECOMMENDED INTERVAL

AUTOMATIC TRANSMISSION FLUID LEVEL DIPSTICK
(CHECK WITH ENGINE RUNNING)

CRANKCASE VENTILATION PCV VALVE
CHANGE AT RECOMMENDED INTERVAL

AIR CLEANER
CHANGE ELEMENT AT RECOMMENDED INTERVAL

BRAKE MASTER CYLINDER
FLUID LEVEL FULL OR 1/4" FROM TOP

ENGINE OIL DRAIN PLUG
CHANGE OIL AT RECOMMENDED INTERVAL

V8 engine service points (© Ford Motor Co.)

10. Remove the support from the transmission and lower the car.
11. Connect engine ground strap and coil primary wire.
12. Connect water temperature gauge wire and the heater hose at coolant outlet housing. Connect accelerator rod at the bellcrank.
13. On cars with automatic transmission, connect the transmission filler tube bracket. Connect the throttle valve vacuum line.
14. On cars with power steering, install the drive belt and power steering pump bracket. Install the bracket retaining bolts. Adjust drive belt to proper tension.
15. Remove plug from the fuel tank line. Connect the flexible fuel line and the oil pressure sending unit wire.
16. Install the pulley, belt spacer, and fan. Adjust belt tension.
17. Install the alternator and the negative battery cable.
18. In vehicles with power brakes, connect vacuum line at intake manifold. On cars with air conditioning, install compressor on mounting bracket.
19. Install radiator. Connect radiator hoses.
20. On cars with automatic transmissions, connect oil cooler lines.
21. Install oil filter. Connect heater hose at water pump, after bleeding the system.
22. Bring crankcase to level with correct grade of oil. Run engine at fast idle and check for leaks. Install air cleaner and make final engine adjustments.
23. Install and adjust hood.
24. Road test car.

Engine Manifolds

Intake and Exhaust Manifold Removal—6-Cylinder

1. Remove the air cleaner. Remove the carburetor linkage and kick down linkage from the engine.
2. Disconnect the fuel line from the carburetor and all vacuum lines from the manifolds.
3. Remove the negative battery cable, then remove the alternator mounting bolts and remove the alternator from the engine with the wires attached.
4. Disconnect the muffler inlet pipe from the engine.
5. Remove the manifold attaching parts from the engine, and remove the two manifolds as an assembly.
6. To separate the manifolds, remove the carburetor and then remove the nuts that secure the manifolds together.
7. Clean all gasket areas and reverse above procedure to install; using all new gaskets.

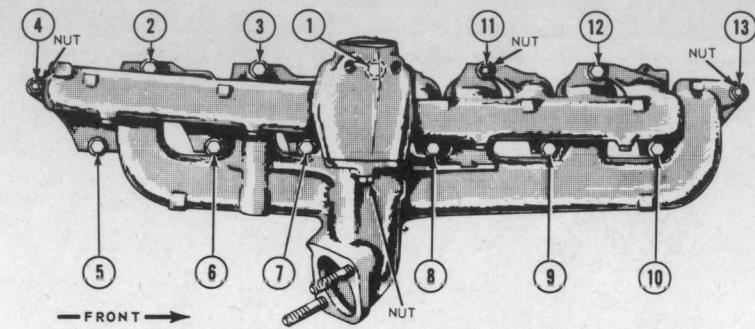

Intake and exhaust manifold torque sequence—240 six cyl. (© Ford Motor Co)

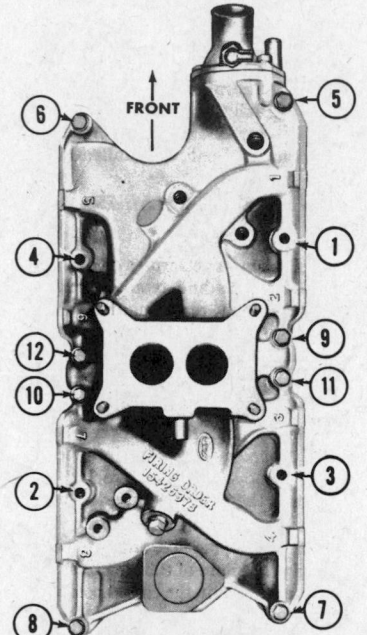

Intake manifold torque sequence—302 V8 (© Ford Motor Co)

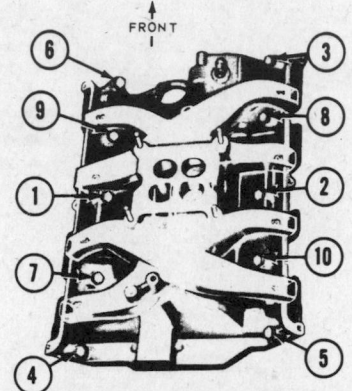

Intake manifold torque sequence—390 and 428 V8 (© Ford Motor Co)

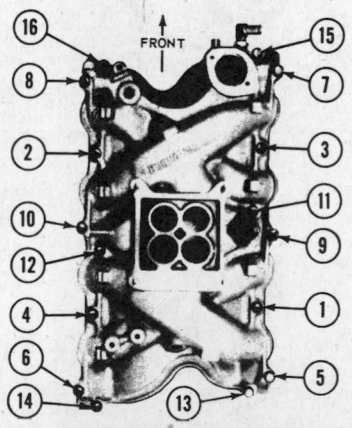

Intake manifold torque sequence—429 and 460 V8 (© Ford Motor Co)

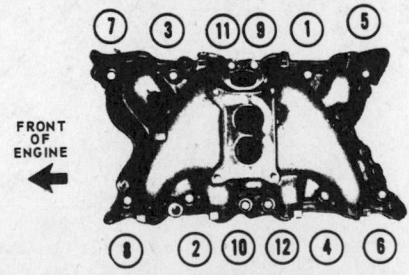

Intake manifold torque sequence—351C, 351M, 400 V8 (© Ford Motor Co)

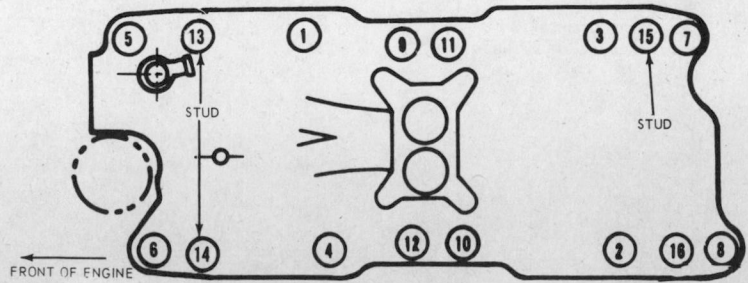

Intake manifold torque sequence—351W V8 (© Ford Motor Co)

Intake Manifold Removal— V8

1. Remove the compressor from its mount. Leave the refrigerant lines attached and set the compressor aside.
2. Drain the cooling system.
3. Disconnect the upper radiator hose from the thermostat housing and the bypass hose from the manifold.
4. Remove the air cleaner and ducts.
5. Remove the distributor cap and wires from the engine. Mark the position of the distributor rotor in relationship to the intake manifold, remove the primary wire from the coil, then remove the distributor hold-down bolt and the distributor. Remove the coil, vacuum solenoid valve and bracket.
6. Remove all vacuum lines from the intake manifold and remove the temperature sending unit wire.
7. Disconnect the fuel line and any vacuum lines from the carburetor.
8. Remove all carburetor linkage and kickdown linkage that attaches to the intake manifold.
9. On 390 and 428 engines, remove the valve covers, the rocker arm assemblies and the pushrods. The rocker arms should be removed by backing off each of the four bolts two turns in sequence from front to back. Keep pushrods in order so that they can be installed in their original position.
10. Remove the manifold attaching bolts and remove the manifold. If it is necessary to pry the manifold to loosen it from the engine, use care not to damage any gasket sealing surfaces.
11. Clean all gasket surfaces and firmly cement new gaskets in place. The gaskets should be securely locked in place before attempting to install the manifold.
12. Reverse procedure to reinstall.

Exhaust Manifold Removal— V8

1. If the right-side manifold is to be removed, disconnect the choke heat tube, remove the air cleaner and ducts.
2. On vehicles with 351C and 400 V8s, to remove the left manifold, remove the oil filter. If equipped with an automatic transmission remove the transmission selector lever cross-shaft from the engine block. If equipped with a manual transmission, disconnect the equalizer shaft bracket and clutch linkage from the engine.
3. Disconnect the manifolds from the muffler inlet pipes.
4. If the manifold attaching bolts are installed with locking washers, bend back the tabs on the washers.
5. Remove the manifold to cylinder head attaching bolts, and remove the manifolds from the car.
6. Clean all gasket surfaces, and reverse above procedure to install; using all new gaskets.

Valve System

Preliminary Valve Adjustment

6-Cylinder

1. Crank the engine until the TDC mark on the crankshaft damper is aligned with timing pointer on the cylinder front cover.
2. Scribe a mark on the damper at this point.
3. Scribe two more marks on the damper, each equally spaced from the first mark (see illustration).
4. With the engine on TDC of the compression stroke, (mark A aligned with the pointer) back off the rocker arm adjusting nut until there is end-play in the pushrod. Tighten the adjusting nut until all clearance is removed, then tighten the adjusting nut one additional turn. To determine when all clearance is removed from the rocker arm, turn the pushrod with the fingers. When the pushrod can no longer be turned, all clearance has been removed.
5. Repeat this procedure for each valve, turning the crankshaft 1/3 turn to the next mark each time and following the engine firing order of 1-5-3-6-2-4.

STEP 1—SET NO. 1 PISTON ON T.D.C. AT END OF COMPRESSION STROKE ADJUST NO. 1 INTAKE AND EXHAUST

STEP 4—ADJUST NO. 6 INTAKE AND EXHAUST

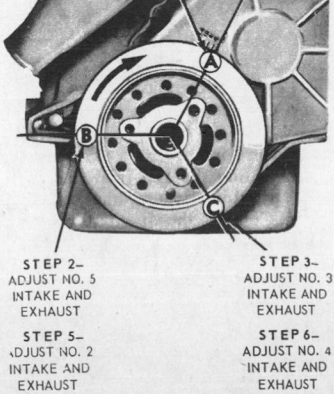

STEP 2— ADJUST NO. 5 INTAKE AND EXHAUST

STEP 3— ADJUST NO. 3 INTAKE AND EXHAUST

STEP 5— ADJUST NO. 2 INTAKE AND EXHAUST

STEP 6— ADJUST NO. 4 INTAKE AND EXHAUST

Position of crankshaft for valve adjustment —6 cylinder
(© Ford Motor Co)

FRONT

Valve locations—240 6 cylinder

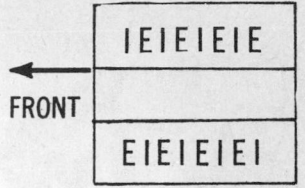

FRONT

Valve locations—302, 351W, 351C, 351M, 400, 429 and 460 V8

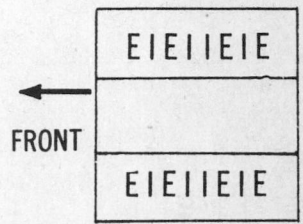

FRONT

Valve locations—390 and 428 V8

All V8

NOTE: The early 302 V8 engine has rocker arm mounting studs which do *not* incorporate a positive stop shoulder on the mounting stud. These engines were originally equipped with this kind of stud. However, due to production differences, it is possible some early 302 engines may be encountered that *are* equipped with positive stop rocker arm mounting studs. Before adjusting the valves, verify that the rocker arm mounting studs do not incorporate a positive stop shoulder. On studs without a positive stop, the shank portion of the stud that is exposed just above the cylinder head is the same diameter as the threaded portion, at the top of the stud, to which the rocker arm retaining nut attaches. If the shank portion of the stud is of greater diameter than the threaded portion, this identifies it as a positive stop rocker arm stud and the adjustment specifications for the 351 engine with adjusting nuts should be used. Only the 302, 351W and 1970-71 429 engines require a preliminary valve adjustment. All other V-8s use either a bolt and fulcrum (351C, 351M, 400, 460 and 1972-73 429) or rocker shafts (390 and 428). High performance versions of any of these V-8s probably will be equipped with rocker arm adjusting nuts.

302, 351W and 1970-71 429
With Rocker Arm Adjusting Nuts

1. Crank the engine until #1 cylinder is at TDC of the compression stroke and the timing pointer is aligned with the mark on the crankshaft damper.
2. Scribe a mark on the damper at this point.

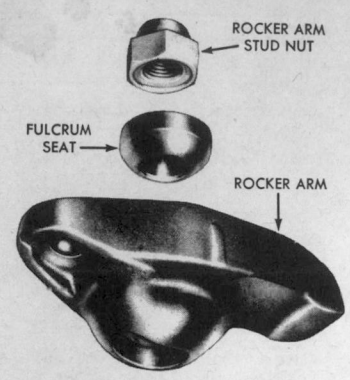

Rocker arm—stud/nut type
(© Ford Motor Co)

3. Scribe three more marks on the damper, dividing the damper into quarters.

4. With the first mark aligned with the timing pointer, adjust the valves on #1 cylinder by backing off the adjusting nut until the pushrod has free play in it. Then, tighten the nut until there is no free play in the rocker arm. This can be determined by turning the pushrod while tightening the nut; when the pushrod can no longer be turned, all clearance has been removed. After the clearance has been removed, tighten the nut an additional ¾ of a turn. (302 V8 w/o positive stop rocker arm studs).

5. Rocker arm adjusting nut tightening specifications are: 302 (with positive stop rocker arm studs) and 351W—tighten the nut until it contacts the rocker shoulder, then torque it to 18-20 ft lbs; 429—tighten the nut until it contacts the rocker shoulder then tighten the nut to 18-22 ft lbs.

6. Repeat this procedure for each valve, turning the crankshaft ¼ turn to the next mark each time and following the engine firing order.

390 and 428 with Rocker Shafts

These engines do not require a preliminary valve adjustment. In the event of cylinder head removal or some operation requiring that the valve train be disturbed, torque the

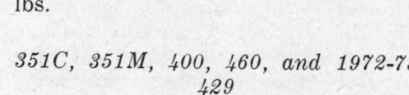

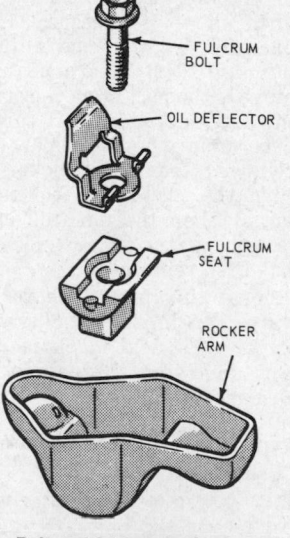

Bolt and fulcrum rocker arm
(© Ford Motor Co)

Chilton's TIME SAVER

Frequently valves become bent or warped, or their seats become blocked with carbon or other material. Left unattended, these situations can cause burnt valves, damaged cylinder heads and other expensive trouble. To detect leaking valves early, perform this test whenever the cylinder head is removed.

1. After removing head, replace spark plugs. Removing spark plugs before removing heads eliminates breakage.

2. Place head on bench with valves, springs, retainers, and keys installed—combustion chambers up.

3. Pour enough gasoline into each combustion chamber to completely cover both valves. Watch combustion chambers for two minutes for any leakage.

Tappet Removal

To remove and replace tappets from 390 and 428 engines without removing the intake manifold, first remove rocker covers and rocker assembly. Then remove pushrods from their bores. Locate tappet or tappets to be moved by shining a light through pushrod bores. Use a magnet or claw tool to seize tappet and withdraw it through pushrod bore. It may be necessary on some tappets to move them over and draw them through a larger adjoining pushrod bore, but tappets should always be replaced in their original holes.

rocker arm shaft supports to 40-45 ft lbs.

351C, 351M, 400, 460, and 1972-73 429

These engines use a bolt and fulcrum rocker arm and require no preliminary valve adjustment. In the event that the valve train is disturbed, install the fulcrum, oil deflector, and tighten the bolt to 18-25 ft. lbs.

Valve Guides

Valve guides on all engines are an integral part of the cylinder head casting. If valve guides become worn, they can be reamed oversize or bronze replacement bushings can be installed. Oversize valves are available with stem diameters .003, .015, and .030 in. larger than standard. If the guides are to be reamed more than .003 in. oversize, they must be reamed in steps starting with .003 in. and progressing until the desired diameter is achieved.

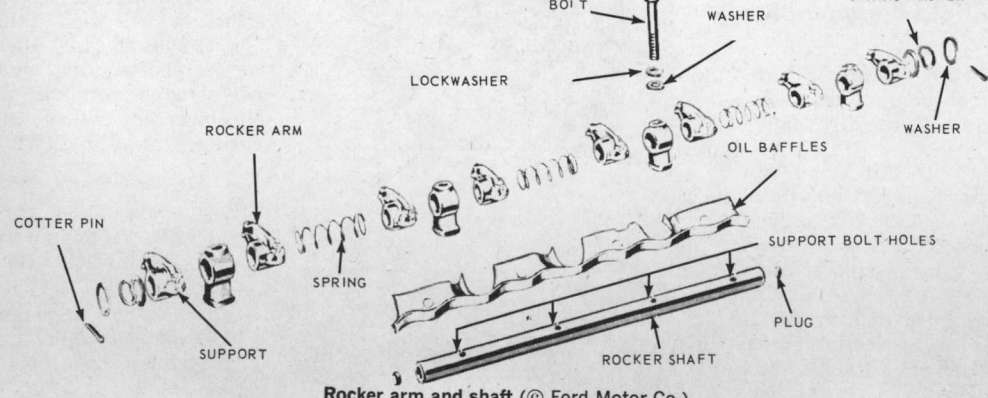

Rocker arm and shaft (© Ford Motor Co.)

NOTE: when valve guides become worn, the excessive clearance between the valve and the head can allow the valve to tap on the cylinder head and emit a noise very similar to the noise a defective valve lifter emits. When checking the valve system to locate a noise, and the lifters are not defective and no excessive clearances exist in the valve train, the valve guides should be checked for wear.

Cylinder Head

6-Cylinder Head Removal

1. Drain coolant and remove air cleaner. Disconnect battery cable at cylinder head.
2. Disconnect exhaust pipe at manifold.
3. Disconnect accelerator retracting spring, choke control cable and accelerator rod at carburetor.
4. Disconnect fuel line and distributor control vacuum line at the carburetor.
5. Disconnect coolant tubes from carburetor spacer. Disconnect coolant and heater hoses.
6. Disconnect distributor control vacuum line at distributor and fuel inlet line at the filter. Remove lines as an assembly.
7. On an engine equipped with positive crankcase ventilation, disconnect the emission exhaust tube.
8. Disconnect spark plug wires at the plugs and the small wire from the temperature-sending unit. On an engine equipped with a Thermactor exhaust emission control system, disconnect the air pump hose at the air manifold assembly. Unscrew the tube nuts and remove the air manifold. Disconnect the anti-backfire valve air and vacuum lines at the intake manifold. On a car equipped with power brakes, disconnect the brake vacuum line at the intake manifold.
9. Remove rocker arm cover.
10. Loosen the rocker arm stud nut so that the rocker arm can be rotated to one side. Remove valve pushrods and keep them in sequence.
11. Remove remaining cylinder head bolts, then remove cylinder head.

6-Cylinder Head Installation

1. Clean head and block surfaces.
2. Apply sealer to both sides of head gasket. Position gasket over guide studs or dowel pins.
   NOTE: apply gasket sealer only to steel shim head gaskets. Steel-asbestos composite head gaskets are to be installed without any sealer.
3. Install new gasket on the exhaust pipe flange.

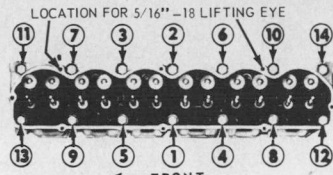

Cylinder head torque sequence—240 six cyl. (© Ford Motor Co)

4. Lift the cylinder head over the guide studs and slide it carefully into place while guiding the exhaust manifold studs into the exhaust pipe flange.
5. Coat cylinder-head attaching bolts with water-resistant sealer and install (but do not tighten), the head bolts.
6. Torque the head, in proper sequence, and in three progressive steps to specifications.
7. Lubricate both ends of the pushrods and insert them in their original bores and sockets.
8. Lubricate valve stem tips and rocker arm pads.
9. Position the rocker arms and tighten the stud nuts enough to hold the pushrods in position. Adjust the valves.
10. Install exhaust pipe-to-manifold nuts and lockwashers. Torque to 17-22 ft. lbs.
11. Connect radiator and heater hoses. Connect coolant tubes at the carburetor spacer.
12. Connect distributor vacuum line and the carburetor fuel line. Connect battery cable to cylinder head.
13. On engines equipped with positive crankcase ventilation, clean components thoroughly and install.
   NOTE: on engines equipped with a Thermactor exhaust emission control system, install the air manifold assembly on the cylinder head. Connect the air pump outlet hose to the air manifold. Connect the anti-backfire valve, air and vacuum lines to the intake manifold.
14. Connect accelerator rod pull-back spring. Connect choke control cable and the accelerator rod at the carburetor.
15. Connect distributor control vacuum line at distributor. Connect

carburetor fuel line at fuel filter.
16. Connect temperature - sending unit wire at sending unit. Connect spark plug wires.
17. Completely fill and bleed the cooling system.
18. Run the engine to stabilize engine temperature. Check for coolant and oil leaks.
19. Adjust engine idle mixture and speed.
20. Install valve rocker arm cover, then the air cleaner.

V8 Head, 390, 428, Removal

1. Remove intake manifold as previously described.
2. Remove any remaining accessories.
3. Disconnect the muffler inlet pipes from the manifolds.
4. Unbolt and remove heads.

V8 Head, 302, 351, 400, 429, and 460 cu. in., Removal

1. Remove the intake manifold and carburetor as an assembly.
2. Remove rocker arm covers.
3. On cars equipped with air conditioning, isolate and remove the compressor.
4. If the left cylinder head is involved on a car with power steering, remove the steering pump and bracket and remove the drive belt. Tie assembly out of the way.
5. If the left cylinder head is involved on a car equipped with a Thermactor exhaust emission control system, disconnect the hose from the air manifold on the left cylinder head.
6. If the right head is involved, remove the alternator mounting bracket bolt and spacer, ignition coil and air cleaner inlet duct from the right cylinder head.
7. If the right cylinder head is to be removed on an engine equipped with a Thermactor exhaust emission control system, remove the air pump and bracket. Disconnect the hose from the right cylinder head.
8. Disconnect the exhaust manifold/s at the exhaust pipe/s.
9. Loosen rocker arm stud nuts so that the arms can rotate to the

Cylinder head torque sequence—all V8 (© Ford Motor Co)

side to clear the pushrods. Remove the pushrods. On 351 engines, remove exhaust manifold to get access to lower cylinder head bolts.

10. Remove cylinder-head bolts and lift off cylinder head.

V8 Head Installation

Installation is the reverse of removal. See valve adjustment under Valve System.

Timing Case

Timing Gear Cover Removal
6-Cylinder Engines

1. Drain the cooling system and the crankcase.
2. Remove the radiator from the car.
3. Loosen and remove all engine drive belts.
4. On vehicles with power steering, disconnect the pump mounting bracket from the cylinder front cover and position the pump and bracket out of the way.
5. On models with air conditioning, remove the condenser mounting bolts and position the condenser out of the way. *Do not disconnect the refrigerant lines.*
6. Disconnect and remove the fan and fan spacer.
7. Remove any accessory drive pulleys from the crankshaft damper. Remove the capscrew and washer from the crankshaft end; then, using a puller, remove the crankshaft damper.
8. Remove the alternator adjusting arm bolt and position the arm out of the way.
9. Remove the starter cable and attaching bolts, and remove the starter.
10. Remove the engine front support insulator to intermediate support bracket nuts on both supports. Remove the engine rear support insulator to crossmember bolt and insulator to transmission extension housing bolts. Raise the transmission and remove the support insulator. Lower the transmission to the crossmember.
11. Raise the engine and place 2 in. thick blocks of wood between both supports and brackets.
12. Remove the oil pan bolts, and lower the oil pan. Reach inside the oil pan and remove the two oil pump to block bolts, and lower the pump and screen into the pan. Turn the crankshaft as required to gain clearance and remove the oil pan.
13. Remove the front cover attaching bolts and remove the cover from the engine.
14. Reverse above procedure to install.

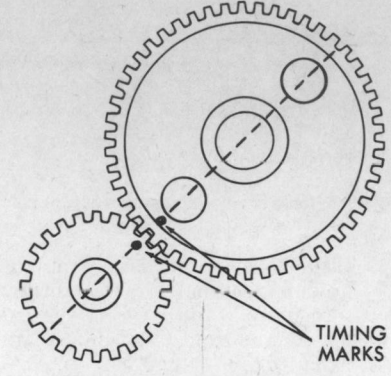

TIMING MARKS

Timing mark alignment—6 cyl.

Timing Gear and/or Camshaft Replacement
6-Cylinder

1. Remove the timing case cover.
2. Mark the location of the grille center support and hood lock assembly in relation to the radiator support. Remove the grille, center support, and hood lock as an assembly.
3. Remove the air cleaner and valve cover.
4. Disconnect the fuel pump outlet line and remove the fuel pump from the engine.
5. Loosen the rocker arm nuts and position the rocker arms to the side so the pushrods can be removed. Keep the pushrods in order so that they can be returned to their original location in the engine.
6. Remove the pushrod cover from the side of the engine, and, using a magnet, remove the lifters from their bores. Keep the lifters in order so they can be returned to their original location in the engine.
7. Rotate the engine until the timing marks are aligned on the timing gears.
8. Remove the camshaft thrust plate screws.
9. Remove the camshaft by pulling it out the front of the engine. Use care not to damage the camshaft lobes or journals while removing the cam from the engine.
10. Place the camshaft/gear assembly in a press and press the cam from the gear.
11. Position new gear on camshaft and press into position.
12. Using a puller, remove the crankshaft timing gear.
13. Using a suitable tool, press the new gear onto the crankshaft.
14. Before installing the camshaft in the engine, coat the lobes with Lubriplate and the journals and all valve train components with heavy oil.
15. Reverse above procedure to install, following recommended torque settings and performing

preliminary valve adjustment before starting engine.

V8 Cover and Chain
Removal

1. Drain the cooling system and crankcase.
2. Disconnect the negative battery cable.
3. If equipped with a fan shroud, disconnect it from the radiator and position it rearward.
4. Remove the radiator. Remove the fuel pump.
5. Remove the fan attaching bolts, remove the fan, fan spacer and shroud from the engine.
6. Loosen and remove all engine drive belts.
7. Remove the power steering pump mounting bracket and position the pump and bracket out of the way.
8. If equipped with air conditioning, remove the compressor and condenser and position them out of the way. *Do not disconnect the refrigerant lines.*
9. Disconnect the alternator adjusting arm from the engine and position it out of the way.
10. If equipped with Thermactor, remove the pump from the engine.
11. Disconnect the heater hose and bypass hose from the water pump.
12. Remove any accessory drive pulleys from the crankshaft damper and remove the crankshaft front bolt and washer.
13. Using a puller, remove the crankshaft damper from the engine.
14. On 390 and 428 V8, use a suitable tool to pull the crankshaft sleeve away from the cylinder front cover. Remove the sleeve from the engine.
15. Remove the front cover attaching bolts and the front oil pan bolts.
16. Remove the front cover and water pump from the engine.
17. Remove the crankshaft front oil slinger.
18. To check timing chain free play, rotate the crankshaft in a clockwise direction until all slack is removed from the left side of the chain. Scribe a mark on the engine parallel to the present position of the chain. Next, rotate the crankshaft in a counterclockwise direction to remove all the slack from the right side of the chain. Force the left side of the chain outward with the fingers and measure the distance between the present position of the chain and the reference mark on the engine. If the distance exceeds ½ in., replace the chain and sprockets.

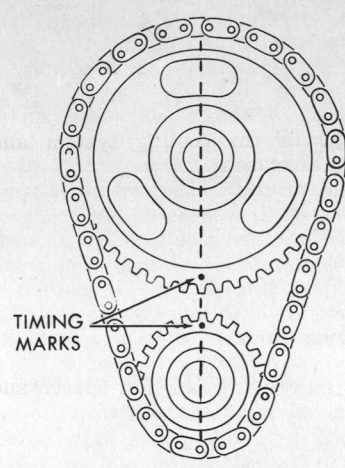

Timing mark alignment—V8

19. To replace the chain and sprockets, crank the engine until the timing marks are aligned as shown in the illustration.
20. Remove the camshaft sprocket attaching bolt and remove the chain and sprockets from the engine by sliding them forward as an assembly.

Installation

1. Position the chain and sprockets on the engine, making sure that the timing marks on the sprockets are aligned.
2. Clean all gasket surfaces. Trim away the exposed portion of the oil pan gasket flush with the front of the block.
3. Cut and position the required portion of a new gasket to the oil pan, applying sealer to both sides of it.
4. Reinstall the front cover, applying oil resistant sealer to the new gasket.
5. Install the components that were removed from the engine by reversing the removal procedure.

Timing Case Oil Seal Replacement

All Models

To replace the oil seal, it is necessary to take off the timing case cover and drive the seal out with a pin punch. Clean out the recess in the cover and install a new seal using a special driving tool.

Coat the new seal with grease to reduce friction when installing and starting the car.

V8 Camshaft Replacement

1. Remove the intake manifold.
2. Remove the cylinder front cover, timing chain and sprockets as outlined previously.
3. Remove the rocker arm covers.
4. On 390 and 428 engines it is necessary to remove the rocker arm shafts to remove the intake manifold. On all other engines with

individual rocker arms, loosen the rocker arm fulcrum bolts or nuts and rotate the rocker arms to the side.
5. Remove the pushrods and lifters and keep them in order so that they can be installed in their original location.
6. Remove the camshaft thrust plate and washer if so equipped. Remove the camshaft from the front of the engine. On certain engine/chassis combinations it may be necessary to remove the grille to gain adequate clearance to remove the camshaft. Use care not to damage the camshaft lobes or journals while removing the cam from the engine.
7. Before installing the camshaft in the engine, coat the lobes with Lubriplate and the journals and all valve train components with heavy oil.
8. Reverse above procedure to install.
9. On all engines with individually mounted rocker arms, a preliminary valve adjustment must be performed before starting the engine.

Piston and Rod Alignment

When installing the assembled piston and rod, positioning is as follows:

240 cu. in.—bearing tang side of rod toward the left; notch on top of piston toward the front.

302, 351W, 429, 460—numbered side of rod outboard; notch on top of piston toward the front.

351H0—numbered side of rod outboard; arrow on top of piston inboard.

351C, 400—numbered side of rod outboard; arrow on top of piston forward.

Engine Lubrication

Oil Pan Removal

6 Cylinder

1. Drain crankcase and cooling system.
2. Disconnect upper hose at outlet elbow and lower hose at radiator. Remove radiator.
3. Disconnect flexible fuel line at fuel pump.
4. With automatic transmission, disconnect kickdown rod at bellcrank assembly. On car with standard transmission, disconnect clutch linkage.
5. Raise car on hoist.
6. Disconnect starter cable at starter. Remove retaining bolts and remove starter.
7. Remove nuts on both engine front support insulator-to-support bracket.

8. Remove bolt and insulator, rear support insulator-to-crossmember and insulator-to-transmission extension housing.
9. Raise transmission, remove support insulator, lower transmission to crossmember.
10. Raise engine with transmission jack and place 3-in. thick wood blocks between both front support insulators and intermediate support brackets.
11. Remove oil pan retaining bolts and oil pump mounting bolts. With oil pump in pan, rotate crankshaft as needed to remove pan.
12. Install in reverse of above.

V8

1. Raise car and place safety stands in position. Drain oil from crankcase. On 429 V8s, disconnect the negative battery cable. On 1970–71 429 V8s, remove bolt attaching vacuum line retaining clip to upper right side of converter housing.
2. Disconnect stabilizer bar links and pull ends down. On models equipped with a fan shroud, remove the shroud from the radiator and position it rearward over the fan. On automatic transmission equipped cars, position oil cooler lines aside.
3. Remove nuts and lockwashers from engine front support insulator-to-intermediate support bracket.
4. Install block of wood on jack and position jack under leading edge of pan.
5. Raise engine approximately 1¼ in. and insert a 1-in. block between insulators and crossmember. Remove floor jack. On 351C, 400, 429, and 460 V8s, remove the starter. On 1972-75 429 and 460 V8s remove the oil filter.
6. Remove oil pan attaching screws and lower pan to frame crossmember.
7. Turn crankshaft to obtain clearance between crankshaft counterweight and rear of pan.
8. Remove oil pump attaching bolts.
9. Position tube and screen out of the way and remove the pan.
10. Install in reverse of above.

Oil Pump

Removal and Installation

1. Remove the oil pan as under the previous "Oil Pan Removal and Installation" procedure.
2. On 302 and 351W V8 applications, remove the oil pump inlet tube and screen assembly.
3. Remove the oil pump attaching bolts. Lower the oil pump, gasket, and intermediate driveshaft

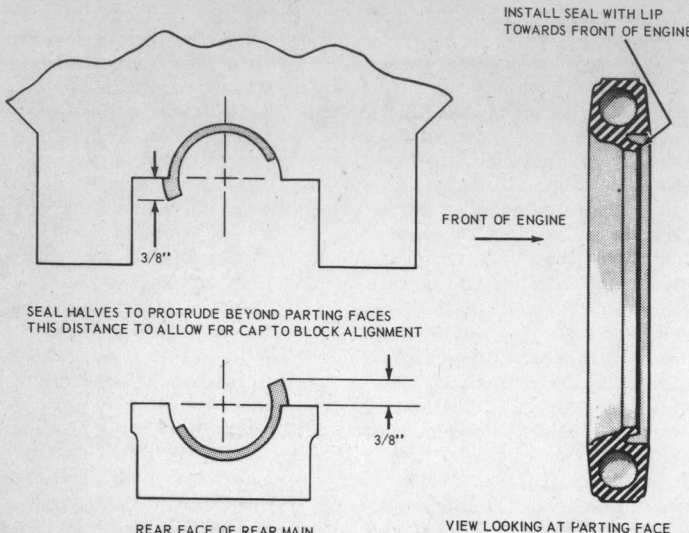

INSTALL SEAL WITH LIP
TOWARDS FRONT OF ENGINE

FRONT OF ENGINE

3/8"

SEAL HALVES TO PROTRUDE BEYOND PARTING FACES
THIS DISTANCE TO ALLOW FOR CAP TO BLOCK ALIGNMENT

3/8"

REAR FACE OF REAR MAIN
BEARING CAP AND CYLINDER BLOCK

VIEW LOOKING AT PARTING FACE
OF SPLIT, LIP-TYPE CRANKSHAFT SEAL

Installing split-lip type rear main oil seal (© Ford Motor Co)

from the crankcase. If not already removed, remove and clean the inlet tube and screen assembly.

4. To install, prime the oil pump by filling either the inlet or outlet port with engine oil. Rotate the pump shaft to distribute the oil within the pump body.

5. Position the intermediate driveshaft into the distributor socket. With the shaft firmly seated in the socket, the stop on the shaft should contact the roof of the crankcase. Remove the shaft and position the stop as necessary.

6. Insert the intermediate driveshaft into the oil pump. Using a new gasket, install the pump and shaft as an assembly. Do not attempt to force the pump into position if it will not seat readily. If necessary, rotate the intermediate driveshaft hex into a new position so that it will mesh with the distributor shaft.

7. Torque the oil pump attaching bolts to 12-15 ft lbs on the six-cylinder engines, 22-32 ft lbs on the 302 and 351W V8, 20-35 ft lbs on the 351C, 351M and 400 V8, and 20-25 ft lbs on the 390, 428, 429, and 460 V8.

8. Clean and install the inlet tube and screen assembly.

9. Install the oil pan as under "Oil Pan Removal and Installation."

Rear Main Bearing Oil Seal Replacement

NOTE: the rear oil seal installed in these engines is a rubber type seal.

1. Remove the oil pan and oil pump if required.

2. Loosen all main bearing cap bolts, lowering crankshaft slightly but not more than 1/32 in.

3. Remove rear main cap, and

remove upper and lower halves of seal. On block half of seal, use seal removing tool or insert a small metal screw into end of seal with which to draw it out.

4. Clean seal grooves with solvent and dip replacement seal in clean engine oil.

5. Install upper seal half in its groove in block with lip toward front of engine by rotating it on seal journal of crankshaft until approximately 3/8 in. protrudes below parting surface.

6. Tighten other main caps and torque to specification.

7. Install lower seal half in rear main cap with lip to front and approximately 3/8 in. of seal protrudes to mate with upper seal.

8. Install rear main cap and torque.

9. Dip side seals in engine oil and install them. Tap seals in last half inch if necessary. Do not cut protruding ends of seals.

CLUTCH

Clutch Pedal Adjustment

1. Disconnect the clutch return spring from the release lever.

2. Loosen the release lever adjusting nut and locknut.

3. Move the clutch release lever rearward until the throwout bearing can be felt to lightly contact the pressure plate fingers.

4. Adjust the rod length until the rod seats in the pocket in the release lever.

5. Insert a feeler gauge of specified thickness between the adjusting nut and swivel sleeve. Tighten the nut against the feeler gauge. Correct feeler gauge thickness is 0.194 in.

6. Tighten the locknut against the

adjusting nut, being careful not to disturb the adjustment.

7. Connect the clutch return spring.

8. Make a final check with the engine running at 3000 rpm, and transmission in neutral. Under this condition, centrifugal weights on release fingers may reduce the clearance. Readjust, if necessary, to obtain at least 1/2 in. free-play while maintaining the 3000 rpm to prevent fingers contacting release bearing.

Clutch and/or Transmission Removal and Installation

1. Raise the vehicle on a hoist.

2. Disconnect the driveshaft from the rear U-joint flange and slide the front yoke from the transmission.

3. Insert a cap or rag in the transmission extension housing to prevent fluid leakage.

4. Disconnect the speedometer cable and shifter linkage from the transmission. On models with a four-speed transmission, remove the shifter mounting bracket from the extension housing.

5. On models with a three-speed transmission, disconnect the transmission mount from the crossmember. If equipped with a four-speed transmission, remove the front parking brake cable from the crossmember and remove the crossmember from the car.

6. Remove the bolts that mount the transmission to the bellhousing. On 429 V8s, the upper left-hand transmission attaching bolt is a seal bolt. Carefully note its location so that it may be returned to its original position.

7. Move the transmission rearward until the input shaft clears the bellhousing and lower it from the car.

8. Disconnect the clutch release lever return spring.

9. If equipped with a one-piece aluminum bellhousing, remove the starter and remove the bellhousing from the engine. If equipped with a cast iron bellhousing, remove only the inspection cover from the bottom of the bellhousing.

10. Loosen the 6 pressure plate attaching bolts evenly to release spring pressure, and remove the clutch assembly from the car.

11. To install, position clutch assembly on flywheel and install each pressure plate attaching bolt finger tight.

12. Insert a transmission pilot shaft or other suitable tool to align the clutch disc with the flywheel and alternately tighten the pressure

plate attaching bolts until the plate is secured to the flywheel.

13. Reverse above procedure to install transmission and driveshaft.

MANUAL TRANSMISSION

Transmissions may be identified by the code on the vehicle certification label. The codes are listed at the beginning of this car section.

Transmission Removal and Installation

See the clutch section.

Shift Linkage Adjustment

1. Place the gear shift lever in the Neutral position.
2. Loosen the two gear shift adjustment nuts on the shift linkage.
3. Insert a 3/16 in. alignment tool through the first and reverse lever, the second and third gear shift lever, and the two holes in the lower casing. An alignment tool can be fabricated from 3/16 in. rod bent to an L shape. The extension that is to be inserted into the levers should be 1 in. in length from the elbow.
4. Manipulate the levers so the alignment tool will move freely through the alignment holes.
5. Tighten the two gear shift rod adjustment nuts.
6. Remove the tool and check linkage operation.

Transmission Lock Rod Adjustment

Models with manual transmissions incorporate a transmission lock rod which prevents the shifter from being moved from the reverse position when the ignition lock is in the OFF position. The lock rod connects the shift tube in the steering column to the transmission reverse lever. The lock rod cannot be properly adjusted until the manual linkage adjustment is correct.

1. With the transmission selector lever in the neutral position, loosen the lock rod adjustment nut on the transmission reverse lever.
2. Insert a .180 in. diameter rod (No. 15 drill bit) in the gauge pin hole located at the 6 o'clock position on the steering column socket casting, directly below the ignition lock.
3. Manipulate the pin until the casting will not move with the pin inserted.
4. Torque the lock rod adjustment nut to 10-20 ft. lbs.

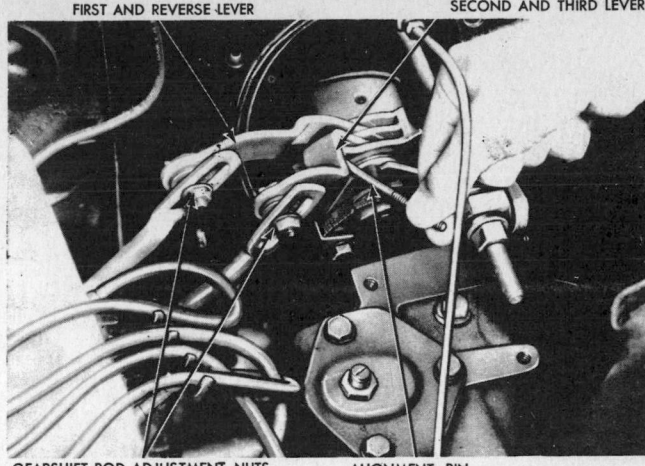

FIRST AND REVERSE LEVER   SECOND AND THIRD LEVER

GEARSHIFT ROD ADJUSTMENT NUTS   ALIGNMENT PIN

Gearshift linkage adjustment 3-speed transmission (© Ford Motor Co)

5. Remove the pin and check the linkage operation.

AUTOMATIC TRANSMISSION

Transmissions may be identified by the code on the vehicle certification label. The codes are listed at the beginning of this car section.

Shift Linkage Adjustment

1. With engine off, loosen clamp at shift lever so shift rod is free to slide.

   On models with a shift cable, remove the nut from the transmission manual lever and disconnect the cable from the transmission.
2. Position selector lever in D1 position (large green dot) on dual range transmissions. On select shift transmission (P R N D 2 1) position lever in D position tightly against the D stop.
3. Shift lever at transmission into D1 detent position on dual range transmissions or into D position on select shift transmissions.

NOTE: D1 position is second from rear on all dual range transmissions. D position is third from rear on all column shift select shift transmissions. D position is fourth from rear on console shift select shift transmissions through 1972.

4. Tighten clamp and nut.

C4 pan gasket

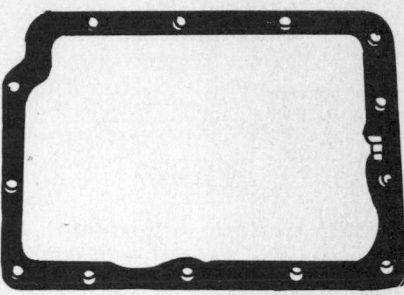

FMX pan gasket

Neutral Start Switch Adjustment

Through 1971

1. With manual linkage properly adjusted, try to engage starter in each position on quadrant. Starter should engage only in neutral or park position.
2. Place shift lever in neutral detent.
3. Disconnect start switch wires at plug connector. Disconnect vacuum hoses, if any. Remove screws securing neutral start switch to steering column and remove switch. Remove actuator lever along with Type III switches.
4. With switch wires facing up, move actuator lever fully to the left and insert gauge pin (No. 43 drill) into gauge pin hole at point A. See accompanying figure. On Type III switch, be sure gauge pin is inserted a full 1/2 in.
5. With pin in place, move actuator lever to right until positive stop is engaged.
6. On Type I and Type II switches, remove gauge pin and insert it at point B. On Type III switches, remove gauge pin, align two holes in switch at point A and reinstall gauge pin.
7. Reinstall switch on steering column. Be sure shift lever is engaged in neutral detent.

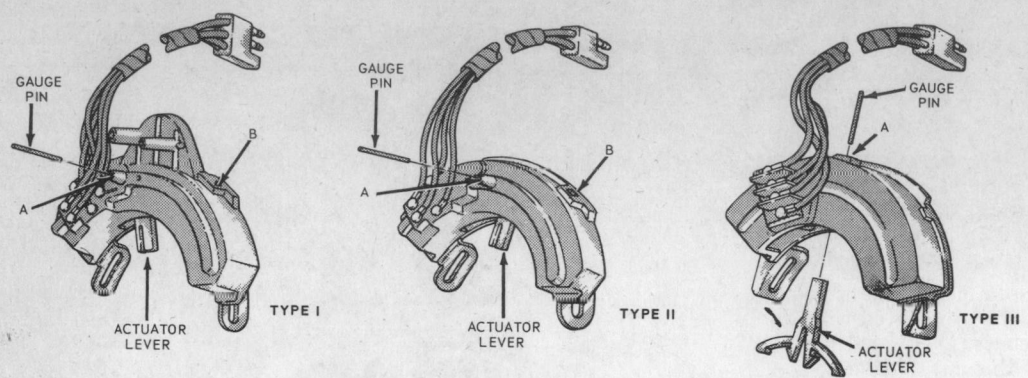

8. Connect switch wires and vacuum hoses and remove gauge pin.
9. Check starter engagement as in Step 1.

1972 and Later

Models with a column shift lever are not equipped with a neutral start switch. Instead, an ignition lock cylinder-to-shift lever interlock prevents these models from being started in any gear other than Park or Neutral.

Throttle Linkage Adjustment

1. Disconnect downshift lever return spring.
2. Hold throttle shaft lever wide open, and hold downshift rod against "through detent stop".
3. Adjust downshift screw to provide 0.050-0.070 in. clearance between screw and throttle shaft lever on models through 1972 and 0.010-0.080 in. on 1973 and later models. On 240 cu. in. engine, tighten locknut.
4. Connect downshift lever return spring.

C-4 Band Adjustment

Intermediate Band

1. Clean all the dirt from the adjusting screw and remove and discard the locknut.
2. Install a new locknut on the adjusting screw using a torque wrench, tighten the adjusting screw to 10 ft lbs.
3. Back off the adjusting screw *exactly 1¾ turns*.
4. Hold the adjusting screw steady and tighten the locknut.

Low-Reverse Band

1. Clean all dirt from around the band adjusting screw, and remove and discard the locknut.
2. Install a new locknut on the adjusting screw. Using a torque wrench, tighten the adjusting screw to 10 ft lbs.
3. Back off the adjusting screw *exactly three full turns*.
4. Hold the adjusting screw steady and tighten the locknut.

C-6 Band Adjustment

Intermediate Band Adjustment

1. Raise the car on a hoist or place it on jack stands.
2. Clean the threads of the intermediate band adjusting screw.
3. Loosen the adjustment screw locknut.
4. Tighten the adjusting screw to 10 ft lbs and back the screw off *exactly 1½ turns*. Tighten the adjusting screw locknut.

FMX, MX, and CW Band Adjustment

Front Band Adjustment

1. Drain the transmission fluid and remove the oil pan, fluid filter screen, and clip.
2. Clean the pan and filter screen and remove the old gasket.
3. Loosen the front servo adjusting screw locknut.
4. Pull back the actuating rod and insert a ¼ in. spacer bar between the adjusting screw and the servo piston stem. Tighten the adjusting screw to 10 in. lbs torque. Remove the spacer bar and tighten the adjusting screw *an additional ¾ turn*. Hold the adjusting screw fast and tighten the locknut securely (20-25 ft lbs).
5. Install the transmission fluid filter screen and clip. Install pan with a new pan gasket.
6. Refill the transmission to the mark on the dipstick. Start the engine, run for a few minutes, shift the selector lever through all positions, and place it in Park. Recheck the fluid level and add fluid if necessary.

Rear Band Adjustment

On certain cars with a console floor shift, the entire console, shift lever and linkage will have to be removed to gain access to the rear band external adjusting screw.

1. Locate the external rear band adjusting screw on the transmission case, clean all dirt from the

threads, and coat the threads with light oil.

NOTE: the adjusting screw is located on the upper right side of the transmission case. Access is often through a hole in the front floor to the right of center under the carpet.

2. Loosen the locknut on the rear band external adjusting screw.
3. Using torque wrench tighten the adjusting screw to 10 ft lbs torque. If the adjusting screw is tighter than 10 ft lbs torque, loosen the adjusting screw and retighten to the proper torque.
4. Back off the adjusting screw *exactly 1½ turns*. Hold the adjusting screw steady while tightening the locknut to the proper torque (35-40 ft lbs).

Pan Replacement, Fluid Change

1. Raise the car on a hoist or jack stands.
2. Place a drain pan under the transmission pan.

NOTE: *On some models of the C4 transmission, the fluid is drained by disconnecting the filler tube from the transmission fluid pan.*

3. Loosen the pan attaching bolts to allow the fluid to drain.
4. When the fluid has stopped draining to the level of the pan flange, remove the pan bolts starting at the rear and along both sides of the pan, allowing the pan to drop and drain gradually.
5. When all the transmission fluid has drained, remove the pan and the fluid filter and clean them.
6. Install the fluid filter screen, a new pan gasket, and the pan on the transmission. Tighten the pan attaching bolts on C4 and C6 transmissions to 12-16 ft lbs. On FMX and CW transmissions, tighten the pan attaching bolts to 10-13 ft lbs.

NOTE: *Be sure to use Type "F" transmission fluid. The use of any other type of fluid will materially affect the service life of the transmission.*

7. Install three quarts of transmission fluid through the filler tube. If the filler tube was removed to drain the transmission, install the filler tube using a new O-ring.

8. Start and run the engine for a few minutes at low idle speed and then at the fast idle speed (about 1,200 rpm) until the normal operating temperature is reached. Do not race the engine.

9. Move the selector lever through all gear positions and place it at the Park position. Check the fluid level, and add fluid until the level is between the "add" and "full" marks on the dipstick. Do not overfill the transmission.

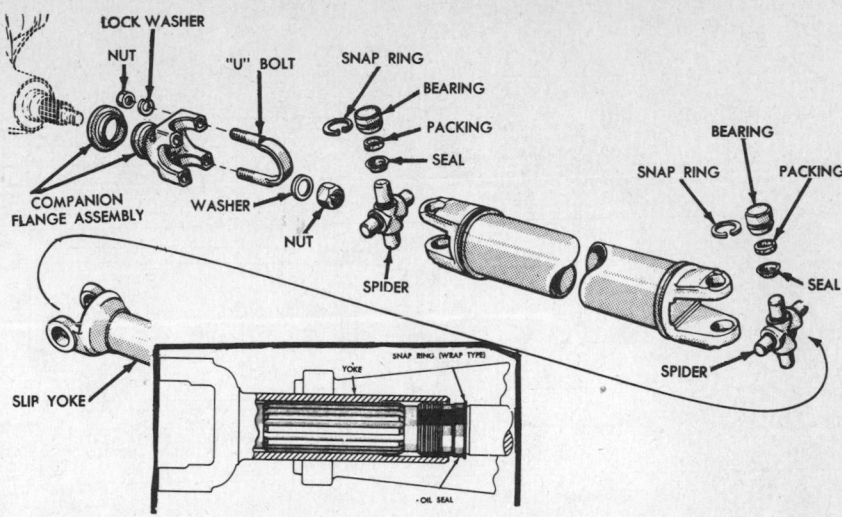

Driveshaft and universal joint (© Ford Motor Co)

U-JOINTS

Rear Joint Removal

The universal joints on all Fords, Mercurys, and 1972-76 Thunderbirds in this section are of the cross- and needle-bearing-type.

The rear universal joint has two pillow blocks which are bolted to the pinion shaft flange.

Take out the four bolts that hold the bearing blocks to the pinion shaft and gently tap off the bearing blocks.

Lower the back end of the driveshaft and the front end can be slid out of the back of the transmission together with the transmission yoke portion of the front universal joint.

Carry the assembly—the front universal joint complete, the driveshaft and the rear universal joint crossover—to the bench and remove the cross from the rear universal joint by taking out the lock rings from the inner side of the bearings. Using a large punch or an arbor press, drive one of the bearings in toward the center forcing out the opposite bearing.

When the bearing is pressed out far enough, grip it with a pair of pliers and pull it out of the driveshaft yoke.

Now, drive the cross in the opposite direction until the remaining bearing has been driven out far enough for a purchase with a pair of pliers.

When both bearings have been taken out, the cross can be lifted from between the two yokes.

Front Joint Removal

Follow the procedure given above for the rear universal joint, but leave the rear universal joint cross in place on the driveshaft if it is not to be removed.

Remove the lock rings from the inner side of two opposite bearings and press on the outer side of one of the bearings, forcing the crossover. This will force the bearing on the opposite side out of its yoke.

Remove the forced-out bearing and press the cross in the opposite direction to force the other bearing out.

Repeat this procedure on the third and fourth bearings.

When installing the new bearings in the universal joint yoke, it is possible to put them in with a driver of some type, but it is recommended that this work be done in an arbor press since a heavy jolt on the needle bearings can very easily misalign them.

Double Cardan Universal Joints

Thunderbirds through 1971 use a driveshaft with a double Cardan U-Joint. Each of the two Cardan joints consist of two universal joints, a centering socket yoke and a center yoke. Bearing cups are retained by injected plastic; but, repair kits contain replacement snap-rings. This driveshaft mounts to the differential pinion flange by means of a circular companion flange.

Replacement

1. Mark the position of the companion flange in relation to the pinion flange so the driveshaft may be returned to its original location.

2. Disconnect the companion flange from the pinion flange.

3. Pull the driveshaft rearward until the front yoke clears the transmission extension housing and remove the driveshaft from the car.

4. Mark the position of the spiders, the center yoke and the centering socket yoke in relation to the companion flange. *The spiders must be assembled with the bosses in their original position to provide proper clearance.*

5. If the universal joints have been previously replaced and are retained with snap-rings, remove the snap-rings.

6. Using a press or large punch, drive one of the bearing caps on

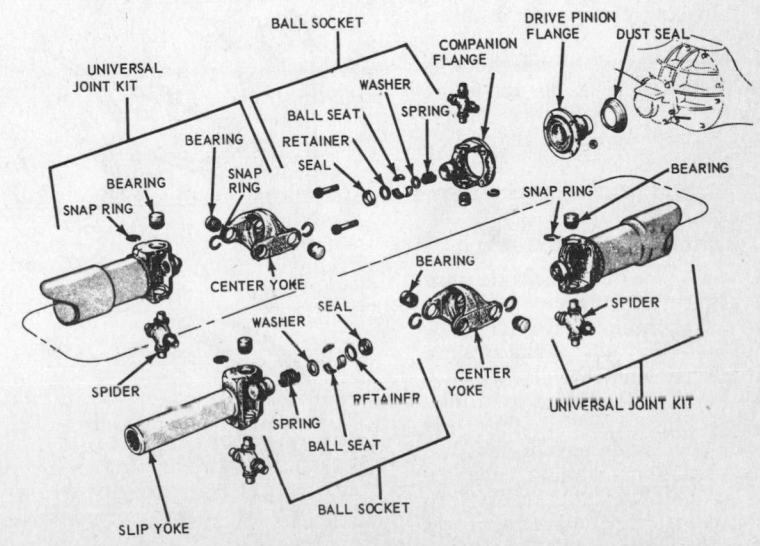

Driveshaft with double Cardan universal joints (© Ford Motor Co)

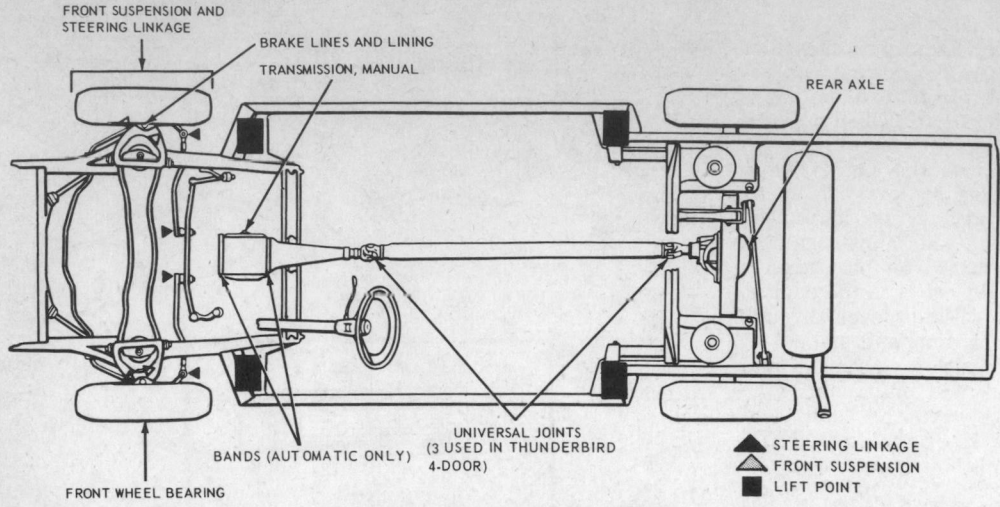

FRONT SUSPENSION AND
STEERING LINKAGE

BRAKE LINES AND LINING

TRANSMISSION, MANUAL

REAR AXLE

UNIVERSAL JOINTS
(3 USED IN THUNDERBIRD
4-DOOR)

BANDS (AUTOMATIC ONLY)

FRONT WHEEL BEARING

▲ STEERING LINKAGE
△ FRONT SUSPENSION
■ LIFT POINT

Ford hoist lifting positions (© Ford Motor Co)

the U-Joint to be replaced toward the center of the driveshaft. Remove the bearing cap opposite the cap being driven as it emerges from the driveshaft. Repeat this procedure until all the bearing caps have been removed, then, remove the spider.

7. To disassemble the ball socket from the yoke, insert a screwdriver into the centering ball socket and pry out the rubber seal. Remove the retainer, three piece ball seat, washer and spring from the ball socket.

8. Reverse above procedure to install, making sure all parts are mounted in their original location.

JACKING, HOISTING

1. Jack car at front spring seats of lower control arms, and at rear axle housing close to differential case.

2. To lift at frame, use adapters so that contact will be made at points shown. Adapters should support at least 12 sq. in.

REAR AXLE

Two basic types of rear axles are used; a removable differential carrier type and an integral carrier type which occurs in two variations; a standard type and the light duty (WER) version. Some integral carrier types and all WER types use C-locks on the inside end of the axle shaft to retain it, while removable carrier axles have no C-locks. To properly identify a C-lock axle, drain the lubricant, remove the rear cover and look for the C-lock on the end of

the axle shaft in the differential side gear bore.

Axle Shaft, Bearing and Seal

Removal and Installation

Removable Carrier Axles, except C-Lock Type

NOTE: *Bearings must be pressed on and off the shaft with an arbor press. Unless you have access to one, it is inadvisable to attempt any repair work on the axle shaft bearing assemblies.*

1. Remove the wheel, tire, and brake drum.

2. Remove the nuts holding the retainer plate to the backing plate. Disconnect the brake line.

3. Remove the retainer and install nuts, finger-tight, to prevent the brake backing plate from being dislodged.

4. Pull out the axle shaft and bearing assembly, using a slide hammer.

NOTE: *If end-play is found to be excessive, the bearing should be replaced. Shimming the bearing is not recommended as this ignores end-play of the bearing itself and could result in improper seating of the bearing.*

5. Using a chisel, nick the bearing retainer in 3 or 4 places. The retainer does not have to be cut, but merely collapsed sufficiently to allow the bearing retainer to be slid from the shaft.

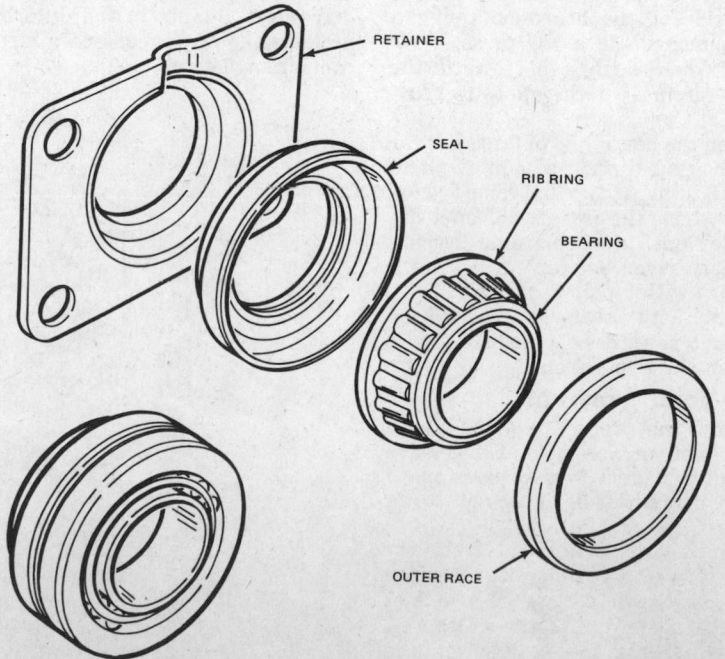

RETAINER

SEAL

RIB RING

BEARING

OUTER RACE

Axle shaft bearing and retainer—removable carrier axle (© Ford Motor Co)

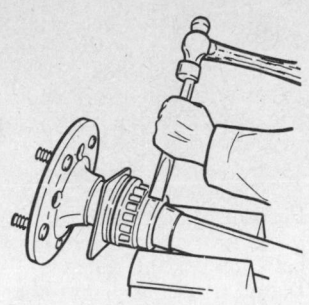

Axle shaft bearing retainer removal
—removable carrier axle
(© Ford Motor Co.)

6. Press off the bearing and install the new one by pressing it into position.
7. Press on the new retainer.
   NOTE: *Do not attempt to press the bearing and the retainer on at the same time.*
8. Assemble the shaft and bearing in the housing, being sure that the bearing is seated properly in the housing.
9. Install the retainer, drum, wheel and tire. Bleed the brakes.

WER and C-Lock Axles

1. Jack up and support the rear of the car.
2. Remove the wheels and tires from the brake drums.
3. Place a drain pan under the housing and drain the lubricant by loosening the housing cover.
4. Remove the nuts securing the brake drums to the axle shaft flanges and remove the drums.
5. Remove the housing cover and gasket.
6. Position jackstands under the rear frame member and lower the axle housing. This is done to give easy access to the inside of the differential.
7. Working through the opening in the differential case, remove the side gear pinion shaft lockbolt and the side gear pinion shaft.
8. Push the axle shafts inward and remove the C-locks from the inner end of the axle shafts.
9. Remove the axle shafts with a slide hammer. Be sure the seal is not damaged by the splines on the axle shaft.
10. Remove the bearing and oil seal from the housing. Two types of bearings are used on some axles, one requiring a press fit and the other a loose fit. A loose fitting bearing does not necessarily indicate excessive wear.
11. Inspect the axle shaft housing and axle shafts for burrs or other irregularities. Replace any worn or damaged parts. A light yellow color on the bearing journal of the axle shaft is normal, and does not require replacement of the axle shaft. Slight pitting and wear is also normal.

Remove the differential pinion shaft lockbolt
—WER axle   (© Ford Motor Co.)

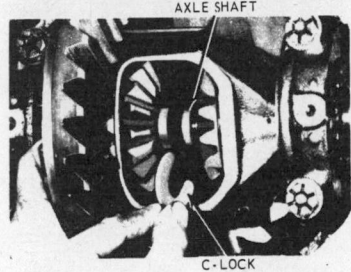

Remove the axle shaft C-locks
—WER axle (© Ford Motor Co.)

12. Lightly coat the wheel bearing rollers with axle lubricant. Install the bearings in the axle housing until the bearing seats firmly against the shoulder.
13. Wipe all lubricant from the oil seal bore, before installing the seal.
14. Inspect the original seals for wear. If necessary, these may be replaced with new seals, which are prepacked with lubricant and do not require soaking.
15. Install the oil seal.

Caution Installation of the seal without the proper tool can cause distortion and seal leakage. Oil seals for the right-side are marked with green stripes and the word RIGHT. Seals for the left-side are marked yellow with the word LEFT. Do not interchange seals from side to side.

16. Carefully slide the axle shafts into place. Be careful that you do not damage the seal with the splined end of the axle shaft. Engage the splined end of the shaft with the differential side gears.
17. Install the axle shaft C-locks on the inner end of the axle shafts and seat the C-locks in the counterbore of the differential side gears.
18. Rotate the differential pinion gears until the differential pinion shaft can be installed. Install the differential pinion shaft lockbolt.
19. Install the brake drum on the axle shaft flange.

20. Install the wheel and tire on the brake drum and tighten the attaching nuts.
21. Clean the gasket surface of the rear housing and install a new cover gasket and the housing cover.
22. Raise the rear axle so that it is in the running position. Add the amount of specified lubricant to bring the lubricant level to the bottom of the filler plug hole.

FRONT SUSPENSION

Shock Absorber Replacement

1. Remove the nut, washer, and bushing from the upper end of the shock absorber.
2. Raise the vehicle and install jackstands under the frame rails.
3. Remove the two bolts securing the shock absorber to the lower control arm and remove the shock absorber.
4. Install a new bushing and washer on the top of the shock absorber and position the unit inside the front spring. Install the two lower attaching bolts.
5. Remove the jackstands and lower the vehicle.
6. Place a new bushing and washer on the shock absorber top stud and install the attaching nut.

Coil Spring and Lower Control Arm Removal and Installation

1. Raise car and support with stands placed back of lower arms.
2. If necessary for clearance or access and equipped with drum brakes, remove the wheel and brake drum as an assembly. Remove the brake backing plate attaching bolts and remove the backing plate from the spindle. Wire the assembly back out of the way.
3. If necessary for clearance or access and equipped with disc brakes, remove the wheel from the hub. Remove two bolts and washers that hold the caliper and brake hose bracket to the spindle. Remove the caliper from the rotor and wire it back out of the way. Then, remove the hub and rotor from the spindle.
4. Disconnect lower end of the shock absorber and push it up to the retracted position.
5. Disconnect stabilizer bar link from the lower arm.
6. Remove cotter pins from the upper and lower ball joint stud nuts.

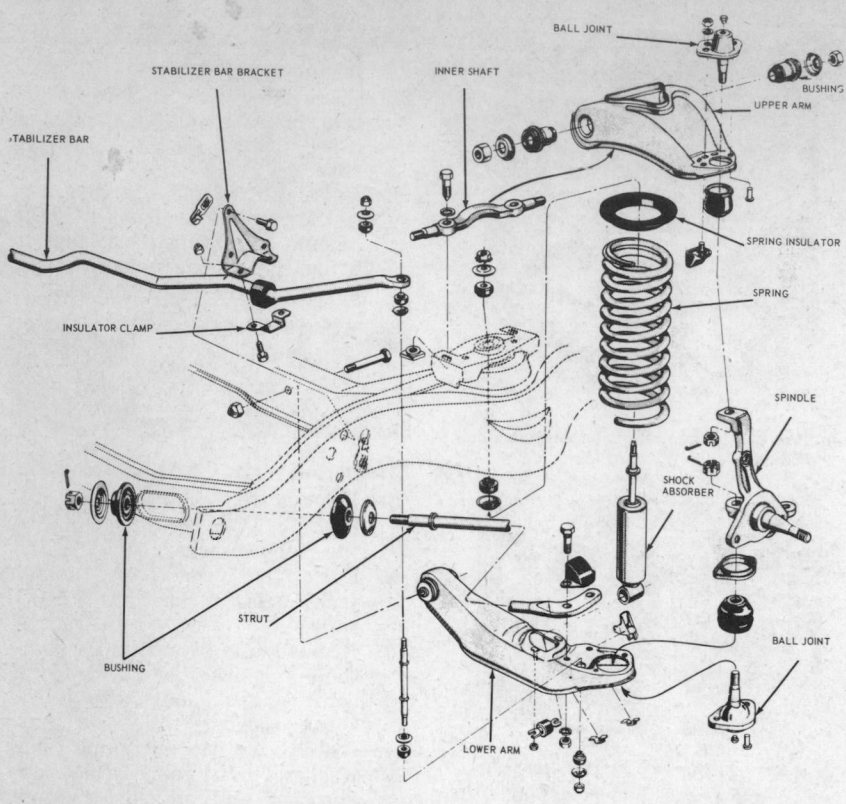

Typical front suspension—1970 (© Ford Motor Co)

upper and lower ball joint studs.

10. Expand the tool until the tool exerts considerable pressure on the studs. Tap the spindle near the lower stud with a hammer to loosen the stud in the spindle. Do not loosen the stud with tool pressure only.

11. Position floor jack under the lower arm and remove the lower ball joint stud nut.

12. Install a spring compressor and lower floor jack and remove the spring and insulator.

13. Remove the A-arm to crossmember attaching parts, and remove the arm from the car.

14. Reverse above procedure to install. If lower control arm was replaced because of damage, check front end alignment.

Lower Ball Joint

Inspection

1. Raise the vehicle by placing a floor jack under the lower arm; or, raise the vehicle on a hoist and place a jack stand under the lower arm and lower the vehicle onto it to remove the preload from the lower ball joint.

2. Adjust the wheel bearings.

3. Have an assistant grasp the wheel top and bottom and apply alternate in and out pressure to the top and bottom of the wheel.

7. Remove two bolts and nuts holding the strut to the lower arm.

8. Loosen the lower ball joint stud

nut two turns. Do not remove this nut.

9. Install spreader tool between the

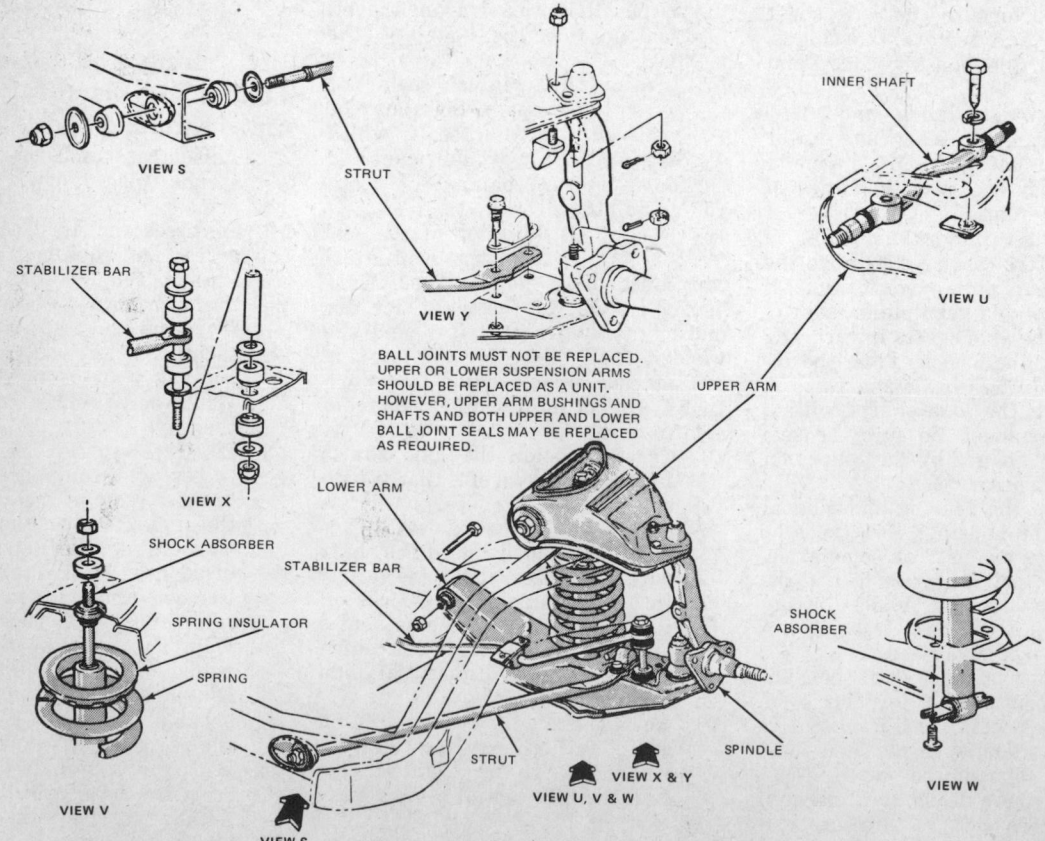

BALL JOINTS MUST NOT BE REPLACED. UPPER OR LOWER SUSPENSION ARMS SHOULD BE REPLACED AS A UNIT. HOWEVER, UPPER ARM BUSHINGS AND SHAFTS AND BOTH UPPER AND LOWER BALL JOINT SEALS MAY BE REPLACED AS REQUIRED.

Typical front suspension, 1976 shown (© Ford Motor Co)

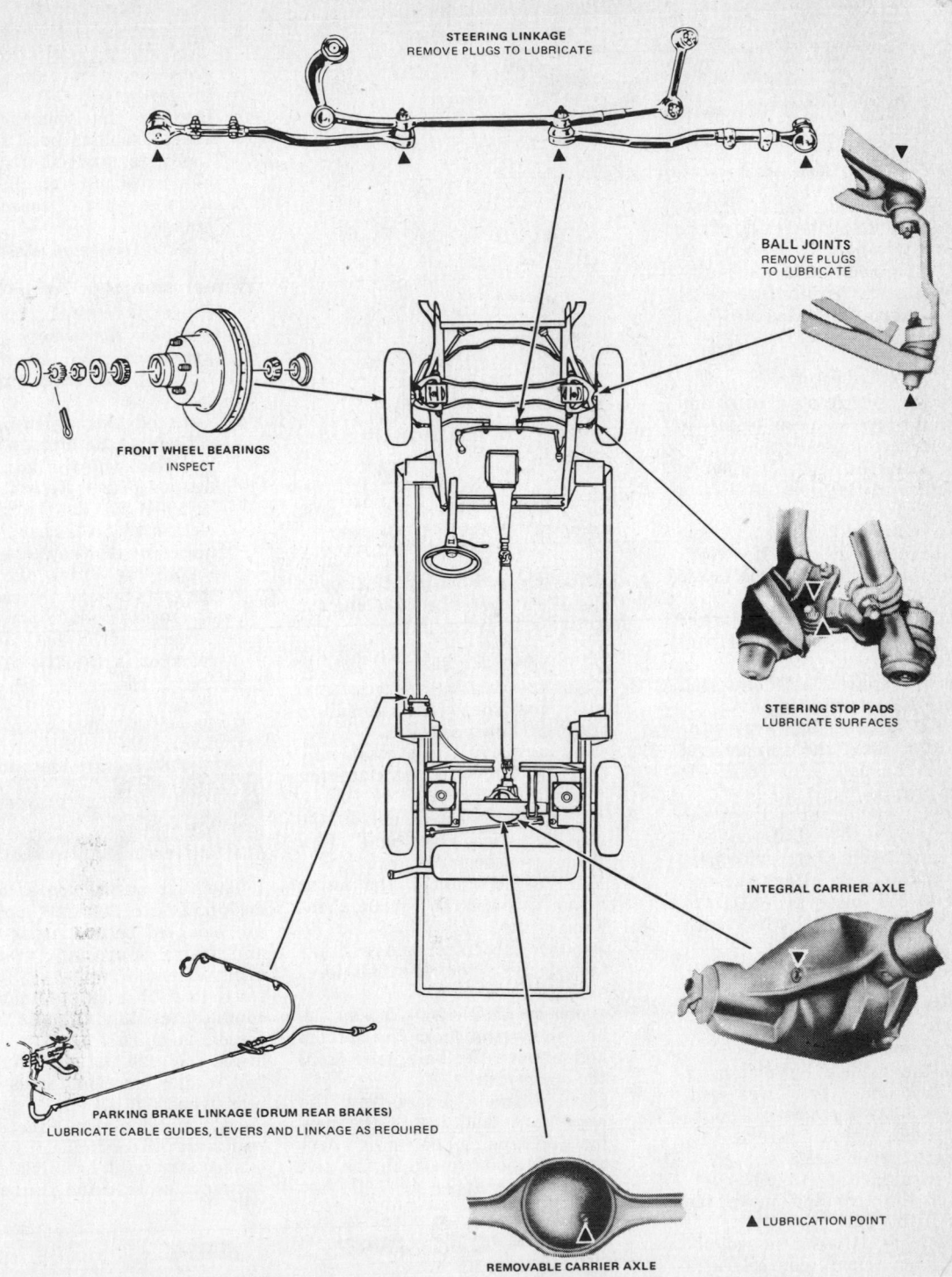

STEERING LINKAGE
REMOVE PLUGS TO LUBRICATE

BALL JOINTS
REMOVE PLUGS
TO LUBRICATE

FRONT WHEEL BEARINGS
INSPECT

STEERING STOP PADS
LUBRICATE SURFACES

INTEGRAL CARRIER AXLE

PARKING BRAKE LINKAGE (DRUM REAR BRAKES)
LUBRICATE CABLE GUIDES, LEVERS AND LINKAGE AS REQUIRED

▲ LUBRICATION POINT

REMOVABLE CARRIER AXLE

Ford and Mercury chassis lubrication points (© Ford Motor Co.)

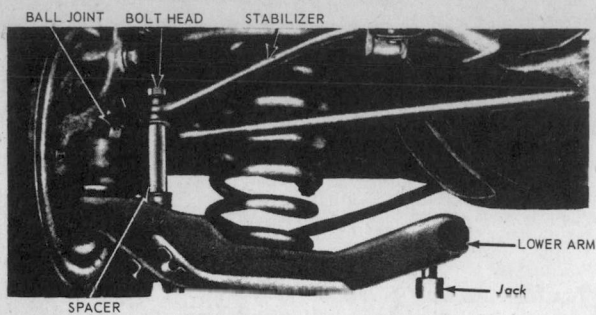

BALL JOINT BOLT HEAD STABILIZER

LOWER ARM

Jack

SPACER

Removing front coil spring (© Ford Motor Co)

4. Radial play of ¼ in. is acceptable measured at the inside of the wheel adjacent to the lower arm.
NOTE: this radial play is multiplied at the outer circumference of the tire and should be measured only at the inside of the wheel.

Replacement

1. Raise the vehicle on a hoist and allow the front wheels to fall to their full down position.
2. Drill a ⅛ in. hole completely through each ball joint attaching rivet.
3. Use a ⅜ in. drill in the pilot hole to drill off the head of the rivet.
4. Drive the rivets from the lower arm.
5. Place a jack under the lower arm and lower the vehicle about 6 in.
6. Remove the lower ball joint stud cotter pin and attaching nut.
7. Using a suitable tool, loosen the ball joint from the spindle and remove the ball joint from the lower arm.
8. Clean all metal burrs from the lower arm and install the new ball joint, using the service part nuts and bolts to attach the ball joint to the lower arm. Do not attempt to rerivet the ball joint once it has been removed.
9. Check front end alignment.

Upper Ball Joint

Inspection

1. Raise the vehicle by placing a floor jack under the lower arm. Do not allow the lower arm to hang freely with the vehicle on a hoist or bumper jack.
2. Have an assistant grasp the bottom of the tire and move the wheel in and out.
3. As the wheel is being moved, observe the upper control arm where the spindle attaches to it. Any movement between the upper part of the spindle and the upper ball joint indicates a bad ball joint which must be replaced.
NOTE: during this check the lower ball joint will be unloaded and may move; this is normal and not an

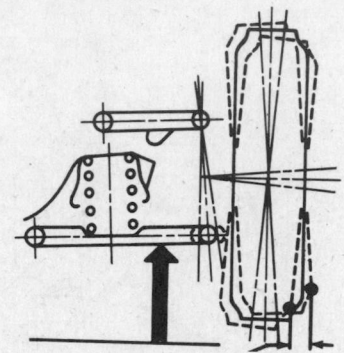

Measuring lower ball joint radial play
(© Ford Motor Co)

indication of a bad ball joint. Also, do not mistake a loose wheel bearing for a defective ball joint.

Replacement

1. Raise the vehicle on a hoist and allow the front wheels to fall to their full down position.
2. Drill a ⅛ in. hole completely through each ball joint attaching rivet.
3. Using a large chisel, cut off the head of each rivet and drive them from the upper arm.
4. Place a jack under the lower arm and lower the vehicle about 6 in.
5. Remove the cotter pin and attaching nut from the ball joint stud.
6. Using a suitable tool, loosen the ball joint stud from the spindle and remove the ball joint from the upper arm.
7. Clean all metal burrs from the upper arm and install the new ball joint, using the service part nuts and bolts to attach the ball joint to the upper arm. Do not

attempt to rerivet the ball joint once it has been removed.
8. Check front end alignment.

Upper Control Arm

Replacement

1. Perform steps 1-12 of the above "Coil Spring and Lower Control Arm Removal and Installation procedure.
2. Remove the upper arm inner shaft attaching bolts and remove the arm and shaft from the chassis as an assembly.
3. Reverse above procedure to install.
4. Adjust front end alignment.

Wheel Bearing Adjustment

1. Raise the front of the vehicle.
2. Remove the wheel cover and grease cap.
3. Remove the cotter pin and nut lock.
4. Back off the adjusting nut and retighten the nut to 17–25 ft. lbs. Back off the adjusting nut again ½ turn. Retighten the nut to 10–15 in. lbs. Install the nut lock so that the castellations are aligned with the cotter pin hole. Install the cotter pin and bend the ends around the castellations of the nut lock to prevent interference with the radio static collector in the grease cap.
5. Install the grease cap and wheel cover.
6. Lower the vehicle.

REAR SUSPENSION

The rear suspension is a coil-link design. Large, low-rate coil springs are mounted between rear axle pads and frame supports. Parallel lower arms extend forward of the spring seats to rubber frame anchor to accommodate driving and breaking forces. A third link is mounted between the axle and the frame to control torque reaction forces from the rear wheels.

Lateral (side sway) motion of the rear axle is controlled by a rubber bushed rear track bar, linked laterally between the axle and frame.

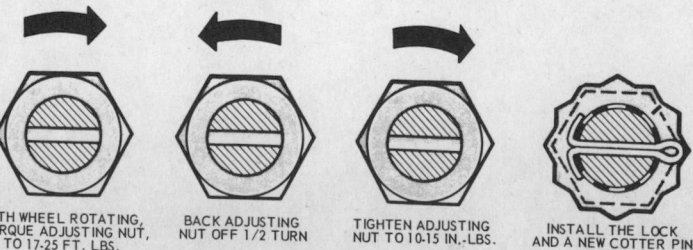

WITH WHEEL ROTATING, TORQUE ADJUSTING NUT, TO 17-25 FT. LBS.

BACK ADJUSTING NUT OFF 1/2 TURN

TIGHTEN ADJUSTING NUT TO 10-15 IN.-LBS.

INSTALL THE LOCK AND A NEW COTTER PIN

Front wheel bearing adjustment (© Ford Motor Co)

Spring Replacement

1. Place car on hoist and lift under rear axle housing. Place jack stands under frame side rails.
2. Disconnect track bar at the rear axle housing bracket.
3. On Ford/Mercury, disconnect the rear of the front-to-rear brake line from the rear brake hose at the No. 4 crossmember bracket. Remove the clip.
4. Disconnect rear shock absorbers from the rear axle housing brackets.
5. Disconnect hose from axle housing vent.
6. Install a spring compressor.
7. Lower hoist with axle housing until coil springs are released.
8. Remove spring lower retainer with bolt, nut, washer and insulator.
9. Remove spring with large rubber insulator pads from car.
10. Install in reverse of above.

Shock Absorber Replacement

Rear shock absorbers on all Fords are straddle-mounted and are held to rubber bushings at both the top and bottom connections. Simply remove the nuts from the top and bottom of the shock absorber and lift the shock absorber off the car.

BRAKES

Starting 1975, these cars are available with improved brake system equipment. A new four-wheel disc brake system combined with the Sure-Track (anti-skid) system is an option on these cars. In addition, a hydraulically assisted Hydro-Boost system is available on some models instead of a vacuum assist brake system.

The Hydro-Boost system uses the power steering pump to pressurize the hydraulic system and is connected to the pump by means of normal power steering hydraulic hoses. The decision to use hydraulic assist instead of vacuum assist was made in order to conserve engine vacuum for emission control equipment and other vacuum assisted power accessories. The rear brake caliper on models with four-wheel disc brakes is of single-piston, sliding caliper design. The parking brake design marks a departure from former practice as the parking brake cable acts directly on the brake pads bringing them into contact with the brake rotor (disc).

No auxiliary parking brake drum assemblies are required with this arrangement.

NOTE: procedure for brake shoe or pad replacement and adjustment as well as wheel and master cylinder overhaul, and brake bleeding can be found in the "Unit Repair Section."

Master Cylinder

Master Cylinder Replacement

Standard Brakes

1. Working under the dash, disconnect the master cylinder pushrod from the brake pedal. The pushrod cannot be removed from the master cylinder.
2. Disconnect the stoplight switch wires and remove the switch from the brake pedal, using care not to damage the switch.
3. Disconnect the brake lines from the master cylinder.
4. Remove the attaching screws master cylinder from the car. from the firewall and remove the
5. Reinstall in reverse of above order, leaving the brake line fittings loose at the master cylinder.
6. Fill the master cylinder, and with the brake lines loose, slowly

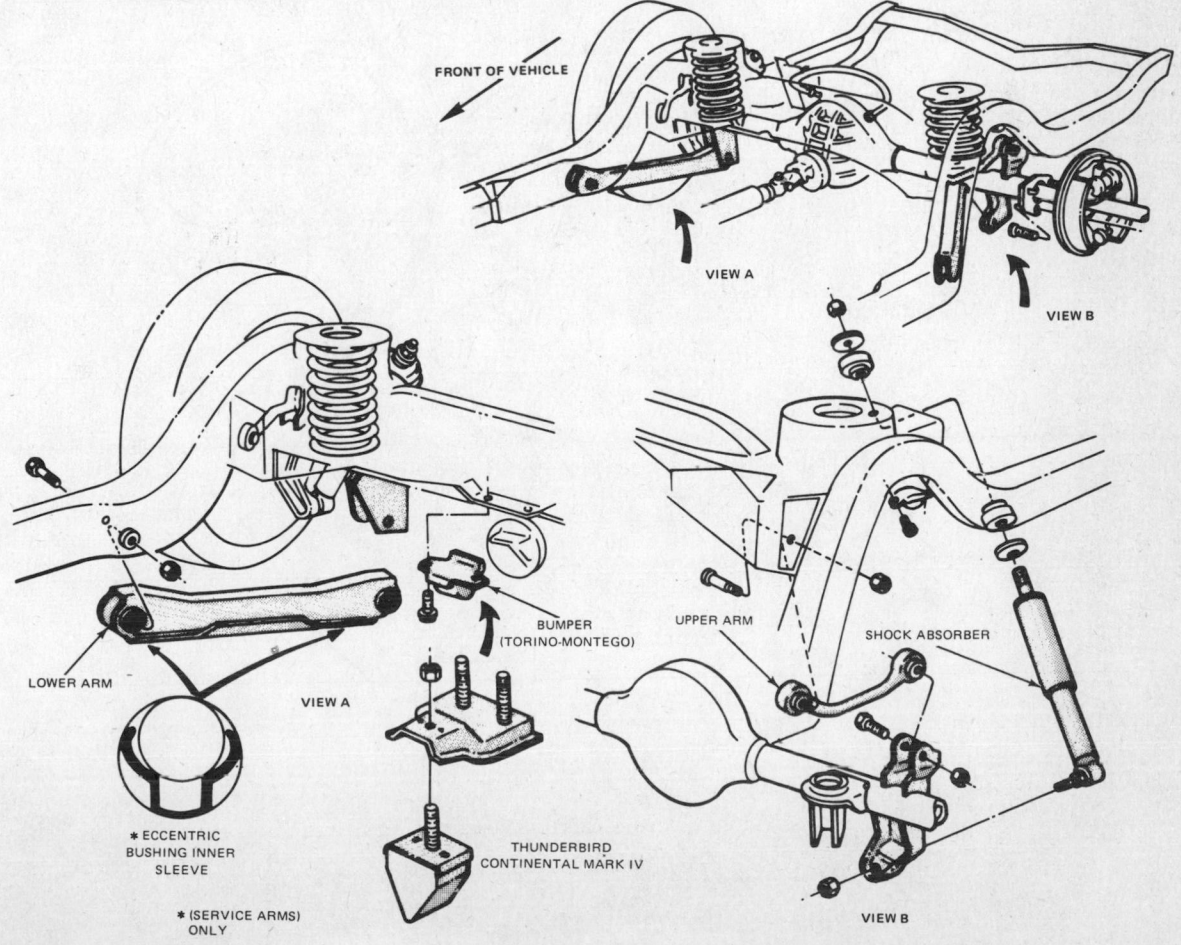

FRONT OF VEHICLE

VIEW A

VIEW B

LOWER ARM

VIEW A

BUMPER (TORINO-MONTEGO)

UPPER ARM

SHOCK ABSORBER

* ECCENTRIC BUSHING INNER SLEEVE

* (SERVICE ARMS) ONLY

THUNDERBIRD CONTINENTAL MARK IV

VIEW B

Rear suspension details (© Ford Motor Co)

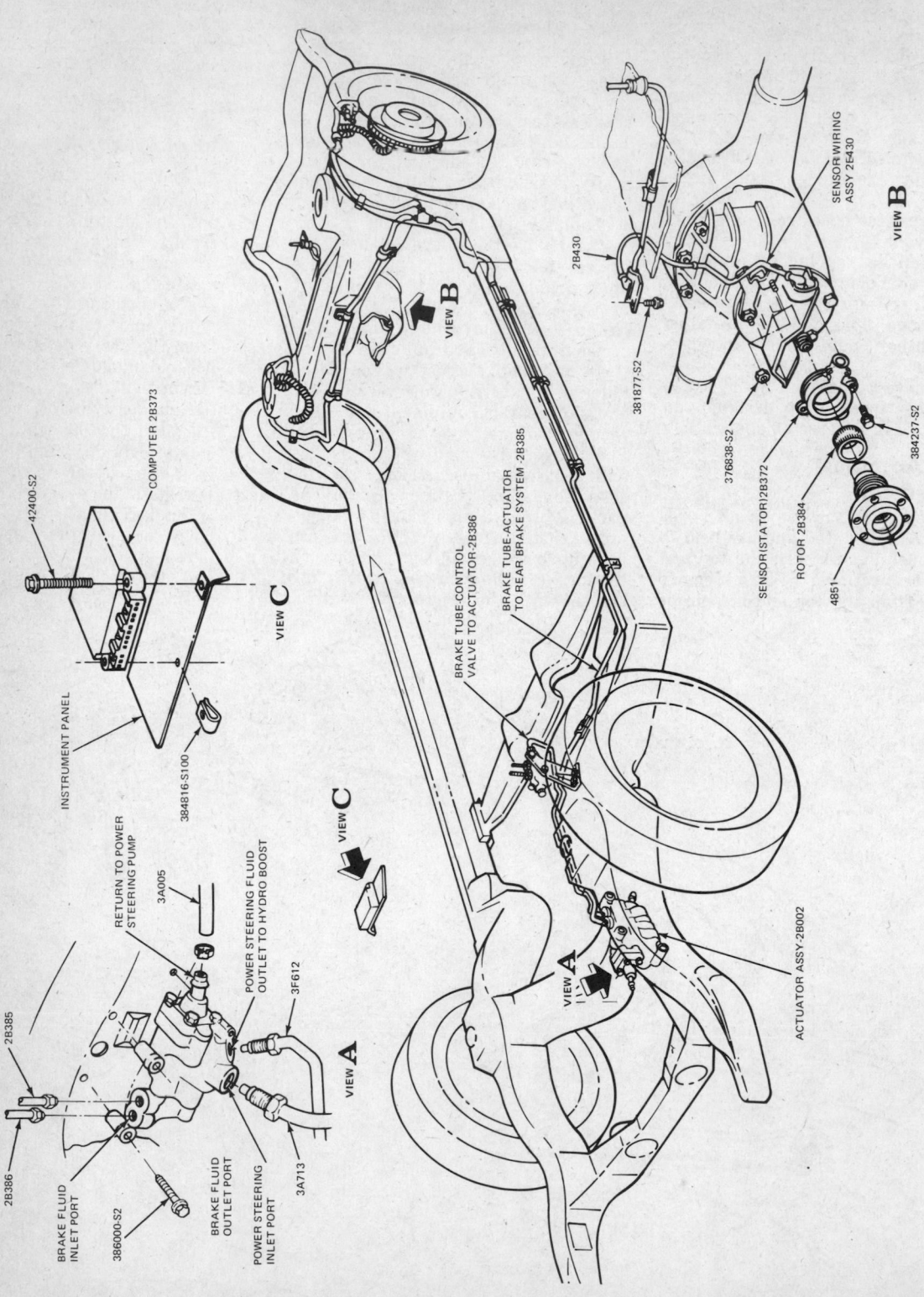

42400-S2

COMPUTER 2B373

INSTRUMENT PANEL

384816-S100

VIEW **C**

RETURN TO POWER STEERING PUMP

3A005

POWER STEERING FLUID OUTLET TO HYDRO BOOST

3F612

VIEW **C**

2B385

2B386

BRAKE FLUID INLET PORT

386000-S2

BRAKE FLUID OUTLET PORT

POWER STEERING INLET PORT

3A713

VIEW **A**

VIEW **B**

BRAKE TUBE-CONTROL VALVE TO ACTUATOR-2B386

BRAKE TUBE-ACTUATOR TO REAR BRAKE SYSTEM -2B385

VIEW **A**

ACTUATOR ASSY.-2B002

2B430

38187T-S2

376838-S2

SENSOR(STATOR)2B372

ROTOR 2B384

4851

384237-S2

SENSOR WIRING ASSY 2E430

VIEW **B**

Sure-Track brake system—1975-76 Thunderbird (© Ford Motor Co.)

bleed the air from the master cylinder using the foot pedal.

Power Brakes (vacuum assist)

1. Disconnect the brake line from the master cylinder.
2. Remove the two nuts and lockwashers that attach the master cylinder to the brake booster.
3. Remove the master cylinder from the booster.
4. Reverse above procedure to reinstall.
5. Fill master cylinder and bleed entire brake system.
6. Refill master cylinder.

Brake Vacuum Booster Removal and Installation

1. Working from inside the car, beneath the instrument panel, remove the booster pushrod from the brake pedal.
2. Disconnect the stop light switch wires and remove the switch from the brake pedal. Use care not to damage the switch during removal.
3. Raise the hood and remove the master cylinder from the booster without disconnecting the brake lines. Carefully position the master cylinder out of the way, being careful not to kink the brake lines.
4. Remove the manifold vacuum hose from the booster.
5. Remove the booster to firewall attaching bolts and remove the booster from the car.
6. Reverse above procedure to reinstall.

Hydro-Boost Accumulator Removal and Installation

1. Open the hood and remove the 2 nuts attaching the master cylinder to the brake booster.
2. Remove the master cylinder from the Hydro-Boost accumulator.
3. Set the master cylinder aside without disturbing the hydraulic lines.
4. Disconnect the pressure, steering and return lines from the accumulator.
5. Plug the lines and ports.
6. Working below the dash, disconnect the Hydro-Boost pushrod from the brake pedal. To do this, disconnect the stoplight switch at the connector. Remove the hairpin retainer. Slide the spotlight switch from the brake pedal pin far enough to clear the switch outer pin hole. Remove the switch from the pin.
7. Loosen the Hydro-Boost attaching nuts and remove the pushrod, washers and bushing from the brake pedal pin.
8. Remove the accumlator.
9. Installation is the reverse of removal.

Parking Brake Adjustment— Rear Drum Brakes

1. Raise the vehicle on an axle hoist with the transmission in Neutral and the parking brake fully released.
2. Tighten the adjusting nut against the cable equalizer until the rear brakes drag when the wheels are turned.
3. Loosen up on the adjustment nut until the brakes are fully released.
4. Tighten the locknut (if used) to 7-10 ft lbs.

Parking Brake Adjustment— Rear Disc Brakes

1. Be sure the parking brake is fully released.
2. Place the transmission in Neutral and raise the vehicle on an axle hoist.
3. Tighten the adjuster nut until the levers on the calipers just begin to move. Loosen the nut just enough to obtain full return to the stop position.
4. Check the operation. Attempt to pull the parking brake levers rearward. If they can be pulled rearward, the parking brake is too tight.

STEERING

Power Steering Pump Removal and Installation

1. Drain the fluid from the pump reservoir by disconnecting the fluid return hose at the pump. Then, disconnect the pressure hose from the pump.
2. Remove the mounting bolts from the front of the pump. On eight cylinder engines, there is a nut on the rear of the pump that must be removed. After removal, move the pump inward to loosen the belt tension and remove the belt from the pulley. Then, remove the pump from the car.
3. To reinstall the pump, position on mounting bracket and loosely install the mounting bolts and nuts. Put the drive belt over the pulley and move the pump outward against the belt until the proper belt tension is obtained. Measure the belt tension with a belt tension gauge for the proper adjustment. Only in cases where

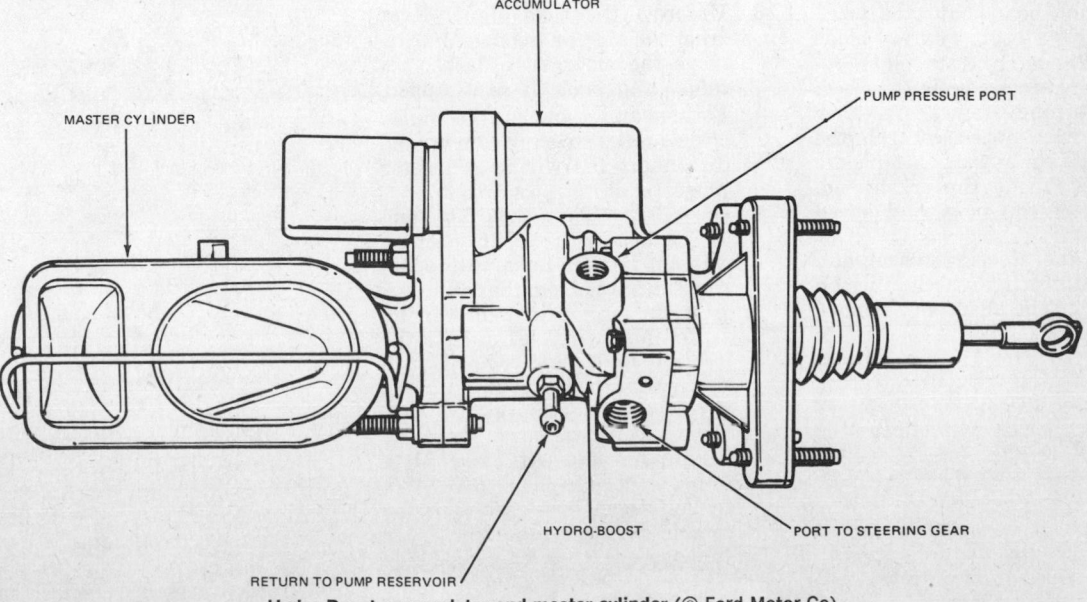

MASTER CYLINDER

ACCUMULATOR

PUMP PRESSURE PORT

PORT TO STEERING GEAR

HYDRO-BOOST

RETURN TO PUMP RESERVOIR

Hydro-Boost accumulator and master cylinder (© Ford Motor Co)

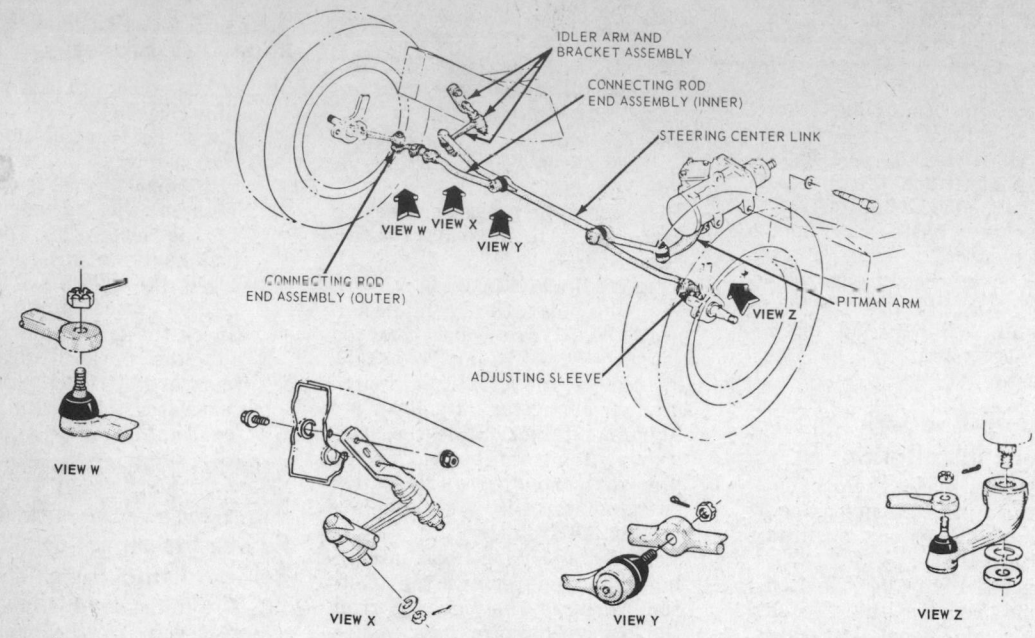

IDLER ARM AND
BRACKET ASSEMBLY

CONNECTING ROD
END ASSEMBLY (INNER)

STEERING CENTER LINK

VIEW W VIEW X

VIEW Y

PITMAN ARM

CONNECTING ROD
END ASSEMBLY (OUTER)

VIEW Z

ADJUSTING SLEEVE

VIEW W

VIEW X   VIEW Y   VIEW Z

Steering linkage (© Ford Motor Co)

a belt tension gauge is not available should the belt deflection method be used. If the belt deflection method is used, be sure to check with a belt tension gauge as soon as possible, since deflection method is not accurate.

4. Tighten the mounting bolts and nuts.

Steering Wheel Removal and Installation

1. Disconnect the negative battery cable.
2. Remove the horn ring or hub cap by pushing it down and rotating it counterclockwise. Remove the retaining screws (from underside of steering wheel) and the crash pad. On 1970 Fords and Mercurys with speed control, the switch bezels must be pried up with a thin knife blade and the center trim plate removed to gain access to the crash pad retaining screws. On later models with speed control, the switches simply snap into plastic retainers inside the crash pad. Disconnect the horn and speed control wires.
3. Remove the steering wheel nut. Install a steering wheel puller on the end of the shaft and remove the wheel.

Caution The use of a knock-off type steering wheel puller or the use of a hammer on the steering shaft will damage the column bearing and, on collapsible columns, the column itself may be damaged.

4. Lubricate the steering shaft bushing with white grease. Transfer all serviceable parts to the new steering wheel.

5. With the front wheels pointing in a straight-ahead direction, and with the alignment marks on steering wheel and the steering shaft lined up, install the steering wheel and locknut.
6. Connect the horn and speed control wires and install the horn ring or hub cap. Install the crash pad and retaining screws.
7. Connect the negative battery cable.

Turn Signal Switch Replacement

1. Disconnect the negative battery cable.
2. Remove the steering wheel as outlined in the "Steering Wheel R&R" section.
3. Unscrew the turn signal lever from the side of the column. Remove the emergency flasher retainer and knob, if so equipped.
4. Locate and remove the finish cover on the steering column and disconnect the wiring connector plugs.
5. On 1970 Thunderbirds, and all models with a tilt steering column, it is necessary to separate the wires from the connector plug in order to remove the switch and wires. First note the location and color code of each wire, prior to removal, with the wire terminal removal tool. Remove the plastic cover from the wiring harness. Attach a piece of heavy cord to the switch wires to pull them down through the column during installation.
6. Remove the retaining clips and screws from the turn signal switch and lift the switch and

wire assembly from the top of the column.
7. Tape the ends of the new switch wires together and transfer the pull cord to these wires.
8. Pull the wires down through the column with the cord and attach the new switch to the column hub.
9. If the switch wires were separated from the connector plug, press the wires into their proper location. Connect the wiring connector plugs and install the finish cover on the column.
10. Install the turn signal lever. Install the emergency flasher retainer and knob, if so equipped.
11. Install the steering wheel as outlined in the "Steering Wheel R&R" section.

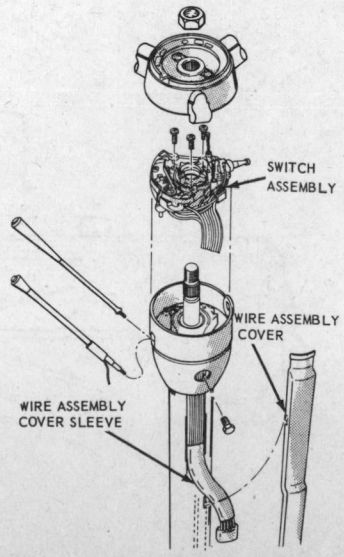

SWITCH
ASSEMBLY

WIRE ASSEMBLY
COVER

WIRE ASSEMBLY
COVER SLEEVE

Turn signal switch—fixed column
(© Ford Motor Co)

12. Connect the negative battery cable and test the operation of the turn signals, horn, emergency flashers, and speed control, if so equipped.

Ignition Lock Cylinder Replacement

1. Disconnect the negative battery cable.
2. On cars with a fixed steering column, remove the steering wheel trim pad and the steering wheel. Insert a stiff wire into the hole located in the lock cylinder housing. On cars with a tilt steering wheel, this hole is located on the outside of the steering column near the emergency flasher button and it is not necessary to remove the steering wheel.
3. Place the gear shift lever in Reverse on standard shift cars and in Park on cars with automatic transmission, and turn the ignition key to the ON position.
4. Depress wire and remove lock cylinder and wire.
5. Insert new cylinder into housing and turn to the OFF position. This will lock the cylinder into position.
6. Reinstall steering wheel and pad if removed.
7. Connect negative battery cable.

Ignition Switch Replacement

1. Disconnect the negative battery cable.
2. Remove the shrouding from the steering column, and detach and lower the steering column from the brake support bracket.
3. Disconnect the switch wiring at the multiple plug.
4. Remove the two nuts that retain the switch to the steering column.
5. On vehicles with column mounted gearshift lever, detach the switch plunger from the switch actuator rod and remove the switch. On vehicles with console mounted gearshift lever, remove the pin connecting the plunger to the actuator and remove the switch.
6. To re-install the switch, place both the lock mechanism at the top of the column and the switch itself in lock position for correct adjustment. To hold the column in the lock position, place the automatic shift lever in PARK or manual shift lever in reverse, and turn to LOCK and remove the key. New switches are held in lock by plastic shipping pins. To pin existing switches, pull the switch plunger out as far as it will go and push it back into the first detent. Insert a 3/32 in. diameter wire in the locking hole in the top of the switch.
7. Connect the switch plunger to the switch actuator rod.
8. Position the switch on the column and install the attaching nuts. Do not tighten them.
9. Move the switch up and down to locate mid-position of rod lash, and then tighten the nuts.
10. Remove the locking pin or wire.
11. Attach the steering column to the brake support bracket and install the shrouding.

INSTRUMENT PANEL

Headlight Switch Replacement

All Except 1970 Mercury and 1972-76 Thunderbird

1. Disconnect the negative battery cable. Remove the knob from the washer switch.

2. On 1971 and later Ford and 1971 and 1973 and later Mercury, remove the instrument panel pad, and instrument cluster. On 1972 Mercurys, remove the instrument panel pad only.
3. Pull the headlight switch control knob to the full ON position and press the release knob on the switch. With the knob depressed, pull the knob and shaft from the switch.
4. Remove the wire connector from the back of the switch and, if equipped with headlight doors, remove the vacuum hoses.
5. Remove the bezel retaining nut and remove the switch from the dash. On 1971-72 Fords and 1971 Mercurys, the switch is attached to the dash with three screws instead of a bezel nut.
6. Reverse above procedure to reinstall. When installing the headlight switch control knob and shaft, turn the shaft in the switch until a distinct click is heard, locking the shaft in place.

Typical headlight switch
(© Ford Motor Co)

1970 Mercury

1. Remove the battery ground cable.
2. Working under the dash, remove the wire connector from the back of the headlight switch. If equipped with headlight doors, remove the vacuum hoses from the switch.
3. Remove the four switch retaining screws and remove the switch from the dash.

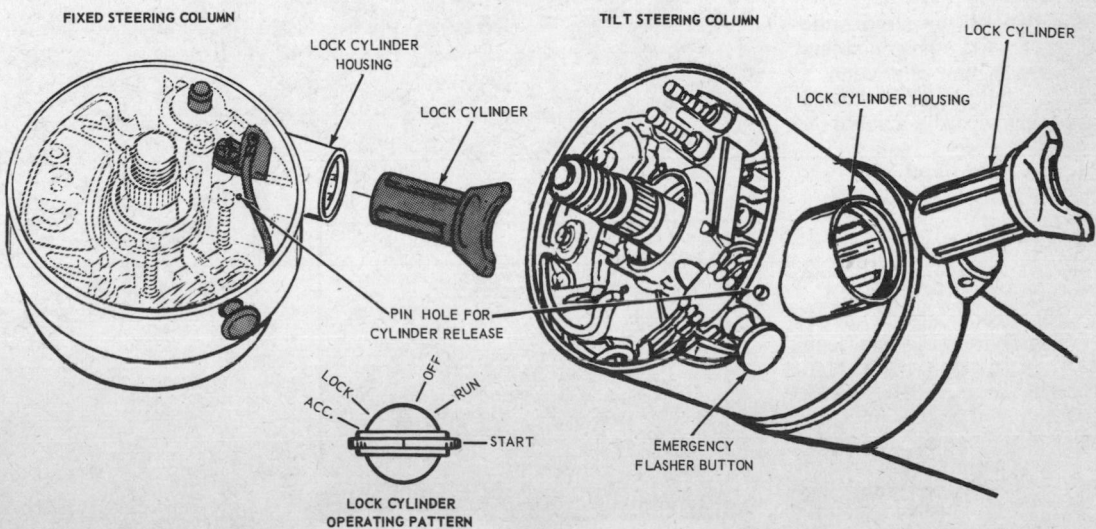

Lock cylinder replacement (© Ford Motor Co)

4. Reverse above procedure to install.

1972-76 Thunderbird

1. Disconnect the negative battery cable.
2. Remove the cluster trim panel.
3. Remove the headlight switch mounting plate.
4. Remove the bezel nut and disconnect the multiple connector.
5. If equipped, remove the vacuum lines.
6. Remove the switch.
7. Reverse the above procedure to install.

WINDSHIELD WIPERS

Motor Removal and Installation

All Ford and Mercury Thunderbird 1972-76

1. Disconnect the negative battery cable.
2. Remove the wiper arm and blade assemblies from the pivot shafts.
3. On 1970 models, remove the cowl grille. Remove the left side cowl grille.
4. Disconnect the wiper links at the wiper output pin by removing the retaining clip.
5. Disconnect the wire leads from the motor. They are located under the dash.
6. Remove the motor attaching bolts from under the dash and remove the motor.
7. Reverse procedure to install.
   NOTE: before installing the wiper arms and blades, operate the wiper motor to ensure the pivot shafts are in the park position when the arms and blades are installed.

Thunderbird, 1971

This motor works by hydraulic pressure taken from the power steering system. During wiper operation, a part of the fluid supply is bypassed through the wiper motor by a valve on the motor.

1. Remove wiper arm and blade assemblies, pivot shaft nuts and bezels.
2. Remove the cowl top panel.
3. Disconnect both pivot shaft links at the wiper motor.
4. Remove carburetor air cleaner.

Caution If the engine has been running recently, watch out for hot fluid in the wiper system.

5. Disconnect the lines at the wiper motor.
6. Remove wiper motor mounting screws.
7. Disconnect the control cable

from the motor, then remove the motor.
8. If replacing the wiper motor, transfer all fittings.
9. Position motor to the bracket area, connect and adjust the control cable.
10. Start the lines in the fittings, position the motor on its mount and install attaching screws. Tighten fittings.
11. Connect the links to the wiper motor arm.
12. Start engine and check operation of wiper motor. Stop engine and bring power steering reservoir to level.
13. Reinstall cowl top panel.
14. Install bezels, nuts and wiper arm assemblies. Install the air cleaner.

Thunderbird, 1970

1. Disconnect the negative battery cable.
2. Disconnect the windshield washer hose. Remove the three retaining bolts and pull the cowl grille from under the two clips.
3. Disconnect the wiper motor leads from the engine side of the firewall and push the wiring and insulating grommet through the hole in the firewall.
4. Remove the four motor to dash retaining bolts.
5. Lift the wiper motor out and, at the same time, pull the wiper arm and blade assembly to the left to gain access to the wiper output pin.
6. Remove the clip and disconnect the wiper links from the motor.
7. Remove the three motor-to-mounting plate bolts and remove the motor.

8. To reinstall, first position the wire harness and grommet in the hole in the firewall, then reverse above procedure.

RADIO

Removal and Installation

1970 Mercury

1. Disconnect battery.
2. Remove radio knobs and remove nut from radio shaft.
3. Remove radio rear support nut and nut retaining radio to instrument panel.
4. Lower radio and disconnect antenna, radio, power, and speaker lead wires.
5. Remove radio. Reverse procedure to install radio.

1970 Ford

1. Remove radio knobs and wiper and washer knobs.
2. Remove lighter and pull off heater switch knobs.
3. Remove ten screws retaining instrument panel trim cover assembly and remove.
4. Remove lower rear radio support bolt.
5. Remove three nuts retaining radio in instrument panel and pull radio halfway out.
6. Disconnect all leads and remove radio.
7. Reverse procedure to install radio.

Thunderbird Through 1971

Use the procedure for the Continental Mark III through 1971.

1971 and Later Ford and Mercury

1. Disconnect the negative battery cable.

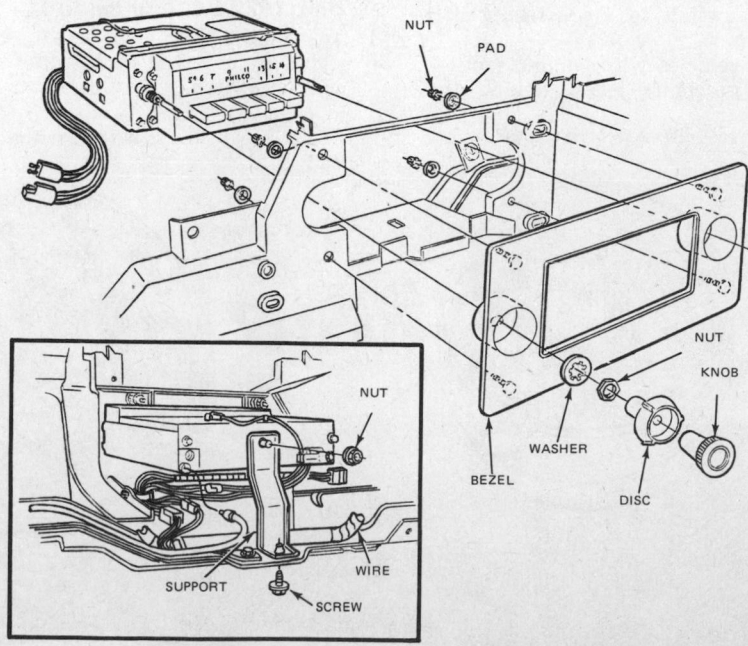

Radio installation—1972-76 Thunderbird (© Ford Motor Co)

2. Remove the radio knobs and the nuts retaining the radio cover bezel.

3. Remove the bezel and the nut retaining the fader control to the bezel.

4. Remove the upper and lower radio support brackets and bolts.

5. Disconnect all leads from the radio.

6. Remove the two nuts retaining the radio to the instrument panel and remove the radio.

7. Reverse above procedure to install.

1972-76 Thunderbird

1. Disconnect the negative battery cable.

2. Remove the knobs from the radio shafts.

3. Remove the radio shaft nuts and the rear support attaching screw.

4. Disconnect the power lead, speaker wires and antenna lead, and remove the radio.

5. Remove the 2 screws attaching the twilight sentinel amplifier. Lower the amplifier.

6. Remove the air conditioning duct from beneath the radio.

7. Disconnect the radio rear support.

8. Reverse the above procedure to install.

HEATER

Vehicles Without Air Conditioning

Heater Core Removal and Installation

Ford and Mercury

1. Partially drain cooling system.
2. Remove heater hoses at core.
3. Remove retaining screws, core cover and seal from plenum.
4. Remove core from plenum.
5. Install in reverse of above, applying a thin coat of silicone to the pads.

Thunderbird Through 1971

1. Remove the hood and air cleaner.
2. Drain the cooling system.
3. Remove the heater hoses and position the hoses and hot water valve out of the way.
4. Disconnect the vacuum hose from the top of the heater case and position it out of the way.
5. Remove the transmission dip stick and tube assembly from the transmission.
6. Disconnect the blower motor lead wires.
7. Remove the heater core case

cover and remove the core from the case.

8. Reverse above procedure to install.

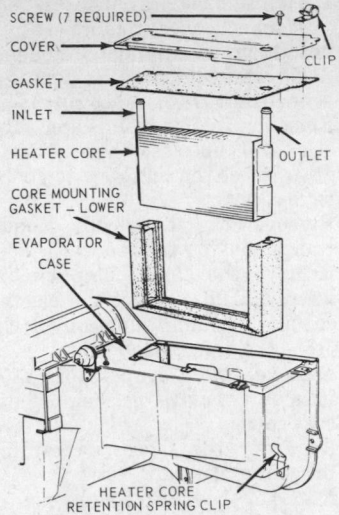

SCREW (7 REQUIRED)
COVER
CLIP
GASKET
INLET
HEATER CORE
OUTLET
CORE MOUNTING
GASKET — LOWER
EVAPORATOR
CASE
HEATER CORE
RETENTION SPRING CLIP

Heater core removal—1973 and later Ford and Mercury (© Ford Motor Co)

1972-76 Thunderbird

1. Drain the coolant and disconnect the hoses from the heater core.
2. Remove the glove box and the heater air outlet register.
3. Remove the mounting screw and disconnect the temperature cable at the blend door crank arm.
4. Remove the blue and red vacuum hoses from the high-low door vacuum motor, the yellow hose from the panel-defrost door motor, and the brown hose at the tee connector to the temperature bypass door motor.
5. Disconnect the wiring connector from the resistor.
6. Remove the 10 retaining screws and the rear half of the plenum case.
7. Remove the heater core tube support bracket mounting nut.
8. Reverse the above procedure to install, taking care to reseal the plenum case halves.

Blower Motor Removal and Installation

Thunderbird Through 1971

1. Working inside the car, remove the right kick panel cover.
2. Remove the screws attaching the fresh air duct and remove the duct from the car.
3. Reach inside the cowl panel and disconnect the blower motor wire leads.
4. Still working inside the cowl panel, remove the one screw attaching the blower motor to the mounting plate. Rotate the motor mounting plate clockwise to disengage it from the heater case.

5. Remove the blower motor and wheel assembly from the car by guiding it out of the opening in the cowl panel.

1972-76 Thunderbird

1. Remove the glovebox and recirc air register and duct assembly.
2. Remove the two, blower lower housing retaining screws.
3. Disconnect the white hose from the outside recirc air door vacuum motor, and remove the vacuum motor from the blower lower housing. Leave the motor actuator connected to the door crank arm.
4. Disconnect the orange lead wire and black ground wire from the blower motor.
5. Remove the six flange screws and separate the blower lower housing from the upper housing. Remove the lower housing from the car.
6. Remove the blower motor and wheel assembly from the lower housing.
7. Reverse the above procedure to install.

Ford and Mercury Through 1972

1. Disconnect the negative battery cable.
2. Disconnect the blower motor wire leads under the hood.
3. Remove any parts mounted on the inside of the right fender apron.
4. Raise the vehicle on a hoist and remove the right front wheel.
5. Remove the fender apron-to-fender attaching bolts and lower the fender apron.
6. Insert a block of wood between the apron and the fender to gain working space.
7. Reach inside the fender apron and remove the blower motor mounting plate attaching screws.
8. Remove the blower motor, wheel and mounting plate from inside the fender as an assembly.
9. Reverse above procedure to install.

1973 and Later Ford and Mercury

1. Disconnect the blower motor lead wire. This is an orange wire located at the rear of the right hood hinge.
2. Remove the mounting screw from the black ground wire located at the upper cowl. Remove both wires from the clip.
3. Remove the right front tire and wheel.
4. In order to get to the blower motor, an access hole must be cut out in the right front fender apron. The pattern for this hole has been outlined on the apron by the factory. It appears as a beaded line.

5. A small indentation or drill dimple is present 1/2 in. from the centerline of the bead. Drill a 1 in. diameter hole at this drill dimple. Be careful not to damage the heater case by overdrilling.
6. Using aircraft snips, cut along the bead to create the opening. Do not use a saber saw.
7. Remove the blower motor mounting plate screws and disconnect the cooler tube from the motor.
8. Remove the motor and wheel assembly out of the heater case and out through the access hole.
9. To install, reverse the removal procedure. Apply rope sealer to the motor mounting plate. Obtain a cover plate from your local Ford parts department, drill 8, 1/8 in. holes in the fender apron and install the cover plate.

Vehicles With Factory Air Conditioning

Heater Core Removal and Installation

Ford and Mercury Through 1972
1. Drain the cooling system.
2. Remove the carburetor air cleaner.
3. Remove the two screws retaining the vacuum manifold to the dash. Disconnect the vacuum hoses as necessary, taking note of their placement, and move the manifold to one side of the heater core cover.
4. Disconnect the heater hoses.
5. Remove the seven attaching screws and the heater core cover.
6. Remove the heater core and pad from the housing.
7. Reverse above procedure to install.

1973 and Later Ford and Mercury
1. Drain the cooling system.
2. Disconnect the heater hoses at the heater core tubes.
3. Remove the seven screws which retain the core cover plate to the core housing and lift off the plate.
4. Pull the heater core and mounting gasket up out of the case. Remove the core mounting gasket.
5. Reverse the above procedure to install, taking care to ensure that the core and gasket seat firmly forward of the core retention spring in the case. Fill the cooling system with the recommended mixture of water and anti-freeze (coolant).

Thunderbird Through 1971
1. Drain the cooling system.
2. Remove the air cleaner. Scribe the outline of the hinges on the hood and remove the hood.

3. On models equipped with hydraulic wipers, disconnect and plug the hydraulic lines at the motor.
4. Disconnect the heater hoses.
5. Disconnect the vacuum supply hose from the top of the housing and remove the oil pressure sender unit from the engine.
6. Remove the transmission dipstick and tube assembly.
7. Disconnect the icing switch multiple connector.
8. Remove the heater-air conditioner housing front cover.
9. Remove the glove compartment liner, and disconnect the electrical and vacuum junction blocks from the inner dash panel.
10. Remove two evaporator stud nuts and remove the heater core case cover.
11. Remove the core retaining bracket and core.
12. Reverse above procedure to install.

1972-76 Thunderbird
See heater core Removal and Installation for non-air-conditioned 1972-76 Thunderbirds.

Blower Motor Removal and Installation

Ford and Mercury Through 1972
1. Remove the battery.
2. Remove the right front wheel.
3. Remove the vacuum tank bolts and fender apron bolts.
4. Move the fender apron inboard.
5. Remove the blower motor attaching screws and vent hose.
6. Pry upward on the hood hinge and remove the blower.
7. Reverse the above procedure to install.

1973 and Later Ford and Mercury
For air-conditioned cars, follow the same procedure outlined under "Blower Motor Removal and Installation" for non-air-conditioned 1973 and later Ford and Mercury.

Thunderbird Through 1971
1. Disconnect the ground cable from the battery.
2. Take out the courtesy light from the lower edge of the instrument panel.
3. Take out the glove box liner.
4. Take off the right cowl side of the trim panel.
5. Take out the six duct mounting flange screws. Reach through the recirculating door opening and take the vacuum hose from the vacuum motor and take out the duct assembly.
6. Disconnect the lead wire from the blower motor.
7. Lift out the motor and wheel assembly through the opening in the cowl side panel.

8. Take out the screw from the motor mounting plate.
9. Rotate the motor mounting plate counter-clockwise until unlocked, then lift out.
10. Reverse the above procedure to install.

1972-76 Thunderbird
See "Blower Motor Removal and Installation" for non-air-conditioned 1972-76 Thunderbirds.

SEAT BELTS

Disabling the Seat Belt/ Starter Interlock

It is now legal to disable the seat belt/starter interlock system. However the warning light portion of the system must be left operational.
1. Apply the parking brake and remove the ignition key.
2. Open the hood and locate the system emergency override switch and connector. It is always under the hood and sometimes on the left fender apron. Remove the connector.
3. Cut the white wire(s) with the pink dots (#33 circuit) and the red wire(s) wth the light blue stripe (#32 circuit).
4. Splice the two (or four) wires together and tape the splice. Use a "butt" connector if available.
NOTE: Do not cut and splice the other connector wires. If the red/ yellow hash wire is spliced to any of the other wires the car will start in gear.
5. Install the connector back on the override switch. Close the hood.
7. Apply the parking brakes, buckle the seat belt, and turn the key to the "ON" position. If the starter cranks in "ON" or any gear selected, the wrong wires have been cut and spliced. Repeat steps 3-6.
8. Unbuckle the belt and try to start the car. If the car doesn't start, repeat steps 3-6. If the car starts, everything is O.K.
9. To stop the warning buzzer from operating, remove it from the connector. Tape the connector to the wiring harness so that it can't rattle.

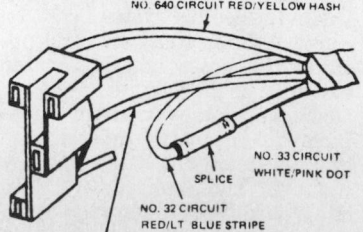

Seat belt interlock disconnect points

(© Ford Motor Co)

INDEX

Lincoln Continental · Mark III · Mark IV · Mark V

Automatic Transmission

in car service **C607, C658**
Downshift rod adjustment C608
Intermediate band adjustment C608
Shift linkage adjustment C608
Pan Removal, fluid
and filter change C609

Brakes **C611, U299**
Hydro-boost booster Removal and
Installation C612
Master cylinder Removal and
Installation C611
Parking brake adjustment C613
Vacuum power brake booster Removal
and Installation C611

Charging System **C599, U2**
Alternator Removal and Installation C599
Regulator Removal and Installation C599

Cooling System **C602, U367**
Radiator Removal and Installation C602
Thermostat Removal and Installation C602
Water pump Removal and Installation C602

Emission Controls **C602, U145**

Engine **C603, U194**
ENGINE REMOVAL AND INSTALLATION C603
CONNECTING RODS AND PISTONS C657
CYLINDER HEAD REMOVAL AND
INSTALLATION C605
LUBRICATION C607
Oil pan Removal and Installation C607
Oil pump Removal and Installation C607
Rear crankshaft oil seal
Removal and Installation C607
MANIFOLDS C604
Exhaust manifold Removal and
Installation C604

Intake manifold Removal and
Installation C604
TIMING CASE COVER, CHAIN AND
SPROCKETS REMOVAL AND
INSTALLATION C606
Camshaft Removal and Installation C607
Oil seal Removal and Installation C607
VALVE SYSTEM C604
Preliminary valve Adjustment C604
Rocker assembly Removal and
Installation C605
Valve guides C604

Front Suspension **C610, U292**

Fuel System **C600, U50**
Fuel filter Removal and Installation C600
Fuel mixture adjustment C601
Fuel pump Removal and Installation C600
Idle speed adjustment C600

Heater **C617**
Blower motor Removal and Installation C617
Heater core Removal and Installation C617

Ignition System **C599, U34**
Contact point replacement
and adjustment C600
Distributor Removal and Installation C599
Firing order C594
Ignition timing C599
Ignition Retiming C599
Solid state ignition tachometer
hookup C600

Instrument Panel **C615, U350**
Light switch Removal and Installation C615

Jacking, Hoisting **C609**

Radio **C616**
Radio Removal and Installation C616

Rear Suspension **C610**
Spring Removal and Installation C610
Shock absorber Removal and
Installation C610

Seat Belts **C618**
Disabling the seat belt starter
interlock C618

Specifications **C594, U359**
Capacities C597
Crankshaft and connecting rod C597
Engine identification code C595
General engine C595
Piston clearance C598
Ring C597
Serial number C595
Torque C597
Tune-up C596
Valve C596
Wheel alignment C598
Year identification C594

Starting System **C599**
Starter Removal and Installation C599

Steering **C613, U328**
Ignition lock Removal and Installation C615
Ignition switch Removal and
Installation C615
Power steering pump Removal and
Installation C614
Tie-rod Removal and Installation C614
Steering wheel Removal and Installation C613
Turn signal switch Removal and
Installation C613

U-Joints **C609**

Windshield Wipers **C615**
Motor Removal and Installation C615

YEAR IDENTIFICATION

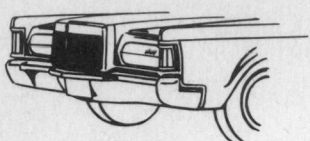

1970-71 Continental Mark III

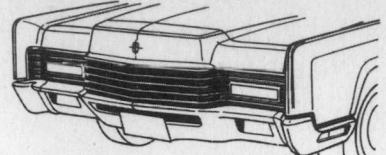

1970 Continental

1971 Continental

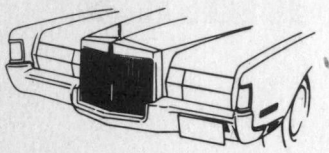

1972 Continental Mark IV

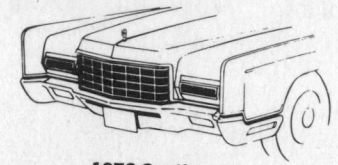

1972 Continental

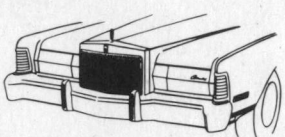

1973 Continental Mark IV

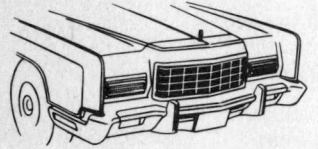

1973 Continental

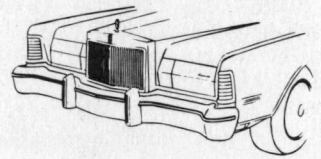

1974 Continental Mark IV

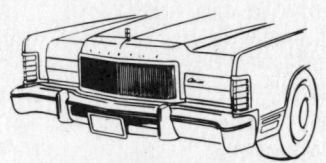

1974 Continental

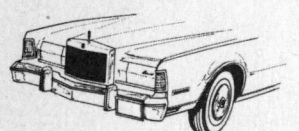

1975 Continental Mark IV

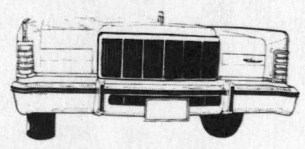

1975 Continental

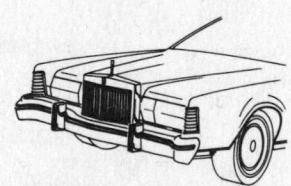

1976 Continental Mark IV

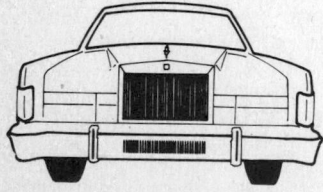

1977 Lincoln Continental

FIRING ORDER

FIRING ORDER
1-5-4-2-6-3-7-8

460 V8

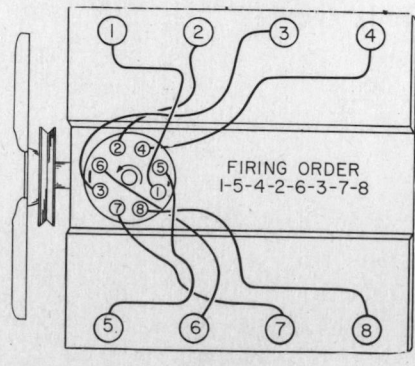

1977 Continental Mark IV

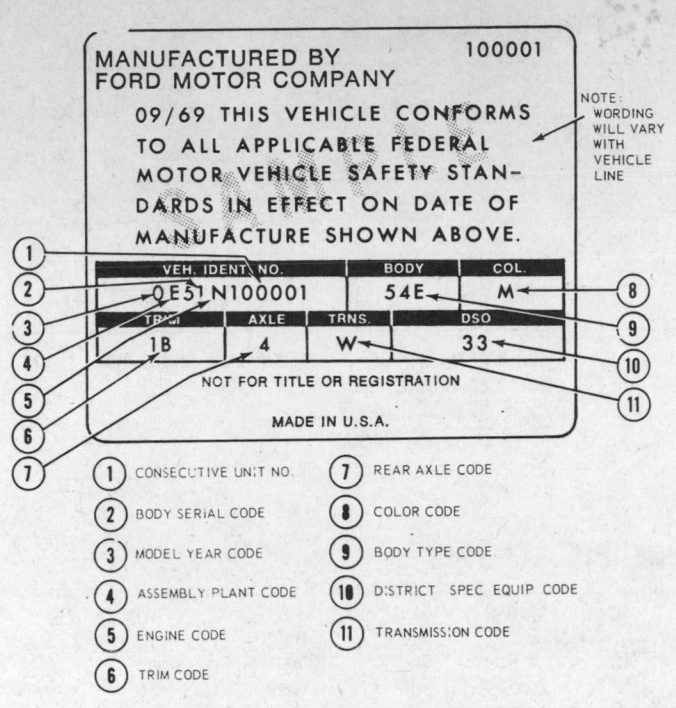

Vehicle certification label—1970-76
((© Ford Motor Co)

(1) CONSECUTIVE UNIT NO.
(2) BODY SERIAL CODE
(3) MODEL YEAR CODE
(4) ASSEMBLY PLANT CODE
(5) ENGINE CODE
(6) TRIM CODE
(7) REAR AXLE CODE
(8) COLOR CODE
(9) BODY TYPE CODE
(10) DISTRICT SPEC EQUIP CODE
(11) TRANSMISSION CODE

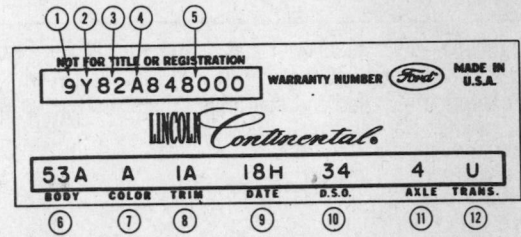

1 Model year code
2 Assembly plant code
3 Body serial code
4 Engine code
5 Consecutive unit number
6 Body type code
7 Color code
8 Trim code
9 Date code
10 District—special equipment code
11 Rear axle code
12 Transmission code

ENGINE IDENTIFICATION

The engine code designation is the 5th digit of the vehicle identification number (V.I.N.) The V.I.N. is stamped on a plate located at the left side of the instrument panel visible through the windshield.

Disp	Bbl	'70	'71	'72	'73	'74	'75	'76	'77
8-Cylinder Models									
400	4								—
460	4	A	A	A	A	A	A	A	Ā

GENERAL ENGINE SPECIFICATIONS

Year	Engine No. Cyl. Displacement Cu. In.	Carburetor Type	Horsepower @ rpm ■	Torque @ rpm (ft lbs) ■	Bore X Stroke (in.)	Advertised Compression Ratio	Oil Pressure @ 2000 rpm
'70	8-460	4 bbl	365 @ 4600	500 @ 2800	4.362 x 3.850	10.50:1	55
'71	8-460	4 bbl	365 @ 4600	500 @ 2800	4.362 x 3.850	10.50:1	35-75
'72	8-460	4 bbl	224 @ 4400	357 @ 2800	4.362 x 3.850	8.50:1	35-75
	8-460 Mark IV	4 bbl	212 @ 4400	342 @ 2800	4.362 x 3.850	8.50:1	35-75
'73	8-460 Continental	4 bbl	224 @ 4400	357 @ 2800	4.362 x 3.850	8.5:1	35-65
	8-460 Mark IV	4 bbl	212 @ 4400	342 @ 2800	4.362 x 3.850	8.5:1	35 65
'74	8-460 Continental	4 bbl	215 @ 4000	350 @ 2600	4.362 x 3.850	8.5:1	35-65
	8-460 Mark IV	4 bbl	220 @ 4000	350 @ 2600	4.362 x 3.850	8.5:1	35-65
'75	8-460 Continental	4 bbl	206 @ 4000①	357 @ 2600②	4.362 x 3.850	8.0:1	35-65
	8-460 Mark IV	4 bbl	194 @ 4000①	347 @ 2600②	4.362 x 3.850	8.0:1	35-65
'76	8-460	4 bbl	202 @ 3800	352 @ 1600	4.362 x 3.850	8.0:1	35-65

GENERAL ENGINE SPECIFICATIONS

Year	Engine No. Cyl. Displacement Cu. In.	Carburetor Type	Horsepower @ rpm ■	Torque @ rpm (ft lbs) ■	Bore X Stroke (in.)	Advertised Compression Ratio	Oil Pressure @ 2000 rpm
'77	8-400 Continental	4 bbl	—	—	4.00 x 4.00	8.0:1	45-75
	8-400 Mark V	4 bbl	—	—	4.00 x 4.00	8.0:1	45-75
	8-460 Continental	4 bbl	—	—	4.362 x 3.850	8.0:1	35-65
	8-460 Mark V	4 bbl	—	—	4.362 x 3.850	8.0:1	35-65

■ Beginning 1972, horsepower and torque are SAE net figures. They are measured at the rear of the transmission with all accessories installed and operating. Since the figures vary when a given engine is installed in different models, some are representative rather than exact.
① 223 @ 4000—California
② 366 @ 2600—California

TUNE-UP SPECIFICATIONS

Year	ENGINE No. Cyl Displacement (cu in.)	hp	SPARK PLUGS Orig. Type	SPARK PLUGS Gap (in.)	DISTRIBUTOR Point Dwell (deg)	DISTRIBUTOR Point Gap (in.)	IGNITION TIMING (deg) ▲ Man Trans	IGNITION TIMING (deg) ▲ ● Auto Trans	VALVES Intake Opens ■ (deg)	Fuel Pump Pressure (psi)	IDLE SPEED (rpm) ▲ Man Trans	IDLE SPEED (rpm) ▲ Auto Trans
'70	8-460	365	BF-42	.034	26-31	.017	—	10B	16	5-7	—	600
'71	8-460	365	BRF-42	.034	26-31	.017	—	4B	16	5-7	—	600
'72	8-460	224	ARF-42	.034	26-30	.017	—	10B(6B)	16	5-7	—	625/500②
'73	8-460	224	ARF-22	.034	26-30	.017	—	6B	16	5-7	—	625/500②
'74-'75	8-460 Mark IV	220	ARF-52	.044	Electronic		—	14B	8	6-7	—	650/500②
	8-460	215	ARF-52	.044	Electronic		—	14B	8	6-7	—	650/500②
'76	8-460	202	ARF-52	.044	Electronic		—	8B(14B)	8	6-7	—	650/600②
	8-460 Mark IV	202	ARF-52	.044	Electronic		—	10B	8	6-7	—	650/600②
'77	8-400	All	AR-52-6	.060	Electronic		—	③	17	7-8	—	③
	8-460		See Underhood Specifications Sticker									

▲ See text for procedure
● Figure in parentheses indicates California engine
■ All figures Before Top Dead Center
① A/C on
② First figure is for idle speed with solenoid energized and automatic transmission in Drive, while second figure is for idle speed with solenoid disconnected and automatic transmission in Neutral

③ See Underhood Specifications Sticker
B Before Top Dead Center
— Not applicable
NOTE: The underhood specifications sticker often reflects tune-up specification changes made in production. Sticker figures must be used if they disagree with those in this chart.

VALVE SPECIFICATIONS

Year	Engine No. Cyl. Displacement (cu in.)	Seat Angle (deg)	Face Angle (deg)	Spring Test Pressure (lbs @ in.)	Spring Installed Height (in.)	STEM TO GUIDE Clearance (in.) Intake	STEM TO GUIDE Clearance (in.) Exhaust	STEM Diameter (in.) Intake	STEM Diameter (in.) Exhaust
'70	8-460	45	46	80 @ 1.81	1 13/16	.0010-.0027	.0010-.0027	.3420	.3420
'71	8-460	45	46	80 @ 1.81	1 13/16	.0010-.0027	.0010-.0027	.3420	.3420
'72	8-460	45	46	80 @ 1.81	1 13/16	.0010-.0027	.0010-.0027	.3420	.3420
'73	8-460	45	44	170 @ 1.39	1 13/16	.0010-.0027	.0010-.0027	.3420	.3420
'74-'77	8-460	45	44	80 @ 1.81	1 13/16	.0010-.0027	.0010-.0027	.3420	.3420
'77	8-400	44½-45	45½	80 @ 1.82	1 13/16	.0010-.0027	.0015-.0032	.3420	.3414

CAPACITIES

Year	ENGINE No. Cyl. Displacement (cu. in.)	Engine Crankcase Add 1 Qt For New Filter	TRANSMISSION Pts To Refill After Draining			Drive Axle (pts)	Gasoline Tank (gals)	COOLING SYSTEM (qts)	
			Manual 3-Speed	4-Speed	Automatic			With Heater	With A/C
'70	8-460	4	—	—	6	5	③	19.5④	19.5④
'71	8-460	4	—	—	6	5	23	19.4	19.4
'72	8-460	4	—	—	6	5	22.5	19.4	19.4
'73	8-460	4	—	—	6	5	22⑤	19.5	19.5
'74	8-460	4	—	—	6	5	26.5⑦	21.5	21.5
'75-'76	8-460	4	—	—	6	5	26.5⑧	⑥	⑥
'77	8-400	4	—	—	6	5	26.5⑧	⑥	⑥
	8-460	4	—	—	6	5	26.5⑧	⑥	⑥

①② Not used
③ Without evaporative emission controls:
    Continental—24.5 gals
    Mark III—24.1 gals
    With evaporative emission controls:
    Continental—23.1 gals
    Mark III—22.5 gals

④ Mark III—19.4 qts
⑤ Mark IV—22.5 gals
⑥ Mark IV—20.5 qts; Lincoln—19.7 qts
⑦ Lincoln—22 gals
⑧ Lincoln—24.2 gals
—— Not applicable

TORQUE SPECIFICATIONS
All readings in ft lbs

Year	Engine Displacement (cu in.)	Cylinder Head Bolts	Rod Bearing Bolts	Main Bearing Bolts	Crankshaft Pulley Bolt	Flywheel to Crankshaft Bolts	MANIFOLD	
							Intake	Exhaust
'70-'77	8-460	130-140①	40-45	95-105	70-90	75-83	25-30	28-33
'77	8-400	95-105②	40-45	95-105	70-90	75-85	③	18-24

① In three steps:
    Step 1—70-80
    Step 2—100-110
    Step 3—130-140

② In two steps:
    Step 1: 75
    Step 2: 95-105

③ 5/16 in. bolt: 21-25
    3/8 in. bolt: 27-33

CRANKSHAFT AND CONNECTING ROD SPECIFICATIONS
All measurements are given in in.

Year	Engine Displacement (cu in.)	CRANKSHAFT				CONNECTING ROD		
		Main Brg. Journal Dia	Main Brg. Oil Clearance	Shaft End-Play	Thrust on No.	Journal Diameter	Oil Clearance	Side Clearance
'70-'77	8-460	2.9998-3.0002	.0005-.0025	.004-.008	3	2.4992-2.5000	.0008-.0026	.010-.020
'77	8-400	2.9994-3.0002	.0009-.0026	.004-.008	3	2.4361-2.4369	.0008-.0026	.010-.020

RING GAP
All measurements are given in inches

Year	Engine No. Cyl. Displacement (cu in.)	Top Compression	Bottom Compression		Year	Engine	Oil Control
'70-'77	8-400, 460	.010-.020	.010-.020		'70	8-460	.010-.035
					'71-'77	8-400, 460	.015-.055

RING SIDE CLEARANCE

All measurements are given in inches

Year	Engine	Top Compression	Bottom Compression
'70-'77	8-400, 460	.002-.004	.002-.004

Year	Engine	Oil Control
'70-'77	8-400, 460	Snug

PISTON CLEARANCE

Year	Engine	Piston to bore clearance (in.)
'69-'73	8-460	.0014-.0022
'74	8-460	.0022-.0030
'75-'77	8-400, 460	.0014-.0022

WHEEL ALIGNMENT SPECIFICATIONS

Year	Model	CASTER Range (deg)	Pref Setting (deg) ■	CAMBER Range (deg)	Pref Setting (deg) ▲	Toe-in (in.)	Steering Axis Inclin. (deg)	WHEEL PIVOT RATIO (deg) Inner Wheel	Outer Wheel
'70	Mark III	½P to 1½P	1	0 to 1P	½P	⅛ to ¼	7¾	20	19.3
'70	Continental	2¼N to ¾N	1½N	⅛P to ⅝P	½P	0 to ¹⁄₁₆	7¾	20	18½
'71	Continental	2½N to ½N	1½N	¼N to 1¼P	½P	0 to ¼	7⅞	20	18½
	Mark III	0 to 2P	1	¼N to 1¼P	½P	¹⁄₁₆ to ⁵⁄₁₆	7¾	20	19¼
'72	Continental	½N to 2½P	1½P①	½N to 1½P	½P②	0 to ¼	7¾	20	18⁷⁄₁₆
'72-'74	Mark IV	0 to 2P	1P①	¼N to 1¼P	½P③	¹⁄₁₆ to ⁵⁄₁₆	7¾	20	17¾
'73-'74	Continental	½N to 2½P	1P	¼N to 1¼P	½P	0 to ¼	9½	20	17¾④
'75-'77	Mark IV, V	¼P-2¾P	2P⑧	⑤	⑥⑦	¹⁄₁₆-⁷⁄₁₆	7¾	20	18.16
'75-'77	Continental	¼P-2¾P	2P⑧	⑤	⑥⑦	0-¼	9½	20	18.16

■ Not to vary more than ½ degree from one side to the other unless otherwise noted

▲ Not to vary more than ¼ degree from one side to the other unless otherwise noted

N Negative   P Positive

① Maximum caster difference between wheels should not exceed 1°

② Maximum camber difference between wheels should not exceed 1°

③ Maximum camber difference between wheels should not exceed ¾°

④ 18½° on Lincoln in 1974

⑤ Left—¼P-1¼P; Right—1½N-1P

⑥ Left—½P; Right—¼P

⑦ Maximum camber difference between wheels should not exceed ± ¾°

⑧ Maximum caster difference between wheels should not exceed — ½ to + 1°

CHARGING SYSTEM

General information on alternator and regulator repair and trouble-shooting is in the Unit Repair Section under the heading Charging and Starting Systems.

Alternator Removal and Installation

1. Disconnect the negative battery cable.
2. Loosen the alternator mounting bolts, remove the alternator to adjusting arm bolt and remove the belt.
3. Remove the alternator mounting bolt and spacer, position the alternator so that the wire connectors can be disconnected and remove the alternator.

NOTE: on alternators with integral regulators mounted on the back of the alternator housing, press the sides of the retainer clip and remove the wire from the regulator.

4. Reverse above procedure to reinstall, applying pressure only to the front of the alternator housing when tightening the drive belt.

Regulator Removal and Installation

1. Disconnect the negative battery cable.
2. Remove the regulator mounting screws and wires, then remove the regulator.
3. On vehicles with integral regulator, remove the alternator to adjusting arm bolt and the drive belt.
4. Swing the alternator down, remove the terminal covers from the regulator and remove the regulator attaching nut.
5. Press the sides of the retainer clip and remove the retaining clip and supply wire. Remove the regulator.
6. Reverse above procedure to reinstall.

STARTING SYSTEM

All Lincoln and Continental models use a starter which mounts an outboard solenoid.

Starter Removal and Installation

1. Disconnect the battery ground cable.
2. Raise the car on a hoist.
3. Disconnect the wires at the solenoid terminals.
4. Loosen the 2 front brace attaching bolts.
5. Remove all other brace attaching bolts and let the brace hang free.
6. Turn the front wheels to full right lock.
7. Remove the bolts securing the steering idler arm to the frame.
8. Unbolt and remove the starter.
9. Installation is the reverse of removal.

IGNITION SYSTEM

Distributor Removal

The distributor is located at the front of the engine between the cylinder banks.

1. Remove the carburetor air cleaner, the ignition primary lead and the vacuum advance lead.
2. Carefully mark the position of the rotor in relation to the body of the distributor, and mark the position of the body of the distributor relative to the chamber cover.
3. Remove the hold-down bolt and lift out distributor. The marks are made so that the distributor can be reinstalled without having to retime the ignition.
4. Installation is the reverse of removal, unless timing has been disturbed. In that case, see "Ignition Retiming."

Ignition Timing

All 1974 and later engines have monolithic timing, set at the factory. The monolithic system uses a timing receptacle on the front of the engine which can be connected to digital read-out equipment, which electronically determines timing. Timing can also be adjusted in the conventional way.

1. Locate the timing mark and pointer. Mark the pointer and timing mark according to the timing specifications of your car.
2. Install a stroboscopic type timing light and tachometer according to the manufacturer's specifications.
3. Disconnect the vacuum line(s) to the distributor and plug them. Loosen the distributor hold-down slightly.
4. Start the engine. Set the idle speed to the figure given on the tune up sticker for timing. If there is no such figure, set the idle speed to the figure given for normal idle.
5. Check the timing mark and pointer alignment with the timing light. To advance the timing, turn the distributor clockwise.
6. Stop the engine, tighten the distributor hold-down, start the car, and check the timing. If necessary, reset the idle.

Ignition Retiming

If the timing relationship has been disturbed, retime the ignition as follows: bring No. 1 cylinder up to the firing position. This can be checked by removing the spark plug, placing your thumb in the spark plug hole and then cranking the engine until the compression is felt. Now, slowly bring the crankshaft around until the T.D.C. mark on the crankshaft pulley lines up with the pointer. This is the approximate firing position for No. 1 cylinder.

Note the placement of the no. one spark plug wire on the distributor cap. Scribe a mark on the distributor body directly below the no. one spark plug wire. Remove the distributor cap, loosen the distributor hold-down, and move the distributor until the mark that you made is directly beneath the tip of the rotor. Install the distributor cap and, working counterclockwise, check to make sure that

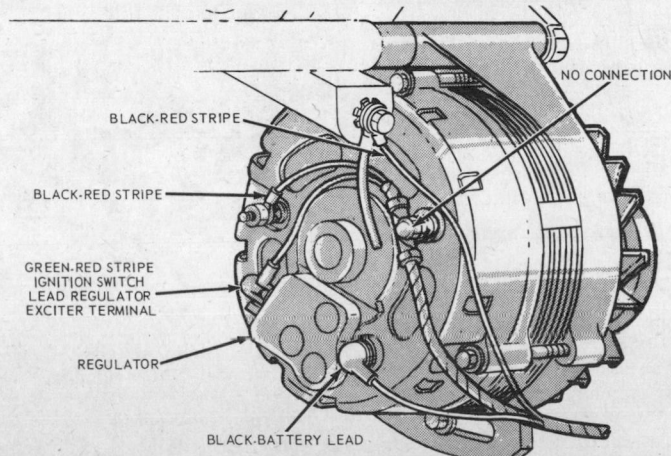

BLACK-RED STRIPE

BLACK-RED STRIPE

GREEN-RED STRIPE
IGNITION SWITCH
LEAD REGULATOR
EXCITER TERMINAL

REGULATOR

NO CONNECTION

BLACK-BATTERY LEAD

Alternator installation with integral regulator
(© Ford Motor Co)

the installation of the spark plug wires corresponds with the firing order of the engine. Check the timing with a timing light.

Contact Point Replacement and Adjustment

Through 1973

1. Unsnap the distributor cap retaining clips and position the cap clear of the breaker plate. Remove the rotor by pulling it straight up.
2. Remove the metal point shield, if so equipped.
3. Disconnect the primary lead and condenser wires from the contact point assembly. On dual-point distributors, remove the jumper strap also.
4. Remove the contact point and condenser retaining screws. Lift the contact point assembly and condenser from the distributor.
5. Lightly lubricate the distributor cam with heat-resistant lubricant.
6. Place the new contact point assembly and condenser in the distributor. Install, but do not tighten, the retaining screws.
7. On all V8 engines, except those equipped with a centrifugal advance distributor, place the ground wire under the contact point assembly screw farthest from the contacts.
8. Turn the engine until the rubbing block on the point assembly is resting on the high point of the distributor cam lobe. Insert a feeler gauge of specified thickness between the contact points and adjust the gap. Tighten the retaining screw and remove the feeler gauge.
9. Connect the primary and condenser wires to the contact point assembly in the same order in which they were removed. On distributors equipped with a metal point shield, the wire should be positioned 180 degrees (180°) from each other, then install the shield.
10. Install the rotor and distributor cap.
11. If a dwell meter is available, check to see that the distributor dwell is within specifications.

Solid State Ignition

Beginning 1974, Lincoln Continental and Mark IV and V are using a solid state or "breakerless" ignition system. This system eliminates the contact breaker points, replacing them with a permanent magnet low voltage generator. For more information, see Electronic Ignition in the Unit Repair section.

Tachometer Connection

The coil connector used with solid state ignition is provided with a cavity for connection of a tachometer, so that the connector doesn't have to be removed to check engine rpm.

Install a tach lead with an alligator clip on its end into the cavity marked "TACH TEST" and connect the other lead to a good ground.

If the coil connector must be removed, pull it out horizontally until it is disengaged from the coil terminal.

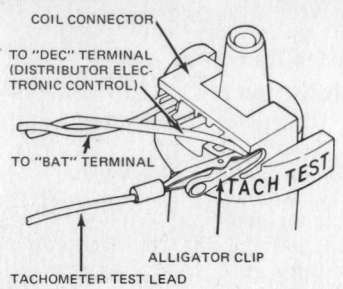

COIL CONNECTOR

TO "DEC" TERMINAL (DISTRIBUTOR ELECTRONIC CONTROL)

TO "BAT" TERMINAL

TACH TEST

ALLIGATOR CLIP

TACHOMETER TEST LEAD

Connecting a tachometer to the electronic ignition coil (© Ford Motor Co)

FUEL SYSTEM

Fuel Pump Replacement

The fuel pump is mounted on the left side of the cylinder front cover.

A separate in-line fuel filter is used. The filter cannot be serviced. Renew it in case of obstruction. This pump is spring loaded in opposition to camshaft eccentric lobe action, and is conventional.

The pump cannot be serviced.

1. Disconnect the inlet and outlet lines at the fuel pump.
2. Remove the attaching bolts and lift the pump off its mount. Remove and discard the gasket.
3. Clean the mounting surfaces of the pad and pump.
4. Apply oil-resistant sealer to both sides of a new gasket. Place the new gasket on the pump flange and hold the pump against the pad. Be sure that the rocker arm is riding on the camshaft eccentric.
5. Install the bolts and connect the fuel lines.
6. Run the engine and check for leaks.

Fuel Filter Removal and Installation

1. Remove the air cleaner.
2. Loosen the hose clamp at the fuel inlet hose connection.
3. Unscrew the filter from the carburetor.
4. Disconnect the filter from the hose and discard the hose clamp.
5. Reverse the above procedure to install, using a new hose clamp. After installation, start the en-

gine and check for fuel leakage.

Idle Speed Adjustment

Through 1973

1. 4300 Carburetor: *Adjust with air cleaner installed.* If it is not possible to adjust carburetor idle speed with the air cleaner installed, the engine idle speed must be rechecked after installing the air cleaner. On models with vacuum controlled heat ducts in the air cleaner, the vacuum line must be plugged if the carburetor is to be adjusted with the air cleaner removed.
2. Run engine at fast idle to equalize operating temperature.
3. Make sure the choke plate is fully released.
4. Turn headlights on high beam.
5. Tape hot idle compensator so that it is fully seated in the closed position.
6. On vehicles equipped with air conditioning, set the idle speed with the air conditioner turned OFF.
7. Remove and plug the vacuum line to the parking brake release, then, set the parking brake and put the transmission in the Drive position.
8. Attach a tachometer of known accuracy to the engine.
9. Adjust the idle speed screw or solenoid to obtain specified rpm. On Carter carburetors, turn the idle speed adjusting screw in to decrease speed and out to increase engine speed. On Autolite carburetors, turn the idle adjusting screw in to increase speed and out to decrease speed. On carburetors through 1971 with an electric solenoid, turn the solenoid plunger to the right to increase idle speed and to the left to decrease it. On 1972-73 carburetors with an electric solenoid, turn the adjusting screw in the solenoid mounting bracket to adjust the idle speed.

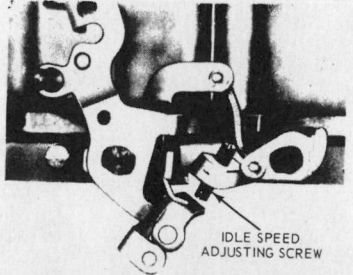

IDLE SPEED ADJUSTING SCREW

Autolite carburetor idle speed adjustment (© Ford Motor Co)

NOTE: There are two engine idle speeds listed for cars with solenoid equipped carburetors. The first or higher speed is adjusted as explained above, the second is adjusted with

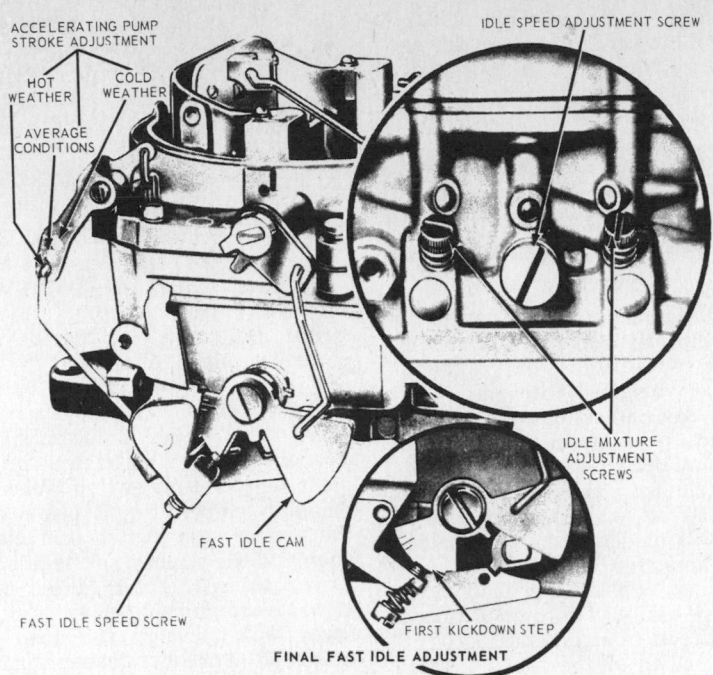

Carter carburetor adjustments
(© Ford Motor Co)

14. Recheck the idle speed.
15. If it is not as specified, readjust the idle to obtain the smoothest idle within the range of the limiter caps.

1975-76

1. Allow the engine to reach normal operating temperature. Check the timing and adjust it, as necessary.
2. Disconnect and plug the distributor vacuum hoses. Remove the top and center hoses from the CSSA coolant temperature operated vacuum valve (in the heater elbow) and connect the two hoses together.
3. Disconnect the EGR vacuum hoses from the carburetor and plug the EGR port. Remove the air cleaner and plug its vacuum hoses. Connect a tachometer.
4. Install the air cleaner and its vacuum hoses. Connect the hoses to the CSSA vacuum valve and the carburetor EGR port.
5. Disconnect the antidieseling solenoid wiring. Set the low idle speed to specification with the low speed adjusting screw (transmission in Neutral).
6. Connect the antidieseling solenoid wiring. Set the curb idle speed to specification by rotating the solenoid body (transmission in Drive).
7. Shift into Neutral and increase the engine speed for a few seconds.
8. Return the engine speed to idle Shift into Drive. Recheck the idle speed. Adjust it, if necessary, by repeating steps 5 and 6.
9. Remove the tachometer. Unplug and connect the distributor vacuum hoses.

the solenoid electrical lead disconnected, and the transmission in Park or Neutral, by turning the adjustment screw on the side of the carburetor.

With the solenoid disconnected, the idle adjusting screw must contact the throttle shaft or the throttle plates may become jammed in the throttle bores of the carburetor when the engine is shut off.

1974

These cars use either the Motorcraft model 4300 4-bbl carburetor or the Carter Thermo-Quad®, which is used only on 1974 California cars.

1. Remove the air cleaner and plug the vacuum line.
2. Set the parking brake.
3. Check the throttle and choke linkage for freedom of movement.
4. Connect a tachometer.
5. Stabilize the engine temperature.
6. Set the ignition timing.
7. Be sure that the choke is fully open.
8. Place automatic transmission in Drive.
9. Turn the solenoid adjusting screw in or out to obtain the higher rpm specified.
10. Disconnect the electrical lead from the throttle solenoid positioner and place the automatic transmission in Neutral.
11. Adjust the "solenoid off" idle speed screw, located on the carburetor body, to obtain the lower specified idle speed.
12. Connect the solenoid wire and allow the plunger to extend.
13. Stop the engine, connect the vacuum line and install the air cleaner.

Fuel Mixture Adjustment

1. On engines with Carter carburetors, turn the mixture screws clockwise until engine idle becomes rough, then, back out adjustment screws until engine reaches highest rpm.
2. On Autolite/Motorcraft carburetors with idle mixture limiter caps, follow the same procedure, but, final adjustment must be made with the caps installed.
3. If adjusting the idle mixture has altered engine idle speed, reset idle speed to specification.

NOTE: The factory recommended procedure for adjusting the idle mixture on 1975 and later models requires the addition of an artificial mixture enrichment substance (propane) to the air intake. This method requires special equipment not available to the general public.

Carter Thermo-Quad® carburetor adjustment points (© Ford Motor Co)

COOLING SYSTEM

Radiator Removal and Installation

1. Drain the cooling system.
2. Disconnect the upper and lower radiator hoses from the radiator.
3. Disconnect the transmission cooler lines from the radiator.
4. If the air conditioner condenser attaches to the radiator, remove the retaining bolts and position the condenser out of the way. *Do not disconnect the refrigerant lines.*
5. If equipped with a fan shroud, disconnect it from the radiator and position it rearward over the fan.
6. Remove the radiator mounting bolts and remove the radiator from the car.
7. Reverse above procedure to install.

Water Pump Removal and Installation

1. Drain cooling system. Remove the fan shroud bolts.
2. Remove bolts retaining fan assembly to water pump.
3. Remove radiator shroud and fan.
4. On air conditioned cars, loosen compressor drive belt.
5. Loosen mounting bolts and remove alternator, power steering and air pump drive belts.
6. Remove water pump pulley.
7. Disconnect radiator lower hose, heater hose, and bypass hose at water pump.
8. Remove water pump bolts and remove water pump.
9. Install in reverse order of removal.

Thermostat Removal and Installation

1. Drain the radiator so that the coolant level is below the thermostat.
2. Remove the coolant outlet housing retaining bolts, pull the elbow away from the manifold, and remove the thermostat and its gasket.
3. Clean the coolant outlet housing and manifold gasket surfaces. Coat a new gasket with water-resistant sealer, and position the gasket on the manifold.
4. Install the thermostat into the outlet with the bridge section facing the outlet.
5. Position the coolant outlet elbow against the intake manifold. Install the retaining bolts, and torque them to specifications.

6. Fill the radiator to the cold fill level, install the cap, start the engine, and check the system for leaks.

EMISSION CONTROLS

1970-71

Lincoln cars used the Thermactor (air pump) System in 1970 in combination with other improvements which are grouped into the IMCO (IMproved Combustion) system. The Thermactor system air manifolds are cast as an integral part of the engine's exhaust manifolds. The Thermactor System continued to be used on all 1971 models and on those 1972 cars designed for California.

Beginning in 1970, some Lincoln cars were equipped with an Evaporative Emisson Control System, a further extension of the IMCO system. The Evaporative Emission Control System became standard on all models in 1971.

1972

1972 California cars are equipped with an addition to the IMCO System, an Electronic Spark Control (ESC) system. This system is composed of an electronic control amplifier, a three-way distributor modulator valve, a speed sensor (found between two sections of the speedometer cable), and a thermal switch (located in the right door pillar of the Lincoln Continental and in the left door pillar of the Continental Mark IV).

The three-way distributor modulator valve is found within the vacuum line connecting the previously discussed ported vacuum switch and the carburetor. It is vented to the atmosphere. The thermal switch is designed to react to a critical temperature range of 50–58° F (outside air temperature). The speed sensor reacts to speeds in excess of 40 mph. The thermal switch dominates over the speed sensor. The impulses from both are fed into the electronic control amplifier.

When the ambient temperature is below 49°F, the ESC system does not operate. When the outside temperature rises above 65°F, the contacts in the temperature switch close. This causes the temperature switch to pass current from the ignition switch to the amplifier. The amplifier then signals the distributor modulator to close and prevent vacuum from reaching the distributor. When the vehicle reaches a speed of 40 mph, the signal from the speed sensor causes the modulator to open and restore normal vacuum advance to the

engine. If the engine should overheat at idle, the ported vacuum switch overrides the ESC system and connects intake manifold vacuum to the distributor.

1973

The 1973 emission control system consists of a new Exhaust Gas Recirculation (EGR) system, and a Delaytd Vacuum Bypass (DVB) spark advance control system.

The DVB system provides two paths by which distributor vacuum can reach the distributor vacuum advance. The system consists of a spark delay valve, a check valve, a solenoid vacuum valve, and an ambient temperature switch. When the ambient temperature is below 49°F, the temperature switch contacts are open and the vacuum solenoid is open (de-energized). Under these conditions, vacuum will flow from the carburetor, through the open solenoid, and to the distributor. Since the spark delay valve resists the flow of carburetor vacuum, the vacuum will always flow through the vacuum solenoid when it is open, since this is the path of least resistance. When the ambient temperature rises above 60°F, the contacts in the temperature switch (which is located in the door post) close. This passes ignition switch current to the solenoid, energizing the solenoid. This blocks one of the two vacuum paths. All distributor vacuum must now flow through the spark delay valve. When carburetor vacuum rises above a certain level on acceleration, a rubber valve in the spark delay valve blocks vacuum from passing through the valve for from 5 to 30 seconds. After this time delay has elapsed, normal vacuum is supplied to the distributor. When the vacuum solenoid is closed (temperature above 60°), the vacuum line from the solenoid to the distributor is vented to atmosphere. To prevent the vacuum that is passing through the spark delay valve from escaping through the solenoid into the atmosphere, a one-way check valve is installed in the vacuum line from the solenoid to the distributor.

The EGR system consists of a control valve, a temperature-controlled vacuum switch, and a special carburetor mounting spacer. A hole that is drilled in the carburetor flange on the intake manifold passes exhaust gases from the manifold crossover passage into the carburetor spacer. A plunger which is attached to the EGR valve normally prevents the exhaust gases from entering the engine. When the engine coolant temperature reaches 125°F, the EGR vacuum valve opens and connects carburetor vacuum to the EGR valve. Under high carburetor vacuum conditions, the EGR valve opens and recirculates exhaust gases into the engine. This lowers peak combustion temperature and reduces oxides of nitrogen.

The spark delay is connected into the distributor vacuum line and closes on hard acceleration to prevent carburetor vacuum from reaching the distributor. After a predetermined number of seconds, the spark delay valve opens and carburetor vacuum is again connected to the distributor.

To meet the standards of the revised California emission controls, all California engines for 1974 will be equipped with the Ford Thermactor system, Exhaust Gas Recirculation (EGR) and the Ford Improved Combustion (IMCO) system.

The Thermactor system keeps hydrocarbon and carbon monoxide emissions at the required level, while the EGR and IMCO systems are designed to reduce oxides of nitrogen.

See the "Unit Repair Section" for troubleshooting procedures for all emission control equipment. On models made after 15 March 1973, the ambient temperature controls were removed from the DVB and EGR systems.

1974

The EGR-CSC system regulates distributor spark advance and EGR valve operation, according to coolant temperature, by sequentially switching vacuum sources. The major components are:
a. 95°F EGR-PVS valve,
b. spark delay valve (SDV), and
c. a vacuum check valve.

When coolant temperature is below 85°F, the EGR-PVS valve admits carburetor EGR port vacuum (at about 2500 rpm) directly to the distributor advance diaphragm through a one-way check valve. At the same time, EGR-PVS valve shuts off carburetor EGR vacuum to the EGR valve and transmission diaphragm.

When coolant temperature is above 95°F, the EGR-PVS valve is actuated and admits carburetor EGR vacuum to the EGR valve and transmission instead of the distributor. At temperatures between 82° and 95°F, the EGR-PVS valve may be open, closed, or in midposition.

The CTAV system (Cold Temperature Actuated Vacuum) consists of an ambient temperature switch, a 3-way vacuum switch, an inline vacuum bleed and a relay. The system is used to more accurately match spark advance to engine requirements in cold ambient temperature conditions. When ambient air temperatures are below 49°F, spark port vacuum is selected for distributor modulation. When ambient temperatures reach 65°F, the system selects EGR vacuum. In between, the system selects

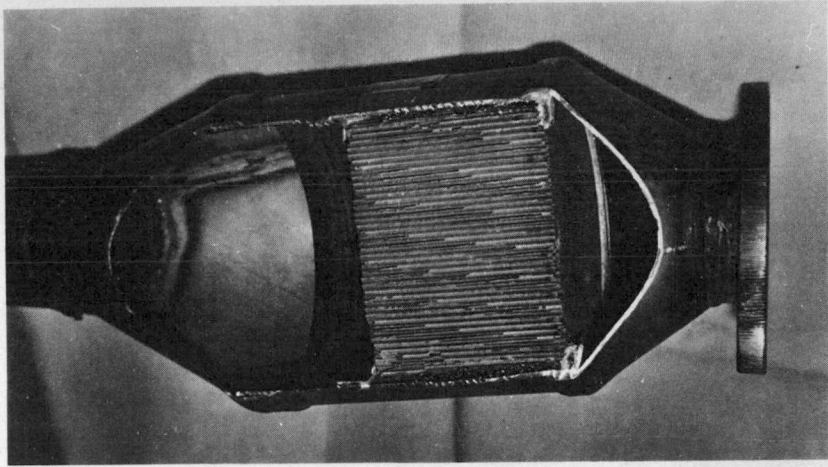

Cutaway view of the catalytic converter
(© Ford Motor Co)

either port, depending on the cycle it is in.

1975-77

Lincoln uses catalytic converters on all models starting 1975. To supply air to the converter, the air injection (Thermactor) system has been modified considerably for the first time since its introduction. For information concerning both air injection changes and catalytic converters, see "Emission Control Systems" in the unit repair section.

A cold start spark advance (CSSA) system has been added to improve cold engine operation. When the coolant temperature is below 125° F. manifold vacuum is routed to the distributor vacuum unit. Above 125° F, carburetor ported vacuum is routed to the distributor through a spark delay valve and coolant temperature operated vacuum valve (PVS).

Another aid to cold engine operation is a "cold weather modulator," which is added to the heated air intake system. When the ambient temperature is below 55° F and the engine is cold, the cold weather modulator prevents the door in the air cleaner snorkle from opening to the fresh air position under hard acceleration. Above 55° F, the door works the same as in other years; i.e., opening under hard acceleration or when the engine has reached normal operating temperatures.

All 1975 engines have spacer entry EGR valves. The EGR valve is mounted on a spacer which is located beneath the carburetor. This replaces the "floor entry" system used on some 1974 engines.

An electric choke was added in 1975 to open the throttle plates sooner in temperatures above 60° F. At temperatures lower than 60°F, there is no current supplied to the choke, and normal thermostatic choke action occurs. At temperatures above 60°, cur-

ren is supplied and the throttle plates are opened within 1½ minutes.

Positive crankcase ventilation (PCV) and evaporative emission control systems are carryovers from previous years.

For system checks and adjustments, see "Emission Control Systems" in the Unit Repair Section.

ENGINE

The 460 cu in. engine has canted valves, stud mounted rocker arms, semi-hemispherical combustion chambers, tunnel ports, a block split at crankshaft centerline. From 1970-76, this engine was used exclusively; in 1977, a 400 cubic inch engine was introduced as the base engine in California only. The 400 cu. in engine is the same one found in other full size Ford and Mercury products.

NOTE: Only service procedures for the 460 engine are given in this section. See the Ford, Mercury, Thunderbird section for 400 engine procedures.

Engine Removal

Engine Removal and Installation is for the engine only, without the transmission attached.
1. Raise the hood, and cover or mask all parts of the car that could be scratched during Removal and Installation procedures.
2. Set the parking brake and raise the car. Put stands beneath the underbody front crossmember.
3. Drain the engine cooling system and the engine oil pan.
4. Scribe the hinge outline on the underside of the hood. Remove hood.
5. If the engine is equipped with an exhaust emission control system, remove the crankcase vent filter from the air cleaner. Re-

move carburetor air cleaner and air inlet duct assembly. Disconnect the battery ground.

6. Remove both engine radiator hoses.
7. Disconnect heater hoses at intake manifold and water pump. Disconnect power brake and power booster line from the intake manifold connection and position it to one side.
8. Disconnect heater vacuum hose from the intake manifold.
9. Disconnect automatic transmission vacuum line at the intake manifold. Disconnect all vacuum lines at the rear of the manifold.
10. Remove transmission tube slotted bracket from the right rear exhaust manifold mounting stud.
11. Disconnect battery ground strap at cylinder block.
12. Disconnect primary wires at the coil. Disconnect wires from temperature-sending unit and the fast idle solenoid (air-conditioned cars).
13. Disconnect wire from oil pressure-sending unit. Detach wiring loom from valve rocker arm cover and position it out of the way.
14. Disconnect transmission fluid lines at the radiator. Remove transmision fluid filter from underbody side member (if car is so equipped).
15. Remove fuel hose mounting bracket from radiator. Remove heat shield from fuel pump.
16. On air-conditioned cars, remove fan drive clutch to water pump pulley retaining bolts. Remove fan drive clutch, fan and compressor pulley from the car as a unit.
17. Remove fan blade and spacer assembly from water pump pulley.
18. On vehicles equipped with air conditioning, disconnect the compressor electrical lead and remove the compressor mounting bracket attaching bolts. Remove the compressor from the engine and position it out of the way without disconnecting the refrigerant lines.

If the compressor refrigerant lines do not have enough slack to position the compressor out of the way without disconnecting the refrigerant lines, the air conditioning system will have to be evacuated by a trained air conditioning serviceman. Under no circumstances should an untrained person attempt to disconnect the air conditioning refrigerant lines.

19. Remove the alternator mounting bolts and position the alternator out of the way without disconnecting the wires.

20. Disconnect the transmission and accelerator linkage at the bellcrank. Secure the linkage to the dash panel for engine clearance purposes. Disconnect speed control cable.
21. Remove access cover from the converter housing. Remove underbody splash shield at lower front of transmission.
22. Remove resonator inlet pipes from the exhaust manifolds.
23. Remove the power steering pump mounting bracket from the engine and position the pump and bracket out of the way.
24. Remove the nuts and washers that hold the engine front support insulators to the underbody side members.
25. Remove the starter attaching bolts. Remove the starter.
26. Detach the oil cooler inlet and outlet transfer line retaining clip from the cylinder block. Remove the block-to-converter housing supports. Remove the converter access plate.
27. Remove the flywheel to converter retaining nuts.
28. Remove lower converter housing to cylinder block retaining bolts.
29. Install a transmission support under the transmission.
30. Remove the upper converter housing to cylinder block retaining bolts.
31. Attach engine lifting eyes to the manifolds.
32. Install lifting sling and attach to chain hoist. With plenty of help, carefully raise and remove engine from car.
33. Install by reversing removal procedure.

Manifold

Intake Manifold Removal and Installation

1. Drain the cooling system.
2. Disconnect the upper radiator hose from the thermostat housing and the bypass hose from the intake manifold.
3. Remove the air cleaner and ducts from the engine.
4. Disconnect the spark plug wires from the spark plugs and remove the distributor cap and wires from the engine as an assembly. Mark the position of the distributor rotor in relation to the intake manifold, remove the primary wire from the coil and the distributor hold-down bolt, then, remove the distributor from the engine.
5. Remove all vacuum lines from the intake manifold and the wire from the temperature sending

unit. Remove the PCV valve and hoses.
6. Disconnect all fuel and vacuum lines from the carburetor.
7. Remove all carburetor and kickdown linkage that attaches to the intake manifold. Remove the air injection supply tubes and check valve at the rear of the cylinder heads. Remove the coil and bracket.
8. Remove the manifold attaching bolts and remove the manifold. If it is necessary to pry the manifold to loosen it from the engine, use care not to damage any gasket sealing surfaces.
9. Clean all gasket surfaces and cement new gaskets firmly in place. The gaskets should be firmly locked in place before attempting to install the manifold.
10. Reverse above procedure to install.

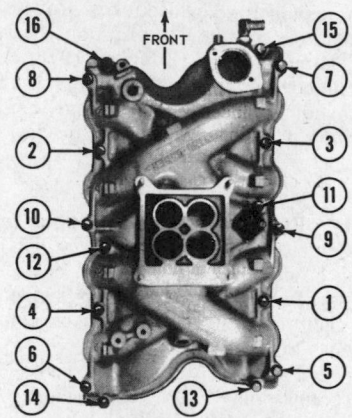

Intake manifold torque sequence
(© Ford Motor Co)

Exhaust Manifold Removal

1. Remove air cleaner and warm air duct assembly to remove right exhaust manifold.
2. Disconnect manifolds at exhaust pipe or catalyst.
3. Remove retaining bolts and washers, and remove manifolds and lifting brackets.

Valve System

Preliminary Valve Adjustment
See Ford section, under 460 V8.

Valve Guides
Lincolns use integral valve guides. Lincoln dealers offer valves with oversize stems for worn guides. To fit these, enlarge valve guide bores with valve guide reamers to an oversize that cleans up wear. As an alternative, some local automotive machine shops will fit replacement guides that use standard stem valves.

TIME SAVER

The following is a method for replacing valve springs, oil seals or spring retainers without removing the cylinder head.

1. Purchase an air chuck with a spark plug hole adaptor.
2. Remove the valve rocker cover. Remove the rocker arm from the valve to be worked on.
3. Remove the spark plug from the cylinder to be worked on.
4. Turn the crankshaft to bring the piston of this cylinder down, away from possible contact with the valve head. Sharply tap the valve retainer to loosen the valve lock.
5. Then turn the crankshaft to bring the piston in this cylinder to the Exact Top of its Compression Stroke.
6. Screw the air chuck fitting. into the spark plug hole.
7. Hook up an air hose to the chuck and turn on the pressure (about 200 psi).
8. With a strong and constant supply of air holding the valve closed, compress the valve spring and remove the lock and retainer.
9. Make the necessary replacements and reassemble.

NOTE: it is important that the operation be performed exactly as stated, in this order. The piston in the cylinder must be on exact top-center to prevent air pressure from turning the crankshaft.

Rocker Arm Assembly

These rocker arms are of the pedestal-mounted-type and are removable, one at a time.

Removal

1. Remove crankcase ventilation regulator valve and hose from valve rocker arm cover. Remove air cleaner and duct assembly. If removing an arm assembly from the left side, take off oil filler cap and air supply hose from valve rocker cover.
2. Disconnect plug wires at spark plugs. Twist, then pull, on molded cap of wire only. Do not pull the wire. Remove wires from bracket on the valve rocker arm covers and pull wires out of the way.
3. Remove rocker arm covers.
4. Remove rocker arm stud nut, fulcrum seat, and rocker arm.

NOTE: rocker arm studs that are broken, or have bad threads, should be replaced.

If the stud is broken, flush with the head, drill and use an easy-out.

When installing the new stud, lubricate the threads, then torque to 65-75 ft. lbs.

Installation

1. Apply lubriplate to top of valve stem.
2. Lubriplate fulcrum seat and socket. Install rocker arm, fulcrum seat and stud nut. Perform preliminary valve adjustment.
3. Adjust valve clearance according to recommendations. See "Preliminary Valve Adjustment."
4. Clean rocker arm covers and cylinder head gasket surfaces.
5. Apply oil-resistant sealer to one side of new cover gaskets. Apply cemented side of gaskets in rim of covers.
6. Position covers on cylinder heads. Install and torque cover bolts to 2½-4 ft. lbs. Two minutes later, retorque attaching bolts to same specifications.
7. Route spark plug wires in brackets on valve rocker covers. Reconnect plug wires.
8. Install heater tube assembly, if disconnected, and fill cooling system.
9. On the right valve rocker arm cover, install crankcase ventilation regulator valve and hose.
10. Install air cleaner and duct, and adjust assembly, if removed. On the left rocker arm cover, install oil filler cap and air supply hose.

Cylinder Head

Removal and Installation

1. Remove the intake manifold/carburetor assembly. See "Intake Manifold" section.
2. Disconnect the exhaust pipe or catalytic converter pipe from the exhaust manifold.
3. Loosen the A/C compressor drivebelt if necessary.
4. Loosen the alternator bolts and remove the alternator/air pump bracket from the cylinder head.
5. Set the A/C compressor out of the way without disconnecting its lines. See "Intake Manifold" for the specific procedure. Remove the compressor support bracket-to water pump nuts. Remove the upper compressor bracket from the cylinder head.
6. If not equipped with A/C, remove the power steering pump bracket from the head. Position the pump and bracket out of the way without disconnecting the power steering lines.
7. Remove the valve covers and rocker assemblies, as detailed above. Remove the rockers in sequence and number them to aid in correct installation.
8. Remove the head bolts. Lift the heads and exhaust manifolds off as assemblies with a hoist.

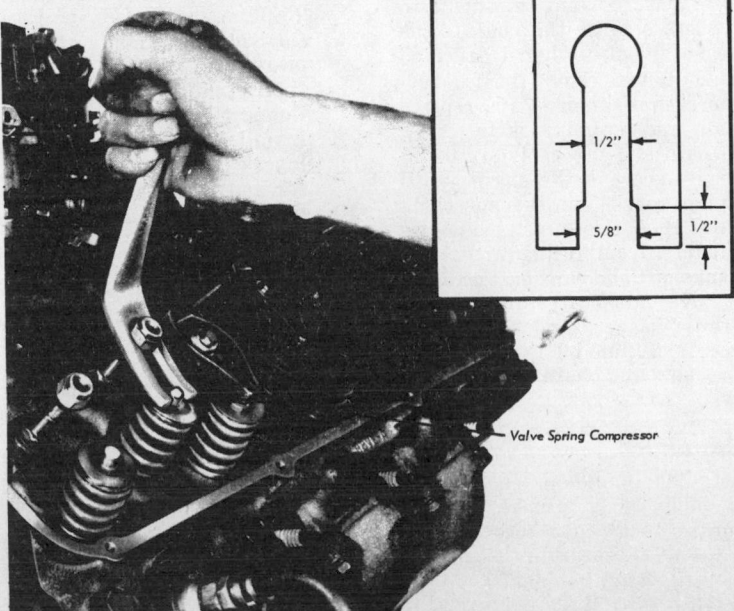

Valve Spring Compressor

1/2"
5/8"
1/2"

Compressing Valve Spring 460 eng.
(© Ford Motor Co.)

NOTE: If necessary, pry the forward corners of the heads at the bosses provided on the block, in order to loosen the head gasket. Be careful not to damage the machined surfaces. Discard the gaskets.

9. If the head is to be machined or disassembled, separate the exhaust manifolds from it.

Installation is as follows:

1. Clean the head, intake manifold, rocker cover, and block gasket surfaces.
2. If the exhaust manifolds were separated from the head, apply graphite grease around the port areas on the manifolds and head. Install the manifold and gasket.
3. Place long cylinder head bolts in the two rear lower bolt holes of the left head. Place a long bolt in the rear lower hole on the right head. Secure the bolts with rubber bands to aid in installation.
4. Fit new head gaskets over the dowels on the block. DO NOT use sealer on the head gasket surfaces.
5. Lower the head on the block. Align the exhaust manifold studs with the exhaust or converter pipe.
6. Install the remaining cylinder head bolts. The long bolts to in the lower row of holes.
7. Tighten the bolts in proper sequence in three stages, to the figures given in the "Torque Specifications" chart.
8. Install the push rod and valve rocker assemblies in their original positions.

NOTE: If any of the valve train components were disturbed, perform the "Preliminary Valve Adjustment" procedure in the Ford section.

For engines through 1971, use the 1969-71 429 procedure. For 1972 and later engines, use the 460 procedure.

9. The remainder of the cylinder head installation procedure is the reverse of removal.

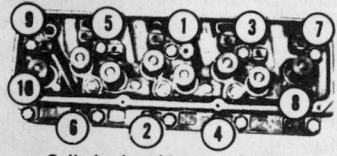

Cylinder head torque sequence
(© Ford Motor Co)

Timing Case Cover, Chain and Sprockets

Removal

1. Drain cooling system and crankcase.

2. Remove oil pan and oil pump.
3. Remove fan blades from water pump shaft.
4. Remove radiator (fan) shroud.
5. Disconnect all radiator hoses at engine. Disconnect oil cooler lines.
6. Remove radiator.
7. Loosen alternator and air pump. Loosen air conditioner idler pulley. Remove drive belts with water pump pulley.
8. Remove and set aside air conditioner compressor (do not open compressor lines to expose the sealed air-conditioner system to atmosphere).
9. Remove crankshaft pulley attaching bolt and washer. Remove damper and remove Woodruff key from crankshaft.
10. If necessary, disconnect power steering pressure line at pump. Drain fluid.
11. Remove steering pump.
12. Loosen by-pass hose at water pump. Disconnect heater hose at pump.
13. Disconnect and plug fuel inlet line at fuel pump. Disconnect fuel line at carburetor fuel pump. Remove fuel pump.
14. Remove front cover-to-block attaching bolts. Remove front cover and water pump as an assembly. Discard gasket.
15. If a new front cover is to be installed, change the water pump at this time.
16. Check timing chain deflection, at this time, by rotating crankshaft in a clockwise direction enough to take up the slack on the right hand side of the chain (as facing the open chain). Establish a reference mark on the block and measure from this point to the left side of the chain. This measurement when deflected should not exceed ½ in. If deflection is more than ½ in., replace chain and both sprockets.
17. If chain and sprockets are being removed, crank the engine until timing marks on the sprockets are at their closest related points and on a center line with both crankshaft and camshaft centers.
18. Remove camshaft sprocket capscrew, washer, and fuel pump eccentric. Slide off timing chain, sprockets and chain as an assembly.

Installation

1. Install chain and sprockets as an assembly with sprocket timing marks directly toward each other and on a centerline with the crankshaft and camshaft.
2. Install fuel pump eccentric, washer, and attaching cap screw. Torque camshaft sprocket attaching

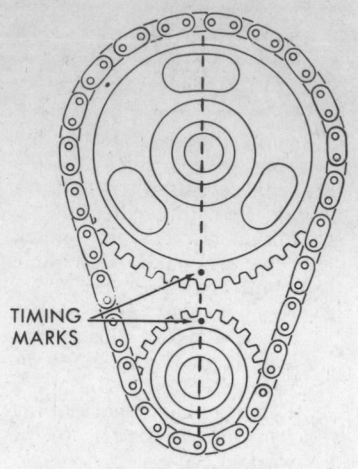

Valve timing alignment marks

screw to 40-45 ft. lbs. Lubricate chain and sprockets with engine oil.
3. After cleaning mating surfaces, coat the areas with oil-resistant sealer and position gasket on cylinder block.
4. Position cover over crankshaft and slide cover on against cylinder block. Coat cover retaining screws with oil-resistant sealer and install screws. Torque attaching screws to 10-13 ft. lbs.
5. Apply Lubriplate® to oil seal rubbing surface of steering pump inner hub. Apply mixture of white lead and oil to crankshaft stub in preparing damper installation. Install power steering pump (if removed).
6. Install crankshaft damper Woodruff key and press on crankshaft damper. Do not hammer damper into place. Install damper retainer screw and washer. Torque to 75-90 ft. lbs.
7. Coat new fuel pump gasket with oil-resistant sealer and place on fuel pump. Install fuel pump. Connect fuel lines to fuel pump.
8. Install oil pump and oil pan.
9. Install air-conditioner compressor and water pump.
10. Install water pump pulley and all drive belts.
11. Position radiator to lower support, position upper support to radiator retaining bolts. Connect air coolant hoses. Connect oil cooler lines.
12. Place fan assembly inside radiator shroud and set in position on water pump hub. Install shroud to radiator screws and tighten. Insert and tighten fan attaching screws.
13. Adjust belt tension. Tighten alternator and air pump retaining bolts and compressor idler pulley.
14. Fill and bleed cooling system Fill crankcase.

15. Run engine at fast idle and check for coolant and oil leaks. Set ignition timing.

Oil Seal Removal and Installation

The front cover oil seal should be replaced whenever the cover is removed.

1. Drive the old oil seal out with a punch.
2. Clean out the oil seal recess.
3. Coat a new oil seal with grease.
4. Install the new seal in the cover. Be sure that the seal spring is in the correct position.

Camshaft Removal and Installation

1. Remove the hood assembly. If the hood is properly aligned, index the hinges to the hood prior to removing the hood, in order to simplify installation.
2. Remove the intake manifold, referring to the procedure under "Intake Manifold Removal and Installation."
3. Remove the distributor and the valve covers.
4. Remove the valve rocker arm shaft assemblies, push rods, and hydraulic lifters from the engine. Back off the rocker arm bolts, turn the rocker arms sideways, and remove the push rods and lifters.
5. Remove the timing chain and camshaft sprocket.
6. Remove the radiator. Remove the grille.
7. If the car is equipped with an air conditioner, cover the left front fender, lift the condenser out of the engine compartment with the lines still attached, and rest it on the covered fender.
8. Remove the camshaft from the front of the cylinder block, taking care not to damage any of the camshaft bearing surfaces.
9. Lubricate the camshaft journals and lobes with engine oil. Install the camshaft in the engine, using care to prevent damage to the camshaft bearings. Care should also be exercised to see that the rear camshaft bearing plug does not become dislodged in the process of installing the camshaft.
10. Reverse the above procedure to complete installation.

Engine Lubrication

Oil Pan Removal and Installation

1. Disconnect the negative battery cable.
2. Disconnect the fan shroud from the radiator and position it rearward over the fan.

3. Drain the crankcase and remove the oil filter.
4. On Mark III and Mark IV models, disconnect the oil cooler lines from the radiator. Remove the bolt that attaches the oil cooler line bracket to the cylinder block.
5. Remove the end attachments of the front stabilizer bar and rotate the ends downward.
6. Remove the starter attaching bolts.
7. Remove the motor mount to chassis attaching bolts and raise the engine several inches.
8. Place blocks of wood between the motor mounts and the chassis.
9. Remove the converter housing to engine block support bracket bolts and remove the brackets.
10. Remove the oil pan attaching bolts and remove the pan from the engine. On Mark III and IV models, it will be necessary to move the oil cooler lines out of position to remove the pan.
11. Clean all gasket mounting surfaces and reverse above procedure to install.

Oil Pump Removal and Installation

1. Remove the oil pan, referring to the procedure for "Oil Pan Removal and Installation."
2. Remove the oil pump mounting bolts and remove the pump from the cylinder block.
3. Prime the oil pump by filling the inlet port with clean engine oil. Rotate the pump shaft so that the oil is evenly distributed within the pump body.
4. Install the distributor intermediate shaft within the oil pump rotor shaft. Apply oil-resistant sealer to the new oil pump mounting gasket and install the gasket on the oil pump.
5. Insert the intermediate shaft into the distributor shaft hex bore. Make sure that the intermediate shaft is properly seated.

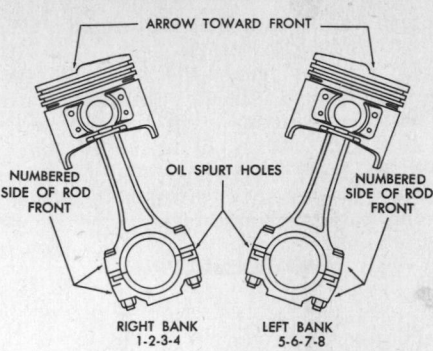

Correct piston and rod positions for 460 engines

Do not attempt to force the pump into position if it does not seat readily, as the intermediate shaft hex may be misaligned with the distributor shaft. To align, rotate the intermediate shaft until it can be seated. Secure the oil pump to the cylinder block and torque the screws to 20–25 ft lbs. As you secure the oil pump, make certain that the gasket is properly installed; leakage resulting from improper gasket installation could cause loss of oil pressure and subsequent engine damage.

6. Install the oil pan and its related parts.

Rear Crankshaft Oil Seal Removal and Installation

See the Ford section for complete procedures.

AUTOMATIC TRANSMISSION

All Lincolns and Continentals use a Ford C6 automatic transmission. This heavy-duty three-speed unit is capable of providing automatic upshifts and downshifts through the three forward gear ratios, in addi-

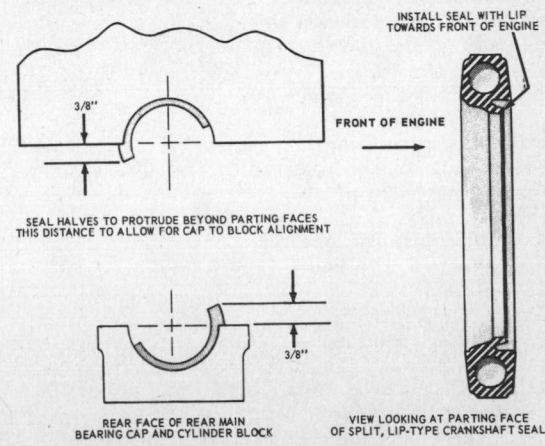

Rear main seal installation (© Ford Motor Co)

tion to offering manual selection of first and second gears.

Only one band—the intermediate band—is used in this transmission. This band, along with the forward clutch, is used to obtain the intermediate gear. The adjustment of this band is the only adjustment required for the C6 transmission.

C6 transmission pan gasket shape

Shift Linkage Adjustment

1. If the car is equipped with a tilt wheel steering, position the column up as far as possible. With the engine off, place the selector lever against the stop in the D1 (large dot) position. Raise the car, and remove linkage splash shield.
2. Disconnect the adjustable link from the transmission manual shift lever on the transmission.
3. Be sure the transmission shift is fully engaged in D1, the second detent from the bottom. The bottom detent is L (low).
4. Loosen locknut on adjustable link, then pull down on the link to hold the selector lever against the D1 stop. Adjust the link by turning the lower end until the hole in the link aligns with the stud on the transmission manual lever. Connect it to the transmission shift lever.
5. Check selector lever through all positions to secure correct adjustment.

Downshift Rod Adjustment

1. Loosen the locknut on the downshift rod. Disconnect rod from the ballstud on the bellcrank assembly by sliding the spring clip off the end of the rod.
2. Pull upward and hold the downshift rod against the transmission internal stop. Adjust length of rod until the hole in the rod is aligned with the ballstud on the bellcrank assembly.
3. Lengthen the downshift rod one turn and position it on the ballstud. Slide the spring clip over the end of the rod to lock the rod to the ballstud. Tighten locknut securely.
4. Be sure the bellcrank outer bracket is against the stop pin. If it is not, lengthen the downshift rod one turn. If the rod is

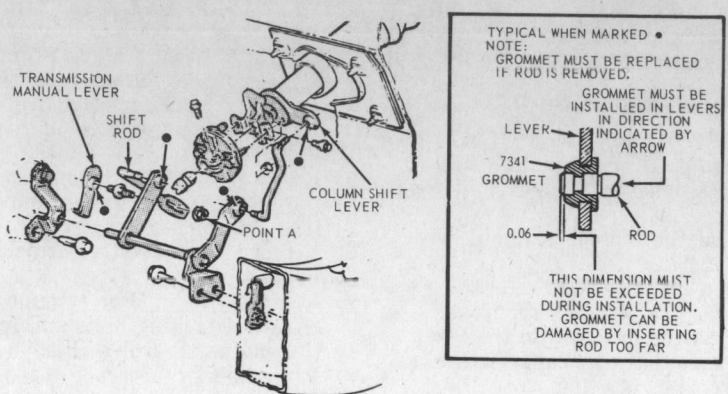

Shift linkage—Lincoln Continental (© Ford Motor Co)

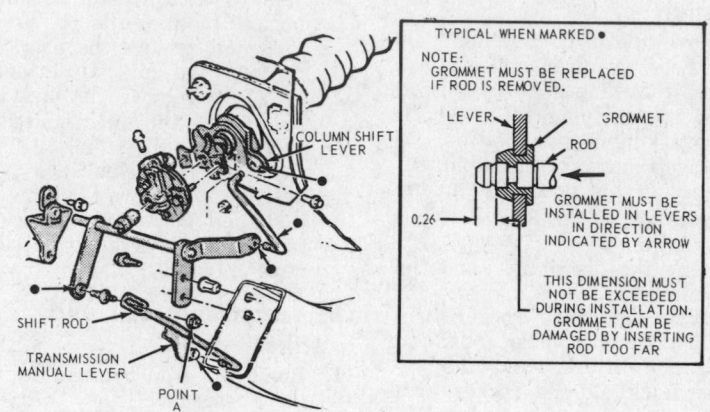

Shift linkage—Mark III (© Ford Motor Co)

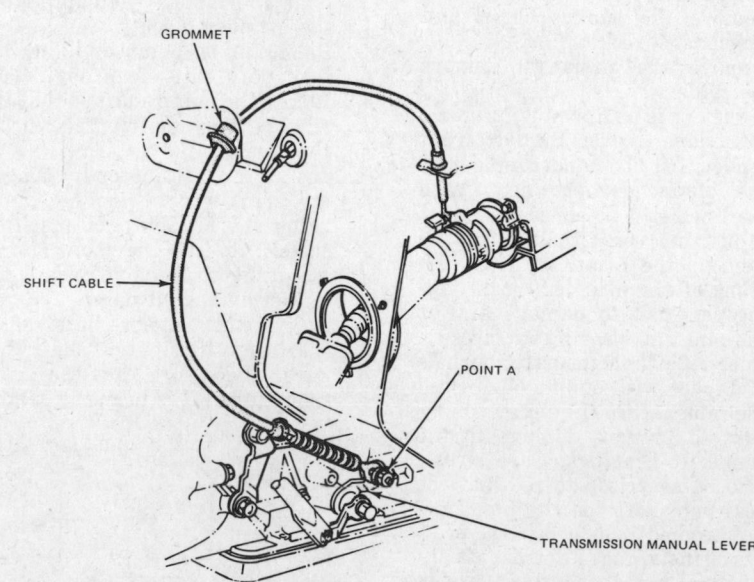

Shift linkage—Mark IV (© Ford Motor Co)

too long, there will be no upshift.

Intermediate Band Adjustment

1. Raise the car on a hoist or place it on jack stands.
2. Clean threads of the intermedi-

ate band adjusting screw.

3. Remove the old locknut and install a new one.
4. Tighten the adjusting screw to 10 ft. lbs., and back the screw off exactly 1 turn (1971 and later models, 1 1/2 turns). Tighten the adjusting screw locknut.

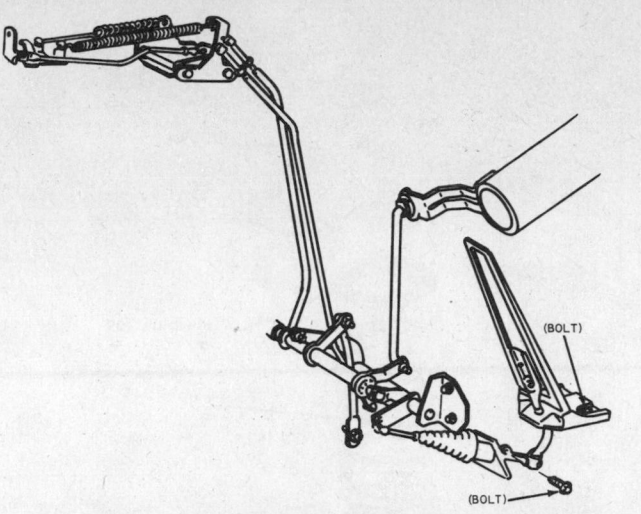

Throttle and downshift linkage—1970 Continental (© Ford Motor Co)

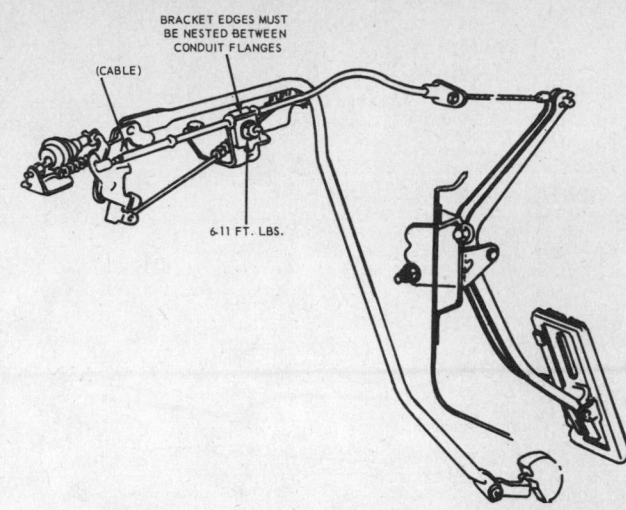

BRACKET EDGES MUST BE NESTED BETWEEN CONDUIT FLANGES

(CABLE)

6-11 FT. LBS.

Throttle and downshift linkage—Mark III (© Ford Motor Co)

Tool-T71P-77370-D

Tool-T71P-77370-H

Intermediate band adjustment
(© Ford Motor Co)

Pan Removal, Fluid and Filter Change

1. Raise the vehicle and support it securely. Place a container beneath the transmission.
2. Loosen the transmission pan bolts and allow the fluid to drain into the container. When the fluid has drained to the transmission pan flange level, remove the bolts, working from the rear, to allow the fluid to drain slowly.
3. Remove the pan and clean it. Discard the gasket.
4. Clean the filter screen.
5. Place a new gasket on the pan. Install the pan.
6. Add three quarts of type F fluid through the filler tube.
7. Run the engine, move the selector lever through all gear ranges. Check the fluid level; add fluid as necessary.

U-JOINTS

All universal joint procedures will be found in the Ford section.

JACKING, HOISTING

See the Ford section.

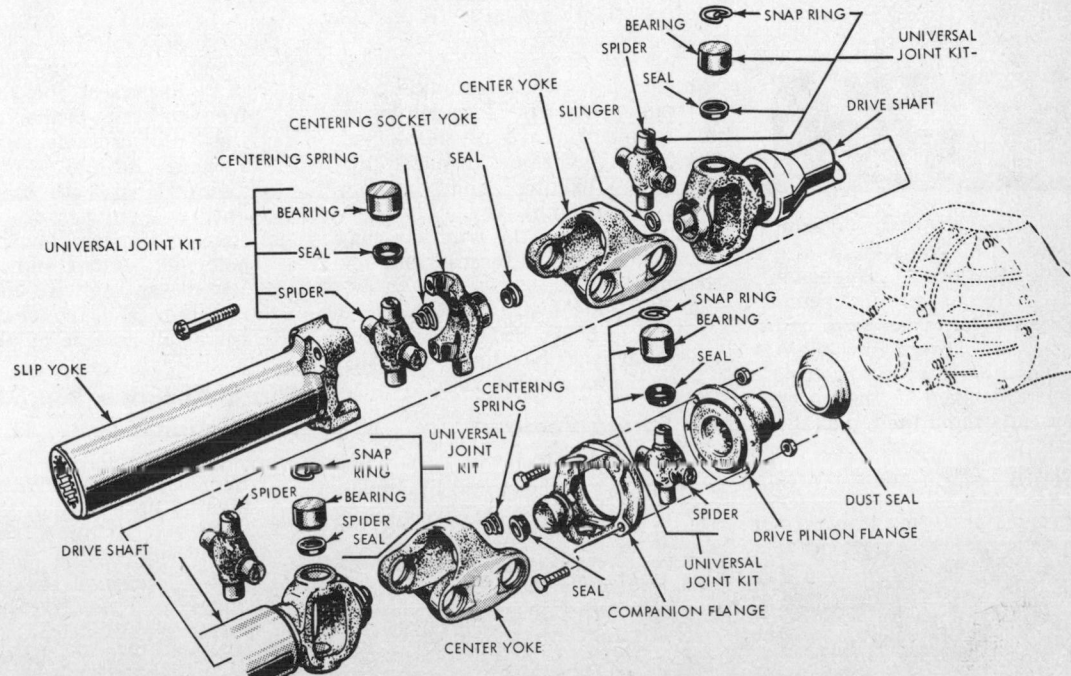

Driveshaft with Dana double Cardan universal joints (© Ford Motor Co)

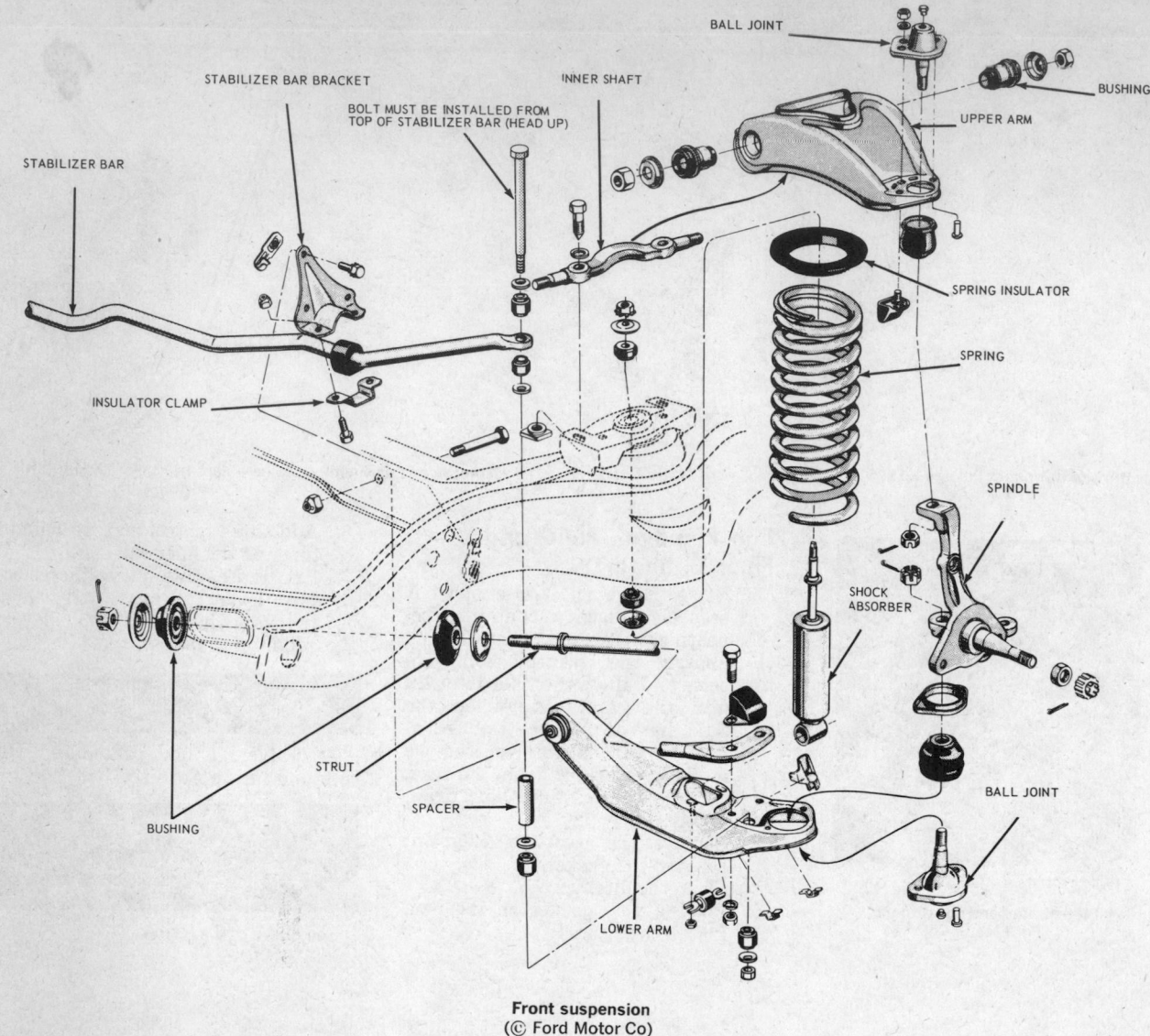

Front suspension
(© Ford Motor Co)

FRONT SUSPENSION

All models have a front suspension system in which the coil springs are supported on the lower suspension member. Each side of this independent front suspension uses two ball joints—upper and lower. Shock absorbers are positioned within the coil springs and are affixed to the lower suspension member and the top of the spring tower.

See the Ford section for all procedures.

REAR SUSPENSION

The rear suspension is a coil-link design. Large, low-rate coil springs are mounted between rear axle pads and frame supports. Parallel lower arms extend forward of the spring seats to rubber frame anchor to accommodate driving and braking forces. A third link is mounted between the axle and the frame to control torque reaction forces from the rear wheels.

Lateral (side sway) motion of the rear axle is controlled by a rubber bushed rear track bar, linked laterally between the axle and frame.

Rear Spring Removal and Installation

1. Place car on hoist and lift under rear axle housing. Place jack stands under frame side rails.
2. Disconnect track bar at the rear axle housing bracket.
3. Disconnect rear shock absorbers from the rear axle housing brackets.
4. Disconnect hose from axle housing vent. On Lincoln Continentals, disconnect the rear of the front-to-back brake tube from the No. 4 crossmember bracket. Remove the clip.
5. Lower hoist with axle housing until coil springs are released.
6. Remove spring lower retainer bolt, nut, washer and insulator.
7. Remove spring with large rubber insulator pads from car.
8. Install in reverse of above.

Shock Absorber Removal and Installation

1. Raise the vehicle.
2. Remove the shock absorber attaching nut, washer, and insulator from the upper stud at the upper side of the spring upper seat. Compress the shock absorber to clear the hole in the spring seat and remove the inner insulator and washer from the upper attaching stud.
3. Remove the self-locking attach-

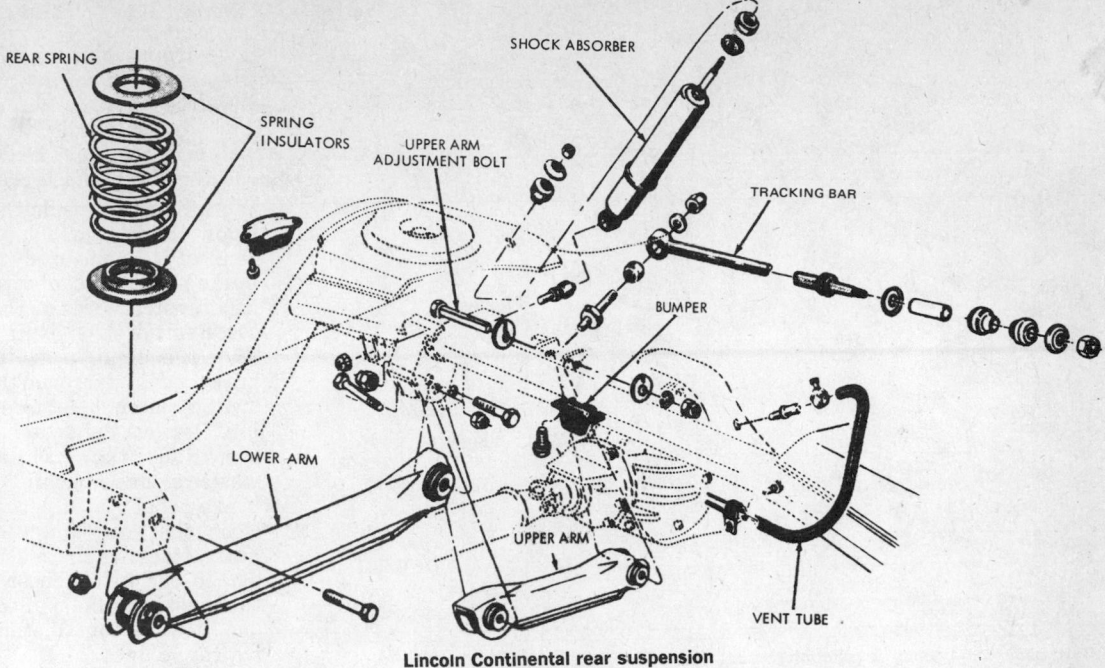

Lincoln Continental rear suspension
(© Ford Motor Co)

ing nut and disconnect the shock absorber lower stud from the mounting bracket on the rear axle housing.

4. Remove the shock absorber from the car.
5. Reverse the above procedure to install the new shock absorber.

BRAKES

Master Cylinder Removal and Installation

1. Disconnect the brake lines from the master cylinder.
2. Remove the two nuts and lockwashers that attach the master cylinder to the brake booster.
3. Slide the master cylinder forward until it clears the booster pushrod, then remove the master cylinder from the car.
4. Reverse above procedure to install; but leave the brake lines loose on the master cylinder.
5. Fill the master cylinder with extra-heavy duty fluid and, using the foot pedal, slowly bleed the air from the master cylinder.
6. Tighten the brake lines, fill the master cylinder, then, bleed the brake system at the front and then the rear wheels.
7. Refill master cylinder.

Vacuum Power Brake Booster Removal and Installation

Through 1974

1. Disconnect the vacuum hose from the booster.

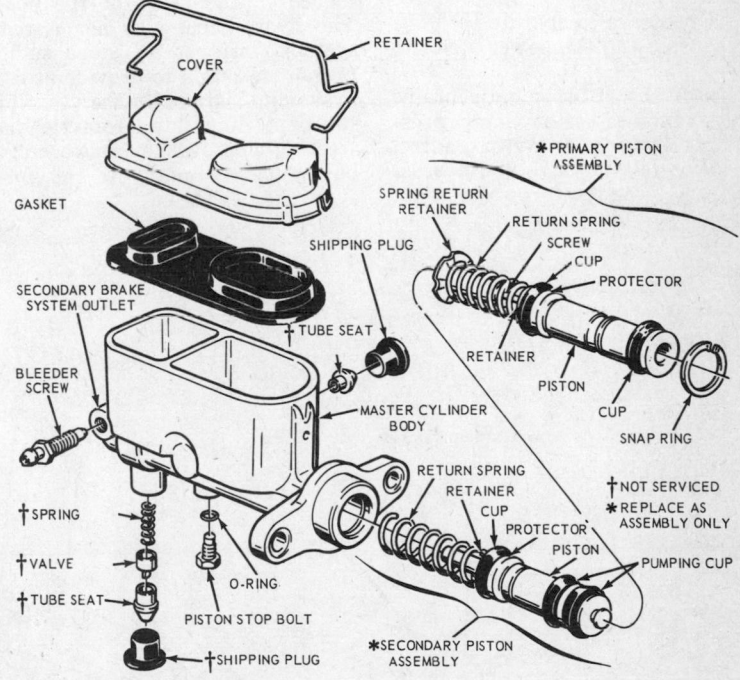

Dual type master cylinder (© Ford Motor Co)

2. Remove the two nuts and lockwashers that mount the master cylinder to the booster and move the master cylinder out of the way with the lines attached. Use care not to kink the brake lines.
3. Working under the dash, disconnect and remove the stop light switch and pushrod from the brake pedal. Use care not to damage the switch during removal.

4. Remove the four booster to firewall attaching nuts from the interior side of the firewall.
5. Remove the booster from under the hood.
6. Reverse above procedure to install.

Hydro-Boost Brake Booster System

A new hydraulically powered brake booster was released as a running

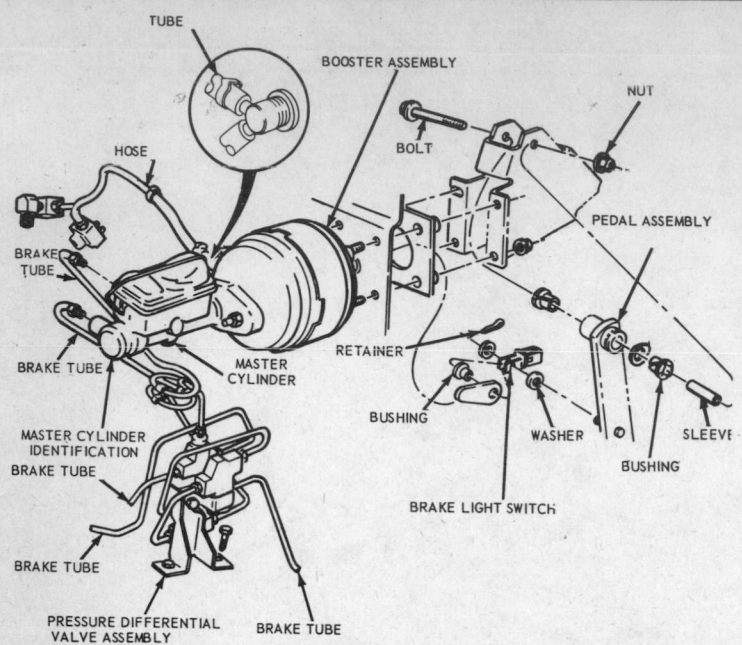

Brake pedal and booster installation (except Hydro-Boost) (© Ford Motor Co)

change in 1974 Lincoln production. The power steering pump provides the fluid pressure to operate both the brake booster and the power steering gear.

The hydro-boost assembly contains a valve which contains pump pressure while braking, a level to control the position of the valve and a boost piston to provide the force to operate

a conventional master cylinder attached to the front of the booster. The hydro-boost also has a reserve system, designed to store sufficient pressurized fluid to provide at least 2 brake applications in the event of insufficient fluid flow from the power steering pump. The brakes can also be applied manually if the reserve system is depleted.

Removal and Installation

The hydro-boost is serviced as an assembly only. Do not attempt to disassemble the booster. Before removing the hydro-boost, discharge the accumulator by making several brake applications until a hard pedal is felt.

1. Working from inside the vehicle, below the instrument panel, disconnect the pushrod from the brake pedal. Disconnect the stoplight switch wires at the connector. Remove the hairpin retainer. Slide the stoplight switch off the brake pedal far enough for the switch outer hole to clear the pin. Remove the switch from the pin. Slide the pushrod, nylon washers and bushing off the brake pedal pin.
2. Open the hood and remove the nuts attaching the master cylinder to the hydro-boost. Remove the master cylinder. Secure it to one side without disturbing the hydraulic lines.
3. Disconnect the pressure, steering gear and return lines from the booster. Plug the lines to prevent the entry of dirt.
4. Remove the nuts attaching the hydro-boost. Remove the booster from the firewall, sliding the pushrod link out of the engine side of the firewall.
5. Install the hydro-boost on the firewall and install the attaching nuts.

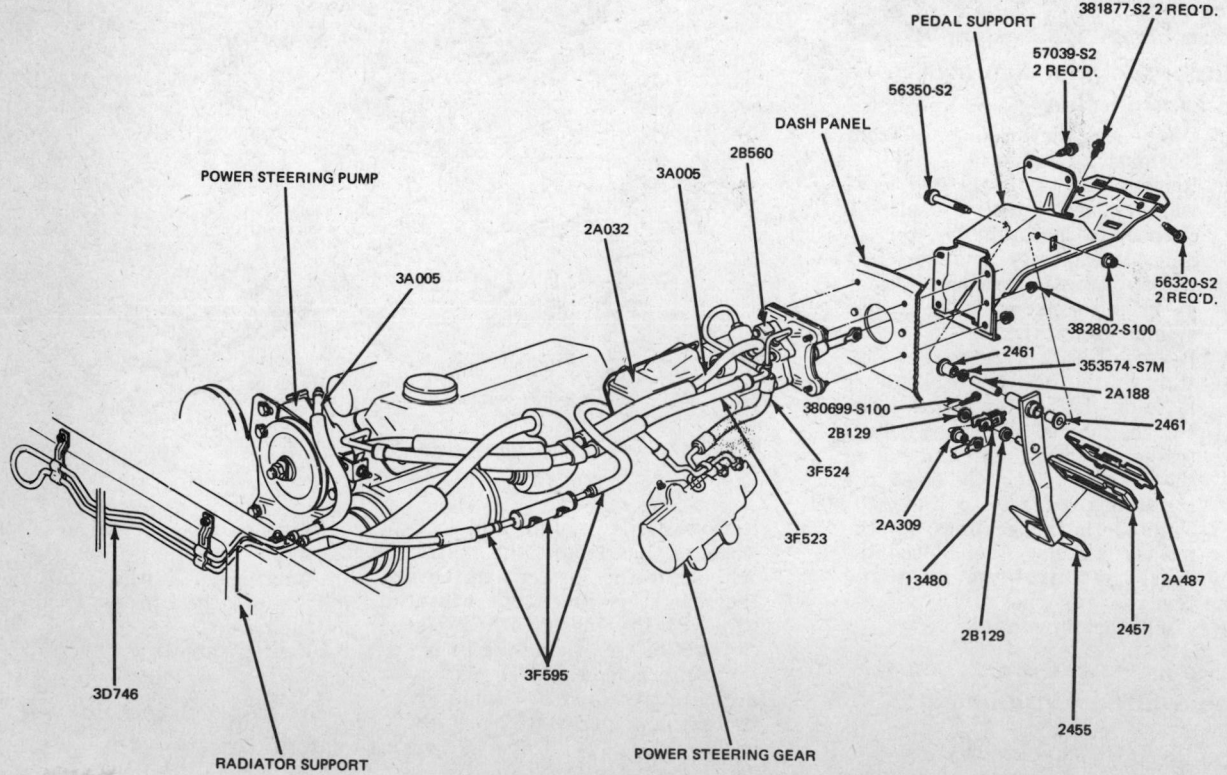

Hydro-Boost system (© Ford Motor Co)

6. Install the master cylinder on the booster.
7. Connect the pressure, steering gear and return lines to the booster.
8. Working below the instrument panel, install the nylon washer, booster pushrod and bushing on the brake pedal pin. Install the switch so that it straddles the pushrod with the switch slot on the pedal pin and the switch outer hole just clearing the pin. Slide the switch completely onto the pin and install the nylon washer. Attach these parts with the hairpin retainer. Connect the stoplight switch wires and install the wires in the retaining clip.
9. Remove the coil wire so that the engine will not start. Fill the power steering pump and engage the starter. Apply the brakes with a pumping action. Do not turn the steering wheel until air has been bled from the booster.
10. Check the fluid level and add as required. Start the engine and apply the brakes, checking for leaks. Cycle the steering wheel.
11. If a whine type noise is heard, suspect fluid aeration.

Parking Brake Adjustment

Through 1973

1. Fully release the parking brake pedal.
2. Raise the car on a hoist.
3. Adjust the pedal cable to about 10 in., measured from the cable attachment at the crossmember to the cable adjusting nut.
4. Depress the parking brake pedal one notch from normal, released position.
5. Loosen locknut on equalizer rod and turn the forward nut inward toward the front of the car until

a moderate drag is felt when turning the rear wheels.
6. Holding forward nut in position, tighten locknut. Lock the adjustment at the equalizer.
7. Release parking brake, and make sure that the brake shoes return to the fully released position.

1974 and Later Rear Drum

1. Make sure that the parking brake is fully released.
2. Place the transmission in Neutral.
3. Raise the vehicle on an axle-type hoist.
4. Tighten the adjusting nut against the cable equalizer or cable adjusting rod to cause rear wheel brake drag. Loosen the adjusting nut until the rear brakes are fully released. There should be no brake drag. Tighten the locknut to 7-10 ft lbs.
5. Lower the vehicle and check the operation of the parking brake.

1975 and Later Rear Disc

1. Fully release the parking brake. Place the transmission selector in Neutral.
2. Raise the vehicle on an axle-type hoist.
3. Tighten the adjusting nut until the levers on the caliper just start to move.
4. Loosen the adjusting nut just enough to obtain complete return of the levers to the "stop" position.
5. Apply and release the parking brakes. Check the caliper levers to see if they are at full stop, by trying to pull them rearward.
6. If the levers can be moved rearward, the adjustment is too tight. Repeat the adjustment.

Brake System Service

Procedures for brake adjustment,

shoe replacement, bleeding of the system, and the overhaul of wheel cylinders, calipers, and master cylinders may be found in the "Unit Repair Section."

STEERING

Steering Wheel Removal and Installation

1. Disconnect the negative battery cable.
2. If the vehicle is equipped with a horn ring, remove it by rotating it counterclockwise. If equipped with a steering wheel crash pad, remove the retaining screws from the underside of the steering wheel and then remove the crash pad. Disconnect the horn and speed control (if so equipped) wires from the inside of the steering wheel center.
3. Remove the steering wheel nut, install a steering wheel puller on the end of the shaft, and remove the steering wheel.

Caution The use of a knock-off type steering wheel puller and a hammer is inadvisable, as they may damage the steering column bearing or (in the case of the collapsible-type steering wheel the column itself.

4. With the front wheels positioned straight ahead, line up the marks on the steering wheel and column and install the steering wheel and the locknut.
5. Connect the horn and speed control wires and install the horn ring if so equipped and the crashpad and retaining screws if so equipped.
6. Connect the negative battery cable.

Turn Signal Switch Removal and Installation

1. Disconnect the negative battery cable.
2. Remove the steering wheel as outlined in the "Steering Wheel Removal and Installation" section.
3. Unscrew the turn signal lever from the side of the column. Remove the emergency flasher retainer and knob.
4. Locate and remove the finish cover on the steering column and disconnect the wiring connector plugs.
5. On all models with a tilt steering column, it is necessary to separate the wires from the connector plug in order to remove the switch and wires. First note the location and color code of each wire, prior to removal.

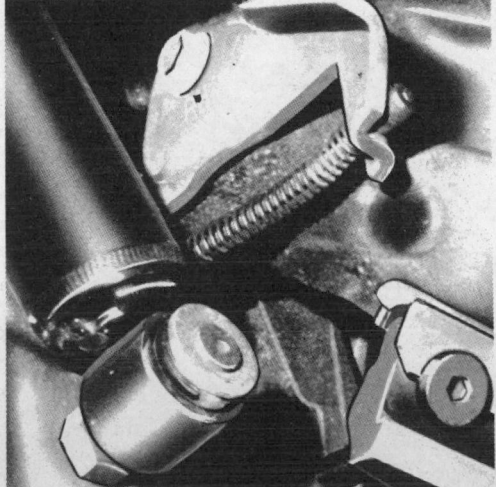
Parking brake cable at the rear disc brake caliper
(© Ford Motor Co)

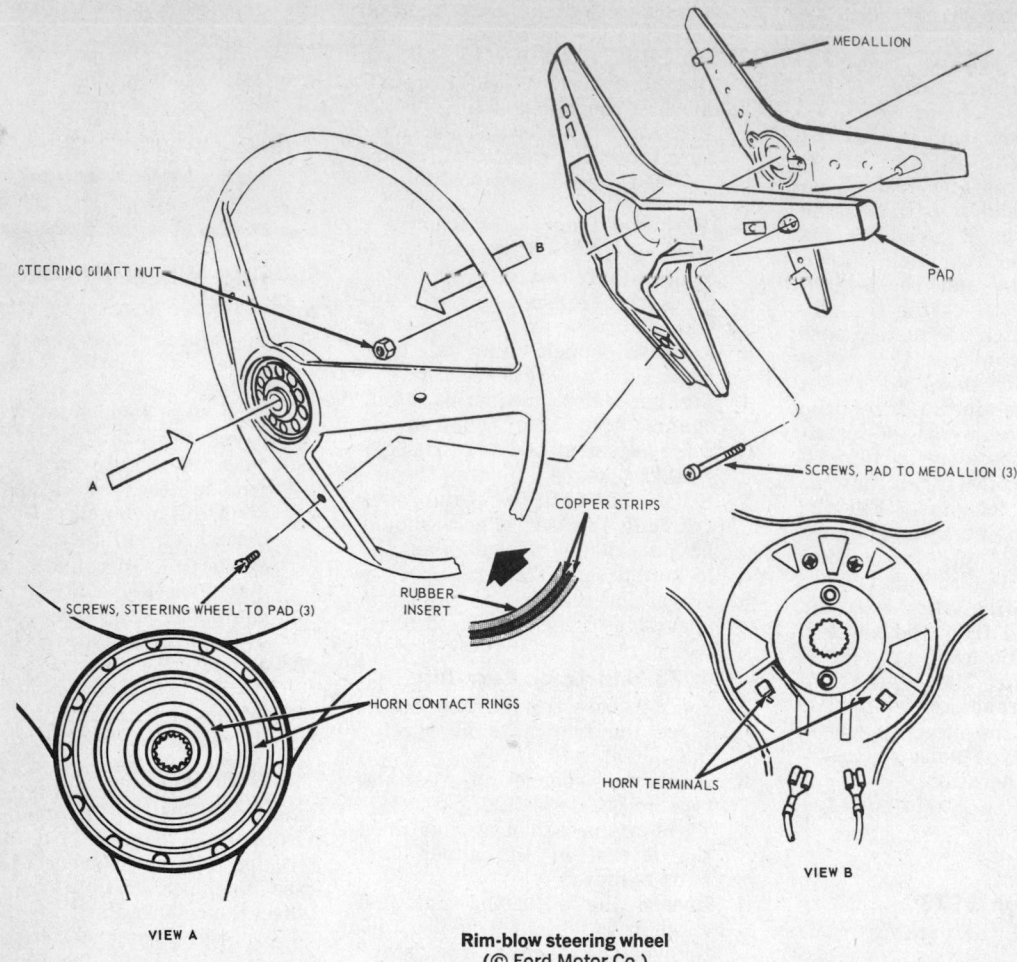

Rim-blow steering wheel
(© Ford Motor Co.)

Remove the plastic cover from the wiring harness. Attach a piece of heavy cord to the switch wires to pull them down through the column during installation.

6. Remove the retaining clips and screws from the turn signal switch and lift the switch and wire assembly from the top of the column.

7. Tape the ends of the new switch wires together and transfer the pull cord to these wires.

8. Pull the wires down through the columns with the cord and attach the new switch to the column hub.

9. If the switch wires were separated from the connector plug, press the wires into their proper location. Connect the wiring connector plugs and install the finish cover on the column.

10. Install the turn signal lever. Install the emergency flasher retainer and knob, if so equipped.

11. Install the steering wheel as outlined in the "Steering Wheel Removal and Installation" section.

12. Connect the negative battery cable and test the operation of

the turn signals, horn, emergency flashers, and speed control, if so equipped.

Power Steering Pump Removal and Installation

See the Ford section for all procedures.

Tie-Rod Removal and Installation

1. Raise the front of the vehicle and install jackstands.
2. Remove the cotter pin and nut from the tie-rod end ball stud.
3. Loosen the tie-rod sleeve clamp bolts. Remove the tie-rod end

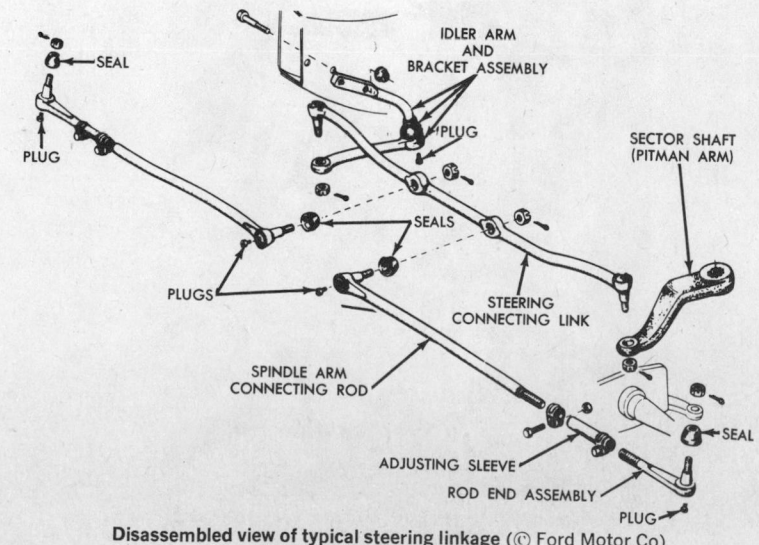

Disassembled view of typical steering linkage (© Ford Motor Co)

from the center link with a puller.

4. Separate the tie-rod end from the sleeve, counting the number of turns required.

Discard all of the tie-rod end assembly parts which were removed from the sleeve. Use all new parts when the tie-rod ends are replaced. Installation is as follows:

1. Thread a new tie-rod end into the sleeve. Turn it in the same number of turns required to remove the old one. Don't tighten the sleeve clamp bolts yet.
2. Install a new seal (if used) on the tie-rod end ball stud.
3. Install the stud and nut. Tighten to 43 ft lbs. Continue tightening the nut until the next slot aligns with the hole in the stud. Secure with a new cotter pin.
4. Check the toe-in and adjust it as necessary.
5. Loosen the sleeve clamps. Oil the clamps, bolts, sleeve, and nuts.
6. Tighten the clamp nuts to 13-18 ft lbs on Mark III models or to 20-22 ft lbs on all other models.

Ignition Lock Removal and Installation

See Ford section

Ignition Switch Removal and Installation

See Ford Section.

INSTRUMENT PANEL

Light Switch Replacement

Continental

1. Disconnect battery.
2. Remove knob and shaft by pressing release knob button on switch housing and with knob in full on position.
3. Remove moulding nut from switch.
4. Remove junction block from switch.
5. Install in reverse of above.

Mark III

1. Disconnect battery ground cable.
2. Remove seven screws holding lower finish panel to lower side of instrument panel.
3. Remove control knob and shaft from headlight switch. This is done by pressing the release button on the underside of the switch (with shaft pulled all the way out).
4. Remove bezel and nut from headlight switch.
5. Remove two screws from switch-to-instrument panel.
6. Remove switch from panel. Disconnect wire multiple connector and vacuum hoses from the switch.

7. Install by reversing removal procedure.

Mark IV, V

1. Remove the instrument cluster trim panel, as explained under "Instrument Cluster Removal and Installation."
2. Remove the lighting switch mounting plate.
3. Remove the bezel nut and disconnect the multiple connector.
4. Remove the vacuum lines and the switch.
5. Reverse this procedure to install.

WINDSHIELD WIPERS

Motor Removal and Installation

Continental, Mark IV and V

1. Disconnect battery.
2. Remove wiper arm and blade assemblies from pivot shafts.
3. Remove left cowl screen for access.
4. Disconnect linkage drive arm from motor output arm crank pin by removing retaining clip.
5. Disconnect two push on wire connectors from the motor.
6. From engine side of dash, remove three bolts that retain motor and remove motor. Reverse

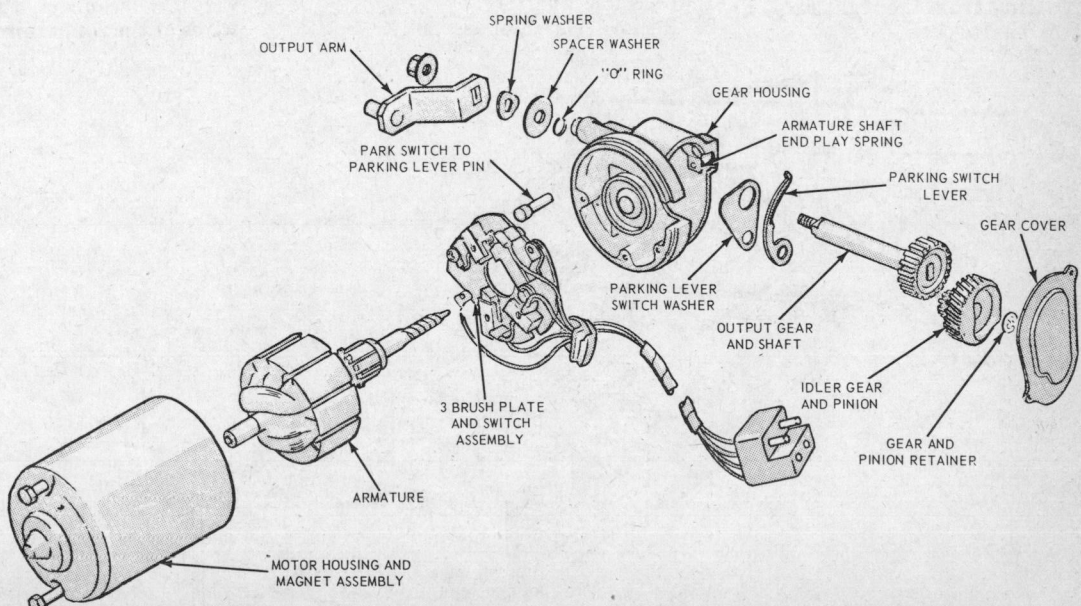

Wiper motor details
(© Ford Motor Co.)

procedure to install. Be sure that output arm is in "park."

1970 Mark III
1. Disconnect battery.
2. Disconnect washer hose, remove three retaining bolts, and pull cowl top grille out from under two clips.
3. Disconnect connector plugs from wiring harness at engine side of dash panel. Push wiring and plugs along with grommet through hole in dash.
4. Remove four motor to cowl retaining bolts. Lift motor out, and at the same time pull wiper arm and blade assembly to left for access to motor crank pin clip. Remove clip and disconnect drive link from motor crank pin. Remove three retaining bolts and separate motor from mounting plate and cover and wiring harness assembly. Reverse procedure to install.

1971 Mark III
See 1971 Thunderbird.

RADIO

Radio Removal and Installation

Mark III
Removal
1. Disconnect ground from battery.
2. Pull knobs off the control shafts.
3. Remove the cover plate located below the steering column.
4. Remove nut from the right radio control shaft.

5. Remove six screws and the trim applique from in front of the radio.
6. Remove the nut and washer from the right radio control shaft.
7. Remove screw attaching the front left side of the radio to the instrument panel.
8. Remove the radio support attaching screw.
9. Disconnect the radio power wires and speaker wires at the connectors.
10. Disconnect the antenna lead-in cable and remove the radio.

Installation
1. Connect the power, speaker, and antenna leads to the radio.
2. Position radio to instrument panel and install the attaching screw at the left front side of the radio.
3. Install the washer and nut on the radio right control shaft.
4. Install radio rear support attaching screw.
5. Position the trim applique to the instrument panel and install the six attaching screws.
6. Install the nut on the radio right control shaft.
7. Install the discs, felt washer and knobs on the radio control shafts.
8. Install cover plate below the steering column.
9. Connect the ground cable to the battery.
10. Check operation of radio and set the push buttons.

Continental
1. Disconnect battery.
2. Remove map light assembly.

3. Remove right and left inspection covers.
4. Remove lower instrument panel pad.
5. Remove glove box, open ashtray, and leave it open.
6. Remove glove box switch.
7. Through glove box opening remove two nuts retaining radio finish panel to instrument panel.
8. Install cover plate below the
9. Remove two screws at top of finish panel. Position panel out and disconnect cigar lighter and light from right panel.
10. Through glove box opening remove nut from lower right corner of center finish panel.
11. Remove radio top support nut and three mounting screws. Pull radio out. Disconnect power leads and antenna cable. Remove radio.
12. Reverse procedure to install.

Mark IV and V
1. Disconnect the negative battery cable.
2. Pull the radio control knobs off the radio shafts. Disconnect and lower the "twilight sentinal" amplifier.
3. Remove the nuts from both radio control shafts. Disconnect the air conditioning ducts.
4. Remove the radio rear support to panel attaching screw. On some 1976 models, this screw was replaced with a rivet. In order to remove the rivet you must drill it out with a 1/4 in. drill bit. When you replace the radio, replace the rivet with a 1/4 in. nut and bolt.
5. Disconnect the radio power wires. Disconnect the speaker wires at the connectors.

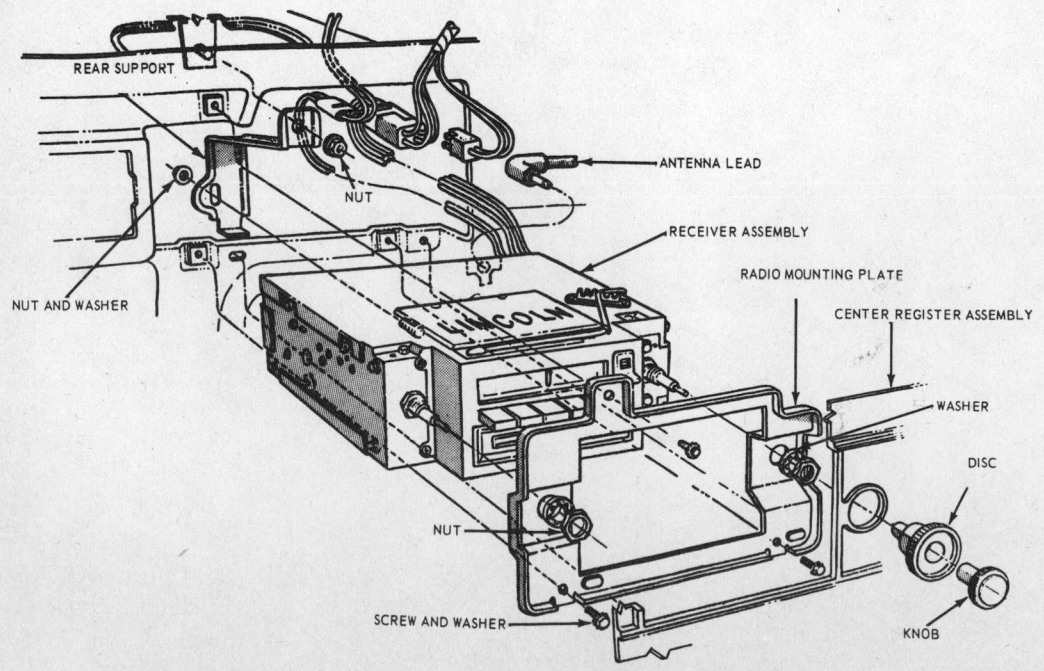

Radio — Continental (© Ford Motor Co)

6. Disconnect the antenna lead and remove the radio.
7. Reverse the above procedure to install.

HEATER

Heater Core Removal

Mark III

1. Remove hood and air cleaner and drain engine coolant.
2. Disconnect both hydraulic lines at wiper motor and position them to one side.
3. Disconnect heater hoses at heater core and position hoses and water valve away from housing.
4. Disconnect vacuum supply hose on top of housing and remove oil pressure sending unit from back of engine.
5. Remove transmission dip stick and tube assembly.
6. Disconnect multiple connector leading to icing switch.
7. Remove evaporator housing front cover. On air-conditioned cars, remove the glove compartment liner and disconnect the electrical and vacuum junction blocks on the inner dash panel.
8. Remove heater core housing cover.
9. Remove heater core retaining bracket and remove heater core. Reverse procedure to install.

Continental Through 1973

1. Drain engine coolant.
2. Disconnect vacuum junction valve from dash panel and move valve and vacuum hoses away from case.
3. Disconnect speed control servo and bracket assembly if so equipped from dash panel and move it away from case.
4. Disconnect multiple connector from blower resistor and remove harness from clip on case.
5. Disconnect heater hoses from heater case and remove hose support clamp from case. Move hoses and water valve away from case.
6. Remove seven case cover to case flange attaching screws and wire harness clip.
7. Remove six cover to back plate stud nuts.
8. Remove one upper case to dash panel mounting screw.
9. Remove two case to dash panel mounting stud nuts, one on inboard mounting flange and one below case on lower flange.
10. Carefully move heater core assembly forward to clear mounting studs and lift up and out of vehicle.

11. Remove two spring clips from core tubes on front of core cover.
12. Remove three screws from core end plate and remove plate.
13. Remove heater core and mounting gasket assembly from core cover and remove gasket from core. Reverse procedure to install.

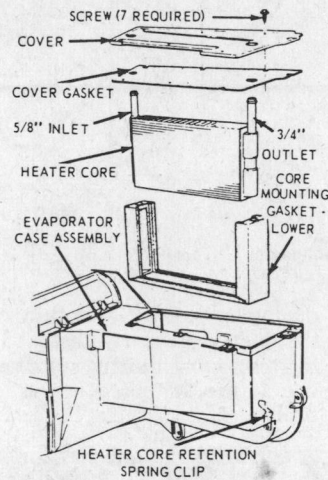

Continental heater core removal
(© Ford Motor Co.)

Mark IV and V

1. Drain the engine coolant and disconnect the heater hoses from the heater core.
2. Remove the glove box.
3. Remove the heater air outlet register from the plenum assembly. It is held in position by two snap-rings.
4. Remove the temperature control cable assembly mounting screw, and disconnect the end of the cable from the blend door crank arm by removing the spring nut.
5. Remove the blue and red vacuum hoses from the high-low door vacuum motor, and the brown hose at the in-line tee connector to the temperature bypass door motor.
6. Disconnect the wire connector from the resistor.
7. Remove 10 screws from around the flange of the plenum case and remove the rear case half of the plenum.
8. Remove the mounting nut from the heater core tube support bracket.
9. Reinstall in the reverse procedure. To provide a positive seal between the front and rear case halves, apply body sealer around the case flanges prior to installation. Be certain that the core mounting gasket is properly installed. Reverse procedure to install.

1974 and Later Continental

1. Drain the engine coolant.
2. Disconnect the heater hoses from the heater core.
3. Remove the heater core cover and gasket.
4. Lift the heater core and lower the mounting gasket out of the evaporator housing.
5. Remove the lower mounting gasket from the heater core.
6. Installation is the reverse of removal.

Blower Motor Removal

Mark III

1. Remove right cowl side trim panel.
2. Remove screws retaining duct to cowl side panel and sound baffle and remove duct.
3. Disconnect lead wire to blower motor.
4. Remove one screw from motor mounting plate, rotate motor mounting plate clockwise to unlock plate from case and remove motor and wheel assembly through opening in cowl side of panel. Reverse procedure to install.

Continental

1. Remove hood.
2. Remove right hood hinge and right fender inner support brace as an assembly.
3. Disconnect blower motor air cooling tube from motor.
4. Disconnect motor lead wire from harness and ground wire from dash panel.
5. Disconnect rear section of right front fender panel apron from fender around wheel opening and remove two lower fender to cowl mounting screws.
6. Separate fender apron from fender wheel opening so that apron can be pushed downward away from blower motor.
7. Remove four blower motor plate screws. Move motor and wheel forward out of blower scroll and remove assembly through opening while applying pressure to fender apron to enlarge opening at hinge area. Reverse procedure to install.

Mark IV and V

1. Remove the glove box for access.
2. Remove the recirculation air register and duct assembly from the blower assembly.
3. Remove the two screws that attach the blower lower housing to the dash panel.
4. Disconnect the white hose from the outside-recirc air door vacuum motor and remove the vacuum motor from the blower lower housing. It is held in place

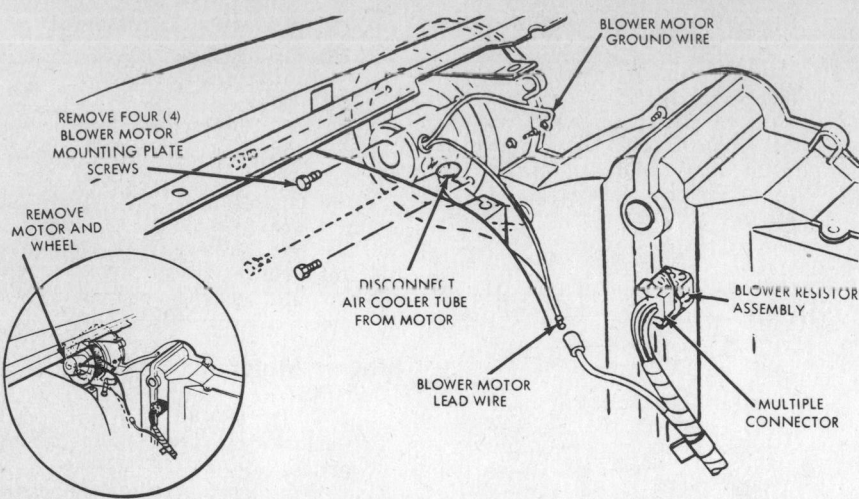

Heater blower removal— Lincoln Continental (© Ford Motor Co)

by two screws. Leave the motor actuator connected to the door crank arm.

5. Disconnect the orange blower motor lead wire from the harness connector, and disconnect the black motor ground wire.
6. Remove the six upper-to-lower blower housing flange screws.
7. Separate the blower lower housing and motor assembly from the upper housing and remove it from beneath the instrument panel.
8. Remove the blower motor and wheel assembly from the lower housing. It is held by four screws.
9. The upper flange of the recirc duct is retained to the blower upper housing with two S-clips that remained on the housing

during removal. Be certain that the duct is properly installed in the two clips during reinstallation. Reverse procedure to install.

SEAT BELTS

Disabling the Seat Belt/Starter Interlock

It is now legal to disable the seat belt/starter interlock system. However the warning light portion of the system must be left operational.

1. Apply the parking brake and remove the ignition key.
2. Open the hood and locate the system emergency override switch and connector. Remove the connector.

3. Cut the white wire(s) with the pink dots (#33 circuit) and the red wire(s) with the light blue stripe (#32 circuit).
4. Splice the two (or four) wires together and tape the splice. Use a "butt" connector if available.

NOTE: Do not cut and splice the other connector wires. If the red/yellow hash wire is spliced to any of the other wires the car will start in gear.

6. Install the connector back on the override switch. Close the hood.
7. Apply the parking brakes, buckle the seat belt, and turn the key to the "ON" position. If the starter cranks in "ON" or any gear selected, the wrong wires have been cut and spliced. Repeat steps 3-6.
8. Unbuckle the belt and try to start the car. If the car doesn't start, repeat steps 3-6. If the car starts, everything is O.K
9. To stop the warning buzzer from operating, remove it from the connector. Tape the connector to the wiring harness so that it can't rattle.

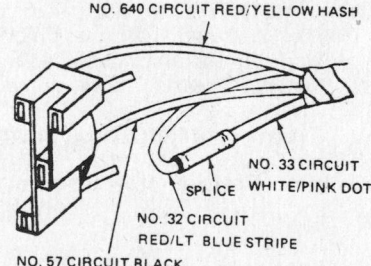

Cut and splice the seat belt/starter interlock wires as shown (© Ford Motor Co)

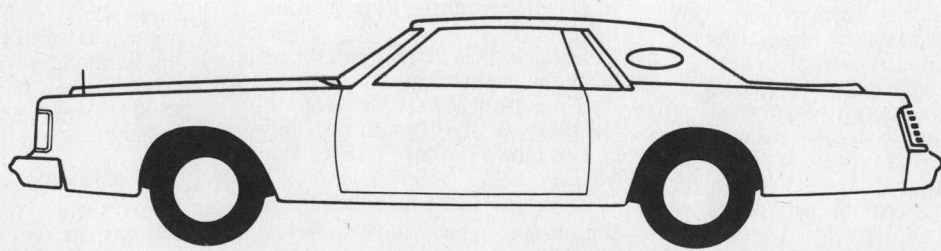

INDEX

Monza · Vega

Automatic Transmission
in car service **C644**
Downshift cable adjustment C646
Band adjustments C647
Shift linkage adjustment C645
Neutral safety switch adjustment C645
Pan Removal and Installation, fluid &
filter change C647
Throttle valve linkage adjustment C646

Brakes **C651, U299**
Master cylinder Removal and
Installation C651
Parking brake adjustment C651
Power booster Removal and Installation C651

Charging System **C625, U2**
Alternator Removal and Installation ... C625

Clutch **C642**
Clutch disc replacement C642
Clutch pedal free-travel adjustment ... C642

Cooling System **C629, U367**
Radiator Removal and Installation C629
Thermostat Removal and Installation ... C630
Water pump Removal and Installation ... C629

Emission Controls **C631, U145**
Air injection reactor C631
Catalytic converter system C633
Controlled combustion system C631
Early-fuel evaporation system C633
Evaporative emission control C631
Exhaust gas recirculation C632
Positive crankcase ventilation C631
Transmission controlled spark C631

Engine **C633, U194**
Engine Removal and Installation C633
CYLINDER HEAD REMOVAL AND
INSTALLATION C637
Rocker arm Removal and Installation ... C638
LUBRICATION C640
Oil pan Removal and Installation C640
Oil pump Removal and Installation C641
Oil pump (front cover) seal Removal and
Installation C641
Rear main oil seal Removal and
Installation C641
MANIFOLDS C635
Exhaust manifold Removal and

Installation C636
Intake manifold Removal and
Installation C635
PISTON AND ROD INSTALLATION C640
TIMING COVER, BELT OR CHAIN, AND
CAMSHAFT C638
Camshaft cover Removal and
Installation C639
Camshaft Removal and Installation C639
Front Cover Removal and Installation .. C638
Timing belt and sprocket Removal
and Installation C638
Timing chain Removal and Installation . C639
VALVE SYSTEM C636
Valve guides C637
Valve lash adjustment C637

Front Suspension **C648, U292**
Ball joint Removal and Installation ... C648
Ball joint inspection C648
Lower control arm Removal and
Installation C649
Shock absorber Removal and
Installation C648
Spring Removal and Installation C649
Upper control arm Removal and
Installation C650
Wheel bearing adjustment C650

Fuel System **C627, U50**
Carburetor adjustments C629
Fuel filter Removal and Installation .. C627
Fuel pump Removal and Installation C627

Heater **C657**
Blower motor Removal and
Installation C657
Heater core Removal and Installation .. C657

Ignition System **C625, U34**
Distributor installation (engine
disturbed) C626
Distributor Removal and Installation .. C626
Firing order C620
HEI timing light and tachometer
connections C625
Point adjustment C626
Ignition timing C627

Instrument Panel **C656, U350**
Headlight switch Removal and
Installation C656

Jacking, Hoisting **C648**

Manual Transmission **C643, U231**
Linkage adjustment C643
Transmission Removal and Installation . C644

Radio **C656**
Radio Removal and Installation C656

Rear Axle **C647, U285**
Axle shaft Removal and Installation ... C647
Oil seal/Axle bearing Removal and
Installation C647

Rear Suspension **C650**
Lower control arm Removal and
Installation C650
Spring Removal and Installation C650
Shock absorber Removal and
Installation C650
Upper control arm Removal and
Installation C650

Seat Belts **C658**
Disabling the interlock system C658

Specifications **C620, U359**
Capacities C623
Crankshaft and connecting rod C624
Engine identification C620
General engine C621
Piston clearance C624
Ring gap and side clearance C624
Torque C623
Tune-up C622
Valve C623
Wheel alignment C625
Year identification C620

Starting System **C625, U2**
Starter Removal and Installation C625

Steering **C651, U328**
Ignition lock cylinder Removal and
Installation C654
Ignition switch Removal and
Installation C653
Power steering pump Removal and
Installation C654
Steering wheel Removal and
Installation C652
Tie rod Removal and Installation C651
Turn signal switch Removal and
Installation C653

U-Joints **C647**
Driveshaft Removal and Installation ... C647

Windshield Wipers **C656**

YEAR IDENTIFICATION

1971-72

1973

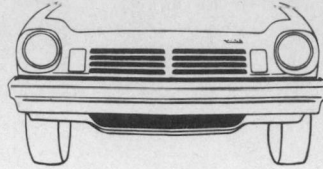

1974

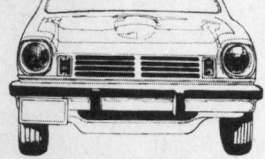

1975 Vega

1975 Monza 2 + 2

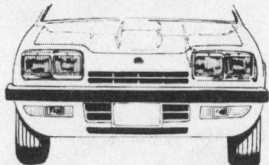

1975 Monza Town Coupe

1976 Vega

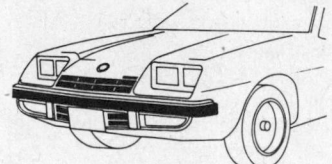

1976 Monza 2 + 2

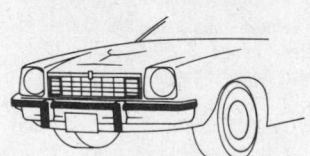

1976 Monza Town Coupe

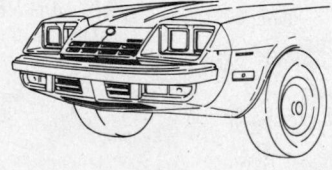

1977 Monza

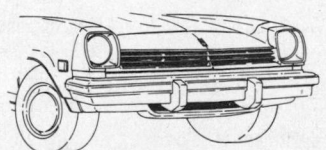

1977 Vega

FIRING ORDER

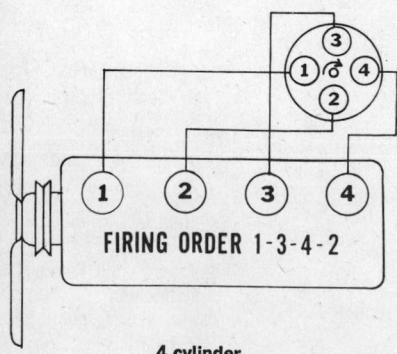

FIRING ORDER 1-3-4-2

4 cylinder

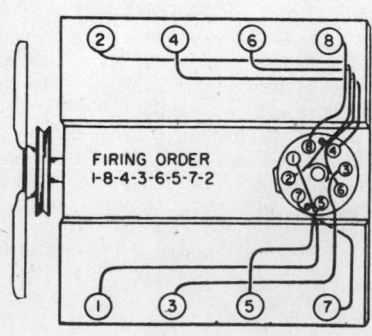

FIRING ORDER 1-8-4-3-6-5-7-2

262, 305 and 350 V8

Model Identification

The vehicle serial number plate is found on top of the instrument panel and is visible through the left side of the windshield. The body number, trim code and paint number are located on the upper right side of the dash panel.

Engine Identification Number

The 4 cylinder engine identification number is located on a machined pad, on the right side of the cylinder block, above the starter motor.

The V8 engine number is located on a pad on the front right-hand side of the cylinder block.

ENGINE IDENTIFICATION

Engine identification is made by means of a letter code stamped on a machined pad, on the right-side, above the starter motor on the OHC four-cylinder engine; or on a pad at the front right-hand side of the cylinder block on V8 engines.

Displacement (cu in.)	Carburetor (No. Bbls.)	1971	1972	1973	1974	1975	1976	1977
4 Cylinder Models								
122 DOHC	EFI					ZCA	ZCA	
140 OHC	1	CHA CHC	CGB CGD CNA CND	CAA CAB CAH CAJ	CAA CAB CAH CAJ ZCR			
140 OHC	2	CHB CHD	CBM CNB CSK	CAC CAD CAK CAL	CAC CAD CAK CAL			
140 OHC	All					CAM CAR CAS CAT CAU CAW CBB CBC CBD CBF	CBK CBL CBS CBT CBU CBW CBX CBY CBZ	
8 Cylinder Models								
262	2					CZA, CZB, CZC, CZD, CZT, CZU, CZW	CGA CGB CZT CZU	
305	2						CPA CPB CPC 9W	
350	2					CHY		

GENERAL ENGINE SPECIFICATIONS

Year	Engine No. Cyl. Displacement (Cu. In.)	Carburetor Type	Horsepower @ rpm ■	Torque @ rpm (ft lbs) ■	Bore X Stroke (in.)	Compression Ratio	Oil Pressure @ 2000 rpm
'71	4-140	1 bbl	90 @ 4600	136 @ 2400	3.501 x 3.625	8.0:1	40
	4-140	2 bbl	110 @ 4800	138 @ 3200	3.501 x 3.625	8.0:1	40
'72	4-140	1 bbl	80 @ 4400	121 @ 2800	3.501 x 3.625	8.0:1	40
	4-140	2 bbl	90 @ 4800	121 @ 3200	3.501 x 3.625	8.0:1	40
'73	4-140	1 bbl	72 @ 4400	100 @ 2000	3.501 x 3.625	8.0:1	40
	4-140	2 bbl	85 @ 4800	115 @ 2400	3.501 x 3.625	8.0:1	40
'74	4-140	1 bbl	75 @ 4400	115 @ 2400	3.501 x 3.625	8.0:1	40
	4-140	2 bbl	85 @ 4400	122 @ 2400	3.501 x 3.625	8.0:1	40

GENERAL ENGINE SPECIFICATIONS

Year	Engine No. Cyl. Displacement (Cu. In.)	Carburetor Type	Horsepower @ rpm ■	Torque @ rpm ■ (ft lbs)	Bore X Stroke (in.)	Compression Ratio	Oil Pressure @ 2000 rpm
'75	4-122	EFI	110 @ 5600	107 @ 4800	3.501 x 3.160	8.5:1	40
	4-140	1 bbl	78 @ 4200	120 @ 2000	3.501 x 3.625	8.0:1	40
	4-140	2 bbl	87 @ 4400	122 @ 2800	3.501 x 3.625	8.0:1	40
	4-140 Calif.	2 bbl	80 @ 4400	116 @ 2800	3.501 x 3.625	8.0:1	40
	8-262	2 bbl	110 @ 3600	200 @ 2000	3.671 x 3.100	8.5:1	32-40
	8-350 Calif.	2 bbl	125 @ 3600	235 @ 2000	4.000 x 3.480	8.5:1	32-40
'76-'77	4-122	EFI	110 @ 5600	107 @ 4800	3.501 x 3.160	8.5:1	27-41
	4-140	1 bbl	70 @ 4400	107 @ 2400	3.501 x 3.625	8.0:1	27-41
	4-140	2 bbl	84 @ 4400	113 @ 3200	3.501 x 3.625	8.0:1	27-41
	8-262	2 bbl	110 @ 3600	195 @ 2000	3.671 x 3.100	8.5:1	32-40
	8-305	2 bbl	140 @ 3800	245 @ 2000	3.736 x 3.480	8.5:1	32-40

■ Beginning 1972, horsepower and torque are SAE net figures. They are measured at the rear of the transmission with all accessories installed and operating. Since the figures vary when a given engine is installed in different models, some are representative rather than exact.

EFI—Electronic Fuel Injection

TUNE-UP SPECIFICATIONS

When analyzing compression test results, look for uniformity among cylinders rather than specific pressures.

Year	ENGINE No. Cyl. Displacement (cu. In.)	hp	SPARK PLUGS Type	Gap (in.)	DISTRIBUTOR Point Dwell (deg)	Point Gap (in.)	IGNITION TIMING (deg) ▲ Man Trans ●	Auto Trans	VALVES Intake Opens ■ (deg) ●	Fuel Pump Pressure (psi)	IDLE SPEED (rpm) ▲ Man Trans *	Auto Trans
'71	4-140①	90	R42TS	.035	31-34	.019	6B	6B	22	3-4½	850/700	650/550
	4-140①	110	R42TS	.035	31-34	.019	6B	10B	25	3-4½	1200/700	650/550
'72	4-140①	80	R42TS	.035	31-34	.019	6B	6B(4B)	22(28)	3-4½	700	700②/550
	4-140①	90	R42TS	.035	31-34	.019	8B	8B	28	3-4½	700	700②/550
'73	4-140①	72	R42TS	.035	31-34	.019	8B	8B	22	3-4½	1000/450	750/450
	4-140①	85	R42TS	.035	31-34	.019	10B	12B	28	3-4½	1200/450	750②/450
'74	4-140①	75	R42TS	.035	31-34	.019	10B(8B)	12B(8B)	22	3-4½	1000/700	750/550
	4-140①	85	R42TS	.035	31-34	.019	10B(8B)	12B(8B)	28	3-4½	1200/700	750②/500
'75	4-122③	All	R43TSX	.060	Electronic		12B	—	38	40	800	—
	4-140①	1 bbl	R43TSX	.060	Electronic		8B	10B	22	3-4½	1200/700	700/550
	4-140①	2 bbl	R43TSX	.060	Electronic		10B	12B	28	3-4½	1200/700	750/600
	8-262	All	R-44TX	.060	Electronic		8B	8B	26	7-8½	800	600
	8-350	All	R-44TX	.060	Electronic		—	6B	28	7-8½	—	600
'76	4-122③	All	R-43LTS	.035	Electronic		12B	—	38	40	600	—
	4-140	1 bbl	R-43TS	.035④	Electronic		8B	10B	34	3-4½	700⑤	750
	4-140	2 bbl	R-43TS	.035④	Electronic		10B	12B	34	3-4½	700	750
	8-262	All	R-45TS	.045	Electronic		6B	8B(TDC)	26	3-4½	800	600
	8-305	All	R-45TS	.045	Electronic		—	8B(TDC)	28	3-4½	—	600
'77	4-140	2 bbl	R-43TS	.035	Electronic		10B	12B	34	3-4½	700	750
	8-305	2 bbl	R-45TS	.045	Electronic		⑥	⑥	28	3-4½	⑥	⑥

▲ See text for procedure
● Figure in parentheses indicates California engine
■ All figures Before Top Dead Center
* Where two figures are separated by a slash, the first figure is for idle speed with solenoid connected, while the second is for idle speed with solenoid disconnected

NOTE: The underhood specifications sticker often reflects tune-up specification changes made in production. Sticker figures must be used if they disagree with those in this chart.

① Adjust mechanical valve lifter clearance to .015 in. for intake, and to .030 in. for exhaust with engine cold
② For air-conditioned vehicles, adjust idle speed to 800 rpm with A/C on
③ Adjust valve clearance to 0.014 in. (intake and exhaust) with engine cold
④ .045 in. for Monza
⑤ 750 rpm for Monza
⑥ See underhood specifications sticker

B Before Top Dead Center
—— Not applicable

CAPACITIES

Year	ENGINE No. Cyl. Displacement (cu. in.)	Engine Crankcase Add 1 Qt For New Filter	TRANSMISSION Pts To Refill After Draining Manual 3-Speed	4/5-Speed	Automatic •	Drive Axle (pts)	Gasoline Tank (gals)	COOLING SYSTEM (qts) With Heater	With A/C
'71	4-140	3	2.4	3	6	2.3	11	6.5	6.5
'72	4-140	3	2.4	3	6①	2.8	11	6.5	6.5
'73	4-140	3	3	3	6②	2.8	11	8.6	9.0
'74	4-140	3	3	3	8	2.8	16	8.6	9.0
'75-'77	4-140, 4-122	3.5	3	3③	8	2.8	16⑤	8.0④	8.0④
	8-262	4.0	—	3③	8	2.8	18.5	18.0	18.0
	8-305, 8-350	4.0	—	3	8	2.8	18.5	18.0	18.0

- • Specifications do not include torque converter
- ① 5 pts with Turbo Hydra-Matic
- ② 8 pts with Turbo Hydra-Matic
- — Not Applicable
- ③ 5-speed uses Dexron® II automatic transmission fluid
- ④ 6.8 qts—4-122
- ⑤ 18.5 gals—Monza 4-140

VALVE SPECIFICATIONS

Year	Engine No. Cyl. Displacement (cu in.)	Seat Angle (deg)	Face Angle (deg)	Spring Test Pressure (lbs @ in.)	Spring Installed Height (in.)	STEM TO GUIDE Clearance (in.) Intake	Exhaust	STEM Diameter (in.) Intake	Exhaust
'71	4-140	46	45	75 @ 1.75	1 ¾	.0010-.0027	.0010-.0027	.3414	.3414
'72	4-140	46	45	75 @ 1.75	1 ¾	.0010-.0027	.0010-.0027	.3414	.3414
'73	4-140	46	45	75 @ 1.75	1 ¾	.0010-.0027	.0010-.0027	.3414	.3414
'74	4-140	46	45	75 @ 1.75	1 ¾	.0010-.0027	.0010-.0027	.3414	.3414
75-'77	4-122	46	45	45 @ 1.30	1.30	.0010-.0027	.0010-.0027	.2791	.2791
	4-140	46	45	75 @ 1.75	1 ¾	.0010-.0027	.0010-.0027	.3414	.3414
	8-262	46	45	80 @ 1.70①	1.70②	.0010-.0027	.0010-.0027	.3414	.3414
	8-305	46	45	80 @ 1.70①	1.70②	.0010-.0027	.0010-.0027	.3414	.3414
	8-350	46	45	80 @ 1.70①	1.70②	.0010-.0027	.0010-.0027	.3414	.3414

① Exhaust—80 @ 1.61
② Exhaust—1.61

TORQUE SPECIFICATIONS

All readings in ft lbs

Year	Engine No. Cyl. Displacement (cu in.)	Cylinder Head Bolts	Rod Bearing Bolts	Main Bearing Bolts	Crankshaft Pulley Bolt	Flywheel to Crankshaft Bolts	MANIFOLD Intake	Exhaust
'71-'77	4-140	60	35	65	80	60	30	30
'75-'76	8-262	65	45	70	60	60	30	20①
'76-'77	8-305	65	45	75	60	60	30	20①
'75	8-350	65	45	75	60	60	30	20①

① Inside bolts—30 ft. lbs

CRANKSHAFT AND CONNECTING ROD SPECIFICATIONS

All measurements are given in inches

| Year | Engine No. Cyl. Displacement (cu in.) | CRANKSHAFT | | | | CONNECTING ROD | | |
		Main Brg. Journal Dia	Main Brg. Oil Clearance	Shaft End-Play	Thrust on No.	Journal Diameter	Oil Clearance	Side Clearance
'71-'72	4-140	2.2983-2.2993	.0029-.0003	.002-.008	4	1.999-2.000	.0007-.0027①	.0085-.0135
'73-'74	4-140	2.2983-2.2993	.0003-.0020②	.002-.007	4	1.999-2.000	.0007-.0038①	.0085-.0135
'75-'77	4-122	2.3011	⑤	.002-.008	4	1.999-2.000	.0007-.0027	.0009-.0013
	4-140	2.3004	.0003-.0029	.002-.008	4	1.999-2.000	.0007-.0027	.0009-.0013
	8-262	2.4502③	④	.002-.007	5	2.098-2.099	.0013-.0035	.008-.014
	8-305	2.4502③	④	.002-.007	5	2.098-2.099	.0013-.0035	.008-.014
	8-350	2.4502③	④	.002-.007	5	2.098-2.099	.0013-.0035	.006-.016

① Maximum service clearance = .004 in.
② .0003-.0027 for No. 2, 3, 4, 5
③ No. 5—2.4508 in.
④ No. 1—.0008-.0020 in.
   No. 2, 3, 4—.0011-.0023 in.
   No. 5—.0017-.0033 in.
⑤ No. 1, 2, 3, 5—.0008-.0034
   No. 4—.0002-.0029

RING GAP

All measurements are given in inches

Year	Engine	Top Compression	Bottom Compression
'71-'77	4-140, 4-122	.015-.025	.009-.019
'75-'76	8-262, 8-350	.010-.020	.010-.020
'76-'77	8-305	.010-.020	.013-.025

Year	Engine	Oil Control
'71-'77	4-140, 4-122	.010-.030
'75-'76	8-262	.010-.025
'75	8-350	.015-.055
'76-'77	8-305	.010-.035

PISTON CLEARANCE

Year	Engine	Piston to Bore Clearance (in.)
'75-'76	4-122	.0020-.0030②
'71-'77	4-140	.0018-.0028①
'75-'76	8-262	.0008-.0018②
'75	8-350	.0007-.0017
'76-'77	8-305	.0017-.0042③

① Measured 1.50 in. from top of piston
② Measured 1.75 in. from top of piston
③ Measured 1.56 in. from top of piston

RING SIDE CLEARANCE

All measurements are given in inches

Year	Engine	Top Compression	Bottom Compression
'71-'77	4-140	.0012-.0027	.0012-.0027
'75-'76	8-262	.0012-.0032	.0012-.0027
'75	8-350	.0012-.0032	.0012-.0027
'76-'77	8-305	.0012-.0032	.0012-.0027

Year	Engine	Oil Control
'71-'77	4-140	.000-.005
'75-'76	8-262	.000-.005
'75	8-350	.000-.005
'76-'77	8-305	.000-.005

WHEEL ALIGNMENT SPECIFICATIONS

Year	Model	CASTER		CAMBER		Toe-in (in.)	Steering Axis Inclin. (deg)	WHEEL PIVOT RATIO (deg)	
		Range (deg)	Pref Setting (deg)	Range (deg)	Pref Setting (deg)			Inner Wheel	Outer Wheel
'71-'73	All	1¼N to ¼N	¾N	¼N to ¾P	¼P	3/16 to 5/16	8.55	—	—
'74	All	1¾N to ¼P	¾N	¾N to 1¼P	¼P	3/16 to 5/16	8.55	—	—
'75-'77	All	1¼N to ¼N	¾N	¼N to ¾P	¼P	0 to ⅛①	8.55	—	—

— Not specified
① 1976 and later—⅛ to 0 toe-out

CHARGING SYSTEM

A 10-SI Series Delcotron alternator is used. This unit features a non-adjustable, integral solid-state regulator mounted inside the slip-ring end frame. Testing procedures for the integrated charging system are found in the Unit Repair Section.

Alternator Removal and Installation

1. Disconnect the battery.
2. Disconnect the alternator wiring.
3. Remove the alternator brace bolt and V-belt.
4. Remove the pivot mount bolt and the alternator.
5. Installation is the reverse of the removal procedure. Adjust the belt tension.

STARTING SYSTEM

The starter is a solenoid actuated Delco-Remy unit similar to other Chevrolet starters except that beginning 1975, the starter has no "R" terminal. The HEI system does not use the solenoid to coil wire. See the Unit Repair Section for testing and overhaul procedures.

Starter Removal and Installation

1. Disconnect the battery ground cable and all wiring at the solenoid terminals. Install each nut on the terminal from which it was removed, as these nuts are not interchangeable.
2. Loosen the front starter bracket and remove the two mounting bolts.
3. Remove the front bracket bolt and rotate the bracket out of the way.
4. Remove the starter from the car, lowering the front end first.
5. To install, reverse the removal procedure. Tighten the mounting bolts, and then install the brace.

IGNITION SYSTEM

The 140 cu in. distributor is mounted in the cylinder head at the rear of the engine and is driven by the camshaft. An unusual feature of this unit is a cup, mounted at the lower end of the driveshaft. This cup is under full engine oil pressure when the engine is running, acting as a vibration damper to reduce driveshaft oscillations. If this cup is not installed after the distributor has been disassembled, engine oil pressure will be lost.

The V8 distributor is mounted at the rear of the engine, gear driven off the camshaft.

Electronic ignition is standard equipment on all 1975 and later models, eliminating the need for point replacement. Two types of HEI distributors are used. V8 distributors combine all ignition components in one unit. The coil is in the distributor cap and connects directly to the rotor. The inline engine distributor has an externally mounted coil.

Timing Light Connections— HEI System

Timing light connections should be made in parallel using an adaptor at the distributor No. 1 terminal.

Tachometer Connections— HEI System

There is a "tach" terminal on the V8 distributor cap and on the 4 cylinder coil. Connect the tachometer to this terminal and ground.

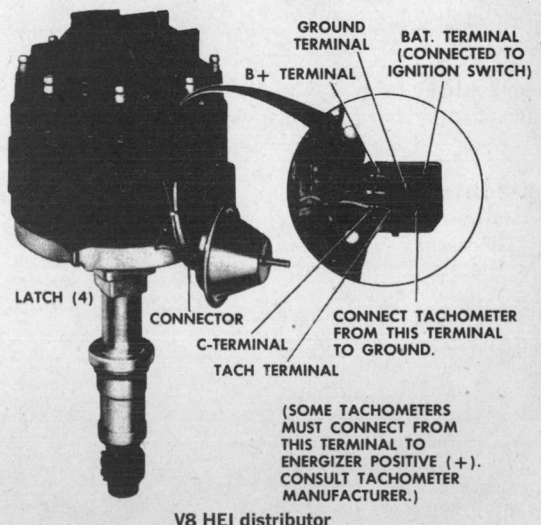

GROUND TERMINAL
BAT. TERMINAL (CONNECTED TO IGNITION SWITCH)
B+ TERMINAL
LATCH (4)
CONNECTOR
C-TERMINAL
TACH TERMINAL
CONNECT TACHOMETER FROM THIS TERMINAL TO GROUND.
(SOME TACHOMETERS MUST CONNECT FROM THIS TERMINAL TO ENERGIZER POSITIVE (+). CONSULT TACHOMETER MANUFACTURER.)

V8 HEI distributor
(© Chevrolet Div., G.M. Corp)

Caution *Grounding the tach terminal could damage the HEI ignition module.*

Distributor Removal

1. Release the cap hold-down screws and remove the cap. On electronic ignition, disconnect the wiring harness connectors at the side of the cap and remove the cap.
2. Disconnect the vacuum line and the primary lead.
3. Mark the distributor housing and the engine in line with the rotor centerline with chalk.
4. Remove the hold-down clamp and distributor.

NOTE: avoid turning the engine while the distributor is removed.

Distributor Installation

1. Turn the rotor approximately ⅛ turn clockwise past the alignment mark.
2. Push the distributor into position, moving the rotor to mesh the gears.
3. Install the clamp bolt.
4. Connect the vacuum line and the primary lead.
5. Install the cap and, if necessary, adjust the timing.

Installation—Engine Disturbed

1. Remove No. 1 spark plug and place a finger over the plug hole. Remove the center coil wire and crank the engine until compression is felt in No. 1 cylinder. Rotate the engine until the timing pointer is aligned with the proper mark.
2. Install the distributor with the vacuum advance pointing toward the front of the engine and the punchmarks on the drive gear in line with the No. 1 cap tower.
3. Install the hold-down clamp and rotate the distributor slightly so that the points are just open. Tighten the clamp bolt.
4. Install the rotor, cap and vacuum line.
5. Connect the primary lead.
6. Check and adjust the ignition timing.

Point Adjustment

Inspect the points for alignment and pitting. If necessary, clean the points with a point file. All the roughness need not be removed. To set the gap, rotate the crankshaft until one of the distributor cam lobes is directly opposite the rubbing block of the point arm (gap at maximum separation). Measure the gap, and if it is not within specifications, loosen the contact point assembly attaching screw and move the assembly to obtain the specified gap. This is done by inserting a screwdriver in the slot

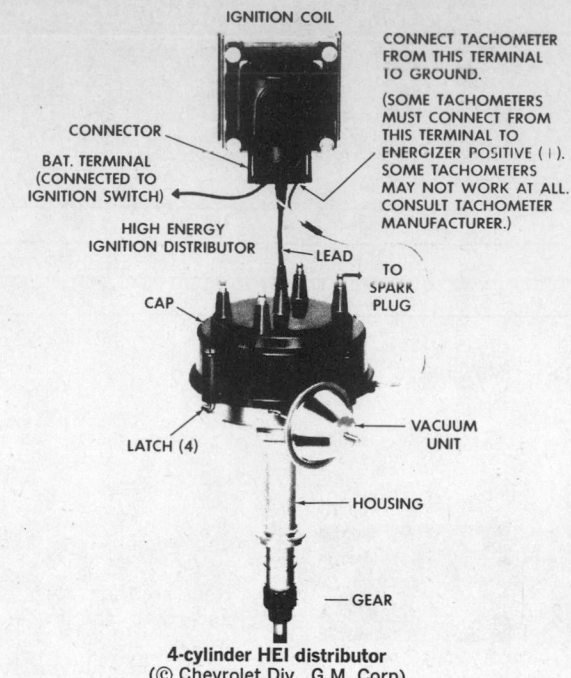

4-cylinder HEI distributor
(© Chevrolet Div., G.M. Corp)

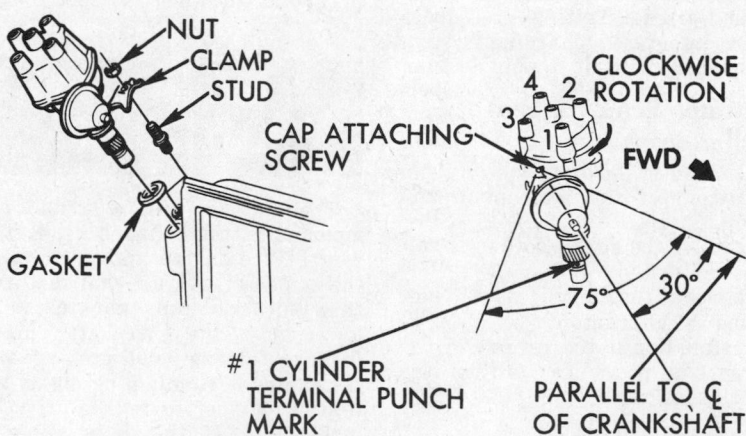

Distributor alignment—4 cylinder (© Chevrolet Div., G.M. Corp)

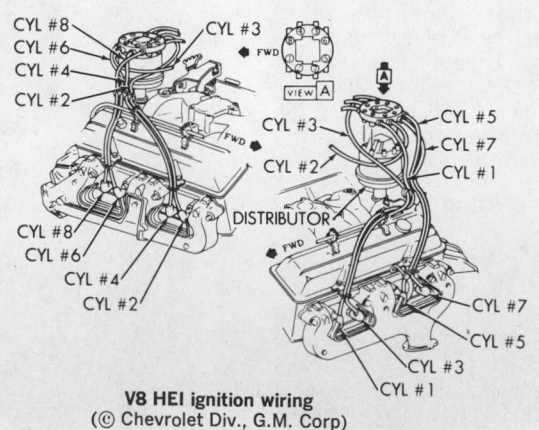

V8 HEI ignition wiring
(© Chevrolet Div., G.M. Corp)

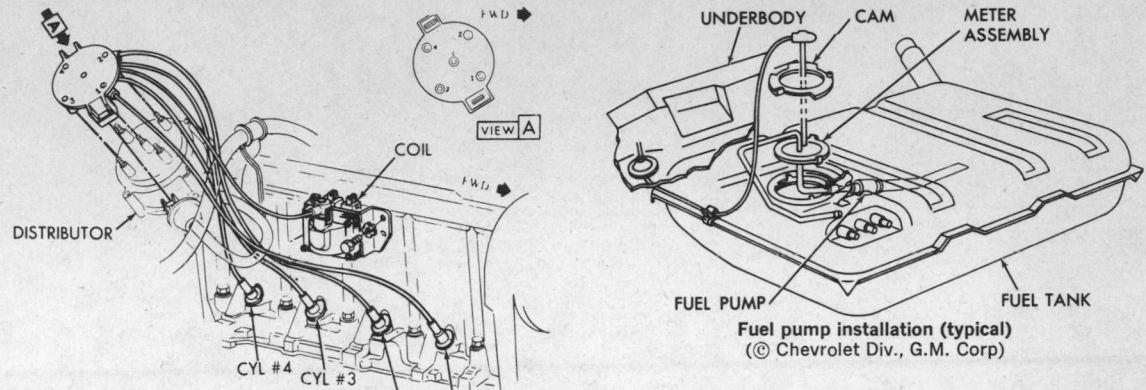

4-cylinder HEI ignition wiring
(© Chevrolet Div., G.M. Corp)

Fuel pump installation (typical)
(© Chevrolet Div., G.M. Corp)

formed by the contact points and the breaker plate and levering the points as required. Tighten the attaching screw.

Check the dwell angle. Check the ignition timing, adjusting it if necessary.

Ignition Timing

The timing marks are on a plate mounted on the front of the block and the timing notch is on the crankshaft pulley.

Timing is set as follows:

1. Bring the engine to normal operating temperature, shut the engine off, and connect a timing light to no. 1 spark plug or no. 1 plug tower on HEI. Clean the timing plate and mark the notch in the pulley with chalk.
2. Disconnect and plug the vacuum line to the distributor.
3. On 4-cylinder engines disconnect the fuel tank line from the evaporative emission canister.
4. If equipped, disconnect the electrical lead from the idle stop solenoid on the carburetor.
5. Start the engine and adjust the carburetor idle screw for an idle speed of 700 rpm or less for 1971-72 models, 1000 rpm or less for 1973-75 4-cylinder models.

NOTE: The idle solenoid is turned to adjust the idle speed on single barrel carburetor models.

6. Aim the timing light at the timing marks. If the notch does not align with the correct value on the scale, loosen the distributor clamp locknut and slowly turn the distributor to adjust.
7. Tighten the clamp locknut. Adjust the carburetor idle speed screw to give the specified idle speed with the solenoid disconnected.
8. Reconnect the idle stop solenoid lead. Increase the engine speed to allow the solenoid to extend and then adjust the solenoid plunger screw to obtain the idle

speed specified with the solenoid connected.

9. Shut the engine off and connect the vacuum and evaporative emission line.

FUEL SYSTEM

Two types of carburetors are used through 1972. Base engines are equipped with a Rochester MV one barrel carburetor. The optional engine is equipped with a Rochester 2GV two barrel carburetor. The MV one barrel continues to be used on the base engine beginning 1973, but the optional engine is equipped with a Holley 5210-C two barrel. The 262 V8 in the Monza 2 + 2 uses a Rochester 2 bbl. Each has an integral fuel filter.

The electric fuel pump is an integral part of the fuel tank unit assembly, which includes the fuel gauge metering unit. The fuel pump is energized by the ignition switch when the key is in the start or on position. After the engine starts, the pump receives current through the oil pressure safety switch as long as there is approximately 2 psi oil pressure.

Fuel Pump Removal and Installation (In-Tank Unit)

1. Disconnect the battery ground cable and siphon the fuel from the tank.
2. Disconnect the gauge sending-unit and pump wires at the rear harness connector.
3. Raise the car. Disconnect the fuel line at the gauge connection.
4. On 1971 models, disconnect the tank vent lines to the vapor separator, which is mounted on the top of the tank. On later models, disconnect the tank vent line to the vapor separator, which is mounted in the tank.
5. Disconnect the gauge wire ground screw from the floorpan.
6. Remove the tank strap bolts and,

very carefully, lower the tank.

7. Use the special wrench, or a suitable substitute, to unscrew the retaining cam ring. Do not strike any part of the tank with a metal tool, such as a hammer; there is a danger of explosion from sparks.
8. Remove the gauge sending-unit and fuel pump assembly.
9. Remove the flat wire conductor from the plastic clip on the fuel tube.
10. While squeezing the clamp, pull the pump straight back ½ in. for access to the terminals. Remove the two nuts, lockwashers, and wires from the pump.
11. Squeeze the clamp and pull the pump straight back to completely remove it from the sending unit.

Caution
Be careful not to bend the circular support bracket.

12. Slide the replacement pump through the circular support bracket until it rests against the rubber coupling. Be sure that the rubber isolator and saran strainer, supplied in the service package, are attached to the pump.
13. Attach the two pump terminals, using lockwashers and nuts. Be sure that the flat conductor is attached to the terminal farthest away from the float arm.
14. Squeeze the clamp and push the pump into the rubber coupling.
15. Replace the flat wire conductor in the plastic clip on the fuel tube.
16. Install the pump and gauge unit into the tank opening. Tighten the cam ring.
17. Install the fuel tank using a reverse of the removal procedure.

Fuel Filter Removal and Installation

Both paper and bronze filters are used on all models.

1. Disconnect the fuel line at the intake fuel filter nut on the carburetor.
2. Remove the intake fuel filter nut.

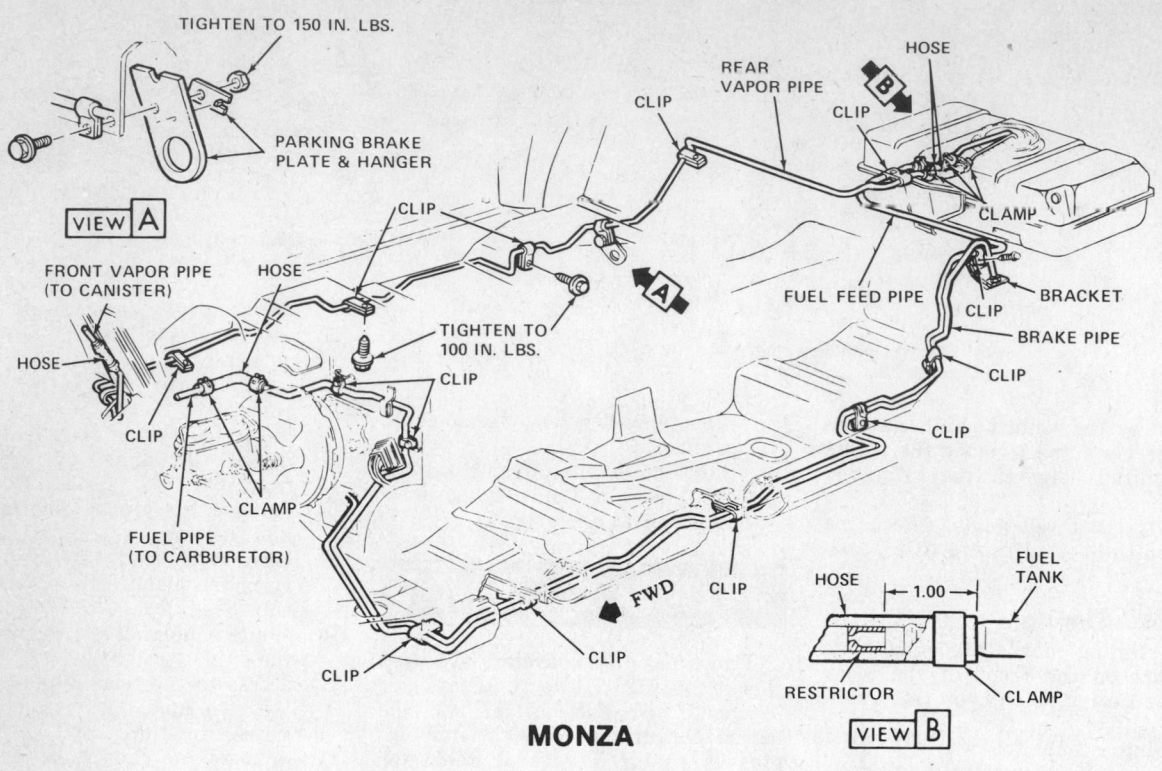

TIGHTEN TO 150 IN. LBS.

PARKING BRAKE PLATE & HANGER

VIEW A

FRONT VAPOR PIPE (TO CANISTER)

HOSE

HOSE

CLIP

CLIP

CLAMP

FUEL PIPE (TO CARBURETOR)

CLIP

TIGHTEN TO 100 IN. LBS.

CLIP

CLIP

FWD

CLIP

REAR VAPOR PIPE

CLIP

HOSE

CLIP

CLAMP

FUEL FEED PIPE

CLIP

BRACKET

BRAKE PIPE

CLIP

CLIP

HOSE

1.00

FUEL TANK

RESTRICTOR

CLAMP

VIEW B

MONZA

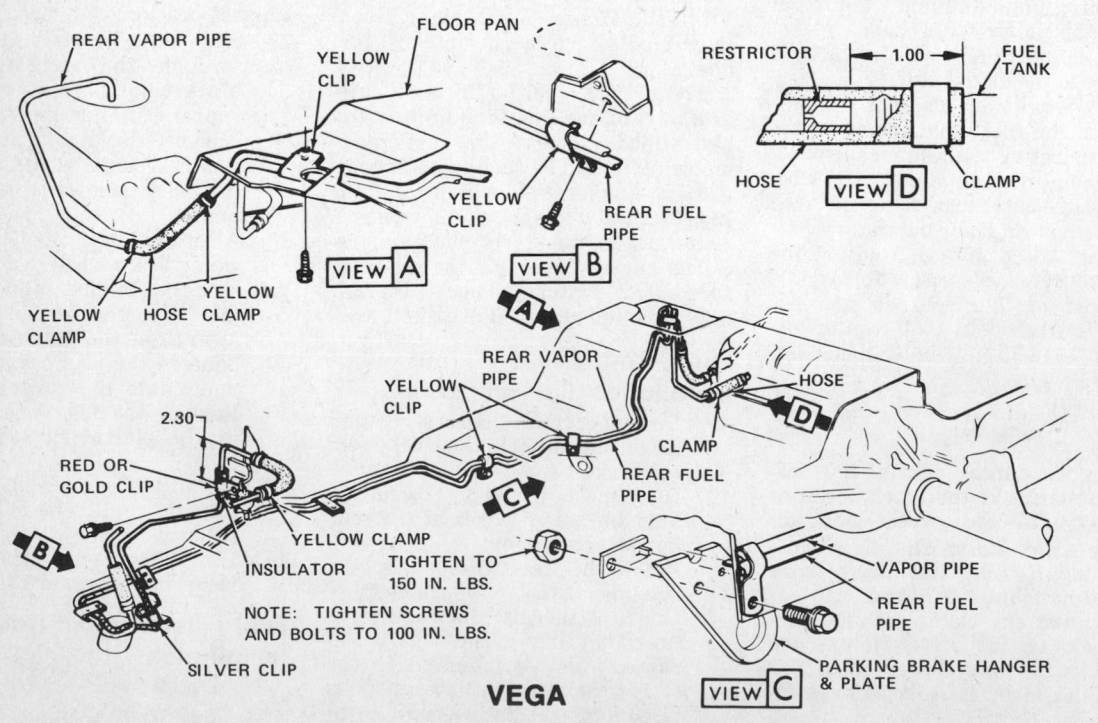

REAR VAPOR PIPE

YELLOW CLIP

FLOOR PAN

YELLOW CLIP

REAR FUEL PIPE

YELLOW CLAMP

HOSE CLAMP

YELLOW CLAMP

VIEW A

VIEW B

RESTRICTOR

1.00

FUEL TANK

HOSE

VIEW D

CLAMP

REAR VAPOR PIPE

YELLOW CLIP

HOSE

CLAMP

REAR FUEL PIPE

2.30

RED OR GOLD CLIP

YELLOW CLAMP

INSULATOR

SILVER CLIP

C

TIGHTEN TO 150 IN. LBS.

NOTE: TIGHTEN SCREWS AND BOLTS TO 100 IN. LBS.

VAPOR PIPE

REAR FUEL PIPE

PARKING BRAKE HANGER & PLATE

VIEW C

VEGA

Fuel feed and evaporation control vapor lines—1976 and later
(© Chevrolet Div., G.M. Corp.)

3. Remove the filter element and spring.
4. Install the element spring and element. Bronze filters are installed with the conical section facing out and with a gasket between the filter element and the fuel intake nut.
5. Install the nut using a new gasket and tighten. Do not overtighten this nut, as it is easily stripped.
6. Install fuel line and tighten the connector.

Carburetor Adjustments

The only carburetor adjustment given here is for idle speed. The idle mixture screw(s) is equipped with a sealed limiter cap(s). Mixture should not be adjusted, except after carburetor overhaul or repair, since it is factory-set to ensure the lowest possible level of exhaust emissions.

Idle stop solenoid adjustment
(© Chevrolet Div., G.M. Corp)

1971-72

1. The engine must be at normal operating temperature and the air cleaner in place. Air conditioning should be on in 1971 models; off in later models.
2. Detach the fuel tank line from the top of the evaporative emission canister.
3. Disconnect the distributor vacuum line and plug the carburetor hose.
4. Disconnect the electrical connector at the idle stop solenoid on the carburetor.
5. Start the engine and adjust the carburetor idle speed screw to obtain the idle speed specified in the "Tune-Up Specifications Chart" (for speed with the solenoid disconnected).
6. Reconnect the idle stop solenoid electrical lead. Speed up the engine to allow the solenoid plunger to extend, then adjust the solenoid plunger screw to obtain the idle speed specified in the "Tune-Up Specifications

Chart" (for speed with the solenoid connected).
7. Stop the engine and reconnect the vacuum line and the evaporative emission canister line.

1973-74

Follow steps 1 through 4 of the 1971-72 procedure, then proceed as follows.

Rochester MV 1-bbl

1. Start the engine and, using a ⅛ in. allen wrench, adjust the idle speed to the figure given in the "Tune-Up Specifications Chart" (for speed with the solenoid disconnected).
2. Check the dwell and ignition timing. Check the idle speed again.
3. Reconnect the electrical wire to the solenoid.
4. Adjust the idle speed (for speed with solenoid connected) by turning the body of the solenoid itself.

Holley 5210-C 2-bbl

1. Start the engine and adjust the idle speed screw for the speed listed in the "Tune-Up Specifications Chart" (speed with solenoid disconnected).
2. Check the dwell and ignition timing. Check the idle speed again.
3. Reconnect the electrical wire to the solenoid.
4. Adjust the screw on the throttle lever (not the same screw as step 1). Set the idle speed to the figure given in the "Tune-Up Specifications Chart" (for speed with the solenoid connected).

1975-77
All Carburetors

1. The engine should be at normal operating temperature, air cleaner ON, choke open and air conditioner OFF.
2. Set the parking brake.
3. Disconnect the fuel tank hose from the vapor canister.
4. Disconnect and plug the vacuum hose. Check and adjust the timing. Reconnect the vacuum hose on Rochester 1MV and 2GC carburetors.
5. Disconnect the electrical connector at the idle stop solenoid.
6. Place automatic transmissions in Drive and manual transmissions in Neutral. On Rochester 1MV carburetors, turn the hex screw in the end of the solenoid body with a ⅛ in. allen wrench to set the low idle speed. On Holley 5210-C and Rochester 2GC models set the low idle speed with the idle screw.
7. Reconnect the electrical connector and crack the throttle slightly.
8. Turn the solenoid in or out to set the curb idle speed.
9. Reconnect the vapor line to the canister.

COOLING SYSTEM

The intake manifold is water heated to provide an even intake temperature. Only early 1971 models have an engine block-drain plug. All 1971 models and models built after March 1973 have a radiator drain petcock. The 1972 models have neither a block drain plug nor a radiator petcock. To drain the cooling system on these models, either the lower radiator hose must be removed or the coolant must be siphoned out.

There are two radiators: a standard type and a larger heavy duty radiator equipped with a fan shroud.

Starting 1973, all models are equipped with a coolant recovery system reservoir. A translucent plastic reservoir allows for hot coolant expansion. When the engine cools, coolant is drawn into the radiator by vacuum. Additional coolant should be added to the reservoir, not the radiator.

Beginning 1976, Monza 2 + 2 models equipped with V8 engine and air conditioning have an auxiliary fan installed forward of the radiator. The fan is operated by a thermostatic switch located on the right rear side of the cylinder head. If engine temperature exceeds approximately 235°F, the switch will close to operate the fan.

Radiator Removal and Installation

1. Drain the radiator.
2. On models with the heavy duty radiator, remove the fan shroud as described below.
3. Disconnect the intake and outlet hoses.
4. Remove the two screws which secure the fan guard to the radiator support, then remove the support and the two radiator pads.
   NOTE: on vehicles with the heavy duty radiator, remove the two upper brackets (instead of the single support).
5. Lift the radiator up and out of the lower brackets.
6. To install, reverse the removal procedure.

Water Pump Removal and Installation

4 Cylinder

The pump bearings are permanently lubricated during manufacture

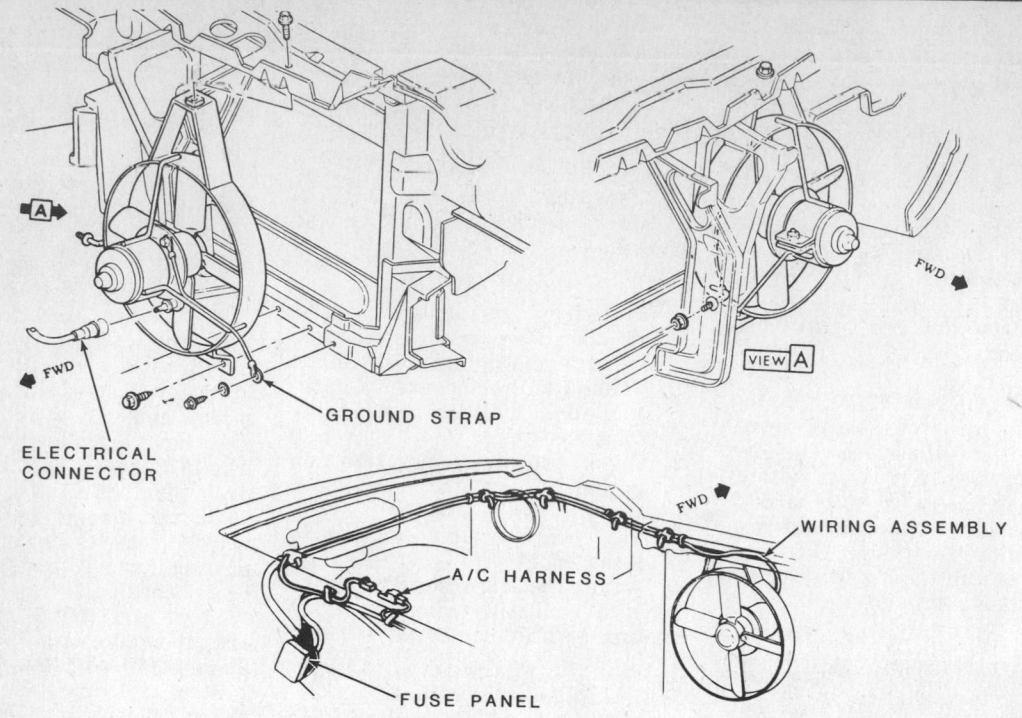

Auxiliary cooling fan—1976 and later Monza 2 + 2 models equipped with V8 engine and air conditioning
(© Chevrolet Div., G.M. Corp)

and do not require periodic maintenance other than keeping the air vent (top of housing) and drain holes (bottom of housing) free of dirt and grease.

The pump components cannot be serviced separately and, in the event of pump failure, the complete assembly must be replaced as a unit, as follows:

1. Raise the hood and install a bolt through the hood hold-open link. tightening the bolts to 20 ft. lbs.
2. Disconnect the negative battery cable.
3. Remove the fan and spacer.

Caution No attempt should be made to repair a bent or damaged fan. The fan assembly must be in proper balance and an improperly balanced fan may cause extensive damage.

4. Loosen, but do not remove, the two lower timing belt cover retaining screws. The holes in the cover are slotted so that the cover is easily removed.
5. Remove the two upper timing belt cover retaining screws and remove the cover.
6. Drain the coolant.
7. Loosen the water pump bolts to relieve the tension on the timing belt.
8. Remove the hoses from the water pump.
9. Remove the water pump bolts, pump and gasket.
10. Thoroughly clean the old gasket material from the pump and block.

11. To install, position the water pump on the block using a new gasket and loosely install the water pump bolts. Make sure that the V grooves of the belt are aligned with the grooves in the water pump.

NOTE: use an anti-seize compound on the water pump bolt threads.

12. A special tool is available to adjust the timing belt. It fits into the round hole in the square lug to the upper right (facing) of the water pump and bears against the pump housing midway between the bolt holes. If this tool is available, apply 15 ft lbs of torque against the water pump (and belt). If the tool is not available, apply a force to the pump in a similar manner. Tighten the pump bolts to 15 ft lbs.
13. Install the radiator and heater hoses to the pump.
14. Install the timing belt cover, lowering the cover lower screw slots over the screws. Loosely tighten the screws against the cover.
15. Install the two upper timing cover screws, then tighten the upper and lower screws to 50 in. lbs.
16. Install the fan spacer and fan, tightening the bolts to 20 ft lbs.
17. Fill the cooling system, connect the battery negative cable, start the engine and check for leaks.
18. Remove the bolt from the hood

hold-open link and close the hood.

V8

1. Drain the coolant from the radiator.
2. Loosen the fan pulley bolts.
3. If necessary, remove the alternator with the drive belt and brackets.
4. If necessary, remove the air pump with the drive belt and brackets.
5. Disconnect the lower radiator hose and the heater hose at the water pump.
6. Remove the fan and pulley.
7. Remove the pump-to-cylinder block and power steering-to-pump bolts and remove the water pump and old gasket.
8. Installation is the reverse of removal. Use a new gasket coated with sealer. Adjust the alternator and air pump drive belt tension. Fill the cooling system, run the engine and check for leaks.

Thermostat Removal and Installation

The thermostat is located in a housing at the cylinder head water outlet adjacent to the intake manifold. On V8 engines, the thermostat is in the water outlet housing in the front of the intake manifold.

4 Cylinder

1. Drain the cooling system.
2. Disconnect the upper radiator hose at the engine.

3. If the alternator is attached to the water outlet, loosen the swivel bolt attachment and move it out of the way.
4. Unbolt the housing and remove the housing, gasket, and thermostat.
5. Replace the thermostat and housing, using a new gasket.
6. Install the alternator and adjust the drive belt. The adjustment procedure is outlined further on in this section.
7. Replace the radiator hose, fill the cooling system, start the engine, and check for leaks.

V8

1. Drain the coolant to a level below that of the water outlet housing.
2. Remove the radiator upper hose.
3. Remove the housing bolts and remove the water outlet housing and gasket.
4. Remove the thermostat.
5. Installation is the reverse of removal. Use a new gasket.

EMISSION CONTROLS

Positive Crankcase Ventilation

All models use the Positive Crankcase Ventilation System (PCV). Some unburned fuel and combustion products leak past the rings during combustion. These gases travel into the crankcase where, if they are not removed, they will combine with the oil to form sludge and also build excessive pressure inside the crankcase. The PCV system removes these gases from the crankcase and routes them to the intake manifold where they are combined with the raw air fuel mixture and reburned in the combustion chamber.

The crankcase gases are drawn from the crankcase by intake manifold vacuum. There is a PCV valve in the line between the crankcase and the intake manifold which regulates the flow of the gases.

Evaporative Emission Control

The Evaporative Emission Control system (EEC) is used on all models. This system limits the amount of gasoline vapor discharged into the air from the gas tank and carburetor. The fuel tank has a non-vented cap. As vapors are generated in the fuel tank, they flow through a liquid vapor separator to a canister where they are stored. Vapors generated by the carburetor after the engine is turned off are also routed to this canister. From the canister, the vapors are routed back to the carburetor where they are burned when the engine is started.

Controlled Combustion System

The Controlled Combustion System (CCS) is used on all models. Essentially the CCS increases combustion efficiency through carburetor and distributor calibrations and by increasing engine operating temperatures.

Carburetors are calibrated leaner and initial ignition timing is retarded. The vacuum advance curve is also altered to decrease emissions.

The CCS also incorporates a higher engine operation temperature. A 195° thermostat is used. Engines that run hotter provide more complete vaporation of fuel and reduce quench area in the combustion chamber. Quench area is the relatively cool area near the cylinder wall and combustion chamber surfaces. Fuel in these areas does not burn properly because of the lower temperatures. This incomplete burning increases emissions.

The CCS uses a thermostatically controlled air cleaner called the Auto-Therm air cleaner. It is designed to keep the temperature of the air entering the carburetor at approximately 100°F. This allows the lean carburetor to work properly, minimizes carburetor icing, and improves engine warm-up characteristics. A sensor unit located on the clean air side of the air filter senses the temperature of the air passing over it and regulates the vacuum supplied to a vacuum diaphragm in the inlet tube of the air cleaner. The colder the air, the greater the amount of vacuum supplied to the vacuum diaphragm. The vacuum diaphragm, depending on the vacuum supplied to it, opens or closes a damper door in the inlet tube of the air cleaner. If the door is open it allows air from the engine compartment to go to the carburetor. If the door is closed, air flows from the heat stove located on the exhaust manifold into the carburetor. In this way, heated air is supplied to the carburetor during cold days and when first starting the engine and warming it up.

Air Injection Reactor System

AIR is used on all 1972 models except non-California cars with single-barrel carburetors. 1975 California cars with the 140 cu. in. engine, Cosworth Vega, and Monza V8 also use an air pump. 1976 49 states 1 bbl four-cylinder engines and California 2 bbl four-cylinder engines also have air injection. Both 1977 engines use air injection.

The Air Injection Reactor (AIR) system was used to treat exhaust emissions. It consists of an air pump, a diverter valve, and tubes and hoses used to inject the air into the exhaust manifolds. The pump, driven by the engine, compresses air which is routed to the exhaust port of each cylinder. The air provides oxygen to further burn any unburned gases that are left over from the combustion process.

The diverter valve closes during engine overrun and deceleration and dumps the output from the air pump to the atmosphere. This prevents backfire due to air being injected when an overly rich mixture is present in the exhaust port.

Transmission Controlled Spark System

The Transmission Controlled Spark (TCS) is used on all 1971–72 models and on all 1973 85 hp engines with manual transmissions. It is also used on all 1973-74 cars built for California with manual transmisions and the Cosworth Vega. 1976 1 bbl four-cylinder engines with manual transmission also have TCS.

The TCS system is used to prevent vacuum advances when the transmission is in low forward gear. The TCS system consists of a temperature-sensing switch, a transmission switch, an idle stop solenoid, and a vacuum advance solenoid.

On 1971–72 cars, the vacuum advance solenoid is normally open, providing full vacuum to the distributor. When the vacuum advance solenoid is energized, the vacuum to the distributor is turned off and the advance unit is vented to the atmosphere.

The transmission switch is located on the transmission and senses when the transmission is in one of the lower gears. When in a lower gear, the switch activates the vacuum advance solenoid, shutting off vacuum advance. There is also an engine-temperature-sensing switch which overrides the transmission switch. It will allow vacuum advance in the lower gears when engine temperature is below 82° F. There is always vacuum advance in high gear and reverse.

On 1972 California models equipped with an automatic transmission, the transmission switch is a dummy switch and will not energize the solenoid. These engines have vacuum advance only when engine temperature is below 82° F.

An idle stop solenoid is used to prevent afterrun when the ignition is turned off. Afterrun is caused by the higher operating temperatures of today's engines and the wider throttle plate openings necessary for emission controls. The loss of spark from turning off the ignition is usually sufficient to stop the engine. However, if the engine has high enough cylinder temperatures, enough air-fuel mixture can pass the wide throttle plate opening and be ignited without the spark plug and the engine will continue to run even after the key is turned off. The idle solenoid is attached to the carburetor to solve this problem. The solenoid has an adjustable plunger and is electrically operated. When the ignition is turned on, the plunger is extended and contacts the carburetor throttle lever, opening the throttle plate wide enough for the engine to idle properly. When the ignition is turned off, the plunger retracts and the throttle lever falls back on the lever stop. When the throttle lever is on its stop the throttle plate opening is very small and will not allow enough air-fuel mixture to pass to run the engine with the ignition off.

On 1973-74 and 1976 cars, the vacuum advance solenoid is normally closed, when (de-energized), venting the vacuum advance circuit to the atmosphere and shutting off vacuum to the distributor advance unit.

When the key is turned on the idle stop solenoid is energized, the plunger extends to touch the throttle lever and maintains idle speed. As long as the engine temperature remains below 93°F, the vacuum advance solenoid is energized and the distributor receives a vacuum supply. The vacuum advance unit functions to give good start-up and drive-away characteristics. When the engine temperature reaches approximately 93°F, the temperature switch breaks

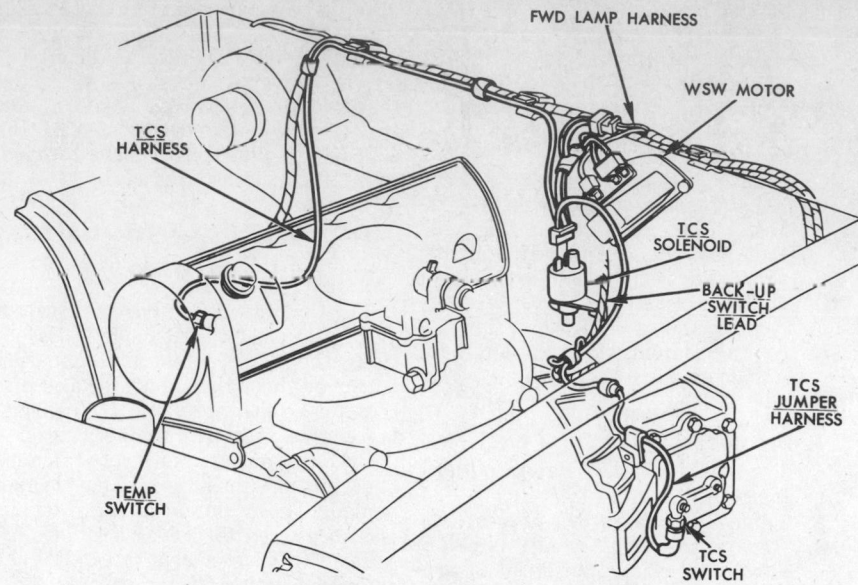

1973-76 TCS electrical components—4 cylinder
(© Chevrolet Div., G.M. Corp)

the circuit, causing the vacuum advance solenoid to de-energize and cut off the vacuum supply. When the engine overheats, the temperature switch completes the circuit to activate the instrument panel warning lamp. Under normal driving conditions, the transmission switch controls the vacuum advance solenoid. In the lower gears, the switch is open and the solenoid de-energized. In high gear, the switch is closed and energizes the solenoid to open the vacuum port to the distributor and permits the advance unit to function. The idle stop solenoid operates as before.

Exhaust Gas Recirculation

Exhaust Gas Recirculation (EGR)

is used beginning 1973 on all models.

EGR is used to reduce oxides of nitrogen (NO_x) that are formed at high operating temperatures.

EGR operates by introducing small amounts of relatively inert exhaust gas into the intake manifold, lowering the peak combustion temperature. The amount of exhaust gas introduced is regulated by the EGR valve. The EGR valve is vacuum modulated. The vacuum to operate the valve is supplied by an orifice just above the throttle valve in the carburetor.

When there is a high vacuum during heavy acceleration, the valve opens to allow exhaust gas into the intake manifold. At idle or cruising speeds the valve is closed and no exhaust gas is introduced into the intake manifold.

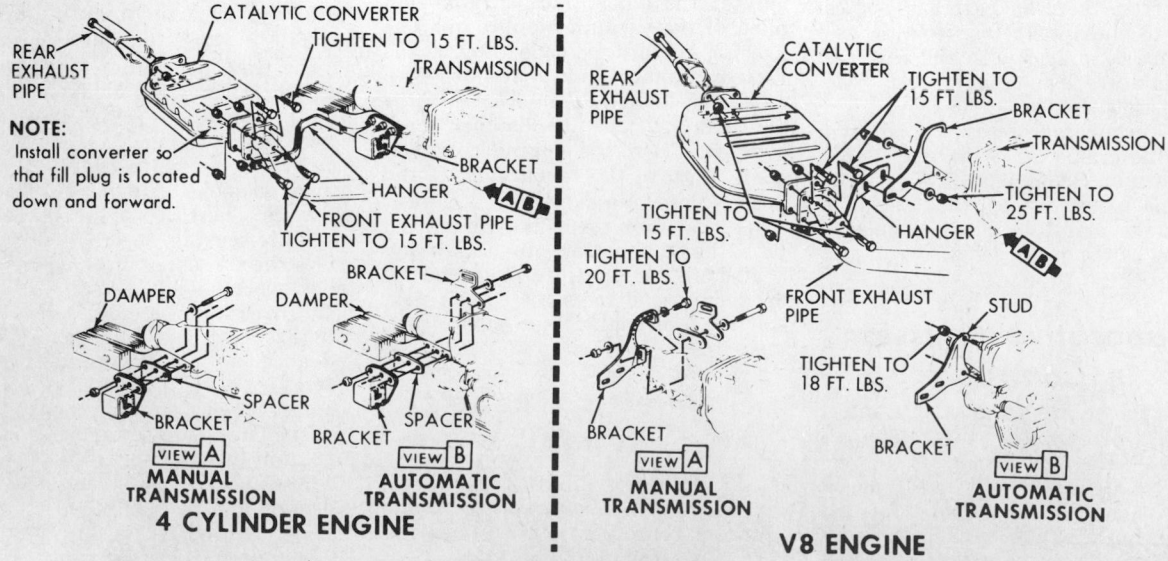

Catalytic converter installation
(© Chevrolet Div., G.M. Corp)

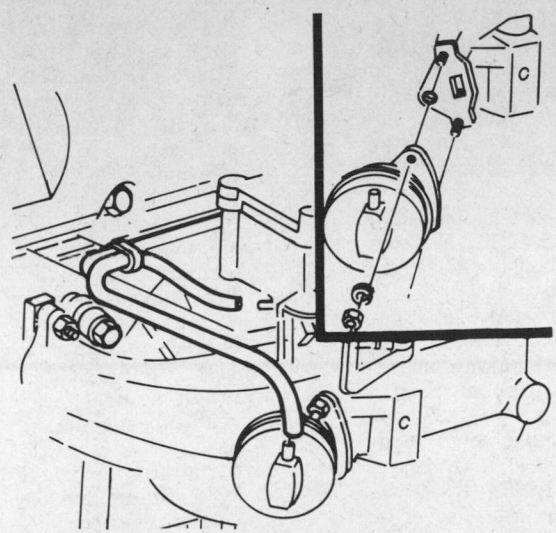

EGR valve mounting—4 cylinder
(© Chevrolet Div., G.M. Corp)

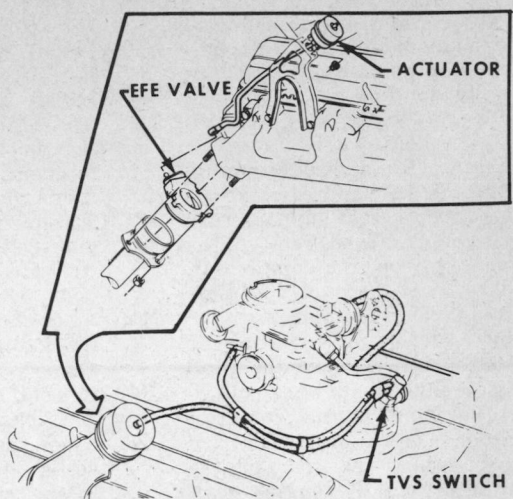

V8 EFE system
(© Chevrolet Div., G.M. Corp)

Catalytic Converter System

The 1975 and later Vega and Monza are equipped with catalytic converters nationwide (including California). It is located between the front and rear exhaust pipes on the right-hand side of the car. A major benefit from the catalytic converter is a large reduction in pollutants, while allowing carburetor settings that provide smoother power, and more spark advance for increased fuel economy and better overall performance.

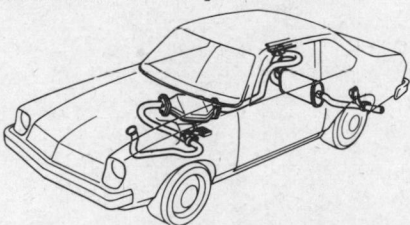

Schematic of typical catalytic exhaust system
(© Chevrolet Div., G.M. Corp)

NOTE: *Unleaded fuel must be used with catalytic converters.*

In addition to the catalytic converters, a restricted fuel inlet is used, which will only accept the smaller fuel nozzles, used to dispense unleaded fuel.

Early Fuel Evaporation (EFE)

Early Fuel Evaporation is used on all V8 models. The system consists of an EFE valve at the exhaust manifold flange, an actuator and a thermal vacuum switch (TVS). The TVS is mounted in the water outlet housing and directly controls vacuum in response to coolant temperatures.

The actuator closes the EFE valve when coolant temperatures are below 180°F., routing hot gases to the base of the carburetor. When coolant temperatures reach 180°F., vacuum to the actuator is cut off releasing an internal spring in the actuator and opening the EFE valve.

For further information concerning emission controls, consult the "Emission Control Systems" Unit Repair Section.

ENGINE

The standard 4 cylinder Vega engine is a single overhead camshaft, four-cylinder design using a die cast aluminum cylinder block and a cast iron cylinder head. The iron-plated aluminum pistons ride directly on honed and electrochemically treated aluminum bores. The cylinder block is cast of an alloy containing silicon which, after suitable etching, provides a proper bore surface for the pistons and rings.

The valve train is completely contained in the head, with a straight-line vertical valve configuration. The camshaft is driven by a timing belt which in turn is driven from a front crankshaft pulley.

The limited production 1975-76 Cosworth Vega uses the basic Vega engine block with a shorter stroke, forged steel crankshaft. Unlike the standard cast iron head, the Cosworth cylinder head is cast aluminum. The dual overhead cams, water pump, and fan are belt driven in a similar manner to the standard engine. The cylinder head is a crossflow design with intake and exhaust manifolds on opposite sides of the head. Each cylinder is serviced by two intake and two exhaust valves. *NOTE: Cosworth Vega engine procedures are not covered in this book.*

The Monza 2 + 2 and Town Coupe are optionally available with the 262 cu in. V8 engine in 1975-76. The 350 cu in. V8 is only available in California in 1975. The 305 V8 is added in 1976 and replaces the 262 cu in. V8 in 1977. This engine is very similar in design to other small block Chevrolet engines.

Engine Removal and Installation

4 Cylinder

1. Raise the hood and install a bolt in the hold-open link.
2. Disconnect the battery cables.
3. Drain the cooling system and disconnect the hoses at the radiator.
4. Disconnect the heater hoses at the water pump and at the heater inlet (bottom hose).
5. Disconnect the following emission hoses:
   a. PCV at the cam cover.
   b. The canister vacuum hose at the carburetor.
   c. PCV vacuum hose at the intake manifold.
   d. Bowl vent at the carburetor.
   e. TCS at the rear of the carburetor.
6. Remove the radiator shroud, radiator, fan, fan spacer and air cleaner.
7. Disconnect the following electrical leads:
   a. Alternator.
   b. Ignition coil.
   c. Starter solenoid.
   d. Oil pressure sending unit.
   e. Temperature sending unit.
   f. TCS switch at the transmission.
   g. TCS solenoid on the firewall.
   h. Ground strap at the firewall.
8. Disconnect:
   a. Powerglide throttle valve linkage or Turbo Hydra-Matic detent cable.
   b. Fuel line at the rubber hose, rearward of the carburetor.

c. Automatic transmission vacuum modulator and air conditioning vacuum line at the intake manifold.

d. Throttle cable at the manifold bellcrank.

9. On cars with air conditioning, disconnect the compressor at the front support, rear support, rear lower bracket and remove the drive belt from the compressor.

NOTE: Do not disconnect any air conditioning lines or fittings.

10. Being careful not to crimp or bend the hoses, move the compressor slightly forward, allowing the front of the compressor to rest on the frame forward brace. Secure the rear of the compressor to the engine compartment so that it does not interfere with the engine removal.

11. If so equipped, disconnect the power steering pump and position it out of the way.

12. Raise the car on a hoist.

13. Disconnect the exhaust pipe at the exhaust manifold.

14. Remove the engine flywheel lower cover or the torque converter underpan.

15. On vehicles equipped with automatic transmission:
    a. Mark the converter-to-flywheel relationship for reassembly.
    b. Remove the converter to flywheel retaining bolts and install a coverter safety strap, to keep the converter from falling out.
    c. Remove the converter housing to engine retaining bolts.
    d. Loosen the engine front mount retaining bolts at the frame attachment and lower the vehicle on the hoist.
    e. Install a floor jack under the transmission and an engine lifting adapter to raise the engine slightly from its mounts.
    f. Remove the engine front mount retaining bolts.
    g. Remove the engine from the vehicle. Pull the engine forward enough to clear the transmission while slowly lifting the engine.

16. On vehicles with manual transmission:
    a. Remove the flywheel housing to engine retaining bolts.
    b. Proceed with Step 15 above. parts d, e, f, and g.

To install engine:

17. Install two guide pins into the upper bolt holes in the engine block. Guide pins can be fabricated by cutting the heads off two bolts and sawing screwdriver slots into them.

18. Lower the engine into place, aligning the engine with the transmission.

19. Install the front mount bolts hand-tight.

20. Install the converter or clutch housing-to-engine bolts, replacing the guide pins. Remove the torque converter retaining strap, if one was used.

21. Torque the clutch housing-to-engine bolts to 25 ft lbs and the converter housing-to-engine bolts to 35 ft lbs.

22. After checking to make sure that the front engine mounts are aligned and not making metal-to-metal contact, tighten them to 20 ft lbs.

23. Align the previously made converter and flywheel marks, and torque the bolts to 35 ft lbs.

24. Install the flywheel dust cover or torque converter underpan.

25. Connect the exhaust pipe at the manifold.

26. If so equipped, install the air conditioning compressor and power steering pump. Adjust the alternator belt.

27. Reconnect:
    a. the accelerator cable,
    b. the automatic transmission vacuum modulator line and the air conditioning vacuum line,
    c. tne fuel line, and

d. the Powerglide transmission throttle valve linkage or the Turbo Hydra-Matic detent cable.

28. Attach the following electrical connections:
    a. alternator
    b. coil
    c. starter solenoid
    d. oil pressure switch
    e. temperature switch
    f. TCS transmission switch
    g. TCS solenoid
    h. engine ground strap

29. Replace the air cleaner and install these hoses:
    a. vent tube at the air cleaner base
    b. carburetor bowl vent
    c. PCV vacuum line
    d. vacuum canister hose

30. Install the radiator, radiator panel or shroud, spacer, and fan.

31. Connect the heater and radiator hoses. Fill the cooling system.

32. Connect the battery cables. Start the engine and check for leaks. Remember to remove the bolt from the hood hold-open link.

V8

1. Raise the hood and install a bolt in the hold-open link.

2. Disconnect the battery cables.

3. Raise and support the car.

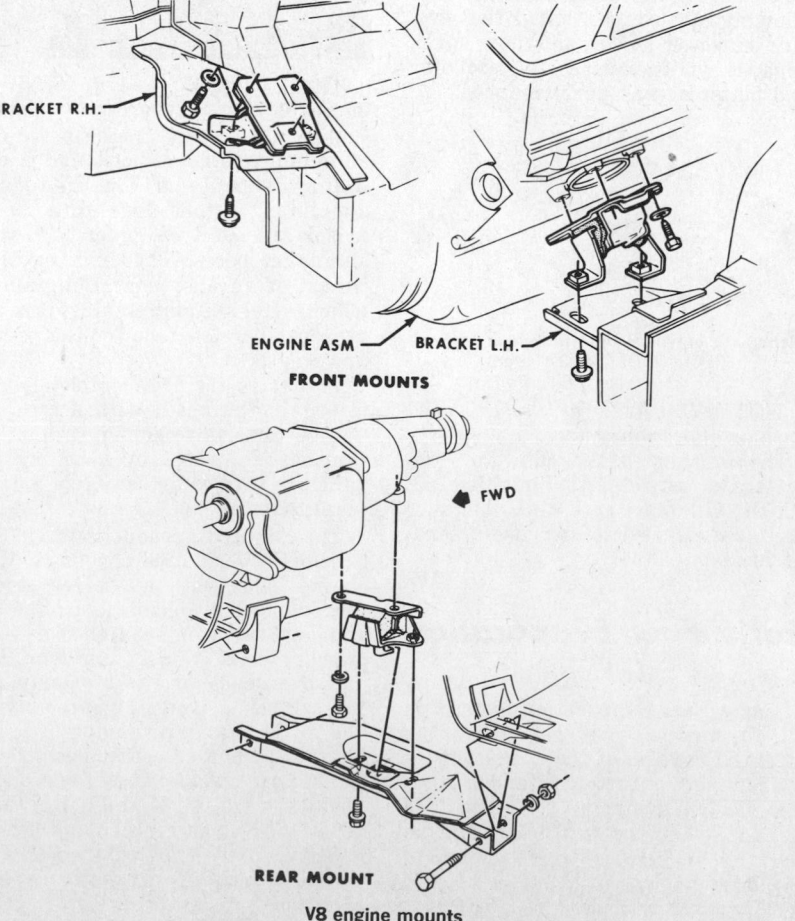

BRACKET R.H.

ENGINE ASM — BRACKET L.H.

FRONT MOUNTS

← FWD

REAR MOUNT

V8 engine mounts
(© Chevrolet Div., G.M. Corp)

4. Drain the coolant, engine and transmission.
5. Disconnect the exhaust pipes at the manifold.
6. Remove the flywheel or converter underpan.
7. On automatic transmissions, remove the converter-to-flywheel retaining bolts and install a converter retaining strap.
8. Remove the accessible converter housing or flywheel housing-to-engine bolts.
9. Remove the transmission cooler lines from the retaining clips on the side of the engine.
10. Remove the engine front mounting bolts at the frame brackets and lower the car.
11. Remove the radiator panel or shroud.
12. Remove the radiator and fan.
13. Disconnect the heater hose from the water pump and manifold.
14. Remove the air cleaner.
15. Disconnect the electrical leads from:
    - alternator
    - distributor
    - starter solenoid
    - oil pressure switch
    - engine temperature switch
    - temperature gauge switch
    - choke secondary pull-off solenoid.
16. Unclip the wiring harness from the rocker cover and position it out of the way.
17. Disconnect the automatic transmission vacuum modulator and air conditioning vacuum line from the manifold.
18. Disconnect the rubber fuel line at the rear of the engine.
19. Disconnect the following:
    - canister vacuum hose at the carburetor
    - accelerator at the carburetor and manifold bracket
    - air conditioning blower delay lead at the rear of the engine.
20. On air conditioned cars, remove the compressor from its mount. Do not disconnect any fittings. Secure the compressor to the fender.
21. Disconnect the power steering pump and lay it aside.
22. Install a floor jack under the transmission.
23. Install a hoist on the engine and raise the engine slightly to take the weight off the engine mounts. Remove the remaining engine to transmission bolts.
24. Remove the engine from the car. To install the engine:
25. Install transmission - to - engine guide pins made from 3/8 in. bolts with the heads cut off, into the engine.
26. Install the engine, aligning the engine with the transmission

housing.
27. Align the engine mounts with the frame brackets and lower the engine onto the brackets. Loosely install the engine mount bolts.
28. Remove the guide pins and install the engine-to-housing bolts. Remove the lifting equipment.
29. Remove the support from transmission and raise and support the car.
30. Remove the converter retaining strap and install and tighten the engine-to-housing bolts.
31. Tighten the engine front mount bolts.
32. Install the converter to the flywheel.
33. Install the flywheel cover or converter underpan.
34. Install the transmission cooler lines in the clips on the side of the block.
35. Connect the exhaust pipe at the manifold and lower the car.
36. Install the air conditioning compressor and power steering pump. Adjust the drive belts.
37. Connect the following:
    - canister vacuum hose to carburetor
    - Accelerator cable at carburetor and manifold bracket
    - air conditioning blower delay lead at side of engine
    - Fuel line to rubber hose at rear of engine
    - air conditioning vacuum line.
38. Install the electrical harness in the clip in the rocker cover and connect the following:
    - alternator
    - distributor
    - starter solenoid
    - oil pressure switch
    - engine temperature switch
    - temperature gauge switch
    - choke secondary pull-off solenoid.
39. Connect the heater hose at the water pump and at the manifold.
40. Install the radiator, fan, radiator panel or shroud, fill the cooling system, add engine oil and fill the transmission.
41. Install the air cleaner.
42. Connect the battery cables, start the engine and check for leaks.

Manifolds

Intake Manifold Removal and Installation
4 Cylinder

1. Raise the hood and install a bolt through the hold-open link.
2. Disconnect the negative battery cable.
3. Drain the cooling system.
4. Remove the EGR tube retaining clamps from both the intake and exhaust manifolds. Remove the

EGR tube by carefully driving it off.
5. Disconnect the heater hose at the fitting on the intake manifold.
6. Disconnect the vent tube at the base of the air cleaner, then remove the air cleaner.
7. Remove the air cleaner silencer.
8. Disconnect:
    a. The choke rod at the carburetor.
    b. PCV valve at the cam cover.
    c. Fuel line at the carburetor.
    d. The carburetor bowl vent line at the carburetor.
    e. Throttle linkage and the transmission throttle valve linkage.
    f. Power steering pump brace at the manifold.
9. Remove the alternator to thermostat housing through-bolt and loosen the alternator swivel bolt. Move the alternator aside to gain access to the manifold bolt.
10. Remove the four intake manifold bolts and remove the manifold.
11. Remove from the manifold:
    a. The carburetor and carburetor linkage.
    b. Pipe plug.
    c. Vacuum fittings.
    d. Hot water nipple.
12. Install the items removed in Step 11 to the new manifold.
13. Clean the gasket surfaces on the manifold and the cylinder head.
14. Position a new gasket over the dowels on the cylinder head, then carefully install the manifold. Make sure that the gasket remains in place.
15. Install the manifold bolts, tightening to 30 ft. lbs. The stud goes in the hole nearest No. 3 intake port.
16. Connect the power steering pump brace to the manifold.
17. Install the alternator to thermostat housing through bolt and adjust the belt tension.
18. Connect:
    a. The choke rod at the carburetor.
    b. The PCV valve at the cam cover.
    c. Fuel line at the carburetor.
    d. Carburetor bowl vent line at the carburetor.
    e. The throttle and transmission throttle valve linkage.
    f. Vacuum connections at the carburetor.
19. Install the air cleaner silencer and secure it to the heat stove tube.
20. Install the air cleaner. Connect the vent tube at the base of the air cleaner.
21. Connect the heater hose to the intake manifold fitting and fill the cooling system.

22. Raise the car. Install the EGR tube on the intake and exhaust manifolds.
23. Install the EGR tube retaining clamps. Lower the car.
24. Connect the negative battery cable and start the engine. Check for leaks and adjust the carburetor.

V8

1. Remove the air cleaner.
2. Drain the radiator.
3. Disconnect:
   a. Battery cables at the battery.
   b. Upper radiator and heater hoses at the manifold.
   c. Crankcase ventilation hoses as required.
   d. Fuel line at the rubber hose.
   e. Accelerator linkage at the pedal lever.
   f. Vacuum hose at the distributor.
   g. Power brake hose at the accelerator bracket.
   h. Ignition coil and temperature sending switch wires.
   i. Air diverter valve line.
   j. Choke pull-off lead.
   k. Air conditioning bracket or power steering brace.
   l. Choke hot and cold air pipes.
4. Remove the distributor cap and scribe the rotor position relative to distributor body.
5. Remove the distributor.
6. If applicable, remove the Delcotron upper bracket.
7. Remove the air pump.
8. Remove the manifold to head attaching bolts, then remove the manifold and carburetor as an assembly.
9. If the manifold is to be replaced, transfer the carburetor (and mounting studs), and other applicable equipment to the new manifold.
10. Before installing the manifold, thoroughly clean the gasket and seal surfaces of the cylinder heads and manifold.
11. Install the manifold end seals, folding the tabs if applicable, and the manifold/head gaskets, using a sealing compound around the water passages. Make sure the gaskets are firmly cemented in place before installing the manifold.
12. When installing the manifold, care should be taken not to dislocate the end seals. It is helpful to use a pilot in the distributor opening. Tighten the manifold bolts to the proper torque in the sequence illustrated.
13. Install the distributor with the rotor in its original location as indicated by the scribe line. If the engine has been disturbed, refer to "Distributor Removal and Installation."

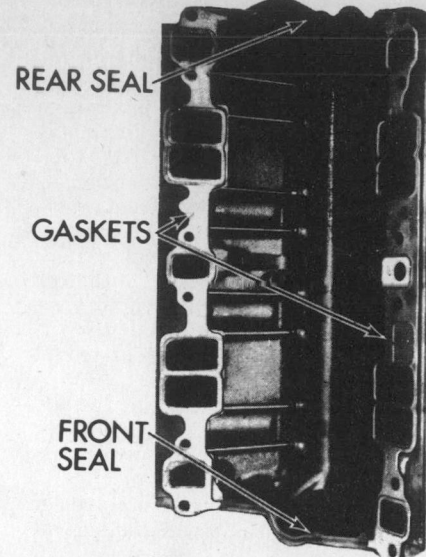

V8 intake manifold gasket and seals
(© Chevrolet Div., G.M. Corp)

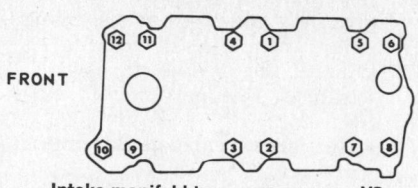

Intake manifold torque sequence—V8

14. If applicable, install the Delcotron upper bracket and adjust the belt tension.
15. Install the air pump. Adjust all drive belts.
16. Connect all components disconnected in Step 3 above.
17. Fill the cooling system, start the engine, check for leaks and adjust the ignition timing and carburetor idle speed and mixture.

Exhaust Manifold Removal and Installation

4 Cylinder

1. From under the car, disconnect the exhaust pipe from the manifold.
2. Remove the intake manifold as described above.
3. Disconnect the oil dipstick bracket at the exhaust manifold.
4. Remove the exhaust manifold bolts, then remove the manifold and carburetor heater assembly.
5. Install the carburetor heater assembly on the new manifold.
6. Install the exhaust manifold and manifold bolts (loosely). The upper bolts are shorter.
7. Tighten the manifold bolts to 30 ft. lbs.
8. Connect the exhaust pipe to the manifold.
9. Connect the oil dipstick bracket to the exhaust manifold.
10. Install the intake manifold.

V8 Right-Side

1. Disconnect the negative battery cable.
2. On air conditioned cars, remove the emission vapor canister. Without disconnecting any lines, remove the air conditioning compressor and place it out of the way.
3. Raise the car and disconnect the exhaust pipe from the manifold. Remove the engine mount-to-frame bolts and slide the engine to the left.
4. Lower the car and disconnect the spark plug wires and temperature sender wire. Remove the alternator and alternator bracket from the exhaust manifold.
5. Remove No. 6 and 8 spark plugs and the six manifold attaching bolts. Remove the spark plug shields from the brackets and bend the brackets upward.
6. Remove the exhaust manifold and EFE valve as an assembly.

Installation is the reverse of removal. On installation, be sure to clean the mating surfaces of the manifold and cylinder head, adjust belt tension where necessary, and align the engine.

V8 Left-Side

1. Disconnect the negative battery cable.
2. Raise the car and disconnect the exhaust pipe from the manifold.
3. Remove the engine mount-to-frame bolts and slide the engine to the right.
4. Remove the two rear manifold bolts, then raise the engine and place a 6 in. piece of 2 x 4 wood block under the left engine mount.
5. Lower the car, remove the air cleaner and dipstick tube bracket nut, and move the dipstick tube aside.
6. Remove the remaining attaching bolts and remove the manifold.
7. To install, clean the mating surfaces of the manifold and cylinder head, install the manifold and the front four attaching bolts, and start the two rear bolts.
8. Install the dipstick tube bracket and air cleaner. Raise the car and remove the block from under the left engine mount.
9. Tighten the two rear manifold attaching bolts and connect the exhaust pipe to the manifold. Align and install the engine mount-to-frame bolts.
10. Lower the car and connect the negative battery cable.

Valve System

The standard 4 cylinder valve train is an overhead camshaft operating mechanical valve tappets (hydraulic starting 1976). The 262, 305, 350 cu in. V-8s use a single camshaft operating hydraulic lifters.

Valve Lash Adjustment

4 Cylinder through 1975

1. Mark the locations of No. one and four spark plug wires on the side of the distributor with chalk. (Refer to the firing order illustration.)
2. Remove the distributor cap, air cleaner, and valve cover.
3. Turn the engine until the rotor points to the No. one position and the points are open. The No. one intake and exhaust, No. two intake and No. three exhaust valves are adjusted at this position. The intake valve is the front valve for each cylinder, and the exhaust valve is the rear one.
4. Insert the correct size feeler gauge between the camshaft lobe and the valve tappet. If the clearance is between 0.014 and 0.017 in. for intakes or 0.029 and 0.032 in. for exhausts, no adjustment is necessary. This is due to the fact that the adjusting mechanism only allows adjustments in increments of 0.003 in.
5. If lash is 0.003 in. or more out of adjustment, insert a 1/8 in. allen wrench into the tappet adjusting screw and turn it one full turn. Turning clockwise tightens; turning counterclockwise loosens.
6. Check the lash again and adjust further if necessary. Always turn the adjuster screw one full turn. You can feel the flat spot by pressing down on the tappet while adjusting.
7. Turn the engine so that the rotor points to no. four. Adjust no. two exhaust, no. three intake, and no. four intake and exhaust valves in this position.
8. Replace the valve cover, air cleaner, and distributor cap.

V8

V8 engines require no periodic valve adjustment. For initial adjustment procedures after overhaul of cylinder head or removal of valve train, see the Camaro section.

Valve Guides

4 Cylinder

Valves with oversize stems are available in three sizes: 0.003 in. o/s, 0.015 in. o/s and 0.030 in. o/s.

V8

Valve guides are integral with the cylinder head. Valve guide bores may be reamed to accommodate oversize valve stems or the guides may be knurled (if wear permits) to allow the retention of standard size valves.

FRONT ← I E I E I E I E

4 cylinder valve arrangement

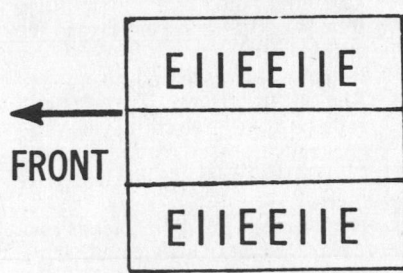

E I I E E I I E

FRONT ←

E I I E E I I E

V8 valve arrangement

Cylinder Head

Cylinder Head Removal and Installation

4 Cylinder

NOTE: Cylinder head gasket removal and installation does not require separating the intake and exhaust manifolds from the cylinder head.

1. Remove the timing belt cover and camshaft cover. Drain the cooling system.
2. Remove the timing belt and camshaft sprocket.
3. Remove the intake and exhaust manifolds.

4. Disconnect the water hose at the thermostat housing (outlet).
5. Remove the cylinder head bolts, then the head and gasket.
NOTE: If the head sticks, bump the starter a few times to loosen it with compression. Do not insert any tools between the head and block to pry them apart.
6. Using a new gasket (smooth side up), carefully position the cylinder head on the block.
7. Install the cylinder head bolts finger-tight. Use an anti-seize compound on the threads. Install the lifting bracket under the second head bolt from the front on the spark plug side. The 6-3/8 in. bolts are installed on the manifold side and the 5-5/8 in. bolts are installed on the spark plug side.
8. Tighten the head bolts to 60 ft. lbs. (in steps), using the illustration.
9. Connect the water hose to the thermostat housing.
10. Install the intake and exhaust manifolds.
11. Install the timing belt and sprocket.
12. Install the front cover and camshaft cover.

V8

1. Drain the coolant.
2. Remove the intake manifold.
3. Remove the exhaust manifolds.
4. Back off the rocker arm nuts and pivot the rocker arms out of the way so that the pushrods can be removed. Identify the pushrods so that they can be reinstalled in their original locations.
5. Remove the cylinder head bolts and cylinder heads.
6. Install using new gaskets. The head gasket is installed with the bead up.
NOTE: coat a STEEL gasket on both sides with sealer. If a STEEL ASBESTOS gasket is used, do not apply sealer. Clean the bolt threads, apply sealing compound and install the bolts finger tight.

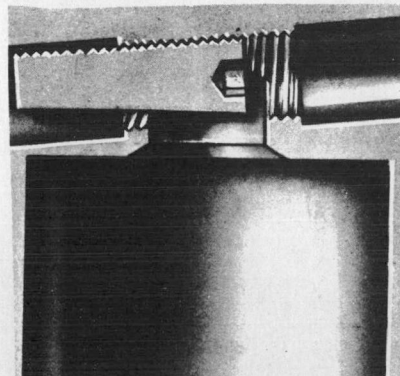

Valve tappet and adjusting screw assembly—4-cylinder   (© Chevrolet Div., G.M. Corp)

4 cylinder head torque sequence
(© Chevrolet Div., G.M. Corp)

7. Tighten the head bolts a little at a time in the sequence illustrated.
8. Install the exhaust and intake manifolds as described previously.
9. Adjust the valves as explained in the Camaro section. Fill the cooling system.

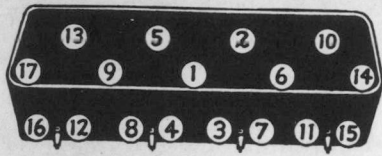

V8 cylinder head torque sequence

Rocker Arm Removal and Installation—V8

Rocker arms are removed by removing the adjusting nut. Be sure to adjust valve lash after replacing rocker arms.

NOTE: when replacing an exhaust rocker, move an old intake rocker to the exhaust rocker arm stud and install the new rocker arm on the intake stud.

Rocker arm studs that have damaged threads or are loose in the cylinder heads may be replaced with new studs available in 0.003 in. and 0.013 in. oversize or the bores may be tapped and screw-in replacement studs used. Do not attempt to install an oversize stud without reaming the stud bore. Studs are press-fit. Lubricate the press-fit area of the stud with hypoid axle lubricant.

NOTE: if engine is equipped with the AIR exhaust emission control system, the interfering components of the system must be removed. Disconnect the lines at the air injection nozzles in the exhaust manifolds.

Timing Cover, Belt, or Chain, and Camshaft

Front Cover Removal and Installation

4 Cylinder

1. Raise the hood and install a bolt in the hood hold-open link.
2. Disconnect the negative battery cable.
3. Remove the fan and spacer.
4. Loosen the two lower cover retaining screws.
5. Remove the two top cover retaining screws and remove the cover, lifting it until the slots clear the lower screws.
6. To install, position the cover, lowering it until the slots are over the lower screws. Loosely

tighten the lower screws.
7. Install the upper screws, then tighten all four screws to 50 in. lbs.
8. Install the spacer and fan, tightening the bolts to 20 ft. lbs.
9. Connect the battery cable and remove the bolt from the hood hold-open link.

V8

NOTE: the timing case cover oil seal may be replaced without removing the case cover.

After gaining access to the oil seal, pry the old seal out of the cover with a screwdriver. Then, lubricate the new seal and drive it into place with a seal installer tool.

1. Remove the fan belt, fan, and pulley.
2. Remove the radiator and shroud.
3. Remove the accessory drive pulley and the torsional damper retaining bolt.
4. Remove the damper from the crankshaft.
5. Remove the water pump.
6. Remove the front cover bolts and remove the front cover and gasket.
7. Clean the gasket mating surfaces.
8. Remove any oil pan gasket material that may still be adhering to the oil pan-engine block joint face.
9. Apply a 1/8 in. bead of silicone sealant or the equivalent to the joint formed by the oil pan and cylinder block, as well as to the entire oil pan front lip.
10. Coat the cover gasket with gasket sealer and install it on the front cover.
11. Loosely install the front cover on the block. Install the 4 top bolts loosely (about 3 turns). Install two 1/4–20x1/2 in. screws in the hole at each side of the front cover and apply a bead of sealant on the bottom of the seal and install it on the cover.
12. Tighten the screws evenly while aligning the dowel pins and holes in the front cover.

13. Remove the 1/4–20x1/2 in. screws and install the rest of the cover screws.
14. Further installation is the reverse of removal. Refill the engine with oil.

Timing Belt and Sprocket Removal and Installation

4 Cylinder

NOTE: This entire procedure isn't necessary to remove only the camshaft sprocket. This can be done simply by removing the upper timing belt cover bolts and pulling the cover forward. It isn't necessary to adjust the timing belt tension.

1. Raise the hood and install a bolt in the hood hold-open link.
2. Disconnect the negative battery cable.
3. Loosen the air conditioner and alternator as necessary and remove the drive belts.
4. Remove the crankshaft pulley and four pulley-to-sprocket bolts. Remove the pulley and damper or washer as applicable.

NOTE: it is not necessary to remove the pulley if only the camshaft sprocket is being removed.

5. Drain the engine coolant and loosen the water pump bolts to relieve the tension on the timing belt.
6. Remove the timing belt lower cover.
7. Remove the timing belt.
8. Align one of the holes in the camshaft timing sprocket with the head bolt behind the sprocket. Using a socket on the head bolt to keep the sprocket from rotating, remove the sprocket retaining bolt and washer.
9. Remove the camshaft sprocket.
10. The crankshaft sprocket may be removed.
11. Pull the crankshaft sprocket with an installation tool. Make sure that the timing mark is facing out and that the key is installed.

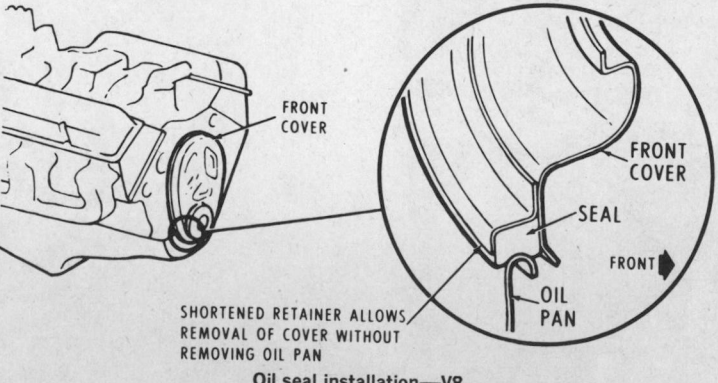

FRONT COVER

FRONT COVER

SEAL

FRONT

OIL PAN

SHORTENED RETAINER ALLOWS REMOVAL OF COVER WITHOUT REMOVING OIL PAN

Oil seal installation—V8
(© Chevrolet Div., G.M. Corp)

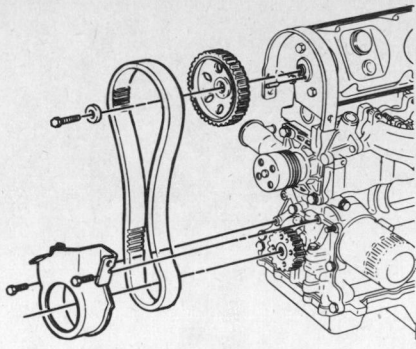

Timing belt and sprockets
(© Chevrolet Div., G.M. Corp)

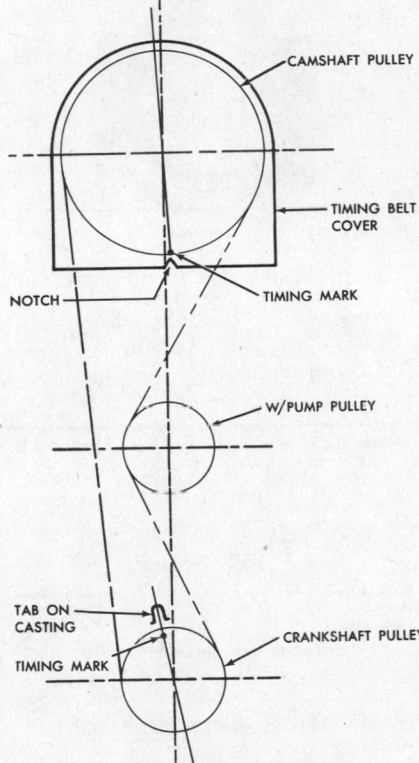

Timing sprocket alignment marks
(© Chevrolet Div., G.M. Corp)

12. To install the camshaft sprocket, align the dowel in the camshaft with the locating hole in the end of the camshaft.
13. Install the sprocket retaining bolt, tightening to 80 ft. lbs.
14. Align the timing mark on the camshaft sprocket with the notch on the timing belt upper cover and the crankshaft sprocket timing mark with the cast rib on the oil pump cover.
15. Install the timing belt on the crankshaft sprocket, then with the back of the belt positioned in the water pump track, install the belt on the camshaft sprocket. Make sure that both sprockets maintain their indexed positions.
16. Install the lower timing belt cover, using anti-seize compound on the threads of the bolts and

tightening them to 50 in. lbs.
17. Adjust the timing belt tension as described under "Water Pump Removal and Installation" above, Steps 11 and 12.
18. Fill the cooling system.
19. Install the accessory drive pulley to the crankshaft sprocket, aligning the tang on the pulley with the keyway on the crankshaft. Install the damper locating dowel in the locating hole of the sprocket.
20. Loosely install the four sprocket bolts, then install the crankshaft (center) bolt. Tighten the crankshaft bolt to 80 ft. lbs. and the four sprocket bolts to 15 ft. lbs.
21. Install the alternator and air conditioning compressor as applicable and adjust the belts.
22. Install the engine front cover, fan and fan spacer.
23. Connect the battery cable and remove the bolt from the hood hold-open link.

Timing Chain Replacement —V8

To replace the chain, remove the radiator core, water pump, the harmonic balancer, and the crankcase front cover. This will allow access to the timing chain. Crank the engine until the timing marks on both sprockets are nearest each other and in line between the shaft centers. Then take out the three bolts that hold the camshaft gear to the camshaft. This gear is a light press fit on the camshaft and will come off easily. It is located by a dowel.

The chain comes off with the camshaft gear.

A gear puller will be required to remove the crankshaft gear.

Without disturbing the position of the engine, mount the new crankshaft gear on the shaft, and mount the chain over the camshaft gear. Arrange the camshaft gear in such a way that the timing marks will line up between the shaft centers and the camshaft locating dowel will enter the dowel hole in the cam sprocket.

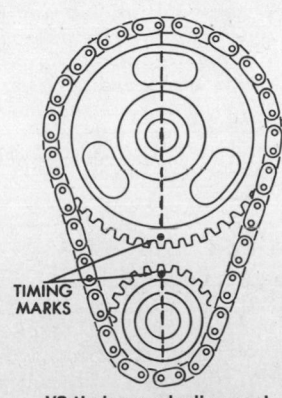

V8 timing mark alignment

Place the cam sprocket, with its chain mounted over it, in position on the front of the car and pull up with the three bolts that hold it to the camshaft. Do not drive the camshaft sprocket onto the shaft. The expansion plug at the rear of the block could be dislodged.

After the gears are in place, turn the engine two full revolutions to make certain that the timing marks are in correct alignment between the shaft centers.

End-play of the V8 camshaft should be zero.

Camshaft Cover Removal and Installation—4 Cylinder

1. Raise the hood and install a bolt in the hood hold-open link.
2. Disconnect the negative battery cable.
3. Remove the air cleaner and the vent tube (at cam cover).
4. Remove the PCV valve from the cam cover.
5. Remove the cam cover screws and the cover.
6. To install, reverse the above procedure. The gasket is reusable. The oil filler cap is at the forward end of the cover. Tighten the cam cover screws to 35 in. lbs.

Camshaft Removal and Installation

4 Cylinder

NOTE: A special valve tappet depressing tool is necessary for camshaft removal. This tool is only available through Chevrolet.

1. Remove the hood.
2. Remove the camshaft timing sprocket.
3. Remove the three screws securing the camshaft seal and retainer assembly and timing cover to the cylinder head.
4. Inspect the seal, prying it out and replacing it if necessary.
5. Remove the camshaft cover.
6. Disconnect the fuel line at the carburetor.
7. Remove:
   a. Idle solenoid from its bracket.
   b. The choke coil, cover and rod assembly.
   c. Ignition distributor.
8. Raise the vehicle on a hoist, disconnect the front engine mounts at the body attachment, raise the front of the engine and install wood blocks, about 1-1/2 in. thick, between the engine mounts and the body.
9. Install camshaft removal tool on the cylinder head to hold down the lifters so that the camshaft may be removed.
   a. Position the tool so that the attaching holes are aligned

with the lower cam cover bolt holes and the tappet levers of the tool are aligned to depress both valves of each cylinder.

b. Back off the bolts in the bottom of the tool so that they are not contacting the bosses beneath the tool.

c. Install the tool attaching bolts, tightening them securely.

d. Tighten the bolts in the bottom of the tool until they just touch the bosses of the cylinder head. Before depressing the tappets, rotate the crankshaft pulley timing mark 90° clockwise from the timing mark on the tab. This assures that the pistons are not at TDC and will prevent valve-to-piston contact.

e. Grease the ball end of the lever depressing bolts and tighten the bolts to depress the tappets.

NOTE: torque the lever bolts to 10 ft. lbs. If more tightening is required, check to see that the tool is properly installed, then proceed cautiously to prevent damaging the depressing lever.

10. Slide the camshaft forward until it clears the head.

NOTE: the camshaft bearings may be removed. It is not necessary to remove the camshaft end plug. Gently tap out the bearings, starting at the forward end. Tap out the rear bearing slowly into the distributor housing, being careful not to unseat the end plug. Crush the rear bearing to remove it from the distributor housing. Install, starting with the rear bearing. The oil holes in the bearings must align with the oil holes in the case. On the first two bearings the oil holes are at 11 o'clock (as seen from the front of the engine) and the oil groove in the number one bearing toward the front of the engine.

11. Install the camshaft with the journals seated in the bores.

12. With the car up on a hoist, raise the front of the engine and remove the wood blocks from the engine mounts.

13. Install the front engine mounts, then lower the vehicle.

14. Using a new gasket, install the timing belt upper cover and retainer plate and seal assembly. Tighten the retaining bolts to 15 ft. lbs.

15. Using a dial indicator, measure the camshaft end-play. If it is not 0.004-0.012 in., select a camshaft retainer (according to cam locator thickness) which will provide more or less end-play as required.

16. Remove the tappet depressing

tool by first releasing the tappet depressing lever bolts, and then removing the tool attaching bolts.

17. Install:
  a. Camshaft timing sprocket.
  b. The timing belt.
  c. Front engine cover.
  d. Distributor.
  e. Vehicle hood.

18. Adjust the valve tappets.

19. Install the camshaft cover.

20. Install and adjust the carburetor choke coil, cover and rod assembly.

21. Connect the carburetor fuel line.

22. Install the idle solenoid to the bracket.

23. Check and adjust the ignition timing.

V8

1. Drain the cooling system and remove the radiator. Remove the hood.

2. Remove the water pump and the timing case cover.

3. Turn the crankshaft until the timing marks on the camshaft and crankshaft gears are aligned.

4. Remove the valve covers and loosen each rocker arm nut enough to turn the rocker to the side and remove the pushrods. Keep the pushrods in order when they are removed from the engine.

5. Remove the distributor cap and mark the position of the rotor relative to the distributor body and the position of the distributor body relative to the engine. Remove the distributor.

6. Remove the intake manifold, then remove the valve lifters from the engine. Keep the lifters in order when they are removed from the engine.

7. Remove the fuel pump.

8. Remove the timing chain and sprockets from the engine.

9. Install two 5/16 in. 18x4 bolts in the holes in the front of the cam and carefully slide it out of the engine.

NOTE: On some engine and model combinations it will be necessary to disconnect the motor mounts and jack up the front of the engine or remove the grille from the car in order to gain adequate clearance in front of the engine to get the camshaft out of the engine.

10. Installation is the reverse of removal.

Piston & Rod Installation

NOTE: 4 cylinder oversize pistons were not supplied initially, since there was no mechanical means available for duplicating the cylinder bore electrochemical etching process. A mechanical honing process has been per-

Piston marking (© Chevrolet Div., G.M. Corp)

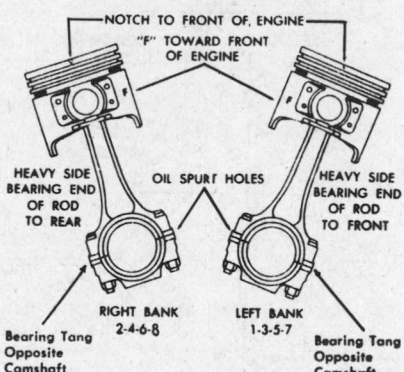

Piston-to-rod relationship—V8

fected and oversize pistons are now available.

The F on the 4 cylinder piston must face toward the front of the engine. On V8s, install the piston with the tang on the connecting rod bearing on the side away from the camshaft. Be sure that the pistons and rods are installed in their original locations or in the cylinder to which it was fitted.

Lubrication

Oil Pan and Baffle Removal and Installation—4 Cylinder

1. Raise the vehicle and drain the engine oil. Raise the front of the engine, being careful not to distort the pan.

2. Support the engine with a jack and remove the frame crossmember and both front crossmember braces.

3. Disconnect the steering idler arm at the frame side rail. On

vehicles with air conditioning, disconnect the idler arm at the relay rod.

4. Mark the position of the steering linkage pitman arm to the steering gear pitman shaft and remove the pitman arm.

NOTE: do not rotate the steering gear pitman shaft while the linkage is disconnected, because the steering wheel alignment will be changed.

5. Remove the flywheel cover or converter underpan.

6. Remove the oil pan bolts, tap the oil pan to break the seal, then remove the pan.

7. Remove the pick-up screen-to-support retaining bolt and the pick-up screen-to-baffle support bolts, then remove the support from the baffle.

8. Remove the bolt which secures the oil drain back tube to the baffle, then rotate the baffle 90° toward the left side of the car and remove the baffle from the pick-up screen.

9. The oil pump screen and pick up tube may be removed as follows:
   a. Remove the two self-locking mounting bolts (in block).
   b. Lightly tap on the U section of the pick-up tube to remove the tube from the casting.
   c. If damaged, the tube and screen assembly are replaced as a unit.
   d. Apply sealing compound to the pick-up tube sealing surface.
   e. Install the tube into its bore, using an open end wrench on the tube boss, tapping the wrench with a mallet. Make sure that the retaining brackets are aligned with the bolt holes.
   f. Using anti-seize compound on the threads, install the retaining bolts. Tighten the bolts to 25 ft. lbs.

10. Install the oil pan and baffle in the reverse order of removal. Use sealing compound on the oil pump gasket surface. Tighten the oil pan bolts to 15 ft. lbs. See "Steering Linkage Removal and Installation" for correct pitman arm and idler arm installation procedure. Tighten frame crossmember and brace bolts to 35 ft. lbs.

Oil Pan Removal and Installation—V8

1. Disconnect the battery.
2. Raise the car and drain the oil.
3. Disconnect the exhaust crossover pipe.
4. Remove the converter housing underpan and splash shield.
5. Scribe marks on each side of the frame crossmember and support the engine. Remove the frame crossmember.
6. Disconnect the steering idler arm at the frame side rail.
7. Disconnect the starter brace and remove the starter.
8. Remove the oil pan bolts and remove the oil pan.
9. Installation is the reverse of removal. Use new gaskets with sealer as a retainer and be sure to match the scribe marks when installing the crossmember. Fill the engine with oil.

Oil Pump Removal and Installation

4 Cylinder

1. Remove:
   a. Front engine cover.
   b. Accessory drive pulley.
   c. Timing belt.
   d. Timing belt lower cover.
   e. Crankshaft sprocket.
2. Raise the vehicle on a hoist and drain the engine oil.
3. Remove the oil pan and baffle.
4. Remove the oil pump bolts and the pump.
5. Inspect the oil pump for wear. The pump gears and body are not serviced separately. Replacement of the entire oil pump is required. Check the pressure regulator for free operation.
6. When installing, clean all gasket surfaces. Be sure that the pump drive key is installed properly. Use anti-seize compound on the threads of the pump mounting bolts, tightening them to 15 ft. lbs. The stud is installed in the upper right (facing pump) and tightened to 30 ft. lbs. Install the oil pan before tightening the timing cover bolts.

V8

1. Remove the oil pan.
2. Remove the bolt holding the oil pump to the rear main bearing cap.
3. Remove the pump and the extension shaft.
4. Installation is the reverse of removal. Align the slot on the top of the extension shaft with the drive tang on the lower end of the distributor driveshaft. The installed position of the oil pump screen should be parallel to the oil pan rails.

Oil Pump (Front Cover) Seal Removal and Installation —4 Cylinder

1. Remove the following:
   a. Engine front cover.
   b. Accessory drive pulley.
   c. Timing belt.
   d. Timing belt lower cover.
   e. Crankshaft timing sprocket.
2. Pry out the old seal, being careful not to damage the housing seal surfaces.
3. Coat the lips of the new seal with oil and apply sealing compound to the outside diameter of the seal.
4. Install the seal with the closed end outward.
5. Install all components removed in Step 1 above.

Rear Main Oil Seal Removal and Installation

4 Cylinder

NOTE: This repair can be made without removing the engine, but the transmission must be removed so that the crankshaft can be lowered.

1. Remove the oil pan and baffle.
2. Remove the rear main bearing cap and discard the lower seal.
3. Loosen the remaining bearing caps to allow the crankshaft to be lowered.
4. Push the upper seal on one end enough so that the other end can be grasped with pliers. Pull out the upper seal.
5. Cut and form a new braided fabric upper seal in the bearing cap. Taper the end of the seal and insert a piece of soft wire through the seal about 1/4 in. from the end. Wrap the wire around the seal to form a secure attachment.
6. Thread the wire through the upper seal groove, then start the seal and pull it into position.
7. Tighten all the bearing caps except the rear cap to 65 ft. lbs.
8. Cut the seal flush to 1/64 in. below the bearing edge, making a clean cut and leaving no raveled edges.
9. Install and cut a seal in the rear main bearing cap.
10. Install the rear main bearing cap and measure the clearance with Plastigage, tightening the cap bolts to 65 ft. lbs. If the

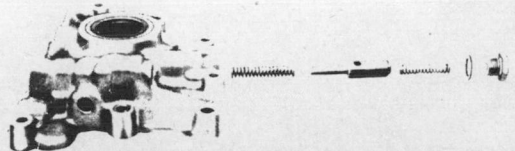

Oil pump pressure regulator (4 cylinder)
(© Chevrolet Div., G.M. Corp)

bearing clearance is within specifications, the seal is properly seated.

11. Install the bearing cap, tightening to 65 ft. lbs.
12. Install rear main bearing cap side sealant. This is available in a kit, complete with plunger applicator, from Chevrolet. Force the compound firmly into place to ensure that there are no air bubbles.
13. Install the oil pan and baffle.

V8

The rear main bearing seal may be replaced without removing the crankshaft. Seals should only be replaced as a pair. Fabrication of a seal installation tool will prevent damaging the bead on the cylinder block. The seal lips should face the front of the engine when properly installed.

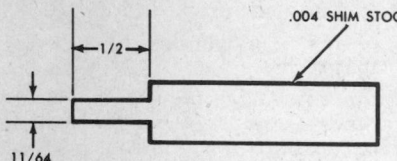

Oil seal installation tool
(© Chevrolet Div., G.M. Corp)

1. Remove the oil pan and pump, and remove the rear main bearing cap.
2. Pry the lower seal out of the bearing cap with a screwdriver, being careful not to gouge the cap surface.
3. Remove the upper seal by lightly tapping on one end with a brass pin punch until the other end can be grasped and pulled out with pliers.
4. Clean the bearing cap, cylinder block, and crankshaft mating surfaces with solvent. Inspect all these surfaces for gouges, nicks, and burrs.
5. Apply light engine oil to the seal lips and bead, but keep the seal ends clean.
6. Insert the tip of the installation tool between the crankshaft and the seal seat of the cylinder block. Place the seal between the tip of the tool and the crankshaft, so that the bead contacts the tip of the tool.
7. Be sure that the seal lip is facing the front of the engine, and work the seal around the crankshaft, using the installation tool to protect the seal from the corner of the cylinder block.
NOTE: do not remove the tool until the opposite end of the seal is flush with the cylinder block surface.
8. Remove the installation tool, being careful not to pull the seal out at the same time.
9. Using the same procedure, install the lower seal into the bearing cap. Use your finger and thumb to lever the seal into the cap.
10. Apply sealer to the cylinder block only where the cap mates to the surface. Do not apply sealer to the seal ends.
11. Install the rear cap and torque the bolts to specifications. Install the oil pan and pump.

Sealant application—V8
(© Chevrolet Div., G.M. Corp)

CLUTCH

Clutch Pedal Free Travel Adjustment

Adjustment for normal clutch wear is accomplished by turning the clutch fork ball stud counterclockwise to give .90 ± .25 in. lash at clutch pedal.

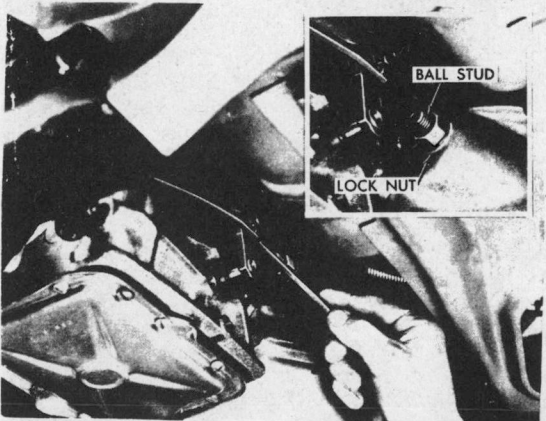

Clutch ball stud adjustment (© Chevrolet Div., G.M. Corp)

1. Remove ball stud cap and loosen locknut on ball stud end located to the right of the transmission on the clutch housing.
2. Adjust ball stud to obtain .90 ± .25 in. free travel.
3. Tighten locknut to 25 ft lbs. being careful not to change adjustment and install ball stud cap.
4. Check operation of clutch.

Clutch Disc Removal and Installation

1. Raise vehicle on hoist.
2. Remove transmission as outlined in this section.
3. Remove clutch fork cover then disconnect clutch return spring and control cable from clutch fork.
4. Remove main drive gear oil seal from clutch release bearing sleeve.
5. Remove flywheel housing lower cover.
6. Remove flywheel housing from engine.
7. To remove the release bearing from clutch fork and sleeve, slide lever off ball stud against spring action. If necessary to replace ball stud, remove cap, locknut and stud from housing.
8. If assembly marks on clutch assembly and flywheel are not dis-

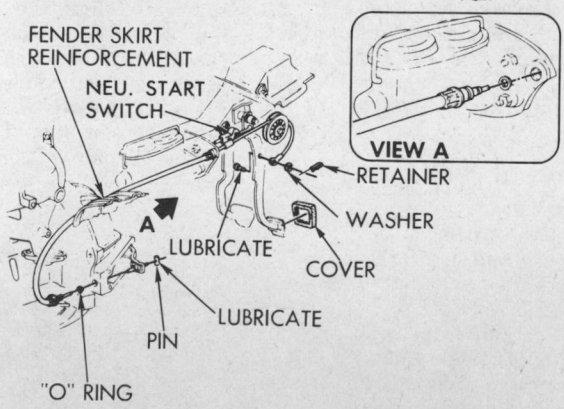

Clutch control cable (© Chevrolet Div., G.M. Corp)

tinguishable, remark with paint or center-punch.

9. Loosen clutch cover to flywheel, attaching bolts one turn at a time until spring pressure is released, to avoid bending clutch cover flange.

10. Support the pressure plate and cover assembly then remove the bolts and clutch assembly.

Caution Do not disassemble the clutch cover, spring and pressure plate for repair. If defective replace complete assembly.

11. Index alignment marks on clutch assembly and flywheel. Place driven plate on pressure plate with long end of splined end facing forward, damper springs inside pressure plate, and insert a dummy clutch gear shaft through the cover and driven plate.

12. Position the complete assembly against the flywheel and insert the dummy shaft into the pilot bearing in the crankshaft.

13. Index the alignment marks and install clutch cover to flywheel bolts finger-tight.

Caution Tighten all bolts evenly and gradually until tight to avoid possible clutch distortion. Torque bolts 18 ft. bs. and remove dummy shaft.

14. Lubricate the clutch fork ball socket and the fingers at the release bearing with a high melting point grease such as graphite grease.

15. Lubricate the recess on the inside of the throwout bearing collar and the fork groove with a light coat of graphite grease. Install fork in housing but not on stud.

16. Install bearing on sleeve, then position clutch fork over bearing in housing and slide fork onto ball stud.

17. Install flywheel housing and lower cover. Tighten bolts to 25 ft. lbs.

18. Install transmission as outlined previously.

19. Adjust clutch as previously outlined.

20. Lower and remove vehicle from hoist.

MANUAL TRANSMISSION

The Opel-made transmissions used in 1971-72 were replaced with Saginaw three and four-speed units in 1973. These are fully synchronized and are similar to those used throughout the Chevrolet line.

A five-speed Borg-Warner T-50 transmission is optional on 1975 and later models. It is also available on the 1976 Cosworth Vega. Fourth gear is direct drive with fifth gear an overdrive. The transmission is shifted by a single shift rail enclosed within the transmission.

Beginning 1976, the "70 mm" four-speed transmission is used on base models. This light weight transmission is also used in the Chevette. Gear shifting is done by an internal shifter shaft.

Linkage Adjustment

1971-72 Four-Speed

The reverse gearshift blocker adjustment can only be made on the four-speed transmission. This adjustment is made at the selector shaft on the left side of the transmission.

1. Shift into second gear.
2. Adjust the selector ring so that the shift lever finger ball has equal clearance on both sides in the intermediate lever hole.
3. Back off the selector ring a quarter turn and tighten the locknut.

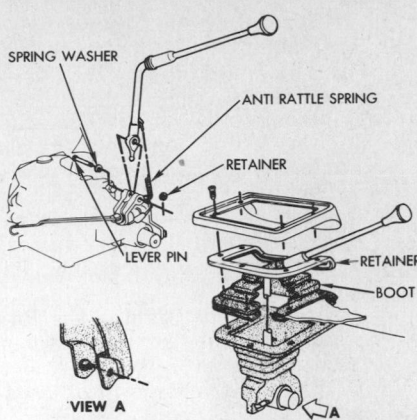

1971-72 shift control lever installation
(© Chevrolet Div., G.M. Corp)

1973 and Later Saginaw Three and Four-Speed

1. Turn the ignition switch to "Off" and place the shift lever in neutral.
2. Raise the car.
3. Loosen the lock nuts on the control rods. Position the transmission side cover levers in their neutral detents.

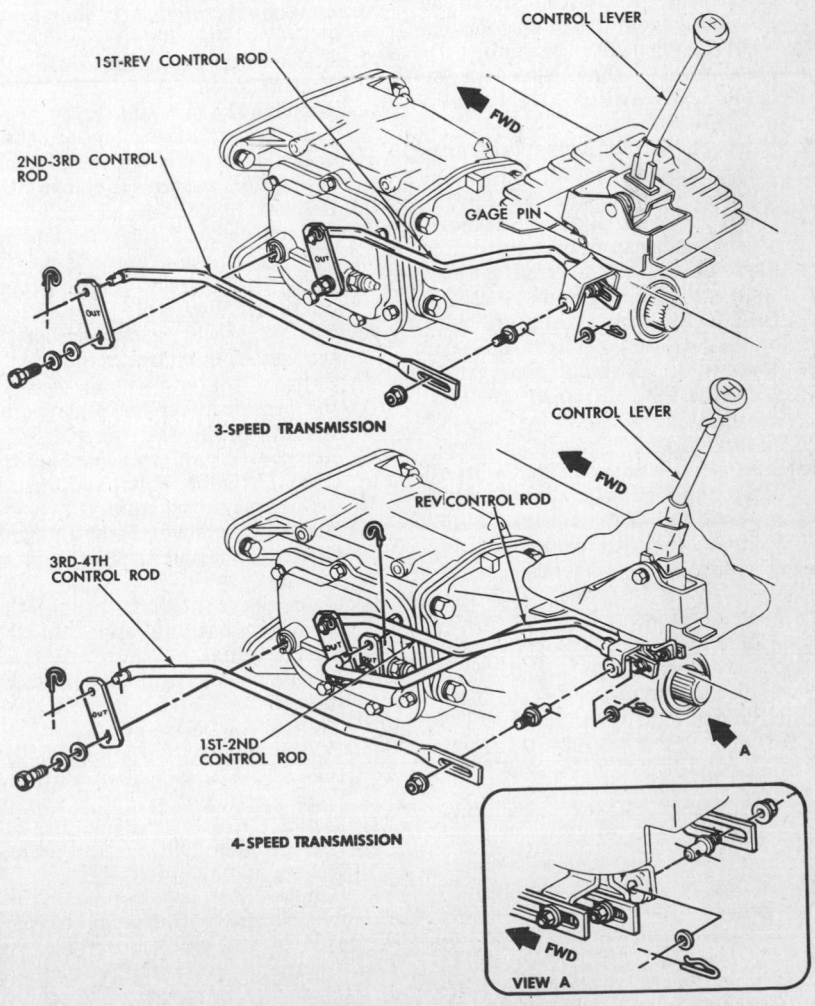

1973 and later three and four-speed linkage
(© Chevrolet Div., G.M. Corp)

4. With the floor shift lever in neutral, align the shifter levers and insert a gauge pin into the levers and bracket.

5. Tighten the First/Reverse (First/Second on four-speed) control rod lock nut against its swivel.

6. Tighten the Second/Third (Third/Fourth on four-speed) control rod lock nut against its swivel.

7. On four-speeds, tighten the Reverse control rod lock nut against its swivel.

NOTE: *All lock nuts are tightened to 120 in. lbs.*

8. Remove the gauge pin and check shifter operation.

Transmission Removal and Installation

1971-72

1. Place transmission shift lever in neutral and pull the boot up.

2. Unhook the antirattle coil spring. Remove the shift finger (lower end of the lever) pin retaining clip and pin. Remove shift lever.

3. Raise the vehicle and drain the lubricant from transmission.

4. Remove driveshaft assembly.

5. Disconnect the speedometer cable, TCS switch and back-up lamp switch.

6. Remove crossmember-to-transmission mount bolts.

7. Support engine with an appropriate jack stand and remove crossmember-to-frame bolts. Remove crossmember from vehicle.

8. Remove transmission to clutch housing upper retaining bolts and install guide pins in holes.

9. Remove lower bolts, then slide transmission rearward and remove from vehicle.

NOTE: inspect throwout bearing support gasket located beneath lip of support. If defective, replace gasket before installing transmission.

10. Lightly lubricate inside diameter of clutch drive gear seal and install seal on drive gear.

11. Position new gasket to face of clutch housing. The gasket can be temporarily retained by a small amount of grease.

12. Position transmission to clutch housing and slide forward, piloting clutch gear in to pilot bearing.

NOTE: make certain main drive gear splines are clean and dry.

13. Install transmission-to-clutch housing retaining bolts and lockwashers.

14. Position crossmember to frame and loosely install retaining bolts. Install crossmember-to-transmission mount bolts. Tighten all retaining bolts to

specifications. Remove engine support.

Caution Check position of engine in front mounts and align as required.

15. Connect speedometer cable, back-up lamp switch and TCS switch.

16. Install driveshaft assembly.

17. Fill transmission to proper level. Lower vehicle.

18. Lubricate shift finger bolt and spherical end of shaft. Install shift lever in shift housing and install bolt. Secure with retaining clip.

19. Install shift lever spring. Position shift lever boot and bezel to floor pan. Install retaining screws.

20. Check operation of transmission.

1973 and Later

Three and Four-Speed

NOTE: *Transmission removal beginning 1975 on Monza and 1976 on Vega will require additional work due to the torque arm rear suspension. The torque arm serves as an upper control arm, is rigidly mounted to the differential, and is mounted to the transmission through a rubber bushing.*

1. Raise the car and drain the transmission.

2. Remove the driveshaft.

3. Disconnect the speedometer cable, TCS switch, and the back-up light switch. Remove the damper.

4. Detach the control rods and levers from the transmission, tie them together, and position them out of the way.

5. Remove the crossmember-to-transmission mounting bolts.

6. Support the engine and remove the crossmember-to-frame bolts. Remove the crossmember.

7. Remove the top transmission-to-clutch housing bolts and install guide pins in the holes.

8. Remove the lower bolts and pull the transmission back and out of the car.

9. Guide the input shaft through the throwout bearing and into the pilot bearing.

10. Install the transmission retaining bolts and lockwashers. Tighten the bolts to 40 ft lbs.

11. Position the crossmember on the frame and install the retaining bolts hand-tight.

12. Install the crossmember-to-transmission bolts and then tighten all bolts to 28 ft lbs.

13. Remove the engine support.

14. Install the transmission control rods to the shifter. Adjust the linkage as previously outlined.

15. Connect the speedometer cable, TCS switch, and back-up light switch.

16. Install the driveshaft.

17. Fill the transmission to the level of the filler plug.

18. Lower the car and check transmission operation.

Five-Speed

1. Remove the shift lever boot bezel and slide the shift boot upward on the shift lever.

2. Remove the foam insulator over the shift lever bolts. Remove the four shift lever bolts and remove the shift lever.

3. Raise the car and remove the driveshaft.

4. Remove the damper assembly, converter bracket, and torque arm bracket. Disconnect the speedometer cable and back-up light switch.

5. Support the transmission with a jack and remove the transmission support.

6. Remove the transmission-to-clutch housing bolts and slide the exhaust bracket forward. Slide the transmission to the rear and remove it.

7. To install, make sure that the main drive gear splines are clean and dry. Position the transmission to the clutch housing and slide it forward.

8. Slide the exhaust bracket into place and install the transmission-to-clutch housing attaching bolts.

9. Install the rear transmission mount and transmission support. Install the converter bracket, damper, and torque arm.

10. Install the driveshaft, connect the speedometer cable and back-up light switch.

11. Fill the transmission with 3 pints of Dexron® II automatic transmission fluid.

12. Lower the car and install the shift lever and foam insulator. Install the shift lever boot and bezel.

13. Check transmission for proper operation.

AUTOMATIC TRANSMISSION

Several automatic transmissions have been available in Vega and Monza models. The aluminum Powerglide is the two-speed unit. The Torque Drive transmission is a Powerglide without the automatic shifting mechanism. Torque Drive was dropped after 1972, while Powerglide was discontinued in mid-1973. A three-speed Turbo Hydra-Matic 350 transmission became available in 1972. Beginning February 1973, a Turbo Hydra-Matic 250 was introduced to replace the 350. The 250 is similar to the 350, except that the intermediate clutch assembly has been replaced by an externally adjustable intermediate band assembly. The 250 can be identified by the band adjusting screw and locknut on the right side of the case. Starting 1976, a new three-speed transmission is offered: Turbo Hydra-Matic 200. The light weight Turbo Hydra-Matic 200 transmission can be identified by the word "METRIC" stamped into the bottom of the fluid pan.

Neutral Safety Switch Adjustment

1. Remove four screws securing floor console.
2. Disconnect the electrical plugs on the back-up, neutral start, and seat belt buzzer (1973 and later) contacts of the neutral safety switch.
3. Place shift lever in Neutral.
4. Remove two screws securing shift indicator plate.
5. Remove two screws securing shift lever curved cover.
6. Remove two screws securing neutral start switch to lever assembly.
   NOTE: screws are hidden beneath lever cover.
7. Tilt switch assembly to right as you lift switch out of lever hole.
8. Make sure shift lever is in Neutral before installing switch assembly.
9. Assemble switch assembly to control lever bracket by inserting drive tang into hole in neutral start switch lever.
   NOTE: When installing the same neutral switch, align the contact support slot with the service adjustment hole in the switch and insert a 3/32 in. drill to hold the switch in neutral. Remove the drill after the switch is fastened to the shift lever mounting bracket.
10. Tighten two mounting screws securing switch assembly to lever bracket.
11. Install curved shift lever cover and secure with two screws.
12. Install shift indicator plate and attach with two screws.
13. Moving control lever out of Neutral will shear the switch plastic locating pin.
14. Plug electrical connectors into switch assembly; apply parking brake and start vehicle—check for starting in Neutral and Park only. Also check for back-up lamps on in reverse.
15. Turn off ignition and install console cover securing with four screws.

Shift Linkage Adjustment
Powerglide, Torque Drive
This adjustment gives about 0.05

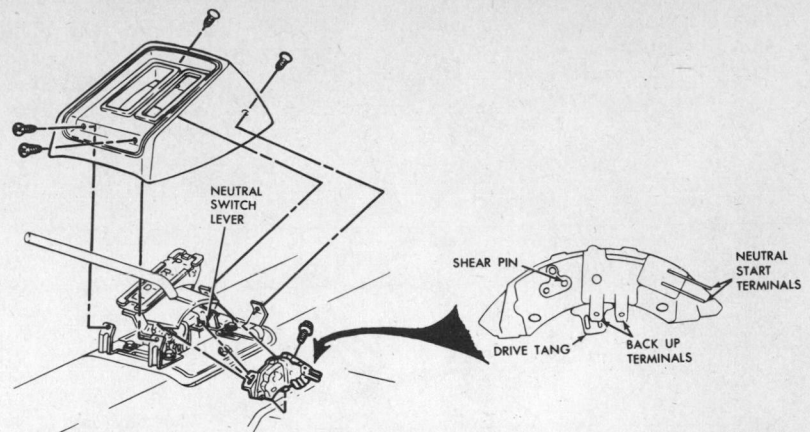

1971-72 neutral safety switch adjustment—1973 and later switch has two additional terminals for seat belt alarm (© Chevrolet Div., G.M. Corp)

in. overtravel in each gear shift position to provide full engagement.

1. Loosen the two shift rod adjusting nuts at the swivel. The swivel is attached to the floor-shift lever lower lever.
2. Turn the shift lever on the transmission all the way clockwise. This is the Park detent position. Turn the lever counterclockwise two detents to the neutral detent position.
3. Make sure that the floorshift is in the neutral position.
4. Push forward lightly on the floorshift assembly lower lever until the floorshift lever can be felt against its neutral detent. Hold the lower lever in place.
5. Hold a 0.073 in. thick spacer in front of the swivel. Tighten the front adjusting nut to clamp the spacer between the nut and swivel.
6. Pull out the spacer and lightly pull back on the floorshift assembly lower lever. Tighten the rear adjusting nut.

1972 Turbo Hydra-Matic

Use the Powerglide and Torque Drive procedure, substituting the following steps:

4. Pull back lightly on the floor-shift assembly lower lever until the floorshift lever can be felt to be against its neutral detent. Hold the lower lever in place.
5. Hold a 0.073 in. thick spacer between the nut and swivel.
6. Pull the spacer out and pull lightly forward on the floorshift assembly lower lever. Tighten the front adjusting nut.
   NOTE: Late 1972 models and all 1973 and later models are equipped with slotted control rods. Adjustment of this linkage is given later.

1973 and Later Turbo Hydra-Matic

1. Loosen the nut and swivel at the transmission lever.
2. Set the transmission lever in Neutral by moving it counterclockwise to the L1 detent and

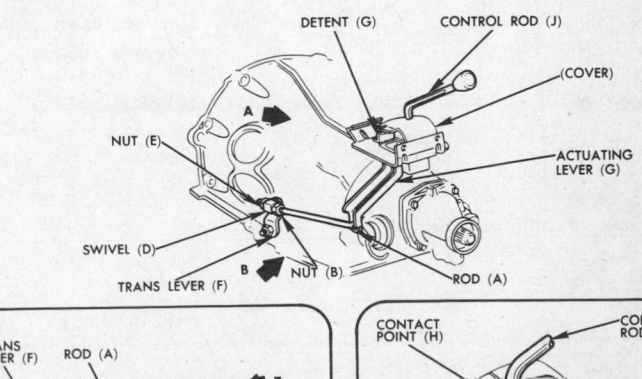

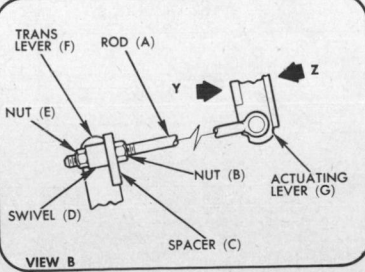

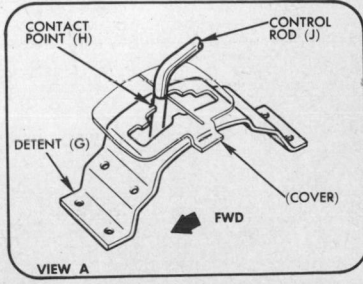

1972 Turbo Hydra-Matic 350 linkage adjustment (© Chevrolet Div., G.M. Corp)

then clockwise three detent positions to Neutral.

3. Position the shift lever in the

Neutral notch of the detent plate.

4. Place the flat of the swivel into

the slot of the control rod. Install the washer and cotter pin.

5. Tighten the locknut. Adjust the neutral safety switch, if necessary.

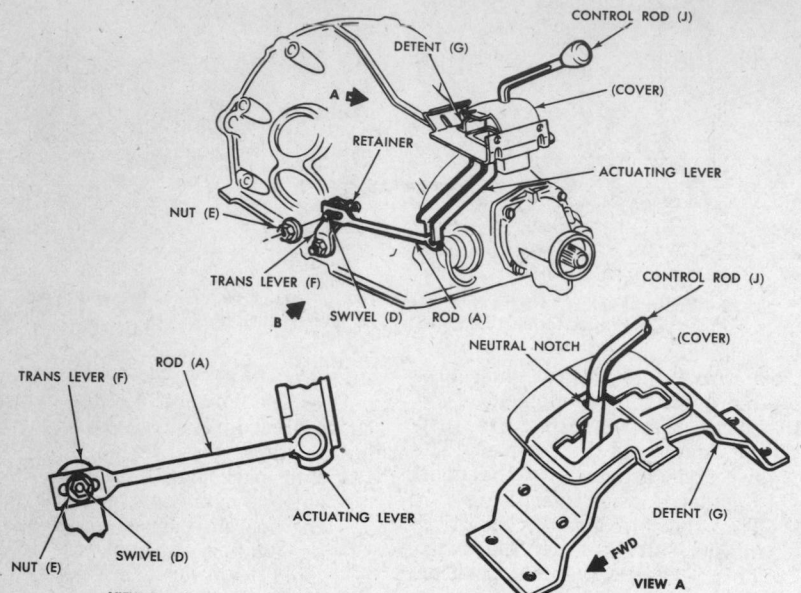

1973-77 Turbo Hydra-Matic linkage
(© Chevrolet Div., G.M. Corp)

Powerglide Throttle Valve Linkage Adjustment

1. Hold the accelerator pedal all the way down.
2. Unclip and detach the rear end of the throttle valve control rod (horizontal rod).
3. The bellcrank lever stud should be all the way forward in the slot at the front of the throttle valve control rod.
4. Hold the lever at the transmission against its internal stop.
5. If the rear end of the throttle valve control rod does not align with the hole in the lever, pull out the retaining clip from the sleeve in the center of the rod. Adjust the sleeve to lengthen or shorten the rod.

NOTE: The sleeve is adjustable one turn at a time.

6. Install the throttle valve control rod in the lever hole and attach the clip.

Turbo Hydra-Matic Downshift Cable Adjustment

1. Remove the air cleaner.
2. Insert a screwdriver on each side of the snap-lock on the bracket at the front of the transmission and pry up to release the lock.
3. Compress the lock tabs and disconnect the snap-lock assembly from the bracket.
4. Position the carburetor lever in the wide open throttle position.
5. Hold the carburetor lever in position and push the snap-lock on the cable down until the top is flush with the cable.

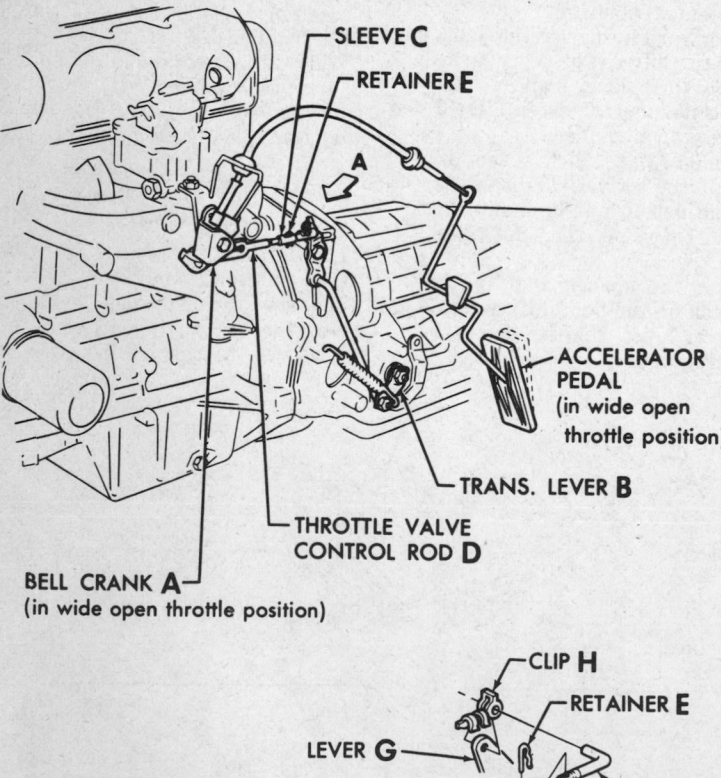

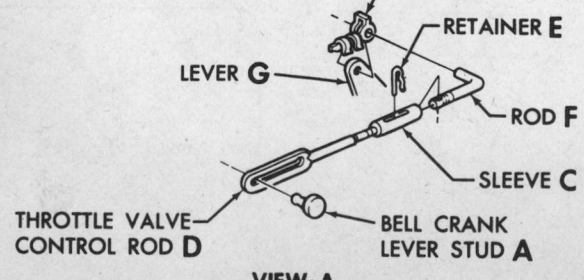

Powerglide throttle valve linkage adjustment (© Chevrolet Div., G.M. Corp)

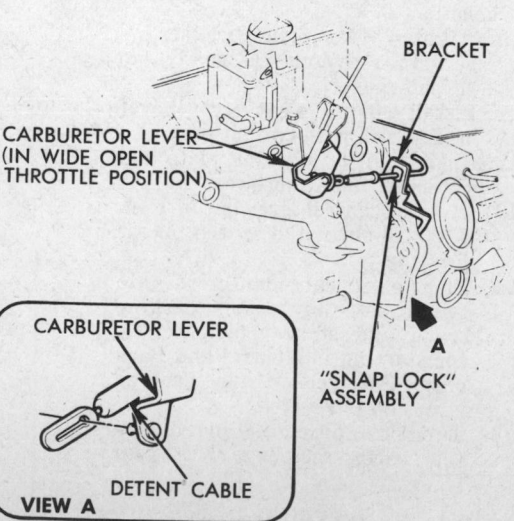

Turbo Hydra-Matic 200, 250 and 350 detent cable adjustment
(© Chevrolet Div., G.M. Corp)

NOTE: The cable should not be lubricated.

6. Install the air cleaner.

Powerglide, Torque Drive Low Band Adjustment

1. Position the shift lever in neutral.
2. Remove the protective cap from the adjusting screw.
3. Loosen the locknut ¼ turn and hold it with a wrench during the entire adjusting procedure.
4. Tighten the adjusting nut to 70 in. lbs, using a 7/32 allen wrench.
5. Back off the adjusting nut exactly three turns for a band used less than 6,000 miles. Back off exactly four turns for a band used 6,000 miles or more.
6. Torque the locknut to 15 ft lbs. and replace the cap.

Turbo Hydra-Matic 250 Intermediate Band Adjustment

1. Position the shift lever in Neutral.
2. Loosen the locknut and tighten the adjusting screw to 30 in lbs.
3. Back the screw out three turns and then tighten the locknut to 15 ft lbs.

Pan Removal and Installation, Fluid and Filter Change

The fluid should be drained with the transmission warm.

1. Support the transmission at the vibration damper. If necessary, remove the crossmember.
2. Prepare a large pan to catch the transmission fluid.
3. Loosen all the pan screws, then pull one corner down to drain most of the fluid.
4. Remove the pan screws and empty out the pan. The pan can be cleaned out with solvent but it must be dried thoroughly before replacement. Be very careful not to leave any lint or threads from rags in the pan.
5. Remove the filter or strainer retaining bolt (two on Turbo Hydra-Matic 200, 250, and 350). A reuseable strainer is used on two-speed transmissions and the Turbo Hydra-Matic 200 and 250. The strainer may be cleaned in solvent and air-dried thoroughly. Filters are to be replaced. Use a new gasket on all other models.
6. Install the new filter or cleaned strainer.
7. Install the pan with a new gasket. Tighten the bolts evenly (12 ft lbs) in a criss-cross pattern.
8. Replace the crossmembers if removed.
9. Add DEXRON® or DEXRON® II transmission fluid through the dipstick tube. Add 6 pints for

Turbo Hydra-Matic 200; 5 pints for Turbo Hydra-Matic 250; and 3 pints for the 350, Torque Drive, and Powerglide.

10. Start the engine and let it idle. Do not race the engine. Shift through all the indicator positions, holding the brakes. Check the fluid level with the engine idling in Park. The level should be between the two dimples on the dipstick, about ¼ in. below the ADD mark. Add fluid as necessary.
11. Check the fluid level after the car has been driven enough to thoroughly warm up the transmission. The level should be at the FULL mark on the dipstick. If the transmission is overfilled, the excess must be drained off. Overfilling causes aerated fluid, resulting in transmission slippage and probable damage.

U-JOINTS

Driveshaft Removal and Installation

1. Raise and support the car. Mark relationship of shaft to companion flange and disconnect the rear universal joint by removing trunnion bearing U-bolts. Tape bearing cups to trunnion to prevent losing the bearing rollers.
2. Withdraw driveshaft front yoke from transmission by moving shaft rearward and passing it under the axle housing. Cover the transmission opening to prevent fluid or oil loss.
3. Inspect yoke seal in the transmission extension, replace if necessary.
4. Insert driveshaft front yoke into transmission extention, making sure that output shaft splines mate with driveshaft yoke splines.
5. Align driveshaft with companion flange using reference marks established in removal procedure. Remove the tape from the U-joint, install the U-bolts to the rear axle flange, and torque them to 15 ft lbs.

REAR AXLE

Vega and Monza axles are the Chevrolet "C-type" with C-locks retaining the axle shafts. All axles are hypoid type, semi-floating with an integral gear carrier and a removable cover plate.

Vega and Monza models both use either a 6½ in. or 7½ in. diameter ring gear.

Axle Shaft Removal and Installation

1. Raise and support the car.
2. Remove the wheel and brake drum.
3. Clean all dirt from the carrier area.
4. Drain the lubricant from the carrier by removing the cover.
5. Remove the differential pinion shaft lockscrew and remove the differential pinion shaft.
6. Push the flanged end of the shaft toward the center of the car and remove the C-lock from the groove in the axle shaft.
7. Pull the axle shaft from the housing. Be careful not to damage the oil seal.
8. Slide the axle shaft into place.
9. Be sure that the splines on the axle shaft engage with the splines in the differential side gears. Be sure the oil seal is not damaged.
10. Install the axle shaft C-lock. Push the shaft outward so that the C-lock seats in the counterbore of the differential side gear.
11. Install the differential pinion shaft and lockscrew.
12. Further installation is the reverse of removal. Fill the axle with fresh lubricant.

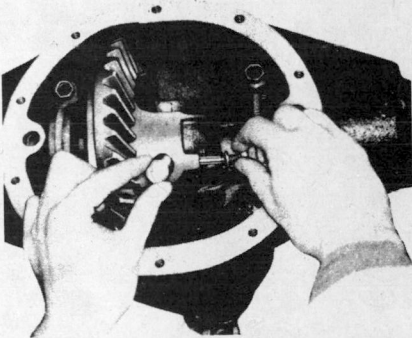

Removing or installing the differential pinion shaft lockpin (© Chevrolet Div., G.M. Corp)

Oil Seal/Axle Bearing Replacement

1. Remove the axle shaft.
2. If replacing the seal only, insert the button end of the axle shaft behind the steel case of the oil seal and pry the seal out of the bore.
3. When removing the bearings, use a slide hammer with care.
4. Lubricate a new bearing with hypoid axle lubricant, and install it with a driver.
5. Lubricate the cavity between the seal lips with high melting point wheel bearing grease and install the seal in the axle housing until it is flush with the end of the housing.
6. Install the axle shaft.

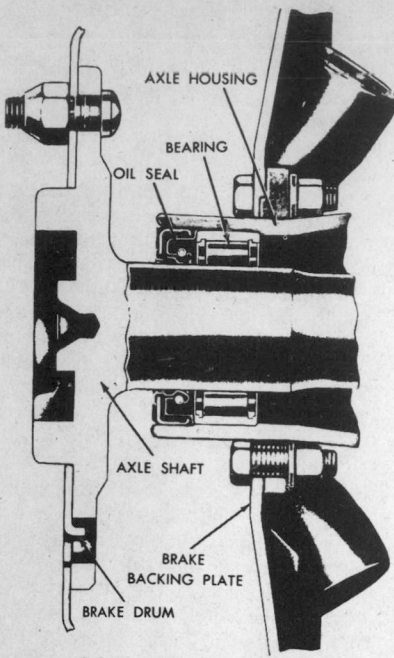

Axle shaft bearing and seal
(© Chevrolet Div., G.M. Corp)

JACKING, HOISTING

The illustration shows the correct jacking and hoist lifting positions.

FRONT SUSPENSION

Vega and Monza suspension utilizes unequal length A-arms with coil springs. The lower control arm bolts to the front end sheet metal with cam bolts which adjust the camber and caster. The upper ball joint is riveted to the upper control arm and the lower ball joint is pressed into the lower control arm.

Shock Absorber Removal and Installation

1. Pry out the access plug in the engine compartment so that the upper mount is visible.
2. Raise the front of the car and safely support it.
3. Turn the wheels for clearance.
4. Hold the upper shock stud with a wrench. Loosen and remove the locknut.
5. Unbolt the lower end and pull the shock down and out.
6. Place the lower retainer and rubber grommet on the shock stud.
7. Put the shock in place and tighten the lower bolts. Torque to 20 ft lbs.
8. Place the upper grommet, retainer, and nut on the shock stud.
9. Hold the stud with a wrench and tighten the nut. Torque to 120 in. lbs.

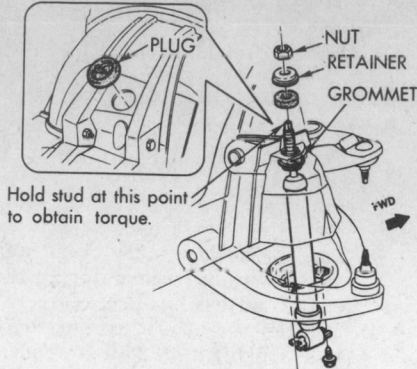

Hold stud at this point to obtain torque.

Front shock absorber mounting
(© Chevrolet Div., G.M. Corp)

Ball Joint Inspection
1971-74

1. Raise the front of the car and support it under the lower control arm. Make sure that the wheel bearings are properly adjusted before making this check.
2. Turn the wheels straight ahead.
3. Grasp and shake the wheel from side to side, horizontally. If there is noticeable looseness, the tie-rod ends are worn.
4. Grasp the top and bottom of the tire and rock it by pushing in on the top and pulling out on the bottom, then pulling out on the top and pushing in on the bottom. A 1/4 in. play indicates worn ball joints.

1975 and Later

The lower ball joints incorporate wear indicators. They can be inspected visually; when the 1/2 in. diameter grease fitting is flush with, or inside the cover surface, replace the ball joint. Inspect the grease fitting with the car supported on its wheels so that the lower ball joint is in a loaded condition. Normal protrusion of the grease fitting is .050 in. beyond the cover surface.

Ball joint tightness can also be checked using the preceding procedure.

Ball Joint Removal and Installation

Upper

1. Jack up the front of the car and support it under the crossmember braces. Remove the wheel.
2. Place a hydraulic jack under the lower control arm.
3. Remove the cotter pin from the ball joint stud. Loosen, but do not remove the nut.
4. The stud may now be pressed out upward. There is a special tool available to do this.
5. Remove the ball joint by grinding off the rivets, or removing the heads of the rivets with a cold chisel.

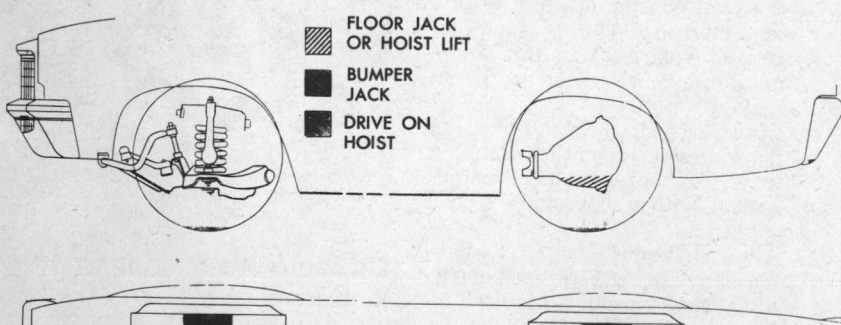

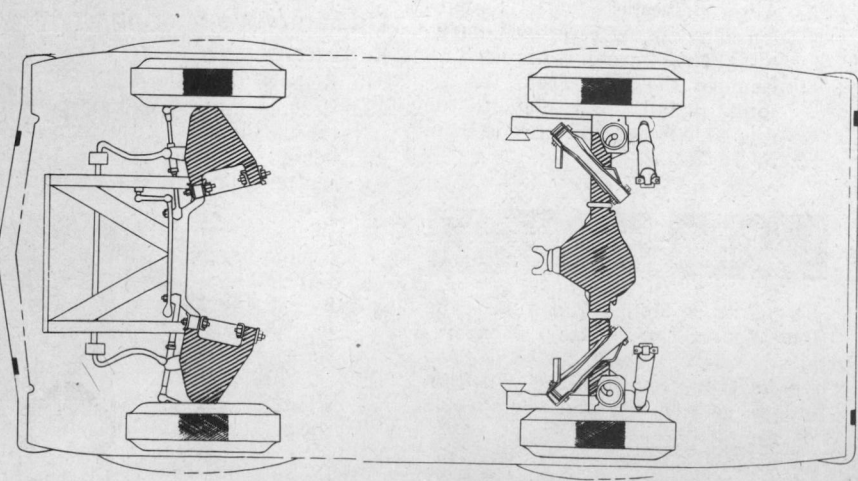

FLOOR JACK OR HOIST LIFT

BUMPER JACK

DRIVE ON HOIST

Lift points (© Chevrolet Div., G.M. Corp)

6. Bolt the new ball joint on, using the nuts and bolts supplied with the replacement joint.

7. Install the stud to the steering knuckle and torque the nut to 30 ft lbs. If the cotter pin hole does not align, tighten the nut ½ of a turn further to line it up. Install a new cotter pin.

8. Install the wheel and lower the car.

Lower

1. Repeat steps one through three of the upper ball joint procedure.

2. The stud may now be pressed out downward. A special tool is available for this purpose.

3. The old joint must be pressed out of the control arm. A tool is available for this operation.

4. Press in the new joint, positioning it so that the grease bleed vent in the rubber boot is facing inward.

5. Install a lubrication fitting in the new joint.

6. Install the stud to the steering knuckle and torque the nut to 60 ft lbs. If the cotter pin hole does not align, tighten it 1/6 of a turn further. Do not loosen the nut to install the cotter pin.

7. Install the wheel and lower the car.

Spring Removal and Installation

1. Raise the front of the car and support it with jackstands placed under the front crossmember braces.

2. Remove the wheel, shock absorbers, and stabilizer bar.

3. Support the lower control arm outer end with a hydraulic floor jack and a block of wood.

4. Securely fasten the spring to the lower control arm with a heavy chain.

5. To detach the tie rod, remove the cotter pin and nut, and tap on the steering arm (not the tie-rod

end) with a hammer. Hold another hammer behind the steering arm to take the force of the tapping. The tie rod should then fall free.

6. Remove the lower ball joint stud from the steering knuckle as described in the "Lower Ball Joint Removal and Installation" procedure.

7. Very cautiously lower the jack until the spring is fully expanded.

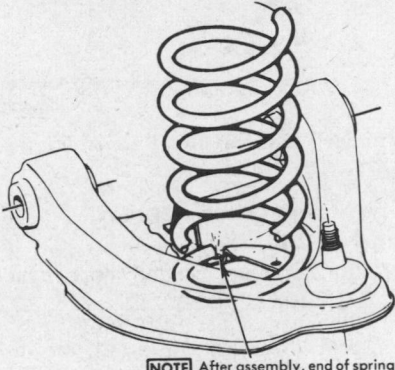

NOTE After assembly, end of spring must be visible through hole.

Front spring positioning
(© Chevrolet Div., G.M. Corp)

8. Place the spring in its pads on the lower control arm and shock tower. Spring insulators are used on 1976 and later models. On these models, make sure that the insulator is indexed with its closed end located at the high point in the spring seat. Secure the spring with a safety chain as in Step 4.

9. Carefully raise the jack.

10. Place the lower ball joint stud in the steering knuckle. Torque the stud nut to 60 ft lbs. If the cotter pin does not align, tighten it further 1/6 of a turn and insert a new cotter pin.

11. Install the tie-rod end to the steering arm. Torque the nut to

35 ft lbs. If the cotter pin hole does not align, tighten further up to a maximum of 50 ft lbs. Insert a new cotter pin.

12. Replace the shock absorber as described in "Shock Absorber Removal and Installation." Do not attach the top end of the shock at this point.

13. Install the stabilizer bar. Tighten the bracket bolts to 30 ft lbs and the control arm bolts to 10 ft lbs.

14. Replace the wheel and lower the car. Install the upper end of the shock absorber.

Lower Control Arm Removal and Installation

1. Raise the front of the car.

2. Remove shock absorber as previously outlined.

3. Remove ball stud from steering knuckle.

4. Remove coil spring using the preceding procedure.

5. Remove the inner pivot cam nuts and bolts.

NOTE: mark the position of the cam bolts before loosening nuts. This step will aid in assembly.

6. Remove the control arm.

7. Install the control arm.

NOTE: be sure that the control arm bushings have the metal caps installed.

8. Install the cam bolts through the control arm bushings.

NOTE: the front cam bolt (camber) must be installed with the head toward the front of the vehicle and the rear cam bolt (caster) must be installed with the head toward the rear of the vehicle.

9. Install the inner cams to the cam bolt.

10. Install the lockwasher and nut.

11. Align the cam bolts with the marks made before removal.

12. Install the coil spring.

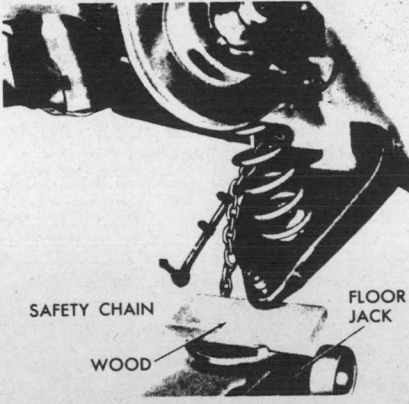

SAFETY CHAIN **FLOOR JACK**

WOOD

Front spring removal
(© Chevrolet Div., G.M. Corp)

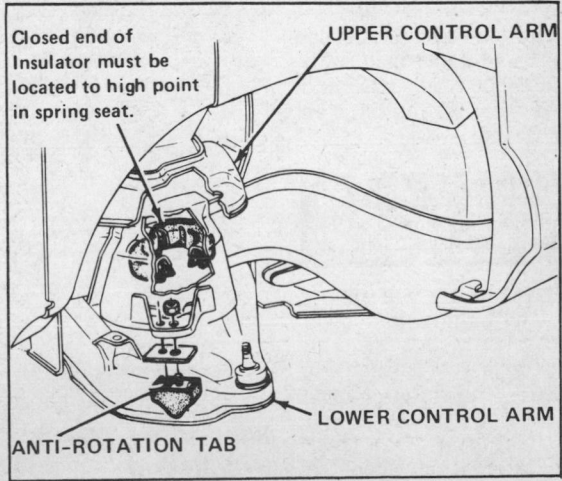

Closed end of Insulator must be located to high point in spring seat.

UPPER CONTROL ARM

LOWER CONTROL ARM

ANTI-ROTATION TAB

Position spring insulators as shown—1976 and later models
(© Chevrolet Div., G.M. Corp)

13. Install the shock absorber.
14. Lower vehicle to the floor.
15. Check front alignment.

Upper Control Arm Removal and Installation

1. Raise vehicle on a hoist and remove the wheel.
2. Support the lower control arm with a floor jack.
3. Remove upper ball stud nut and remove ball stud from steering knuckle.
4. Remove control arm pivot bolts and remove control arm from vehicle.
5. Install upper control arm to vehicle at inner pivot.

NOTE: the inner pivot bolts must be installed with the bolt heads to the front (on the front bushing) and to the rear, (on the rear bushing).

6. Install the inner pivot nuts.
7. Position the control arm in a horizontal plane and tighten the inner pivot nuts.
8. Install ball stud to steering knuckle. Tighten nut and install cotter pin.
9. Install tire and wheel assembly and lower vehicle.

Wheel Bearing Adjustment

1. Jack up the front of the car and support it with jackstands.
2. Remove the dust cap with a pair of slip-joint pliers.
3. Remove and discard the cotter pin. Loosen the spindle nut. Tighten it snugly to seat the bearings, and then loosen the nut again.
4. Rotate the wheel and tighten the spindle nut to 12 ft lbs. which is roughly equivalent to finger tightness.
5. Back the nut off one flat and insert a new cotter pin. If the hole does not line up, back the nut off ½ flat or less to align the hole.
6. Check that the wheel turns freely, and then lock the cotter pin.
7. Bearing end-play should be between 0.001 and 0.008 in. (1971-73) or 0.001-0.005 in. (1974 and later). Tap the dust cap back on and lower the car.

REAR SUSPENSION

Vegas (1971-75) use a coil spring rear suspension with upper and lower control arms.

A new torque arm rear suspension is used on 1975 and later Monza models and 1976 and later Vegas using lower control arms and a track bar to control lateral movement. A torque arm is used to control rear axle wind-up. A stabilizer bar is

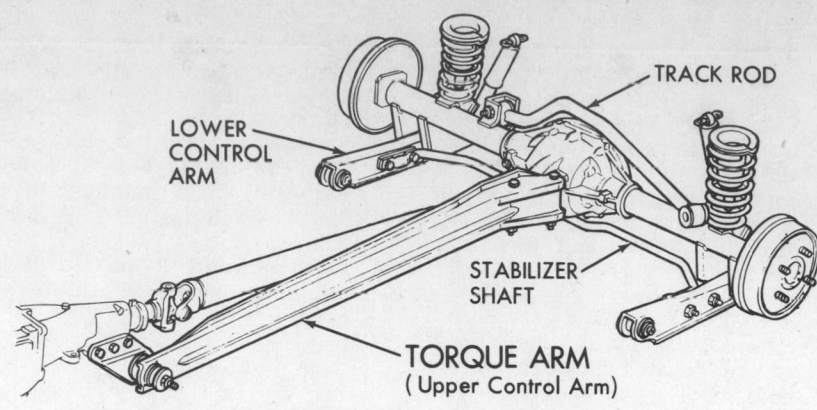

Monza, 1976 and later Vega rear suspension
(© Chevrolet Div., G.M. Corp)

standard and the upper control arms have been eliminated.

Shock Absorber Removal and Installation

1. Raise the vehicle and support the rear axle.
2. Remove upper attaching bolts and lower attaching nut, retainer, and cushion on early 1971 models or the through-bolt on later models.
3. Remove the shock absorber.
4. Install retainer and rubber grommet onto shock.
5. Place shock absorber into installed position and install upper retaining bolts. Torque to 18 ft. lbs.
6. On early models, install cushion, retainer and nut onto lower shock absorber attachment.
7. On later models, install the through-bolt and a rubber grommet on each side of the shock eye. Torque the nut to 80 in. lbs (42 ft lbs—1974 and later models).
8. Lower the car.

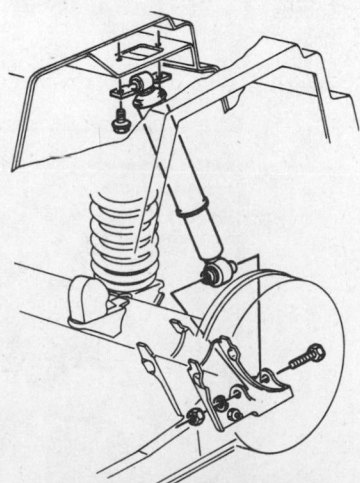

Rear shock absorber mounting
(© Chevrolet Div., G.M. Corp)

Rear Spring Removal and Installation

1. Raise vehicle and support the rear axle, with a hydraulic jack.

2. Disconnect both shock absorbers from lower brackets.
3. Lower axle and remove springs and spring insulators.

NOTE: one or both springs may be removed at this point.

Caution When lowering axle do not stretch brake hose running from frame to axle.

4. Install insulators on top and bottom of springs and position on axle.
5. Raise axle and reconnect shock absorbers. Torque the bottom stud or bolt nuts to 80 in. lbs (42 ft lbs—1974 and later models).
6. Lower the vehicle.

Upper Control Arm Removal and Installation

Caution If both control arms are to be replaced, remove and replace one control arm at a time to prevent the axle from rolling or slipping sideways.

1. Raise vehicle on hoist and support the rear axle.
2. Remove control arm front and rear bolts and remove arm.
3. Press out the bushing.
4. Before bushing installation, observe that holes in control arm have different diameters.
5. Install small end of bushing in largest hole.
6. Press bushing into control until bushing flange seats on control arm.
7. Install control arm front and rear attaching bolts. Torque to 60 ft. lbs.

NOTE: car must be at curb height when tightening pivot bolts.

8. Remove support from axle.
9. Lower vehicle and remove from hoist.

Lower Control Arm Removal and Installation

Caution If both control arms are to be replaced, remove and replace one control arm at a time to prevent the axle from rolling or slipping sideways.

1. Raise vehicle on hoist.
2. Support rear axle.
3. Disconnect stabilizer bar if so equipped.
4. Remove control arm front and rear attaching bolts and remove control arm.
5. Replacement of these bushings is the same procedure as that described for the Upper Control Arm above.
6. Place control arm into position and install front and rear bolts. Torque to 80 ft. lbs.
7. Attach stabilizer bar and restraint cable, if so equipped.
8. Remove support from axle.
9. Lower vehicle.

BRAKES

Front disc brakes are standard equipment on all models with power brakes available beginning 1975. The disc is 10 in. in diameter and 0.5 in. thick. 1976 and later Monza models use a vented disc which is 0.88 in. thick. Hub and disc are one-piece and the assembly is mounted to a one-piece steering knuckle and steering arm. The disc caliper design is similar to the single-piston Delco-Moraine disc brake used on other Chevrolet vehicles.

Rear brakes are drum-type, 9 in. in diameter. Unlike most other brake designs, the rear brakes are not automatically adjusted when the brakes are applied, but are adjusted when the parking brake is applied. For this reason, consistent parking in gear without using the parking brake is not recommended. Starting 1976, 9.5 in. diameter self-adjusting rear drum brakes are used on all Vega and Monza models. Adjustment occurs automatically when the brakes are applied during a reverse stop.

The tandem master cylinder pushrod is not adjustable, thus eliminating a pedal free travel adjustment.

Both front and rear hydraulic systems are routed to and from a distribution valve. Any significant change in the pressure difference between the front and rear systems moves a piston which activates a warning light switch, indicating pressure failure in one of the systems.

Master Cylinder Removal and Installation

1. Disconnect the master cylinder from the brake pedal by detaching the clip and pin.
2. Disconnect the two hydraulic lines at the master cylinder, plugging or covering the ends of the lines.
3. Remove master cylinder attaching nuts and remove the master cylinder.
4. Reverse the removal procedure to install. Torque the mounting nuts to 24 ft lbs.
5. Bleed the hydraulic system.

Power Booster Removal and Installation

1. Remove the vacuum hose from the check valve.
2. Remove the master cylinder-to-power booster nuts.
3. Remove the brake line distribution and switch mounting bolt from the fender skirt.
4. Pull forward on the master cylinder until the cylinder clears the power booster.
5. Carefully remove the master cylinder with the brake lines attached and set the master cylinder aside. Support the cylinder so that there is no stress on the brake lines. The master cylinder should be moved the minimum distance necessary.
6. Unbolt the power booster from the firewall.
7. Remove the brake pedal pushrod from the pedal pin.
8. Remove the power brake booster.
9. Installation is the reverse of removal. Be sure the brake lines are properly routed to provide sufficient clearance.

Parking Brake Adjustment

1. Raise and support the rear of the car.
2. Apply the parking brake one notch from the fully released position.
3. Loosen the adjusting locknut and tighten the adjusting nut until a slight drag is felt when the rear wheels are rotated.
4. Tighten the locknut securely.
5. The rear wheels should rotate freely when the parking brake is fully released.
6. Lower the vehicle.

STEERING

Tie Rod Removal and Installation

1. Place vehicle on hoist.
2. Remove cotter pins from ball studs and remove special nuts.
3. To remove outer ball stud, tap on steering arm at tie rod end with a hammer while using a heavy hammer or similar tool as a backing.
4. Remove inner ball stud from relay rod using same procedure as described in Step 3.
5. To remove tie rod ends from tie rod, loosen clamp bolts and unscrew end assemblies.
6. If the tie rod ends were removed, lubricate the tie rod threads with chassis lube and install ends on tie rod making sure both ends are threaded an equal distance from the tie rod.
7. Make sure that threads on ball studs and in ball stud nuts are perfectly clean and smooth. Check condition of ball stud seals; replace if necessary.

NOTE: if threads are not clean and smooth, ball studs may turn in tie rod ends when attempting to tighten nut.

8. Install ball studs in steering arms and relay rod.
9. Install ball stud nut, tighten and install new cotter pins. Lubricate tie rod ends.
10. Remove vehicle from hoist.
11. Adjust toe-in.

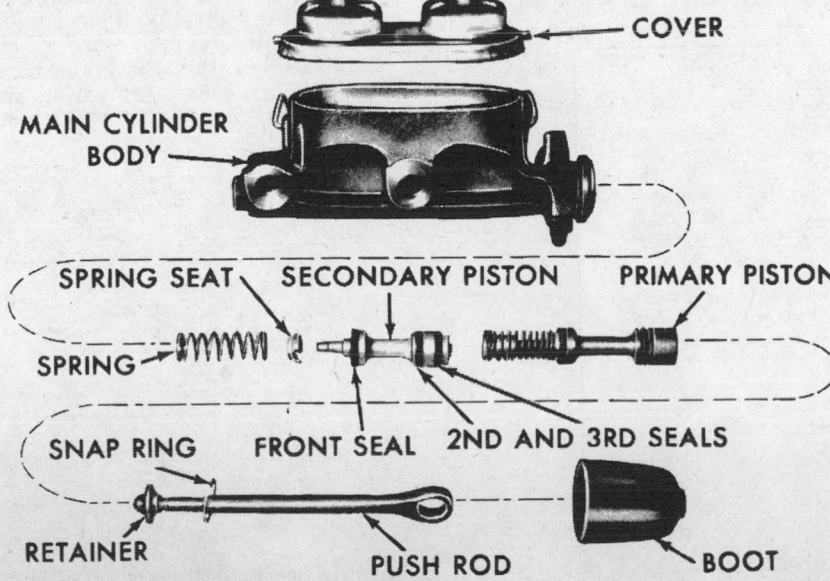

COVER

MAIN CYLINDER BODY

SPRING SEAT   SECONDARY PISTON   PRIMARY PISTON

SPRING

SNAP RING   FRONT SEAL   2ND AND 3RD SEALS

RETAINER   PUSH ROD   BOOT

Brake master cylinder (© Chevrolet Div., G.M. Corp)

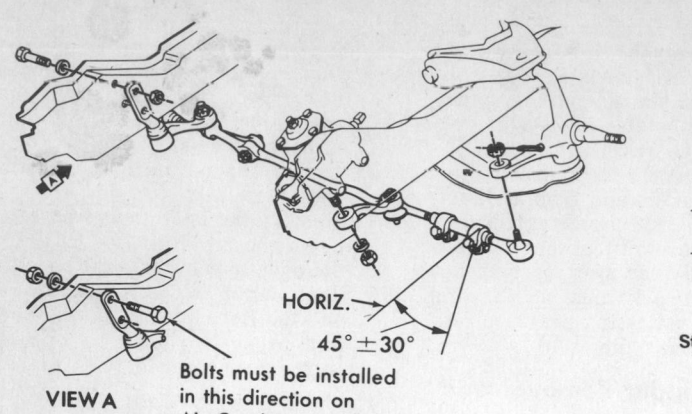

Steering linkage (© Chevrolet Div., G.M. Corp)

VIEW A

HORIZ.

45° ± 30°

Bolts must be installed in this direction on Air Conditioned Models

INSULATOR
EYELET
SPRING
SHAFT NUT
WHEEL

Standard steering wheel assembly—1975 and later models have a snap-ring in front of the nut (© Chevrolet Div., G.M. Corp)

Caution Before tightening the tie rod adjusting sleeve clamp bolts, be sure that the following conditions have been met:

a. The sleeve clamps must be positioned between the locating dimples at either end of the sleeve.

b. The clamps must be positioned within the angular travel as illustrated.

c. The relationship of the clamp slot with the slit in the sleeve should be maintained as shown.

d. Both inner and outer tie rod ends must rotate for full travel in the same direction.

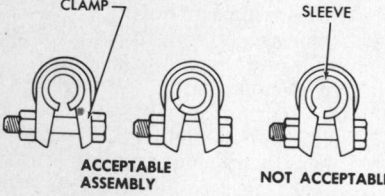

CLAMP
SLEEVE
ACCEPTABLE ASSEMBLY
NOT ACCEPTABLE

Tie-rod clamp installation—Vega through 1974 (© Chevrolet Div., G.M. Corp)

The position of each tie rod end must be maintained as the clamps are tightened to ensure free movement of each joint.

e. All procedures for alignment, adjustment and assembly of tie rods applies to each side.

Steering Wheel Removal and Installation

Standard Wheel

1. Disconnect the battery ground cable.
2. Remove the two screws from the back of the wheel, allowing the shroud (horn actuator bar) to be removed.
3. Set the wheel straight ahead. Mark the relationship of the wheel to the shaft and remove the snap-ring (1975 and later) and nut.
4. Remove the steering wheel with a puller, using the two threaded holes in the wheel.
5. Install the wheel, aligning the previously made marks. Make

sure that the turn signal switch is in the neutral position. Torque the nut to 30 ft lbs.

6. Make sure that the lower horn insulator, eyelet, and spring are in place.
7. Position the shroud, seating the pin on the right side of the wheel in the hole in the shroud.
8. Replace the two screws in the rear of the wheel. Connect the battery cable.

GT and Sport Wheel

1. Disconnect the battery ground cable.
2. Pry off the horn button. Set the wheel in the straight ahead position.
3. Mark the relationship of the wheel to the shaft.
4. Remove the three screws and the upper horn insulator, receiver, and round belleville spring. Remove the snap-ring (1975 and later) and nut.
5. Remove the steering wheel with a puller, utilizing the two threaded holes in the wheel.
6. Replace the wheel, aligning the marks previously made. Make sure that the turn signal switch is in the neutral position. Torque the nut to 30 ft lbs.
7. Make sure that the lower horn insulator, eyelet, and spring are in place.

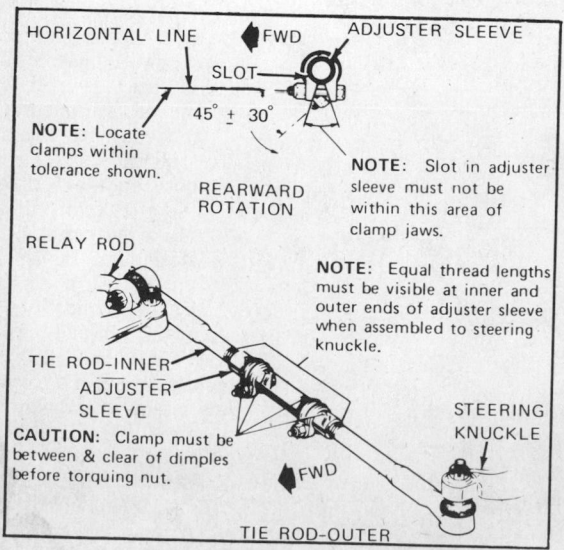

HORIZONTAL LINE
FWD
ADJUSTER SLEEVE
SLOT
45° ± 30°
NOTE: Locate clamps within tolerance shown.
REARWARD ROTATION
NOTE: Slot in adjuster sleeve must not be within this area of clamp jaws.
RELAY ROD
NOTE: Equal thread lengths must be visible at inner and outer ends of adjuster sleeve when assembled to steering knuckle.
TIE ROD-INNER
ADJUSTER SLEEVE
CAUTION: Clamp must be between & clear of dimples before torquing nut.
STEERING KNUCKLE
FWD
TIE ROD-OUTER

Tie-rod clamp positioning—1975 and later models (© Chevrolet Div., G.M. Corp)

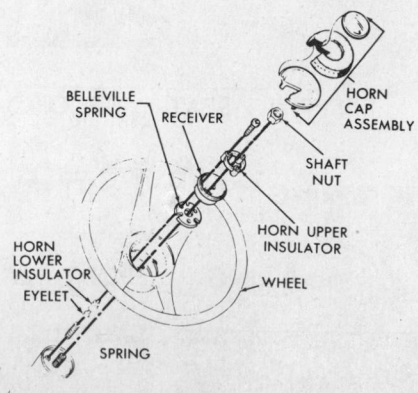

BELLEVILLE SPRING
RECEIVER
HORN CAP ASSEMBLY
SHAFT NUT
HORN UPPER INSULATOR
HORN LOWER INSULATOR
WHEEL
EYELET
SPRING

Optional steering wheel assembly—1975 and later models have a snap-ring in front of the nut (© Chevrolet Div., G.M. Corp)

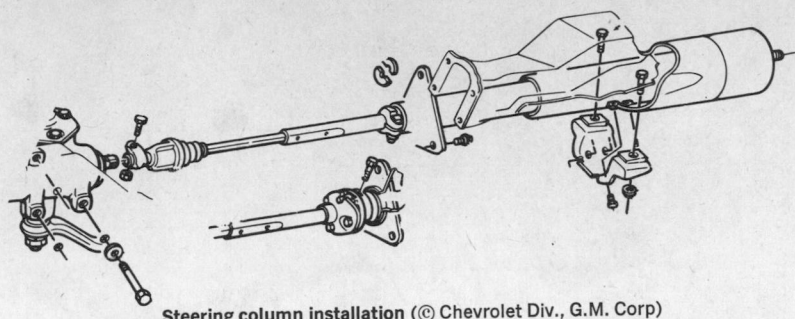

Steering column installation (© Chevrolet Div., G.M. Corp)

8. Install the belleville spring, receiver, upper horn insulator, and the three screws.
9. Install the horn button and connect the battery cable.

Turn Signal Switch Removal and Installation

Standard Column

1. Remove the steering wheel as outlined above.
2. Loosen the three captive screws and lift the cover off the shaft.
3. The lockplate must be depressed with a special tool. Depress the lockplate and remove the wire snap-ring from the shaft.
4. Remove the cancelling cam, upper bearing pre-load spring, and thrust washer from the shaft.
5. Remove the turn signal lever screw and the lever.
6. Push the hazard knob in and unscrew it.
7. Unplug the switch connector from the column and wrap the upper part of the connector with tape.
8. Remove the three switch mounting screws and pull the switch straight up. Guide the wiring connector through the column.
9. Tape the new switch connector. Feed the connector down through the column housing and under the mounting bracket.
10. Install the three switch mounting screws.
11. Replace the hazard flasher knob and the turn signal lever. The turn signal switch should be in neutral and the hazard flasher knob out.
12. Place the thrust washer, upper bearing preload spring, and cancelling cam on the shaft.
13. Place the lockplate and a new snap-ring on the shaft. Press the lockplate down as in step three and install the new snap-ring.
14. Replace the cover and its three screws.
15. Install the steering wheel.

Tilt Column

1. Remove the steering wheel.
2. Remove the cover from the steering shaft. The screws have plastic retainers on the back of the cover. It is not necessary to completely remove the screws.
3. Remove the turn signal lever screw and lever.
4. Push the hazard warning knob in and remove the knob.
5. Depress the shaft lockplate and remove the retaining snap-ring. Remove the lockplate.
6. Slide the turn signal cancelling cam and upper bearing preload spring off the end of the shaft.
7. Remove the column mounting bracket and gently lower the column. Support the column.
8. Remove the signal switch wire protective cover and strip the wires from the protector. Do not damage the wires. Disconnect the switch connector from the bracket. Tape the wires close to the connectors to facilitate removal.
9. Remove the switch mounting screws and pull the switch straight up, guiding the wiring harness through the column.
10. Tape a new turn signal switch wiring harness and connector and feed the harness through the housing. Push the hazard warning switch in to aid in installation.
11. Reinstall the protective signal switch wire cover.

12. Install the column bracket and raise the column into position.
13. Install the mounting screws and clip the connector to the bracket on the steering column jacket.
14. Install the hazard warning knob and turn signal level.
15. Be sure the switch is in the neutral position and the hazard warning knob is out. Slide the upper bearing preload spring and cancelling cam onto the shaft.
16. Install the lockplate on the end of the shaft. Compress the lockplate and install a new snap-ring.
17. Reinstall the cover on the end of the shaft.
18. Install the steering wheel.

Ignition Switch Removal and Installation

The ignition switch is mounted on top of the column jacket under the dashboard, completely inaccessible unless the steering column is lowered. The energy-absorbing column is fragile when disconnected and should not be subjected to any shock or excess pressure. Since the column will distort under its own weight, make sure that it is fully supported along its entire length while it is disconnected from the dashboard.

1. Disconnect the battery ground cable.
2. Remove the steering wheel.
3. On manual steering columns, remove the pot joint coupling clamp bolt.
4. On power steering columns, remove the flexible coupling pinch bolt.
5. Move the front seat back out of the way.
6. Remove the three floor pan bracket screws.
7. Remove the two column-to-instrument panel nuts and carefully lower the column far enough to allow the harness

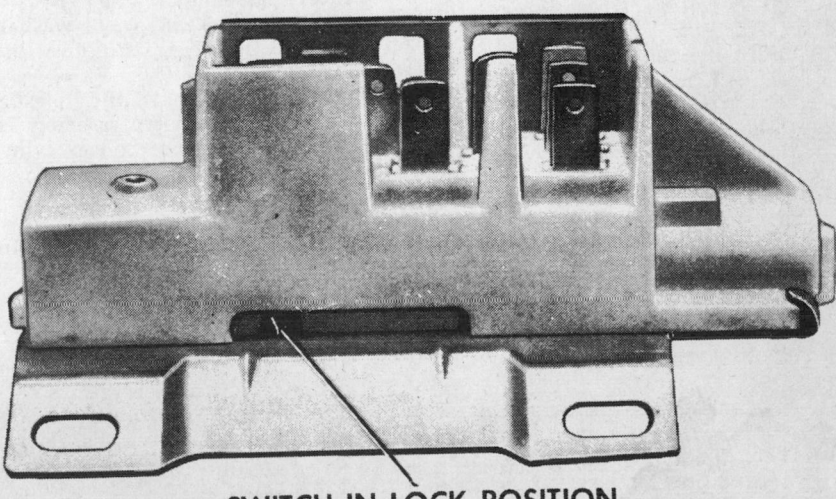

SWITCH IN LOCK POSITION
Ignition switch in lock (© Chevrolet Div., G.M. Corp)

plugs to be disconnected.

8. Disconnect the turn signal and ignition switch harnesses.
9. Place the ignition switch in LOCK position.
10. Remove the two switch screws and the switch assembly.
11. When installing, make sure that the switch is in LOCK position.
12. Install the rod to the switch and the switch to the column. Do not use mounting screws longer than the original ones because they could interfere with the ability of the column to collapse.

NOTE: the following is a mandatory column installation procedure, and must be followed exactly to prevent severe column damage.

13. On power steering models, place the pot joint clamp over the lower end of the pot joint and assemble the intermediate shaft assembly (pot joint, intermediate shaft and flex coupling) to the steering gear stub shaft, aligning the flat on the stub shaft with the flat in the pot joint.
14. Position the column in the vehicle.
15. On manual steering models, place the pot joint clamp over the lower end of the pot joint and assemble the pot joint to the steering gear wormshaft with the flat in the pot joint. On power steering models, align the steering shaft flat with the flat in the flex coupling. When the shaft is bottomed against the coupling reinforcement, install and tighten bolt to 30 ft lbs.
16. Connect the turn signal and ignition switch wiring harnesses.
17. Loosely install the steering column bracket to instrument panel stud nuts.
18. Align the pot joint clamp with the groove across the end of the pot joint. Install bolt and nut, tightening nut to 55 ft. lbs.

NOTE: bolt must pass through the shaft undercut.

19. With the vehicle on the ground, tighten instrument panel nuts to 19 ft lbs.
20. Slide the toe plate down the column to the floorboard and install the three screws.

NOTE: on power steering models, alignment flange on the toe plate must be engaged with the front of the toe pan before driving screws. On manual steering models, no side load is allowed during installation of the attaching screws. A side load could cause misalignment.

21. On manual steering models: remove the alignment spacers. The minimum allowable clearance between the O.D. of the steering shaft and the I.D. of the column jacket lower plastic

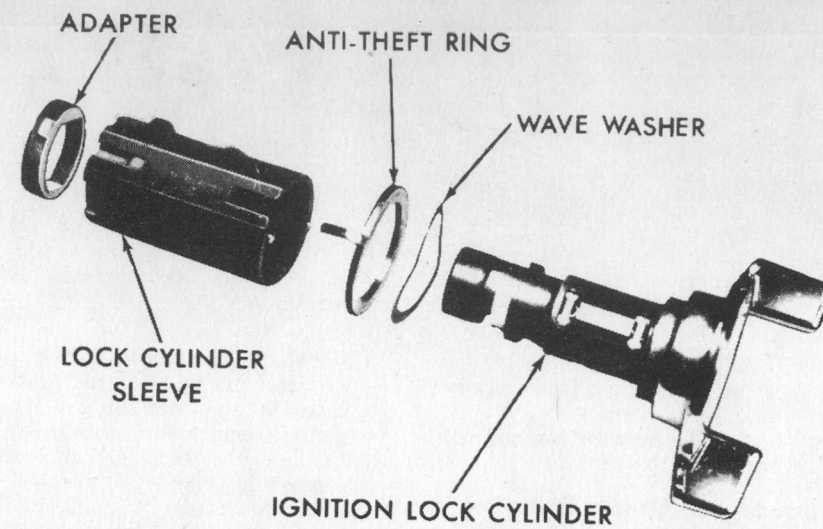

Ignition lock assembly (© Chevrolet Div., G.M. Corp)

bushing after installation is 0.18 in.

22. Install the steering wheel.
23. Connect the battery ground cable.

Ignition Lock Cylinder Removal and Installation

1. Place the lock cylinder in the "On" position.
2. Remove the turn signal switch and steering wheel as previously described.
3. Insert a thin-bladed screwdriver into the rectangular slot inside the column housing. Keep the screwdriver to the right side of the slot and break the housing casting flash loose. Depress the spring latch at the lower end of the lock cylinder. The lock cylinder can be removed with the latch depressed.
4. Place the key part way into the new lock cylinder assembly. If the key is in all the way, the sleeve assembly cannot be installed. Place the wave washer and antitheft ring onto the cylinder.
5. Make sure that the plastic keeper in the sleeve assembly is protruding. Align the lock cylinder lock bolt, the antitheft ring tab, and the slot in the sleeve.
6. Push the sleeve onto the cylinder. Push the key all the way in and rotate the cylinder clockwise.
7. Clamp the tabs of the lock in a padded vise.
8. Place the adaptor ring on the cylinder with the serrations out. The adaptor ring tab should be against the step in the sleeve. The key must be free to rotate 120°.
9. Tap the adaptor into place so that the cylinder extends

through it about 1/16 in.
10. Use a small, flat-tipped punch, at least 1/8 in. in diameter, to stake the cylinder over the adaptor ring in four places just outside the four dimples.
11. Check the lock for proper operation.
12. Hold the sleeve and turn the tabs clockwise against the stop. Insert the assembly into the housing, aligning the key on the sleeve with the slot in the housing bore.
13. Hold a 0.070 in. drill bit between the lock rim and the housing. Turn the cylinder counterclockwise while pushing in lightly.
14. When the cylinder is felt to go into place, push the cylinder in until the retainer pops into place, securing the cylinder.
15. Remove the drill. Check the operation of the lock.
16. Install the turn signal switch and the steering wheel.

Power Steering Pump Removal and Installation

1. On 1975 and later Monzas, remove the radiator and fan shroud.
2. Disconnect the pressure and return hoses at the pump. Cap the ends to prevent leakage and contamination.
3. Remove the drive belt.
4. Unbolt and remove the pump.
5. Reverse the removal procedure to install the pump.
6. Fill the reservoir. Turn the pulley counterclockwise to bleed the pump until no more bubbles appear in the reservoir.
7. Install the drive belt and adjust its tension.
8. If removed, install the radiator and fan shroud and fill the cooling system.

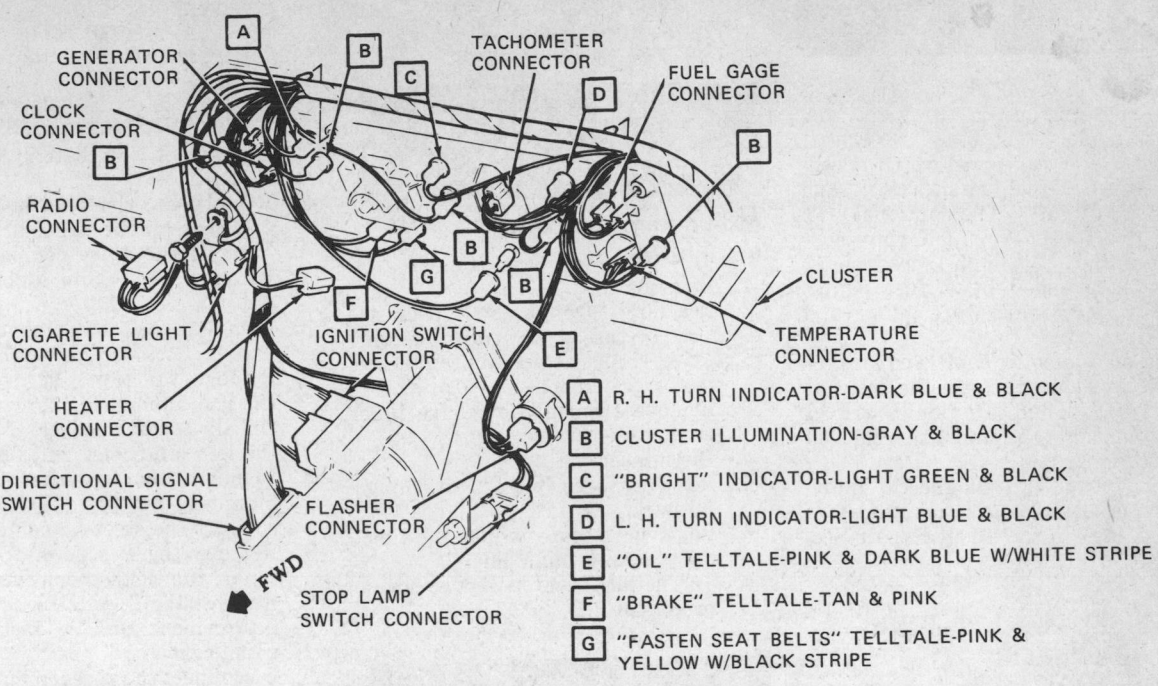

GENERATOR CONNECTOR

CLOCK CONNECTOR

RADIO CONNECTOR

CIGARETTE LIGHT CONNECTOR

HEATER CONNECTOR

DIRECTIONAL SIGNAL SWITCH CONNECTOR

IGNITION SWITCH CONNECTOR

FLASHER CONNECTOR

FWD

STOP LAMP SWITCH CONNECTOR

TACHOMETER CONNECTOR

FUEL GAGE CONNECTOR

CLUSTER

TEMPERATURE CONNECTOR

A R. H. TURN INDICATOR-DARK BLUE & BLACK
B CLUSTER ILLUMINATION-GRAY & BLACK
C "BRIGHT" INDICATOR-LIGHT GREEN & BLACK
D L. H. TURN INDICATOR-LIGHT BLUE & BLACK
E "OIL" TELLTALE-PINK & DARK BLUE W/WHITE STRIPE
F "BRAKE" TELLTALE-TAN & PINK
G "FASTEN SEAT BELTS" TELLTALE-PINK & YELLOW W/BLACK STRIPE

Instument cluster wiring—1975 Vega GT and Monza 2 + 2
(© Chevrolet Div., G.M. Corp.)

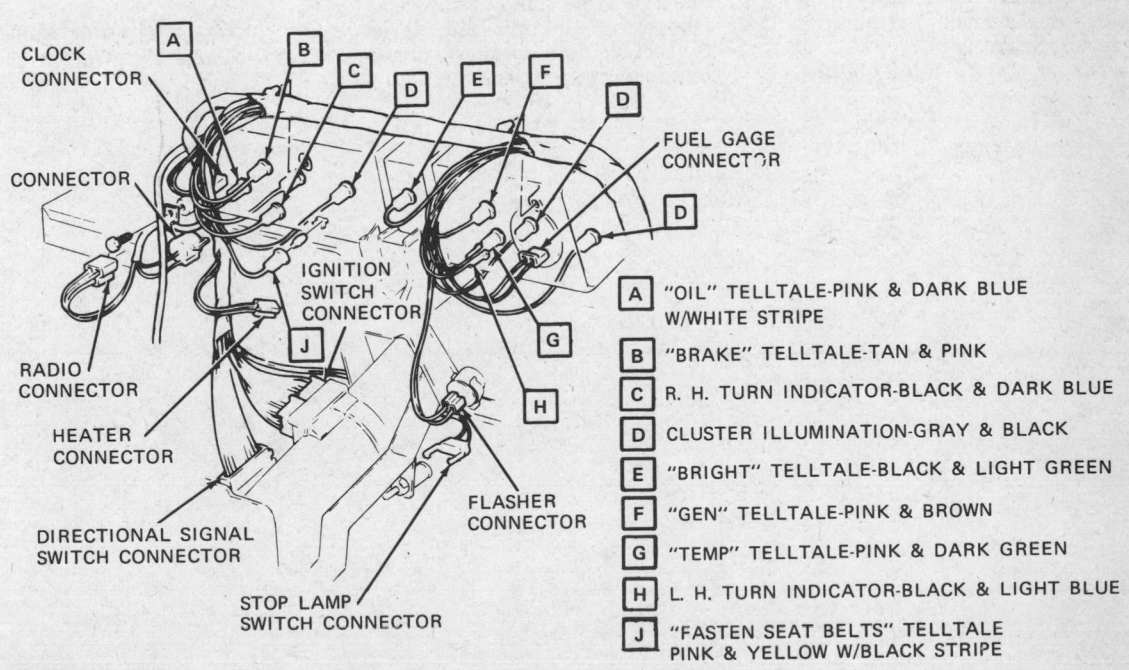

CLOCK CONNECTOR

CONNECTOR

RADIO CONNECTOR

HEATER CONNECTOR

DIRECTIONAL SIGNAL SWITCH CONNECTOR

IGNITION SWITCH CONNECTOR

STOP LAMP SWITCH CONNECTOR

FLASHER CONNECTOR

FUEL GAGE CONNECTOR

A "OIL" TELLTALE-PINK & DARK BLUE W/WHITE STRIPE
B "BRAKE" TELLTALE-TAN & PINK
C R. H. TURN INDICATOR-BLACK & DARK BLUE
D CLUSTER ILLUMINATION-GRAY & BLACK
E "BRIGHT" TELLTALE-BLACK & LIGHT GREEN
F "GEN" TELLTALE-PINK & BROWN
G "TEMP" TELLTALE-PINK & DARK GREEN
H L. H. TURN INDICATOR-BLACK & LIGHT BLUE
J "FASTEN SEAT BELTS" TELLTALE PINK & YELLOW W/BLACK STRIPE

Instument cluster wiring—standard 1975 Vega
(© Chevrolet Div., G.M. Corp.)

INSTRUMENT PANEL

There are two basic instrument panel designs used on Vega and Monza models. The standard cluster consists of a full-panel-width speedometer with fuel gauge, clock and indicator lights. The optional GT model has a separate 7,000 rpm tachometer and 130 mph speedometer units, surrounded by a fuel gauge, clock, water temperature gauge and ammeter.

The speedometer cable and instruments are removed from the front of the panel. All indicator bulbs are ¼ turn twist-in type and are removed from the rear.

Descriptive and diagnostic information on dash gauges and indicators is contained in the "Unit Repair Section."

Headlight Switch Removal and Installation

1. Disconnect the battery ground cable.
2. Pull the light switch to ON position.
3. Reach up under the instrument panel and depress the switch retainer button while pulling on the knob.
4. Remove the knob and shaft, then remove the ferrule nut with a large screwdriver.
5. Disconnect the multi-contact connector, prying gently with a small screwdriver.
6. Connect the new switch and reverse the removal procedure to complete the replacement.

WINDSHIELD WIPERS

Motor Removal and Installation

1. Raise hood.
2. Reaching through cowl opening, loosen the two transmission drive link attaching nuts to motor crankarm.
3. Remove transmission drive link from motor crankarm.
4. Disconnect wiring.
5. Remove three motor attaching screws.
6. Remove motor while guiding crankarm through hole.
7. To install, reverse the removal procedure.

RADIO

Radio Removal and Installation

Vega

1. Remove battery ground cable.
2. Remove knobs, controls, washers and nuts from radio bushings.
3. Disconnect antenna lead, power connector, and speaker connectors from rear of receiver.
4. Remove two screws securing radio mounting bracket to instrument panel lower reinforcement and lift out radio receiver.
5. To install, reverse the removal procedure.

1975 Monza

1. Disconnect the battery ground cable.
2. Remove the clock set stem knob and instrument panel bezel.
3. Remove the glove compartment.
4. Remove the radio knobs and nuts.
5. Remove the instrument panel pad.
6. Remove the lower screws from the radio mounting bracket.
7. On air conditioned cars, remove the left lap cooler and duct.
8. Remove the steering column mounting bracket and lower and support the steering column.
9. Remove the 3 screws from the top of the instrument cluster.
10. Remove the 3 bolts from the reinforcement on the instrument panel carrier.
11. Disconnect the speedometer drive cable from the speedometer head.
12. Pull the instrument panel slightly forward and disconnect the electrical and antenna leads.
13. Remove the radio from the instrument panel.
14. Installation is the reverse of removal.

1976 and Later Monza

1. Disconnect the negative battery cable.

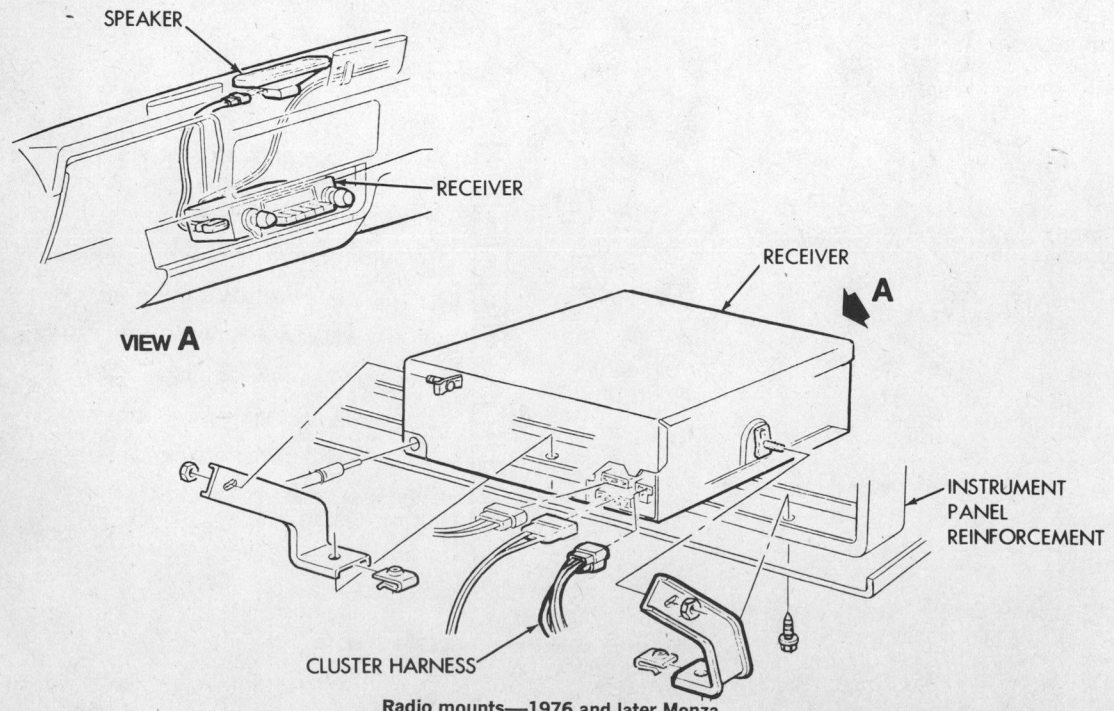

VIEW A

Radio mounts—1976 and later Monza
(© Chevrolet Div., G.M. Corp)

2. Remove the knobs, bezels, nuts, and washers from the radio control shafts.
3. Remove the two screws attaching the radio to the instrument panel reinforcement.
4. With mounts still attached, lower the radio and disconnect the electrical leads.
5. Installation is the reverse of removal.

HEATER

Blower Motor Removal and Installation

1. Disconnect the battery ground cable.
2. On 1976 and later models, remove the coolant recovery tank attaching screws and move the tank aside; draining the tank is unnecessary.
3. Disconnect the blower motor lead wire. Disconnect the motor cooling tube on air-conditioned models.
4. Scribe the blower motor flange to case position.
5. Remove the blower to case attaching screws and remove the blower wheel and motor assembly. Pry the flange gently if the sealer is retaining the assembly.
6. Remove the blower wheel retaining nut and separate the motor and wheel.
7. To install, reverse Steps 1-5, lining up the match-marks on the motor flange and case which were made at removal.

NOTE: assemble the blower wheel to the motor with the open end of the blower away from the motor. Reseal the motor flange, if necessary.

Heater Core Removal and Installation

W/O Air Conditioning

1. Disconnect the battery ground cable.
2. Disconnect the blower motor lead wire.
3. Place a pan under the vehicle. Disconnect the heater hoses at the core connections and secure the ends of the hoses in a raised position.
4. Remove the coil bracket to **dash** panel stud nut and move the coil out of the way.
5. Remove the blower intake to dash panel screws and nuts and remove the blower intake, blower motor and wheel as an assembly.
6. Remove the core retaining strap screws and remove the core from the vehicle.

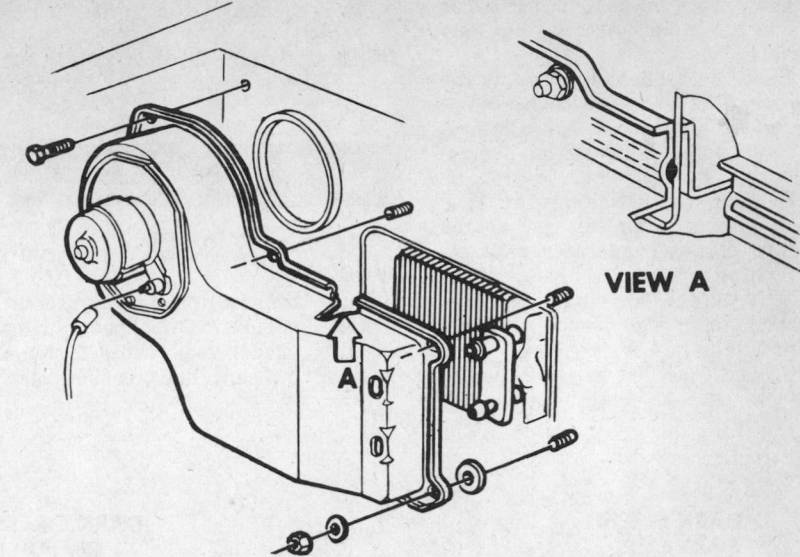

VIEW A

Heater installation (© Chevrolet Div., G.M. Corp)

7. To install, reverse Steps 1-6.
NOTE: be sure that the blower intake sealer is intact, replace if necessary.

With Air Conditioning
Vega and 1975 Monza

1. Disconnect the battery ground cable.
2. Disconnect the heater hoses at the core and plug them.
3. Remove the firewall selector stud nuts.
4. Disconnect the left-side flexible dash outlet hose from the center distributor duct.
5. Remove the right-side dash outlet assembly.
6. Remove the instrument bezel and center outlet as an assembly.
7. Remove the ash tray and retainer.
8. Remove the radio as previously outlined.
9. Remove the control-to-dash screws and lower the control assembly.
10. Remove the cigarette lighter. Remove the screw retaining the right side of the dash reinforcement.
11. Pry out the center duct-to-dash clip. Remove the center duct-to-selector duct screws and remove the center duct. Turn the duct clockwise and pull down and to the left to remove.
12. Remove the defroster duct-to-selector duct screw. Remove the remaining selector duct-to-dash screws and pull the duct back far enough to allow the electrical and vacuum lines to be disconnected.
13. Disconnect the lines and the control cable and remove the selector duct assembly.

14. Pry off the temperature door bellcrank, being careful not to bend the arm or damage the selector case.
15. Remove the temperature door. Remove the backing plate and temperature door cable retainer screws.
16. Remove the heater core and backing plate as an assembly. Remove the core retaining straps and withdraw the core.
17. Reverse the removal procedure to install the core.

1976 and Later Monza

1. Disconnect the negative battery cable.
2. Remove the floor outlet duct. Remove the glove box and door.
3. Remove the right and left-side dash outlets by prying them out with a putty knife or similar tool.
4. Remove the instrument panel pad. Disconnect the vacuum hoses at the valves on the left end of the heater-evaporator.
5. Remove the insulation tray below the instrument cluster. Loosen the console and slide it rearward.
6. Lower the steering column by removing the attaching nuts. Rest the steering column on the driver's seat.
7. Remove the instrument panel-to-dash attaching screws, place a protective cover over the steering column, and lower the instrument panel onto the steering column. Disconnect the speedometer cable, radio electrical leads, and control head connectors.
8. As an assembly, remove the right-side instrument panel and lap cooler. Remove the modular duct-to-heater-evaporator screw and remove the modular duct.

9. Disconnect the temperature door bowden cable and wiring harness.
10. Remove the heater hoses at the core tubes and place the hoses upright. Plug the core tubes to prevent coolant spillage on heater-evaporator removal.
11. Remove the three heater case stud nuts. Remove the heater core case-to-evaporator case attaching screws.
12. Drive on the case studs to remove them from the firewall and remove the heater core case.
13. Remove the heater core-to-case screws and remove the heater core.
14. Installation is the reverse of removal.

SEAT BELTS

Disabling the Interlock System

Since the requirement for the interlock system was dropped during the 1975 model year, those systems installed on cars built earlier may now be legally disabled. The seat belt warning light is still required.
1. Disconnect the negative battery cable.
2. Locate the interlock harness connector with orange, yellow and green leads under the left side of the instrument panel on or near the fuse block. 1974 Vegas have the connector under the parking brake cable cover.
3. Cut and tape the ends of the green wire on the body side of the connector.
4. Remove the buzzer from the fuse block or connector.

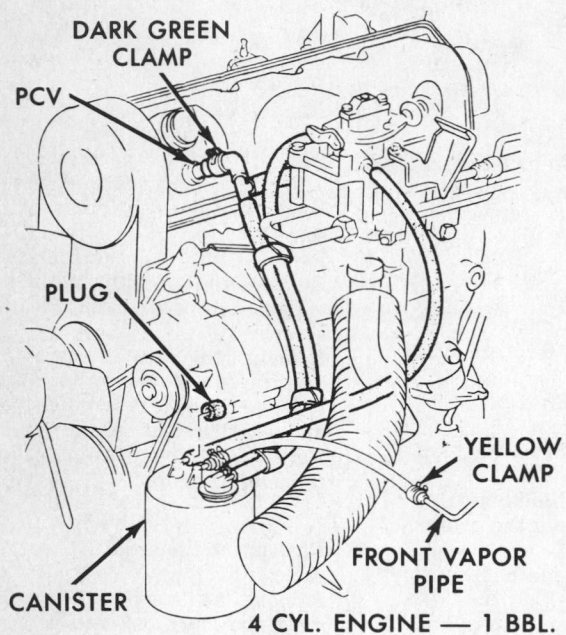

4 CYL. ENGINE — 1 BBL.

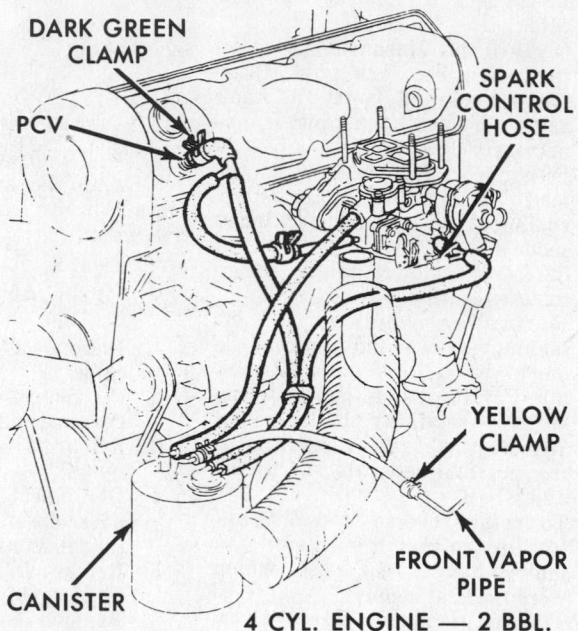

4 CYL. ENGINE — 2 BBL.

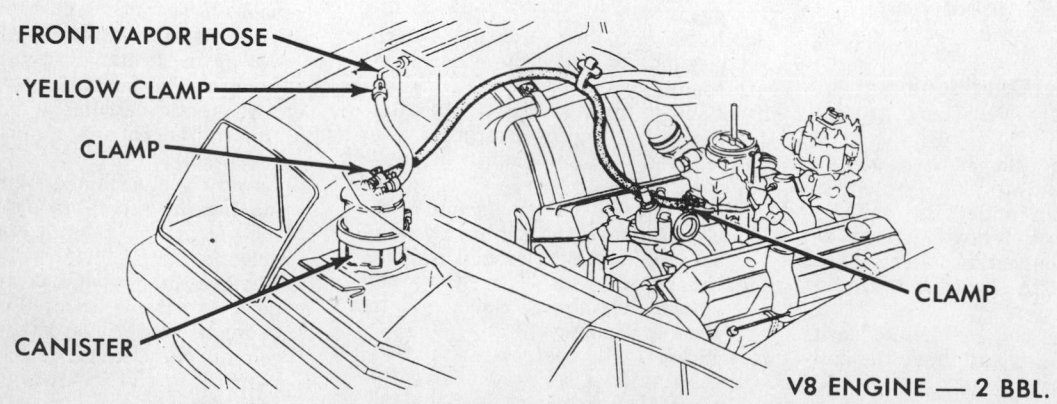

V8 ENGINE — 2 BBL.

Evaporation control canister and connections—1976 and later
(© Chevrolet Div., G.M. Corp.)

INDEX

Oldsmobile · Cutlass · F-85 · 4-4-2 · Omega · Starfire

Automatic Transmission
in car service **C694**
Downshift linkage adjustment C696
Intermediate band adjustment C696
Neutral safety switch C695
Pan Removal and Installation, fluid &
filter change C696
Shift linkage adjustment C695

Brakes **C702, U299**
Master cylinder Removal and
Installation C703
Parking brake adjustment C702
Power brake unit Removal and
Installation C703

Charging System **C673, U2**
Alternator Removal and Installation ... C673
Regulator Removal and Installation C673

Clutch **C692**
Clutch pedal adjustment C692
Clutch Removal and Installation C692

Cooling System **C677, U367**
Radiator Removal and Installation C677
Thermostat Removal and Installation .. C677
Water pump Removal and Installation .. C677

Emission Controls **C679, U145**

Engine **C683, U194**
ENGINE REMOVAL AND INSTALLATION ... C683
CYLINDER HEAD REMOVAL AND
INSTALLATION C686
LUBRICATION C691
Oil pan Removal and Installation C691
Oil pump Removal and Installation C691
Rear main bearing oil seal C691
MANIFOLDS C683
Combination manifold C685
Exhaust manifold removal C684
Intake manifold removal C683
TIMING CASE AND CAMSHAFT C686
Camshaft Removal and Installation C688

Timing chain replacement and
valve timing C688
Timing gear replacement C687
VALVE SYSTEM C685
Rocker arm replacement C685
Valve adjustment C686

Front Suspension **C699, U292**
Shock absorber Removal and
Installation C699
Lower ball joint inspection and removal C699
Lower control arm and/or
spring Removal and Installation C701
Upper ball joint inspection and removal C700
Upper control arm Removal and
Installation C700
Wheel bearing adjustment C701

Fuel System **C675, U50**
Fuel filter Removal and Installation C675
Fuel pump removal C675
Idle speed and mixture adjustment C675

Heater **C706**
Blower motor Removal and Installation
with A/C C707
Blower motor Removal and Installation
without A/C C706
Heater core Removal and Installation
with A/C C707
Heater Core Removal and Installation
without A/C C706

Ignition System **C673, U34**
Contact point replacement C674
Distributor Removal and Installation ... C673
Firing order C661
HEI timing light and tachometer hookup C674
Ignition timing C674

Instrument Panel **C705, U350**
Headlight switch replacement C705

Jacking, Hoisting **C698**

Manual Transmission **C693, U231**
Shift linkage adjustment C693
Transmission Removal and Installation C693

Radio **C705**
Radio Removal and Installation C705

Rear Axle **C697, U285**
Axle shaft, bearing and seal Removal
and Installation C697

Rear Suspension **C701**
Leaf spring replacement C702
Coil spring replacement C702
Shock absorber replacement C701

Seat Belts **C708**
Disabling the seat belt/starter
Interlock and buzzer C708

Specifications **C660, U359**
Capacities C667
Crankshaft and connecting rod C670
Engine identification code C662
General engine C663
Piston clearance C671
Ring gap and side clearance C670
Torque C668
Tune-up C664
Valve C669
Wheel alignment C671
Year identification C660

Starting System **C673, U2**
Starter Removal and Installation C673

Steering **C703, U328**
Ignition switch and/or lock
cylinder replacement C704
Steering wheel Removal and
Installation C703
Turn signal switch replacement C703
Power steering pump removal C704
Steering linkage C704

U-Joints **C696**
Driveshaft Removal and Installation ... C696

Windshield Wipers **C705**
Motor Removal and Installation C705

YEAR IDENTIFICATION

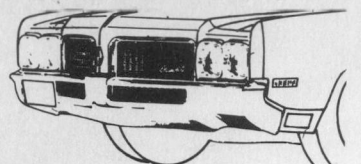

1970 Delta 88

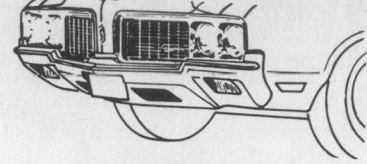

1970 F85

1970 98 Series

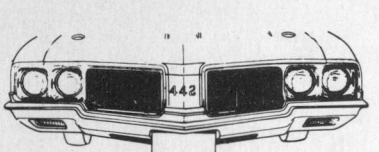

1970 4-4-2

1971 Delta 88

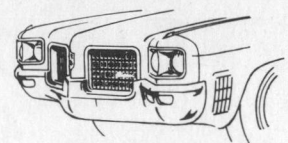

1971 98

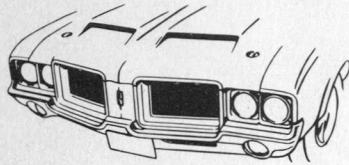

1971 4-4-2

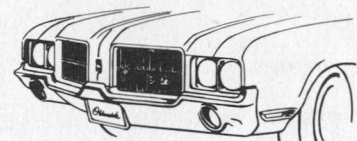

1971 Cutlass Supreme

1972 Delta 88

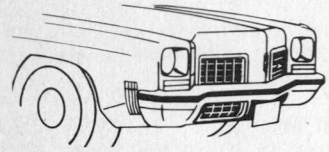

1972 98

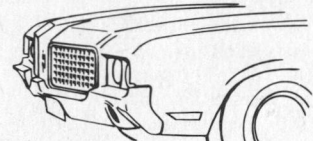

1972 Cutlass Supreme

1972 Cutlass S

1973 Delta 88

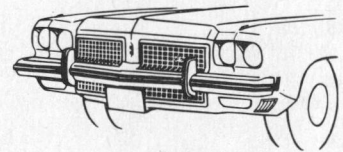

1973 98

1973 Cutlass Supreme

1973 Cutlass S

1973 Omega

1974 Delta 88

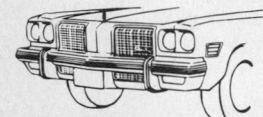

1974 98

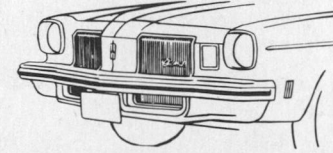

1974 Cutlass

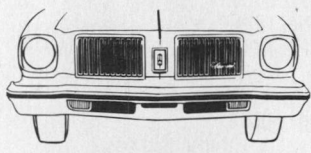

1974 Omega

1975 Delta 88

1975 98

1975 Cutlass S

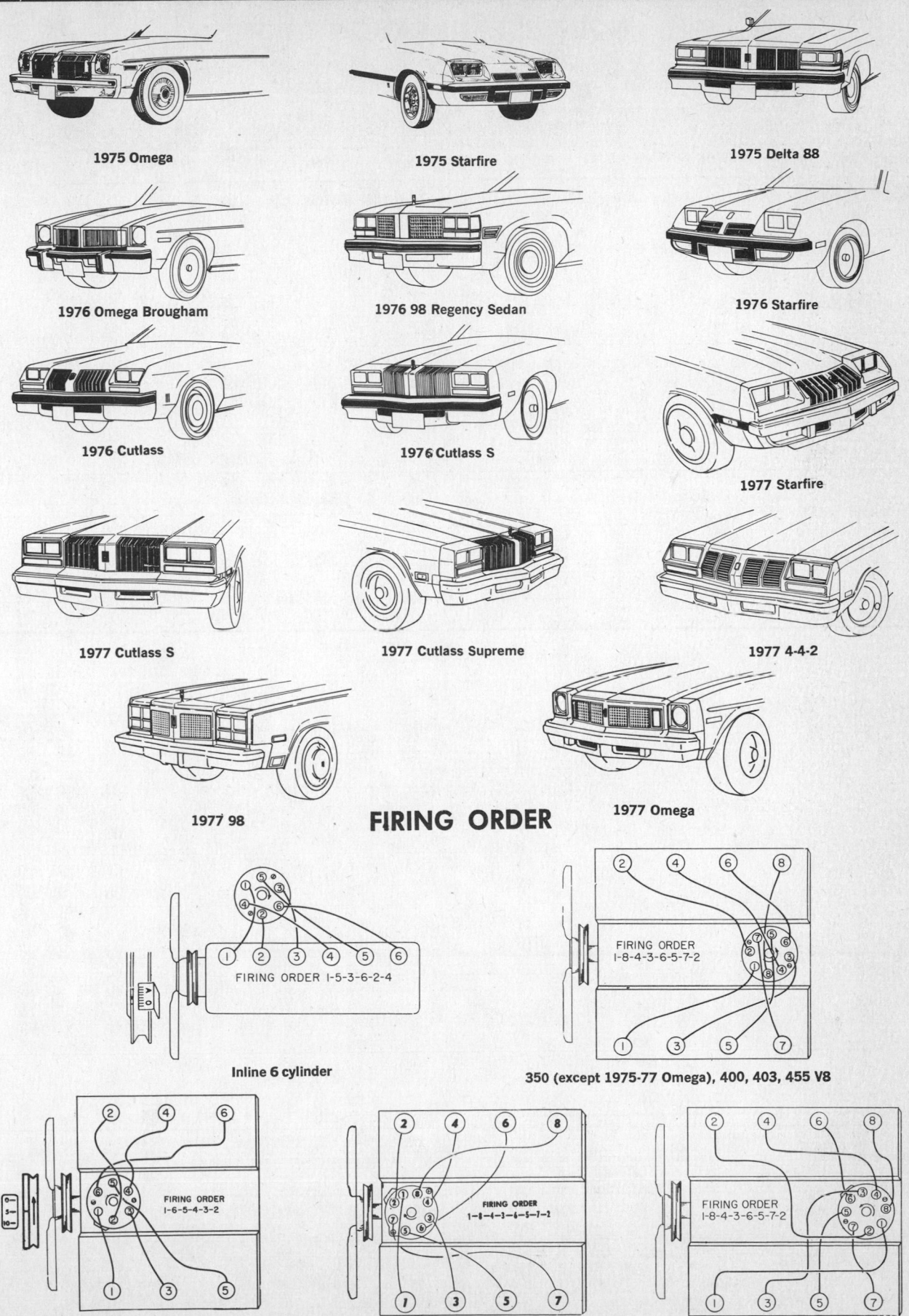

1975 Omega

1975 Starfire

1975 Delta 88

1976 Omega Brougham

1976 98 Regency Sedan

1976 Starfire

1976 Cutlass

1976 Cutlass S

1977 Starfire

1977 Cutlass S

1977 Cutlass Supreme

1977 4-4-2

1977 98

FIRING ORDER

1977 Omega

FIRING ORDER 1-5-3-6-2-4

Inline 6 cylinder

FIRING ORDER 1-8-4-3-6-5-7-2

350 (except 1975-77 Omega), 400, 403, 455 V8

FIRING ORDER 1-6-5-4-3-2

V6 engine

FIRING ORDER 1-8-4-1-6-5-7-2

1975-76 Omega 350 V8

FIRING ORDER 1-8-4-3-6-5-7-2

302 V8

ENGINE IDENTIFICATION CODE

The engine identification code is stamped on a machined pad on the right side of the cylinder block behind the distributor on inline sixes. It is stamped on the front of the engine, below the right cylinder head on V6 and 1975-76 Omega 350. It is stamped at the top right side of the engine on the OHC 4. Most engines also have a tape either on the oil fill tube or the front of the valve cover, giving the engine code.

Disp	Bbl	Hp■	'70	'71	'72	'73	'74	'75	'76	'77
4-Cylinder Models										
140	2	All							BS BK BL BT	
6-Cylinder Models										
231	2	All						FP FS FR	FH FI FJ FO	
250	1	All	VB VF	VB VF		CCA CCB CCC CCD	CCA CCB CCC CCD	CJU CJT CJL	CCC CCD CCF CCH CCJ	
8-Cylinder Models										
260	2	110						QA QB QC QD QK QN QE QJ QP TE TJ TP TT	QA QD QK QN QB QC Q7 Q8 QP QT TE TJ TP TT TA TD TK TN T2 T3 T4 T5	
350	2	145				QS QT				
350	2	160			QA QB QC	QN QQ QP QO QS QT				
8-Cylinder Models										
350	4	160, 170, 180, 200#	QD QE QJ QK	QB QC QD QL QO QU QW TB TC TL	QB QC QL QO QU QW TB TC TL TO	QL QO QU QW QX TL TO TW TX Q6	Q2 Q3 Q5 TL TO TX TW TY Q4			

Disp	Bbl	Hp■	'70	'71	'72	'73	'74	'75	'76	'77
8-Cylinder Models										
350	4					TO QA QE QJ QK				
350	2	240, 250	QA QI QJ TC TD TL	QA QI QJ TC TD TE						
350	4	310	QN QP QV							
350	4	325	QD QX							
350	4①	155, 165					RW RX PA PB	PE PF PM PN PA PB		
350	2①	140, 145					RS RT	PA PB		
455	4	190, 210, 230#				UA UB UC UD UL UN UR VA VB VC VD VL	UB UC UD UE UP VB VC VD VE VP	UE UD UB UC U3 U5 U6 U7 U8 VE VD VB V3 V5		
455	4	225, 230, 250		US UT UU UV	UA UB UD US UT UV UU					
455	4	270		UA UB UD UE						
455	4	275				UV, UX				
455	2	280		UC						

ENGINE IDENTIFICATION CODE (con't.)

Disp	Bbl	Hp■	'70	'71	'72	'73	'74	'75	'76	'77
8-Cylinder Models										
455	2	280		UD UE						
455	4	300			UL UN UO					
455	2	310	UC UD UJ							
455	2	320	TX TY							
455	4	320		TD TN TQ TU TV TW UN UO						
455	4	340		TB TL						

Disp	Bbl	Hp■	'70	'71	'72	'73	'74	'75	'76	'77
8-Cylinder Models										
455	4	340		TS TT						
455	4	350		US UT						
455	4	365	TP TQ TU TV TW UN UO TS TT							

① 1975-76 Omega only

■ Beginning 1972, horsepower figures are SAE net. They are measured at the rear of the transmission with all accesories installed and operating. Since the figures vary when a given engine is installed in different models, some are representative rather than exact.

\# With dual exhaust

GENERAL ENGINE SPECIFICATIONS

Year	Engine No. Cyl. Displacement (cu. in.)	Carburetor Type	Horsepower @ rpm ■	Torque @ rpm (ft lbs) ■	Bore X Stroke (in.)	Compression Ratio	Oil Pressure @ 2000 rpm
'70	6-250	1 bbl	155 @ 4200	240 @ 2000	3.875 x 3.530	8.50:1	30-45
	8-350	2 bbl	250 @ 4400	355 @ 2600	4.057 x 3.385	9.00:1	30-45
	8-350	4 bbl	310 @ 4800	390 @ 3200	4.057 x 3.385	10.25:1	30-45
	8-350	4 bbl	325 @ 5400	360 @ 3600	4.057 x 3.385	10.50:1	30-45
	8-455	2 bbl	310 @ 4200	490 @ 2400	4.125 x 4.250	9.00:1	30-45
	8-455	2 bbl	320 @ 4200	500 @ 2400	4.126 x 4.250	10.25:1	30-45
	8-455	4 bbl	365 @ 4600	510 @ 3000	4.126 x 4.250	10.25:1	35-45
	8-455	4 bbl	365 @ 5000	500 @ 3200	4.126 x 4.250	10.50:1	35-50
	8-455	4 bbl	370 @ 5200	500 @ 3600	4.126 x 4.250	10.50:1	35-50
	8-455	4 bbl	390 @ 5000	500 @ 3200	4.126 x 4.250	10.25:1	30-45
'71	6-250	1 bbl	145 @ 4200	230 @ 2000	3.875 x 3.530	8.00:1	30-45
	8-350	2 bbl	240 @ 4200	350 @ 2400	4.057 x 3.385	8.50:1	30-45
	8-350	4 bbl	260 @ 4600	360 @ 3200	4.057 x 3.385	8.50:1	30-45
	8-455	2 bbl	280 @ 4000	445 @ 2000	4.126 x 4.250	8.50:1	30-45
	8-455	4 bbl	320 @ 4400	460 @ 2800	4.126 x 4.250	8.50:1	30-45
	8-455	4 bbl	340 @ 4600	460 @ 3200	4.126 x 4.250	8.50:1	30-50
	8-455	4 bbl	350 @ 4700	460 @ 3200	4.126 x 4.250	8.50:1	30-50
'72	8-350	2 bbl	160 @ 4000	275 @ 2400	4.057 x 3.385	8.50:1	30-45
	8-350①	2 bbl	175 @ 4000	295 @ 2600	4.057 x 3.385	8.50:1	30-45
	8-350	4 bbl	180 @ 4000	275 @ 2800	4.057 x 3.385	8.50:1	30-45
	8-350①	4 bbl	200 @ 4400	300 @ 3200	4.057 x 3.385	8.50:1	30-45
	8-455	4 bbl	225 @ 3600	360 @ 2600	4.126 x 4.250	8.50:1	30-50
	8-455①	4 bbl	250 @ 4200	370 @ 2800	4.126 x 4.250	8.50:1	30-50
	8-455	4 bbl	270 @ 4400	370 @ 3200	4.126 x 4.250	8.50:1	30-50
	8-455	4 bbl	300 @ 4700	410 @ 3200	4.126 x 4.250	8.50:1	30-50

GENERAL ENGINE SPECIFICATIONS

Year	Engine No. Cyl. Displacement (cu. in.)	Carburetor Type	Horsepower @ rpm ■	Torque @ rpm (ft lbs) ■	Bore X Stroke (in.)	Compression Ratio	Oil Pressure @ 2000 rpm
'73	6-250	1 bbl	100 @ 3600	175 @ 1600	3.875 x 3.530	8.50:1	30-45
	8-350	2 bbl	160 @ 3800	275 @ 2400	4.057 x 3.385	8.50:1	30-45
	8-350	4 bbl	180 @ 3800	275 @ 2800	4.057 x 3.385	8.50:1	30-45
	8-455	4 bbl	225 @ 3600	360 @ 2600	4.126 x 4.250	8.50:1	30-50
	8-455	4 bbl	250 @ 4000	370 @ 2800	4.126 x 4.250	8.50:1	30-50
'74	6-250	1 bbl	100 @ 3600	175 @ 1600	3.875 x 3.530	8.00:1	30-45
	8-350	4 bbl	160 @ 3800	275 @ 2400	4.057 x 3.385	8.50:1	30-45
	8-350	4 bbl	180 @ 3800	275 @ 2800	4.057 x 3.385	8.50:1	30-45
	8-350①	4 bbl	200 @ 4200	300 @ 3200	4.057 x 3.385	8.50:1	30-45
	8-455	4 bbl	210 @ 3600	350 @ 2400	4.126 x 4.250	8.50:1	30-50
	8-455①	4 bbl	230 @ 4000	370 @ 2800	4.126 x 4.250	8.50:1	30-50
'75	6-231	2 bbl	110 @ 4000	175 @ 2000	3.800 x 3.400	8.00:1	37②
	6-250	1 bbl	100 @ 3600	175 @ 1600	3.875 x 3.530	8.50:1	36-41
	8-260	2 bbl	110 @ 3400	205 @ 1600	3.550 x 3.385	8.50:1	30-45
	8-350 Omega	2 bbl	145 @ 3200	270 @ 2000	3.800 x 3.850	8.00:1	37②
	8-350 Omega	4 bbl	165 @ 3800	260 @ 2200	3.800 x 3.850	8.00:1	37②
	8-350	4 bbl	160 @ 3800	275 @ 2400	4.057 x 3.385	8.50:1	30-45
	8-455	4 bbl	190 @ 3400	350 @ 2400	4.126 x 4.250	8.50:1	30-45
'76-'77	4-140	2 bbl	85 @ 4400	122 @ 2400	3.500 x 3.625	8.00:1	40
	6-231	2 bbl	105 @ 3400	185 @ 2000	3.800 x 3.400	8.00:1	37②
	6-250	1 bbl	105 @ 3800	185 @ 1200	3.875 x 3.530	8.25:1	36-41
	8-260	2 bbl	110 @ 3400	205 @ 1600	3.550 x 3.385	8.00:1	30-45
	8-302	2 bbl	—	—	—	—	—
	8-350 Omega	2 bbl	140 @ 3200	280 @ 1800	3.800 x 3.850	8.00:1	37②
	8-350 Omega	4 bbl	155 @ 3400	280 @ 1800	3.800 x 3.850	8.00:1	37②
	8-350	4 bbl	170 @ 3800	275 @ 2400	4.057 x 3.385	8.50:1	30-45
	8-403	4 bbl	—	—	4.351 x 3.385	—	30-45
	8-455	4 bbl	190 @ 3400	350 @ 2000	4.126 x 4.250	8.50:1	30-45

■ Beginning 1972, horsepower and torque are SAE net figures. They are measured at the rear of the transmission with all accessories installed and operating. Since the figures vary when a given engine is installed in different models, some are representative rather than exact.
① Dual exhaust
② @ 2500 rpm

Oldsmobile 88, 98 TUNE-UP SPECIFICATIONS

When analyzing compression test results, look for uniformity among cylinders rather than specific pressures.

Year	ENGINE No. Cyl Displacement (cu in.)	hp	SPARK PLUGS Orig. Type	Gap (in.)	DISTRIBUTOR Point Dwell (deg)	Point Gap (in.)	IGNITION TIMING (deg) ▲ Man Trans *	Auto Trans ●	VALVES Intake Opens ■ (deg) ●	Fuel Pump Pressure (psi)	IDLE SPEED (rpm) ▲ Man Trans	Auto Trans ●
'70	8-350	250	R-46S	.030	28-32	.016	8B	8B	16	5½-6½	675	575
	8-455	310	R-46S	.030	28-32	.016	8B	8B	20	5½-6½	675	575
	8-455	365	R-45S	.030	28-32	.016	—	8B	20	5½-6½	—	575
'71	8-350	240	R-46S	.040	28-32	.016	—	10B	14	5½-6½	—	600
	8-455	280	R-46S	.040	28-32	.016	—	8B	20	5½-6½	—	600
	8-455	320	R-46S	.040	28-32	.016	—	8B	20	5½-6½	—	600

Oldsmobile 88, 98 TUNE-UP SPECIFICATIONS (cont'd)

When analyzing compression test results, look for uniformity among cylinders rather than specific pressures.

Year	Engine No. Cyl Displacement (cu in.)	hp	Spark Plugs Type	Gap (in.)	Distributor Point Dwell (deg)	Point Gap (in.)	Ignition Timing (deg) ▲ Man Trans * ●	Auto Trans	Valves Intake Opens ■ (deg) ●	Fuel Pump Pressure (psi)	Idle Speed (rpm) ▲ Man Trans ●	Auto Trans
'72	8-350	160	R-46S	.040	28-32	.016	—	8B	16	5½-6½	—	650/600
	8-350	180	R-46S	.040	28-32	.016	—	12B	22	5½-6½	—	600
	8-455	225	R-46S	.040	28-32	.016	—	8B	20	5½-6½	—	650/600
'73	8-350	160	R-46S	.040	30	.016	—	12B	16	5½-6½	—	700/550
	8-455	225	R-46S	.040	30	.016	—	8B	20	5½-6½	—	650/550
'74	8-350	180	R-46S	.040	30	.016	—	12B	16	5½-6½	—	650/550
	8-455	210	R-46S	.040	30	.016	—	8B	20	5½-6½	—	650/550
	8-455	230	R-46SX	.080	Electronic		—	8B	20	5½-6½	—	650/550
'75	8-350	170	R-46SX	.080	Electronic		—	20B	16	5½-6½	—	650/550
	8-455	190	R-46SX	.080	Electronic		—	16B	20	5½-6½	—	650/550
'76	8-350	170	R-46SX	.080	Electronic		—	20B	16	5½-6½	—	650②/550(600)
	8-455	190	R-46SX	.080	Electronic		—	16B①	20	5½-6½	—	650②/550(600)
'77	All		See Underhood Specifications Sticker									

① 18B with 2.4:1 axle ratio in 98
② A/C on and compressor clutch wires disconnected
▲ See text for procedure
* Set V8 timing through 1974 at 1100 rpm without A/C and at 850 rpm with A/C. See sticker for timing rpm on later models.
■ All figures are in degrees Before Top Dead Center

● Figures in parentheses apply to California engines. Where two idle speed figures appear separated by a slash, the first is idle speed with solenoid energized, the second is idle speed with solenoid disconnected.
B Before Top Dead Center
— Not applicable
NOTE: The underhood specifications sticker often reflects tune-up specification changes made in production. Sticker figures must be used if they disagree with those in this chart.

F-85, Cutlass, Omega, Starfire, Vista Cruiser, 4-4-2 TUNE-UP SPECIFICATIONS

When analyzing compression test results, look for uniformity among cylinders rather than specific pressures.

Year	Engine No. Cyl Displacement (cu in.)	hp	Spark Plugs Orig. Type	Gap (in.)	Distributor Point Dwell (deg)	Point Gap (in.)	Ignition Timing (deg) ▲ Man Trans * ●	Auto Trans	Valves Intake Opens ■ (deg) ●	Fuel Pump Pressure (psi)	Idle Speed (rpm) ▲ Man Trans ●	Auto Trans
'70	6-250	155	R-46T	.035	31-34	.019	TDC	4B	16	4-5	830-750	630-600
	8-350	250	R-46S	.030	28-32	.016	10B	10B	16	5½-6½	750	575
	8-350	310	R-45S	.030	28-32	.016	10B	10B	16	5½-6½	650	575
	8-350	325	R-43S	.030	28-32	.016	14B	14B	40	5½-6½	750	625
	8-455	320	R-45S	.030	28-32	.016	—	8B	20	5½-6½	—	575
	8-455	365③	R-44S	.030	28-32	.016	—	12½	20	5½-6½	—	600
	8-455	365④	R-45S	.030	28-32	.016	—	8B	24	5½-6½	—	575
	8-455	365⑤	R-44S	.030	28-32	.016	12B	12B	24②	5½-6½	700	650
	8-455	370⑤	R-44S	.030	28-32	.016	8B	8B	56	5½-6½	700	650
'71	6-250	145	R-46TS	.035	31-34	.019	4B	4B	16	4-5	600⑧	575⑧
	8-350	240	R-46S	.040	28-32	.016	10B	10B	14	5½-6½	750	600
	8-350	260	R-45S⑥	.040	28-32	.016	10B	12B	14②	5½-6½	750	600
	8-455	280	R-46S	.040	28-32	.016	—	8B	20	5½-6½	—	600
	8-455	320	R-46S	.040	28-32	.016	—	8B	20	5½-6½	—	600
	8-455	340	R-45S	.040	28-32	.016	10B	10B	24②	5½-6½	750	600
	8-455	350	R-45S	.040	28-32	.016	12B	10B	56	5½-6½	750	600

F-85, Cutlass, Omega, Starfire, Vista Cruiser, 4-4-2   TUNE-UP SPECIFICATIONS (cont'd)

When analyzing compression test results, look for uniformity among cylinders rather than specific pressures.

Year	ENGINE No. Cyl Displacement (cu in.)	hp	SPARK PLUGS Orig. Type	Gap (in.)	DISTRIBUTOR Point Dwell (deg)	Point Gap (in.)	IGNITION TIMING (deg) ▲ Man	Trans * ● Auto Trans	VALVES Intake Opens ■ (deg) ●	Fuel Pump Pressure (psi)	IDLE SPEED (rpm) ▲ Man Trans	● Auto Trans
'72	8-350	160	R-46S	.040	28-32	.016	8B	8B(6B)	16(22)	5½-6½	750	650/550
	8-350	180	R-46S	.040	28-32	.016	8B	12B	16(22)	5½-6½	750	600
	8-455	250	R-46S	.040	28-32	.016	10B	8B	30⑦	5½-6½	750	600
	8-455	270	R-46S	.040	28-32	.016	10B	8B	30⑦	5½-6½	750	600
	8-455	300	R-45S	.040	28-32	.016	12B	10B	56	5½-6½	750	650
'73	6-250	100	R-46T	.035	33	.019	6B	6B	16	4-5	700/450	600/450
	8-350	160	R-46S	.040	30	.016	—	14B	22	5½-6½	—	650/550
	8-350	180	R-46S	.040	30	.016	—	12B	22	5½-6½	—	650/550
	8-350	180	R-45S	.040	30	.016	—	12B	22	5½-6½	1000/600	—
	8-455	225	R-45S	.040	30	.016	10B	8B	28	5½-6½	1000/750	650/550
'74	6-250	100	R-46T	.035	33	.019	8B	8B	16	4-5	850/450	600/450
	8-350	160, 180	R-46S	.040	30	.016	—	12B	22	5½-6½	—	650/550
	8-350	200	R-46S	.040	30	.016	—	14B	22	5½-6½	—	650/550
	8-455	210	R-46S	.040	30	.016	—	8B	22	5½-6½	—	650/550
	8-455	230	R-46SX	.080	Electronic		—	8B	22	5½-6½	—	650/550
'75	6-231	110	R-44SX	.060	Electronic		12B	12B	17	4½-5¾	800/600	650/500
	6-250	100	R-46TX	.060	Electronic		10B	10B	16	4-5	800/425	600/425
	8-260	110	R-46SX	.080	Electronic		16B	18B(16B)⑨	22	5½-6½	750	650/550
	8-350 Omega	145	R-45TSX	.060	Electronic		—	12B	19	4½-5¾	—	600
	8-350 Omega	165	R-45TSX	.060	Electronic		—	12B	19	4¼-5¾	—	600
	8-350	170	R-46SX	.080	Electronic		—	20B	16	5½-6½	—	600/650
	8-455	190	R-46SX	.080	Electronic		—	16B	20	5½-6½	—	650/550 (600)
'76	4-140	85	R-43TS	.035	Electronic		10B	12B	34	3-4½	700(1000/700)	750/600 (750/700)
	6-231	105	R-44SX	.060	Electronic		12B	12B	17	3-4½	800/600	600
	6-250	105	R-46TS	.035	Electronic		6B	10B	16	4-5	850/425	550(600)/425
	8-260	110	R-46SX	.080	Electronic		16B(14B)	18B(16B)⑨	14	5½-6½	750	650⑩/550
	8-350 Omega	140, 155	R-45TSX	.060	Electronic		—	12B	19	4¼-5¾	—	600
	8-350	170	R-46SX	.080	Electronic		—	20B⑪	16	5½-6½	—	650⑩/550(600)
	8-455	190	R-46SX	.080	Electronic		—	16B	20	5½-6½	—	650⑩/550(600)
'77	All				See Underhood Specifications Sticker							

▲ See text for procedure
■ All figures Before Top Dead Center
● Figure in parentheses indicates California engine. Where two idle speed figures appear separated by a slash, the second is with the idle speed solenoid disconnected.
* Set V8 timing through 1974 at 1100 rpm without A/C and at 850 rpm with A/C. See sticker for timing rpm on later models.

① Not used
② Figure is 30 degrees for manual transmission
③ Cutlass
④ Vista Cruiser
⑤ 442

⑥ R-46S for automatic transmission
⑦ Figure is 44 degrees for manual transmission
⑧ Without A/C
    550—automatic transmission
    500—manual transmission
⑨ 14B—Omega, California
⑩ A/C on and compressor clutch wires disconnected
⑪ 22B with 2.4:1 axle
B Before Top Dead Center
TDC Top Dead Center
— Not applicable
N.A. Not Available
NOTE: The underhood specifications sticker often reflects tune-up specification changes made in production. Sticker figures must be used if they disagree with those in this chart.

Oldsmobile 88, 98   CAPACITIES

Year	ENGINE No. Cyl. Displacement (Cu. In.)	Engine Crankcase Add 1 qt For New Filter*	TRANSMISSION Pts To Refill After Draining Manual 3-Speed	4/5-Speed	Automatic ●	Drive Axle (pts)	Gasoline Tank (gals)	COOLING SYSTEM (qts) With Heater	With A/C
'70	8-350	4	4.9	—	6	3.7	25	17.5	18
	8-455	4	4.9	—	6	5.3	25	17.5	18
'71	8-350	4	—	—	6	4.3	24[1]	17.5	18
	8-455	4	—	—	6	5.4	24[1]	17.5	18
'72	8-350	4	—	—	6	4.3	24[2]	16.2	16.7
	8-455	4	—	—	6	5.4	24[2]	17	17.5
'73	8-350	4	—	—	6	4.3	26	16.2[4]	16.2[4]
	8-455	4	—	—	6	5.4	26[3]	17.0[5]	17.5[5]
'74	8-350	4	—	—	6	4.3	26	21[5]	21[5]
	8-455	4	—	—	6	5.5	26[3]	21[6]	21.5[6]
'75	8-350	4	—	—	6	5.5	26	20[5]	20[5]
	8-455	4	—	—	6	5.5	26[3]	21[6]	21.5[6]
'76-'77	8-350, 403	4	—	—	6	5.4	26[3]	20	22.5
	8-455	4	—	—	6	5.4	26[3]	21[6]	21.5[6]

- Specifications do not include torque converter
- [1] 22.7 gals with station wagon
- [2] 23 gals on station wagon
- [3] 22 gals on station wagon
- [4] With heavy duty cooling system—21.5 qts
- [5] With heavy cooling system—22.5 qts
- [6] With heavy duty cooling system—23.5 qts
- —— Not applicable

Oldsmobile F-85, Cutlass, Omega, Starfire, Vista Cruiser, 4-4-2   CAPACITIES

Year	ENGINE No. Cyl. Displacement (Cu. In.)	Engine Crankcase Add 1 qt For New Filter*	TRANSMISSION Pts To Refill After Draining Manual 3-Speed	4/5-Speed	Automatic ●	Drive Axle (pts)	Gasoline Tank (gals)	COOLING SYSTEM (qts) With Heater	With A/C
'70	6-250	4	3.5	—	6	3.7	20[2]	12.2	12.2
	8-350	4	3.5	2.25	6	3.7	20[2]	15.2	15.7
	8-455	4	3.5	2.25	6	3.7	20[2]	17.5	18
	8-455 4-4-2	4	5	2.25	6	3.7	20	16.2	17.2
'71	6-250	4	3.5	—	6	4.25	20[3]	12.2	12.2
	8-350	4	3.5	2.25	6	4.25	20[3]	15.2	15.7
	8-455	4	3.5	—	6	4.25	20[3]	17.5	18
	8-455 4-4-2	4	4.5	2.5	6	4.25	20	16.2	17.2
'72	8-350	4	3.5	2.25	6	4.25[1]	20[2]	15.2	15.7
	8-455	4	—	—	6	4.25[1]	23	17	17.5
'73	6-250	4	3.5	—	6	4.25	21	12.5	—
	8-350	4	3.5	2.25	6	4.25[1][5]	22[4]	15.9[7]	[6][7]
	8-455	4	—	2.25	6	4.25[1][5]	22	17.0[8]	18[8]
'74	6-250	4	3.5	—	6	4.25	21	15.5	—
	8-350	4	—	—	6	4.25[5]	22[4]	20.0[9]	20.0[10]
	8-455	4	—	—	6	5.50	22	21.0[11]	21.5[11]

Oldsmobile F-85, Cutlass, Vista Cruiser, Omega, Starfire   CAPACITIES

Year	ENGINE No. Cyl. Displacement (Cu. In.)	Engine Crankcase Add 1 qt For New Filter *	TRANSMISSION Pts To Refill After Draining 3-Speed	Manual 4-Speed	Automatic ●	Drive Axle (pts)	Gasoline Tank (gals)	COOLING SYSTEM (qts) With Heater	With A/C
'75	6-231	4	——	2.5	6	2.75	18.5	13.3	13.8⑫
	6-250	4	3.5	——	6	4.25	22④	17.0⑬	17.0⑩
	8-260	4	3.5	——	6	4.25	22④	23.5⑨	23.5⑩⑪
	8-350	4	——	——	6	4.25⑤	22④	20.0⑨	22.5⑩
	8-455	4	——	——	6	5.50	22	21.0⑪	21.5⑪
'76-'77	4-140	3½	——	2.5⑭	6	2.75	18.5	8.5	——
	6-231	4	——	3⑭	6	3.5	18.5	13.5	14
	6-250 Omega	4	3.5	——	6	3.5	21	15.5	16.5
	6-250 Cutlass	4	——	——	6	4.25	22	17	17
	8-260 Omega	4	3.5	3.5	6	3.5	21	23	23.5
	8-260 Cutlass	4	——	3.5	6	4.25	22	23.5	26
	8-350 Omega	4	——	——	6	3.5	21	21.5	22
	8-350, 403	4	——	——	6	4.25⑤	22	20	22.5
	8-455	4	——	——	6	5.4	22	21.0⑪	21.5⑪

- ● Specifications do not include torque converter
- * Add ½ qt. on 4-140
- ① Limited slip differential—5.4 pts
- ② Station wagon 23 gals
- ③ Station wagon 22 gals
- ④ Omega 21 gals
- ⑤ Vista Cruiser—5.5 pts

- ⑥ Omega—16.5 qts
  Cutlass—16 qts
- ⑦ Heavy duty cooling—21 qts
- ⑧ Heavy duty cooling—22 qts
- ⑨ Omega—18.5 qts
- ⑩ Omega—19.5 qts
- ⑪ Heavy duty cooling—23.5 qts
- ⑫ California—14.25 qts
- ⑬ Omega—15.5 qts
- ⑭ 3 pts with 70 mm 4-speed, 3½ with 5-speed
- —— Not applicable

TORQUE SPECIFICATIONS

All readings in ft lbs

Year	Engine	Cylinder Head Bolts	Rod Bearing Bolts	Main Bearing Bolts	Crankshaft Damper or Pulley Bolt	Flywheel to Crankshaft Bolts	MANIFOLD Intake	Exhaust
'70-'72	6-250	95	35	65	Press fit	60	25	30
	8-All	80	42	120②	160 min	③	35	25
'73-'74	6-250	95	35	65	Press fit	60	25	30
	8-All	85	42	120②	160 min	③	40	25
'75	6-231	75	40	115	140 min	55	45	25
	6-250	95	35	65	Press fit	60	①	④
	8-350 Omega	80	40	115	140 min	60	45	28
	8-260, 350, 455	85	42	120②	200-310	③	40	25
'76-'77	4-140	60	35	65	80	60	30	30
	6-231	80	40	115	175	60	45	25
	6-250	95	35	65	Press fit	60	①	④
	8-350 Omega	80	40	115	175	60	45	25
	8-260, 350, 403, 455	85	42	120②	200-310	③	40	25

- ① Intake manifold integral with cylinder head
- ② 8-260, 350—80 on No. 1-4, 120 on No. 5
- ③ A.T. 60 ft lbs.; M.T. 90 ft lbs.
- ④ Inner bolts—30 ft lbs.; outer bolts—20 ft lbs. minimum

VALVE SPECIFICATIONS

Year	Engine No. Cyl. Displacement (cu in.)	Seat Angle (deg)	Face Angle (deg)	Spring Test Pressure (lbs @ in.)	Spring Installed Height (in.)	STEM TO GUIDE Clearance (in.) Intake	Exhaust	STEM Diameter (in.) Intake	Exhaust
'70	6-250	46	45	186 @ 1.27	1 21/32	.0010-.0027	.0010-.0027	.3414	.3414
	8-350	45	46	187 @ 1.27	1 21/32	.0010-.0027	.0015-.0032	.3429	.3424
	8-455	45	46	187 @ 1.27	1 21/32	.0010-.0027	.0015-.0032	.3429	.3424
	8-455 4-4-2	①	④	187 @ 1.27⑤	1 21/32	.0010-.0027	.0015-.0032	.3429	.3424
'71	6-250	46	45	186 @ 1.27	1 21/32	.0010-.0027	.0010-.0027	.3414	.3414
	8-350	45	46	187 @ 1.27	1 21/32	.0010-.0027	.0015-.0032	.3424	.3424
	8-455	45	46	187 @ 1.27	1 21/32	.0010-.0027	.0015-.0032	.3429	.3424
	8-455 4-4-2	①	④	187 @ 1.27⑤	1 21/32	.0010-.0027	.0015-.0032	.3429	.3424
'72	8-350	⑥	⑦	187 @ 1.27	1 21/32	.0010-.0027	.0015-.0032	.3429	.3424
	8-350 Calif.	45	46	198 @ 1.23	1 21/32	.0010-.0027	.0015-.0032	.3429	.3424
	8-455 98	⑥	46	187 @ 1.27	1 21/32	.0010-.0027	.0015-.0032	.3429	.3424
	8-455	①	④	206 @ 1.19	1 21/32	.0010-.0027	.0015-.0032	.3429	.3424
'73	6-250	46	45	186 @ 1.27	1 21/32	.0010-.0027	.0010-.0027	.3413	.3413
	8-350	②	⑲	187 @ 1.27	1 21/32	.0010-.0027	.0015-.0032	.3429	.3424
	8-455	②	⑲	187 @ 1.27	1 21/32	.0010-.0027	.0015-.0032	.3429	.3424
	8-455 Cutlass M.T.	⑮	⑯	206 @ 1.19	1 21/32	.0010-.0027	.0015-.0032	.3429	.3424
'74	6-250	46	45	186 @ 1.27	1 21/32	.0010-.0027	.0015-.0032	.3413	.3413
	8-350	②	⑲	187 @ 1.27	1 21/32	.0010-.0027	.0015-.0032	.3429	.3424
	8-455	②	⑲	187 @ 1.27	1 21/32	.0010-.0027	.0015-.0032	.3429	.3424
'75	6-231	45	45	168 @ 1.33	1 47/64	.0015-.0035	.0015-.0032	.3407	.3407
	6-250	46	45	186 @ 1.27	1 21/32	.0010-.0027	.0015-.0032	.3413	.3413
	8-260	②	⑲	186 @ 1.27	1 47/64	.0010-.0027	.0015-.0032	.3427	.3424
	8-350 Omega	45	46	180 @ 1.34③	1 47/64	.0015-.0035	.0015-.0032	.3725	.3728
	8-350	②	⑲	187 @ 1.27	1 21/32	.0010-.0027	.0015-.0032	.3429	.3424
	8-455	②	⑲	187 @ 1.27	1 21/32	.0010-.0027	.0015-.0032	.3429	.3424
'76-'77	4-140	46	45	190 @ 1.31	1 3/4	.0010-.0030	.0010-.0040	.3414	.3414
	6-231	45	45	168 @ 1.33	1 47/64	.0015-.0032	.0015-.0032	.3408	.3408
	6-250	46	45	175 @ 1.26	1 21/32	.0010-.0027	.0015-.0032	.3413	.3413
	8-260	②	⑲	187 @ 1.27	1 47/64	.0010-.0027	.0015-.0032	.3428	.3423
	8-350 Omega	45	45	180 @ 1.34③	1 47/64	.0015-.0035	.0015-.0032	.3725	.3726
	8-350, 403	②	⑲	187 @ 1.27	1 21/32	.0010-.0027	.0015-.0032	.3429	.3424
	8-455	②	⑲	187 @ 1.27	1 21/32	.0010-.0027	.0015-.0032	.3429	.3424

① Intake 30°, exhaust 45°
② Intake 45°, exhaust 31°
③ Exhaust 177 @ 1.45
④ Intake 30°, exhaust 46°
⑤ With air induction—302 @ 1.17
⑥ Intake 45°, exhaust 30°
⑦ Intake 46°, exhaust 30°

⑧⑨⑩⑪⑫⑬ not used
⑭ Cutlass
⑮ Intake 31°, exhaust 45°
⑯ Intake 30°, exhaust 44°
⑰⑱ not used
⑲ Intake 44°, exhaust 30°

CRANKSHAFT AND CONNECTING ROD SPECIFICATIONS

All measurements are given in inches

Year	Engine No. Cyl. Displacement (cu in.)	Main Brg. Journal Dia	CRANKSHAFT Main Brg. Oil Clearance	Shaft End-Play	Thrust on No.	Journal Diameter	CONNECTING ROD Oil Clearance	Side Clearance
'70-'73	6-250	2.3004	.0003-.0029	.002-.006	7	1.999-2.000	.0007-.0027	.007-.016
	8-350	2.4990⑥	.0005-.0021①	.004-.008	3	2.1238-2.1248	.0004-.0033⑦	④
	8-455	2.9998	.0005-.0021②	.004-.008	3	2.4988-2.4998	.0004-.0033	④⑤
'74	6-250	2.2988	.0035⑧	.002-.006	7	1.999-2.000	.0035	.009-.014
	8-350	2.4990⑨	.0005-.0021①	.004-.008	3	2.1238-2.1248	.0004-.0033	.006-.020
	8-455	2.9998	.0005-.0021②	.004-.008	3	2.4988-2.4998	.0004-.0033	.006-.020
'75-'77	4-140	2.2980	.0035⑧	.002-.007	4	1.9990	.0040 max	.008-.014
	6-231	2.4995	.0004-.0015	.004-.008	2	2.0000	.0005-.0026	.006-.027
	6-250	2.2988	.0035⑧	.002-.006	7	1.999-2.000	.0035	.009-.014
	8-260	2.4990⑨	.0005-.0021①	.004-.008	3	2.1238-2.1248	.0004-.0033	.006-.020
	8-350 Omega	3.0000	.0004-.0015	.003-.009	3	1.9991-2.000	.0005-.0026	.006-.027
	8-350, 403	2.4990⑨	.0005-.0021①	.004-.008	3	2.1238-2.1248	.0004-.0033	.006-.020
	8-455	2.9998	.0005-.0021②	.004-.008	3	2.4988-2.4998	.0004-.0033	.006-.020

① No. 5—.0015-.0031
② No. 5—.0020-.0034
③ Not used
④ 1970—.002-.013; 1971—.002-.011; 1972-73—.006-.020
⑤ 1970-73 W-30—.002-.021
⑥ 1973—2.50 in.
⑦ 1973—.0005-.0026
⑧ No. 1—.0020 in. max.
⑨ No. 1—2.4993 in.

RING SIDE CLEARANCE

All measurements are given in inches

Year	Engine	Top Compression	Bottom Compression
'70-71	6-250	.0020-.0038	.0020-.0038
'70-71	8-All	.0018-.0033	.0018-.0038
'72-'77	8-260, 350, 403, 455	.0020-.0040	.0020-.0040
'73-'77	6-250	.0012-.0027	.0012-.0032
'75-'77	6-231, 8-350 (Omega)	.0015-.0050	.0015-.0050
'76-'77	4-140	.0010-.0030	.0010-.0030

Year	Engine	Oil Control
'70-'77	6-250	.000-.005
'70-'77	8-260, 350, 403	.0006-.0096
'70-'76	8-455	.0021-.0031
'75-'77	6-231, 8-350 (Omega)	.0035-.0095
'76-'77	4-140	.0010-.0060

RING GAP

All measurements are given in inches

Year	Engine	Top Compression	Bottom Compression
'70-'71	6-250, 8-350	.010-.020	.010-.020
'70-'71	8-455	.013-.023	.013-.023
'72-'77	8-350, 403, 455	.010-.023	.010-.023
'73-'77	6-250	.010-.020	.010-.020
'75-'77	6-231, 8-350 (Omega)	.010-.020	.010-.020
'76-'77	4-140	.015-.026	.009-.020

Year	Engine	Oil Control
'70-'77	6-250, 8-260, 350, 403, 455	.015-.055
'75-'77	6-231, 8-350 (Omega)	.015-.035
'76-'77	4-140	.010-.031

PISTON CLEARANCE

Year	Engine	Piston-to-Bore Clearance (in.)
'70-'74	6-250	.0025 max
	8-350, 455	.0010-.0020①
'75-'77	6-231, 8-350 (Omega)	.0013-.0035
	4-140	.0050 max
	6-250	.0025 max
	8-260	.0010-.0020
	8-350, 403, 455	.0010-.0020

① 1972 W-30 455—.0025-.0035 in.

WHEEL ALIGNMENT SPECIFICATIONS

Year	Model	CASTER Range (deg)	CASTER Pref Setting (deg)	CAMBER Range (deg)	CAMBER Pref Setting (deg)	Toe-in (in.)	Steering Axis Inclin. (deg)	WHEEL PIVOT RATIO (deg) Inner Wheel	WHEEL PIVOT RATIO (deg) Outer Wheel
'70	F-85 Series	½N to 2N	1¼N①	¼N to ½P	⅛P	⅛ to ³/₁₆	9	20	18³/₅
	88 & 98 Series	½N to 1½N	1¼N①	¼N to ½P	⅛P	⅛ to ³/₁₆	11	20	18³/₁₀④
'71-'72	F-85 Series	¾N to 1¾N	1¼N	¾N to ¾P*	¼P*	¹/₁₆N to ¹/₁₆P	8	20	19②
	88 & 98 Series	½P to 1½P	1P	¾N to ¾P*	¼P*	¹/₁₆N to ¹/₁₆P	10½③	20	18½
'73	Omega	½N to 1½P	½P	½N to 1P	½P	¹/₁₆ to ⁵/₁₆	9	—	—
	Cutlass	¾N to 1¾N	1¼N	⑤	⑤	¹/₁₆	10½	20	19②
	88 & 98 Series	0 to 2P	1P	¾N to ¾P*	¼P*	¹/₁₆ to ¹/₁₆	9½	20	18½
'74	Omega	½N to 1½P	½P	½N to 1P	¼P	¹/₁₆ to ⁵/₁₆	9	—	—
	Cutlass	1N to 1P	0	⑥	⑥	0 to ⅛	10½	20	19②
	Cutlass Salon	1P to 3P	2P	⑥	⑥	0 to ⅛	10½	20	19②
	88, 98 Series	0 to 2P	1P	⑥	⑥	¹/₁₆ to ³/₁₆	9½	20	18½
'75-'77	Starfire	1¾N to ¼P	¾N	½N to 1P	¼P	0 to ⅛	9	—	—
	Omega	0 to 2P⑧	1P⑦	0 to 1½P	¾P	0 to ⅛	10½	—	—
	Cutlass	1P to 3P	2P	⑨	⑩	0 to ⅛	10½	20	19②
	88, 98 Series	½P to 2½P	1½P	⑨	⑩	0 to ⅛	10½	20	18½

* Left side camber to be ½° more positive than right side
① Power steering—¾N
② Power steering—18
③ 9.6 for 1972 88 & 98 Series
④ 17⁷/₁₀ for power steering
⑤ 1°P—LH; ½°N—RH: ± ¾°
⑥ IP ± ½—LH; ½P ± ½—RH

⑦ 1N with manual steering
⑧ 2N to 0 with manual steering
⑨ ¼P to 1¾P—LH,
   ¼N to 1¼P—RH
⑩ 1P—LH, ½P—RH
—Not specified
N Negative   P Positive

New fuse block with mini-fuses is used on 1977 88 and 98
(© Oldsmobile Div., G.M. Corp.)

NOTE: Service procedures related to the Starfire OHC 4-cylinder engine may be found in the Monza, Vega car section.

CHARGING SYSTEM

The charging system consists of the Delco-Remy Delcotron AC generator and a conventional relay-type regulator. The Delcotron in the 442 model was equipped with a built in transistorized regulator unit. This regulator is a completely electronic sealed unit and cannot be adjusted. A capacitor mounted in the end frame keeps down high voltages and suppresses radio noise. All 1973 and later models have this integral alternator/regulator.

See "Charging and Starting Systems" in the Unit Repair Section for charging system test and component overhaul procedures.

Alternator

Removal

NOTE: Before removing the alternator, disconnect the battery ground cable.

1. Disconnect the wiring from the alternator.
2. Remove the mounting bolt, adjusting bolt, and drive belt.
3. Lift out the alternator.

Installation

To install, reverse the removal procedure, connect the battery ground cable and tighten the alternator belt. Determine belt tension at a point halfway between the pulleys by pressing on the belt with moderate thumb pressure. If the distance between the pulleys (measured at the pulley center) is 13–16 in., the belt should deflect ½ in. at the halfway point or ¼ in. if the distance is 7–10 in.

Regulator

All 4-4-2 models through 1971 and all 1973 and later models are equipped with an alternator containing a built-in transistorized regulator. This is a completely sealed unit that cannot be adjusted or disassembled. All other models through 1972 are equipped with a conventional, externally mounted regulator which should be removed and installed in the following manner:

Removal

1. Disconnect the electrical connector from the regulator.
2. Remove the attaching screws and the regulator.

Installation

To install, reverse the removal procedure.

STARTING SYSTEM

See "Charging and Starting Systems" in the Unit Repair Section for starter motor service procedures, including overhaul and starter drive replacement.

Starter Removal and Installation

All Except V6

1. Disconnect battery and carefully raise the car.
2. Remove upper support attaching bolts.
3. Remove the V8 flywheel housing cover.
4. Remove two starter mounting bolts.
5. Lower starter, disconnect wiring, and remove starter. If equipped with dual exhausts, it may be necessary to remove the left-hand exhaust pipe.
6. Install by reversing the above procedure.

V6—Automatic Transmission

1. Disconnect the battery and raise the car.
2. Disconnect and plug the fluid cooler lines from the transmission.
3. Remove the upper support bolts.
4. Take off the flywheel housing cover.
5. Unfasten the two starter securing bolts and lower the starter.
6. Disconnect the wiring after noting its position for installation.

Starter installation is the reverse of removal.

V6—Manual Transmission

1. Disconnect the battery ground cable. Raise and support the front of the car.
2. Unbolt the front crossmember from the body and from the braces. Loosen the brace bolts so that the braces hang down. Remove the crossmember.
3. Unbolt and lower the starter. Disconnect the wiring.
4. Reverse the procedure for installation.

IGNITION SYSTEM

A high energy ignition (HEI) system was offered as an option on some engines in 1974 and made standard equipment beginning 1975. The HEI distributor replaces the points and condenser with a timing wheel, magnetic pick-up, and control module. On V6 and V8 engines, the coil is built into the distributor cap; on inline engines, the coil is mounted separately. For further description, as well as service procedures for HEI, see the "Electronic Ignition" unit repair section.

Distributor Removal

1. Remove distributor cap, primary (or feed) wire and vacuum line at the distributor. On inline engines, disconnect the feed wire from the coil.
2. Scribe a mark on the distributor body, locating the position of the rotor, and scribe another mark on the distributor body and engine block, showing the position of the body in the block.
3. Remove the hold-down screw and lift the distributor out of the block.

Note: Do not crank the engine with the distributor removed; this will change the timing.

Distributor Installation

If engine has *not* been disturbed (cranked) after removing the distributor, perform the following procedure for installation:

1. Turn the rotor until it is about ⅛ turn past the locating mark previously made on the distributor housing.
2. Push the distributor down into the block. It may be necessary to turn the rotor slightly until the shaft engages in the block. The mark on the distributor housing must line up with the mark made on the engine block.
3. Tighten the hold-down bolt until it is snug and then connect the vacuum advance line.
4. Connect the primary wire to the coil or, on HEI, connect the feed wire and install the distributor cap.
5. Check the timing and adjust it as necessary. Tighten the hold-down bolt.

If engine has been disturbed (cranked) after removing distributor, perform the following procedure for installation:

1. Crank the engine until no. one piston is at the top of its compression stroke. The compression stroke can be determined by removing the spark plug from the no. one cylinder and placing your thumb over the hole while an assistant slowly cranks the engine. Crank until compression is felt at the hole and then continue cranking slowly until the timing mark on the crankshaft pulley lines up with the 0° timing mark.

2. Position the distributor in the block but do not allow it to engage with its drive gear. Observe the position of the vacuum control unit on the distributor. If the distributor is located correctly, the vacuum unit will be positioned normally so that the vacuum hose can be easily connected to it.

3. Position the distributor rotor so that it aligns with the no. one spark plug in the distributor cap.

4. Install the distributor, making sure the distributor shaft engages the oil pump shaft, thereby allowing the distributor to fully contact the engine block.

5. Install the hold-down clamp and tighten the bolt until it is snug.

6. Turn the distributor slightly until the points just open, then tighten the bolt.

7. Install the distributor cap.

8. Attach all wires and the vacuum advance hose.

9. Check the timing and adjust it as necessary.

Contact Point Replacement

V8 Engines

1. Remove the distributor cap and rotor.

2. V8 distributors were equipped with a two-piece metal shield to suppress radio static. Remove the two attaching screws and the shield.

3. Remove the two wiring terminals from the retainer.

4. Remove the mounting screws and lift out the contact points and condenser.

5. Install the new contact points and condenser and tighten the mounting screws.

6. Install the primary and condenser wire terminals in the retainer. If the replacement point set has a snap-lock type retainer, the terminals can be pushed in to provide plenty of clearance between the shield (if so equipped) and the terminals to prevent accidental short circuiting. If the contact points have a screw type retainer, insufficient clearance may exist between the terminals and the shield, possibly causing a short circuit. To prevent this possibility, insert terminals in the retainer and bend them slightly toward the distributor cam. Make sure the wiring does not interfere with the other components.

7. Inspect the cam lubricator wick and replace or rotate it if it is worn out or dry. Using a feeler gauge, check and adjust the point gap.

8. If so equipped, install the two-piece shield and tighten the mounting screws.

9. Install the rotor, making sure that the round peg goes in the round hole and the square peg into the square hole.

10. Install the distributor cap.

11. Set the points to specifications with a dwell meter while the engine is running.

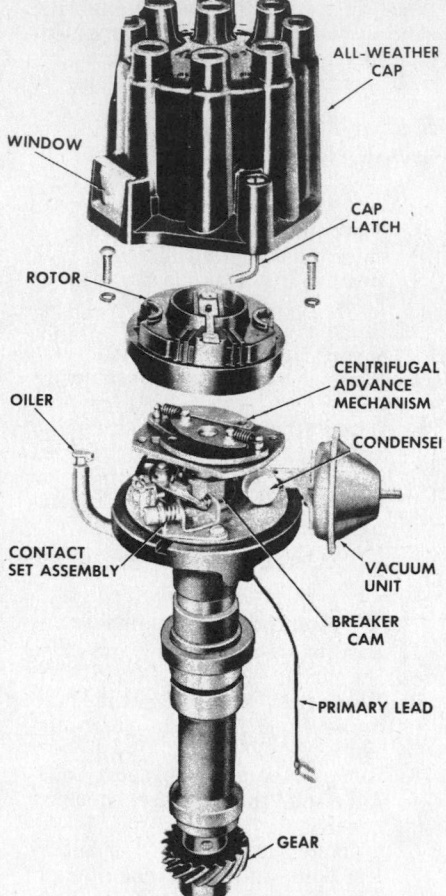

Distributor details, externally adjusted type—V8
(© Oldsmobile Div, G.M. Corp)

Inline 6

1. Remove the distributor cap retaining screws and lift off the distributor cap. Remove the rotor.

2. Disconnect the primary and condenser leads from the quick-disconnect terminal.

3. Remove the attaching screw and lift the contact point set from the distributor.

4. Withdraw the condenser retaining screw and remove the condenser.

5. Install the new condenser and tighten its retaining screw.

6. Install the new point set but do not fully tighten its attaching screw.

7. Connect the condenser and primary leads to the quick-disconnect terminal.

8. If necessary, align the contacts by bending the stationary contact bracket only. *Never bend the movable contact arm to correct alignment.*

9. Attach a remote starter switch to the electrical system. Crank the engine, rotating the distributor cam until the rubbing block of the movable contact arm rests on a peak of the cam lobe. It is also possible to turn the engine manually.

10. Insert the proper thickness feeler gauge between the contact points. If necessary, increase or decrease the gap by inserting a screwdriver in the "V" notch of the stationary contact base and using the screwdriver to move the stationary contact.

11. Tighten the point set attaching screw and recheck the gap setting.

12. Install the new rotor and replace the distributor cap. Check the point dwell and the ignition timing.

Ignition Timing

1. Disconnect the vacuum advance hose from the distributor and plug it.

2. Remove the air cleaner and tape over the vacuum hose fitting.

3. Connect the tachometer and adjust the engine speed to specifications.

4. Connect a timing light, loosen the distributor mounting bolt, and turn the distributor until the specified timing is obtained.

5. Tighten the mounting bolt and recheck timing to see if it changed during tightening.

6. Unplug the vacuum advance hose and connect it to the distributor.

7. Remove the tape from the vacuum hose fitting and install and connect the hose, if so equipped.

8. Install the V6 and V8 air cleaner.

Timing Light and Tachometer Hook-Up for HEI

1. Use an adapter between the No. 1 spark plug and No. 1 spark plug lead, when connecting a timing light. Connect the timing light to the adapter; DO NOT pierce the spark plug lead. Because of the higher voltage used in the HEI system, any break in the insulation will cause electricity to jump to the nearest ground, making the No. 1 plug misfire.

2. The tachometer terminal is next to the ignition switch connector on the cap of V6 and V8 distributors or next to the ignition switch connector on the coil on inline six engines.

3. Most new tachometers can be

used. Tachometers without a relay can't be used. Check the tach's instructions if you aren't sure. If you don't have the instructions, hook up the tach and check the readings on both the high and low rpm scales. If they agree, the tach is OK; if they don't, use another tach.

4. There is no way of adjusting dwell, since this is controlled by the electronic module.

5. If you want to crank the engine without starting it, disconnect the ignition switch wire at the distributor cap (V8 or V6) or at the coil (inline engines).

Idle Speed and Mixture Adjustments

1970 1-bbl

Adjust only with the air cleaner removed.

1. Run the engine to attain the normal operating temperature and remove the air cleaner. Disconnect the air vacuum hose from the base of the carburetor and plug the fitting.

2. Disconnect the vacuum advance hose from the distributor and plug the end of the hose. Plug the carburetor hot idle compensator so it is closed.

adjust the throttle stop screw to obtain the lower of the two idle speeds in the specifications.

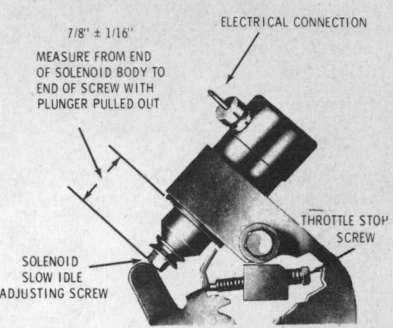

7/8" ± 1/16"
MEASURE FROM END OF SOLENOID BODY TO END OF SCREW WITH PLUNGER PULLED OUT
ELECTRICAL CONNECTION
THROTTLE STOP SCREW
SOLENOID SLOW IDLE ADJUSTING SCREW

Adjusting throttle closing solenoid—1-bbl
(© Oldsmobile Div, G.M. Corp)

1971 and 1973-76 1-bbl

NOTE: 1971 and some later models are equipped with a CEC solenoid. This solenoid does not function as an idle speed solenoid and it should not be adjusted during a routine carburetor adjustment.

1. Run the engine to the normal operating temperature, making sure that the choke is fully open.

2. Set the parking brake and block the drive wheels.

3. Disconnect the fuel tank hose from the vapor canister and the EGR valve hose.

4. Disconnect the distributor vacuum hoses from the CEC solenoid and plug the hose leading to the carburetor.

5. Set the dwell and timing.

6. Turn off the air conditioner and place automatic transmissions in Drive and manual transmissions in Neutral.

7. Connect a tachometer to the engine and, on 1971 models, turn the idle speed adjusting screw to obtain the correct speed.

8. Turn the *throttle* stop solenoid plunger inward or outward to obtain the higher of the two idle speeds listed in the specifications tables by turning the large hex nut. On later models, adjustment is made by turning the entire solenoid. Disconnect the lead wire from the solenoid and insert a 1/8 in. allen wrench into the end of the solenoid to obtain the lower of the two idle speeds listed. On models with an automatic transmission, this shut-off speed adjustment should be made with the transmission in Park.

9. Idle mixture is set by increasing the idle speed to about 100 rpm over that specified, cutting the tab off the limiter cap, and turning the mixture screw counterclockwise until the maximum possible speed is reached. The idle speed should then be

GROUND TERMINAL
C- TERMINAL
B+ TERMINAL
BATT. TERMINAL (CONNECTED TO IGNITION SWITCH)
LATCH (4)
CONNECT TACHOMETER FROM THIS TERMINAL TO GROUND.
CONNECTOR
SOME TACHOMETERS MUST CONNECT FROM THIS TERMINAL TO ENERGIZER POSITIVE (+). CONSULT TACHOMETER MANUFACTURER.

HEI distributor connections
(© Oldsmobile Div., GM Corp.)

FUEL SYSTEM

See "Dash Gauges and Indicators" in the Unit Repair Section for a discussion of fuel gauge operation.

Fuel Pump Removal and Installation

1. Disconnect the fuel lines.
2. Remove the two mounting bolts.
3. Remove the pump and gasket.
Installation is the reverse of removal.

Fuel Filter Removal and Installation

All carburetors have a fuel filter which is integral with the carburetor body. To replace the filter element, remove the fuel inlet line, then remove the inlet fitting and pull out the filter element. Be careful when tightening the brass fitting because the threads are easily stripped.

3. Apply the parking brake and set blocks in front of the rear wheels.

4. If so equipped, turn off the air conditioner.

5. If the car has an automatic transmission, place the selector lever in Drive, or in neutral if it has a manual transmission.

6. The choke must be fully opened and the fast idle cam follower must be off the cam.

7. The solenoid wire must be connected and the throttle stop screw should not touch the throttle lever.

8. Adjust the idle mixture to obtain the highest rpm possible. Adjust the throttle solenoid plunger to obtain an idle speed 25 rpm above the higher of the two idle speeds in the tune-up specifications.

9. Turn the idle mixture screw inward to lower the idle speed to the cutrect rpm.

10. Disconnect the solenoid wire and

reset to 100 rpm over that specified. Turn the mixture screw clockwise until the idle speed drops down to the normal specified idle speed.

2-bbl and 4-bbl through 1974

Adjust with air cleaner removed.

1. Warm up engine and leave it running.
2. Remove air cleaner, disconnect air cleaner hose at the intake manifold and plug the fitting.
3. Make sure the choke is open and the air conditioner is off. Set the parking brake and block the drive wheels.
4. Disconnect the hoses from the vapor canister and the EGR valve, depending on equipment. Plug the hoses, except on 1970-72 models which are equipped with 4-bbl carburetors. On 1973-75 4-bbl models, plug the holes.
5. Disconnect the distributor vacuum hose at the distributor and plug the hose.
6. Set the dwell and timing.
7. On models without a throttle solenoid or vacuum actuator, turn the idle speed adjusting screw inward or outward to obtain the idle speed listed in the specifications.
8. On models with a throttle solenoid or vacuum actuator, turn the solenoid plunger inward or outward to obtain the higher of the two idle speeds listed in the tune-up specifications. After this adjustment has been made, disconnect the electric lead from the solenoid or the vacuum hose from the vacuum actuator. Plug the vacuum hose after disconnecting it. On models with an automatic transmission, place the transmission in Park. Adjust the throttle stop screw to obtain an idle speed which corresponds with the lower of the two idle speeds listed in the specifications.

NOTE: idle mixture screws have been preset at the factory and capped. Remove the caps only in the case of major overhaul, throttle body removal or when all other possible causes of poor idle condition have been thoroughly checked.

9. To adjust the idle mixture, stop the engine, connect a CO (carbon monoxide) meter to the exhaust system and turn the idle mixture screws until they are lightly seated. Back out the idle mixture screws 6 full turns, then start engine and adjust the screws equally to obtain a good idle at the specified rpm with a maximum CO reading of 0.6 percent on the 1971 2-barrel models and 0.3 percent on 1972-73 models, 0.3 percent on 1971-73 4-barrel

and 0.2 percent on 1974 models. Temporarily install the air cleaner and check that the CO concentration does not exceed the specified level, readjusting idle mixture screws if necessary.
10. Install new idler limiter caps.
11. Reinstall and reconnect everything which was removed or disconnected in Steps 1 through 5.

1975-76 Idle Speed—2-bbl and 4-bbl

1. Run the engine until it reaches normal operating temperature.
2. Remove the air cleaner and disconnect its vacuum hose from the intake manifold. Plug the manifold fitting. Disconnect and plug the evaporative emission hose at the air cleaner.
3. Make sure that the choke is opened and that the A/C is turned off. Apply the parking brake and block the drive wheels.
4. Disconnect and plug the vapor canister and EGR valve vacuum lines.
5. Adjust the timing to specifications.
6. Adjust the curb idle by doing the following:
   a. 231-V6—(vacuum line connected to the distributor) adjust the anti-dieseling solenoid (energized) screw to the specified idle rpm.
   b. 260-V8—(vacuum line connected to the distributor; except California with A/T) adjust the curb idle screw to obtain specified rpm. On cars with manual transmissions, depress the dashpot and turn it to obtain 0.040 in clearance between its stem and the throttle lever.
   c. Omega 350-V8—(vacuum line connected to the distributor) adjust the curb idle screw to the specified rpm. Adjust the dashpot, on California cars, by turning it toward the throttle lever until it just touches it, then 2½ more turns toward the lever.
   d. 350-V8 (except Omega) and 455-V8—(distributor vacuum line disconnected and plugged) turn the curb idle screw to obtain specified rpm.
7. On 231-V6 engines, adjust the antidieseling solenoid in Neutral (M/T) or Drive (A/T) with the solenoid wiring disconnected, to the lower of the two idle speed figures in the "Tune-Up Specifications" chart.
8. On 260, 350 (except Omega) and 455 V8s, adjust the idle speed-up solenoid, on cars with air conditioning, as follows:
   a. Turn the A/C on.

   b. Disconnect the compressor wiring at the compressor.
   c. Place the transmission in Drive, with the parking brake applied and the drive wheels blocked.
   d. Adjust the idle speed to 650 rpm.
   e. Reconnect the compressor wiring.
9. Install the air cleaner and all vacuum hoses that were disconnected. Remove the tachometer and the timing light.

260 V8 antidieseling solenoid

1975-76 Idle Mixture—2-bbl and 4-bbl

Idle mixture is preset at the factory and should not normally require adjustment. However, in cases of high idle emissions, carburetor overhaul, or poor idle quality (which can't be traced to other causes), it is possible to remove the limiter caps and adjust the mixture.

2-bbl—231-V6, 350-V8 (Omega)

1. Allow the engine to reach normal operating temperature. Apply the parking brake, block the drive wheels, and place the transmission in Neutral (M/T) or Drive (A/T).
2. Disconnect the vapor canister hose at the air cleaner. Disconnect and plug the EGR valve and distributor vacuum unit.
3. Adjust the idle rpm to specifications.
4. Cut the tabs off the limiter caps.
5. Turn the mixture screws outward equally until maximum rpm is obtained. If a speed of at least 80 rpm above curb idle can't be obtained, reset the idle speed screw until it can. If the mixture screws aren't balanced or if the carburetor was overhauled, seat the mixture screws *lightly* and back each out 5 full turns.
6. Turn the mixture screws back in, equally, until the specified idle speed is obtained.
7. Disconnect the tachometer and reconnect all vacuum lines.

2-bbl—260-V8

1. Allow the engine to reach normal operating temperature. Remove the air cleaner, disconnect

the air cleaner vacuum hose from the manifold, and plug the fitting.

5. Disconnect the EGR valve vacuum hose from the carburetor. Leave the distributor vacuum hose connected.

NOTE: On cars with manual transmissions the distributor vacuum hose comes from the same carburetor port. Disconnect the EGR hose while leaving the distributor vacuum hoses connected. On California cars the distributor has no vacuum hose.

6. Connect a timing light and set the timing to specifications.
7. Remove the limiter caps. Back each mixture screw out as follows:
Manual transmission—6 turns
Automatic transmissions—5 turns
8. Set the engine idle to the following initial specifications:
Manual transmission—1075 rpm
Automatic (in Drive)—610 rpm
California Automatic (in Drive)—700 rpm
9. Turn each mixture screw 1/2-turn at-a-time until the specified curb idle speed is reached.
10. Adjust the A/C idle speed-up solenoid, if so equipped, and the throttle closing dashpot, as outlined under "1975-76 Idle Speed 2-bbl and 4-bbl".
11. Connect all vacuum hoses which were removed and install the air cleaner. Disconnect the timing light and tach.

4-bbl—350-V8 and 455-V8

1. Allow the engine to reach normal operating temperature. Remove the air cleaner; disconnect and plug its vacuum hoses.
2. Make sure that the choke is opened and the A/C turned off. Apply the parking brake and block the drive wheels.
3. Disconnect the vacuum hoses from the EGR valve and vapor canister. Don't disconnect the distributor hose.
4. Break the tabs off the idle mixture screws.
5. Connect a tachometer. Connect a vacuum gauge to the intake manifold.
6. Turn the idle mixture screws out equally until the idle speed will go no higher. Note the vacuum gauge reading.

NOTE: If the carburetor has been overhauled or if the mixture screws aren't balanced, lightly seat both screws and then turn each out 3 full turns (4 full turns—California).

7. Set the idle speed to 580 rpm (625 rpm—California).
8. Adjust the idle speed to specifications by turning the mixture screws in equally. The vacuum

gauge reading should not drop more than 2 in. Hg from the figure obtained in step 6. If it does, repeat the procedure.

9. On California cars, check the CO level with an accurate CO meter. The level should be less than 0.5%. If not, repeat the procedure.
10. Install the air cleaner and connect all vacuum hoses.

COOLING SYSTEM

Detailed information on cooling system capacity is in the Capacities table. Information on the water temperature light or gauge is in the Unit Repair Section.

Radiator Removal and Installation

All—Except 1975 and Later Omega

1. Drain the cooling system.
2. Remove the upper radiator baffle and slide the shroud back over the fan.
3. Unfasten the upper and lower hoses from the radiator.
4. Disconnect the overflow hose or the optional coolant recovery system hose.
5. On models equipped with an automatic transmission, disconnect and cap the lines which run to the fluid cooler.
6. Unfasten the radiator's securing bolts and move the radiator upward to disengage it from its supports. Remove the radiator from the car.

NOTE: It may be necessary to rotate the fan blades in order to keep them out of the way.

Installation is the reverse of removal. Refill the cooling system.

1975 and later Omega

NOTE: On models with air conditioning, it will be necessary to discharge the A/C system in order to remove the radiator. Unless you have the special tools and knowledge necessary for this task, it is recommended that it be left to qualified service personnel only.

1. Disconnect the battery and drain the radiator.
2. Remove the upper radiator baffle and slide the shroud back over the fan.
3. On models with an automatic transmission, disconnect and cap the fluid cooler lines.
4. Remove the upper and lower radiator hoses. Disconnect the coolant recovery system hose.
5. On models with A/C, discharge the system. To gain working clearance, disconnect the upper

A/C condenser line. See the "NOTE" at the beginning of this procedure.

6. Unfasten its mounting bolts and lift the radiator out of the car.

Installation is the reverse of removal. Check the coolant and transmission fluid levels.

Water Pump Removal and Installation

1. Drain the cooling system.
2. Unfasten the heater, bypass, and lower radiator hoses from the pump.
3. Loosen the drive belts. Remove the fan and pulley, complete with the fan clutch, if so equipped.

NOTE: Keep the fan in an upright position during removal to prevent the silicone fluid from leaking out of the fan clutch.

4. Unfasten the bolts which secure the water pump and remove it.

NOTE: On six-cylinder engines, pull the pump straight out, to prevent impeller damage.

Installation is as follows:

1. Apply a thin coating of sealer to the pump housing gasket mounting surface.
2. Place a *new* gasket on the housing.
3. Install the pump assembly. Lightly oil the self-tapping bolts and tighten them to 13 ft lbs.
4. Torque the 5/16 in. bolts to 10 ft lbs.
5. Install the fan assembly and tighten the bolts which secure it to the pump to 20 ft lbs.

NOTE: On 1970-73 models which have a clutch-operated fan, torque the bolts to 15 ft lbs, on 1974 and later models, tighten the bolts to 20 ft lbs.

6. Install the drive belts and adjust their tension.
7. Refill the cooling system.

Thermostat Replacement

1. Remove the hoses from the thermostat housing.

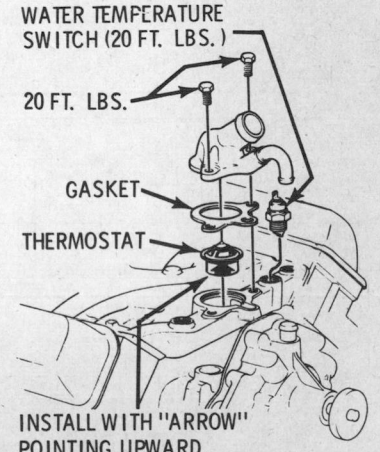

WATER TEMPERATURE SWITCH (20 FT. LBS.)

20 FT. LBS.

GASKET

THERMOSTAT

INSTALL WITH "ARROW" POINTING UPWARD.

Typical thermostat installation
(© Oldsmobile Div., GM Corp.)

LOW COOLANT INDICATOR   DIAGNOSIS - STARFIRE

LOW COOLANT INDICATOR INOPERATIVE (INDICATOR BULB DOES NOT LIGHT WHEN IGNITION IN START POSITION - BULB CHECK)

Bulb known good. Connect a jumper wire from black/yellow stripe wire at low coolant module (from ignition switch) to ground.

Turn ignition to start position and low coolant bulb should light. (Bulb check) Turn ignition on.   Disconnect probe wire (YELLOW/BLACK STRIPE) at radiator, indicator lamp should light.

LOW COOLANT INDICATOR INOPERATIVE (INDICATOR BULB LIGHTS WHEN IGNITION IN START POSITION - BULB CHECK)

Connect test lamp to ground and probe PINK wire at low coolant module.

INDICATOR LAMP OFF

Connect a jumper from yellow wire (from low coolant module to indicator bulb) to ground.

INDICATOR LAMP ON

Connect a jumper from the black/yellow stripe wire at the ignition switch to ground.

INDICATOR LAMP OFF

Repair open in black/yellow stripe wire from low coolant module to ignition switch.

INDICATOR LAMP ON

Replace ignition switch.

LAMP ON

Connect test lamp to 12 volts and probe BLACK wire at low coolant module.

LAMP OFF

Locate and repair open circuit in PINK wire from low coolant module to harness junction.

LAMP ON

Disconnect module connector and connect test lamp to 12 volts and probe YELLOW/BLACK STRIPE wire at low coolant module to radiator probe.

LAMP OFF

Locate and repair open circuit in BLACK wire from low coolant module to ground.

INDICATOR LAMP OFF

Check gauges fuse.

INDICATOR LAMP ON

Replace low coolant module.

LOW COOLANT INDICATOR OPERATION

Transistor circuits change battery DC voltage to a low AC voltage. This is connected to the base of TR3, and to the radiator sensor.

Coolant provides the ground circuit from the sensor to the Radiator and to Chassis ground. This keeps the base of TR3 grounded and TR3 remains turned off to keep the indicator lamp off.

If the coolant level drops below the Radiator Probe, the base of TR3 is no longer grounded, so TR3 turns ON, to provide a ground for the Coolant Indicator Lamp.

Use of an a.c. signal at the Radiator Probe prevents sensor erosion.

A Bulb Check feature is provided by a GROUND terminal at the ignition switch, when in the START position.

LAMP ON

Locate and repair short circuit in YELLOW/BLACK STRIPE wire from low coolant module to radiator probe.

LAMP OFF

Replace low coolant module.

LOW COOLANT INDICATOR LAMP STAYS ON ALL THE TIME

Remove lead from radiator probe and connect to a good ground.

FUSE OK

Connect test lamp to ground and probe PINK wire at low coolant module.

FUSE BLOWN

Locate and repair short circuit in PINK feed wire in gauges circuit.

INDICATOR LAMP OFF

Replace radiator probe.

INDICATOR LAMP ON

Connect a jumper wire from the radiator probe terminal (YELLOW/BLACK STRIPE wire) of the low coolant module to ground.

LAMP ON

Locate and repair open circuit in yellow stripe wire from indicator bulb to low coolant module.

LAMP OFF

Locate and repair open circuit in PINK wire from fuse panel to low coolant module.

INDICATOR LAMP OFF

Locate and repair open circuit in YELLOW/BLACK STRIPE wire from low coolant module to radiator probe.

INDICATOR LAMP ON

Remove low coolant module connector.

LOW COOLANT INDICATOR OPERATES BUT INDICATOR LAMP FLICKERS

Replace low coolant module.

INDICATOR LAMP ON

Repair short in YELLOW wire from low coolant module to indicator lamp.

INDICATOR LAMP OFF

Connect test lamp to 12 volts and probe BLK/YEL STR wire to ignition switch at low coolant module connector (module disconnected).

LOW COOLANT INDICATOR SCHEMATIC

IGNITION SWITCH BULB CHECK

BLACK/YELLOW STRIPE

YELLOW

PINK

YELLOW/BLACK STRIPE

BLACK

R1 R4 R2 R3 R5 C3

C1 C2 R6 TR3 D1 C4

TR1 TR2

LOW COOLANT MODULE

PINK

GAUGES FUSE

RADIATOR PROBE

TEST LAMP OFF

Replace low coolant module.

TEST LAMP ON

Repair short in BLK/YEL STR wire from low coolant module to ignition switch.

2. Remove the bolts, water outlet, and gasket from the thermostat housing.
3. Install the new thermostat and gasket in the engine. The thermostat may be etched with the word "front"; if so, "front" must face the radiator.
4. Connect the hoses and refill the cooling system.

EMISSION CONTROLS

NOTE: See "Emission Control Systems" in the Unit Repair Section, for testing and adjustment of the various system components.

1970

Thermostatic Vacuum Switch

All F-85/Cutlass models (including 4-4-2) equipped with the 455 cu in. engine (except some W-30 cars) used a thermostatic vacuum switch to advance engine timing for cooling engine operation during idle.

Transmission-Controlled Spark (TCS)

TCS is new for 1970, consisting of a temperature switch (6 cyl only), a solenoid valve, and a transmission switch. This system allows vacuum-controlled spark advance to the distributor only when the transmission is in high gear or when a six-cylinder's engine temperature is below 85°F or above 220° F. A vacuum line runs from the carburetor to the TCS solenoid (mounted on the intake manifold) and on to the vacuum advance unit on the distributor. A pressure-sensitive switch is located on the side of the transmission case (automatic transmission) and is electrically connected to the TCS solenoid at the intake manifold.

When the transmission is in any other gear than high gear, the transmission switch is closed and the circuit to the TCS solenoid is complete. This causes the solenoid to close and prevents carburetor vacuum from reaching the distributor. When the transmission enters high gear, hydraulic pressure opens the transmission switch, and the circuit to the solenoid opens. This permits carburetor vacuum to pass to the distributor and advance the spark. On six-cylinder engines, the temperature sending switch is electrically connected to the solenoid through a relay. At engine temperatures below 85° F or above 220° F, this switch opens up and stops current from reaching the solenoid, thereby permitting vacuum to pass through to the distributor and advancing the spark. The system used on models that are equipped with a manual transmission is identical, except that the transmission switch is manually actuated by the transmission linkage.

Evaporative Control System

California law requires that all 1970 model cars sold in that state be equipped with an evaporative control system as a means of preventing fuel vapor loss to the atmosphere. The system consists of a special fuel tank, a liquid/vapor separator, a carbon canister, and a special gas cap. A gas tank baffle limits tank capacity by 1 gal to provide room for expansion of fuel. The liquid/vapor separator is mounted to the underbody near the tank. Its purpose is to separate the liquid fuel from the vapors.

A vapor line connects to the separator output and runs to the front of the car where it attaches to a carbon-filled canister mounted on the front fender inner panel. Fuel vapors from the separator are stored here and then withdrawn by manifold vacuum through a hose to the intake

manifold where they are reburned.

Caution The pressure/vacuum cap used with this system cannot be replaced by a cap of any other design.

1971

The distributor vacuum control switch (replaces thermostatic vacuum switch) and limiter caps for the idle mixture screws are new for 1971. The other equipment is carried on from 1970.

Distributor Vacuum Control Switch

This switch combines the functions of a TCS solenoid with those of a thermostatic vacuum switch. All cars having air conditioning, heavy-duty cooling systems, and all F-85 models (Cutlass, 4-4-2) equipped with the 455 cu in. engine use this switch assembly, while all other models use a TCS solenoid. This vacuum control switch allows vacuum to reach the distributor when the transmission is in third or fourth gear or when coolant temperatures are high at idle. Operating the car in first or second gear energizes the solenoid which raises the solenoid plunger to block off port C thereby shutting off the vacuum supply from the carburetor. By blocking off port C, port V (vent) is opened to the atmosphere to drain any vacuum that might be present in the vacuum advance unit. In third or fourth gear, the transmission switch opens and current to the solenoid stops and the solenoid plunger drops to seal off the vent port (V). This allows vacuum from the carburetor to enter the switch at port C and out port D (distributor) to the distributor vacuum advance. When coolant temperatures reaches 210° F, expansion within the intake manifold moves the plunger upward to seal off the vent (V) port and opening up the manifold (MT) port to manifold vacuum. At 218–224° F, full manifold vacuum is directed to port D (distributor) and on to the vacuum advance unit on the distributor. This advances the spark and cools coolant temperatures, regardless of transmission position.

Limiter Caps

Beginning 1971, limiter caps (plastic caps) were placed over the idle mixture screws on the carburetor. Mixture is pre-set at the factory.

Evaporative Control System

In 1971, this system was standard for all models, not just California cars. The system remains basically the same as that used in 1970.

1972

1972 cars contain the same emission control equipment as 1971 cars with the following exceptions:

Thermostatic vacuum switch
(© Oldsmobile Div, G.M. Corp)

DISTRIBUTOR

THERMOSTATIC VACUUM SWITCH

CARBURETOR

MANIFOLD TEE

(HOSE) WATER OUTLET TO SWITCH

HOSE TO INTAKE BLEED VALVE

THERMOSTATIC VACUUM SWITCH

(HOSE) SWITCH TO WATER PUMP

HOSE THERMOSTATIC VACUUM SWITCH TO DISTRIBUTOR

C679

Transmission-Controlled Spark Solenoid

For 1972, this switch is used only on Cutlass models equipped with 350 cu in. two-barrel engines and no air conditioning. On all other models equipped with TCS, the vacuum cut-off solenoid is contained in the distributor vacuum control switch.

Idle Solenoid

The two-barrel and four-barrel carburetors are now equipped with an idle solenoid or a vacuum actuator. Both controls help to create a higher idle speed as a means of reducing emissions.

1973

Exhaust Gas Recirculation

All 1973 models are equipped with Exhaust Gas Recirculation (EGR). This system routes a portion of the engine exhaust gases back into the engine to dilute the incoming air/fuel mixture. By reducing the amount of combustible material in the combustion chamber, peak combustion temperature and the corresponding formation of oxides of Nitrogen (NO_x) are lowered.

An internal intake manifold passage conducts gases from the intake manifold crossover passage to the air/fuel passages in the manifold on V8 engines. In 6-cylinder engines, a drilled hole passes the exhaust gases to the intake manifold. The EGR control valve is attached to the intake manifold and normally blocks the exhaust gases from entering the engine. The EGR valve contains a spring-loaded diaphragm which is controlled by carburetor vacuum. On V8s, the EGR valve vacuum hose contains a low-temperature cut-off valve which blocks carburetor vacuum from the control valve until the ambient temperature around the intake manifold has reached 50-60°F. The black and white plastic cut-off valve must always be installed with the side marked "EGR" facing the EGR valve.

Models equipped with a 350 2-bbl engine use the same port on the carburetor as a source for both EGR and distributor vacuum.

V8s made on or after 15 March 1973 have a black plastic cover over the EGR low temperature cut-off valve, so that the valve is dependent upon engine, rather than air, temperature.

Thermal Vacuum Switch

All V8 engines are equipped with a Thermal Vacuum Switch (TVS). Vacuum hoses from the carburetor, intake manifold, and distributor connect to this switch which is controlled by engine coolant temperature. During normal engine operation, vacuum from the carburetor passes through the TVS to the distributor. If the engine should overheat while idling, the TVS connects intake manifold vacuum to the distributor which helps to lower the coolant temperature.

On models equipped with a 350 2-bbl engine, the intake manifold vacuum hose to the TVS contains a vacuum reducing valve. The purpose of this valve is to limit the amount of vacuum supplied to the distributor by the intake manifold to 9 in. Hg. This valve is required on this engine because of the fact that the distributor and EGR valve normally share the same vacuum port on the carburetor. Since the vacuum from this source is divided between two sources, the distributor is calibrated to operate on a maximum of about 7 in. Hg.

Thermal Check and Delay Valve

All 350 and 455 cu in. 4-bbl carburetor engines, except for the 350 engine equipped with manual transmission, have a thermal check and delay valve. This valve is in the vacuum line which runs between the carburetor spark port and the TVS.

When the underhood (or engine

Distributor vacuum unit

Carburetor

Spark delay valve

EGR valve

Low-temperature cut-off valve

To intake manifold

Coolant temperature operated vacuum valve (or TVS switch)

1973 350 4 bbl and 455 V8 emission controls

block) temperature is below 50°F full carburetor-ported vacuum is supplied to the distributor vacuum unit. Above 50°F, the valve blocks full vacuum for up to 40 seconds.

If ported vacuum drops, the valve opens, causing the distributor vacuum advance to be retarded. As vacuum increases, the valve closes, blocking full vacuum again.

Cars made from 15 March 1973 have a cover over the valve so that it is more dependent upon engine block temperature.

Air Injection Reactor

All six-cylinder engines are equipped with Air Injection Reactor (AIR). A belt-driven air pump supplies air to an injection manifold which has a nozzle positioned behind each exhaust valve. Injection of air at this point causes combustion of any unburned hydrocarbons in the exhaust manifold rather than allowing them to escape into the atmosphere. An antibackfire (diverter) valve controls the flow of air from the pump to prevent backfires resulting from an overly rich mixture under closed throttle conditions. A check valve functions to prevent hot exhaust gas backflow into the pump and hoses in case of pump failure or when the antibackfire valve is working.

Combined Emission Controls

All Omegas equipped with a six-cylinder engine and a manual transmission are equipped with a CEC valve. This system is basically a Transmission Controlled Spark (TCS) system. The CEC solenoid is mounted on the side of the carburetor and the carburetor vacuum line to the distributor passes through it. This switch, which is normally closed, is energized to allow vacuum advance only under the following conditions: when engine coolant temperature is below 93° F, for a period of 20 seconds after the engine is started, or when the transmission is in third gear. When any of the above conditions exist, a complete circuit is made from the ignition switch through either the temperature switch, time-delay relay, or transmission switch to the CEC solenoid. This energizes the solenoid and causes its plunger to extend, uncovering the carburetor vacuum port to the distributor and raising the idle speed of the engine.

1974

Exhaust Gas Recirculation

The 1974 exhaust gas recirculation (EGR) system remains basically the same as that used on cars made after 15 March 1973 (see above). However, a backpressure transducer valve (BPV) has been added to the EGR

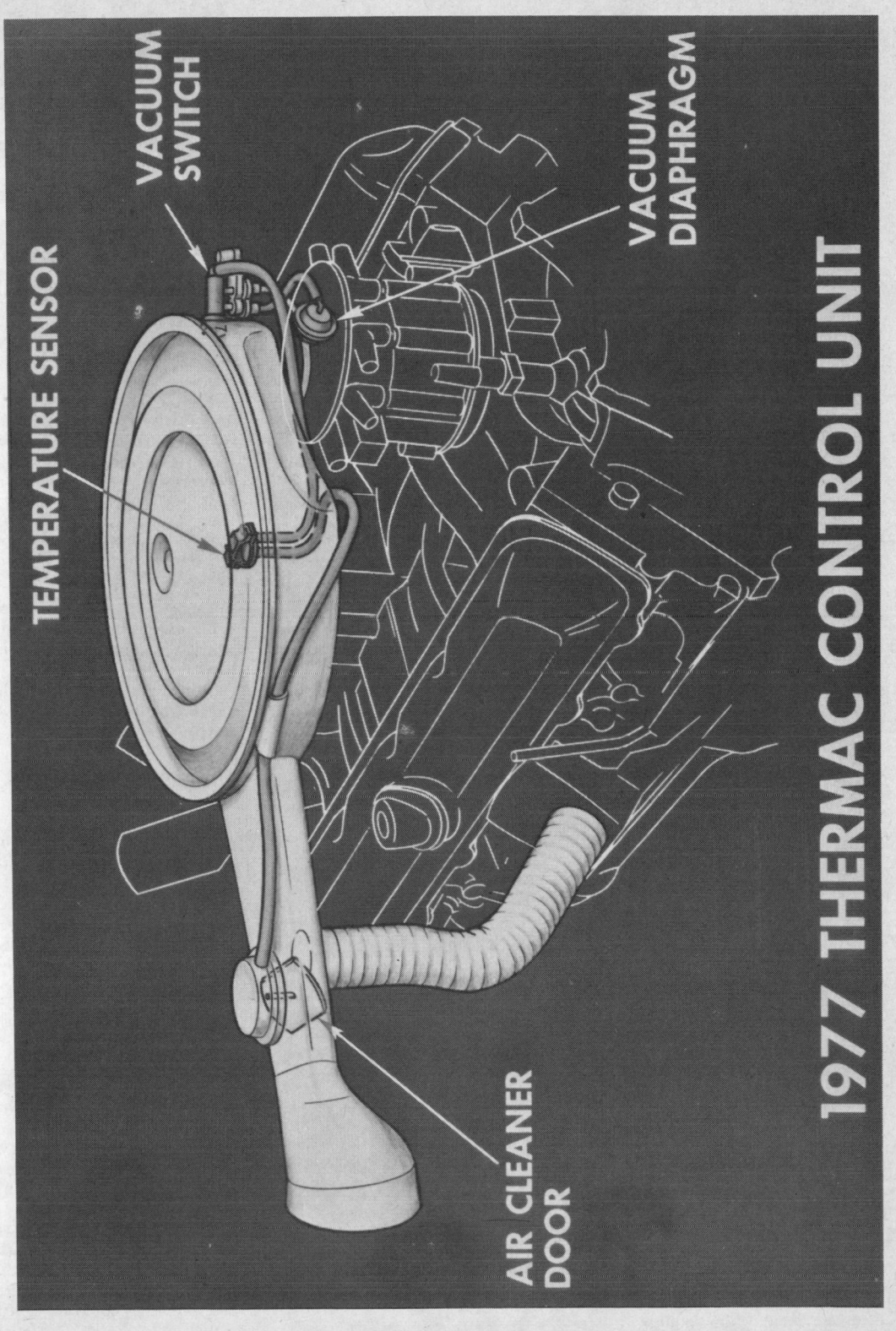

1977 Oldsmobile thermostatically controlled air cleaner unit
(© Oldsmobile Div., G.M. Corp.)

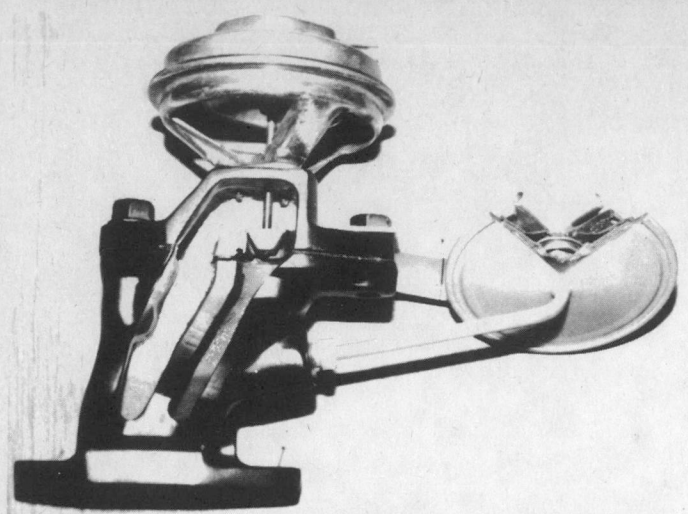

1974-75 EGR valve with backpressure transducer valve (BPV) is used on California V8s

Early fuel evaporation (EFE) valve and vacuum motor

system used on V8 engines which are sold in California.

The bottom of the BPV diaphragm is open to exhaust pressure. At idle, the lack of exhaust backpressure allows the spring above the diaphragm to open an air bleed, which prevents vacuum from reaching the EGR valve. When there is backpressure in the exhaust system, i.e., above idle, the diaphragm is forced up against the spring, closing the air bleed, which allows the EGR valve to get normal vacuum.

On 1974 inline six-cylinder engines, a thermostatically controlled vacuum switch (valve) controls the EGR valve's vacuum supply. When coolant temperature is below 100°F, the switch is closed, blocking vacuum to the EGR valve; above 100°F, the switch opens, allowing the EGR valve to function. The vacuum switch is threaded into the water outlet.

TCS System—Inline 6 Engine

The transmission controlled spark system, used on Omega models with six-cylinder engines and manual transmissions, is similar to the CEC system used in 1973.

The only difference is that the CEC solenoid has been replaced by a vacuum advance solenoid, which is attached to the coil bracket.

The transmission switch, temperature switch, and time-delay relay remain as before.

Distributor Vacuum Valve

A distributor vacuum valve (DVV) is used on all 350 and 455 cu in. engines sold in California and on some of the 455 cu in. engines which are sold nationally.

The DVV switches the distributor vacuum advance unit's vacuum source from the carburetor spark port to the EGR port. Below 7 in. Hg,

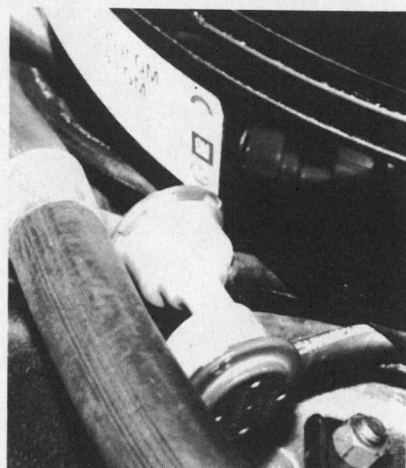

The distributor vacuum valve (DVV) is used on some V8s in 1974-75

the vacuum unit operates from the spark port. Above 7 in. Hg, the vacuum supply is switched by the DVV from the spark port to the EGR port.

Other Emission Control Systems

The rest of the emission control systems used on 1974 Oldsmobile V8 engines remain the same as those described above for 1973.

EGR temperature sensor is located under black metal cover which is just above water pump

1975-76

Catalytic Converter

All Oldsmobiles use catalytic converters to reduce hydrocarbon/carbon monoxide (HC/CO) emissions. See the Emission Control Unit Repair section for details.

Early Fuel Evaporation (EFE)

The early fuel evaporation (EFE) system is basically a vacuum-operated heat riser valve.

When the engine is cold, the EFE valve is closed by a vacuum motor, forcing the exhaust gases up around a plate underneath the carburetor, which heats the incoming mixture to aid in quicker warm-ups.

When the engine is warm, the vacuum for the EFE vacuum motor is blocked off, and spring tension pulls the heat valve to the opened position.

Vacuum to the EFE vacuum motor is controlled by either a coolant temperature operated vacuum valve, or by an oil temperature sensor and solenoid, depending upon engine application.

EFE is not used on all engines.

Dual Vacuum Break Choke

A dual vacuum break choke is used on inline six and 4-bbl V8 engines.

The secondary vacuum break pulls the choke to almost wide-open position, once the engine has reached a specified temperature. Vacuum to the secondary break is controlled by a coolant temperature operated vacuum valve (V8) or by a solenoid and electrical thermoswitch on inline sixes.

When the coolant temperature is below the specified level, vacuum is blocked to the secondary choke break. As soon as the specified temperature is reached, vacuum is sent to the break, which, in turn, opens the choke plate.

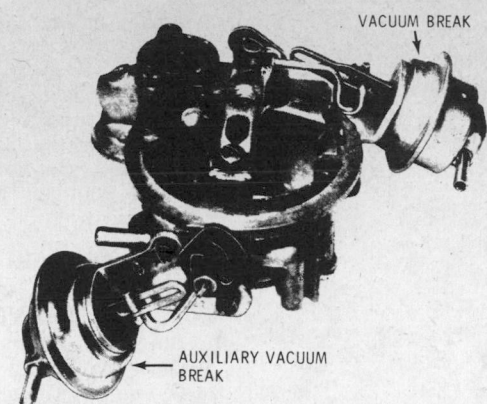

VACUUM BREAK

AUXILIARY VACUUM BREAK

Some 1975 and later carburetors have two choke vacuum breaks
(© Oldsmobile Div., G.M. Corp.)

Thermostatic Air Cleaner Thermal Valve

The thermostatic air cleaner (TAC) thermal valve is located on the air cleaner housing. When the engine is cold, the valve restricts the vacuum supplied to the air cleaner door vacuum motor which slows the operation of the door down. Under wide-open throttle conditions, the door does not "jump" to the full cold air position, thus eliminating the flat spot during cold engine acceleration.

At normal operating temperatures, the thermal valve opens and the air cleaner vacuum motor is allowed to operate in the usual manner.

Temperature Compensated Spark Advance

All V6 engines and most V8s have a temperature compensated spark advance to improve cold engine operation, and fuel economy.

When the engine is below a specified temperature, a coolant temperature operated vacuum valve supplies full manifold vacuum to the distributor vacuum advance unit.

When the coolant goes above the specified temperature, the vacuum valve switches the direct manifold vacuum supply off. This leaves only a manifold vacuum line which has a spark delay valve in it running to the distributor; reducing the amount of vacuum advance at normal operating temperature.

Other Emission Control Systems

Most of the other emission control systems remain as they were in 1974, except for the folowing changes:
1. Air injection (AIR) is used on some engines.
2. Transmission controlled spark (TCS) is not used.
3. The EGR temperature valve and its cover have been moved to above the water pump on some V8s.
4. The bowl vent on 4-bbl carburetors is opened to the charcoal canister when the engine is shut off. This helps to improve hot starting characteristics.

ENGINE

NOTE: Service procedures for the Starfire OHC 4-cylinder engine may be found in the Monza, Vega car section.

Engine Removal

1. Disconnect the negative battery cable. Remove the air cleaner assembly and heat pipe.
2. Scribe the outline of the hood hinges on the hood and remove the hood.
3. Drain the cooling system and disconnect the radiator and heater hoses from the engine.
4. Disconnect the engine ground strap from the cylinder head. Remove the fan shroud.
5. Disconnect and tag all vacuum lines and electrical leads from the engine.
6. Disconnect the throttle linkage. Disconnect the fuel line from the fuel pump. Remove the clutch equalizer on manual transmission cars.
7. If the car is equipped with an automatic transmission, disconnect the cooler lines from the radiator. If equipped with power steering or air conditioning, remove the pump and bracket or compressor and bracket from the engine *without disconnecting the lines.*

Caution Disconnecting the air conditioner lines could result in personal injury or damage to the A/C system.

8. Remove the radiator. Remove the fan, if necessary to gain working clearance. Raise the car.
9. Disconnect the exhaust pipes from the exhaust manifolds. Remove the motor mount thru-

bolts. Remove the starter.
10. On models equipped with an automatic transmission, remove the torque converter cover. Match-mark the flywheel and converter. Turn the crankshaft pulley to gain access to the three torque converter-to-flywheel attaching bolts and remove the bolts.
11. Remove the transmission or clutch housing-to-engine bolts, place a jack under the transmission, and raise the transmission slightly. On the Starfire, it is recommended that the manual transmission be removed with the engine.
12. Attach a chain hoist to the engine and remove the engine from the car.
13. Reverse the above procedure to install the engine.

Engine Manifolds

Intake Manifold Removal and Installation
V6, 1975 and Later Omega 350 V8

1. Disconnect the battery and drain the cooling system.
2. Remove the air cleaner assembly.
3. Disconnect the upper radiator hose from the intake manifold.
4. Disconnect the accelerator and downshift (A/T) linkages from the carburetor. Remove the linkage bracket from the manifold.
5. Disconnect the following:
   a. Power brake line from manifold
   b. Fuel line from carburetor
   c. Choke pipe from housing
   d. Transmission modulator line
   e. Antidieseling solenoid wire (if used)
   f. Distributor leads
   g. Vacuum lines from distributor, TVS, and EFE
   h. Coolant by-pass hose from manifold
6. On V6 engines remove the distributor cap and rotor to gain access to the left-hand front manifold bolt. Remove the spark plug leads, as well.
7. Remove the throttle linkage springs.
8. Unfasten the bolts and remove the intake manifold.

Installation is the reverse of removal. Use a new gasket and seals. Coat the ends of the seals with a nonhardening silicone sealer. The pointed end of the seal should be a snug fit aginst the block and head. When installing the manifold, start with the Nos. 1 and 2 bolts, slowly tightening them until *snug*. Continue with the rest of the bolts in the sequence illustrated, tightening them in sev-

Intake manifold bolt tightening sequence—231 V6
(© Oldsmobile Div., GM Corp.)

Intake manifold bolt tightening sequence
—1975-77 Omega 350 V8
(© G.M. Corp)

eral stages to the correct torque specification.

302 V8

1. Drain the coolant from the radiator and from both sides of the block. It is possible to drain the block through the radiator drain, by hoisting the rear of the car 15-18 in. off the ground.
2. Remove the air cleaner assembly, complete with all hoses.
3. Without removing the radiator hose, remove the outlet elbow bolts, and set the elbow out of the way.
4. Disconnect the vacuum lines and electrical leads from the various emission control devices.
5. Remove the spark plug lead harness from the intake manifold
6. Disconnect the power brake vacuum line at the carburetor. Disconnect the distributor vacuum solenoid hose from the carburetor.
7. Unfasten the fuel line from the carburetor.
8. Remove the PCV hose from the manifold.
9. Separate the accelerator cable from the carburetor. Remove the throttle control bracket screws.
10. Remove the EGR valve assembly.
11. Unfasten its bolts and remove the intake manifold. Be careful not to lose the O-ring which goes between the manifold and the timing chain cover.

Installation is the reverse of removal. Use new intake manifold gaskets, securing them with the plastic retainers. Use a new O-ring between the manifold and timing chain cover, if the old one was lost or damaged. Tighten the manifold bolts to specifications in several stages.

260, 350, 403, 455 V8

1. Remove the carburetor air cleaner, drain the radiator.
2. Disconnect the upper radiator hose, by-pass hose, and heater hose from the manifold.
3. Disconnect the throttle linkage, vacuum and gas lines from the carburetor.
4. Remove the bolts that hold the intake manifold to the two cylinder heads.
5. The coil can be left on the intake manifold if the wires are disconnected through 1974.
6. Remove the generator and air conditioning compressor brackets if necessary.

Caution Do not disconnect the A/C lines. Severe personal injury or damage to the A/C system could result.

7. Disconnect the temperature gauge wire.

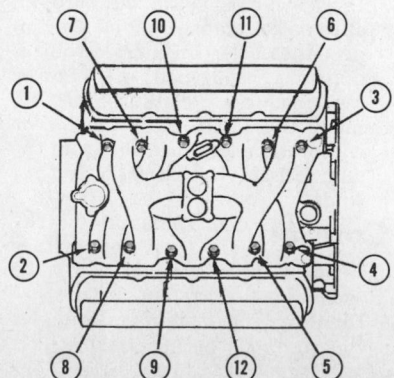

Intake manifold bolt tightening sequence—260, 350 (except 1975-77 Omega), 403, and 455
(© Oldsmobile Div, G.M. Corp)

NOTE: On the 455 cu. in. engine it will be necessary to remove the oil filler tube.

Install in the reverse order of removal, tightening all bolts first to 15 ft. lbs., then to the figure specified in the torque chart, in the sequence illustrated. Coat all gasket surfaces with sealer.

Exhaust Manifold Removal
V6, 1975 and later Omega 350 V8

1. Raise the car and support it securely with jackstands.
2. Disconnect the crossover pipe if necessary.
3. When removing the left manifold from the Omega, remove the left front engine mount thru-bolt and loosen the right thru-bolt. Raise the engine.
4. When removing the exhaust manifolds from the Starfire, disconnect the choke tube on the right side and the EFE pipe on the left side.
5. Remove the exhaust pipe-to-manifold flange bolts and the manifold-to-head bolts.
6. Remove the manifold(s).

Installation is the reverse of removal. Torque the manifold bolts to specification.

1975 and Later Inline 6

1. Remove the air cleaner assembly.
2. Remove the power steering pump and/or the air injection pump brackets. Leave the power steering pump hoses connected and set the pump out of the way.
3. Remove the EFE valve bracket.
4. Disconnect the throttle linkage and springs.
5. Disconnect the exhaust pipe from the manifold flange.
6. Unfasten the manifold bolts and remove the exhaust manifold. Discard the gasket.

Installation is as follows:

1. Clean the manifold and cylinder head gasket surfaces. Put a new gasket on the manifold.
2. Clean and oil all the exhaust manifold-to-head bolts. Hold the manifold in place while loosely installing the bolts.
3. Torque all exhaust manifold-to-head bolts in the sequence, in several stages to the correct torque specifications.
4. The rest of installation is the reverse of removal.

260, 350 (Except 1975 and Later Omega), 403, 455 V8

1. Disconnect the negative battery cable and remove the air cleaner.
2. Remove the bolts from the exhaust manifold flanges on both sides and take off the crossover pipe.

3. On the right side, remove generator and bracket.
4. Remove the hot air pipe and shroud if so equipped.
5. Disconnect the exhaust pipe from the manifold.
6. Remove the bolts that hold the exhaust manifold to the cylinder head and lift off the exhaust manifolds.

On some models with the 455 cu. in. engine, the starter will have to be removed to work on the left-hand exhaust manifold. On air-conditioned models with the 455 cu in. and 350 cu in. (1971 and later) engines, the front wheel will have to be removed in order to gain access to the right-hand manifold through the opening in the fender inner panel. When installing, tighten the manifold-to-head attaching bolts to 25 ft. lbs. on models through 1973, tightening those in the center first. On 1974 and later engines, tighten the bolts to the following specifications:

> 5/16 in.—25 ft lbs
> 3/8 in.—35 ft lbs
> 7/16 in.—50 ft lbs

302 V8

Tab locks are used on front and rear pairs of bolts on each exhaust manifold. When removing bolts, straighten tabs from beneath car using long handled screw driver. When installing tab locks, bend tabs against sides of bolt not over top of bolt.

Left-Side Manifold

1. If the car is equipped with power steering, disconnect the power steering pump but leave it attached to its hoses and pull it up out of the way.
2. Remove the generator belt, the generator and the mounting bracket as an assembly.
3. From underneath the vehicle, disconnect the exhaust crossover pipe flange.
4. If the car is equipped with power brakes, the rear bolts of the manifold are difficult to reach but they can be removed with a box wrench.
5. Remove the bolts that hold the manifold to the left cylinder head and take off the manifold.

Right-Side Manifold

From underneath the vehicle, disconnect the upper flange from the right manifold. This is the upper flange where the cross manifold, exhaust pipe and right manifold join.

From underneath the vehicle, remove the bolts that hold the manifold to the head on the back two flanges. The front flange can be removed from the top of the car with a box wrench.

Combination Manifold

Inline 6 Models through 1974

This engine uses a combined intake and exhaust manifold, equipped with thermostatic heat-riser valve.

1. Remove the air cleaner assembly.
2. Detach the throttle cable and lever at the bellcrank. Unfasten the throttle return spring.
3. Detach the fuel and vacuum lines from the carburetor.
4. Remove the PCV hose and valve from the grommet on the valve cover. Disconnect the air supply hose from the check valve on the air injection manifold (right-hand side of engine), if so equipped.
5. Detach the downpipe from the exhaust manifold flange. Discard the old packing.
6. Unfasten the manifold securing bolts and remove the clamps.
7. Remove the manifold assembly and throw the old gasket away.
8. If it is necessary to separate the manifolds, unfasten the single bolt and two nuts at the center of the assembly.

Installation is performed in the reverse order of removal.

Before reinstalling the manifold, thoroughly clean out the ports to prevent turbulence, particularly in the intake manifold. Use a new gasket and packing during installation.

1975 and Later Inline 6

These inline 250 cu in. sixes use a cylinder head which has the intake manifold cast integrally with it. The intake manifold is removed along with the cylinder head and cannot be separated from it.

Valve System

Hydraulic lifters are used on all engines. Valve guides are not replaceable, but may be reamed oversize. Occasionally a valve guide bore will be oversize as manufactured. These are marked on the inboard side of the cylinder heads on the machined surface just above the intake manifold.

Rocker Arm Replacement

V8—260, 350, 403, 455 (Except 1975 and Later Omega 350)

Remove the valve covers. Remove the two bolts that attach the rocker arm pivot to the cylinder head. Remove the rocker arms in pairs. Install the pairs of rocker arms for each cylinder only when the lifters are off the cam lobe and the valves are closed. Lubricate all pivot and rocker arm wear points with white grease. Torque the hardened flanged retaining bolts to 25 ft. lbs.

Valve adjustment—inline 6
(© Oldsmobile Div., GM Corp.)

Inline 6 and 302 V8

1. Remove the valve cover.
2. Remove the attaching nut from the rocker arm to be removed, and lift the rocker arm nut, ball, and the rocker arm from the engine.
3. If more than one rocker arm is being removed, repeat step two until all the arms have been removed. Keep the nuts, balls, and arms in order when they are removed so they can be installed in their original location.
4. Install the rocker arm and ball on their stud after coating wear points with white grease.
5. Make sure the pushrod is installed in the lifter and the end of the rocker arm, and tighten the rocker arm attaching nut finger-tight.
6. Adjust the valves on inline-6 only.

V6 and 1975 and Later Omega 350 V8

1. Remove the rocker arm cover.
2. Remove the rocker arm shaft assembly bolts and the assembly.
3. Remove the nylon arm retainers by breaking them below their head with a chisel.
4. Remove the rocker arms.

Installation is performed in the following order:

NOTE: Each pair of rocker arms must be installed so that the external rib on each arm points away from the rocker arm shaft bolt that is located between each pair of rocker arms. On V6 engines, the service replacement rocker arms are marked "R" and "L" for right and left side installation; don't interchange.

1. Install the rocker arms on the shaft and lubricate them with oil.
2. Center each arm on the 1/4 in. hole in the shaft. Install new nylon rocker arm retainers in the holes using a 1/2 in. drift.
3. Locate the push rods in the rocker arms and insert the

shaft-to-cylinder head bolts. Tighten the bolts a little at a time until they are tight.

4. Install the rocker cover and use a new gasket.

Valve Adjustment

V8 and V6

These valves cannot be adjusted. If there is excessive clearance in the valve train, look for worn pushrods, rocker arms, valve springs, or collapsed or stuck valve lifters.

Inline 6

This procedure is given for all General Motors cars using the 250 cu. in. inline six in the Camaro, Chevelle, Monte Carlo, Nova, car section.

Cylinder Head

Cylinder Head Removal and Installation

Caution Do not disconnect the A/C lines. Severe personal injury or system damage could result.

V8 Except 1975 and Later Omega 350

1. Drain the cooling system.
2. Remove the intake manifold and carburetor as an assembly.
3. Remove exhaust manifolds.
4. Loosen or remove any accessory brackets which interfere.
5. Remove the valve cover. Loosen any accessory brackets which are in the way.
6. Remove rocker arm bolts, pivots, rocker arms and pushrods. Scribe the pivots and identify the rocker arms and pushrods so that they may be installed in their original locations.

NOTE: On some models equipped with a 455 cu in. engine and air conditioning, disconnect the right motor mount and jack up the right front corner of the engine to remove the no. 8 pushrod. When the above models are also equipped with power brakes, it is necessary to disconnect the booster and turn it sideways to remove no. 7 pushrod.

7. Remove cylinder head bolts and cylinder head(s).
8. Install in the reverse order of removal. It is recommended that the head gasket be coated on both sides with sealer. Dip head bolts in oil before installing. Tighten all head bolts in the correct sequence to 60-70 ft. lbs., then again in sequence to the specified torque. See Specifications at the beginning of this section for correct head bolt torque. Retorque the bolts after engine is warmed-up.

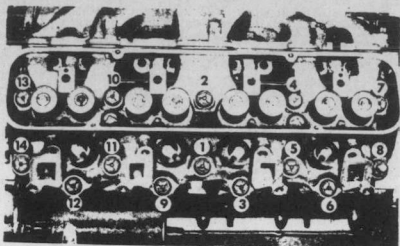

302 V8
(© Oldsmobile Div., G.M. Corp.)

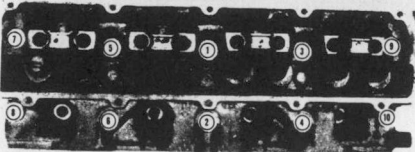

260, 350 (except 1975-77 Omega), 400, 403, 455 V8

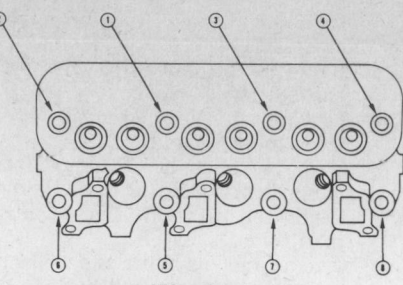

V6 engine
(© Buick Div, G.M. Corp)

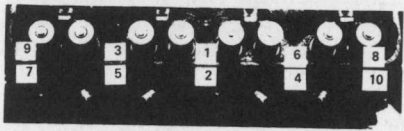

1975-77 Omega 350 V8

V6, 1975 and Later Omega 350 V8

1. Disconnect the battery.
2. Drain the coolant.
3. Remove the air cleaner.
4. Remove the air conditioning compressor, *but do not disconnect any lines.*
5. Remove the intake manifold.
6. When removing the right cylinder head, loosen the alternator belt and remove the alternator.
7. When removing the left cylinder head, remove the dipstick, power brake hose, power steering pump and AIR pump if so equipped.
8. Disconnect the plug wires.
9. Disconnect the exhaust manifold from the head being removed.
10. Remove the rocker arm cover and rocker shaft assembly. Lift out the push rods.

NOTE: When removing the head on Omega models, it will be necessary to disconnect the crossover pipe, remove its support, remove the left front engine mount thrubolt, and raise the engine to gain working clearance.

11. Remove the cylinder head bolts.
12. Remove the cylinder head and gasket.
13. Reverse the above steps to install. Torque the head bolts to specifications in three steps.

Inline 6

1. Drain cooling system (including block) and remove manifold as-

sembly and valve mechanism.

2. Remove fuel and vacuum line from retaining clip and disconnect wires from temperature sending units and EFE solenoid (1975 and later).
3. Disconnect upper radiator hose and battery ground strap.
4. Remove coil.
5. Remove cylinder head bolts, then head and gasket.

Install in the reverse order of removal. Use sealer on the head bolts prior to installation. Do not use gasket sealer when using a composition steel-asbestos head gasket. Retorque the head bolts after the engine has warmed up.

Inline 6 cylinder—through 1974

Timing Case and Camshaft

Front Cover Removal and Installation

V8 Engines Except 1975 and Later Omega 350, 302 V8

The timing case cover and the

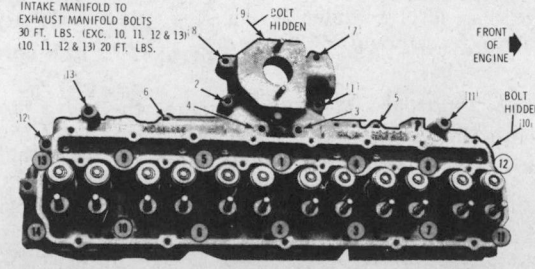

INTAKE MANIFOLD TO
EXHAUST MANIFOLD BOLTS
30 FT. LBS. (EXC. 10, 11, 12 & 13)
(10, 11, 12 & 13) 20 FT. LBS.

HEAD BOLTS
95 FT. LBS.

Cylinder head/intake manifold—1975 and later inline 6
(© Oldsmobile Div., G.M. Corp.)

water pump housing are a one-piece casting.

1. Drain the cooling system and disconnect the radiator and heater hoses, remove the radiator core, the fan blades and pulley.
2. Remove the vibration damper and crankshaft pulley.
3. Place a jack under the engine, take a light load on the jack and remove the two bolts that attach the front of the engine to the frame.
4. Drain the oil and remove the oil pan (see Engine Lubrication section).
5. Remove the front cover attaching bolts and remove the cover, timing indicator and water pump from the front of the engine.
6. Install in the reverse order of removal using a new gasket with sealing compound. Tighten self-tapping water pump attaching screws to 13 ft. lbs., 5/16 in. front cover attaching bolts to 25 ft. lbs. and the four bottom bolts (cover plate) to 35 ft. lbs. Torque the pulley hub bolt to 160 ft lbs, crankshaft pulley bolts to 20 ft lbs (10 ft lbs for 1972 and later), and fan bolts to 20 ft lbs.

V6, 1975 and Later Omega 350 V8

1. Drain cooling system and remove radiator, shroud, fan, pulleys, and belts.
2. Remove crankshaft pulley, fuel pump and distributor.
3. Remove Delcotron and power steering pump, if necessary
4. Loosen and slide rearward front clamp on thermostat by-pass hose. Remove harmonic balancer.
5. Remove bolts attaching timing chair cover to cylinder block and oil pan to timing chain cover bolts. Remove timing chain cover assembly and gasket. Clean cover thoroughly, being careful not to damage the gasket surface.
6. Turn the crankshaft so that the timing marks on the sprockets are adjacent to each other on a line with the shaft centers.
7. Remove crankshaft oil slinger.
8. Remove bolt, special washer, distributor drive gear, and fuel pump eccentric from camshaft.
9. Pry camshaft and crankshaft sprockets forward until camshaft sprocket is free. Then remove both sprockets and chain.
   If oil seal appears worn or has been leaking, replace as follows:
10. Use a punch to drive out the old seal and retainer. Drive from front to rear of the timing chain cover.
11. Coil new packing around opening so that ends are at top. Drive in retainer. Stake the retainer in at

least three places. Size the packing by rotating a hammer handle, etc. around the packing until the balancer hub fits through the packing.
   If engine has been disturbed since chain and sprockets were removed:
12. Turn crankshaft until No. 1 piston is at top dead center.
13. Mount sprocket temporarily and turn camshaft so that timing mark is straight down.
14. Assemble chain and sprockets and mount on shafts with their timing marks closest to each other.
15. Mount slinger on sprocket with the concave side to the front.
16. Reinstall fuel pump eccentric, distributor drive gear, special washer, and bolt on camshaft. Reinstall Woodruff key with oil groove forward.
17. Remove oil pump cover and pack the space around the oil pump gears full of petroleum jelly, leaving no air spaces. Reinstall oil pump cover with new gasket. This step is very important. If it is not done the oil pump will not begin to pump oil as soon as the engine is started.
18. Reinstall timing chain cover with new gasket.

Keep engine speed low for a short time after installation of a new oil seal.

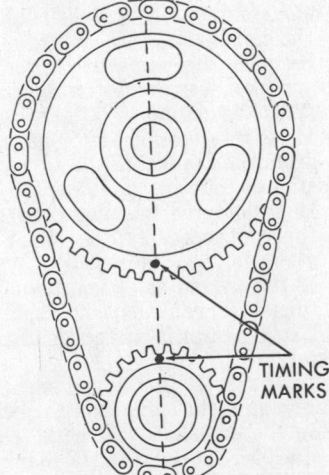

Timing marks—except Inline 6 cylinder

302 V8

1. Perform steps 1 and 2 of the "V8 Engines Except 1975 and later Omega 350, 302 V8" timing chain cover removal procedure.
2. Remove the water and fuel pumps.
3. Remove the 4 oil pan-to-timing chain cover bolts.
4. Remove all the cover-to-block bolts and nuts. Remove the cover-to-intake manifold bolt.

5. Pull the cover forward, enough to clear its mounting studs, and remove it.
6. Pull the O-ring out of its intake manifold water passage.
7. Remove the timing chain cover gasket. Clean the gasket surfaces on the block and cover thoroughly.
8. Replace the front oil pan gasket, if damaged. Cement it to the oil pan.

Installation is the reverse of removal. Use a new cover gasket and manifold O-ring. Tighten the cover-to-oil pan bolts to 12 ft lbs. harmonic balancer to 160 ft lbs, and the fan bolts to 20 ft lbs. Refill the cooling system and check for leaks.

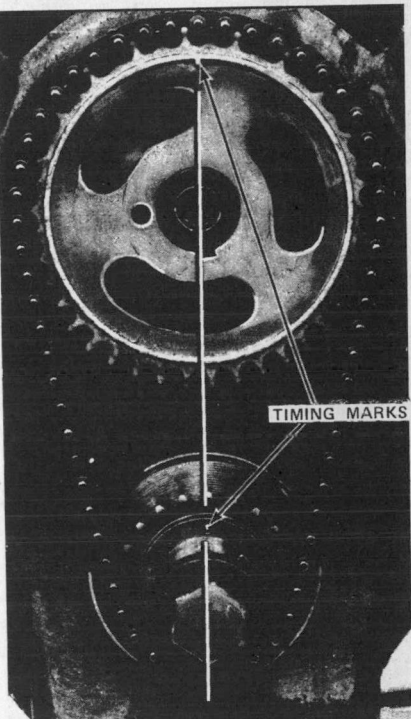

302 V8 timing marks
(© G.M. Corp.)

Inline 6

1. Remove the crankshaft pulley. Remove the oil pan.
2. Remove the timing case cover attaching bolts.
3. Remove the cover and gasket. Pry the old seal out of the front side of the cover with a large screwdriver.
4. Install the new seal so that the open end of the seal is toward the inside of the cover. When reinstalling, be careful that cover is positioned to center seal on the shaft.
5. Tighten the screws and the two bolts inside the engine to 6-7½ ft. lbs.

Timing Gear Replacement
Inline 6

Timing gears are arranged so that

(unless deliberately disturbed) the valve timing will remain as set at the factory. Unless the gears are badly worn or seriously damaged, the valve timing will remain constant within reasonable limits.

If it becomes necessary to remove the timing gear, proceed in the following order:

1. Remove the camshaft.
2. Place the camshaft and gear assembly in an arbor press. Using an adapter, press the camshaft from the gear.

Caution The thrust plate should be positioned so that the Woodruff key and shaft do not damage it during removal.

3. If the crankshaft gear requires replacement, remove it with a gear puller. Replace it using a drift of the proper size.

Installation is performed in the reverse order of removal. The clearance between the camshaft and the thrust plate should be 0.001-0.005 in. Install the camshaft as outlined below.

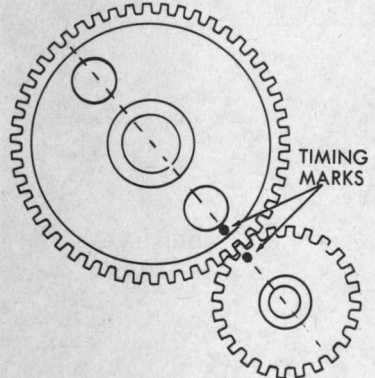

Timing marks—Inline 6 cylinder

Timing Chain Replacement and Valve Timing

V8 Except 1975 and Later Omega 350

1. Remove the timing case cover and take off the camshaft gear.

NOTE: the fuel pump operating cam is bolted to the front of the camshaft sprocket and the sprocket is located on the camshaft by means of a dowel.

2. Remove the oil slinger, timing chain, and the camshaft sprocket. If the crankshaft sprocket is to be replaced, remove it also at this time.
3. Reinstall the crankshaft sprocket being careful to start it with the keyway in perfect alignment since it is rather difficult to correct for misalignment after the gear has been started on the shaft. Turn the timing mark on the crankshaft gear until it points directly toward the center of the camshaft. Mount the tim-

ing chain over the camshaft gear and start the camshaft gear up on to its shaft with the timing marks as close as possible to each other and in line between the shaft centers. Rotate the camshaft to align the shaft with the new gear.

A dowel pin is used for alignment. Secure the camshaft gear and check to see that the mark on the crankshaft sprocket and the mark on the camshaft sprocket are as described above.

V6, 1975 and Later Omega 350 V8

1. Remove the timing chain cover.
2. Make sure that the timing marks on the crankshaft and the camshaft sprockets are aligned. This will make installing the parts easier.

NOTE: It is not necessary to remove the timing chain dampers (tensioners) unless they are worn or damaged and require replacement.

3. Remove the front crankshaft oil slinger.
4. Remove the bolt and the special washer that hold the camshaft distributor drive gear and fuel pump eccentric at the forward end of the camshaft. Remove the eccentric and the gear from the camshaft.
5. Alternately pry forward the camshaft sprocket and then the crankshaft sprocket until the camshaft sprocket is pried from the camshaft.
6. Remove the camshaft sprocket, sprocket key, and timing chain from the engine.
7. Pry the crankshaft sprocket from the crankshaft.

Install as follows:

1. If the engine has not been disturbed proceed to Step 4 for installation procedures.
2. If the engine has been disturbed turn the crankshaft so that the No. 1 piston is at top dead center.
3. Temporarily install the sprocket key and the camshaft sprocket on the camshaft. Turn the camshaft so that the index mark of the sprocket is downward. Remove the key and sprocket from the camshaft.
4. Assemble the timing chain and sprockets. Install the keys, sprockets, and chain assembly on the camshaft and crankshaft so that the index marks of both the sprockets are aligned.

NOTE: It will be necessary to hold the spring loaded timing chain damper out of the way while installing the timing chain and sprocket assembly.

5. Install the front oil slinger on the crankshaft with the inside

diameter against the sprocket (concave side toward the front of the engine).

6. Install the fuel pump eccentric on the camshaft and the key, with the oil groove of the eccentric forward.
7. Install the distributor drive gear on the camshaft. Secure the gear and eccentric to the camshaft with the retaining washer and bolt.
8. Torque the bolt to 40-55 ft lbs.

Camshaft Removal and Installation

Inline 6

1. Remove the valve lifters and the crankcase front cover.
2. Remove the radiator, evaporator (A/C only), and grille from the front of the car.
3. Remove the fuel pump.
4. Align the timing gear marks on the crankshaft and the camshaft gears, then remove the thrust plate bolts.
5. Remove the camshaft and gear assembly from the engine. Support the shaft during removal to prevent damage to the camshaft bearing.
6. Check the camshaft journals with a micrometer to determine if they are out-of-round. If the journals exceed .001 in. out-of-round, replace the camshaft. Check the assembly for signs of wear or damage.
7. Insert the camshaft and gear assembly in the engine, being careful not to damage the shaft.
8. Turn the crankshaft and camshaft gears so that the valve timing marks align. Push the camshaft into position and install and torque the thrust plate bolts to 7 ft lbs.
9. Check camshaft and crankshaft gear run-out with a dial indicator. Camshaft gear run-out should not exceed .004 in. and crankshaft gear run-out should not be above .003 in.
10. If run-out is excessive, clean off any burrs from the shaft and make another measurement. If run-out is still excessive, replace the gear.
11. Using a dial indicator, check the backlash at several points between the camshaft and crankshaft gear teeth. Backlash should be .004-.006 in.
12. Install the fuel pump.
13. Install the grille, radiator, A/C condenser, and crankcase front cover.
14. Install the valve lifters.

1970 V8

1. Disconnect the battery.

2. Drain and remove the radiator.
3. Remove the grille and any other obstructing sheet metal.
4. If the car is air conditioned, move the condenser out of the way but *do not disconnect any of the refrigerant lines.*
5. Remove the fuel pump and crankcase front cover.
6. Remove the oil slinger, timing chain and gears.
7. To facilitate proper installation of the distributor, mark the exact location of the distributor in relation to the block. Remove the distributor.
8. Remove the intake manifold.
9. Remove the rocker arm assemblies, pushrods, and lifters.
10. Carefully remove the camshaft from the block.
11. Inspect the camshaft assembly for excessive wear or damage.
12. Liberally coat camshaft with heavy engine oil prior to installation.
13. Carefully insert the camshaft into the engine.
14. Install the lifters, pushrods, rocker arm assemblies, and valve covers.
15. Install the intake manifold.
16. Install the timing chain and gears, oil slinger, and front cover.
17. Install the fuel pump, radiator, air conditioning condenser, and any front-end sheet metal that may have been removed.
18. Install the distributor to agree with the location markings made before removal.

1971 and later V8 Except 1975 and later Omega 350

1. Disconnect the battery.
2. Drain and remove the radiator.
3. Disconnect the fuel line at the fuel pump.
4. Disconnect the throttle cable.
5. Remove the generator belt, loosen the generator bolts, and move the generator to one side.
6. Remove the power steering pump from its brackets and move it out of the way.
7. Remove the air conditioning compressor from its brackets and move the compressor out of the way *without disconnecting the lines.*
8. Disconnect the hoses from the water pump.
9. Disconnect the electrical and vacuum connections.
10. Mark the distributor as to location in the block. Remove the distributor.
11. Raise the car and drain the oil pan.
12. Remove the exhaust crossover pipe and starter motor.

13. Disconnect the exhaust pipe at the manifold.
14. Remove the harmonic balancer and pulley.
15. Support the engine and remove the front motor mounts.
16. Remove the flywheel inspection cover.
17. Remove the engine oil pan.
18. Support the engine by placing wooden blocks between the exhaust manifolds and the front crossmember.
19. Remove the engine front cover.
20. Remove the valve covers.
21. Remove the intake manifold, oil filler pipe, and temperature sending switch.
22. Mark the lifters, pushrods, and rocker arms as to location so that they may be installed in the same position. Remove these parts.
23. If the car is equipped with air conditioning, remove the condenser attaching bolts and move the condenser to one side.

NOTE: Do not remove the A/C lines from the condenser.

24. Remove the fuel pump eccentric, camshaft gear, oil slinger, and timing chain.
25. Carefully remove the camshaft from the engine.
26. Inspect the shaft for signs of excessive wear or damage.
27. Liberally coat camshaft and bearings with heavy-weight engine oil and insert them into the engine.
28. Align the timing marks on the camshaft and crankshaft gears. See "Timing Chain Replacement and Valve Timing" for details.
29. Install the distributor using the locating marks made during removal. If any problems are encountered, see "Distributor Installation" in the "Ignition" Section.
30. To install, reverse the removal procedure but pay attention to the following points:
   a. Install the timing indicator before installing the power steering pump bracket.
   b. Install the flywheel inspection cover after installing the starter.
   c. Replace the engine oil and radiator coolant.

V6, 1975 and Later Omega 350 V8

1. Remove the engine, if necessary to gain working clearance.
2. Remove the intake manifold and carburetor assembly.
3. Remove the distributor.
4. Remove the fuel pump.
5. Remove the alternator, drive belts, cooling fan, fan pulley, and water pump.

6. Remove the crankshaft pulley and the vibration damper.
7. Remove the oil pump.
8. Remove the timing chain cover.
9. Remove the timing chain and the camshaft sprocket, along with the distributor drive gear and the fuel pump eccentric.
10. Remove the rocker arm assemblies.

NOTE: The push rods need not be removed. But if they are, be sure that they are replaced in their original positions.

11. Lift the tappets up so that they are not in contact with the camshaft. Use wire clips or clip-type clothes pins to hold the tappets up.
12. Carefully guide the camshaft forward out of the engine. Avoid marring the bearing surfaces.
13. Install in reverse order of the above procedure.

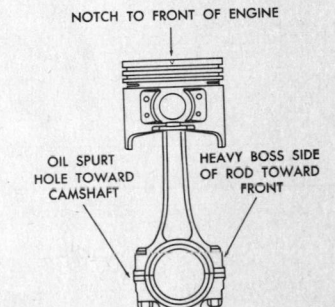

Piston and rod assembly—Inline 6 cylinder

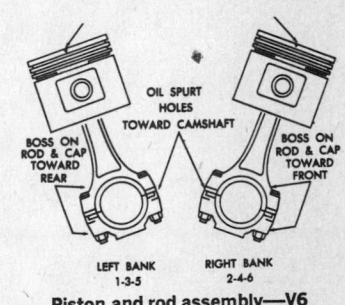

Piston and rod assembly—V6

Piston and rod assembly—V8

1977 Oldsmobile 403 V8 engine (© Oldsmobile Div., G.M. Corp.)

Engine Lubrication

Oil Pan Removal and Installation

All 1970 Olds and F-85 with 350 and 455 Engines; All V8 F-85, Cutlass, Olds, and Omega Except 455 Cutlass Through 1972

1. Disconnect the negative battery cable and remove the dipstick.
2. On 88 and 98 models, remove the upper radiator support and fan shroud attaching screws.
3. Raise the car on a hoist and drain the crankcase.
4. On F-85, Cutlass, 442 and Vista Cruiser models, disconnect the exhaust pipe from the right exhaust manifold. On 88 and 98 models lower the relay rod by disconnecting the idler arm or pitman arm.
5. Disconnect the engine mounts and carefully jack the front of the engine up as far as possible using a suitable tool. The special lifting tool bolts to the front of the block.
6. Remove crossover pipe and starter.
7. Remove oil pan attaching bolts, rotate the crankshaft until the No. 1 crankshaft throw is up, then remove the oil pan.
8. When installing, apply sealer to both sides of pan gasket and install on block. Install the front and rear (rubber) seals. Install the pan, tightening 5/16 in. bolts to 15 ft. lbs. and 1/4 in. bolts to 10 ft. lbs.
9. Reverse Steps 1 through 6 to complete installation.

455 V8 F-85 and Cutlass through 1972

1. Disconnect the negative battery cable and disconnect the fan shroud.
2. Raise the car on a hoist and drain the crankcase.
3. Remove the driveshaft.
4. Disconnect the exhaust pipe and starter.
5. Install a rear engine support bar and remove the flywheel housing inspection cover.
6. Disconnect modulator line, speedometer cable, oil cooler lines, solenoid wire and linkage.
7. Remove transmission crossmember, transmission and flywheel.
8. Raise the front of the engine.
9. Remove the right engine mount and raise the engine 2 in. Install a wedge block.
10. Loosen the left engine mount-to-block bolts enough to allow for the removal of the oil pan bolts.
11. Remove the oil pan bolts, free the pan from the block and disconnect the oil pump.
12. Remove the oil pan and pump.
13. To install, clean all gasket surfaces and apply sealer to both sides of the pan gaskets. Install the gaskets on the block.
14. Install front and rear (rubber) seals.
15. Hold the oil pan in approximate position and install the oil pump, tightening bolts to 35 ft. lbs.
16. Install the oil pan, tightening 5/16 in. bolts to 15 ft. lbs. and 1/4 in. bolts to 10 ft. lbs.
17. Install the flywheel.
18. Remove the wedge block and tighten engine mount to engine block bolts to 50 ft. lbs.
19. Remove front engine support tool and install the transmission.
20. Install transmission crossmember and remove the rear engine support tool.
21. Connect modulator lines, speedometer cable, oil cooler lines, solenoid wire and linkage.
22. Connect the starter and exhaust pipe.
23. Install the driveshaft.
24. Lower car and fill the crankcase.
25. Connect the fan shroud and connect the battery negative cable.

V6

1. Raise the car and support it with jackstands.
2. Drain the oil.
4. Remove the flywheel/torque converter cover.
5. Remove the crossover pipe.
6. Remove the oil pan bolts and the oil pan.

Installation is the reverse of removal. Apply non-hardening silicone sealer to several places around the oil pan gasket, before installing it on the block.

Inline 6

1. Disconnect battery negative cable, fuel flex line at the fuel pump and starter leads at the starter.
2. Remove upper radiator support and bracket to upper hose. On cars with air conditioning, remove the fan and clutch assembly.
3. Remove front motor mount bracket to motor mount bolts.

4. Raise the car on a hoist and drain crankcase.
5. Disconnect automatic transmission linkage and remove flywheel cover and starter.
6. Disconnect exhaust pipe at the manifold.
7. Position timing mark notch at the 6 o'clock position.
8. Raise the engine with a jack at the crankshaft damper and remove the right engine mount with bracket.
9. Remove the oil pan attaching bolts and the oil pan. It may be necessary to raise the engine further to get the pan out. Be careful not to damage cowl mounted parts.
10. To install, reverse the above procedure. Use new gaskets.

Oil Pump

The oil pump is mounted to the bottom of the block and is accessible only by removing the oil pan.

On V8 engines, remove the oil pan, then unbolt and remove the oil pump and screen as an assembly. On the OHV 6 the pickup tube has a bolt-attached bracket.

Rear Main Bearing Oil Seal

V6 and V8 except 302 V8

The crankshaft need not be removed to replace the rear main bearing upper oil seal.

1. Drain the crankcase and remove the oil pan and rear main bearing cap.
2. Using a blunt-ended tool, drive the upper seal into its groove on each side until it is tightly packed. This is usually 1/4-3/4 in.
3. Cut pieces of new seal 1/16 in. longer than required to fill the grooves and install, packing into place.
4. Carefully trim any protruding seal, being sure not to scratch or damage the bearing surface.
5. Install a new seal in the bearing cap and install cap, tightening bolts to 120 ft. lbs. Install the oil pan.

302 V8

1. Remove the oil pan, baffle, and oil pump.
2. Remove the rear main bearing cap.

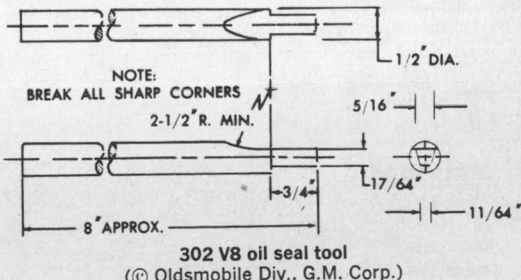

NOTE:
BREAK ALL SHARP CORNERS
2-1/2" R. MIN.
1/2" DIA.
5/16"
3/4"
17/64"
11/64"
8" APPROX.

302 V8 oil seal tool
(© Oldsmobile Div., G.M. Corp.)

3. Make a seal tool.

4. Insert the tool against one end of the oil seal in the block and drive the seal gently into the groove ¾ in. Repeat on the other end of the seal.

5. Form a new seal in the cap. Cut four pieces ⅜ in. long from this seal.

6. Work two of the pieces into each of the gaps which have been made at the end of the seal in the block. Do not cut off any material to make them fit.

7. Form a new seal in the bearing cap.

8. Apply a 1/16 in. bead of sealer across to the external cork groove.

9. Reassemble the cap and torque to specifications.

Inline 6

The rear main bearing oil seal is of moulded design and can be replaced (both halves) without removal of the crankshaft.

NOTE: always replace both halves as a unit. Install with the lip facing toward front of the engine.

1. With oil pan and pump removed, remove the rear main bearing cap.

2. Remove oil seal from the groove by lifting the end tab, then clean seal groove.

3. Lubricate the lip and O.D. of a new seal with engine oil. Keep oil off the parting line surface.

4. Insert seal into cap and roll into place with fingers. Use light pressure on the seal to prevent cutting the O.D. of the seal with the sharp edges of the groove. Be sure the tabs of the seal are properly located in the cross grooves.

5. To remove upper half of seal, use a small hammer to tap a brass pin punch on one end of seal until it protrudes far enough to be removed with pliers.

6. Lubricate the lip and O.D. of a new seal with engine oil. Keep oil off parting line surface. Gradually push with a hammer handle, while turning crankshaft, until seal is rolled into place. Be careful that seal bead on O.D. of seal is not cut.

7. Install rear main bearing cap (with new seal) and torque to specifications. Be sure cross seal tabs are in place and properly seated.

CLUTCH

Clutch Pedal Adjustment

Through 1972

The clutch pedal should be adjusted so that there is ¾ to 1 in.

free-play at the clutch pedal before the throwout bearing engages the clutch fingers. This adjustment is made under the car at the adjustable clutch rod just in front of the throwout fork. Loosen the jam nut and turn the adjusting screw until the desired clearance is obtained, then tighten the jam nut.

1973 and Later—Omega, Cutlass

The clutch pedal free-play should be adjusted to the following specifications, which are measured from the center of the clutch pedal pad:

Cutlass—¾-1¼ in.
Omega—⅞-1½ in.

To adjust free-play, proceed in the following manner:

1. Loosen the locknut on the push rod swivel.

2. Detach the pedal return spring.

3. Turn the equalizer assembly until the clutch pedal seats against the rubber bumper on the dash brace.

4. Push the outer end of the clutch fork rearward, so that the throwout bearing just contacts the clutch plate.

5. Remove the retaining clip from the lower push rod swivel and install the swivel in the *upper* gauge hole. Install the retaining clip.

6. Lengthen the push rod until there is no lash.

7. Remove the retaining clip and reinstall the swivel in the *lower* hole on the equalizer lever.

8. Tighten the locknut against the swivel. Be sure that the rod length remains unchanged.

9. Install the pedal return spring and check pedal free-play.

1975 Starfire

Adjustment for normal clutch wear is accomplished by turning the clutch fork ball stud counterclock-

wise to give 11/16 to 1⅛ in. lash at clutch pedal.

1. Remove the ball stud cap and loosen the locknut on ball stud end located to the right of the transmission on the clutch housing.

2. Adjust the ball stud to obtain 11/16 to 1⅛ in. free travel.

3. Tighten the locknut to 30 ft lbs. being careful not to change adjustment and install ball stud cap.

4. Check the operation of clutch.

1976 and Later Starfire

1. Remove the clutch fork return spring.

2. Loosen the cable end nut (pin).

3. Push the clutch fork forward until the throwout bearing can be felt to contact the release fingers, while pulling on the end of the clutch cable so that the pedal arm is up against the rubber stop. Tighten the cable end nut (pin) until it touches the fork. Tighten it another quarter turn so that it can drop into the fork groove.

4. Replace the return spring. Pedal play should now be 11/16-1⅛ in.

Clutch Replacement
Omega and Cutlass

1. Remove the transmission.

2. Detach the clutch return spring and clutch release rod assembly.

3. Remove the throwout bearing.

4. Without removing the starter from the engine, remove the flywheel housing.

NOTE: The release yoke, boot and ball stud will remain in the housing.

5. Scribe a mark opposite the "X" mark on the flywheel cover.

6. Loosen the pressure plate evenly, one turn at a time.

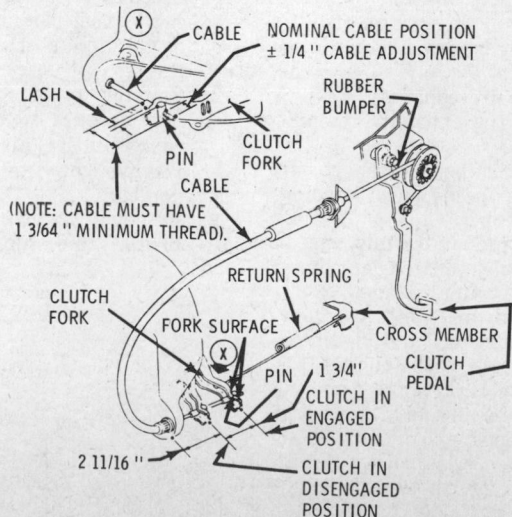

Starfire clutch cable installation and adjustment
(© Oldsmobile Div., GM Corp.)

Clutch installation is performed in the following order:

Caution Do not lubricate the splines as the lubricant will be forced on to the damper, resulting in clutch rattle.

1. Install the clutch disc/cover assembly and finger-tighten its securing bolts.

   NOTE: Align the mark made during removal with the "X" mark on the flywheel cover.

2. Use a clutch arbor or an old input shaft to align the disc by inserting it through the disc and into the pilot bearing.

3. Tighten every other bolt until the cover assembly is within ¼ in. of the flywheel.

4. Repeat step 3 for the three remaining bolts.

5. Tighten the first three bolts to the torque figure given below and then tighten the remaining three bolts to the same figure.

   1970—17 ft lbs
   1971 and later—30 ft lbs

6. Remove the arbor. Lubricate the inside groove of the throwout bearing and the release yoke ball stud with wheel bearing grease.

7. Install the throwout bearing.

8. Install the flywheel housing and the transmission. Adjust clutch free-play as outlined above.

Starfire

1. Raise vehicle on hoist.

2. Remove transmission as outlined in this section.

3. Remove clutch fork cover then disconnect clutch return spring and control cable from clutch fork.

4. Remove flywheel housing lower cover.

5. Remove flywheel housing from engine.

6. To remove the release bearing from clutch fork and sleeve, slide lever off ball stud against spring action. If necessary to replace ball stud, remove cap, locknut and stud from housing.

7. If assembly marks on clutch assembly and flywheel are not visible remark with paint or centerpunch.

8. Loosen clutch cover-to-flywheel attaching bolts one turn at a time until spring pressure is released, to avoid bending clutch cover flange.

9. Support the pressure plate and cover assembly then remove the bolts and clutch assembly.

Caution Do not disassemble the clutch cover, spring and pressure plate for repair. If defective replace complete assembly.

10. Index alignment marks on clutch assembly and flywheel. Place driven plate on pressure plate with long end of splined end facing forward, damper springs inside pressure plate, and insert a dummy clutch gear shaft through the cover and driven plate.

11. Position the complete assembly against the flywheel and insert the dummy shaft into the pilot bearing in the crankshaft.

12. Index the alignment marks and install clutch cover to flywheel bolts finger-tight.

Caution Tighten all bolts evenly and gradually until tight to avoid possible clutch distortion. Torque bolts 18 ft. lbs. and remove dummy shaft.

13. Lubricate the clutch fork ball socket and the fingers at the release bearing with a high melting point grease such as graphite grease.

14. Lubricate the recess on the inside of the throwout bearing collar and the fork groove with a light coat of graphite grease. Install fork in housing but not on stud.

15. Install bearing on sleeve, then position clutch fork over bearing in housing and slide fork onto ball stud.

16. Install flywheel housing and lower cover. Tighten bolts to 30 ft lbs.

17. Install transmission as outlined.

18. Adjust clutch as previously outlined.

19. Lower and remove vehicle from hoist.

MANUAL TRANSMISSION

The standard 3-speed transmission in all models is the Saginaw unit. The optional heavy-duty 3-speed offered in the Cutlass-size body through 1971 is the Muncie transmission. The Saginaw and Muncie 3-speeds are very similar in appearance, but the Saginaw has only one case bolt boss casting "ear" at the center top of the side cover, while the Muncie has two such "ears." The standard 4-speed transmission in all models is the Saginaw unit. The optional heavy-duty 4-speed offered in the Cutlass-size body through 1973 is the Muncie transmission. On the Saginaw, all three shift rods go to levers on the side cover, while on the Muncie, one rod (reverse) goes to a lever on the case extension housing. Some Starfires with the OHC 4-cylinder engine use the GM 70 mm 4-speed transmission, which has no external shift linkage.

The 5-speed transmission is the Warner T-50 unit. There is no shift linkage adjustment necessary or possible on the GM 70 mm 4-speed or the Warner T-50 5-speed.

See the Capacities Table at the beginning of this section for manual transmission refill capacities. For manual transmission overhaul procedures, see the Unit Repair Section.

Transmission Removal and Installation

1. Disconnect throttle linkage and raise car. If applicable, disconnect T.C.S. switch.

2. Remove driveshaft.

3. Support the rear of the engine. Remove the catalytic converter and/or brackets, if they are in the way.

4. On console equipped floorshifts, disconnect shifter assembly at transmission, allowing this unit to remain in car. On regular floorshifts, remove floor pan seal. Insert a feeler gauge between the shift lever and its point of attachment. This will release a pin allowing the lever to be removed. Remove the 5-speed shift lever. Remove the shifter with transmission.

5. Disconnect parking brake cables and remove the cross member. Remove the Starfire torque arm.

6. Disconnect speedometer cable and back-up light switch.

7. Remove transmission upper and lower bolts.

Caution During removal, use aligning studs to support the transmission, otherwise distortion of the clutch driven plate will result.

8. Slide transmission rearward and remove. On models equipped with dual exhaust, it may be necessary to disconnect left exhaust pipe at the manifold.

9. Install by reversing procedure above.

Shift Linkage Adjustment

Column Shift

1. With the transmission in reverse loosen the swivel bolts on the shift rods at the transmission.

2. Check that the shift rods move freely in the swivels, then push up on the reverse shift rod until the detent in the column is felt and tighten the swivel bolt for the first-reverse rod.

3. With transmission in neutral, insert a 3/16 in. rod through the second-third shift lever and into the alignment hole. Tighten the swivel bolt for the second-third shift lever.

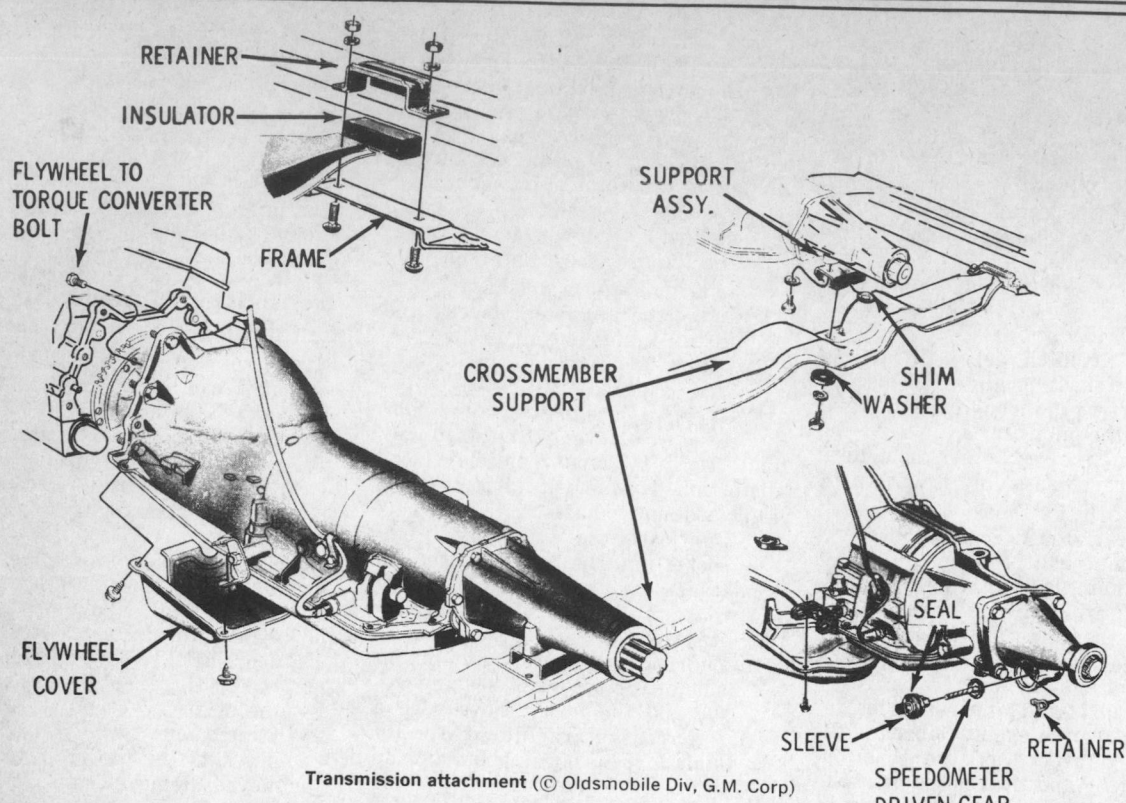

RETAINER

INSULATOR

FLYWHEEL TO
TORQUE CONVERTER
BOLT

FRAME

SUPPORT
ASSY.

CROSSMEMBER
SUPPORT

SHIM
WASHER

FLYWHEEL
COVER

SEAL

SLEEVE

SPEEDOMETER
DRIVEN GEAR

RETAINER

Transmission attachment (© Oldsmobile Div, G.M. Corp)

4. Lower the car and check the shift operation.
5. Place transmission in Reverse and the ignition in LOCK position. Check that the key can be removed, the wheel not turned and the transmission will not shift out of Reverse.
6. Turn the ignition to RUN position and place the transmission in second gear. Check that the ignition key cannot be removed and that the steering wheel will turn.

Cutlass 3- and 4-Speed Floor Shift

The linkage adjustment procedure is the same as that described above

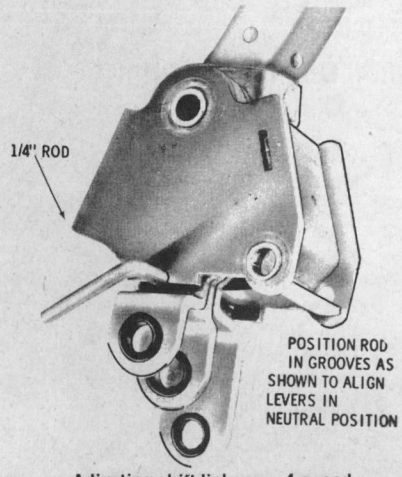

1/4" ROD

POSITION ROD IN GROOVES AS SHOWN TO ALIGN LEVERS IN NEUTRAL POSITION

Adjusting shift linkage—4-speed
(© Oldsmobile Div, G.M. Corp)

for the column shift type, with the exception that the shift levers are aligned with a ¼ in. rod.

Omega 3-Speed Floorshift

1. Place the shift lever in Neutral.
2. Loosen the swivel nuts on the shift rods and detach the rods from the shifter assembly.
3. Insert a ¼ in. pin in the locating gauge hole on the shifter.
4. Adjust the swivel so that free pin length is obtained.
5. Tighten the swivel nuts and attach the shift rods back to the shifter.
6. Position the shift lever in Reverse and turn the ignition key to LOCK.
7. Loosen the equalizer clamp screw and pull the backdrive rod down lightly against the stop.
8. Tighten the clamp screw.
9. Perform steps 5-6 of the "Column Shift" adjustment.

Starfire 4-Speed Floorshift (Saginaw Transmission)

1. Turn the ignition switch to "Off" and place the shift lever in Neutral.
2. Loosen the locknuts on the control rods. Position the transmission side cover levers in their neutral detents.
3. With the floor shift lever in Neutral, align the shifter levers and insert a gauge pin into the levers and bracket.
4. Tighten the First/Second control rod locknut against its swivel.

5. Tighten the Third/Fourth control rod locknut against its swivel.
6. Tighten the Reverse control rod locknut against its swivel.
7. Remove the gauge pin and check shifter operation.

AUTOMATIC TRANSMISSION

All Oldsmobile models use the Turbo Hydra-Matic automatic transmission. 1976 and later Starfires and Omegas with 260 cu. in. or smaller engines use the Turbo Hydra-Matic 200. This transmission is readily identified by the word METRIC stamped on the pan. Starfires with the OHC 4-cylinder engine use the Turbo Hydra-Matic 250. This transmission is similar to the 200, but has an intermediate band adjusting screw on the right side of the case. The Turbo Hydra-Matic 350 is the standard automatic transmission on most models. It can readily be identified by its downshift cable between the carburetor accelerator linkage and the transmission. The Turbo Hydra-Matic 375B, introduced in 1976 on a few 88 models, is externally similar to the 350, differing only in torque capacity and extension housing and output shaft length. The Turbo Hydra-Matic 375 and 400 are used in the larger cars and with the larger engines. They are identical externally, differing only in torque capacity. The 375 and 400 may be identified by their electrical downshift switch on the accelerator pedal linkage.

Shift Linkage Adjustment

Column Shift

1. Put the column shift lever in Neutral (Park for 1970).
2. Loosen the adjusting clamp on the linkage to the transmission.
3. Hold the column shift lever against the stop, but don't raise the lever.
4. Tighten the clamp screw after making sure that the lever on the transmission is engaged in the detent.
5. Check that the key cannot be removed and the steering wheel is not locked with the key in Run and the transmission in Reverse. Check that the key can be removed and the steering wheel and transmission linkage is locked, when the key is in Lock and the transmission in Park.

Floorshift

The 1975 Starfire uses a rod operated linkage, which is adjusted at the bottom of the shifter. All other models use a cable linkage, adjusted at the transmission.

1. Set the Starfire floorshift lever in Neutral. Set all other models in Park, with the key in Lock.
2. Loosen the adjusting clamp on the linkage.
3. Make sure that the lever on the transmission is engaged in the detent.
4. Tighten the clamp screw.
5. Check that the key cannot be

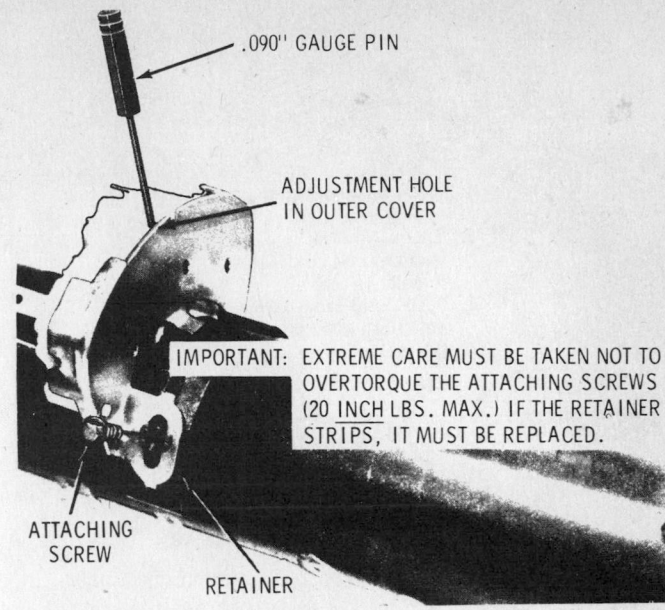

IMPORTANT: EXTREME CARE MUST BE TAKEN NOT TO OVERTORQUE THE ATTACHING SCREWS (20 INCH LBS. MAX.) IF THE RETAINER STRIPS, IT MUST BE REPLACED.

.090" GAUGE PIN

ADJUSTMENT HOLE IN OUTER COVER

ATTACHING SCREW

RETAINER

Neutral safety switch adjustment (© Oldsmobile Div, G.M. Corp)

removed and the steering wheel is not locked with the key in Run and the transmission in Reverse. Check that the key can be removed and the steering wheel and transmission linkage is locked, when the key is in Lock and the transmission in Park.

Neutral Safety Switch

Column-Mounted Switch, 1971 and later Console-Mounted Switch

1. Place the gear selector in the appropriate range:
   1970 Column—Drive (D)
   1971 and later Column—Neutral (N)
   1971 and later Console—Park (P)
   Starfire Console—Neutral (N)
2. Loosen the switch securing screws.
   NOTE: Remove the center console first, if necessary.
3. Fit a 0.090 in. gauge pin into the outer hole on the switch cover.
4. Move the switch until the gauge pin drops into the alignment hole on the inner slide. Tighten the switch securing screws; then remove the gauge pin.

1970 Console-Mounted Switch

1. Remove the center console assembly.

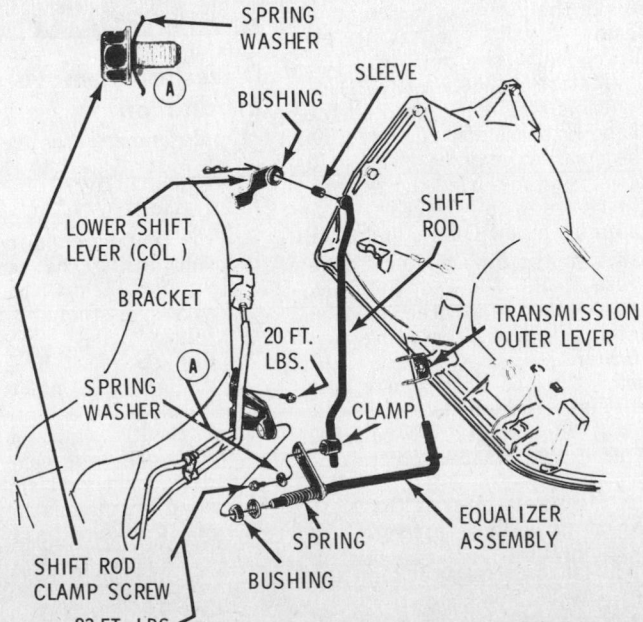

SPRING WASHER

Ⓐ

BUSHING

SLEEVE

LOWER SHIFT LEVER (COL.)

BRACKET

SPRING WASHER

Ⓐ

20 FT. LBS.

SHIFT ROD

SHIFT ROD CLAMP SCREW

23 FT. LBS.

SPRING

BUSHING

CLAMP

TRANSMISSION OUTER LEVER

EQUALIZER ASSEMBLY

SHIFT ROD ADJUSTMENT

1. WITH SHIFT ROD CLAMP SCREW LOOSENED, SET TRANSMISSION OUTER LEVER IN NEUTRAL POSITION.

2. HOLD UPPER SHIFT LEVER AGAINST NEUTRAL POSITION STOP IN UPPER STEERING COLUMN. (DO NOT RAISE LEVER.)

3. TIGHTEN SCREW IN CLAMP ON LOWER END OF SHIFT ROD TO SPECIFIED TORQUE.

4. CHECK OPERATION:

   A. WITH KEY IN "RUN" POSITION AND TRANSMISSION IN "REVERSE" BE SURE THAT KEY CANNOT BE REMOVED AND THAT STEERING WHEEL IS NOT LOCKED.

   B. WITH KEY IN "LOCK" POSITION AND SHIFT LEVER IN "PARK", BE SURE THAT KEY CAN BE REMOVED, THAT STEERING WHEEL IS LOCKED, AND THAT THE TRANSMISSION REMAINS IN PARK WHEN THE STEERING COLUMN IS LOCKED.

Column shift linkage adjustment—1971-76 (© Oldsmobile Div., GM Corp.)

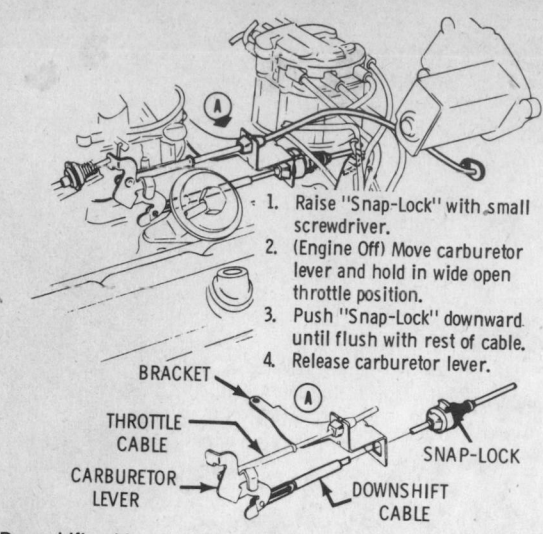

1. Raise "Snap-Lock" with small screwdriver.
2. (Engine Off) Move carburetor lever and hold in wide open throttle position.
3. Push "Snap-Lock" downward until flush with rest of cable.
4. Release carburetor lever.

BRACKET
THROTTLE CABLE
CARBURETOR LEVER
SNAP-LOCK
DOWNSHIFT CABLE

Downshift cable adjustment, Turbo Hydra-Matic 350—Omega V8
(© Oldsmobile Div., GM Corp.)

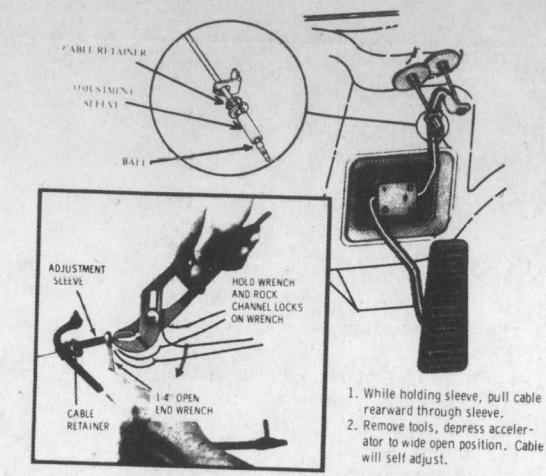

CABLE RETAINER
ADJUSTMENT SLEEVE
BALL
ADJUSTMENT SLEEVE
HOLD WRENCH AND ROCK CHANNEL LOCKS ON WRENCH
CABLE RETAINER
1/4" OPEN END WRENCH

1. While holding sleeve, pull cable rearward through sleeve.
2. Remove tools, depress accelerator to wide open position. Cable will self adjust.

Downshift cable adjustment, Turbo Hydra-Matic 350—Cutlass V8
(© Oldsmobile Div., GM Corp.)

2. Position the gear selector lever against the neutral stop.
3. Adjust the switch so that the car will start only when the gear selector lever is in Park (P) or Neutral (N).

Downshift Linkage Adjustment
Turbo Hydra-Matic 200, 250, 350, 375B

The downshift cable on all except Cutlass-size body cars is adjusted by removing the spring horseshoe clip holding the outer cable on the engine bracket, holding the carburetor wide open with the engine off, and replacing the clip. On Cutlass-size body cars, the adjustment is made by pulling on the end of the cable inside the car with pliers, while holding the adjusting sleeve in place, then floorboarding the accelerator with the engine off.

Turbo Hydra-Matic 375, 400

The downshift switch is adjusted by pushing the switch plunger forward until it is flush with the switch housing, then floorboarding the accelerator with the engine off.

Turbo Hydra-Matic 250 Intermediate Band Adjustment

Only the Turbo Hydra-Matic 250 requires periodic band adjustment. This adjustment is required at fluid change intervals, or whenever slippage is evident.
1. Position the shift lever in Neutral.
2. Loosen the locknut on the right side of the transmission and tighten the adjusting screw to 30 in lbs.
3. Back the screw out three turns and then tighten the locknut.

Pan Removal, Fluid and Filter Change

The fluid should be drained with the transmission warm.
1. Support the Starfire transmission at the vibration damper. Remove the crossmember. This may not be necessary on the Turbo Hydra-Matic 200.
2. Prepare a large pan to catch the transmission fluid.
3. Loosen all the pan screws, then pull one corner down to drain most of the fluid.
4. Remove the pan screws and empty out the pan. The pan can be cleaned out with solvent but it must be dried thoroughly before replacement. Be very careful not to leave any lint or threads from rags in the pan.
5. Remove the filter or strainer retaining bolt (two on Turbo Hydra-Matic 250, 350, and 375B). A reuseable strainer is used on the Turbo Hydra-Matic 200 and 250. The strainer may be cleaned in solvent and air-dried thoroughly. Filters are to be replaced.
6. Assemble a new O-ring and filter to the intake pipe on the Turbo Hydra-Matic 375 and 400. Use a new gasket on all other models.
7. Install the new filter or cleaned strainer.
8. Install the pan with a new gasket. Tighten the bolts evenly (12 ft lbs) in a criss-cross pattern.
9. Replace the Starfire crossmember.
10. Add DEXRON or DEXRON II transmission fluid through the dipstick tube. Add 4 qts for Turbo Hydra-Matic 250, 3 for all others.
11. Start the engine and let it idle. Do not race the engine. Shift through all the indicator positions, holding the brakes. Check the fluid level with the engine idling in Park. The level should be between the two dimples on the dipstick, about 1/4 in. below the ADD mark. Add fluid as necessary.
12. Check the fluid level after the car has been driven enough to thoroughly warm up the transmission. The level should be at the FULL mark on the dipstick. If the transmission is overfilled, the excess must be drained off. Overfilling causes aerated fluid, resulting in transmission slippage and probable damage.

U-JOINTS

Driveshaft Removal and Installation

1. Matchmark the relationship of the driveshaft to the differential flange.
2. Unbolt the straps or flange. Tape the bearing caps in place to prevent losing the bearing rollers. Support the driveshaft to prevent excessive strain on the universal joints.
3. Pull the shaft back and remove it. Be careful not to damage the splines at the transmission end.
4. If the transmission splined slip yoke does not have a vent hole at the center, it should be lubricated for installation with engine oil. If it does have a vent hole, it should be lubricated with special grease. Slide the slip yoke into place.
5. Align the matchmarks and tighten the bolts. Strap bolts should be tightened to 14 ft lbs through

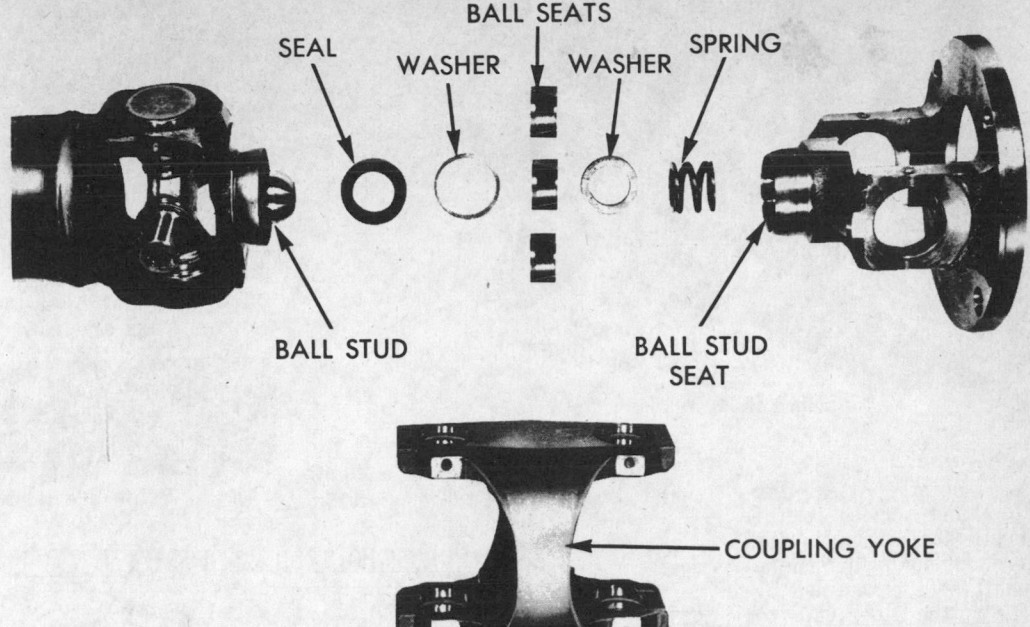

SEAL · WASHER · BALL SEATS · WASHER · SPRING · BALL STUD · BALL STUD SEAT · COUPLING YOKE

Constant velocity joint (© Oldsmobile Div, G.M. Corp)

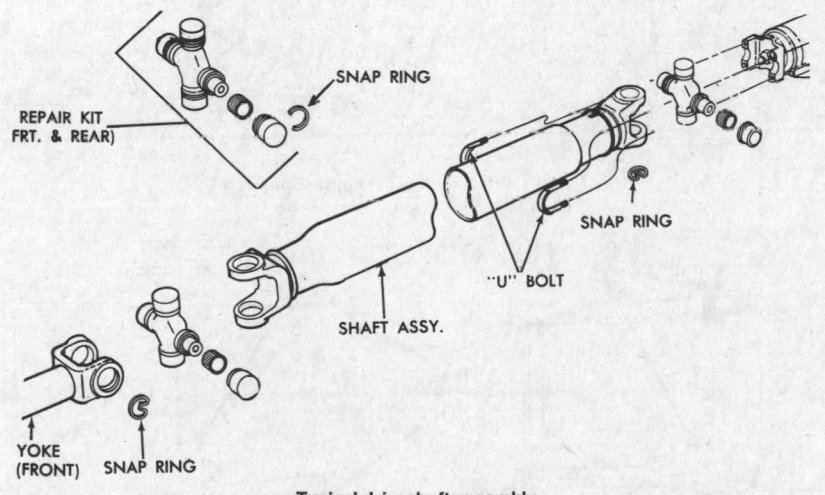

SNAP RING · REPAIR KIT FRT. & REAR) · SNAP RING · "U" BOLT · SHAFT ASSY. · YOKE (FRONT) · SNAP RING

Typical driveshaft assembly
(© Oldsmobile Div, G.M. Corp)

1974 and 20 ft lbs for 1975 and later. Flange bolts should be tightened to 75 ft lbs through 1974 and 95 ft lbs for 1975 and later.

REAR AXLE

AXLE, SHAFT, BEARING AND SEAL

Removal and Installation

These cars use two different types of drive axle, the C- and the non C-type. Axle shafts in the C-type are retained by C-shaped locks, which fit grooves at the inner end of the shaft. Axle shafts in the non C-type are retained by the brake backing plate,

which is bolted to the axle housing. Bearings in the C-type axle consist of an outer race, bearing rollers and a roller cage, retained by snap-rings. The non C-type axle uses a unit roller bearing (inner race, rollers and outer race), which is pressed onto the shaft up to a shoulder. When servicing axles, it is imperative to determine the axle type.

NOTE: All Starfires and Omegas use the C-type axles. Other models may use either kind.

Non C-Type

Caution Before attempting any service to the drive axle or axle shafts, remove the axle carrier cover and visually determine if the axle shafts are retained by C-shaped locks at the inner end, or by the brake backing plate at the

outer end. If the shafts are *not* retained by C-locks, proceed as follows.

Design allows for maximum axle shaft end-play of 0.022 in., which can be measured with a dial indicator. If end-play is found to be excessive, the bearing should be replaced. Shimming the bearing is not recommended as this ignores end-play of the bearing itself and could result in improper seating of the bearing.

1. Remove the wheel, tire and brake drum.
2. Remove the nuts holding the retainer plate to the backing plate. Disconnect the brake line.
3. Remove the retainer and install nuts, fingertight, to prevent the brake backing plate from being dislodged.
4. Pull out the axle shaft and bearing assembly, using a slide hammer.
5. Using a chisel, nick the bearing retainer in three or four places. The retainer does not have to be cut, merely collapsed sufficiently, to allow the bearing retainer to be slid from the shaft.
6. Press off the bearing and install the new one by pressing it into position.
7. Press on the new retainer.

NOTE: do not attempt to press the bearing and the retainer on at the same time.

8. Assemble the shaft and bearing in the housing, being sure that the bearing is seated properly in the housing.
9. Install the retainer, drum, wheel and tire. Bleed the brakes.

CHISEL RETAINER BUT DO NOT MARK SHAFT ON BEARING SURFACE

SHAFT — SEAL — BEARING — RETAINER (OUTER)

Cutting Bearing Retainer

C-Type

Caution Before attempting any service to the drive axle or axle shafts, remove the carrier cover and visually determine if the axle shaft(s) are retained by C-shaped locks at the inner ends or by a brake backing plate at the outer end. If they *are* retained by C-shaped locks, proceed as follows.

1. Raise the vehicle and remove the wheels.
2. The differential cover has already been removed (see Caution note above). Remove the differential pinion shaft lockscrew and the differential pinion shaft.
3. Push the flanged end of the axle shaft toward the center of the vehicle and remove the C-lock from the end of the shaft.
4. Remove the axle shaft from the housing, being careful not to damage the oil seal.
5. Remove the oil seal by inserting the button end of the axle shaft behind the steel case of the oil seal. Pry the seal loose from the bore.
6. Seat the legs of the bearing puller behind the bearing. Seat a washer against the bearing and hold it in place with a nut. Use a slide hammer to pull the bearing.
7. Pack the cavity between the seal lips with wheel bearing lubricant and lubricate a new wheel bearing with same.
8. Use a suitable driver and install the bearing until it bottoms against the tube. Install the oil seal.
9. Slide the axle shaft into place. Be sure that the splines on the shaft do not damage the oil seal. Make sure that the splines engage the differential side gear.
10. Install the axle shaft C-lock on the inner end of the axle shaft and push the shaft outward so that the C-lock seats in the differential side gear counterbore.
11. Position the differential pinion shaft through the case and pin-

ions, aligning the hole in the case with the hole for the lockscrew.

12. Install the pinion shaft lockscrew.
13. Use a new gasket and install the carrier cover. Be sure that the gasket surfaces are clean before installing the gasket and cover.
14. Fill the axle with lubricant to the bottom of the filler hole.
15. Install the brake drum and wheels and lower the car. Check for leaks and road test the car.

JACKING, HOISTING

Lifting Points are illustrated.

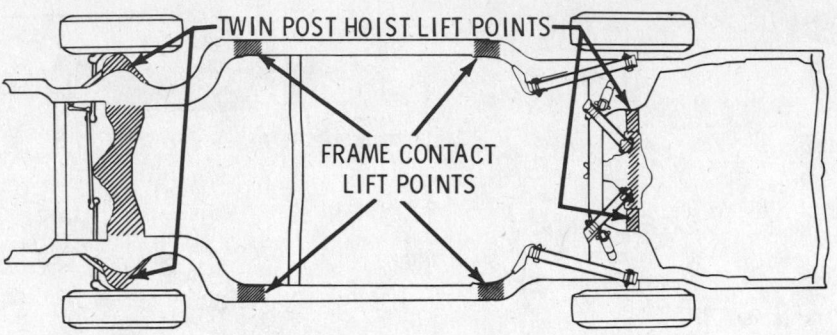

TWIN POST HOIST LIFT POINTS

FRAME CONTACT LIFT POINTS

Cutlass, 88, and 98 hoist contact points
(© Oldsmobile Div., G.M. Corp.)

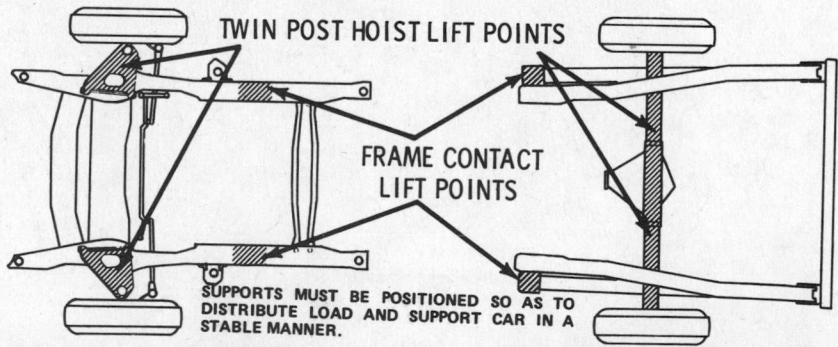

TWIN POST HOIST LIFT POINTS

FRAME CONTACT LIFT POINTS

SUPPORTS MUST BE POSITIONED SO AS TO DISTRIBUTE LOAD AND SUPPORT CAR IN A STABLE MANNER.

Omega hoisting points (© Oldsmobile Div, G.M. Corp)

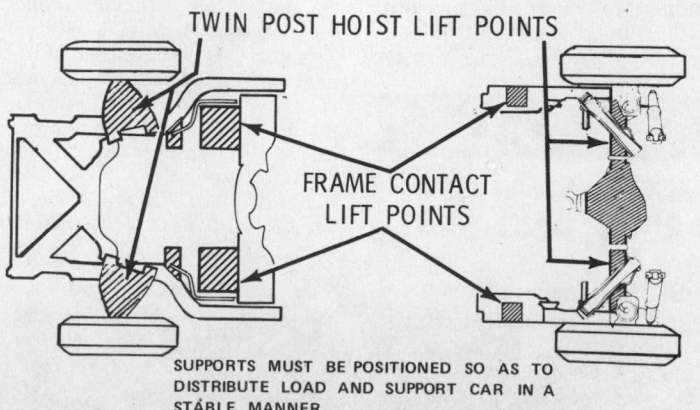

TWIN POST HOIST LIFT POINTS

FRAME CONTACT LIFT POINTS

SUPPORTS MUST BE POSITIONED SO AS TO DISTRIBUTE LOAD AND SUPPORT CAR IN A STABLE MANNER.

Starfire hoisting points
(© Oldsmobile Div., GM Corp.)

FRONT SUSPENSION

Shock Absorber Replacement —All Models

1. Remove the two bolts and lock-washers securing the shock to the lower control arm.
2. Remove the upper nut, retainer, and grommet from the shock.

NOTE: On Starfires, remove the access plug from the inner fender panel first.

3. To install, reverse the removal procedure.

Lower Ball Joint

Inspection

Cutlass and F-85 through 1973 88 and 98 through 1972

1. Jack up the car and place floor stands under the left and right control arms as near as possible to the lower ball joints. Make sure the car sits steadily on the floor stands.
2. Position a dial indicator so that its button contacts the inside lip of the wheel rim.
3. Place a 2 x 4 (about 6 in. tall) vertically between the lower control arm and the steering knuckle. Insert a pry bar between the wood and the steering knuckle nut and pry gently up and down. The dial indicator reading must not exceed .125 in. and there should be no deflection on the

1971-72 88 and 98 models. Repeat this procedure for the other side.

4. After completing this vertical check, remove the wood block and reposition the dial indicator button to contact the outer lip of the wheel rim.
5. Push in on the top of the tire while pulling out on the bottom and observe the dial indicator reading. Reverse this push-pull procedure and check the reading. This procedure (horizontal check) enables you to check both upper and lower ball joints. The gauge reading should not exceed .125 in.
6. Do the same on the other side.

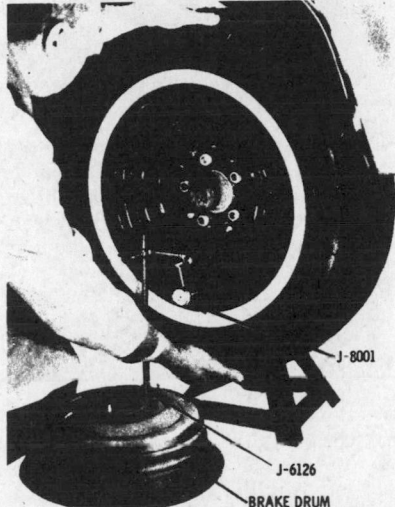

J-8001
J-6126
BRAKE DRUM

Ball joint horizontal check
(© Oldsmobile Div, G.M. Corp)

1973-74 Omega

NOTE: The lower ball joint used on the Omega is not internally pre-loaded but rather, is seated by the car's weight. Therefore, some looseness may be apparent when the lower control arm is raised with a jack; this looseness does not necessarily mean that the joint is defective or worn.

1. Use a jack placed underneath the lower control arm to support vehicle weight.
2. Measure the distance between the grease fitting and the threaded stud.
3. Raise the tire by means of a lever, to seat the ball stud, and measure the distance again.
4. If the difference between the two measurements is greater than 1/16 in., the ball joint is worn and should be replaced.
5. Shake the wheel and observe the end of the stud or the nut on the knuckle boss for *excessive* looseness. Replace any parts which are defective.

1973-74 88 and 98, 1974 Cutlass and All 1975 and Later Models

These lower ball joints contain a visual wear indicator. The lower ball joint grease plug screws into the wear indicator which protrudes from the bottom of the ball joint housing. As long as the wear indicator extends out of the ball joint housing, the ball joint is not worn. If the tip of the wear indicator is parallel with, or recessed into the ball joint housing, the ball joint is defective.

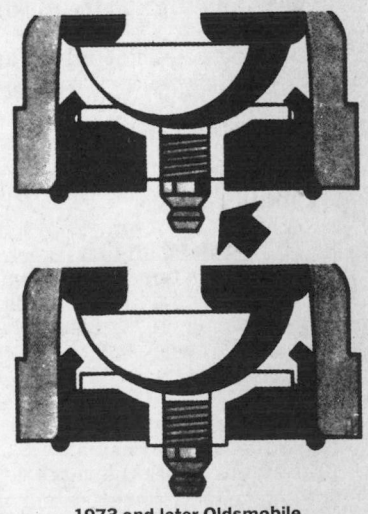

1973 and later Oldsmobile ball joint wear indicator

Removal and Installation

1. Raise car and support the frame with floor stands.
2. Remove the tire and wheel.
3. Place a floor jack under the control arm spring seat.

Caution Leave the jack under the spring seat dur-

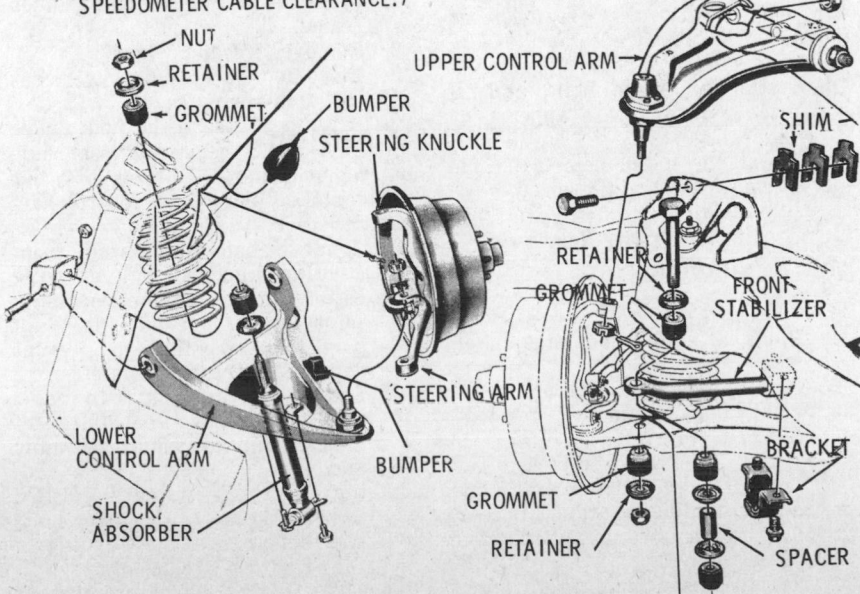

COTTER PIN MUST NOT BE BENT OVER LOWER BALL JOINT STUD. BEND DOWN OR TO SIDE. (NECESSARY FOR SPEEDOMETER CABLE CLEARANCE.)

NUT
RETAINER
GROMMET
BUMPER
STEERING KNUCKLE
LOWER CONTROL ARM
SHOCK ABSORBER
STEERING ARM
BUMPER

SHIM AS REQUIRED TO OBTAIN CASTER & CAMBER SPECIFICATION AFTER SUSPENSION IS ASSEMBLED TO FRAME.

UPPER CONTROL ARM
SHIM
RETAINER
GROMMET
FRONT STABILIZER
GROMMET
RETAINER
SPACER
BRACKET

Front suspension—88 and 98 (© Oldsmobile Div, G.M. Corp)

ing removal and installation, in order to keep the spring and control arm positioned.

4. Remove the cotter pin from the ball joint stud and, using a ball joint stud removal tool, separate the ball joint from the steering knuckle.
5. Raise the control arm to relieve tension and remove the stud nut.
6. If the backing plate blocks removal of the ball joint, loosen the backing plate bolts to obtain the necessary clearance.
7. Hold the brake assembly out of way by placing a wooden block between the frame and the upper control arm.
8. Using a screwdriver or chisel, remove the ball joint seal.
9. Using a suitable tool, remove the ball joint.
10. Press in a new ball joint until it bottoms on the lower control arm.

NOTE: On disc brake cars, make sure the grease purge on the seal faces away from the brakes.

11. On Cutlass, Omega, and F-85, install the ball joint stud into the steering knuckle, torque the nut to 70 ft lbs (through 1973) or 95 ft lbs (1974 and later), and install the cotter pin.
12. On 88 and 98, reassemble the suspension and torque the ball joint stud nut to 70 ft lbs (1970) 90 ft lbs (1971-74) or to 105 ft lbs (1975 and later). Install the cotter pin and bend it to the side of the nut. On the Starfire tighten the nut to 65 ft lbs.
13. If applicable, tighten the backing plate bolts.
14. Install the ball joint fitting and lube until grease appears at the seal.
15. Install the tire and wheel assembly.

Upper Ball Joint

Inspection

To inspect the upper ball joints, follow steps 1 and 4-6 of the "Cutlass and F-85 through 1973, 88 and 98 through 1972" lower ball joint inspection procedure.

Removal and Installation

1. Raise the front of car and place floor stands under the lower control arm between the spring seats and the ball joints.

Caution Leave the jack under the spring seat during removal and installation, in order to keep the spring and control arm positioned.
2. Remove the wheel.
3. Remove the cotter pin from the upper ball joint stud and loosen the upper ball joint nut.

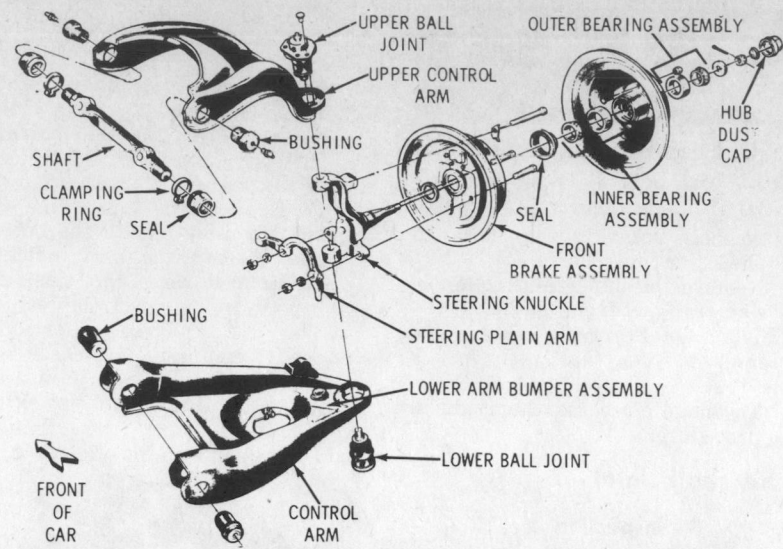

Front suspension—F85 and Cutlass (Omega similar) (© Oldsmobile Div, G.M. Corp)

4. Using a ball joint remover tool, break the stud loose and remove the nut and pull the stud out of the knuckle. Support the steering knuckle to prevent damage to the brake line.
5. Using a ⅛ in. diameter drill bit, drill into each of the four rivet heads a depth of ¼ in.
6. Drill off the rivet heads with a ½ in. diameter bit.
7. Punch out the rivets and remove the ball joint.
8. To install, place the new ball joint in the upper control arm and secure it with four bolts and nuts. Tighten the nuts to 8 ft lbs.
9. Connect the ball joint-to-steering knuckle. Torque the nut to 40 ft lbs minimum (through 1974) or to 70 ft lbs (1975 and later). On Starfires, 35 ft lbs (min).

NOTE: When replacing ball joints, use only high-quality replacement parts and bolts and nuts specified to be strong enough to endure the stress.

10. Install the grease fitting and lubricate until grease appears at the seal.
11. Install the speedometer cable (if so equipped) and the wheel.

Upper Control Arm Removal and Installation

1970 F-85

1. Raise car and place stands under frame.
2. Remove tire and wheel.
3. Place floor jack under lower control arm spring seat.

Caution Leave the jack under the spring seat during removal and installation, in order to keep the spring and control arm positioned.
4. Remove ball joint stud from steering knuckle, by removing cotter pin and nut and with an

appropriate tool, press joint loose from knuckle. For left-side arm removal, it may be necessary to move the steering gear out of the way. When installing a gear, torque bolts to 70 ft lbs.
5. Support hub assembly and remove upper arm by sliding shaft off end of bolts.

NOTE: mark or locate alignment shims for easier reassembly.

6. Attach arm assembly to frame using original shims. Torque to 55 ft lbs.
7. Install ball joint. Torque nut to 40 ft lbs (minimum). Install a grease fitting and lubricate.
8. Install hub, drum and wheel assembly and lower car to floor.

All Models Except 1970 F-85

1. Raise car and place stands under frame.
2. Remove tire and wheel.
3. Place floor jack under lower control arm spring seat.

Caution Leave the jack under the spring seat during removal and installtion, in order to keep the spring and control arm positioned.
4. Remove ball joint stud from steering knuckle, by removing cotter pin and nut and pressing joint loose from knuckle. Support hub assembly to prevent damage to the brake line.
5. Loosen the pivot shaft-to-frame nuts and remove the alignment shims. Support hub assembly and remove upper arms by sliding shaft off end of bolts. On Starfires, remove the pivot bolts and remove the control arm from the car; there are no shims.

NOTE: mark or locate alignment shims for easier reassembly.

6. It is necessary to remove upper

control arm attaching bolts to gain clearance to remove arm assembly.

7. Remove control arm from car.
8. To reinstall, position bolts loosely in frame and install pivot shaft on bolts.
9. Install lock washers and nuts and with brass drift, drive attaching bolts into frame.
10. Install alignment shims (except Starfire) placing them in position from which they were removed. Torque nuts, 75 ft lbs (through 1971 except F-85) and 80 ft lbs for all 1972 and later models except 1972 Cutlass and F-85. Torque to 50 ft lbs for 1971-72 Cutlass and F-85 models. Torque to 65 ft lbs on Starfire.
11. Connect ball joint stud and torque to specifications.
12. Install wheel and tire and lower car to floor.

Lower Control Arm and/or Spring Removal and Installation

1. Raise front of car and support by stands under frame.
2. Remove tire and wheel.
3. Disconnect stabilizer link from lower arm, if so equipped.
4. Remove shock absorber.
5. Place floor jack under lower arm, between spring seat and ball joint. Using a spring compressor, compress spring.
6. Disconnect lower control arm ball joint from knuckle.
7. Slowly lower floor jack until spring is fully extended and remove spring.
8. To reinstall, tape insulator to top of spring.
9. While holding spring and insulator against pilot in front cross bar, tilt spring so it will pivot in lower arm. Rotate spring so bottom coil will index with edge of hole in arm spring seat. Spring

should not cover any portion of hole.
10. With floor jack positioned between seat and ball joint, raise arm until ball joint is tight in knuckle. Install ball joint nut and tighten to the torque specified in the lower ball joint removal and installation procedure.
11. Install shock absorber.
12. Connect stabilizer link.
13. Install wheel and lower car.

Wheel Bearing Adjustment

1. Tighten the adjusting nut to 30 ft lbs, while turning the wheel.
2. Back off on the nut ½ turn.
3. Finger-tighten the nut and install the cotter pin or the retaining ring.

NOTE: If the cotter pin cannot be installed, back off on the nut until the slot aligns with the serrations on the nut. Do not back off on the nut more than 1/24 of a turn.

4. Once adjusted, the front wheel bearings should have 0.001-0.008 in. end-play.

REAR SUSPENSION

Shock Absorber Replacement

All Except Omega and Starfire

To replace the rear shock absorber, first raise the car and support the rear axle to prevent stretching of the brake hose. Then remove the nut from the lower end of the shock and tap the shock free from the bracket. To disconnect the shock at the top, remove the bolt or bolts and remove the shock.

Omega and Starfire

1. Raise the vehicle and support the rear axle housing.
2. Remove the lower shock mounting bolt from the shock absorber eye.
3. Unfasten the upper mounting bracket bolts and remove the shock.

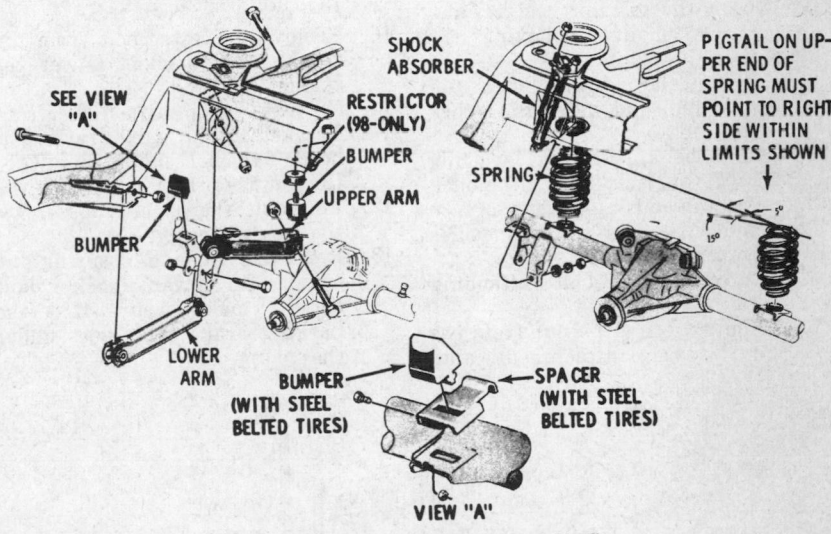

Coil spring rear suspension—except Starfire
(© Oldsmobile Div., GM Corp.)

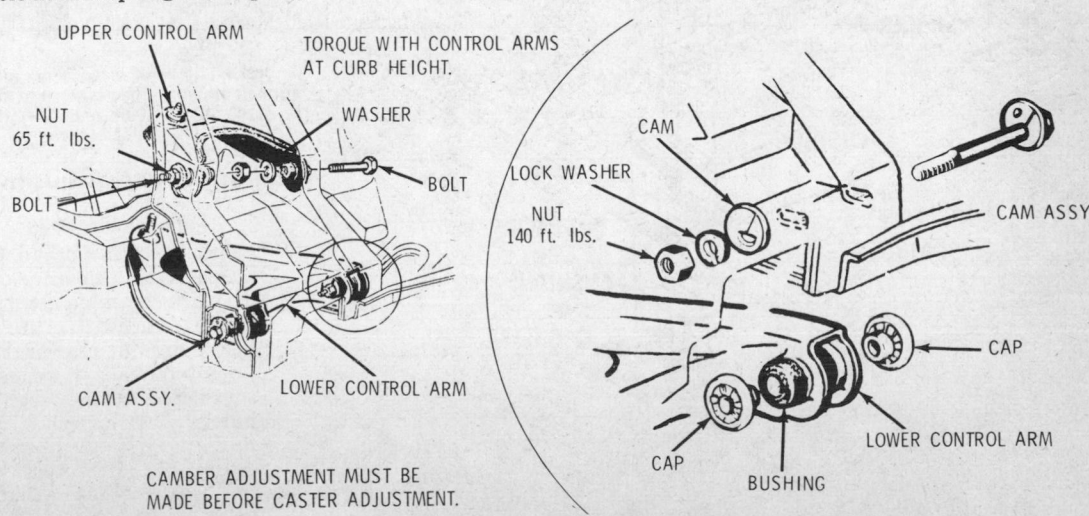

CAMBER ADJUSTMENT MUST BE MADE BEFORE CASTER ADJUSTMENT.

Starfire front suspension (© Oldsmobile Div., GM Corp.)

Installation is the reverse of removal, except that the upper attaching bolts should remain loose while the lower (eye) bolt is being tightened.

Coil Spring Replacement

1. Raise the rear axle housing on a floor jack and raise and support the rear frame on jackstands.
2. Disconnect the bottom shock absorber mounts.
3. Disconnect the brake line.
4. Detach the upper suspension arms at the axle housing. Lower the axle housing until the springs are completely extended.
5. Remove the springs. Reverse the procedure for installation.

NOTE: If a spring compressor is used, the suspension arms need not be detached.

Leaf Spring Replacement
88 Wagon

1. Lift the rear of the car by the axle housing and support the car on floor stands.
2. Loosen the tailpipe and resonator if you are removing the right-side spring.
3. Remove the lower shock absorber nut and move the shock out of the way.
4. Relax the springs by lowering the lift or jack. Leave the jack under the housing for support.
5. Remove the bolts and shackles from the rear of the spring.
6. Remove the U-bolt attaching nuts.
7. Remove ONLY the nut from the front spring attachment and, while holding the spring up, remove the bolt from the front of the spring and remove the spring.
8. Remove the insulators and shim from the spring.
9. To install, reverse the removal procedure.

Omega

1. Raise the rear of the car on stands.
2. Support the rear axle to take its weight off the springs.
3. Disconnect the bottom of the shock absorber.
4. Loosen the front spring eye bolt.
5. Unbolt the spring front bracket from the underbody.
6. Lower the axle slightly and remove the front bracket from the spring.
7. Pry the parking brake cable out of its retainer bracket on the axle spring mounting plate.
8. Unbolt the spring from the axle.
9. Remove the spring plate and cushion between the axle and the spring.
10. Remove the lower bolt from the rear spring shackle. Lower the spring.
11. On installation, attach the front bracket to the spring eye. The head of the bolt should be toward the center of the car.
12. Assemble the shackle loosely to the rear spring eye.
13. Raise the rear end of spring and install the lower shackle bolt loosely, making sure that the parking brake cable goes under the spring.
14. Raise the front end of the spring and loosely attach the front bracket to the underbody. Make sure that the bracket tab goes into its slot.
15. Make sure that the upper and lower spring cushions are aligned properly. The upper one has locating ribs and the lower one, a locating dowel.
16. Install the spring lower mounting plate over the locating dowel and loosely install the nuts. Don't forget the parking brake cable bracket.
17. Attach the bottom of the shock absorber.
18. Attach the parking brake cable to the bracket on the lower spring plate.
19. Let the vehicle weight down on the springs. Tighten all the bolts. Torques are: rear shackle bolts —40-60 ft lbs, front bracket screws—25-35 ft lbs, front eye bolt—65-80 ft lbs, and axle bolts —35-50 ft lbs.

BRAKES

Information on brake adjustments, lining replacement, bleeding procedure, master and wheel cylinder overhaul is in the Unit Repair Section.

A brake pad with a warning indicator that squeals when the pad is worn to service limits is used on all 1974 and later models with disc brakes

Parking Brake Adjustment

Through 1971

1. Release parking brake. Check for proper pedal clearance.
2. Adjust rear cables by tightening equalizer adjusting nut to obtain heavy drag at rear brakes.
3. Loosen equalizer adjusting nut seven full turns. Tighten locknut.

1972 and Later

1. Set the parking brake exactly three clicks (one on Starfire, two on Omega).

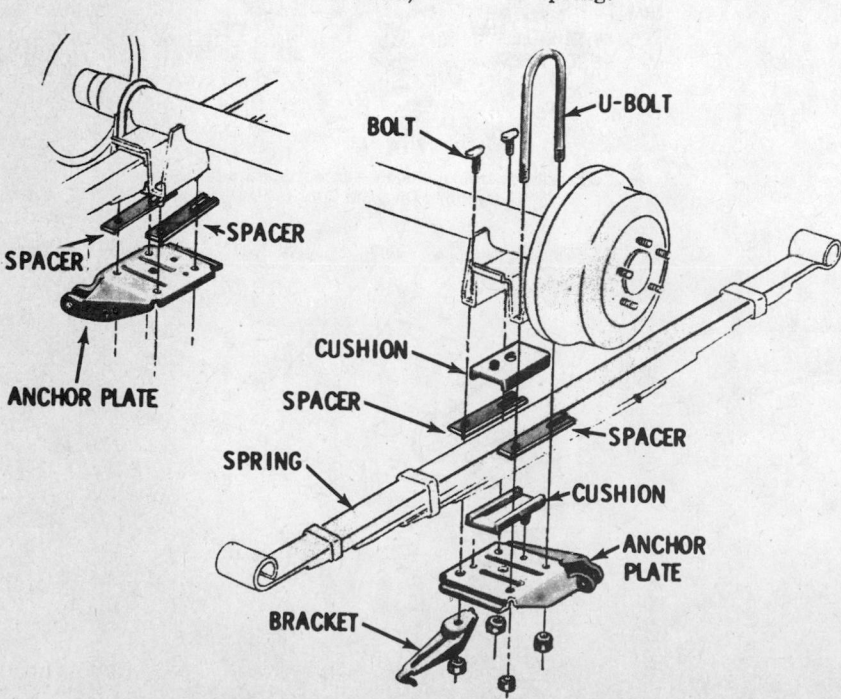

BOLT

U-BOLT

SPACER

SPACER

SPACER

ANCHOR PLATE

CUSHION

SPACER

SPACER

SPRING

CUSHION

ANCHOR PLATE

BRACKET

Omega leaf spring rear suspension—Custom Cruiser similar
(© Oldsmobile Div, G.M. Corp)

2. Loosen the locknut at the rear of the equalizer adjusting nut. Then tighten the adjusting nut until the rear wheels can barely be turned backward (using two hands) but lock up when moved forward. Tighten the nut against the adjusting nut.

3. With the parking brake disengaged the rear wheels should turn freely in either direction with *no brake drag.*

Master Cylinder Removal and Installation

NOTE: Be sure that the area where the master cylinder is mounted is clean, before beginning removal.

1. Disconnect and cap or plug hydraulic lines.
2. If there is no power booster unit, remove the pushrod - to - pedal clevis pin.
3. Remove the attaching bolts and master cylinder.
4. Install in the reverse order of removal. Fill with fluid and bleed.

Power Brake Unit Removal and Installation

The master cylinder and power booster are removed as a unit. Disconnect vacuum and hydraulic lines. Disconnect the pushrod from the brake pedal. Remove the vacuum unit mounting stud nuts and remove the assembly. Install in the reverse order of removal, tightening the mounting nuts to 28 ft. lbs. Fill the master cylinder reservoir with fluid.

STEERING

CAUTION: Some 1974 and later models have the A.C.R.S. system (air bags). Special servicing information and safety precautions for these cars are given in the Buick car section.

Steering Wheel Removal and Installation

1. Disconnect the battery ground cable.
2. Remove the round center cap horn button by pulling out. If the center horn bar has screws at the back of the wheel spokes, remove them and lift it off. If there are no screws, pull down and out on the horn bar to remove.
3. Detach the horn contact wire.
4. Remove the shaft spring clip on 1975 and later models.
5. Remove the steering wheel nut. If there are no alignment marks, make some.
6. Remove the steering wheel with a puller.
7. Align the marks on replacement. Torque the nut to 35 ft lbs.

CAUTION: Do not hammer on the steering shaft. The energy-absorbing

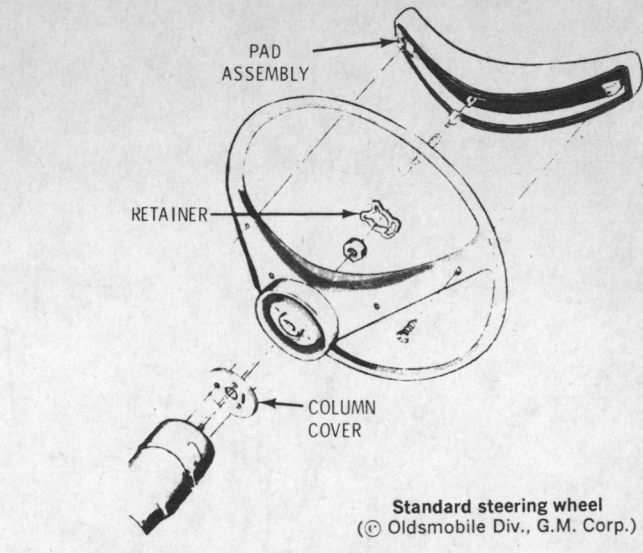

Standard steering wheel
(© Oldsmobile Div., G.M. Corp.)

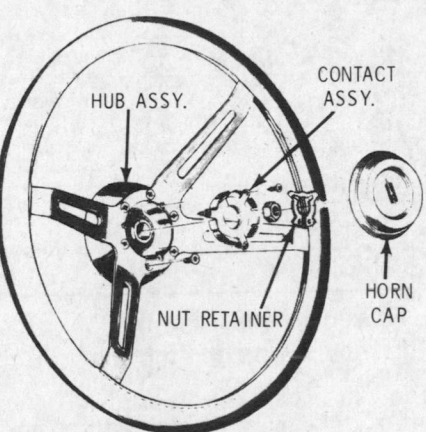

Sport steering wheel
(© Oldsmobile Div., G.M. Corp.)

column will be damaged and require replacement.

Turn Signal Switch Replacement

Except Tilt and Telescopic Column

1. Disconnect the battery.
2. Remove the steering wheel.
3. Remove the cover from the shaft. Plastic keepers under the cover are not necessary for installation.
4. Depress the lockplate and remove the snap-ring from the shaft.
5. Remove the lockplate and cancelling cam.
6. Remove the upper bearing preload spring.
7. Remove the turn signal lever.
8. Remove the four-way flasher knob.
9. Remove the three screws from the switch.
10. Disconnect the turn signal connector from the wiring harness.

NOTE: On 1975 and later models,

it will be necessary to perform steps 10 through 13 of the "Turn Signal Switch Replacement/Tilt and Telescope Column," before proceeding with the next step.

11. Tape the turn signal wires at the connector and carefully remove the turn signal switch, wiring, and protector from the column as a unit.
12. To install, reverse the removal procedure using a new shaft snap-ring. When replacing screws (especially cover screws), make sure they are of the same size.

Tilt and Telescopic Column

1. Disconnect negative battery cable.
2. Remove the steering wheel.
3. Remove the screws and lift the cover from the shaft. Plastic keepers are not necessary for installation.
4. Compress the lockplate and pry the snap-ring from shaft.
5. Remove the lockplate and cancelling cam.
6. Remove the upper bearing preload spring.
7. Remove the turn signal lever and the four-way flasher knob.
8. Lift up on the tilt lever and position the housing in its central position.
9. Remove the switch attaching screws.
10. Remove the lower trim cap from the instrument panel and disconnect the turn signal connector from the harness.
11. Remove the four bolts securing the bracket assembly to the jacket.
12. On cars (except Starfire) with automatic transmission, loosen the screw holding the shift indicator needle and disconnect the clip from the link.

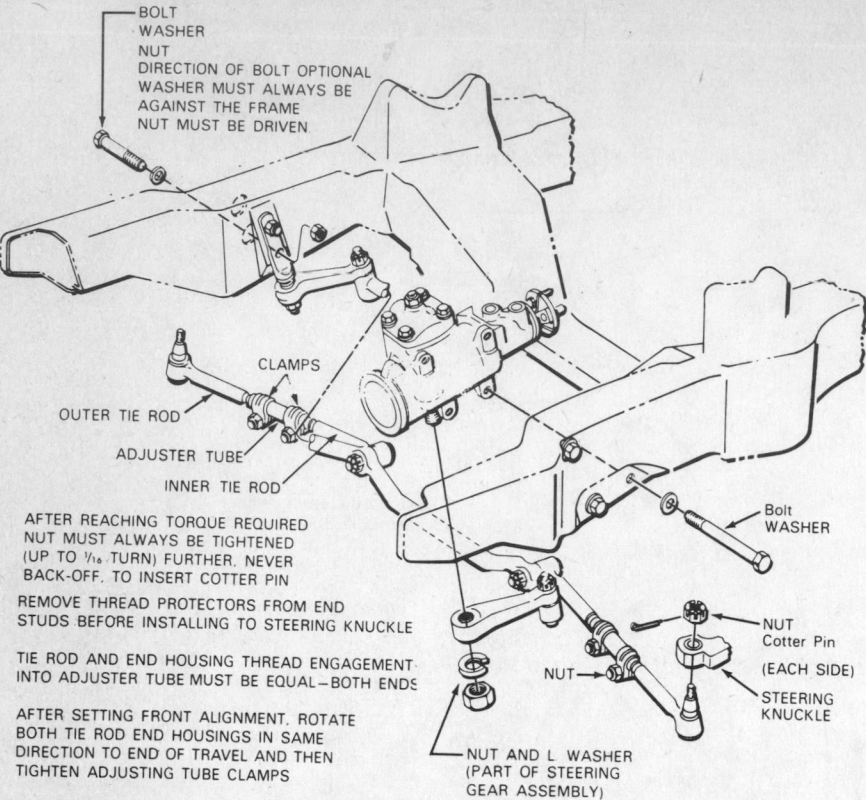

BOLT
WASHER
NUT
DIRECTION OF BOLT OPTIONAL
WASHER MUST ALWAYS BE
AGAINST THE FRAME
NUT MUST BE DRIVEN

CLAMPS

OUTER TIE ROD

ADJUSTER TUBE

INNER TIE ROD

Bolt
WASHER

AFTER REACHING TORQUE REQUIRED
NUT MUST ALWAYS BE TIGHTENED
(UP TO 1/16 TURN) FURTHER. NEVER
BACK-OFF. TO INSERT COTTER PIN

REMOVE THREAD PROTECTORS FROM END
STUDS BEFORE INSTALLING TO STEERING KNUCKLE

TIE ROD AND END HOUSING THREAD ENGAGEMENT
INTO ADJUSTER TUBE MUST BE EQUAL—BOTH ENDS

AFTER SETTING FRONT ALIGNMENT, ROTATE
BOTH TIE ROD END HOUSINGS IN SAME
DIRECTION TO END OF TRAVEL AND THEN
TIGHTEN ADJUSTING TUBE CLAMPS

NUT

NUT
Cotter Pin
(EACH SIDE)

STEERING
KNUCKLE

NUT AND L WASHER
(PART OF STEERING
GEAR ASSEMBLY)

Typical Steering linkage
(© Oldsmobile Div., GM Corp.)

13. Remove the two nuts from the column support bracket while holding the column in position. Remove the bracket assembly and wire protector from the wiring, then loosely install the bracket-to-support column.
14. Tape the turn signal wires at the connector to keep them flat and parallel. -
15. Carefully remove the turn signal switch and wiring from the column.
16. To install, reverse the removal procedure, making sure that screws of the same size are used.

Power Steering Pump Removal and Installation

1. Remove the drive belt.
2. Use a puller to remove the pump pulley.
3. Detach and cap the hoses.
4. Remove the pump and mounting bracket.
5. Reverse the procedure for installation. Bleed the system of air by turning the wheels from side to side without hitting the stops, with the wheels off the floor and the engine running.

Ignition Switch and/or Lock Cylinder Replacement

Ignition Switch

1. Disconnect negative battery cable.
2. Place ignition switch in Run position (1970), Off-Unlocked (1971 and later), or Acc (1971 and later tilt wheel).
3. Remove toe pan cover (if applicable) and loosen toe clamp bolts.
4. Remove lower instrument panel trim and toe pan trim panel.
5. Remove automatic transmission shift indicator needle.
6. Remove steering column dash bracket and let steering wheel rest on the driver's seat.
7. Remove two switch attaching screws and lift switch off actuator rod.
8. Disconnect wiring.
9. To install, check that lock cylinder is still in Run position (1970), Off-Unlocked (1971 and later), or Acc (1971 and later tilt wheel), and move sliding portion of switch until switch hole is positioned correctly. Hold the switch in this position with a 0.090 in. pin.
10. Connect the wiring to the switch.
11. Position switch over actuator rod, install attaching screws and remove the 0.090 in. pin.
12. Reverse Steps 1 through 6 to complete installation.

Lock Cylinder

1. Disconnect the negative battery cable.
2. Remove the steering wheel. See the special procedure for cars equipped with air bags.
3. On models equipped with a tilt and travel steering column, pry up the three tabs on the plastic lock cover.

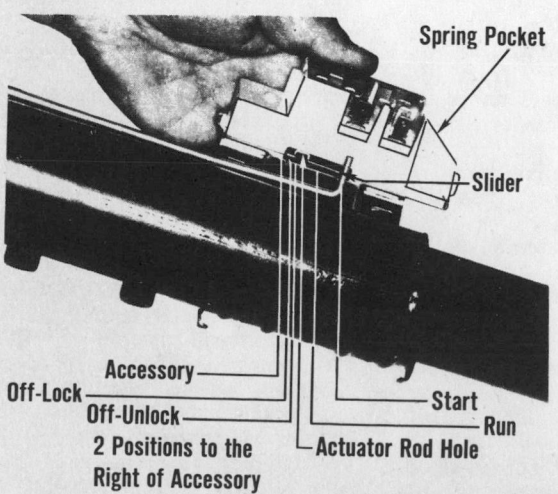

Spring Pocket

Slider

Accessory

Off-Lock

Off-Unlock

Start

Run

Actuator Rod Hole

2 Positions to the
Right of Accessory

Ignition switch in "Off-Unlocked" position, 1971 and later
(© Oldsmobile Div, G.M. Corp)

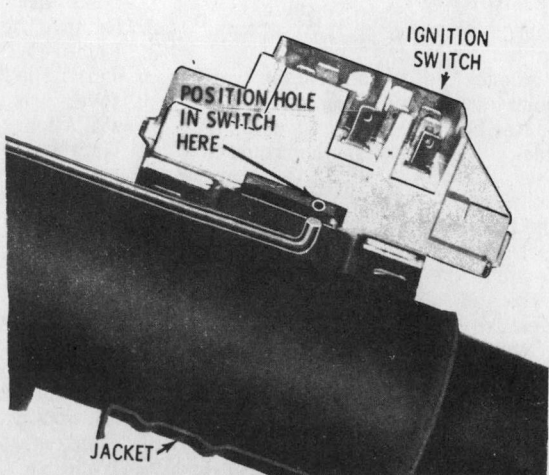

IGNITION
SWITCH

POSITION HOLE
IN SWITCH
HERE

JACKET

Ignition switch in "RUN" position—1970
(© Oldsmobile Div, G.M. Corp)

4. On models with a standard or tilt column remove the three screws that attach the lock cover and remove it. The plastic keepers on the underside of the cover can be discarded after the cover is removed.
5. Depress the steering wheel lock plate and pry the snap-ring from the steering shaft.
6. Remove the lock plate, cancelling cam, and upper bearing spring.
7. Position the turn signal lever in the right turn position and unscrew the turn signal lever.
8. Push the hazard warning knob in and unscrew the knob.
9. Remove the turn signal switch retaining screws and pull the switch up out of the way.
10. On 1970 models, insert the ignition key into the cylinder and turn it to the "Acc" position. On 1971 and later models, turn the key to the "Run" position.
11. Insert a long thin screwdriver into the slot in the upper bearing housing and depress the release tab while pulling the cylinder from the column.
12. Insert the new lock cylinder into the column after aligning the key on the cylinder with the keyway in the column.
13. Press inward on the cylinder while turning it clockwise.
14. Reverse the procedure to complete installation.

INSTRUMENT PANEL

Headlight Switch Replacement

F-85/Cutlass, Omega, 88 and 98 Through 1973
1. Disconnect the battery.
2. On 1971-73 88 and 98 models and 1973 and later Cutlass models with air conditioning remove the left-hand control panel from the dash. On 1973 and later Cutlass without air conditioning, remove the column trim cover.
3. Pull the switch to "ON" position, then depress the spring-loaded button on the switch body and pull knob out of the switch.
4. Remove the escutcheon.
5. Remove the switch from behind the panel and disconnect the multiple connector.
6. Install in the reverse order of the above procedure.

Starfire
1. Disconnect the negative (—) battery lead.
2. Remove the left-hand bottom air conditioning outlet or panel lower insulator as necessary.
3. Working underneath the dash,

depress the switch shaft retainer. Remove the shaft and knob assembly.
4. Unfasten the switch bezel nut and remove the switch.
5. Disconnect the switch multiconnector by prying it with a small screwdriver at the side of the switch.
Installation is the reverse of removal.

1974 and Later 88 and 98
1. Disconnect the negative (—) battery lead.
2. Remove the heater/AC control assembly from the panel, but don't disconnect its leads and vacuum lines.
3. Remove the bezel nut from the switch.
4. Pull the switch out through the heater/AC control opening.
5. Disconnect the wiring and remove the switch.
Installation is the reverse of removal.

WINDSHIELD WIPERS

Motor Removal and Installation

1970 88 and 98
1. Disconnect the wiring and the washer hoses.
2. Remove the three motor attaching screws and the access hole plug.
3. Loosen the two linkage crankarm attaching nuts through the access hole.
4. Hold the motor with one hand and, with the other hand, move the wiper arm halfway through its travel. This will center the crankarm in the hole in the dash.
5. Remove the motor, guiding the crankarm through the hole.
6. Reverse the above steps to install.

1970 F-85/Cutlass
1. Remove the three cowl screen attaching screws from the left side of the cowl screen and lift the screen.
2. Loosen the two nuts securing the linkage crankarm to the pivot arm through the cowl opening.
3. Disconnect the wiring and washer hoses.
4. Remove the three motor securing screws and, guiding the crankarm through the hole in the dash, remove the motor.
5. Reverse the above steps to install.

1971 and Later
1. Remove the cowl screen or grille.
2. Loosen the linkage drive link-to-crankarm attaching nuts, and remove the link from the arm.
3. Disconnect the wiring and washer hoses.
4. Remove the three motor attaching screws, guide the crankarm through the hole in the dash, and remove the motor.
5. Reverse the above steps to install.

RADIO

Removal and Installation

F-85 and Cutlass through 1972, 1970 88 and 98, Omega
1. Disconnect battery.
2. If equipped with air conditioning, remove cool air manifold if necessary.
3. Remove defroster manifold if necessary.
4. Remove radio knobs, washers or rear speaker control.
5. Remove radio attaching nuts and escutcheons.
6. Disconnect all wiring and antenna lead-in.
7. Remove radio support bracket attaching screw(s), if applicable.
8. Remove radio from rear of instrument panel.
9. Install by reversing removal procedure.

1971-73 88 and 98
1. Disconnect the negative battery cable.
2. Unfasten the nut which secures the radio to its mounting brace.
3. Detach the speaker and antenna leads from the radio.
4. Unfasten the radio ground strap screw.
5. Use a thin-bladed screwdriver to carefully pry out the map and flood light lens assembly.
6. Unfasten the four right-hand control panel securing screws. Withdraw the control panel from the dash.
7. Turn the radio knobs until the notch at the base of the knob appears. Insert a pointed object under the retainer and release it. Pull the knobs off the shafts.
8. Remove the inside knobs and nuts from the shafts.
9. Unfasten the nut which secures the radio attaching brace to the control panel.
Installation is the reverse of removal.

1973 and Later Cutlass
1. Detach the cable from the negative battery terminal.

2. Remove the four screws which secure the steering column cover and separate it from the instrument panel.
3. Pull the knobs off the radio.
4. Unfasten the nuts from the front of the radio.
5. Remove its four retaining screws and then gently pull the right-hand control panel up and out.
6. Unfasten the radio support bracket screw.
7. Remove the four ashtray housing screws and take the housing off the tie-bar.
8. Disconnect the antenna and speaker wiring from the radio.
9. Remove the radio from behind the control panel.

Installation is the reverse of removal.

1974 and Later 88 and 98

1. Disconnect the negative (—) cable from the battery. Remove the lower trim panel on 1976 and later models.
2. Detach the wiring harness and antenna lead from the radio.
3. On 1974-75 models, unfasten the throttle cable and remove the accelerator linkage, complete with support bracket.
4. Remove the screw which secures the radio bracket to the tie-bar.
5. Pull the knobs off the shafts and unfasten the securing nuts from the shafts.
6. Lower the radio and remove it from behind the dash panel.

Installation is the reverse of removal.

1975 Starfire

1. Disconnect the battery.
2. Remove the clock set knob.
3. Remove the screws securing the instrument cluster bezel and remove the bezel.
4. Remove the glove compartment.
5. Remove the screws securing the instrument panel crash pad and remove the pad.
6. Pull the knobs off the radio shafts and unfasten the shaft retaining nuts.
7. Remove the two bottom screws from the radio bracket.
8. On models with A/C, remove the left lap cooler and duct.
9. Remove the two steering column bracket nuts and lower the column so that it rests on the driver's seat. Remove the screw which secures the cluster to the carrier, from the steering column bracket.
10. Unfasten the instrument cluster screws, wiring, speedometer cable, and pull the cluster out toward the driver's seat.
11. Remove the lower radio support-to-dash screw.

12. Working through the cluster opening, remove the radio leads and antenna cable.
13. Remove the radio.

Installation is the reverse of removal.

1976 and Later Starfire

1. Disconnect the battery ground cable.
2. Pull off the knobs and bezels.
3. Remove the shaft nuts and washers.
4. Remove the panel lower insulator assembly.
5. Detach the antenna lead from the back of the radio.
6. Remove the heater outlet duct on air conditioned cars.
7. Remove the two screws holding the radio to the panel brace.
8. Lower the radio, detach the speaker and power leads, and remove the mounts from the radio.
9. Reverse the procedure for installation.

HEATER

Blower Motor and Heater Core Removal and Installation without Air Conditioning

1970 88 and 98, Omega

To remove the heater case and core, remove the glove box. Disconnect the wiring, vacuum lines and defroster hoses from the heater case. Drain the radiator enough so that the heater hoses can be disconnected. Remove the blower assembly attaching screws and remove the heater case from inside the car. Remove the heater core from the case. Install in the reverse of the above procedure.

To remove the blower motor, disconnect the blower feed wire. Remove the fender filler panel bolts and move the filler panel forward and inward. Remove the blower assembly attaching nuts and screws. Push the heater case studs back so that they do not protrude through the firewall. Push down on the inner fender panel and remove the blower assembly. Remove the blower motor attaching screws and remove the blower. When installing, use a bead of sealer around the heater inlet.

1971 and later 88 and 98

To remove the heater case and core, disconnect the battery and remove the four heater case to firewall attaching nuts. Drain the radiator enough so that the heater hoses may be disconnected. Disconnect the control cables and vacuum hose. Remove the defroster duct to case attaching screw and the right half of the right hand dash trim panel. Remove the

heater case from the car. The heater core may now be removed from the case. Install in reverse order of removal.

To remove the blower motor on models through 1974, disconnect the battery and remove the right front wheel. Remove the canister or battery. Remove the three filler plate to radiator support screws, the filler plate to wheelhouse attaching screws and the filler plate. Remove the blower attaching screws and the connector. Remove the blower. Installation is the reverse of the removal procedure.

To remove the blower motor on 1975 and later models, cut a flap through the inner fender for access. Seal the flap securely after installation.

F-85, Cutlass

To remove the heater blower and inlet assembly, remove the right front fender filler panel. Disconnect the blower motor wiring. Remove the attaching nuts and screws and remove the heater assembly. The blower motor may be removed from the inlet assembly by removing the attaching screws. Installation is the reverse of the removal procedure.

To remove the core from the heater case, drain the radiator, disconnect the heater hoses and remove the attaching nuts. On models through 1972, to gain access to the lower nut it will be necessary to disconnect the right fender at the bottom and wedge it away from the body. Disconnect the wiring and the three control cables and remove the case assembly from the dash. Remove the core retainer and core. Install in reverse of the above procedure.

Starfire

NOTE: To remove only the blower motor, perform steps 1 through 4. Skip step 3.

1. Disconnect the battery ground cable.
2. Disconnect the blower motor lead wire.
3. Place a pan under the vehicle. Disconnect the heater hoses at the core connections and secure the ends of the hoses in a raised position.
4. Remove the blower intake to dash panel screws and nuts and remove the blower intake, blower motor and wheel as an assembly.
5. Remove the core retaining strap screws and remove the core from the vehicle.
6. To install, reverse removal.

NOTE: Be sure that the blower intake sealer is intact, replace if necessary.

Blower Motor Removal and Installation with Air Conditionng

F-85, Cutlass, 1970 88 and 98

NOTE: On models through 1972 it will be necessary to remove the inner fender (fill) panel to reach the blower.

1. Disconnect the wiring.
2. Remove the screws securing the motor to the case.
3. Remove the motor.
4. Reverse the above steps to install.

1971-74 88 and 98

1. Raise the car and remove the right front wheel and tire.
2. Remove the charcoal canister.
3. Unfasten the bolts which attach the radiator supports to the filler panel.
4. Remove the wheel arch securing bolts.
5. Take the right-hand wheel arch filler panel off.
6. Unfasten the blower motor mounting screws, remove the motor and disconnect its wiring.

Installation is performed in the reverse order of removal.

1975 and Later 88 and 98

1. Remove the right front wheel.
2. Cut a flap for access through the inner fender.
3. Remove the blower motor mounting screws and remove the motor.
4. Reverse the procedure for installation. Seal the flap securely.

Omega

The blower motor removal procedure for A/C equipped Omega models is similar to that for those models without A/C, except that the fender fill panel must be unbolted and moved forward and inward.

Starfire

NOTE: This procedure requires discharging and changing the A/C system. Do not attempt it unless you have the special tools and knowledge necessary to perform this task.

1. Disconnect the battery.
2. Disconnect the blower relay.
3. Carefully discharge the refrigerant from the system. There may be enough clearance to get the blower motor by the A/C line on 1976 and later models. If so, discharging is not necessary.
4. Disconnect the O-ring and the A/C lines.
5. Remove the screws securing the blower motor. Remove the motor.

Installation is the reverse of removal. Apply a bead of sealer to the flange before installing the blower motor. Recharge the A/C system.

Heater Core Removal and Installation with Air Conditioning

1970 88 and 98

1. Working inside the car, remove the right and left duct hoses from the heater box. The hoses are sometimes stapled into place with three staples and there are tabs that snap into holes in the hoses.
2. Remove the manifold assembly from the front of the heater box.
3. Disconnect the wiring and vacuum hoses.
4. Remove the screws and/or nuts securing the heater box to the firewall. Fasteners may be located on both sides of the firewall.
5. Drain the radiator and disconnect the heater hoses from the heater core.
6. Remove the heater box and remove the core from the box by removing the top half of the heater box.
7. Reverse the above steps to install.

1971-73 88 and 98

1. Working inside the car, remove the air distribution hoses from the heater box. Hoses are sometimes held in place by staples. There are also tabs that snap into holes in the end of the hoses.
2. Remove the manifold from the front of the heater box. It is held in place by two screws and a tab.
3. Disconnect the wiring, vacuum hoses, and cables.
4. Disconnect the defroster manifold from the top of the heater box.
5. Working from outside the car, drain the radiator and disconnect the heater hoses.
6. Remove the heater box stud nuts and remove the heater box from the firewall.
7. Remove the heater core from the heater box.
8. Reverse the above steps to install.

1974 and Later 88 and 98

1. Drain the radiator.
2. Remove the heater case securing nuts. Disconnect the heater hoses.
3. Remove the instrument panel trim pad.
4. Remove the heater case-to-firewall bolts from inside the car.
5. Remove the bottom air duct.
6. Remove the instrument panel crash pad. Unfasten the leads from the clock and glovebox light.
7. Remove the upper right-hand trim panel.

8. Separate the air distribution manifold and defroster duct from the heater case.
9. Remove the lower dash trim panel.
10. Lift out the heater case and disconnect the hoses and cables from it.
11. Remove the core from the case.

Installation is the reverse of removal.

F-85, Cutlass

1. Working inside the car, remove the defroster adapter from the upper right side of the heater box.
2. Remove the manifold attached to the front of the heater box. It is secured by two screws and a metal tab. Remove the glovebox, first, if necessary.
3. Disconnect the vacuum hoses, cables, and wiring.
4. Working outside the car, drain the radiator and disconnect the heater hoses from the heater core.
5. Remove the nuts from the heater box studs and remove the heater box.
6. Remove the heater core from the heater box.
7. Reverse the above steps to install.

Omega

1. Disconnect the battery and drain the cooling system.
2. Detach the upper heater hose at the core tube.
3. Remove all accessible heater core and case securing nuts.
4. Unfasten the right-hand front fender filler panel bolts and lower the panel, in order to gain access to the lower heater hose clamp.
5. Unfasten the hose clamp and detach the hose from the lower heater core tube.
6. Unfasten the lower nut which secures the right-hand heater case/core assembly.
7. Plug both of the core tubes to prevent coolant from leaking.
8. Remove the glovebox and its door.
9. Take the vacuum diaphragm assembly off the right-hand kick-panel.
10. Remove the outlet from the bottom of the heater case.
11. Separate the cold air duct from the heater case.
12. Unfasten the screws which secure the extension to the heater case. Remove the extension from the case.
13. Detach the cables and the wiring from the case. Remove the core and case as an assembly.
14. Remove the core from the case.

Installation is performed in the reverse order of removal.

1975 Starfire

NOTE: This procedure requires discharging and charging the A/C system. Do not attempt it unless you have the special tools and knowledge necessary to perform this task.

1. Disconnect the battery.
2. Remove the glovebox.
3. Remove the right-hand air outlet duct.
4. Remove the instrument cluster bezel and the instrument panel crash pad.
5. Remove the left-hand air outlet deflector and feed duct.
6. Remove its retaining screws and lower the steering column so that it rests on the driver's seat.
9. Unfasten the instrument cluster screws, leads, speedometer cable, and remove the cluster. Remove the radio.
10. Remove the defroster and center distribution ducts.
11. Carefully discharge the refrigerant from the system.
12. Place a container beneath them and then remove the heater hoses from the core pipes. Plug the hoses.
13. Clean the external surfaces and fittings of the VIR assembly.
14. Disconnect the compressor intake line, oil bleed line, and condenser outlet line. Plug ALL open connections.
15. Loosen the evaporator intake and outlet connections. Remove the VIR mounting clamp screw and remove the clamp. Slide the VIR off the evaporator outlet line and then off the intake line. Remove and throw all the old O-rings away. Plug ALL open connections.

16. Remove the heater distributor case stud-to-firewall nuts. Remove the distributor case assbly, after disconnecting all electrical leads and vacuum hoses from it.
17. Separate the heater case from the distributor and the core from the case.

Installation is the reverse of removal. Charge the A/C system and add coolant, as required.

1976 and Later Starfire

1. Disconnect the battery ground cable.
2. Remove the three nuts from the engine compartment side of the cover plate.
3. Disconnect the heater hoses and fasten them in a raised position to prevent coolant loss. Plug the core tubes.
4. Remove the heater floor outlet.
5. Remove the glove box and door.
6. Remove the right and left instrument panel outlets.
7. Unscrew and move the console back.
8. Remove the instrument panel pad. Remove the column nuts and let the wheel rest on the seat. Remove the instrument panel screws and lower the panel onto the steering column.
9. Remove the right instrument panel and lower outlet as an assembly.
10. Disconnect the vacuum hoses at the left end of the heater case.
11. Remove the modular duct to heater case screw and the two heater case to evaporator case screws. Pry off the retaining clips at the defroster outlets and move the duct back.
12. Pull the heater case away from the firewall until the core tubes

clear, then disconnect the temperature cable.
13. Remove the core to case screws and remove the core.
14. Reverse the procedure for installation. Torque the steering column nuts to 25 ft lbs.

SEAT BELTS

Disabling the Seat Belt/Starter Interlock and Buzzer

The seat belt/starter interlock was used only on early production 1975s. It is now legal to disable the seat belt/starter interlock, but *not* the warning light. To do this, proceed as follows:

1. Disconnect the negative (−) battery cable.
2. Locate the interlock harness connector, which is on or near the fuse block. The connector has orange, yellow, and green leads running to it.
3. Cut and tape the green lead on the body harness side of the interlock connector.
4. a. On Cutlass, 88, and 98 without low coolant warning and heavy duty cooling: disconnect the buzzer or beeper from the fuse panel and remove it.
   b. On Cutlass, 88, and 98 with low coolant warning and heavy duty cooling: cut the yellow wire behind the connector and tape its ends.
   c. On Omega and Starfire: remove the buzzer from its connector on the wiring harness.
5. Check the battery cable.
6. Check system operation by starting the car with the seat belt unfastened.

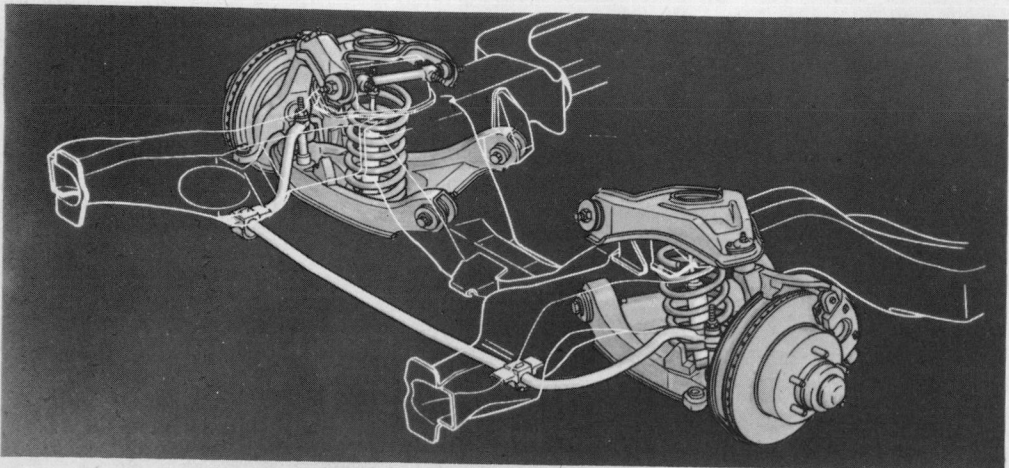

1977 88 and 98 front suspension (© Oldsmobile Div., G.M. Corp.)

INDEX

Oldsmobile Toronado

Automatic Transmission C717

Brakes **C723, U299**
  Master cylinder Removal and
    Installation C723
  Parking brake adjustment C723
  Power booster Removal and
    Installation C723

Charging System .... See Oldsmobile Section

Cooling System .... See Oldsmobile Section

Differential Removal and Installation C717

Drive Axles **C719**
  Drive axle Removal and Installation
    —left side C719
  Drive axle Removal and Installation
    —right-side C719

Emission Controls ...... See Oldsmobile Section

Engine **C713, U194**
  Engine Removal and Installation C713
  LUBRICATION C716
  Oil pan Removal and Installation C716
  Oil pump Removal and Installation C717
  Rear main oil seal replacement C717
  MANIFOLDS C715
  Exhaust manifold Removal and
    Installation C715
  TIMING COVER, CHAIN, AND
    CAMSHAFT C715

Camshaft Removal and Installation C716
Timing cover Removal and Installation ..C715
Timing chain Removal and
  Installation C716

Front Suspension **C720**
  Ball joint vertical check C721
  Ball joint horizontal check C721
  Disc Removal and Installation C720
  Front end alignment C722
  Lower ball joint Removal and
    Installation C722
  Lower control arm Removal and
    Installation C721
  Torsion bar crossmember Removal and
    Installation C785
  Torsion bar Removal and Installation ...C720
  Upper control arm Removal and
    Installation C721
  Wheel hub Removal and Installation C720

Fuel System .... See Oldsmobile Section

Heater **C726**
  Blower motor Removal and Installation C726
  Heater core Removal and Installation ...C726

Ignition System .... See Oldsmobile Section
  Firing order C764

Instrument Panel **C726, U350**
  Headlight switch Removal and
    Installation C726

Radio **C726**
  Radio Removal and Installation C726

Rear Suspension **C722**
  Coil spring Removal and Installation C723
  Leaf spring Removal and Installation C723
  Spindle Removal and Installation C722
  Wheel bearing adjustment C722

Seat Belts **C726**
  Disabling the interlock system C726

Specifications **C710, U359**
  Alternator and regulator C767
  Battery and starter C767
  Brakes C768
  Capacities C711
  Car serial no. location C710
  Crankshaft and connecting rod C712
  Engine identification code C710
  General engine C711
  Piston clearance C713
  Ring gap and side clearance C713
  Torque C712
  Tune-up C711
  Valve C712
  Wheel alignment C713
  Year identification C710

Starting System .... See Oldsmobile Section

Steering **C723, U328**

Windshield Wipers **C726**

YEAR IDENTIFICATION

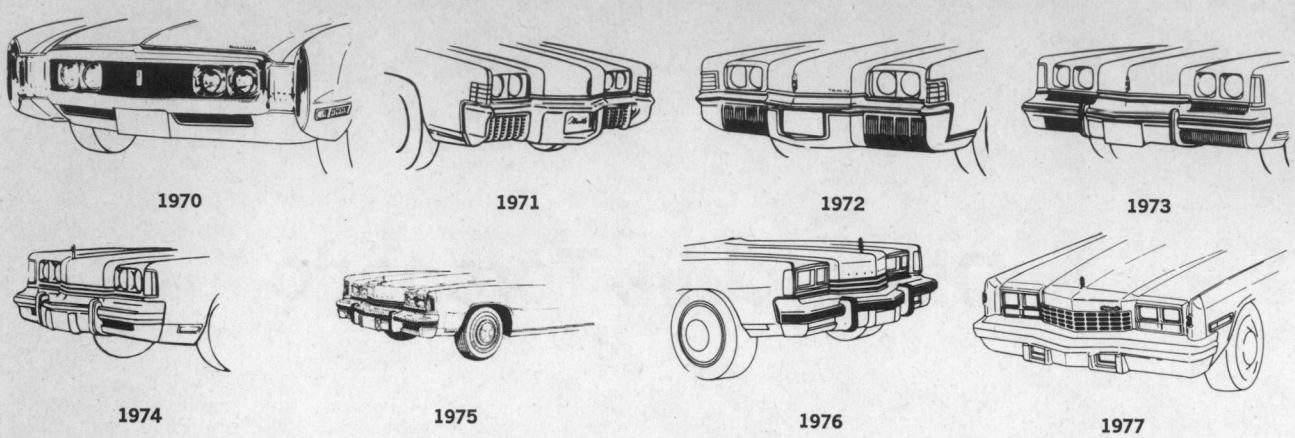

1970　　1971　　1972　　1973

1974　　1975　　1976　　1977

FIRING ORDER

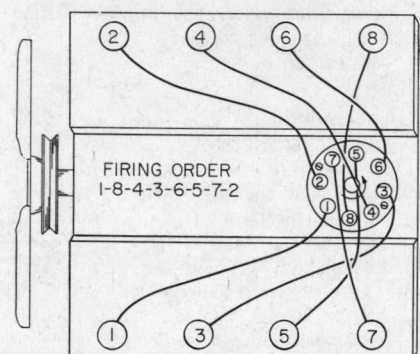

FIRING ORDER
1-8-4-3-6-5-7-2

CAR SERIAL NUMBER LOCATION AND ENGINE IDENTIFICATION

Vehicle Identification Number

The vehicle identification plate is located on the left side of the dashboard, visible through the windshield.

Engine Identification

The engine identification number is found on a tape attached to the oil filler tube.

ENGINE IDENTIFICATION CODE

The engine identification code is located on tape attached directly to the front of the oil filler tube.

Disp	Bbl	'70	'71	'72	'73	'74	'75	'76	'77
403	4								—
455	4				UQ UV VO VP UV	UO UP VO VP	UP VP	UP VP	
455	4		UU						
455	4			UU UV					
455	4	US UT							
455	4								
455	4	UV UW							

GENERAL ENGINE SPECIFICATIONS

Year	Engine No. Cyl. Displacement Cu. In.	Carburetor Type	Horsepower @ rpm ■	Torque @ rpm (ft lbs) ■	Bore X Stroke (in.)	Compression Ratio	Oil Pressure @ 1500 rpm
'70	8-455	4 bbl	375 @ 4600	510 @ 3000	4.126 x 4.250	10.25:1	38
	8-455	4 bbl	400 @ 3200	500 @ 3200	4.126 x 4.250	10.25:1	38
'71	8-455	4 bbl	350 @ 4400	465 @ 2800	4.126 x 4.250	8.50:1	38
'72	8-455	4 bbl	265 @ 4200	375 @ 2800	4.126 x 4.250	8.50:1	38
'73	8-455	4 bbl	250 @ 4000	375 @ 2800	4.126 x 4.250	8.50:1	38
'74	8-455	4 bbl	230 @ 3800	370 @ 2800	4.126 x 4.250	8.50:1	38
'75-'76	8-455	4 bbl	215 @ 3600	370 @ 2400	4.126 x 4.250	8.50:1	38
'77	8-403	4 bbl	——→	——	4.351 x 3.385	——	——

■ Beginning 1972, horsepower and torque are SAE net figures. They are measured at the rear of the transmission with all accessories installed and operating. Since the figures vary when a given engine is installed in different models, some are representative rather than exact.

TUNE-UP SPECIFICATIONS

When analyzing compression test results, look for uniformity among cylinders rather than specific pressures.

	ENGINE No. Cyl.	SPARK PLUGS		DISTRIBUTOR		IGNITION TIMING (deg) ▲		VALVES Intake Opens	Fuel Pump Pressure	IDLE SPEED (rpm) ▲	
Year	Displacement (cu in.)	Orig. Type	Gap (in.)	Point Dwell (deg)	Point Gap (in.)	Man Trans	* Auto Trans	(deg) ●	(psi)	Man Trans	● Auto Trans
'70	8-455	45S	.030	28-32	.016	—	8B	22B	5½-6½	—	600
	8-455①	44S	.030	28-32	.016	—	12B	24B	5½-6½	—	600
'71	8-455	46S	.040	28-32	.016	—	10B	22B	5½-6½	—	600
'72	8-455	46S	.040	28-32	.016	—	8B	20B	5½-6½	—	650/550
'73	8-455	R46S	.040	30	.016	—	8B	20B	5½-6½	—	650/550
'74	8-455	R46S	.040	30	.016	—	10B	20B	5½-6½	—	650/550
'74	8-455	R46SX	.080	Electronic		—	10B	20B	5½-6½	—	650/550
'75	8-455	R46SX	.080	Electronic		—	12B	20B	5½-6½	—	650/550 (650/600)②
'76	8-455	R46SX	.080	Electronic		—	14B(12B)	20B	5½-6½	—	650/550 (650/600)②
'77	All	See Underhood Specifications Sticker									

* Set timing with carburetor adjusted to 1100 rpm, unless sticker specifies otherwise.
▲ See text for procedure
● Where two figures appear separated by a slash, the first is idle speed with solenoid energized, the second is idle speed with solenoid disconnected. Figure in parentheses indicates California engine.

① Air Injection Reactor System
② Solenoid energized (higher) idle speed is set with A/C on and compressor clutch wires disconnected.
B Before Top Dead Center
— Not applicable

CAPACITIES

Year	ENGINE No. Cyl. Displacement (cu. in.)	Engine Crankcase Add 1 Qt For New Filter	TRANSMISSION Pts To Refill After Draining			Drive Axle (pts)	Gasoline Tank (gals)	COOLING SYSTEM (qts)	
			Manual 3-Speed	4-Speed	Automatic ●			With Heater	With A/C
'70	8-455	5	——	——	8	4	24	18	18.5
'71	8-455	5	——	——	8	4	24	18	18.5
'72	8-455	5	——	——	8	4	25	19.5	20
'73	8-455	5	——	——	8	4	26	19.5	20
'74	8-455	5	——	——	8	4	26	21	21.5

● Does not include torque converter   —— Not applicable

CAPACITIES

Year	ENGINE No. Cyl. Displacement (cu. in.)	Engine Crankcase Add 1 Qt For New Filter	TRANSMISSION Pts To Refill After Draining			Drive Axle (qts)	Gasoline Tank (gals)	COOLING SYSTEM (qts)	
			Manual 3-Speed	4-Speed	Automatic •			With Heater	With A/C
'75-'76	8-455	5	—	—	8	4	26	21.5	21.5
'77	8-403	5	—	—	8	4	26	21.5	21.5

• Does not include torque converter   — Not applicable

VALVE SPECIFICATIONS

Year	Engine No. Cyl. Displacement (cu in.)	Seat Angle (deg)	Face Angle (deg)	Spring Test Pressure (lbs @ in.)	Spring Installed Height (in.)	STEM TO GUIDE Clearance (in.)		STEM Diameter (in.)	
						Intake	Exhaust	Intake	Exhaust
'70	8-455	45	46	187 @ 1.27	1 21/32	.0010-.0027	.0015-.0032	.3429	.3424
'71	8-455	45	46	187 @ 1.27	1 21/32	.0010-.0027	.0015-.0032	.3429	.3424
'72	8-455	45	46	197 @ 1.23	1 21/32	.0010-.0027	.0015-.0032	.3429	.3424
'73	8-455	45	46	197 @ 1.23	1 21/32	.0010-.0027	.0015-.0032	.3429	.3424
'74	8-455	45	46	197 @ 1.23	1 21/32	.0010-.0027	.0015-.0032	.3429	.3424
'75-'76	8-455	45①	44①	187 @ 1.27	1 39/64	.0010-.0027	.0015-.0032	.3429	.3424
'77	8-403	45①	44①	—	—	.0010-.0027	.0015-.0032	.3429	.3424

① Exhaust valve seat 31°
  Exhaust valve face 30°

TORQUE SPECIFICATIONS

All readings in ft lbs

Year	Engine No. Cyl. Displacement (cu in.)	Cylinder Head Bolts	Bearing Bolts Rod	Bearing Bolts Main	Crankshaft Damper or Pulley Bolt	Flywheel to Crankshaft Bolts	MANIFOLD	
							Intake	Exhaust
'70-'74	8-455	80	42	120	160	60	35	25
'75-'76	8-455	85	42	120	200-310	60	40	25
'77	8-403	85	42	80①	200-310	60	40	25

① 120 on no. 5

CRANKSHAFT AND CONNECTING ROD SPECIFICATIONS

All measurements are given in inches

Year	Engine No. Cyl. Displacement (cu in.)	CRANKSHAFT Main Brg. Journal Dia	Main Brg. Oil Clearance	Shaft End-Play	Thrust on No.	CONNECTING ROD Journal Diameter	Oil Clearance	Side Clearance
'70	8-455	2.9998	.0005-.0021①	.004-.008	3	2.4988-2.4998	.0004-.0033	.002-.013
'71	8-455	2.9998	.0005-.0021①	.004-.008	3	2.4988-2.4998	.0004-.0033	.002-.011
'72-'76	8-455	2.9998	.0005-.0021①	.004-.008	3	2.4988-2.4998	.0004-.0033	.006-.020
'77	8-403	2.4990②	.0005-.0021③	.004-.008	3	2.1238-2.1248	.0004-.0033	.006-.020

① No. 5—.0020-.0034
② No. 1—2.4993
③ No. 5—.0015-.0031

RING GAP

All measurements are given in inches

Year	Engine	Top Compression	Bottom Compression		Year	Engine	Oil Control
'70-'71	8-455	.013-.023	.013-.023		'70-'76	8-455	.015-.055
'72-'76	8-455	.010-.023	.010-.023		'77	8-403	.015-.055
'77	8-403	.010-.023	.010-.023				

RING SIDE CLEARANCE

All measurements are given in inches

Year	Engine	Top Compression	Bottom Compression		Year	Engine	Oil Control
'70-'71	8-455	.0018-.0033	.0018-.0038		'70-'76	8-455	.0021-.0031
'72-'76	8-455	.0020-.0040	.0020-.0040		'77	8-403	.0006-.0096
'77	8-403	.0020-.0040	.0020-.0040				

PISTON CLEARANCE

Year	Engine	Piston-to-bore Clearance (in.)
'70-'76	8-455	.001-.002
'77	8-403	.001-.002

WHEEL ALIGNMENT SPECIFICATIONS

Year	CASTER Range (deg)	Pref Setting (deg)	CAMBER Range (deg)	Pref Setting (deg)	Toe-in (in.)	Steering Axis Inclin. (deg)	WHEEL PIVOT RATIO (deg) Inner Wheel	Outer Wheel
'70	1½N to 2½N	2N	¼N to ½P	⅛P	0 ± 1/16	11	20	18⅕
'71-'74	1½N to 2½N	2N	¼N to ¾P① ¾N to ¼P②	¼P① ¼N②	0 ± 1/16	11	—	—
'75-'77	1N to 1P	0	¼N to ¾P① ¾N to ¼P②	¼P① ¼N②	0 ± 1/16	11	—	—

N Negative   P Positive

① Left side
② Right side

NOTE: Service procedures for the Charging System, Starting System, Ignition System, Fuel System, Cooling System, and Emission Controls on the Toronado can be found in the Oldsmobile section.

ENGINE

NOTE: Any engine procedures not given here are the same as those given in the Oldsmobile section.

Engine Removal and Installation

1. Drain radiator.
2. Remove hood, marking hinge for reassembly.
3. If equipped with a fan shroud, unhook the strap and remove the clips holding the seal to the venturi ring. Move the seal toward the radiator.
4. Disconnect battery.
5. Disconnect radiator hoses and cooler lines, heater hoses, vacuum hoses, engine to body ground strap, fuel hose from fuel pump, wiring and accelerator cable. Remove the air cleaner, hot air pipe, air conditioner compressor and power steering pump without disconnecting lines and set them aside.
6. Remove coil, throttle control switch bracket, radiator support and radiator.
7. Raise the car.
8. Disconnect exhaust pipes at manifold. Loosen, but do not remove, upper left flywheel cover attaching bolt (this will require a long extension).
9. Disconnect wires and remove starter.
10. Remove torque converter cover and remove three bolts securing the converter to flywheel. Scribe

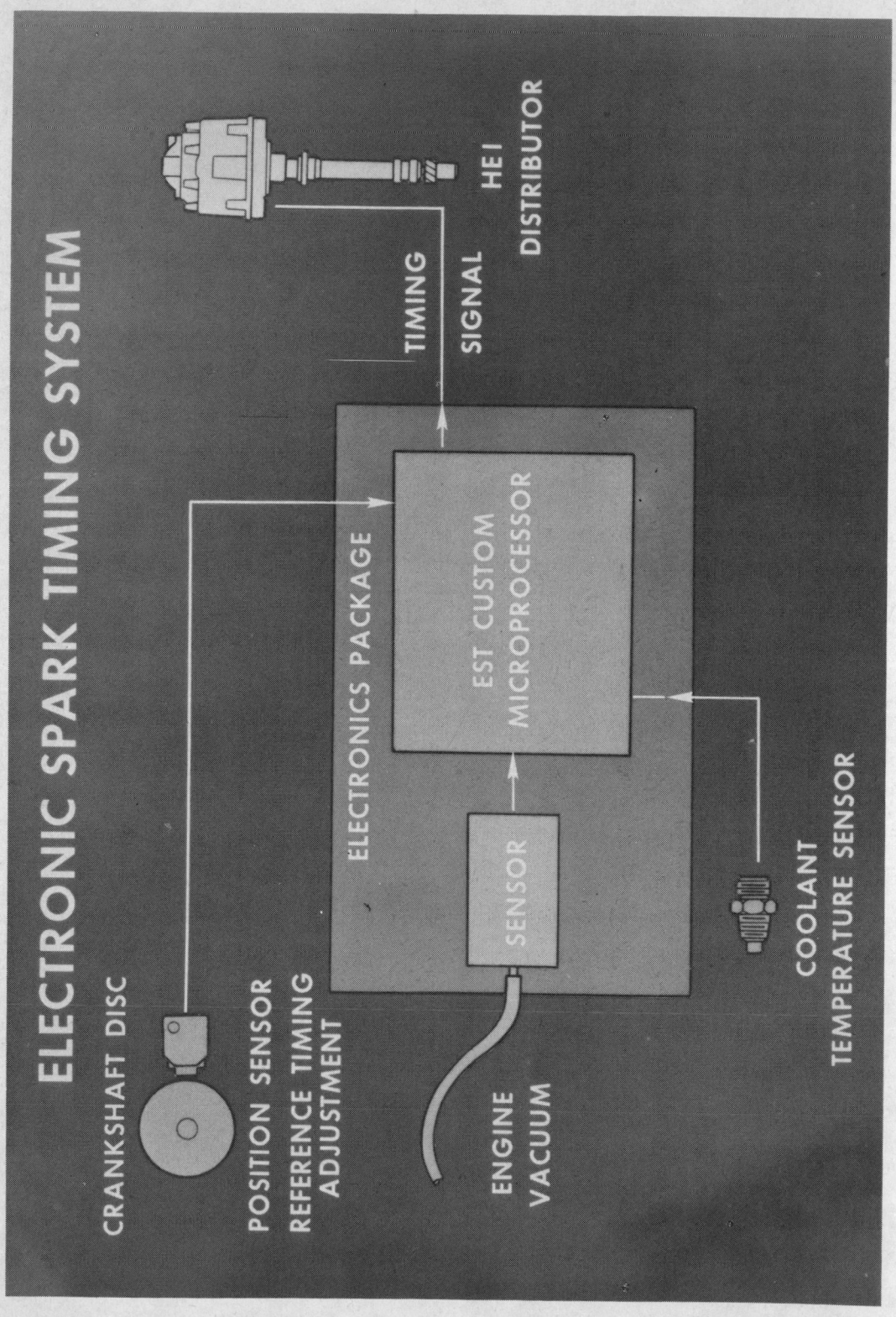

Electronic spark timing control system used on 1977 Toronado 403 V8
(© Oldsmobile Div., G.M. Corp.)

marks on converter and flywheel for reassembly.

11. Support the final drive assembly.
12. Remove two attaching bolts from right output shaft support bracket and one through bolt attaching final drive to engine block on the left side. Scribe around the washers for correct reassembly.
13. Remove engine mount to crossmember nuts and front engine mount nuts. Remove the lower right engine-to-transmission attaching bolt.

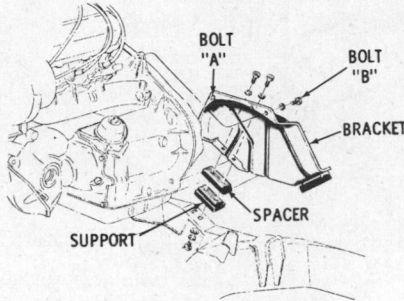

Engine mount attachment
(© Oldsmobile Div., G.M. Corp)

14. Lower the car.
15. Support the final drive assembly with a chain stretched under and across the final drive assembly and attached to holes in the frame members.
16. Support engine by using a lifting fixture.
17. Remove five remaining transmission-to-engine bolts.
18. Lift the engine from the car.

Caution
If car is to be moved, install converter holding tool.

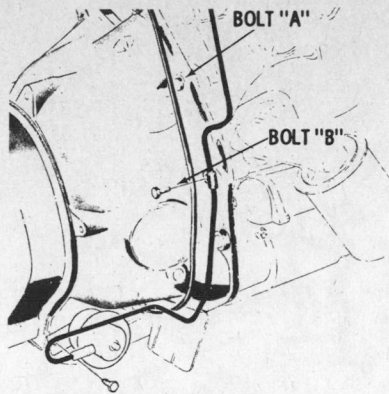

Transmission to engine attachment
(© Oldsmobile Div., G.M. Corp)

19. To install, reverse removal procedure.

Manifolds

Exhaust Manifold Removal and Installation

Left Side

1. Remove the air cleaner and the carburetor heat box on the manifold.
2. Remove the lower alternator bracket; raise the front of the car and support it securely.
3. Remove the exhaust pipe.
4. Lower the car and remove the manifold attaching bolts. Remove the manifold from above.
5. To install, reverse the removal procedure using the correct torque for the manifold attaching bolts. (See illustration for the correct torque specifications.)

Right Side

1. Raise the car and support it securely.

2. Remove the exhaust pipe and the right front wheel.
3. Remove the attaching bolts and lower the manifold down and out from under the vehicle.
4. To install, reverse the removal procedure.

Timing Cover, Chain, and Camshaft

Timing Cover Removal and Installation

In order to remove the front cover, on 1971 and later models, the engine must be removed from the car.

1. Drain the cooling system. Disconnect the upper and lower radiator, heater and bypass hoses.
2. Remove the radiator, belts, fan and fan pulley, crankshaft pulley and the harmonic balancer.
3. Remove the engine.
4. Remove the timing cover attaching bolts and pull off the cover. Also, remove the timing pointer and the water pump.
5. Before assembly, remove all old gaskets and install a new timing cover gasket.
6. Position the front cover, timing pointer and the water pump.
7. Lubricate the attaching bolts and install.
8. Install the harmonic balancer on the crankshaft after lubrication. Replace the engine.
9. Connect all cooling hoses.
10. Install the crankshaft pulley.
11. Install the fan and the fan pulley.
12. Install the drive belts and adjust.
13. Fill the crankcase and the radiator.
14. Run the engine and check for leaks.

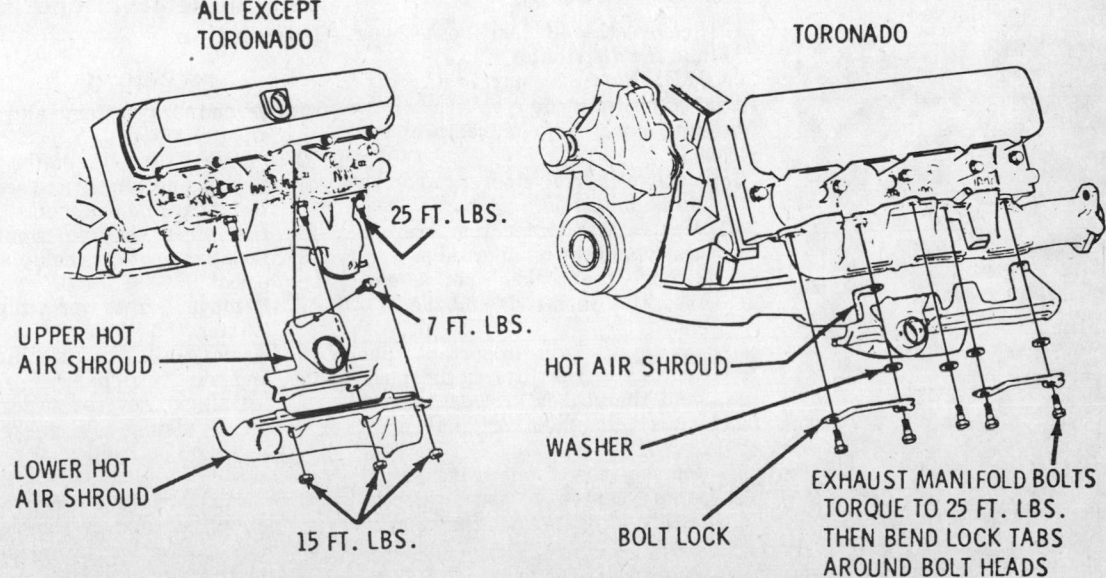

Exhaust manifold components and torque requirements (© Oldsmobile Div., G.M. Corp)

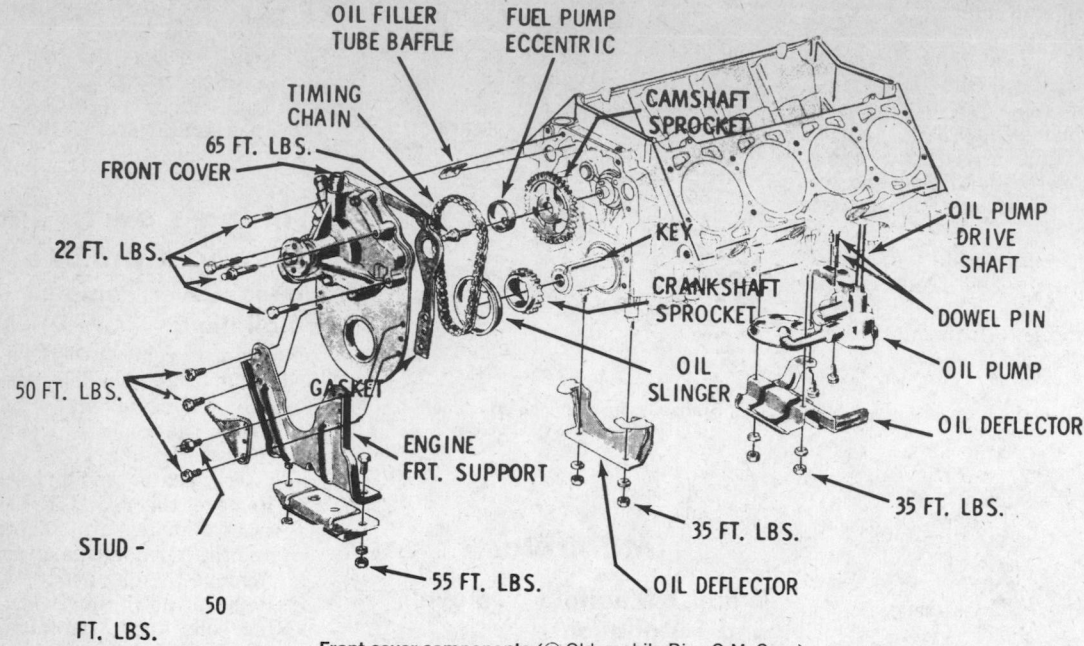

OIL FILLER
TUBE BAFFLE

FUEL PUMP
ECCENTRIC

CAMSHAFT
SPROCKET

TIMING
CHAIN

65 FT. LBS.

FRONT COVER

22 FT. LBS.

KEY

CRANKSHAFT
SPROCKET

OIL PUMP
DRIVE
SHAFT

DOWEL PIN

OIL PUMP

50 FT. LBS.

GASKET

OIL
SLINGER

OIL DEFLECTOR

ENGINE
FRT. SUPPORT

STUD -

35 FT. LBS.

35 FT. LBS.

50
FT. LBS.

55 FT. LBS.

OIL DEFLECTOR

Front cover components (© Oldsmobile Div., G.M. Corp)

Timing Chain Removal and Installation

NOTE: 1971 and later models require that the engine be removed before performing the chain removal procedure.

1. Remove the front engine cover.
2. Remove the fuel pump eccentric, oil slinger, cam sprocket and timing chain.

NOTE: It is necessary to use a puller to remove the crankshaft sprocket.

4. To install, align the camshaft and crankshaft sprockets. The camshaft sprocket aligning mark must be in the 6 o'clock position while the crankshaft sprocket must be in the 12 o'clock position.

65 FT. LBS.

ALIGN
TIMING MARKS

Timing chain alignment
(© Oldsmobile Div., G.M. Corp)

NOTE: This alignment brings No. 6 cylinder to top dead center. Turn the crankshaft one full turn to bring No. 1 to top dead center.

5. Position the fuel pump eccentric with the flat side against the gear. Using a brass hammer, place the key against the gear until it bottoms.
6. Install the oil slinger. Replace the cover.

Camshaft Removal and Installation

NOTE: The removal and installation of the camshaft on 1971 and later models requires the removal of the engine since the oil pan and the front cover must be removed.

1. Remove the oil pan, front cover and the distributor.

NOTE: Before removing the distributor, position the No. 1 piston at top dead center of its compression stroke.

2. Remove the valve covers and the intake manifold.
3. Remove the water temperature sensor and the oil filler tube.
4. Remove the rocker arm assemblies, the push rods and the lifters.

Caution It is important that the lifters, the push rods, and the rocker arm assemblies be replaced in their original positions.

5. Remove the front cover, fuel pump eccentric, camshaft sprocket, oil slinger and the timing chain.
6. Remove the camshaft by carefully sliding it from the front of the engine. Use caution not to

damage the camshaft bearings during this procedure. Keep the camshaft parallel with the crankshaft as it is removed.

7. Before installing the camshaft, coat both the cam lobes and the bearings with camshaft grease. Install the camshaft and align the timing marks on the camshaft and crankshaft sprockets as outlined in the Timing Chain Removal and Installation section.
8. Install the distributor.
9. Reverse the removal procedure to complete the installation.

Engine Lubrication

Oil Pan Removal and Installation

1970

1. Disconnect battery and remove dipstick.
2. Remove upper radiator support screws and fan shroud screws.
3. Hoist car and drain oil.
4. Disconnect engine mounts and jack front of engine up as far as possible.
5. Remove crossover pipe and starter.
6. Remove oil pan attaching bolts and remove oil pan.
7. Install in reverse order of removal, using new gaskets with sealer on both sides.

1971 and Later

The engine must be removed from the vehicle in order to remove the oil pan.

1. Remove engine assembly.
2. Remove dipstick.

3. Drain oil and remove filter assembly.
4. Remove the front engine mount and bracket.
5. Remove oil pan attaching bolts and remove oil pan.
6. Apply a good sealer to both sides of pan gaskets and install on block.
7. Install front and rear seal.
8. Install the pan. Torque 5/16 in. bolts to 15 ft. lbs. and ¼ in. bolts to 10 ft. lbs.
9. Reinstall mount and oil filter assembly.
10. Reinstall engine and fill crankcase.

Oil Pump Removal and Installation

Remove the oil pan as described above. Remove the oil baffle. Remove the oil pump to rear main bearing cap attaching bolts, then remove the pump and drive shaft extension.

Rear Main Bearing Oil Seal Replacement

Whether or not the engine must be removed from the vehicle in order to replace the rear main bearing oil seal depends upon the removal of the oil pan. See "Oil Pan Removal and Installation". Remove the oil pan and rear main bearing cap. Using a blunt-ended tool, drive the upper seal into its groove on each side until it is tightly packed. This is usually ¼—¾ in. Cut pieces of the old bearing cap seal 1/16 in. longer than the distance each side of the upper seal was compressed. Install these pieces into each side of the upper seal seat, packing them into place. Carefully trim any protruding seal, being sure not to scratch or damage the bearing surface. Install a new seal in the bearing cap and install the cap, tightening bolts to the specified torque. Install the oil pan.

AUTOMATIC TRANSMISSION

The Toronado uses a Turbo Hydra-Matic 425 automatic transmission. This is the Turbo Hydra-Matic 400 used in the larger Oldsmobiles, adapted to the front-drive car.

All Turbo Hydra-Matic 425 in-car service procedures are the same as those given for the Turbo Hydra-Matic 400 in the Oldsmobile car section. Only the fluid refill capacity is different.

Differential

Removal

1. Disconnect battery.

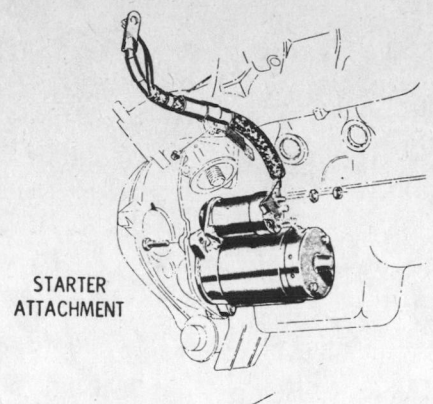

STARTER ATTACHMENT

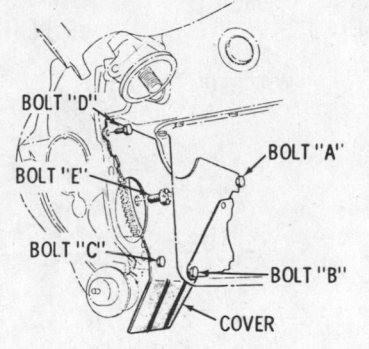

BOLT "D"
BOLT "A"
BOLT "E"
BOLT "C"
BOLT "B"
COVER

Transmission to converter attachment
(© Oldsmobile Div., G.M. Corp)

2. See illustration. Remove bolts A, B, and C. Nut D must be removed with a special wrench. *NOTE: it may be necessary to remove the transmission filler tube to gain clearance.*
3. Hoist the car. If a two post hoist is used, the car must be supported with floor stands at the front frame rails and the front post lowered.
4. Disconnect right and left drive axles from the output shafts.

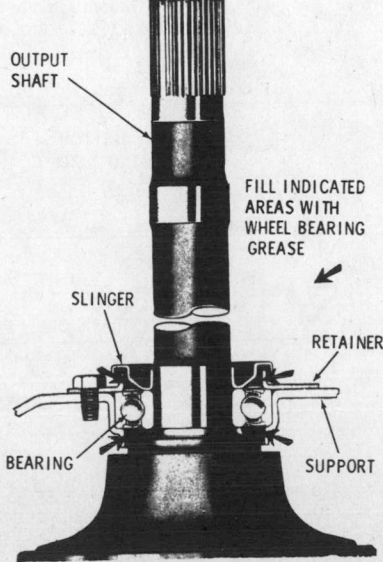

OUTPUT SHAFT

FILL INDICATED AREAS WITH WHEEL BEARING GREASE

SLINGER

RETAINER

BEARING

SUPPORT

Assembly of right-hand output shaft
(© Oldsmobile Div., G.M. Corp)

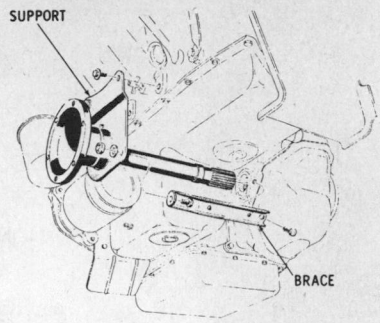

SUPPORT

BRACE

Right-hand output shaft
(© Oldsmobile Div., G.M. Corp)

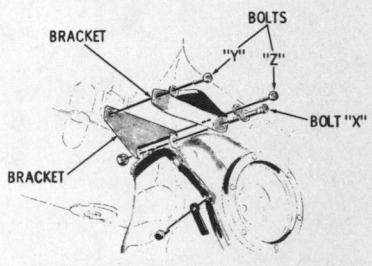

BRACKET
BOLTS "Y" "Z"
BOLT "X"
BRACKET

Disconnecting final drive from engine
(© Oldsmobile Div., G.M. Corp)

5. Remove engine oil filter.
6. Disconnect brace from final drive, then disconnect right-hand output shaft assembly from engine.
7. Remove output shaft assembly from final drive.
8. See illustration. Remove bolt X and loosen bolts Y and Z.
9. Remove final drive cover and allow lubricant to drain.
10. Position transmission lift with adapter for final drive. Install an anchor bolt through final drive housing and lift pad.
11. See illustration. Remove bolts E, F, and G, and nut from H.
12. Move transmission lift toward front of car to disengage final drive splines from transmission. Some transmission fluid will be lost.
13. Lower transmission lift and remove final drive from lift.
14. Using a 9/16 in. socket, remove the left output shaft retainer bolt, then pull output shaft from final drive.
15. Remove transmission to final drive gasket.

Installation

1. Apply special seal lubricant to both output shaft seals.
2. Install the left output shaft into the final drive. Retain with bolt and torque to 40 ft. lbs. (45 ft. lbs. 1975 and later)
3. Position final drive on transmission lift and install an anchor bolt through the housing and lift pad.
4. Apply a thin film of special seal lubricant on the transmission

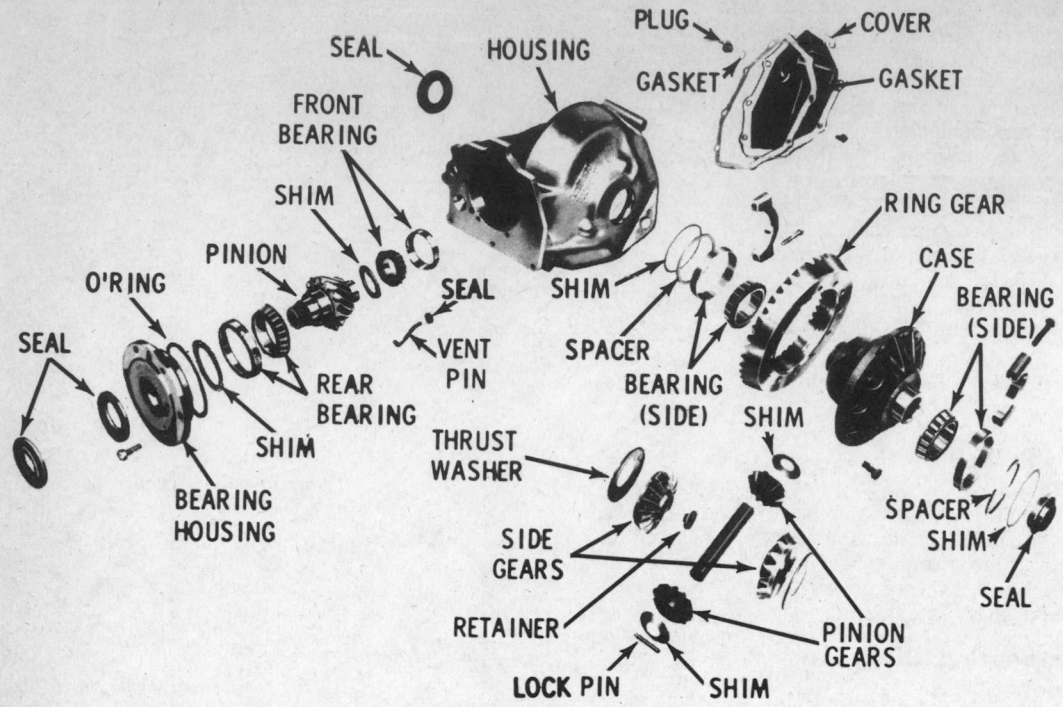

Final drive components (© Oldsmobile Div., G.M. Corp)

side of the new final drive to transmission gasket. Then position gasket on the transmission.

5. Raise the transmission lift. Align the two bolt studs D and H on the transmission with their mating holes in the final drive. Move final drive until it mates with the transmission.

Caution It may be necessary to rotate the left output shaft to align the splines on the final drive with the splines of the transmission output shaft.

6. Install bolts E, F, and G and nut H finger tight.
7. Install bolt X and torque to 75 ft. lbs (100 ft lbs—1974) (110 ft. lbs—1975 and later). Tighten and torque bolts Y and Z to 50 ft lbs. (55 ft lbs—1975 and later).
8. Loosen and remove lift from final drive.
9. Position a new cover gasket on the final drive, then install cover. Torque cover bolts to 30 ft. lbs.
10. Install right output shaft into final drive, indexing splines of output shaft with splines of final drive. Install mounting bracket and brace bolts and tighten.
11. Connect drive axles to output shafts using new bolts. Tighten the bolts to 75 ft lbs.
12. Install oil filter.
13. Raise hoist, remove stands and lower car.
14. If filler tube was removed, attach a new O-ring and install filler tube.

15. Install bolts A, B, and C and nut D. Torque all final drive to transmission bolts to 25 ft.

lbs., 50 ft lbs (1974 and later). Torque nuts to about 25 ft lbs. or 50 ft lbs (1974 and later).

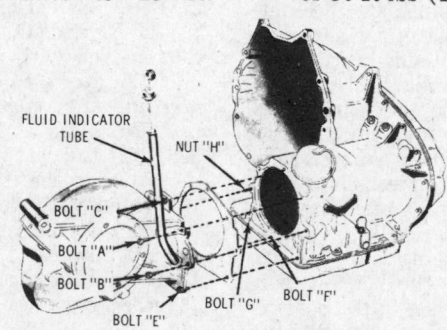

Transmission-to-final drive attachment
(© Oldsmobile Div., G.M. Corp)

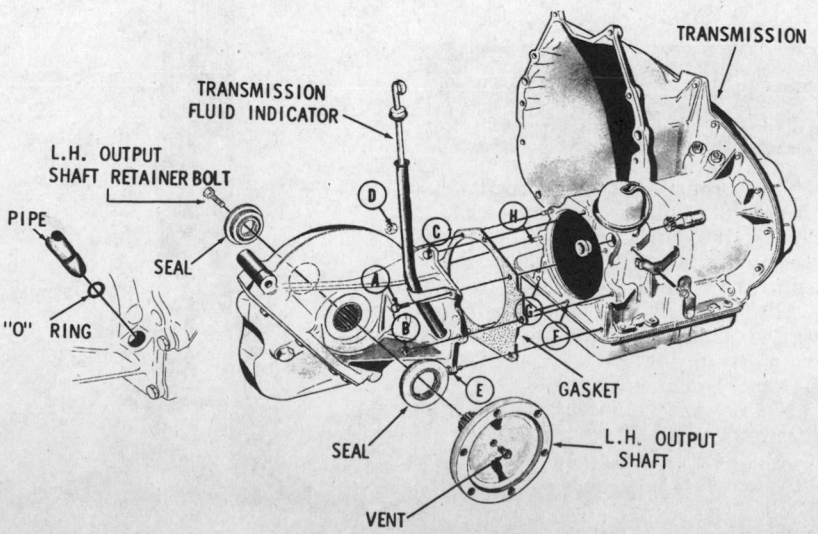

Transmission attachment bolts
(© Oldsmobile Div., G.M. Corp)

16. Connect battery.
17. Fill final drive.
18. Check engine oil level. Start engine and check transmission fluid level.
19. Check for any oil leaks.

DRIVE AXLES

Drive axles are flexible assemblies and consist of an axle shaft with an inner and outer constant velocity joint. The right axle shaft has a torsional damper mounted in the center. The inner constant velocity joint has complete flexibility, plus inward and outward movement. The outer constant velocity joint has complete flexibility but doesn't allow for inward and outward movement.

Drive Axle Removal —Right Side

1. Hoist car under lower control arms.
2. Remove drive axle cotter pin, nut and washer.
3. Remove oil filter.
4. Remove inner constant velocity joint attaching bolts.
5. Push inner constant velocity joint outward enough to disengage the right-hand final drive output shaft, then move rearward.
6. Remove right-hand output shaft bracket bolts to engine and final drive.
7. Remove right-hand output shaft and drive axle assembly.

Caution Care must be exercised so that constant velocity joints do not turn to full extremes, and that seals are not damaged against shock absorber or stabilizer bar.

Drive Axle Installation —Right Side

1. Carefully place righthand drive axle assembly into lower control arm and enter outer race splines into knuckle.
2. Lubricate final drive output shaft seal, with special seal lubricant.
3. Install right-hand output shaft into final drive and attach the support bolts to engine and brakes. Torque the bolts to 55 ft. lbs.
4. Move right-hand drive axle assembly toward front of car and align with right-hand output shaft. Install attaching bolts and torque to 75 ft. lbs.
5. Install oil filter.
6. Install washer and nut on drive axle. Torque to 140 ft. lbs. (200 ft. lbs. 1975 and later), then insert cotter pin.
7. Remove floor stands and lower hoist.

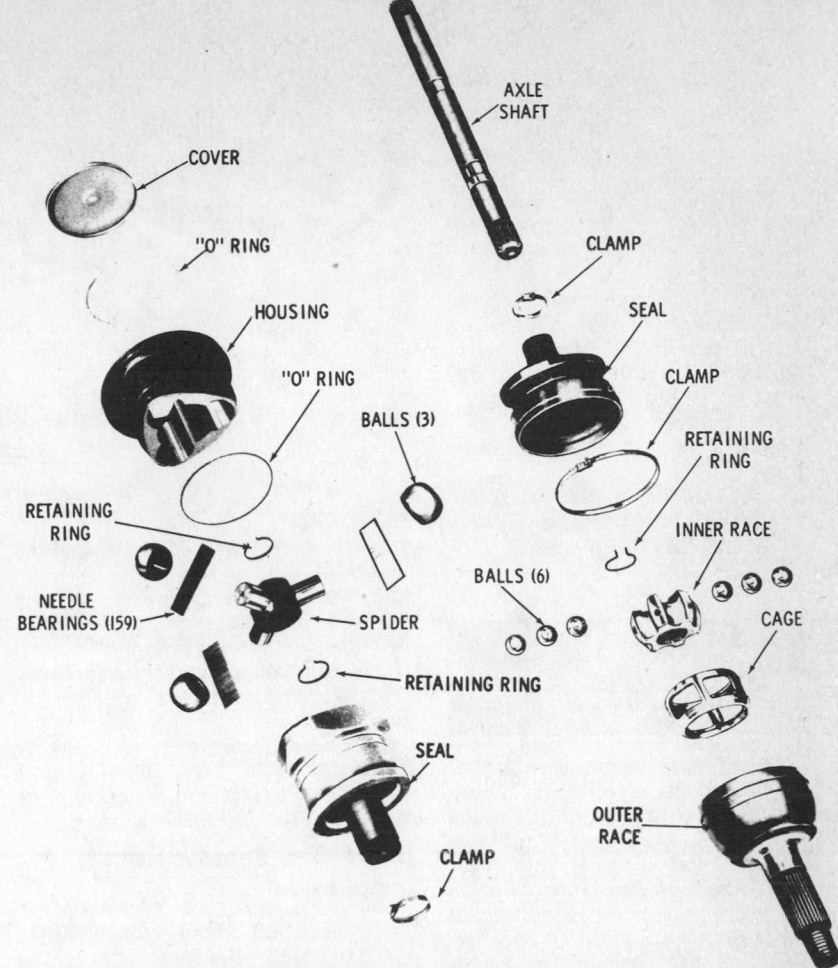

Exploded view of the left drive axle assembly
(© Oldsmobile Div., G.M. Corp)

8. Check engine oil level.

Drive Axle Removal —Left Side

1. Hoist car under lower control arms.
2. Remove wheel and, if equipped with drum brakes, remove drum. If equipped with disc brakes, remove disc.
3. Remove drive axle cotter pin, nut and washer.
4. Remove tie-rod end cotter pin and nut.
5. Remove the tie-rod end from the knuckle with a puller.
6. Remove bolts from drive axle assembly and left output shaft. Insert a spacer between the axle shaft and lower control arm.
7. Remove upper control arm ball joint cotter pin and nut.
8. Using hammer and brass drift, drive on knuckle until upper ball joint stud is free.
9. Using puller, remove lower ball joint from knuckle. Care must be exercised so that ball joint does not damage drive axle seal.
10. Remove knuckle and support, so that brake hose is not damaged.

11. Carefully guide drive axle assembly outboard.
NOTE: Care must be exercised so that constant velocity joints do not turn to full extremes and that seals are not damaged against shock absorber or stabilizer bar.

Drive Axle Installation —Left Side

1. Carefully guide left-hand drive axle assembly onto lower control arm and into position on spacer.
2. Insert lower control ball joint stud into knuckle and attach nut. Do not torque.
3. Center left-hand drive axle assembly in opening of knuckle and insert upper ball joint stud.
4. Place brake hose clip over upper ball joint stud and install nut. Do not torque.
5. Insert tie-rod end stud into knuckle and attach nut. Torque to 35 ft lbs. on models through 1974 and 40 ft lbs on 1975 and later models. Install cotter pin and crimp.
6. Align inner constant velocity joint with output shaft and in-

stall attaching bolts. Torque to 65 ft. lbs. (75 ft lbs 1975 and later).

7. Torque upper and lower ball joint stud nuts to 50 ft. lbs. upper —60 ft lbs, lower (95 ft lbs, 1975 and later) Install cotter pins and crimp.

NOTE: Upper ball joint cotter pin must be crimped toward upper control arm to prevent interference with outer constant velocity joint seal.

8. Install drive axle washer and nut. Torque to 150 ft lbs on models through 1974 and 200 ft lbs on 1975 and later models. Install cotter pin and crimp.
9. Install wheel.
10. Remove floor stands and lower hoist.
11. Check camber, caster and toe-in and adjust if necessary. Refer to Front End Alignment.

FRONT SUSPENSION

The front suspension consists of control arms, stabilizer bar, shock absorbers and a right and left torsion bar. Torsion bars are used in place of conventional coil springs. The front end of the torsion bar is attached to the lower control arm. The rear of torsion bar is mounted into an adjustable arm at the torsion bar crossmember. The carrying height of the car is controlled by this adjustment.

Wheel Hub
Removal and Installation

1. Remove drive axle cotter pin, nut and washer. Remove the brake disc.
2. Position access slot in hub as-

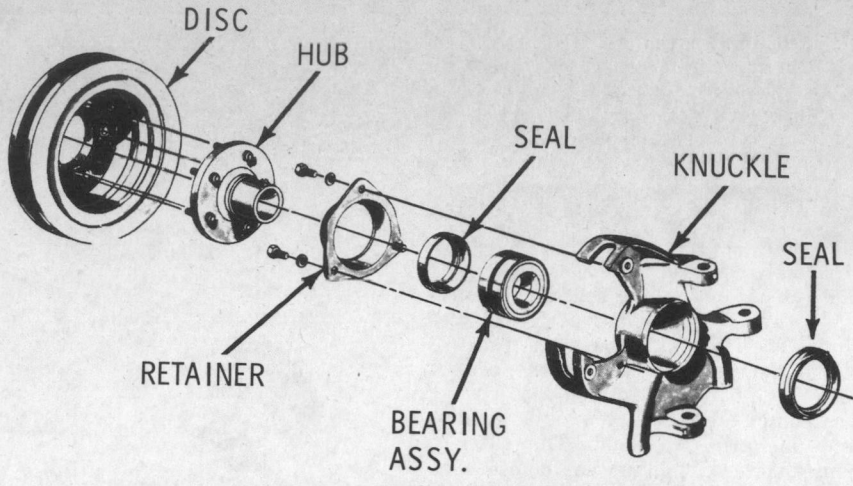

Exploded view of the hub assembly
(© Oldsmobile Div., G.M. Corp)

sembly so each of the attaching bolts can be removed.
3. Install a front hub puller and slide hammer.
4. Remove hub assembly.
5. To install, reverse removal procedure. Tighten the axle nut to 140 ft lbs.

NOTE: O.D. of bearing must be lubricated with E.P. chassis lubricant. Use care when installing hub assembly over drive axle splines.

Brake Disc Removal and Installation

1. Siphon off about two-thirds of the fluid in the front reservoir of the master cylinder. Do not empty the reservoir or it will be necessary to bleed the system.
2. Hoist the car and remove the wheel.
3. Position piston compressor tool on the caliper and tighten the screw until the piston bottoms and the shoes are backed off the disc.

4. Remove the two caliper to knuckle attaching bolts and carefully lift the caliper from the disc. Support it so that the hose is not kinked or stretched.
5. Mark the hub and disc so that they will be correctly positioned when installed, then pull evenly on the disc to remove.
6. To install, reverse the above procedure. Make sure that the disc is positioned according to the marks made during removal. Tighten the caliper attaching bolts to 35 ft. lbs. Fill the front reservoir of the master cylinder with new fluid and check the action of the brakes.

Torsion Bar Removal and Installation
1970

1. Hoist car and support at lift points.
2. Place torsion bar remover and installer so that center screw is seated in dimple of torsion adjusting arm.
3. Remove torsion bar adjusting bolt, counting number of turns necessary.
4. Turn center screw of tool until torsion bar is completely relaxed.
5. Disconnect stabilizer link.
6. Disconnect shock absorber from lower control arm.
7. Remove bolts from lower control arm to frame.
8. Pry lower control arm from frame and move forward until torsion bar and adjusting arm can be removed.
9. Lubricate both ends of torsion bar for approximately 3 in. with extreme pressure chassis lubricant.
10. Position adjusting arm into crossmember, insert torson bar into adjusting arm and lower control arm, then position lower control arm into frame brackets and install nuts and bolts loosely.

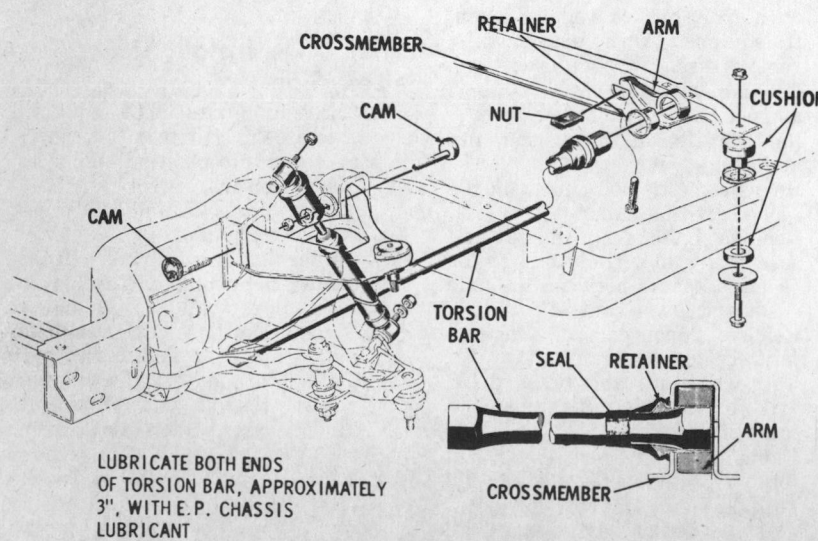

Front suspension
(© Oldsmobile Div., G.M. Corp)

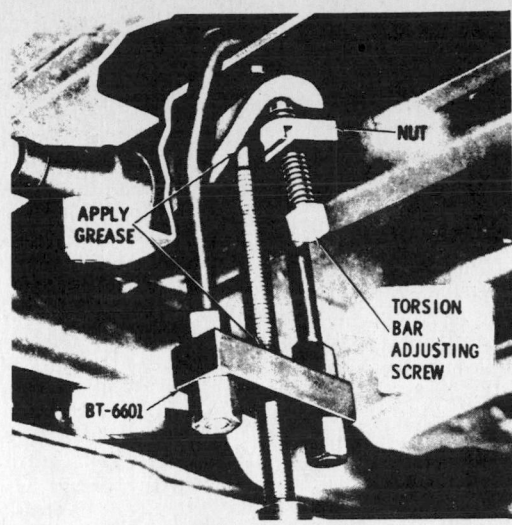

Torsion bar removal
(© Oldsmobile Div., G.M. Corp)

4. Turn center screw of tool until torsion bar is completely relaxed.
5. Disconnect shock absorber and stabilizer link from lower control arm.
6. Remove drive axle nut. Remove the bolt and nut from the front of the frame brace. Loosen the rear bolt and move the brace out.
7. Remove cotter pin and nut from lower ball joint stud.
8. Remove ball joint stud from knuckle, using puller.
9. Push drive axle in and pull knuckle outward to gain clearance, then remove lower control arm from knuckle and torsion bar.
10. Install by reversing removal procedure. Check and adjust ride height if necessary.

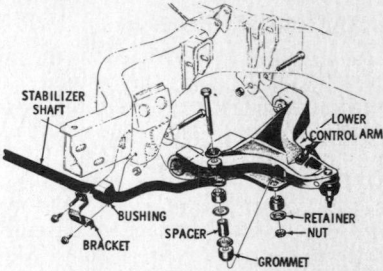

Lower control arm and related components
(© Oldsmobile Div., G.M. Corp)

11. Connect shock to lower control arm, tightening nut to 80 ft. lbs.
12. Connect stabilizer bar to lower control arm. Torque nut to 15 ft. lbs. and cut off bolt ¼ in. below nut.
13. Place torsion bar remover and installer over crossmember and tighten center screw.
14. Raise hoist under lower control arms.
15. Torque lower control arm bushing nuts to 90 ft. lbs.
16. Check ride height and adjust if necessary.

1971 and Later

1. Raise the car and support the frame.
2. Disconnect the parking brake cable at the equalizer and pull it through the support.
3. Install a torsion bar remover tool, remove the torsion bar adjusting bolt and nut, noting the number of turns to remove, and relax the torsion bar. Do the same on the other torsion bar.
4. Remove the bolts and retainer from the torsion bar crossmember. Move the crossmember back until the bars are free and the adjusting arms can be removed. You may have to slide the torsion bars forward.
5. Disconnect the exhaust system hangers.
6. Reverse the procedure for installation.

Upper Control Arm Removal

NOTE: The upper control arm is serviced as an assembly, less bushings.

1. Hoist car under lower control arm and remove wheel.
2. Remove upper shock attaching bolt.
3. Remove cotter pin and nut on upper ball joint.

4. Disconnect brake hose clamp from ball joint stud.
5. Separate upper ball joint stud from steering knuckle.
6. Remove upper control arm cam assemblies and remove control arm from car by guiding shock absorber through access hole in arm.

Upper Control Arm Installation

1. Guide upper control arm over shock absorber and install bushing ends into frame horns.
2. Install cam assemblies.
3. Install ball joint stud into knuckle.
4. Install brake hose clip onto ball joint stud.
5. Install ball joint nut. Torque to 50 ft. lbs. (60 ft lbs—1975 and later) and insert cotter pin and crimp.
NOTE: Cotter pin must be crimped toward upper control arm to prevent interference with outer constant velocity joint seal.
6. Install upper shock, attaching bolt and nut. Torque to 75 ft. lbs, 90 ft. lbs for 1972 and later models.
7. Install wheel.
8. Lower hoist.
9. Check camber, caster and toe-in, and adjust if necessary.

Lower Control Arm Removal and Installation

1. Hoist car and support at lift points. Remove wheel assembly.
2. Place torsion bar remover and installer over crossmember so that center screw is seated in dimple of torsion adjusting arm.
3. Remove torsion bar adjusting bolt and nut, counting the number of turns necessary.
NOTE: This number of turns will be used when installing, to obtain initial ride height.

Ball Joint Vertical Check

1. Raise the car and position floor stands under the left and right lower control arm, as near as possible to each lower ball joint. Car must be stable and should not rock on floor stands.
2. Position dial indicator to register vertical movement at wheel hub.
3. Place a pry bar between the lower control arm and the outer race of the constant velocity joint and pry down on the bar. Care must be used so that the drive axle seal is not damaged. The vertical reading must not exceed .125 in.

Ball Joint Horizontal Check Through 1971

1. Place car on floor stands, as outlined in Step 1 in the Vertical Check.
2. Position dial indicator at the rim of the wheel, to indicate side play.
3. Grasp wheel with the hands, top and bottom, and push in on the bottom of the tire while pulling out at the top. Read gauge, then reverse the push-pull procedure. Horizontal deflection on the gauge should not exceed .125 in. at the wheel rim. This procedure checks both the upper and lower ball joints.

Lower Ball Joint Removal

1. Remove the steering knuckle.
2. Drill the top rivet head off.
3. Drill the side rivets just deep enough to remove the rivet head.
4. Using a hammer and punch. drive the rivets out of the control arm.

Lower Ball Joint Installation

1. Install service ball joint into control arm and torque bolts and nut. Side bolts are torqued to 25 ft lbs while the upper nut is tightened to 45 ft lbs. Stake the upper nut.
2. Install knuckle.
3. Check the nut to drive axle outer joint clearance. If necessary, grind a maximum of 1/16 in. from the nut.

Front End Alignment

Ride height is controlled by the adjustment setting of the torsion bar adjusting bolt. Clockwise rotation of the bolt increases the front height. It is very important that this height be made correct before front end alignment. Car must be on a level surface, gas tank full or a compensating weight added. Front seat must be all the way to the rear and tires inflated properly. All doors must be closed with no passengers or additional weight.

NOTE: If any excess weight is normally carried in the car, i.e., tool boxes, salesmans samples, etc., it should remain in the car in its normal location.

1. Check rocker panel to ground dimension. Front and rear reading to ground should be as follows. Front to rear and side to side should be within ¾ in.

	Front	Rear
1970	8 in.	8 in.
1971-74	8¾ in.	9 in.
1975-77	9 in.	9¼ in.

2. Align car on wheel alignment equipment as follows:
3. Loosen nuts on inboard side of upper control arm cam bolts.
4. Check camber and adjust if necessary by turning the front cam bolt in or out to correct ½ of the incorrect reading found when checked. Turn the rear cam bolt in the same direction the front bolt was turned to correct the remaining ½ of the incorrect setting.
5. Take the caster reading.
   A. Turn front bolt so camber changes ¼ of the number of degrees caster change needed for correct reading.
   B. Turn the rear cam bolt so camber returns to the original proper setting.
   C. Recheck caster reading.

NOTE: If you should run out of cam in the attempt to gain correct reading:
   A. Turn front cam bolt so high part of cam is pointing up.
   B. Turn rear cam bolt so high part of cam bolt is pointing down.
This is the location to start from. A correct setting should be obtainable with the above procedure.
   D. Torque upper control arm cam nuts to 95 ft. lbs. through 1974, 110 ft. lbs. for 1975 and later; hold head of bolt securely with a back-up wrench. Any movement of cam will affect final setting and you will have to recheck caster and camber adjustment.
6. Toe-in adjustment is as follows:
   A. Center steering wheel and raise car.
   B. Loosen tie rod clamp nuts, and turn the tie-rod adjusting sleeves to obtain the proper toe-in setting.
   C. Tighten tie rod end nuts. Torque nuts 24 ft. lbs. Position tie rod clamps so openings of clamps are facing up.

REAR SUSPENSION

Some 1971-75 models are equipped with True-Track Braking (JL9 option). This is an electrically controlled rear brake equalizing system. The wheel speed sensors are mounted under the spindles, each with a driveshaft which runs through the spindle to attach to the grease cap. Care must be taken when removing the rear spindle or the rear assembly not to break the sensor wiring or damage the sensor unit.

All 1971 and later models have a straight tubular axle housing instead of the I-beam drop axle used on 1970 models.

Spindle Removal and Installation

1. Support the rear of the car with stands.
2. Remove the wheel, drum and hub assembly.
3. Disconnect the brake line fitting at the wheel cylinder.
4. If equipped with JL9, disconnect the wiring at the sensor.
5. Remove the four spindle attaching bolts and tie the backing plate out of the way.
6. On 1971 and later models, pull the spindle with a slide hammer.
7. On 1970 models, place a jack under the axle and remove the four bolts from the center spring clamp assembly. Remove the rubber insulator and lower the axle enough with the jack to provide working room for the spindle removal. Either drive the spindle out from behind or use a pulling tool.
8. To install, reverse the removal procedure. Install spindle with the keyway up, tightening the four bolts progressively one turn at a time. Adjust the rear wheel bearing.

Wheel Bearing Adjustment

For the rear wheel tapered roller bearings to be correctly adjusted, the following precautions should be taken:

1. The cones must be a slip fit on the spindle.
2. Inside of cones should be lubricated to make sure the cone creeps on the spindle.
3. Spindle nut must be a free-running fit on the threads.
4. Adjustment of rear wheel bearings should be made by continuously revolving the wheel while torquing the nut as follows:
   A. Torque adjusting nut to 25-30 ft. lbs. to seat all components thoroughly.
   B. Back off nut one-half turn, then retighten finger tight.
   C. If unable to insert cotter pin at this position, back off to nearest castellation.

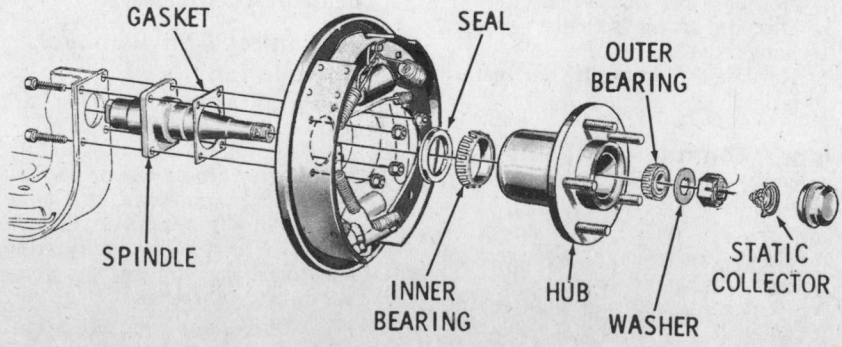

Rear hub assembly
(© Oldsmobile Div., G.M. Corp)

D. End-play should be 0.001-0.005 in.

Leaf Spring Removal and Installation, 1970

1. Raise car and support on frame pad. With jack under axle, remove wheel.
2. Remove nut only from front of rear spring.
3. Remove two attaching nuts on rear shackle (outer). Remove rear shackle (outer).
4. Remove four attaching bolts on center clamp assembly.
5. Lift center clamp up, shock will hold it in position.
6. Lower jack until axle is free from spring.
7. Remove shackle assembly from spring and body.
8. Remove bolt from front of rear spring and remove spring.
9. If spring bushing is worn, remove and replace it.
10. To install, reverse removal procedure.
    A. Front bushing is a press fit. Replacement will require an arbor press.
    B. Torque resonator bracket attaching bolts to 14 ft. lbs.
    C. Torque four spring center clamp assembly bolts to 30 ft. lbs.
    D. Install wheel, torque to 115 ft. lbs.
    E. Remove all supports and, with car on the ground, torque rear shackle bolts to 40 ft. lbs. and front spring bolt to 75-80 ft. lbs.

Coil Spring Removal and Installation, 1971 and Later

1. With the car supported with floor stands, position a hoist under the tube assembly and raise it enough to relieve the tension on the shock absorber.
2. Disconnect the shock absorbers at the tube assembly.
3. Carefully lower the tube assembly until the springs are fully extended.

Caution Do not stretch the brake hydraulic hose.

NOTE: For 1973 and later models, the factory recommends that a spring compressor be used to compress the spring for removal and installation.

4. Remove the springs and insulators.
5. When installing, place the insulator on top of the spring and install the spring with the identification tag next to the tube assembly on 1971 models. The top end of the spring should point to the right side of the car on 1972 and later models.
6. Hoist the tube assembly and connect the shock absorber.

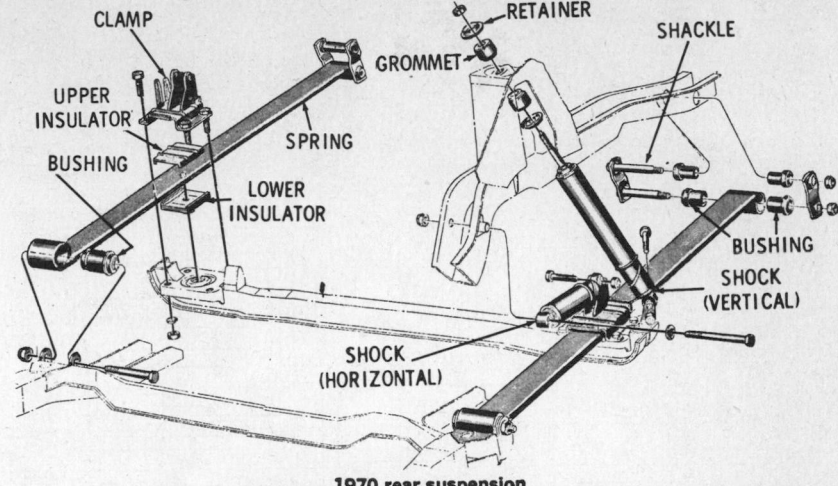

1970 rear suspension
(© Oldsmobile Div., G.M. Corp)

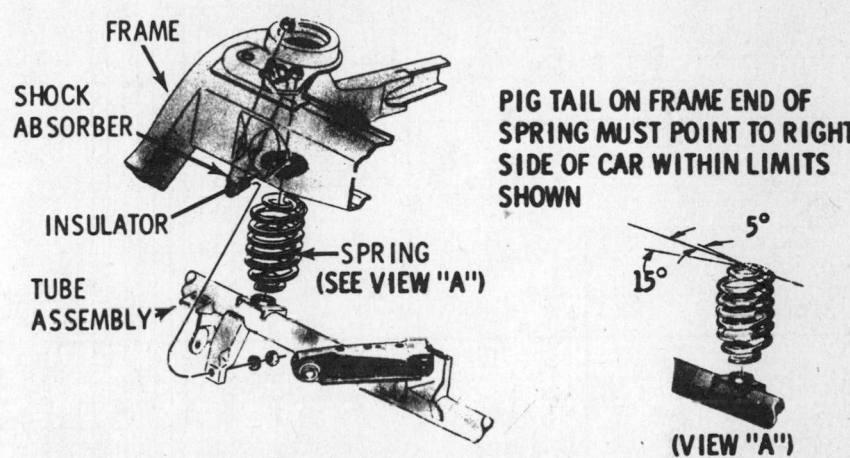

PIG TAIL ON FRAME END OF SPRING MUST POINT TO RIGHT SIDE OF CAR WITHIN LIMITS SHOWN

5°
15°

(VIEW "A")

Rear suspension—1971 and Later
(© Oldsmobile Div., G.M. Corp)

BRAKES

Parking Brake Adjustment

Through 1971

1. Release the parking brake.
2. Tighten the equalizer adjusting nut until heavy resistance is felt when rotating the rear wheels forward, then back off the adjusting nut seven full turns.

1972 and Later

1. Depress the parking brake pedal exactly three clicks.
2. Tighten the adjusting nut at the cable equalizer until the rear wheels can just be turned rearward using 2 hands, but are locked in forward rotation.
3. With the parking brake off, the rear wheels should rotate freely in either direction with no drag.

Master Cylinder Removal and Installation

1. Disconnect and plug hydraulic lines, and drain the cylinder.
2. Remove the attaching nuts and remove the master cylinder from the power unit.

Power Booster Removal and Installation

1. From inside the car, detach the brake pushrod from the brake pedal.
2. Detach the vacuum hose at the vacuum cylinder and disconnect the hydraulic line from the front of the slave cylinder.
3. Remove the four nuts that hold the vacuum unit up to the toe-board and remove the unit.
4. Install in reverse order of removal. Bleed system.

STEERING

CAUTION: Some 1974 and later models may have A.C.R.S. (air bags). See the Buick section for special precautions and procedures.

All steering system procedures are the same as those given in the Oldsmobile section for 88 and 98 models.

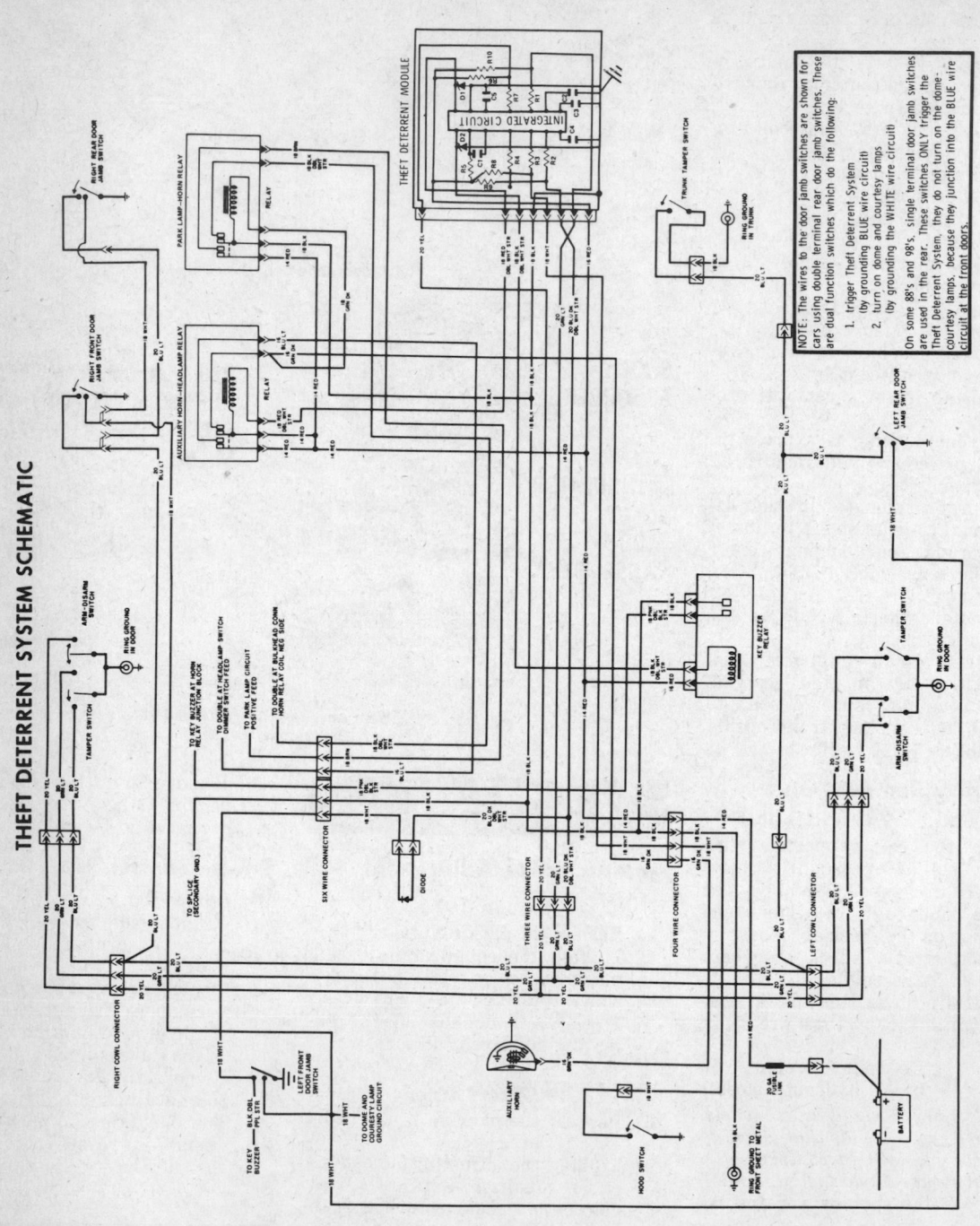

THEFT DETERRENT SYSTEM SCHEMATIC

(© Oldsmobile Div., G.M. Corp.)

HEADLAMP ON WARNING SYSTEM DIAGNOSIS

WARNING BUZZER INOPERATIVE (WARNING LIGHT O.K.)

Check operation of buzzer with key.

KEY BUZZER OPERATES

1. Remove ignition key.
2. Open left front door.
3. Turn headlamps ON.

KEY BUZZER DOES NOT OPERATE

Trouble is in key buzzer wiring or horn relay. REFER TO KEY BUZZER DIAGNOSIS

HEADLAMP ON WARNING RELAY CLICKS

1. Leave headlamps ON.
2. Ground one lead of a 12 volt test light.
3. Touch the other test light lead to the pink/dbl. black stripe wire in connector at warning relay (Under dash).

HEADLAMP ON WARNING RELAY DOES NOT CLICK

1. Repair loose connection in brown wire at warning relay.
2. If relay still does not operate, repair loose ground on relay case.
3. If ground OK, replace relay.

LAMP ON

Check brown and black/dbl. purple stripe wire connections at warning relay.

LAMP OFF

Repair open circuit in pink/dbl. black stripe wire, relay to turn signal connector.

Brown and black/dbl. purple stripe wire connections are good.

Brown and black/dbl. purple stripe wire connections are bad.

Replace warning relay.

Repair as necessary.

NOTE:
1. If warning bulb comes on with key in ignition switch and door open with headlamps OFF, trouble is diode in black/dbl. purple stripe wire (warning relay to door switch). REPLACE DIODE AND WIRING.
2. HEADLAMP ON WARNING SYSTEM operates all the time when there is a short circuit to ground in door switch wiring. LOCATE AND REPAIR.
3. HEADLAMP ON WARNING SYSTEM will be completely inoperative if there is an open circuit to door switch. LOCATE AND REPAIR.

WARNING LIGHT INOPERATIVE (WARNING BUZZER O.K.) BULB KNOWN GOOD

1. Remove ignition key.
2. Turn headlamps ON.
3. Disconnect brown wire at warning relay. (Under dash)
4. Ground one lead of a 12 volt test light.
5. Touch the other test light lead to the brown wire connector at the warning bulb.

LAMP ON

1. Repeat Steps 1,2 and 3 above.
2. Ground one end of a jumper wire.
3. Touch the other end to the black/dbl. purple stripe wire connector at the warning bulb.

LAMP OFF

1. Repair open circuit in brown wire, warning relay to warning bulb.
2. Reconnect brown wire at warning relay.

WARNING BULB COMES ON

1. Repair open circuit in black/dbl. purple stripe wire, warning bulb to warning relay.
2. Reconnect brown wire at warning relay.

WARNING BULB STAYS OFF

1. Clean warning bulb contacts.
2. Reconnect brown wire at warning relay.

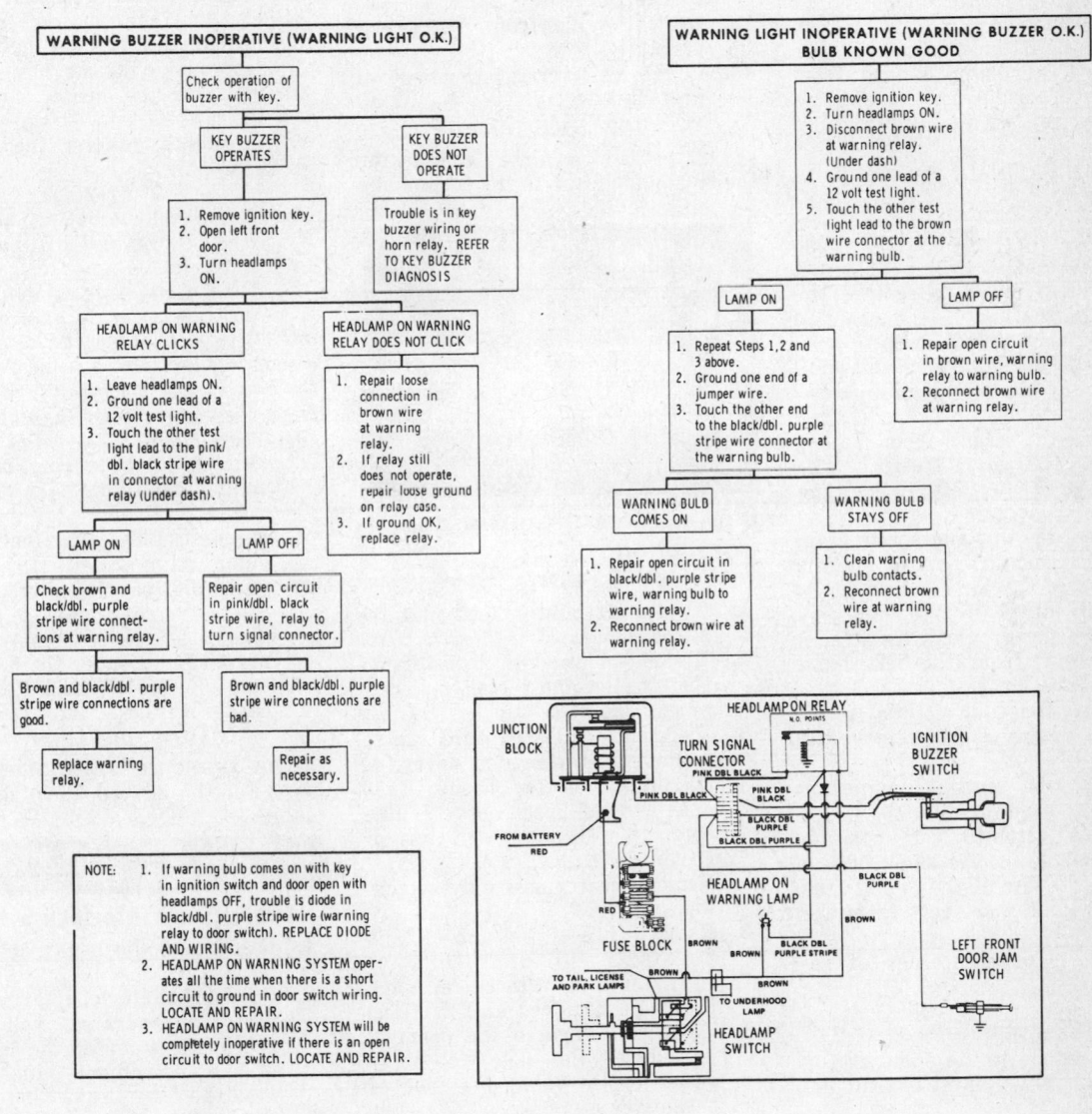

INSTRUMENT PANEL

Headlight Switch Replacement

1970

1. Remove lower left-hand trim panel.
2. Remove knob by first pulling the knob out to the headlight position, then depressing the spring-loaded button on switch body. Then, pull knob out of switch assembly.
3. Remove escutcheon nut.
4. Remove headlamp switch from rear of control panel.
5. Disconnect wiring and vacuum hoses.
6. Installation is the reverse of removal.

1971-73

The left hand control panel must be removed in order to remove the headlight switch.

1. Disconnect the battery.
2. Pry the floor lamp lens and lamp assembly out with a thin screwdriver.
3. Remove the screws from the left side of the lower steering trim and from the left hand trim panel.
4. Remove the nut and screw from the temperature cable on the bottom of the air conditioner or heater control.
5. Remove the ground wire attaching screw from the left hand panel lower brace.
6. Remove the four control panel attaching screws and remove the panel.
7. Remove the multiple connector from the headlight switch.
8. Pull the switch to "ON" position and push in on the small button on the switch, then pull the switch knob and shaft from the switch.
10. Install in reverse order of removal.

1974 and Later

This procedure is the same as for the 88 and 98, given in the Oldsmobile section.

RADIO

Removal and Installation

1970

1. Disconnect battery.
2. Remove both lower cluster panels.
3. Remove steering column attaching nuts and lower bracket.
4. Remove shift indicator needle.
5. Disconnect speedometer cable.

6. Remove attaching nuts from cluster lower brackets, leaving brackets attached to the instrument panel.
7. Remove two upper instrument panel screws and lay cluster assembly on steering column.
8. Remove radio knobs, washers or rear seat speaker control.
9. Remove radio attaching nuts and escutcheons.
10. Disconnect all wiring and antenna lead-in.
11. Remove lower radio support bracket attaching nut.
12. Remove radio from instrument panel.
13. Install by reversing the removal procedure.

1971 and Later

This procedure is the same as for the 88 and 98, given in the Oldsmobile section.

WINDSHIELD WIPERS

This procedure is the same as for the 88 and 98, given in the Oldsmobile section.

HEATER

Blower Motor Removal and Installation

1970

1. Disconnect blower feed and resistor wiring.
2. Disconnect vacuum hoses from the air inlet and forced vent diaphragms.
3. Disconnect temperature cable from temperature door lever.
4. Disconnect heater hoses. Keep open ends of hoses above engine coolant level to prevent loss of coolant.
5. Remove heater assembly attaching screws.
6. Remove heater assembly from the cowl.
7. If heater core is to be removed, it can be removed at this time.
8. To install, reverse the removal procedure. Be sure to apply sealer to the mounting face of the heater assembly.

1971-74

1. Remove the right front fender filler panel.
2. Disconnect the blower electrical wiring.
3. Remove the five nuts and two screws which secure the inlet assembly to the dash.
4. Remove the inlet assembly and the blower motor. The fan may be removed from the shaft by releasing the nut and lockwasher.
5. To install, reverse the removal procedure.

1975 and Later

This procedure is the same as that given for the 88 and 98 in the Oldsmobile section.

Heater Core Removal and Installation

1970

1. Remove the glove box.
2. Disconnect the wiring, vacuum lines, and the defroster hoses from the heater case.
3. Drain the radiator below the level of the heater. Remove the heater hoses and gasket.
4. Remove the blower assembly screws and also the heater case from inside the car.
5. Separate the heater core from the case.
6. To install, reverse the removal procedure.

1971-73

1. Disconnect the battery and drain the radiator and disconnect the heater hoses.
2. Remove the four attaching nuts.

NOTE: In order to gain access to one of the nuts, it may be necessary to disconnect the right front fender at the bottom and block the fender away from the body so that the nut may be removed through the opening.

3. Disconnect the wiring, the three control cables, and the defroster duct.
4. Disconnect the right half of the right trim panel. If equipped with air conditioning, remove the instrument panel tie bar.
5. The case assembly may be removed from under the dash. The core may be separated from the case if it is defective.

1974 and Later

This procedure is the same as that given for the 88 and 98 in the Oldsmobile section.

SEAT BELTS

Disabling the Interlock System

1. Disconnect the negative battery cable.
2. Locate the interlock harness connector with orange, yellow and green wires under the left side of the instrument panel on or near the fuse block.
3. Cut and tape the green wire on the body harness side of the connector.
4. If not equipped with the low coolant warning and heavy duty cooling system, disconnect and remove the buzzer from the fuse panel.
5. If equipped with the low coolant warning and heavy duty cooling system, cut the yellow wire behind the connector and tape the ends.
6. Reconnect the battery and check the operation of the system.

Pontiac · Grand Prix

Automatic Transmission
in-car service **C749**
Downshift cable adjustment C751
Low band adjustment two-speed (M-35) C751
Neutral safety/backup light switch
adjustment C751
Pan Removal and Installation, fluid
& filter change C751
Shift linkage adjustment C750
Throttle valve linkage adjustment C749

Brakes **C756, U299**
Master cylinder removal C756
Parking brake adjustment C756
Power brake booster Removal and
Installation C756

Charging System **C738, U2**
Alternator Removal and Installation ... C738
Voltage regulator Removal and
Installation C738

Clutch **C749**

Cooling System **C741, U367**
Radiator Removal and Installation C741
Thermostat Removal and Installation ... C741
Water pump Removal and Installation ... C741

Emission Controls **C741, U145**

Engine **C743, U194**
Engine removal and installation C745
CYLINDER HEAD REMOVAL AND
INSTALLATION C746
LUBRICATION C748
Oil pan Removal and Installation C748
Oil pump Removal and Installation C749
Rear main bearing oil seal
Removal and Installation C748
MANIFOLDS C745
Exhaust manifold Removal and
Installation C745
Intake manifold Removal and
Installation C745
PISTONS AND CONNECTING RODS C748
TIMING COVER, CHAIN, AND CAMSHAFT ..C746
Camshaft Removal and Installation C747
Timing case cover Removal and
Installation and seal replacement .. C746

Timing chain and sprocket Removal and
Installation C747
VALVE SYSTEM C745
Rocker arm Removal and Installation ...C745
Valve guides C746

Front Suspension **C754, U292**
Ball joint inspection C754
Ball joint replacement C754
Spring Removal and Installation C755
Lower ball joint Removal and
Installation C755
Shock absorber Removal and
Installation C754
Upper ball joint Removal and
Installation C754
Wheel bearing adjustment C755

Fuel System **C739, U50**
Fuel filter Removal and Installation C739
Fuel pump Removal and Installation C739
Idle speed and mixture adjustment C739

Heater **C758**
CARS WITH factory installed A/C C758
Blower motor Removal and
Installation C758
Heater core Removal and Installation ...C760
CARS WITHOUT factory installed A/C C758
Blower Motor Removal and
Installation C758
Heater Core Removal and
Installation C758

Ignition System **C738, U34**
Contact point and condenser
replacement and adjustment C739
Distributor Removal and Installation ... C738
Firing order C728
Ignition timing C739

Instrument Panel **C758, U350**
Headlight switch replacement C758

Jacking, Hoisting **C753**

Manual Transmission **C749, U231**

Radio **C758**
Removal and installation C758

Rear Axle **C753, U285**

Rear Suspension **C755**
Coil spring replacement C756
Leaf spring replacement C756
Shock absorber Removal and
Installation C755

Seat Belts **C760**
Disabling the interlock system C760

Specifications **C728, U359**
Capacities C733
Crankshaft and connecting rod C736
Engine identification C729
General engine C730
Piston ring C736
Piston clearance C737
Serial number location C729
Torque C735
Tune-up C731
Valve C734
Wheel alignment C737
Year identification C728

Starting System **C738**
Starter Removal and Installation C738

Steering **C756, U328**
Ignition switch replacement C757
Lock cylinder replacement C757
Power steering pump Removal and
Installation C757
Steering wheel Removal and
Installation C757
Tie-rod end Removal and Installation ... C756
Turn signal switch Removal and
Installation C757

U-Joints **C752**
Constant-velocity rear U-joint
Removal and Installation C753
Driveshaft Removal and Installation C752
U-joint Removal and Installation all front
and single rear U-Joints C752

Windshield Wipers **C758**
Motor Removal and Installation C758

YEAR IDENTIFICATION

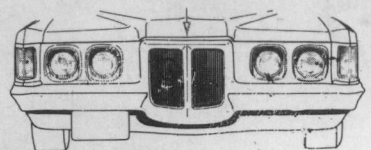

1970 Grand Prix

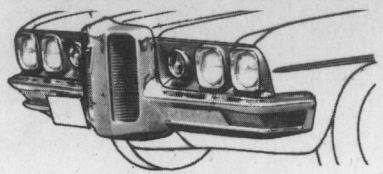

1970 Catalina

1971 Pontiac

1971 Grand Prix

1972 Pontiac

1972 Grand Prix

1973 Catalina

1973 Grand Prix

1974 Catalina

1974 Grand Prix

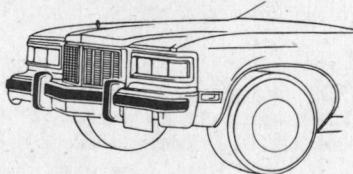

1974 Grand Ville

1975 Grand Prix

1975 Grandville Brougham, Grand Safari

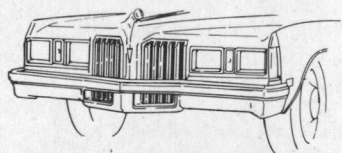

1976 Bonneville Brougham

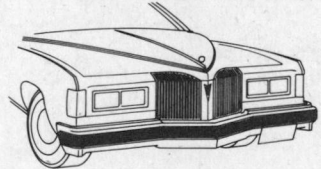

1976 Grand Prix

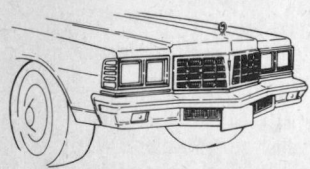

1977 Bonneville Brougham

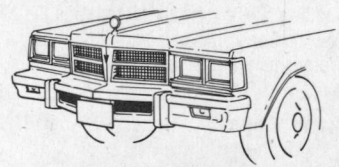

1977 Catalina

1977 Grand Prix

FIRING ORDER

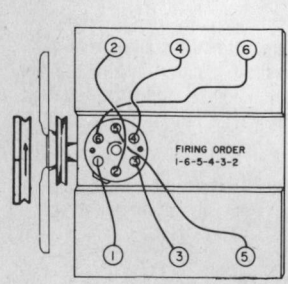

V6

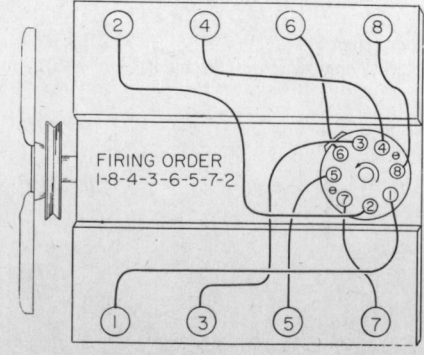

301, 350, 400, 455 Pontiac-design V8

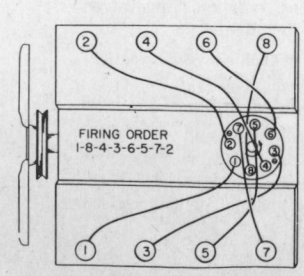

350, 403 Oldsmobile-design V8

CAR SERIAL NUMBER

Car serial number is located on the upper left-hand side of the instrument panel, visible through the windshield. The number is interpreted as follows:

Through 1971

First digit: Car division
Second and third digits: Series number

Fourth and fifth digits: Body style code
Sixth digit: Year manufactured
Seventh digit: Plant
Eighth digit: Engine used (1 = V8)
Ninth to thirteenth digits—sequential serial number

1972 and later

First digit: 2, for Pontiac division

Second digit: Series letter
Third and fourth digits: Body style
Fifth digit: Engine identification letter
Sixth digit: Last digit of model year
Seventh digit: Assembly plant letter
Eighth through thirteenth digits: Sequential serial number

ENGINE IDENTIFICATION

Engine identification is made by a letter/number code located on the machined face of the cylinder block, below and in front of the right-hand cylinder head on all Pontiac-made V8 engines. Oldsmobile-made 350 and 403 V8s, starting 1977, are identified by a tape on the oil filler tube.

Disp.	Bbl.	Hp.*	1970	1971	1972	1973	1974	1975	1976	1977
6 Cylinder Models										
231	2	—								
8 Cylinder Models										
301	2	—								
350	2	255	W7 X7							
350	2	250		WR XR YU						
350	2	150, 155, 175#				Y7 ZR			XH XN YA YK YP YL	
350	4	175							ZX	
400	2	265	YB	WS XX						
400	2	290	WE YD							
									YC YJ	
400	2	175, 200#			XX ZX		AH YH YJ	YH		
400	2	170, 185#				Y1 Y4 YZ ZK				
400	4	340								
400	4	350	WX XH							
400	4	330	XZ							
400	4	300		WK WT YS	YS					
400	4	200, 250#							Y6	
400	4	200, 230#				Y3 YN YT ZN			Y7 ZA	

ENGINE IDENTIFICATION—cont'd

Disp.	Bbl.	Hp.*	1970	1971	1972	1973	1974	1975	1976	1977
400	4	185, 200, 225 #					AT YT YZ ZT	YT ZT YM		
403	4	—								
455	2	280		WG YG						
455	2	185, 200 #			YH ZH					
455	4	360	YH							
455	4	370	WG XF							
455	4	325		WJ YC						
455	4	220, 250 #			YA YC					
455	4	200, 215, 250 #				YA YC YD YK ZA ZC	AU YR YU YW YX YY ZU ZW ZX	YW YU ZU ZW	Y3 Y4 Y8 ZB Z3 Z4	
455SD	4	310				Y8				

* All 1972 and later horsepower ratings are SAE net.
SD Super Duty
With dual exhaust

GENERAL ENGINE SPECIFICATIONS

Year	Engine No. Cyl. Displacement (cu in.)	Carburetor Type	Horsepower @ rpm ■	Torque @ rpm (ft lbs) ■	Bore X Stroke (in.)	Compression Ratio	Oil Pressure @ 2000 rpm
'70	8-350	2 bbl	255 @ 4600	355 @ 2800	3.8762 x 3.750	8.8:1	35
	8-400	2 bbl	265 @ 4600	397 @ 2400	4.1212 x 3.750	8.8:1	35
	8-400	2 bbl	290 @ 4600	428 @ 2500	4.1212 x 3.750	10.0:1	35
	8-400	4 bbl	330 @ 4800	445 @ 2900	4.1212 x 3.750	10.0:1	35
	8-455	4 bbl	360 @ 4300	500 @ 2700	4.1522 x 4.210	10.0:1	35
	8-455 HO	4 bbl	370 @ 4600	500 @ 3100	4.1522 x 4.210	10.25:1	35
'71	8-350	2 bbl	250 @ 4400	350 @ 2400	3.8762 x 3.750	8.0:1	35
	8-400	2 bbl	265 @ 4400	400 @ 2400	4.1212 x 3.750	8.2:1	35
	8-400	4 bbl	300 @ 4800	400 @ 3600	4.1212 x 3.750	8.2:1	35
	8-455	2 bbl	280 @ 4400	455 @ 2000	4.1522 x 4.210	8.2:1	35
	8-455	4 bbl	325 @ 4400	455 @ 3200	4.1522 x 4.210	8.2:1	35
'72	8-400	2 bbl	175 @ 4000	310 @ 2400	4.1212 x 3.750	8.2:1	35
	8-400 DE	2 bbl	200 @ 4000	325 @ 2400	4.1212 x 3.750	8.2:1	35
	8-400	4 bbl	200 @ 4000	295 @ 2800	4.1212 x 3.750	8.2:1	35
	8-400 DE	4 bbl	250 @ 4400	325 @ 3200	4.1212 x 3.750	8.2:1	35
	8-455	2 bbl	185 @ 4000	350 @ 2000	4.1522 x 4.210	8.2:1	35
	8-455 DE	2 bbl	200 @ 4000	370 @ 2000	4.1522 x 4.210	8.2:1	35
	8-455	4 bbl	220 @ 3600	350 @ 2400	4.1522 x 4.210	8.2:1	35
	8-455 DE	4 bbl	250 @ 3600	370 @ 2400	4.1522 x 4.210	8.2:1	35

GENERAL ENGINE SPECIFICATIONS

Year	Engine No. Cyl. Displacement (Cu. In.)	Carburetor Type	Horsepower @ rpm ■	Torque @ rpm (ft lbs) ■	Bore X Stroke (in.)	Compression Ratio	Oil Pressure @ 2000 rpm
'73	8-350	2 bbl	150 @ 4000	270 @ 2000	3.8762 x 3.750	7.6:1	55-60①
	8-350 DE	2 bbl	175 @ 4400	280 @ 2400	3.8762 x 3.750	7.6:1	55-60①
	8-400	2 bbl	170 @ 3600	320 @ 2000	4.1212 x 3.750	8.0:1	55-60①
	8-400 DE	2 bbl	185 @ 4000	320 @ 2400	4.1212 x 3.750	8.0:1	55-60①
	8-400	4 bbl	200 @ 4000	310 @ 2400	4.1212 x 3.750	8.0:1	55-60①
	8-400 DE	4 bbl	230 @ 4400	325 @ 3200	4.1212 x 3.750	8.0:1	55-60①
	8-455	4 bbl	215 @ 3600	350 @ 2400	4.1522 x 4.210	8.0:1	55-60①
	8-455 DE	4 bbl	250 @ 2800	370 @ 2800	4.1522 x 4.210	8.0:1	55-60①
	8-455 S.D. DE	4 bbl	310 @ 4000	390 @ 3600	4.1522 x 4.210	8.4:1	75-80①
'74	8-400	2 bbl	175 @ 3600	315 @ 2000	4.1212 x 3.750	8.0:1	55-60①
	8-400	4 bbl	200 @ 4000	320 @ 2400	4.1212 x 3.750	8.0:1	55-60①
	8-400 DE	4 bbl	225 @ 4400	330 @ 2800	4.1212 x 3.750	8.0:1	55-60①
	8-455	4 bbl	215 @ 3600	355 @ 2400	4.1522 x 4.210	8.0:1	55-60①
	8-455 DE	4 bbl	250 @ 4000	380 @ 2800	4.1522 x 4.210	8.0:1	55-60①
'75	8-400	2 bbl	175 @ 3600	315 @ 2000	4.1212 x 3.750	7.6:1	55-60①
	8-400	4 bbl	200 @ 4000	320 @ 2400	4.1212 x 3.750	7.6:1	55-60①
	8-455	4 bbl	215 @ 3600	355 @ 2400	4.1522 x 4.210	7.6:1	55-60①
'76	8-350	2 bbl	155 @ 4000	280 @ 2000	3.8750 x 3.530	7.6:1	55-60①
	8-350	4 bbl	175 @ 4000	280 @ 2000	3.8750 x 3.530	7.6:1	55-60①
	8-400	2 bbl	170 @ 4000	305 @ 2000	4.1212 x 3.750	7.6:1	55-60①
	8-400	4 bbl	185 @ 3600	310 @ 1600	4.1212 x 3.750	7.6:1	55-60①
	8-455	4 bbl	200 @ 3500	330 @ 2000	4.1522 x 4.210	7.6:1	55-60①
'77	6-231	2 bbl	105 @ 3200	185 @ 2000	3.8000 x 3.4000	8.0:1	37②
	8-301	2 bbl	135 @ 4000	250 @ 1600	4.0000 x 3.0000	8.2:1	35-40①
	8-350	4 bbl	170 @ 4000	280 @ 1800	3.8762 x 3.7500	7.6:1	55-60①
	8-350③	4 bbl	170 @ 3800	275 @ 2000	4.0570 x 3.3850	8.0:1	30-45④
	8-400	4 bbl	180 @ 3600	325 @ 1600	4.1212 x 3.7500	7.6:1	55-60①
	8-403③	4 bbl	200 @ 3600	330 @ 2400	4.3510 x 3.3850	8.0:1	—

■ Beginning 1972, horsepower and torque are SAE net figures. They are measured at the rear of the transmission with all accessories installed and operating. Since the figures vary when a given engine is installed in different models, some are representative rather than exact.

HO High output
DE Dual exhaust
S.D. Super Duty
① Above 2600 rpm
② At 2400 rpm
③ Oldsmobile design
④ At 1500 rpm
GP Grand Prix

TUNE-UP SPECIFICATIONS

When analyzing compression test results, look for uniformity among cylinders rather than specific pressures.

	ENGINE			SPARK PLUGS		DISTRIBUTOR		IGNITION TIMING (deg) ▲		VALVES Intake Opens	Fuel Pump Pressure (psi)	IDLE SPEED ● (rpm) ▲	
Year	No. Cyl Displacement (cu in.)	hp	Orig. Type ●	Gap (in.)	Point Dwell (deg)	Point Gap (in.)	Man Trans ●	Auto Trans	■ (deg) ●		Man Trans	Auto Trans
'70	8-350	255	R-46S	.035	28-32	.016	9B	9B	22	5-6½	800	650
	8-400	265	R-46S④	.035	28-32	.016	9B	9B	30/22	5-6½	800	650
	8-400	290	R-46S④	.035	28-32	.016	9B	9B	30/22	5-6½	800	650
	8-400	330	R-46S	.035	28-32	.016	9B	9B	30	5-6½	950	650
	8-455	360	R-45S	.035	28-32	.016	9B	9B	31/23	5-6½	950	650
	8-455	370	R-45S	.035	28-32	.016	9B	9B	23	5-6½	950	650

TUNE-UP SPECIFICATIONS

When analyzing compression test results, look for uniformity among cylinders rather than specific pressures.

Year	ENGINE No. Cyl Displacement (cu in.)	hp	SPARK PLUGS Orig. Type ●	Gap (in.)	DISTRIBUTOR Point Dwell (deg)	Point Gap (in.)	IGNITION TIMING (deg) ▲ Man Trans ●	Auto Trans	VALVES Intake Opens ■ (deg) ●	Fuel Pump Pressure (psi)	IDLE SPEED ● (rpm) ▲ Man Trans	Auto Trans
'71	8-350	250	R-47S	.035	28-32	.016	12B	12B	26B/30B	5-6½⑤	800	600
	8-400	265	R-47S	.035	28-32	.016	—	8B	26B	5-6½⑤	—	600
	8-400	300	R-46S	.035	28-32	.016	12B	12B	23B	5-6½⑤	1000/600	700
	8-455	280	R-46S	.035	28-32	.016	—	12B	30B	5-6½⑤	—	650
	8-455	325	R-46S	.035	28-32	.016	—	12B	23B	5-6½⑤	—	650
	8-455	335	R-46S	.035	28-32	.016	12B	12B	31B	5-6½⑤	1000/600	700
'72	8-400	175	R-46TS	.035	28-32	.016	—	10B	26	5-6½	—	625
	8-400	200	R-45TS	.035	28-32	.016	8B	10B	23	5-6½	1000/600	700/500
	8-400	250	R-45TS	.035	28-32	.016	10B	10B	23	5-6½	1000/600	700/500
	8-455	185	R-45TS	.035	28-32	.016	—	10B	30	5-6½	—	625
	8-455	200	R-45TS	.035	28-32	.016	—	10B	23	5-6½	—	625
	8-455	220	R-45TS	.035	28-32	.016	—	10B	23	5-6½	—	650/500
	8-455	250	R-45TS	.035	28-32	.016	—	10B	23	5-6½	—	650/500
'73	8-350	150	R-46TS	.040	28-32	.016	—	12B	26/30	5-6½	—	650
	8-350	175	R-46TS	.040	28-32	.016	—	12B	26/30	5-6½	—	650
	8-400	170	R-46TS	.040	28-32	.016	—	12B	26	5-6½	—	650
	8-400	185	R-46TS	.040	28-32	.016	—	12B	26	5-6½	—	650
	8-400	200	R-45TS	.040	28-32	.016	—	12B	26	5-6½	—	650
	8-400	230	R-45TS	.040	28-32	.016	—	12B	26	5-6½	—	650
	8-455	215	R-45TS	.040	28-32	.016	—	12B	23	5-6½	—	650
	8-455	250	R-45TS	.040	28-32	.016	—	12B	23	5-6½	—	650
	8-455 S.D.	310	R-45TS	.040	28-32	.016	—	12B	42	5-6½	—	750/500
'74	8-400 2 bbl	175	R-46TS	.040	29-31	.016	—	12B (10)	26	5-6½	—	650 (625)
	8-400 4 bbl	All	R-45TS	.040	29-31	.016	—	12B (10)	30	5-6½	—	650 (625)
	8-455 4 bbl	All	R-45TS	.040	29-31	.016	—	12B (10)	23	5-6½	—	650 (625)
'75	8-400 2 bbl	All	R-46TSX	.060	Electronic		—	16B	26	5-6½	—	650
	8-400 4 bbl	All	R-45TSX	.060	Electronic		—	16B (12)	30	5-6½	—	650
	8-455	All	R-45TSX	.060	Electronic		—	16B (10)	23	5-6½	—	650 (625)
'76	8-350	155	R-46TSX	.060	Electronic		—	16B	22	7-8½	—	550
	8-350	175	R-46TSX	.060	Electronic		—	16B	26	7-8½	—	600
	8-400	170	R-46TSX	.060	Electronic		—	16B	26	7-8½	—	550
	8-400	185	R-45TSX	.060	Electronic		—	16B	30	7-8½	—	575
	8-455	200	R-45TSX	.060	Electronic		—	16B	33	7-8½	—	550 (600)
'77	6-231	105	R-46TSX (R-45TSX)	.060	Electronic		—	12B	17	4¼-5¾	—	600
	8-301	135	R-46TSX	.060	Electronic		—	12B	27	7-8½	—	550,650②
	8-350	170	R-45TSX	.060	Electronic		—	16B	29	7-8½	—	575,650②
	8-350③	170	R-46SX (R-46SZ)	.080	Electronic		—	20B@1100	16	5½-6½	—	600,550②
	8-400	180	R-45TSX	.060	Electronic		—	16B	29	7-8½	—	575,600②
	8-403③	200	R-46SX (R-46SZ)	.080	Electronic		—	20B@1100	—	5½-6½	—	600,550②

▲ See text for procedure
● Figure in parentheses indicates California engine. Where two idle speeds appear separated by a slash, the second is with the solenoid disconnected.
■ All figures are in degrees Before Top Dead Center. Where two figures appear, the first represents timing with manual transmission, the second with automatic transmission.
① Not used
② Second figure is for air conditioned cars; to be set with A/C on
③ Oldsmobile design

④ AC-R-45S with automatic transmission
⑤ 6½-8 with A/C
B Before Top Dead Center
— Not applicable

S.D. Super Duty
NOTE: The underhood specifications sticker often reflects tune-up specification changes made in production. Sticker figures must be used if they disagree with those in this chart.

Pontiac — CAPACITIES

Year	ENGINE No. Cyl. Displacement (Cu. In.)	Engine Crankcase Add 1 Qt For New Filter	TRANSMISSION Pts To Refill After Draining Manual 3-Speed	4-Speed	Automatic ●	Drive Axle (pts)	Gasoline Tank (gals) ▲	COOLING SYSTEM (qts) With Heater	With A/C
'70	8-350	5	2.8	——	6	4.5	26	19.6	19.6
	8-400	5	2.8	——	7.5	4.5	26	18	18
	8-455	5	2.8	——	7.5	4.5	26	17.2	17.2
'71	8-350	5	2.8	——	6	4.5	23.5	20.2	21
	8-400	5	2.8	——	7.5	4.5	23.5	18.6	19.6
	8-455	5	2.8	——	7.5	4.5	23.5	17.9	19
'72	8-400	5	——	——	7.5	5.5	25	18.6	19.6
	8-455	5	——	——	7.5	5.5	25	17.9	19
'73	8-350	5	——	——	7.5	4.25①	25.8	21.9	23.3
	8-400	5	——	——	7.5	4.25①	25.8	21.9	24.3
	8-455	5	——	——	7.5	4.25①	25.8	21.2	22.2
'74	8-400	5	——	——	7.5	4.25①	25.8	21.9	24.3
	8-455	5	——	——	7.5	4.25①	25.8	21.2	22.2
'75	8-400	5	——	——	7.5	5.31②	25.8	21.6	22.4
	8-455	5	——	——	7.5	5.31②	25.8	19.8	22.3
'76	8-400	5	——	——	7.5	5.5	25.8	21.6	22.4
	8-455	5	——	——	7.5	5.5	25.8	22.1	22.1
'77	6-231	4	——	——	7.5	4.25	20	12.8	—
	8-301	5	——	——	6	4.25	20	20.9	—
	8-350③	4	——	——	6	3.5	20	15.1	—
	8-403③	4	——	——	7.5	4.25	24.5	16.3	—

● Specifications do not include torque converter
—— Not applicable

① 5 pts with 8.875 in. ring gear
② 4.25 pts with 8.50 in. ring gear
③ Oldsmobile design

▲ Station wagon fuel tank (gals)
'70   24
'71   22.5
'72   23
'73-'76   22
'77   22.5

Grand Prix — CAPACITIES

Year	ENGINE No. Cyl. Displacement (Cu. In.)	Engine Crankcase Add 1 Qt For New Filter	TRANSMISSION Pts To Refill After Draining Manual 3-Speed	4-Speed	Automatic ●	Drive Axle (pts)	Gasoline Tank (gals)	COOLING SYSTEM (qts) With Heater	With A/C
'70	8-400	5	2.8	——	7.5	3①	24.5	18.7	21.1
	8-455	5	2.8	——	7.5	3①	24.5	17.5	19.9
'71	8-400	5	2.8	2.5	7.5	3①	23.5	18.6	19.6
	8-455	5	2.8	——	7.5	3①	23.5	17.9	19
'72	8-400	5	——	——	7.5	3①	26	18.7	19.7
	8-455	5	——	——	7.5	3①	26	18.1	19.2

Grand Prix   CAPACITIES

Year	ENGINE No. Cyl. Displacement (Cu. In.)	Engine Crankcase Add 1 Qt For New Filter	TRANSMISSION Pts To Refill After Draining Manual 3-Speed	4-Speed	Automatic ●	Drive Axle (pts)	Gasoline Tank (gals)	COOLING SYSTEM (qts) With Heater	With A/C
'73	8-400	5	—	—	7.5	4.25	25	23.1	22.9
	8-455	5	—	—	7.5	4.25	25	21.3	22.5
'74	8-400	5	—	—	7.5	4.25	25	23.1	22.9
	8-455	5	—	—	7.5	4.25	25	21.3	22.5
'75	8-400	5	—	—	7.5	5.31	25	21.6	24.0
	8-455	5	—	—	7.5	5.31	25	20.2	22.2
'76	8-350	5	—	—	7.5	3②	25	21.6	22
	8-400	5	—	—	7.5	3②	25	22.2	22.2
	8-455	5	—	—	7.5	3②	25	22.2	22.2
'77	8-301	5	—	—	7.5	4.25	25	22	—
	8-350	5	—	—	7.5	4.25	25	21	—
	8-350③	4	—	—	7.5	4.25	25	16.2	—
	8-400	5	—	—	7.5	4.25	25	19.5	—
	8-403③	4	—	—	7.5	4.25	25	17.3	—

● Specifications do not include torque converter
① 5 pts with 8.875 in. ring gear
— Not applicable or specified

② 4.9 with optional axle
③ Oldsmobile design

VALVE SPECIFICATIONS

Year	Engine No. Cyl. Displacement (cu in.)	Seat Angle (deg) ■	Face Angle (deg) ●	Spring Test Pressure▲ (lbs @ in.)	Spring Installed Height (in.)	STEM TO GUIDE Clearance (in.) Intake	Exhaust	STEM Diameter (in.) Intake	Exhaust
'70	8-350	45	44	63 @ 1.58	1 37/64	.0016-.0033	.0021-.0038	.3416	.3411
	8-400	45	44	63 @ 1.58	1 37/64	.0016-.0033	.0021-.0038	.3416	.3416
	8-455 Man.	30	29	63 @ 1.58	1 37/64	.0016-.0033	.0021-.0038	.3416	.3411
	8-455 Auto	45	44	66 @ 1.56	1 9/16	.0016-.0033	.0021-.0038	.3416	.3411
	8-455 HO	30	45	66 @ 1.56	1 9/16	.0016-.0033	.0021-.0038	.3416	.3411
'71	8-350	45	44	61 @ 1.59	1 19/32	.0016-.0033	.0021-.0038	.3416	.3411
	8-400 2 bbl	45	44	61 @ 1.59	1 19/32	.0016-.0033	.0021-.0038	.3416	.3411
	8-400 4 bbl	30	29	65 @ 1.57	1 9/16	.0016-.0033	.0021-.0038	.3416	.3411
	8-455 2 bbl	45	44	61 @ 1.59	1 19/32	.0016-.0033	.0021-.0038	.3416	.3411
	8-455 4 bbl	30	29	65 @ 1.57	1 9/16	.0016-.0033	.0021-.0038	.3416	.3411
'72	8-400 2 bbl	45	44	61 @ 1.59	1 19/32	.0016-.0033	.0021-.0038	.3416	.3411
	8-400 4 bbl	30	29	65 @ 1.57	1 9/16	.0016-.0033	.0021-.0038	.3416	.3411
	8-455 2 bbl	45	44	61 @ 1.59	1 19/32	.0016-.0033	.0021-.0038	.3416	.3411
	8-455 4 bbl	30	29	65 @ 1.57	1 9/16	.0016-.0033	.0021-.0038	.3416	.3411
'73	8-350	45	44	61 @ 1.59	1 19/32	.0016-.0033	.0021-.0038	.3416	.3411
	8-400 2 bbl	45	44	61 @ 1.59	1 19/32	.0016-.0033	.0021-.0038	.3416	.3411
	8-400 4 bbl	30	29	65 @ 1.57	1 9/16	.0016-.0033	.0021-.0038	.3416	.3411
	8-455 2 bbl	45	44	61 @ 1.59	1 19/32	.0016-.0033	.0021-.0038	.3416	.3411
	8-455 4 bbl	30	29	65 @ 1.57	1 9/16	.0016-.0033	.0021-.0038	.3416	.3411
	8-455 S.D.	45	44	70 @ 1.82	1 9/16	.0016-.0033	.0021-.0038	.3416	.3416
'74	8-400	30	29	65 @ 1.57	1 9/16	.0016-.0033	.0021-.0038	.3416	.3411
	8-455 2 bbl	45	44	61 @ 1.59	1 19/32	.0016-.0033	.0021-.0038	.3416	.3411
	8-455 4 bbl	30	29	65 @ 1.57	1 9/16	.0016-.0033	.0021-.0038	.3416	.3411

VALVE SPECIFICATIONS

Year	Engine No. Cyl. Displacement (cu in.)	Seat Angle (deg) ■	Face Angle (deg) ●	Spring Test Pressure▲ (lbs @ in.)	Spring Installed Height (in.)	STEM TO GUIDE Clearance (in.) Intake	Exhaust	STEM Diameter (in.) Intake	Exhaust
'75	8-400 2 bbl	45	44	65 @ 1.57	1 9/16	.0016-.0033	.0021-.0038	.3416	.3411
	8-400 4 bbl	45	44	65 @ 1.57	1 19/32	.0016-.0033	.0021-.0038	.3416	.3411
	8-455	45	44	65 @ 1.57	1 9/16	.0016-.0033	.0021-.0038	.3416	.3411
'76	8-350	30	29	66 @ 1.56	1 19/32	.0016-.0033	.0021-.0038	.3416	.3411
	8-400 2 bbl	30	29	70 @ 1.54	1 19/32	.0016-.0033	.0021-.0038	.3416	.3411
	8-400 4 bbl	30	29	70 @ 1.54	1 9/16	.0016-.0033	.0021-.0038	.3416	.3411
	8-455	30	29	65 @ 1.57	1 9/16	.0016-.0033	.0021-.0038	.3416	.3411
'77	6-231	45	45	164 @ 1.34④	1 47/64	.0015-.0035	.0015-.0032	.3407	.3407
	8-301	46	45	166 @ 1.30	1 21/32	.0010-.0027	.0010-.0027	.3422	.3422
	8-350 ①	45②	46③	187 @ 1.27	1 31/32	.0010-.0027	.0015-.0032	.3429	.3424
	8-350	30	29	131 @ 1.19	1 19/32	.0016-.0033	.0021-.0038	.3416	.3411
	8-400	30	29	131 @ 1.19	1 19/32	.0016-.0033	.0021-.0038	.3416	.3411
	8-403 ①	—	—	—	—	—	—	—	—

■ Intake valve seat angles are shown. All exhaust valve seat angles are 45° unless otherwise indicated.
● Intake valve face angles are shown. All exhaust valve face angles are 44° unless otherwise indicated.
① Oldsmobile design

② Exhaust 55
③ Exhaust 60
④ Exhaust—182 @ 1.34
HO High output
S.D. Super Duty

▲INNER SPRING TEST PRESSURE

'70	8-350	35 @ 1.54
	8-400	35 @ 1.54
	8-455 Man.	35 @ 1.54
	8-455 Auto.	38 @ 1.52
	8-455 HO	38 @ 1.52
'71	8-350	33 @ 1.55
	8-400 2 bbl	33 @ 1.55
	8-400 4 bbl	37 @ 1.53
	8-455 2 bbl	33 @ 1.55
	8-455 4 bbl	37 @ 1.53
'72	8-400 2 bbl	33 @ 1.55
	8-400 4 bbl	37 @ 1.53

'73	8-350	33 @ 1.55
	8-400 2 bbl	33 @ 1.55
	8-400 4 bbl	37 @ 1.53
	8-455	37 @ 1.53
	8-455 S.D.	40 @ 1.75
'74	8-400 2 bbl	33 @ 1.55
	8-400 4 bbl	37 @ 1.53
	8-455	37 @ 1.53
'75-'76	8-350	33 @ 1.55
	8-400	41 @ 1.50
	8-455	36 @ 1.53
'77	8-350	39 @ 1.51
	8-400	40 @ 1.51

TORQUE SPECIFICATIONS

All readings in ft lbs

Year	Engine	Cylinder Head Bolts	Rod Bearing Bolts	Main Bearing Bolts	Crankshaft Pulley Bolt	Flywheel to Crankshaft Bolts	MANIFOLD Intake	Exhaust
'70-'76	All	95	43②	100①	160	95	40	30
'77	6-231	75	40	115	150	55	45	25
	8-301, 350, 400	95	43	100①	160	95	40	30
	8-350, 403③	85	42	80①	160 min	90	40	25

① Rear main—120   ② 63 ft lbs on 455 S.D. engine   ③ Oldsmobile design

CRANKSHAFT AND CONNECTING ROD SPECIFICATIONS

All measurements are given in inches

Year	Engine No. Cyl. Displacement (cu in.)	CRANKSHAFT Main Brg. Journal Dia	Main Brg. Oil Clearance	Shaft End-Play	Thrust on No.	CONNECTING ROD Journal Diameter	Oil Clearance	Side Clearance
'70	8-350	3.000	.0002-.0017	.0035-.0085	4	2.250	.0005-.0025	.012-.017
	8-400	3.000	.0002-.0017	.0035-.0085	4	2.250	.0005-.0025	.012-.017
	8-455	3.250	.0005-.0021	.0035-.0085	4	2.250	.0005-.0026	.012-.017
'71-'75	8-400	3.000	.0002-.0017	.0035-.0085①	4	2.250	.0005-.0025	.012-.017
	8-455	3.250	.0005-.0021	.0035-.0085①	4	2.250	.0010-.0031	.012-.017
'75	8-455 S.D.	3.250	.0010-.0026	.0030-.0090	4	2.250	.0015-.0031	.019-.027
'76	8-350, 400	3.000	.0002-.0017	.0030-.0090	4	2.250	.0005-.0025	.012-.017
	8-455	3.250	.0005-.0021	.0030-.0090	4	2.250	.0005-.0025	.012-.017
'77	6-231	2.500	.0004-.0015	.004-.008	2	2.000	.0002-.0023	.006-.022
	8-301	3.000	.0002-.0020	.004-.008	4	2.250	.0005-.0026	.006-.022
	8-350, 400	3.000	.0002-.0017	.0035-.0085	4	2.250	.0005-.0026	.002-.017
	8-350, 403②	2.500	.0005-.0021③	.0040-.0080	3	2.124	.0005-.0026	.006-.020

* Total for two rods
① 1972 and later models—0.003-0.009 in.
② Oldsmobile design
③ No. 5—.0015-.0031

RING GAP

All measurements are given in inches

Year	Engine No. Cyl.	Compression Top	Compression Bottom
'70-'76	8-350, 400, 455	.010-.030	.010-.030
'77	6-231	.015-.023	.015-.023
	8-301	—	—
	8-350	.019	.019
	8-350, 403①	.010-.020	.010-.020

Year	Engine No. Cyl.	Oil Control
'70-'76	8-350, 400, 455	.015-.055
'77	6-231	.015-.035
	8-350, 400	.035
	8-350, 403①	.015-.055

① Oldsmobile design

RING SIDE CLEARANCE

All measurements are given in inches

Year	Engine	Top Compression	Bottom Compression
'70-'77	8-301, 350, 400, 455	.0015-.0050	.0015-.0050
'77	6-231	.0030-.0050	.0030-.0050
	8-350, 403①	.0020-.0040	.0020-.0040

Year	Engine	Oil Control
'70-'77	8-301, 350, 400, 455	.0015-.0050
'77	6-231	.0035 max
	8-350, 403①	.0006-.0096

① Oldsmobile design

PISTON CLEARANCE

Year	Engine No. Cyl. Displacement (cu. in.)	Clearance (in.) Piston-to-Bore
'70-'72	8-350	.0025-.0033
	8-400	.0025-.0033
	8-455	.0025-.0033
	8-400 Ram Air	.0055-.0061
'73	8-350	.0029-.0037
	8-400	.0029-.0037
	8-455	.0025-.0033
	8-455 S.D.	.0060-.0068
'74-'77	6-231	.0008-.0014
	8-301, 350, 400	.0029-.0037
	8-350, 403①	.0008-.0018
	8-455	.0021-.0029

① Oldsmobile design, available starting 1977

WHEEL ALIGNMENT SPECIFICATIONS

Year	Model	CASTER Range (deg)	CASTER Pref Setting (deg)	CAMBER Range (deg)	CAMBER Pref Setting (deg)	Toe-in (in.)	Steering Axis Inclin.	WHEEL PIVOT RATIO (deg) Inner Wheel	WHEEL PIVOT RATIO (deg) Outer Wheel
'70	All	1N to 2N	1½N	0 to ½P	¼P	0 to ⅛	8½	20	18
'71	Grand Prix	1N to 2N	1½N	½N to ½P	0	¹⁄₁₆ to ³⁄₁₆	8½	20	18
	Catalina, Grand Ville & Bonneville	½P to 1½P	1P	¼P to 1¼P	¾P	⅛ to ¼	8½	20	18
'72	Grand Prix	1N to 2N	1½N	¼N to ¾P	¼P	0 to ⅛	9	20	18
	Catalina, Grand Ville & Bonneville	1N to 2N	1½N	¼N to ¾P	¼P	0 to ⅛	8½	20	18
'73-'74	Grand Prix	2½P to 3½P	3P	½P to 1½P (LH) / 0 to 1P (RH)	1P / ½P	0 to ⅛	10½	20	18¹³⁄₁₆ (LH) / 19³⁄₁₆ (RH)
	Pontiac	½P to 1½P	1P	½P to 1½P (LH) / 0 to 1P (RH)	1P / ½P	0 to ⅛	10½	20	18½
'75-'77	Grand Prix	2½P to 3½P	3P	½P to 1½P (LH) / 0 to 1P (RH)	1P / ½P	0 to ⅛	10⅓	——	——
'75-'76	Pontiac	1P to 2P	1½P	½P to 1P (LH) / 0 to 1P (RH)	1P / ½P	0 to ⅛	10⅓	——	——
'77	Pontiac	2½P to 3½P	3P	——	¾P	0 to ⅛	10⅓	——	——

—— Not specified
N Negative   P Positive
LH lefthand side   RH righthand side

CHARGING SYSTEM

Alternator Removal and Installation

1. Disconnect the battery cables.
2. Remove the alternator wires or connector.
3. Loosen adjusting bolts.
4. Remove V-belt and through-bolt.
5. Remove alternator.
6. To install, reverse the removal procedure. Adjust the belt tension so that the longest span of belt between pulleys can be depressed about ½ in. in the middle by moderate thumb pressure.

Caution Pull out on the alternator by hand to avoid damage to the housing and overtightening, which could damage the bearings.

Tighten first the adjuster bolt, then the pivot bolt.

1970 Voltage Regulator Removal and Installation

1. Disconnect the battery cables.
2. Disconnect the wiring from the voltage regulator.
3. Remove the screws holding the regulator to the firewall or front bulkhead depending on the car.
4. Reverse the removal procedures to install.

1971 and later Voltage Regulator Removal and Installation

The voltage regulator is inside the alternator. See "Charging and Starting Systems" in the "Unit Repair Section."

STARTING SYSTEM

A detailed discussion of starters can be found in the Unit Repair Section under Charging and Starting Systems.

Starter Removal and Installation

1. Disconnect positive cable from battery.
2. Raise front of car and support on stands.
3. Pull cable and wire loom down to hang free.
4. Disconnect brace, starting 1971.
5. Remove mounting screws and starter motor with cable and solenoid wires.
6. Remove wires from starter.
7. To reinstall reverse the above, first installing the wires to solenoid.

IGNITION SYSTEM

All distributors through 1973 have a Radio Frequency Interference Shield (R.F.I.) covering the circuit breaker plate assembly. The shield must be removed to install points or condenser, but dwell angle may be set through an opening in the shield. A unitized point and condenser set was introduced in 1974. It was installed as original equipment in some cases. The R.F.I. shield isn't required when the unitized point and condenser set is used.

A unitized electronic ignition system is optional on late 1971 and 1972-74 models having the 455 cu. in. V8 with four-barrel carburetor. This system replaces the ignition coil, distributor, amplifier, wiring and spark plug wires used with previous transistorized systems.

Starting 1975, Pontiac is using High Energy Electronic ignition on all models. It is also used in place of the unitized system on some 1974 models. It is triggered by a magnetic pulse, and transistor controlled. There is a capacitor in the distributor for radio noise suppression.

This system may not be compatible with all tachometers, so check the instruction sheet for the tachometer before attempting to hook it up to a car with electronic ignition. There is a terminal on the distributor which is marked TACH; connect a tachometer from this terminal to a suitable ground. Some tachometers may connect from this terminal to the battery positive terminal.

Troubleshooting of the Ignition System can be found in the "Unit Repair Section" under "Electronic Ignition Systems."

Distributor Removal and Installation

1. Disconnect the coil wire connector. On HEI systems, disconnect the ignition switch battery feed wire from the distributor cap.
2. Remove distributor cap.
3. Crank engine so that rotor points to No. 1 cylinder plug tower and timing mark on crankshaft pulley are indexed with pointer.

NOTE: Observe the position of the rotor and make marks on the distributor housing and on the block that line up with tip of the rotor. Make sure these marks line up upon reassembly. If the engine is disturbed, these marks can be used for reassembly.

4. Remove distributor vacuum line.
5. Remove distributor hold-down bolt and clamp. Do not disturb the engine after the distributor has been removed.
6. Lift the distributor out of its bore. Notice the slight rotation of the rotor as the distributor is removed from the block.
7. Installation procedure is the reverse of the removal procedure. However, before inserting the distributor into the block, the rotor should be moved slightly to one side. This is necessary because of the helical cut of the gears. As the distributor seats in its bore, the rotor will rotate slightly so that the reference

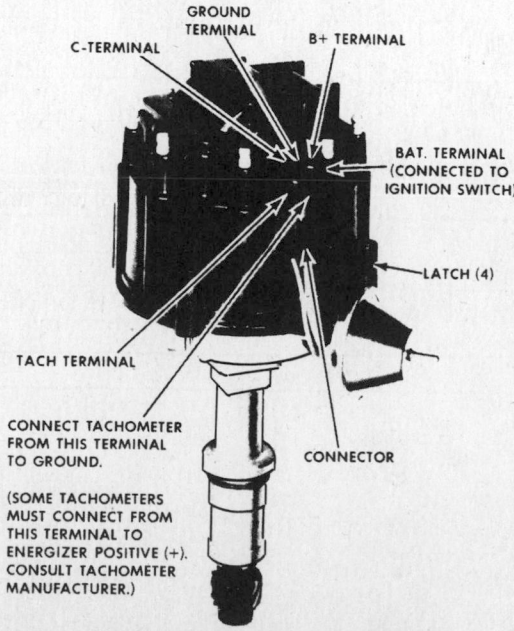

GROUND TERMINAL

C-TERMINAL

B+ TERMINAL

BAT. TERMINAL (CONNECTED TO IGNITION SWITCH)

LATCH (4)

TACH TERMINAL

CONNECT TACHOMETER FROM THIS TERMINAL TO GROUND.

(SOME TACHOMETERS MUST CONNECT FROM THIS TERMINAL TO ENERGIZER POSITIVE (+). CONSULT TACHOMETER MANUFACTURER.)

CONNECTOR

High Energy Ignition system distributor
(© Pontiac Div., G.M. Corp)

marks will once again be in line. Retime the engine with a timing light.

Installation If Engine Has Been Disturbed

1. With no. 1 piston on the compression stroke, rotate the crankshaft until the pulley timing mark indexes with the stationary mark at TDC.
2. Replace the distributor to block gasket.
3. Install the distributor in the block. The rotor should point toward the contact in the cap for no. 1 cylinder. Move the rotor slightly to the side because as the distributor is pressed into its bore it will rotate a small amount.
4. Install the distributor clamp and clamp bolt.
5. Install the vacuum line, rotor, cap, and coil wire.
6. Retime the engine with a timing light.

Ignition Timing

Timing marks are located on the front engine cover and on the harmonic balancer or pulley.

1. Disconnect and plug the distributor vacuum advance hose.
2. Make sure the dwell is adjusted. *NOTE: It may be necessary to put a small amount of white paint or chalk on the timing marks to make them more visible.*
3. Connect a timing light to no. 1 spark plug.
4. Loosen the distributor clamp.
5. Start the engine and rotate the distributor until the correct marks line up. Tighten the distributor clamp and recheck the timing.
6. Reconnect the vacuum hose.

Contact Point and Condenser Replacement and Adjustment

1. Remove the distributor cap and the rotor.
2. Remove the R.F.I. shield, if so equipped.
3. Remove the screws holding the points in place.
4. Remove the condenser lead and primary lead from the points. Loosen the clamp and slide the condenser out.
5. Install a new set of points and tighten the attaching screws. Adjust the point gap if the point set isn't preset. Install the condenser.
6. Connect the condenser and primary leads, to the points.
7. Apply a very small amount of grease to the breaker cam.
8. Install the R.F.I. shield; the half covering the points should be installed first. You don't need the

shield if the unitized point and condenser set is being used.
9. Install the rotor and distributor cap.
10. Set the dwell with the engine running.

FUEL SYSTEM

A non-repairable fuel pump is used.

Information on the fuel gauge will be found in the Unit Repair Section.

Fuel Pump Removal and Installation

1. Disconnect the input and output lines from the fuel pump.
2. Remove the bolts which hold the fuel pump and lift off the pump and gasket.
NOTE: on some models equipped with power steering it is possible, but somewhat difficult, to reach the mounting bolts with the steering pump in place. It may help to slack off on the power steering pump, remove its mounting bolts and, with it still connected to its lines, lift it up out of the way.
3. Reverse the procedure for installation.

Fuel Filter Replacement

1. Disconnect fuel line connection at inlet of carburetor.
2. Remove inlet fuel filter nut from carburetor using a box wrench.
3. Remove filter element and spring.
4. The element should allow air to pass freely.
5. Install element spring and new element into carburetor. Bronze elements are installed with small section of cone facing outward.
6. Install new gasket on fitting nut and install nut.
7. Install fuel line and tighten securely. Start engine and check for leaks.

Idle Speed and Mixture Adjustments

1970

Adjust with air cleaner installed.
1. On California cars, remove fuel filler cap.
2. Disconnect and plug distributor vacuum advance hose.
3. Plug hot idle compensator on all automatic transmission V8s with Quadrajet (4MV). Also plug compensator on all V8 2-BBL. with automatic and A/C.
4. With automatic in Drive, Manual in Neutral, adjust curb idle speed as follows:
5. Back out mixture screws 3-5 turns from lightly seated positions.

6. Adjust carburetor idle speed screw to obtain 850 rpm for manual 350 and 400 2-BBL., 1,050 rpm for manual 400 and 455 4-BBL., or 675 rpm for all automatic 350, 400, 455 engines.
7. Lean mixture screws equally (turn in) to obtain 800 rpm for manual 350 and 400 2-BBL., 950 rpm for manual 400 and 455 4-BBL., or 650 rpm for all automatic 350, 400, 455 engines.

1971-72

Adjust with air cleaner installed.

The Combination Emission Control (C.E.C.) valve was introduced in 1971. This valve is energized through the transmission switch to increase idle speed under conditions of high gear deceleration and to provide full vacuum spark advance during high gear operation. The valve is de-energized at curb idle and in the lower gears to prevent carburetor vacuum from reaching the distributor and advancing ignition timing under these conditions, the result of which is lower exhaust emission. *The valve need not be adjusted unless the solenoid or throttle body is removed, or the carburetor overhauled.*

1. Disconnect carburetor "EVAP" hose from vapor storage canister.
2. Disconnect and plug carburetor-to-vacuum (distributor vacuum) solenoid hose at solenoid. Disconnect throttle solenoid wire on 4-BBL. manual transmission engines.
3. Set dwell and timing (in that order) at specified idle speed.
4. Adjust carburetor speed screw to obtain specified idle speed, automatic in Drive, manual in Neutral.
5. On 4-BBL. manual transmission models, reconnect throttle solenoid wire, manually extend solenoid screw and adjust to specified idle rpm.
6. Place automatic in Park, manual in Neutral and check fast idle speed with screw on top step of cam. Adjust fast idle screw to obtain 1,700 rpm.
NOTE: 2 BBL. carburetors are not adjustable for fast idle.
7. Reconnect distributor vacuum and vapor storage hoses.

Idle Mixture If Carburetor Is Rebuilt

If the carburetor has been overhauled, or the plastic locks removed from the mixture screws, the following procedure must be used to adjust idle speed and mixture.

1. Turn in mixture screws until lightly seated, then back out 3½ turns.
2. Start engine and adjust carburetor idle speed screw to obtain a

FUEL BOWL
VENT TO AIR
CLEANER

PUMP
LEVER

VACUUM
BREAK
DIAPHRAGM

SECONDARY VALVES
ACTUATING ROD

TO VACUUM
MODULATOR
(AUTO. ONLY)

IDLE SPEED
SCREW

VACUUM PURGE
TO CANNISTER

PUMP LEVER
RETAINING PIN

IDLE MIXTURE LIMITER

4 bbl carburetor idle mixture and idle speed screws (© Pontiac Div, G.M. Corp)

speed 25 rpm above specified idle (automatic), 75 rpm higher for 2-BBL. V8 (manual), or 100 rpm higher for 4-BBL. V8 (manual).

3. Turn mixture screws in equally until specified idle speed is obtained. At this point a CO meter should be employed to adjust mixture. A reading of 0.2% or less must be maintained.

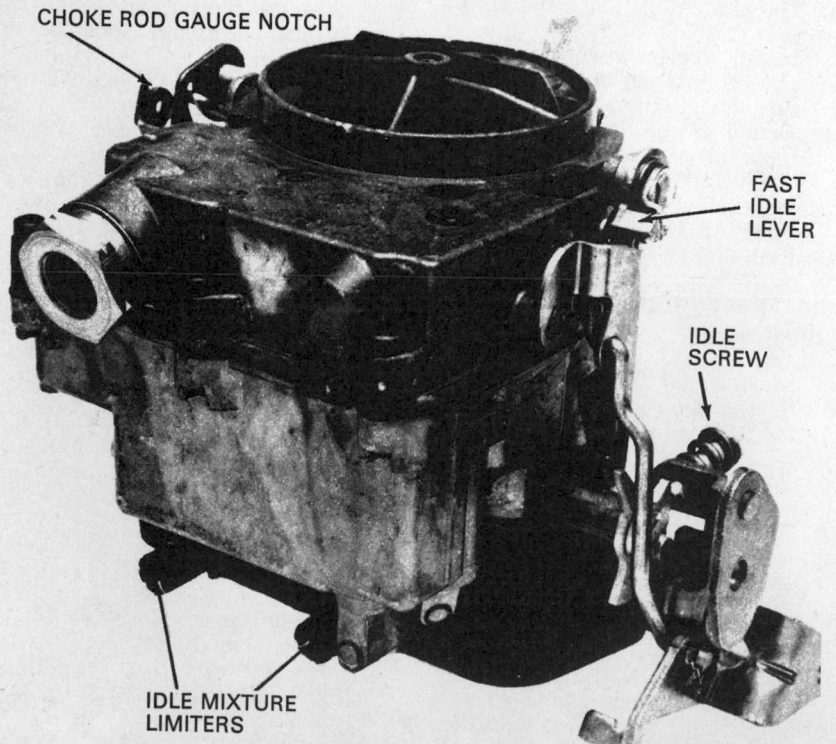

CHOKE ROD GAUGE NOTCH

FAST
IDLE
LEVER

IDLE
SCREW

IDLE MIXTURE
LIMITERS

2 bbl carburetor idle mixture and idle speed screws (© Pontiac Div, G.M. Corp)

4. Shut off engine and install new limiter caps, with tabs against full rich stops.
5. Adjust fast idle speed, as described previously.

1973-74

Idle Speed

1. Disconnect and plug the carburetor hose from the vapor canister.

2. Disconnect and plug the distributor and EGR valve vacuum hoses. Plug any open vacuum tubes on the carburetor.
3. Check the dwell and timing.
4. Disconnect the idle stop solenoid wire.
5. Adjust the carburetor idle speed screw to the low rpm specified in the Tune-Up Specifications chart.
6. Reconnect the solenoid wire and adjust the solenoid plunger screw to obtain the specified idle speed.

NOTE: *You might have to work the throttle linkage by hand first, since the solenoid isn't always powerful enough to move it.*

7. On four-barrel carburetors, check the fast idle speed with the fast idle speed screw on the top step of the fast idle cam. Adjust the speed by turning the fast idle screw. Fast idle speed is 1,500 rpm for all engines.

NOTE: *The fast idle speed screw is not the same one used in Step 5. You can't make this adjustment on two-barrel carburetors.*

Idle Mixture

1. Set the parking brake and block the wheels.
2. Disconnect and plug the carburetor hose from the vapor canister in the engine compartment. Disconnect and plug the distributor vacuum hose.
3. If the idle mixture limiter caps are intact and a CO meter is available, attempt to obtain an idle setting of 0.2% CO by adjusting the mixture screws. If

this doesn't work, remove the caps and proceed to the next step.

NOTE: The engine must be at normal operating temperature.

4. Remove the idle mixture limiter caps. If you have a CO meter, adjust the mixture screws equally to get a reading of 0.2% CO.
5. Run the screws in until they are lightly seated, then back them out six turns for 1973 and seven for 1974.
6. Turn the air conditioner off, place the automatic transmission in Drive (block the wheels), place the manual transmission in Neutral, leave the air cleaner off and plug the air cleaner manifold vacuum fitting. Adjust the idle speed screw or the idle stop solenoid to obtain the following temporary idle speed.

Engine	Year	rpm
8-350, 2 bbl.	1973	700
8-400, 2 bbl.	1973	700
8-400, 455, 4 bbl.	1973	700
8-400, 2 bbl.	1974	720
8-400, 2 bbl., Calif.	1974	690
8-400, 4 bbl.	1974	720
8-400, 4 bbl., Calif.	1974	685
8-455, 4 bbl.	1974	680
8-455, 4 bbl., Calif.	1974	675

7. Turn the mixture screws in equally to get the highest idle speed. Then set the speed back to that listed in Step 6.
8. Turn the mixture screws in equally until the engine speed drops to the normal idle speed given in the Tune-Up Specifications chart.
9. Install the air cleaner. If the idle speed changes, adjust the mixture screws slightly to compensate.

1975-76

1. The adjustment must be made with the engine at normal operating temperature, with the air conditioner off, and the air cleaner removed. The air cleaner vacuum fitting in the manifold should be plugged. Automatic transmissions should be in Drive and manual transmissions in neutral.
2. Set the parking brake and block the wheels.
3. On all models, disconnect and plug the hose going to the carburetor from the vapor cannister. On 1975 350 V8 2-bbl, detach and plug the distributor vacuum hose to block vacuum advance. Disconnect and plug the EGR hose to the carburetor at the

EGR valve end.

4. Use pliers to break off the plastic idle mixture screw limiter caps. Turn in the mixture screws until they seat lightly, then back them out five turns.
5. Adjust the idle speed screw or idle solenoid screw to get the "before lean drop idle" speed listed on the underhood specifications sticker. The tachometer hookup for the HEI ignition system is covered earlier under Ignition System.
6. Adjust the mixture screws equally (quarter-turn increments are recommended) to obtain the highest possible idle speed. Check the adjustment by shifting into Neutral, running the engine at 2,000 rpm for 5-10 seconds, returning to idle, shifting back into Drive, and letting the speed stabilize for 10 seconds.
7. Return the idle speed to that set in Step 5.
8. Repeat Steps 6 and 7, until no further speed increase is possible.
9. Turn in the mixture screws equally until the normal idle speed is reached.
10. Place the automatic transmission in Park and the manual in neutral. Check the tune-up sticker and adjust the fast idle with the fast idle speed screw. If there is no speed shown, you do not have to adjust the fast idle. For 4MC carburetors, adjust with the fast idle speed screw on the high step of the cam.
11. If there is an idle speed-up solenoid, place the transmission in Drive, disconnect the terminal connector at the air conditioner compressor clutch and adjust the solenoid to give 675 RPM; when finished reconnect the terminal connector.
12. If there is a dashpot, adjust it so that at idle, there is .040 in. clearance between the tip of the plunger (compressed) and the throttle lever.
13. Replace and connect the air cleaner. Use the mixture screws to make any slight idle speed correction necessary.
14. Replace the distributor and canister hoses.

COOLING SYSTEM

Radiator Removal and Installation

1. Drain the radiator.
2. On Grand Prix, remove the fan.
3. Disconnect the upper and lower radiator hoses.

4. If equipped with automatic transmission, disconnect the cooling lines and plug them to prevent excessive fluid loss.
5. Remove the radiator upper bracket bolts and remove the bracket.
6. Remove the radiator and shroud assembly by lifting straight up.
7. Reverse the above steps to install the radiator.

Water Pump Removal and Installation

This is a centrifugal type waterpump. It is die cast, with sealed bearings, and is pressed together. Therefore, it is serviced as a unit.

NOTE: It is sometimes more convenient to remove the radiator than to leave it in place. This depends on the working space available and the options on the car such as air conditioning and power steering.

1. Disconnect the battery and drain the radiator.
2. Loosen the alternator and remove the fan belt.
3. Remove the power steering and air conditioning belts, if so equipped.
4. Remove the fan and water pump pulley.
5. Remove the front alternator bracket.
6. Remove the heater hose and radiator hose at the pump.
7. Remove the water pump retaining bolts and remove the pump.
8. Install the pump by reversing above steps. Make sure the gasket surfaces are clean and smooth. Always use a gasket sealer on both sides of the gasket. Torque the retaining bolts to 15 ft lbs.

Thermostat Replacement

1. Drain coolant to below thermostat level.
2. Disconnect the upper hose and remove water outlet assembly.
3. Replace by reversing the above steps. Clean gasket surfaces and use a gasket sealer and a new gasket. Torque attaching bolts to 30 ft. lbs.
4. Refill to 3 in. below filler neck and bleed cooling system.

EMISSION CONTROLS

There are three types of emissions to be controlled: crankcase emissions, carburetor and gas tank vapor emissions, and exhaust emissions. See the "Unit Repair Section" for troubleshooting and repair information.

1970

Crankcase emissions are controlled by the Closed Positive Crankcase Ventilation System, and exhaust emissions by the engine Controlled Combustion System (C.C.S.), in conjunction with the new Transmission Controlled Spark System (T.C.S.).

In addition, cars sold in California are equipped with an Evaporation Control System that limits the amount of gasoline vapor discharged into the atmosphere (usually from the carburetor and fuel tank).

The T.C.S. system consists of a transmission switch, a solenoid valve, and a temperature switch. Under normal conditions, the system permits the vacuum distributor (spark) advance to operate only in high gear (both manual and automatic transmissions) and reverse.

The transmission switch is located on the transmission and senses when the transmission is in one of the lower gears. When in a lower gear, the switch activates the vacuum solenoid valve. This valve is located in the vacuum line that runs from the carburetor to the distributor, and it prevents vacuum from going to the distributor advance when it is activated. There is also an engine-temperature sensing switch which overrides the transmission switch. It will allow vacuum advance in the lower gears when engine temperature is below 85° or above 220°. There is always vacuum advance in high gear and reverse.

1971

In 1971, the Combination Emission Control System (C.E.C.) was introduced. It uses the C.C.S. of 1969 and incorporates several but not all of the features in the T.C.S. of 1970. Although distributor vacuum advance is eliminated in the lower gears, as in the T.C.S. system, it is eliminated in a different manner. A C.E.C. solenoid valve is used to regulate distributor vacuum advance and the T.C.S. valve is eliminated.

The C.E.C. solenoid valve is mounted on the carburetor. Vacuum from the intake manifold passes through a port at the base of the solenoid before it reaches the distributor. When the solenoid receives an electrical signal from the transmission or temperature switches, the plunger extends, opening the solenoid's vacuum port, which allows vacuum to the distributor. At the same time the plunger head contacts the carburetor throttle lever increasing engine speed. When the solenoid is de-energized the spring-loaded plunger returns to its unextended position closing the vacuum port and allowing the throttle lever to rest against the idle speed adjusting screw.

The C.E.C. solenoid valve is energized by two switches and one relay.

The time delay relay is used to energize the C.E.C. solenoid and provide vacuum advance for the first 15 seconds after the ignition is turned on. This happens regardless of engine temperature. After the 15 seconds, the solenoid is again regulated by the temperature switch and the transmission switch.

One of the controlling switches is an engine temperature switch. It allows vacuum advance in all gears, by energizing the C.E.C. solenoid, when engine temperature is below 82° or above 220°. Between these temperatures, the C.E.C. solenoid is controlled by the transmission switch.

The other switch is the transmission switch. When the transmission is in the lower gears, this switch keeps the C.E.C. solenoid in the de-energized position eliminating vacuum advance. In high gear, the solenoid is energized by the transmission switch, and vacuum advance is supplied.

Engine dieseling is controlled by use of lower throttle plate openings (lower idle speeds).

On A/C, automatic transmission cars, a solid-state timing device engages the A/C compressor for about three seconds after the ignition is turned off. The load from the compressor effectively stalls the engine and prevents dieseling or over-run.

An evaporation control system was added to all cars in 1971. This system limits the amount of gasoline vapor discharged into the air from the gas tank and carburetor. The fuel tank has a non-vented cap. As vapors are generated in the fuel tank, they flow through a liquid vapor separator to a canister where they are stored. From the canister the vapors are routed to the carburetor where they are burned when the engine is running.

1972

All models use the new Speed Control Spark System, (S.C.S.).

Every engine and transmission combination uses the Auto-therm air cleaner, P.C.V. system, and the evaporation control system of 1971.

The S.C.S. system uses a solenoid valve in the vacuum line running between the carburetor and the distributor. This valve is the same as the Transmission Controlled Spark Valve used in 1970. The difference in this system is that the valve is regulated by vehicle speed using a speed control spark switch, instead of by a transmission switch. The S.C.S. solenoid valve is energized below 38 mph in any gear, under normal operating temperature, allowing no vacuum advance. Above 38 mph, in any gear, or any time engine temperature is higher or lower than normal operating temperature, the solenoid valve is de-energized allowing full vacuum advance to the distributor.

Normally S.C.S. engine operating temperatures range from 95° to 230°. An engine temperature sensing switch is located in the head and de-energizes the solenoid until operating temperature is reached regardless of vehicle speed.

1973

The Controlled Combustion System (C.C.S.) is standard on all engines. The Air Injection Reactor (A.I.R.) is used on all 350 engines with manual transmissions and 350/400 California engines. A combination of the Transmission Controlled Spark and Exhaust Gas Re-Circulation (E.G.R.) is found on all V8 engines.

E.G.R. is a system used to reduce nitrous oxide (NO_x) emissions. It functions by allowing a small amount of exhaust gas into the air fuel mixture in the intake manifold, under certain conditions.

The EGR-TCS system consists of a temperature switch which senses when the engine temperature is under 71° or over 230°, a second temperature switch sensing engine temperature between 140° and 230°, an EGR solenoid, a vacuum advance solenoid, a transmission switch, and a time delay relay.

The under 71° and over 230° switch is mounted on the left cylinder head. The 140° to 230° switch is mounted in the right cylinder head. The time delay relay is mounted on the vacuum advance solenoid.

The 71° to 230° switch grounds the circuit for the solenoids below 71° and above 230°. The 140° switch passes current to the transmission switch when engine temperature is between 140° and 230°. The transmission switch then grounds the circuit for the solenoids in first gear only. Between 71° and 140° the temperature switches are both open and the solenoids are in the normal positions.

The vacuum advance solenoid is normally closed, allowing no vacuum advance. The EGR solenoid is normally open, allowing exhaust gas recirculation.

Below 71° there is a complete circuit and both solenoids are energized, allowing vacuum advance and cutting off EGR.

From 71° to 140° there is an open circuit, the solenoids return to their normal positions and vacuum advance is cut off and EGR is allowed.

From 140° to 230°, in first gear, there is an open circuit and the solenoids are in their normal positions. The time delay relay maintains the open circuit for 33 to 55 seconds after the transmission shifts into second gear. However, after the time delay in second and third gear, the solenoids are energized to allow vacuum advance and cut off EGR.

Over 235° the solenoids are energized, vacuum advance occurs and there is no EGR.

A mid-year redesign of the emission control system was necessitated by newly-announced Federal standards. On cars equipped with A.I.R., air is not supplied to nos. 3 and 6 cylinders. This is done by internal changes in the cylinder heads. Mid-year A.I.R. cylinder heads can usually be identified by the absence of a drilled passage and metal sealing ball at the nos. 3 and 6 cylinder locations.

The new engines have a relocated vacuum source for the air cleaner. Vacuum is supplied through a tee in the hose feeding vacuum to the distributor vacuum spark thermal valve.

The mid-year EGR system operates basically on the same principle as the 1973 system, except for two major differences:

1. The EGR and TCS systems now work completely independent of each other.
2. A new EGR thermal vacuum valve is used to sense the temperature of the intake manifold coolant. Below 95°F, no EGR; above 95°F, ported EGR.

In the TCS system, full vacuum advance is provided below 62°F. When the temperature rises above 62°F, the distributor vacuum spark thermal valve closes and from this point on the distributor solenoid must be energized to get vacuum advance. The upper temperature limit for vacuum advance cut-in is now 240°F.

The Start-Up Relay Switch gives full advance (ported for manual transmission) in any gear for 20 seconds after all engine starts. After the 20 seconds has elapsed, the switch breaks ground and the distributor solenoid is de-energized, shutting off the vacuum advance.

1974

The A.I.R. system is carried over from 1973 and is used on all 400 cu in 2 bbl California engines.

The EGR/TCS system is once again together, as in pre-1973½ systems, and consists of a thermal vacuum valve, vacuum advance solenoid, EGR valve, hot coolant switch, cold feed switch and a time-delay relay for engine starting. The system is found on all V8s.

On the EGR/TCS system, the distributor spark-EGR thermal vacuum valve senses the temperature of the air/fuel mixture inside the intake manifold. Below 62°F, EGR is off and full vacuum advance is provided. When the temperature rises above 62°F, EGR is on (operated by a port above the throttle blade, so that it only comes on above idle). From this point on the distributor vacuum advance solenoid must be energized by the other components and switches to provide vacuum advance.

When the cylinder head metal temperature goes above 125°, 140°, 155°F (depending on use), the cold feed switch closes. This sends the 12V current to the TCS switch looking for a ground. The TCS switch provides a ground only when the transmission shifts into high gear. There is no time delay after shifting into high gear.

Any time the coolant temperature goes over 240°F, the hot coolant switch provides a ground for the distributor solenoid. Since the hot coolant switch will ground whether the TCS switch does or not, vacuum advance will be supplied to the distributor in any gear when the coolant temperature reaches 240°F or above.

There is a distributor vacuum spark delay valve on some models, between the distributor solenoid and the distributor acting as a restrictor on vacuum supplied to the distributor. This merely slows down the rate vacuum is initially supplied to the distributor. Full vacuum is eventually supplied.

The function of the start-up relay switch is identical to 1973½.

1975-77

The Controlled Combustion System (C.C.S.) is continued on all non-California engines. It introduces preheated carburetor intake air during engine warmup.

The Air Injection Reactor (A.I.R.), or air pump system is continued in some applications.

E.G.R. (Exhaust Gas Recirculation) is used with the exhaust gas introduced into the intake mixture in the intake manifold and modulated by an exhaust backpressure modulating valve.

A hot air choke is used to provide quick response to engine warmup.

All models have high energy ignition (H.E.I.) to prevent any possible catalyst damage caused by ignition miss. Refer to the "Electronic Ignition" Unit Repair Section for details.

Oxidizing catalytic converters are used on all models to control hydrocarbons and carbon monoxide. Refer to the "Emission Control" Unit Repair Section for details on this system.

All engines have outside air intakes. The cooler outside air improves driveability.

The Early Fuel Evaporation System has a heat valve in the exhaust manifold which, during warm-up, forces the exhaust gases to flow under the carburetor heating the mixture. When the engine reaches normal temperature the valve opens and exhaust gases are routed normally.

The Evaporative Emission Control System is carried over from the previous year.

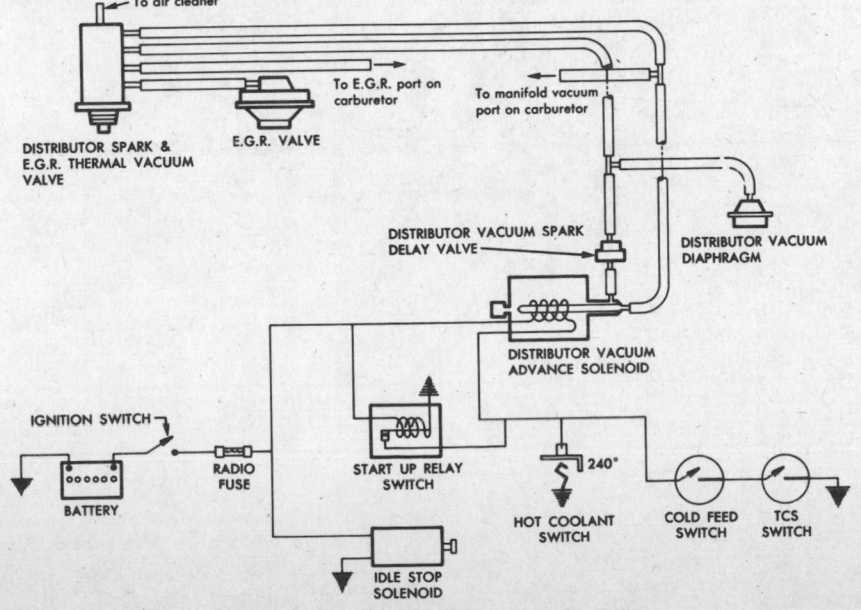

1974 emission control system—schematic diagram
(© Pontiac Div., G.M. Corp)

ENGINE

Engines used in Pontiacs through 1976 are all of Pontiac design. These are 350, 400, and 455 V8s. A new 301 Pontiac V8 was introduced in 1977, as was a 231 V6 of Buick design, and 350 and 403 V8s of Oldsmobile design.

NOTE: Service procedures for the 231 V6 are given in the Astre car section. Refer to the Oldsmobile section for procedures on the Oldsmobile design 350 and 403 V8s.

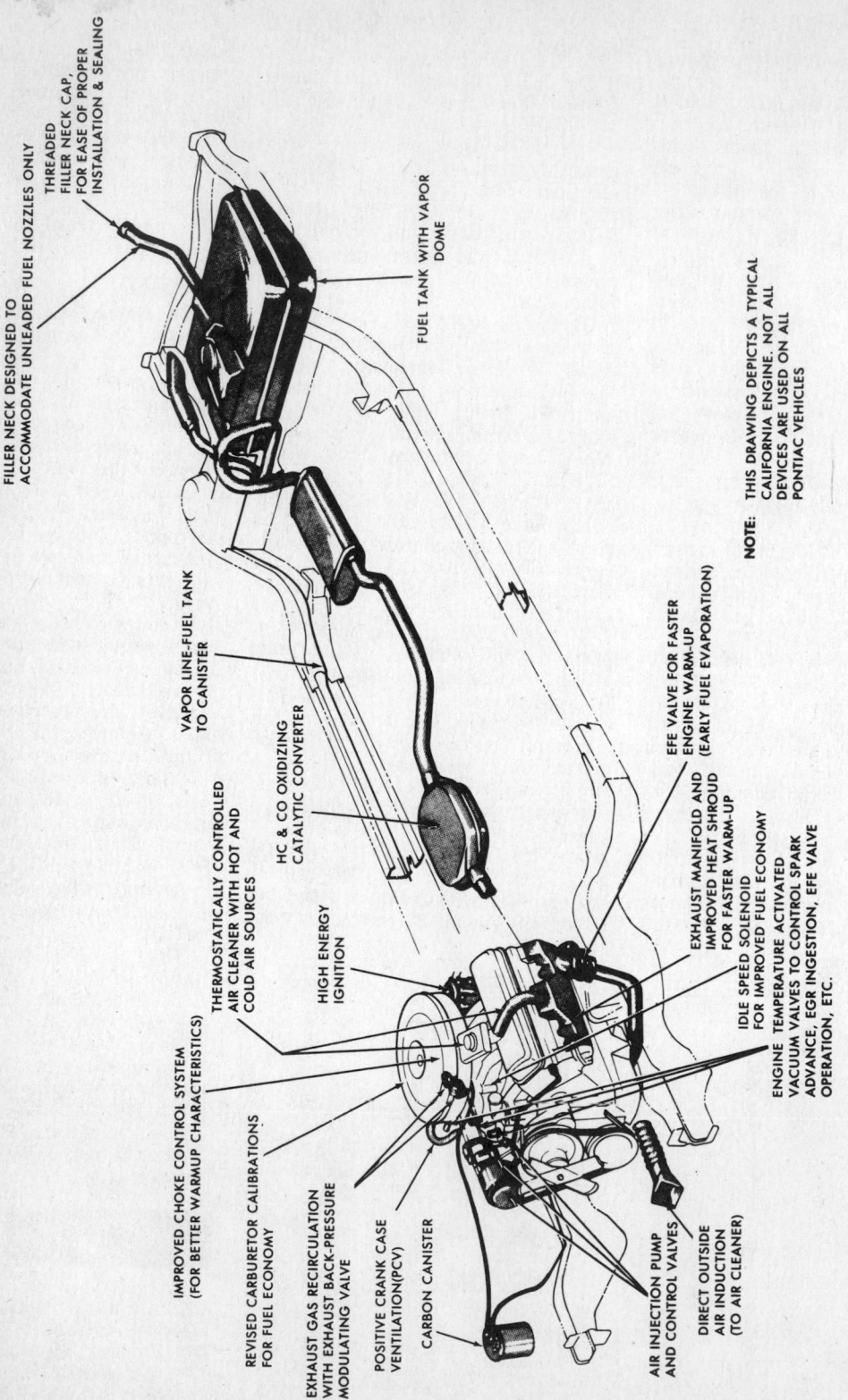

1976 PONTIAC EMISSION CONTROL SYSTEMS

FILLER NECK DESIGNED TO
ACCOMMODATE UNLEADED FUEL NOZZLES ONLY

THREADED
FILLER NECK CAP,
FOR EASE OF PROPER
INSTALLATION & SEALING

FUEL TANK WITH VAPOR
DOME

VAPOR LINE-FUEL TANK
TO CANISTER

HC & CO OXIDIZING
CATALYTIC CONVERTER

THERMOSTATICALLY CONTROLLED
AIR CLEANER WITH HOT AND
COLD AIR SOURCES

HIGH ENERGY
IGNITION

EFE VALVE FOR FASTER
ENGINE WARM-UP
(EARLY FUEL EVAPORATION)

EXHAUST MANIFOLD AND
IMPROVED HEAT SHROUD
FOR FASTER WARM-UP

IDLE SPEED SOLENOID
FOR IMPROVED FUEL ECONOMY

ENGINE TEMPERATURE ACTIVATED
VACUUM VALVES TO CONTROL SPARK
ADVANCE, EGR INGESTION, EFE VALVE
OPERATION, ETC.

IMPROVED CHOKE CONTROL SYSTEM
(FOR BETTER WARMUP CHARACTERISTICS)

REVISED CARBURETOR CALIBRATIONS
FOR FUEL ECONOMY

EXHAUST GAS RECIRCULATION
WITH EXHAUST BACK-PRESSURE
MODULATING VALVE

POSITIVE CRANK CASE
VENTILATION(PCV)

CARBON CANISTER

AIR INJECTION PUMP
AND CONTROL VALVES

DIRECT OUTSIDE
AIR INDUCTION
(TO AIR CLEANER)

NOTE: THIS DRAWING DEPICTS A TYPICAL
CALIFORNIA ENGINE. NOT ALL
DEVICES ARE USED ON ALL
PONTIAC VEHICLES

(© Pontiac Div., G.M. Corp)

Engine Removal and Installation

1. Disconnect battery cables and remove battery.
2. Drain cooling system.
3. Scribe alignment marks around hood hinges and remove hood.
4. Disconnect engine wiring and all ground straps. Disconnect the thermal feed switch from the left rear cylinder head on all 1973 and later cars.
5. Remove air cleaner and fan shroud, then disconnect radiator and heater hoses.
6. Remove the radiator.
7. Remove power steering pump and A/C compressor from brackets and swing units aside without disconnecting hoses.

Caution If the compressor refrigerant lines do not have enough slack to position the compressor out of the way without disconnecting the refrigerant lines, the air conditioning system will have to be removed by a trained air-conditioning specialist. Under no conditions should an untrained person attempt to disconnect the air conditioning refrigerant lines. These lines contain pressurized Freon, which can be extremely dangerous to the untrained.

8. Remove fan and fan pulley.
9. Disconnect accelerator linkage or cable and remove bracket.
10. Disconnect transmission vacuum modulator line (automatic) and power brake vacuum line.

Caution Do not bend the metal transmission modulator line.

11. Jack up car and support on axle stands.
12. Drain engine oil, disconnect fuel lines at pump and exhaust pipes from manifolds.
13. Disconnect starter wires and remove starter motor on manual transmission cars.
14. If equipped with automatic transmission: remove converter cover and three converter retaining bolts. Slide converter rearward.
15. If equipped with manual transmission: disconnect clutch linkage and remove cross-shaft and flywheel housing cover.
16. Remove four lower bellhousing bolts—two per side.
17. Disconnect auto transmission filler tube support and starter wire shield.
18. Remove the two front motor mount bolts, then lower car to floor.
19. Support auto transmission with a wood-padded jack, then remove the two remaining bellhousing bolts from above.
20. Jack up auto transmission slightly, attach a chain hoist and remove the engine.
21. To install, reverse removal procedure. Note that there are dowel pins in the block that have matching holes in the bellhousing. These dowel pins must be in almost perfect alignment with their holes before the engine and bellhousing will go together. Do not lower the engine completely while the jack is supporting the transmission.

Manifolds

Exhaust Manifold Removal and Installation

Tab locks are used on front and rear pairs of bolts on each exhaust manifold. When removing bolts, straighten tabs from beneath car using long handled screw driver. When installing tab locks, bend tabs against sides of bolt, not over top of bolt.

Left-Side Manifold

1. If the car is equipped with power steering, disconnect the power steering pump but leave it attached to its hoses and pull it up out of the way.
2. Remove the alternator belt, the alternator and the mounting bracket as an assembly.
3. From underneath the vehicle, disconnect the exhaust crossover pipe flange.
4. If the car is equipped with power brakes, the rear bolts of the manifold are difficult to reach but they can be removed with a box wrench.
5. Remove the bolts that hold the manifold to the left cylinder head and take off the manifold.

Right-Side Manifold

From underneath the vehicle, disconnect the upper flange from the right manifold. This is the upper flange where the cross manifold, exhaust pipe and right manifold join.

From underneath the vehicle, remove the bolts that hold the manifold to the head on the back two flanges. The front flange can be removed from the top of the car with a box wrench.

Intake Manifold Removal and Installation

1. Drain coolant from petcocks on radiator and on each side of block. Remove the EGR valve where necessary before removing the manifold.
   NOTE: most of the coolant can be drained from block through radiator drain by raising rear end of car approximately 15-18 in. off floor.
2. Remove air cleaner.
3. Remove water outlet fitting bolts and position fitting out of way, leaving radiator hose attached.
4. Disconnect heater hose from fitting.
5. Disconnect electrical wires and vacuum hoses from all emission switches and solenoids.
6. Remove spark plug wire brackets from manifold.
7. On cars equipped with power brakes, remove power brake vacuum pipe from carburetor.
8. Disconnect distributor to carburetor vacuum hoses.
9. Disconnect fuel line connecting carburetor and fuel pump.
10. Disconnect crankcase vent hose from intake manifold.
11. Disconnect throttle rod from carburetor.
12. Remove screws retaining throttle control bracket assembly.
13. Remove intake manifold retaining bolts and nuts, and remove manifold and gaskets. Make sure that O-ring seal between intake manifold and timing chain cover is retained and installed during assembly.
14. Reverse procedure to install. Use plastic gasket retainers to prevent manifold gaskets from slipping out of place.

Valve System

All Pontiac design V8 engines use a ball pivot type valve train and hydraulic valve lifters.

Rocker Arm Removal and Installation

1. Remove the valve covers.
2. Remove the rocker arm nut and rocker arm ball.
3. Lift the rocker arm off the

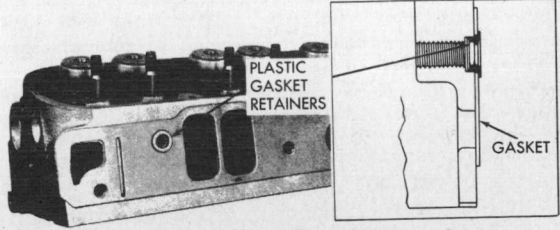

Plastic manifold retainers used on Pontiac-design V8s
(© Pontiac Div, G.M. Corp)

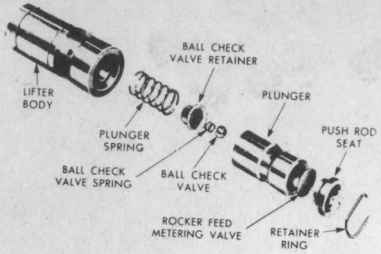

Hydraulic lifter
(© Pontiac Div, G.M. Corp)

rocker arm stud. Always keep the rocker arm assemblies together and assemble them on the same stud.

4. Remove the pushrod from its bore. Make sure the rods are returned to their original bore, with the same end in the block.
5. Reverse the removal procedure to install the rocker arms. Tighten the ball retaining nuts to 20 ft lbs.

Valve Guides

Pontiac engines have integral valve guides. Pontiac offers valves with oversize stems for worn guides (0.001, 0.003 and 0.005 in. being available for most engines). To fit these, enlarge valve guide bores with valve guide reamers to an oversize that cleans up wear.

As an alternate procedure, some local automotive machine shops fit replacement guides that use standard stem valves.

Cylinder Head

Cylinder Head Removal

1. Drain the cooling system including the block. Remove intake manifold, valley cover, and rocker arm cover.
2. Loosen all rocker arm retaining nuts and pivot rockers off pushrods.
3. Remove pushrods and place in order. The pushrods must be replaced in the same position with the same end in the block.
4. On all but the left head of the 455 S.D. engine, remove the exhaust pipe-to-manifold attaching bolts. In order to remove the left head of the 455 S.D., it is necessary to remove the exhaust manifold attaching nuts and drop the manifold. Remove the inner panel of the carburetor heat stove from the two center cylinder head bolts.
5. Remove battery ground strap and engine ground strap on left head; engine ground strap and automatic transmission filler tube bracket on right head.
6. Remove cylinder head bolts and head, with exhaust manifold attached.

NOTE: left head must be maneuvered to clear power steering and power brake units.

Cylinder Head Installation

1. Check head surface for straightness, then place a new head gasket on block.

NOTE: bolts are of three different lengths on all V8s. When bolts are properly installed, they will project an equal distance from head.

2. Install all bolts and tighten evenly to specified torque. Tighten to specifications in three stages.

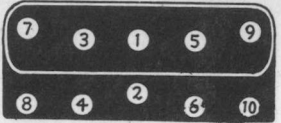

Pontiac-design 301, 350, 400, 455 V8 cylinder head tightening sequence

3. Install pushrods in original positions.
4. Position rocker arms over pushrods. Tighten the rocker arm ball retaining nut to 20 ft lbs.
5. Replace rocker arm cover.
6. Replace the valley cover.
7. Replace ground straps, oil filler tube bracket, intake manifold.
8. Install exhaust pipe flange nuts. On 455 S.D. engine, install left head exhaust manifold, with new gasket.

Timing Cover, Chain, and Camshaft

Timing Case Cover Removal and Installation and Seal Replacement

1. Drain radiator and cylinder block.
2. Loosen alternator adjusting bolts.
3. Remove fan, fan pulley, accessory drive belts, and water pump.
4. Disconnect radiator hoses.
5. Remove fuel pump.
6. Remove harmonic balancer bolt and washer.
7. Remove harmonic balancer.

NOTE: do not pry on rubber-mounted balancers. If only seal is to be replaced, proceed to Step 12.

8. Remove front four oil pan to timing cover bolts.
9. Remove timing cover bolts and nuts and cover to intake manifold bolt.
10. Pull cover forward and remove.
11. Remove O-ring from recess in intake manifold, then clean all gasket surfaces.
12. To replace seal, pry it out of the cover using a screwdriver. Install the new seal with lip inwards.

NOTE: seal can be replaced with cover installed.

13. To install, reverse removal procedure, making sure all gaskets are replaced. Tighten four oil pan bolts to 12 ft. lbs., and fan pulley bolts to 20 ft. lbs.

TIME SAVER

The following is a method for replacing valve springs, oil seals or spring retainers without removing the cylinder head.

1. Obtain a spark plug hole air chuck adaptor from an auto parts store.
2. To this adaptor add an air chuck so that the hose from an air compressor can be attached. This assembly will be used later to pressurize the cylinder.
3. Remove the valve rocker cover. Remove the rocker arm from the valve to be worked on.
4. Remove the spark plug from the cylinder to be worked on.
5. Turn the crankshaft to bring the piston of this cylinder down, away from

possible contact with the valve head. Sharply tap the valve retainer to loosen the valve lock.

6. Then turn the crankshaft to bring the piston in this cylinder to the Exact Top of its Compression Stroke.
7. Screw in the chuck-equipped tool.
8. Hook up an air hose to the chuck and turn on the pressure (about 200 lbs.).
9. With a strong and constant supply of air holding the valve closed, compress the valve spring and remove the lock and retainer.
10. Make the necessary replacements and reassemble.

NOTE: it is important that the operation be performed exactly as stated, in this order. The piston in the cylinder must be on exact top-center to prevent air pressure from turning the crankshaft.

Timing Chain and Sprocket Removal and Installation

1. Remove the timing case cover and fuel pump cam.
2. Turn the crank and camshaft (if the chain is broken) until the two timing marks are in line.
3. Using a puller, draw the sprocket off the front of the crankshaft.
4. Install the chain and sprockets with the timing marks aligned.
5. Secure the camshaft sprocket in position, with pump cam in place.

NOTE: when reassembling the timing case cover, extra care should be taken to make sure that the oil seal between the bottom of the timing case cover and the front of the oil pan is still a good one. Plenty of gasket cement should be used, at this point, to prevent oil leaks.

Camshaft Removal and Installation

1. Drain cooling system and remove air cleaner.
2. Disconnect all water hoses, vacuum lines and spark plug wires.
3. Disconnect accelerator linkage, temperature gauge wire, and fuel lines. Remove the radiator.
4. Remove hood latch brace.
5. Remove PCV hose, then remove rocker covers. Remove the water pump.

NOTE: on air-conditioned models, remove alternator and bracket.

6. Remove distributor, then remove intake manifold.
7. Remove valve tappet cover.

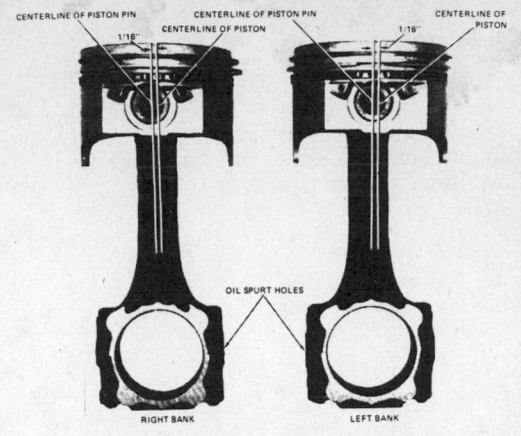

Pontiac-design 301, 350, 400, 455 V8 piston and rod assembly
(© Pontiac Div, G.M. Corp)

8. Loosen rocker arm nuts and pivot rockers out of the way.
9. Remove pushrods and lifters (keep them in proper order).
10. Remove harmonic balancer, fuel pump, and four oil pan to timing cover bolts.
11. Remove timing cover and gasket, then remove fuel pump eccentric and bushing.
12. Align timing marks, then remove timing chain and sprockets.
13. Remove camshaft thrust plate.
14. Remove camshaft by pulling

straight forward, being careful not to damage cam bearings in the process.

NOTE: it may be necessary to jack up the engine slightly to gain clearance, especially if motor mounts are worn.

15. Install new camshaft, with lobes and journals coated with heavy (SAE 50-60) oil, into the engine, being careful not to damage cam bearings.

NOTE: most specialty cams come with a special "break-in" lubricant for the lobes and journals; if such lu-

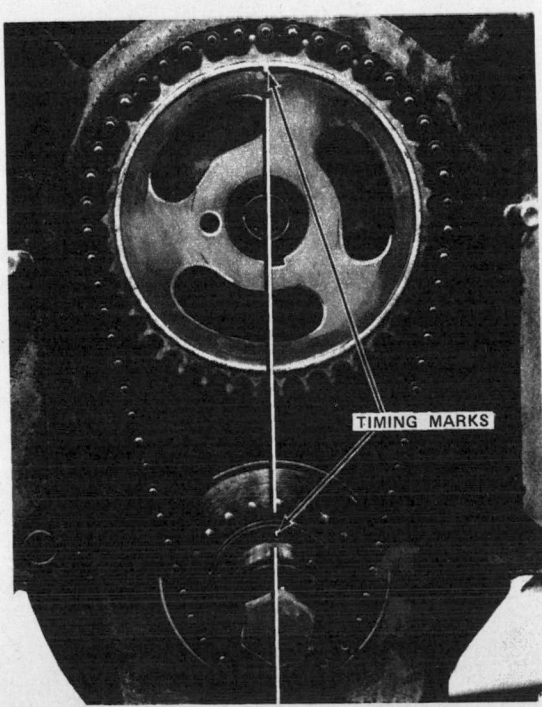

Pontiac-design 301, 350, 400, 455 V8 timing marks
(© Pontiac Div., G.M. Corp)

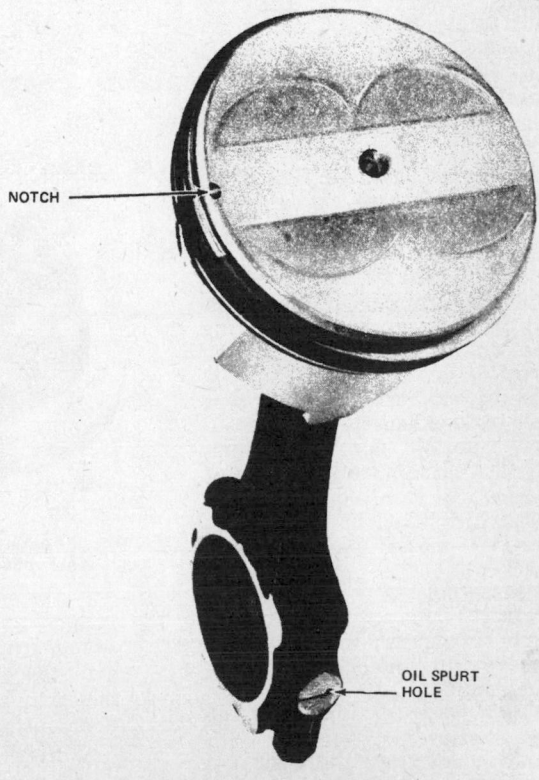

Piston and rod assembly
(© Pontiac Div, G.M. Corp)

bricant is available, use it instead of heavy oil.

16. Install camshaft thrust plate and tighten bolts to 20 ft. lbs.
17. To install, reverse steps 1-12, tightening sprocket bolts to 40 ft. lbs., timing cover bolts and nuts to 30 ft. lbs., and oil pan bolts to 12 ft. lbs.

Piston and Connecting Rod

The letter F, or the notch in the edge of the piston, goes to the front of the engine in all cases. The oil spurt holes on the connecting rod lower ends must face the camshaft. Some 1973, and all 1974 and later, engines don't have these holes. These connecting rods have three dimples on one side of the rod and a single dimple on the connecting rod cap. The dimples must face to the rear on the right bank, and forward on the left.

Lubrication

Oil Pan Removal and Installation

1. Disconnect battery cables.
2. Remove fan shroud and the power steering belt, then tilt the steering pump upward.
3. Remove the fan and pulley.
4. Disconnect engine ground straps. Drain radiator.
5. On A/C cars, remove compressor from brackets and swing aside WITHOUT DISCONNECTING HOSES.
6. Check all wiring, fuel lines and hoses for clearance, and disconnect the thermal feed switch from the left rear cylinder head, on 1973 and later models, as the engine must be raised. Disconnect the radiator hose at the water pump.
7. Jack up car and drain engine oil.
8. Disconnect the steering idler arm from the frame and remove the Pitman arm from the steering box on 1971 and later Grand Prix.
9. Remove exhaust crossover pipe on single-exhaust cars; disconnect manifold flanges on dual-exhaust cars. Wire pipes out of the way to gain working room.
10. Remove flywheel housing cover, starter motor and motor bracket.
11. Attach a hoist to the front of the engine.
12. Support engine on hoist and remove front motor mount bolts and mounts.
13. Loosen rear motor mount at transmission or, better still, remove it entirely and allow extension housing to rest on crossmember.

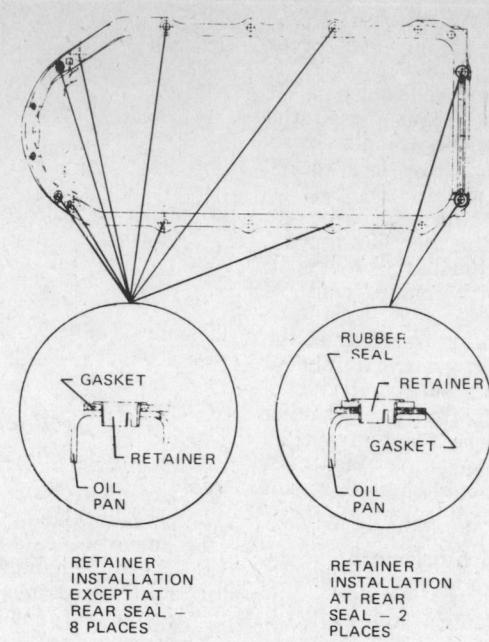

TOP VIEW OF OIL PAN

RETAINER INSTALLATION EXCEPT AT REAR SEAL – 8 PLACES

RETAINER INSTALLATION AT REAR SEAL – 2 PLACES

1972 and later Pontiac-design V8 oil pan gasket installation
(© Pontiac Div., G.M. Corp)

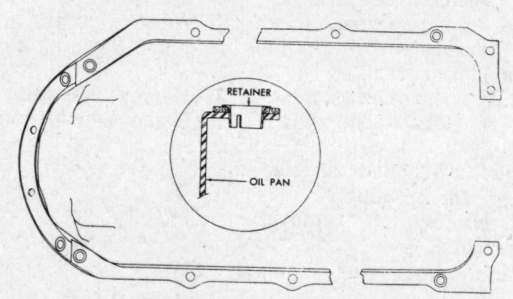

Oil pan gasket retainers
(© Pontiac Div., G.M. Corp)

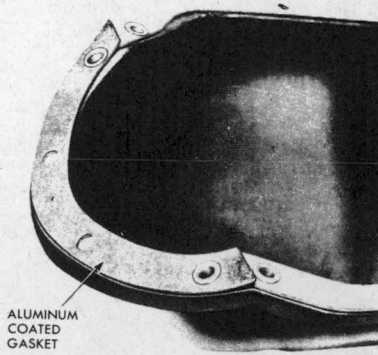

ALUMINUM COATED GASKET

Front oil pan gasket overlapping side gaskets
(© Pontiac Div., G.M. Corp)

14. Remove oil pan bolts, then raise engine straight up about 4½ in. until top of transmission is hitting floor pan. On some models, it also helps to move engine forward about 1½ in.
15. Rotate oil pan forward to clear oil pump, then remove oil pan.
16. Place wood blocks between engine and motor mount brackets for safety.
17. To install, reverse removal procedure. Clean all gasket surfaces thoroughly. Use gasket cement and a new gasket.

Rear Main Bearing Oil Seal Replacement

1. Remove the oil pan, baffle, and oil pump.
2. Remove the rear main bearing cap.
3. Make a seal tool.
4. Insert the tool against one end of the oil seal in the block and drive the seal gently into the groove ¾ in. Repeat on the other end of the seal.
5. Form a new seal in the cap. Cut four pieces ⅜ in. long from this seal.
6. Work two of the pieces into each of the gaps which have been made at the end of the seal in the block. Do not cut off any material to make them fit.

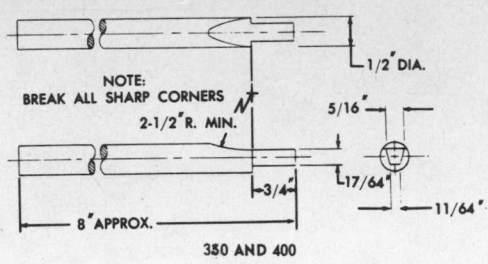

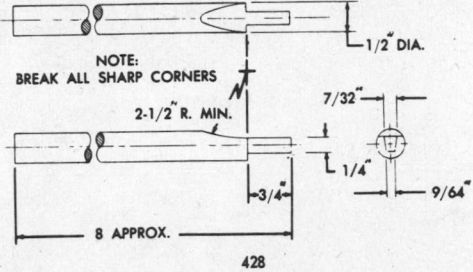

Pontiac V8 upper rear main bearing seal tool—the lower one is for 455, upper for 301, 350, and 400
(© Pontiac Div., G.M. Corp)

7. Form a new seal in the bearing cap.
8. Apply a 1/16 in. bead of sealer from the center of the seal across to the external gasket groove.
9. Reassemble the cap and torque to specifications.

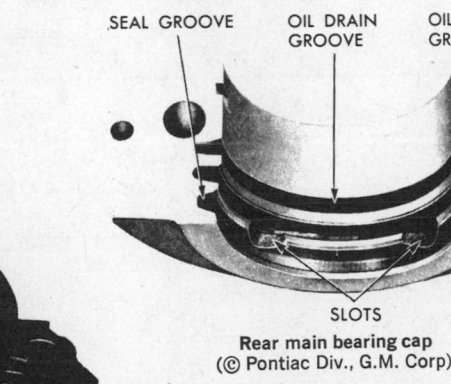

Rear main bearing cap
(© Pontiac Div., G.M. Corp)

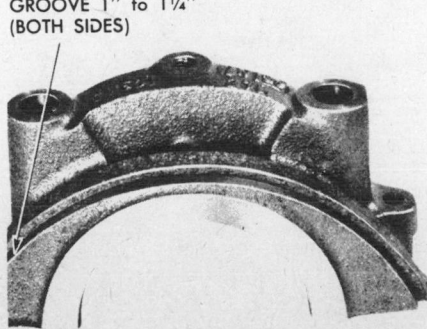

Forming a new crankshaft seal
(© Pontiac Div., G.M. Corp)

Rear main bearing oil seal positioned in bearing cap
(© Pontiac Div., G.M. Corp)

Oil Pump Removal and Installation

1. Remove engine oil pan.
2. Remove pump attaching screws and carefully lower the pump, while removing the pump drive shaft.
3. Reinstall in reverse order.

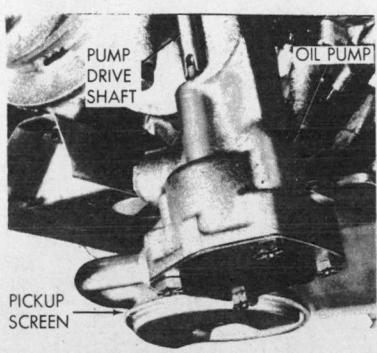

Oil pump and pump drive shaft
(© Pontiac Div., G.M. Corp)

CLUTCH

See the Astre section for clutch procedures. No manual transmissions are available after 1971.

MANUAL TRANSMISSION

In 1970, there were three different transmissions available. They were: a three speed Dearborn unit, standard in all full size Pontiacs except the Grand Prix; a three speed Muncie standard in the Grand Prix, and a four speed Muncie available only in the Grand Prix. The four speed Muncie was available in wide and close ratios in 1970; the code letters were painted on top of the case, DJ for the wide ratio and DP for the close ratio. In 1971, the four speed used in the Grand Prix was only available with a wide ratio, code letters WT.

See the Astre section for manual transmission procedures. No manual transmissions are available after 1971.

Step-by-step repair procedures are covered in the Unit Repair Section.

AUTOMATIC TRANSMISSION

The M-35 two-speed automatic was available with the smaller engines through 1971. The three-speed automatics are the M-38 and M-40 (Turbo Hydra-Matic 350 and 400). The M-38 has a downshift cable between the carburetor throttle linkage and the transmission, while the heavier-duty M-40 has an electrical downshift switch on the accelerator pedal linkage. The M-40 is used exclusively, starting 1972.

Throttle Valve (TV) Linkage Adjustment, M-35 Two-Speed

1. Remove air cleaner.
2. Disconnect accelerator linkage at carburetor.
3. Disconnect return spring and T.V. rod return spring.
4. Pull upper T.V. rod forward until through detent. At same time, open throttle at carburetor to full throttle position. Full throttle must be reached at the same time the ball stud contacts end of slot in upper T.V. rod.
5. If necessary, adjust upper swivel. Tolerance is ± 1/32 in.
6. Reconnect return springs and linkage, then install air cleaner.

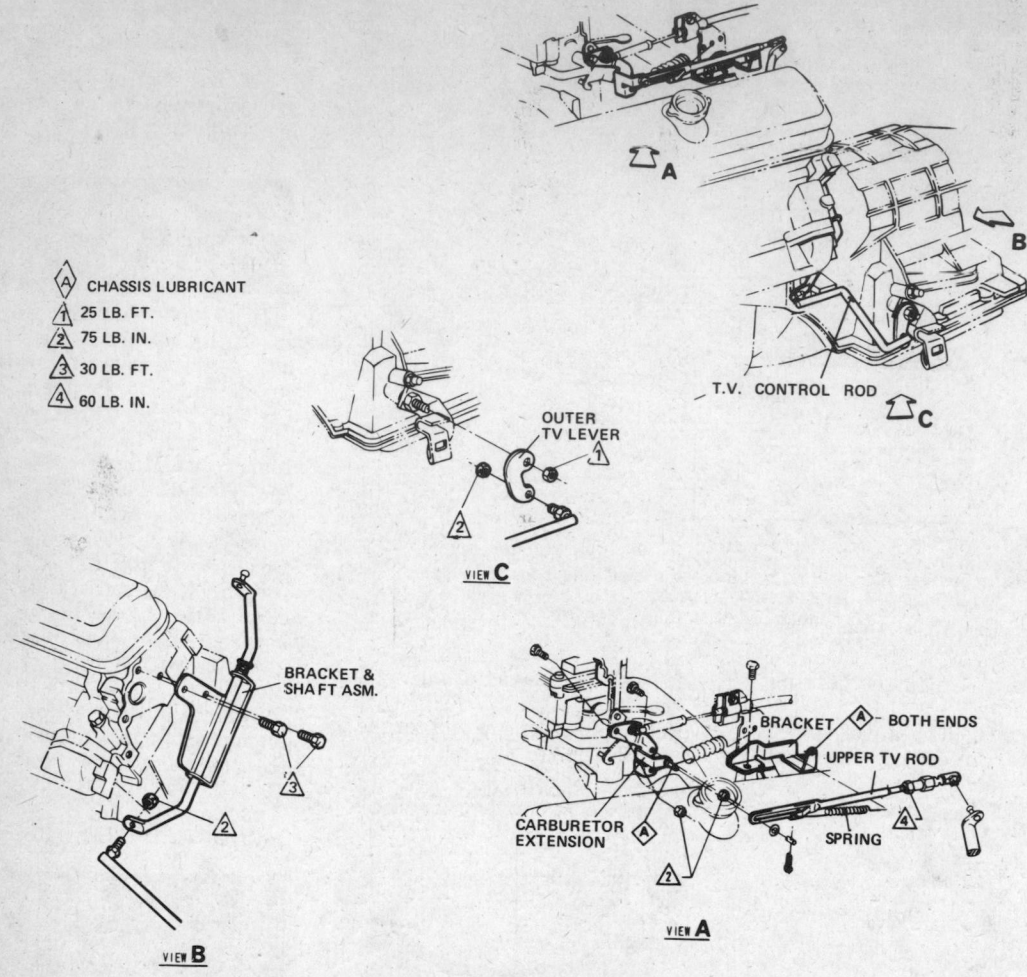

A CHASSIS LUBRICANT
1 25 LB. FT.
2 75 LB. IN.
3 30 LB. FT.
4 60 LB. IN.

Throttle valve linkage adjustment—Catalina with M-35 transmission through 1972
(© Pontiac Div., G.M. Corp)

Shift Linkage Adjustment

Column Shift

1. Loosen screw on adjusting swivel clamp.
2. Place gearshift lever in Park (Neutral starting 1976) and lock ignition.
3. Place transmission shift lever in Park detent (Neutral starting 1976).
4. Push up on gearshift control rod until lash is taken up in steering column lock mechanism, then tighten screw on swivel clamp.

Floorshift

1. Disconnect shift cable from transmission shift lever by removing nut from pin.
2. Adjust column lock (as in Step 4, above).
3. Unlock ignition and rotate transmission shift lever into Neutral (Park starting 1976).
4. Place console lever in Neutral (Park starting 1976) and move against forward stop.
5. Assemble shift cable and pin to transmission shift lever so that

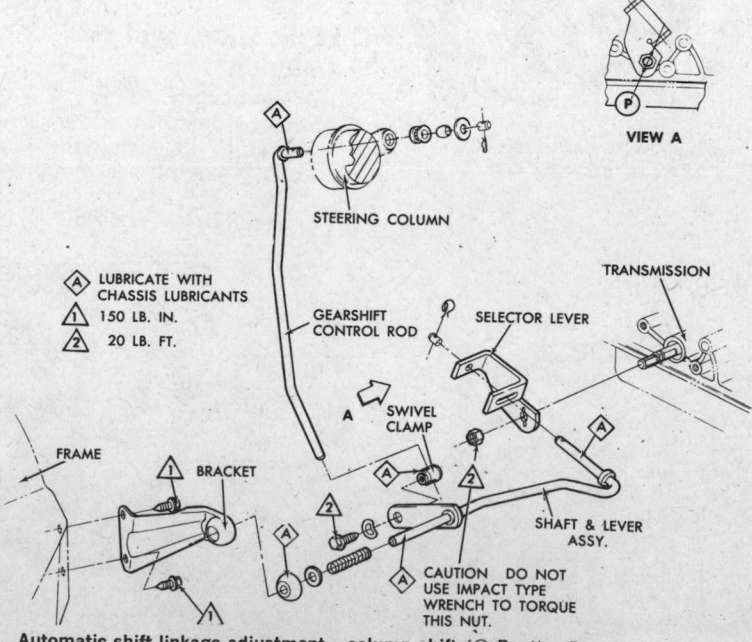

Automatic shift linkage adjustment—column shift (© Pontiac Div., G.M. Corp)

no binding exists, then tighten nut.

Turbo Hydra-Matic 350 Downshift Cable Adjustment

1. With the engine off and the throttle valves closed, release the snap-lock at the carburetor end of the cable.
2. Hold the carburetor in the wide open throttle position.
3. Push the snap-lock back into place.

Low Band Adjustment, Two-Speed (M-35)

1. Place shifter lever in neutral and raise the vehicle.
2. Remove the adjusting screw protecting cap.
3. Loosen the adjusting screw locknut 1/4 turn.

Caution Be sure to hold the adjusting screw locknut ¼ turn loose during the adjusting procedure.

4. Tighten the adjusting screw to 70 in. lbs and then back off exactly four complete turns for a band with 6,000 miles or more of use; three turns for a band with less than 6,000 miles of use.
5. Tighten the locknut, and install the protective cap.

Neutral Safety/Backup Light Switch Adjustment

Through 1971

NOTE: The switch is on the steering column. This procedure applies to switches marked "ADJUST" and "RESET".

Caution After the switch has been adjusted, before starting the engine to test the shifting pattern, make sure the brakes are securely locked. This is necessary because a misadjusted switch will allow the engine to start in any of the forward or reverse gears.

1. Place the shifter lever in Park.
2. Loosen the switch retaining screws. Make sure the switch drive tang is engaged in the shifter tube slot and that it stays engaged during adjustment.
3. Rotate the switch in its slot until it is in the Park position and tighten the screws.
4. After observing the above caution, check the shifter pattern by placing the shifter lever in neutral. If the transmission does not shift into neutral, place the lever back in Park and rotate the switch slightly until the shift pattern is correct.
5. If it is possible to move the shift lever a large distance without having the transmission respond, check for a worn switch drive

tang or bad electrical contacts inside the switch. In either case replace the switch.

1972 and later Floorshift, 1971 and later Column Shift

NOTE: This procedure applies to all switches with an adjusting pin hole in the back.

1. Place the shift lever in Neutral, except for 1971 models which must be placed in Drive. 1972 floorshift models must be in Park.
2. Loosen the switch mounting screws.
3. Move the switch until you can insert a 0.092 in. diameter adjusting pin into the hole in the back of the switch about ⅜ in.
4. Tighten the screws and remove the pin.
5. Step on the brake pedal and check that the engine will start only in Neutral or Park.

Pan Removal and Installation, Fluid and Filter Change

1. Let the engine warm up to normal operating temperature, then raise the car on a lift. On the M-35 transmission, remove the drain

plug and let the fluid drain into a suitable container. On all others, remove the pan attaching bolts and let the fluid drain over the edge of the pan, being careful not to let the hot fluid spill.
2. Remove the pan on the M-35. Discard the pan gasket on all models.
3. The M-35 has a suction screen which should be cleaned and reused. Remove the two retaining bolts, the screen and gasket. Clean and replace them using a new gasket.
4. On all other models, the filter is not reused. When the pan has been removed, remove the filter retaining bolts, filter and gasket (350). On the 400 transmission, the intake pipe is removed along with the transmission and the O ring gasket discarded.
5. Make sure all the old gasket material has been removed, then install the new gasket and filter.
6. Replace the pan and gasket. Add 3 pints of Dexron transmission fluid for the M-35, 3 for the 350, and 7 for the 400.
7. Start the car in Park with the parking brake on and let it idle. Shift through all the indicator

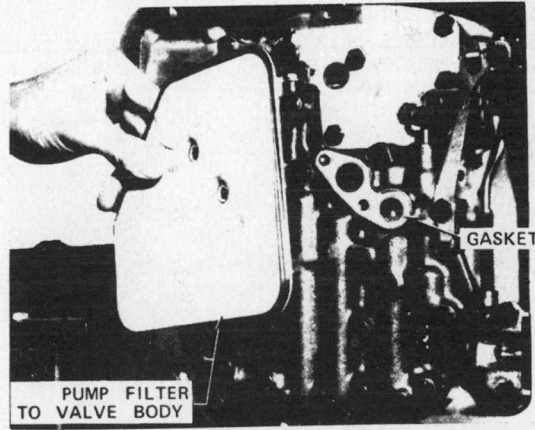

Removing the Turbo Hydra-Matic 350 transmission filter
(© Pontiac Div., G.M. Corp)

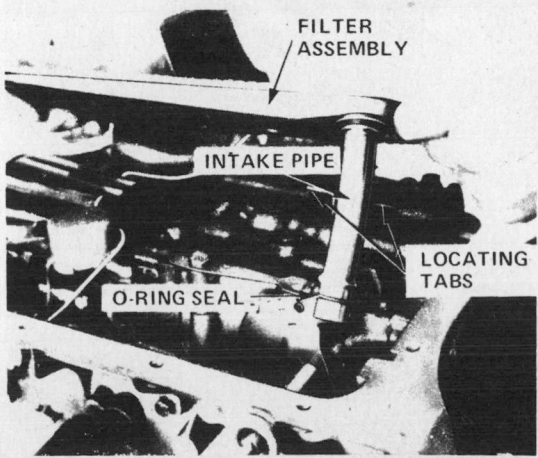

Removing the filter, intake pipe and O ring on Turbo Hydra-Matic 400 transmission
(© Pontiac Div., G.M. Corp)

positions and back to Park. The fluid level should be between the two dimples on the dipstick, about ¼ in. below the ADD mark. Be very cautious not to overfill. Check the level again after the transmission is throughly warm. The level should then be at FULL HOT.

U-JOINTS

Two basic designs are used; one is a typical solid shaft with two joints. Starting 1971, a constant velocity joint is used at the rear on all Pontiac models except the Grand Prix and station wagons.

There are two types of cross-and-bearing U-joints. One type held with a C-shaped lock ring; the other held with a lock plate.

Driveshaft Removal and Installation

1. Mark the driveshaft rear yoke and the differential flange to assure correct alignment upon reassembly.
2. Remove the bolts and straps (or four bolts on double cardan U-joint) from the differential flange. If the bearing cups are loose, tape them together so the needle rollers don't fall out.
3. Remove the driveshaft assembly by first sliding the driveshaft

forward to disengage the differential flange, then sliding the shaft downward and rearward to disengage the front splined yoke from the transmission output shaft.

4. Installation is the reversal of removal. Be sure to align the match mark made before disassembly.

Front and Single Rear U-Joint Replacement

Removal

1. Remove the driveshaft.
   NOTE: The universal may have snap-rings that are used to retain the bearing cups in the yokes. These snap-rings may be located at the outside of each yoke or in a groove at the base or open end of each bearing cap. In both cases, there are four snap-rings for each universal joint and they must be removed before proceeding further.
2. Support the splined yoke (front universal) or the journal (rear universal) in such a manner that will allow the fixed yoke on the driveshaft to be moved. Support the opposite end so that the driveshaft will be in a horizontal position.
3. Using a piece of pipe or similar tool with a large enough diameter, apply force to the fixed yoke until the bearing is almost completely pushed out of the yoke

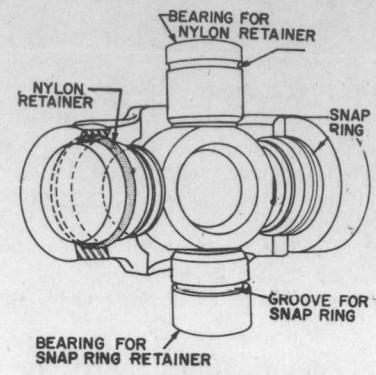

U-joint locking methods
(© Pontiac Div., G.M. Corp)

and into the pipe. Remove the bearing completely by inserting a spacer between the seal and the bearing cup and finish pressing the bearing out of its yoke, or by tapping around the circumference of the exposed portion of the bearing with a punch and small hammer.

NOTE: The plastic which retains factory-installed bearings will be sheared when the bearing cup is pressed out. Be sure to remove the remains of the plastic retainer from the ears of the yoke. It is easier to remove the remains if a small pin or punch is first driven through the injection holes in the yoke. Failure to remove all of the plastic may prevent the bearing cups from being pressed into place and the bearing retainers from being properly seated.

4. Remove the rest of the bearings following the same procedure.

Installation

1. Install a bearing ¼ of the way into one side of the splined yoke (front universal) or fixed yoke (rear universal).
2. Insert the journal into the yoke so that an arm of the journal seats into the bearing.
3. Press the bearing in the remaining distance and snap the bearing retainer into place.

Installing snap-ring retainer
(© Pontiac Div., G.M. Corp)

4. Install the opposite bearing. Do not allow the bearing rollers to jam. Continually check for free movement of the journal in the bearings as they are pressed into the yoke.

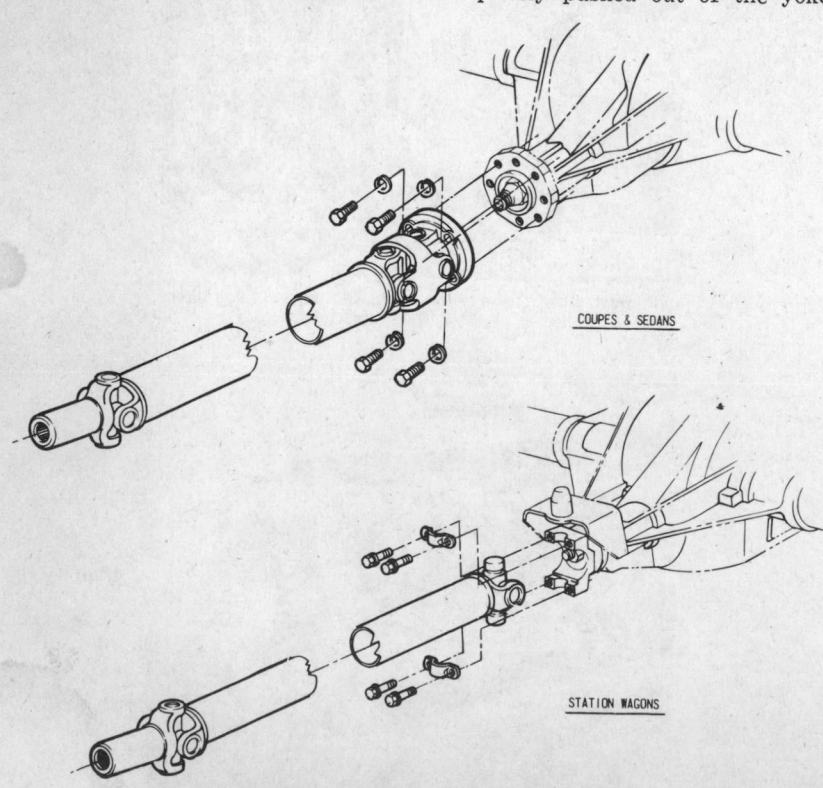

COUPES & SEDANS

STATION WAGONS

1971 and later Pontiac U-joint and driveshaft construction.
Grand Prix is similar to station wagon
(© Pontiac Div., G.M. Corp)

5. Install the rest of the bearings in the same manner.

Constant-Velocity Rear U-Joint Replacement

Removal

1. Using a punch, mark the link yoke and the adjoining yokes before disassembly to ensure proper reassembly and driveshaft balance.

NOTE: It is easier to remove the universal joint bearings from the flange yoke first. The first pair of flange yoke universal joint bearings to be removed is the pair in the link yoke.

2. With the driveshaft in a horizontal position, solidly support the link yoke (a 1 7/8 in. pipe will do).

3. Apply force to the bearing cup on the opposite side with a 1⅛ in. pipe or a socket the size of the bearing cup. Use a vise or press to apply force. Force the cup inward as far as possible.

NOTE: In the absence of a press, a heavy vise may be used, but make sure that the universal to be removed is at a right angle to the jaws of the vise. Do not cock the bearing cups in their bores.

4. Remove the pieces of pipe and complete the removal of the protruding bearing cup by tapping around the circumference of the exposed portion of the bearing with a small hammer.

5. Reverse the position of the pieces of pipe and apply force to the exposed journal end. This will force the other bearing cup out of its bore and allow removal of the flange.

NOTE: There is a ball joint located between the two universals. The ball portion of this joint is on the inner end of the flange yoke. Prior to 1973, the ball was not replaceable. Beginning 1973, the ball, as well as the ball seat parts, is replaceable. Care must be taken not to damage the ball. The ball portion of this joint is on the driveshaft. To remove the seat, pry the seal out with a screwdriver.

6. To remove the journal from the flange, use steps two through five.

7. Remove the universal joint bearings from the driveshaft using the steps from two through five. The first pair of bearing caps that should be removed is the pair in the link yoke.

Installation

1. Examine the ball stud seat and ball stud for scores or wear. Worn seats can be replaced with a kit. A worn ball, however, requires the replacement of the entire shaft yoke and flange assembly. Clean the ball seat cavity and fill it with grease. Install the spring, washer, ball seats, and spacer, if removed.

2. Install the universal joints opposite the order in which they were disassembled.

3. Install a bearing ¼ of the way into one side of the yoke.

4. Insert the journal into the yoke so that an arm of the journal seats into the bearing.

5. Press the bearing in the remaining distance and install its snapring.

6. Install the opposite bearing. Do not allow the bearing rollers to jam. Continually check for free movement of the journal in the bearings as they are pressed into the yoke.

7. Install the rest of the bearings in the same manner.

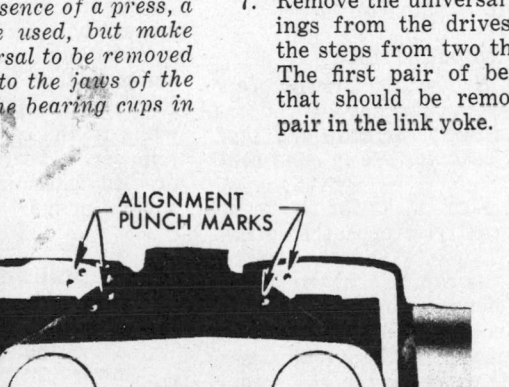

Match marks for double cardan joint
(© Pontiac Div., G.M. Corp)

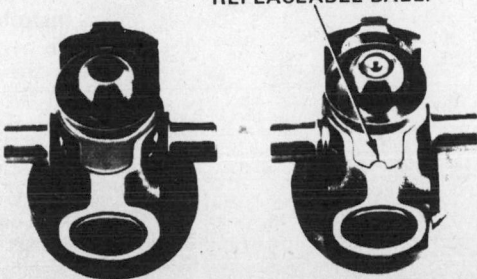

THIS NOTCH IDENTIFIES DRIVE SHAFT WITH REPLACEABLE BALL.

SOLID BALL   REPLACEABLE BALL

Solid and replaceable U-joint balls
(© Pontiac Div., G.M. Corp)

Journal installation
(© Pontiac Div., G.M. Corp)

REAR AXLE

For axle shaft, bearing and seal removal and installation procedures, refer to the Astre section.

JACKING, HOISTING

Jack car at front spring seats of lower control arms and, at rear, at axle housing.

When using frame lift, use side rails at points shown on diagram. Be sure that adapters are properly supporting these designated areas.

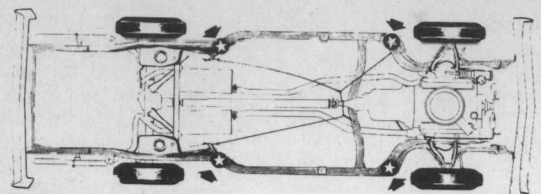

Hoist contact lifting points

FRONT SUSPENSION

Shock Absorber Replacement

1. Remove the nut, retainer and grommet which attach the upper end of the shock absorber to the frame bracket.

NOTE: The shock absorber stud may turn while loosening the nut. If necessary, use pliers or a wrench to hold the top of the stud while removing the nut. Do not grasp the shaft as any marks on the shaft will cause rapid failure of the shock.

2. Raise the car to allow removal of the shock down through the lower control arm.
3. Remove the two shock absorber lower attaching screws and remove the shock through the lower control arm.
4. Reverse the above steps to install. Make sure all grommets and washers are in the correct position. Tighten the stud nut to 10 ft lbs.

Ball Joint Inspection

Through 1972

NOTE: Before performing this inspection, make sure the wheel bearings are adjusted correctly and that the A-arm bushings are in good condition.

1. Jack the car up under the front lower control arm at the spring seat.
2. Raise the car until there is 1-2 in. of clearance under the wheel.
3. Insert a bar under the wheel and pry upward. If the wheel raises more than 1/8 in. the ball joints are worn. Determine if the upper or lower ball joint is worn by visual inspection while prying on the wheel.

NOTE: Due to the distribution of forces in the suspension, the lower ball joint is usually the defective joint.

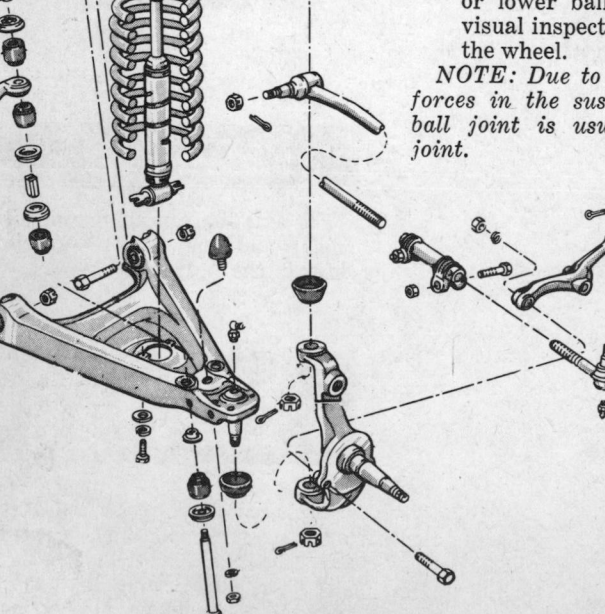

Typical front suspension
(© Pontiac Div., G.M. Corp)

1973 and later

Beginning 1973, lower ball joints contain a visual wear indicator. The lower ball joint grease plug screws into the wear indicator which protrudes from the bottom of the ball joint housing. As long as the wear indicator extends out of the ball joint housing, the ball joint is not worn. If the tip of the wear indicator is parallel with, or recessed into the ball joint housing, the ball joint is defective.

Ball Joint Replacement

Ball joints are riveted to the control arms on 1970 Pontiacs.

The service joint comes with specially hardened bolts and nuts that replace the rivets. It is extremely important that only these special fasteners are installed—standard bolts are not strong enough for this application. Tighten service bolts to 9 ft. lbs. for upper joints, 16 ft. lbs. for lower joints.

All 1971 and later Pontiac and all Grand Prix models have their lower ball joints pressed into the control arms. The entire control arm can be removed and the joint pressed out using a large bench vise, or the old joint can be pressed from the arm while in the car using a screw-type remover. The new joint must be pressed into place, in any case, to avoid damage.

Upper Ball Joint Replacement

Removal

1. Raise the car and support the lower control arm.
2. Remove the ball joint stud nut and cotter pin. Using a ball joint removing tool, break the taper holding the steering knuckle to the ball joint stud and move the steering knuckle out of the way.
3. Remove the rivets securing the ball joint to the control arm by chiseling or drilling the rivet heads and drive out the rivets with a punch.
4. Remove the ball joint from the control arm.

Installation

1. Install the new ball joint assembly using the special bolts supplied with the ball joint. Torque to 9 ft lbs.
2. Insert the ball stud in the steering knuckle and tighten the nut to 40 ft lbs. (50 ft lbs., 1975 and later). Insert a new cotter pin.
3. Install the wheel and tire.
4. Lower the car.

NOTE: It may be necessary to adjust the wheel alignment after installing a new ball joint.

Lower Ball Joint Replacement, 1970 Except Grand Prix

Removal

NOTE: Jack the car securely under the lower control arm.

1. Remove the hub and backing plate assembly or, if equipped with disc brakes, hub and brake caliper.
2. Remove the ball joint stud from the steering knuckle using a ball joint removal tool.
3. Remove the ball joint assembly from the lower control arm by chiseling or drilling the rivet heads and drive out the rivets with a punch.

Installation

1. Installation is the same as the upper ball joint installation procedures.

1971 and Later, All Grand Prix

Removal

1. Raise the car under the lower control arm.
2. Remove the hub and backing plate or, if equipped with disc brakes, the rotor and caliper assembly, remove the stud nut and cotter pin.
3. Remove the ball joint stud from the steering knuckle using a ball joint removal tool.
4. Pry the ball joint seal and retainer off the joint.
5. Press the ball joint out of the lower control arm. This is a very heavy press fit.

Installation

1. Press, do not hammer, a new ball joint into place and reverse steps 1 to 4 to install.

Spring Removal and Installation

1. Jack up car and support on jack stands at frame side rails.
2. Remove shock absorber.
3. Disconnect stabilizer bar at lower control arm.
4. Support lower control arm with a hydraulic floor jack, then remove the two inner control arm to front crossmember bolts.
5. Carefully lower the control arm, allowing the spring to relax.
6. Reach in and remove spring.
7. To install, reverse removal procedure. Tighten pivot bolts to 110 ft. lbs., nuts to 80 ft. lbs. (1972-74—bolts to 120 ft lbs; nuts to 90 ft lbs) (1975 and later, bolts to 105 ft lbs; nuts to 95 ft lbs.) with car resting on wheels.

Wheel Bearing Adjustment

1. Lift the wheel off the ground by jacking under the lower control arm.
2. Remove the dust cap from the hub.
3. Remove the cotter pin and discard.
4. Snug up the spindle nut to seat the bearings (12 ft. lbs.). Then back off the nut 1/4-1/2 turn.
5. Retighten the nut by hand until it is finger-tight.
6. Loosen the nut until the nearest hole in the spindle lines up with a slot in the spindle nut, and insert a new cotter pin. When the bearing is properly adjusted there will be 0.001-0.005 in. endplay.

NOTE: Under no circumstances is the final bearing nut adjustment to be even finger-tight.

7. Replace the dust cover and lower the car.

REAR SUSPENSION

Shock Absorber Replacement

1. Raise the car at the axle housing. Remove the wheel on station wagons.
2. Remove the nut, retainer, and grommet, or nut, and lock washer, which attach the lower end of the shock absorber to its mounting.
3. Remove the two shock absorber

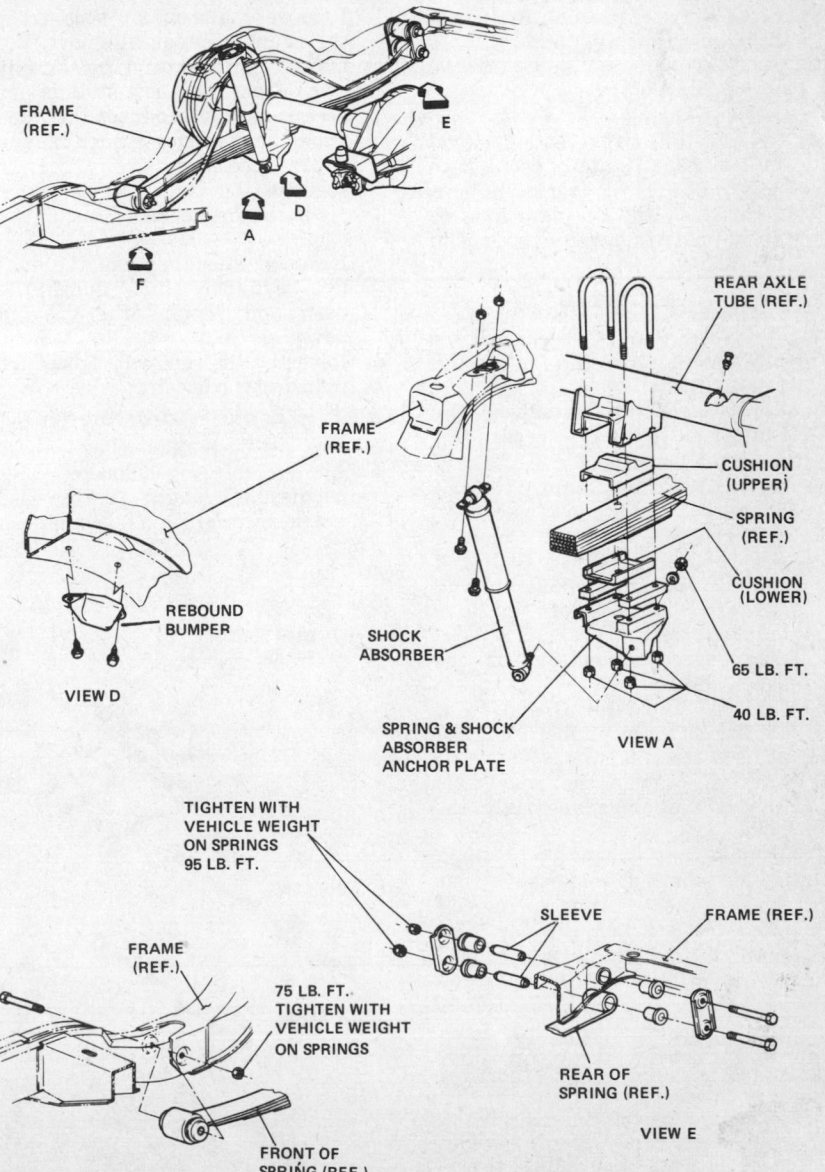

FRAME (REF.)

E

D

A

F

FRAME (REF.)

REBOUND BUMPER

VIEW D

SHOCK ABSORBER

SPRING & SHOCK ABSORBER ANCHOR PLATE

REAR AXLE TUBE (REF.)

CUSHION (UPPER)

SPRING (REF.)

CUSHION (LOWER)

65 LB. FT.

40 LB. FT.

VIEW A

TIGHTEN WITH VEHICLE WEIGHT ON SPRINGS 95 LB. FT.

SLEEVE

FRAME (REF.)

FRAME (REF.)

75 LB. FT. TIGHTEN WITH VEHICLE WEIGHT ON SPRINGS

FRONT OF SPRING (REF.)

VIEW F

REAR OF SPRING (REF.)

VIEW E

1971-76 Pontiac station wagon leaf spring rear suspension
(© Pontiac Div., G.M. Corp)

upper attaching screws and remove the shock absorber.

4. Reverse the removal procedures to install.

Leaf Spring Replacement, 1971-76 Station Wagon

1. Jack up car at axle housing. Make sure you don't crush exhaust pipe.
2. Support car at both frame side rails, using axle stands.
3. Remove nut and lockwasher from lower shock stud.
4. Move shock out of the way.
5. Remove spring anchor plate nuts, then remove anchor plate and cushion.
6. Jack axle housing up and remove upper cushion.
7. Loosen upper and lower spring shackle nuts.
8. Loosen front spring eye bolt.
9. Remove front eye bolt and carefully lower spring.
10. Support spring and remove lower shackle pin.
11. Remove spring.
12. To install, reverse removal procedure. Tighten front eye bolt to 80 ft. lbs., shackle nuts to 95 ft. lbs., anchor plate nuts to 40 ft. lbs., and lower shock nut to 65 ft. lbs.

Coil Spring Replacement

1. Raise the rear of the car. Place jackstands under the frame side rails.
2. Remove the clip attaching the brake hose to the rear crossmember on Pontiacs. On 1972 and later Grand Prix, remove the clip and disconnect the brake hose.
3. Support the rear axle housing with a floor jack. On 1973 and later Grand Prix, make sure to support the nose of the axle housing.
4. Disconnect the bottom of the shock absorbers.
5. On 1973 and later Grand Prix, disconnect the upper control arms at the axle.
6. Carefully lower the rear axle until the springs are fully extended.
7. Remove the springs.
8. On installation, make sure that the end of the bottom spring coil is to the rear of the car. The brake system will have to be bled of air on 1973 and later Grand Prix.

BRAKES

Information on brake adjustment, lining replacement, bleeding procedure, master and wheel cylinder overhaul can be found in the Unit Repair Section.

C756

Master Cylinder Removal and Installation

The master cylinder is located in the engine compartment just above the steering column.

From under the dash, disconnect the brake pedal from the master cylinder on Bendix power brakes and non-power brakes. Delco power booster pushrods are not connected to the master cylinder. From under the hood, disconnect the hydraulic lines and the stoplight wire.

Remove the bolts which hold the master cylinder to the cowl panel and lift off the master cylinder.

The unit is installed in reverse order of removal. Bleed the brakes after installation.

Power Brake Booster Removal and Installation

1. Remove the vacuum hose from the front housing. Remove the master cylinder and position it away from the booster. It is not necessary to disconnect the lines from the master cylinder if it is not to be repaired.
2. Remove the clevis pin retainer from the brake pedal inside the car.
3. Remove the nuts from the vacuum cylinder studs under the dash and remove the vacuum power section.
4. Reverse the removal procedure to install the booster.

Parking Brake Adjustment

1. Jack up both rear wheels.
2. Apply parking brake, 5-7 notches through 1970, 4-8 notches for 1971-72, 8 notches for 1973-74 models, from full release. 1975 and later models should be adjusted 3 notches from full release, except the station wagons which should be 6 notches.
3. Loosen equalizer locknut. Adjust until the rear wheels can be rotated backward but not forward, using two hands.
4. Tighten the locknut.
5. Fully release the parking brake and rotate rear wheels; no drag should be felt in either direction.

STEERING

Tie-Rod End Replacement

1. Loosen the tie-rod adjuster sleeve clamp nuts.
2. Remove the tie-rod stud nut cotter pin and nut.
3. Remove the tie-rod stud from the steering arm or intermediate rod. This is a taper fit. Removal is accomplished by using a ball joint removal tool.
4. Unthread the tie rod from the adjuster sleeve. Outer tie rods have right-hand threads and inner tie rods have left-hand threads. Count the number of turns the tie rod must be rotated to remove it from the adjusting sleeve. This will allow a reasonably accurate toe-in realignment upon reassembly.
5. Reverse the removal procedures to install. Clean rust and dirt from the threads. Check the alignment and adjust if necessary.

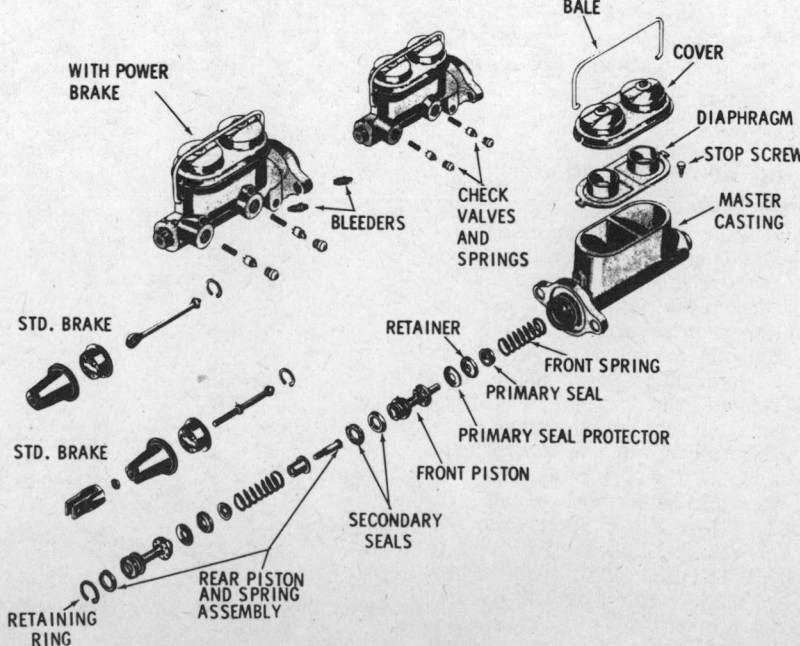

Dual type master cylinder (Delco) (© Pontiac Div., G.M. Corp)

Power Steering Pump Removal and Installation

1. Disconnect the hoses at the pump. Plug the lines and the pump to prevent loss of fluid.
2. Remove the drive pulley attaching nut.
3. Loosen the bracket-to-pump mounting bolts and remove the drive belt.
4. Slide the pulley from the shaft. Do not hammer on the pulley.
5. Remove the bracket-to-pump mounting bolts and remove the pump.
6. Reverse the removal steps to install.

Steering Wheel Removal and Installation

1. On deluxe models, remove the screws holding the trim cover to the wheel or, if equipped with a horn button, lift the button off.
2. Remove the steering wheel snapring and nut from the steering shaft.
3. Position the wheels in the straight-ahead position and make match marks on the steering shaft and steering wheel.
4. Using a puller, remove the steering wheel.

Caution Don't pound on the steering wheel or the steering shaft. The collapsible column could be damaged enough to require replacement.

5. Disconnect the horn wire insulator by rotating the insulator counterclockwise to unlock position and then pull up.
6. Reverse the removal procedures to install. Make sure the match marks are lined up when installing the wheel. Tighten the nut to 30 ft lbs.

Turn Signal Switch Replacement

1. Remove the steering wheel.
2. Loosen the three cover screws and lift cover off the shaft. Do not remove the screws completely.
3. Depress the lockplate downward and remove the snap-ring.
4. Slide the upper bearing spring and turn signal cam off the shaft. Remove the thrust washer.
5. Remove the turn signal lever screw and lever.
6. Push the hazard warning switch in and remove the knob.
7. Lower the steering column (on models through 1974) and disconnect the switch wiring.

Caution The steering column must be supported at all times to prevent damage.

8. Remove the turn signal switch mounting screws and pull the

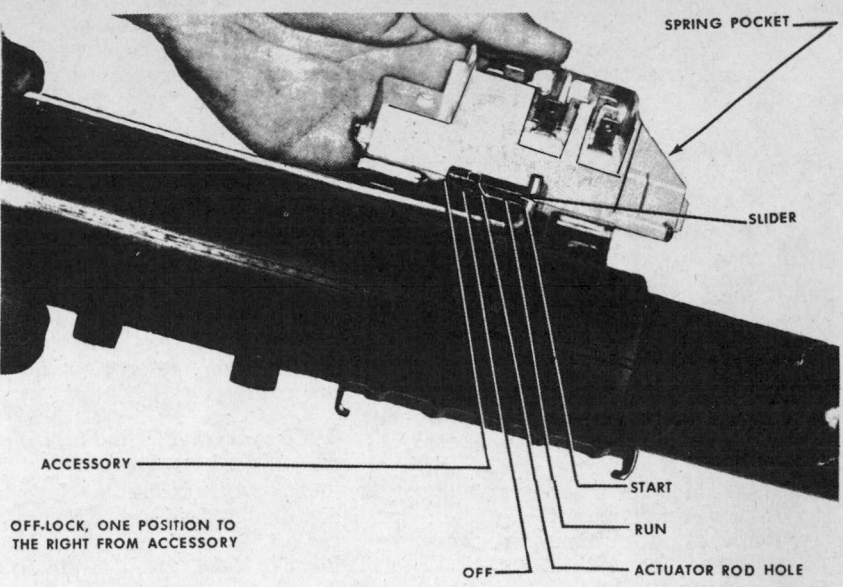

ACCESSORY

OFF-LOCK, ONE POSITION TO THE RIGHT FROM ACCESSORY

SPRING POCKET

SLIDER

START

RUN

ACTUATOR ROD HOLE

OFF

Installing ignition switch (© Pontiac Div., G.M. Corp)

switch straight up with the wire protector and remove it from the housing.

9. Reverse the removal procedures to install.

Ignition Switch Replacement

1. Disconnect battery.
2. Loosen toe pan screws on steering column.
3. Remove column to instrument panel trim plates and attaching nuts.
4. Lower column and disconnect switch wire connectors.

Caution The steering column must be supported at all times to prevent damage.

5. Remove switch attaching screws and remove switch.
6. To replace move key lock to LOCK position.
7. Move actuator rod hole in switch to LOCK position.
8. Install switch with rod in hole.
9. Position and reassemble steering column in reverse of disassembly procedure.

Switch Adjustment—Standard Column

1. Place switch in OFF position.
2. Position switch on column, then move slider to extreme left (toward wheel).
3. Move slider back two positions to the right of ACCESSORY position.
4. Place key in any run position and shift transmission into any position but Park for automatics. Put it in Reverse for manual.
5. Position lock toward ACCESSORY with a light finger pressure and secure switch.

Switch Adjustment—Tilt Column

1. Place key in ACCESSORY position; leave key in lock.
2. Loosen switch mounting screws.
3. Push switch upward toward wheel to make certain it is in ACCESSORY detent.
4. Hold key in full counter clockwise ACCESSORY position and tighten switch mounting screws.
5. Switch is properly adjusted if: it will go into ACCESSORY position, the key can be removed when in lock, and switch will go into START position.

Lock Cylinder Replacement

1. Remove steering wheel.
2. Pull turn signal switch up far enough to allow access to spring latch slot.
3. Place key in RUN position, insert a thin screwdriver into the slot next to the switch mounting screw boss and depress spring latch.

NOTE: There is a casting flash over this slot if the lock has not been removed before. It is sometimes necessary to use substantial force to remove it. Be careful not to damage anything beneath the flash when penetrating the slot.

4. Remove lock from housing.
5. To install, first hold lock cylinder sleeve and rotate knob clockwise against stop.

Caution If lock cylinder is forced beyond its normal latched position, complete disassembly of upper bearing assembly will be necessary to free it.

6. Lay a 1/16 in. drill on housing surface next to housing bore. This isn't necessary for 1975 and later models.

7. Insert cylinder into housing bore, aligning keyway, and push in to abutment.
8. Rotate knob counterclockwise, pushing in slightly, until cylinder mates with sector.
9. Push in until spring latch pops into groove, then remove drill.

INSTRUMENT PANEL

Headlight Switch Replacement

1. Disconnect the battery. Pull the knob all the way out. From under dash depress button on switch and remove knob and shaft.
2. Remove retaining nut.
3. Remove wire connector from switch and remove switch.
4. Reverse procedure to install.

WINDSHIELD WIPERS

Motor Removal and Installation

1. Disconnect electrical and hose connections at wiper.
2. Disconnect wiper crank from wiper linkage, through cowl opening.
3. Remove wiper motor mounting screws, then remove the motor from the firewall.
4. Install by reversing removal procedure. Motor must be in park position.

RADIO

Removal and Installation

1970

1. Disconnect battery.
2. Remove lower air conditioning duct if equipped.
3. Remove two radio control knobs and hex nuts.
4. Remove ash tray and bracket.
5. Remove upper air conditioning duct, if so equipped.
6. Disconnect all radio connections.
7. Remove screws holding radio brace to lower edge of instrument panel and remove radio.
8. Reverse procedure to install.

1971-76 Pontiac

1. Disconnect battery, then remove radio knobs and hex nuts.
2. Remove upper and lower instrument panel trim plates and lower front radio bracket.
3. Remove glove box and discon-

nect radio connections.
4. Loosen side brace screw and slide radio toward front seat.
5. To install, reverse removal procedure.

1971-72 Grand Prix

1. Disconnect battery and remove lower A/C duct.
2. Remove control knobs and hex nuts, then remove support bracket bolt.
3. Disconnect electrical leads and remove radio.
4. To install, reverse removal procedure.

1973 and Later Grand Prix

1. Disconnect the battery.
2. Remove the knobs, bezels, and right-hand hex nut from the radio.
3. Remove the four retaining screws and the radio trim plate.
4. Remove the two side (one front beginning 1974) retaining screws and the radio mounting bracket retaining screw (below radio).
5. Remove radio and bracket as an assembly; disconnect radio connections and antenna lead-in while radio is pulled out.
6. Reverse the above steps to install.

HEATER

Cars Without A/C

Pontiac Through 1976

Blower Motor Removal and Installation

1. Jack up front of car and remove right front wheel.
2. Cut access hole along stamped outline on right fender skirt, using an air chisel.
3. Disconnect blower power wire.
4. Remove blower.
5. To install, reverse removal procedure, covering access hole with a metal plate secured with sealer and sheet metal screws.

Heater Core Removal and Installation

1. Drain radiator.
2. Disconnect heater hoses at air inlet assembly.
NOTE: the water pump hose goes to right-hand heater core pipe, the other hose (from rear of right cylinder head) goes to the left-hand heater core pipe.
3. Remove nuts from core studs on firewall (under hood). Remove the glove compartment.
4. From inside the car, remove the defroster nozzle retaining screw from the heater case and pull the

heater assembly from the firewall.
5. Disconnect control cables, vacuum hoses and wires, then remove heater assembly.
6. Remove the core.
7. To install, reverse removal procedure, making sure core is properly sealed during installation.

Grand Prix

Blower Motor Removal and Installation

1. Disconnect power wire.
2. Remove motor retaining screws.
3. Remove motor.
4. To install, reverse removal procedure.

Heater Core Removal and Installation

Same as 1970-76 Pontiac.

Cars With A/C

Grand Prix

Blower Motor Removal and Installation

This procedure is the same as for cars without air conditioning.

Blower Motor Removal and Installation, 1973 Grand Prix w/o V.I.R.

On some 1973 Grand Prix models without the V.I.R. (Valves In Receiver) system, removal and replacement of the blower motor may be hindered by the position of the POA (evaporator pressure regulator valve) valve-to-compressor tube. If this tube is positioned so that the blower motor cannot be removed:

1. Disconnect the blower motor feed wire and cooling tube.
2. Remove the six blower retaining screws.
3. Loosen the fitting on the POA valve-to-compressor tube at the POA valve just enough to allow the tube to be turned (approx. $\frac{1}{4}$ to $\frac{1}{2}$ turn).

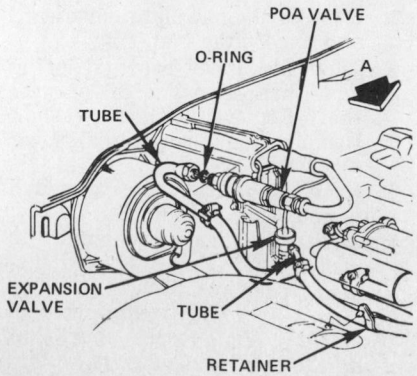

POA valve location
(© Pontiac Div., G.M. Corp)

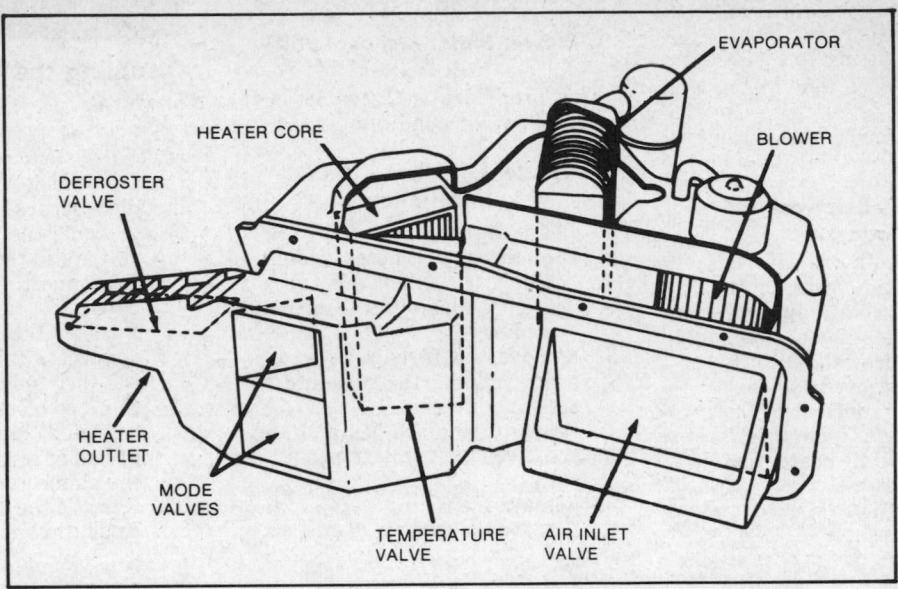

Module for A/C cars.

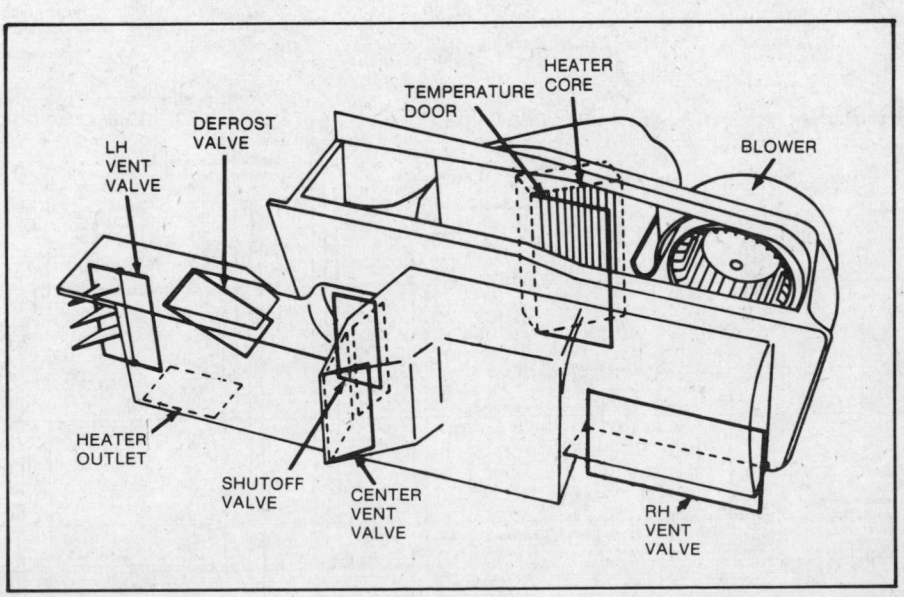

Module for non-A/C cars.

Full size 1977 Pontiacs use a new modular heater/air conditioning system
to make service easier (© Pontiac Div., G.M. Corp.)

Caution This procedure should be done only by a trained air-conditioning specialist. Escaping refrigerant (Freon) could cause severe injury, even blindness.

4. Reposition the lower portion of the tube to allow clearance when removing the blower motor. Retighten the fitting to 20-33 ft lb.
5. Remove the blower motor and impeller.
6. To install, reverse the removal procedure.

Heater Core Removal and Installation

1. Drain the radiator.
2. Disconnect the heater hoses.
3. Remove the retaining nuts from the core case studs on the engine side of the firewall.
4. Remove the glove box.
5. Remove the defroster duct retaining screw from the heater case and pull the heater assembly from the firewall.
6. Disconnect the heater control cables and wires.

7. Remove the core tube seal and core assembly retaining strips and remove the core.
8. Reverse the above steps to install.

Pontiac Through 1976

Blower Motor Removal and Installation

This procedure is the same as for cars without air conditioning.

Heater Core Removal and Installation

1. Drain the coolant.
2. Disconnect the hoses from the heater core. Plug the tubes to prevent damage to the carpeting on removal.
3. Remove the three nuts and one screw holding the core and case assembly in place.
4. Remove the glove box and upper and lower instrument panel trim plates.
5. Remove the radio.
6. Remove the cold air duct.

7. Remove the heater outlet duct.
8. Remove the screw holding the defroster duct to the heater case.

SEAT BELTS

Disabling the Interlock System

Since the requirement for the interlock system was dropped during the 1975 model year, those systems installed on cars built earlier may now be legally disabled. The seat belt warning light is still required.

1. Disconnect the negative battery cable.
2. Locate the interlock harness connector under the left side of the instrument panel on or near the fuse block.
3. Cut and tape the ends of the green wire on the body side of the connector.
4. Remove the buzzer from the fuse block or connector.

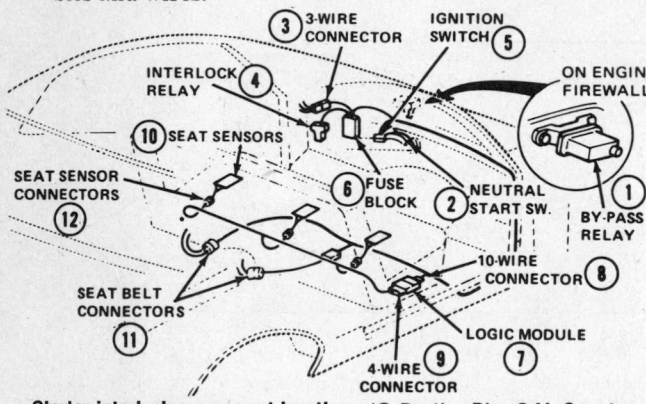

Starter interlock component locations (© Pontiac Div., G.M. Corp.)

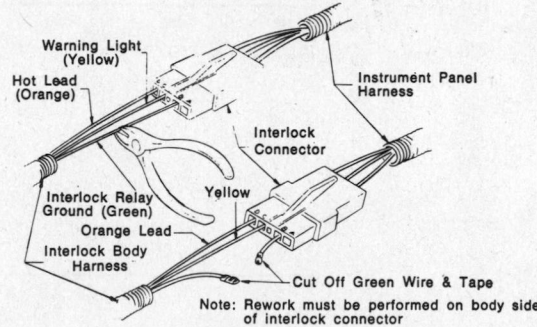

Disabling the seat belt interlock system (© Pontiac Div., G.M. Corp)

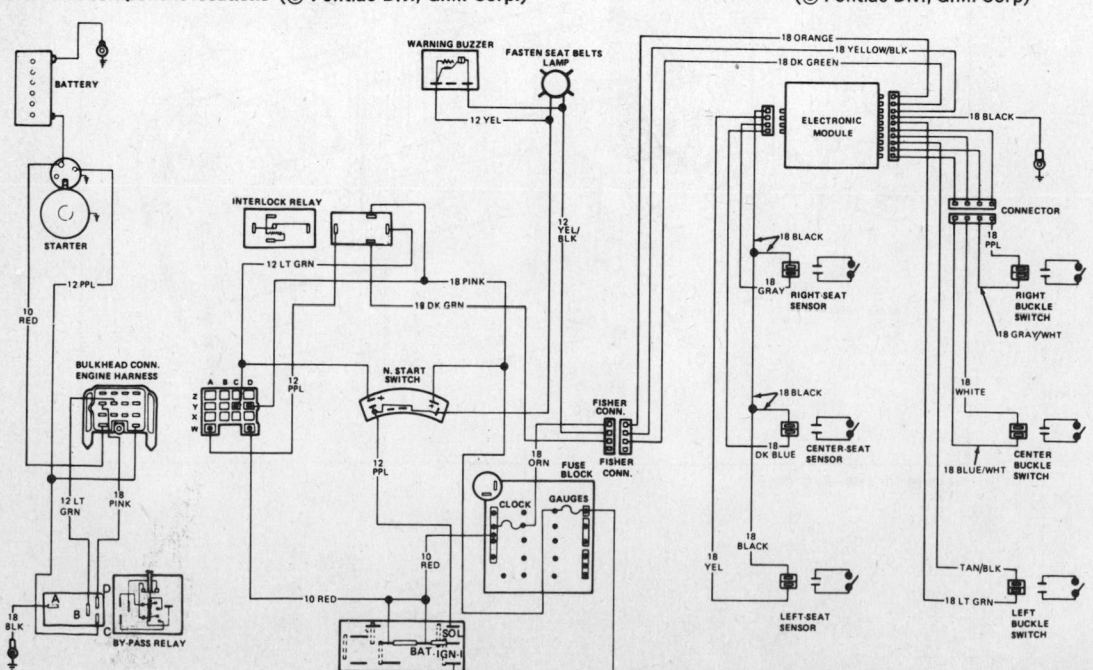

Seat belt/starter interlock schematic (© Pontiac Div., G.M. Corp)

Unit Repair Section

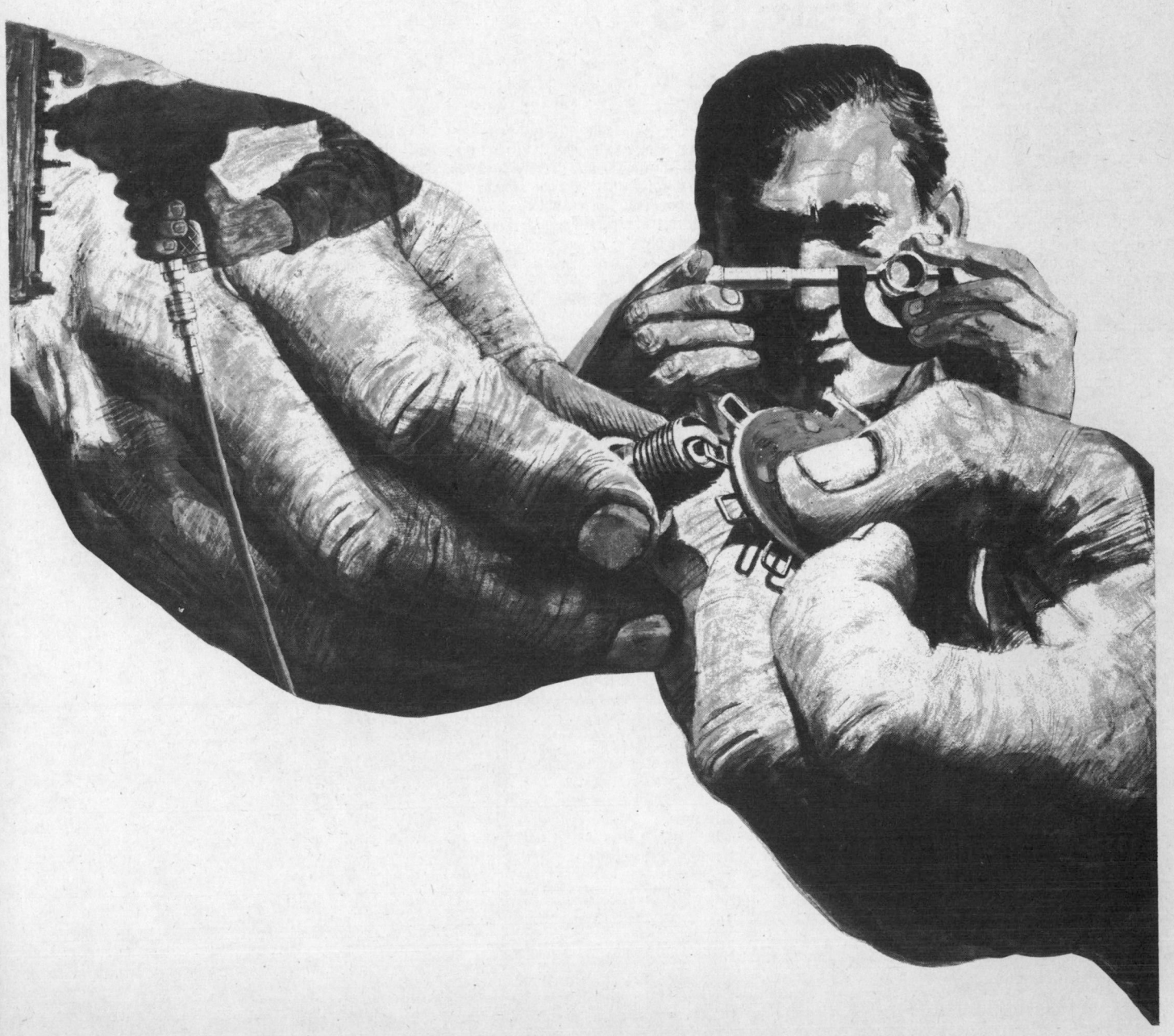

INDEX

Charging and Starting Systems

Testing the Battery **U3**
Selection U3
Replacing U3
Preparation U3
Troubles—Causes and Corrections U3
Specific gravity test—hydrometer U4
Testing polarity U4
Testing Delco 'sealed top" battery U4
Ohmmeter U5
Ammeter U5
Voltmeter U5
Boost Charging Rates U5

Testing the Starting Motor **U5**
Testing the starter circuit U5
Cranking voltage U5
Amperage draw U5
Voltage drop—grounded side U6
Voltage drop-battery side U7

Starter Motor and System Service **U7**
Diagnosis U7
Magnetic switches U7
Solenoids without relays U7
Solenoids with separate relays U7

Solenoids with Built-in relays U8
Neutral Safety switches U8
Troubleshooting neutral Safety switches .. U8
Neutral safety/backup light switch U9
Reduction Gear starter motor
(Chrysler Corporation) U9
Disassembly U9
Assembly U11
Direct drive starter motor
(Chrysler Corporation) U11
Disassembly U11
Assembly U12
Autolite/Motorcraft positive engagement
starter motor (Ford Motor Co.) U12
Disassembly U13
Assembly U13
Autolite/Motorcraft solenoid acuated
starter motor (Ford Motor Co.) U14
Disassembly U14
Assembly U14
Delco-Remy starter motor
(General Motors Corp.) U15
Disassembly U15
Assembly U16

**AC Generator (Alternator)
and System Service** **U17**
Preliminary changing system
inspection U17
Chrysler isolated field alternator
(electronic regulator) U17
Troubleshooting U17
Delcotron 5.5 Series 1D and 6.2 Series 2D
(General Motors Corp.) U20
Troubleshooting U20
Delcotron 10-SI Series 100
(General Motors Corp.) U23
Troubleshooting U23
Autolite Motorcraft alternator with
external regulator (Ford Motor Co.) U25
Troubleshooting U26
Autolite alternator with integral
regulator (Ford Motor Co.) U27
Troubleshooting U29
The Motorola system U31
Troubleshooting U32
The Prestolite system U33
Troubleshooting U33

Testing the Battery

Selection of Battery

The modern car battery (with very few exceptions) is a 12-volt lead-acid unit having a particular ampere hours capacity, depending upon the required work load (radio, air conditioning, electric windows, tailgate, telephone, etc.).

Batteries come in different forms as specified and designed by the car manufacturer and are matched to the car's electrical needs.

The prime purpose of the battery is to supply a source of energy for cranking the car engine. It also provides the necessary power for the ignition system. A battery can, for a limited time, supply adequate current to satisfy electrical demands during periods when requirements exceed generator output.

Replacing a Battery

The most convenient and popular way to store new batteries is in a dry state. They are charged (with special equipment) at the time of manufacture. A dry charged unit will hold this charge almost indefinitely, in the absence of moisture.

Before deciding on a particular battery, consider some of the essentials that may put the replacement battery in a different category from that of the unit originally supplied with the vehicle. When the original battery wears out, resistance in the wiring circuits is probably much increased, and the starter may be less efficient, along with the ignition system. There is also the likelihood that electrical accessories have been added.

All of the above reasons are justification for choosing a battery of greater capacity than the one supplied by the manufacturer.

Preparation

After the electrical needs have been considered, and a selection made, place the new battery on a bench or work table. Never activate a battery installed in the car. Remove vent caps from all the cells.

Fill each cell carefully, using sulfuric acid and distilled water (electrolyte) at a strength of 1.250-1.265 specific gravity to about 3/8 in. above the top of the separators, or to indicated level mark.

Place a battery type thermometer in one of the center cells. Check specific gravity of the electrolyte with a battery hydrometer. The battery temperature must be above 80°F. and specific gravity must be above 1.250 prior to installing the battery. In charging 12-volt batteries, set charging rate at 35 amperes (6-volt batteries at 70 amperes) until electrolyte has reached 80° F. and electrolyte gravity is 1.250 or higher.

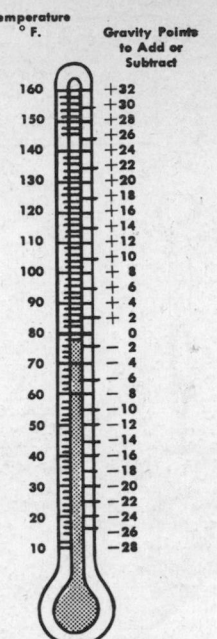

Temperature
° F.

Gravity Points
to Add or
Subtract

160 +32
+30
150 +28
+26
140 +24
+22
130 +20
+18
120 +16
+14
110 +12
+10
100 + 8
+ 6
90 + 4
+ 2
80 0
70 − 2
− 4
60 − 6
− 8
50 − 10
− 12
40 − 14
− 16
30 − 18
− 20
20 − 22
− 24
10 − 26
− 28

Hydrometer temperature correction chart
(© Chrysler Corp)

Lower charging rates also may be used to obtain 80° F. and 1.250 specific gravity. When charging, do not allow electrolyte temperature to exceed 125° F. Normally, 10-15 minutes charging will be sufficient; however, in colder climates a little longer is O.K.

When the battery is removed from the charger, top up if necessary, with electrolyte, and replace the vent plugs.

When installing, make sure that both ends of the battery cables are clean and securely tightened, observing correct polarity.

Start engine and make sure that the generator is charging with lights and all accessories on.

Caution
Be careful not to install or charge the battery with cables reversed. Damage to battery and generator can result, especially if the car is equipped with an alternator or transistorized radio.

Caution
Because electrolyte is extremely corrosive to metals and many other materials, do not pour into sinks or drains. If battery acid is spilled on battery during filling or charging, or on bench or clothing, immediately flush it off with generous amounts of water and baking soda or ammonia.

Battery Troubles—Causes

1. Battery too small for the job (accessories, etc.).
2. Tired battery (worn out).
3. Corroded battery connections.
4. Generator not charging.
5. Generator charging rate too low.
6. Regulator defective.
7. Regulator out of adjustment.
8. Regulator has poor ground.
9. Alternator inoperative.
10. Loose generator or alternator drive belt.
11. Constant drain of current due to short circuit.

Battery Troubles—Corrections

1. Battery capacity may be less than requirements demand. Additional accessories, too frequent use of starter, low operational speeds, require a greater source of electrical supply. Install a larger capacity battery.
2. Either age or abuse is the usual cause of a tired battery. No amount of charging will offer more than temporary relief. Install a new battery of proper capacity if plates are sulfated.
3. Corroded battery posts and connections result from the chemical reaction between dissimilar metals and battery electrolyte. Excessive corrosion at a battery post is usually an indication of the failure of a seal between the post and the battery cover. Clean post and cable clamp, seal post-to-battery cover with rubber cement or other plastic material, then coat post with petroleum jelly, install cable clamp and tighten.
4. Generator not charging can be caused by a defective generator or other system component. Check entire charging system and correct the fault.
5. Low generator charging rate may be caused by a loose drive belt, loose or poor battery post connections, high resistance in charging circuit or a poor or improperly adjusted regulator.
6. Regulator may be defective because of burned points in the regulator or any open circuit in the control system.
7. Regulator out of adjustment.
8. A possible cause of trouble in DC systems is a poor regulator ground in any of the externally grounded (Type A) field circuit or, in heavy-duty (Type B) circuits, the internally grounded field within the generator.
9. The alternator may be inoperative because of damaged diodes, poor internal connections, open, grounded, or shorted field circuit, grounded or shorted stator windings.
10. A loose generator drive belt will cause low, or partial charging. Correct by adjusting drive belt.
11. A constant drain of current from the battery may be caused by frayed insulation on any live wire in the electrical system.

This can cause a short circuit. There is also the possibility of a light (in the trunk, glove box, under the hood. etc.) or other electric accessory remaining on after the ignition is turned off. To correct the situation:

First, with a sensitive ammeter, determine whether or not there is a current drain by opening the circuit at either battery post connection, hooking the ammeter in series, and checking for current drain.

Second, if the meter registers a drain, isolate the leak by reconnecting the battery, then, one by one, check each circuit at the fuse block. This is a tedious but unavoidable procedure and consists of removing each fuse and testing that circuit with the prods of an ammeter (in series). The circuit which activates the meter is the guilty one; identify the trouble spot by elimination. Correct the trouble by correcting the short or replacing the switch or other electrical component.

In the event that the fuse block test does not indicate the trouble, check the circuits which are protected with circuit breakers, (headlamps, parking lamps, seat and window controls, etc.).

Specific Gravity Test— Hydrometer

Before attempting any electrical checks, it is important to check the condition of the battery.

While not technically exact, a practical measurement of the chemical condition of the battery is indicated by measuring the specific gravity of the acid (electrolyte) contained in each cell. The electrolyte in a fully charged battery is usually between

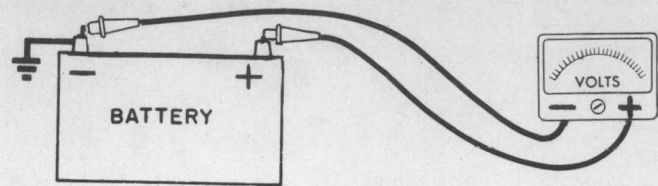

Battery polarity test

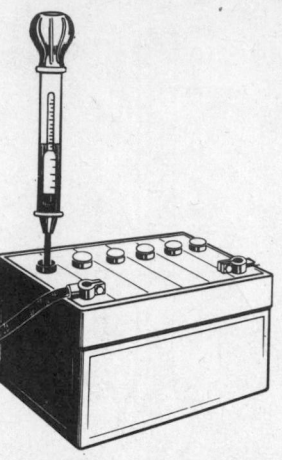

Testing battery specific gravity

1.260 and 1.280 times as heavy as pure water at the same temperature (80°F.). Variations in the specific gravity readings for a fully charged battery may differ. Therefore, it is most important that all battery cells produce an equal reading.

As a battery discharges, a chemical change takes place within each cell. The sulfate factor of the electrolyte combines chemically with the battery plates, reducing the weight of the electrolyte. A reading of the specific gravity of the acid, or electrolyte, of any partially charged battery, will therefore be less than that taken in a fully charged one.

The hydrometer is the instrument in general use for determining the specific gravity of liquids. The battery hydrometer is readily available from many sources, including local auto replacement parts stores. The following chart gives an indication of specific gravity value, related to battery charge condition. If, after charging, the specific gravity between any two cells varies more than 50 points (.050), the battery is probably bad.

Specific Gravity Reading	Charged Condition
1.260-1.280	Fully charged
1.230-1.250	Three-quarter charged
1.200-1.220	One-half charged
1.170-1.190	One-quarter charged
1.140-1.160	Just about flat
1.110-1.130	All the way down

Testing Battery Polarity

Battery polarity is very important, especially since the introduction of AC generators. Permanent damage to the diodes of alternators (AC generators) will result from reversing polarity.

To determine battery polarity, turn the voltmeter selector to the high reading scale. Connect voltmeter leads to the battery posts. If the gauge needle moves in the correct direction, the positive lead of the meter is on the positive (+) post of the battery. If the gauge needle moves in the wrong direction, polarity is reversed.

Testing the Delco "Sealed Top" Battery

Some GM cars come equipped with a "sealed top" battery which does not require the usual maintenance. Because the battery has a greater

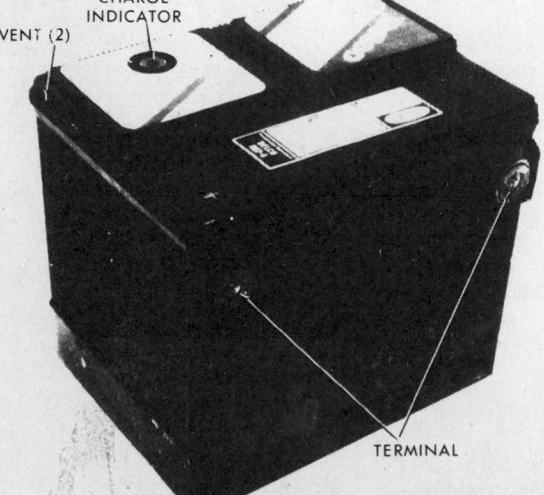

Delco sealed top battery
(© G.M. Corp.)

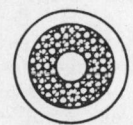 **DARKENED INDICATOR WITH GREEN DOT**

    - FULLY CHARGED

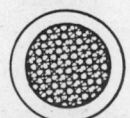 **DARKENED INDICATOR NO GREEN DOT**

    - NEEDS CHARGING

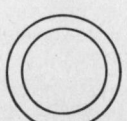 **LIGHTENED INDICATOR**

    - REPLACE BATTERY

Delco sealed battery indicator conditions
(© G.M. Corp.)

amount of electrolyte and a reduced need for water, the top of the battery has no filler caps and is sealed. A small vent is provided at one edge of the battery top.

There are two types of sealed batteries used: one has a charge indicator eye and the other does not. Both types may be tested in the following manner:

1. Check the condition of the battery case. If the case is damaged so that loss of electrolyte is possible, the battery must be replaced.
2. If the battery has a charge indicator eye, check the following:
   a. If the eye is dark, the battery has enough electrolyte. If the eye is light, the electrolyte level is too low and the battery must be replaced.
   b. If a green dot appears in the middle of the eye, the battery is sufficiently charged; go on to Step 4. If there is no green dot visible, charge the battery as in Step 3.
3. Charge the battery if there is no green dot visible in the eye, or if it is the type without an eye, at the following rates:

Amps	Time
75	40 min
50	1 hr
25	2 hr
10	5 hr

Caution

Do not charge the battery for more than 50 ampere-hours. If the green dot appears or electrolyte squirts out of the vent, stop the charge and go on with Step 4.

4. Either disconnect the high-tension coil wire or the engine harness (electronic ignition) and crank the starter motor for 15 seconds, to remove the surface charge.
5. Connect a voltmeter and a 230 amp load across the battery terminals.
6. Take a voltmeter reading after the load has been connected for 15 seconds, then disconnect the load.

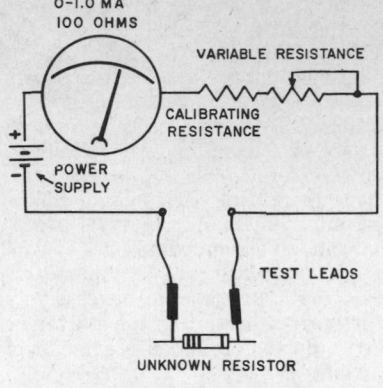

Ohmmeter circuit

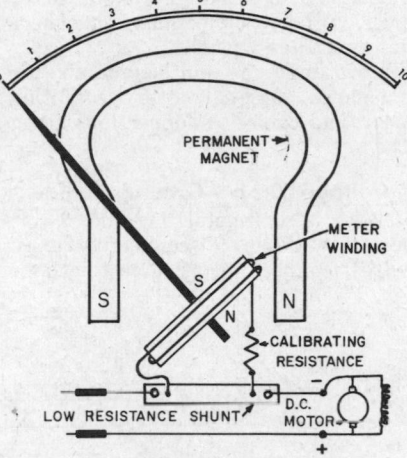

Ammeter circuit

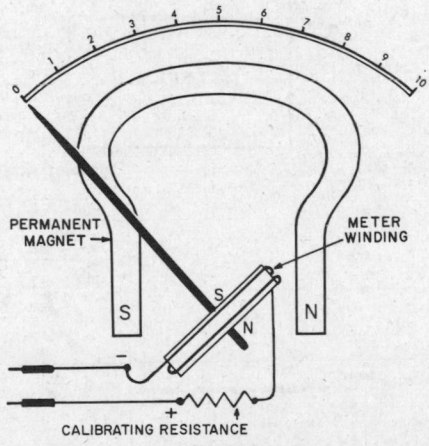

Voltmeter circuit

7. Consult the following chart. If the battery voltage is that specified (or more) for the given ambient temperature, the battery is good. If the voltage falls below that specified, then the battery is bad and must be replaced.

Ambient Temperature (°F)	Minimum Voltage
70 (or above)	9.6
60	9.5
50	9.4
40	9.3
30	9.1
20	8.9
10	8.7
0	8.5

Know Your Instruments

Ohmmeter

An ohmmeter is used to measure electrical resistance in a unit or circuit. The ohmmeter has a self-contained power supply. In use, it is connected across (or in parallel with) the terminals of the unit being tested.

Ammeter

An ammeter is used to measure current (amount of electricity) flowing through a unit, or circuit. Ammeters are always connected in the line (in series) with the unit or circuit being tested.

Voltmeter

A voltmeter is used to measure voltage (electrical pressure) pushing the current through a unit, or circuit. The meter is connected across the terminals of the unit being tested. The meter reading will be the difference in pressure (voltage drop) between the two sides of the unit.

Boost Charging Rates

12-volt Battery: 1,000 ampere minutes (50 amps. x 20 min.)

6-volt Battery: 1,800 ampere minutes (60 amps. x 30 min.)

NOTE: *Not all charger clips will fit the newer side-terminal batteries. If your clips don't fit, adapters are available from your local parts store.*

Testing the Starting Motor

Testing the Starter Circuit

The starter circuit should be divided and tested in four separate phases:

1. Cranking voltage check.
2. Amperage draw.
3. Voltage drop—grounded side.
4. Voltage drop—battery side.

NOTE: *The battery must be in good condition for this test to have significance. To accurately check battery condition, use equipment designed to measure its capacity under a load. Instructions accompanying the equipment should be followed.*

Cranking Voltage

Turn voltmeter selector to 8-10 volt scale for cars equipped with 6-volt systems, and to the 16-20 volt scale for cars equipped with 12-volt systems.

Connect voltmeter leads to the battery posts (observe polarity and reverse meter leads if necessary). Remove the high tension wire from the distributor cap and ground it to prevent starting. Now, turn the key. Observe both voltmeter reading and cranking speed. The cranking speed should be even, and at a satisfactory rate of speed, with a voltmeter reading of 4.8 volts or more for 6-volt systems, and at least 9.6 volts for 12-volt systems.

Amperage Draw

The amount of current the starter

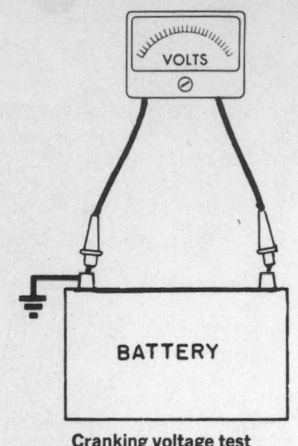

Cranking voltage test

Starter current indicator

current draw should be about one-half the amount registered for the 6-volt system.

More accurate but complex equipment is available from many name brand manufacturers. This equipment consists of a combination voltmeter, ammeter, and carbon pile rheostat. When using this equipment, follow the equipment manufacturer's procedures and recommendations.

High amperage and lazy performance would suggest an excessively tight engine, friction in the starter or starter drive, grounded starter field or armature.

Normal amperage and lazy performance suggest high resistance, or possibly poor connections somewhere in the starter circuit.

Low amperage and lazy or no performance suggest battery condition poor, bad cables or connections along the line.

Voltage Drop—Grounded Side

With a voltmeter on the 3-volt scale, without disconnecting any wires, connect negative test lead of

the voltmeter to a prod secured in the grounded battery post. The positive test lead is connected to a cleaned, bare metal portion of the starter motor housing. Close the starter switch and note the voltmeter reading. If the reading is the same as battery reading, the ground circuit is open somewhere between the battery and the starter. In many cases the reading will be very small. The reading shown will indicate voltage drop (loss) between battery ground post and starter housing. The drop should not exceed 0.2 volt. If the voltage drop is above the specified amount, the next step is to isolate and correct the cause. It can be a bad cable or connection anywhere in the battery-to-starter ground circuit. A check of this type should progress along the various points of possible trouble, between the battery ground post and the starter motor housing, until the trouble spot has been located.

NOTE: due to the design of the Chrysler reduction gear starter, testing is limited to measuring voltage drop to starter cable connection.

motor draws is usually (but not always) associated with the mechanical problems involved in cranking the engine. (Mechanical trouble in the engine, frozen or worn starter parts, misaligned starter or starter components, etc.) Because starter motor amperage draw is directly influenced by anything restricting the free turning of the engine, or starter, it is important that the engine and all components be at operating temperatures.

To measure starter current draw, remove the high tension wire from the center of the distributor cap and ground it.

NOTE: *On cars with electronic ignition, disconnect the control box from the distributor (harness).*

A very simple and inexpensive starter current indicator is available at auto stores. This indicator is an induction type gauge and shows, without disconnecting any wires, starter current draw.

Place the yoke of the meter directly over the insulated starter supply cable (cable must be straight for a minimum of 2 in.). Close the starter switch for about 20 seconds, watch the meter dial and record the average reading. If the indicator swings in the wrong direction, reverse the position of the meter. On 6-volt systems, normal draw for small to medium size engines is 150 to 225 amperes. Larger and high compression engines may draw as much as 400 amperes. On 12-volt systems, the

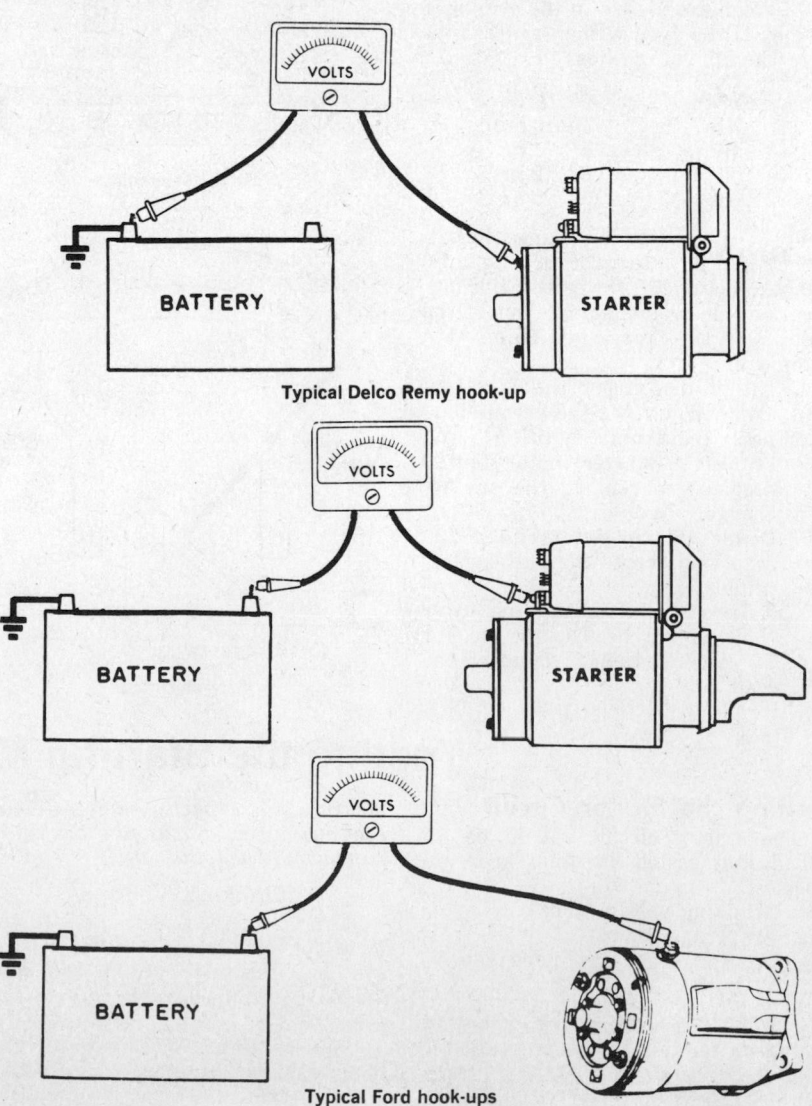

Typical Delco Remy hook-up

Typical Ford hook-ups

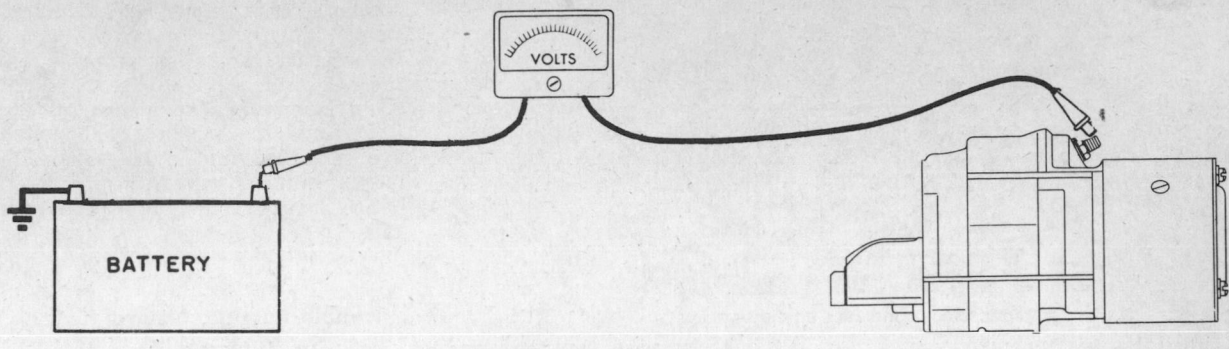

Typical Chrysler hook-up

Voltage Drop—Battery Side

Bad starter cranking may result from poor connections or faulty components of the battery or hot phase of the starter motor circuit. To check this phase of the circuit, without disconnecting any wires, connect one lead of a voltmeter to a prod secured in the hot post of the battery and the other voltmeter lead to the field terminal of the starting motor. The meter should be set to the 16-20 volt scale. Before closing the starter switch, the voltmeter reading will be that of the battery. After closing the

starter switch, change the selector on the voltmeter to the 3-volt scale. With a jumper wire between the relay battery terminal and the relay starter switch terminal, crank the engine. If the starting motor cranks the engine, the relay (solenoid) is operating.

While the engine is being cranked, watch the voltmeter. It should not register more than 0.5 volt. If more than this, check each part of the circuit for voltage drop to isolate the trouble, (high resistance).

Without disturbing the voltmeter-

to-battery hook-up, move the free voltmeter lead to the battery terminal of the relay (solenoid), and crank the engine. The voltmeter should show no more than 0.1 volt.

If this reading is correct, move the same voltmeter lead to the starting motor terminal of the relay (solenoid). While the engine is being cranked, the voltmeter should show no more than 0.3 volt. If it does, the trouble lies in the relay.

If the reading is correct, the trouble is in the cable or connections between the relay and the starting motor.

Starter Motor And System Service

Diagnosis

Starter Won't Crank the Engine

1. Dead battery.
2. Open starter circuit, such as:
   A. Broken or loose battery cables.
   B. Inoperative starter motor solenoid.
   C. Broken or loose wire from starter switch to solenoid.
   D. Poor solenoid or starter ground.
   E. Bad starter switch, (ignition, dash button or carburetor).
   F. Defective seat belt interlock system—1974-75 cars only.
3. Defective starter internal circuit, such as:
   A. Dirty or burnt commutator.
   B. Stuck, worn or broken brushes.
   C. Open or shorted armature.
   D. Open or grounded fields.
4. Starter motor mechanical faults, such as:
   A. Jammed armature end bearings.
   B. Bar bearing, allowing armature ture to rub fields.
   C. Bent shaft.
   D. Broken starter housing.
   E. Bad starter worm or drive mechanism.
   F. Bad starter drive or flywheel driven gear.
5. Engine hard or impossible to crank, such as:
   A. Hydrostatic lock, water in combustion chamber.
   B. Crankshaft seizing in bearings.

C. Piston or ring seizing.
D. Bent or broken connecting rod.
E. Seizing of connecting rod bearing.
F. Flywheel jammed or broken.
G. In some remote cases, an incandescent particle in the combustion chamber of a hot engine will prevent starting. This condition acts like a low battery or ignition timing so far advanced that the engine kicks back. The piston refuses to pass over top center. A two or three minute wait is generally enough to cool the troubled spot and temporarily clear the fault.

Starter Spins Free, Won't Engage

1. Sticking or broken drive mechanism.

Magnetic Switches

Magnetic switches serve only to make contact for the starter motor. Usually, such switches are located on the inner fender panel, although they are found mounted on the starter in a few cases.

Magnetic Switches with Two Control Terminals

On this type of magnetic switch current is supplied from the ignition switch or transmission neutral button to one of the magnetic switch control terminals. The other control

terminal is connected to the transmission neutral safety switch (on the transmission) where it is grounded.

Magnetic Switches with Ignition Resistor By-Pass Terminals

Used with 12-volt systems. All normally use a magnetic switch with a single control terminal. The second terminal is an ignition resistor by-pass terminal.

Solenoids Without Relays

This type of starter solenoid is always mounted on the starter. Makes electrical contact for the starter and pulls the starter and drive clutch into mesh with the flywheel. The Chrysler reduction gear starter has this solenoid embodied in the starter housing.

There is only one control terminal on the solenoid.

The ignition by-pass terminal is usually marked R or IGN, if it is used.

Solenoids With Separate Relays

The solenoid itself is always mounted on the starter. In addition to making contact for the starter, it

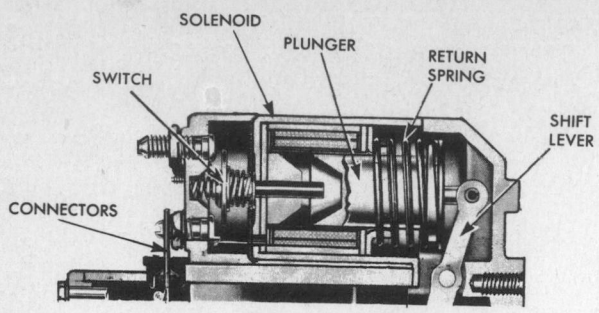

Starter solenoid mounted on starter motor

also pulls the starter drive clutch gear into mesh with the flywheel. A single control terminal is used on the solenoid itself. The relay is usually found mounted to the inner fender panel or on the firewall.

Solenoids With Built-In Relays

These units are always mounted on the starter and are connected, through linkage, to the starter drive clutch. The relay portion is a square box built into and integral with the front end of the solenoid assembly.

Neutral Safety Switches

The purpose of the neutral safety switch is to prevent the starter from cranking the engine except when the transmission is in Neutral or Park.

NOTE: *Fords starting 1971 and Cadillacs starting 1974 with a column mounted automatic transmission selector and steering column lock do not have a neutral safety switch; instead the key can only be turned to the "START" position when the selector is in Park or Neutral.*

On some cars, the neutral safety switch is located on the transmission. It serves to ground the solenoid or magnetic switch, whichever is used.

On other cars the neutral safety switch is located either at the bottom of the steering column, where it contacts the shift mechanism, on the steering column, underneath the dash, or on the shift linkage (console).

NOTE: *Some recent cars with*

manual transmissions have a safety switch mounted on the clutch linkage to prevent starter operation unless the pedal is depressed.

On most cars, the neutral safety switch and the back-up light switch are combined into a single switch mechanism.

See the car sections for specific details.

Troubleshooting Neutral Safety Switches—Quick Test

If the starter fails to function and the neutral safety switch is to be checked, a jumper can be placed across its terminals. If the starter then functions the safety switch is defective.

In the case of neutral safety switches with one wire, this wire must be grounded for testing purposes. If the starter works with the wire grounded, the switch is defective.

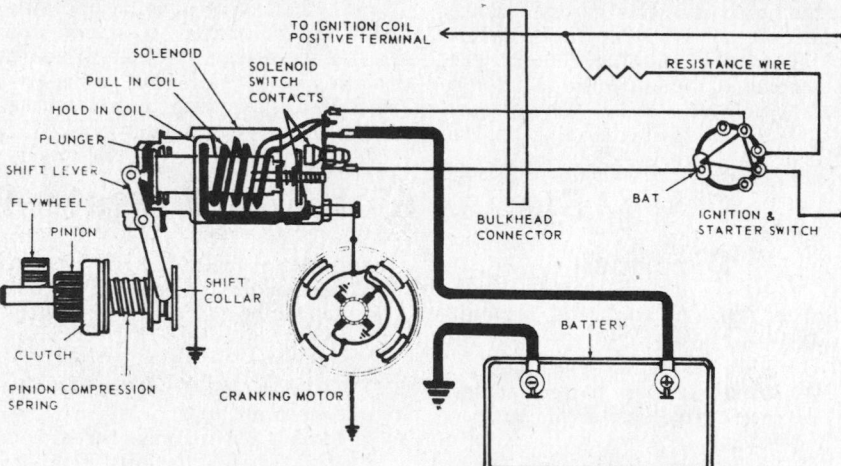

G.M. starter circuit (© G.M. Corp)

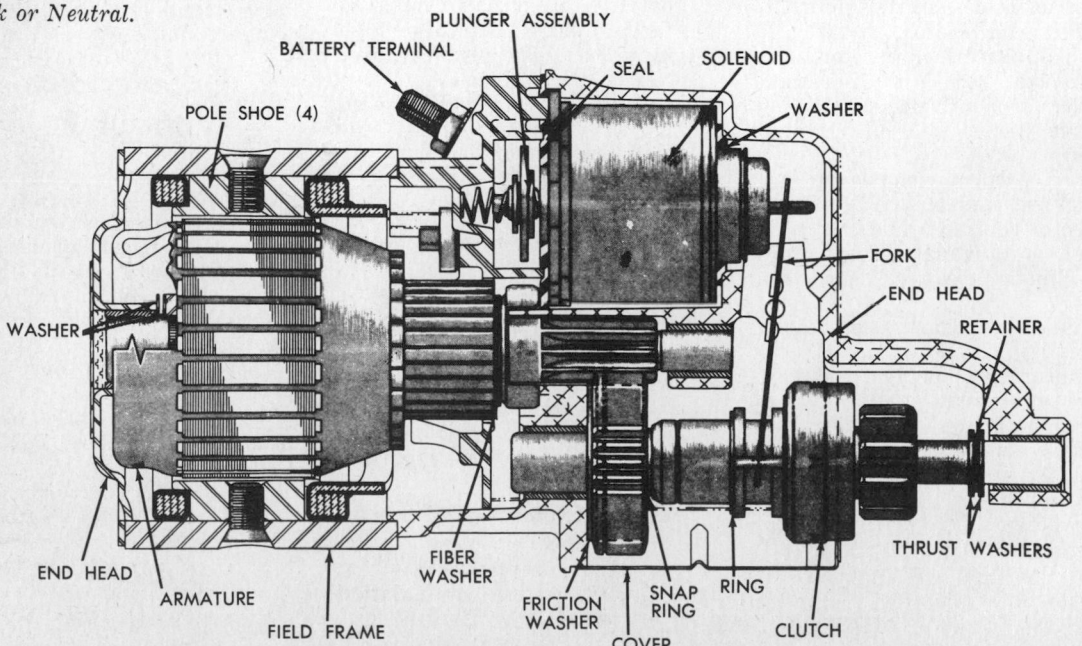

Reduction gear starter motor (© Chrysler Corp)

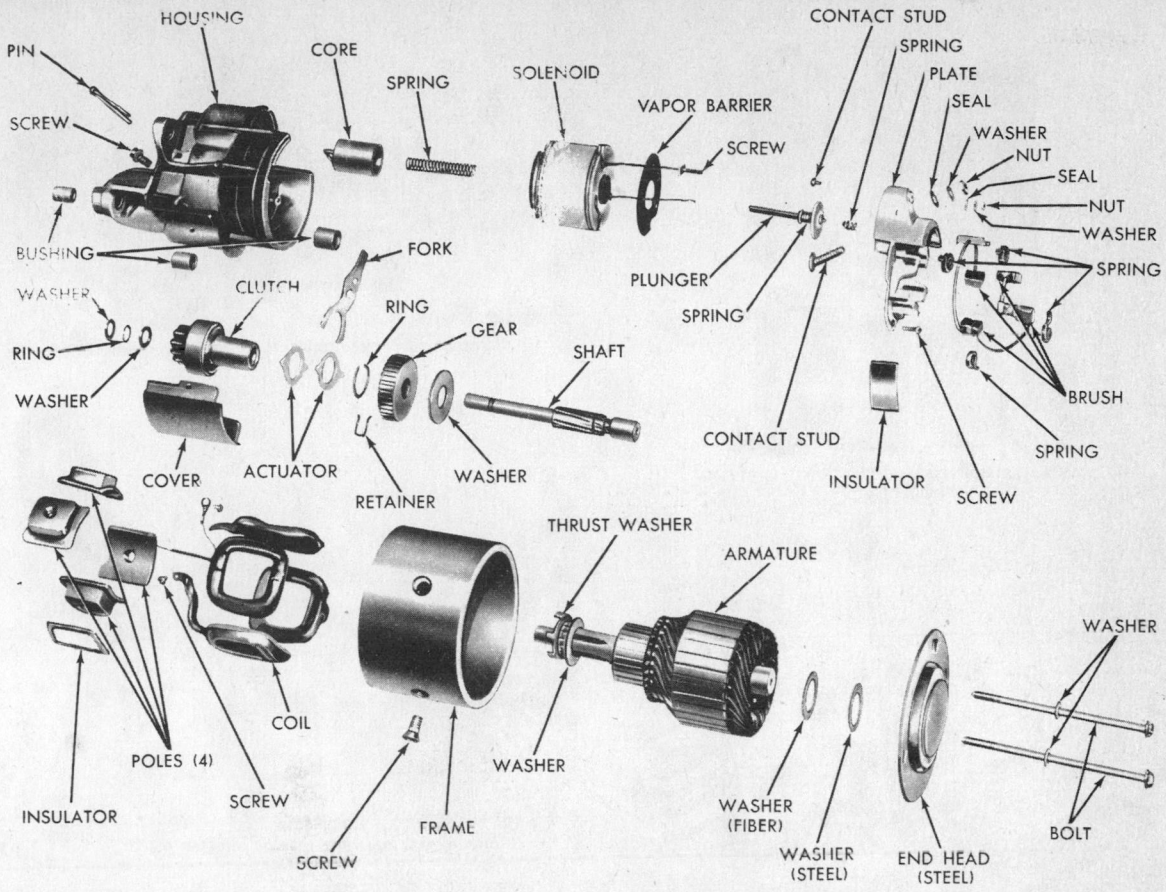

Reduction gear motor—exploded view (© Chrysler Corp)

Neutral Safety Switch—
Back-Up Light Switch

When the neutral safety switch is built in combination with the back-up light switch, the easiest way to tell which terminals are for the back-up lights is to take a jumper and cross every pair of wires. The pair of wires which light the back-up lamps should be ignored when testing the neutral safety switch. Once the back-up light wires have been located, jump the other pair of wires to test the neutral safety switch. If the starter functions only when the jumper is placed across these two wires, the neutral safety switch is defective or requires adjustment.

Reduction-Gear Starter Motor

(Chrysler Corporation)

The housing is die-cast aluminum. A 3.5 to 1 reduction, combined with the starter to ring gear ratio, results in a total gear reduction of about 45 to 1.

NOTE: the high-pitched sound is caused by the higher starter speed.

The positive shift solenoid is enclosed in the starter housing and is energized through the ignition switch. When ignition switch is turned to start, the solenoid plunger engages drive gear through a shifting fork. At the completion of travel, the plunger closes a switch to revolve the starter.

The tension of the spring-type shifting prevents a butt-tooth lock up and motor will not start before total shift.

An overrunning clutch prevents motor damage if key is held on after engine starts.

No lubrication is required due to Oilite bearings.

1975 and later Chrysler Corporation cars with large V-8s (360 cu. in. and up) use a larger reduction gear starter motor. It is similar to the previous models but is more powerful and has a 2:1 gear reduction rather than the 3.5:1 unit. The clutch drive unit in the new starter has been enlarged to handle the increased load as have the rest of the components. While the new starter is outwardly similar to the old one, parts are not interchangeable; however removal, installation, disassembly and assembly procedures are unchanged.

Disassembly

1. Support assembly in a vise equipped with soft jaws. Do not clamp. Care must be used not to distort or damage the die cast aluminum.
2. Remove the thru-bolts and the end housing.

3. Carefully pull the armature up and out of the gear housing, and the starter frame and field assembly. Remove the steel and fiber thrust washer.

NOTE: on eight cylinder engines the starting motors have the wire of the shunt field coil soldered to the brush terminal. Six cylinder engines have the four coils in series and do not have a wire soldered to the brush terminal. One pair of brushes is connected to this terminal. The other pair of brushes is attached to the series field coils by means of a terminal screw. Carefully pull the frame and field assembly up just enough to expose the terminal screw and the solder connection of the shunt field at the brush terminal. Place two wood blocks between the starter frame and starter gear housing to facilitate removal of the terminal screw and unsoldering of the shunt field wire at the brush terminal.

4. Support the brush terminal with a finger behind terminal and remove screw.
5. On eight cylinder engine starters unsolder the shunt field coil lead from the brush terminal and housing.
6. The brush holder plate with terminal, contact and brushes is serviced as an assembly.

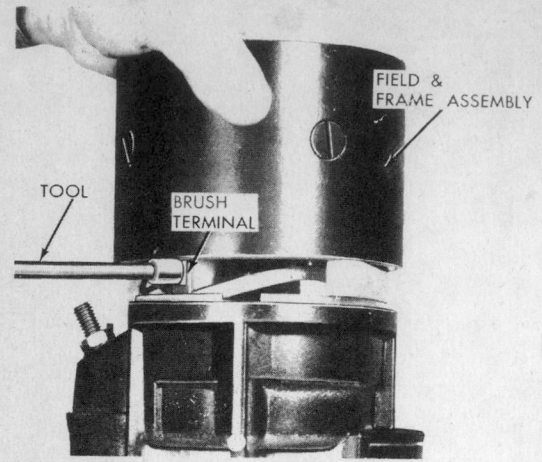

Removing terminal screw—reduction gear motor
(© Chrysler Corp)

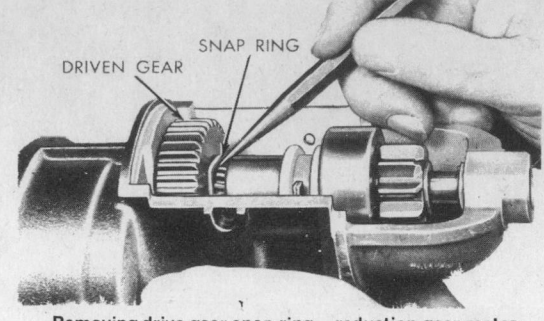

Removing drive gear snap-ring—reduction gear motor
(© Chrysler Corp)

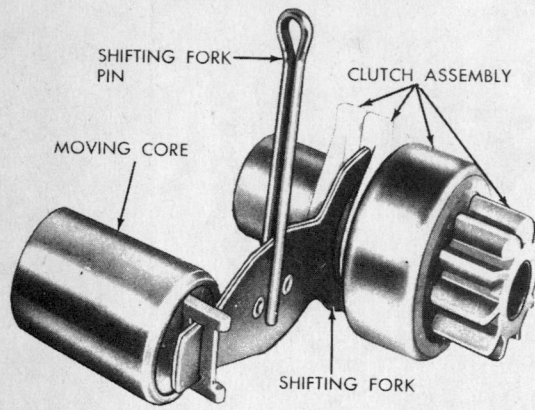

Shift fork and clutch arrangement—reduction gear motor
(© Chrysler Corp)

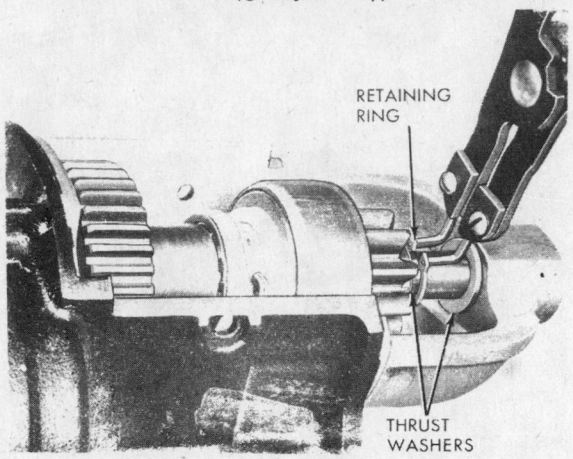

Removing retainer ring—reduction gear motor
(© Chrysler Corp)

7. Clean all old sealer from around plate and housing.

8. Remove the brush holder attaching screw.

9. On the shunt type, unsolder the solenoid winding from the brush terminal.

10. Remove 11/32 in. nut, washer and insulator from solenoid terminal.

11. Remove brush holder plate with brushes as an assembly.

12. Remove gear housing ground screw.

13. The solenoid assembly can be removed from the well.

14. Remove nut, washer and seal from starter battery terminal and remove terminal from plate.

15. Remove solenoid contact and plunger from solenoid and remove the coil sleeve.

16. Remove the solenoid return spring, coil retaining washer, retainer and the dust cover from the gear housing.

17. Release the snap-ring that locates the driven gear on pinion shaft.

CAUTION: *The snap-ring is under tension; to prevent it from flying off, place a cloth over it prior to removal.*

18. Release front retaining ring.

19. Push pinion shaft toward the rear and remove snap-ring, thrust washers, clutch and pinion, and two shift fork nylon actuators.

20. Remove driven gear and friction washer.

21. Pull shifting fork forward and remove moving core.

22. Remove fork retainer pin and shifting fork assembly. The gear housing with bushings is serviced as an assembly.

Replacement of Brushes

1. Brushes that are worn more than one-half the length of new brushes, or are oil-soaked, should be replaced.

2. When resoldering the shunt field and solenoid lead, make a strong, low-resistance connection using a high-temperature solder and resin flux. Do not use acid or acid-core solder. Do not break the shunt field wire units when removing and installing the brushes.

Starter Clutch and Pinion Gear Inspection

1. Do not immerse the starter clutch unit in a cleaning solvent. The outside of the clutch and pinion must be cleaned with a cloth so as not to wash the lubricant from the inside of the clutch.

2. Rotate the pinion. The pinion gear should rotate smoothly and in one direction only. If the starter clutch unit does not function properly, or if the pinion is worn, chipped, or burred, replace the starter clutch unit.

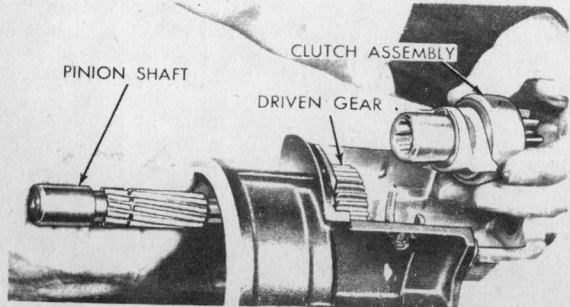

Removing clutch assembly—reduction gear motor
(© Chrysler Corp)

Commutator Inspection

1. Inspect the commutator and the surface contacted by the brushes when the starter is assembled, for flat spots, out-of-roundness, or excessive wear.
2. Reface the commutator if necessary, removing only a sufficient amount of metal to provide a smooth, even surface.
3. Using light pressure, clean the grooves of the face of the commutator with a pointed tool. Neither remove any metal or widen the grooves.

Assembly

1. The shifter fork consists of two spring steel plates held together by two rivets. Before assembling the starter, check the plates for side movement. After lubricating between the plates with a small amount of SAE 10 engine oil, they should have about 1/16 in. side movement to insure proper pinion gear engagement.
2. Position the shift fork in the drive housing and install the shifting fork retainer pin. One tip of the pin should be straight and the other bent at a 15 degree angle away from the housing. The fork and retainer pin should operate freely after bending the tip of the pin.
3. Install the solenoid moving core and engage the shifting fork.
4. Place the pinion shaft into the drive housing and install the friction washer and drive gear.
5. Install the clutch and pinion assembly, thrust washer, and retaining washer.
6. Engage the shifting fork with the clutch actuators.

Caution
The friction washer must be positioned on the shoulder of the splines of the pinion shaft before the driven gear is positioned.

7. Install the driven gear snap ring.
8. Install the pinion shaft retaining ring.

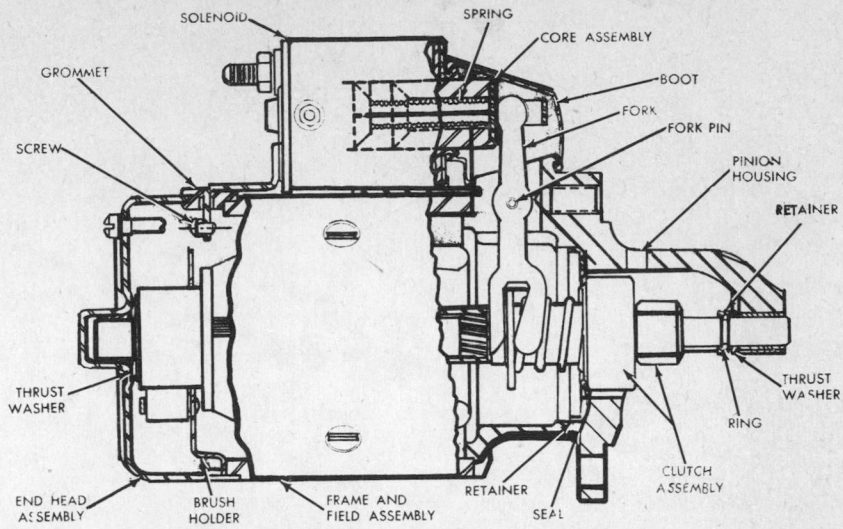

Chrysler direct drive starter motor (© Chrysler Corp)

9. The starter solenoid return spring can now be inserted in the movable core.
10. Install the solenoid contact plunger assembly into the solenoid and reform the double wires so they can be curved around the contactor. This will allow the terminal stud to enter the brush holder properly.

Caution
The contactor must not touch these double wires after assembly is complete.

11. Assemble the battery terminal stud in the brush holder.
12. Position the seal on the brush holder plate.
13. Run the solenoid lead wire through the hole in the brush holder and attach the solenoid stud, insulating washer, flat washer, and nut.
14. Wrap the solenoid lead wire tightly around the brush terminal post and solder it.
15. Fix the brush holder to the solenoid attaching screws.
16. Gently lower the solenoid coil and brush plate into the gear housing.
17. Position the brush plate assembly into the starter gear housing, install the nuts, and tighten.
18. Solder the shunt coil lead wire to the starter brush terminal.

19. Install the brush terminal screw.
20. Position the field frame on the gear housing and start the armature into the housing, carefully engaging the splines on the shaft with the reduction gear by rotating the armature.
21. Install the fiber thrust washer and the steel washer on the armature shaft.
22. Replace the starter end housing and starter through bolts; tighten securely.

Direct Drive Starter Motor
(Chrysler Corporation)

NOTE: *The direct drive starter was last used in 1973.*

Disassembly

1. Remove through bolts and tap commutator end head from frame.
2. Remove thrust washers from armature shaft.
3. Lift brush holder springs and remove brushes from holders.
4. Remove brush holder plate.
5. Disconnect the field coil wires at the solenoid connector, and remove the solenoid screws.

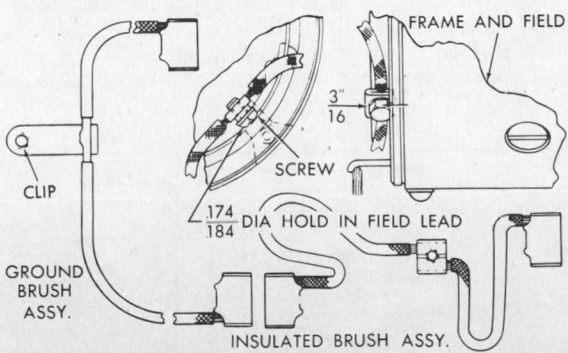

Brush lead arrangement—Chrysler direct drive motor
(© Chrysler Corp)

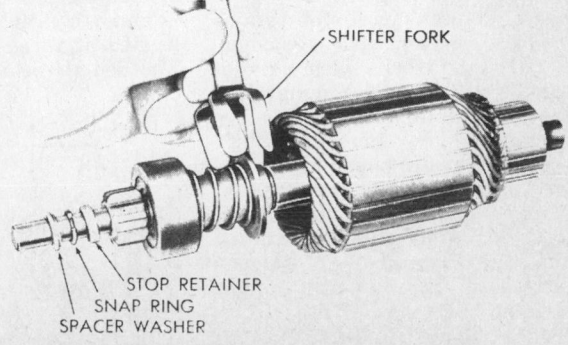

Removing shift fork—direct drive motor
(© Chrysler Corp)

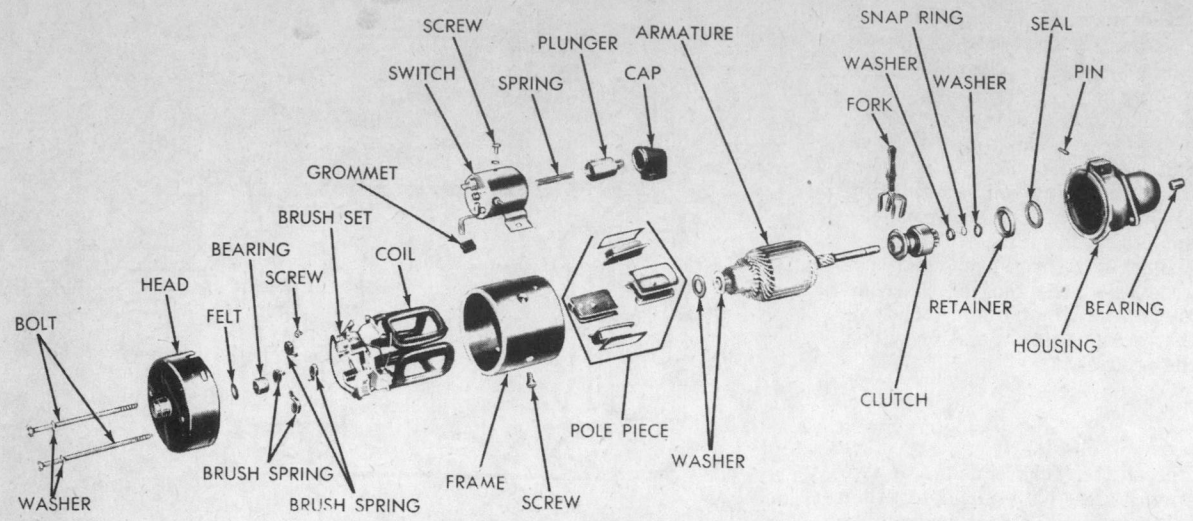

Chrysler direct drive motor—exploded view (© Chrysler Corp)

6. Remove solenoid and boot.
7. Drive out shift fork pivot pin.
8. Remove drive end pinion housing and spacer washer.
9. Remove shift fork from starter drive.
10. Slide overrunning clutch pinion gear toward commutator, drive stop retainer toward clutch pinion gear and remove the now-exposed snap-ring.
11. Remove overrunning clutch drive from armature shaft.
12. If field coils are good, stop disassembly at this point. If field coils must be replaced, remove ground brushes terminal screw and remove brushes, terminal and shunt wire. Remove pole shoe screws, using a ratchet-type impact driver and special wide screwdriver blade, then remove field coils.
13. Replacement of the brushes, inspection of the starter clutch and pinion, and inspection of the commutator procedures are the same as the reduction-gear starter procedures.

Assembly

1. Install field coils into frame, if removed.
2. Lubricate armature shaft and splines with engine oil.
3. Install starter drive, stop retainer, lock ring and spacer washer.
4. Install shift fork, with *narrow* leg of fork toward commutator.
5. Install pinion housing onto armature shaft, indexing shift fork with slot in housing.
6. Install shift fork pivot pin.
7. With clutch drive, shift fork, and pinion housing assembled onto the armature, slide armature into frame until pinion housing indexes with slot.
8. Install solenoid and boot, tightening bolts to 60-70 in. lbs.
9. Connect field coil wires to solenoid connector, making sure they do not touch frame.
10. Install brush holder plate, indexing tang in frame hole.
11. Place brushes in holders, making sure field coil wires do not interfere.
12. Install thrust washers on commutator end of armature shaft to obtain a maximum of 0.010 in. end-play.
13. Install commutator end head and through bolts. Tighten bolts to 40-50 in. lbs.
14. Measure drive gear pinion clearance; it should be 1/8 in. Adjust by moving solenoid fore and aft as required.

Autolite / Motorcraft Positive Engagement Starter Motor

(Ford Motor Co.)

This starting motor is a series-parallel wound, four pole, four brush unit. It is equipped with an overrunning clutch drive pinion, which is engaged with the flywheel ring gear by an actuating lever, operated by a movable pole piece. This pole piece is hinged to the starter frame and can drop into position through an opening in the frame.

Three conventional field coils are located at three pole piece positions. The fourth field coil is designed to

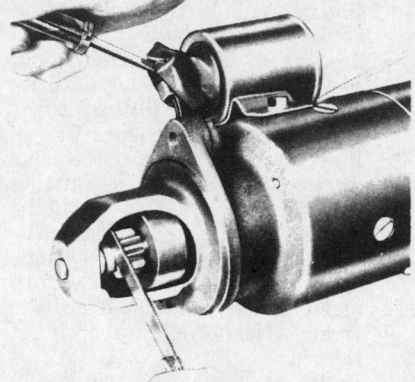

Checking drive pinion clearance—direct drive motor (© Chrysler Corp)

serve also as an engaging coil and a hold-in coil for the operation of the drive pinion.

When the ignition switch is turned to the start position, the starter relay is energized and current flows from the battery to the starter motor terminal. This prime surge of current first flows through the starter engaging coil, creating a very strong magnetic field. This magnetism draws the movable pole piece down toward the starter frame, which then causes the lever attached to it to move the starter pinion into engagement with the flywheel ring gear.

When the movable pole shoe is fully seated, it opens the field coil, grounding contacts, and the starter is then in normal operation. A hold-

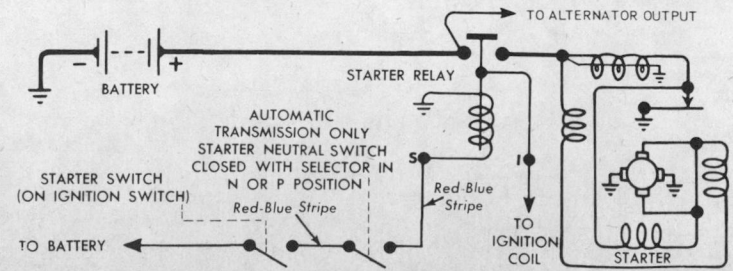

Ford positive engagement starter circuit (© Ford Motor Co)

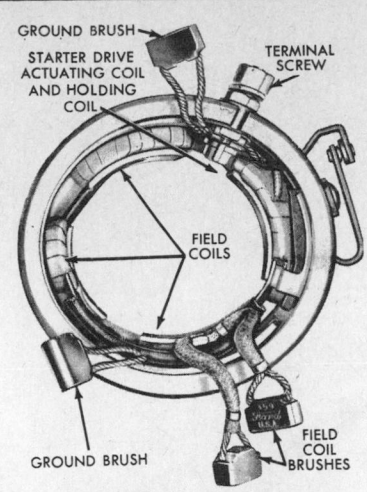

Autolite field coil assembly

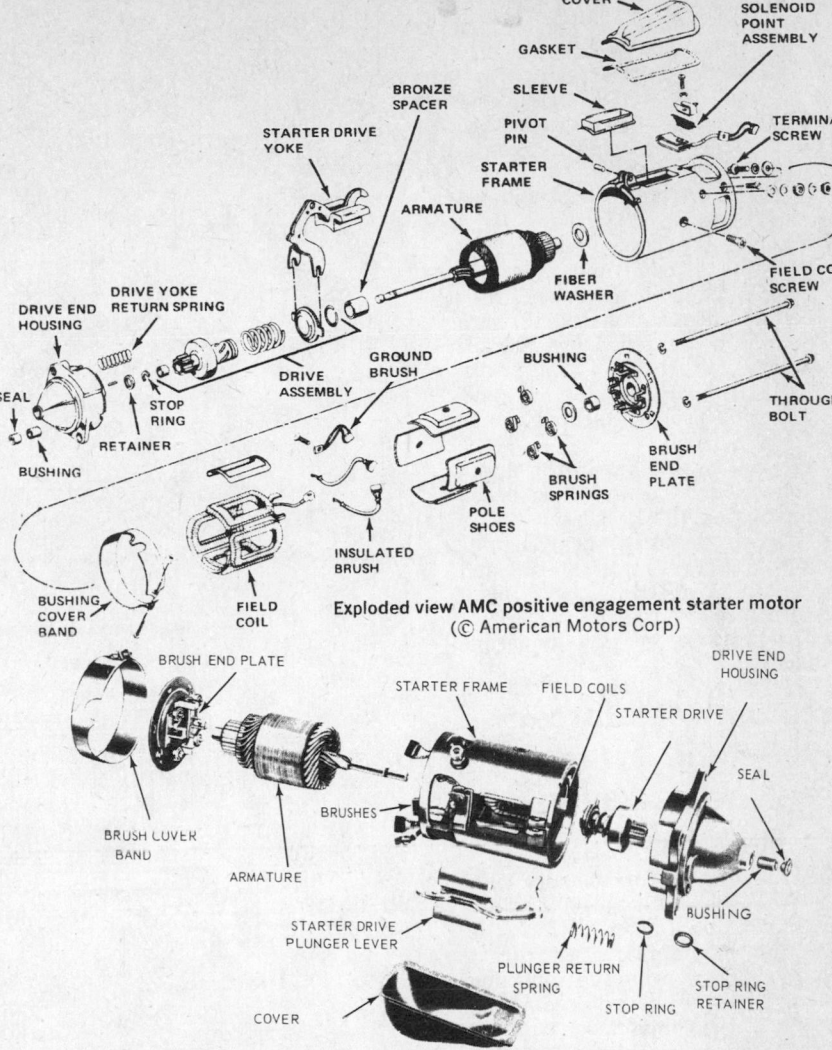

Exploded view AMC positive engagement starter motor
(© American Motors Corp)

Exploded view Ford positive engagement starter motor
(© Ford Motor Co)

ing coil is used to hold the movable pole shoe in the fully seated position during the engine cranking operation.

Cars equipped with automatic transmissions have a starter neutral switch circuit control. This is to prevent operation of the starter if the selector lever is not in Neutral or Park.

This type starter is used on both Ford and American Motors products since 1970.

Disassembly

1. Remove brush cover band and starter drive gear actuating lever cover. Observe the brush lead locations for reassembly, then remove the brushes from their holders.
   NOTE: factory brush length is ½ in.; wear limit is ¼ in.
2. Remove the through bolts, starter drive gear housing and the drive gear actuating lever return spring.
3. Remove the pivot pin retaining the starter gear actuating lever and remove the lever and the armature.
4. Remove the stop ring retainer. Remove and discard the stop ring holding the drive gear to the armature shaft; then remove the drive gear assembly.
5. Remove the brush end plate.
6. Remove the two screws holding the ground brushes to the frame.
7. On the field coil that operates the starter drive gear actuating lever, bend the tab up on the field retainer and remove the field coil retainer.
8. Remove the three coil retaining screws. Unsolder the field coil leads from the terminal screw, then remove the pole shoes and coils from the frame (use a 300 watt iron).
9. Remove the starter terminal nut, washer, insulator and terminal from the starter frame.

10. Check the commutator for run-out. If the commutator is rough, has flat spots, or is more than 0.005 in. out of round, reface the commutator. Clean the grooves in the commutator face.
11. Inspect the armature shaft and the two bearings for scoring and excessive wear. Replace if necessary.
12. Inspect the starter drive. If the gear teeth are pitted, broken, or excessively worn, replace the starter drive.

Assembly

1. Install starter terminal, insulator, washers and retaining nut in the frame. (Be sure to position the slot in the screw perpendicular to the frame end surface.)
2. Position coils and pole pieces, with the coil leads in the terminal screw slot, then install the retaining screws. As the pole screws are tightened, strike the

frame several sharp hammer blows to align the pole shoes. Tighten, then stake the screws.
3. Install solenoid coil and retainer and bend the tabs to hold the coils to the frame.
4. Solder the field coils and solenoid wire to the starter terminal, using rosin-core solder and a 300 watt iron.
5. Check for continuity and ground connections in the assembled coils.
6. Position the solenoid coil ground terminal over the nearest ground screw hole.
7. Position the ground brushes to the starter frame and install retaining screws.
8. Position the brush end plate to the frame, with the end plate boss in the frame slot.
9. Lightly Lubriplate the armature shaft splines and install the starter drive gear assembly on the shaft. Install a new retaining stop ring and stop ring retainer.

10. Position the fiber thrust washer on the commutator end of the armature shaft, then position the armature in the starter frame.

11. Position the starter drive gear actuating lever to the frame and starter drive assembly, and install the pivot pin.

    NOTE: fill drive gear housing bore ¼ full of grease.

12. Position the drive actuating lever return spring and the drive gear housing to the frame, then install and tighten the through bolts. Do not pinch brush leads between brush plate and frame. Be sure that the stop ring retainer is properly seated in the drive housing.

13. Install the brushes in the brush holders and center the brush springs on the brushes.

14. Position the drive gear actuating lever cover on the starter and install the brush cover band with a new gasket.

15. Check starter no-load amperage draw.

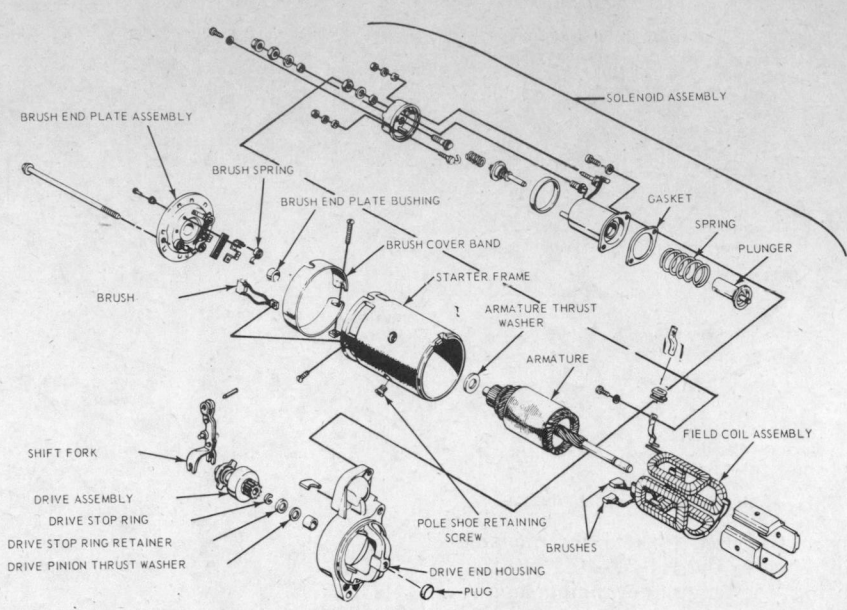

Ford solenoid actuated starter motor (© Ford Motor Co)

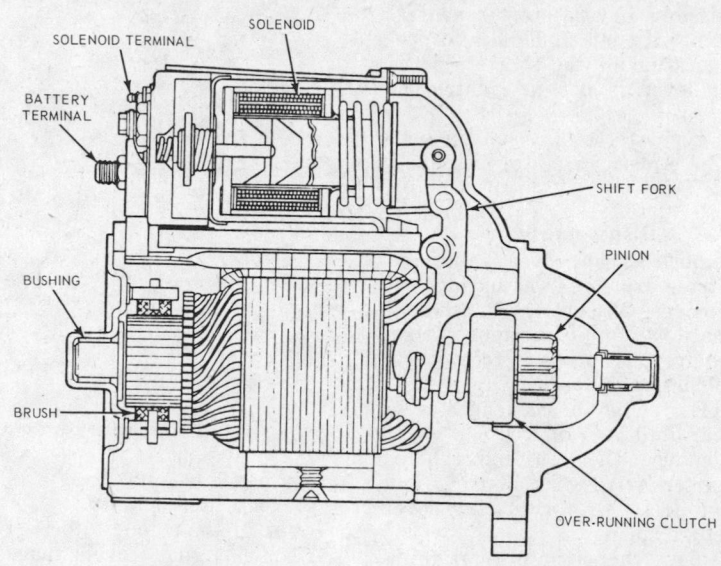

Ford solenoid actuated starter motor (© Ford Motor Co)

Autolite/Motorcraft Solenoid Actuated Starter Motor

(Ford Motor Co.)

This starter motor, usually used with late-model 429 and 460 engines, is a four-brush, four-field, four-pole wound unit. The frame encloses a wound armature, which is supported at the drive end by caged needle bearings and at the commutator end by a sintered copper bushing. The four pole shoes are retained to the frame by one pole screw apiece, and on each pole shoe is wound a ribbon-type field coil connected in series-parallel.

The solenoid is mounted to a flange on the starter drive housing, which encloses the entire shift mechanism and solenoid plunger. The solenoid, following standard industry practice, utilizes two windings—a pull-in winding and a hold-in winding.

Disassembly

1. Disconnect the copper strap from the solenoid starter terminal, remove the remaining screws and remove the solenoid.

2. Loosen the retaining screw and slide the brush cover band back far enough to gain access to the brushes.

3. Remove the brushes from their holders, then remove the through bolts and separate the drive end housing from the frame and brush end plate.

    NOTE: factory brush length is ½ in., wear limit ¼ in.

4. Remove the solenoid plunger and shift fork. These two items can be separated from each other by removing the roll pin.

5. Remove the armature and drive assembly from the frame. Remove the drive stop ring and slide the drive off the armature shaft.

6. Remove the drive stop ring retainer from the drive housing.

7. Inspection of the commutator, armature and bearings, and pinion gear procedures is the same as the positive engagement starter procedures.

Assembly

1. Lubricate the armature shaft splines with Lubriplate, then install drive assembly and a new stop ring.

2. Lubricate shift lever pivot pin with Lubriplate, then position solenoid plunger and shift lever assembly in the drive housing.

3. Place a new retainer in the drive housing. Apply a small amount of Lubriplate to the drive end of the armature shaft, then place armature and drive assembly into the drive housing, indexing the shift lever tangs with the drive assembly.

4. Apply a small amount of Lubriplate to the commutator end of the armature shaft, then position the frame and field assembly to the drive housing.

5. Position the brush plate assembly to the frame, making sure it properly indexes. Install through bolts and tighten to 45-85 in. lbs.

6. Install brushes into their holders and make sure leads are not touching any interior starter components.

7. Place the rubber gasket between the solenoid mount and the frame surface.
8. Place the starter solenoid in position with metal gasket and spring, install heat shield (if so equipped) and install solenoid screws.
9. Connect copper strap and install cover band.

Delco-Remy Starter Motor

(General Motors Corp.)

There are many different versions of the Delco-Remy starter, depending upon application. In general, six-cylinder engines use a unit having four field coils in series between the terminal and armature. Standard V8 engines use, depending on displacement, one of three types: one has two field coils in series with the armature and parallel to each other; another has two field coils in parallel between the field terminal and ground, and another has three field coils in series with the armature and one field connected between the motor terminal and ground. Heavy-duty starter motors, such as used on some of the largest G.M. high-output engines (over 400 cu. in.) have series compound windings. On the 1975 and later Delco starter, the terminal that connects the starter solenoid to the ignition coil has been removed as it is unnecessary with the High Energy Ignition System.

In spite of these differences, all Delco-Remy starters are disassembled and assembled in essentially the same manner.

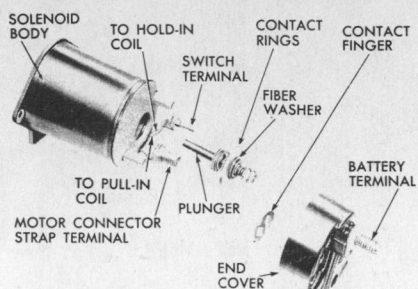

SOLENOID BODY — TO HOLD-IN COIL — SWITCH TERMINAL — CONTACT RINGS — CONTACT FINGER — FIBER WASHER — TO PULL-IN COIL — PLUNGER — BATTERY TERMINAL — MOTOR CONNECTOR STRAP TERMINAL — END COVER

Delco-Remy starter solenoid
(© Chevrolet Div., G.M. Corp.)

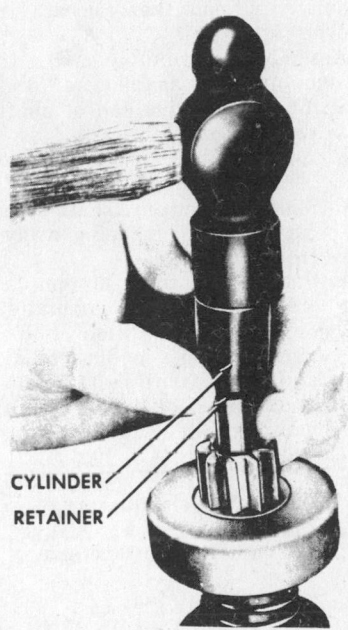

CYLINDER
RETAINER

Driving retainer off snap ring —Delco-Remy motor
(© Chevrolet Div., G.M. Corp)

Disassembly

1. Detach the field coil connectors from the motor solenoid terminal.
   NOTE: on models so equipped, remove solenoid mounting screws.
2. Remove the through bolts.
3. Remove commutator end frame, field frame and armature assembly from drive housing.
4. Remove the overrunning clutch from the armature shaft as follows:
   a. Slide the two-piece thrust collar off the end of the armature shaft.
   b. Slide a standard ½ in. pipe coupling or other spacer onto the shaft so that the end of the coupling butts against the edge of the retainer.
   c. Tap the end of the coupling with a hammer, driving retainer towards armature end of snap-ring.
   d. Remove snap-ring from its groove in the shaft using pliers. Slide retainer and clutch from armature shaft.
5. Disassemble brush assembly from field frame by releasing the V-spring and removing the support pin. The brush holders, brushes and springs now can be pulled out as a unit and the leads disconnected.
6. On models so equipped, separate solenoid from lever housing.

Cleaning and Inspection

1. Clean parts with a rag, but do not immerse the parts in a solvent. Immersion in a solvent will dissolve the grease that is packed in the clutch mechanism and damage the armature and field coil insulation.

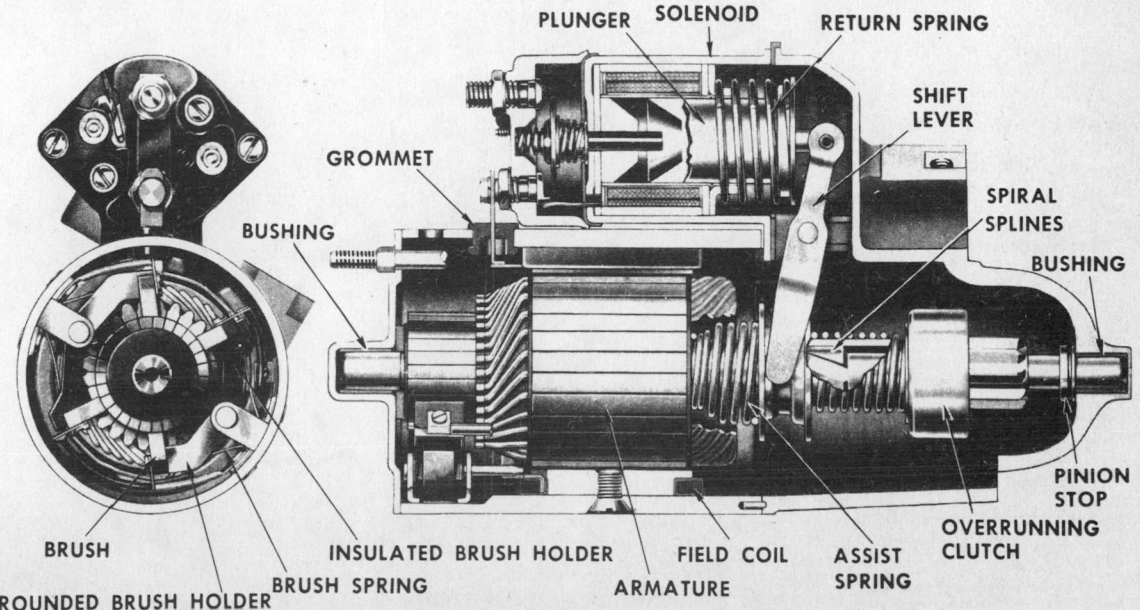

PLUNGER — SOLENOID — RETURN SPRING — SHIFT LEVER — SPIRAL SPLINES — BUSHING — PINION STOP — OVERRUNNING CLUTCH — ASSIST SPRING — ARMATURE — FIELD COIL — INSULATED BRUSH HOLDER — BRUSH SPRING — GROUNDED BRUSH HOLDER — BRUSH — GROMMET — BUSHING

Typical Delco-Remy starter motor using an assist spring—light duty Chevrolet illustrated
(© Chevrolet Div., G.M. Corp)

2. Test overrunning clutch action. The pinion should turn freely in the overrunning direction and must not slip in the cranking direction. Check pinion teeth to see that they have not been chipped, cracked, or excessively worn. Replace the unit if necessary.

3. Inspect the armature commutator. If the commutator is rough or out of round, it should be turned down and undercut.

Caution Undercut the insulation between the commatator bars by 1/32 in.

This undercut must be the full width of the insulation and flat at the bottom; a triangular groove will not be satisfactory. Some starter motor models use a molded armature commutator design and no attempt to undercut the insulation should be made or serious damage may result to the commutator.

Assembly

1. Install brushes into holders. Install solenoid, if so equipped.
2. Assemble insulated and grounded brush holder together using the V-spring and position the assembled unit on the support pin. Push holders and spring to bottom of support and rotate spring to engage the slot in support. Attach ground wire to grounded brush and field lead wire to insulated brush, then repeat for other brush sets.

3. Assemble overrunning clutch to armature shaft as follows:
   a. Lubricate drive end of shaft with silicone lubricant.
   b. Slide clutch assembly onto shaft with pinion outward.
   c. Slide retainer onto shaft with cupped surface facing away from pinion.
   d. Stand armature up on a wood surface, commutator downwards. Position snapring on upper end of shaft and drive it onto shaft with a small block of wood and a hammer. Slide snap-ring into groove.
   e. Install thrust collar onto shaft with shoulder next to snap-ring.
   f. With retainer on one side of

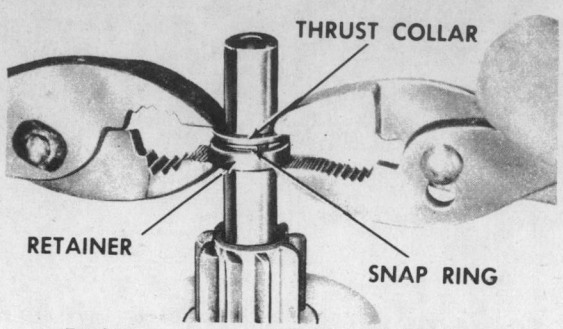

Forcing snap ring into retainer—Delco-Remy motor
(© Chevrolet Div., G.M. Corp)

snap-ring and thrust collar on the other side, squeeze together with two sets of pliers until ring seats in retainer. On models without thrust collar, use a washer. Remember to remove washer before continuing.

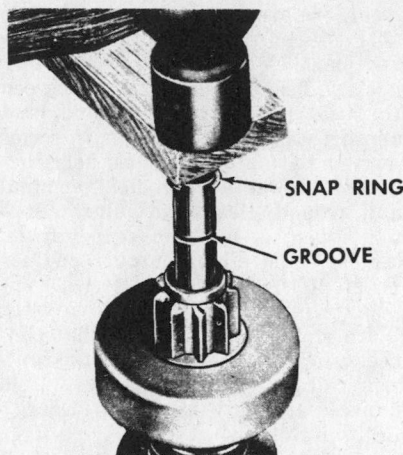

Forcing snap ring over armature shaft—Delco-Remy motor
(© Chevrolet Div., G.M. Corp)

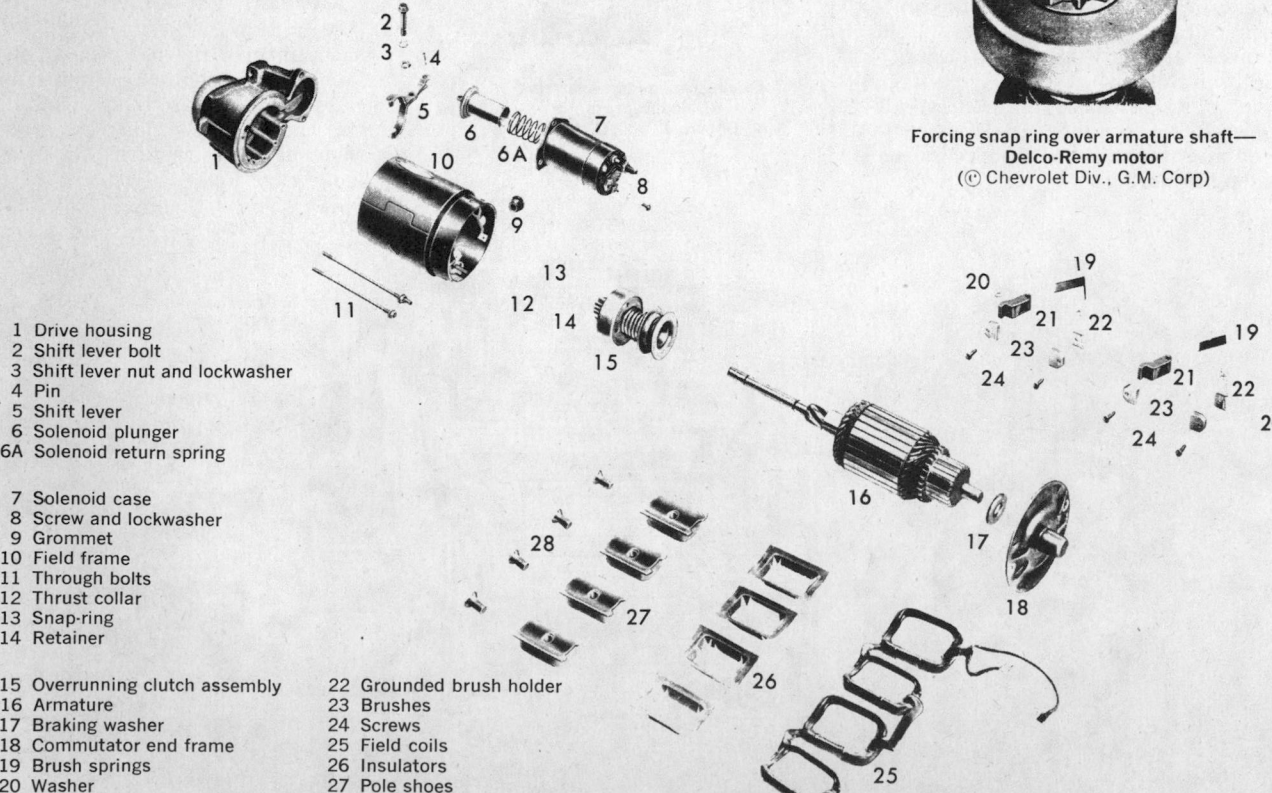

1 Drive housing
2 Shift lever bolt
3 Shift lever nut and lockwasher
4 Pin
5 Shift lever
6 Solenoid plunger
6A Solenoid return spring

7 Solenoid case
8 Screw and lockwasher
9 Grommet
10 Field frame
11 Through bolts
12 Thrust collar
13 Snap-ring
14 Retainer

15 Overrunning clutch assembly
16 Armature
17 Braking washer
18 Commutator end frame
19 Brush springs
20 Washer
21 Insulated brush holders

22 Grounded brush holder
23 Brushes
24 Screws
25 Field coils
26 Insulators
27 Pole shoes
28 Screws

Typical Delco-Remy starter motor exploded view—light duty Chevrolet illustrated
(© Chevrolet Div., G.M. Corp)

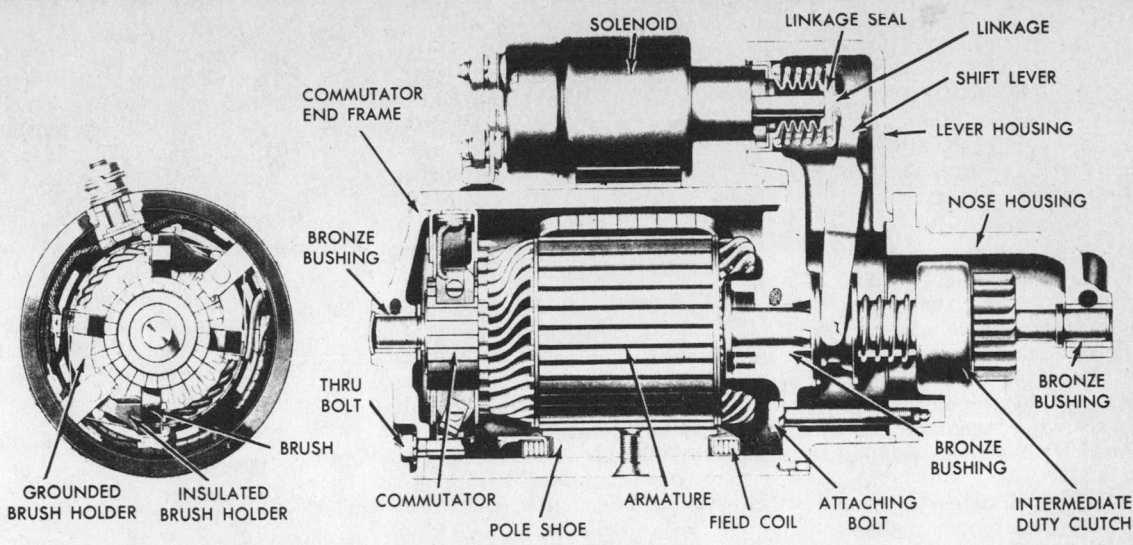

Typical Delco-Remy starter motor as used on intermediate models—Chevrolet application illustrated (© Chevrolet Div., G.M. Corp)

4. Lubricate drive end bushing with silicone lubricant, then slide armature and clutch assembly into place, at the same time engaging shift lever with clutch.
5. Position field frame over armature and apply sealer (silicone) between frame and solenoid case. Position frame against

drive housing, making sure brushes are not damaged in the process.

6. Lubricate commutator end bushing with silicone lubricant, place a leather brake washer on the armature shaft and slide commutator end frame onto shaft.

Install through bolts and tighten to 65 in. lbs.
7. Reconnect field coil connector/s to the solenoid motor terminal. Install solenoid mounting screws, if so equipped.
8. Check pinion clearance; it should be 0.010-0.140 in. on all models.

AC Generator (Alternator) And System Service

Preliminary Charging System Inspection

NOTE: before performing any tests on the charging systems, these precautions should be taken to ensure the accuracy of the tests in this section.

1. Check the condition of the alternator belt and tighten it if necessary.
2. Clean the battery cable connections at the battery. Make sure that the connections between the battery wires and the battery clamps are good. Reconnect the negative terminal only, and proceed to the next step.
3. With the key off, insert a test light between the positive terminal on the battery and the disconnected positive battery terminal clamp. If the test light comes on, there is a short in the electrical system of the car. The short has to be repaired before proceeding. If the light fails to glow, reconnect the clamp and proceed to the next step.
NOTE: alternators with transistorized regulators sometimes draw a slight current even when the key is turned off. To properly check these systems for a short, the regulator must be disconnected. Also, on cars equipped with an electric clock, disconnect the lead wire from the clock.

4. Check the charging system wiring for breaks or shorts.
5. Check the battery to make sure that it is fully charged and in good condition.

Chrysler Isolated Field Alternator (Electronic Regulator)

The Chrysler isolated field alternator replaced the grounded brush alternator in 1970 and derived its name from its construction. Both of the brushes are insulated from ground and there is no heat sink connection, thereby isolating the internal field.

Troubleshooting

NOTE: see the "Preliminary Charging System Inspection" section before proceeding further. Make sure that the continuous running blower, if equipped, is disconnected. This blower will run with the key turned on even if the blower controls are off unless disconnected.

Fusible Links

Chrysler Corporation cars have a single fusible link which is connected between the starter relay and the junction block. Failure of this link will cause all electrical systems to stop functioning.

Charging System Operation

NOTE: if the current indicator is to give an accurate reading, the battery cables must be of the same gauge and length as the original equipment.

1. With the engine running and all electrical systems off, place a current indicator over the positive battery cable.
2. If a charge of about 5 amps is recorded, the charging system is working. If a draw of about 5 amps is recorded the system is not working. The needle moves toward the battery when a charge condition is indicated and away from the battery when a draw condition is indicated. If a draw is indicated, proceed to the next testing procedure. If an overcharge of 10-15 amps is indicated, check for a faulty regulator.

Ignition Switch-to-Regulator Circuit Check

1. Disconnect the regulator wires at the regulator.
2. Turn the key on but do not start the engine.
3. Using a voltmeter or test light, check for voltage across the I and F terminals. If there is current present, the circuit is good. If there is no current, check for bad connections, a bad ballast

resistor, a bad ammeter, broken wires, or bad ground at the alternator or voltage regulator. Also, check for voltage from the I wire to ground; current should be present. Check for voltage from the F terminal to ground; current should be present.

Isolation Test

This test determines whether the regulator or alternator is bad if everything else in the circuit was OK.

1. Disconnect, at the alternator, the wire that runs between one of the alternator field connections and the voltage regulator.
2. Run a jumper wire from the disconnected alternator terminal to ground.
3. Connect a voltmeter to the battery. The positive voltmeter lead connects to the positive battery terminal, and the negative lead goes to the negative terminal. Record the reading.
4. Make sure that all electrical systems are turned off. Start the engine. Do not race the engine.
5. Gradually raise engine speed to 1500–2000 rpm. There should be an increase of one to two volts on the voltmeter. If this is true, the alternator is good and the voltage regulator should be repaired. If there is no voltage increase, the alternator is faulty.

NOTE: *the following tests require the use of a carbon pile and an ammeter.*

Charging Circuit Resistance Test

1. Disconnect battery ground cable.
2. Disconnect the lead from the alternator output (BATT.) terminal.
3. Hook up an ammeter as follows:
   a. Connect the positive lead to the alternator output terminal.
   b. Connect the negative lead to the lead just disconnected from the alternator output terminal.
4. Hook up voltmeter as follows:
   a. Connect the positive voltmeter lead to the lead just disconnected from the alternator output terminal.
   b. Connect the negative voltmeter lead to the positive battery post.
5. Disconnect the lead from the alternator field (FLD.) terminal.
6. Connect a jumper wire between alternator field terminal and ground.
7. Hook up a tachometer to the engine.
8. Connect the battery ground cable, then connect carbon pile to battery terminals.
9. Start the engine and allow to idle.

10. Slowly adjust the engine speed and carbon pile until the ammeter registers 20 amps.
11. The voltmeter reading will now show the voltage drop in the charging circuit. There should not be more than 0.7 volt drop.
12. If the voltage drop exceeds 0.7 volt, stop the engine, clean and tighten all circuit connections, then repeat the test.

Current Output Test

1. The ammeter and carbon pile hookup should remain the same as for the circuit resistance test.
2. Connect the voltmeter negative lead to the battery negative post.
3. Move the positive voltmeter lead to the alternator "BATT" post.
4. Start the engine and adjust speed to 1250 rpm.

CAUTION: *Reduce the engine speed to idle immediately after starting the engine. Adjust the carbon pile and engine speed incrementally until 1250 rpm is reached.*

5. Note voltmeter and ammeter readings. Maintain a 15 volt reading by adjusting the carbon pile control.
6. Compare ammeter reading with manufacturer's specifications. The reading should be no less than specified, 3 amps.
7. If below specifications, internal trouble is indicated. Remove the alternator for further testing.

Electronic Voltage Regulator Test

1. Make sure battery terminals are clean and battery is charged.
2. Connect the positive lead of a test voltmeter to ignition Terminal No. 1 of the ballast resistor.

On 1975 and later Dart and Valiant, connect the positive lead of the voltmeter to the terminal on the ballast resistor which has a blue or black wire connected to it. On all other 1975 and later models, connect the voltmeter to the battery.

NOTE: *Don't remove the connector from the ballast resistor terminal.*

3. Connect the negative voltmeter lead to a good *body* ground.
4. Start engine and allow it to idle at 1250 rpm, all lights and accessories turned off. Voltage should be as follows:

Ambient Temp. ¼ in. from Regulator	Voltage
-20°F.	14.3-15.3
80°F.	13.8-14.4
140°F.	13.3-14.0

5. If the voltage is *below* specifications, check the following:
   a. Voltage regulator ground—check voltage drop between regulator cover and ground.
   b. Harness wiring—disconnect regulator plug (ign. switch off), then turn on ign. switch and check for battery voltage at the terminal having the blue and green leads. *Wiring harness must be disconnected from the regulator when checking individual leads.* If no voltage is present in either lead, the problem is in the car wiring or alternator field.
6. If Step 5 tests showed no malfunctions, install a new regulator and repeat Step 4.

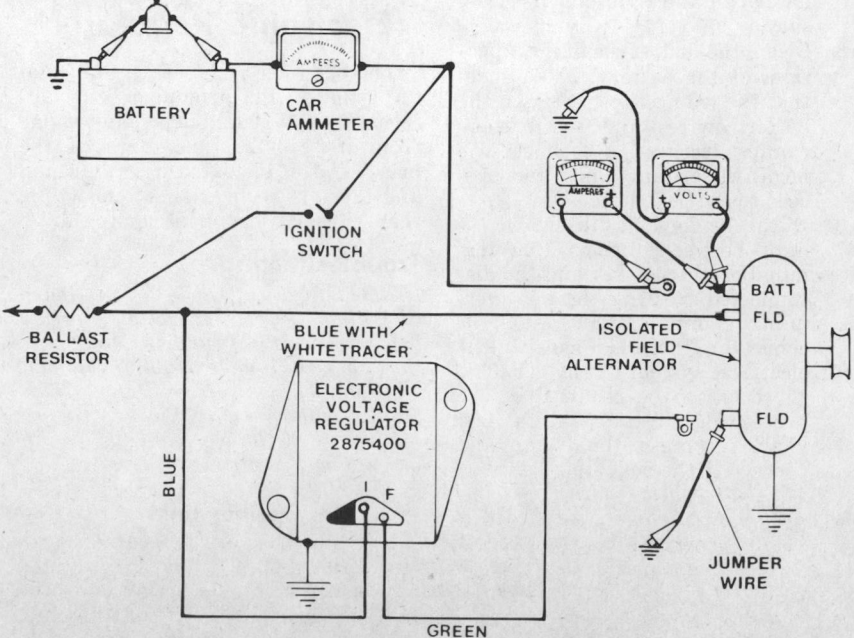

Current output test hook-up—Chrysler isolated field alternator

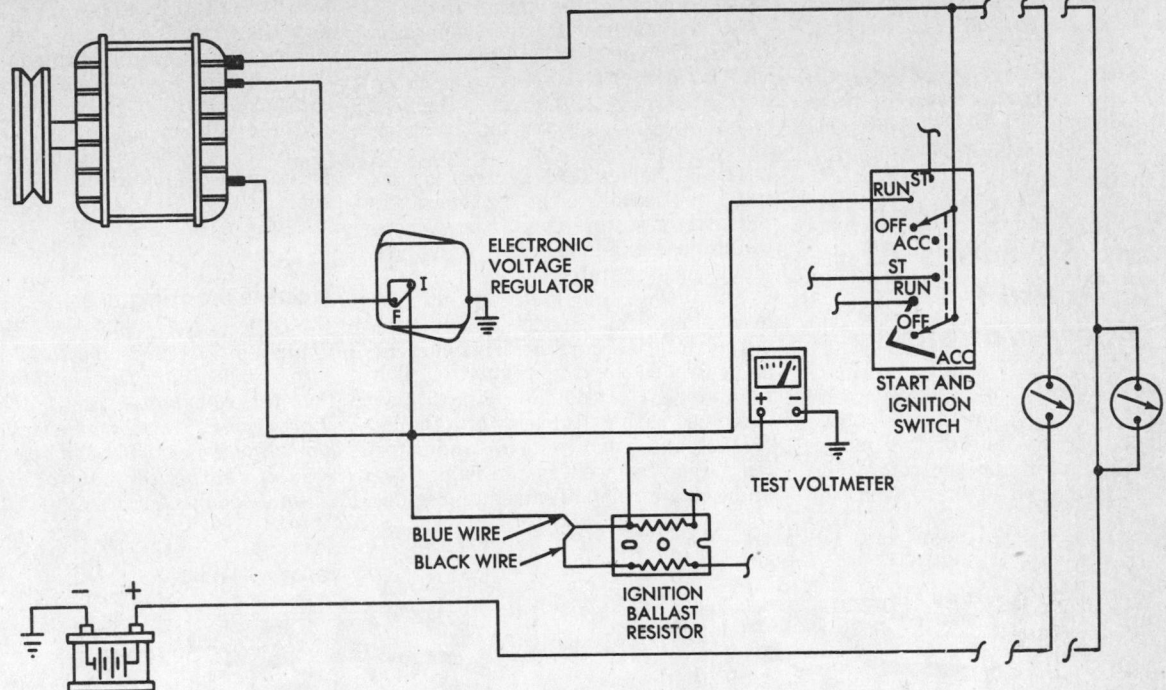

Voltage Regulator Test hook-up; right ammeter gauge for Monaco, Fury, Chrysler and Imperial, left for all other models
(© Chrysler Corp)

7. If voltage is *above* specifications (Step 4), or fluctuates, check the following:

   a. Ground between regulator and body, and between body and engine.

   b. Ignition switch circuit between switch and regulator.

8. If voltage is still more than ½ volt above specifications, install a new regulator and repeat Step 4.

Field-Loads Relay Test

On all Chrysler Corporation cars beginning 1975 except Dart and Valiant, the charging system wiring circuit has been redesigned to protect the battery from overcharging by the addition of an ignition switch operated field-loads relay. This unit reduces voltage drop between charging system components, making the regulator more sensitive to battery requirements and decreasing the possibility of overcharging.

1. Disconnect the wiring harness connector at the voltage regulator. Ground the negative lead of the voltmeter.

2. Turn the ignition switch on but don't start the engine.

3. Measure the voltage at the terminals of the disconnected wiring harness connector with the positive lead of the voltmeter. Voltage here should be the same as at the battery.

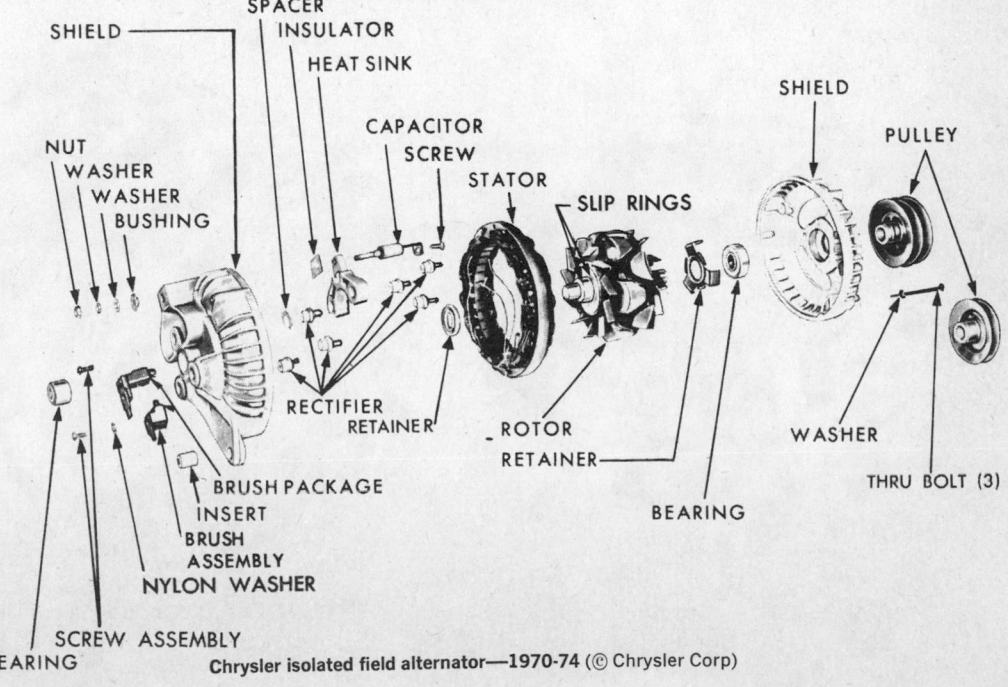

Chrysler isolated field alternator—1970-74 (© Chrysler Corp)

4. If there is battery voltage at the terminals, the unit is working properly.

5. If battery voltage is not obtained, check all wiring and connections for damage. If they are alright, the unit must be replaced.

Delcotron 5.5 Series 1D and 6.2 Series 2D (General Motors Corporation)

Description

The Delcotron continuous output AC generator consists of two major parts—the stator and the rotor. The stator is composed of many turns of wire on the inside of a laminated core that is attached to the generator frame. The rotor is mounted on bearings at each end. Two brushes carry current through slip rings to the field coils, which are wound on the rotor shaft.

The 5.5 Series 1D Delcotron is similar in operation to the 6.2 Series 2D perforated stator Delcotron. Where differences exist, the two units are mentioned separately.

Six diodes, mounted on internal heat sinks, change the AC current output into DC current. This current is controlled by the regulator. The regulator is a double-contact unit combined with a field relay or a triple-contact unit containing an indicator lamp relay as well as the field relay and voltage relay. Transistor regulators were also used in production intermittently.

On high-output Delcotron units, the regulator incorporates a field discharge diode.

These alternators were last used in 1972. Starting 1973, the Delco 10-SI became the standard GM alternator.

Troubleshooting

NOTE: *See the "Preliminary Charging System Inspection" section before proceeding further. Make sure that the continuous running blower, if equipped, is disconnected. This blower will run with the key on and even if the blower control is off, it is not disconnected.*

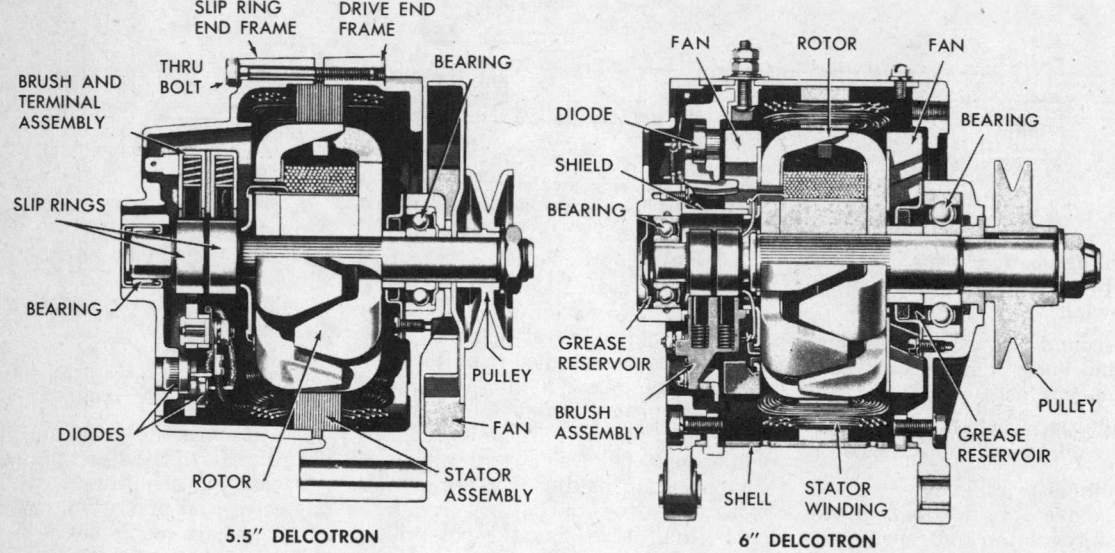

5.5" DELCOTRON · 6" DELCOTRON

5.5 and 6.2 Delcotron models—cross sectional views (© Chevrolet Div., G.M. Corp)

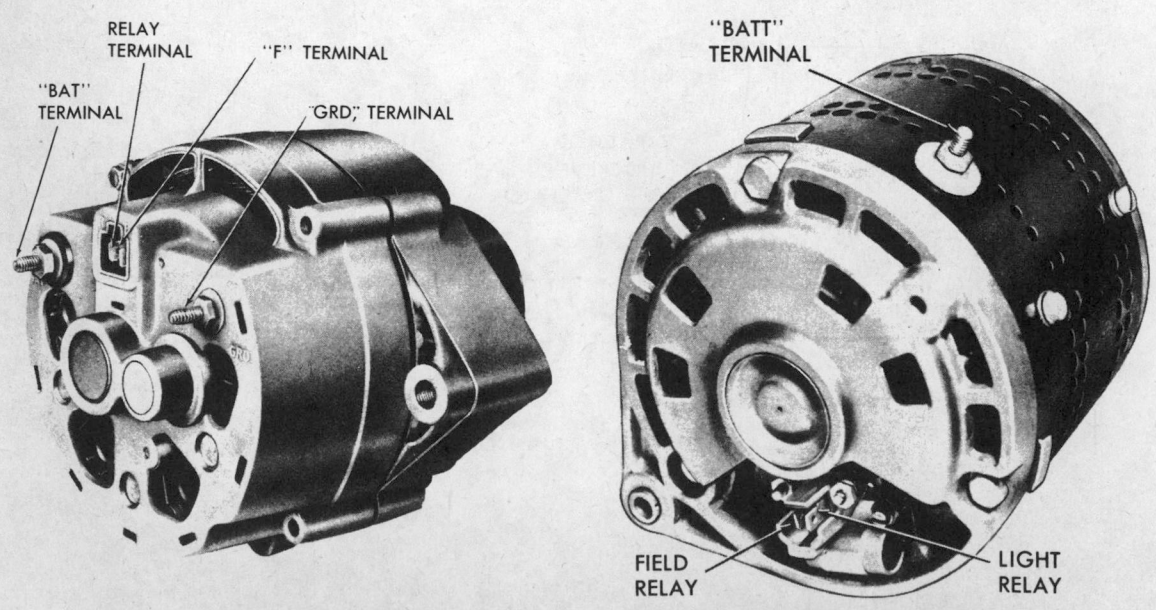

5.5" ALUMINUM DELCOTRON · 6.2" PERFORATED STATOR DELCOTRON

5.5 and 6.2 Delcotron models (© Chevrolet Div., G.M. Corp)

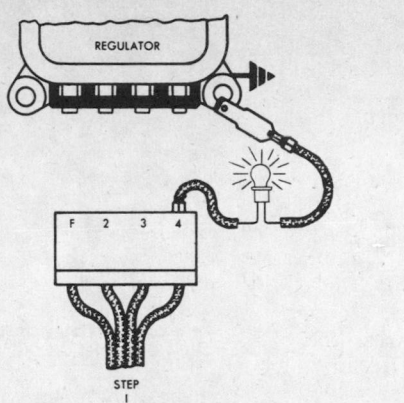
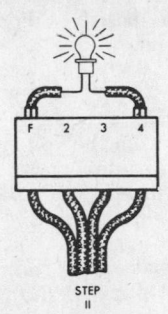
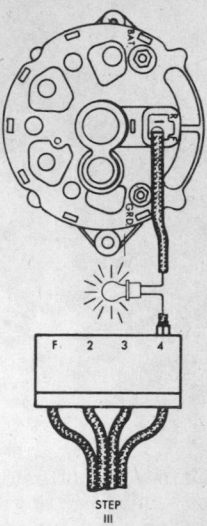

Initial field excitation circuit test hook-ups (© Chevrolet Div., G.M. Corp)

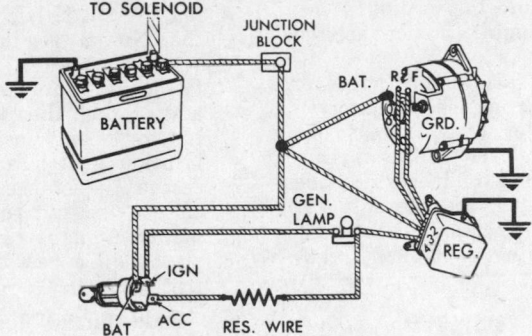

Typical Delcotron circuit diagram
(© Chevrolet Div., G.M. Corp)

Indicator Light Circuit Check:

Check the indicator light for normal operation:

Ignition Switch Condition	Light Condition	Engine Condition
Off	Off	Stopped
On	On	Stopped
On	Off	Running

If the alternator light is operating properly, proceed to the next section. If one of the following conditions exists, proceed as directed:

A. *Ignition Switch off, light stays on:* disconnect leads from number 1 and 2 terminals. If the light remains on, there is a short between these two leads. If the lamp goes out, replace the rectifier bridge.

B. *Ignition switch on, light off, engine not running:* This condition can be caused by the defects listed in A., by reversal of number 1 and 2 leads at the alternator, or by an open circuit. If the circuit is open proceed as follows:

1. Connect a voltmeter from no. 2 alternator terminal to ground. If a reading is obtained, proceed to the next step. If a zero reading is obtained, repair the circuit between no. 2 terminal and the battery. If the light comes on, no further testing is necessary.

2. With the ignition switch on and with no. 1 and 2 terminals disconnected at the alternator, momentarily ground no. 1 terminal lead.

Caution *Do not ground no. 2 Lead.* If the light still doesn't light, check for a blown fuse or fusible link, burned out bulb, defective bulb socket, or an open no. 1 lead circuit between generator and ignition switch.

3. If the lamp lights, remove the ground at no. 1 terminal, and with no. 1 and 2 terminals connected to the alternator, insert a screwdriver into the test hole at the back of the alternator to ground the winding.

4. If the light does not come on, check the connection between the wiring harness and no. 1 terminal of the alternator. If the connection is alright, disassemble the alternator and check the brushes, slip rings, and field winding.

5. If a light now comes on, and a reading was obtained in step 1, replace the regulator.

C. *Switch on, Light on, Engine Running.* The causes for this condition are covered in Charging System Tests, Low Charging Rate.

Fusible Links

There are four fusible links on all GM cars.

1. The 14 gauge wire that runs from the junction block to the positive battery terminal serves as a fusible link.
2. There is a second link in the circuit between the horn relay and the ignition switch.
3. A third link is in the wire running to the No. 3 voltage regulator terminal. It's purpose is to protect the regulator contacts and the alternator field circuit.
4. The fourth link is connected between the main junction block and the horn relay.

These links must be inspected before proceeding with troubleshooting.

Charging System Operation

NOTE: *If the current indicator is to give an accurate reading, the battery cables must be the same gauge and length as the original equipment.*

1. With the engine running and all electrical systems turned off, place a current indicator over the positive battery cable.
2. If a charge of about 5 amps is recorded, the charging system is working. If a draw of about 5 amps is recorded, the system is not working. The needle moves toward the battery when a charge condition is indicated, and away from the battery when a draw condition is indicated. If a draw is indicated, proceed with further testing. If an excessive charge (10–15 amps) is indicated, check for an overcharge, caused by a faulty regulator.

Indicator Light Circuit Testing

The indicator light is important in AC charging systems, for it provides initial field excitation current to the alternator. The light goes out when the field relay closes, which applies

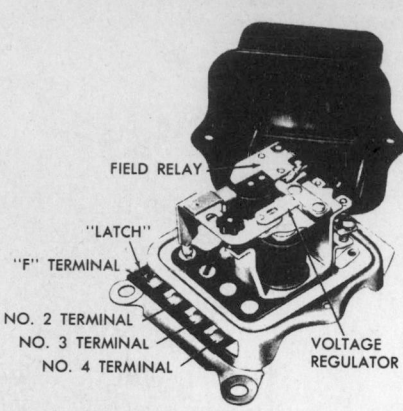

FIELD RELAY

"LATCH"

"F" TERMINAL

NO. 2 TERMINAL
NO. 3 TERMINAL
NO. 4 TERMINAL

VOLTAGE
REGULATOR

Mechanical voltage regulator
(© Chevrolet Div., G.M. Corp)

battery current to both sides of the bulb. If the light does not go on when key is turned, the bulb could be faulty, there could be an open circuit in the wiring or a positive diode in the alternator could be shorted to ground.

1. Disconnect plug from regulator and connect a test light between terminal No. 4 (in plug) and ground. Turn on ignition switch and observe the light. If light does not go on, check bulb, socket or wiring between switch and regulator plug. If light goes on, check regulator, wiring between regulator F terminal and alternator, or Delcotron itself.
2. Disconnect jumper wire at ground end and reconnect to F terminal in plug. Turn on ignition for a second and note light. If light goes on, problem is in regulator. If light does not go on, problem is in wire between F terminals (regulator and alternator).
3. Disconnect light at plug F terminal and reconnect the free end to F terminal at alternator. Turn on ignition switch for a second and note light. If light goes on, the problem is an open circuit in the wire connecting the regulator and alternator F terminals. If light does not go on, the alter-

nator field windings are defective.

If the indicator light does not extinguish when engine is started, check for a loose drive belt, faulty field relay, faulty alternator, open parallel resistance wire (usually shows up at idle). If the light stays on with the key turned off, an alternator positive diode is shorted to ground.

Isolation Test

1. Disconnect the wiring harness from the voltage regulator. With a jumper wire connect the F wire to the no. 3 wire in the wire harness plug.
2. Connect a voltmeter across the battery terminals, the positive voltmeter lead to the positive battery terminal, and the negative lead to the negative terminal. Record the reading.
3. Start the engine. Do not race the engine.
4. Gradually raise engine speed to 1500-2000 rpm. The reading on the voltmeter should increase one to two volts over the initial reading. If there is no increase in the reading, repair the alternator. If there is an increase in the voltmeter reading, replace the regulator.

Field Relay Test

1. Connect a voltmeter between the No. 2 terminal and the ground on the regulator.
2. Start the engine and run at about 1500-2000 RPM.
3. If voltmeter reads zero, check circuit connecting regulator terminal No. 2 and Delcotron R terminal.
4. If voltage exceeds closing voltage (field relay), and light remains on, field relay is faulty and must be checked.

Field Relay Adjustment

1. Connect a voltmeter between No. 2 regulator terminal and ground.
2. To adjust, connect a 50 ohm

Adjusting field relay closing voltage
(© Chevrolet Div., G.M. Corp)

rheostat between wiring harness terminal No. 3 and regulator terminal No. 2, after disconnecting the spade lug on the end of the No. 2 regulator terminal wire. Connect a voltmeter between regulator terminal No. 2 and ground, then turn the resistor to "open" position, turn off ignition switch and slowly decrease resistance until relay closes (noting voltage at this point). Voltage can be adjusted by bending heel iron as illustrated.

Field Circuit Resistance Testing

The resistance wire is an integral part of the ignition wiring harness. The wire cannot be soldered; any connections must be made using crimp-type connectors. Resistance is 10 ohms, 6¼ watts.

1. Connect a voltmeter between the wiring harness terminal No. 4 and ground.
2. Turn on ignition switch, needle must indicate or resistor is open.

Delcotron Current Output Test

NOTE: disconnect battery ground cable while making test connections, then reconnect cable after completing Step 5. Disconnect battery ground

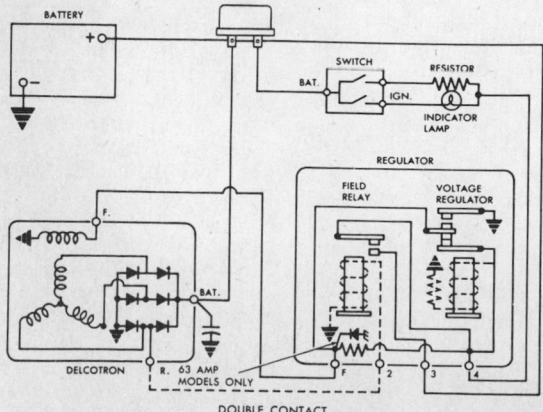

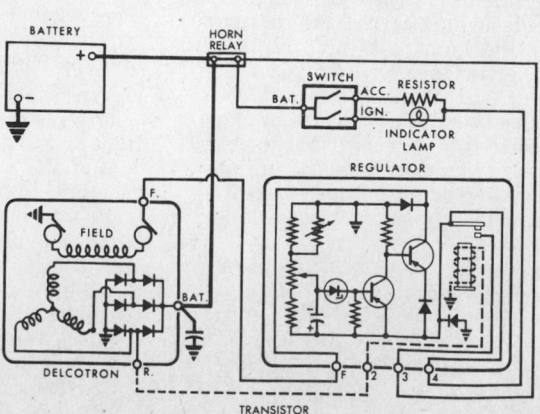

Voltage regulator circuit diagrams (© Chevrolet Div., G.M. Corp)

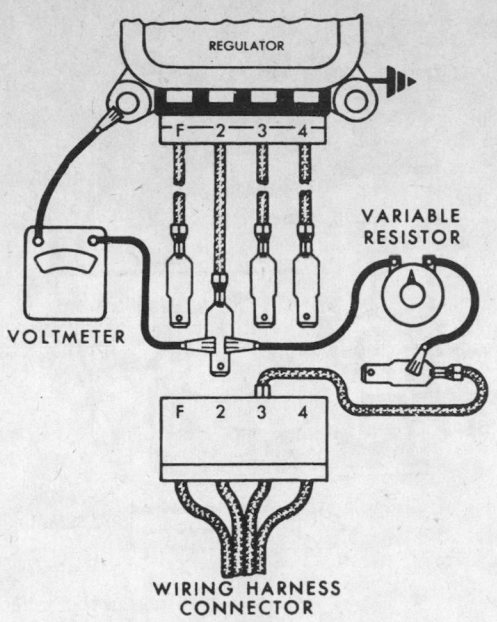

Testing field relay closing voltage
(© Chevrolet Div., G.M. Corp)

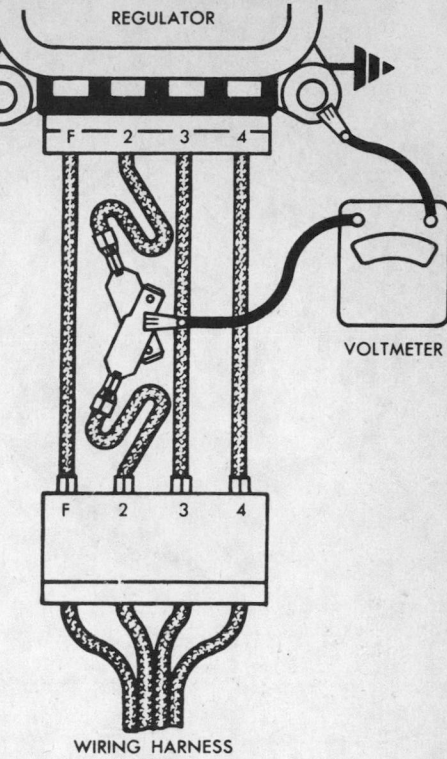

Testing field relay
(© Chevrolet Div., G.M. Corp)

cable again before removing test set-up. This test yields the same information as the isolation test but requires the use of an ammeter and a carbon pile.

1. Disconnect lead from BAT. terminal of Delcotron.
2. Hook an ammeter to the lead just disconnected, and to the BAT. terminal of the Delcotron.
3. Hook up the voltmeter leads to the BAT. terminal and a good ground on the alternator.
4. Disconnect the lead from the FR. terminal of the Delcotron.
5. Hook up a jumper wire between BAT. and F terminals of the Delcotron.
6. With a carbon pile load control hooked up to the battery posts, start the engine and set engine to 1,500 rpm, while adjusting carbon pile to obtain 14 volts. With a 6.2 in. alternator, only 600-800 rpm is required.

Caution Be careful not to exceed the recommended regulator voltage setting. This is controlled by the carbon pile load.

7. Ammeter should read within 10% of rated output, as stamped on frame of each unit.

Delcotron 10-SI Series 100 (General Motors Corp.)

This system is an integrated AC generating system containing a built-in voltage regulator. Removal and replacement is essentially the same as for the standard AC generator.

The regulator is mounted inside the slip ring end frame. All regulator

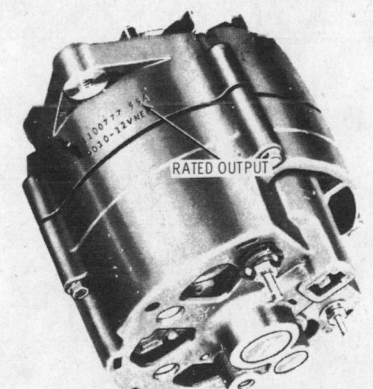

Delcotron rated output is stamped on the case
(© Oldsmobile Div., G.M. Corp)

components are enclosed in an epoxy molding, and the regulator cannot be adjusted. Rotor and stator tests are the same as for the 5.5 Delcotron, covered previously.

This alternator became standard equipment on all GM cars in 1973, and is also used in some American Motors cars starting 1975.

Troubleshooting

NOTE: *See the "Preliminary Charging System Inspection" section before proceeding further. Make sure that the continuous running blower, if equipped, is disconnected. This*

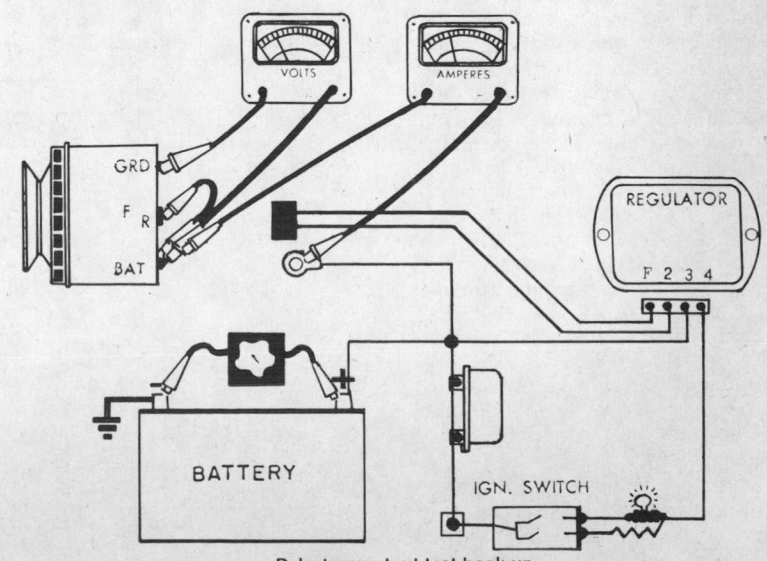

Delcotron output test hook-up

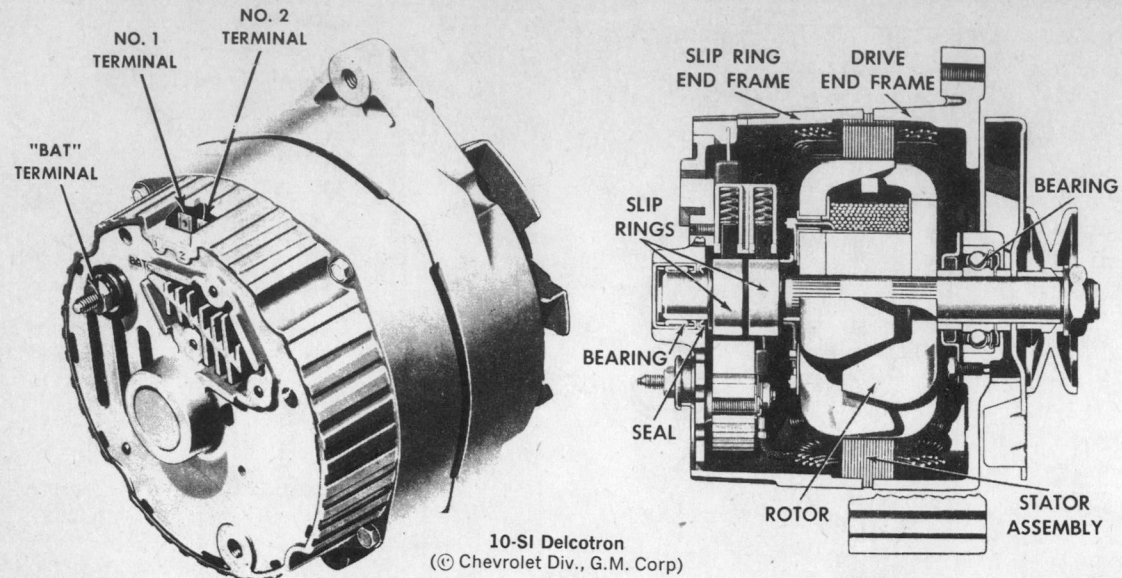

NO. 1 TERMINAL

NO. 2 TERMINAL

"BAT" TERMINAL

SLIP RING END FRAME

DRIVE END FRAME

SLIP RINGS

BEARING

BEARING

SEAL

ROTOR

STATOR ASSEMBLY

10-SI Delcotron
(© Chevrolet Div., G.M. Corp)

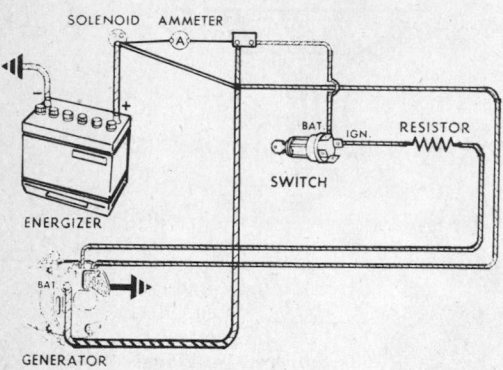

SOLENOID   AMMETER

ENERGIZER

BAT   IGN.   RESISTOR

SWITCH

BAT

GENERATOR

10-SI basic wiring diagram
(© Chevrolet Div., G.M. Corp)

blower will run with the key on even if the blower control is off, unless disconnected.

Charging System Test—Low Charging Rate

1. After battery condition, drive belt tension, and wiring terminals and connections have been checked, charge the battery fully and perform the following test:
2. Connect a test voltmeter between the alternator BAT. terminal and ground, ignition switch on. Connect the voltmeter in turn to alternator terminals No. 1 and No. 2, the other voltmeter lead being grounded as before. A zero reading indicates an open circuit between the battery and each connection at the alternator. If this test discloses no faults in the wiring, proceed to Step 3.
3. Connect the test voltmeter to the alternator BAT. terminal (the other test lead to ground), start the engine and run at 1,500-2,000 rpm with all lights and electrical accessories turned on. If the voltmeter reads 12.8 volts or greater, the alternator is

good and no further checks need be made. If the voltmeter reads less than 12.8 volts, ground the field winding by inserting a screwdriver into the test hole in the end frame.

Caution Do not force tab more than ¾ in. into end frame.

a. If voltage increases to 13 volts or more, the regulator unit is defective.

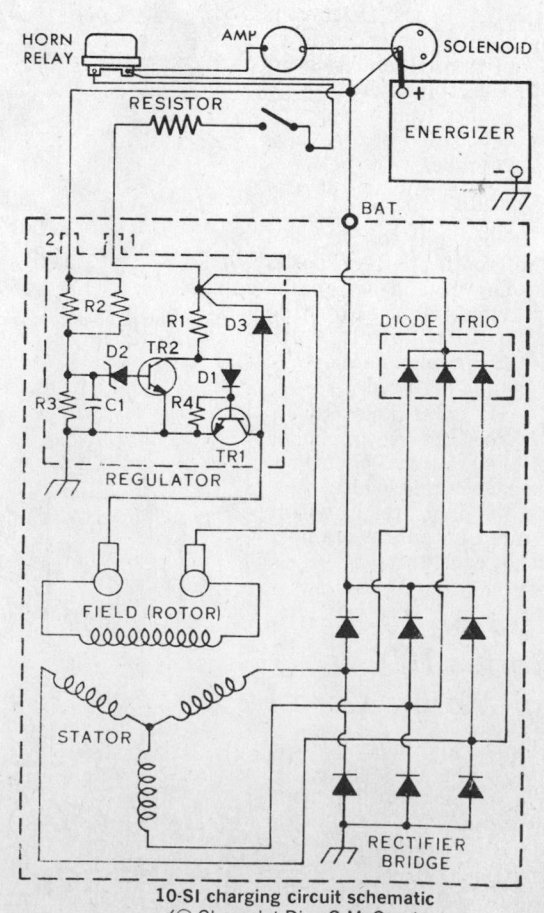

HORN RELAY   AMP   SOLENOID

RESISTOR

ENERGIZER

BAT.

R2   R1   D3   DIODE TRIO

D2   TR2   D1

R3   C1   R4   TR1

REGULATOR

FIELD (ROTOR)

STATOR

RECTIFIER BRIDGE

10-SI charging circuit schematic
(© Chevrolet Div., G.M. Corp)

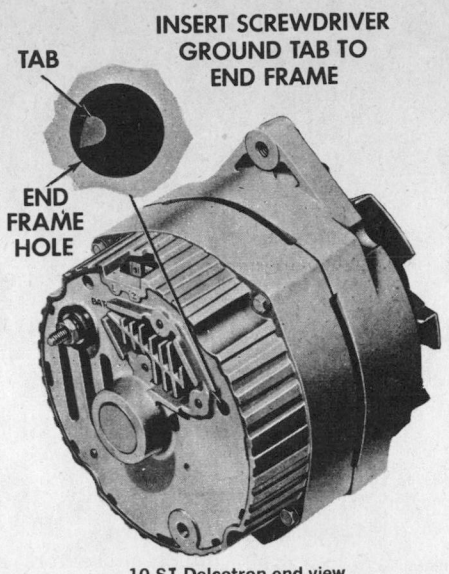

TAB

INSERT SCREWDRIVER GROUND TAB TO END FRAME

END FRAME HOLE

10-SI Delcotron end view
(© Chevrolet Div., G.M. Corp)

b. If voltage does not increase significantly, generator is defective.

Charging System Test—High Charging Rate

1. With the battery fully charged, connect a voltmeter between alternator terminal no. 2 and ground. If the reading is zero, no. 2 circuit from the battery is open.

2. If no. 2 circuit is OK, but an obvious overcharging condition still exists, proceed as follows:
   a. Remove the alternator and separate the end frames.
   b. Connect a low-range ohmmeter between the brush lead clip and the end frame, as illustrated (test no. 1), then reverse the lead connections. If both readings are zero, either the brush lead clip is grounded or the regulator is defective. A grounded brush lead clip can be due to a damaged insulating sleeve or omission of the insulating washer.

Alternator Output Test

1. Disconnect the battery ground cable.

2. Disconnect the wire from the battery terminal on the alternator.

3. Connect your ammeter black (negative) lead to the wire removed in step 2, and the ammeter red (positive) lead to the battery terminal on the alternator.

4. Reconnect the battery ground cable, and turn on all electrical accessories. If the battery is fully charged, bump the starter a few times to discharge it partially.

5. Start the engine and run it to obtain a maximum current reading on the ammeter.

6. If the current is within 10 amps of the rated output of the alternator, the alternator is working properly; if the current is not within 10 amps, insert a screwdriver in the test hole in the end frame and use it to ground the tab in the test hole against the side of the hole.

7. If the current is now within 10 amps of the rated output, remove the alternator and have the voltage regulator replaced; if it is still below 10 amps of rated output, remove the alternator and have it tested further.

Autolite/Motorcraft Alternator with External Regulator (Ford Motor Co.)

The Autolite/Motorcraft charging system is a negative ground system.

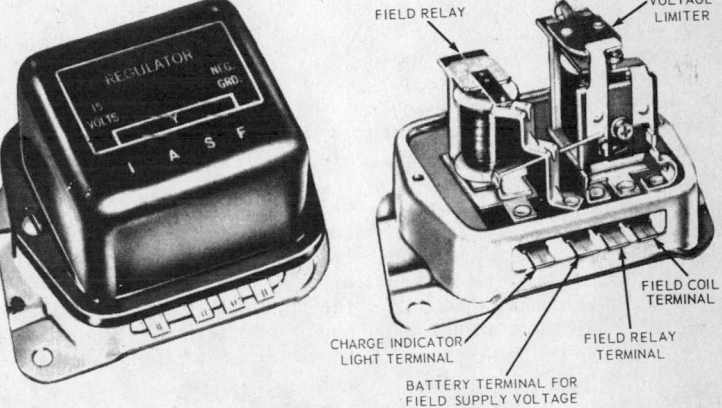

External electro-mechanical regulator
(© Ford Motor Co)

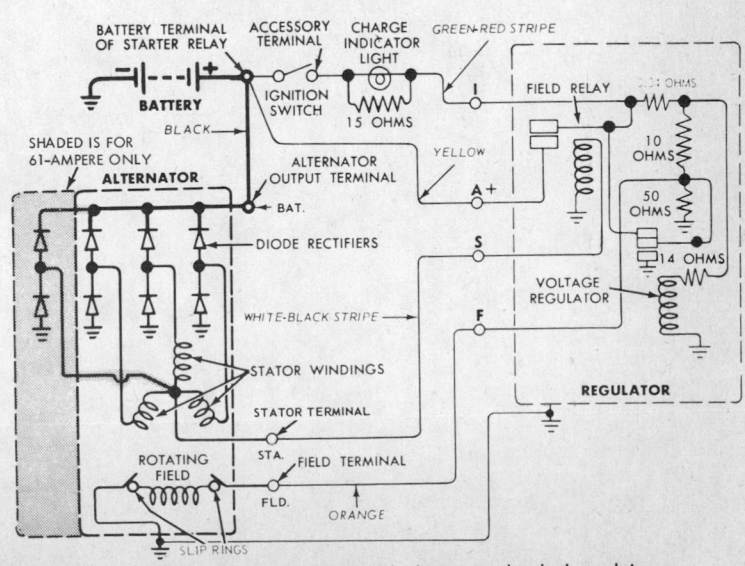

Charging system schematic with electro-mechanical regulator and charging light
(© Ford Motor Co)

U25

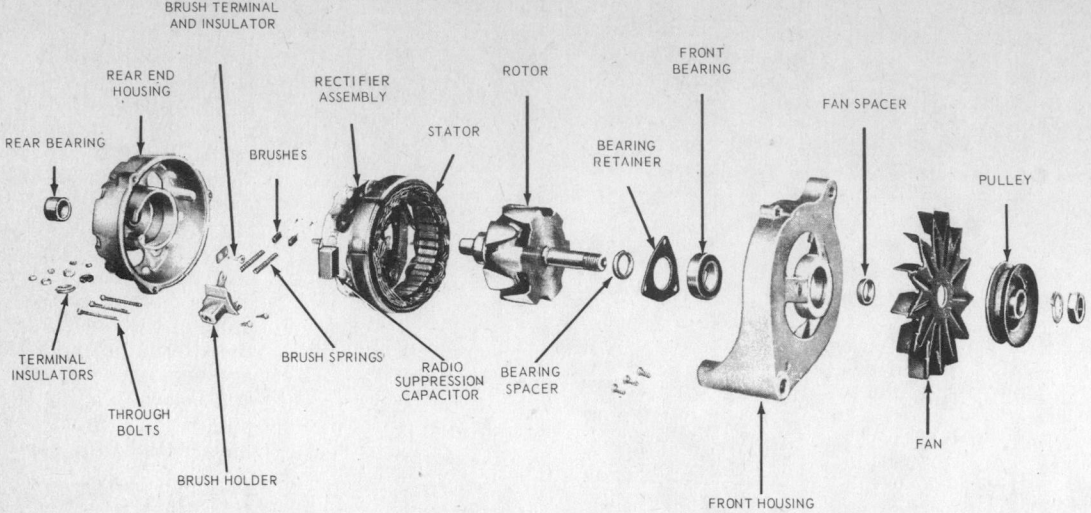

Typical disassembled Autolite alternator—except 65 amp unit (© Ford Motor Co)

It includes an alternator, an electro-mechanical or transistorized regulator, a charge indicator, and a storage battery.

Caution Some 1974 and later Continental Mark IVs and Thunderbirds may have two alternators. The second alternator is a high voltage (120 volt) unit which is used to operate a special heated windshield and rear window. This alternator and its wiring are completely isolated from the regular charging system, and all of its connections are marked with warning tags. DO NOT attempt to service the alternator or its wiring and DO NOT confuse its wiring with that of the regular charging system. Because this system can produce a severe electrical shock, its service should be left to an authorized facility.

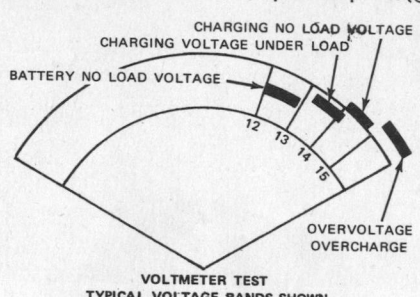

VOLTMETER TEST
TYPICAL VOLTAGE BANDS SHOWN
Voltmeter readings isolation test
(© Ford Motor Co)

Ford alternators with external voltage regulators are available in two different types, rear terminal and side terminal. Both types provide the same function, the only difference aside from terminal mounting, is in the internal wiring. Ford side ter-minal alternators are also used in American Motors cars starting 1976. All procedures are the same for both alternators, regardless of application.

Troubleshooting

NOTE: See the "Preliminary Charging System Inspection" section before proceeding further.

Charging System Tests Using a Voltmeter

This test series will determine which element of the charging system is malfunctioning.
1. Connect the leads of a voltmeter to the battery clamps.
2. Check the voltage.
3. Connect a tachometer and run the engine at about 1,500 RPM with no electrical load.

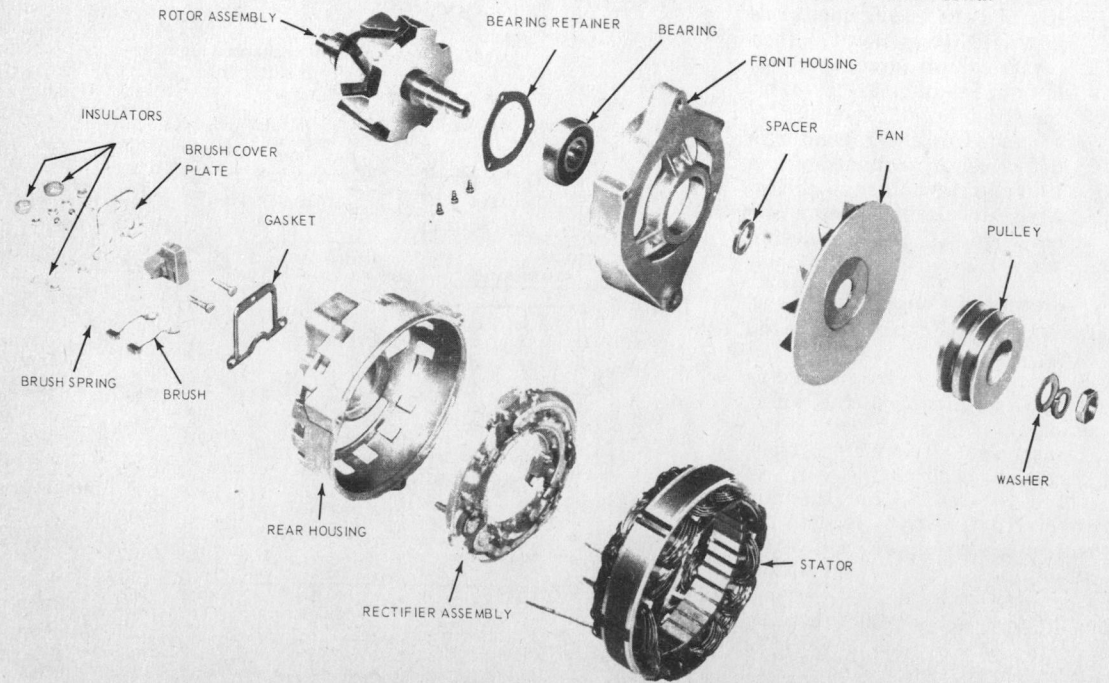

Disassembled view of 65 amp Autolite alternator (used through 1972)
(© Ford Motor Co)

4. The voltage should increase 1 V but should not be more than 2 V above the previously recorded voltage.
5. With the engine running, turn on the heater and/or air conditioner blower motor (high speed) and the headlights (high beam).
6. Increase the engine speed to 2000 RPM.
7. The voltmeter should now indicate a minimum of 0.5 V above the first recorded battery voltage.
8. If the voltmeter indicates more than 2 volts above the battery voltage, stop the engine and check the regulator and alternator ground connections. Clean and tighten these connections and repeat the test.
9. If the overvoltage condition still exists, disconnect the wiring plug from the regulator and repeat the test.
10. If the overvoltage condition ceases replace or adjust the voltage regulator and repeat the test. If the problem is in the regulator, replacing or adjusting it should provide a normal reading.
11. If overvoltage still exists with the regulator plug disconnected, repair the short in the wiring harness between the alternator and regulator; then replace the regulator and wiring plug and repeat the test.
12. If the voltmeter reading does not increase 1 V check for battery voltage at the alternator battery terminal and the regulator plug 'A' terminal. If there is no voltage, repair the wiring and repeat the test.
13. If the voltage does not increase by 1 V, the field circuit must be checked to determine if it is grounding. The field circuit should be checked with the regulator wiring plug disconnected and an ohmmeter connected between the 'F' terminal of the plug and the battery ground. There should be between 4 and 250 ohms resistance.
14. Check for an open wire in the regulator by connecting an ohmmeter between the 'I' and 'F' terminals of the regulator. There should be no resistance between the two terminals. If there is about 10 ohms, the connector wire inside the regulator is shorted.

Field Circuit and Alternator Tests
1. If the field circuit is ok, disconnect the regulator wiring plug at the regulator and connect the jumper wire from the 'A' to the 'F' terminals on the plug.
2. Repeat the test procedure. If there is still a problem (under

voltage), remove the jumper wire and leave the plug disconnected.
3. Connect a jumper wire to the FLD and BAT terminals on the alternator and repeat the test. If the tests are now satisfactory, repair the wiring harness between the alternator and regulator. If there is no defect in the harness, replace the alternator, and repeat the test.

Diode Tests on Car
1. Disconnect the electric choke and voltage regulator plug.
2. Connect a jumper between the 'A' and 'F' terminals of the plug; connect a voltmeter to the battery clamps, start the engine and let it run at idle.
3. Read and record the voltmeter reading; move the voltmeter lead to the 'S' terminal in the wiring harness and note the reading.
4. If the voltmeter reads ½ of battery voltage, the diodes are ok.
5. If the voltmeter reads approximately 1.5 V, the alternator has a shorted negative diode, or a grounded stator winding.
6. If the voltmeter reads about 1.5 V less than battery voltage, the alternator has a shorted positive diode.
7. If the voltmeter reads 1.0-1.5 V less than ½ battery voltage, there is an open positive diode; if it is 1.0-1.5 V more than ½ battery charge, there is an open negative diode.

After the test is complete, reconnect the choke.

Fusible Links
1. Check the fusible link located between the starter relay and the alternator. Replace the link if it is burned or open.
2. Ford, Mercury, Torino, Montego, Maverick, Comet, Bobcat, and Pinto all have two fusible links between the starter relay and the alternator. Be sure to check both of them for damage.

Charging System Operation
NOTE: if the current indicator is to give an accurate reading, the battery cables must be of the same gauge and length as the original equipment.
1. With the engine running, and all electrical systems turned off, place a current indicator over the positive battery cable.
2. If a charge of about 5 amps is recorded, the charging system is working. If a draw of about 5 amps is recorded, the system is not working. The needle moves toward the battery when a charge condition is indicated, and away from the battery when

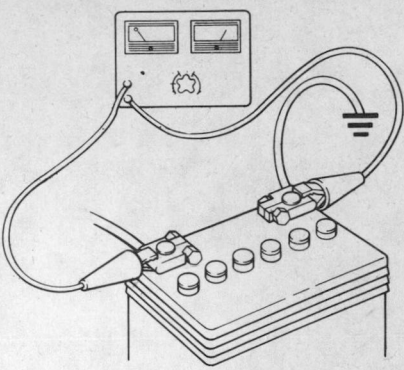

Voltmeter connections isolation test and ignition circuit test
(© Ford Motor Co)

a draw condition is indicated. If a draw is indicated, continue to the next testing procedure. If an overcharge of 10-15 amps is indicated, check for a faulty regulator or a bad ground at the regulator or the alternator.

Testing the Ignition Switch to Regulator Circuit
1. Disconnect the regulator wiring harness from the regulator.
2. Turn on the key. Using a test light or voltmeter, check for voltage between the I wire and ground. Check for voltage between the A wire and ground. If voltage is present at this part of the system, the circuit is OK. If there is no voltage at the I wire, check for a burned-out charge indicator bulb, a burned-out resistor, or a break or short in the wiring. If there is no voltage present at the A wire, check for a bad connection at the starter relay or a break or short in the wire.

Voltage Regulator Adjustments
Ford alternators with external voltage regulators can use either an electromechanical regulator or a transistorized voltage regulator. The electromechanical regulator is not adjustable, and has to be replaced as a unit when faulty; the transistorized voltage regulator is adjustable by means of a screw located in the transistor circuit board. The cover of the electromechanical regulator is held in place by non-removable rivets, while the transistorized regulator cover is held on by Phillips head screws.

To adjust, remove the cover of the regulator, and using a fiber or plastic rod, turn the adjusting screw clockwise to increase the voltage setting or counterclockwise to decrease the voltage setting.

Autolite Alternator with Integral Regulator

Description
In 1970 some vehicles were

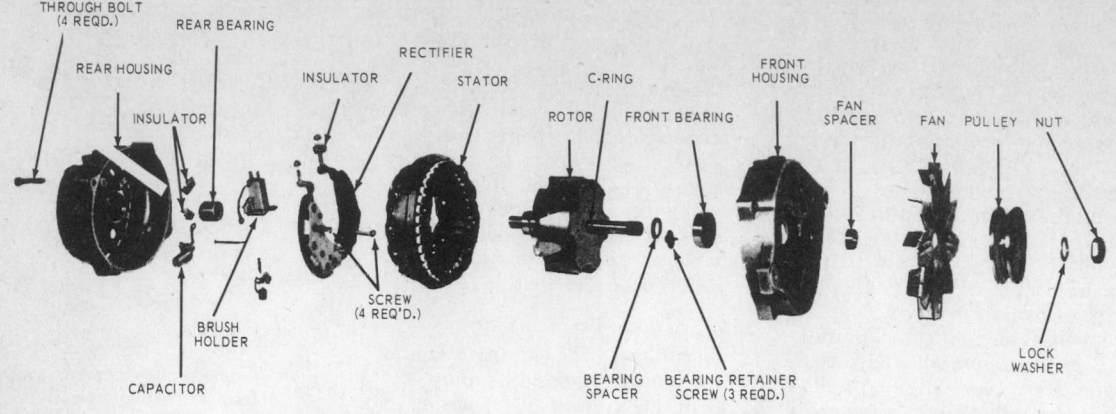

THROUGH BOLT (4 REQD.)
REAR BEARING
REAR HOUSING
INSULATOR
INSULATOR
RECTIFIER
STATOR
C-RING
ROTOR
FRONT BEARING
FRONT HOUSING
FAN SPACER
FAN
PULLEY
NUT
BRUSH HOLDER
CAPACITOR
SCREW (4 REQ'D.)
BEARING SPACER
BEARING RETAINER SCREW (3 REQD.)
LOCK WASHER

Ford side terminal alternator—exploded view (© Ford Motor Co)

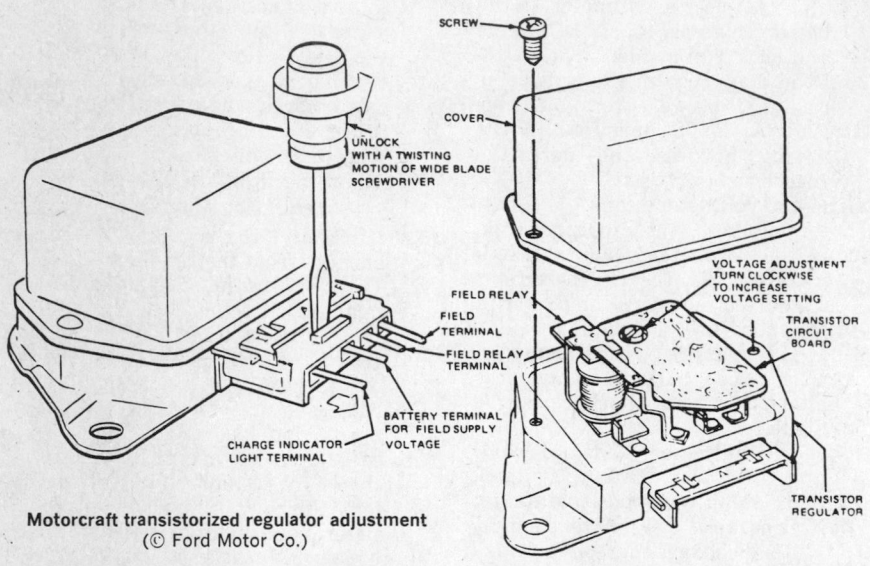

SCREW
COVER
UNLOCK WITH A TWISTING MOTION OF WIDE BLADE SCREWDRIVER
FIELD RELAY
FIELD TERMINAL
FIELD RELAY TERMINAL
BATTERY TERMINAL FOR FIELD SUPPLY VOLTAGE
CHARGE INDICATOR LIGHT TERMINAL
VOLTAGE ADJUSTMENT TURN CLOCKWISE TO INCREASE VOLTAGE SETTING
TRANSISTOR CIRCUIT BOARD
TRANSISTOR REGULATOR

Motorcraft transistorized regulator adjustment
(© Ford Motor Co.)

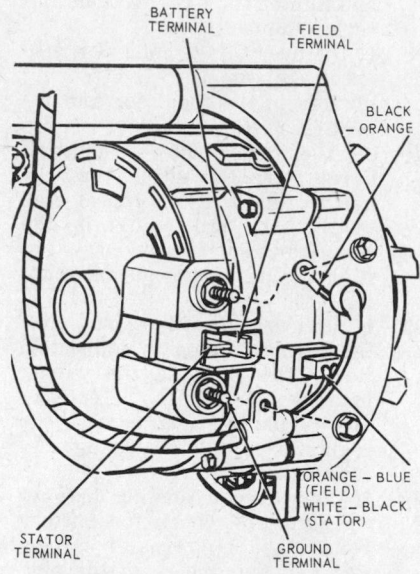

BATTERY TERMINAL
FIELD TERMINAL
BLACK – ORANGE
ORANGE – BLUE (FIELD)
WHITE – BLACK (STATOR)
GROUND TERMINAL
STATOR TERMINAL

Wiring connections—Ford side terminal alternator (© Ford Motor Co)

equipped with an Autolite alternator having an integral regulator mounted to the rear end housing. The regulator is a hybrid unit featuring use of solid state integrated circuits. These circuits may consist of transis-

tors, diodes and resistors. The unusual feature of this type of microelectronic circuit is that the entire circuit is within a silicone crystal approximately 1/8 in. square. Because of the small size of the circuit, it is not

repairable or adjustable and must be replaced as a unit if found to be defective. It should be noted that the size of the regulator housing is dic-

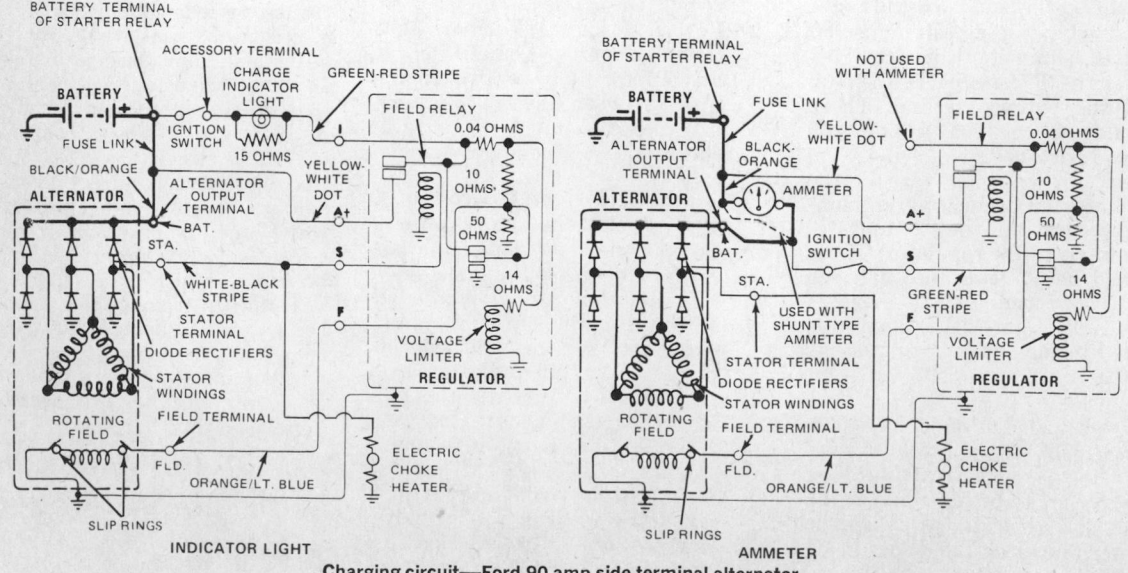

BATTERY TERMINAL OF STARTER RELAY
ACCESSORY TERMINAL
CHARGE INDICATOR LIGHT
GREEN-RED STRIPE
BATTERY
IGNITION SWITCH
15 OHMS
FUSE LINK
BLACK/ORANGE
ALTERNATOR
ALTERNATOR OUTPUT TERMINAL
BAT.
STA.
WHITE-BLACK STRIPE
STATOR TERMINAL
DIODE RECTIFIERS
STATOR WINDINGS
ROTATING FIELD
FIELD TERMINAL
FLD.
ORANGE/LT. BLUE
SLIP RINGS
FIELD RELAY
0.04 OHMS
YELLOW-WHITE DOT
10 OHMS
50 OHMS
A+
S
14 OHMS
F
VOLTAGE LIMITER
REGULATOR
ELECTRIC CHOKE HEATER

INDICATOR LIGHT

BATTERY TERMINAL OF STARTER RELAY
NOT USED WITH AMMETER
BATTERY
ALTERNATOR OUTPUT TERMINAL
FUSE LINK
BLACK-ORANGE
YELLOW-WHITE DOT
AMMETER
IGNITION SWITCH
ALTERNATOR
BAT.
STA.
USED WITH SHUNT TYPE AMMETER
GREEN-RED STRIPE
STATOR TERMINAL
DIODE RECTIFIERS
STATOR WINDINGS
ROTATING FIELD
FIELD TERMINAL
FLD.
ORANGE/LT. BLUE
SLIP RINGS
FIELD RELAY
0.04 OHMS
10 OHMS
50 OHMS
A+
S
14 OHMS
F
VOLTAGE LIMITER
REGULATOR
ELECTRIC CHOKE HEATER

AMMETER

Charging circuit—Ford 90 amp side terminal alternator
(© Ford Motor Co)

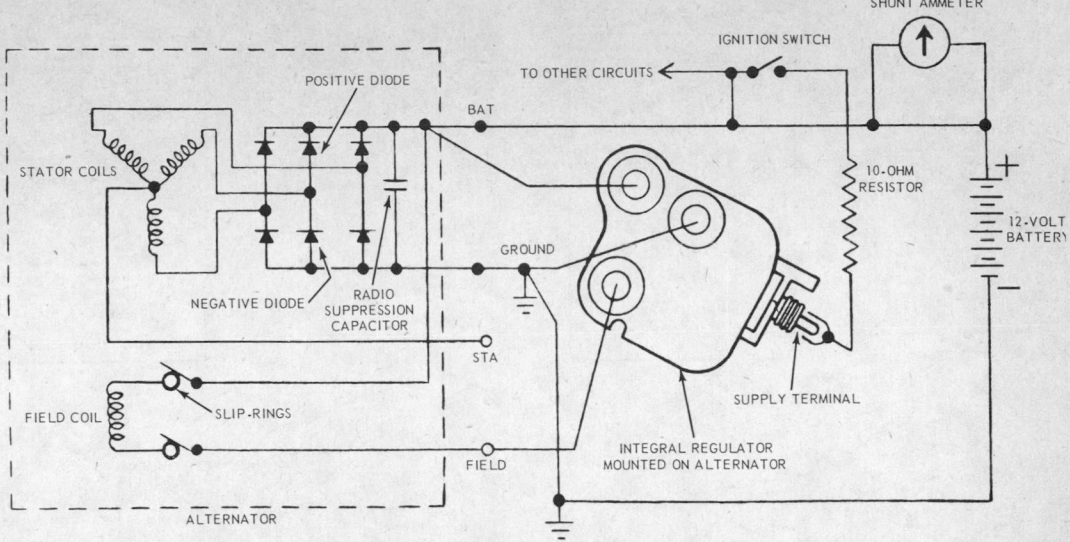

Charging system schematic with integral regulator
(© Ford Motor Co)

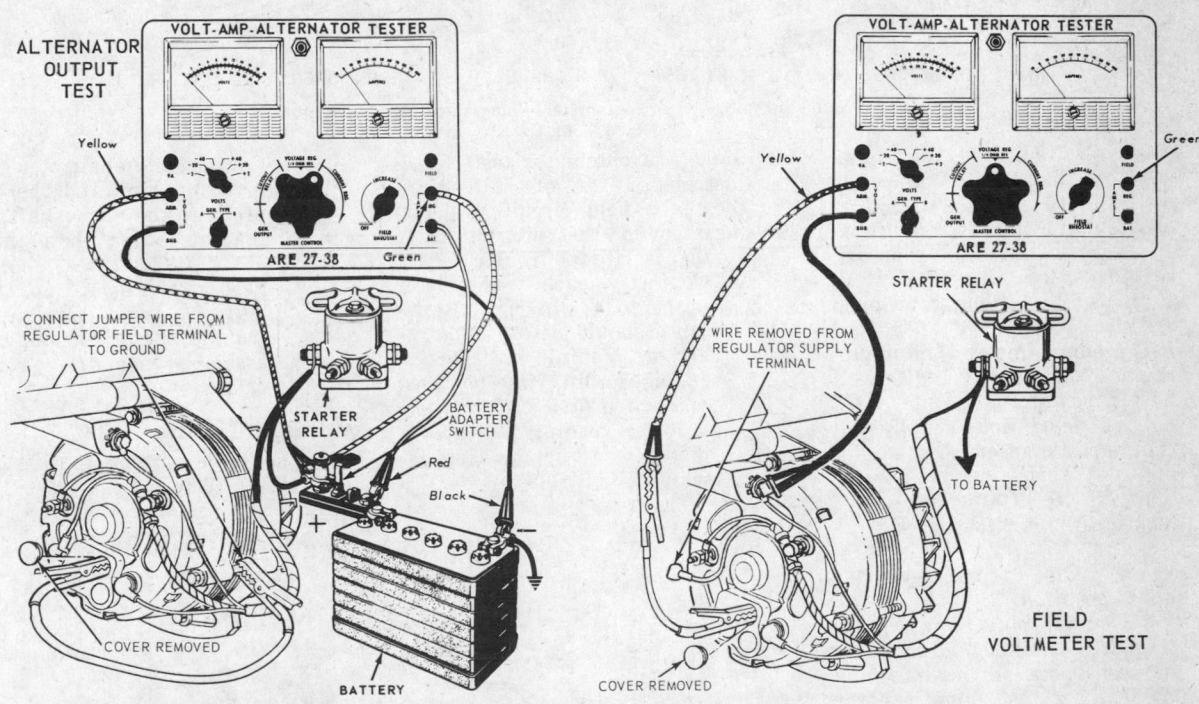

Output test hook-up—integral regulator alternator
(© Ford Motor Co)

Field voltmeter test hook-up—integral regulator alternator
(© Ford Motor Co)

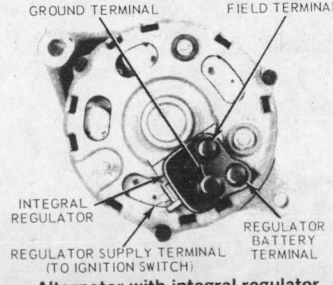

Alternator with integral regulator
(© Ford Motor Co)

tated only by the fact that some means of connecting the regulator to the alternator is necessary. Overhaul is the same as for other Autolite alternators.

Troubleshooting

NOTE: see the "Preliminary Charging System Inspection" section before proceeding further.

Fusible Links

1. Check the fusible link located between the starter relay and the alternator. Replace the link if it is burned or open.

Output Test

1. Place transmission in Neutral or Park.
2. Remove the positive battery cable and install a battery adapter switch in the line.

3. Attach one lead of a test voltmeter to the negative battery post and the other test lead to the circuit side of the adapter switch.
4. Connect a test ammeter to each side of the adapter switch, so that charging current will go through the ammeter when the switch is opened.
5. Connect a jumper wire between the alternator frame and the integral regulator field terminal (cover plug removed).
6. Close adapter switch, start engine and open adapter switch.
7. Running engine at 2,000 rpm, observe voltmeter and ammeter.

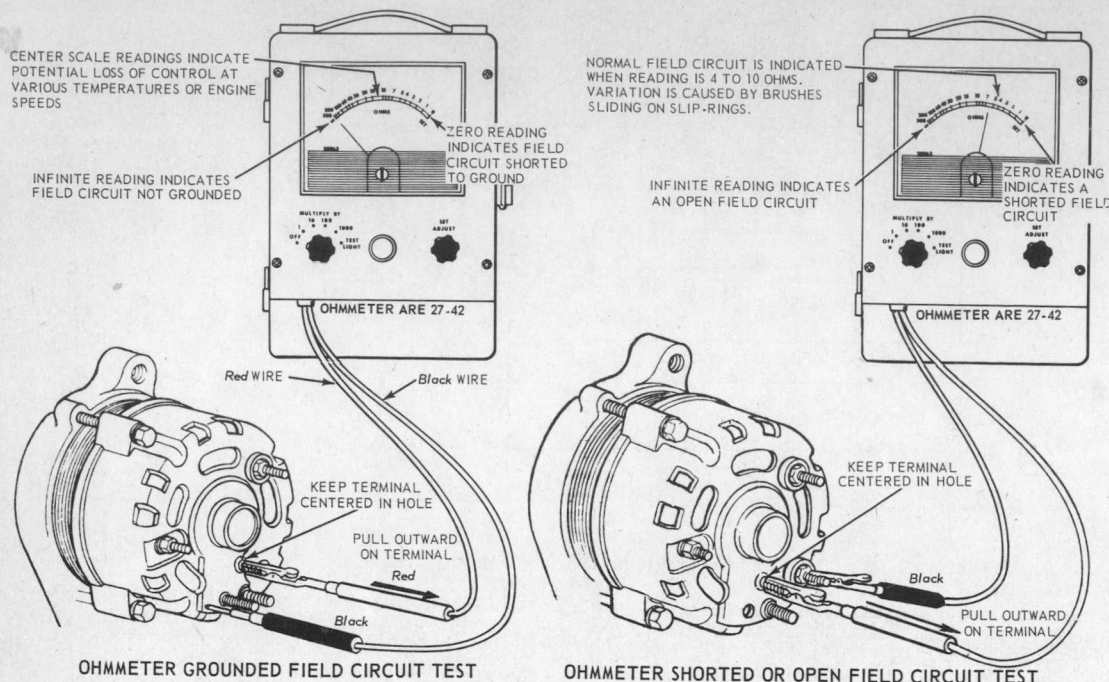

CENTER SCALE READINGS INDICATE POTENTIAL LOSS OF CONTROL AT VARIOUS TEMPERATURES OR ENGINE SPEEDS

INFINITE READING INDICATES FIELD CIRCUIT NOT GROUNDED

ZERO READING INDICATES FIELD CIRCUIT SHORTED TO GROUND

OHMMETER ARE 27-42

NORMAL FIELD CIRCUIT IS INDICATED WHEN READING IS 4 TO 10 OHMS. VARIATION IS CAUSED BY BRUSHES SLIDING ON SLIP-RINGS.

INFINITE READING INDICATES AN OPEN FIELD CIRCUIT

ZERO READING INDICATES A SHORTED FIELD CIRCUIT

OHMMETER ARE 27-42

Red WIRE   Black WIRE

KEEP TERMINAL CENTERED IN HOLE

PULL OUTWARD ON TERMINAL

Red

Black

KEEP TERMINAL CENTERED IN HOLE

Black

PULL OUTWARD ON TERMINAL

OHMMETER GROUNDED FIELD CIRCUIT TEST   **OHMMETER SHORTED OR OPEN FIELD CIRCUIT TEST**

Field circuit test hook-ups with ohmmeter—integral regulator alternator
(© Ford Motor Co)

At 15 volts indicated, the ammeter should read 50-57 amps. If so, and there is still a no-charge condition, the regulator is probably faulty and must be replaced. An output 2-8 amps. below 50 amps. usually indicates an open diode rectifier, while an output 10-15 amps. below minimum specifications usually indicates a shorted diode. An alternator with a shorted diode usually will whine at idle speed.

Field Test (Voltmeter)

1. Turn ignition switch to OFF position.
2. Remove wire from regulator supply terminal.
3. Remove cover plug from regulator field terminal and connect one test voltmeter lead to this terminal. A ¼ ohm resistor should be in the circuit.
4. Connect the other test voltmeter lead to a good engine ground.
5. The voltmeter should read 12 volts. If *no* voltage is present, the field circuit is open or grounded.
6. If voltmeter reads more than 1 volt, but still less than battery voltage, there is probably a partial ground in the alternator field circuit and the circuit should be checked with an ohmmeter.

Field Test (Ohmmeter)

1. Disconnect battery ground cable; remove alternator from car.
2. Remove the regulator from the alternator (covered later).

3. Make the ohmmeter tests as illustrated. If any of the tests indicates a field circuit problem, disassemble the alternator to further isolate the trouble.
a. Contact each ohmmeter probe to a slip ring. Resistance should be 4-5 ohms. A higher reading indicates a damaged slip ring soldered connection or a broken wire. A lower reading indicates a shorted wire or slip ring assembly.

b. Contact one ohmmeter probe to a slip ring and the other probe to the rotor shaft. Any reading other than infinite ohms indicates a short to ground. If neither of these tests (A and B) isolates the trouble, the brushes or brush assembly are the probable cause.

Voltage Limiter Test

1. Check the battery specific gravity. If it is not at least 1.230,

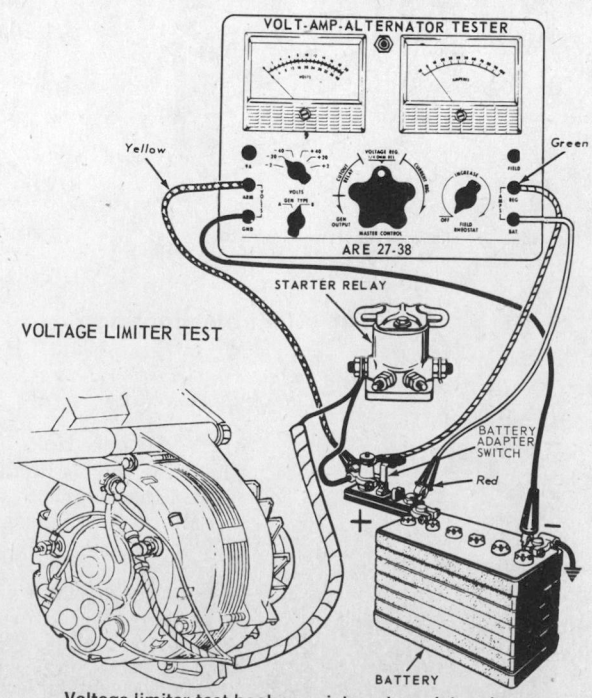

VOLT-AMP-ALTERNATOR TESTER

Yellow   Green

ARE 27-38

STARTER RELAY

VOLTAGE LIMITER TEST

BATTERY ADAPTER SWITCH

Red

BATTERY

Voltage limiter test hook-up—integral regulator alternator
(© Ford Motor Co)

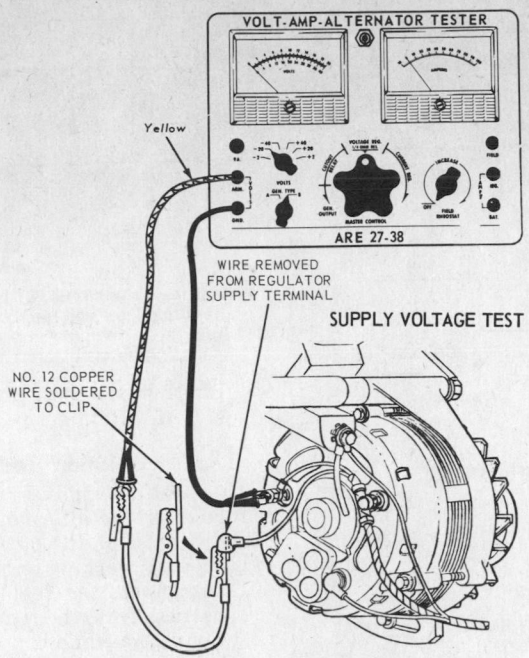

VOLT-AMP-ALTERNATOR TESTER

ARE 27-38

Yellow

WIRE REMOVED FROM REGULATOR SUPPLY TERMINAL

SUPPLY VOLTAGE TEST

NO. 12 COPPER WIRE SOLDERED TO CLIP

Supply voltage test hook-up—integral regulator alternator
(© Ford Motor Co)

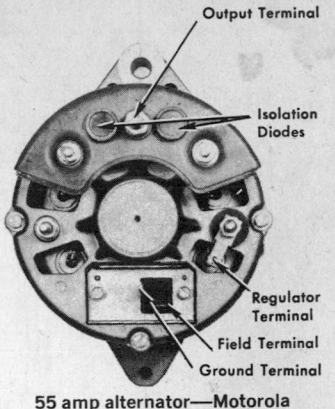

Output Terminal

Isolation Diodes

Regulator Terminal

Field Terminal

Ground Terminal

55 amp alternator—Motorola
(© American Motors Corp)

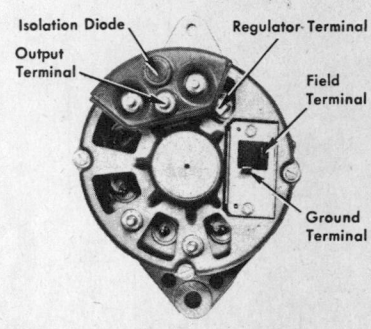

Isolation Diode

Output Terminal

Regulator Terminal

Field Terminal

Ground Terminal

35 amp alternator—Motorola
(© American Motors Corp)

charge the battery or install a charged battery for the test.

2. Make sure all lights and accessories are turned off, including such items as dome lights and radio.

3. Make the test connections as illustrated.

4. Place transmission in Neutral or Park, close battery adapter switch and start the engine.

5. Open the battery adapter switch and operate engine at 2,000 rpm for 5 minutes. The voltmeter should read 13.3-15.3 volts.

6. If voltage does not rise above 12 volts, perform a regulator supply voltage test to determine whether or not the regulator is getting voltage from the battery. Before replacing a regulator, check the wiring of the entire charging system for shorts, opens, or high resistance connections.

Regulator Supply Voltage Test

The regulator is "turned on" by the application of battery voltage through a 10 ohm resistor wire. If the supply circuit is defective, the regulator will not function and the alternator will not put out current.

1. Connect a 12-volt test light or voltmeter between the regulator supply lead and ground.

2. Turn on the ignition switch. The test light should glow or the voltmeter indicate. If not, the supply circuit should be checked back to the battery, especially the resistance wire.

The Motorola System

The Motorola alternator is designed to pass all the DC current through an isolation diode, or diodes, mounted in an external aluminum heat sink.

Due to the nature of the alternator, residual magnetism is at near zero when the unit is at rest. It is, therefore, necessary to provide some small current to excite the field prior to generating current. With Motorola, this priming current is supplied by means of a 75 ohm resistance unit between the ignition coil and the alternator (inside the regulator). It is quite important that this resistance unit be checked and found satisfactory before proceeding with subsequent tests.

The charge indicator light on some cars operates in the same way as this resistor by furnishing the necessary initial field starting current. If this resistor circuit is open (a burned out indicator lamp) on some models, the alternator will not function. On later models, a resistor is placed in parallel with the bulb to provide excitation current if the bulb burns out.

The regulator is a sealed unit and should require no adjustment. It is therefore, recommended that non-functioning regulators be replaced.

This unit was last used on American Motors cars in 1975.

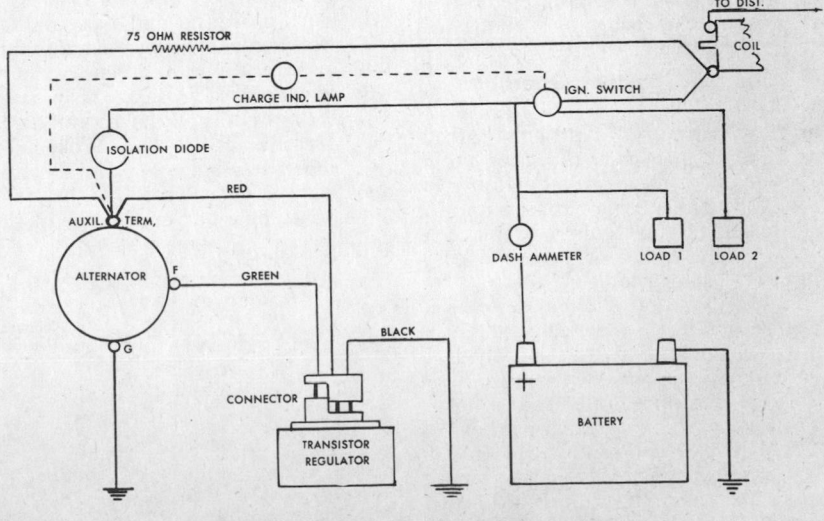

Typical Motorola alternator system charging circuit
(© American Motors Corp)

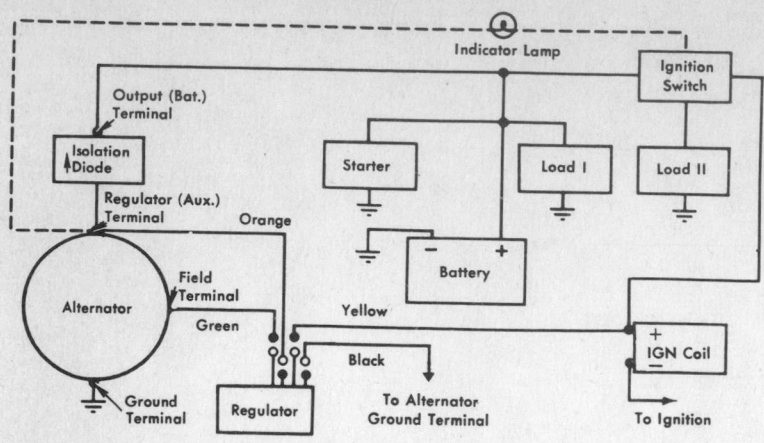

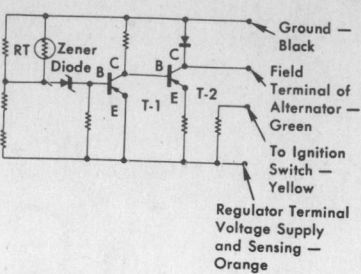

Motorola circuit diagram—1970 American Motors illustrated
(© American Motors Corp)

Voltage regulator circuit. RT is a thermistor that regulates voltage according to temperature
(© American Motors Corp)

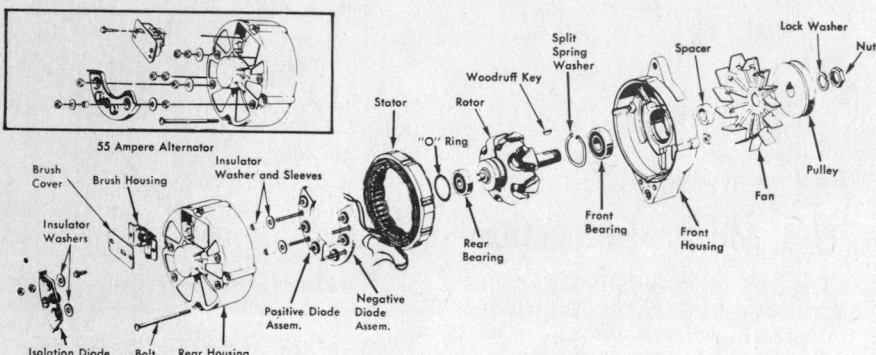

Motorola alternator—exploded view
(© American Motors Corp)

Troubleshooting

NOTE: see the "Preliminary Charging System Inspection" section before proceeding further.

Fusible Link Test

There are many fuse links in the car, however, the fuse link located in the wiring between the battery terminal of the horn relay to the main wire harness is the only one that concerns the charging system. This link protects the entire wiring harness. If it fails, all the electrical systems will fail to function.

Charging System Operation

NOTE: if the current indicator is to give an accurate reading, the battery cables must be of the same gauge and length as the original equipment.

1. With the engine running and all electrical systems off, place a current indicator over the positive battery cable.
2. If a charge of about 5 amps is recorded, the charging system is working. If a draw of about 5 amps is recorded, the system is not working. The needle moves toward the battery when a charge condition is indicated, and away from the battery when a draw condition is indicated. If a draw is indicated, continue to the next testing procedure. If an overcharge of 10-15 amps is indicated, check for a faulty regulator, or a bad ground at the regulator or the alternator.

Testing the Ignition Switch to Regulator Circuit

1. Disconnect the regulator wires from the regulator.
2. Turn on the key. Using a test light or voltmeter, check for current between the voltage supply wire and ground. This wire is usually orange and has another wire connected to it, usually blue or orange with a tracer.
3. If current is present, this part of the system is OK. If no voltage is present, check for broken or shorted wiring, a bad indicator bulb, a bad fuse in the fuse panel, or a bad connection at the

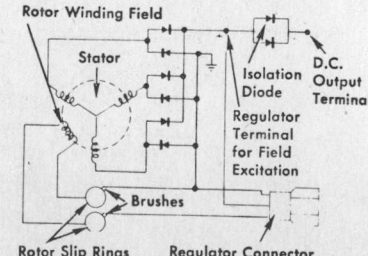

Alternator circuit—40 and 55 amp models
(© American Motors Corp)

ignition switch or on the battery side of the starter relay.

Isolation Test

This test determines whether the regulator or the alternator is faulty, after the rest of the circuit is found to be in good working order.

1. Disconnect the regulator wiring harness from the regulator.
2. Connect a jumper wire from the voltage supply wire from the battery, orange, to the field wire for the alternator, green.
3. Connect a voltmeter to the battery. The positive voltmeter lead goes to the positive terminal and the negative lead to the negative terminal. Record the reading on the voltmeter.
4. Turn off all of the electrical systems and start the engine. Do not race the engine.
5. Gradually increase engine speed to 1500-2000 rpm. The voltmeter reading should increase above the previously recorded battery voltage reading by at least one to two volts. If there is no increase, the alternator is not working correctly. If there is an increase the voltage regulator needs to be replaced.

Field Current Draw Test

1. With battery disconnected, disconnect the wires from the alternator output terminal and the alternator field terminal.
2. With a field rheostat in the open position, connect its leads to the disconnected alternator output wire and to the positive lead of the test ammeter.
3. Connect the negative ammeter lead to the alternator field terminal.
4. Connect the positive voltmeter lead to the alternator field terminal.
5. Connect the negative voltmeter lead to the alternator ground terminal.
6. Reconnect the battery.
7. Start and run the engine at fast idle.
8. Adjust field rheostat to closed position, then note the voltmeter and ammeter readings.

9. Adjust field rheostat control to the open position.
10. Compare the readings obtained in Step 8 with manufacturers' specifications.
11. If readings are zero, there is an indication of trouble in the field coil, or the connections between field coil and slip ring.
12. If readings are low, there is probable trouble in the slip rings or brushes.
13. If readings are high, the field coil is probably shorted.
14. If readings are normal, on an alternator which failed to produce its rated output, the probable cause lies in the stator or diodes. Replace the alternator in this case.

Alternator Output Test beginning 1971 (Alternator In Car)

1. Connect a voltmeter to the battery.
2. Start the engine and turn the lights on low beam.
3. Run the engine at 1000 RPM and observe the voltage reading for two minutes. If the voltage remains above 13 V, the alternator and regulator are ok. If not, proceed to the Regulator Bypass Test to determine which component is at fault.

Field Draw (Amperage) Test, beginning 1971

This test determines if there is an open or short circuit in the alternator brush circuit.
1. Disconnect the voltage regulator.
2. Connect an ammeter between the positive battery post and the green wire leading to the insulated brush terminal of the alternator. Ground the black wire.
3. Turn the alternator rotor slowly by hand. The ammeter should indicate between 1½ and 3 amperes. If the reading varies, the slip rings require cleaning. If the amperage is too high, remove the brush assembly and do continuity and isolation tests on it. Check the rotor field windings if the field draw is too low or high after testing the brush assembly and cleaning the slip rings.

Alternator Output (Regulator Bypass) Test, beginning 1972

This test will determine whether the alternator or voltage regulator is at fault for a no or low charge condition.
1. Disconnect the voltage regulator and perform the Field Draw Test. After completing it, disconnect the ammeter.
2. Connect the voltmeter to the battery and start the engine and run it at idle.
3. Connect an ammeter between the battery positive post and the insulated brush on the alternator.
4. Observe the voltage reading while slowly increasing the engine RPM. If 16 volts can be obtained, the alternator is not bad. Do not exceed sixteen volts or component damage may occur. It may take a few minutes for a dead battery to achieve a reading of 16 volts.
5. If the reading does not reach 16 volts then the fault is in the alternator.

Diode Trio Test, beginning 1971 (on car)

This test will check the field diode assembly for marginal defects which may not affect alternator performance but may cause the dash indicator light to glow.
1. Do the Regulator Bypass Test. If 16 volts can not be obtained from the alternator, this test's results will not be valid.
2. Start and idle the engine. Connect a voltmeter to the alternator (if no reading is obtained, switch the test leads).
3. Turn on the lights and blower (heater) unit and let them operate for about 2 minutes, then turn them off.
4. Check the meter reading. A good diode will read from zero to 0.2 volts. A reading above this indicates that the diodes are deteriorating. It is not necessary to replace them until the reading is above 0.6 volts.
5. If the meter pulsates, either the diode trio, the positive diode, or the soldered connections between them is beginning to break down. In either case the alternator will have to be disassembled and the diode tested.

6. If the reading is over 0.6 V. but the alternator output is alright, remove the diode trio for a bench test.
7. If the reading is less than 0.6 V. and the diode trio appears to be functioning properly, and the indicator light still glows, check the wiring connections for corrosion.

The Prestolite System

Prestolite alternators incorporate an *isolation diode*, mounted as a component part of the internal positive heat sink assembly. Such alternators are almost identical to late model Motorola units in operation. Test procedures for the Motorola alternator also apply to the diode-equipped Prestolite.

The Prestolite alternator was last used in American Motors cars in 1970.

Troubleshooting

NOTE: see the "Preliminary Charging System Inspection" section before proceeding further.

For troubleshooting procedures see the Motorola Troubleshooting section.

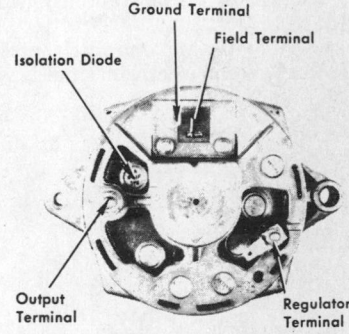

Prestolite alternator—diode type
(© American Motors Corp)

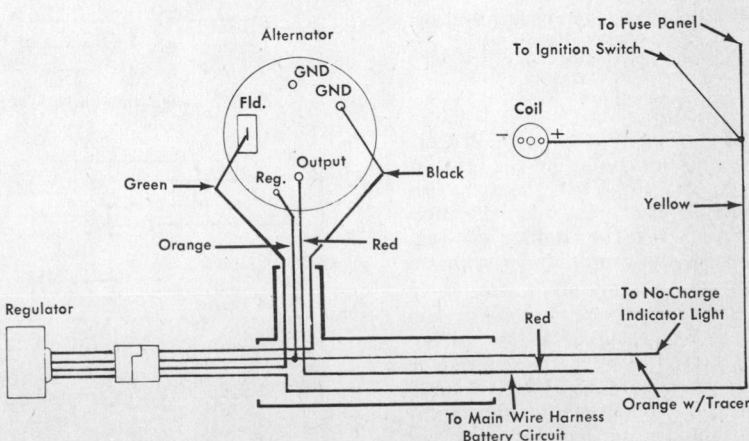

Prestolite wiring diagram

INDEX

Introduction

Ford-Motorcraft Solid-State Ignition
System U34

Delco-Remy Magnetic Pulse System U37

Delco-Remy Unit Ignition System U40

Delco-Remy High Energy Ignition (HEI)
System U41

Chrysler Electronic Ignition System U44

AMC Breakerless Inductive Discharge (BID)
Ignition System U47

Introduction

The rise to prominence of electronic ignition systems is due to the superiority of electronic ignition over conventional ignition systems in several major areas. These systems totally remove one area of maintenance from the ignition system; the troublesome ignition points and condenser. Since the electronic system produces a higher voltage than the conventional system, the electronic ignition system can usually fire a fouled spark plug. In the area of high performance, the electronic ignition system is far superior in that its voltage does not deteriorate as quickly at high engine speeds as the conventional ignition system.

As automotive emission laws became stricter, the maintenance-free electronic ignition systems gained favor among automotive manufacturers. Since these systems do not contain ignition points which wear, ignition performance does not deteriorate with mileage. This, plus the fact that these systems can usually fire a fouled plug, helps to keep down exhaust emissions after a car leaves the factory. Evidence on the manufacturer's acceptance of these systems is the fact that all 1973 and later Chrysler Corporation cars as well as all 1975 domestic cars have electronic ignition as standard equipment.

Ford-Motorcraft Solid-State Ignition System

The Ford-Motorcraft Solid-State Ignition System is a pulse triggered, breakerless, transistor controlled ignition system available on some late model 1973 460 V8 Lincolns; all 1974 models sold in the 49 states with a 400 or 460 V8; all 1974 six-cylinder and V8 models sold in California; and is standard equipment on all 1975 Ford Motor Company models. The system utilizes most of the standard ignition components, but substitutes an amplifier module and magnetic pick-up assembly for the conventional ignition contact points.

magnetic field built up in the ignition coil is allowed to collapse, inducing a high voltage into the secondary windings of the coil. High voltage is produced each time the field is thus built up and collapsed.

The high voltage flows through the coil high tension lead to the distribu-

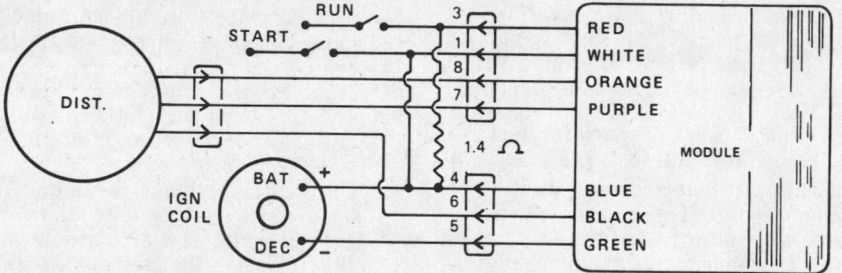

Electronic module schematic—solid-state ignition
(© Ford Motor Co)

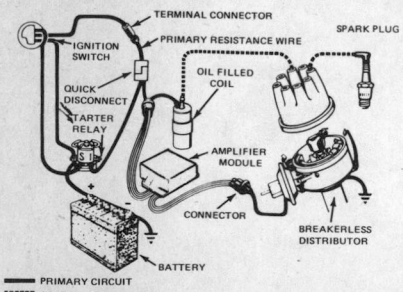

Ford-Motorcraft Solid-State Ignition System —basic wiring
(© Ford Motor Co)

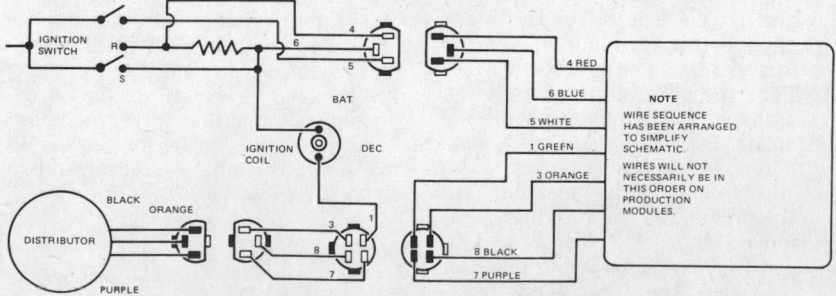

Electronic module schematic—solid-state ignition, 1975
(© Ford Motor Co.)

Operation

With the ignition switch "on", the primary circuit is on and the ignition coil is energized. When the armature "spokes" approach the magnetic pick-up coil assembly, they induce a voltage which tells the amplifier to turn the coil primary current off. A timing circuit in the amplifier module will turn the current on again after the coil field has collapsed. When the current is "on", it flows from the battery through the ignition switch, the primary windings of the ignition coil, and through the amplifier module circuits to ground. When the current is off, the

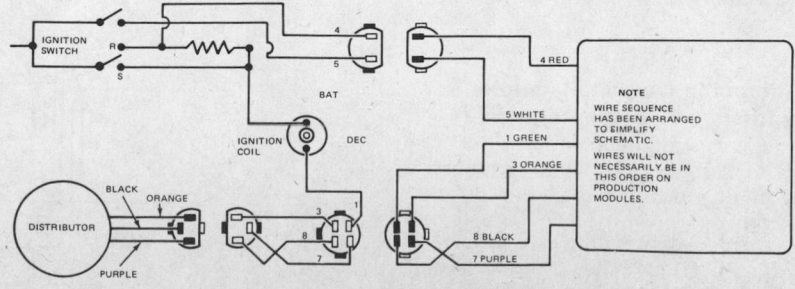

Electronic module schematic—solid-state ignition, 1976 and later
(© Ford Motor Co.)

tor cap where the rotor distributes it to one of the spark plug terminals in the distributor cap. This process is repeated for every power stroke of the engine.

Ignition system troubles are caused by a failure in the primary and/or the secondary circuit; incorrect ignition timing; or incorrect distributor advance. Circuit failures may be caused by shorts, corroded or dirty terminals, loose connections, defective wire insulation, cracked distributor cap or rotor, defective pick-up coil assembly or amplifier module, defective distributor points, fouled spark plugs, or by improper dwell angle.

If an engine starting or operating trouble is attributed to the ignition system, start the engine and verify the complaint. On engines that will not start, be sure that there is gasoline in the fuel tank and that fuel is reaching the carburetor. Then locate the ignition system problem by an oscilloscope test or by a spark intensity test.

Primary Circuit Testing

A breakdown or energy loss in the primary circuit can be caused by: defective primary wiring, loose or corroded connections, inoperative or de-

fective magnetic pick-up coil assembly, or defective amplifier module.

A complete test of the primary circuit consists of checking the circuits in the ignition coil, the magnetic pick-up coil assembly and the amplifier module. Wiring harness checks will be included as a part of basic component circuit tests.

Always inspect connectors for dirt, corrosion or poor fit before assuming you have spotted a possible problem.

Troubleshooting

Make sure that the battery is fully charged before beginning tests. Perform a Spark Intensity Test. If no spark is observed, make sure that the high tension coil wire is good. Disconnect the three-way and four-way connectors at the electronic module.

The first trouble isolation test will be conducted on the harness terminals, with the electronic module disconnected from the circuit. The pin or socket numbers shown in the schematic correspond to those shown in the diagnosis tables.

Make the following tests using a sensitive volt-ohmmeter. These tests will direct you to the proper follow-up test to determine the actual problem.

If the circuit checks good at all these test points, connect a known good electronic module in place of the vehicle module and again perform the spark intensity test. If the substitution corrects the malfunction again reconnect the vehicle module and perform the spark intensity test. If the malfunction still exists, the problem is in the module and it must be replaced. If the problem is gone, it may be in the wiring connectors.

If the substitute module does not correct the problem, reconnect the original module and make repairs elsewhere in the system.

Module Bias Test

Measure the voltage at the indicated point to engine ground with the ignition key "on." If the voltage observed is less than battery voltage, repair the voltage feed wiring to the module for running conditions (rewire).

Battery Source Test

1. Connect the voltmeter leads from the battery terminal at the coil to engine ground, without disconnecting the coil from the circuit.
2. Install a jumper wire from the DEC terminal of the coil to a good engine ground.
3. Turn the lights and all accessories off.
4. Turn the ignition switch "on".
5. If the voltmeter reading is between 4.9 and 7.9 volts, the primary circuit from the battery is satisfactory.
6. If the voltmeter reading is less than 4.9 volts, check the following:
   a. The primary wiring for worn insulation, broken strands, and loose or corroded terminals.
   b. The resistance wiring for defects.
7. If the voltmeter reading is greater than 7.9 volts, the resistance wire should be replaced after verifying a defect.

Cranking Test

Measure the voltage at the indicated point to engine ground with the engine cranking. If the voltage observed is not 8 to 12 volts, repair the voltage feed to the module for starting conditions (white wire).

Starting Circuit Test

If the reading is not between 8 and 12 volts on models through 1974 the ignition by-pass circuit is open or grounded from either the starter solenoid or the ignition switch to Pin 5. On 1975 and later models, the switch by-pass circuit is open or grounded from either the starter solenoid or the switch to socket 5, if the reading

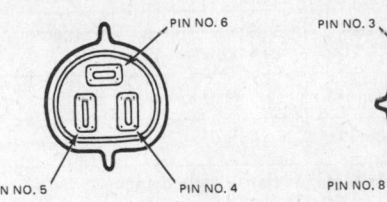
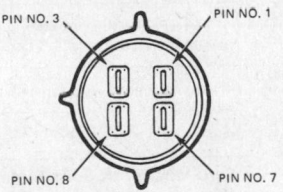

Electronic module connectors—harness side through 1974
(© Ford Motor Co)

TROUBLE ISOLATION TESTS

	TEST VOLTAGE BETWEEN	SHOULD BE	IF NOT, CONDUCT
KEY ON	Pin # 3 and Engine Ground	Battery Voltage	Module Bias Test
	Pin # 5 and Engine Ground	Battery Voltage	Battery Source Test
CRANKING	Pin # 1 and Engine Ground	8 to 12 volts	Cranking Test
	Pin # 5 and Engine Ground	8 to 12 volts	Starting Circuit Test
	Pin # 7 and Pin # 8	½ volt A.C. or D.C. volt wiggle	Distributor Hardware Test

	TEST RESISTANCE BETWEEN	SHOULD BE	IF NOT, CONDUCT
KEY OFF	Pin # 7 and Pin # 8 Pin # 6 and Engine Ground Pin # 7 and Engine Ground Pin # 8 and Engine Ground	400 to 800 ohms 0 ohms more than 70,000 ohms more than 70,000 ohms	Magnetic Pick-up (Stator) Test
	Pin # 3 and Coil Tower Pin # 5 and Pin # 4	7000 to 13000 ohms 1.0 to 2.0 ohms	Coil Test
	Pin # 5 and Engine Ground	more than 10.0 ohms	Short Test
	Pin # 3 and Pin # 4	1.0 to 2.0 ohms	Resistance Wire

Ford-Motorcraft Solid-State Ignition System diagnosis through 1974
(© Ford Motor Co)

is under 6 volts. Check the primary connections at the coil.

Distributor Hardware Test

1. Disconnect the three-wire weatherproof connector at the distributor pigtail.
2. Connect a D.C. voltmeter on a 2.5 volt scale to the two parallel blades. With the engine cranking, the meter needle should oscillate.
3. Remove the distributor cap and check for visual damage or misassembly.
   a. Sintered iron armature (4, 6 or 8-toothed wheel) must be tight on the sleeve, and the roll pin aligning the armature must be in position.
   b. Sintered iron stator must not be broken.
   c. Armature must rotate when the engine is cranked.
4. If the hardware is alright, but the meter doesn't oscillate, replace the magnetic pick-up assembly.

Magnetic Pick-Up Tests

1. Resistance of pick-up coil measured between two parallel pins in the distributor connector must be 400-800 ohms.
2. Resistance between the third blade (ground) and the distributor body must be zero ohms.
3. Resistance between either parallel blade and engine ground must be greater than 70,000 ohms.
4. If any test fails, the distributor stator assembly is defective and must be replaced.
5. If the above readings are not the same as measured in the original test, check for a defective harness. If the readings are the same, proceed.
6. If these tests check alright, the signal generator portion of the distributor is working properly.

Ignition Coil Test

The breakerless ignition coil must be diagnosed separately from the rest of the ignition system.
1. Primary resistance must be 1.0-2.0 ohms, measured from the BAT to the DEC terminals.
2. Secondary resistance must be 7,000-13,000 ohms, measured from the BAT or DEC terminal to the center tower of the coil.
3. If resistance tests are alright, but the coil is still suspected, test the coil on a coil tester by following the test equipment manufacturer's instructions for a standard coil. If the reading differs from the original test, check for a defective harness.

Short Test

If the resistance from Pin 5 to ground is less than 4 ohms, check for

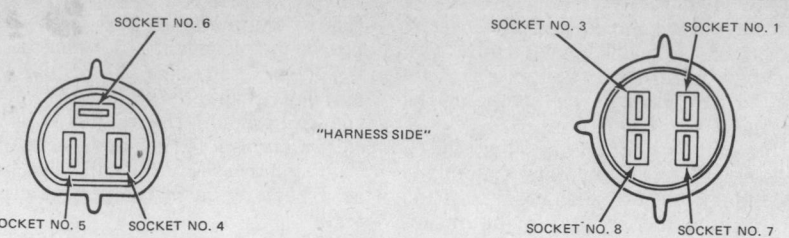

Electronic module connectors—harness side, 1975 and later
(© Ford Motor Co.)

	TEST VOLTAGE BETWEEN	SHOULD BE	IF NOT, CONDUCT
KEY ON	Socket # 4 and Engine Ground	Battery Voltage ± 0.1 Volt	Module Bias Test
	Socket # 1 and Engine Ground	Battery Voltage ± 0.1 Volt	Battery Source Test
CRANKING	Socket # 5 and Engine Ground	8 to 12 volts	Cranking Test
	Jumper # 1 to # 8 Read # 6	more than 6 volts	Starting Circuit Test
	Pin # 7 and Pin # 3	1/2 volt minimum A.C. or any D.C. volt wiggle	Distributor Hardware Test

	TEST VOLTAGE BETWEEN	SHOULD BE	IF NOT, CONDUCT
KEY OFF	Socket # 7 and # 3 Socket # 8 and Engine Ground Socket # 7 and Engine Ground Socket # 3 and Engine Ground	400 to 800 ohms 0 ohms more than 70,000 ohms	Magnetic Pick-up (Stator) Test
	Socket # 4 and Coil Tower Socket # 1 and Pin # 6	7000 to 13000 ohms 1.0 to 2.0 ohms	Coil Test
	Socket # 1 and Engine Ground	more than 4.0 ohms	Short Test
	Socket # 4 and Pin # 6	1.0 to 2.0 ohms	Resistance Wire Test

Ford-Motorcraft Solid-State ignition system diagnosis, 1975
(© Ford Motor Co.)

	TEST VOLTAGE BETWEEN	SHOULD BE	IF NOT, CONDUCT
KEY ON	Socket No. 4 and Engine Ground	Battery Voltage ± 0.1 Volt	Battery Source Test
	Socket No. 1 and Engine Ground	Battery Voltage ± 0.1 Volt	Battery Source Test
CRANKING	Socket No. 5 and Engine Ground	8 to 12 volts	Check Supply Circuit (starting) through Ignition Switch
	Jumper No. 1 to No. 8 Read No. 6	more than 6 volts	Starting Circuit Test
	Pin No. 3 and Pin No. 8	1/2 volt minimum A.C. or any D.C. volt wiggle	Distributor Hardware Test

	TEST VOLTAGE BETWEEN	SHOULD BE	IF NOT, CONDUCT
KEY OFF	Socket No. 8 and No. 3 Socket No. 7 and Engine Ground Socket No. 8 and Engine Ground Socket No. 3 and Engine Ground	400 to 800 ohms 0 ohms more than 70,000 ohms more than 70,000 ohms	Magnetic Pick-up (Stator) Test
	Socket No. 4 and Coil Tower	7000 to 13,000 ohms	Coil Test
	Socket No. 1 and Engine Ground	more than 4.0 ohms	Short Test

Ford-Motorcraft Solid-State ignition system diagnosis, 1976 and later
(© Ford Motor Co.)

a short to ground at the DEC terminal of the ignition coil or in the wiring to that terminal.

Resistance Wire Test

Replace the resistance wire if it does not show a resistance of 1.3-1.4 ohms.

Adjustments

The air gap between the armature and magnetic pick-up coil in the distributor is not adjustable, nor are there any adjustments for the amplifier module. Inoperative components are simply replaced. Any attempt to connect components outside the vehicle may result in component failure.

Component Replacement

Magnetic Pick-up Assembly Removal and Installation

1. Remove the distributor cap and rotor and disconnect the distributor harness plug.
2. Using a small gear puller or two screwdrivers, lift or pry the armature from the advance plate sleeve. Remove the roll pin.
3. Remove the large wire retaining clip from the base plate annular groove.
4. Remove the snap-ring which secures the vacuum advance link to the pick-up assembly.
5. Remove the magnetic pick-up assembly ground screw and lift the assembly from the distributor.
6. Lift the vacuum advance arm off the post on the pick-up assembly and move it out against the distributor housing.
7. Place the new pick-up assembly in position over the fixed base plate and slide the wiring in position through the slot in the side of the distributor housing.
8. Install the fine wire snap-ring securing the pick-up assembly to the fixed base plate.

Ford-Motorcraft Solid-State Ignition distributor disassembled
(© Ford Motor Co)

9. Position the vacuum advance arm over the post on the pick-up assembly and install the snap-ring.
10. Install the grounding screw through the tab on the wiring harness and into the fixed base plate.
11. Install the armature on the advance plate sleeve making sure that the roll pin is engaged in the matching slots.
12. Install the distributor rotor cap.
13. Connect the distributor wiring plug to the vehicle harness.

Delco-Remy Magnetic Pulse System

Components

The Delco-Remy magnetic pulse, fully transistorized ignition system uses a magnetic pulse distributor having no breaker points. This system switches power electronically rather than with ignition contact points. Instead of the familiar cam and breaker plate assembly, this distributor uses a rotating iron timer core and a magnetic pickup assembly. The magnetic pickup assembly consists of a bearing plate on which are sandwiched a ceramic ring-type permanent magnet, two pole pieces and a pick-up coil. The pole pieces are doughnut shaped steel plates with accurately spaced internal teeth, one tooth for each cylinder of the engine.

A critically important part is the iron timer core. It has a number of equally spaced projections or vanes and is attached to, and rotates with, the distributor shaft.

The transistor control unit, the switchbox of the system, is mounted in an aluminum case and contains three transistors, a zener diode, a condenser and five small resistors. The zener diode is a circuit protection device. Remaining components control and switch ignition-coil current electronically; there are no moving parts in the control unit.

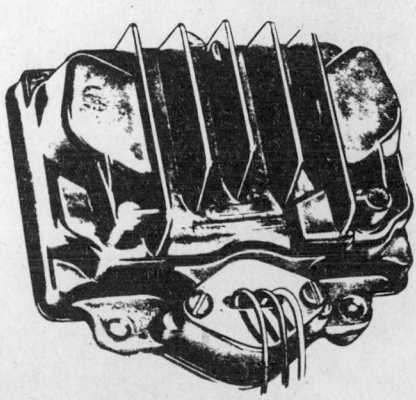

Delco-Remy amplifier unit
(© Chevrolet Div., G.M. Corp)

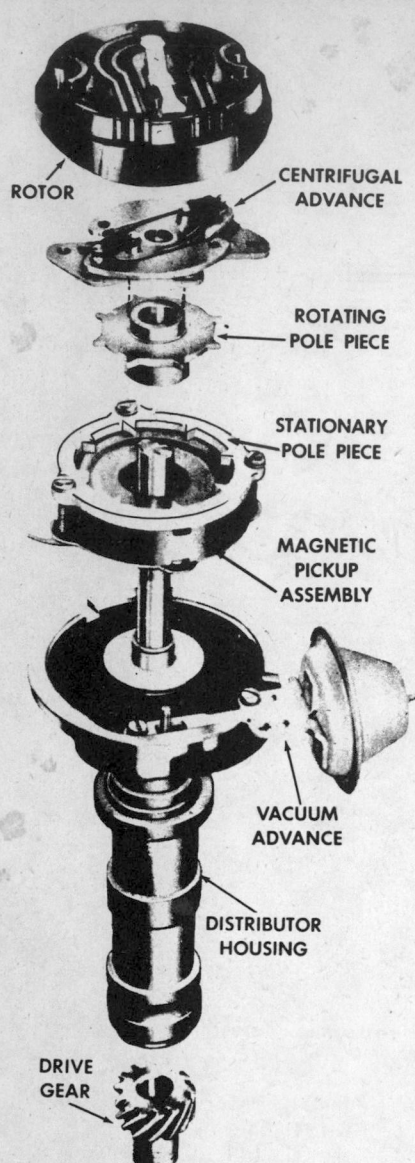

Delco-Remy pulse distributor exploded view
(© Chevrolet Div., G.M. Corp)

The ignition coil is of standard design except for a special winding. The external primary resistor is a ceramic type, similar to those used on various conventional systems.

The system was last used in 1972.

Operation

The ignition primary circuit is connected from the battery, through the ignition switch, through the ignition pulse amplifier assembly, through the primary side of the ignition coil, and back to the amplifier housing where it is grounded externally. The secondary circuit is the same as in conventional ignition systems: the secondary side of the coil, the coil wire to the distributor, the rotor, the spark plug wires and the spark plugs.

The magnetic pulse distributor is also connected to the ignition pulse amplifier. As the distributor shaft rotates, the distributor rotating pole piece turns inside the stationary pole piece. As the rotating pole piece turns inside the stationary pole piece, the eight teeth on the rotating pole piece align with the eight teeth on the stationary pole piece eight times during each distributor revolution (two crankshaft revolutions since the distributor runs at one-half crankshaft speed). As the rotating pole piece teeth move close to, and align with, the teeth on the stationary pole piece, the magnetic rotating pole piece induces voltage into the magnetic pole piece through the stationary pole piece. This voltage pulse is sent to the ignition pulse amplifier from the magnetic pole piece. When the pulse enters the amplifier, it signals the ignition pulse amplifier to interrupt the ignition primary circuit. This causes the primary circuit to collapse and begins the induction of the magnetic lines of force from the primary side of the coil into the secondary side of the coil. This induction provides the required voltage to fire the spark plugs.

The advantages of this system are that the transistors in the ignition pulse amplifier can make and break the primary ignition circuit much faster than conventional ignition points, and higher primary voltage can be utilized since this system can be made to handle higher voltage without adverse effects, whereas ignition breaker points cannot. The shorter switching time of this system allows longer coil primary circuit saturation time and longer induction time when the primary circuit collapses. This increased time allows the primary circuit to build up more current and the secondary circuit to discharge more current.

Troubleshooting

Cautions

1. Don't use 18 volts or 24 volts for emergency starting.
2. Never crank engine with coil high-tension lead or more than three spark plug leads disconnected.
3. Don't short circuit between coil positive terminal and ground.

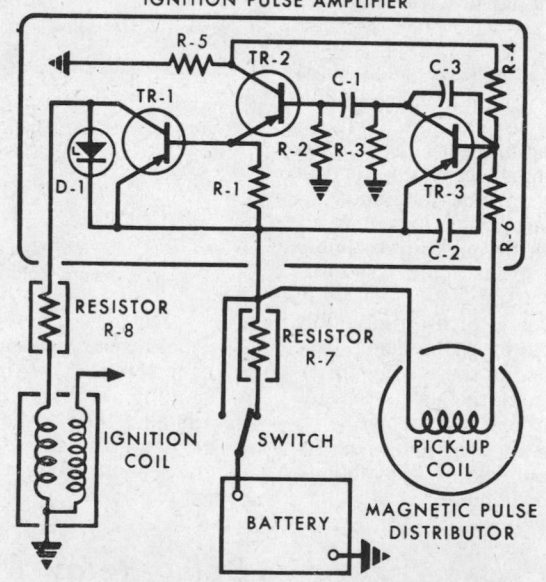

Delco-Remy amplifier schematic
(© Chevrolet Div., G.M. Corp)

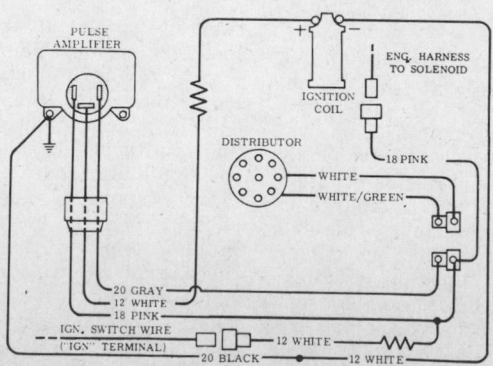

Delco-Remy circuit diagram
(© Chevrolet Div., G.M. Corp)

4. On any repair that necessitates replacement of control unit or ignition resistor, perform complete charging system check before releasing the unit. Basic cause of trouble may be high or uncontrolled charging rate.

Engine Surge or Intermittent Miss

Since there are so many possible causes for this problem, all other possible defects must be ruled out before the specialized components of the electronic ignition system are judged defective.

As a general rule, a miss or surge that is caused by an ignition problem will be much more pronounced than a similiar problem that is caused by carburetion. Also, carburetion is usually affected by temperature more than the ignition system is. A carburetor or intake manifold vacuum leak is often compensated for by the choke when the engine is cold. When the engine warms up and the choke is released, the engine surge will show up.

If the ignition system is found to be the source of the problem, first check all connections in the system to make sure that they are *clean and tight*. Check the coil and spark plug high-tension wires with an ohmmeter to be sure they have the correct resistance. Check the inside and outside of the distributor cap and the tower on the ignition coil for cracks which would allow the high voltage intended for the spark plugs to short to ground.

If none of the above checks uncovers a defective component, the distributor pick-up coil leads may be reversed in the connector, or the pickup coil itself may have an intermittent open.

Engine Will Not Start or Is Hard to Start

1. Disconnect a spark plug wire from one spark plug and hold the wire 1/4 in. from a good ground with a pair of insulated pliers.
2. Crank the engine over and observe whether a spark jumps from the plug wire to ground.
3. *If spark occurs*, the problem is not in the ignition system.
4. *If spark does not occur*, reconnect the spark plug wire that was disconnected and connect a tachometer between the positive (+) coil primary terminal and the pink wire in the three-wire connector to the ignition pulse amplifier.
5. Crank the engine over and observe the tachometer.
6. *If the tachometer needle deflects* while cranking the engine, perform "Ignition Distributor Test" to locate the problem.
7. *If the tachometer needle does not deflect* while cranking the engine, perform "Circuit Resistance Test" to pinpoint the problem.

Circuit Resistance Test
Ignition Distributor Check

1. Disconnect the distributor leads from the engine wiring harness.
2. Connect the two leads of an ohmmeter to the distributor leads at the connector.
3. Rotate the magnetic pick-up assembly in the distributor through full vacuum advance travel and read the ohmmeter. If the reading is not within a range of 500-700 ohms, replace the magnetic pick-up assembly.
4. If the reading is within the 500-700 ohms range, disconnect one ohmmeter lead from the distributor connector and connect it to a good ground. If the reading is less than infinity (needle moves to end of scale), replace the magnetic pick-up assembly.
5. If the reading is infinite, and there was no spark when the spark plug wire was disconnected from the plug, the amplifier is defective.

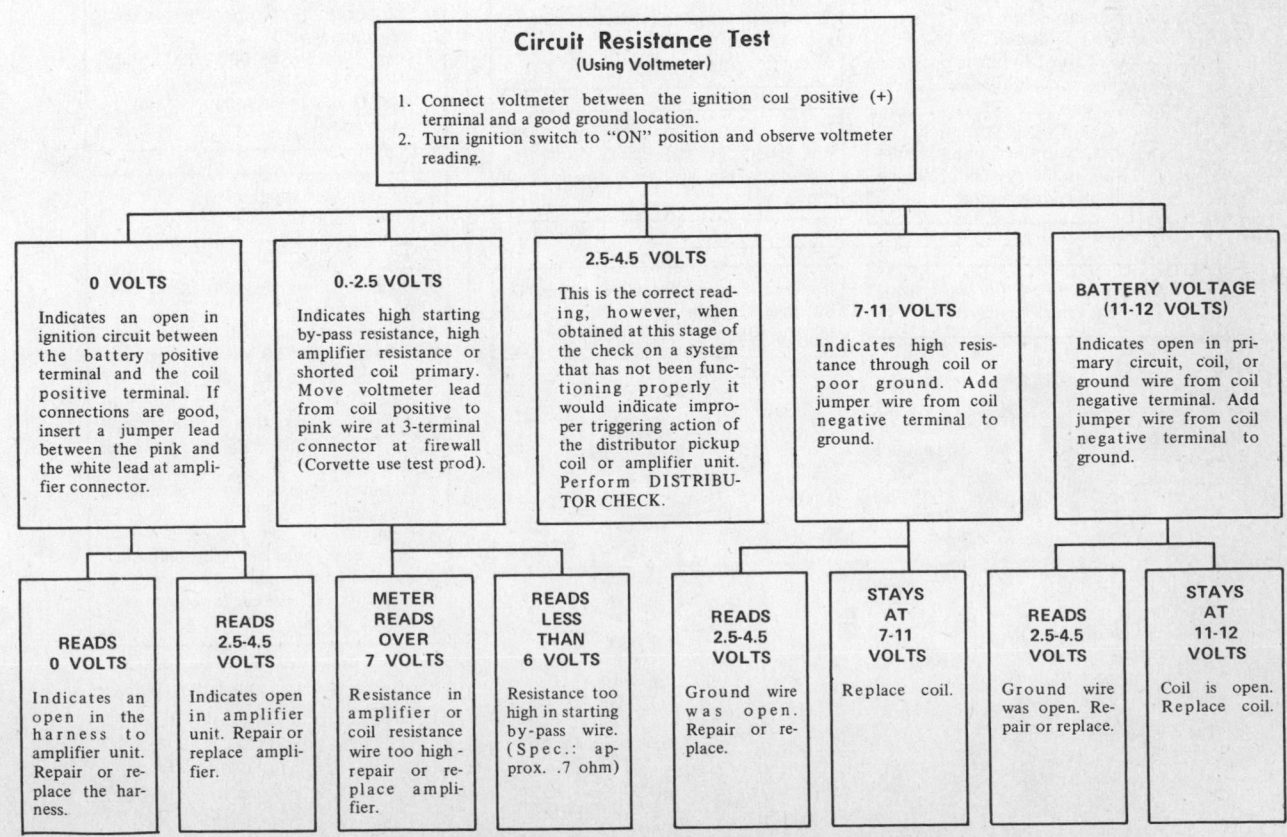

Magnetic Pulse System (© Chevrolet Div., G.M. Corp)

Delco-Remy Unit Ignition System

This system is almost identical to the Delco-Remy Magnetic Pulse System. The ignition primary circuit passes through the electronic module (called the ignition pulse amplifier in Delco-Remy system) and is interrupted when a signal is sent to the control module from the distributor. The main difference between the two systems is that, in the Unitized System, the ignition coil and control module are attached to the distributor body, making a compact, one-piece ignition system. It is optional equipment on some 1972-74 model Pontiacs with V8 engines.

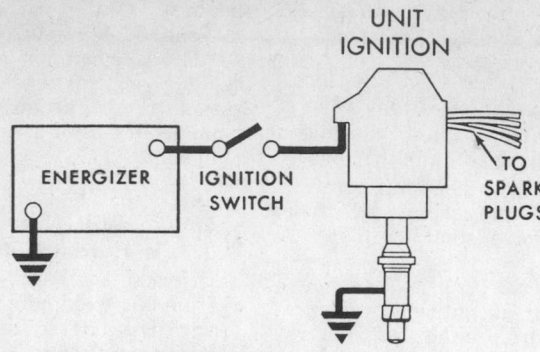

Unit Ignition System wiring diagram
(© Pontiac Div., G.M. Corp)

UNIT IGNITION SYSTEM TROUBLESHOOTING

Insure that black and pink leads are connected as shown in Fig. 1. Tighten both bolts, Fig. 1. Loose bolts may cause poor performance and radio interference.

ON THE VEHICLE

ENGINE WILL NOT RUN

1. Check ignition switch connector, Fig. 1.
2. Connect voltmeter from ignition switch connector to ground.
3. Turn on ignition switch.
4. If reading is zero, circuit is open between connector and ignition switch. Repair if needed.
5. If reading is battery voltage, hold one spark lead with insulating pliers about ¼ in. from dry area of engine block while cranking engine.

If sparking occurs, trouble most likely is not ignition. Check fuel system.

ENGINE WILL START BUT NOT RUN, AND ENGINE MISS OR SURGE.

1. Insure that fuel system is satisfactory.
2. Check spark plug leads for arcing or leakage to ground.
3. Check spark plugs.

If no defects are found, follow procedure under "On the Bench" with Unit Ignition System initially either on or off the vehicle.

If no spark, follow procedure under "On the Bench," with Unit Ignition System initially either on or off the engine.

ON THE BENCH

1. Disassemble unit (Fig. 2).
2. Inspect coil, eight inserts, shell and rotor for arc-over or leakage.

1. Connect ohmmeter, Fig. 3.
2. Parts A and B each should be practically zero. If infinite on either reading, replace coil.
3. Part C should be 6000-9000 ohms. If outside range, replace coil.
4. Part D should be infinite. If not, replace coil.

1. Connect test stand vacuum source to vacuum unit.
2. Connect ohmmeter Parts A and B. Fig. 4.
3. Observe ohmmeter throughout vacuum range.
4. If Part A reads less than 650 ohms, or more than 850 ohms at any time, replace pickup coil, per Step 7 below.
5. If Part B reads other than infinite at any time, replace pickup coil, per step 7 below.
6. If vacuum unit is inoperative, replace per Step 7 below.
7. Remove unit from engine, drive pin from gear, remove rotor and shaft assembly from housing, remove shim and then "C" washer to replace pickup coil or vacuum unit (Fig. 5).

If no defects have been found, remove two attaching screws and replace module.

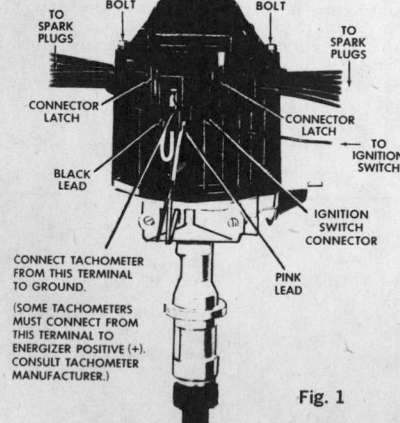

Fig. 1

Unit Ignition System test hook-up
(© PONTIAC Div., G.M. Corp)

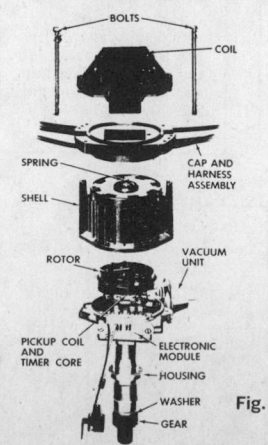

Fig. 2

Unit Ignition System exploded view
(© Pontiac Div., G.M. Corp)

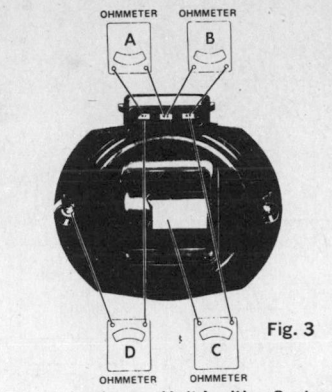

Fig. 3

Coil test hook-up—Unit Ignition System
(© Pontiac Div., G.M. Corp)

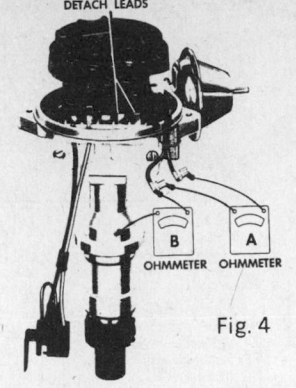

Fig. 4

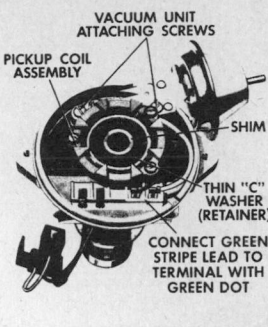

Fig. 5

Delco-Remy High Energy Ignition (HEI) System

Components

The Delco-Remy High Energy Ignition (HEI) System is a breakerless, pulse triggered, transistor controlled, inductive discharge ignition system available as an option on 1974 model Oldsmobiles, Buicks, and Cadillacs with V8 engines. Starting 1975, HEI is used on all GM passenger car engines as standard equipment.

It is similar in operation to the Magnetic Pulse System and is identical to the Unit Ignition System except for the arrangement of components within the distributor. On V6 and V8 engines, the ignition coil is located within the distributor cap, connecting directly to the rotor. The major difference between the HEI System and the Unit Ignition System is that the HEI System is a full 12 volt system, while the Unit Ignition System incorporates a resistance wire to limit the voltage to the coil except during periods of starter motor operation.

Operation

The magnetic pick-up assembly located inside the distributor contains a permanent magnet, a pole piece with internal teeth, and a pick-up coil. When the teeth of the rotating timer core and pole piece align, an induced voltage in the pick-up coil signals the electronic module to open the coil primary circuit. As the primary current decreases, a high voltage is induced in the secondary windings of the ignition coil, directing a spark through the rotor and high voltage leads to fire the spark plugs. The dwell period is automatically controlled by the electronic module and is increased with increasing engine rpm. The HEI System features a longer spark duration which is instrumental in firing lean and EGR diluted fuel/air mixtures. The condenser (capacitor) located within the HEI distributor is provided for noise (static) suppression purposes only and is not a regularly replaced ignition system component.

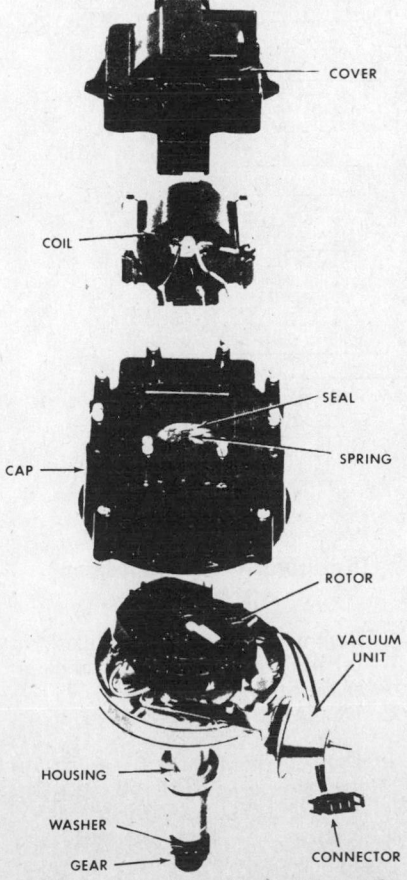

HEI distributor internal parts, V6 and V8
(© Buick Div., G.M. Corp)

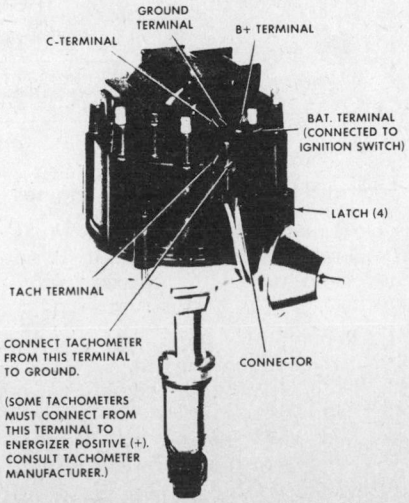

High Energy Ignition System distributor, V6 and V8
(© Oldsmobile Div., G.M. Corp)

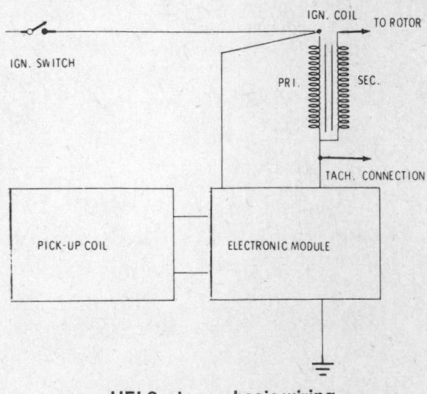

HEI System—basic wiring
(© Oldsmobile Div., G.M. Corp)

Major Repair Operations (distributor in engine)

Ignition Coil Replacement V6 and V8 Engines

1. Disconnect the feed and module wire terminal connectors from the distributor cap.
2. Remove the ignition set retainer.
3. Remove the 4 coil cover-to-distributor cap screws and the coil cover.

U41

HIGH ENERGY IGNITION DIAGNOSIS

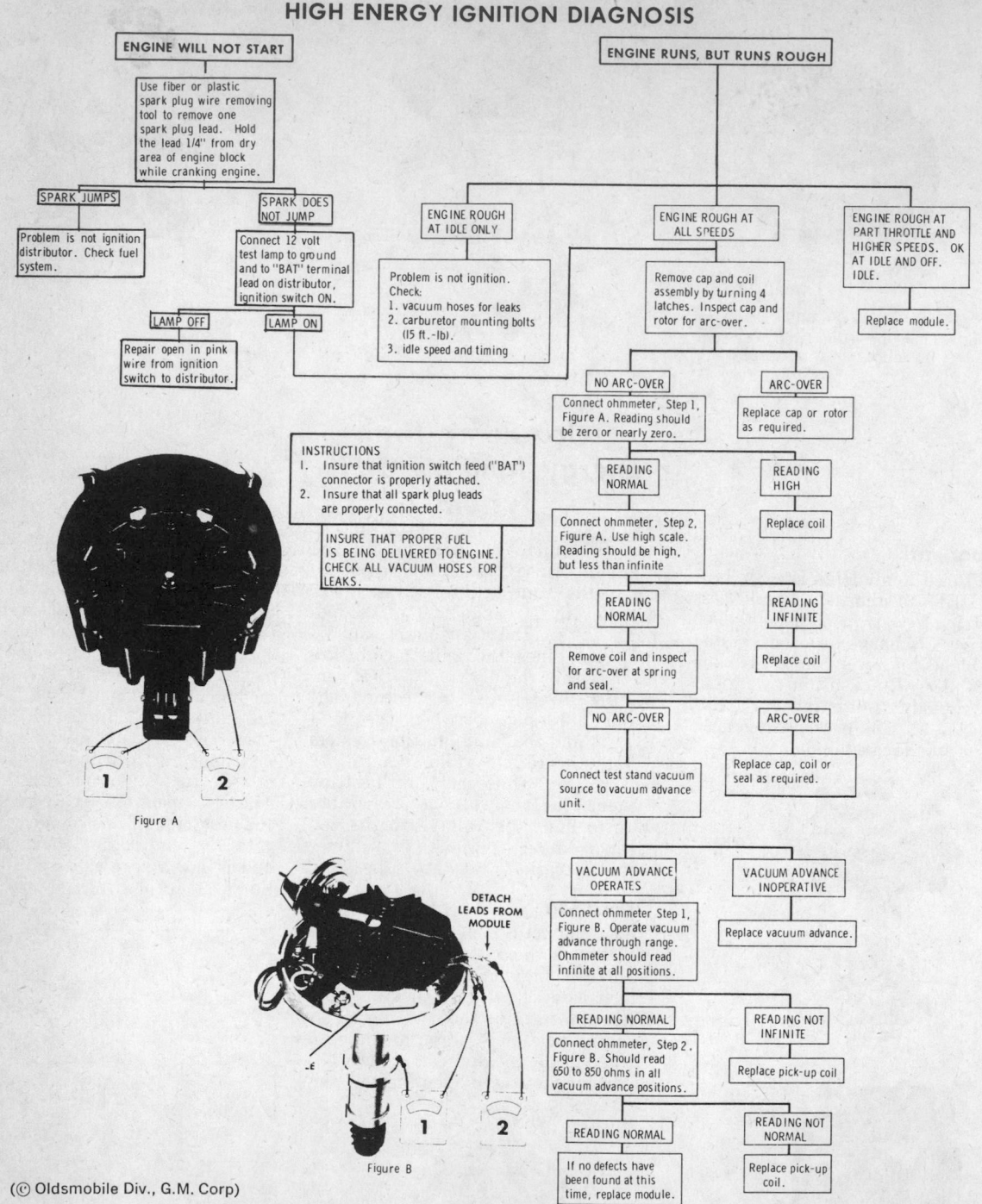

ENGINE WILL NOT START

Use fiber or plastic spark plug wire removing tool to remove one spark plug lead. Hold the lead 1/4" from dry area of engine block while cranking engine.

SPARK JUMPS

Problem is not ignition distributor. Check fuel system.

SPARK DOES NOT JUMP

Connect 12 volt test lamp to ground and to "BAT" terminal lead on distributor, ignition switch ON.

LAMP OFF

Repair open in pink wire from ignition switch to distributor.

LAMP ON

ENGINE RUNS, BUT RUNS ROUGH

ENGINE ROUGH AT IDLE ONLY

Problem is not ignition. Check:
1. vacuum hoses for leaks
2. carburetor mounting bolts (15 ft.-lb).
3. idle speed and timing

ENGINE ROUGH AT ALL SPEEDS

Remove cap and coil assembly by turning 4 latches. Inspect cap and rotor for arc-over.

ENGINE ROUGH AT PART THROTTLE AND HIGHER SPEEDS. OK AT IDLE AND OFF. IDLE.

Replace module.

NO ARC-OVER

Connect ohmmeter, Step 1, Figure A. Reading should be zero or nearly zero.

ARC-OVER

Replace cap or rotor as required.

READING NORMAL

Connect ohmmeter, Step 2, Figure A. Use high scale. Reading should be high, but less than infinite

READING HIGH

Replace coil

READING NORMAL

Remove coil and inspect for arc-over at spring and seal.

READING INFINITE

Replace coil

NO ARC-OVER

Connect test stand vacuum source to vacuum advance unit.

ARC-OVER

Replace cap, coil or seal as required.

VACUUM ADVANCE OPERATES

Connect ohmmeter Step 1, Figure B. Operate vacuum advance through range. Ohmmeter should read infinite at all positions.

VACUUM ADVANCE INOPERATIVE

Replace vacuum advance.

READING NORMAL

Connect ohmmeter, Step 2, Figure B. Should read 650 to 850 ohms in all vacuum advance positions.

READING NOT INFINITE

Replace pick-up coil

READING NORMAL

If no defects have been found at this time, replace module.

READING NOT NORMAL

Replace pick-up coil.

INSTRUCTIONS
1. Insure that ignition switch feed ("BAT") connector is properly attached.
2. Insure that all spark plug leads are properly connected.

INSURE THAT PROPER FUEL IS BEING DELIVERED TO ENGINE. CHECK ALL VACUUM HOSES FOR LEAKS.

Figure A

DETACH LEADS FROM MODULE

Figure B

(© Oldsmobile Div., G.M. Corp)

---

4. Remove the 4 coil-to-distributor cap screws.
5. Using a blunt drift, press the coil wire spade terminals up out of distributor cap.
6. Lift the coil up out of the distributor cap.
7. Remove and clean the coil spring, rubber seal washer and coil cavity of the distributor cap.
8. Coat the rubber seal with a dielectric lubricant furnished in the replacement ignition coil package.
9. Reverse the above procedures to install.

Four and Inline Six Cylinder Engines

On 4 and inline 6 cylinder engines, a separate ignition coil is used. To remove and install it, proceed as follows:

1. Remove the ignition switch-to-coil lead from the coil.
2. Unfasten the distributor leads from the coil.
3. Remove the screws which secure the coil to the engine and lift it off.

Installation is the reverse of removal.

Distributor Cap Replacement
All Engines

1. Remove the feed and module wire terminal connectors from the distributor cap.
2. Remove the retainer and spark plug wires from the cap.
3. Depress and release the 4 distributor cap-to-housing retainers and lift off the cap assembly.
4. Remove the 4 coil cover screws and cover (V8 and V6 only).
5. Using a finger or a blunt drift, push the spade terminals up out

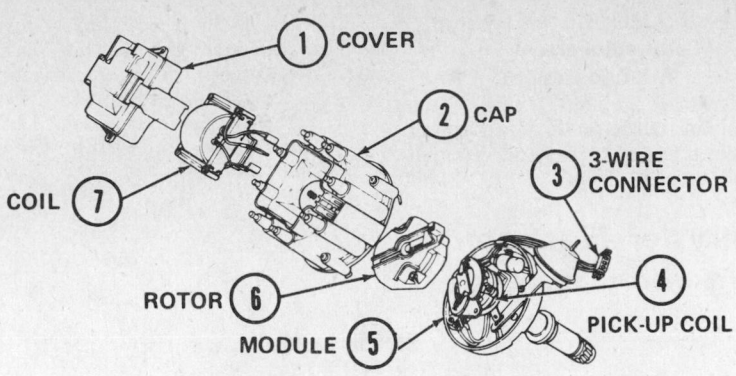

V6 and V8 HEI distributor components
(© Buick Div., G.M. Corp.)

of the distributor cap (V8 and V6 only).

6. Remove all 4 coil screws and lift the coil, coil spring and rubber seal washer out of the cap coil cavity (V8 and V6 only).

7. Using a new distributor cap, reverse the above procedures to assemble being sure to clean and lubricate the rubber seal washer with dielectric lubricant.

Rotor Replacement
All Engines

1. Disconnect the feed and module wire connectors from the distributor.

2. Depress and release the 4 distributor cap to housing retainers and lift off the cap assembly.

3. Remove the two rotor attaching screws and rotor.

4. Reverse the above procedure to install.

Vacuum Advance Replacement
All Engines

1. Remove the distributor cap and rotor as previously described.

2. Disconnect the vacuum hose from the vacuum advance unit. Remove the module.

3. Remove the two vacuum advance retaining screws, pull the advance unit outward, rotate and disengage the operating rod from its tang.

4. Reverse the above procedure to install.

Module Replacement
All Engines

1. Remove the distributor cap and rotor as previously described.

2. Disconnect the harness connector and pick-up coil spade connectors from the module (note their positions).

3. Remove the two screws and module from the distributor housing.

4. Coat the bottom of the new module with dielectric lubricant. Reverse the above procedure to install. Be sure that the leads are installed correctly.

Distributor Removal
All Engines

1. Disconnect the ground cable from the battery.

2. Disconnect the feed and module terminal connectors from the distributor cap. (Don't use a screwdriver).

3. Disconnect the hose at the vacuum advance.

4. Depress and release the 4 distributor cap-to-housing retainers and lift off the cap assembly.

5. Using crayon or chalk, make locating marks on the rotor and module and on the distributor housing and engine for installation purposes.

6. Loosen and remove the distributor clamp bolt and clamp, and lift distributor out of the engine. Noting the relative position of the

rotor and module alignment marks, make a second mark on the rotor to align it with the one mark on the module.

Distributor Installation
All Engines

1. With a new O-ring on the distributor housing and the second mark on the rotor aligned with the mark on the module, install the distributor, taking care to align the mark on the housing with the one on the engine. It may be necessary to lift the distributor and turn the rotor slightly to align the gears and the oil pump driveshaft.

2. With the respective marks aligned, install the clamp and bolt finger-tight.

3. Install and secure the distributor cap.

4. Connect the feed and module connectors to the distributor cap.

5. Connect a timing light to the engine and plug the vacuum hose.

6. Connect the ground cable to the battery.

7. Start the engine and set the timing.

8. Turn the engine off and tighten the distributor clamp bolt. Disconnect the timing light and unplug and connect the hose to the vacuum advance.

Service Procedures (distributor removed)

Driven Gear Replacement
All Engines

1. With the distributor removed, use a 1/8 in. pin punch and tap out the driven gear roll pin.

2. Hold the rotor end of shaft and rotate the driven gear to shear any burrs in the roll pin hole.

3. Remove the driven gear from the shaft.

4. Reverse the above procedure to install.

Mainshaft Replacement
All Engines

1. With the driven gear and rotor

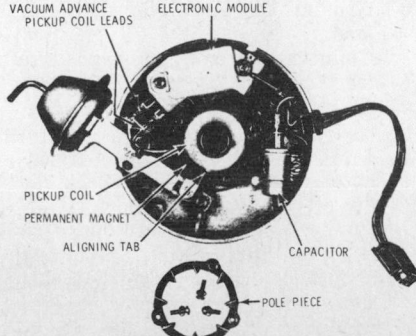

HEI System—pole piece removal
(© Oldsmobile Div., G.M. Corp)

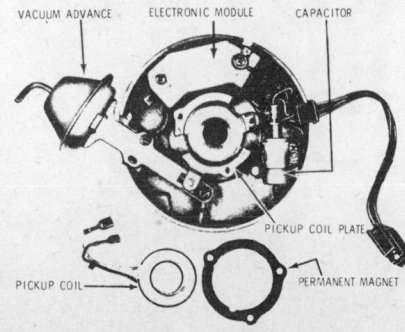

HEI System—coil and magnet removal
(© Oldsmobile Div., G.M. Corp)

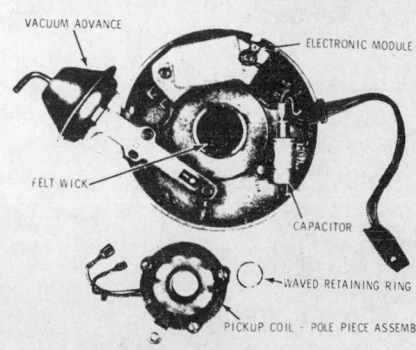

HEI System—pick-up coil removal
(© Oldsmobile Div., G.M. Corp)

removed, gently pull the main-shaft out of the housing.

2. Remove the advance springs, weights and slide the weight base plate off the mainshaft.

3. Reverse the above procedure to install.

Pole Piece, Magnet or Pick-up Coil Replacement
All Engines

1. With the mainshaft out of its housing, remove the 3 retaining screws, pole piece and magnet and/or pick-up coil.

2. Reverse the removal procedure to install making sure that the pole piece teeth do not contact the timer core teeth by installing and rotating the mainshaft. Loosen the 3 screws and realign the pole piece as necessary.

Chrysler Electronic Ignition System

Components

This system consists of a special pulse-sending distributor, an electronic control unit, a two-element ballast resistor, and a special ignition coil.

The distributor does not contain breaker points or a condenser, these parts being replaced by a distributor reluctor and a pick-up unit.

Operation

The ignition primary circuit is connected from the battery, through the ignition switch, through the primary side of the ignition coil, to the control unit where it is grounded. The secondary circuit is the same as in conventional ignition systems: the secondary side of the coil, the coil wire to the distributor, the rotor, the spark plug wires, and the spark plugs.

The magnetic pulse distributor is also connected to the control unit. As the distributor shaft rotates, the distributor reluctor turns past the pick-up unit. As the reluctor turns past the pick-up unit, each of the eight (or six) teeth on the reluctor pass near the pick-up unit once during each distributor revolution (two crankshaft revolutions since the distributor runs at one-half crankshaft speed). As the reluctor teeth move close to the pick-up unit, the magnetic rotating reluctor induces voltage into the magnetic pick-up unit. This voltage pulse is sent to the ignition control unit from the magnetic

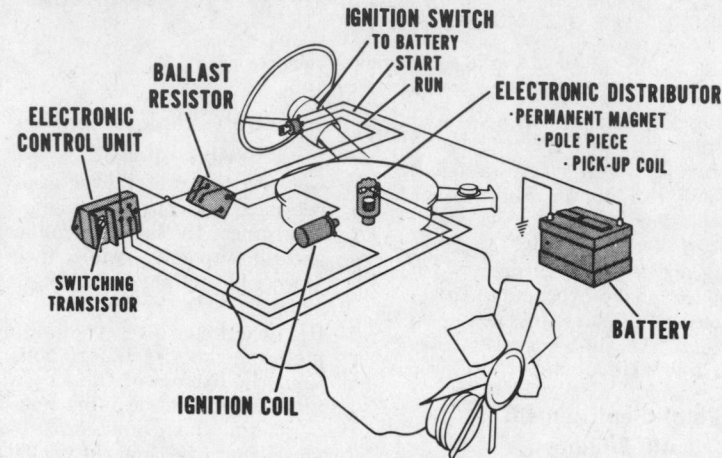

Chrysler system wiring diagram (© Chrysler Corp)

pick-up unit. When the pulse enters the control unit, it signals the control unit to interrupt the ignition primary circuit. This causes the primary circuit to collapse and begins the induction of the magnetic lines of force from the primary side of the coil into the secondary side of the coil. This induction provides the required voltage to fire the spark plugs.

The advantages of this system are that the transistors in the control unit can make and break the primary ignition circuit much faster than conventional ignition points can, and higher primary voltage can be utilized, since this system can be made to handle higher voltage without adverse effects, whereas ignition

breaker points cannot. The quicker switching time of this system allows longer coil primary circuit saturation time and longer induction time when the primary circuit collapses. This increased time allows the primary circuit to build up more current and the secondary circuit to discharge more current.

System Test

A voltmeter with a 20,000 ohm/volt rating and a 1½ volt battery powered ohmmeter are required. Car battery voltage must be at least 12 volts.

1. Remove the wiring plug from the control unit.

CAUTION: *Make sure the ignition switch is off when removing or replacing the control unit connector.*

2. Turn the ignition switch on.

3. Ground the negative voltmeter lead.

4. Connect the voltmeter positive lead to the harness connector cavity No. 1 (shown on the schematic). Voltage should be within 1 volt of battery voltage with all accessories off. If not, check the circuit through to the battery.

5. Connect the voltmeter positive lead to cavity No. 2. Voltage should be within 1 volt of battery voltage with all accessories off. If not, check the circuit through to the battery.

6. Connect the voltmeter positive lead to cavity No. 3. Voltage

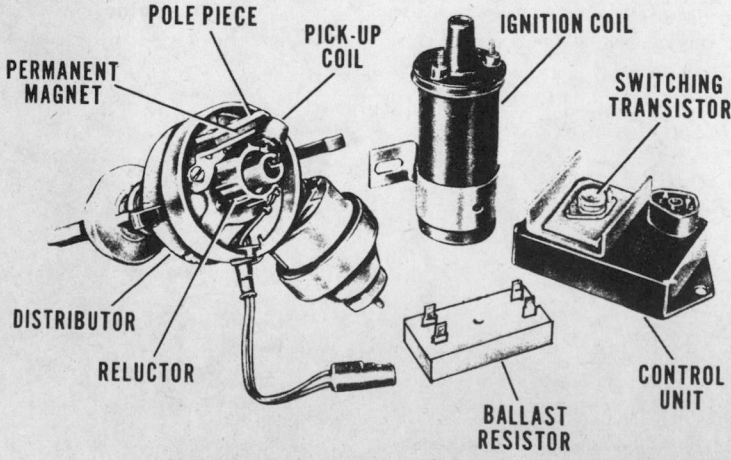

Chrysler system components (© Chrysler Corp)

should be within 1 volt of battery voltage with all accessories off. If not, check the circuit through to the battery.

7. Turn the ignition switch off.
8. Connect the ohmmeter leads to cavities No. 4 and 5. The resistance should be 150-900 ohms. If it isn't, detach the dual lead connector from the distributor. Check the resistance at the dual lead connector. If it still isn't within the range, replace the distributor pick-up coil.
9. Connect one ohmmeter lead to a ground and the other to either distributor connector. If the ohmmeter shows a reading, replace the distributor pick-up coil.
10. Connect one ohmmeter lead to a ground and the other to the control unit pin No. 5. The ohmmeter should show continuity. If not, remove and remount the control unit and check again. Replace the control unit if no continuity can be established.
11. Make sure the ignition switch is off and replace the control unit connector plug and the distributor plug.
12. Check the air gap adjustment, as shown later.
13. Remove the center wire from the distributor cap. Very cautiously, using insulated pliers and a very heavy glove, hold the cable about 3 16 in. from the engine block and have the starter operated. If there is no spark, replace the control unit. Try the test again. If there is still no spark, replace the coil.

Pick-Up Coil Replacement

1972-74

1. Remove the distributor.
2. Remove the pick-up coil mounting screw.
3. Remove the wires from the retainers on the upper plate and distributor housing.
4. Remove pick-up coil from the upper plate.
5. Position the pick-up coil on the pivot of the upper plate and install the mounting screw. Do not tighten.
6. Insert the wires into the appropriate retainers in the distributor.
7. Install the distributor.
8. Set the air gap.

1975 and Later

1. Remove the distributor from the engine.
2. Using two small pry-bars or screwdrivers (maximum 7 16 in. wide), pry the reluctor off the shaft from the bottom.

Caution Do not damage the teeth on the reluctor.

TROUBLESHOOTING CHRYSLER ELECTRONIC IGNITION

Condition	Possible Cause	Correction
ENGINE WILL NOT START (Fuel and carburetion known to be OK)	a) Dual Ballast	Check resistance of each section: Compensating resistance: .50-.60 ohms @ 70°-80°F Auxiliary Ballast: 4.75-5.75 ohms Replace if faulty. Check wire positions.
	b) Faulty Ignition Coil	Check for carbonized tower. Check primary and secondary resistances: Primary: 1.41-1.79 ohms @ 70°-80°F Secondary: 9,200-11,700 ohms @ 70°-80°F Check in coil tester.
	c) Faulty Pickup or Improper Pickup Air Gap	Check pickup coil resistance: 400-600 ohms Check pickup gap: .010 in. feeler gauge should not slip between pickup coil core and an aligned reluctor blade. No evidence of pickup core striking reluctor blades should be visible. To reset gap, tighten pickup adjustment screw with a .008 in. feeler gauge held between pickup core and an aligned reluctor blade. After resetting gap, run distributor on test stand and apply vacuum advance, making sure that the pickup core does not strike the reluctor blades.
	d) Faulty Wiring	Visually inspect wiring for brittle insulation. Inspect connectors. Molded connectors should be inspected for rubber inside female terminals.
	e) Faulty Control Unit	Replace if all of the above checks are negative. Whenever the control unit or dual ballast is replaced, make sure the dual ballast wires are correctly inserted in the keyed molded connector.
ENGINE SURGES SEVERELY (Not Lean Carburetor)	a) Wiring	Inspect for loose connection and/or broken conductors in harness.
	b) Faulty Pickup Leads	Disconnect vacuum advance. If surging stops, replace pickup.
	c) Ignition Coil	Check for intermittent primary.
ENGINE MISSES (Carburetion OK)	a) Spark Plugs	Check plugs. Clean and regap if necessary.
	b) Secondary Cable	Check cables with an ohmmeter, or observe secondary circuit performance with an oscilloscope.
	c) Ignition Coil	Check for cabonized tower. Check in coil tester.
	d) Wiring	Check for loose or dirty connections.
	e) Faulty Pickup Lead	Disconnect vacuum advance. If miss stops, replace pickup.
	f) Control Unit	Replace if the above checks are negative.

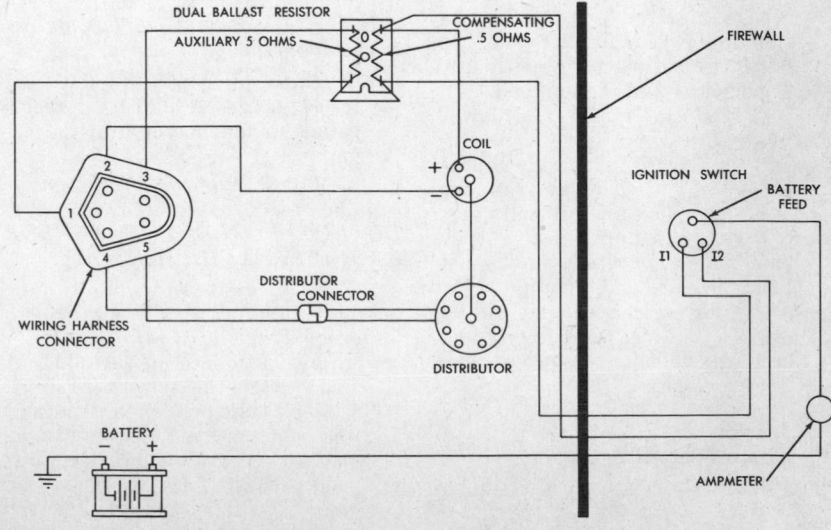

Chrysler corporation electronic ignition system schematic
(© Chrysler Corp.)

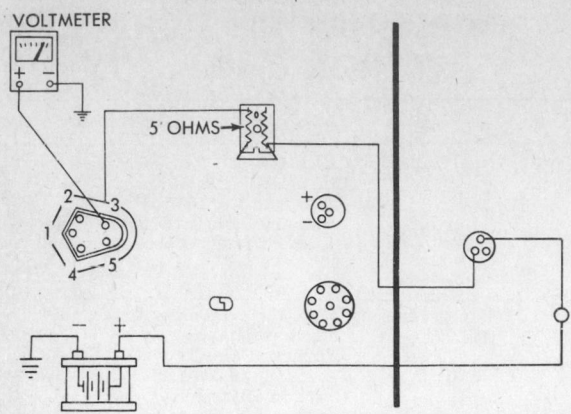

Circuit to be checked out if voltage at plug cavity No. 3 is not within 1 volt of battery voltage (© Chrysler Corp.)

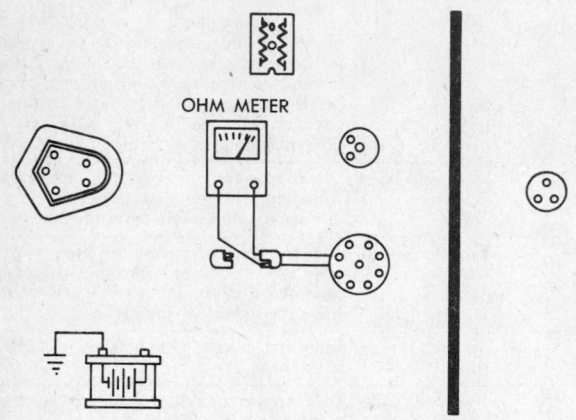

Checking the resistance at the dual lead connector
(© Chrysler Corp.)

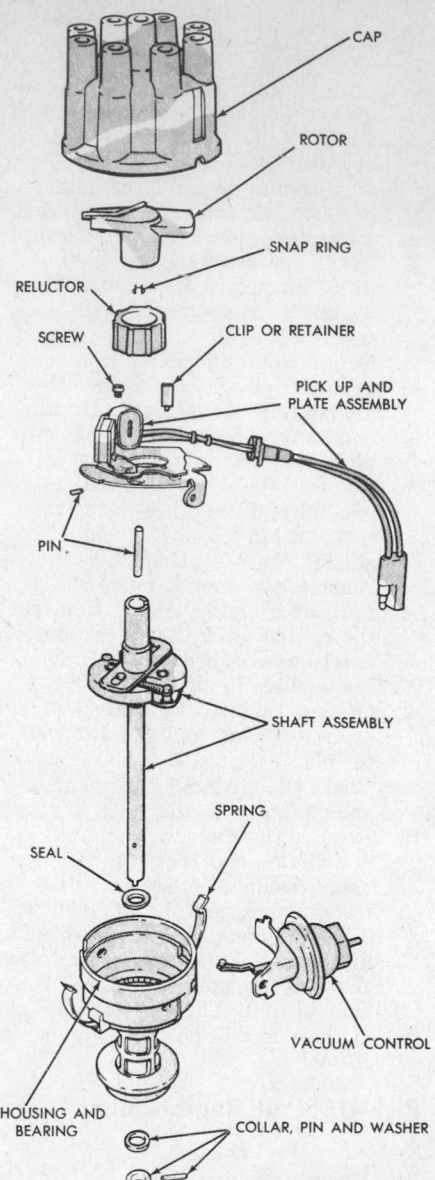

Chrysler Electronic Ignition distributor
disassembled—V8
(© Chrysler Corp)

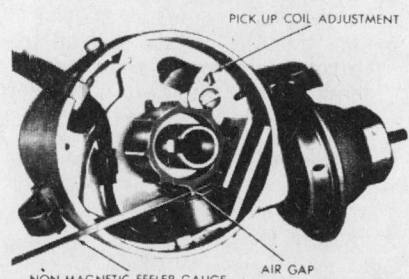

Air gap adjustment—Chrysler Electronic
Ignition distributor (© Chrysler Corp)

3. Unfasten the vacuum advance-to-distributor housing screws. Remove the vacuum unit, after disconnecting the arm from the upper plate.
4. Unfasten the pick-up coil wires from the distributor housing.
5. Unfasten the two screws which secure the lower plate to the distributor housing. Lift out the lower plate together with the upper plate and pick-up coil.
6. Separate the upper and lower plates by depressing the retaining clip on the underside of the plate and slide it away from the stud. The pick-up coil will come off with the upper plate; they cannot be separated; they must be serviced as an assembly.

Installation is the reverse of removal. Place a small amount of distributor grease on the support pins on the lower plate.

Air Gap Adjustment
1. Align one reluctor tooth with the pick-up coil tooth.
2. Loosen the pick-up coil hold-down screw.
3. Insert a 0.008 in. nonmagnetic feeler gauge between the reluctor tooth and the pick-up coil tooth.
4. Adjust the air gap so that contact is made between the reluctor tooth, the feeler gauge, and the pick-up coil tooth.
5. Tighten the hold-down screw.
6. Remove the feeler gauge.
NOTE : *No force should be required in removing the feeler gauge.*
7. Check the air gap with a 0.010 in. feeler gauge. A 0.010 in. feeler gauge should not fit into the air gap.
CAUTION : *A 0.010 in. feeler gauge can be forced into the air gap.* DO NOT FORCE THE FEELER GAUGE INTO THE AIR GAP.
NOTE : *Lean burn engines have two pick-up air gaps. The gap is .008 in. for start, and .012 in. for run.*
8. Apply vacuum to the vacuum unit and rotate the governor shaft. The pick-up pole should not hit the reluctor teeth. The gap was not properly adjusted if any hitting occurs. If hitting occurs on only one side of the reluctor, the distributor shaft is probably bent, and the governor and shaft assembly should be replaced.

AMC Breakerless Inductive Discharge (BID) Ignition System

Components

The AMC breakerless inductive discharge (BID) ignition system consists of five components:

Control unit
Coil
Breakerless distributor
Ignition cables
Spark plugs

The control unit is a solid-state, epoxy-sealed module with waterproof connectors. The control unit has a built-in current regulator, so no separate ballast resistor or resistance wire is needed in the primary circuit. Battery voltage is supplied to the ignition coil positive (+) terminal when the ignition key is turned to the "ON" or "START" position; low voltage is also supplied by the control unit.

The coil used with the BID system requires no special service. It works just like the coil in a conventional ignition system.

The distributor is conventional, except for the lack of points, condenser and cam. Advance is supplied by both a vacuum unit and a centrifugal advance mechanism. A standard cap, rotor, and dust shield are used.

In place of the points, cam, and condensor, the distributor has a sensor and trigger wheel. The sensor is a small coil which generates an electromagnetic field when excited by the oscillator in the control unit.

Standard spark plugs and ignition cables are used.

Operation

When the ignition switch is turned on, the control unit is activated. The control unit then sends an oscillating signal to the sensor which causes the sensor to generate a magnetic field. When one of the trigger wheel teeth enters this field, the strength of the oscillation in the sensor is reduced. Once the strength drops to a predetermined level, a demodulator circuit operates the control unit's switching transistor. The switching transistor is wired in series with the coil primary circuit; it switches the circuit off when it gets the demodulator signal.

From this point on, the BID ignition system works in the same manner as a conventional ignition system.

Troubleshooting

1. Check all of the BID ignition system electrical connections.
2. Disconnect the coil-to-distributor high tension lead from the distributor cap.

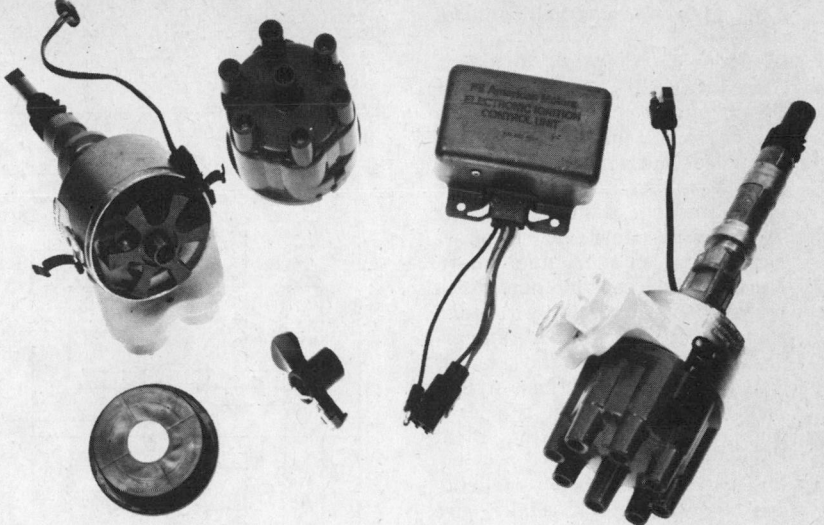

Components of the BID electronic ignition system (© AMC)

3. Using insulated pliers and a heavy glove, hold the end of the lead ½ in. away from a ground. Crank the engine. If there is a spark, the trouble is not in the ignition system. Check the distributor cap, rotor, and wires.
4. If there was no spark in step 3, connect a test light with a No. 57 bulb between the positive coil terminal (+) and a good ground. Have an assistant turn the ignition switch to "ON" and "START" (Do not start the engine). The bulb should light (battery voltage) in both positions; if it doesn't, the fault lies in the battery-to-coil circuit. Check the ignition switch and related wiring.
5. If the test light lit in step 4, disconnect the coil-to-distributor leads at the connector and connect the test light between the positive (+) and negative (−) coil terminals.
6. Turn the ignition switch on. If the test light doesn't come on, check the control unit's ground lead. If the ground lead is in good condition, replace the control unit.
7. If the bulb lights in step 6, leave the test light in place and short the terminals on the coil-to-distributor connector together with a jumper lead, (connector separated) at the coil side of the connector. If the light stays on, replace the control unit.
8. If the test light goes out, remove it. Check for a spark, as in step 2, each time that the coil-to-dis-

tributor connector terminals are shorted together with the jumper lead. If there is a spark, replace the control unit; if there is no spark, replace the coil.

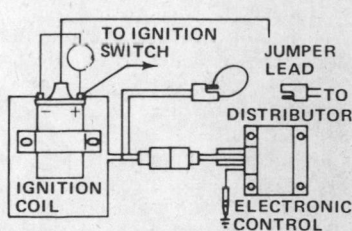

Short the terminals shown with a jumper lead for steps 7 and 8 (© AMC)

Coil Testing

Test the coil with a conventional coil checker or an ohmmeter. Primary resistance should be 1-2 ohms and secondary resistance should be 9-15 kilohms. The open output circuit should be more than 20 kilovolts. Replace the coil if it doesn't meet specifications.

Sensor Testing

Check the sensor resistance by connecting an ohmmeter to its leads. Resistance should be 1.8 ohms (±10%) at 77°-200° F. Replace the sensor if it doesn't meet these specifications.

Distributor Overhaul

NOTE: *If you must remove the sensor from the distributor for any reason, it will be necessary to have the special sensor positioning gauge in order to align it properly during installation.*

1. Scribe matchmarks on the dis-

tributor housing, rotor, and engine block. Disconnect the leads and vacuum lines from the distributor. Remove the distributor. Unless the cap is to be replaced, leave it connected to the spark plug cables and position it out of the way.

2. Remove the rotor and dust cap.
3. Place a small gear puller over the trigger wheel, so that its jaws grip the inner shoulders of the wheel and not its arms. Place a thick washer between the gear puller and the distributor shaft to act as a spacer; do not press against the smaller inner shaft.
4. Loosen the sensor hold-down screw with a small pair of needle-nosed pliers; it has a tamper-proof head. Pull the sensor lead grommet out of the distributor body and pull out the leads from around the spring pivot pin.
5. Release the sensor securing spring by lifting it. Make sure that it clears the leads. Slide the sensor off the bracket. *Remember, a special gauge is required for sensor installation.*
6. Remove the vacuum advance unit securing screw. Slide the vacuum unit out of the distributor. Remove it only if it is to be replaced.
7. Clean and dry the vacuum unit and sensor backets. Lubrication of these parts is not necessary.

BID distributor assembly is as follows:

1. Install the vacuum unit, if it was removed.
2. Assemble the sensor, sensor guide, flat washer, and retaining screw. Tighten the screw only far enough to keep the assembly together; don't allow the screw

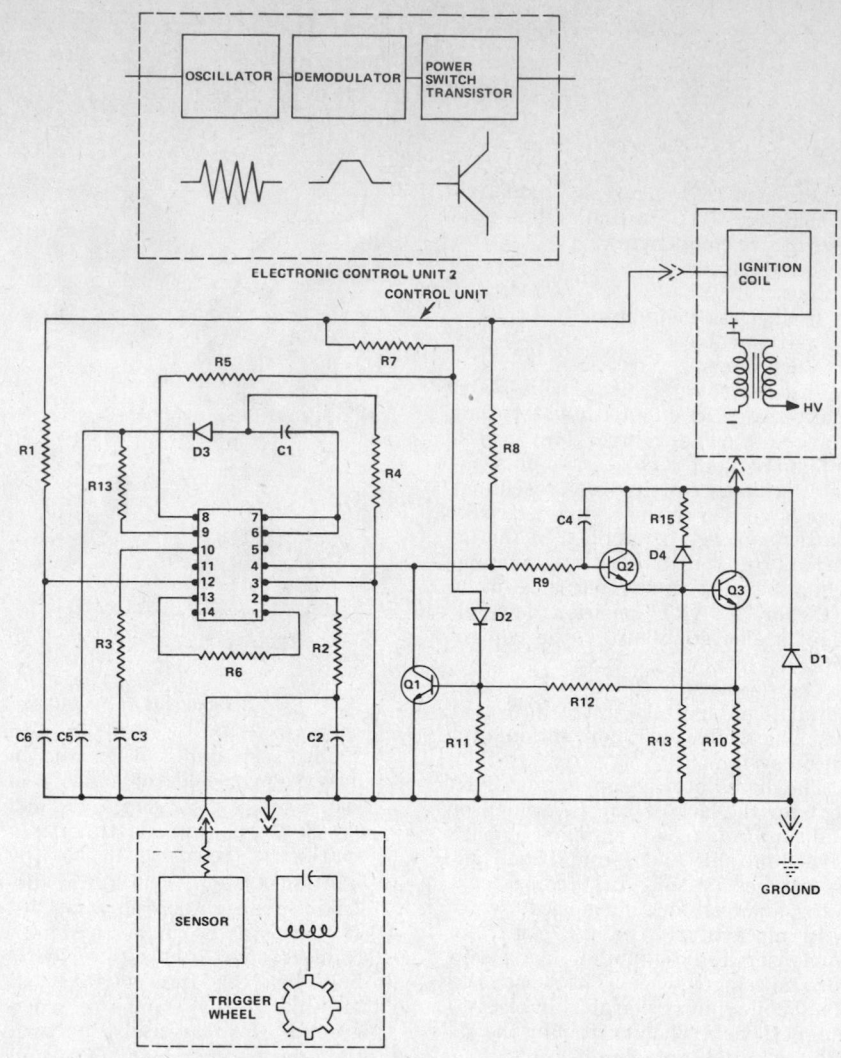

BID ignition system schematic (© AMC)

to project below the bottom of the sensor.

NOTE: *Replacement sensors come with a slotted-head screw to aid in assembly. If the original sensor is being used, replace the tamper-proof screw with a conventional one. Use the original washer.*

3. Secure the sensor on the vacuum advance unit bracket, making sure that the tip of the senor is placed in the notch on the summing bar.
4. Position the spring on the sensor and route the leads around the spring pivot pin. Fit the sensor lead grommet into the slot on the distributor body. Be sure that the lead can't get caught in the trigger wheel.
5. Place the special sensor positioning gauge over the distributor shaft, so that the flat on the shaft is against the large notch on the gauge. Move the sensor until the sensor core fits into the small notch on the gauge.

Tighten the sensor securing screw with the gauge in place (through the round hole in the gauge).

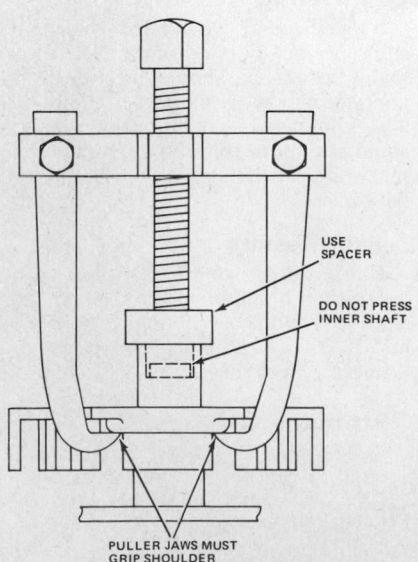

Removing the trigger wheel (© AMC)

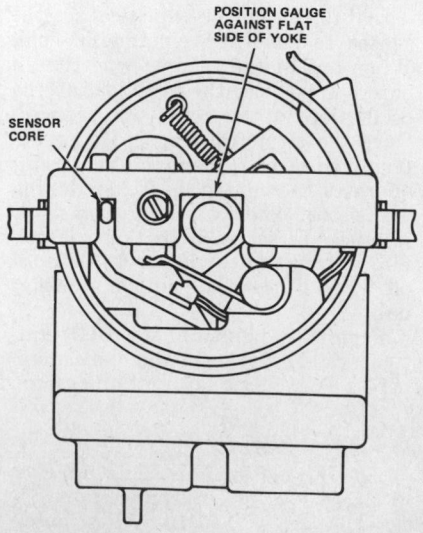

Using the special gauge to align the sensor coil (© AMC)

6. It should be possible to remove and install the gauge without any side movement of the sensor. Check this and remove the gauge.

7. Position the trigger wheel on the shaft. Check to see that the sensor core is centered between the trigger wheel legs and that the legs don't touch the core.

8. Bend a piece of 0.050 in. gauge wire, so that it has a 90° angle and one leg ½ in. long. Use the gauge to measure the clearance between the trigger wheel legs and the sensor boss. Press the trigger wheel on the shaft until it just touches the gauge. Support the shaft during this operation.

9. Place 3 to 5 drops of SAE 20 oil on the felt lubricator wick.

10. Install the dust shield and rotor on the shaft.

11. Install the distributor on the engine using the matchmarks made during removal and adjust the timing. Use a new distributor mounting gasket.

1 Cap
2 Rotor
3 Dust shield
4 Trigger wheel
5 Felt lubricator
6 Sensor assembly
7 Distributor body
8 Vacuum unit screw
9 Vacuum advance unit
10 Shim
11 Drive gear
12 Pin

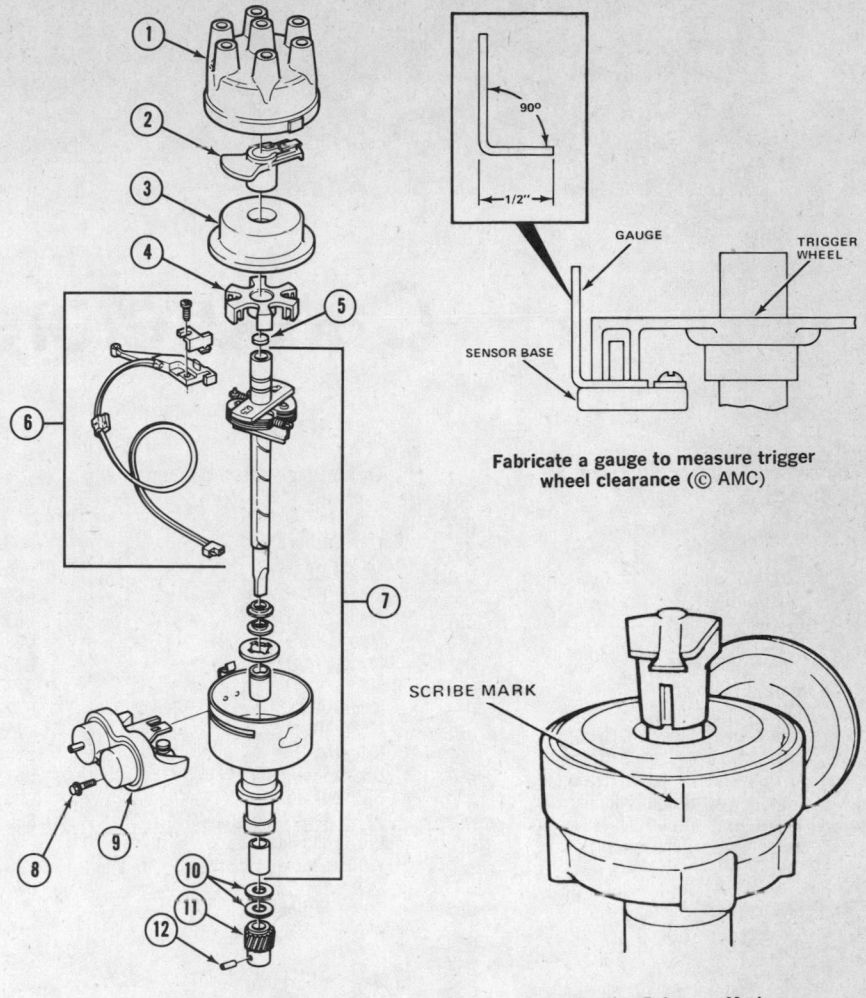

Fabricate a gauge to measure trigger wheel clearance (© AMC)

BID distributor components (© AMC)

Rotor Position Reference Mark

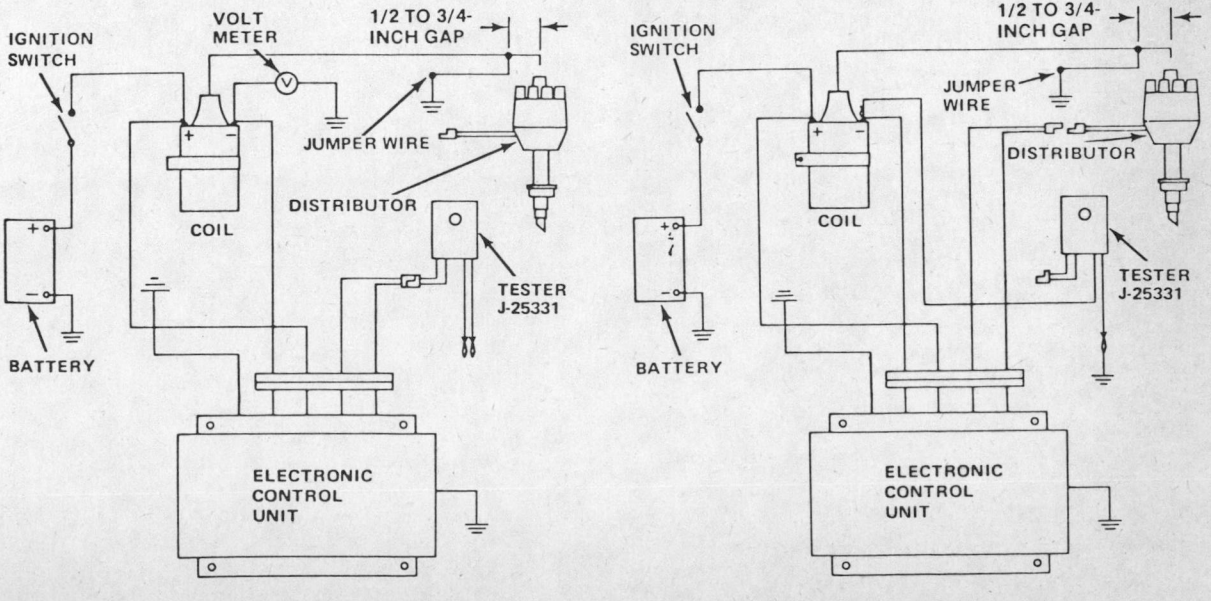

Voltmeter Connected to Coil Negative Terminal

Tester Connected to Coil Negative Terminal

INDEX

Carburetors

Carburetor Functions, Principles, and Circuits ... U51

Functions ... U51
  Metering ... U51
  Atomization ... U51
  Distribution ... U51
Principles ... U51
  Vacuum ... U51
  Venturi Principle ... U51
Carburetor Circuits ... U51
  Float circuit ... U51
  Idle and low speed circuit ... U51
  High speed partial load circuit ... U52
  High speed full power circuit ... U52
  Full power circuit (mechanical) ... U52
  Full power circuit (vacuum) ... U52
  Accelerator pump circuit ... U52
  Choke ... U52

Troubleshooting ... U53

Engine cranks—No start ... U53
Engine stalls ... U54
Engine hesitates on Acceleration ... U55
Engine feels sluggish or flat on
  Acceleration ... U55
Carburetor flooding ... U56
Rough engine idle or stalling ... U56
Engine runs unevenly or surges ... U56
Poor economy ... U57

Lack of high speed performance or
  power ... U57

Carter Carburetors ... U58

Model BBS ... U58
Model BBD ... U61
Model YF, YFA ... U65
Model RBS ... U68
Model WCD ... U70
Model WGD ... U71
Model AVS ... U72
Model TQ ... U75
Model AFB ... U79
BBS specifications ... U61
BBD specifications ... U64
YF, YFA specifications ... U66
RBS specifications ... U69
WCD automatic choke specifications ... U70
AVS specifications ... U74
TQ specifications ... U78
AFB specifications ... U80

Holley Carburetors ... U81

Model 1920 ... U81
Model 1945 ... U82
Model 2210 ... U83
Model 2245 ... U85
Model 2300 ... U87
Model 5210 ... U93

Model 4150, 4160 ... U94
One and Two barrel specifications ... U90
5210 specifications ... U94
4150 and 4160 specifications ... U98

Ford, Autolite, Motorcraft Carburetors ... U99

Model 1250 ... U99
Models 2100, 2150 ... U101
Model 5200 ... U106
Model 4300, 4350 ... U110
Model 1250 specifications ... U100
Model 2100, 2150 specifications ... U103
Model 5200 specifications ... U109
Model 4300, 4350 specifications ... U114

Rochester Carburetors ... U116

Model 1ME ... U116
Model MV ... U118
Model 2GC, 2GV ... U123
Model 2MC ... U131
Model 4MC, M4MC, M4MCA,
  M4ME, M4MEA, 4MV ... U134
1ME specifications ... U117
2GC, 2GV specifications ... U126
2MC specifications ... U132
Model 4MC, M4MC, M4MCA,
  M4ME, M4MEA, 4MV ... U137

CARBURETOR FUNCTIONS, PRINCIPLES, AND CIRCUITS

Functions

Gasoline is the source of fuel for power in the automobile engine and the carburetor is the mechanism which automatically mixes liquid fuel with air in the correct proportions to provide the desired power output from the engine. The carburetor performs this function by metering, atomizing, and mixing fuel with air flowing through the engine.

A carburetor also regulates the volume of air-to-fuel mixture which enters the engine. It is the carburetor's regulation of the mixture flow which gives the operator control of the engine speed.

Metering

The automotive internal combustion engine operates efficiently within a relatively small range of air-to-fuel ratios. It is the function of the carburetor to meter the fuel in exact proportions to the air flowing into the engine, so that the optimum ratio of air-to-fuel is maintained under all operating conditions. Regulations governing exhaust gas emissions have made the proper metering of fuel by the carburetor an increasingly important factor. Too rich a mixture will result in poor economy and increased emissions, while too lean a mixture will result in loss of power and generally poor performance.

Carburetors are matched to engines so that metering can be accomplished by using carefully calibrated metering jets which allow fuel to enter the engine at a rate proportional to the engine's ability to draw air.

Atomization

The liquid fuel must be broken up into small particles so that it will more readily mix with air and vaporize. The more contact the fuel has with the air, the better the vaporization. Atomization can be accomplished in two ways: air may be drawn into a stream of fuel which will cause a turbulence and break the solid stream of fuel into smaller particles; or a nozzle can be positioned at the point of highest air velocity in the carburetor and the fuel will be torn into a fine spray as it enters the air stream.

Distribution

The carburetor is the primary device involved in the distribution of fuel to the engine. The more efficiently fuel and air are combined in the carburetor, the smoother the flow of vaporized mixture through the intake manifold to each combustion chamber. Hence, the importance of the carburetor in fuel distribution.

Principles

Vacuum

All carburetors operate on the basic principle of pressure difference. Any pressure less than atmospheric pressure is considered vacuum or a low pressure area. In the engine, as the piston moves down on the intake stroke with the intake valve open, a partial vacuum is created in the intake manifold. The farther the piston travels downward, the greater the vacuum created in the manifold. As vacuum increases in the manifold, a difference in pressure occurs between the carburetor and cylinder. The carburetor is positioned in such a way that the high pressure above it, and the vacuum or low pressure beneath it, causes air to be drawn through it. Fuel and air always move from high to low pressure areas.

Venturi Principle

To obtain greater pressure drop at the tip of the fuel nozzle so that fuel will flow, the principle of increasing the air velocity to create a low pressure area is used. The device used to increase the velocity of the air flowing through the carburetor is called a venturi. A venturi is a specially designed restriction placed in the air flow. In order for the air to pass through the restriction, it must accelerate causing a pressure drop or vacuum as it passes.

Carburetor Circuits

Float Circuit

The float circuit includes the float, float bowl, and a needle valve and seat. This circuit controls the amount of gas allowed to flow into the carburetor.

As the fuel level rises, it causes the float to rise which pushes the needle valve into its seat. As soon as the valve and seat make contact, the flow of gas is cut off from the fuel inlet. When the level of fuel drops, the float sinks and releases the needle valve from its seat which allows the gas to flow in. In actual operation, the fuel is maintained at practically a constant level. The float tends to hold the needle valve partly closed so that the incoming fuel just balances the fuel being withdrawn.

Idle and Low Speed Circuit

When the throttle is closed or only slightly opened, the air speed is low and practically no vacuum develops in the venturi. This means that the fuel nozzle will not feed. Thus, the carburetor must have another circuit to supply fuel during operation with a closed or slightly opened throttle.

This circuit is called the idle and low speed circuit. It consists of passages in which air and gas can flow beneath the throttle plate. With the throttle plate closed, there is high vacuum from the intake manifold.

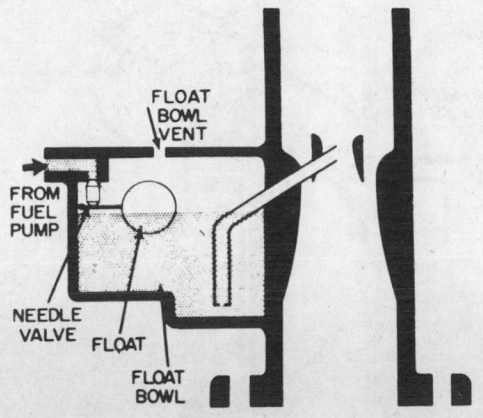

Float circuit
(© United Delco Div., G.M. Corp)

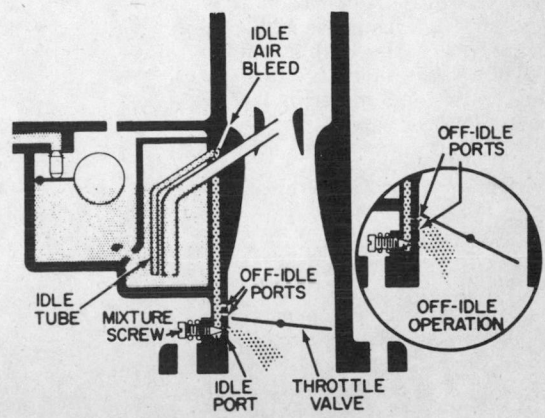

Idle and low speed circuit
(© United Delco Div., G.M. Corp)

Atmospheric pressure pushes the air/fuel mixture through the passages of the idle and low speed circuit and past the tapered point of the idle adjustment screw, which regulates engine idle mixture volume.

High Speed Partial Load Circuit

When the throttle plate is opened sufficiently, there is little difference in vacuum between the upper and lower part of the air horn. Thus, little air/fuel mixture will discharge from the low speed and idle circuit. However, under this condition enough air is moving through the air horn to produce vacuum in the venturi to cause the main nozzle or high speed nozzle to discharge fuel. The circuit from the float bowl to the main nozzle is called the high speed partial load circuit. A nearly constant air/fuel ratio is maintained by this circuit from part to full-throttle.

High Speed Full Power Circuit

For high-speed, full-power, wide-open throttle operation, the air/fuel mixture must be enriched; this is done either mechanically or by intake manifold vacuum.

Full Power Circuit (Mechanical)

This circuit includes a metering rod jet and a metering rod. The rod has two steps of different diameters and is attached to the throttle linkage.

When the throttle is wide open, the metering rod is lifted bringing the smaller diameter of the rod into the jet. When the throttle is partly closed, the larger diameter of the metering rod is in the jet. This restricts fuel flow to the main nozzle but adequate amounts of fuel do flow for part-throttle operation.

Full Power Circuit (Vacuum)

This circuit is operated by intake manifold vacuum. It includes a vacuum diaphragm or piston linked to a valve.

When the throttle is opened so that intake manifold vacuum is reduced, the spring raises the diaphragm or piston. This allows more fuel to flow in, either by lifting a metering rod or by opening a power valve.

Accelerator Pump Circuit

For acceleration, the carburetor must deliver additional fuel. A sudden inrush of air is caused by rapid acceleration or applying full throttle.

When the throttle is opened, the pump lever pushes the plunger down and this forces fuel to flow through the accelerator pump circuit and out the pump jet. This fuel enters the air passage through the carburetor to supply additional fuel demands.

Choke

When starting an engine, it is necessary to increase the amount of fuel delivered to the intake manifold. This increase is controlled by the choke.

The choke consists of a valve in the top of the air horn controlled mechanically by an automatic device. When the choke valve is closed, only a small amount of air can get past it. When the engine is cranked, a fairly high vacuum develops in the air horn. This vacuum causes the main nozzle to discharge a heavy stream of fuel. The quantity delivered is sufficient to produce the correct air/fuel mixture needed for starting the engine. The choke is released either manually or by heat from the engine.

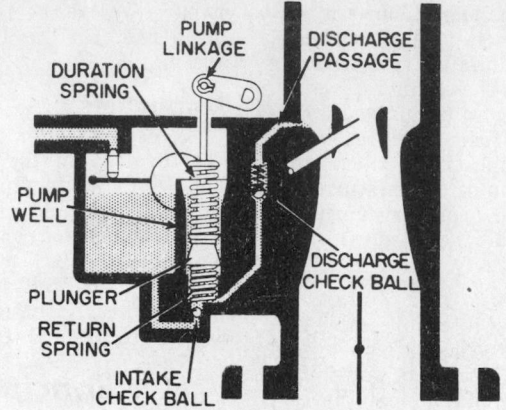

Accelerator pump circuit
(© United Delco Div., G.M. Corp)

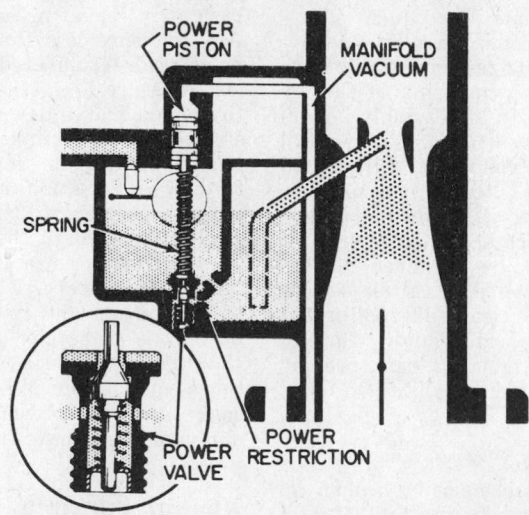

Power circuit
(© United Delco Div., G.M. Corp)

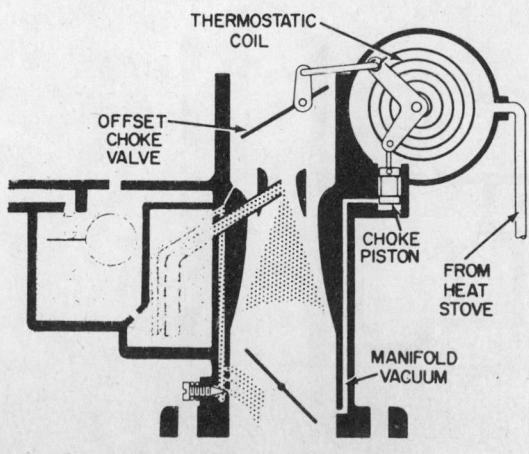

Choke system
(© United Delco Div., G.M. Corp)

TROUBLESHOOTING

NOTE: Carburetor problems cannot be isolated effectively unless all other engine systems are functioning correctly and the engine is properly tuned.

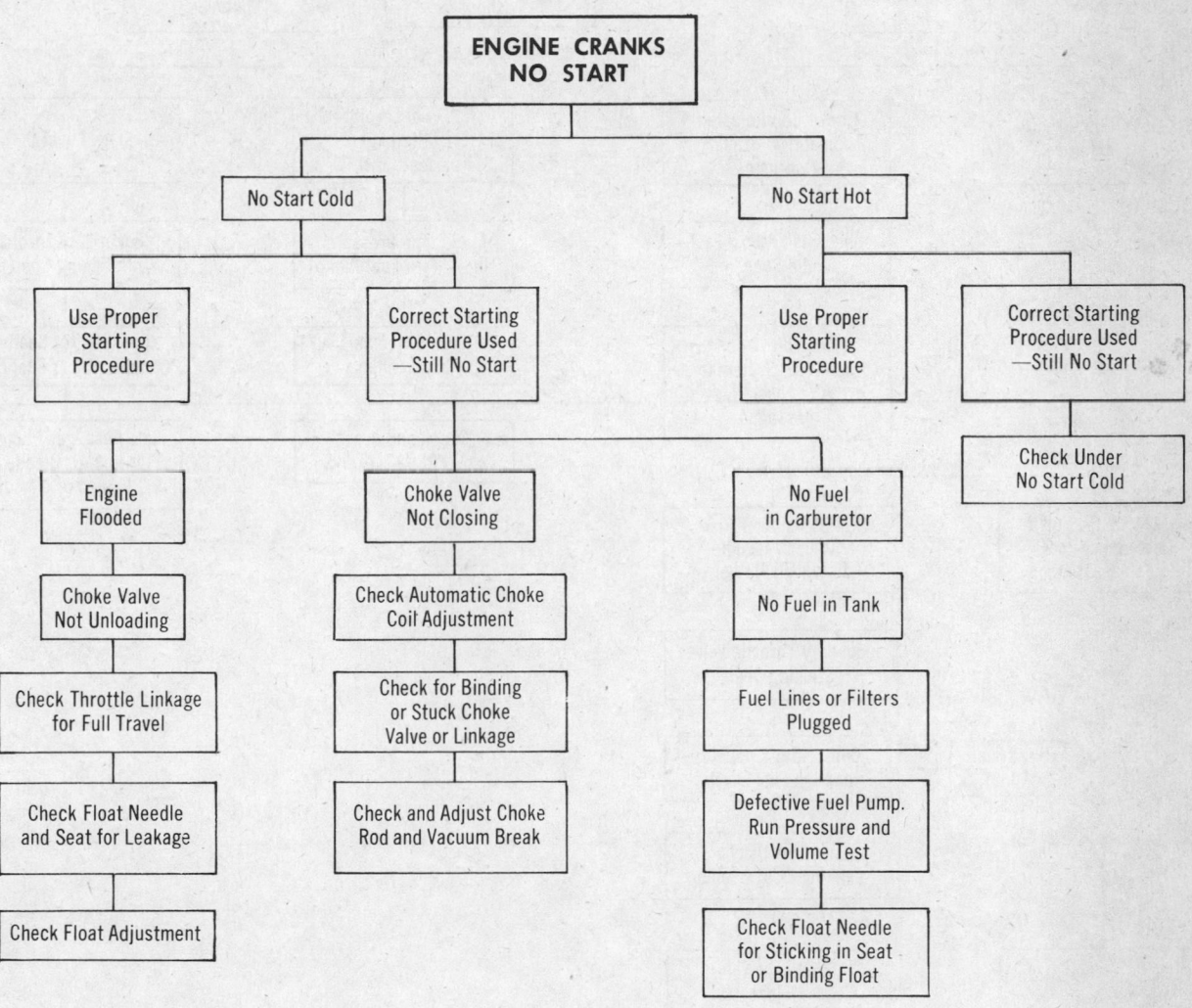

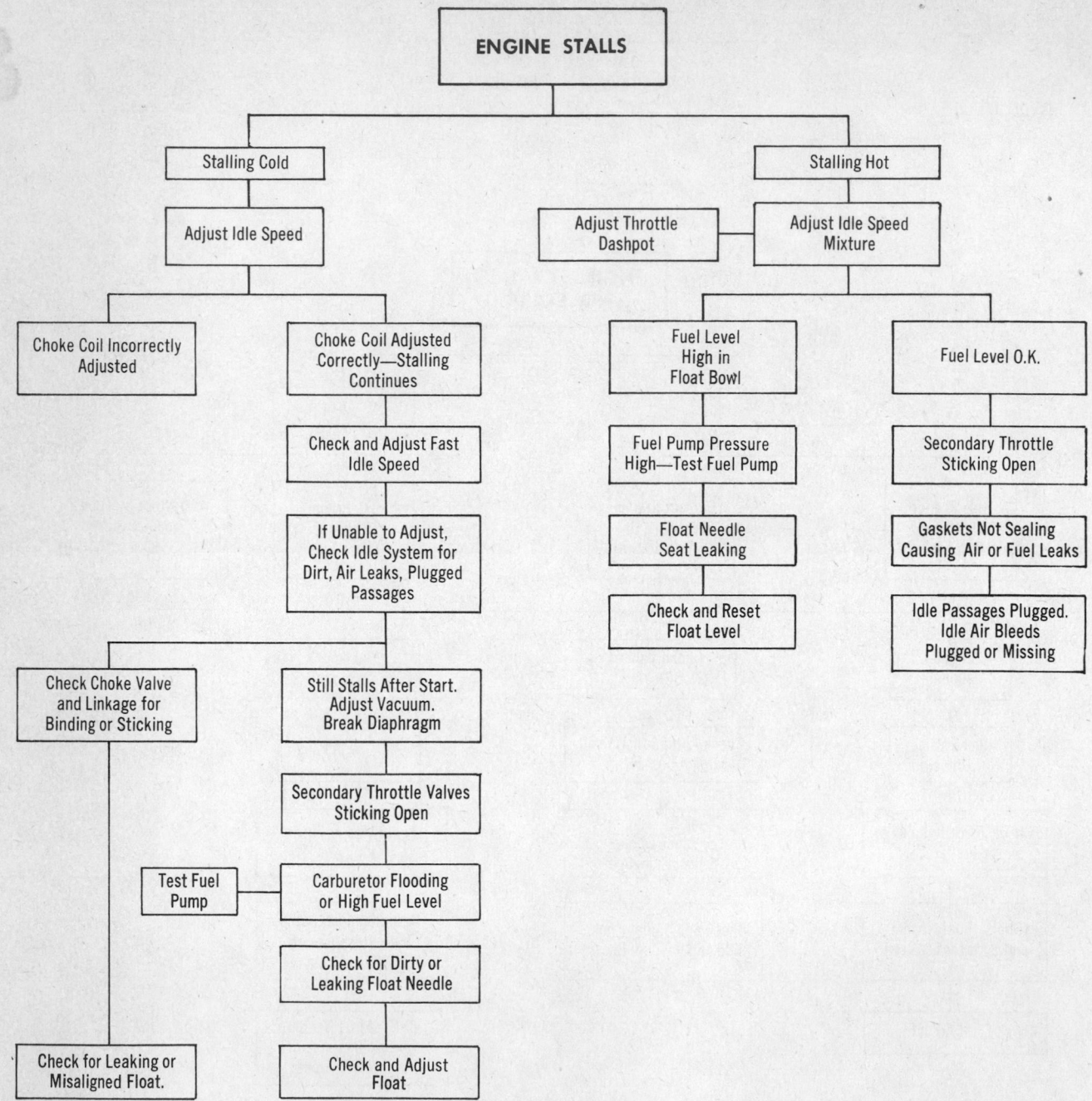

ENGINE STALLS

Stalling Cold

Adjust Idle Speed

Choke Coil Incorrectly Adjusted

Choke Coil Adjusted Correctly—Stalling Continues

Check and Adjust Fast Idle Speed

If Unable to Adjust, Check Idle System for Dirt, Air Leaks, Plugged Passages

Check Choke Valve and Linkage for Binding or Sticking

Still Stalls After Start. Adjust Vacuum. Break Diaphragm

Secondary Throttle Valves Sticking Open

Test Fuel Pump

Carburetor Flooding or High Fuel Level

Check for Dirty or Leaking Float Needle

Check for Leaking or Misaligned Float.

Check and Adjust Float

Stalling Hot

Adjust Throttle Dashpot

Adjust Idle Speed Mixture

Fuel Level High in Float Bowl

Fuel Pump Pressure High—Test Fuel Pump

Float Needle Seat Leaking

Check and Reset Float Level

Fuel Level O.K.

Secondary Throttle Sticking Open

Gaskets Not Sealing Causing Air or Fuel Leaks

Idle Passages Plugged. Idle Air Bleeds Plugged or Missing

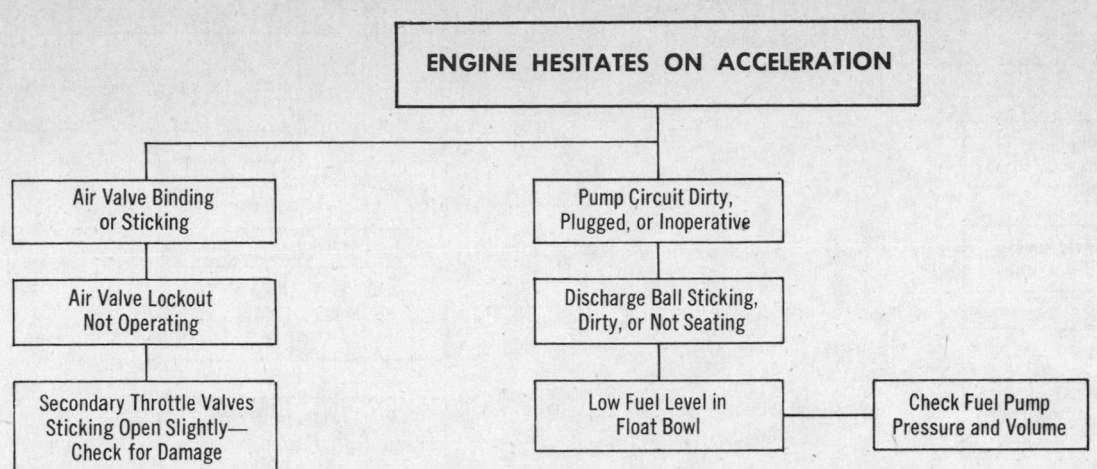

ENGINE HESITATES ON ACCELERATION

Air Valve Binding or Sticking

Air Valve Lockout Not Operating

Secondary Throttle Valves Sticking Open Slightly— Check for Damage

Pump Circuit Dirty, Plugged, or Inoperative

Discharge Ball Sticking, Dirty, or Not Seating

Low Fuel Level in Float Bowl

Check Fuel Pump Pressure and Volume

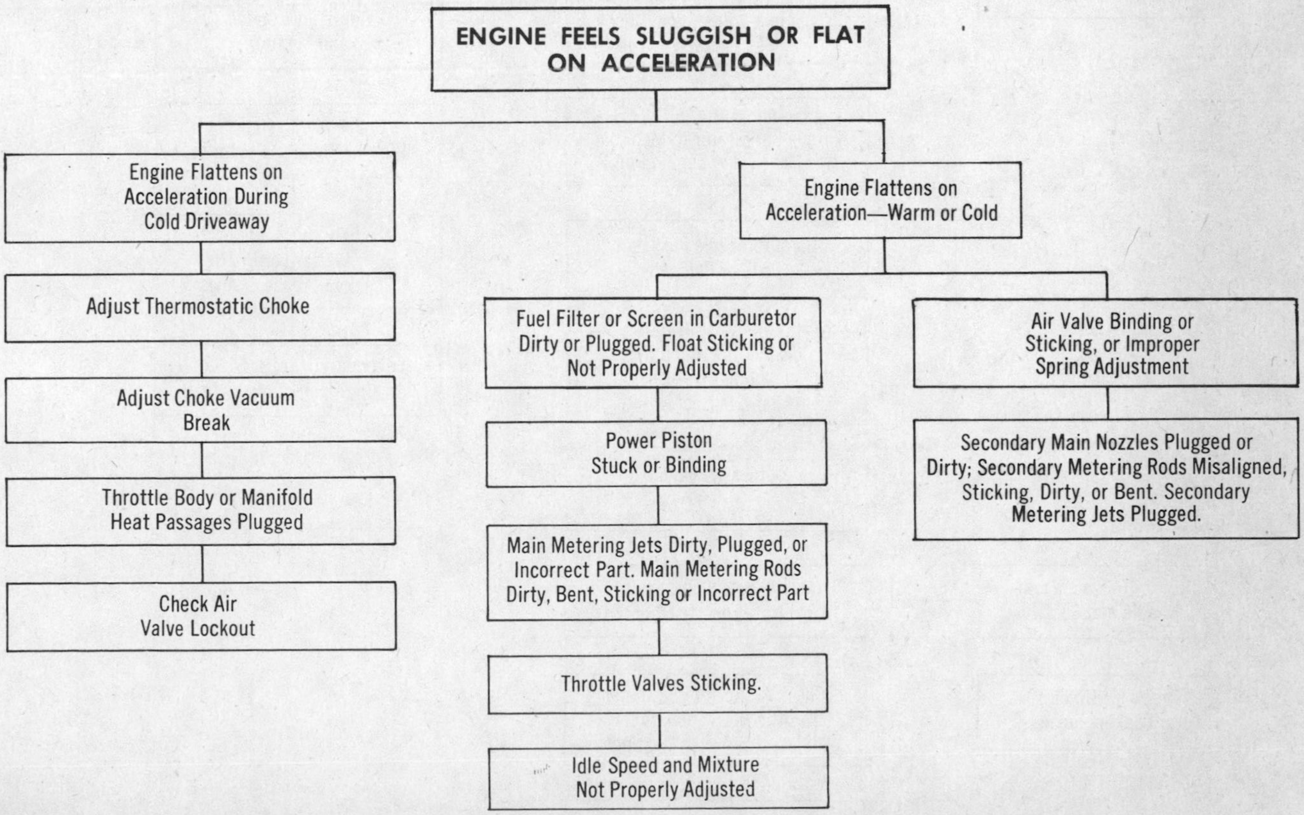

ENGINE FEELS SLUGGISH OR FLAT ON ACCELERATION

Engine Flattens on Acceleration During Cold Driveaway

Adjust Thermostatic Choke

Adjust Choke Vacuum Break

Throttle Body or Manifold Heat Passages Plugged

Check Air Valve Lockout

Engine Flattens on Acceleration—Warm or Cold

Fuel Filter or Screen in Carburetor Dirty or Plugged. Float Sticking or Not Properly Adjusted

Power Piston Stuck or Binding

Main Metering Jets Dirty, Plugged, or Incorrect Part. Main Metering Rods Dirty, Bent, Sticking or Incorrect Part

Throttle Valves Sticking.

Idle Speed and Mixture Not Properly Adjusted

Air Valve Binding or Sticking, or Improper Spring Adjustment

Secondary Main Nozzles Plugged or Dirty; Secondary Metering Rods Misaligned, Sticking, Dirty, or Bent. Secondary Metering Jets Plugged.

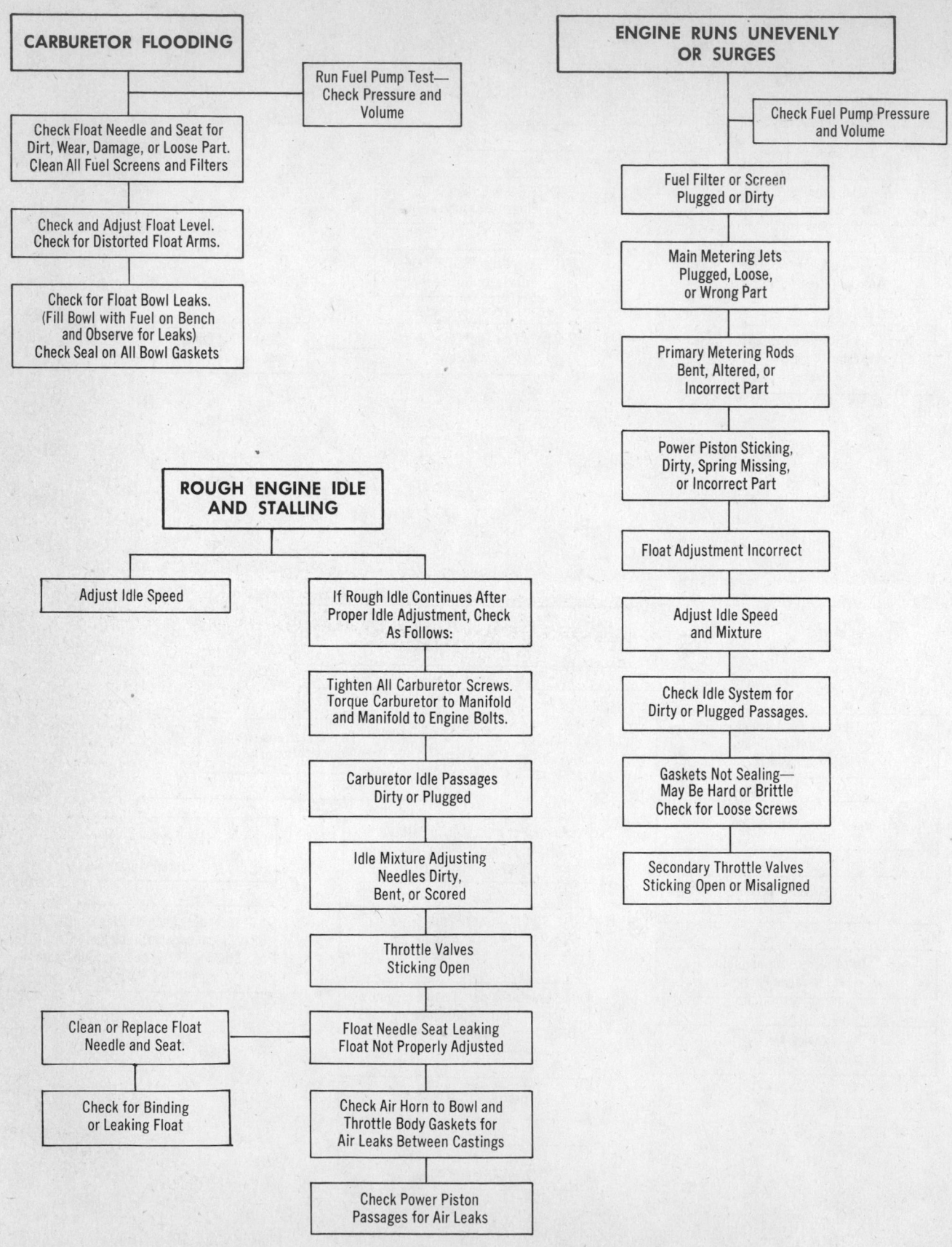

CARBURETOR FLOODING

Run Fuel Pump Test—
Check Pressure and
Volume

Check Float Needle and Seat for
Dirt, Wear, Damage, or Loose Part.
Clean All Fuel Screens and Filters

Check and Adjust Float Level.
Check for Distorted Float Arms.

Check for Float Bowl Leaks.
(Fill Bowl with Fuel on Bench
and Observe for Leaks)
Check Seal on All Bowl Gaskets

**ROUGH ENGINE IDLE
AND STALLING**

Adjust Idle Speed

If Rough Idle Continues After
Proper Idle Adjustment, Check
As Follows:

Tighten All Carburetor Screws.
Torque Carburetor to Manifold
and Manifold to Engine Bolts.

Carburetor Idle Passages
Dirty or Plugged

Idle Mixture Adjusting
Needles Dirty,
Bent, or Scored

Throttle Valves
Sticking Open

Clean or Replace Float
Needle and Seat.

Float Needle Seat Leaking
Float Not Properly Adjusted

Check for Binding
or Leaking Float

Check Air Horn to Bowl and
Throttle Body Gaskets for
Air Leaks Between Castings

Check Power Piston
Passages for Air Leaks

**ENGINE RUNS UNEVENLY
OR SURGES**

Check Fuel Pump Pressure
and Volume

Fuel Filter or Screen
Plugged or Dirty

Main Metering Jets
Plugged, Loose,
or Wrong Part

Primary Metering Rods
Bent, Altered, or
Incorrect Part

Power Piston Sticking,
Dirty, Spring Missing,
or Incorrect Part

Float Adjustment Incorrect

Adjust Idle Speed
and Mixture

Check Idle System for
Dirty or Plugged Passages.

Gaskets Not Sealing—
May Be Hard or Brittle
Check for Loose Screws

Secondary Throttle Valves
Sticking Open or Misaligned

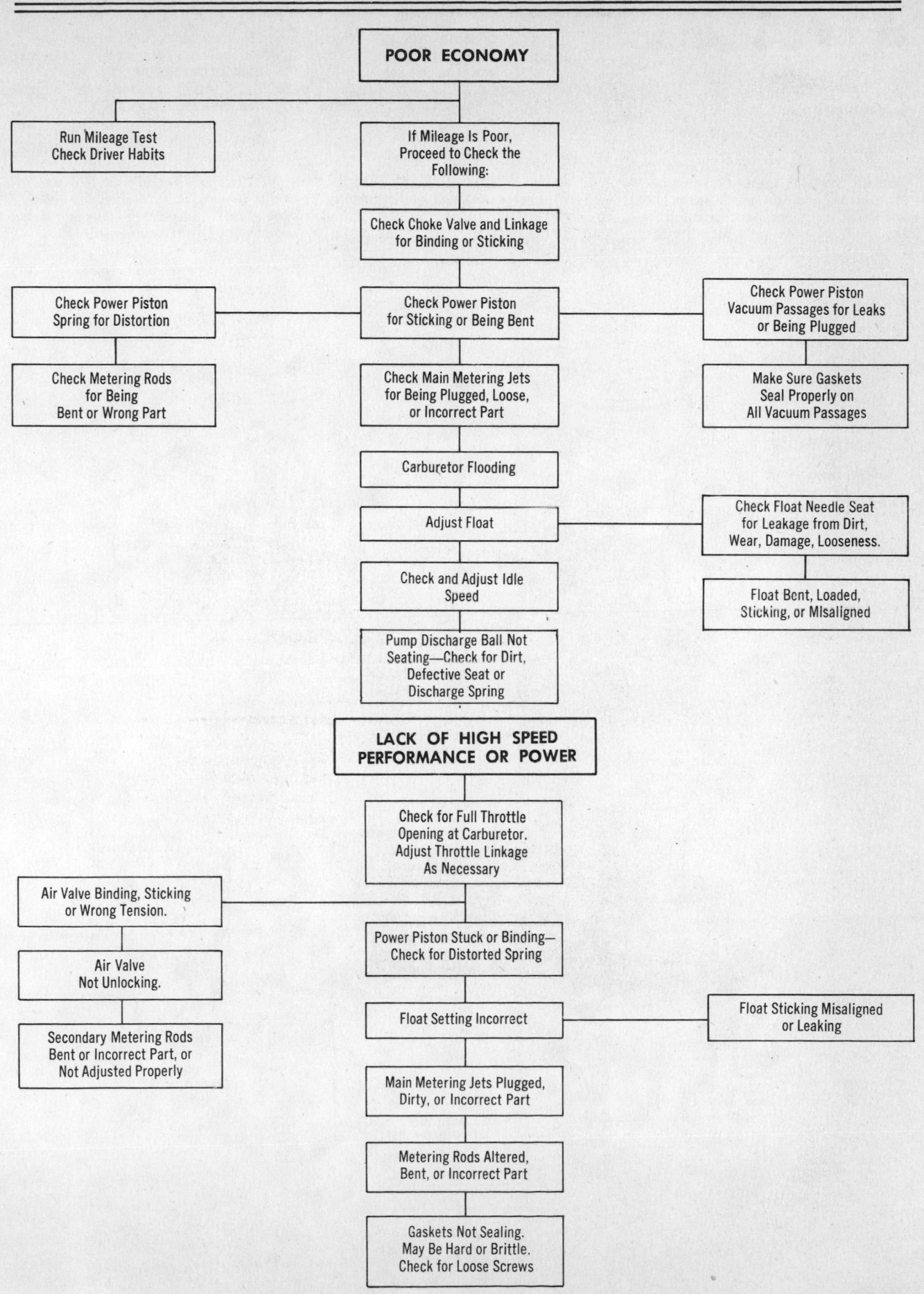

POOR ECONOMY

Run Mileage Test
Check Driver Habits

If Mileage Is Poor,
Proceed to Check the
Following:

Check Choke Valve and Linkage
for Binding or Sticking

Check Power Piston
Spring for Distortion

Check Power Piston
for Sticking or Being Bent

Check Power Piston
Vacuum Passages for Leaks
or Being Plugged

Check Metering Rods
for Being
Bent or Wrong Part

Check Main Metering Jets
for Being Plugged, Loose,
or Incorrect Part

Make Sure Gaskets
Seal Properly on
All Vacuum Passages

Carburetor Flooding

Adjust Float

Check Float Needle Seat
for Leakage from Dirt,
Wear, Damage, Looseness.

Check and Adjust Idle
Speed

Float Bent, Loaded,
Sticking, or Misaligned

Pump Discharge Ball Not
Seating—Check for Dirt,
Defective Seat or
Discharge Spring

**LACK OF HIGH SPEED
PERFORMANCE OR POWER**

Check for Full Throttle
Opening at Carburetor.
Adjust Throttle Linkage
As Necessary

Air Valve Binding, Sticking
or Wrong Tension.

Power Piston Stuck or Binding—
Check for Distorted Spring

Air Valve
Not Unlocking.

Float Setting Incorrect

Float Sticking Misaligned
or Leaking

Secondary Metering Rods
Bent or Incorrect Part, or
Not Adjusted Properly

Main Metering Jets Plugged,
Dirty, or Incorrect Part

Metering Rods Altered,
Bent, or Incorrect Part

Gaskets Not Sealing.
May Be Hard or Brittle.
Check for Loose Screws

CARTER CARBURETORS
Model BBS

Introduction

The BBS series carburetor is a standard Ball and Ball single throat model. It uses ECS (Evaporation Control System) on its newer models. It also uses a spring staged choke which is a device incorporated into the choke mechanism which limits the choke blade closing torque when cranking the engine at temperatures below zero. Thus, the spring staging of the choke is a better match for the engine's starting requirements at low temperatures.

Float Level Adjustments

1. Invert the main body so that the weight of each float is forcing the needle against the seat.
2. If the proper gauge is not available, measure from the surface of the bowl to the crown of each float at the center.
3. Adjustment is listed in the specifications chart.
4. To adjust, bend the lip of the float lever in or out until adjustment is correct.

NOTE: On the ECS BBS carburetor, it is necessary to check or set the accelerator pump travel before checking the bowl vent valve opening.

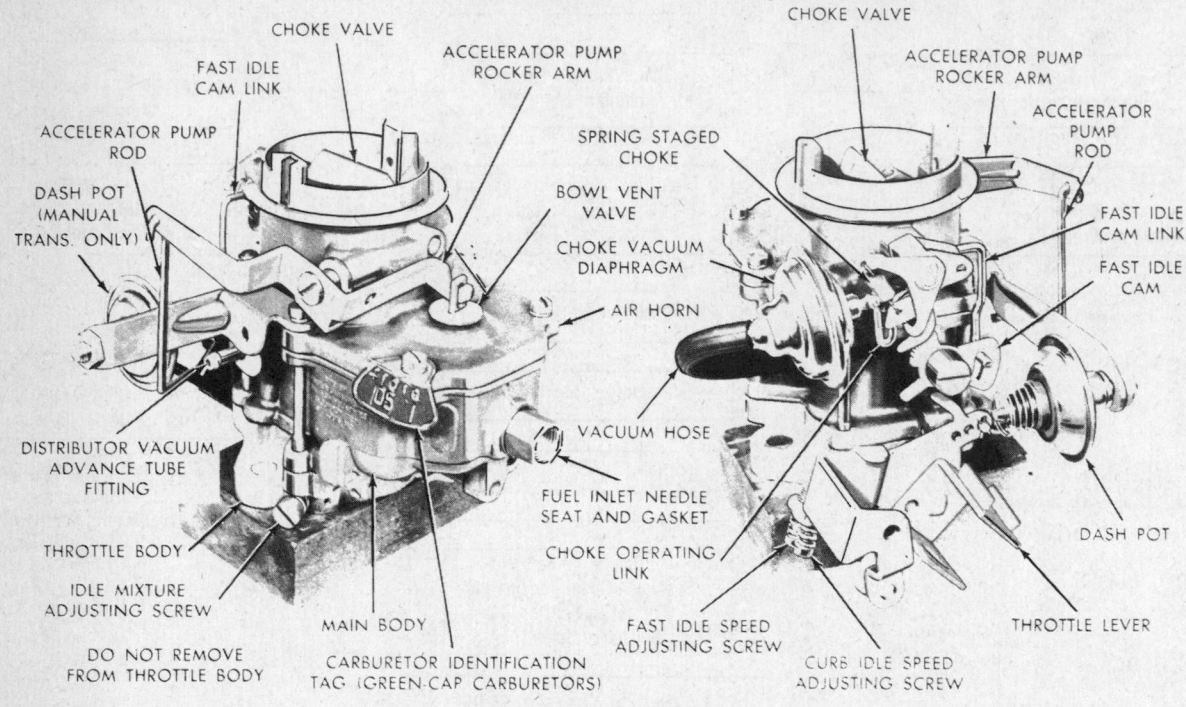

BBS carburetor assembly

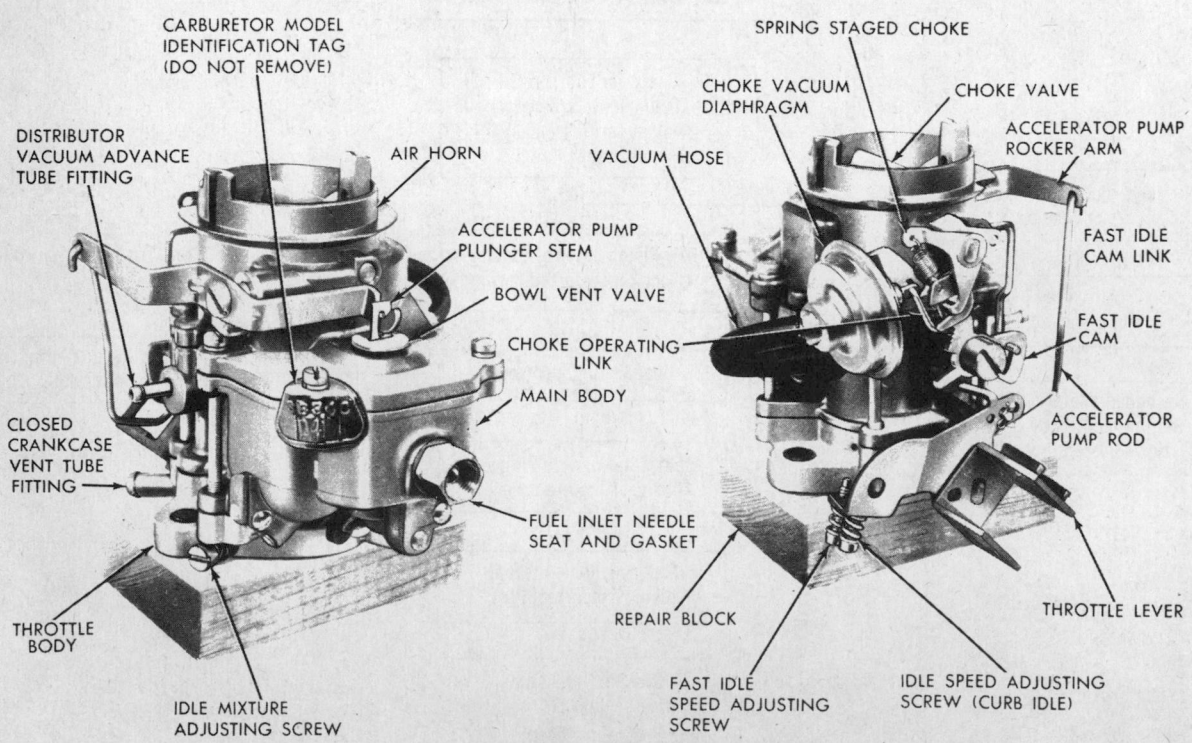

BBS carburetor assembly

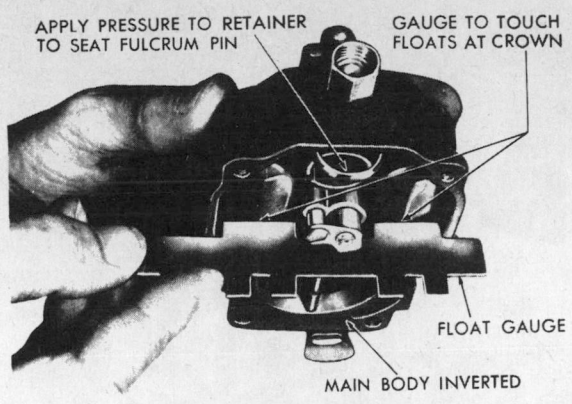

APPLY PRESSURE TO RETAINER
TO SEAT FULCRUM PIN

GAUGE TO TOUCH
FLOATS AT CROWN

FLOAT GAUGE

MAIN BODY INVERTED

BBS float level adjustment

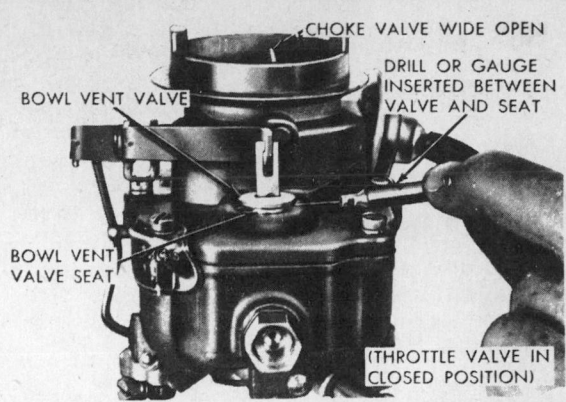

CHOKE VALVE WIDE OPEN

DRILL OR GAUGE
INSERTED BETWEEN
VALVE AND SEAT

BOWL VENT VALVE

BOWL VENT
VALVE SEAT

(THROTTLE VALVE IN
CLOSED POSITION)

BBS pump and bowl vent adjustment

Pump and Bowl Vent Adjustment

1. Back off the idle adjusting screw.
2. Open the choke valve so that when the throttle valve is closed, the fast idle adjusting screw will not contact the fast idle cam.
3. Be sure that the pump operating rod is in the center hole in the throttle lever.
4. Make sure that the bowl vent clip on the pump stem is in the center groove.
5. Close the throttle valve tightly.
6. Insert a drill of the specified size between the bowl vent and the air horn.
7. To adjust, bend the pump operating rod at the lower angle.

Pump and Bowl Vent Adjustment (ECS)

1. With the throttle valve at curb idle, measure the distance from the top of the casting to the top of the bowl vent valve stem.
2. See specifications for the distance.
3. If an adjustment is necessary, bend the lower tang on the bowl vent valve operating lever at the pivot until the correct opening has been obtained.

Accelerator Pump Adjustment

1. Be sure that the accelerator pump rod is in the outer hole of the throttle lever.
2. Close the throttle valve to curb idle.
3. Place a straightedge on the air cleaner mounting surface.
4. Measure the distance between the straight edge and the top of the accelerator pump plunger.
5. See the Specifications Chart for the proper distance.
6. If an adjustment is necessary, bend the accelerator pump until the correct pump angle has been obtained.

Fast Idle Cam Adjustment

1. With the fast idle speed adjusting screw contacting the second highest step on the fast idle cam, move the choke valve toward the closed position with light pressure on the choke shaft lever.
2. Insert the specified gauge between the top of the choke valve and the wall of the air horn. Refer to the Specifications Chart.
3. An adjustment will be necessary if a slight drag is not obtained as the drill shank is being removed.
4. Adjust by bending the fast idle link at an angle, until the correct valve opening has been obtained.

Choke Vacuum Kick Adjustment

NOTE: The test can be made on or off the vehicle.

1. If the adjustment is to be made with the engine running, back off the fast idle speed screw until the choke can be closed to the kick position with the engine at curb idle. (Note the number of screw turns required so that the fast idle can be returned to the original adjustment.)
2. If an auxiliary vacuum source is to be used, open the throttle valve (engine not running) and move the choke to the closed position. Release the throttle first, then release the choke.

   When using an auxiliary vacuum source, disconnect the vacuum hose from the carburetor and connect it to the hose from the vacuum supply with a small length of tube to act as a fitting. Removal of the hose from the diaphragm may require sufficient force to damage the system. Apply a vacuum of 15 or more in. of mercury.
3. Insert the gauge between the top of the choke valve and the wall of the air horn. Refer to the Specifications Chart.
4. Apply sufficient closing pressure on the lever to which the choke

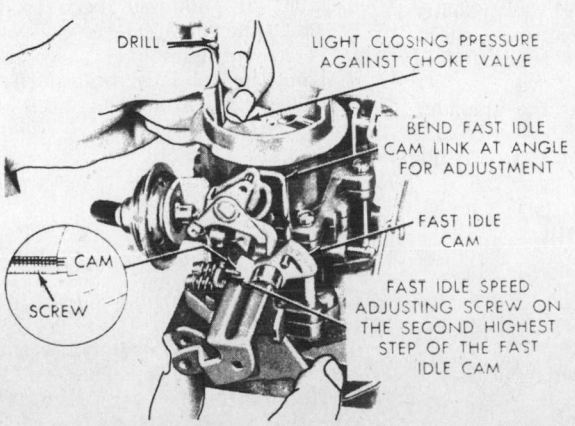

DRILL

LIGHT CLOSING PRESSURE
AGAINST CHOKE VALVE

BEND FAST IDLE
CAM LINK AT ANGLE
FOR ADJUSTMENT

FAST IDLE
CAM

FAST IDLE SPEED
ADJUSTING SCREW ON
THE SECOND HIGHEST
STEP OF THE FAST
IDLE CAM

CAM

SCREW

BBS fast idle cam adjustment

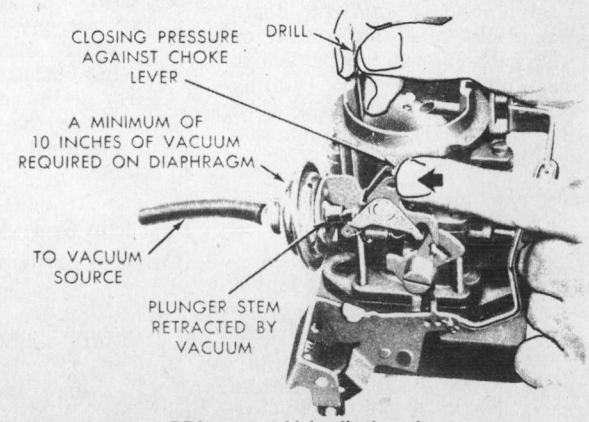

CLOSING PRESSURE
AGAINST CHOKE
LEVER

DRILL

A MINIMUM OF
10 INCHES OF VACUUM
REQUIRED ON DIAPHRAGM

TO VACUUM
SOURCE

PLUNGER STEM
RETRACTED BY
VACUUM

BBS vacuum kick adjustment

U59

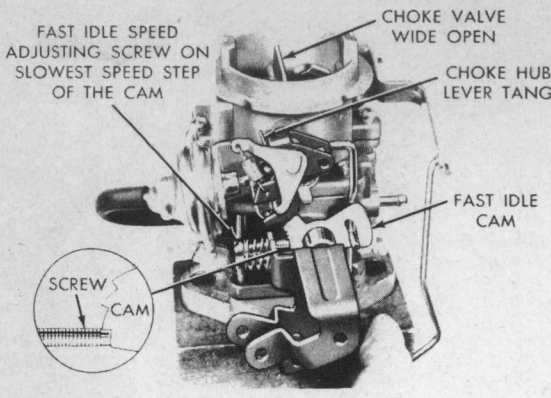

FAST IDLE SPEED ADJUSTING SCREW ON SLOWEST SPEED STEP OF THE CAM

CHOKE VALVE WIDE OPEN

CHOKE HUB LEVER TANG

FAST IDLE CAM

SCREW CAM

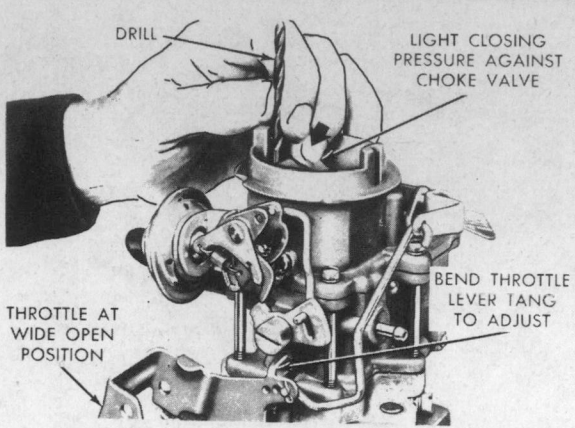

DRILL

LIGHT CLOSING PRESSURE AGAINST CHOKE VALVE

THROTTLE AT WIDE OPEN POSITION

BEND THROTTLE LEVER TANG TO ADJUST

BBS choke unloader adjustment (wide open kick)

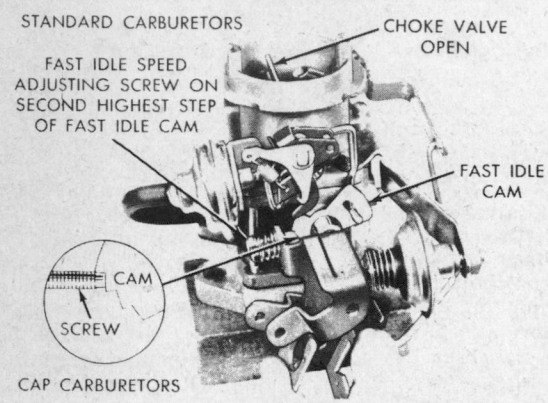

STANDARD CARBURETORS

FAST IDLE SPEED ADJUSTING SCREW ON SECOND HIGHEST STEP OF FAST IDLE CAM

CHOKE VALVE OPEN

FAST IDLE CAM

CAM SCREW

CAP CARBURETORS

BBS fast idle speed adjustment (on the vehicle)

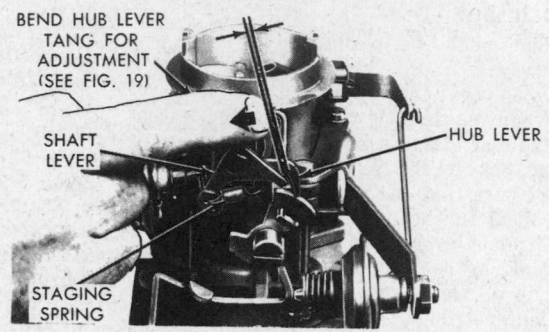

BEND HUB LEVER TANG FOR ADJUSTMENT (SEE FIG. 19)

SHAFT LEVER

HUB LEVER

STAGING SPRING

BBS spring staged choke adjustment

rod attaches, to provide a minimum choke valve opening without distortion of the diaphragm link.

NOTE: The cylindrical stem of the diaphragm extends as the internal spring is compressed. This spring must be fully compressed for proper measurement of the vacuum kick adjustment.

5. Adjustment is necessary if a slight drag is not obtained when removing the gauge. Shorten or lengthen the diaphragm link to obtain the correct choke valve opening. Length changes should be made by carefully opening or closing the U-bend provided in the link. Improper bending causes contact between the U-section and the diaphragm assembly.

NOTE: Do not apply a twisting or bending force to diaphragm.

6. After completing adjustments, reinstall the vacuum hose on the correct carburetor fitting.
7. Return the fast idle screw to its original location if it was disturbed. Make the following check. With no vacuum applied to the diaphragm, the choke

valve should move freely between the open and closed positions. If the movement is not free, examine the linkage for misalignment or interferences caused by the bending operation.

Choke Unloader (Wide Open Kick) Adjustment

1. With the throttle valve in the wide open position, insert a drill gauge between the upper edge of the choke valve and the inner wall of the air horn. Refer to the Specifications Chart.
2. With a finger lightly pressing against the shaft lever, a slight drag should be felt as the drill is being withdrawn.
3. Adjust by bending the unloader tang on the throttle lever until the correct opening has been obtained.

Fast Idle Speed Adjustment (On the Vehicle)

1. With the engine off and transmission in Neutral, open the throttle slightly.
2. Close the choke valve until the fast idle screw can be positioned on the second highest speed step of the fast idle cam.

3. Start engine and let the idle speed stabilize. Turn the fast idle speed screw in or out to obtain a fast idle of 1800 RPM.
4. To provide the correct throttle closing torque, reposition the fast idle speed screw on the cam after each adjustment.

Spring Staged Choke Adjustment

1. Push the hub lever to the closed choke position.
2. There should be between 0.010-0.040 in. distance between the shaft and the hub levers.
3. If an adjustment is necessary, bend the hub lever tang until the correct opening has been obtained.

Choke Adjustment

1. Loosen the mounting post locknut.
2. Turn the mounting post with a screwdriver until the index mark on the disc is positioned as listed in the specifications chart.
3. Hold in this position with a screwdriver and tighten with the locknut.

CARTER BBS SPECIFICATIONS

CHRYSLER PRODUCTS

Year	Model ②	Float Level (in.)	Accelerator Pump Travel (in.)	Bowl Vent (in.)	Choke Unloader (in.)	Fast Idle Cam Position ①	Choke Vacuum Kick ①
1970	4715S	1/4	——	1/32	3/16	48	35
	4716S	1/4	——	1/32	3/16	48	48
	4717S	1/4	5/16	9/32	3/16	48	35
	4718S	1/4	5/16	9/32	3/16	48	48
1971	4955S	1/4	5/16	17/64	3/16	48	35
	4956S	1/4	5/16	17/64	3/16	48	35

① Indicates the drill bit number.
② Model numbers located on tag or casting
Note: Automatic choke setting 2 Rich for all BBS

Model BBD

Introduction

The BBD carburetor is a two barrel unit. It has been equipped with CAS (Cleaner Air System) packages and now uses ECS (Evaporation Control System) on the newer models. It is also equipped with a dashpot on some applications.

Accelerator Pump Adjustment

383 Cu. In. V8

1. Back off the idle adjusting screw. Open the choke valve so that the fast idle cam allows the throttle valves to finally close. Be sure that the pump connector rod is installed in the center hole of the throttle lever.

2. With the throttle valves closed tightly, measure the distance between the top of the air horn and the end of the pump plunger shaft. If the dimension is not as specified, bend the pump connector rod at an angle on the rod until the correct setting is obtained.

1974 and Later

1. Back off the idle adjusting screw. Open the choke valve so that the fast idle cam allows the throttle valves to close. Be sure that the accelerator pump "S" link is in the outer hole of the pump arm.

2. Turn the idle adjusting screw in two complete turns after it contacts the stop.

3. With the throttle valves closed tightly, measure the distance between the top of the air horn and the top of the pump plunger shaft. If the dimension is not as specified, loosen the pump arm adjusting lockscrew (near the plunger shaft) and rotate the sleeve to obtain the correct dimension.

Fast Idle Cam Position Adjustment

1. With the fast idle speed adjusting screw contacting the second highest speed step on the fast idle cam, move the choke valve toward the closed position with light pressure on the choke shaft

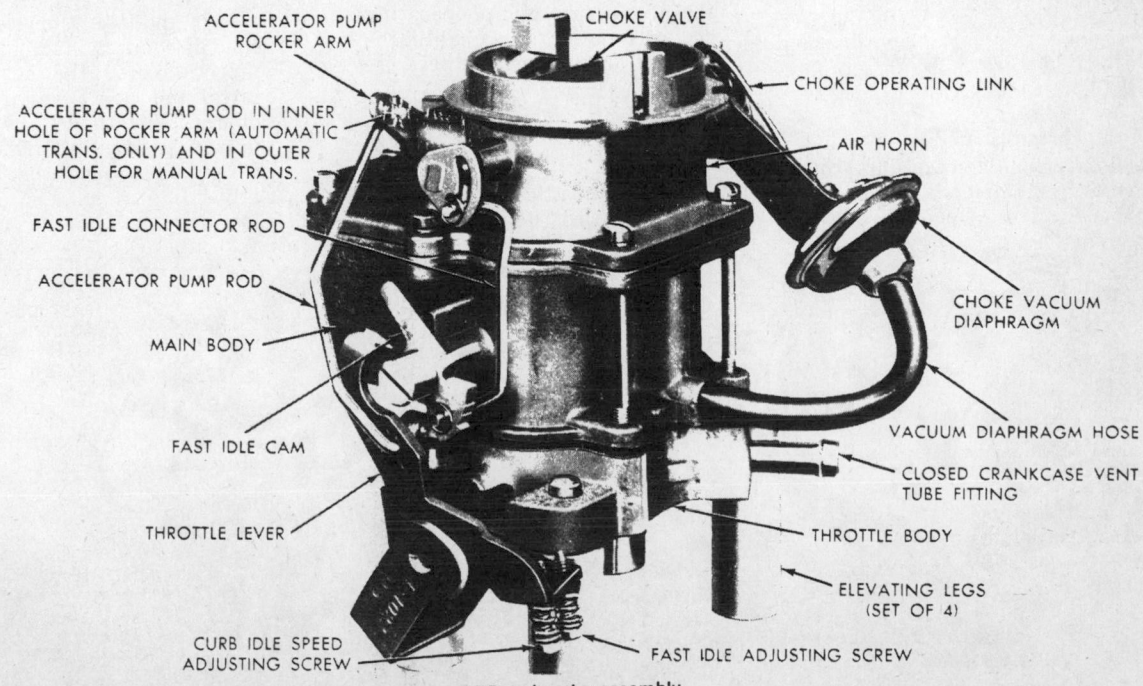

ACCELERATOR PUMP ROCKER ARM

ACCELERATOR PUMP ROD IN INNER HOLE OF ROCKER ARM (AUTOMATIC TRANS. ONLY) AND IN OUTER HOLE FOR MANUAL TRANS.

FAST IDLE CONNECTOR ROD

ACCELERATOR PUMP ROD

MAIN BODY

FAST IDLE CAM

THROTTLE LEVER

CURB IDLE SPEED ADJUSTING SCREW

CHOKE VALVE

CHOKE OPERATING LINK

AIR HORN

CHOKE VACUUM DIAPHRAGM

VACUUM DIAPHRAGM HOSE

CLOSED CRANKCASE VENT TUBE FITTING

THROTTLE BODY

ELEVATING LEGS (SET OF 4)

FAST IDLE ADJUSTING SCREW

BBD carburetor assembly

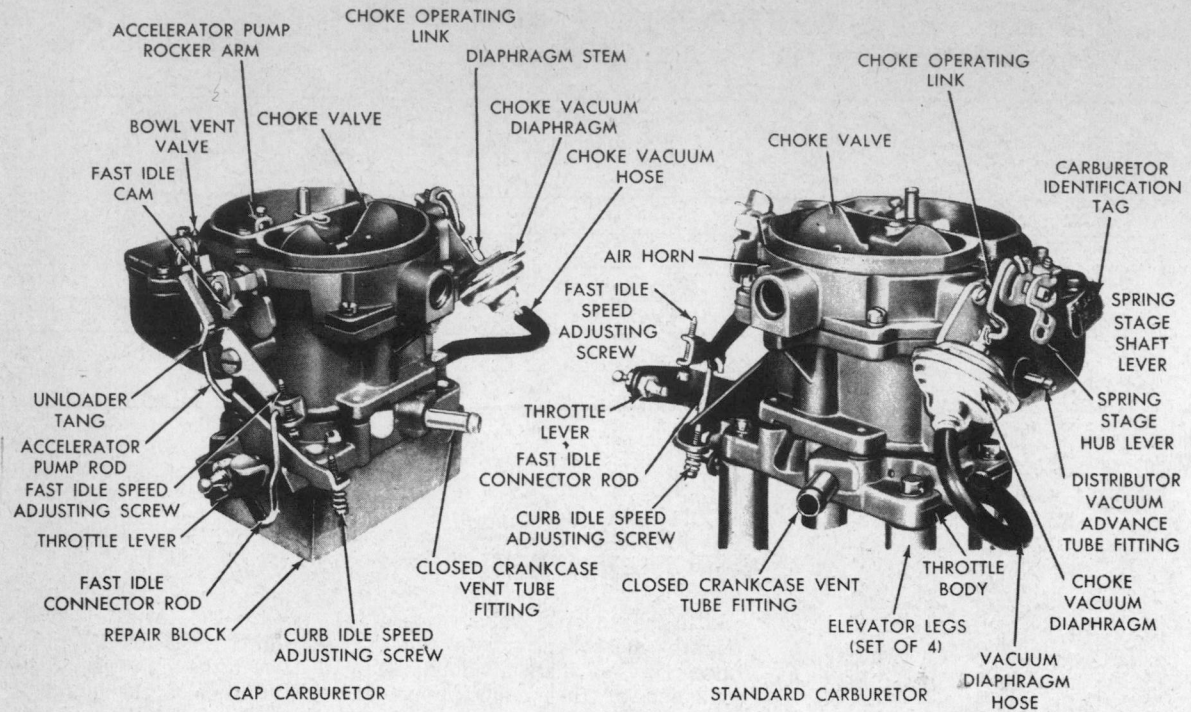

BBD carburetor assembly

lever. On AMC, remove the choke cover and hold the bi-metallic coil tang in the closed position.

2. Insert the specified drill (refer to Specifications), between the choke valve and the wall of the **air horn**. An adjustment will be necessary if a slight drag is not obtained as the drill is being removed.

3. If an adjustment is required, bend the fast idle connector rod at the lower angle.

Accelerator Pump & Bowl Vent (ECS)

Through 1973

1. Back off the idle speed adjusting screw to completely close the throttle valves. Open the choke

valve so that the fast idle cam allows the throttle valves to seat in the bores.

2. Be sure that the accelerator pump operating rod is in the medium stroke hole in the throttle lever.

3. Close the throttle valves tightly. Measure the distance between the air cleaner gasket surface and the top of the accelerator pump rod. This measurement should be .200 in.

4. To adjust the pump travel, bend the accelerator pump operating rod at a lower angle, until the correct pump travel has been obtained.

Choke Unloader (Wide Open Kick)

1. Hold the throttle valves in the wide open position. Insert the

specified drill (see Specifications) between the upper edge of the choke valve and the inner wall of the air horn.

2. With a finger lightly pressing against the valve, a slight drag should be felt as the drill is being withdrawn. If an adjustment is necessary, bend the unloader tang on the throttle lever until the correct opening has been obtained.

Fast Idle Speed (On Vehicle)

1. On 1974 and later Chrysler products, disconnect and plug the connections for the heated air control and OSAC valve or distributor. With the engine off and the transmission in Park or Neutral position, open the throttle slightly.

2. Close the choke valve until the

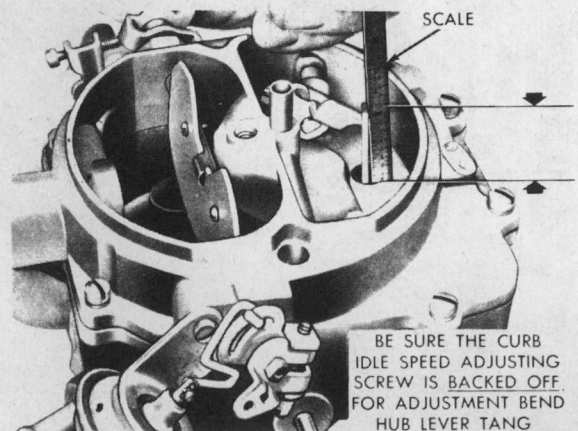

BBD accelerator pump adjustment

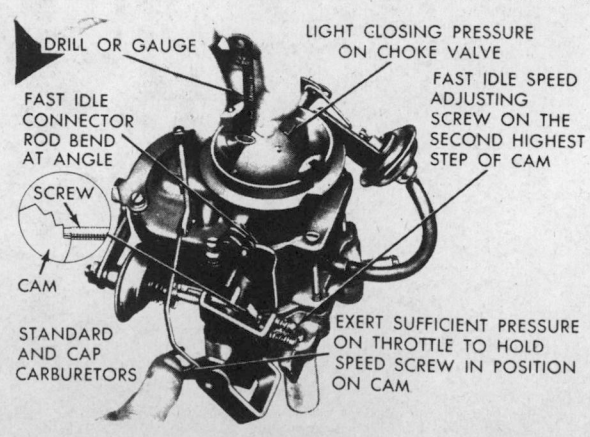

BBD fast idle cam position adjustment

fast idle screw can be positioned on the second highest speed step (highest speed step, 1974 and later Chrysler products) of the fast idle cam.

3. Start the engine and let the idle stabilize. Turn the fast idle speed screw in or out to obtain the specified speed.
4. Stopping the engine between adjustments is not necessary. However, reposition the fast idle speed screw on the cam after each speed adjustment to provide the correct throttle closing torque.

Vacuum Kick Adjustment

Chrysler Products

1. If the adjustment is to be made with the engine running, disconnect the fast idle linkage to allow the choke to close to the kick position with engine at curb idle. If an auxiliary vacuum source is to be used, open the throttle valves (engine not running) and move the choke to the closed position. Release the throttle first, then release the choke.
2. When using an auxiliary vacuum source, disconnect the vacuum hose from the carburetor and connect it to the hose from the vacuum supply with a small length of tube to act as a fitting. Removal of the hose from the diaphragm may require sufficient force to damage the system. Apply a vacuum of 10 (15 beginning 1973) or more in. of mercury.
3. Insert the specified drill (refer to Specifications) between the choke valve and the wall of the air horn. Apply sufficient closing pressure on the lever to which the choke rod attaches to provide a minimum choke valve opening without distortion of the diaphragm link. Note that the cylindrical stem of the diaphragm will extend as the internal spring is compressed. This spring must be fully compressed for proper measurement of the vacuum kick of adjustment.
4. An adjustment will be necessary if a slight drag is not obtained as the drill is being removed. Shorten or lengthen the diaphragm link to obtain the correct choke opening. Length changes should be made carefully by bending (opening or closing) the

U-bend provided in the diaphragm link.

Caution Do not apply twisting or bending force to the diaphragm.

5. Reinstall the vacuum hose on the correct carburetor fitting. Return the fast idle linkage to its original condition if it was disturbed, as suggested in Step 1.
6. Make the following check: With no vacuum applied to the diaphragm, the choke valve should move freely between the open and closed positions. If its movement is not free, examine the linkage for misalignment or interference caused by the bending operation. Repeat the adjustment if necessary to provide proper link operation.

Float Level

Chrysler Products

1. Invert the carburetor so that the weight of the floats is the only force on the needle and seat.
2. Use a T-scale to check the float level. Measure the area from the surface of the fuel bowl to the crown of each float at center.

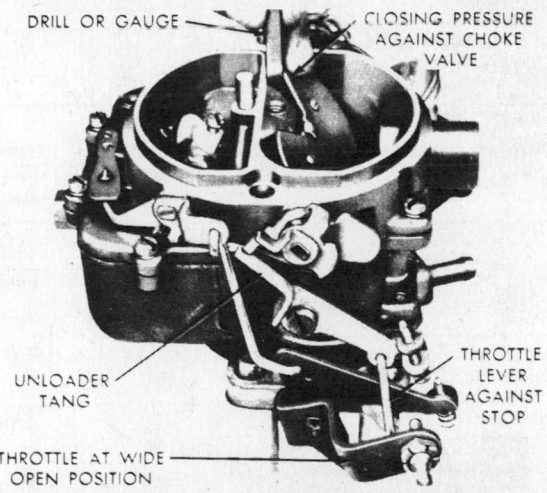

BBD choke unloader adjustment (wide open kick)

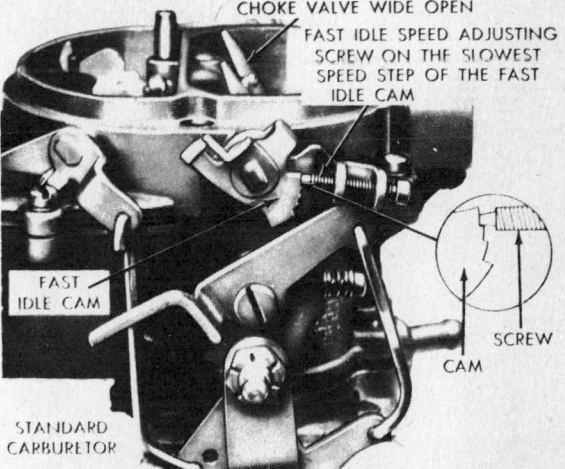

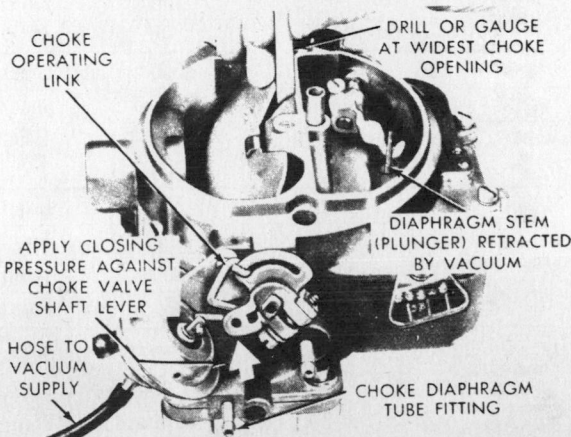

BBD vacuum kick adjustment

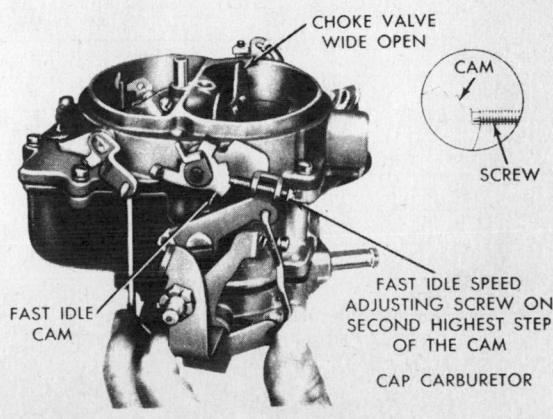

BBD fast idle adjustment on the vehicle

3. To adjust, hold the floats on the bottom of the bowl and bend the float lip to give the specified dimension.

American Motors Products
1. Remove the air horn.
2. Hold the float lip gently against the needle to raise the float.
3. Place a straightedge across the float bowl to measure the float level at the top of the float.
4. To adjust, bend the float lip, being careful not to exert pressure on the synthetic needle tip.

Bowl Vent Adjustment

383 Cu. In. V8
1. Open the choke valve so that the fast idle cam allows the valves to close to curb idle.
2. Be sure that the pump operating rod is in the long stroke hole in the throttle lever. Remove the bowl vent valve cover if it was not previously done.
3. On ECS units, close the throttle

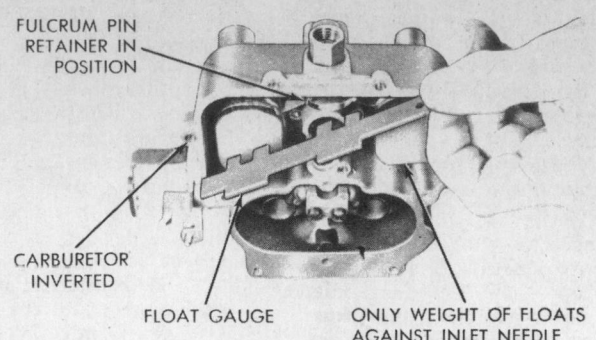

FULCRUM PIN RETAINER IN POSITION

CARBURETOR INVERTED

FLOAT GAUGE

ONLY WEIGHT OF FLOATS AGAINST INLET NEEDLE

BBD float level adjustment

valves tightly. Using a narrow ruler, measure the distance from the top of the bowl vent valve to the top of the air horn casting.

With the throttle valves closed (curb idle), there should be the specified clearance between the bowl vent valve and the seat on the air horn. Measure at the outermost or the longest dimension.
4. To adjust, bend the lift arm until the correct clearance has been obtained.

Dashpot Adjustment

American Motors Products
1. Make sure that the idle speed adjustment is correct.
2. Hold the dashpot plunger in against the stop.
3. Measure the clearance between the plunger and the throttle lever with the throttle in idle position. It should be .104 in.
4. Adjust by turning the fast idle screw.

CARTER BBD SPECIFICATIONS
CHRYSLER PRODUCTS

Year	Model ④	Float Level (in.)	Accelerator Pump Travel (in.)	Bowl Vent (in.)	Choke Unloader (in.)	Choke Vacuum Kick ①	Fast Idle Cam Position ①	Fast Idle Speed (rpm)	Automatic Choke Adjustment
1970	4721S	1/4	——	1/32	1/4	20	41	1600	Index
	4722S	1/4	——	1/32	1/4	20	41	2000	Index
	4723S	1/4	——	15/64	1/4	20	41	1600	Index
	4724S	1/4	——	15/64	1/4	20	41	2000	Index
	4725S	11/32	1	1/32	1/4	20	28	1700	2 Rich
	4726S	11/32	1	1/32	1/4	28	28	1700	2 Rich
	4727S	11/32	1	1/8	1/4	20	28	1700	2 Rich
	4728S	11/32	1	3/16	1/4	28	28	1700	2 Rich
	4894S	11/32	1	1/32	1/4	28	28	1700	2 Rich
	4895S	1/4	——	1/32	1/4	20	41	1700	Index
1971	4957S	1/4	0.200②	13/64	1/4	20	41	1600	Index
	4958S	1/4	0.200②	13/64	1/4	20	41	1900	Index
	4961S	5/16	1	3/16	1/4	20	20	1900	2 Rich
	4962S	5/16	1	3/16	1/4	28	28	1700	2 Rich
1972	6149S	1/4	0.225③	15/64	1/4	25	41	1700	Fixed
	6150S	1/4	0.225③	15/64	1/4	25	41	1900	Fixed
	6151S	1/4	0.225③	15/64	1/4	25	41	1800	Fixed
	6152S	1/4	0.225③	15/64	1/4	25	41	2000	Fixed
1973	6316SA	1/4	0.242③	——	1/4	24	41	1700	Fixed
	6317SA	1/4	0.242③	——	1/4	30	41	1700	Fixed
	6343SA	1/4	0.242③	——	1/4	24	41	1700	Fixed
	6344SA	1/4	0.242③	——	1/4	24	41	1700	Fixed

CARTER BBD SPECIFICATIONS
CHRYSLER PRODUCTS

Year	Model ④	Float Level (in.)	Accelerator Pump Travel (in.)	Bowl Vent (in.)	Choke Unloader (in.)	Choke Vacuum Kick ①	Fast Idle Cam Position ①	Fast Idle Speed (rpm)	Automatic Choke Adjustment
1974	6464S	¼	0.500③	——	.325	25	41	1700	Fixed
	6465S	¼	0.500③	——	.325	35	41	1500	Fixed
	6466S	¼	0.500③	——	.325	25	41	1700	Fixed
	6467S	¼	0.500③	——	.325	35	41	1500	Fixed
1975	8000S	¼	0.500③	——	0.280	0.130	0.070	1500	Fixed
	8064S	¼	0.500③	——	0.310	0.070	0.070	1500	Fixed
	8001S	¼	0.500③	——	0.310	0.110	0.070	1500	Fixed
	8003S	¼	0.500③	——	0.310	0.110	0.070	1500	Fixed
	8066S	¼	0.500③	——	0.280	0.130	0.070	1500	Fixed
	8062S	¼	0.500③	——	0.310	0.110	0.070	1500	Fixed
1976	8071S	¼	0.500③	——	0.280	0.130	0.070	1500	Fixed
	8069S	¼	0.500③	——	0.310	0.070	0.070	1200	Fixed
	8070S	¼	0.500③	——	0.310	0.110	0.070	1500	Fixed
	8077S	¼	0.500③	——	0.280	0.110	0.070	1250	Fixed
	8072S	¼	0.500③	——	0.310	0.070	0.070	1500	Fixed

AMERICAN MOTORS

Year	Model	Float Level (in.)	Accelerator Pump Travel (in.)	Bowl Vent (in.)	Choke Unloader (in.)	Choke Vacuum Kick ①	Fast Idle Cam Position ①	Fast Idle Speed (rpm)	Automatic Choke Adjustment
1976	8067	¼	0.500	——	0.250	——	0.095	1700	2 Rich
	8073	¼	0.500	——	0.250	——	0.095	1700	1 Rich

① Indicates the drill bit number.
② Throttle closed
③ At idle
④ Model numbers located on the tag or casting

Model YF, YFA

Introduction

The YF carburetor is a single barrel downdraft carburetor with a diaphragm type accelerator pump and diaphragm operated metering rods.

Float Adjustment

1. Invert the air horn assembly and check the clearance from the top of the float to the surface of the air horn with a T-scale. The air horn should be held at eye level when gauging and the float arm should be resting on the needle pin.
2. Do not exert pressure on the nee-

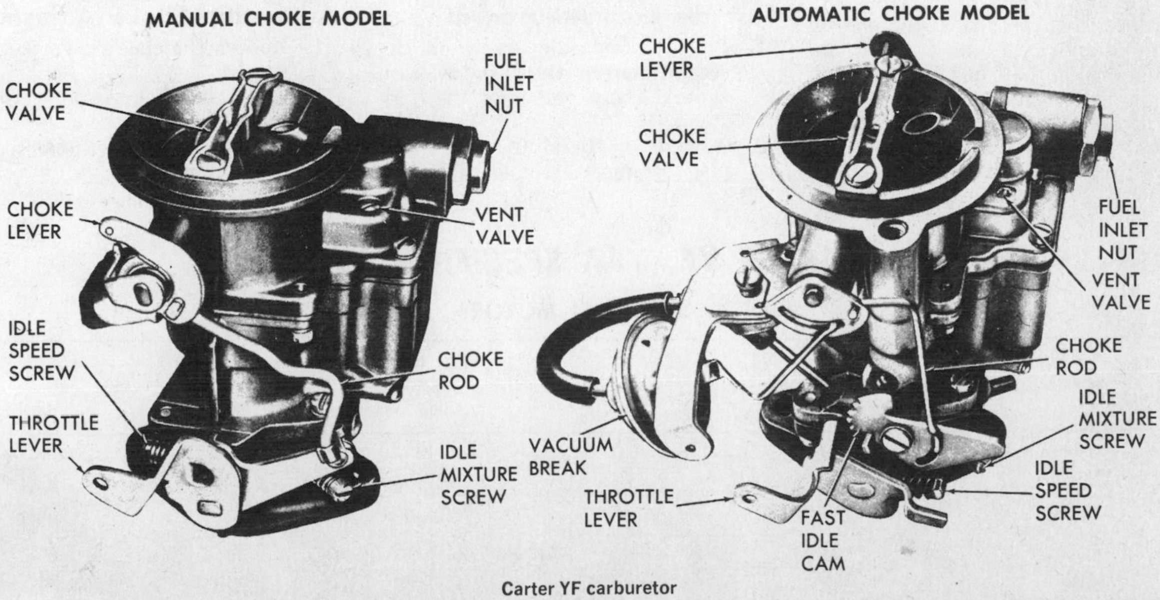

MANUAL CHOKE MODEL

AUTOMATIC CHOKE MODEL

Carter YF carburetor

GAUGE BETWEEN FLOAT AND AIR HORN

BEND HERE

YF float level adjustment

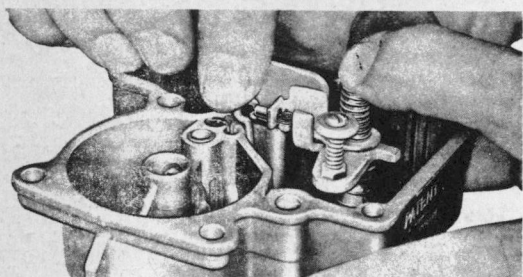

YF metering rod adjustment

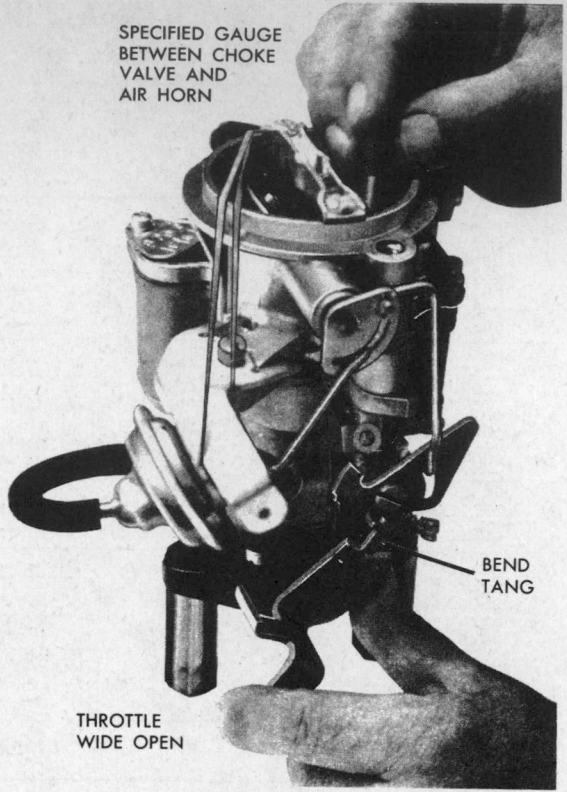

SPECIFIED GAUGE BETWEEN CHOKE VALVE AND AIR HORN

BEND TANG

THROTTLE WIDE OPEN

YF choke unloader adjustment

dle valve when measuring or adjusting the float. Bend the float arm as necessary to adjust the float level.

Caution Do not bend the tab at the end of the float arm as it prevents the float from striking the bottom of the fuel bowl when empty.

Metering Rod Adjustment

1. Remove the air horn. Back out the idle speed adjusting screw until the throttle plate is seated fully in its bore.
2. Press down on the upper end of the diaphragm shaft until the diaphragm bottoms in the vacuum chamber.
3. The metering rod should contact the bottom of the metering rod well and lifter link at the outer end nearest the springs and at the supporting link.
4. On models not equipped with an adjusting screw, adjust by bending the lip of the metering rod arm to which the metering rod is attached.
5. On models with an adjusting screw, turn the screw until the metering rod just bottoms in the body casting. For final adjustment, turn the screw one additional turn clockwise.

Fast Idle Cam Adjustment

1. Put the fast idle screw on the second step of the fast idle cam against the shoulder of the high step.
2. Adjust by bending the choke plate connecting rod to obtain the specified clearance between the lower edge of the choke plate and the air horn wall.

Choke Unloader Adjustment

1. With the throttle valve held wide open and the choke valve held in the closed position, bend the unloader tang on the throttle lever to obtain the specified clearance between the lower edge of the choke valve and the air horn wall.

Automatic Choke Adjustment

1. Loosen the choke cover retaining screws.
2. Turn the choke over so that the index mark on the cover lines up with the specified mark on the choke housing.

CARTER YF, YFA SPECIFICATIONS

AMERICAN MOTORS

Year	Model ①	Float Level (in.)	Idle Vent (in.)	Fast Idle Cam (in.)	Unloader (in.)	Choke
1970	4767S	29/64	0.052	2300 RPM	0.300	Index
	4768S	29/64	0.052	2300 RPM	0.325	Index
	4769S	29/64	0.055	2300 RPM	0.300	Index
	4770S	29/64	0.055	2300 RPM	0.300	Index
	4978S	29/64	0.055	2300 RPM	0.300	1 Rich

CARTER YF, YFA SPECIFICATIONS

AMERICAN MOTORS

Year	Model ①	Float Level (in.)	Idle Vent (in.)	Fast Idle Cam (in.)	Unloader (in.)	Choke
1971	6038S	$^{29}/_{64}$	——	2300 RPM	0.300	Index
	6093S	$^{29}/_{64}$	——	2300 RPM	0.300	Index
	6094S	$^{29}/_{64}$	——	2300 RPM	0.300	1 Rich
	6095S	$^{29}/_{64}$	——	2300 RPM	0.300	Index
	6096S	$^{29}/_{64}$	——	2300 RPM	0.300	1 Rich
1972	6199S	$^{29}/_{64}$	——	1600 RPM	0.300	Index
	6200S	$^{29}/_{64}$	——	1600 RPM	0.300	Index
1973	All	$^{29}/_{64}$	——	Index mark	0.275	1 Rich
1974	All	0.476	——	0.190	0.275	1 Rich
1975	All	0.476	——	0.190	0.275	1 Rich
1976	7083, 7085, 7112	0.476	——	0.185	0.275	1 Rich
	7084, 7086	0.476	——	0.185	0.275	2 Rich

FORD MOTOR CO.

Year	Model ①	Float Level (in.)	Idle Vent (in.)	Fast Idle Cam (in.)	Unloader (in.)	Choke
1970	D0AF-A	$^3/_8$	——	0.029	0.250	Index
	D0AF-B	$^3/_8$	——	0.025	0.250	1 Lean
	D0DF-L	$^3/_8$	——	0.036	0.250	Index
	D0DF-M	$^3/_8$	——	0.031	0.250	Index
	D0DF-N	$^7/_{32}$	——	0.035	0.280	Index
	D0DF-R	$^7/_{32}$	——	0.036	0.280	1 Rich
	D0DF-S	$^7/_{32}$	——	0.035	0.280	Index
	D0DF-T	$^3/_8$	——	0.031	0.250	Index
	D0DF-U	$^7/_{32}$	——	0.036	0.280	1 Rich
	D0DF-V	$^3/_8$	——	0.036	0.250	Index
1971	D1DF-EA	$^3/_8$	——	0.105	0.250	Index
	D1DF-GA, HA	$^3/_8$	——	0.170	0.250	Index
	D1DF-JA, LA	$^3/_8$	——	0.140	0.250	Index
	D1DF-KA, MA	$^3/_8$	——	0.140	0.250	Index
	D1DF-PA	$^3/_8$	——	0.190	0.250	Index
	D1DF-RA	$^3/_8$	——	0.220	0.250	Index
1972	D2DF-AA	$^3/_8$	——	0.105	0.280	Index
	D2DF-BA	$^3/_8$	——	0.170	0.250	Index
	D2DF-CA	$^3/_8$	——	0.170	0.250	Index
	D2DF-DA	$^3/_8$	——	0.140	0.250	1 Rich
	D2DF-EA	$^3/_8$	——	0.140	0.250	1 Rich
	D2AF-JA	$^3/_8$	——	0.220	0.250	1 Lean
1973	D3DF-AA	$^3/_8$	——	0.170	0.250	Index
	D3DF-CA	$^3/_8$	——	0.140	0.250	1 Rich
1974	D4DE-JA	$^3/_8$	——	0.140	0.250	1 Rich
	D4DE-JB	$^3/_8$	——	0.140	0.250	Index
	D4DE-ABA	$^3/_8$	——	0.170	0.250	Index
	D4DE-KA	$^3/_8$	——	0.140	0.250	1 Rich
	D4DE-KB	$^3/_8$	——	0.140	0.250	Index
	D4DE-EA	$^3/_8$	——	0.140	0.250	Index

CARTER YF, YFA SPECIFICATIONS

FORD MOTOR CO.

Year	Model ①	Float Level (in.)	Idle Vent (in.)	Fast Idle Cam (in.)	Unloader (in.)	Choke
1975	D5DE-EA	3/8	——	0.140	0.250	2 Rich
	D5DE-MA	3/8	——	0.140	0.250	2 Rich
	D5DE-ZA	3/8	——	0.140	0.250	2 Rich
	D5DE-DA	3/8	——	0.140	0.250	2 Rich
	D5DE-GA	3/8	——	0.140	0.250	2 Rich
1976	D6BE-AA	25/32	——	0.140	0.250	1 Rich
	D6BE-BB	25/32	——	0.140	0.250	2 Rich
	D5DE-DB	25/32	——	0.140	0.250	2 Rich
	D5DE-MB	25/32	——	0.140	0.250	2 Rich
	D6DE-AB	25/32	——	0.140	0.250	Index
	D6DE-BB	25/32	——	0.140	0.250	Index

① Model number located on the tag or casting

Model RBS

Introduction

The Carter RBS is a single barrel carburetor made from aluminum casting. It is equipped with a vacuum piston automatic choke. The 1973 and later models use an EGR (Exhaust Gas Recirculation) system.

Float Level Adjustment

1. After removing the bowl and the bowl gasket, invert the carburetor so that only the weight of the float is pressing down on the needle and seat assembly.
2. Measure the vertical distance from the casting to the projections at the outer ends of the float.
3. Measure both ends of the float and, if adjustment is necessary, it can be done by holding the lip

end of the float bracket with needle nose pliers and bending the float bracket at its narrowest point.

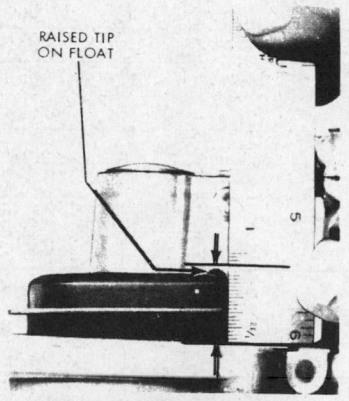

RAISED TIP ON FLOAT

RBS float level adjustment

Float Drop Adjustment

With the air horn upright and the float hanging free, measure the vertical distance from the main body casting surface of the fuel bowl to the outer ends of the float on the top side. Adjust by bending the tab at the end of the float arm. The proper setting is 1.250 in.

Accelerator Pump Adjustment

NOTE: The accelerator pump adjustment must be made before adjusting the bowl vent or the choke unloader.

The pump stroke is measured as the difference in height between the measured height with the throttle valve fully closed and fully open. To adjust, open or close the pump connector link at the offset portion.

PUMP ARM

CONNECTOR LINK

RBS accelerator pump adjustment

Bowl Vent Adjustment

After adjusting the accelerator pump stroke, close the throttle valve completely and measure the distance between the vent valve and the carburetor casting. To adjust, bend the connector rod at the accelerator pump end.

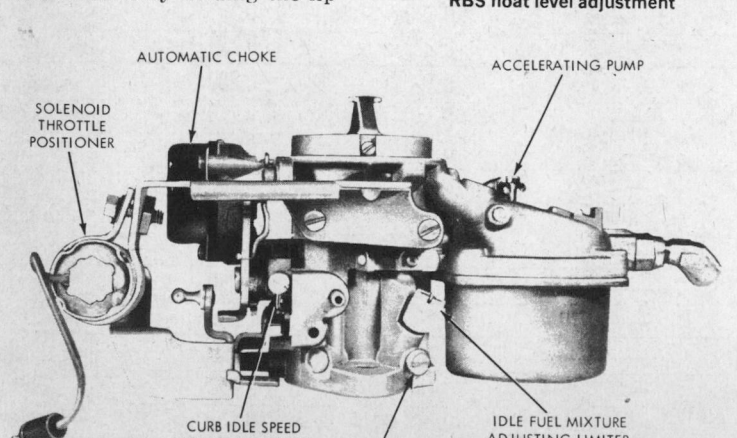

AUTOMATIC CHOKE

ACCELERATING PUMP

SOLENOID THROTTLE POSITIONER

CURB IDLE SPEED ADJUSTING SCREW

IDLE FUEL MIXTURE ADJUSTING LIMITER

IDLE PASSAGE PLUG (DO NOT TURN)

RBS carburetor assembly

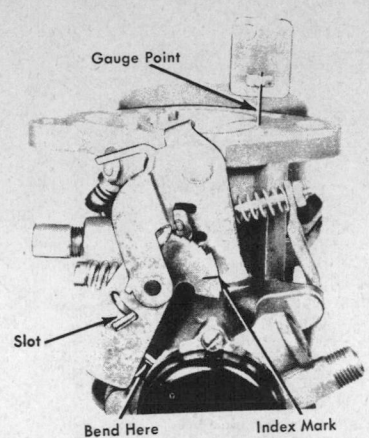

RBS fast idle cam adjustment

Fast Idle Cam Adjustment

1970

With the choke valve tightly closed and the choke connector rod in the upper end of the slot in the cam, align the cam index with the center of the fast idle tang. Adjust by bending the choke connector rod at the offset portion.

Beginning 1971

Place the fast idle screw on the second step of the fast idle cam and against the shoulder of the high step. Specified clearance should exist between the lower edge of the choke valve and the air horn wall. If adjustment is needed, bend the choke plate connecting rod.

Choke Unloader Adjustment

With the throttle valve wide open, the clearance between the upper edge of the valve and the inner air horn wall should be to specification. If it is not, adjust by bending the tang on the throttle lever.

Fast Idle Speed Adjustment

1. Revolve the fast idle cam until the tang on the throttle lever is aligned with the mark on the cam.
2. Proper clearance should exist between the throttle valve and the carburetor bore on the idle port side.
3. If adjustment is required, close the choke valve fully and put the fast idle connector rod against the end of the slot in the cam. Bend the connector rod at the offset portion to align the marks.

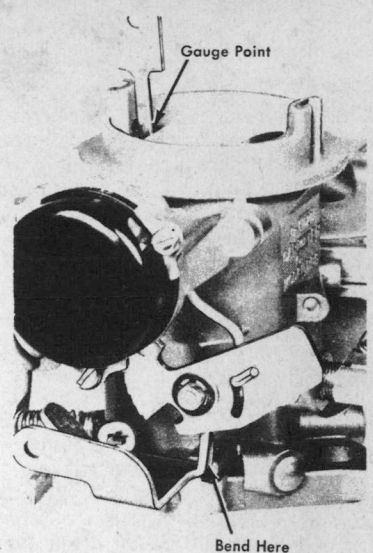

RBS choke unloader adjustment

Automatic Choke Adjustment

1. Loosen the choke cover retaining screws.
2. Turn the choke cover so that the index mark on the cover lines up with the specified mark on the choke housing.

CARTER RBS SPECIFICATIONS

FORD MOTOR CO.

Year	Model ①	Float Level (in.)	Bowl Vent (in.)	Accelerator Pump (in.)	Fast Idle (rpm)	Fast Idle Throttle Plate (in.)	Choke Unloader (in.)	Choke
1970	D0ZF-C	9/16	—	0.400③	See Text	0.040	0.250	Index
	D0ZF-D	9/16	—	0.400③	See Text	0.046	0.252	1 Rich
	D0ZF-F	9/16	—	0.400③	See Text	—	0.252	1 Rich
1971	D1ZF-HA, LA	9/16	—	0.400③	0.115②	—	0.250	Index
	D1ZF-NA, KA	9/16	—	0.400③	0.115②	—	0.250	1 Rich
1972	D2OF-LA	9/16	—	0.400③	0.115②	—	0.250	Index
	D2OF-MA	9/16	—	0.400③	0.115②	—	0.250	1 Rich
	D2OF-SA	9/16	—	0.400③	0.115②	—	0.250	1 Rich
1973	D3OF-BA	9/16	—	0.420③	0.115②	—	0.250	Index
	D3OF-CA	9/16	—	0.400③	0.115②	—	0.250	Index
1974	D4DE-BB	9/16	—	—	0.115②	—	0.250	Index
	D4DE-SB	9/16	—	—	0.115②	—	0.250	Index
	D4DE-AAA	9/16	—	—	0.115②	—	0.250	1 Lean
	D4DE-AB	9/16	—	—	0.115②	—	0.250	Index

① Model numbers located on a tag or on the casting
② At kickdown
③ Closed throttle.

Model WCD

Introduction

This is a two barrel carburetor using a single needle valve even though two floats are provided. On several of these units, the floats operate independently of each other so that the highest float always controls the fuel level. This is necessary when the carburetor is mounted with the float centerline parallel to the centerline of the engine.

Float Adjustment

(Lateral)

1. Invert the bowl cover.
2. Remove the bowl cover gasket.
3. Place the float gauge directly under the floats with the notched portions of the gauge fitted over the edges of the casting.
4. The sides of the float should barely touch the vertical uprights of the float gauge. A gauge is normally included in a rebuilding kit.
5. Adjustment is made by bending the arms of the floats.

WCD float level adjustment

(Vertical)

1. With the float gauge in the same position as for the lateral adjustment, the floats should just clear the horizontal portion of the gauge.
2. The vertical distance between the top center of the float and the machined surface of the casting must be 7/32 in.
3. Adjust by bending the float arms as required.
4. To install the bowl cover gasket, remove the floats, install the gasket, and reinstall the floats.

Pump Adjustment

1. Install the pump connector link in the outer hole (long stroke) of the pump arm with the ends extending away from the countershaft arm.
2. Back out the throttle lever set screw until the throttle valves seat in the carburetor bores.
3. Be sure that the fast idle adjustment screw does not hold the throttle open.
4. Hold a straightedge across the top of the dust cover boss at the pump arm.
5. The flat on top of the pump arm should be parallel to the straightedge.

WCD pump adjustment

6. Adjust by bending the throttle connector rod to the upper angle.

Metering Rod Adjustment

1. Complete the pump adjustment.
2. Back out the throttle lever set screw to allow the valves (throttle) to seat in the bores of the carburetor.
3. Loosen the metering rod clamp screw.
4. With the metering rod in place, press down on the vacumeter link until the metering rods bottom in the carburetor body casting.
5. While holding the rods in a downward position, revolve the metering rod arm until the finger on the arm contacts the lip of the vacumeter link.
6. Hold in place and carefully tighten the clamp screw.

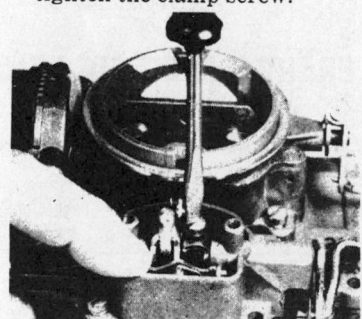

WCD metering rod adjustment

Fast Idle Cam Adjustment

1. Loosen the choke lever clamp screw on the choke shaft.
2. Insert a 0.010 in. feeler gauge between the lip of the fast idle cam and the boss of the flange casting.
3. Hold the choke valve tightly closed and take the slack out of the linkage by pressing the choke lever toward the closed position.
4. With the choke valve in the closed position, tighten the fast idle adjusting screw to obtain the specified clearance.
5. Be sure that the fast idle adjusting screw is on the high step of the cam or index mark while making this adjustment.

Choke Unloader Adjustment

1. With the throttle valves wide

WCD fast idle cam adjustment

open, there should be clearance between the upper edge of the choke valve and the inner wall of the air horn.
2. Adjust by bending the unloader lip on the throttle shaft lever.
3. Adjustment is 3/16 in.

WCD choke unloader adjustment

Automatic Choke Adjustment

1. Loosen the choke cover retaining screws.
2. Turn the cover so that the index mark on the cover lines up with the specified mark on the choke housing.
3. See the Specifications Chart for the proper mark alignment.

WCD AUTOMATIC CHOKE SPECIFICATIONS

Year	Model ①	Choke
1970	4816S	Index
	4817S	Index
	4950S	Index

① Model numbers located on the tag or the casting

Model WGD

Introduction

The WGD carburetor is the same basic carburetor as the WCD, the only difference being that the WGD has only one float. The choke is operated by a thermostatic coil. This carburetor is used mainly on 1972 Pontiacs. It carries model number 6311S.

Float Adjustment

1. With the air horn inverted, check to see that the float is parallel with the outer edge of the air horn casting.
2. Adjust by bending the float arm. Next, place the gauge between the air horn and the center of the float. The distance should be 5/16 in.
3. Adjust the float level by bending the float arm until the float touches the gauge. The float should not have excessive clearance at the hinge pin and must operate freely.

NOTE: When adjusting the float, care must be exercised to avoid pressing the flared tip needle into the needle seats as a false setting will result. Allow only the float weight to seat the needle when gauging.

Pump Adjustment

1. Back out the throttle stop screw.
2. Turn the fast idle cam to "hot" position and fully close the throttle valves.
3. Place a ¼ in. gauge or a similar straightedge across the dust cover boss. The dust cover boss should be parallel with the top surface of the pump arm.
4. Adjust by bending the pump rod at the offset.

Metering Rod Adjustment

NOTE: This adjustment should be made after the pump adjustment. No metering rod gauges are necessary.

1. Back out the throttle screw and fully close the throttle valves. Press down on the vacuum piston link until the metering rods bottom.

WGD metering rod adjustment

2. While holding the rods down and the metering arm tongue against the lip of the vacuum piston link, carefully tighten the metering arm set screw.

WGD fast idle cam adjustment

Fast Idle Cam Adjustment

1. Open the throttle to clear the fast idle cam and close the choke valve.
2. With the choke valve held fully closed and the stop on the fast idle cam against the casting, there should be 0.005 in. minimum clearance between the inner and outer choke levers.
3. Adjust by bending the outer lever lug as required.

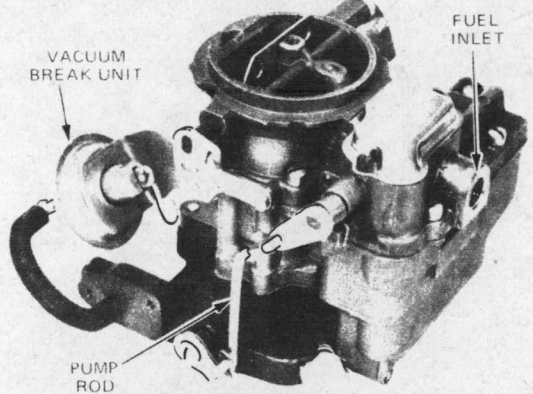

WGD carburetor assembly

WGD float level adjustment

WGD choke unloader adjustment

WGD pump adjustment

NOTE: With the choke fully closed, the tang on the fast idle cam must clear the stop on the throttle body flange.

Unloader Adjustment

1. Hold the choke closed lightly.
2. Fully open the throttle, forcing the choke valve open.
3. Check the clearance between the upper edge of the choke valve and the wall of the air horn. The clearance should be 3/16 in.

4. Adjust by bending the unloader arm as required.

Fast Idle Speed Adjustment

1. With the carburetor on the engine, rotate the fast idle cam until the fast idle tang contacts the cam's high step.
2. With the engine at normal operating temperature, adjust the fast idle tang to obtain an engine speed of 1500 rpm.

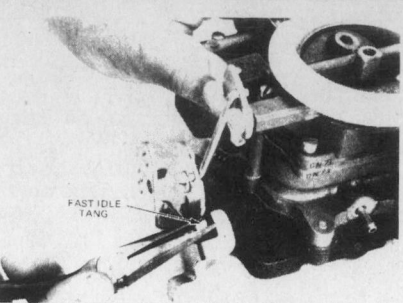

WGD fast idle speed adjustment

Model AVS

Introduction

The AVS carburetor is very similar to the AFB carburetor. AVS means Air Valve Secondary. It employs a spring loaded air valve located above the secondary fuel nozzles. This system gives smooth response whenever the secondaries are opened. Venturi clusters are used in the primary side for fuel control in the idle and economy ranges.

Float Alignment

1. The sides of the float should be parallel to the edge of the casting with minimum clearance between the lever and the air horn lugs without binding.
2. To adjust, bend the float arm lever.

Float Level Adjustment

1. With the air horn inverted, the air horn gasket in place, and the float needle seated, slide the float gauge between the top of the float, at the outer edge, and the air horn gasket. Refer to the Specifications Chart.
2. Check the other float in the same manner.
3. Adjust by bending the float arm. After bending the arm, recheck the float alignment.

Float Drop Adjustment

1. The dimension listed in the Specifications Chart should exist between the tops of the floats, at the outer end, and the air horn gasket.
2. To adjust, bend the stop tabs on the float brackets.

Pump Adjustment

1. With the throttle valves closed tightly, the dimension listed in the Specifications Chart should be from the top of the air horn to the top of the pump plunger

shaft with the throttle connector rod in the inner hole of the pump arm.
2. To adjust, bend the throttle connector rod at an angle.

Fast Idle Cam Adjustment

1. With the fast idle speed adjusting screw contacting the second highest speed step on the fast idle cam, move the choke valve toward the closed position with light pressure on the choke shaft lever.
2. Insert the drill gauge between the choke valve and the wall of the air horn. Refer to the Specifications Chart.
3. An adjustment will be necessary if a slight drag is not obtained as the drill is beginning to be removed.
4. Adjust by bending the fast idle connector rod at an angle.

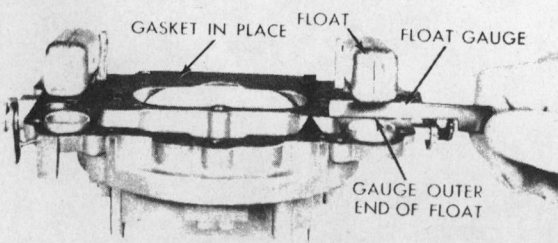

AVS float alignment

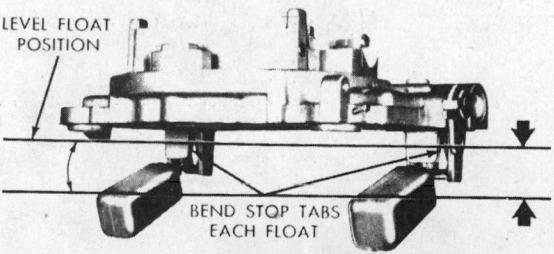

AVS float drop adjustment

AVS float level adjustment

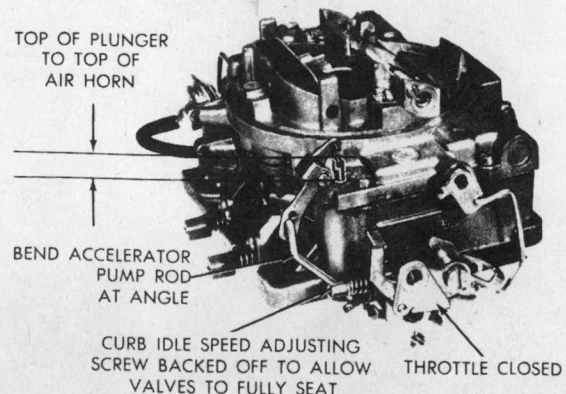

AVS pump adjustment

Choke Unloader Adjustment

1. With the throttle valves wide open there should be 1/4 in. clearance between the upper edge of the choke valve and the inner wall of the air horn.
2. To adjust, bend the unloader tang on the fast idle cam.

Bowl Vent Adjustment

1970 Without ECS

1. With the throttle valves tightly closed, insert a drill gauge between the air horn and the valve at the smallest opening. Refer to the Specifications Chart.

2. Adjust by bending the tang on the pivot end of the lever.

ECS Equipped

1. Remove the bowl vent valve and check the hole plug in the air horn.
2. With the throttle valves at closed curb idle position, insert a nar-

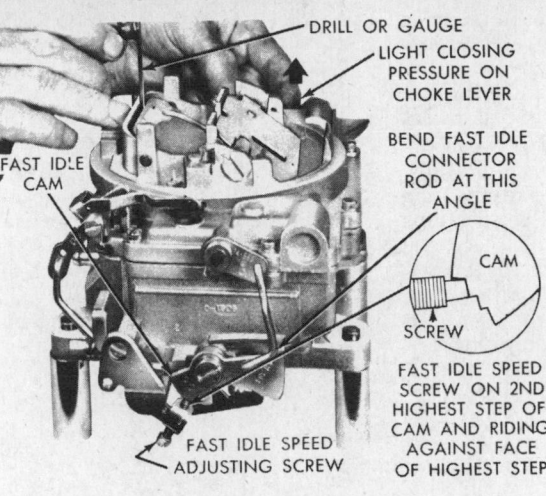

DRILL OR GAUGE
LIGHT CLOSING PRESSURE ON CHOKE LEVER
FAST IDLE CAM
BEND FAST IDLE CONNECTOR ROD AT THIS ANGLE
CAM
SCREW
FAST IDLE SPEED ADJUSTING SCREW
FAST IDLE SPEED SCREW ON 2ND HIGHEST STEP OF CAM AND RIDING AGAINST FACE OF HIGHEST STEP

AVS fast idle cam adjustment

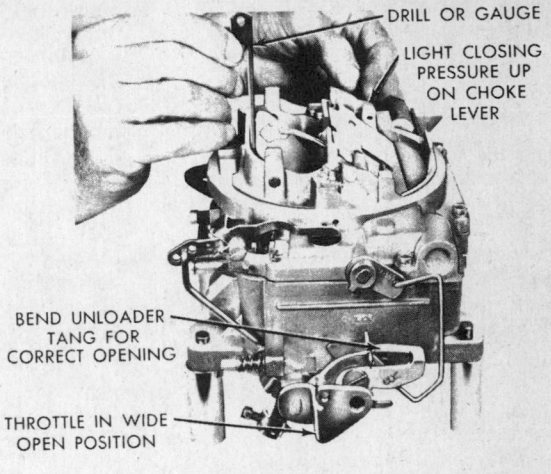

DRILL OR GAUGE
LIGHT CLOSING PRESSURE UP ON CHOKE LEVER
BEND UNLOADER TANG FOR CORRECT OPENING
THROTTLE IN WIDE OPEN POSITION

AVS choke unloader adjustment

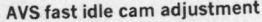

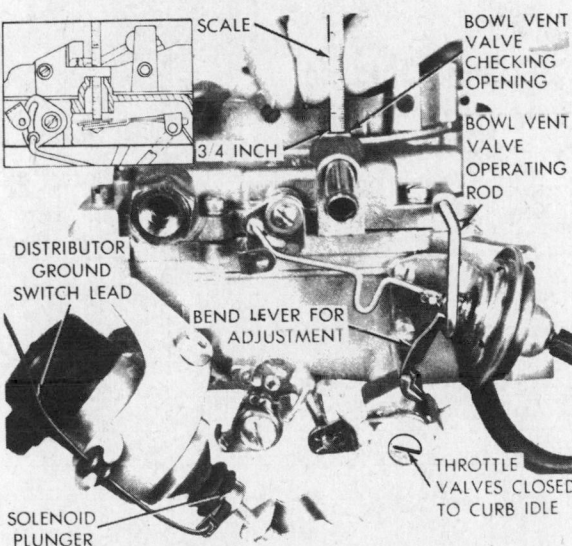

SCALE
BOWL VENT VALVE CHECKING OPENING
3/4 INCH
BOWL VENT VALVE OPERATING ROD
DISTRIBUTOR GROUND SWITCH LEAD
BEND LEVER FOR ADJUSTMENT
SOLENOID PLUNGER
THROTTLE VALVES CLOSED TO CURB IDLE

AVS bowl vent adjustment

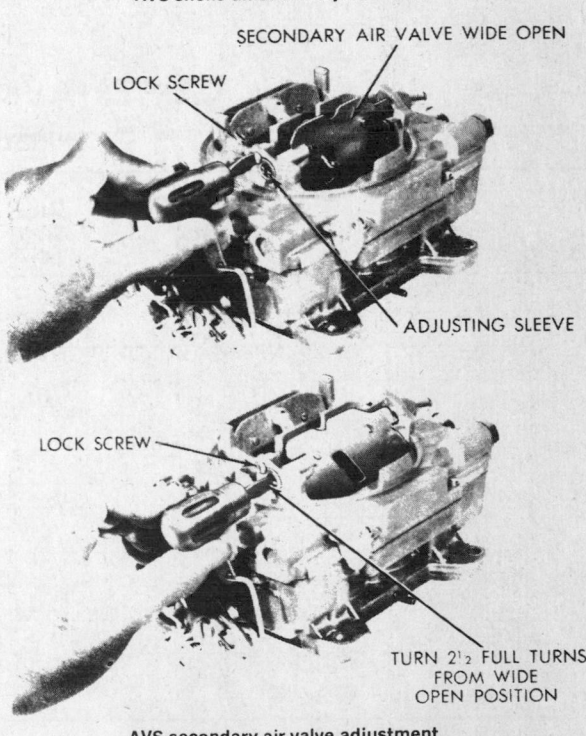

SECONDARY AIR VALVE WIDE OPEN
LOCK SCREW
ADJUSTING SLEEVE

LOCK SCREW
TURN 2 1/2 FULL TURNS FROM WIDE OPEN POSITION

AVS secondary air valve adjustment

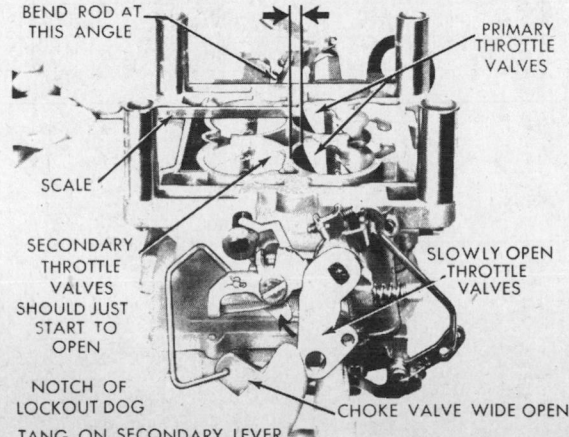

BEND ROD AT THIS ANGLE
PRIMARY THROTTLE VALVES
SCALE
SECONDARY THROTTLE VALVES SHOULD JUST START TO OPEN
SLOWLY OPEN THROTTLE VALVES
NOTCH OF LOCKOUT DOG
TANG ON SECONDARY LEVER
CHOKE VALVE WIDE OPEN

AVS secondary throttle lockout

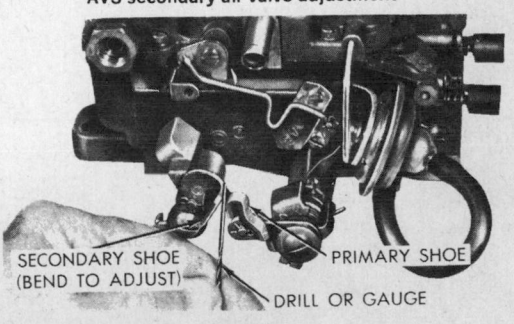

SECONDARY SHOE (BEND TO ADJUST)
PRIMARY SHOE
DRILL OR GAUGE

AVS closing shoe adjustment

row ruler down through the hole. Allow the ruler to rest lightly on top of the valve.

3. Measure from the top of the valve to the top of the air horn casting at the opening. Refer to the Specifications Chart.
4. Adjust by bending the bowl vent operating lever.
5. Install the plug and rap lightly on the seat, using a hammer.

Secondary Air Valve Adjustment

1. Loosen the lock screw and allow the air valve to position itself at the wide open position.
2. From the wide open position turn the slotted sleeve 2½ turns counterclockwise.
3. Hold the sleeve in this position

with your fingers, then tighten the lock screw securely.
4. Check the valve for freedom of movement.

Secondary Throttle Lever Adjustment

1. Block the choke valve in the wide open position and invert the carburetor.
2. Slowly open the primary throttle valves until the specified measurement is obtained between the lower edge of the primary valve and the bore opposite the idle port. Refer to the Specifications Chart.
3. At this measurement, the secondary valves should just start to open.
4. Adjust by bending the secondary

throttle operating rod at the angle.

Closing Shoe Adjustment

1. With the primary and secondary throttle valves closed, bend the secondary closing shoe to obtain 0.020 in. clearance between the positive closing shoes on the primary and secondary throttle levers.
2. To adjust, bend the shoe on the secondary lever.

Secondary Throttle Lockout

1. Crack the throttle valves and manually open and close the choke valve. The tang on the secondary throttle lever should freely engage in the notch of the lockout dog.
2. To adjust, bend the tang on the secondary throttle lever.

CARTER AVS SPECIFICATIONS

CHRYSLER PRODUCTS

Year	Carb. Model ①	Float Level (in.)	Float Drop (in.)	Accelerator Pump (in.)	Bowl Vent (in.)	Fast Idle Cam (in.) ②	Secondary Throttle Lever (In.)
1970	4732S*	5/16	1/2	7/16	3/64	50	19/64
	4734S*	5/16	1/2	7/16	3/64	50	19/64
	4736S*	5/16	1/2	7/16	3/64	50	19/64
	4737S*	7/32	1/2	7/16	3/64	50	23/64
	4738S	7/32	1/2	7/16	3/64	50	23/64
	4739S	7/32	1/2	7/16	3/64	50	23/64
	4740S	7/32	1/2	7/16	3/64	50	23/64
	4741S	7/32	1/2	7/16	3/64	50	23/64
	4933S	7/32	1/2	7/16	3/64	50	19/64
	4934S	7/32	1/2	7/16	1/8	50	19/64
	4935S	7/32	1/2	7/16	1/8	50	19/64
	4936S	7/32	1/2	7/16	3/4	50	19/64
	4937S	7/32	1/2	7/16	3/4	50	19/64
1971	4966S	7/32	1/2	7/16	3/4	50	23/64
	4967S	7/32	1/2	7/16	3/4	50	23/64
	4968S	7/32	1/2	7/16	3/4	50	23/64
	6125S	7/32	1/2	7/16	3/4	50	23/64

① Model numbers are located on a tag or on the casting
② Indicates drill bit number.
NOTE: Accelerator pump adjustment is 7/16 in. for all AVS carburetors. Choke setting on 1970 models is on the index except when marked (*) which is 2 notches rich. 1971 models should be 2 rich.

Model TQ

Introduction

The TQ (Thermo-Quad) has a fuel bowl made of phenolic resin. This acts as a heat insulator. Fuel is kept 20 degrees cooler than in metal carburetors. It also has a suspended design metering system which aids in cooling. All the calibration points are in the upper aluminum casting or air horn and are in effect suspended in the cavities in the main body.

Float Adjustment

1. With the bowl cover inverted, the gasket installed, and the floats resting on the seated needle, the dimension of each float from the bowl cover gasket to the bottom side of the float should be as shown in the specifications chart.

2. To adjust, bend the float lever.

Secondary Throttle Linkage

1. Block the choke valve in the wide open position and invert the carburetor.
2. Slowly open the primary throttle valves until the secondary valves start to open. Measure between the lower edge of the primary valve and its bore.
3. If it is necessary to adjust, bend the secondary throttle operating rod at the lower angle until the correct dimension is obtained.

Secondary Air Valve Opening

1. With the air valve in the closed position, the opening along the air valve at its long side must be at its maximum and parallel

with the air horn gasket surface.
2. With the air valve wide open, the opening of the air valve at the short side and the air horn must match the dimensions in the Specifications Charts. The corner of the air valve is notched for adjustment. Bend the corner with a pair of pliers to give proper opening.

Accelerator Pump Adjustment

Through 1975

1. Move the choke valve wide open to release the fast idle cam.
2. Back off the idle speed adjusting screw until the throttle valves are seated in the bores.
3. Be sure that the throttle connector rod is in the center (three

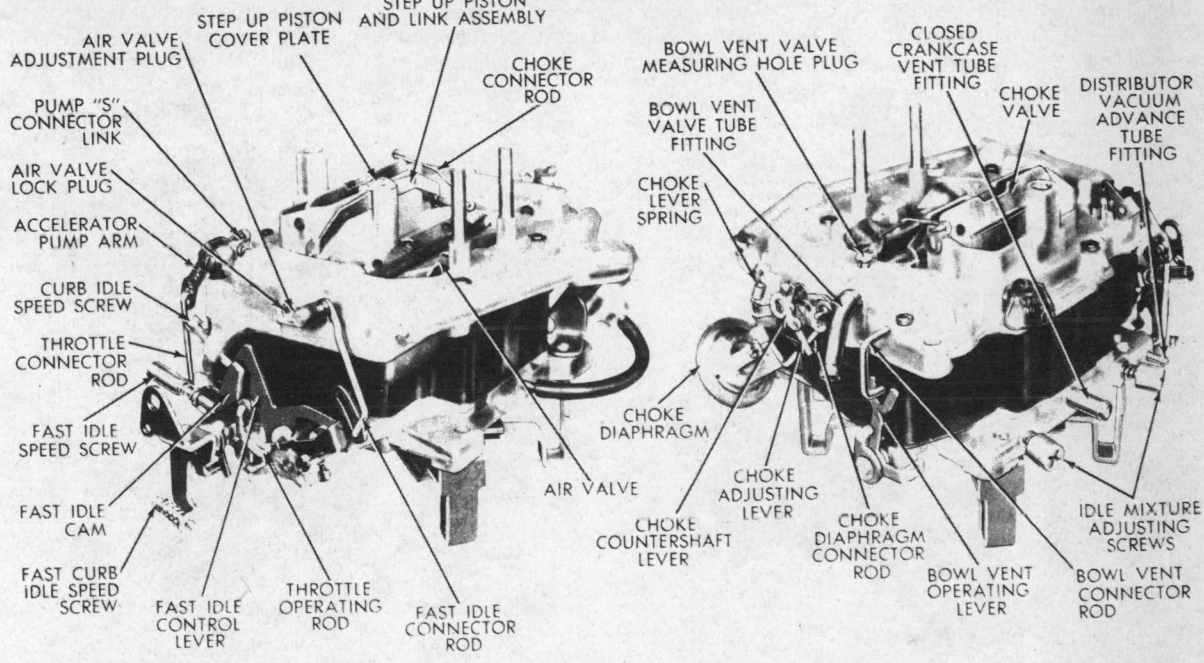

TQ carburetor assembly

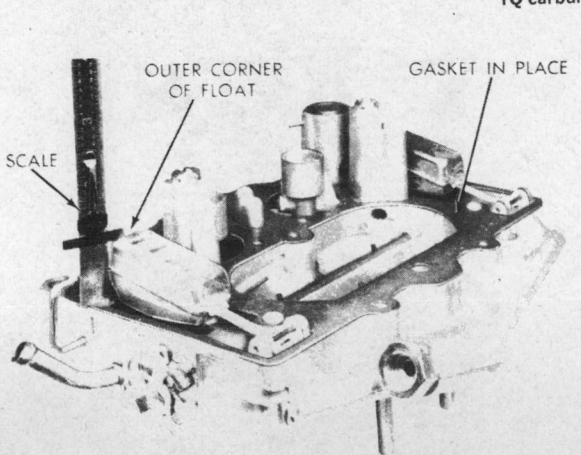

TQ float adjustment

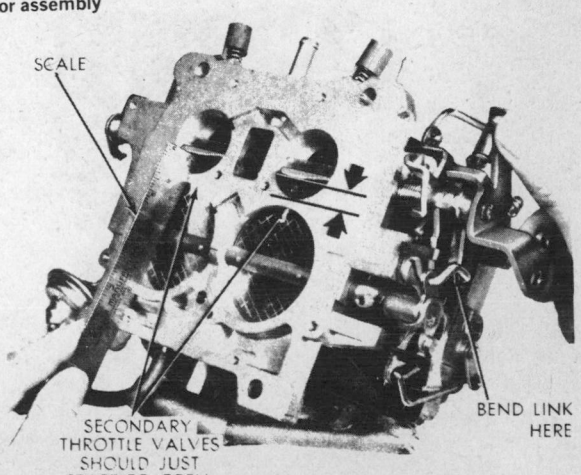

TQ secondary throttle adjustment

holes) or the inner (two holes) hole of the pump arm.

4. Close the throttle valve tightly and measure the distance between the top of the bowl cover and the end of the plunger shaft. The dimension should be as shown in the Specifications Chart.

5. Bend the throttle connector rod at the lower angle to adjust.

1976 and Later

1. Make sure the throttle connector rod is in the center hole (three holes) or inner holes (two holes) of the pump arm.

2. Measure the height of the accelerator pump plunger at curb idle.

3. Adjust plunger height by bending the throttle connector rod.

Choke Control Lever

1. Disconnect the diaphragm rod.

2. Close the choke by pushing on the choke lever with the throttle partly open.

3. Measure the vertical distance from the top of the rod hole in the control lever down to the carburetor base. The dimensions should be as shown in the Specifications Chart.

4. To adjust, bend the link which connects the two choke shafts.

Vacuum Kick Adjustment

1. With the engine running, back off the fast idle speed screw until the choke can be closed to the kick position at idle.

2. Count the number of screw turns so that the fast idle can be turned back to the original adjustment.

3. Insert the specified drill between the long side, lower edge, of the choke valve and the air horn wall.

4. Apply sufficient pressure on the choke control lever to provide a minimum choke valve opening. The spring connecting the control lever to the adjustment lever

must be fully extended for proper adjustment.

5. Bend the tang to change contact with the end of the diaphragm rod. Do not adjust the diaphragm rod. A slight drag should be felt as the drill is being removed.

Fast Idle Cam Linkage

1. With the fast idle screw on the second fastest step of the cam against the shoulder of the first step, there should be 0.110 in. (.100 beginning 1974) between the air horn wall and edge of the choke valve.

2. To adjust, bend the fast idle connector rod at the lower angle.

Secondary Throttle Lockout

1. Move the choke control lever to the open choke position.

2. Measure the clearance between the lockout lever and the stop.

3. Bend the tang on the fast idle

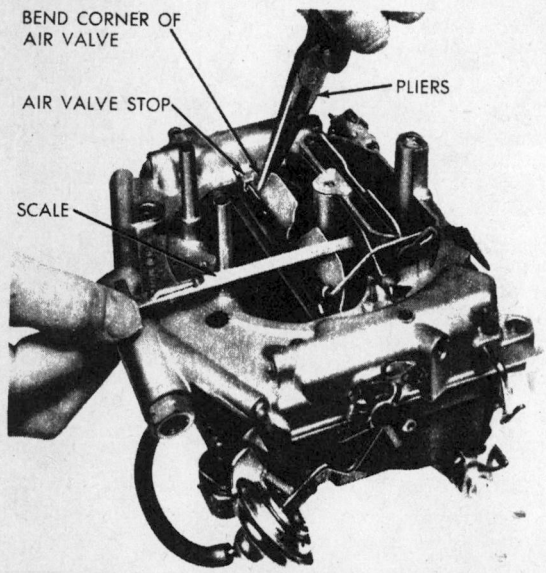

TQ secondary air valve adjustment

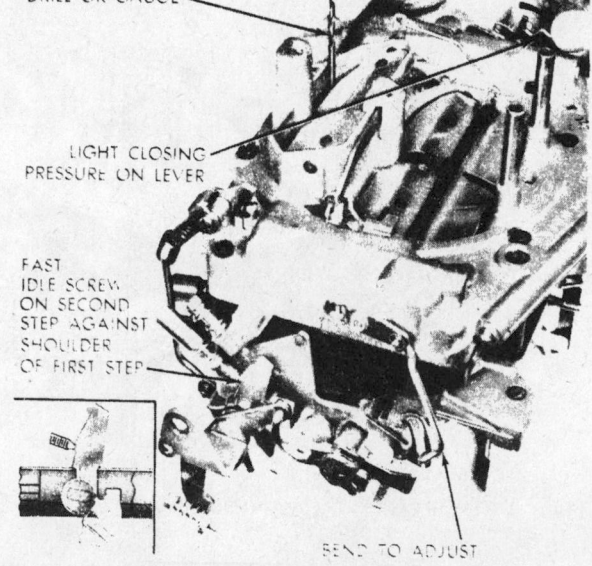

TQ adjusting fast idle cam linkage

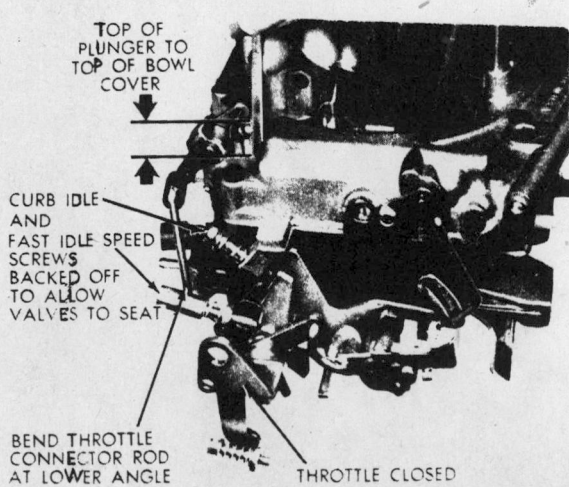

TQ accelerator pump adjustment

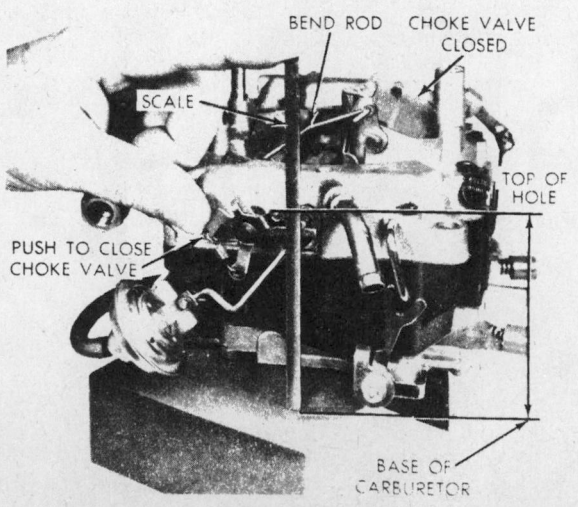

TQ choke control lever

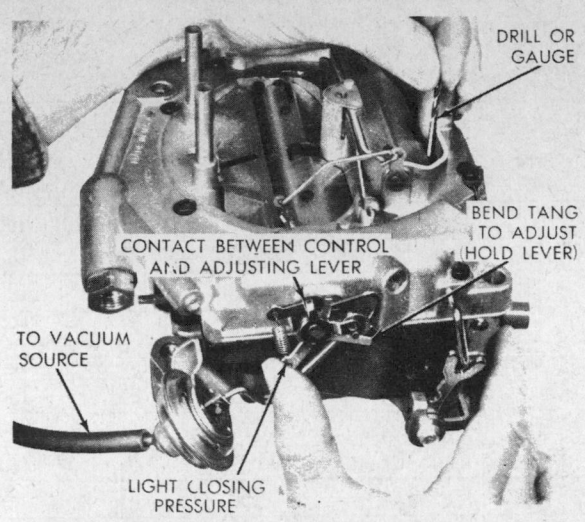

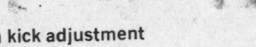

TQ vacuum kick adjustment

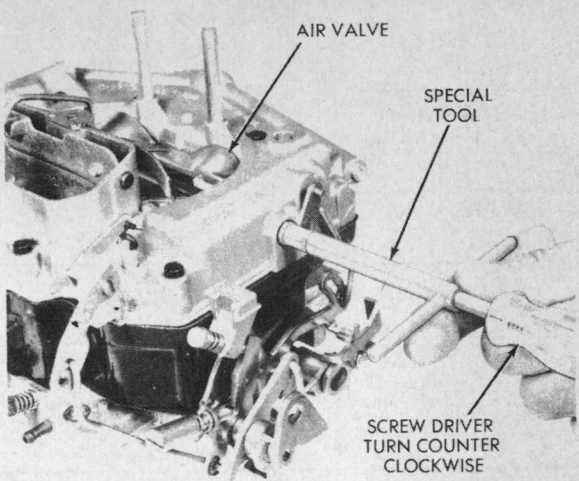

TQ air valve spring tension adjustment

control lever to provide the proper clearance. The reading should be 0.010 to 0.030 for models through 1972, and 0.060 to 0.090 in. beginning 1973.

Bowl Vent Valve Adjustment

1. Remove the bowl vent valve checking hole plug in the bowl cover.
2. With the throttle valve in the idle position insert a narrow ruler down through the hole.
3. Allow the ruler to rest lightly on the top of the valve. Measure from the top of the valve to the top of the bowl cover at the opening. The correct dimension should be 13/16 in.

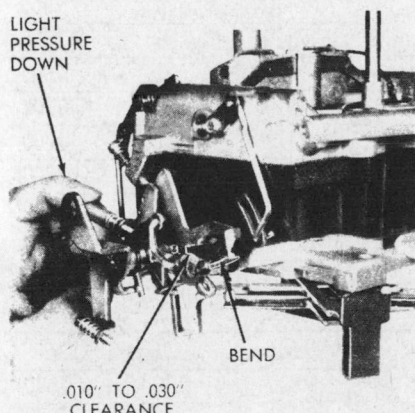

Adjusting the TQ secondary throttle lockout

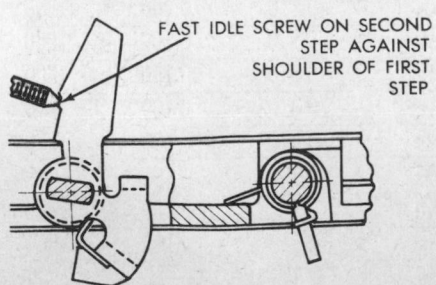

TQ fast idle cam adjustment

4. Bend the bowl vent operating lever at the notch to adjust.
5. Install a new plug.

Fast Idle Speed Cam

1. Disconnect and plug the heated air, OSAC valve, or distributor connections on 1974 and later models. With the engine off and the transmission in Park or Neutral, open the throttle slightly.
2. Close the choke valve until the fast idle screw can be positioned on the second step of the cam against the shoulder of the first step.
3. Start the engine and adjust the screw to obtain the specified fast idle speed.

Choke Unloader Adjustment

1. Hold the throttle valves in the wide open position and insert the specified drill between the long side of the choke valve and inner wall of the air horn.
2. With a finger pressing lightly

against the choke control lever, a slight drag should be felt as the drill is being withdrawn.
3. To adjust, bend the tang on the fast idle lever.

Secondary Air Valve Spring Tension

1. Loosen the air valve lock plug and allow the air valve to position itself in the wide open position.
2. With a long screwdriver that will enter the center of tool C-4152 positioned on the air valve adjustment plug, turn the plug counterclockwise until the air valve contacts the stop lightly, then an additional 1¼ turn.
3. Hold the adjustment plug with the screwdriver and tighten the lock plug with the tool. Make sure the adjustment does not move and that the air valve moves freely.

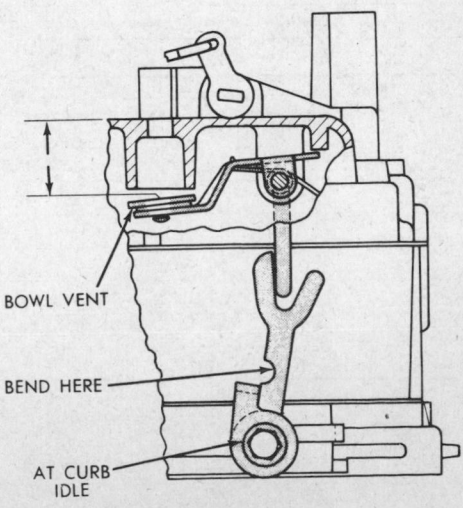

TQ bowl vent adjustment

CARTER TQ SPECIFICATIONS

CHRYSLER PRODUCTS

Year	Model ①	Float Setting (in.)	Secondary Throttle Linkage (in.)	Secondary Air Valve Opening (in.)	Secondary Air Valve Spring (turns)	Accelerator Pump (in.)	Choke Control Lever (in.)	Choke Unloader (in.)	Vacuum Kick (Drill Size)	Fast Idle Speed (rpm)
1971	4972S	1	11/32	31/64	1 1/4	31/64	5 41/64	0.190	35	1800
	4973S	1	11/32	31/64	1 1/4	31/64	5 41/64	0.190	35	1800
1972	6090S	1	②	31/64	1	31/64	3 3/8	0.190	28	1900
	6138S	1	②	29/64	1	9/16	3 3/8	0.190	21	1900
	6139S	1	②	29/64	1	31/64	3 3/8	0.190	28	1900
	6140S	1	②	31/64	1	9/16	3 3/8	0.190	21	1900
	6165S	1	②	31/64	1	9/16	3 3/8	0.190	21	2000
	6166S	1	②	31/64	1	31/64	3 3/8	0.190	28	2100
1973	6318S	1 1/16	②	29/64	1 1/4	35/64	3 3/8	0.190	21	1300
	6319S	1 1/16	②	29/64	1 1/4	31/64	3 3/8	0.190	21	1800
	6320S	1 1/16	②	31/64	1 1/4	35/64	3 3/8	0.190	21	1300
	6321S	1 1/16	②	31/64	1 1/4	31/64	3 3/8	0.190	21	1800
	6322S	1 1/16	②	31/64	1 1/4	31/64	3 3/8	0.190	21	1700
	6324S	1 1/16	②	31/64	1 1/4	31/64	3 3/8	0.190	21	1800
	6339S	1 1/16	②	29/64	1 1/4	35/64	3 3/8	0.190	21	1700
	6340S	1 1/16	②	29/64	1 1/4	31/64	3 3/8	0.190	21	1800
	6341S	1 1/16	②	29/64	1 1/4	35/64	3 3/8	0.190	21	1700
	6342S	1 1/16	②	29/64	1 1/4	31/64	3 3/8	0.190	21	1700
	6410S	1 1/16	②	31/64	1 1/4	31/64	3 3/8	0.190	21	1700
	6411S	1 1/16	②	31/64	1 1/4	31/64	3 3/8	0,190	21	1700
1974	6488S	1	②	1/2	1 1/4	35/64	3 3/8	.310	21	1800
	6452S	1	②	1/2	1 1/4	35/64	3 3/8	.310	4	1900
	6453S	1	②	1/2	1 1/4	31/64	3 3/8	.310	21	1900
	6454S	1	②	1/2	1 1/4	35/64	3 3/8	.310	4	1900
	6455S	1	②	1/2	1 1/4	31/64	3 3/8	.310	21	1900
	6489S	1	②	1/2	1 1/4	31/64	3 3/8	.310	21	2000
	6496S	1	②	1/2	1 1/4	31/64	3 3/8	.310	21	2000
	6456S	1	②	1/2	1 1/4	35/64	3 3/8	.310	4	1700
	6457S	1	②	1/2	1 1/4	31/64	3 3/8	.310	21	1800
	6459	1	②	1/2	1 1/4	31/64	3 3/8	.310	21	1800
	6460S	1	②	1/2	1 1/4	31/64	3 3/8	.310	21	1700
	6461S	1	②	1/2	1 1/4	31/64	3 3/8	.310	21	1700
	6462S	1	②	1/2	1 1/4	31/64	3 3/8	.310	21	1700
	6463S	1	②	1/2	1 1/4	31/64	3 3/8	.310	21	1700
1975	9004S	29/32	②	1/2	1 1/4	35/64	3 3/8	0.310	0.100	1600
	9002S	29/32	②	1/2	1 1/4	35/64	3 3/8	0.310	0.100	1600
	9046S	29/32	②	1/2	1 1/4	35/64	3 3/8	0.310	0.100	1800
	9008S	29/32	②	1/2	1 1/4	35/64	3 3/8	0.310	0.100	1800
	9053S	29/32	②	1/2	1 1/4	35/64	3 3/8	0.310	0.100	1800
	9009S	29/32	②	1/2	1 1/4	35/64	3 3/8	0.310	0.100	1600
	9010S	29/32	②	1/2	1 1/4	35/64	3 3/8	0.310	0.100	1600
	9011S	29/32	②	1/2	1 1/4	35/64	3 3/8	0.310	0.100	1600
	9012S	29/32	②	1/2	1 1/4	35/64	3 3/8	0.310	0.100	1800
1976	9002S	29/32	②	33/64	1 1/4	33/64	3 3/8	0.310	0.100	1700
	9055S	29/32	②	33/64	1 1/4	33/64	3 3/8	0.310	0.100	1700
	9074S	29/32	②	33/64	1 1/4	33/64	3 3/8	0.310	0.100	1600
	9057S	29/32	②	33/64	1 1/4	33/64	3 3/8	0.310	0.100	1600

CARTER TQ SPECIFICATIONS

CHRYSLER PRODUCTS

Year	Model ①	Float Setting (in.)	Secondary Throttle Linkage (in.)	Secondary Air Valve Opening (in.)	Secondary Air Valve Spring (turns)	Accelerator Pump (in.)	Choke Control Lever (in.)	Choke Unloader (in.)	Vacuum Kick (Drill Size) (in.)	Fast Idle Speed (rpm)
1976	9054S	29/32	②	33/64	1 1/4	33/64	3 3/8	0.310	0.100	1800
	9058S	29/32	②	33/64	1 1/4	31/64	3 3/8	0.310	0.100	1600
	9059S	29/32	②	33/64	1 1/4	31/64	3 3/8	0.310	0.100	1600
	9066S	29/32	②	33/64	1 1/4	33/64	3 3/8	0.310	0.100	1600
	9062S	29/32	②	33/64	1 1/4	33/64	3 3/8	0.310	0.100	1600
	9052S	29/32	②	33/64	1 1/4	33/64	3 3/8	0.310	0.100	1600

① Model numbers located on the tag or on the casting
② Adjust link so primary and secondary stops both contact at same time
NOTE: All choke settings are fixed except 1971 which is 2 notches rich

Model AFB

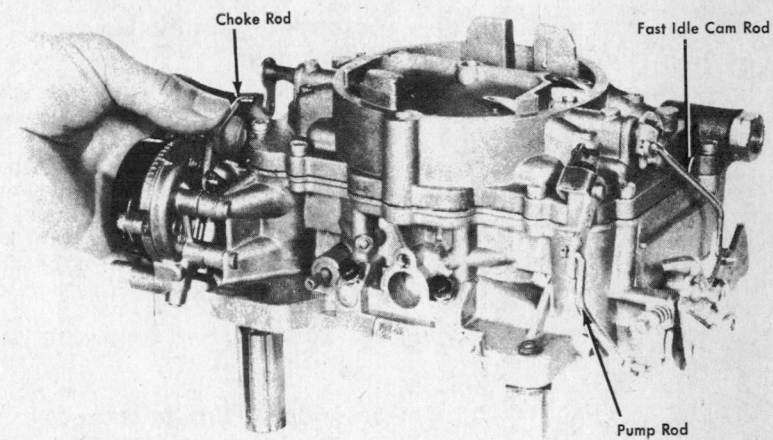

AFB carburetor assembly

Introduction

The Carter AFB (Aluminum Four-Barrel) carburetor has four barrels. All the major castings are of aluminum and the venturi assemblies are replaceable. For better performance in cornering and stopping, one fuel bowl feeds the primary and secondary on the left. The other bowl feeds the primary and secondary on the right. Thermostatic spring coil chokes are used on most models.

Float Alignment

1. Sight down the side of the float to determine if it is parallel to the outer edge of the air horn casting.
2. To adjust, bend the float lever accordingly.
3. To bend the lever, apply pressure on the end of the float with your fingers while supporting the float lever with your thumb.
4. After aligning the float, remove as much clearance as possible between the arms of the float lever and the lugs on the air horn by bending the float lever.
5. The arms of the float lever should be parallel to the inner surfaces of the lugs on the air horn. The floats must operate freely without excess clearance on the hinge pin.

Float Level Adjustment

1. With the air horn inverted, the bowl cover in place, and the needle seated, clearance between the top of the float (at outer edge) and the air horn gasket should be as listed in the Specifications Chart.
2. To adjust, bend the float arm. Adjust both floats and recheck the float alignment.

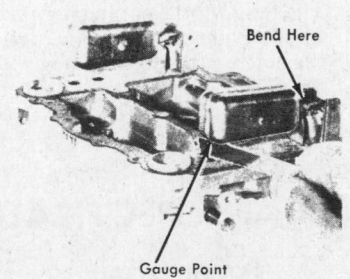

AFB float level adjustment

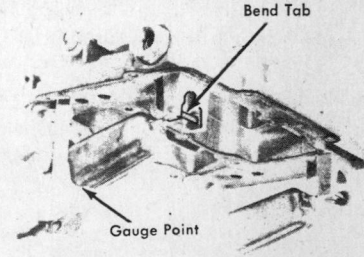

AFB float drop adjustment

Float Drop Adjustment

1. With the bowl cover held in the upright position, measure between the outer end of each float, the distance between the top of the floats and the bowl cover gasket as listed in the Specifications Chart.
2. To adjust, bend the tabs on the float brackets.

Pump Adjustment

1. Back out the idle speed screw

AFB pump adjustment

until the throttle valve seats in the carburetor bores with the choke off.

2. The distance from the top of the bowl cover to the top of the pump plunger shaft should be as listed in the Specifications Chart. To adjust, bend the throttle connector rod at its lower angle.

Fast Idle Speed Cam Position Adjustment

1. With the fast idle speed adjusting screw contacting the second highest speed step on the fast idle cam, move the choke valve toward the closed position with light pressure on the choke shaft lever.
2. Insert a drill gauge between the choke valve and the wall of the air horn. Refer to the Specifications Chart.
3. Adjustment is necessary if a slight drag is not obtained as the drill is being removed.
4. Adjust by bending the fast idle connector rod at the lower angle.

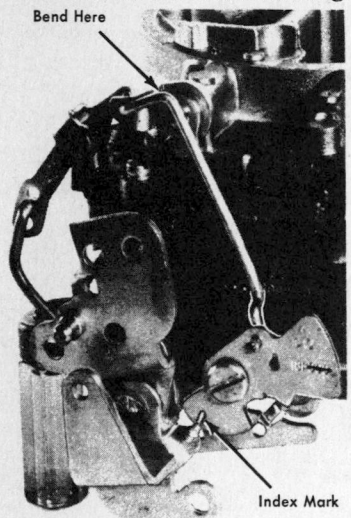

AFB fast idle linkage adjustment

Choke Unloader Adjustment

1. With the throttle wide open, the clearance between the upper edge of the choke valve and the inner wall of the air horn should be as listed in the Specifications Chart.
2. To adjust, bend the unloader tang on the throttle shaft lever.

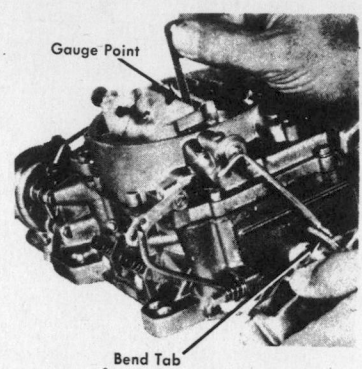

AFB choke unloader adjustment

Secondary Throttle Lever Adjustment

1. Block the choke valve wide open and invert the carburetor. The secondary throttle valves should just start to open when the primary throttle valves are opened to the clearance (listed in the Specifications Chart) between the lower edge of the throttle valve and the carburetor bore.
2. To adjust, bend the throttle connecting rod.

Secondary Throttle Lockout

1. Crack the throttle valves and manually open and close the choke valve.
2. The tang on the secondary throttle lever should freely engage in the notch of the lockout dog.
3. To adjust, bend the tang on the throttle lever. Refer to the Specifications Chart.

AFB secondary throttle lever adjustment

Bowl Vent Valve Adjustment

1970 Without ECS

1. With the throttle valves tightly closed, insert the drill gauge between the air horn and the valve at the smallest opening. Refer to the Specifications Chart.
2. Adjust by bending the adjusting tang on the pivot end of the lever.

ECS Equipped

1. Remove the bowl vent valve and checking the hole plug in the air horn.
2. With the throttle valves in the closed curb idle position, insert a narrow ruler down through the hole.
3. Allow the ruler to rest lightly on top of the valve.
4. Measure from the top of the valve to the top of the air horn casting at the opening. Refer to the Specifications Chart.
5. Adjust by bending the bowl vent valve operating lever.
6. Install a new plug and rap lightly to seat it, using a hammer.

Automatic Choke Adjustment

1. Loosen the choke cover retaining screws.
2. Turn the choke cover so that the index mark on the cover lines up with the specified mark on the choke housing.

CARTER AFB SPECIFICATIONS

CHRYSLER PRODUCTS

Year	Carb. Model ①	Float Level (in.)	Float Drop (in.)	Accelerator Pump Travel (in.)	Fast Idle ②	Choke Unloader (in.)	Secondary Throttle Lever (in.)	Secondary Throttle Lockout (in.)	Bowl Vent (in.)	Choke
1970	4742S	7/32	3/4	7/16	—	—	17/64	0.020	—	—
	4745S	7/32	3/4	7/16	50	1/4	17/64	0.020	3/4③	2 Rich
	4746S	7/32	3/4	7/16	50	1/4	17/64	0.020	3/4③	2 Rich
1971	4969S	7/32	3/4	31/64	—	1/4	17/64	0.020	3/4③	—
	4970S	7/32	3/4	31/64	50	1/4	17/64	0.020	3/4③	—
	4971S	7/32	3/4	31/64	50	—	17/64	0.020		—

① Model numbers are located on a tag or on the casting
② Indicates drill bit number. See Mechanic's Data
③ At curb idle

Holley Carburetors

Model 1920

On these units, the choke valve in the carburetor bore is connected to a well-type automatic choke.

The accelerator pump is a diaphragm, spring-driven type operated by a lever connected to the throttle shaft.

A two-stage power valve, mounted in the metering body and actuated by manifold vacuum, delivers additional fuel for full power and high speed operation.

This carburetor is used on 1971-73 six-cylinder engines.

Float Level Adjustment

NOTE: Do not allow the float tab to contact the float needle head during the adjustment procedure as the rubber tip of the needle can be compressed, giving a false reading.

Units through 1972

1. With the carburetor inverted, slide the special float gauge into position and test the setting on the "touch" leg of the gauge. The float should just touch the gauge.
2. Reverse the gauge and test the "no touch" leg. The float should just clear the gauge.
3. To adjust, bend the float tab which touches the head of the fuel inlet needle, using needle nose pliers.
4. This adjustment corresponds to a wet fuel level of 27/32 in., measured through the economizer opening from the top of the bowl.

1973 Units

1. With the carburetor inverted, measure from the top of the float to the upper wall of the main body with the gauge against the cast rib, approximately 2 in. from the float hinge pin.
2. Be sure that the gauge is parallel with the top of the float. Refer to the Specifications Chart for the proper dry float setting.
3. Adjust by bending the float tab which touches the head of the fuel needle using needle nosed pliers.

Float Bowl Vent Valve Adjustment

1. With the throttle valve closed, the bowl vent should be adjusted

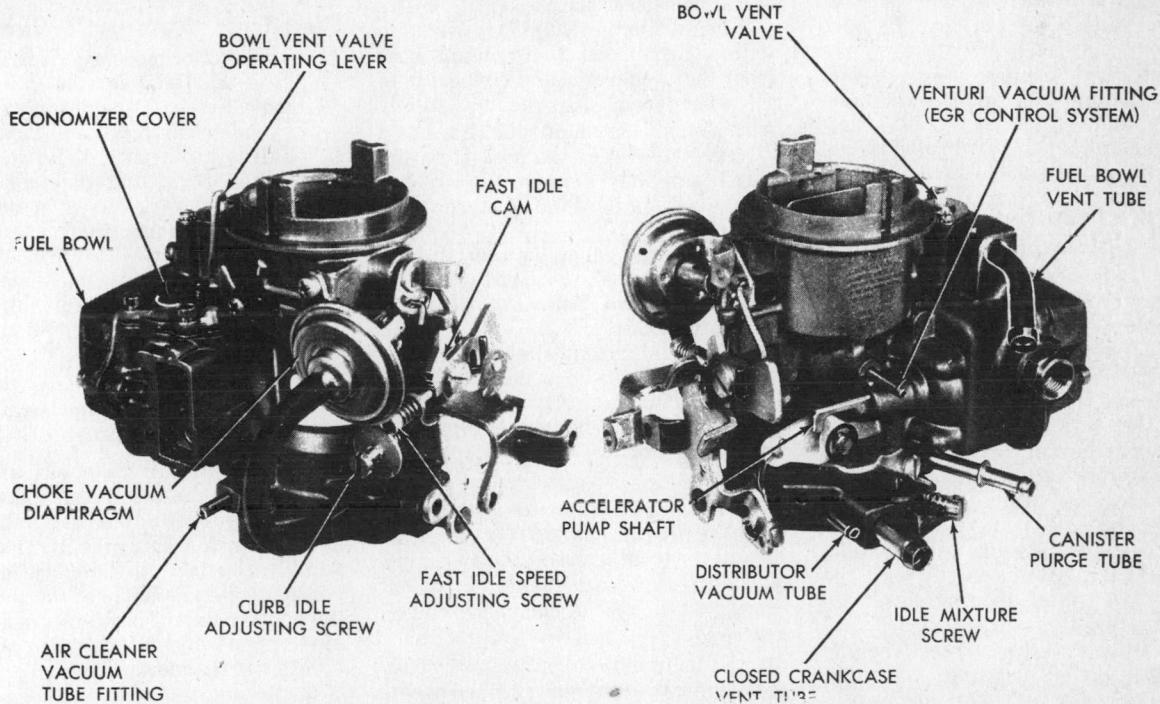

Carburetor assembly—Holley 1920

Adjusting the float level—Holley 1920

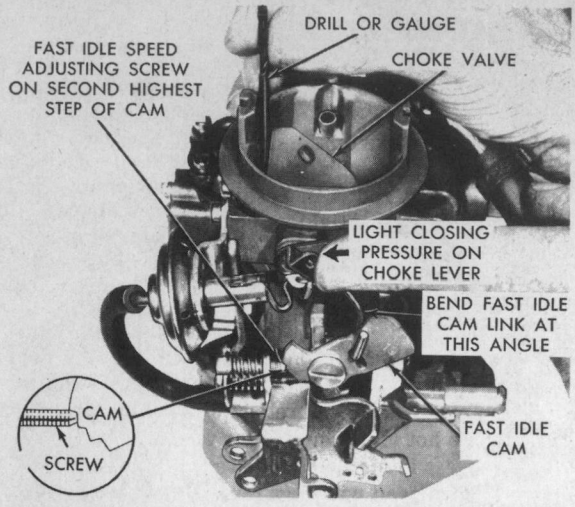

FAST IDLE SPEED ADJUSTING SCREW ON SECOND HIGHEST STEP OF CAM

DRILL OR GAUGE

CHOKE VALVE

LIGHT CLOSING PRESSURE ON CHOKE LEVER

BEND FAST IDLE CAM LINK AT THIS ANGLE

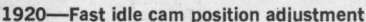
CAM SCREW

FAST IDLE CAM

1920—Fast idle cam position adjustment

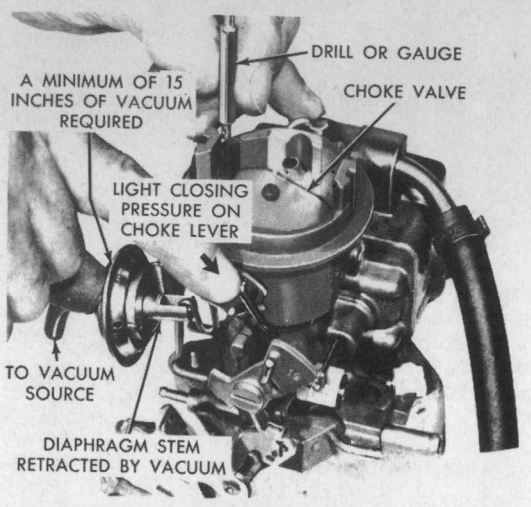

A MINIMUM OF 15 INCHES OF VACUUM REQUIRED

DRILL OR GAUGE

CHOKE VALVE

LIGHT CLOSING PRESSURE ON CHOKE LEVER

TO VACUUM SOURCE

DIAPHRAGM STEM RETRACTED BY VACUUM

Adjusting the choke vacuum kick—Holley 1920

so that the shank of a drill of the size listed in the Specifications Chart can be inserted between the bowl vent stem and the bowl vent rod.

2. Adjust by bending the bowl vent operating lever up or down as required.

3. Be sure that the vent rod does not bind in the guide after adjusting.

Fast Idle Cam Position and Choke Unloader Adjustment

1. With the fast idle speed adjusting screw contacting the second highest step on the fast idle cam, move the choke valve toward the closed position with light pressure on the choke shaft lever.

2. Insert the specified gauge between the top of the choke valve and the wall of the air horn. Refer to the Specifications Chart.

3. Adjust by bending the fast idle link at the lower angle, until the correct valve opening has been obtained.

NOTE: When the correct fast idle cam position adjustment has been made, the choke unloader (wide open kick) adjustment has also been obtained. No further adjustment is required.

Choke Vacuum Kick

NOTE: The test can be made on or off the vehicle.

1. If adjustments are to be made with the engine running, back off the fast idle speed screw until the choke can be closed to the kick position with the engine at curb idle.

2. Note the number of screw turns required so that fast idle can be returned to its original adjustment.

3. If an auxiliary vacuum source is to be used, open the throttle valve (engine not running) and move the choke to the closed position. Release the throttle first, then release the choke.

When using an auxiliary vacuum source, disconnect the vacuum hose from the carburetor and connect it to the hose from the vacuum supply with a small length of tube to act as a fitting. Removal of the hose from the diaphragm may damage the system. Apply a vacuum of 15 or more in. of mercury.

4. Insert the gauge between the top of the choke valve and the wall of the air horn. Refer to the Specifications Chart.

5. Apply sufficient closing pressure on the lever to which the choke rod attaches to provide a minimum choke valve opening without distortion of the diaphragm link.

NOTE: The cylindrical stem of the diaphragm extends as the internal spring is compressed. This spring must be fully compressed for proper measurement of the vacuum kick adjustment.

6. Adjustment is necessary if a slight drag is not obtained when removing the gauge. Shorten or lengthen the diaphragm link to obtain the correct choke valve opening. Length changes should be made by carefully opening or closing the U-bend in the link.

NOTE: Do not apply a twisting or bending force to the diaphragm.

7. After completion of adjustment, reinstall the vacuum hose onto the correct carburetor fitting.

8. Return the fast idle screw to its original location if disturbed. Make the following check. With no vacuum applied to the diaphragm, the choke valve should move freely between the open and closed positions. If the movement is not free, examine the linkage for misalignment or interfer-

ences caused by the bending operation.

Well-Type Automatic Choke

1. To function properly, it is important that all parts be clean and move freely. Other than an occasional cleaning, the choke requires no attention. However, it is important that the choke control unit work freely in the well and at the choke shaft.

2. Move the choke rod up and down to check for free movement on the pivot. If the unit binds, a new choke unit should be installed.

NOTE: This type of choke is serviced only as a unit. Do not attempt to repair or change the setting.

When installing the choke unit, be certain that the coil housing does not contact the sides of the well in the exhaust manifold. Any contact at this point will affect choke operation. Do not lubricate any parts of the choke or the control unit. This causes an accumulation of dirt which will result in binding of the mechanism.

Model 1945

The model 1945 carburetor is a concentric downdraft single barrel carburetor with an internal float bowl which completely surrounds the venturi. The unit uses dual nitrophyl floats which permit operation at extreme angles. It is used on 1974 and later six-cylinder engines.

Float Adjustment

1. Remove the float bowl cover and invert the bowl. Hold the retaining spring in place.

2. Place a straightedge across the surface of the bowl. It should just clear the toes of the floats by the specified measurement.

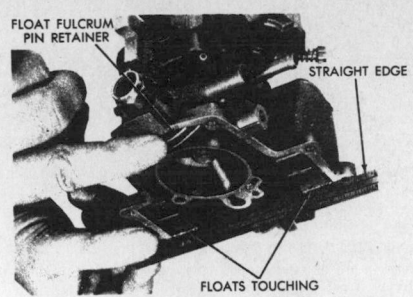

Checking the float adjustment—Holley 1945

3. If adjustment is necessary, bend the float tang to obtain the correct adjustment.

Fast Idle Adjustment

1. Remove the air cleaner and disconnect the vacuum lines to the heated air control and the OSAC (Orifice Spark Advance Control) valve. If there is no OSAC valve, disconnect the hose to the distributor and the EGR hose. Cap all carburetor vacuum fittings.
2. With the engine off, transmission in Neutral and the parking brake set, open the throttle and close the choke.
3. Close the throttle. This will place the fast idle speed screw on the highest step.
4. Move the fast idle cam until the screw drops to the second highest speed step.
5. Start the engine and stabilize the engine speed. Rotate the idle speed screw to obtain the specified setting. See Specifications Chart.

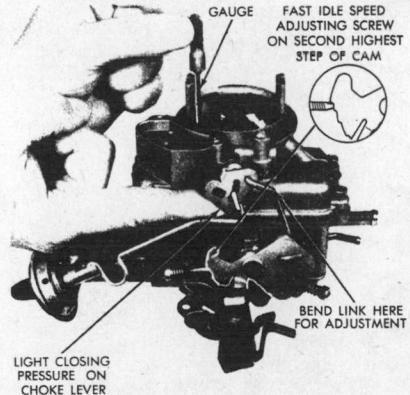

Checking the fast idle adjustment--Holley 1945

Choke Unloader Adjustment

1. Hold the throttle valves wide-open and insert the specified gauge between the upper edge of the choke valve and the inner wall of the air horn.
2. Place slight pressure against the control lever and attempt to remove the gauge. There should be a slight drag as the gauge is being withdrawn. If adjustment is necessary, bend the unloader

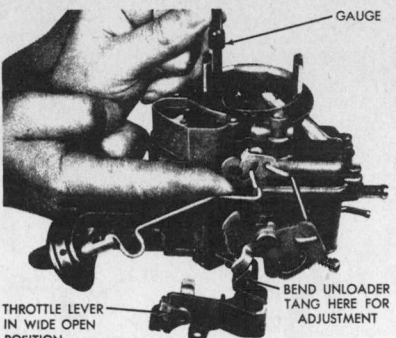

Choke unloader adjustment—Holley 1945

tang on the throttle lever until the correct opening has been obtained.

Choke Vacuum Kick Adjustment

1. With the engine running, back off the fast idle screw to allow the choke to close to the kick position with the engine at curb idle. Note the number of turns. If the adjustment is made with the engine stopped, open the throttle and move the choke to the closed position. Release the throttle first and then the choke.
2. If an auxiliary vacuum source is used, disconnect the vacuum hose from the carburetor and connect it to the hose from the vacuum supply with an extra length of tube. Apply a vacuum of 15 or more in. of mercury.
3. Insert the correct gauge (see Specifications Chart) between the choke valve and the wall of the air horn. Close and hold the choke rod lever with light pressure. The cylindrical stem of the diaphragm will extend as the internal spring is compressed. This spring must be fully compressed for proper measurement of the vacuum kick.
4. If adjustment is necessary, shorten or lengthen the diaphragm link to obtain the correct opening.

Caution Do not twist or bend the diaphragm.

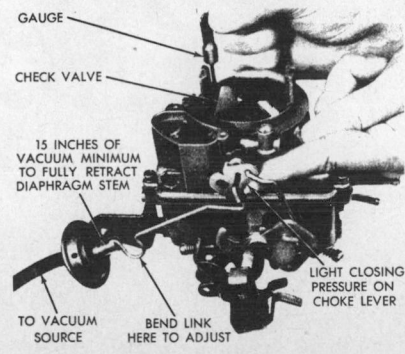

Choke vacuum kick adjustment—Holley 1945

5. Install the vacuum hose on the correct carburetor fitting and connect the fast idle linkage.
6. Check the operation in the following manner. With no vacuum applied to the diaphragm, the choke valve should move freely between the open and closed positions. If there is binding, examine the linkage for misalignment or interferences caused by bending.

Model 2210

This carburetor is a two-barrel unit but can be considered as two carburetors built side by side into one unit, utilizing the same fuel and air inlets. Each throat of the carburetor has its own throttle valve and main metering systems and are supplemented by the float, accelerating, idle, and power systems. The 1970 version is equipped with a distributor ground switch which retards the distributor when the carburetor is at curb idle, resulting in better emission control.

The 1971 version is equipped with a hot idle compensator valve which is a thermostatically operated air bleed to relieve an over-rich condition at idle. Units beginning 1971 have a bowl vent valve tube which works in conjunction with the vent valve. In 1973, an extra port for use with the (EGR) Exhaust Gas Recirculation system was added.

This carburetor is used on some 1971 383 and all 1972-73 400 two-barrel engines.

Float Adjustment

1. Invert the air horn so that the weight of the float only is forcing the needle against the seat.
2. Measure the clearance between the top of the float and the float stop.
3. Be sure the drill gauge is perfectly level when measuring. Adjust by bending the float lip toward or away from the needle, using a narrow blade screwdriver, until the correct clearance of the setting has been obtained.

Float Drop Adjustment

1. Check the float drop by holding the air horn in an upright position.
2. The bottom edge of the float should be parallel to the underside surface of the air horn.
3. Adjust by bending the tang on the float arm.

Fast Idle Cam Position Adjustment

1. With the fast idle speed adjusting screw contacting the second highest step on the fast idle cam,

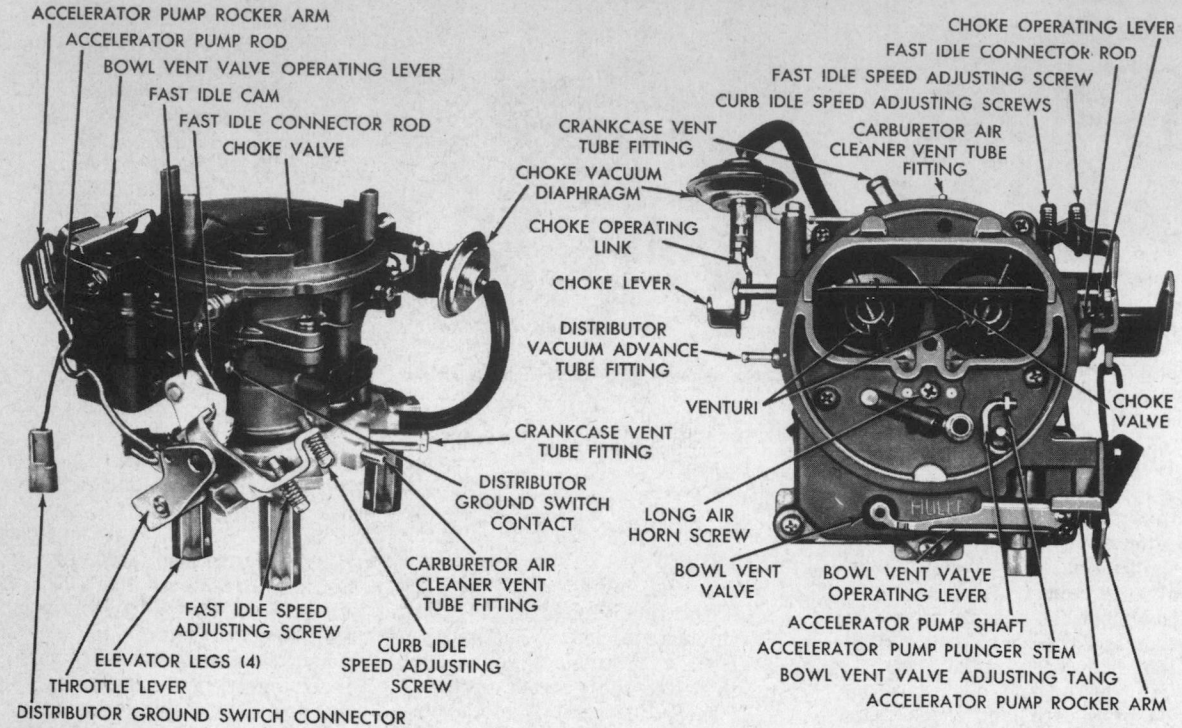

Carburetor assembly—Holley 2210

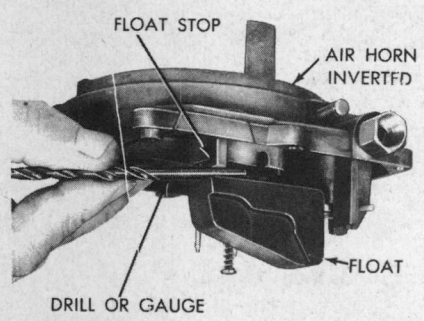

Checking the float adjustment—Holley 2210

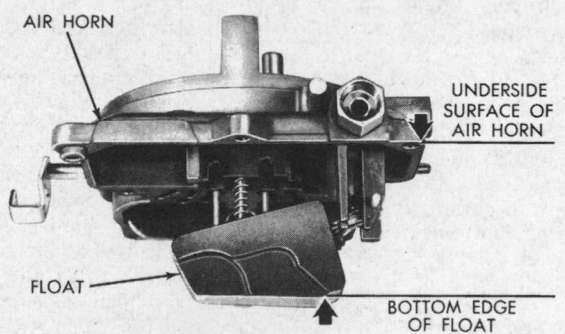

FLOAT SHOULD BE PARALLED

Checking the float drop—Holley 2210

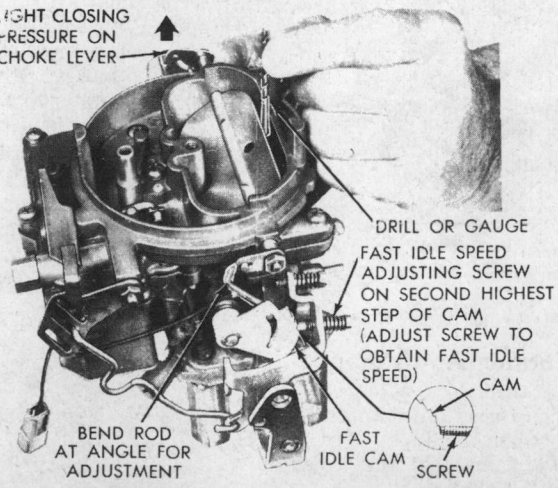

2210—Fast idle cam position adjustment

move the choke valve toward the closed position with light pressure on the choke shaft lever.

2. Insert the specified gauge between the top of the choke valve and the wall of the air horn. Refer to the Specifications Chart.

3. An adjustment will be necessary if a slight drag is not obtained as the drill shank is being removed.

4. Adjust by bending the fast idle link at the angle.

Choke Vacuum Kick Adjustment

NOTE: The test can be made on or off the vehicle.

1. If the adjustment is to be made with the engine running, disconnect the fast idle linkage to allow the choke to close to the kick position.

2. If an auxiliary vacuum source is to be used, open the throttle valve (engine not running) and move the choke to the closed position. Release the throttle first, then release the choke.

When using an auxiliary vacuum source, disconnect the vacuum hose from the carburetor and connect it to the hose from the vacuum supply with a small length of tube to act as a fitting. Removal of the hose from the

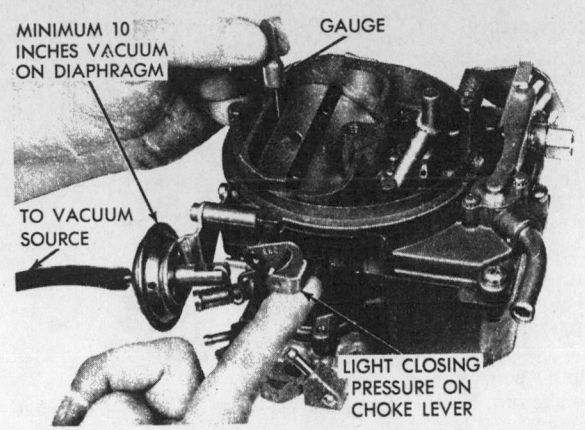

2210—Vacuum kick adjustment

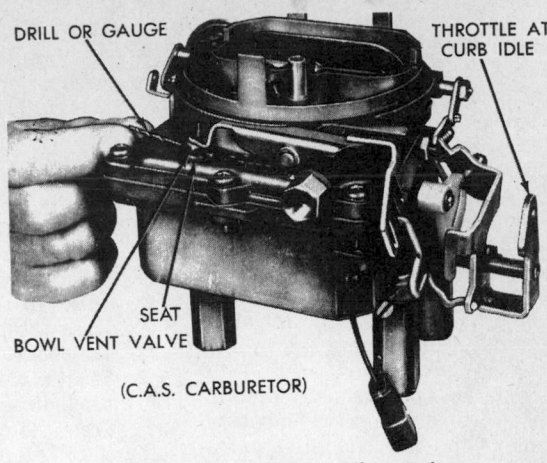

(C.A.S. CARBURETOR)

2210—Choke unloader adjustment

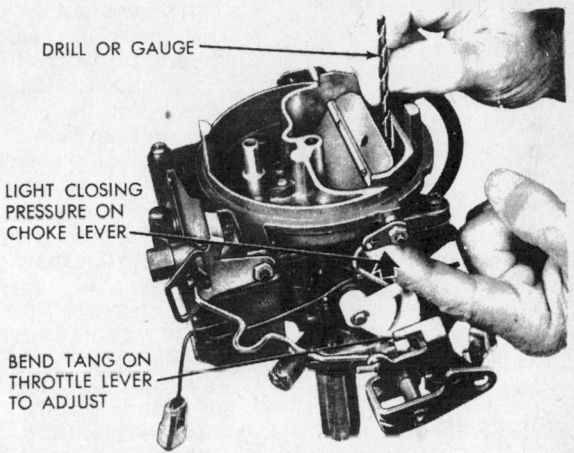

2210—Bowl vent valve adjustment

diaphragm may require forces which could damage the system. Apply a vacuum of 10 or more in. of mercury.

3. Insert the gauge between the top of the choke valve and the wall of the air horn. Refer to the Specifications Chart.

4. Apply sufficient closing pressure on the lever to which the choke rod attaches, to provide a minimum choke valve opening without distortion of the diaphragm link.

NOTE: The cylindrical stem of the diaphragm extends as the internal spring is compressed. This spring must be fully compressed for proper measurement of the vacuum kick adjustment.

5. Adjustment is necessary if a slight drag is not obtained when removing the gauge. Shorten or lengthen the diaphragm link to obtain the correct choke valve opening. Length changes should be made by carefully opening or closing the U-bend provided in the link. Improper bending causes contact between the U-section and the diaphragm assembly.

NOTE: Do not apply a twisting or bending force to diaphragm.

6. After completing adjustments, reinstall the vacuum hose on the correct carburetor fitting.

7. Return the fast idle linkage to its original location if it was disturbed. Make the following check. With no vacuum applied to the diaphragm, the choke valve should move freely between the open and closed positions. If the movement is not free, examine the linkage for misalignment or interferences caused by the bending operation.

Choke Unloader (Wide Open Kick) Adjustment

1. With the throttle valve in the wide open position, insert a drill gauge between the upper edge of

the choke valve and the inner wall of the air horn. Refer to the Specifications Chart.

2. With a finger lightly pressing against the shaft lever, a slight drag should be felt as the drill is being withdrawn.

3. Adjust by bending the unloader tang on the throttle lever until the correct opening has been obtained.

Accelerator Pump Adjustment

1. Back off the curb idle speed adjusting screw.

2. Open the choke valve so that the fast idle cam allows the throttle valves to be completely seated in the bores.

3. Be sure that the pump connector rod is installed in the correct slot of the accelerator pump rocker arm. The slot for manual transmissions is next to the retaining nut.

4. Close the throttle valves tightly. Measure the distance between the top of the air horn and the end of the plunger shaft. Refer to the Specifications Chart.

5. Adjust by bending the pump operating rod at the loop of the rod.

Bowl Vent Valve Clearance Adjustment

1. With the throttle valves at curb idle, it should be possible to insert a gauge between the bowl vent valve plunger stem and the operating rod. Refer to the Specifications Chart.

2. Adjust by bending the tang on the pump lever to change the arc of contact with the throttle lever.

Model 2245

The model 2245 carburetor is a two barrel unit used on 1974 and later Chrysler products with 360 or 400 cubic inch engines. The carburetor uses 4 fuel metering systems. The Idle and idle enrichment System provides the correct mixture for idle and high-speed performance; the Accelerator Pump System furnishes additional fuel during acceleration; the Main Metering System gives an economical mixture for normal cruising conditions; and the Power Enrichment System enriches the mixture when high power output is desired.

Float Adjustment

1. Invert the air horn so that the

weight of the float is forcing the metering needle against its seat.

2. Measure the distance from the top of the float and the float stop. The clearance should be the same as given in the Specifications Chart. Make certain that the gauge is level when making the measurement.

3. If adjustment is necessary, bend the float adjusting tab toward or away from the needle until the correct clearance is obtained. A narrow-bladed screwdriver may be used to bend the tab.

4. Check the float drop by holding the air horn upright. The bottom edge of the float should be parallel to the underside of the air horn. If an adjustment is necessary, bend the tang on the float arm.

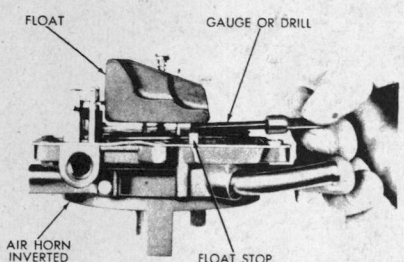

Adjusting the float—Holley 2245

Fast Idle Cam Position Adjustment

1. Position the fast idle speed adjusting screw on the second highest notch on the fast idle cam. Move the choke valve toward the closed position by applying light pressure on the choke shaft lever.

2. Insert the correct gauge (see Specifications Chart) between the top of the choke vale and the wall of the air horn. An adjustment will be necessary if there is not a slight drag when the gauge is removed.

3. If an adjustment is necessary, bend the fast idle connector rod at the angle.

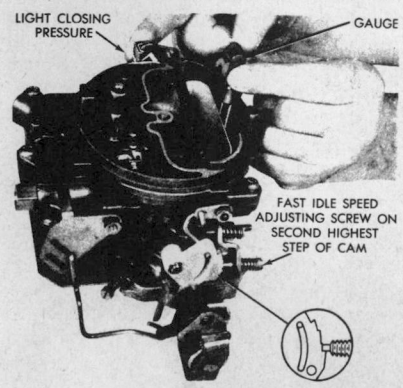

Adjusting the fast idle cam—Holley 2245

Vacuum Kick Adjustment

1. The adjustment must be made with some type of vacuum source. If the adjustment is made with the engine running, disconnect the fast idle linkage to allow the choke to close to the kick position with the engine at curb idle. If an auxiliary vacuum source is to be used, open the throttle valves and move the choke to the closed position. Release the throttle first and then the choke.

2. If an auxiliary vacuum source is used, disconnect the vacuum hose from the carburetor and connect it to the hose from the vacuum supply with a small length of extra hose. Apply a vacuum of 15 or more in. of mercury.

3. Insert the correct gauge (see Specifications Chart) between the top of the choke valve and the wall of the air horn. Apply pressure to the lever to which the choke rod attaches without distorting the diaphragm link. The cylindrical stem of the diaphragm will extend as the internal spring is compressed. This spring must be fully compressed for proper measurement of the vacuum kick adjustment.

4. If a slight drag is not felt when the gauge is removed, adjustment is necessary. Adjust the diaphragm link to obtain the correct choke valve opening. Adjustments can be made by carefully opening or closing the U-bend in the link.

Caution Do not twist or bend the diaphragm.

5. Connect the vacuum hose to the correct carburetor fitting. Replace the linkage.

6. Make the following check. With no vacuum source attached to the diaphragm, the choke valve should move freely between open and closed positions. If the movement is not free, examine the linkage for misalignment or interferences caused by the bending operation.

Choke Unloader (Wide Open Kick) Adjustment

1. Place the throttle valves in the wide-open position and insert the proper gauge (see Specifications Chart) between the upper edge of the choke valve and the inner wall of the air horn.

2. While holding pressure on the shaft lever, a slight drag should be felt as the gauge is removed.

3. If an adjustment is necessary, bend the unloader tang on the throttle lever until the correct opening has been obtained.

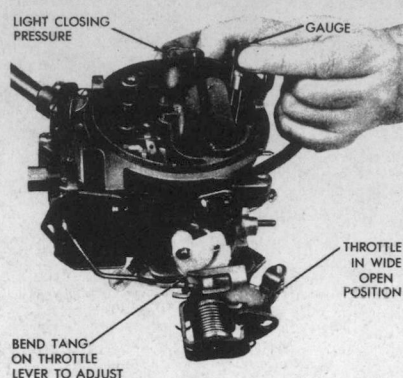

Adjusting the choke unloader—Holley 2245

Accelerator Pump Adjustment

Through 1975

1. Back off the curb idle adjusting screw and open the choke valve so that the fast idle cam allows the throttle valves to be completely seated in their bores.

NOTE: Make certain that the pump connector rod is placed in the correct slot of the accelerator pump rocker arm. On manual transmission models, it is the first slot next to the retaining nut.

2. Close the throttle valves and measure the distance from the top of the air horn to the end of the plunger shaft. See Specifications Chart.

3. If adjustment is needed, bend the pump operating rod at its loop until the correct setting has been obtained.

1976 and Later

1. Make sure that the pump connector rod is in the first slot next to the retaining nut of the pump arm on 360 engines, and in the second slot for the 400.

2. Measure the drop of the pump plunger between curb idle and wide open throttle.

3. Adjust the travel by bending the operating rod.

Bowl Vent Valve Clearance

1. With the throttle valves set at curb idle, insert the specified gauge between the bowl vent valve plunger stem and the operating rod.

Adjusting the bowl vent clearance—Holley 2245

2. If the gauge does not fit, bend the tang on the pump lever until the correct clearance has been obtained.

Model 2300

The 2300 carburetor is used only in a triple installation through 1972. This system utilizes two types of Holley two-barrels, one mounted in the center and the two secondaries mounted fore and aft. The secondary units contain all the regulatory systems with the exception of chokes, power enrichment valve, accelerating pump, idle system and spark advance. The throttle operation of the primary carburetor is conventional whereas the secondary units are equipped with throttle control vacuum diaphragms for the purpose of opening the secondary throttles which close mechanically. The choke used only on the primary unit is controlled by a temperature sensing choke coil mounted on the intake manifold, over the exhaust crossover passage.

The only adjustments required on the secondary units are the float level and the wet fuel level. All other adjustments are made on the primary unit.

Float Adjustment

1. Make a preliminary float adjustment by inverting the fuel bowl and turning the adjustable needle and seat until the float is centered in the bowl.
2. Do not fully tighten the lock screw. Snug the screw to temporarily retain adjustment.

NOTE: Final adjustment of the float is made on the vehicle.

Wet Fuel Level

1. With the car level and the engine idling, remove the sight plug from the fuel bowl.

NOTE: The fuel pump pressure must be at least 5 psi.

2. The fuel level should be in line with the threads at the bottom of the sight plug hole. Fuel should dribble out slowly.

Caution *Use a cloth to catch the excess fuel. Discard it safely.*

3. To adjust, loosen the lock screw and turn the adjusting nut as required to raise or lower the fuel level.

Automatic Choke Control Lever Setting

Adjustment of the choke control lever is necessary to provide the correct relationship between the choke valve, the thermostatic coil spring, and the fast idle cam. It should be checked and adjusted (if necessary), as preparation of the choke system linkage before making the Vacuum Kick, Cam Position, or Unloader adjustment. These three adjustments must be made after adjustment of the choke control lever.

NOTE: Improper bending of the choke rod will result in binding.

Chevrolet

1. Close the choke rod by applying slight pressure on the choke control lever; the thermostatic choke rod should be even with the top of the choke rod hole.
2. Adjust by bending the choke rod at the upper angle.

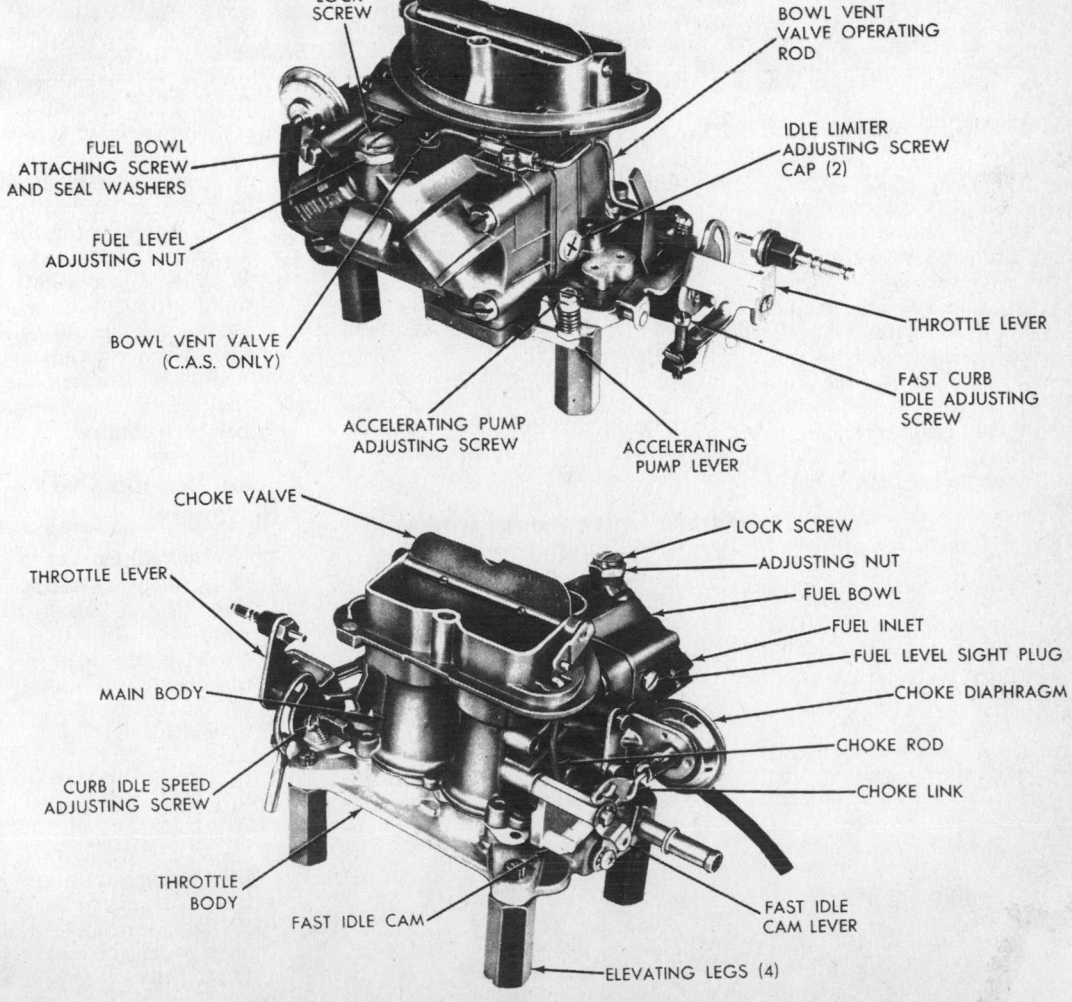

Carburetor assembly—Holley 2300

Adjusting 2300 fuel level on vehicle

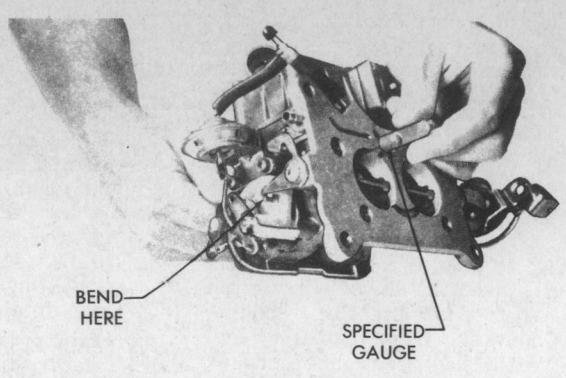

2300—Fast idle cam adjustment, Chevrolet

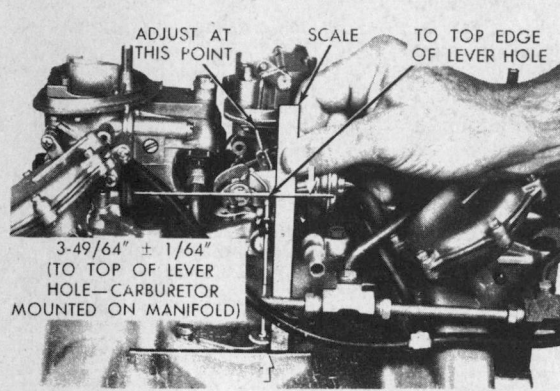

Adjusting the 2300 choke control lever

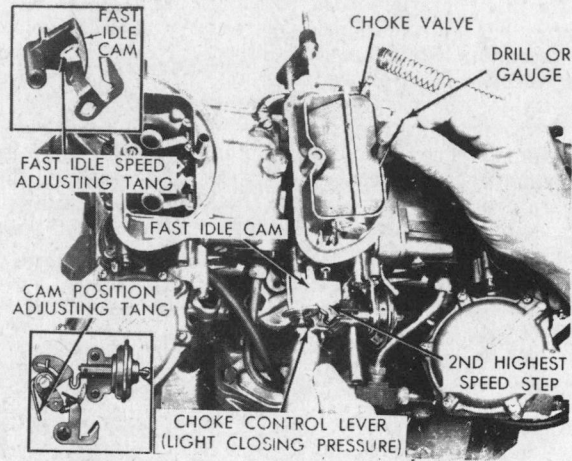

2300—Fast idle cam position adjustment, Chrysler

Chrysler

1. Open the throttle to mid-position; close the choke valve by applying slight pressure on the choke control lever.
2. The top of choke rod hole in the control lever should be 3 49/64 in. above the choke pad with the carburetor on the engine, or 1 23/32 in. above the carburetor base with the carburetor on a bench.
3. Adjust by bending the choke shaft rod.

Fast Idle Cam Position Adjustment

Chevrolet

1. With the throttle slightly open, close the choke plate positioning fast idle lever against the top step of the fast idle cam.
2. Adjust the fast idle screw to obtain the clearance listed in the Specifications Chart between the throttle valve and the bore on the idle transfer slot side of the carburetor.
3. Adjust by bending the idle lever.

Chrysler

1. With the fast idle speed adjusting screw contacting the second highest step on the fast idle cam,

move the choke valve toward the closed position with light pressure on the choke control lever.
2. Insert the specified gauge between the top of the choke valve and the wall of the air horn. Refer to the Specifications Chart.
3. An adjustment will be necessary if a slight drag is not obtained as the drill shank is being removed.
4. Adjust by bending the cam position adjusting tang.

Choke Unloader Adjustment (Wide Open Kick)

Chevrolet

1. Hold the throttle lever in the wide open throttle position with a rubber band.
2. Hold the choke valve toward the closed position against the unloader tang of the throttle shaft, then measure the opening between the choke valve lower edge and the main body. Refer to the Specifications Chart.
3. Adjust by bending the choke rod (at the off-set bend).

Chrysler

1. Hold the throttle valves in the wide-open position.
2. Insert the specified drill between

the upper edge of the choke valve and the inner wall of the air horn. Refer to the Specifications Chart.
3. With a finger lightly pressing against the choke control lever, a slight drag should be felt as the drill is being withdrawn.
4. Adjust by bending the indicated tang until the correct opening has been obtained.

Choke Vacuum Kick Adjustment

Chevrolet

1. With the choke valve closed, hold the vacuum break against the stop.
2. Measure the distance between the choke valve lower edge and the main body. Refer to the Specifications Chart.

Chrysler

NOTE: The test can be made on or off the vehicle.
1. If adjustment is to be made with the engine running, position the fast idle tang (cam position adjustment) to allow the choke to close to the kick position.
2. If an auxiliary vacuum source is to be used, open the throttle valve (engine not running) and

move the choke to the closed position. Release the throttle first, then release the choke.

When using an auxiliary vacuum source, disconnect the vacuum hose from the carburetor and connect it to the hose from the vacuum supply with a small length of tube to act as a fitting. Removal of the hose from the diaphragm may require forces which damage the diaphragm. Apply a vacuum of 10 or more in. of mercury.

3. Insert the gauge between the top of the choke valve and the wall of the air horn. Refer to the Specifications Chart.

4. Apply sufficient closing pressure on the lever to which the choke rod attaches to provide a minimum choke valve opening without distortion of the diaphragm link.

NOTE: The cylindrical stem of the diaphragm extends as the internal spring is compressed for proper measurement of the vacuum kick adjustment.

5. Adjustment is necessary if a slight drag is not obtained when removing the gauge. Shorten or lengthen the diaphragm link to obtain the correct choke valve opening. Length changes should be made by carefully opening or closing the U-bend provided in the link. Improper bending causes contact between the U-section and the diaphragm assembly.

NOTE: Do not apply a twisting or bending force to the diaphragm.

6. After completion of adjustment, reinstall the vacuum hose onto the correct carburetor fitting.

7. Return the fast idle screw to its original location if it was disturbed. Make the following check. With no vacuum applied to the diaphragm, the choke valve should move freely between the open and closed positions. If the movement is not free, examine the linkage for misalignment or interferences caused by the bending operation.

Fast Idle Speed Adjustment (On Vehicle)

1. Open the throttle slightly with the engine off. Close the choke valve until the fast idle screw tang can be positioned on the second highest-speed step of the fast idle cam.

2. Start the engine and determine the stabilized speed.

3. Bend the fast idle tang by use of a screwdriver placed in the tang slot to secure the specified speed. Refer to the Specifications Chart.

NOTE: Bend it only in a direction perpendicular to the contact surface of the cam. Movement in any other direction changes the cam position adjustment. Bend it only when the tang is clear of the cam. Stopping the engine between adjustments is not necessary. However, reposition the fast idle tang on the cam after each speed adjustment to provide correct throttle closing torque.

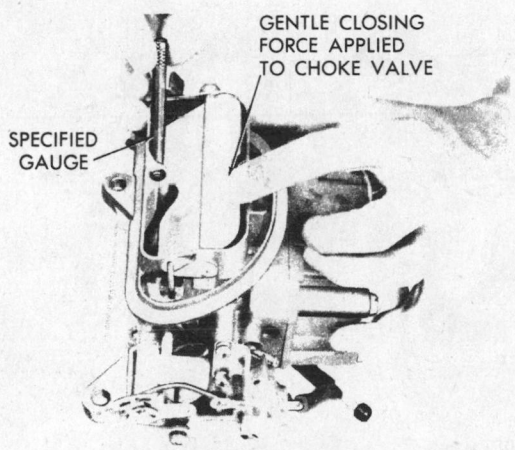

2300—Choke unloader adjustment—wide open kick, Chevrolet

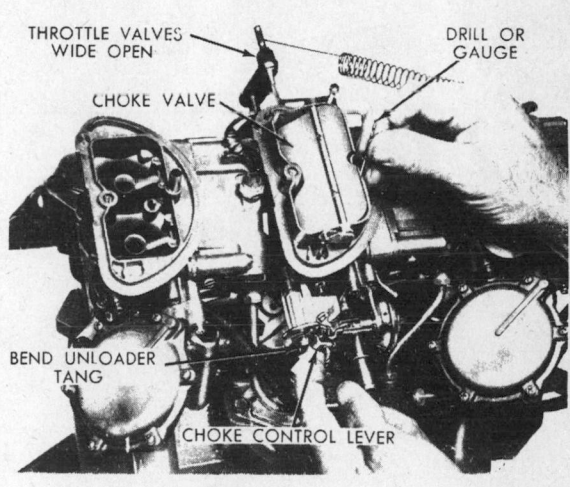

2300—Choke unloader adjustment—wide open kick, Chrysler

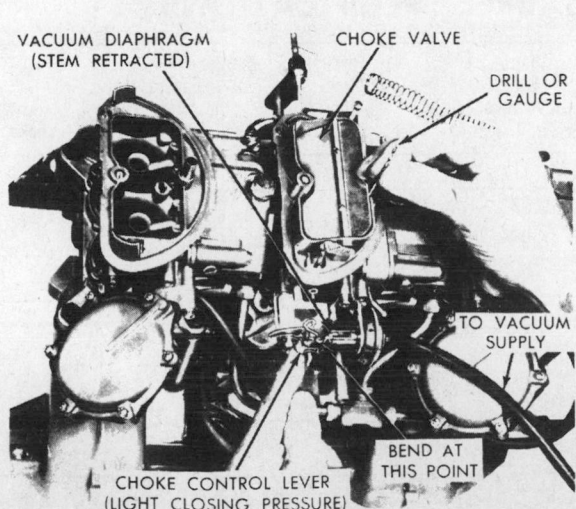

2300—Choke vacuum kick adjustment, Chrysler

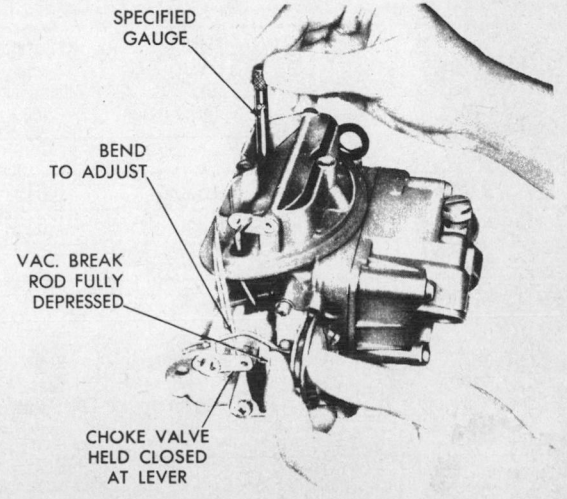

2300—Choke vacuum kick adjustment, Chevrolet

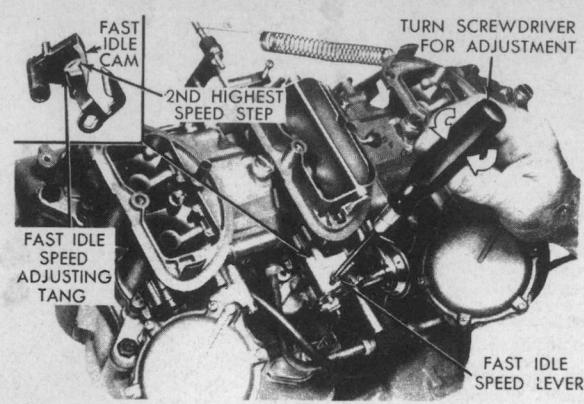

2300—Fast idle speed adjustment on the vehicle

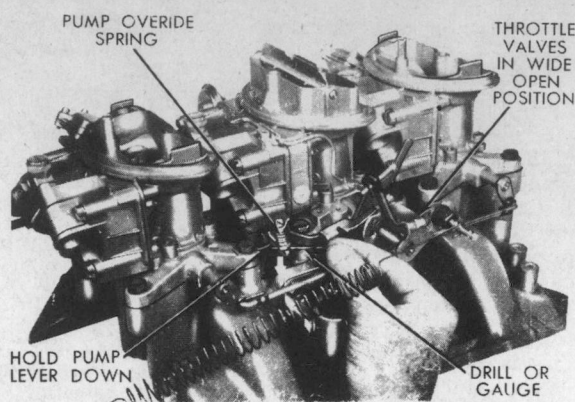

Checking the 2300 accelerator pump lever adjustment, Chrysler

Accelerator Pump Adjustment

1. With the throttle lever in the wide open position and the pump lever fully compressed (down), measure the clearance between the spring adjusting nut and the arm of the pump lever. Refer to Specifications Chart. It should be a minimum of 0.015 in. and a maximum of 0.063 in.

2. Adjust by turning the nut or screw as required while holding the opposite end. (The pump operating lever is not threaded.) There should be no free movement of the pump lever when the throttle is at curb idle.

Bowl Vent Valve Adjustment

1. With the throttle valves at fast curb idle, insert the drill gauge between the bowl vent valve and the bowl vent rod with the fast curb idle speed properly set. Refer to the Specifications Chart.

2. Adjust by bending the rod to change the arc of contact with the throttle lever, until the correct clearance has been obtained.

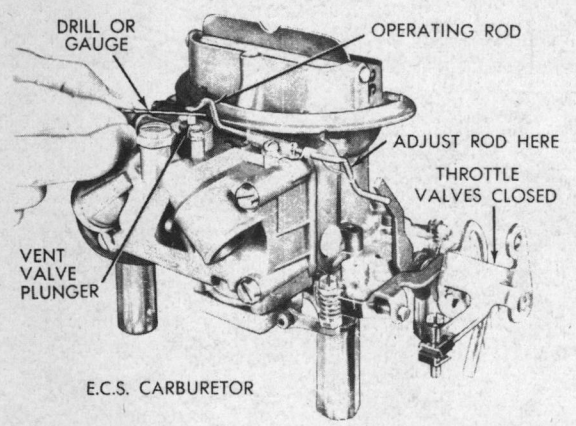

E.C.S. CARBURETOR

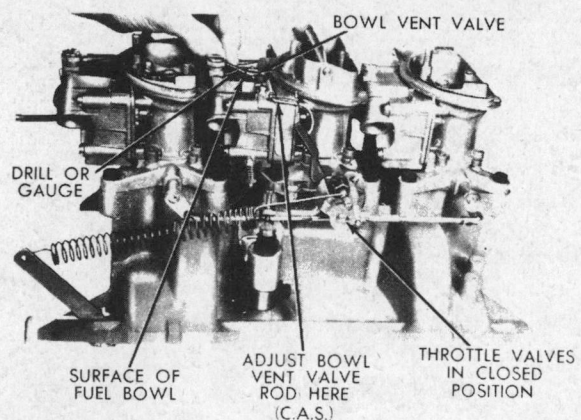

Checking the 2300 bowl vent valve adjustment

HOLLEY ONE AND TWO BARREL SPECIFICATIONS

Year	Carb. Part No. ⑦	Float Level Dry (in.)	Accelerator Pump Adjustment (in.)	Bowl Vent Clearance (in.)	Fast Idle On Car (rpm)	Choke Unloader Clearance (in.)	Choke
CHEVROLET							
1970	R4055-A	0.350	0.015	0.085	2200	0.250	⑥
	R4056-A	0.350	0.015	0.085	2200	0.250	⑥
	A3659-A	0.350	—	—			

Year	Carb. Part No. ⑦	Float Level (in.)	Accelerator Pump Adjustment (in.)	Bowl Vent Clearance (in.)	Fast Idle (rpm)	Choke Unloader Clearance (in.)	Vacuum Kick (in.)	Fast Idle Cam Position (in.)	Choke
CHRYSLER PRODUCTS									
1970	R-4351-A	See Text	⑥	$3/32$	1600②	⑤	#39	#52	2 Rich
	R-4352-A	See Text	⑥	$3/32$	1800②	⑤	#50	#52	2 Rich

HOLLEY ONE AND TWO BARREL SPECIFICATIONS

CHRYSLER PRODUCTS

Year	Carb. Part No. ⑦	Float Level (in.)	Accelerator Pump Adjustment (in.)	Bowl Vent Clearance (in.)	Fast Idle (rpm)	Choke Unloader Clearance (in.)	Vacuum Kick (in.)	Fast Idle Cam Position (in.)	Choke
1970	R-4353-A	See Text	⑥	3/32	1600②	⑤	#39	#52	2 Rich
	R-4354-A	See Text	⑥	3/32	1800②	⑤	#50	#52	2 Rich
	R-4355-A	See Text	⑥	3/32	1700②	⑤	#39	#52	2 Rich
	R-4363-A	See Text	⑥	3/32	1700②	⑤	#39	#52	2 Rich
	R-4371-A	0.200	——	5/64	1700②	11/64	#28	#35	2 Rich
	R-4175-AF	③	——	——	——	——	——	——	——
	R-4144-A	③	0.015	0.101	1800	5/32	#50	#53	2 Rich
	R-4365-AR	③	——	——	——	——	——	——	——
	R-4374-A	③	0.015	0.101	2200	5/32	#28	#53	2 Rich
	R-4375-A	③	0.015	0.101	2200	5/32	#28	#53	2 Rich
	R-4376-A	③	0.015	0.101	1800	5/32	#50	#53	2 Rich
	R-4382-AF	③	——	——	——	——	——	——	——
	R-4383-AR	③	——	——	——	——	——	——	——
1971	R-4655-A	See Text	——	1/32	1600	9/32	#39	#52	2 Rich
	R-4656-A	See Text	——	1/32	1900	9/32	#39	#52	2 Rich
	R-4659-A	See Text	——	1/32	1800	9/32	#39	#52	2 Rich
	R-6363-A	See Text	——	1/64	2000	9/32	——	——	2 Rich
	R-6364-A	See Text	——	1/64	1900	9/32	——	——	2 Rich
	R-4373-A	0.200	9/16	5/64	1700	11/64	0.141	0.110	2 Rich
	R-4665-A	0.200	9/16	0.015	1800	1/4	#28	#35	2 Rich
	R-4666-A	0.200	9/16	0.015	1800	1/4	#30	#35	2 Rich
	R-4669-A	③	0.015-0.063	0.102	1800	5/32	0.141	0.060	2 Rich
	R-4670-A	③	0.015-0.063	0.102	1800	5/32	0.700	0.060	2 Rich
	R-4671-A	③	——	——	——	——	——	——	——
	R-4672-A	③	——	——	——	——	——	——	——
	R-4789-A	③	——	——	——	——	——	——	——
	R-4790-A	③	——	——	——	——	——	——	——
	R-4791-A	③	0.015	0.101	2600	5/32	#28	#53	On Index
	R-4792-A	③	0.015	0.101	2800	5/32	#39	#53	On Index
1972	R-6153-A	See Text	——	0.015	2000	⑤	0.100	0.064	Fixed
	R-6154-A	See Text	——	0.015	2000	⑤	0.100	0.064	Fixed
	R-6155-A	See Text	——	0.015	2000	⑤	0.100	0.064	Fixed
	R-6156-A	See Text	——	0.015	1900	⑤	0.100	0.064	Fixed
	R-6159-A	See Text	——	0.015	1900	⑤	0.100	0.064	Fixed
	R-6363-A	See Text	——	0.015	2000	⑤	0.100	0.064	Fixed
	R-6364-A	See Text	——	0.015	1900	⑤	0.100	0.064	Fixed
	R-6365-A	See Text	——	0.015	2000	⑤	0.100	0.064	Fixed
	R-6366-A	See Text	——	0.015	2000	⑤	0.100	0.064	Fixed
	R-6162-A	0.180	0.285	0.015	1900	0.170	0.100	0.064	Fixed
	R-6164-A	0.180	0.250	0.015	2000	0.170	0.100	0.064	Fixed
	R-6368-A	0.180	0.285	0.015	1900	0.170	0.100	0.110	Fixed
	R-6370-A	0.180	0.285	0.015	2000	0.170	0.100	0.110	Fixed
	R-6404-A	③	0.015-0.063	0.015	1800	0.150	0.070	0.060	Fixed
	R-6405-A	③	——	——	——	——	——	——	——
	R-6406-A	③	——	——	——	——	——	——	——
1973	R-6447-A	0.260	——	0.015	2000	⑤	0.100	0.065	Fixed

HOLLEY ONE AND TWO BARREL SPECIFICATIONS

CHRYSLER PRODUCTS

Year	Carb. Part No. ⑦	Float Level (in.)	Accelerator Pump Adjustment (in.)	Bowl Vent Clearance (in.)	Fast Idle (rpm)	Choke Unloader Clearance (in.)	Vacuum Kick (in.)	Fast Idle Cam Position (in.)	Choke
1973	R-6448-A	0.260	——	0.015	1700	⑤	0.080	0.045	Fixed
	R-6593-A	0.260	——	0.015	2000	⑤	0.100	0.065	Fixed
	R-6594-A	0.260	——	0.015	1700	⑤	0.100	0.065	Fixed
	R-6595-A	0.260	——	0.015	2000	⑤	0.100	0.065	Fixed
	R-6596-A	0.260	——	0.015	1700	⑤	0.100	0.065	Fixed
	R-6452-A	0.180	0.250	0.015	1900	0.170	0.150	0.110	Fixed
	R-6454-A	0.180	0.250	0.015	1800	0.170	0.150	0.110	Fixed
	R-6472-A	0.180	0.250	0.015	1800	0.170	0.150	0.110	Fixed
	R-6575-A	0.180	0.250	0.015	1900	0.170	0.150	0.110	Fixed
1974	R-6721-A	3/64	11/16	——	1600	0.250	0.140	0.080	Fixed
	R-6722-A	3/64	13/16	——	1800	0.250	0.090	0.080	Fixed
	R-6723-A	3/64	11/16	——	1600	0.250	0.140	0.080	Fixed
	R-6724-A	3/64	3/4	——	1800	0.250	0.080	0.080	Fixed
	R-6725-A	3/64	3/4	——	1600	0.250	0.140	0.080	Fixed
	R-6726-A	3/64	3/4	——	1800	0.250	0.090	0.080	Fixed
	R-6731-A	0.180	0.255	0.015	1800	0.170	0.150	0.110	Fixed
	R-6990-A	0.180	0.255	0.015	1600	0.170	0.150	0.110	Fixed
	R-7139-A	0.180	0.255	0.015	1600	0.170	0.150	0.110	Fixed
1975	R-7329-A	3/64	2-7/32	——	1700	0.250	0.130	0.080	Fixed
	R-7017-A	3/64	2-7/32	——	1600	0.250	0.130	0.080	Fixed
	R-7018-A	3/64	2-21/64	——	1700	0.250	0.090	0.080	Fixed
	R-7019-A	3/64	2-7/32	——	1600	0.250	0.130	0.080	Fixed
	R-7020-A	3/64	2-21/64	——	1700	0.250	0.090	0.080	Fixed
	R-7029-A	3/64	2-7/32	——	1600	0.250	0.130	0.080	Fixed
	R-7210-A	3/64	2-21/64	——	1700	0.250	0.090	0.080	Fixed
	R-7226-A	3/16	1/4	0.015	1600	0.170	0.150	0.110	Fixed
	R-7211-A	3/16	1/4	0.015	1600	0.170	0.150	0.110	Fixed
	R-7027-A	3/16	1/4	0.015	1600	0.170	0.150	0.110	Fixed
1976	R-7356A	⑨	2-7/32	1/16	1600	0.250	0.110	0.080	Fixed
	R-7357A	⑨	2-21/32	1/16	1700	0.250	0.100	0.080	Fixed
	R-7360A	⑨	2-7/32	——	1600	0.250	0.110	0.080	Fixed
	R-7361A	3/64	2-21/32	——	1700	0.250	0.100	0.080	Fixed
	R-7362A	3/64	2-7/32	——	1600	0.250	0.110	0.080	Fixed
	R-7363A	3/64	2-21/32	——	1700	0.250	0.100	0.080	Fixed
	R-7364A	3/16	17/64	0.025	1600	0.170	0.150	0.110	Fixed
	R-7366A	3/16	17/64	0.025	1600	0.170	0.150	0.110	Fixed

① Not used
② Engine hot and on the highest step of the cam
③ Center the float in the bowl with the bowl inverted for preliminary adjustment; then set wet level to bottom of sight plug opening
④ Not used
⑤ Unloader automatically set when the fast idle cam is adjusted

⑥ Seasonal setting, the long stroke hole for winter, the short stroke hole for summer
⑦ Located on the tag attached to the carburetor or on the casting
⑧ Engine hot and screw on the second step of the cam
⑨ Flush with top of bowl cover gasket
—— Not applicable

Model 5210

The Holley 5210 is a progressive two barrel carburetor with a new automatic choke system which is activated by a water heated thermostatic coil. It also has an exhaust gas recirculation system with the valve located in the intake manifold. It is used on General Motors four-cylinder engines.

Float Level

1. With the carburetor air horn inverted, and the float tang resting lightly on the inlet needle, insert the specified drill bit between the air horn and the float.
2. Bend the float tang if an adjustment is needed.

Float Drop

1. With the air horn right side up, measure between the air horn and the top of the float.
2. Bend the float tang if an adjustment is needed.

Fast Idle Cam Adjustments

1. Place the fast idle screw on the second step of the fast idle cam and against the shoulder of the high step.
2. Place the specified drill or gauge on the downstream side of the choke plate.
3. To adjust, bend the choke lever tang.

Choke Plate Pulldown Adjustment

1. Remove the three hex headed screws and ring which retain the choke cover.

Caution Do not remove the choke water housing screw if adjusting on the car. Pull the choke water housing and bimetal cover assembly back out of the way.

2. Push the diaphragm shaft against the stop.
3. Insert the specified size drill bit on the downstream side of the primary choke plate.

4. Take the slack out of the linkage and turn the adjusting screw with a 5/32 in. Allen wrench.

Fast Idle Speed Adjustment

Through 1975

1. Engine temperature must be normal with the air cleaner off. Disconnect and plug the vacuum advance line to the distributor.
2. Position the fast idle screw on the top step (second step for 1975) of the fast idle cam.

3. Adjust the fast idle speed to specifications.
4. Adjustments are made by turning the fast idle screw in or out.

1976 and Later

1. The engine must be at normal operating temperature with the air cleaner off.
2. With the engine running, position the fast idle screw on the high step of the cam.
3. Adjust the speed by turning the fast idle screw.

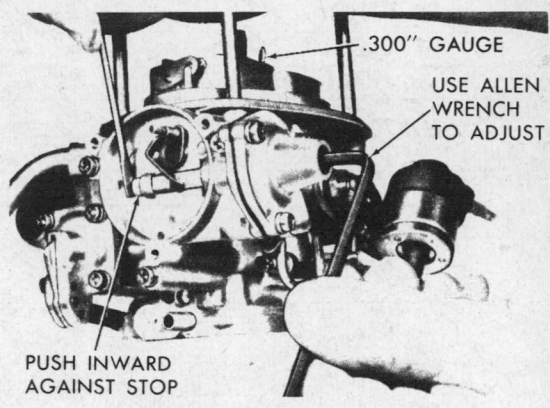

5210—Choke plate pulldown adjustment

Adjusting 5210 fast idle

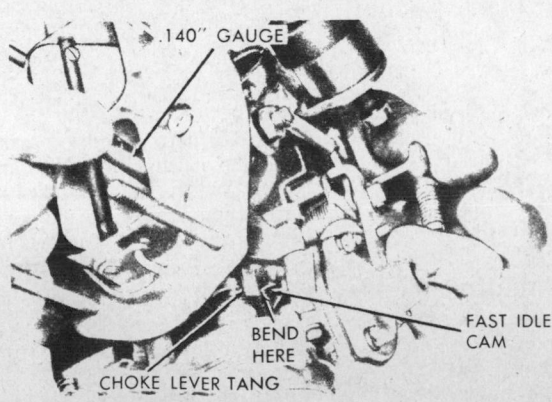

Adjusting 5210 fast idle cam

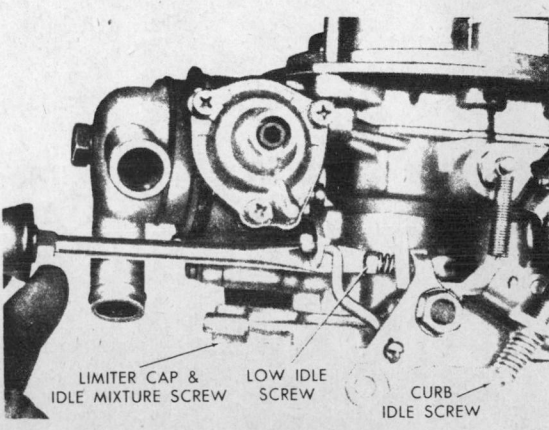

5210—Idle adjustment

HOLLEY 5210 SPECIFICATIONS

CHEVROLET Monza, Vega

Year	Carb. Part No. ① ②	Float Level (Dry) (in.)	Float Drop (in.)	Pump Position	Fast Idle Cam (in.)	Choke Plate Pulldown (in.)	Fast Idle Setting (rpm)	Choke Setting
1973	R-6477A	0.420	1	#3	0.140	0.300	2000	1 Rich
	R-6478A	0.420	1	#2	0.140	0.300	2200	2 Rich
	R-6580A	0.420	1	#2	0.140	0.300	2200	2 Rich
	R-6581A	0.420	1	#3	0.140	0.300	2000	1 Rich
1974	338179	0.420	1	#3	0.140	0.300	2000⑥	2½ Rich
	338181	0.420	1	#3	0.140	0.300	2000⑥	2½ Rich
	338168	0.420	1	#2	0.140	0.300	2200⑥	3½ Rich
	338170	0.420	1	#2	0.140	0.300	2200⑥	3½ Rich
1975	348659, 348663,	0.420	1	#2	0.110	0.325	1600⑥	3 Rich
	348661, 348665	0.420	1	#2	0.110	0.275	1600⑥	3 Rich
	348660, 348664	0.420	1	#2	0.110	0.300	1600⑥	4 Rich
	348662, 348666	0.420	1	#2	0.110	0.275	1600⑥	4 Rich
1976	366829, 366831	0.420	——	#3	0.320	0.313	2200	2 Rich
	366833, 366841	0.420	——	#3	0.320	0.268	2200	2 Rich
	366830, 366832	0.420	——	#2	0.320	0.288	2200	3 Rich
	366834, 366840	0.420	——	#2	0.320	0.268	2200	3 Rich

Oldsmobile Starfire

Year		Float Level (Dry) (in.)	Float Drop (in.)	Pump Position	Fast Idle Cam (in.)	Choke Plate Pulldown (in.)	Fast Idle Setting (rpm)	Choke Setting
1976	Manual	0.420	——	#3	0.320	0.313③	2200	2 Rich
	Automatic	0.420	——	#2	0.320	0.288③	2200	3 Rich

Pontiac Astre, Sunbird

Year		Float Level (Dry) (in.)	Float Drop (in.)	Pump Position	Fast Idle Cam (in.)	Choke Plate Pulldown (in.)	Fast Idle Setting (rpm)	Choke Setting
1975	Manual	0.420	1	#3	0.140	0.300	2000⑥	2½ Rich
	Automatic	0.420	1	#2	0.140	0.400	2200⑥	3½ Rich
1976	Manual	0.410	1	#3	0.320	0.313③	2200⑥	2 Rich
	Automatic	0.410	1	#2	0.320	0.288③	2200⑥	3 Rich

① Located on tag attached to the carburetor, or on the casting or choke plate
② Beginning 1974, GM identification numbers are used in place of the Holley numbers

③ 0.268 in California
④ Not used
⑤ Not used
⑥ With no vacuum to the distributor

Model 4150, 4160

The 4150 and 4160 are four barrel carburetors which contain all the basic systems in the primary sides. The secondary sides of these units contain a fuel transfer and bypass system which richens the mixture when needed.

Some 4150 models have a central fuel inlet whereas other units have a side inlet.

Model 4160 Adjustments (Chrysler Products)

Bowl Vent Valve Adjustment
1. With the throttle valves at curb idle, it should be possible to insert a 0.015 in. gauge between the bowl vent valve plunger stem and the operating rod.

2. If an adjustment is necessary, bend the rod to change the arc of contact with the throttle lever until the correct clearance has been obtained.

Accelerator Pump Adjustment
1. With the throttle valves open wide and the pump lever held down, it should be possible to insert a 0.015 in. feeler gauge between the adjusting nut and the lever.

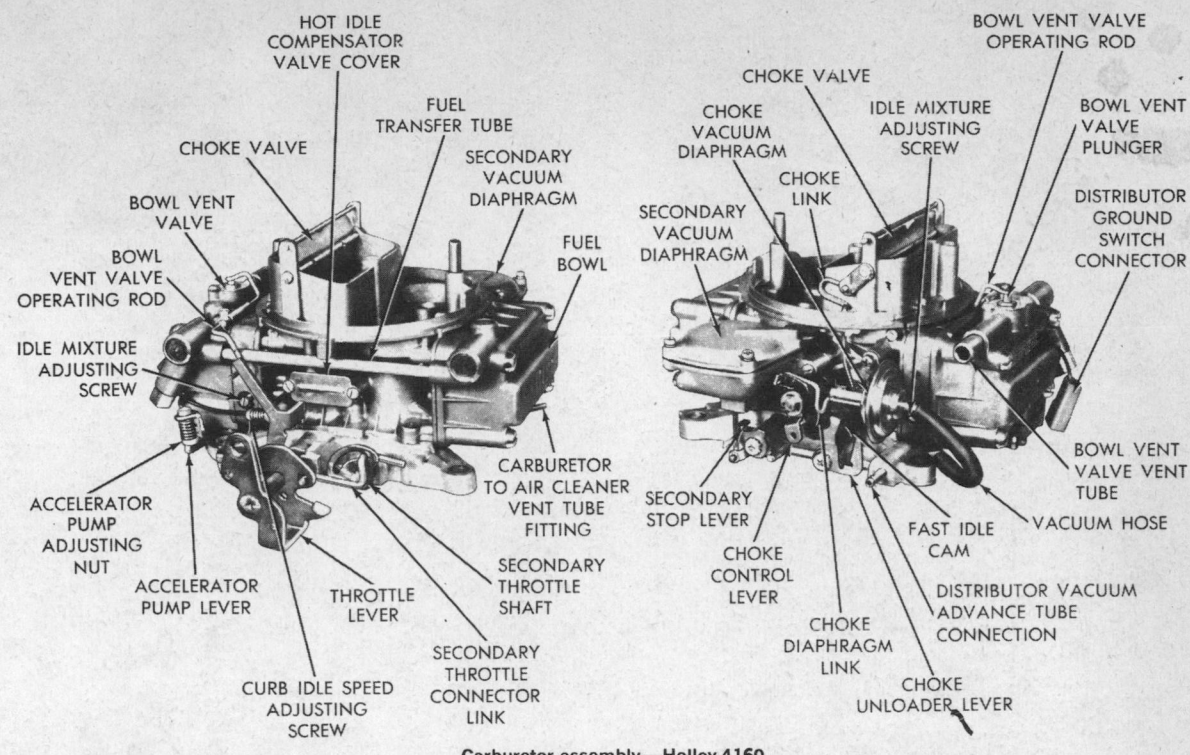

Carburetor assembly—Holley 4160

2. If an adjustment is necessary, adjust the pump override screw until the correct clearance has been obtained.
3. There must be no free movement of the pump lever when the throttle is at curb idle.

Choke Lever Adjustment

1. Open the throttle to the mid position.
2. Close the choke valve by exerting slight pressure on the choke control lever.
3. The top of the choke rod hole in the control lever should be 2¾ in. above the choke assembly with the carburetor on the engine. With the carburetor on the bench, the measurement should be 1-9/16 in. above the carburetor base.
4. To adjust, bend the choke shaft rod at the top bend.

Caution Improper bending will cause binding of the rod. Check for free movement between the open and closed position.

Choke Unloader Adjustment (Wide Open Kick)

1. Adjust the choke control lever.
2. Hold the throttle valves in the wide-open position. Insert the specified drill between the upper edge of the choke valve and the inner wall of the air horn.
3. With a finger pressed against the choke control lever, a slight drag should be felt as the drill is being withdrawn. If an adjustment is

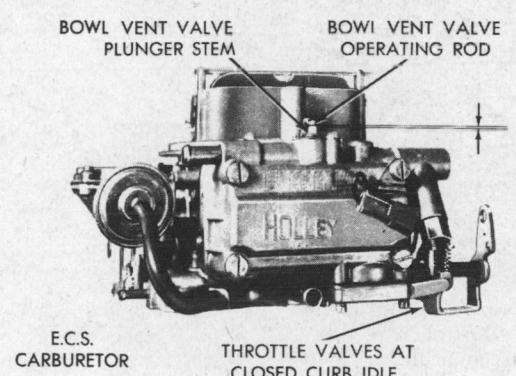

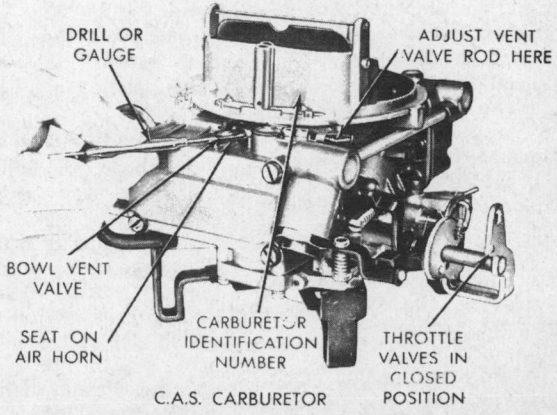

Checking the 4160 bowl vent valve clearance, Chrysler

to be made, bend the flat tang that contacts the bottom of the fast idle cam until the correct opening has been obtained.

Fast Idle Speed Adjustment

1. With the engine off and the transmission in Neutral, open the throttle slightly.

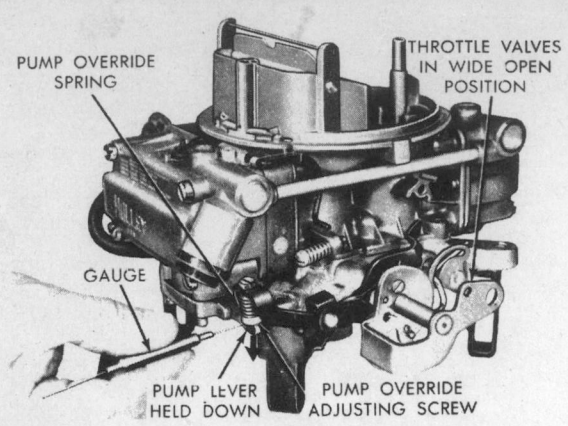

Checking 4160 accelerator pump lever clearance, Chrysler

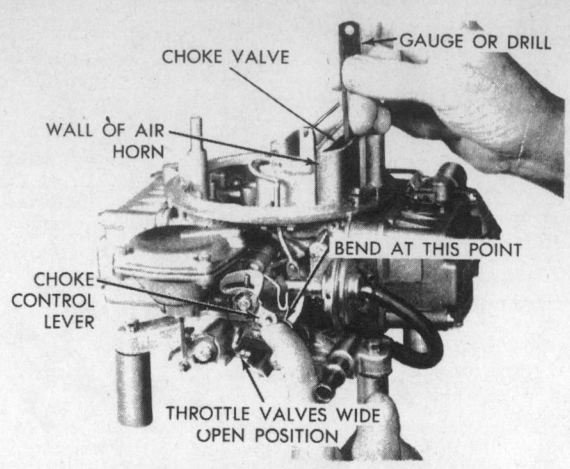

4160 Choke unloader adjustment, Chrysler

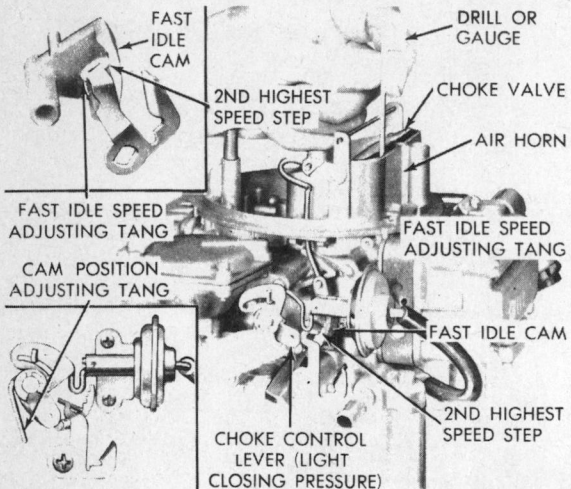

4160—Fast idle cam position adjustment, Chrysler

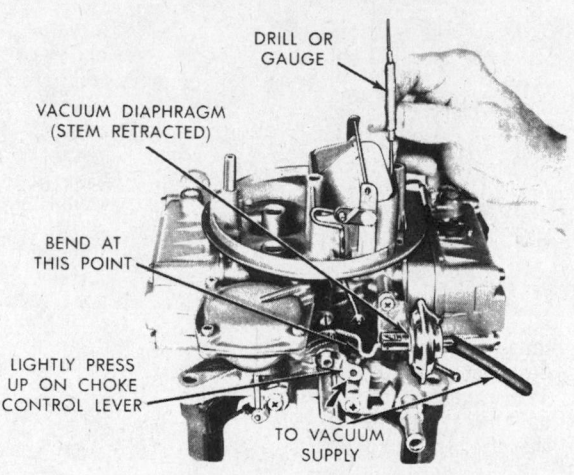

4160—Vacuum kick adjustment, Chrysler

2. Close the choke valve until the fast idle screw tang can be positioned on the second highest step of the fast idle cam.
3. Start the engine and determine the stabilized speed. Bend the fast idle tang by use of a screwdriver placed in the tang slot to secure the specified speed.

Caution Bend only in a direction perpendicular to the contact surface of the cam. Movement in any other direction will change the cam position adjustment described earlier.

4. Reposition the fast idle tang on the cam after each speed adjustment, to provide the correct throttle closing torque.

Fast Idle Cam Position Adjustment

1. Adjust the choke control lever.
2. With the fast idle speed adjusting tang contacting the second highest speed step on the fast idle cam, move the choke valve toward the closed position with light pressure on the choke control lever.

3. Insert a 0.060 in. drill bit between the choke valve and the wall of the air horn. An adjustment will be necessary if a slight drag is not obtained as the drill is being removed.
4. To adjust, bend the adjusting tang until the correct choke valve opening has been obtained.

Vacuum Kick Adjustment

1. Start the engine and position the fast idle tang to allow choke closure to the kick position.
2. Insert the specified drill between the choke valve and the wall of the air horn. Apply sufficient closing pressure on the lever to which the choke rod attaches to provide a minimum choke valve opening without distortion of the diaphragm link.

NOTE: The cylindrical stem of the diaphragm will extend as an internal spring is compressed. This spring must be fully compressed for proper measurement of the vacuum link adjustment.

4. An adjustment will be necessary if a slight drag is not obtained as

the drill is being removed. Shorten or lengthen the diaphragm link to obtain the correct choke opening. Length changes should be made by carefully opening or closing the bend provided in the diaphragm link.

Caution Do not apply twisting or bending force to the diaphragm.

5. With no vacuum applied to the diaphragm, the choke valve should move freely between the open and closed positions. If the movement is not free, examine the linkage for misalignment or interference caused by the bending operation. Repeat the adjustment if necessary to provide the proper link operation.

Model 4150 Adjustments (General Motors)

Float Adjustment

1. A preliminary float adjustment can be made by inverting the

primary fuel bowl and turning the adjustable needle seat until the top of the float is the specified distance from the top of the fuel bowl.

2. Repeat Step 1 for the secondary float.

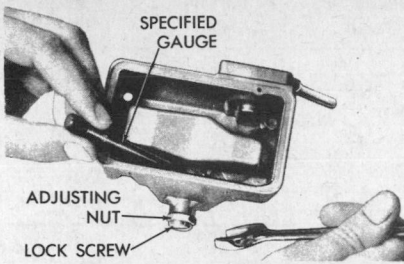

Preliminary 4150 float adjustment, GM

Secondary Throttle Valve Stop Screw

1. Back off the adjustment screw until the throttle plates are fully closed.
2. Turn the adjustment screw until it just touches the throttle lever and then make ½ turn more to position the valves.

Air Vent Valve Adjustment

1. Back off the idle speed screw until the throttle valves are fully closed.
2. Check the clearance between the choke valve and the seat.

3. Bend the air valve rod to adjust.
4. Turn the idle screw in until contact is made with the throttle lever, then turn the screw in 1½ additional turns for preliminary idle speed adjustments.

Fast Idle Cam Adjustment

1. Open the throttle slightly, close the choke plate, and position the fast idle lever against the top step of the fast idle cam.
2. Adjust the fast idle to give the 0.025 in. opening on the throttle plates on the idle transfer slot side of the carburetor.
3. Bend the fast idle lever to adjust.

Accelerator Pump Adjustment

1. Hold the throttle lever in the wide-open position with a rubber band; hold the pump lever fully compressed down; then measure the clearance between the spring adjusting nut and the arm of the pump lever.
2. Clearance should be 0.015 in.; adjust by turning the nut or screw as required while holding the opposite end.
3. After the adjustment is made,

rotate the throttle lever to fully closed and partly open again. Any movement of the throttle lever should be noticed at the operating lever spring end, indicating the correct pump tip-in.

Choke Unloader Adjustment

1. Hold the throttle lever in the wide-open position with a rubber band.
2. Hold the choke valve toward the closed position against the unloader tang of the throttle shaft, then measure the opening between the choke valve lower edge and the main body.
3. To adjust, bend the choke rod at the offset end. Recheck after adjusting.

Vacuum Break Adjustment

1. Hold the choke valve closed with a rubber band attached to the linkage.
2. Hold the vacuum break in against the stop.
3. Measure the distance between the choke valve lower edge and the main body.
4. Bend the vacuum break link to adjust.

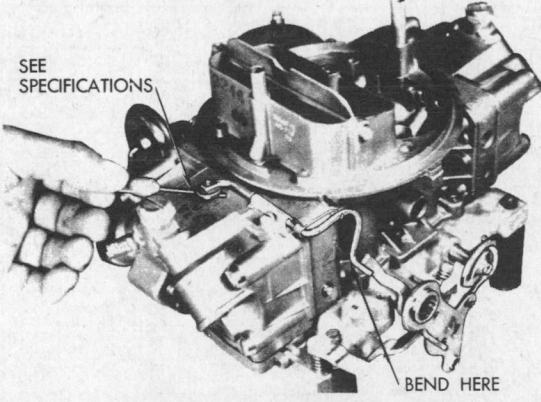

4150—Air vent valve adjustment, GM

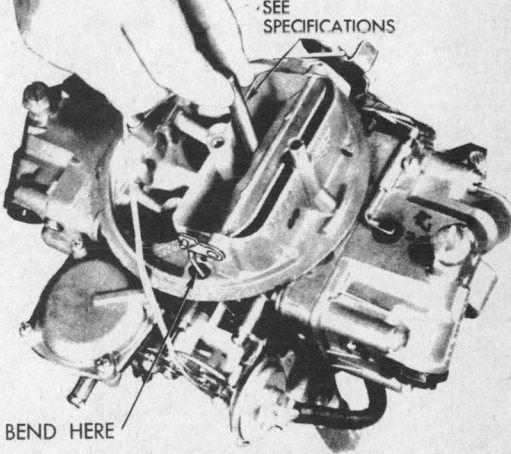

4150—Choke unloader adjustment, GM

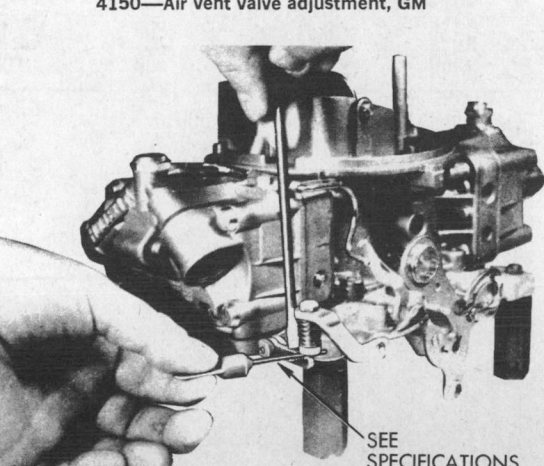

4150—Accelerator Pump adjustment, GM

4150—Fast idle cam adjustment, GM

HOLLEY 4150 and 4160 SPECIFICATIONS

CHEVROLET

Year	Carb. Part No. ①	Float Level (Dry) (in.)	Accelerator Pump Lever Adjustment (in.)	Choke Setting (in.)	Choke Unloader Clearance (in.)	Bowl Vent Clearance (in.)	Fast Idle On Car (rpm)	Choke Vacuum Break (in.)
1970	R4053-A	⑥	0.015	⑧	0.350	——	2200	0.300
	R4296-A	⑥	0.015	⑧	0.350	——	2200	0.350
	R4346	⑥	0.015	⑧	0.350	——	2200	0.300
	R4492-A	⑥	0.015	⑧	0.350	——	2200	0.350
	R4557-A	⑥	0.015	⑧	0.350	——	2200	0.350
1971	R4800-A	⑩	0.015	1.320⑪	0.350	——	2200	0.350
	R4801-A	⑩	0.015	1.320⑪	0.350	——	2200	0.350
	R4802-A	⑩	0.015	1.320⑪	0.350	——	2200	0.350
	R4803-A	⑩	0.015	1.320⑪	0.350	——	2200	0.350
1972	R6238-A	⑩	0.015	1.320⑪	0.350	——	2350	0.350
	R6239-A	⑩	0.015	1.320⑪	0.350	——	2350	0.350

CHRYSLER PRODUCTS

Year	Carburetor Part No. ①	Float Level (Dry) (in.)	Minimum Pump Clearance (in.)	Choke Setting	Choke Unloader Clearance (in.)	Bowl Vent Valve Clearance (in.)	Fast Idle Speed (rpm)	Vacuum Kick (in.)
1970-71	R-4360-A	⑦	0.015	2 Rich	25 Drill	72 Drill	1600	46 Drill
	R-4366-A	⑦	0.015	2 Rich	25 Drill	5/64	1600	46 Drill
1971	R-4668-A	⑦	0.015	2 Rich	25 Drill	0.015	1700	46 Drill
	R-4735-A	⑦	0.015	2 Rich	25 Drill	0.015	1700	46 Drill
	R-6191-A	⑦	0.015	2 Rich	25 Drill	0.015	1800	18 Drill
	R-6193-A	⑦	0.015	2 Rich	25 Drill	0.015	1800	18 Drill
1972	R-6160-A	⑫	0.015	Fixed	0.150	0.015	1600	0.080
	R-6252-A	⑫	0.015	Fixed	0.150	0.015	1800	0.140
	R-6253-A	⑫	0.015	Fixed	0.150	0.015	1600	0.080
	R-6254-A	⑫	0.015	Fixed	0.150	0.015	1800	0.140
	R-6255-A	⑫	0.015	Fixed	0.150	0.015	1600	0.080
	R-6256-A	⑫	0.015	Fixed	0.150	0.015	2000	0.140
	R-6257-A	⑫	0.015	Fixed	0.150	0.015	1800	0.080
	R-6290-A	⑫	0.015	Fixed	0.150	0.015	1500	0.080

① Located on tag attached to carburetor, or on the casting or choke plate
② Not used
③ Not used
④ Not used
⑤ No. 5 Step on cam
⑥ Primary 0.350 in., secondary 0.500 in.
⑦ Primary 15/64 in., secondary 17/64 in.
⑧ Top of rod even with bottom of hole
⑨ No. 2 Step on cam
⑩ Float centered in bowl
⑪ Not used
⑫ Primary 0.110 in., secondary 0.204 in.

Ford, Autolite, Motorcraft Carburetors

Model 1250

The model 1250 is a single barrel downdraft carburetor designed for use on the 1600 cc Pinto engine. It is equipped with a diaphragm type accelerator pump and a water heated thermostatic choke.

Choke Plate Pulldown

1. Remove the thermostatic spring and the water housing.
2. Push in on the vacuum piston until the vacuum inner bleed slot is fully exposed.
3. Take a length of 0.040 in. wire and insert it into this slot. Raise the piston to trap the wire.
4. Partially open the throttle valve so that the choke plate may be moved toward the closed position.
5. Close the choke plate until its movement is stopped.
6. Check the clearance between the bottom of the choke plate and the inside wall of the carburetor body.
7. If the specified clearance is not present, bend the extension of the choke thermostat lever to adjust it.

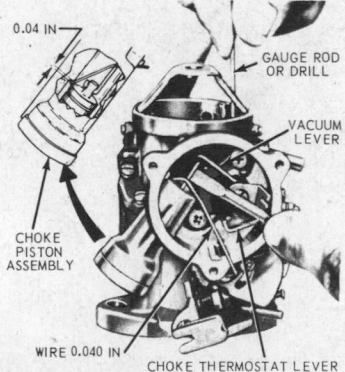

Choke plate pulldown adjustment
(© Ford Motor Co)

Dechoke

1. Open the throttle valve fully and measure the clearance between the bottom of the choke plate and the carburetor body.
2. If adjustment is necessary, bend the tang on the fast idle cam.

Accelerator Pump Stroke

1. Back out the throttle stop screw so that the throttle plate may be fully closed.
2. Depress the plunger of the accelerator pump diaphragm and check the clearance between the operating lever and the plunger with the proper gauge.

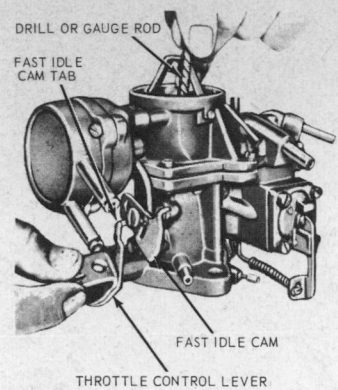

Dechoke adjustment—Autolite 1 barrel
(© Ford Motor Co)

3. To adjust, bend the gooseneck of the pump push rod. Closing the gooseneck will lengthen the stroke and expanding it will shorten the stroke.
4. Reset the throttle valve stop screw.

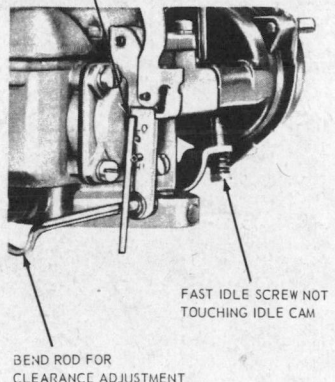

Accelerator pump adjustment
(© Ford Motor Co)

Fast Idle

1. After adjusting the choke plate pulldown, hold the choke plate in the closed position.

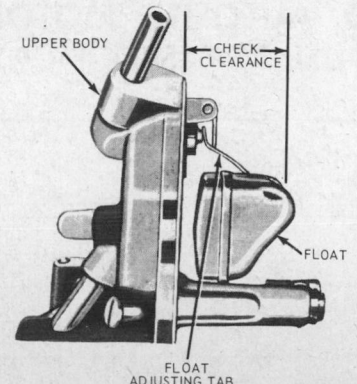

2. Make sure the fast idle tab is on the second step of the fast idle cam.
3. Install the thermostatic spring and water housing. Locate the spring in the center slot and accurately align the marks on the housing.
4. Connect a tachometer to the engine.
5. Run the engine until the normal operating temperature is reached.
6. Put the fast idle tab on the second step of the fast idle cam and check engine speed. If adjustment is needed, bend the tab which contacts the fast idle cam.

Float Level

1. Disconnect all connections to the carburetor upper body including the fuel line, decel valve hose, choke fast idle pivot screw, and the thermostatic housing. Remove the upper carburetor body.
2. With the upper carburetor body held so that the float hangs down, measure the distance from the bottom of the float to the upper body gasket. To adjust, bend the tab which contacts the needle valve and seat assembly.
3. Invert the carburetor so that the float rests on the carburetor body. Again measure the distance from the bottom of the float to the body gasket. Adjust by bending the tab which rests on the needle valve housing.

Vent Valve Adjustment

1. Adjust the vent valve only after the accelerator pump has been properly adjusted.
2. Set the linkage in the hot idle position.
3. The groove in the vent valve should now be even with the open end of the vent.
4. Bend the arm on the vent valve actuating lever to align the groove with the edge of the bore.

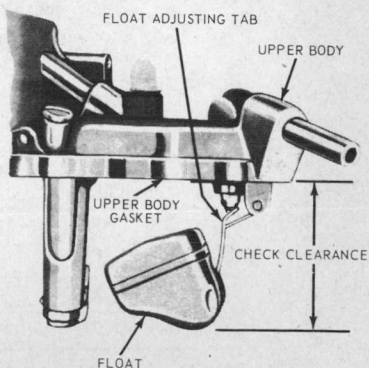

Adjusting float level—Model 1250
(© Ford Motor Co)

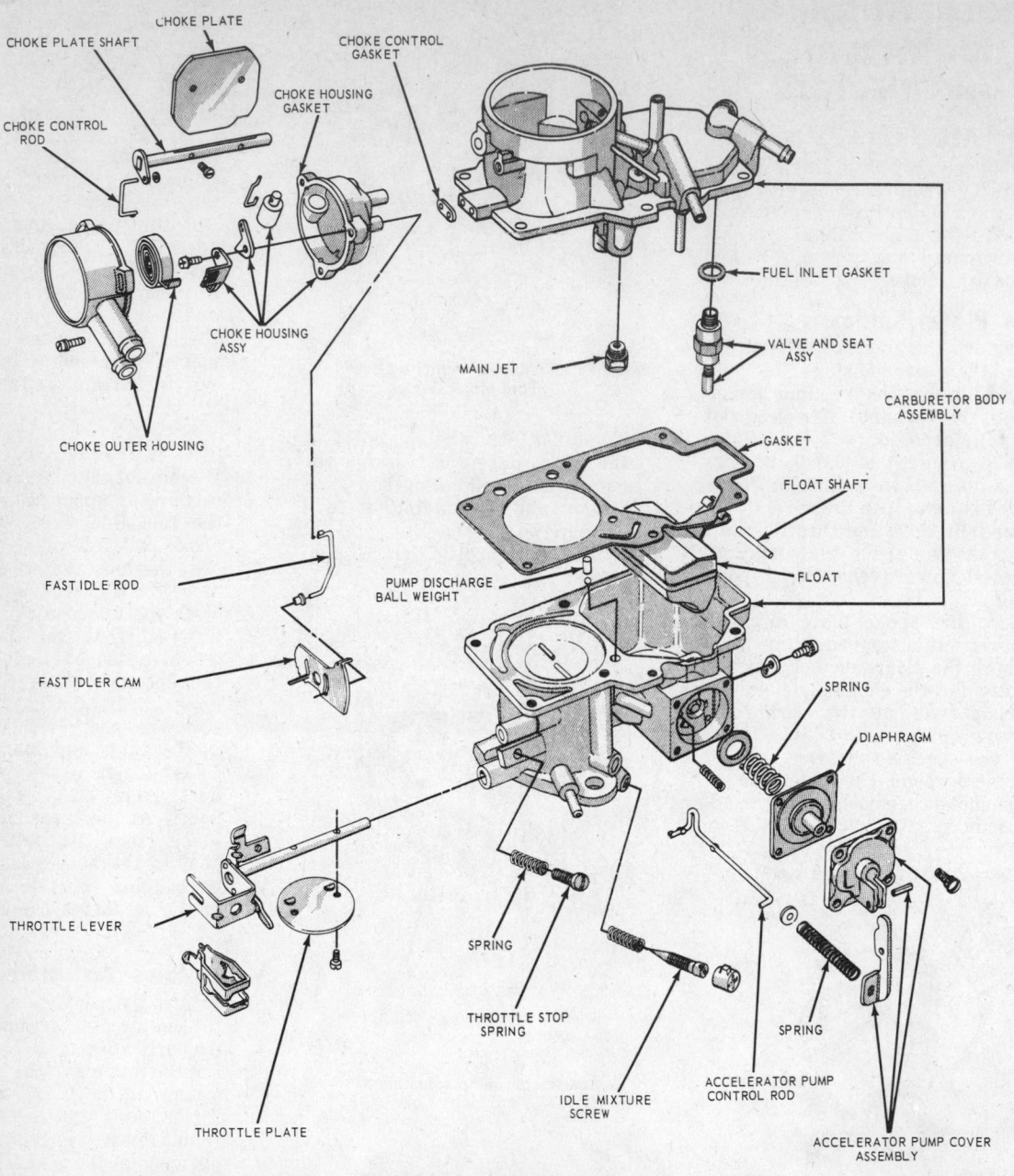

CHOKE PLATE SHAFT
CHOKE PLATE
CHOKE CONTROL GASKET
CHOKE CONTROL ROD
CHOKE HOUSING GASKET
CHOKE HOUSING ASSY
CHOKE OUTER HOUSING
FUEL INLET GASKET
MAIN JET
VALVE AND SEAT ASSY
CARBURETOR BODY ASSEMBLY
GASKET
FLOAT SHAFT
FLOAT
FAST IDLE ROD
PUMP DISCHARGE BALL WEIGHT
FAST IDLER CAM
SPRING
DIAPHRAGM
THROTTLE LEVER
SPRING
THROTTLE STOP SPRING
IDLE MIXTURE SCREW
ACCELERATOR PUMP CONTROL ROD
SPRING
THROTTLE PLATE
ACCELERATOR PUMP COVER ASSEMBLY

Disassembled Model 1250 carburetor (© Ford Motor Co)

FORD, AUTOLITE, MOTORCRAFT
MODEL 1250 SPECIFICATIONS

Pinto

Year	(9510)* Carburetor Identification	Float Level (in.)	Pump (in.)	Fast Idle (rpm)	Choke Plate Pulldown (in.)	Dechoke (in.)	Choke Setting
1971	711-BDA	①	0.085	1700	0.120	0.210	Index
	711-BDB	①	0.070	1700	0.075	0.210	Index
1972	721F-KFA	②	0.070	1700	0.075	0.210	Index
1973	731F-KAA	②	0.085	—	0.075	—	Index

* Basic carburetor number ② Body vertical—1.200
① Body vertical—1.160-1.200
Body horizontal—1.350-1.370

Models 2100, 2150

The Model 2100 and 2150 two barrel carburetor are basically the same in construction. Adjustments are performed in the same manner for all carburetors.

The air horn assembly covers the main body and houses the choke plate and the internal fuel bowl vents. The throttle plate, accelerator pump assembly, power valve assembly, and fuel bowl are contained in the main body. The automatic choke is also attached to the main body. On the 2100 and 2150 two barrel, each bore contains a main and booster venturi, a main fuel discharge, an accelerating pump discharge, an idle fuel discharge, and a throttle plate.

Float Level (Dry)

The dry float level measurement is a preliminary check and must be followed by a wet float level measurement with the carburetor mounted on the engine.

1. With the air horn removed and the fuel inlet needle seated lightly, gently raise the float and measure the distance between the main body gasket surface (gasket removed) and the top of the float. This measurement should be taken near the center of the float, at a point 1/8 in. from the free end of the float.
2. If necessary, bend the float tab to obtain the correct level.

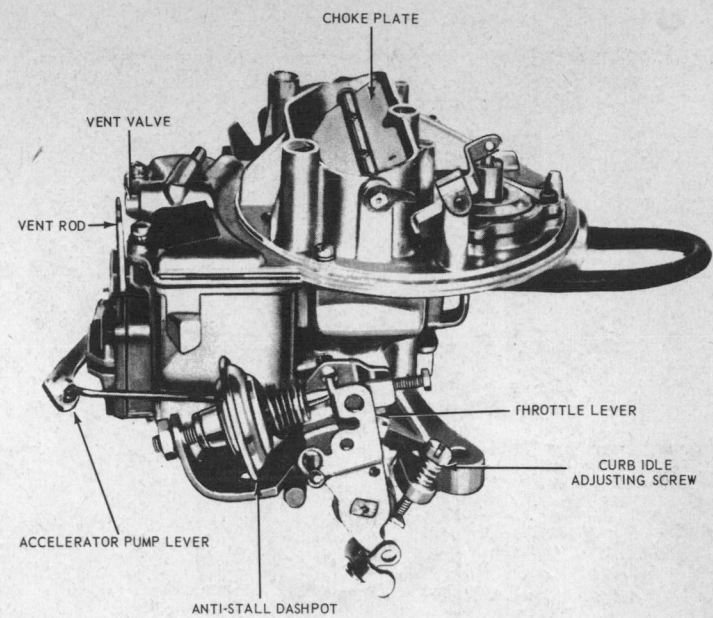

Model 2100 two barrel carburetor
(© Ford Motor Co)

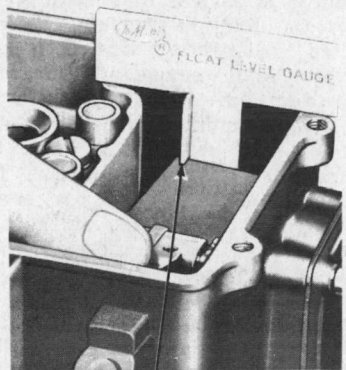

FLOAT SHOULD JUST
TOUCH AT THIS POINT
Checking float level (dry)
(© Ford Motor Co)

Float Level (Wet)

1. Remove the screws that hold the air horn to the main body and break the seal between the air horn and main body. Leave the air horn and gasket loosely in place on top of the main body.
2. Start the engine and allow it to idle for at least three minutes.
3. After the engine has idled long enough to stabilize the fuel level, remove the air horn assembly.
4. With the engine idling, use a T-scale to measure the distance from the top of the fuel bowl ma-

chined surface to the surface of the fuel. The scale must be held at least 1/4 in. away from any vertical surface to ensure proper measurement.
5. If any adjustment is required, stop the engine to avoid a fire from fuel spraying on the engine.
6. Bend the float tab upward to raise the level and downward to lower the level.

Caution Be sure to hold the fuel inlet needle off its seat when bending the float tab so as not to damage the Viton® tip.

7. Each time the float level is changed, the air horn must be temporarily positioned and the engine started to stabilize the fuel level before again checking it.

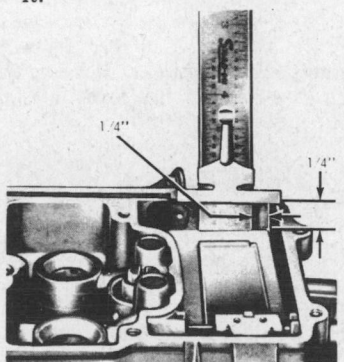

Fuel level measurement (wet)
(© Ford Motor Co)

Choke Plate Pulldown
Model 2100 through 1974

1. Loosen the screws on the choke cover and rotate the cover 1/4 turn clockwise (rich), then tighten the screws.

2. Operate the throttle to allow full closing of the choke plate.
3. Press down on the choke modulator arm until the choke modulator diaphragm is bottomed and then measure the distance from the lower edge of the choke plate to the inside air horn wall.
4. Adjustment is achieved by turning the diaphragm stop screw on the underside of the air horn.
5. Turn the screw clockwise to decrease clearance and counterclockwise to increase clearance.

NOTE: Do not reset the choke cover until the fast idle cam adjustment is made.

Model 2150 beginning 1975

1. Remove the air cleaner assembly.
2. Set the throttle on the top step of the fast idle cam.
3. Noting the position of the choke housing cap, loosen the retaining screws and rotate the cap 90 degrees in the rich (closing) direction.
4. Activate the pull-down motor by manually forcing the pull-down control diaphragm link in the direction of applied vacuum or by applying vacuum to the external vacuum tube.
5. Using a drill gauge of the specified diameter, measure the clearance between the choke plate and the center of the air horn wall nearest the fuel bowl.
6. To adjust, reset the diaphragm stop on the end of the choke pull-down diaphragm.

NOTE: Loctite® was applied to the adjusting screw during manufacture and this will have to be loosened before the adjustment can be made.

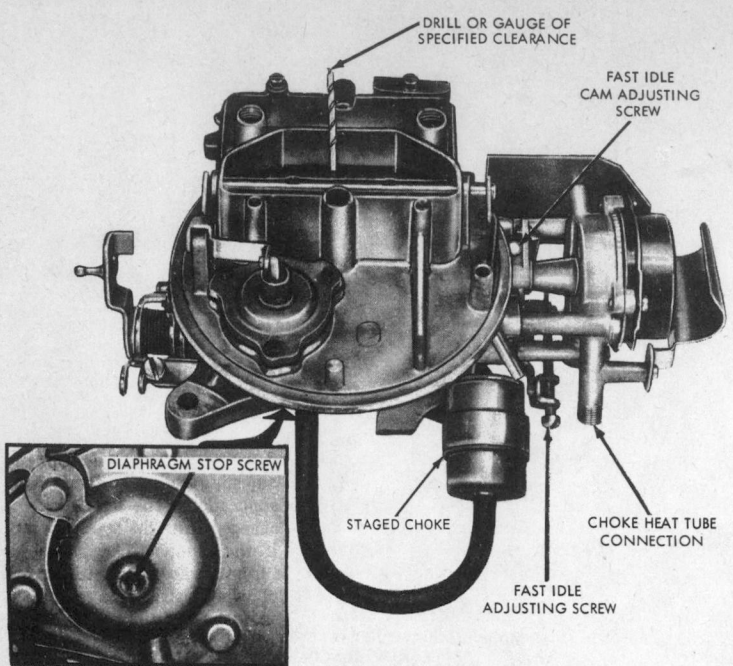

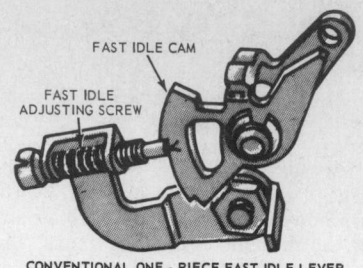

CONVENTIONAL ONE - PIECE FAST IDLE LEVER

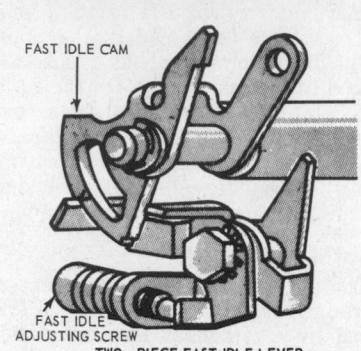

TWO - PIECE FAST IDLE LEVER
FOR 351-C ENGINE

Adjusting choke plate pulldown
(© Ford Motor Co)

Fast idle adjustment
(© Ford Motor Co)

Heat the area around the screw with an electric soldering gun until the Loctite® softens enough to permit the screw to turn freely.

7. After adjusting, reset the choke housing cap to the specified notch. Check and reset fast idle speed, if necessary. Install the air cleaner.

Electric Choke Operating Test

2150

1. Remove the air cleaner and make sure all vacuum hoses, solenoids and electric choke wires are properly connected.
2. Check the throttle system, choke plate, choke linkage and fast idle cam to make sure that nothing is binding.
3. Disconnect the lead on the choke cap and hook up a test light to it. The test light should glow all the time the engine is running. If it doesn't glow, either the alternator or the wire itself is bad.
4. Next, connect the light series with the wire and the terminal on the choke cap. If the light doesn't glow, replace the choke cap assembly.

Fast Idle Cam

1. Push down on the fast idle cam lever until the fast idle screw is in contact with the second step of the fast idle cam and against the shoulder of the high step.
2. The specified clearance should be present between the lower edge

of the choke plate and the air horn wall.
3. The adjustment is made by turning the fast idle cam lever screw.
4. The choke cover may now be replaced and indexed according to specification.

Choke Unloader (Dechoke)

1. With the throttle held completely open, move the choke plate to the closed position.
2. Measure the distance between the lower edge of the choke plate and the air horn wall.
3. Adjust by bending the tang on the fast idle speed lever which is located on the throttle shaft.

NOTE: Final unloader adjustment must be performed on the car and the throttle should be opened by using the accelerator pedal of the car. This is to be sure that full throttle operation is achieved.

Accelerator Pump

The accelerator pump operating rod must be positioned in the proper holes of the accelerator pump lever and the throttle over-travel lever to assure correct pump travel. If adjusting is required, additional holes are provided in the throttle over-travel lever.

Dashpot Adjustment

With the throttle set at the curb idle position, fully depress the dashpot stem and measure the distance between the stem and the throttle lever. Adjust by loosening the locknut and turning the dashpot.

Fast Idle

Adjust the fast idle setting with the engine at operating temperature. If the engine is equipped with a spark delay valve, remove it and reroute the partial throttle vacuum signal line directly to the advance side of the distributor. If the distributor is a dual diaphragm type, leave the manifold vacuum line connected to the retard side of the distributor, and remove and plug the line to the advance side. Remove the EGR vacuum line at the valve, and plug it. On AMC cars, plug the spark port on the carburetor. The fast idle screw should be resting against the second step of the fast idle cam on all except those 1975 and later models used with a 302 cu. in. engine. These have the screw set on the high step of the fast idle cam. Adjust the fast idle speed by turning the fast idle screw.

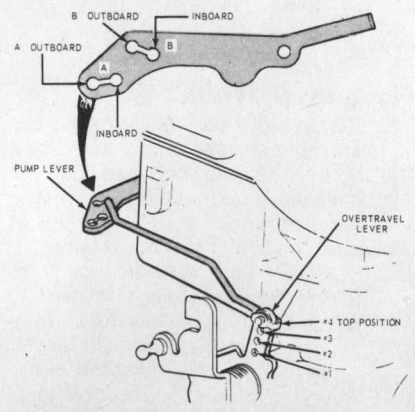

Accelerator pump stroke adjustment
(© Ford Motor Co)

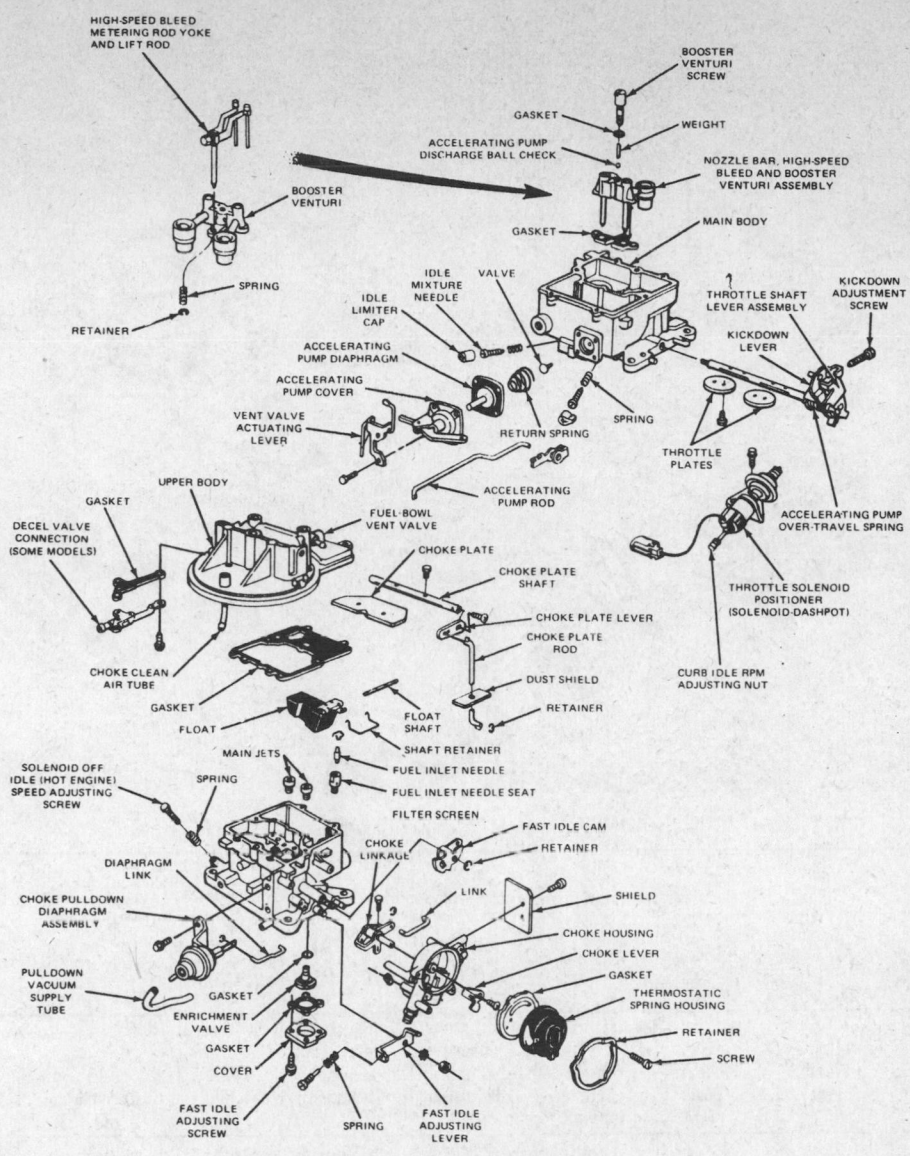

Exploded view—Motorcraft 2150-2V

FORD, AUTOLITE, MOTORCRAFT MODELS 2100, 2150 SPECIFICATIONS

American Motors

Year	(9510)* Carburetor Identification	Dry Float Level (in.)	Wet Float Level (in.)	Pump Setting Hole #①	Choke Plate Pulldown (in.)	Fast Idle Cam Linkage Clearance (in.)	Fast Idle (rpm)	Dechoke (in)	Choke Setting	Dashpot (in.)
1970	0DA2	3/8	13/16	3	0.300	0.170	1600	0.200	2 Rich	1/8
	0DM2	3/8	13/16	3	0.260	0.170	1600	0.200	Index	1/8
	0RA2	3/8	13/16	3	0.350	0.170	1600	0.200	1 Rich	1/8
1971	1DA2	3/8	13/16	3	0.190	0.170	1600	0.200	2 Rich	1/8
	1DM2	3/8	13/16	3	0.190	0.170	1600	0.200	1 Rich	1/8
	1RA2	3/8	13/16	3	0.190	0.170	1600	0.200	2 Rich	1/8
1972	2DA2	3/8	3/4	3A	0.130	0.120	1600	0.200	2 Rich	9/64
	2DM2	3/8	3/4	3A	0.140	0.130	1600	0.200	1 Rich	7/64
	2RA2	3/8	3/4	3A	0.130	0.120	1600	0.200	2 Rich	—
1973	3DA2	3/8	3/4	3A	0.120	0.110	1600	0.250	2 Rich	—
	3DM2	3/8	3/4	3A	0.130	0.130	1600	0.250	1 Rich	9/64
	3RA2	3/8	3/4	3A	0.120	0.110	1600	0.250	2 Rich	—

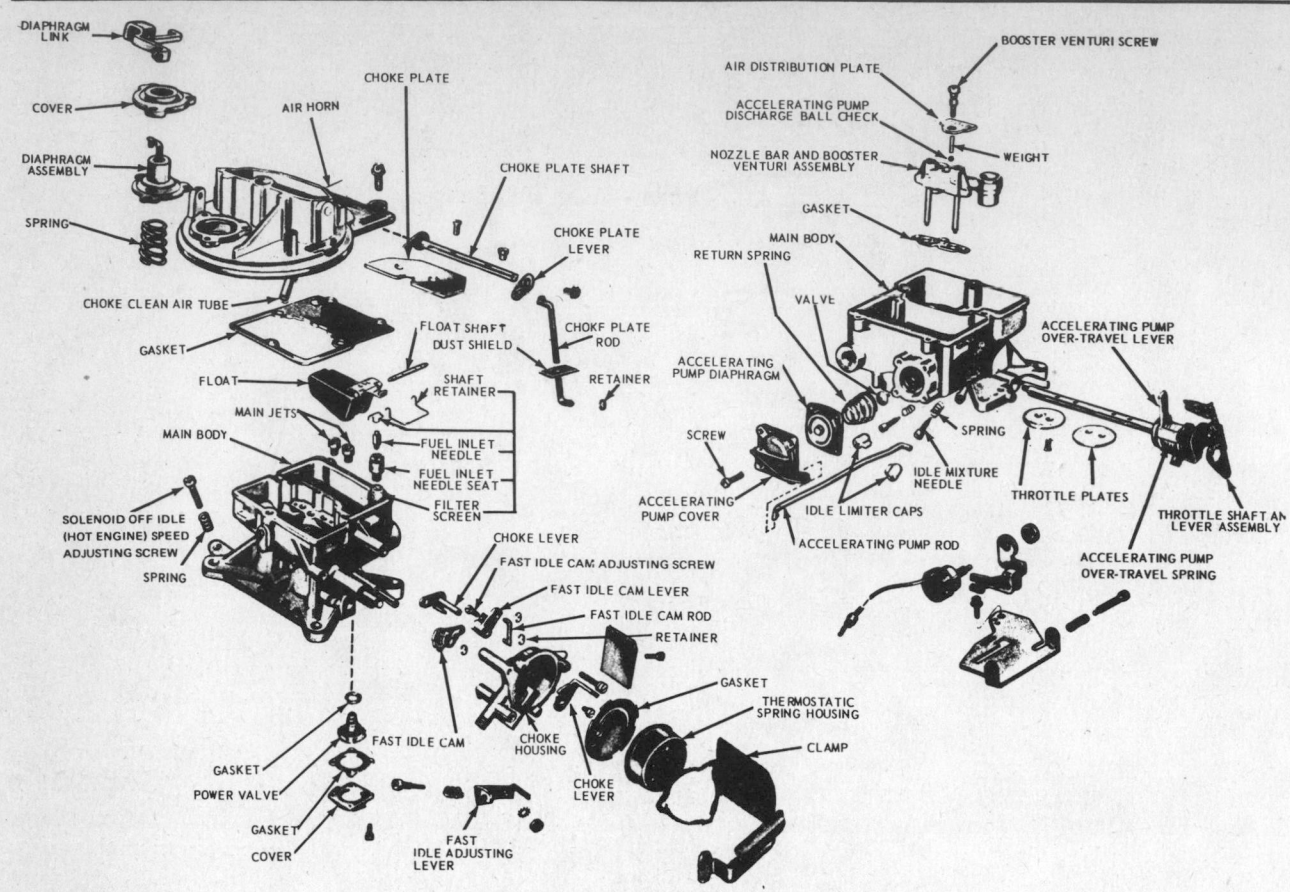

Model 2100D carburetor—disassembled (© Ford Motor Co)

American Motors

Year	(9510)* Carburetor Identification	Dry Float Level (in.)	Wet Float Level (in.)	Pump Setting Hole # ①	Choke Plate Pulldown (in.)	Fast Idle Cam Linkage Clearance (in.)	Fast Idle (rpm)	Dechoke (in)	Choke Setting	Dashpot (in.)
1974	4DA2, 4DA2-E	25/64	25/32	3A	0.140	0.130	1600	0.250	1 Rich	——
	4DM2	25/64	25/32	3A	0.130	0.130	1600	0.250	2 Rich	9/64
	4RA2, 4RAC2	25/64	25/32	3A	0.140	0.130	1600	0.250	1 Rich	——
1975	5DA2	13/32	3/4	——	0.140	0.130	1600	0.250	1 Rich	——
	5DMS	13/32	3/4	——	0.130	0.130	1600	0.250	2 Rich	3/32
	5RAS	13/32	3/4	——	0.140	0.130	1600	0.250	1 Rich	——
1976	6DA2	13/32	3/4	——	0.140	0.130	1600	0.250	1 Rich	——
	6DM2	35/64	15/16	——	0.130	0.120	1600	0.250	2 Rich	——
	6RA2	13/32	3/4	——	0.140	0.130	1600	0.250	1 Rich	——

Ford Products

1970	D0AF-C	7/16	13/16	3	0.150	0.130	1400	0.060	1 Rich	——
	D0AF-D	7/16	13/16	3	0.150	0.130	1500	0.060	1 Rich	1/8
	D0AF-U	7/16	13/16	3	0.150	0.130	1500	0.060	1 Rich	——
	D0AF-E	7/16	13/16	3	0.230	0.190	1300	0.190	2 Lean	——
	D0AF-F	7/16	13/16	3	0.200	0.170	1600	0.170	2 Lean	1/8
	D0AF-V	7/16	13/16	3	0.200	0.170	1600	0.170	2 Lean	——
	D0OF-K	7/16	13/16	3	0.220	0.190	1500	0.190	Index	——
	D0OF-L	7/16	13/16	3	0.190	0.130	1500	0.130	1 Rich	1/8
	D0OF-M	7/16	13/16	3	0.190	0.130	1500	0.130	1 Rich	——

Ford Products

Year	(9510)* Carburetor Identification	Dry Float Level (in.)	Wet Float Level (in.)	Pump Setting Hole #①	Choke Plate Pulldown (in.)	Fast Idle Cam Linkage Clearance (in.)	Fast Idle (rpm)	Dechoke (in)	Choke Setting	Dashpot (in.)
1971	D1YF-DA	7/16	13/16	3	0.200	0.160	1500	0.060	Index	——
	D1MF-JA	7/16	13/16	3	0.190	0.160	1500	0.060	1 Rich	1/8
	D1MF-FA	7/16	13/16	3	0.200	0.160	1500	0.060	1 Rich	1/8
1972	D2AF-FB	7/16	13/16	3	0.140	0.130	1500	0.030	Index	1/8
	D2AF-GB	7/16	13/16	3	0.140	0.130	1500	0.030	Index	1/8
	D2AF-HA	7/16	13/16	2	0.150	0.130	1400	0.060	1 Rich	1/8
	D2GF-AA	7/16	13/16	2	0.150	0.130	1400	0.060	1 Rich	1/8
	D2GF-BA	7/16	13/16	2	0.150	0.130	1400	0.060	1 Rich	——
	D2MF-FB	7/16	13/16	4	0.180	0.150	1500	0.060	1 Rich	——
	D2OF-KA	7/16	13/16	2	0.150	0.130	1400	0.060	1 Rich	——
	D2OF-VB	7/16	13/16	3	0.190	0.160	1400	0.030	2 Rich	——
	D2WF-CA	7/16	13/16	3	0.190	0.160	1400	0.030	2 Rich	——
	D2ZF-FA	7/16	13/16	2	0.150	0.130	1400	0.060	1 Rich	——
	D2ZF-LA	7/16	13/16	3	0.240	0.210	1500	0.030	1 Rich	——
1973	D3AF-CE	7/16	13/16	3A	②	②	1500	②	1 Rich	——
	D3AF-DC	7/16	13/16	3A	②	②	1500	②	3 Rich	——
	D3GF-AF	7/16	13/16	2A	②	②	1400	②	3 Rich	——
	D3GF-BB	7/16	13/16	2A	②	②	1250	②	3 Rich	——
	D3ZF-EA	7/16	13/16	2A	②	②	1400	②	1 Rich	——
	D3AF-KA	7/16	13/16	3A	②	②	1500	②	3 Rich	——
	D3MF-AE	7/16	13/16	3A	②	②	1500	②	3 Rich	——
	D3MF-BA	7/16	13/16	3A	②	②	1500	②	3 Rich	——
1974	D4AE-DA	7/16	13/16	2A	②	②	1500	②	1 Rich	——
	D4AE-EA	7/16	13/16	2A	②	②	1500	②	3 Rich	——
	D4AE-FA	7/16	13/16	3A	②	②	1500	②	3 Rich	——
	D4AE-GA	7/16	13/16	3A	②	②	1500	②	3 Rich	——
	D4DE-LA	7/16	13/16	2A	②	②	1500	②	3 Rich	——
	D4DE-RB	7/16	13/16	2A	②	②	1500	②	3 Rich	——
	D4OE-FA	7/16	13/16	2A	②	②	1500	②	3 Rich	——
	D4AE-HB	7/16	13/16	3A	②	②	1500	②	3 Rich	——
	D4DE-NB	7/16	13/16	2	②	②	1500	②	3 Rich	——
	D4DE-PA	7/16	13/16	2	②	②	1500	②	3 Rich	——
	D4OE-CA	7/16	13/16	2	②	②	1500	②	3 Rich	——
	D4ME-BA	7/16	13/16	3A	②	②	1500	②	3 Rich	——
	D4ME-CA	7/16	13/16	3A	②	②	1500	②	3 Rich	——
1975	D5ZE-AC	3/8	3/4	2	0.145	②	1500	②	2 Rich	——
	D5ZE-BC	3/8	3/4	2	0.145	②	1500	②	2 Rich	——
	D5ZE-CC	3/8	3/4	3	0.145	②	1500	②	2 Rich	——
	D5ZE-DC	3/8	3/4	2	0.145	②	1500	②	2 Rich	——
	D5DE-AA	7/16	13/16	2	0.140	②	1500	②	3 Rich	——
	D5DE-BA	7/16	13/16	2	0.140	②	1500	②	3 Rich	——
	D5DE-JA	7/16	13/16	2	0.140	②	1500	②	3 Rich	——
	D5ZE-JA	7/16	13/16	2	0.140	②	1500	②	3 Rich	——
	D5OE-AA	7/16	13/16	2	0.140	②	1500	②	3 Rich	——
	D5OE-DA	7/16	13/16	2	0.140	②	1500	②	3 Rich	——
	D5DE-HA	7/16	13/16	3	0.140	②	1500	②	3 Rich	——
	D5DE-UA	7/16	13/16	2	0.140	②	1500	②	3 Rich	——
	D5OE-BA	7/16	13/16	3	0.125	②	1500	②	3 Rich	——

Ford Products

Year	(9510)* Carburetor Identification	Dry Float Level (in.)	Wet Float Level (in.)	Pump Setting Hole #①	Choke Plate Pulldown (in.)	Fast Idle Cam Linkage Clearance (in.)	Fast Idle (rpm)	Dechoke (in)	Choke Setting	Dashpot (in.)
1975	D50E-CA	7/16	13/16	3	0.125	②	1500	②	3 Rich	——
	D50E-GA	7/16	13/16	2	0.125	②	1500	②	3 Rich	——
	D5AE-AA	7/16	13/16	3	0.125	②	1500	②	3 Rich	——
	D5AE-EA	7/16	13/16	3	0.125	②	1500	②	3 Rich	——
	D5ME-BA	7/16	13/16	2	0.125	②	1500	②	3 Rich	——
	D5ME-FA	7/16	13/16	2	0.125	②	1500	②	3 Rich	——
1976	D5ZE-BE	3/8	3/4	2	0.105	②	1600③	②	3 Rich	——
	D6ZE-AA	3/8	3/4	2	0.100	②	1600③	②	3 Rich	——
	D6ZE-BA	3/8	3/4	2	0.100	②	1600③	②	3 Rich	——
	D6ZE-CA	13/32	3/4	2	0.110	②	1600③	②	3 Rich	——
	D6ZE-DA	3/8	3/4	3	0.110	②	1600③	②	3 Rich	——
	D5DE-AEA	7/16	13/16	2	0.160	②	2000④	②	3 Rich	——
	D5DE-AFA	7/16	13/16	2	0.160	②	2000④	②	3 Rich	——
	D5WE-FA	7/16	13/16	2	0.160	②	2000④	②	3 Rich	——
	D6ZE-JA	7/16	13/16	2	0.160	②	2000④	②	3 Rich	——
	D6OE-AA	7/16	13/16	3	0.160	②	2000④	②	3 Rich	——
	D6OE-BA	7/16	13/16	3	0.160	②	2000④	②	3 Rich	——
	D6OE-CA	7/16	13/16	3	0.160	②	2000④	②	3 Rich	——
	D6WE-AA	7/16	13/16	2	0.160	②	1350⑤	②	3 Rich	——
	D6WE-BA	7/16	13/16	2	0.160	②	1350⑤	②	3 Rich	——
	D6AE-HA	7/16	13/16	2	0.160	②	1350⑤	②	3 Rich	——
	D6ME-AA	7/16	13/16	2	0.160	②	1350⑤	②	3 Rich	——

* Basic carburetor number for Ford products
① With link in inboard hole of pump lever
② Electric choke; see procedure in text
③ Figure given is for manual transmission; for automatics add 100 RPM.
④ Figure given is for 49 states Granada and Monarch; for Calif. Granada and Monarch and all Torino, Montego and Cougar models, figure is 1400 RPM.
⑤ Figure given is for 49 states model; Calif. specification is 1150 RPM.

Model 5200

The 5200 carburetor is a two-stage, two-venturi carburetor in which the secondary venturi is the larger. The secondary system is mechanically operated. It is used with 2000, 2300 and 2800 cc Pinto, Bobcat and Mustang II engines.

Fast Idle Cam

1. Insert a 5/32 in. drill between the lower edge of the choke plate and the air horn wall.
2. With the fast idle screw held on the second step of the fast idle cam, measure the clearance between the tang of the choke lever and the arm on the fast idle cam.
3. Bend the choke lever tang to adjust it if it is not up to specification.

Choke Plate Pulldown

1. Remove the choke thermostatic spring cover.

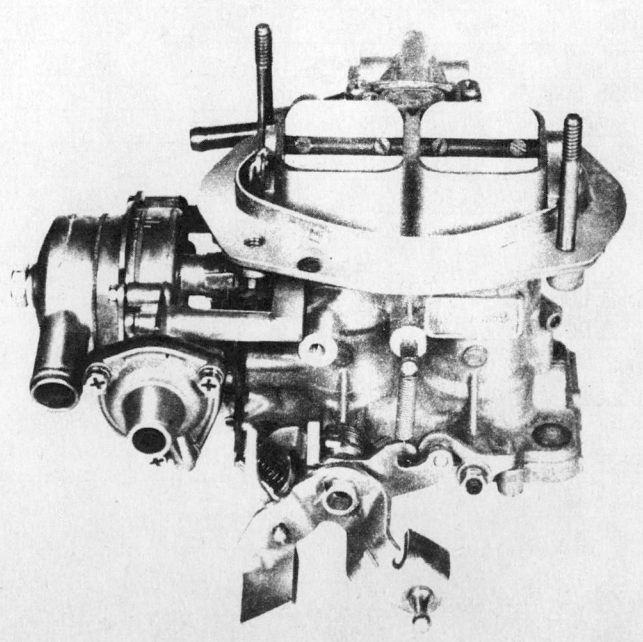

Model 5200 carburetor (ⓒ Ford Motor Co)

2. Pull the water cover and the thermostatic spring cover assembly out of the way.
3. Set the fast idle cam on the high step.

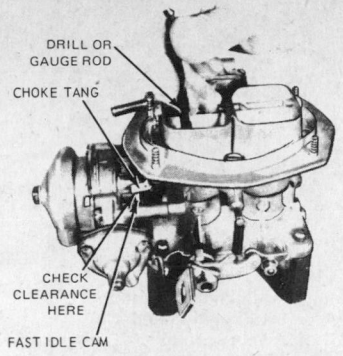

Fast idle cam adjustment
(© Ford Motor Co)

4. Push the diaphragm stem against its stop and insert the specified gauge between the lower edge of the choke valve and the air horn wall.
5. Apply sufficient pressure to the upper edge of the choke valve to take up any slack in the choke linkage.
6. Turn the adjusting screw in or out to adjust the choke plate-to-air horn clearance.

Dechoke (Unloader) Adjustment

1. Hold the throttle in the wide open position.
2. Remove any slack from the choke linkage by applying pressure to the upper edge of the choke valve.
3. Measure the distance from the lower edge of the choke valve to the air horn wall.
4. Make adjustments by bending the tab on the fast idle lever where it touches the fast idle cam.

Fast Idle

Set the fast idle speed with the fast idle screw positioned on the second step of the fast idle cam and with the engine at operating temperature.

On 1975-76 models, you must also remove the EGR line at the valve and plug it. If the car is equipped with a spark delay valve, remove the valve and route the distributor advance vacuum signal directly to the distributor advance diaphragm. On all manual transmission models, remove and plug the vacuum line to the dis-

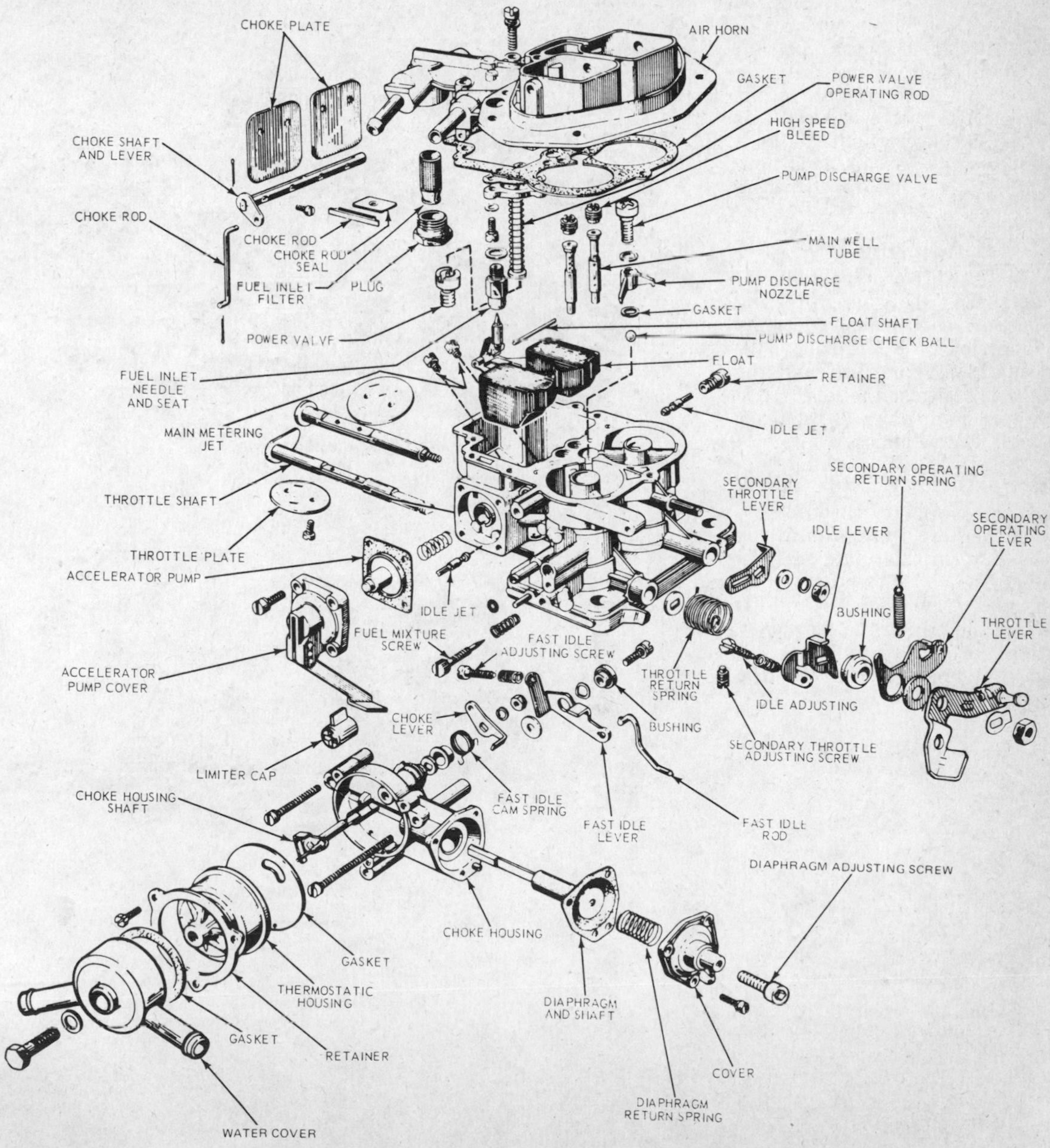

Model 5200 carburetor—exploded view (© Ford Motor Co)

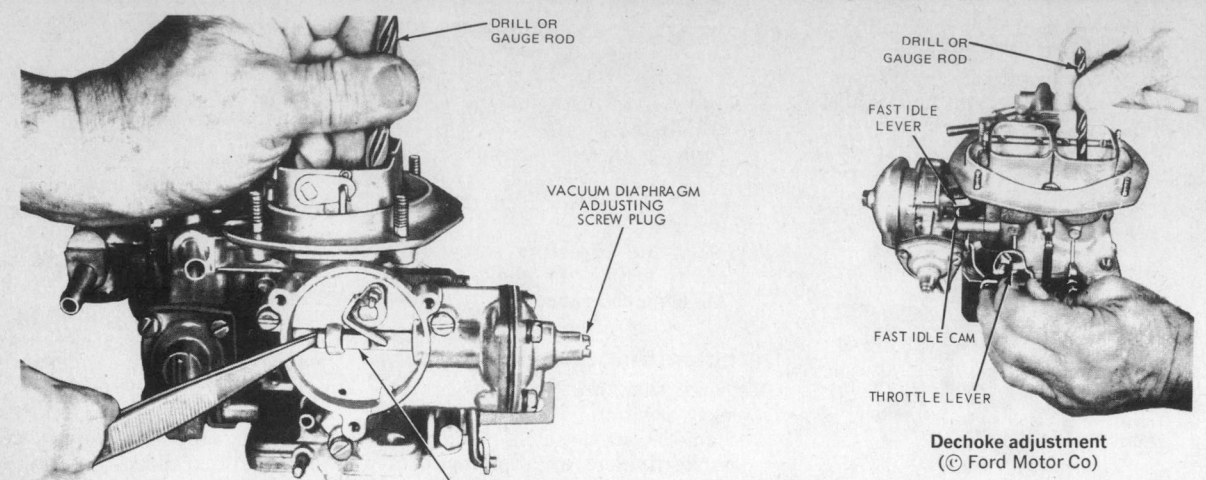

Choke plate pulldown adjustment
(© Ford Motor Co)

Dechoke adjustment
(© Ford Motor Co)

tributor. If the distributor also has a retard diaphragm, leave the hose connected to it alone. If the engine has a deceleration valve, remove this hose at the carburetor and plug it. Finally, if the car has air conditioning it must be off before adjusting the fast idle.

Float Level Adjustment

With the bowl cover held upside down and the float tang resting lightly on the spring loaded fuel inlet needle, measure the clearance between the edge of the float and the bowl cover. To adjust the level, bend the float tang up or down as required. Adjust both floats equally.

Secondary Throttle Stop Screw

1. Turn the secondary throttle stop screw counterclockwise until the secondary throttle plate seats in its bore.
2. Turn the screw clockwise until it touches the tab on the secondary throttle lever.
3. Add ¼ turn clockwise and the stop is adjusted.

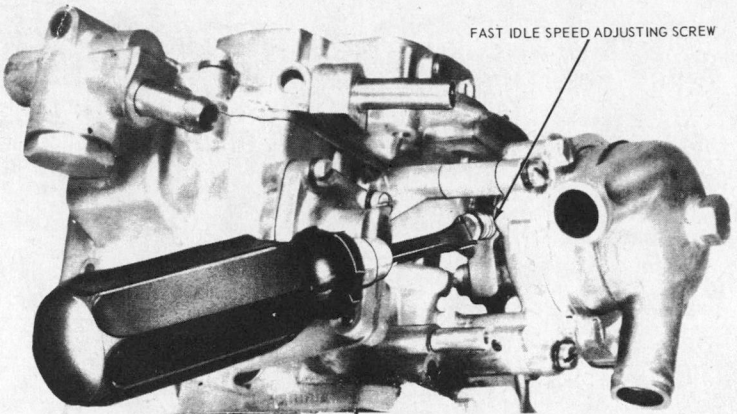

Fast idle adjustment
(© Ford Motor Co)

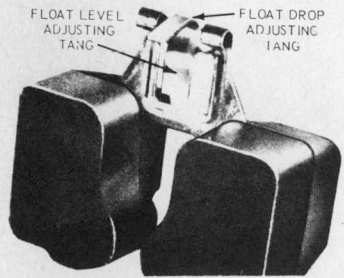

Float adjustment
(© Ford Motor Co)

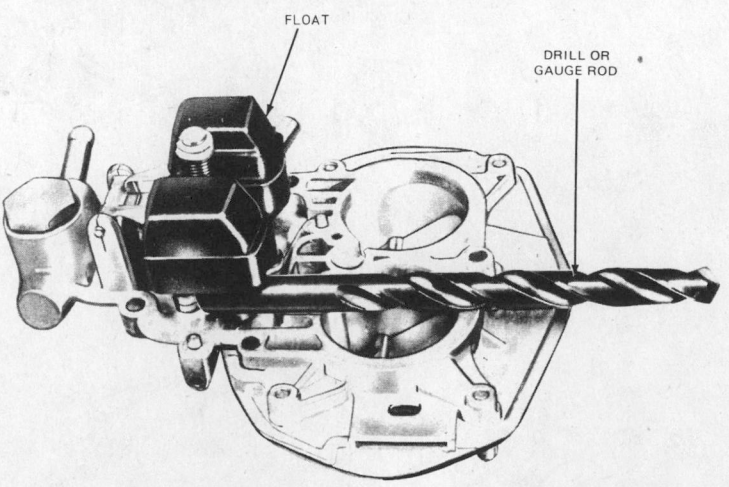

Checking float level
(© Ford Motor Co)

FORD, AUTOLITE, MOTORCRAFT MODEL 5200 SPECIFICATIONS

Year	(9510)* Carburetor Identification	Dry Float Level (in.)	Pump Hole Setting	Choke Plate Pulldown (in.)	Fast Idle Cam Linkage (in.)	Fast Idle (rpm)	Dechoke (in.)	Choke Setting	Dashpot
1971	D12F-AA	0.420	Lower	0.236	0.010	1800	0.256	Index	—
	D12F-BA	0.420	Lower	0.236	0.010	1600	0.256	Index	—
	D12F-CA	0.420	Lower	0.236	0.010	1800	0.256	Index	—
	D12F-DA	0.420	Lower	0.236	0.010	1800	0.256	1 Rich	—
	D12F-EA	0.420	Lower	0.236	0.010	1600	0.256	1 Rich	—
	D12F-FA	0.420	Lower	0.236	0.010	1800	0.256	1 Rich	—
1972	D22F-AB	0.420	3	0.236	0.156	1800	0.256	1 Lean	—
	D22F-BB	0.420	2	0.236	0.079	1600	0.256	1 Lean	—
	D22F-CB	0.420	3	0.236	0.156	1800	0.256	1 Lean	—
	D22F-DB	0.420	2	0.236	0.079	1600	0.256	1 Lean	—
	D22F-EA	0.420	3	0.236	0.156	1800	0.256	Index	—
	D22F-GA	0.420	3	0.236	0.156	1800	0.256	Index	—
1973	D32F-CA	0.420	2	0.158	0.158	1800	0.256	Index	—
	D32F-BD	0.420	2	0.158	0.118	1600	0.256	1 Lean	—
1974	D42E-AA	0.460	2	0.280	0.158	1800	0.255	Index	—
	D42E-BA	0.460	2	0.280	0.158	1800	0.255	1 Rich	—
	D42F-EA	0.460	2	0.236	0.158	1800	0.255	Index	—
	D42F-GA	0.460	2	0.236	0.158	1800	0.255	Index	—
	D4ZE-CA	0.430	2	0.195	0.195	1800	0.256	1 Rich	—
	D4ZE-BC	0.430	2	0.195	0.195	1800	0.255	1 Rich	—
	D4ZE-DC	0.430	2	0.195	0.195	1800	0.255	1 Rich	—
	D42E-EB	0.460	2	0.158	0.158	1800	0.255	Index	—
	D42E-CD	0.460	2	0.280	0.158	1800	0.255	Index	—
	D42E-AC	0.460	2	0.280	0.158	1800	0.255	Index	—
	D42E-KA	0.460	2	0.280	0.158	1800	0.255	1 Rich	—
1975	D52E-AA	0.460	2	0.200	0.100	1800	0.260	1 Lean	—
	D52E-BA	0.460	2	0.200	0.100	1800	0.260	1 Lean	—
	D52E-CA	0.460	2	0.200	0.100	1800	0.260	1 Lean	—
	D52E-DB	0.460	2	0.200	0.100	1800	0.260	1 Lean	—
	D5ZE-EA	0.460	2	0.200	0.100	1800	0.260	1 Lean	—
	D5ZE-FA	0.460	2	0.200	0.100	1800	0.260	1 Lean	—
	D5ZE-GA	0.460	2	0.200	0.100	1800	0.260	1 Lean	—
	D5ZE-HB	0.460	2	0.200	0.100	1800	0.260	1 Lean	—
1976	D6EE-BA	0.460	2	0.200	0.100	1500①	0.260	1 Lean	—
	D6EE-CA	0.460	2	0.270	0.160	1500①	0.260	1 Lean	—
	D6EE-DA	0.460	2	0.200	0.100	1500①	0.260	1 Lean	—
	D6ZE-EA	0.460	2	0.270	0.160	1500①	0.260	1 Lean	—

* Basic carburetor number
① Figure given is for all manual transmissions; for automatic trans.
   the figures are: (49 states) 2000 RPM; (Calif.) 1800 RPM.

Model 4300, 4350

The model 4300 and 4350 4 barrel carburetor is composed of three main assemblies: the air horn, the main body, and the throttle body. The air horn assembly serves as the fuel bowl cover as well as the housing for the choke valve and shaft. It contains the accelerator pump linkage, fuel inlet seat, float and lever, booster venturi, and internal fuel bowl vents.

The main body houses the fuel metering passages, accelerator pump mechanism, and the power valve.

The throttle body contains the primary and secondary throttle valves and shafts, the curb idle adjusting screw, the fast idle adjusting screw, the idle mixture adjusting screws, and the automatic choke assembly.

Float Adjustment

1. Adjustments to the fuel level are best made with the carburetor removed from the engine and the carburetor cleaned upon disassembly.
2. Invert the air horn assembly and remove the gasket from the surface.
3. Use a T-scale to measure the distance from the floats to the air horn casting. Position the scale horizontally over the flat surface of both floats at the free ends and parallel to the air horn casting. Hold the lower end of the vertical scale in full contact with the smooth surface of the air horn.

Caution The end of the vertical scale must not come into contact with any gasket sealing ridges while measuring the float level.

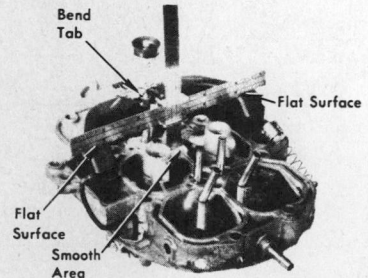

Checking float level using a T-scale
(© American Motors Co)

4. The free end of each float should just touch the horizontal scale, if one float is lower than the other; twist the float and lever assembly slightly to correct.
5. Adjust the float level by bending the tab which contacts the needle and seat assembly.

NOTE: The illustrations in this section show an alternate method of adjusting the floats on the model 4300 carburetor.

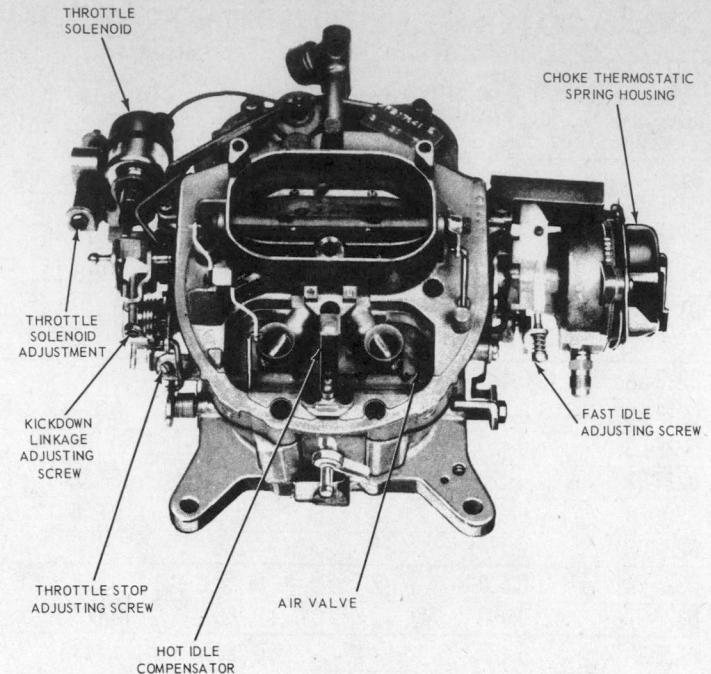

Top view—Model 4300 carburetor
(© Ford Motor Co)

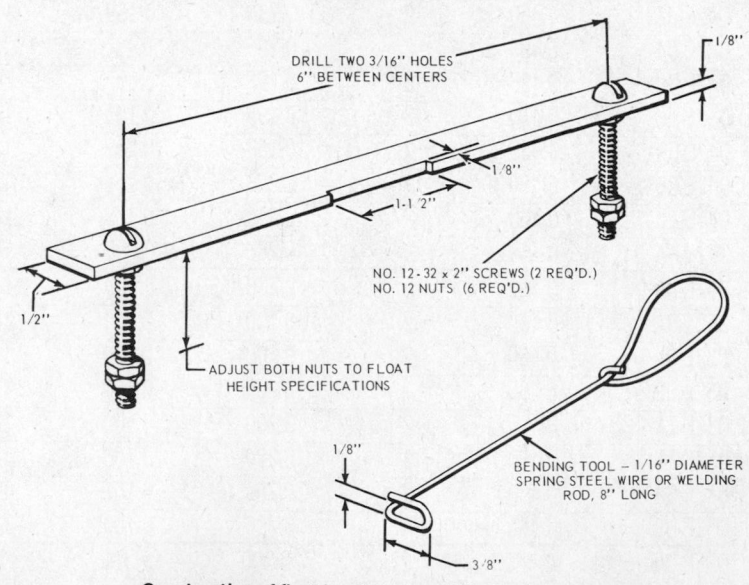

Construction of float level gauge and float arm bending tool
(© Ford Motor Co)

The procedure includes the fabrication of a gauge and a bending device. After fabricating the gauge, it is possible to adjust it to the specified dimensions and insert it into the air horn outboard holes. Both pontoons should just touch the gauge.

A float tab bending tool is also shown and may be used in the following manner.

To raise the float: insert the open end of the bending tool to the RIGHT side of the float lever tab and between the needle and float hinge. Raise the float lever off of the needle and bend the tab downward.

To lower the float: insert the bending tool to the LEFT side of the float lever tab between the needle and float hinge, support the float lever, and bend the tab upward.

Electric Choke Operating Test

4350

1. Remove the air cleaner and make sure all vacuum hoses, solenoids and electric choke wires are properly connected.
2. Check the throttle system, choke plate, choke linkage and fast idle cam to make sure that nothing is binding.
3. Disconnect the lead on the choke cap and hook up a test light to it. The test light should glow all the

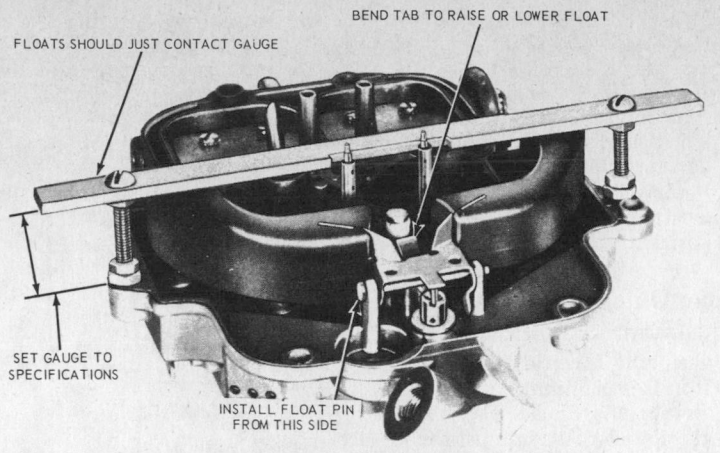

Measuring float level
(© Ford Motor Co)

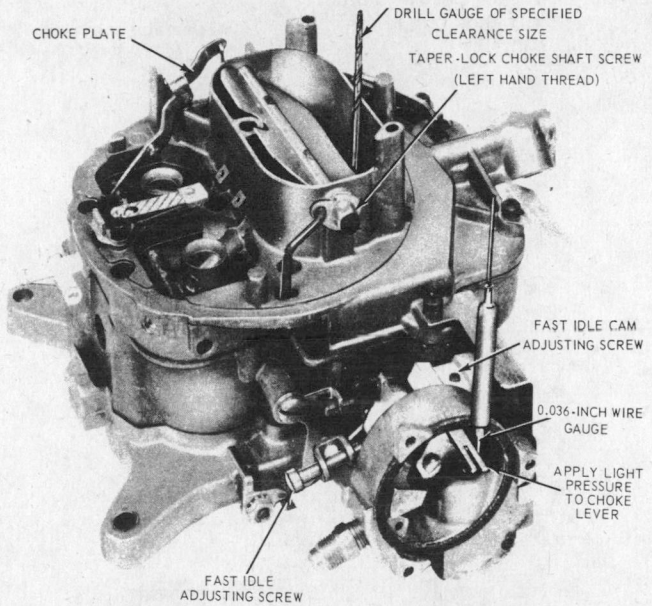

Choke plate pulldown and fast idle cam adjustment
(© Ford Motor Co)

wire in place by exerting light pressure in a rearward direction on the choke piston lever. Check the distance from the lower edge of the choke valve to the air horn wall.

6. Adjustment is done by loosening the hex head screw (left-hand thread) on the choke valve shaft and prying the link away from the shaft. Use a drill gauge 0.010 in. under the specified clearance between the lower edge of the choke valve and the air horn wall. Hold the choke valve against the gauge and maintain a light rearward pressure on the choke lever.

7. With the choke piston snug against the 0.036 in. wire and the choke valve against the drill, tighten the hex screw on the choke valve shaft. The use of a gauge 0.010 in. undersize compensates for tolerance in the linkage.

8. Use the correct size gauge for final measurement.

9. Replace the housing on the thermostatic spring.

Delayed Choke Pulldown

The 4350 is also equipped with a vacuum-diaphragm operated delayed choke pulldown that opens the choke to a wider setting after about 6-18 seconds of engine operation.

1. With the throttle set on the fast idle cam, note the position of the index marks on the cap. Loosen the retaining screws and rotate the cap ninety degrees (¼ turn), in the closing (rich) direction.

2. Disconnect the vacuum supply hose from the port on the delayed choke pulldown diaphragm as-

time the engine is running. If it doesn't glow, either the alternator or the wire itself is bad.

4. Next, connect the light series with the wire and the terminal on the choke cap. If the light doesn't glow, replace the choke cap assembly.

Choke Plate Pulldown

1. Remove the air cleaner and choke thermostatic spring housing.

2. Bend a wire gauge (0.036 in. diameter) at a 90 degree angle about ⅛ in. from one end.

3. Block the throttle open so that the fast idle screw does not contact the fast idle cam.

4. Insert the bent end of the wire gauge between the lower edge of the piston slot and the upper edge of the right hand slot in the choke housing.

5. Pull the choke piston lever counterclockwise until the gauge is snug in the piston slot. Hold the

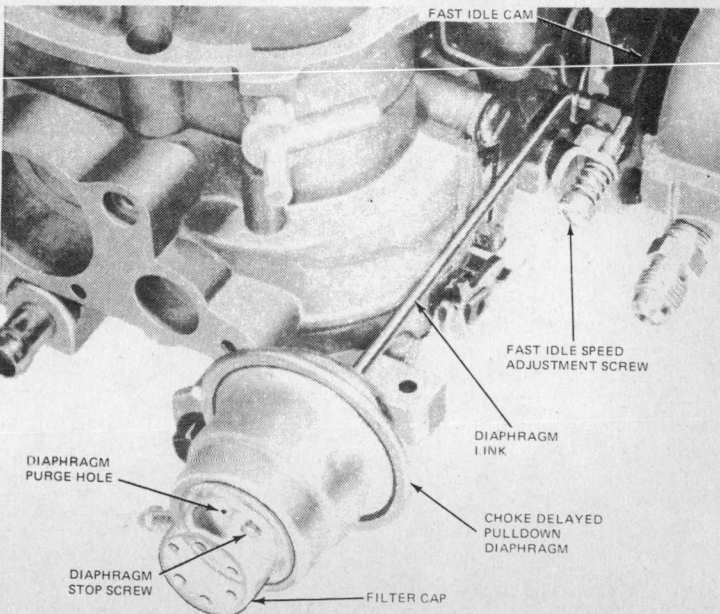

Motorcraft 4350 delayed choke assembly (© Ford Motor Co.)

sembly. After removing the filter cap, place a piece of tape over the purge hole, and apply vacuum to the port.

3. Measure the dimension at the lower edge of the choke plate at the center of the air horn. To adjust this figure, turn the stop screw on the delayed choke pulldown diaphragm.

Fast Idle Cam Adjustment

1. Loosen the screws on the choke thermostatic spring cover and rotate the housing ¼ turn counter clockwise. Tighten the screws.
2. Open the throttle and allow the choke valve to close completely.
3. Push down on the fast idle cam counterweight until the fast idle screw is in contact with the second step of the cam and against the high step.

4. Measure the clearance between the lower edge of the choke plate and the air horn wall.
5. Adjust by turning the fast idle cam adjusting screw (inward to increase clearance, outward to decrease clearance).
6. Return the housing on the thermostatic spring to its original position.

Choke Unloader (Dechoke) Adjustment

1. Open the throttle fully and hold it in this position.
2. Rotate the choke plate toward the closed position until the pawl on the fast idle speed lever contacts the fast idle cam.
3. Check the clearance between the lower edge of the choke plate and the air horn wall.

4. Adjust by bending the pawl on the fast idle speed lever forward to increase the clearance and backward to decrease the clearance.

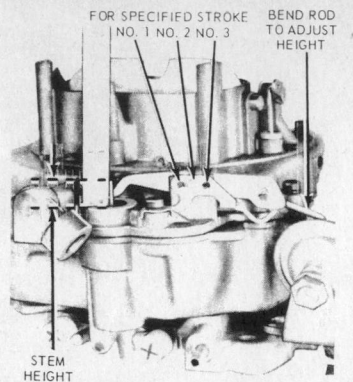

Accelerator pump adjustment
(© Ford Motor Co)

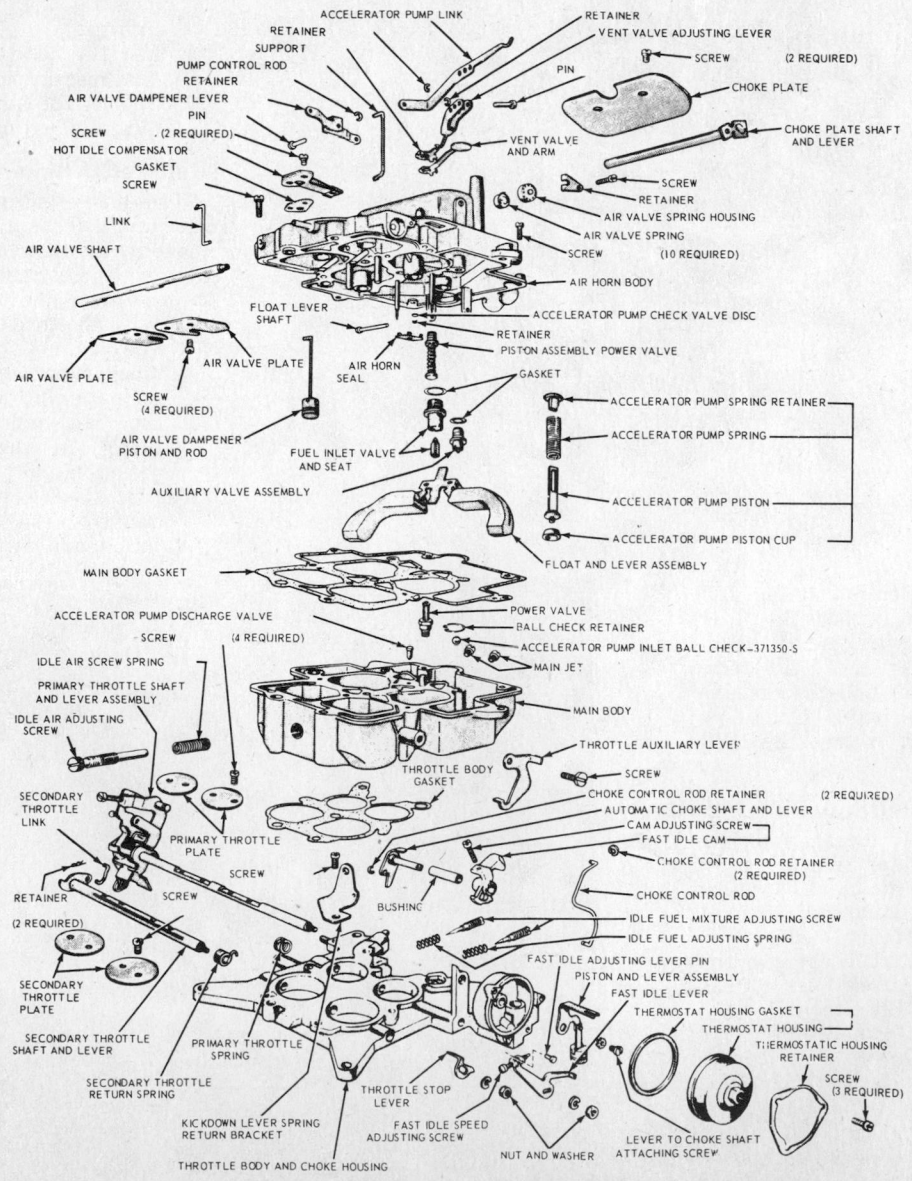

Model 4300 carburetor—disassembled
(© Ford Motor Co)

Accelerator Pump Stroke Adjustment

Model 4300 through 1974

The accelerator pump should not need adjustment as its stroke is preset in compliance with exhaust emission control standards. If for any reason the stroke must be altered, it may be done by repositioning the external link in the desired holes.

Model 4350 beginning 1975

The accelerator pump adjustment is preset at the factory for reduced exhaust emissions. Adjustment is provided only for different engine installations. The adjustment is internal, with three piston-to-shaft pin positions in the pump piston.

To check that the shaft pin is located in the specified piston hole, remove the carburetor air horn and invert it. Disconnect the accelerator pump from the operating arm by pressing downward on the spring and sliding the arm out of the pump shaft slot. Disassemble the spring and nylon keeper retaining the adjustment pin. If the pin is not in its specified hole, remove it, reposition the shaft to the correct hole in the piston assembly and reinstall the pin. Then, slide the nylon retainer over the pin and position the spring on

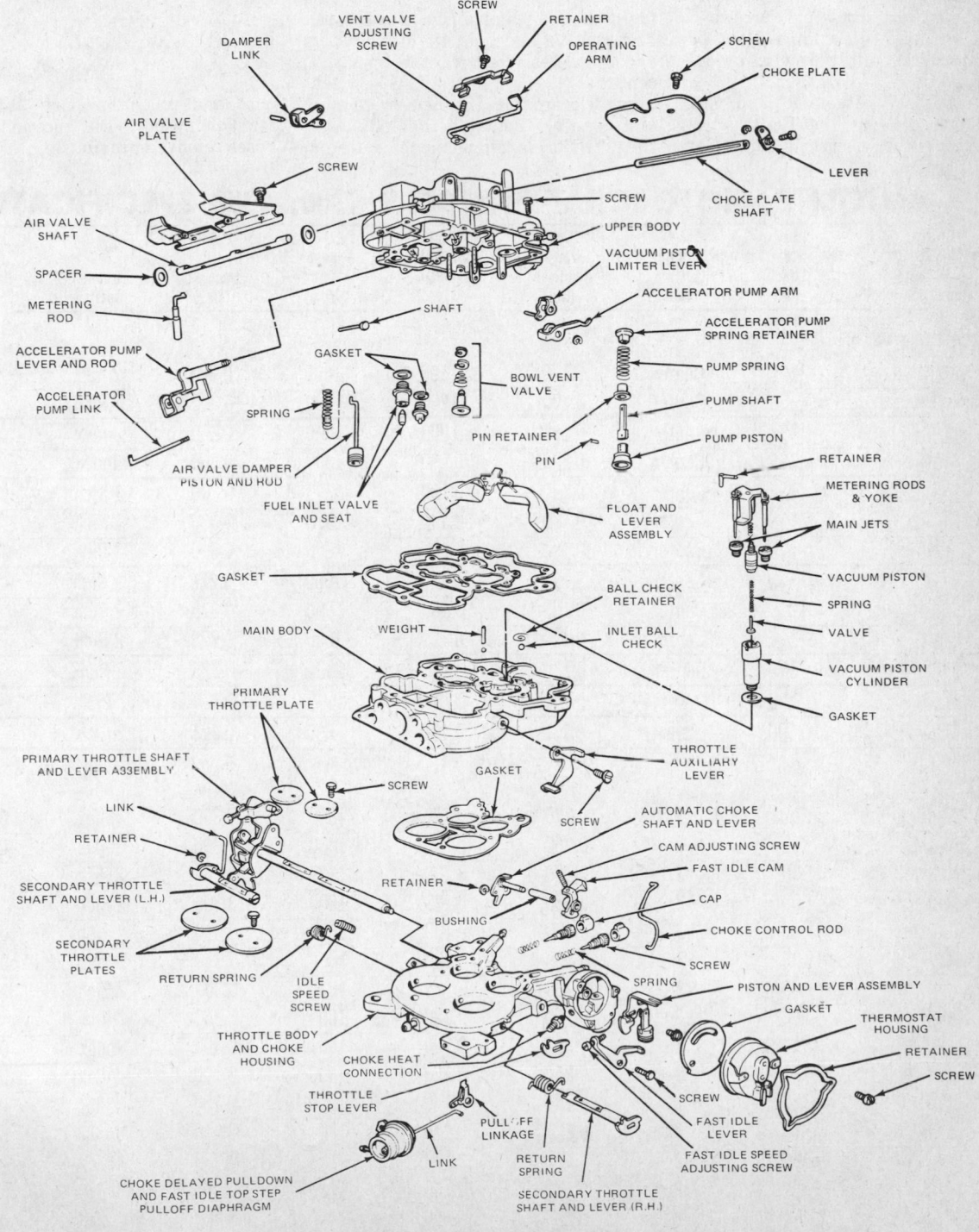

Exploded view—Motorcraft 4350-4V

the shaft. Finally, compress the spring on the shaft and install the pump on the pump arm.

NOTE: *Under no circumstances should you adjust the stroke of the accelerator pump by turning the vacuum limiter lever adjusting nut. This adjustment is preset at the factory and modification could result in poor cold driveability.*

Fast Idle Speed

The fast idle speed is adjusted with the engine at operating temperature and the fast idle screw on the second step of the fast idle cam. Adjust by turning the fast idle screw in or out as required.

On AMC cars, disconnect and plug the vacuum line at the EGR valve, and remove the electrical connector

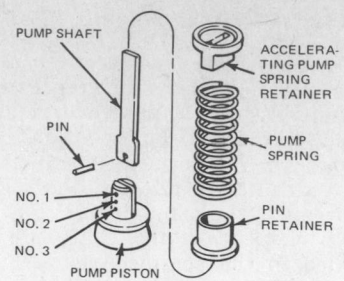

Accelerator Pump stroke adjustment— -Motorcraft 4350-4V

from the TCS valve. On Ford cars, first remove and plug the distributor vacuum lines. Remove the top and center CSSA system PVS switch hoses (located in the heater elbow) and connect them together. Remove the EGR hose from the carburetor

Fast idle adjustment (© Ford Motor Co)

port and plug the port. When the fast idle speed is set, reconnect those hoses removed previously.

FORD, AUTOLITE, MOTORCRAFT MODELS 4300, 4350 SPECIFICATIONS

Year	(9510)* Carburetor Identification ①	Dry Float Level (in.)	Pump Setting Hole	Choke Plate Pulldown (in.)	Fast Idle Cam Linkage (in.)	Fast Idle (rpm)	Dechoke (in.)	Choke Setting	Dashpot (in.)
American Motors									
1970	0WA4	13/16	Center	0.170	0.190	1600	0.300	2 Rich	1/8
	0WM4	13/16	Center	0.190	0.200	1600	0.300	2 Rich	1/16
1971	1TA4	13/16	Center	0.190	0.200	1600	0.300	Index	1/8
	1TM4	13/16	Center	0.170	0.190	1600	0.300	Index	1/16
1972	2RA4	13/16	Center	0.190	0.190	1600	0.300	1 Rich	9/64
	2TA4	13/16	Center	0.190	0.190	1600	0.300	1 Rich	9/64
	2TM4	13/16	Center	0.190	0.190	1600	0.300	1 Rich	9/64
1973	3TA4	13/16	Center	0.190	0.160	1600	0.275	2 Rich	9/64
	3TA4 (Police)	15/16	Center	0.190	0.160	1600	0.275	2 Rich	9/64
	3TM4	13/16	Center	0.190	0.160	1600	0.275	2 Rich	9/64
1974	4TA4, 4TM4	13/16	Center	0.170	0.160	1600	0.325	2 Rich	9/64
1975	5TA4	0.90	Lower	0.140	0.160	1600	0.325	2 Rich	—
1976	6TA4	0.090	Lower	0.130	0.135	1600	0.325	2 Rich	—
Ford Products									
1970	D0AF-K	49/64	2	0.220	0.170	1300	0.300	Index	0.070
	D0AF-L	25/32	2	0.250	0.220	1400	0.300	Index	0.070
	D0AF-M	1.00	3	0.160	0.120	1600	0.300	2 Rich	0.080
	D0AF-R	1.00	3	0.160	0.120	1600	0.300	2 Rich	—
	D0AF-AD	1.00	3	0.160	0.120	1600	0.300	2 Rich	0.080
	D0AF-AJ	1.00	3	0.160	0.120	1600	0.300	2 Rich	0.080
	D0AF-AE	1.00	3	0.160	0.120	1600	0.300	2 Rich	—
	D0AF-AK	1.00	3	0.160	0.120	1600	0.300	2 Rich	—
	D0AF-AB	25/32	2	0.250	0.220	1400	0.300	Index	0.070
	D0AF-AL	25/32	2	0.250	0.220	1400	0.300	Index	0.070
	D0AF-AG	25/32	2	0.220	0.170	1300	0.300	Index	0.070
	D0AF-AM	25/32	2	0.220	0.170	1300	0.300	Index	0.070
	D0AF-AN	49/64	2	0.225	0.170	1350	0.300	Index	0.070
	D0OF-B	13/16	2	0.180	0.160	1250	0.300	Index	—
	D0OF-C	13/16	2	0.200	0.180	1400	0.300	Index	0.080
	D0OF-D	13/16	2	0.180	0.160	1250	0.300	Index	—

FORD, AUTOLITE, MOTORCRAFT MODELS 4300, 4350 SPECIFICATIONS

Year	(9510)* Carburetor Identification ①	Dry Float Level (in.)	Pump Setting Hole	Choke Plate Pulldown (in.)	Fast Idle Cam Linkage (in.)	Fast Idle (rpm)	Dechoke (in.)	Choke Setting	Dashpot (in.)
Ford Products									
1970	D0OF-H	13/16	2	0.200	0.180	1400	0.300	Index	——
	D0OF-Y	13/16	2	0.180	0.160	1250	0.300	Index	——
	D0OF-Z	13/16	2	0.180	0.160	1250	0.300	Index	——
	D0OF-AA	13/16	2	0.200	0.180	1400	0.300	Index	——
	D0OF-AB	13/16	2	0.180	0.160	1250	0.300	Index	——
	D0OF-AC	13/16	2	0.200	0.180	1400	0.300	Index	0.080
	D0OF-AD	13/16	2	0.200	0.180	1400	0.300	Index	——
	D0OF-AE	13/16	2	0.180	0.160	1250	0.300	Index	——
	D0SF-A	25/32	2	0.220	0.170	1300	0.300	Index	0.070
	D0SF-D	25/32	2	0.220	0.170	1300	0.300	Index	0.070
	D0SF-E	25/32	2	0.220	0.170	1300	0.300	Index	0.070
	D0VF-A	25/32	2	0.230	0.170	1250	0.300	Index	0.100
1971	D1AF-MA	49/64	2	0.220	——	1350	——	Index	1/16
	D10F-EA	13/16	2	0.180	0.160	1250	——	Index	——
	D10F-AAA	13/16	2	0.200	0.180	1400	——	Index	——
	D1SF-AA	49/64	2	0.220	——	1350	——	Index	1/16
	D1VF-AA	49/64	2	0.220	0.170	1250	——	1 Rich	0.100
1972	D2AF-AA	49/64	1	0.220	0.200	1350	——	2 Rich	——
	D2AF-LA	49/64	1	0.215	0.190	1900	——	2 Rich	——
	D2SF-AA	49/64	1	0.220	0.200	1350	——	2 Rich	——
	D2SF-BA	49/64	1	0.220	0.200	1350	——	2 Rich	——
	D2VF-AA	49/64	1	0.230	0.200	1250	——	Index	——
	D2VF-BA	49/64	1	0.230	0.200	1250	——	Index	——
	D2ZF-AA	13/16	1	0.200	0.180	1200	——	Index	——
	D2ZF-BB	13/16	1	0.200	0.200	1200	——	Index	——
	D2ZF-DA	13/16	1	0.200	0.200	1200	——	Index	——
	D2ZF-GA	13/16	1	0.200	0.180	1200	——	Index	——
1973	D3VF-DA	0.76	1	0.210	0.190	1350	——	Index	——
	D3ZF-AC	0.82	1	0.180	0.180	1300	——	Index	——
	D3ZF-BC	0.82	1	0.170	0.170	1300	——	INR	——
	D3ZF-DC	0.82	1	0.180	0.180	1300	——	Index	——
	D3AF-HA	0.76	1	0.210	0.200	1350	——	Index	——
	D3AF-EB	0.88	1	0.200	0.200	1900	——	Index	——
1974	D4AE-AA	3/4	1	0.230	0.200	1900	——	Index	——
	D4AE-NA, D4VE-AB	3/4	1	0.220	0.200	1250	——	Index	——
	D4TE-ATA	13/16	1	0.220	0.180	1250	——	Index	——
	D40E-AA	13/16	1	0.180	0.180	1800	——	Index	——
1975	D5VE-AD	15/16	1	②	0.160	1600	0.300	2 Rich	——
	D5VE-BA	15/16	1	②	0.160	1600	0.300	2 Rich	——
	D5AE-CA	31/32	1	②	0.160	1600	0.300	2 Rich	——
	D5AE-DA	31/32	1	②	0.160	1600	0.300	2 Rich	——
1976	D6AE-CA	1.00	2	0.140③	0.140	1350	0.30	2 Rich	——
	D6AE-FA	1.00	2	0.140③	0.140	1350	0.30	2 Rich	——
	D6AE-DA	1.00	2	0.160④	0.160	1350	0.30	2 Rich	——

* Basic carburetor number for Ford products.
① The identification tag is on the bowl cover.
② Initial—0.160 in. Delayed—0.190 in.
③ Initial Figure given; delayed—0.190
④ Initial Figure given; delayed—0.210

Rochester Carburetors

Model 1ME

This is a new Rochester Monojet carburetor, designed for use on the Chevette. It is a single bore down-draft unit with a triple venturi. Some models have a hot idle compensator. The 1ME has an integral automatic choke system with an electrically heated choke coil.

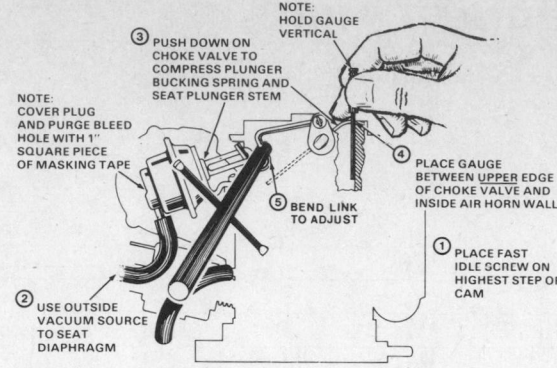

1ME Vacuum break adjustment (© Chevrolet Div., G.M. Corp.)

Float Level Adjustment

1. Remove the top of the carburetor.
2. Hold the float retaining pin in place and push down on the float arm at the outer end against the top of the float needle valve.
3. Measure the distance from the bump on the top of the float at the end to the bowl gasket surface, without the gasket.
4. To adjust, bend the float arm at the point where it joins the float.

Metering Rod Adjustment

1. Remove the top of the carburetor.
2. Back out the idle stop solenoid and rotate the fast idle cam so that the fast idle screw does not contact the cam.
3. With the throttle valve completely closed, make sure the power piston is all the way up.
4. Insert the specified size gauge between the bowl gasket surface with no gasket and the lower surface of the metering rod holder, next to the metering rod.
5. To adjust, carefully bend the metering rod holder.

Fast Idle Speed Adjustment

1. The engine should be at normal temperature with the air cleaner in place. Disconnect and plug the EGR valve vacuum line.
2. Make sure that the curb idle speed is as specified.
3. Place the fast idle screw on the highest cam step with the engine running.
4. Adjust the fast idle speed screw to the correct fast idle speed.

Fast Idle Cam Adjustment

1. Hold the fast idle speed screw on the second cam step against the shoulder of the high step.
2. Hold the choke valve closed with a finger.
3. Insert the specified gauge between the center upper edge of the choke valve and the airhorn wall.
4. Bend the linkage rod at the upper angle to adjust.

Vacuum Break Adjustment

1. Place the fast idle speed screw on the highest cam step.
2. Tape over the bleed hole in the diaphragm unit. Apply suction by mouth to seat the diaphragm.
3. Push down on the choke valve with a finger.
4. Insert the gauge between the

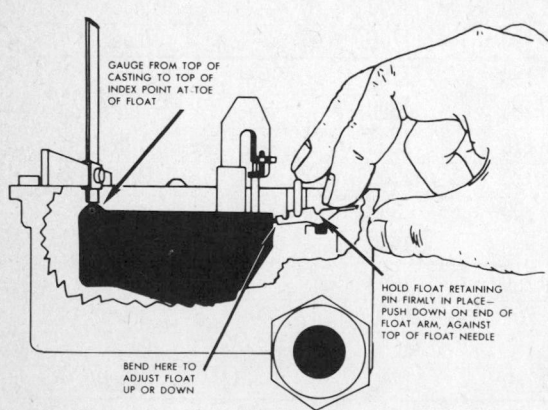

1ME Float level adjustment (© Chevrolet Div., G.M. Corp.)

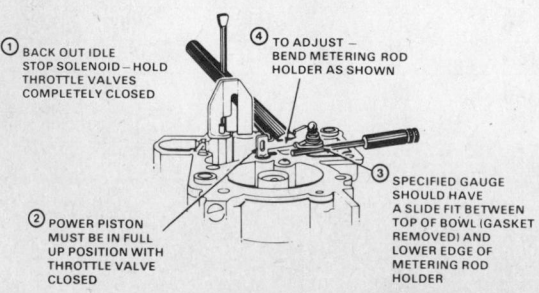

1ME Metering rod adjustment (© Chevrolet Div., G.M. Corp.)

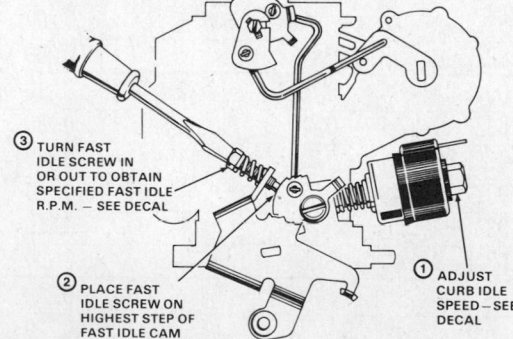

1ME Fast idle speed adjustment (© Chevrolet Div., G.M. Corp.)

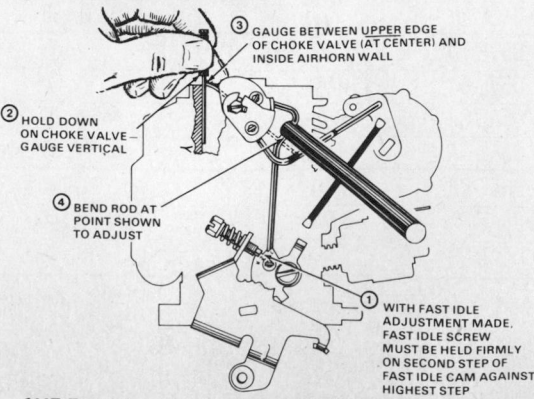

1ME Fast idle cam adjustment (© Chevrolet Div., G.M. Corp.)

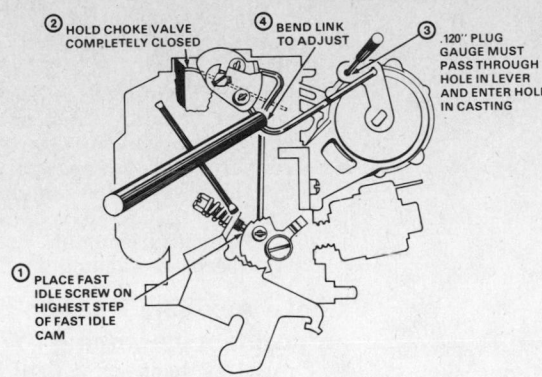

1ME Choke coil lever adjustment (© Chevrolet Div., G.M. Corp.)

1ME Electric choke adjustment (© Chevrolet Div., G.M. Corp.)

upper edge of the choke valve and the airhorn wall.
5. Bend the link to adjust.

Choke Unloader Adjustment

1. Hold the throttle valve wide open.
2. Hold down the choke valve with a finger and insert the specified gauge between the upper edge of the choke valve and the airhorn wall.
3. Bend the linkage tang to adjust.

Choke Coil Lever Adjustment

1. Place the fast idle speed screw on the highest cam step.
2. Hold the choke valve closed.
3. Insert a 0.120 in. gauge through the hole in the arm on the choke housing and into the hole in the casting.
4. Bend the link to adjust.

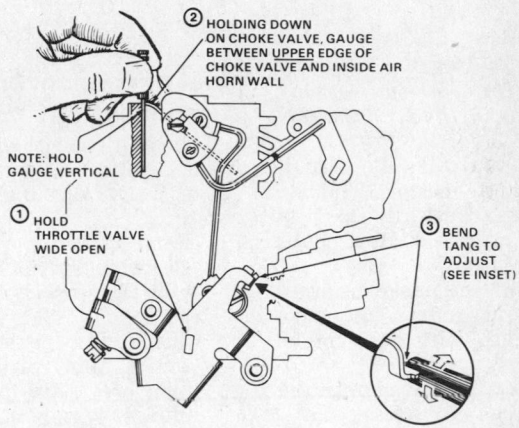

1ME Choke unloader adjustment (© Chevrolet Div., G.M. Corp.)

Electric Choke Adjustment

1. Place the fast idle cam follower on the high step.
2. Loosen the three retaining screws and rotate the cover counterclockwise until the choke valve just closes.
3. Align the index mark on the cover with the specified housing mark.
4. Tighten the three screws.

1ME CARBURETOR SPECIFICATIONS

CHEVROLET CHEVETTE

Year	Carburetor Identification① Number	Float Level (in.)	Metering Rod (in.)	Fast Idle Speed (rpm)	Fast Idle Cam (in.)	Vacuum Break (in.)	Choke Unloader (in.)	Choke Setting (notches)
1976	17056030, 17056036, 17056031, 17056037	5/32	0.072	2000②	0.065	0.070	0.165	3 Rich
	17056032, 17056034, 17056033, 17056035	5/32	0.073	2000③	0.045	0.070	0.200	3 Rich
	17056330, 17056331	5/32	0.072	2000	0.065	0.070	0.165	3 Rich
	17056332, 17056333, 17056334	5/32	0.073	2000	0.045	0.070	0.200	3 Rich
	17056335	5/32	0.073	2000	0.045	0.120	0.200	3 Rich

① Stamped on float bowl, next to fuel inlet nut
② 2200 rpm for the first two numbers
③ 2200 rpm for the last two numbers

Model MV

The model MV carburetor is a single bore, down-draft carburetor with an aluminum throttle body, automatic choke, internally balanced venting, and a hot idle compensating system for cars equipped with automatic transmissions. Newer models are also equipped with Combination Emission Control valves (C.E.C.) and an Exhaust Gas Recirculation (EGR) system. An electrically operated idle stop solenoid replaces the idle stop screw of older models.

The MV carburetor is used on General Motors inline four and six cylinder cars.

Fast Idle Adjustment

NOTE: *The fast idle adjustment must be made with the transmission in Neutral.*

1. Disconnect and plug the distributor vacuum line on 1976 and later models. Position the fast idle lever on the high step of the fast idle cam.
2. Be sure that the choke is properly adjusted and in the wide open position with the engine warm.
3. Bend the fast idle lever until the specified speed is obtained.

Choke Rod (fast idle cam) Adjustment

NOTE: *Adjust the fast idle before making choke rod adjustments.*

1. Place the fast idle cam follower on the second step of the fast idle cam and hold it firmly against the rise to the high step.
2. Rotate the choke valve in the direction of a closed choke by applying force to the choke coil lever.
3. Bend the choke rod to give the specified opening between the lower edge (upper edge starting 1976) of the choke valve and the inside air horn wall.

NOTE: *Measurement must be made at the center of the choke valve.*

Choke Vacuum Break Adjustment

The adjustment of the vacuum break diaphragm unit insures correct choke valve opening after engine starting.

1. Remove the air cleaner on vehicles with Therm AC air cleaner; plug the sensor's vacuum take off port.
2. Using an external vacuum source, apply vacuum to the vacuum break diaphragm until the plunger is fully seated.

3. When the plunger is seated, push the choke valve toward the closed position.
4. Holding the choke valve in this position, place the specified gauge between the lower edge (upper edge starting 1976) of the choke valve and the air horn wall.
5. If the measurement is not correct, bend the vacuum break rod.

Choke Auxiliary Vacuum Break Adjustment (beginning 1975)

This adjustment is required in addition to the preceding vacuum break adjustment, beginning 1975.

1. Using an external source of vacuum, apply vacuum to the auxiliary vacuum break diaphram until the plunger is seated fully.
2. Place the cam follower on the highest step of the fast idle cam.
3. With the diaphragm seated, insert the specified gauge between the upper edge of the choke valve and the inner air horn wall.
4. To adjust the clearance, bend the link between the vacuum break and the choke lever.

NOTE: *The auxiliary vacuum break diaphragm is on the same side of the carburetor as the throttle stop solenoid.*

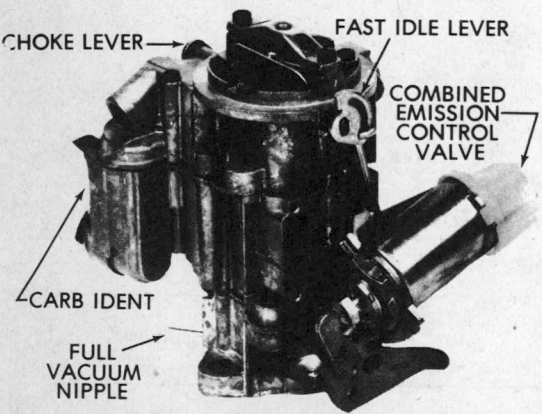

Rochester Monojet Carburetor
(© Buick Div., G.M. Corp)

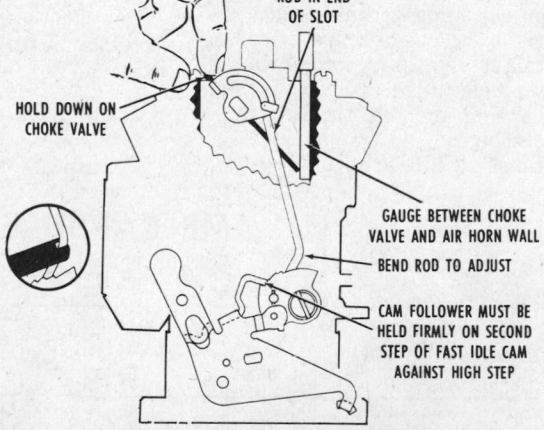

Fast Idle Cam Adjustment through 1975
(© Chevrolet Div., G.M. Corp)

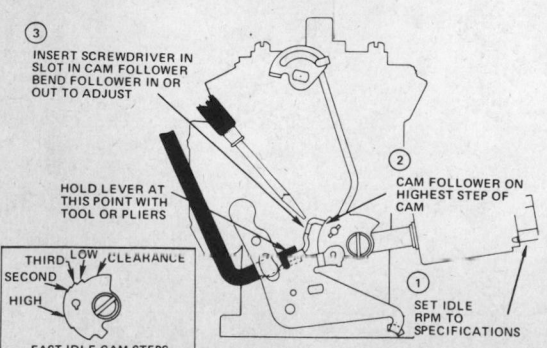

Fast Idle Adjustment
(© Chevrolet Div., G.M. Corp)

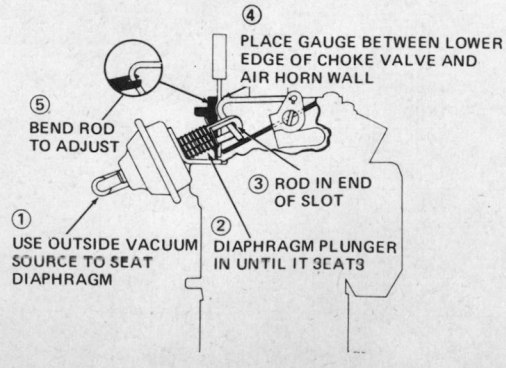

Vacuum Break Adjustment through 1975
(© Chevrolet Div., G.M. Corp)

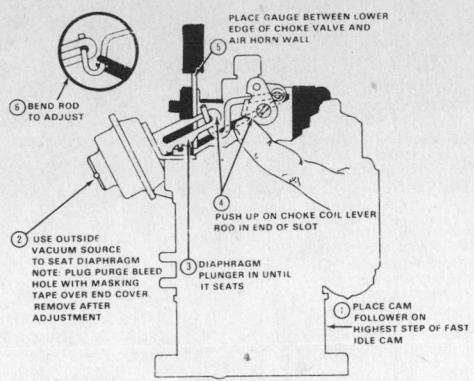

Primary vacuum break adjustment, beginning 1975
(© Chevrolet Div., G.M. Corp.)

PLACE GAUGE BETWEEN LOWER
EDGE OF CHOKE VALVE AND
AIR HORN WALL

⑥ BEND ROD
TO ADJUST

② USE OUTSIDE
VACUUM SOURCE
TO SEAT DIAPHRAGM
NOTE: PLUG PURGE BLEED
HOLE WITH MASKING
TAPE OVER END COVER
REMOVE AFTER
ADJUSTMENT

④ PUSH UP ON CHOKE COIL LEVER
ROD IN END OF SLOT

③ DIAPHRAGM
PLUNGER IN UNTIL
IT SEATS

① PLACE CAM
FOLLOWER ON
HIGHEST STEP OF FAST
IDLE CAM

④ PLACE SPECIFIED
GAUGE BETWEEN UPPER
EDGE OF CHOKE VALVE AND
INNER AIR HORN WALL

② USE OUTSIDE
VACUUM SOURCE TO
SEAT DIAPHRAGM

③ DIAPHRAGM
PLUNGER
IN UNTIL SEATED

⑤ BEND LINK
TO ADJUST

① CAM FOLLOWER
ON HIGHEST STEP
OF CAM

Auxiliary vacuum break adjustment, beginning 1975
(© Chevrolet Div., G.M. Corp.)

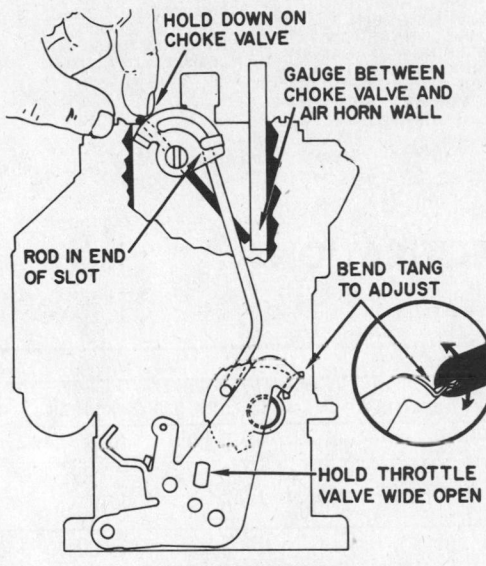

HOLD DOWN ON
CHOKE VALVE

GAUGE BETWEEN
CHOKE VALVE AND
AIR HORN WALL

ROD IN END
OF SLOT

BEND TANG
TO ADJUST

HOLD THROTTLE
VALVE WIDE OPEN

Adjusting Choke Unloader
(© Chevrolet Div., G.M. Corp)

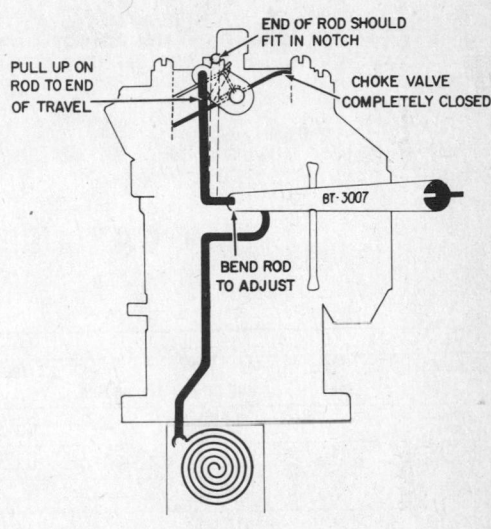

PULL UP ON
ROD TO END
OF TRAVEL

END OF ROD SHOULD
FIT IN NOTCH

CHOKE VALVE
COMPLETELY CLOSED

BT-3007

BEND ROD
TO ADJUST

Choke Coil Rod Adjustment
(© Pontiac Div., G.M. Corp)

Choke Unloader Adjustment

1. Apply pressure to the choke valve and hold it in the closed position.
2. Open the throttle valve to the wide open position.
3. Check the dimension between the lower edge (upper edge starting 1976) of the choke plate and the air horn wall; if adjustment is needed, bend the unloader tang on the throttle lever.

Choke Coil Rod Adjustment

1. Disconnect the thermostatic coil rod from the upper choke lever and hold the choke valve closed.
2. Push down on the coil rod to the end of its travel.
3. The top of the rod should be even with the bottom hole in the choke lever.
4. To make adjustments, bend the rod.

Float Adjustment

1. Hold the float retainer in place and the float arm against the top of the float needle by pushing down on the float arm at the outer end toward the float bowl casting.
2. Using an adjustable T scale, measure the distance from the toe of the float to the float bowl gasket surface.

   NOTE: The float bowl gasket should be removed and the gauge held on the index point on the float for accurate measurement.
3. Adjust the float level by bending the float arm up or down at the float arm junction.

Metering Rod Adjustment

1. Hold the throttle valve wide open and push down on the metering rod against spring tension, then remove the rod from the main metering jet.
2. In order to check adjustment, the slow idle screw must be backed out and the fast idle cam rotated so that the fast idle cam follower does not contact the steps on the cam.
3. With the throttle valve closed, push down on the power piston until it contacts its stop.
4. With the power piston depressed, swing the metering rod holder over the flat surface of the bowl casting next to the carburetor bore.
5. Insert a specified size drill between the bowl casting sealing bead and the lower surface of the metering rod holder. The drill should slide smoothly between both surfaces.
6. If adjustment is needed, carefully bend the metering rod holder up or down at the point shown. After adjustment, reinstall the metering rod.

Idle Vent Adjustment

1. The engine idle must be set at the specified RPM and the choke valve held wide open so that the

fast idle cam follower is not contacting the cam.

NOTE: If the carburetor is off the car, a preliminary idle setting can be made by turning the idle speed screw in 1½ turns from the closed throttle valve position.

2. With the throttle stop screw held against the idle stop screw, the idle vent valve should be open to specification. To check, a drill of specified size may be inserted between the top of the air horn casting and the bottom surface of the valve.

3. If adjustment is necessary, turn the slotted vent valve head with a screwdriver. Turning the head clockwise *increases* the clearance.

NOTE: On models equipped with an idle stop solenoid, the solenoid must be activated when checking and adjusting the valve.

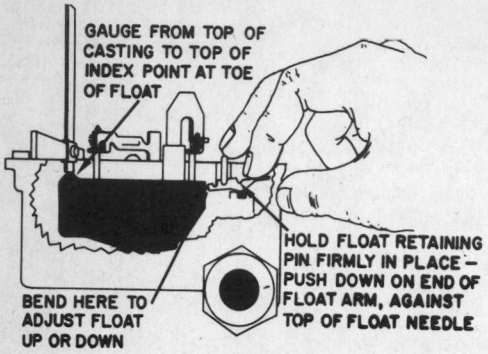

Float Level
(© Pontiac Div., G.M. Corp)

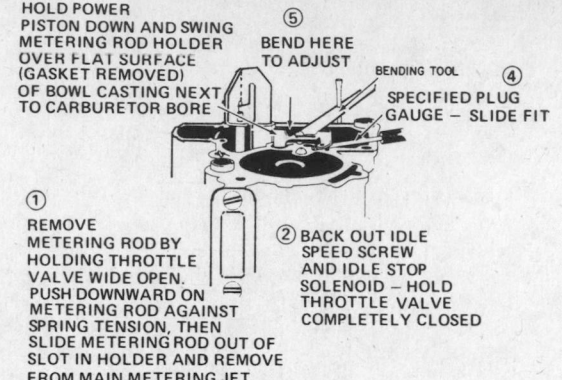

Metering Rod Adjustment
(© Chevrolet Div., G.M. Corp)

MV CARBURETOR SPECIFICATIONS

BUICK

Year	Carburetor Identification①	Float Level (in.)	Metering Rod (in.)	Pump Rod	Idle Vent (in.)	Vacuum Break (in.)	Auxiliary Vacuum Break (in.)	Fast Idle Off Car (in.)	Choke Rod (in.)	Choke Unloader (in.)	Fast Idle Speed (rpm)
1970	7040014	¼	0.070	——	0.050	0.245	——	——	0.170	0.350	650
	7040015	¼	0.140	——	0.050	0.275	——	——	0.200	0.350	900
	7040017	¼	0.070	——	——	0.230	——	0.100	0.190	0.350	900
1971	7041014	¼	0.080	——	0.050	0.225	——	——	0.160	0.500	500
	7041017	¼	0.080	——	0.050	0.225	——	——	0.180	0.350	550
1974	Automatic	¼	0.080	——	——	0.300	——	——	0.245	0.500	1800②
	Manual	¼	0.080	——	——	0.350	——	——	0.275	0.500	1800②
1975	7045012	¹¹/₃₂	0.080	——	——	0.200	0.215	——	0.160	0.275	1700②
	7045013	¹¹/₃₂	0.080	——	——	0.350	0.312	——	0.275	0.275	1800②
	7045314	¹¹/₃₂	0.080	——	——	0.275	0.312	——	0.230	0.275	1700②

① The Carburetor identification number is stamped on the float bowl, next to the fuel inlet nut.
② In Neutral or Park

CHEVROLET

Year	Carburetor Identification①	Float Level (in.)	Metering Rod (in.)	Pump Rod	Idle Vent (in.)	Vacuum Break (in.)	Auxiliary Vacuum Break (in.)	Fast Idle Off Car (in.)	Choke Rod (in.)	Choke Unloader (in.)	Fast Idle Speed (rpm)
1970	7040014	¼	0.070	——	——	0.200	——	0.110	0.170	0.350	2400②
	7040017	¼	0.090	——	——	0.160	——	0.100	0.190	0.350	2400②
1971	7041014	¼	0.080	——	——	0.200	——	0.100	0.160	0.350	——
	7041017	¼	0.080	——	——	0.230	——	0.100	0.180	0.350	——
	7041023	¹/₁₆	——	——	——	0.200	——	0.110	0.120	0.350	——
1972	7042014	¼	0.080	——	——	0.190	——	——	0.125	0.500	2400②
	7042017	¼	0.078	——	——	0.225	——	——	0.150	0.500	2400②
	7042984	¼	0.078	——	——	0.190	——	——	0.125	0.500	2400②
	7042987	¼	0.076	——	——	0.225	——	——	0.150	0.500	2400②

CHEVROLET

Year	Carburetor Identification[1]	Float Level (in.)	Metering Rod (in.)	Pump Rod	Idle Vent (in.)	Vacuum Break (in.)	Auxiliary Vacuum Break (in.)	Fast Idle Off Car (in.)	Choke Rod (in.)	Choke Unloader (in.)	Fast Idle Speed (rpm)
1973	7043014	1/4	0.080	——	——	0.300	——	——	0.245	0.500	1800[2]
	7043017	1/4	0.080	——	——	0.350	——	——	0.275	0.500	1800[2]
1974	7044014	3/10	0.079	——	——	0.275	——	——	0.230	0.500	1800[2][3]
	7044017	3/10	0.072	——	——	0.350	——	——	0.275	0.500	1800[2][3]
	7044314	3/10	0.073	——	——	0.300	——	——	0.245	0.500	1800[2][3]
1975	7045013	11/32	0.080	——	——	0.200	0.215	——	0.160	0.215	1800[4]
	7045012	11/32	0.080	——	——	0.350	0.312	——	0.275	0.275	1800[4]
	7045314	11/32	0.080	——	——	0.275	0.312	——	0.230	0.275	1800[4]
1976	17056012	11/32	0.084	——	——	0.140	0.265	——	0.100	0.260	2200[5]
	17066013	11/32	0.082	——	——	0.140	0.325	——	0.140	0.260	2100
	17056016	11/32	0.080	——	——	0.140	WFO	——	0.115	0.260	2200[5]
	17056018	11/32	0.084	——	——	0.140	0.265	——	0.100	0.260	2200[5]
	17056314	11/32	0.083	——	——	0.150	0.325	——	0.135	0.260	1700

[1] The carburetor identification number is stamped on the float bowl, next to the fuel inlet nut.
[2] High step of cam.
[3] Without vacuum advance.
[4] 1700 rpm with automatic transmission in neutral.
[5] 2100 rpm with integral intake manifold.

CHEVROLET VEGA, MONZA

Year	Carburetor Identification[1]	Float Level (in.)	Metering Rod (in.)	Pump Rod (in.)	Vacuum Break (in.)	Auxiliary Vacuum Break (in.)	Fast Idle Off Car (in.)	Choke Rod (in.)	Choke Unloader (in.)	Fast Idle Speed (rpm)
1971	Manual	1/16	——	——	0.200	——	0.110	0.120	0.350	2400[1]
	Automatic	1/16	——	——	0.140	——	0.110	0.080	0.350	2400[2]
1972	Manual	1/8	——	——	0.200	——	0.110	0.130	0.375	2400[2]
	Automatic	1/16	——	——	0.120	——	0.110	0.070	0.375	2800[2]
1973	Manual	0.06	——	——	0.140	——	——	0.110	0.375	2000[3]
	Automatic	0.06	——	——	0.120	——	——	0.085	0.375	2200[3]
1974	Manual	0.06	——	——	0.130	——	——	0.080	0.375	2000[3]
	Automatic	0.06	——	——	0.130	——	——	0.080	0.375	2200[3]
1975	Manual	1/8	——	——	0.100	0.450	——	0.080	0.375	2000
	Automatic	1/8	——	——	0.100	0.450	——	0.080	0.375	2200
1976	Manual	1/8	——	——	0.060	0.450	——	0.045	0.215	1200
	Automatic	1/8	——	——	0.060	0.450	——	0.045	0.215	750

[1] The carburetor identification number is stamped on the float bowl, next to the fuel inlet nut.
[2] TCS disconnected for full vacuum advance.
[3] No vacuum to distributor.

OLDSMOBILE

Year	Carburetor Identification[1]	Float Level (in.)	Metering Rod (in.)	Pump Rod	Idle Vent (in.)	Vacuum Break (in.)	Auxiliary Vacuum Break (in.)	Fast Idle Off Car (in.)	Choke Rod (in.)	Choke Unloader (in.)	Fast Idle Speed (rpm)
1970	7040014	1/4	0.070	——	——	0.200	——	——	0.170	0.350	900[3]
	7040017	1/4	0.070	——	——	0.225	——	——	0.190	0.350	750[3]
1971	7041014	1/4	0.070	——	——	0.200	——	——	0.160	0.350	900[3]
	7041019	1/4	0.070	——	——	0.225	——	——	0.180	0.350	750[3]
1973-74	Manual	1/4	0.080	——	——	0.350	——	——	0.275	0.500	[2]
	Automatic	1/4	0.080	——	——	0.300	——	——	0.245	0.500	[2]

Rochester Carburetors

OLDSMOBILE

Year	Carburetor Identification①	Float Level (in.)	Metering Rod (in.)	Pump Rod	Idle Vent (in.)	Vacuum Break (in.)	Auxiliary Vacuum Break (in.)	Fast Idle Off Car (in.)	Choke Rod (in.)	Choke Unloader (in.)	Fast Idle Speed (rpm)
1975	Manual	¹¹/₃₂	0.080	——	——	0.350	0.312	——	0.275	0.275	1800②
	Automatic	¹¹/₃₂	0.080	——	——	0.200	0.215		0.160	0.275	1800②
1976	4-140 Man.	⅛	——	——	——	0.055	0.450	——	0.045	0.215	——
	4-140 Auto.	⅛	——	——	——	0.060	0.450	——	0.045	0.215	——
	17056012	¹¹/₃₂	——	——	——	0.140	0.265	——	0.100	0.265	——
	17056013	¹¹/₃₂	——	——	——	0.165	0.320	——	0.140	0.265	——
	17056014	¹¹/₃₂	——	——	——	0.140	0.265	——	0.100	0.265	——
	17056015	¹¹/₃₂	——	——	——	0.165	0.320	——	0.140	0.265	——
	17056018	¹¹/₃₂	——	——	——	0.140	0.260	——	0.100	0.265	——
	17056314	¹¹/₃₂	——	——	——	0.165	0.320	——	0.135	0.265	——

① The carburetor identification number is stamped on the float bowl, next to the fuel inlet nut.
② Preset
③ Low step of cam.

PONTIAC

Year	Carburetor Identification①	Float Level (in.)	Metering Rod (in.)	Pump Rod	Idle Vent (in.)	Vacuum Break (in.)	Auxiliary Vacuum Break (in.)	Fast Idle Off Car (in.)	Choke Rod (in.)	Choke Unloader (in.)	Fast Idle Speed (rpm)
1970	7040014	¼	0.100	——	——	0.200	——	——	0.170	0.350	——
	7040017	¼	0.100	——	——	0.230	——	——	0.190	0.350	——
1971	7041014	¼	0.080	——	——	0.200	——	——	0.160	0.350	——
	7041017	¼	0.078	——	——	0.225	——	——	0.180	0.350	——
1972	7042014	¼	0.080	——	——	0.200	——	——	0.160	0.500	2400②
	7042017	¼	0.080	——	——	0.230	——	——	0.180	0.500	2400②
	7042984	¼	0.080	——	——	0.200	——	——	0.160	0.500	2400②
	7042987	¼	0.080	——	——	0.230	——	——	0.180	0.500	2400②
1973	7043014	¼	0.080	——	——	0.300	——	——	0.245	0.500	2400②
	7043017	¾	0.080	——	——	0.350	——	——	0.275	0.500	2400②
1974	7044041	0.354	0.079	——	——	0.275	——	——	0.230	0.500	1800②
	7044017	0.354	0.072	——	——	0.350	——	——	0.275	0.500	1800②
	7044314	0.354	0.073	——	——	0.300	——	——	0.245	0.500	1800②
1975	7045012	¹¹/₃₂	0.080	——	——	0.200	0.215	——	0.160	0.275	1800②
	7045013	¹¹/₃₂	0.080	——	——	0.350	0.312	——	0.275	0.275	1800②
	7045014	¹¹/₃₂	0.080	——	——	0.257	0.312	——	0.230	0.275	1800②
	Astre Man.	⅛	——	——	——	0.130	——	——	0.080	0.375	2000③
	Astre Auto.	⅛	——	——	——	0.130	——	——	0.080	0.375	2000③
1976	4-140 Man.	⅛	——	——	——	0.055	0.450	——	0.045	0.215	——
	4-140 Auto.	⅛	——	——	——	0.060	0.450	——	0.045	0.215	——
	6-250 Man.	¹¹/₃₂	——	——	——	0.165	0.320	——	0.140	0.265	——
	6-250 Auto	¹¹/₃₂	——	——	——	0.140	0.265	——	0.100	0.265	——
	6-250 Calif.	¹¹/₃₂	——	——	——	0.150	0.260	——	0.135	0.265	——

① The carburetor identification number is stamped on the float bowl, next to the fuel inlet nut.
② High step of cam.
③ No vacuum to the distributor

Model 2GC, 2GV

This two barrel carburetor is used on General Motors cars and on some 1971 Chrysler Corp vehicles. The newer carburetors use a plastic float and a longer needle and seat to provide better fuel control.

Fast Idle Adjustment

1. On 2GC and 2GV models, except on some Oldsmobile and Chrysler Corp cars, the fast idle is set automatically when the curb idle and mixture is set.
2. Some Oldsmobile 2GC carburetors have a screw to adjust the fast idle.
3. On Chrysler Corp cars, follow this procedure: with engine off and the transmission in Neutral, open the throttle slightly. Close the choke valve until the fast idle screw can be positioned on the second step of the fast idle cam. Start the engine to determine speed. Turn the fast idle screw to obtain the specified RPM.

Choke Rod (fast idle cam)

1. Turn in the idle cam stop screw until it just contacts the bottom

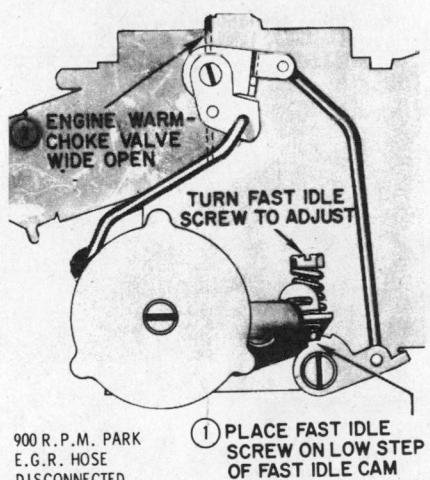

900 R.P.M. PARK
E.G.R. HOSE
DISCONNECTED
AND PLUGGED

① PLACE FAST IDLE
SCREW ON LOW STEP
OF FAST IDLE CAM

ENGINE WARM—
CHOKE VALVE
WIDE OPEN

TURN FAST IDLE
SCREW TO ADJUST

Fast Idle Speed Setting
(© Oldsmobile Div., G.M. Corp)

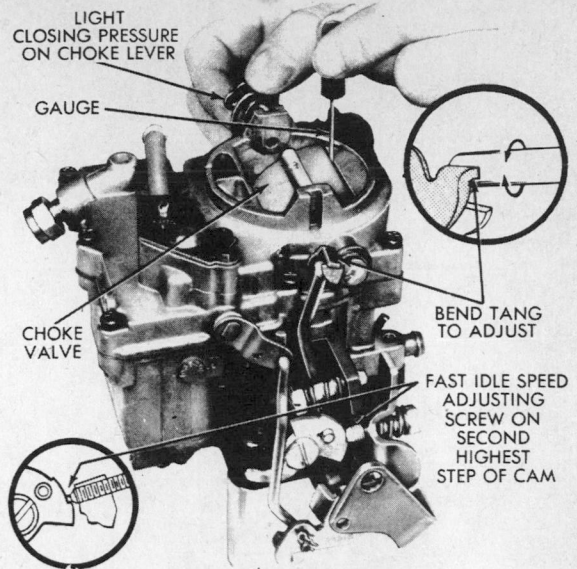

LIGHT
CLOSING PRESSURE
ON CHOKE LEVER

GAUGE

CHOKE
VALVE

BEND TANG
TO ADJUST

FAST IDLE SPEED
ADJUSTING
SCREW ON
SECOND
HIGHEST
STEP OF CAM

Fast Idle Cam Setting
(© Dodge Div., Chrysler Corp)

step of the fast idle cam. Then turn the screw one full turn.
2. Place the idle screw on the second step of the fast idle cam against the shoulder of the high step.
3. Hold the choke valve closed and check the clearance between the upper edge of the choke valve and the air horn wall.
4. Adjust the clearance by bending the tang on the choke lever.

Intermediate Choke Rod Adjustment (Beginning 1975)

1. Remove the thermostatic cover coil, gasket, and inside baffle plate assembly.
2. Place the idle speed screw on the highest step of the fast idle cam.
3. Close the choke valve by pushing up on the intermediate choke lever.
4. The edge of the coil lever inside the choke housing must line up with the edge of a 0.120 in. drill bit inserted into the hole inside the choke housing.

5. Adjust by bending the intermediate choke rod at the first bend from the bottom of the rod.

Vacuum Break Adjustment

1. Remove the air cleaner. Vehicles with a Therm AC air cleaner should have the sensor's vacuum take-off port plugged.
2. Using an external vacuum source, apply vacuum to the vacuum break diaphragm until the plunger is fully seated.
3. When the plunger is seated, push the choke valve toward the closed position. For 1975 and later models, place the idle speed screw on the high step of the fast idle cam.
4. Holding the choke valve or coil lever inside the choke housing in the closed position, place the specified size gauge between the upper (lower, through 1974) edge of the choke valve and the air horn wall.
5. If the measurement is not correct, bend the vacuum break rod.

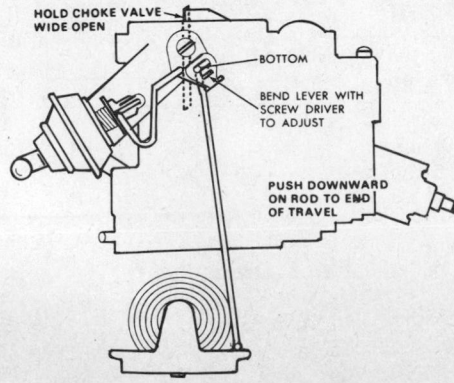

HOLD CHOKE VALVE
WIDE OPEN

BOTTOM

BEND LEVER WITH
SCREW DRIVER
TO ADJUST

PUSH DOWNWARD
ON ROD TO END
OF TRAVEL

Choke Coil Rod Adjustment
(© Chevrolet Div., G.M. Corp)

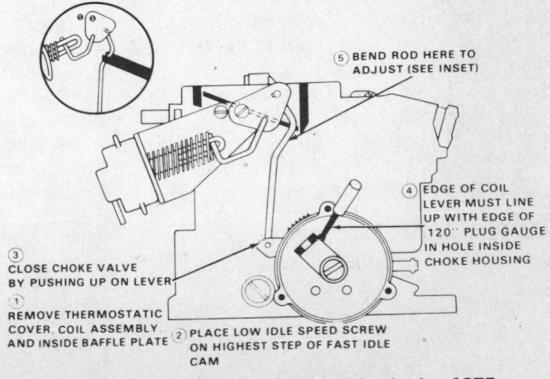

⑤ BEND ROD HERE TO
ADJUST (SEE INSET)

④ EDGE OF COIL
LEVER MUST LINE
UP WITH EDGE OF
120° PLUG GAUGE
IN HOLE INSIDE
CHOKE HOUSING

③ CLOSE CHOKE VALVE
BY PUSHING UP ON LEVER

① REMOVE THERMOSTATIC
COVER COIL ASSEMBLY
AND INSIDE BAFFLE PLATE

② PLACE LOW IDLE SPEED SCREW
ON HIGHEST STEP OF FAST IDLE
CAM

Intermediate choke rod adjustment, beginning 1975
(© Chevrolet Div., G.M. Corp.)

U123

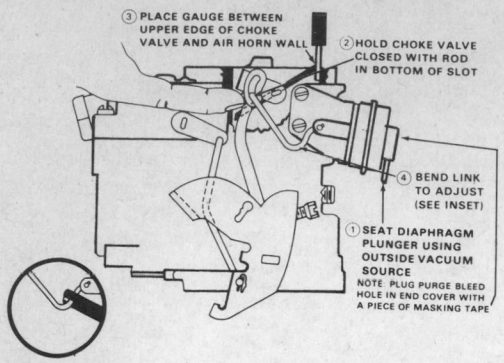

Primary vacuum break adjustment, beginning 1975
(© Buick Div., G.M. Corp.)

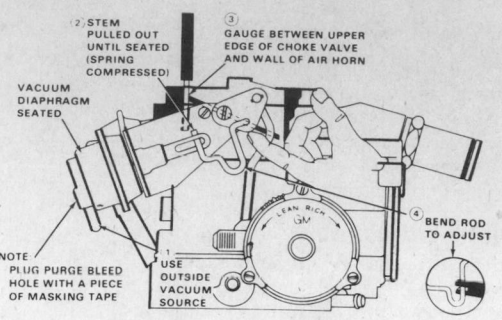

Auxiliary vacuum break adjustment, beginning 1975
(© Buick Div., G.M. Corp.)

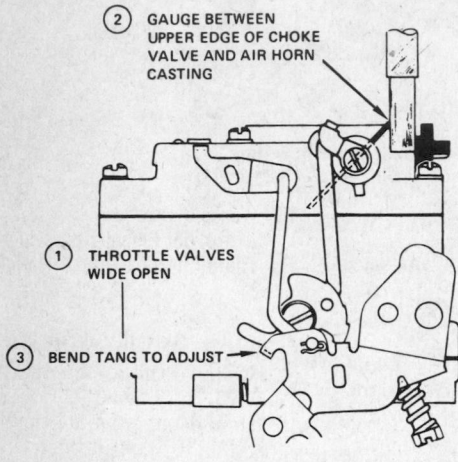

Choke Unloader Adjustment
(© Chevrolet Div., G.M. Corp)

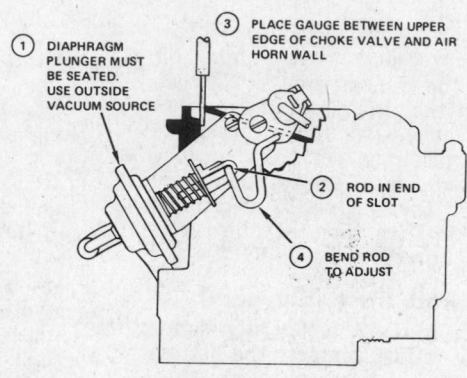

Vacuum Break Adjustment
(© Chevrolet Div., G.M. Corp)

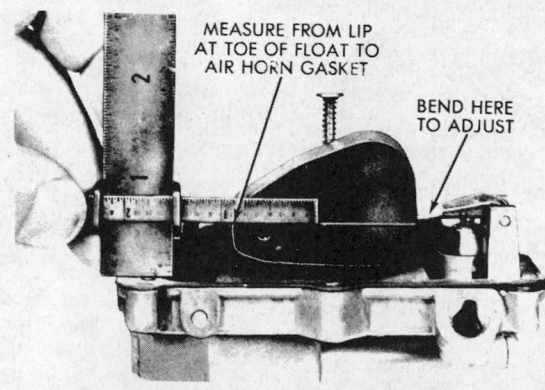

Float Level Measurement, Plastic Float
(© Dodge Div., Chrysler Corp.)

Auxiliary Vacuum Break (Beginning 1975)

1. Seat the auxiliary vacuum diaphragm by applying an outside source of vacuum. Tape over the vacuum bleed hole so the vacuum will not bleed down.
2. Place the idle speed screw on the high step of the fast idle cam.
3. Hold the choke coil lever inside the choke housing towards the closed choke position.
4. Rotate the inside choke coil lever until the spring in the diaphragm plunger is seated. Measure the distance between the upper edge of the choke valve and the air horn wall.
5. Adjust by bending the auxiliary vacuum break rod at the bottom of the U-shaped bend. Remove the piece of tape from the auxiliary vacuum diaphragm.

Choke Unloader Adjustment

1. Hold the throttle valves wide open.
2. Close the choke valve.
3. Bend the unloader tang to obtain the proper clearance between the upper edge of the choke valve and air horn wall.

Choke Coil Rod Adjustment

1. Hold the choke valve completely open.
2. Disconnect the coil rod from the upper lever and push down on the rod to the end of its travel.
3. When the rod is all the way down, the top of the rod should line up with the bottom of the slotted hole on the choke valve linkage.
4. Adjust by bending the lever.

Float Level

With the air horn assembly upside down, measure the distance from the air horn gasket to the lip at the toe of the float. Bend the float arm to adjust to specifications.

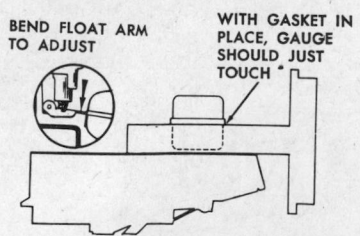

Float Level Measurement, Metal Float

Float Drop

Holding the air horn assembly upright, measure the distance from the gasket to the lip at the toe of the float. If correction is necessary, bend the float tang at the rear, next to the needle and seat.

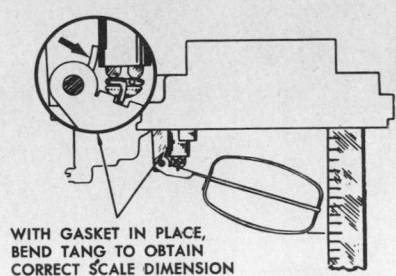

WITH GASKET IN PLACE,
BEND TANG TO OBTAIN
CORRECT SCALE DIMENSION

Float Drop, Metal Float

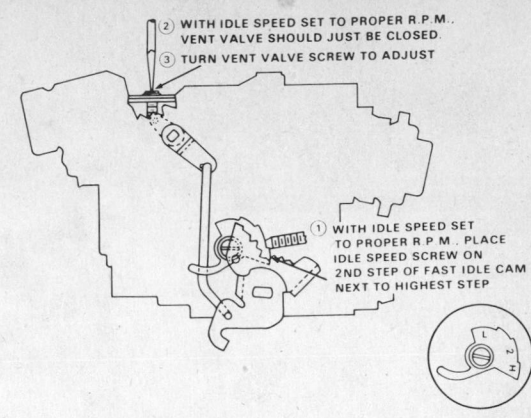

② WITH IDLE SPEED SET TO PROPER R.P.M.,
VENT VALVE SHOULD JUST BE CLOSED.
③ TURN VENT VALVE SCREW TO ADJUST

① WITH IDLE SPEED SET
TO PROPER R.P.M., PLACE
IDLE SPEED SCREW ON
2ND STEP OF FAST IDLE CAM
NEXT TO HIGHEST STEP

Bowl vent valve adjustment (© Buick Div., G.M. Corp.)

Accelerator Pump Rod

1. Back out the idle speed screw and completely close the throttle valves.
2. Place the pump gauge across the air cleaner mounting surface.
3. With the T-scale set to the specified height, the lower leg of the gauge should just touch the top of the accelerator pump rod.
4. Bend the pump rod to adjust.

Bowl Vent Valve Adjustment

NOTE: Check and adjust, if necessary, the pump rod clearance and curb idle speed before adjusting the bowl vent valve.

1. Remove the two bowl vent valve cover attaching screws in the top of the air horn and remove the cover and gasket. Remove the bowl vent valve spring.
2. Place the idle speed screw on the second step of the fast idle cam next to the highest step. In this position, the bowl vent valve should just be closed.

3. If the vent valve is just closed with the idle speed screw on the second step of the fast idle cam, rotate the fast idle cam so that the idle speed screw is on the next lower step. In this position, the vent valve should just begin to open.
4. If it is necessary to adjust the bowl vent valve, turn the adjustment screw in the top of the valve, to obtain the conditions mentioned in Steps 2 and 3.

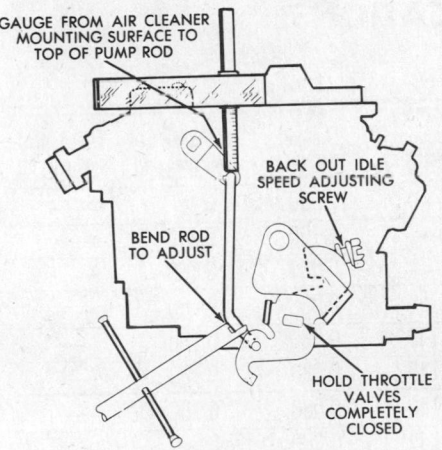

GAUGE FROM AIR CLEANER
MOUNTING SURFACE TO
TOP OF PUMP ROD

BACK OUT IDLE
SPEED ADJUSTING
SCREW

BEND ROD
TO ADJUST

HOLD THROTTLE
VALVES
COMPLETELY
CLOSED

Accelerator Pump Rod
(© Dodge Div., Chrysler Corp)

BEND TANG TO ADJUST
FOR PROPER IDLE VENT
SETTING

OPEN THROTTLE VALVES
TO POINT WHERE VENT VALVE
JUST CLOSES ON ITS SEAT

LEG OF GAUGE MARKED VENT TO JUST TOUCH

Idle Vent Adjustment

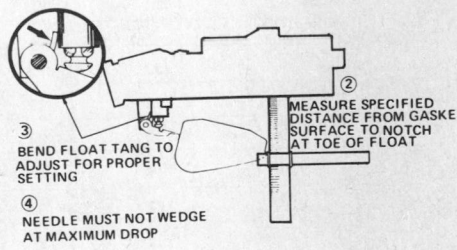

① AIR HORN RIGHT SIDE UP TO ALLOW
FLOAT TO HANG FREE (GASKET IN PLACE)

② MEASURE SPECIFIED
DISTANCE FROM GASKET
SURFACE TO NOTCH
AT TOE OF FLOAT

③ BEND FLOAT TANG TO
ADJUST FOR PROPER
SETTING

④ NEEDLE MUST NOT WEDGE
AT MAXIMUM DROP

Float Drop, Plastic Float

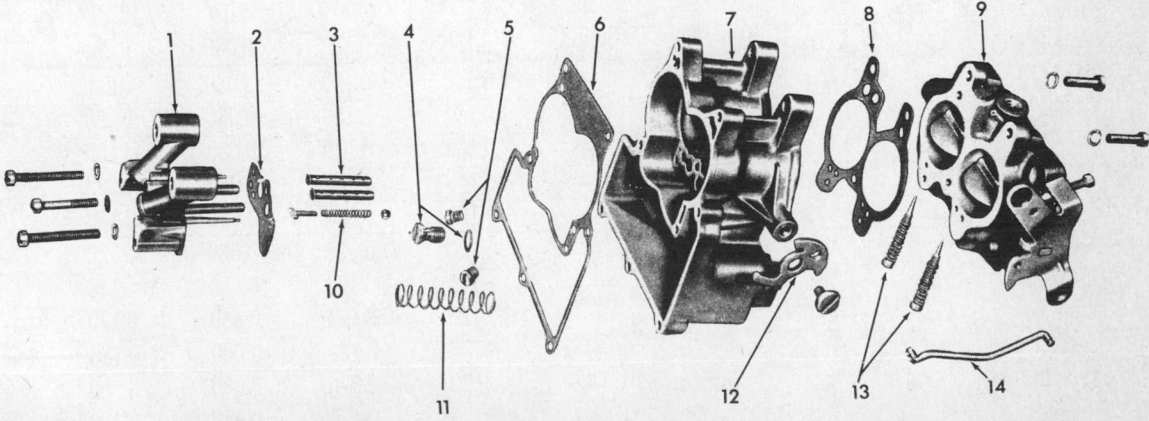

Float Bowl, Exploded View

1. Cluster assembly
2. Gasket
3. Splash shield—main well
4. Power valve assembly
5. Main jets

6. Air horn gasket
7. Bowl assembly
8. Throttle body-to-bowl gasket
9. Throttle body assembly

10. Pump discharge check assembly
11. Accelerator pump spring
12. Fast idle cam
13. Idle mixture screws
14. Choke rod

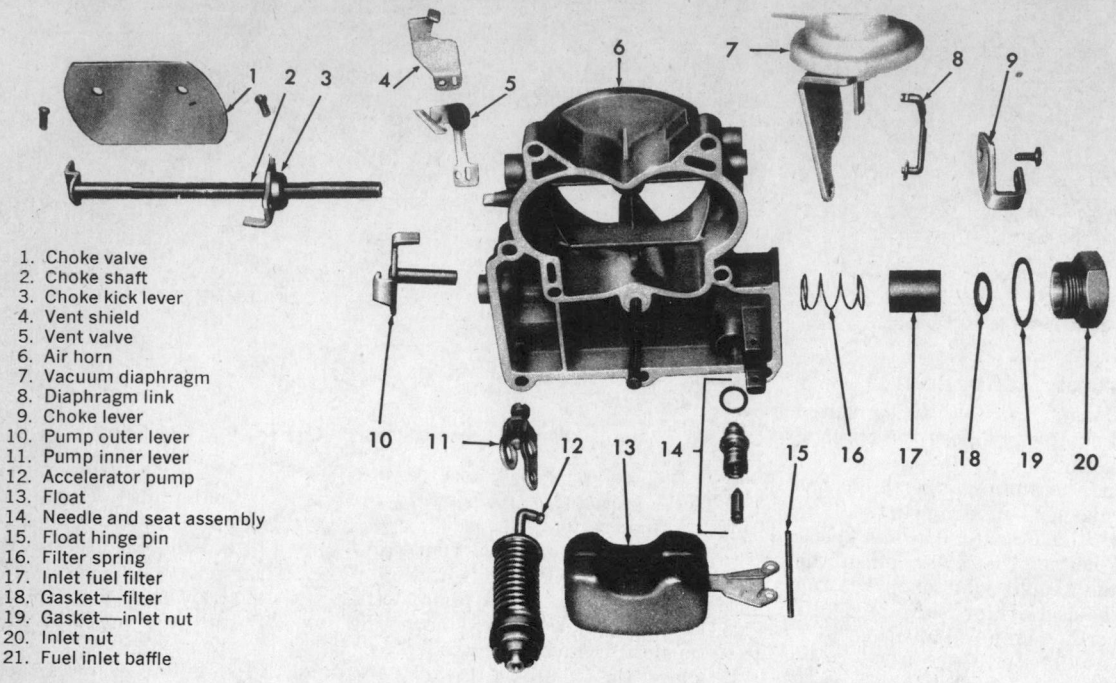

1. Choke valve
2. Choke shaft
3. Choke kick lever
4. Vent shield
5. Vent valve
6. Air horn
7. Vacuum diaphragm
8. Diaphragm link
9. Choke lever
10. Pump outer lever
11. Pump inner lever
12. Accelerator pump
13. Float
14. Needle and seat assembly
15. Float hinge pin
16. Filter spring
17. Inlet fuel filter
18. Gasket—filter
19. Gasket—inlet nut
20. Inlet nut
21. Fuel inlet baffle

Air horn, exploded view, 2GC, 2GV

2GC, 2GV CARBURETOR SPECIFICATIONS

BUICK

Year	Carburetor Identification①	Float Level (in.)	Float Drop (in.)	Pump Rod (in.)	Idle Vent (in.)	Vacuum Break (in.)	Auxiliary Vacuum Break (in.)	Choke Rod (in.)	Choke Unloader (in.)	Fast Idle Speed (rpm)
1970	7040142	$15/32$	$1\ 7/32$	$1\ 13/32$	——	0.150	——	0.080	0.180	——
	7040143	$15/32$	$1\ 7/32$	$1\ 15/32$	——	0.190	——	0.100	0.200	——
	7040446	$15/32$	$1\ 7/32$	$1\ 13/32$	——	0.150	——	0.080	0.180	——
1971	7040143	$15/32$	$1\ 7/8$	$1\ 15/32$	——	0.160	0.140	0.080	0.180	——
	7041142	$15/32$	$1\ 7/8$	$1\ 15/32$	——	0.150	0.140	0.080	0.180	——
	7041442	$15/32$	$1\ 7/8$	$1\ 15/32$	——	0.150	0.140	0.080	0.180	——
1972	7042142	$15/32$	$1\ 7/8$	$1\ 15/32$	——	0.150	0.140	0.080	0.180	——
	7042143	$15/32$	$1\ 7/8$	$1\ 15/32$	——	0.160	0.140	0.080	0.180	——
	7042842	$15/32$	$1\ 7/8$	$1\ 15/32$	——	0.150	0.140	0.080	0.180	——
1973	7043142	$15/32$	$1\ 9/32$	$1\ 15/32$	——	0.140	0.120	0.080	0.180	——
	7043143	$15/32$	$1\ 9/32$	$1\ 15/32$	——	0.150	0.120	0.080	0.200	——
1974	7044142	$15/32$	$1\ 9/32$	$1\ 15/32$	——	0.140	0.120	0.080	0.180	——
	7044442	$15/32$	$1\ 9/32$	$1\ 15/32$	——	0.140	0.120	0.080	0.180	——
	7044141	$15/32$	$1\ 9/32$	$1\ 15/32$	——	0.160	0.120	0.080	0.180	——
	7044144	$15/32$	$1\ 9/32$	$1\ 15/32$	——	0.140	0.120	0.080	0.180	——
	7044444	$15/32$	$1\ 9/32$	$1\ 15/32$	——	0.140	0.120	0.080	0.180	——
1975	7045145	$15/32$	$1\ 9/32$	$1\ 15/32$	——	0.120	0.120	0.080	0.120	——
	7045146	$15/32$	$1\ 9/32$	$1\ 15/32$	——	0.120	0.120	0.080	0.120	——
	7045147	$15/32$	$1\ 9/32$	$1\ 15/32$	——	0.120	0.120	0.080	0.120	——
	7045148	$15/32$	$1\ 9/32$	$1\ 15/32$	——	0.120	0.120	0.080	0.120	——
	7045149	$15/32$	$1\ 9/32$	$1\ 15/32$	——	0.120	0.120	0.080	0.120	——
	7045446	$15/32$	$1\ 9/32$	$1\ 15/32$	——	0.120	0.120	0.080	0.120	——
	7045448	$15/32$	$1\ 9/32$	$1\ 15/32$	——	0.120	0.120	0.080	0.120	——
	7045449	$15/32$	$1\ 9/32$	$1\ 15/32$	——	0.120	0.120	0.080	0.120	——
	7045143	$15/32$	$1\ 9/32$	$1\ 15/32$	——	0.140	0.120	0.080	0.140	——
	7045140	$15/32$	$1\ 9/32$	$1\ 15/32$	——	0.140	0.120	0.080	0.140	——

BUICK

Year	Carburetor Identification[1]	Float Level (in.)	Float Drop (in.)	Pump Rod (in.)	Idle Vent (in.)	Vacuum Break (in.)	Auxiliary Vacuum Break (in.)	Choke Rod (in.)	Choke Unloader (in.)	Fast Idle Speed (rpm)
1976	17056447	7/16	1 9/32	1 19/32	——	0.130	0.100	0.080	0.140	——
	17056145	13/32	1 9/32	1 19/32[2]	——	0.110	0.100	0.080	0.140	
	17056148	7/16	1 9/32	1 19/32	——	0.120	0.100	0.080	0.140	
	17056149	7/16	1 9/32	1 19/32	——	0.120	0.100	0.080	0.140	
	17056448	7/16	1 9/32	1 19/32	——	0.130	0.110	0.080	0.140	
	17056449	7/16	1 9/32	1 19/32	——	0.130	0.110	0.080	0.140	
	17056143	15/32	1 9/32	1 19/32	——	0.140	0.100	0.080	0.180	
	17056140	15/32	1 9/32	1 19/32	——	0.140	0.100	0.080	0.180	

[1] The carburetor identification number is stamped on the float bowl, next to the fuel inlet nut.

[2] 1¾ in. on Skyhawk.

CHEVROLET

Year	Carburetor Identification[1]	Float Level (in.)	Float Drop (in.)	Pump Rod (in.)	Idle Vent (in.)	Vacuum Break (in.)	Auxiliary Vacuum Break (in.)	Choke Rod (in.)	Choke Unloader (in.)	Fast Idle Speed (rpm)
1970	7040110	27/32	1 3/4	1 1/8	0.020	0.100	——	0.060	0.215	——
	7040112	27/32	1 3/4	1 1/8	0.020	0.100	——	0.060	0.215	
	7040101	27/32	1 3/4	1 1/8	0.020	0.125	——	0.060	0.160	
	7040103	27/32	1 3/4	1 1/8	0.020	0.125	——	0.060	0.225	
	7040114	23/32	1 3/8	1 17/32	0.020	0.200	——	0,085	0.325	
	7040116	23/32	1 3/8	1 17/32	0.020	0.200	——	0.085	0.325	
	7040113	23/32	1 3/8	1 17/32	0.020	0.215	——	0.085	0.275	
	7040115	23/32	1 3/8	1 17/32	0.020	0.215	——	0.085	0.275	
	7040118	23/32	1 3/8	1 17/32	0.020	0.215	——	0.085	0.325	
	7040120	23/32	1 3/8	1 17/32	0.020	0.215	——	0.085	0.325	
	7040117	23/32	1 3/8	1 17/32	0.020	0.215	——	0.085	0.325	
	7040119	23/32	1 3/8	1 17/32	0.020	0.215	——	0.085	0.325	
1971	7041024	1/16	——	——	——	0.140	——	0.080	0.350	——
	7041101	13/16	1 3/4	1 3/64	——	0.110	——	0.075	0.215	——
	7041110	13/16	1 3/4	1 3/64	——	0.080	——	0.040	0.215	——
	7041102	25/32	1 3/8	1 5/32	——	0.170	——	0.100	0.325	——
	7041114	25/32	1 3/8	1 5/32	——	0.170	——	0.100	0.325	——
	7041113	23/32	1 3/8	1 5/32	——	0.180	——	0.100	0.325	——
	7041127	23/32	1 3/8	1 5/32	——	0.180	——	0.100	0.325	——
	7041117	23/32	1 3/8	1 5/32	——	0.170	——	0.100	0.325	——
	7041118	23/32	1 3/8	1 5/32	——	0.170	——	0.100	0.325	——
	7041181	5/8	1 3/4	1 3/8	——	0.120	——	0.080	0.180	——
	7041182	5/8	1 3/4	1 3/8	——	0.120	——	0.080	0.180	——
1972	7042111	23/32	1 9/32	1 1/2	——	0.180	——	0.100	0.325	——
	7042113	23/32	1 9/32	1 1/2	——	0.180	——	0.100	0.325	——
	7042831	23/32	1 9/32	1 1/2	——	0.180	——	0.100	0.325	——
	7042833	23/32	1 9/32	1 1/2	——	0.180	——	0.100	0.325	——
	7042112	23/32	1 9/32	1 1/2	——	0.170	——	0.100	0.325	——
	7042114	23/32	1 9/32	1 1/2	——	0.170	——	0.100	0.325	——
	7042118	23/32	1 9/32	1 1/2	——	0.190	——	0.100	0.325	——
	7042832	23/32	1 9/32	1 1/2	——	0.170	——	0.100	0.325	——
	7042834	23/32	1 9/32	1 1/2	——	0.170	——	0.100	0.325	——
	7042838	23/32	1 9/32	1 1/2	——	0.190	——	0.100	0.325	——

CHEVROLET

Year	Carburetor Identification[1]	Float Level (in.)	Float Drop (in.)	Pump Rod (in.)	Idle Vent (in.)	Vacuum Break (in.)	Auxiliary Vacuum Break (in.)	Choke Rod (in.)	Choke Unloader (in.)	Fast Idle Speed (rpm)
1972	7042100	25/32	1 31/32	1 5/16	——	0.080	——	0.040	0.215	——
	7042820	25/32	1 31/32	1 5/16	——	0.080	——	0.040	0.215	——
	7042101	25/32	1 31/32	1 5/16	——	0.110	——	0.075	0.215	——
	7042821	25/32	1 31/32	1 5/16	——	0.110	——	0.075	0.215	——
1973	7043100	21/32	1 9/32	1 5/16	——	0.080	——	0.150	0.215	——
	7043101	21/32	1 9/32	1 5/16	——	0.080	——	0.150	0.215	——
	7043120	21/32	1 9/32	1 5/16	——	0.080	——	0.150	0.215	——
	7043105	21/32	1 9/32	1 5/16	——	0.080	——	0.150	0.215	——
	7043114	19/32	1 9/32	1 7/16	——	0.130	——	0.245	0.325	——
	7043113	19/32	1 9/32	1 7/16	——	0.140	——	0.200	0.250	——
	7043112	19/32	1 9/32	1 7/16	——	0.130	——	0.245	0.325	——
	7043111	19/32	1 9/32	1 7/16	——	0.140	——	0.200	0.250	——
	7043118	19/32	1 9/32	1 7/16	——	0.130	——	0.245	0.325	——
1974	7044111	19/32	1 9/32	1 9/32	——	0.140	——	0.200	0.250	1600[2]
	7044112	19/32	1 9/32	1 3/16	——	0.130	——	0.245	0.325	1600[2]
	7044113	19/32	1 9/32	1 9/32	——	0.140	——	0.200	0.250	1600[2]
	7044114	19/32	1 9/32	1 3/16	——	0.130	——	0.245	0.325	1600[2]
	7044115	19/32	1 9/32	1 9/32	——	0.140	——	0.200	0.250	1600[2]
	7044116	19/32	1 9/32	1 3/16	——	0.130	——	0.245	0.325	1600[2]
	7044118	19/32	1 9/32	1 3/16	——	0.130	——	0.245	0.325	1600[2]
	7044123	19/32	1 9/32	1 9/32	——	0.140	——	0.200	0.250	1600[2]
	7044124	19/32	1 9/32	1 3/16	——	0.130	——	0.245	0.320	1600[2]
1975	7045105	19/32	1 7/32	1 19/32	——	0.130	——	0.375	0.350	——
	7045106	19/32	1 7/32	1 19/32	——	0.130	——	0.380	0.350	——
	7045111	21/32	31/32	1 5/8	——	0.130	——	0.400	0.350	——
	7045112	21/32	31/32	1 5/8	——	0.130	——	0.400	0.350	——
	7045114	21/32	31/32	1 5/8	——	0.130	——	0.400	0.350	——
	7045115	21/32	31/32	1 5/8	——	0.130	——	0.400	0.350	——
	7045123	21/32	31/32	1 5/8	——	0.130	——	0.400	0.350	——
	7045124	21/32	31/32	1 5/8	——	0.130	——	0.400	0.350	——
	7045405	21/32	1 7/32	1 19/32	——	0.130	——	0.380	0.350	——
	7045406	21/32	1 7/32	1 19/32	——	0.130	——	0.380	0.350	——
1976	17056108	9/16	1 9/32	1 21/32	——	0.140	——	0.260	0.325	——
	17056110	9/16	1 9/32	1 21/32	——	0.140	——	0.260	0.325	——
	17056111	9/16	1 9/32	1 21/32	——	0.140	——	0.260	0.325	——
	17056112	9/16	1 9/32	1 21/32	——	0.140	——	0.260	0.325	——
	17056113	9/16	1 9/32	1 21/32	——	0.140	——	0.260	0.325	——
	17056114	21/32	31/32	1 11/16	——	0.130	——	0.260	0.325	——
	17056410	9/16	1 9/32	1 11/16	——	0.140	——	0.260	0.325	——
	17056412	9/16	1 9/32	1 11/16	——	0.140	——	0.260	0.325	——

[1] The carburetor identification number is stamped on the float bowl, next to the fuel inlet nut.

[2] This setting is with the low idle at 500 rpm with the clutch fan disengaged.

CHEVROLET VEGA, MONZA

Year	Carburetor Identification①	Float Level (in.)	Float Drop (in.)	Pump Rod (in.)	Idle Vent (in.)	Vacuum Break (in.)	Auxiliary Vacuum Break (in.)	Choke Rod (in.)	Choke Unloader (in.)	Fast Idle Speed (rpm)
1971	Manual	5/8	1 3/4	1 3/8	——	0.120	——	0.080	0.180	2400②
	Automatic	5/8	1 3/4	1 3/8	——	0.120	——	0.080	0.180	2400②
1972	Manual	19/32	1 7/8	1 1/16	——	0.100	——	0.080	0.215	2400②
	Automatic	19/32	1 7/8	1 1/16	——	0.085	——	0.060	0.215	2800②
1975	7045101, 7045105	19/32	1 7/32	1 19/32	——	0.130	——	0.375	0.350	——
	7045401, 7045405	21/32	1 7/32	1 19/32	——	0.130	——	0.380	0.350	——
	7045102, 7045106	19/32	1 7/32	1 19/32	——	0.130	——	0.375	0.350	——
	7045406	21/32	1 7/32	1 19/32	——	0.130	——	0.380	0.350	——
1976	17056101	17/32	1 9/32	1 5/8	——	0.130	——	0.260	0.325	——
	17056102	17/32	1 9/32	1 5/8	——	0.130	——	0.260	0.325	——
	17056104	17/32	1 5/32	1 5/8	——	0.140	——	0.260	0.325	——
	17056404	9/16	1 3/16	1 21/32	——	0.140	——	0.260	0.325	——

① The carburetor identification number is stamped on the float bowl, next to the fuel inlet nut.
② TCS disconnected for full vacuum advance.

CHEVROLET VEGA, MONZA

Year	Carburetor Identification①	Float Level (in.)	Float Drop (in.)	Pump Rod (in.)	Idle Vent (in.)	Vacuum Break (in.)	Auxiliary Vacuum Break (in.)	Choke Rod (in.)	Choke Unloader (in.)	Fast Idle Speed (rpm)
1971	7041180	21/32	1 3/4	1 5/64	——	41 drill	——	——	29 drill	1800

① The carburetor identification number is stamped on the float bowl, next to the fuel inlet nut.

OLDSMOBILE

Year	Carburetor Identification①	Float Level (in.)	Float Drop (in.)	Pump Rod (in.)	Idle Vent (in.)	Primary Vacuum Break (in.)	Secondary Vacuum Break (in.)	Automatic Choke (Notches)	Choke Rod (in.)	Choke Unloader (in.)	Fast Idle Speed (rpm)
1970	7040154	9/16	1 3/8	1 11/32	——	0.160	——	Index	0.140	0.170	——
	7040155	9/16	1 3/8	1 11/32	——	0.160	——	1 Lean	0.140	0.170	——
	7040156	9/16	1 3/8	1 11/32	——	0.160	——	Index	0.140	0.170	——
	7040158	9/16	1 3/8	1 11/32	——	0.160	——	Index	0.140	0.170	——
	7040159	9/16	1 3/8	1 11/32	——	0.160	——	Index	0.140	0.170	——
1971	7041155	9/16	1 3/8	1 11/32	——	0.200	——	1 Lean	0.140	0.170	——
	7041156	9/16	1 3/8	1 11/32	——	0.200	——	Index	0.140	0.170	——
	7041159	9/16	1 3/8	1 11/32	——	0.215	——	Index	0.140	0.170	——
1972	7042155	17/32	1 3/8	1 3/8	——	0.200	——	1 Lean	0.160	0.170	——
	7042156	17/32	1 3/8	1 3/8	——	0.200	——	Index	0.160	0.170	——
1973	All	15/32	1 9/32	1 11/32	——	0.200	——	Index	0.160	0.250	——
1975	7045143	15/32	1 9/32	1 19/32	——	0.140	0.120	1 Rich	0.080	0.080	Preset
	7045147	7/16	1 9/32	1 19/32	——	0.120	0.120	1 Lean	0.080	0.140	1800②
	7045149	7/16	1 9/32	1 19/32	——	0.120	0.120	1 Rich	0.080	0.140	1800②
	7045160	9/16	1 7/32	1 11/32	——	0.145	0.265	1 Rich	0.085	0.180	Preset
	7045161	9/16	1 7/32	1 11/32	——	0.145	0.265	1 Rich	0.085	0.180	Preset
	7045449	7/16	1 9/32	1 19/32	——	0.120	0.120	1 Lean	0.080	0.140	Preset

Rochester Carburetors

OLDSMOBILE

Year	Carburetor Identification①	Float Level (in.)	Float Drop (in.)	Pump Rod (in.)	Idle Vent (in.)	Primary Vacuum Break (in.)	Secondary Vacuum Break (in.)	Automatic Choke (Notches)	Choke Rod (in.)	Choke Unloader (in.)	Fast Idle Speed (rpm)
1976	17056143	$^{15}/_{32}$	1 $^5/_{32}$	1 $^{11}/_{32}$	——	0.140	0.100	1 Rich	0.080	0.180	——
	17056145	$^7/_{16}$	1 $^5/_{32}$	1 $^{19}/_{32}$	——	0.110	0.100	1 Rich	0.080	0.140	——
	17056149	$^7/_{16}$	1 $^5/_{32}$	1 $^{19}/_{32}$	——	0.120	0.100	1 Rich	0.080	0.140	——
	17056447	$^7/_{16}$	1 $^5/_{32}$	1 $^{19}/_{32}$	——	0.130	0.110	1 Rich	0.080	0.140	——
	17056449	$^7/_{16}$	1 $^5/_{32}$	1 $^{19}/_{32}$	——	0.130	0.110	1 Rich	0.080	0.140	——

① The carburetor identification number is stamped on the float bowl, next to the fuel inlet nut.
② In Park
③ In Neutral

PONTIAC

Year	Carburetor Identification①	Float Level (in.)	Float Drop (in.)	Pump Rod (in.)	Idle Vent (in.)	Primary Vacuum Break (in.)	Secondary Vacuum Break (in.)	Automatic Choke (Notches)	Choke Rod (in.)	Choke Unloader (in.)	Fast Idle Speed (rpm)
1970	7040060	$^{11}/_{16}$	1 $^3/_4$	1 $^{11}/_{32}$	——	0.180	——	——	0.085	0.180	——
	7040062	$^9/_{16}$	1 $^3/_4$	1 $^{11}/_{32}$	——	0.150	——	——	0.085	0.180	——
	7040064	$^{11}/_{16}$	1 $^3/_4$	1 $^{11}/_{32}$	——	0.150	——	——	0.085	0.180	——
	7040066	$^{11}/_{16}$	1 $^3/_4$	1 $^{11}/_{32}$	——	0.170	——	——	0.085	0.180	——
	7040071	$^9/_{16}$	1 $^3/_4$	1 $^{11}/_{32}$	——	0.160	——	——	0.085	0.180	——
	7040072	$^9/_{16}$	1 $^3/_4$	1 $^{11}/_{32}$	——	0.150	——	——	0.085	0.180	——
	7040460	$^{11}/_{16}$	1 $^3/_4$	1 $^{11}/_{32}$	——	0.150	——	——	0.085	0.180	——
	7040461	$^{11}/_{16}$	1 $^3/_4$	1 $^{11}/_{32}$	——	0.150	——	——	0.085	0.180	——
	7040462	$^9/_{16}$	1 $^3/_4$	1 $^{11}/_{32}$	——	0.150	——	——	0.085	0.180	——
	7040463	$^9/_{16}$	1 $^3/_4$	1 $^{11}/_{32}$	——	0.150	——	——	0.085	0.180	——
	7040466	$^{11}/_{16}$	1 $^3/_4$	1 $^{11}/_{32}$	——	0.170	——	——	0.085	0.180	——
	7040471	$^9/_{16}$	1 $^3/_4$	1 $^{11}/_{32}$	——	0.160	——	——	0.085	0.180	——
1971	7041060	$^{11}/_{16}$	1 $^3/_4$	1 $^{11}/_{32}$	——	0.125	——	——	0.085	0.180	——
	7041061	$^{11}/_{16}$	1 $^3/_4$	1 $^{11}/_{32}$	——	0.125	——	——	0.085	0.180	——
	7041062	$^9/_{16}$	1 $^3/_4$	1 $^{11}/_{32}$	——	0.105	——	——	0.085	0.180	——
	7041063	$^9/_{16}$	1 $^3/_4$	1 $^{11}/_{32}$	——	0.105	——	——	0.085	0.180	——
	7041064	$^{11}/_{16}$	1 $^3/_4$	1 $^{11}/_{32}$	——	0.130	——	——	0.085	0.180	——
	7041070	$^{11}/_{16}$	1 $^3/_4$	1 $^{11}/_{32}$	——	0.125	——	——	0.085	0.180	——
	7041072	$^9/_{16}$	1 $^3/_4$	1 $^{11}/_{32}$	——	0.105	——	——	0.085	0.180	——
	7041074	$^{11}/_{16}$	1 $^3/_4$	1 $^{11}/_{32}$	——	0.130	——	——	0.085	0.180	——
	7041171	$^9/_{16}$	1 $^3/_4$	1 $^{11}/_{32}$	——	0.140	——	——	0.085	0.180	——
1972	7042060	$^5/_8$	1 $^9/_{32}$	1 $^{11}/_{32}$	——	0.122	——	——	0.085	0.180	——
	7042061	$^5/_8$	1 $^9/_{32}$	1 $^{11}/_{32}$	——	0.122	——	——	0.085	0.180	——
	7042062	$^9/_{16}$	1 $^9/_{32}$	1 $^{11}/_{32}$	——	0.105	——	——	0.085	0.180	——
	7042064	$^5/_8$	1 $^9/_{32}$	1 $^{11}/_{32}$	——	0.150	——	——	0.085	0.180	——
	7042100	$^{25}/_{32}$	1 $^{31}/_{32}$	1 $^5/_{16}$	——	0.080	——	——	0.040	0.215	——
	7042101	$^{25}/_{32}$	1 $^{31}/_{32}$	1 $^5/_{16}$	——	0.100	——	——	0.075	0.215	——
1973	7043062	$^{21}/_{32}$	1 $^9/_{32}$	1 $^5/_{16}$	——	0.167	——	——	0.085	0.180	——
	7043063	$^{21}/_{32}$	1 $^9/_{32}$	1 $^5/_{16}$	——	0.167	——	——	0.085	0.180	——
	7043071	$^{23}/_{32}$	1 $^9/_{32}$	1 $^5/_{16}$	——	0.195	——	——	0.085	0.180	——
	7043072	$^{23}/_{32}$	1 $^9/_{32}$	1 $^5/_{16}$	——	0.167	——	——	0.085	0.180	——
	7043060	$^{21}/_{32}$	1 $^9/_{32}$	1 $^5/_{16}$	——	0.157	——	——	0.085	0.180	——
	7043061	$^{21}/_{32}$	1 $^9/_{32}$	1 $^5/_{16}$	——	0.157	——	——	0.085	0.180	——
	7043066	$^{21}/_{32}$	1 $^9/_{32}$	1 $^5/_{16}$	——	0.180	——	——	0.085	0.180	——
	7043067	$^{21}/_{32}$	1 $^9/_{32}$	1 $^5/_{16}$	——	0.180	——	——	0.085	0.180	——
	7043070	$^{23}/_{32}$	1 $^9/_{32}$	1 $^5/_{16}$	——	0.157	——	——	0.085	0.180	——

PONTIAC

Year	Carburetor Identification①	Float Level (in.)	Float Drop (in.)	Pump Rod (in.)	Idle Vent (in.)	Primary Vacuum Break (in.)	Secondary Vacuum Break (in.)	Automatic Choke (Notches)	Choke Rod (in.)	Choke Unloader (in.)	Fast Idle Speed (rpm)
1974	7043060	0.670	1 3/4	1 5/16	——	0.157	——	1 Lean	0.085	0.180	——
	7043062	0.670	1 3/4	1 5/16	——	0.167	——	1 Lean	0.085	0.180	——
	7043070	0.670	1 3/4	1 5/16	——	0.157	——	1 Lean	0.085	0.180	——
	7043071	0.670	1 3/4	1 5/16	——	0.195	——	1 Lean	0.085	0.180	——
	7043072	0.670	1 3/4	1 5/16	——	0.167	——	1 Lean	0.085	0.180	——
	7044063	0.670	1 3/4	1 5/16	——	0.157	——	1 Lean	0.085	0.180	——
	7044066	0.670	1 3/4	1 5/16	——	0.177	——	1 Lean	0.085	0.180	——
	7044067	0.670	1 3/4	1 5/16	——	0.177	——	1 Lean	0.085	0.180	——
1975	7045160	9/16	1 7/32	1 3/4	0.025	0.145	0.265	1 Rich	0.085	0.180	
	7045162	9/16	1 7/32	1 13/16	0.025	0.145	0.260	1 Rich	0.085	0.180	
	7045171	9/16	1 7/32	1 13/16	0.025	0.145	0.260	1 Rich	0.085	0.180	
	7045143	15/32	1 7/32	1 13/16	0.025	0.140	0.120	1 Rich	0.080	0.180	
1976	6-231 Man.	7/16	1 9/32	1 19/32	——	0.110	0.100	1 Rich	0.080	0.140	——
	6-231 Auto.	7/16	1 9/32	1 19/32	——	0.120	0.100	1 Rich	0.080	0.140	——
	6-231 Calif.	7/16	1 9/32	1 19/32	——	0.130	0.110	1 Rich	0.080	0.140	——
	8-350 Ventura	15/32	1 9/32	1 11/32	——	0.140	0.100	1 Rich	0.080	0.180	——
	8-350, 400 Auto.	9/16	1 9/32	1 11/32	——	0.165	0.285	1 Rich	0.085	0.180	——

① The carburetor identification number is stamped on the float bowl, next to the fuel inlet nut.

Model 2MC

The Rochester model 2MC carburetor is a two-barrel single stage carburetor which incorporates the design features of the primary side of the standard Rochester Quadrajet four-barrel carburetor. It is used on small displacement (260) V8s.

Fast Idle

1. Place the fast idle lever on the high step of the fast idle cam.
2. Make sure that the choke valve is wide open and the engine warm.
3. Turn the fast idle screw to get the proper fast idle rpm.

Fast Idle Cam (Choke Rod) Adjustment

1. Adjust the fast idle speed.
2. Place the cam follower lever on the second step of the fast idle cam, holding it firmly against the rise of the high step.
3. Close the choke valve by pushing upward on the choke coil lever inside the choke housing.
4. Gauge between the upper edge of the choke valve and the inside of the air horn wall.
5. Bend the tang on the intermediate choke lever to adjust.

Pump Adjustment

1. With the fast idle cam follower off the steps of the fast idle cam, back out the idle speed screw until the throttle valves are completely closed.
2. Place the pump rod in the proper hole of the lever.
3. Measure from the top of the choke valve wall, next to the vent stack, to the top of the pump stem.
4. Bend the pump lever to adjust.

Choke Coil Lever Adjustment

1. Remove the choke cover and thermostatic coil from the choke housing.
2. Push up on the coil tang (counter-clockwise) until the choke valve is closed.
3. Insert a 0.120 in. plug gauge in the hole in the choke housing.
4. The lower edge of the choke coil lever should just contact the side of the plug gauge.
5. Bend the choke rod to adjust.

Vacuum Break Adjustment

1. Place the cam follower on the highest step of the fast idle cam.
2. Seat the vacuum break diaphragm by using an outside vacuum source.

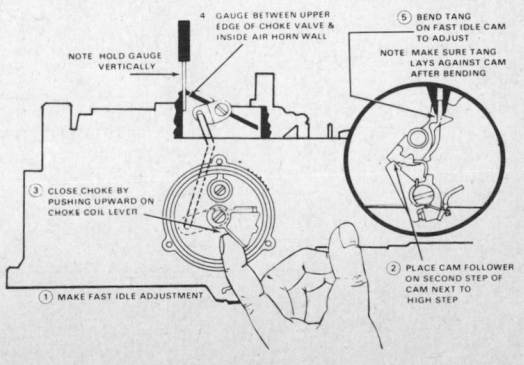

Fast idle cam (choke rod) adjustment (© Buick Div., G.M. Corp.)

3. Remove the choke cover and thermostatic coil and push up on the coil lever inside the choke housing until the tang on the vacuum break lever contacts the tang on the vacuum break plunger stem. Do not compress the backing spring for lean adjustment. Compress the bucking spring for rich adjustment.

4. With the choke rod in the bottom of the slot in the choke lever, gauge between the upper edge of the choke valve and the inside wall of the air horn.

5. Bend the link rod at the vacuum break plunger stem to adjust the lean setting. Bend the link rod at the opposite end from the diaphragm to adjust the rich setting.

Unloader Adjustment

1. With the choke valve completely closed, hold the throttle valves wide open.
2. Measure between the upper edge of the choke valve and air horn wall.
3. Bend the tang on the fast idle lever to obtain the proper measurement.

Idle Speed-Up Solenoid Adjustment

1. With the engine at normal operating temperature and the air conditioning turned on, the solenoid should be electrically energized (plunger stem extended).
2. Adjust the plunger screw to obtain the specified idle speed.
3. Turn off the air conditioner. The solenoid plunger should move away from the tang on the throttle lever.
4. Adjust the curb idle speed with the idle speed screw, if necessary.

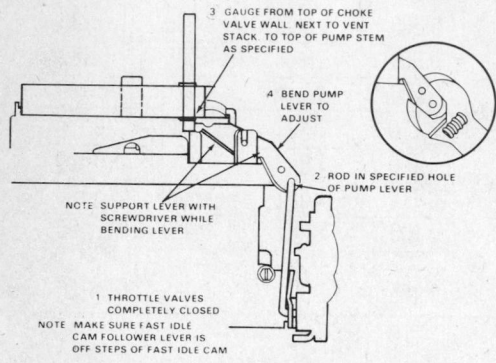

Pump adjustment (© Buick Div., G.M. Corp.)

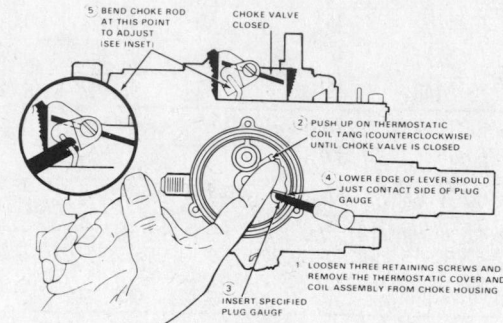

Choke coil lever adjustment (© Buick Div., G.M. Corp.)

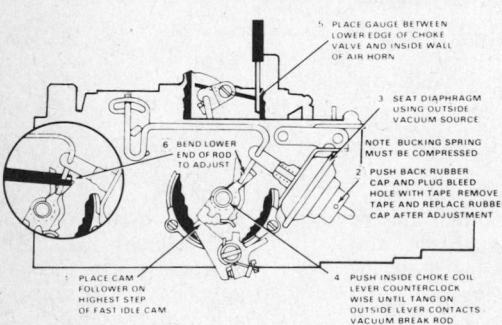

Vacuum break adjustment (© Buick Div., G.M. Corp.)

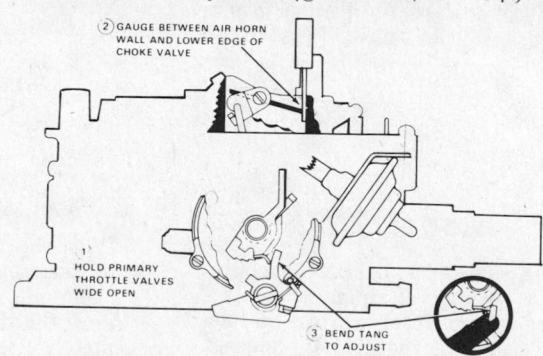

Unloader adjustment (© Buick Div., G.M. Corp.)

2MC CARBURETOR SPECIFICATIONS

BUICK

Year	Carburetor Identification ①	Float Level (in.)	Choke Rod (in.)	Choke Unloader (in.)	Vacuum Break Lean (in.)	Vacuum Break Rich (in.)	Pump Rod (in.)	Choke Coil Lever (in.)
1975	7045156	5/32	0.130	0.285	0.235	0.150	9/32 ②	0.120
	7045248	5/32	0.130	0.285	0.235	0.150	9/32 ②	0.120
	7045358	3/16	0.130	0.285	0.300	0.150	5/16 ③	0.120
	7045354	3/16	0.130	0.285	0.300	0.150	5/16 ③	0.120
1976	17056156	1/8	0.105	0.210	0.175	0.110	9/32 ②	0.120
	17056158	1/8	0.105	0.210	0.175	0.110	9/32 ②	0.120
	17056458	1/8	0.105	0.210	0.175	0.110	3/16 ③	0.120
	17056454	1/8	0.105	0.210	0.175	0.110	3/16 ③	0.120

① The carburetor identification number is stamped on the float bowl, next to the fuel inlet nut.
② Inner hole.
③ Outer hole.

OLDSMOBILE

Year	Carburetor Identification①	Float Level (in.)	Choke Rod (in.)	Choke Unloader (in.)	Vacuum Break Lean (in.)	Vacuum Break Rich (in.)	Pump Rod (in.)	Choke Coil Lever (in.)
1975	7045297	3/16	0.130	0.300	0.300	0.150	9/32②	0.120
	7045354	3/16	0.130	0.300	0.300	0.150	5/16③	0.120
	7045358	3/16	0.130	0.300	0.300	0.150	5/16③	0.120
	7045156	5/32	0.130	0.300	0.300	0.150	9/32②	0.120
	7045598	5/32	0.130	0.300	0.300	0.150	3/16②	0.120
	7045298	5/32	0.130	0.300	0.300	0.150	3/16②	0.120
	7045356	5/32	0.130	0.300	0.300	0.150	3/16②	0.120
1976	17056156	1/8	0.105	0.210	0.175	0.110	9/32②	0.120
	17056157	1/8	0.105	0.210	0.175	0.110	3/16③	0.120
	17056158	1/8	0.105	0.210	0.175	0.110	9/32②	0.120
	17056454	1/8	0.105	0.210	0.210	0.110	3/16③	0.120
	17056455	1/8	0.120	0.210	0.210	0.130	9/32②	0.120
	17056456	1/8	0.105	0.210	0.210	0.110	3/16③	0.120
	17056457	1/8	0.105	0.210	0.245	0.110	3/16③	0.120
	17056458	1/8	0.105	0.210	0.210	0.110	3/16③	0.120
	17056459	1/8	0.105	0.210	0.210	0.110	3/16③	0.120

① The carburetor identification number is stamped on the float bowl, next to the fuel inlet nut.
② Inner hole
③ Outer hole

PONTIAC

Year	Carburetor Identification①	Float Level (in.)	Choke Rod (in.)	Choke Unloader (in.)	Vacuum Break Lean (in.)	Vacuum Break Rich (in.)	Pump Rod (in.)	Choke Coil Lever (in.)
1975	7045156	5/32	0.130	0.275	0.230	0.150	9/32②	0.120
	7045297	3/16	0.130	0.275	0.275	0.180	9/32②	0.120
	7045298	5/32	0.130	0.275	0.275	0.150	9/32②	0.120
	7045598	5/32	0.160	0.275	0.230	0.150	9/32②	0.120
	7045356	5/32	0.160	0.275	0.275	0.180	9/32②	0.120
1976	8-260 Man.	1/8	0.105	0.210	0.175	0.110	3/16③	0.120
	8-260 Auto.	1/8	0.105	0.210	0.175	0.110	9/32②	0.120
	8-260 Calif.	1/8	0.105	0.210	0.210	0.110	3/16③	0.120

① The carburetor identification number is stamped on the float bowl, next to the fuel inlet nut.
② Inner hole
③ Outer hole

Model 4MC, M4MC, M4MCA, M4ME, M4MEA, 4MV

The Rochester Quadrajet carburetor is a two stage, four-barrel downdraft carburetor. The designation MC, MV, or ME refers to the type of choke system the carburetor is designed for. The MV model is equipped with a manifold mounted thermostatic choke coil. The MC model has a choke housing and coil mounted on the side of the float bowl. ME models have an electric choke.

The primary side of the carburetor is equipped with 1⅜ diameter bores and a triple venturi with plain tube nozzles. During off idle and part throttle operation, the fuel is metered through tapered metering rods operating in specially designed jets positioned by a manifold vacuum responsive piston.

The secondary side of the carburetor contains two 2¼ bores. An air valve is used on the secondary side for metering control and supplements the primary bores.

The secondary air valve operates tapered metering rods which regulate the fuel in constant proportion to the air being supplied.

Fast Idle

1. Position the fast idle lever on the high step of the fast idle cam, the second step on the 1974 454 cu. in. engine only.
2. Be sure that the choke is wide open and the engine warm. Plug the EGR vacuum hose. Disconnect the vacuum hose to the front vacuum break unit, if there are two.
3. Turn the fast idle screw to gain the proper fast idle rpm.

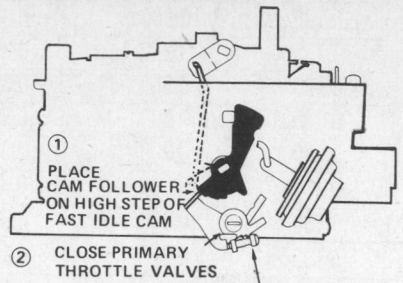

① PLACE CAM FOLLOWER ON HIGH STEP OF FAST IDLE CAM

② CLOSE PRIMARY THROTTLE VALVES

③ TURN SCREW IN TO SPECIFIED FAST IDLE RPM TO ADJUST

Fast Idle Adjustment
(© Chevrolet Div., G.M. Corp)

Choke Rod (Fast idle cam)

1. Adjust the fast idle and place the cam follower on the second step of the fast idle cam.
2. Close the choke valve by exerting counterclockwise pressure on the external choke lever. On 1975 and later models, remove the coil assembly from the choke housing and push on the choke coil lever.
3. Insert a gauge of the proper size between the lower (upper beginning 1975) edge of the choke valve and the inside air horn wall.
4. To adjust models through 1974, bend the choke rod. To adjust 1975 and later models, bend the tang on the fast idle cam. Be sure that the tang rests against the cam after bending.

Primary Vacuum Break (Through 1974)

1. Fully seat the vacuum break diaphragm using an outside vacuum source.
2. Open the throttle valve enough to allow the fast idle cam follower to clear the fast idle cam.
3. The end of the vacuum break rod should be at the outer end of the slot in the vacuum break diaphragm plunger.
4. The specified clearance should register from the lower end of the choke valve to the inside air horn wall.
5. If the clearance is not correct, bend the vacuum break link at the point shown in the illustration.

Primary Vacuum Break Adjustment (Beginning 1975)

1. Loosen the three retaining screws and remove the thermostatic cover and coil assembly from the choke housing.
2. Place the cam follower lever on the highest step of the fast idle cam.
3. Seat the front vacuum diaphragm using an outside vacuum source.
4. Push up on the inside choke coil lever until the tang on the vacuum break lever contacts the tang on the vacuum break plunger.

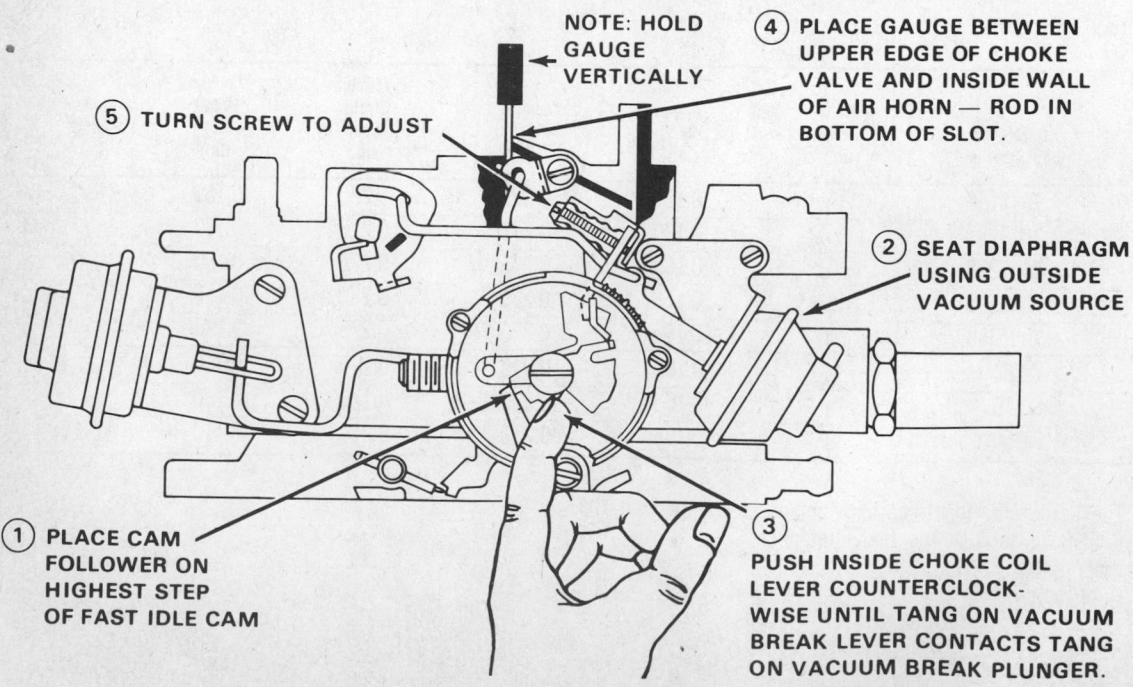

NOTE: HOLD GAUGE VERTICALLY

⑤ TURN SCREW TO ADJUST

④ PLACE GAUGE BETWEEN UPPER EDGE OF CHOKE VALVE AND INSIDE WALL OF AIR HORN — ROD IN BOTTOM OF SLOT.

② SEAT DIAPHRAGM USING OUTSIDE VACUUM SOURCE

① PLACE CAM FOLLOWER ON HIGHEST STEP OF FAST IDLE CAM

③ PUSH INSIDE CHOKE COIL LEVER COUNTERCLOCKWISE UNTIL TANG ON VACUUM BREAK LEVER CONTACTS TANG ON VACUUM BREAK PLUNGER.

Front vacuum break adjustment, beginning 1975 (© Buick Div., G.M. Corp.)

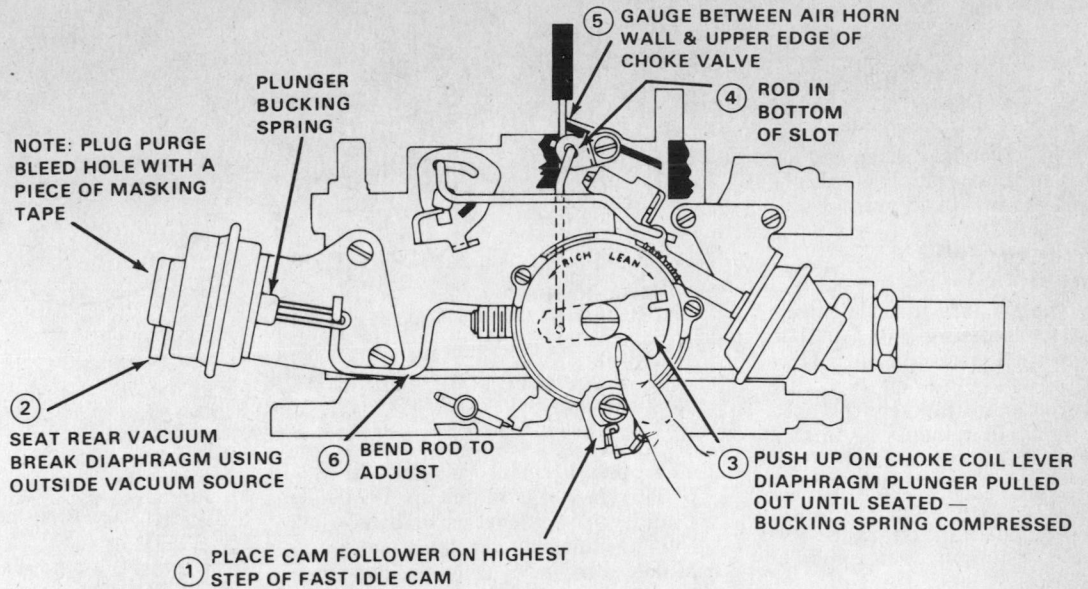

Rear vacuum break adjustment, beginning 1975 (except 454 cu in.)
(© Buick Div., G.M. Corp.)

5. Place the proper size gauge between the upper edge of the choke valve and the inside of the air horn wall.

6. To adjust, turn the adjustment screw on the vacuum break plunger lever.

7. Install the vacuum hose to the vacuum break unit.

Secondary Vacuum Break (Through 1974)

1. Using an outside vacuum source, seat the auxiliary vacuum break diaphragm plunger.

2. Rotate the choke lever in the closed position until the spring loaded diaphragm plunger is fully extended.

3. Holding the choke valve closed, check the distance between the lower edge of the choke valve and the air horn wall.

4. To adjust to specifications, bend the vacuum break link.

Secondary Vacuum Break Adjustment (Beginning 1975)

1. Remove the thermostatic cover and coil assembly from the choke housing.

2. Place the cam follower on the highest step of the fast idle cam.

3. Tape over the bleed hole in the rear vacuum break diaphragm and seat the diaphragm using an outside vacuum source.

4. Close the choke by pushing up on the choke coil lever inside the choke housing.

5. With the choke rod in the bottom of the slot in the choke lever, measure between the upper edge of the choke valve and the air horn wall with a wire type gauge.

NOTE: On 1975 454 cu. in. engines only, the choke valve should be held wide open.

6. To adjust, bend the vacuum break rod at the first bend near the diaphragm.

7. Remove the tape covering the bleed hole of the diaphragm and connect the vacuum hose.

Choke Unloader

1. Push up on the vacuum break lever to close the choke valve, and fully open the throttle valves.

2. Measure the distance from the lower (upper beginning 1975) edge of the choke valve to the air horn wall.

3. To adjust, bend the tang on the fast idle lever.

Choke Coil Rod

1. Close the choke valve by rotating the choke coil lever counterclockwise.

2. Disconnect the thermostatic coil rod from the upper lever.

3. Push down on the rod until it contacts the bracket of the coil.

4. The rod must fit in the notch of the upper lever.

5. If it does not, it must be bent on the curved portion just below the upper lever.

Secondary Closing Adjustment

This adjustment assures proper closing of the secondary throttle plates.

1. Set the slow idle as per instructions in the appropriate car section. Make sure that the fast idle cam follower is not resting on the fast idle cam and the choke valve is wide open.

2. There should be 0.020 in. clear-

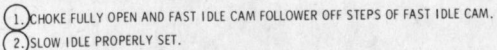

1. CHOKE FULLY OPEN AND FAST IDLE CAM FOLLOWER OFF STEPS OF FAST IDLE CAM.
2. SLOW IDLE PROPERLY SET.
3. MAKE SURE THROTTLE LEVER TANG IS AGAINST SECONDARY THROTTLE ROD OPERATING LEVER AS SHOWN IN 3.
4. GAUGE BETWEEN ROD AND END OF SLOT AS SHOWN IN 4.
5. TO ADJUST, OPEN THROTTLE SLIGHTLY AND BEND TANG

Secondary Closing Adjustments (© Odsmobile Div., G.M. Corp)

ance between the secondary throttle actuating rod and the front of the slot on the secondary throttle lever with the closing tang on the throttle lever resting against the actuating lever.

3. Bend the secondary closing tang on the primary throttle actuating rod or lever to adjust.

Secondary Opening Adjustment

1. Open the primary throttle valves until the actuating link contacts the upper tang on the secondary lever.
2. With two point linkage, the bottom of the link should be in the center of the secondary lever slot.
3. With three point linkage, there should be 0.070 in. clearance between the link and the middle tang.
4. Bend the upper tang on the secondary lever to adjust as necessary.

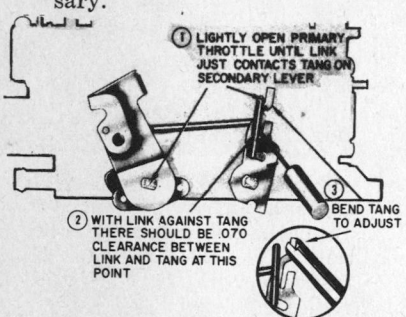

Secondary Opening Adjustments
(© Oldsmobile Div., G.M. Corp)

Float Level

With the air horn assembly removed, measure the distance from the air horn gasket surface (gasket removed) to the top of the float at the toe (1/16 in. back from the toe on 1975 models; 3/16 in. back on 1976 and later models).

NOTE: Make sure the retaining pin is firmly held in place and that the tang of the float is firmly against the needle and seat assembly.

Bend the float arm to adjust.

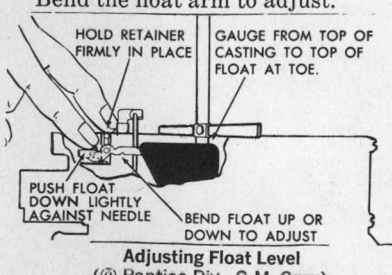

Adjusting Float Level
(© Pontiac Div., G.M. Corp)

Secondary Metering Rod Adjustment

1. With the air valves fully closed, measure from the top of each metering rod to the top of the air horn casting.

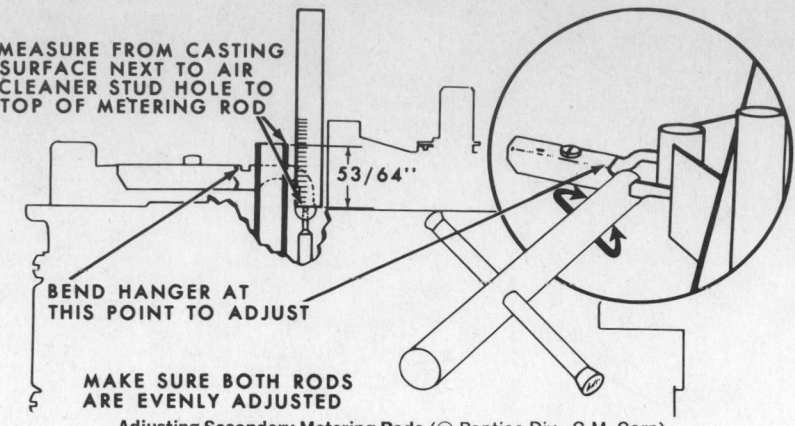

MEASURE FROM CASTING SURFACE NEXT TO AIR CLEANER STUD HOLE TO TOP OF METERING ROD

53/64"

BEND HANGER AT THIS POINT TO ADJUST

MAKE SURE BOTH RODS ARE EVENLY ADJUSTED

Adjusting Secondary Metering Rods (© Pontiac Div., G.M. Corp)

2. The measurement should be 5 3/64 in., 2 7/32 in. on 1974 Cadillac; if not, correct by bending the metering rod hanger. Make sure both rods are adjusted correctly.

Accelerator Pump

1. Close the primary throttle valves by backing out the slow idle screw and making sure that the fast idle cam follower is off the steps of the fast idle cam.
2. Bend the secondary throttle closing tang away from the primary throttle lever, if necessary, to insure that the primary throttle valves are fully closed.
3. With the pump in the appropriate hole in the pump lever, measure from the top of the choke valve wall to the top of the pump stem.
4. To adjust, bend the pump lever.
5. After adjusting, readjust the secondary throttle tang and the slow idle screw.

Idle Vent Adjustment

After adjusting the accelerator pump rod as specified above, open the primary throttle valve enough to just close the idle vent. Measure from the

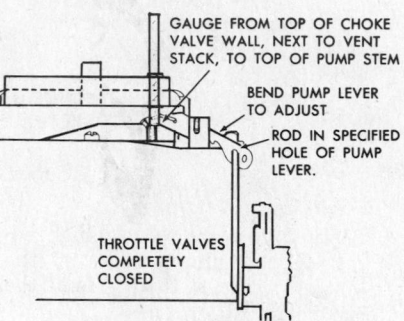

GAUGE FROM TOP OF CHOKE VALVE WALL, NEXT TO VENT STACK, TO TOP OF PUMP STEM

BEND PUMP LEVER TO ADJUST

ROD IN SPECIFIED HOLE OF PUMP LEVER.

THROTTLE VALVES COMPLETELY CLOSED

Accelerator Pump Rod Adjustment
(© Pontiac Div., G.M. Corp)

top of the choke valve wall to the top of the pump plunger stem. If adjustment is necessary, bend the wire tang on the pump lever.

Air Valve Spring Adjustment

To adjust the air valve spring windup, loosen the Allen head lockscrew and turn the adjusting screw counterclockwise to remove all spring tension. With the air valve closed, turn the adjusting screw clockwise the specified number of turns after the torsion spring contacts the pin on the shaft. Hold the adjusting screw in this position and tighten the lockscrew.

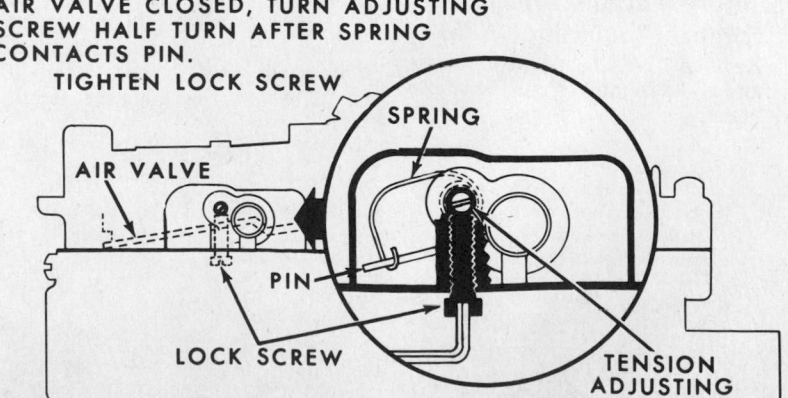

WITH LOCK SCREW LOOSENED AND WITH AIR VALVE CLOSED, TURN ADJUSTING SCREW HALF TURN AFTER SPRING CONTACTS PIN.
TIGHTEN LOCK SCREW

SPRING

AIR VALVE

PIN

LOCK SCREW

TENSION ADJUSTING SCREW

Air Valve Spring Setting (© Pontiac Div., G.M. Corp)

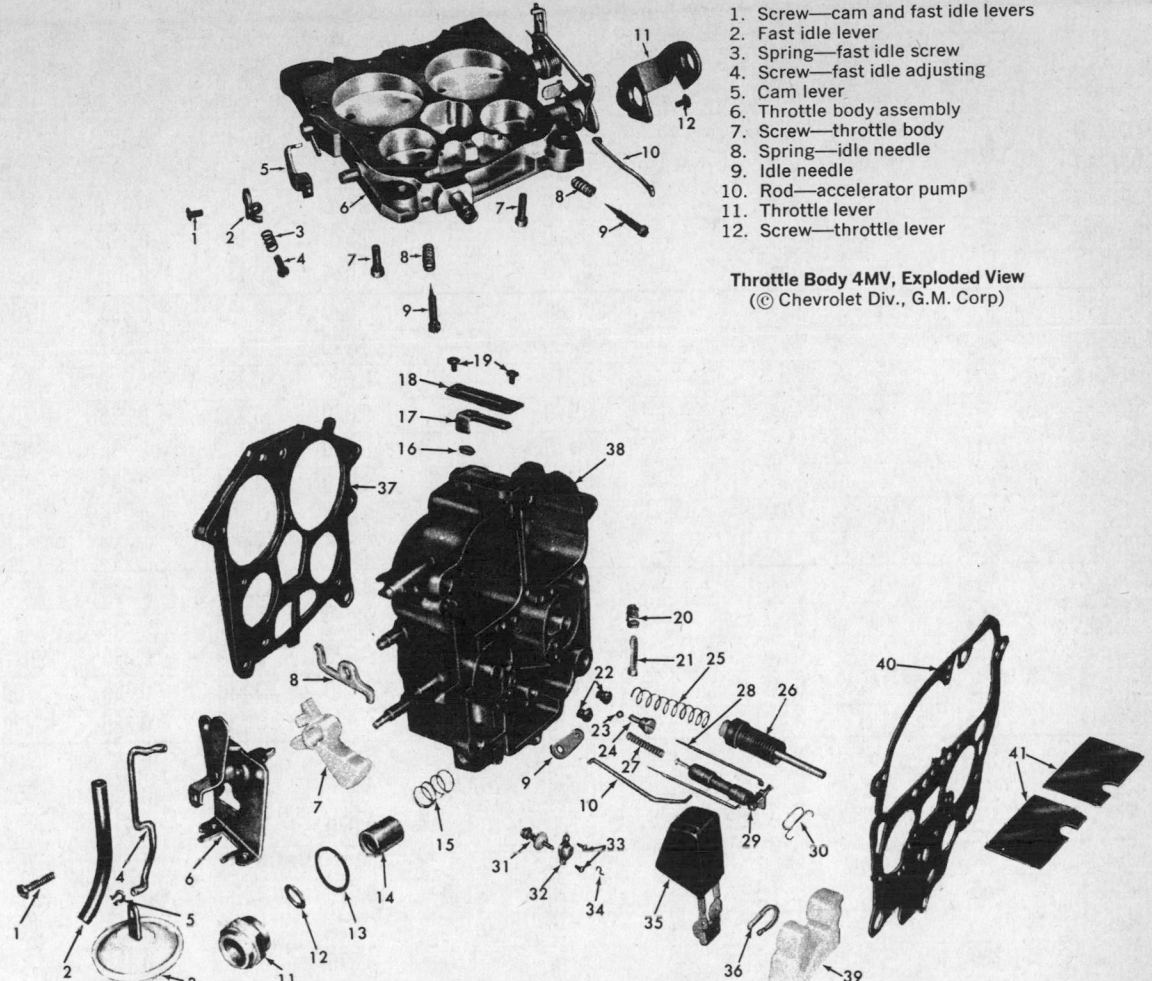

1. Screw—cam and fast idle levers
2. Fast idle lever
3. Spring—fast idle screw
4. Screw—fast idle adjusting
5. Cam lever
6. Throttle body assembly
7. Screw—throttle body
8. Spring—idle needle
9. Idle needle
10. Rod—accelerator pump
11. Throttle lever
12. Screw—throttle lever

Throttle Body 4MV, Exploded View
(© Chevrolet Div., G.M. Corp)

Exploded View 4MV Float Bowl (© Chevrolet Div., G.M. Corp)

1. Screw—choke control	15. Spring—fuel filter	29. Power piston assembly—primary
2. Hose—vacuum break	16. Gasket—idle compensator	30. Spring—metering rod primary
3. Vacuum break	17. Idle compensator assembly	31. Float needle and diaphragm assembly
4. Link—vacuum break	18. Cover—idle compensator	32. Retainer—float needle assembly
5. Clip—vacuum break rod	19. Screw—idle compensator cover	33. Screw—float needle retainer
6. Bracket assembly—choke control	20. Spring—idle speed screw	34. Pull clip—float needle
7. Cam—fast idle	21. Screw—idle speed	35. Float assembly
8. Lever—secondary lock out	22. Jet—primary	36. Hinge pin—float assembly
9. Lever—choke intermediate	23. Ball—pump discharge	37. Gasket—throttle body
10. Rod—choke	24. Retainer—pump discharge ball	38. Float bowl assembly
11. Nut—fuel inlet	25. Spring—pump return	39. Insert—float bowl
12. Gasket—fuel filter	26. Pump assembly	40. Gasket—air horn
13. Gasket—fuel inlet nut	27. Spring—power piston	41. Baffle—float bowl
14. Filter—fuel inlet	28. Metering rod—primary	

4MC, M4MC, M4MCA, M4ME, M4MEA, 4MV CARBURETOR SPECIFICATIONS

BUICK

Year	Carburetor Identification①	Float Level (in.)	Air Valve Spring (turn)	Pump Rod (in.)	Idle Vent (in.)	Primary Vacuum Break (in.)	Secondary Vacuum Break (in.)	Secondary Opening (in.)	Choke Rod (in.)	Choke Unloader (in.)	Fast Idle Speed ④ (rpm)
1970	7040240	3/8	1/2	9/32	——	0.180	——	0.020	0.130	0.335	650
	7040243	3/8	1/2	9/32	——	0.215	——	0.020	0.130	0.335	720
	7040244	5/16	1/2	13/32	——	0.170	——	0.020	0.130	0.335	650
	7040245	5/16	1/2	13/32	——	0.215	——	0.020	0.130	0.335	720
	7040246	5/16	1/2	9/32	——	0.200	——	0.020	0.130	0.335	650
	7040247	3/8	1/2	9/32	——	0.160	——	0.020	0.130	0.335	650

Rochester Carburetors

BUICK

Year	Carburetor Identification①	Float Level (in.)	Air Valve Spring (turn)	Pump Rod (in.)	Idle Vent (in.)	Primary Vacuum Break (in.)	Secondary Vacuum Break (in.)	Secondary Opening (in.)	Choke Rod (in.)	Choke Unloader (in.)	Fast Idle Speed④ (rpm)
1971	7041242	3/8	1/2	1/4	——	0.200	——	0.020	0.130	0.335	650
	7041243	13/32	1/2	1/4	——	0.215	——	0.020	0.130	0.335	720
	7041245	15/32	1/2	9/32	——	0.170	——	0.020	0.130	0.335	820
	7041540	3/8	1/2	1/4	——	0.180	——	0.020	0.130	0.335	650
	7041544	15/32	1/2	9/32	——	0.170	——	0.020	0.130	0.335	650
1972	7042240	3/8	1/2	1/4	——	0.180	——	0.020	0.130	0.335	700
	7042242	3/8	1/2	1/4	——	0.200	——	0.020	0.130	0.335	700
	7042243	13/32	1/2	1/4	——	0.215	——	0.020	0.130	0.335	920
	7042244	15/32	1/2	9/32	——	0.170	——	0.020	0.130	0.335	700
	7042245	15/32	1/2	9/32	——	0.170	——	0.020	0.130	0.335	820
	7042940	3/8	1/2	1/4	——	0.180	——	0.020	0.130	0.335	700
	7042942	3/8	1/2	1/4	——	0.200	——	0.020	0.130	0.335	700
	7042944	15/32	1/2	9/32	——	0.170	——	0.020	0.130	0.335	700
1973	7043240	13/32	7/16	7/16	——	0.215	——	0.020	0.130	0.335	700
	7043243	13/32	7/16	7/16	——	0.215	——	0.020	0.130	0.335	920
	7043242	13/32	7/16	7/16	——	0.200	——	0.020	0.130	0.335	920/700③
	7043244	15/32	11/16	0.306	——	0.170	——	0.020	0.130	0.335	700
	7043245	15/32	11/16	0.410	——	0.170	——	0.020	0.130	0.335	820
1974	7044240	13/32	7/16	1/4	——	0.215	0.160	0.070	0.130	0.335	700
	7044540	13/32	7/16	1/4	——	0.215	0.160	0.070	0.130	0.335	700
	7044242	13/32	7/16	1/4	——	0.200	0.180	0.070	0.130	0.335	700
	7044241	13/32	7/16	1/4	——	0.215	0.160	0.070	0.130	0.335	700
	7044244	15/32	11/16	0.306	——	0.170	0.150	0.070	0.130	0.335	700
	7044544	15/32	11/16	0.306	——	0.170	0.150	0.070	0.130	0.335	700
	7044546	15/32	11/16	0.306	——	0.170	0.150	0.070	0.130	0.335	700
	7044246	15/32	11/16	0.306	——	0.170	0.150	0.070	0.130	0.335	700
1975	7045240	7/16	7/16	9/32	——	0.135	0.120	②	0.095	0.240	1800
	7045548	7/16	7/16	9/32	——	0.135	0.120	②	0.095	0.240	1800
	7045244	5/16	3/4	15/32	——	0.130	0.115	②	0.095	0.240	1800
	7045246	5/16	3/4	15/32	——	0.130	0.115	②	0.095	0.240	1800
	7045544	5/16	3/4	15/32	——	0.145	0.130	②	0.095	0.240	1800
	7045546	5/16	3/4	15/32	——	0.145	0.130	②	0.095	0.240	1800
1976	17056240	15/32	7/16	3/8	——	0.135	0.120	②	0.095	0.250	1800
	17056540	15/32	7/16	3/8	——	0.135	0.120	②	0.095	0.250	1800
	17056244	5/16	3/4	3/8	——	0.130	0.120	②	0.095	0.250	1800
	17056246	5/16	3/4	3/8	——	0.130	0.120	②	0.095	0.250	1800
	17056544	5/16	3/4	3/8	——	0.130	0.130	②	0.095	0.250	1800
	17056546	5/16	3/4	3/8	——	0.130	0.130	②	0.095	0.250	1800

① The carburetor identification number is stamped on the float bowl, near the secondary throttle lever.
② No measurement necessary; see text
③ Manual/Automatic
④ On low step of cam, automatic in Drive through 1974; on high step of cam, automatic in Park starting 1975.

CADILLAC

Year	Carburetor Identification①	Float Level (in.)	Air Valve Spring (turn)	Pump Rod (in.)	Primary Vacuum Break (in.)	Secondary Vacuum Break (in.)	Secondary Opening (in.)	Choke Rod (in.)	Choke Unloader (in.)	Fast Idle Speed② (rpm)
1970	7047030	1/4	1/2	11/32	0.230	——	0.020	0.090	0.300	——
1971	7041766	1/4	1/2	11/32	0.300	——	0.020	0.090	0.310	——
	7041777	23/64	1/2	11/32	0.300	——	0.020	0.090	0.310	——

CADILLAC

Year	Carburetor Identification[1]	Float Level (in.)	Air Valve Spring (turn)	Pump Rod (in.)	Primary Vacuum Break (in.)	Secondary Vacuum Break (in.)	Secondary Opening (in.)	Choke Rod (in.)	Choke Unloader (in.)	Fast Idle Speed[2] (rpm)
1972	7047231	15/64	1/2	11/32	0.140	——	0.020	0.090	0.312	——
	7047232	23/64	1/2	11/32	0.140	——	0.020	0.090	0.312	——
1973	7047331	1/4	1/2	11/32	0.200	——	0.020	0.090	0.015	——
	7047332	23/64	1/2	11/32	0.205	——	0.020	0.090	0.015	——
1974	7044230	1/4	3/8	1/4	0.185	——	0.020	0.110	0.312	1200-1500
	7044232	23/64	1/2	1/4	0.200	——	0.020	0.110	0.312	1200-1500
	7044530	1/4	3/8	1/4	0.185	——	0.020	0.110	0.312	1200-1500
	7044532	23/64	1/2	1/4	0.200	——	0.020	0.110	0.312	1200-1500
	7044234	1/4	7/16	11/32	0.185	——	0.020	0.110	0.312	1200-1500
	7044235	23/64	9/16	11/32	0.200	——	0.020	0.110	0.312	1200-1500
	7044233	19/64	3/8	11/32	0.185	——	0.020	0.110	0.312	1200-1500
1975	7045230	15/32	7/16	3/8	0.160	0.130	0.015	0.080	0.215	1200-1250
	7045530	15/32	1/2	3/8	0.230	0.230	0.015	0.080	0.215	1200-1250
1976	7056232	13/32	3/8	3/8	0.160	0.160	0.160	0.080	0.230	1400
	7056230	13/32	3/8	3/8	0.160	0.160	0.160	0.080	0.230	1400
	7056530	7/16	3/8	9/32	0.160	0.160	0.160	0.080	0.230	1400

[1] The carburetor identification number is stamped on the float bowl, near the secondary throttle lever.
[2] On second step of cam.

CHEVROLET

Year	Carburetor Identification[1]	Float Level (in.)	Air Valve Spring (turn)	Pump Rod (in.)	Idle Vent (in.)	Primary Vacuum Break (in.)	Secondary Vacuum Break (in.)	Secondary Opening (in.)	Choke Rod (in.)	Choke Unloader (in.)	Fast Idle Speed (rpm)
1970	7040202	1/4	7/16	5/16	——	0.245	——	——	0.100	0.450	——
	7040203	1/4	7/16	5/16	——	0.275	——	——	0.100	0.450	——
	7040207	1/4	13/16	5/16	——	0.275	——	——	0.100	0.450	——
	7040200	1/4	13/16	5/16	——	0.245	——	——	0.100	0.450	——
	7040201	1/4	13/16	5/16	——	0.275	——	——	0.100	0.450	——
	7040204	1/4	13/16	5/16	——	0.245	——	——	0.100	0.450	——
	7040205	1/4	13/16	5/16	——	0.275	——	——	0.100	0.450	——
1971	7041200	1/4	7/16	——	——	0.260	——	——	0.100	——	——
	7041202	1/4	7/16	——	——	0.260	——	——	0.100	——	——
	7041204	1/4	7/16	——	——	0.260	——	——	0.100	——	——
	7041212	1/4	7/16	——	——	0.260	——	——	0.100	——	——
	7041201	1/4	7/16	——	——	0.275	——	——	0.100	——	——
	7041203	1/4	7/16	——	——	0.275	——	——	0.100	——	——
	7041205	1/4	7/16	——	——	0.275	——	——	0.100	——	——
	7041213	1/4	7/16	——	——	0.275	——	——	0.100	——	——
1972	7042220	1/4	7/16	3/8	——	0.250	——	——	0.100	0.450	——
	7042216	1/4	7/16	3/8	——	0.250	——	——	0.100	0.450	——
	7042215	1/4	7/16	3/8	——	0.250	——	——	0.100	0.450	——
	7042217	1/4	7/16	3/8	——	0.250	——	——	0.100	0.450	——
	7042202	1/4	1/2	3/8	——	0.215	——	——	0.100	0.450	——
	7042203	1/4	1/2	3/8	——	0.215	——	——	0.100	0.450	——
	7042902	1/4	1/2	3/8	——	0.215	——	——	0.100	0.450	——
	7042903	1/4	1/2	3/8	——	0.215	——	——	0.100	0.450	——

Rochester Carburetors

CHEVROLET

Year	Carburetor Identification①	Float Level (in.)	Air Valve Spring (turn)	Pump Rod (in.)	Idle Vent (in.)	Primary Vacuum Break (in.)	Secondary Vacuum Break (in.)	Secondary Opening (in.)	Choke Rod (in.)	Choke Unloader (in.)	Fast Idle Speed (rpm)
1973	7043202	$7/32$	$1/2$	$13/32$	——	0.250	——	——	0.430	0.450	——
	7043203	$7/32$	$1/2$	$13/32$	——	0.250	——	——	0.430	0.450	——
	7043212	$7/32$	1	$13/32$	——	0.250	——	——	0.430	0.450	——
	7043213	$7/32$	1	$13/32$	——	0.250	——	——	0.430	0.450	——
	7043200	$1/4$	$11/16$	$13/32$	——	0.250	——	——	0.430	0.450	——
	7043201	$1/4$	$11/16$	$13/32$	——	0.250	——	——	0.430	0.450	——
1974	7044202	$1/4$	$7/8$	$13/32$②	——	0.230	——	——	0.430	0.450	1600③-1300④
	7044203	$1/4$	$7/8$	$13/32$②	——	0.230	——	——	0.430	0.450	1600③-1300④
	7044206	$1/4$	$7/8$	$13/32$②	——	0.230	——	——	0.430	0.450	1600③-1300④
	7044207	$1/4$	$7/8$	$13/32$②	——	0.230	——	——	0.430	0.450	1600③-1300④
	7044223	$3/8$	$7/16$	$13/32$②	——	0.220	——	——	0.430	0.450	1600③-1300④
	7044201	$3/8$	$7/16$	$13/32$②	——	0.250	——	——	0.430	0.450	1600③-1300④
	7044500	$3/8$	$7/16$	$13/32$②	——	0.250	——	——	0.430	0.450	1600③-1300④
	7044208	$1/4$	1	$13/32$②	——	0.230	——	——	0.430	0.450	1600③-1300④
	7044209	$1/4$	1	$13/32$②	——	0.230	——	——	0.430	0.450	1600③-1300④
	7044210	$1/4$	1	$13/32$②	——	0.230	——	——	0.450	0.450	1600③-1300④
	7044211	$1/4$	1	$13/32$②	——	0.230	——	——	0.430	0.450	1600③-1300④
	7044502	$1/4$	$7/8$	$13/32$②	——	0.230	——	——	0.430	0.450	1600③-1300④
	7044503	$1/4$	$7/8$	$13/32$②	——	0.230	——	——	0.430	0.450	1600③-1300④
	7044506	$1/4$	$7/8$	$13/32$②	——	0.230	——	——	0.430	0.450	1600③-1300④
	7044507	$1/4$	$7/8$	$13/32$②	——	0.230	——	——	0.430	0.450	1600③-1300④
	7044221	$3/8$	$7/16$	$13/32$	——	0.250	——	——	0.430	0.450	1600③-1300④
	7044225	$3/8$	$7/16$	$13/32$	——	0.220	——	——	0.430	0.450	1600③-1300④
	7044226	$1/4$	$3/4$	$13/32$	——	0.230	——	——	0.430	0.450	1600③-1300④
	7044505	$3/8$	$7/16$	$13/32$	——	0.250	——	——	0.430	0.450	1600③-1300④
	7044526	$1/4$	$3/4$	$13/32$	——	0.230	——	——	0.430	0.450	1600③-1300④
1975	7045200	$17/32$	$9/16$	0.275	——	0.200	0.550	——	0.300	0.325	1000
	7045202	$15/32$	$7/8$	0.275	——	0.180	0.170	——	0.300	0.325	1600
	7045203	$15/32$	$7/8$	0.275	——	0.180	0.170	——	0.300	0.325	1600
	7045206	$15/32$	$7/8$	0.275	——	0.180	0.170	——	0.300	0.325	1600
	7045207	$15/32$	$7/8$	0.275	——	0.180	0.170	——	0.300	0.325	1600
	7045208	$15/32$	$7/8$	0.275	——	0.180	0.170	——	0.300	0.325	1600
	7045209	$15/32$	$7/8$	0.275	——	0.180	0.170	——	0.300	0.325	1600
	7045210	$15/32$	$7/8$	0.275	——	0.180	0.170	——	0.300	0.325	1600
	7045211	$15/32$	$7/8$	0.275	——	0.180	0.170	——	0.300	0.325	1600
	7045222	$15/32$	$7/8$	0.275	——	0.180	0.170	——	0.300	0.325	1600
	7045223	$15/32$	$7/8$	0.275	——	0.180	0.170	——	0.300	0.325	1600
	7045224	$15/32$	$3/4$	0.275	——	0.180	0.170	——	0.325	0.325	1600
	7045228	$15/32$	$3/4$	0.275	——	0.180	0.170	——	0.325	0.325	1600
	7045502	$15/32$	$7/8$	0.275	——	0.180	0.170	——	0.300	0.325	1600
	7045503	$15/32$	$7/8$	0.275	——	0.180	0.170	——	0.300	0.325	1600
	7045504	$15/32$	$7/8$	0.275	——	0.180	0.170	——	0.300	0.325	1600
	7045506	$15/32$	$7/8$	0.275	——	0.180	0.170	——	0.300	0.325	1600
	7044507	$15/32$	$7/8$	0.275	——	0.180	0.170	——	0.300	0.325	1600
1976	17056202	$13/32$	$7/8$	$9/32$	——	0.185	——	——	0.325	0.325	1600
	17056203	$13/32$	$7/8$	$9/32$	——	0.170	——	——	0.325	0.325	1600
	17056206	$13/32$	$7/8$	$9/32$	——	0.185	——	——	0.325	0.325	1600
	17056207	$13/32$	$7/8$	$9/32$	——	0.170	——	——	0.325	0.325	1600
	17056210	$13/32$	1.0	$9/32$	——	0.185	——	——	0.325	0.325	1600
	17056211	$13/32$	$3/4$	$9/32$	——	0.185	——	——	0.325	0.325	1600

CHEVROLET

Year	Carburetor Identification①	Float Level (in.)	Air Valve Spring (turn)	Pump Rod (in.)	Idle Vent (in.)	Primary Vacuum Break (in.)	Secondary Vacuum Break (in.)	Secondary Opening (in.)	Choke Rod (in.)	Choke Unloader (in.)	Fast Idle Speed (rpm)
1976	17056228	13/32	7/8	9/32	——	0.185	——	——	0.325	0.325	1600
	17056502	13/32	7/8	9/32	——	0.185	——	——	0.325	0.325	1600
	17056506	13/32	3/4	9/32	——	0.185	——	——	0.325	0.325	1600
	17056528	13/32	7/8	9/32	——	0.185	——	——	0.325	0.325	1600
	17056200	13/32	7/8	9/32	——	0.240	0.160	——	0.190	0.270	1600

① The carburetor identification number is stamped on the float bowl, near the secondary throttle lever.
② Without vacuum advance.
③ With automatic transmission; vacuum advance connected and EGR disconnected and the throttle positioned on the high step of cam.
④ With manual transmission; without vacuum advance and the throttle positioned on the high step of cam.

FORD

Year	Carburetor Identification①	Float Level (in.)	Air Valve Spring	Pump Rod (in.)	Idle Vent (in.)	Vacuum Break (in.)	Secondary Opening (in.)	Choke Rod (in.)	Choke Unloader (in.)	Fast Idle Speed (rpm)
1970	D0OF-A	5/8	0.030	5/16	——	0.140	——	0.130	0.300	750②
	D0OF-B	5/8	0.030	5/16	——	0.190	——	0.166	0.300	1850③
	D0OF-E	5/8	0.030	5/16	——	0.190	——	0.166	0.300	1850③
	D0OF-F	5/8	0.030	5/16	——	0.140	——	0.130	0.300	750②
1971	D0OF-A	11/32	0.030	5/16	——	0.140	——	0.130	0.300	1800③
	D0OF-E	11/32	0.030	5/16	——	0.190	——	0.166	0.300	2000③

① The carburetor identification tag is located at the rear of the carburetor on one of the air horn screws.
② Third step of cam.
③ Second step of cam.

OLDSMOBILE

Year	Carburetor Identification①	Float Level (in.)	Air Valve Spring (turn)	Pump Rod (in.)	Idle Vent (in.)	Primary Vacuum Break (in.)	Secondary Vacuum Break (in.)	Secondary Opening (in.)	Choke Rod (in.)	Choke Unloader (in.)	Fast Idle Speed (rpm)
1970	7040250	1/4	1/2	3/8	——	0.200	——	——	0.120	0.200	——
	7040251	1/4	3/4	3/8	——	0.200	——	——	0.120	0.200	——
	7040252	1/4	3/4	3/8	——	0.200	——	——	0.120	0.200	——
	7040253	1/4	3/4	3/8	——	0.275	——	——	0.120	0.200	——
	7040255	1/4	3/4	3/8	——	0.325	——	——	0.120	0.200	——
	7040256	1/4	3/4	3/8	——	0.325	——	——	0.120	0.200	——
	7040257	1/4	3/4	3/8	——	0.200	——	——	0.120	0.200	——
	7040258	1/4	3/4	3/8	——	0.200	——	——	0.120	0.200	——
1971	7041250	1/4	1/2	3/8	——	0.200	——	——	0.120	0.200	——
	7041251	1/4	3/4	3/8	——	0.200	——	——	0.120	0.200	——
	7041252	1/4	3/4	3/8	——	0.200	——	——	0.120	0.200	——
	7041253	1/4	3/4	3/8	——	0.200	——	——	0.120	0.200	——
	7041257	1/4	3/4	3/8	——	0.200	——	——	0.120	0.200	——
1972	7042250	1/4	1/2	3/8	——	0.230	——	——	0.120	0.200	——
	7042251	1/4	3/4	3/8	——	0.215	——	——	0.120	0.200	——
	7042252	1/4	3/4	3/8	——	0.215	——	——	0.120	0.200	——
	7042953	1/4	3/4	3/8	——	0.275	——	——	0.120	0.200	——

OLDSMOBILE

Year	Carburetor Identification①	Float Level (in.)	Air Valve Spring (turn)	Pump Rod (in.)	Idle Vent (in.)	Primary Vacuum Break (in.)	Secondary Vacuum Break (in.)	Secondary Opening (in.)	Choke Rod (in.)	Choke Unloader (in.)	Fast Idle Speed (rpm)
1973	7043256	1/4	3/4	——	——	0.200	——	——	0.120	0.300	——
	7043257	1/4	1/2	——	——	0.200	——	——	0.120	0.300	——
	7043255	1/4	3/4	——	——	0.200	——	——	0.120	0.300	——
	7043251	1/4	3/4	——	——	0.200	——	——	0.120	0.300	——
	7043253	1/4	3/4	——	——	0.275	——	——	0.120	0.300	——
	7043252	1/4	3/4	——	——	0.200	——	——	0.120	0.300	——
	7043259	1/4	3/4	——	——	0.215	——	——	0.120	0.300	——
1974	7043250	1/4	1/2	3/8	——	0.200	——	0.070	0.120	0.300	1000②
	7043251	1/4	3/4	3/8	——	0.200	——	0.070	0.120	0.300	1000②
	7043252	1/4	3/4	3/8	——	0.200	——	0.070	0.120	0.300	1000②
	7043254	1/4	3/4	3/8	——	0.275	——	0.070	0.120	0.300	1000②
	7043255	1/4	1/2	3/8	——	0.200	——	0.070	0.120	0.300	1000②
	7043256	1/4	1/2	3/8	——	0.200	——	0.070	0.120	0.300	1000②
	7043259	1/4	3/4	3/8	——	0.215	——	0.070	0.120	0.300	1000②
	7043282	1/4	3/4	3/8	——	0.215	——	0.070	0.120	0.300	1000②
	7044557	1/4	3/4	3/8	——	0.200	——	0.070	0.120	0.300	1000②
	7044558	1/4	3/4	3/8	——	0.200	——	0.070	0.120	0.300	1000②
	7044559	1/4	3/4	3/8	——	0.275	——	0.070	0.120	0.300	1000②
1975	7045183	3/8	1/2	9/32	——	0.190	0.140	——	0.135	0.235	③
	7045250	3/8	1/2	9/32	——	0.250	0.180	——	0.170	0.300	③
	7045483	3/8	1/2	9/32	——	0.275	0.180	——	0.135	0.235	③
	7045550	3/8	1/2	9/32	——	0.275	0.180	——	0.135	0.235	③
	7045264	17/32	1/2	9/32	——	0.150	0.260	——	0.130	0.235	③
	7045184	3/8	3/4	9/32	——	0.190	0.140	——	0.135	0.235	③
	7045185	3/8	3/4	9/32	——	0.275	0.140	——	0.135	0.235	③
	7045251	3/8	3/4	9/32	——	0.190	0.140	——	0.135	0.235	③
	7045484	3/8	3/4	9/32	——	0.190	0.140	——	0.135	0.235	③
	7045485	3/8	3/4	9/32	——	0.190	0.180	——	0.160	0.235	③
	7045551	3/8	3/4	9/32	——	0.190	0.140	——	0.135	0.235	③
	7045246	5/16	3/4	3/8	——	0.130	0.115	——	0.095	0.240	③
	7045546	5/16	3/4	3/8	——	0.145	0.130	——	0.095	0.240	③
1976	17056246	5/16	3/4	3/8	——	0.130	0.120	——	0.095	0.250	——
	17056250	13/32	1/2	9/32	——	0.190	0.140	——	0.130	0.230	——
	17056251	13/32	3/4	9/32	——	0.190	0.140	——	0.130	0.230	——
	17056252	13/32	3/4	9/32	——	0.190	0.140	——	0.130	0.230	——
	17056253	13/32	1/2	9/32	——	0.190	0.140	——	0.130	0.230	——
	17056255	13/32	3/4	9/32	——	0.190	0.140	——	0.130	0.230	——
	17056256	13/32	3/4	9/32	——	0.190	0.140	——	0.130	0.230	——
	17056257	13/32	3/4	9/32	——	0.190	0.140	——	0.130	0.230	——
	17056258	13/32	1/2	9/32	——	0.190	0.140	——	0.130	0.230	——
	17056259	13/32	1/2	9/32	——	0.190	0.140	——	0.130	0.230	——
	17056546	5/16	3/4	3/8	——	0.130	0.130	——	0.095	0.250	——
	17056550	13/32	1/2	9/32	——	0.190	0.140	——	0.130	0.230	——
	17056551	13/32	3/4	9/32	——	0.190	0.140	——	0.130	0.230	——
	17056552	13/32	3/4	9/32	——	0.200	0.140	——	0.130	0.230	——
	17056553	13/32	1/2	9/32	——	0.190	0.140	——	0.130	0.230	——
	17056556	13/32	3/4	9/32	——	0.190	0.140	——	0.130	0.230	——

① The carburetor identification number is stamped on the float bowl, next to the secondary throttle lever.
② On low step.
③ 1800 rpm on Omega and 400 cu. in. engines with the cam follower on the highest step of the fast idle cam; 900 rpm on all others with the fast idle cam follower on the lowest step of the fast idle cam.

PONTIAC

Year	Carburetor Identification[1]	Float Level (in.)	Air Valve Spring (turn)	Pump Rod (in.)	Idle Vent (in.)	Primary Vacuum Break (in.)	Secondary Vacuum Break (in.)	Secondary Opening (in.)	Choke Rod (in.)	Choke Unloader (in.)	Fast Idle Speed (rpm)
1970	7040262	9/32	7/16	——	——	0.400	——	——	0.100	——	——
	7040263	9/32	7/16	——	——	0.400	——	——	0.100	——	——
	7040264	9/32	7/16	——	——	0.400	——	——	0.100	——	——
	7040267	9/32	7/16	——	——	0.400	——	——	0.100	——	——
	7040268	9/32	7/16	——	——	0.400	——	——	0.100	——	——
	7040270	9/32	7/16	——	——	0.245	——	——	0.100	——	——
	7040273	9/32	7/16	——	——	0.245	——	——	0.100	——	——
	7040274	9/32	7/16	——	——	0.400	——	——	0.100	——	——
1971	7041262	9/32	7/16	——	——	0.240	——	——	0.100	——	——
	7041263	9/32	7/16	——	——	0.240	——	——	0.100	——	——
	7041264	9/32	7/16	——	——	0.240	——	——	0.100	——	——
	7041267	9/32	1/2	——	——	0.370	——	——	0.100	——	——
	7041268	9/32	1/2	——	——	0.430	——	——	0.100	——	——
	7041270	9/32	1/2	——	——	0.430	——	——	0.100	——	——
	7041271	9/32	7/16	——	——	0.240	——	——	0.100	——	——
	7041273	9/32	1/2	——	——	0.370	——	——	0.100	——	——
1972	7042262	1/4	7/16	13/32	——	0.290	——	——	0.100	——	——
	7042263	1/4	11/16	13/32	——	0.290	——	——	0.100	——	——
	7042264	1/4	5/8	13/32	——	0.290	——	——	0.100	——	——
	7042270	1/4	7/16	7/16	——	0.290	——	——	0.100	——	——
	7042273	1/4	7/16	7/16	——	0.290	——	——	0.100	——	——
1973	7043263	13/32	5/8	13/32	——	0.290	——	——	0.100	——	——
	7043264	13/32	1/2	13/32	——	0.290	——	——	0.100	——	——
	7043274	13/32	9/16	13/32	——	0.290	——	——	0.100	——	——
	7043262	13/32	3/8	13/32	——	0.290	——	——	0.100	——	——
	7043265	13/32	9/16	13/32	——	0.290	——	——	0.100	——	——
	7043272	13/32	3/8	13/32	——	0.290	——	——	0.100	——	——
1974	7043263	25/64	5/8	0.410	——	0.290	——	0.020	0.205	0.310	1500
	7044262	25/64	3/8	0.410	——	0.260	——	0.020	0.205	0.310	1500
	7044266	25/64	1/2	0.410	——	0.260	——	0.020	0.205	0.310	1500
	7044267	25/64	3/8	0.410	——	0.260	——	0.020	0.205	0.310	1500
	7044268	25/64	1/2	0.410	——	0.260	——	0.020	0.205	0.310	1500
	7044269	25/64	1/2	0.410	——	0.290	——	0.020	0.205	0.310	1500
	7044270	25/64	3/4	0.410	——	0.290	——	0.020	0.205	0.310	2000
	7044272	25/64	3/8	0.315	——	0.290	——	0.020	0.205	0.310	1500
	7044273	25/64	3/4	0.410	——	0.290	——	0.020	0.205	0.310	2000
	7044274	25/64	9/16	0.315	——	0.290	——	0.020	0.205	0.310	1500
	7044560	25/64	3/8	0.410	——	0.260	——	0.020	0.205	0.310	1500
	7044568	25/64	1/2	0.410	——	0.260	——	0.020	0.205	0.310	1500
1975	7045246	5/16	1/2	15/32	——	0.130	0.115	——	0.095	0.240	1800
	7045546	5/16	1/2	15/32	——	0.145	0.130	——	0.095	0.240	1800
	7045263	1/2	1/2	9/32	——	0.150	0.260	——	0.130	0.230	1800
	7045264	1/2	1/2	9/32	——	0.150	0.260	——	0.130	0.230	1800
	7045268	1/2	3/8	9/32	——	0.150	0.260	——	0.130	0.230	1800
	7045269	1/2	3/8	9/32	——	0.160	0.265	——	0.130	0.230	1800
	7045274	1/2	1/2	9/32	——	0.150	0.260	——	0.130	0.230	1800
	7045260	1/2	1/2	9/32	——	0.150	0.260	——	0.130	0.230	1800
	7045262	1/2	1/2	9/32	——	0.150	0.260	——	0.130	0.230	1800
	7045266	1/2	1/2	9/32	——	0.150	0.260	——	0.130	0.230	1800

PONTIAC

Year	Carburetor Identification①	Float Level (in.)	Air Valve Spring (turn)	Pump Rod (in.)	Idle Vent (in.)	Primary Vacuum Break (in.)	Secondary Vacuum Break (in.)	Secondary Opening (in.)	Choke Rod (in.)	Choke Unloader (in.)	Fast Idle Speed (rpm)
1975	7045562	$\frac{1}{2}$	$\frac{1}{2}$	$\frac{9}{32}$	——	0.150	0.260	——	0.130	0.230	1800
	7045564	$\frac{1}{2}$	$\frac{1}{2}$	$\frac{9}{32}$	——	0.150	0.2€0	——	0.130	0.230	1800
	7045568	$\frac{1}{2}$	$\frac{1}{2}$	$\frac{9}{32}$	——	0.150	0.260	——	0.130	0.230	1800
	7045566	$\frac{1}{2}$	$\frac{1}{2}$	$\frac{9}{32}$	——	0.150	0.260	——	0.130	0.230	1800
1976	8-350 Ventura	$\frac{5}{16}$	$\frac{3}{4}$	$\frac{3}{8}$	——	0.130	0.120	——	0.095	0.250	1800
	8-350 Ventura, Calif.	$\frac{5}{16}$	$\frac{3}{4}$	$\frac{3}{8}$	——	0.130	0.130	——	0.095	0.250	1800
	8-350	$\frac{17}{32}$	$\frac{1}{2}$	$\frac{3}{8}$	——	0.160	0.250	——	0.125	0.230	1800
	8-400 Auto.	$\frac{17}{32}$	$\frac{1}{2}$	$\frac{3}{8}$	——	0.160	0.250	——	0.125	0.230	1800
	8-400 Man.	$\frac{17}{32}$	$\frac{5}{8}$	$\frac{3}{8}$	——	0.170	0.250	——	0.125	0.230	1800
	8-400 Calif.	$\frac{17}{32}$	$\frac{1}{2}$	$\frac{3}{8}$	——	0.150	0.260	——	0.130	0.230	1800
	8-455 Auto.	$\frac{17}{32}$	$\frac{1}{2}$	$\frac{3}{8}$	——	0.160	0.250	——	0.125	0.230	1800
	8-44 Man.	$\frac{17}{32}$	$\frac{1}{2}$	$\frac{3}{8}$	——	0.160	0.250	——	0.125	0.230	1800
	8-455 Calif.	$\frac{17}{32}$	$\frac{1}{2}$	$\frac{3}{8}$	——	0.170	0.250	——	0.120	0.230	1800

① The carburetor identification number is stamped on the float bowl, near the secondary throttle lever.

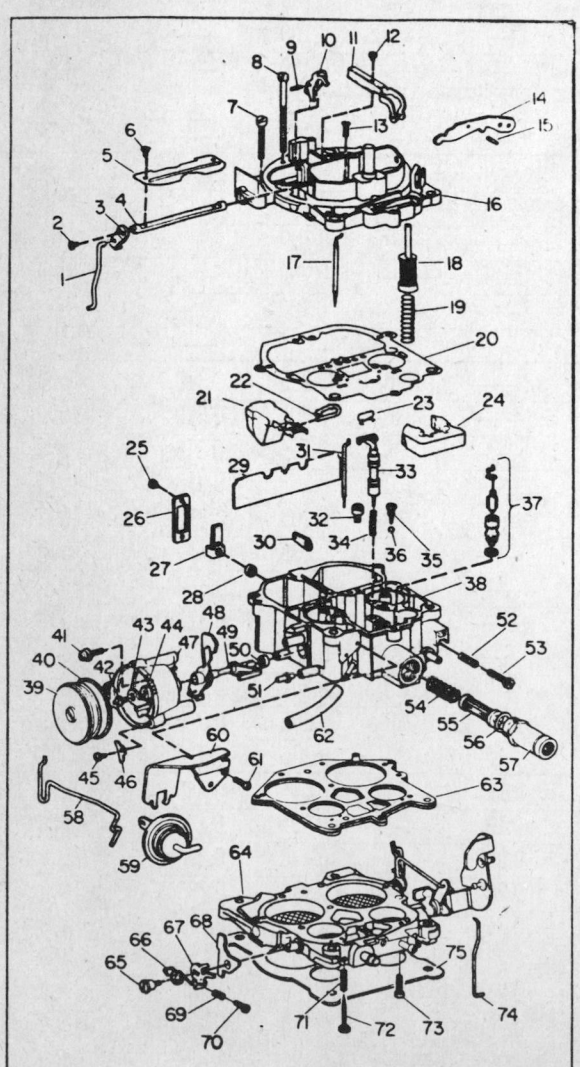

1. Choke rod
2. Choke lever screw
3. Choke lever
4. Choke shaft
5. Choke valve
6. Choke valve screw
7. Short air horn screw
8. Long air horn screw
9. Roll pin
10. Lever
11. Secondary metering rod holder
12. Secondary metering rod holder screw
13. Air horn screw
14. Pump actuating lever
15. Pump lever roll pin
16. Air horn assembly
17. Secondary metering rod
18. Pump assembly
19. Pump return spring
20. Air horn gasket
21. Float assembly
22. Float assembly hinge pin
23. Primary metering rod retainer spring
24. Float bowl
25. Idle compensator cover screw
26. Idle compensator cover
27. Idle compensator
28. Idle compensator seal
29. Float bowl baffle
30. Choke rod lever
31. Primary metering rod
32. Primary main metering jet
33. Power piston assembly
34. Power piston spring
35. Pump discharge ball retainer
36. Pump discharge ball
37. Needle and seat assembly, gasket
38. Float bowl assembly
39. Thermostatic cover and coil assembly
40. Thermostatic cover gasket
41. Choke housing-to-bowl screw
42. Choke coil lever screw
43. Choke coil lever
44. Intermediate choke shaft
45. Stat cover screw
46. Stat cover retainer
47. Choke housing
48. Fast idle cam
49. Inter choke shaft lever assembly
50. Intermediate choke shaft seal
51. Choke housing-to-bowl seal
52. Idle adjust screw spring
53. Idle adjusting screw
54. Filter relief spring
55. Fuel inlet filter
56. Filter nut gasket
57. Fuel inlet filter nut
58. Vacuum break rod
59. Vacuum break diaphragm assembly
60. Vacuum break control bracket
61. Bracket attaching screw
62. Vacuum control hose
63. Throttle body-to-bowl gasket
64. Throttle body assembly
65. Cam and fast idle lever screw
66. Fast idle lever spring
67. Fast idle lever
68. Cam follower lever
69. Fast idle screw spring
70. Fast idle adjusting screw
71. Idle mixture needle spring
72. Idle mixture needle
73. Throttle body-to-bowl attaching screw
74. Pump rod
75. Flange gasket

Exploded view of Quadrajet

Emission Control Systems

Introduction U146
  Positive Crankcase Ventilation (PCV)
    Systems U146
  Air Injection System U146
  Thermostatically Controlled Air Cleaner U146
  Distributor Controls U146
    Engine Vacuum Controls U146
    Transmission-Controlled Spark (TCS)
    System U146
    Speed-Controlled Spark (SCS)
    Systems U146
  Carburetor Controls U147
  Evaporative Emission Control Systems U147
  Exhaust Gas Recirculation (EGR) U147
  Catalytic Converters U147
  Vacuum-Operated Heat Risers U147

Troubleshooting U147
  Positive Crankcase Ventilation (PCV)
    System U147
    Valve Tests U147
  Air Injection Systems U148
    Air Pump Tests U148
    Antibackfire Valve Tests U148
    California Chevette Valve Tests U149
    Check Valve Test U150
    Ford Differential Vacuum Valve Test .. U150
    Ford Solenoid Vacuum Valve Tests U150
    Ford Vacuum Reservoir Check U150
    Air Injection Diagnosis Chart U151
  Thermostatically Controlled Air Cleaner U151
    Air Door Tests U151
    Vacuum Motor Tests U151
    Cold Weather Modulator Tests U152
  Distributor Controls U152
    Dual Diaphragm Distributor Tests U152
    Timing Retard Solenoid Test U152
    Timing Advance Solenoid Test U152
    Deceleration Valve Tests,
    Adjustments U153
    Coolant Temperature Operated Vacuum
    Valve Tests U154
    AMC Coolant Temperature Switch
    Test U155
    Ford Spark Delay Valve Tests U155
    Ford Dual Delay Valve Tests U155
    Ford Retard-Air Cleaner Delay Valve
    Test U156
    Ford Vacuum Check Valve Test U156
    Chrysler Orifice Spark Advance Control
      (OSAC) Valve Test U156
    Chrysler Thermal Ignition Control
    Valve U156
    Oldsmobile, Vega, and Buick Spark Delay
    Valve Test U156

Pontiac and Olds Vacuum Retard Delay
  Valve Tests U157
Pontiac, Olds, and Buick Distributor
  Vacuum Valve (DVV) Test U157
1974 Oldsmobile Distributor Vacuum
  Valve Test U157
Oldsmobile Vacuum Reducing valve
  Test U157
Transmission Controlled Spark System
  Tests U157
  Ford U157
  American Motors U159
  Chrysler Corporation U159
  GM except 1973 Pontiac U160
  1973 Pontiac Combination TCS-EGR
  System U163
  Vacuum Advance Solenoid and
  Transmission Switch Usage
  Chart U163
Speed Controlled Spark System Tests U164
  Ford Distributor Modulator System U164
  Distributor Modulator System
  Troubleshooting Chart U165
Ford Electronic Spark Control (ESC)
  System U166
  Chrysler Corporation System U167
  American Motors and Pontiac U167
  Cadillac U168
Ford Temperature Activated Vacuum
  System (TAV) Tests U169
Ford Cold Temperature Activated
  Vacuum System (CTAV) Tests U170
Ford Cold Start Spark Advance
  System (CSSA) Tests U170
Ford Cold Lock Out Spark System
  Test U170
Ford Delay Valve Bypass System
  Check U171
Carburetor Controls U171
  Antidieseling Solenoid Tests U171
  Solenoid/Dashpot Test U172
  A/C Operated Antidieseling Device
  Tests U172
  GM Idle Speed Increase Solenoid
  Operation U172
  CEC Solenoid Operation U172
  Electrically Assisted Choke Tests U172
    Ford and AMC U172
    Chrysler Corporation U173
    General Motors U173
  GM Secondary Choke Break Tests
  and Adjustments U174
  Chrysler Corp. Coolant Control Idle
  Enrichment (CCIE) System Test U175
  Ford Fuel Deceleration Valve U176
  Ford Speed Modulated Fuel Decel

System Test U177
GM Choke Hot Air Modulator System U178
Evaporative Emission Control Systems U178
Exhaust Gas Recirculation (EGR)
  Systems U179
  GM EGR Valve Tests U179
  GM Dual Diaphragm EGR Valve Test .. U179
  GM Backpressure Transducer Valve
  (BPV) Test U180
  Cadillac Electronic Fuel Injection
  EGR Test U180
  Chrysler Corp. EGR Floor Jet Service U180
  Chrysler Corp. Proportional EGR
  System Tests U180
  Chrysler Corp. EGR Delay System
  Test U181
  Chrysler Corp. EGR Service Reminder
  Light U182
  Ford EGR System Tests U182
  Ford High Speed EGR Modulator
  System Tests U183
  Ford EGR System Component Tests U183
  American Motors EGR System Tests ... U184
Catalytic Converters U185
  Testing the Converter U185
  Recharging or Changing Converters ... U185
  Converter Removal U186
  Catalyst Damage U186
  Chrysler Corp. Catalyst Protection
  System Test U186
  Replacing the Catalyst U186
    Chrysler and Ford U186
    GM and AMC U187
Vacuum-Operated Heat Risers U187
  Ford Vacuum Exhaust Heat Valve
  System Tests U187
  GM Early Fuel Evaporation (EFE)
  System Tests U188
Roll-Over Spill Protection U189
Chrysler Corporation Lean Burn System U189
  Operation U190
  Equipment U190
  Troubleshooting U190
    Engine Not Running—Will Not Start
    (Start Pickup Tests) U190
    Engine Running Badly (Run Pickup
    Tests) U191
    Start Timer Advance Test U191
    Throttle Advance Test U191
    Vacuum Transducer Vacuum
    Advance Test U192
    Coolant Switch Test U192
  Basic Timing Setting U192
  Idle Speed and Mixture Adjustment ... U193
  Component Removal and Overhaul U193
  Pickup Gap Specifications U193

Introduction

With emission level maintenance standards getting stricter on both the State and Federal levels, proper testing and adjustment of emission control systems are becoming increasingly important. Much confusion results from the many types and combinations of emission control systems currently in use.

To ease some of the confusion, the emission control systems section in this book has been divided into two parts. The first part is found in each of the individual car sections. It explains which system and components each make and model uses. Component R&R is also given where it is available.

The second part, below, covers testing and adjustment of the emission control systems and their individual components. Many of the components are similar (or the same) from one manufacturer to another and therefore the testing procedures are the same. Thus, one test may be used for several different manufacturers or models. Where components, although similar, differ significantly the tests are different.

For the sake of added clarity, a general description of the various types of emission control systems follows.

Positive Crankcase Ventilation (PCV) Systems

A simple valve, operated by intake manifold vacuum, is used to meter the flow of air and vapors through the crankcase. Air is drawn in through the carburetor air cleaner. When the car is decelerating or the engine is idling, high manifold vacuum closes the valve; this restricts the flow of crankcase vapor into the intake manifold. During acceleration or at a constant speed, the intake manifold vacuum drops, the valve spring forces the valve open and more vapors flow into the intake manifold from the crankcase. If a backfire occurs the valve closes, preventing the vapor in the crankcase from being ignited. If the vapor is ignited, an explosion will result.

Air Injection System

On most engines, a belt-driven air pump supplies air to an injector manifold which has a nozzle positioned behind each exhaust valve. On some engines with catalytic converters, the air from the pump is routed directly from the pump to the head pipe. Injection of air at this point causes combustion of any unburned hydrocarbons in the exhaust manifold rather than allowing them to escape into the atmosphere. An antibackfire valve controls the flow of air from the pump to prevent backfires resulting from an overly rich mixture under closed throttle conditions. A check valve, sometimes an integral part of the air injection manifold, functions to prevent hot exhaust gas backflow into the pump and hoses in case of pump failure or when the antibackfire valve is working.

On some engines, the air injection system also supplies air to aid in the operation of the catalytic converter. (see "Catalytic Converter" section.)

Thermostatically Controlled Air Cleaner

Thermostatically controlled air cleaners are used to improve operation of the engine and to prevent carburetor icing during warm-up in cold weather.

A movable door in the air cleaner snorkle allows air to be drawn in from either a manifold heat stove (cold operation) or from under the hood (normal operation). The door may be operated by a bimetallic spring or a vacuum motor. Doors of both types may use a vacuum override to provide cold air intake during periods of hard acceleration when stove-heated air is normally being supplied.

Distributor Controls

There are three basic types of distributor controls:
1. Engine vacuum controls
2. Transmission-controlled spark —transmission gear selected and/or temperature.
3. Speed-controlled spark—vehicles speed and/or temperature.

It is easier to consider these three types separately, although some of them perform similar functions and may be used in conjunction with one another.

Engine Vacuum Controls

Many small valves and solenoids fall into this class of emission controls. Some distributors are equipped with a dual-diaphragm vacuum unit which retards the spark during closed throttle deceleration and idle. On some distributors, solenoids may be used to either advance or retard the timing under predetermined conditions.

A deceleration valve may be used to provide maximum vacuum advance when the car is slowing down, by sending intake manifold vacuum to the distributor vacuum unit. By doing this, emissions may be better controlled during deceleration.

Because emission-controlled engines run hotter, it is often necessary to use a coolant temperature vacuum valve to provide additional vacuum advance when the engine is overheated. The valve is threaded into an engine coolant passage. If the engine overheats, the additional vacuum advance causes the engine speed to increase; allowing it to cool down quite rapidly. A similar valve may also be used to determine the temperature at which a TCS, SCS, or EGR system operates (see below).

A spark delay valve is installed on some engines to prevent the vacuum advance from working immediately under heavy acceleration.

On some engines a temperature activated valve may also control distributor vacuum. This valve may be part of the spark delay valve.

Transmission-Controlled Spark (TCS) System

Many variations of transmission-controlled spark (TCS) systems are used to control vehicle emissions. The basic components of these systems are: a transmission switch, which is operated either by oil pressure (automatic transmissions) or by the gear selected (manual transmission); and a vacuum solenoid. The solenoid allows vacuum to be supplied to the distributor vacuum unit or ports it into the atmosphere. Usually vacuum is supplied only in high gear and is ported in the lower gears. However, few TCS systems are quite this simple.

For example, most TCS systems use some type of temperature switch to control their operation, i.e., the system will not function below a specified air or engine temperature. In some cases it will not work above a specified temperature either. Some cars use a coolant temperature-operated vacuum valve in conjuction with the TCS system.

Various reversing and time delay relays may also be used, depending upon the needs of the engine and transmission.

Speed-Controlled Spark (SCS) Systems

Speed-controlled spark (SCS) systems perform a similar function to the transmission-controlled systems above. Many of the components are the same and used in similar way in both of the systems. The major difference lies in the switch which is activated by the speed, rather than the gear.

In its simplest form, this switch is nothing more than a centrifugal switch, connected to the speedometer drive, which completes the SCS circuit at or above a predetermined speed. A more complicated type of switch uses a small speedometer gear (or speedometer cable) driven pulse generator to send a signal to an amplifier, which, in turn, completes the

SCS system circuit at predetermined speed.

Once the circuit has been completed, vacuum is allowed to flow to the distributor vacuum unit. When the circuit is not energized, vacuum is ported into the atmosphere.

Like the transmission-controlled spark systems, SCS systems use temperature switches and various relays.

Carburetor Controls

Because of the increase in engine speed necessary to control emissions at idle, dieseling has become a problem. As a result, many carburetors use a solenoid to allow the throttle to close when the ingition is shut off, thus reducing engine speed which, in turn, prevents dieseling.

To prevent dieseling on some air-conditioned cars, a signal from an amplifier engages the A/C compressor clutch momentarily when the engine is shut off. This puts a load on the engine, thus slowing it down.

Some carburetors have enrichment circuits which are controlled by coolant temperature. This provides a richer mixture when the engine is cold, making the engine less likely to stall.

Dashpots are used on many engines to reduce emissions during deceleration. This is done by slowing down throttle closing. The dashpot may be combined with the anti-dieseling solenoid in some aplications.

Compensators may also be used on the carburetor to provide a more uniform mixture under different temperature and altitude conditions.

On some vehicles, with catalytic converters, a solenoid is used to hold the throttle open slightly when the vehicle is decelerating and the engine speed is above 2,000 rpm. This prevents catalyst damage from too rich a mixture.

Evaporative Emission Control Systems

To control emissions resulting from fuel evaporation, all cars made after 1971 use a closed fuel supply system. Instead of fuel vapor being vented into the atmosphere, it goes into a vapor/liquid separator and is routed from there, either directly through a charcoal storage canister, or into the crankcase. To prevent vapor loss at other points, the carburetor has controlled vents and a PCV system (see above) is used along with the evaporative emission control system.

Exhaust Gas Recirculation (EGR)

Exhaust gas recirculation (EGR) systems are used to reduce NO_x emissions by lowering peak flame temperature during combustion. Exhaust gases are routed into the intake manifold via floor jets, intake manifold passages, and/or an EGR control valve. This valve may be located either on the intake manifold or on a special carburetor spacer.

Some EGR systems use coolant temperature-operated vacuum valves or air temperature-operated valves to determine when they function. In addition, a vacuum amplifier (mechanical) may be provided if a weak vacuum signal is being supplied to the EGR valve.

Catalytic Converters

Starting 1975, all domestic cars sold in California are equipped with catalytic converters, as are many of the cars sold in the rest of the U.S. The converters are used to oxidize hydrocarbons (HC) and carbon monoxide (CO). They are necessary because of even stricter emission standards for the 1975 models.

The catalysts are made of noble metals (platinum and palladium) which are bonded to either a mono-lithic (one-piece) element or to individual pellets. The catalyst causes the HC and CO to break down without taking part in the reaction; hence, a catalyst life of 50,000 miles is expected.

Some engines equipped with the converters require an air injection pump to supply air for the reaction; others will not.

Vacuum-Operated Heat Risers

Starting 1975, some Ford and GM engines have a vacuum-operated heat riser (manifold heat valve). These valves replace the bimetallic spring operated valves which have been previously used.

TROUBLESHOOTING

NOTE: For model usage, a description of, as well as, available removal and installation procedures for the components of emission control systems, consult the individual car repair sections. This section covers tests and adjustments only.

Positive Crankcase Ventilation (PCV) System

Valve Tests

1. See if any deposits are present in the carburetor passages, the oil filler cap, or the hoses. Clean these as required.
2. Connect a tachometer, as instructed by its manufacturer, to the engine.
3. With the engine idling, do one of the following:
   a. Remove the PCV valve hose from the crankcase or the oil filler connection.
   b. On cars with the PCV valve located in a grommet on the valve cover, remove both the valve and the grommet.

NOTE: If the valve and the hoses are not clogged-up, a hissing sound should be present.

4. Check the tachometer reading. Place a finger over the valve or hose opening (a suction should be felt).
5. Check the tachometer again. The engine speed should have dropped at least 50 rpm. It should return to normal when the finger is removed from the opening.

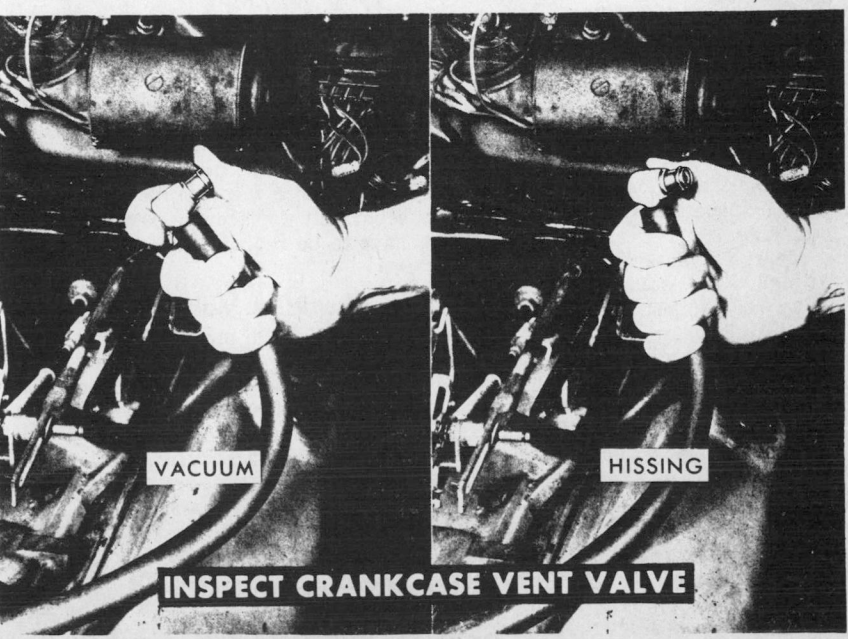

VACUUM   HISSING

INSPECT CRANKCASE VENT VALVE

Testing PCV valve (© Chrysler Corp)

6. If the engine does not change speed or if the change is less than 50 rpm, the hose is clogged or the valve is defective. Check the hose first. If the hose is not clogged replace, do not attempt to repair, the PCV valve.

7. Test the new valve in the above manner, to make sure that it is operating properly.

NOTE: There are several commercial PCV valve testers available. Be sure that the one used is suitable for the valve to be tested, as the testers are not universal. Follow the manufacturer's instructions.

Air Injection Systems

Air Pump Tests

Caution Do not hammer on, pry, or bend the pump housing while tightening the drive belt or testing the pump.

Belt Tension and Air Leaks

1. Before proceeding with the tests, check the pump drive belt tension to see if it is within specifications.

2. Turn the pump by hand. If it has seized, the belt will slip, producing noise. Disregard any chirping, squealing, or rolling sounds from inside the pump; these are normal when it is turned by hand.

3. Check the hoses and connections for leaks. Hissing or a blast of air is indicative of a leak. Soapy water, applied lightly around the area in question, is a good method for detecting leaks.

Air Output Tests

1. Disconnect the air supply hose at the antibackfire valve.

2. Connect a vacuum gauge, using a suitable adaptor, to the air supply hose.

NOTE: If there are two hoses plug the second one up.

3. With the engine at normal operating temperature, increase the idle speed and watch the vacuum gauge.

4. The air flow from the pump should be steady and fall between 2–6 psi. If it is unsteady or falls below this, the pump is defective and must be replaced.

Pump Noise Diagnosis

The air pump is normally noisy; as engine speed increases, the noise of the pump will rise in pitch. The rolling sound the pump bearings make is normal, however if this sound becomes objectionable at certain speeds, the pump is defective and will have to be replaced.

A continual hissing sound from the air pump pressure relief valve at idle,

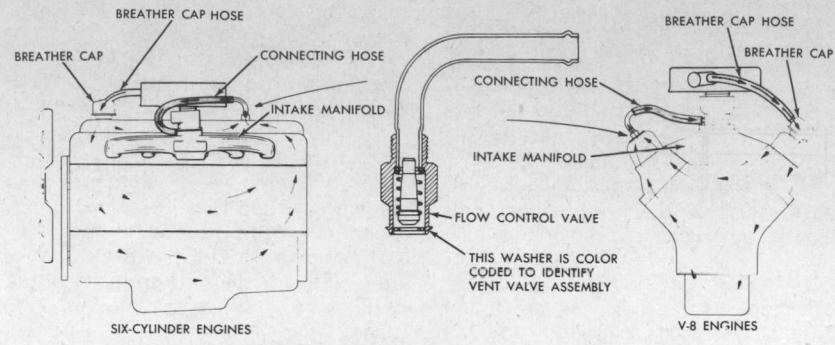

Fully closed ventilation system (© Chrysler Corp)

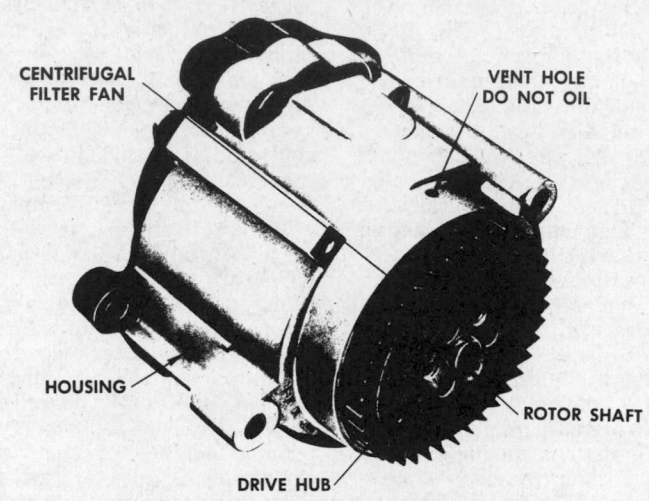

Identifying the external parts of an air pump (© G.M. Corp)

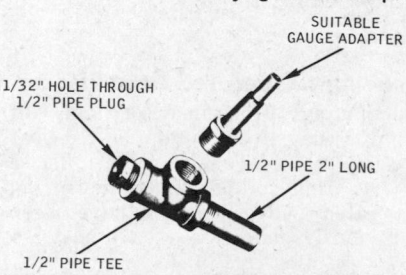

Making an air pump-to-vacuum gauge adapter (© Ford Motor Co)

indicates a defective valve. Replace the relief valve.

If the pump rear bearing fails, a continual knocking sound will be heard. Since the rear bearing is not separately replaceable, the pump will have to be replaced as an assembly.

Antibackfire Valve Tests

There are different types of antibackfire valves used with air injection systems. A by-pass (diverter) valve is used on most current engines, while most older engines use a gulp type antibackfire valve. Test procedures for both types are given below.

To protect the catalyst, 1975 and later Ford cars have a slightly different arrangement used when the car is equipped with a catalytic converter. The by-pass valve allows air to flow to the exhaust ports when high manifold vacuum is applied to it. Since

there is no manifold vacuum, the by-pass valve dumps the air from the pump into the atmosphere at wide-open throttle. To prevent backfiring, during deceleration, when manifold vacuum is high, a vacuum differential valve (VDV) is used to block the vacuum signal to the by-pass valve, causing it to dump the air from the pump.

A solenoid which is connected to a temperature sensor in the air cleaner, blocks vacuum to the by-pass valve when the choke is on; shutting the entire air injection system off when the engine is cold.

On 351M and 400 cu in. engines, a coolant temperature operated vacuum valve is used to block vacuum to the by-pass valve if the engine overheats.

By-pass (Diverter) Valve (except '75 and later Ford)

1. Detach the hose, which runs from the by-pass valve to the check valve, at the by-pass valve hose connection.

2. Connect a tachometer to the engine. With the engine running at normal idle speed, check to see that air is flowing from the by-pass valve hose connection.

3. Speed the engine up, so that it is running at 1,500–2,000 rpm. Allow the throttle to snap shut. The flow of air from the by-pass valve at the check valve hose

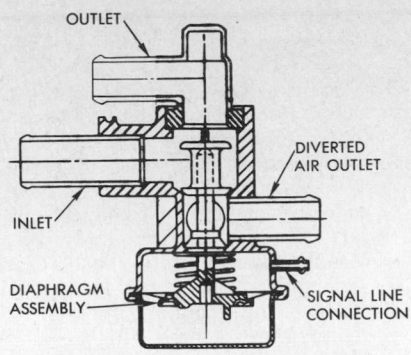

VALVE IN OPEN POSITION

GM type air by-pass (diverter) valve

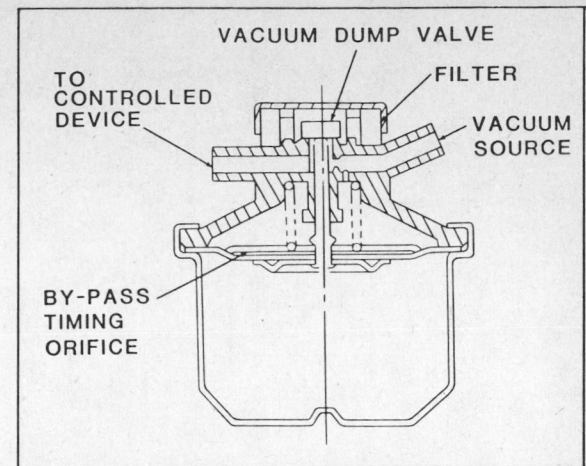

Chevette vacuum differential valve
(© G.M. Corp.)

connection should stop momentarily and air should then flow from the exhaust port on the valve body or the silencer assembly.

4. Repeat step three several times. If the flow of air is not diverted into the atmosphere from the valve exhaust port or if it fails to stop flowing from the hose connection, check the vacuum lines and connections. If these are tight, the valve is defective and requires replacement.

5. A leaking diaphragm will cause the air to flow out both the hose connection and the exhaust port at the same time. If this happens, replace the valve.

By-Pass Valve—1975 and later Ford

1. Allow the engine to reach normal operating temperature. Put the transmission in Neutral (N) or Park (P) and apply the parking brake.

2. Stop the engine. Remove the by-pass valve-to-check valve hose from the by-pass valve. On V6s and V8s, remove both hoses.

3. Install a tachometer and start the engine.

4. Hold your hand over the by-pass valve hose connection(s) and increase the engine speed to 1500 rpm. Air should flow from the hose connection(s).

5. Remove and plug the by-pass valve vacuum hose. Increase the engine speed to 1500 rpm. No air should flow from the hose connections. Instead, air should flow out the exhaust ports in the silencer cover.

6. If the by-pass valve fails the preceeding tests, replace it.

7. Stop the engine. Remove the tachometer and reconnect all hoses. If you are going to perform the air injection decel valve test, leave the tachometer in place.

California Chevette Valve Tests

Chevettes sold in California do not use the bypass valve, but use three valves in combination. They are: the vacuum differential valve, the differential vacuum delay and separator valve, and an air bypass valve.

Vacuum Differential Valve

1. Check the condition of all the vacuum lines.

2. With the engine at idle, no air should be escaping from the muffler or the by-pass valve. Open and close the throttle quickly, air should discharge from the muffler for about a second.

3. If this does not happen, recheck the lines involved; if they are good, replace the vacuum differential valve.

Differential Delay and Separator Valve

1. Start the engine and let it idle in neutral.

2. Disconnect the black VAC line coming from the engine to the valve. After about 30 seconds air should be discharged from the muffler. If air starts discharging immediately, the valve was installed wrong. Turn it around; the black side should be connected to engine vacuum.

3. Reconnect the black line, the air should stop discharging. If it does not, replace the valve.

Air By-Pass Valve

1. Check all the lines, make sure they are connected properly and without kinks.

2. Disconnect the vacuum line from the engine; air should be discharged from the muffler. Reconnect the line, air should stop coming from the muffler.

3. If the valve does not operate as shown in step 2, replace it.

Large canister is 1975-76 Ford air by-pass valve; smaller valve below it is vacuum differential valve (VDV)

U149

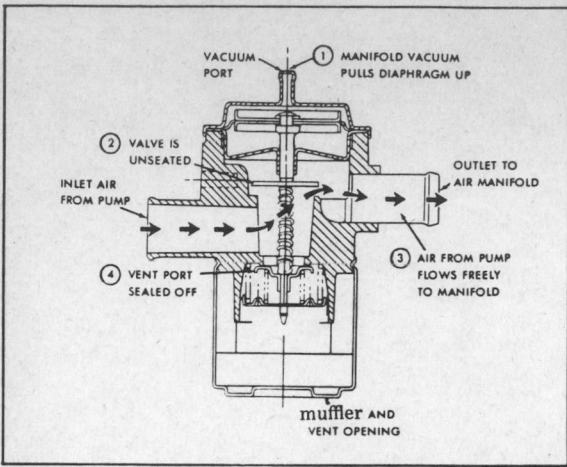

Chevette air by-pass valve
(© G.M. Corp.)

Check Valve Test

1. Before starting the test, check all of the hoses and connections for leaks.
2. Detach the air supply hose(s) from the check valve(s).
3. Insert a suitable probe into the check valve and depress the plate. Release it; the plate should return to its original position against the valve seat. If binding is evident, replace the valve.
4. Repeat step three if two valves are used.
5. With the engine running at normal operating temperature, gradually increase its speed to 1,500 rpm. Check for exhaust gas leakage. If any is present, replace the valve assembly.

NOTE: Vibration and flutter of the check valve at idle speed is a normal condition and does not mean that the valve should be replaced.

You can also check the condition of the check valve by blowing through it toward the air manifold; air should be able to pass in this direction. Apply suction to the same place; a check valve in working order will not permit air to flow back.

1975-76 Ford Differential Vacuum Valve Test

The differential vacuum valve is only used on air injection systems on models with catalytic converters.

Perform the by-pass valve test prior to this test.

1. Allow the engine to reach normal operating temperature. Put transmission in Park (P) or Neutral (N) and apply the parking brake.
2. Stop the engine. Remove the by-pass valve-to-check valve hose at the by-pass valve end. On V6s and V8s, remove both hoses.
3. Install a tachometer and start the engine.
4. Hold your hand over the by-pass valve hose connection(s) and in-

Vacuum solenoid for VDV/air by-pass system —1975 Ford (© Ford Motor Co)

crease engine speed to 2500 rpm. Release the throttle. Air flow from the hose connections should stop momentarily and then start again. When the hose connection air flow stops, air should start coming out the by-pass valve silencer ports.
5. If the by-pass valve isn't working correctly in step 4, check to see that the decel valve is getting a vacuum signal.
6. If the decel valve is getting vacuum, and the by-pass valve is known to be working OK, replace the decel valve.
7. Stop the engine. Remove the test equipment and reconnect the hoses.

1975-76 Ford Air Injection System Solenoid Vacuum Valve Tests

Air injection system solenoid vacuum valves are used only on models with catalytic converters. There are two types of solenoid vacuum: type I is normally closed and type II is normally open. Check the vehicle's tune-up specifications decal to determine which type is used.

Type I (Normally Closed)

1. Allow the engine to reach normal operating temperature. Be sure that the air cleaner temperature is above 65°F.

2. Allow the engine to idle, Detach the vacuum hose from the by-pass valve. Air should flow from the by-pass valve silencer exhaust ports. Connect the by-pass valve vacuum hose.
3. If the air is exhausted out the silencer cover exhaust ports, the solenoid vacuum hose connections are OK. The vacuum supply hose should always go to the bottom solenoid fitting (type I).
4. Detach the vacuum supply hose from the solenoid. Place your finger over the end of the hose. Vacuum should be felt. It not, check the hose and manifold vacuum fitting. Reconnect the vacuum hose.
5. Unfasten the solenoid vacuum valve wiring.
6. Connect one terminal of the solenoid vacuum valve to a 12V power source. Ground the other terminal. Air should *not* come out the by-pass valve exhaust ports.
7. Disconect the 12V power source and ground wires. Reconnect the solenoid valve wiring.
8. Air still should not come out of the by-pass valve exhaust ports.
9. If the solenoid vacuum valve doesn't operate as outlined, replace it.

Type II (Normally Open)

1. Do steps 1 through 3 of the type I solenoid vacuum valve test.

NOTE: The vacuum supply hose should be connected to the black nozzle on type II valves.

2. Unfasten the wiring from the solenoid vacuum valve.
3. Connect one terminal of the vacuum valve to a 12V power source. Ground the other terminal.
4. Air should flow from the by-pass valve exhaust ports.
5. Disconnect the 12V power source and ground wires. Reconnect the solenoid vacuum valve wiring.
6. Air should *stop* flowing out of the by-pass valve exhaust ports. If it dosen't operate as outlined replace the solenoid vacuum valve.

1975-76 Ford Vacuum Reservoir Check

A vacuum reservoir is required on some air injection systems when used with a catalytic converter. To check it:

1. Detach the soleniod vacuum valve-to-reservoir hose from the reservoir fitting.
2. Connect a vacuum gauge to the reservoir fitting.
3. Disconect the manifold vacuum hose from the reservoir and connect an external vacuum source in its place.
4. Apply a 14 in. Hg vacuum to the

AIR INJECTION SYSTEM DIAGNOSIS CHART

Problem	Cause	Cure
1. Noisy drive belt	1a Loose belt 1b Seized pump	1a Tighten belt 1b Replace
2. Noisy pump	2a Leaking hose 2b Loose hose 2c Hose contacting other parts 2d Diverter or check valve failure 2e Pump mounting loose 2g Defective pump	2a Trace and fix leak 2b Tighten hose clamp 2c Reposition hose 2d Replace 2e Tighten securing bolts 2g Replace
3. No air supply	3a Loose belt 3b Leak in hose or at fitting 3c Defective anti-backfire valve 3d Defective check valve 3e Defective pump	3a Tighten belt 3b Trace and fix leak 3c Replace 3d Replace 3e Replace
4. Exhaust backfire	4a Vacuum or air leaks 4b Defective anti-backfire valve 4c Sticking choke 4d Choke setting rich	4a Trace and fix leak 4b Replace 4c Service choke 4d Adjust choke

reservoir and trap it. The vacuum should not drop more than 1 in. Hg in 1 min.

5. Remove the test equipment and reconnect the vacuum lines.

Thermostatically Controlled Air Cleaner

Air Door Tests

Non-Vacuum-Operated and 1970-71 Ford Vacuum-Operated

1. Unfasten the temperature sensing valve and snorkle assembly from the air cleaner. Place it in a container of cold water. Make sure that the thermostat is completely covered with water.
2. Place a thermometer, of known accuracy, in the water. Heat the water slowly and watch the temperature.
3. At 105° F, or less, the door should be closed (manifold heat position).
4. Continue heating the water until it reaches 130° F. The door should be fully open to the outside air position.
5. If the door does not open at or near this temperature, check it for binding or a detached spring. If neither of this situations exist, the sensor is defective and must be replaced.

NOTE: This usually means that the entire snorkle assembly must be replaced.

Vacuum-Operated Door— Except 1970-71 Ford

1. Either start with a cold engine or remove the air cleaner from the engine for at least half an hour. While cooling the air cleaner, leave the engine compartment hood open.
2. Tape a thermometer, of known accuracy, to the inside of the air cleaner so that it is near the temperature sensor unit. Install the air cleaner on the engine but do not fasten its securing nut.
3. Start the engine. With the engine cold and the outside temperature less than 80° F., the door should be in the "heat on" position (closed to outside air).

NOTE: Due to the position of the air cleaner on some cars, a mirror may be necessary when observing the position of the air door.

4. Operate the throttle lever rapidly to ½–¾ of its opening and release it. The air door should open to allow outside air to enter and then close again, except on some 1975 Ford models with a cold weather modulator.
5. Allow the engine to warm up to normal temperature. Watch the door. When it opens to the outside air, remove the cover from the air cleaner. The temperature should be over 80°F and no more than 130°F; 115°F is about normal. If the door does not work within these temperature ranges, or fails to work at all, check for linkage or door binding.

If binding is not present and the air door is not working, proceed with the vacuum tests, given below. If these indicate no faults in the vacuum motor and the door is not working, the temperature sensor is defective and must be replaced.

Vacuum Motor Tests

1970-71 Ford

1. Detach the hose from the vacuum override motor. Connect a vacuum gauge to the hose.
2. With the engine at idle, the vacuum gauge should read 15 in. Hg or better. If it is less than this, check the vacuum lines and connections for leaks.
3. If the vacuum is at specification, install the hose back on the vacuum motor.
4. With the underhood temperature below 100°F, check the air door position. If the air door is less than halfway to the "heat on" position and no components are binding, remove the vacuum motor for bench-testing.
5. Connect the motor to an *alternate* vacuum source. If the rod on the motor moves at least ½ in., reinstall it and check for a defective thermostat bulb.
6. If the rod does not move at all or if it moves less than ½ in., the motor is defective and should be replaced.

GM, AMC, and Ford (1972-on)

NOTE: Be sure that the vacuum hose that runs between the temperature switch and the vacuum motor is not pinched by the retaining clip under the air cleaner. This could prevent the air door from closing.

1. Check all of the vacuum lines and fittings for leaks. Correct any leaks. If none are found, proceed with the test.
2. Remove the hose which runs from the sensor to the vacuum motor. Run a hose directly from the manifold vacuum source to the vacuum motor.
3. If the motor closes the air door, it is functioning properly and the temperature sensor is defective.
4. If the motor does *not* close the door and no binding is present in its operation, the vacuum motor is defective and must be replaced.

NOTE: If an alternate vacuum source is applied to the motor, insert a vacuum gauge in the line by using a

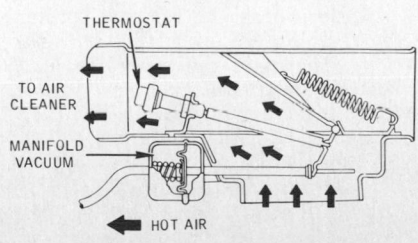

Duct and valve assembly in "heat on" position — warm-up

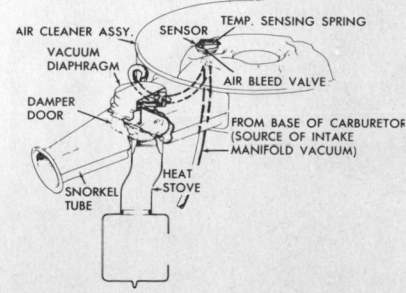

Components of the thermostatically controlled air cleaner (© G.M. Corp)

T-fitting. *Apply at least 9 in. Hg of vacuum in order to operate the motor.*

Chrysler Corp.

1. Remove the air cleaner from the carburetor and allow it to cool to 90°F. Connect a vacuum source to the sensor as well as a vacuum gauge.
2. Apply 20 in. Hg to the sensor, the door should be in the "heat on" (up) position. If it remains in the "off" position, test the vacuum motor.
3. Connect the motor to a vacuum source. In addition to the vacuum gauge, a hose clamp and a bleed valve are necessary. Connect them in the following order:
   a. Vacuum source
   b. Hose clamp (or shut-off valve)
   c. Bleed valve
   d. Vacuum gauge
   e. Vacuum motor
4. Apply 20 in. Hg vacuum to the motor. Use the hose clamp to block the line, so that the motor will retain the vacuum. The door operating motor should retain this amount of vacuum for five minutes. Release the hose clamp.
NOTE: If the vacuum cannot be built up to the specified amount, the diaphragm has a leak and the valve will require replacement.

Testing the vacuum motor—Chrysler heated air intake system (© Chrysler Corp)

1975-76 Ford cold weather modulator is mounted in the air cleaner (© Ford Motor Co.)

5. By slowly closing the bleed valve, check the operation of the door. The door should start to raise at not less than 5 in. Hg and should be fully raised at no more than 9 in. Hg.
6. If the vacuum motor fails any of the tests in steps 3–5, it is defective. Replace it with a new unit.
7. If the door works properly but fails to pass step two, the sensor is a fault and should be replaced.
NOTE: If the engine has a dual snorkle air cleaner, check the right side as in steps 3–5, above. However, there is no temperature sensor on the right-side door.

Cold Weather Modulator Tests

1975-77 Ford

Some 1975-77 Ford models use a cold weather modulator to prevent the air door from being opened under hard acceleration, when the temperature is below 55°F.

Check the vehicle's tune-up specifications decal, to see if the cold weather modulator is used, before beginning this test:
1. Stop the engine.
2. Cool the modulator unit in the air cleaner to below 40°F with areosol circuit test spray or equivalent.

Caution Do not spray the modulator with the engine running. If the spray is drawn into the carburetor, poisonous PHOS-GENE gas will come out the tailpipe. Perform this test only in a well ventilated area.

3. Apply at least 16 in. Hg with an external vacuum source to the vacuum motor side of the modulator. Trap the vacuum.
4. The modulator must hold at least 14 in. Hg vacuum for one minute. If it doesn't, replace the modulator.
5. Use a heat gun or run the engine to warm the modulator to at least 70°F.
6. Perform step 3. This time the modulator should not hold the vacuum. Replace it, if it does.

Distributor Controls
Dual Diaphragm Distributor Tests

1. Connect a timing light to the engine. Check the ignition timing.
NOTE: Before proceeding with the tests, disconnect any spark control devices, distributor vacuum valves, etc. If these are left connected, inaccurate results may be obtained.
2. Remove the retard hose from the distributor and plug it. Increase the engine speed. The timing should advance. If it fails to do so, then the vacuum unit is faulty and must be replaced.

3. Check the timing with the engine at normal idle speed. Unplug the retard hose and connect it to the vacuum unit. The timing should instantly be retarded from 4–10°. If this does not occur, the retard diaphragm has a leak and the vacuum unit must be replaced.

Timing Retard Solenoid Test

A timing retard solenoid is used on some Chrysler Corp. products up to, and including the 1971 model year.
1. Connect a timing light to the engine and check the timing.
2. Detach the solenoid ground lead near its carburetor end. Timing should advance at least 5° and there should be an increase in engine speed.

Detach the timing retard solenoid leads at the carburetor end (© Chrysler Corp)

3. Reconnect the ground lead. Timing should be retarded to the original position noted and the engine should slow down. Repeat the test several times.
4. If the timing does not behave in the manner indicated, the solenoid is defective and must be replaced; it cannot be adjusted or repaired.

Timing Advance Solenoid Test

NOTE: A timing advance solenoid is used on Chrysler products in 1972. It should not be confused with the retard solenoid, above. It is used only on the 400 cu. in. 4-bbl engine in 1973–1974.
1. Attach a tachometer to the engine.
2. Detach the vacuum advance line from the distributor advance unit.
3. Run the engine at normal idle and check engine rpm with the tachometer.
4. Detach the solenoid lead wire at its connection, which is about 6 in. away from it. Run a jumper wire from the battery to the disconnected lead from the solenoid.
5. When the two leads are touched, the engine speed should increase by 50 rpm or, if a timing light is used, the timing should advance 7–8°.
NOTE: Do not touch the jumper wire to the solenoid lead for more than 30 seconds, or the solenoid will overheat.

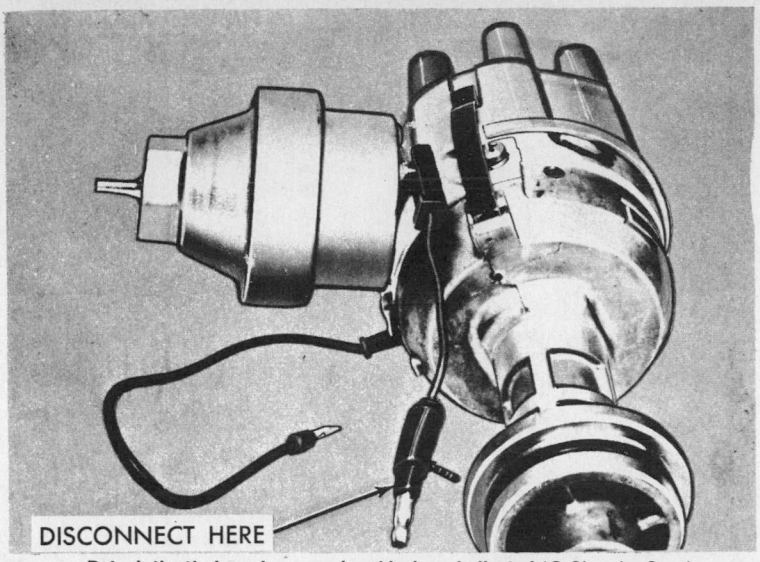

DISCONNECT HERE

Detach the timing advance solenoid where indicated (© Chrysler Corp)

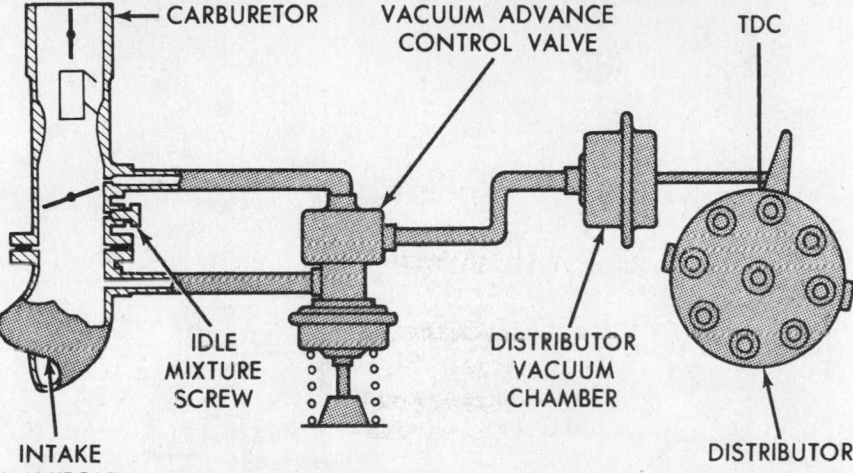

CARBURETOR — VACUUM ADVANCE CONTROL VALVE — TDC — IDLE MIXTURE SCREW — DISTRIBUTOR VACUUM CHAMBER — INTAKE MANIFOLD — DISTRIBUTOR

Carburetor/deceleration (control) valve/distributor relationship

6. If the engine speed does not increase or the timing advance, the solenoid is defective and must be replaced. Remember to reconnect it when through testing.

Deceleration Valve Tests

NOTE: Timing, idle speed and air/fuel mixture should be at proper specifications before starting this test.

1. Connect a vacuum gauge to the distributor vacuum advance line, by using a T-connection which has about the same inside diameter as the line. Do not clamp the line shut.
2. If the carburetor is equipped with a dashpot, tape its plunger down so that it cannot touch the throttle lever at idle.
3. Speed the engine up to about 2,-000 rpm and retain this speed for about five seconds.
4. Release the throttle, allowing the engine to return to normal idle.
5. The vacuum reading should rise to about 15–16 in. Hg and stay there for one second. It should

take about three seconds for the vacuum to return to its normal 6 in. Hg reading. These specifications do not apply to American Motors cars. See note under "De-

celeration Valve Adjustment for American Motors Cars."

6. If the valve does not retain its high reading for about one second or if it takes over three seconds for the reading to return to normal, the valve should be adjusted, as outlined below.

To check for a leaking valve diaphragm, proceed as follows:

1. Remove the vacuum gauge and connect it to the manifold vacuum line with a T-connection.
2. Clamp the valve-to-distributor vacuum line and, with the engine at normal idle speed, check the vacuum reading.
3. Clamp the line shut between the deceleration valve and the T-connection. Check the vacuum gauge reading again.
4. If the second reading is higher than the first, the valve diaphragm is leaking and the valve should be replaced.

Ford V6 Deceleration Valve Test

1. Install a vacuum gauge between the solenoid valve and the decel valve. Raise the rear wheels, start the engine and put it in gear.
2. If you do not get a vacuum gauge reading below eleven miles an hour, connect a set of jumper wires from the solenoid terminals to the battery and a ground. Shift the transmission into neutral and run the engine at 1500 RPM. There should be no vacuum reading. If there is, replace the deceleration valve.
3. With the ignition switch turned on, check for battery voltage to the solenoid. If you do not get any, check for an open circuit in the line; check for a good ground also.

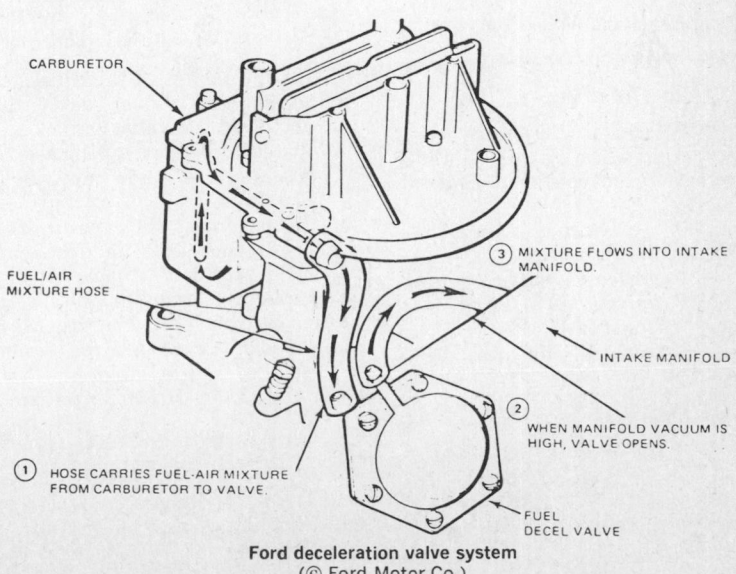

CARBURETOR — FUEL/AIR MIXTURE HOSE — ③ MIXTURE FLOWS INTO INTAKE MANIFOLD. — INTAKE MANIFOLD — ② WHEN MANIFOLD VACUUM IS HIGH, VALVE OPENS. — ① HOSE CARRIES FUEL-AIR MIXTURE FROM CARBURETOR TO VALVE. — FUEL DECEL VALVE

Ford deceleration valve system
(© Ford Motor Co.)

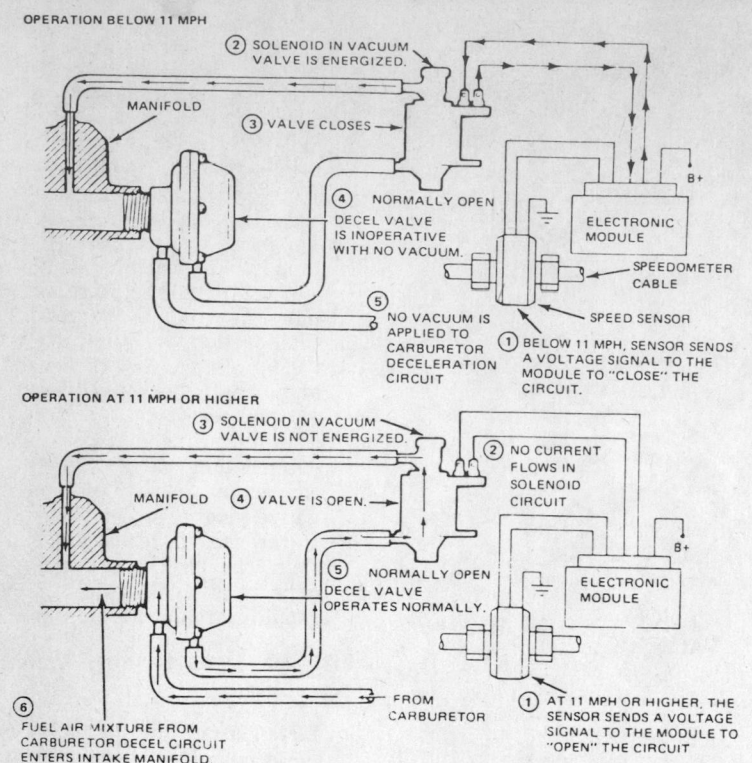

OPERATION BELOW 11 MPH

② SOLENOID IN VACUUM VALVE IS ENERGIZED.

MANIFOLD

③ VALVE CLOSES

④ NORMALLY OPEN DECEL VALVE IS INOPERATIVE WITH NO VACUUM.

ELECTRONIC MODULE

B+

SPEEDOMETER CABLE

SPEED SENSOR

⑤ NO VACUUM IS APPLIED TO CARBURETOR DECELERATION CIRCUIT

① BELOW 11 MPH, SENSOR SENDS A VOLTAGE SIGNAL TO THE MODULE TO "CLOSE" THE CIRCUIT.

OPERATION AT 11 MPH OR HIGHER

③ SOLENOID IN VACUUM VALVE IS NOT ENERGIZED.

MANIFOLD

④ VALVE IS OPEN.

② NO CURRENT FLOWS IN SOLENOID CIRCUIT

B+

⑤ NORMALLY OPEN DECEL VALVE OPERATES NORMALLY.

ELECTRONIC MODULE

FROM CARBURETOR

① AT 11 MPH OR HIGHER, THE SENSOR SENDS A VOLTAGE SIGNAL TO THE MODULE TO "OPEN" THE CIRCUIT.

⑥ FUEL AIR MIXTURE FROM CARBURETOR DECEL CIRCUIT ENTERS INTAKE MANIFOLD.

Ford speed modulated deceleration system
(© Ford Motor Co.)

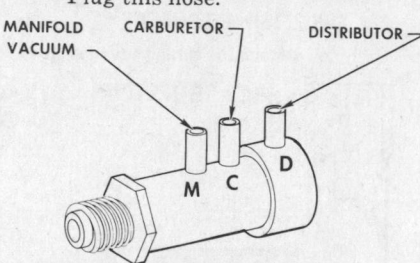

MANIFOLD VACUUM CARBURETOR DISTRIBUTOR

M C D

Typical GM coolant temperature-operated vacuum valve (© G.M. Corp)

4. Check the speed sensor for continuity by connecting an ohmmeter between the leads. Resistance should be 40 ohms. If the resistance varies, replace the speed sensor.

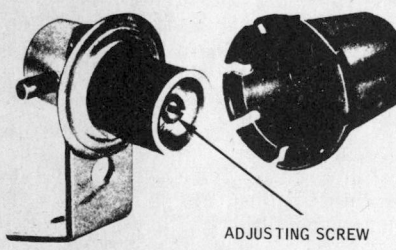

ADJUSTING SCREW

Adjustment of the deceleration valve
(© Ford Motor Co)

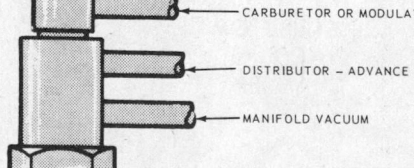
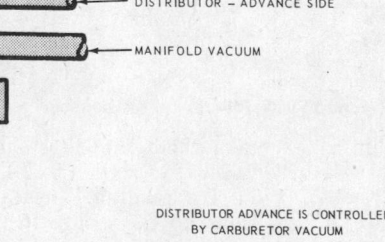

WITHOUT FILTER

CARBURETOR OR MODULATOR VACUUM

DISTRIBUTOR – ADVANCE SIDE

MANIFOLD VACUUM

WITH FILTER

MANIFOLD VACUUM

DISTRIBUTOR– RETARD SIDE

FILTER

DISTRIBUTOR ADVANCE IS CONTROLLED BY CARBURETOR VACUUM

DISTRIBUTOR RETARD IS CONTROLLED BY MANIFOLD VACUUM

Basic hose routing for temperature-operated vacuum valve

Deceleration Valve Adjustments

If the deceleration valve test indicated a need for adjustments, proceed as follows:

1. Remove the cover to gain access to the adjusting screw.
2. If an *increase* in valve opening time is desired, turn the adjusting screw counterclockwise.
3. If a *decrease* in time is desired, turn the adjusting screw clockwise.

NOTE: Each complete turn of the adjusting screw equals ½ in. Hg. Thus, if the vacuum reading at the end of three seconds is 7½ in. Hg, it will take three turns of the screw to return it to the proper 6 in. Hg. reading.

tions. *If a malfunction of the distributor control system occurs, remember to check the vacuum valve.*

1. Check all of the vacuum hoses for proper installation and routing.
2. Connect a tachometer to the engine.
3. Run the engine until it reaches normal operating temperature but do not allow it to overheat. Be sure that the choke is open.
4. On Chrysler Corp., cars, detach the distributor solenoid ground lead at the carburetor (if so equipped).
5. Check engine rpm with the carburetor at curb idle.
6. Detach the vacuum line from the intake manifold at the valve end. Plug this hose.

4. After finishing the adjustments, retest the valve, as outlined above. If the valve cannot be adjusted to proper specifications, it is defective and must be replaced.

NOTE: On 1970 American Motors cars equipped with a deceleration valve, the test and adjustment procedures are the same, but the specifications are different. Operate the engine at 2,000 rpm for ten seconds; the vacuum reading range should fall between 4 (low)–20 (high) in. Hg.

Coolant Temperature Operated Vacuum Valve Tests

NOTE: On some cars equipped with distributor control systems, this valve also is used to override the control system under overheating condi-

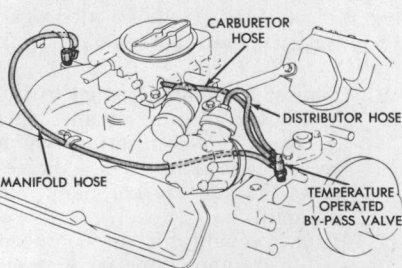

CARBURETOR HOSE

DISTRIBUTOR HOSE

MANIFOLD HOSE

TEMPERATURE OPERATED BY-PASS VALVE

Basic hose routing for temperature-operated vacuum valve

7. Check the idle speed; there should be no change. If the idle speed drops 100 rpm or more, the valve is defective and must be replaced.
8. Check the coolant level and radiator cap. Reconnect the intake

manifold hose to the temperature valve.

9. Cover the radiator to increase the coolant temperature. Then do one of the following:
   a. If the car is equipped with a temperature gauge, run the engine until the gauge registers near the top of the "Normal" range.
   b. On cars equipped with warning lights, run the engine until the red temperature light comes on.

Caution Do not run the engine at an abnormally high temperature for any longer than is required to test the valve. It is not necessary, nor desirable, to overheat an engine when the car uses a temperature gauge, i.e., the gauge should never be allowed to register "H" (Hot) when testing the valve.

10. If the engine speed has increased by at least 100 rpm, the valve is functioning properly. If there is little or no increase in engine speed, the valve is faulty and must be replaced.
11. Uncover the radiator and allow the car to cool by running the engine at idle.
12. On Chrysler products, remember to connect the distributor solenoid wire.

AMC Coolant Temperature Switch Test

This switch on all 1976 49 states engines admits manifold vacuum to the distributor below a specified temperature.

1. Connect a vacuum gauge to the center port of the gauge.
2. At below 160°F, you should be reading intake manifold vacuum. Above 160°, ported vacuum from the carburetor should be registered. This vacuum varies with the position of the throttle plates.

Ford Spark Delay Valve Tests

NOTE: If the distributor vacuum line contains a cut-off solenoid, it must be open during this test.

1. Detach the vacuum line from the distributor at the spark delay valve end. Connect a vacuum gauge to the valve, in its place. On some 1975 models, the valve has a "CARB" nipple also; leave it alone.
2. Connect a tachometer to the engine. Start the engine and rapidly increase its speed to 2,000 rpm with the transmission in neutral.
3. As soon as the engine speed is increased, the vacuum gauge reading should drop to zero.
4. Hold the engine speed at a steady 2,000 rpm. It should take longer than two seconds for the

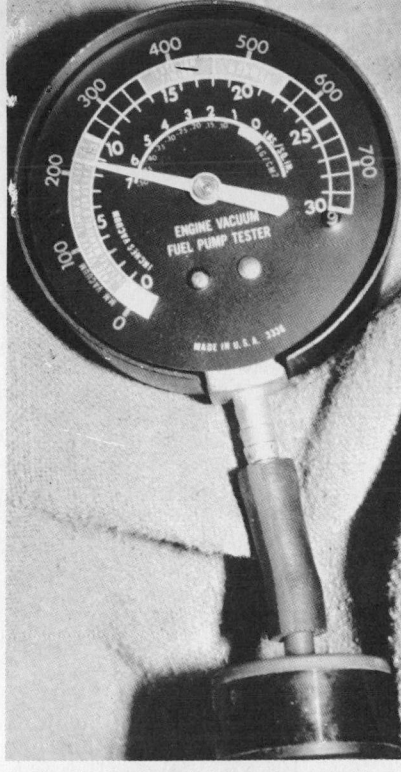

Testing the Ford spark delay valve—the black side should be connected to the vacuum source

gauge to register 6 in. Hg. If it takes less than two seconds, the valve is defective and must be replaced.

5. If it takes longer than the number of seconds specified in the chart below for the gauge to reach 6 in. Hg, disconnect the vacuum gauge from the spark delay valve. Disconnect the hose which runs from the spark delay valve to the carburetor at the valve end. Connect the vacuum gauge to this hose.
6. Start the engine and increase its speed to 2,000 rpm. The gauge should indicate 10–16 in. Hg. If it

does not, there is a blockage in the carburetor vacuum port or else the hose itself is plugged or broken. If the gauge reading is within specification, the valve is defective.

7. Reconnect all vacuum lines and remove the tachometer, once testing is completed.

Spark Delay Valve Color Code (Ford)

Color (With Black)	1972 Time Delay Maximum (sec)	1973-76 Time Delay Maximum (sec)
Gray	—	4
Green	20	20
Blue	15	16
Red	40	28
White	5	12
Yellow	10	14
Orange	—	24
Brown	—	5

Ford Dual Delay Valve Tests

1. Either obtain an external source or use the engine to provide a constant source of 10 Hg. of vacuum for this test.
2. Connect a 2 foot section of vacuum hose to the distributor nipple of the delay valve and the other end to a vacuum gauge.
3. Connect the black side of the delay valve and the *carb* nipple of the delay valve to the vacuum source.
4. Apply 10 in. Hg. of vacuum to the black side of the valve while preventing vacuum from being applied to the CARB nipple.
5. Next, apply vacuum to the CARB nipple and see how long it takes for the gauge to read 8 in. Hg. Replace it if the delay is incorrect.

White and Brown	5 seconds
White and Green	20 seconds

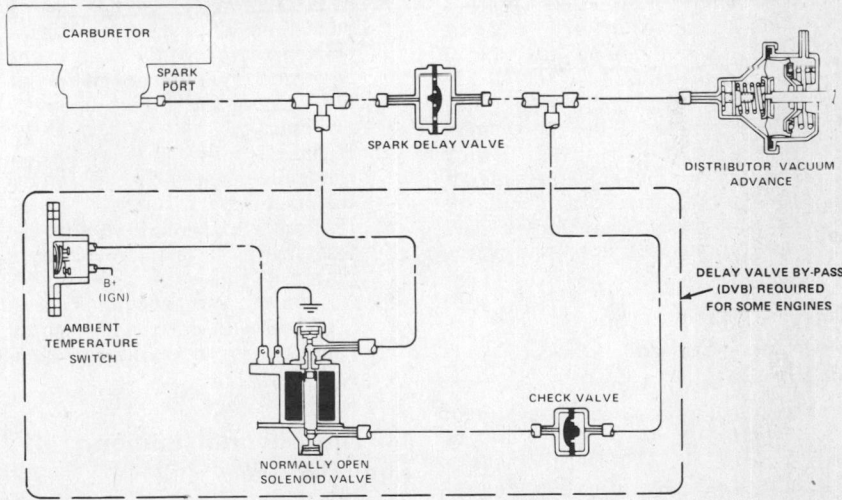

Ford spark delay valve circuit (© Ford Motor Co)

Ford Retard-Air Cleaner Delay Valve Test

1. Connect a steady (either engine or external), vacuum of 10 Hg. to the colored (not white or black) side of the delay valve.
2. Connect a vacuum gauge and two feet of vacuum line to the white side of the valve.
3. With the vacuum applied, check the number of seconds needed to read from 0-8 in. Hg. If the times do not match those in the following chart, replace the valve.

Air Cleaner-Retard Delay Valve Chart

VALVE COLOR	I.D. NO.	TIME IN SECONDS MIN.	MAX.
White/Brown	2	2	2
White/Green	20	9	20
Black/White	5	4	12
Black/Yellow	10	5.8	14
Black/Blue	15	7	16
Black/Green	20	9	20
White/Red	40	15	28

Ford Vacuum Check Valve Test

1. Apply a source of 5 in. HG to the check side of the check valve and trap it there. Check with a vacuum gauge; after 30 seconds, there should not be less than 4 in. Hg. vacuum.
2. Connect a gauge to the side where you connected the vacuum source in the first step. Apply vacuum to the opposite side of the valve. The reading should be the same as the amount of vacuum applied. If not, replace the valve.

Chrysler Orifice Spark Advance Control (OSAC) Valve

NOTE: Air temperature around the car must be above 68°F for this test because the OSAC valve has a temperature sensor in it. Valves produced from around 1 March 1973 do not have an ambient temperature

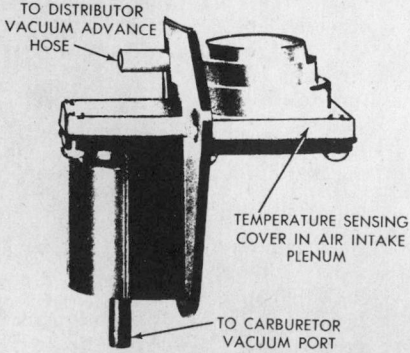

TO DISTRIBUTOR VACUUM ADVANCE HOSE

TEMPERATURE SENSING COVER IN AIR INTAKE PLENUM

TO CARBURETOR VACUUM PORT

Chrysler orifice spark advance control (OSAC) valve (© Chrysler Corp)

sensor built into them. They may be identified by their white gasket (old OSAC valves had a black one) and a pasted-on label with the part number (3755499) on it. 1974 and later models have the OSAC valve located in the air cleaner, rather than on the firewall.

1. Check the vacuum hoses and connections for any signs of leaks or plugging.
2. Detach the vacuum line which runs from the distributor to the OSAC valve at the distributor end. Connect a vacuum gauge to this line.
3. Connect a tachometer to the engine. Rapidly open the throttle and then stabilize the engine speed at 2,000 rpm in neutral. When the throttle is rapidly opened the vacuum gauge reading should drop to zero.
4. With the engine speed at a steady 2,000 rpm, it should take about 15 seconds for the vacuum level to rise and then stabilize.
NOTE: The length of time may vary slightly with different engines; 15 seconds is an approximate figure.
5. If the vacuum level rises immediately, the valve is defective and must be replaced.
6. If there is no increase in vacuum at all, disconnect the hose which runs from the carburetor to the OSAC valve at the valve and connect a vacuum gauge to this hose. Speed the engine up to 2,000 rpm.
7. If there is no vacuum reading on the gauge, check for a clogged carburetor port, filters or hoses.
8. If there is a vacuum reading, the valve is defective and must be replaced.
9. Reconnect the vacuum hoses, after disconnecting the vacuum gauge. Disconnect the tachometer.

Chrysler Thermal Ignition Control Valve

1. Check the hose connections and routing; also check the coolant level of the radiator.
2. Hook up a tachometer and bring the engine to normal operating

temperature. Adjust the idle to 600 RPM.
3. Disconnect and plug the hose from the number 2 valve port.
4. If the idle speed drops 100 RPM or more, replace the valve; if not, reconnect the hose and proceed to the next step.
5. Cover the front of the radiator to increase the temperature, but do not overheat the engine.
6. Idle the engine until the temperature is about 225° F, or when the indicator needle reaches the top of the normal bar. If the speed has not increased 100 RPM or more, the valve should be replaced.

1973-76 Oldsmobile, Vega and Buick Spark Delay Valve

NOTE: The ambient temperature must be 50°F or above, for this test. 1974 2bbl. Vegas with A/T made before Dec. 7, 1973 use a spark delay valve, as well as 1975 models.

1. Disconnect the vacuum lines from the spark delay valve, after removing its cover.
2. Connect a vacuum gauge to the "TVS" port on the valve and a *hand-operated* vacuum pump (with a gauge attached) to the "CARB" port.
3. Operate the hand pump to create a vacuum. The vacuum gauge on the TVS side should show a slight hesitation before registering.
4. The gauge reading on the pump should drop slightly, taking 3-4 seconds for it to balance with the reading on the other gauge.
5. If Steps 3 and 4 are negative, replace the valve.
6. Remove the vacuum gauge from the TVS side of the valve.
7. Cover the "TVS" port on the valve with your finger and operate the pump to create a vacuum of 15 in. Hg.
8. The reading on the pump gauge should remain steady, if the valve leaks down, i.e., the gauge reading drops, replace the valve.
9. Remove your finger, the reading on the gauge should drop slowly. If the reading goes to zero rapidly, replace the valve.

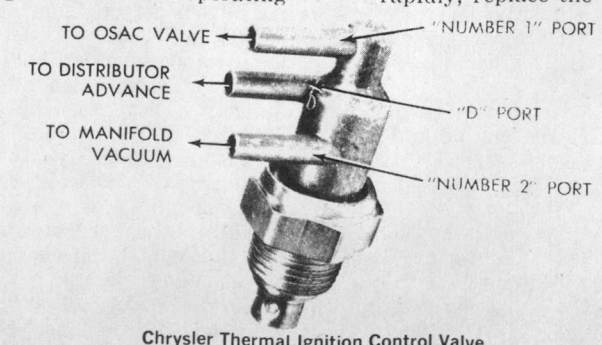

TO OSAC VALVE — "NUMBER 1" PORT
TO DISTRIBUTOR ADVANCE
TO MANIFOLD VACUUM
"D" PORT
"NUMBER 2" PORT

Chrysler Thermal Ignition Control Valve (© Chrysler Corp.)

This part of the test applies only to 1973-74 models:

10. Use ice to cool the valve to below 40°F. Connect the vacuum gauge and the hand pump as in Step 2.
11. Operate the pump to create a vacuum; this time there should be no delay before the gauge readings balance. If there is a delay, replace the valve.
12. Reconnect the vacuum lines, in the correct order, to the valve after completing the test. Replace the cover.

1975-76 Pontiac (All V8) and Olds (V8-400) Vacuum Retard Delay Valve Tests

1. Check the vacuum retard delay valve installation. The side labeled "DIST" should face the distributor.
2. Disconnect and plug the hose which runs to the No. 1 port on the coolant temperature operated vacuum valve (located on the manifold water crossover) at its vacuum source. Plug the vacuum source.
3. Using a T-connector, hook up a vacuum gauge in the line between the spark delay valve and the distributor vacuum advance unit.
4. Stop the engine and watch the vacuum gauge.
5. It should take the gauge reading 2 to 5 seconds to drop from 15 to 5 in Hg. If the vacuum drop is within specifications, everything is OK; disconnect the vacuum gauge and connect the vacuum lines. If the vacuum drops too fast, proceed with the rest of the test.
6. Remove and plug the line which runs to the No. 2 port on the coolant temperature operated vacuum valve.
7. Repeat steps 4 and 5. If the vacuum reading now drops slowly, replace the coolant temperature operated vacuum valve. If the reading still drops rapidly, replace the delay valve (unless there is a second coolant temperature operated vacuum valve).
8. On engines with two vacuum valves, disconnect and plug the vacuum line which runs from the "D" port of the valve on the right cylinder head.
9. Repeat steps 4 and 5. If the vacuum reading now drops slowly, replace the valve on the right cylinder head. If it still drops fast replace the delay valve.
10. Remove the vacuum gauge and reconnect the vacuum lines.

1976 Pontiacs are using a spark restrictor disc instead of the valve used previously. This restrictor is used during warm-up and on sudden acceleration or deceleration. During regular engine operation (warmed up engine), this restrictor is bypassed.

1975-76 Pontiac, Oldsmobile, and Buick Distributor Vacuum Valve (DVV)

1. Remove the hose from the distributor vacuum advance unit. Connect a vacuum gauge to the hose.
2. Using a T-connector, hook up a second vacuum gauge to the "C" or "CARB" port on the DVV.
3. At idle the gauge should register 10 in. Hg at the distributor hose.
4. Replace the DVV if the gauge registers more or less than 10 in Hg. or 7 in. Hg. on 260 V8 automatic transmission.
5. With the engine idling in Park (P), open the throttle slowly and watch the gauges.
6. The vacuum at the distributor should remain at 10 in. Hg. while that at the "CARB" port should slowly increase.
7. As the gauge at the "CARB" port goes over 10 in. Hg. (7 in. Hg. on 260 V8). The distributor gauge will read the same as the throttle is opened further. The maximum reading should be about 15 in. Hg.
8. If the DVV doesn't work right, replace it.

1974 Oldsmobile Distributor Vacuum Valve (DVV)

NOTE: The distributor vacuum valve (DVV) is used on all California V8s and on all Toronado models.

1. Remove the air cleaner from the carburetor and plug up the manifold vacuum fitting.
2. Place the transmission in Park and block the wheels.
3. Start the engine and allow it to reach normal running temperature. Be sure that the air conditioner is turned off.
4. Remove the vacuum line from the "D" port of the coolant temperature operated vacuum valve.

Install a vacuum gauge on the "D" port.
5. Connect another vacuum gauge to the hose at the carburetor EGR port with a T-fitting.
6. Slowly open the throttle; the reading on the gauge connected to the "D" port should raise, and level off at one of the following:
   Toronado—8 in. Hg
   All California—7 in. Hg
7. The second gauge (at the EGR port) should then reach the same figure given in Step 6. If this does not happen, replace the DVV.
8. After completing the test, disconnect both vacuum gauges, then install the vacuum lines and the air cleaner.

1973-74 Oldsmobile Vacuum Reducing Valve Test

1. Allow the engine to warm up.
2. Disconnect the line which runs from the vacuum reducing valve to the coolant temperature operated vacuum valve at the temperature valve end. Plug the nipple on the temperature valve to prevent a vacuum leak.
3. Connect a vacuum gauge to the line, after being sure that the line is neither plugged nor pinched.
4. With the engine at idle, the vacuum gauge should register no more than 9 in Hg—1973; 11-12 in. Hg—1974; or 13—13.5 in. Hg—1975. If the reading is higher than this, replace the vacuum reducing valve.

Transmission Controlled Spark System Tests
1970-73 Ford

NOTE: When performing the following tests, be sure that the temperature switch is kept above 65°F, except as noted. On models equipped with a spark delay valve, the spark delay valve must be removed for this test to be valid.

Manual Transmission System Test

1. Connect a vacuum gauge between the distributor and the

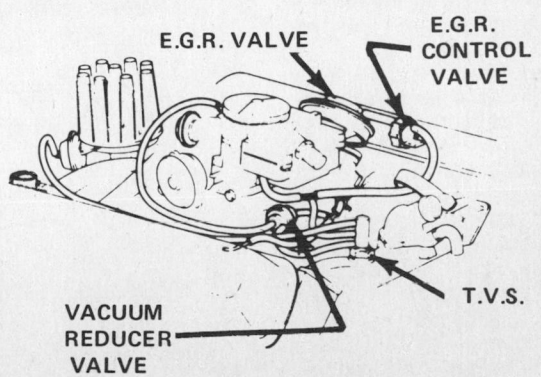

Oldsmobile vacuum reducing valve location (© G.M. Corp)

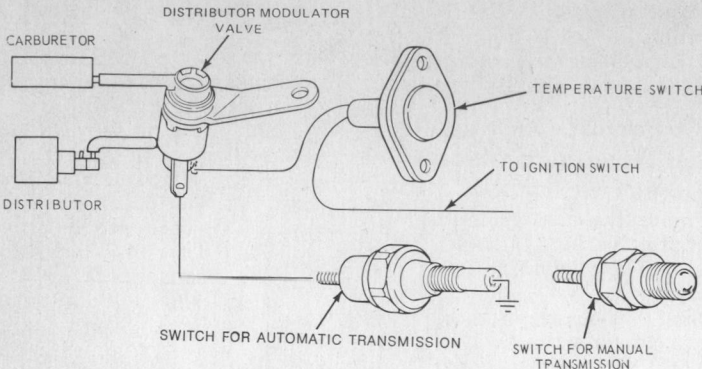

Ford transmission controlled spark system (© Ford Motor Co).

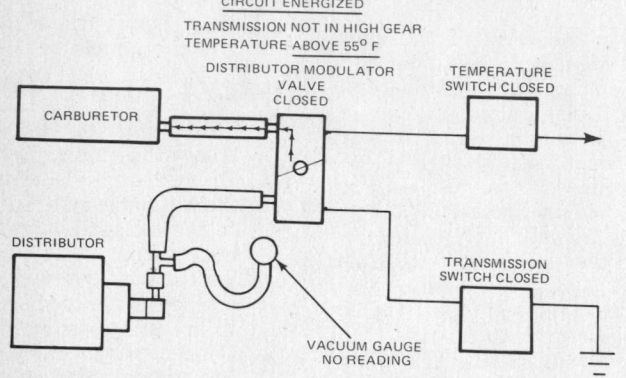

CIRCUIT ENERGIZED
TRANSMISSION NOT IN HIGH GEAR
TEMPERATURE ABOVE 55° F

Testing the transmission-controlled spark system with the circuit energized (© Ford Motor Co)

Automatic Transmission System Test

1. Connect a vacuum gauge between the distributor and the distributor modulator valve using a T-connection. Start the engine.
2. When the transmission is in Park or neutral, the vacuum gauge should read zero.
3. Apply the brakes and shift into Reverse. Increase the engine speed. The gauge may or may not register a vacuum.
4. If no vacuum is present, detach a wire from the distributor modulator valve and shift into neutral. Increase engine speed to between 1,000–1,500 rpm. This time the gauge should definitely show a vacuum reading.
5. If vacuum still is not present, disconnect the two vacuum lines from the distributor modulator valve and join them, using a nipple, to bypass the valve. Repeat step four.
6. If there is vacuum now, proceed with the rest of the tests. If no vacuum is present, check for loose, pinched, or plugged hoses. When finished, reconnect the wire to the valve.
7. Detach the transmission switch lead from the distributor modulator valve. Connect the lead in series with a test lamp and the positive terminal of the battery.
8. Start the engine and apply the

distributor modulator valve, using a T-connector.

2. Start the engine. With the transmission in neutral, the vacuum gauge should read zero.
3. Increase engine speed to between 1,000–1,500 rpm with the clutch pedal depressed. The vacuum reading should remain at zero.
4. With the clutch still depressed, place the transmission in high gear. Increase engine speed, as before. The vacuum gauge should now read at least 6 in. Hg. If it does not, proceed further with testing. Remember to shift into netural or stop the engine before engaging the clutch.
5. Unfasten the transmission switch lead from the distributor modulator terminal. Connect the lead in series with a low amperage test lamp and the positive side of the battery.
6. Move the gear shift lever through all of the gears. The test lamp should remain on until high gear is entered.
7. If the lamp stays on when the transmission is in high, either the switch is defective or the circuit is grounded. If it fails to come on at all, the switch is defective or the circuit has a loose wire.
8. If the transmission switch is functioning properly but the system check indicates that some-

thing is still wrong, proceed with the temperature switch test below.

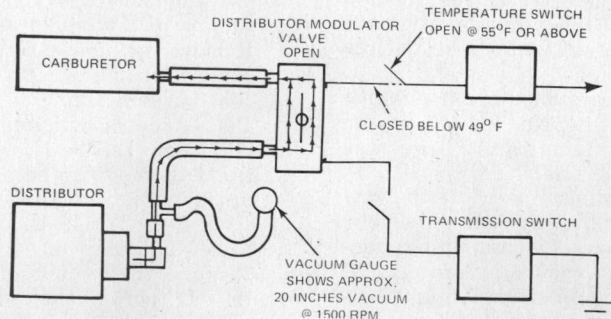

CIRCUIT DE-ENERGIZED
TRANSMISSION IN HIGH GEAR (OR REVERSE-AUTOMATIC)
TEMPERATURE SWITCH CAN BE OPEN OR CLOSED DEPENDING ON TEMPERATURE

Testing the transmission-controlled spark system with the circuit de-energized (© Ford Motor Co)

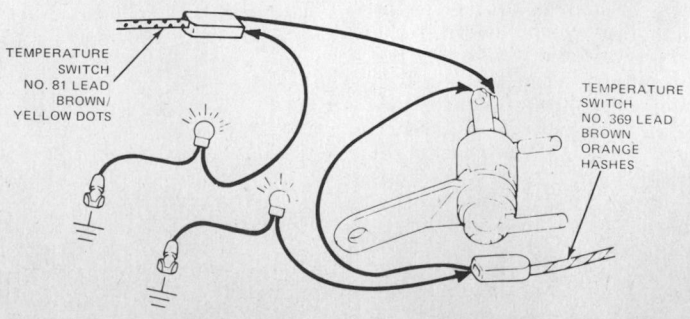

Using a test lamp to check the temperature of the transmission switch (© Ford Motor Co)

brakes. Move the transmission selector through all of the positions on the quadrant.

9. The lamp should go out only when Reverse is selected. If it stays on in Reverse or fails to come on at all, either the switch is defective or the wiring is faulty.

10. If the transmission switch and wiring are in proper order, but vacuum still is not present, it will be necessary to test the temperature switch.

Temperature Switch Tests

NOTE: Cars made after 15 March 1973 do not use ambient temperature switches with TCS systems.

1. Detach the temperature switch lead from its terminal or the distributor modulator valve. Connect the lead to a grounded test lamp.

2. Remove the temperature switch from either the right or left door pillar. Warm the switch by holding it in the palm of the hand. The lamp should come on once 65°F is reached.

3. Using ice, or an aerosol spray circuit cooler, cool the switch to below 49°F. The test lamp should go out.

4. If the lamp fails to go on or off when it should, the switch is defective and must be replaced.

5. If the temperature switch is functioning properly, and no vacuum was present in the system test, the distributor modulator valve is defective.

Distributor Modulator Valve Test

1. Perform the above system test.

2. If the other components, i.e., the transmission switch and the temperature switch, are functioning properly and vacuum is present when it should not be, or vice versa, the fault probably lies in the distributor modulator valve.

3. Before replacing the valve, however, remember to check for clogged, pinched, or loose vacuum hoses, as these could result in similar symptoms.

American Motors

NOTE: All 1973 V8s and 1973 sixes from 15 March on, as well as all 1974 and later engines with TCS, use a coolant temperature operated vacuum valve to shut the TCS system off below 160°F. For 1975 and later, this system was only used on California engines.

Manual Transmission Test

The transmission-controlled spark (TCS) system used on American Motors cars equipped with manual transmissions is similar to the one used by Ford for their cars with manual transmissions.

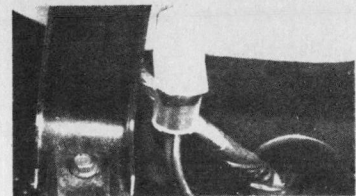
Location of American Motors ambient temperature switch on the front upper crossmember
(© American Motors Corp)

The major difference is in the temperature switch (not used after 15 March 1973). The American Motors switch is located on the front upper crossmember and closes at 63°F. Also, American Motors refers to the "distributor modulator valve" (Ford) as the "solenoid vacuum valve."

Bearing these differences in mind, test the American Motors system in the same manner as outlined under "Ford—Manual Transmission," above.

NOTE: For the test procedures to be used when a 1972–73½ car is equipped with an automatic transmission, consult the "Speed Controlled Spark" section, below.

1973½-74 Automatic Transmission

NOTE: The spark control system used on AMC cars, equipped with automatic transmissions and made after 15 March 1973, is controlled by a switch which operates on transmission governor oil pressure. Test procedures for cars made before this date may be found in the "Speed Controlled Spark Systems" section, below.

1. Disconnect the electrical lead from the terminal of the governor pressure switch.

NOTE: The switch may easily be reached with the hood opened. On sixes, the switch is located on the right rear of the cylinder block; on V8s, it is attached to a bracket at the rear of the right-hand rocker cover.

2. Connect a 12V test light in series, between the lead and the terminal on the switch.

Caution *Use a low amperage test light, so that the switch contacts will not be damaged.*

3. Raise the car, block the front wheels (if they are not off the ground), and securely support it

Late 1973 and later solenoid vacuum valve (top) and transmission governor pressure switch (bottom)—AMC V8

so that the rear wheels are free to turn.

4. Apply the service brakes. Start the engine. The test light should glow.

5. Place the gear selector in Drive (D), release the brake pedal and slowly depress the gas pedal.

6. Watch the speedometer and the test light; between 33-37 mph the switch should open and the test light should go out.

7. If the light does not go out within this speed range, adjust the switch by turning the 1/16 in. allen screw on the switch terminal. Turn the screw clockwise to increase or counterclockwise to decrease the switch cut-out speed. The switch should be adjusted to open at 35 mph.

8. If the switch cannot be adjusted to specification, replace it.

9. If the switch is working properly, but the TCS system is not working, the solenoid vacuum valve is probably defective.

Chrysler

1971-72 Manual Transmission

NOTE: For testing procedures to be used on Chrysler products that are equipped with an automatic transmission, see Speed Control Spark.

1. Turn the ignition switch to the "on" position. Place the transmission selector lever in the "neutral" position.

2. Disconnect the wire from the B+ terminal on the ignition system ballast resistor while holding the solenoid vacuum valve.

3. When the wire is disconnected, the valve should be felt to de-energize.

4. Reconnect the wire to the ballast resistor, the valve should be felt to energize. If the solenoid vacuum valve does not react this way, either the vacuum valve or the transmission switch is defective, or voltage is not present at the ballast resistor. Connect a test light to the B+ terminal of the resistor to check for voltage.

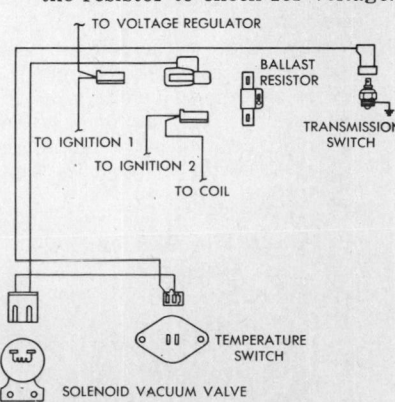
NOₓ (TCS) system schematic—manual transmission (© Chrysler Corp)

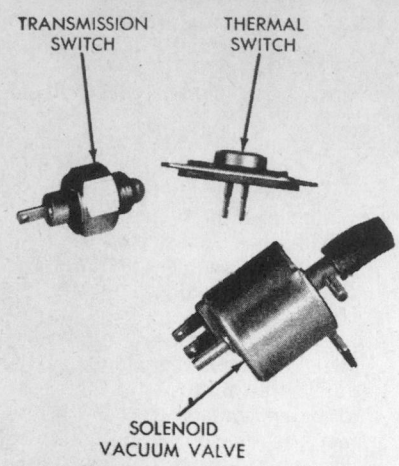

SOLENOID
VACUUM VALVE

NO$_x$ (TCS) system components—
manual transmission (© Chrysler Corp)

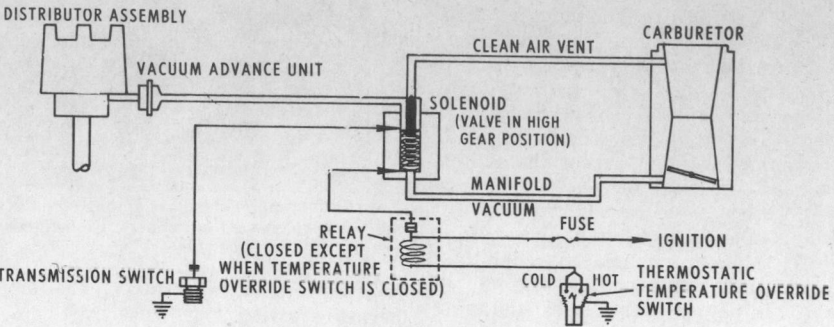

A typical transmission controlled spark system (© General Motors Corp)

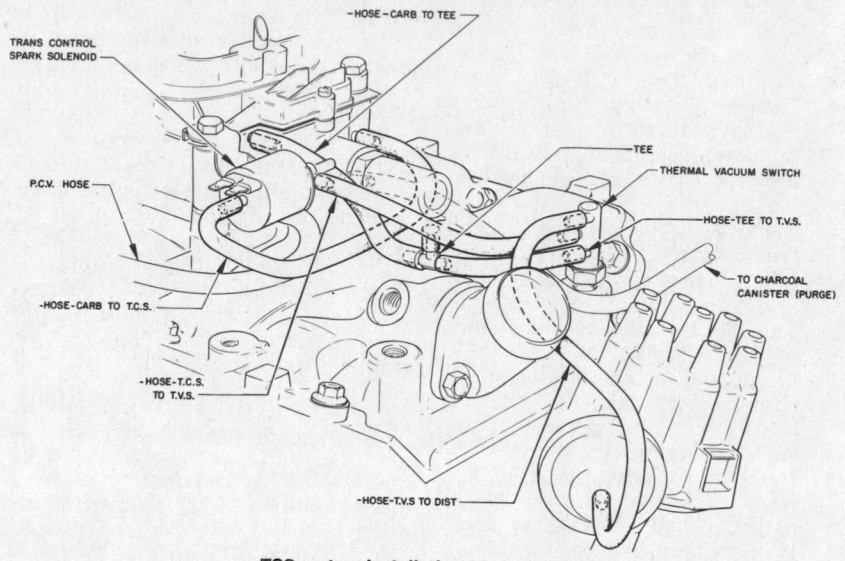

TCS system installation (© G.M. Corp)

5. To test the solenoid vacuum valve, disconnect the wiring connector from the solenoid. Run a jumper wire from the piggyback connector on the ballast resistor to one of the terminals on the solenoid vacuum valve. Connect another jumper wire from the other terminal on the solenoid vacuum valve to a good ground. When the ignition switch is turned to the "on" position, the vacuum valve should be felt to energize. If the vacuum valve does not energize, it is defective. If the vacuum valve does energize, but did not energize in Steps 2–4, proceed to Step 6. Connect the lead wires to the vacuum valve.

6. Disconnect the lead wire from the transmission switch. Connect a jumper wire from the just disconnected switch lead to a good ground. When the ignition switch is turned to the "on" position the solenoid vacuum valve should be felt to energize. If the switch does energize when the lead wire to the switch was connected to ground, but failed to energize in Steps 2–4, the transmission switch is either defective or it has a bad ground. If the transmission switch is attached to the transmission with 180 in. lbs torque, it is correctly grounded.

7. If the vacuum valve energized in Step 5, but did not energize in Step 6, the lead wire from the ballast resistor to the vacuum valve is defective.

GM Except All 1973 Pontiac Models

NOTE: The components used on the GM transmission-controlled spark (TCS) systems vary from model to model. For a description of the components used for each model, see the appropriate Car Sections. GM did not use TCS in 1975; in 1976 its use is limited to the 2300 cc. engine with manual transmission.

SYSTEM TEST

1. Connect a vacuum gauge to the vacuum source for the vacuum solenoid. With the transmission in neutral and the engine idling, vacuum should be present.

2. If there is no vacuum present, check for a clogged vacuum port, damaged vacuum lines or loose hose connections.

3. Disconnect the vacuum guage and reconnect the vacuum line.

4. Detach the vacuum line from the distributor vacuum unit and connect it to the vacuum gauge. This is the line which contains the vacuum advance solenoid or CEC solenoid.

5. With engine temperature above 95°F and the transmission in neutral, run the engine for at least 25 seconds. The vacuum gauge should read zero.

NOTE: All 1971 Cadillacs have a by-pass circuit to provide vacuum advance in both Park and neutral.

6. Do one of the following:
   a. Manual transmission — Depress the clutch pedal and move the shift lever through the gears. Increase engine speed in each gear, enough to cause vacuum advance. A vacuum should be present only in High gear.

   NOTE: On 1970–71 models with four-speed transmissions, vacuum should also be present in third gear.

   b. Automatic transmission — Raise the rear wheels of the car off the ground. Support the car and block the front wheels, so that it cannot roll forward. Place the transmission in Drive and speed the engine up enough so that the transmission will shift into high gear; vacuum should only be present when the transmission enters high gear, and not while it is in lower gears.

   NOTE: Some cars are equipped with a time-delay device, so it may take 20–25 seconds before vacuum is present once the proper gear has been reached. Do not run the engine any longer than necessary to complete the test.

7. If no vacuum is present when it should be or if it is present when it should not be, first check the TCS system fuse (if so equipped) and then proceed with the individual tests outlined below.

VACUUM ADVANCE SOLENOID TESTS

NOTE: There are several different types of vacuum advance solenoids used on GM cars; look at the chart below to determine proper model usage.

Type A—Normally Opened

1. Disconnect the vacuum line from the vacuum advance solenoid to the distributor vacuum unit, at the distributor end. Connect a vacuum gauge to the line after making sure that it is not broken or clogged.
2. Detach the electrical leads from the solenoid. With the engine running, the vacuum gauge should register a vacuum. If it does not, the solenoid is faulty and must be replaced.
3. Using care to observe the proper polarity, connect one solenoid terminal to a 12 V power source. Using a jumper wire, connect the transmission switch terminal on the vacuum solenoid to ground. The solenoid should energize and the vacuum gauge reading should return to zero. If vacuum is still present, the solenoid is jammed and should be replaced.
4. If the solenoid is not defective, connect it in the original manner and go on to the next appropriate test.

Type B—Normally Closed

1. Disconnect the line which runs from the vacuum advance solenoid to the distributor vacuum unit. Connect a vacuum gauge to this line, after making sure that it is neither plugged nor broken.

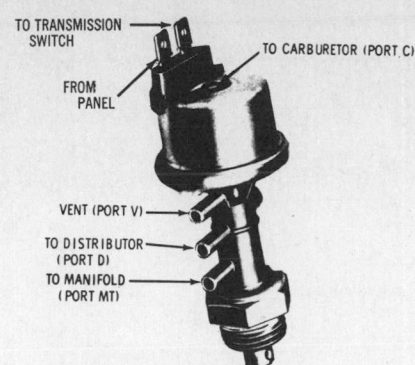

The combination vacuum advance solenoid and coolant temperature operated vacuum valve

2. Detach both electrical leads from the solenoid. The gauge should indicate zero vacuum. If it does not, the solenoid is defective and must be replaced.
3. Using care to observe proper polarity, connect the "hot" lead of the solenoid to a 12 V power source. Ground the other lead. Vacuum should now be present in the line. If it is not, the solenoid is defective and needs to be replaced.
4. If the solenoid is not defective, connect it in the original manner and go on with the next applicable test.

Type C—CEC Solenoid and Relays

The test for the CEC solenoid is similar to that for the Type B vacuum advance solenoid, above, expect that a vacuum guage is not needed. With 12 V applied to the CEC solenoid, its plunger should extend. With no power applied to the solenoid, the plunger should retract. If it fails to do either properly, the solenoid is

defective and must be replaced. If it is not defective, reconnect it.

NOTE: A defective CEC solenoid will also affect the operation of the throttle. For further details, see "Carburetor Modifications," below.

Models made prior to 1972 which are equipped with a CEC solenoid, use a reversing relay to provide proper switching action for the solenoid. To test relay operation:

1. Bypass the relay by grounding its single wire connector.
2. If the CEC solenoid plunger will now extend, and it did not extend in the above test, the reversing relay is defective.

A time-delay relay is used on some models equipped with a CEC solenoid to provide vacuum advance for 15–20 seconds after the ignition is switched on. To check its operation, proceed as follows:

1. Disconnect the electrical lead from the temperature switch.
2. Allow the relay to cool. Turn the ignition on. The CEC solenoid should energize (plunger extend) for about 15–20 seconds and then go off.
3. If it fails to go off, detach the blue lead from the time-delay relay. If the CEC solenoid now de-energizes, then the relay is faulty and must be replaced.

If none of the CEC system components which were tested are defective, go on to the next applicable test.

VACUUM DELAY RELAY TESTS

This relay is a solid-state unit which is used on some 1972 models. (It is not used with the CEC solenoid and should not be confused with the *time*-delay relay, above.) It is located underneath the dashboard, inside the passenger compartment. To test it proceed in the following manner:

1. Turn the ignition on. Then, using a lower amperage test lamp, check to see that the relay is getting power. If it is not, check its wiring.
2. Disconnect and ground the black lead.
3. Wait for 26 seconds. The vacuum advance solenoid should then energize. If it does not, the relay is faulty and must be replaced. If it does, reconnect the vacuum delay relay and proceed with the next applicable test.

TEMPERATURE SWITCH TEST

1. Connect a vacuum gauge to the vacuum advance solenoid to the distributor vacuum unit.
2. Allow the engine to cool to around 75°F and then start it. The gauge should indicate the presence of a vacuum.
3. If it does not, ground the lead from the cold terminal of the temperature switch.

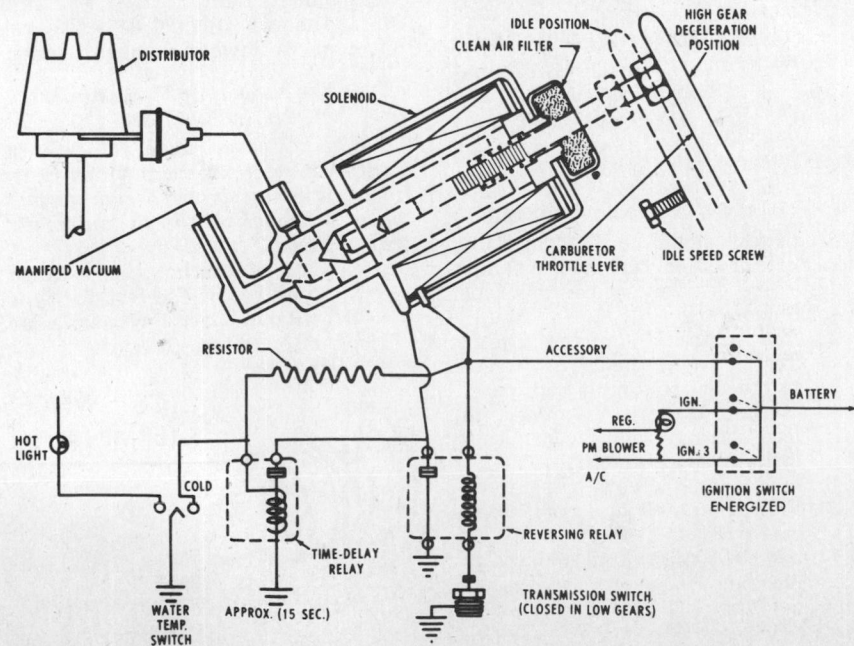

1970-71 CEC System (© G.M. Corp)

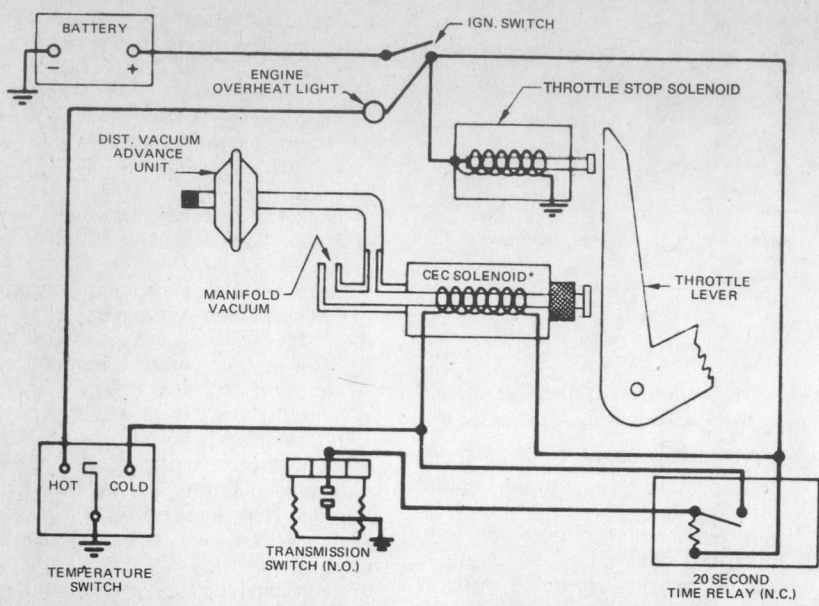

Location of the manual transmission switch (© G.M. Corp)

1972-73 CEC system without the reversing relay (© G.M. Corp)

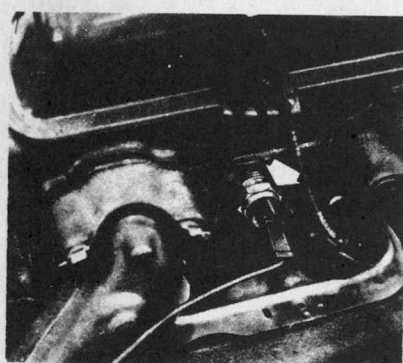

The temperature sensing switch is usually threaded into the cylinder head (© G.M. Corp)

4. On temperature controls with an additional hot terminal, repeat step 3—this time grounding the hot terminal.
5. If vacuum is not present when either terminal is grounded, the temperature switch is defective. If vacuum still is not present, reconnect the temperature switch leads and vacuum line. Proceed with the next applicable test.

TCS RELAY TEST—VEGA
1971–72

1. Test the TCS relay with the engine warm and the ignition on.
2. Ground the vacuum advance solenoid with the black lead. The solenoid should energize.
3. Keep the solenoid engaged in this manner. Ground the terminal which has the green and white wire running to it.
4. The vacuum advance solenoid should de-energize. If it remains energized, the TCS solenoid is faulty and must be replaced. If it is functioning properly, remove the jumpers and proceed with the next applicable test.

Location of the Vega TCS relay (© G.M. Corp)

TRANSMISSION SWITCH TESTS
NOTE: There are several different types of transmission switches used on GM cars. Check the chart below for proper model usage and then proceed with the applicable test.

Type D—Normally Opened
This test should be performed last, once all the other TCS system components are known to be in proper working order.

1. Repeat steps 4–6 of the "System Test." There should be vacuum to the distributor in high gear.
2. If there is none, disconnect the lead from the transmission switch and ground it.
3. If vacuum is now present, i.e., the vacuum advance solenoid has energized, then the transmission switch is faulty and must be replaced.

Type E—Manual Transmission/ Normally Closed
NOTE: Some models with manual

transmissions use a two-terminal transmission switch. Before proceeding with the test, ground the extra terminal.

1. Detach the switch connector at the side of the transmission.
2. Connect a test lamp in series with the switch and 12 V power source.

Caution Do not use a bulb any larger than 0.8 amp (no. 1893); the switch contacts will be damaged at a higher amperage.

3. With the engine and ignition off, move the gear shift lever through all of the gears. The test lamp should remain lighted in every gear except third and fourth (if so equipped).
NOTE: On 1972 models with four-speed transmissions, the lamp should remain lighted in third gear and not go out until fourth is selected.
4. If the test lamp fails to go out when it should, the switch is defective.
5. If the test lamp fails to come on at all, the switch is broken or the wiring is faulty.
6. If the switch is not defective, reconnect it when finished testing.

Type F—Automatic Transmission/ Normally Closed
NOTE: Vegas, made for sale in California in 1972, have a non-functional, dummy transmission switch when equipped with an automatic transmission.

1. Connect a test lamp as detailed in steps 1–2 of the test for type E switch above. Pay particular attention to the "Caution."

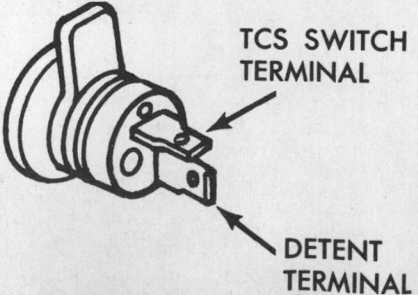

The terminals on the Turbo Hydra-Matic 400 transmission switch (© G.M. Corp)

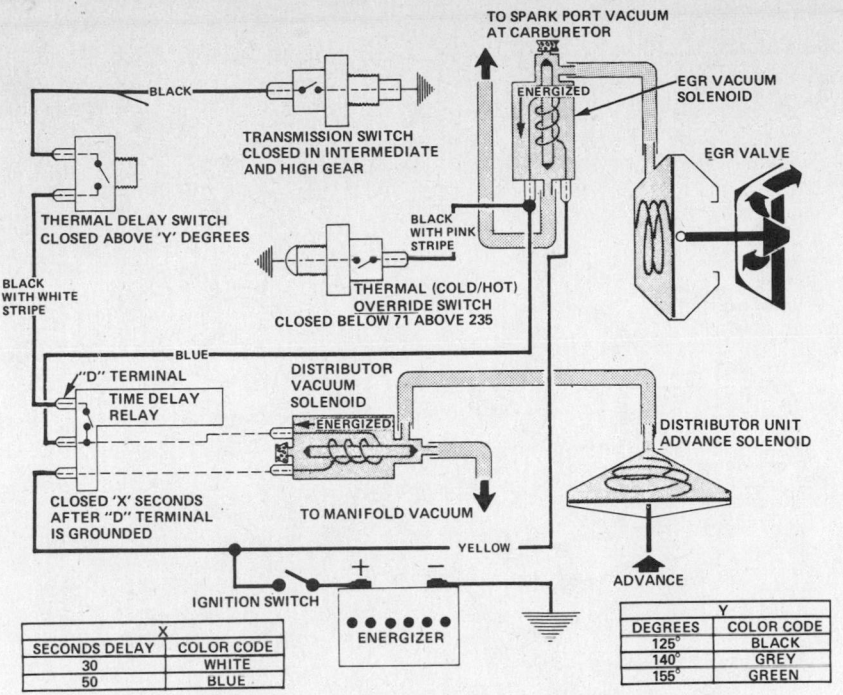

TO SPARK PORT VACUUM
AT CARBURETOR

BLACK

TRANSMISSION SWITCH
CLOSED IN INTERMEDIATE
AND HIGH GEAR

ENERGIZED

EGR VACUUM
SOLENOID

EGR VALVE

THERMAL DELAY SWITCH
CLOSED ABOVE 'Y' DEGREES

BLACK WITH PINK
STRIPE

BLACK
WITH WHITE
STRIPE

THERMAL (COLD/HOT)
OVERRIDE SWITCH
CLOSED BELOW 71 ABOVE 235

BLUE

"D" TERMINAL

TIME DELAY
RELAY

DISTRIBUTOR
VACUUM
SOLENOID

ENERGIZED

DISTRIBUTOR UNIT
ADVANCE SOLENOID

CLOSED "X" SECONDS
AFTER "D" TERMINAL
IS GROUNDED

TO MANIFOLD VACUUM

YELLOW

ADVANCE

IGNITION SWITCH

+   −

ENERGIZER

X	
SECONDS DELAY	COLOR CODE
30	WHITE
50	BLUE

Y	
DEGREES	COLOR CODE
125°	BLACK
140°	GREY
155°	GREEN

Early 1973 Pontiac TCS-EGR system (© G.M. Corp)

2. Raise the rear wheels of the car so they are off of the ground and support the car so that it cannot move forward.

3. Start the engine. Shift the transmission into Drive. Increase engine speed so that the transmission shifts into high gear, the test lamp should go out when the transmission enters high gear.

4. Allow the engine to return to idle and apply the brakes. Shift into Reverse. The light should go out again, except on cars equipped with Powerglide or Torque Drive.

5. In all other gears the lamp should remain on. If it does not or if it fails to go out when it should, replace the switch.

1973 Pontiac Combination T.C.S.-E.G.R. System

System Test

1. Apply parking brake, and securely block wheels. Connect a vacuum gauge to the distributor end of the vacuum line that runs from the T.C.S. solenoid to the distributor. Observe the position of the stem under the E.G.R. valve, this should be in the closed position.

2. The engine must be "overnight" cold with the ambient temperature below 71°. If this condition cannot be duplicated, follow the instructions below, skipping step four, and then use the "Simulated Temperature Switch Test" which follows the normal testing procedures.

3. Depress accelerator to set choke and place throttle linkage on fast idle cam. Start the engine and allow throttle to remain on fast idle cam.

4. Vacuum gauge should indicate a high manifold vacuum and E.G.R. valve should remain fully closed.

5. When the engine reaches 71°, manifold vacuum should disappear and the E.G.R. valve should open.

6. Shut off the engine. Raise the rear of the car and place it on jackstands so wheels are off the floor. Release parking brake. Put automatic transmission in Drive, manual transmission in highest gear. Place throttle on fast idle cam. Make sure automatic transmission shifts out of first gear.

7. When engine temperature reaches 140° (well before coolant flows through radiator), the E.G.R. valve should close fully, and manifold vacuum should again show on the vacuum gauge. Shift transmission out of gear for several seconds, then put it back in gear. Vacuum should disappear and E.G.R. valve should open. 33–55 seconds. after the transmission shifts out of first gear, vacuum should come back and the E.G.R. valve should close.

8. Restrict the flow of air across the radiator core. Shift the transmission into neutral. Vacuum will disappear, and E.G.R. valve will open. At 235° (before temperature light comes on) vacuum should be restored and the E.G.R. valve should close.

VACUUM ADVANCE SOLENOID AND TRANSMISSION SWITCH USAGE

Make	Year	Model	Vacuum Advance Solenoid	Transmission Switch
			Test Section Used For:	
Buick	1970–74	All V8	A	E, F
	1974	L6	B	D
Cadillac	1970–71	All	A	F
Chevrolet	1970	All	A	E, F
	1971	L6, V8	C	E, F
		Vega	A	E, F
	1972–73	L6	C	D
		V8	C	D
	1974	V8	B	D
	1972	Vega	A	E, F①
	1973–74	Vega	B	D
	1974	L6	B	D
	1976	2300 cc (4 cyl.)	B	D
Pontiac	1970–71	All	A	E, F
	1972–73	L6	C	D
	1974	L6	B	D
	1972	V8	A	E, F
	1974	V8	B	D
	1976	2300 cc (4 cyl.)	B	D
Oldsmobile	1971–73	V8	A	E, F
	1973	L6	C	D
	1974	L6	B	D
	1976	2300 cc (4 cyl.)	B	D

①—The transmission switch is not operative on Vegas sold in California when equipped with an automatic transmission.

NOTE: If the EGR valve is not operating properly, perform steps 5-7 of the GM EGR valve test, below.

Simulated Temperature Switch Test

If the other parts of the system function, but conditions would not permit testing the low temperature function, remove the temperature sensor from the rear of the left head as follows:

1. Allow engine to cool until radiator cap can be safely removed, then remove the cap.
2. Place a clean container under the drain cock and begin draining coolant.
3. Disconnect wiring and loosen switch at rear of left cylinder head to check for presence of coolant. As soon as switch can be removed without loss of coolant, close the radiator drain cock and remove the switch. Test the switch as follows:
   1. Prepare a container of cold water or water and ice. Check with a thermometer to make sure temperature is below 60°.
   2. Immerse the threaded portion of the switch in the water, and allow it to cool until it has reached the temperature of the water.
   3. Remove the switch from the bath and immediately check for continuity between the electrical prong and the threaded portion of the switch. Replace a switch which shows no continuity under these conditions.

Symptoms and Appropriate Checks

1. System responds normally at operating temperatures but does not supply advance and deny EGR below 71° and/or above 235°. Operate engine at fast idle with transmission in neutral until normal operating temperature is reached. Jump the switch at the rear of the left cylinder head by grounding the wire which goes to the switch. If this produces vacuum and shuts off the EGR valve, replace the switch. Otherwise, check for defects in the wiring between this switch and the solenoids.
2. System responds to temperature changes, but does not provide vacuum advance and deny EGR after transmission shifts to second gear. Operate engine at fast idle with transmission in Neutral until operating temperature is reached. Ground the switch on the right side of the transmission, by grounding the wire connected to it. Keep wire grounded one minute. If this produces vacuum advance and denies EGR, replace the transmission switch. Otherwise, bypass the switch on the right cylinder head and ground the wire

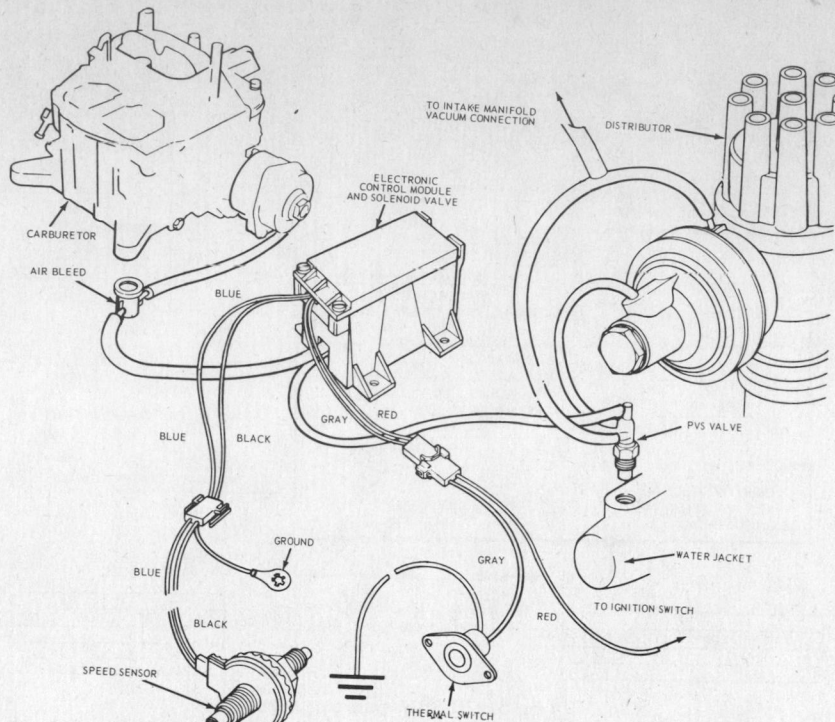

Distributor modulator system details (© Ford Motor Co)

to the transmission switch. If this produces vacuum advance and denies EGR after one minute, replace the sensor in the right head. Otherwise, the Time Delay Relay or associated wiring is defective. Bypass each to locate the defective component.

3. System responds normally except that EGR is denied and vacuum advance established as soon as transmission shifts to second gear. Replace Time Delay Relay.
4. Only one function responds as required, or system provides EGR and denies vacuum advance at all times; check wiring. Replace if defective. Otherwise, solenoid(s) are at fault.

Speed Controlled Spark Systems

Ford Distributor Modulator System—1970-71

System Tests

Check the distributor vacuum advance on an analyzer (distributor modulator system bypassed if distributor is left in engine for test). If it is functioning correctly, proceed with the tests outlined below.

1. Disconnect the distributor vacuum advance line from the carburetor and connect a vacuum gauge to vacuum line fitting on the carburetor. Run the engine at 1,500 rpm and take a vacuum reading. Make a note of the result. Disconnect the vacuum

gauge and attach the vacuum line back on the carburetor.

2. Using a short length of rubber hose to bypass the distributor modulator control box, connect the distributor vacuum advance unit directly to the carburetor. Disconnect the vacuum line from the distributor vacuum advance unit and connect it to the vacuum gauge.
3. Run the engine at 1,500 rpm again. The vacuum gauge reading should be similar to that obtained above. If it is zero or much less than in step one, check for pinched or leaking vacuum lines.
4. Remove the hose used to bypass the distributor modulator and reconnect the vacuum lines as originally found. Leave the vacuum gauge connected to the distributor vacuum line, however.
5. Raise the rear wheels off the ground and support the car so that it cannot roll forward. Run the engine at idle until normal operating temperature is reached.
6. Remove the thermal switch from the door pillar. Hold the switch in the palm of the hand long enough to bring its temperature above 60° F.
7. Place the transmission selector in Drive. Accelerate to 35 mph. By the time this speed is reached, the vacuum gauge should show a reading.
8. If the vacuum gauge shows a

reading below 20–35 mph, or if it does not show a reading above 35 mph, proceed with the individual component tests as required.

NOTE: Remember to check the coolant temperature operated vacuum valve, if so equipped, as possible cause of trouble. The test procedures may be found above.

Power Supply Test

1. Switch the ignition on. Take a voltage reading at the red lead which runs to the control module.
2. If the voltmeter reads zero, check for a blown system fuse or faulty wiring.

ELECTRONIC CONTROL MODULE
JUMPER WIRE
TO IGNITION SWITCH

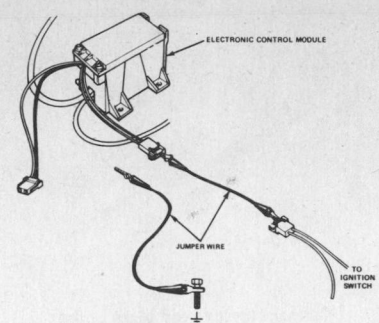

Connect the grey (or white) wire to ground by using a jumper lead
(© Ford Motor Co)

3. If the voltmeter registers normal battery voltage, the module is getting the proper power. Proceed with the next test.

Thermal Switch Test

1. Disconnect the thermal switch at its multiconnector.
2. Connect an ohmmeter to the grey (or white) and black leads coming from the switch.
3. Warm the switch by holding it in the palm of the hand until it is above 68° F. There should be no reading (zero) on the ohmmeter. If there is a reading the switch is defective and needs to be replaced.

DISTRIBUTOR MODULATOR SYSTEM TROUBLESHOOTING CHART

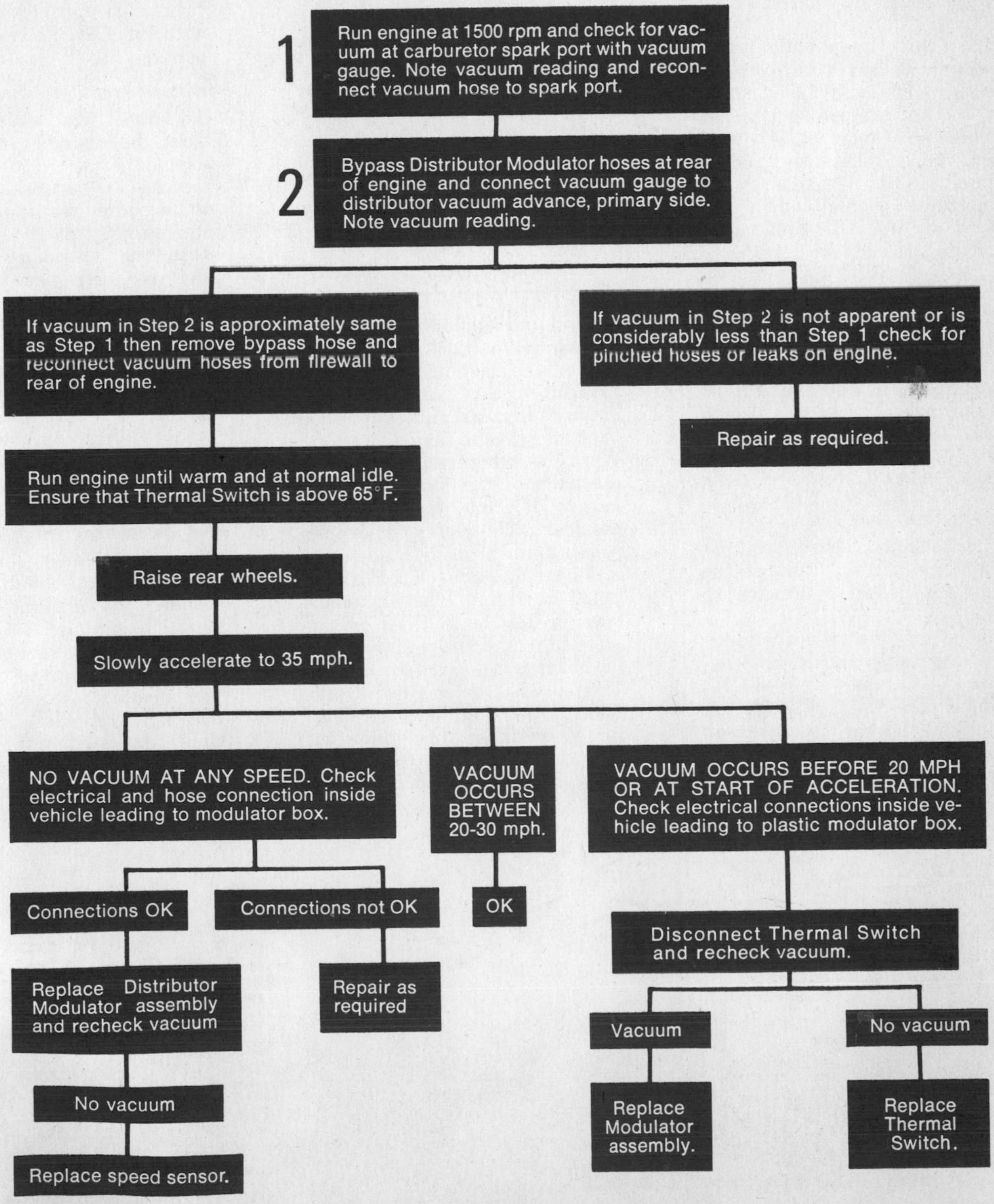

1
Run engine at 1500 rpm and check for vacuum at carburetor spark port with vacuum gauge. Note vacuum reading and reconnect vacuum hose to spark port.
2
Bypass Distributor Modulator hoses at rear of engine and connect vacuum gauge to distributor vacuum advance, primary side. Note vacuum reading.
If vacuum in Step 2 is approximately same as Step 1 then remove bypass hose and reconnect vacuum hoses from firewall to rear of engine.
If vacuum in Step 2 is not apparent or is considerably less than Step 1 check for pinched hoses or leaks on engine.
Repair as required.
Run engine until warm and at normal idle. Ensure that Thermal Switch is above 65°F.
Raise rear wheels.
Slowly accelerate to 35 mph.
NO VACUUM AT ANY SPEED. Check electrical and hose connection inside vehicle leading to modulator box.
VACUUM OCCURS BETWEEN 20-30 mph.
VACUUM OCCURS BEFORE 20 MPH OR AT START OF ACCELERATION. Check electrical connections inside vehicle leading to plastic modulator box.
Connections OK
Connections not OK
OK
Disconnect Thermal Switch and recheck vacuum.
Replace Distributor Modulator assembly and recheck vacuum
Repair as required
Vacuum
No vacuum
No vacuum
Replace Modulator assembly.
Replace Thermal Switch.
Replace speed sensor.

4. Chill the switch, using ice or cold water, to below 50° F. There should now be a reading (resistance indicated) on the meter. If there is no reading, the switch is defective and should be replaced.
5. If the temperature switch is functioning properly, proceed with the next test.

Control Module Test

1. Disconnect the thermal switch multiconnector from the module. Use a jumper lead to connect the two red wires leading from the two halves of multiconnector.
2. Attach a vacuum gauge to the distributor vacuum line fitting on the carburetor. Run the engine at fast idle and note the reading. Disconnect the gauge and reconnect the vacuum line to the port.
3. Connect the vacuum gauge to the vacuum hose that runs to the distributor vacuum advance unit.
4. Use another jumper lead to connect the grey (or white) wire, which runs from the control module to the thermal switch connector, to ground.
5. Run the engine at fast idle again and note the vacuum reading. It should be almost the same as that taken at the carburetor port.
6. If the reading is zero or lower than that at the carburetor port, the module is defective and must be replaced.
7. If the module is functioning properly, reconnect it and go on with the next test.

Speed Sensor Test

1. Detach the speed sensor leads at its multiconnector. Connect the test prods of an ohmmeter to them.
2. With the sensor at room temperature, the meter should read between 40–60 ohms.
3. Test for continuity between the black lead and the speed sensor case. There should be no meter reading.
4. The speed sensor is defective if

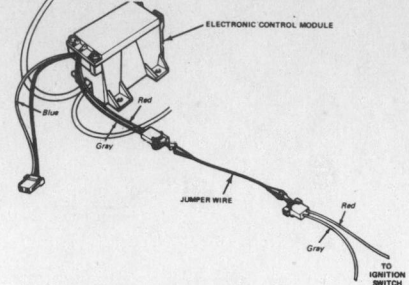

Connect the two red wires of the multiconnector by using a jumper lead
(© Ford Motor Co)

the reading in step 2 does not fall within specifications or if a reading is obtained between the case and the black lead.

Ford Electronic Spark Control (ESC)—1972-73

This system replaces the distributor modulator system, above. The test procedures for the two systems are somewhat different and should not be interchanged, except as noted.

NOTE: Vehicles made on or after 15 March 1973 do not use a temperature switch.

System Test

1. Raise the rear wheels off the ground and support the car so it cannot roll forward.
2. Detach the vacuum hose on the primary side of the distributor vacuum advance unit. Connect a vacuum gauge to the hose.
3. Warm the temperature sensor in the palm of the hand, after removing it from its location on the door pillar (left or right, depending upon model). Be sure it is heated to above 65°F.
4. Start the engine. Place the transmission selector in Drive. Accelerate until the speed specified in the chart is reached (see below). This speed is determined by the color of the amplifier case. Wait for 40 seconds; this allows the time delay valve to work (if so equipped). At this point vacuum should be present.

Amplifier Case Color	Vacuum Advance Cut-in Speed (mph)
Black	23
White	28
Blue	33
Grey	35

5. If there is no vacuum, first check for a clogged carburetor vacuum port.
6. Then check the vacuum lines to see if they are pinched, clogged or misrouted.

NOTE: Remember to check the coolant temperature-operated vacuum valve, if so equipped, as a possible source of the malfunction. The test procedures for it are given above.

7. If the above checks indicate that the problem does not lie in the vacuum supply system, proceed with the ESC individual component tests.

Distributor Modulator Solenoid Test

1. Disconnect the electrical leads from the distributor modulator solenoid.
2. Increase engine speed. If there is no vacuum reading, with the gauge connected as in the System Test, the solenoid is defective and must be replaced. Reconnect the electrical leads to the distributor modulator solenoid and allow the engine to slow down.
3. If vacuum occurs below the specified cut-in speeds (see the chart in step 4, above), the solenoid is not being energized and the trouble lies elsewhere in the system. Proceed with the next test.

Temperature Switch Tests

1. Disconnect the temperature switch at the multiconnector. Connect an ohmmeter to the switch terminals.
2. Warm the switch by placing it in the palm of the hand. The ohmmeter should show a reading. If it does not, the switch is defective.
3. Chill the switch to 49°F or below, by using ice or cold water. There should be no reading (zero) on the ohmmeter. If a re-

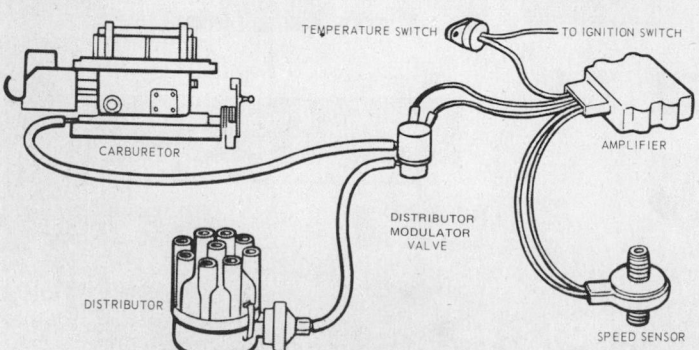

Components of the Ford ECS system (© Ford Motor Co)

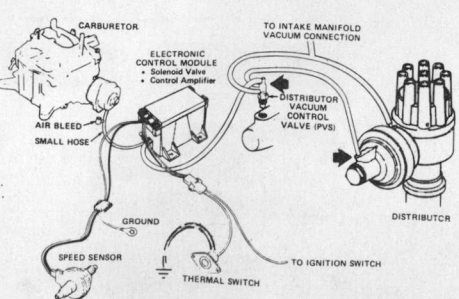

Arrows show the vacuum gauge hook-up points used during control module tests
(© Ford Motor Co)

sistance is indicated, the temperature switch is defective.

4. Replace the switch if defective. If it is not, proceed with the next test.

Power Supply Test

1. Ground one side of a low-amperage test lamp and connect the other side to the temperature switch connector of the instrument panel wiring (red/yellow hash lead).

2. Turn on the ignition. The lamp should light. If it fails to do so, check the wiring to the ignition switch or check the ignition switch itself.

3. If the ESC system is getting power, proceed with the next test.

Speed Sensor Test

This test is exactly the same as that for the speed sensor used in the distributor modulator system.

Perform the speed sensor test as outlined in the "Distributor Modulator" section, above.

Amplifier

If everything else in the ESC system is functioning properly, the fault lies with the amplifier module. Replace the amplifier and repeat the "System Test".

Chrysler Corp.

1971-72 Automatic Transmission System Test

1. Warm the engine to normal operating temperature. Be sure the ambient temperature is well above 70°F.

2. T-connect a vacuum gauge between the distributor and the solenoid vacuum valve.

3. Raise the car on a lift, with the wheels hanging free.

4. Disconnect the vacuum line at the vacuum switch on the control unit.

5. Start the engine and run at a speed above 850 rpm. Vacuum gauge should read zero.

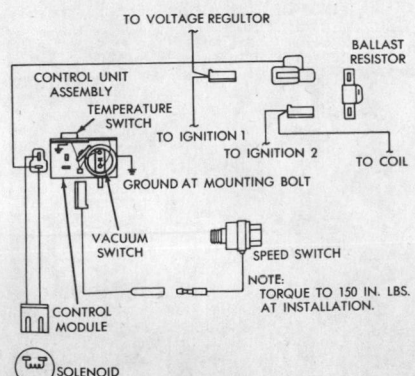

NOx (SCS) system schematic
—automatic transmission (© Chrysler Corp)

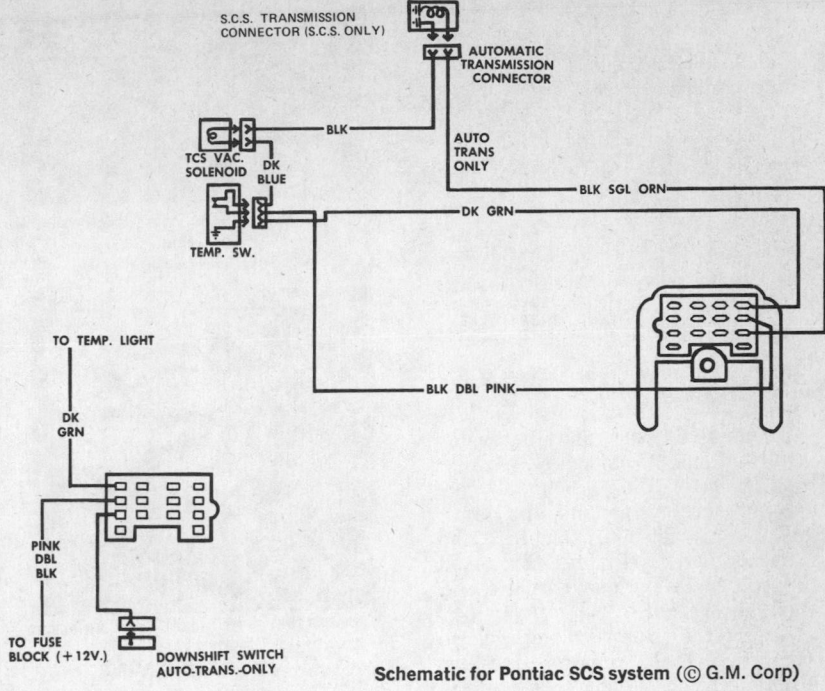

Schematic for Pontiac SCS system (© G.M. Corp)

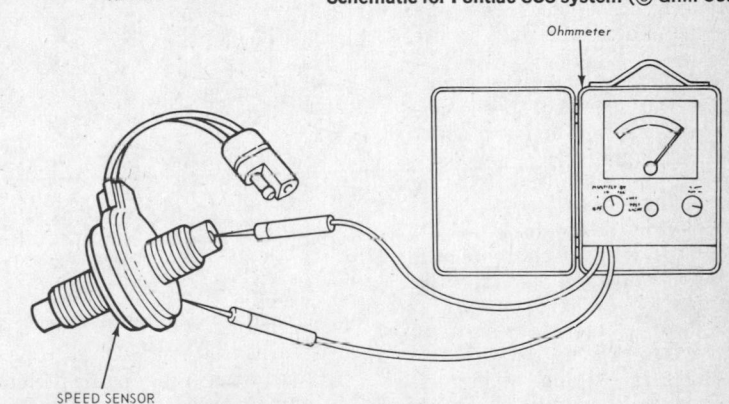

Using an ohmmeter to see if the speed sensor is grounded to the case (© Ford Motor Co)

6. Disconnect the wire from the control unit. The vacuum gauge should read normal advance unit operating vacuum. Reconnect the wire. The gauge should drop to zero.

7. Unplug and reconnect the vacuum line to the vacuum switch. Disconnect the wire from the control unit to the speed switch. The gauge should read normal advance unit operating vacuum.

8. Place transmission in Drive. Sharp acceleration should cause the gauge reading to drop sharply to zero. Do not exceed 40 mph.

9. Accelerate above 30 mph. The gauge should read normal vacuum advance unit operating vacuum.

10. If solenoid valve did not operate during the tests, replace control unit.

American Motors (1972-early '73) and Pontiac

NOTE: Although American Motors calls all of their spark control systems "Transmission - Controlled Spark" (TCS), the one used with automatic transmissions is really a speed-controlled spark system (SCS). American Motors cars made on or after 15 March 1973 do not use an SCS system, but have, instead, a transmission controlled spark (TCS) system. Consult the appropriate section above for system testing.

System Test

This test should be performed with the air temperature above 65°F and the coolant temperature above 160°F (American Motors V8) or with the engine temperature between 95° and 230°F (Pontiac).

1. Raise the rear wheels off the ground and support the car so it cannot roll forward.

2. Disconnect the vacuum hose which runs between the distributor vacuum unit or the coolant temperature vacuum override valve (1972–73 American Motors) and the vacuum advance

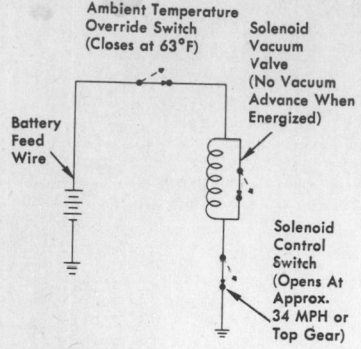

Schematic for the American Motors SCS (or TCS) system (© American Motors Corp)

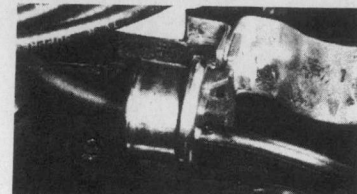

American Motors vacuum advance solenoid location
(© American Motors Corp)

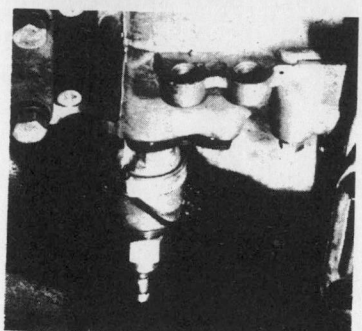

Transmission switch location on American Motors cars
(© American Motors Corp)

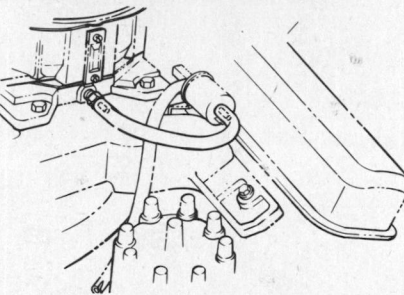

Pontiac vacuum solenoid location
(© G.M. Corp)

solenoid at the distributor or valve end. Connect a vacuum gauge to the hose.

3. Start the engine and shift into Drive. Accelerate to until the speedometer registers the speed specified in the chart at the end of this section.

4. Until the specified speed is reached, the vacuum reading should be zero. Once this speed is reached, vacuum should be present.

5. If no vacuum is registered at or above the specified speed, check the vacuum lines and connections first. Examine the carburetor port to be sure that it is not clogged.

NOTE: Remember to check the coolant temperature vacuum override valve, if so equipped, as its failure could cause a loss of vacuum. Test procedures for it are given earlier in this section.

6. If there is nothing wrong with the vacuum supply, disconnect the gauge, reconnect the hose and proceed with the next test.

Transmission Switch Tests

1. Leave the rear wheels of the car off the ground as in the system test above.

2. Disconnect the transmission switch leads. Connect a low-amperage test lamp in series with the switch and the positive side of the battery.

3. Accelerate to the specified speed (see chart below) and watch the test lamp. It should remain on until the specified speed is reached. If the lamp fails to go out or if it does not light at all, the switch is defective and must be replaced.

4. If the switch is working properly, reconnect it and go on with the next test.

Vacuum Advance Solenoid Test

1. Disconnect the vacuum advance solenoid leads. Connect a vacuum gauge to the solenoid hose as in the system test.

2. Place the transmission in neutral

and start the engine. Increase engine speed. The gauge should indicate the presence of a vacuum.

3. Connect the hot lead to a 12 V power source. Ground the other lead. Increase the engine speed again. The solenoid should energize, resulting in a vacuum reading of zero.

4. Replace the vacuum advance solenoid if it is faulty. If it is not, reconnect the wiring and go on with the next appropriate test.

Ambient Temperature Override Switch—American Motors

1. Disconnect the ambient temperature switch leads.

2. Replace the switch in the circuit with a jumper wire.

3. Repeat the system test. If the vacuum gauge now reads zero or below the specified speed, i.e., the solenoid energizes, the temperature switch is defective.

4. If the switch proves not to be defective when tested in step 3, reconnect it after removing the jumper lead.

5. Cool the switch, using either ice, cold water, or an aerosol spray

circuit tester, to below 63°F. Repeat the system test. If there is no vacuum below the specified speed, the switch is stuck closed and must be replaced.

Engine Temperature Switch—Pontiac

If vacuum advance is present when it should not be, i.e., below the speed specified in the chart, the temperature switch is defective if the other SCS System components are functioning properly and the engine temperature is 95–230°F. Replace it and repeat the system test.

If, on the other hand, vacuum is not being supplied when it should be, with the engine temperature below 95°F or above 230°F, and the other components are functioning properly, the fault again lies in the temperature switch. Replace it and repeat the system test with the engine below 95°F (cold). Vacuum advance should be present at all speeds.

Cadillac

The Cadillac speed-controlled spark system used on *rear-wheel-drive* models (all models except Eldorado) may be tested in a similar manner to the American Motors and Pontiac systems above.

NOTE: *Since Cadillac does not use this component, the temperature switch tests are unnecessary.*

Cadillac recommends a road test procedure because the front wheels of the Eldorado should not be raised off the ground for test purposes. The procedure outlined below may be used for rear-wheel-drive Cadillac models, as well.

Caution Never test the SCS system used on the Eldorado with its front (drive) wheels off the ground. Working near the front wheels while they are rotating could result in personal injury or vehicle damage.

1. Unfasten the double connector at the vacuum advance solenoid. Install a low-amperage test lamp, with long leads, between the wires on the connector.

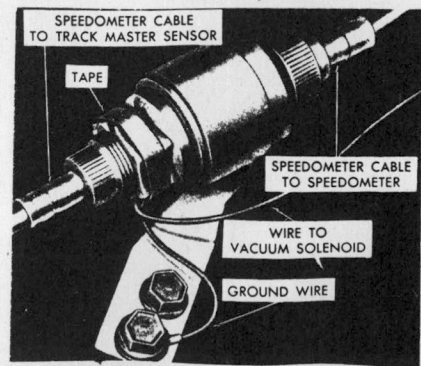

Speed control switch when used with
Track-Master (except Eldorado) (© G.M. Corp)

2. Tape the test lamp to the car so that it is visible to the driver (hood, fender, cowl, etc.,) and close the hood.

3. Road-test the car while watching the test lamp (and traffic). Once 33 mph (± 2 mph) is reached, the test lamp should go out. Slow down; when 25 mph is reached, the lamp should come back on again.

4. If the test lamp fails to operate as indicated, jump the black wire to ground with the ignition turned on. If the lamp comes on now, replace the speed sensor switch and repeat step three. If the lamp does not come on, remove the jumper and proceed with the next step.

5. Install a jumper between one of the solenoid terminals and ground. Momentarily connect the other solenoid terminal to the positive (+) side of the battery.

6. The solenoid should energize when this is done, i.e., a "click" should be heard. If the solenoid fails to operate it is defective.

7. If both the solenoid and transmission switch are functioning properly, reconnect the leads to the solenoid and check for faulty wiring.

1973 Ford Temperature Activated Vacuum System (TAV)

System Test

1. Disconnect the vacuum line from the primary port of the distributor. Connect a vacuum gauge to the line by means of a T-fitting. Connect the other end of the T-fitting to the distributor.

2. Be sure that the air temperature is above 65°F. Hot water may be used to warm the temperature switch, which is located in the front door pillar.

3. Place the transmission in Park or Neutral. Start the engine.

4. Run the engine at idle; the vacuum gauge should read zero.

5. Increase the engine speed to 1,500 rpm or slightly more. The gauge should read 5 in. Hg or better.

6. If there is no vacuum reading, check for leaking, plugged, or pinched lines and fittings.

7. Detach the EGR port hose and plug up the carburetor line. The vacuum gauge should read zero.

8. If it does not, check the lines and then proceed with the three-way vacuum valve test, below. If it does, go on to Step 9.

9. Next, detach one of the power leads from the three-way vacuum valve.

10. Speed the engine up to 1,500 rpm or more. The vacuum gauge

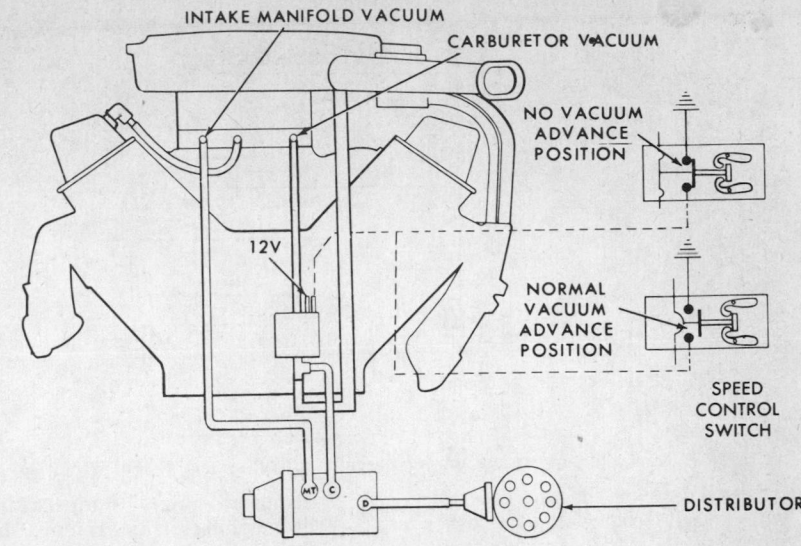

Cadillac SCS system (© G.M. Corp)

SCS VACUUM ADVANCE

Make	Year	No vacuum advance below	With engine temperature (deg F)
American Motors	1971	30 mph	All temperatures①
	1972–73	34 mph	above 160①②
Cadillac	1972	33±2 mph	All temperatures
Pontiac	1972	38 mph	Between 95–230

①—Air temperature above 68°F
②—V8 only

should now read 6 in. Hg or better.

11. If the system fails to function as outlined, check the ambient temperature switch, the EGR valve, or the three-way vacuum valve.

12. If everything is functioning properly, reconnect the leads and vacuum lines after disconnecting the vacuum gauge.

Temperature Switch Test

Test the door-mounted ambient temperature switch, as outlined under "Ford Electronic Spark Control—1972–73," above. The switch is in either the left or right front door pillar.

Three-way Vacuum Valve Test

1. Remove the three-way vacuum valve from the car.

2. Connect a vacuum gauge to the horizontal port at the *bottom* of the valve.

3. Apply a vacuum source to the horizontal port at the *top* of the valve.

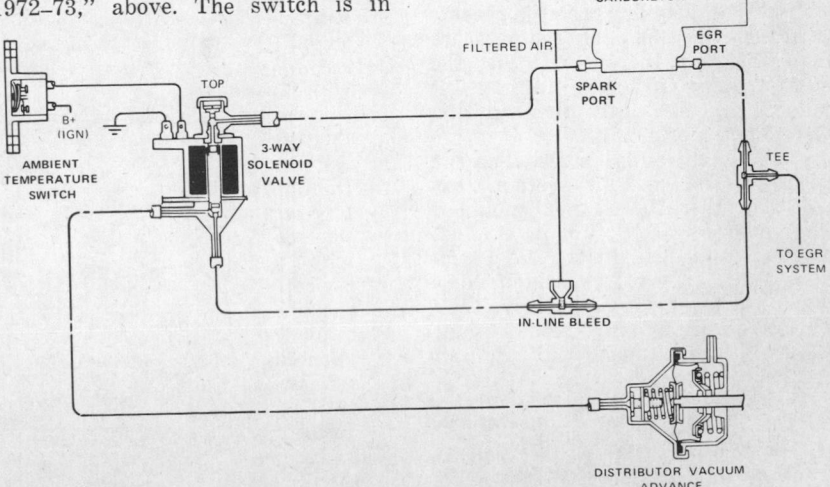

The temperature activated vacuum system used on some 1973 Fords (© Ford Motor Co)

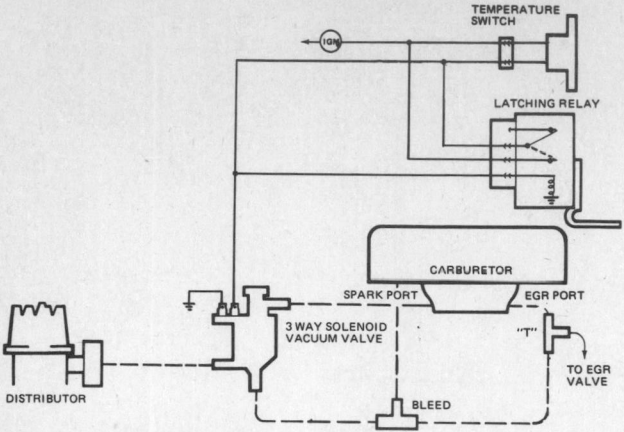

Late 1973-76 Ford cold temperature activated vacuum (CATV) system (© Ford Motor Co)

4. Ground one of the valve terminals while connecting the other terminal to a 12V power supply. The vacuum gauge should read zero.
5. With the valve energized, connect the vacuum source to the bottom *vertical* port. The vacuum gauge should now indicate an amount of vacuum equal to the output of the vacuum source.
6. Disconnect the leads from the valve. The vacuum gauge reading should return to zero.
7. If the valve fails to function as outlined, replace it. If it is functioning correctly, check the EGR valve operation as detailed in the appropriate section below.

1973½-76 Ford Cold Temperature Activated Vacuum System (CTAV)

The cold temperature activated vacuum (CTAV) system is similar to the temperature activated system used on 1973 vehicles made before 15 March (see the previous section). On CTAV equipped vehicles, the temperature sensor has been moved from the door pillar to the air cleaner housing, and a latching relay has been added. The latching relay prevents variations in ambient temperature from affecting the system; once the CTAV system has been activated it cannot recycle until the ignition system has been shut off.

The CTAV system is tested in the same way as the TAV system. (except for the air cleaner mounted temperature switch). Follow the test procedure outlined in the TAV section. If all of the CTAV system components are working properly, then the latching relay must be defective; replace it and repeat the "System Test".

Air Cleaner-Mounted Temperature Switch—Normally Closed

The normally closed temperature switch may be identified by its rectangular connector.

1. Disconnect the temperature switch connector and remove the switch from the air cleaner.
2. Warm the switch in the palm of your hand.
3. Conect a self-powered test light between the terminals of the switch connector. The test light should glow.
4. Cool the switch with ice or aerosol circuit testing spray. The light should go off.
5. If the switch doesn't work as outlined, replace it.

Air Cleaner-Mounted Temperature Switch—Normally Opened

The normally opened temperature switch may be identified by its round connector.

1. Perform steps 1 and 2 of the test for the normally closed switch.
2. Connect a self-powered test light between the terminals on the switch connector. The test light should stay off.
3. Cool the switch with ice or aerosol circuit testing spray. The test light should come on.
4. If the switch doesn't work as outlined, replace it.

1975-76 Ford Cold Start Spark Advance (CSSA) System

System Test

1. Allow the engine to reach normal operating temperature. Stop the engine.
2. If the engine is equipped with a spark delay valve (SDV), remove it and test it separately. Use a fiitting to connect the two halves of the vacuum hose together where the SDV was mounted.
3. Using a T-fitting, connect a vacuum guage to the distributor vacuum unit.
4. Block the wheels, set the parking brake, place the transmission in Neutral (N), and start the engine. Open the throttle halfway and then allow it to close.
5. The vacuum guage should register a rise and then a fall in vacuum. If it doesn't, check for plugged vacuum fittings, and/or loose or misrouted hoses. If everything else checks out OK, then test the two coolant temperature operated vacuum valves (PVS) as outlined elsewhere in this section.
6. Remove the T-fitting and vacuum gauge. Install the SDV, if so equipped.

1975-76 Ford Cold Lock out Spark System Check

(single and dual delay valves)

1. Remove the spark delay valve and check it.
2. On the dual delay valve, connect a gauge to the line removed from the manifold vacuum source; install a connector between the spark port line and the distributor line. On a single delay valve, install a connector in place of the valve and connect a vacuum gauge using a 'T' fitting to the primary side of the distributor.

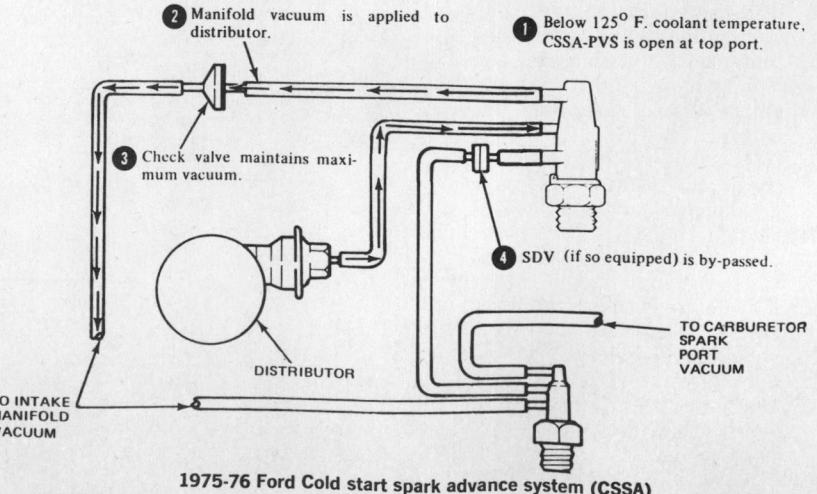

2 Manifold vacuum is applied to distributor.

3 Check valve maintains maximum vacuum.

1 Below 125° F. coolant temperature, CSSA-PVS is open at top port.

4 SDV (if so equipped) is by-passed.

TO CARBURETOR SPARK PORT VACUUM

TO INTAKE MANIFOLD VACUUM

DISTRIBUTOR

1975-76 Ford Cold start spark advance system (CSSA)
(© Ford Motor Co.)

A typical anti-dieseling solenoid installation (© G.M. Corp)

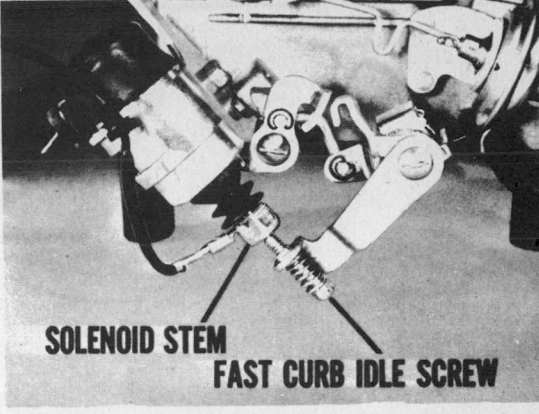

SOLENOID STEM
FAST CURB IDLE SCREW

When the anti-dieseling solenoid is energized, its plunger should make contact with the (fast) curb idle screw (© Chrysler Corp)

3. Start the engine and open and close the throttle. There should be a vacuum reading on the gauge. If not check all lines and fittings of the system.

4. On dual delay valve systems only, remove the gauge from the line and plug it. Then connect the gauge to the primary and secondary side of the distributor in turn. Start the engine, open the throttle and check for a vacuum reading. If you do not get one in either case, check the lines and fittings.

1975-76 Ford Delay Valve By-Pass System Check

1. Remove the air cleaner.
2. Remove the spark delay valve and check it.
3. Install a connector in place of the valve. Remove the vacuum line at the distributor, install a 'T' fitting and vacuum gauge.
4. Idle the engine in Neutral and open and close the throttle. The gauge should rise and fall as the throttle is opened and closed. If not check the lines and fittings.
5. Stop the engine and remove the vacuum gauge and its fittings. Reinstall the spark delay valve and vacuum hoses.
6. Remove the vacuum check valve and check it.
7. Install the vacuum gauge and connector in the vacuum hose from the PVS switch. Idle the engine, then momentarily open the throttle half way. If the vacuum reading is 2 in. Hg. or less, the PVS switch is alright; if vacuum reading is more than 2 in. Hg., replace the PVS switch.

Carburetor Controls

Antidieseling Solenoid Tests

NOTE: Antidieseling solenoids are also referred to as, "throttle stop" or "idle stop" solenoids.

Combined antidieseling solenoid/dashpot used on some 1975-76 Ford products

Caution 1975 only Chrysler Corp. cars that are equipped with catalytic converters have an additional solenoid; this is NOT an anti-dieseling solenoid, and no attempt to adjust the idle speed with it should be made. See "Catalytic Converters" for its operation.

1. Turn the ignition key on and open the throttle. The solenoid plunger should extend (solenoid energize).
2. Turn the ignition off. The plunger should retract, allowing the throttle to close.

NOTE: With the antidieseling solenoid de-energized, the carburetor idle speed adjusting screw must make contact with the throttle shaft to pre-vent the throttle plates from jamming in the throttle bore when the engine is turned off.

3. If the solenoid is functioning properly and the engine is still dieseling, check for one of the following:
   a. High idle or engine shut off speed;
   b. Engine timing not set to specification;
   c. Binding throttle linkage;
   d. Too low an octane fuel being used.

Correct any of these problems, as necessary.

4. If the solenoid fails to function as outlined in steps 1–2, disconnect the solenoid leads; the solenoid should de-enegerize. If it

does not, it is jammed and must be replaced.

5. Connect the solenoid to a 12 V power source and to ground. Open the throttle so that the plunger can extend. If it does not, the solenoid is defective.

6. If the solenoid is functioning correctly and no other source of trouble can be found, the fault probably lies in the wiring between the solenoid and the ignition switch or in the ignition switch itself. Remember to reconnect the solenoid when finished testing.

NOTE: On some 1970–71 Ford models, dieseling may occur when the engine is turned off because of feedback through the alternator warning light circuit. A diode kit is available from Ford to cure this problem. A failure of this diode may also lead to a similar problem.

Solenoid/Dashpot

Some 1975 Ford products use a combination antidieseling solenoid and dashpot. The antidieseling solenoid operation is tested in the same manner as any other antidieseling solenoid. See the previous section for the correct testing procedure.

A/C Operated Antidieseling Device Tests

1. Run the engine and turn off all of the air conditioning controls.

2. Turn the engine off. The air conditioner compressor clutch should engage for several seconds to slow the engine down.

3. If the compressor clutch engagement does not occur, check the wiring for a loose connection, at either the compressor or the antidieseling relay.

4. Check to see that the relay is properly grounded to its mounting. Examine the air conditioner fuse(s) to see that they are not blown.

5. Start the engine and turn on the air conditioner. The clutch should engage. If it does not, the problem lies in the air conditioner circuit.

6. If the car is equipped with a blocking relay, remove it for bench-testing. Connect a 12 V test lamp between the two outboard connectors. Ground the mounting bracket. Connect a 12 V power source to the center terminal. The lamp should come on. If it does not, the blocking relay is defective and must be replaced.

7. If all of the other components are functioning properly, the antidieseling relay is defective and requires replacement.

GM Idle Increase Solenoid

Many 1976 GM engines (especially on cars equipped with air conditioning), use an idle stop solenoid to increase the idle speed when the air conditioning is turned on. This solenoid is *not* an anti-dieseling solenoid and is not used to set the idle. To determine if the engine is equipped with this type of solenoid, or an antidieseling solenoid, check the tune-up specifications sticker and follow the instructions there.

Some 1976 Pontiac engines without air conditioning, sold in California are equipped with a non functional idle stop solenoid. Do not attempt to connect it.

CEC Solenoid Operation

The CEC solenoid is used on some GM models. It has two functions; one is to regulate distributor vacuum and the other is operate as a throttle positioner. When the solenoid is energized, the throttle blade is held off its seat by a plunger located at one end of the CEC solenoid. This provides higher engine rpm during deceleration, thus reducing exhaust emissions.

Because of its dual function, failure of this valve can lead to higher emission levels or an idle which is considerably faster than normal. If the CEC solenoid is suspected of not working properly, follow the complete set of test procedures for it in "Distributor Controls," above.

NOTE: On 1971 Buicks, the CEC solenoid is divided into two separate

parts: a regular TCS solenoid and a solenoid to hold the throttle open during high gear deceleration. Testing and service should be carried out in the same manner as they would be for a regular CEC valve.

Electrically Assisted Choke

Ford and AMC

1. Detach the electrical lead from the choke cap.

2. Use a jumper lead to connect the terminal on the choke cap and the wire terminal, so that the electrical circuit is still completed.

3. Start the engine.

4. Hook up a test light between the connector on the choke lead and ground.

5. The test light should glow. If it does not, current is not being supplied to the electrically assisted choke.

6. Connect the test light between the terminal on the alternator and the terminal on the choke cap. If the light now glows, replace the lead, since it is not passing current to the choke assist.

Caution Do not ground the terminal on the alternator while performing Step 6.

7. If the light still does not glow, the fault lies somewhere in the electrical system. Check the system out.

NOTE: Steps 8 through 12 do not apply to 1975 models equipped with 2300 four-cylinder engines.

If the electrically assisted choke receives power but still does not appear to be functioning properly, reconnect the choke lead and proceed with the rest of the test.

8. Tape the bulb end of the thermometer to the metallic portion of the choke housing.

9. If the electrically assisted choke operates below 55°F, it is defective and must be replaced.

10. Allow the engine to warm up to between 80 and 110°F; at these temperatures the choke should operate for about 1½ minutes.

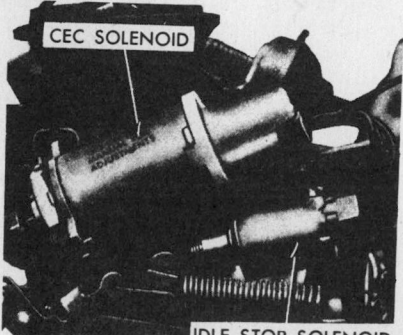

A typical CEC solenoid mounting (© G.M .Corp)

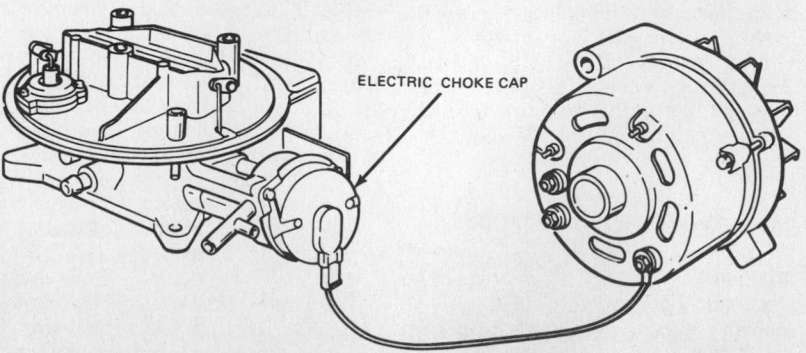

Ford and AMC electrically assisted choke hook-up (© Ford Motor Co)

11. If it does not operate for this length of time, check the bi-metallic spring to see if it is connected to the tang on the choke lever.

12. If the spring is connected and the choke is not operating properly, replace the cap assembly.

Chrysler Corp.

Caution Do not immerse the choke heating element in any type of liquid, especially solvent, for any reason.

NOTE: A short circuit in the choke wiring or in the heater will show up as a short in the ignition system.

1. Disconnect the electrical leads from the choke control switch before starting the engine.

2. Connect a test light between the smaller of the two terminals on the choke control switch and a ground.

3. Start the engine and run it until it reaches normal operating temperature.

4. Apply power from a 12V source to the terminal marked "BAT" on the choke control switch.

5. The test light should light for at least a few seconds or for as long as five minutes. If the light does not come on at all, glows dimly, or if it stays on longer than five minutes, replace the switch.

6. Disconnect the test light and reconnect the electrical leads to the choke switch, if it is functioning properly.

7. Detach the lead (B+) from the choke switch which runs to the choke heating element.

8. Connect the lead from an ohmmeter to the crimped section at the choke end of the wire, which was removed in Step 7.

Caution Do not connect the ohmmeter to the metallic heater housing.

9. Ground the other ohmmeter test lead to the engine manifold.

10. The meter should indicate a resistance of 4–6 ohms (1973) or 4–12 ohms (1974-76).

11. If the reading is not within specifications, or if it indicates an opened (zero resistance) or a shorted (infinite resistance) heater coil, replace the heater assembly.

NOTE: The electrically assisted choke does not change any carburetor service procedures. If any parts of the electrically assisted choke are defective, they must be replaced. Adjustment is not possible.

Chrysler Dual Stage Choke

Some 1976 Chrysler engines are equipped with a choke that has two levels for improved cold weather

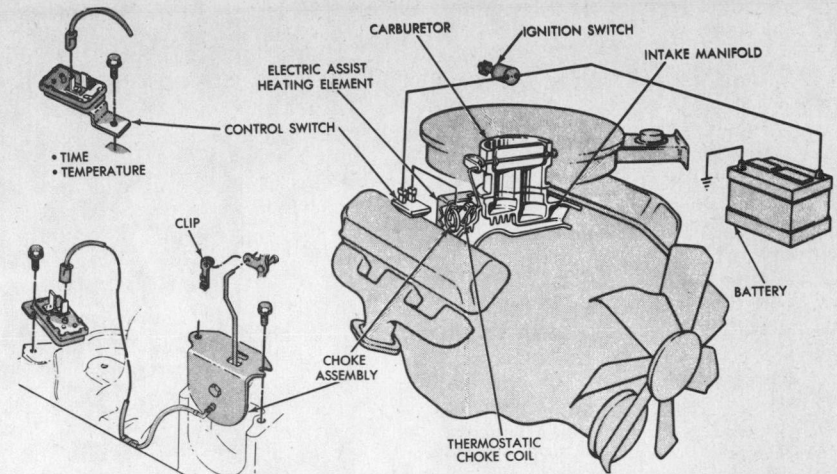

Chrysler electrically assisted choke system components (© Chrysler Corp)

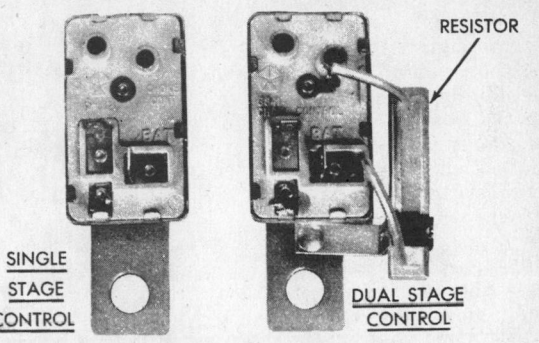

Chrysler single and dual stage choke control switches
(© Chrysler Corp.)

warm-up. It can be identified by the resistor attached to one side.

1. Before you start this test, check the intensity of the test light by connecting it between the terminals of the battery.

2. Remove the 'BAT' connector from the choke control switch, and then connect the test light between the small terminal and ground.

3. Start the engine and let it warm up, reconnect the 'BAT' electrical connector.

4. The light must go on with the same intensity as in step 1. If it does come on with the same intensity, it must not stay on for any longer than five minutes; if it fails in either intensity or duration, replace the unit.

1975-76 GM

Starting in 1975 on Cadillac, some General Motors engines use an electric choke. Cadillacs, some Quadrajets (see the Carburetor Section for details), and Chevettes use an electric choke in 1976.

1. At an engine compartment temperature of approximately 70° F (cold engine) the choke should open wide in approximately 1-1/2 minutes. The easiest way to make this test is to move the air cleaner to one side, open the

throttle to allow the choke to close, and run a hot wire from the positive battery post to the choke terminal. Then time how long it takes the choke to open.

2. Off the car, the choke coil can be tested by connecting a hot wire to the coil terminal, and a ground wire to the choke grounding plate. Starting at a room temperature of 60–70°F the choke coil should rotate 45 degrees within 54–90 seconds after the connection is made. If not, the choke is defective, and the entire choke cover must be replaced.

3. If the choke coil is in good condition, but will not operate on the engine, it could be caused by:

a. Broken or disconnected wire between oil pressure switch and choke coil.

b. Poor ground between choke cover grounding plate and housing.

c. Broken or disconnected wire in circuit from battery to oil pressure switch.

d. Burned out fuse in fuse block.

e. Defective oil pressure switch.

f. No oil pressure to switch. This could be caused by blocked oil passageways or sludged oil.

4. Repairs are limited to replacement.

1975 and later GM Secondary Choke Break Systems

System Test—2300-4

1. Start with a cold engine and allow it to idle.
2. The secondary vacuum break (1-bbl) or pull-off solenoid (2-bbl) should not operate.
3. Pull the connector off the temperature switch on the right side of the engine. The secondary vacuum break or solenoid should open the choke. If not, proceed with component checks.

NOTE: If the engine stalls in step 3 connect the temperature switch and depress the gas pedal before restarting the engine.

4. On a warm engine the secondary break or pull-off solenoid should be holding the choke in a nearly opened position when the engine is running.
5. Remove the connector on the temperature switch and ground the green wire with white stripe. The solenoid or vacuum break should de-engergize and you should be able to open the throttle and move the choke to the fully closed position.
6. Stop the engine and close the choke.
7. Start the engine. The choke should immediately be pulled open. If not, proceed with the component tests.

System Adjustments—2300-4

The amount of choke opening by the secondary vacuum break or pull-off solenoid is adjusted by bending its linkage. Choke plate-to-air horn wall clearances should be 0.450 in.

None of the other components are adjustable. If they are defective, they must be replaced.

Temperature Switch Test—2300-4

The switch is threaded into the water jacket on the right side of the engine. The green wire with the white stripe is the lead for the choke.

1. Connect a self-powered test light to the choke terminal and ground.
2. At normal operating temperature the light should stay off.
3. On a cold engine (below 93°F—automatic, or 120°F—manual) the light should come on.
4. If not, the switch is defective. Replace it.

Relay Test—2300-4 (2-bbl)

1. With the relay bracket pointing toward you and the terminals pointing up, connect the lower left terminal to a 12-volt power source.

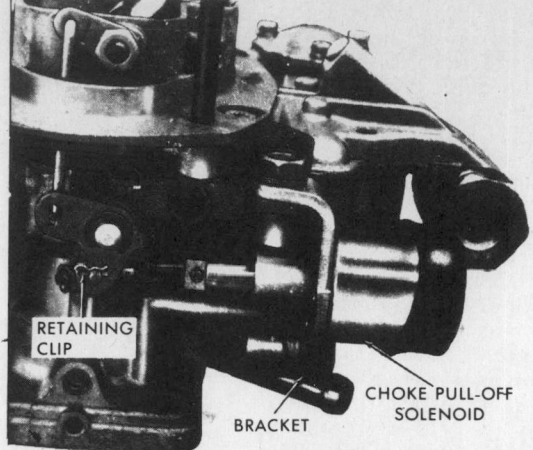

Choke pull-off solenoid—GM 2300 OHC 4-cylinder engine with 2-bbl carburetor
(© Pontiac Div., GM Corp.)

The secondary choke vacuum break is the one on the left

2. Ground the relay bracket.
3. Connect a 12 volt non-powered test light between the upper left terminal and the relay bracket.
4. The test light should light. If not, the relay is defective.
5. Connect a jumper wire between the upper right terminal and the relay bracket. The light should go off. If not, the relay is defective.

Vacuum Solenoid Test—2300-4 (1-bbl)

1. Connect a vacuum gauge to the carburetor side of the solenoid.
2. Conect engine vacuum or an auxiliary source of vacuum to the other side.
3. Apply vacuum. The solenoid should hold the vacuum and not leak down. The gauge should register no vacuum.
4. Apply 12 volts to one solenoid terminal; ground the other. The solenoid should open and the gauge should indicate vacuum.
5. If the solenoid doesn't operate as outlined, replace it.

Testing Choke Pull-Off Solenoid—2300-4 (2-bbl)

1. Connect a 12-volt power source

to the solenoid lead. Ground the body of the solenoid.
2. When the connection is completed, the solenoid stem should retract into the body. You should be unable to pull it out with your fingers.
3. If the stem is fully extended, it might be necessary to give it a push to make it retract.
4. Break the connections. You should be able to pull the solenoid out with your fingers.

NOTE: Don't expect the stem to jump out on its own. It is designed so that the choke linkage must pull it out.

5. If the solenoid dosen't operate as outlined, replace it.

System Test—GM 250-6 And Chevrolet V8 (4-bbl)

If the engine temperature is above 70°F, a timer starts as soon as the ignition switch is turned on. If you turn the ignition on but do not start the engine within 35 seconds, you will be attempting to start the engine with a wide-opened choke. To start the engine now, it will be necessary to turn the ignition off and start the engine immediately.

1. With the engine warmed-up and running, shut the ignition off.

2. Start the engine. It should take about 35 seconds for the secondary vacuum break to operate. If it doesn't the system is defective.

3. To simulate a cold engine, ground the temperature switch lead. Disconnect the lead from the temperature switch; there should be two terminals. Ground each terminal individually until you find the one that operates the red, "HOT" warning light on the dash. The *other* terminal is the timer terminal.

4. Ground the timer terminal with a jumper lead. Start the engine and watch the secondary vacuum break, for at least one miunte. The break should not operate. If it does, proceed with the component tests.

5. Leave the engine running and disconect the ground wire. About 35 seconds later the vacuum break should operate. If, not, proceed with the component tests.

6. The simulated cold test will not check temperature switch operation. The temperature switch will either have to be checked on a cold engine or by removing it, as outlined below.

Temperature Switch Test— GM 250-6 and Chevrolet V8 (4-bbl)

1. Turn the ignition switch on.
2. Remove the connector from the temperature switch and ground each terminal. One terminal will cause the red "HOT" warning light to come on; the *other* terminal works the timer.
3. With the engine temperature below 70°F, connect a self-powered test light between the temperature switch timer terminal and ground. The light should come on.
7. With the engine temperature above 70°F, the light should go off.

NOTE: If necessary, remove the temperature switch to cool it. Relieve cooling system pressure first.

8. Replace the temperature switch if it doesn't work as outlined.

Vacuum Solenoid Test—GM 250-6 and Chevrolet V8 (4-bbl)

The solenoid for the secondary choke break system is the one next to the choke vacuum diaphragm. The one on the heat valve bracket is for the EFE system.

1. Remove the connector from the choke vacuum solenoid.
2. Connect one of the solenoid terminals to a 12 volt power source and ground the other terminal.
3. If the solenoid doesn't "click" on (energize) when the connection is made in step 2, the solenoid is defective. Replace it.

---

4. Leave the solenoid connected as in step 2. Disconnect the hose from the choke secondary vacuum break and connect a vacuum gauge to it.
5. With the engine running and the solenoid energized, the gauge should read zero.
6. Disconnect the jumper wires and the gauge should show full manifold vacuum.
7. Replace the solenoid if it is defective.

Timer Test—GM 250-6 and Chevrolet V8 (4-bbl)

If the secondary choke break vacuum solenoid and temperature switch are OK, and the system is not working, the problem is probably in the timer. Replace it and perform the system test again.

Adjusting the Secondary Choke Vacuum Diaphragm—GM 250-6 and Chevrolet V8 (4-bbl)

1. Disconnect the vacuum hose from the secondary choke break vacuum diaphragm.
2. Connect a hand-operated vacuum pump with a gauge to the diaphragm.
3. Cover the diaphragm bleed hole with your finger. Apply vacuum to the diaphragm. It should hold vacuum and not leak down. If it leaks it is defective.
4. Note the position of the choke cover and then remove it. Put the follower lever on the highest step of the fast idle cam.
5. Tape the bleed hole in the diaphragm. Make sure you tape it completely with a non-porous tape or it will leak and the diaphragm will not pull in. Use a hand pump to apply vacuum to the diaphragm. Apply enough vacuum to pull the diaphragm in all the way. It may take a few seconds for the diaphragm to make a full stroke.
6. Push the lever on the inside of the choke coil housing toward the closed position (up).
7. The choke rod should be in the bottom of the slot in the choke lever, and the choke plate wide-open.
8. If not, bend the rod at the first bend (next to the vacuum break diaphragm), until the choke plate is wide-open.
9. Remove the tape, install the hose and put the choke cover back in its original position.

System Test—400-V8 Olds and All Pontiac V8

1. Remove the air cleaner from the carburetor and move it to one side, so that you can watch the choke. Don't disconnect any of the air cleaner vacuum hoses.

NOTE: If necessary, remove the secondary choke break thermal vacuum valve from the air cleaner, but leave its hoses connected.

2. Start the engine and watch the choke. The main vacuum break (front) should partially open the choke.
3. If the air temperature is above 62°F the secondary (rear) vacuum break should (slowly) open the choke a bit further.
4. To check cold operation, remove the thermal vacuum from the air cleaner and drop it in an ice bath. Leave the vacuum hoses connected.
5. Witl the engine idling, you should see the vacuum break link move out, as the valve cools off.
6. If the system doesn't work as outlined, proceed with the component tests.

Testing the Vacuum Break—400-V8 400-V8 Olds and All Pontiac V8

1. Disconnect the vacuum hose from the secondary break vacuum unit. Connect the unit directly to manifold vacuum.
2. It should take less than 20 seconds for the vacuum break link to make a full stroke.
3. If is takes longer than 20 seconds, the vacuum break is defective and must be replaced.

Thermal Vacuum Valve Test— 400-V8 Olds and All Pontiac V8

1. Connect a hand-operated vacuum pump with a gauge to the thermostatic vacuum valve (TVV) nipple marked "S". Connect another vacuum gauge to the nipple marked "E".
2. Warm the valve in your hand to above 62°F.
3. Apply vacuum to the TVV. Both gauges should read within 1 in. Hg of each other.
4. Cool the valve in an ice bath. Apply vacuum to it. Below 62° F, the vacuum gauge on the "E" nipple should read zero.
5. If the valve doesn't work as outlined, replace it.

1975 and later Chrysler Coolant Control Idle Enrichment (CCIE) System

California System Test

NOTE: The engine coolant temperature must be below 80°F for this test.

1. Disconnect the vacuum line, which runs from the two-nozzle coolant temperature operated vacuum valve to the CCIE valve on the carburetor, at the air

Hose with air bleed runs to carburetor idle enricher as part of Chrysler CCIE system

bleed (on the vacuum valve side).

2. Connect a vacuum gauge to this line and start the engine.
3. The vacuum gauge should register manifold vacuum. If it does not, check the lines and fittings to see if they are pinched or plugged.
4. If everything is in good condition, replace the coolant temperature operated vacuum valve.
5. If the valve is OK, then run the engine until the coolant temperature goes above 90°F. Above this temperature, the vacuum gauge should read zero; if it does not, replace the vacuum valve.
6. Check the air bleed and the vacuum line which runs from it to the carburetor. Replace either if it is plugged.
7. Remove the vacuum gauge and connect the vacuum lines.

Federal (except California) System Test

NOTE: The engine coolant temperature must be below 150°F for this test.

1. Disconnect the vacuum line which runs from the two-nozzle coolant temperature operated vacuum valve to the CCIE valve on the carburetor, at the air bleed (on the vacuum valve side).
2. Connect a vacuum gauge to the disconnected line.
3. Start the engine, the gauge should register manifold vacuum for about 35 seconds, and then drop to zero.
4. If there is no vacuum, stop the engine. Check the vacuum lines and fittings. If these are in good shape, check the EGR delay timer and solenoid as detailed in the appropriate section.
5. If the delay timer, solenoid, fittings, and lines check out OK, then replace the two-nozzle cool-

ant temperature operated vacuum valve.

6. If there was vacuum present long after 35 seconds in Step 3, then check the EGR delay timer and solenoid.
7. Start the engine and allow the coolant to warm-up to above 150°F, then stop the engine.
8. Start the engine again; there should be no vacuum reading on the gauge. If there is, replace the coolant temperature operated vacuum valve.
9. Check the air bleed and the vacuum line from it to the carburetor. Replace either if it is plugged.
10. Remove the vacuum gauge and connect the vacuum lines.

Ford Fuel Deceleration Valve—1971-76

Diaphragm Test

With the engine running, cover the small hole in the base of the valve. If the engine idle smoothes out or the speed decreases, the diaphragm is leaking and must be replaced.

Poppet Valve Test

If the engine idles excessively high, and it is not caused by improper carburetor adjustment, throttle linkage bind, or throttle plate bind, the poppet valve in the decel valve may be defective. With the engine running, disconnect the air-fuel line from the carburetor to the decel valve at the decel valve. Seal the opening where the line was disconnected. If the engine speed decreases noticeably, the poppet valve is hanging open and must be replaced.

Adjustment—1971-73

1. Install a vacuum gauge in the hose between the carburetor and the decel valve, using a T-fitting.
2. Attach a tachometer and run the engine at 3000 rpm.
3. Release the throttle and observe the time required for the vacuum gauge to drop to 0. Correct decel valve timing is 3-5 seconds on 1600 cc engines and 1½-5 seconds on 2000 cc engines.
4. The time delay can be adjusted by turning the nylon adjuster at the top of the decel valve body; clockwise to reduce the time, counterclockwise to increase.

To gain access to the adjuster, unscrew the covering cap. Do not use a screwdriver to adjust the decel valve. It is recommended that a special tool be made from a ⅜ in. allen wrench. If the valve cannot be adjusted within specifications, it must be replaced as an assembly.

1974 Adjustment

1. Operate the engine to make sure that it is at normal operating

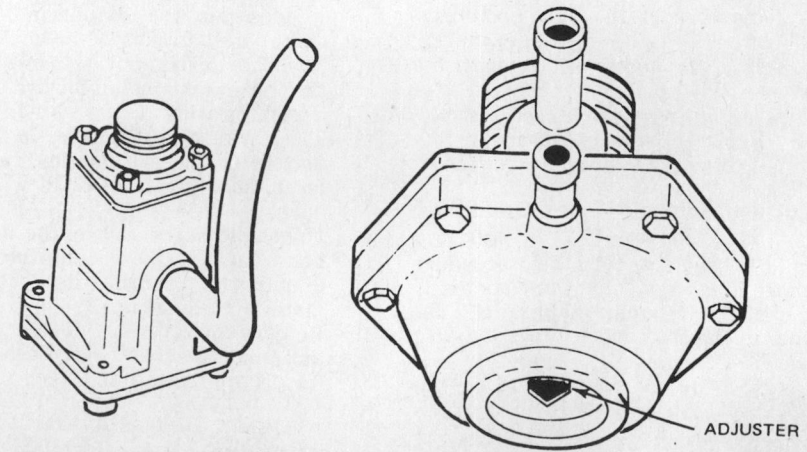

THIS VALVE DISCONTINUED FOR 1975

THIS TYPE USED IN 1975 IS NOW ADJUSTABLE.

ADJUSTER

The two types of Ford fuel decel valves
(© Ford Motor Co.)

temperature when performing the tests.

2. Attach a tachometer to the engine.
3. Disconnect the ruber hose between the decel valve and the carburetor at the decel valve and plug the nipple on the valve.
4. Make sure that the ignition timing, CO or idle mixture and idle speed are set to the correct specifications.
5. Increase the engine speed to 3000 rpm and hold for about 5 seconds, then release the throttle to make sure that the engine returns to normal idle speed.
6. Unplug the decel valve and install a vacuum gauge with a T-fitting into the hose between the decel valve and the carburetor.
7. On the 2300 cc engines, make sure that a 3/16 in. vacuum hose is conected between the small nipple on the valve to a manifold vacuum source.
8. Increase engine speed to 3000 rpm then release the throttle and measure the time required for the vacuum gauge reading to drop to 0. This should take 2-5 seconds.
9. The decel valve on the 2300 cc engine must be replaced if the time delay is not within specifications.
10. On the 2000 cc and 2800 cc engines the decel valve can be adjusted as required to meet the time specifications. Adjust the decel valve in the same manner as for models through 1973.

If the valve closes too soon, emission levels will be high. If the valve closes too late (stays open too long), engine speed will be excessive.

Advanced initial timing and/ or too rich a mixture can cause the decel valve to remain open too long.

NOTE: The vacuum readings must not exceed 18.5 in. Hg for engines with dual-diaphragm distributors, or 19.5 in. Hg with single diaphragm distributor.

1975-76 Adjustment

NOTE: On models with a speed modulated fuel decel system, perform the system test (below) before adjusting the decel valve.

1. Allow the engine to reach normal operating temperature. Connect a tachometer and timing light. Set the timing and idle to specifications.
2. Remove the air cleaner assembly. Inspect the vacuum hoses.
3. Disconnect and plug the carburetor-to-decel valve hose at the carburetor end.
4. Place the transmission in Neutral (N) and apply the parking brake.
5. Increase the engine speed to 3000 rpm and hold for 5 seconds. Release the throttle. The engine should return to normal idle immediately. If not, check for a binding throttle or throttle linkage.
6. Unplug the decel valve-to-carburetor vacuum hose. Using a T-fitting, install a vacuum gauge in it.
7. Increase the engine speed to 300 rpm and hold it for 5 seconds. Release the throttle. It should take 2 to 3.5 seconds for the vacuum to return to zero.
8. If the time in step 7 was incorrect, adjust the decel valve. Rotate the adjuster with a ¼ in.

allen key. Clockwise rotation of the adjuster reduces time and counterclockwise rotation increases time. Replace the valve if it can't be adjusted to specifications.
9. Disconnect the tachometer, vacuum gauge and timing light. Reconnect the vacuum hose.

Ford Speed Modulated Fuel Decel System
1975-76 Test (V6 only)

1. Raise the rear wheels of the vehicle off the ground and support it securely. Block the front wheels if they remain on the ground.
2. Using a T-fitting, install a vacuum gauge in the hose which runs between the fuel decel valve and the solenoid vacuum valve. Position the gauge so that it's visible from the driver's seat.
3. Start the engine and engage First gear or Drive (D). Bring the vehicle's indicated speed up to 11 mph. If the gauge shows vacuum below 11 mph and no vacuum above 11 mph, the system is working correctly. Disconnect the test equipment and lower the vehicle.
4. If there was no vacuum indicated at all in step 3, disconnect the solenoid vacuum valve leads. Connect the solenoid directly to battery voltage and a ground.
5. Run the engine at 1500 rpm with the transmisson in Neutral. If the gauge shows vacuum, replace the solenoid vacuum valve.
6. If there was no vacuum reading in step 5, connect a voltmeter or test light between the normal

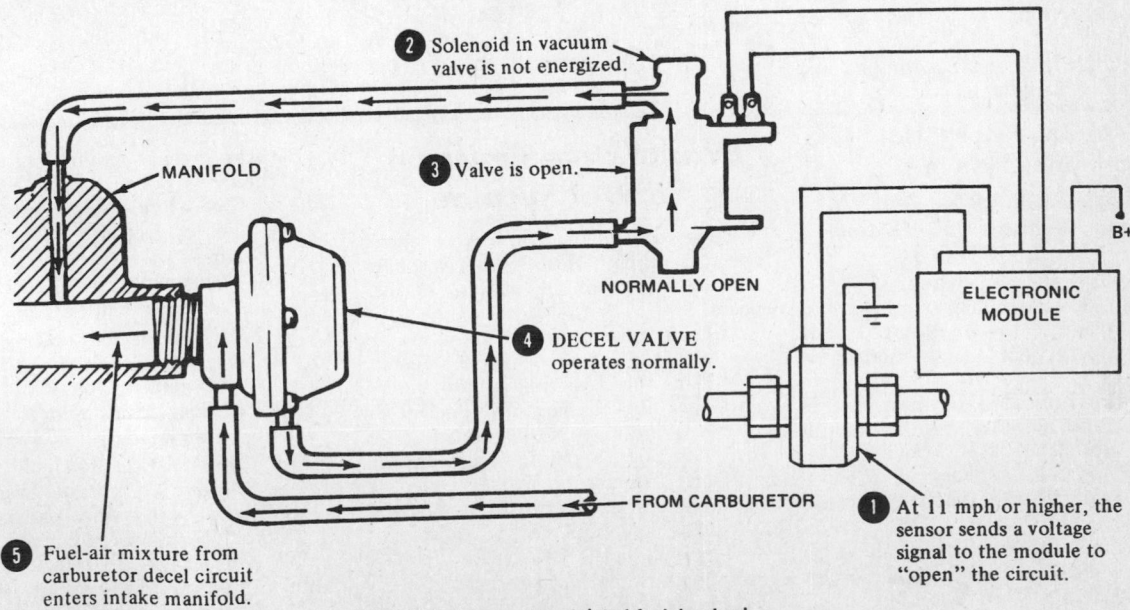

2 Solenoid in vacuum valve is not energized.

MANIFOLD

3 Valve is open.

NORMALLY OPEN

B+

ELECTRONIC MODULE

4 DECEL VALVE operates normally.

FROM CARBURETOR

5 Fuel-air mixture from carburetor decel circuit enters intake manifold.

1 At 11 mph or higher, the sensor sends a voltage signal to the module to "open" the circuit.

1975-76 Ford speed modulated fuel decel valve
(© Ford Motor Co.)

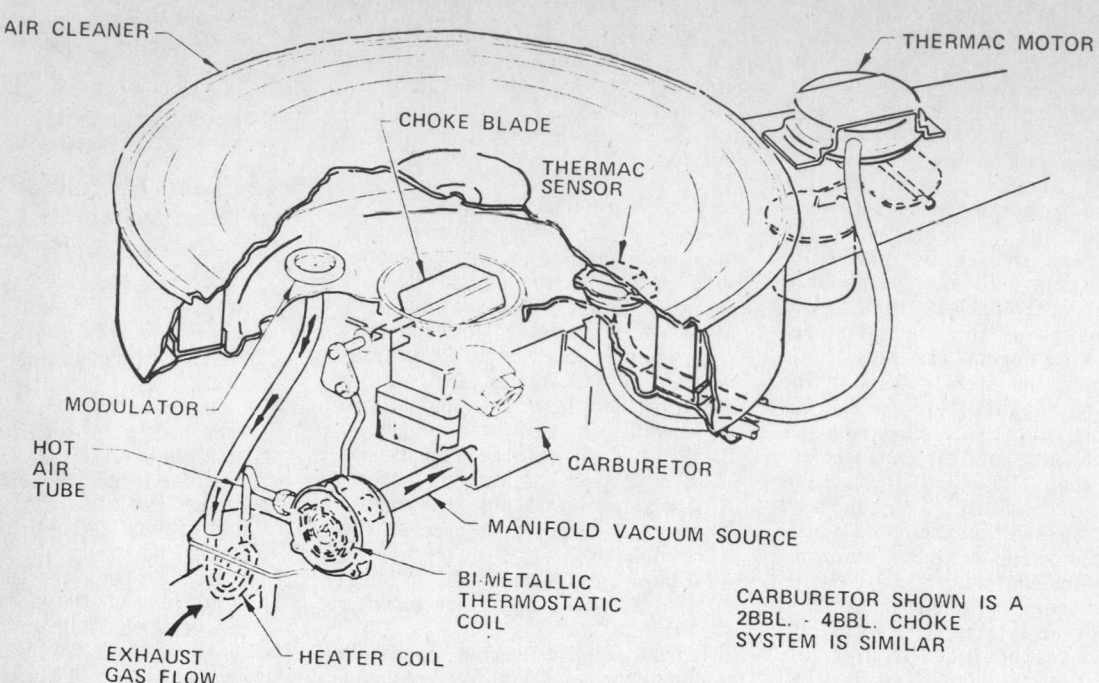

Choke hot air modulator system—1975 and later GM
(© Oldsmobile Div., GM Corp.)

source of B+ (battery) voltage and the solenoid vacuum valve terminal. Ground the other terminal. Turn the ignition on. Voltage should be indicated. If not, check for an opened circuit.

7. If voltage was indicated in step 6, check the speed sensor (in the speedometer cable) with an ohmmeter. Replace the speed sensor if it shorted (infinite reading) or open (zero reading). If it is OK, check for a poor ground.

8. If everything else is working correctly, replace the electronic module and test the system again.

9. Remove the test equipment and lower the vehicle.

1975-76 GM Choke Hot Air Modulator System

Testing—All Buick V8 and V6, Omega, Ventura 350-V8 and Starfire 231-V6

1. Remove the air cleaner top.
2. Tape a thermometer of known accuracy to the inside of the air cleaner, near the modulator valve.
3. If the indicated temperature is less than 68°F, the valve should be closed.
4. If the temperature is greater than 68°F, the valve should be open.
5. Replace the modulator valve if does not work within ±7° of 68°F.
6. Remove the thermometer.

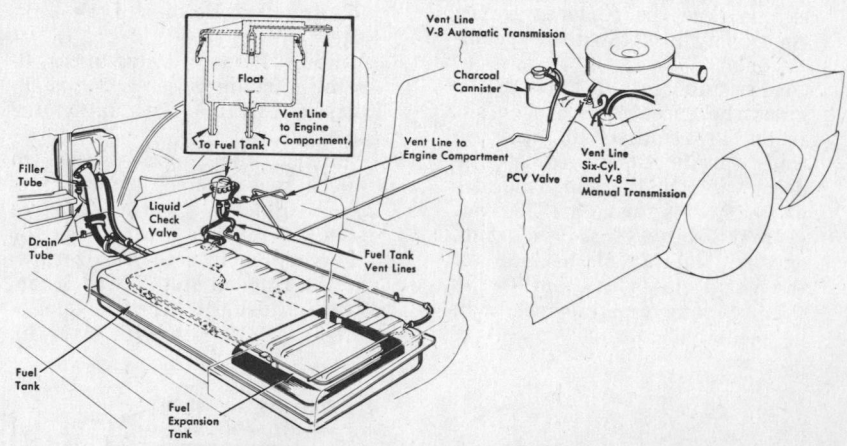

Vapor emission control system components (© American Motors Corp)

Evaporative Emission Control System

There are several things to check for if a malfunction of the evaporative emission control system is suspected.

1. Leaks may be traced by using an infrared hydrocarbon tester. Run the test probe along the lines and connections. The meter will indicate the presence of a leak by a high hydrocarbon (HC) reading. This method is much more accurate than a visual inspection which would indicate only the presence of a leak large enough to pass liquid.

2. Leaks may be caused by any of the following, so always check these areas when looking for them:
   a. Defective or worn lines;
   b. Disconnected or pinched lines;
   c. Improperly routed lines;
   d. A defective filler cap.

NOTE: If it becomes necessary to replace any of the lines used in the evaporative emission control system, use only those hoses which are fuel resistant or are marked "EVAP."

3. If the fuel tank has collapsed, it may be the fault of clogged or pinched vent lines, a defective vapor separator, or a plugged or incorrect fuel filler cap.

4. To test the filler cap, clean it and place it against the mouth. Blow into the relief valve housing. If

the cap passes pressure with light blowing or if it fails to release with hard blowing, it is defective and must be replaced.

NOTE: Replace the cap with one marked "pressure/vacuum" only. An incorrect cap will render the system inoperative or damage its components.

Exhaust Gas Recirculation (EGR) Systems

1972 Buick and 1973-76 GM EGR Valve Tests

NOTE: Skip steps 1-4 when checking early 1973 Pontiacs with combined EGR/TCS systems. Start with step 5. See TCS section above for further tests.

1. Start the engine. Allow it to warm up and reach normal idle speed.

NOTE: Some models are equipped with a temperature switch. This temperature switch may be coolant, block, or ambient temperature operated. Be sure that under-hood temperature is above 50-70°F, before testing the EGR valve.

2. Increase the engine speed to 1,200-1,500 rpm and watch the EGR valve shaft. The shaft should move upward at this speed.

3. Allow the engine to return to normal idle; the valve shaft should go down.

4. If the shaft fails to raise in step two, check the vacuum line which runs from the carburetor port to the valve. Make sure that it is not loose, clogged, or pinched. On models with temperature controls, disconnect the temperature switch and connect the two pieces of the vacuum hose. If the EGR valve now works, replace the temperature switch. If none of these conditions are present, proceed with the next step.

NOTE: On some models the temperature switch may operate other emission control systems as well. If more than one system is out, the fault probably lies in this switch. On 1976 California Cadillacs (without fuel injection), a five port thermal vacuum switch control the EGR, and the EFE system. If both systems are inoperative, check the switch first.

5. Test the valve diaphragm by disconnecting the vacuum line and applying an outside vacuum source to the valve. The shaft should raise between 8-10 in. Hg. It should retain the pressure and not leak down.

6. If the valve shaft is frozen in the

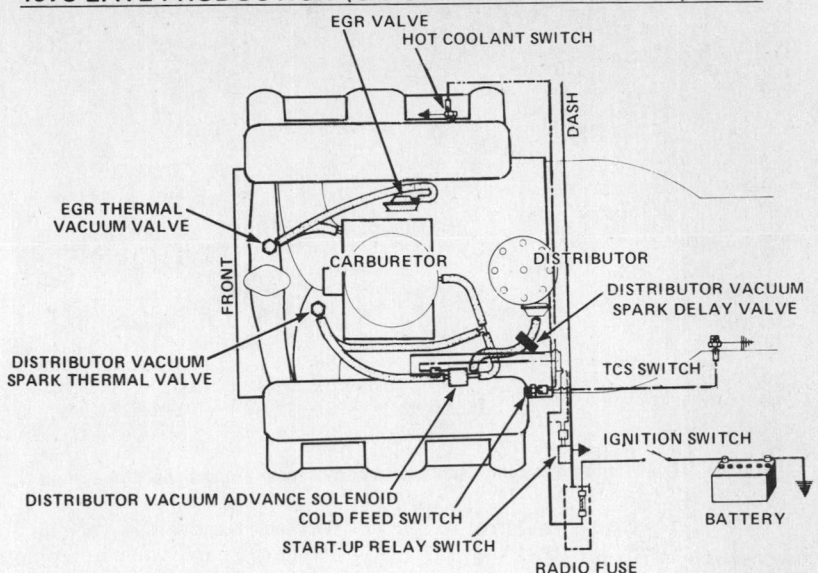

raised position, the valve is defective.

7. If the valve fails any of the above tests, it is defective. Replace it as an assembly; the valve cannot be disassembled and repaired.

8. In some cases the valve may be cleaned with a wire brush or in a spark plug cleaning machine, to loosen deposits which may cause the valve to stick.

NOTE: If the engine is to be tested by "shorting out" the cylinders when it is equipped with an EGR valve, first disconnect the vacuum hose at the valve and plug it. Failure to do this will cause uneven idling and indicate false test results.

1973½-75 Pontiac EGR System

NOTE: Pontiac models made on or after 15 March 1973 use separate systems for TCS and EGR. For TCS system checking procedures, see the appropriate section above.

The testing procedure for the Pontiac EGR valve is basically the same as that outlined for the other GM cars, in the preceding section. However, there are several points which should be noted:

1. The engine must be warmed up until the coolant temperature is above 95°F.

2. The air cleaner must be removed in order to see the EGR valve shaft. Plug the manifold vacuum fitting.

3. If the EGR valve is not getting vacuum, check the vacuum hoses, then check the mixture thermal vacuum valve and/or the coolant temperature operated vacuum valve as outlined in the appropriate section above. The

valve should work when the coolant temperature is above 95°F.

1976 Pontiac EGR

Instead of a temperature switch as used on other GM engines, Pontiac is using a snap disc valve in the intake manifold on all except the Ventura series and LeMans w/260 V-8.

1. Connect a vacuum source to the EGR side of the valve and a gauge to the carburetor side.

2. With the engine cold, there should be no vacuum; with the engine warm (above 68° F), vacuum registered on the gauge should be within 1 in. of the amount you applied to the EGR side.

1974 GM Dual Diaphragm EGR Valve

A dual diaphragm EGR valve is used on some GM V8s which are sold in California. The dual diaphragm valve may be identified by the two vacuum hoses which run to it. To test, proceed as follows:

1. Shut the engine off.

2. Disconnect the *lower* vacuum line from the EGR valve.

3. Connect a hand-operated vacuum pump, which has a built in vacuum gauge, to the lower port on the EGR valve.

4. Draw about 14 in. Hg with the pump. There should be no drop in the gauge reading for at least 30 seconds.

5. If the vacuum gauge shows a drop within 30 seconds, replace the EGR valve.

6. If the valve is good, disconnect the pump and connect the vacuum line to the lower port.

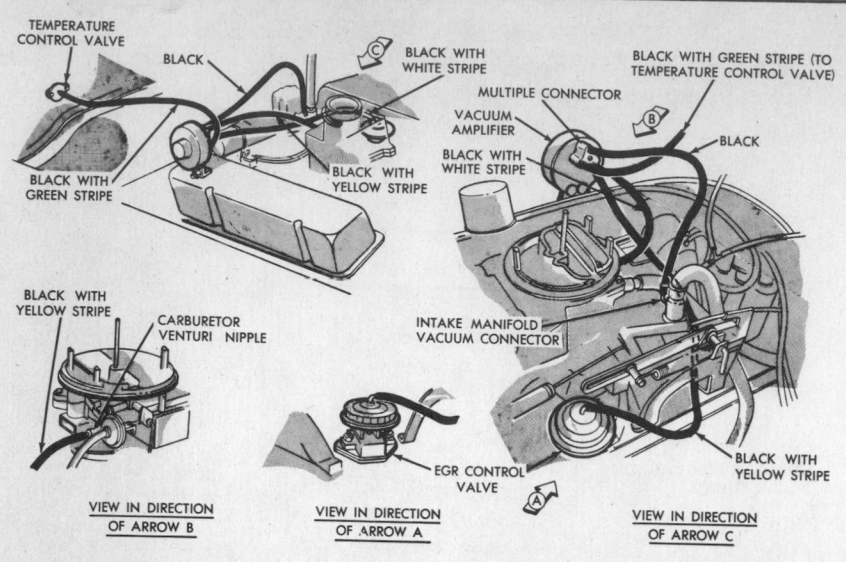

Typical hose routing and component layout of a Chrysler Proportional EGR system

1974-76 GM Backpressure Transducer Valve (BPV)

1. Take the air cleaner off of the carburetor and plug the manifold vacuum fitting.
2. Block the drive wheels, place the transmission in Park, and turn the air conditioner off.
3. Start the engine and allow it to reach normal operating temperature. Place the cam follower on the high step of the fast idle cam.
4. Connect a vacuum gauge to the carburetor side of the BPV. Note the reading. Reconnect the vacuum line.
5. Connect a vacuum gauge to the EGR valve side of the BPV with a T-fitting. The gauge should read 1.7-3.2 in. Hg; if it does not, replace the BPV.
6. With the vacuum gauge still con-nected, remove the vacuum line from the EGR valve and plug it; the gauge should read the same as in Step 4. If it does not read within 2-3 in. Hg of the figure obtained in Step 4, replace the BPV.
7. Remove the vacuum gauge, connect the vacuum lines, and replace the air cleaner.

1975-76 Cadillac with Electronic Fuel Injection

On models with electronic fuel injection (EFI) vacuum for the EGR valve is controlled by the fuel injection system.

A solenoid in the EGR valve vacuum line blocks its vacuum signal when coolant temperature is below 130°F. The solenoid is controlled by the fuel injection system computer.

The EGR valve is tested as outlined under "1972 Buick and 1973-75 GM EGR Valve Tests", except that the vacuum hose should be removed from the solenoid and its two halves joined. If the vacuum solenoid or its control circuit is suspected of faulty operation, they must be tested as part of the fuel injection system. Fuel injection system testing requires the use of a special factory checker.

The backpressure transducer valve (BPV) used with the fuel injection EGR system is tested by using the procedure outlined in the "1974-75 GM Backpressure Transducer Valve" test section.

Chrysler Corp. EGR Floor Jet Service—1972-73

All six-cylinder engines have one floor jet, while all V8s have two.

1. Turn the engine off. Remove the air cleaner assembly from the carburetor.
2. Hold the choke and throttle valves open. Shine a flashlight through the carburetor to inspect the floor jet(s). The jet(s) is/are in satisfactory condition if the passage shows an open path to the orifice.
3. If the jet (s) is/are clogged, completely remove the carburetor. Withdraw the jet and clean it.

Caution Use care when handling the jets. They have very thin walls and are, therefore, easily damaged. Because they are made out of stainless steel, they are not magnetic and cannot be retrieved readily if dropped into the manifold.

4. Install the jet(s) and tighten to 25 ft lbs. Install the carburetor and attach the air cleaner.

NOTE: "Shorting out" cylinders on engines equipped with floor jets is not a reliable test proceedure. The unburned mixture is circulated to the other cylinders, causing the engine speed to fluctuate. Because of this, false test results may be obtained.

Chrysler Corp. 1973 (early) Proportional EGR System Tests

NOTE: Air temperature should be above 68°F for this test.

1. Check all of the vacuum hoses which run between the carburetor, intake manifold, EGR valve, and the vacuum amplifier (if so equipped). Replace the hoses and tighten the connections, as required.
2. Allow the engine to warm up. Connect a tachometer to it. Start with the engine idling in neutral and rapidly increase the engine speed to 2,000 rpm.
3. If the EGR valve stem moves (watch the groove on the stem),

Floor jet location in Chrysler Corp V8s—sixes use only one jet (© Chrysler Corp)

the valve and the rest of the system are functioning properly. If the stem does not move, proceed with the rest of the EGR system tests.

4. Disconnect the vacuum supply hose from the EGR valve. Apply a vacuum of at least 10 in. Hg to the valve with the engine warmed-up and idling and the transmission in neutral.

NOTE: A source of more than adequate vacuum is the intake manifold vacuum connection. Run a hose from the EGR valve directly to the connection.

5. When vacuum is applied to the EGR valve, the engine speed should drop at least 150 rpm. In some cases the engine may even stall. If the engine does not slow down and the EGR valve does not operate, the valve is defective or dirty. Replace it or remove the deposits from it.

NOTE: Always replace the EGR valve gasket with a new one when the valve is removed for service, even if the valve itself is not replaced.

6. If the EGR valve is functioning properly, reconnect its vacuum line and test the temperature control valve.

7. Disconnect the vacuum hose which runs to the temperature control valve and plug it. Repeat steps 2–3. If the EGR valve now functions, the temperature control valve is defective and must be replaced.

8. If everything else is functioning properly, the EGR system does not work and the engine is equipped with a vacuum amplifier (see the chart below), the amplifier is at fault. Replace it and repeat the system test.

NOTE: Before replacng the amplifier, check the vacuum port in the carburetor. If it is clogged, clean it with solvent; do not use a drill.

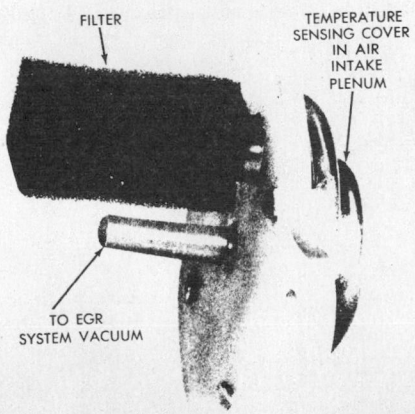

The temperature sensing valve used prior to 15 March 1973 on Chrysler EGR systems

(© Chrysler Corp)

The late 1973-76 EGR temperature control valve is located on the top tank of the radiator on most Chrysler products

Engine	Vacuum amplifier used on:
225—6	All
318—V8	California only
360—V8	All
440—V8	All non-high-performance engines

Chrysler Corp. 1973 (late)-76 Proportional EGR System Tests

NOTE. This system is used starting with cars made on or after 15 March 1973. It replaces the system tested in the above section.

1. Perform Steps 1-6 of the 1973 proportional EGR system tests, detailed in the above section.
2. Depressurize the cooling system. Remove the coolant temperature operated EGR vacuum valve (CCEGR) from the top tank of the radiator. On 1975 360-V8 2-bbl engines, remove the CCEGR valve from the front of the block.
3. Place the CCEGR valve in an ice bath so that its threaded portion is covered. Cool it to less than 40°F.
4. Connect a hand-operated vacuum pump and gauge to the valve nipple which had the blue or yellow striped hose attached to it.
5. Apply at least 10 in. Hg. vacuum to the valve. The gauge should show no more than a 1 in. Hg. drop in vacuum in 1 minute.
6. If the reading drops off more than this, replace the CCEGR valve.
7. Proceed with step 8 in the preceding section.

Chrysler Corp. 1974-76 EGR Delay System

NOTE: Not all engines use an EGR delay timer; some 1975 engines also

used the EGR delay timer to control the coolant control idle enrichment (CCIE) system as well.

1. Unfasten the distributor-to-coil lead.
2. Disconnect the vacuum line which runs from the delay solenoid to the vacuum amplifier at the amplifier end.
3. Turn the car's ignition switch to "START" and then release it, so that it returns to "RUN"
4. Suck on the end of the disconnected hose; the hose should be blocked.
5. After about 35 seconds from the time that the ignition switch was turned to "START", the solenoid should open, allowing air to flow through the line that you are sucking on.
6. If the system isn't working, disconnect the solenoid and connect it directly to a 12-volt power source, making and breaking the circuit several times. If the solenoid works, replace the delay timer.
7. If the solenoid doesn't work, replace the solenoid.
8. Reconnect the vacuum lines and the coil after completing the test.

1976 Chrysler EGR Time Delay System

1. Check the wiring for proper connections, and remove the terminal connector from the time delay solenoid valve.
2. Connect a test light across the connector terminals, then start the engine.
3. The light should go on and remain on for 30-40 seconds.
4. If it does not go on, or remains on too long, replace the time delay unit. Retest using a new unit, but make sure the test light is not

drawing too much current. It should not draw any more than 0.5 amps, and be about the size of a dash panel light.

Chrysler Corp. 1975-76
EGR Reminder Light

NOTE: This light is designed to remind the driver that regularly scheduled service is due; it does not mean that the EGR system is not working properly.

1. After checking the EGR system for proper operation, slide the rubber boot on the EGR reminder odometer up, out of the way.
2. Reset the odometer with a small screwdriver.
3. Slide the boot back down over the odometer. The light will come on again when the next 15,000 mile check-up is due.

1973 Ford EGR System Tests

1. Allow the engine to warm up, so that the coolant temperature has reached at least 135°F.
2. Disconnect the vacuum hose which runs from the temperature cut-in valve to the EGR valve at the EGR valve end. Connect a vacuum gauge to this hose with a T-fitting.
3. Increase engine speed. The gauge should indicate a vacuum. If no vacuum is present, check the following:
   a. The carburetor—look for a clogged vacuum port.
   b. The vacuum hoses—including the vacuum hoses to the transmission modulator.
   c. The temperature cut-in valve —if no vacuum is present at its outlet with the engine temperature above 135°F and vacuum available from the carburetor, the valve is defective.
4. If all of the above tests are positive, check the EGR valve itself.
5. Connect an outside vacuum source and a vacuum gauge to the valve.
6. Apply vacuum to the EGR valve. The valve should open at 3–10 in. Hg, the engine idle speed should slow down, and the idle quality should become more rough.
7. If this does not happen, i.e., the EGR valve remains closed, the EGR valve is defective and must be replaced.
8. If the valve stem moves but the idle remains the same, the valve orifice is clogged and must be cleaned.

NOTE: If an outside vacuum source is not available, disconnect the hose which runs between the EGR valve and the temperature cut-in valve and plug the hose connections on the cut-in valve. Connect the EGR valve hose to a source of intake mani-

Black cylinder (under steering shaft) is the EGR maintenance warning odometer used on 1975-76 Chrysler products

fold vacuum and watch the idle. The results should be the same as in steps 6–7, above.

Vacuum Modulator—Bench Test

NOTE: The vacuum modulator is used only with an automatic transmission.

1. Remove the vacuum modulator from the car.
2. Connect the modulator to an outside vacuum source: a distributor tester, for example.

NOTE: The vacuum source should be adjusted to supply 18 in. Hg, with the end of the vacuum line blocked off.

3. Connect the vacuum line from the vacuum source to the EGR port on the vacuum modulator.
4. The vacuum modulator should hold the 18 in. Hg reading. If it does not, then the diaphragm is leaking and must be replaced.

Temperature Cut-In Valve— Bench Test

1. Remove the valve from the engine.
2. Connect an outside source of vacuum to the top port on the valve.

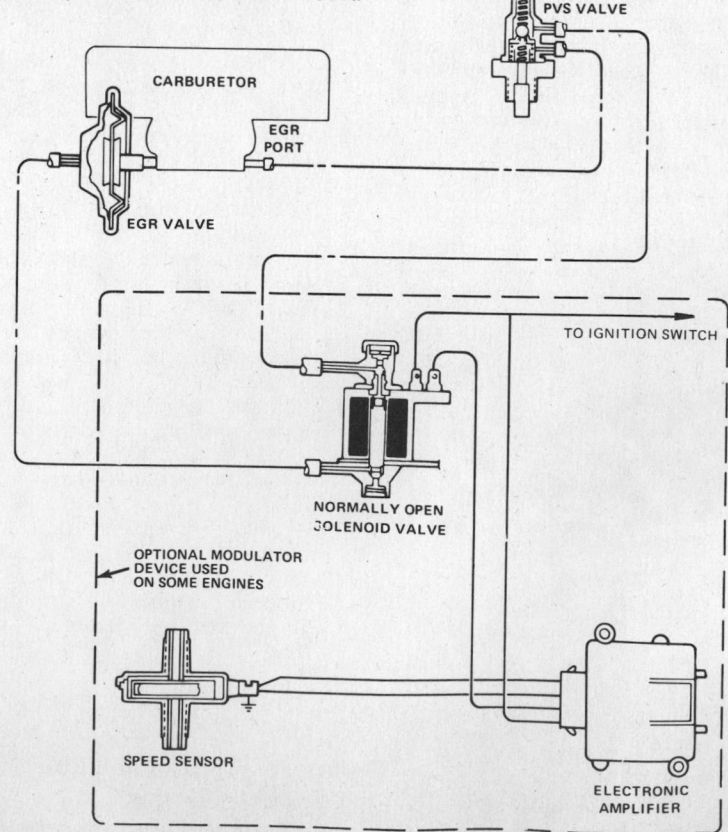

Ford exhaust gas recirculation (EGR) system (© Ford Motor Co)

Leave the bottom port vented to the atmosphere.

3. Use ice or an aerosol spray to cool the valve below 60°F.

4. Apply 20 in. Hg vacuum to the valve. The valve should hold a minimum of 19 in. Hg vacuum for five minutes without leaking down.

5. Leave the vacuum source connected to the valve and place it, along with a high temperature thermometer, into a non-metallic, heat-resistant container full of water.

6. Heat the water. The vacuum in the valve should drop to zero once the temperature of the water reaches about 125°F.

7. Replace the valve if it fails either of the tests.

1973 Ford High Speed EGR Modulator—System Tests

NOTE: Before beginning this test, check the EGR valve and the other related components as outlined in the section above.

1. Detach the line from the EGR valve. Connect a vacuum gauge to the line, using a T-fitting, and reconnect the EGR valve.

NOTE: Position the vacuum gauge so that it can be seen from the driver's seat.

2. Raise the rear wheels of the car off the ground, supporting it so that it cannot roll forward.

3. Start the engine and allow it to warm up at *fast* idle for 3–4 minutes.

4. Return the engine to normal idle; the vacuum gauge reading should return to zero.

5. Place the transmission in Third gear (manual) or Drive (automatic). Increase the engine speed; vacuum should also increase.

6. At an indicated speed of approximately 67 mph, the vacuum gauge reading should drop to zero.

If the system is functioning properly, lower the car, disconnect the vacuum gauge, and reconnect the vacuum lines. If the system is malfunctioning, proceed with the tests below.

Power Supply Tests

Caution Do not use a self-powered test light; damage to the amplifier could result.

1. Check the electrical leads which run to and from the vacuum solenoid valve with a low-amperage test light. The car should be running so that power is being supplied to the system.

2. If there is no current at the valve, trace the wiring back to its power source to determine the reason for the failure.

---

3. If there is current at the valve, remove the power connector from the amplifier and check for current at the connector. If there is none, replace the wiring between the amplifier and the vacuum valve.

Speed Sensor Tests

1. Check the resistance of the speed sensor by touching its leads with the test prods of an ohmmeter. The ohmmeter should read 40–60 ohms.

2. Replace the speed sensor if its resistance is not within specifications.

3. Check the connector on the speed sensor to be sure that it is tight. If the ground interlock loop between the connectors is loose, the circuit will not be grounded and the speed sensor will appear not to be functioning.

Vacuum Solenoid Valve Tests

1. Disconnect the leads from the vacuum solenoid valve which run to the amplifier.

Caution Never connect a jumper lead or a self-powered test light to the valve while it is still connected to the amplifier; damage to the amplifier could result.

2. Connect a vacuum gauge to the EGR valve port on the vacuum valve.

3. With the valve disconnected from the amplifier, connect the valve directly to a 12V power source (the battery) with jumper leads.

4. With the transmission in Neutral and current flowing to the valve, increase the engine speed to 1,500 rpm. The vacuum gauge should read zero. If it does not, replace the valve.

5. Disconnect the 12V power source from the valve. The gauge should show a vacuum reading with the engine speed at 1,500 rpm.

If the valve is not functioning properly, replace it. If it is functioning properly and the system still is not, the only other possible source of trouble is the amplifier; replace it.

NOTE: There is no way to test amplifier operation other than by process of elimination or by substitution. Attempts to check it will probably lead to its failure, if it is not already defective.

1974–76 Ford EGR System— Component Tests

1. Perform Steps 5-8 of the "1973 Ford EGR System Test". Replace the EGR valve and gasket, if necessary.

2. Connect a vacuum gauge to the EGR port on the carburetor, after

---

disconnecting the EGR vacuum hose.

3. With the engine running (warmed-up), quickly open the throttle halfway. Allow the throttle to close.

4. If the vacuum gauge shows a quick rise and fall in vacuum, the EGR port is not clogged. No reading indicates a clogged port; if there is no reading, clean the port.

5. Check the coolant temperature operated vacuum valve (PVS) which controls the EGR system vacuum, when the engine is cold, as outlined in the appropriate section. Check the vacuum hoses for correct routing.

If everything else is in good working order, proceed with the vacuum amplifier tests (if so equipped):

6. Run the engine until normal operating temperature is reached.

7. Check the vacuum amplifier connections to be sure that they are tight and that the hoses are routed properly.

8. Remove the hose which runs from the EGR valve to the vacuum amplifier at the EGR valve end. Connect a vacuum gauge to this hose; the gauge *must* read in increments of 1 in. Hg or less.

9. Disconnect the venturi vacuum hose at the carburetor port.

10. With the engine at curb idle, the vacuum gauge should read either zero or show a small reading.

11. Increase the engine speed to 1500-2000 rpm, then allow it to return to idle.

12. If the vacuum reading increases more than 1 in. Hg or if it does not return to the same figure indicated in Step 10, replace the amplifier.

13. Reconnect the venturi hose to the carburetor port.

14. With the engine at curb idle, there should be no great increase in vacuum above the figure obtained in Step 10 (more than 0.5 in. Hg). If the vacuum increases greatly, check the idle speed, it is probably too high.

15. Unfasten the external reservoir hose from the amplifier and plug it.

16. Rapidly increase the engine speed to 1500-2000 rpm. The vacuum gauge reading should increase by at least 4 in. Hg; if it does not, replace the amplifier.

17. After completing the tests, remove the gauge and connect the vacuum hoses.

18. Check the external vacuum amplifier reservoir, if so equipped, by following the procedure outlined below.

External Amplifer Reservoir
Without Check Valve

1. Disconnect the reservoir-to-amp-

lifier hose. Connect a vacuum gauge to it.

2. Using an external vacuum source, apply at least 14 in. Hg to the reservoir.
3. Trap the vacuum in the reservoir.
4. The vacuum should drop no more than 1 in. Hg in 1 minute. If it does, replace the reservoir.

With External Check Valve

1. Connect an external vacuum source and gauge to the amplifier side of the T-fitting in the reservoir-to-check valve hose.
2. Apply and trap 15 in. Hg to the line. Vacuum should leak down no more than 1 in. Hg in 1 minute. If it doesn't the system is OK. If it does, proceed with the rest of the test.
3. Remove the reservoir hose at the T-fitting and apply 15 in. Hg to the reservoir. Trap the vacuum in the reservoir.
4. The vacuum should drop no more than 1 in. Hg in 1 minute. If it does, replace the reservoir.
5. Remove the check valve hose. Apply 15 in. Hg vacuum to the check valve and trap it.
6. The vacuum should drop no more than 1 in. Hg in 1 minute. Replace the check valve if it does otherwise.
7. Remove the vacuum pump, and gauge. Reconnect the hoses.

Two-Nipple EGR/PVS

1. Disconnect the hoses from the EGR coolant temperature operated vacuum valve (PVS).
2. Connect a vacuum gauge to one of the nipples and an external vacuum source to the other (it dosn't matter which).
3. If the engine is cold, start it and allow the coolant temperature to reach at least 135°F.
4. If the vacuum dosen't indicate vacuum with the engine warm when vacuum is applied, the PVS is defective. Replace it.
5. If vacuum is indicated, the PVS is OK.

Three-Nipple EGR/PVS

1. Disconnect the EGR vacuum hose from the carburetor port. Connect the hose to either manifold vacuum or an auxiliary vacuum source.
2. Remove the vacuum hose from the EGR valve and connect a vacuum gauge to the hose.
3. If the engine is cold, start it and allow the coolant temperature to reach at least 135°F.
4. If the gauge doesn't indicate vacuum the PVS is defective and should be replaced.
5. If the gauge indicates vacuum the PVS is OK. Remove the

gauge and reconnect the vacuum lines.

Four Nipple EGR/PVS

1. Disconnect the vacuum hoses at the PVS valve and keep them in order. Connect a vacuum gauge to either the D or M port; then connect a vacuum supply to the other one.
2. Start the engine and warm it up. If you do not get a vacuum reading, the valve is ok; if you do get a reading, replace the valve.
3. Repeat Step 1 using the E and S ports. If you get a vacuum here, the valve is good; if you do not, replace the valve.

1973 American Motors EGR System Test

NOTE: Start the test with the engine cold.

1. Disconnect the vacuum line at the EGR valve. Connect a vacuum gauge to the vacuum line.
2. Heat the low ambient compensator (located in front of the radiator) in the palm of the hand, until it is above 60°F.
3. Start the engine; increase engine speed. There should be no vacuum reading on the gauge. Allow the engine to warm up to at least 125°F (160°F—304 V8/manual). With the ambient temperature compensator above 60°F and the engine coolant temperature above 125°F (160°F), vacuum should be present when the engine speed is increased.
4. Using a trouble light or some other suitable heat source, heat the *high* temperature compensator (mounted on the firewall) to above 115°F. Speed the engine up; the vacuum reading should be zero or quite low.
5. Cool the *high* temperature compensator to below 115°F, using ice; the gauge should now show a strong vacuum reading.
6. Using ice, cool the *low* ambient compensator to below 60°F; the vacuum reading should decrease.
7. If vacuum is present when it should not be, while one of the components is being tested, replace the component and repeat the system test.
8. If *no* vacuum is present when it should be, check the vacuum lines. If the lines are satisfactory, replace the suspect component and repeat the system test. Disconnect the vacuum gauge when the tests are completed.
9. Connect the EGR valve directly to the carburetor port or some other source of vacuum. Speed up the engine; the valve stem should move upward (8-10 in.

Hg). Allow the engine to slow down; the valve stem should move down. If the valve is defective, replace it. Reconnect the vacuum lines.

NOTE: The following components were dropped from the EGR system on, or after 15 March 1973:

1. *High temperature compensator— All engines.*
2. *Low temperature compensator— All engines.*
3. *Coolant temperature override switch — Six-cylinder engines only.*

Those steps of the test procedure which deal with these components are not required on models made after 15 March 1973.

1974-76 American Motors EGR System

EGR Valve Tests—All Engines

1. Start the engine and allow it to reach normal operating temperature.
2. Compress the EGR valve diaphragm by hand; the engine speed should drop by about 200 rpm.

Caution

Be careful when depressing the valve diaphragm, the area around the valve gets very hot.

3. If the engine speed doesn't drop, but the engine is idling smoothly, the EGR passage to the intake manifold is plugged and must be cleaned.
4. If the engine idle is poor, and lifting the diaphragm has no effect on its speed, the EGR valve is probably plugged or defective. Clean or replace it, as necessary.
5. Insert a T-fitting in the EGR valve vacuum line and connect a vacuum gauge to the fitting.
6. Increase the engine speed slowly, while watching the vacuum gauge; at the same time either watch or feel the valve diaphragm.
7. The valve should start to open between 1.8-3.2 in. Hg and be fully opened at 3.8-7.3 in. Hg.
8. At wide-open throttle, the diaphragm should be fully depressed with no sign of leakage. Replace the valve if it is defective.

EGR Coolant Temperature Operated Vacuum Valve—All Engines

NOTE: Engine coolant temperature must be below 100°F before beginning this test.

1. Be sure that the lines are routed correctly and are not pinched, plugged, or leaking.
2. Unfasten the vacuum line from the EGR valve. Connect a vacuum gauge to this line.
3. Start the engine and increase its speed to 1500 rpm. The vacuum

The coolant temperature override switch is the only control for EGR vacuum used on AMC V8s after 15 March 1973

gauge should read zero; if it does not, replace the coolant temperature operated vacuum valve.

4. Allow the engine to run until the coolant temperature reaches 115°F or more.
   NOTE: At 115°F, the needle on the car's temperature gauge should be halfway between "C" and the beginning of the band.
5. Increase the engine speed to 1500 rpm again. The vacuum gauge should show ported vacuum; if it doesn't, replace the vacuum valve.

Exhaust Backpressure Sensor Test—California Engines and all 1976 engines

1. Check all vacuum lines and fittings. Make sure that the vacuum line to the EGR valve is connected to the coolant temperature operated vacuum valve nipple with the 0.030 in. restriction.
2. Install a vacuum gauge, using a T-fitting, in the line which runs from the EGR valve to the backpressure sensor.
3. Start the engine and allow it to warm-up. With the engine at curb idle the vacuum gauge should read zero.
4. If vacuum is present, check the vacuum lines to be sure that manifold vacuum is *not* being used instead of carburetor ported vacuum. If the correct ported vacuum is being used, check to be sure that the throttle plate isn't sticking opened.
5. Increase the engine speed to 2000 rpm, while watching for one of the following:
   a. If the coolant temperature is less than 115°F (black), or 160°F (yellow), the gauge should read zero.
   b. If the coolant temperature is above 115°F (black), or 160°F (yellow), the gauge should show ported vacuum.
6. If vacuum is not shown when it should be, or vice versa, check the coolant temperature operated vacuum valve, as previously outlined.

7. If everything else is in good working order, remove the backpressure sensor. Check to see that the spacer port and tube are not blocked. Clean them with a spiral wire brush, as necessary. If this doesn't solve the problem, replace the backpressure sensor.

Catalytic Converters

Testing the Converter

At the present time there is no known way to reliably test catalytic converter operation in the field. The only reliable test is a 12 hour and 40 minute "soak test" (CVS) which must be done in a laboratory.

An infrared HC/CO tester is not sensitive enough to measure the higher tailpipe emissions from a partially-failed converter. Thus, a bad converter may allow enough HC and CO emissions to escape, so that the car is not in compliance with Federal (or state) standards, but still will not cause the needle on the HC/CO tester to move off zero.

You can check a converter for physical damage, such as a ripped skin or crushed shell. You can test for a plugged converter the same way you test for a plugged muffler. You can look for pellets coming out of the tailpipe, which means the pellets are breaking up. All such physical damage means the converter must be repaired, replaced, or recharged. But when it comes to testing the actual efficiency of the converter, or measuring the amount of HC and CO that it removes from the exhaust, forget it.

If you have a car with high HC or CO coming out the tailpipe, the problem has to be in the engine. If you took the converter off most 1975 cars, they would still be as clean as the 1974 cars. The converter removes so little HC and CO from the exhaust that even with the converter taken off, the car would still pass state or

CATALYTIC CONVERTER

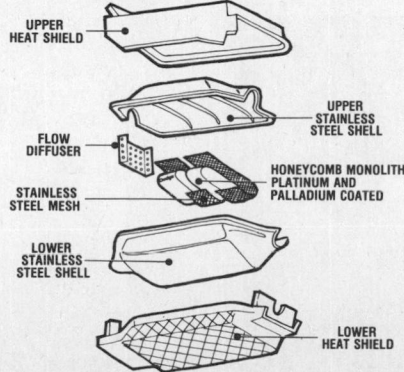

UPPER HEAT SHIELD

FLOW DIFFUSER

STAINLESS STEEL MESH

LOWER STAINLESS STEEL SHELL

UPPER STAINLESS STEEL SHELL

HONEYCOMB MONOLITH PLATINUM AND PALLADIUM COATED

LOWER HEAT SHIELD

Typical monolithic catalytic converter construction
(© Chrysler Corp)

city emission control laws. The converter was put on the 1975 cars so they would pass the EPA and California laboratory test, which is much more severe than any state or city used car standards, including California.

If you discover the car has high tailpipe emissions, or if the car gets a citation for high emissions, it's easy to jump to the conclusion that the converter is to blame. *Do not replace or recharge a converter because of high tailpipe emissions.* The problem is in the engine, not the converter.

Following are the most common causes of high tailpipe emissions, as measured on an infra-red tester.

High HC	Missing cylinder
	Lean mixture screws
	Extreme flooding
High CO	Rich mixture screws
	Dirty air cleaner
	High float level

The only domestic car maker who gives idle CO settings is Chrysler. The mixture screws are set with the air pump disconnected, which reduces the efficiency of the converter and causes enough CO to go through that you get a reading. American Motors and General Motors use the lean drop method of setting idle mixture, and Ford uses the speed increase method of adding propane.

Recharging or Changing Converters

Because the converter cannot be tested in the field, many people wonder what should be done to it. We have established the following guidlines.

1. The car manufacturer requires it.
2. The converter is damaged beyond repair.
3. The law requires it.
4. The catalyst dosen't work.

So far, there is no requirement by either the car manufacturer or the law to change or recharge the converter according to mileage or time. General Motors and American Motors converters can be repaired if the bottom cover is damaged by installing a replacement cover.

We know of only two ways to tell if the catalyst isn't working. If *you* see pellets or pieces of the catalyst coming out the tailpipe, the catalyst is breaking up, and the converter must be recharged or changed. The other indication is the catalyst that melts and plugs the exhaust. In that case, you have to do something immediately, because the car probably won't run.

Leaded fuel will reduce the efficiency of the converter while the leaded fuel is being used. After the leaded fuel has been used up, and the car runs again on non-leaded fuel, the converter will recover its efficiency to a degree. How much the converter recovers depends on how long it was run on leaded fuel. How much efficiency is reduced you have no way of knowing.

Converter Removal

A new car dealer is prohibited by federal law from tampering with emission controls. If the catalyst melts or breaks up, he must replace or recharge the converter. An independent shop's work on emission controls is regulated by state and local laws. Before you remove a converter make sure that you are not breaking any state or local laws.

Catalyst Damage

Converters operate best at an internal temperature of 600-1500°F. At 1700°F or higher, the catalyst begins to melt or break up. The converter generates its own heat, according to how many hydrocarbons are fed through it. Hydrocarbons are nothing more than raw, liquid fuel, so any excess of fuel will cause the converter to overheat. The following conditions will cause extra fuel to go through the converter, and may damage it.

1. Fast idle for a long time.
2. A missing plug or plugs, for a long time.
3. An extremely rich mixture for a long time.

How long is a long time? Only the converter knows. Garage testing may overheat the converter if carried on too long. Any testing that requires shorting out one or more cylinders will put raw fuel through the converter.

There is nothing wrong with these tests, as long as they are done quickly. The same applies to dynamometer tests. It isn't necessary to hold the engine at full throttle for more than a few seconds. There is no reason for changing normal dynamometer procedures. However, if you are doing experimental work that requires a lot of dyno running, the converter could overheat. For extensive experimental work, we suggest removing the converter temporarily and putting a length of empty tubing in its place. On the dyno, you can remove the converter (if it isn't welded) and put your exhaust collector over the end of the exhaust pipe.

The following check list shows possible causes for catalyst damage:

Excessive vibration
Rich mixtures
Leaded fuel
Spark plug misfire
Excessive fast idle
Running out of gas (causes misfire)
Fuel additives
Carbon solvents
Misuse of engine (turning key off at speed)
Total ignition failure at speed

Catalyst Protection System Testing

Chrysler Corp. (1975 only)

1. Start the engine and allow it to warm up.
2. Connect a tachometer to the engine.
3. Increase the engine speed to 2,500 rpm; the solenoid plunger should extend.
4. Release the throttle, once the engine speed has dropped below 2,000 rpm; the plunger should retract.
5. If the solenoid doesn't work properly, disconnect it from the speed switch and connect it to a 12 volt power source. If the plunger extends, the solenoid is working and the speed switch is defective. Replace the speed switch.
6. If the plunger does not extend, the solenoid is defective and must be replaced.
7. With the solenoid connected to the 12 volt power source (energized) so that its plunger is out, adjust the engine speed to 1,500 rpm.

Caution *Do not* adjust the curb idle speed with the catalyst protection system solenoid. This is not an antidieseling solenoid. If the curb idle speed is adjusted with this solenoid, it wil be far above 2,000 rpm once the solenoid has been energized, creating a hazardous driving situation. The only way to stop an engine which has been adjusted in this manner, is to shut it off and not restart it until the solenoid has been correctly adjusted.

8. Reconnect the solenoid to the speed switch and disconnect the tachometer, once the proper setting has been obtained.

Replacing the Catalyst

Chrysler and Ford

The catalyst used in Ford and Chrysler products is the monolithic (one-piece) type which cannot be removed from the converter for replacement.

If the catalyst fails, it will be necessary to replace the entire converter assembly with a new one. To do so, proceed as follows:

Caution Allow the converter assembly to cool completely before attempting to service it; catalyst temperatures can reach 1500°-1600°F.

1. If a grass shield is used, remove the bolts which secure it and lower the shield from underneath the vehicle.
2. Unbolt the converter assembly at the mounting flanges, just as you would a normal exhaust pipe from the manifold.

NOTE: Support the exhaust pipe while the converter is removed.

3. Replace the old converter with a new unit which is the exact same size, part number, and type (or its *exact* equivalent) as was originally installed.
4. Remove the plastic plugs from the ends of the converter (if used) and install it in the reverse order of removal, being sure to use new gaskets to ensure a leak-free fit.
5. Install the grass shields.

Speed switch for Chrysler catalyst protection system

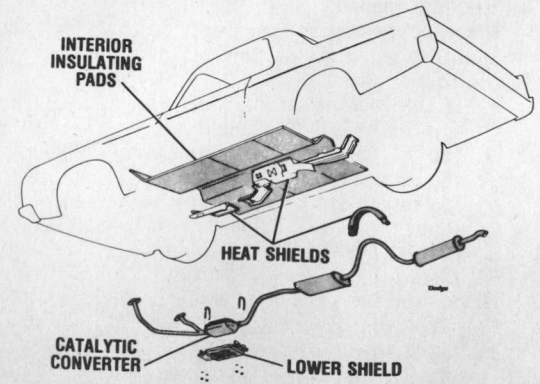
Typical Chrysler catalytic converter mounting   (© Chrysler Corp)

INTERIOR INSULATING PADS

HEAT SHIELDS

CATALYTIC CONVERTER — LOWER SHIELD

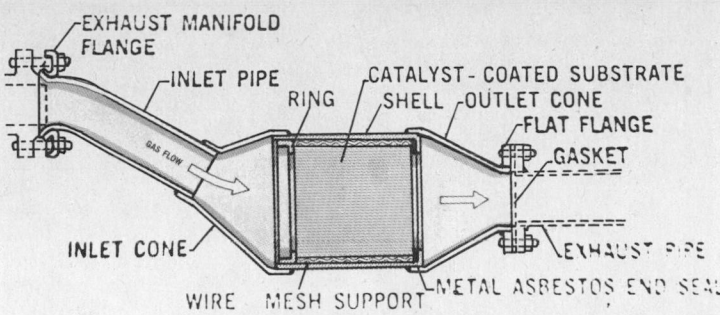

Ford monolithic converter—cutaway view
(© Ford Motor Co)

This special vibrator is used in filling the
GM catalytic converter
(© Cadillac Div, G.M. Corp)

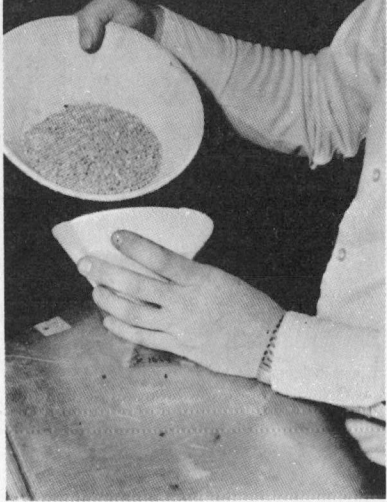

Filling the GM converter
(© Cadillac Div, G.M. Corp)

GM and AMC

General Motors and American Motors cars use pellets in their converters, which may be replaced without replacing the whole catalytic converter assembly.

To replace the pellets, proceed as follows:

Caution Allow the converter assembly to cool completely before attempting to service it; catalyst temperatures can reach 1500°F.

1. Using a ¾ in. allen wrench, loosen, but do not remove the converter fill plug.
2. Remove the four nuts and bolts at each converter flange. Lower the converter being careful to note the position of, and saving any gaskets used.
3. Loosely install the upper rear flange nuts and bolts, to secure the exhaust system to the hanger while the converter is removed.
4. Place the converter on the workbench and remove the fill plug. Drain the old pellets into a container and discard them.
5. Inspect the converter housing for signs of damage. Replace the assembly, if necessary.

6. Clamp the special vibrator to the converter flange on the opposite end from the fill plug, with the mounting nuts and bolts.
7. Place the converter on a 30° angle with the fill plug end up. Fill the converter with new catalyst pellets through a funnel.
8. When it appears that the converter is full, connect the air supply to the vibrator and continue to add pellets in small amounts. Pack the pellets in tightly with your fingers.
9. Once the pellets are flush with the fill plug, remove the air supply from the vibrator. Coat the fill plug with an anti-seize compound and tighten it 50 ft lbs (GM) or 40 ft lbs (AMC).
10. Remove the vibrator.
11. Install the converter assembly on the car in the reverse order of removal, being sure to use all necessary gaskets. Tighten the flange nuts and bolts.

NOTE: GM makes a kit to replace the bottom converter cover should it become torn or damaged.

Vacuum-Operated Heat Risers

These valves are similar to the spring-operated heat risers used on American cars for many years. The old valve was operated by a bimetal spring. The type of valve is operated by a vacuum motor (diaphragm) which, in turn, is controlled by a vacuum valve that is temperature-sensitive. In some applications the vacuum is controlled by a solenoid that is hooked up to a temperature switch.

1975 and later Ford Vacuum Exhaust Heat Valve

Valve Test

1. With the engine off, look at the rod which connects the diaphragm with the valve lever. The

Emptying the pellets from a GM catalytic converter
(© Cadillac Div, G.M. Corp)

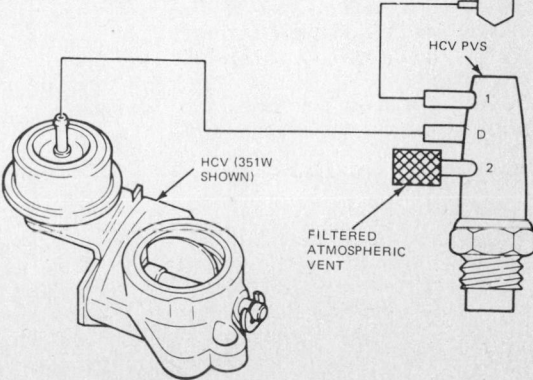

1975-76 Ford vacuum operated heat riser
(© Ford Motor Co.)

U187

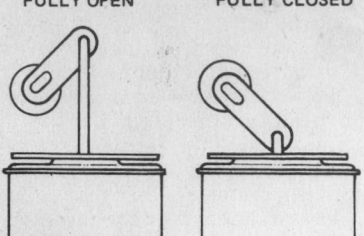

FULLY OPEN   **FULLY CLOSED**

Ford vacuum operated heat riser rod operation
(© Ford Motor Co.)

rod should be fully extended (no vacuum applied).

2. Connect a hand-operated vacuum pump with a gauge to the diaphragm unit.
3. Apply vacuum. Check the results against the chart below:

Engine	Valve starts to close (in. Hg)	Valve Closed (in. Hg)
302, 351W	1-3	6 or less
351M, 400	3-6	10 or less

4. If the valve rod doesn't extend fully when no vacuum is applied and doesn't close fully when vacuum is applied, tap the valve and apply heat riser lubricant to free it.
5. Apply 15-20 in. Hg vacuum to the diaphragm and trap it. If the vacuum leaks down more 2 in. Hg in one minute, replace the valve assembly.

Coolant Temperature Operated Vacuum Valve

1. Start with the engine cold.
2. Remove the vacuum line from the top nipple. Connect a hand-operated vacuum pump to the nipple.
3. Plug the middle nipple. Apply vacuum. The valve should hold the vacuum without leaking down.
4. With the engine at normal operating temperature, leave the middle nipple open and apply vacuum. The valve should hold vacuum and not leak down.
5. With the engine hot, remove the vacuum pump and connect the hose. Attach a hose to the middle nipple and blow through it. Air should come out through the valve vent.
6. If the valve doesn't work as outlined, replace it with a new one.

GM Early Fuel Evaporation (EFE) System

Starting in 1975, all 250-6, all 231-V6, and most GM V8 engines use a vacuum-operated heat riser valve. GM calls this system "Early Fuel Evaporation" or "EFE" for short.

With the exception of the 250-6 and the 1975 Chevrolet 454-V8, all engines use a coolant temperature op-

EFE vacuum solenoid
(© Pontiac Div., GM Corp.)

erated vacuum valve (EFE/TVV) to control vacuum to the EFE valve vacuum motor. The 250-6 and 1975 454-V8 use an oil temperature switch and vacuum solenoid, instead.

EFE Valve Test—All Engines

1. Inspect the manifold heat riser valve and linkage for damage and binding. Check for plugged, cracked, or misrouted vacuum hoses.
2. Connect external vacuum source and vacuum gauge to the EFE valve vacuum motor, after disconnecting the vacuum hose from from it.
3. Apply at least 10 in. Hg vacuum to the motor. The valve should move freely. The motor should hold the plunger in the retracted position for 1 minute without the aplication of additonal vacuum.
4. If the vacuum motor leaks down in less the 1 minute or fails to operate the EFE valve (linkage not binding), replace it.
5. If the valve or linkage binds, use heat riser lubricant on it. If the valve can't be freed by tapping it loose and lubricating it, replace the assembly.

EFE Vacuum Solenoid Test— 250-6 and Chevrolet 454-V8

1. Disconnect the engine harness wiring plug from the solenoid. Use a short jumper wire to connect one of the solenoid terminals to ground. Run a hot wire from the positive battery terminal to the other terminal.
2. The solenoid should click when the wire is connected. If not, the solenoid is defective.
3. To check for correct vacuum switching of the solenoid, con-

nect an engine manifold vacuum hose to the nozzle that points straight down in the opposite direction from the wire terminals. Connect a vacuum gauge to the nozzle that points out to the side of he solenoid.

4. With the engine running, energize the solenoid as described above. Full manifold vacuum should appear on the gauge.
5. De-energize the solenoid and the vacuum should drop to zero. If not, the solenoid is defective.
6. The manifold vacuum hose must connect to the bottom end nozzle, not to the side nozzle. If the hoses are hooked up backwards, the EFE valve may stay closed after the engine warms up.
7. Repairs are limited to replacement. Test the new solenoid to be sure it sends vacuum to the EFE actuator when energized. If it allows vacuum through when de-energized, it's the wrong solenoid.

Oil Temperature Switch Test— 250-6 and 1975 Chevrolet 454-V8

1. Disconnect the oil temperature switch harness wiring.
2. Connect a self-powered test light between the switch terminal and ground.
3. If the engine is cold (below 150 —250-6 or 100°F—454-V8), the test light should come on.
4. Run the engine. When it reaches normal operating temperature, the light should go out.
5. Replace the switch if it doesn't work as outlined.

EFE Coolant Temperature Operated Vacuum Valve Tests

5-Nozzle Valve

This valve may be identified by the nozzle on top and four nozzles down the side. A vent is also located on the other side.

1. Remove the vacuum hose from the top (vertical) nozzle and cap it.
2. Connect a hand-operated vacuum pump to the top nozzle on the side and a vacuum gauge to the next lower nozzle.
3. On a cold engine vacuum should register on the gauge.
4. Allow the engine to warm up to above 120°F.
5. The gauge should register zero. The valve should hold vacuum and not leak down.
6. Remove the vacuum gauge from the lower nozzle and blow through it. Air should come out of the vent.
7. Replace the valve if it doesn't work as outlined.

4-Nozzle Valve

This valve may be identified by the one vertical nozzle on top and the three nozzles down the side. There is also a vent on the side opposite the three nozzles.

1. Remove the hose from the top (vertical) nozzle. Connect a hand-operated vacuum pump to it.
2. Connect a vacuum gauge to the top nozzle on the side (marked "HV").
3. On a warm engine, about 120°F, the vertical nozzle should be closed and you should be able to get a reading on the hand pump gauge. The gauge connected to the "HV" nozzle should read zero.
4. Remove the vacuum gauge and blow through the "HV" nozzle; air should come out the vent.
5. Relieve the cooling system pressure and remove the coolant temperature operated vacuum valve.
6. Cool the valve in an ice bath.

Below 120°F, you should get a reading on the gauge attached to the HV nozzle. The vacuum should not leak down.

7. Replace the valve if it doesn't work as outlined.

2-Nozzle Valve

This valve may be identified by the two nozzles on the one side with a vent on the opposite side.

1. Disconnect the vacuum hose from the top nozzle. Connect a hand-operated vacuum pump to the nozzle.
2. Connect a vacuum gauge to the lower nozzle.
3. On a cold engine the vacuum gauge on the lower nozzle should register when the vacuum is applied to the upper nozzle. The vent should be closed.
4. Warm the engine up, so that the coolant is above one of the following:

   Chevrolet V8—180°F
   Cadillac V8—150°F
   All other V8—120°

5. Apply vacuum to the uper nozzle. The gauge on the lower nozzle should register zero.
6. Remove the vacuum gauge from the lower nozzle. Blow through the nozzle, air should come out the vent.
7. Replace the valve if it doesn't work as outlined.

EFE Check Valve Test

Some engines have a check valve in the EFE vacuum line.

1. Remove the vacuum hose from the tappered end of the check valve.
2. Connect a hand-operated vacuum pump with gauge to the check valve. Apply vacuum and trap it.
3. The vacuum should not leak down. Replace the check valve if vacuum leaks down more than 0.5 in. Hg. in one minute.

Roll-Over Spill Protection

Federal Law requires that all 1976 and later cars sold in the U.S. be equipped with protection against fuel spilling or continuing to be fed to the engine in the event of a roll-over. This means that a check valve must be installed in the fuel system of all new cars to contain any fuel that might escape in a roll-over type accident. These check valves are one way valves, permitting the normal flow of fuel, but if the car should turn over, the valve cuts off the flow of fuel. Chrysler and GM mount these check valves in the fuel filter. When replacing the filter, do not use a filter for an earlier car; it will not contain the check valve. Ford and AMC mount the valve in the fuel pump.

Chrysler's Lean Burn System

This system, new for 1976, is based on the principle that lower NO$_x$ emissions would occur if the air fuel ratio inside the cylinder area was raised from its current point (15.5:1) to a much leaner point (18:1). In order to make the engine workable, a solution to the problems of carburetion and timing had to be found, since a lean running engine is not the most efficient in terms of driveability. Chrysler adapted a conventional Thermo-Quad carburetor to handle the added air coming in, but the real advance of the system is the Spark Control Computer mounted on the air cleaner. Since a lean burning engine demands precise ignition timing, additional spark control was needed for the distributor. The computer supplies this control by providing an infinitely variable advance curve. Input data is fed instantaneously to the computer by a series of seven sensors located in the engine compartment which monitor timing, water temperature, air temperature, throttle position, idle/off-idle operation, and intake manifold vacuum. The program schedule module of the spark control computer receives the information from the sensors, processes it, and then directs the ignition control module to advance or retard the timing as necessary. This whole process is going on continuously as the engine is running, taking only a thousandth of a second to complete a circuit from sensor to distributor. The components of the system are as follows: Modified Thermo-Quad carburetor; Spark Control Computer, consisting of two interacting modules, the Program Schedule Module which is responsible for translating input data, and the Ignition Control Module which transmits data to the distributor to advance or retard the timing. Sensors:

Start pick-up sensor, located inside the distributor, supplies a signal to the computer providing a fixed timing

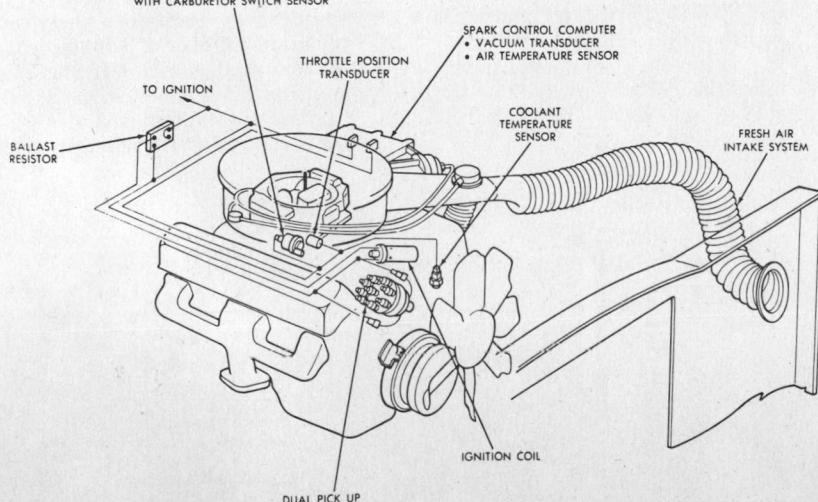

Components of the Chrysler Lean Burn System (© Chrysler Corp.)

point that is only used for starting the car. It also has a back-up function of taking over engine timing in case the run pick-up fails. Since the timing in this pick-up is fixed at one point, the car will be able to run but not very well. The run pick-up sensor, also located in the distributor, provides timing data to the computer once the engine is running. It also monitors engine speed, and helps the computer decide when the piston is reaching the top of its compression stroke.

Coolant Temperature Sensor, located on the water pump housng, informs the computer when the coolant temperature is below 150°. Air Temperature Sensor, inside the computer itself, monitors the temperature of the air coming in the air cleaner.

Throttle Position Transducer, located on the carburetor, monitors the position and rate of change of the throttle plates. When the throttle plates start to open and as they continue to open toward full throttle, more and more spark advance is called for by the computer. If the throttle plates are opened quickly, even more spark advance is given for about one second. The amount of maximum advance is determined by the temperature of the air coming into the air cleaner. Less advance under acceleration will be given if the air entering the air cleaner is hot, while more advance will be given if the air is cold.

Carburetor Switch Sensor, located on the end of the idle stop solenoid, tells the computer if the engine is at idle or off-idle.

Vacuum Transducer, located on the computer, monitors the amount of intake manifold vacuum; the more vacuum, the more spark advance to the distributor. In order to obtain this spark advance in the distributor, the Carburetor switch sensor has to remain open for a specified amount of time, during which time the advance will slowly build up to the amount indicated as necessary by the vacuum transducer. If the carburetor switch should close during that time, the advance to the distributor will be cancelled. From here the computer will start with an advance countdown if the carburetor switch is reopened with a certain amount of time. The advance will continue from a point decided by the computer. If the switch is reopened after the computer has counted down to "no advance," the vacuum advance process must start over again.

Operation

When you turn the ignition key on, the start pick-up sends its signal to the computer, which relays back information for more spark advance during cranking. As soon as the engine starts, the run pick-up takes

over, and receives more advance for about one minute. This advance is slowly eliminated during the one minute warm up period. While the engine is cold, (coolant temperature below 150° as monitored by the coolant temperature sensor), no more advance will be given to the distributor until it reaches normal operating temperature. At this point, normal operation of the system will begin.

In normal operation, the basic timing information is related by the run pick-up to the computer along with input signals from all the other sensors. From this data, the computer determines the maximum allowable advance or retard to be sent to the distributor for any situation.

If either the run pick-up or the computer should fail, the back up system of the start pick-up takes over. This supplies a fixed timing signal to the distributor which allows the car to be driven until it can be repaired. In this mode, very poor fuel economy and performance will be experienced. If the start pick-up or the ignition control module section of the computer should fail, the car will not start or run.

Equipment

Some of the procedures in this section refer to an adjustable timing light. This is also known as a spark advance tester, i.e., a device that will measure how much spark advance is present going from one point, a base figure, to another. Since precise timing is very important to the Lean Burn System, do not attempt to perform any of the tests calling for an adjustable timing light without one. In places where a regular timing light can be used, it will be noted in the text.

Troubleshooting

1. Remove the coil wire and hold it cautiously about 1/4 in. away from an engine ground, then have someone crank the engine while you check for spark.
2. If you have a good spark, slowly move the coil wire away from the engine and check for arcing at the coil while cranking.

3. If you have good spark and it is not arcing at the coil, check the rest of the parts of the ignition system. Check the Engine Trouble Shooting Section of this book.

Engine Not Running—Will Not Start

(Start Pick-Up Tests)

1. Check the battery specific gravity; it must be at least 1.220 to deliver the necessary voltage to fire the plugs.
2. Remove the terminal connector from the coolant switch, and put a piece of paper or plastic between the curb idle adjusting screw and the carburetor switch. This is unnecessary if the screw and switch are not touching.
3. Connect the negative lead of a voltmeter to a good engine ground, turn the ignition switch to the "run" position and measure the voltage at the carburetor switch terminal. If you receive a reading of more than five volts, go on to Step 7; if not, proceed to the next step.
4. Turn the ignition switch "off" and disconnect the double terminal connector from the bottom of the Spark Control Computer. Turn the ignition switch back to the "run" position and measure the voltage at the terminal number 4; if the voltage is not within 1 volt of the voltage you received in Step 3, check the wiring between terminal 3 and the ignition switch. If the voltage is correct, go on to the next step.
5. Turn the ignition switch "off" and disconnect the single connector from the bottom of the Spark Control Computer. Using an ohmmeter, check for continuity between terminal 11 and the carburetor switch terminal. There should be continuity present. If not, check the wiring.
6. Check for continuity between terminal number 2 (double connector(and ground. If there is continuity, replace the Spark Control Computer; if not check the wiring, and if the engine still

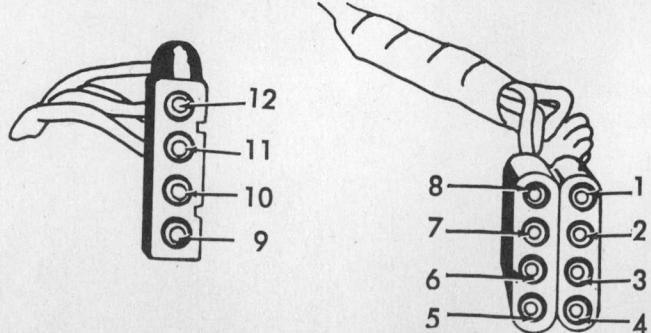

Single and dual connectors with numbered terminals, at the bottom of the Spark Control Computer (© Chrysler Corp.)

will not start, proceed to the next step.

7. Turn the ignition switch to the run position and check for voltage at terminals 7 and 8 of the double connector. If you received voltage within 1 volt of that recorded in Step 3, proceed to the next step. If you did not on terminal 7, check the wiring between it and the ignition switch and check the 5 ohm side of the ballast resistor. If you did not on terminal 8, check the wiring, and the primary windings of the coil and the $\frac{1}{2}$ ohm side of the ballast resistor.

8. Turn the ignition switch "off" and with an ohmmeter, measure resistance between terminals 5 and 6 of the dual connector. If you do not receive a reading of 150-900 ohms disconnect the start pick-up leads at the distributor and measure the resistance going into the distributor. If you get a reading of 150-900 ohms here, the wiring between terminals 5 and 6 and the distributor is faulty. If you still do not get a reading between 150-900 ohms, replace the start pickup. If you received the proper reading when you initially checked terminals 5 and 6, proceed to the next step.

9. Connect one lead of an ohmmeter to a good engine ground and with the other lead, check the continuity of both start pick-up leads going into the distributor. If there is not continuity, go on to the next step. If you do get a reading, replace the start pick-up.

10. Remove the distributor cap and check the air gap of the start pick-up coil. Adjust if necessary and proceed to the next step.

11. Replace the distributor cap, and start the engine. If it still will not start, replace the Spark Control Computer. If the engine still does not start, put the old one back and retrace your steps, pay-

ing close attention to any wiring which may be shorted.

Engine Running Badly

(Run Pick-Up Tests)

1. Start the engine and let it run for a couple of minutes. Disconnect the start pick-up lead. If the engine still runs, leave this test and go on to the Start Timer Advance Test. If the engine stops, proceed to step 2.

2. Reconnect the start pick-up, turn the ignition switch off and disconnect the dual connector from the bottom of the spark control computer.

3. Using an ohmmeter, measure the resistance between terminals 3 and 5 of the dual connector. Resistance should be 150-900 ohms. If it is, proceed to the next step. If not, disconnect the run pick-up leads from the distributor. Measure the resistance going into the distributor. If the resistance is now between 150-900 ohms, there is bad wiring between terminals 3 and 5 of the double connector plug and the distributor connector terminal. If the resistance is still not within 150-900 ohms, replace the run pick-up and try to start the engine. If the engine still fails to start, go on to step 4.

4. Disconnect the run pick-up coil from the distributor. Use an ohmmeter to check for continuity at each of the leads going into the distributor. If there is continuity shown, replace the pick-up coil and repeat Step 1. If you do not get a reading of continuity, proceed to the next step.

5. Remove the distributor cap, check the gap of the run pick-up and adjust it if necessary.

6. Reinstall the distributor cap, check the wiring and try to start the car. If it does not start, replace the Spark Control Computer and try again. If it still

does not start repeat the test paying close attention to all wiring connections.

Start Timer Advance Test

1. Hook up an *adjustable* timing light to the engine.

2. Have an assistant start the engine, place his foot firmly on the brake, then open and close the throttle and place the transmission in Drive.

3. Locate the timing signal immediately after the transmission is put in drive. The meter on the timing light should show about 5-9° advance. This advance should slowly decrease to the basic timing signal after about one minute. If it did not, increase the 5-9°, or return after one minute, replace the Spark Control Computer. If it did operate properly, proceed to the next test.

Throttle Advance Test

Before performing this test, the throttle position transducer must be adjusted. The adjustments are as follows:

1. The air temperature sensor inside the Spark Control Computer must be cool (below 135°). If the engine is at operating temperature, either turn it off and let it cool down or remove the top of the air cleaner and inject a spray coolant into the computer over the air temperature sensor for about 15 seconds. If steps 2-5 take longer than 3-4 minutes, recool the sensor.

2. Start the engine and wait about 90 seconds, then connect a jumper wire between the carburetor switch terminal and a ground.

3. Disconnect the electrical connector from the transducer and check the timing, adjusting if necessary. Reconnect the electrical connector to the transducer and recheck the timing.

4. If the timing is more advanced than specified on the tune-up decal, loosen the transducer lock

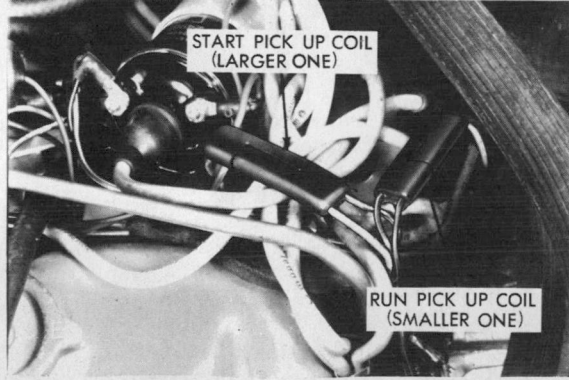

Distributor pick-up connector identification
(© Chrysler Corp.)

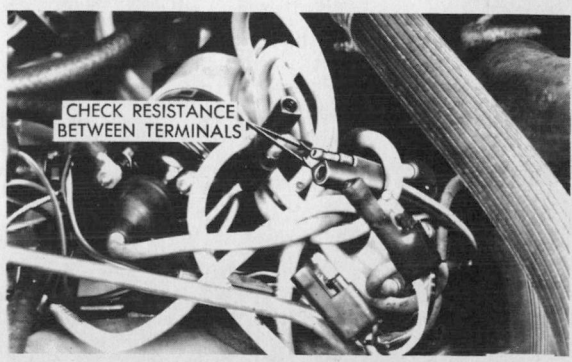

Checking the 'run' pick-up at the distributor leads
(© Chrysler Corp.)

nut and turn the transducer clockwise until it comes within limits, then turn it an additional ½ turn clockwise and tighten the locknut.

5. If the timing is at the specified limits, loosen the locknut and turn the transducer counterclockwise until the timing just begins to advance. At that point, turn the transducer ½ turn clockwise and tighten the locknut. After this step you are ready to begin the throttle advance test.

6. Turn the ignition switch off and disconnect the single connector from the bottom of the Spark Control Computer.

7. With an ohmmeter, measure the resistance between terminals 9 and 10 of the single connector. The measured resistance should be between 50-90 ohms. If it is, go on to the next step. If not, remove the connector from the throttle position transducer and measure the resistance at the transducer terminals. If you now get a reading of 50-90 ohms, check the wiring between the computer terminal and the transducer terminal. If you do not get the 50-90 reading, replace the transducer and proceed to the next step.

8. Reconnect the wiring and turn the switch to the run position without starting the engine. Hook up a voltmeter, negative lead to an engine ground, and touch the positive lead to one terminal of the transducer while opening and closing the throttle all the way. Do the same thing to the other terminal of the transducer. Both terminals should show a 2 volt change when opening and closing the throttle. If not proceed to the next step.

9. Position the throttle linkage on the fast idle cam and ground the carb switch with a jumper wire. Disconnect the wiring connector from the transducer and connect it to a transducer that you know is good.

10. Move the core of the transducer all the way in, start the engine, wait about 90 seconds and then move the core out about an inch.

11. Adjust the timing light so that it registers the basic timing signal. The timing light should show the additional amount of advance as given in the specifications table in this section. If it is within the specifications, move the core back into the transducer, and the timing should go back to the original position. If the timing did advance and return, go on to the next step. If it did not advance and/or return, replace the Spark Control Computer and try this test over again. If it still fails, replace the transducer.

12. Reset the timing light meter, and have an assistant move the transducer core in and out 5-6 times quickly. The timing should advance 7-12° for about a second and then return to the base figure. If it did not, replace the Spark Control Computer; if you did not get the 2 volt change in reading in step 8, replace the transducer.

13. Remove the test transducer (from step 9) and reconnect all wiring.

Transducer Advance Specifications

Core Moved out 1″	7-12° @ 75°F
	4-7° @ 104°F
Moved 5-6 Times	7-12°F
	(one second duration each time)

Vacuum Advance Test (Vacuum Transducer)

1. Hook up an adjustable timing light.

2. Turn the ignition switch to the run position, but do not start the engine. Disconnect the idle stop solenoid wire and the wiring connector from the coolant switch. Push the solenoid plunger in all the way, and while holding the throttle linkage open, reconnect the solenoid wire. The solenoid plunger should pop out when the throttle linkage is released, it should also hold the linkage in place. If it does not, replace the idle stop solenoid.

3. Start the engine and let it warm up; make sure the transmission is in Neutral and the parking brake is on.

4. Place a small piece of plastic or paper between the carburetor switch and the curb idle adjusting screw; if the screw is not touching the switch make sure the fast idle cam is not on or binding; the linkage is not binding, or the throttle stop screw is not overadjusted. Adjust the timing light for the basic timing figure. The meter of the timing light should show 2-5° of advance with a minimum of 16 in. of vacuum at the vacuum transducer (checked with a vacuum gauge). If this advance is not present, replace the Spark Control Computer and try the test again. If the advance is present, let the engine run for about 6-9 minutes then go on to the next step.

5. After the 6-9 minute waiting period, adjust the timing light so that it registers the basic timing figure. The timing light meter should now register 32-35° of additional engine advance. If the advance is not shown, replace the Spark Control Computer and repeat the test; if it is shown, proceed to step 6.

6. Remove the insulator (paper or plastic) that was installed in step 4; the timing should return to its base setting. If it does not, make sure the curb idle adjusting screw is not touching the carburetor switch. If that is alright, turn the engine off and check the wire between terminal 11 of the single connector (from the bottom of tht Spark Control Computer), and the carburetor switch terminal for a bad connection. If it turns out alright, and the timing still will not return to its base setting, replace the Spark Control Computer.

Coolant Switch Test

1. Connect one lead of the ohmmeter to a good engine ground, the other to the black wire with a tracer in it. Disregard the orange wire if there is one on the switch.

2. If the engine is cold (below 150°) there should be continuity present in the switch. With the thermostat open, and the engine warmed up, there should be no continuity. If either of the conditions in this step are not met, replace the switch.

Lean Burn Timing

This procedure is to set the basic timing as shown on the tune-up sticker in the engine compartment.

1. Connect a jumper wire between the carburetor switch terminal and the ground. Connect a standard timing light to the number 1 cylinder.

2. Block the wheels and set the parking brake. If the car has an automatic release type parking brake, remove and plug the vacuum line which controls it from the fitting on the rear of the engine.

3. Start and warm the engine up; raise engine speed above 1500 RPM for a second, then drop the speed and let it idle for a minute or two.

4. With the engine idling at the speed specified on the sticker and the transmission in Drive, adjust the timing to the figure given on the tune-up decal.

Idle Speed and Mixture

1. Follow the first three steps under the Lean Burn Timing section, then insert an exhaust gas analyzer into the tailpipe.

2. Place the transmission in Drive with the air conditioning and headlights off. Adjust the idle speed to that shown on the tune-up sticker by turning the idle speed solenoid screw.

3. Adjust the carbon monoxide level to 0.1% with the mixture screws while trying to keep hydrocarbons to a minimum and the idle speed to specification.

4. Place the transmission in Neutral; disconnect the wire at the idle stop solenoid and adjust the curb idle speed screw to obtain 650 RPM. Reconnect the wire.

5. Remove the air cleaner cover and lift and support the air cleaner assembly high enough to gain access to the fast idle adjustment screw.

6. Place the fast idle speed screw on the highest step of the cam and adjust the fast idle speed to that shown on the tune-up sticker.

7. Drop the idle back down to the curb idle position and turn the ignition switch off. Reconnect any hoses or electrical connections taken off in the procedure.

8. If the procedure has to be performed a second time, make sure you start from the beginning, or the readings will be inaccurate.

Removal and Overhaul

None of the components of the Lean Burn System (except the carburetor) may be taken apart and repaired. When a part is known to be bad, it should be replaced.

The Spark Control Computer is held on by mounting screws inside the air cleaner. To remove the Throttle Position Transducer, loosen the locknut and unscrew it from the mounting bracket, then unsnap the core from the carburetor linkage.

Pick-up Gaps

Start Pick-up	(set to)	0.008
	(check at)	0.010
Run Pick-up	(set to)	0.012
	(check at)	0.014

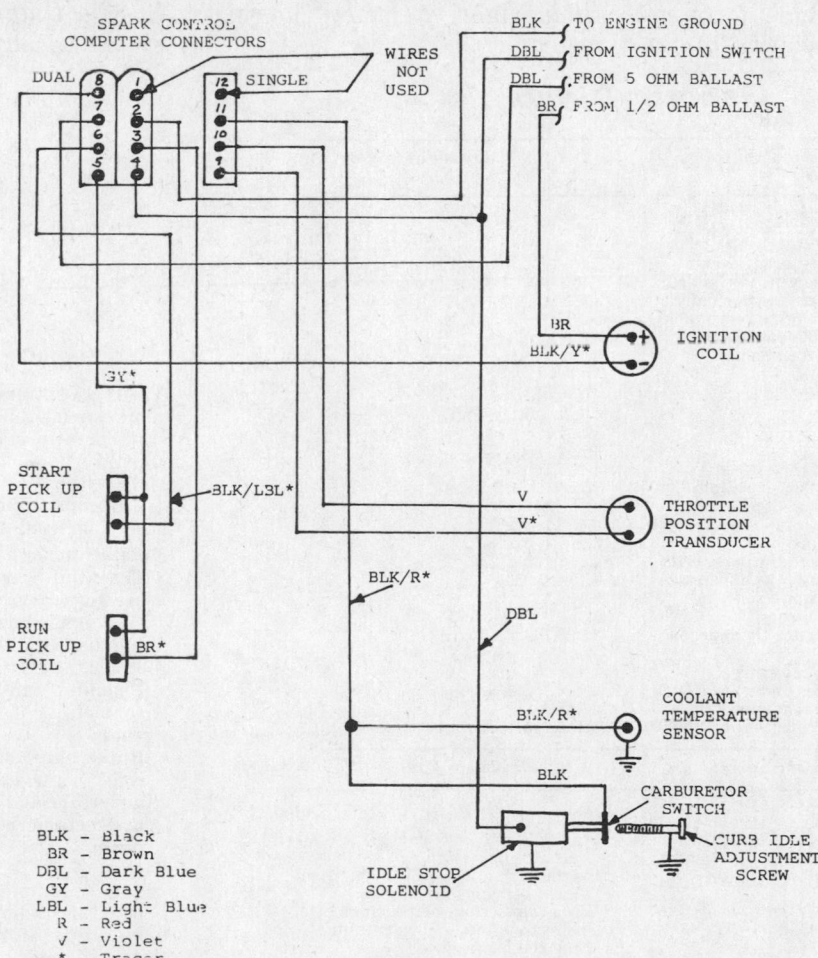

Lean Burn System wiring diagram
(© Chrysler Corp.)

Engine Troubleshooting

The following section is designed to aid in the rapid diagnosis of engine problems. The systematic format is used to diagnose problems ranging from engine starting difficulties to the need for engine overhaul. It is assumed that the user is equipped with basic hand tools and test equipment (tach-dwell meter, timing light, voltmeter, and ohmmeter).

Troubleshooting is divided into two sections. The first, *General Diagnosis*, is used to locate the problem area. In the second, *Specific Diagnosis*, the problem is systematically evaluated.

General Diagnosis

PROBLEM: Symptom	Begin diagnosis at Section Two, Number ——
Engine won't start:	
Starter doesn't turn	1.1, 2.1
Starter turns, engine doesn't	2.1
Starter turns engine very slowly	1.1, 2.4
Starter turns engine normally	3.1, 4.1
Starter turns engine very quickly	6.1
Engine fires intermittently	4.1
Engine fires consistently	5.1, 6.1
Engine runs poorly:	
Hard starting	3.1, 4.1, 5.1, 8.1
Rough idle	4.1, 5.1, 8.1
Stalling	3.1, 4.1, 5.1, 8.1
Engine dies at high speeds	4.1, 5.1
Hesitation (on acceleration from standing stop)	5.1, 8.1
Poor pickup	4.1, 5.1, 8.1
Lack of power	3.1, 4.1, 5.1, 8.1
Backfire through the carburetor	4.1, 8.1, 9.1
Backfire through the exhaust	4.1, 8.1, 9.1
Blue exhaust gases	6.1, 7.1
Black exhaust gases	5.1
Running on (after the ignition is shut off)	3.1, 8.1
Susceptible to moisture	4.1
Engine misfires under load	4.1, 7.1, 8.4, 9.1
Engine misfires at speed	4.1, 8.4
Engine misfires at idle	3.1, 4.1, 5.1, 7.1, 8.4

PROBLEM: Symptom	Probable Cause
Engine noises: ①	
Metallic grind while starting	Starter drive not engaging completely
Constant grind or rumble	*Starter drive not releasing, worn main bearings
Constant knock	Worn connecting rod bearings
Knock under load	Fuel octane too low, worn connecting rod bearings
Double knock	Loose piston pin
Metallic tap	*Collapsed or sticky valve lifter, excessive valve clearance, excessive end play in a rotating shaft
Scrape	*Fan belt contacting a stationary surface
Tick while starting	S.U. electric fuel pump (normal), starter brushes
Constant tick	*Generator brushes, shreaded fan belt
Squeal	*Improperly tensioned fan belt
Hiss or roar	*Steam escaping through a leak in the cooling system or the radiator overflow vent
Whistle	*Vacuum leak
Wheeze	Loose or cracked spark plug

①—It is extremely difficult to evaluate vehicle noises. While the above are general definitions of engine noises, those starred (*) should be considered as possibly originating elsewhere in the car. To aid diagnosis, the following list considers other potential sources of these sounds.

Metallic grind:
 Throwout bearing; transmission gears, bearings, or synchronizers; differential bearings, gears; something metallic in contact with brake drum or disc.

Metallic tap:
 U-joints; fan-to-radiator (or shroud) contact.

Scrape:
 Brake shoe or pad dragging; tire to body contact; suspension contacting undercarriage or exhaust; something non-metallic contacting brake shoe or drum.

Tick:
 Transmission gears; differential gears; lack of radio suppression; resonant vibration of body panels; windshield wiper motor or transmission; heater motor and blower.

Squeal:
 Brake shoe or pad not fully releasing; tires (excessive wear, uneven wear, improper inflation); front or rear wheel alignment (most commonly due to improper toe-in).

Hiss or whistle:
 Wind leaks (body or window); heater motor and blower fan.

Roar:
 Wheel bearings; wind leaks (body and window).

Specific Diagnosis

This section is arranged so that following each test, instructions are given to proceed to another, until a problem is diagnosed.

INDEX

Group		Topic
1	*	Battery
2	*	Cranking system
3	*	Primary electrical system
4	*	Secondary electrical system
5	*	Fuel system
6	*	Engine compression
7	**	Engine vacuum
8	**	Secondary electrical system
9	**	Valve train
10	**	Exhaust system
11	**	Cooling system
12	**	Engine lubrication

*—The engine need not be running.
**—The engine must be running.

SAMPLE SECTION

Test and Procedure	Results and Indications	Proceed to
4.1—Check for spark: Hold each spark plug wire approximately ¼" from ground with gloves or a heavy, dry rag. Crank the engine and observe the spark.	If no spark is evident:	4.2
	If spark is good in some cases:	4.3
	If spark is good in all cases:	4.6

DIAGNOSIS

1.1—Inspect the battery visually for case condition (corrosion, cracks) and water level.	If case is cracked, replace battery:	1.4
	If the case is intact, remove corrosion with a solution of baking soda and water (CAUTION: *do not get the solution into the battery*), and fill with water:	1.2

1.2—Check the battery cable connections: Insert a screwdriver between the battery post and the cable clamp. Turn the headlights on high beam, and observe them as the screwdriver is gently twisted to ensure good metal to metal contact.	If the lights brighten, remove and clean the clamp and post; coat the post with petroleum jelly, install and tighten the clamp:	1.4
	If no improvement is noted:	1.3

Testing battery cable connections using a screwdriver

1.3—Test the state of charge of the battery using an individual cell tester or hydrometer.

Spec. Grav. Reading	Charged Condition
1.260-1.280	Fully Charged
1.230-1.250	Three Quarter Charged
1.200-1.220	One Half Charged
1.170-1.190	One Quarter Charged
1.140-1.160	Just About Flat
1.110-1.130	All The Way Down

State of battery charge

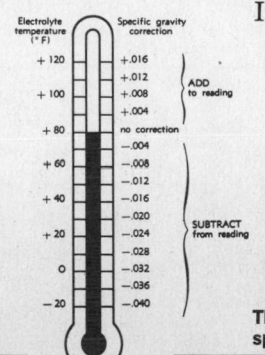

If indicated, charge the battery. NOTE: *If no obvious reason exists for the low state of charge (i.e., battery age, prolonged storage), the charging system should be tested:*   1.4

The effect of temperature on the specific gravity of battery electrolyte

Test and Procedure	Results and Indications	Proceed to
1.4—Visually inspect battery cables for cracking, bad connection to ground, or bad connection to starter.	If necessary, tighten connections or replace the cables:	2.1

Tests in Group 2 are performed with coil high tension lead disconnected to prevent accidental starting.

Test and Procedure	Results and Indications	Proceed to
2.1—Test the starter motor and solenoid: Connect a jumper from the battery post of the solenoid (or relay) to the ignition switch post of the solenoid (or relay).	If starter turns the engine normally:	2.2
	If the starter buzzes, or turns the engine very slowly:	2.4
	If no response, replace the solenoid (or relay).	3.1
	If the starter turns, but the engine doesn't, ensure that the flywheel ring gear is intact. If the gear is undamaged, replace the starter drive.	3.1
2.2—Determine whether ignition override switches are functioning properly (clutch start switch, neutral safety switch), by connecting a jumper across the switch(es), and turning the ignition switch to "start".	If starter operates, adjust or replace switch:	3.1
	If the starter doesn't operate:	2.3
2.3—Check the ignition switch "start" position: Connect a 12V test lamp between the starter post of the solenoid (or relay) and ground. Turn the ignition switch to the "start" position, and jiggle the key.	If the lamp doesn't light when the switch is turned, check the ignition switch for loose connections, cracked insulation, or broken wires. Repair or replace as necessary:	3.1
	If the lamp flickers when the key is jiggled, replace the ignition switch.	3.3

Checking the ignition switch "start" position

Test and Procedure	Results and Indications	Proceed to
2.4—Remove and bench test the starter, according to specifications in the car section.	If the starter does not meet specifications, repair or replace as needed:	3.1
	If the starter is operating properly:	2.5
2.5—Determine whether the engine can turn freely: Remove the spark plugs, and check for water in the cylinders. Check for water on the dipstick, or oil in the radiator. Attempt to turn the engine using an 18″ flex drive and socket on the crankshaft pulley nut or bolt.	If the engine will turn freely only with the spark plugs out, and hydrostatic lock (water in the cylinders) is ruled out, check valve timing:	9.2
	If engine will not turn freely, and it is known that the clutch and transmission are free, the engine must be disassembled for further evaluation:	Next Chapter

Tests and Procedures	*Results and Indications*	*Proceed to*
3.1—Check the ignition switch "on" position: Connect a jumper wire between the distributor side of the coil and ground, and a 12V test lamp between the switch side of the coil and ground. Remove the high tension lead from the coil. Turn the ignition switch on and jiggle the key.	If the lamp lights:	3.2
	If the lamp flickers when the key is jiggled, replace the ignition switch:	3.3
	If the lamp doesn't light, check for loose or open connections. If none are found, remove the ignition switch and check for continuity. If the switch is faulty, replace it:	3.3

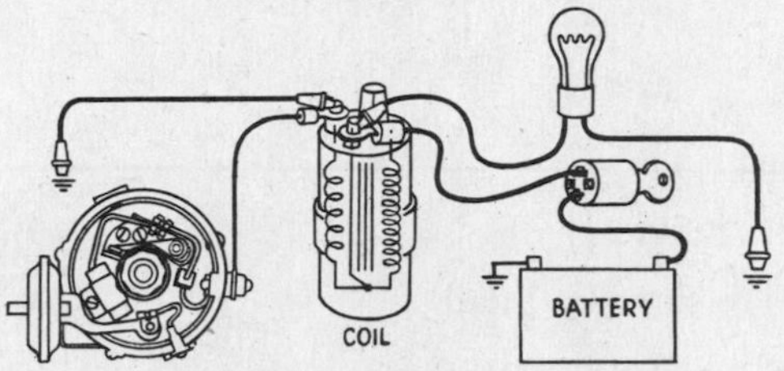

Checking the ignition switch "on" position

3.2—Check the ballast resistor or resistance wire for an open circuit, using an ohmmeter.	Replace the resistor or the resistance wire if the resistance is zero.	3.3
3.3—Visually inspect the breaker points for burning, pitting, or excessive wear. Gray coloring of the point contact surfaces is normal. Rotate the crankshaft until the contact heel rests on a high point of the distributor cam, and adjust the point gap to specifications.	If the breaker points are intact, clean the contact surfaces with fine emery cloth, and adjust the point gap to specifications. If pitted or worn, replace the points and condenser, and adjust the gap to specifications: NOTE: *Always lubricate the distributor cam according to manufacturer's recommendations when servicing the breaker points.*	3.4
3.4—Connect a dwell meter between the distributor primary lead and ground. Crank the engine and observe the point dwell angle.	If necessary, adjust the point dwell angle: NOTE: *Increasing the point gap decreases the dwell angle, and vice-versa.*	3.6
	If dwell meter shows little or no reading:	3.5

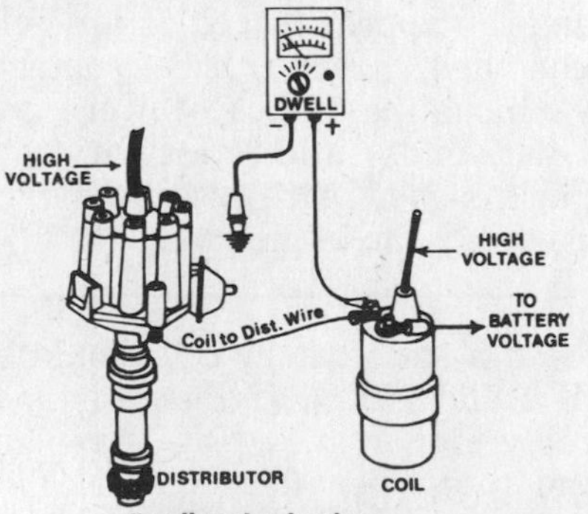

Dwell meter hook-up

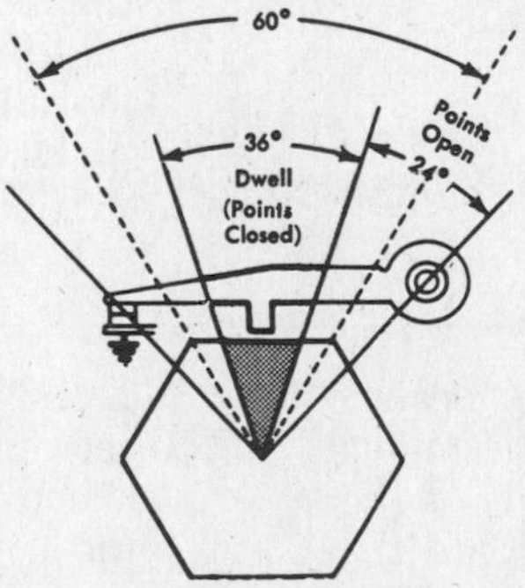

Dwell angle

3.5—Check the condenser for short: Connect an ohmmeter across the condenser body and the pigtail lead.	If any reading other than infinite resistance is noted, replace the condenser:	3.6

Checking the condenser for short

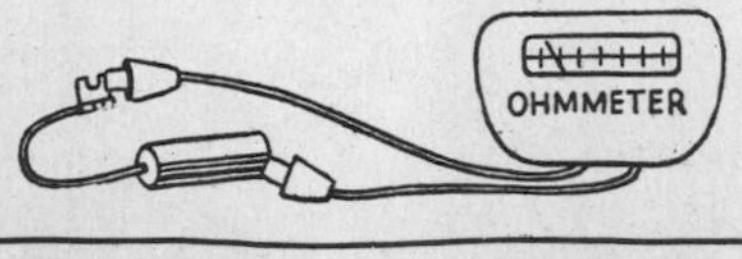

Test and Procedure	Results and Indications	Proceed to
3.6—Test the coil primary resistance: Connect an ohmmeter across the coil primary terminals, and read the resistance on the low scale. Note whether an external ballast resistor or resistance wire is utilized. **Testing the coil primary resistance**	Coils utilizing ballast resistors or resistance wires should have approximately 1.0Ω resistance; coils with internal resistors should have approximately 4.0Ω resistance. If values far from the above are noted, replace the coil:	4.1
4.1—Check for spark: Hold each spark plug wire approximately $\frac{1}{4}''$ from ground with gloves or a heavy, dry rag. Crank the engine, and observe the spark.	If no spark is evident: If spark is good in some cylinders: If spark is good in all cylinders:	4.2 4.3 4.6
4.2—Check for spark at the coil high tension lead: Remove the coil high tension lead from the distributor and position it approximately $\frac{1}{4}''$ from ground. Crank the engine and observe spark. CAUTION: *This test should not be performed on cars equipped with transistorized ignition.*	If the spark is good and consistent: If the spark is good but intermittent, test the primary electrical system starting at 3.3: If the spark is weak or non-existent, replace the coil high tension lead, clean and tighten all connections and retest. If no improvement is noted:	4.3 3.3 4.4

4.3—Visually inspect the distributor cap and rotor for burned or corroded contacts, cracks, carbon tracks, or moisture. Also check the fit of the rotor on the distributor shaft (where applicable).	If moisture is present, dry thoroughly, and retest per 4.1:
	
	 If burned or excessively corroded contacts, cracks, or carbon tracks are noted, replace the defective part(s) and retest per 4.1:
	
	 If the rotor and cap appear intact, or are only slightly corroded, clean the contacts thoroughly (including the cap towers and spark plug wire ends) and retest per 4.1:
	    If the spark is good in all cases:
	    If the spark is poor in all cases:
		4.1
		
		 4.1
		
		 4.6
		 4.5

4.4—Check the coil secondary resistance: Connect an ohmmeter across the distributor side of the coil and the coil tower. Read the resistance on the high scale of the ohmmeter. **Testing the coil secondary resistance**	The resistance of a satisfactory coil should be between $4K\Omega$ and $10K\Omega$. If the resistance is considerably higher (i.e., $40K\Omega$) replace the coil, and retest per 4.1: NOTE: *This does not apply to high performance coils.*	4.1

Test and Procedure	Results and Indications	Proceed to
4.5—Visually inspect the spark plug wires for cracking or brittleness. Ensure that no two wires are positioned so as to cause induction firing (adjacent and parallel). Remove each wire, one by one, and check resistance with an ohmmeter.	Replace any cracked or brittle wires. If any of the wires are defective, replace the entire set. Replace any wires with excessive resistance (over 8000Ω per foot for suppression wire), and separate any wires that might cause induction firing.	4.6
4.6—Remove the spark plugs, noting the cylinders from which they were removed, and evaluate according to the chart below.	See below.	See below.

	Condition	Cause	Remedy	Proceed to
	Electrodes eroded, light brown deposits.	Normal wear. Normal wear is indicated by approximately .001″ wear per 1000 miles.	Clean and regap the spark plug if wear is not excessive: Replace the spark plug if excessively worn:	4.7
	Carbon fouling (black, dry, fluffy deposits).	If present on one or two plugs: Faulty high tension lead(s). Burnt or sticking valve(s).	Test the high tension leads: Check the valve train: (Clean and regap the plugs in either case.)	4.5 9.1
		If present on most or all plugs: Overly rich fuel mixture, due to restricted air filter, improper carburetor adjustment, improper choke or heat riser adjustment or operation.	Check the fuel system:	5.1
	Oil fouling (wet black deposits)	Worn engine components. NOTE: *Oil fouling may occur in new or recently rebuilt engines until broken in.*	Check engine vacuum and compression: Replace with new spark plug	6.1
	Lead fouling (gray, black, tan, or yellow deposits, which appear glazed or cinder-like).	Combustion by-products.	Clean and regap the plugs: (Use plugs of a different heat range if the problem recurs.)	4.7

	Condition	Cause	Remedy	Proceed to
	Gap bridging (deposits lodged between the electrodes).	Incomplete combustion, or transfer of deposits from the combustion chamber.	Replace the spark plugs:	
	Overheating (burnt electrodes, and extremely white insulator with small black spots).	Ignition timing advanced too far.	Adjust timing to specifications:	8.2
		Overly lean fuel mixture.	Check the fuel system:	5.1
		Spark plugs not seated properly.	Clean spark plug seat and install a new gasket washer: (Replace the spark plugs in all cases.)	4.7
	Fused spot deposits on the insulator.	Combustion chamber blow-by.	Clean and regap the spark plugs:	4.7
	Pre-ignition (melted or severely burned electrodes, blistered or cracked insulators, or metallic deposits on the insulator).	Incorrect spark plug heat range.	Replace with plugs of the proper heat range:	4.7
		Ignition timing advanced too far.	Adjust timing to specifications:	8.2
		Spark plugs not being cooled efficiently.	Clean the spark plug seat, and check the cooling system:	11.1
		Fuel mixture too lean.	Check the fuel system:	5.1
		Poor compression.	Check compression:	6.1
		Fuel grade too low.	Use higher octane fuel:	4.7

Test and Procedure	Results and Indications	Proceed to
4.7—Determine the static ignition timing: Using the flywheel or crankshaft pulley timing marks as a guide, locate top dead center on the *compression* stroke of the No. 1 cylinder. Remove the distributor cap.	Adjust the distributor so that the rotor points toward the No. 1 tower in the distributor cap, and the points are just opening:	4.8
4.8—Check coil polarity: Connect a voltmeter negative lead to the coil high tension lead, and the positive lead to ground (NOTE: *reverse the hook-up for positive ground cars*). Crank the engine momentarily. **Checking coil polarity**	If the voltmeter reads up-scale, the polarity is correct:	5.1
	If the voltmeter reads down-scale, reverse the coil polarity (switch the primary leads):	5.1

Test and Procedure	*Results and Indications*	*Proceed to*
5.1—Determine that the air filter is functioning efficiently: Hold paper elements up to a strong light, and attempt to see light through the filter.	Clean permanent air filters in gasoline (or manufacturer's recommendation), and allow to dry. Replace paper elements through which light cannot be seen:	5.2
5.2—Determine whether a flooding condition exists: Flooding is identified by a strong gasoline odor, and excessive gasoline present in the throttle bore(s) of the carburetor.	If flooding is not evident:	5.3
	If flooding is evident, permit the gasoline to dry for a few moments and restart.	
	If flooding doesn't recur:	5.6
	If flooding is persistant:	5.5
5.3—Check that fuel is reaching the carburetor: Detach the fuel line at the carburetor inlet. Hold the end of the line in a cup (not styrofoam), and crank the engine.	If fuel flows smoothly:	5.6
	If fuel doesn't flow (NOTE: *Make sure that there is fuel in the tank*), or flows erratically:	5.4
5.4—Test the fuel pump: Disconnect all fuel lines from the fuel pump. Hold a finger over the input fitting, crank the engine (with electric pump, turn the ignition or pump on), and feel for suction.	If suction is evident, blow out the fuel line to the tank with low pressure compressed air until bubbling is heard from the fuel filler neck. Also blow out the carburetor fuel line (both ends disconnected):	5.6
	If no suction is evident, replace or repair the fuel pump:	5.6
	NOTE: *Repeated oil fouling of the spark plugs, or a no-start condition, could be the result of a ruptured vacuum booster pump diaphragm, through which oil or gasoline is being drawn into the intake manifold (where applicable).*	
5.5—Check the needle and seat: Tap the carburetor in the area of the needle and seat.	If flooding stops, a gasoline additive (e.g., Gumout) will often cure the problem:	5.6
	If flooding continues, check the fuel pump for excessive pressure at the carburetor (according to specifications). If the pressure is normal, the needle and seat must be removed and checked, and/or the float level adjusted:	5.6
5.6—Test the accelerator pump by looking into the throttle bores while operating the throttle.	If the accelerator pump appears to be operating normally:	5.7
	If the accelerator pump is not operating, the pump must be reconditioned. Where possible, service the pump with the carburetor(s) installed on the engine. If necessary, remove the carburetor. Prior to removal:	5.7
5.7—Determine whether the carburetor main fuel system is functioning: Spray a commercial starting fluid into the carburetor while attempting to start the engine.	If the engine starts, runs for a few seconds, and dies:	5.8
	If the engine doesn't start:	6.1

Test and Procedures	*Results and Indications*	*Proceed to*
5.8—Uncommon fuel system malfunctions: See below:	If the problem is solved:	6.1
	If the problem remains, remove and recondition the carburetor.	

Condition	*Indication*	*Test*	*Usual Weather Conditions*	*Remedy*
Vapor lock	Car will not restart shortly after running.	Cool the components of the fuel system until the engine starts.	Hot to very hot	Ensure that the exhaust manifold heat control valve is operating. Check with the vehicle manufacturer for the recommended solution to vapor lock on the model in question.
Carburetor icing	Car will not idle, stalls at low speeds.	Visually inspect the throttle plate area of the throttle bores for frost.	High humidity, 32-40 F.	Ensure that the exhaust manifold heat control valve is operating, and that the intake manifold heat riser is not blocked.
Water in the fuel	Engine sputters and stalls; may not start.	Pump a small amount of fuel into a glass jar. Allow to stand, and inspect for droplets or a layer of water.	High humidity, extreme temperature changes.	For droplets, use one or two cans of commercial gas dryer (Dry Gas) For a layer of water, the tank must be drained, and the fuel lines blown out with compressed air.

Test and Procedure	*Results and Indications*	*Proceed to*
6.1—Test engine compression: Remove all spark plugs. Insert a compression gauge into a spark plug port, crank the engine to obtain the maximum reading, and record.	If compression is within limits on all cylinders:	7.1
	If gauge reading is extremely low on all cylinders:	6.2
	If gauge reading is low on one or two cylinders:	6.2
	(If gauge readings are identical and low on two or more adjacent cylinders, the head gasket must be replaced.)	

Testing compression
(© Chevrolet Div. G.M. Corp.)

Maxi. Press. Lbs. Sq. In.	*Min. Press. Lbs. Sq. In.*	*Maxi. Press. Lbs. Sq. In.*	*Min. Press. Lbs. Sq. In.*	*Max. Press. Lbs. Sq. In.*	*Min. Press. Lbs. Sq. In.*	*Max. Press. Lbs. Sq. In.*	*Min. Press. Lbs. Sq. In.*
134	101	162	121	188	141	214	160
136	102	164	123	190	142	216	162
138	104	166	124	192	144	218	163
140	105	168	126	194	145	220	165
142	107	170	127	196	147	222	166
146	110	172	129	198	148	224	168
148	111	174	131	200	150	226	169
150	113	176	132	202	151	228	171
152	114	178	133	204	153	230	172
154	115	180	135	206	154	232	174
156	117	182	136	208	156	234	175
158	118	184	138	210	157	236	177
160	120	186	140	212	158	238	178

Compression pressure limits
(© Buick Div. G.M. Corp.)

Test and Procedure	Results and Indications	Proceed to
6.2—Test engine compression (wet): Squirt approximately 30 cc. of engine oil into each cylinder, and retest per 6.1.	If the readings improve, worn or cracked rings or broken pistons are indicated:	Next Chapter
	If the readings do not improve, burned or excessively carboned valves or a jumped timing chain are indicated:	7.1
	NOTE: *A jumped timing chain is often indicated by difficult cranking.*	
7.1—Perform a vacuum check of the engine: Attach a vacuum gauge to the intake manifold beyond the throttle plate. Start the engine, and observe the action of the needle over the range of engine speeds.	See below.	See below

	Reading	Indications	Proceed to
	Steady, from 17-22 in. Hg.	Normal.	8.1
	Low and steady.	Late ignition or valve timing, or low compression:	6.1
	Very low	Vacuum leak:	
	Needle fluctuates as engine speed increases.	Ignition miss, blown cylinder head gasket, leaking valve or weak valve spring:	6.1, 8.3
	Gradual drop in reading at idle.	Excessive back pressure in the exhaust system:	10.1
	Intermittent fluctuation at idle.	Ignition miss, sticking valve:	8.3, 9.1
	Drifting needle.	Improper idle mixture adjustment, carburetors not synchronized (where applicable), or minor intake leak. Synchronize the carburetors, adjust the idle, and retest. If the condition persists:	7.2
	High and steady.	Early ignition timing:	8.2

Test and Procedure	Results and Indications	Proceed to
7.2—Attach a vacuum gauge per 7.1, and test for an intake manifold leak. Squirt a small amount of oil around the intake manifold gaskets, carburetor gaskets, plugs and fittings. Observe the action of the vacuum gauge.	If the reading improves, replace the indicated gasket, or seal the indicated fitting or plug: If the reading remains low:	8.1 7.3
7.3—Test all vacuum hoses and accessories for leaks as described in 7.2. Also check the carburetor body (dashpots, automatic choke mechanism, throttle shafts) for leaks in the same manner.	If the reading improves, service or replace the offending part(s): If the reading remains low:	8.1 6.1
8.1—Check the point dwell angle: Connect a dwell meter between the distributor primary wire and ground. Start the engine, and observe the dwell angle from idle to 3000 rpm.	If necessary, adjust the dwell angle. NOTE: *Increasing the point gap reduces the dwell angle and vice-versa.* If the dwell angle moves outside specifications as engine speed increases, the distributor should be removed and checked for cam accuracy, shaft endplay and concentricity, bushing wear, and adequate point arm tension (NOTE: *Most of these items may be checked with the distributor installed in the engine, using an oscilloscope*):	8.2
8.2—Connect a timing light (per manufacturer's recommendation) and check the dynamic ignition timing. Disconnect and plug the vacuum hose(s) to the distributor if specified, start the engine, and observe the timing marks at the specified engine speed.	If the timing is not correct, adjust to specifications by rotating the distributor in the engine: (Advance timing by rotating distributor opposite normal direction of rotor rotation, retard timing by rotating distributor in same direction as rotor rotation.)	8.3
8.3—Check the operation of the distributor advance mechanism(s): To test the mechanical advance, disconnect all but the mechanical advance, and observe the timing marks with a timing light as the engine speed is increased from idle. If the mark moves smoothly, without hesitation, it may be assumed that the mechanical advance is functioning properly. To test vacuum advance and/or retard systems, alternately crimp and release the vacuum line, and observe the timing mark for movement. If movement is noted, the system is operating.	If the systems are functioning: If the systems are not functioning, remove the distributor, and test on a distributor tester:	8.4 8.4
8.4—Locate an ignition miss: With the engine running, remove each spark plug wire, one by one, until one is found that doesn't cause the engine to roughen and slow down.	When the missing cylinder is identified:	4.1

Test and Procedure	Results and Indications	Proceed to
9.1—Evaluate the valve train: Remove the valve cover, and ensure that the valves are adjusted to specifications. A mechanic's stethoscope may be used to aid in the diagnosis of the valve train. By pushing the probe on or near push rods or rockers, valve noise often can be isolated. A timing light also may be used to diagnose valve problems. Connect the light according to manufacturer's recommendations, and start the engine. Vary the firing moment of the light by increasing the engine speed (and therefore the ignition advance), and moving the trigger from cylinder to cylinder. Observe the movement of each valve.	See below	See below

Observation	Probable Cause	Remedy	Proceed to
Metallic tap heard through the stethoscope.	Sticking hydraulic lifter or excessive valve clearance.	Adjust valve. If tap persists, remove and replace the lifter:	10.1
Metallic tap through the stethoscope, able to push the rocker arm (lifter side) down by hand.	Collapsed valve lifter.	Remove and replace the lifter:	10.1
Erratic, irregular motion of the valve stem.*	Sticking valve, burned valve.	Recondition the valve and/or valve guide:	Next Chapter
Eccentric motion of the pushrod at the rocker arm.*	Bent pushrod.	Replace the pushrod:	10.1
Valve retainer bounces as the valve closes.*	Weak valve spring or damper.	Remove and test the spring and damper. Replace if necessary:	10.1

*—When observed with a timing light.

Test and Procedure	Results and Indications	Proceed to
9.2—Check the valve timing: Locate top dead center of the No. 1 piston, and install a degree wheel or tape on the crankshaft pulley or damper with zero corresponding to an index mark on the engine. Rotate the crankshaft in its direction of rotation, and observe the opening of the No. 1 cylinder intake valve. The opening should correspond with the correct mark on the degree wheel according to specifications.	If the timing is not correct, the timing cover must be removed for further investigation:	

Test and Procedure	Results and Indications	Proceed to
10.1—Determine whether the exhaust manifold heat control valve is operating: Operate the valve by hand to determine whether it is free to move. If the valve is free, run the engine to operating temperature and observe the action of the valve, to ensure that it is opening.	If the valve sticks, spray it with a suitable solvent, open and close the valve to free it, and retest.	
	If the valve functions properly:	10.2
	If the valve does not free, or does not operate, replace the valve:	10.2
10.2—Ensure that there are no exhaust restrictions: Visually inspect the exhaust system for kinks, dents, or crushing. Also note that gasses are flowing freely from the tailpipe at all engine speeds, indicating no restriction in the muffler or resonator.	Replace any damaged portion of the system:	11.1
11.1—Visually inspect the fan belt for glazing, cracks, and fraying, and replace if necessary. Tighten the belt so that the longest span has approximately ½″ play at its midpoint under thumb pressure.	Replace or tighten the fan belt as necessary:	11.2

Checking the fan belt tension
(© Outboard Marine Corp.)

Test and Procedure	Results and Indications	Proceed to
11.2—Check the fluid level of the cooling system.	If full or slightly low, fill as necessary:	11.5
	If extremely low:	11.3
11.3—Visually inspect the external portions of the cooling system (radiator, radiator hoses, thermostat elbow, water pump seals, heater hoses, etc.) for leaks. If none are found, pressurize the cooling system to 14-15 psi.	If cooling system holds the pressure:	11.5
	If cooling system loses pressure rapidly, re-inspect external parts of the system for leaks under pressure. If none are found, check dipstick for coolant in crankcase. If no coolant is present, but pressure loss continues:	11.4
	If coolant is evident in crankcase, remove cylinder head(s), and check gasket(s). If gaskets are intact, block and cylinder head(s) should be checked for cracks or holes.	
	If the gasket(s) is blown, replace, and purge the crankcase of coolant:	12.6
	NOTE: Occasionally, due to atmospheric and driving conditions, condensation of water can occur in the crankcase. This causes the oil to appear milky white. To remedy, run the engine until hot, and change the oil and oil filter.	

Test and Procedure	*Results and Indication*	*Proceed to*
11.4—Check for combustion leaks into the cooling system: Pressurize the cooling system as above. Start the engine, and observe the pressure gauge. If the needle fluctuates, remove each spark plug wire, one by one, noting which cylinder(s) reduce or eliminate the fluctuation. **Radiator pressure tester** (ⓒ American Motors Corp.)	Cylinders which reduce or eliminate the fluctuation, when the spark plug wire is removed, are leaking into the cooling system. Replace the head gasket on the affected cylinder bank(s).	
11.5—Check the radiator pressure cap: Attach a radiator pressure tester to the radiator cap (wet the seal prior to installation). Quickly pump up the pressure, noting the point at which the cap releases. **Testing the radiator pressure cap** (ⓒ American Motors Corp.)	If the cap releases within ± 1 psi of the specified rating, it is operating properly: If the cap releases at more than ± 1 psi of the specified rating, it should be replaced:	11.6 11.6
11.6—Test the thermostat: Start the engine cold, remove the radiator cap, and insert a thermometer into the radiator. Allow the engine to idle. After a short while, there will be a sudden, rapid increase in coolant temperature. The temperature at which this sharp rise stops is the thermostat opening temperature.	If the thermostat opens at or about the specified temperature: If the temperature doesn't increase: (If the temperature increases slowly and gradually, replace the thermostat.)	11.7 11.7
11.7—Check the water pump: Remove the thermostat elbow and the thermostat, disconnect the coil high tension lead (to prevent starting), and crank the engine momentarily.	If coolant flows, replace the thermostat and retest per 11.6: If coolant doesn't flow, reverse flush the cooling system to alleviate any blockage that might exist. If system is not blocked, and coolant will not flow, recondition the water pump.	11.6 —
12.1—Check the oil pressure gauge or warning light: If the gauge shows low pressure, or the light is on, for no obvious reason, remove the oil pressure sender. Install an accurate oil pressure gauge and run the engine momentarily.	If oil pressure builds normally, run engine for a few moments to determine that it is functioning normally, and replace the sender. If the pressure remains low: If the pressure surges: If the oil pressure is zero:	— 12.2 12.3 12.3

Test and Procedure	Results and Indications	Proceed to
12.2—Visually inspect the oil: If the oil is watery or very thin, milky, or foamy, replace the oil and oil filter.	If the oil is normal:	12.3
	If after replacing oil the pressure remains low:	12.3
	If after replacing oil the pressure becomes normal:	—
12.3—Inspect the oil pressure relief valve and spring, to ensure that it is not sticking or stuck. Remove and thoroughly clean the valve, spring, and the valve body.	If the oil pressure improves:	—
	If no improvement is noted:	12.4

Oil pressure relief valve
(© British Leyland Motors)

Test and Procedure	Results and Indications	Proceed to
12.4—Check to ensure that the oil pump is not cavitating (sucking air instead of oil): See that the crankcase is neither over nor underfull, and that the pickup in the sump is in the proper position and free from sludge.	Fill or drain the crankcase to the proper capacity, and clean the pickup screen in solvent if necessary. If no improvement is noted:	12.5
12.5—Inspect the oil pump drive and the oil pump:	If the pump drive or the oil pump appear to be defective, service as necessary and retest per 12.1:	12.1
	If the pump drive and pump appear to be operating normally, the engine should be disassembled to determine where blockage exists:	Next Chapter
12.6—Purge the engine of ethylene glycol coolant: Completely drain the crankcase and the oil filter. Obtain a commercial butyl cellosolve base solvent, designated for this purpose, and follow the instructions precisely. Following this, install a new oil filter and refill the crankcase with the proper weight oil. The next oil and filter change should follow shortly thereafter (1000 miles).		

Engine Rebuilding

This section describes, in detail, the procedures involved in rebuilding a typical engine. The procedures specifically refer to an inline engine, however, they are basically identical to those used in rebuilding engines of nearly all design and configurations. Procedures for servicing atypical engines (i.e., horizontally opposed) are described in the appropriate section, although in most cases, cylinder head reconditioning procedures described in this chapter will apply.

The section is divided into two sections. The first, Cylinder Head Reconditioning, assumes that the cylinder head is removed from the engine, all manifolds are removed, and the cylinder head is on a workbench. The camshaft should be removed from overhead cam cylinder heads. The second section, Cylinder Block Reconditioning, covers the block, pistons, connecting rods and crankshaft. It is assumed that the engine is mounted on a work stand, and the cylinder head and all accessories are removed.

Procedures are identified as follows:

Unmarked—Basic procedures that must be performed in order to successfully complete the rebuilding process.

Starred (*)—Procedures that should be performed to ensure maximum performance and engine life.

Double starred (**)—Procedures that may be performed to increase engine performance and reliability. These procedures are usually reserved for extremely heavy-duty or competition usage.

In many cases, a choice of methods is also provided. Methods are identified in the same manner as procedures. The choice of method for a procedure is at the discretion of the user.

The tools required for the basic rebuilding procedure should, with minor exceptions, be those

TORQUE (ft. lbs.)*

U.S.

Bolt Diameter (inches)	Bolt Grade (SAE)				Wrench Size (inches)	
	1 and 2	5	6	8	Bolt	Nut.
1/4	5	7	10	10.5	3/8	7/16
5/16	9	14	19	22	1/2	9/16
3/8	15	25	34	37	9/16	5/8
7/16	24	40	55	60	5/8	3/4
1/2	37	60	85	92	3/4	13/16
9/16	53	88	120	132	7/8	7/8
5/8	74	120	167	180	15/16	1
3/4	120	200	280	296	1-1/8	1-1/8
7/8	190	302	440	473	1-5/16	1-5/16
1	282	466	660	714	1-1/2	1-1/2

Metric

Bolt Diameter (mm)	Bolt Grade				Wrench Size (mm) Bolt and Nut
	5D	8G	10K	12K	
6	5	6	8	10	10
8	10	16	22	27	14
10	19	31	40	49	17
12	34	54	70	86	19
14	55	89	117	137	22
16	83	132	175	208	24
18	111	182	236	283	27
22	182	284	394	464	32
24	261	419	570	689	36

*—Torque values are for lightly oiled bolts. CAUTION: Bolts threaded into aluminum require much less torque.

General Torque Specifications

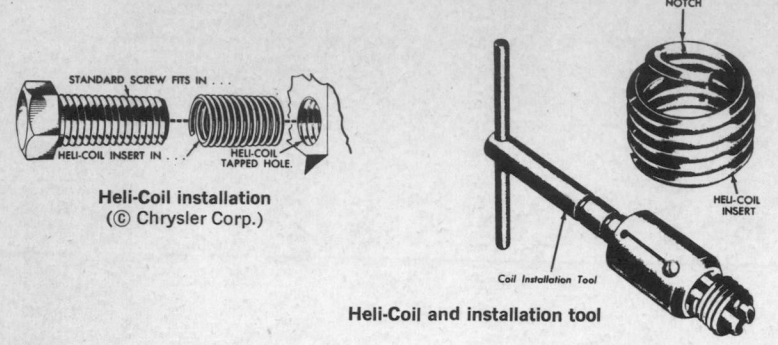

Heli-Coil installation
(© Chrysler Corp.)

Heli-Coil and installation tool

Heli-Coil Insert			Drill	Tap	Insert. Tool	Extracting Tool
Thread Size	Part No.	Insert Length (In.)	Size	Part No.	Part No.	Part No.
1/2 -20	1185-4	3/8	17/64(.266)	4 CPB	528-4N	1227-6
5/16-18	1185-5	15/32	Q(.332)	5 CPB	528-5N	1227-6
3/8 -16	1185-6	9/16	X(.397)	6 CPB	528-6N	1227-6
7/16-14	1185-7	21/32	29/64(.453)	7 CPB	528-7N	1227-16
1/2 -13	1185-8	3/4	33/64(.516)	8 CPB	528-8N	1227-16

Heli-Coil Specifications

included in a mechanic's tool kit. An accurate torque wrench, and a dial indicator (reading in thousandths) mounted on a universal base should be available. Bolts and nuts with no torque specification should be tightened according to size (see chart). Special tools, where required, all are readily available from the major tool suppliers (i.e., Craftsman, Snap-On, K-D). The services of a competent automotive machine shop must also be readily available.

When assembling the engine, any parts that will be in frictional contact must be pre-lubricated, to provide protection on initial start-up. Vortex Pre-Lube, STP, or any product specifically formulated for this purpose may be used. NOTE: *Do not use engine oil.* Where semi-permanent (locked but removable) installation of bolts or nuts is desired, threads should be cleaned and coated with Loctite. Studs may be permanently installed using Loctite Stud and Bearing Mount.

Aluminum has become increasingly popular for use in engines, due to its low weight and excellent heat transfer characteristics. The following precautions must be observed when handling aluminum engine parts:

—Never hot-tank aluminum parts.

—Remove all aluminum parts (identification tags, etc.) from engine parts before hot-tanking (otherwise they will be removed during the process).

—Always coat threads lightly with engine oil or anti-seize compounds before installation, to prevent seizure.

—Never over-torque bolts or spark plugs in aluminum threads. Should stripping occur, threads can be restored according to the following procedure, using Heli-Coil thread inserts:

Tap drill the hole with the stripped threads to the specified size (see chart). Using the specified tap (NOTE: *Heli-Coil tap sizes refer to the size thread being replaced, rather than the actual tap size*), tap the hole for the Heli-Coil. Place the insert on the proper installation tool (see chart). Apply pressure on the insert while winding it clockwise into the hole, until the top of the insert is one turn below the surface. Remove the installation tool, and break the installation tang from the bottom of the in-

sert by moving it up and down. If the Heli-Coil must be removed, tap the removal tool firmly into the hole, so that it engages the top thread, and turn the tool counter-clockwise to extract the insert.

Snapped bolts or studs may be removed, using a stud extractor (unthreaded) or Vise-Grip pliers (threaded). Penetrating oil (e.g., Liquid Wrench) will often aid in breaking frozen threads. In cases where the stud or bolt is flush with, or below the surface, proceed as follows:

Drill a hole in the broken stud or bolt, approximately 1/2 its diameter. Select a screw extractor (e.g., Easy-Out) of the proper size, and tap it into the stud or bolt. Turn the extractor counter-clockwise to remove the stud or bolt.

Magnaflux and Zyglo are inspection techniques used to locate material flaws, such as stress cracks. Magnafluxing coats the part with fine magnetic particles, and subjects the part to a magnetic field. Cracks cause breaks

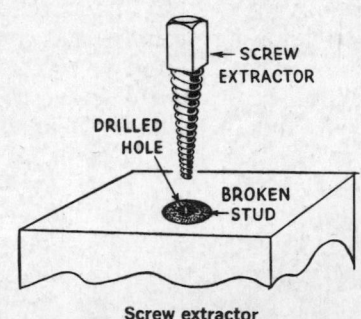

Screw extractor

in the magnetic field, which are outlined by the particles. Since Magnaflux is a magnetic process, it is applicable only to ferrous materials. The Zyglo process coats the material with a fluorescent dye penetrant, and then subjects it to blacklight inspection, under which cracks glow bright-

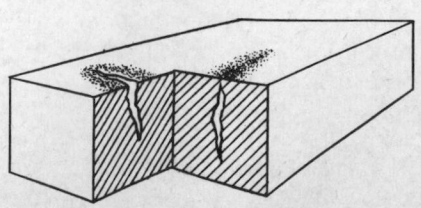

Magnaflux indication of cracks

ly. Parts made of any material may be tested using Zyglo. While Magnaflux and Zyglo are excellent for general inspection, and locating hidden defects, specific checks of suspected cracks may be made at lower cost and more readily using spot check dye. The dye is sprayed onto the suspected area, wiped off, and the area is then sprayed with a developer. Cracks then will show up brightly. Spot check dyes will only indicate surface cracks; therefore, structural cracks below the surface may escape detection. When questionable, the part should be tested using Magnaflux or Zyglo.

CYLINDER HEAD RECONDITIONING

Procedure	*Method*
Identify the valves:  **Valve identification** (© SAAB)	Invert the cylinder head, and number the valve faces front to rear, using a permanent felt-tip marker.
Remove the rocker arms:	Remove the rocker arms with shaft(s) or balls and nuts. Wire the sets of rockers, balls and nuts together, and identify according to the corresponding valve.
Remove the valves and springs:	Using an appropriate valve spring compressor (depending on the configuration of the cylinder head), compress the valve springs. Lift out the keepers with needlenose pliers, release the compressor, and remove the valve, spring, and spring retainer.
Check the valve stem-to-guide clearance: 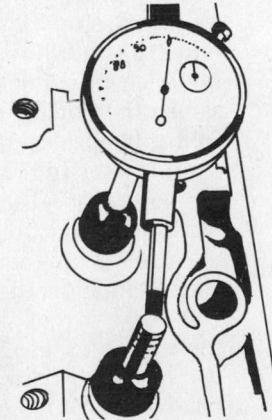 **Checking the valve stem-to-guide clearance** (© American Motors Corp.)	Clean the valve stem with lacquer thinner or a similar solvent to remove all gum and varnish. Clean the valve guides using solvent and an expanding wire-type valve guide cleaner. Mount a dial indicator so that the stem is at 90° to the valve stem, as close to the valve guide as possible. Move the valve off its seat, and measure the valve guide-to-stem clearance by moving the stem back and forth to actuate the dial indicator. Measure the valve stems using a micrometer, and compare to specifications, to determine whether stem or guide wear is responsible for excessive clearance.
De-carbon the cylinder head and valves: 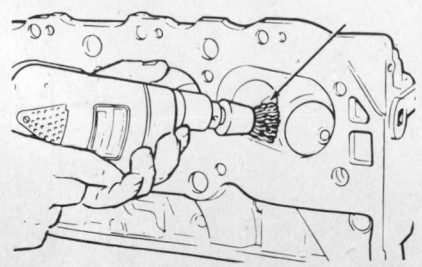 **Removing carbon from the cylinder head**	Chip carbon away from the valve heads, combustion chambers, and ports, using a chisel made of hardwood. Remove the remaining deposits with a stiff wire brush. NOTE: *Ensure that the deposits are actually removed, rather than burnished.*

Procedure	Method
Hot-tank the cylinder head:	Have the cylinder head hot-tanked to remove grease, corrosion, and scale from the water passages. NOTE: *In the case of overhead cam cylinder heads, consult the operator to determine whether the camshaft bearings will be damaged by the caustic solution.*
Degrease the remaining cylinder head parts:	Using solvent (i.e., Gunk), clean the rockers, rocker shaft(s) (where applicable), rocker balls and nuts, springs, spring retainers, and keepers. Do not remove the protective coating from the springs.
Check the cylinder head for warpage: 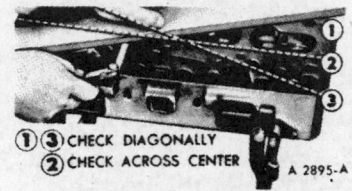 **Checking the cylinder head for warpage** (© Ford Motor Co.)	Place a straight-edge across the gasket surface of the cylinder head. Using feeler gauges, determine the clearance at the center of the straight-edge. Measure across both diagonals, along the longitudinal centerline, and across the cylinder head at several points. If warpage exceeds .003″ in a 6″ span, or .006″ over the total length, the cylinder head must be resurfaced. NOTE: *If warpage exceeds the manufacturers maximum tolerance for material removal, the cylinder head must be replaced.* When milling the cylinder heads of V-type engines, the intake manifold mounting position is altered, and must be corrected by milling the manifold flange a proportionate amount.
** Porting and gasket matching: 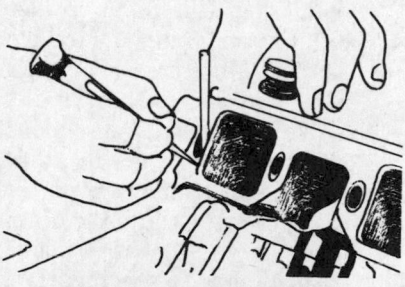 **Marking the cylinder head for gasket matching** (© Petersen Publishing Co.) 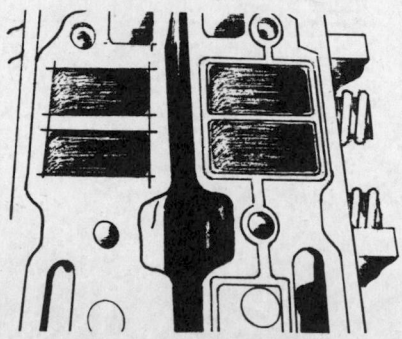 **Port configuration before and after gasket matching** (© Petersen Publishing Co.)	** Coat the manifold flanges of the cylinder head with Prussian blue dye. Glue intake and exhaust gaskets to the cylinder head in their installed position using rubber cement and scribe the outline of the ports on the manifold flanges. Remove the gaskets. Using a small cutter in a hand-held power tool (i.e., Dremel Moto-Tool), gradually taper the walls of the port out to the scribed outline of the gasket. Further enlargement of the ports should include the removal of sharp edges and radiusing of sharp corners. Do not alter the valve guides. NOTE: *The most efficient port configuration is determined only by extensive testing. Therefore, it is best to consult someone experienced with the head in question to determine the optimum alterations.*

Procedure	*Method*

** Polish the ports:

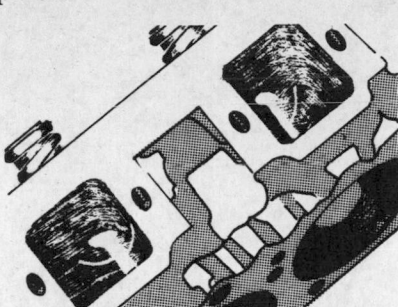

Relieved and polished ports
(© Petersen Publishing Co.)

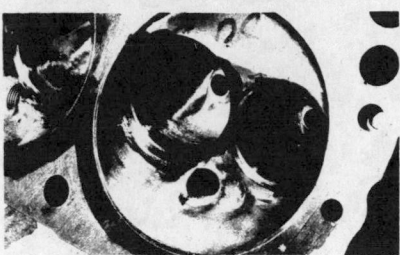

Polished combustion chamber
(© Petersen Publishing Co.)

** Using a grinding stone with the above mentioned tool, polish the walls of the intake and exhaust ports, and combustion chamber. Use progressively finer stones until all surface imperfections are removed. NOTE: *Through testing, it has been determined that a smooth surface is more effective than a mirror polished surface in intake ports, and vice-versa in exhaust ports.*

* Knurling the valve guides:

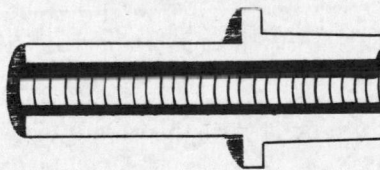

Cut-away view of a knurled valve guide
(© Petersen Publishing Co.)

* Valve guides which are not excessively worn or distorted may, in some cases, be knurled rather than replaced. Knurling is a process in which metal is displaced and raised, thereby reducing clearance. Knurling also provides excellent oil control. The possibility of knurling rather than replacing valve guides should be discussed with a machinist.

Replacing the valve guides: NOTE: *Valve guides should only be replaced if damaged or if an oversize valve stem is not available.*

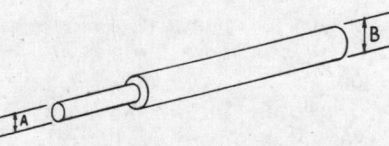

A-VALVE GUIDE I.D.
B-SLIGHTLY SMALLER THAN VALVE GUIDE O.D.

Valve guide removal tool

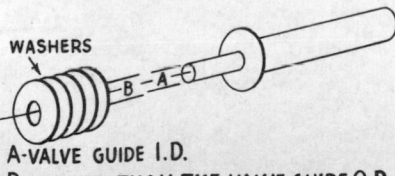

WASHERS

A-VALVE GUIDE I.D.
B-LARGER THAN THE VALVE GUIDE O.D.

Valve guide installation tool (with washers used during installation)

Depending on the type of cylinder head, valve guides may be pressed, hammered, or shrunk in. In cases where the guides are shrunk into the head, replacement should be left to an equipped machine shop. In other cases, the guides are replaced as follows: Press or tap the valve guides out of the head using a stepped drift (see illustration). Determine the height above the boss that the guide must extend, and obtain a stack of washers, their I.D. similar to the guide's O.D., of that height. Place the stack of washers on the guide, and insert the guide into the boss. NOTE: *Valve guides are often tapered or beveled for installation.* Using the stepped installation tool (see illustration), press or tap the guides into position. Ream the guides according to the size of the valve stem.

Procedure	Method
Replacing valve seat inserts :	Replacement of valve seat inserts which are worn beyond resurfacing or broken, if feasible, must be done by a machine shop.

Resurfacing (grinding) the valve face :

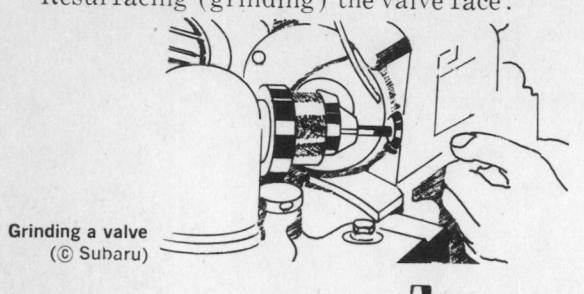

Grinding a valve
(© Subaru)

Using a valve grinder, resurface the valves according to specifications. CAUTION: *Valve face angle is not always identical to valve seat angle.* A minimum margin of 1/32" should remain after grinding the valve. The valve stem tip should also be squared and resurfaced, by placing the stem in the V-block of the grinder, and turning it while pressing lightly against the grinding wheel.

CHECK FOR
BENT STEM

DIAMETER

FOR DIMENSIONS,
REFER TO
SPECIFICATIONS

VALVE
FACE
ANGLE

THIS LINE
PARALLEL
WITH
VALVE HEAD

1/32'' MINIMUM

Critical valve dimensions
(© Ford Motor Co.)

Resurfacing the valve seats using reamers :

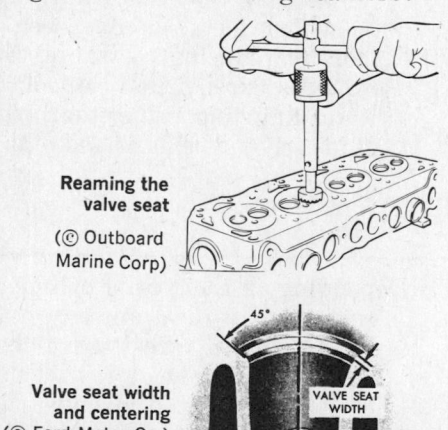

Reaming the valve seat

(© Outboard Marine Corp)

45°

VALVE SEAT
WIDTH

Valve seat width and centering
(© Ford Motor Co.)

A 2897-A

Select a reamer of the correct seat angle, slightly larger than the diameter of the valve seat, and assemble it with a pilot of the correct size. Install the pilot into the valve guide, and using steady pressure, turn the reamer clockwise. CAUTION: *Do not turn the reamer counter-clockwise.* Remove only as much material as necessary to clean the seat. Check the concentricity of the seat (see below). If the dye method is not used, coat the valve face with Prussian blue dye, install and rotate it on the valve seat. Using the dye marked area as a centering guide, center and narrow the valve seat to specifications with correction cutters. NOTE: *When no specifications are available, minimum seat width for exhaust valves should be 5/64", intake valves 1/16".* After making correction cuts, check the position of the valve seat on the valve face using Prussian blue dye.

---

* Resurfacing the valve seats using a grinder :

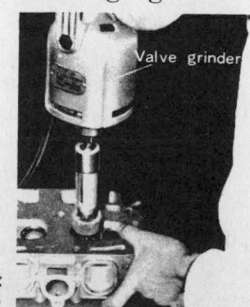

Valve grinder

Grinding a valve seat
(© Subaru)

Select a pilot of the correct size, and a coarse stone of the correct seat angle. Lubricate the pilot if necessary, and install the tool in the valve guide. Move the stone on and off the seat at approximately two cycles per second, until all flaws are removed from the seat. Install a fine stone, and finish the seat. Center and narrow the seat using correction stones, as described above.

Procedure	*Method*

Checking the valve seat concentricity :

Checking the valve seat concentricity using a dial gauge (© American Motors Corp.)

Coat the valve face with Prussian blue dye, install the valve, and rotate it on the valve seat. If the entire seat becomes coated, and the valve is known to be concentric, the seat is concentric.

---

* Install the dial gauge pilot into the guide, and rest the arm on the valve seat. Zero the gauge, and rotate the arm around the seat. Run-out should not exceed .002″.

---

* Lapping the valves : NOTE : *Valve lapping is done to ensure efficient sealing of resurfaced valves and seats. Valve lapping alone is not recommended for use as a resurfacing procedure.*

Hand lapping the valves

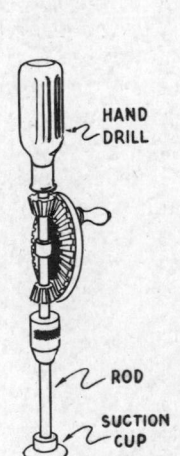

HAND DRILL

ROD

SUCTION CUP

Home made mechanical valve lapping tool

* Invert the cylinder head, lightly lubricate the valve stems, and install the valves in the head as numbered. Coat valve seats with fine grinding compound, and attach the lapping tool suction cup to a valve head (NOTE : *Moisten the suction cup*). Rotate the tool between the palms, changing position and lifting the tool often to prevent grooving. Lap the valve until a smooth, polished seat is evident. Remove the valve and tool, and rinse away all traces of grinding compound.

** Fasten a suction cup to a piece of drill rod, and mount the rod in a hand drill. Proceed as above, using the hand drill as a lapping tool. CAUTION : *Due to the higher speeds involved when using the hand drill, care must be exercised to avoid grooving the seat.* Lift the tool and change direction of rotation often.

Check the valve springs :

Checking the valve spring free length and squareness (© Ford Motor Co.)

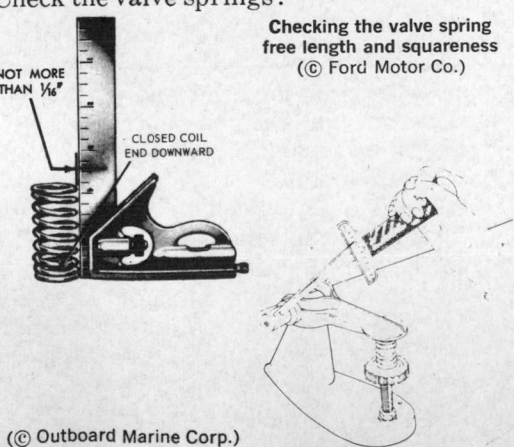

NOT MORE THAN 1/16″

CLOSED COIL END DOWNWARD

(© Outboard Marine Corp.)

Place the spring on a flat surface next to a square. Measure the height of the spring, and rotate it against the edge of the square to measure distortion. If spring height varies (by comparison) by more than 1/16″ or if distortion exceeds 1/16″, replace the spring.

** In addition to evaluating the spring as above, test the spring pressure at the installed and compressed (installed height minus valve lift) height using a valve spring tester. Springs used on small displacement engines (up to 3 liters) should be ± 1 lb. of all other springs in either position. A tolerance of ± 5 lbs. is permissible on larger engines.

Procedure	*Method*
* Install valve stem seals:  **Valve stem seal installation** (© Ford Motor Co.) SEAL	* Due to the pressure differential that exists at the ends of the intake valve guides (atmospheric pressure above, manifold vacuum below), oil is drawn through the valve guides into the intake port. This has been alleviated somewhat since the addition of positive crankcase ventilation, which lowers the pressure above the guides. Several types of valve stem seals are available to reduce blow-by. Certain seals simply slip over the stem and guide boss, while others require that the boss be machined. Recently, Teflon guide seals have become popular. Consult a parts supplier or machinist concerning availability and suggested usages. NOTE: *When installing seals, ensure that a small amount of oil is able to pass the seal to lubricate the valve guides; otherwise, excessive wear may result.*
Install the valves:	Lubricate the valve stems, and install the valves in the cylinder head as numbered. Lubricate and position the seals (if used, see above) and the valve springs. Install the spring retainers, compress the springs, and insert the keys using needlenose pliers or a tool designed for this purpose. NOTE: *Retain the keys with wheel bearing grease during installation.*
Checking valve spring installed height: 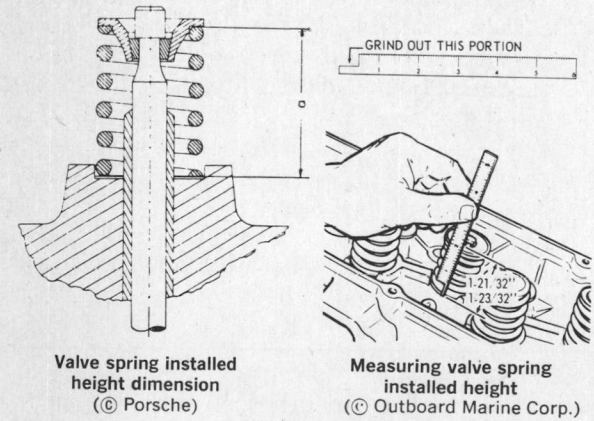 GRIND OUT THIS PORTION **Valve spring installed height dimension** (© Porsche) **Measuring valve spring installed height** (© Outboard Marine Corp.)	Measure the distance between the spring pad and the lower edge of the spring retainer, and compare to specifications. If the installed height is incorrect, add shim washers between the spring pad and the spring. CAUTION: *Use only washers designed for this purpose.*
** CC'ing the combustion chambers:	** Invert the cylinder head and place a bead of sealer around a combustion chamber. Install an apparatus designed for this purpose (burette mounted on a clear plate; see illustration) over the combustion chamber, and fill with the specified fluid to an even mark on the burette. Record the burette reading, and fill the combustion chamber with fluid. (NOTE: *A hole drilled in the plate will permit air to escape*). Subtract the burette reading, with the combustion chamber filled, from the previous reading, to determine combustion chamber volume in cc's. Duplicate this procedure in all combustion

Procedure	*Method*

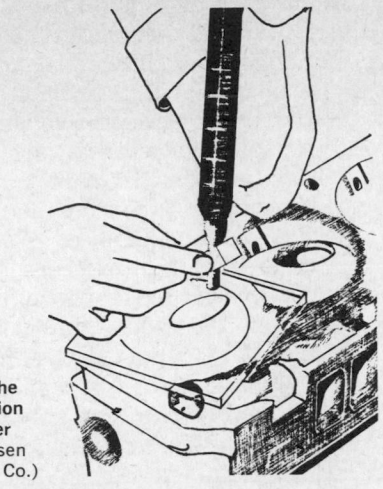

CC'ing the combustion chamber
(© Petersen Publishing Co.)

chambers on the cylinder head, and compare the readings. The volume of all combustion chambers should be made equal to that of the largest. Combustion chamber volume may be increased in two ways. When only a small change is required (usually), a small cutter or coarse stone may be used to remove material from the combustion chamber. NOTE: *Check volume frequently.* Remove material over a wide area, so as not to change the configuration of the combustion chamber. When a larger change is required, the valve seat may be sunk (lowered into the head). NOTE: *When altering valve seat, remember to compensate for the change in spring installed height.*

Inspect the rocker arms, balls, studs, and nuts (where applicable):

SMALL FRACTURES

Stress cracks in rocker nuts
(© Ford Motor Co.)

Visually inspect the rocker arms, balls, studs, and nuts for cracks, galling, burning, scoring, or wear. If all parts are intact, liberally lubricate the rocker arms and balls, and install them on the cylinder head. If wear is noted on a rocker arm at the point of valve contact, grind it smooth and square, removing as little material as possible. Replace the rocker arm if excessively worn. If a rocker stud shows signs of wear, it must be replaced (see below). If a rocker nut shows stress cracks, replace it. If an exhaust ball is galled or burned, substitute the intake ball from the same cylinder (if it is intact), and install a new intake ball. NOTE: *Avoid using new rocker balls on exhaust valves.*

Replacing rocker studs:

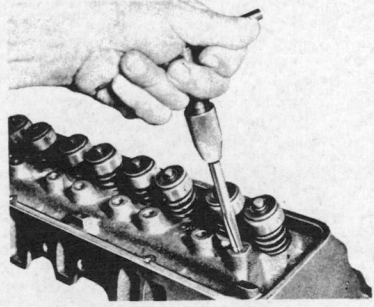

Reaming the stud bore for oversize rocker studs
(© Buick Div. G.M. Corp.)

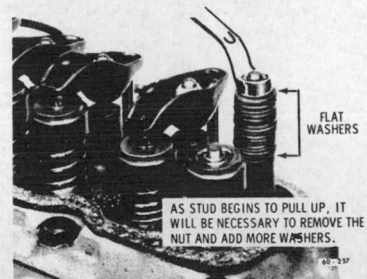

FLAT WASHERS

AS STUD BEGINS TO PULL UP, IT WILL BE NECESSARY TO REMOVE THE NUT AND ADD MORE WASHERS.

Extracting a pressed in rocker stud
(© Buick Div. G.M. Corp.)

In order to remove a threaded stud, lock two nuts on the stud, and unscrew the stud using the lower nut. Coat the lower threads of the new stud with Loctite, and install.

Two alternative methods are available for replacing pressed in studs. Remove the damaged stud using a stack of washers and a nut (see illustration). In the first, the boss is reamed .005-.006″ oversize, and an oversize stud pressed in. Control the stud extension over the boss using washers, in the same manner as valve guides. Before installing the stud, coat it with white lead and grease. To retain the stud more positively, drill a hole through the stud and boss, and install a roll pin. In the second method, the boss is tapped, and a threaded stud installed. Retain the stud using Loctite Stud and Bearing Mount.

Procedure	*Method*
Inspect the rocker shaft(s) and rocker arms (where applicable):  **Disassembled rocker shaft parts arranged for inspection** (© American Motors Corp.) 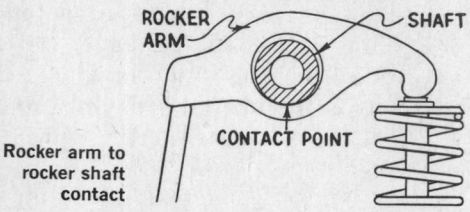 **Rocker arm to rocker shaft contact**	Remove rocker arms, springs and washers from rocker shaft. NOTE: *Lay out parts in the order they are removed.* Inspect rocker arms for pitting or wear on the valve contact point, or excessive bushing wear. Bushings need only be replaced if wear is excessive, because the rocker arm normally contacts the shaft at one point only. Grind the valve contact point of rocker arm smooth if necessary, removing as little material as possible. If excessive material must be removed to smooth and square the arm, it should be replaced. Clean out all oil holes and passages in rocker shaft. If shaft is grooved or worn, replace it. Lubricate and assemble the rocker shaft.
Inspect the camshaft bushings and the camshaft (overhead cam engines):	See next section.
Inspect the pushrods:	Remove the pushrods, and, if hollow, clean out the oil passages using fine wire. Roll each pushrod over a piece of clean glass. If a distinct clicking sound is heard as the pushrod rolls, the rod is bent, and must be replaced.
	* The length of all pushrods must be equal. Measure the length of the pushrods, compare to specifications, and replace as necessary.
Inspect the valve lifters: 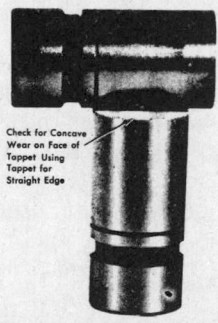 **Checking the lifter face** (© American Motors Corp.)	Remove lifters from their bores, and remove gum and varnish, using solvent. Clean walls of lifter bores. Check lifters for concave wear as illustrated. If face is worn concave, replace lifter, and carefully inspect the camshaft. Lightly lubricate lifter and insert it into its bore. If play is excessive, an oversize lifter must be installed (where possible). Consult a machinist concerning feasibility. If play is satisfactory, remove, lubricate, and reinstall the lifter.
* Testing hydraulic lifter leak down: 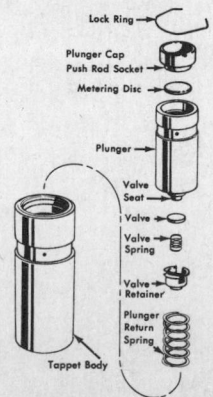 **Exploded view of a typical hydraulic lifter** (© American Motors Corp.)	Submerge lifter in a container of kerosene. Chuck a used pushrod or its equivalent into a drill press. Position container of kerosene so pushrod acts on the lifter plunger. Pump lifter with the drill press, until resistance increases. Pump several more times to bleed any air out of lifter. Apply very firm, constant pressure to the lifter, and observe rate at which fluid bleeds out of lifter. If the fluid bleeds very quickly (less than 15 seconds), lifter is defective. If the time exceeds 60 seconds, lifter is sticking. In either case, recondition or replace lifter. If lifter is operating properly (leak down time 15-60 seconds), lubricate and install it.

CYLINDER BLOCK RECONDITIONING

Procedure	Method

Checking the main bearing clearance:

Plastigage installed on main bearing journal
(© Chevrolet Div. G.M. Corp.)

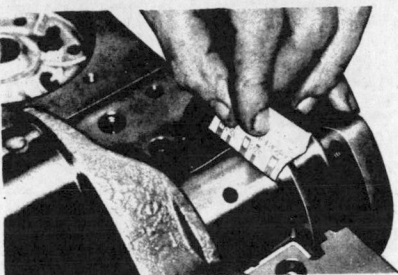

Measuring Plastigage to determine main bearing clearance
(© Chevrolet Div. G.M. Corp.)

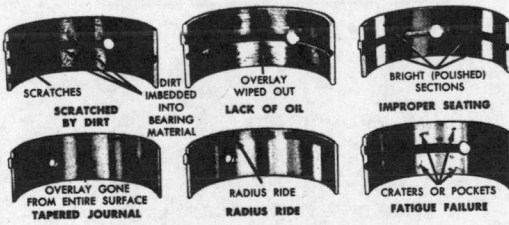

SCRATCHES — SCRATCHED BY DIRT — DIRT IMBEDDED INTO BEARING MATERIAL — OVERLAY WIPED OUT — LACK OF OIL — BRIGHT (POLISHED) SECTIONS — IMPROPER SEATING — OVERLAY GONE FROM ENTIRE SURFACE — TAPERED JOURNAL — RADIUS RIDE — RADIUS RIDE — CRATERS OR POCKETS — FATIGUE FAILURE

Causes of bearing failure
(© Ford Motor Co.)

Invert engine, and remove cap from the bearing to be checked. Using a clean, dry rag, thoroughly clean all oil from crankshaft journal and bearing insert. NOTE: *Plastigage is soluble in oil; therefore, oil on the journal or bearing could result in erroneous readings.* Place a piece of Plastigage along the full length of journal, reinstall cap, and torque to specifications. Remove bearing cap, and determine bearing clearance by comparing width of Plastigage to the scale on Plastigage envelope. Journal taper is determined by comparing width of the Plastigage strip near its ends. Rotate crankshaft 90° and retest, to determine journal eccentricity. NOTE: *Do not rotate crankshaft with Plastigage installed.* If bearing insert and journal appear intact, and are within tolerances, no further main bearing service is required. If bearing or journal appear defective, cause of failure should be determined before replacement.

* Remove crankshaft from block (see below). Measure the main bearing journals at each end twice (90° apart) using a micrometer, to determine diameter, journal taper and eccentricity. If journals are within tolerances, reinstall bearing caps at their specified torque. Using a telescope gauge and micrometer, measure bearing I.D. parallel to piston axis and at 30° on each side of piston axis. Subtract journal O.D. from bearing I.D. to determine oil clearance. If crankshaft journals appear defective, or do not meet tolerances, there is no need to measure bearings; for the crankshaft will require grinding and/or undersize bearings will be required. If bearing appears defective, cause for failure should be determined prior to replacement.

Checking the connecting rod bearing clearance:

Plastigage installed on connecting rod bearing journal
(© Chevrolet Div. G.M. Corp.)

Connecting rod bearing clearance is checked in the same manner as main bearing clearance, using Plastigage. Before removing the crankshaft, connecting rod side clearance also should be measured and recorded.

* Checking connecting rod bearing clearance, using a micrometer, is identical to checking main bearing clearance. If no other service

Procedure	*Method*

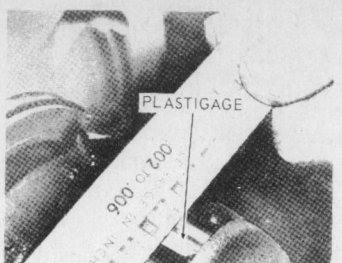

**Measuring Plastigage to determine
connecting rod bearing clearance**
(© Outboard Marine Corp.)

is required, the piston and rod assemblies need not be removed.

Removing the crankshaft:

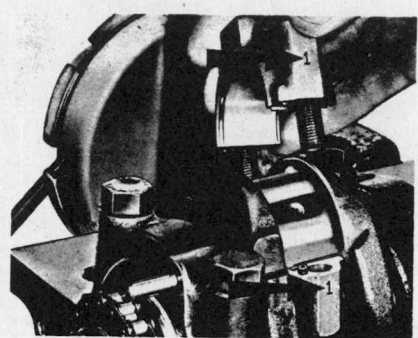

Connecting rod matching marks
(© Ford Motor Co.)

Using a punch, mark the corresponding main bearing caps and saddles according to position (i.e., one punch on the front main cap and saddle, two on the second, three on the third, etc.). Using number stamps, identify the corresponding connecting rods and caps, according to cylinder (if no numbers are present). Remove the main and connecting rod caps, and place sleeves of plastic tubing over the connecting rod bolts, to protect the journals as the crankshaft is removed. Lift the crankshaft out of the block.

Remove the ridge from the top of the cylinder:

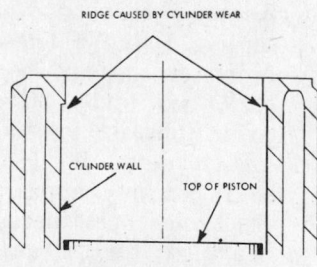

Cylinder bore ridge
(© Pontiac Div. G.M. Corp.)

In order to facilitate removal of the piston and connecting rod, the ridge at the top of the cylinder (unworn area; see illustration) must be removed. Place the piston at the bottom of the bore, and cover it with a rag. Cut the ridge away using a ridge reamer, exercising extreme care to avoid cutting too deeply. Remove the rag, and remove cuttings that remain on the piston. CAUTION: *If the ridge is not removed, and new rings are installed, damage to rings will result.*

Removing the piston and connecting rod:

Removing the piston
(© SAAB)

Invert the engine, and push the pistons and connecting rods out of the cylinders. If necessary, tap the connecting rod boss with a wooden hammer handle, to force the piston out. CAUTION: *Do not attempt to force the piston past the cylinder ridge* (see above).

Procedure	Method
Service the crankshaft:	Ensure that all oil holes and passages in the crankshaft are open and free of sludge. If necessary, have the crankshaft ground to the largest possible undersize.
	** Have the crankshaft Magnafluxed, to locate stress cracks. Consult a machinist concerning additional service procedures, such as surface hardening (e.g., nitriding, Tuftriding) to improve wear characteristics, cross drilling and chamfering the oil holes to improve lubrication, and balancing.
Removing freeze plugs:	Drill a hole in the center of the freeze plugs, and pry them out using a screwdriver or drift.
Remove the oil gallery plugs:	Threaded plugs should be removed using an appropriate (usually square) wrench. To remove soft, pressed in plugs, drill a hole in the plug, and thread in a sheet metal screw. Pull the plug out by the screw using pliers.
Hot-tank the block:	Have the block hot-tanked to remove grease, corrosion, and scale from the water jackets. NOTE: *Consult the operator to determine whether the camshaft bearings will be damaged during the hot-tank process.*
Check the block for cracks:	Visually inspect the block for cracks or chips. The most common locations are as follows: Adjacent to freeze plugs. Between the cylinders and water jackets. Adjacent to the main bearing saddles. At the extreme bottom of the cylinders. Check only suspected cracks using spot check dye (see introduction). If a crack is located, consult a machinist concerning possible repairs.
	** Magnaflux the block to locate hidden cracks. If cracks are located, consult a machinist about feasibility of repair.
Install the oil gallery plugs and freeze plugs:	Coat freeze plugs with sealer and tap into position using a piece of pipe, slightly smaller than the plug, as a driver. To ensure retention, stake the edges of the plugs. Coat threaded oil gallery plugs with sealer and install. Drive replacement soft plugs into block using a large drift as a driver.
	* Rather than reinstalling lead plugs, drill and tap the holes, and install threaded plugs.

Procedure	*Method*

Check the bore diameter and surface:

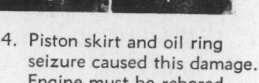

1, 2, 3 Piston skirt seizure resulted in this pattern. Engine must be rebored

4. Piston skirt and oil ring seizure caused this damage. Engine must be rebored

 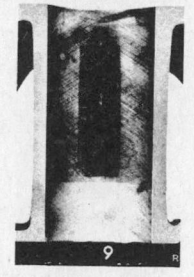

5, 6 Score marks caused by a split piston skirt. Damage is not serious enough to warrant reboring

7. Ring seized longitudinally, causing a score mark 1 3/16" wide, on the land side of the piston groove. The honing pattern is destroyed and the cylinder must be rebored

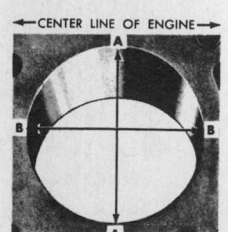 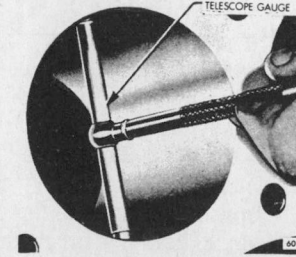

8. Result of oil ring seizure. Engine must be rebored

9. Oil ring seizure here was not serious enough to warrant reboring. The honing marks are still visible

Cylinder wall damage
(© Daimler-Benz A.G.)

Visually inspect the cylinder bores for roughness, scoring, or scuffing. If evident, the cylinder bore must be bored or honed oversize to eliminate imperfections, and the smallest possible oversize piston used. The new pistons should be given to the machinist with the block, so that the cylinders can be bored or honed exactly to the piston size (plus clearance). If no flaws are evident, measure the bore diameter using a telescope gauge and micrometer, or dial gauge, parallel and perpendicular to the engine centerline, at the top (below the ridge) and bottom of the bore. Subtract the bottom measurements from the top to determine taper, and the parallel to the centerline measurements from the perpendicular measurements to determine eccentricity. If the measurements are not within specifications, the cylinder must be bored or honed, and an oversize piston installed. If the measurements are within specifications the cylinder may be used as is, with only finish honing (see below). NOTE: *Prior to submitting the block for boring, perform the following operation(s).*

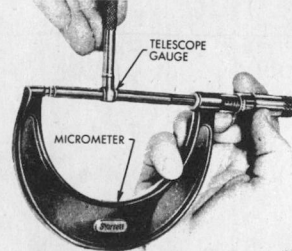 

Cylinder bore measuring positions
(© Ford Motor Co.)

Measuring the cylinder bore with a telescope gauge
(© Buick Div. G.M. Corp.)

Determining the cylinder bore by measuring the telescope gauge with a micrometer
(© Buick Div. G.M. Corp.)

Measuring the cylinder bore with a dial gauge
(© Chevrolet Div. G.M. Corp.)

Procedure	*Method*
Check the block deck for warpage:	Using a straightedge and feeler gauges, check the block deck for warpage in the same manner that the cylinder head is checked (see Cylinder Head Reconditioning). If warpage exceeds specifications, have the deck resurfaced. NOTE: *In certain cases a specification for total material removal (Cylinder head and block deck) is provided. This specification must not be exceeded.*
* Check the deck height:	The deck height is the distance from the crankshaft centerline to the block deck. To measure, invert the engine, and install the crankshaft, retaining it with the center main cap. Measure the distance from the crankshaft journal to the block deck, parallel to the cylinder centerline. Measure the diameter of the end (front and rear) main journals, parallel to the centerline of the cylinders, divide the diameter in half, and subtract it from the previous measurement. The results of the front and rear measurements should be identical. If the difference exceeds .005″, the deck height should be corrected. NOTE: *Block deck height and warpage should be corrected concurrently.*
Check the cylinder block bearing alignment: 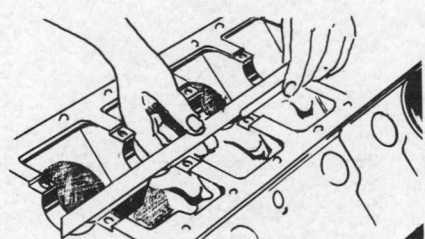 **Checking main bearing saddle alignment** (ⓒ Petersen Publishing Co.)	Remove the upper bearing inserts. Place a straightedge in the bearing saddles along the centerline of the crankshaft. If clearance exists between the straightedge and the center saddle, the block must be align-bored.
Clean and inspect the pistons and connecting rods: 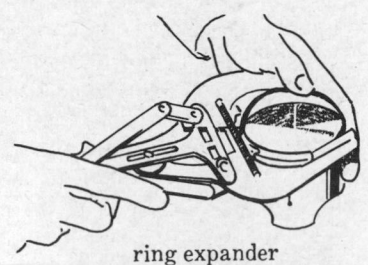 ring expander **Removing the piston rings** (ⓒ Subaru)	Using a ring expander, remove the rings from the piston. Remove the retaining rings (if so equipped) and remove piston pin. NOTE: *If the piston pin must be pressed out, determine the proper method and use the proper tools; otherwise the piston will distort.* Clean the ring grooves using an appropriate tool, exercising care to avoid cutting too deeply. Thoroughly clean all carbon and varnish from the piston with solvent. CAUTION: *Do not use a wire brush or caustic solvent on pistons.* Inspect the pistons for scuffing, scoring, cracks, pitting, or excessive ring groove wear. If wear is evident, the piston must be replaced. Check the connecting rod length by measuring the rod from the inside of the large end to the inside of the small end using calipers (see

Procedure	*Method*

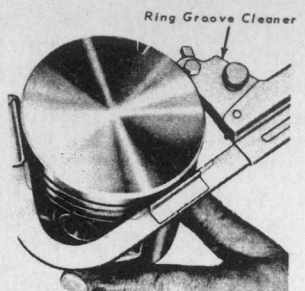
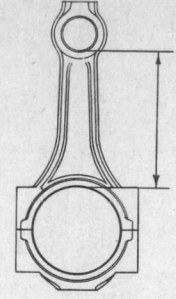

Cleaning the piston ring grooves
(© Ford Motor Co.)

Connecting rod
length checking
dimension

illustration). All connecting rods should be equal length. Replace any rod that differs from the others in the engine.

* Have the connecting rod alignment checked in an alignment fixture by a machinist. Replace any twisted or bent rods.

* Magnaflux the connecting rods to locate stress cracks. If cracks are found, replace the connecting rod.

Fit the pistons to the cylinders:

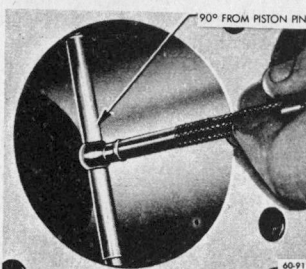

Measuring the cylinder
with a telescope gauge
for piston fitting
((© Buick Div.
G.M. Corp.)

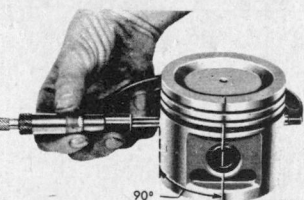

Measuring the piston
for fitting
(© Buick Div.
G.M. Corp.)

Using a telescope gauge and micrometer, or a dial gauge, measure the cylinder bore diameter perpendicular to the piston pin, 2½" below the deck. Measure the piston perpendicular to its pin on the skirt. The difference between the two measurements is the piston clearance. If the clearance is within specifications or slightly below (after boring or honing), finish honing is all that is required. If the clearance is excessive, try to obtain a slightly larger piston to bring clearance within specifications. Where this is not possible, obtain the first oversize piston, and hone (or if necessary, bore) the cylinder to size.

Assemble the pistons and connecting rods:

Installing piston pin lock rings
(© Nissan Motor Co., Ltd.)

Inspect piston pin, connecting rod small end bushing, and piston bore for galling, scoring, or excessive wear. If evident, replace defective part(s). Measure the I.D. of the piston boss and connecting rod small end, and the O.D. of the piston pin. If within specifications, assemble piston pin and rod. CAUTION: *If piston pin must be pressed in, determine the proper method and use the proper tools; otherwise the piston will distort.* Install the lock rings; ensure that they seat properly. If the parts are not within specifications, determine the service method for the type of engine. In some cases, piston and pin are serviced as an assembly when either is defective. Others specify reaming the piston and connecting rods for an oversize pin. If the connecting rod bushing is worn, it may in many cases be replaced. Reaming the piston and replacing the rod bushing are machine shop operations.

Procedure	*Method*

Clean and inspect the camshaft:

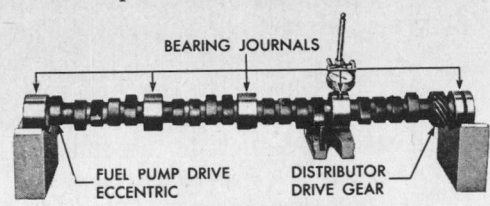

**Checking the camshaft
for straightness**
(ⓒ Chevrolet Motor
Div. G.M. Corp.)

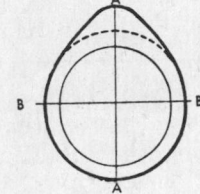

Camshaft lobe measurement
(ⓒ Ford Motor Co.)

Degrease the camshaft, using solvent, and clean out all oil holes. Visually inspect cam lobes and bearing journals for excessive wear. If a lobe is questionable, check all lobes as indicated below. If a journal or lobe is worn, the camshaft must be reground or replaced. NOTE: *If a journal is worn, there is a good chance that the bushings are worn.* If lobes and journals appear intact, place the front and rear journals in V-blocks, and rest a dial indicator on the center journal. Rotate the camshaft to check straightness. If deviation exceeds .001″, replace the camshaft.

* Check the camshaft lobes with a micrometer, by measuring the lobes from the nose to base and again at 90° (see illustration). The lift is determined by subtracting the second measurement from the first. If all exhaust lobes and all intake lobes are not identical, the camshaft must be reground or replaced.

Replace the camshaft bearings:

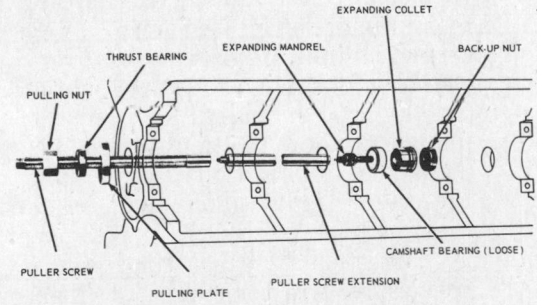

Camshaft removal and installation tool (typical)
(ⓒ Ford Motor Co.)

If excessive wear is indicated, or if the engine is being completely rebuilt, camshaft bearings should be replaced as follows: Drive the camshaft rear plug from the block. Assemble the removal puller with its shoulder on the bearing to be removed. Gradually tighten the puller nut until bearing is removed. Remove remaining bearings, leaving the front and rear for last. To remove front and rear bearings, reverse position of the tool, so as to pull the bearings in toward the center of the block. Leave the tool in this position, pilot the new front and rear bearings on the installer, and pull them into position. Return the tool to its original position and pull remaining bearings into position. NOTE: *Ensure that oil holes align when installing bearings.* Replace camshaft rear plug, and stake it into position to aid retention.

Finish hone the cylinders:

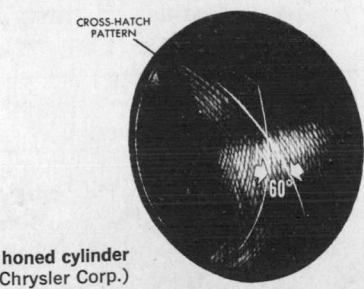

Finish honed cylinder
(ⓒ Chrysler Corp.)

Chuck a flexible drive hone into a power drill, and insert it into the cylinder. Start the hone, and move it up and down in the cylinder at a rate which will produce approximately a 60° cross-hatch pattern (see illustration). NOTE: *Do not extend the hone below the cylinder bore.* After developing the pattern, remove the hone and recheck piston fit. Wash the cylinders with a detergent and water solution to remove abrasive dust, dry, and wipe several times with a rag soaked in engine oil.

U225

Procedure	*Method*
Check piston ring end-gap: 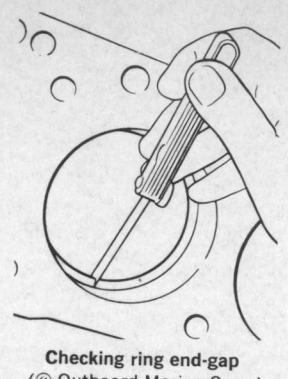 **Checking ring end-gap** (© Outboard Marine Corp.)	Compress the piston rings to be used in a cylinder, one at a time, into that cylinder, and press them approximately 1″ below the deck with an inverted piston. Using feeler gauges, measure the ring end-gap, and compare to specifications. Pull the ring out of the cylinder and file the ends with a fine file to obtain proper clearance. CAUTION: *If inadequate ring end-gap is utilized, ring breakage will result.*
Install the piston rings: 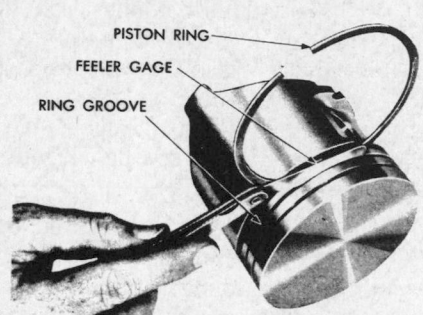 **Checking ring side clearance** (© Chrysler Corp.) 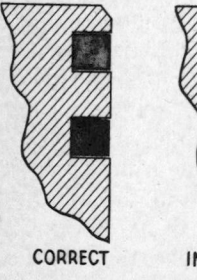 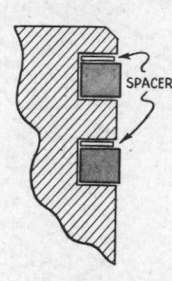 **CORRECT** **INCORRECT** SPACER **Piston groove depth** **Correct ring spacer installation**	Inspect the ring grooves in the piston for excessive wear or taper. If necessary, recut the groove(s) for use with an overwidth ring or a standard ring and spacer. If the groove is worn uniformly, overwidth rings, or standard rings and spacers may be installed without recutting. Roll the outside of the ring around the groove to check for burrs or deposits. If any are found, remove with a fine file. Hold the ring in the groove, and measure side clearance. If necessary, correct as indicated above. NOTE: *Always install any additional spacers above the piston ring.* The ring groove must be deep enough to allow the ring to seat below the lands (see illustration). In many cases, a "go-no-go" depth gauge will be provided with the piston rings. Shallow grooves may be corrected by recutting, while deep grooves require some type of filler or expander behind the piston. Consult the piston ring supplier concerning the suggested method. Install the rings on the piston, lowest ring first, using a ring expander. NOTE: *Position the ring markings as specified by the manufacturer (see car section).*
Install the camshaft:	Liberally lubricate the camshaft lobes and journals, and slide the camshaft into the block. CAUTION: *Exercise extreme care to avoid damaging the bearings when inserting the camshaft.* Install and tighten the camshaft thrust plate retaining bolts.
Check camshaft end-play: 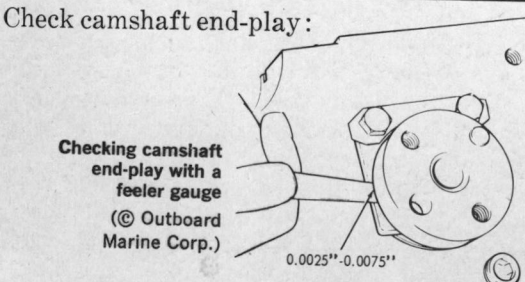 **Checking camshaft end-play with a feeler gauge** (© Outboard Marine Corp.) 0.0025″-0.0075″	Using feeler gauges, determine whether the clearance between the camshaft boss (or gear) and backing plate is within specifications. Install shims behind the thrust plate, or reposition the camshaft gear and retest end-play.

Procedure	*Method*

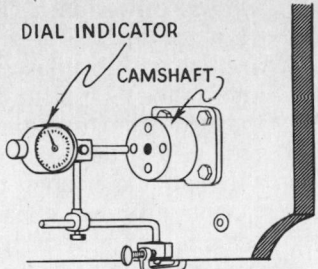

Checking camshaft end-play with a dial indicator

* Mount a dial indicator stand so that the stem of the dial indicator rests on the nose of the camshaft, parallel to the camshaft axis. Push the camshaft as far in as possible and zero the gauge. Move the camshaft outward to determine the amount of camshaft end-play. If the end-play is not within tolerance, install shims behind the thrust plate, or reposition the camshaft gear and retest.

Install the rear main seal (where applicable):

Seating the rear main seal
(© Buick Div. G.M. Corp.)

Position the block with the bearing saddles facing upward. Lay the rear main seal in its groove and press it lightly into its seat. Place a piece of pipe the same diameter as the crankshaft journal into the saddle, and firmly seat the seal. Hold the pipe in position, and trim the ends of the seal flush if required.

Install the crankshaft:

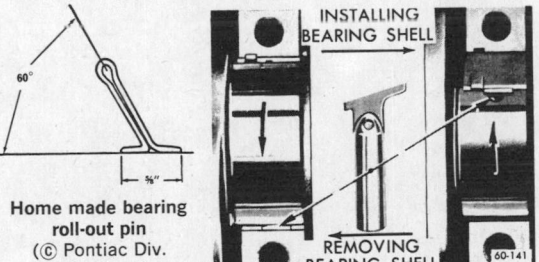

Home made bearing roll-out pin
(© Pontiac Div. G.M. Corp.)

Removal and installation of upper bearing insert using a roll-out pin
(© Buick Div. G.M. Corp.)

Thoroughly clean the main bearing saddles and caps. Place the upper halves of the bearing inserts on the saddles and press into position. NOTE: *Ensure that the oil holes align.* Press the corresponding bearing inserts into the main bearing caps. Lubricate the upper main bearings, and lay the crankshaft in position. Place a strip of Plastigage on each of the crankshaft journals, install the main caps, and torque to specifications. Remove the main caps, and compare the Plastigage to the scale on the Plastigage envelope. If clearances are within tolerances, remove the Plastigage, turn the crankshaft 90°, wipe off all oil and retest. If all clearances are correct, remove all Plastigage, thoroughly

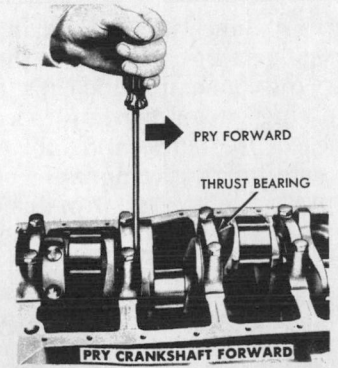

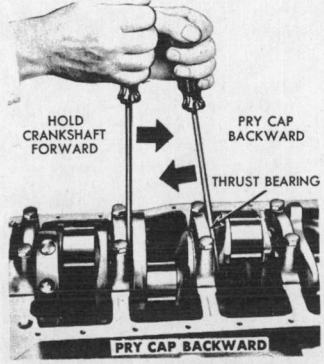

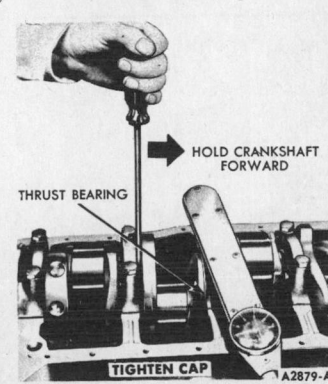

Aligning the thrust bearing
(© Ford Motor Co.)

Procedure	*Method*

lubricate the main caps and bearing journals, and install the main caps. If clearances are not within tolerance, the upper bearing inserts may be removed, without removing the crankshaft, using a bearing roll out pin (see illustration). Roll in a bearing that will provide proper clearance, and retest. Torque all main caps, excluding the thrust bearing cap, to specifications. Tighten the thrust bearing cap finger tight. To properly align the thrust bearing, pry the crankshaft the extent of its axial travel several times, the last movement held toward the front of the engine, and torque the thrust bearing cap to specifications. Determine the crankshaft end-play (see below), and bring within tolerance with thrust washers.

Measure crankshaft end-play:

Checking crankshaft end-play with a dial indicator
(© Ford Motor Co.)

Checking crankshaft end-play with a feeler gauge
(© Outboard Marine Corp.)

Mount a dial indicator stand on the front of the block, with the dial indicator stem resting on the nose of the crankshaft, parallel to the crankshaft axis. Pry the crankshaft the extent of its travel rearward, and zero the indicator. Pry the crankshaft forward and record crankshaft end-play. NOTE: *Crankshaft end-play also may be measured at the thrust bearing, using feeler gauges* (see illustration).

Install the pistons:

Press the upper connecting rod bearing halves into the connecting rods, and the lower halves into the connecting rod caps. Position the piston ring gaps according to specifications (see car section), and lubricate the pistons. Install a ring compresser on a piston, and press two long (8″) pieces of plastic tubing over the rod bolts. Using the plastic tubes as a guide, press the pistons into the bores and onto the crankshaft with a wooden hammer handle. After seating the rod on the crankshaft journal, remove the tubes and install the cap finger tight. Install the remaining pistons in the same man-

Procedure *Method*

Tubing used as guide when installing a piston
(© Oldsmobile Div. G.M. Corp.)

ner. Invert the engine and check the bearing clearance at two points (90° apart) on each journal with Plastigage. NOTE: *Do not turn the crankshaft with Plastigage installed.* If clearance is within tolerances, remove *all* Plastigage, thoroughly lubricate the journals, and torque the rod caps to specifications. If clearance is not within specifications, install different thickness bearing inserts and recheck. CAUTION: *Never shim or file the connecting rods or caps.* Always install plastic tube sleeves over the rod bolts when the caps are not installed, to protect the crankshaft journals.

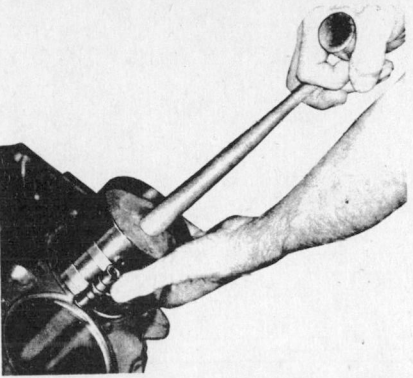

Installing a piston
(© Chevrolet Div. G.M. Corp.)

Check connecting rod side clearance:

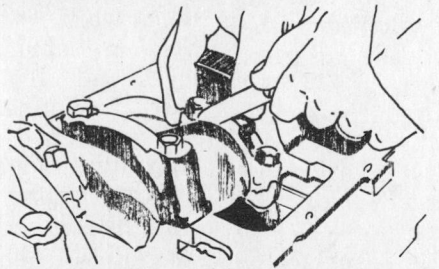

Checking connecting rod side clearance
(© Chevrolet Div. G.M. Corp.)

Determine the clearance between the sides of the connecting rods and the crankshaft, using feeler gauges. If clearance is below the minimum tolerance, the rod may be machined to provide adequate clearance. If clearance is excessive, substitute an unworn rod, and recheck. If clearance is still outside specifications, the crankshaft must be welded and reground, or replaced.

Inspect the timing chain:

Visually inspect the timing chain for broken or loose links, and replace the chain if any are found. If the chain will flex sideways, it must be replaced. Install the timing chain as specified. NOTE: *If the original timing chain is to be reused, install it in its original position.*

Procedure	*Method*

Check timing gear backlash and runout:

Checking camshaft gear backlash
(© Chevrolet Div. G.M. Corp.)

Checking camshaft gear runout
(© Chevrolet Div. G.M. Corp.)

Mount a dial indicator with its stem resting on a tooth of the camshaft gear (as illustrated). Rotate the gear until all slack is removed, and zero the indicator. Rotate the gear in the opposite direction until slack is removed, and record gear backlash. Mount the indicator with its stem resting on the edge of the camshaft gear, parallel to the axis of the camshaft. Zero the indicator, and turn the camshaft gear one full turn, recording the runout. If either backlash or runout exceed specifications, replace the worn gear(s).

Completing the Rebuilding Process

Following the above procedures, complete the rebuilding process as follows:

Fill the oil pump with oil, to prevent cavitating (sucking air) on initial engine start up. Install the oil pump and the pickup tube on the engine. Coat the oil pan gasket as necessary, and install the gasket and the oil pan. Mount the flywheel and the crankshaft vibrational damper or pulley on the crankshaft. NOTE: *Always use new bolts when installing the flywheel.* Inspect the clutch shaft pilot bushing in the crankshaft. If the bushing is excessively worn, remove it with an expanding puller and a slide hammer, and tap a new bushing into place.

Position the engine, cylinder head side up. Lubricate the lifters, and install them into their bores. Install the cylinder head, and torque it as specified in the car section. Insert the pushrods (where applicable), and install the rocker shaft(s) (if so equipped) or position the rocker arms on the pushrods. If solid lifters are utilized, adjust the valves to the "cold" specifications.

Mount the intake and exhaust manifolds, the carburetor(s), the distributor and spark plugs. Adjust the point gap and the static ignition timing. Mount all accessories and install the engine in the car. Fill the radiator with coolant, and the crankcase with high quality engine oil.

Break-in Procedure

Start the engine, and allow it to run at low speed for a few minutes, while checking for leaks. Stop the engine, check the oil level, and fill as necessary. Restart the engine, and fill the cooling system to capacity. Check the point dwell angle and adjust the ignition timing and the valves. Run the engine at low to medium speed (800-2500 rpm) for approximately ½ hour, and re-torque the cylinder head bolts. Road test the car, and check again for leaks.

Follow the manufacturer's recommended engine break-in procedure and maintenance schedule for new engines.

Manual Transmissions

Applicability Chart

| Make | Model | TYPE | |
		3-Spd	4/5 Spd
American Motors	1970-72	16, 17	18
	1973	16	18
	1974	4, 16	18
	1975-77	4, 19, 16	
Apollo, Skylark	1973-77	10	
Barracuda, Challenger	1970-72	1, 2	3
	1973-74	1	3
Buick, Oldsmobile	1970-71	4	
Buick Special, Regal, Century, GS	1970-71	9, 10	11
	1972	10	11
	1973-77	10	
Camaro	1970-73	9, 10	11, 12
	1974-77	10	12, 18
Chevelle	1970-74	9, 10	11, 12
	1975-77	10	
Chevrolet	1970-73	9, 10	
Chrysler	1970-71	1	
Comet, Maverick, Granada, Monarch	1970-77	4	
Corvette	1970-73		11, 12
	1974-77		12, 18
Cougar	1970-73	4	8
Dart, Demon, Aspen, Volare, Valiant Duster	1970-74	1, 2	3
	1975-77	1, 4	3
Dodge, Coronet, Charger, Plymouth, Belvedere, Satellite, Fury	1970-72	1, 2	3
	1973-74	1	3
	1975-77	1	
Fairlane, Falcon, Ford, Mercury, Montego, Mustang, Torino	1970-74	4	8
Firebird	1970-71	9, 10	11
	1972-73	9, 10	11, 12
	1974	9, 10	11, 12, 18
	1975-77	10	12, 18
Monte Carlo	1970-71	9	11
	1972-73	9	
Monza, Skyhawk, Starfire, Sunbird	1975-77	10	12, 15, 20
Mustang II	1974-77		7
Nova	1970-74	9, 10	11, 12
	1975-77	10	12

Applicability Chart

Make	Model	TYPE 3-Spd	TYPE 4/5 Spd
Oldsmobile F-85, Cutlass, 4-4-2	1970-71	9, 10	11
	1972-73	10	11
	1974-77	10	20
Omega	1973-77	10	20
Pinto, Bobcat	1971-73 1600 cc		6
	1971-77 All others		5
Pontiac	1970-71	4, 9	11
Tempest, GTO, LeMans	1970-74	9, 10	11, 12
	1975-77	10	20
Vega, Cosworth Vega, Chevette, Astre	1971-72	13	14
	1973-75	10	12
	1976-77	10	15, 20
Ventura	1971-77	10	11, 12, 20

Type Numbers Refer to Sections in Text

See Car Sections for Identification

Section Page Numbers

Transmission	Type	Page No.
Diagnosis		
Chrysler Corporation		
A-230 Fully Synchronized Chrysler 3-Speed	1	U233
A-390 Fully Synchronized Chrysler 3-Speed	4	U244
A-903, A-250 Chrysler 3-Speed	2	U237
A-833 Chrysler 4-Speed and Overdrive-4	3	U239
Ford Motor Company		
3.03 Fully Synchronized Ford 3-Speed	4	U244
Pinto, Bobcat German 4-Speed	5	U247
Pinto British 4-Speed	6	U250
Mustang II American 4-Speed	7	U252
Ford 4-Speed	8	U255
General Motors Corporation		
Muncie Fully Synchronized 3-Speed	9	U259
Saginaw Fully Synchronized 3-Speed	10	U261
Muncie 4-Speed	11	U263
Saginaw 4-Speed	12	U265
Vega 3-Speed	13	U267
Vega 4-Speed	14	U269
70 mm. 4-Speed	15	U272
Warner Gear, American Motors		
Warner T-14, T-15 Fully Synchronized 3-Speed	16	U274
Warner T-96 3-Speed	17	U275
AMC 150T Fully Synchronized 3-Speed	4	U244
Warner T-10 4-Speed	18	U277
AMC Overdrive	19	U279
Warner T-50 5-Speed	20	U282

Manual Transmissions

Diagnosis

Jumping out of High Gear

1. Misalignment of transmission case or clutch housing.
2. Worn pilot bearing in crankshaft.
3. Bent transmission shaft.
4. Worn high speed sliding gear.
5. Worn teeth in clutch shaft.
6. Insufficient spring tension on shifter rail plunger.
7. Bent or loose shifter fork.
8. End-play in clutch shaft.
9. Gears not engaging completely.
10. Loose or worn bearings on clutch shaft or mainshaft.

Sticking in High Gear

1. Clutch not releasing fully.
2. Burred or battered teeth on clutch shaft.
3. Burred or battered transmission main-shaft.
4. Frozen synchronizing clutch.
5. Stuck shifter rail plunger.
6. Gearshift lever twisting and binding shifter rail.
7. Battered teeth on high speed sliding gear or on sleeve.
8. Lack of lubrication.
9. Improper lubrication.
10. Corroded transmission parts.
11. Defective mainshaft pilot bearing.

Jumping out of Second Gear

1. Insufficient spring tension on shifter rail plunger.
2. Bent or loose shifter fork.
3. Gears not engaging completely.
4. End-play in transmission mainshaft.
5. Loose transmission gear bearing.
6. Defective mainshaft pilot bearing.
7. Bent transmission shaft.
8. Worn teeth on second speed sliding gear or sleeve.

9. Loose or worn bearings on transmission mainshaft.
10. End-play in countershaft.

Sticking in Second Gear

1. Clutch not releasing fully.
2. Burred or battered teeth on sliding sleeve.
3. Burred or battered transmission main-shaft.
4. Frozen synchronizing clutch.
5. Stuck shifter rail plunger.
6. Gearshift lever twisting and binding shifter rail.
7. Lack of lubrication.
8. Second speed transmission gear bearings locked will give same effect as gears stuck in second.
9. Improper lubrication.
10. Corroded transmission parts.

Jumping out of Low Gear

1. Gears not engaging completely.
2. Bent or loose shifter fork.
3. End-play in transmission mainshaft.
4. End-play in countershaft.
5. Loose or worn bearings on transmission mainshaft.
6. Loose or worn bearings in countershaft.
7. Defective mainshaft pilot bearing.

Sticking in Low Gear

1. Clutch not releasing fully.
2. Burred or battered transmission main-shaft.
3. Stuck shifter rail plunger.
4. Gearshift lever twisting and binding shifter rail.
5. Lack of lubrication.
6. Improper lubrication.
7. Corroded transmission parts.

Jumping out of Reverse Gear

1. Insufficient spring tension on shifter rail plunger.
2. Bent or loose shifter fork.
3. Badly worn gear teeth.

4. Gears not engaging completely.
5. End-play in transmission mainshaft.
6. Idler gear bushings loose or worn.
7. Loose or worn bearings on transmission mainshaft.
8. Defective mainshaft pilot bearing.

Sticking in Reverse Gear

1. Clutch not releasing fully.
2. Burred or battered transmission main-shaft.
3. Stuck shifter rail plunger.
4. Gearshift lever twisting and binding shifter rail.
5. Lack of lubrication.
6. Improper lubrication.
7. Corroded transmission parts.

Failure of Gears to Synchronize

1. Binding pilot bearing on mainshaft, will synchronize in high gear only.
2. Clutch not releasing fully.
3. Detent springs weak or broken.
4. Weak or broken springs under balls in sliding gear sleeve.
5. Binding bearing on clutch shaft.
6. Binding countershaft.
7. Binding pilot bearing in crankshaft.
8. Badly worn gear teeth.
9. Scored or worn cones.
10. Improper lubrication.
11. Constant mesh gear not turning freely on transmission mainshaft. Will synchronize in that gear only.

Gears Spinning When Shifting into Gear from Neutral

1. Clutch not releasing fully.
2. In some cases an extremely light lubricant in transmission will cause gears to continue to spin for a short time after clutch is released.
3. Binding pilot bearing in crankshaft.

Type-1
A-230 Fully Synchronized Chrysler 3-Speed

Application (V8)
Aspen, 1976-77
Barracuda, 1970-74
Challenger, 1970-74
Charger, 1970-74
Chrysler, 1970-71
Dart, 1970-77
Dodge, 1970-77
Plymouth, 1970-77
Valiant, 1970-77
Volare, 1976-77

Disassembly

Shift Housing and Mechanism

1. Shift to second gear.
2. Unbolt and remove side cover with shift mechanism.
   If shaft O-ring seals need replacement:
3. Pull shift forks out of shafts.
4. Remove nuts and operating levers from shafts.
5. Deburr shafts. Remove shafts.

Drive Pinion Retainer and Extension Housing

1. Unbolt pinion bearing retainer from front of transmission case. Remove retainer and gasket. Pry off retainer oil seal.
   For clearance:
2. With a brass drift, tap drive pinion as far forward as possible. Rotate cut away part of second gear next to countershaft gear. Shift second-third synchronizer sleeve forward.

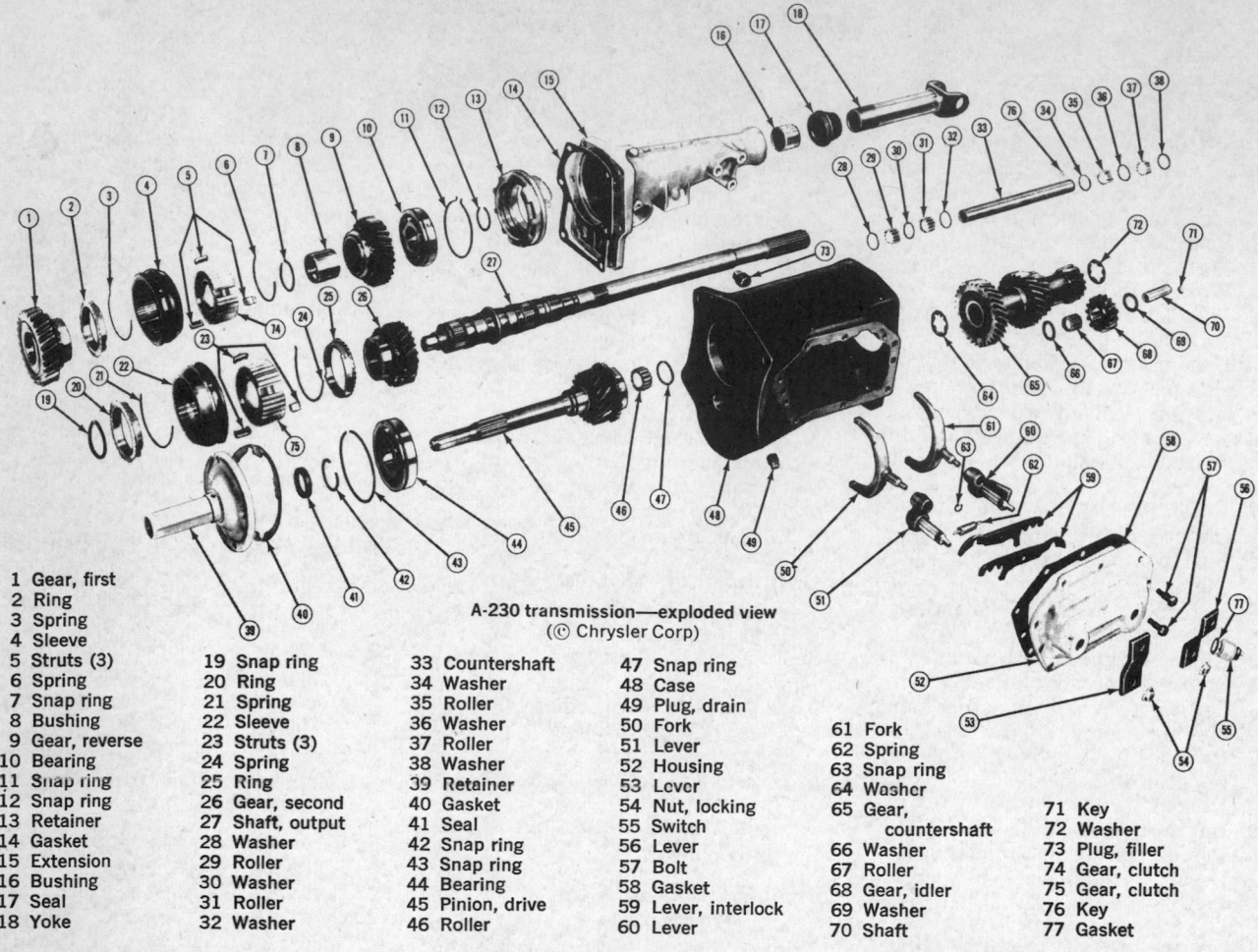

A-230 transmission—exploded view
(© Chrysler Corp)

1 Gear, first
2 Ring
3 Spring
4 Sleeve
5 Struts (3)
6 Spring
7 Snap ring
8 Bushing
9 Gear, reverse
10 Bearing
11 Snap ring
12 Snap ring
13 Retainer
14 Gasket
15 Extension
16 Bushing
17 Seal
18 Yoke

19 Snap ring
20 Ring
21 Spring
22 Sleeve
23 Struts (3)
24 Spring
25 Ring
26 Gear, second
27 Shaft, output
28 Washer
29 Roller
30 Washer
31 Roller
32 Washer

33 Countershaft
34 Washer
35 Roller
36 Washer
37 Roller
38 Washer
39 Retainer
40 Gasket
41 Seal
42 Snap ring
43 Snap ring
44 Bearing
45 Pinion, drive
46 Roller

47 Snap ring
48 Case
49 Plug, drain
50 Fork
51 Lever
52 Housing
53 Lever
54 Nut, locking
55 Switch
56 Lever
57 Bolt
58 Gasket
59 Lever, interlock
60 Lever

61 Fork
62 Spring
63 Snap ring
64 Washer
65 Gear, countershaft
66 Washer
67 Roller
68 Gear, idler
69 Washer
70 Shaft

71 Key
72 Washer
73 Plug, filler
74 Gear, clutch
75 Gear, clutch
76 Key
77 Gasket

3. Remove speedometer pinion adapter retainer. Work adapter and pinion out of extension housing.
4. Unbolt extension housing. Break housing loose with plastic hammer and carefully remove.

Idler Gear and Mainshaft

1. Insert dummy shaft in case to push reverse idler shaft and key out of case.
2. Remove dummy shaft and idler gear together to prevent losing rollers.
3. Remove both tanged idler gear thrust washers.
4. Remove mainshaft assembly through rear of case.

Countershaft Gear and Drive Pinion

1. Using a mallet and dummy shaft, tap the countershaft rearward enough to remove key. Drive countershaft out of case, maintaining contact between countershaft and dummy shaft so that washers will not drop out.
2. Lower countershaft gear to bottom of case.
3. Remove snap-ring from pinion bearing outer race (outside

front of case).
4. Drive pinion shaft into case with plastic hammer. Remove assembly through rear of case.
5. If bearing is to be replaced, remove snap-ring and press off bearing.
6. Lift countershaft gear and dummy shaft out through rear of case.

Mainshaft

1. Remove snap-ring from front end of mainshaft along with second gear stop ring. Remove second gear from mainshaft.
2. Spread snap-ring in mainshaft bearing retainer. Slide retainer back off the bearing race.
3. Remove snap-ring at rear of mainshaft. Support front side of reverse gear. Press bearing off mainshaft. Be careful not to let parts drop when bearing clears shaft.
4. Remove from press. Remove mainshaft bearing and reverse gear from shaft.
5. Remove snap-ring from rear of shaft. Slide first-reverse synchronizer assembly off splines and remove rearward. Remove stop-ring and first gear through the rear.

Inspection

1. Clean all parts with solvent.
2. Dry with compressed air.

Case

1. Check for cracks, stripped threads, and burrs or nicks on machined surfaces. Dress off any burrs with a fine file. Stripped threads may be repaired by use of Helicoil inserts.

Ball Bearings

1. Do not spin bearings with air pressure; turn slowly by hand to avoid damage.
2. Lubricate with light engine oil.
3. Check for pitting.
4. Check fit on shafts.

Needle Bearings

1. Check rollers for flats or brinelling.
2. Check roller spacers for wear or galling.

Gears

1. Check gear splines on synchronizer clutch gears and stop-rings for chipping or worn teeth.
2. Be sure the clutch sleeve slides easily on clutch gear.
3. Check countershaft gear and all

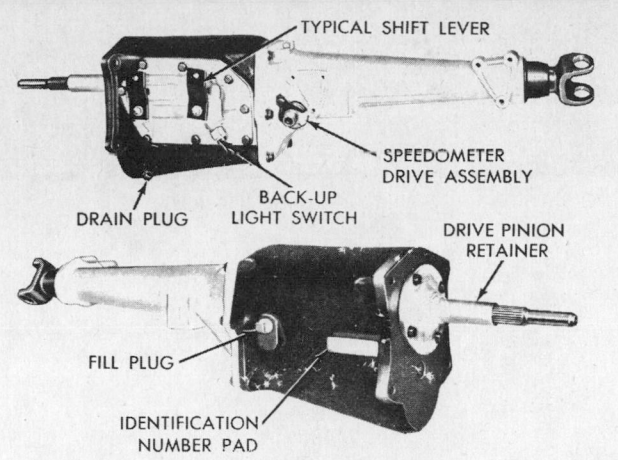

TYPICAL SHIFT LEVER

SPEEDOMETER DRIVE ASSEMBLY

BACK-UP LIGHT SWITCH

DRAIN PLUG

DRIVE PINION RETAINER

FILL PLUG

IDENTIFICATION NUMBER PAD

Side views of A-230 transmission
(© Chrysler Corp)

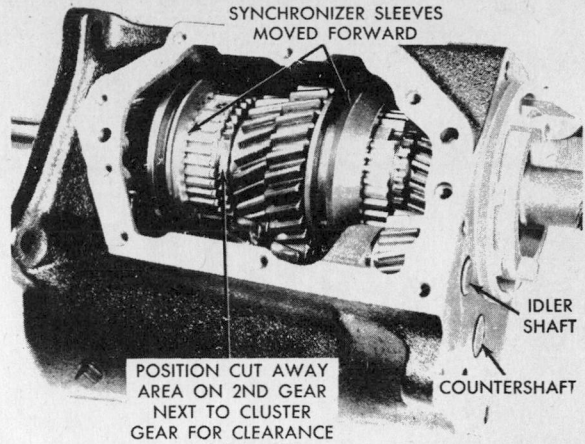

SYNCHRONIZER SLEEVES MOVED FORWARD

IDLER SHAFT

COUNTERSHAFT

POSITION CUT AWAY AREA ON 2ND GEAR NEXT TO CLUSTER GEAR FOR CLEARANCE

Positioning second gear and shift sleeves for clearance
(© Chrysler Corp)

gear teeth for chipping, broken teeth, or excessive wear. Stone off small nicks or burrs.

4. If oil seal contact area on drive pinion shaft is pitted, rusted, or scratched, replace the pinion.

Synchronizer Stop Rings

1. Check for cracks or wear.
2. Check new rings for good fit on gear cones with minimum wobble.

Mainshaft

1. Check mainshaft gear and bearing mating surfaces for galling or excessive wear.
2. Check snap-rings for burred edges. Remove burrs with a fine file.
3. Check synchronizer clutch gear splines on shaft for burrs.

Assembly

Countershaft Gear

1. Slide dummy shaft into countershaft gear.
2. Slide one roller thrust washer over dummy shaft and into gear, followed by 22 greased rollers.
3. Repeat Step 2, adding one roller thrust washer on end.
4. Repeat steps 2 and 3 at other end of countershaft gear. There is a total of 88 rollers and 6 thrust washers.
5. Place greased front thrust washer on dummy shaft against gear with tangs forward.
6. Grease rear thrust washer and stick it in place in the case, with tangs rearward. Place countershaft gear assembly in bottom of transmission case until drive pinion is installed.

Pinion Gear

1. Press new bearing on pinion shaft with snap-ring groove forward. Install new snap-ring.

2. Install 15 rollers and retaining ring in drive pinion gear.
3. Install drive pinion and bearing assembly into case.
4. Install the countershaft gear assembly by positioning it and thrust washers so countershaft can be tapped into position. Be careful to keep the countershaft against the dummy shaft to keep parts from falling between them. Install key in countershaft.
5. Tap drive pinion forward for clearance.

Mainshaft

1. Place a stop-ring flat on the bench. Place a clutch gear and a sleeve on top. Drop the struts in their slots and snap in a strut spring placing the tang inside

one strut. Turn the assembly over and install second strut spring, tang in a different strut.

2. Slide first gear and stop-ring over rear of mainshaft and against thrust flange between first and second gears on shaft.
3. Slide first-reverse synchronizer assembly over rear of mainshaft, indexing hub slots to first gear stop-ring lugs.
4. Install first-reverse synchronizer clutch gear snap-ring on mainshaft.
5. Slide reverse gear and mainshaft bearing into place. Press bearing on shaft, supporting inner race of bearing. Be sure snap-ring groove on outer race is forward.
6. Install bearing retaining snap-ring on mainshaft. Spread

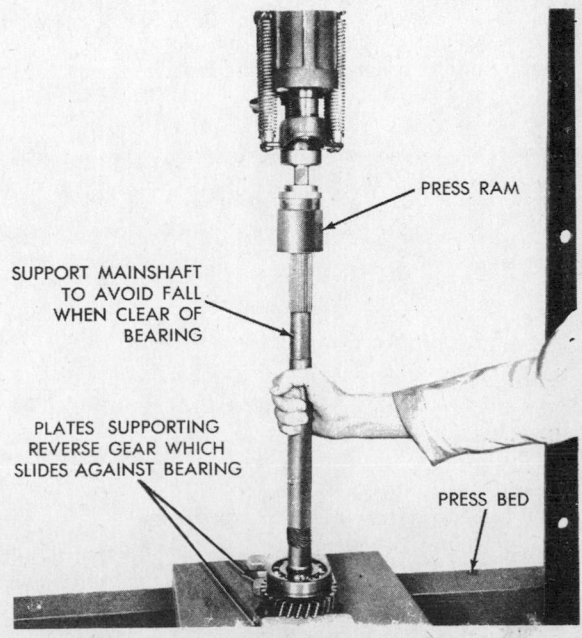

PRESS RAM

SUPPORT MAINSHAFT TO AVOID FALL WHEN CLEAR OF BEARING

PLATES SUPPORTING REVERSE GEAR WHICH SLIDES AGAINST BEARING

PRESS BED

Pressing off mainshaft bearing
(© Chrysler Corp)

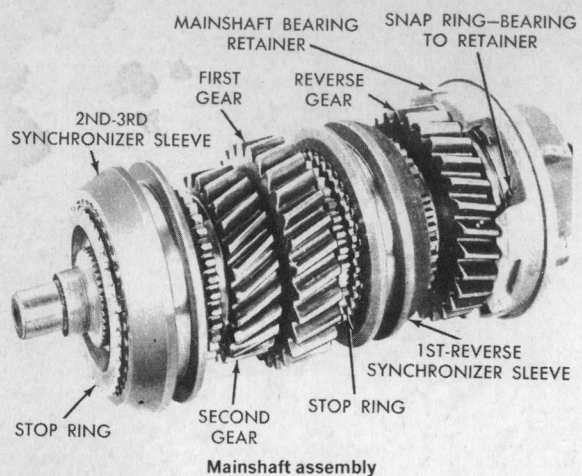

Mainshaft assembly
(© Chrysler Corp)

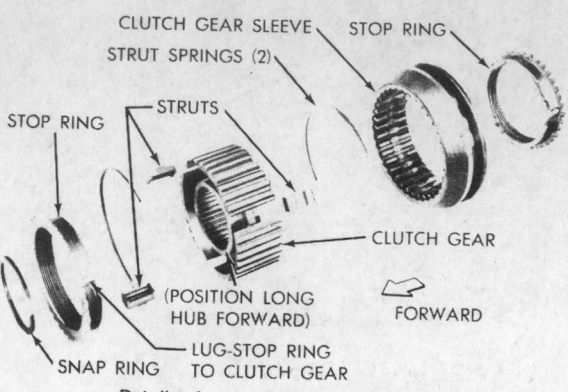

Details of second-third synchronizer
(© Chrysler Corp)

snap-ring in retainer groove and slide it over the bearing. Seat ring in groove.

7. Place second gear over front of mainshaft with thrust surface against flange.

8. Install stop-ring and second-third synchronizer assembly against second gear. Install second-third synchronizer clutch gear snap-ring on shaft.

9. Move second-third synchronizer sleeve forward as far as possible. Install front stop-ring, inside the sleeve with lugs indexed to struts. Coat the stop-ring with grease to hold it in position.

10. Rotate cut-out on second gear toward countershaft gear to provide clearance.

11. Insert mainshaft assembly into case. Tilt assembly to clear cluster gears and insert pilot rollers in drive pinion gear. If assembly is correct, the bearing retainer will bottom to the case without force. If not, check for a misplaced strut, pinion roller, or stop-ring.

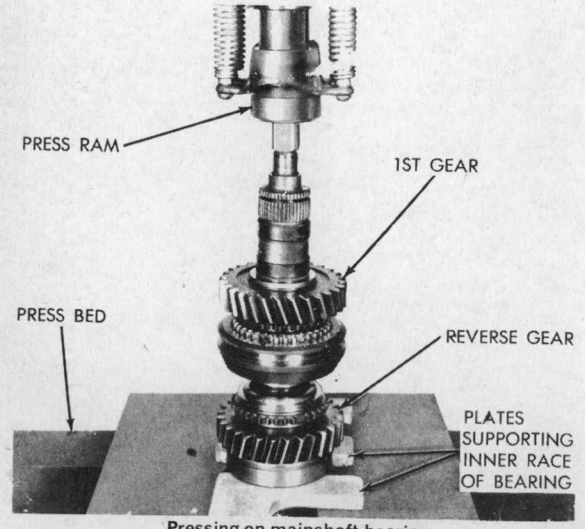

Pressing on mainshaft bearing
(© Chrysler Corp)

Reverse Idler Gear

1. Place dummy shaft into idler gear. Insert 22 greased rollers.
2. Position reverse idler thrust washers in case with grease.
3. Position idler gear and dummy shaft in case. Install idler shaft and key.

Extension Housing

1. Remove extension housing yoke seal. Drive bushing out from inside housing.
2. Align oil hole in bushing with oil slot in housing. Drive bushing into place. Drive new seal into housing.
3. Install extension housing and gasket to hold mainshaft and bearing retainer in place.

Drive Pinion Bearing Retainer

1. Install outer snap-ring on drive pinion bearing. Tap assembly back until snap-ring contacts case.
2. Install a new seal in retainer bore.

3. Position main drive pinion bearing retainer and gasket on front of case. Coat threads with sealing compound, install bolts, torque to 30 ft. lbs.

Gearshift Mechanism and Housing

1. If removed, place two interlock levers on pivot pin with spring hangers offset toward each other, so that spring installs in a straight line. Place E-clip on pivot pin.
2. Grease and install new O-ring seals on both shift shafts. Grease housing bores. Push each shaft into its bore.
3. Install spring on interlock lever hangers.
4. Rotate each shift shaft fork bore to vertical position. Install shift forks through bores and under both interlock levers.
5. Position second-third synchronizer sleeve to rear, in second gear position. Position first-reverse synchronizer sleeve to middle of travel, in neutral position. Place shift forks in the same positions.
6. Install gasket and gearshift mechanism. The bolt with the extra long shoulder must be installed at the center rear of the case. Torque bolts to 15 ft. lbs.
7. Install speedometer drive pinion gear and adapter. Range number on adapter, which represents the number of teeth on the gear, should be in 6 o'clock position.

Exhaust Emission Control System Switch

Some models have a switch in the shift cover, adjacent to the 2-3 shift lever. It is actuated by a flat on the 2-3 shift lever, when in third gear. If vehicle is not equipped with Emission System, a plug is installed in the mounting hole. Torque the switch or plug to 15 ft. lbs.

Type-2
A-903 Chrysler
3-Speed

Application
Charger/Coronet (6 Cyl.),
   1970-72
Challenger (6 Cyl.), 1970-72

Barracuda (6 Cyl.), 1970-72
Dart (6 Cyl.), 1970-72
Dodge (6 Cyl.), 1970-72

Belvedere/Satellite (6 Cyl.),
   1970-72
Plymouth (6 Cyl.), 1970-72
Valiant (6 Cyl.), 1970-72

A-250 Chrysler
3-Speed

Application
Dart, (6 Cyl.), 1973-74
Valiant, (6 Cyl.), 1973-74

Disassembly

1. Remove output shaft yoke.
2. Remove the bolts that attach the extension housing to the transmission case. Remove the housing.
3. Remove extension housing oil seal.
4. Remove the transmission case cover. Measure synchronizer float with feeler gauges on A-903 models. This measurement is taken between the end of a synchronizer pin and the opposite synchronizer outer ring. This measurement should be .060-.117 in.

5. Remove the attaching bolts and remove the main drive pinion bearing retainer. Then grasp the pinion shaft and pull the assembly out of the case.

CAUTION: Be careful not to bind the inner synchronizer ring on the drive pinion clutch teeth.

6. Remove the snap-ring that locks the main drive pinion bearing onto the pinion shaft. Remove the bearing washer, press the shaft out of the bearing and remove the oil slinger.
7. Remove the snap-ring from the pilot bearing in the end of the drive pinion and remove the 14 rollers.
8. With the transmission in reverse, remove the outer center bearing snap-ring, then partially

remove the mainshaft.
9. Cock the mainshaft, then remove the clutch sleeve, the outer synchronizer rings, the front inner ring and the second-third shift box.
10. Remove clutch gear retaining snap ring and slide the clutch gear off the end of the mainshaft.
11. Slide the second-speed gear, stop-ring and synchronizer spring off the mainshaft.
12. Remove the low and reverse sliding gear and shift fork, as the mainshaft is completely withdrawn from the case.
13. Check cluster gear end-play. End-play should be .005-.022 in. This measurement will determine thrust washer value at reassembly.

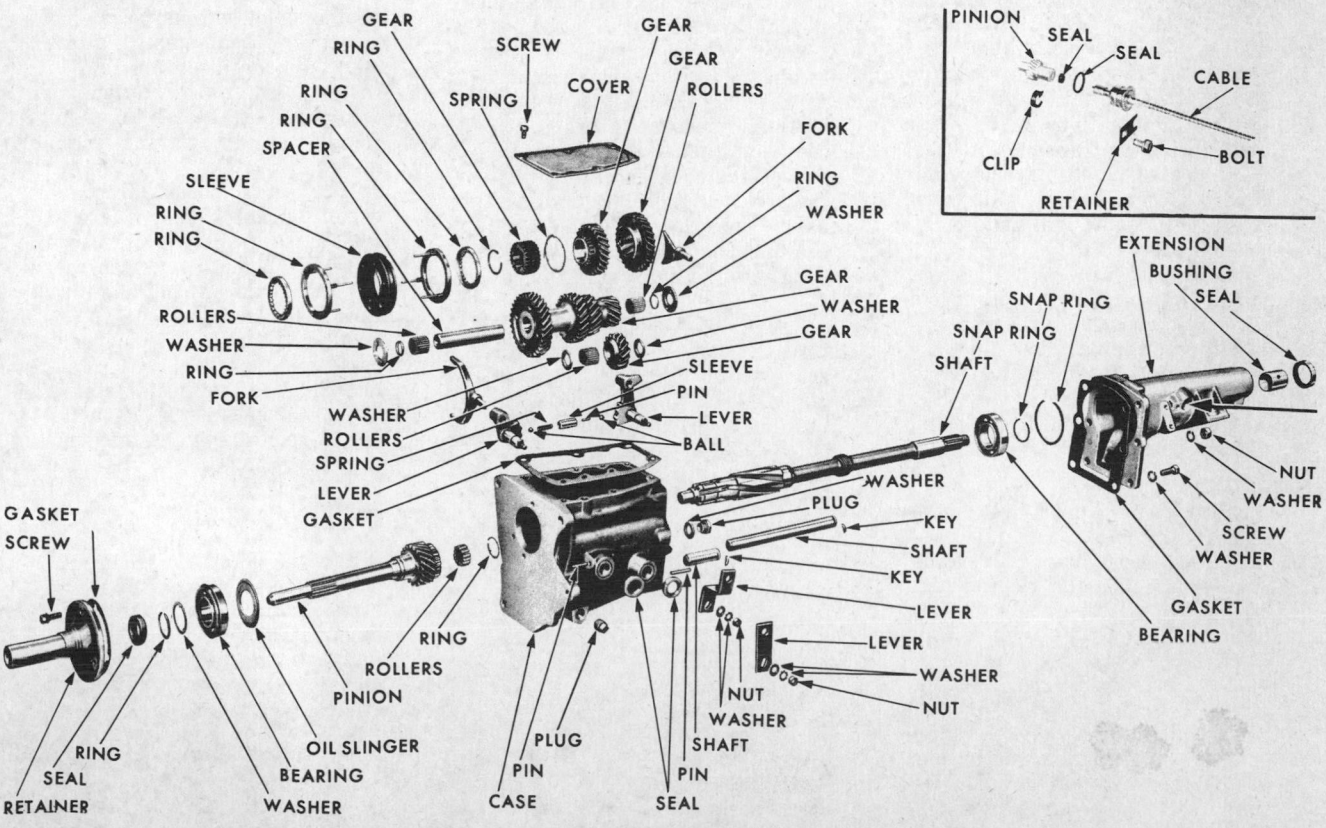

A-903, A-250 Chrysler transmission

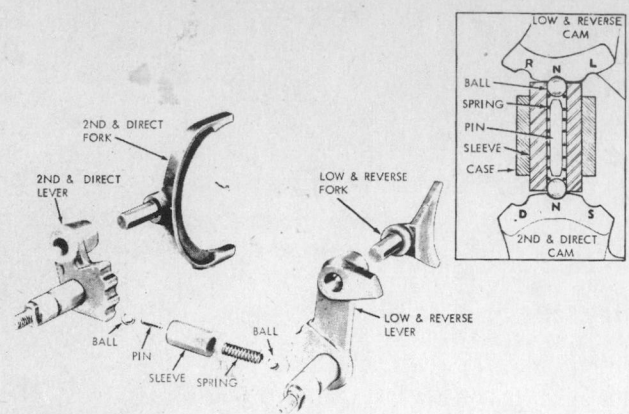

Shift forks and levers

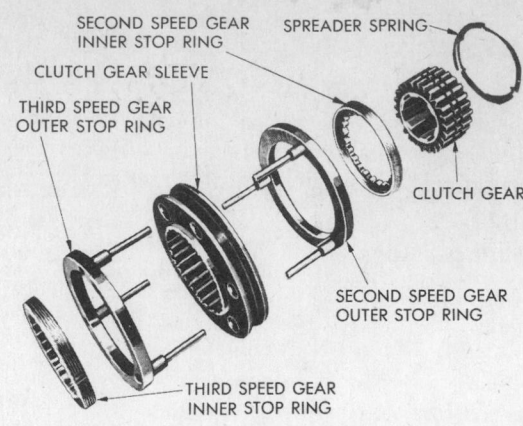

Synchronizer assembly

14. Drive the countershaft rearward, removing key, and out of the case.
15. Lift the gear cluster and thrust washers out of the case. Remove the needle bearings, (22 each end) and spacer from the cluster.
16. Drive the reverse idler shaft toward the rear and out of the case. Remove key.
17. Lift the reverse idler gear, thrust washers and 22 needle bearings out of the case.
18. Remove gearshift operating levers from their respective shafts. On an A-250 transmission, remove the tapered pins retaining the shift shafts to the case with a hammer and an 1/8 in. punch. Drive out the front pin to the front and the rear pin to the rear.
19. Drive out tapered retaining pin from either of the two lever shafts, then withdraw the shaft from inside the transmission case. (The detent balls are spring-loaded, as the shaft is being withdrawn, the balls will fall to the bottom of the case.)
20. Remove the interlock sleeve, spring, pin and both balls from the case. Drive out the remaining tapered pin, then slide the lever shaft out of the transmission.
21. Remove the lever shaft seals and discard them.

Assembly
1. Install two new shift lever shaft seals in the case.
2. Carefully insert low and reverse lever shaft into the rear of the case, through the seal and into position. Lock with a tapered pin. Turn lever until the center detent is in line with the interlock bore.
3. Slide the interlock sleeve in its bore in the case, followed by one of the interlock balls. Then, install interlock spring and pin.
4. Place the remaining interlock ball on top of the interlock spring.
5. Depress the interlock ball and at the same time install the second and high lever shaft into the fully seated position, with the center detent aligned with the detent ball. Secure the shaft with the remaining tapered pin.
6. Install the operating levers and secure to the shafts with nuts. Torque the nuts to 18 ft. lbs.

Countershaft (Cluster) Gear
1. Slide the dummy shaft and tubular spacer into the bore of the countergear.
2. Grease and install 22 bearing rollers into each end of the countergear bore in the area around the arbor. Install the bearing retaining rings at each end of the gear, covering the bearings. If countershaft gear end-play measured over .022 in. at disassembly, install new thrust washers.
3. Install a thrust washer at each end of the countergear and over the arbor. Install the countergear assembly in the case, making sure the tabs on the thrust washers slide into the grooves in the case.

Reverse Idler Gear
1. Coat the bore of the reverse idler gear with grease, then slide dummy shaft into the bore, then install 22 bearing rollers in the bore and around the dummy shaft.
2. Install a new thrust washer at each end of the gear and over the arbor.
3. With the beveled end of the teeth forward, slide the gear into position in the case. Install the reverse idler shaft in its bore in the rear of the case. Install Woodruff key and align with the keyway in the case.
4. Align the idler gear with the shaft, then drive the shaft into the case and gear until the key seats in recess.

Mainshaft
1. Install rear bearing on mainshaft and install selective fit snap-ring.
2. Hold low and reverse sliding gear in position with shift fork. Insert mainshaft with rear bearing through rear of case and into the sliding gear. Both shift forks are offset toward rear of the case.
3. Place synchronizer spreader ring, and then rear stop ring, on synchronizer splines of second speed gear. Install second speed gear on mainshaft, with shims if required. Shims should be installed to correct excessive synchronizer float. If synchronizer float is below minimum, as measured on disassembly, shorten all six synchronizer pins.
4. Install synchronizer clutch gear on mainshaft. Install snap-ring.
5. Install second and direct fork in lever shaft with offset toward rear of transmission. Hold synchronizer clutch gear sleeve and two outer rings together, with pins in holes in clutch gear sleeve. Engage second and direct fork with clutch gear sleeve.
6. While holding synchronizer parts and fork in position, slide mainshaft forward, starting synchronizer clutch gear into clutch gear sleeve and mainshaft rear bearing into the case bore. Synchronizer parts must be correctly positioned before mainshaft is positioned.
7. While holding synchronizer parts in position, tap mainshaft forward until rear bearing bottoms in the case bore.
8. Install mainshaft rear bearing selective fit snap-ring into groove in case bore.

Drive Pinion (Clutch Shaft)
1. Slide the oil slinger over the pinion shaft and down against the gear.

2. Slide the bearing over the pinion shaft (ring groove away from the gear), then press to a firm seat against the oil slinger and gear.
3. Install the keyed washer, then the snap-ring. Four thicknesses of snap-ring are available to eliminate end-play. Install the large snap-ring onto the race of the ball bearing.
4. Install 14 greased bearing rollers in the bore of the pinion shaft gear. Install bearing roller retaining ring in the pinion gear bore.
5. Install third gear outer stop-ring and third gear inner stop-ring onto the mainshaft. Guide the drive pinion through the front of the case and engage the inner

stop-ring with the clutch teeth, then seat the bearing so the large snap-ring is hard against the case.
6. Install a new seal in the pinion bearing retainer.
7. Install the gasket on the retainer and install with attaching bolts torqued to 30 ft. lbs.

Extension Housing

1. Install a new rear mainshaft bushing, and a new oil seal.
2. Protect the oil seal with thimble-type seal protector, and with gasket attached, slide the extension housing over the mainshaft and down against the case. Attach with bolts torqued to 50 ft. lbs.

Type-3
A-833 Chrysler
4-Speed and
Overdrive-4

Application

Aspen, 1976-77
Barracuda, 1970-74
Challenger, 1970-74
Charger, 1970-74
Dart, 1970-77
Dodge, 1970-74
Plymouth, 1970-74
Valiant, 1970-77
Volare, 1976-77

This unit is used by Chrysler Corporation cars and varies somewhat with car application. However, illustrations and repair procedures may be considered as typical. Starting 1976, there is an overdrive four speed available as an option on some models. This transmission is similar in design to the A-833 Chrysler four speed but repair procedures are different.

Disassembly

NOTE: Steps 1-11 apply to both 4-Speed and Overdrive-4.
1. If available, mount transmission in a repair stand.
2. Disconnect gearshift control rods from the shift control levers and the transmission operating levers.
3. Remove the two gearshift control housing mounting bolts.
4. Remove gearshift control housing from the transmission extension housing or mounting bracket (if so equipped).
5. Remove the gearshift control housing mounting bracket bolts, then, remove the bracket (if so equipped).
6. Remove back-up light switch (if so equipped).

7. Remove output companion flange nut and washer, then pull the flange from the mainshaft (output shaft).
8. Remove gearshift housing-to-transmission case attaching bolts.
9. With all levers in the neutral detent position, pull housing out and away from the case.
NOTE: if first and second, or third and fourth shift forks remain in engagement with the synchronizer sleeves, work the sleeves and remove forks from the case.
10. Remove nuts, lock washers and flat washers that hold first-second, and third-fourth-speed shift operating levers to the shafts.
11. Disengage shift levers from the flats on the shafts and remove levers. Remove the E-ring on the overdrive four speed.

4—Speed

NOTE: Steps 12-37 apply only to the 4-Speed; Overdrive-4 disassembly follows.
12. Remove gearshift lever shafts out of the housing, allowing detent balls to fall free. Remove seals and discard.
13. Slide interlock sleeve, interlock pin and spring from the housing.
14. Remove main drive pinion bearing retainer attaching bolts, then slide retainer and gasket from the main drive shaft. Remove the pinion oil seal.
15. Remove the attaching bolts that hold the tailshaft extension housing to the transmission case.
16. Slide the third-fourth synchronizer sleeve slightly forward, slide the reverse idler gear to the center of its shaft, then, using a

soft hammer, tap rearward on the extension housing. Slide housing and mainshaft assembly out and away from the case.
17. Remove the snap-ring that holds the third-fourth synchronizer clutch gear and sleeve. Then, slide third-fourth synchronizer assembly from the end of the mainshaft.
18. Slide third speed gear and stop-ring from the mainshaft.
NOTE: do not separate third-fourth-speed synchronizer clutch gear, sleeve, shift plates or spring unless replacement is required.
19. With long-nose pliers, compress the snap-ring that retains the mainshaft center bearing in the extension housing.
20. With snap-ring compressed, pull the mainshaft assembly and bearing out of the extension housing.
21. Remove and discard extension housing rear oil seal.
22. Remove rear bearing from the mainshaft by inserting steel plates on the front side of first-speed gear, then, with an arbor press, force the rear bearing from the mainshaft.
23. Remove the snap-ring that holds the mainshaft bearing onto the shaft.
24. Remove mainshaft bearing, retainer ring, first-speed gear, and first-speed stop-ring.
25. Remove the snap-ring that holds the first and second clutch sleeve gear and clutch to the mainshaft.
26. Slide the first and second clutch sleeve gear and clutch from the mainshaft.
NOTE: do not dismantle the clutch unless inspection reveals need for parts replacement.

3. Install flange assembly and secure with new washer and nut. Torque the nut to 140 ft. lbs.
4. Grease the cover gasket, and install gasket on cover. Torque attaching bolts to 12 ft. lbs.
5. Install drain plug and back-up light switch (if so equipped) and tighten securely. Refill transmission to proper level.

Exhaust Emission Control Switch

Some models have a switch mounted above the 2-3 shift lever, for emission control. In the absence of a switch a plug is substituted. Torque the plug or switch to 15 ft. lbs.

1 Bearing retainer
2 Bearing retainer gasket
3 Bearing retainer oil seal
4 Inner bearing snap-ring
5 Outer bearing snap-ring
6 Pinion bearing
7 Transmission case
8 Filler plug
9 2nd speed gear
10 Stop ring
11 Shift strut springs
12 Clutch gear
13 Shift struts (3)
14 Shift strut spring
15 Snap-ring
16 1st and 2nd clutch sleeve gear
17 Stop ring
18 1st speed gear
19 Bearing retainer ring
20 Rear bearing
21 Snap-ring
24 Baffle
25 Case to extension housing gasket
26 Lockwasher

27 Bolt
28 Extension housing
29 Mainshaft yoke bushing
30 Oil seal
31 Main drive pinion
33 Needle bearing rollers
34 Snap-ring
35 Stop ring
36 Snap-ring
37 Shift strut spring
38 Clutch gear
39 Shift strut spring
40 Clutch sleeve
41 Stop ring
42 3rd speed gear
43 Mainshaft (output)
44 Shift struts (3)
45 Woodruff key
46 Countershaft
47 Gear thrustwasher (1)
48 Needle roller bearing thrustwasher
49 Needle bearing rollers
50 Bearing spacer
51 Countershaft gear (cluster)

52 Needle bearing rollers
53 Needle roller bearing thrustwasher
54 Gear thrustwasher (1)
55 Backup light switch
56 Backup light switch gasket
57 Plug
58 Reverse detent ball spring retainer
59 Gasket
60 Reverse detent ball spring
61 Rerverse detent ball
62 Woodruff key
63 Reverse idler gear shaft
64 Reverse idler gear bushing
65 Reverse idler gear
66 Reverse shifter fork
67 Reverse lever
68 Reverse lever shaft oil seal
69 Reverse operating lever
70 Flatwasher
71 Lockwasher

72 Nut
73 Gearshift control housing
74 1st and 2nd operating lever
75 Flatwasher
76 Lockwasher lever
77 Lever nut
78 Lever lockwasher
79 Lever flatwasher
80 3rd and 4th operating lever
81 Switch
82 Gasket
83 Interlock lever (2)
84 E-ring
85 Spring
86 Oil seal (2)
87 3rd and 4th lever
88 Ist and 2nd lever
89 3rd and 4th speed fork
90 1st and 2nd speed fork
91 Drain plug
92 Shift control housing gasket

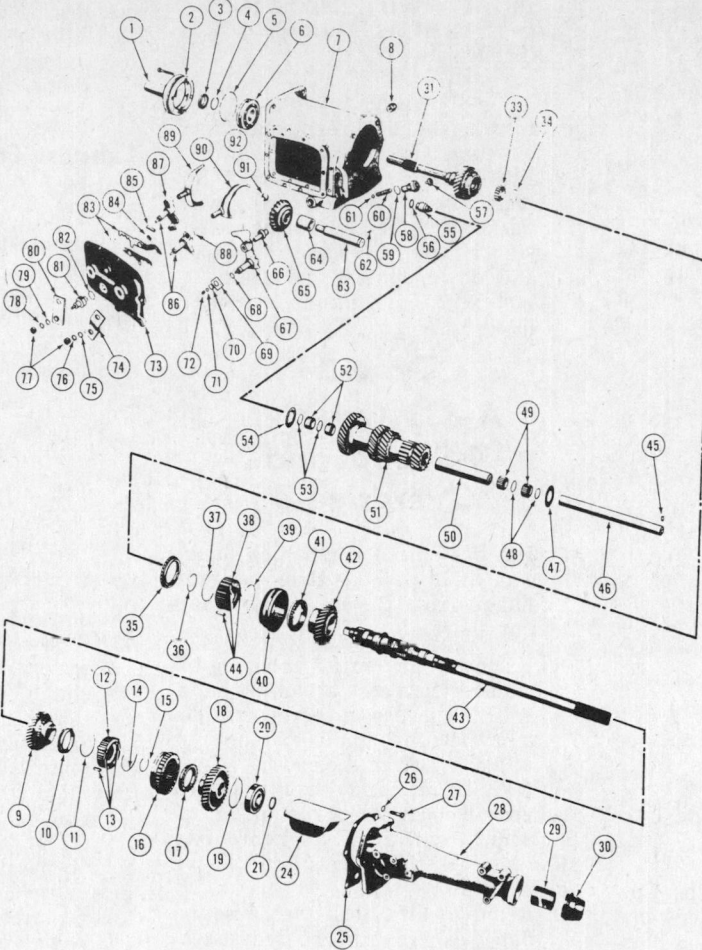

A-833 4-speed transmission disassembled

27. With a feeler gauge, measure countershaft gear end-play. This measurement should be .015-.025 in. If measurement is greater than specified, a new thrust washer of desirable thickness must be installed at assembly.
28. Drive the reverse idler gear shaft, from front to rear, far enough out of the case to permit removal of the reverse idler gear.
29. Remove idler gear shaft from the case, then remove the Woodruff key from the shaft.
30. Remove reverse gearshift lever detent spring retainer, gasket, plug and detent ball spring from the rear of the case.
31. Push the reverse gearshift lever shaft into the case, and remove. Lift the detent ball from the bottom of the case.

32. Remove the shift fork from the shaft and detent plate.
33. Using a countershaft dummy, drive the countershaft from the gear and case, allowing the countergear and dummy assembly to rest on the bottom of the case.
34. Remove the main drive pinion bearing outer snap-ring, then with a soft hammer, drive the main drive pinion into the case and remove.
35. Remove the main drive pinion bearing outer snap-ring, then, with an arbor press, remove the bearing from the main drive pinion. Remove the oil slinger.
36. Lift the countergear cluster from the bottom of the case.
37. Remove the countergear dummy shaft, 76 bearing rollers, thrust washers and tubular spacer from

the center of the countergear.

Overdrive—4

1. Remove the bolt and retainer holding the speedometer pinion adapter in the extension housing, then remove the pinion adapter.
2. Remove the bolts attaching the extension housing to the transmission case.
3. Rotate the extension housing on the output shaft to expose the rear of the countershaft. Install one bolt to hold the extension in place.
4. Drill a hole in the countershaft extension plug at the front of the case.
5. Reaching through this hole, push the countershaft to the rear to expose the Woodruff key; when exposed, remove it. Push the

EXTENSION BOLT

EXTENSION INVERTED

COUNTER SHAFT

EXPANSION PLUG

CASE—UPRIGHT

Rotating the extension housing on an Overdrive-4 (© Chrysler Corp.)

countershaft forward against the expansion plug, and using a brass drift, tap the countershaft forward until the expansion plug is removed.

6. Using a countershaft arbor, push the countershaft out the rear of the case, but don't let the countershaft out the rear of the case, but don't let the countershaft washers fall out of position. Lower the cluster gear to the bottom of the transmission case.

7. Remove the bolt and rotate the extension back to the normal position.

8. Remove the drive pinion attaching bolts and slide the retainer and gasket from the pinion shaft, then pry the pinion or seal from the retainer. When installing the new seal, don't nick or scratch the seal bore in the retainer or the surface on which the seal bottoms.

9. Using a brass drift, tap the pinion and bearing assembly forward and remove through the front of the case.

10. Slide the third and overdrive synchronizer sleeve slightly forward, slide the reverse idler gear to the center of its shaft, and tap the extension housing rearward. Slide the housing and mainshaft assembly out and away from the case.

11. Remove the snap ring holding the third and overdrive synchronizer clutch gear and sleeve assembly to the mainshaft, then remove the synchronizer assembly.

12. Slide the overdrive gear and stop ring off the mainshaft. Using pair of long nose pliers, compress the snap ring holding the mainshaft bearing in the extension housing. With it compressed, pull the mainshaft assembly and bearing out of the extension housing.

13. Remove the snap ring holding the mainshaft on the shaft. The bearing is removed by inserting steel plates on the front side of the first speed gear, then pressing the mainshaft through the bearing being careful not to damage the gear teeth.

14. Remove the bearing, retainer ring, first speed gear and stop ring from the shaft.

15. Remove the first and second clutch gear and sleeve assembly from the mainshaft.

16. Remove the drive pinion bearing inner snap ring, then using an arbor press, remove the bear-

ing. Remove the snap ring and bearing rollers from the cavity in the drive pinion.

17. Remove the countershaft gear from the bottom of the case, then remove the arbor, needle bearings, thrust washers and spacers from the center of the counter shaft gear.

18. Remove the reverse gearshift lever detent spring retainer, gasket, plug, and detent ball spring from the rear of the case.

19. The reverse idler gear shaft is a tight fit in the case and will have to ge pressed out.

20. If there is oil leakage visible around the reverse gearshift lever shaft, push the lever shaft in and remove it from the case. Remove the detent ball from the bottom of the transmission case and remove the shift fork from the shaft and detent plate.

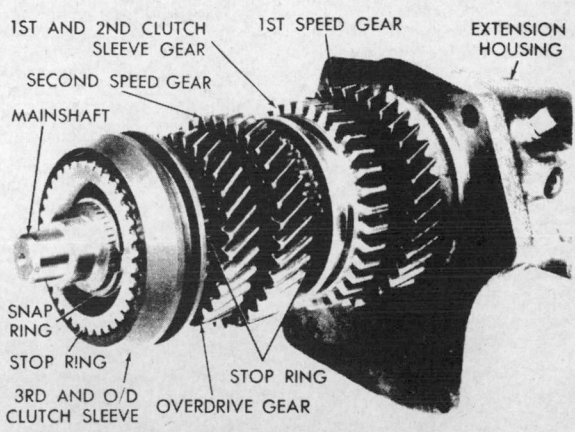

1ST AND 2ND CLUTCH SLEEVE GEAR

1ST SPEED GEAR

EXTENSION HOUSING

SECOND SPEED GEAR

MAINSHAFT

SNAP RING

STOP RING

3RD AND O/D CLUTCH SLEEVE

STOP RING

OVERDRIVE GEAR

Overdrive-4 Mainshaft gear identification (© Chrysler Corp.)

Assembly

4-Speed

1. Slide the second-speed gear over the mainshaft (synchronizer cone toward rear) and down into position against the shoulder on the shaft.
2. Slide first and second clutch sleeve gear assembly (including second gear stop-ring) over the mainshaft. Be sure shift fork groove is toward the front and down into position against second-speed gear, (stop-ring must be indexed with the shift plates). Install a new snap-ring to secure.
3. Slide low gear stop-ring over the shaft and down into position and index with the shift plates.
4. Slide first-speed gear, (synchronizer cone toward clutch sleeve gear) over the mainshaft and down into position against the clutch sleeve gear.
5. Install the mainshaft bearing retainer ring, followed by the mainshaft center bearing. Using an arbor or other suitable tool, press the bearing down into position. Install new snap-ring.
6. Slide the rear bearing over the mainshaft and drive, or press, into position.
7. Install partially assembled mainshaft into the extension housing far enough to engage the retaining ring in the slot in the extension housing. Compress the retaining ring and, at the same time, seat the mainshaft in the extension housing.
8. Slide third-speed gear over the mainshaft, synchronizer cone forward, followed by third gear stop-ring.
9. Install third and fourth-speed synchronizer clutch gear assembly onto the mainshaft (shift fork groove toward rear) down against third-speed gear. Be sure to index the rear stop-ring with the clutch shift plates.
10. Install retaining snap-ring, then, using heavy grease, position the front stop-ring over the clutch gear, indexing the ring slots with the shift plates.

NOTE: if above indexing of the stop-rings and the positioning of the gears and clutches is ignored at this point, damage will most likely result when mating the extension housing to the transmission case.

11. Grease the bore of the countergear at each end, then install the roller bearing tubular spacer (centered). Insert the countergear dummy shaft.
12. Grease each bearing roller, then install 19 bearing rollers at each end of the gear. Now, install a flat spacer onto each end of the dummy shaft and into the gear, followed by 19 more bearing rollers and a spacer ring into each end of the countergear.
13. Grease the tanged thrust washers and install them, one over each end of the dummy shaft, with the tangs toward the case (away from the gear).
14. Lay the countergear assembly into the bottom of the case.
15. To install the main drive pinion, slide the bearing oil slinger over the main drive pinion shaft, then, press the main drive pinion bearing on the pinion shaft. (Be sure the outer snap-ring groove is toward the front). Seat bearing all the way, against shoulder on gear.
16. Install a new inner snap-ring into the bearing retainer groove of the shaft.
17. Now, install the outer snap-ring into the main drive pinion bearing. Then, insert and tap the main drive pinion and bearing assembly into the front of the case.
18. Start the countershaft into its bore at the rear of the case. Raise the countergear cluster assembly until the gear bore is aligned with the countershaft bore in the case. (Be sure the thrust washer tangs are in place in the case recesses.)
19. Press the countershaft into the countergear, washer and bearings assembly while displacing the dummy shaft. Install Woodruff key into countershaft, then continue pressing the countershaft and key into its bore and recess.

NOTE: countergear end-play should not exceed .029 in.

20. Install a new oil seal onto the reverse gearshift lever shaft.
21. Lubricate and carefully install the lever shaft into the bore in the case. Insert reverse fork into the lever.
22. Install reverse shift detent ball and spring retainer gasket and retainer. Tighten securely.
23. Start reverse idler gear shaft into the end of the case, and press in far enough to position the reverse idler gear on the protruding end of the shaft. At the same time, engage the shifter groove with the reverse shift fork.
24. With reverse idler gear properly positioned, install Woodruff key into the sliding gear shaft, then finish seating the shaft and key flush with the end of the case.
25. Grease, then position a new gasket on the end of the extension housing.
26. Center reverse sliding gear on its

shaft, then carefully insert the mainshaft assembly into the case. (Be sure of the indexing of third and fourth-speed stop-rings and shifter plates.)
27. Move third and fourth-speed clutch sleeve slightly toward the front, and, at the same time, align the end of the mainshaft with the main drive pinion. Push in on the extension housing assembly until it is entirely seated against the rear of the case.
28. Install extension-to-case attaching bolts and torque to 50 ft. lbs.
29. Install back-up light switch (if so equipped).
30. Move reverse sliding gear ahead to neutral position.
31. Slide interlock sleeve into position in the gearshift housing. Lubricate and slide a new seal over a shifter shaft and down into its groove.
32. Install the gearshift lever shaft into position in the housing, then install the gearshift operating lever onto the flats of the shaft, (lever pointing up). Install flat washer, Lockwasher and nut. Tighten securely.
33. Place a detent ball in the sleeve, followed by the poppet spring and interlock pin.
34. Lubricate and slide a new seal over the other shifter shaft and down into its groove.
35. As with the first gearshift lever shaft, push the shaft into position in the housing, then install the operating lever onto the flats of the shaft (lever pointing up). Install flat washer, lockwasher and nut and tighten securely.
36. Place remaining detent ball on the poppet spring, compress the ball and spring with a small screwdriver, then, push the shafts in until seated. Turn the shafts until the balls drop into the neutral position detent.
37. Place transmission on its side, gearshift cover opening up.
38. Install a shift fork onto each synchronizer sleeve collar, and, with both sleeves in neutral position, install the shift housing and new gasket.
39. Install attaching bolts and tighten to 12 ft. lbs. (The center bolt on each side of the cover is a pilot bolt and should be installed first.)
40. Lubricate and install a new oil seal in the main drive pinion retainer bore, then install the retainer and gasket. Install attaching bolts, torqued to 15-20 ft. lbs.
41. Install gearshift control and rod assembly on the extension housing, then, secure rods with washers and clips.
42. Install output companion flange,

washer and nut. Torque to 175 ft. lbs.

Overdrive-4

Follow the first four steps only if you removed the reverse shaft in the disassembly procedure.

1. Install a new oil seal O-ring on the lever shaft and coat the shaft with grease; insert it into its bore and install the reverse fork in the lever.
2. Install the reverse detent spring and gasket and torque to 50 ft. lbs; insert the ball and spring and install the plug and gasket which are torqued to 24 ft. lbs.
3. Place the reverse idler gear shaft in position in the end of the case and drive it in far enough to position the reverse idler gear on the protruding end of the shaft with the fork slot toward the rear. While doing this, engage the slot with the reverse shift fork.
4. With the reverse idler gear correctly positioned, drive the reverse gear shaft into the case far enough to install the woodruff key. Drive the shaft in flush with the end of the transmission case. Install the back-up light switch and gasket.

Countershaft Gear and Drive Pinion

5. Coat the inside bore of the countershaft gear with a thin film of grease and install the roller bearing spacer with an arbor, into the gear; center the spacer and arbor.
6. Install the roller bearings and a spacer ring on each end.
7. Replace worn thrust washers; coat the new ones with grease and install them over the arbor with the tang side toward the case boss.
8. Install the countershaft assembly into the case and allow the gear assembly to sit on the bottom of the case so that the thrust washers won't come out of position.
9. Press the drive pinion bearing on the pinion shaft. Make sure the outer snap ring groove is toward the front and the bearing is seated against the shoulder on the gear.
10. Install a new snap ring on the shaft to hold the bearing in place; make sure the snap ring is seated and that there is minimum end play.
11. Place the pinion shaft in a soft-jawed vise and install the roller bearings in the cavity of the shaft. Coat them with grease and install the retaining ring.
12. Install a new oil seal in the bore.

Extension Housing Bushing

13. Remove the yoke seal from the extension housing.
14. Drive out the old bushing and slide in a new one, aligning the oil hole in the bushing with the slot in the housing.
15. Place a new seal in the opening of the extension housing and then drive the bushing into place.

Mainshaft

Assemble the synchronizer as follows:

1. Place a stop ring flat on a bench followed by the clutch gear and sleeve; drop the struts in their sleeves and snap in a strut spring placing the tang inside one strut. Install the second strut spring tang in a different strut after turning the assembly over.
2. Slide the second speed gear over the mainshaft with the synchronizer cone toward the rear and down against the shoulder on the shaft.
3. Slide the first and second gear synchronizer assembly including stop rings with lugs indexed in the hub slots, over the mainshaft down against the second gear cone and hold it there with a new snap ring. Slide the next snap ring over the shaft and index the lugs into the clutch hub slots.
4. Slide the first speed gear with the synchronizer cone toward the clutch sleeve just installed over the mainshaft and into position against the clutch sleeve gear.
5. Install the mainshaft bearing retaining ring followed by the mainshaft rear bearing; press the bearing down into position and install a new snap ring to secure it. Make sure that there is not much end play in the assembly before proceeding.
6. Install the partially assembled mainshaft into the extension housing far enough to engage the bearing retaining ring in the slot in the extension housing.

Compress the ring with pliers so that the mainshaft ball bearing can move in and bottom against its thrust shoulder in the extension housing. Release the ring and make sure that it is seated.

7. Slide the overdrive gear over the mainshaft with the synchronizer cone toward the front followed by the gears' snap ring.
8. Install the third-overdrive gear synchronizer clutch gear assembly on the mainshaft against the overdrive gear. Make sure to index the rear stop ring with the clutch gear struts.
9. Install the snap ring and position the front stop ring over the clutch gear again lining up the ring lugs with the struts; coat a new extension gasket with grease and place it in position.
10. Slide the reverse idler gear to the center of its shaft and move the third-overdrive synchronizer as far forward as possible without losing the struts.
11. Insert the mainshaft assembly in the case tilting it as necessary. Place the third-overdrive sleeve in the neutral detent.
12. Rotate the extension on the mainshaft to expose the rear of the countershaft and install one bolt to hold it in position.
13. Install the drive pinion and bearing assembly through the front of the case and position it in the front bore. Install the outer snap ring in the bearing groove and tap lightly into place. If it doesn't bottom easily, check to see if a strut, pinion roller or stop ring is out of position.
14. Turn the transmission upside down while holding the countershaft gear to prevent damage. Then lower the countershaft gear assembly into position making sure that the teeth mesh with the drive pinion gear.
15. Start the countershaft into the bore at the rear of the case and push until it is in about halfway; then install the Woodruff key and push it in until it is flush with the end of the rear case.
16. Rotate the extension back to normal position and install the bolts; rotate the transmission and install the drive pinion bearing retainer and gasket. Coat the threads with sealing compound and tighten the attaching bolts to 30 ft lbs.
17. Install a new expansion in its bore.

Gearshift Housing and Mechanism

18. Install the interlock levers on the pivot pin and secure with the E-ring. Install the spring with a pair of pliers.
19. Grease and install new O-ring seals on both shift shafts; grease the housing bores and push the shafts through.
20. Install the operating levers and tighten the retaining nuts to 18 ft lbs; make sure the third-overdrive lever points down.
21. Rotate each shift shaft fork bore straight up and install the third-overdrive shift fork in its bore and under both interlock levers.
22. Position both synchronizer sleeves in neutral and place the first and second gear shift fork in the groove of the first and second gear synchronizer sleeve. Turn the transmission on its right side and place the gearshift

housing gasket in place holding it there with grease.

23. As the shift housing is lowered in place, guide the third-over-drive shift fork into its synchronizer groove then lead the shaft of the first and second shift fork into its bore in the first and second shift lever.

24. Raise the interlock lever with a screwdriver to allow the first and second shift fork to slip under the levers. The shift housing will now seat against the case.

25. Install the bolts lightly and shift through all the gears to check for proper operation.

26. The reverse shift lever and the first and second gear shift lever have cam surfaces which mate in reverse position to lock the first and second lever, the fork and synchronizer in the neutral position. To check for proper operation, put the transmission in reverse, and, while turning the input shaft, move the first and second lever in each direc-

tion. If it locks up or becomes harder to turn, select a new shift lever size with more or less clearance. If there is too little cam clearance, it will be difficult or impossible to shift into reverse.

27. Grease the reverse shaft, install the operating lever and nut, and install the speedometer drive pinion gear and adapter, making sure the range number is in the straight down position.

Type-4
3.03 Fully Synchronized Ford 3-Speed

Application
Buick LeSabre, Centurion, 1970-71
Buick Wildcat, 1970
Comet, 1971-77
Cougar, 1970-72

Fairlane, 1970
Ford, 1970-71
Granada, 1975-77
Maverick, 1970-77
Mercury, 1970-71

Monarch, 1975-77
Montego, 1970-74
Mustang, 1970-73
Oldsmobile, 1970-71
Pontiac, 1970-71
Torino, 1971-75

A-390 Fully Synchronized Chrysler 3-Speed

Application
Dart (6 Cyl.), 1975-76
Dodge (6 Cyl.), 1975-77
Plymouth (6 Cyl.), 1975-77
Valiant (6 Cyl.), 1975-76

AMC 150T Fully Synchronized 3-Speed

Application
American Motors (Hornet, Matador, Pacer) 1975-76

Disassembly

1. Drain the lubricant, then remove the cover bolts and the case cover.

2. Remove the five attaching screws, then remove the extension housing from the transmission case. Remove a long spring which retains the detent plug in the case. Remove the detent plug with a small magnet.

3. Remove the four attaching screws, then remove the front bearing retainer from the case.

4. Remove the filler plug. Working through the filler plug hole, drive the roll pin out of the case and countershaft with a small punch.

5. With a dummy shaft, push the countershaft out of the rear of the case until the countershaft cluster gear can be lowered to the bottom of the case. Remove the countershaft from the rear of the case.

6. Remove the snap-ring. Lift the input gear and shaft from the front of the case. Press the shaft out of the bearing.

7. Remove the snap-ring that holds the speedometer gear onto the shaft. Slide the speedometer gear off the output shaft. Remove the

speedometer gear lockball.

8. Remove the snap-ring that holds the output shaft bearing on the shaft. With a puller, remove the bearing from both the case and shaft.

9. Place both shaft levers in the neutral position.

10. Remove the set screw that holds the detent springs and plugs in the case. Remove a detent spring and plug from the case.

11. Remove the set screw that holds the first and reverse shift fork to the shift rail. Slide first and reverse shift rail out through the rear of the case.

12. Rotate the first and reverse shift fork upward, then lift it from the case.

13. Remove the set screw that holds the second and third shift fork to the shift rail. Rotate the shift rail 90°.

14. With a magnet, lift the interlock plug from the case.

15. Tap on the inner end of the second and third shift rail to remove the expansion plug from the front of the case. Remove the shift rail.

16. Remove second and third detent plug and spring from the detent

bore.
NOTE: on 1971-72 RAT model transmissions, pull the input gear and shaft forward until the gear contacts the case. On all other models, remove the input gear and shaft through the front of the case.

17. Rotate the second and third shift fork upward, then lift it from the case.

18. Lift the output shaft out through the top of the case.

19. Working through the front bearing opening, drive the reverse idler shaft out through the rear of the case.

20. Lift the reverse idler gear and two thrust washers from the case.

21. Lift the countershaft gear and thrust washers from the case.

22. Remove the countershaft-to-case retaining pin and any needle bearings which may have fallen into the case.

23. Remove the shift levers and shafts from the case. Discard the O-rings.

24. Remove the snap-ring from the front of the output shaft, then slide the synchronizer and the second-speed gear from the shaft.

25. Remove the next snap-ring and thrust washer from the output

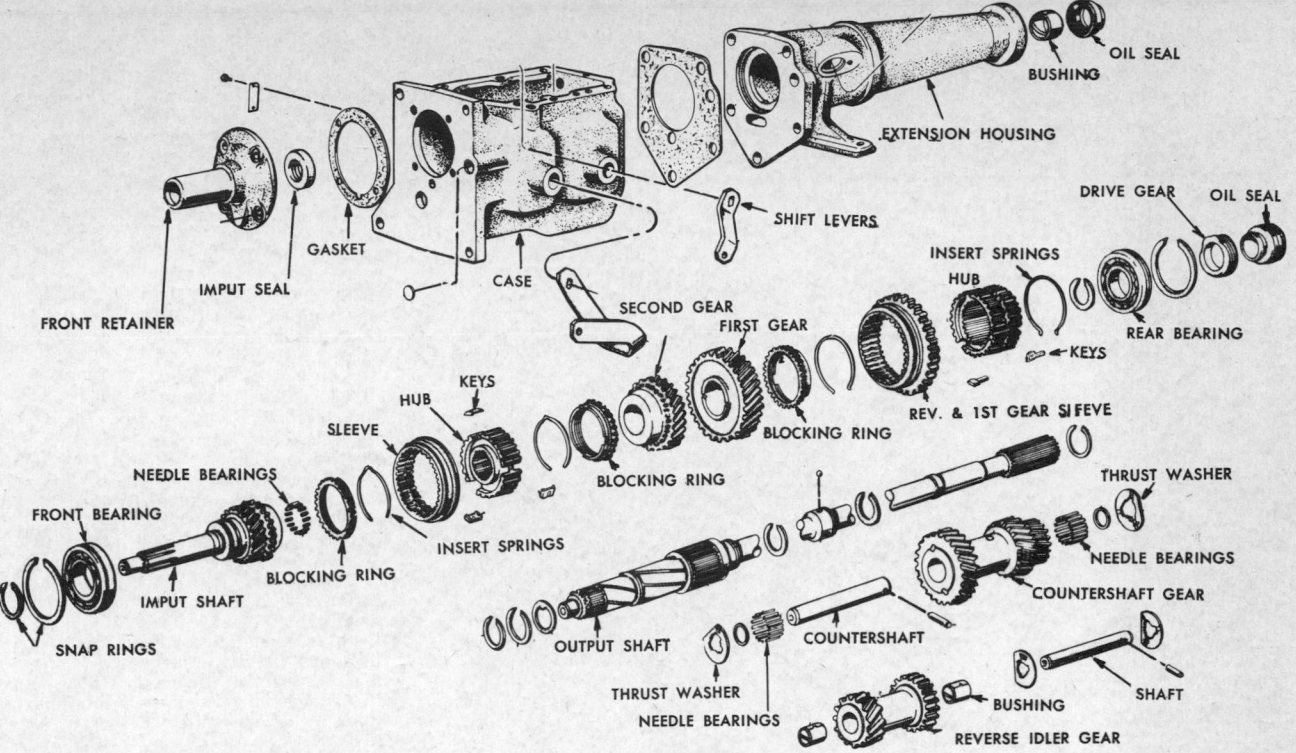

3.03 Ford 3-speed transmission disassembled (© Ford Motor Co)

shaft, then slide the first gear and blocking ring off the shaft.

26. Remove the next snap-ring from the output shaft, then press off the first-reverse synchronizer hub from the shaft.

27. Remove the dummy shaft, 50 bearing rollers and the two retainer washers from the countershaft gear.

28. Disassemble the synchronizers.

Assembly

1. Coat the bore in each end of the countershaft gear with grease. Hold the dummy shaft in the gear and install 25 bearing rollers and a retainer washer in each end of the gear. Install the countershaft

gear, thrust washers and dummy shaft in the case. End-play is controlled with variable thickness thrust washers to .004-.018 in. Let the gear cluster assembly lie in the bottom of the case.

2. Install the idler gear, thrust washers and shaft in the case. Make sure that the thrust washer with the flat side, is at the web end and that the spur gear is toward the rear of the case. Idler gear end-play should be .004-.018 in.

3. Install an insert spring into the groove of the first and reverse synchronizer hub. Be sure that the spring covers all insert grooves. Start the hub in the

sleeve, being sure the alignment marks are properly indexed. Position the three inserts in the hub and be sure the small end is over the spring and that the shoulder is on the inside of the hub. Slide the sleeve and reverse gear onto the hub until the detent is engaged. Install the other insert spring in the front of the hub to hold the inserts against it.

4. Install one insert spring into a groove of the second-third synchronizer hub. With the alignment marks on the hub and sleeve aligned, start the hub into the sleeve. Place the three inserts on top of the retaining spring and push the assembly to-

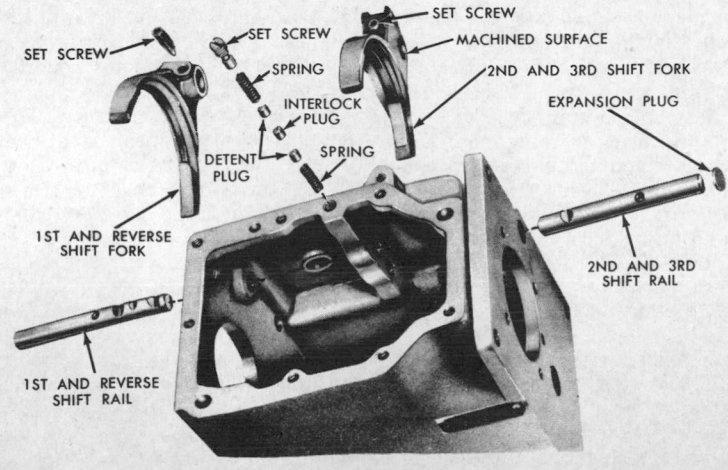

Shift rail and forks

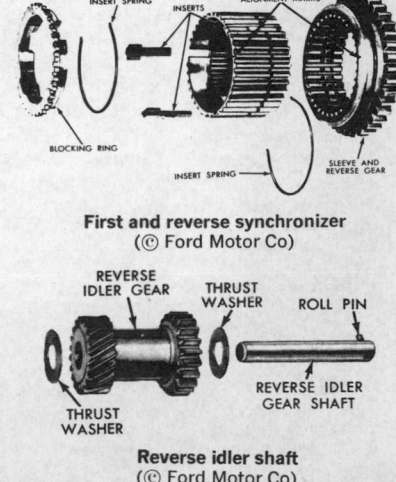

First and reverse synchronizer
(© Ford Motor Co)

Reverse idler shaft
(© Ford Motor Co)

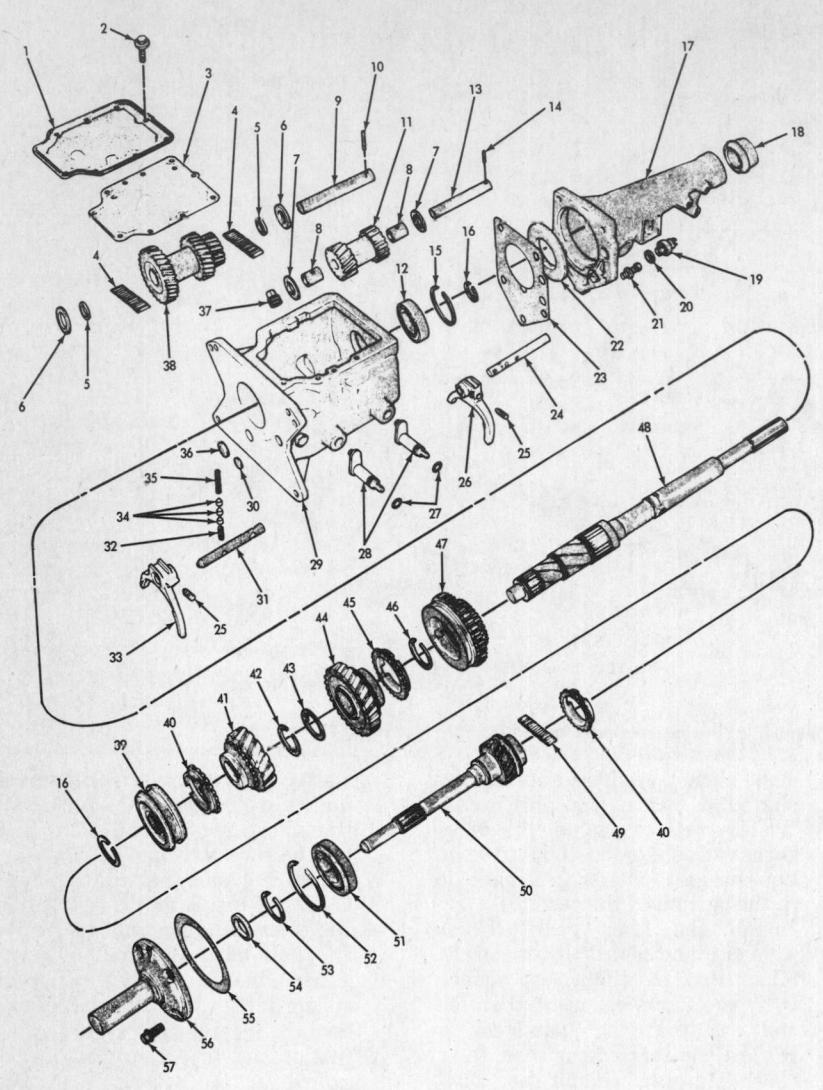

1 Cover, Case
2 Screw, Case Cover
3 Gasket, Case Cover
4 Roller, Countershaft Brg.
5 Washer, Countershaft Brg.
6 Washer, Countershaft Thrust
7 Washer, Reverse Idler Thrust
8 Bushing, Reverse Idler
9 Countershaft
10 Pin, Countershaft Roll
11 Gear, Reverse Idler
12 Bearing, Output Shaft
13 Shaft, Reverse Idler
14 Pin, Reverse Idler Stop
15 Snap Ring, Output Shaft Brg., Outer
16 Snap Ring, Output Shaft, Inner
17 Extension
18 Seal, Extension
19 Switch, Back-Up Lamp
20 Gasket, Back-Up Lamp Switch
21 Screw, Extension
   Lockwasher, Extension Screw
22 Retainer, Output Shaft Brg.
23 Gasket, Extension
24 Rail, Gearshift First and Reverse
25 Screw, Fork Set
26 Fork, Gearshift First and Reverse
27 Seal, Gearshift Lever Shaft Oil
28 Lever, Gearshift
29 Case
30 Plug
31 Rail, Gearshift Second and Third
32 Spring, Gearshift Detent Pin
33 Fork, Gearshift Second and Third
34 Pin, Gearshift Detent
35 Spring, Gearshift Detent Pin
36 Plug
37 Plug, Case Filler
38 Gear, Countershaft
39 Synchronizer Assy., Second and
   Third
40 Ring, Synchronizer Second and
   Third Stop
41 Gear, Second Speed
42 Snap Ring, Low Speed Gear
   Thrust Washer
43 Washer, Low Speed Gear Thrust
44 Gear, Low Speed
45 Ring, Synchronizer Low Stop
46 Snap Ring, Synchronizer Low and
   Reverse Clutch Gear
47 Synchronizer Assy., Low and
   Reverse
48 Shaft, Output
49 Roller, Output Shaft Pilot
50 Shaft, Input
51 Bearing, Input Shaft
52 Snap Ring, Bearing, Outer
53 Snap Ring, Bearing, Inner
54 Seal, Bearing Retainer Oil
55 Gasket, Bearing Retainer
56 Retainer, Bearing
57 Screw, Bearing Retainer

Exploded view of Chrysler A-390 fully synchronized three speed

gether. Install the remaining insert spring, so that the spring ends cover the same slots as do the other spring. Do not stagger the springs. Place a synchronizer blocking ring in each end of the synchronizer sleeve.

5. Lubricate the output shaft splines and machined surfaces with transmission lubricant.

6. Press the first and reverse synchronizer hub onto the output shaft, with the teeth end of the gear facing toward the rear end of the shaft. Secure it with the snap-ring.

7. Place the blocking ring on the tapered machined surface of the first gear.

8. Slide the first gear onto the output shaft, with the blocking ring toward the rear of the shaft. Rotate the gear to engage the three notches in the blocking ring with the synchronizer inserts. Secure the first gear with the thrust washer and snap-ring.

9. Slide the blocking ring onto the tapered, machined surface of the second gear. Slide the second gear, with blocking ring and the second and third gear synchronizer, onto the mainshaft. The tapered machined surface of the second gear must be toward the front of the shaft. Secure the synchronizer with a snap-ring.

10. Install new O-rings onto the two shift lever shafts. Lubricate the shafts with transmission fluid and install them into the case. Secure each shift lever onto its

shaft.

11. Coat the bore of the input shaft with a light coat of grease. Install the 15 bearing rollers into the bore.

NOTE: on RAT models (1971-72) install the input gear and bearing through the top of the case. On other models the input shaft is installed through the front of the transmission.

12. Position the output shaft assembly in the case.

13. Place a detent plug spring and a plug in the case. Place a second and third-speed shift fork in the synchronizer groove. Rotate the fork into position and install the second and third-speed shift rail. Move the rail inward until the detent plug engages the forward

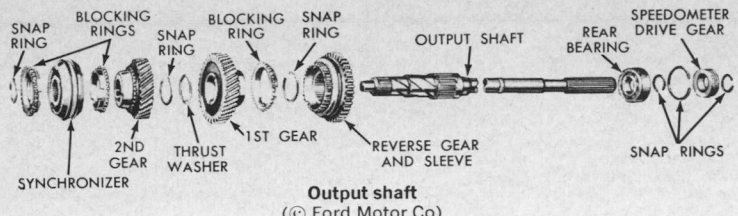

SNAP RING — BLOCKING RINGS — SNAP RING — BLOCKING RING — SNAP RING — OUTPUT SHAFT — REAR BEARING — SPEEDOMETER DRIVE GEAR

2ND GEAR — THRUST WASHER — 1ST GEAR — REVERSE GEAR AND SLEEVE — SNAP RINGS

SYNCHRONIZER

Output shaft
(© Ford Motor Co)

notch (second). Secure the fork to the shaft with a set screw. Move the synchronizer to the neutral position.

14. Install the interlock plug in the case.

15. Place first and reverse shift fork in the groove of the first and reverse synchronizer. Rotate the fork into position and install the first and reverse shift rail. Move the rail inward until the center notch is aligned with the detent bore. Secure the fork to the shaft with a set screw. Install the remaining detent plug and spring. Secure the detent spring with the slotted head set screw. Tighten set screw until the head is flush with the case.

16. Install a new expansion plug in the case front.

17. Install the input shaft and gear in the front of the case.

18. Place front bearing retainer (with new gasket in place) on the case with the oil return groove at the bottom. Torque attaching screws to 30 ft. lbs.

19. Install the large snap-ring on the rear bearing. Place the bearing on the output shaft, with the snapring end toward the rear of the shaft. Press bearing into place and secure with a snap-ring.

20. Hold the speedometer drive gear lock ball in the detent and slide the speedometer gear into place. Secure the gear with a snap-ring.

21. Lift the countershaft gear cluster up into place, and, by entering the countershaft at the rear of the case, push the dummy shaft out of the gear and transmission case. Before the countershaft is com-

pletely in place, align the roll pin hole in the shaft with the hole in the case.

NOTE: on all eight-cylinder vehicles and Ford six-cylinder models the countershaft is a press fit in the case. On Ford six-cylinder models with RAN transmissions, there is a radial clearance of .020 in. at front bore and .010 in. at rear.

22. Working through the filler hole, install a roll pin into the case and countershaft.

23. Install filler and drain plugs in the case.

24. Coat a new extension housing gasket with sealer and install it on the case.

25. Apply sealer to attaching screws and secure extension housing to the case by torqueing the screws to 42 to 50 ft. lbs.

26. With transmission in gear, pour lubricant over the entire gear train while rotating the input or output shaft.

27. Install the transmission cover, with a new sealer-coated gasket in place, and torque the nine attaching screws to 14-19 ft lbs.

28. Check operation of transmission in all of the gear positions.

Type-5
Ford 4-Speed
(German Design)
Types 71 WG, 72 WG, 74 WT, 75 WT

Application
Pinto, 1971-77

NOTE: cars equipped with this transmission are identified by a transmission ID code suffix of AD, BA, or AE. The transmission ID code appears on a tag located under the left extension housing-to-case bolt.

Transmission Disassembly

1. Remove the clutch release bearing and detach the clutch housing.

2. Drain the lubricant and remove the cover and gasket from the case.

3. Remove the threaded plug, spring and shift rail detent plunger from the front of the case.

4. Drive the access plug from the rear of the case. Drive the interlock retaining pin from the case and remove the interlock plate.

5. Remove the roll pin from the selector lever arm.

6. Tap the front end of the shift rail, to displace the plug at the rear of the extension housing. Remove the shift rail from the

rear of the extension housing.

7. Remove the selector arm and shift fork from the case.

8. Remove the extension housing attaching bolts. Loosen the extension housing and rotate the

housing to align the countershaft with the cutaway in the extension housing flange.

9. Drive the countershaft rearward until the shaft clears the front of the case. Install a dummy shaft in the case and gear until the countershaft gear can be

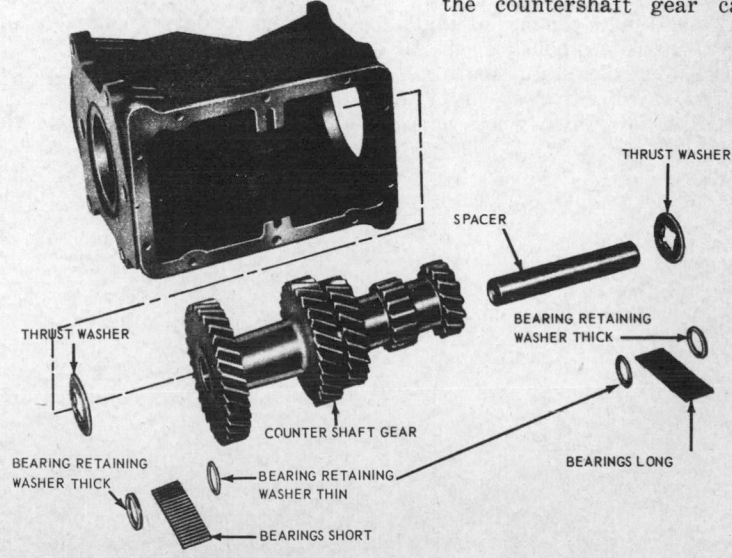

THRUST WASHER — SPACER — BEARING RETAINING WASHER THICK — BEARINGS LONG — THRUST WASHER — COUNTER SHAFT GEAR — BEARING RETAINING WASHER THIN — BEARING RETAINING WASHER THICK — BEARINGS SHORT

Countershaft gear disassembled (© Ford Motor Co)

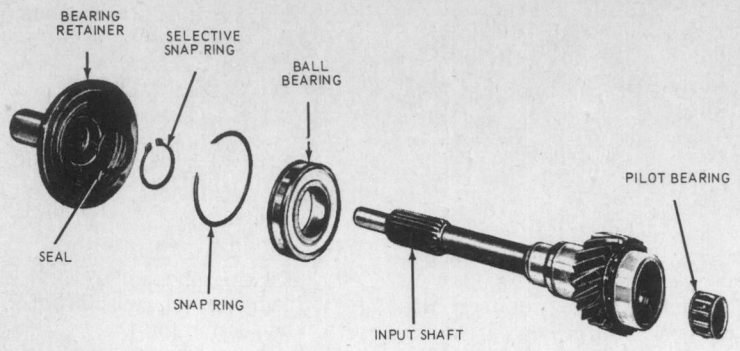

**Input shaft disassembled
—Types 71WG-AD and 72WG-AE**
(© Ford Motor Co)

lowered to the bottom of the case. Remove the countershaft.

10. Lift the extension housing and mainshaft from the case as an assembly.

11. Remove the input shaft bearing retainer attaching bolts. Remove the input shaft and bearing retainer from the case as an assembly.

12. Remove the reverse idler gear and shaft from the rear of the case.

13. Remove the bearing retainers, bearings, dummy shaft and spacer from the countershaft gear.

14. Remove the pilot bearing and bearing retainer from the input shaft gear.

15. Do not remove the ball bearing from the input shaft unless replacement is necessary.

16. Pry the input shaft seal out of the bearing retainer.

17. Lift the fourth gear blocker ring from the front of the output shaft.

18. Remove the snap-ring from the forward end of the output shaft.

19. Support third gear on press plates and place the output shaft and extension housing in a press. Press the output shaft out of the third-fourth speed synchronizer and third gear, while supporting the extension housing and output shaft from beneath. Remove the snap-ring and washer and remove second gear and the blocker ring from the output shaft.

20. Disassemble the synchronizer assembly by pulling the sleeve from the hub and removing the inserts and spring.

21. Remove the snap-ring which retains the output shaft bearing to the extension housing.

22. Use a plastic hammer and tap the output shaft assembly from the extension housing.

23. Position press plates behind first gear and place the assembly in a press. The first and second speed synchronizer are serviced as an assembly. No attempt should be made to separate the hub from the shaft. The only serviceable parts are the springs and inserts. If the hub or sleeve is worn, the shaft and synchronizer must be replaced as an assembly.

24. Drive the shift rail bushing from the rear of the extension housing, using a 9/16 in. socket. Do not remove serviceable bushings.

25. Pry the shift rail seal from the rear of the case.

26. Remove the remaining shaft linkage from the case. Do not remove the seat belt sensing switch unless it is damaged.

Transmission Assembly

1. Install a new shift rail seal in the rear of the case.

2. If the shift rail bushing was removed, drive a new one into position with a 9/16 in. socket.

3. Slide the synchronizer hub over the shaft, making sure that the shift fork groove is toward the front of the shaft. The sleeve and hub are select fit and must be assembled with the etch marks in the same relative locations. Locate an insert in each of three slots in the hub. Oil all parts, and install an insert spring inside the sleeve. The spring tab must locate in a section of an insert. Fit the other spring to the opposite face, making sure that the tab locates in the same insert. Both springs should be in the same rotational direction. The tab end of one spring should be aligned with the tab of the spring on the opposite side.

4. Assemble a blocker ring on the first gear side of the first-second synchronizer. Lubricate the cone surface of first gear and all output shaft gear journals, and slide the cone onto the output shaft, so that the cone surface engages the blocker ring.

5. Position the spacer on the output shaft, larger diameter rearward.

6. Install a snap-ring (selected from the chart) which will come closest to removing all end-play from the output shaft bearing.

Part No.	Thickness	Identification
D1FZ-7030-A	0.0679-	Color Coded—Copper
D1FZ-7030-B	0.0689-	Letter—W
D1FZ-7030-C	0.0699-	Letter—V
D1FZ-7030-D	0.0709-	Letter—U
D1FZ-7030-E	0.0719-	None
D1FZ-7030-F	0.0728-	Color Coded—Blue
D1FZ-7030-G	0.0738-	Color Coded—Black
D1FZ-7030-H	0.0748-	Color Coded—Brown

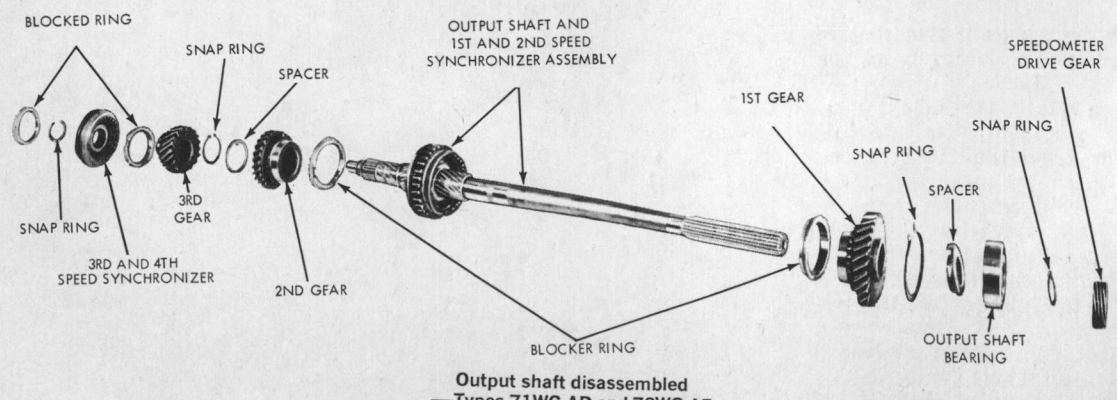

**Output shaft disassembled
—Types 71WG-AD and 72WG-AE**
(© Ford Motor Co)

Position the output shaft bearing on the shaft and press the bearing into place. Secure the bearing with the thickest snap-ring that will fit the groove.

7. Slide the synchronizer over the hub and locate an insert in each of three slots in the sleeve. The sleeve and hub must be assembled with the etch marks in the same relative locations. Lightly oil all parts. Complete assembly of the synchronizer by following directions in previous Step 3.

8. Position second gear and the blocker ring on the output shaft, dog teeth facing rearward. Install the washer and snap-ring. Position third gear on the output shaft, dog teeth forward. Lubricate the gear cones and assemble a blocker ring on third gear cone.

9. Position the third-fourth synchronizer assembly on the output shaft, hub boss facing forward.

10. Install press plates against the boss on the synchronizer hub.

11. Place the entire unit in a press, extension end up, and press the synchronizer assembly onto the output shaft as far as possible.

12. Retain the third-fourth synchronizer assembly to the output shaft with a snap-ring. Pull up on the synchronizer so that the snap-ring is tight in the groove.

13. Lubricate the gear cone and place the blocker ring on the input shaft gear cone.

14. Press the speedometer drive gear onto the shaft.

15. Lubricate the bearing bore of the extension housing. Install the output shaft in the housing. It may be necessary to tap the shaft while holding the synchronizer sleeves firmly. Secure the shaft to the housing with the snap-ring previously installed.

16. Press the bearing on the input shaft. The snap-ring groove must be toward the front of the shaft. Use the thickest snap-ring that will fit.

17. Slide the spacer and dummy shaft into the countershaft gear. Position a thin bearing retaining washer on each end of the dummy shaft. Lubricate the roller bearings and load long bearings in the small end of the gear and short bearings in the long end of the gear. 19 needle bearings are used at either end of the gear on 71 WG and 72 WG series transmissions, and 21 needle bearings at either end of the gear on 74 WT series transmissions. Place a thick retaining washer over each end of the dummy shaft. Grease the thrust

Installing speedometer driven gear
(© Ford Motor Co)

washers and place one on each end of the dummy shaft. The tabs must be in the same relative position to engage the slots in the case when the gear is lowered. Loop a piece of rope around each end of the gear and carefully install the gear and rope through the rear of the case. Lower the gear in place.

18. Lubricate the reverse idler gear shaft. Position the selector lever relay on the pivot pin. Secure with a spring clip. Hold the gear in the lever, long hub toward the rear of the case, and slide the reverse idler shaft into place. Seat the shaft in the case with a brass hammer.

19. Install a new seal in the input shaft bearing retainer. Install the input shaft in the case with a new bearing retainer O-ring. Tap on the outer race of the bearing to seat the outer snap-ring.

Caution Use a soft hammer and do not tap on the input shaft itself.

20. Carefully slide third-fourth synchronizer sleeve into fourth speed position.

21. Place a new gasket on the extension housing.

22. Lubricate and install the input shaft pilot bearing on the shaft. Slide the extension housing and output shaft into place, being careful not to disturb the fourth speed synchronizer.

23. Align the cutaway in the extension housing flange with the countershaft bore in the rear of the case.

24. Lift the countershaft gear into place and install the countershaft, making sure that the thrust washers remain in place. The flat on the countershaft should be parallel to the top of the case. Tap the shaft with a brass hammer until the front of the shaft is flush with the case.

25. Rotate the extension housing to align the bolt holes and loosely install the attaching bolts. Make sure that the rail slides freely in its bore. Binding is remedied by slightly rotating the extension housing to free the rail, then pushing the housing into the case. Apply sealer to the attaching bolts and torque to 33-36 ft lbs. Place the shift forks in the synchronizer sleeves. Install the interlock lever and new retaining pin. Lubricate the shift rail oil seal and slide the shift rail through the extension housing, case and second and first speed shift forks. Position the selector arm on the rail and slide the rail through third and fourth speed shift fork. Slide the shift rail through the front of the case until the center detent bore is aligned with the detent plunger bore. Install a new retaining pin in the selector arm.

26. Install the detent plunger, spring and plug with sealer.

27. Install a new access plug in the rear of the case.

28. Position a new oil seal with tension spring and lip facing in the direction of the case.

29. Drive the seal in until it bottoms.

30. Position a new O-ring in the groove in the case. Position the

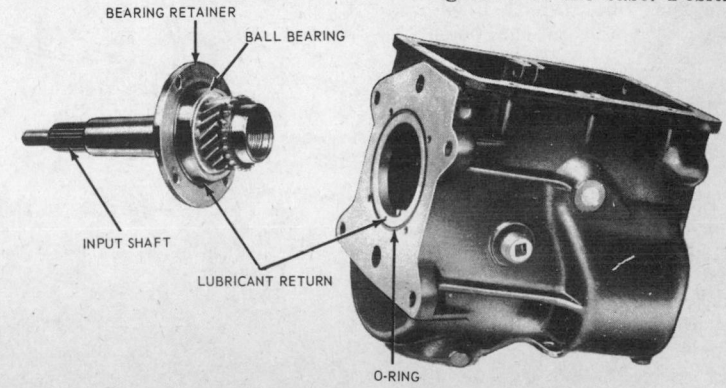

Installing input shaft gear (© Ford Motor Co)

input shaft bearing retainer with the groove in the retainer aligned with the oil passage in the case. Install the retaining bolts finger-tight.

31. Install the flywheel housing and tighten the retaining bolts and the front bearing retainer at-taching bolts. Coat the retainer with grease.
32. Install the clutch release arm and bearing.
33. Install a new extension housing plug, using sealer.
34. Install a new cover gasket and cover, with the vent to the rear. Apply sealer to the left front cover attaching bolt. Torque to 8-10 ft lbs.
35. Install a new seat belt sensing switch if the old one was re-moved.

Type-6
Ford 4-Speed
(British Design)
Types 71 WG, 72 WG

Application

Pinto, 1971-73

NOTE: cars equipped with this transmission are identified by a trans-mission ID code suffix of BB or BC. The transmission ID code appears on a tag located under the left extension housing-to-case bolt.

Transmission Disassembly

1. Remove four bolts and top cover plate.
2. Pry plug from rear of extension housing.
3. Remove plunger screw from right side of case.
4. Working through the top cover opening, use a punch to remove the pin securing the shift selec-tor arm to the shift shaft.
5. Pull the shift shaft rearward, being careful not to drop the shift selector arm and the inter-lock plate.
6. Move the first-second and third-fourth gear synchronizer hubs toward the input shaft bearing.
7. If necessary, remove the shift shaft plunger spring from the case. The plunger screw was re-moved in Step 3.
8. Remove the pin from the third-fourth shift fork. Remove the fork.
9. Unbolt extension housing from case. With a plastic hammer, tap the extension housing slightly rearward. Rotate the housing until the countershaft lines up with the notch in the housing flange.
10. Tap the countershaft rearward with a brass drift until it is just clear of the front of the case. Push the countershaft out with a dummy shaft. Lower the cluster gear to the bottom of the case.
11. Remove extension housing and output shaft assembly. The third-fourth synchronizer sleeve must be pushed forward for clearance.
12. Unbolt front bearing retainer from case. Remove retainer and gasket.
13. Remove input shaft oil seal.
14. Remove the snap ring around the input shaft bearing. Tap the input shaft gear and bearing as-sembly out of the transmission with a brass drift. Remove the needle roller bearing from the recess in the end of the input shaft gear.
15. Remove the cluster gear, two thrust washers, and the dummy shaft from the case. Remove 20 needle rollers and a retaining washer from each end of the cluster gear.
16. Assemble a nut, a flat washer, and a sleeve on a 5/16 in. x 24 UNF threaded bolt. Screw the bolt into the reverse idler shaft and tighten to pull out the shaft.
17. Remove the low-reverse shift fork from the lever pin inside the case. Do not remove the pin.

Component Disassembly

Third-Fourth Synchronizer

1. Remove fourth gear blocking ring from input shaft gear side of assembly.
2. Remove synchronizer hub snap-ring from forward end of output shaft and discard.
3. Support third gear. Press the output shaft out of the third-fourth gear synchronizer and third gear. Be careful not to drop the output shaft.
4. Pull the sleeve off the hub. Remove the inserts and springs.
5. Check all parts for wear. Syn-chronizer hub and sleeve should be replaced if worn or damaged.

First-Second Synchronizer

1. Remove plug in extension hous-ing. Remove speedometer driven gear.
2. Remove snap-ring holding out-put shaft bearing to extension housing. With a plastic hammer, tap output shaft assembly out of housing.
3. Remove snap-ring holding speed-ometer drive gear. Pull off gear. Remove snap-ring holding output shaft bearing.
4. Support low and reverse sliding gear. Press low and reverse slid-ing gear, spacer, and output shaft bearing from the output shaft.
5. Remove snap-ring holding first-second synchronizer assembly to output shaft.
6. Support second gear. Press sec-ond gear and first-second syn-

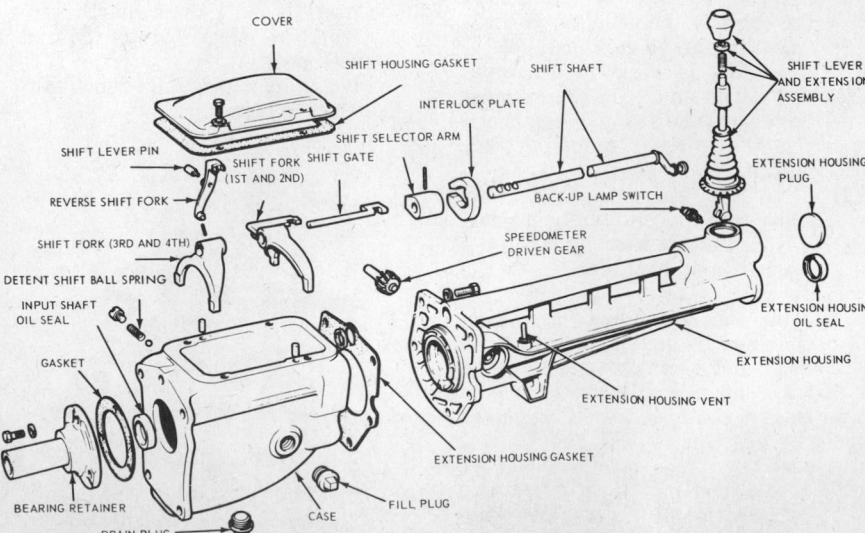

British 4-speed transmission disassembled—Types 71WG-BC and 72WG-BB
(© Ford Motor Co)

chronizer assembly from output shaft.

7. Dismantle synchronizer assembly. Replace synchronizer hub or sleeve if worn or damaged. The output shaft bearing must be replaced.

Input Shaft and Gear

1. Remove and discard input shaft snap-ring.
2. Press off input shaft bearing.

Component Assembly

Third-Fourth Synchronizer

1. Slide gear over hub. Locate an insert in each slot.
2. Install a synchronizer spring inside the sleeve beneath the inserts; the spring tang should fit into an insert. Install the other spring on the opposite side, fitting the tang into the same insert. When viewed from the edge, the springs should run in opposite directions.
3. Place the third gear on the output shaft with the dog teeth forward. Assemble the blocking ring on the third gear cone.
4. Place the synchronizer assembly on the output shaft with the boss forward.
5. Support the hub. Press the hub on the output shaft and install a new snap-ring.

First-Second Synchronizer

1. Install the second gear on the output shaft with the cone and dog teeth to the rear.
2. Slide the synchronizer sleeve over the hub. Place an insert in each of the three slots.
3. Install synchronizer springs as for third-fourth synchronizer assembly.
4. Install a blocking ring to cone on second gear.
5. Install synchronizer assembly on output shaft with the gear teeth on the periphery of the synchronizer sleeve forward. Slide low and reverse sliding gear to the rear of the synchronizer hub.
6. Support the sliding gear. Press synchronizer assembly onto output shaft as far as possible.
7. Secure the synchronizer assembly with snap-ring.
8. Place a blocking ring on first gear side of first-second synchronizer assembly on output shaft. Install first gear, cone side forward.
9. Place the spacer with the larger diameter adjacent to first gear.
10. Select a snap-ring of the proper size to hold the output shaft bearing into the bearing recess with no end float.
11. Position the selected snap-ring loosely on the output shaft next

Removing low-reverse sliding gear, spacer and output shaft bearing
(© Ford Motor Co)

to the spacer.

12. Support the bearing inner race. Press the bearing onto the shaft.
13. Select the thickest snap-ring that fits the groove to hold the bearing to the output shaft.
14. Locate output shaft ball bearing in shaft indent, push speedometer drive gear onto output shaft. Install new snap-ring.
15. Heat the end of the extension housing. Do not use a torch. A pan of hot water is recommended.
16. Install the output shaft into the extension housing. Install the snap-ring securing the output shaft bearing to the housing.
17. Replace the speedometer driven gear. Install a new plug, using sealer.

Input Shaft and Gear

1. Support the input shaft bearing inner race. Press the bearing onto the shaft.

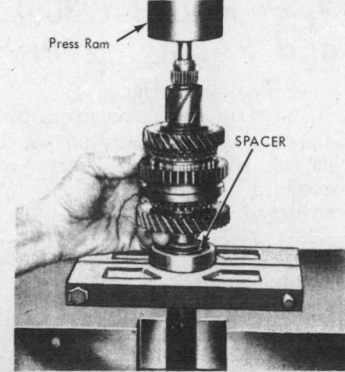

Replacing output shaft bearing
(© Ford Motor Co)

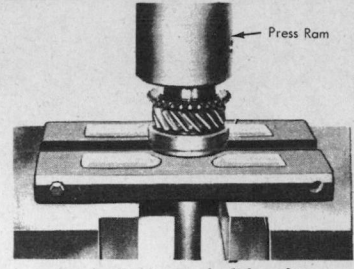

Replacing input shaft bearing
(© Ford Motor Co)

2. Install the snap-ring securing the bearing to the input shaft.

Transmission Assembly

1. Slide the low-reverse lever onto the lever pin inside the case.
2. Push the idler shaft into the case. Place the reverse idler gear on the shaft. Locate the low-reverse lever in the gear groove. Tap the reverse idler shaft into position with a soft hammer.
3. Slide a dummy shaft into the cluster gear. Push a retainer washer into the gear bore. Grease and install 20 needle rollers and the second retaining washer. Install the washers and rollers at the other end of the gear. Grease and install the thrust washers with their convex side into the gear recess.
4. Place the cluster gear in the bottom of the case. Position the thrust washers with the flat upward.
5. Place the input shaft and gear in the case. Using a brass drift, tap bearing outer race into place. Be careful not to damage the dog teeth on the input shaft gear with the cluster gear. Install the bearing snap-ring.
6. Place the input shaft needle bearing in the input shaft gear recess.
7. Drive a new oil seal into the input shaft retainer. Cover the input shaft splines. Install a new gasket on the transmission front face. Check that the retainer oil groove is lined up with the oil passage in the case. Coat the bolts with sealer and install them with lock-washers.
8. Locate the fourth gear blocking ring on the input shaft gear cone.
9. Install a new oil seal in the shift shaft aperture. Drive the seal in with a socket.
10. Install a new sealer coated gasket to the extension housing.
11. Pull the third-fourth synchronizer sleeve forward. Slide the extension housing and output shaft into position. Align the cutaway on the extension housing with the countershaft aperture in the rear face of the case.

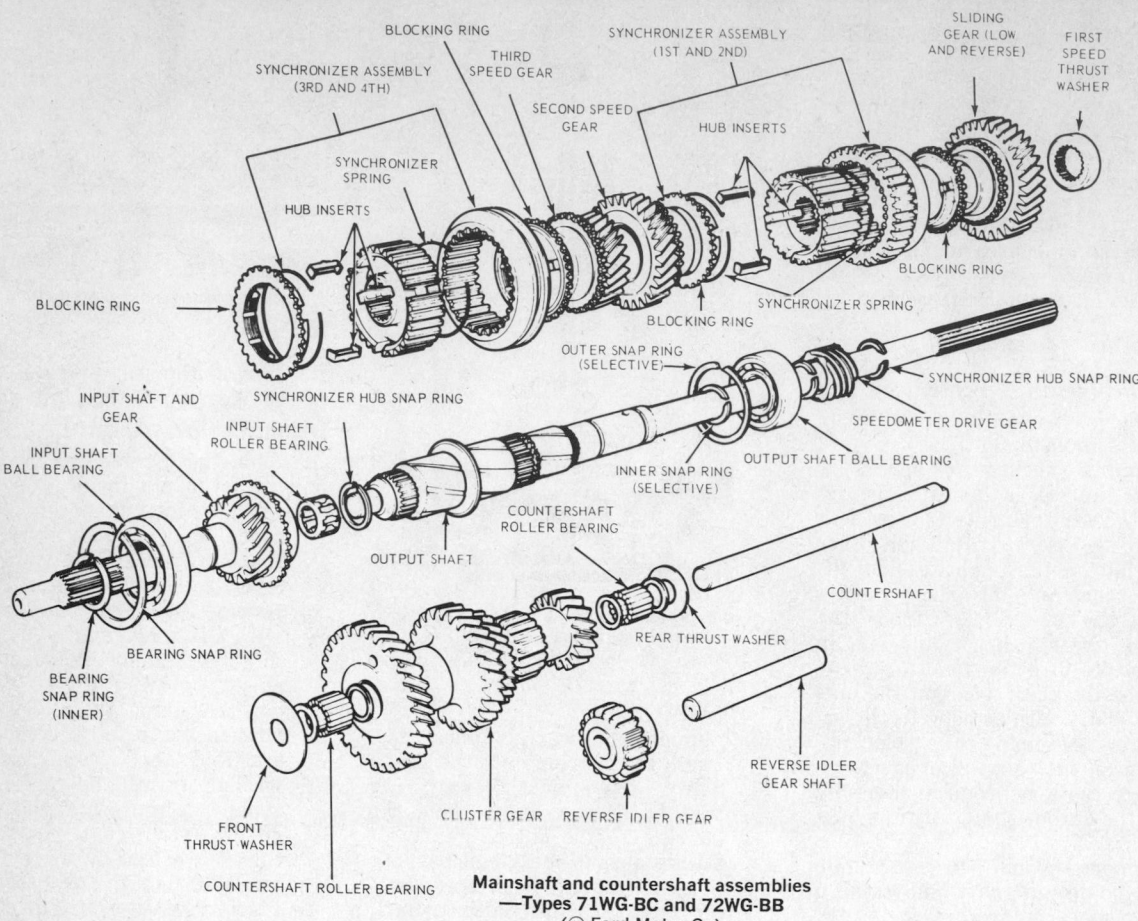

Mainshaft and countershaft assemblies —Types 71WG-BC and 72WG-BB
(© Ford Motor Co)

12. Using loops of cord, lift the cluster gear into mesh with the output and input shaft gears. Take care not to drop the countershaft thrust washers.

13. Tap the countershaft into place, driving out the dummy shaft, ensuring that the lug on the rear of the countershaft fits into the recess on the extension housing flange.

14. Push the extension housing onto the transmission case. Apply sealer to bolts. Torque to 30-35 ft. lbs.

15. Replace both shift forks. Secure third-fourth fork with a new pin.

16. Position shift forks to synchronizer sleeves. Move synchronizer hubs into neutral positions.

17. Grease shift shaft oil seal in rear of case. Slide shift shaft through extension housing. Position shift selector arm and interlock plate so that interlock plate locates in cutouts in shift forks. Pass the shift shaft through the shift selector arm and forks until the pin holes are aligned.

18. Replace the plunger ball and spring. Replace the retaining screw, using sealer.

19. Install the pin through the shift selector arm and shift shaft.

20. Apply sealer to plug. Tap plug into rear of extension housing.

21. Install top cover and gasket.

22. Refill transmission with 2.8 pints SAE 80 oil.

Type-7
Ford 4-Speed
Types RAD-B (2300)
and RAD-C (2800)

Application
Mustang II, 1974-77

Transmission Disassembly

1. Drain the lubricant by removing the lower extension housing bolt.

2. Drive the access plug from the rear of the extension housing. Remove the nut and washer securing the offset lever assembly. Remove the offset lever assembly.

3. Remove the remaining extension housing bolts and washers. Remove the extension from the case and discard the old gasket.

4. Remove the cap screws retaining the cover to the case. Remove the cover, shifter fork, shift rod assembly, and discard the old cover gasket.

5. Remove the bolts and washers attaching the front bearing retainer to the case. Remove the front bearing retainer and gasket.

6. Remove the spring clip retaining the reverse lever assembly to the pivot bolt. Remove the pivot and the reverse lever assembly.

7. Support the countershaft gear with a wire hook. To remove the countershaft, insert a dummy shaft in from the front of the case until the cluster gear falls to the bottom of the case. Then, remove the countershaft from the rear of the case. Lower the cluster gear to the bottom of the case.

8. Remove the input shaft from the front of the case.

9. Remove the snap-ring securing the speedometer drive gear on the output shaft. Slide the gear

off and remove the lock ball from the shaft.

10. Remove the snap-ring retaining the output shaft bearing on the shaft. Use the outer snap-ring to pull the output shaft bearing from the shaft and case, then remove the snap-ring from the bearing. Carefully lift the output shaft and gear train assembly from the top of the case.

11. Slide out the reverse idler gear shaft through the rear of the case and remove reverse gear.

12. Remove the cluster gear and dummy shaft assembly from the bottom of the case. Remove the cluster gear thrust washers.

13. Clean and inspect all parts. If the back-up light switch was damaged, remove it at this time.

Component Disassembly

Cover Assembly

1. Remove the detent screw, spring and plunger.

2. Pull the shifter shaft rod rearward, rotating it counterclockwise.

3. Remove the spring pin retaining the manual selector and interlock

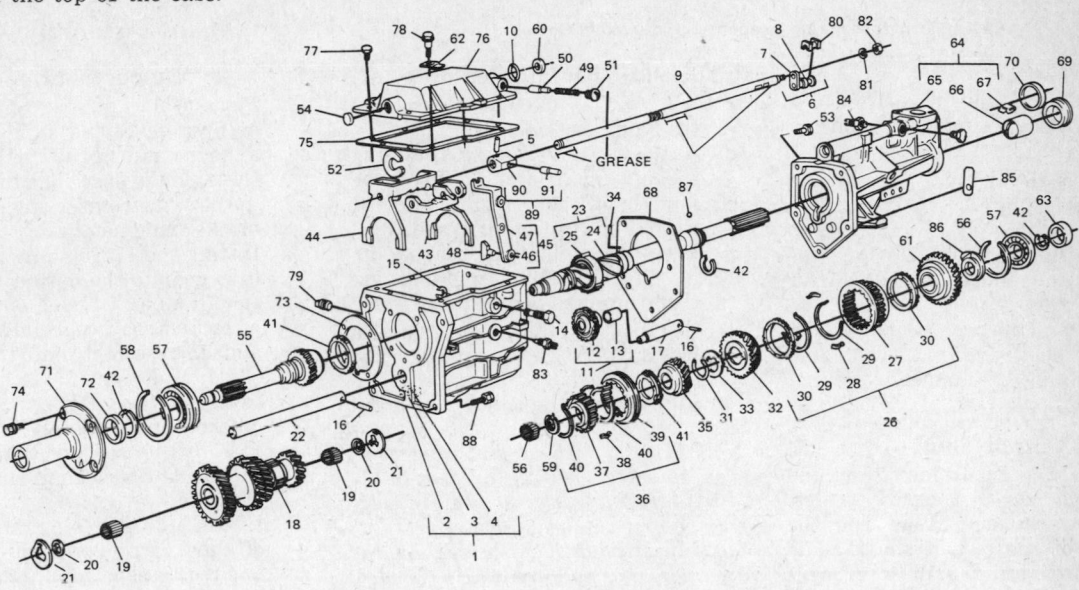

RAD transmission disassembled (© Ford Motor Co)

1 Case assembly—transmission
2 Case—transmission
3 Magnet—transmission case chip
4 Nut spring 9/64
5 Pin—3/16 diameter x 13/16 rolled spring
6 Lever assembly—transmission gearshift shaft offset
7 Lever transmission gearshift shaft offset
8 Pin—transmission gearshift shaft offset lever
9 Shaft—transmission shifter
10 Seal—O-ring
11 Gear & bush assembly—transmission reverse idler sliding
12 Gear—transmission reverse idler sliding
13 Bushing—transmission reverse idler gear
14 Pin—transmission reverse gear selector fork pivot
15 Ring—7/16 retaining
16 Pin—1/4 x 1 spring
17 Shaft—transmission reverse idler gear
18 Gear—transmission countershaft
19 Roller—transmission countershaft bearing
20 Washer—208/.918 flat
21 Washer—transmission countershaft gear thrust
22 Countershaft—transmission
23 Shaft assembly—transmission output
24 Shaft—transmission output
25 Hub—transmission synchronizer 1st & 2nd gear cluster
26 Shaft and gear assembly—transmission output
27 Gear—transmission reverse sliding
28 Insert—transmission synchronizer hub
29 Spring—transmission synchronizer retaining
30 Ring—transmission synchronizer blocking
31 Ring—transmission 2nd speed gear retaining snap
32 Gear—transmission 2nd speed
33 Washer—transmission 2nd speed gear thrust
34 Pin—1/8 x 1/4 rolled spring
35 Gear—transmission 3rd speed
36 Synchronizer assembly—3rd & 4th speed
37 Hub—transmission synchronizer   ; 4th gear clutch
38 Insert—transmission synchronizer hub
39 Sleeve—transmission 3rd & 4th gear clutch hub
40 Spring—transmission synchronizer retaining
41 Ring—transmission synchronizer blocking
42 Ring—transmission m/d gear bearing shaft snap
43 Fork—transmission 1st & 2nd gear shift
44 Fork—transmission 3rd & 4th gear shift
45 Lever assembly—transmission reverse gear shaft relay

46 Retaining   transmission reverse gear shaft relay lever
47 Lever—transmission reverse gear shaft relay
48 Fork—transmission reverse gear shift
49 Spring—transmission shifter interlock
50 Plunger—transmission meshlock
51 Screw—m12 x 10 round head flat
52 Plate—transmission gear selector interlock
53 Screw & washer assembly—m10 x 30 hex head
54 Plug—3/4 diameter welch type
55 Shaft—transmission input
56 Roller—transmission mainshaft bearing
57 Bearing assembly—transmission m/d gear ball
58 Ring—m/d gear bearing retaining snap
59 Ring—1.00 retaining
60 Seal—transmission shift shaft
61 Gear—transmission 1st speed
62 Clip—spark control switch wire retaining
63 Gear—speedometer drive
64 Extension assembly—transmission
65 Extension—transmission
66 Bushing—transmission extension
67 Stop—transmission gear shift lever reverse
68 Gasket—transmission extension
69 Seal assembly—transmission extension oil
70 Plug—transmission extension
71 Retainer—transmission input shaft gear bearing
72 Seal assembly—transmission input shaft oil
73 Gasket—transmission input shaft bearing retainer
74 Bolt—M8 x 20 hex head-lock
75 Gasket—transmission case cover
76 Cover—transmission case
77 Screw—m6 x 20 hex head
78 Bolt—m6 x 32 hex washer HD shoulder
79 Plug—1/2-14 pipe (filler)
80 Bushing—transmission gear shift damper
81 Washer—spring lock
82 Nut—hexagon
83 Switch assembly—back-up lamp
84 Switch assembly—transmission seat belt warning sensor
85 Tag—transmission service identification
86 Washer—transmission 1st gear thrust
87 Ball—.25 diameter
88 Screw & lockwasher assembly—m12 x 40
89 Arm assembly—transmission control selector
90 Arm—transmission control selector
91 Pin—transmission gear shift

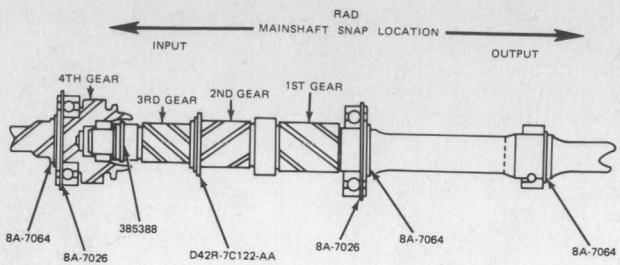

RAD mainshaft snap-ring locations (© Ford Motor Co)

to the shifter shaft.

4. Remove the shifter shaft from the cover taking care not to damage the seal.
5. Remove the manual selector and interlock plate.
6. Remove the first and second speed shifter fork. Remove the third and fourth speed shifter fork.
7. Clean and inspect all parts. Replace the shifter shaft seal and welch plug, if damaged.

Output Shaft

1. Scribe alignment marks on the synchronizer and blocker rings. Remove the snap-rings from the front of the output shaft. Slide the third and fourth speed synchronizer assembly, blocker rings and third gear off the shaft.
2. Remove the next snap-ring and the second gear thrust washer from the shaft. Slide second gear and the blocker ring off the shaft, taking care not to lose the sliding gear from the first and second speed synchronizer assembly. The first and second speed synchronizer hub cannot be removed from the output shaft.
3. Remove the first gear thrust washer (oil slinger) from the rear of the output shaft. Remove the spring pin retaining first gear onto the shaft.
4. Slide first gear off the output shaft, and remove the first speed blocker ring. Take care not to lose the sliding gear from the first and second speed synchronizer assembly.
5. Clean and inspect all parts.

Countershaft Gear Bearing Replacement

1. Remove the dummy shaft, bearing retainer washers and needle bearings from the countershaft gear. Clean and inspect the parts.
2. Coat the bore at each end of the countershaft gear with grease to retain the needle bearings.
3. While holding the dummy shaft in the gear, install the needle bearings and retainer washers in each end of the gear.

Input Shaft Bearing Replacement

1. Remove the roller bearings from the input shaft.
2. Remove the snap-ring retaining the input shaft bearing. Press the input shaft out of the bearing. Clean and inspect all parts.
3. Press the input shaft bearing onto the input shaft, making sure that the snap-ring groove faces the front of the shaft. Install a new snap-ring to retain the bearing on the shaft.
4. Lightly coat the bore of the input shaft with grease.
NOTE: *If a thick film of grease, such as wheel bearing grease, is applied to the shaft, the lubrication holes may become clogged, thereby preventing transmission oil from reaching the bearings, possibly resulting in premature bearing failure.*
5. Install the roller bearings in the bore.

Synchronizer Replacement

1. Scribe alignment marks on the hub and sleeve of the synchronizer.
2. Push the synchronizer sleeve from each synchronizer hub.
NOTE: *The first and second speed synchronizer hub cannot be removed from the output shaft.*
3. Separate the inserts and insert springs from the hubs, taking care not to mix the parts of the first and second speed synchronizer with that of the third and

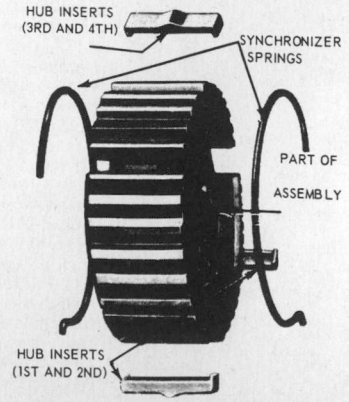

RAD synchronizer spring rotation
(© Ford Motor Co)

fourth speed synchronizer. Clean and inspect all parts.
4. Position the sleeve on the hub, making sure that the alignment marks scribed prior to disassembly are aligned.
5. Position the 3 inserts on the hub. Install the insert springs, taking care to seat the bent tab in one of the inserts. The springs must face in opposite directions.

Component Assembly

Output Shaft

1. Place a blocker ring on the cone of first gear, and slide the gear and ring assembly onto the output shaft. Make sure that the inserts in the synchronizer engage in the blocker ring notches.
2. Install the spring pin retaining first gear to the output shaft.
3. Install a blocker ring on the cone of second gear, and slide the gear and ring assembly onto the output shaft. Make sure that the inserts in the synchronizer engage in the blocker ring notches.
4. Install the second gear thrust washer and new snap-ring on the shaft.
5. Install a blocker ring on the cone of third gear, and slide the gear and ring assembly onto the output shaft. Install the third and fourth speed synchronizer. Make sure that the inserts in the synchronizer engage in the blocker ring notches.
6. Install a new third and fourth gear synchronizer snap-ring.
7. Place the first gear thrust washer (oil slinger) on the shaft and on the spring pin retaining first gear.
CAUTION: *The oil grooves must be positioned against the gear.*

Cover Assembly

1. Install the third and fourth speed shifter fork into the cover.
2. Install the first and second speed shifter fork into the cover. Lubricate the shifter shaft bore with grease.
3. Install the manual selector arm through the interlock plate, and position the two pieces into the cover, with the wide leg of the interlock plate towards the inside of the transmission case.
4. Align the shifter shaft in the cover, and insert the shaft through the shifter forks and manual selector. Coat the shifter shaft with a light coating of grease.
5. Align the pin holes in the manual selector arm and shifter shaft. Install the spring pin flush with the surface of the selector arm.
6. Install the detent plunger, spring, and plug. Tighten the plug to 8-12 ft lbs.

7. Check the operation of the shift forks in each gear position.

Transmission Assembly

1. Position the reverse idler gear and shaft in place.
2. Coat the surfaces of the countershaft thrust washer with a thin film of grease and position in the case. Position the cluster gear assembly in the bottom of the case.
3. Position the output shaft assembly into the case through the cover opening. With the snap-ring groove facing rearward, place the rear bearing on the output shaft. Place the transmission in the vertical position and install the bearing. Position the first gear thrust washer on the roll pin carefully, holding it tightly during bearing installation. Install the rear bearing snap-rings.
4. Return the transmission to the horizontal position. Install the input shaft and blocker ring through the front of the case. Make sure that the blocker ring

notches engage the synchronizer insert.

5. Install the front bearing retainer using a new gasket. Apply gasket sealer to the bolt threads and tighten to 11-15 ft lbs.
6. Place the transmission in the vertical position. Align the countershaft gear bore and thrust washers with the bore in the case. Install the countershaft from the rear of the case.
7. Install the reverse idler gear lever assembly, taking care to insert the fork in the reverse idler gear groove.
8. Apply gasket sealer to the reverse lever pivot bolt threads and install the bolt. Align the lever on the pivot bolt and torque the bolt to 15-25 ft lbs. Install the reverse lever retaining spring clip to the reverse gear pivot bolt. Tilt the transmission forward and pour a light coating of gear lube over the gear train.
9. Using a new cover gasket, install

the cover assembly. Install the bolts and wiring clips and tighten to 7-10 ft lbs.
NOTE: *The two shouldered locating bolts must be installed first.*
Position the shift rail into first or third gear position.

10. Insert the speedometer drive gear lock ball into its hole. While holding the ball, slide the speedometer drive gear into place and secure it with a new snap-ring.
11. Using a new gasket, install the extension housing to the case. Using gasket sealer on the bolts, tighten them to 18-27 ft lbs. Take care not to damage the extension yoke seal.
12. Install the offset lever assembly onto the shift shaft, securing the assembly with a nut and flat washer. Tighten to 14-20 ft lbs.
13. Insert the gearshift lever into place. Check its operation in each gear position.
14. Install the access plug into the rear of the extension housing, using a soft mallet.

Type-8
Ford 4-Speed

Fairlane V8, 1970
Falcon V8, 1970
Ford, 1970-71

Mercury, 1970
Montego, 1970-73

Application
Cougar, 1970-73
Mustang V8, 1970-73
Torino V8, 1970-73

Disassembly

1. Remove retaining clips and flat washers from the shift rods at the levers.
2. Remove shift linkage control bracket attaching screws and remove shift linkage and control bracket.
3. Remove cover attaching screws. Then lift cover and gasket from the case.
4. Remove extension housing attaching screws. Then, remove extension housing and gasket.
5. Remove input shaft bearing retainer attaching screws. Then, slide retainer from the input shaft.
6. Working a dummy shaft in from the front of the case, drive the countershaft out the rear of the case. Let the countergear assembly lie in the bottom of the case.
7. Locate first - second - speed gear shift lever in neutral. Locate third fourth-speed gear shift lever in third-speed position.
8. Remove the lockbolt that holds the third-fourth-speed shift rail detent spring and plug the left side of the case. Remove spring and plug with a magnet.
9. Remove the detent mechanism set screw from top of case. Then,

remove the detent spring and plug with a small magnet.

10. Remove attaching screw from the third-fourth-speed shift fork. Tap lightly on the inner end of the shift rail to remove the expansion plug from front of case. Then, withdraw the third-fourth-speed shift rail from the front. (Do not lose the interlock pin from rail.)

11. Remove attaching screw from the first and second-speed shift fork. Slide the first-second shift rail from the rear of case.
12. Remove the interlock and detent plugs from the top of the case with a magnet.
13. Remove the snap-ring or disengage retainer that holds the speedometer drive gear to the

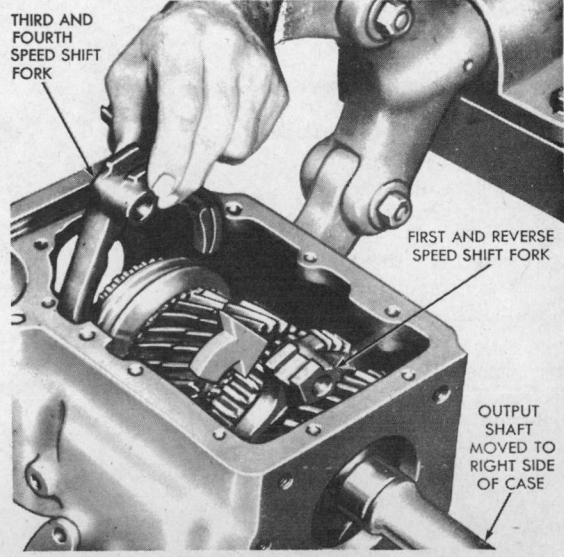

THIRD AND FOURTH SPEED SHIFT FORK

FIRST AND REVERSE SPEED SHIFT FORK

OUTPUT SHAFT MOVED TO RIGHT SIDE OF CASE

Removing shift forks
(© Ford Motor Co)

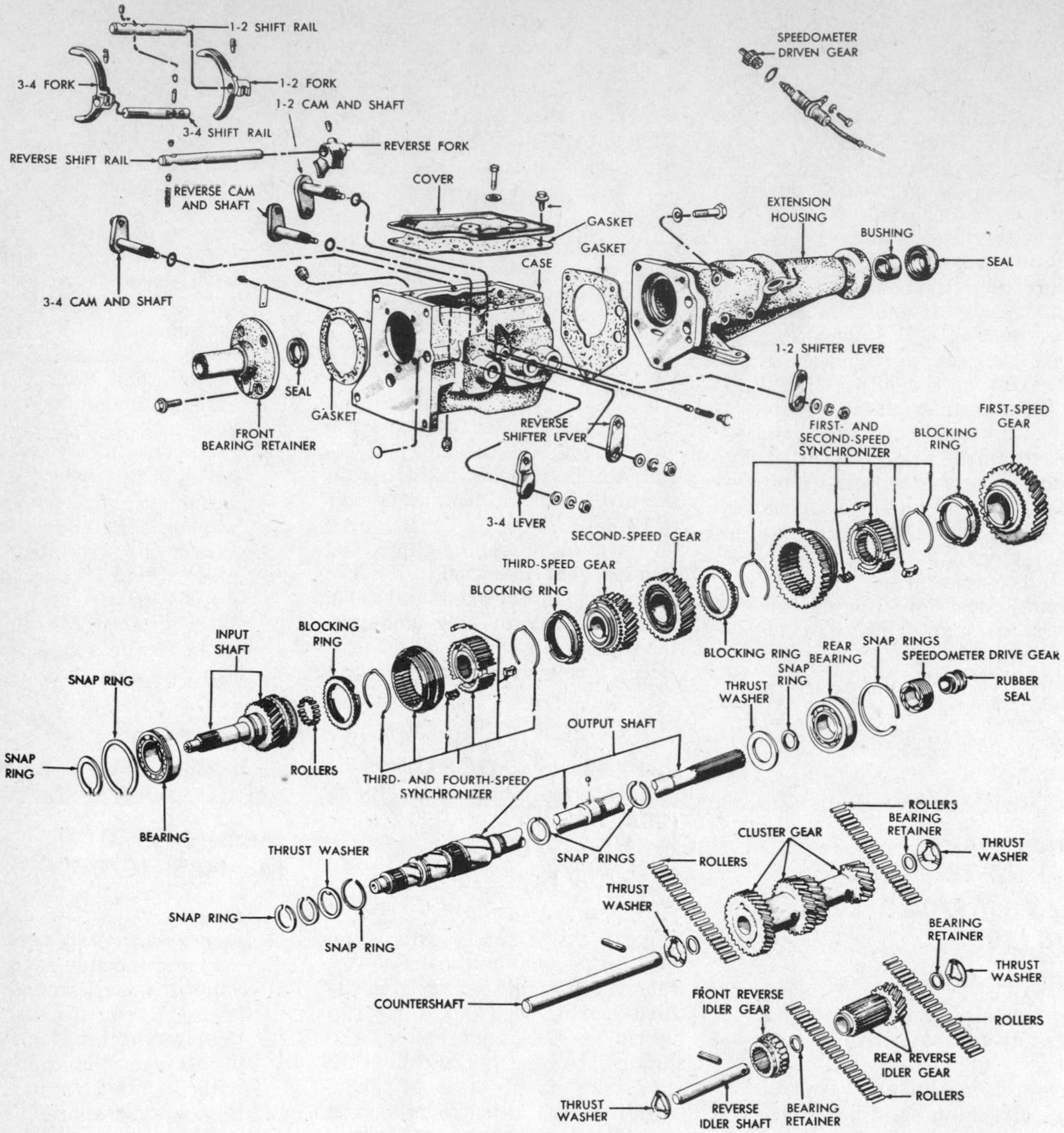

Ford 4-speed transmission disassembled (© Ford Motor Co)

output shaft. Slide the gear from the shaft, then remove speedometer gear drive ball.

14. Remove the snap-ring used to hold the output shaft bearing to the shaft. Remove output shaft bearing.

15. Remove the input shaft bearing and blocking ring from the front of the case.

16. Move output shaft to the right side of case. Then, maneuver the forks to permit lifting them from the case.

17. Support first-speed gear to prevent it sliding from the shaft, then lift output shaft from the case.

18. Remove reverse gear shift fork attaching screw. Rotate the reverse shift rail 90°, then, slide the shift rail out the rear of the case. Lift out the reverse shift fork.

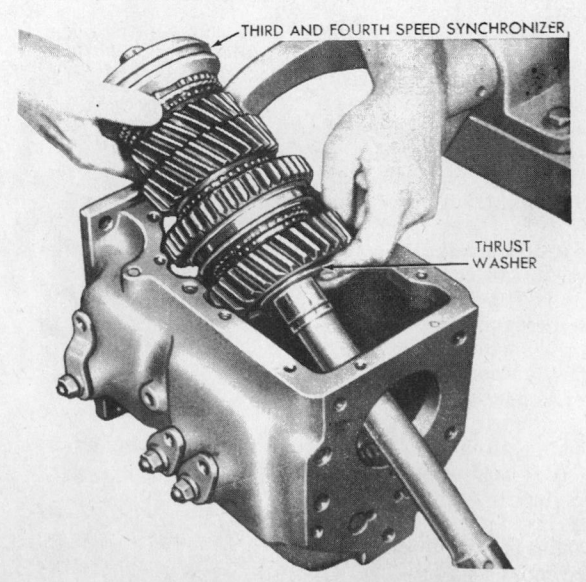

Removing output shaft
(© Ford Motor Co)

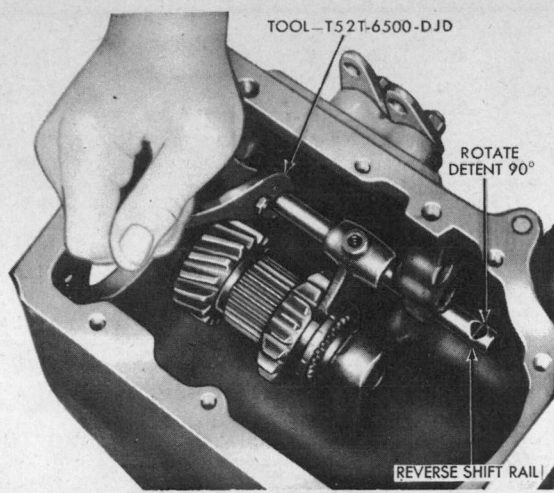

TOOL—T52T-6500-DJD

ROTATE DETENT 90°

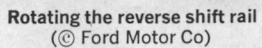

REVERSE SHIFT RAIL

Rotating the reverse shift rail
(© Ford Motor Co)

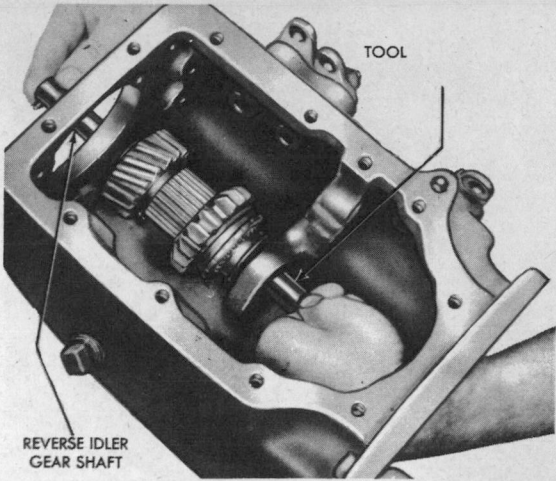

TOOL

REVERSE IDLER GEAR SHAFT

Removing reverse idler shaft
(© Ford Motor Co)

19. Remove the reverse detent plug and spring from the case with a magnet.
20. Using a dummy shaft, remove the reverse idler shaft from the case.
21. Lift reverse idler gear and thrust washers from the case. Be careful not to drop the bearing rollers or the dummy from the gear.
22. Lift the countergear, thrust washers, rollers and dummy shaft assembly from the case.
23. Remove the snap-ring from the front of the output shaft. Then, slide the third-fourth synchronizer blocking ring and the third-speed gear from the shaft.
24. Remove the next snap-ring and the second-speed gear thrust washer from the shaft. Slide the second-speed gear and the blocking ring from the shaft.
25. Remove the snap-ring, then slide the first-second synchronizer, blocking ring and the first-speed gear from the shaft.
26. Remove the thrust washer from rear of the shaft.

Unit Repairs

Cam and Shaft Seals

1. Remove attaching nut and washers from each shift lever, then remove the three levers.
2. Remove the three cams and shafts from inside the case.
3. Replace the old O-rings with new ones that have been well-lubricated.
4. Slide each cam and shaft into its respective bore in the transmission.
5. Install the levers and secure them with their respective washers and nuts.

Input Shaft Bearing

1. Remove the snap-ring that holds the bearing to the shaft.
2. Press the shaft gear from the bearing.
3. Press a new bearing onto the input shaft.
4. Secure the bearing with a snap-ring.

Synchronizers

1. Push the synchronizer hub from each synchronizer sleeve.
2. Separate the inserts and springs from the hubs. Do not mix parts of the first-second with parts of third-fourth synchronizers.
3. To assemble, position the hub in the sleeve. Be sure the alignment marks are properly indexed.
4. Place the three inserts into place on the hub. Install the insert springs so that the irregular surface (hump) is seated in one of the inserts. Do not stagger the springs.

Countershaft Gear

1. Dismantle the countershaft gear assembly.
2. Assemble the gear by coating each end of the countershaft gear bore with grease.
3. Install dummy shaft in the gear. Then install 21 bearing rollers and a retainer washer in each end of the gear.

Reverse Idler Gear

1. Dismantle reverse idler gear.
2. Assemble reverse idler gear by coating the bore in each end of reverse idler gear with grease.
3. Hold the dummy shaft in the gear and install the 22 bearing rollers and the retainer washer into each end of the gear.
4. Install the reverse idler sliding gear on the splines of the reverse idler gear. Be sure the shift fork groove is toward the front.

Input Shaft Seal

1. Remove the seal from the input shaft bearing retainer.
2. Coat the sealing surface of a new seal with lubricant, then press the new seal into the input shaft bearing retainer.

Assembly

1. Grease the countershaft gear thrust surfaces in the case. Then, position a thrust washer at each end of the case.
2. Position the countershaft gear, dummy shaft, and roller bearings in the case.
3. Align the gear bore and thrust washers with the bores in the case. Install the countershaft.
4. With the case in a horizontal position, countershaft gear end-play should be from .004-.018 in. Use thrust washers to obtain play within these limits.
5. After establishing correct end-play, place the dummy shaft in the countershaft gear and allow the gear assembly to remain on the bottom of the case.
6. Grease the reverse idler gear thrust surfaces in the case, and position the two thrust washers.
7. Position the reverse idler gear, sliding gear, dummy, etc. in place. Make sure that the shift fork groove in the sliding gear is toward the front.
8. Align the gear bore and thrust washers with the case bores and install the reverse idler shaft.
9. Reverse idler gear end-play should be .004-.018 in. Use selective thrust washers to obtain play within these limits.
10. Position reverse gear shift rail detent spring and detent plug in the case. Hold the reverse shift fork in place on the reverse idler sliding gear and install the shift rail from the rear of the case. Lock the fork to the rail with the Allen head set screws.
11. Install the first-second synchronizer onto the output shaft. The

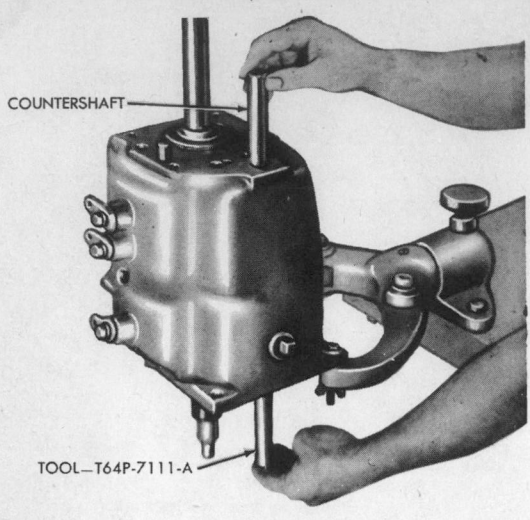

Installing countershaft
(© Ford Motor Co)

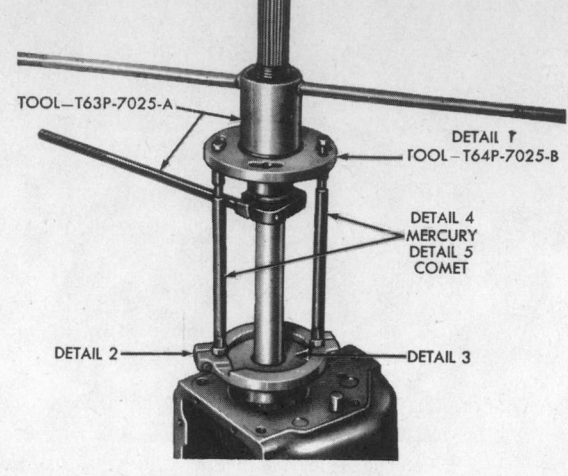

Installing output shaft bearing
(© Ford Motor Co)

first and reverse synchronizer hub are a press fit and should be installed with gear teeth facing the rear of the shaft.

12. Slide second-speed gear onto the front of the shaft with the synchronizer coned surface toward the rear.

13. Install the second-speed gear thrust washer and snap-ring.

14. Slide the third-speed gear onto the shaft with the synchronizer coned surface front.

15. Coat the cone of third-speed gear with grease. Place a blocking ring on the third-speed gear.

16. Slide the third-fourth speed gear synchronizer onto the shaft. Be sure that the inserts in the synchronizer engage the notches in the blocking ring. Install the snap-ring onto the front of the output shaft.

17. Coat the cone of second-speed gear with grease and position the blocking ring on the gear.

18. Slide the first-second speed synchronizer onto the rear of the output shaft. Be sure that the inserts engage the notches in the blocking ring and that the shift fork groove is toward the rear.

19. Coat the coned surface of first-speed gear with grease and position the blocking ring on it.

20. Slide the first-speed gear onto the rear of the output shaft. Be sure that the notches in the blocker ring engage the synchronizer inserts.

21. Install heavy thrust washer onto the rear of the output shaft.

22. Lower the output shaft assembly into the case.

23. Position the first-second speed shift fork and the third-fourth-speed shift fork in place on their respective gears. Rotate them into place.

24. Place a detent plug in the detent bore. Place the reverse shift rail into neutral position.

25. Coat the third-fourth-speed shift rail interlock pin with grease, then position it in the shift rail.

26. Align the third-fourth-speed shift fork with the shift rail bores and slide the shift rail into place. Be sure that the three detents are facing the outside of the case. Place the front synchronizer into third-fourth-speed position and install the set screw into the third-fourth-speed shift fork. Move the synchronizer to neutral position. Install the third-fourth-speed shift rail detent plug, spring and bolt into the left side of the transmission case. Place the interlock plug (tapered ends) in the detent bore.

27. Align first-second-speed shift fork with the case bores and slide the shift rail into place. Lock the fork with the set screw. Install the detent plug and spring into the detent bore. Thread the set screw into the case until the head is flush with the case.

28. Coat the input gear bore with a small amount of grease. Then install the 15 bearing rollers.

29. Place the input shaft gear in the case. Be sure that the output shaft pilot enters the roller bearing of the input shaft gear.

30. With a new gasket on the input bearing retainer, dip attaching

bolts in sealer, install bolts and torque to 30-36 ft. lbs.

31. Install the output shaft bearing, then install the snap-ring to hold the bearing.

32. Position the speedometer gear drive ball in the output shaft and slide the speedometer drive gear into place. Secure gear with snap-ring.

33. Align the countershaft gear bore and thrust washers with the bore in the case. Install the countershaft.

34. With a new gasket in place, install and secure the extension housing. Dip the extension housing screws in sealer, then torque screws to 42-50 ft. lbs.

35. Install the filler plug (torque 10-20 ft. lbs.) and the drain plug (torque 20-30 ft. lbs.), the drain plug is magnetic.

36. Pour in four pints of mild E.P. gear oil over the entire gear train while rotating the input shaft.

37. Place each shift fork in all positions to make sure they function properly.

38. With a new cover gasket in place, install the cover. Dip attaching screws in sealer, then torque screws to 14-19 ft. lbs.

39. Coat the third-fourth speed shift rail plug bore with sealer. Install a new plug.

40. Secure each shift rod to its respective lever with a spring washer, flat washer and retaining pin.

41. Position the shift linkage control bracket to the extension housing. Install and torque the attaching screws to 12-15 ft. lbs.

Type-9
Muncie Fully Synchro-
nized 3-Speed

Application
Camaro, 1970-74
Chevelle, 1970-74
Chevrolet, 1970-73

Firebird, 1970-74
GTO, 1970-74
Monte Carlo, 1970-74

Nova, 1970-74
Olds F-85, 4-4-2, 1970-71
Pontiac Grand Prix, 1970-71
Tempest, 1970-71

Transmission Disassembly

1. Remove side cover and shift forks.
2. Unbolt extension. Rotate extension to line up groove in extension flange with reverse idler shaft. Drive reverse idler shaft and key out of case with a brass drift.
3. Move second-third synchronizer sleeve forward. Remove extension housing and mainshaft assembly.
4. Remove reverse idler gear from case.
5. Remove third speed blocker ring from clutch gear.
6. Expand snap-ring which retains mainshaft rear bearing. Tap gently on end of mainshaft to remove extension.
7. Remove clutch gear bearing retainer and gasket.
8. Remove snap-ring. Remove clutch gear from inside case by gently tapping on end of clutch gear.
9. Remove oil slinger. Remove 16 mainshaft pilot bearings from clutch gear cavity.
10. Slip clutch gear bearing out front of case. Aid removal with a screwdriver between case and bearing outer snap-ring.
11. Drive countershaft and key out to rear.
12. Remove countergear and two tanged thrust washers.

Mainshaft Disassembly

1. Depress speedometer drive gear retaining clip. Slide off gear. Some speedometer drive gears, made of metal, must be pulled off.
2. Remove rear bearing snap-ring.
3. Support reverse gear and press on rear of mainshaft to remove reverse gear, thrust washer, and

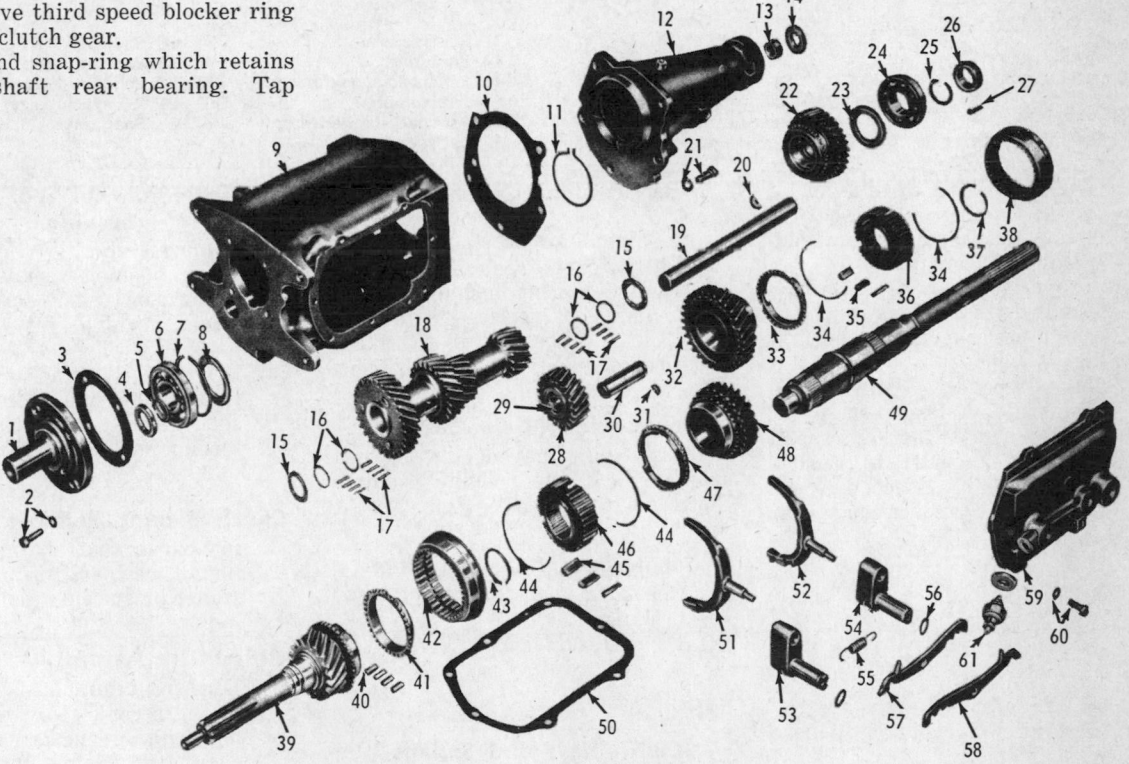

Muncie 3-speed transmission disassembled (© G.M. Corp)

1 Bearing retainer	17 Needle bearings	35 Synchronizer keys	49 Mainshaft
2 Bolt and lock washer	18 Countergear	36 1st and reverse synchronizer	50 Gasket
3 Gasket	19 Countershaft	hub assembly	51 2nd and 3rd shifter fork
4 Oil seal	20 Woodruff key	37 Snap ring	52 1st and reverse shifter fork
5 Snap ring (bearing-to-main drive gear)	21 Bolt (extension-to-case)	38 1st and reverse synchronizer collar	53 2-3 shifter shaft assembly
6 Main drive gear bearing	22 Reverse gear	39 Main drive gear	54 1st and reverse shifter shaft assembly
7 Snap ring bearing	23 Thrust washer	40 Pilot bearings	55 Spring
8 Oil slinger	24 Rear bearing	41 3rd speed blocker ring	56 O-ring seal
9 Case	25 Snap ring	42 2nd and 3rd synchronizer collar	57 1st and reverse detent cam
10 Gasket	26 Speedometer drive gear	43 Snap ring	58 2nd and 3rd detent cam
11 Snap ring (rear bearing-to-extension)	27 Retainer clip	44 Synchronizer key spring	59 Side cover
12 Extension	28 Reverse idler gear	45 Synchronizer keys	60 Bolt and lock washer
13 Extension bushing	29 Reverse idler bushing	46 2nd and 3rd synchronizer hub	
14 Oil seal	30 Reverse idler shaft	47 2nd speed blocker ring	
15 Thrust washer	31 Woodruff key	48 2nd speed gear	
16 Bearing washer	32 1st speed gear		
	33 1st speed blocker ring		
	34 Synchronizer key spring		

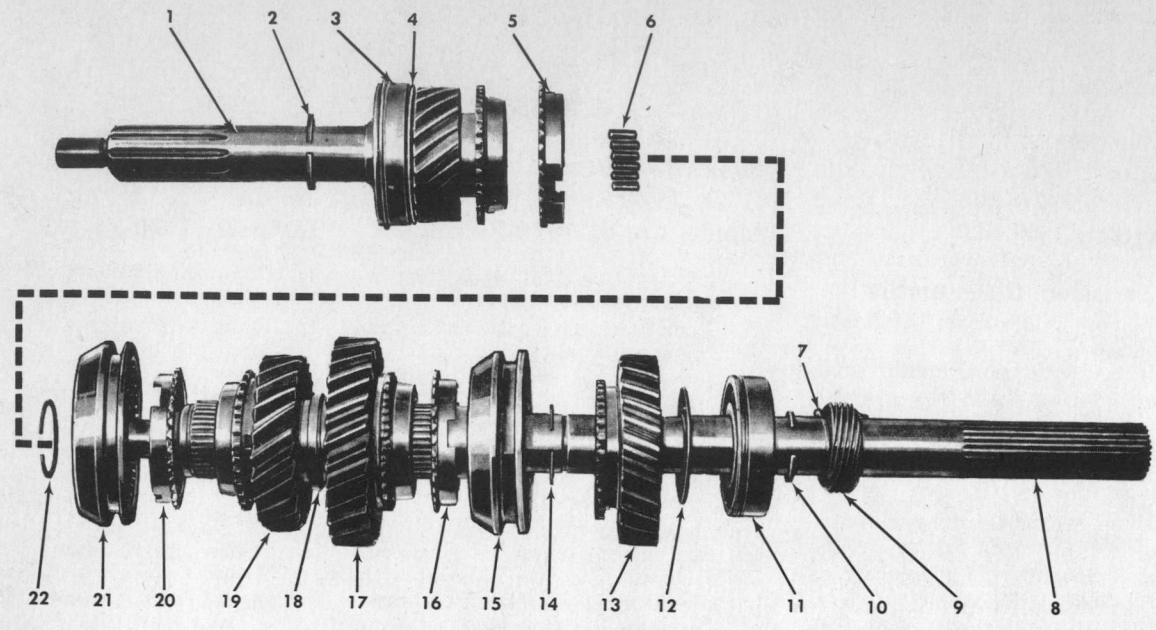

Clutch gear and mainshaft assembly (© G.M. Corp)

1 Clutch gear	7 Retaining clip	13 Reverse gear	18 Shoulder (part of mainshaft)
2 Snap ring	8 Mainshaft	14 Snap ring	19 2nd speed gear
3 Clutch gear bearing	9 Speedo drive gear	15 1st speed synchronizer	20 2nd speed blocker ring
4 Oil slinger	10 Snap ring	assembly	21 2-3 synchronizer assembly
5 3rd speed blocker ring	11 Rear bearing	16 1st speed blocker ring	22 Snap ring
6 Mainshaft pilot bearings (16)	12 Reverse gear thrust washer	17 1st speed gear	

rear bearing. Be careful not to cock the bearing on the shaft.
4. Remove first and reverse sliding clutch hub snap-ring.
5. Support first gear. Press on rear of mainshaft to remove clutch assembly, blocker ring, and first gear.
6. Remove second and third speed sliding clutch hub snap-ring.
7. Support second gear. Press on front of mainshaft to remove clutch assembly, second speed blocker ring, and second gear from shaft.

Inspection
1. Wash all parts in solvent.
2. Air dry.

Case
1. Check for cracks.
2. Check faces for burrs. Remove with a fine file.
3. Check bearing bores for damage. If they are damaged, replace case.

Front and Rear Bearings
1. Do not spin bearings with air pressure; turn them slowly by hand.
2. Lubricate bearings with light oil. Turn slowly to check for roughness.

Bearing Rollers
1. Check for wear; replace if worn.
2. Check countershaft and reverse idler shaft.

3. Replace all worn washers.

Gears
1. Check for wear, chips, or cracks.
2. If reverse gear bushing is worn or damaged, replace entire gear.
3. Check to see that both clutch sleeves slide freely on their hubs.

Reverse Idler Gear Bushing
This bushing may not be serviced separately. If the bushing requires replacement, replace the gear.

Countergear Anti-Lash Plate
1. Check the plate teeth for wear or damage.
2. Do not disassemble.

Repair

Clutch Keys and Springs
Keys and springs may be replaced if worn or broken, but the hubs and sleeves must be kept together as originally assembled.
1. Mark hub and sleeve for reassembly.
2. Push hub from sleeve. Remove keys and springs.
3. Place three keys and two springs, one on each side of hub, so all three keys are engaged by both springs. The tanged end of the springs should not be installed into the same key.
4. Slide the sleeve onto the hub, aligning the marks.

Extension Oil Seal and Bushing
1. Remove seal.
2. Using bushing remover and installer, or other suitable tool, drive bushing into extension housing.
3. Drive new bushing in from rear. Lubricate inside of bushing and seal. Install new oil seal with extension seal installer or suitable tool.

Clutch Bearing Retainer Oil Seal
1. Pry old seal out.
2. Install new seal using seal installer or suitable tool. Seat seal in bore.

Mainshaft Assembly
1. Turn front of mainshaft up.
2. Install second gear with clutching teeth up; the rear face of the gear butts against the flange on the mainshaft.
3. Install a blocking ring with clutching teeth downward. All three blocking rings are the same.
4. Install second and third synchronizer assembly with fork slot down. Press it onto mainshaft splines. Both synchronizer assemblies are identical but are assembled differently. The second-third speed hub and sleeve is assembled with the sleeve fork slot toward the thrust face of the hub; the first-reverse hub and sleeve, with the fork slot op-

posite the thrust face. Be sure that the blocker ring notches align with the synchronizer assembly keys.

5. Install synchronizer snap-ring. Both synchronizer snap-rings are the same.
6. Turn rear of shaft up.
7. Install first gear with clutching teeth upward; the front face of the gear butts against the flange on the mainshaft.
8. Install a blocker ring with clutching teeth down.
9. Install first and reverse synchronizer assembly with fork slot up. Press it onto mainshaft splines. Be sure blocker ring notches align with synchronizer assembly keys and both synchronizer sleeves face front of mainshaft.
10. Install snap-ring.
11. Install reverse gear with clutching teeth down.
12. Install steel reverse gear thrust washer with flats aligned.
13. Press rear ball bearing onto shaft with snap-ring slot down.
14. Install snap-ring.
15. Install speedometer drive gear and retaining clip.

Transmission Assembly

1. Place a row of 29 roller bearings, a bearing washer, a second row of 29 bearings, and a second bearing washer at each end of the countergear. Hold in place with grease.
2. Place countergear assembly through rear case opening with a tanged thrust washer, tang away from gear, at each end. Install countershaft and key from rear of case. Be sure that thrust washer tangs are aligned with notches in case.
3. Place reverse idler gear in case. Do not install reverse idler shaft yet.
4. Expand snap-ring in extension. Assemble extension over mainshaft and onto rear bearing. Seat snap-ring.
5. Load 16 mainshaft pilot bearings into clutch gear cavity. Assemble third speed blocker ring onto clutch gear clutching surface with teeth toward gear.
6. Place clutch gear assembly, without front bearing, over front of mainshaft. Make sure

that blocker ring notches align with keys in second-third synchronizer assembly.
7. Stick gasket onto extension housing with grease. Assemble clutch gear, mainshaft, and extension to case together. Make sure that clutch gear teeth engage teeth of countergear anti-lash plate.
8. Rotate extension housing. Install reverse idler shaft and key.
9. Torque extension bolts to 45 ft. lbs.
10. Install oil slinger with inner lip facing forward. Install front bearing outer snap-ring to bearing. Slide bearing into case bore.
11. Install snap-ring to clutch gear stem. Install bearing retainer and gasket. Torque bolts to 20 ft. lbs. Retainer oil return hole must be at 6 o'clock.
12. Shift both synchronizer sleeves to neutral positions. Install side cover, aligning shifter forks with synchronizer sleeve grooves.
13. Torque side cover bolts to 20 ft. lbs.

Type-10
Saginaw Fully Synchronized 3-Speed

Application
Apollo, 1973-77
Astre, 1975-77
Buick Special, Skylark, Century, 1970-77
Camaro, 1970-77

Chevelle, 1970-77
Chevrolet, 1970-73
Firebird, 1970-77
Monza, 1976-77
Nova, 1970-77

Olds F-85, Cutlass, 1970-77
Olds 4-4-2, 1972
Omega, 1973-77
Tempest, 1970-77
Ventura, 1971-77
Vega, 1973-77

Transmission Disassembly

1. Remove side cover assembly and shift forks.
2. Remove clutch gear bearing retainer.
3. Remove clutch gear bearing to gear stem snap-ring. Pull clutch gear outward until a screwdriver can be inserted between bearing and case. Remove clutch gear bearing.
4. Remove speedometer driven gear and extension bolts.
5. Remove reverse idler shaft snap-ring. Slide reverse idler gear forward on shaft.
6. Remove mainshaft and extension assembly.
7. Remove clutch gear and third speed blocker ring from inside case. Remove 14 roller bearings from clutch gear.
8. Expand the snap-ring which retains the mainshaft rear bearing. Remove the extension.
9. Using a dummy shaft, drive the countershaft and key out the

rear of the case. Remove the gear, two tanged thrust washers, and dummy shaft. Remove bearing washer and 27 roller bearings from each end of countergear.
10. Use a long drift to drive the reverse idler shaft and key through the rear of the case.
11. Remove reverse idler gear and tanged steel thrust washer.

Mainshaft Disassembly

1. Remove second and third speed sliding clutch hub snap-ring from mainshaft. Remove clutch assembly, second speed blocker ring, and second gear from front of mainshaft.
2. Depress speedometer drive gear retaining clip. Remove gear. Some units have a metal speedometer drive gear which must be pulled off.
3. Remove rear bearing snap-ring.
4. Support reverse gear. Press on rear of mainshaft. Remove re-

verse gear, thrust washer, spring washer, rear bearing, and snap-ring. When pressing off the rear bearing, be careful not to cock the bearing on the shaft.
5. Remove first and reverse sliding clutch hub snap-ring. Remove clutch assembly, first speed blocker ring, and first gear.

Inspection
1. Wash all parts in solvent.
2. Air dry.

Case
1. Check for cracks.
2. Check faces for burrs. Remove with a fine file.
3. Check bearing bores for damage. If they are damaged, replace case.

Front and Rear Bearings
1. Do not spin bearings with air pressure; turn them slowly by hand.
2. Lubricate bearings with light oil. Turn slowly to check for

1 Thrust washer—front
2 Bearing washer
3 Needle bearings
4 Countergear
5 Needle bearings
6 Bearing washer
7 Thrust washer—rear
8 Counter shaft
9 Woodruff key
10 Bearing retainer
11 Gasket
12 Oil seal

13 Snap ring—bearing to case
14 Snap ring—bearing to gear
15 Clutch gear bearing
16 Case
17 Clutch gear
18 Pilot bearings
19 3rd speed blocker ring
20 Retainer "E" ring
21 Reverse idler gear
22 Reverse idler shaft
23 Woodruff key
24 Snap ring—hub to shaft
25 2-3 synchronizer sleeve
26 Synchronizer key spring
27 2-3 synchronizer hub
   assembly

34 1-2 synchronizer sleeve
35 Snap ring—hub to shaft
36 Reverse gear
37 Thrust washer
38 Spring washer

39 Rear bearing
40 Snap ring—bearing to shaft
41 Speedometer drive gear
42 Clip
43 Gasket
44 Snap ring—rear bearing to
   extension
45 Extension
46 Oil seal

47 Gasket
48 2-3 shift fork
49 1st and reverse shift fork
50 2-3 shifter shaft assembly
51 1st and reverse shifter
   shaft assembly
52 "O" ring seal
53 "E" ring
54 Spring
55 2nd and 3rd detent cam
56 1st and reverse detent cam
57 Side cover
58 TCS switch

28 2nd speed blocker ring
29 2nd speed gear
30 Mainshaft
31 1st speed gear
32 1st speed blocker ring
33 1-2 synchronizer hub
   assembly

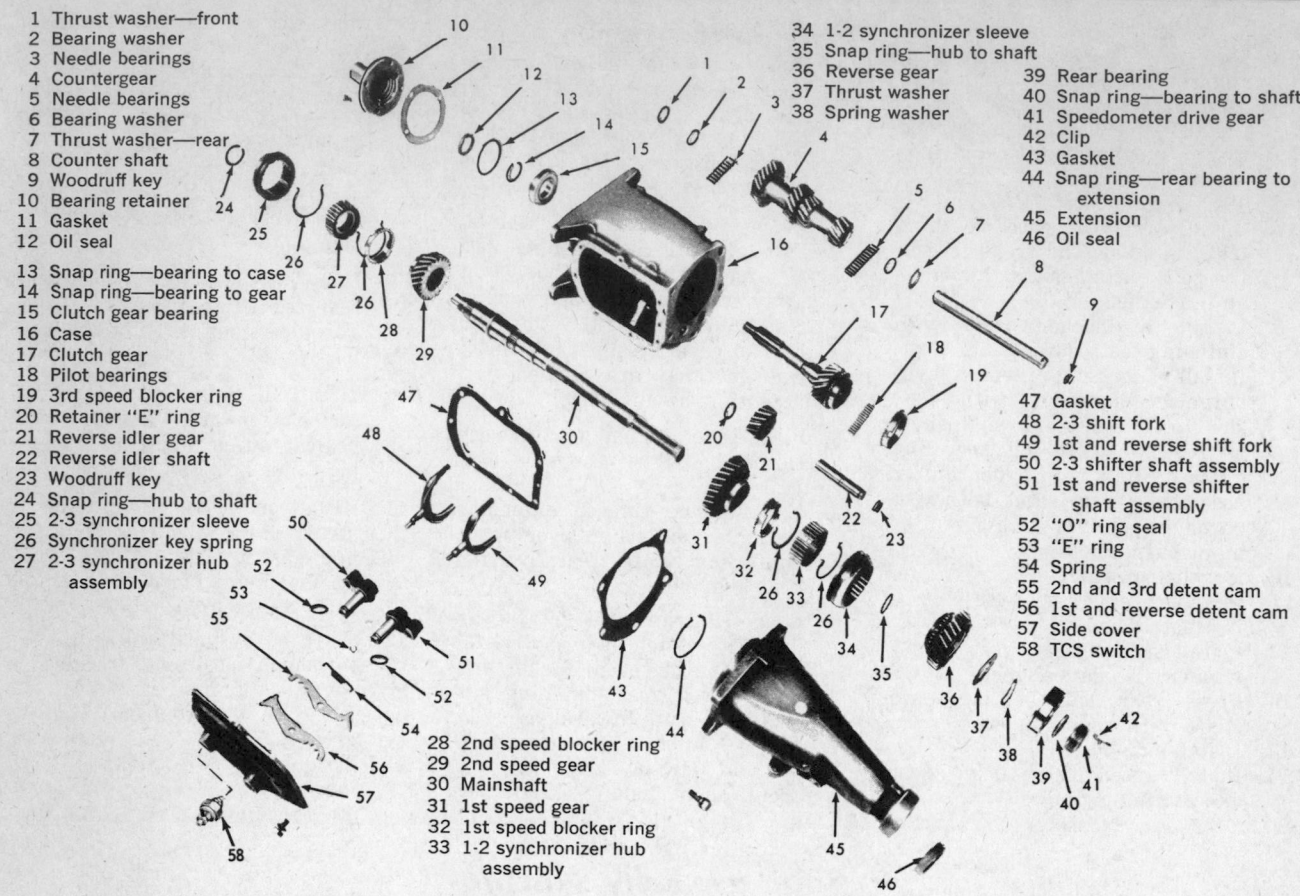

Saginaw transmission—exploded view (© G.M. Corp)

roughness.

Bearing Rollers

1. Check for wear; replace if worn.
2. Check countershaft and reverse idler shaft for wear or damage.
3. Replace all worn washers.

Gears

1. Check for wear, chips, or cracks.
2. If reverse gear bushing is worn or damaged, replace entire gear.
3. Check that both clutch sleeves slide freely on their hubs.

Reverse Idler Gear Bushing

This bushing may not be serviced separately. If the bushing requires replacement, replace the gear.

Countergear Anti-Lash Plate

1. Check the plate teeth for wear or damage.
2. Do not disassemble unit.

Repair

Clutch Keys and Springs

Keys and springs may be replaced if worn or broken, but the hubs and sleeves are matched pairs and must be kept together.

1. Mark hub and sleeve for reassembly.
2. Push hub from sleeve. Remove keys and springs.
3. Place three keys and two springs, one on each side of hub, in position, so all three keys are engaged by both springs. The tanged end of the springs should not be installed into the same key.
4. Slide the sleeve onto the hub, aligning the marks.

NOTE: a groove around the outside of the synchronizer hub marks the end that must be opposite the fork slot in the sleeve when assembled.

Extension Oil Seal and Bushing

1. Remove seal.
2. Using bushing remover and installer tool, or other suitable tool, drive bushing into extension housing.
3. Drive new bushing in from the rear. Lubricate inside of bushing and seal. Install new oil seal with extension seal installer tool or other suitable tool.

Clutch Bearing Retainer Oil Seal

1. Pry old seal out.
2. Install new seal using seal installer or suitable tool. Seat seal in bore.

Mainshaft Assembly

1. Turn front of mainshaft up.
2. Install second gear with clutching teeth up; the rear face of the gear butts against the flange on the mainshaft.
3. Install a blocker ring with clutching teeth down. All three blocker rings are the same.
4. Install second and third speed synchronizer assembly with fork slot down. Press it onto mainshaft splines. Both synchronizer assemblies are the same. Be sure that blocker ring notches align with synchronizer assembly keys.
5. Install synchronizer snap-ring. Both synchronizer snap-rings are the same.
6. Turn rear of shaft up.
7. Install first gear with clutching teeth up; the front face of the gear butts against the flange on the mainshaft.
8. Install a blocker ring with clutching teeth down.
9. Install first and reverse synchronizer assembly with fork slot down. Press it onto mainshaft splines. Be sure blocker ring notches align with synchronizer assembly keys.
10. Install snap-ring.
11. Install reverse gear with clutch-

Clutch gear and mainshaft assembly (© G.M. Corp)

1 Clutch gear
2 Clutch gear bearing
3 3rd speed blocker ring
4 Mainshaft pilot bearings (14)
5 Snap ring
6 2-3 synchronizer assembly
7 2nd speed blocker ring

8 2nd speed gear
9 Shoulder (part of main shaft)
10 1st speed gear
11 1st speed blocker ring
12 1st speed synchronizer assembly
13 Snap ring

14 Reverse gear
15 Reverse gear thrust washer
16 Spring washer
17 Rear bearing
18 Snap ring
19 Speedo drive gear and clip
20 Mainshaft

semble third speed blocker ring onto clutch gear clutching surface with teeth toward gear.

6. Place clutch gear, pilot bearings, and third speed blocker ring assembly over front of mainshaft assembly. Be sure blocker rings align with keys in second-third synchronizer assembly.

7. Stick extension gasket to case with grease. Install clutch gear, mainshaft, and extension together. Be sure clutch gear engages teeth of countergear anti-lash plate. Torque extension bolts to 45 ft. lbs.

ing teeth down.
12. Install steel reverse gear thrust washer and spring washer.
13. Press rear ball bearing onto shaft with snap-ring slot down.
14. Install snap-ring.
15. Install speedometer drive gear and retaining clip. Press on metal speedometer drive gear.

Transmission Assembly

1. Using dummy shaft, load a row of 27 roller bearings and a thrust washer at each end of countergear. Hold in place with grease.
2. Place countergear assembly into case through rear. Place a tanged thrust washer, tang away from gear, at each end. Install countershaft and key, making sure that tangs align with notches in case.
3. Install reverse idler gear thrust washer, gear, and shaft with key from rear of case. Be sure thrust washer is between gear and rear of case with tang toward notch in case.
4. Expand snap-ring in extension. Assemble extension over rear of mainshaft and onto rear bearing. Seat snap-ring in rear bearing groove.
5. Install 14 mainshaft pilot bearings into clutch gear cavity. As-

8. Place bearing over stem of clutch gear and into front case bore. Install front bearing to clutch gear snap-ring.
9. Install clutch gear bearing retainer and gasket. The retainer oil return hole must be at the bottom. Torque retainer bolts to 10 ft. lbs.
10. Install reverse idler gear shaft E-ring.
11. Shift synchronizer sleeves to neutral positions. Install cover, gasket, and forks, aligning forks with synchronizer sleeve grooves. Torque side cover bolts to 10 ft. lbs.
12. Install speedometer driven gear.

Type-11
Muncie 4-Speed

Application
Buick Special, GS, 1970-72
Camaro, 1970-74
Chevelle, 1970-74
Corvette, 1970-74

Firebird, 1970-74
GTO, 1971-74
Monte Carlo, 1970-71

Nova, 1970-74
Olds F-85, Cutlass, 4-4-2, 1969-73
Pontiac GP, 1970-71
Tempest, 1970-74

Disassembly

1. Remove side cover and shift controls after draining.
2. Remove bolts and bolt lock strips from front bearing retainer and remove retainer and gasket.
3. Lock up transmission by shifting into two gears and remove main drive gear retaining nut.
NOTE: this nut may have left-hand threads.
4. Return gears to neutral and remove lock pin from reverse shifter lever boss and pull shaft out about ⅛ in. This will disengage reverse shift fork from reverse gear.
5. Remove extension case attaching bolts. Tap extension with soft hammer toward rear. When idler shaft is out as far as it will go, move extension to left so reverse fork clears gear and remove ex-

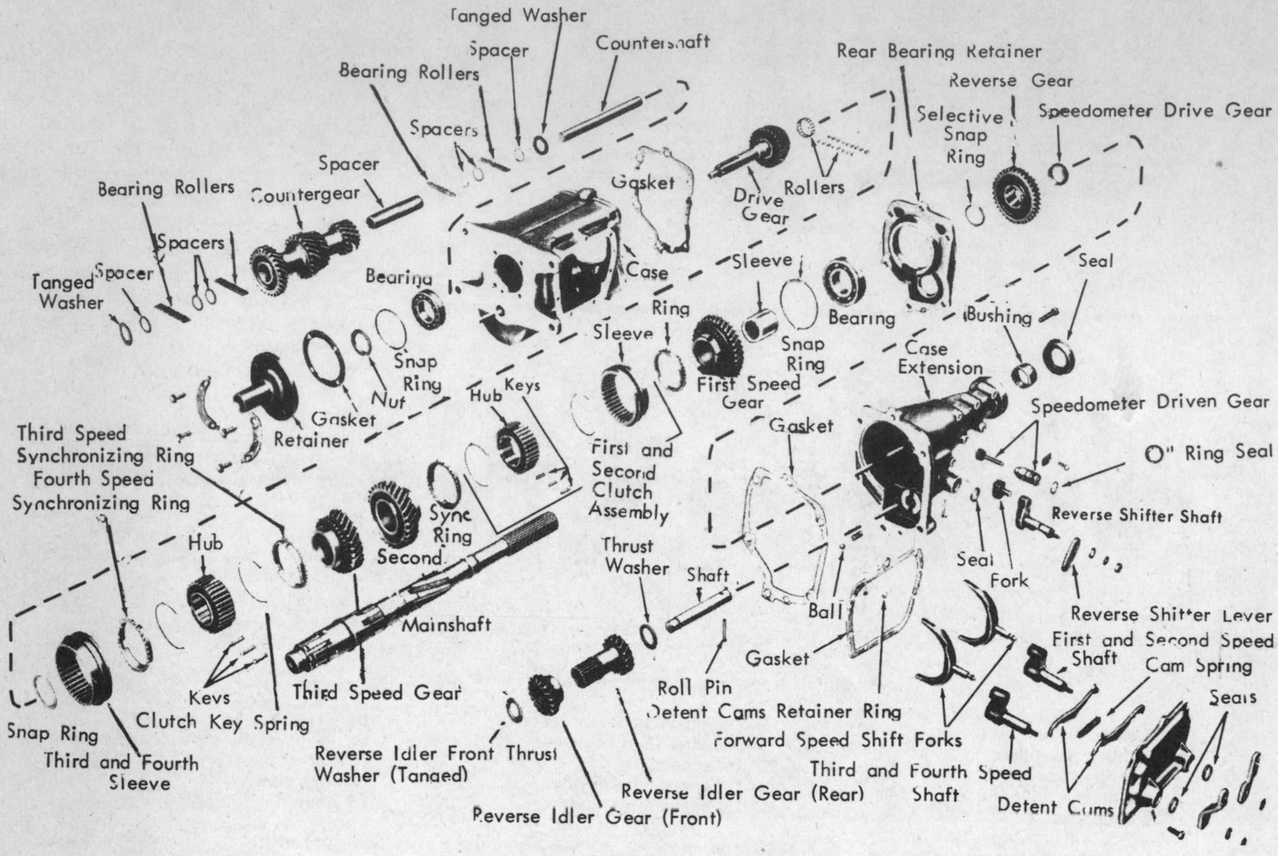

Tanged Washer
Spacer
Countershaft
Rear Bearing Retainer
Reverse Gear
Selective Snap Ring
Speedometer Drive Gear
Bearing Rollers
Spacers
Gasket
Drive Gear
Rollers
Spacer
Bearing Rollers
Countergear
Case
Sleeve
Spacers
Ring
Bearing
Seal
Tanged Washer
Spacer
Sleeve
Snap Ring
Bushing
Case Extension
Bearing
Snap Ring
First Speed Gear
Nut
Hub
Keys
Gasket
Speedometer Driven Gear
Retainer
Gasket
First and Second Clutch Assembly
Third Speed Synchronizing Ring
Fourth Speed Synchronizing Ring
Sync Ring
"O" Ring Seal
Hub
Second
Thrust Washer
Shaft
Reverse Shifter Shaft
Mainshaft
Seal
Fork
Ball
Reverse Shifter Lever
First and Second Speed Shaft
Cam Spring
Seals
Keys
Third Speed Gear
Gasket
Clutch Key Spring
Roll Pin
Detent Cams Retainer Ring
Snap Ring
Third and Fourth Sleeve
Reverse Idler Front Thrust Washer (Tanged)
Forward Speed Shift Forks
Third and Fourth Speed Shaft
Reverse Idler Gear (Rear)
Detent Cams
Reverse Idler Gear (Front)

Muncie 4-speed transmission disassembled

tension and gasket.

6. Remove reverse idler gear, flat washer, shaft and roll spring pin.
7. Remove speedometer and reverse gears.

NOTE: slide third-fourth synchronizer clutch sleeve to fourth-speed gear position (forward) before trying to remove mainshaft assembly from case.

8. Remove rear bearing retainer and mainshaft assembly from case by tapping bearing retainer with soft hammer.
9. Unload bearing rollers from main drive gear and remove fourth-speed synchronizer blocking ring.
10. Lift front half of reverse idler gear with tanged thrust washer from case.
11. Press main drive gear down from bearing.
12. Tap front bearing and snap-ring from case.
13. From front of case, press out countershaft. Then, remove the countershaft gear and both tanged washers.
14. Remove the rollers (112), six spacers and roller spacer from countergear.
15. Remove mainshaft front snap-ring and slide third and fourth-speed clutch and third-speed gear and synchronizer ring from front of mainshaft.

16. Spread rear bearing retainer snap-ring and press mainshaft out of retainer.
17. Remove mainshaft snap-ring. Support second-speed gear and press on rear of mainshaft to remove rear bearing, first-speed gear and sleeve, first-speed synchronizing ring, first-second-speed synchronizer clutch, second-speed synchronizer ring and second-speed gear.

After thoroughly cleaning case and all parts, make thorough inspection and replace required parts. In checking bearings do not spin at high speeds, but rather clean and rotate by hand to detect roughness and unevenness. Spinning can damage balls and races.

Removing countershaft
(© G.M. Corp)

Assembly

Mainshaft

1. From rear of shaft, assemble second-speed gear (hub of gear toward rear of shaft).
2. Install first-second synchronizer clutch assembly onto mainshaft (sleeve taper toward rear, hub to front); together with a synchronizer ring on each side of clutch assembly so that keyways line up with clutch keys.
3. Press first-speed sleeve onto mainshaft. (A 1¾ in. or 1⅝ in. ID pipe cut to convenient length makes a suitable tool).
4. Install first-speed gear (hub toward front) and press onto the rear bearing with snap-ring grooves toward front of transmission. Be sure bearing is firmly seated.
5. Choose selective fit snap-ring (.087, .090, .093 or .096 in.) and install it into groove in mainshaft behind rear bearing. Maximum clearance of snap-ring and rear face should be between zero and .005 in.

NOTE: always use new snap-ring.

6. Install third-speed gear (hub to front of transmission) and third-speed gear synchronizing ring (notches to front).
7. Install third and fourth-speed

gear clutch assembly with both sleeve taper and hub toward front.

8. Install snap-ring onto mainshaft in front of third and fourth-speed clutch, with ends of snap-ring seated behind spline teeth.

9. Install rear bearing retainer. Spread snap - ring in plate, to allow ring to drop around rear bearing, and press on the end of mainshaft until snap - ring engages the groove in rear bearing.

10. Install reverse gear (shift collar to rear).

11. Install speedometer drive gear.

Countergear

1. Install roller spacer into counter gear.

2. With heavy grease to assist, install a spacer in either end of countergear, 28 roller bearings, then a spacer and 28 more rollers. Then, install another spacer. In the other end of the countergear, do the same.

3. Insert dummy shaft into counter gear.

Transmission

1. Rest case on side with cover opening toward mechanic. Install countergear tanged thrust washers in place, holding with heavy grease. Make sure tangs are in proper notches.

2. Set countergear in place. Use care not to disturb tanged washers.

3. Position transmission case so that it rests on front face.

4. Lubricate and insert countershaft in rear. Turn countershaft so flat on end of shaft is horizontal and facing bottom of case.
   NOTE: the flat of shaft must be horizontal and toward bottom to mate with rear bearing retainer when installed.

5. Align countergear with shaft in rear and hole in front of case (pushing dummy shaft out front of case) until flat of shaft is flush with rear of case. Be sure thrust washers remain in place.

6. Check end-play in countergear (dial indicator should be used).

If end-play is more than .025 in. install new thrust washer.

7. Install cage and 17 roller bearings into main drive gear. Use heavy grease to hold bearings.

8. Install main drive gear with bearings through side opening of case and into position in front bore.

9. Place gasket in position on rear bearing retainer.

10. Install fourth-speed synchronizing ring onto main drive gear (notches toward rear).

11. Position tanged thrust washer for reverse idler on machined face. Position front reverse idler gear next to thrust washer (hub facing toward rear of case).

Caution Before attempting to install mainshaft to case, slide the third-fourth synchronizer clutch sleeve forward into fourth-speed detent position.

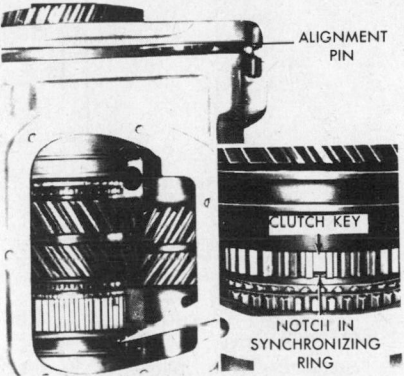

Installing mainshaft assembly
(© G.M. Corp)

12. Lower mainshaft assembly into case. Be sure notches on fourth-speed synchronizer ring correspond to keys in clutch assembly.

13. With guide pin in rear bearing retainer aligned with hole in rear of case, tap rear bearing retainer into position with soft hammer.

14. From rear of case, insert reverse idler gear, engaging splines with portion of front gear in case.

15. Place gasket in position on rear face of bearing retainer.

16. Install remaining flat washer on reverse idler shaft.

17. Install reverse idler shaft, roll pin, and thrust washer into gears and front boss of case. Make sure to pick up front tanged thrust washer.

18. Pull reverse shifter shaft to left side of extension and rotate shaft to bring reverse shift fork forward in extension (reverse detent position). Start extension onto transmission case, while slowly pushing in on shifter shaft to engage the shift fork with the reverse gear shift collar. Then, pilot the reverse idler shaft into the extension housing, permitting the extension to slide into the transmission case.

19. Install extension and retainer-to-case attaching bolts.

20. Push or pull reverse shifter shaft to line up grooves in the shaft with the holes in the boss and drive in the lockpin. Install shift lever.

21. Press bearing onto main drive gear (snap-ring groove in front), and into case until several main drive gear retaining nut threads are exposed.

22. Lock transmission by shifting into two gears. Install main drive gear retaining nut onto the gear shaft and draw it up tight. Be sure bearing is completely seated against shoulder. Torque retaining nut to 40 ft. lbs. and lock in place by staking into main drive gear shaft hole with punch. Do not damage shaft threads.

23. Install main drive gear bearing retainer, gasket attaching bolts and boltlock retainers. Use a suitable seal on bolts. Tighten to 20 ft. lbs.

24. Shift mainshaft third-fourth sliding clutch sleeve into neutral position and first-second sliding clutch into second gear (forward) detent position. Shift side cover third-fourth shift lever into neutral detent and first-second shift lever into second gear detent position.

25. Install side cover, with gasket, and carefully position in place. A dowel pin provides proper alignment position. Install bolts and tighten evenly to avoid distortion. Torque to 20 ft. lbs.

Type-12
Saginaw 4-Speed

Application
Astre, 1975
Camaro, 1970-77
Chevelle, 1970-74

Corvette, 1970-77
Firebird, (V8) 1972-77
Monza, 1975-77
Nova, 1970-77

Skyhawk, 1975-77
Starfire, 1975-77
Tempest, 1970-74
Vega, 1973-75

Disassembly

1. Remove the side cover and shift forks after draining the transmission.

2. Remove the clutch gear bearing retainer. Remove the bearing-to-gear stem snap-ring and pull out on the clutch gear until a screwdriver can be inserted between the bearing, large snap-ring, and

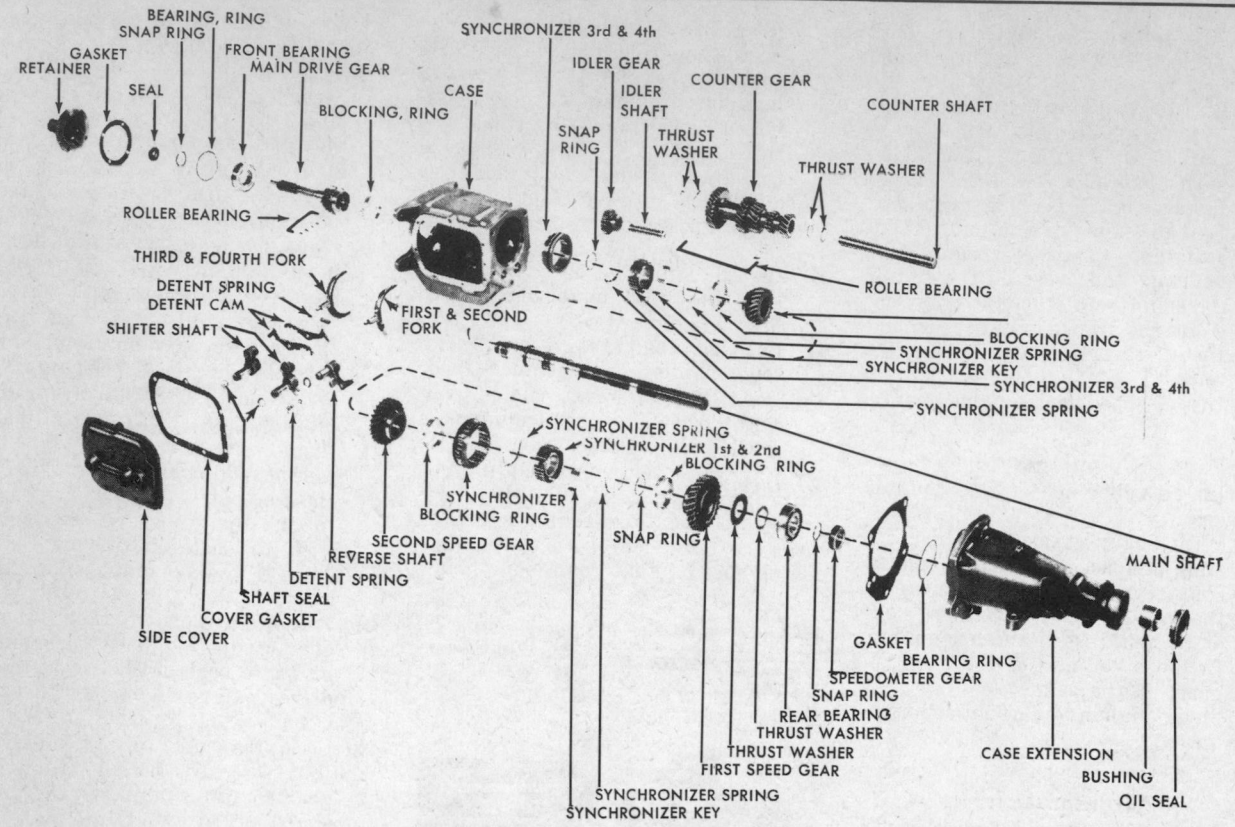

BEARING, RING
SNAP RING
GASKET
RETAINER
FRONT BEARING
MAIN DRIVE GEAR
SEAL
SYNCHRONIZER 3rd & 4th
IDLER GEAR
COUNTER GEAR
COUNTER SHAFT
BLOCKING, RING
CASE
SNAP RING
IDLER SHAFT
THRUST WASHER
THRUST WASHER
ROLLER BEARING
THIRD & FOURTH FORK
DETENT SPRING
DETENT CAM
SHIFTER SHAFT
FIRST & SECOND FORK
ROLLER BEARING
BLOCKING RING
SYNCHRONIZER SPRING
SYNCHRONIZER KEY
SYNCHRONIZER 3rd & 4th
SYNCHRONIZER SPRING
SYNCHRONIZER SPRING
SYNCHRONIZER 1st & 2nd
BLOCKING RING
SYNCHRONIZER
BLOCKING RING
SECOND SPEED GEAR
REVERSE SHAFT
DETENT SPRING
SNAP RING
SHAFT SEAL
COVER GASKET
SIDE COVER
MAIN SHAFT
GASKET
SPEEDOMETER GEAR
SNAP RING
REAR BEARING
THRUST WASHER
THRUST WASHER
FIRST SPEED GEAR
CASE EXTENSION
BUSHING
OIL SEAL
BEARING RING
SYNCHRONIZER SPRING
SYNCHRONIZER KEY

Saginaw 4-speed transmission disassembled

case to pry the bearing off.

NOTE: the clutch gear bearing is a slip-fit on the gear and in the case. Removal of the bearing will provide clearance for clutch gear and mainshaft removal.

3. Remove the rear extension attaching bolts and remove the clutch gear, mainshaft, and extension as an assembly.
4. Spread the snap-ring which holds the mainshaft rear bearing and remove the extension case.
5. Remove the countershaft and its woodruff key by driving out of the rear of the case with a pipe or an old countershaft. Remove the countergear assembly and bearings.
6. Using a long drift, drive the reverse idler shaft and woodruff key through the rear of the case.
7. Expand and remove the third and fourth-speed sliding clutch hub snap-ring from the mainshaft. Remove the clutch assembly, third gear blocker ring, and third-speed gear from the front of the mainshaft.
8. Press in the speedometer gear retaining clip and slide the gear off the mainshaft. Remove the rear bearing snap-ring from its groove in the mainshaft.
9. With first gear supported on press plates, press first gear, thrust washer, spring washer, rear bearing, and snap-ring from

the rear of the mainshaft.

Caution Be careful to center the gear, washers, bearings, and snap-ring when pressing the rear bearing.

10. Expand and remove the first and second sliding clutch hub snap-ring from the mainshaft and remove the clutch assembly, second-speed blocker ring, and second-speed gear from the rear of the mainshaft.

After thoroughly cleaning all parts and the transmission case, inspect and replace all damaged or worn parts. When checking the bearings, do not spin them at high speeds. Clean and rotate the bearings by hand to detect roughness and unevenness. Spinning can damage balls and races.

Assembly

Mainshaft

Install the following parts with the

front of the mainshaft facing up:

1. Install the third-speed gear with the clutching teeth up; the rear face of the gear will abut with the mainshaft flange.
2. Install a blocking ring, clutching teeth down, over the third-speed gear synchronizing surface.

NOTE: all four blocker rings are the same.

3. Press the third and fourth synchronizer assembly, fork slot down, onto the mainshaft splines until it bottoms.

Caution The blocker ring notches must align with the synchronizer assembly keys.

4. Install the synchronizer hub-to-mainshaft snap-ring. (Both synchronizer snap-rings are the same.)

Install the following parts with the rear of the mainshaft up:

5. Install the second-speed gear with the clutching teeth up; the front face of the gear will abut

Removing clutch gear, mainshaft, and extension housing
(© G.M. Corp).

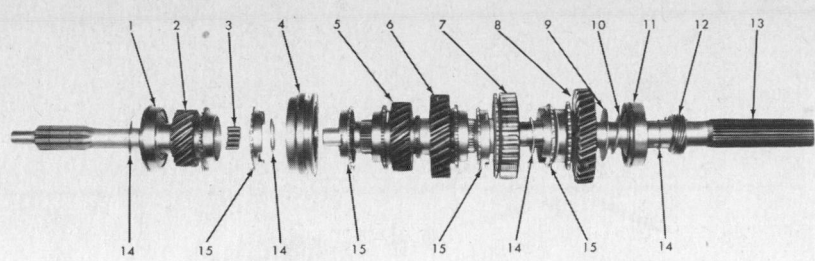

Clutch gear and mainshaft assembly
(© G.M. Corp)

1 Clutch gear bearing	8 First speed gear
2 Clutch gear	9 Thrust washer
3 Mainshaft pilot bearings	10 Spring washer
4 3-4 synchronizer assembly	11 Rear bearing
5 Third speed gear	12 Speedo drive gear
6 Second speed gear	13 Mainshaft
7 1-2 synchronizer and reverse gear assembly	14 Snap-ring
	15 Synchronizing "blocker" ring

with the flange on the mainshaft.

6. Install a blocking ring, clutching teeth down, over the second-speed gear synchronizing surface.

7. Press the first and second synchronizer assembly, fork slot down, onto the mainshaft.

Caution The blocker ring notches must align with the synchronizer assembly keys.

8. Install the synchronizer hub-to-mainshaft snap-ring.

9. Install a blocker ring with the notches down so they align with the first/second synchronizer assembly keys.

10. Install first gear with the clutching teeth down. Install the first gear thrust washer and spring washer.

11. Press the rear ball bearing and snap-ring, slot down, onto the mainshaft. Install the snap-ring. Install the speedometer gear and clip.

Transmission

1. Using a dummy countergear shaft, load a row of roller bearings (27) and bearing thrust washers at each end of the countergear. Grease can be used to hold the bearings in place.

2. Position the countergear assembly into the case through the rear opening. Place a tanged thrust washer at each end of the countergear.

3. Install the countergear shaft and woodruff key from the rear of the case. Make sure that the shaft engages both thrust wash-

ers and that the tangs align with their notches in the case.

4. Install the reverse idler gear and shaft and the woodruff key. Install the extension-to-rear bearing snap-ring.

5. Install the fourteen mainshaft pilot bearings into the clutch opening and install the fourth-speed blocker ring onto the clutching surface of the clutch gear (clutching teeth toward the gear.)

6. Assemble the clutch gear, pilot bearings, and fourth-speed blocker ring unit over the front of the mainshaft. Do not assemble the bearing to the gear at this point.
   Be sure that the blocker ring notches line up with third/fourth synchronizer assembly keys.

7. Install the extension-to-case gasket and secure it with grease. Insert the clutch gear, mainshaft, and extension into the case as a unit. Install the extension-to-case bolts (apply sealer to the bottom bolt) and torque to 45 ft lbs.

8. Install the outer snap-ring on the front bearing and place the bearing over the stem of the clutch gear and into the case bore.

9. Install the snap-ring to the clutch gear stem. Install the clutch gear bearing retainer and gasket to the case, with the retainer oil return hole at the bottom.

10. Place the synchronizer sleeves into neutral positions and install the cover, gasket, and fork assemblies to the case. Be sure the forks align with their synchronizer sleeve grooves. Torque the cover bolts to 22 ft lbs.

Type-13

Vega 3-Speed

Application
Vega, 1971-72

Transmission Disassembly

1. Remove the shift lever boot. Remove the TCS switch and back-up light switch.

2. Remove the cotter pins from each end of the shift control rod. Remove washers and shift control rod.

3. Remove retaining rings, wave rings, and selector ring from selector shaft. Slide the selector lever and shift idler lever shaft from the intermediate shift lever assembly while simultaneously removing the selector ring.

4. Remove the transmission case cover and gasket.

5. Invert the transmission to drain the oil.

6. Remove the rear extension attaching bolts and rotate the extension until the countergear shaft is exposed.

7. From the front of the transmission, remove the countergear shaft. Lift the countergear from the case. Do not lose the lockball.

8. Engage second gear to prevent the second-third fork pin from binding against the case. Use a ⅛ in. pin punch to remove all lockpins.

9. Drive the lockpins from both shifter forks. Place the transmission in third gear and be sure that the second-third intermediate lever engages the shifter shaft. This will allow the intermediate levers to pivot as the shifter shaft is removed.

10. Insert a long narrow drift

through the bolt hole at the rear of the case and drive the second-third shifter shaft from the case. Remove the fork.

11. Drive the first-reverse shifter shaft from the front of the case and remove the fork from the case.

12. Remove the selector shaft intermediate lever lockpins.
   Remove the shaft and levers from the case.

13. Remove the snap-ring from the rear bearing retainer groove and slide the rear extension from the mainshaft assembly.

14. Remove the clutch drive gear from the case.

15. Position first-reverse sliding gear to the rear of the hub shaft and remove the mainshaft assembly from the case. Remove

1. Rear extension to case bolts
2. Back-up lamp switch and seal ring
3. Shift idler lever spring
4. Intermediate lever bushing snap-ring
5. Intermediate lever bushing
6. Shift idler lever
7. Rear extension
8. Rear extension gasket
9. Reverse idler gear shaft and lockball
10. Reverse idler gear and bushing assembly
11. 2-3 speed shifter shaft
12. 2-3 speed shift fork and spiral pin
13. Cotter pin
14. Waved washer

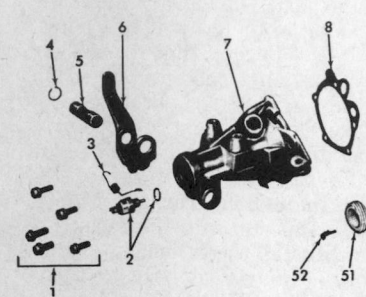
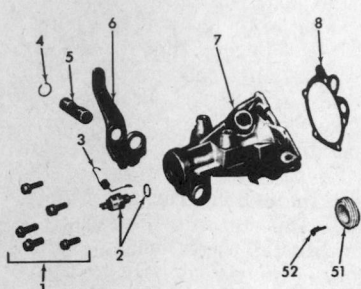
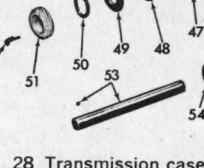

15 Shift selector rod	28 Transmission case	43 1st-reverse synchronizer hub
16 Washer	29 2-3 speed synchronizer assembly retaining ring	44 1st-reverse synchronizer sleeve
17 Selector shaft	30 2-3 speed synchronizer sleeve	45 Rear bearing to extension locking ring
18 Selector shaft seal	31 Synchronizer spring	46 1st-reverse key stop-ring
19 2-3 intermediate shift lever and spiral pin	32 2-3 synchronizer hub	47 Mainshaft rear bearing
20 1st-reverse intermediate shift lever and spiral pin	33 2-3 synchronizer keys	48 Rear bearing spacer
21 Cover gasket	34 Synchronizer spring	49 Belleville washer
22 Cover assembly	35 2nd gear synchronizer ring	50 Rear bearing retaining ring
23 Cover-to-case screws	36 2nd speed gear	51 Speedo drive gear
23a Clutch drive gear seal	37 Mainshaft	52 Speedo drive clip
24 Clutch drive gear assembly	38 1st speed gear	53 Countergear shaft and lockball
25 Mainshaft pilot bearing assembly	39 1st speed gear synchronizer ring	54 Countergear thrust washer
26 Pilot bearing spacer ring	40 Synchronizer spring	55 Countergear bearing washer
27 3rd gear synchronizer ring	41 1st-reverse synchronizer keys	56 Countergear roller bearings (24)
	42 Synchronizer spring	

57 Countergear
58 Countergear bearing washer
59 Countergear roller bearings (24)
60 Countergear thrust washers
61 1st-reverse shift shaft
62 1st-reverse shift fork and spiral pin
63 Intermediate lever shaft and pin
64 TCS switch and gasket
65 2-3 shift detent ball, spring and hole plug
66 1st-reverse shift detent ball, spring and hole plug
67 Pivot pin lockring
68 Shift selector rod
69 Selector lever pivot pin
70 Oil filler plug
71 Selector shaft oil seal
72 Selector shaft lockring
73 Selector shaft ring
74 Belleville washer
75 Selector shaft lockring

Exploded view (inverted) of Vega 3-speed transmission
(© Chevrolet Div., G.M. Corp)

the lockpins and detent balls from the bottom of the case.

16. Drive the plugs and springs from the shift rail detent holes.

17. Remove the reverse idler gear and shaft from the case.

Mainshaft Disassembly

NOTE: the synchronizer hubs and sliding sleeves are a select assembly and kept together as originally assembled. Keys and springs may be replaced.

1. Remove the snap-ring from in front of the clutch hub.

2. Depress the retaining clip and slide the speedometer drive gear from the shaft.

3. Remove the snap-ring, spacer and Belleville washer from the shaft.

4. Support first gear and press the mainshaft until the bearing and synchronizers are free on the shaft. Remove all loose parts from the shaft.

5. Support second speed gear and press and shaft until second-third synchronizer assembly and second speed gear are free.

Inspection

1. Examine the shaft, bearing gear and hubs for excessive wear. Examine for chips, nicking or scoring. Wash ball bearings in solvent and blow dry. Replace worn synchronizer rings, clutch keys and hubs. Oil all parts with SAE 90 transmission fluid during assembly.

Mainshaft Assembly

1. From the front of the mainshaft, install the second speed gear. The gear must turn freely on the shaft.

2. Install the second-third synchronizer onto second speed gear cone.

3. Install front and rear synchronizer key springs into second-third

speed synchronizer hubs, so that hooked spring ends are in the same slot and raised ends are against the blocker rings.

4. Install sliding sleeve and keys on clutch hub. Arrows must point to front of shaft.

5. Press second-third speed synchronizer hub onto the mainshaft. Secure with a snap-ring.

6. Install both clutch key springs into first-reverse speed synchronizer hub. Hooks of both springs must rest in the same hub slot and raised spring ends should be positioned opposite each other against the blocker rings.

7. Assemble the sliding gear and keys on hub assembly with longer key flat and fork groove on gear toward the rear of the shaft.

8. From the rear of the mainshaft, slide on first gear. Gear must turn freely.

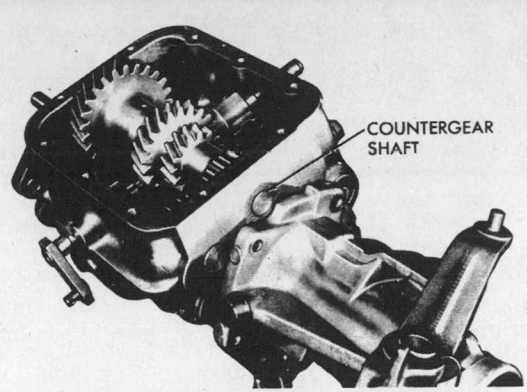

Counter gear shaft exposed for removal
(© Chevrolet Div., G.M. Corp)

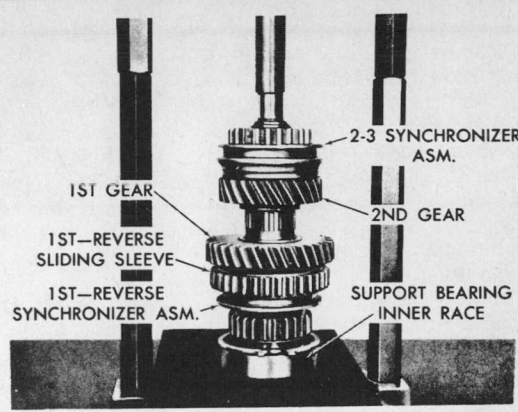

Assembling mainshaft components
(© Chevrolet Div., G.M. Corp)

9. Place first-reverse speed synchronizer ring onto first speed gear cone.
10. Slide the first-reverse synchronizer assembly onto the mainshaft. Slide the stop-ring, rear extension retaining ring and rear bearing onto the shaft. Support the rear bearing inner race and press the components together.

Caution Align slots with synchronizer keys. The clutch drive bearing is used to service the mainshaft rear bearing. Install replacement bearing with shield side toward rear of shaft.

11. Place spacer and Belleville washer on the mainshaft. Secure with a snap-ring.
12. Position the speedometer drive gear retaining clip on shaft and install the speedometer drive gear.
13. Install the mainshaft into the extension housing up to the stop. Secure with a retaining ring.

Transmission Assembly

1. Install a new gasket on the rear extension and slide mainshaft assembly into the case. Install one or two bolts to keep the extension from rotating.
2. Coat the pilot roller bearing with grease. From the front, slide the lockring and pilot roller bearing onto the mainshaft.
3. Install the blocker ring on clutch drive gear, and install the gear into the transmission case, up to the snap-ring stop.

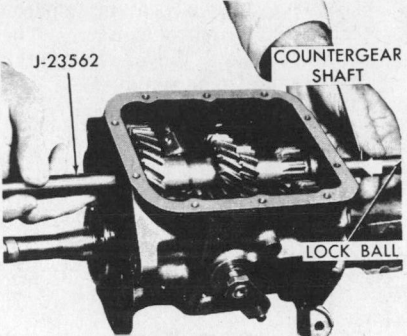

Installing countergear shaft
(© Chevrolet Div., G.M. Corp)

4. Insert the first-reverse speed shifter shaft at the front of the case with the notches down, pushing it through the shifter fork. Position the fork shoulder toward the front of the case. Drive the lockpin in place.

NOTE: all lockpins should be installed protruding 1/16 in. to 5/16 in. above the fork or lever.

5. Insert the second-third speed shifter shaft, from the front of the case, with the notches down, pushing it through the shifter fork shoulder toward the front. Install the lockpin.
6. Install the selector shaft in the case. Push it through the second-third speed intermediate lever and the first-reverse lever. Install lockpins.
7. Install both lockballs and springs into the bores in the case and drive in the plugs.
8. Remove the rear extension bolt(s), pull back on the extension and rotate the extension until the bore for the reverse idler gear is exposed.
9. Install the lockball into the shaft from the rear of the case and install the shaft into the gear. Drive the shaft into place.
10. Using a dummy shaft, install a spacer at each end of the countergear. Hold them in place with heavy grease.
11. Coat the thrust washer with grease and stick it to the case. The lugs of the thrust washers must engage the slots in the case.
12. Turn the case extension until the countergear bore is exposed.
13. Place the lockball in the shaft. From the rear of the transmission, insert the shaft so that the thrust washer is held in position. Hold the opposite thrust washer in position with a short drift.
14. Insert the countergear into the case.
15. Insert the shaft into the countergear and push out the dummy shaft. Align the lockball with the groove in the case and tap the shaft into the case.
16. Align the rear bearing retainer and tighten the bolts.
17. Install the case cover gasket, cover and screws.
18. Install the gearshift linkages in reverse sequence to removal.

NOTE: start the idler lever shaft into the shift control simultaneously when installing selector ring.

Type-14

Vega 4-Speed

Application
Vega, 1971-72

Transmission Disassembly

1. Follow Steps 1-7 under early Vega 3-Speed transmission for removal of gearshift linkage, case cover and countergear shaft and countergear.
2. Drive out intermediate shift lever pin and remove intermediate lever. Use a 1/8 in. pin punch to drive out all pins.
3. Slide the reverse shaft to rear of the case so that the scallop in the selector shaft will clear the reverse shaft.
4. Shift transmission to neutral. Push in on the selector shaft and turn so that the lockpins are in

the vertical position. Drive the lockpin out of the third-fourth speed intermediate lever cam and then from the first-second speed intermediate lever cam. Remove the selector shaft.

5. Pry the selector shaft seal rings out of the case.

6. Remove the lockball plugs with a slide hammer. Remove the thrust springs and balls.

7. Place the transmission in first gear and drive the lockpins out of the shifter forks and selector levers. Remove the first-second lever pin first.

8. From the rear of the transmission drive out the first-second shifter shaft with a brass drift. Remove the fork from the sliding sleeve.

9. Tap the third-fourth shifter shaft rearward until the fork can be removed from the shaft, then drive out the third-fourth shifter shaft through the front of the case.

10. Remove the clutch drive gear from the case.

11. Remove the rear extension and mainshaft from the case.

12. Push the reverse idler gear shaft toward the rear. Be sure that the lockball is not lost, and remove the reverse idler gear and shaft from the case.

13. From the front of the transmission, drive out the reverse shifter shaft with a brass drift. Remove the shifter fork from the case.

Mainshaft Disassembly

1. Remove the snap-ring from the rear bearing retainer groove and remove the mainshaft assembly from the rear bearing retainer.

2. Depress the retaining clip and remove the speedometer driven gear.

3. Remove needle bearing, spacer ring and synchronizer ring. The sliding sleeve, keys and clutch keys can also be removed.

NOTE: the synchronizer hubs and sliding sleeves are a select assembly and should be kept together as originally assembled.

4. Remove the snap-ring from in front of the synchronizer hub.

5. Remove the snap-ring, spacer and Belleville washer from the shaft.

6. Support second gear and press the mainshaft until the bearing and synchronizers are free on the shaft. Remove all loose parts.

7. Remove third speed synchronizer hub snap-ring. Support third gear and press the mainshaft until the synchronizer and third gear are free.

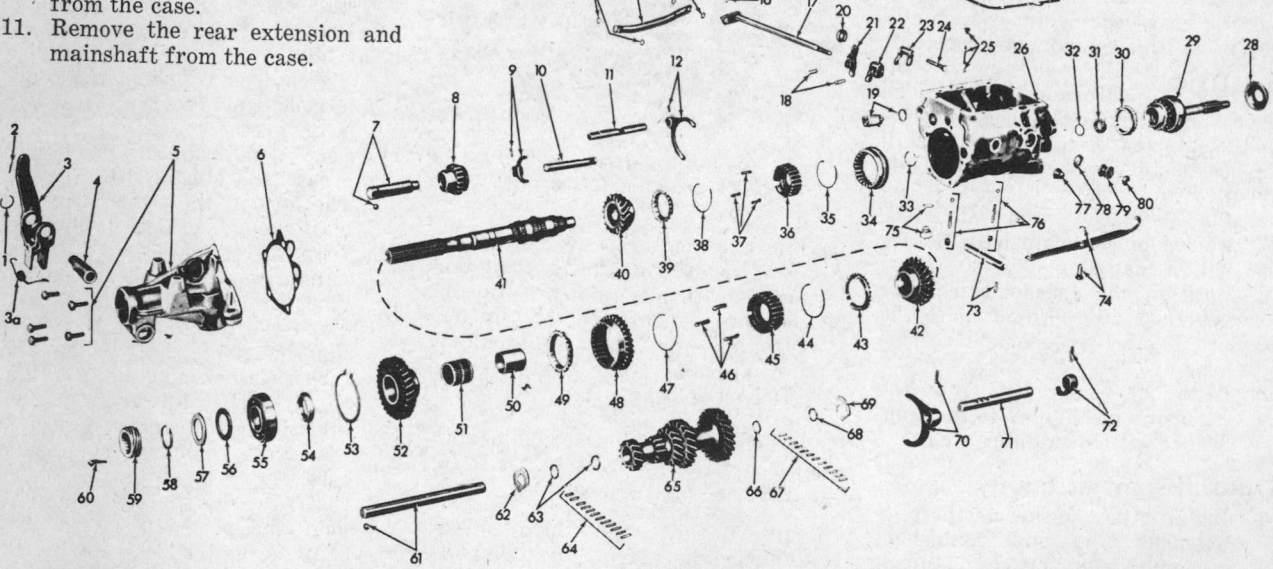

9 Reverse idler gear shift fork and spiral pin	26 Transmission case	45 1st-2nd synchronizer hub	63 Countergear bearing washers
10 Reverse idler gear shifter shaft	27 Cover gasket, cover, and screws	46 1st-2nd synchronizer keys	64 Countergear roller bearings (24)
11 3-4 speed shifter shaft	28 Clutch drive gear to housing seal	47 Synchronizer spring	65 Countergear
12 3-4 speed shift fork and spiral pin	29 Clutch drive gear assembly	48 1st-2nd synchronizer sleeve	66 Countergear bearing washer
13 Washers	30 4th gear synchronizer ring	49 1st speed synchronizer ring	67 Countergear roller bearings (24)
14 Shift control rod	31 Mainshaft pilot bearing assembly	50 1st speed gear bushing	68 Countergear bearing washer
15 Washers	32 Pilot bearing spacer ring	51 1st gear needle bearing assembly	69 Countergear thrust washer
16 Cotter pin	33 3-4 speed synchronizer assembly retaining ring	52 1st speed gear	70 1st-2nd shift fork and spiral pin
17 Selector shaft	34 3-4 speed synchronizer sleeve	53 Rear bearing to extension locking ring	71 1st-2nd shift shaft
18 Spiral pins	35 Synchronizer spring	54 Rear bearing spacer ring (front)	72 1st-2nd selector lever cam and spiral pin
19 Back-up lamp switch and seal ring	36 3-4 synchronizer hub		73 Intermediate lever shaft and pin
20 Selector shaft oil seal	37 3-4 synchronizer keys	55 Mainshaft rear bearing	74 Shift selector rod, pivot pin and lock ring
21 3rd-4th speed intermediate shifter lever	38 Synchronizer spring	56 Rear bearing spacer (rear)	75 TCS switch and gasket
22 1st-2nd intermediate shift lever	39 3rd speed gear synchronizer ring	57 Belleville washer	76 Shifter shaft detent balls, springs and hole plugs
23 Reverse intermediate lever	40 3rd speed gear	58 Rear bearing retaining ring (brg.-to-mainshaft)	77 Oil filler plug
24 Reverse intermediate lever pin	41 Mainshaft	59 Speedo drive gear	78 Selector shaft oil seal
25 Reverse shifter shaft detent ball, spring and cap	42 2nd speed gear	60 Speedo drive clip	79 Selector shaft adjusting ring
	43 2nd speed synchronizer ring	61 Countergear shaft and lockball	80 Selector shaft locknut
	44 Synchronizer spring	62 Countergear thrust washer	

Exploded view (inverted) of Vega 4-speed transmission (© Chevrolet Div., G.M. Corp)

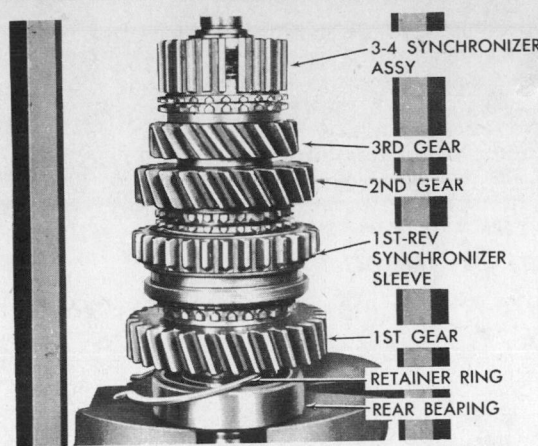

3-4 SYNCHRONIZER ASSY

3RD GEAR

2ND GEAR

1ST-REV SYNCHRONIZER SLEEVE

1ST GEAR

RETAINER RING

REAR BEARING

Assembling mainshaft components
(© Chevrolet Div., G.M. Corp)

Inspection

1. See inspection of components under early Vega 3-Speed transmission.

Mainshaft Assembly

1. From the front of the mainshaft, install the third speed gear. Gear must turn freely.
2. Install the third speed synchronizer ring onto the third speed gear cone.
3. Install the rear clutch key spring into the third-fourth speed synchronizer hub so that the hooked spring rests in one of the slots and the raised end is toward the blocker ring.
4. Press the third-fourth speed clutch hub onto the mainshaft.
5. Secure the third-fourth synchronizer hub with a snap-ring.
6. From the rear of the mainshaft slide on the second speed gear. Gear must turn freely.
7. Place the second speed synchronizer ring on the second speed gear cone.
8. Install both synchronizer key springs into the first-second speed synchronizer hub, so that the spring hooks rest in the same hub slot and the other spring ends are positioned cp-

posite each other and toward the blocker rings. Install the sliding gear and keys on the hub.

9. Slide the first-second speed synchronizer hub, needle bearing and inner sleeve onto the mainshaft. Slide the spacer, rear extension retaining ring and rear bearing onto the shaft.
10. Support the rear bearing inner race and press the components together.

NOTE: align the slots in the synchronizer rings with the synchronizer keys.

11. Install the spacer and Belleville washer on the mainshaft and secure with snap-ring.

NOTE: the concave side of the Belleville washer should face the bearing.

12. Position the speedometer gear retaining clip on the shaft and install the gear.
13. Place the mainshaft assembly into the rear bearing retainer up to the stop. Secure with a snap-ring.
14. Assemble the third-fourth speed synchronizer assembly on hub with the raised end of the key springs toward the blocker ring.

NOTE: arrows on the keys point toward the shifter fork groove.

Transmission Assembly

1. Install a new gasket onto the rear extension.
2. Slide the mainshaft assembly into the transmission case.
3. From the front, slide the spacer ring and needle bearing onto the mainshaft. Coat the needle bearing and roller with grease.
4. Install the synchronizer blocker ring on the clutch drive gear and install the gear into the case up to the stop.
5. Insert the first-second shifter shaft at the front of the case with the notches down, pushing it first through the L shaped selector dog. Push the first-second speed selector shaft through the shifter fork, positioning the shoulder toward the front of the case. Drive the lockpins in. Install selector dog pin first.

NOTE: all lockpins should protrude 1/16 in. to 5/64 in.

6. Insert the third-fourth speed shifter shaft from the front of the case. The notches should be down and it is pushed through the third-fourth speed shifter fork, positioning the shoulder toward the front. Install lockpin.
7. Install the reverse shifter shaft from the rear of the case with the notches up. Push it through the reverse shifter fork and install the lockpin. Position the shoulder of the shift fork toward the front of the case.
8. Insert the selector shaft into the case, through the third-fourth speed intermediate lever and through the first-second speed intermediate lever. Install lockpins.
9. Place the transmission in neutral and rotate the selector shaft to engage the levers with the shifter shafts.
10. Engage reverse speed intermediate levers with third-fourth speed intermediate lever and install pivot pin. Reverse speed intermediate lever end-play on the

CLUTCH KEY SPRINGS

CLUTCH HUB

Installing synchronizer key springs
(© Chevrolet Div., G.M. Corp)

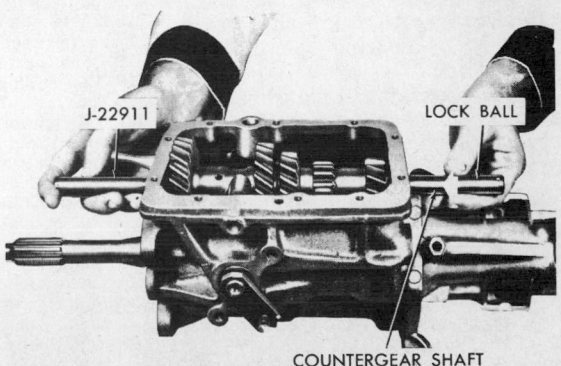

J-22911

LOCK BALL

COUNTERGEAR SHAFT

Installing counter gear shaft
(© Chevrolet Div., G.M. Corp)

11. pin should be .004-.012 in.
11. Insert both lockballs and springs into their bores. Drive in plugs.
12. Turn the transmission case extension until the bore for the reverse idler gear shaft is exposed.

13. Place the lockball into the shaft and from the rear of the case, install the shaft into the gear.
14. Simultaneously, position the reverse idler gear and reverse shifter fork. The shifter fork groove of the reverse idler gear

and the shoulder of the shifter fork should be toward the front of the mainshaft.
15. Follow Steps 10-18 under Transmission Assembly for early Vega 3-Speed transmission.

Type-15
70 mm. 4-Speed

Chevette, 1976-77
Monza, 1976-77

Sunbird, 1976-77
Vega, 1976-77

Application
Astre, 1976-77

Disassembly

1. Place the transmission so that it is resting on the bellhousing.
2. Drive the spring pin from the shifter shaft arm assembly and shifter shaft, then remove the shifter shaft arm assembly.
3. Remove the five bolts holding the extension housing to the transmission case and remove the extension.
4. Press down on the speedometer gear retainer and remove the gear and retainer from the mainshaft.
5. Remove the snap rings from the shifter shaft and using a slide hammer with the proper adapter, remove the reverse shifter shaft cover, shifter shaft detent cap, the spring and ball, and the interlock lock pin.
6. Pull the reverse lever shaft outward to disengage the reverse idler; remove the idler shaft with the gear attached.
7. Remove the snap ring on the reverse gear and reverse countershaft gear; when finished remove the gears.
8. Turn the transmission on its side and remove the clutch gear bearing retainer bolts, the retainer and gasket.
9. Remove the snap ring holding the clutch gear ball bearing to the bell housing; and then remove the bolts holding the bellhousing to the case.
10. Turn the transmission so that it rests on the bellhousing again and expand the snap ring in the mainshaft bearing opening. Remove the case by lifting it off the mainshaft. Make sure that the mainshaft assembly, the countergear, and shifter shaft assembly stay with the bell housing.
11. Lift the entire mainshaft assembly complete with shifter forks and countergear from the bellhousing.

Mainshaft

12. Separate the shift shaft assembly and countergear from the mainshaft.

1 Bearing retainer bolts
2 Bearing retainer
3 Bearing retainer gasket
4 Bearing retainer seal
5 Snap ring
6 Bearing outer snap ring
7 Shifter shaft stop plug
8 Bell housing to case bolts
9 Clutch gear bearing

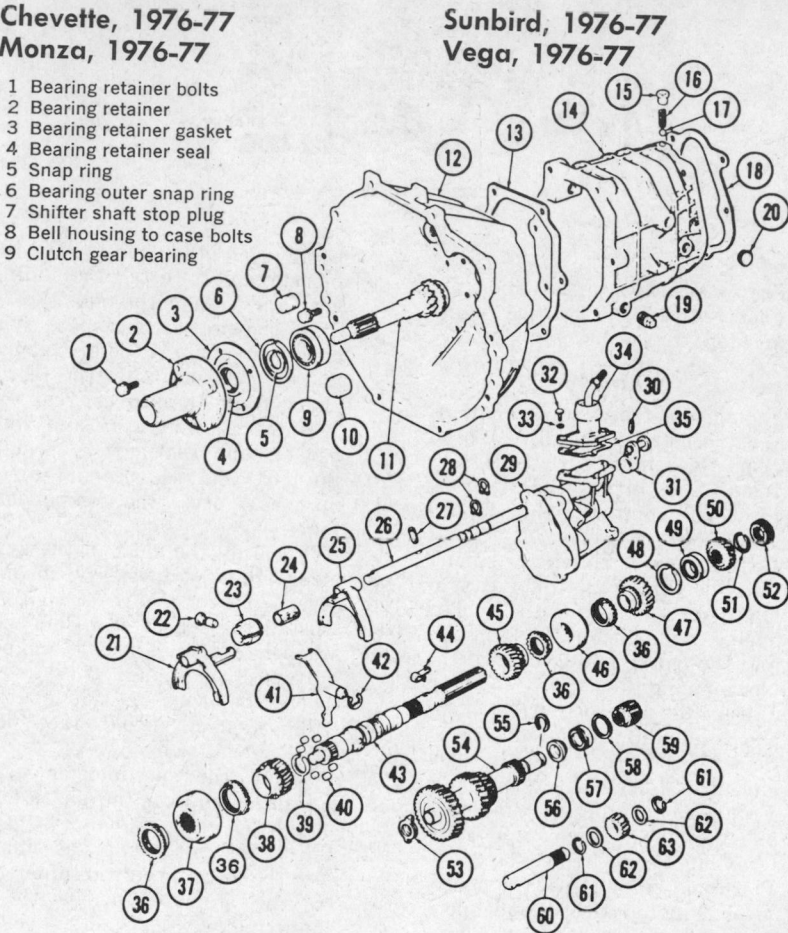

Exploded view of GM 70 mm. transmission (© G.M. Corp.)

10 Countergear front needle bearings
11 Clutch gear
12 Bell housing
13 Bellhousing to case gasket
14 Case
15 Shifter shaft detent cap
16 Shifter shaft detent spring
17 Shifter shaft detent ball
18 Case to extension gasket
19 Magnet plug
20 Reverse lever cap
21 3-4 Shift forks
22 Interlock lock pin
23 Detent bushing
24 Detent lever
25 1-2 shift fork
26 Shifter shaft
27 Detent lever pin
28 Shifter shaft snap rings
29 Extension housing
30 Shifter shaft arm spring pin
31 Shifter shaft arm
32 Shift lever to extension bolts
33 Shift lever to extension washer
34 Shift lever assembly
35 Shift lever to extension gasket
36 Blocker rings

37 3-4 synchronizer assembly
38 3rd speed gear
39 Snap ring hub to shaft
40 Clutch gear bearings
41 Reverse lever assembly
42 Reverse lever snap ring
43 Main shaft
44 Speedometer gear retainer
45 2nd speed gear
46 1-2 synchronizer assembly
47 1st speed gear
48 Bearing outer snap ring
49 Rear bearing
50 Reverse gear
51 Snap ring reverse gear
52 Speedometer gear
53 Countergear thrust washer
54 Countergear
55 Snap ring
56 Inner bearing race
57 Countergear bearing
58 Bearing outer snap ring
59 Reverse gear on countergear
60 Idler gear shaft
61 Thrust washer idler gear
62 Snap ring idler gear
63 Reverse idler gear

13. Remove the clutch gear and blocker ring from the mainshaft. When doing this, make sure you don't lose any of the clutch gear roller bearings.
14. Remove the snap ring in front of third-fourth gear synchronizer hub and remove the hub, using an arbor press if necessary.
15. Remove the retaining ring and the third speed gear, then using press plates, remove the ball bearing from the rear of the mainshaft. Remove the remaining parts from the mainshaft keeping them in order for later reassembly.

Assembly

Synchronizer Keys and Springs

1. The synchronizer hubs and sliding sleeves are an assembly and should be kept together as originally assembled; the keys and springs can be replaced.
2. Mark the position of the hub and sleeve for reassembly.
3. Push the hub from the sliding sleeve; the keys will fall out and the springs can be easily removed.
4. Place the new springs in position with one on each side of the hub so that the three keys are engaged by both springs.
5. Place the keys in position and while holding them in position, slide the sleeve into the hub aligning the marks made during disassembly.

Extension Oil Seal

6. Pry the old seal from rear of the extension, then drive the bushing from the extension housing.
7. Coat the inside diameter of the seal and bushing with transmission fluid and install them.

Drive Gear Bearing Oil Seal

8. Pry out the old seal, and install a new one making sure that it bottoms properly in its bore.

Mainshaft

9. With the mainshaft turned up, install the second speed gear with the clutching teeth upward; the rear face of the gear will butt against the flange of the mainshaft.
10. Install a blocker ring with the clutching teeth down over the second speed gear.
11. Install the first and second synchronizer assembly with the fork slot down; press it on the splines on the mainshaft until it bottoms. Make sure the notches of the blocker ring align with the keys of the synchronizer assembly.

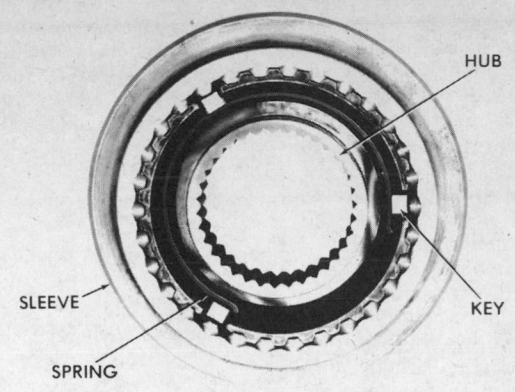

GM 70 mm. synchronizer assembly (© G.M. Corp.)

12. Install the snychronizer hub to the mainshaft snap ring, then install a blocker ring with the notches down so that they align with the keys of the first and second gear synchronizer assembly.
13. Install the first speed gear with the clutching teeth down; install the rear ball bearing with the snap ring groove down and press into place on the mainshaft.
14. Turn the mainshaft up and install the third speed gear with the clutching teeth going up; the front face of the gear will butt against the flange on the mainshaft.
15. Install a blocker ring with the clutching teeth down, over the synchronizer surface of the third speed gear.
16. Install the third and fourth gear synchronizer assembly with the fork slot down; make sure the notches of the blocker ring align with the keys of the synchronizer assembly.
17. Install the synchronizer hub to mainshaft snap ring; install a blocker ring with the notches down so that they align with the keys of the third and fourth gear synchronizer assembly.

Components to Transmission Case

18. Using a press, install the shielded ball bearing to the clutch gear shaft with the snap ring groove up.
19. Install the snap ring on the clutch gear shaft; place the pilot bearings into the clutch gear cavity, using heavy grease to hold them in place.
20. Assemble the clutch gear to the mainshaft and then install the detent lever to the shift shaft with the roll pin.
21. Slide the first and second gear shifter so that it engages the detent lever.
22. Assemble the third and fourth gear shifter fork to the detent bushing and slide the assembly on the shift shaft to place it below the first and second shifter fork arm.
23. Install the shifter assembly to the synchronizer sleeve grooves

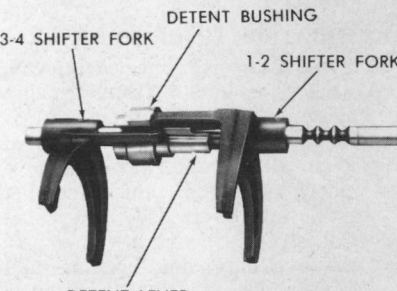

GM 70 mm. shift forks assembled
(© G.M. Corp.)

GM 70 mm. countergear and mainshaft assembled to the bellhousing (© G.M. Corp.)

on the mainshaft.

24. With the front of the bellhousing resting on wooden blocks, place a thrust washer over the hole for the countergear shaft. The thrust washer must be placed in the holes in the bellhousing.
25. Mesh the countershaft gears to the mainshaft gears and install this into the bellhousing.
26. Turn the bellhousing on its side, and install the snap ring to the ball bearing on the clutch gear; then install the bearing retainer to the bellhousing. Make sure you use sealant on the four retaining bolts.
27. Turn the bellhousing so that it is resting on the blocks again, and install the reverse lever to the case using grease to hold it in place. When it's installed, the screwdriver slot should be parrallel to the front of the case.
28. Install the reverse lever snap ring; install the roller bearing to the countergear opening with the snap ring groove inside of the case.
29. Install the gasket on the bellhousing with rubber sealant. Before installing the case, make sure the synchronizers are in the neutral position, the detent bushing slot is facing outward, and the reverse lever is flush with the inside wall of the case.
30. Expand the snap ring in the opening of the mainshaft case and let it slide over the bearing.
31. Install the interlock lock pin to hold the shifter shaft in place; install the idler shaft so it will enage with the reverse lever inside the shaft.
32. Install the cover over the screwdriver arm to hold the reverse lever in place.
33. Install the detent ball, spring and cap in the transmission case, then install the reverse gear with the chamfer on the gear teeth up. Push the reverse gear on the splines and hold it there with a snap ring.
34. Install the smaller reverse gear on the counter gear shaft with the shoulder resting against the countergear bearing and hold it there with a snap ring.
35. Install the snap ring, thrust washer and reverse idler gear with the chamfer of the gear teeth facing down, to the idler shaft. Hold it there with the thrust washer and snap ring.
36. Install the snap rings on the shifter shaft and engage the speedometer gear retainer in the hole in the mainshaft with the retainer loop toward the front; slide the speedometer gear over the mainshaft and into position.
37. Place the extension housing and gasket on the transmission case and install the two pilot bolts (one in the top right hand corner; the other in the bottom left hand corner) and then the other three bolts. The pilot bolts *must* be installed first to prevent splitting the transmission case.
38. Assemble the shifter shaft arm over the shifter shaft to a position aligned with the drilled hole near the end of the shaft; drive spring pin into shifter shaft arm and shaft to hold these parts.
39. Turn the transmission on its side and install the two pilot bolts, and then the four retaining bolts.

Type-16
Warner T-14, T-15 Fully Synchronized 3-Speed

T-14 Application
American Motors (6 Cyl.), 1970-74, (Gremlin) 1976-77

Transmission Disassembly

1. Remove cover, front bearing cap, gasket, and two front bearing snap rings.
2. Align notch in clutch shaft third gear with countergear. Remove clutch shaft and front bearing. A puller may be needed.
3. Pull off front bearing.
4. Remove extension housing and gasket. Using oil seal remover and slide hammer, remove extension housing oil seal. Remove extension housing bushing. Install new bushing, aligning oil groove with housing slot.
5. Remove snap-ring, speedometer drive gear, and locating ball.
6. Remove two rear bearing snap-rings and pull off rear bearing.
7. Move mainshaft aside. Remove both shift forks.
8. Push front synchronizer toward rear. Tilt front of mainshaft up and out through top of case.
9. If necessary, remove the transmission controlled spark switch assembly.
10. Drive out roll pins. Push shift shafts into case. Remove shift shafts and detent assembly.
11. Tap reverse idler shaft and countershaft rearward. Remove shaft lockplate. Drive reverse idler shaft from case. Use dummy shaft to drive out countershaft.

Mainshaft Disassembly

1. From front of shaft, remove front snap-ring, second-third synchro-clutch assembly, and second gear.
2. From rear of shaft, remove reverse gear, rear snap-ring, rear synchro-clutch assembly, and low gear.

Inspection

1. Check gears for worn, chipped, or cracked teeth. Check fit to mainshaft.
2. Check bearings for smoothness and excessive play.
3. Check roller bearings for wear or damage.
4. Slide synchro-clutch and friction rings on gear cones and clutch shaft. Replace rings if taper is worn or pitted. There should be no play between hub and shaft splines.
5. Check case for cracks or damaged bearing bores.

T-15 Application
American Motors, 1970-74

Mainshaft Assembly

1. Install low gear and friction ring; friction ring hub to the rear.
2. Install low synchro-gear into synchro-collar so deep end of gear faces low gear. Install synchro-plates (dogs) and retainer ring with large end of plates toward low gear.
3. Place synchro-clutch assembly on mainshaft with synchro-collar groove toward low gear. Install the thickest snap-ring that will fit in groove.
4. Measure clearance between first gear and collar on mainshaft. The clearance should be .003-.012 in. for the T-14; .003-.014 in. for the T-15.
5. Place second gear and the friction ring on the front of the mainshaft with the gear hub and ring forward. Place second synchro-gear into synchro-collar with deep end of gear facing rear of shaft.
6. Hold synchro-clutch assembly with one synchro-plate, or dog, in 12 o'clock position. Install tang of retainer ring into the dog

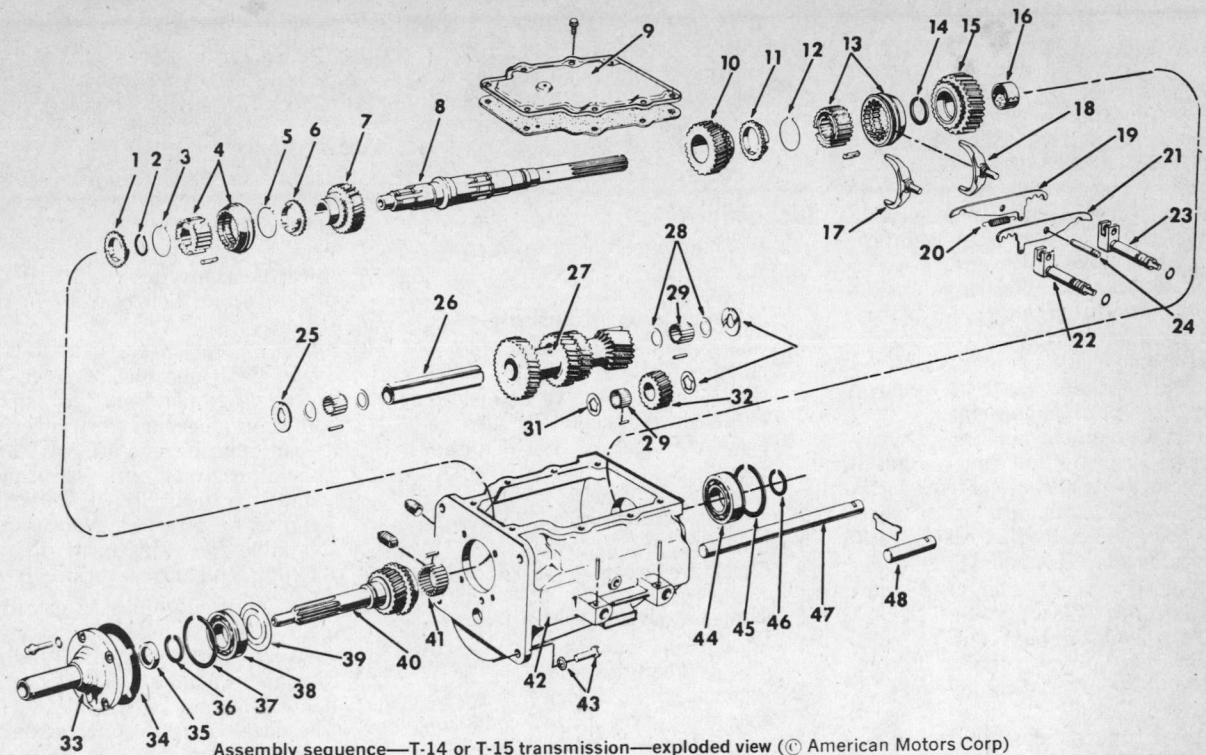

Assembly sequence—T-14 or T-15 transmission—exploded view (© American Motors Corp)

1 Synchro ring	13 1st-rev. synchro assy	25 Thrust washer	37 Lock ring
2 Snap-ring	14 Snap-ring	26 Spacer	38 Front bearing
3 Retaining ring	15 Reverse gear	27 Countergear	39 Washer
4 2-3 synchro assy	16 Bushing	28 Washer	40 Clutch shaft
5 Retaining ring	17 2nd-3rd fork	29 Rollers	41 Rollers
6 Synchro ring	18 1st-rev. fork	30 Washer	42 Case
7 2nd gear	19 1st-rev. lever	31 Washer	43 Case-to-bellhousing
8 Mainshaft	20 Interlock spring	32 Idler gear	bolt (1)
9 Cover	21 2nd-3rd lever	33 Bearing cap	44 Rear bearing
10 1st gear	22 2nd-3rd shaft	34 Gasket	45 Snap-ring
11 Synchro ring	23 1st-rev. shaft	35 Front seal	46 Snap-ring
12 Retaining ring	24 Interlock pin	36 Snap ring	47 Countershaft
			48 Idler shaft

at 12 o'clock and install ring clockwise. On opposite side, start with the same dog and install ring clockwise.

7. Place second synchro assembly on shaft with deep end to rear. Install the thickest snap-ring that will fit into the groove.

8. Measure clearance between second gear and collar on mainshaft. It must be .003-.018 in.

9. Install reverse gear on rear of mainshaft.

Transmission Assembly

1. Install dummy shaft in countergear. Install spacer washers and roller bearings.

2. Place countergear in case. Align thrust washers at each end. Insert countershaft.

3. Install rollers in reverse idler gear. Hold rollers with petroleum jelly. Place gear in case. Position thrust washers. Insert shaft. Install shaft lockplate.

4. Insert shifter shafts in case. Position low-reverse lever to inside of case. Locate notches on top of levers to rear of case stud. Align shift detent assembly with shifter shafts and case stud. Push detent assembly and shifter shafts into place. Install shaft roll pins.

5. If removed, install the transmission controlled spark switch.

6. Place front synchronizer in second shift position. Place mainshaft assembly in case to one side.

7. Pull detent levers up. Place shift forks in shifting assembly.

8. Install mainshaft pilot end support in case. Install front bearing cap. Drive rear bearing into thickest rear bearing snap-ring with a 1¼ x 17 in. pipe. Install support and bearing cap.

9. Install locating ball, speedometer drive gear, and snap-ring.

10. Press front bearing onto clutch shaft.

11. Place rollers in clutch shaft. Hold with petroleum jelly.

12. Place friction ring on mainshaft. Slide clutch shaft into position from front.

13. Install thickest front bearing snap-ring that will fit in groove, gasket and cap. Align cap lubrication hole with hole in case.

14. Install extension housing. Install oil seal. Install shift lever, gaskets, and cover.

Type-17
Warner T-96 3-Speed

Application
American Motors, 1970-72 (6 Cyl.)

Disassembly

1. Remove top cover.

2. Remove front bearing cap, clutch shaft snap-ring, and bearing lockring.

3. Use a bearing puller and a thrust yoke to remove front bearing.

4. Remove oil slinger.

5. Remove extension housing. Replace rear bearing oil seal and extension housing bushing if necessary.

6. Remove speedometer drive gear snap-ring, drive gear, and retaining ball.

7. Move mainshaft assembly to rear ½ in. Lower front of clutch shaft and raise rear of countergear. Remove clutch shaft.

8. Check 21 roller bearings inside rear of clutch shaft for wear, pitting, or scoring.

9. Remove second-third shifter fork. Tilt mainshaft to remove synchro-clutch snap-ring.

10. Remove synchro-clutch. second gear, and low and reverse gear.

11. Remove low-reverse shifter fork.

12. Remove mainshaft and rear bearing from rear of case. Press rear bearing from shaft.

13. Remove reverse idler shaft and countershaft lockplate.

14. Drive countershaft out to rear with a dummy shaft. Lower dummy shaft and countergear to bottom of case.

15. Drive reverse idler shaft out to rear. Remove gear. Remove countergear.

16. Note position of reverse idler shaft thrust washers; check for wear or damage.

17. Remove outer shift levers and shifter shaft lockpin. Remove shifter shafts from inside case. Remove two interlock ball bearings. Remove interlock sleeve, pin, and spring. Remove shifter shaft O-rings.

Inspection

1. Wash all parts in solvent.
2. Air dry.

Gears and Mainshaft

1. Check for worn, cracked, or chipped teeth.
2. Check fit of gears to mainshaft. If gears are replaced, also replace the gear with which they mesh.

Bearings

1. Check for cracked races.
2. Check for worn or scored balls.

Synchro-Clutch and Friction Rings

1. Slide rings on cones of second gear and clutch shaft.
2. Replace rings if there is excessive wear or a pitted condition on the taper.

Case

1. Check for evidence of bearings turning in their bores.
2. Check for cracks.

Assembly

1. Install new shift shaft O-rings.
2. Install low-reverse shift shaft interlock sleeve, ball bearing, and spring.
3. Install second-third shift shaft. Place second ball bearing in position.
4. Place shifter mechanism in any gear. With one end of interlock sleeve against shifter shaft quadrant, measure clearance between opposite end of sleeve and the other quadrant. Clearance should be .001-.007 in. Selective lengths of interlock sleeves are available for adjustment. Install lockpins and shift levers.
5. Install dummy shaft in countergear. Install needle bearings, spacer, and washers. Install thrust washers. The bronze front washer must index with the case. Install countergear assembly in bottom of case.
6. Install reverse idler gear with chamfered side of teeth to front. Drive reverse idler shaft in from rear.

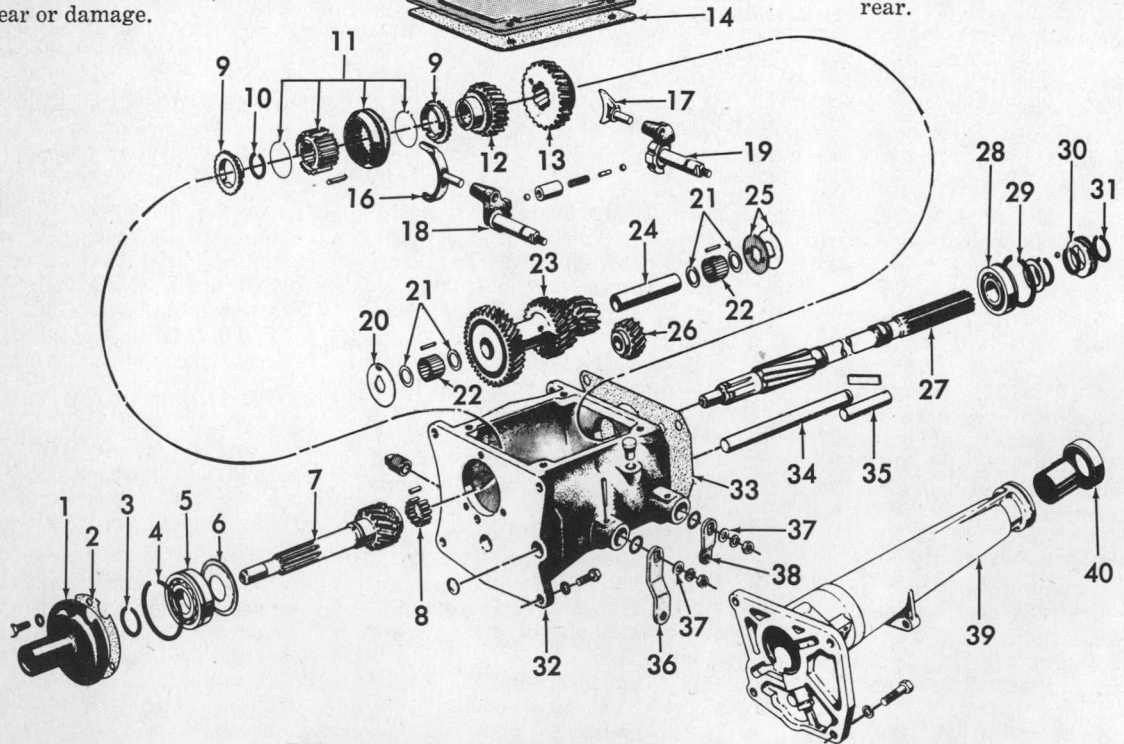

T-96 transmission—exploded view (© American Motors Corp)

1 Bearing cap	11 Synchronizer	21 Bearing washers	31 Snap-ring
2 Gasket	12 Second gear	22 Bearing rollers	32 Case
3 Snap-ring	13 First and reverse gear	23 Countershaft gear	33 Extension gasket
4 Lock ring	14 Cover gasket	24 Countershaft spacer	34 Countershaft
5 Bearing	15 Cover	25 Thrust washer	35 Reverse idler shaft
6 Retaining washer	16 Second and third fork	26 Reverse idler gear	36 Second and third lever
7 Clutch shaft	17 First and reverse fork	27 Mainshaft	37 Shift lever seal
8 Bearing rollers	18 Second and third shaft	28 Rear bearing	38 First and reverse lever
9 Friction ring set	19 First and reverse shaft	29 Lock ring	39 Extension
10 Snap-ring	20 Thrust washer	30 Speedometer drive gear	40 Extension seal

7. Drive countershaft into place. Install lockplate.
8. Press rear bearing on mainshaft. Install snap-rings. Place mainshaft in case.
9. Install shifter forks. Install

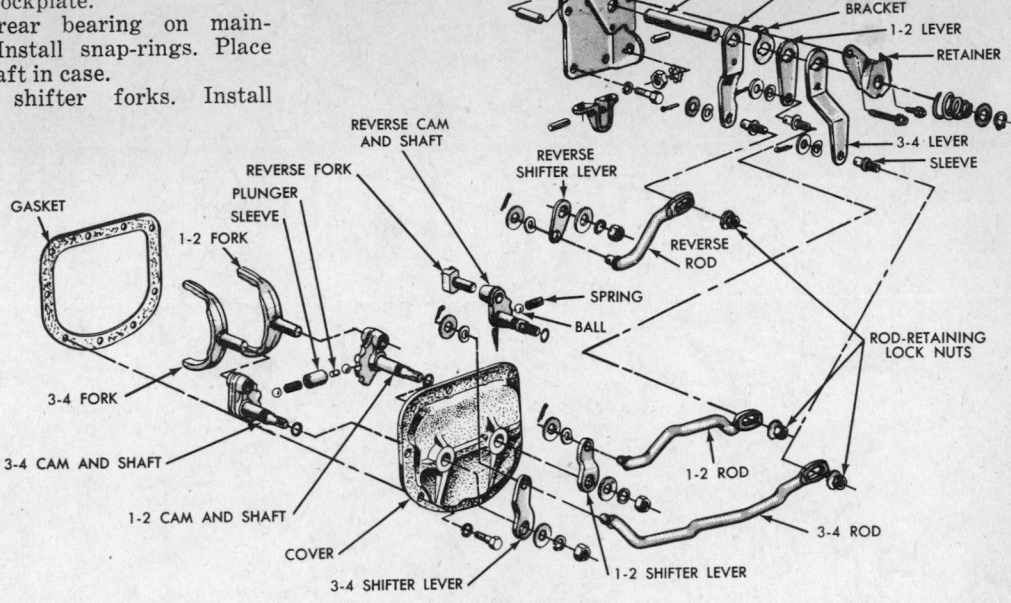

Linkage and cover

first-reverse sliding gear, second gear, and synchro-clutch assembly, hub forward.
10. Install thickest mainshaft front snap-ring that will fit in groove.
11. There should be .003-.010 in. clearance between second gear and the mainshaft shoulder, with the synchro-clutch hub pressed against the snap-ring.
12. Hold the 21 clutch shaft bearings in place with petroleum jelly. Install front friction ring

and clutch shaft on mainshaft.
13. Simultaneously install the mainshaft rear bearing, align the shifter forks and gears, and guide the mainshaft into the clutch shaft.
14. Install the thickest rear mainshaft snap-ring that will fit in the groove.
15. Install retaining ball, speedometer drive gear, and snap-ring.
16. Install extension housing with a new oil seal.

17. Place oil slinger on clutch shaft with concave side to rear. Install front bearing using thrust yoke. Install thickest snap-ring that will fit in the groove.
18. Install bearing cap and a new gasket.
19. Check clearance of synchro-clutch friction rings. Both clearances should be .036-.100 in.
20. Check transmission operation in all gears; then install the case cover and gasket.

Type-18
Warner T-10 4-Speed

Camaro, 1974-77
Corvette, 1974-77
Firebird, 1974-77

Application
American Motors, 1970-74

Disassembly

1. Drain transmission, mount in adequate stand. Then remove the side cover and shift controls.
2. Remove four bolts from front bearing retainer, then remove retainer and gasket.
3. Remove output shaft companion flange.
4. Drive lockpin up from reverse shifter lever boss, then pull shift-shaft out about 1/8 in. to disengage shifter fork from reverse gear.
5. Remove five bolts from the case extension and tap the extension (with soft hammer) rearward. When idler gear shaft is out as far as it will go, move extension to the left so the reverse fork clears the reverse gear. Remove extension and gasket.
6. Remove rear bearing snap-ring from mainshaft.

7. Remove case extension oil seal.
8. Remove speedometer drive gear with puller.
9. Remove the reverse gear, reverse idler gear and tanged thrust washer.
10. Remove self-locking bolt holding the rear bearing retainer to transmission case.
11. Remove the entire mainshaft assembly.
12. Unload bearing rollers from main drive gear and remove fourth-speed synchronizer blocking ring.
13. Lift the front half of reverse idler gear and its thrust washer from the case.
14. Remove the main drive gear snap-ring and remove spacer washer.
15. With soft hammer, tap main drive gear toward rear and out of front bearing.

16. From inside the case, tap out front bearing and snap-ring.
17. From the front of the case, tap out the countershaft, using dummy shaft.
18. Then lift out the countergear assembly with both tanged washers.
19. Dismantle the countergear, consisting of 80 rollers, six .050 in. spacers and a roller tubular spacer.
20. Remove mainshaft front snap-ring and slide third and fourth-speed clutch assembly, third-speed gear and synchronizer ring, second and third-speed gear thrust bearing, second-speed gear and second-speed synchronizer ring from front of mainshaft.
21. Spread rear bearing retainer snap-ring and press mainshaft out of retainer.
22. Remove the mainshaft rear snap-

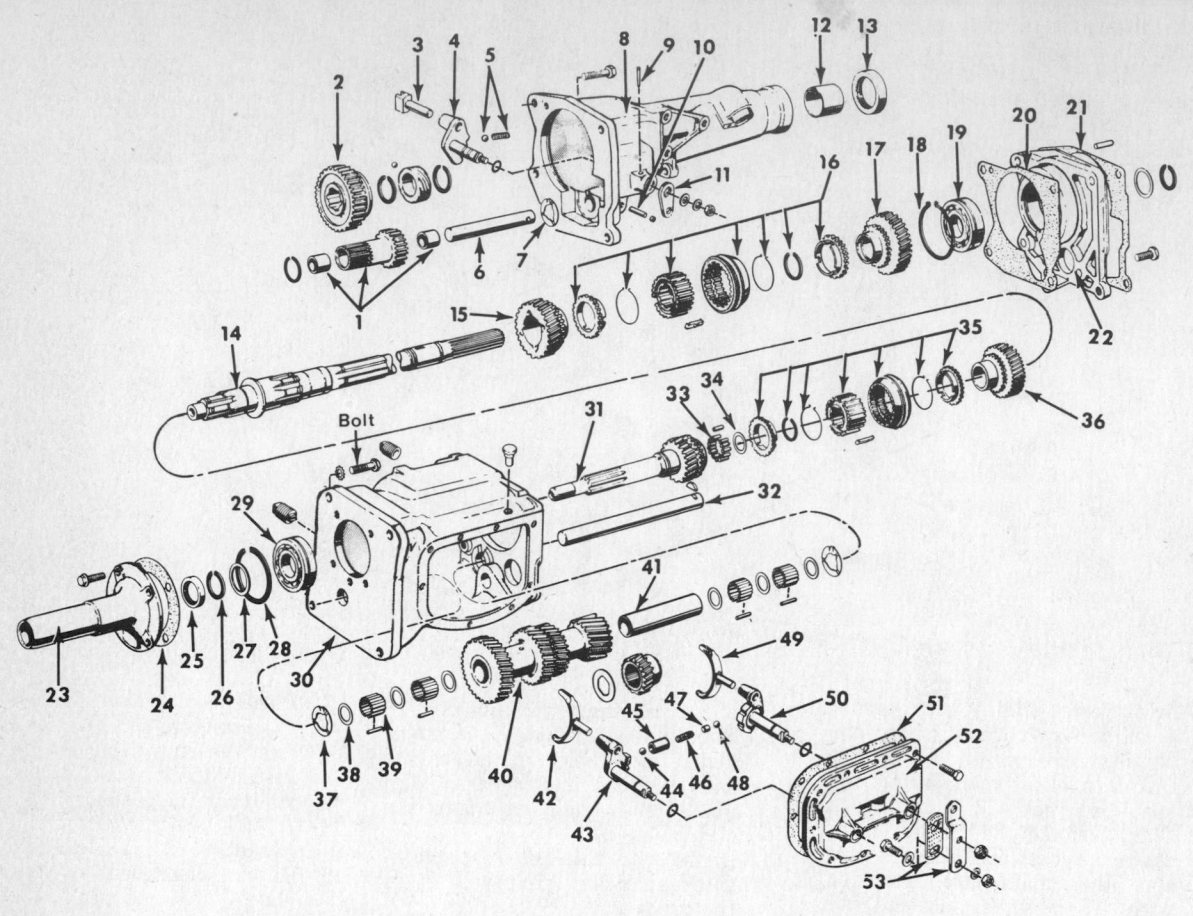

Warner T-10 transmission disassembled (American Motors application)

1 Reverse idler gear	12 Bushing	23 Front bearing cap	34 Roller spacer	44 Poppet ball
2 Reverse gear	13 Seal	24 Gasket	35 Synchro assy	45 Interlock sleeve
3 Reverse fork	14 Mainshaft	25 Seal	36 3rd gear	46 Poppet spring
4 Reverse shaft	15 2nd gear	26 Snap-ring	37 Countergear washer	47 Interlock
5 Poppet ball and spring	16 Synchro assy	27 Washer	38 Roller bearing washer	48 Poppet ball
6 Idler shaft	17 1st gear	28 Lock ring	39 Rollers	49 1st-2nd fork
7 Thrust washer	18 Snap-ring	29 Front bearing	40 Countergear	50 1st-2nd shaft
8 Reverse housing	19 Adapter bearing	30 Case	41 Spacer	51 Cover gasket
9 Reverse pin	20 Adapter	31 Clutch shaft	42 3rd-4th fork	52 Cover
10 Lock pin	21 Gasket	32 Countershaft	43 3rd-4th shaft	53 Shift levers
11 Reverse lever	22 Adapter	33 Rollers		

ring.

23. Support first and second-speed clutch assembly and press on rear of mainshaft to remove shaft from rear bearing, first-speed gear, and synchromesh ring, first and second-speed clutch sliding sleeve and first-speed gear bushing.

Assembly

Mainshaft

1. From the rear of the mainshaft, assemble first and second-speed clutch assembly to mainshaft (sliding clutch sleeve taper toward the rear, hub to the front) and press the first-speed gear bushing onto the shaft.

2. Install first-speed gear synchronizing ring so notches in ring align with keys in hub.

3. Install first-speed gear (hub toward front) and the first-speed gear thrust washer. Be sure the grooves in the washer are facing first-speed gear.

4. Press on the rear bearing, with the snap-ring groove toward the front of the transmission. Be sure the bearing is firmly seated against the shoulder on the mainshaft.

5. Install the selective fit snap-ring onto the mainshaft behind the rear bearing. Use the thickest ring that will fit between the rear face of the bearing and the front face of the snap-ring.

6. From the front of the mainshaft, install the second-speed gear synchronizing ring so that notches in the ring correspond with the keys in the hub.

7. Install the second-speed gear (hub toward the back) and install the second and third-speed gear thrust bearing.

8. Install third-speed gear (hub to

front) and third-speed gear synchronizing ring (notches front).

9. Install third and fourth-speed gear clutch assembly (hub and sliding sleeve) with taper front, being sure keys in the hub correspond with notches in third-speed gear synchronizing ring.

10. Install snap-ring (.086-.088 in. thickness) into groove in mainshaft, in front of the third and fourth-speed clutch assembly.

11. Install rear bearing retainer plate. Spread the snap-ring on the plate to allow the snap-ring to drop around the rear bearing and press on the end of the mainshaft until the snap-ring engages the groove in the rear bearing.

12. Install reverse gear (shift collar to the rear).

13. Press speedometer drive gear onto the mainshaft. Position the speedometer gear to get a measurement of 4½ in. from the center

of the gear to the flat surface of the rear bearing retainer.

14. Install special snap-ring into the groove at the rear of the mainshaft.

Countergear

1. Install countergear dummy and tubular roller bearing spacer into the countergear.
2. Using heavy grease to hold the rollers, install 20 bearing rollers in either end of the countergear, two spacers, 20 more rollers, then one spacer. Install the same combination of rollers and spacers in the other end of the countergear.
3. Set the countergear assembly in the bottom of the transmission case, be sure the tanged thrust washers are in their proper position.

Main Drive Gear

1. Press bearing (snap-ring groove front) onto main drive gear until the bearing fully seats against the shoulder on the gear.
2. Install spacer washer and selective fit snap-ring in the groove in the main drive gear shaft.
   NOTE: variable thickness snaprings are available to obtain a prescribed clearance of .000-.005 in. between the rear face of the snap ring and the front face of the spacer washer.

Transmission

1. Install main drive gear and bearing assembly through the side cover opening and into position in the transmission front bore. After assembly is in place, install snapring into groove in front bearing.
2. Lift countergear and thrust washers into place. Install Woodruff

key into end of countershaft, then from the rear of the case, press the countershaft in until the end of the shaft is flush with rear of transmission case and the dummy shaft is displaced. Endplay in the countergear must not exceed .025 in.

3. Install the 14 bearing rollers into the grease-coated end of the main drive gear.
4. Using heavy grease, position gasket on front face of rear bearing retainer. Install the fourth-speed synchronizing ring onto main drive gear with clutch key notches toward rear of transmission.
5. Position the reverse idler gear thrust washer on the machined face of the gear cast in the case for the reverse idler shaft. Position the front reverse idler gear on top of the thrust washer, hub facing toward rear of case.
6. Lower the mainshaft assembly into the case, with the notches of the fourth-speed synchronizing ring corresponding to the keys in the clutch assembly.
7. Install self-locking bolt, holding the rear bearing retainer to the transmission case. Torque to 20-30 ft. lbs.
8. From the rear of the case, insert the rear reverse idler gear, engaging the splines with the portion of the gear within the case.
9. Grease gasket, and place in position on the rear face of the rear bearing retainer.
10. Install remaining tanged thrust washer into place on reverse idler shaft, being sure the tang on the thrust washer is in the notch in the idler thrust face of the extension.

11. Place the two clutches in neutral position.
12. Pull reverse shifter shaft to left side of extension and rotate shaft to bring reverse fork to extreme forward position in extension. Line up forward and reverse idler gears.
13. Start the extension onto the transmission case by inserting reverse idler shaft through reverse idler gears. Push in on shifter until shift fork engages reverse gear shift collar. When the fork engages, rotate the shifter shaft to move reverse gear rearward. This will allow the extension to slide onto the transmission case.
14. Install three extension and retainer to case attaching bolts and torque to 35-45 ft. lbs. Install two extension to retainer attaching bolts and torque to 20-30 ft. lbs. Use sealer on the lower, right attaching bolt.
15. Adjust reverse shift shaft so that groove in shaft lines up with hole in boss. Drive in lockpin from top of boss.
16. Install the main drive gear bearing retainer and gasket, being sure the oil well lines up with the oil outlet hole. Install four sealer-coated attaching bolts and torque to 15-20 ft. lbs.
17. Install a shift fork into each clutch sleeve.
18. With both clutches in neutral, install side cover gasket and lower side cover into place.
19. Install attaching bolts and torque to 10-20 ft. lbs. Use sealer on the lower right bolt.
20. Install first and second, and third and fourth shift levers, lockwashers and nuts.

Type-19
AMC Overdrive

Application
American Motors (6 Cyl. Gremlin, Hornet, Pacer), 1975-77

This unit uses an electrical solenoid valve to actuate a hydraulic circuit which engages and disengages a planetary gear system. Overdrive is available only in high gear.

NOTE: To make removal of the overdrive unit from the transmission easier, drive the car with overdrive engaged, then disengage it with the clutch pedal down. You can drain the transmission and overdrive by removing the transmission bottom extension housing bolt.

Disassembly

1. Use a ¼ in. thick (or less) open end wrench to remove the solenoid valve.
2. At the front of the unit, remove the self-locking nuts holding the clutch piston apply bars to the thrust bearing cover pins. Discard the nuts; they can't be reused.
3. Remove the nuts and lockwashers from the case studs. Remove the copper gaskets used under the two top nuts. Separate the main and rear cases.
4. Remove the loose clutch return springs and the clutch brake ring and gaskets from the main case. If the brake ring is stuck, tap it with a plastic hammer; don't pry on it.
5. Remove the main case lower pan, gasket, filter, and pressure plug.

A new gasket will be needed.

6. Use a spanner pin tool (one can be fabricated) to unscrew the pressure filter plug and remove the pressure filter and aluminum washer.
7. Use the spanner tool to unscrew the pump body plug and the non-return valve ball seat spring, check ball, and seat. Remove the O-ring from the plug.
8. Use pliers to carefully take the clutch apply pistons from their bores. Remove the piston O-rings.

Note: Don't remove the lubrication relief valve yet.

9. Pull the pump body up and slide the plunger out. Remove the body from the case, taking note of the flat side which must align

with a lubrication feed hole. Remove the drive cam and key from the pump strap. Don't take apart the pump strap and plunger.

10. Now remove the relief valve piston plug with the spanner tool and take out the piston and spring. Remove the plug O-ring. Don't try to take the spring off the valve piston. Use a magnet or needlenose pliers to remove the relief valve and spring assembly. Don't try to remove the spring from the valve. A special tool is available to remove the relief valve sleeve and body; it is a hook device that pulls the valve body and sleeve out together. Don't jerk the body and sleeve out; they can easily be damaged. Remove all the valve body, sleeve, and plug O-rings.

11. In the rear case, remove the sliding clutch, sun gear, and thrust bearing cover assembly from the mainshaft annulus gear. Remove the pinion carrier assembly from the gear.

12. Remove the sun gear snap-ring and the sliding clutch ring lock. Push the sun gear out of the hub.

13. Support the thrust bearing cover and gently drive the clutch hub from the bearing.

14. Remove the thrust bearing snap-ring and press the bearing from the cover, using an arbor press. Don't remove the thrust bearing cover bolts.

15. Remove the overrunning clutch snap-ring and the brass oil slinger.

16. Remove the overrunning clutch. Remove the mainshaft thrust washer from the recess in the annulus gear.

17. Pry the expansion plug out of the rear case. Place the rear case face down on two wood blocks, and using snap-ring pliers through the expansion plug hole, expand the mainshaft bearing snap-ring while tapping the mainshaft out of the case with a mallet.

18. Hold the splined end of the mainshaft and remove the drive gear locknut. Remove the speedometer drive gear tab washer and the gear. Press off the mainshaft bearing.

19. Pry the rear case oil seal out and remove the mainshaft bearing snap-ring. Don't remove the disc washer or rear bushing; the rear case must be replaced if these are damaged.

Assembly

1. Lubricate the mainshaft bearing with the lubricant to be used in the transmission and overdrive (SAE 80 gear lubricant is recommended). Put the bearing on the mainshaft with the snap-ring groove on the rear. Seat the bearing with a length of pipe.

2. Install the speedometer drive gear with the shoulder side toward the mainshaft bearing. Install a new drive gear washer on top of the gear with the tab in the mainshaft slot and finger tighten the drive gear locknut. Hold the mainshaft splines and torque the locknut to 55 ft lbs. Bend the washer against the nut in two places.

3. Put a new mainshaft bearing snap-ring in the groove in the rear case.

4. Place the mainshaft upright and lower the rear case over it. Tap the case with a soft hammer to start the bearing. Expand the snap-ring and tap the case down until the bearing and snap-ring are seated.

5. Lubricate the lip of the new rear case oil seal and install the seal. Install a new expansion plug in the case.

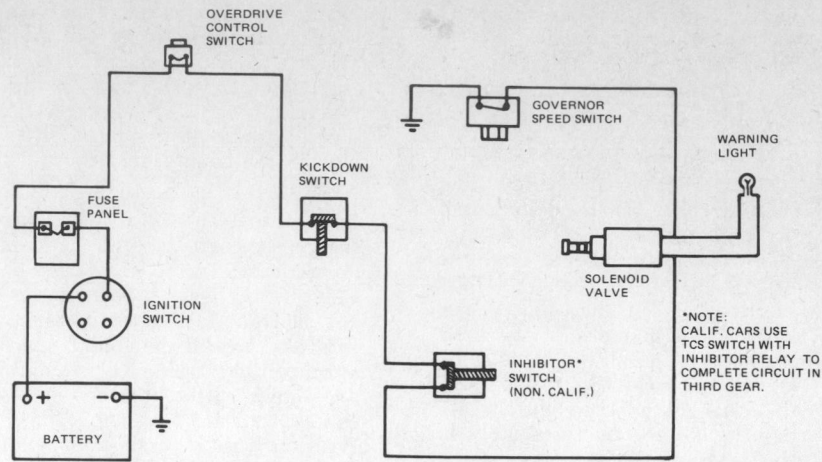

AMC overdrive electrical circuit

6. Lubricate the mainshaft thrust washer and place it in the recess in the annulus gear.

7. Assemble and lubricate the overrunning clutch. Install it in the bore of the annulus gear. Install the brass oil slinger, shoulder out, and the snap-ring.

8. Lubricate the pinion carrier assembly and install it in the annulus gear.

9. Press the thrust bearing into the thrust bearing cover and install the snap-ring. Lubricate the bearing. Position the bearing and clutch hub. Tap the cover to start the bearing onto the hub. Turn the assembly over, support the thrust bearing cover, and drive the hub into the bearing.

10. Install the sun gear into the sliding clutch hub. Install the ring lock, sharp edge up, and the snap-ring.

11. Engage the sun gear into the pinion gear and install the sliding clutch assembly onto the mainshaft annulus gear. Make sure the sliding clutch is seated and

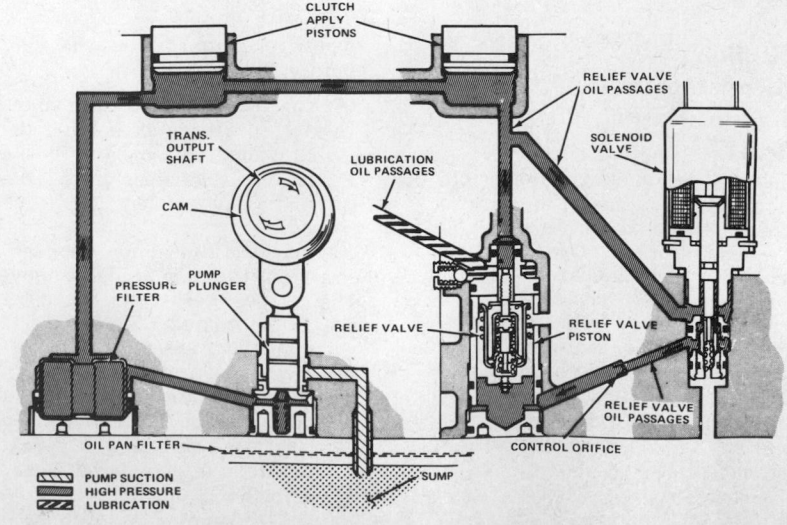

AMC overdrive hydraulic circuit, engaged

1 Gasket Transmission to Adapter
2 Adapter, Transmission
3 Nut, Self Locking, Main Case Stud
4 Washer, Lock
5 Gasket, Main Case to Transmission Adaptor
6 Key, Pump Strap Cam Drive
7 Cam, Pump Strap
8 Strap, Pump
9 Bar, Clutch Piston Apply
10 Piston, Clutch Apply
11 Seal, Clutch Apply Piston O-Ring
12 Stud, Main Case to Transmission Adapter
13 Main Case
14 Gasket, Clutch Brake Ring (front)
15 Brake Ring, Clutch
16 Gasket, Clutch Brake Ring (rear)
17 Ring, Sun Gear Snap
18 Ring Lock, Sliding Clutch
19 Ring, Thrust Bearing Snap
20 Bearing, Thrust
21 Cover, Thrust Bearing
22 Clutch, Sliding
23 Sun Gear
24 Assembly, Pinion Carrier
25 Bolt, Thrust Bearing Cover (4 reqd.)
26 Spring, Clutch Return (4 reqd.)
27 Solenoid Valve
28 Washer, Solenoid Valve
29 Seal, Solenoid Valve O-Ring
30 Seal, Solenoid Valve O-Ring
31 Gasket, Main Case Pressure Plug
32 Plug, Main Case Pressure
33 Ring, Overrunning Clutch Snap
34 Slinger, Overrunning Clutch Oil
35 Assembly, Overrunning Clutch
36 Washer, Mainshaft Thrust
37 Bushing, Mainshaft Support (Included in Mainshaft)
38 Main Shaft and Annulus Gear
39 Ring, Mainshaft Bearing Snap
40 Washer, Speedometer Drive Gear Tab
41 Nut, Speedometer Drive Gear Lock
42 Gear, Speedometer Drive
43 Bearing, Mainshaft
44 Bolt, Speedometer Adapter Clamp
45 Clamp, Speedometer Adapter
46 Adapter, Speedometer to Governor Speed Switch
47 Adapter, Speedometer Driven Gear
48 Gear, Speedometer Driven
49 Plug, Expansion
50 Bushing, Rear Case (included in Case)
51 Seal, Rear Case Oil
52 Nut, Self Locking, Main Case to Rear Case Stud
53 Washer, Lock
54 Rear Case
55 Stud, Main Case to Rear Case
56 Washer, Disc (not removed: included in rear case)
57 Seal, Speedometer Adapter O-Ring
58 Seal, Speedometer Adapter Oil
59 Seal, Relief Valve Body O-Ring (Inner)
60 Body, Relief Valve
61 Seal, Relief Valve Body O-Ring (Outer)
62 Assembly, Relief Valve and Spring
63 Spring, Relief Valve Residual Pressure

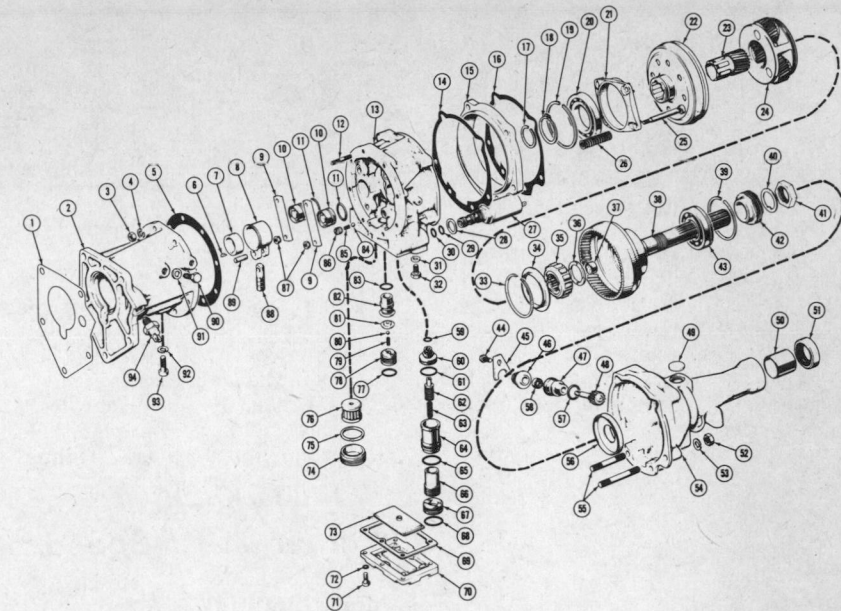

Exploded view, AMC overdrive

64 Sleeve, Relief Valve
65 Seal, Relief Valve Sleeve O-Ring
66 Piston, Relief Valve
67 Plug, Relief Valve Piston
68 Seal, Relief Valve Piston Plug O-Ring
69 Gasket, Oil Pan
70 Oil Pan
71 Bolt, Oil Pan
72 Washer, Lock
73 Filter, Oil Pan
74 Plug, Pressure Filter
75 Washer, Pressure Filter (Aluminum)
76 Filter, Pressure
77 Seal, Pump Body O-Ring
78 Plug, Pump Body

79 Spring, Non-return Valve Ball-seat
80 Ball, Non-return Valve Check
81 Seat, Non-return Valve
82 Body, Pump Plunger
83 Seal, Pump Plunger Body O-Ring
84 Ball, Lubrication Relief Valve Check
85 Spring, Lubrication Relief Valve
86 Plug, Lubrication Relief Valve
87 Nut, Self Locking, Clutch Piston Apply Bar
88 Plunger, Pump
89 Pin, Pump Plunger
90 Bolt, Gearshift Lever Retainer to Adapter
91 Washer, Lock
92 Washer, Lock
93 Bolt, Rear Support Cushion to Adapter
94 Switch, Back-up Light

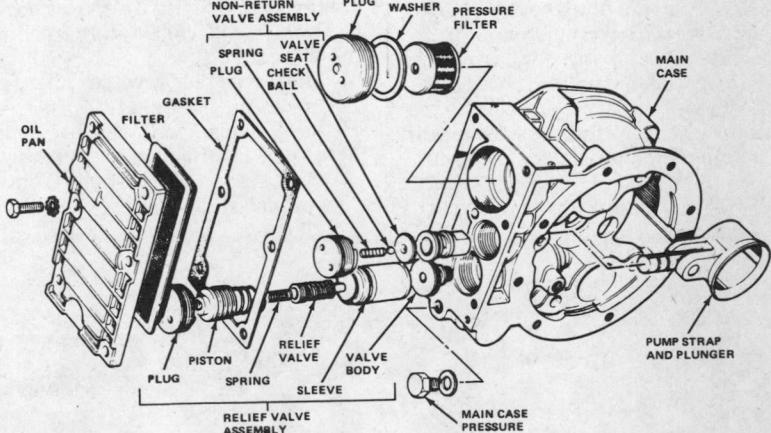

Lower main case details

the gears fully engaged. Turning the shaft will make it easier.

12. Lubricate the clutch apply pistons, install new O-rings, and install the pistons with the counterbored end out.

13. Lubricate the relief valve components and install new O-rings. Insert the relief valve body into the case, align the sleeve hole with the bore oil hole and insert it with the O-ring end up. Push the sleeve firmly into the bore, install the valve and spring assembly in the body, install the residual pressure spring in the valve and spring assembly. Install the piston in the valve sleeve and install the plug, tightening it to 16 ft lbs.

14. Install the pressure filter, aluminum washer, and plug, torquing to 16 ft lbs.

15. Lubricate the pump plunger assembly, pump body, and non-return valve seat. Install new O-rings. Align the pump body flat with the main case bore oil hole and insert the body halfway. Insert the pump plunger into the

body, then push the body completely into the case bore. Place the non-return valve seat on top of the body with the check ball seat up. Place the ball in the seat. Install the non-return valve ball seat spring. Install the plug and spring, tightening to 16 ft lbs.

16. Install the main case pressure

plug, gasket, pan filter, new gasket, and cover. Tighten the pan bolts to 6 ft lbs and the plug to 16 ft lbs.

17. Place the rear case front up and install new clutch return springs on the thrust bearing cover bolts.

18. Install the first clutch brake ring gasket on the rear case. Install the clutch brake ring into the rear case with the tapered surface to the rear. Install the second new clutch brake ring gasket on the brake ring. Make sure the gaskets and the brake ring are aligned with the stud holes in the rear case.

19. Use sealer on the case studs.

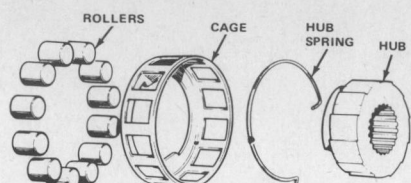

Overrunning clutch components

Lower the main case onto the rear case, aligning the thrust bearing cover bolts with the bolt holes in the main case.

20. Install the six nuts, four lockwashers, and two copper gaskets (on the upper studs). Tighten

the nuts in a criss-cross pattern to 11 ft lbs.

21. Install the clutch apply bars on the thrust bearing cover bolts and fasten with new locknuts, tightened to 8 ft lbs.

22. Install the solenoid valve.

23. Lubricate the new drive cam and install it and the key on the output shaft. Install the snap-ring.

24. Pour about a pint of lubricant in through the access hole in the front of the main case. On installation, tighten the overdrive case to adapter nuts to 18 ft lbs. Check the lubricant level at the transmission filler plug; the two units have a common lubricant supply.

Type-20
Warner T50 5-Speed

Application
Astre, 1976-77
Cosworth Vega, 1976-77
Cutlass (260), 1976-77

LeMans (260), 1976-77
Monza, 1976-77
Omega (260), 1976-77
Skyhawk, 1976-77

Starfire, 1976-77
Sunbird, 1976-77
Vega, 1976-77
Ventura, (260), 1976-77

NOTE: A wave washer has been added to one end of the cluster gear assembly to take up minor vibration that was apparent on early units in service. This wave washer may not be on some T50 gearboxes, especially those installed on non-air conditioned cars.

Disassembly
Drain the unit and remove it from the vehicle.

1. Remove the selector lever pivot. Remove the plug poppet spring and mesh lock plunger.

2. Drive the spring pin from the shifter head and shift rail.

3. Remove the six bolts which retain the transmission case and extension housing to the center support.

4. Slide the case forward from the transmission.

5. Disassembly may be completed on a bench; however, a holding fixture will simplify the job by supporting the transmission.

6. Remove the extension housing by sliding it rearward. The shifter head, shift rail and selector are not fastened to the housing and should not be permitted to drop out and be damaged.

NOTE: The needle rollers are not always retained in the needle race. Catch loose needles as they fall out during disassembly so that they can be replaced in the mating race during assembly.

7. Remove the reverse idler gear from the idler shaft.

8. Press down on the speedometer gear retainer tab and remove the gear and retainer from the output shaft.

9. Remove the snap ring, thrust

washer, first speed gear, and blocking ring from the output shaft.

10. Remove the snap ring from behind the synchronizer hub.

11. Move the shift rail to locate the pawl to permit removal of the first and reverse shift link.

12. Slide the first and reverse synchronizer, shift fork, and rail rearward from the transmission.

13. Position the interlock pawl in a position to permit the second and third speed shift link and shift fork to be removed.

14. Position the interlock pawl in a position to permit the fourth and fifth shift fork and link to be removed.

15. Remove the snap ring, thrust washer and slide reverse gear rearward from output shaft.

16. Remove the center support from

T-50 interlock pawl and retaining plate (© G.M. Corp.)

Removing the T-50 center support (© G.M. Corp.)

1 Oil seal
2 Bushing
3 Pin
4 Shifter head
5 Threaded plug
6 Poppet spring
7 Mesh lock plunger
8 Breather assy.
9 Selector lever pivot
10 Wiring harness clip
11 Name plate
12 Back-up light bracket
13 Cup plug
14 Extension housing with bushing
15 Switch
16 ⅜"—16 X 3¼" hex HD bolt
17 Switch
18 Needle bearing
19 Shift rail
20 Spring pin
21 Rail selector end
22 First & reverse shift fork
23 Shift fork pad
24 First reverse shift link
25 Gasket
26 3/16"—18 plug
27 Speedometer gear
28 Speedometer gear retaining clip
29 Snap ring
30 Thrust washer
31 1st speed gear
32 Snap ring
33 Blocking ring
34 Synchronizer spring
35 Shift plate
36 Clutch hub
37 Clutch sleeve
38 Reverse gear & bushing assy.
39 Bushing
40 Selector arm—optional
41 Spring pin
42 Interlock pawl

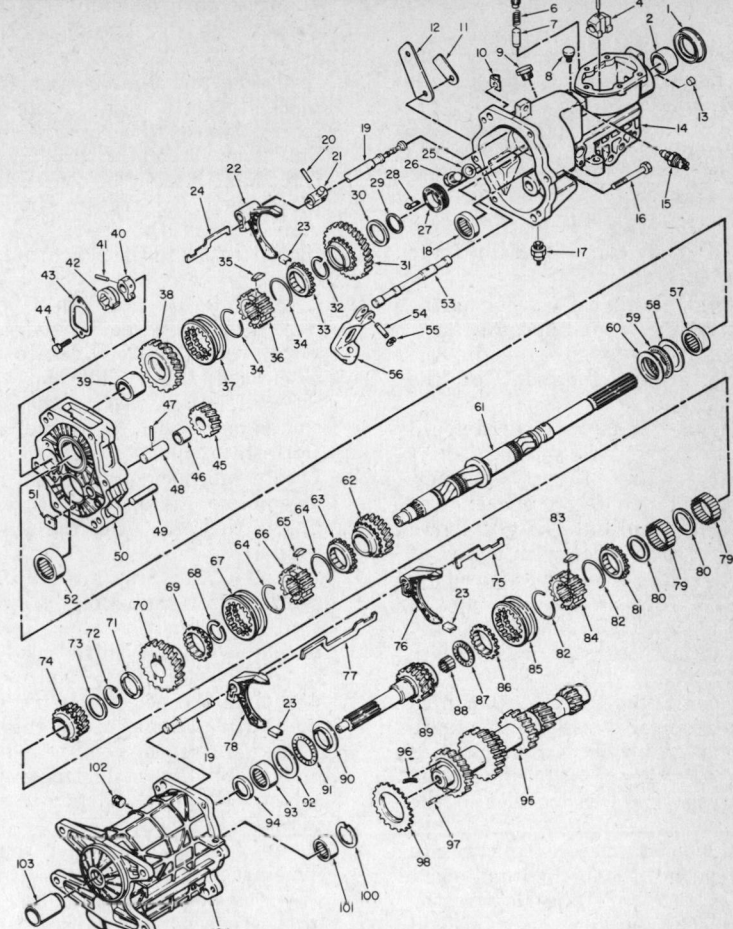

Exploded view of the T-50 5-speed (© G.M. Corp.)

the output shaft and cluster gear.

17. Remove the needle thrust race and bearing from the output shaft.

18. Remove the cluster gear from the remaining gears.

19. Remove the output shaft from the input shaft.

20. The remaining components may be removed one at a time from the output shaft.

Synchronizer and Bearing Disassembly

1. Check the clutch sleeves to see if they slide freely on their hubs. These are a selective fit and should be kept together to ensure a free sliding fit with maximum backlash of 0.002 in.

2. If the keys and springs are worn or broken, they should be replaced as follows: mark the hub and sleeve so they can be correctly reassembled, then push the hub from the sleeve and remove the keys and springs. Place one spring on each side of the hub so the springs overlap the slots in the hub and the opening in the springs are not op-

posite each other. Place the shift keys in the slots of the hub with the smaller edge and the springs in the grooves of the keys. Press down on the keys and install the sleeve onto the hub, aligning the marks made previously.

3. Remove the drive gear bearing and seal from the transmission case.

4. Install a new seal into the case and drive it in until it bottoms.

5. Remove the countergear bearing from the case; replace if necessary.

6. Support the center support on two wooden blocks and drive the mainshaft bearing from the support; replace if necessary.

7. With the center still supported, remove the retaining plate and interlock pawl, and drive the countergear bearing out of the center support. Replace if necessary.

8. Remove the countergear bearing, the extension housing oil seal and the extension housing bushing; Replace as necessary.

Assembly

1. Assemble the 27 tooth third

speed gear with the coned end up over the output shaft and against the shaft shoulder.

NOTE: Synchronizer assemblies are similiar except hub splines differ. The hub and sleeve are a selective fit to obtain a free sliding fit with .002 inch maximum backlash. Keep mated parts together to insure correct sliding fit and blacklash.

2. Assemble the three shift plates in the second and third synchronizer hub slots. Assemble the sleeve over the hub and shifter plates. The chamfer on one end of the sleeve may be assembled to either end of the hub. Hook an end of one synchronizer spring over one shift plate and wrap the spring around the inside of the hub. Hook the other synchronizer spring over the other end of the shift plate the first spring was hooked over and wrapped inside of the hub in a direction opposite to the first spring. Eight to fifteen pounds force should be required to shift a new sleeve from detent position.

3. Assemble the blocker rings with the slots aligned with the shift

plates of the synchronizer assembly.

4. Assemble the synchronizer and blocker rings over the output shaft and position them on the face of the third speed gear.

5. Assemble a snap ring in the shaft groove ahead of the synchronizer hub.

6. Assemble the 34 tooth second speed gear coned end into the blocker ring.

7. Assemble a thrust washer on the face of the second speed gear.

8. Assemble a snap ring in the shaft groove in front of the thrust washer.

9. Assemble the 22 tooth fifth speed gear over the output shaft against the thrust washer. Assemble one needle spacer over the shaft and into the gear bore. Follow the spacer with a row of 47 needles, a second spacer, a second row of needles, and a third spacer. Use petroleum jelly to retain these parts as they are assembled.

10. Assemble the fourth and fifth synchronizer with the 27 tooth hub as described in Steps 2, 3 and 4. Assemble a needle thrust bearing on the front face of the hub.

11. Assemble 19 needle rollers into the second step of the input shaft bore and carefully lower the shaft with needles over the end of the output shaft. Petroleum jelly or low melting point grease should hold needles in position.

12. Mesh the cluster gear teeth with the teeth of the input shaft gear and the gears assembled to output shaft as the cluster gear. The input shaft and output shaft are positioned to assemble the center support.

13. Assemble a needle thrust washer and thrust plate over the output shaft against the shaft shoulder.

14. Assemble the interlock pawl into the center support bore. Assemble retaining plate and two 1/4 — 20 × 3/4 hex head self tapping screws.

15. Assemble the needle rollers into the races in the center support. Petroleum jelly low melting point grease should be used to retain the needles during assembly.

NOTE: *Some needles are locked in the cage and others are not.*

16. Assemble the center support over the output shaft and cluster gear.

17. Assemble the 35 tooth reverse gear and bushing assembly over the output shaft and rest it on the center support.

18. Assemble the 19 tooth reverse idler gear and bushing over the reverse idler shaft.

19. Replace worn or damaged shift pads on all shift forks if necessary.

20. Assemble the fourth and fifth link into shift fork. Locate the interlock pawl to permit the shift link to be assembled through the right hand slot of the center support when the transmission is viewed from the rear. Engage the shift fork in the synchronizer collar.

21. Locate interlock pawl in a position to permit the second and third speed shift link to be assembled in the middle slot with the shift assembled to the link and engaged with the second and third shift collar.

22. Locate interlock pawl to permit assembling the first and reverse link in the left slot of the center support.

23. Assemble the first and reverse synchronizer assembly as described in Step 3.

24. Assemble reverse shift link into the shift fork.

25. Assemble the selector arm over the shift rail to a position aligned with the drilled hole near the middle of the rail. Drive the spring pin into the arm and rail to retain these parts.

26. Assemble the shift rail through the shift fork from front to rear with the pocket notches located to the rear of the transmission.

27. Engage the shift fork with first and reverse synchronizer sleeve and assemble these parts by sliding the synchronizer hub over the output shaft as the shift rail is assembled through the interlock pawl, the second and third shift fork and the fourth and fifth shift fork.

28. Assemble a blocking ring and the 38 tooth first speed gear over the output shaft behind the first and reverse synchronizer assembly.

29. Assemble a thrust washer and snap ring over the output shaft

T-50 fourth and fifth gear shift linkage
(© G.M. Corp.)

behind the first speed gear.

30. Engage the speedometer gear retainer in the hole provided in the output shaft with the retainer looped forward, slide the speedometer gear over the output shaft and in a position over the retainer until the retainer ends snaps up to lock the gear in position.

31. Slide the rail selector end with the hole located to the rear of the transmission over the end of the shift rail. Drive a spring pin into the selector and rail to retain these parts.

32. Assemble the selector lever to the shorter shift rail. Use a pin and two retainer clips to hold these parts together.

33. Press a new oil seal into the extension housing.

34. Assemble the loose needles in the extension housing race, use petroleum jelly or low melting point grease to retain the needles.

35. Assemble the selector lever and shift rail into the hole provided in the extension housing. Assemble the shifter head onto the rail as the rail becomes exposed in the housing opening. Do not drive the spring pin in at this time.

36. Replace the oil seal and needle rollers in the transmission case.

37. Apply a continuous 1/32 inch bead of silicone sealer or an approved equivalent to the transmission case and extension housing faces.

38. Extend the rail end into the extension housing to engage the rail selector end as the extension housing is assembled over the output shaft and brought into contact with the center support rear face.

39. Assemble the lipped thrust race, needle thrust washer and flat thrust race over the input shaft. Assemble the case to the front side of the center support. Assemble the six 3/8 — 16 × 3 1/4 hex head bolts to retain the extension housing and transmission case to center support.

40. Drive the spring pin into the shifter head and shift rail.

41. Assemble the transmission mesh lock plunger, poppet spring and threaded plug.

42. Assemble the selector lever pivot, with Loctite or equivalent applied to the threads, into the extension housing.

43. Assemble the switches into the extension housing.

The fluid capacity of the T50 unit is 55 fl. ozs. Use Dexron automatic transmission fluid.

Introduction

The rear axle must transmit power through 90°. To accomplish this, straight cut bevel gears or spiral bevel gears were used. This type of gear is satisfactory for differential side gears, but since the centerline of the gears must intersect, they rapidly became unsuited for ring and pinion gears. The lowering of the driveshaft brought about a variation of the bevel gear, which is called the hypoid gear. This type of gear does not require a meeting of the gear centerlines and can therefore be underslung, relative to the centerline of the ring gear.

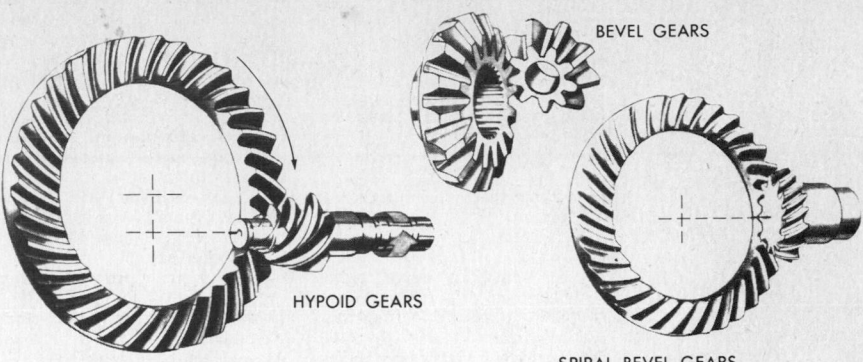

HYPOID GEARS

BEVEL GEARS

SPIRAL BEVEL GEARS

Hypoid gear application
(© Chevrolet Div., G.M. Corp)

Bevel gear application
(© Chevrolet Div., G.M. Corp)

Gear Ratios

The drive axle of a vehicle is said to have a certain axle ratio. This number (usually a whole number and a decimal fraction) is actually a comparison of the number of gear teeth on the ring gear and the pinion gear. For example, a 4.11 rear means that theoretically, there are 4.11 teeth on the ring gear and one tooth on the pinion. Actually, on a 4.11 rear, there are 37 teeth on the ring gear and nine teeth on the pinion gear. By dividing the number of teeth on the pinion gear into the number of teeth on the ring gear, the numerical axle ratio (4.11) is obtained. This also provides a good method of ascertaining exactly which axle ratio one is dealing with.

Differential Operation

The differential is an arrangement of gears that permits the rear wheels to turn at different speeds when cornering and divides the torque between the axle shafts. The differential gears are mounted on a pinion shaft and the gears are free to rotate on this shaft. The pinion shaft is fitted in a bore in the differential case and is at right angles to the axle shafts.

Power flow through the differential is as follows. The drive pinion, which is turned by the driveshaft, turns the ring gear. The ring gear, which is bolted to the differential case, rotates the case. The differential pinion forces the pinion gears against the side gears. In cases where both wheels have equal traction, the pinion gears do not rotate on the pinion shaft, because the input force of the pinion gear is divided equally between the two side gears. Consequently the pinion gears revolve with the pinion shaft, although they do not revolve on the pinion shaft itself. The side gears, which are splined to the axle shafts, and meshed with the pinion gears, rotate the axle shafts.

When it becomes necessary to turn a corner, the differential becomes effective and allows the axle shafts to rotate at different speeds. As the inner wheel slows down, the side gear splined to the inner wheel axle shaft also slows down. The pinion gears act as balancing levers by maintaining equal tooth loads to both gears while allowing unequal speeds of rotation at the axle shafts. If the vehicle speed remains constant, and the inner wheel slows down to 90 percent of vehicle speed, the outer wheel will speed up to 110 percent.

GENERAL DRIVE AXLE DIAGNOSTIC GUIDE

(Also see following text for further differential diagnosis.)

CONDITION	POSSIBLE CAUSE	CORRECTION
REAR WHEEL NOISE	(a) Loose Wheel.	(a) Tighten loose wheel nuts.
	(b) Spalled wheel bearing cup or cone.	(b) Check rear wheel bearings. If spalled or worn, replace.
	(c) Defective or brinelled wheel bearing.	(c) Defective or brinelled bearings must be replaced. Check rear axle shaft end-play.
	(d) Excessive axle shaft end-play.	(d) Readjust axle shaft end-play.
	(e) Bent or sprung axle shaft flange.	(e) Replace bent or sprung axle shaft.
SCORING OF DIFFERENTIAL GEARS AND PINIONS	(a) Insufficient lubrication.	(a) Replace scored gears. Scoring marks on the pressure face of gear teeth or in the bore are caused by instantaneous fusing of the mating surfaces. Scored gears should be replaced. Fill rear axle to required capacity with proper lubricant.
	(b) Improper grade of lubricant.	(b) Replace scored gears. Inspect all gears and bearings for possible damage. Clean and refill axle to required capacity with proper lubricant.
	(c) Excessive spinning of one wheel.	(c) Replace scored gears. Inspect all gears, pinion bores and shaft for scoring, or bearings for possible damage.
TOOTH BREAKAGE (RING GEAR AND PINION)	(a) Overloading.	(a) Replace gears. Examine other gears and bearings for possible damage. Avoid future overloading.
	(b) Erratic clutch operation.	(b) Replace gears, and examine remaining parts for possible damage. Avoid erratic clutch operation.
	(c) Ice-spotted pavements.	(c) Replace gears. Examine remaining parts for possible damage. Replace parts as required.
	(d) Improper adjustment.	(d) Replace gears. Examine other parts for possible damage. Be sure ring gear and pinion backlash is correct.

Rear Axle Noise	(a) Insufficient lubricant.	(a) Refill rear axle with correct amount of the proper lubricant. Also check for leaks and correct as necessary.
	(b) Improper ring gear and pinion adjustment.	(b) Check ring gear and pinion tooth contact.
	(c) Unmatched ring gear and pinion.	(c) Remove unmatched ring gear and pinion. Replace with a new matched gear and pinion set.
	(d) Worn teeth on ring gear or pinion.	(d) Check teeth on ring gear and pinion for contact. If necessary, replace with new matched set.
	(e) End-play in drive pinion bearings.	(e) Adjust drive pinion bearing preload.
	(f) Side play in differential bearings.	(f) Adjust differential bearing preload.
	(g) Incorrect drive gearlash.	(g) Correct drive gear lash.
	(h) Limited-Slip differential — moan and chatter.	(h) Drain and flush lubricant. Refill with proper lubricant.
Loss of Lubricant	(a) Lubricant level too high.	(a) Drain excess lubricant.
	(b) Worn axle shaft oil seals.	(b) Replace worn oil seals with new ones. Prepare new seals before replacement.
	(c) Cracked rear axle housing.	(c) Repair or replace housing as required.
	(d) Worn drive pinion oil seal.	(d) Replace worn drive pinion oil seal with a new one.
	(e) Scored and worn companion flange.	(e) Replace worn or scored companion flange and oil seal.
	(f) Clogged vent.	(f) Remove obstructions.
	(g) Loose carrier housing bolts or housing cover screws.	(g) Tighten bolts or cover screws to specifications and fill to correct level with proper lubricant.
Overheating of Unit	(a) Lubricant level too low.	(a) Refill rear axle.
	(b) Incorrect grade of lubricant.	(b) Drain, flush and refill rear axle with correct amount of the proper lubricant.
	(c) Bearings adjusted too tightly.	(c) Readjust bearings.
	(d) Excessive wear in gears.	(d) Check gears for excessive wear or scoring. Replace as necessary.
	(e) Insufficient ring gear-to-pinion clearance.	(e) Readjust ring gear and pinion backlash and check gears for possible scoring.

Limited-Slip Differential Operation

Limited-slip differentials provide driving force to the wheel with the best traction before the other wheel begins to spin. This is accomplished through clutch plates or cones. The clutch plates or cones are located between the side gears and inner wall of the differential case. When they are squeezed together through spring tension and outward force from the side gears, three reactions occur. Resistance on the side gears causes more torque to be exerted on the clutch packs or clutch cones. Rapid one-wheel spin cannot occur, because the side gear is forced to turn at the same speed as the case. Most important, with the side gear and the differential case turning at the same speed, the other wheel is forced to rotate in the same direction and at the same speed as the differential case. Thus driving force is applied to the wheel with the better traction.

Differential Diagnosis

The most essential part of rear axle service is proper diagnosis of the problem. Bent or broken axle shafts or broken gears pose little problem, but isolating an axle noise and correctly interpreting the problem can be extremely difficult, even for an experienced mechanic.

Any gear driven unit will produce a certain amount of noise, therefore, a specific diagnosis for each individual unit is the best practice. Acceptable or normal noise can be classified as a slight noise heard only at certain speeds or under unusual conditions. This noise tends to reach a peak at 40-60 mph, depending on the road condition, load, gear ratio and tire size. Frequently, other noises are mistakenly diagnosed as coming from the rear axle. Vehicle noises from tires, transmission, driveshaft, U-joints and front and rear wheel bearings will often be mistaken as emanating from the rear axle. Raising the tire pressure to eliminate tire noise (although this will not silence mud or snow treads), listening for noise at varying speeds and road conditions and listening for noise at drive and coast conditions will aid in diagnosing alleged rear axle noises.

External Noise Elimination

It is advisable to make a thorough road test to determine whether the noise originates in the rear axle or whether it originates from the tires, engine transmission, wheel bearings or road surface. Noise originating from other places cannot be corrected by overhauling the rear axle.

Road Noise

Brick roads or rough surfaced concrete, may cause a noise which can be mistaken as coming from the rear axle. Driving on a different type of road, (smooth asphalt or dirt) will determine whether the road is the cause of the noise. Road noise is usually the same on drive or coast conditions.

Tire Noise

Tire noise can be mistaken as rear axle noises, even though the tires on the front are at fault. Snow tread and mud tread tires or tires worn unevenly will frequently cause vibrations which seem to originate elsewhere; *temporarily, and for test purposes only*, inflate the tires to 40-50 lbs. This will significantly alter the noise produced by the tires, but will not alter noise from the rear axle. Noises from the rear axle will normally cease at speeds below 30 mph on coast, while tire noise will continue at lower tone as car speed is decreased. The rear axle noise will usually change from drive conditions to coast conditions, while tire noise will not. Do not forget to lower the tire pressure to normal after the test is complete.

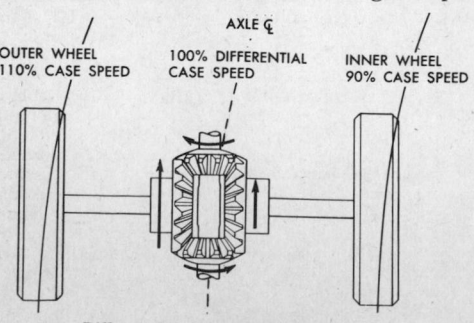

AXLE ℄

OUTER WHEEL 110% CASE SPEED   100% DIFFERENTIAL CASE SPEED   INNER WHEEL 90% CASE SPEED

Differential action during cornering
(© Chevrolet Div., G.M. Corp)

Engine and Transmission Noise

Engine and transmission noises also seem to originate in the rear axle. Road test the vehicle and determine at which speeds the noise is most pronounced. Stop the car in a quiet place to avoid interfering noises. With the transmission in neutral, run the engine slowly through the engine speeds corresponding to the car speed at which the noise was most noticeable. If a similar noise was produced with the car standing still, the noise is not in the rear axle, but somewhere in the engine or transmission.

Front Wheel Bearing Noise

Front wheel bearing noises, sometimes confused with rear axle noises, will not change when comparing drive and coast conditions. While holding the car speed steady, lightly apply the footbrake. This will often cause wheel bearing noise to lessen, as some of the weight is taken off the bearing. Front wheel bearings are easily checked by jacking up the wheels and spinning the wheels. Shaking the wheels will also determine if the wheel bearings are excessively loose.

Rear Axle Noises

If a logical test of the vehicle shows that the noise is not caused by external items, it can be assumed that the noise originates from the rear axle. The rear axle should be tested on a smooth level road to avoid road noise. It is not advisable to test the axle by jacking up the rear wheels and running the car.

True rear axle noises generally fall into two classes; gear noise and bearing noises, and can be caused by a faulty driveshaft, faulty wheel bearings, worn differential or pinion shaft bearings, U-joint misalignment, worn differential side gears and pinions, or mismatched, improperly adjusted, or scored ring and pinion gears.

Rear Wheel Bearing Noise

A rough rear wheel bearing causes a vibration or growl which will continue with the car coasting or in neutral. A brinelled rear wheel bearing will also cause a knock or click approximately every two revolutions of the rear wheel, due to the fact that the bearing rollers do not travel at the same speed as the rear wheel and axle. Jack up the rear wheels and spin the wheel slowly, listening for signs of a rough or brinelled wheel bearing.

Differential Side Gear and Pinion Noise

Differential side gears and pinions seldom cause noise, since their movement is relatively slight on straight ahead driving. Noise produced by these gears will be more noticeable on turns.

Pinion Bearing Noise

Pinion bearing failures can be distinguished by their speed of rotation, which is higher than side bearings or axle bearings. Rough or brinelled pinion bearings cause a continuous low pitch whirring or scraping noise beginning at low speeds.

Side Bearing Noise

Side bearings produce a constant rough noise, which is slower than the pinion bearing noise. Side bearing noise may also fluctuate in the above rear wheel bearing test.

Gear Noise

Two basic types of gear noise exist. First, is the type produced by bent or broken gear teeth which have been forcibly damaged. The noise from this type of damage is audible over the entire speed range. Scoring or damage to the hypoid gear teeth generally results from insufficient lubricant, improper lubricant, improper breakin, insufficient gear backlash, improper ring and pinion gear alignment or loss of torque on the drive pinion nut. If not corrected, the scoring will lead to eventual erosion or fracture of the gear teeth. Hypoid gear tooth fracture can also be caused by extended overloading of the gear set (fatigue fracture) or by shock overloading (sudden failure). Differential and side gears rarely give trouble, but common causes of differential failure are shock loading, extended overloading and differential pinion seizure at the cross-shaft, re-

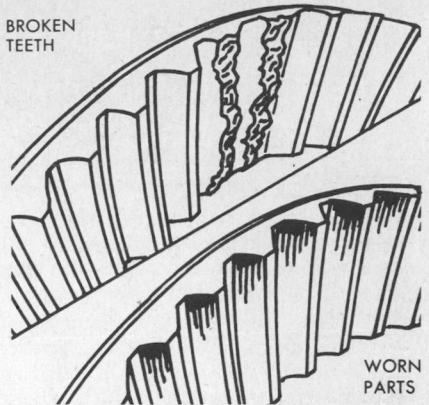

Two types of damage which cause gear noise
(© Chevrolet Div., G.M. Corp)

sulting from excessive wheel spin and consequent lubricant breakdown.

The second type of gear noise pertains to the mesh pattern between the ring and pinion gears. This type of abnormal gear noise can be recognized as a cycling pitch or whine audible in either drive, float or coast conditions. Gear noises can be recognized as they tend to peak out in a narrow speed range and remain constant in pitch, whereas bearing noises tend to vary in pitch with vehicle speeds. Noises produced by the ring and pinion gears will generally follow the pattern below.

A. Drive Noise: Produced under vehicle acceleration.
B. Coast Noise: Produced while the car coasts with a closed throttle.
C. Float Noise: Occurs while maintaining constant car speed (just enough to keep speed constant) on a level road.

NOISE DIAGNOSIS CHART

PROBLEM	CAUSE
1. Identical noise in Drive or Coast conditions	1. Road noise Tire noise Front wheel bearing noise
2. Noise changes on a different type of road	2. Road noise Tire noise
3. Noise tone lowers as car speed is lowered	3. Tire noise
4. Similar noise is produced with car standing and driving	4. Engine noise Transmission noise
5. Vibration	5. Rough rear wheel bearing Unbalanced or damaged driveshaft Unbalanced tire Worn universal joint in driveshaft Misaligned drive shaft at companion flange Excessive companion flange runout
6. A knock or click approximately every two revolutions of rear wheel	6. Brinelled rear wheel bearing
7. Noise most pronounced on turns	7. Differential side gear and pinion wear or damage
8. A continuous low pitch whirring or scraping noise starting at relatively low speed	8. Damaged or worn pinion bearing
9. Drive noise, coast noise or float noise	9. Damaged or worn ring and pinion gear
10. Clunk on acceleration or deceleration	10. Worn differential cross-shaft in case
11. Clunk on stops	11. Insufficient grease in driveshaft slip yoke
12. Groan in Forward or Reverse	12. Improper differential lubricant
13. Chatter on turns	13. Improper differential lubricant Worn clutch plates
14. Clunk or knock during operation on rough roads.	14. Excessive end-play of axle shafts to differential cross-shaft

D. Drive, Coast
and Float
Noise: These noises will vary in tone with speed and be very rough or irregular if the differential or pinion shaft bearings are worn.

Bearing Diagnosis

This section will help in the diagnosis of bearing failure and the causes. Bearing diagnosis can be very helpful in determining the cause of rear axle failure.

When disassembling a rear axle, the general condition of all bearings should be noted and classified where possible. Proper recognition of the cause will help in correcting the problem and avoiding a repetition of the failure.

Some of the common causes of bearing failure are:

a. Abuse during assembly or disassembly.
b. Improper assembly methods.
c. Improper or inadequate lubrication.
d. Bearing contact with dirt or water.
e. Wear caused by dirt or metal chips.
f. Corrosion or rust.
g. Seizing due to overloading.
h. Overheating.
i. Frettage of the bearing seats.
j. Brinelling from impact or shock loading.
k. Manufacturing defects.
l. Pitting due to fatigue.

To avoid damage to the bearing from improper handling, it is best to treat a used bearing the same as a new bearing. Always work in a clean area with clean tools. Remove all outside dirt from the housing before exposing a bearing and clean all bearing seats before installing a bearing.

Caution Never spin a bearing, either by hand or with compressed air, as this will lead to almost certain bearing failure.

Limited-Slip Differential Diagnosis

Lubrication

The use of proper lubricant is very important in limited-slip type drive axles. The forces applied when cornering tend to apply the clutch pack or clutch cones. The use of the wrong lubricant can cause the clutch services to grab and chatter while turning. Always follow the manufacturer's recommendations regarding drive axle lubrication. When chatter is encountered, the differential lubricant should be drained and refilled with the specified lubricant.

Testing

The clutch operation on all limited-slip type axles can be tested as follows. Refer to the manufacturer in question.

American Motors "Twin-Grip"

1. With the engine off and the transmission in neutral, jack up one rear wheel.
2. Block the other wheel to prevent it from moving.
3. With a socket and torque wrench on the axle shaft nut, turn the raised wheel forward.
4. The torque required to move the wheel should be 70–100 ft lbs for 8⅞ in. axles or 80–120 ft lbs for 7-9/16 in. axles.
5. A breakaway torque which is less than the specified figure, indicates a need for repair or replacement.

Cadillac Controlled Differential

This unit should not be serviced. If a malfunction exists that cannot be cured by changing the fluid, remove the unit and install a new one.

Chrysler Corp. Sure-Grip

1. Place the vehicle on a hoist with the engine off and the automatic transmission in Park (manual transmission in low gear).
2. Attempt to rotate the wheel by hand, by gripping the tire.
3. If it is extremely difficult, if not impossible, to rotate either wheel the Sure-Grip differential can be assumed to be performing satisfactorily.
4. If it is relatively easy to continuously turn either rear wheel, the unit should be removed and replaced.

Caution The Sure-Grip differential is serviced as a unit only. Under no circumstances should the unit be disassembled and reinstalled.

Ford Motor Company Equa-Lok

1. Jack up one rear wheel and remove the wheel cover.
2. Block the other wheel front and rear to prevent the car from moving.
3. Using a 200 ft lbs capacity torque wrench on one of the wheel lug nuts, measure the torque required to continuously rotate the wheel. The breakaway torque reading can be disregarded. The minimum torque to continuously rotate the wheel should be as follows.
   All axles except integral carrier type: 75 ft lbs
   Integral carrier type axles: 50 ft lbs
4. If the minimum torque is not as specified, the differential should be checked for improper assembly.

Ford Motor Company Traction-Lok

1. Follow the procedure for the Ford Motor Company Equa-Lok rear. The minimum torque to continuously rotate the wheel (disregarding the breakaway torque) should be at least 40 ft lbs.

General Motors Corp. (except Cadillac) Positraction

1. Place the transmission in neutral.
2. Raise one rear wheel off the floor and block the other rear wheel (front and rear) to prevent the car from moving.
3. Install a torque wrench and extension on the lug nut and note the torque required to continuously rotate one rear wheel. Disregard the breakaway torque figure, as this may be a great deal higher.
4. The minimum torque to continuously rotate the rear wheel should be at least 35 ft lbs. If it is not, the rear axle is in need of service.

General Diagnosis

Improper operation of a limited-slip type rear axle is generally indicated by clutch slippage or grabbing, which will sometimes produce a whirring or chatter sound. Occasionally, this condition is induced by improper lubrication. Check the unit for the wrong type of lubricant or lubricant which has broken down or become contaminated. Replace the lubricant with the type specified by the manufacturer.

During normal operation, i.e., straight-ahead driving, both wheels are rotating at equal speeds, and the driving force is distributed equally between both wheels. When cornering, the inside wheel delivers extra driving force, causing slippage in both clutch packs. Therefore, if the wheel rotation of both rear wheels is not equal, the unit will constantly be functioning as if the car were cornering. This will cause constant slippage and lead to eventual failure of the unit. It is important that there be no excessive differences in wheel and tire size, wear pattern, or tire pressures between both rear wheels. Swerving on acceleration is an indication of one or more of the above conditions. Before attempting an overhaul or replacement operation, check both rear wheels for identical tire sizes, tire pressure, tire tread depth, and wear pattern.

Drive Axle Disassembly Analysis

Testing the Gear Tooth Contact Pattern

Once it has been established that

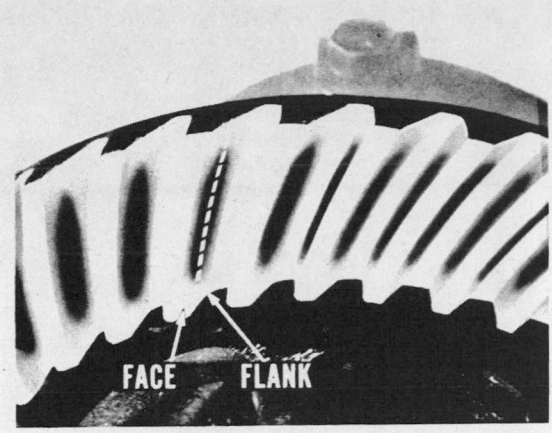

Gear tooth face and flank showing oval gear tooth
contact pattern
(© Chrysler Corp)

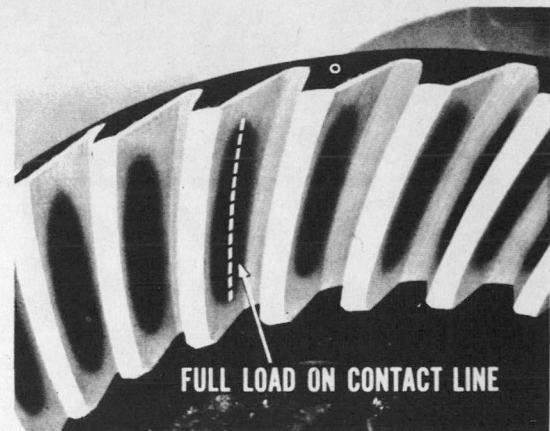

Gear tooth contact pattern showing load centered
on gear tooth
(© Chrysler Corp)

the differential is indeed in need of service, the worst procedure is to simply plunge ahead and remove the differential and disassemble the parts. Prior to disassembly, a tooth contact pattern test should be made. However, it is worthwhile to first know the nomenclature associated with hypoid gear teeth.

The thick end of the tooth is called the heel and the thin end of the tooth is called the toe. The base half of the tooth is called the flank and the other end of the tooth is known as the face. The imaginary line at the halfway point between the face and flank is known as the pitch line. The space between the meshed pinion and ring gear teeth is known as backlash.

A gear tooth contact pattern can be made with the carrier in or out of the housing depending on the type of carrier. On integral carrier models, the lubricant must be drained and the rear cover removed. The ring gear will now be exposed and the test can be made with the carrier still in the housing. On removable carrier models, drain the lubricant and remove the carrier from the housing. The test can be made on the bench.

Unlike simple spur gears, hypoid gear teeth leave a complex pattern on the ring gear. When hypoid gears turn, the line contact between pinion and ring gear teeth has the same wiping motion as with spur gear teeth. Because of the complicated movement of hypoid gear teeth, the contact area takes an oval shape as opposed to the rectangular shape left by spur gear teeth. Actually, the tooth contact test shows where each gear tooth has been wiped by the movement of the contact line, so that you can tell whether the gears are set correctly. With a properly adjusted ring and pinion (with properly adjusted pinion depth and backlash) the tooth contact will be close to center. In this case, the load is borne by the strongest part of the tooth. If the gear setting is off, the contact line may reach any part of the edge of a tooth, and the metal will be overloaded at that point. When overload occurs, rapid deterioration of the gears will follow.

Preparing the Test

Coat the drive gear teeth with red or white lead. The white lead will show the pattern in better contrast on new gears. If either lead is not available, substitute a metallic base artists' oil color such as zinc white or titanium white. The tooth coating material must be smooth and firm enough to spread without running. A consistency somewhat like toothpaste works well. If it is necessary to thicken the material, add a small amount of cup grease.

NOTE: prussian blue dye does not work well, since the blue tends to smear the pattern.

Thoroughly clean the ring gear and pinion before applying the testing material. Any gear lube left on the teeth will make the pattern quite unreadable. Coat the drive and coast sides of all the ring gear teeth, but leave the pinion gear teeth clean. Do not apply the coating too thickly as the pattern will be smeared.

Because the axle gears are normally easy to rotate, turning resistance must be applied to produce pressure between the pinion and ring gear teeth to make a legible pattern. On a removable carrier type axle, insert a large screwdriver between the carrier housing and the differential case rim. Apply the load squarely against the case rim while prying out against the upper or lower section of the carrier housing. On integral carrier models, apply the parking brake to a point where it requires approximately 50 ft lbs to turn the pinion with a torque wrench. Since the

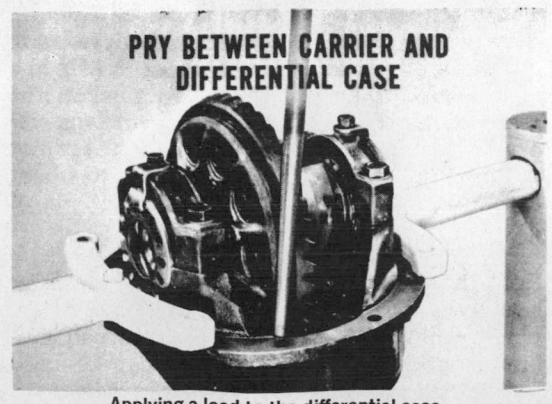

PRY BETWEEN CARRIER AND
DIFFERENTIAL CASE

Applying a load to the differential case
(© Chrysler Corp)

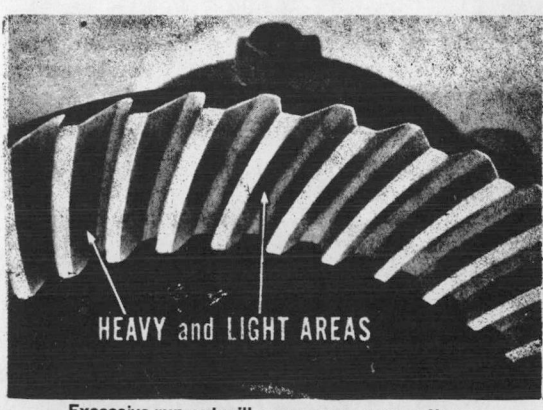

HEAVY and LIGHT AREAS

Excessive run-out will cause an uneven pattern
(© Chrysler Corp)

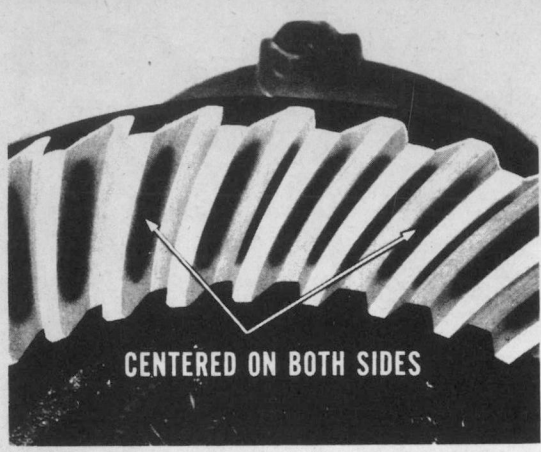

Gear tooth contact pattern showing load centered
on gear tooth
(© Chrysler Corp)

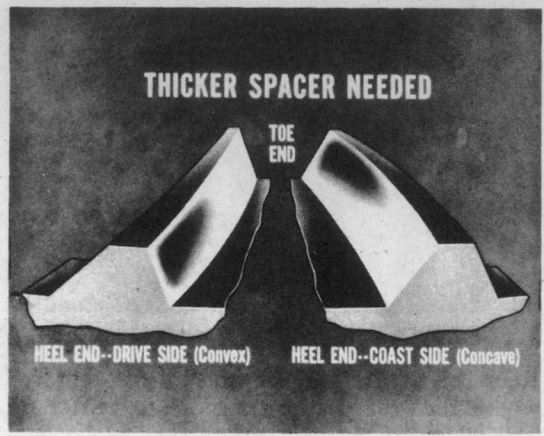

Tooth contact patterns high on the tooth side
(© Chrysler Corp)

shape and position of the contact pattern will vary, depending on the load, try to use the same load for each test or the results can be misleading. This is especially true when testing after an overhaul.

Once the gears have a load applied, obtain a tooth contact pattern by rotating the ring gear and pinion one complete turn in each direction. This will produce a constant pattern on the coast and drive side of each tooth. Do not rotate the ring gear more than one revolution in each direction as this will tend to obscure the pattern.

NOTE: if the pattern does not look right on the first try, recoat the gear teeth and try again.

Making a good gear tooth test takes a little practice; so if it is not right, try again.

Interpreting Gear Tooth Contact Patterns

The tooth contact pattern should be the same on every tooth. If the pattern shows heavy and light areas on different teeth, check the ring gear and differential case for excessive run-out.

Note: run-out can be cured in many cases by removing the ring gear from the case, rotating it 90° or 180°, and remounting it.

Since you can only apply test load pressure to the gears, the contact pattern will be less distinct toward the tooth ends. But, when the ring gear and pinion are under operating loads in the vehicle, the tooth contact area spreads out, especially towards the heel end of the tooth. For this reason, do not try to "get by" with a tooth contact pattern that is centered, but favors the heel end of the teeth. This will only lead to overloading at the heel ends of the gear teeth. On the other hand, a contact pattern which is reasonably centered, but favors the toe end of the teeth, is acceptable.

Assuming that the tooth contact pattern is even on all teeth, the main problem is to get the most distinct part of the pattern centered on both the drive and coast sides of the ring gear teeth. The contact patterns should be nearly opposite each other on both sides of each tooth. In some cases, the pattern will be centered on the drive side and off center on the coast side, or vice versa. The off center pattern can be moved to a more

acceptable position by slightly altering the backlash. This procedure will not seriously affect the other pattern. More often, however, the pattern will be off center on both sides of the teeth. The basic cause of this condition is an improperly adjusted pinion.

Adjusting Pinion Depth

It is necessary to understand that an incorrect pinion depth setting moves the contact pattern away from the center on both sides of the tooth in opposite directions. This means that when you install a thicker or thinner washer under the pinion head you bring the pattern into the center of the tooth from opposite ends.

When the contact pattern is high on the heel end of the drive side and low on the toe end of the coast side, a thicker washer is needed to bring the pinion in, toward the center of the drive gear. Increasing the thickness of the spacer washer will bring the pattern in, toward the center of the drive gear teeth, and also will move the pattern down from the tooth face. However, this movement is less than the in-or-out movement.

When tooth contact is low on the toe end of the drive side and high on the heel end of the coast side, the pin-

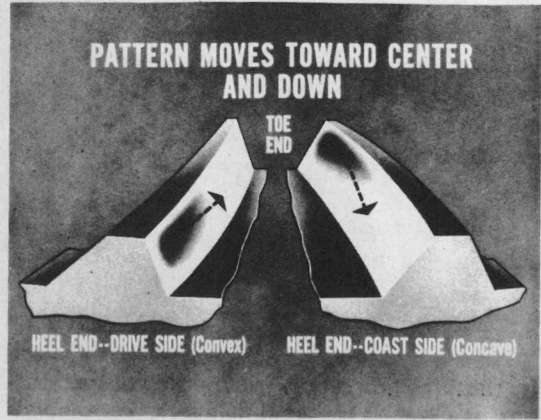

A thicker spacer moves the pattern in and down
(© Chrysler Corp)

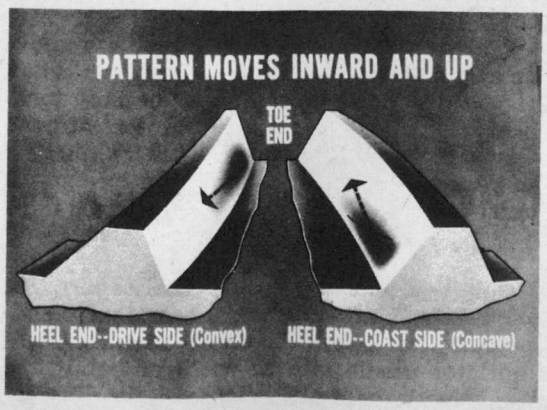

A thinner spacer will move the pattern up and inward
(© Chrysler Corp)

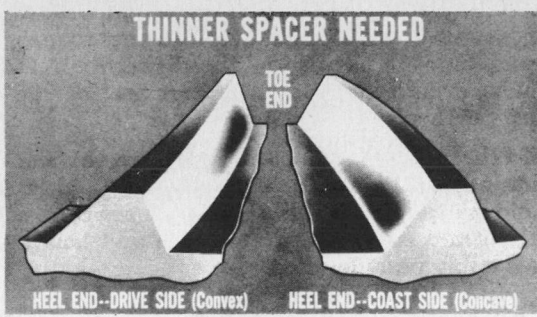

Gear contact pattern low on tooth side
(© Chrysler Corp)

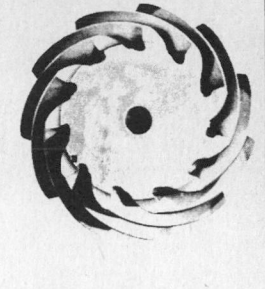
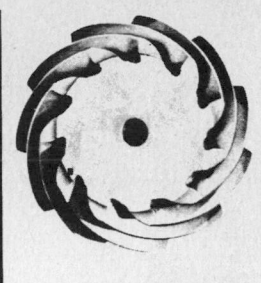

One example of pinion markings
(© Chrysler Corp)

ion must be moved out, by installing a thinner washer under the pinion head. This will move the pattern inward toward the center, and will also result in slight movement of the pattern up from the tooth flank.

A factory service facility will use special tools and gauge blocks to determine the thickness of the spacer under the pinion head. In the absence of such specialized equipment, the following procedure may be used. Bear in mind that with the "hit-or-miss" method, each time you are wrong with the pinion depth, the unit must be disassembled, the spacer thickness changed, and the unit must be completely set up again.

Gather a handful of spacers to cover any thickness and several collapsible pinion spacers (if the unit uses them). Assemble the unit following the procedures in the overhaul section. If the original gear set is being reused, and the tooth contact pattern is reasonably correct, install a new spacer of the same thickness as the old one. This will provide a reasonable starting point. If the gear contact pattern test indicates a need for movement of the pinion, use a new spacer 0.001–0.002 in. thicker or thinner, depending on the direction the pinion must go. If a new gear set is being used, the thickness of the spacer will have to be determined in the following manner. Compare the markings on the old and new pinion.

It will usually be marked with a number preceded by a plus (+) or minus (−) sign. This number indicates the production deviation from the nominal pinion, which are known as "zero pinions." In service, zero pinions are rare. Assume that the old pinion is marked with a plus two (+2). Assume that the new pinion is marked with a +3. By comparing the pinion markings, find the numerical difference between the two pinions, in this case +1. With a micrometer, measure the thickness of the original spacer. We will assume that the old spacer is 0.030 in. thick. If the numerical difference between pinions is a positive number (+1) the spacer should be 0.001 in. thinner than the original spacer, or 0.029 in. total. If the numerical difference is a negative number (say, −1) then the spacer should be increased by 0.001 in., to 0.031 in. total. This will only provide a reasonable beginning point.

It is rare that this method works out the first time. Assemble the pinion, differential, and ring gear with the spacer of calculated thickness. The side bearing preload, backlash, pinion nut torque, and pinion rotating torque must all be set correctly. Obtain a gear tooth pattern on the ring gear teeth and analyze the results. Small deviations from the acceptable pattern can usually be made by varying the backlash within the

limits of specifications. If the gear tooth contact pattern is off, the unit must be disassembled and another spacer installed. This spacer must be of suitable thickness to compensate for the contact pattern test.

NOTE: without special tools, there is absolutely no way of determining exactly how much to increase or decrease the thickness of the pinion shim; it must be estimated.

After estimating the thickness of the new shim, assemble the unit again, setting all preloads and backlash. Check the contact pattern again and act accordingly. If the unit uses a collapsible spacer, be sure a new one is installed each time it is disassembled. Crushed spacers can not be used again. It is well to note that the unit may have to be assembled and disassembled several times before an acceptable contact pattern is obtained.

Adjusting Backlash

The tooth contact pattern can be altered slightly, by varying the backlash adjustment within the limits of the specifications. The backlash adjustment can be used to alter a pattern which is slightly off center on either side of the tooth, but should not be used as a substitute for pinion depth adjustment. This adjustment must always be made after the pinion depth has been adjusted.

Checking differential bearing end-play
(© Chrysler Corp)

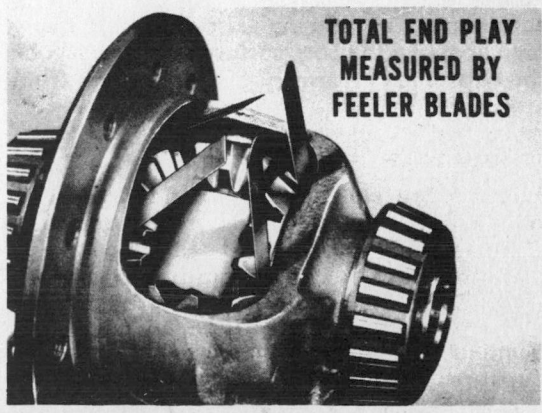

Checking total differential end-play
(© Chrysler Corp)

Front End Alignment

SERVICE PROCEDURE INDEX

Section Numbers Refer to Sections in Text

Manufacturer	Car	Year	Caster, Camber, and Toe-in	Manufacturer	Car	Year	Caster, Camber, and Toe-in
American Motors					Ford Granada; Mercury Monarch	1975-77	3
	American Motors (all except Pacer)	1970-77	3		Ford (full-size); Mercury (full size)	1970-77	7
	Pacer	1975-77	9		Ford Thunderbird; Lincoln Continental		
					Mk III, Mk IV	1970-77	7
Chrysler Corporation					Lincoln Continental	1970-77	7
	Plymouth Valiant, Duster, Barracuda;						
	Dodge Dart, Demon, Challenger	1970-77	4	**General Motors**			
	Plymouth Volare; Dodge Aspen	1976-77	5		Chevrolet Chevette	1976-77	6
	Plymouth Belvedere, Satellite, Road Runner,				Chevrolet Vega, Monza, Pontiac Astre, Sunbird;		
	GTX; Dodge Coronet, Charger	1970-72	4		Oldsmobile Starfire; Buick Skyhawk	1971-77	9
	Plymouth Satellite, Fury (1975-76 only);				Chevrolet Nova; Pontiac Ventura; Oldsmobile		
	Dodge Coronet, Charger; Chrysler Cordoba	1973-77	5		Omega; Buick Apollo	1970-77	1
	Plymouth Fury; Dodge Polara, Monaco	1970-73	4		Chevrolet Chevelle, Monte Carlo; Pontiac		
	Plymouth Fury (1974 only), Gran Fury;				Tempest, Le Mans, GTO, Grand Prix;		
	Dodge Monaco, Gran Monaco	1974-77	5		Oldsmobile F-85, Cutlass, 4-4-2; Buick Special,		
	Chrysler, Chrysler Imperial	1970-73	4		Skylark, GS, Century, Riviera	1970-77	1
	Chrysler (full-size), Imperial	1974-77	5		Chevrolet Camaro; Pontiac Firebird	1970-77	1
					Chevrolet Corvette	1970-77	1
Ford Motor Company					Chevrolet (full-size)	1970	3
	Ford Pinto, Mustang II; Mercury Bobcat	1971-77	8		Chevrolet (full-size)	1971-77	1
	Ford Falcon, Fairlane, Torino;				Pontiac (full-size); Oldsmobile (full-size);		
	Mercury Montego	1970-71	3		Buick (full-size)	1970-77	1
	Ford Torino; Mercury Montego	1972-77	7				See Car
	Ford Mustang; Mercury Cougar	1970-73	3		Oldsmobile Toronado; Cadillac Eldorado	1970-77	Section
	Ford Elite; Mercury Cougar	1974-77	7		Cadillac (except Eldorado, Seville)	1970-77	2
	Ford Maverick; Mercury Comet	1971-77	3		Cadillac Seville	1976-77	1

Section Page Numbers

Wheel Alignment	U293
Diagnosis	U294
Caster, Camber, and Toe-In Adjustment	U295
Section 1	U295
2	U295
3	U295
4	U296
5	U296
6	U296
7	U297
8	U297
9	U298

Wheel Alignment

Front wheel alignment is the position of the front wheels relative to each other and to the vehicle. It is determined, and must be maintained to provide safe, accurate steering, directional stability, and minimum tire wear. Many factors are involved in wheel alignment, and adjustments are provided to return those that might change due to normal wear to their original value. The factors which determine wheel alignment are dependent on one another; therefore, when one of the factors is adjusted, the others must be adjusted to compensate.

Descriptions of these factors and their effects on the car are provided below. Adjustment specifications for each model year are given at the beginning of each Car Section.

Camber

Camber angle is the number of degrees that the centerline of the wheel is inclined from the vertical when viewed from the front. A small degree of positive camber reduces loading of the outer wheel bearing, and allows for easier steering.

Caster

Caster angle is the number of degrees that a line drawn through the steering knuckle pivots is inclined from the vertical, toward the front or rear of the car. A small degree of positive caster improves directional stability and decreases susceptibility to crosswinds or road surface deviations.

Steering Axis Inclination

Steering axis inclination is the number of degrees that a line drawn through the steering knuckle pivots is inclined to the vertical, when viewed from the front of the car. This, in combination with caster, is responsible for directional stability and self-centering of the steering. As the steering knuckle swings from lock to lock, the spindle generates an arc (see illustration), the high point being the straight ahead position of the wheel. Due to this arc, as the wheel turns, the front of the car is raised. The weight of the car acts against this lift, and attempts to return the spindle to the high point of the arc, resulting in self-centering when the steering wheel is released, and straight line stability.

Included Angle

Included angle is the sum of the camber angle and the steering axis inclination. This angle is determined by the design of the steering knuckle forging and must remain constant. Therefore, if a different camber

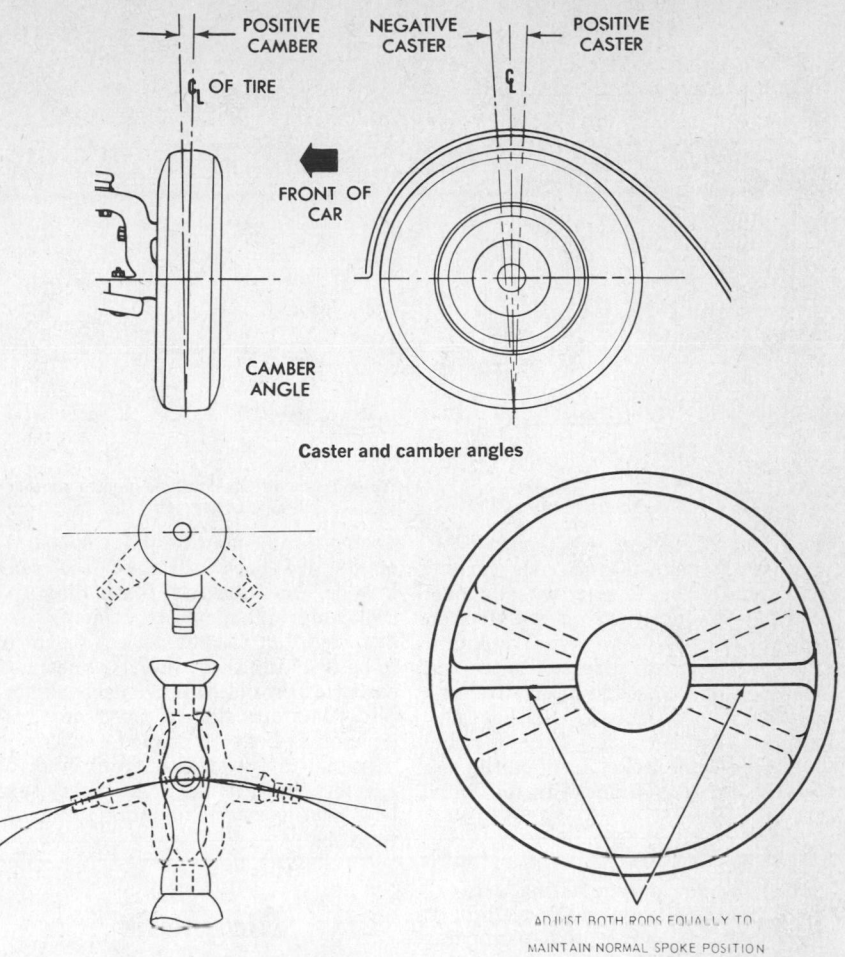

Caster and camber angles

Arc generated by the spindle as the steering knuckle turns

Steering wheel spoke alignment

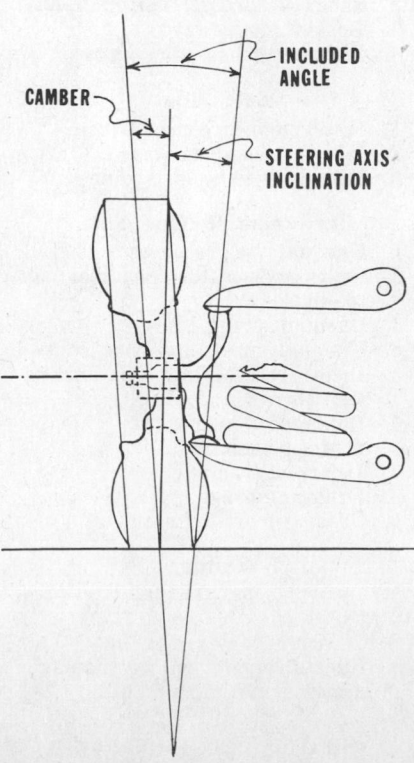

Camber, steering axis, and included angle

angle is necessary to make the included angle on both sides identical, a bent spindle or steering knuckle is indicated. When indicated, the damaged suspension member must be replaced, to permit accurate front wheel alignment. Since steering knuckle damage is most commonly due to impact on the lower portion of the wheel (i.e., hitting curb), the side with the greater included angle (camber angle same on each side) will often be found to have a bent spindle.

Toe-In

Toe-in is the difference of the distance between the centers of the front and rear of the front wheels measured at spindle height. It is most commonly measured in inches, but is occasionally referred to as an angle between the wheels. Toe-in is necessary to compensate for the tendency of the wheels to deflect rearward while in motion. Due to this tendency, the wheels of a vehicle with properly adjusted toe-in are traveling straight forward when the vehicle itself is traveling straight forward, resulting in directional stability and minimum tire wear.

Steering wheel spoke misalignment is often an indication of incorrect

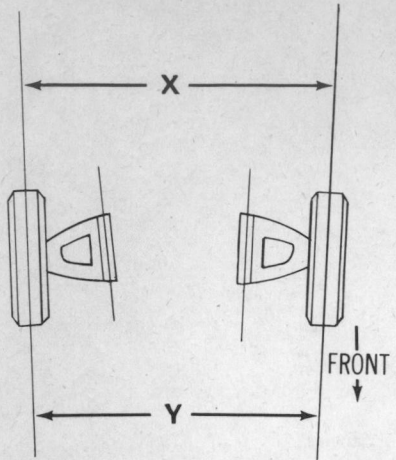

X-Y=Toe-In

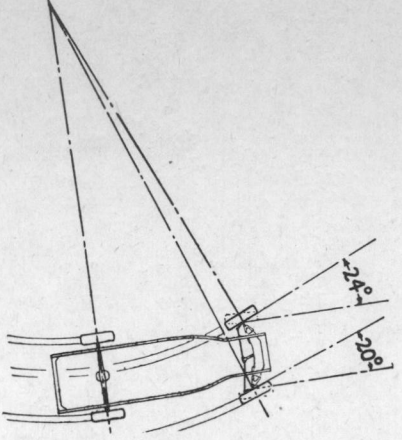

Toe-out. Inside wheel turns a greater number of degrees

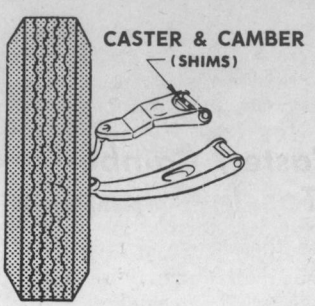

CASTER & CAMBER (SHIMS)

Location of caster and camber adjustments for type 1
(© Snap-On Tools Corp)

front end alignment. Care should be exercised when aligning the front end to maintain steering wheel spoke position. When adjusting the tie rod ends, adjust each an equal amount (in the opposite direction) to increase or decrease toe-in. If, following toe-in adjustment, further adjustments are necessary to center the steering wheel spokes, adjust the tie rod ends an equal amount in the same direction.

Steering Radius

When a car is negotiating a turn, the outer wheel follows the path of a circle of a larger radius than the inner wheel. For this reason, the inner wheel must be steered to a somewhat larger angle than the outer wheel. This value (known as the Ackerman effect) is designed into the steering linkage; therefore, if alignment is adjusted properly, and the steering radius (or toe-out on turns) appears to be incorrect, it is indicated that the steering arms or the linkage is bent.

Tracking

Tracking is the relationship between the paths traveled by the front and rear wheels when the vehicle is traveling in a straight line. When a car is tracking correctly, the path of the rear wheels will duplicate, or evenly straddle the path of the front wheels. Observing the car from the rear as it is driven away in a straight line will often make incorrect tracking evident.

If incorrect tracking is indicated, check as follows: Drop a plumb line from each lower ball joint, and from a point at each end of the rear axle, and mark the points on the ground with chalk. Measure these points from front to rear and diagonally. If the diagonal measurements are different (a tolerance of +¼″ is acceptable), but the longitudinal measurements are the same, the frame is swayed (diamond shaped). If the di-

agonal and longitudinal measurements are both different, the rear axle is misaligned. If both diagonal and longitudinal measurements are different, but the car does not appear to be tracking incorrectly, a kneeback condition is indicated. Kneeback implies that one side of the front suspension is bent or pushed back. It is possible to align the front end to specifications, and, if kneeback exists, have very poor handling characteristics.

Diagnosis

Hard Ride
1. Excessive tire pressure
2. Shock absorbers malfunctioning
3. Broken spring
4. Worn suspension bushings

Soft Ride
1. Insufficient tire pressure
2. Worn shock absorbers
3. Collapsed or weak spring

Car Veers to One Side
1. Unequal tire pressures
2. Incorrect caster, camber or toe-in
3. Unequal spring rates
4. Unequal shock absorber control
5. Incorrect steering axis inclination (bent spindle)
6. Damaged suspension components or bushings
7. Incorrect tracking
8. Dragging brake
9. Grease on brake lining

Wander
1. Incorrect or unequal tire pressures
2. Incorrect caster or toe-in
3. Excessively worn or damaged suspension components

Hard or Erratic Steering
1. Insufficient tire pressure
2. Lack of lubrication

3. Binding or damaged steering column, steering gear, or linkage
4. Loose power steering pump belt, or poor pump operation
5. Worn or damaged suspension components

Tires Wear in Center
1. Excessive tire pressure

Tires Wear on Both Edges
1. Insufficient tire pressure

Tires Wear Evenly on One Edge
1. Incorrect camber or toe-in
2. Bent or damaged suspension components

Tires Wear Unevenly on One Edge
1. Insufficient tire pressure
2. Incorrect camber or toe-in
3. Out of round wheel and/or tire
4. Loose steering linkage
5. Severe cornering

Tires Wear Unequally
1. Unequal tire pressure
2. Unequal tire size
3. Incorrect toe-in or camber
4. Loose or bent steering linkage

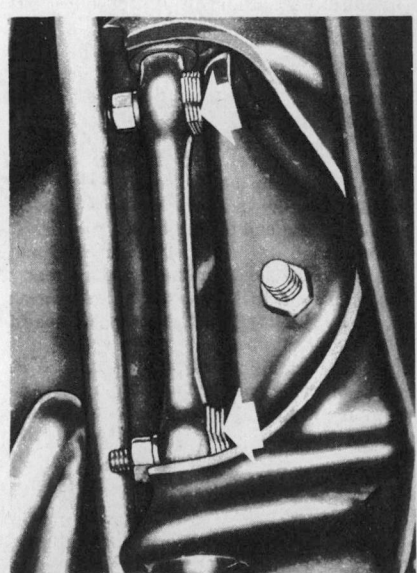

Typical type 1 caster and camber adjusting shim location
(© Chevrolet Div, G.M. Corp)

Squeal on Cornering
1. Insufficient tire pressure
2. Incorrect toe-in or camber
3. Severe cornering

Caster, Camber and Toe-In Adjustment

Use the Service Procedure Index at the start of this section to relate these section numbers to makes and models.

Section 1

Caster and Camber are controlled by shims between the frame bracket and the upper suspension arm pivot shaft.

To adjust caster, remove shims from the front bolt and replace them at the rear bolt, or vice versa. To adjust camber, add or remove the same number of shims from each bolt.

Keep in mind when loosening the bolts that the upper suspension arm is supporting the weight of the vehicle. Loosen the bolts only a sufficient amount to remove the shims.

Adjust toe-in by loosening the clamps on the sleeves at the outer ends of the tie-rod, and turning the sleeves an equal amount in the opposite direction, to maintain steering wheel spoke alignment while adjusting toe-in.

Section 2

Caster is adjusted by lengthening or shortening the struts at the frame crossmember. To adjust, turn both nuts an equal number of turns in the same direction. Lengthening the strut increases negative caster. One turn of the nuts changes caster approximately ½°.

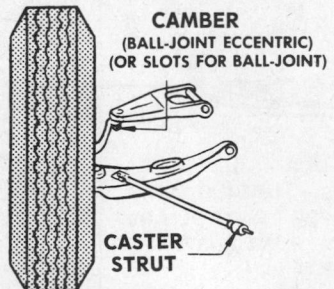

CAMBER
(BALL-JOINT ECCENTRIC)
(OR SLOTS FOR BALL-JOINT)

CASTER STRUT

Location of caster and camber adjustments for type 2
(© Snap-On Tools Corp)

Camber is adjusted by turning the camber eccentric located in the steering knuckle upper support. Turning the eccentric changes the camber by moving the steering knuckle in or out. Loosen the ball joint stud locknut and tap the knuckle to free the eccentric, being careful not to strike the brake line or ball joint seal. Turn the ec-

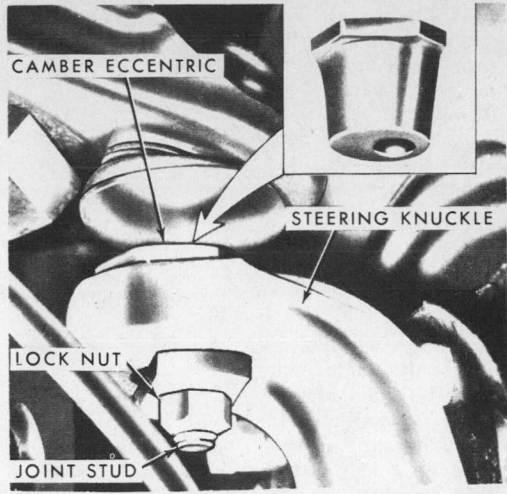

Details of type 2 camber adjustment
(© Cadillac Div, G.M. Corp)

centric until camber is within specifications. The stud must be positioned to the rear of the eccentric in order to maintain correct steering geometry. Tighten the ball joint stud nut to 60 ft. lbs.

Adjust toe-in by loosening the clamp bolts, and turning the adjuster sleeves at the outer ends of the tie rod. Turn each sleeve an equal amount in the opposite direction, in order to maintain steering wheel spoke alignment.

Section 3

Caster is adjusted by lengthening or shortening the struts at the frame crossmember. To adjust, turn both nuts an equal number of turns in the same direction. Caster adjustments

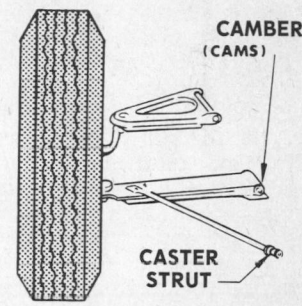

CAMBER
(CAMS)

CASTER STRUT

Location of caster and camber adjustments for type 3
(© Snap-On Tools Corp)

should be within ¼° of the opposing side of the car.

To adjust camber, loosen the lower control arm pivot bolt and rotate the eccentrics.

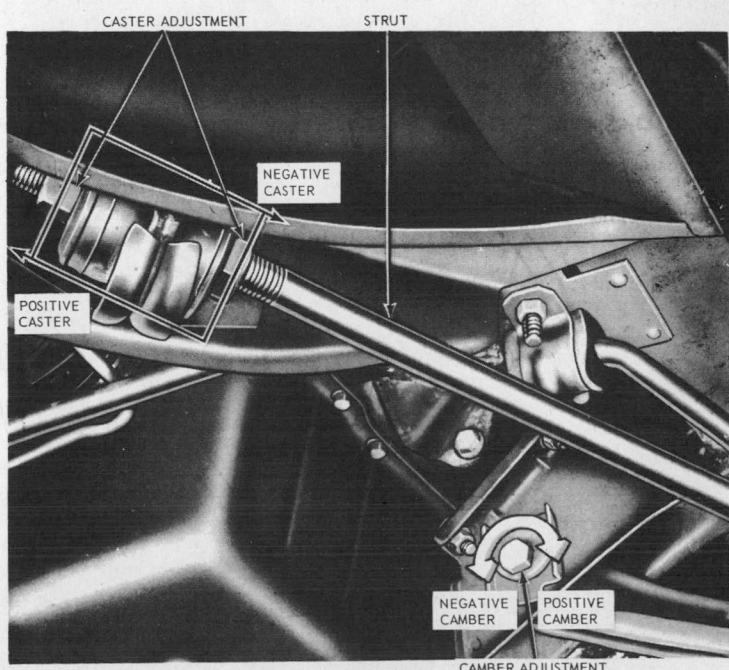

Type 3 caster and camber adjustment points
(© Ford Motor Co)

Adjust toe-in by loosening the clamp bolts, and turning the adjuster sleeves at the outer ends of the tie rod. Turn each sleeve an equal amount in the opposite direction, in order to maintain steering wheel spoke alignment.

Section 4

Front end height should be checked, as explained in the car section, before front end alignment.

Caster and camber are controlled by eccentric (cam) bolts. The cam bolts are located at the ends of the upper control arm shafts on all models except the Imperial. They are on the underside of the upper control arm pivot bar attaching bracket on the Imperial. To adjust the caster, loosen the eccentric (cam) bolt nuts and turn either of the eccentric bolts. Camber is adjusted by turning both eccentrics an equal amount. Recheck caster after setting camber. Torque the eccentric (cam) bolts to 65–70 ft lbs (all Chrysler Corp. except Imperial), and 160 ft lbs (Imperial).

To adjust toe-in, loosen the tie rod clamp bolts and turn the adjuster sleeves at the outer ends of the tie-rod an equal amount in opposite directions so that steering wheel spoke alignment is maintained.

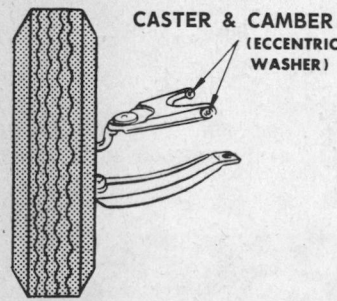

CASTER & CAMBER (ECCENTRIC WASHER)

Location of caster and camber adjustment for type 4 (except Imperial)
(© Snap-On Tools Corp)

Section 5

Front end height should be checked, as explained in the car section, before front end alignment.

Caster and camber are controlled by the positioning of the upper control arm pivot bar adjusting bolts. To adjust caster, loosen one of the pivot bar adjusting bolts or nuts and slide one end of the bar either inboard or outboard in its elongated mounting hole in the cross-member. Camber is adjusted by loosening both the pivot bar adjusting bolts or nuts and sliding both ends of the bar an equal amount.

NOTE: Chrysler recommends the use of a special pry bar no. C-4196 for the adjusting operation on the upper control arm pivot bar.

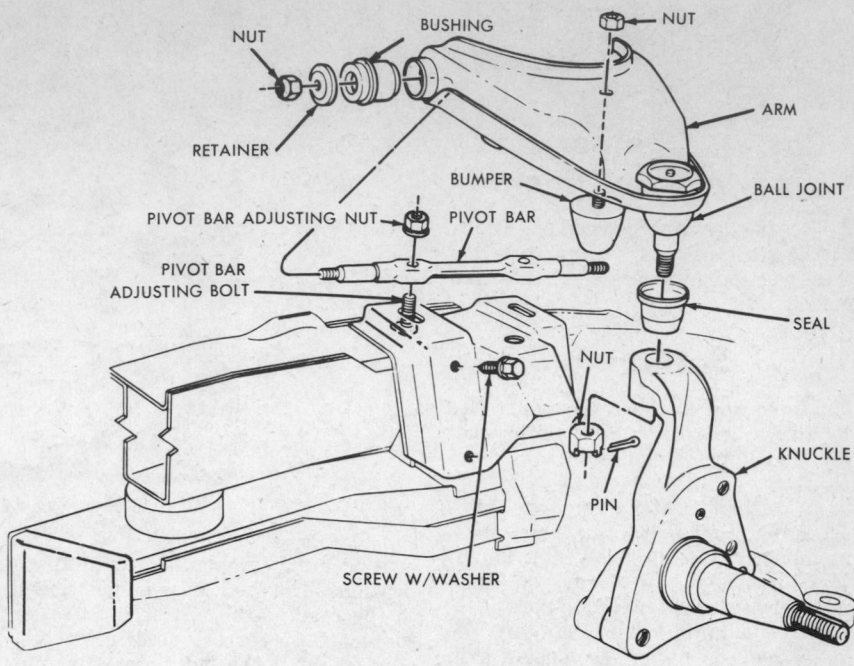

Type 5 upper control arm showing location of pivot bar and pivot bar adjusting nut and bolt
(© Chrysler Corp)

Type 5 caster and camber adjusting pry bar
(© Chrysler Corp)

Recheck caster after setting camber. Torque the pivot bar adjusting bolts or nuts to 160 ft lbs.

To adjust toe-in, loosen the tie rod clamp bolts and turn the adjuster sleeves at the outer ends of the tie rod an equal amount in opposite directions, so that steering wheel spoke alignment is maintained.

Section 6

Caster and camber are not fully adjustable, but they may be corrected. Camber can be increased by approximately one degree by removing the

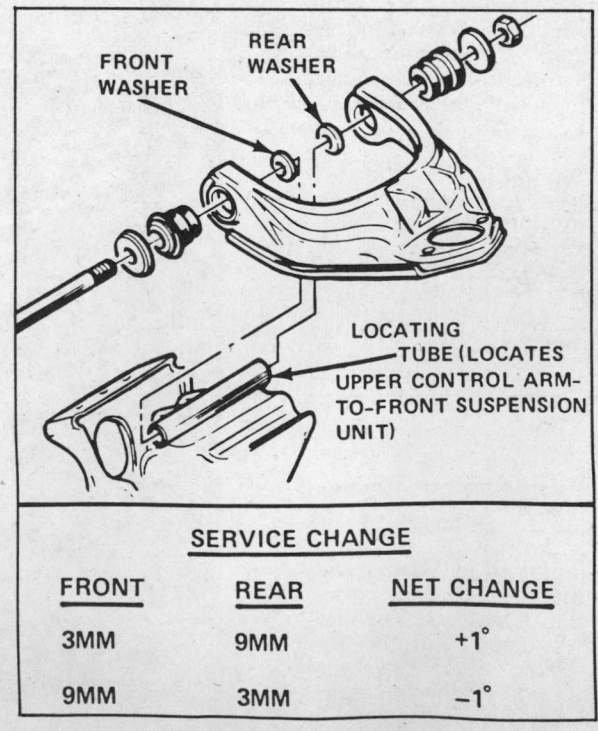

FRONT	REAR	NET CHANGE
3MM	9MM	+1°
9MM	3MM	−1°

SERVICE CHANGE

Type 6 caster adjustment
(© Chevrolet Div., G.M. Corp.)

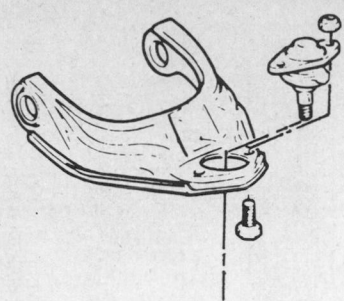

NOTE: TO INCREASE CAMBER, DISCONNECT UPPER BALL JOINT, ROTATE 180° TO POSITION "FLAT" OF FLANGE INBOARD, THEN RECONNECT BALLJOINT.

Type 6 camber adjustment
(© Chevrolet Div., G.M. Corp.)

upper ball joint, turning it around, and reinstalling it with the flat on the upper flange on the inboard side of the control arm. Caster can be changed one degree by changing the position of the washers between the legs of the upper control arm. Placing the thinner washer in front will increase caster, while placing it at the back will reduce caster.

Toe-in is adjusted by loosening the nuts at the steering knuckle end of each tie-rod and the rubber cover at the other end, then turning the rod.

Section 7

Install Ford tool T69P-3000-A or its equivalent on the frame rail, position the hooks around the upper control arm pivot shaft, and tighten the adjusting nuts of the tool slightly. Loosen the pivot shaft retaining bolts to permit adjustment.

To adjust caster, loosen or tighten either the front or rear adjusting nut. After adjusting caster, adjust camber by loosening or tightening both nuts an equal amount. Tighten the shaft retaining bolts to specifications, remove the tool, and recheck the adjustments.

Adjust toe-in by loosening the clamp bolts, and turning the adjuster sleeves at the outer ends of the tie-rod. Turn the sleeves an equal amount in the opposite direction, to maintain steering wheel spoke alignment.

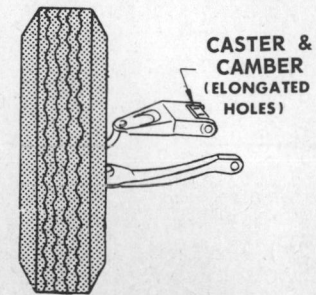

CASTER & CAMBER (ELONGATED HOLES)

Location of caster and camber adjustments for type 7
(© Snap-On Tools Corp)

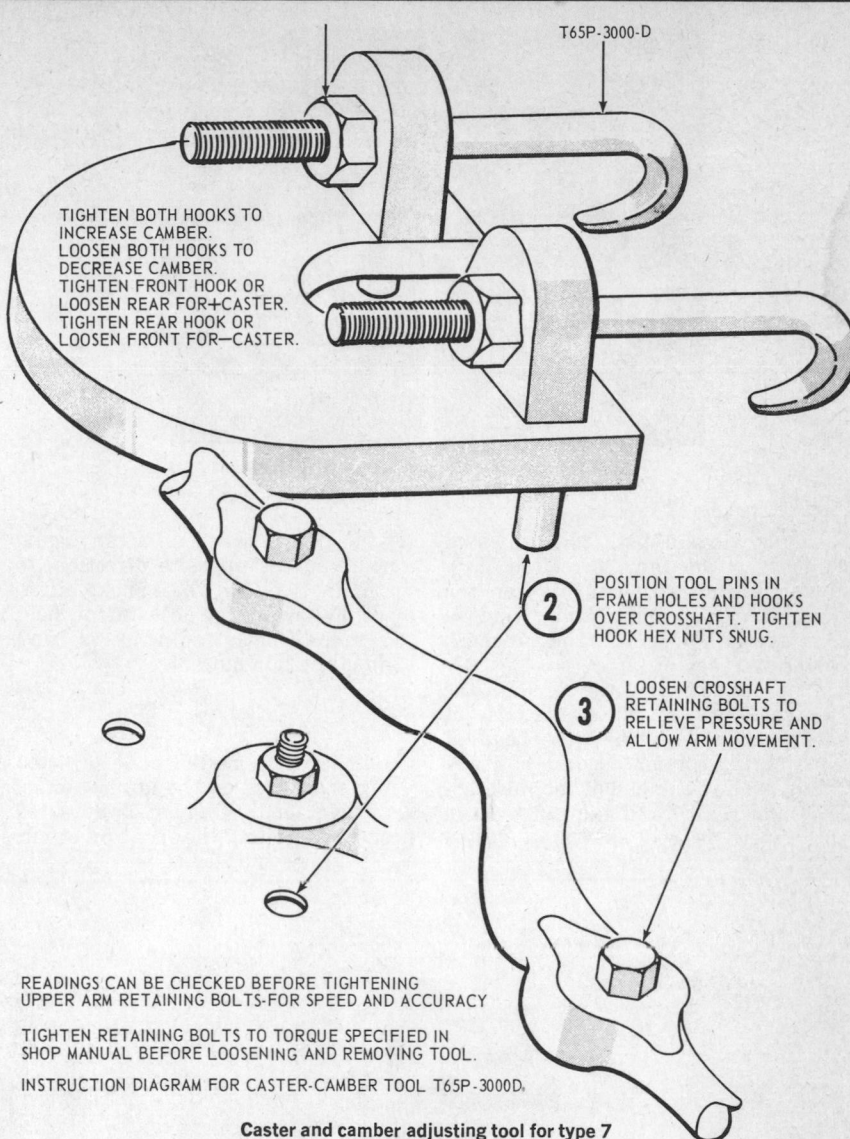

T65P-3000-D

TIGHTEN BOTH HOOKS TO INCREASE CAMBER. LOOSEN BOTH HOOKS TO DECREASE CAMBER. TIGHTEN FRONT HOOK OR LOOSEN REAR FOR +CASTER. TIGHTEN REAR HOOK OR LOOSEN FRONT FOR —CASTER.

2 — POSITION TOOL PINS IN FRAME HOLES AND HOOKS OVER CROSSHAFT. TIGHTEN HOOK HEX NUTS SNUG.

3 — LOOSEN CROSSHAFT RETAINING BOLTS TO RELIEVE PRESSURE AND ALLOW ARM MOVEMENT.

READINGS CAN BE CHECKED BEFORE TIGHTENING UPPER ARM RETAINING BOLTS-FOR SPEED AND ACCURACY

TIGHTEN RETAINING BOLTS TO TORQUE SPECIFIED IN SHOP MANUAL BEFORE LOOSENING AND REMOVING TOOL.

INSTRUCTION DIAGRAM FOR CASTER-CAMBER TOOL T65P-3000D

Caster and camber adjusting tool for type 7
(© Ford Motor Co)

Section 8

Position one Ford tool T74P-3000 or its equivalent at each end of the upper control arm, pivot shaft with the leg of the tools through the holes in the sheet metal (see illustration).

Turn the adjusting bolts until they are solidly contacting sheet metal, and loosen the pivot shaft retaining bolts.

Caster is adjusted by turning the front and rear adjusting bolts in the opposite direction. Camber is ad-

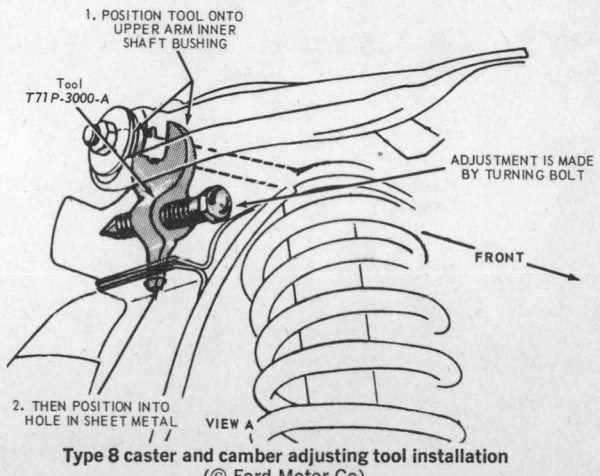

1. POSITION TOOL ONTO UPPER ARM INNER SHAFT BUSHING

Tool T71P-3000-A

ADJUSTMENT IS MADE BY TURNING BOLT

FRONT

2. THEN POSITION INTO HOLE IN SHEET METAL   VIEW A

Type 8 caster and camber adjusting tool installation
(© Ford Motor Co)

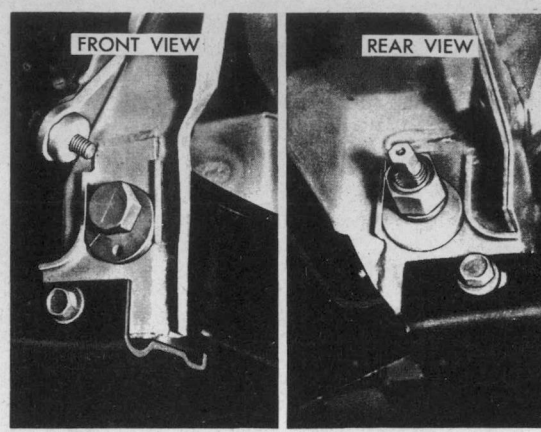

Type 9 camber (left) and caster (right) adjustments
(© Chevrolet Div, G.M. Corp)

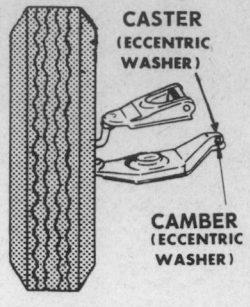

Location of caster and camber adjustments
for type 9
(© Snap-On Tools Corp)

justed by turning both bolts an equal amount in the same direction. Following the adjustments, tighten the pivot shaft retaining bolts, remove the adjusting tools, and recheck caster and camber.

Prior to adjusting toe-in, align the straight ahead marks at the base of the steering wheel and the head of the steering column. Loosen both the clamp at the outer end of the rack bellows and the tie rod jam nuts. Turn the inner tie rod shafts to adjust toe-in. Turn the shafts an equal amount in the opposite direction, to maintain steering wheel spoke alignment. Following the adjustment, hold the inner shafts with pliers, and tighten the jam nuts.

Section 9

Camber and caster are adjusted using eccentrics on the lower control arm pivot bolts. Camber is adjusted first, by loosening the front pivot nut and rotating the eccentric. Tighten the front, and loosen the rear pivot nuts. Adjust caster by rotating the rear eccentric, and tighten the rear pivot nut while holding the bolt in position. Recheck camber and caster.

To adjust toe-in, loosen the clamps on the adjusting sleeves at the outer ends of the tie rod, and turn each sleeve an equal amount in the opposite direction, to maintain steering wheel spoke alignment while adjusting toe-in.

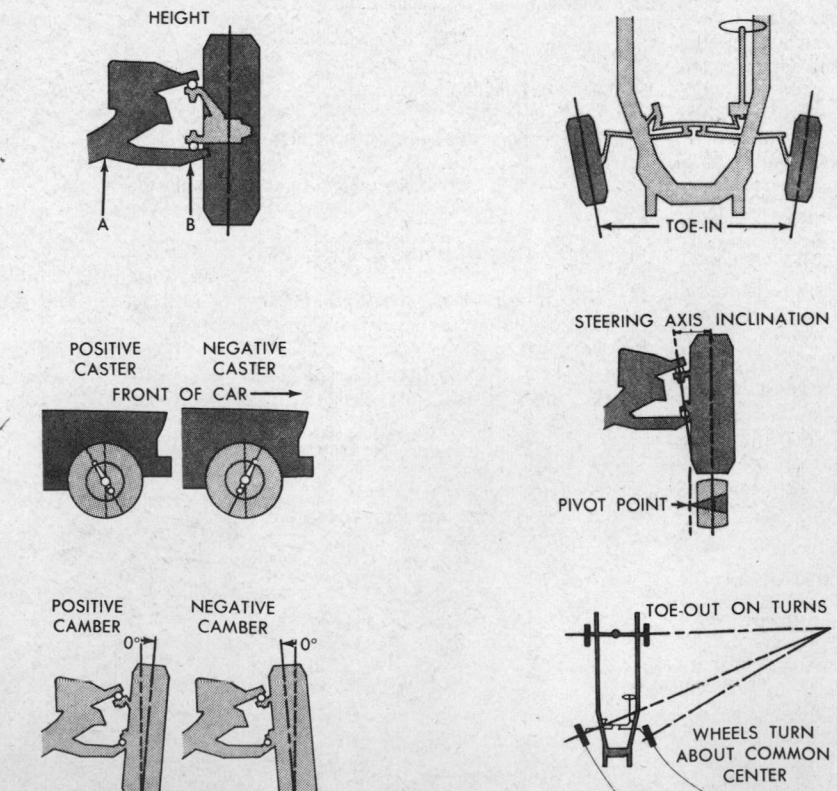

(© Chrysler Corp)

Brakes

Brake Diagnosis Chart U300

Drum Brakes (Duo-Servo Self Adjusting
Type) U300
 Drum Brake Application Chart U299
 Star and Screw Adjuster Type Drum
  Brake Service U300
  Adjustment U300
  Testing Adjuster U300
  Brake Shoe Removal U301
  Brake Shoe Installation U302
 Expanding Strut Adjuster Type Drum
  Brake Service U303
  Adjuster Disassembly U303
  Adjuster Assembly U303
  Shoe Replacement U304
 Pin and Slot Adjuster Type Brake
  Service U304
  Shoe Replacement U304

Disc Brakes U305
 Disc Brake Application and Specifications
  Chart U306
 Description and Inspection U305
 Bendix 4 Piston Disc Brake Service .. U305
  Pad Replacement U305
  Caliper Assembly Service U305
  Caliper Alignment (American Motors) .. U308
 Delco-Moraine 4 Piston Disc Brake
  Service U308
  Pad Replacement U308
  Caliper Assembly Service U309

Kelsey-Hayes 4 Piston Disc Brake
  Service U309
  Pad Replacement U309
 Caliper Assembly Service U309
 Delco-Moraine Single Piston Disc Brake
  Service U310
  Pad Replacement U310
  Caliper Assembly Service U311
 Kelsey-Hayes Single Piston Disc Brake
  (Chrysler Corporation) Service U311
  Pad Replacement U311
   Floating Caliper U311
   Sliding Caliper U311
  Caliper Removal and Installation .. U311
  Caliper Assembly Service U312
   Floating Caliper U312
   Sliding Caliper U313
 Kelsey-Hayes Single Piston Disc Brake
  (American Motors) Service U313
  Pad Replacement, 1975 and Later
   Sliding Caliper U313
  Sliding Caliper Assembly Service, 1975
   and Later U314
 Kelsey-Hayes Single Piston Floating
  Caliper Disc Brake (Ford) Service .. U315
  Pad Replacement U315
  Caliper Assembly Service U315
 Ford Single Piston Sliding Caliper Brake
  Service U316
  Pad Replacement U316
  Caliper Assembly Service U317
 Disc Service—All Cars U317
  Disc Replacement U317

 Lateral Runout U317
 Parallelism U318
 Rear Disc Brakes—Imperial U318
  Pad Replacement and Caliper Service U318
  Parking Brake Service U318
 Rear Disc Brakes—Chevrolet Corvette U319
  Pad Replacement and Caliper Service U319
  Parking Brake Service U319
 Rear Disc Brakes—Ford Motor Company U319
  Caliper Removal and Installation .. U320
  Caliper Overhaul U321

Hydraulic Cylinders and Valves U322
 Master Cylinder Service U322
 Wheel Cylinder Service U323
 Proportioning Valves U323
 Metering Valves U324
 Pressure Differential Warning Valves . U324

Brake Hydraulic System Bleeding U325
 Gravity Bleeding Procedure U325
 Pressure Bleeding Disc Brakes U325

Power Brakes U325
 Vacuum Operated Booster U325
  Power Brake Booster Troubleshooting U325
  Overhaul U325
 Hydro-Boost U325
  Hydro-Boost System Checks U326
  Hydro-Boost Tests U326
  Hydro-Boost Troubleshooting U327
  Overhaul U327

DRUM BRAKE APPLICATION CHART

Car and Years	Brake Type	Self-Adjuster Type
AMERICAN MOTORS		
1970-77 all models	Duo-Servo	Star & Screw
CHRYSLER CORP.		
1970-77 all models	Duo-Servo	Star & Screw
FORD MOTOR CO.		
1970-77 all models	Duo-Servo	Star & Screw
GENERAL MOTORS CORP.		
1970-77 all models except below	Duo-Servo	Star & Screw
1971-75 Astre, Monza, Skyhawk, Starfire, Vega	Duo-Servo	Expanding Strut
1976-77 Chevette	Duo-Servo	Pin and Slot

Brakes
Brake Diagnosis Chart

Condition	Mechanical	Hydraulic	Vacuum (Power Unit)
Low pedal (Excessive pedal travel to apply brakes)	FGIMfg	T	k
Spongy Pedal (A springy sensation of pedal upon application)	I	PQU	
Hard Pedal (Excessive pedal pressure needed to stop vehicle)	AFGKVaf	RTUW	cehk
Fading Pedal (A falling away of pedal under steady foot pressure)	I	PQSTW	
Grabbing or Pulling	ADEGHIKL NVXYZa	RW	k
Noise (Squealing, clicking or scraping noise)	FGHILMN		
Chatter or Shudder (May be accompanied by brake roughness or pedal pumping)	DGILNO		
Dragging Brakes (Slow or incomplete release of brakes)	ABCFGHK LVafg	RUTW	k

A. Pedal linkage binding. (Check by bleeding one wheel cylinder using light pedal effort. Observe for smooth full travel of pedal)

B. Parking brake cables and linkage sticking, dirty or corroded.

C. Parking brake improperly adjusted (too loose or too tight).

D. Wheel bearings loose.

E. Front wheel alignment or uneven tire tread.

F. Brake shoes improperly adjusted. Automatic adjuster parts corroded, distorted or broken.

G. Brake linings or disc pads worn, contaminated or distorted.

H. Shoe return spring weak, broken, improperly installed.

I. Drums cracked, thin (beyond 0.060" of original specifications), scored, hard spotted, or out of round.

K. Brake support plate ledges rusted or grooved.

L. Support plate loose, worn, or distorted.

M. Disc brake pad "knock back" (loose or worn wheel bearings or steering parts).

N. Caliper not aligned with disc or loose.

O. Disc has excessive lateral runout. Excessively out of parallel.

P. Hydraulic system fluid has air in it, improper quality (low boiling point).

Q. Hoses and lines soft or weak (expanding under pressure).

R. Hose sand lines kinked, collapsed, dented, or clogged.

S. Hoses and lines loosely connected, ruptured, or damaged (causing leakage).

T. Master cylinder primary cup worn or damaged, bore worn, rough, corroded.

U. Master cylinder check valve faulty, or compensator port blocked.

V. Wheel or caliper cylinder pistons frozen or seized.

W. Wheel or caliper cylinder cups swollen, worn or damaged seals; bores rough or corroded.

X. Wheel or caliper cylinders mismatched (size).

Y. Check tire pressure.

Z. Rear wheels (both) grabbing. Rear brake line proportioning valve defective—replace.

a. Power unit valve rod linkage binding.

c. Vacuum lines loose, broken, collapsed. Engine vacuum low.

e. Vacuum check valve defective or sticking.

f. Power unit hydraulic pushrod improperly adjusted.

g. Air trapped in hub cavity of master cylinder. Inspect and remove master cylinder boot if installed.

h. Air filter dirty, clogged.

k. Corrosion or lack of lubrication in power cylinder. Control valve, power cylinder, piston or diaphragm defective.

Servicing Drum Brakes

Refer to the Drum Brake Application Chart for adjuster applications.

Star and Screw Adjuster

The duo-servo brake, with star and screw type self-adjusters, is used on most late-model American cars. The same basic brake unit has been used on all cars. General Motors cars use a rod-operated lever to turn the star-wheel, while all others use a cable-operated lever. This is the only difference, other than size, between units used on different models.

Adjustment

1. Remove the access slot plug from the backing plate or front of drum on GM cars. On some late-model GM cars, there is no access slot in the backing plate or in the front of the drums. It has been filled in and must be punched out to gain access to the adjuster. Complete the adjustment and cover the hole with a plug to prevent entrance of dirt and water.

2. Using a brake adjusting spoon or screwdriver, pry downward on the end of the tool (starwheel teeth moving up) to tighten the brakes, or upward on the end of the tool (starwheel teeth moving down) to loosen the brakes.

   NOTE: it will be necessary to use a small screwdriver to hold the adjusting lever away from the starwheel. Be careful not to bend the adjusting lever.

3. When the brakes are tight almost to the point of being locked, back off on the starwheel until the wheel is able to rotate freely. The starwheel on each set of brakes (front or rear) must be backed off the same number of turns to prevent brake pull from side to side.

4. When all four brakes are adjusted, check brake pedal travel and then make several stops, while backing the car up, to equalize all the wheels.

Testing Adjuster

1. Raise the vehicle on a hoist, with a helper in the car, to apply the brakes.

2. Loosen the brakes by holding the adjuster lever away from the

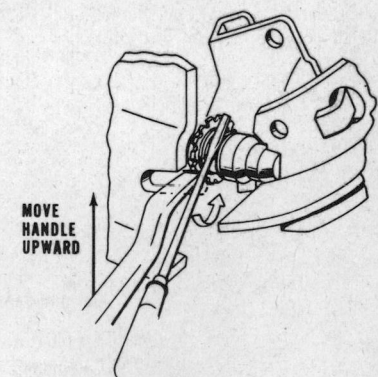

MOVE HANDLE UPWARD

Self-adjuster method. Push the self-adjusting lever out of the way with a small screwdriver or ice pick to back off star wheel.

starwheel and backing off the starwheel approximately 30 notches.

3. Spin the wheel and brake drum in reverse and apply the brakes. The movement of the secondary shoe should pull the adjuster lever up, and when the brakes are released the lever should snap down and turn the star-wheel.

4. If the automatic adjuster doesn't work, the drum must be removed and the adjuster components inspected carefully for breakage, wear, or improper installation.

Brake Shoe Removal

NOTE: if you are not thoroughly familiar with the procedures involved in brake replacement, disassemble and assemble one side at a time, leaving the other wheel intact, as a reference.

1. Remove the brake drum.
2. Place the hollow end of a brake spring service tool on the brake shoe anchor pin and twist it to disengage one of the brake retaining springs. Repeat this operation to remove the other spring. On GM cars, grasp the secondary shoe return spring with a pair of pliers and lift upward on the spring to disengage it from the automatic adjuster link.

Caution Be careful that the springs do not slip off the tool during removal, as the springs could break loose and cause personal injury.

3. Reach behind the brake backing plate and place a finger on the end of one of the brake hold-down mounting pins. Using a pair of pliers, grasp the washer on the top of the hold-down spring that corresponds to the pin that you are holding. Push

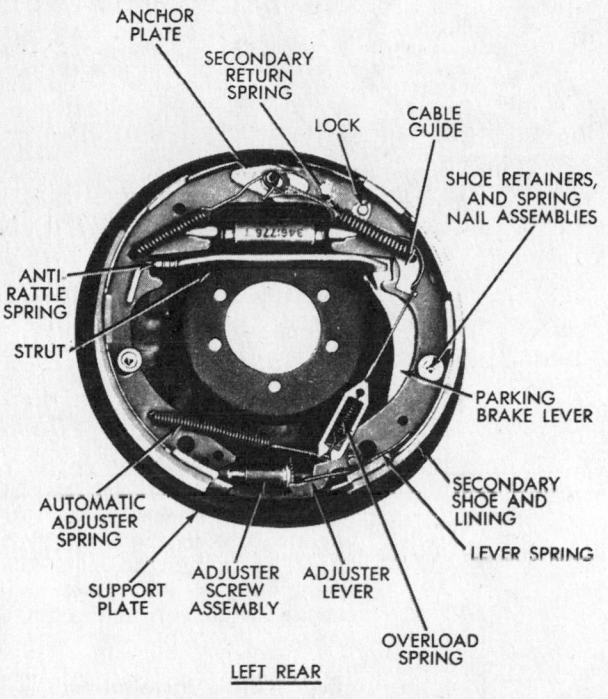

Bendix duo-servo self-adjusting brake—Chrysler Corp. 11 in. type

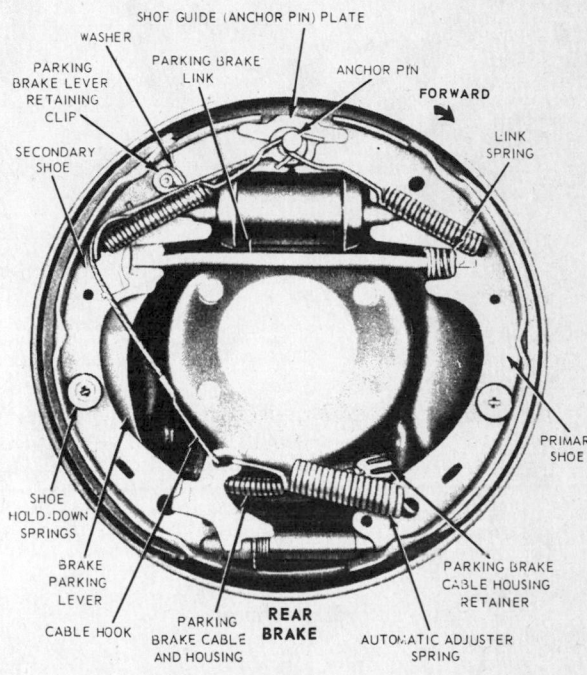

Bendix duo-servo self-adjusting brake—Ford type

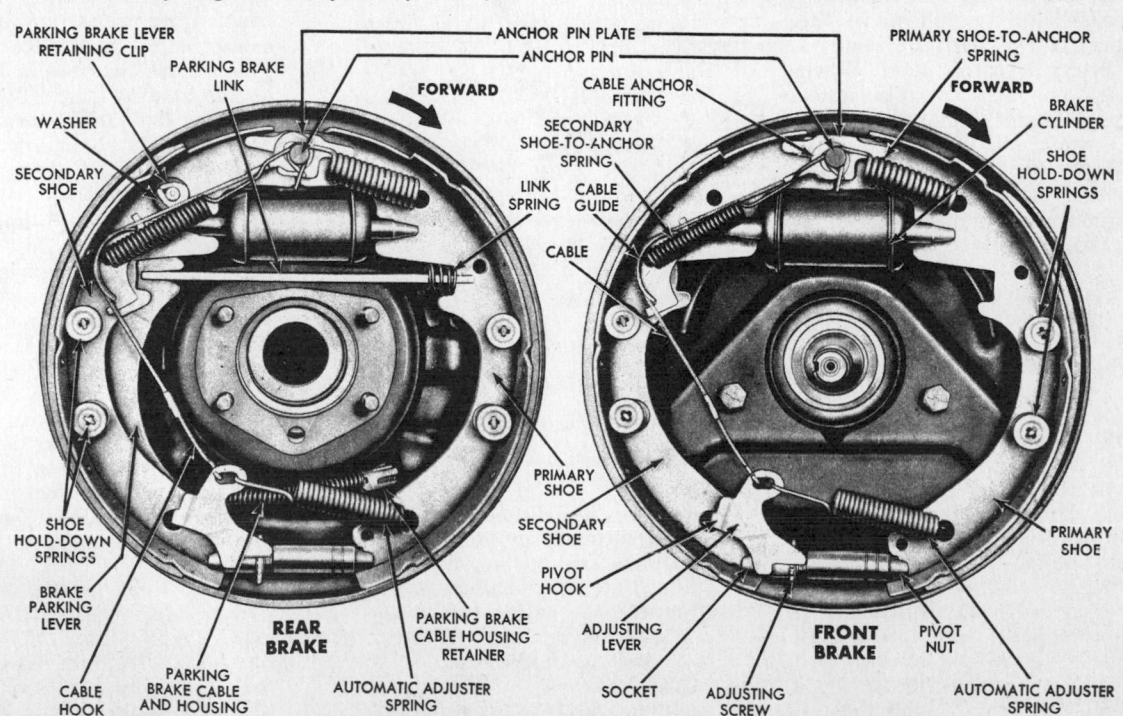

Bendix duo-servo self-adjusting brakes

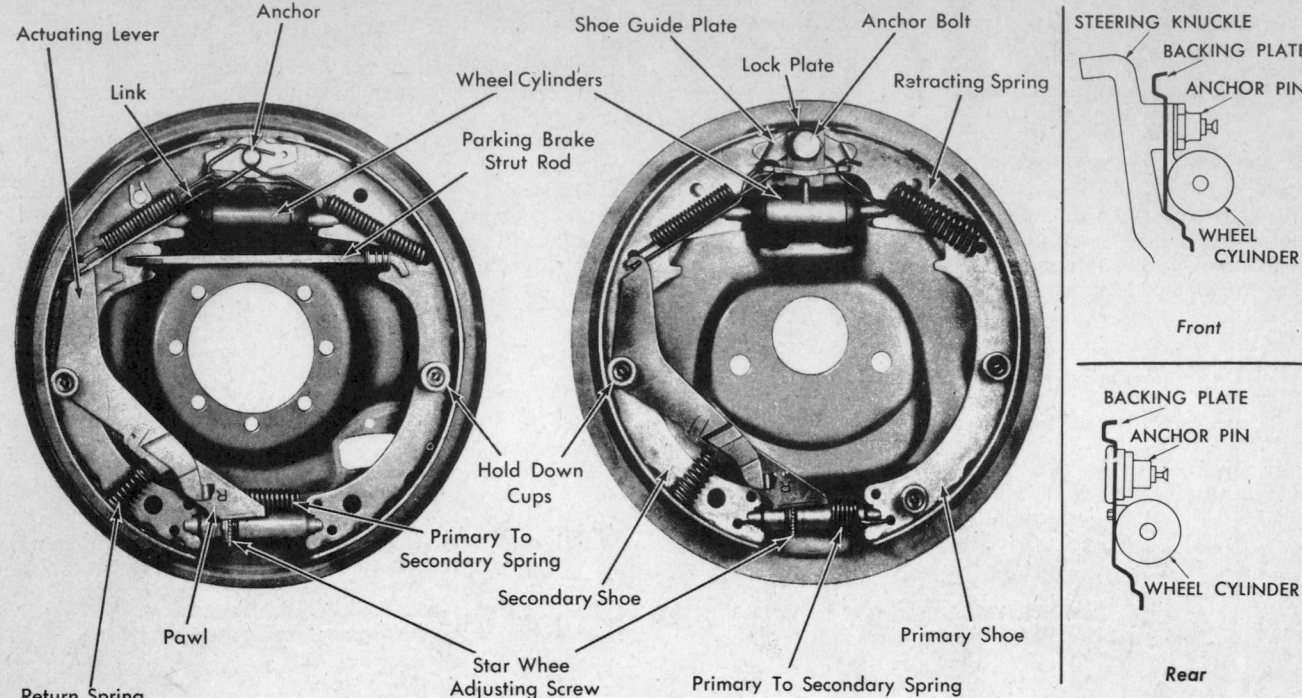

Bendix duo-servo self-adjusting brake—G.M. type

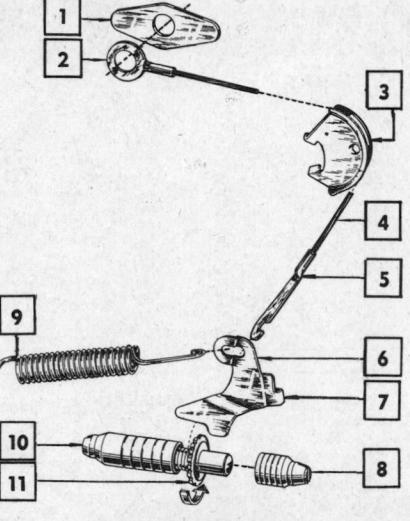

1 Shoe guide plate
2 Cable anchor fitting
3 Cable guide
4 Cable
5 Cable hook
6 Lever
7 Pivot hook
8 Socket
9 Spring—automatic adjuster
10 Pivot nut
11 Adjusting screw

Self-adjusting brake components

down on the pliers and turn them 90° to align the slot in the washer with the head on the spring mounting pin. Remove the spring and washer and repeat this operation on the hold-down spring of the other brake shoe.

4. Step 4 varies according to manufacturer:

On Ford and American Motors cars, place the tip of a screwdriver on the top of the brake adjusting screw and move the screwdriver upward to lift up on the brake adjusting lever. When there is enough slack in the automatic adjuster cable, disconnect the loop on the top of the cable from the anchor. Grasp the top of each brake shoe and move them outward to disengage from the wheel cylinder and parking brake link (if working on rear wheels). When the brake shoes are clear, lift them from the backing plate. Twist the shoes slightly and the automatic adjuster assembly will disassemble itself.

On GM cars, remove the automatic adjuster link. Remove the automatic adjuster lever, pivot, and override spring from the secondary spring as an assembly. Move the top of each brake shoe outward to clear the wheel cylinder pins and parking brake link (rear brakes). Lift the brakes from the backing plate and remove the adjusting screw.

On Chrysler cars, slide the automatic adjuster cable from the

anchor pin and disengage it from the adjusting lever. Remove the cable, overload spring, and cable guide. Disconnect the automatic adjuster lever return spring and remove the spring and lever. Move the top of the brake shoes outward to clear the wheel cylinder pins and parking brake link (rear brakes). Lift the brakes

from the backing plate and remove the adjusting screw.

5. If you are working on rear brakes, grasp the end of the brake cable spring with a pair of pliers and, using the brake lever as a fulcrum, pull the end of the spring away from the lever. Disengage the cable from the brake lever.

Brake Shoe Installation

1. If you are working on rear brakes, the brake cable must be connected to the secondary brake shoe before the shoe is installed on the backing plate. To do this, transfer the parking brake lever from the old secondary shoe to the new one. This is accomplished by spreading the bottom of the horseshoe clip and disengaging the lever. Position the lever on the new secondary shoe and install the spring washer and the horseshoe clip. Close the bottom of the clip after installing it. Grasp the metal tip of the parking brake cable with a pair of pliers. Position a pair of side cutters on the end of the cable coil spring and, using the pliers as a fulcrum, pull the coil spring back with the side cutters. Position the cable in the parking brake lever.

2. Apply a light coating of high-temperature grease to the brake shoe contact points on the backing plate. Position the primary brake shoe on the front of the backing plate and install the hold-down spring and washer

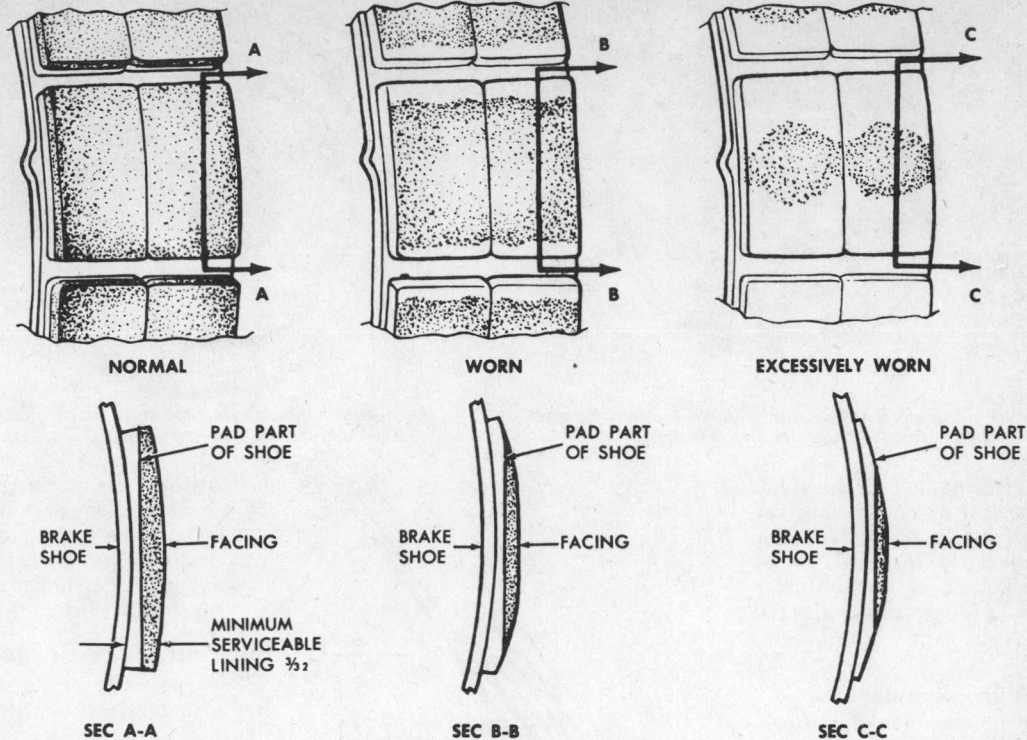

NORMAL   WORN   EXCESSIVELY WORN

SEC A-A   **SEC B-B**   **SEC C-C**

Metallic brake linings—Pontiac and Chevrolet

over the mounting pin. Install the secondary shoe on the rear of the backing plate.

3. If working on rear brakes, install the parking brake link between the primary brake shoe and the secondary brake shoe.

4. Step 4 varies according to manufacturer:

On Ford and American Motors cars, install the automatic adjuster cable loop end on the anchor pin. Make sure that the crimped side of the loop faces the backing plate.

On GM cars, assemble the automatic adjuster lever, pivot, and override spring and install to the secondary spring as an assembly.

On Chrysler, install the automatic adjuster lever and return spring. Install the adjuster overload spring and cable. One end of the cable engages with the adjusting lever while the other slips over the anchor pin underneath the primary and secondary return springs.

5. Install the return spring in the primary brake shoe and, using the tapered end of a brake spring service tool, slide the top of the spring onto the anchor pin.

Caution Be careful to make sure that the spring does not slip off the tool during installation, as the spring could break loose and cause personal injury.

6. Install the automatic adjuster cable guide in the secondary brake shoe, making sure that the flared hole in the cable guide is inside the hole in the brake shoe. Fit the cable into the groove in the top of the cable guide.

7. Install the secondary shoe return spring through the hole in the cable guide and the brake shoe. Using the brake spring tool, slide the top of the spring onto the anchor pin.

8. Clean the threads on the adjusting screw and apply a *light* coating of high-temperature grease to the threads. Screw the adjuster closed, then open it one-half turn.

9. Install the adjusting screw between the brake shoes with the star wheel nearest to the secondary shoe. Make sure that the star wheel is in a position that is accessible from the adjusting slot in the backing plate.

10. Install the short, hooked end of the automatic adjuster spring in the proper hole in the primary brake shoe.

11. Connect the hooked end of the automatic adjuster cable and the free end of the automatic adjuster spring in the slot in the top of the automatic adjuster lever.

12. Pull the automatic adjuster lever (the lever will pull the cable and spring with it) downward and to the left, and engage the pivot hook of the lever in the hole in the secondary brake shoe.

13. Check the entire brake assembly to make sure everything is installed properly. Make sure that the shoes engage the wheel cylinder properly and are flush on the anchor pin. Make sure that the automatic adjuster cable is flush on the anchor pin and in the slot on the back of cable guide. Make sure that the adjusting lever rests on the adjusting screw star wheel. Pull upward on the adjusting cable until the adjusting lever is free of the star wheel, then release the cable. The adjusting lever should snap back into place on the adjusting screw star wheel and turn the wheel one tooth.

14. Expand the brake adjusting screw until the brake drum will just fit over the brake shoes.

15. Install the wheel and drum and adjust the brakes. (See "Brake Adjustment.")

Expanding Strut Adjuster

Duo-servo brakes with expanding strut adjusters are used exclusively on 1971-75 GM subcompact cars.

Adjuster Disassembly

1. Remove the adjuster assembly from the wheel.
2. Separate the rod assembly from the adjuster locks.
3. Slide the rod off from the strut.

Adjuster Assembly

1. Assemble the adjuster lock to the strut, making sure that the index hole in the lock is lined up and

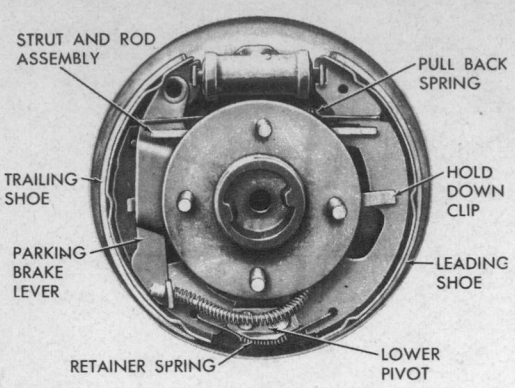

Bendix duo-servo self-adjusting brake—expanding strut type (© Chevrolet Div., G.M. Corp)

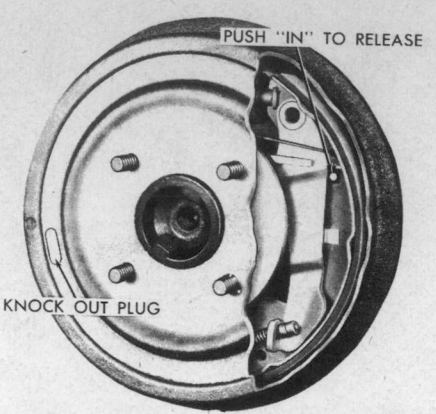

Release adjuster to remove drum on expanding strut rear brakes (© Chevrolet Div., G.M. Corp)

seated with the hole in the strut.

2. Slide the rod assembly onto the strut and over the adjuster locks. When properly installed, ½ of the index hole in the adjuster lock should be covered by the rod assembly.

Shoe Replacement

1. If the drum does not slip off easily, it will be necessary to knock out the metal plug in the drum and push in on the adjuster rod so that the spring will pull the shoes away from the drum. Remove the drum. The adjuster rod is at the 2 o'clock position on the left wheel and at the 10 o'clock position on the right wheel.
2. Release all tension from the parking brake equalizer.
3. Remove the parking brake cable from the lever next to the shoe. Allowing the lever to swing forward will engage the adjuster rod and change the adjustment position.
4. Remove the pull-back spring.
5. Remove the shoes from under the clips and lift out with the strut and adjuster assembly attached.
6. Separate the shoes, and remove the strut and adjuster assembly.
7. Remove the parking brake lever.
8. Remove the shoe hold-down clips only if they are broken or worn.
9. Using white grease, lubricate the six contact surfaces on the backing plate. Do not allow any grease to contact the brake linings.
10. Install the parking brake lever to the rear brake shoe and install the parking brake strut and adjuster. The rear shoe can be identified as having a hole for the parking brake lever and one for the adjusting rod.
11. Connect both shoes with the lower spring.
12. Install both shoes with the spring onto the backing plate, placing the spring under the

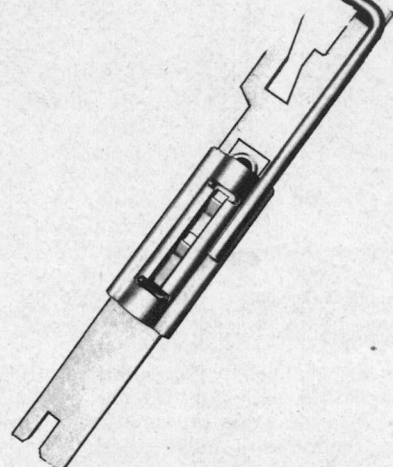

Adjuster properly positioned for installation— expanding strut rear brakes (© Chevrolet Div., G.M. Corp)

shoe anchor. Position the lever and adjuster assembly.
13. Engage the wheel cylinder links with the shoes.
14. Engage the parking brake strut to the leading shoe and install the pull-back spring.
15. Connect the parking brake cable to its lever, being careful not to activate the adjuster.
16. Install the drums and wheels, and adjust the parking brake equalizer. Lower the vehicle to the floor.

17. Adjust the parking brake and service brake by pulling and releasing the handle several times.
18. Seal the adjuster hole in the drum with a rubber or plastic replacement plug.

Pin and Slot Adjuster

The duo-servo brake with pin and slot adjusters is a new design for the Chevette.

Shoe Replacement

1. Remove the brake drum.
2. Loosen the equalizer to let all tension from the parking brake cable.
3. Unhook the parking brake cable from the lever.
4. Use pliers to remove the long shoe pull back spring at the top.
5. Use pliers to remove the shoe hold down springs and retainers from the middle of each shoe.
6. Separate the shoes at the top and remove them.
7. Check that the adjusters work properly; it should take 29-36 ft. lbs. torque to turn the adjusters. The adjusters and backing plate must be replaced as an assembly.
8. Lubricate the shoe contact surfaces on the backing plate and all pivot points with brake lubricant. Lubricate the parking brake cable.

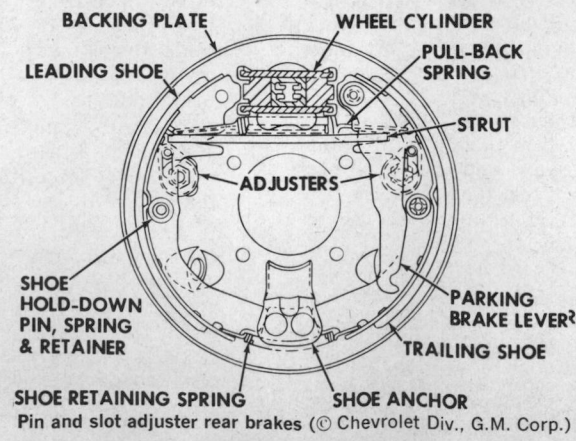

Pin and slot adjuster rear brakes (© Chevrolet Div., G.M. Corp.)

9. Lubricate the pivot end of the parking brake lever and attach the lever to the shoe.
10. Connect the shoes at the bottom with the retaining spring.
11. Place the shoes in position and fasten the front shoe with the hold down spring and retainer. Be sure that the adjuster peg is in the shoe slot.
12. Install the parking brake lever to front shoe strut. Fasten down the rear shoe with the hold down spring and retainer. Be sure that the adjuster peg is in the shoe slot.
13. Install the shoe pull back spring.
14. Attach the end of the parking brake cable to the lever.
15. Replace the drum. Adjust the brakes by applying the brake several times until the pedal is firm. Check the fluid level frequently. Adjust the parking brake.

Servicing Disc Brakes

Description and Inspection

Caliper disc brakes can be divided into three types: the four-piston, fixed-caliper type; the single-piston, floating-caliper type, and the single-piston sliding-caliper type. Refer to the Disc Brake Chart for applications.

In the four piston type (two in each side of the caliper) braking effect is achieved by hydraulically pushing both shoes against the disc sides.

With the single piston floating-caliper type the inboard shoe is pushed hydraulically into contact with the disc, while the reaction force thus generated is used to pull the outboard shoe into frictional contact (made possible by letting the caliper move slightly along the axle centerline).

In the sliding caliper (single piston) type, the caliper assembly slides along the machined surfaces of the anchor plate. A steel key located between the machined surfaces of the caliper and the machined surfaces of the anchor plate is held in place with either a retaining screw or two cotter pins. The caliper is held in place against the anchor plate with one or two support springs.

Disc pads (lining and shoe assemblies) should be replaced in axle sets (both wheels) when the lining on any pad is worn to 1/16 in. at any point. *If lining is allowed to wear past 1/16 in. minimum thickness severe damage to disc may result. Note:*

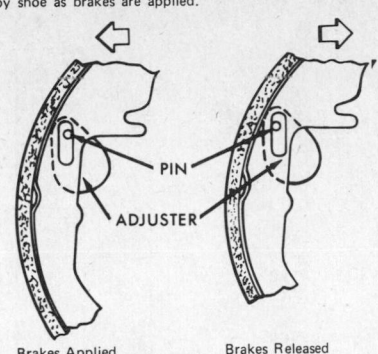

Adjuster remains in new position as brakes are released—shoe travel stops at contact with adjuster pin.

Adjuster is rotated outward by shoe as brakes are applied.

PIN

ADJUSTER

Brakes Applied   Brakes Released

Pin and slot adjuster operation
(© Chevrolet Div., G.M. Corp.)

state inspection specifications take precedence over these general recommendations. Note that disc pads in floating caliper type brakes may wear at an angle, and measurement should be made at the narrow end of the taper. Tapered linings should be replaced if the taper exceeds 1/8 in. from end to end (the difference between the thickest and thinnest points).

Caution To prevent costly paint damage, remove some brake fluid (don't re-use) from the reservoir and install the reservoir cover before replacing the disc pads. When replacing the pads, the piston is depressed and fluid is forced back through the lines to squirt out of the fluid reservoir.

When the caliper is unbolted from the hub do not let it dangle by the

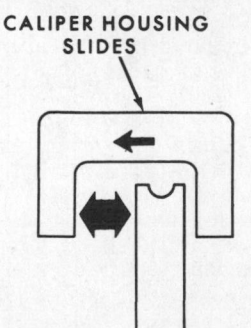

CALIPER HOUSING SLIDES

Floating caliper disc brake operation

CALIPER HOUSING STATIONARY

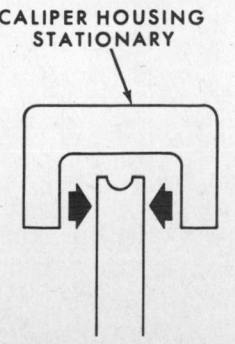

Fixed caliper disc brake operation

brake hose; it can be rested on a suspension member or wired onto the frame. All disc brake systems are inherently self-adjusting and have no provision for manual adjustment.

Bendix 4 Piston Brake

Pad Replacement
1. Raise the vehicle on a hoist and remove the front wheels.
   See CAUTION under Delco-Moraine 4 Piston Brake.
2. Working on one side at a time only, remove the caliper mounting bolts and slide the caliper off of the disc.
   NOTE: on American Motors cars the shims under the mounting bolts must be replaced exactly as removed. Remove the lower bolt, shake out the shims, and tag them as "lower." Remove the upper shims and tag them as "upper."
3. Remove the disc pads and inspect the caliper for damaged or leaking seals and casting cracks.
4. To install new pads insert the curved edge first (tabs, if any, should be up) and position the steel plate against the pistons.
5. Spread the pads apart until the pistons are bottomed in their bores and slide the caliper assembly over the disc.
6. Align the mounting holes and install shims (if used) and mounting bolts. Torque to specifications.
7. Check brake fluid level and pump the brake pedal to seat the linings against the disc. Replace the wheels and road test the vehicle.

Servicing the Caliper Assembly
1. Raise the vehicle on a hoist and remove the front wheels.
2. Working on one side at a time only, disconnect the hydraulic inlet line from the caliper and plug the end. Remove the caliper mounting bolts and shims (if used) and slide the caliper off of the disc.
3. Remove the disc pads from the caliper. If the old ones are to be reused, mark them so that they can be reinstalled in their original positions.
4. Open the caliper bleed screw and drain the fluid. Clean the outside of the caliper and mount it in a vise with padded jaws.

Caution When cleaning any brake components, use only brake fluid or denatured alcohol. Never use a mineral-based solvent, such as gasoline or paint thinner, since it will swell and quickly deteriorate rubber parts.

DISC BRAKE APPLICATIONS AND SPECIFICATIONS

Manufacturer/Model/Year	CALIPER SPECIFICATIONS				HYDRAULIC CONTROLS		MANUFACTURER'S DISC SPECIFICATIONS			
	Fixed Caliper Four Piston	Floating or Sliding Caliper Single Piston	Mounting Bolts Torque ft lbs	Bridge Bolts Torque ft lbs	Proportioning Valve	Metering Valve	Original Thickness (in.)	Resurfacing Min. Thickness (in.) ⑧	Parallel Variation (in.)	Runout Maximum (in.)
AMERICAN MOTORS										
All 1970	Bendix	—		100-110	Yes	no	.500	.450	.0005	.005
All 1971-74	—	Kelsey-Hayes floating	upper: 105/lower: 85	30-35②	yes	yes	1.000	.940	.0005	.005
All 1975-77	—	Kelsey-Hayes sliding	80	—	no	yes	1.190	1.120	.0005	.003
CHRYSLER CORPORATION										
Valiant, Dart 1970-72	Kelsey-Hayes	—	50-80	70-80	yes	yes	.810	.780	.0005	.0025
Valiant, Dart 1973-77; Volare, Aspen 1976-77	—	Kelsey-Hayes sliding	adapter: 75-100 (thru 1974) 95-125 (1975 on)	—	yes	no (thru 1975) yes (1976 on)	1.000-1.010	.940	.0005	.0025⑨
Intermediates, Barracuda, Challenger 1970-72	—	Kelsey-Hayes floating	adapter: 75-100 pin: 30-35	—	yes	yes	1.000-1.010	.980 (1970) .940	.0005	.0025
Intermediates, Cordoba, Charger SE, Barracuda, Challenger 1973-77	—	⑪ Kelsey-Hayes floating	adapter: 75-100 (thru 1974) 95-125 (1975 on) pin: 25-35 (thru 1975) 25-40 (1976 on)	—	yes⑦	yes	1.000-1.010	.940	.0005	.0025⑨
Full Size Models, Imperial 1970-72	—	Kelsey-Hayes floating	adapter: 75-100 pin: 30-35	—	no (1970-77) yes⑦	yes	1.250	1.200 (1970) 1.180	.0005	.0025
Full Size Models, Imperial 1973-77	—	Kelsey-Hayes sliding	adapter: 75-100 (through 1974) 95-125 (1975 on)	—	yes⑦	yes	1.250	1.180	.0005	.0025⑨
FORD MOTOR COMPANY										
Mustang, Cougar 1970-73	—	Kelsey-Hayes floating	upper: 100-140 lower: 55-75	25-35②	yes	yes	.935	.875	.0007	.002
Fairlane, Montego, Torino 1970-71	—	Kelsey-Hayes floating	upper: 120 lower: 170	25-35②	yes	no	.935	.875	.0007	.002
Ford, Mercury, Lincoln Mark III, Thunderbird 1970-72; Mark III 1970-71	—	Kelsey-Hayes floating	upper: 125 lower: 105	25-35②	yes	yes	1.180	1.120	.0007	.003
Pinto 1971-73	—	Ford sliding	—	—	yes	no	.750	.685	.0007	.003
Montego, Torino 1972-73	—	Ford sliding	—	—	yes	yes	1.180	1.120	.0005	.003
Mark IV, Thunderbird 1972-73	—	Ford sliding	—	—	yes	yes	1.180	1.120	.0005	.003
All 1974-77	—	Ford sliding	—	—	yes	yes	1.180	1.120	.0005	.003⑩
GENERAL MOTORS										
Buick (full size) 1970-77	—	Delco-Moraine	35	—	yes no (1970)	yes	1.290	1.230 (1973-74) 1.215	.0005	.004

Model	Year		Caliper	Guide Pin Torque ②			Original Thickness	Min. Thickness	Runout	Parallelism
Buick Special, Century	1970-77	—	Delco-Moraine 35	—	no	no	1.040	.965	.0005	.004
Buick Skyhawk	1975-77	—	Delco-Moraine —	—	yes	no	.500 (thru 1975) / .880	.455 (thru 1975) / .815	.0005	.005
Buick Appollo, Skylark	1975-77	—	Delco-Moraine 35	—	yes	yes	1.040	.980	.0005	.005
Cadillac	1970-77	—	Delco-Moraine 30	—	no (1970) yes	yes	1.250	1.220	.0005	.0025
Cadillac Eldorado	1970-77	—	Delco-Moraine 30	—	yes	yes	1.210	1.190	.0005	.008 (on hub)
Cadillac Seville	1976-77	—	Delco-Moraine 30	—	yes	yes	1.030	.980	.0005	.005
Chevrolet (full size)	1970-77	—	Delco-Moraine 35	—	no (1970) yes	yes	1.250 (1970) / 1.285 (1971-72) / 1.280	1.215 (thru 1972) / 1.230	.0005	.002
Corvette	1970-77	—	Delco-Moraine 70	front: 130 rear: 60	yes (HD)	no	1.250	1.230	.0005	.002
Chevelle, Nova, Camaro	1970-77	—	Delco-Moraine 35	—	yes	yes	1.000 (1970) / 1.035	.965 (1970) / .980	.0005	.002
Chevrolet Vega, Monza	1971-77	—	Delco-Moraine —	—	yes	no	.500 ③ / .880 ③	.470 / .830 ③	.0005	.005
Chevette	1976-77	—	Delco-Moraine —	—	no	no	.500	⑧	.0005	.003
Oldsmobile 88, 98	1970-77	—	Delco-Moraine 40	—	yes	yes	1.250 (1970) / 1.280 (1971-74) / 1.290	1.215 (1971-73) / 1.230	.0005	.005
Oldsmobile Toronado	1970-77	—	Delco-Moraine 40	—	yes	yes	1.205 (thru 1974) / 1.245	1.185 (thru 1974) / 1.170	.0005	.002
Oldsmobile F-85, Cutlass, 4-4-2	1970-77	—	Delco-Moraine 35	—	yes	no	1.035	.980	.0005	.004
Omega	1973-77	—	Delco-Moraine 40	—	yes	yes	1.040	.965	.0005	.005
Oldsmobile Starfire	1975-77	—	Delco-Moraine —	—	yes	no	.500 (1975) / .880	.400 (1975) / .820	.0005	.005
Pontiac (full size)	1970-77	—	Delco-Moraine 35	—	no (1970) yes	yes	1.230 (1970) / 1.250 (1971-72) / 1.285	1.195 (1970) / 1.230 (1971-72) / 1.215	.0005	.002 (1971-72) / .004
Pontiac Tempest, LeMans, Firebird	1970-77	—	Delco-Moraine 35	—	yes	yes	1.005 (thru 1972) / 1.035	.960	.0007	.004
Pontiac Ventura	1971-77	—	Delco-Moraine 35	—	yes	yes	1.035	.965	.0007	.004
Pontiac Astre, Sunbird	1975-77	—	Delco-Moraine —	—	yes	no	.500 ③ / .880 ③	.470 / .830 ③	.0005	.005

① Not used.
② Caliper guide pin torque.
③ Larger figure for 1976 and later Monza, Sunbird.
④ ⑤ ⑥ Not used.
⑦ No proportioning valve on wagons.
⑧ Resurfacing minimum thickness is cast on the disc on late models.
⑨ .004 in. runout—1975 and later.
⑩ .004 in. runout—rear discs.
⑪ 1976 Cordoba and Charger SE made before Jan. 1976 use Kelsey-Hayes sliding caliper as on Volare, Aspen.

5. Remove the bridge bolts, separate the caliper halves, and remove the two O-ring seals from the transfer holes.

6. Pry the lip on each piston dust boot from its groove and remove the piston assemblies and springs from the bores. If necessary, air pressure may be used to force the pistons out of the bores, using care to prevent them from popping out of control.

7. Remove the boots and seals from the pistons and clean the pistons in brake fluid. Blow out the caliper passages with an air hose.

8. Inspect the cylinder bores for scoring, pitting, or corrosion. Corrosion is a pitted or rough condition not to be confused with staining. Light rough spots may be removed by rotating crocus cloth, using finger pressure, in the bores. Do not polish with an in and out motion or use any other abrasive.

9. If the pistons are pitted, scored, or worn, they must be replaced. A corroded or deeply scored caliper should also be replaced.

10. Check the clearance of the pistons in the bores using a feeler gauge. Clearance should be 0.002-0.006 in. If there is excessive clearance the caliper must be replaced.

11. Replace all rubber parts and lubricate with brake fluid. Install the seals and boots in the grooves in each piston. The seal should be installed in the groove closest to the closed end of the piston with the seal lips facing the closed end. The lip on the boot should be facing the seal.

12. Lubricate the piston and bore with brake fluid. Position the piston return spring, large coil first, in the piston bore.

13. Install the piston in the bore, taking great care to avoid damaging the seal lip as it passes the edge of the cylinder bore.

14. Compress the lip on the dust boot into the groove in the caliper. Be sure the boot is fully seated in the groove, as poor sealing will allow contaminants to ruin the bore.

15. Position the O-rings in the cavities around the caliper transfer holes, and fit the caliper halves together. Install the bridge bolts (lubricated with brake fluid) and be sure to torque to specification.

16. Install the disc pads in the caliper and remount the caliper on the hub (see Disc Pad Replacement). Connect the brake line to the caliper and bleed the brakes (see Brake Bleeding). Replace the wheels. Recheck the brake fluid level, check the brake pe-

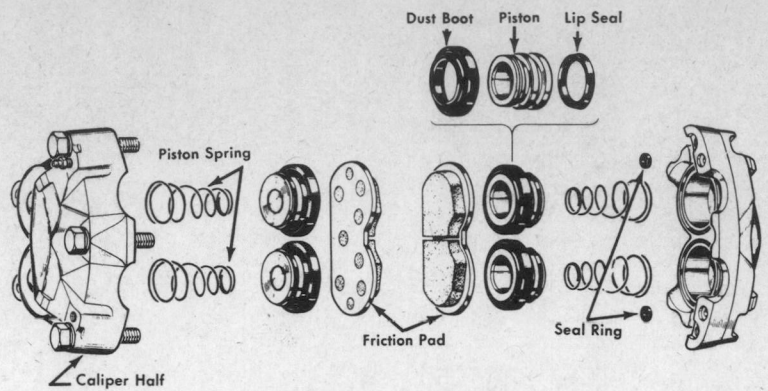

Bendix four piston disc brake (© American Motors Corp)

dal travel, and road test the vehicle.

Caliper Alignment Procedure for American Motors Cars

1. Check dimension "C" on either side of the disc (rotor). Both measurements should be within 0.010 in. of each other.

2. Check dimension "D" at both ends of the caliper. The measurements between the caliper reference surface and disc at both ends of the caliper should be within 0.005 in. of each other.

3. Add or remove shims as required to bring the dimensions to within the tolerance limits.

Delco-Moraine 4 Piston Brake

Pad Replacement

1. Raise the car and remove the front wheels.

Caution To prevent paint damage from brake fluid, be sure to remove part of brake fluid (don't re-use) from master cylinder and to keep the master cylinder covered. Do not allow cylinder to drain too low or air will be pumped into system.

2. Remove and discard the cotter pin from the end of the pad retaining pin. Remove the retaining pin or pins. If old pads are to be re-used, mark them so that they can be returned to their original positions.

3. Push one pad back so that it is as far away from the disc as possible. Remove that pad and replace it with a new one. Replace the second pad in the same manner. Pistons are spring loaded so it will be difficult to insert the new pad. To facilitate this job, use a stiff, long-bladed putty knife to hold back the pistons while inserting the new pad. If this fails to work, it may be necessary to release some of the fluid pressure by loosening the bleeder screw. This will require

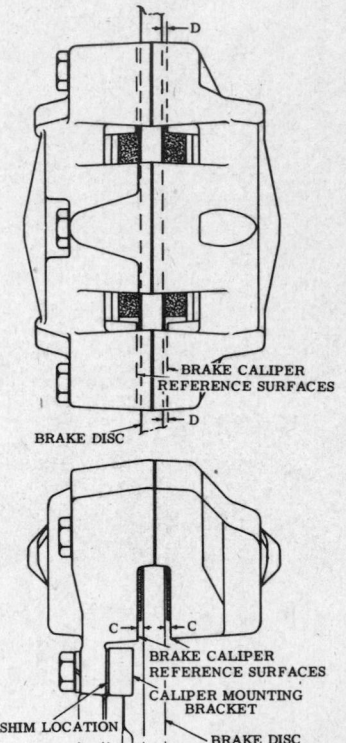

Alignment of caliper to disc—American Motors Cars

bleeding air from the system later.

NOTE: pads are interchangeable from inboard to outboard and right to left on all cars except the Corvette. Disc pads for the Corvette have more metal showing (in relation to the lining centerline) at one end of the pad, and this end must be towards the front of the car. To remove Corvette pads lift straight out, to remove all others swivel one end up and lift out. Shims (if any) between the pads and pistons should be replaced in the exact position as removed.

4 With new pads in place install the retaining pin and lock it in place with a new cotter pin.

5. Replace the wheels, check the brake fluid level, check brake pedal travel, and road test the car.

Servicing the Caliper Assembly

See Bendix 4 Piston Brake—Servicing the Caliper Assembly. Procedure is identical except that:

1. When the pistons are installed in the caliper, a small screwdriver must be used to "tuck" the lip of the piston seal into the caliper bore (Step 13).
2. Corvette rear disc brakes have only one transfer hole and O-ring (Step 5).
3. Each piston boot has a retaining ring. It can be pried out using the piston as a fulcrum. When installing the ring in the piston bore make sure it is seated evenly flush or below the machined face of the caliper (Steps 6 & 13).
4. Piston to bore clearance should be from 0.0045-0.010 in. (except Corvette rear which is 0.0035-0.009 in. (Step 10).
5. The piston seal lip faces toward the spring end of the piston, and the fold in the piston boot faces toward the seal (Step 14).
6. Slide the caliper over the disc. A putty knife can be used to hold back the pistons so that the caliper can be completely lowered into position. The caliper should be positioned carefully to avoid tearing the rubber boot on the edge of the disc. Secure the caliper to the mounting bracket and torque to specifications. Install the pads as instructed earlier (Step 16).
7. When the brake hose is connected it should not be twisted or touch other parts at any time during suspension or steering travel (Step 16).

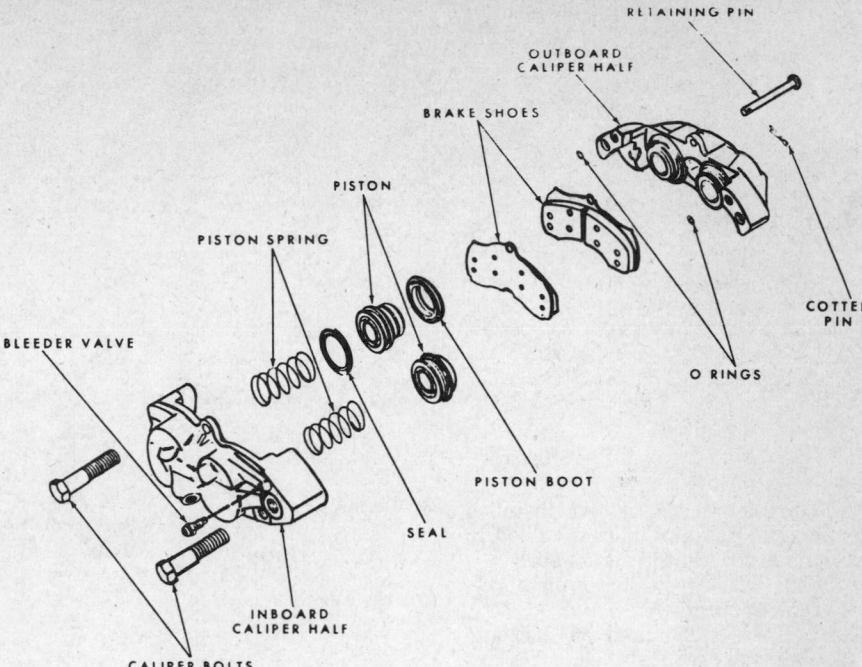

Delco Moraine four piston disc brake (© Chevrolet Div., G.M. Corp)

Kelsey-Hayes 4 Piston Brake

Pad Replacement

See CAUTION under Delco-Moraine 4 Piston Brake.
1. Raise the car and remove the front wheels.
2. Remove the retainer bolts and the retainer(s).
3. Using two pairs of pliers, grasp the outer ends of one of the pads and pull straight out. Push the two pistons into their bores using a flat metal bar and install a new disc pad. Repeat for the second pad.

4. Install the retainer(s) and bolts.
5. Replace the wheels, check the brake fluid level, check brake pedal travel, and road test the car.

Servicing the Caliper Assembly

See Bendix 4 Piston Brake—Servicing the Caliper Assembly. Procedure is identical except that:
1. This unit does not use internal transfer passages with O-rings, an external crossover line is used instead. It must be removed before the caliper is disassembled.

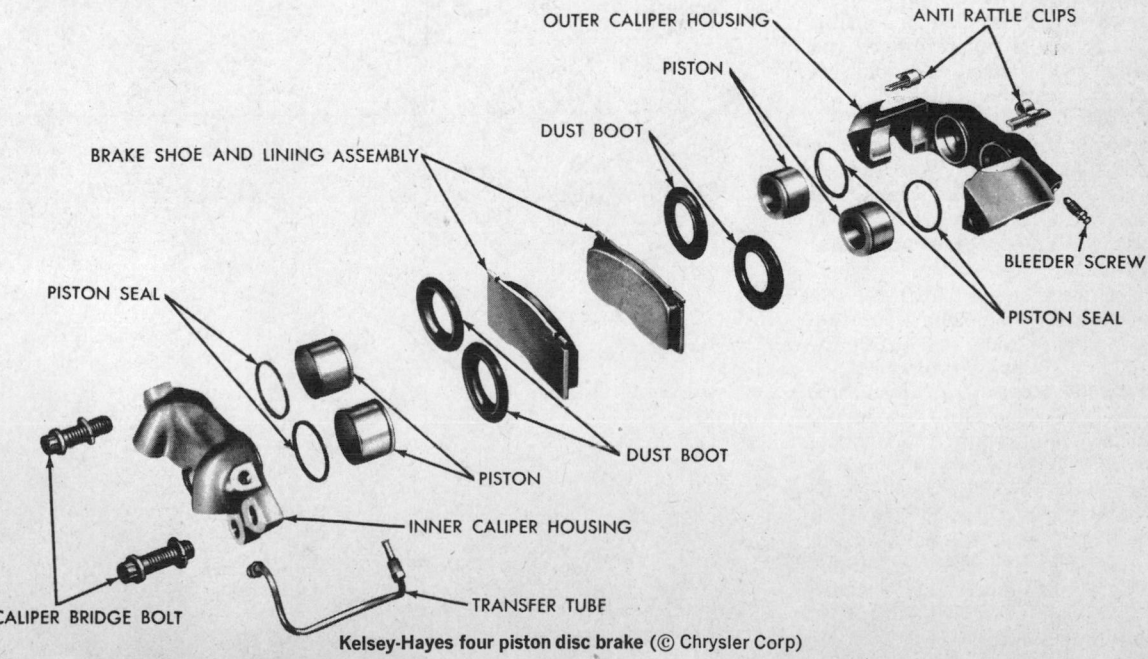

Kelsey-Hayes four piston disc brake (© Chrysler Corp)

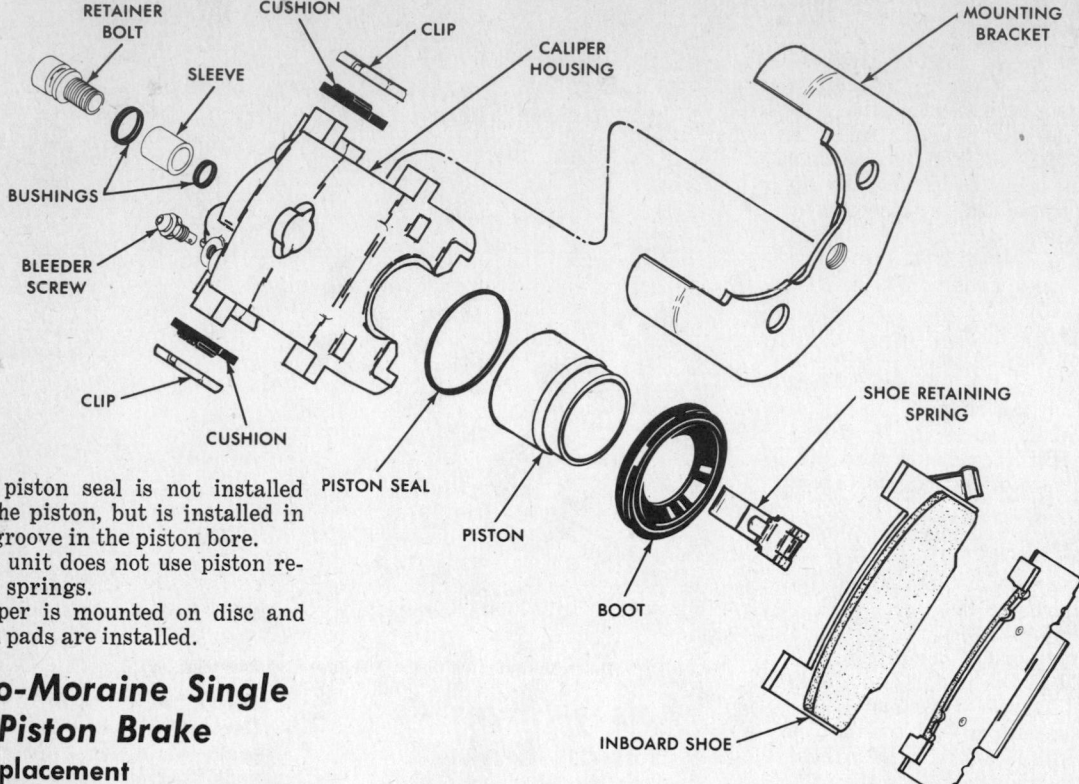

2. The piston seal is not installed on the piston, but is installed in the groove in the piston bore.
3. This unit does not use piston return springs.
4. Caliper is mounted on disc and then pads are installed.

Delco-Moraine Single Piston Brake

Pad Replacement

See CAUTION under Delco-Moraine 4 Piston Brake.

1. Drain about ⅔ of the fluid from the master cylinder. Discard the fluid. Raise the vehicle on a hoist and remove the front wheels.
2. Place a "C" clamp on the caliper so that the solid side of the clamp rests against the back of the caliper and the screw end rests against the metal part of the outboard shoe. Tighten the clamp until the caliper moves enough to bottom the piston in the bore. Remove the clamp.
3. Remove the caliper mounting bolts or guide pin retainers and guide pins (throw the old retainers away) and lift the caliper away from the disc.
4. Remove the disc pads (mark them as to location) and inspect the caliper for fluid leaks and damage. Lubricate with silicon and install new sleeves and bushings in caliper ears.
5. Place the inboard pad in the caliper so that the bottom edge contacts the piston, and press the pad flat against the piston.
   NOTE: most cars use a spring to locate the pad. The clip-type spring must be assembled onto the pad before the pad is placed over the piston.
6. Place the outboard pad in the caliper so that the two ears on the pad fit over the ears on the caliper. Squeeze the ears on the pad tight around the caliper ears with a pair of pliers, except on subcompact cars.

Delco-Moraine single piston disc brake used on Chevette (© Chevrolet Div., G.M. Corp.)

7. Position the caliper assembly onto the disc, align the mounting holes, and make sure that the brake line isn't twisted.
8. Install the mounting bolts (making sure that they pass under the retaining ears on the inboard shoe) and torque to specification. On models with guide pins, install the mounting pins with new retainers.
9. On Chevette, clinch the outboard

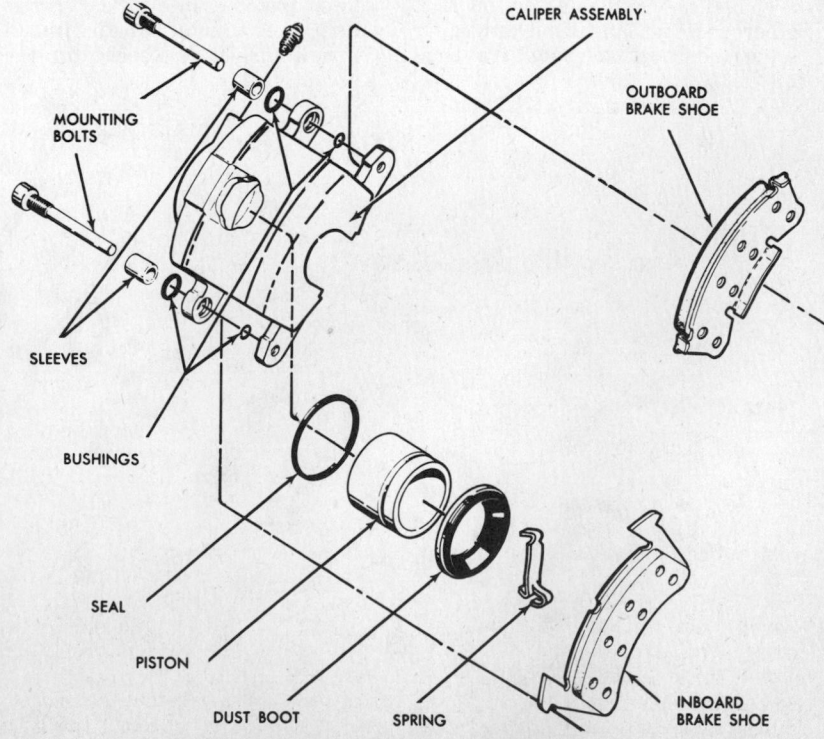

Delco-Moraine single piston disc brake (© Chevrolet Div., G.M. Corp)

shoe tabs to the caliper with a pair of channel lock pliers.

10. Check the brake fluid level and pump the brake pedal to seat the linings against the disc. Replace the wheels and road test the car.

Servicing the Caliper Assembly

See CAUTION under Delco-Moraine 4 Piston Brake.

1. Raise the vehicle on a hoist and remove the front wheels.
2. Working on one side at a time only, disconnect the brake hose from the steel brake line and cap the fittings. Remove the U-shaped retainer from the hose fitting (if applicable).
3. Remove the caliper mounting bolts or guide pin retainers and guide pins (throw the old retainers away) and lift the caliper away from the disc.
4. Clean the holes and the bushing grooves in the caliper ears, and wipe all dirt from the mounting bolts. If the bolts are corroded or damaged they should be replaced.
5. Remove the shoe support springs (if applicable) from the piston.
6. Remove the sleeves from the ears of the caliper with a suitable drift pin. Remove the rubber bushings from the grooves in the caliper ears.
7. Remove the brake hose, drain the brake fluid, and clean the outside of the caliper.
8. Pad the inside of the caliper with towels and direct compressed air into the brake fluid inlet hole to remove the piston.

Caution To prevent damage to the piston use just enough air pressure to ease it out of the bore. Do not attempt to catch or protect the piston with the hand since this may cause serious injury.

9. Use a screwdriver to pry the boot out of the caliper. Avoid scratching the bore.
10. Remove the piston seal from its groove in the caliper bore. *Do not use a metal tool of any type for this operation.*
11. Blow out all passages in the caliper and bleeder valve. Clean the piston and piston bore with fresh brake fluid.
12. Examine the piston for scoring, scratches, or corrosion. If any of these conditions exist the piston must be replaced, as it is plated and cannot be refinished.
13. Examine the bore for the same defects. Light rough spots may be removed by rotating crocus cloth, using finger pressure, in the bore. Do not polish with an in and out motion or use any other abrasive.

14. Lubricate the piston bore and the new rubber parts with fresh brake fluid. Position the seal in the piston bore groove.
15. Lubricate the piston with brake fluid and assemble the boot into the piston groove so that the fold faces the open end of the piston.
16. Insert the piston into the bore, taking care not to unseat the seal.
17. Force the piston to the bottom of the bore. (This will require a force of 50-100 lbs.). Seat the boot lip around the caliper counterbore. Proper seating of the boot is very important for sealing out contaminants.
18. Install the brake hose into the caliper using a new copper gasket.
19. Lubricate the new sleeves and rubber bushings. Install the bushings in the caliper ears. Install the sleeves so that the end toward the disc pad is flush with the machined surface.

NOTE: lubrication of the sleeves and bushings is essential to ensure the proper operation of the sliding caliper design.

20. Install the shoe support spring (if applicable) in the piston.
21. Install the disc pads in the caliper and remount the caliper on the hub (see Disc Pad Replacement).
22. Reconnect the brake hose to the steel brake line. Install the retainer clip. Bleed the brakes (see Brake Bleeding).
23. Replace the wheels, check the brake fluid level, check the brake pedal travel, and road test the vehicle.

Kelsey-Hayes Single Piston Brake (Chrysler)

See CAUTION under Delco-Moraine 4 Piston Brake. Refer to the Disc Brake Chart for sliding and floating caliper applications.

Pad Replacement

Floating Caliper

1. Raise the vehicle on a hoist and remove front wheels.
2. Working on only one brake at a time, remove the caliper guide pins (and positioners, on AMC) which attach caliper to adapter. Lift the caliper away from the disc.
3. Remove (and discard) the inner bushings (and positioners, on AMC) from the guide pins, and the outboard bushings from the caliper.
4. Slide the disc pads out of the caliper, and carefully push the piston back into the bore.

5. Compress the flanges of the new outboard bushings and work them into position from the outboard side of the caliper.
6. Slide the new disc pads into position (outboard pad in the retaining spring) and carefully slide the caliper assembly over the rotor.
7. Compress the flanges of the new inner bushings and install them. Install new positioners on the guide pins with the open ends out on AMC models.
8. Install the guide pins from the inboard side and press in while threading pin into adapter. *Use extreme care to avoid crossing threads.* Tighten to specifications. Be sure the tabs of the positioners are over the machined surfaces of the caliper on AMC models.
9. Check the brake fluid level and pump the brake pedal to seat the linings against the disc. Replace the wheels and road test the car.

Sliding Caliper

1. Jack up the car and remove the wheel and tire.
2. Remove the caliper retaining clips and anti-rattle springs.
3. Remove the caliper from the disc by slowly sliding the caliper and brake pad assembly out and away from the disc.
4. Remove the outboard pad from the caliper by prying between the pad and the caliper fingers. Remove the inboard pad from the caliper support by the same method.

NOTE: Safety-wire the caliper to the suspension while removing the inboard pad.

5. Push the pistons to the bottom of their bores. This may be done with a pair of large pliers or by placing a flat metal bar against the pistons and depressing the pistons with a steady force. This operation is much easier with the cover removed from the master cylinder.
6. Slide the new pads into the caliper and caliper support. The ears of the pad should rest on the bridges of the caliper.
7. Install the caliper on the disc and install the caliper retaining clips and anti-rattle springs. Install the retaining screws. Pump the brake pedal until it is firm.
8. Check the fluid level in the master cylinder and add fluid as needed.
9. Install the wheel and tire.

Caliper Removal and Installation

1. Raise the car and support it securely with jackstands.

U311

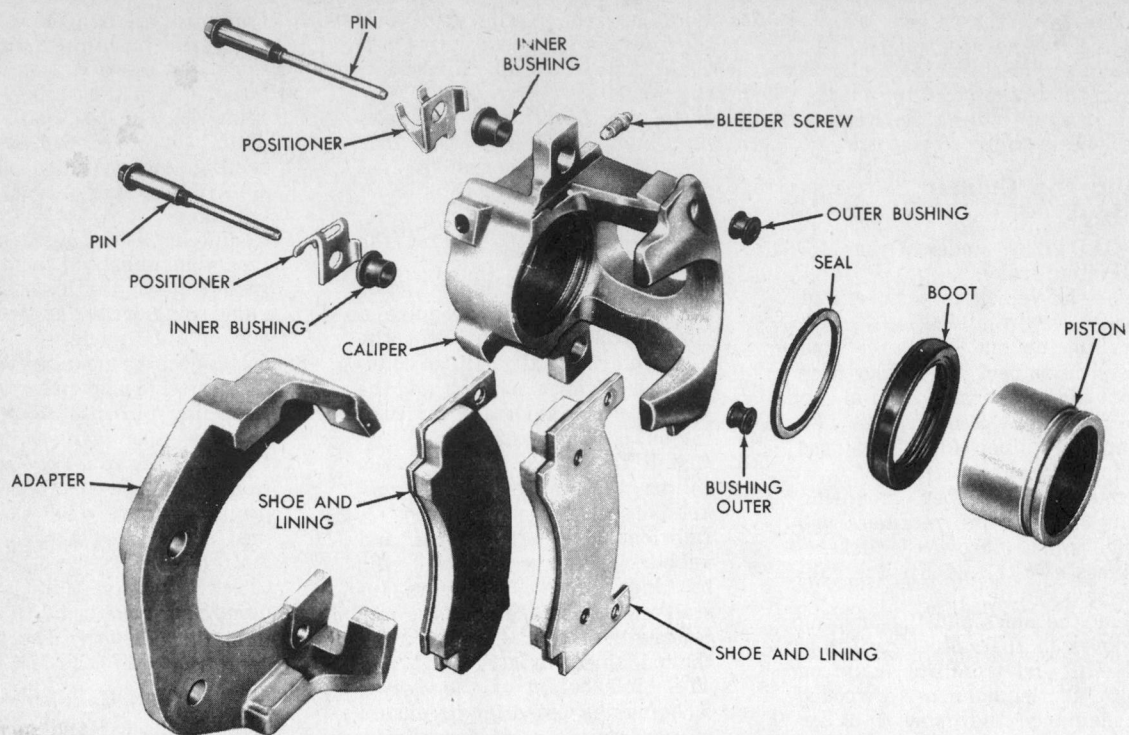

Kelsey-Hayes single piston floating disc brake—Chrysler (© Chrysler Corp)

2. Remove the wheel and tire assembly from the car.
3. Detach the brake hose from the frame mounting bracket. Disconnect the intermediate hose bracket on Volare/Aspen. Plug the brake tube to prevent fluid loss.
4. a. On floating caliper, remove the guide pins (and positioners, on AMC) attaching the caliper to the adapter.
   b. On sliding caliper, remove the screw, clip, and anti-rattle spring attaching the caliper to the adapter.
5. Slide the caliper assembly away from the disc. Hold the outboard pad while doing this so that it can't fall out.
6. Remove the pads if the caliper is being overhauled.
7. Install the calipers. Connect the brake hose and bleed the brake system.

Servicing the Caliper Assembly

Floating Caliper

1. Remove the caliper assembly from the car *without* disconnecting the hydraulic line.
2. Support the caliper assembly on the upper control arm and surround it with shop towels to absorb any brake fluid. Slowly depress the brake pedal until the piston is pushed out of its bore.

Caution Do not use compressed air to force the piston from its bore; injury could result.

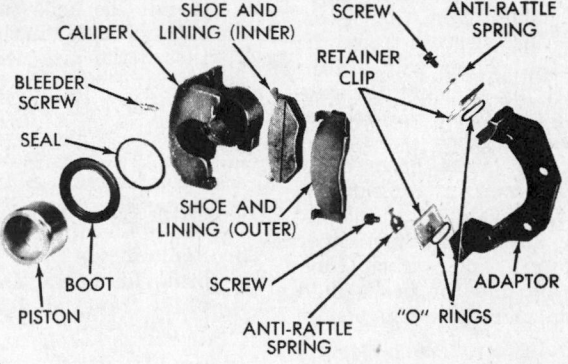

Kelsey-Hayes single piston sliding caliper disc brake—Chrysler (© Chrysler Corp)

3. Disconnect the brake line from the caliper and plug it to prevent fluid loss.
4. Mount the caliper in a soft-jawed vise and clamp lightly. Do not tighten the vise too much or the caliper will become distorted.
5. Work the dust boot out with your fingers.
6. Use a small pointed *wooden* or *plastic* stick to work the piston seal out of the groove in the bore. Discard the seal.

Caution Using a screwdriver or other metal tool could scratch the piston bore.

7. Using the same wooden or plastic stick, press the outer bushings out of the housing. Discard the old bushings. Remove the inner bushings in the same manner. Discard them as well.
8. Clean all parts in denatured alco-

hol or brake fluid. Blow out all bores and passages with compressed air.
9. Inspect the piston and bore for scoring or pitting. Replace the piston if necessary. Bores with light scratches or corrosion may be cleaned with crocus cloth. Bores with deep scratches may be honed if you do not increase the bore diameter more than 0.002 in. Replace the housing if the bore must be enlarged beyond this.

NOTE: Black stains are caused by piston seals and are harmless.

10. If the bore had to be honed, clean its grooves with a stiff, non-metallic rotary brush. Clean the bore twice by flushing it out with brake fluid and drying it with a soft, lint-free cloth.

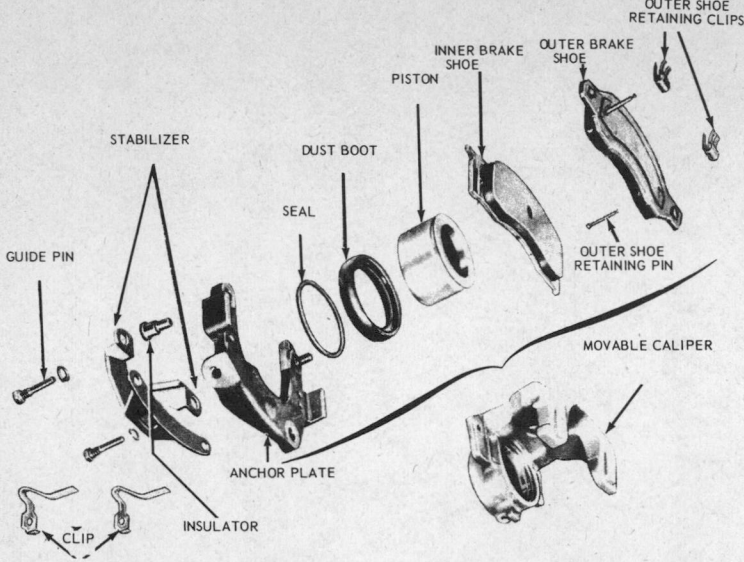

Kelsey-Hayes single piston disc brake—Ford (© Ford Motor Co)

Caliper assembly is as follows:

1. Clamp the caliper in a soft-jawed vise; do not overtighten.
2. Dip a new piston seal in brake fluid or the lubricant supplied with the rebuilding kit. Position the new seal in one area of its groove and gently work it into place with clean fingers, so that it is correctly seated. Do not use an old seal.
3. Coat a new boot with brake fluid or lubricant (as above), leaving a generous amount inside.
4. Insert the boot in the caliper and work it into the groove, using your fingers only. The boot will snap into place once it is correctly positioned. Run your forefinger around the inside of the boot to make sure that it is correctly seated.
5. Install the bleed screw in its hole and plug the fluid inlet on the caliper.
6. Coat the piston with brake fluid or lubricant. Spread the boot with your fingers and work the piston into the boot.
7. Depress the piston; this will force the boot into its groove on the piston. Remove the plug and bottom the piston in the bore.
8. Compress the flanges of new guide pin bushings and work them into place by pressing *in* on the bushings with your fingertips, until they are seated. Make sure that the flanges cover the housing evenly on all sides.
9. Install the caliper on the car as previously outlined.

Sliding Caliper

The overhaul procedure for these calipers is identical to that for the floating caliper, except that there are no guide pin bushings to be removed or installed.

Kelsey-Hayes Single Piston Brake (American Motors)

For disc brake service procedures for 1971-74 AMC models, see the floating caliper service sections for "Kelsey-Hayes Single Piston Brake (Chrysler)."

Pad Replacement—1975 and later Sliding Caliper

CAUTION: To prevent paint damage from leaking brake fluid, remove about 2/3 of the brake fluid from the larger reservoir (supplying the front brakes), in the master cylinder and keep the cylinder reservoir covered. Do not allow the reservoir level to get too low or air will enter the hydraulic system, necessitating bleeding. Do not reuse the removed brake fluid.

1. Remove the hub caps and loosen the front wheel lug nuts slightly. Firmly apply the parking brake and block the rear wheels.
2. Raise the front of the car and install jackstands beneath the front jacking points or lower control arms. Remove the front wheels.
3. Working on only one caliper at a time, bottom the caliper piston in its bore by carefully inserting a screwdriver between the piston and the inboard shoe and prying back on the piston.

NOTE: Take care not to damage the rubber piston seals. If the piston cannot be bottomed with a screwdriver, a large C-clamp will suffice.

4. Using a ¼ in. hex key or allen wrench, remove the caliper support key retaining screw.
5. Remove the caliper support key and support spring using a drift

pin and hammer. Lift the caliper assembly off its anchor plate and over the rotor (disc.).

NOTE: Do not allow the caliper to hang by its flexible brake hose. Use a piece of heavy wire to suspend the caliper from the coil spring until you are ready to reinstall it.

6. Remove the inboard brake shoe from the anchor plate. Remove the inboard brake shoe anti-rattle spring from the inboard shoe, noting its position for reassembly.
7. Remove the outboard brake shoe from the caliper, rapping lightly with a hammer, if necessary, to free it from the caliper.
8. Wipe the inside of the caliper free of all accumulated brake pad dust, road dirt and other foreign material with a clean, dry rag.

NOTE: Do not blow the caliper clean with compressed air as this may dislodge the rubber dust cover.

Check the piston seals for evidence of leakage from the piston bore, and overhaul the caliper if necessary. Clean all rust and dirt from the abutment (sliding), surfaces of the caliper and caliper anchor plate using a wire brush and crocus cloth. Then, lightly grease the sliding surfaces with white grease to ensure that the sliding motion of the caliper is not impaired.

9. Install the inboard brake shoe anti-rattle spring on the rear flange of the inboard brake shoe, making sure that the looper section of the clip is facing away from the rotor.
10. Install the assembled inboard brake shoe and anti-rattle spring in the caliper anchor plate, taking care not to dislodge the anti-rattle spring during installation.
11. Install the outboard brake shoe in the caliper, making sure to seat the shoe flange fully, into the outboard arms of the caliper.
12. Install the caliper assembly over the rotor and into position in the anchor plate. Exercise extreme care when installing the caliper not to tear or dislodge the piston dust cover on the inboard brake shoe.
13. Align the caliper assembly with the abutment surfaces of the anchor plate and insert the caliper support key and support spring between the abutment surfaces at the rearward end of the caliper and anchor plate. Then, using a hammer and drift pin, drive the caliper support key and spring into position. Install the support key retaining screw and tighten to 15 ft lbs.

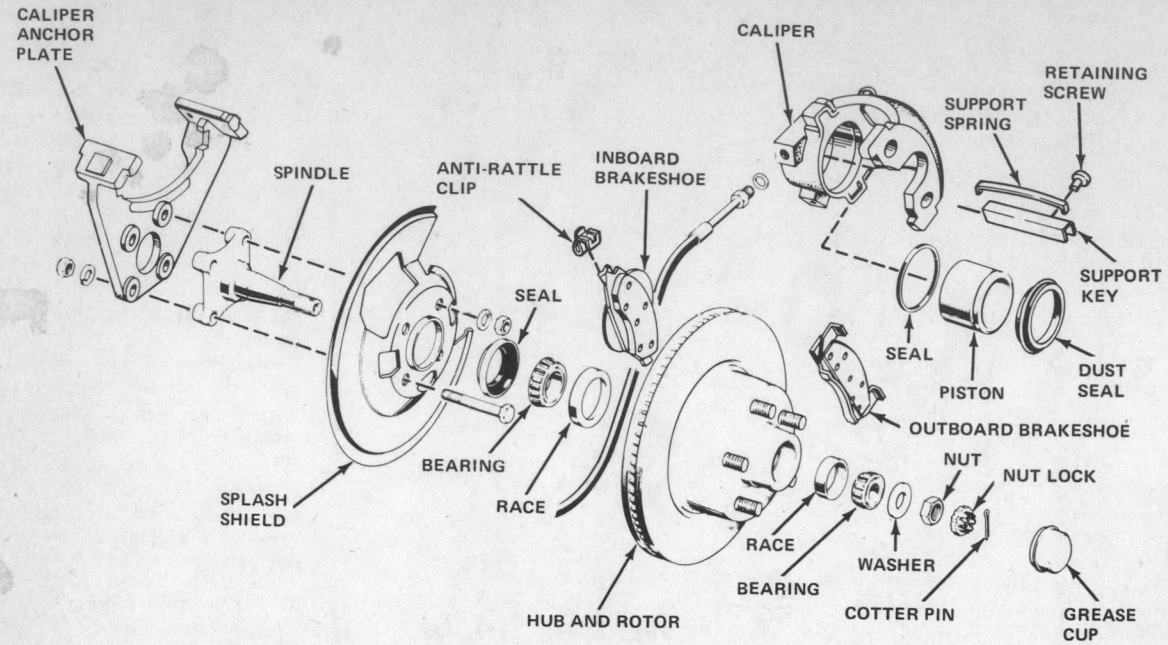

Kelsey-Hayes single piston sliding caliper disc brake—AMC (© American Motors Corp.)

14. Fill the master cylinder reservoir to within ¼ in. of the rim. Press the brake pedal firmly several times to seat the shoes.
15. Install the wheels and lower the car. Road-test the car after rechecking the fluid level and checking for firm brake pedal.

Servicing the 1975 and later Sliding Caliper Assembly

1. Remove the caliper as in Steps 1-7 of "Disc Pad Replacement."
2. Place a clean piece of paper on your work area to put the parts of the caliper on while it is being disassembled.
3. Drain the brake fluid from the caliper by opening the bleeder plug.

4. Place the caliper assembly in a vise with padded jaws.
CAUTION: Do not overtighten the vise; too much pressure will cause distortion of the caliper bore.
5. Using compressed air, remove the piston from the caliper bore. Be careful not to damage the piston or the bore. Leave the dust boot in the caliper groove while the piston is being removed.
6. Take the caliper out of the vise and withdraw the dust boot.
7. Work the piston seal out of its groove in the piston bore with a small, pointed wooden or plastic stick. Do not use a screwdriver or other metallic tool to remove the seal as it could damage the bore. Throw the old seal away.

8. Unscrew the bleeder plug.
9. Clean all of the parts in brake fluid (*do not use solvent*) and wipe them dry with a clean, lint-free cloth. Dry the passages and bores with compressed air.

Check the cylinder bore for scoring, pitting, and/or corrosion. If the caliper bore is deeply scored or corroded, replace the entire caliper.

If it is only lightly scored or stained, polish with crocus cloth. Use finger-pressure to rotate the crocus cloth in the cylinder bore. Any black stains found in the bore are caused by seals and are harmless.

CAUTION: Do not slide the crocus cloth in and out of the bore. Do not use any other type of abrasive material.

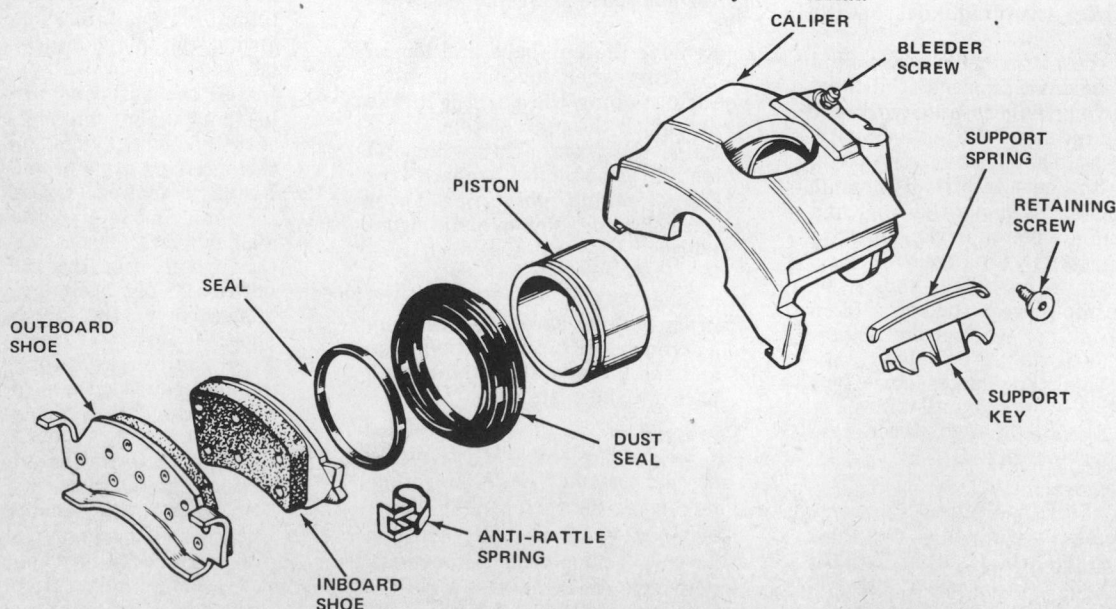

Caliper details—AMC sliding caliper disc brake (© American Motors Corp.)

Check the piston. If it is pitted, scored, or worn, it should be replaced with a new one.

Check the piston-to-bore clearance with a feeler gauge. It should be 0.002-0.006 in. If it is more than this, replace the caliper assembly.

Assembly and installation are as follow:

1. Dip a new piston seal in clean brake fluid. Position the seal in one area of the groove in the cylinder bore and gently work it into place around the groove until it is seated. Be sure that your fingers are clean before touching the seal.

   CAUTION: Never reuse an old piston seal.

2. Coat a new piston boot with clean brake fluid. Work it into the outer groove of the bore with your fingers until it snaps into place. Don't worry if the boot seems too large for the groove; once seated, it will fit properly. Check the boot, by running your forefinger around the inside of it, to be sure that it is correctly installed.

3. Coat the piston with plenty of brake fluid. Spread the boot with your fingers and insert the piston into it.

4. Depress the piston until it bottoms in the bore.

   CAUTION: Apply uniform force to the piston or it will crack.

5. Install the caliper assembly as in Steps 9-15 of "Pad Replacement."

Kelsey-Hayes Single Piston Floating Caliper Brake (Ford)

Pad Replacement

1970-71 Thunderbird, Continental Mark III 1970-72 Ford, Mercury, Lincoln

1. Check brake fluid level in the large (primary) reservoir of the master cylinder. Remove enough fluid so that this reservoir is only half full. Do not re-use this fluid, throw it away.

2. Remove the wheel and tire assembly.

3. Remove the inboard pad hold down clips.

4. Using a small screwdriver, remove the retaining clips from the outboard pad and remove the pad.

5. Remove the caliper locating pins (2) from the back of the caliper.

6. Remove the upper stabilizer.

7. Remove the caliper assembly from the anchor plate and detach the outboard pad and retaining pins from the caliper.

8. Using a piece of wire, hang the caliper from the upper control arm.

9. Remove the caliper locating pin insulators from the anchor plate.

10. Remove the inboard pad and inspect the disc surfaces for wear.

11. Install the inboard pad to the anchor plate. Insert new locating pin insulators into the anchor plate.

    NOTE: when replacing pads, install new stabilizer, insulators, shoe clips and pins. It may help to wet insulators with water before installing.

12. Install the inboard pad hold down clips and tighten bolts.

13. The piston must be fully retracted into the cylinder before the caliper and pad assembly will fit over the disc. Retracting the piston can be made easier by fabricating a retracting tool using a bolt, a nut, a used outer brake pad and a retaining spring.

14. Position the tool onto the caliper holding it in place with the retaining spring. Gradually turn in on the bolt pausing to allow the piston to pull in the seal. Make sure the piston is fully bottomed in the cylinder to create proper clearance between the pads. Inspect piston dust boot and replace if cracked. See Servicing the Caliper Assembly for replacement procedures.

15. Install the outer brake pad, retaining pins and new retainer clips.

16. Join the caliper assembly to the anchor plate.

17. Install the stabilizers to caliper.

18. Check the brake fluid level and pump the brake pedal to seat the pads against the disc. Install the wheels and road test the car.

1970 Fairlane 1970-71 Torino, 1970-71 Montego, 1970-73 Mustang and Cougar

1. Make sure large master cylinder reservoir is only half full.

2. Remove the front wheel and tire.

3. Disconnect and plug the brake line if necessary.

4. Remove the caliper locating pins and stabilizer bolts.

5. Lift caliper off disc. If working on both wheels, mark calipers right or left.

6. Remove the inboard pad hold down clips and the pin insulators from the anchor plate.

7. Remove the inboard pad.

8. Using a small screwdriver, lift the outer pad retaining clips off the retaining pins. Remove the outer pad.

9. Insert new caliper locating pin insulators in the anchor plate.

10. Install the inboard pad retaining clips.

11. Using a piston retracting tool (see steps 13 & 14 of Disc Pad Replacement for Ford, Mercury, etc.), push the piston completely into its cylinder.

12. Install outer pad and retaining clips.

13. Install the caliper onto the disc being careful not to pinch the piston boot between the inner pad and the piston.

14. Attach a new stabilizer to the caliper with clean locating pins.

15. Attach the stabilizer to the anchor plate.

16. Connect brake hose (if previously disconnected) using new copper washers, one on each side of the hose fitting. Bleed brakes.

17. Check the brake fluid level and pump the brake pedal to seat the pads against the disc. Install the wheels and road test the car.

Servicing the Caliper Assembly

1. Raise the vehicle on a hoist and remove the front wheels.

2. Disconnect and plug the brake line.

3. Remove the lockwires from the two caliper mounting bolts and remove the bolt. Lift the caliper off the disc.

4. Remove and discard the locating pin insulators. Replace all rubber parts at reassembly.

5. Remove the retaining clips with a screwdriver and slide the outboard pad and retaining pins out of the caliper. Remove the inboard pad. Loosen the bleed screw and drain the brake fluid.

6. Remove the two small bolts and caliper stabilizers.

7. Remove the inboard pad retaining clips and bolts.

8. Clean and inspect all parts, and reinstall on anchor plate. Do not tighten stabilizer bolts at this time.

9. Remove the piston by applying compressed air to the fluid inlet hole. Use care to prevent the piston from popping out of control.

Caution Do not attempt to catch the piston with the hand. Use folded towels to cushion it.

10. Remove the piston boot. Inspect the piston for scoring, pitting, or corrosion. The piston must be replaced if there is any visible damage or wear.

11. Remove the piston seal from the cylinder bore. *Do not use any metal tools for this operation.*

12. Clean the caliper with fresh brake fluid. Inspect the cylinder bore for damage or wear. Light defects can be removed by rotating crocus cloth around the bore. Do not use any other type of abrasive.

13. Lubricate all new rubber parts in brake fluid. Install the piston seal in the cylinder groove. Install the boot into its piston groove.

14. Install the piston, open end out, into the bore while working the boot around the outside of the piston. Make sure boot lip is seated in the piston groove.

15. Slide the anchor plate assembly onto the caliper housing and reinstall the locating pins. Tighten pins to specification. Tighten stabilizer anchor plate bolts. Perform Steps 4-8 of Disc Pad Replacement.

16. Connect the brake line and bleed the brakes (see Brake Bleeding).

17. Install the front wheels, recheck the brake fluid level, and road test the car.

Ford Single Piston Sliding Caliper Brake

Pad Replacement

All Models except Pinto through 1973

1. Raise the car, safely support it and remove the tire and wheel assembly.
2. Remove the retaining screw from the caliper retaining key.
3. Using a hammer and drift, remove the caliper retaining key and support spring from the anchor plate. Be careful not to damage key.
4. Push the caliper down against the anchor plate and rotate the upper end off the anchor plate.
5. Remove the inboard pad from the anchor plate. Do not lose the anti-rattle clip. Tap lightly on the outer pad to free it from the caliper. If the original pads are to be reused, mark them as to location for correct installation.
6. Clean all components and inspect for damage, leakage and excessive wear.

NOTE: *if the pads on one wheel are replaced it is necessary to replace those on the other wheel to maintain equal braking action.*

7. When installing new pads, use a 4 in. c-clamp and a block of wood measuring 1-¾ in. x 1 in. x ¾ in. thick. This will aid in seating the piston in its cylinder so that the caliper will fit over the new pads when installed.
8. Install the anti-rattle clip on the lower inboard pad support located on the anchor plate (on the lower end of the inner pad, starting 1974). The loop of the clip must be toward the inside of the plate. Place the inner pad on the anchor plate.

9. Install the outer pad with the upper flanges over the shoulders on the caliper legs. If the old pads are reused, be certain they are installed in their original positions.
10. If previously used, remove the C-clamp from the caliper since the piston will remain seated in its cylinder.
11. Position the caliper assembly lower V-groove on the anchor plate lower abutment surface.
12. Pivot the caliper housing upward toward the disc until the outer edge of the piston dust boot is about ¼ in. from the upper edge of inboard pad.
13. Place a piece of thin cardboard between the inboard pad and the lower half of the piston dust boot to prevent pinching of the boot when rotating the caliper onto the disc.
14. Continue to rotate the caliper onto the disc until a slight resistance is felt.
15. Gradually remove the cardboard as the caliper rotates onto the disc. Complete the rotation onto the disc and completely remove the cardboard.
16. Slide the caliper up against the upper anchor plate abutment and center it over the lower anchor plate abutment.
17. Install the caliper support spring and key into the opening between the lower end of the caliper and the lower anchor plate abutment. The hole in the slot must be centered over the threaded hole in the anchor plate.

18. Install the key retaining screw and torque to 12-16 ft. lbs.
19. Check the brake fluid level and pump the brake pedal to seat the pads against the disc. Install the wheels and road test the car.

Pinto through 1973

1. Raise car and support safely. Remove wheel and tire assembly.
2. Remove the two cotter pins from the retaining key.
3. Using a hammer and drift, carefully remove the key.
4. Push in on the caliper assembly and lift it away from the anchor plate.

NOTE: do not stretch or twist the brake hose.

5. Using wire, temporarily suspend the caliper assembly from the upper suspension arms.
6. If brake pads are to be reused, mark them as to correct location.
7. Remove the pads from the anchor plate.
8. Clean the caliper, anchor plate and disc and inspect them for leakage, damage or excessive wear.

NOTE: *if the shoes are replaced on one wheel they must also be replaced on the other wheel to maintain balanced brake action.*

9. When installing new pads, it is necessary to compress the piston in its cylinder to provide enough clearance for the caliper to fit over the pads. To perform this, place a block of wood (1-¾" x 1" x ¾" thick) on the piston and clamp down on it with a 4 in. C-clamp.

DUST SHIELD

ANCHOR PLATE

CALIPER ASSEMBLY

KEY RETAINER SCREW

KEY

CALIPER SUPPORT SPRING

OUTER BRAKE SHOE AND LINING ASSEMBLY

HUB AND ROTOR ASSEMBLY

Ford Sliding caliper disc brake—all models except Pinto through 1973
(© Ford Motor Co)

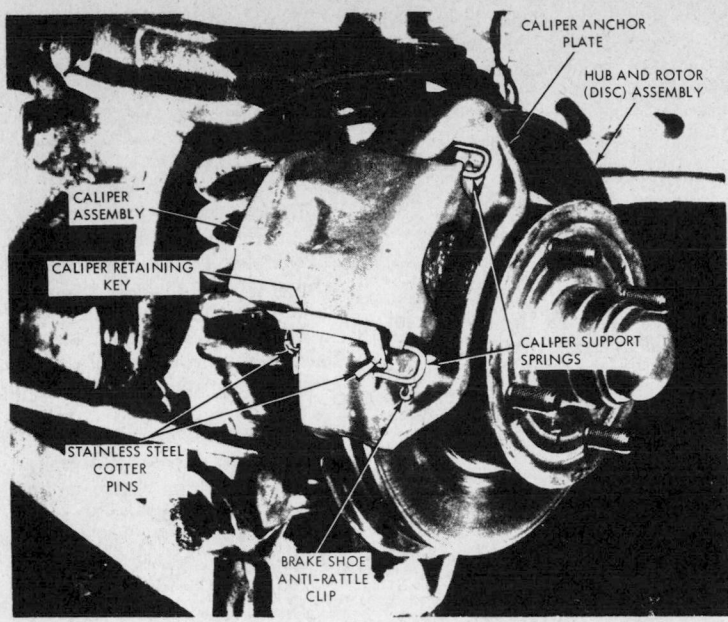

CALIPER ANCHOR PLATE

HUB AND ROTOR (DISC) ASSEMBLY

CALIPER ASSEMBLY

CALIPER RETAINING KEY

CALIPER SUPPORT SPRINGS

STAINLESS STEEL COTTER PINS

BRAKE SHOE ANTI-RATTLE CLIP

Ford sliding caliper disc brake—Pinto through 1973 (© Ford Motor Co)

10. Place pads and anti-rattle clips in anchor plate.
11. Remove the C-clamp from the piston and remove the wire holding the caliper to the suspension arm.
12. Place the caliper on the anchor plate so that the lower edge of the caliper is on top of the rear caliper support spring.
13. Pivot the caliper over the pads until the upper edge of the caliper can be pushed over the forward caliper support spring.
14. Using a heavy screwdriver, hold the caliper over the upper support spring and against the anchor plate. Insert the retaining key.
15. Install two new stainless steel cotter pins in the key.
16. Check the brake fluid level and pump the brake pedal to seat the pads against the disc. Install the wheels and road test the car.

Servicing the Caliper Assembly

All Models except Pinto through 1973

To service the caliper on these models, follow the instructions listed for the same models under Pad Replacement. The instructions are identical with one exception—caliper service requires you to disconnect and connect the brake hose from the caliper and bleed the brakes. If it is necessary to remove and install piston, follow steps 6-12 of Pinto through 1973.

Pinto through 1973

1. Raise the car and support safely. Remove the wheel and tire assembly.
2. Disconnect the brake hose from the caliper.
3. Remove the two cotter pins from the retaining key.
4. Using a drift and hammer, remove the retaining key.
5. Press inward on the caliper assembly and lift it away from the anchor plate.
6. Remove the piston by applying air pressure to the caliper fluid port.
IMPORTANT: to prevent piston damage and possible personal injury, place a cloth over the piston before applying air pressure.
7. If the piston is seized in its cylinder, tap lightly around the piston while applying air pressure.
8. Remove and discard the piston dust boot and seal.
9. Clean (using alcohol) and inspect all parts for damage or excessive wear. Replace the piston if pitted or scored or if the chrome plating is worn off.
10. Lightly coat a new piston seal with clean brake fluid and seat it in the piston groove.
11. Install a new dust boot with its flange in the outer groove of the cylinder.
12. Coat the piston with fluid and install in the cylinder. Spread the dust boot over the piston while inserting it in cylinder and seat it in the piston groove.
13. Place the caliper on the anchor plate so that the lower edge of the caliper can be pushed over the forward caliper support spring.
14. Using a heavy screwdriver, hold the caliper over the upper support spring and against the anchor plate. Insert the retaining key.

15. Install two new stainless steel cotter pins in the key.
16. Connect the brake hose and bleed the brakes.
17. Check the brake fluid level and pump the brake pedal to seat the pads against the disc. Install the wheels and road test the car.

Servicing the Disc— All Cars

Disc Replacement

1. Raise the vehicle on a hoist and remove the wheel.
2. Remove the caliper mounting bolts. Slide the caliper away from the disc and suspend it using a wire loop. On some cars, it is advisable to install a cardboard spacer between the pads to prevent the piston from coming out of its cylinder.
3. Remove the wheel bearing nut from the spindle and remove the outer wheel bearing roller assembly from the hub.
   On Ford sliding caliper brakes, remove the wheel bearing adjusting nut and pull the hub and disc assembly outward enough to loosen the washer and outer wheel bearing. Push the assembly back onto the spindle and remove the washer and outer wheel bearing from the spindle.
4. Remove the hub and disc assembly from the spindle.
5. Installation of hub and disc is in reverse order of removal.

Caution Alignment of the caliper assembly depends on proper sequence of bolt installations on some cars. Check caliper installation procedure under Disc Pad Replacement of proper brake type.
NOTE: the disc is removable from the hub on the Eldorado, Toronado, and Corvette (rear only).

To separate the rear disc and hub on a Corvette the three hub-to-disc attaching rivets must be drilled out. This can be done with the hub and rotor mounted on the car. It is not necessary to install new rivets when the disc is installed.

Lateral Runout

Lateral runout is the movement of the disc from side to side (wobble) as it rotates. Excessive runout will result in brake chatter, pedal pumping, excessive pedal travel, or vibration during braking.
To check lateral runout:
1. Tighten the spindle nut until there is no end-play in the bearings, just loose enough to allow wheel to turn.
2. Fasten a dial indicator to the suspension so that the point con-

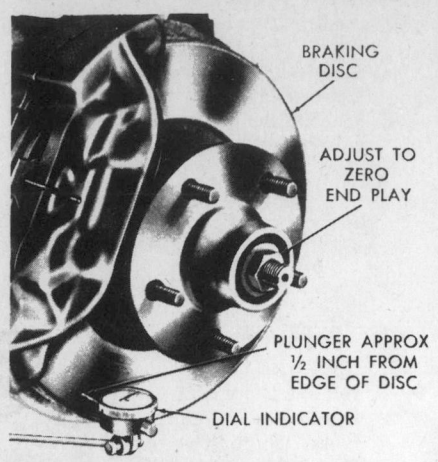

BRAKING DISC

ADJUST TO ZERO END PLAY

PLUNGER APPROX ½ INCH FROM EDGE OF DISC

DIAL INDICATOR

Checking disc runout
(© Chrysler Corp)

tacts the disc face about ½ in. from the outer edge.

3. Set the dial to zero. Turn the disc through one complete revolution and check the indicator as the disc moves.

If the runout is more than the allowable maximum the disc and hub assembly should be replaced. Be sure to readjust the spindle nut if its setting was changed while checking the disc.

Parallelism

Parallelism refers to the variations in thickness of the disc. Excessive variation can cause pedal vibration and front end vibration during braking. Parallelism can be checked by measuring thickness at four or more equally spaced points around the braking surface of the disc. All measurements must be made at the same distance from the outer edge of the disc. The disc and hub should be replaced if variations in thickness ex-

ceed specification. Do not forget to adjust the spindle nut to specification if its setting was changed while checking the disc.

Rear Disc Brakes— Imperial

Pad Replacement and Caliper Service

The sliding caliper which is used on the rear of 1974-75 Imperial models is serviced in the same manner as the Kelsey-Hayes sliding caliper which is used on the front. Disc brake pad changing and caliper removal procedures are identical, except that the rear caliper has a dust shield, which must be removed prior to caliper removal.

Parking Brake

The disc used on the rear of 1974-75 Imperial has a 7 in. internal parking brake drum. The brake assembly itself is mounted on the rear axle flange and disc adapter.

See the car section for parking brake adjustment procedures.

Rear Disc/Drum Removal and Installation

1. Remove the caliper assembly. See the procedure for removing the sliding caliper from the front wheels of Chrysler products. Do not disconnect the caliper from the brake lines; safety wire it to the rear spring.
2. Remove the inboard pad.
3. Take the plug out of the parking brake adjuster access hole. Insert a brake adjusting tool into the hole and engage the notches on the starwheel. Pry down with

the tool to release the adjustment.
4. Pull the disc/drum assembly off the studs.

Installation is the reverse of removal.

Drum Inspection

Measure drum runout and diameter. Variation in drum diameter should not exceed 0.006 in. Reface drums which exceed these specifications. Do not remove more than 0.060 in. from the standard drum diameter. The maximum allowable diameter of 7.090 in. is stamped on the drum.

Parking Brake Shoe Removal and Installation

1. Remove the caliper and disc/drum assembly.
2. Remove the lower brake shoe return spring.
3. Spread the shoes slightly and remove the starwheel adjuster assembly.
4. Remove the upper shoe return spring.
5. Move the shoes off the support and remove the retainers, springs and nails. Remove the shoes.

Installation is as follows:

1. Lubricate the shoe tab contact area on the support plate with special brake grease.
2. Position the shoes on the support plate and install the nails, springs, and retainers.
3. Install the upper shoe return spring.
4. Install the starwheel adjuster. The starwheel goes forward on the left side and rearward in the right side.
5. Install the lower shoe return spring.

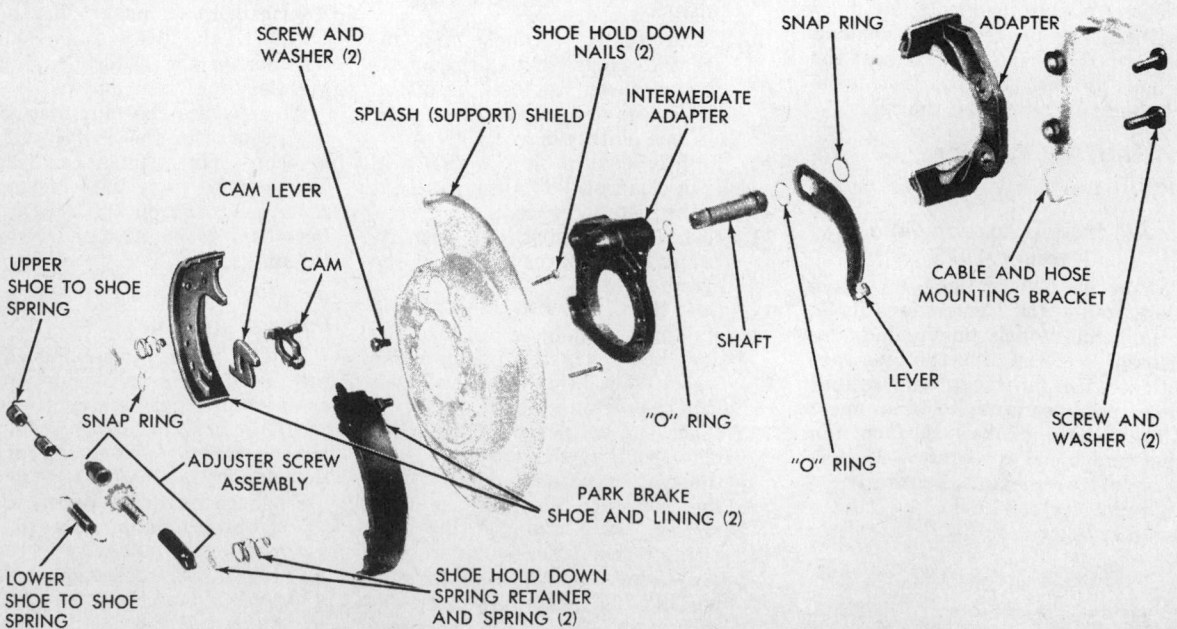

UPPER SHOE TO SHOE SPRING

SNAP RING

CAM LEVER

CAM

SCREW AND WASHER (2)

SPLASH (SUPPORT) SHIELD

SHOE HOLD DOWN NAILS (2)

INTERMEDIATE ADAPTER

SNAP RING

ADAPTER

SHAFT

CABLE AND HOSE MOUNTING BRACKET

"O" RING

LEVER

"O" RING

SCREW AND WASHER (2)

ADJUSTER SCREW ASSEMBLY

PARK BRAKE SHOE AND LINING (2)

SHOE HOLD DOWN SPRING RETAINER AND SPRING (2)

LOWER SHOE TO SHOE SPRING

Rear wheel parking brake components—Imperial (© Chrysler Corp)

6. Install the disc/drum and caliper.

Lever, Cam and Shaft Removal and Installation

1. Detach the parking brake cable from the inner operating lever and separate the snap ring retainer from the shaft. Remove the operating lever.
2. Remove the inner shaft snapring and the cam lever. Remove the cam.
3. Pull out the shaft.

Installation is the reverse of removal. Lubricate the shaft with brake grease.

Rear Disc Brakes— Chevrolet Corvette

Pad Replacement and Caliper Service

The Corvette uses Delco-Moraine four-piston fixed caliper disc brakes on the rear wheels, as well as on the front. Rear disc brake pad replacement and caliper service procedures are the same as those for "Delco-Moraine 4 Piston Brake."

Parking Brakes

The discs used on the rear of the Corvette have integral drums which are used as parking brakes only. See the "Chevrolet-Corvette" section for parking brake adjustment procedures.

Corvette Parking Brake Shoe Removal and Installation

1. Jack the car up and remove the rear wheels and tires.
2. Remove the brake caliper from the disc. Do not disconnect the brake line, but remove the line clip from the control arm and hang the caliper above the disc with wire.
3. Drill the disc retaining rivets out and remove the disc from the axle hub. It is not necessary to replace the rivets when the disc is reinstalled.
4. Insert a screwdriver into the adjusting hole and turn the screw several times to expand the shoes.
5. Push the brake shoes forward until the front shoe hold-down spring can be seen through the adjusting hole.
6. Insert a pair of needle-nosed pliers through the hole and grasp the hold-down pin. Depress the spring with a screwdriver inserted from the side and turn the pin 90° to free the spring and retainer. Remove the spring and retainer.
7. Repeat this operation on the rear brake shoe.
8. Retract the shoes by turning the adjuster screw. Pull the shoes

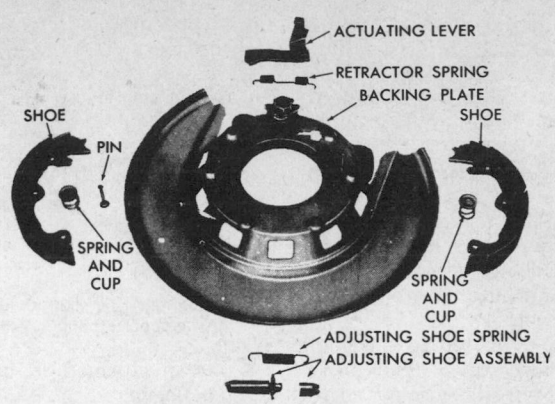

Rear wheel parking brake components— Corvette (© Chevrolet Div., GM Corp)

from the adjuster and remove the adjuster and spring.
9. Separate the shoes at the anchor pin and lift the shoes up and out of the housing, while allowing the straight part of the return spring to go between the outer tip of the anchor pin and the axle flange plate.
10. Lightly lubricate the backing plate shoe contact surfaces, anchor pin, and adjusting screw threads.
11. Install the return spring on the replacement shoes and position the shoes on the anchor pin.
12. Install the adjuster spring and adjuster. Turn the adjuster screw to expand the shoes.
13. Turn the axle shaft flange so that the adjustment hole aligns with the front hold-down spring pin.
14. Push the shoe forward and over the hold-down pin.
15. Install the spring and retainer over the hold-down pin and using needle-nosed pliers and a screwdriver as in step 6, depress the spring and twist the pin 90°.
16. Repeat the above step on the rear shoe. Another pair of needle-nosed pliers will have to be utilized to hold the pin in position, as head of this pin is not accessible.
17. Turn the adjuster screw to retract the shoes.
18. Install the brake disc onto the studs, making sure that the adjustment holes in the disc and flange align.
19. Install the caliper.
20. Adjust the parking brake as described above.
21. Install the tire and wheel and lower the car.

Burnishing New Parking Brake Linings

Perform this procedure after new parking brake shoes have been installed:
1. Adjust the parking brakes.

2. Drive the car at a steady 50 mph and apply the parking brake lever 10 to 12 notches (until a light drag is felt).
3. Hold this speed with the brake applied for 50-60 seconds and then release the brake.

Rear Disc Brakes— Ford Motor Co.

Starting 1975, rear disc brakes are standard equipment on Continental Mark IV models and are optional on Lincoln, Ford, Mercury, Thunderbird, Granada, and Monarch.

The rear sliding caliper assembly is similar to the one used on the front, except for the parking brake mechanism and a bigger anti-rattle spring. The parking brake lever on the caliper is cable-operated by depressing (or releasing) the parking brake pedal under the dash panel.

When the pedal is depressed, the cable rotates the parking brake lever (on the back of the caliper) and the operating shaft (inside the caliper). Three steel balls, which are located in pockets on the opposing heads of the shaft and thrust screw, roll between ramps formed in the pockets. The motion of the balls forces the thrust screw away from the shaft which, in turn, forces the piston and pad assembly against the disc to create braking action.

An automatic adjuster in the piston compensates for pad wear by moving the thrust screw.

Pad Replacement

NOTE: This procedure requires the use of a special service tool.
1. Raise the car and support it with jackstands. Block the front wheels if they remain on the ground.
2. Remove the wheel and tire.
3. Disconnect the cable from the caliper parking brake lever. Be careful not to kink or cut the cable and return spring.

4. Unfasten the setscrew which secures the caliper key. Use a hammer and soft brass drift (if necessary) to slide the support spring and retaining key out of the anchor plate.

5. Push the caliper against the anchor plate and rotate its upper end away from the plate. If a ridge of rust on the disc prevents caliper removal, scrape the rust away with a putty knife or similar blunt tool.

6. If the disc is scored to the point that the caliper still can't be removed, loosen the caliper end retainer ½-turn, after removing the retaining screw and caliper parking brake lever. Also, be sure to matchmark the caliper housing and end retainer to ensure that the retainer is only given ½-turn.

Caution Turning the end retainer more than ½-turn could cause internal fluid leaks in the caliper, which would make caliper rebuilding necessary.

7. Wire the caliper assembly out of the way to avoid stretching or kinking the brake hose.

8. Remove the inner pad assembly from the retaining clip. Tap lightly on the outer pad to free it from the caliper.

9. Mark the pads for proper installation if they are not going to be replaced. Used pads must be returned to the same side from which they were removed.

10. If the pad is worn to within 1/8 in. of the shoe surface, replace all of the pads on both rear brakes. Do not replace just one pad or one set of pads; uneven braking will result.

NOTE: Pad replacement requires the use of a special tool to bottom the piston in its bore.

11. Inspect the caliper for leaks. Clean any rust off the caliper and anchor plate sliding surfaces or inner brake pad abutment surfaces on the anchor plate.

Installation is as follows:

1. If the end retainer was loosened in order to remove the caliper, perform the following:
   a. Install the caliper on the anchor plate and secure it with the key, but do not install the pads.
   b. Tighten the retainer end to 75-95 ft lbs.
   c. Install the caliper parking brake lever with the arm pointing rearward and down. This allows the cable to pass under the axle.
   d. Tighten the lever retaining screw to 16-22 ft lbs. Check for free rotation of the lever.
   e. Remove the caliper.

2. The following special steps must

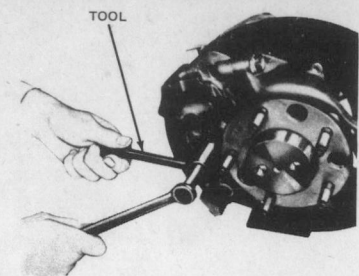

Adjusting the rear caliper piston depth with the special tool (© Ford Motor Co)

be performed if new pads are being installed:
   a. Remove the disc and install the caliper less the pads. Use only the key to retain the caliper.
   b. Seat the special tool firmly against the piston by holding the shaft rotating the tool handle.
   c. Loosen the handle ¼-turn. Hold the handle and rotate the tool shaft clockwise until the caliper piston bottoms (it will continue to turn after it bottoms).
   d. Rotate the handle until the piston is firmly seated.
   e. Remove the caliper and install the disc.

3. Confirm that the brake pad anti-rattle clip is correctly positioned in the lower inner brake pad support, the clip loop should face the inside of the anchor plate.

4. Fit the inner pad assembly on the anchor plate, with the lining facing the disc.

5. Install the outer brake pad with its lower flanges against the caliper leg abutments and its upper flanges against the machined shoulder surfaces.

6. Lubricate the caliper and anchor plate sliding surfaces with special brake lubricant. Keep the lubricant off the pad and disc.

7. Position the caliper housing lower groove against the anchor plate lower abutment surfaces. Rotate the housing until it is completely over the disc. Be careful not to damage the dust boot.

8. Slide the caliper outward until the inner pad is seated firmly against the disc. Measure the outer pad-to-disc clearance. It should be 1/16 in. or less. If it is more, adjust the piston *outward* with the special tool (See step 2). Each ¼-turn of the piston is about 1/16 in. of piston movement.

Caution If piston clearance is more than 1/16 in., the adjuster may pull out of the piston when the service brakes are applied, causing adjuster failure.

9. Center the caliper over the lower anchor plate abutment, while holding it over the upper abutment.

10. Install the retaining spring and key in the keyway and slide them into the opening at the lower end of the caliper and anchor plate abutment. Center the semi-circular slot in the key over the anchor plate setscrew hole. Tighten the setscrew to 12-16 ft lbs.

11. Attach the parking brake cable to the lower lever end.

12. If the caliper was completely removed (lines disconnected), bleed the hydraulic system. Run the engine and lightly pump the service brake pedal 40 times; allow one second between brake applications. Check the parking brake for too much travel or too light operating effort. Repeat the pumping and adjust the cable, if necessary.

13. Install the wheel and tire, remove the jackstand and lower the car.

14. Make sure that the service brake pedal feels firm and then road-test the car. Check parking brake operation.

Caliper Removal and Installation

Perform all of the necessary procedures in the disc brake pad removal and installation section, and do the following:

1. Prior to removing the caliper, disconnect the rear brake pipe fitting from the hose end at the frame bracket.

2. Plug the brake pipe.

3. Unfasten the horseshoe clip from the hose fitting and separate the hose from the bracket. On Granadas and Monarchs, remove the hose bracket from the spring seat.

4. On Lincoln and Mercury models, unscrew the hose fitting from the caliper. On Mark IV, Granada, Monarch, and Thunderbird models, unfasten the hollow retaining nut which secures the fitting to the caliper.

When installing the caliper, perform the following additional steps.

1. On Lincoln and Mercury models, put a new gasket on the fitting and screw the fitting into the caliper port; tighten to 20-30 ft lbs. On Mark IV, Granada, Monarch, and Thunderbird models, put new gaskets on either side of the fitting outlet and insert the hollow securing bolt through the washers and fitting; tighten to 17-20 ft lbs. On Granada and Monarch be sure to fit the hose pin in the hole on the caliper.

2. Fit the upper end of the flexible hose in the bracket and install

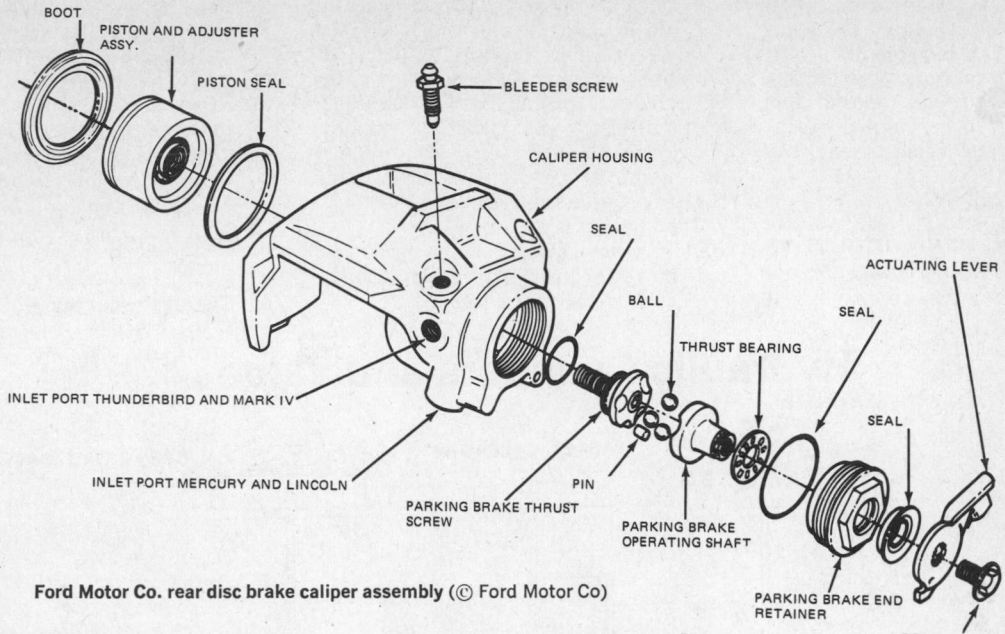

Ford Motor Co. rear disc brake caliper assembly (© Ford Motor Co)

the horseshoe clip. Do not twist or coil the brake hose; keep the stripe on the hose straight. On Granada and Monarch, install the hose bracket on the spring seat.

3. Unplug the pipe. Connect the hose to the pipe and tighten the fitting to 10-15 ft lbs.

4. Bleed the brake system.

Caliper Overhaul

1. Remove the caliper assembly from the car.

2. Remove the retaining screw, parking brake lever, and caliper end retainer.

3. Pull out the operating shaft, thrust bearing, and balls from the caliper.

4. Using either a magnet or tweezers, extract the thrust screw anti-rotation pin.

5. Using a ¼ in. Allen key, rotate the thrust screw counterclockwise to remove it.

6. Push the piston/adjuster assembly out of its bore from behind.

NOTE: A special tool is available to do this. Use care not to scratch the bore or press on the piston adjuster can while removing the piston.

7. Remove and discard the following:
   a. Piston seal
   b. Boot
   c. Thrust screw O-ring seal
   d. End retainer O-ring
   e. End retainer lip seal

8. Clean all metal parts in isopropyl alcohol. Dry them with compressed air. Be sure that no foreign material remains in the caliper.

9. Inspect the caliper bores. The thrust screw bore must be smooth and show no sign of pitting.

10. If the piston is pitted, scored, or the plating worn off, replace the piston/adjuster as an assembly. The adjuster can should not be loose, high, or damaged; if it is, replace the piston/adjuster assembly. If brake adjustment is incorrect, replace the piston/adjuster assembly.

NOTE: The piston and the adjuster must be replaced as an assembly. No attempt to repair the adjuster should be made.

11. If in doubt about adjuster operation; check it as follows:
   a. Install the thrust screw in the piston/adjuster.
   b. Pull the two pieces apart about ¼ in. and release them.
   c. When the pieces are pulled apart, the brass drive ring should remain stationary, causing the nut to turn.
   d. When the pieces are released, the nut should remain stationary and the drive ring rotate.
   e. Replace the piston/adjuster if it fails to operate in this manner.

12. Inspect all bearing, sliding, rotating and rolling surfaces for wear, pitting or brinnelling. Replace any parts necessary. A polished appearance on ball paths or bearing surfaces is OK, as long as there is no sign of wear into the surface.

Assembly is as follows:

1. Coat a new piston seal with clean brake fluid. Seat the seal in the groove of the bore. Be sure it is not twisted.

2. Seat the flange of a new dust boot squarely in the caliper bore outer groove.

3. Coat the piston/adjuster assembly with clean brake fluid.

Spread the dust boot over the piston and install the piston. Seat the dust boot in the piston/adjuster groove.

4. Lay the caliper assembly (rear of bore up) in a soft-jawed vise. Do not tighten the vise; housing distortion will result.

5. Fill the piston/adjuster assembly up to the bottom edge of thrust screw bore with clean brake fluid.

6. Install a new O-ring in the thrust screw groove, after coating it with clean brake fluid. Use a ¼ in. Allen key to install the thrust screw in the piston adjuster assembly, until its top surface is flush with the bottom of the threaded bore. Align the notches on the thrust screw with those on the caliper housing. Install the anti-rotation pin.

7. Install one ball in each of the three thrust screw pockets. Coat all components of the parking brake mechanism with a liberal amount of silicone grease.

8. Install the parking brake operating shaft over the balls. Coat the thrust bearing with silicone grease and fit it on the shaft.

9. Install a new lip seal and O-ring on the caliper end retainer. Coat both seals with a light film of silicone grease and install the end retainer on the caliper; tighten it to 75-90 ft lbs. Hold the operating shaft so that it is securely seated against the parking brake mechanism during end retainer installation. If the lip seal is dislocated, reseat it.

10. Install the parking brake lever over its keyed spline, so that it points down and rearward.

Torque the lever securing screw to 16-22 ft lbs. Check the lever for freedom of movement.
11. Support the caliper and bottom the piston with the special tool as in steps 2b through d of the disc brake pad replacement procedure.
12. Install the caliper.

Disc Removal and Installation
1. Remove the caliper assembly and wire it out of the way, unless it

is to be serviced. Do not remove the anchor plate.
2. If corrosion makes identification difficult, mark the raised (not the braking) surface of the disc "RIGHT" or "LEFT" prior to removal.
3. Remove the securing nuts and take the disc off the axle shaft.
   Installation is as follows:
1. If a new disc is being used, remove its protective coating with carburetor degreaser.

2. Identify the left and right discs before installation. The words "LEFT" and "RIGHT" are cast into the inner surface of the raised section of the disc. This is important, since the cooling vanes cast into the disc must face in the direction of forward rotation.
3. Install the two disc securing nuts.
4. Install the caliper.

Hydraulic Cylinders and Valves

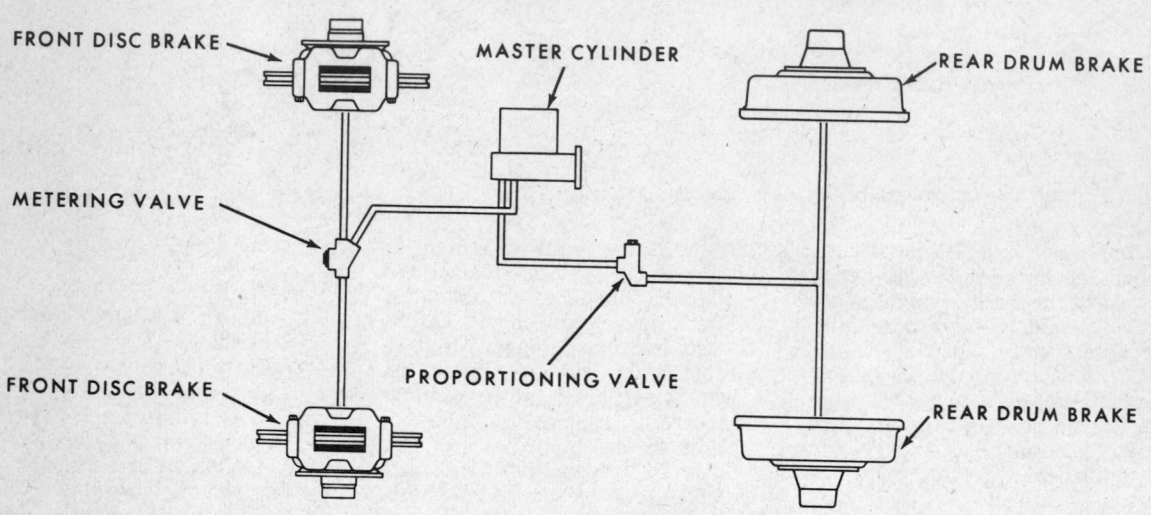

Disc brake hydraulic system

Master Cylinders

Dual master cylinders, used on all cars, are actually two single master cylinders operating in the same bore. They are designed so that the front and rear brakes have separate hydraulic systems. Malfunction in either system has no effect on the other system but is immediately evident to the driver because of the additional pedal travel required to actuate the remaining half of the brake system. Service procedure for single master cylinders is identical, except that there is only one piston assembly and no stop screw. Some master cylinders have bleed screws on the outlet flanges and may be bled without disturbing the wheel cylinders.

Servicing Master Cylinders
1. Remove the cylinder from the car and drain the brake fluid.
2. Mount the cylinder in a vise so that the outlets are up and remove the seal from the hub.
3. Remove the stop screw from the bottom of the front reservoir.
4. Remove the snap-ring from the front of the bore and remove the primary piston assembly.
5. Remove the secondary piston assembly using compressed air or a

piece of wire. Cover the bore opening with a cloth to prevent damage to the piston.
6. Clean metal parts in brake fluid and discard rubber parts.
7. Inspect the bore for damage or wear, and check pistons for

damage and proper clearance in the bore.
8. If the bore is only slightly scored or pitted it may be honed. Always use hones that are in good condition and completely clean the cylinder with brake fluid

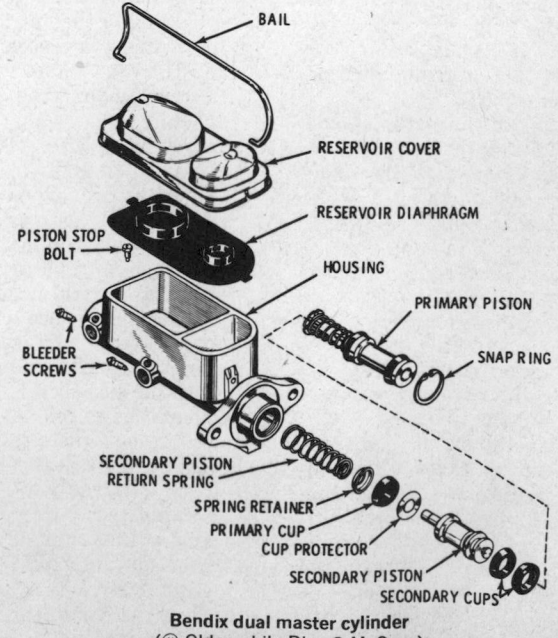

Bendix dual master cylinder
(© Oldsmobile Div., G.M. Corp)

when honing is completed. If any evidence of contamination exists in the master cylinder the entire hydraulic system should be flushed and refilled with clean brake fluid. Blow out passages with compressed air.

9. Install new secondary seals in the two grooves in the flat end of the front piston. The lips of the seals will be facing away from each other.

10. Install a new primary seal and the seal protector on opposite end of the front piston with the lips of the seal facing outward.

11. Coat the seals with brake fluid. Install the spring on the front piston with the spring retainer in the primary seal.

12. Insert the piston assembly, spring end first, into the bore and use a wooden rod to seat it.

13. Coat the rear piston seals with brake fluid and install them into the piston grooves with the lips facing the spring end.

14. Assemble the spring onto the piston and install the assembly into the bore spring first. Install the snap-ring.

15. Hold the piston train at the bottom of the bore and install the stop screw. Install a new seal on the hub. Bench-bleed the cylinder or install and bleed the cylinder on the car.

Wheel Cylinders

Servicing Wheel Cylinders

1. Raise the vehicle on a hoist and remove the wheel and drum from the brake to be serviced.

2. Remove the brake shoes and clean the backing plate and wheel cylinder.

3. Disconnect the brake line from the brake hose. Remove the brake hose retainer clip at the frame bracket and remove the hose from the wheel cylinder. (On rear brakes it will only be necessary to remove the line from the cylinder.)

4. Remove the cylinder mounting bolts and remove the cylinder.

5. Remove the boots from the cylinder ends and discard. Remove the pistons, remove and discard the seal cups, and remove the expanders and spring.

6. Inspect the bore and pistons for damage or wear. Damaged pistons should be discarded, as they cannot be reconditioned. Slight bore roughness can be removed using a brake cylinder hone or crocus cloth. (Cloth should be rotated in the bore under finger pressure. Do not slide lengthwise). Use only lint-free cloth for cleaning.

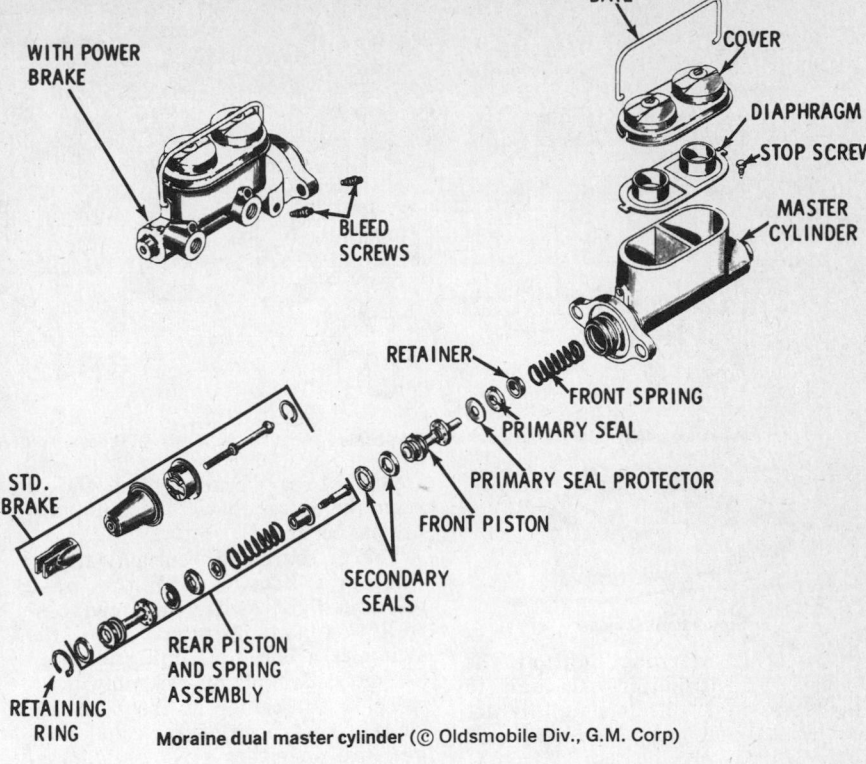

Moraine dual master cylinder (© Oldsmobile Div., G.M. Corp)

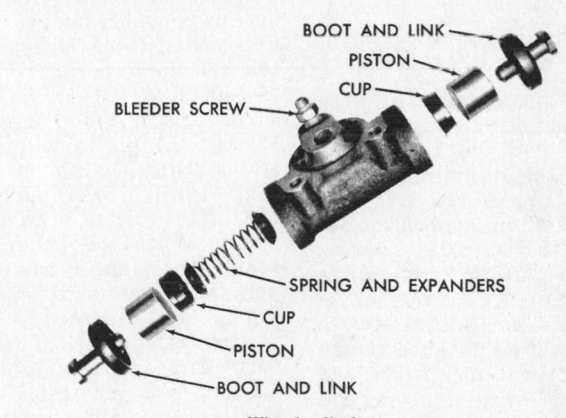

Wheel cylinder
(© Chevrolet Div., G.M. Corp)

7. Clean the cylinder and internal parts *using only brake fluid or denatured alcohol.*

8. Insert the spring expander assembly. Lubricate all rubber parts using only fresh brake fluid.

9. Install new cups with the seal lips facing inwards.

10. Install the pistons and rubber boots. Install the cylinder on the car in reverse order of removal. Bleed the cylinder (see Brake Bleeding).

Proportioning Valves

On vehicles equipped with front disc and rear drum (or rear disc) brakes a proportioning valve is an important part of the system. It is installed in the hydraulic line to the rear brakes. Its function is to maintain the correct proportion between line pressures to the front and rear brakes. It prevents early lock-up of rear brakes and provides balanced braking during hard stops. *No attempt at adjustment of this valve should be made, as adjustment is pre-set and tampering will result in uneven braking action.*

To assure correct installation when replacing the valve, the outlet to the rear brakes is stamped with the letter "R". Replacement is a simple job requiring no special instructions.

Beginning with 1971 models, General Motors and American Motors installed a combination valve on their front disc (rear drum) brake cars. This valve combines in one unit, a metering valve, a proportioning valve and a pressure differential warning valve. Mounted on top of the unit is an electrical terminal which connects

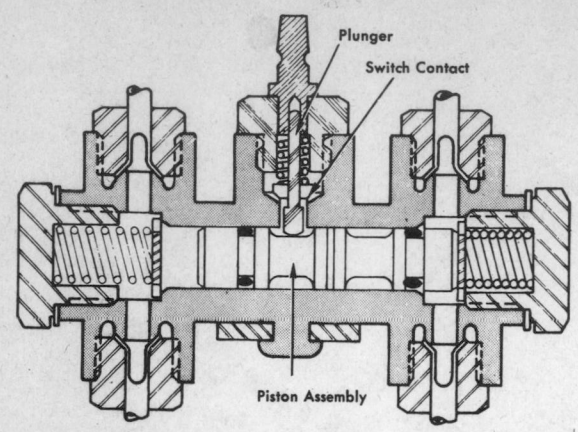

Pressure differential warning valve—ON position

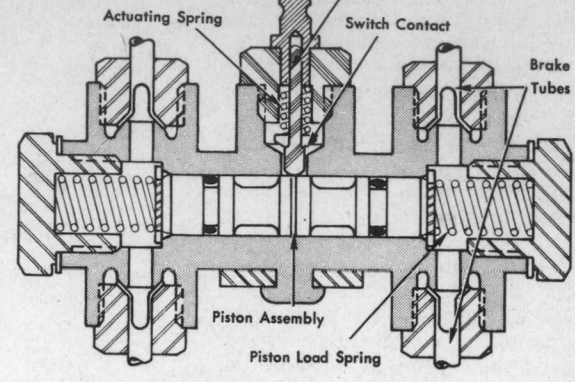

Pressure differential warning valve—OFF position

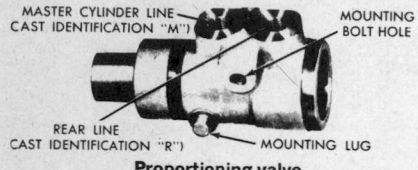

Proportioning valve

to the brake warning light on the dash. Ford introduced this unit to their cars in 1972. This unit is not serviceable and must be replaced if faulty.

Metering Valves

On some vehicles equipped with disc brakes a metering valve is used. This valve is installed in the hydraulic line to the front brakes, and functions to delay pressure buildup to the front brakes on application. It provides balanced braking during mild stops. Its purpose is to reduce front brake pressure until rear brake pressure builds up adequately to overcome the rear brake shoe return springs. In this way disc brake pad life is extended because it prevents the front disc brakes from carrying all or most of the braking load at low operating line pressures.

The metering valve can be checked very simply. With the car stopped, gently apply the brakes. At about one inch of travel a very small change in pedal effort (like a small bump) will be felt if the valve is operating properly. Metering valves are not serviceable, and must be replaced if defective.

Pressure Differential Warning Valves

Since the introduction of dual master cylinders to the hydraulic brake system, a pressure differential warning signal has been added. This signal consists of a warning light on the dashboard activated by a differential pressure switch located below the master cylinder. The signal indicates a loss of fluid pressure in either the

front or rear brakes, and should warn the driver that a hydraulic failure has occurred.

The pressure differential warning valve is a housing with the brake warning light switch mounted centrally on top. Directly below the switch is a bore containing a piston assembly. The piston assembly is located in the center of the bore and kept in that position by equal fluid pressure on either side. Fluid pressure is provided by two brake lines, one coming from the rear brake system and one from the front brakes. If a leak develops in either system (front or rear), fluid pressure to that side of the piston will decrease or stop causing the piston to move in that direction. The plunger on the end of the switch engages with the piston. When the piston moves off center, the plunger moves and triggers the switch to activate the warning light on the dash.

After repairing and bleeding any part of the hydraulic system the warning light may remain on due to the pressure differential valve remaining in the off-center position. All cars except a few American Motors models have a self-centering valve. After repairs or bleeding have been performed, center the valve by

applying moderate pressure on the brake pedal. This will turn out the light.

NOTE: front wheel balancing of cars equipped with disc brakes may also cause a pressure differential in the front branch of the system.

To centralize the valve on 1970 (drum and disc) and 1971-1974 (drum only) American Motors cars, perform the following procedure:

1. Before repairing or bleeding the brakes, disconnect the switch terminal wire and remove the nylon switch terminal, contact plunger spring, and nylon plunger with contact.
2. If the light had come on and actuated the valve, spring pressure may hold the plunger. To release the plunger, apply a small amount of brake pedal pressure.

NOTE: location of the leak can be determined by the position of the plunger in its bore. The top of the plunger will lean to the side (front or rear) which has the low pressure.

3. Make the repair and bleed the brakes. Install the spring and plunger in the valve with the contact down.
4. Install the nylon terminal and connect the warning light wire to the terminal.

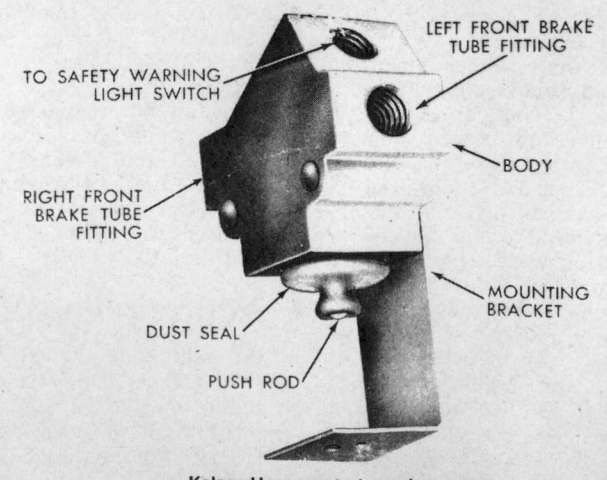

Kelsey-Hayes metering valve

5. Replace the valve assembly if any fluid leaks from the center terminal opening while removing the terminal.

IMPORTANT: the switch assembly is non-serviceable, replace if faulty.

Brake Bleeding

The purpose of bleeding brakes is to expel air trapped in the hydraulic system, and there are two methods of accomplishing this. The quickest and easiest of the two is pressure bleeding, but special pressure equipment is needed to externally pressurize the hydraulic system. The other, more commonly used method is gravity bleeding.

Gravity Bleeding Procedure

NOTE: when bleeding brakes on American Motors cars (1970 drum and disc, 1971-74 drum only), it is necessary to remove warning light switch terminal and plunger. For details, see Pressure Differential Warning Valves.

1. Clean the bleed screw at each wheel.
2. Attach a small rubber hose to one of the bleed screws and place the end in a container of brake fluid.
3. Top up the master cylinder with brake fluid. (Check often during bleeding). Pump up the brake pedal and hold.
4. Open the bleed screw about one-quarter turn, press the brake pedal to the floor, close the bleed screw and slowly release the pedal. Continue until no more air bubbles are forced from the cylinder on application of the brake pedal.
5. Repeat procedure on remaining wheel cylinders.

Master cylinders equipped with bleed screws may be bled independently. When bleeding the Bendix-type dual master cylinder it is necessary to solidly cap one reservoir section while bleeding the other to prevent pressure loss through the cap vent hole.

Disc brakes may be bled in the same manner as drum brakes, except that:

1. It usually requires a longer time to bleed a disc brake thoroughly.
2. The disc should be rotated to make sure that the piston has returned to the unapplied position when bleeding is completed and the bleed screw closed.

Pressure Bleeding Disc Brakes

NOTE: see NOTE under Gravity Bleeding Procedure.

Pressure bleeding disc brakes will close the metering valve and the front brakes will not bleed. For this reason it is necessary to manually hold the metering valve open during pressure bleeding. Never use a block or clamp to hold the valve open, and never force the valve stem beyond its normal position. Two different types of valves are used. The most common type requires the valve stem to be held in while bleeding the brakes, while the second type requires the valve stem to be held out (.060 in. minimum travel). Determine the type by visual inspection.

Power Brakes

Vacuum Operated Booster

Power brakes operate just as standard brake systems except in the actuation of the master cylinder pistons. A vacuum diaphragm is located on the front of the master cylinder and assists the driver in applying the brakes, reducing both the effort and travel he must put into moving the brake pedal.

The vacuum diaphragm housing is connected to the intake manifold by a vacuum hose. A check valve is placed at the point where the hose enters the diaphragm housing, so that during periods of low manifold vacuum brake assist vacuum will not be lost.

Depressing the brake pedal closes off the vacuum source and allows atmospheric pressure to enter on one side of the diaphragm. This causes the master cylinder pistons to move and apply the brakes. When the brake pedal is released, vacuum is applied to both sides of the diaphragm, and return springs return the diaphragm and master cylinder pistons to the released position. If the vacuum fails, the brake pedal rod will butt against the end of the master cylinder actuating rod, and direct mechanical application will occur as the pedal is depressed.

The hydraulic and mechanical problems that apply to conventional brake systems also apply to power brakes, and should be checked for if the tests and chart below do not reveal the problem.

Test for a system vacuum leak as described below:

1. Operate the engine at idle with the transmission in Neutral without touching the brake pedal for at least one minute.

2. Turn off the engine, and wait one minute.
3. Test for the presence of assist vacuum by depressing the brake pedal and releasing it several times. Light application will produce less and less pedal travel, if vacuum was present. If there is no vacuum, air is leaking into the system somewhere.

Test for system operation as follows:

1. Pump the brake pedal (with engine off) until the supply vacuum is entirely gone.
2. Put a light, steady pressure on the pedal.
3. Start the engine, and operate it at idle with the transmission in Neutral. If the system is operating, the brake pedal should fall toward the floor if constant pressure is maintained on the pedal.

Power brake systems may be tested for hydraulic leaks just as ordinary systems are tested, except that the engine should be idling with the transmission in Neutral throughout the test.

Power Brake Booster Troubleshooting Chart

The following items are in addition to those listed in the "Brake Diagnosis Chart" at the front of the Hydraulic Brake Section. Check those items first.

Hard Pedal

1. Faulty vacuum check valve
2. Vacuum hose kinked, collapsed, plugged, leaky, or improperly connected.
3. Internal leak in unit
4. Damaged vacuum cylinder
5. Damaged valve plunger
6. Broken or faulty springs
7. Broken plunger stem

Grabbing Brakes

1. Damaged vacuum cylinder
2. Faulty vacuum check valve
3. Vacuum hose leaky or improperly connected
4. Broken plunger stem

Pedal Goes to Floor

Generally, when this problem occurs, it is not caused by the power brake booster. In rare cases, a broken plunger stem may be at fault.

Overhaul

Due to complex repair procedure and the need for special tools, it is suggested that the unit be replaced with a new or rebuilt unit or be taken to a shop with adequate facilities.

Hydro-Boost

Hydro-boost was first offered as a mid-year option on 1974 Continental Mark IV models. Starting 1975, it became standard on all Ford Motor

Company cars equipped with four wheel disc brakes.

Hydro-boost differs from conventional power brake systems, in that it operates from power steering pump fluid pressure, rather than intake manifold vacuum.

The hydro-boost unit contains a spool valve with an open center which controls the strength of pump pressure when braking occurs. A lever assembly controls the valve's position. A boost piston provides the force necessary to operate the conventional master cylinder on the front of the booster.

A reserve of at least two assisted brake applications is supplied by a spring-loaded accumulator, which retains power steering fluid under pressure.

The brakes can be operated without assist, once the reserve is depleted.

Hydro-Boost System Checks

1. A defective hydro-boost cannot cause any of the following conditions:
   a. Noisy brakes
   b. Fading pedal
   c. Pulling brakes
   If any of these occur, check elsewhere in the brake system.
2. Check the fluid level in the master cylinder. It should be within ¼ in. of the top. If it isn't, add only DOT-3 or DOT-4 brake fluid until the correct level is reached.
3. Check the fluid level in the power steering pump. The engine should be at normal running temperature and stopped. The level should register on the pump dipstick. Add power steering fluid to bring the reservoir level up to the correct level. Low fluid level will result in both poor steering and stopping ability.

Caution

The brake hydraulic system uses brake fluid only, while the power steering and hydro-boost systems use power steering fluid only. Don't mix the two.

4. Check the power steering pump belt tension, and inspect all of the power steering/hydro-boost hoses for kinks or leaks.
5. Check and adjust the engine idle speed, as necessary.
6. Check the power steering pump fluid for bubbles. If air bubbles are present in the fluid, bleed the system:
   a. Fill the power steering pump reservoir to specifications with the engine at normal operating temperature.
   b. With the engine running, rotate the steering wheel through its normal travel 3 or 4 times, without holding the wheel against the stops.
   c. Check the fluid level again.
7. If the problem still exists, go on to the hydro-boost test sections and toubleshooting chart.

Hydro-Boost Tests

Functional Test

1. Check the brake system for leaks or low fluid level. Correct as necessary.
2. Place the transmission in Neutral and stop the engine. Apply the brakes 4 or 5 times to empty the accumulator.
3. Keep the pedal depressed with moderate (25-30 lbs) pressure and start the engine.
4. The brake pedal should fall slightly and then push back up against your foot. If no movement is felt, the hydro-boost system is not working.

Accumulator Leak Test

1. Run the engine at normal idle. Turn the steering wheel against one of the stops; hold it there for no longer than 5 seconds. Center the steering wheel and stop the engine.

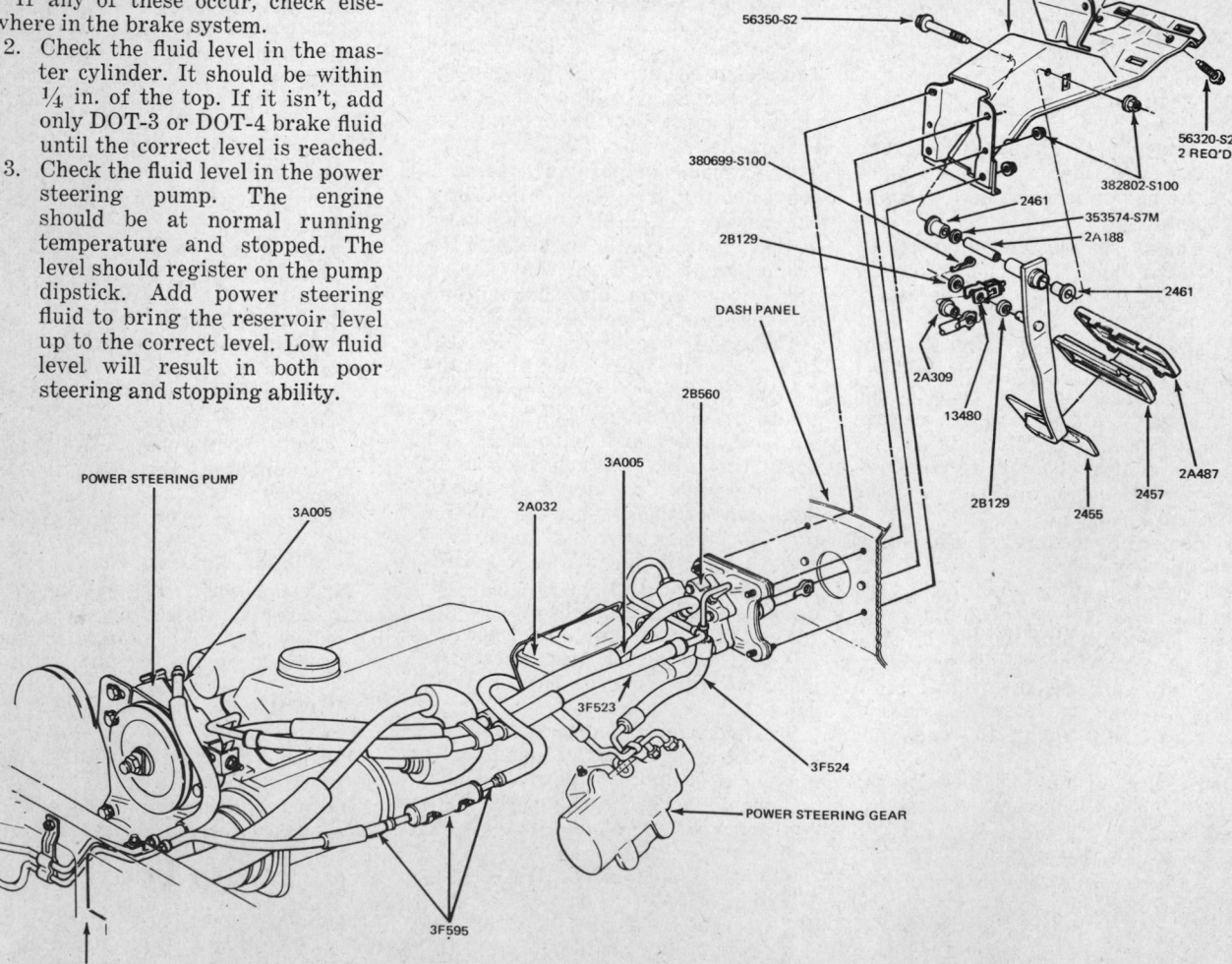

Hydro-boost component and related system locations (© Ford Motor Co)

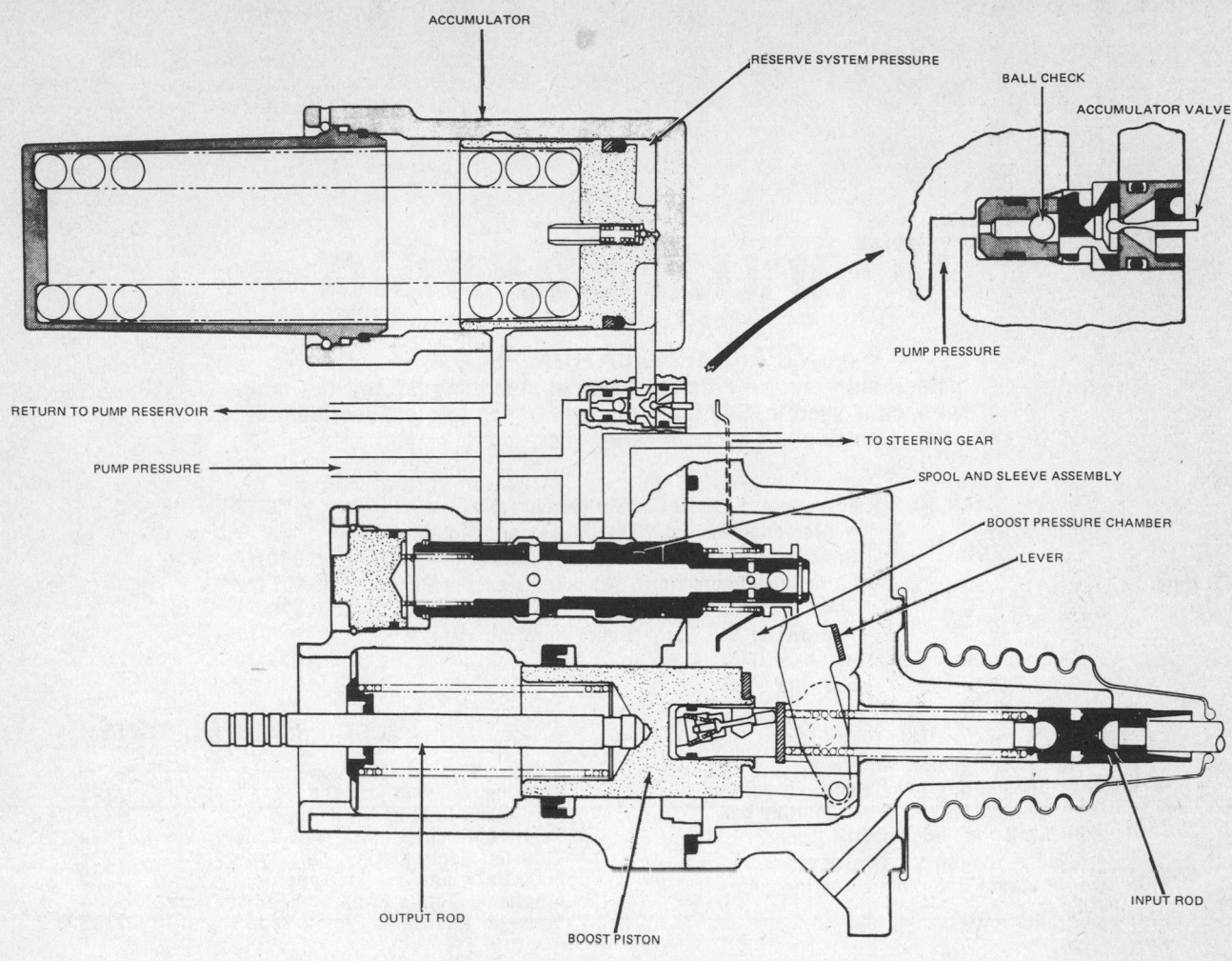

ACCUMULATOR

RESERVE SYSTEM PRESSURE

BALL CHECK

ACCUMULATOR VALVE

PUMP PRESSURE

RETURN TO PUMP RESERVOIR

TO STEERING GEAR

PUMP PRESSURE

SPOOL AND SLEEVE ASSEMBLY

BOOST PRESSURE CHAMBER

LEVER

OUTPUT ROD

INPUT ROD

BOOST PISTON

Cutaway view of the hydro-boost power brake unit and accumulator (© Ford Motor Co)

2. Keep applying the brakes until a "hard" pedal is obtained. There should be a minimum of 2 power assisted brake applications when pedal pressure of 20-25 lbs is applied.

3. Start the engine and allow it to idle. Rotate the steering wheel against the stop. Listen for a light "hissing" sound; this is the accumulator being charged. Center the steering wheel and stop the engine.

4. Wait one hour and apply the brakes several times without starting the engine. As in step 2, there should be at least two stops with power assist. If not, the accumulator is defective and must be replaced.

Caution Do not attempt to disassemble the accumulator. It can be serviced as a unit only. Do not puncture the accumulator housing.

Hydro-Boost Troubleshooting Chart

High Pedal and Steering Effort (Idle)

1. Loose broken power steering pump belt.
2. Low power steering fluid level
3. Leaking hoses or fittings
4. Low idle speed
5. Hose restriction
6. Defective power steering pump

High Pedal Effort (Idle)

1. Binding pedal/linkage
2. Fluid contamination
3. Defective hydro-boost unit

Poor Pedal Return

1. Binding pedal linkage
2. Restricted booster return line
3. Internal return system restriction

Pedal Chatter/Pulsation

1. Power steering pump drivebelt slipping
2. Low power steering fluid level
3. Defective power steering pump
4. Defective hydro-boost unit

Brakes Oversensitive

1. Binding pedal/linkage
2. Defective hydro-boost unit

Noise

1. Low power steering fluid level
2. Air in the power steering fluid
3. Loose power steering pump drivebelt
4. Hose restrictions

Overhaul

Neither the hydro-boost unit nor the accumulator can be dismantled and serviced. If either unit is defective, it must be replaced as a complete assembly. Attempts to disassemble the accumulator could result in personal injury.

Manual Steering

GEAR APPLICATION INDEX

Listed below are the different types of steering gear and the make of car each is used in. Section numbers refer to the text sections that cover that particular type of steering gear.

Gear Type	Section	Make	Year
A	2	Ford Motor Co. and Lincoln-Mercury Division All models except Pinto, Bobcat, and Mustang II	1970-77
B	3	General Motors Corp., All models except Chevette	1970-77
		American Motors Corp., All models except Pacer	1970-77
C	4	Chrysler Corp., All models	1970-77
D	5	Ford Motor Co., Pinto, Bobcat, and Mustang II	1970-77
E	6	American Motors Pacer	1975-77
F	7	Chevette	1976-77

Gear Types

A Ford steering gear, recirculating ball
B Saginaw steering gear, recirculating ball
C Chrysler steering gear, recirculating ball
D Ford Rack and pinion steering gear
E AMC rack and pinion steering gear
F Chevette rack and pinion steering gear

Section Page Numbers

	Manual Steering Diagnosis	U329
1	Steering Gear Alignment	U329
2	Ford Recirculating Ball Type	U329
3	Saginaw Recirculating Ball Type	U330
4	Chrysler Recirculating Ball Type	U331
5	Ford Rack and Pinion Type	U332
6	American Motors Rack and Pinion Type	U334
7	Chevette Rack and Pinion Type	U335

Power Steering

APPLICATION INDEX

Section Numbers Refer to Sections in Text

Make	Year	Gear Type	Sections
American Motors			
All except Pacer	1970-77	D	2,6
Pacer	1975-77	G	2,10
Chrysler Corporation			
All	1970-77	C	2,7
Ford Motor Company			
Maverick, Comet	1970-77	A	2,4
Granada, Monarch	1976-77	A	2,4
Falcon, Mustang, Cougar	1970	A	2,4
Mustang, Cougar	1971-73	D	2,6
Cougar	1974-77	E	2,8
Fairlane, Torino	1970-71	A	2,4
Torino, Montego	1972-77	E	2,8
Ford, Mercury, Thunderbird, Lincoln	1970-77	E	2,8
Mustang II, Pinto, Bobcat	1971-77	F	2,9
General Motors			
All except Corvette	1970-77	D	2,6
Corvette	1970-77	B	2,5

Gear Type

A—Bendix linkage-Type (Ford Non-Integral System)
B—Saginaw linkage-Type
C—Chrysler Full-Time (constant control type)
D—Saginaw rotary-Type
E—Ford torsion bar (Ford Integral System)
F—Ford integral rack and pinion
G—AMC rack and pinion

Section Page Numbers

	Preliminary	U336
1	General Diagnosis	U336
2	Preliminary Tests	U337
3	Power Steering Pumps	U337
4	Bendix Linkage-Type System (Ford Non-Integral System)	U345
5	Saginaw Linkage-Type System	U346
6	Saginaw Rotary-Type	U346
7	Chrysler Full-Time (constant control type)	U347
8	Ford Torsion Bar (Ford Integral System)	U348
9	Ford Integral Rack and Pinion (Ford Integral System)	U348
10	American Motors Rack and Pinion	U348
	Specifications	U349

MANUAL STEERING
Manual Steering Diagnosis

Condition	Possible Cause	Correction
Hard steering	(a) Low or uneven tire pressure.	(a) Inflate tires to recommended pressures.
	(b) Insufficient lubricant in the steering gear housing or in steering linkage.	(b) Lubricate as necessary.
	(c) Steering gear shaft adjusted too tight.	(c) Adjust according to instructions.
	(d) Front wheels out of line.	(d) Align the wheels. See the Front Suspension Section.
	(e) Steering column misaligned.	(e) See the Car Section for alignment procedures.
Excessive play or looseness in the steering wheel	(a) Steering gear shaft adjusted too loose or badly worn.	(a) Replace worn parts and adjust according to instructions.
	(b) Steering linkage loose or worn.	(b) Replace worn parts. See the Front Wheel Alignment Section.
	(c) Front wheel bearings improperly adjusted.	(c) Adjust according to instructions.
	(d) Steering arm loose on steering gear shaft.	(d) Inspect for damage to the gear shaft and steering arm, replace parts as necessary.
	(e) Steering gear housing attaching bolts loose.	(e) Tighten attaching bolts to specifications.
	(f) Steering arms loose at steering knuckles.	(f) Tighten according to specifications.
	(g) Worn ball joints.	(g) Replace the ball joints as necessary. See the Front Suspension Section.
	(h) Worm shaft bearing adjustment too loose.	(h) Adjust worm bearing preload according to instructions.

Section 1
Steering Gear Alignment

Before any steering gear adjustments are made, it is recommended that the front end of the car be raised and a thorough inspection be made for stiffness or lost motion in the steering gear, steering linkage and front suspension. Worn or damaged parts should be replaced, since a satisfactory adjustment of the steering gear cannot be obtained if bent or badly worn parts exist.

It is also very important that the steering gear be properly aligned in the car. Misalignment of the gear places a stress on the steering worm shaft, therefore a proper adjustment is impossible. To align the steering gear, loosen the mounting bolts to permit the gear to align itself. Check the steering gear mounting seat, and if there is a gap at any of the mounting bolts, proper alignment may be obtained by placing shims where excessive gap appears. Tighten the steering gear bolts. Alignment of the gear in the car is very important and should be done carefully so that a satisfactory, trouble-free gear adjustment may be obtained.

Section 2
Ford Recirculating Ball Type

Steering Worm and Sector Gear Adjustments

The ball nut assembly and the sector gear must be adjusted properly to maintain a minimum amount of steering shaft end-play and a minimum amount of backlash between the sector gear and the ball nut. There are only two adjustments that may be done on this steering gear and they should be done as given below:

1. Disconnect the pitman arm from the steering pitman-to-idler arm rod.
2. Loosen the locknut on the sector shaft adjustment screw and turn the adjusting screw counterclockwise.
3. Measure the worm bearing preload by attaching an in. lbs. torque wrench to the steering wheel

nut. With the steering wheel off center, note the reading required to rotate input shaft about 1½ turns either side of center. If the torque reading is not about 3-8

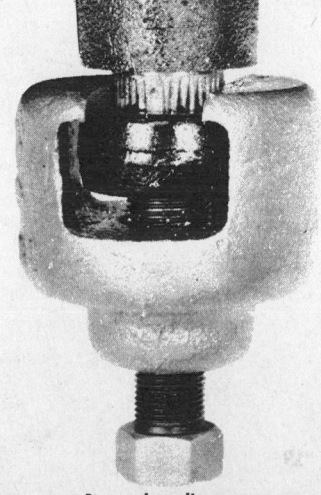

Removing pitman arm
(© Ford Motor Co)

Inch-Pound Torque Wrench

Checking steering gear preload
(© Ford Motor Co)

U329

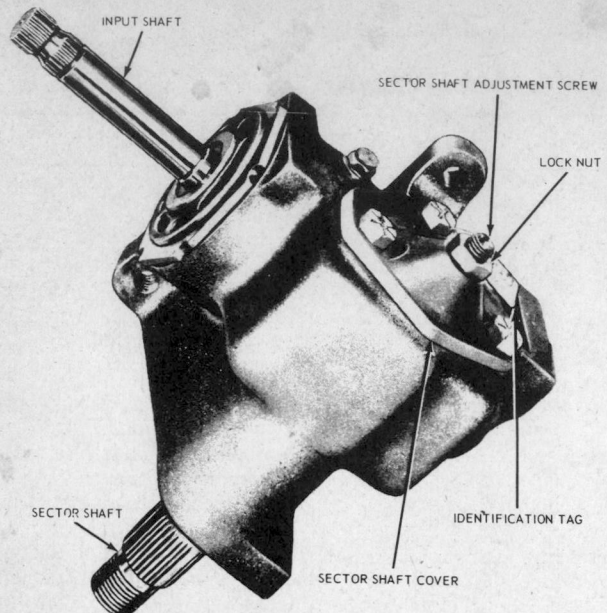

Ford manual steering gear, recirculating ball type
(© Ford Motor Co)

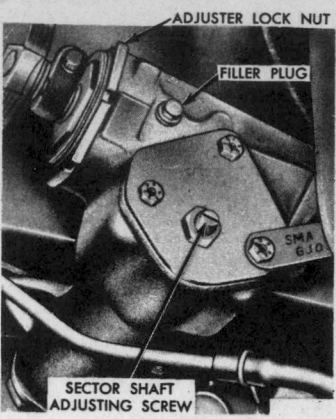

Steering gear adjustments
(© Ford Motor Co)

in. lbs., adjust the gear as given in the next step.

4. Loosen the steering shaft bearing adjuster locknut and tighten or back off the bearing adjusting screw until the preload is within the specified limits.

5. Tighten the steering shaft bearing adjuster locknut to 60-80 ft lbs, and recheck the preload torque.

6. Turn the steering wheel slowly to either stop. Turn *gently* against the stop to avoid possible damage to the ball return guides. Then rotate the wheel 2¾ turns (2 turns with 16:1 ratio) to center the ball nut on Maverick, Comet, Granada, and Monarch; 3¼ turns on larger models.

7. Turn the sector adjusting screw clockwise until the proper torque (7-13 in. lbs.) is obtained that is necessary to rotate the worm gear past its center (high spot).

8. While holding the sector adjusting screw, tighten the sector screw adjusting locknut to 32-40 ft. lbs. and recheck the backlash adjustment.

9. Connect the pitman arm to the steering arm-to-idler arm rod.

Section 3
Saginaw Recirculating Ball Type

The steering gear is of the recirculating ball nut type. The ball nut, mounted on the worm gear, is driven by means of steel balls which circulate in helical grooves in both the worm and nut. Ball return guides attached to the nut serve to recirculate the two sets of balls in the grooves. As the steering wheel is turned to the right, the ball nut moves upward. When the wheel is turned to the left, the ball nut moves downward.

The sector teeth on the pinion shaft and the ball nut are designed so that they fit the tightest when the steering wheel is straight ahead. This mesh action is adjusted by an adjusting screw which moves the pinion shaft endwise until the teeth mesh properly. The worm bearing adjuster provides proper preloading of the upper and lower bearings.

Before doing the adjustment procedures given below, refer to Section 1 to ensure that the steering problem is not caused by faulty suspension components, bad front end alignment, etc. Then, proceed with the following adjustments.

Worm Bearing Preload Adjustment

Caution Do not turn steering wheel hard against stops as damage to ball nut assembly may result. Use a torque wrench calibrated to 50 in. lbs or less.

1. Disconnect the steering linkage ball stud from the pitman arm.

2. Loosen the pitman shaft adjusting screw locknut and back off adjusting screw a few turns.

3. Install an in. lbs torque wrench to the steering wheel attaching

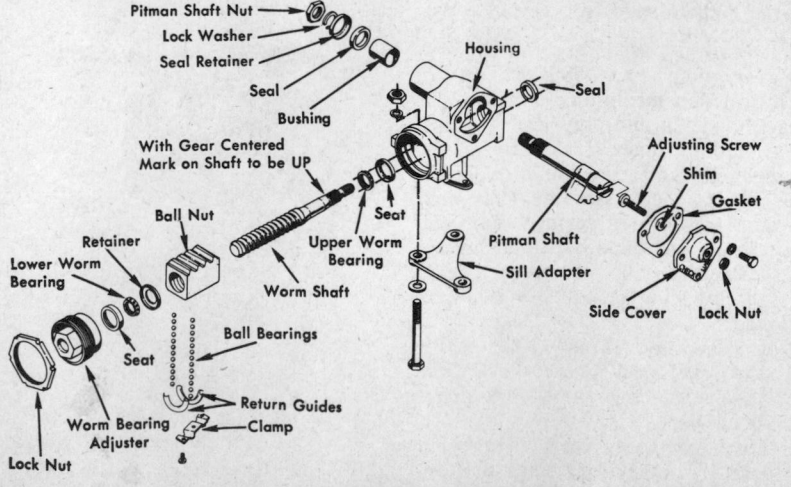

Saginaw steering gear, recirculating ball type (© American Motors Corp)

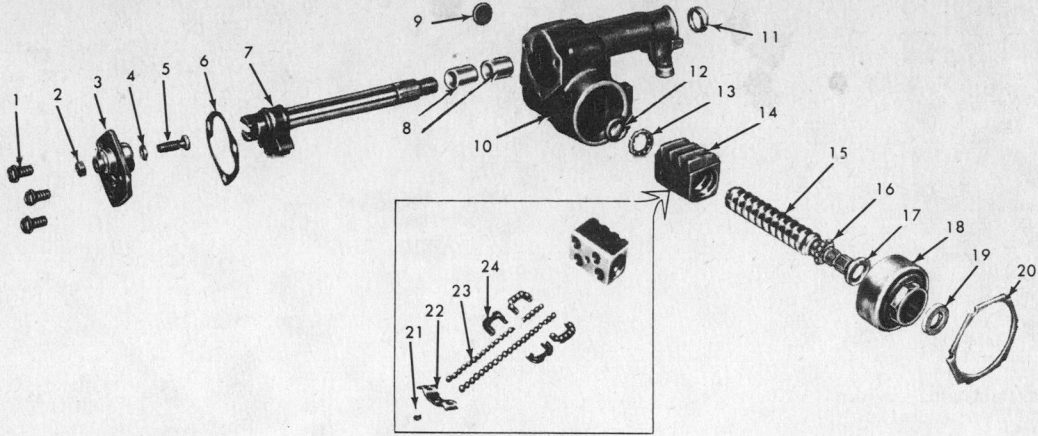

1. Side Cover Screws
2. Lash Adjuster Locknut
3. Side Cover and Bushing
4. Lash Adjuster Shim
5. Lash Adjuster Screw
6. Side Cover Gasket
7. Pitman Shaft
8. Pitman Shaft Bushings

9. Expansion Plug
10. Steering Gear Housing
11. Pitman Shaft Seal
12. Worm Bearing Race—Lower
13. Worm Bearing—Lower
14. Ball Nut
15. Wormshaft
16. Worm Bearing—Upper

17. Worm Bearing Race—Upper
18. Adjuster Plug
19. Wormshaft Seal
20. Adjuster Plug Locknut
21. Clamp Screw
22. Ball Guide Clamp
23. Balls
24. Ball Guides

Corvette steering gear, recirculating ball type (© G.M. Corp)

nut and measure the pull needed to move the steering wheel when off the high point. The pull should be between 4 and 6 in. lbs on GM cars and 5 and 8 in. lbs on AMC vehicles.

4. To adjust the worm bearing, loosen the worm bearing adjuster locknut with a brass drift and turn the adjuster screw until the proper pull is obtained. When adjustment is correct, tighten the adjuster locknut, and recheck with the torque wrench.

Sector and Ball Nut Backlash Adjustment

1. After the worm bearing preload has been adjusted correctly, loosen the pitman shaft adjusting screw locknut and turn the pitman shaft adjusting screw until a pull of 5 to 9 in. lbs on GM cars and 4 to 10 in. lbs on AMC cars is required to turn the steering wheel through the center of its travel. When the adjustment is correct, tighten the pitman shaft

adjusting screw locknut and recheck the adjustment.

NOTE: This torque is in addition to Worm bearing preload torque. Total torque required to turn the worm shaft should not exceed 16 in. lbs.

2. Turn the steering wheel to the center of its turning limits (pitman arm disconnected). If the steering wheel is removed, the mark on the steering shaft should be at top center.

3. Connect the ball stud to the pitman arm, tightening the attaching nut to 45-35 ft. lbs.

Section 4
Chrysler Recirculating Ball Type

This steering gear is quite similar to the Saginaw recirculating ball design. The main differences are adjustment and torque specifications. Refer to the introduction in Section 3 before proceeding with the adjustments below.

Worm Bearing Pre-load Adjustment

1. Remove the steering gear arm and lockwasher from the sector shaft, using a suitable gear puller.
2. Remove the horn button or horn ring.
3. Loosen the cross-shaft adjusting screw locknut, and back out the adjusting screw about two turns.
4. Turn the steering wheel two complete turns from the straight ahead position, and place an in.

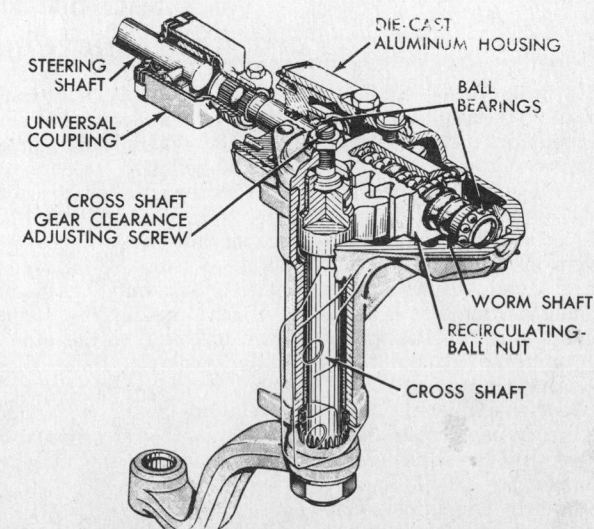

Chrysler steering gear, recirculating ball type
(© Chrysler Corp)

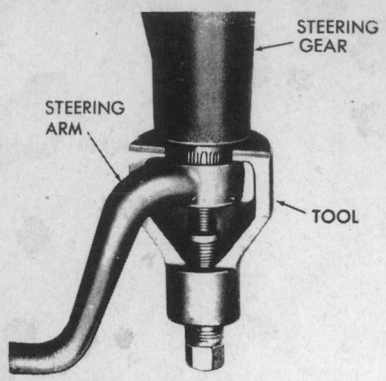

Removing steering gear arm
(© Chrysler Corp)

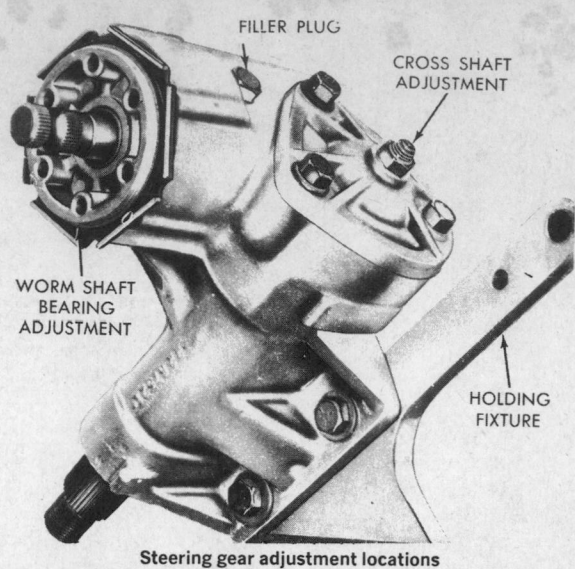

Steering gear adjustment locations
(© Chrysler Corp)

lb torque wrench on the steering shaft nut.

5. Rotate the steering shaft at least one turn toward the straight ahead position while measuring the torque on the torque wrench. The torque should be between $1\frac{1}{8}$ and $4\frac{1}{2}$ in. lbs. to move the steering wheel. If torque is not within these limits, loosen the worm shaft bearing adjuster locknut and turn the adjuster clockwise to increase the preload or counterclockwise to decrease the preload. When the preload is correct, hold the adjuster screw steady and tighten the locknut. Recheck preload.

Ball Nut Rack and Sector Mesh Adjustment

NOTE: this adjustment can be accurately made only after proper preloading of worm bearing.

1. Turn steering wheel gently from one stop to the other. counting the number of turns. Turn the steering wheel back exactly half way, to the center position.

2. Turn the cross-shaft adjusting screw clockwise to remove all lash between ball nut rack and the sector gear teeth, then tighten adjusting screw locknut to 35 ft. lbs.

3. Turn the steering wheel about $\frac{1}{4}$ turn away from the center or high spot position. With the torque wrench on the steering wheel nut measure the torque required to turn the steering wheel through the high spot at the center position. The reading should be between 8 and 11 in. lbs. This is the total of the worm shaft bearing preload and the ball nut rack and sector gear mesh load. Readjust the cross-shaft adjustment screw if necessary to obtain a correct torque reading.

4. After completing the adjust-

ments, place the front wheels in a straight ahead position, and with the steering wheel and steering gear centered, install the steering arm on cross-shaft. Tighten the steering arm retaining nut to 180 ft. lbs.

Cross-Shaft Oil Seal Replacement

1. Remove the steering gear arm retaining nut and lockwasher.
2. Remove seal with a seal puller or other appropriate tool.
3. Place a new oil seal onto the splines of the cross-shaft with the lip of the seal facing the housing.
4. Remove the tool, and install the steering gear arm, lockwasher, and retaining nut. Tighten the nut to 180 ft. lbs. torque.

Section 5
Ford Rack and Pinion Type

The steering gear input shaft is connected to the steering shaft. A pinion gear is machined on the input shaft and engages the rack. Rotation of the input shaft pinion causes the rack to move from side to side.

A tie rod is attached at both ends of the rack by a moveable joint. The unit is sealed at each end with a rubber bellows. The steering gear is filled with SAE-90 oil at initial assembly and checking or refilling is not required unless leakage is evident.

Replacement of the inner tie rods, rack, housing, or upper pinion bearing, necessitates removal of the steering gear assembly.

It is important to remember that when the front wheels are off the ground, the steering wheel should not be moved quickly or forcefully from

lock to lock. This could cause a build-up of hydraulic pressure within the assembly which could damage or blow off the bellows.

With the front suspension and linkage in good condition and gear in proper adjustment, there should be no more than $\frac{3}{8}$ in. free-play measured at the rim of the steering wheel.

When turning the steering wheel from one stop to the other in a stationary vehicle, there should be no knock produced by the steering gear.

All repair and adjustment procedures require the removal of the rack and pinion gear from the vehicle.

Support Yoke to Rack Adjustment

1. Clean the exterior of the gear

thoroughly and place it, using the mounting pads, in a soft-jawed vise, with the yoke cover up.

2. Remove the yoke cover, gasket, shims, and yoke spring.
3. Clean the cover and housing flange areas thoroughly.
4. Reinstall the yoke and cover, omitting the gasket, shims, and spring. Tighten the cover bolts lightly, until the cover just touches the yoke.
5. Measure the gap between the cover and the housing flange with a feeler gauge. With the gasket, add selected shims to give a combined shim pack thickness of 0.005-0.006 in. more than the gap.
6. Remove the cover.
7. Assemble the gasket next to the

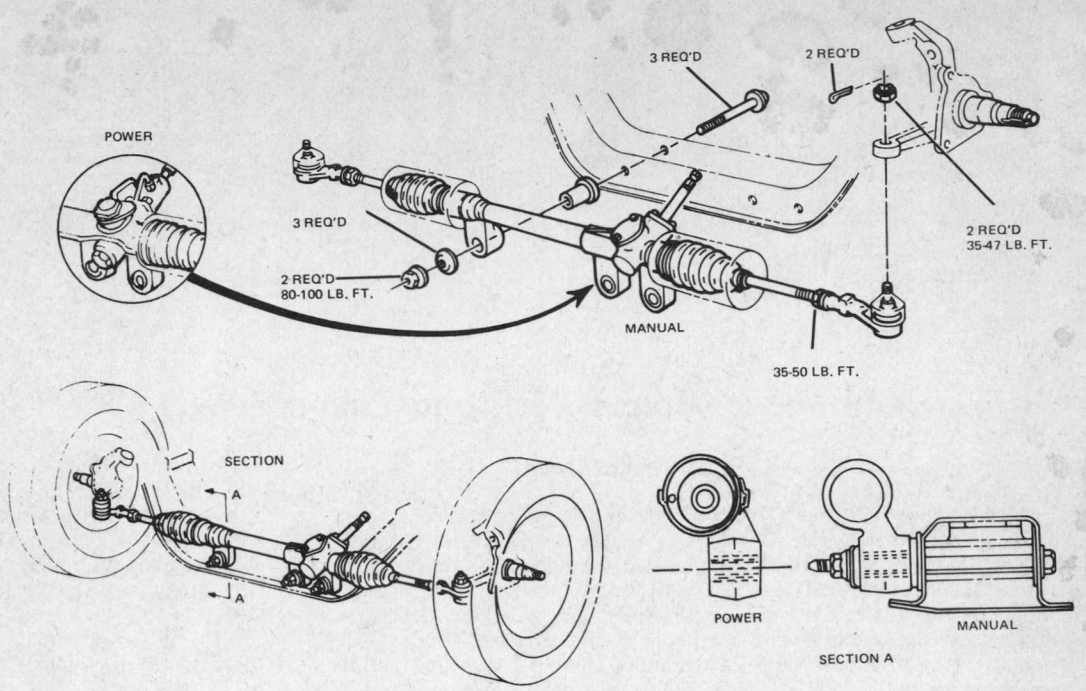

POWER

3 REQ'D

2 REQ'D

3 REQ'D

2 REQ'D
35-47 LB. FT.

2 REQ'D
80-100 LB. FT.

MANUAL

35-50 LB. FT.

SECTION

A

A

SECTION A

POWER

MANUAL

Mustang II rack and pinion steering gear (© Ford Motor Co)

housing flange and then assemble the selected shims, spring, and cover.

8. Add a sealant to cover the bolt threads and torque to 7-10 ft lbs through 1972, and 15-20 ft lbs on later models.

9. Check to see that gear operates smoothly without binding or slackness.

Pinion Bearing Preload Adjustment

1. Loosen the attaching bolts of the yoke cover to relieve spring pressure on the rack.

2. Remove the pinion cover and clean area thoroughly. On some later models, beginning 1974, the input shaft passes through the pinion cover. The adjustment is made at this point rather than at a bottom cover.

3. Remove the gasket and shims. On later models, remove the spacer and shims.

4. Install a new gasket and fit shims until shim pack is flush with the

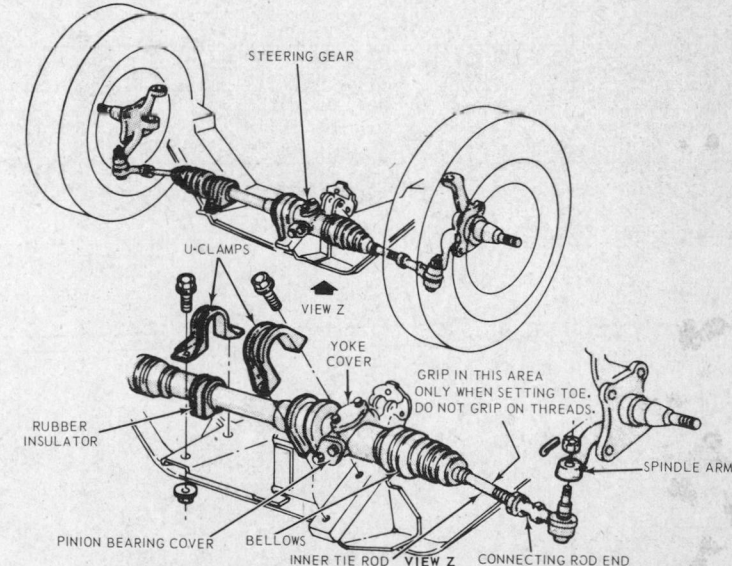

STEERING GEAR

U-CLAMPS

VIEW Z

YOKE COVER

GRIP IN THIS AREA ONLY WHEN SETTING TOE. DO NOT GRIP ON THREADS.

RUBBER INSULATOR

SPINDLE ARM

PINION BEARING COVER   BELLOWS

INNER TIE ROD   VIEW Z   CONNECTING ROD END

Pinto steering gear assembly, rack and pinion type (© Ford Motor Co)

gasket. On later models, the top of the spacer should be flush with the gasket. Check with a straight-edge using light pressure. Install the thinnest of the selected shims first, then the 0.093 in. shim and cover.

5. Add one 0.005 in. shim to the pack, next to the pinion cover, in order to preload the bearing.

6. Add sealant to the bolt threads and install. Torque to 15-20 ft. lbs.

7. Torque yoke cover bolts to 7-10 ft lbs through 1972, and 15-20 ft lbs on later models.

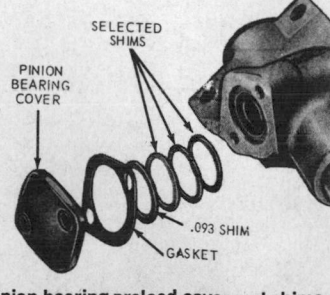

SELECTED SHIMS

PINION BEARING COVER

.093 SHIM

GASKET

Pinion bearing preload cover and shims (© Ford Motor Co)

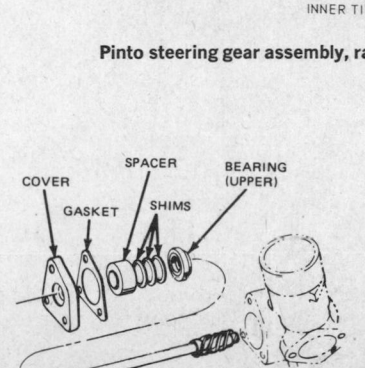

COVER

GASKET

SPACER

SHIMS

BEARING (UPPER)

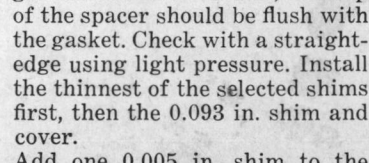

Pinion bearing preload is adjusted at the upper cover on later models (© Ford Motor Co)

Input Shaft Seal Replacement

1. Clean the area around the input shaft end-seal. Do not scratch or damage the pinion shaft.
2. Pry the pinion seal from its bore.
3. Lubricate the new pinion seal and install it over the shaft.
4. Use a piece of tubing to engage the outer flange of the seal and press or tap the seal into place so it is flush with shoulder of the bore.

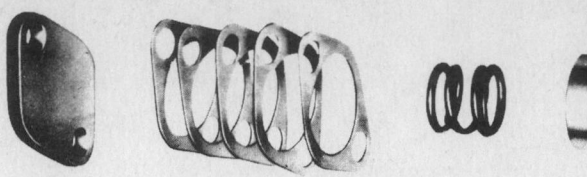

Support yoke assembly
(© Ford Motor Co)

Section 6
American Motors Rack and Pinion Type

The rack and pinion design combines the steering gear and linkage into one compact assembly. The steering gear consists of a tube and housing assembly which contains the pinion shaft and steering rack. The steering linkage consists of two inner tie rod assemblies, two adjuster tube assemblies, and two tie rod ends. The inner tie rods are covered with rubber boots, connected with a pressure-equalizing breather tube.

Boot Replacement

1. Raise and support the car.
2. Cut off the original boot clamps.
3. Loosen the adjusting tube clamp bolts, matchmark the tubes and tie rods, and unscrew the tube from the tie rods.
4. Remove the old boots and install the new ones. Align the holes with the breather tube.

5. Position the boot clamps with the ear ¾ in. from the breather tube Compress the clamps.
6. Install the adjuster tubes. Tighten the clamp bolts to 22 ft lbs. Make sure that at least three threads are visible at each end of the adjuster tube. The number of threads per side should not differ by more than three.
7. Toe-in must be checked.

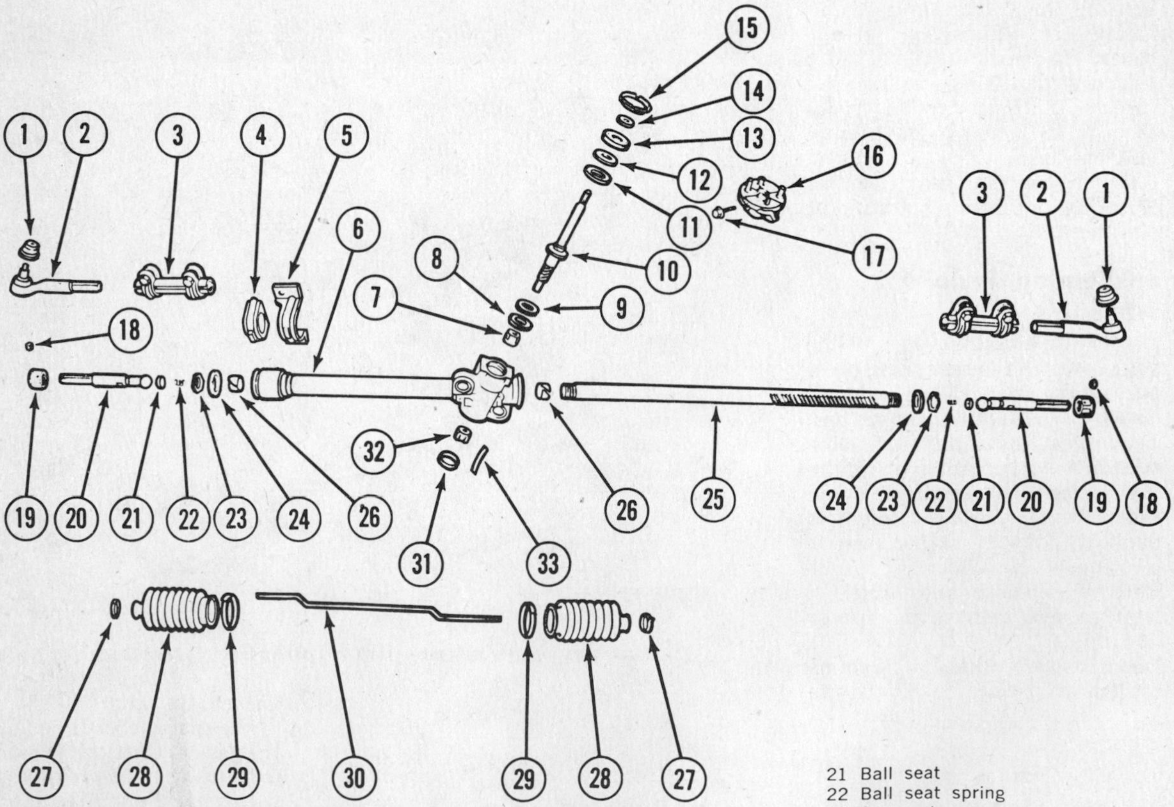

1	Tie rod seal	11	Upper thrust bearing	21	Ball seat
2	Tie rod end	12	Upper thrust bearing race	22	Ball seat spring
3	Adjuster tube	13	Adjuster plug	23	Jam nut
4	Mounting grommet	14	Pinion shaft seal	24	Shock dampener ring
5	Mounting clamp	15	Adjuster plug locknut	25	Steering rack
6	Tube and housing assembly	16	Flexible coupling	26	Rack bushing
7	Upper pinion bushing	17	Pinch bolt	27	Boot retainer
8	Lower thrust bearing race	18	Set screw	28	Boot
9	Lower thrust bearing	19	Tie rod housing	29	Boot clamp
10	Pinion shaft	20	Inner tie rod	30	Breather tube
				31	Contraction plug
				32	Lower pinion bushing
				33	Preload spring

Exploded view of the American Motors Pacer manual rack and pinion steering gear
(© American Motors Corp)

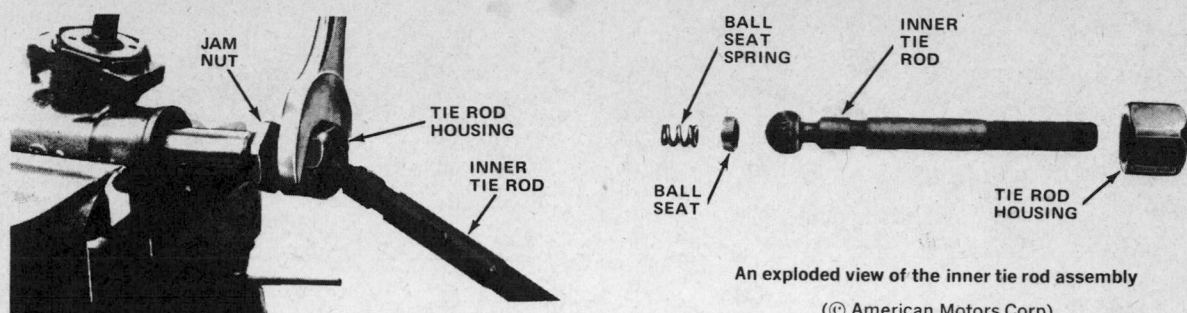

Removing the tie rod housing and inner tie rod
(© American Motors Corp)

An exploded view of the inner tie rod assembly
(© American Motors Corp)

Mounting Clamp and Grommet Replacement

1. Raise and support the car.
2. Remove the boot clamps, adjusting tubes, and boots as in Steps 1-3 of Boot Replacement.
3. Loosen both mounting clamp to front crossmember bolts, then remove them.
4. Remove the clamps and grommets with a twisting, pulling motion.
5. Install the replacement clamps and grommets, aligning the grommet holes with the breather tube.
6. Install the mounting bolts and tighten them to 50 ft lbs.
7. Replace the boots and adjuster tubes as in Steps 4-7 of Boot Replacement.

Tie Rod End and Adjuster Tube Replacement

1. Raise and support the car.
2. Turn the wheels to the stop in the direction of the tie rod end to be removed. Jack the lower control arm up at least 2 in. Remove the cotter pin and nut at the tie rod end. Remove the tie rod end from the steering arm using a tie rod end removal tool.
3. Matchmark the positions of the adjusting tubes and tie rod ends.
4. Install the new tie rod ends and adjuster tubes. Torque the clamp bolts to 22 ft lbs. and the tie rod end nuts to 50 ft lbs. Replace the cotter pins. Make sure that at least three threads are visible at each end of the adjuster tube. The number of threads per side should not differ by more than three.
5. Toe-in must be checked.

Inner Tie Rod Housing, Tie Rod, Ball Seat, and Spring Replacement

1. Raise and support the car.
2. Disconnect the tie rod ends as in Step 2 of Tie Rod End and Adjuster Tube Replacement.
3. Matchmark the adjuster clamps and inner tie rods. Loosen the clamp bolts and unscrew the adjuster tube and tie rod end from the inner tie rods.
4. Cut off the large boot clamps and move the boots aside.
5. Slide the plastic shock dampener rings off the jamnuts and loosen the jamnuts.
6. Loosen the setscrews in the tie rod housings. Unscrew the housings from the rack. Remove the inner tie rods, tie rod housings, ball seats, and springs.
7. Use waterproof EP lithium base chassis grease on all the replacement inner tie rod assembly surfaces. Pack the tie rod housing with the grease.
8. Install the ball seat springs and ball seats.
9. Assemble the inner tie rods and housings and install them on the rack. Tighten the tie rod housing to 25 ft lbs while rocking the inner tie rod to prevent grease lock. Back the housing off 1/8 turn; the tie rod should rock and rotate freely in the housing. Tighten the tie rod housing setscrews to 60 in lbs.
10. Hold the tie rod end housings with an end wrench and tighten the jamnuts to 100 ft lbs. Slide the shock dampener rings over the jamnuts.
11. Install the boot and clamps as in Steps 4 and 5 of Boot Replacement.
12. Screw the adjuster tube and tie rod end assembly onto the inner tie rod, aligning the matchmarks.
13. Replace the tie rod ends in the steering arms and torque the nuts to 50 ft lbs. Replace the cotter pins.

Section 7
Chevette Rack and Pinion Type

The Chevette rack and pinion system incorporates both the steering gear and linkage assembly in one package. The pinion and most of the rack are in an aluminum housing. The pinion is supported by and turns in a sealed ball bearing at the top and a pressed in roller bearing at the bottom.

Wear is compensated for by an adjuster spring which forces the rack against the pinion teeth. The inner tie rod assemblies are threaded and staked to the rack. The unit must be removed from the car to remove the inner tie rod assemblies, which have a spring loaded spherical joint to allow both rocking and rotating movement.

Any service other than replacement of the outer tie rods or the boots requires removal of the unit from the car. Torque for the outer tie rod jam nuts is 50 ft lbs.

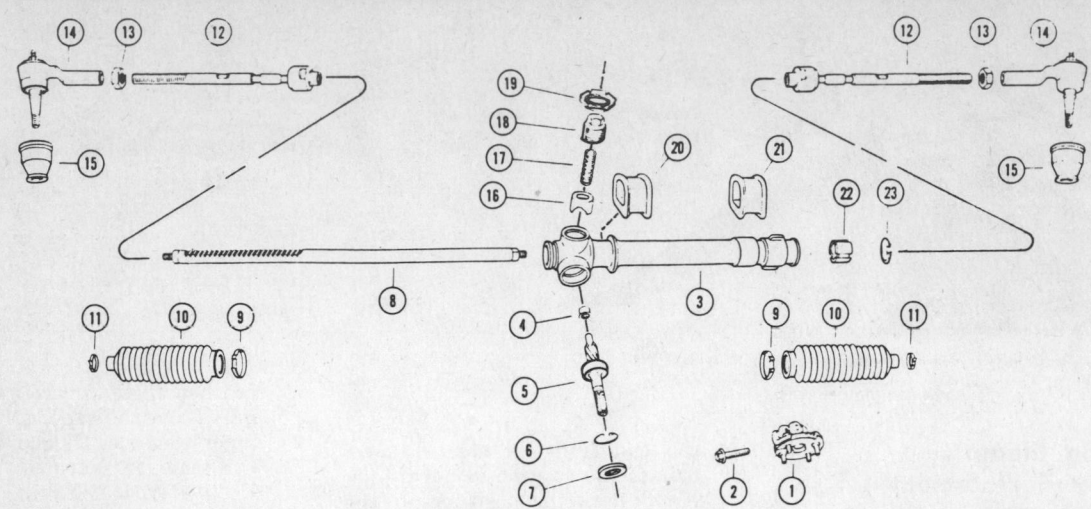

1 Coupling and steering flange assembly
2 Pinch bolt
3 Housing assembly
4 Roller bearing assembly
5 Bearing and pinion assembly
6 Retaining ring
7 Steering pinion seal
8 Steering rack

9 Boot clamp
10 Boot
11 Boot clamp
12 Inner tie rod assembly
13 Jam nut
14 Outer tie rod assembly
15 Tie rod seal
16 Rack bearing

17 Adjuster spring
18 Adjuster plug
19 Adjuster plug locknut
20 Left mounting grommet
21 Right mounting grommet
22 Rack bushing
23 Retaining ring

Chevette rack and pinion steering (© Chevrolet Div., G.M. Corp.)

Power Steering

Preliminary

Before investigating any power steering system, first be sure of the general condition of the systems around it. Simple items such as tire pressure, loose belts, or faulty front end parts can have great effect on the function of the power steering system. After a common-sense general inspection has been made, consult Section 1 and proceed from there. Specific listings of make, model and year will be found in the Application Index.

Section 1 General Diagnosis

Hard Steering

1. Improper tire pressure.
2. Loose pump drive belt.
3. Low or incorrect hydraulic fluid.
4. Loose, bent or poorly lubricated front end parts.
5. Improper front end alignment, especially caster.
6. Bind in steering column or mechanism.
7. Air in hydraulic system.
8. Low pump output or leaks in system.
9. Obstruction in lines.
10. Pump valves sticking or out of adjustment.

Loose Steering

1. Loose wheel bearings.
2. Faulty shocks.
3. Worn Pitman arm or front end components.
4. Loose steering gear mountings or linkage points.
5. Steering mechanism worn or improperly adjusted.
6. Valve spool improperly adjusted.

Veer or Wander

1. Improper tire pressure.
2. Improper front end alignment.
3. Dragging brakes.
4. Bent frame.
5. Improper rear end alignment.
6. Faulty shocks or springs.
7. Loose or bent front end components.
8. Play in Pitman arm.
9. Loose wheel bearings.
10. Binding Pitman arm.
11. Spool valve sticking or improperly adjusted.

Wheel Oscillation

1. Improper tire pressure.
2. Loose wheel bearings.
3. Improper front end alignment.
4. Bent spindle.
5. Worn, bent or broken front end components.
6. Tires out of round or imbalanced.

Noises

1. Loose belts.
2. Low fluid, air in system.
3. Foreign matter in system.
4. Improper lubrication.
5. Interference or chafing in front end.
6. Steering gear mountings loose.
7. Incorrect adjustment or wear in mechanism.
8. Faulty valves or wear in pump.

Section 2
Preliminary Tests

NOTE: The following tests are generally applicable to most power steering systems. If the specification required is not listed, then that test is only generally applicable to that system.

Turning Effort

Check the effort required to turn the steering wheel after aligning the front wheels and inflating the tires to the proper pressure.

1. With the vehicle on dry pavement and the front wheels straight ahead, set the parking brake and turn the engine on.

2. After a short warm-up period turn the steering wheel back and forth several times to warm the steering fluid.

3. Attach a spring scale to the steering wheel rim and measure the pull required to turn the steering wheel one complete revolution in each direction. The effort needed to turn the steering wheel should not exceed the limits given in the specifications.

NOTE: this test may be done with torque wrench on the steering wheel nut. See the section on Manual Steering for a discussion of this test.

Checking the Oil Flow and Pressure Relief Valve in the Pump Assembly

When the wheels are turned hard right or hard left, against the stops, the oil flow and pressure relief valves come into action. If these valves are working, there should be a slight buzzing noise. Do not hold the wheels in the extreme position for over three or four seconds because, if the pressure relief valve is not working, the pressure could get high enough to damage the system.

Section 3
Power Steering Pumps

The power steering pump supplies all the power assist used in power steering systems of all designs. There are various designs of pumps used by the automobile manufacturers but all pumps supply power to operate the steering systems with the least effort. All power steering pumps have a reservoir tank built onto the pump. These pumps are driven by belts turned by pulleys on the front of the crankshaft.

With the engine at idle speed, the pump supplies high fluid pressure. When the car is moving straight ahead, less pressure is needed and the excess is relieved through a pressure relief and flow control valve. The pressure relief part of the valve is inside the flow control part and is basically the same for all pumps. The flow control valve regulates the constant flow of fluid from the pump to meet the demands of the steering gear. The pressure relief valve limits the hydraulic pressure built up when the steering gear is turned against its stops.

During all pump disassembly work, make sure all work is done on a clean work surface. Clean the outside of the pump thoroughly and do not allow dirt of any kind to get inside the pump. Do not immerse the shaft oil seal in solvent.

When replacing the rotor shaft seal, be extremely careful not to scratch sealing surfaces.

Vane Type Power Steering Pump Overhaul

The vane type power steering pump is used in Saginaw steering systems. The operation is basically the same as that of the roller type pumps. Centrifugal force moves a number of vanes outward against the pump ring, pumping the fluid to the control valve.

Application
1970-77 All GM cars
1970-77 Chrysler cars*
1972-77 All AMC cars
1972-77 Thunderbird and Lincoln with 429-460 V8
1973-77 Mercury with 429-460 V8
1974-77 Ford with 460 V8

* Varies with car line; visual identification is necessary.

Disassembly

1. Clean the outside of the pump in a non-toxic solvent before disassembling, and remove it from the engine.

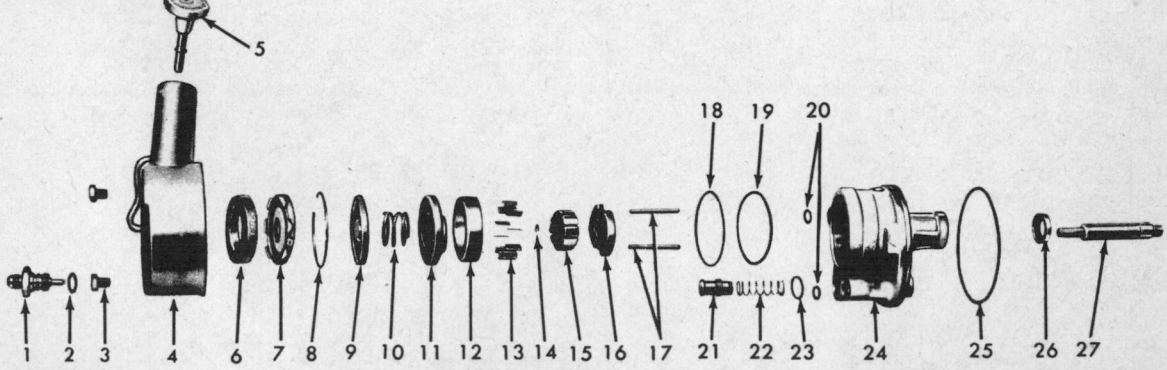

1 Union
2 Seal
3 Mounting studs
4 Reservoir
5 Dip stick and cover
6 Element (Chevy II and Corvette)
7 Filter assembly (Chevy II and Corvette)
8 End plate retaining ring
9 End plate
10 Spring
11 Pressure plate
12 Pump ring
13 Vanes
14 Drive shaft retaining ring
15 Rotor
16 Thrust plate
17 Dowel pins
18 End plate O-ring
19 Pressure plate O-ring
20 Mounting stud O-ring seals
21 Flow control valve
22 Flow control valve spring
23 Flow control valve O-ring seal
24 Pump housing
25 Reservoir O-ring seal
26 Shaft seal
27 Shaft

Vane type pump, exploded view (© Chevrolet Motor Div., G.M. Corp)

Power Steering

2. Mount the pump in a vise, being careful not to distort the front hub of the pump. Remove pulley retaining nut and remove pulley.
3. Remove the union and seal.
4. Remove the reservoir retaining studs and separate the reservoir from the housing.
5. Remove the mounting bolt O-rings and the union O-rings.
6. Remove the filter and filter cage; discard the filter element.
7. Remove the end plate retaining ring by compressing the retaining ring and then prying it out with a screwdriver. The retaining ring may be compressed by inserting a small punch in the 1/8 in. diameter hole in the housing and pushing in until the ring clears the groove.
8. Remove the end plate. The end plate is spring-loaded and should rise above the housing level. If it is stuck inside the housing, gentle tapping should free the plate.
9. Remove the shaft Woodruff key and tap the end of the shaft gently to free the pressure plate, pump ring, rotor assembly, and thrust plate. Remove these parts as one unit.
10. Remove the end plate O-ring. Separate the pressure plate, pump ring, rotor assembly, and thrust plate.

Inspection

Clean all metal parts in a non-toxic solvent and inspect them as noted below:
1. Check the flow control valve for free movement in the housing bore. If the valve is sticking, see if there is dirt or roughness in the bore.
2. Check the cap screw in the end of the flow control valve for looseness. Tighten if necessary, being careful not to damage the machined surfaces.
3. Inspect the pressure plate and pump plate surfaces for flatness, cracks, or scores. Do not mistake the normal wear marks for scoring.

Removing impeller unit
(© Chevrolet Motor Div., G.M. Corp)

Removing end plate ring
(© Chevrolet Motor Div., G.M. Corp)

Installing thrust plate
(© Chevrolet Motor Div., G.M. Corp)

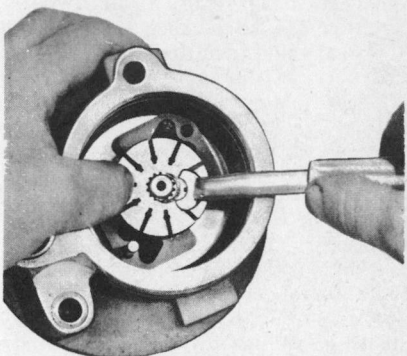

Installing shaft snap ring
(© Chevrolet Motor Div., G.M. Corp)

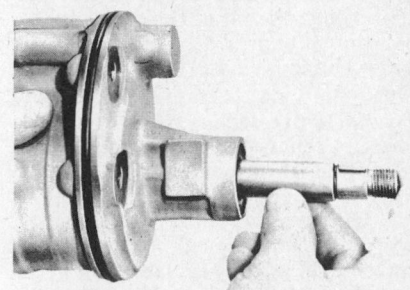

Shaft installation
(© Chevrolet Motor Div., G.M. Corp)

Installing vanes
(© Chevrolet Motor Div., G.M. Corp)

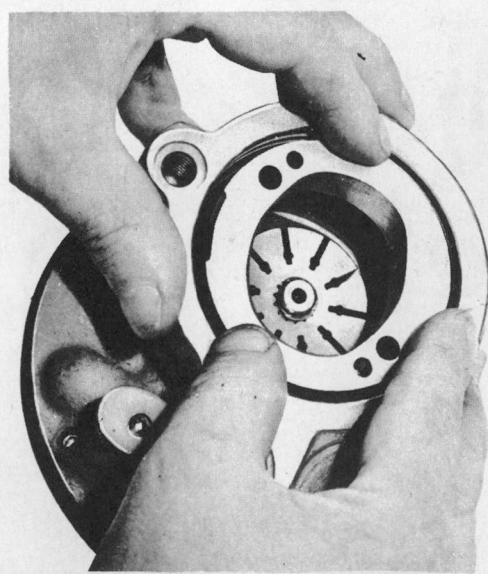

Installing pump ring
(© Chevrolet Motor Div., G.M. Corp)

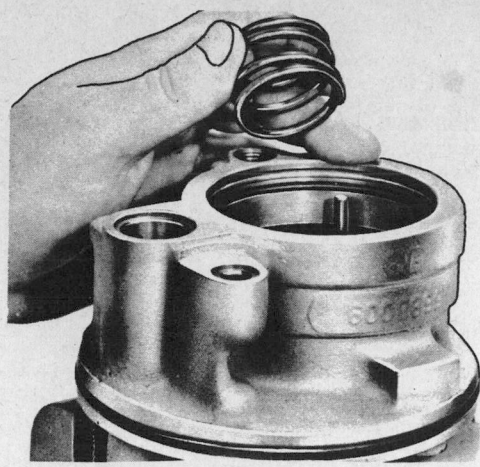

Installing pressure plate spring
(© Chevrolet Motor Div., G.M. Corp)

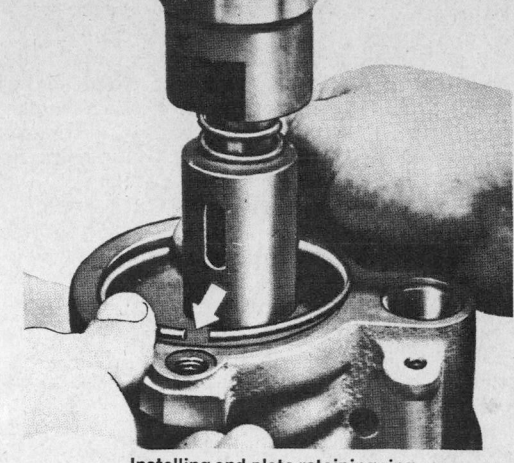

Installing end plate retaining ring
(© Chevrolet Motor Div., G.M. Corp)

4. Check the vanes in the rotor assembly for free movement. See that they were installed with the radiused edge toward the pump ring.
5. If the flow control valve plunger is defective, install a new part. It is factory calibrated and supplied as a unit.
6. Check the driveshaft for worn splines, cracks, bushing material pick-up, etc.
7. Check the reservoir, studs, casting, etc. for burrs and other defects that would impair operation.
8. Use new O-rings when assembling.

Assembly

1. Install a new shaft seal in the housing and insert the shaft at the hub end of housing, splined end entering mounting face side.
2. Install the thrust plate on the dowel pins with the ported side facing the rear of the pump housing.
3. Install the rotor on the shaft, making sure it moves freely on the splines. Countersunk side must be toward the pulley.
4. Install the shaft retaining ring. Install the pump ring on the dowel pins with the direction of rotation arrow to the rear of the pump housing. Rotation is clockwise as seen from the pulley.
5. Install the vanes in the rotor slots with the radius edge towards the outside.
6. Lubricate the outside diameter and chamfer of the pressure plate with petroleum jelly so as not to damage the O-ring and install the plate on the dowel pins with the ported face toward the pump ring. Seat the pressure plate by placing a large socket on top of the plate and pushing down with hand.
7. Install the pressure plate spring in the center groove of the plate.

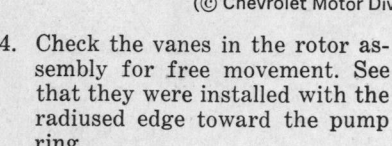

Correct vane assembly
(© Chevrolet Motor Div., G.M. Corp)

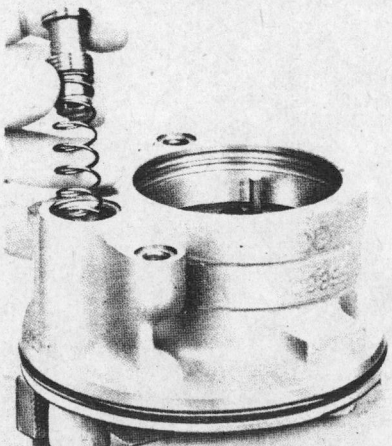

Installing flow control valve
(© Chevrolet Motor Div., G.M. Corp)

8. Install the end plate O-ring. Lubricate the outside diameter and chamfer of the end plate with petroleum jelly so as not to damage the O-ring and install the end plate in the housing using an arbor press. Install the end plate retaining ring while pump is in the arbor press. Be sure the ring is in the groove and the ring gap is positioned properly.
9. Install the flow control spring and plunger, hex head screw end in bore first. Install the filter cage, new filter stud seals and union seal.
10. Place the reservoir in the normal position and press down until the reservoir seats on the housing. Check the position of the stud seals and the union seal.
11. Install the studs, union, and driveshaft Woodruff key. Support the shaft on the opposite side of the key when tapping the key into place.

Roller Type Power Steering Pump Overhaul

Application
1970-77 Chrysler cars*
1970-71 AMC V8

* Varies with car line; visual identification is necessary.

The roller type power steering pump is similar to other constant flow centrifugal force pumps. A star-shaped rotor forces 12 steel rollers against the inside surface of a cam ring. As the rollers follow the eccentric pattern of the cam ring, fluid is drawn into the inlet ports and exhausted through the discharge ports while the rollers are forced into vee shaped cavities of the rotor, forcing fluid into the high pressure circuit. A flow control valve permits a regulated amount of fluid to return to the intake side of the pump when excess output is produced during high speed operation. This reduces the power needed to drive the pump and minimizes temperature build-up.

Under high pressure demand (such as turning the wheels against the stops), the pressure built up in the steering gear exerts force on the spring end of the flow control valve. This end of the valve contains the pressure relief valve. High pressure lifts the relief valve ball from its seat, allowing fluid to flow through a trigger orifice located in the front land of the flow control valve. This reduces pressure on the spring end of the valve which then opens and allows the fluid to return to the intake side of the pump. This action limits the maximum pressure output of the pump to a safe level. On Chrysler cars, this type can be identified by its rounded body; the vane type pump uses an oval body.

Disassembly

1. Remove pump from engine, drain reservoir, and clean outside of pump. Clamp the pump in a vise at the mounting bracket.
2. Remove the drive pulley.
3. Remove the shaft seal.
4. Remove the pump from the vise and remove the bracket mounting bolts. Remove the bracket.
5. Remove the reservoir and place the pump in a soft-faced vise with the shaft down. Discard the

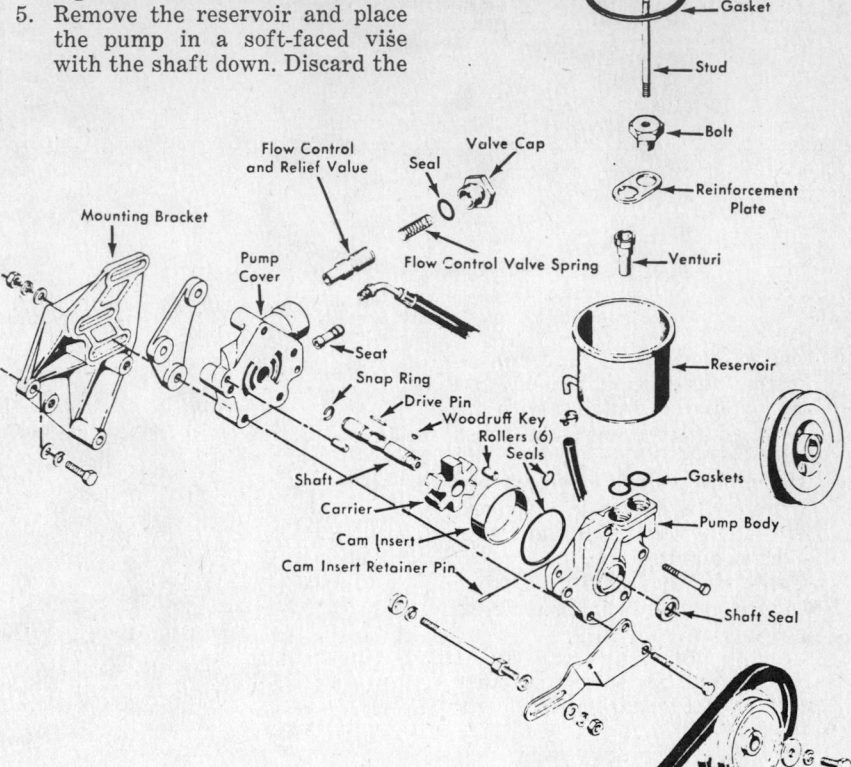

1970-71 AMC roller type power steering pump (© American Motors Corp)

mounting bolt and the reservoir O-rings.

6. Move the end cover retaining ring around until one end of the ring lines up with the hole in the pump body. Insert a small punch in the hole and push it in far enough to bend the ring so a screwdriver can be inserted to pry the ring loose.

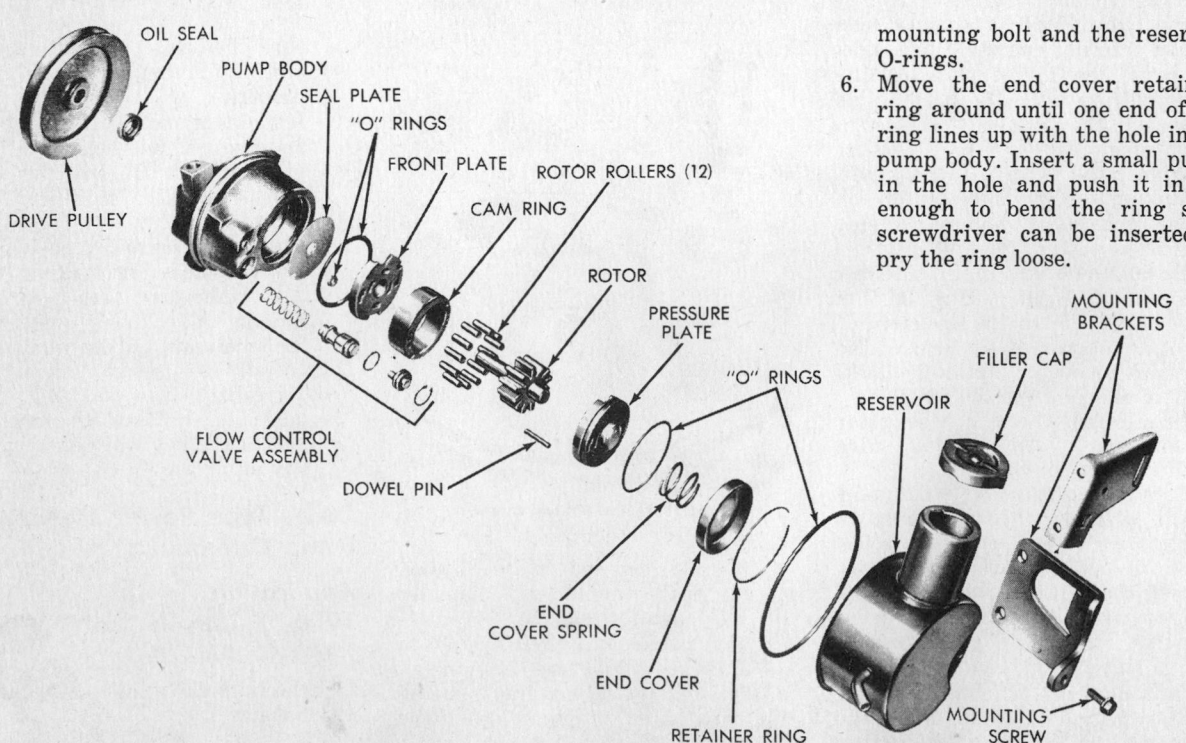

Chrysler 1.06 power steering pump, disassembled view (© Chrysler Corp)

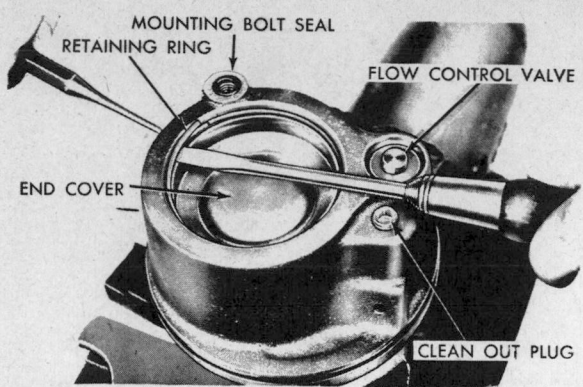

Removing end cover retaining ring
(© Chrysler Corp)

7. Remove the end cover and spring from the housing. It may be necessary to tap the cover gently to loosen it.
8. Remove the pump from the vise and turn the pump over so the rotating group may come out of the housing. Tap the end of the driveshaft to loosen these parts. Lift the pump body off the rotating group. Check that the seal plate is removed from the bottom of the housing bore.
9. Discard the O-rings from the pressure plate and end cover.
10. Remove the snap ring, bore plug, flow control valve and spring from the housing. Discard the O-ring. If necessary to disassemble the flow control valve for cleaning, see the procedure for disassembly.

Inspection

1. Remove the clean out plug with an Allen wrench.
2. Wash all metal parts in clean, non-toxic solvent. Blow out all passages with compressed air and air dry all cleaned parts.
3. Inspect the driveshaft for excessive wear and the seal area for nicks or scoring. Replace if necessary.
4. Inspect the end plates, rollers, rotor and cam ring for nicks, burrs, or scratches. If any of the components are damaged enough to cause poor operation of the pump, all the internal parts may have to be replaced to prevent later failures.
5. Inspect the pump body drive shaft bushing for excessive wear. Replace the pump body and bushing as one assembly.

Assembly

1. Install the 1/8 in. pipe clean out plug, tightening it to 80 in. lbs.
2. Place the pump body on a clean flat surface and drive a new shaft seal into the bore.
3. Install a new lubricated end cover O-ring into the groove in the pump bore.

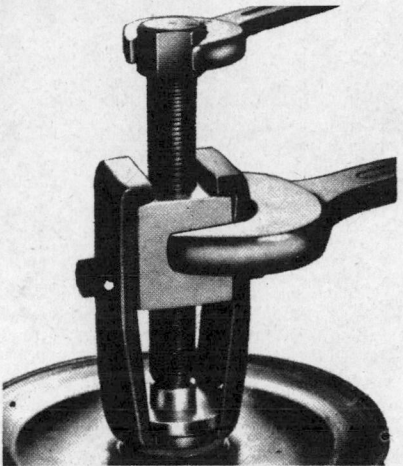

Removing drive pulley
(© Chrysler Corp)

Installing seal plate
(© Chrysler Corp)

4. Lubricate and install a new O-ring on the pump body to reservoir joint.
5. Install a new fiber gasket and brass seal plate on bottom of housing floor, taking care to align correctly. Align the notch in the seal plate with the dowel pin hole in the housing.
6. Carefully install the front plate with the chamfered edge down in the pump bore. Align the index notch in the plate with the dowel pin hole in the housing.

Caution Be extremely careful to align the dowel pin properly. Pump can be completely assembled with the dowel pin improperly seated in the housing and positioned improperly in the end plates.

Installing cam ring
(© Chrysler Corp)

7. Place the dowel pin in the cam ring and position the cam ring inside the pump bore. Notch in the cam ring must be facing up (away from the pulley end of pump housing). If the cam ring has two notches, one machined and one cast, install with machined notch up. If dowel pin protrudes above cam ring surface by more than 3/16 in., the dowel pin is not seated in the index hole in the housing.
8. Install the rotor and shaft in the cam ring and carefully install the 12 steel rollers in the rotor. Lubricate the rotor, rollers, and the inside surface of the cam ring with power steering fluid. Rotate the shaft by hand to be sure all the rollers are seated and are not sticking or binding.
9. Position the pressure plate by carefully aligning the index notch on the plate with the dowel pin and inserting a clean drill (number 13 to 16) in the cam ring oil hole next to the dowel pin notch until it bottoms on the housing floor.
10. Lubricate and install a new O-ring on the pressure plate. Position the pressure plate in the pump bore so that the dowel pin is in the index notch on the plate and the drill extends through the oil passage in the pressure plate. Seat the pressure plate on the cam ring using a clean 1 1/8 in. socket and a soft-faced hammer to tap it gently. Remove the drill and inspect the plate at both oil passage slots to be sure that the plate is squarely seated on the cam ring.
11. Place the large coil spring over the raised portion of the installed pressure plate.
12. Place the end cover, lip edge facing up, over the spring. Press the end cover down below the retaining ring groove. Install the retaining ring in the groove. Be sure the end cover chamfer is squarely seated against the snap ring.
13. Replace the reservoir mounting bolt seal.

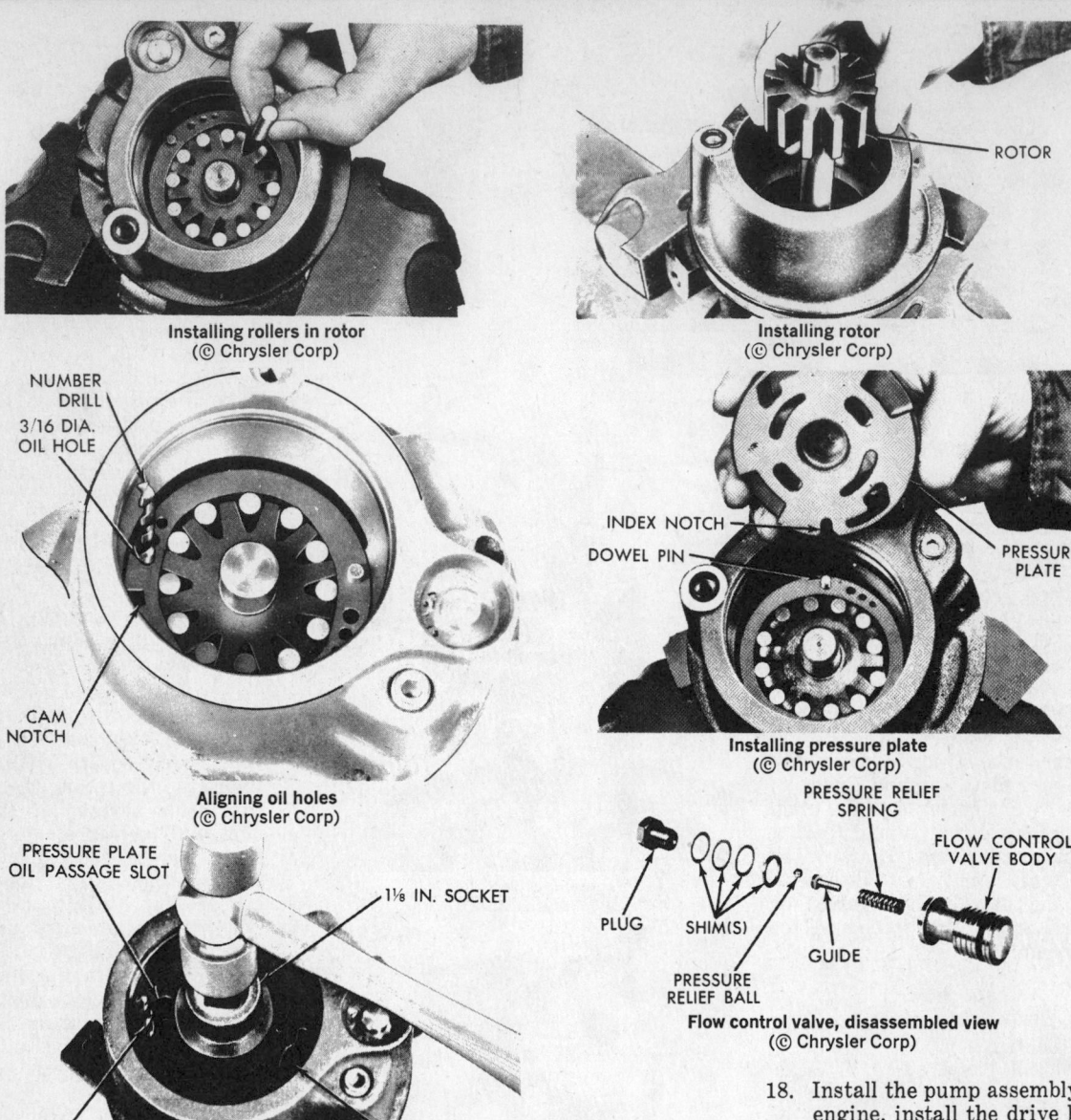

Installing rollers in rotor
(© Chrysler Corp)

Installing rotor
(© Chrysler Corp)

NUMBER DRILL
3/16 DIA. OIL HOLE
CAM NOTCH

Aligning oil holes
(© Chrysler Corp)

INDEX NOTCH
DOWEL PIN
PRESSURE PLATE

Installing pressure plate
(© Chrysler Corp)

PRESSURE PLATE OIL PASSAGE SLOT
1⅛ IN. SOCKET
NUMBER DRILL
OIL PASSAGE SLOT

Seating pressure plate
(© Chrysler Corp)

PLUG
SHIM(S)
PRESSURE RELIEF BALL
GUIDE
PRESSURE RELIEF SPRING
FLOW CONTROL VALVE BODY

Flow control valve, disassembled view
(© Chrysler Corp)

14. Lubricate the flow control valve assembly with power steering fluid and insert the valve spring and valve in the bore. Install a new O-ring on the bore plug, lubricate with fluid, and carefully install in the bore. Install the snap ring with the sharp edge up. *Do not depress the bore plug more than 1/16 in. below the snap-ring groove.*

15. Place the reservoir on the pump body and visually align the mounting bolt hole. Tap the reservoir down on the pump with a plastic-faced hammer.

16. Remove the pump from the vise and install the mounting brackets on the pump. Tighten to 18 ft. lbs.

17. Install the drive pulley by using the installer tool as follows. Place the pulley on the end of the shaft and thread the installer tool into the ⅜ in. threaded hole in the end of the shaft. Put the installer shaft in a vise and tighten the drive nut against the thrust bearing, pressing the pulley on the shaft until it is flush with the end of the shaft. *Do not try to press the pulley on the shaft without the special installer tool since the pump will be damaged by any other installation procedure.* A small amount of driveshaft end-play will be seen when the pulley is installed. This end-play is necessary and will be minimized by a thin coat of oil between the rotor and the end plates when the pump is operating.

18. Install the pump assembly on the engine, install the drive belt and hoses (use new O-ring on pressure hose), and check for leaks.

Flow Control Valve Disassembly

1. After removing the pump from the engine and the reservoir from the pump, remove the snap-ring and plug from the flow bore. Discard the O-ring.

2. Depress the control valve against the spring pressure and allow the valve to spring out of the bore. If the valve is stuck in the bore or it did not come out far enough, it may be necessary to tap the housing lightly.

3. If the valve has dirt or foreign particles on it or in its bore, the rest of the pump needs cleaning. The hoses should be flushed and the steering gear valve body reconditioned. If the valve bore is badly scored, replace the pump body and the flow control valve.

4. Remove any nicks or burrs by gently rubbing the valve with crocus cloth. Clamp the valve

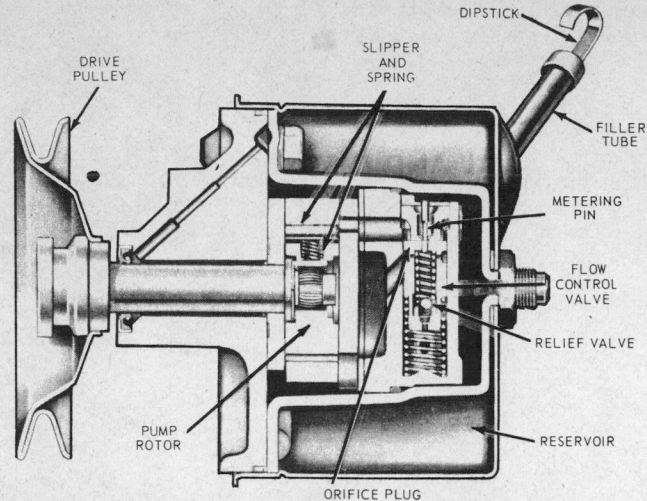

Ford-Thompson power steering pump, sectional view
(© Ford Motor Co)

placement unit that uses a number of spring-loaded slippers in the pump rotor to force oil from the inlet side to the flow control valve. Openings in the metering pin allow a flow of about two gpm. of fluid to the steering gear before the flow control valve directs the excess fluid to the inlet side of the pump again. Maximum pressure in the pump is limited by the pressure relief valve which opens when the oil pressure exceeds the maximum pressure limits.

The slipper type power steering pump discussed in this section is used in some Ford cars and is called the Ford-Thompson or TRW power steering pump.

Application
1970-71 All Ford Cars
1972-77 All except Thunderbird, Lincoln, Ford and Mercury

Disassembly

1. Drain as much fluid from the pump as possible after removing the pump from the car.
2. Install a ⅜-16 in. capscrew in the end of the pump shaft to avoid damaging the shaft. Install the pulley remover tool on the pulley hub and place the pump and remover tool in a vise as shown. Hold the pump steady and turn the tool nut counterclockwise to draw the pulley off the shaft. *The pulley must be removed without in and out pressure on the pump shaft to avoid damaging the internal thrust washers.*
3. Remove the pump reservoir by installing the pump in a holding

land in a soft-jawed vise and remove the hex head ball seat and shims. Note the number and gauge (thickness) of the shims on the ball seat. They must be re-installed at the same shim thickness to keep the same value of relief pressure.
5. Remove the valve from the vise and remove the pressure relief ball, guide, and spring.

Flow Control Valve Assembly

1. Insert the spring, guide and pressure relief ball in the end of the flow control valve.
2. Install the hex head plug using the same number and thickness shims that were removed. Tighten the plug to 80 in. lbs.
3. Lubricate the valve with power steering fluid and insert the flow control valve spring and valve in the housing bore. Install a new O-ring on the bore plug, lubricate with fluid and carefully install into the bore. Install the snap ring. *Do not depress the bore plug more than 1/16 in. beyond the snap-ring groove.*

Slipper Type Power Steering Pump Overhaul

The slipper type power steering pump is a belt-driven constant dis-

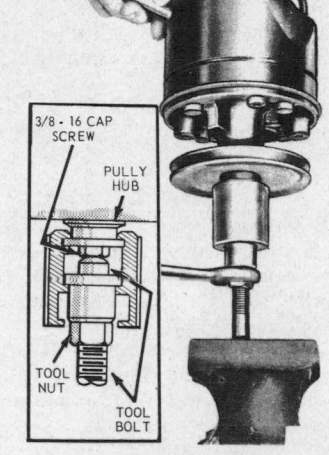

Removing drive pulley
(© Ford Motor Co)

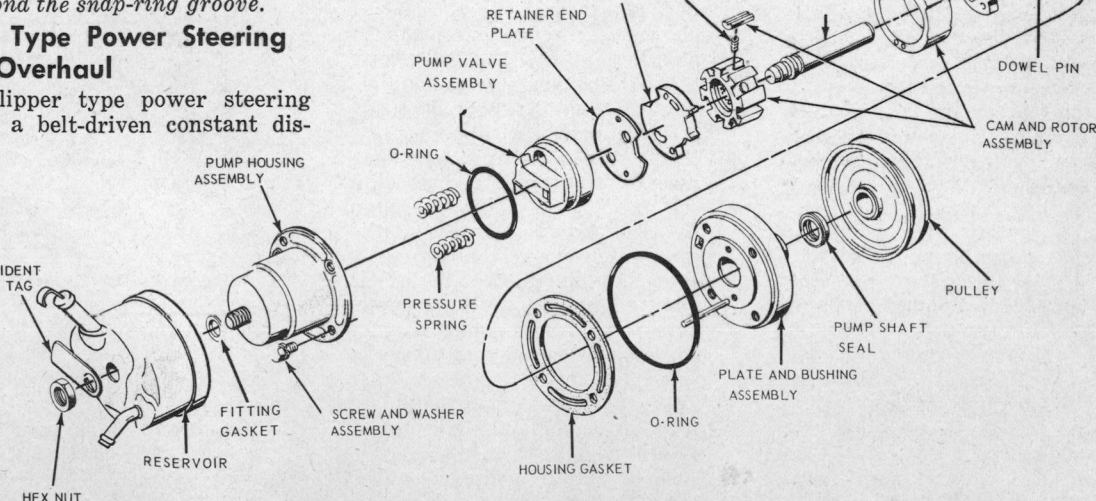

Ford-Thompson power steering pump, disassembled view (© Ford Motor Co)

Removing pump reservoir
(© Ford Motor Co)

fixture in a vise with the reservoir facing up.

4. Remove the outlet fitting hex nut and any other attaching parts from the reservoir case.

5. Invert the pump so the reservoir is now facing down. Using a wooden block, remove the reservoir by tapping around the flange until the reservoir is loose. Remove the reservoir O-ring seal and the outlet fitting gasket from the pump.

6. Again invert the pump assembly in the vise, remove the pump housing holding bolts, and the pump housing.

7. Remove the housing cover, the O-ring seal, and the pressure springs from inside the pump housing. Remove the pump cover gasket and discard it.

8. Remove the retainer end plate and upper pressure plate. In some pumps, the end plate and the upper pressure plate are one unit.

9. Remove the loose-fitting dowel pin. Be careful not to bend the fixed dowel pin which remains in the housing plate assembly.

10. Remove the rotor assembly, being careful not to let the slippers and springs fall out of the rotor. It may not be necessary to disassemble the rotor assembly unless the lower pressure plate, housing plate, rotor shaft and/or seal is to be replaced. However, the rotor assembly may be disassembled by removing the slippers and springs from the cam ring.

11. Clean any rust, dirt, burrs, or scoring from the pulley end of the rotor shaft before removing the shaft from the housing plate. The shaft must come out without restrictions to avoid scoring or damaging the bushing. Remove the pump rotor shaft.

12. Remove the lower pressure plate.

13. Remove the rotor shaft seal after first wrapping a piece of 0.005 in. shim stock around the

shaft and pushing it into the inside of the seal until it touches the bushing. With a sharp tool, pierce the seal body and pry the seal out. *Do not damage the bushing, housing, or the shaft.* Install a new seal using the tool shown and a soft-faced hammer.

14. If the pump has a flow control valve, disassemble according to instructions given in the section on the roller type power steering pump.

Inspection

1. Wash all metal parts in clean, non-toxic solvent. Blow out all oil passages with compressed air and air dry all cleaned parts.

2. Inspect the driveshaft for excessive wear and the seal area for nicks or scoring. Replace if necessary.

3. Inspect the pressure plates, slippers, rotor, and cam ring for nicks, burrs, or scratches. If any of the parts are damaged enough to cause poor operation or binding of the pump, replace the defective part.

4. Inspect the driveshaft bushing in the pump body for excessive wear. Replace if necessary.

Assembly

1. With the pump assembly in the holding fixture, install the lower pressure plate on the anchor pin with the chamfered slots at the center hole facing up.

2. Lubricate the rotor shaft with power steering fluid and insert the shaft into the lower pressure plate and housing plate.

3. Assemble the rotor, slippers, and springs by wrapping a piece of wire around the rotor, installing the springs, and sliding a slipper into each groove of the rotor over the springs. Then, insert the assembly into the cam ring. Be sure the flat side of the slippers are toward the left side as shown. (Ford-Thompson power steering pump). Be sure that the springs are installed straight and are not cocked to one side under the slippers.

4. Install the cam ring and rotor assembly on the driveshaft with the fixed dowel passing through the first hole to the left of the cam notch when the arrow on the cam outside diameter is pointing toward the lower pressure plate. If the cam and rotor assembly does not seat properly, turn the rotor shaft slightly until the spline teeth mesh, allowing the cam and rotor to drop into position.

5. Insert the loose-fitting dowel through the cam insert and lower pressure plate into the

Pump gasket locations
(© Ford Motor Co)

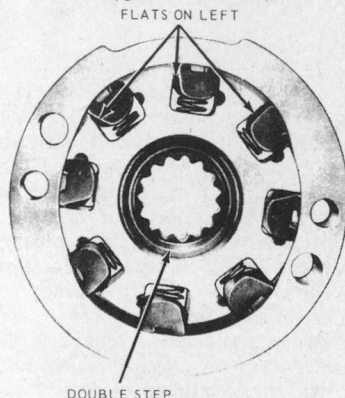

Correct slipper installation, Ford-Thompson power steering pump
(© Ford Motor Co)

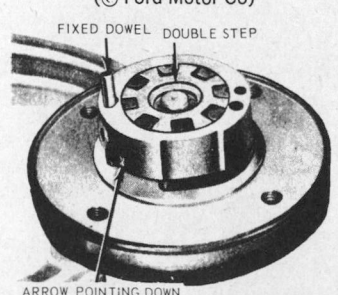

Cam and rotor installation
(© Ford Motor Co)

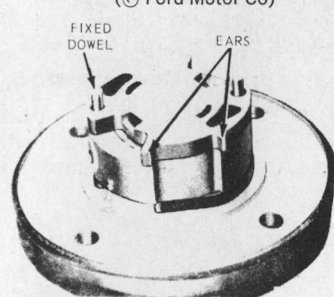

Upper pressure plate installation
(© Ford Motor Co)

hole in the housing plate assembly. When both dowels are installed properly, they will be the same height.

6. Install the upper pressure plate so the tapered notch is facing down against the cam insert. The fixed dowel should pass through the round dowel hole

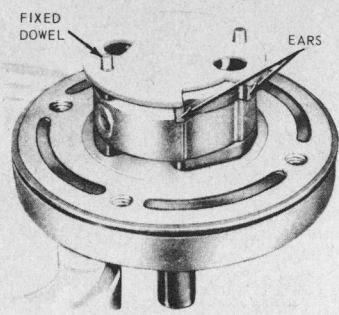

Retainer end plate installation
(© Ford Motor Co)

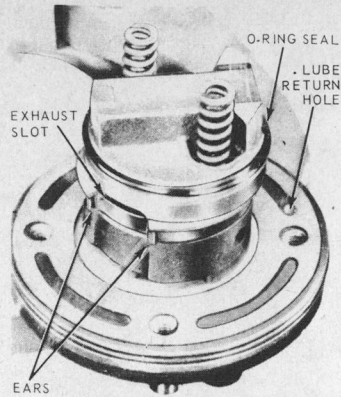

Valve and pressure spring installation
(© Ford Motor Co)

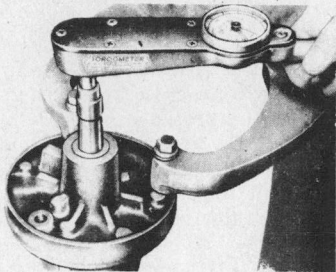

Checking pump rotational torque
(© Ford Motor Co)

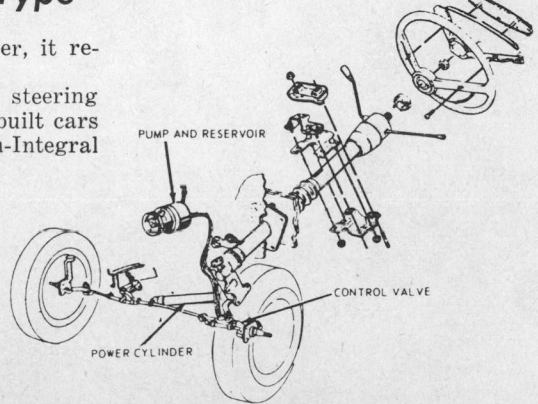

Low pressure plate installed
(© Ford Motor Co)

and the loose dowel through the long hole. The slot between the ears on the outside of the pressure plate should match the notch on the cam insert.

7. Install the retainer end plate so the slot on the end plate matches the notches on the upper pressure plate and the cam insert.

8. Install the pump valve assembly O-ring seal on the pump valve assembly. *Do not twist the seal.*

9. Place the pump valve assembly on top of the retainer end plate with the large exhaust slot on the pump valve in line with the outside notches of the cam, upper pressure plate, and retainer end plate. All parts must be fully seated. If correctly installed, the relief valve stem will be in line with the lube return hole in the pump housing plate.

10. Put small amounts of vaseline on the pump housing plate to hold the cover gasket in place. Install the cover gasket.

11. Insert the pressure plate springs into the pockets in the pump valve assembly.

12. Block the intake hole in the housing.

13. Lubricate the inside of the housing and the housing cover seal with power steering fluid. Make and install two studs for use as positioning guides, one in the bolt hole nearest the drain hole and the other in the bolt hole on the opposite side of the housing plate.

14. Align the small lube hole in the housing rim and the lube hole in the housing plate. Install the housing, using a steady, even, downward pressure. *Do not jar the pressure spring out of position.* Remove the guide studs and loosely install the housing retaining bolts finger tight. Remove the block from the intake hole.

15. Tighten the retaining bolts evenly to 28-32 ft. lbs. until the housing flange contacts the gasket.

16. Install a ⅜-16 hex head screw into the end of the rotor shaft. Check the amount of torque needed to rotate the shaft. If the torque is more than 15 in. lbs., loosen the retaining bolts slightly and rotate the rotor shaft. Then, retighten the retaining bolts evenly. *Do not use the pump if the shaft torque exceeds 15 in. lbs.*

17. Remove pump from the bench holding fixture and shake the assembly back and forth. If there is a rattle, the pressure springs have fallen out of their seats and must be reinstalled.

18. Install the reservoir O-ring seal on the housing plate without twisting it. Lubricate the seal and install the reservoir, aligning the notch in the reservoir flange with the notch in the outside edge of the pump housing plate and bushing assembly. Using a soft-faced hammer, tap at the rear outer corners of the reservoir. Inspect the assembly to be sure the reservoir is fully seated on the housing plate.

19. Install the identification tag (if any) on the outlet valve fitting. Install the outlet valve fitting nut and tighten to 43-45 ft. lbs.

20. Turn the pump assembly over and install the pulley with the tool used to remove it. Draw the pulley onto the shaft until it is flush with the shaft end. *Do not exert inward and outward pressures on the shaft to avoid damaging the internal thrust areas.*

Section 4
Bendix Linkage-Type

The Bendix linkage-type power steering system is a hydraulically controlled linkage-type system composed of an integral pump and fluid reservoir, a control valve, a power cylinder, connecting fluid lines, and the steering linkage. The hydraulic pump, which is driven by a belt turned by the engine, draws fluid from the reservoir and provides fluid pressure through hoses to the control valve and the power cylinder. There is a pressure relief valve to limit the pressures within the steering system to a safe level. After the fluid has passed from the pump to the control valve and the power cylinder, it returns to the reservoir.

The Bendix linkage-type steering system when used in Ford-built cars is called the Ford Non-Integral Power Steering System.

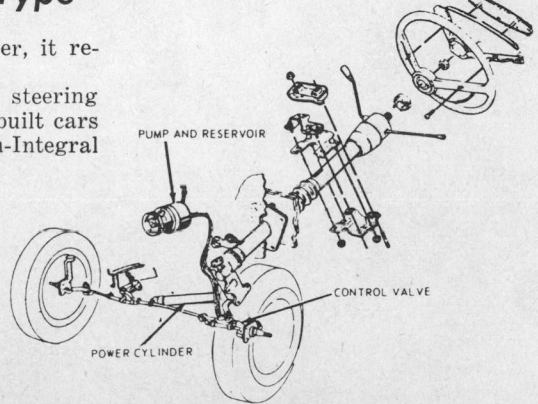

Bendix linkage-type power steering system (© Ford Motor Co)

Section 5
Saginaw Linkage-Type System

The Corvette is the only car which uses the Saginaw linkage type power steering. The design of this system is similiar to the Saginaw rotary type power steering, but on the Corvette, a constant ratio gear is used rather than a variable ratio gear. There are no in-car adjustments possible with this system.

Section 6
Saginaw Rotary-Type

The rotary type power steering gear is designed with all components in one housing.

The power cylinder is an integral part of the gear housing. A double-acting piston allows oil pressure to be applied to either side of the piston. The one-piece piston and power rack is meshed to the sector shaft.

The hydraulic control valve is composed of a sleeve and valve spool. The spool is held in the neutral position by the torsion bar and spool actuator. Twisting of the torsion bar moves the valve spool, allowing oil pressure to be directed to either side of the power piston, depending on the directional rotation of the steering wheel, to give power assist.

On many General Motors cars a modified version of the system provides variable ratio steering for easier and safer control. The steering gear ratio will vary from a high ratio of about 16:1 while steering straight ahead to a lower gear ratio of about 12.4:1 while making a full turn to either side.

Power Steering Unit
Checking Steering Effort

Run the engine to attain normal operating temperatures. With the wheels on a dry floor, hook a pull scale to the spoke of the steering wheel at the outer edge. The effort required to turn the steering wheel should be 3½-5 lbs. If the pull is not within these limits, check the hydraulic pressure.

Pressure Test

To check the hydraulic pressure, disconnect the pressure hose from the gear. Now connect the pressure gauge between the pressure hose from the pump and the steering gear housing. Fill the fluid reservoir to the proper level. Run the engine and turn the wheel to a full right and a full left turn to the wheel stops to attain normal operating temperatures (150°F-170°F).

Hold the wheel in this position only momentarily.

The initial pressure gauge reading should be 80-125 psi. If the pressure reading is less than the minimum pressure needed for proper operation, check for hose restrictions. Close the valve at the gauge. Do not close the valve for more than 5 seconds. The pressure reading should be within 50 psi of 1350 to 1450 psi (870-1000 psi on Corvette), 1200 to 1300 with 6-cyl-inder engines). If the pressure is 100 psi or more below specifications, the pump is defective and needs repair. If the pressure reading is within 50 psi of the minimum specifications, the pump is normal and needs only an adjustment of the power steering gear or flow control valve.

If the maximum pressure specification still cannot be obtained by turning the steering wheel against the stops momentarily, then the steering gear is leaking internally and must be disassembled and repaired.

Worm Bearing Preload and Sector Mesh Adjustments

NOTE: The steering gear must be out of the car to adjust it on 1974 and later models. On earlier models only the over-center preload (sector shaft) can be adjusted with the steering gear in the car.

Disconnect the Pitman arm from the sector shaft, then completely back off on the sector shaft adjusting screw on the sector shaft cover.

Center the steering on the high point, then attach an in. lb torque wrench to the steering wheel attaching nut. The torque required to keep the wheel moving for one complete turn

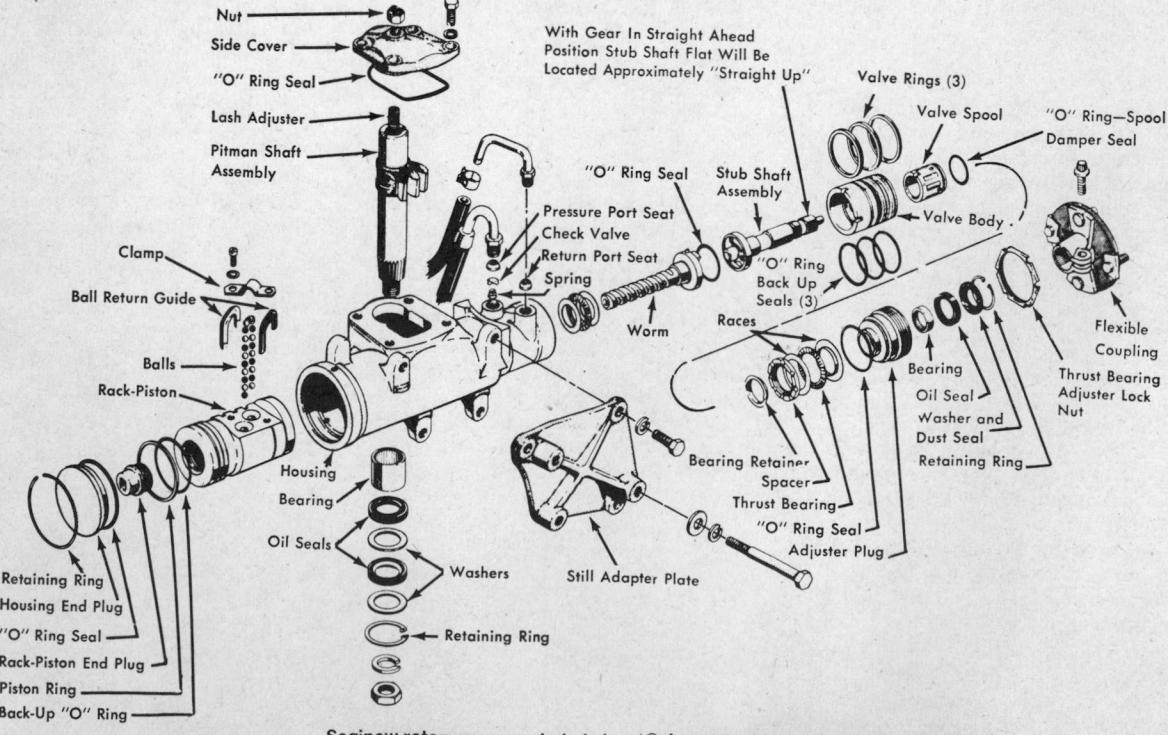

Saginaw rotary gear, exploded view (© American Motors Corp)

should be ½-2 in. lbs.

If the torque is not within these limits, loosen the thrust bearing locknut and tighten or back off on the valve sleeve adjuster plug to bring the preload within limits. Tighten the thrust bearing locknut and recheck the preload.

Slowly rotate the steering wheel several times, then center the steering on the high point. Now, turn the sector shaft adjusting screw until a steering shaft torque of 3-6 in. lbs more is required to move the worm through the center point. Tighten the sector shaft adjusting screw locknut to 35 ft lbs and recheck the sector mesh adjustment. Total steering gear preload should be 14 in. lbs or less.

Install the pitman arm and draw the arm into position with the nut.

Section 7
Chrysler Full-Time (Constant Control Type)

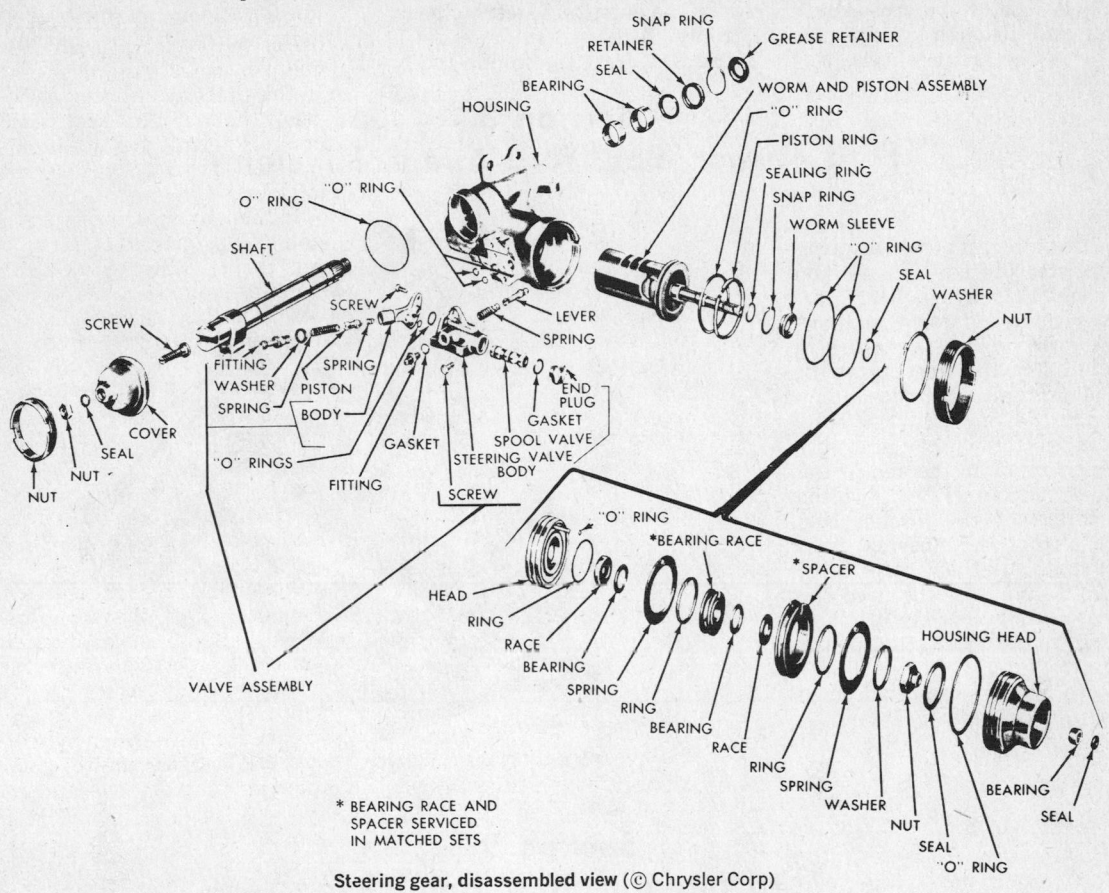

Steering gear, disassembled view (© Chrysler Corp)

The power steering gear system for Chrysler Corporation cars is called the Constant Control type. This system consists of a hydraulic pressure pump, a power steering gear and connecting hoses.

The power steering gear housing contains a gear shaft and sector gear, a power piston with gear teeth milled into the side of the piston which is in constant mesh with the gear shaft sector teeth, a worm shaft which connects the steering wheel to the power piston through a coupling. The worm shaft is geared to the piston through recirculating ball contact.

A pivot lever is fitted into the spool valve at the upper end and into a drilled hole in the center thrust bearing race at the lower end. The center thrust bearing race is held firmly against the shoulder of the worm shaft by two thrust bearings, bearing races and an adjusting nut. The pivot lever pivots in the spacer which is held in place by the pressure plate.

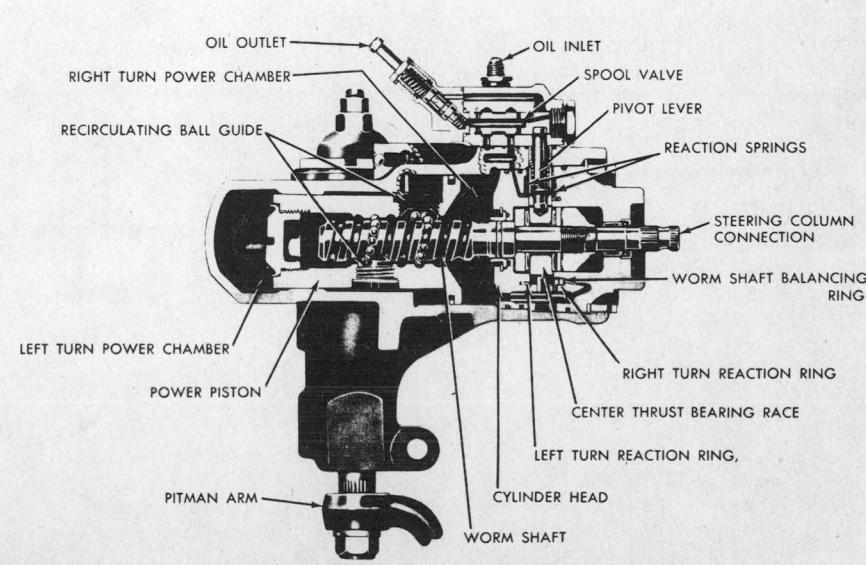

Chrysler power steering gear (© Chrysler Corp)

When the steering wheel is turned to the left the worm shaft moves out of the power piston a few thousandths of an inch, the center thrust bearing race moves the same distance since it is clamped to the worm shaft. The race thus tips the pivot lever and moves the spool valve down, allowing oil under pressure to flow into the left-turn power chamber and force the power piston down. As the power piston moves, it rotates the cross-shaft sector gear and, through the steering linkage, turns the front wheels.

On a right turn the worm shaft moves into the power piston, the center thrust bearing race thus tips the pivot lever and moves the spool valve up, allowing oil under pressure to flow into the right power chamber and force the power piston up.

Pressure Test

Connect the pressure test hoses with the pressure gauge installed between the pump and steering gear.

Now, fill the reservoir to the level mark, then start the engine and bleed the system. Allow the engine to idle until the fluid in the reservoir is between 150° F. and 170° F. Now turn the steering wheel to the extreme right and check the pressure reading, then turn to the extreme left and check the reading again. The gauge reading should be equal in each direction. If not, it indicates excessive internal leakage in the unit.

The pressure should agree with the specifications in Pump Section for satisfactory power steering operation.

Section 8
Ford Torsion Bar (Ford Integral System)

In the Ford integral power steering system, the steering unit is a torsion bar type which is hydraulically assisted. It includes a worm and one piece rack piston which is meshed to the gear teeth on the steering sector shaft. The unit also includes a hydraulic rotary valve sleeve assembly, input shaft and torsion bar assembly which are mounted on the end of the worm shaft and operated by the twisting action of the torsion bar. The combining of the steering gear, the power unit, and the control valve into one unit eliminates the need for all external hoses except the pressure and return hoses from the power steering pump.

There are no in-car adjustments possible with this unit.

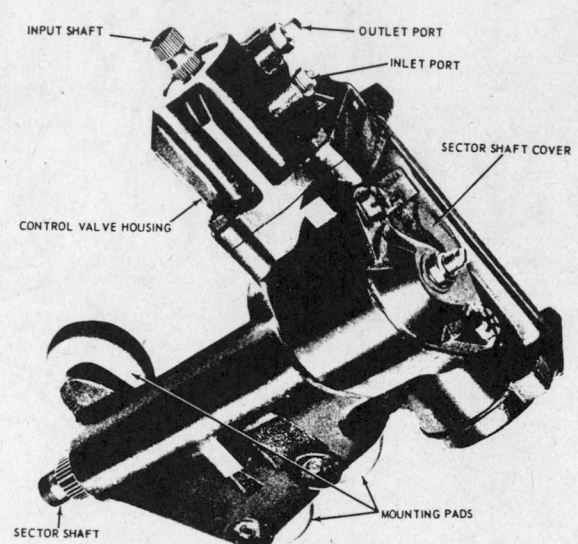

Power steering gear (© Lincoln-Mercury Div., Ford Motor Co)

Section 9
Ford Integral Rack and Pinion

This system was developed to provide a power steering system for those small Ford Motor Company cars equipped with rack and pinion steering.

It consists of a hydraulic mechanical unit which uses an integral piston and rack design to provide power assisted steering Internal valves both direct and control the pump flow in response to steering conditions. The unit consists of a rotary fluid control valve integrated to the input shaft

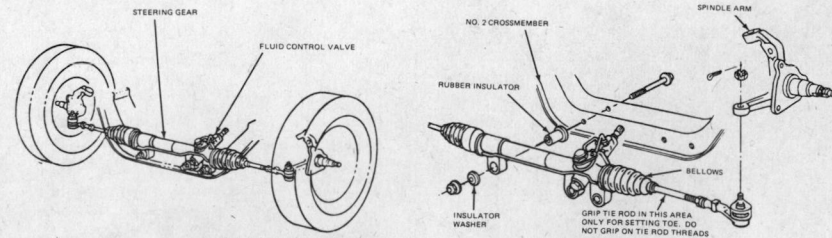

Ford integral rack and pinion steering gear installation
(© Ford Motor Co)

and a boost cylinder integrated with the rack.

There are no in-car adjustments possible on this unit.

Section 10
American Motors Pacer Rack and Pinion

The Pacer rack and pinion power steering system consists of an integral tube and housing assembly which contains the steering rack and piston, the pinion shaft and valve body assembly, and the adjuster plug assembly. In operation, the fluid under pressure from the power steering pump is sent through the inlet hose to the steering gear housing and into the valve body. The valve body then directs the fluid to either side of the power cylinder to provide a power assist for the wheels. There are no in-car adjustments possible on this system.

Chrysler Pump

Type	Constant displacement—1.06 cu. in. per revolution	Constant displacement—.94 cu. in per revolution
Maximum pressure	1200 to 1300 PSI	950 to 1075 PSI
Pump output High level Low level Type of fluid	2.5 to 3.0 gpm 1.4 to 1.8 gpm Power steering—Part No. 2084329 or equivalent. Do not use Type "A" Transmission fluid	2.1 to 2.6 gpm Power steering—Part No. 2084329 or equivalent Do not use Type "A" Transmission fluid

Pump Torques

Location	Ft. Lbs.
High pressure hose fittings	13
Pump bracket bolts	23
Flow control valve plug	7
Bracket mounting bolts	30
⅛ in. pipe clean out plug	7

Ford Power Steering Pump Service Specifications

Description	Ford—Thompson	Eaton
Pump Rotor Shaft End Play	.017 in. Max.—.003 in. Min.	
Max. Torque Allowed to Rotate Rotor Shaft	15 In-Lb.	
Stamped Housing-to-Plate Assy. Screw and Washer Assy.	28-32 Ft.-Lb.	

Description	Ford—Thompson	Eaton
Stamped Housing-to-Plate Assy. Washer head hex bolt		38-47 Ft.-Lb.
Reservoir-to-Stamped Housing Nut	43-47 Ft.-Lb.	
Cam Ring-to-Pressure Plate Screw		20 In-Lb.
Housing-to-Cover Screw		15-20 Ft.-Lb.

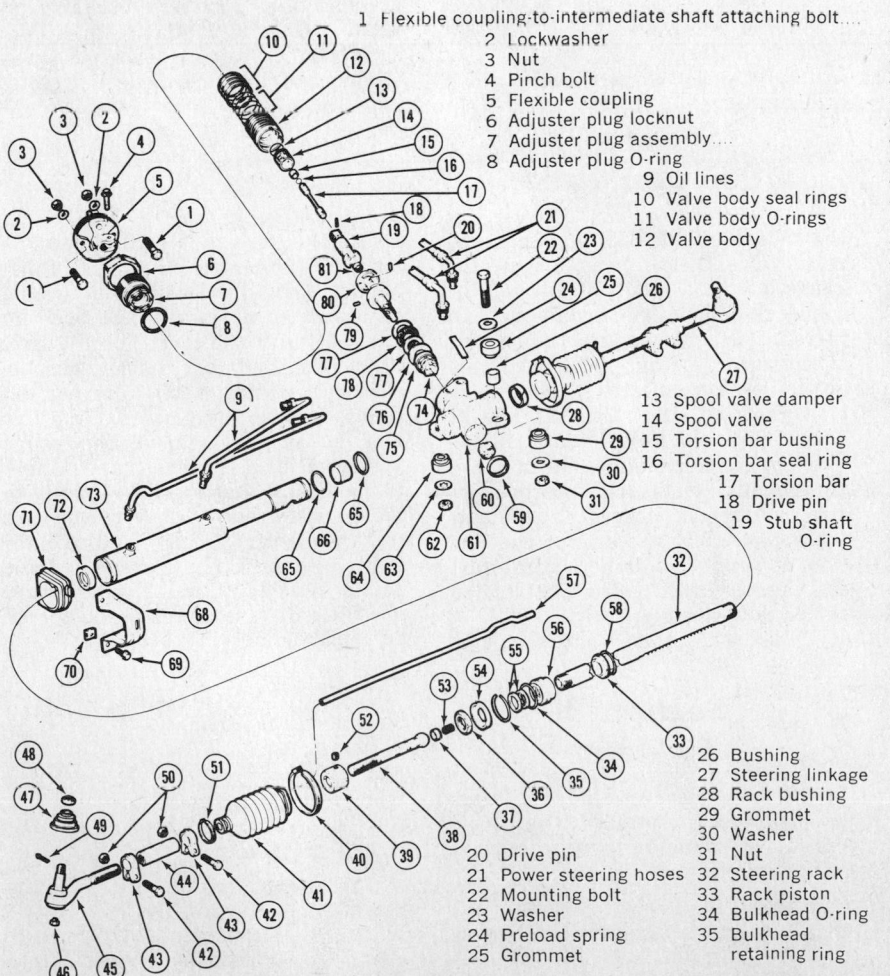

1 Flexible coupling-to-intermediate shaft attaching bolt
2 Lockwasher
3 Nut
4 Pinch bolt
5 Flexible coupling
6 Adjuster plug locknut
7 Adjuster plug assembly
8 Adjuster plug O-ring
9 Oil lines
10 Valve body seal rings
11 Valve body O-rings
12 Valve body
13 Spool valve damper
14 Spool valve
15 Torsion bar bushing
16 Torsion bar seal ring
17 Torsion bar
18 Drive pin
19 Stub shaft O-ring
20 Drive pin
21 Power steering hoses
22 Mounting bolt
23 Washer
24 Preload spring
25 Grommet
26 Bushing
27 Steering linkage
28 Rack bushing
29 Grommet
30 Washer
31 Nut
32 Steering rack
33 Rack piston
34 Bulkhead O-ring
35 Bulkhead retaining ring
36 Jam nut
37 Ball seat
38 Inner tie rod
39 Inner tie rod housing
40 Boot clamp
41 Boot
42 Adjuster tube clamp bolt
43 Adjuster tube clamp
44 Adjuster tube
45 Tie rod end
46 Lube plug
47 Tie rod end seal
48 Tie rod end nut
49 Cotter pin
50 Adjuster tube clamp nut
51 Boot clamp
52 Tie rod housing set screw
53 Ball seat spring
54 Shock dampener ring
55 Bulkhead seals
56 Bulkhead
57 Breather tube
58 Rack piston seal ring
59 Contraction plug
60 Lower pinion bushing
61 Housing
62 Nut
63 Washer
64 Grommet
65 Plastic injection ring
66 Locating bushing
67 Plastic injection ring
68 Mounting clamp
69 Bolt
70 Mounting clip
71 Mounting grommet
72 Inner rack seal
73 Tube and power cylinder
74 Upper pinion bushing
75 Pinion shaft seal
76 Support washer
77 Conical thrust bearing race
78 Thrust bearing
79 Drive pin
80 Shaft cap
81 Torsion bar bushing

Exploded view of the American Motors Pacer power rack and pinion steering gear
(ⓒ American Motors Corp)

Dash Gauges and Indicators

INDEX

Introduction
Section 1, Bourdon tube gauges U350
Section 2, Bi-Metal Gauges U350
Section 3, Magnetic Gauges U351
Section 4, Warning Lights U353
Section 5, Ammeters U354
Section 6, Voltmeters U354

There are various systems used to indicate values of heat, pressure, current flow and fuel supply. The following are the more popular systems used.

Bourdon Tube

This gauge consists of a flattened tube that is bent to form a curve. The curve tends to straighten under internal pressure caused by engine oil pressure. The curved tube is geared or linked to an indicator needle which may be read on a calibrated scale.

Bourdon tube oil pressure gauges are used on some Corvettes and the optional instrument panels on some Chevrolet sport models. This type of gauge may be easily distinguished from the electrical type by the small copper or nylon tube running from the gauge to the engine.

Bi-Metallic or Thermal

This gauge is activated by the dif-

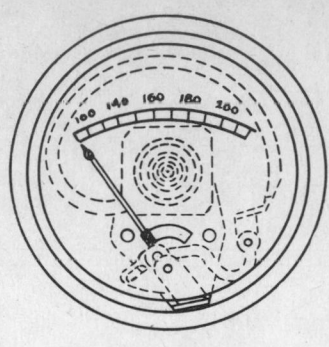

Bourdon tube gauge

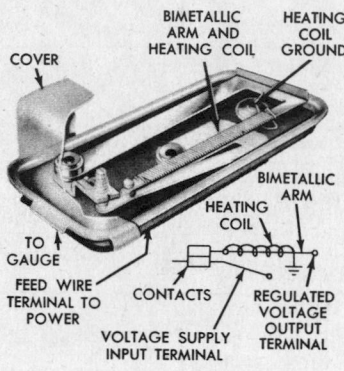

Constant voltage regulator

ference in the expansion factors of a bi-metal bar. A sending unit, consisting of a variable resistance conductor, influences current flow to a voltage limiter, or directly to a heating element coiled around a bi-metal bar in the gauge. A bi-metallic gauge pointer will move slowly to its gauging position.

Magnetic

In this system, the indicator needle is moved by changing the balance between the magnetic pull of two coils built in the gauge. When the ignition switch is in the "off" position, the pointer may rest any place on the gauge dial. Balance is controlled by the action of a sending unit or a tank unit containing a rheostat, the value of which varies with temperature, pressure or movement of a float arm. A magnetic gauge will snap to its position when turned on.

Warning Lights

This system is quite popular and may be used to indicate heat, low pressure or as a battery discharge indicator. General Motors uses a two-light temperature indicator version of this unit in some models.

Section 1
Bourdon Tube

Oil Pressure

The gauge is the pressure expansion type and is activated by oil pressure developed by the oil pump, acting directly on the mechanism of the gauge. The gauge is connected by a small tube to the main oil passage in the engine oiling system. This design registers the full pressure of the oil pump.

Testing

A gauge pointer that flutters is usually an indication that oil has entered the gauge tube. The tube should contain trapped air to cushion

the pulsations of the oil pump and relief valve. Oil can work up into the gauge line as a result of a gauge or tube leak or improper installation. To correct this condition, renew the unit or correct the leak; then, with the gauge line disconnected at both ends, blow the line clear. Connect line at gauge first and then at the engine.

If the gauge reads too low or reads no pressure, test for a possible obstruction by disconnecting the line at the gauge. Hold the end of the line over an empty container, then start the engine. After a few bubbles, oil should flow steadily.

If oil does not flow satisfactorily,

first make sure that the oil level is correct and that the oil pump is functioning. Should the engine oil system be operating correctly, the problem is either with the gauge or the line. Check the line for kinks, leaks, or blockage which would prevent oil from reaching the gauge. If the line is unobstructed, remove the gauge unit from the instrument panel. Check to make sure that the hole leading to the Bourdon tube is clear and be sure that the lever linkage and pointer gears operate freely. If none of these points is at fault, the Bourdon tube itself is defective and the gauge must be replaced.

Section 2
Bi-Metal

Fuel

Bi-metal or thermal type gauges operate on the principle of constant applied voltage and are sensitive only to changes originating at the sending unit.

The fuel gauge system consists of a sending unit, located in the fuel tank, and a registering unit mounted

in the instrument cluster. The sending unit is a rheostat that varies its resistance depending on the amount of fuel in the tank.

Testing the Dash Gauge

Caution Gauge systems using constant voltage regulators should not be grounded while testing. An excess of 5 volts is likely

to burn out the unit.

To safely test this type of voltage regulated system:

1. Have the ignition switch in the "off" position.
2. Connect the terminals of four, series-connected, D-type flashlight batteries (total of six volts) to the terminals of the

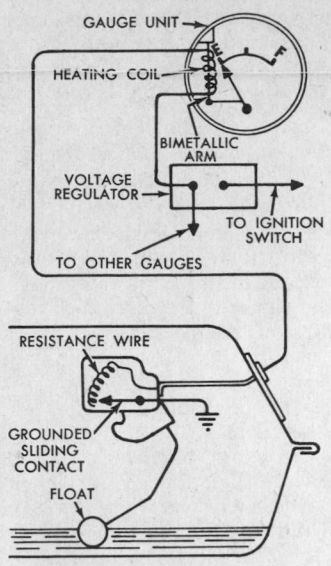

Bi-metallic fuel gauge system

gauge to be tested. Three volts should cause the gauge to read approximately half-scale.

If the gauge reads half-full and was not working properly before, the sending unit in the tank is probably defective.

If the gauge is inaccurate or does not register, replace it.

If both the fuel gauge and temperature gauge are in error, in the same manner, the constant voltage regulator is probably at fault.

While working under the dash, be careful not to ground any of the gauges. A full flow of current through the regulator to ground is likely to burn out the regulator.

Testing the Sending Unit

If the dash gauge test shows that unit to be satisfactory, the sending unit or gauge system wiring is faulty. Substitute a jumper wire between the gauge and the tank unit. If the gauge now functions, replace the wire. If the gauge still does not function correctly, replace the tank sending unit.

Oil Pressure

Oil pressure gauges of the bi-metal type operate on the same principle as

gas gauges. They are activated by temperature and the difference in the expansion factors of a bi-metal bar.

The pressure sending unit consists of a pressure-activated variable resistor. This sealed unit is usually screwed into the engine oil pressure circuit. As pressure is applied to one side of a diaphragm, linkage advances a contact arm across the coils of a resistor. This action reduces resistance in the gauge circuit, thus increasing current flow and heat to the bi-metal arm in the gauge. The gauge is calibrated to read oil pressure in psi.

Run the engine and have an assistant watch the dash gauge. If the gauge reads zero, turn off the engine and remove the sending unit from the engine block. Restart the engine and allow it to idle for a minute. If there is oil pressure, oil should surge from the sending unit hole. If no oil flows from the hole, the problem is with the engine lubricating system. If oil flows, the fault lies with the sending unit, the wiring, or the dash gauge.

Check the gauge by grounding the connecting wire for an instant with the ignition switch turned on. A good gauge will go to the top of its scale.

Caution Grounding the connecting wire for any longer than a moment will damage the dash units.

If the gauge did not move when grounded, check the wiring to the dash unit for continuity. If the wiring is not faulty and the gauge doesn't register when grounded, replace the gauge. If the gauge functions when grounded, replace the sending unit.

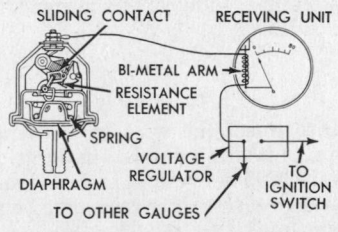

Bi-metallic oil gauge circuit

Temperature

The temperature gauge consists of a sending unit, mounted in the cyl-

inder head or block, and a remote resistor unit (temperature gauge) mounted on the instrument panel. The principle of operation is essentially the same as the bi-metallic fuel gauge, the exception being that the resistance of the sending unit is influenced by engine temperature instead of tank fuel level, as with the fuel gauge.

The temperature sending unit is constructed with a coil spring and sensing disc. Current passing through this coil encounters increased resistance, proportional to an increase in temperature. The gauge registers this resistance change and is calibrated to indicate the temperature.

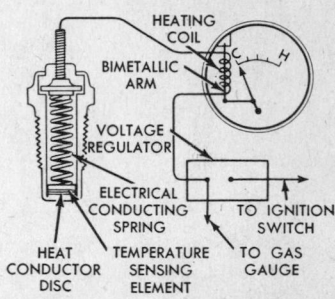

Bi-metallic temperature gauge

Testing the Dash Gauge

Connect four D-cells (total of 6 volts) in series with the dash gauge, with the ignition switched off. A good gauge will register 1/2 on the scale. Replace the gauge if it does not move.

Testing the Sending Unit

Bring the engine to normal operating temperature (check with a thermometer). If the gauge doesn't register, disconnect the connecting wire from the engine sending unit and ground the connecting wire for an instant and have an assistant observe the gauge.

Caution Grounding the wire for any longer than a moment will damage the dash units.

If the gauge shows no reading, replace the connecting wire. If the gauge registers when grounded, replace the sending unit.

Section 3
Magnetic

Fuel

The magnetic fuel gauge consists of two units, the dash unit and the sending unit in the fuel tank. One terminal of the dash unit is connected to the ignition switch so that the system is active only when the ignition is on. With the ignition off, the pointer may come to rest at any position on the dial.

The gauge pointer is moved by varying the magnetic pull of two coils in the unit. The magnetic pull is controlled by the action of the tank unit which contains a variable rheostat, the value of which varies with movement of a float and arm.

When the ignition switch is on and the tank unit arm is in the full position, the current flow to ground

is through the resistor, battery coil and the ground coil. Because the ground coil has more windings than the battery coil, it builds up a stronger magnetic field and the pointer is pulled to the full position.

When the tank unit arm is in the empty position, the current flow is through the resistor, the battery coil and the wire to ground at the tank

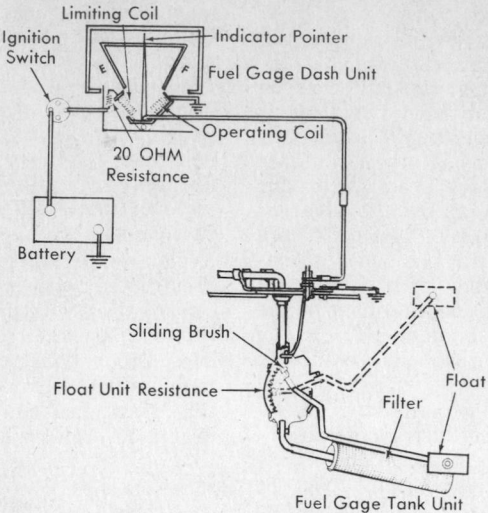

Magnetic fuel gauge circuit

unit. The pointer is thus pulled to the empty position. The resistor in series with the battery coil balances resistance between the two coils in the dash unit.

Testing the Dash Gauge

Disconnect the wire from the tank unit. Using a tank unit of known accuracy, clip a test wire from the body of the test unit to ground. Clip another test wire from the connector of the test unit to the tank unit wire. With the ignition on, moving the float arm through its entire range should cause the gauge to respond proportionally. If the dash gauge does not correspond to the movement of the test unit and the wiring to the gauge is OK, the dash unit is bad.

Testing the Tank Unit

If tests indicate that the trouble lies in the tank unit, remove the unit and check for mechanical failure. The unit may have either a ruptured or binding float.

An electrical check for circuit continuity may be made throughout the unit's range.

Temperature

The temperature gauge system consists of a magnetic dash unit and a resistance-type sending unit screwed into the water jacket of the cylinder head or the engine block.

The dash unit has two magnetic poles. One of the windings is connected to the ignition switch and ground. This electromagnet exerts a steady pull to hold the gauge pointer to the left or "cold" position when the ignition is on.

The other winding in the dash unit connects to a ground through the engine sending unit. This electromagnet exerts a steady pull on the gauge pointer toward the right, or "hot"

side of the gauge. The strength of this pull is dependent upon the current allowed to pass through the engine unit (sending unit) resistor.

The sending unit, located in the engine cooling system, contains a flat disc (thermistor) that changes resistance as its temperature varies.

NOTE: this sending unit, while similar in appearance, is different and is not interchangeable with the unit used in systems using bi-metal or thermal dash gauges. The resistance of the thermistor disc is maximum when the temperature is cold and minimum when hot. The decrease in resistance allows more current to flow through the electromagnet connected to the engine unit. The resulting increase in magnetic pull causes the gauge pointer to move to the right, or "hot" side.

Tests

1. Disconnect the wire at the sending unit and turn on the ignition switch. The gauge hand should stay against the cold side stop pin.

2. Ground the wire disconnected from the sending unit. With the ignition switch still on, the gauge hand should swing across the dial to the hot stop pin.

Corrective Measures

If the gauge hand does not stay to the left, either the wire is grounded between the dash unit and the engine unit or the dash unit is defective.

Test further by disconnecting the sending unit wire at the gauge. Turn on the ignition. If the gauge hand stays on the left-hand stop pin, replace the disconnected wire. If the gauge still moves, replace the gauge.

If the gauge hand does not swing across the dial, there is an open circuit in the wire between the sending unit and gauge, the gauge is defective, or current is not reaching the dash gauge.

Test further by grounding the sending unit terminal of the dash gauge and turning on the ignition. If the gauge hand now moves, replace the disconnected wire. If the gauge hand does not move, connect a test lamp into the circuit. If the test lamp does not light, test the wire between the ignition switch and the dash unit by connecting the lamp to the accessory terminal at the ignition switch and ground. The test lamp should light.

If the gauge hand operates correctly, but the gauge does not indicate temperature correctly, either the sending unit is defective or the dash gauge is out of calibration. Replace sending unit with one of known accuracy. If gauge reading is still incorrect, replace the gauge.

If the gauge hand is at maximum at all times, and tests 1 and 2 indicate that the wiring and the dash unit are good, the sending unit must be replaced.

If the gauge hand will not move, the dash unit is bad, or incorrectly installed. Correct the installation or replace the gauge.

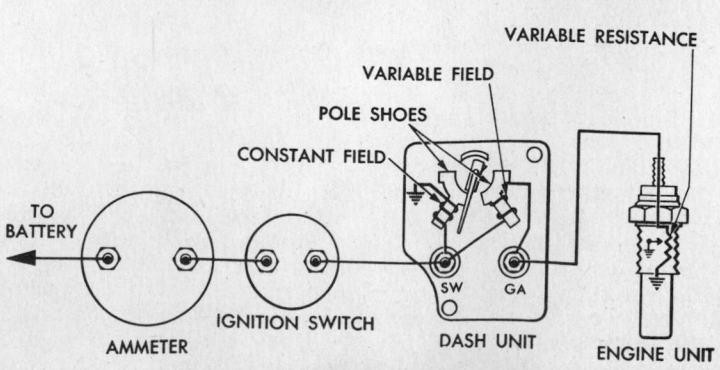

Magnetic temperature gauge

Section 4
Warning Lights

Oil Pressure

The warning or indicator light system supplies the driver with a visual signal of low engine oil pressure. The light usually lights at pressures below 5 psi.

The low pressure warning light is wired in series with an oil pressure sending unit. The sending unit is tapped into the main oil gallery and is sensitive to oil pressure. The unit contains a diaphragm, spring linkage and electrical contacts. When the ignition switch is on, the warning light circuit is energized and the circuit is completed through the closed contacts in the sending unit. When the engine starts, oil pressure will compress the diaphragm, opening the contact points and breaking the circuit.

Tests

The light should light when the engine is not running and the ignition switch is turned on. If the light does not go on, first substitute a new bulb. If there is still no light, check the wire from the light to the switch. If the wire is not at fault, disconnect the wire at the sending unit and ground it. Replace the sending unit if the light now lights.

Temperature

This system employs a heat sending unit with either one or two sets of contacts. Some systems use a green light to indicate subnormal, and a red light to warn of abnormal heat. The more common system, however, uses a simple make-and-break heat-sensitive sending unit screwed into the engine cooling system, and wired in series with the hot indicator light in the instrument panel.

The two-light system uses a bi-metal element mounted between two signal circuits. Normal operating temperature (somewhere between 120°F. and 250°F.) will cause the bi-metal bar to assume a position of no contact between the low and the high temperature circuit. When the ignition switch is turned on, with a cold engine, the cold (green) circuit is complete. If the engine becomes hot enough to move the bi-metal bar so that it touches the contacts of the hot circuit, the hot (red) light comes on. This hot signal indicates that temperatures are in the area of 250°F. in the sealed cooling system.

Tests

Use the same testing procedure given for oil pressure.

Charge Indicator

A light is used to indicate general charging system operation. When

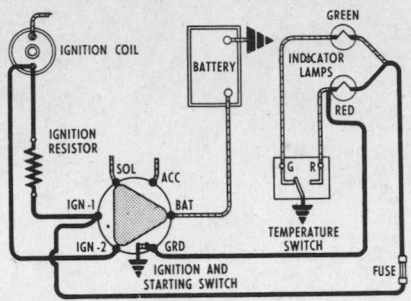

Cold and hot temperature indicator circuit

output is below battery potential, a red light is shown. When output is above battery potential, other factors (wiring, voltage regulator, etc.) being normal, the light is out.

The charge indicator bulb is connected to the charging circuit, obtaining its ground through the voltage regulator. When the output rises above battery potential, the current flow causes the light to go out.

When an alternator is used, it is necessary to supply a small amount of excitation current to the alternator field, due to the small amount of residual magnetism. Current can be supplied from the battery, through the indicator light, and to the regulator terminal on the alternator. This current has a value of about 12 volts at .25 amperes and will cause the indicator light to come on when the ignition switch is turned on. Most

systems have a resistor in parallel with the bulb to provide excitation if the bulb burns out and to prevent the light from glowing dimly during normal operation.

When the alternator starts to generate, an output voltage is developed at the regulator terminal. When this voltage exceeds the battery voltage, current will pass from the alternator to the battery and to the system. This current is flowing in the reverse direction of the voltage supplied by the battery. The current flow coming from the alternator exceeds the battery current by a regulated 1 or 2 volts. This is not enough to light the indicator light, therefore, the light will go out when the alternator is supplying sufficient current.

If the alternator output current should drop below battery voltage, current will begin to flow in the opposite direction. If it exceeds 2 or 3 volts, the light will glow indicating that the alternator is not operating properly.

Coolant Level Indicator

Some GM models have a warning light which comes on if the coolant level in the radiator drops below a predetermined level. The coolant level indicator consists of three units; a sending unit which is threaded into the side tank of the radiator, a module which is mounted behind the instrument cluster, and a warning light.

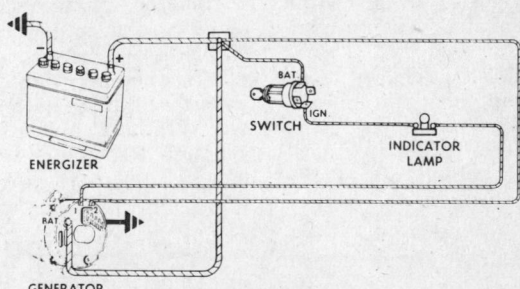

Charging indicator light circuit

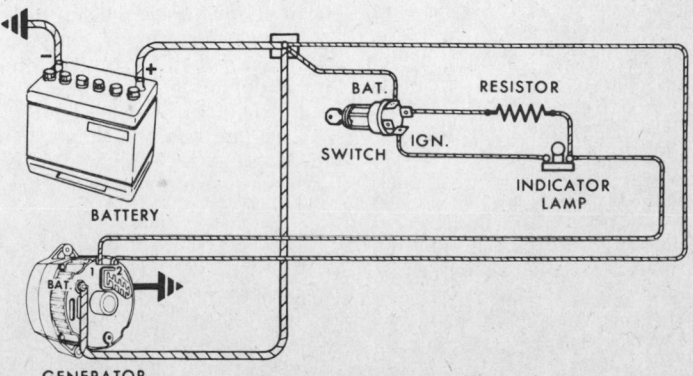

Simplified typical charging system schematic showing the resistor wired in parallel with the charge indicator lamp (© Cadillac Div., G.M. Corp.)

As a bulb test, the light is wired so that it comes on when the key is turned to the "START" position.

Light Doesn't Come On

Perform the following checks if the warning light won't come on when the key is turned to the "START" position:

1. With the ignition switch in the "ON" position, unfasten the lead from the coolant level sending unit. If the light comes on replace the sending unit.
2. If the light didn't come on in step 1, check the light in the indicator and replace it, if necesary.
3. If the bulb is OK, check the wiring between the sending unit and module, and then between the module and light. If the wiring is not "open", replace the module.

Light Won't Go Out

Perform the following checks if the light won't go out when the coolant is at the specified level:

1. Detach the lead from the coolant

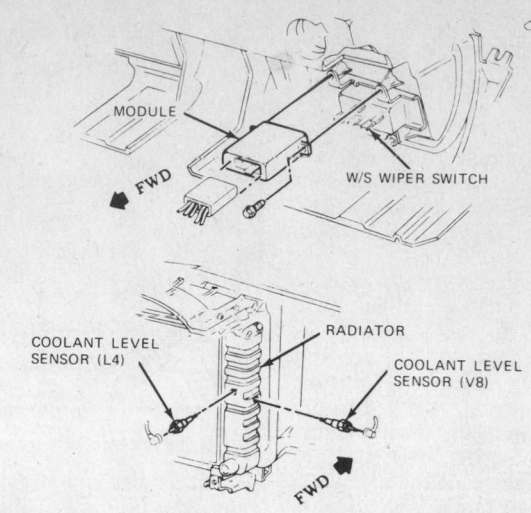

Coolant level sending unit and module (© Chevrolet Div., G.M. Corp.)

level sending unit and ground the lead connector with a jumper wire. Turn the ignition switch to the "ON" position.
2. If the light doesn't come on, replace the sending unit. If the light remains on disconnect the jumper wire and proceed with the next step.
3. Check for a short in the sending unit-to-module wiring. If there is no short, replace the module.

Section 5
Ammeters

The automotive ammeter is a gauge or meter used to indicate direction and relative value of current flow. This type of charge indicator is usually equipped with a dampening device to reduce pointer fluctuation during current surge from the voltage regulator. An ammeter is always wired in series with the circuit being monitored.

The meter will show charge when the battery is being charged and discharge when the battery is being discharged. It merely gives an indication of the state of charge of the battery, since it shows a relatively high charging rate when the battery is low, and a low charging rate when the battery is near full charge. An ammeter does not give a complete report of battery condition, whereas a voltmeter does. Just after cranking the engine, the meter will swing toward the charge side for a short time, if lights and accessories are turned off. As the energy spent in cranking is restored to the battery, the pointer will gradually move back toward center but should stay on the charge side. If the battery charge is low, however, the indicator will show a high charging rate for an indeterminate length of time.

The ammeter does not show the charging rate of the generator.

At speeds above 30-35 mph, with all lights and accessories on, the indicator should show a reading somewhere on the charge side, depending on the state of the battery. Above this speed, the indicator should never show a discharge reading; if it does, the generator and regulator should be tested. See "Charging and Starting Systems" for troubleshooting.

Section 6
Voltmeters

A voltmeter is used on some cars, instead of an ammeter. The voltmeter indicates regulated voltage, which shows the charging system's ability to keep the battery charged. A voltmeter is always wired in parallel with the circuit being monitored. Voltmeter readings that are continuously high or low, may indicate a defective regulator, broken or slipping alternator drivebelt, a faulty alternator, or a defective battery. For testing and service of these items, see "Charging and Starting Systems".

If a faulty voltmeter is suspected, check the voltage regulator output with a test voltmeter of known accuracy (See "Charging and Starting Systems"). If the voltage indicated on the test instrument is within specifications, and disagrees with the car's voltmeter reading, replace the car's voltmeter.

BRAKE DIAGNOSIS

Problems

● Most probable causes
✔ Possible causes

Causes	Brake Tell-Tale Glows During Stop	Brakes Chatter (Roughness)	Brakes Squeak During Application	Scraping Noise from Brakes	Uneven Braking Action (Front to Rear)	Uneven Braking Action (Pulls to Side)	Brakes Drag	Brakes Slow to Release	Brakes Slow to Respond	Excessive Braking Action	Excessive Brake Pedal Effort	Pedal Travel Gradually Increases	Excessive Brake Pedal Travel
Leaking Brake Line or Connection	●				✔							●	✔
Leaking Wheel Cylinder or Piston Seal	✔					✔					✔	●	✔
Leaking Master Cylinder	✔											●	✔
Restricted Brake Fluid Passage					✔	✔	✔	✔	✔		✔	✔	
Air In Brake System	●				✔								●
Contaminated or Improper Brake Fluid	✔						✔	✔	✔				
Faulty Metering Valve (Disc Only)	✔					✔		✔	✔	✔	✔		✔
Sticking Wheel Cylinder or Caliper Pistons						✔	✔	✔	✔		✔		✔
Improperly Adjusted Master Cylinder Push Rod	✔						●	✔					✔
Leaking Vacuum System									✔		●		
Restricted Air Passage In Power Unit									✔	●	✔		
Improperly Assembled Power Unit								●	✔	✔	✔	✔	
Damaged Power Unit								✔	✔	✔	✔		
Brake Assembly Attachments—Missing or Loose		✔		✔	✔	✔	✔					✔	
Brake Pedal Linkage Interference or Binding							●	●	✔		✔		
Worn Out Brake Lining—Replace			✔	✔	✔	✔					✔		
Uneven Brake Lining Wear—Replace	✔			✔	✔	✔							✔
Glazed Brake Lining—Sand Lightly			✔		✔	✔			✔		●		
Incorrect Lining Material—Replace		✔	●		✔	✔			✔	✔	✔		
Contaminated Brake Lining—Replace		✔	✔	✔	●	●				✔	●		
Linings Damaged By Abusive Use—Replace			✔	✔	✔	✔					●	✔	
Excessive Brake Lining Dust—Remove with Air			✔		●	●					●	✔	
Brake Drums or Rotors Heat Spotted or Scored		●	✔		✔	✔					✔		
Out-of-Round or Vibrating Brake Drums		●											
Out-of-Parallel Brake Rotors		●											
Excessive Rotor Run-Out		✔											
Faulty Automatic Adjusters	✔					✔	✔	✔				●	✔
Weak or Incorrect Brake Shoe Return Springs			✔	●	✔	✔	●	✔			✔		
Drums Tapered or Threaded				●									
Incorrect Wheel Cylinder Sizes						✔	✔				✔	✔	
Improperly Adjusted Parking Brake								✔					
Incorrect Front End Alignment							●						
Incorrect Tire Pressure						✔	✔						
Incorrect Wheel Bearing Adjustment		✔		✔									✔
Loose Front Suspension Attachments		✔		●		✔							
Out-of-Balance Wheel Assemblies		●											
Driver Riding Brake Pedal							✔		✔		✔	✔	✔
Faulty Proportioning Valve									✔	✔	✔	✔	
Insufficient Brake Shoe Pad Lubricant			●	●	✔			✔	✔				

DISC BRAKE DIAGNOSIS

Problems

● Most probable causes
✔ Possible causes

Causes	Excessive Pedal Travel	Hard Pedal	Grabbing or Pulling	Fading Pedal	Noise and Chatter	Dragging Brakes
Master Cylinder Fluid Low	●		✔	✔		
Air in Hydraulic System	●		✔			
Hoses Soft or Weak	●			✔		
Caliper Seals Soft or Broken	●		●		✔	●
Power Brake Malfunctioning		●				
Lining Soiled With Brake Fluid		●	●			
Lines or Hoses Kinked or Collapsed		●	●			●
Caliper Pistons Frozen or Seized		●	●		✔	●
Master Cylinder Cups Swollen		●				●
Master Cylinder Bore Rough		●	●	●		
Caliper Cylinder Bore Rough or Worn		●	●	●	✔	●
Pedal Push Rod and Linkage Binding		●	✔			
Metering Valve Not Working		●	●			
Hydraulic Connections Loose or Ruptured	✔		✔	●		
Caliper Cylinder Seals Worn or Damaged	✔			●	✔	●
Bleed Screw Open	✔			●		
Lines or Hoses Ruptured	✔			●		
Disc Has Excessive Internal Runout					●	✔
Disc Out of Parallel			✔		●	✔
Disc Has Casting Imperfections					●	✔
Restricted Port in Master Cylinder		✔				●
Residual Pressure Check Valve		✔				●
Push Rod on Master Cylinder Out of Adjustment		✔				●
Caliper Loose			●		✔	
Poor Quality Brake Fluid				●		
Poor Quality Brake Lining				●	●	

AIR CONDITIONING DIAGNOSIS

Problems

● Most probable causes
✔ Possible causes

Causes	Compressor Discharge Pressure Too High	Compressor Discharge Pressure Too Low	P.O.A. Valve Inlet Pressure Too High	P.O.A. Valve Inlet Pressure Too Low	Nozzle Outlet Temperature Too High	Nozzle Outlet Temperature Too Low	Blown Thermal Limiter	Evaporator Pressure Too Warm	Compressor Clutch Slips	Water Blowing Out Discharge Nozzle	Compressor Pressure Too High	Compressor Not Operating	Water Drains Onto Floor
Engine Overheated	●							✔			✔	✔	
Overcharge of Refrigerant or Air in System	●							✔			✔	✔	
Restriction in Condenser	●							✔		✔	✔		
Restriction in Receiver-Dehydrator		●			✔			✔		✔			
Restriction in Any High Pressure Line	●	✔			✔			✔		✔	✔		
Condenser Air Flow Blocked	●							✔		✔	✔		
P.O.A. Valve Inlet Pressure Too High	●												
Insufficient Refrigerant		●			✔	●		●					✔
Defective Compressor		●	✔					✔		✔	✔	●	
Plug in Refrigerant System	✔	●	✔	✔				✔				✔	
P.O.A. Valve Inlet Pressure Too Low		●					✔	✔					✔
P.O.A. Valve Stuck Open							✔	✔	✔				✔
Capillary Tube to Evaporator Tube Contact	✔		●				✔	✔	●		✔		
Expansion Valve Inoperative	✔	✔	●	✔	●			●	✔	●		✔	
Inlet Screen Plugged or Valve Fails		✔			●		✔	✔				✔	
Restriction in System Hoses or Tubes	✔				●	✔	✔	✔	✔			✔	
Poor Seal Evaporator to Evaporator Inlet Case		✔		✔		●							
Poor Seal Evaporator to Heater Case		✔		✔		●							
Defective or Missing Evaporator Drain Hose										●			●
Air Ducts Not Properly Connected		✔		✔		●	✔						
Vacuum Hoses Not Connected Properly						●	✔						
P.O.A. Valve Faulty			●			●	●						
Low Charge or Discharged System		✔	✔	✔	✔			●			✔		✔
Thermal Limiter Improperly Installed									●				✔
Thermal Limiter Blown												●	
Faulty Superheat Shut Off Switch									●			✔	
Head Pressure Too High											●		
Pulley Wobbles											●		
Loose Compressor Drive Belt		✔	✔		✔						●		●
Defective Clutch or Coil		✔	✔		✔						●		●
Restriction in Suction Line		✔	✔		✔						●		✔
Defective Suction Throttling Valve	✔	✔	●								✔		
Defective Expansion Valve	✔		●	✔	✔		✔				✔		
Plugged or Kinked Evaporator Drain Hose												●	
Broken Compressor Drive Belt												●	
No Power to Clutch									✔			●	
Faulty Switch or Wiring											✔	●	

COOLING SYSTEM DIAGNOSIS

Problems

● Most probable causes
✔ Possible causes

Causes	External Leakage	Internal Leakage	Poor Circulation	Overheating	Overflow Loss	Corrosion	Temp Too Low (Slow Engine Warm Up)	Water Pump Noisy
Hose Leaking	●				●			
Water Pump Leaking	●				●			
Damaged Gasket	●	●			●			
Leaking Heater Core	●				✔			
Cracked Cylinder Block	●	●			✔			
Faulty Pressure Cap	●	●			●	●		
Oil Cooler Fittings Loose	●	●			✔			
Faulty Head Gasket	●	●			✔			
Loose Cylinder Head Bolts	●	●			✔			
Cracked Valve Port			●		✔			
Cracked Cylinder Wall			●		✔			
Leaking Oil Cooler			●					
Low Coolant Level				●	●			
Collapsed Radiator Hose				●	●			
Fan Belt Loose				●	✔			✔
Air Leak Through Bottom Hose	✔			●				
Faulty Thermostat				●			●	
Water Pump Impeller Broken				●				●
Restricted Radiator Core				●	●			
Restricted Engine Water Jacket				●				
Incorrect Ignition Timing				●				
Inaccurate Temperature Gauge				●			●	
Excessive Engine Idling				●				
Frozen Coolant				●				
Faulty Vacuum By Pass Valve			✔	●				
Overfilling					●			
Blown Head Gasket	✔				●			
Coolant Foaming					●			
Insufficient Corrosion Inhibitor				✔	✔	●		
Extended Use of Anti-Freeze				✔	✔	●		
High Mineral and Lime Content of Coolant				✔	✔	●		
Faulty Temperature Sending Unit							●	
Faulty Heater Controls				✔			●	
Defective Seal								●
Bearing Corroded								●

SI Metric Tables

The following tables are given in SI (International System) metric units. SI units replace both customary (English) and the older gravimetric units. The use of SI units as a new worldwide standard was set by the International Committee of Weights and Measures in 1960. SI has since been adopted by most countries as their national standard.

These tables are general conversion tables which will allow you to convert customary units, which appear in the text, into SI units.

The following are a list of SI units and the customary units, used in this book, which they replace:

To measure:	Use SI units:	Which replace (customary units):
mass	kilograms (kg)	pounds (lbs)
temperature	Celsius (°C)	Fahrenheit (°F)
length	millimeters (mm)	inches (in.)
force	newtons (N)	pounds force (lbs)
capacities	liters (l)	pints/quarts/gallons (pts/qts/gals)
torque	newton-meters (N·m)	foot pounds (ft lbs)
pressure	kilopascals (kPa)	pounds per square inch (psi)
volume	cubic centimeters (cm^3)	cubic inches (cu in.)
power	kilowatts (kW)	horsepower (hp)

If you have had any prior experience with the metric system, you may have noticed units in this chart which are not familiar to you. This is because, in some cases, SI units differ from the older gravimetric units which they replace. For example, newtons (N) replace kilograms (kg) as a force unit, kilopascals (kPa) replace atmospheres or bars as a unit of pressure, and, although the units are the same, the name Celsius replaces centigrade for temperature measurement.

If you are not using the SI tables, have a look at them anyway; you will be seeing a lot more of them in the future.

ENGLISH-METRIC CONVERSION (MASS)

lbs	kg	oz	kg
0.1	0.04	0.1	0.003
0.2	0.09	0.2	0.005
0.3	0.14	0.3	0.008
0.4	0.18	0.4	0.011
0.5	0.23	0.5	0.014
0.6	0.27	0.6	0.017
0.7	0.32	0.7	0.020
0.8	0.36	0.8	0.023
0.9	0.41	0.9	0.024
1	0.4	1	0.03
2	0.9	2	0.06
3	1.4	3	0.08
4	1.8	4	0.11
5	2.3	5	0.14
6	2.7	6	0.17
7	3.2	7	0.20
8	3.6	8	0.23
9	4.1	9	0.26
10	4.5	10	0.28
11	5.0	11	0.31
12	5.4	12	0.34
13	5.9	13	0.37
14	6.4	14	0.40
15	6.8	15	0.42

ENGLISH-METRIC CONVERSION
(Temperature)

Fahrenheit (F)		Celsius (C)		Fahrenheit (F)		Celsius (C)		Fahrenheit (F)		Celsius (C)	
°F	°C	°C	°F	°F	°C	°C	°F	°F	°C	°C	°F
−40	−40	−38	−36.4	80	26.7	18	64.4	215	101.7	80	176
−35	−37.2	−36	−32.8	85	29.4	20	68	220	104.4	85	185
−30	−34.4	−34	−29.2	90	32.2	22	71.6	225	107.2	90	194
−25	−31.7	−32	−25.6	95	35.0	24	75.2	230	110.0	95	202
−20	−28.9	−30	−22	100	37.8	26	78.8	235	112.8	100	212
−15	−26.1	−28	−18.4	105	40.6	28	82.4	240	115.6	105	221
−10	−23.3	−26	−14.8	110	43.3	30	86	245	118.3	110	230
−5	−20.6	−24	−11.2	115	46.1	32	89.6	250	121.1	115	239
0	−17.8	−22	−7.6	120	48.9	34	93.2	255	123.9	120	248
1	−17.2	−20	−4	125	51.7	36	96.8	260	126.6	125	257
2	−16.7	−18	−0.4	130	54.4	38	100.4	265	129.4	130	266
3	−16.1	−16	3.2	135	57.2	40	104	270	132.2	135	275
4	−15.6	−14	6.8	140	60.0	42	107.6	275	135.0	140	284
5	−15.0	−12	10.4	145	62.8	44	112.2	280	137.8	145	293
10	−12.2	−10	14	150	65.6	46	114.8	285	140.6	150	302
15	−9.4	−8	17.6	155	68.3	48	118.4	290	143.3	155	311
20	−6.7	−6	21.2	160	71.1	50	122	295	146.1	160	320
25	−3.9	−4	24.8	165	73.9	52	125.6	300	148.9	165	329
30	−1.1	−2	28.4	170	76.7	54	129.2	305	151.7	170	338
35	1.7	0	32	175	79.4	56	132.8	310	154.4	175	347
40	4.4	2	35.6	180	82.2	58	136.4	315	157.2	180	356
45	7.2	4	39.2	185	85.0	60	140	320	160.0	185	365
50	10.0	6	42.8	190	87.8	62	143.6	325	162.8	190	374
55	12.8	8	46.4	195	90.6	64	147.2	330	165.6	195	383
60	15.6	10	50	200	93.3	66	150.8	335	168.3	200	392
65	18.3	12	53.6	205	96.1	68	154.4	340	171.1	205	401
70	21.1	14	57.2	210	98.9	70	158	345	173.9	210	410
75	23.9	16	60.8	212	100.0	75	167	350	176.7	215	414

ENGLISH-METRIC CONVERSION (Length)

Inches	Decimals	Milli-meters	Inches to millimeters inches	mm	Inches	Decimals	Milli-meters	Inches to millimeters inches	mm
1/64	0.015625	0.3969	0.0001	0.00254	33/64	0.515625	13.0969	0.6	15.24
1/32	0.03125	0.7937	0.0002	0.00508	17/32	0.53125	13.4937	0.7	17.78
3/64	0.046875	1.1906	0.0003	0.00762	35/64	0.546875	13.8906	0.8	20.32
1/16	0.0625	1.5875	0.0004	0.01016	9/16	0.5625	14.2875	0.9	22.86
5/64	0.078125	1.9844	0.0005	0.01270	37/64	0.578125	14.6844	1	25.4
3/32	0.09375	2.3812	0.0006	0.01524	19/32	0.59375	15.0812	2	50.8
7/64	0.109375	2.7781	0.0007	0.01778	39/64	0.609375	15.4781	3	76.2
1/8	0.125	3.1750	0.0008	0.02032	5/8	0.625	15.8750	4	101.6
9/64	0.140625	3.5719	0.0009	0.02286	41/64	0.640625	16.2719	5	127.0
5/32	0.15625	3.9687	0.001	0.0254	21/32	0.65625	16.6687	6	152.4
11/64	0.171875	4.3656	0.002	0.0508	43/64	0.671875	17.0656	7	177.8
3/16	0.1875	4.7625	0.003	0.0762	11/16	0.6875	17.4625	8	203.2
13/64	0.203125	5.1594	0.004	0.1016	45/64	0.703125	17.8594	9	228.6
7/32	0.21875	5.5562	0.005	0.1270	23/32	0.71875	18.2562	10	254.0
15/64	0.234375	5.9531	0.006	0.1524	47/64	0.734375	18.6531	11	279.4
1/4	0.25	6.3500	0.007	0.1778	3/4	0.75	19.0500	12	304.8
17/64	0.265625	6.7469	0.008	0.2032	49/64	0.765625	19.4469	13	330.2
9/32	0.28125	7.1437	0.009	0.2286	25/32	0.78125	19.8437	14	355.6
19/64	0.296875	7.5406	0.01	0.254	51/64	0.796875	20.2406	15	381.0
5/16	0.3125	7.9375	0.02	0.508	13/16	0.8125	20.6375	16	406.4
21/64	0.328125	8.3344	0.03	0.762	53/64	0.828125	21.0344	17	431.8
11/32	0.34375	8.7312	0.04	1.016	27/32	0.84375	21.4312	18	457.2
23/64	0.359375	9.1281	0.05	1.270	55/64	0.859375	21.8281	19	482.6
3/8	0.375	9.5250	0.06	1.524	7/8	0.875	22.2250	20	508.0
25/64	0.390625	9.9219	0.07	1.778	57/64	0.890625	22.6219	21	533.4
13/32	0.40625	10.3187	0.08	2.032	29/32	0.90625	23.0187	22	558.8
27/64	0.421875	10.7156	0.09	2.286	59/64	0.921875	23.4156	23	584.2
7/16	0.4375	11.1125	0.1	2.54	15/16	0.9375	23.8125	24	609.6
29/64	0.453125	11.5094	0.2	5.08	61/64	0.953125	24.2094	25	635.0
15/32	0.46875	11.9062	0.3	7.62	31/32	0.96875	24.6062	26	660.4
31/64	0.484375	12.3031	0.4	10.16	63/64	0.984375	25.0031	27	690.6
1/2	0.5	12.7000	0.5	12.70					

ENGLISH-METRIC CONVERSION (FORCE)

lbs	N	lbs	N	lbs	N	oz	N
0.01	0.04	4	17.8	25	111.2	1	0.3
0.02	0.09	5	22.2	26	115.6	2	0.6
0.03	0.13	6	26.7	27	120.1	3	0.8
0.04	0.18	7	31.1	28	124.6	4	1.1
0.05	0.22	8	35.6	29	129.0	5	1.4
0.06	0.27	9	40.0	30	133.4	6	1.7
0.07	0.31	10	44.5	31	137.9	7	2.0
0.08	0.36	11	48.9	32	142.3	8	2.2
0.09	0.40	12	53.4	33	146.8	9	2.5
0.1	0.4	13	57.8	34	151.2	10	2.8
0.2	0.9	14	62.3	35	155.7	11	3.1
0.3	1.3	15	66.7	36	160.1	12	3.3
0.4	1.8	16	71.2	37	164.6	13	3.6
0.5	2.2	17	75.6	38	169.0	14	3.9
0.6	2.7	18	80.1	39	173.5	15	4.2
0.7	3.1	19	84.5	40	177.9	16	4.4
0.8	3.6	20	89.0	41	182.4	17	4.7
0.9	4.0	21	93.4	42	186.8	18	5.0
1	4.4	22	97.9	43	191.3	19	5.3
2	8.9	23	102.3	44	195.7	20	5.6
3	13.4	24	106.8	45	200.2	21	5.8

ENGLISH-METRIC CONVERSION (FORCE)

lbs	N	lbs	N	lbs	N	oz	N
46	204.6	75	333.6	104	462.6	22	6.1
47	209.1	76	338.1	105	467.1	23	6.4
48	213.5	77	342.5	106	471.5	24	6.7
49	218.0	78	347.0	107	476.0	25	7.0
50	224.4	79	351.4	108	480.4	26	7.2
51	226.9	80	355.9	109	484.8	27	7.5
52	231.3	81	360.3	110	489.3	28	7.8
53	235.8	82	364.8	111	493.8	29	8.1
54	240.2	83	369.2	112	498.2	30	8.3
55	244.6	84	373.6	113	502.6	31	8.6
56	249.1	85	378.1	114	507.1	32	8.9
57	253.6	86	382.6	115	511.5	33	9.2
58	258.0	87	387.0	116	516.0	34	9.4
59	262.4	88	391.4	117	520.4	35	9.7
60	266.9	89	395.9	118	524.9	36	10.0
61	271.3	90	400.3	119	529.3	37	10.3
62	275.8	91	404.8	120	533.8	38	10.6
63	280.2	92	409.2	121	538.2	39	10.8
64	284.6	93	413.7	122	542.7	40	11.1
65	289.1	94	418.1	123	547.1	41	11.4
66	293.6	95	422.6	124	551.6	42	11.7
67	298.0	96	427.0	125	556.0	43	12.0
68	302.5	97	431.5	126	560.5	44	12.2
69	306.9	98	435.9	127	564.9	45	12.5
70	311.4	99	440.4	128	569.4	46	12.8
71	315.8	100	444.8	129	573.8	47	13.1
72	320.3	101	449.3	130	578.3	48	13.3
73	324.7	102	453.7	131	582.7	49	13.6
74	329.2	103	458.2	132	587.2	50	13.9

ENGLISH-METRIC CONVERSION (CAPACITIES)

gals	liters	qts	liters	pts	liters
0.1	0.38	0.1	0.10	0.1	0.05
0.2	0.76	0.2	0.19	0.2	0.10
0.3	1.1	0.3	0.28	0.3	0.14
0.4	1.5	0.4	0.38	0.4	0.19
0.5	1.9	0.5	0.47	0.5	0.24
0.6	2.3	0.6	0.57	0.6	0.28
0.7	2.6	0.7	0.66	0.7	0.33
0.8	3.0	0.8	0.76	0.8	0.38
0.9	3.4	0.9	0.85	0.9	0.43
1	3.8	1	1.0	1	0.5
2	7.6	2	1.9	2	1.0
3	11.4	3	2.8	3	1.4
4	15.1	4	3.8	4	1.9
5	18.9	5	4.7	5	2.4
6	22.7	6	5.7	6	2.8
7	26.5	7	6.6	7	3.3
8	30.3	8	7.6	8	3.8
9	34.1	9	8.5	9	4.3
10	37.8	10	9.5	10	4.7

ENGLISH-METRIC CONVERSION (CAPACITIES)

gals	liters	qts	liters	pts	liters
11	41.6	11	10.4	11	5.2
12	45.4	12	11.4	12	5.7
13	49.2	13	12.3	13	6.2
14	53.0	14	13.2	14	6.6
15	56.8	15	14.2	15	7.1
16	60.6	16	15.1	16	7.6
17	64.3	17	16.1	17	8.0
18	68.1	18	17.0	18	8.5
19	71.9	19	18.0	19	9.0
20	75.7	20	18.9	20	9.5
21	79.5	21	19.9	21	9.9
22	83.2	22	20.8	22	10.4
23	87.0	23	21.8	23	10.9
24	90.8	24	22.7	24	11.4
25	94.6	25	23.6	25	11.8
26	98.4	26	24.6	26	12.3
27	102.2	27	25.5	27	12.8
28	106.0	28	26.5	28	13.2
29	110.0	29	27.4	29	13.7
30	113.5	30	28.4	30	14.2

ENGLISH-METRIC CONVERSION (Torque)

ft lbs	N-m	ft lbs	N-m	ft lbs	N-m	ft lbs	N-m
0.1	0.1	20	27.1	48	65.1	76	103.0
0.2	0.3	21	28.5	49	66.4	77	104.4
0.3	0.4	22	29.8	50	67.8	78	105.8
0.4	0.5	23	31.2	51	69.2	79	107.1
0.5	0.7	24	32.5	52	70.5	80	108.5
0.6	0.8	25	33.9	53	71.9	81	109.8
0.7	1.0	26	35.2	54	73.2	82	111.2
0.8	1.1	27	36.6	55	74.6	83	112.5
0.9	1.2	28	38.0	56	75.9	84	113.9
1	1.3	29	39.3	57	77.3	85	115.2
2	2.7	30	40.7	58	78.6	86	116.6
3	4.1	31	42.4	59	80.0	87	118.0
4	5.4	32	43.4	60	81.4	88	119.3
5	6.8	33	44.7	61	82.7	89	120.7
6	8.1	34	46.1	62	84.1	90	122.0
7	9.5	35	47.4	63	85.4	91	123.4
8	10.8	36	48.8	64	86.8	92	124.7
9	12.2	37	50.7	65	88.1	93	126.1
10	13.6	38	51.5	66	89.5	94	127.4
11	14.9	39	52.9	67	90.8	95	128.8
12	16.3	40	54.2	68	92.2	96	130.2
13	17.6	41	55.6	69	93.6	97	131.5
14	18.9	42	56.9	70	94.9	98	132.9
15	20.3	43	58.3	71	96.3	99	134.2
16	21.7	44	59.7	72	97.6	100	135.6
17	23.0	45	61.0	73	99.0	101	136.9
18	24.4	46	62.4	74	100.3	102	138.3
19	25.8	47	63.7	75	101.7	103	139.6

ENGLISH-METRIC CONVERSION (Torque)

ft lbs	N-m	ft lbs	N-m	ft lbs	N-m	ft lbs	N-m
104	141.0	150	203.4	196	265.7	242	328.1
105	142.4	151	204.7	197	267.1	243	329.5
106	143.7	152	206.1	198	268.4	244	330.8
107	145.1	153	207.4	199	269.8	245	332.2
108	146.4	154	208.8	200	271.2	246	333.5
109	147.8	155	210.2	201	272.5	247	334.9
110	149.1	156	211.5	202	273.9	248	336.2
111	150.5	157	212.9	203	275.2	249	337.6
112	151.8	158	214.2	204	276.6	250	339.0
113	153.2	159	215.6	205	277.9	251	340.3
114	154.6	160	216.9	206	279.3	252	341.7
115	155.9	161	218.3	207	280.6	253	343.0
116	157.3	162	219.6	208	282.0	254	344.4
117	158.6	163	221.0	209	283.4	255	345.7
118	160.0	164	222.4	210	284.7	256	347.1
119	161.3	165	223.7	211	286.1	257	348.4
120	162.7	166	225.1	212	287.4	258	349.8
121	164.0	167	226.4	213	288.8	259	351.2
122	165.4	168	227.8	214	290.1	260	352.5
123	166.8	169	229.1	215	291.5	261	353.9
124	168.1	170	230.5	216	292.9	262	355.2
125	169.5	171	231.8	217	294.2	263	356.6
126	170.8	172	233.2	218	295.6	264	357.9
127	172.2	173	234.6	219	296.9	265	359.3
128	173.5	174	235.9	220	298.3	266	360.6
129	174.9	175	237.3	221	299.6	267	362.0
130	176.2	176	238.6	222	301.0	268	363.4
131	177.6	177	240.0	223	302.4	269	364.7
132	179.0	178	241.3	224	303.7	270	366.1
133	180.3	179	242.7	225	305.1	271	367.4
134	181.7	180	244.0	226	306.4	272	368.8
135	183.0	181	245.4	227	307.8	273	370.1
136	184.4	182	246.8	228	309.1	274	371.5
137	185.7	183	248.1	229	310.5	275	372.9
138	187.1	184	249.5	230	311.8	276	374.2
139	188.5	185	250.8	231	313.2	277	375.6
140	189.8	186	252.2	232	314.6	278	376.9
141	191.2	187	253.5	233	315.9	279	378.3
142	192.5	188	254.9	234	317.3	280	379.6
143	193.9	189	256.2	235	318.6	281	381.0
144	195.2	190	257.6	236	320.0	282	382.3
145	196.6	191	259.0	237	321.3	283	383.7
146	198.0	192	260.3	238	322.7	284	385.0
147	199.3	193	261.7	239	324.0	285	386.4
148	200.7	194	263.0	240	325.4	286	387.8
149	202.0	195	264.4	241	326.8	287	389.1

ENGLISH-METRIC CONVERSION (TORQUE)

in lbs	N-m	in lbs	N-m	in lbs	N-m	in lbs	N-m
0.1	0.01	5	0.56	18	2.03	31	3.50
0.2	0.02	6	0.68	19	2.15	32	3.62
0.3	0.03	7	0.78	20	2.26	33	3.73
0.4	0.04	8	0.90	21	2.37	34	3.84
0.5	0.06	9	1.02	22	2.49	35	3.95
0.6	0.07	10	1.13	23	2.60	36	4.07
0.7	0.08	11	1.24	24	2.71	37	4.18
0.8	0.09	12	1.36	25	2.82	38	4.29
0.9	0.10	13	1.47	26	2.94	39	4.41
1	0.11	14	1.58	27	3.05	40	4.52
2	0.23	15	1.70	28	3.16	41	4.63
3	0.34	16	1.81	29	3.28	42	4.74
4	0.45	17	1.92	30	3.39	43	4.86

ENGLISH-METRIC CONVERSION (PRESSURE)

Psi	kPa	Psi	kPa	Psi	kPa	Psi	kPa
0.1	0.7	28	193.0	64	441.3	100	689.5
0.2	1.4	29	200.0	65	448.2	101	696.4
0.3	2.1	30	206.8	66	455.0	102	703.3
0.4	2.8	31	213.7	67	461.9	103	710.2
0.5	3.4	32	220.6	68	468.8	104	717.0
0.6	4.1	33	227.5	69	475.7	105	723.9
0.7	4.8	34	234.4	70	482.6	106	730.8
0.8	5.5	35	241.3	71	489.5	107	737.7
0.9	6.2	36	248.2	72	496.4	108	744.6
1	6.9	37	255.1	73	503.3	109	751.5
2	13.8	38	262.0	74	510.2	110	758.4
3	20.7	39	268.9	75	517.1	111	765.3
4	27.6	40	275.8	76	524.0	112	772.2
5	34.5	41	282.7	77	530.9	113	779.1
6	41.4	42	289.6	78	537.8	114	786.0
7	48.3	43	296.5	79	544.7	115	792.9
8	55.2	44	303.4	80	551.6	116	799.8
9	62.1	45	310.3	81	558.5	117	806.7
10	69.0	46	317.2	82	565.4	118	813.6
11	75.8	47	324.0	83	572.3	119	820.5
12	82.7	48	331.0	84	579.2	120	827.4
13	89.6	49	337.8	85	586.0	121	834.3
14	96.5	50	344.7	86	592.9	122	841.2
15	103.4	51	351.6	87	599.8	123	848.0
16	110.3	52	358.5	88	606.7	124	854.9
17	117.2	53	365.4	89	613.6	125	861.8
18	124.1	54	372.3	90	620.5	126	868.7
19	131.0	55	379.2	91	627.4	127	875.6
20	137.9	56	386.1	92	634.3	128	882.5
21	144.8	57	393.0	93	641.2	129	889.4
22	151.7	58	399.9	94	648.1	130	896.3
23	158.6	59	406.8	95	655.0	131	903.2
24	165.5	60	413.7	96	661.9	132	910.1
25	172.4	61	420.6	97	668.8	133	917.0
26	179.3	62	427.5	98	675.7	134	923.9
27	186.2	63	434.4	99	682.6	135	930.8

ENGLISH-METRIC CONVERSION (Pressure)

Psi	kPa	Psi	kPa	Psi	kPa	Psi	kPa
136	937.7	189	1303.1	242	1668.5	295	2034.0
137	944.6	190	1310.0	243	1675.4	296	2040.8
138	951.5	191	1316.9	244	1682.3	297	2047.7
139	958.4	192	1323.8	245	1689.2	298	2054.6
140	965.2	193	1330.7	246	1696.1	299	2061.5
141	972.2	194	1337.6	247	1703.0	300	2068.4
142	979.0	195	1344.5	248	1709.9	301	2075.3
143	985.9	196	1351.4	249	1716.8	302	2082.2
144	992.8	197	1358.3	250	1723.7	303	2089.1
145	999.7	198	1365.2	251	1730.6	304	2096.0
146	1006.6	199	1372.0	252	1737.5	305	2102.9
147	1013.5	200	1378.9	253	1744.4	306	2109.8
148	1020.4	201	1385.8	254	1751.3	307	2116.7
149	1027.3	202	1392.7	255	1758.2	308	2123.6
150	1034.2	203	1399.6	256	1765.1	309	2130.5
151	1041.1	204	1406.5	257	1772.0	310	2137.4
152	1048.0	205	1413.4	258	1778.8	311	2144.3
153	1054.9	206	1420.3	259	1785.7	312	2151.2
154	1061.8	207	1427.2	260	1792.6	313	2158.1
155	1068.7	208	1434.1	261	1799.5	314	2164.9
156	1075.6	209	1441.0	262	1806.4	315	2171.8
157	1082.5	210	1447.9	263	1813.3	316	2178.7
158	1089.4	211	1454.8	264	1820.2	317	2185.6
159	1096.3	212	1461.7	265	1827.1	318	2192.5
160	1103.2	213	1468.7	266	1834.0	319	2199.4
161	1110.0	214	1475.5	267	1840.9	320	2206.3
162	1116.9	215	1482.4	268	1847.8	321	2213.2
163	1123.8	216	1489.3	269	1854.7	322	2220.1
164	1130.7	217	1496.2	270	1861.6	323	2227.0
165	1137.6	218	1503.1	271	1868.5	324	2233.9
166	1144.5	219	1510.0	272	1875.4	325	2240.8
167	1151.4	220	1516.8	273	1882.3	326	2247.7
168	1158.3	221	1523.7	274	1889.2	327	2254.6
169	1165.2	222	1530.6	275	1896.1	328	2261.5
170	1172.1	223	1537.5	276	1903.0	329	2268.4
171	1179.0	224	1544.4	277	1909.8	330	2275.3
172	1185.9	225	1551.3	278	1916.7	331	2282.2
173	1192.8	226	1558.2	279	1923.6	332	2289.1
174	1199.7	227	1565.1	280	1930.5	333	2295.9
175	1206.6	228	1572.0	281	1937.4	334	2302.8
176	1213.5	229	1578.9	282	1944.3	335	2309.7
177	1220.4	230	1585.8	283	1951.2	336	2316.6
178	1227.3	231	1592.7	284	1958.1	337	2323.5
179	1234.2	232	1599.6	285	1965.0	338	2330.4
180	1241.0	233	1606.5	286	1971.9	339	2337.3
181	1247.9	234	1613.4	287	1978.8	240	2344.2
182	1254.8	235	1620.3	288	1985.7	341	2351.1
183	1261.7	236	1627.2	289	1992.6	342	2358.0
184	1268.6	237	1634.1	290	1999.5	343	2364.9
185	1275.5	238	1641.0	291	2006.4	344	2371.8
186	1282.4	239	1647.8	292	2013.3	345	2378.7
187	1289.3	240	1654.7	293	2020.2	346	2385.6

Turn Signal Flasher and Fuse Box Location Chart

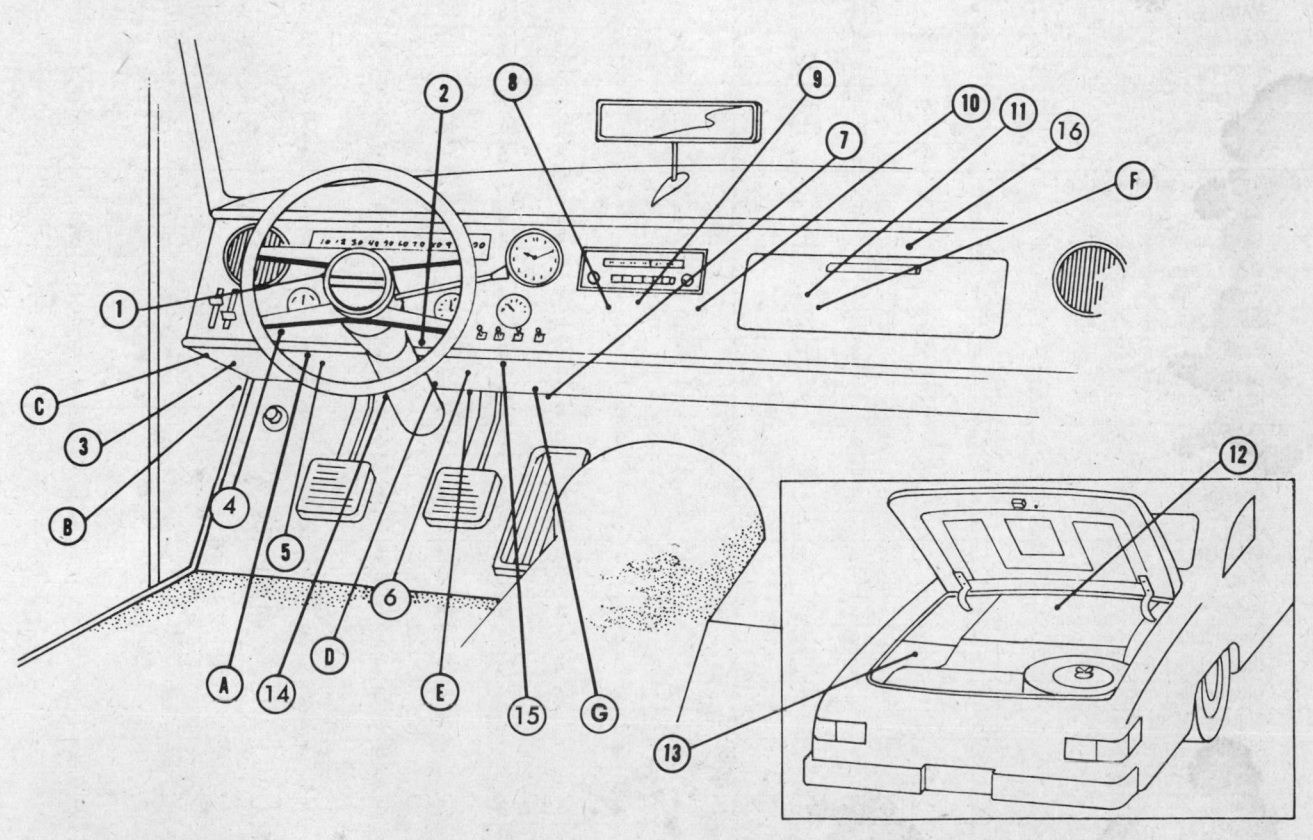

TURN SIGNAL FLASHER, HAZARD WARNING FLASHER, AND FUSE BLOCK LOCATION

	1970 TSF	1970 HWF	1971 TSF	1971 HWF	1972 TSF	1972 HWF	1973 TSF	1973 HWF	1974 TSF	1974 HWF	1975 TSF	1975 HWF	1976-77 TSF	1976-77 HWF	Through 1973 Fuse Block Location	1974 Fuse Block Location	1975-77 Fuse Block Location
American Motors																	
Ambassador	2	3	2	3	2	3	2	3	2	3	—	—	—	—	C	F	—
AMX	2	3	—	—	—	—	—	—	—	—	—	—	—	—	C	—	—
Hornet, Gremlin	3	3	3	3	3	3	3	3	3	2	3	2	3	2	C	C	C
Javelin	3	3	3	3	3	3	3	3	3	3	—	—	—	—	C	C	C
Rebel, Matador	2	3	2	3	2	3	2	3	2	3	3	1	3	1	C	F	F
Pacer	—	—	—	—	—	—	—	—	—	—	2	14	2	14	—	—	F
Chrysler Corporation																	
Barracuda	8	6	8	6	10	6	8	6	6	6	—	—	—	—	D	G	—
Challenger	8	6	8	6	10	6	8	6	6	6	—	—	—	—	A	G	—
Chrysler	5	4	5	4	5	5	5	5	5	5	14	5	14	5	A	A	A
Cordoba	—	—	—	—	—	—	—	—	—	—	4	15	4	15	—	—	A
Dart, Aspen	8	6	8	6	10	6	8	6	8	6	5	5	5	5	D	D	A
Dodge	5	6	5, 10	—	5, 10	5	8	6	8	6①	4③	15④	4③	15①	A	D②	A
Imperial	5	4	5	4	5	5	5	6	5	5	14	5	—	—	F	A	A
Plymouth	4, 8	6	5, 10	—	5, 10	5	8	6	8	6①	4③	15①	4③	15④	A	D②	A
Valiant, Volare	8	6	8	6	10	6	8	5	8	6	5	5	5	5	A	D	A
Ford Motor Company																	
Comet	—	—	5	5	5	5	5	5	5	5	5	3	5	3	E	E	E
Cougar	8	10	11	6	8	10	8	10	3	3	3	3	3	3	E	C	C
Fairlane, Torino, Elite	6	5	5	5	5	5	5	5	3	3	3	3	3	3	E	C	C
Ford	11	3	8	3	8	3	8	3	8	3	3	3	3	3	E	C	A
Granada, Monarch	—	—	—	—	—	—	—	—	—	—	6	14	6	14	—	—	C
Lincoln Continental	3	3	6	6	3	3	3	3	3	5	10	5	10	5	F	A	E
Mark III, IV, V	11	3	11	3	3	3	3	3	3	3	3	5	3	5	F	C	A
Maverick	6	—	5	5	5	5	5	5	5	5	5	3	5	3	E	E	E
Mercury	11	3	8	3	8	3	8	3	8	3	3	3	3	3	E	C	A
Montego	6	5	5	5	5	5	5	5	3	3	3	3	3	3	E	C	C
Mustang	10	8	11	6	8	10	8	10	—	—	—	—	—	—	E	—	—
Mustang II	—	—	—	—	—	—	—	—	7	7	7	7	7	7	—	G	G
Pinto, Bobcat	—	—	10	10	10	10	10	10	10	10	16	16	16	16	E	E	E
Thunderbird	3	11	11	6	3	3	3	3	3	5	3	3	3	3	F	C	C
General Motors Corporation																	
Buick	3	3	3	3	3	3	3	3	3	3	3	3	3	3	—	—	B
Buick Apollo, Skylark	—	—	—	—	—	—	5	3	5	3	3	3	3	3	B	B	B
Buick Special, Skylark, Regal	3	3	4	3	4	3	4	3	14	3	14	3	14	3	C	C	C
Buick Skyhawk	—	—	—	—	—	—	—	—	—	—	3	3	3	3	C	C	B
Cadillac, Eldorado	14	14	14	3	14	3	14	3	14	3	6	3	6	3	B	B	B
Cadillac Seville	—	—	—	—	—	—	—	—	—	—	5	6	5	6	—	—	E
Camaro	8	3	8	3	8	3	8	3	8	3	14	5	14	5	A	A	A
Chevelle	1	3	7	3	7	3	4	3	4	3	14	5	14	5	A	A	A
Chevette	—	—	—	—	—	—	—	—	—	—	—	—	3	3	—	—	C
Chevrolet	10	3	7	3	7	3	6	3	6	3	14	5	14	5	A	A	A
Nova	10	3	7	3	7	3	10	3	10	3	14	5	14	5	A	A	A
Corvette	11	3	11	3	11	3	11	3	6	3	14	5	14	5	A	A	A
Monza	—	—	—	—	—	—	—	—	—	—	14	3	14	3	—	—	C
Vega	—	—	5	3	5	3	5	3	5	3	14	3	14	3	C	C	C
Oldsmobile	1	3	4	3	4	3	4	3	5	3	5	5	5	5	C	C	A
Oldsmobile F-85, Cutlass	3	3	4	3	4	3	4	3	14	3	14	3	14	3	C	C	C
Oldsmobile Omega	—	—	—	—	—	—	5	3	6	3	6	5	6	5	C	C	A
Oldsmobile Starfire	—	—	—	—	—	—	—	—	—	—	14	3	14	3	—	—	C
Oldsmobile Toronado	4	3	4	3	4	3	4	3	5	3	5	5	5	5	C	C	A
Pontiac Astre, Sunbird	—	—	—	—	—	—	—	—	—	—	14	3	14	3	—	—	C
Pontiac	3	3	3	3	3	3	3	3	3	3	5	3	5	3	C	C	B
Firebird	3	3	3	3	3	3	3	3	3	3	5	3	5	3	C	C	B
Tempest, GTO, Grand Am	3	3	3	3	3	3	3	3	3	3	5	3	5	3	C	C	B
Ventura	—	—	3	3	3	3	3	3	3	3	5	3	5	3	C	C	B

①—5 on Monaco, Fury
②—A on Monaco, Fury and Gran Fury
③—14 on Gran Fury, Monaco
④—5 on Gran Fury, Monaco
TSF—Turn Signal Flasher
HWF—Hazard Warning Flasher